343

477.10; extravagant etc. (inordinate) 31.9; opinionated etc. (bigoted) 606.7.

504. Madman, Eccentric
(See also 503. Insanity, Eccentricity)

1. *n.* madman, crazy etc. 503.12 person, lunatic, dement, crackbrain, crackskull [rare], cracked wit, bedlam, bedlamite, candidate for bedlam, Tom o' Bedlam, phrenetic, noncompos, psychopath, psychopathic case; demoniac, energumen; loon, loony, nut, bat, coot, goof, crackpot, screwball [all slang]; maniac, raving lunatic; madcap; monomaniac, crank [coll.]; kleptomaniac, kleptomanist; phobiac [rare], phobic, phobe; automaniac; dipsomaniac; paranoiac; hypochondriac etc. 837.5; idiot, imbecile etc. (fool) 501.

2. *n.* fanatic, fan [slang], energumen, infatuate, devotee, bug [slang], nut [slang], enthusiast, rhapsodist, seer, highflier *or* highflyer; zealot, zealotist; faddist, fadmonger; dogmatist etc. 474.4; opinionist etc. 606.3.

3. *n.* eccentric, erratic, maggot-pate [obs.]; freak, character, crank [all coll.]; crackpot, nut, screwball, queer bird, odd *or* queer card, queer case, odd *or* queer fish, rum customer, queer potato [all slang].

505. Memory
(See 506. Oblivion)

1. *n.* memory, memoria, memento [joc.], remembrance, rememorance [rare], recollection, recall [rare], mental reproduction *or* recurrence; recognition, recognizance [now rare], reidentification; mirror of the mind, mind's eye, eye of the mind; tablets of the memory, Memory's halls *or* pictures; corner *or* recess of the memory, inmost recesses of the memory.
"that inward eye" (Wordsworth), "the warder of the brain" (Shakespeare), "the treasury and guardian of all things" (Cicero), "storehouse of the mind, garner of facts and oration etc. (celebration) 883.

2. *n.* retentivity, retentiveness, retention; retentive memory etc. *below.*

3. *n.* good memory, faithful *or* trustworthy memory, exact *or* correct memory, ready *or* prompt memory, retentive memory, tenacious memory, capacious memory; memory for faces, camera eye.

4. *n.* remembering, recalling etc. *v.*; recalling to the memory, rememoration [obs.], recollection, reminiscence, retrospect, retrospection, looking back, looking back on things past, review, review *or* contemplation of the past, reconsideration, reflection; afterthought etc. (mature thought) 451.2.

5. *n.* reminder, remindal; remembrance, remembrancer; jogger [coll.], flapper; prompt, prompter, prompting; mnemonic device, mnemonic, mnemonicon; token of remembrance, memento, token, souvenir, keepsake, relic; word to the wise, suggestion etc. (hint, tip), 527.3, 4.

6. *n.* memorandum (*pl.* memoranda), memo [coll.], memoir, memorial [obs. exc. Law], commonplace; memorandum book, memo book [coll.], notebook, pocketbook, engagement book, promptbook, commonplace book, adversaria; memory book [U.S.], scrapbook, album; birthday book, address book.

7. *n.* memorial, testimonial etc. (monument) 551.4.

8. *n.* memories, memorabilia, memoranda, memoirs, memorials.

9. *n.* mnemonics, mnemotechny, mnemotechnics, mnemonization, art of memory improvement, artificial memory; Mnemosyne [Gr. Myth.].

10. *v.* remember, rememorate [obs.], member [obs. exc. dial.], mem [slang], recollect, recomember [dial. U.S.], recall, call *or* recall to mind *or* remembrance, call ~, summon *or* conjure up, mind, renind [obs.], think back, carry one's thoughts back, look back *or* backwards, look back upon, look back upon

---

504. Who is yonder poor maniac?—SOUTHEY. There is a pleasure, sure, / In being mad, which none but madmen know.—DRYDEN. 'Tis the times' plague, when madmen lead the blind.—SHAKESPEARE. Every madman thinks all other men mad.—PUBLILIUS.
505. Memory is the diary that we all carry about with us.—WILDE. O call back yesterday, bid time return.—SHAKESPEARE. Fresh and lasting . . . in remembrance.—SHAKESPEARE. Beasts and babies remember, that is, recognize: man alone recollects.—COLERIDGE. A man of great memory without learning hath a rock and a spindle and no staff to spin.—G. HERBERT. Lay it where childhood's dreams are twined / In Memory's mystic band.—CARROLL. Music, when soft voices die, / Vibrates in the memory.—SHELLEY. *Parsque est me-*

PETER MARK ROGET
(1779–1869)

PETER MARK ROGET was the only son of John Roget, who hailed from Geneva and later had oversight of the French Protestant Church in Threadneedle Street, London, where Peter was born in 1779. His father died a few years later, and his mother removed to Edinburgh, where the son entered the university there at the age of fourteen. He was graduated M.D. from the medical school at the early age of nineteen and distinguished himself by valuable research work on such subjects as consumption and the effects of laughing gas. In 1802 he went to Geneva, his father's home, in company with the sons of a wealthy merchant of Manchester, to whom he acted as tutor. The disturbances caused by the breach of the Peace of Amiens interrupted their tour and Roget was for a time held a prisoner at Geneva. He succeeded in getting away, however, at the end of 1803 and became private physician to the Marquis of Lansdowne.

In 1805 he became physician to the Manchester Infirmary and made a name for himself there by giving courses of lectures on scientific subjects. He combined in an unusual degree exact knowledge with a power of apt and vivid presentation, and this work he continued for well-nigh fifty years after his removal to London in 1808. He became honorary physician to the Northern Dispensary and lectured assiduously on medical and other subjects in various parts of the metropolis. A testimony to his versatility is afforded by the fact that he was asked by the Government to make an inquiry into the water supply of London, and in 1828 he published a report on the subject. For three years he held the post of Fullerian Professor of Physiology at the London Institution.

Dr. Roget was made a Fellow of the Royal Society in 1815, and served as secretary of the organization for over twenty years. He was appointed Examiner in Physiology in the University of London. He wrote various papers on physiology and health, among them *On Animal and Vegetable Physiology*, a Bridgewater treatise, 1834; a work on phrenology in two volumes, 1838; *The Economic Chess-Board*, 1846; and *Electricity, Galvanism*, 1848.

These activities would be more than enough for most men, but Roget's insatiable thirst for knowledge and his appetite for work led him into yet other fields. He was no high-and-dry scientist who thought that learning was the prerogative of the elect. His aim was to broadcast it as widely as possible, and to this end he founded the Society for the Diffusion of Knowledge and wrote for it a series of popular manuals. He also devised a slide rule. He spent much time in attempting to perfect a calculating machine, and showed remarkable ingenuity in inventing and solving chess problems.

However, the one work that extended and perpetuated his fame on two continents was one which he probably regarded as a side issue. In the year 1852 he brought out his *Thesaurus of English Words and Phrases Classified and Arranged so as to Facilitate the Expression of Ideas and Assist in Literary Composition*. A second edition followed the next year, a third two years later, and still others in the next few years. The work was extended and corrected by his son. In 1911 the THOMAS Y. CROWELL COMPANY published the first edition prepared by the noted lexicographer and orientalist C. O. Sylvester Mawson. The edition of 1922— virtually a new book—was again the work of Dr. Mawson and the first to be called "International Edition." The long series of subsequent improved and enlarged editions finds its climax in the present revision in which the Publishers and Editors have spared neither effort nor expense to live up to and even better the standards of so remarkable a tradition.

Peter Roget died in West Malvern, on September 17, 1869, at the age of ninety.

Introduction xii

content to accept them at the value of their present currency, and have no concern with their etymologies, or with the history of their transformations; far less do I venture to thread the mazes of the vast labyrinth into which I should be led by any attempt at a general discrimination of synonyms. The difficulties I have had to contend with have already been sufficiently great, without this addition to my labors.

The most cursory glance over the pages of a dictionary will show that a great number of words are used in various senses, sometimes distinguished by slight shades of difference, but often diverging widely from their primary signification, and even, in some cases, bearing to it no perceptible relation. It may even happen that the very same word has two significations quite opposite to one another. This is the case with the verb *to cleave*, which means *to adhere tenaciously*, and also *to separate by a blow*. *To propugn* sometimes expresses *to attack;* at other times *to defend*. *To let* is *to hinder*, as well as *to permit*. *To ravel* means both *to entangle* and *to disentangle*. *Shameful* and *shameless* are nearly synonymous. *Priceless* may either mean *invaluable* or *of no value*. *Nervous* is used sometimes for *strong*, at other times for *weak*. The alphabetical Index at the end of this work sufficiently shows the multiplicity of uses to which, by the elasticity of language, the meaning of words has been stretched, so as to adapt them to a great variety of modified significations in subservience to the nicer shades of thought, which, under peculiarity of circumstances, require corresponding expression. Words thus admitting of different meanings have therefore to be arranged under each of the respective heads corresponding to these various acceptations. There are many words, again, which express ideas compounded of two elementary ideas belonging to different classes. It is therefore necessary to place these words respectively under each of the generic heads to which they relate. The necessity of these repetitions is increased by the circumstance, that ideas included under one class are often connected by relations of the same kind as the ideas which belong to another class. Thus we find the same relations of *order* and of *quantity* existing among the ideas of *Time* as well as those of *Space*. Sequence in the one is denoted by the same terms as sequence in the other; and the measures of time also express the measures of space. The cause and the effect are often designated by the same word. The word *Sound*, for instance, denotes both the impression made upon the ear by sonorous vibrations, and also the vibrations themselves, which are the cause or source of that impression. *Mixture* is used for the act of mixing, as well as for the product of that operation. *Taste* and *Smell* express both the sensations and the qualities of material bodies giving rise to them. *Thought* is the act of thinking; but the same word denotes also the idea resulting from that act. *Judgment* is the act of deciding, and also the decision come to. *Purchase* is the acquisition of a thing by payment, as well as the thing itself so acquired. *Speech* is both the act of speaking and the words spoken; and so on with regard to an endless multiplicity of words. Mind is essentially distinct from Matter; and yet, in all languages, the attributes of the one are metaphorically transferred to those of the other. Matter, in all its forms, is endowed by the figurative genius of every language with the functions which pertain to intellect; and we perpetually talk of its phenomena and of its powers, as if they resulted from the voluntary influence of one body on another, acting and reacting, impelling and being impelled, controlling and being controlled, as if animated by spontaneous energies and guided by specific intentions. On the other hand, expressions, of which the primary signification refers exclusively to the properties and actions of matter, are metaphorically applied to the phenomena of thought and volition, and even to the feelings and passions of the soul; and speaking of a *ray of hope*, a *shade of doubt,* a *flight of fancy,* a *flash of wit,* the *warmth of emotion,* or the *ebullitions of anger,* we are scarcely conscious that we are employing metaphors which have this material origin.

impartial; extravagant was simple *digressive;* and to *prevent* was properly to *precede* and *assist*. The old translations of the Scriptures furnish many striking examples of the alterations which time has brought in the signification of words. Much curious information on this subject is contained in Trench's *Lectures on the Study of Words*.

our SENTIMENT AND MORAL POWERS; including our *Feelings, Emotions, Passions,* and *Moral and Religious Sentiments*.[1]

The further subdivisions and minuter details will be best understood from an inspection of the tabular Synopsis of Categories prefixed to the Work, in which are specified the several *topics* or *heads of signification*, under which the words have been arranged. By the aid of this table, the reader will, with a little practice, readily discover the place which the particular topic he is in search of occupies in the series; and on turning to the page in the body of the work which contains it, he will find the group of expressions he requires, out of which he may cull those that are most appropriate to his purpose. For the convenience of reference, I have designated each separate group or heading by a particular number; so that if, during the search, any doubt or difficulty should occur, recourse may be had to the copious alphabetical Index of words at the end of the volume, which will at once indicate the number of the required group.[2]

The object I have proposed to myself in this work would have been but imperfectly attained if I had confined myself to a mere catalogue of words, and had omitted the numerous phrases and forms of expression composed of several words, which are of such frequent use as to entitle them to rank among the constituent parts of the language.[3] Very few of these verbal combinations, so essential to the knowledge of our native tongue, and so profusely abounding in its daily use, are to be met with in ordinary dictionaries. These phrases and forms of expression I have endeavored diligently to collect and to insert in their proper places, under the general ideas that they are designed to convey. Some of these conventional forms, indeed, partake of the nature of proverbial expressions; but actual proverbs, as such, being wholly of a didactic character, do not come within the scope of the present work; and the reader must therefore not expect to find them here inserted.[4] ...

It is hardly possible to find two words having in all respects the same meaning, and being therefore interchangeable; that is, admitting of being employed indiscriminately, the one or the other, in all their applications. The investigation of the distinctions to be drawn between words apparently synonymous forms a separate branch of inquiry, which I have not presumed here to enter upon; for the subject has already occupied the attention of much abler critics than myself, and its complete exhaustion would require the devotion of a whole life. The purpose of this work, it must be borne in mind, is, not to explain the signification of words, but simply to classify and arrange them according to the sense in which they are now used, and which I presume to be already known to the reader. I enter into no inquiry into the changes of meaning they may have undergone in the course of time.[5] I am

---

[1] It must necessarily happen in every system of classification framed with this view, that ideas and expressions arranged under one class must include also ideas relating to another class; for the operations of the *Intellect* generally involve also those of the *Will*, and vice versa; and our *Affections* and *Emotions*, in like manner, generally imply the agency both of the *Intellect* and of the *Will*. All that can be effected, therefore, is to arrange the words according to the principal or dominant idea they convey. *Teaching*, for example, although a Voluntary act, relates primarily to the Communication of Ideas, and is accordingly placed at No. 537, under Class IV, Division (II). On the other hand, *Choice, Conduct, Skill,* etc., although implying the co-operation of Voluntary with Intellectual acts, relate principally to the former, and are therefore arranged under Class V.

[2] It often happens that the same word admits of various applications, or may be used in different senses. In consulting the Index the reader will be guided to the number of the heading under which that word, in each particular acceptation, will be found, by means of *supplementary words;* which words, however, are not to be understood as explaining the meaning of the word to which they are annexed, but only as assisting in the required reference....

[3] For example:—To take time by the forelock;—to turn over a new leaf;—to show the white feather;—to have a finger in the pie;—to let the cat out of the bag;—to take care of number one;—to kill two birds with one stone, etc.

[4] See Trench, *On the Lessons in Proverbs.*

[5] Such changes are innumerable: for instance, the words *tyrant, parasite, sophist, churl, knave, villain,* anciently conveyed no opprobrious meaning. *Impertinent* merely expressed *irrelative;* and implied neither *rudeness* nor *intrusion,* as it does at present. *Indifferent* originally meant

Introduction

on this ground, also, that the present work founds a claim to utility. The review of a catalogue of words of analogous signification, will often suggest by association other trains of thought, which, presenting the subject under new and varied aspects, will vastly expand the sphere of our mental vision. Amidst the many objects thus brought within the range of our contemplation, some striking similitude or appropriate image, some excursive flight or brilliant conception, may flash on the mind, giving point and force to our arguments, awakening a responsive chord in the imagination or sensibility of the reader, and procuring for our reasonings a more ready access both to his understanding and to his heart.

It is of the utmost consequence that strict accuracy should regulate our use of language, and that every one should acquire the power and the habit of expressing his thoughts with perspicuity and correctness. Few, indeed, can appreciate the real extent and importance of that influence which language has always exercised on human affairs, or can be aware how often these are determined by causes much slighter than are apparent to a superficial observer. False logic, disguised under specious phraseology, too often gains the assent of the unthinking multitude, disseminating far and wide the seeds of prejudice and error. Truisms pass current, and wear the semblance of profound wisdom, when dressed up in the tinsel garb of antithetical phrases, or set off by an imposing pomp of paradox. By a confused jargon of involved and mystical sentences, the imagination is easily inveigled into a transcendental region of clouds, and the understanding beguiled into the belief that it is acquiring knowledge and approaching truth. A misapplied or misapprehended term is sufficient to give rise to fierce and interminable disputes; a misnomer has turned the tide of popular opinion; a verbal sophism has decided a party question; an artful watchword, thrown among combustible materials, has kindled the flame of deadly warfare, and changed the destiny of an empire.

In constructing the following system of classification of the ideas which are expressible by language, my chief aim has been to obtain the greatest amount of practical utility. I have accordingly adopted such principles of arrangement as appeared to me to be the simplest and most natural, and which would not require, either for their comprehension or application, any disciplined acumen, or depth of metaphysical or antiquarian lore. Eschewing all needless refinements and subtleties, I have taken as my guide the more obvious characters of the ideas for which expressions were to be tabulated, arranging them under such classes and categories as reflection and experience had taught me would conduct the inquirer most readily and quickly to the object of his search. Commencing with the ideas expressing abstract relations, I proceed to those which relate to space and to the phenomena of the material world, and lastly to those in which the mind is concerned, and which comprehend intellect, volition, and feeling; thus establishing six primary Classes of Categories.

1. The first of these classes comprehends ideas derived from the more general and ABSTRACT RELATIONS among things, such as *Existence, Resemblance, Quantity, Order, Number, Time, Power.*

2. The second class refers to SPACE and its various relations, including *Motion,* or change of place.

3. The third class includes all ideas that relate to the MATERIAL WORLD; namely, the *Properties of Matter,* such as *Solidity, Fluidity, Heat, Sound, Light,* and the *Phenomena* they present, as well as the simple *Perceptions* to which they give rise.

4. The fourth class embraces all ideas of phenomena relating to the INTELLECT and its operations; comprising the *Acquisition,* the *Retention,* and the *Communication of Ideas.*

5. The fifth class includes the ideas derived from the exercise of VOLITION; embracing the phenomena and results of our *Voluntary and Active Powers;* such as *Choice, Intention, Utility, Action, Antagonism, Authority, Compact, Property,* etc.

6. The sixth and last class comprehends all ideas derived from the operation of

vista of collateral ideas, which could not, without an extended and obtrusive episode, have been unfolded to his view; and often will the judicious insertion of a happy epithet, like a beam of sunshine in a landscape, illumine and adorn the subject which it touches, imparting new grace and giving life and spirit to the picture.

Every workman in the exercise of his art should be provided with proper implements. For the fabrication of complicated and curious pieces of mechanism, the artisan requires a corresponding assortment of various tools and instruments. For giving proper effect to the fictions of the drama, the actor should have at his disposal a well-furnished wardrobe, supplying the costumes best suited to the personages he is to represent. For the perfect delineation of the beauties of nature, the painter should have within reach of his pencil every variety and combination of hues and tints. Now, the writer, as well as the orator, employs for the accomplishment of his purposes the instrumentality of words; it is in words that he clothes his thoughts; it is by means of words that he depicts his feelings. It is therefore essential to his success that he be provided with a copious vocabulary, and that he possess an entire command of all the resources and appliances of his language. To the acquisition of this power no procedure appears more directly conducive than the study of a methodized system such as that now offered to his use.

The utility of the present work will be appreciated more especially by those who are engaged in the arduous process of translating into English a work written in another language. Simple as the operation may appear, on a superficial view, of rendering into English each of its sentences, the task of transfusing, with perfect exactness, the sense of the original, preserving at the same time the style and character of its composition, and reflecting with fidelity the mind and the spirit of the author, is a task of extreme difficulty. The cultivation of this useful department of literature was in ancient times strongly recommended both by Cicero and by Quintilian, as essential to the formation of a good writer and accomplished orator. Regarded simply as a mental exercise, the practice of translation is the best training for the attainment of that mastery of language and felicity of diction which are the sources of the highest oratory, and are requisite for the possession of a graceful and persuasive eloquence. By rendering ourselves the faithful interpreters of the thoughts and feelings of others, we are rewarded with the acquisition of greater readiness and facility in correctly expressing our own; as he who has best learned to execute the orders of a commander, becomes himself best qualified to command.

In the earliest periods of civilization, translators have been the agents for propagating knowledge from nation to nation, and the value of their labors has been inestimable; but, in the present age, when so many different languages have become the depositories of the vast treasures of literature and of science which have been accumulating for centuries, the utility of accurate translations has greatly increased and it has become a more important object to attain perfection in the art.

The use of language is not confined to its being the medium through which we communicate our ideas to one another; it fulfills a no less important function as an *instrument of thought;* not being merely its vehicle but giving it wings for flight. Metaphysicians are agreed that scarcely any of our intellectual operations could be carried on, to any considerable extent, without the agency of words. None but those who are conversant with the philosophy of mental phenomena can be aware of the immense influence that is exercised by language in promoting the development of our ideas, in fixing them in the mind, and in detaining them for steady contemplation. Into every process of reasoning, language enters as an essential element. Words are the instruments by which we form all our abstractions, by which we fashion and embody our ideas, and by which we are enabled to glide along a series of premises and conclusions with a rapidity so great as to leave in the memory no trace of the successive steps of the process; and we remain unconscious how much we owe to this potent auxiliary of the reasoning faculty. It is

As a general rule, I have deemed it incumbent on me to place words and phrases which appertain more especially to one head, also under the other heads to which they have a relation, whenever it appeared to me that this repetition would suit the convenience of the inquirer, and spare him the trouble of turning to other parts of the work; for I have always preferred to subject myself to the imputation of redundance, rather than incur the reproach of insufficiency.[1] When, however, the divergence of the associated from the primary idea is sufficiently marked, I have contented myself with making a reference to the place where the modified signification will be found. But in order to prevent needless extension, I have, in general, omitted *conjugate words*[2] which are so obviously derivable from those that are given in the same place, that the reader may safely be left to form them for himself. This is the case with adverbs derived from adjectives by the simple addition of the terminal syllable *-ly;* such as *closely, carefully, safely,* etc., from *close, careful, safe,* etc., and also with adjectives or participles immediately derived from the verbs which are already given. In all such cases, an "etc." indicates that reference is understood to be made to these roots. . . .

There are a multitude of words of a specific character which, although they properly occupy places in the columns of a dictionary, yet, having no relation to general ideas, do not come within the scope of this compilation, and are consequently omitted.[3] The names of objects in Natural History, and technical terms belonging exclusively to Science or to Art, or relating to particular operations, and of which the signification is restricted to those specific objects, come under this category. Exceptions must, however, be made in favor of such words as admit of metaphorical application to general subjects, with which custom has associated them, and of which they may be cited as being typical or illustrative. Thus, the word *Lion* will find a place under the head of *Courage,* of which it is regarded as the type. *Anchor,* being emblematic of *Hope,* is introduced among the words expressing that emotion; and in like manner, *butterfly* and *weathercock,* which are suggestive of fickleness, are included in the category of *Irresolution.*

With regard to the admission of many words and expressions, which the classical reader might be disposed to condemn as vulgarisms, or which he, perhaps, might stigmatize as pertaining rather to the slang than to the legitimate language of the day, I would beg to observe, that, having due regard to the uses to which this work was to be adapted, I did not feel myself justified in excluding them solely on that ground, if they possessed an acknowledged currency in general intercourse. It is obvious that, with respect to degrees of conventionality, I could not have attempted to draw any strict lines of demarcation; and far less could I have presumed to erect any absolute standard of purity. My object, be it remembered, is not to regulate the use of words, but simply to supply and to suggest such as may be wanted on occasion, leaving the proper selection entirely to the discretion and taste of the employer.[4] If a novelist or a dramatist, for example, proposed to

[1] Frequent repetitions of the same series of expressions, accordingly, will be met with under various headings. For example, the word *Chance* has two significations, distinct from one another: the one implying the *absence of an assignable cause;* in which case it comes under the category of the relation of Causation, and occupies the No. 156: the other, the *absence of design,* in which latter sense it ranks under the operations of the Will, and has assigned to it the place No. 621. I have, in like manner, distinguished *Sensibility, Pleasure, Pain, Taste,* etc., according as they relate to *Physical,* or to *Moral Affections;* the former being found at Nos. 375, 377, 378, 390, etc., and the latter at Nos. 822, 827, 828, 850, etc.

[2] By "*conjugate* or *paronymous* words is meant, correctly speaking, different parts of speech from the same root, which exactly correspond in point of meaning."—*A Selection of English Synonyms,* edited by Archbishop Whately.

[3] [This rule was not in all cases rigorously observed by the author; and later editors have included such words in the interest of the general writer.]

[4] [In keeping with the trend of the times the editors of subsequent editions have progressively increased the space given over to colloquialisms, dialect terms and slang. The present edition is almost as complete with respect to these much-neglected groups of words in our language as with regard to standard expressions. All substandard or nonstandard terms, however, have been specially marked with appropriate labels.]

Introduction

delineate some vulgar personage, he would wish to have the power of putting into the mouth of the speaker expressions that would accord with his character; just as the actor, to revert to a former comparison, who had to personate a peasant, would choose for his attire the most homely garb, and would have just reason to complain if the theatrical wardrobe furnished him with no suitable costume....

I have admitted a considerable number of words and phrases borrowed from other languages, some of which may be considered as already naturalized; while others, though avowedly foreign, are frequently employed in English composition, particularly in familiar style, on account of their being peculiarly expressive, and because we have no corresponding words of equal force in our own language.[1] The rapid advances which are being made in scientific knowledge, and consequent improvement in all the arts of life, and the extension of those arts and sciences to so many new purposes and objects, create a continual demand for the formation of new terms to express new agencies, new wants, and new combinations. Such terms, from being at first merely technical, are rendered, by more general use, familiar to the multitude, and having a well-defined acceptation, are eventually incorporated into the language, which they contribute to enlarge and to enrich. *Neologies* of this kind are perfectly legitimate, and highly advantageous; and they necessarily introduce those gradual and progressive changes which every language is destined to undergo.[2] ...

A work constructed on the plan of classification I have proposed might, if ably executed, be of great value, in tending to limit the fluctuations to which language has always been subject, by establishing an authoritative standard for its regulation. Future historians, philologists, and lexicographers, when investigating the period when new words were introduced, or discussing the import given at the present time to the old, might find their labors lightened by being enabled to appeal to such a standard, instead of having to search for data among the scattered writings of the age. Nor would its utility be confined to a single language; for the principles of its construction are universally applicable to all languages, whether living or dead. On the same plan of classification there might be formed a French, a German, a Latin, or a Greek Thesaurus, possessing, in their respective spheres, the same advantages as those of the English model.[3] Still more useful would be a conjunction of these methodized compilations in two languages, the French and English, for instance; the columns of each being placed in parallel juxtaposition. No means yet devised would so greatly facilitate the acquisition of the one language, by those who are acquainted with the other: none would afford such ample assistance to the translator in either language; and none would supply such ready and effectual means of instituting an accurate comparison between them, and of fairly appreciating their respective merits and defects. In a still higher degree would all those advantages be combined and multiplied in a *Polyglot Lexicon* constructed on this system.

Metaphysicians engaged in the more profound investigation of the Philosophy of Language will be materially assisted by having the ground thus prepared for them, in a previous analysis and classification of our ideas; for such classification of ideas is the true basis on which words, which are their symbols, should be classi-

---

[1] All these words and phrases are printed in Italics.

[2] Thus, in framing the present classification, I have frequently felt the want of substantive terms corresponding to abstract qualities or ideas denoted by certain adjectives; and have been often tempted to invent words that might express these abstractions: but I have yielded to this temptation only in the four following instances; having framed from the adjectives *irrelative, amorphous, sinistral,* and *gaseous,* the abstract nouns *irrelation, amorphism, sinistrality,* and *gaseity.* I have ventured also to introduce the adjective *intersocial,* to express the active voluntary relations between man and man. [Note that all these words have become fairly generally accepted.]

[3] [Similar works in other languages have since appeared, notably *Dictionnaire Idéologique* by T. Robertson (Paris, 1859); *Deutscher Sprachschatz* by D. Sanders (Hamburg, 1878), and *Deutscher Wortschatz, oder Der passende Ausdruck* by A. Schelling (Stuttgart, 1892).]

fied.[1] It is by such analysis alone that we can arrive at a clear perception of the relation which these symbols bear to their corresponding ideas, or can obtain a correct knowledge of the elements which enter into the formation of compound ideas, and of the exclusions by which we arrive at the abstractions so perpetually resorted to in the process of reasoning, and in the communication of our thoughts.

Lastly, such analyses alone can determine the principles on which a strictly *Philosophical Language* might be constructed. The probable result of the construction of such a language would be its eventual adoption by every civilized nation; thus realizing that splendid aspiration of philanthropists,—the establishment of a Universal Language. However utopian such a project may appear to the present generation, and however abortive may have been the former endeavors of Bishop Wilkins and others to realize it,[2] its accomplishment is surely not beset with greater difficulties than have impeded the progress to many other beneficial objects, which in former times appeared to be no less visionary, and which yet were successfully achieved, in later ages, by the continued and persevering exertions of the human intellect. Is there at the present day, then, any ground for despair, that at some future stage of that higher civilization to which we trust the world is gradually tending, some new and bolder effort of genius towards the solution of this great problem may be crowned with success, and compass an object of such vast and paramount utility? Nothing, indeed, would conduce more directly to bring about a golden age of union and harmony among the several nations and races of mankind than the removal of that barrier to the interchange of thought and mutual good understanding between man and man, which is now interposed by the diversity of their respective languages.

P. M. ROGET.

[1] The principle by which I have been guided in framing my verbal classification is the same as that which is employed in the various departments of Natural History. Thus the sectional divisions I have formed, correspond to Natural Families in Botany and Zoology, and the filiation of words presents a network analogous to the natural filiation of plants or animals.

The following are the only publications that have come to my knowledge in which any attempt has been made to construct a systematic arrangement of ideas with a view to their expression. The earliest of these, supposed to be at least nine hundred years old, is the AMERA CÓSHA, or *Vocabulary of the Sanscrit Language,* by Amera Sanha, of which an English translation, by the late Henry T. Colebrooke, was printed at Serampoor, in the year 1808. The classification of words is there, as might be expected, exceedingly imperfect and confused, especially in all that relates to abstract ideas or mental operations. This will be apparent from the very title of the first section, which comprehends "*Heaven, Gods, Demons, Fire, Air, Velocity, Eternity, Much*"; while *Sin, Virtue, Happiness, Destiny, Cause, Nature, Intellect, Reasoning, Knowledge, Senses, Tastes, Odors, Colors,* are all included and jumbled together in the fourth section. A more logical order, however, pervades the sections relating to natural objects, such as *Seas, Earth, Towns, Plants,* and *Animals,* which form separate classes; exhibiting a remarkable effort at analysis at so remote a period of Indian literature.

The well-known work of Bishop Wilkins, entitled, *An Essay towards a Real Character and a Philosophical Language,* published in 1668, had for its object the formation of a system of symbols which might serve as a universal language. It professed to be founded on a "scheme of analysis of the things or notions to which names were to be assigned"; but notwithstanding the immense labor and ingenuity expended in the construction of this system, it was soon found to be far too abstruse and recondite for practical application.

In the year 1797, there appeared in Paris an anonymous work, entitled "PASIGRAPHIE *ou premiers éléments du nouvel art-science d'écrire et d'imprimer une langue de manière à être lu et entendu dans toute autre langue sans traduction,*" of which an edition in German was also published. It contains a great number of tabular schemes of categories; all of which appear to be excessively arbitrary and artificial, and extremely difficult of application, as well as of apprehension.

[2] "The Languages," observes Horne Tooke, "which are commonly used throughout the world, are much more simple and easy, convenient and philosophical, than Wilkins's scheme for a *real character;* or than any other scheme that has been at any other time imagined or proposed for the purpose."—Επεα Πτερόεντα, p. 125.

SYNOPSIS OF CATEGORIES

Classes: I. ABSTRACT RELATIONS; II. SPACE; III. MATTER; IV. INTELLECT; V. VOLITION; VI. AFFECTIONS

CLASS ONE: Abstract relations
- Section I. Existence
    1. Being in the Abstract
        - 1. Existence. 2. Nonexistence.
    2. Being in the Concrete
        - 3. Substantiality. 4. Unsubstantiality.
    3. Formal Existence
        - Internal conditions
            - 5. Intrinsicality.
        - External conditions
            - 6. Extrinsicality.
    4. Modal Existence
        - Absolute
            - 7. State.
        - Relative
            - 8. Circumstance.
- Section II. Relation
    1. Absolute Relation
        - 9. Relation. 10. Irrelation. 11. Consanguinity. 12. Correlation. 13. Identity. 14. Contrariety. 15. Difference.
    2. Continuous Relation
        - 16. Uniformity. 16a. Nonuniformity.
    3. Partial Relation
        - 17. Similarity. 18. Dissimilarity. 19. Imitation. 20. Nonimitation. 21. Copy. 22. Prototype.
    4. General Relation
        - 23. Agreement. 24. Disagreement.
- Section III. Quantity
    1. Simple Quantity
        - 25. Quantity. 26. Degree.
    2. Comparative Quantity
        - 27. Equality. 28. Inequality. 29. Mean. 30. Compensation.
        - Quantity by Comparison with a Standard
            - 31. Greatness. 32. Smallness.
        - Quantity by Comparison with a Similar Object
            - 33. Superiority. 34. Inferiority.
        - Changes in Quantity
            - 35. Increase. 36. Decrease.
    3. Conjunctive Quantity
        - 37. Addition. 38. Deduction. 39. Adjunct. 39a. Decrement. 40. Remainder. 41. Mixture. 42. Simpleness. 43. Junction. 44. Disjunction. 45. Bond.

CLASS ONE (*Continued*)

    46. Coherence. 47. Incoherence. 48. Combination. 49. Decomposition.

  4. Concrete Quantity

    50. Whole. 51. Part. 52. Completeness. 53. Incompleteness. 54. Composition. 55. Exclusion. 56. Component. 57. Extraneousness.

Section IV. Order

  1. Order in General

    58. Order. 59. Disorder. 60. Arrangement. 61. Derangement.

  2. Consecutive Order

    62. Precedence. 63. Sequence. 64. Precursor. 65. Sequel. 66. Beginning. 67. End. 68. Middle. 69. Continuity. 70. Discontinuity. 71. Term.

  3. Collective Order

    72. Assemblage. 73. Dispersion. 74. Focus.

  4. Distributive Order

    75. Class. 76. Inclusion. 77. Noninclusion. 78. Generality. 79. Speciality.

  5. Order as Regards Categories

    80. Rule. 81. Multiformity. 82. Conformity. 83. Unconformity.

Section V. Number

  1. Number in the Abstract

    84. Number. 85. Numeration. 86. List.

  2. Determinate Number

    87. Unity. 87a. Zero. 88. Accompaniment. 89. Duality. 90. Duplication. 91. Bisection. 92. Triality. 93. Triplication. 94. Trisection. 95. Quaternity. 96. Quadruplication. 97. Quadrisection. 98. Five, etc. 99. Quinquesection, etc.

  3. Indeterminate Number

    100. Plurality. 101. Fraction. 102. Numerousness. 103. Fewness. 104. Repetition. 105. Infinity.

Section VI. Time

  1. Absolute Time

    106. Time. 107. Timelessness. 108. Period. 109. Course. 109a. Interim. 110. Durability. 111. Transience. 112. Perpetuity. 113. Instantaneity. 114. Chronometry. 115. Anachronism.

  2. Relative Time

    i. Time with Reference to Succession

      116. Priority. 117. Posteriority. 118. Present Time. 119. Different Time. 120. Synchronism. 121. Futurity. 122. Preterition.

    ii. Time with Reference to a Particular Period

      123. Newness. 124. Oldness.

    Divisions of the Day

      125. Morning; Noon. 126. Evening; Night

Synopsis

CLASS ONE (*Continued*)

Divisions of the Year
126a. Season.

Time of Life
127. Youth. 128. Age. 129. Youngling. 130. Elder. 131. Adulthood.

iii. Time with Reference to an Effect or Purpose
132. Earliness; Punctuality. 133. Lateness. 134. Timeliness. 135. Untimeliness.

3. Recurrent Time
136. Frequency. 137. Infrequency. 138. Regularity of Recurrence; Periodicity. 139. Irregularity of Recurrence.

Section VII. Change

1. Simple Change
140. Change. 141. Permanence. 142. Cessation. 143. Continuance. 144. Conversion. 145. Reversion. 146. Revolution. 147. Substitution. 148. Interchange.

2. Complex Change
149. Changeableness. 150. Stability.

Present Events
151. Eventuality.

Future Events
152. Imminence.

Section VIII. Causation

1. Constancy of Sequence in Events
153. Cause. 154. Effect. 155. Attribution. 156. Chance.

2. Connection between Cause and Effect
157. Potence. **158. Impotence.** 158a. Electricity. **159. Strength.** 159a. Virility. 160. Weakness. 160a. Effeminacy.

3. Power in Operation
161. Production. 162. Destruction. 163. Reproduction. 164. Producer. 165. Destroyer. 166. Ancestry. 167. Posterity. 168. Productiveness. 169. Unproductiveness. 170. Agency. 171. Energy. 172. Inertness. 173. Violence. 174. Moderation.

4. Indirect Power
175. Influence. 175a. Noninfluence. 176. Tendency. 177. Liability.

5. Combination of Causes
178. Concurrence. 179. Counteraction.

CLASS TWO: Space

Section I. Space in General

1. Abstract Space
180. Space. 180a. Inextension. 181. Region. 182. Country. 183. The Country.

2. Relative Space
184. Location. 185. Dislocation.

3. Existence in Space
186. Presence. 187. Absence. 188. In-

Synopsis

CLASS TWO (*Continued*)

habitant. 189. Abode. 190. Contents. 191. Receptacle.

Section II. Dimensions

1. General Dimensions

192. Size. 193. Littleness. 194. Expansion. 195. Contraction. 196. Distance. 197. Nearness. 198. Interval. 199. Contiguity.

2. Linear Dimensions

200. Length. 201. Shortness. 202. Breadth; Thickness. 203. Narrowness; Thinness. 204. Layer. 205. Filament. 206. Height. 207. Lowness. 208. Depth. 209. Shallowness. 210. Summit. 211. Base. 212. Verticality. 213. Horizontality. 214. Pendency. 215. Support. 216. Parallelism. 217. Obliquity. 218. Inversion. 219. Crossing.

3. Centrical Dimensions

i. General Centrical Dimensions

220. Exteriority. 221. Interiority. 222. Centrality. 223. Covering. 224. Lining. 225. Investment. 226. Divestment. 227. Circumjacence. 228. Interjacence. 229. Circumscription. 230. Outline. 231. Edge. 232. Enclosure. 233. Limit.

ii. Special Centrical Dimensions

234. Front. 235. Rear. 236. Side. 237. Contraposition. 238. Dextrality. 239. Sinistrality.

Section III. Form

1. General Form

240. Form. 241. Formlessness. 242. Symmetry. 243. Distortion.

2. Special Form

244. Angularity. 245. Curvature. 246. Straightness. 247. Circularity. 248. Convolution. 249. Rotundity.

3. Superficial Form

250. Convexity. 251. Flatness. 252. Concavity. 253. Sharpness. 254. Bluntness. 255. Smoothness. 256. Roughness. 257. Notch. 258. Fold. 259. Furrow. 260. Opening. 261. Closure. 262. Perforator. 263. Stopper.

Section IV. Motion

1. Motion in General

264. Motion. 265. Quiescence. 266. Travel. 267. Navigation. 267a. Aeronautics. 268. Traveler. 269. Mariner. 269a. Aeronaut. 270. Transference. 271. Carrier. 272. Vehicle. 273. Ship. 273a. Aircraft.

2. Degrees of Motion

274. Velocity. 275. Slowness.

3. Motion Conjoined with Force

276. Impulse. 277. Recoil.

Synopsis

CLASS TWO (*Continued*)

4. Motion with Reference to Direction

278. Direction. 279. Deviation. 280. Precession. 281. Sequence. 282. Progression. 283. Regression. 284. Propulsion. 285. Traction. 286. Approach. 287. Recession. 288. Attraction. 289. Repulsion. 290. Convergence. 291. Divergence. 292. Arrival. 293. Departure. 294. Ingress. 295. Egress. 296. Reception. 297. Ejection. 298. Eating. 299. Excretion. 300. Insertion. 301. Extraction. 302. Passage. 303. Overrunning. 304. Shortcoming. 305. Ascent. 306. Descent. 307. Elevation. 308. Depression. 309. Leap. 310. Plunge. 311. Circuity. 312. Rotation. 313. Evolution. 314. Oscillation. 315. Agitation.

CLASS THREE: Matter

Section I. Matter in General

316. Materiality. 317. Immateriality. 318. World. 319. Gravity. 320. Levity.

Section II. Inorganic Matter

1. Solid Matter

321. Density. 322. Rarity. 323. Hardness. 324. Softness. 325. Elasticity. 326. Inelasticity. 327. Toughness. 328. Brittleness. 329. Texture. 330. Pulverulence. 331. Friction. 332. Lubrication.

2. Fluid Matter

i. Fluids in General

333. Fluidity. 334. Gaseity. 335. Liquefaction. 336. Vaporization.

ii. Specific Fluids

337. Water. 338. Air. 339. Moisture. 340. Dryness. 341. Ocean. 342. Land. 343. Inlet; Gulf. 343a. Lake; Pool. 344. Plain. 345. Marsh. 346. Island.

iii. Fluids in Motion

347. Flow. 348. Stream. 349. Wind. 350. Conduit. 351. Air Passage.

3. Imperfect Fluids

352. Semiliquidity. 353. Bubble; Cloud. 354. Pulpiness. 355. Unctuousness. 356. Oil. 356a. Resin.

Section III. Organic Matter

1. Vitality

i. Vitality in General

357. Organic Matter. 358. Inorganic Matter. 359. Life. 360. Death. 361. Killing. 362. Corpse. 363. Interment.

ii. Special Vitality

364. Animality. 365. Vegetation. 366. Animals. 367. Vegetables. 368. Zoology. 369. Botany. 370. Animal Culture.

CLASS THREE (*Continued*)

        371. Agriculture. 372. Mankind.
        373. Male. 374. Female.

2. Sensation
   i. Sensation in General
        375. Physical Sensibility. 376. Physical Insensibility. 377. Physical Pleasure.
        378. Physical Pain.
   ii. Special Sensation
     (1) Touch
        379. Touch. 380. Sensations of Touch.
        381. Numbness.
     (2) Heat
        382. Heat. 383. Cold. 384. Calefaction.
        385. Refrigeration. 386. Heater.
        387. Cooler. 388. Fuel. 389. Thermometer.
     (3) Taste
        390. Taste. 391. Insipidity. 392. Pungency. 392a. Tobacco. 393. Condiment.
        394. Savoriness. 395. Unsavoriness.
        396. Sweetness. 397. Sourness.
     (4) Smell
        398. Odor. 399. Inodorousness.
        400. Fragrance. 401. Fetor.
     (5) Sound
       a. Sound in General
        402. Sound. 403. Silence. 404. Loudness.
        405. Faintness.
       b. Specific Sounds
        406. Snap. 407. Roll. 408. Resonance.
        408a. Nonresonance. 409. Sibilation.
        410. Stridor. 411. Cry. 412. Ululation.
       c. Musical Sounds
        413. Concord. 414. Discord. 415. Music.
        416. Musician. 417. Musical Instruments.
       d. Perception of Sound
        418. Hearing. 419. Deafness.
     (6) Light
       a. Light in General
        420. Light. 421. Darkness. 422. Dimness. 423. Luminary. 424. Shade.
        425. Transparency. 426. Opacity.
        427. Semitransparency.
       b. Specific Light
        428. Color. 429. Colorlessness.
        430. Whiteness. 431. Blackness.
        432. Grayness. 433. Brownness.
        434. Redness. 435. Greenness. 436. Yellowness. 437. Purpleness. 438. Blueness.
        439. Orange. 440. Variegation.
        440a. Discoloration.
       c. Perception of Light
        441. Vision. 442. Blindness. 443. Defective Vision. 444. Spectator. 445. Optical Instruments. 446. Visibility.
        447. Invisibility. 448. Appearance.
        449. Disappearance.

Synopsis

CLASS FOUR: Intellect
    Division (I) Formation of Ideas
        Section I. Operations of Intellect in General
            450. Intellect. 450a. Absence of Intellect.
            451. Thought. 452. Incogitance.
            453. Idea. 454. Topic.
        Section II. Precursory Conditions and Operations of Intellect
            455. Curiosity. 456. Incuriosity.
            457. Attention. 458. Inattention.
            459. Care. 460. Neglect. 461. Inquiry.
            462. Answer. 463. Experiment.
            464. Comparison. 465. Discrimination.
            465a. Indiscrimination. 466. Measurement.
        Section III. Materials for Reasoning
            467. Evidence. 468. Counterevidence.
            469. Qualification.
            Degrees of Evidence
            470. Possibility. 471. Impossibility.
            472. Probability. 473. Improbability.
            474. Certainty. 475. Uncertainty.
        Section IV. Reasoning Processes
            476. Reasoning. 477. Sophistry.
            477a. Intuition. 478. Demonstration.
            479. Confutation.
        Section V. Results of Reasoning
            480. Judgment. 481. Misjudgment.
            481a. Discovery. 482. Overestimation.
            483. Underestimation. 484. Belief.
            485. Unbelief; Doubt. 486. Credulity.
            487. Incredulity. 488. Assent. 489. Dissent. 490. Knowledge. 491. Ignorance.
            492. Scholar. 493. Ignoramus.
            494. Truth. 495. Error. 496. Maxim.
            497. Absurdity.
            Faculties
            498. Intelligence; Wisdom. 499. Unintelligence; Folly. 500. Sage. 501. Fool.
            502. Sanity. 503. Insanity. 504. Madman.
        Section VI. Extension of Thought
          1. Extension of Thought to the Past
            505. Memory. 506. Oblivion.
          2. Extension of Thought to the Future
            507. Expectation. 508. Inexpectation.
            509. Disappointment. 510. Foresight.
            511. Prediction. 512. Omen. 513. Oracle.
        Section VII. Creative Thought
            514. Supposition. 515. Imagination.
    Division (II). Communication of Ideas
        Section I. Nature of Ideas Communicated
            516. Meaning. 517. Unmeaningness.
            518. Intelligibility. 519. Unintelligibility.
            520. Equivocalness. 521. Figure of Speech.
            522. Interpretation. 523. Misinterpretation. 524. Interpreter.
        Section II. Modes of Communication
            525. Manifestation. 526. Latency.
            527. Information. 528. Concealment.

CLASS FOUR (*Continued*)

529. Disclosure. 530. Ambush; Hiding. 531. Publication. 532. News. 532a. Telephone and Wireless Communication. 533. Secret. 534. Messenger. 535. Affirmation. 536. Negation. 537. Teaching. 538. Misteaching. 539. Learning. 540. Teacher. 541. Learner. 542. School. 543. Veracity. 544. Falsehood. 545. Deception. 545a. Undeception. 546. Untruth. 547. Dupe. 548. Deceiver. 549. Exaggeration.

Section III. Means of Communicating Ideas
1. Natural Means of Communicating Ideas

550. Indication. 551. Record. 552. Obliteration. 553. Recorder. 554. Representation. 555. Misrepresentation.

Arts of Design

556. Graphic Arts. 557. Sculpture. 558. Engraving. 559. Artist.

2. Conventional Means of Communicating Ideas
i. Language Generally

560. Language. 561. Letter. 562. Word. 563. Barbarianism; Colloquialism. 564. Nomenclature. 565. Misnomer; Anonymity. 566. Phrase. 567. Grammar. 568. Ungrammaticism.

Style; Mode of Expression

569. Diction. 570. Perspicuity. 571. Imperspicuity. 572. Conciseness. 573. Diffuseness. 574. Vigor. 575. Feebleness. 576. Plainness. 577. Ornament. 578. Elegance. 579. Inelegance.

ii. Spoken Language

580. Voice. 581. Aphonia. 582. Speech. 583. Imperfect Speech. 584. Loquacity. 585. Taciturnity. 586. Allocution. 587. Response. 588. Interlocution. 589. Soliloquy.

iii. Written Language

590. Writing. 591. Printing. 592. Correspondence. 593. Book. 594. Description. 595. Dissertation. 596. Compendium. 597. Poetry. 598. Prose. 599. Drama.

CLASS FIVE: Volition
Division (I). Individual Volition
Section I. Volition in General
1. Acts of Volition

600. Will. 601. Necessity. 602. Willingness. 603. Unwillingness. 604. Resolution. 604a. Perseverance. 605. Irresolution. 606. Obstinacy. 607. Tergiversation. 608. Caprice. 609. Choice. 609a. Choicelessness. 610. Rejection. 611. Predetermination. 612. Impulse. 613. Habit. 614. Want of Habit.

Synopsis

CLASS FIVE (*Continued*)

2. Causes of Volition
615. Motive. 616. Dissuasion. 617. Allurement. 618. Bribery. 619. Pretext

Section II. Prospective Volition

1. Conceptional Volition
620. Intention. 621. Chance. 622. Pursuit. 623. Avoidance. 624. Abandonment. 625. Business. 626. Plan. 627. Way. 628. Mid-course. 629. Circuit. 630. Requirement.

2. Subservience of Volition to Ends

a. Actual Subservience
631. Instrumentality. 632. Means. 633. Instrument. 634. Equipment. 635. Materials. 636. Store. 637. Provision. 638. Waste. 639. Sufficiency. 640. Insufficiency. 641. Redundance.

b. Degree of Subservience
642. Importance. 643. Unimportance. 644. Utility. 645. Inutility. 646. Expedience. 647. Inexpedience. 648. Goodness. 649. Badness. 650. Perfection. 651. Imperfection. 652. Cleanness. 653. Uncleanness. 654. Health. 655. Disease. 656. Salubrity. 657. Insalubrity. 658. Improvement. 659. Deterioration. 660. Restoration. 661. Relapse. 662. Remedy. 663. Bane.

c. Contingent Subservience
664. Safety. 665. Danger. 666. Safeguard; Refuge. 667. Source of Danger. 668. Warning. 669. Alarm. 670. Preservation. 671. Escape. 672. Deliverance.

3. Precursory Measures
673. Preparation. 674. Nonpreparation. 675. Essay. 676. Undertaking. 677. Use. 678. Disuse. 679. Misuse.

Section III. Voluntary Action

1. Simple Voluntary Action
680. Action. 681. Inaction. 682. Activity 683. Inactivity. 684. Haste. 685. Leisure. 686. Exertion. 687. Repose. 688. Fatigue. 689. Refreshment. 690. Agent. 691. Workshop.

2. Complex Voluntary Action
692. Conduct. 693. Direction. 694. Director. 695. Advice. 696. Council. 697. Precept. 698. Skill. 699. Unskillfulness. 700. Proficient. 701. Bungler. 702. Cunning. 703. Artlessness.

Section IV. Antagonism

1. Conditional Antagonism
704. Difficulty. 705. Facility.

2. Active Antagonism
706. Hindrance. 707. Aid. 708. Opposition. 709. Co-operation. 710. Opponent. **711. Auxiliary. 712. Party. 713. Discord.**

CLASS FIVE (*Continued*)

714. Concord. 715. Defiance. 716. Attack. 717. Defense. 718. Retaliation. 719. Resistance. 720. Contention. 721. Peace. 722. Warfare. 723. Pacification. 724. Mediation. 725. Submission. 726. Combatant. 727. Arms. 728. Arena.

Section V. Results of Action

729. Completion. 730. Noncompletion. 731. Success. 732. Failure. 733. Trophy. 734. Prosperity. 735. Adversity. 736. Mediocrity.

Division (II). Intersocial Volition

Section I. General Intersocial Volition

737. Authority. 738. Laxity. 739. Severity. 740. Lenity. 741. Command. 742. Disobedience. 743. Obedience. 744. Compulsion. 745. Master. 746. Servant. 747. Insignia of Authority. 748. Freedom. 749. Subjection. 750. Liberation. 751. Restraint. 752. Prison; Shackle. 753. Jailer. 754. Prisoner. 755. Commission. 756. Abrogation. 757. Resignation. 758. Consignee. 759. Deputy.

Section II. Special Intersocial Volition

760. Permission. 761. Prohibition. 762. Consent. 763. Offer. 764. Refusal. 765. Request. 766. Deprecation. 767. Petitioner.

Section III. Conditional Intersocial Volition

768. Promise. 769. Compact. 770. Conditions. 771. Security. 772. Observance. 773. Nonobservance. 774. Compromise.

Section IV. Possessive Relations

1. Property in General

775. Acquisition. 776. Loss. 777. Possession. 777a. Nonpossession. 778. Participation. 779. Possessor. 780. Property. 781. Retention. 782. Relinquishment.

2. Transfer of Property

783. Transfer. 784. Giving. 785. Receiving. 786. Apportionment. 787. Lending. 788. Borrowing. 789. Taking. 790. Restitution. 791. Theft. 792. Thief. 793. Booty.

3. Interchange of Property

794. Barter. 795. Purchase. 796. Sale. 797. Merchant. 798. Merchandise. 799. Mart.

4. Monetary Relations

800. Money. 801. Treasurer. 802. Treasury. 803. Wealth. 804. Poverty. 805. Credit. 806. Debt. 807. Payment. 808. Nonpayment. 809. Expenditure. 810. Receipt. 811. Accounts. 812. Price. 813. Discount. 814. Dearness. 815. Cheapness. 816. Liberality.

Synopsis

CLASS FIVE (*Continued*)

817. Economy. 818. Prodigality. 819. Parsimony.

CLASS SIX: Affections

Section I. Affections Generally

820. Affection. 821. Feeling. 822. Sensibility. 823. Insensibility. 824. Excitation. 825. Excitability. 826. Inexcitability.

Section II. Personal Affections

1. Passive Affections

827. Pleasure. 828. Pain. 829. Pleasurableness. 830. Painfulness. 831. Content. 832. Discontent. 833. Regret. 834. Relief. 835. Aggravation. 836. Cheerfulness. 837. Sadness. 838. Rejoicing. 839. Lamentation. 840. Amusement. 841. Weariness. 842. Wit. 843. Dullness. 844. Humorist.

2. Discriminative Affections

845. Beauty. 846. Ugliness. 847. Ornamentation. 848. Blemish. 849. Simplicity. 850. Taste. 851. Vulgarity. 852. Fashion. 853. Affectation. 854. Fop. 855. Ridiculousness. 856. Ridicule. 857. Laughingstock.

3. Prospective Affections

858. Hope. 859. Hopelessness. 860. Fear. 861. Courage. 862. Cowardice. 863. Rashness. 864. Caution. 865. Desire. 866. Indifference. 867. Dislike. 868. Fastidiousness. 869. Satiety.

4. Contemplative Affections

870. Wonder. 871. Unastonishment. 872. Prodigy.

5. Extrinsic Affections

873. Repute. 874. Disrepute. 875. Nobility. 876. Commonalty. 877. Title. 878. Pride. 879. Humility. 880. Vanity. 881. Modesty. 882. Ostentation. 883. Celebration. 884. Boasting. 885. Arrogance; Insolence. 886. Servility. 887. Bluster.

Section III. Sympathetic Affections

1. Social Affections

888. Friendship. 889. Enmity. 890. Friend. 891. Enemy. 892. Sociality. 893. Insociality. 894. Courtesy. 895. Discourtesy. 896. Congratulation. 897. Love. 898. Hate. 899. Favorite. 900. Resentment. 901. Ill-humor. 902. Love-making; Endearment. 903. Marriage. 904. Celibacy. 905. Divorce; Widowhood.

2. Diffusive Affections

906. Benevolence. 907. Malevolence. 908. Malediction. 909. Threat. 910. Misanthropy. 911. Philanthropist. 912. Benefactor. 913. Evildoer.

CLASS SIX (Continued)

3. Special Sympathetic Affections
914. Pity. 914a. Pitilessness. 915. Condolence.

4. Retrospective Sympathetic Affections
916. Gratitude. 917. Ingratitude.
918. Forgiveness. 919. Revenge.
920. Jealousy. 921. Envy.

Section IV. Moral Affections

1. Moral Obligations
922. Right. 923. Wrong. 924. Dueness. 925. Undueness. 926. Duty. 927. Dereliction of Duty.

2. Moral Sentiments
928. Respect. 929. Disrespect. 930. Contempt. 931. Approbation. 932. Disapprobation. 933. Flattery. 934. Detraction. 935. Commender. 936. Detractor. 937. Vindication. 938. Accusation.

3. Moral Conditions
939. Probity. 940. Improbity. 941. Justice. 941a. Injustice. 942. Unselfishness. 943. Selfishness. 944. Virtue. 945. Vice. 946. Innocence. 947. Guilt. 948. Good Person. 949. Bad Person. 950. Penitence. 951. Impenitence. 952. Atonement.

4. Moral Practice
953. Temperance. 954. Intemperance. 954a. Sensualist. 955. Asceticism. 956. Fasting. 957. Gluttony. 958. Sobriety. 959. Drunkenness. 960. Purity. 961. Impurity. 962. Libertine.

5. Moral Institutions
963. Legality. 964. Illegality. 965. Jurisdiction. 966. Tribunal. 967. Judge. 968. Lawyer. 969. Lawsuit. 970. Acquittal. 971. Condemnation. 972. Punishment. 973. Reward. 974. Penalty. 975. Scourge.

Section V. Religious Affections

1. Superhuman Beings and Regions
976. Deity. 977. Angel. 978. Satan. 979. Mythic and Pagan Deities. 980. Evil Spirits. 980a. Specter. 981. Heaven. 982. Hell.

2. Religious Doctrines
983. Theology. 983a. Orthodoxy. 984. Heterodoxy. 985. Revelation (Biblical). 986. Sacred Writings (non-Biblical).

3. Religious Sentiments
987. Piety. 988. Impiety. 989. Irreligion. 990. Worship. 991. Idolatry.

4. Occult Arts and Sciences
992. Sorcery. 993. Spell. 994. Esoteric Sciences.

5. Religious Institutions
995. Churchdom. 996. Clergy. 997. Laity. 998. Rite. 999. Canonicals. 1000. Temple.

HOW TO USE THE BOOK

Always turn first to the Index Guide

The text part of the book consists of comprehensive lists of related words and phrases. In one of these lists is the answer to your problem. The Index Guide can direct you to the list you need.

TO FIND THE MOST FITTING WORD FOR A GIVEN IDEA
Look under any related term in the Index Guide for a reference to the desired list.

Example: Suppose you are looking for a term to describe the performance of a poor public speaker. The idea has something to do with "bad taste." The Index Guide tells you that **bad taste** in connection with "language" is listed in section 579.1.

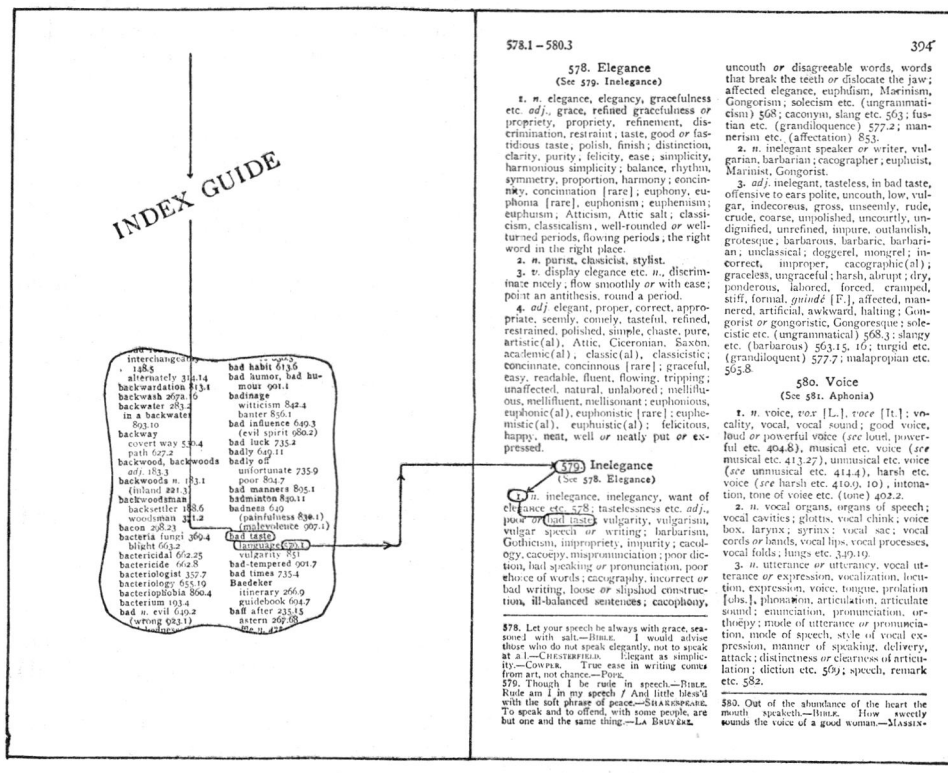

Turning to that section you find a variety of terms, one or several of which are applicable to your speaker. Now you can complain about his *vulgarity,* his *poor diction,* his *slipshod constructions,* and so on.

xxviii

xxix   **How to Use the Book**

TO FIND A BETTER WORD TO TAKE THE PLACE OF ONE THAT IS GIVEN

                    Look under the less satisfactory term in the Index Guide
                           for references to suitable lists.

Example: Suppose you wish to describe somebody's behavior as "foolish" but you feel that that term is somewhat flat. Under the word **foolish** in the Index Guide you find several references. "Foolish" in the sense of "absurd" looks more promising than "foolish" in the sense of "silly" which would seem to apply to the person

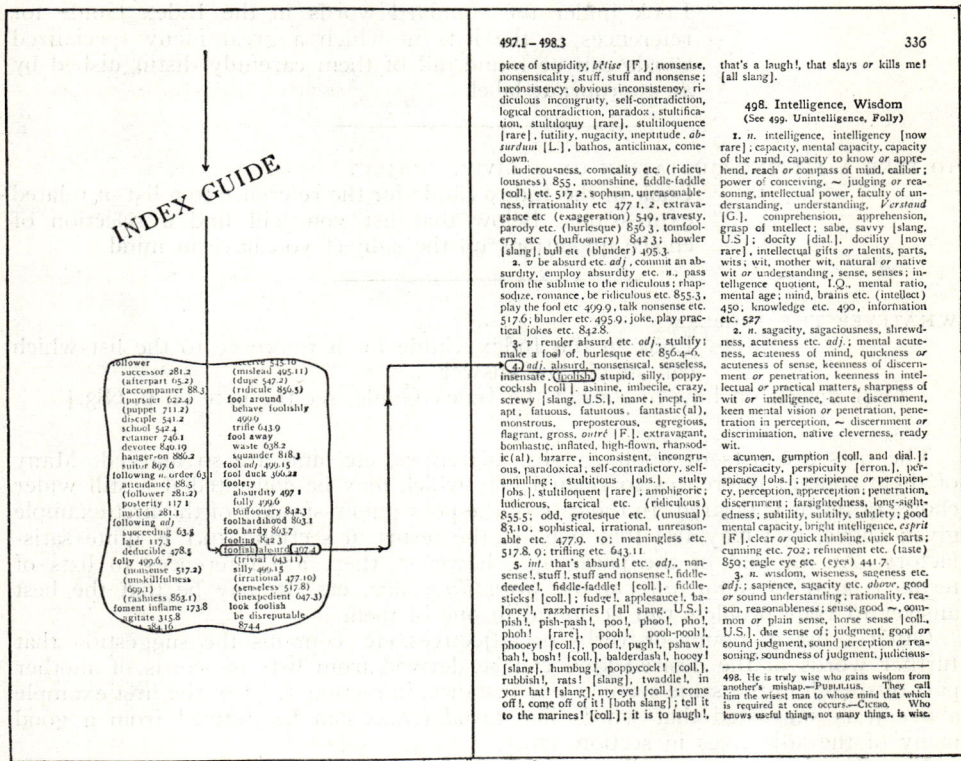

himself rather than to his behavior. The reference number 497.4 takes you to a list of adjectives from among which you can choose the most appropriate one. Now you can state that the person's behavior was *absurd, stupid, crazy, preposterous, bizarre,* and the like.

TO FIND THE CORRECT WORD FOR SOMETHING VAGUELY REMEMBERED IN ITS ASSOCIATIONS

                    Look under an associated term in the Index Guide for a
                           reference to the required list.

Example: Suppose you recall vaguely that a certain individual holds some sort of an academic title. Looking up **doctor** in the Index Guide you find a reference to "academic degree 877.3." Reading through that paragraph you may suddenly feel reminded of the title you are looking for. Now you can give the person his *B.Ed.* (Bachelor of Education), his *LL.D.* (Doctor of Laws), or whatever else he happens to have earned.

How to Use the Book

TO FIND WORDS SUGGESTIVE OF NEW IDEAS ON A GIVEN SUBJECT
> Look under related terms in the Index Guide for references to the appropriate lists.

TO FIND WORDS WITH PECULIAR CONNOTATIONS AS COLLOQUIALISMS, SLANG, DIALECT, ARCHAIC OR OBSOLETE EXPRESSIONS, BRITICISMS, MILITARY AND NAVAL OR OTHERWISE TECHNICAL TERMS, ETC.
> Look under the standard words in the Index Guide for references to the lists in which a great many specialized words can be found, all of them carefully distinguished by an appropriate label.

TO FIND A FITTING QUOTATION ON A GIVEN SUBJECT
> Look in the Index Guide for the reference to a list of related expressions. Below that list you will find a selection of choice quotations on the subject you have in mind.

WHATEVER THE PROBLEM
> Look in the Index Guide for a reference to the list which can supply the answer.

[For details on how to consult the Index Guide, see the note on p. 683.]

The lists are lists of nouns, verbs, adjectives, etc. and are so marked. Many of them contain references to related lists which may be consulted if a still wider choice of terms is desired. In the case of the poor public speaker of the first example given above, you may feel that none of the terms in section 579.1 is quite satisfactory. At the end of the paragraph, however, there are references to lists of terms related to *slang, affectation, grandiloquence,* etc. It may be that the best answer to your problem can be found in one of them.

Often a list of nouns or verbs or adjectives etc. contains the suggestion that further words of the desired kind can be derived from lists of words of another part of speech in the same section. For instance, in section 579.1 of the first example above it is suggested that words like *tastelessness* can be derived from a good many of the adjectives in section 579.3.

Note that there are generally several lists of the same part of speech in one section but that the parts of speech appear always in the order *n., v., adj., adv., prep., conj., int.*

It is often helpful to look through the lists of various parts of speech in a given section, for by changing the construction one had in mind one may be able to express one's thought more cogently with the help of a noun or a verb or the like instead of the adjective or whatever else one had intended to use.

At times it is profitable to extend one's search to lists of terms expressing the opposite of the original idea. Instead of saying, for instance, that something is *clear,* it may be better to say that it is not *obscure.* References to sections dealing with opposite ideas will be found immediately below the sectional captions. (In the same place there are often references to correlated sections.)

Note. The order of sections in this book follows the "logical" structure set up by Peter Roget. It may be of interest to study this structure in the Synopsis of Categories on pp. xvi to xxvii. A thorough grasp of the principle of Roget's classification can facilitate the use of the book, for reference to the desired lists of synonyms may occasionally be made from the Synopsis taken as an index of subjects and sections instead of from the complete Index Guide.

THESAURUS
OF ENGLISH WORDS AND PHRASES

1. Existence
(See 2. Nonexistence)

1. *n.* existence, being, entity, *ens* [L.], essence, *esse* [L.], subsistence *or* subsistency; hypaxis [rare]; automaton; life etc. 359; substantiality etc. 3; presence etc. (existence in space) 186; coexistence etc. 120.

2. *n.* reality, actuality, actual existence, factuality, fact, the real know [slang, U.S.], positive fact, matter of fact, plain matter of fact, "plain, plump fact" (Browning), naked fact, undeniable fact, brute fact [coll.], stubborn fact, sober *or* grim reality, no joke, not a dream; true state, what's what [coll.]; basics, essentials, fundamentals, basic *or* essential facts, brass tacks [coll.], cases [slang, U.S.], turkey [coll., U.S. and Can.]; complete facts, whole story [coll.]; *fait accompli* [F.]; truth etc. 494.1; the real McCoy [slang, U.S.] etc. (the real thing) 494.4; certainty etc. 474.

3. *n.* (science of existence) ontology, metaphysics, cosmology.

4. *v.* exist, be, have being etc. *n.*, subsist, stand, obtain, prevail, be the case, be no buts about it [coll.]; have place, rank; coexist, coincide, contemporize; postexist, pre-exist; pass the time, vegetate; live, breathe etc. 359.6; abide, endure etc. (be permanent) 141.4; be present etc. 186.8.

5. *v.* become, come into existence etc. *n.*, see the light, see the light of day; arise etc. (begin) 66.5, 6; come forth etc. (appear) 446.2.

6. *v.* consist in, lie in, be comprised in, be contained in, be constituted by.

7. *adj.* existing etc. *v.*, existent, in existence etc. *n.*; subsistent, subsistential; extant, prevalent, current, afloat, on foot; under the sun, on the face of the world; living etc. 359.10; present etc. 186.13.

8. *adj.* real, actual, factual; positive, absolute; self-existing, self-existent; essential; unideal, unimagined; authentic, valid etc. (true) 494.10–494.14; substantial etc. 3.4; tangible etc. 316.8.

9. *adv.* actually, really etc. *adj.*; in fact, in point of fact, as a matter of fact, *de facto* [L.], *ipso facto* [L.], in actuality, in reality; no buts about it [coll.], nothing else but [slang]; unquestionably, undoubtedly etc. (certainly) 474.16; really-truly [coll.], indeed etc. (truly) 494.15.

2. Nonexistence
(See 1. Existence)

1. *n.* nonexistence, inexistence, existlessness, nonsubsistence, nonentity, *non esse* [L.], nonbeing, nullity, nothingness, oblivion, nirvana; nihility, nihilism; neg-

---

1. *Cogito ergo sum* [I think, therefore I am]. —DESCARTES. To be, or not to be: that is the question.—SHAKESPEARE. Facts are stubborn things.—SMOLLET. To live is not merely to breathe, it is to act.—ROUSSEAU. I abhor the dull routine of existence.—A. CONAN DOYLE. Facts do not cease to exist because they are ignored.—HUXLEY. You can't alter facts by filming them over with dead romances.—DRINKWATER. Fact is stranger than fiction.

2. And through my Self, the deepest of the seas, / I strive to thee, Nirvana.—LANIER. Into the darkness they go, the wise and the lovely.—MILLAY.

ativeness, negation, negation of being; abeyance *or* abeyancy; vacuity, blank, void etc. (absence) 187; unsubstantiality etc. 4.

2. *n.* nothing, *nil* [L.], *nihil* [L.], *nichts* [G.], nix [slang], luke [slang], naught *or* nought, none, nothing *or* none whatever, nothing at all, nothing on earth *or* under the sun, none in the world, no such thing; never a one, ne'er a one, nary one [dial.] ; no thing, no degree, no part, no quantity, not a blessed one [coll.], not a particle etc. 32.2; no one, nobody, not a soul; lowest point, nadir, scratch [chiefly coll.], point of commencement; goose egg [sports slang], cipher etc. (zero) 87a; thing of naught etc. 4.2.

3. *n.* annihilation, obliteration etc. (extinction) 162.2.

4. *v.* not exist etc. 1.4, have no existence etc. 1.1, be null and void etc. *adj.*

5. *v.* cease to exist etc. 1.4, become extinct etc. *adj.*, come to nothing etc. *n.*, cease, vanish, disappear, evaporate, fade, fade out *or* away, fleet [arch.], fly, sink, dissolve, melt away, die out *or* away, pass away, pass out of the picture [coll.], peter out [coll.], peg out [slang], go, be no more, leave no trace, "leave not a rack behind" (Shakespeare); perish etc. 162.5 ; die etc. 360.6.

6. *v.* render null etc. *adj.*, nullify; annihilate, obliterate etc. (destroy) 162.4; abrogate etc. 756.3.

7. *adj.* nonexistent, inexistent, nonsubsistent, existless ; null, void, null and void; minus, missing, omitted, negative ; blank etc. (absent) 187.10, 11.

8. *adj.* unreal, not real etc. 1.8; potential, virtual ; vain ; unsubstantial, chimerical etc. 4.5, 6; visionary, fabulous, ideal etc. (imaginary) 515.12–14; supposititious etc. 514.9.

9. *adj.* unborn, uncreated, unbegotten, unconceived, unproduced, unmade.

10. *adj.* extinct, no more, napoo [slang], gone, all gone, all [dial., U.S.], all over with, all up [coll.], all U.P. [slang], done for [coll.], dead and done for [coll.], exhausted, petered out [coll.], gone phut [slang, U.S.], lost, departed; destroyed, perished etc. 162.7; defunct etc. (dead) 360.8.

11. *adv.* none etc. 101.

---

3. And the Word was made flesh and dwelt among us.—BIBLE.   Beware lest you lose the substance by grasping at the shadow.—AESOP.

3. Substantiality
(See 4. Unsubstantiality)

1. *n.* substantiality, substantialness, substantivity ; concreteness, tangibility ; objectivity, objective reality ; hypostasis, substratum (*pl.* substrata), groundwork, foundation ; corporeity etc. (materiality) 316; essential nature, vital part etc. (essence) 5.2 ; reality etc. (existence) 1.

2. *n.* something, thing ; an existence, a being ; creature, critter [dial.] ; body, flesh and blood, person ; substance, object etc. (matter) 316.2, 3.

3. *n.* (totality of existences) *plenum* [L.] etc. (world) 318.

4. *adj.* substantial, substantive ; physical, bodily, personal ; hypostatic(al) ; practical, effective; right, sober; well-founded, well-grounded, sound, solid, sturdy, stable ; as big as life [coll.] ; corporeal, tangible etc. (material) 316.8; real etc. (existent) 1.7, 8.

5. *adv.* substantially, bodily etc. *adj.*; essentially etc. (intrinsically) 5.8.

4. Unsubstantiality
(See 3. Substantiality)

1. *n.* unsubstantiality, insubstantiality, unsubstantialness etc. *adj.*, unsubstantiation; incorporeity etc. (immateriality) 317; nothingness etc. (inexistence) 2.

2. *n.* thing of naught, nullity, nihility, nonentity, obscurity; *nominis umbra* [L.], *vox et praeterea nihil* [L.] ; cipher, "an O without a figure" man of straw, (Shakespeare); lay figure, puppet, dummy; fagot *or* faggot voter [polit. cant, Eng.] ; all talk, all talk and no cider [coll., U.S.], all moonshine, all stuff and nonsense, all tommyrot [slang] ; flash in the pan, blank cartridge, dud [slang] ; matter of no importance *or* consequence,

---

4. Who warms himself with unsubstantial hopes.—SOPHOCLES.   Out of nothing nothing can come, and nothing can become nothing.—PERSIUS.   Nothing hath no savour.—BECON.   We know not substance ; 'mid the shades shadows ourselves we live and die.—R. BURTON.   I have heard that two negatives make an affirmative ; but I never heard that two nothings ever made anything.—DUKE OF BUCKINGHAM.   Its glory is all moonshine.—W. SHERMAN.   *Ex nihilo nihil* [Nothing from nothing].

a nobody etc. (unimportance) 643.3–6; nothing etc. 2.2.

3. *n.* (something unsubstantial) shadow, air, thin air, mockery, "such stuff as dreams are made on" (Shakespeare); illusion, phantom etc. (optical illusion) 443.9; fantasy, dream etc. (imagination) 515; *ignis fatuus* [L.] etc. (luminescence) 420.11; bubble etc. 353; incorporeal, incorporeal being etc. 317.2.

4. *n.* inanity, fatuity, fool's paradise.

5. *adj.* unsubstantial, insubstantial; baseless, groundless, ungrounded, without foundation; nominal; eviscerated; slight, fragile etc. (frail) 160.11; vacuous, blank etc. (empty) 187.11; unreal etc. 2.8; incorporeal etc. (immaterial) 317.6; inane, fatuitous etc. (nugatory) 158.11.

6. *adj.* chimerical, ethereal, airy, made of empty air, gaseous, vaporous, imponderable, tenuous, gossamery, illusory, shadowy, vague, *in nubibus* [L.]; cloud-built, cloud-formed; dreamy, dreamlike; visionary etc. (imaginary) 515.12–14; spectral etc. 980a.4.

5. Intrinsicality
(See 6. Extrinsicality)

1. *n.* intrinsicality, intrinsicalness etc. *adj.*, inbeing, inherence, inhesion, immanence, indwelling; subjectiveness, subjectivity; egohood, egoity [rare]; interiority etc. 221.

2. *n.* essence, quintessence, elixir, substance; essential, principle, fundamental; true being, intrinsic truth, inmost nature, inmost heart *or* soul, inner *or* esoteric reality, essential nature, true inwardness, center of life, vital principle, essential *or* vital part; essential quality, suchness; quid, quiddity; soul, spirit, *spiritus* [L.]; heart, heart's core, heart of hearts, secret *or* inmost recesses of the heart, cockles of the heart; breast, bosom; gist, jet, nub [coll., U.S.], pith, core, kernel, nucleus, flower, backbone; marrow, sap; lifeblood, heartblood, heart's blood; important part etc. (salient point) 642.4; existence etc. 1; truth etc. 494.

3. *n.* nature, constitution, character, quality, property, crasis, diathesis, aspect; temper, temperament; disposition, habit, frame, cast, cue, mood, humor, spirit, tone, grain, vein, streak, stripe; type, sort etc. (kind) 75.2; characteristic etc. (particularity) 79.2; tendency etc. 176.

4. *n.* capacity, endowment; size, speed [both slang]; capability etc. 157.2.

5. *v.* be intrinsic etc. *adj.*, be *or* run in the blood, be born so, be built that way [slang, U.S.].

6. *adj.* intrinsic(al), immanent, native, inherent, innate, inborn, inbred, incarnate, indwelling, infixed, inwrought, ingrained, implanted, ingenerate, ingenit *or* ingenite [obs.], indigenous, congenital, connate; genetous, genetic; derived from within, subjective, nonobjective; idiocratic(al), idiosyncratic(al).

native, natural, normal; essential, fundamental, elementary, primary, basic, basal, underlying, original, radical; instinctive, bred in the bone, running in the blood, in the grain etc. *n.;* hereditary, inherited, to the manner born, coeval with birth; hematobious; syngenetic, syngenic; thoroughbred, purebred, blue-blooded, hot-blooded [turf cant]; virtual; inward etc. (internal) 221.9.

7. *adj.* characteristic etc. (peculiar) 79.8, (indicative) 550.21.

8. *adv.* intrinsically, essentially etc. *adj.*; at bottom, in the main, in effect, practically, virtually, substantially, per se, *au fond* [F.]; fairly; truly etc. 494.15.

6. Extrinsicality
(See 5. Intrinsicality; also
57. Extraneousness)

1. *n.* extrinsicality, extrinsicalness, objectiveness etc. *adj.*; *non ego* [L.]; accident, contingency, accessory; modality; extraneousness etc. 57; exteriority etc. 220.

---

5. *Magnos homines virtute metimur non fortuna* [We estimate men as great not by their wealth but by their virtue].—Nepos. His own character is the arbiter of every one's fortune.—Publilius. Who is it that can tell me who I am?—Shakespeare. Vital spark of heavenly flame.—Pope. Character is higher than intellect.—Emerson. What is bred in the bone will never come out of the flesh.—Pilpay. Dust thou art, to dust returnest, / Was not spoken of the soul.—Longfellow. The all-important factor in national greatness is national character.—T. Roosevelt. Temper my spirit, O Lord, / Burn out its alloy.—Untermeyer.

6. Outside show is a poor substitute for inner worth.—Aesop. These but the trappings and the suits of woe.—Shakespeare.

2. *adj.* extrinsic(al), derived from without, objective, added extrinsically, adventitious, ascititious, adscititious, accidental, fortuitous, casual, incidental, nonessential *or* unessential, supervenient, accessory, contingent, subsidiary; modal; extraneous etc. 57.4; outward etc. (exterior) 220.7; circumstantial etc. 8.5.

7. State

1. *n.* state, condition, estate, lot, case; form, shape [coll.], trim, fig [coll.], fettle, whack [slang], order, commission [coll.], kilter *or* kelter [coll. or dial.], way [coll.]; fashion, style; mode, modality; complexion, light, tone, tenor, turn; character, disposition, temper, mood; constitution, make-up [coll.] etc. 240; plight etc. (predicament) 8.3.

2. *v.* fare, do, be in ∼, possess *or* enjoy a state etc., *n.*, be on a footing; come to pass.

3. *adj.* conditional, modal, formal; structural etc. 240.9.

4. *adv. etc.* conditionally, provisionally; provided etc. 8.8.

8. Circumstance

1. *n.* circumstance, situation, position, status, standing, footing, posture, attitude, place, point; phase, phasis; terms; regime; occurrence, go [coll.].

2. *n.* occasion, juncture, conjuncture; contingency etc. (event) 151.1.

3. *n.* predicament, plight, pass, pickle [chiefly coll.]; fix, kettle of fish, go, how-do-you-do, how-de-do, to-do [all coll.]; corner, hole etc. (bad predicament) 704.2; emergency, exigency etc. (crisis) 134.4; condition etc. (state) 7.

4. *n.* bearings, how the land lies.

5. *adj.* circumstantial, given, conditional, provisional, limitative; contingent, incidental; critical, crucial; modal; adventitious etc. (extrinsic) 6.2; detailed, minute etc. (special) 79.7.

6. *adv.* thus, thusly [coll.], in such wise, thuswise, this-a-way [dial.], thus and thus, thus and so, so, so fashion [dial., U.S.], just like that.

7. *adv. etc.* accordingly, that being the case, such being the case, that being so, *quae cum ita sint* [L.]; in *or* under the circumstances *or* conditions, according to circumstances *or* the occasion, as matters stand, as the matter stands, as the case may be, as it may be, as it may happen *or* turn out, *pro re nata* [L.], as things go, as times go, as the wind blows; therefore etc. (hence) 155.5; consequently etc. 154.7; seeing that etc. (since) 155.8.

8. *conj. etc.* provided, it being provided, on condition, on *or* upon condition that, with the stipulation *or* understanding; if, if so, if so be [arch. and dial.], if case be [arch.], if it be so, if it so happen *or* turn out; in case, just in case, in case that, granting ∼, allowing *or* supposing that, in such a case, ∼ contingency *or* event; unless, except, without [now chiefly dial.].

9. Relation

(See 10. Irrelation; also 12. Correlation)

1. *n.* relation, relationship, relative position; bearing, reference, concern, dependence *or* dependency, interest, applicability; apposition, appositeness etc. *adj.*; connection, tie-in [slang], association, alliance, cognation, affinity, rapport, homogeneity, homology; approximation etc. (nearness) 197; kinship, filiation etc. (consanguinity) 11; correlation etc. 12; analogy etc. (similarity) 17; relevance etc. 23.2; ratio, proportion etc. (comparative relation) 464.

2. *n.* link, tie, bond of union etc. (bond) 45.

3. *v.* be related etc. *adj.*, have a relation etc. *n.*, connect, relate to, refer to, bear upon, regard, concern, touch, affect, interest, have to do with, tie in with [slang], pertain to, appertain to, belong to, answer to, correspond to.

4. *v.* relate, associate, connect, bring

---

7. No one lives content with his condition.—HORACE. When in disgrace with fortune and men's eyes / I all alone beweep my outcast state.—SHAKESPEARE. Along the cool sequester'd vale of life / They kept the noiseless tenor of their way.—GRAY. It is a condition that confronts us—not a theory.—CLEVELAND. Between the devil and the deep sea.
8. Men's plans should be regulated by the circumstances, not circumstances by the plans.—LIVY. Fearful concatenation of circumstances.—D. WEBSTER. Circumstances alter cases.—HALIBURTON. Circumstances are beyond the control of man; but his conduct is in his own power.—DISRAELI.
9. Thereby hangs a tale.—SHAKESPEARE. A man is a bundle of relations, a knot of roots.—EMERSON.

into relation with, bring to bear upon; parallel, parallelize, draw a parallel; link etc. 43.5, 6; compare etc. 464.2.

5. *adj.* relative, relational; relating to, belonging to etc. *v.*; relative to, in relation with, referable *or* referrible to, pertinent *or* appurtenant to, in common with; correlative etc. 12.6, 7.

6. *adj.* related, connected, implicated, associated, affiliated, allied; germane, apposite; collateral, connate [rare], cognate, connatural, affinitive, paronymous, equiparant; congener [rare], congenerous, congeneric(al); in relation etc. *n.*, in touch with; *en rapport* [F.], in rapport; kindred, akin etc. (consanguineous) 11.7.

7. *adj.* approximative, approximating, much of a muchness [coll.]; proportional, proportionate, proportionable; allusive, allusory [obs.]; comparative, comparable etc. 464.5, 6.

8. *adj.* relevant, applicable, pertinent etc. (apt) 23.10; in the same category etc. 75; like etc. 17.10–16.

9. *adv. etc.* relatively etc. *adj.*, in a relative manner, in relation *or* respect to; not absolutely; pertinently etc. 23.13; comparatively etc. 464.7.

10. *prep. etc.* with relation to, with reference to, with regard to, in *or* with respect to, in respect to *or* of, in connection with, *à propos* [F.] *or* apropos of, speaking of; as respects, as regards, as to, as for; in point of, on the part of, on the score of, in the matter of, *in re* [L.], *quoad hoc* [L.]; concerning, touching etc. *v.*; about, anent; concerning which, in regard to which, on which; whereon, whereanent [chiefly Scot.], whereto, whereunto, wherein, whereof; thereof [obs.], therein, thereto, thereunto, thereover, thereon [rare], thereby; under the head of etc. (class) 75; by the way etc. 134.11.

10. Irrelation
(See 9. Relation)

1. *n.* irrelation, unrelatedness etc. *adj.*, irrelevance *or* irrelevancy, impertinence, nonpertinence, inapplicability, inconnection, inconsequence, independence, incommensurability; disquiparancy, dis-

quiparation; dissociation, disassociation; disagreement etc. 24; unconformity etc. 83; disconnection etc. (disjunction) 44; heterogeneity, multifariousness etc. 81.

2. *n.* misrelation, misapplicability, misreference, misalliance.

3. *v.* not concern etc. 9.3, have no concern with, have no relation to, have no bearing upon, have no business with *or* there, have nothing to do with.

4. *v.* introduce irrelevantly, drag in, work in, lug in, worm in, smuggle in, foist in, run in, drag *or* lug in by the head and shoulders; interject, intrude etc. 228.8, 10; insert etc. 300.5.

5. *adj.* irrelative, unrelated, disrelated, irrelate [rare]; independent, irrespective [rare], unallied; unconnected, disconnected; adrift, away from the point; isolated, insular; arbitrary; extraneous, strange, outlandish, exotic [rare], alien; foreign, furrin [dial.], foreignistic [coll.]; not comparable, incommensurable, incommensurate; discordant etc. 24.6, 7; different etc. 15.7; heterogeneous, multifarious etc. (multiform) 81.2, 3.

6. *adj.* irrelevant, inconsequent, inapplicable, impertinent, not pertinent etc. 23.10, inapposite; unessential, inessential, nonessential; accidental; without connection, *à propos de bottes* [F.], beside the mark, ~ point, ~ purpose *or* question, aside *or* away from the purpose, ~ question, ~ transaction *or* point, nothing to the point, *nihil ad rem* [L.], not to the purpose, traveling out of the record; disquiparant, not equiparant; inapt etc. 24.7; misplaced etc. (uncongenial) 24.8; illogical etc. 477.10.

7. *adj.* remote, farfetched, out-of-the-way, forced, neither here nor there, quite another thing; detached, apart; segregated, segregate.

8. *adj.* incidental, parenthetical, *obiter dictum* [L.], episodic.

9. *adv. etc.* irrelevantly, irrespectively etc. *adj.*; without reference *or* regard to; *a se* [L.].

10. *adv.* incidentally, parenthetically etc. *adj.*; by the way etc. 134.11.

11. Consanguinity

Relation of Kindred.—1. *n.* consanguinity, kinship, kindred; relation, rela-

---

10. I do desire we may be better strangers.—Shakespeare.   She stood in tears amid the alien corn.—Keats.   But that's another story.—Kipling.

11. And hath made of one blood all nations of men.—Bible.   A little more than kin and

tionship; blood relation *or* relationship, blood, ties of blood, cognation, agnation, connation [obs.]; filiation, affiliation; alliance, connection, family connection *or* tie; nepotism; ancestry etc. 166; posterity etc. 167; family likeness etc. (connaturalness) 17.2.

2. *n.* brotherhood, fraternity; sisterhood, sorority [rare]; cousinhood, cousinage [obs.].

3. *n.* kinsmen, kinsfolk, kinfolk [dial.], kinfolks [dial.], kinspeople [U.S.], kindred, kinnery [slang], kin, kith [arch.], kith and kin, kith and kind [dial.], folks [coll.], relatives, relations, people, connections; near relation, distant relation; german, germane; consanguine [rare], consanguinean; blood, blood relation *or* relative; one's own flesh and blood; next of kin.

brother, bub [coll., U.S.], bud [dial. and coll.], buddy [coll., U.S.], br'er [dial., South, U.S.], blood brother, brother-german; sister, sis [coll.], sissy [coll.], blood sister, sister-german; uncle, nunks *or* nunky [slang], nuncle [dial.]; aunt, nephew, niece; cousin, cousin-german, first ~, second etc. cousin, cousin once (twice etc.) removed, country cousin; in-law [coll.], brother-in-law, sister-in-law, mother-in-law, father-in-law; father, mother etc. (parent) 166.5–9; son, daughter etc. (offspring) 167.4.

4. *n.* race, generation [obs.], gens [Rom. Hist.], people, family, house, clan, tribe, nation; nationality, gentility; stock, lineage, strain etc. (extraction) 166.4; Caucasian, Caucasian race etc. *adj.*; Scandinavian, Jew etc. (nationalities) 188.9.

5. *n.* family, household, homefolks [coll.].

6. *v.* be related etc. *adj.*, claim relationship with etc. *n.*

7. *adj.* consanguineous, consanguine, consanguinean; related, kindred, akin, sib [Scot. or arch.], of the blood, cognate, agnate, connate [rare]; allied, affiliated; collateral; fraternal, sororal [rare]; intimately *or* closely related, remotely *or* distantly related; affinal; german, germane; connatural etc. 17.13.

8. *adj.* racial, tribal, national, family, lineal; phyletic, phylogenetic; gentile, gentilic, gentilitian, gentilitial, gentilitious; Caucasian, Aryan, Mongolian, Indian, American, European, Asiatic, African, Ethiopian; Negro, Negroid; Malay, Malayan; Jewish, Hebrew; Scandinavian, Mexican etc. (nationality) 188.11.

12. Correlation
(See also 9. Relation)

1. *n.* correlation, corelation, double relation, correlativity, correlativism; mutual relation, mutuality, commutuality; correspondence *or* correspondency; interrelation, interconnection, interdependence.

2. *n.* reciprocation, reciprocal relation, reciprocalness etc. *adj.*, reciprocity, reciprocality; *quid pro quo* [L.]; interchange etc. 148; exchange etc. (barter) 794; alternation etc. (reciprocating motion) 314.3; retaliation etc. 718.

3. *n.* reciprocator, reciprocatist; each other, one another.

4. *v.* correlate, be correlative etc. *adj.*, correspond; interrelate, interconnect, interdepend.

5. *v.* reciprocate, be reciprocative etc. *adj.*, interact, interwork; exchange, counterchange etc. (interchange) 148.3; alternate etc. 314.10; retaliate etc. 718.2.

6. *adj.* correlative, interrelative, interrelated, interconnected, interdependent; mutually related, mutual, commutual; common; correspondent, corresponding etc. *v.*, equivalent; complemental, complementary; relative etc. 9.5.

7. *adj.* reciprocal, reciprocative, reciprocate [rare], reciprocally related; alternate; interchangeable etc. 148.4.

8. *adv.* reciprocally etc. *adj.*; by turns etc. 148.5; *vice versa* [L.] etc. (contrarily) 14.7.

---

less than kind.—SHAKESPEARE. The greater the kindred is, the less the kindness.—LYLY. And so do his sisters and his cousins and his aunts.—GILBERT. I was blood-sister to the clod, blood-brother to the stone.—W. V. MOODY. Blood is thicker than water.

12. We are interested in others when they are interested in us.—PUBLILIUS. My true love hath my heart and I have his.—SIDNEY. There is a reciprocal pleasure in governing and being governed.—JOHNSON. Independence? That's middle class blasphemy. We are all dependent on one another, every soul of us on earth.—SHAW.

13. Identity

(See 14. Contrariety, 15. Difference; also 17. Similarity, 23. Agreement, 27. Equality)

1. *n.* identity, identicalness, oneness etc. *adj.*; unity, coincidence, coalescence, homoousia; synonymity, synonymy; identification; equality etc. 27; connaturalness etc. (similarity) 17; individuality, self etc. 79.2, 4.

2. *n.* sameness, selfsameness; sameliness etc. (regularity) 16.2; wearisome sameness etc. (tedium) 841.3; similarity etc. 17; equivalence etc. 27.2.

3. *n.* same, selfsame, very same, one and the same, the identical same, no other, very *or* actual thing; *ipsissima verba* [L.], the very words; counterpart etc. (analogue) 17.5; facsimile etc. (copy) 21.

4. *v.* be identical etc. *adj.,* coincide, ditto [coll.], coalesce.

5. *v.* identify, recognize *or* establish the identity of, treat *or* render as identical *or* the same; diagnose, diagnosticate [rare]; recognize etc. 481a.6.

6. *adj.* identical, same etc. *n.,* ilk [arch.], self [obs.]; one, one and the same, all one; homoousian, homoousious [rare].

7. *adj.* coincident, coincidental, coinciding; coalescent, coalescing; indistinguishable, undistinguishable; synonymous, synonymic(al); equivalent etc. (equal) 27.8, 9; alike, analogous, etc. 17.10–15.

8. *adv. etc.* identically etc. *adj.,* on all fours with; *ibidem* [L.], *ibid.* [L.]; in the same manner, ditto, same here [coll.].

14. Contrariety

(See 13. Identity; also 15. Difference)

1. *n.* contrariety, contrariness etc. *adj.,* contrast, antithesis, opposition, contradiction, contradistinction; antagonism, repugnance, antipathy, clashing, collision, conflict; inversion etc. 218; difference etc. 15; contraposition etc. 237; counteraction etc. 179.

2. *n.* the contrary, opposite, direct opposite, antithesis, reverse, inverse, converse, obverse, the other extreme, antipode, antipodes [pl. used as sing.], antipole, counterpole, counterpoint; foil; *vis-à-vis* [F.]; counterpart etc. (analogue) 17.5.

3. *v.* be contrary etc. *adj.,* contrast with, antithesize [rare], contradict, contravene, counteract, counterwork; go *or* act contrary to, go *or* run counter to, fly in the face of, be *or* play at cross-purposes; oppose, be opposed to, be *or* run in opposition to; differ *toto caelo* [L.]; differ etc. 15.5; be unlike etc. 18.2.

4. *v.* invert, reverse, retrograde [rare], transpose; invaginate, intussuscept; turn the tables etc. 218.4.

5. *adj.* contrary, contrarious [arch.], contrariant [rare]; opposite, *vis-à-vis* [F.], counter, antithetic(al), contrasted, converse, reverse, inverse, adverse, averse, oppositional, opposing, opposed, anti [coll.], dead against; antipodal, antipodean, antipodic; antagonistic(al), repugnant, hostile, inimical, conflicting, clashing, inconsistent, contradictory, at cross-purposes; negative; subcontrary; contrapositive etc. 237.6; different etc. 15.7; inverted etc. 218.6; counteractive etc. 179.5.

6. *adj.* diametrically opposite *or* different, differing *toto caelo* [L.], as opposite as black and white, ~ as light and darkness, ~ as fire and water, ~ as the poles etc.; "hyperion to a satyr" (Shakespeare); quite the contrary *or* reverse, *tout au contraire* [F.], just the other way, no such thing.

7. *adv.* contrarily, conversely etc. *adj.*; contra, contrariwise, against the grain, *à rebours* [F.]; in reverse English [coll., U.S.], *per contra* [L.], on *or* to the contrary, nay rather; by contraries, by way of opposition; *vice versa* [L.]; on the other hand etc. (in compensation) 30.7, 8; differently etc. 15.10; inversely etc. 218.8; otherwise etc. 18.6; reciprocally etc. 148.5; counteractively etc. 179.6.

---

13. When I had lost one shaft, / I shot his fellow of the selfsame flight / The selfsame way.
—SHAKESPEARE.   The self-same song ...
—KEATS.
14. All concord's born of contraries.—JONSON. Every sweet has its sour; every evil its good.—EMERSON.   Good and evil ben two contraries.
—CHAUCER.   And yet you incessantly stand on your head.—CARROLL.

15. Difference
(See 13. Identity; also 14. Contrariety, 18. Dissimilarity, 24. Disagreement)

1. *n.* difference, diff [slang], odds, dissimilitude, otherness etc. *adj.*, variance, variation, variety, heterogeneity, diversity, divergence, deviation, departure, disaccord, inconformity, incompatibility, inconsistence *or* inconsistency; discongruity, incongruity, incongruence; discordance *or* discordancy, dissonance *or* dissonancy; inharmoniousness, inharmony; discrepancy, discrepance [rare], discrepation [rare]; distinction, distinctity [rare]; moods and tenses; dissimilarity etc. 18; disagreement etc. 24; disparity etc. (inequality) 28; antithesis etc. (contrariety) 14; differentiation etc. (discrimination) 465.

2. *n.* nicety, subtlety, *nuance* [F.], refinement, delicacy, nice ~, fine ~, delicate *or* subtle distinction, shade of difference; differentia, differential.

3. *n.* different thing, different story [coll.], something else, something else again [coll.]; apple off another tree, another pair of shoes, another order of cat [slang], horse of a different *or* another color, bird of another feather; nothing of the kind, no such thing, no such a thing [dial. *or* coll.], quite another thing, *lucus a non lucendo* [L.], *tertium quid* [L.]; this, that, or the other.

4. *n.* modification, alteration etc. (change) 140.

5. *v.* be different etc. *adj.*, differ, vary, ablude [obs.], mismatch, discept [rare], discrepate [rare], divaricate, diverge, deviate, depart; diverge from, depart from etc.; disagree with, disaccord with, conflict with, clash with, jar with; differ *toto caelo* or *longo intervallo* [L.]; contrast with etc. 14.3; be unlike etc. 18.2.

6. *v.* differentiate, difference; sever, severalize; specialize, particularize; disequalize, desynonymize, despecificate; distinguish etc. (discriminate) 465.2, 3; compare etc. 464.2; modify etc. (change) 140.6.

7. *adj.* differing etc. *v.*, different; varied, variant; diverse, divers [arch.]; divergent; deviative, widely apart, distinct, distinguished, separate, heterogeneous, disaccordant, inconformable, irreconcilable, incompatible, incongruous, discrepant, discordant, dissonant, inharmonious, unmatched; dissimilar etc. 18.4, 5; disagreeing etc. 24.6; contrary etc. 14.5, 6; unequal etc. 28.3; ununiform etc. 16a.2; variform, diversified etc. 81.2, 3; unrelated etc. 10.5.

8. *adj.* differentiative, differential; distinctive, characteristic, peculiar; diacritic(al); diagnostic; distinguishing, discriminative etc. 465.4.

9. *adj. etc.* other, another, not the same, else, otherwise, other than *or* from, othersome.

10. *adv.* differently etc. *adj.*, in a different manner; otherwise etc. 18.6; contrarily etc. 14.7.

11. *phr.* what's the difference?, what's the diff? [slang], what's the odds?

16. Uniformity
(See 16a. Nonuniformity, 81. Multiformity)

1. *n.* uniformity, uniformness, evenness, steadiness etc. *adj.*; stability, continuity, permanence, persistence *or* persistency; consistence *or* consistency, consonance, accordance, unity; connature, connaturality [both rare]; homogeneity, homology; conformity etc. 82; agreement etc. 23; similarity etc. 17.

2. *n.* regularity, constancy, evenness, even tenor, sameness, sameliness, samesomeness [dial.], monotony; undeviation, unvariation, invariability; clockwork precision; wearisome sameness etc. (tedium) 841.3; routine etc. (habit) 613; periodicity etc. 138.

3. *v.* be uniform etc. *adj.*, run through; accord with etc. (agree) 23.7; conform etc. 82.4.

4. *v.* render uniform etc. *adj.*, bring into uniformity etc. *n.*, uniform, assimi-

---

15. *Quot homines tot sententiae* [As many opinions as men].—TERENCE. It is difference of opinion that makes horse races.—TWAIN. You must wear your rue with a difference.—SHAKESPEARE. O, the difference of man and man!—SHAKESPEARE. A distinction without a difference.—FIELDING. Like—but oh! how different!—WORDSWORTH. Strange! all this difference should be / 'Twixt Tweedledum and Tweedledee.—BYROM. It takes all sorts to make a world. *Il y a fagots et fagots* [There are fagots and fagots].

16. *Ab uno disce omnes* [From one learn to know all].—VERGIL. Consistence, thou art a jewel.—ANON. A foolish consistency is the hobgoblin of little minds.—EMERSON. Constant dropping wears the stone.

late, make alike etc. (*See* alike etc. 17.10); level, smooth, dress.

5. *adj.* uniform, even, equable, constant, steady, level, regular; samely, samesome [dial.]; monotonous, humdrum, dingdong, singsong, jog-trot [coll.]; unchanging, unchanged, undeviating, unvarying, unvaried, invariable, undiversified; homogeneous, homogenetic, homogenetical, homogenic, homogeneal [rare]; homologous, homologic(al); consistent, of a piece, connatural; alike etc. (similar) 17.10–16; in harmony with etc. (agreeing) 23.9; methodical, systematic etc. (orderly) 58.7; measured etc. 466.13; stable etc. 150.6; wearisomely uniform etc. (tedious) 841.8; conformable to rule etc. 82.9.

6. *adv. etc.* uniformly etc. *adj.*; uniformly with etc. (conformably) 82.12.

7. *adv.* invariably, without exception, never otherwise; constantly, continually, right along [coll., U.S.]; regularly, regular [chiefly dial.]; by clockwork; in a rut *or* groove; always etc. (perpetually) 112.5; generally etc. 78.15; commonly etc. (habitually) 613.13.

16a. Nonuniformity
(See 16. Uniformity)

1. *n.* nonuniformity, ununiformity, ununiformness; irregularity, unevenness; divarication, divergence, deviation, heteromorphism, heterogeneity; diversity etc. (multiformity) 81, (dissimilarity) 18; unconformity etc. 83; roughness etc. 256.

2. *adj.* ununiform, nonuniform; irregular, uneven, "of every shape that was not uniform" (Lowell); different etc. 15.7; dissimilar etc. 18.4, 5; multifarious, diversified etc. 81.2, 3; rough etc. 256.12.

3. *adv.* ununiformly etc. *adj.*, in all manner of ways, every which way *or* everywhichway [coll., U.S.]; here, there, and everywhere.

17. Similarity
(See 18. Dissimilarity; also 13. Identity, 27. Equality)

1. *n.* similarity, resemblance, likeness, alikeness, similitude, semblance, consimilarity [rare], homogeneity, affinity, approximation, parallelism; analogy, analogicalness; correspondence, homoiousia, parity; agreement etc. 23; sameness etc. (identity) 13; uniformity etc. 16; equivalence etc. 27.2; comparability etc. 464.

2. *n.* connaturalness, connature [rare], connaturality [rare]; family likeness *or* resemblance, family favor; isogamy, isogametism; brotherhood etc. (consanguinity) 11.

3. *n.* assonance, alliteration, rhyme *or* rime, pun, paronomasia.

4. *n.* a similar, simile [obs.]; the like, the like *or* likes of [coll.]; suchlike, such.

5. *n.* analogue, congener, correlative, correlate, equivalent, correspondent, parallel, counterpart, complement, pendant, match, double, dub [slang, U.S.], twin, fellow, companion, mate, brother, sister; second self, *alter ego* [L.]; couple, pair; two of a kind, birds of a feather, *Arcades ambo* [L.], *gens de même famille* [F.], *par nobile fratrum* [L.]; *et hoc genus omne* [L.]; chip of *or* off the old block, second edition; synonym etc. 516.3; inverse etc. (opposite) 14.2; same etc. 13.3; copy etc. 21.

6. *n.* perfect likeness, speaking likeness, striking resemblance, image, very image, portrait, picture, very picture, living picture [coll.], dead rap [slang], fetch [dial.], dead *or* very fetch [dial.], moral [slang], ringer *or* dead ringer [slang]; spit, spitting image, spit and image, ~ picture *or* likeness, dead spit [all dial.].

7. *v.* be similar etc. *adj.*, resemble, bear resemblance, put one in mind of [chiefly coll.], have all the earmarks of, look like, favor [coll.], feature [dial.], take after, follow, savor *or* smack of; approximate, approach; parallel, match, span [U.S.]; not tell which from tother [slang]; hunt *or* run in couples; be comparable etc. 864.4.

8. *v.* render similar etc. *adj.*, similarize

16a. Of every shape that was not uniform.—LOWELL.   Oh, how various is the scene / Allowed to Man for his demesne.—HOFFENSTEIN.
17. They say we are / Almost as like as eggs.—SHAKESPEARE.   For the Colonel's Lady and Judy O'Grady / Are sisters under their skins.—KIPLING.   Though analogy is often misleading, it is the least misleading thing we have.—BUTLER.   As lyke as one pease is to another.—LYLY.   Birds of a feather flock together.   *Tel père tel fils* [Like father like son].

[rare], assimilate, approximate, bring near; connaturalize, make alike.

9. *v.* assonate, alliterate, rhyme *or* rime, pun.

10. *adj.* similar, like, alike, resembling etc. *v.*; comparable etc. 464.6; coincident etc. 13.7; relevant etc. 9.8; uniform etc. 16.5.

11. *adj.* analogous, analogical; parallel, of a piece; homoiousian, homoiousious [rare]; twin; equivalent etc. 27.9.

12. *adj.* such as, suchlike *or* such like, so; -like [as *crazy-like*; dial.].

13. *adj.* connatural, correlative, cognate; corresponding, correspondent; congeneric, congenerous; allied to, tarred with the same brush [coll.]; *instar omnium* [L.]; akin etc. (consanguineous) 11.7.

14. *adj.* approximative, much the same, much at one, much of a muchness [coll.], nearly the same, same but different [joc.], "like—but oh! how different!" (Wordsworth); near, close, something like; *quasi* [L.], near- [as *near-silk*; coll.]; pseudo etc. (spurious) 545.13.

15. *adj.* exactly like, the very picture *or* image of, for all the world like, ridiculously like; *comme deux gouttes d'eau* [F.], as like as two peas, "as lyke as one pease is to another" (Lyly), "as like as eggs" (Shakespeare), cast in the same mold; lifelike, speaking, true to life *or* nature; strict, servile etc. (faithful) 21.5.

16. *adj.* assonant, assonantal; alliterative, alliterate, alliteral, alliterated; rhyming *or* riming, rhymy *or* rimy [rare].

17. *adv. etc.* as if, *quasi* [L.], just as, just as if, so to speak, in a manner of speaking [coll.], as it were, as if it were, as though, in a way; kind of, sort of [both coll.]; *veluti in speculum* [L.].

18. Dissimilarity
(See 17. Similarity; also 15. Difference, 28. Inequality)

1. *n.* dissimilarity, dissimilitude, unlikeness etc. *adj.,* dissemblance, diversity, disparity, divergence, variation; dissimilation; oögamy, heterogamy; difference etc. 15; nonuniformity etc. 16a, novelty etc. 123; originality etc. 20.1.

2. *v.* be unlike etc. *adj.,* bear little *or* no resemblance to, not compare with; differ etc. 15.5; contrast with etc. 14.3.

3. *v.* render unlike etc. *adj.,* dissimilate, dissimilarize [rare]; vary etc. (change) 140.6.

4. *adj.* dissimilar, dissimilatory, dissimilative; unlike, unalike; disparate, divergent, varied; nonidentical, unidentical; of a different kind etc. 75.2; of a sort, of sorts [both coll.]; unmatched, odd, out [as *out sizes*]; different etc. 15.7; unique, original etc. (unusual) 83.10, 11; novel etc. 123.10; at variance etc. (disagreeing) 24.6–8; diversified etc. (multiform) 81.2, 3; ununiform etc. 16a.2.

5. *adj.* far from it, far other [coll.], nothing of the kind, quite another thing, no such thing, no such a thing [coll.]; cast in a different mold, as like a dock as a daisy, "very like a whale" (Shakespeare); as different as chalk from cheese, as different as Macedon and Monmouth; not comparable to, not able to touch, not able to reach [coll.].

6. *adv.* otherwise, otherways [obs. exc. dial.], othergates [obs. exc. dial. Eng.], otherguess [rare], otherguise [obs.], otherhow [rare]; elsewise, elseways [dial.], elsehow [dial.]; alias; differently etc. 15.10; contrarily etc. 14.7; on the other hand etc. 30.8.

19. Imitation
(See 20. Nonimitation; also 21. Copy)

1. *n.* imitation, imitating, copying, etc. *v.*; reproduction, duplication, reduplication, repetition; quotation; transcription; mimeography; an imitation etc. (copy) 21; representation etc. 554.

2. *n.* mockery, mimicry, apery; parrotry, parrotism.

3. *n.* simulation, pretense, sham, fakement [coll.], semblance etc. (dissimula-

---

18. *Dis aliter visum* [To the gods it has seemed otherwise].—Vergil.   No more like my father / Than I to Hercules.—Shakespeare.

19. Men often applaud an imitation, and hiss the real thing.—Aesop.   Fair Portia's counterfeit.—Shakespeare.   The sound must seem an echo to the sense.—Pope.   To admire on principle is the only way to imitate without loss of originality.—Coleridge.   Genius borrows nobly.—Emerson.   Quotation confesses inferiority.—Emerson.   Play the sedulous ape to men of letters.—Stevenson.   He wrapped himself in quotations.—Kipling.   By necessity, by proclivity, and by delight, we all quote.—Emerson.   *Tel maître tel valet* [Like master like man].

tion) 544.2; counterfeiting, forgery, plagiarism etc. (falsification) 544.1; personation etc. (representation) 554; imposture etc. (deception) 545.1.

4. *n.* imitator, mimic, mimicker, mime [rare], mimer, mimester [rare], mocker, mockie [crim. slang, U.S.]; mockingbird, cuckoo; parrot, polly, poll-parrot *or* polly-parrot [coll.]; ape, monkey; echo, echoer, echoist; copyist, copier, copycat [coll.]; counterfeiter, forger, plagiarist.

5. *v.* imitate, copy, mirror, reflect, ditto [coll.], reproduce, repeat, do like, do a [slang, U.S.], go like [coll.]; duplicate, dupe [printers' slang]; double, dub [slang, U.S.]; echo, re-echo; match, parallel; facsimile, squeeze [cant]; transcribe; mimeograph.

6. *v.* mock, mimic, mime, copycat [coll.], ape, take off, hit off, pipe off [slang], borrow, steal one's stuff [slang, U.S.].

7. *v.* simulate, assume, convey an impression of, register [slang], go through the motions [slang], act the part, put on an act [slang, U.S.], make a show of; sham, feign etc. (dissemble) 544.6; counterfeit, forge etc. (falsify) 544.3; represent, personate etc. 554.7, 8; act etc. (drama) 599.26.

8. *v.* caricature, parody, burlesque, travesty, hit *or* take off on.

9. *v.* paraphrase, translate etc. (interpret) 522.6, 7.

10. *v.* emulate, follow, follow *or* tread in the steps *or* footsteps of, walk in the shoes of, put oneself in another's shoes, follow in the wake of, follow the example of, follow suit [coll.], take pattern by, take after, copy after, model after *or* on, take a leaf out of another's book.

11. *adj.* imitated etc. *v.*, modeled after *or* on; literal.

12. *adj.* imitation, imitative; mock, mimic, apish, make-believe; pseudo, quasi [L.], near- [as *near-silk*; coll., U.S.], ape- [as *ape-ware*; slang, U.S.], trick [as *trick decorations*; slang]; borrowed, secondhand; imitable; counterfeit, sham etc. (spurious) 545.13; representative etc. 554.9.

13. *adj.* caricatural, burlesque, parodic(al).

14. *adv.* literally, *literatim* [L.], to the letter, according to the letter, *au pied de la lettre* [F.], verbally, verbatim, *verbatim et literatim* [L.], *ipsissimus verbis* [L.],

totidem verbis [L.], in the same words, word for word, *mot à mot* [F.]; *sic* [L.], thus; exactly, precisely etc. (accurately) 494.16; faithfully etc. 772.6; by heart etc. 505.22.

20. Nonimitation
(See 19. Imitation)

1. *n.* nonimitation, no imitation etc. 21; originality, authenticity, creativeness; novelty etc. 123; uniqueness etc. 83.3.

2. *n.* an original etc. (prototype) 22; sulphite [slang], eccentric etc. (nonconformist) 83.4.

3. *adj.* unimitated, uncopied, unexampled, unreproduced, untranslated; unmatched, unparalleled; firsthand; archetypal, prototypal, prototypical; primordial; genuine etc. (authentic) 494.12; rare, unique, original etc. (unusual) 83.10, 11; novel etc. 123.10.

4. *adj.* inimitable etc. (supreme) 33.8.

21. Copy
(See 22. Prototype; also 19. Imitation)

Result of Imitation.—1. *n.* copy, imitation, likeness, resemblance, semblance, similitude, image, form [obs.], icon; effigy, *effigies* [L.]; ectype; representation, adumbration, study; *pasticcio* [It.]; "counterfeit presentment" (Shakespeare), fakement [coll.]; take-off [coll.], hit-off [slang], pipe-off [slang]; near-silk, near-leather, near-antique [all coll., U.S.]; ape-ware [slang, U.S.]; revise, revision; rewrite, rewriting, rescript; fair copy, faithful copy etc. *adj.*; portrait etc. (picture) 556.9; counterfeit etc. (spurious article) 545.6; perfect likeness etc. 17.6; same etc. 13.3; typescript etc. (writing) 590.3; printed matter etc. (print) 591.2.

2. *n.* duplicate, duplication, dupe

---

20. Not picked from the leaves of any author, but bred amongst the weeds and tares of mine own brain.—T. BROWNE. The merit of originality is not novelty; it is sincerity.—CARLYLE. Originality provokes originality.—GOETHE. Wrapped in the solitude of his own originality. —C. PHILLIPS. A thought is often original, though you have uttered it a hundred times.— HOLMES.

21. The only good copies are those which make us see the absurdity of bad originals.— LA ROCHEFOUCAULD. Parody might indeed be defined as the worshipper's half-holiday.— CHESTERTON.

[printers' slang]; ditto [coll.], reproduction, replica, model, counterpart; double, dub [slang, U.S.]; cast, casting; facsimile, facsimile impression, squeeze [cant]; transcript, transcription; apograph, transfer, tracing, counterscript, offprint, reprint, second edition; carbon, carbon copy; canned editorial *or* music [slang]; reflected counterpart, reflex, reflexion, reflection; shadow, echo; chip of *or* off the old block.

3. *n.* caricature, take-off [coll.], burlesque, parody; travesty, *travesti* [F.]; extravaganza; cartoon.

4. *n.* paraphrase, metaphrase, version, translation etc. (rendering) 522.2.

5. *adj.* faithful, close, exact, strict, conscientious, servile; lifelike etc. (similar) 17.15.

22. Prototype
(See 21. Copy)

Thing Copied.—1. *n.* prototype, original, model, pattern, paradigm, precedent, standard, criterion, rule, module, scantling [obs.], type, mirror; archetype, antitype; protoplast, protoplasm, proplasm [rare]; exemplar, example, ensample [rare]; model house, model [coll.]; artist's model, dressmaker's model, lay figure; imitatee; fugler, fugleman *or* flugelman; guide; keynote; beau ideal etc. (paragon) 650.2.

2. *n.* copy, text; design etc. (outline) 626.2.

3. *n.* die, mold, matrix, last, mint, seal, stamp, punch, intaglio, negative.

4. *v.* prototype, example, serve as *or* set an example etc. *n.*

23. Agreement
(See 24. Disagreement; also 13. Identity, 83. Conformity)

1. *n.* agreement, accord, accordance; concord, concordance; whack [slang], harmony, *rapport* [F.], concert, concinnity, assonance, consonance *or* consonancy, conformance, conformation, conformity, line, keeping, consistence *or* consistency, coherence, unison, union, congruence *or* congruency, congruity, congeniality, compatibility, affinity, correspondence, coincidence, parallelism, apposition; synchronization, sync *or* sink [motion-picture slang]; uniformity etc. 16; concurrence etc. 178; similarity etc. 17; assent etc. 488.

2. *n.* fitness, aptness etc. *adj.*; relevance *or* relevancy, pertinence *or* pertinency; aptitude, coaptation, propriety, applicability, admissibility, commensurability; cognation etc. (relation) 9; relevant instance, case in point etc. (example) 82.2; timeliness etc. 134.

3. *n.* adaptation, adaption; adjustment, graduation, accommodation, assimilation; reconciliation, reconcilement.

4. *n.* mutual agreement, understanding, mutual *or* cordial understanding, *entente cordiale* [F.], gentleman's agreement; go [coll.], whiz *or* whizz [slang, U.S.]; compact etc. 769.

5. *n.* general agreement, consensus, consension, consentaneity, consentaneousness, concentus, unanimity; like-mindedness, meeting of minds; cooperation etc. 709; concurrence etc. 178.

6. *n.* very thing, just the thing, quite the thing, the thing, the article [slang, U.S.], the idea [coll.], the ticket [coll.]; right man in the right place, round peg in a round hole.

7. *v.* agree, be accordant etc. *adj.*, accord, harmonize, chime, correspond, tally, respond, meet, do, suit, fit, befit, gee [slang and dial.], jibe [coll., U.S.], hitch [coll.], go with, conform with, assimilate, adapt itself to, become adapted, fit together, dovetail, square *or* quadrate with, fall *or* chime in with, consort *or* comport with; homologate, homologize, hit it off with, cotton, hitch horses [all coll.]; fit like a glove, fit to a T *or* tittle; synchronize, sync *or* sink [motion-picture slang].

be self-consistent, be logically consistent; hang *or* hold together, hold up, hold water [all coll.]; conform etc. 82.4;

---

22. For each man to be a standard to himself is most excellent for the good, but for the bad it is the worst of all things.—HOMER. I do not give you to posterity as a pattern to imitate, but as an example to deter.—JUNIUS. A precedent embalms a principle.—DISRAELI. Follow the copy though it fly out of the window.—PRINTER'S SAYING. *Exempla sunt odiosa* [Examples are odious].

23. *Auxilia humilia firma consensus facit* [Unanimity makes humble help strong].—PUBLILIUS. *Concordia discors* [Inharmonious harmony].—HORACE. They agree like bells, they want nothing but hanging.—MERITON. Finally, be ye all of one mind.—BIBLE. If the cap fits, put it on. When in Rome, do as the Romans do.

come to an agreement etc. (assent) 488.6–8; concur etc. 178.2, 3; be expedient etc. 646.3.

8. *v.* render accordant etc. *adj.,* bring into accordance etc. *n.,* accord, agree, assimilate, similarize, harmonize, reconcile, adapt, accommodate, fit, suit; homologize, homologate; arrange, dress, regulate; readjust, readapt; fadge, dovetail, square; adjust etc. (render equal) 27.7; pacify etc. 723.4.

9. *adj.* agreeing, suiting etc. *v.*; in accordance with, in harmony with, in unison with etc. *n.*; in rapport, *en rapport* [F.]; in accord, in step; accordant, concordant, consonant, harmonious, agreeable, becoming, consistent, congenial, compatible, conformable, reconcilable, answerable, correspondent, commensurate, proportionate; consentient, consentaneous, consentive [rare], consensual, concentual; congruent, congruous; at one, at one with, on all fours with, of a piece; of one mind, of the same mind, likeminded; synchronized, synchronal, synchronous, in synchronization, in sync *or* sink [motion-picture slang]; self-consistent; concurrent etc. 178.4; uniform etc. 16.5.

10. *adj.* apt, apposite, pertinent, appurtenant, pat, happy, felicitous, germane, *ad rem* [L.], in point, to the point *or* purpose, bearing upon, applicable, relevant, admissible.

11. *adj.* fit, adapted, *in loco* [L.], *à propos* [F.] *or* apropos, appropriate, seasonable, sortable, suitable, idoneous [rare]; meet etc. (expedient) 646.4.

12. *adj.* at home, in one's proper element.

13. *adv. etc.* pertinently etc. *adj., à propos* [F.] *or* apropos of; relatively etc. 9.9.

24. Disagreement
(See 23. **Agreement**; also 15. **Difference**, 83. **Unconformity**)

1. *n.* disagreement, discord, discordance *or* discordancy; disaccord, disaccordance, inaccordance; dissonance, dis-

---

24. Fill'd the air with barbarous dissonance.—MILTON. All discord, harmony not understood.—POPE. That which is agreeable to the nature of one thing, is many times contrary to the nature of another.—L'ESTRANGE. A round peg in a square hole.

sidence; disunity, disunion; incongruity, incongruence; discongruity, discongruence; disharmony, unharmoniousness etc. *adj.*; misalliance, *mésalliance* [F.]; jarring, clashing etc. *v.*; dissension, misunderstanding, bickering etc. (personal discord) 713; conflict etc. (opposition) 708; unconformity etc. 83.

2. *n.* disparity, disproportionateness etc. *adj.,* disproportion, dissimilitude, inequality, variance, difference, divergence, repugnance; discrepance [rare], discrepancy, discrepation [rare].

3. *n.* unfitness, unsuitability, inapplicability etc. *adj.*; inaptitude, impropriety, inconsistency, inconcinnity; misjoining, misjoinder; mismatch, mismatchment; syncretism; irrelevance etc. (irrelation) 10.

4. *n.* misfit, ass in lion's skin, jackdaw in peacock's feathers, *asinus ad lyram* [L.], fish out of water; square peg, square peg in a round hole; failure etc. 732.4.

5. *v.* disagree, not jibe [coll., U.S.] etc. 23.7; be *or* run at cross-purposes, be out of harmony, disaccord, conflict, clash, jar, jostle, collide, swear at [slang]; come amiss; mismatch, mismate; *humano capiti cervicem jungere equinam* [L.]; dispute, quarrel etc. (discord) 713.6; interfere etc. (intrude) 228.10; not hear to [coll.] etc. (dissent) 489.4; differ etc. 15.5.

6. *adj.* disagreeing etc. *v.,* discordant, disaccordant, discrepant, divergent, variant, at variance, at odds, at war, hostile, antagonistic, repugnant, inaccordant, out of accord etc. 23.1, out of whack [slang], clashing, clashy [coll.], jarring, factious, dissident, unconsonant, incompatible, irreconcilable, inconsistent; incongruent, incongruous; unharmonious, disharmonious; intrusive; disproportionate, disproportioned; unconformable, exceptional etc. 83.9, 10; dissentient etc. 489.5; contentious etc. 901.9; differing etc. 15.7; dissimilar etc. 18.4.

7. *adj.* inapt, unapt; inappropriate, unappropriate [rare], malappropriate [rare], *mal à propos* [F.]; unseasonable, ill-timed, untimely; improper, ill-adapted, infelicitous, inadmissible, unbecoming; unsuited, unsuitable, dissuitable [rare]; unfit, unfitting, unbefitting; out of character, out of keeping, out of proportion, out of joint, out of tune, out of place, out

of season, out of time, out of its element; inapposite etc. (irrelevant) 10.6.

8. *adj.* uncongenial, unsympathetic; ill-assorted, ill-sorted; mismatched, misjoined, mismated, misplaced; unaccommodating, irreducible, uncommensurable.

9. *adv.* discordantly etc. *adj., à tort et à travers* [F.].

10. *prep.* in disagreement with, in defiance of, in contempt of, in opposition to, at cross-purposes with; in spite of, regardless of etc. (notwithstanding) 30.8.

25. Quantity

Absolute Quantity.—1. *n.* quantity, amount, quantum, feck [Scot. and dial.], mass, bulk, substance, magnitude, amplitude, extent, sum; measure, measurement; strength, force, numbers; size etc. (dimensions) 192; number etc. 84.

2. *n.* a quantity, amount, sum, measure, portion, stock, batch, lot, dose, deal, grist [coll., U.S.], gob [chiefly dial. and slang], boiling [slang], jag *or* jagg [dial. U.S.], swad [slang, U.S.], chance [dial. U.S.]; armful, handful, yaffle [dial.], mouthful, spoonful, cupful, capful, etc.; quota, quotiety [rare], quotum; great quantity etc. 31.3; small quantity etc. 32.2; pittance etc. 640.5.

3. *n.* (science of quantity) quantitative analysis, gravimetric analysis, volumetric analysis etc. (mathematics) 85.2.

4. *n.* (logic) category, general conception, universal predicament.

5. *v.* quantify, rate, fix; modify, qualify; measure etc. 466.10.

6. *adj.* quantitative, quantitive, quantic, quantical, quantified, quantitied [rare].

7. *adj.* some, any, more or less.

8. *adv.* to the amount *or* tune of . . . [coll.].

26. Degree

Relative Quantity.—1. *n.* degree, grade, step, *pas* [F.], round, rung, stair, point, mark, peg; notch, cut, hole [all coll.]; extent, measure, amount, ratio, stint *or* stent, standard, height, pitch, reach, remove, compass, amplitude, range, scale, scope, caliber; gradation, graduation; shadow, shade; rank, sphere, stage, station, status, stand, standing, footing; period, interval, line [Mus.], space [Mus.]; rate, way, sort; intensity, strength etc. (greatness) 31.

2. *v.* graduate, gradation, mark with degrees, divide into grades; change gradually, pass by degrees, shade off; calibrate, measure; rectify.

3. *adj.* comparative, relative; within the bounds etc. (limit) 233.

4. *adj.* gradual, gradational, gradatory [rare], shading off.

5. *adv.* by degrees, degreewise [Mus.]; gradually, gradatim; step by step, grade by grade, *di grado in grado* [It.], bit by bit, little by little, inch by inch, drop by drop; by slow degrees, by inches, by little and little; in some degree *or* measure, to some extent; to such an extent, *pro tanto* [L.], for so much, inasmuch; to whatever extent, whatever; however, howe'er, howsoever, howsomever [dial. or vulg.].

27. Equality

(See 28. Inequality; also 13. Identity, 17. Similarity)

Sameness of Quantity or Degree.—1. *n.* equality, parity, coextension, symmetry, balance, poise; evenness, monotony, level.

2. *n.* equivalence *or* equivalency, equipollence, equipoise, equilibrium, equiponderance; par, quits; distinction without a difference, six of one and half a dozen of the other, not a pin to choose; coequality, coevality [rare], isonomy, isopolity, isotropy, parallelism, owelty [Law]; sameness etc. (identity) 13; likeness etc. (similarity) 17.

3. *n.* equalization, equation, equaling; equilibration, co-ordination, adjustment, readjustment; halves, halvers [obs. exc. dial. and slang]; compensation etc. 30.

4. *n.* tie, draw, drawn game *or* battle, dead heat, neck-and-neck race, nose finish [turf slang], standoff [coll.], level, even Stephen [slang, U.S.], even break [slang]; tied score, knotted score [slang].

---

26. Who shines in the second rank is eclipsed in the first.—VOLTAIRE.   Curs of low degree.—GOLDSMITH.

27. All men are created equal.—DECLARATION OF INDEPENDENCE.   One man is as good as another—and a great dale betther, as the Irish philosopher said.—THACKERAY.   All mankind are equalized by death.—HOOD.   We shall not produce equality by turning everything upside down.—A. P. HERBERT.   What's sauce for the goose is sauce for the gander.

5. *n.* equal, match, ditto [coll.], peer, compeer, equivalent, equipollent, coequal, parallel, countervail [obs.]; mate, fellow etc. (analogue) 17.5; synonym etc. 516.3.

6. *v.* be equal etc. *adj.*, equal, match, fellow with, correspond, cope with [obs.], reach, touch; keep pace *or* step with, run abreast; come *or* amount to, come up to, check with *or* up with [coll.], stack up with [slang], match up with; be *or* lie on a level with, balance, parallel; come *or* amount to the same thing, ditto [coll.], even, even off, break even [slang]; tie, knot the score [slang].

7. *v.* render equal, equalize, equate, equivalent [rare], square, level, dress, balance, strike a balance, poise, adjust, trim; handicap, give points; fit, accommodate; establish *or* restore equality *or* equilibrium, re-equalize, readjust; stretch on the bed of Procrustes; adapt etc. (render accordant) 23.8; compensate etc. 30.4.

8. *adj.* equal, even, even Stephen [slang, U.S.], level, coequal, symmetric(al), co-ordinate; equiparant, equiparate [rare]; horse and horse [slang], hank and hank [Naut.]; square, hunky [slang, U.S.]; on even terms, on a par with, on a level with, on a footing with; up to the mark, up to the notch [coll.] etc. (*see* mark, notch etc. 26.1).

9. *adj.* equivalent, tantamount, corresponding; quits, on *or* upon a par; homologous, homologic(al), resolvable into, convertible; much at one, much the same as, as good as, as broad as long, neither more nor less; fifty-fifty [slang, U.S.], half-and-half, on or to the halvers [slang]; all one, all the same; equipollent, equiponderant, equiponderous, equibalanced; equalized etc. *v.*, drawn, tied; isochronal, isochronous, isoperimetric(al); isobath, isobathic; identical etc. 13.6, 7; synonymous etc. 516.11; similar etc. 17.10–16.

10. *adv.* equally etc. *adj.*, at the same rate, with equal step, *pari passu* [L.], to the same degree, *ad eundem* [L.]; to all intents and purposes, other things being equal, *caeteris paribus* [L.]; to a standoff [coll.].

28. Men are made by nature unequal. It is vain, therefore, to treat them as if they were equal.—Froude. Inequality is as dear to the American heart as liberty itself.—Howells. When people have to obey other people's or-

28. Inequality
(See 27. Equality; also 15. Difference)

Difference of Quantity or Degree.—1. *n.* inequality, unequality, inequation; inequalness [rare], unevenness etc. *adj.*; disparity, imparity [rare]; odds; inclination of the balance, partiality; casting weight, makeweight; inadequation [arch.], inadequacy, shortcoming; superiority etc. 33; inferiority etc. 34; difference etc. 15.

2. *v.* be unequal etc. *adj.*, countervail, turn the scale; have *or* give the advantage; kick the beam, be found wanting; topple, topple over; overmatch etc. 33.5, 6; not come up to etc. 34.4.

3. *adj.* unequal, inequal [rare], uneven, irregular, disparate, partial, inadequate; ill-matched, ill-balanced; overbalanced, unbalanced; top-heavy, lopsided; disquiparant; odd; differing etc. 15.7.

4. *adj.* unequaled, unparalleled, unmatched, matchless, fellowless [rare], unrivaled, unique, unapproached, inimitable, transcendent, unpeered, peerless, nonpareil, unexampled, unpatterned [rare]; not to be compared to, not a circumstance to [coll., U.S.], not a marker on [coll.].

5. *adv.* unequally etc. *adj.*, unequal; *haud passibus aequis* (Vergil).

29. Mean

1. *n.* mean, golden mean, *juste-milieu* [F.], medium (*pl.* media), happy medium, intermedium [obs.], average, balance, normal, rule, run, *meden agan* [Gr. μηδὲν ἄγαν], *ariston metron* [Gr. ἄριστον μέτρον]; middle term, *mezzo termine* [It.]; middle state, middle ground; generality; middle etc. 68; middle of the road, neutrality etc. (mid-course) 628;

ders, equality is out of the question.—Gilbert.
29. *Est modus in rebus* [There is a mean in (all) things].—Horace. Keep the golden mean.—Publilius. Give me neither poverty nor riches.—Bible. Measure is a merry mean.—J. Russell. Not below mediocrity, nor above it.—Johnson. *Medium tenuere beati* [Happy are they who have kept a middle course].

compromise etc. 774; moderation etc. 174; *aurea mediocritas* [L.] etc. (mediocrity) 736.

2. *v.* average, split the difference, take the average etc. *n.*, reduce to a mean etc. *n.*, strike a balance, pair off.

3. *adj.* mean, medium, intermediate, intermediary, medial; average, ordinary, normal, standard; middle etc. 68.5; mediocre etc. 736.3; neutral etc. 628.3.

4. *adv.* mediumly etc. *adj.*, in the mean, *in medias res* [L.]; in the middle etc. (midway) 68.6.

5. *adv.* on an average, in the long run; taking one *or* one thing with another, taking all things together, taking all in all, taking it for all in all; *communibus annis* [L.], in round numbers; generally etc. 78.15.

30. Compensation

1. *n.* compensation, recompense, recompensation [obs. exc. Scot. Law]; indemnification, indemnity; measure for measure; commutation, substitution; neutralization, nullification; counteraction etc. 179; retaliation etc. 718; equalization etc. 27.3; compromise etc. 774; atonement etc. 952.

2. *n.* setoff, offset, counterpoise, counterbalance, counterweight, makeweight, casting weight, ballast; equivalent, *quid pro quo* [L.]; countervail [obs.], countervailing; cross debt, cross demand, counterclaim; amends etc. (atonement) 952.

3. *n.* pay etc. (payment) 807, (reward) 973; bribe etc. 618.2; gift etc. 784.3.

4. *v.* compensate, compense [rare], make compensation, make good, make up for, recompense, indemnify; cover, fill up; neutralize, nullify, rob Peter to pay Paul; equalize etc. 27.7; make amends, redeem etc. (atone) 952.4; pay, reward etc. 973.3; repay etc. 807.9.

5. *v.* offset, set off, counteract, countervail, counterpoise, counterbalance, balance; outbalance, overbalance; hedge;

square, square up; give and take, get it coming and going [slang].

6. *adj.* compensating, countervailing etc. *v.*; compensative, compensatory; recompensive, amendatory, indemnificatory, reparative; in the opposite scale; equivalent etc. (equal) 27.8, 9.

7. *adv.* in compensation *or* return, in consideration, for a consideration.

8. *adv., prep.* notwithstanding, but, all the same [coll.], yet, still, however, howe'er; nevertheless, natheless *or* nathless [arch.]; although, though, howbeit, albeit; mauger *or* maugre [arch.], at all events, at any rate; in spite of, spite of [coll.], in despite of, despite; regardless of, without regard to; be that as it may, for all that, even so, on the other hand, at the same time, *quoad minus* [L.], *quand même* [F.], however that may be; after all, after all is said and done; taking one thing with another etc. (average) 29.5; in defiance of etc. 708.6; contrarily etc. 14.7; in disagreement with etc. 24.10; excepting etc. 55.7; otherwise etc. 18.6.

31. Greatness
(See **32. Smallness**; also **192. Size**)

1. *n.* greatness, largeness, vastness etc. *adj.*; magnitude, immensity, enormity, muchness; might, strength, intensity, fullness, amplitude, bigness etc. (size) 192; numerousness etc. 102; boundlessness etc. (infinity) 105.

2. *n.* eminence, distinction, consequence, prominence, grandeur, dignity, notability, nobility; fame etc. (repute) 873; importance etc. 642; pre-eminence etc. (superiority) 33.

3. *n.* great quantity, quantity *or* quantities, abundance *or* abundancy, profusion, volume, world *or* worlds, sea, ocean *or* oceans, mass; mint, peck, pack, plenty [all chiefly coll.]; lot *or* lots, considerable, deal, good *or* great deal, quite a little; sight, galore, pot, raft *or* rafts, slew, slews, whole slew, heap *or* heaps, pile *or* piles, loads, stack *or* stacks, batch, mess, wad *or* wads, hunk [all coll.]; peck, bushel; load, carload, cartload, wagonload, shipload; flood, spring tide; ac-

---

30. *Saepe creat molles aspera spina rosas* [Often the sharp thorn produces delicate roses].—OVID.   It is a comfort that the medal has two sides.—JEFFERSON.   Every sweet has its sour; every evil its good.—EMERSON.   White shall not neutralize the black, nor good compensate bad in man.—BROWNING.   Robbing Peter to pay Paul.

31. Some are born great, some achieve greatness, and some have greatness thrust upon them.—SHAKESPEARE.   The great man is the man who does a thing for the first time.—A.

cumulation, collection, bunch etc. (assemblage) 72; hoard, stock etc. (store) 636.1, 2; greater part etc. 50.3; host, quite a few etc. (multitude) 102.5.

lump, gob or gobs, heap sight [all slang or dial.]; swad, smear or whole smear, fat lot, oodle or oodles [all slang]; chance, quite a chance, right smart chance, scad or scads, slather or slathers, lashings, lavish, power [all dial.].

4. *v.* be great etc. *adj.*; run high, soar, tower, loom, bulk, bulk large, rise or carry to a great height, know no bounds; tower above, rise above, transcend; ascend, mount.

5. *v.* enlarge etc. (increase) 35.3, (expand) 194.5–8.

6. *adj.* great, grand, large, tall [slang, U.S.], considerable, mickle [arch.], goodly, noble, precious, mighty, full, intense, strong, sound, passing [obs.], heavy, plenary, deep, high; signal, at its height, in the zenith; sad, grave, serious; big, bulky etc. (sizable) 192.11–15; ample, abundant etc. (plenty) 639.7; many etc. 102.5; important etc. 642.10–14; greater etc. 33.7.

7. *adj.* extensive, wholesale, sweeping, wide, broad, liberal, far-stretched, far-reaching, fargoing, far-embracing, far-extending, far-flying, far-ranging, far-flung, far-spread, far-spreading, widespread, indiscriminate; far-famed, far-heard; world-wide, prevalent, universal etc. 78.10, 11; abundant etc. 639.7.

8. *adj.* vast, immense, enormous, magnitudinous [rare], stupendous, prodigious, gigantic, colossal, titanic, towering; Atlantean, Herculean, Cyclopean; astonishing, appalling, incredible; fabulous; whopping, whacking, banging, thumping, thundering, roaring, slapping, swingeing, rousing [all coll.]; whaling, spanking, whooping, howling, staving [all slang]; fearful, frightful, dreadful, horrible, terrible, terrific [all coll.]; huge etc. (size) 192.15; unlimited etc. (infinite) 105.3; marvelous etc. (wonderful) 870.7; unsurpassed etc. (supreme) 33.8.

9. *adj.* inordinate, excessive, extravagant, exorbitant, outrageous, preposterous, unconscionable, monstrous; overdone, overwrought, overgrown.

10. *adj.* inexpressible, unutterable, indescribable, ineffable, unspeakable, beyond expression, nameless, unnamable.

11. *adj.* undiminished, unabated, unreduced, unrestricted; undivided etc. 50.7.

12. *adj.* absolute, utter, downright, thorough, thoroughgoing, thoroughpaced, out-and-out, stark, desperate, profound, positive, pronounced, decided, unequivocal, essential, consummate, perfect, finished, complete, extreme; arrant, unmitigated, flagrant, tall [slang, U.S.], glaring, stark-staring, rank, crass, gross.

13. *adj.* remarkable, of mark, marked, pointed, veriest; notable, noticeable, noteworthy; extraordinary etc. (unusual) 83.10.

14. *adj.* august, eminent, distinguished, grand, dignified, sublime, majestic etc. (reputable) 873.15–19.

15. *adv.* (in a great or high degree) greatly, largely etc. *adj.*; much, mickle [arch.], muchly [obs. exc. slang], very much, so very much, ever so much, ever so, never so, so, pretty much or well, no end [coll., U.S.], no end of, not a little, a deal [coll.]; by much, by far, far and away, far and wide, widely; to a large or great extent, in a great measure, on a large scale, by wholesale; like or as all creation [coll.], like or as all get-out [slang, U.S.], like or as all possessed [coll., U.S.]; very, quite, plenty [coll.], real [coll.], right [dial. and coll.], pretty, jolly [coll., Eng.], gallows [dial.], parlous [coll.], right smart [dial., U.S.].

considerably, considerable [obs. exc. dial.], exceedingly, tremendously, extravagantly, richly, intensely, acutely, exquisitely, preciously, precious [coll.], powerfully or powerful [dial. and coll.], mightily, mighty [chiefly coll.], almightily or almighty [slang], mortally [coll.], mortal [chiefly dial.], properly [chiefly slang], proper [dial. and coll.].

16. *adv.* (in a positive degree) absolutely, positively, truly, verily, indeed, decidedly, unequivocally, unconditionally, assuredly, certainly, essentially, fundamentally, radically, downright, purely, seriously, in all conscience; for a certainty, for fair [slang]; for the most part, in the main.

SMITH. The sense of greatness keeps a nation great.—W. WATSON. Too huge for mortal tongue, or pen of scribe.—KEATS.

There is no great and no small / To the soul that maketh all.—EMERSON. Great things are made of little things.—BROWNING. *A*

17. *adv.* (in a complete degree) fully, thoroughly, throughout etc. (completely) 52.13–15; totally, altogether, entirely etc. (wholly) 50.10; abundantly, amply etc. (sufficiently) 639.8.

18. *adv.* (in a supreme degree) supremely, pre-eminently, superlatively etc. (superiority) 33.10.

19. *adv.* (in an extreme degree) extremely, in the extreme, most, *à outrance* [F.], *à toute outrance* [F.]; indefinitely, immeasurably, incalculably, infinitely; beyond compare or comparison, beyond measure or all bounds; to the utmost etc. (utterly) 52.14.

20. *adv.* (in an excessive degree) excessively, immoderately, unreasonably, monstrously, preposterously, grossly, inordinately, exorbitantly, woundily *or* woundy [arch.], superabundantly, overly [chiefly Scot. and U.S.], enormously, out of all proportion, out of sight [coll.]; too, too-too [slang].

21. *adv.* (in a marked degree) remarkably, particularly, singularly; curiously, oddly, uncommonly, uncommon [dial. and coll.], unusually, extraordinarily, peculiarly, strangely, queerly; famously, egregiously, prominently, glaringly, notably, signally, strikingly, pointedly, emphatically; wonderfully [coll.], wonderful [dial.], wondrous, amazingly, amazing [dial.], surprisingly, astonishingly, incredibly, marvelously, awfully [coll.], awful [dial. and coll.], stupendously.

22. *adv.* (in a violent degree) violently, furiously, terrifically [coll.], severely, desperately, desperate [dial. and coll.], with a vengeance; all to pieces, all to sticks *or* sticks and staves, all to smash, all to smithereens [all coll.].

23. *adv.* (in a painful or distressing degree) painfully, sadly, sorely, bitterly, piteously, grievously, miserably, cruelly, woefully, lamentably, balefully, dolorously, distressingly; shockingly, frightfully [coll.], awfully [coll.], awful [dial. and coll.], dreadfully [coll.], dreadful [dial. and coll.], terribly [coll.], terrible [dial. and slang], horribly [coll.], horrible [slang], abominably [coll.], something awful, ~ fierce *or* terrible [slang], the worst way [slang].

24. *adv.* (in an infamous degree) cursedly, confoundedly, damnably, devilishly [coll.], deucedly [slang], dashedly [coll.], darned [coll.], blamed *or* blame [coll.], plaguily [coll.], plaguy [coll.], infernally [coll.], hellishly, hell-firedly *or* hell-fired [slang], all-firedly *or* all-fired [slang], bally [slang, Eng.], bloody [slang, Eng.], bleeding [slang, Eng.], beastly [coll.].

32. Smallness
(See 31. Greatness; also 193. Littleness)

1. *n.* smallness, littleness, picayunishness [U.S.] etc. *adj.*; tenuity; diminutiveness etc. (small size) 193; paucity, fewness etc. (small number) 103; insignificance etc. (unimportance) 643; inextension etc. 180a.

2. *n.* small quantity, finite quantity, modicum, minimum; vanishing point; material point, atom, particle, electron, molecule, corpuscle, point, speck, flyspeck, dot, mote, jot, iota, hooter [dial. and slang], hoot [slang], ace; look, thought, idea, dab [dial. and coll.], dablet [coll.], drab [coll.], canch [dial.], dight [dial.], whit, tittle, shade, shadow, suspicion; spark, scintilla, gleam, glim [Scot.]; touch, cast.

grain, scruple, granule, globule, minim, sup, sip, sop, spice, drop, droplet, driblet, sprinkling, dash, *morceau* [F.] screed [Scot.], smack, taste, smell, lick, tinge, tincture; inch, patch, scantling, cantle, cantlet, gobbet, dole, pittance, mite [chiefly coll.], bit, little bit [coll.], *soupçon* [F.], small dose, homeopathic dose [coll.]; morsel, crumb, scrimption [dial.], smidge *or* smidgen [dial., U.S.], smitch [coll.], snitch [coll.].

scrap, tatter, flitter [coll.], smither [coll.], smithereen [coll.], shivereen [Scot. and North. Eng.], smatter [Scot.], shred, tag, splinter, rag; seed, fritter, shive; snip, snippet; snick, snack [dial.]; snatch, slip; chip, chipping; shiver [dial. and coll.], sliver, clipping, paring, shaving, hair; nutshell; thimbleful, spoonful, handful, capful, mouthful; mere nothing, next to nothing, hardly anything, just enough to swear by, a drop in the bucket *or* ocean, the shadow of a shade, the suspicion of a suspicion; minutiae, details;

---

maximis ad minima [From the greatest things to the least].

32. Always the Gods give small things to the small.—CALLIMACHUS. For the proverb

fragment, fraction etc. (small part) 51; animalcule etc. 193.2-4; trifle etc. (unimportant thing) 643.3; a few etc. 103.2.

3. *n.* minutiae etc. (particulars) 79.3, (trivia) 643.4.

4. *v.* be small etc. *adj.*, lie in a nutshell; cut no ice [slang], not amount to a hill of beans [coll.]; be found wanting, kick the beam.

5. *v.* diminish etc. (decrease) 36; contract etc. 195.4.

6. *adj.* small, little, dinky [slang], puny; minute, miniature, minikin; diminutive etc. (small in size) 193.8.

7. *adj.* limited, conditioned, circumscribed, bounded, finite; part-way, halfway.

8. *adj.* inconsiderable, insignificant, picayunish [U.S.], moderate, modest, light, slender, slight, sparse, homeopathic [coll.]; scant, scanty; scrimp, scrimpy [coll.]; skimp, skimpy [coll.], skimping [chiefly coll.]; middling, tolerable, passable, indifferent, fair, fairish, fair to middling [coll.], soso *or* so-so [coll.], no great shakes [coll.]; below *or* under par, below *or* under the mark; shallow, depthless, cursory, superficial, skin-deep; short, brief, low; at a low ebb, at low-water mark; meager, scarce etc. (insufficient) 640.9, 10; few etc. 103.3; trivial, petty, paltry etc. (unimportant) 643.10-12.

9. *adj.* inappreciable, evanescent etc. (infinitesimal) 193.10.

10. *adj.* dainty, delicate, puny, tender; subtle, subtile; fragile etc. (frail) 160.11.

11. *adj.* mere, simple, sheer, stark, bare, plain.

12. *adv.* (in a small degree) smally [rare], slightly etc. *adj.*; to a small extent, on a small scale; imperfectly, faintly, feebly, weakly, miserably, wretchedly; insufficiently etc. 640.13.

13. *adv.* (in a certain or limited degree) partially, partly, in part; to a certain degree *or* extent, to such an extent, *pro tanto* [L.]; comparatively, relatively; simply, only, purely, merely; at least, at the least; at most, at the most; in ever so small a degree, ever so little, as little as may be, *tant soit peu* [F.]; thus far, within bounds, in a manner, in a manner of speaking [coll.], after a fashion.

14. *adv.* (in some degree) in some measure, to some extent, somewhat, some [coll.], something [chiefly coll.], something like [coll.], rather, ratherish [coll.], kind of [coll.], sort of [coll.], pretty; moderately, passably, tolerably, tolerable [dial.], middling [coll.], middling of [dial.], soso *or* so-so [coll.], pretty well, well enough; imperfectly etc. 651.5.

15. *adv. etc.* almost, most [coll. and dial.], nearly, near, nigh, nigh about, nigh on *or* upon [dial.], well-nigh, near *or* close upon, pretty near, around [coll.], *peu s'en faut* [F.]; near the mark, within an ace *or* inch of, on the brink of; not quite, all but.

16. *adv. etc.* scarcely, hardly, barely, only just, no more than.

17. *adv. etc.* (in an uncertain degree) about, thereabouts, somewhere about *or* near, around, *circa* [L.], nearly, approximately, say; the same more or less, the same little more or less.

18. *adv.* (in no degree) noway *or* noways, nowise, in no wise, in no respect, by no means, by no manner of means, on no account, at no hand, not at all, not by a darn sight *or* long shot [slang], not in the least, not much [coll.], not a bit, not a bit of it, not a whit, ~ jot, ~ shadow etc. *n.*

33. Superiority
(See 34. Inferiority)

1. *n.* superiority, pre-eminence, pre-eminency [now rare]; precedence, priority, lead, transcendence *or* transcendency; ascendance *or* ascendence, ascendancy *or* ascendency, prestige, prepotence *or* prepotency, prepollence *or* prepollency; prevalence *or* prevalency, prevailment [all rare]; predominance *or* predominancy, predomination; preponderance *or* preponderancy, preponderation [rare]; excellence etc. 648; importance etc. 642; greatness etc. 31; majority etc. 100.2; perfection etc. 650.

2. *n.* advantage, vantage; upper *or* whip

---

saith that many small maken a great.—CHAUCER. The microscope cannot find the animalcule which is less perfect for being little.—EMERSON. Let a man once overcome his selfish terror at his own finitude, and his finitude is, in one sense, overcome.—SANTAYANA.

33. No two men can be half an hour together but one shall acquire an evident superiority over the other.—JOHNSON. You're a better man than I am, Gunga Din!—KIPLING. No man can ever end with being superior who will not

hand, odds, inside track [coll.]; edge, bulge, jump, drop, deadwood, pull over [all slang]; superior *or* commanding position, vantage ground, ~ point *or* post, advantage ground [rare], eminence [obs.], height; leverage etc. (influence) 175.

3. *n.* supremacy, supremeness etc. *adj.*, supremity [rare]; primacy, paramountcy, the highest degree, *ne plus ultra* [L.]; leadership, headship, sovereignty etc. (dominion) 737.2, 3; the highest position, crest, maximum, climax etc. (summit) 210.

4. *n.* a superior, higher-up [slang]; superior being, superman, superhuman [rare], Triton among the minnows; ace, crackajack [slang, U.S.], heavyweight [coll., U.S.]; superioress [of a convent] etc. (clergy) 996.12; top sawyer [coll.] etc. 642.6; master etc. 745.

5. *v.* be superior etc. *adj.*, possess superiority etc. *n.*, exceed, excel, transcend, rival, cap; top, overtop, o'ertop; overpass, override, overmatch; preponderate, predominate, prevail; distance, surpass, pass, be ahead of; beat, beat hollow *or* all hollow [coll.], play the leading part, play first fiddle, beat the band [slang], cut out [coll.], come it all over [slang], have it all over [coll.], skin [slang], skin a mile [slang].

outdo, outpoint, outprize [obs. exc. dial.], outstrip, outplay, outrival, outrank, out-Tory, out-Herod Herod; get ahead of, outweigh, outbalance, overweigh, overbalance, overbear; eclipse, throw into the shade, take the shine out of [coll.], put one's nose out of joint [coll.]; precede, take precedence, come *or* rank first, come to the front, lead, lead the way, lead the dance, take the lead; beat *or* surpass all others, beat all creation [coll.], bear the palm, bear away the bell, bring home the bacon [coll., U.S.], take the cake [slang, U.S.]; break the record, reach a new high [coll.].

6. *v.* have the advantage *or* ascendancy, have superiority over, have the upper *or* whip hand, have the pull over [slang], have the edge on, ~ bulge on, ~ deadwood on, ~ jump *or* drop on [all slang], have the inside track [coll.], have

the better *or* best of, have on the hip; change the preponderance, turn the scale *or* balance, turn the tables; gain the ascendancy etc. 731.8.

7. *adj.* superior, greater, better, major, higher, upper, over, above; surpassing, exceeding etc. *v.*; ascendant, in the ascendant, in ascendancy; eminent, distinguished, marked; more than a match for, one (*or* two, three, etc.) up on [slang].

8. *adj.* supreme, greatest, banner [chiefly coll.], highest, maximal, maximum, utmost, uppermost, top, topmost, tiptop [coll.], top-notch [coll.], top-hole [slang, chiefly Eng.], A 1, A one, A number 1 [coll.], of the first water; paramount, chief, main, principal, leading, dominant, predominant, hegemonic(al), crowning, capital, cardinal; prime, primary; pre-eminent, supereminent; ruling, overruling.

peerless, matchless, unmatched, unrivaled, unparagoned, unparalleled, unequaled, unapproached, unsurpassed, unexcelled, champion [chiefly coll.]; inimitable, incomparable, beyond compare *or* comparison, *ne plus ultra* [L.], easily first, *facile princeps* [L.], second to none, *nulli secundus* [L.], *sans pareil* [F.], without equal *or* parallel, superlative, transcendent *or* transcendental; sovereign, suzerain; *plus royaliste que le roi* [F.]; best etc. 648.9; perfect etc. 650.5.

9. *adv.*, *prep.* beyond, more, over; over *or* above the mark, above par; in advance of, upwards of, over and above, in addition to; at the top of the scale, at its height.

10. *adv.* (in a superior or supreme degree) eminently, egregiously [obs. exc. humorous], prominently, remarkably; pre-eminently, surpassingly, superlatively, supremely, of all things, the most, to crown all, *par excellence* [F.]; principally, especially, particularly, peculiarly, mainly, in the main, in the first place, before everything else, above all, to crown all; *a fortiori* [L.], even, yea, still more, all the more.

34. Inferiority
(See 33. Superiority)

1. *n.* inferiority, subordinacy, subordinancy [obs.], subordinance [obs.], sub-

---

begin with being inferior.—S. SMITH. Inferiors revolt in order that they may be equal, and equals that they may be superior.—ARISTOTLE.

34. Exaggerated sensitiveness is an expression of the feeling of inferiority.—ADLER.

ordination, subjacency [rare], secondariness etc. *adj.*; deficiency, inadequacy, inadequation [arch.], imperfection; poorness, smallness, littleness, meanness, baseness, shabbiness; back seat [coll.], second fiddle; lowest degree, minimum; shortcoming etc. 304.

2. *n.* (personal inferiority) juniority, minority; subservience, subjection; inferiority complex; commonalty etc. 876.

3. *n.* an inferior, underling, understrapper, subordinate, subsidiary, subaltern, sub [coll.], secondary, second fiddle, second-stringer [slang, U.S.], bottom sawyer [coll.]; henchman, liege etc. (servant) 746.

4. *v.* be inferior etc. *adj.*, fall *or* come short of, not come up to, not pass, want, be found wanting, kick the beam; concede superiority, hand it to [slang], yield the palm, retire into the shade, hide its diminished head, play second fiddle, take a back seat [coll.]; be unequal to etc. 28.2; be smaller etc. 195.5.

5. *adj.* inferior, deterior [rare], smaller, less, lesser, lower, subordinate, subaltern, sub, secondary, minor, junior, humble; not fit to hold a candle to, not a marker on *or* to [slang], not a circumstance to [coll., U.S.], not a patch on [coll.]; in the shade, thrown into the shade; left a mile [coll.], not in it [slang], out of the picture [coll.]; weighed in the balance and found wanting; beat, skinned etc. (*see* skin etc. 33.5); deficient, second-rate etc. (imperfect) 651.4; unimportant etc. 643.10–12; small etc. 32.6–11; bad etc. 649.8.

6. *adj.* most inferior, lowest; least, smallest etc. (*see* little, small etc. 193.8).

7. *adv., prep.* less, under, below, short of, under *or* below the mark, under par, at a low ebb; at the bottom of the scale, at the bottom of the heap [slang, U.S.]; at a disadvantage.

35. Increase
(See 36. Decrease; also 37. Addition, 194. Expansion)

1. *n.* increase, increasement [rare]; augmentation, enlargement, extension, increment, accretion, aggrandizement, accumulation; enhancement, reinforcement, redoubling, intensification, aggravation, magnification, exaggeration; exacerbation, exacerbescence [obs.]; advance, appreciation, rise *or* raise [as in price], boost [slang, U.S.], hike [slang], up [coll.]; flood tide, spring tide; dilation, inflation etc. (expansion) 194; accession etc. (addition) 37; spread etc. (dispersion) 73; improvement etc. 658.

2. *n.* gain, produce, product, profit, getting, gettings, take [slang, U.S.], take-in [coll.], rake-off [slang, U.S.], booty, plunder, superlucration [obs.], cleanup [slang].

3. *v.* increase, make greater, augment, add to, enlarge, largify [dial.], eke [arch. and dial.], extend, aggrandize; greaten [arch.], biggen [chiefly dial., Eng.], lengthen, heighten, deepen, thicken; enhance, strengthen, reinforce, amplify, intensify, step up [coll.], aggravate, magnify, exaggerate; double, redouble, triple etc.; expand, distend, inflate; raise, exalt, boost [slang], hike *or* hike up [slang], jack *or* jack up [coll.], up [coll.]; add fuel to the flame, *oleum addere camino* [L.]; add etc. 37.3, 4; spread etc. (disperse) 73.3; improve etc. 658.6.

4. *v.* be increased, become greater, increase, grow, augment, advance, appreciate [coll. exc. in value], look up [coll.], wax, get ahead, gain strength, run *or* shoot up; multiply, prolificate, be prolific *or* fruitful; rise, mount etc. (ascend) 305.4; enlarge, expand etc. (become larger) 194.5–7.

5. *adj.* increased, enlarged etc. *v.*; undiminished, unreduced etc. (*see* diminish, reduce etc. 36.3, 4); additional etc. (added) 37.7.

6. *adj.* increasing, growing, crescent, crescive [rare], lengthening, multiplying, intensifying, intensive, intensitive [rare], incretionary [rare]; on the increase, crescendo.

7. *adv.* increasingly etc. *adj.*, crescendo.

Weighed in the balance and found wanting. 35. *Vires acquirit eundo* [It gains strength as it goes].—Vergil. He enlargeth the nations, and straiteneth them again.—Bible. They go from strength to strength.—Bible. The Fraction of Life can be increased in value not so much by increasing your numerator as by lessening your denominator.—Carlyle. We are here to add what we can to, not to get what we can from, Life.—Osler. Tall oaks from little acorns grow.—D. Everett.

36. Decrease

(See 35. Increase; also 38. Deduction, 195. Contraction)

1. *n.* decrease, decrescence, diminishment, diminution, lessening etc. *v.*, alleviation, mitigation, curtailment, cut, reduction, step-down [coll.], rebatement [rare], abatement, letup [coll.], declension; attenuation, extenuation; decrement, waste, loss, shrinkage, depreciation, wear and tear, erosion, consumption; subtraction etc. 38; contraction etc. 195; abridgment etc. (shortening) 201.2; moderation etc. 174.

2. *n.* subsidence, decline, slump [coll.], lapse, wane, reflux, ebb, ebb tide, neap tide, ebbing; catabasis [Med.].

3. *v.* decrease, diminish, lessen, grow less; subside, decline, wane, ebb, bate, abate, let up, languish, dwindle, melt *or* die away, tail off, drop off, fall off, fall away, fall to a low ebb, run low; waste, wear, waste *or* wear away, crumble, erode, consume, consume away, tabefy [rare]; retire into the shade, hide its diminishing head; shrink etc. (contract) 195.4; descend etc. 306.4.

4. *v.* reduce, render less, lessen, decrease, diminish, minish [rare], minify [rare], minimize, belittle; dwarf, bedwarf; bate, abate; deliquesce, ease, remit; attenuate, extenuate, weaken; lower, step down [coll.], tune down [coll.]; take from, take away; fritter away; compress, constrict etc. (contract) 195.4; abbreviate, curtail etc. (shorten) 201.4; mitigate etc. (moderate) 174.5; subtract, pare etc. (deduct) 38.4-6; reduce weight etc. 203.8.

5. *adj.* decreased, decreasing etc. *v.*; decrescent, reductive; deliquescent, contractive; decrescendo.

6. *adv.* decreasingly etc. *adj.*, decrescendo, on the wane etc. *n.*

37. Addition

(See 38. Deduction; also 35. Increase, 39. Adjunct)

1. *n.* addition, additory, adjection [rare], accession, reinforcement; superaddition, superposition, superjunction, superfetation; annexation, joining etc. (junction) 43; augmentation, increment etc. (increase) 35; appendage, affix etc. (adjunct) 39; interjection etc. 228.2; insertion etc. 300.

2. *n.* computation, adding, footing, totaling, casting, reckoning, calculation, summation; count, cast, total, tottle [dial.], tot *or* tot-up [coll., chiefly Eng.]; plus sign, plus; sum, gross amount etc. (all) 50.2.

3. *v.* add, annex, affix, plus [coll.], clap on, saddle on, tack on, tuck on [slang], hitch on [coll.], slap on [coll.], append, tag, adject [rare], attach, hitch up [coll.], postfix, adjoin [rare]; superadd, superpose, superimpose; fix a burden upon, burden, encumber, saddle with; interpose etc. (interject) 228.8; infix, ingraft etc. (insert) 300.5, 6.

4. *v.* reinforce, restrengthen, recruit, add to, swell the ranks of; fortify, buttress etc. (strengthen) 159.8; enlarge, augment etc. (increase) 35.3.

5. *v.* compute, add, add up, foot up, count up, total, tottle [dial.], tot *or* tot up [coll.], cast, cast up, sum, sum up, count up, reckon, reckon up [coll.], calculate, figure, figure out *or* up, enumerate, numerate, number, cipher; figure in [coll.], include in a reckoning.

6. *v.* become added, accrue; supervene, advene.

7. *adj.* added, annexed etc. *v.*; additional, supplemental, supplementary, supplement; suppletive [rare], suppletory; addititious, adjectitious [obs.], adscititious, ascititious, subjunctive, supervenient [rare], extraneous; extra, plus, further, fresh, more, new, ulterior, other, remanent [chiefly Scot.], auxiliary, supernumerary, contributary, accessory; spare, surplus; additive, additory; increased etc. 35.5.

8. *adv.* additionally etc. *v.*, in addition, also, and also, and eke [arch.], and all [coll.], as well, too, else, besides, to boot, into the bargain, at that [coll.], over and above, on top of . . . , beyond, plus, overplus, extra, on the side [slang], more, moreover, *au reste* [F.], further, furthermore, yet, similarly, likewise; item.

---

36. What a falling off was there!—SHAKESPEARE. Who liveth in the palace hall / Waneth fast and spendeth all.—EMERSON. My days are like a shadow that declineth; and I am withered like grass.—BIBLE.

37. *Adde parvum parvo magnus acervus erit* [Add little to little and there will be a great heap].—OVID. This pluralistic view of a world of additive constitution.—W. JAMES.

9. *prep.* by the addition of, with, withal [chiefly arch.], including, inclusive of, as well as, not to mention, let alone [coll.], along *or* together with, coupled with, in conjunction with; jointly etc. 43.14.

10. *conj. etc.* and, and also, also [coll.], in addition to, plus, added *or* linked to, along *or* together with, as well as, as at the same time, in addition to being, with the addition *or* increment of, with an addition, attended by.

11. *phr.* et cetera, et caetera, etc.; and so on, and so forth, and others, and others of the same *or* similar kind, and other things, and everything else, and everything [coll.], and the rest, and all [coll.], and all that [coll.], and suchlike, and the like, and all like that [slang], and stuff like that [slang], and whatnot, and I don't know what [coll.], and what have you [slang]; *cum multis aliis* [L.].

6. *v.* cut off, retrench, amputate, mutilate; truncate, detruncate, obtruncate; prune, pare, peel, clip, crop, dock, lop, nip, snub, shear, shave, skive, mow; clip off, shave off etc.; abrade, scrape off, file off, rub off, grind off; pollard.

7. *v.* geld, castrate, cut [dial. and coll.], alter [coll.], spay [a female], capon *or* caponize [a cock], emasculate, evirate [rare], unman, effeminize, eunuchize, sterilize.

8. *adj.* deducted etc. *v.*, deductive, deducible, subtractive, ablatitious [rare].

9. *adj.* tailless, acaudal, acaudate.

10. *adv.* in deduction etc. *n.*

11. *prep.* minus, less, short of, out [slang], diminished by, with the subtraction *or* deduction of, with the rejection of, without, lacking, leaving *or* left out, excepting, except, with the exception of, barring, bar, save, save and except, exclusive of, excluding.

38. Deduction
(See 37. Addition; also 36. Decrease, 39a. Decrement)

1. *n.* deduction, subtraction, subduction, removal; sublation [rare], ablation, abstraction; retrenchment; abrasion; abbreviation, curtailment etc. 201.2; reduction etc. (decrease) 36; decrement, rebate etc. (thing deducted) 39a.

2. *n.* excision, recision [rare], abscission; amputation, mutilation; truncation, detruncation, obtruncation.

3. *n.* (mathematics) subtraction, takeaway [slang]; subtrahend, subtract [obs.]; minuend; subtraction *or* minus sign, minus.

4. *v.* deduct, deduce, subduct, reduct [dial.], subtract, minus [coll.], take from, take away, remove, withdraw, abstract, discount; rebate [obs.], bate [obs. exc. fig.]; detract; decimate; diminish etc. (reduce) 36.4; curtail etc. (shorten) 201.4.

5. *v.* excise, abscind [rare], cut out, retrench [rare], extirpate, expunge, erase, wipe out, rub out, blot out, strike out, cancel; delete, dele; thin, thin out, weed; discard etc. 678.3.

---

38. If we take a farthing from a thousand pounds, it will be a thousand pounds no longer. —GOLDSMITH. And take from seventy springs a score. / It only leaves me fifty more.— HOUSMAN.

39. Adjunct
(See also 37. Addition)

Thing Added.—**1.** *n.* adjunct, addition, additament, *additum* [L.], addendum (*pl.* addenda), affix, appendage, and [coll.], annex, *annexe* [F.], annexation, augment, augmentation, accession, increment, reinforcement, supernumerary, appurtenance, appurtenant, accessory, item, adjective, expletive, complement, supplement, continuation, extension; pendant, rider, offshoot, episode, side issue, corollary; codicil, subscript, postscript, prefix, suffix, appendix; accompaniment etc. 88; insertion etc. 300.3.

2. *n.* tab, tag, flap, lug, lapel, apron, fly, tuck, lap, lappet, skirt; embroidery, frills *or* frillery [coll.]; trappings, traps [coll.]; *cortège* [F.] *or* cortege, retinue; afterpart etc. 65.2.

3. *n.* (building) wing, addition, annex, *annexe* [F.], extension, ell *or* L.

4. *adj.* winged, alate, alated.

39a. Decrement
(See also 38. Deduction)

Thing Deducted.—*n.* decrement, discount, deduction, eduction, tare, offtake, take-off [slang], drawback, draft *or* draught, reprise; rebate, rebatement; defect, loss, shrinkage, waste; afterglow.

40. Remainder

Thing Remaining.—1. *n.* remainder, remainders, remains, remanence, remnant, remanet [rare], residue, residuum (*pl.* residua), rest, balance [coll.], relicts [rare], relics [poetic], leavings, leftovers; oddments, odds and ends, scraps, orts, candle ends, rags; parings, cheeseparings, scobs, raspings, filings, shavings, sawdust; chaff, straw, stubble; detritus, debris *or* débris, ruins; skeleton, fossil, shadow; stump, butt [as of a cigar], rump, fag end; plugs [publishers' slang]; castoff skin etc. 223.13.

2. *n.* dregs, sordes, grounds, lees, mother [obs.], dross, sprue, slag, draff, recrement, scoria (*pl.* scoriae), feces *or* faeces, residue etc. *above*; *caput mortuum* [L.; old Chem.]; sediment, settlement, settlings, bottoms, deposit; heeltap *or* heeltaps; precipitate, precipitation, sublimate [Chem.]; alluvium, alluvion, diluvium; silt, loess, moraine; sweepings; scourings, offscourings; scum, offscum, froth; ash, ember, cinder, sinter, clinker, coal, carbon, charcoal, lava; soot, smut; refuse, waste etc. (rubbish) 645.4; feculence, scurf etc. (offal) 653.6; condensation etc. 321.3.

3. *n.* result, resultant, eliminant [Math.]; educt, eduction.

4. *n.* surplus, surplusage, overplus, superplus [obs. exc. Scot.], overage, overset, leftover, redundant, balance [commercial slang], carry-over; survival, survivance [rare]; excess, superfluity etc. (redundance) 641.

5. *v.* remain, be left etc. *adj.*, survive, subsist.

6. *adj.* remaining, left, leftover, surplus, remanent, supplementary, over, odd, surviving; unconsumed, unused; residuary, residual; sedimentary, sedimental; exceeding, over and above; supernumerary, spare, to spare; outlying, outstanding; superfluous etc. (redundant) 641.5

41. Mixture

(See 42. Simpleness; also 43. Junction)

1. *n.* mixture, admixture, admixtion; commixture, commixtion [obs.]; intermixture, immixture, minglement, eucrasy [Med.], fusion, interfusion, intertanglement, interlacement, interlacery, intertexture; interlarding, interlardation; amalgamation, alloyage; levigation; matrimony, marriage; intermarriage, interbreeding; junction etc. 43; multiformity etc. 81; combination etc. 48.

2. *n.* imbuement, impregnation, infusion, diffusion, suffusion, transfusion, infiltration, permeation, pervasion, penetration; seasoning, sprinkling; adulteration, sophistication, corruption; interpolation etc. (interjection) 228.2.

3. *n.* (thing mixed) tinge, tincture, touch, dash, smack, sprinkling, spice, seasoning, infusion, *soupçon* [F.].

4. *n.* (compound resulting from mixture) mixture, admixture etc. *above* 41.1; compound, combination, combo [slang, U.S.], composition, compo [slang, U.S.], *tertium quid* [L.]; miscellany, *mélange* [F.], medley, varied assortment, mess, muss [coll., U.S.], mux [dial.], mix-up [coll.], mix [chiefly coll.], hash, hodgepodge, hotchpotch, hotchpot, chowchow, *pasticcio* [It.], patchwork, odds and ends, all sorts, omnium-gatherum [coll.], what the cat brought in [coll. U.S.], Noah's ark; salad, sauce, mash, gallimaufry, ollapodrida, olio, salmagundi, potpourri, stew, mulligan [slang, U.S.]; amalgam, alloy; brass, pewter; paste, magma; texture; mingled yarn; mosaic etc. (variegation) 440; jumble etc. (confusion) 59.2.

5. *n.* mongrel, crossbreed, cross, hybrid; mustee *or* mestee [W. Ind. and Ind.], métis, métisse [F.], mestizo [Sp.], (*fem. mestiza*); half-breed, half blood, half-caste; mulatto, high yellow [coll., U.S.], sepian [slang, U.S.], kelt *or* keltch [dial. and slang, U.S.], three-quarter kelt *or* keltch [dial. and slang, U.S.]; quadroon, quarteroon, quarteron; quinteroon, quinteron, quintroon; octoroon, octoon [rare]; sambo *or* zambo, cafuzo, Eurasian, Americanadian [coll.], fustee [W. Ind.], ladino, marabou, sacatra [U.S.]; griffe *or* griffin [local, U.S.], griffado, *grifado* [Sp.]; zebrule *or* zebrula, zebrass, cattalo, mule; pomato, citrange, tangelo,

---

40. Round the decay / Of that colossal wreck, boundless and bare / The lone and level sands stretch far away.—SHELLEY. It is strange that men should see sublime inspiration in the ruins of an old church and see none in the ruins of a man.—CHESTERTON.
41. There is also a mixture of good and evil wisely distributed by God.—ATTERBURY. "The time has come," the Walrus said, / "To talk of many things: / Of shoes—and ships—and sealing-wax— / Of cabbages—and kings.—

plumcot; drop of black blood, touch of the tar brush [coll.].

6. *v.* mix, commix, immix, intermix, mingle, commingle, immingle; intermingle, bemingle, scramble; throw together, pound together; stir up, hash up [chiefly coll.]; mix up with, associate with; amalgamate, alloy; mix thoroughly, levigate; knead, brew; cross, crossbreed, interbreed, intermarry, hybridize, miscegenate; put together, join etc. 43.5; blend, fuse, etc. (combine) 48.3; intertwine, interweave etc. (interlace) 219.8; interlard etc. (interject) 228.8, 9; mix up, shuffle etc. (derange) 61.2–5; variegate etc. 440.4.

7. *v.* be mixed etc., get among, be entangled with.

8. *v.* imbue, infuse, suffuse, transfuse, instill, infiltrate, saturate, impregnate, lace [as tea], fortify [a beverage], flavor, dash, tinge, tincture, entincture, season, sprinkle, besprinkle; medicate, drug, dope *or* dope up [slang]; attemper, dilute, cut [coll.]; adulterate, sophisticate, corrupt, doctor *or* doctor up [coll.], hocus [coll.]; infect, contaminate; pervade etc. 186.12; interfuse etc. (interpenetrate) 228.9.

9. *adj.* mixed etc. *v.*, implex [rare], composite, medley, linsey-woolsey, chowchow, heterogeneous, miscellaneous; promiscuous, indiscriminate; half-and-half, fifty-fifty [slang, U.S.]; variegated etc. 440.5–10.

10. *adj.* mongrel, hybrid, amphibious, crossbred, crossed; half-blooded, half-breed, half-bred, half-caste.

11. *prep.* among, amongst, 'mongst; amid, mid *or* 'mid, amidst, midst *or* 'midst, in the midst of, in the thick of; with, together with.

42. Simpleness
(See 41. Mixture)

Freedom from Mixture.—**1.** *n.* simpleness, simplicity, purity, homogeneity; homozygousness, homozygosity.

2. *n.* elimination, riddance, shut [dial.], exclusion, rejection, ejection, expulsion, evacuation; purification, defecation etc. (cleaning) 652.2.

3. *v.* simplify, render simple etc. *adj.*, reduce to simplicity etc. *n.*, disinvolve, disintricate; disentangle etc. 60.9.

4. *v.* eliminate, exclude, count out, reject, eject, expel, abstract, discard, get rid of, get shut of [dial.], bilge [sea slang], chuck [slang]; clear, clear away, clear the decks; weed *or* weed out [chiefly coll.], pick out; sift, winnow etc. (refine) 652.10; purge, purify etc. (clean) 652.9.

5. *adj.* simple, uniform, of a piece, single, homogeneous; pure, *pur et simple* [F.], pure and simple, Attic, clear, sheer, neat; plain, homespun.

6. *adj.* unmixed, unmingled, unblended, uncombined, uncompounded, incomposite [rare], incomplex; unadulterated, unsophisticated, unalloyed, untinged, unfortified; elemental, elementary; free *or* exempt from, exclusive.

7. *adv.* simply, purely, singly etc. *adj.*; solely, only, alone.

43. Junction
(See 44. Disjunction; also 41. Mixture, 48. Combination)

1. *n.* junction, joining, meeting etc. *v.*; joinder, union, accouplement, concurrence, connection, hookup [spec. coll.], tie-up [coll.], tie-in [coll.]; conjunction, conjuncture, conjugation; annexion, annexation, annexment [rare]; subjunction; ligation, alligation [rare]; compagination, structure; interrelation, interconnection, intertexture, interdigitation, interjoinder.

blending, inosculation, anastomosis, confluence, concatenation, interlinking, interlocking, infibulation; restriction, astriction; coalescence, symphysis; concourse, consolidation, alliance, coalition, combine [coll.]; coupling, copulation [Chem.]; communication, intercourse; reunion, reune [coll.]; marriage etc. 903; assemblage etc. 72; combination etc. 48; mixture etc. 41; coherence etc. 46, addition etc. 37.

2. *n.* coition, coitus, copulation, copula [chiefly Law], sexual congress, sexual connection *or* conjunction, intercourse,

---

CARROLL. I like a bit of a mongrel myself, whether it's a man or a dog; they're the best for everyday.—SHAW.

43. In every union there is a mystery—a certain invisible bond which must not be disturbed.—AMIEL. What therefore God hath joined together, let not man put asunder.—BIBLE. Were there not an identity in the

sexual intercourse; procreation etc. (generation) 161.2; fructification etc. 168.1.

3. *n.* joint, jint [dial.], joining, juncture, connection, articulation; pivot, hinge, elbow, knee; weld, welded joint; splice, node [Bot.], suture, stitch, raphe; hitch, gilligan hitch [coll., West. U.S.]; closure, seam, commissure [Tech.]; gore, gusset; miter, mortise, dovetail; intersection, decussation; chiasm, chiasma; osculation, osculature [rare]; link, bond, knot etc. 45.

4. *n.* joiner [spec. coll., U.S.], annexationist.

5. *v.* join, unite, unify, combine, incorporate, compound, conjoin, connect, meet, associate, consolidate, league, link, band; put together, lay together, clap together, hang together, hold together, lump together, piece together, tack together, fix together, bind up together, roll into one; embody, re-embody; reunite, reune [coll.]; bridge over, span; mingle, etc. (mix) 41.6; enlist etc. (become a member) 712.8; unite with etc. (league) 48.3, 4; relate etc. 9.4.

6. *v.* attach, fix, affix, saddle on, fasten, bind, secure, immobilize [rare], clinch, make fast etc. *adj.*; tie, pinion, string, strap, hitch, hook up [coll.], lash, leash, truss, bandage, swathe, swaddle, gird, girth, cinch, harness; tie up, tether, moor, picket, stake out; forefoot [slang, West. U.S.], hog-tie [coll., U.S.], put a half nelson on [coll.], get a strangle hold on.

sew, lace, stitch, tack, knit; splice, bend [Naut. slang]; button, buckle; lock, latch; belay, brace, grapple; hook, link, yoke, poke [coll., U.S.], couple, acouple, copulate [Chem.], bracket; chain, pin, nail, screw, bolt, hasp, clasp, clamp, rivet; fuse, fuse together; wedge, rabbet, mortise, miter, jam, dovetail, enchase, set; graft, ingraft; inosculate, anastomose; tighten, trice up, screw up; append, annex etc. (add) 37.3; glue, weld etc. (cement) 46.7; fetter, shackle etc. (bind) 751.7.

7. *v.* intertwine, interlink etc. (interlace) 219.8.

8. *v.* copulate, unite in sexual intercourse, have sexual congress etc. *n.*, come together; board, jazz, niggle [all slang];
fructify etc. 168.2; procreate etc. (generate) 161.10.

9. *v.* be joined etc. join etc. *above* 43.5; hang *or* hold together; stick, cohere etc. 46.5, 6.

10. *adj.* joined, united etc. *v.*; copulate, joint, conjoint, conjunct, corporate, compact, concurrent, coincident, correal [civil Law]; hand-in-hand, intimate; unseparated etc. 46.10.

11. *adj.* fast, secure, firm, fixed, close, tight, taut, set, sound; intervolved [rare].

12. *adj.* inseparable, indissoluble, indiscerptible, insecable [obs.], inseverable.

13. *adj.* conjunctive, conjunctival; connective, combinative, copulative [Gram.]; unifying etc. 87.9.

14. *adv.* jointly, conjointly etc. *adj.*; in conjunction, ~ union etc. *n.*, hand in hand; with . . . , together etc. 88.9, 10.

15. *adv.* fast, close, firm; firmly, securely etc. *adj.*

44. Disjunction
(See 43. Junction; also 49. Decomposition)

1. *n.* disjunction, disconnection, disconnectedness, etc. *adj.*, inconnection; disunity, disunion; disassociation, dissociation, disengagement, disjointure; separation, parting etc. *v.*, detachment, segregation, abstraction; divorce, divorcement; isolation, insulation, insularity; oasis, island; division, subdivision; section, resection; dislocation, luxation; partibility, separability; separatism; *disjecta membra* [L.]; discontinuity etc. 70; incoherence etc. 47; apportionment etc. 786; dispersion etc. 73; bisection etc. 91; interval etc. 198; divergence etc. 291; irrelation etc. 10.

2. *n.* sunderance, severance, disseverance, discerption, diremption, scission, fission, cleavage, splitment [slang]; abscission, rescission [obs.]; abstriction, abjunction; laceration, dilaceration; disruption, abruption, cataclasm; avulsion, divulsion; elision, syncope; circumcision.

3. *n.* fissure, cut, fracture etc. (cleft) 198.2, 3.

4. *n.* dissection, dissecting etc. *v.*; analysis, resolution, breakup, diaeresis, dismemberment; anatomy, anat [Med.

---

substance, men and women might join, but they could never unify.—COLERIDGE.   Seas but join the regions they divide.—POPE.

44. Even as a splitted bark, so sunder we.—SHAKESPEARE.   It went to pieces all at once. — / All at once and nothing first.—HOLMES.

slang]; disintegration etc. (decomposition) 49.

5. *n.* separatist etc. (apostate) 607.5; dissenter etc. 489.3; heretic etc. 984.12, 13; insurgent etc. 742.3.

6. *v.* be disjoined etc., come *or* fall off, come *or* fall to pieces, get loose, peel off.

7. *v.* disjoin, disconnect, disengage, disunite, dissociate; separate, divide, part, dispart, divorce, detach, remove, rescind, cut off, cut adrift; segregate, set *or* keep apart, isolate, insulate; section, sectionize [rare]; disjoint, dislocate, throw out of joint *or* gear; loose, unloose, undo, unbind, untie, unchain, unlock, unattach etc. (*see* attach etc. 43.6); unfetter, set free etc. (liberate) 750.2, 3; disentangle etc. 60.9; loosen etc. 47.2; discontinue etc. 70.3; bisect etc. 91.4; diverge etc. 291.2.

8. *v.* sunder, sever, dissever, abscind [rare], incise; cut, cleave, saw, snip, nip, rive, rend, tear, slit, split, chip, chop, hack, whack [coll.], hew, slash, slice, slish [dial. or rare], carve, whittle, haggle, hackle, gash; crack, snap; break, burst, bust [dial. and inelegant]; cut ~, rend etc. asunder, cut in two, rend in twain.

9. *v.* separate into parts, disintegrate, decompose, divellicate [rare], segment, break up, cut up, whack up [coll.], take ~, pull ~, pick *or* tear to pieces, tear to rags *or* tatters, tear piecemeal, pull in pieces, decimate, reduce to fragments, shatter; smithereen, break to smithers *or* smithereens, break all to smithers *or* smithereens [all coll.], shiver, shivereen [dial.], break into shivereens [dial.]; flinderate, break to flinderation *or* all to flinderation [all slang], splinter; smash, crush; crunch, craunch, cranch; lacerate, scramble [obs.], mangle, mutilate, mince, hash.

dissect, anatomize, analyze, separate into its elements *or* integrant parts; dismember, dislimb, disbranch; subdivide, divide and redivide, separate into subdivisions; comminute etc. (pulverize) 330.6, 7.

10. *v.* partition, parcel, portion, apportion, allocate, divide, divvy *or* divvy up [slang], split, split up, whack up [coll.], demarcate [rare]; graduate, grade; district, chapter, canton.

11. *v.* part, part company, separate, disperse, disband, split up, split out [coll.], divide, break it up [slang], leave,

take leave, quit, go away; alienate, estrange, break with, split [coll.]; demobilize, demob [slang].

12. *adj.* disjoined, divided, disconnected etc. *v.*; disjoint, disjunct, disjunctive; detached, unconnected, unattached, unassociated, unannexed; separate, disparate, withdrawn, abstract [arch.], apart, asunder, far between; loose, free, adrift; distinct, distinctive [rare]; discrete, discretive; isolated, insular; cut, reft, rift [obs.], cleft, split; lobate, lobulate, lobulated, lobulose; digitate, digitated; bipartite, biparted [rare]; multipartite, multisegmental, multisegmentate; straggling, straggly; secant; discontinuous etc. 70.4; fractional etc. (partial) 51.8; alone etc. 87.8.

13. *adj.* divisible, dividuous [rare], discerptible [rare], partible, separable, severable, scissile, abjunctive; dissoluble, dissolvable.

14. *adv.* separately etc. *adj.*, severally, one by one; apart, adrift, asunder, in twain; in the abstract, abstractly.

15. *adv.* to pieces, to smithers etc. *v.*; to smash, to sticks, to sticks and staves; all to pieces etc.

45. Bond

Connecting Medium.—**1.** *n.* bond, bond of union, privity [Law], vinculum (*pl.* vincula), tie, link, connection, connective [spec. Tech.], connective link, interconnection, intermedium, nexus; bridge, steppingstone; neck, isthmus, jugulum [Zool.]; ridge, fold, frenum [Anat.], ligation; hyphen, dash; junction etc. 43.

2. *n.* fastening, fastener, fast, tie, clinch, clamp, holdfast; catch, detent, click, pawl; clip, clasp, hasp, buckle, button; hook, hook and eye; latch, latchet; bolt, bar; lock, padlock; copula, coupler, couple, coupling, union; bonder [masonry], bondstone, binding stone; girder, tie beam; anchor, moorings; guy, guy rope; band, bandage, brace, roller, fillet; with, withe, withy.

belt, girth, surcingle, cinch [U.S.], bellyband, girdle, cestus [Zool. or Gr. and Rom. Antiq.]; garter, suspenders, braces

---

45. Blest be the tie that binds.—FAWCETT. Together linkt with adamantine chains.—SPENSER. It is too hard a knot for me t'untie.—SHAKESPEARE.

[Eng.]; hawser, halser [obs.], bow ~, head ~, quarter ~, breast or stern fast; noose, hempen bridle [slang]; lasso, lariat, *reata* or *riata* [Sp.]; lass rope, throw rope, ketch rope, lazo [all slang, West. U.S.]; thong, boondoggle [slang, U.S.], whang [Scot. and dial.]; braid, inkle, sennit [Naut.], oxreim [S. Afr.]; lace, lacing; harness, gear, tackle; bridle, halter, freno [West. U.S.]; yoke, poke [local, U.S.]; link, loop, tag, ring, terret, hank [Naut.], *larigo* [Sp.]; grappling iron or hook, grapple iron or hook, grapnel, grappler; connection, juncture etc. (joint) 43.3; suspender etc. 214.3; prop etc. (support) 215.2; shackle, rein etc. (means of restraint) 752.2; grip etc. 781.2.

3. *n.* knot, bend, tie, hitch; slipknot, slide knot, running knot, running bowline, anchor knot, weaver's hitch *or* knot, becket knot, wall knot, Blackwall hitch, timber knot, bowknot, bowline, bowline knot, surgeon's knot, builder's knot, stunner hitch, carrick bend, cat's paw, studding-sail halyard bend, tack bend, stopper knot, clinch, clinch inside *or* outside, clove hitch, cuckold's neck, stevedore's knot, square knot, diamond knot, Englishman's tie, figure-of-eight knot, fisherman's bend, flat knot.

Flemish knot, French shroud knot, German knot, single knot, double hitch, shroud knot, sheet bend, sheepshank, granny knot, half crown, half hitch, harness hitch, hawser bend, hawser fastening, heaving-line bend, round turn and half hitch, round seizing, rope-yarn knot, rolling hitches, reeving-line bend, reef knot, prolonge knot, overhand knot, outside clinch, inside clinch, lanyard knot, loop knot, magnus hitch, manrope knot, open hand knot, netting knot, midshipman's hitch, mesh knot, Matthew Walker knot, marling hitch, marlinespike hitch, Gordian knot.

4. *n.* ligature, ligament, *ligamentum* [L.]; line, leader, tendon, sinew, thew; cable, wire; strap, strop; chain, catena; funicle, funiculus; umbilical cord, spermatic cord; lines, reins, jerk line [West. U.S.]; cord, string, rope etc. (filament) 205.

5. *n.* pin, corking pin [obs. exc. dial.], drawing pin [Eng.], hairpin; nail, spike, brad, rivet, screw, staple, peg, skewer; tack, thumb tack; dowel, doll [coll.], duledge [Mil.]; thole, tholepin; treenail, trenail; toggle [Naut.], kevel [Naut.], cleat, bollard; tooth [Carp.], stub tenon; stake, stob [dial.], post, snubbing post.

6. *n.* cement, glue, adhesive, stickum [slang.], fish glue, mucilage, mastic, paste, library paste, gluten, gum, solution, size, wafer, solder, lute, putty, lime; birdlime, viscum, viscin; mortar, stucco etc. (plaster) 223.19.

46. Coherence
(See 47. Incoherence)

1. *n.* coherence, coherency, cohesion, adherence, adhesion; cementation, conglutination, agglutination; sticking, soldering etc. *v.*; concretion, accretion, solidification, set, congelation, coagulation; conglomeration, agglomeration, aggregation, consolidation; connection, dependence; junction etc. 43.

2. *n.* tenacity, tenaciousness, adhesiveness, cohesiveness, stick-to-itiveness [coll.], glutinousness, glutinosity, viscidity, viscosity, stickiness, toughness; stay [coll.], stay-putness [slang]; inseparability, inseparableness, indivisibility; retention etc. 781.

3. *n.* (something adhesive or tenacious) adhesive, adherent, adherer; adhesive plaster, plaster; bur *or* burr, cocklebur, clotbur, bramble, brier, prickle, thorn, sticker [coll.]; claw, talon; pincers, nippers, vise; bulldog, leech; sirup, molasses; varnish, casein, resin; remora, clog, drag; parasite etc. (sycophant) 886.2; glue etc. (cement) 45.6.

4. *n.* conglomerate, conglomeration, agglomerate, agglomeration; concrete etc. (solid) 321.4, 5.

5. *v.* cohere, adhere, stick, stick together, stay, stay put, cling, cleave, hold, close with, hold ~, hang *or* grow together; take hold of, clasp, grasp, hug; join etc. 43.9.

6. *v.* hold fast, hold on like old Billy Hell [slang], stick close, stick like a leech, stick like wax, stick like the paper on the wall, stick like a wet shirt, stick closer than a brother, cling like ivy, cling like

46. Held in cohesion by unresting cells.—MASEFIELD. Only throw dirt enough and some of it is sure to stick.—T. HUGHES. This cold, congealed blood / That glues my lips.—SHAKESPEARE.

a bur, adhere like a remora, adhere like Dejanira's shirt.

7. *v.* cement, agglutinate, conglutinate, glue, solution [coll.], paste, gum, lute, belute [rare]; solder, weld, braze, ferruminate [rare].

8. *v.* agglomerate, conglomerate; consolidate, coagulate etc. (solidify) 321.7.

9. *adj.* coherent, adherent, adhesive, cohesive, stickable, stick-to-itive [coll.], tenacious; cohering, adhering etc. *v.*; tough, sticky etc. (viscid) 352.8; compact, inseparable etc. (dense) 321.8–10.

10. *adj.* unseparated, undivided, sessile; inseparable, compact etc. 321.8–10; combined etc. 48.5, 6; united etc. 43.10.

47. Incoherence
(See 46. Coherence)

1. *n.* incoherence, nonadhesion, noncohesion; looseness etc. *adj.*, laxity, relaxation; immiscibility; rope of sand; disjunction etc. 44.

2. *v.* loosen, slacken, relax; unglue etc. (*see* glue etc. 46.7); detach etc. (disjoin) 44.7.

3. *adj.* nonadhesive, noncohesive; incoherent, detached, loose, slack, lax, relaxed, flapping, streaming, baggy, disheveled; immiscible; uncombined etc. (*see* combined etc. 48.5), segregated, like grains of sand.

48. Combination
(See 49. Decomposition; also 43. Junction, 54. Composition)

1. *n.* combination, combo [slang, U.S.], union, unification, alliance, aggregation, coadunation, synthesis, synizesis, synaeresis, incorporation, amalgamation, embodiment, coalescence, coalition, crasis, fusion, inosculation, absorption; blend, blendure [rare], blending etc. *v.*; centralization; impregnation; junction etc. 43; mixture etc. 41.

2. *n.* compound, alloy, composition etc. (mixture) 41.4.

3. *v.* combine, unite, unify, incorporate, consolidate, inosculate, consubstantiate, alloy, amalgamate, syncretize, agglutinate, absorb, blend, merge, melt into one, coalesce, solidify, contemper, centralize, put *or* lump together; fuse, interfuse; impregnate; embody, re-embody; link etc. (join) 43.5, 6; interlink etc. (interlace) 219.8; intermix, intermingle etc. (mix) 41.6.

4. *v.* league, interleague [rare]; federate, confederate, federalize; associate, consociate; fraternize, fraternate [rare]; club, club together [coll.], band together, bunch, bunch up [coll.], gang, gang up [coll.], amalgamate, unionize, form *or* cement a union, ally, form an alliance, go cahoots *or* in cahoots [slang], join together, join forces, join *or* unite with, hitch horses [coll.], hook up with [slang], join up with [coll.], throw in with [slang], tie up *or* in with [slang]; couple, pair, pair off, partner, go in partnership, go in partners [coll.], team with, team up with [coll.]; syndicate; co-operate etc. 709.4; form a party etc. 712.7.

5. *adj.* combined etc. *v.*, coadunate, conjunctive, conjugate; joint, conjoint; indiscrete; impregnated, ingrained, imbued, inoculated; unseparated etc. 46.10.

6. *adj.* leagued, enleagued, in league, in cahoots [slang]; allied, amalgamated, incorporated, confederated etc. *v.*; federal, federative, federate, confederate; corporate, corporative, corporational, co-operative etc. 709.7.

49. Decomposition
(See 48. Combination; also 44. Disjunction)

1. *n.* decomposition, disintegration, dissolution, catalysis [rare], resolution, breakup, diaeresis; erosion, crumbling etc. *v.*; wear, wear and tear; decay etc. 659.2; dissection etc. (disjunction) 44; waste etc. 638.

2. *n.* (physics) electrolysis, electrolyzation; hydrolysis, proteolysis, thermolysis, catalysis.

3. *v.* decompose, become decomposed etc. *adj.*, undergo decomposition etc. *n.*, disintegrate, decompound [rare], dissolve, break up, come *or* fall to pieces, crumble, crumble into dust, erode, con-

---

47. Well of soft incoherence.—L. BACON.
48. Strength united is the greater.—BACON. A threefold cord is not quickly broken.—BIBLE. Great is the strength of feeble arms combined.—HOMER. All your strength is in your union.—LONGFELLOW. *E pluribus unum* [From many, one]. U.S. MOTTO.
49. It went to pieces all at once, — / Just as bubbles do when they burst.—HOLMES. A sorry breaking-up.—T. MOORE. Constant dropping wears the stone.

sume, consume ~, wear *or* waste away, tabefy [rare]; decay etc. 659.7; analyze, dissect etc. (separate into its integrant parts) 44.9; comminute etc. (pulverize) 330.6, 7.

4. *v.* (physics) electrolyze, hydrolyze, thermolyze, catalyze.

5. *adj.* decomposed, decomposing, disintegrated etc. *v.*; catalytic, analytical; resolvent, separative; solvent; decayed etc. 659.13.

50. Whole
(See 51. Part; also 52. Completeness)

1. *n.* whole, totality, teetotality *or* T-totality [coll.], entirety, integrity, collectivity; integration [Tech.], embodiment; organic unity, compages [*sing.* and *pl.*], compaction [rare]; complete unity, integer, integral [spec. Math.]; unity etc. 87; completeness etc. 52.

2. *n.* all, the whole etc. *above*; entire [rare], general [arch.], everything, aggregate, assemblage, the complete assemblage, one and all, the devil and all [coll.], the altogether [joc.] *ensemble* [F.], *tout ensemble* [F.]; complex, *complexus* [L.]; total, teetotal *or* T-total [coll.], tote [coll.], tot, tottle [dial.], sum, sum total, amount, whole *or* gross amount, stick [sporting slang]; length and breadth, alpha and omega, beginning and end, be-all; lock, stock and barrel.

whole boodle *or* caboodle, the boodle, the caboodle, whole kit *or* kit and caboodle, the kit and caboodle, whole jimbang *or* jingbang, whole shoot *or* shooting match, the shooting match, whole boiling, whole smear, the shebang, whole shebang, whole business *or* works, the business, the works, whole toot and scramble *or* stumble, whole show, whole squeeze [all slang]; everyone etc. 78.5; summation etc. (calculation) 37.2.

3. *n.* principal part, greater ~, major ~, best ~, main etc. part, main squeeze [slang, U.S.], almost *or* nearly all; bulk, heft [coll., U.S.], mass, lump, tissue, staple, body, gross; trunk, torso, bole, hull, hulk, skeleton; lion's share, Benjamin's mess, big *or* long end [slang];

essential part etc. (salient point) 642.4.

4. *v.* form a whole, constitute a whole; integrate, embody, amass.

5. *v.* total, be in its totality, amount *or* come to, add up to, tottle [dial.], tot *or* tot up to [coll.], tote *or* tote up to [coll.], reckon up to [coll.], pile up to, aggregate [coll.], come to in its aggregate.

6. *adj.* whole, total, teetotal *or* T-total [coll.], entire, integral [rare], integrate [rare], gross; one, individual; complete etc. 52.9.

7. *adj.* undivided, unbroken, uncut, unsevered, unclipped, uncropped, unshorn, undiminished, unreduced, undemolished, undissolved, undestroyed, unbruised; seamless; intact.

8. *adj.* indivisible, inseparable etc. 321.10.

9. *adj.* comprehensive, wholesale etc. (extensive) 31.

10. *adv.* wholly, entirely, totally etc. *adj.*; *in toto* [L.], *toto caelo* [L.], all, altogether, on all counts, all put together, collectively, in a body, bodily, as a whole, in the aggregate, in the lump, in the gross, in the mass, *en masse* [F.], *en bloc* [F.], by wholesale; one and indivisible; completely, throughout etc. 52.13–15.

11. *adv.* on the whole, in the long run, all in all, to all intents and purposes, by and large, in all respects, in the main, mainly, substantially, effectually.

12. *adv.* for all, for all in all, for the total amount, for the stick [sporting slang].

51. Part
(See 50. Whole)

1. *n.* part, portion, fragment, fraction, frustum [rare], division, parcel [Law or arch.], dole [dial., Eng.], ward, sector, segment, section, cantle, cantlet, moiety; subdivision, detachment; item, detail, particular; dose, go [coll.], jag [dial., U.S.], slug [slang], rare [slang, U.S.], aught, any; installment; dividend, divvy [slang]; share etc. (allotment) 786.2; role etc. 599.7; principle part etc. 50.3; essential part etc. 642.4.

2. *n.* (part of writing) section, chapter, verse, article, clause, phrase, paragraph, passage, number, book; fascicle,

---

50. All are but parts of one stupendous Whole, / Whose body Nature is, and God the soul.— POPE.   The be-all and the end-all here.— SHAKESPEARE.   *Tout bien ou rien* [All or nothing].

51. Fools! they know not how much half exceeds the whole.—HESIOD.

fascicule *or* fasciculus; *livraison* [F.], serial.

3. *n.* piece, bit, snatch, snack, whack [slang], cut, cutting, clipping, paring, shaving, rasher, snip, chip, collop, slice, canch [dial.], crumb, scale, scrap, swatch [cant], tatter, shred, stitch, splinter, flinder, flitter [coll.], shiver [dial. and coll.]; shivereen [Scot. and North. Eng.], smither *or* smithereen [coll.]; lump, gob [dial. and slang], chunk [coll.], hunk [coll.], hunch, hank [dial.], whang [Scot. and dial.]; stump, butt; particle, morsel etc. (small quantity) 32.2; lamina etc. (layer) 204.2.

4. *n.* member, limb, branch, bush, bough, twig, sprig, spray, switch; runner, tendril, sarmentum [*pl.* sarmenta]; offshoot, ramification, scion, spur, arm, leg, wing; lobe, lobule; joint, link; component, component part etc. 56.

5. *n.* compartment; department etc. (class) 75; county etc. (region) 181.

6. *n.* oddments, odds and ends; leftovers, detritus etc. (remains) 40; debris *or* débris, refuse etc. (rubbish) 645.4.

7. *v.* part, divide, disconnect etc. (disjoin) 44.7–11.

8. *adj.* partial, fractional, fragmentary, portional [rare], sectional, aliquot [Math.], multifid; divided, divisible etc. (disjunction) 44.12, 13; incomplete etc. 53.4, 5; imperfect etc. 651.4.

9. *adv.* partly, partially, in part; incompletely etc. 53.6; somewhat etc. (in a limited degree) 32.13, 14.

10. *adv.* piecemeal, piece by piece, part by part, bit by bit, little by little, inch by inch, foot by foot, drop by drop; by degrees, by *or* in installments, by *or* in snatches, by inches, by driblets, dribslike [dial. and slang]; in lots, in small lots; in compartments; in detail.

52. Completeness
(See 53. Incompleteness; also 50. Whole, 729. Completion)

1. *n.* completeness, wholeness, entireness etc. *adj.*; entirety, totality, teetotality *or* T-totality [coll.], allness [rare], universality; integrity, integrality [rare]; unity, solidity, solidarity; indivisibility, indiscerptibility; whole, all etc. 50; completion etc. 729.

2. *n.* fullness, full; plenitude, amplitude; abundance etc. (plenty) 639.2.

3. *n.* fill, full [coll.], full supply *or* measure, "good measure, pressed down, and shaken together, and running over" (Bible), full house [slang], impletion; saturation, saturity [obs.]; high water, high tide, flood tide, springtide; load, lading, jag [chiefly dial.], lug [coll.]; bumper, brimmer; cupful, basketful etc.; bellyful [vulgar], skinful [coll.], mouthfull [in *say a mouthful*; slang]; crush, cram [coll.], jam-up [slang]; sufficiency, plenty etc. 639; redundance etc. 641.

4. *n.* consummation, limit, ideal, extreme, extremity, acme, climax, maximum, the nines [coll.], the nth [coll.], utmost, uttermost, utmost extent, highest degree, *ne plus ultra* [L.]; the whole length *or* way, the whole figure [coll.], the whole hog [slang]; the whole hog or none [slang], all or nothing; all creation, all forty, all get out [all slang].

5. *n.* complement, supplement, makeweight; filling up etc. *v.*

6. *v.* be complete etc. *adj.*; come to a head, etc. (reach completion) 729.4.

7. *v.* render complete etc. *adj.,* implete [rare], fill, charge, load, lade, freight, weight, pile, stuff, wad, pad, pack; replenish, replete [rare]; supply deficiencies, fill in, make up, make good, piece *or* eke out; fill up, fill to the brim, fill the measure of, capacitate [coll.]; saturate, satiate [obs.]; complete etc. (accomplish) 729.2; overload etc. 641.4; sate etc. 869.4.

8. *v.* be thorough etc. *adj.,* do thoroughly, go all lengths, go to all lengths, go the limit [coll.], go the whole length *or* way, go the whole hog [slang], go the whole figure [slang].

9. *adj.* complete, entire, solid, intact, with all its parts, all-sided; whole, undivided etc. 50.6, 7; perfect etc. 650.5.

10. *adj.* thorough, thoroughgoing, fully realized, exhaustive, comprehensive, radical, sweeping; unqualified, unmitigated, whole-hog [slang], out-and-out, outright, utter, regular [coll.], consummate, perfect [chiefly coll.], precious [chiefly coll.], absolute, downright, plumb [chiefly coll.], total, sheer, veritable, dead, blue [slang]; unconditional, unrestricted, free.

---

52. That ye may be perfect and entire, wanting nothing.—BIBLE. *Totus in toto, et totus in qualibet parte* [Complete as a whole, and complete in every part].

11. *adj.* full, replete, ample, plump, good, plenary, pleny [naut.], flush; brimming, brimful; topfull, chock-full, chokefull, chuck-full, chock *or* chuck [coll.], crammed, cram-full; cram-jam-full, cramp-full, jam-full, jam-packed, pack-jammed, jam-up, chug-full, full-up [all slang]; bursting, ready to burst; capacitive, capacitative, capacitated [coll.]; as full as an egg is of meat, as full as a vetch; saturated, fraught, laden, full-laden, full-fraught, full-charged, heavy-laden, packed like sardines *or* herrings; crawling *or* oozing with . . . , replete with . . . ; crowded, packed etc. 72.13; overful etc. 641.6; satiated etc. 869.6; plenty etc. 639.7.

12. *adj.* completing etc. *v.,* completive, completory; adscititious, ascititious; supplemental, supplementary.

13. *adv.* completely, fully, entirely, thoroughly etc. *adj.; à fond* [F.], to *or* in entirety, to the limit, all, all over [spec. coll.], in full measure; altogether, totally etc. (wholly) 50.10; perfectly etc. 650.6.

14. *adv.* utterly, to the utmost, *à outrance* [F.], *à toute outrance* [F.], to the full, to the limit, to the backbone, to *or* up to the nines [coll.], to the nth [coll.], to the nth degree, to the sky *or* skies, to the top of one's bent, for all there is in it [coll.], for fair [slang], to a fare-you-well *or* fare-ye-well [coll.], as far as possible, out of sight [slang, U.S.], as . . . as can be, than which there is no whicher [slang]; with a vengeance, with a witness [coll.]; hollow, all hollow; quite, fair [dial.], stark, stock [coll.], clean, clean as a whistle, plumb [chiefly coll., U.S.], plain *or* just plain [dial. and coll.]; absolutely etc. 31.16, 17; extremely etc. 31.19.

15. *adv.* throughout, all out, from first to last, from beginning to end, from one end to the other, fore and aft, from cover to cover, inside and out, from here out [coll.], to the end, to the end of the chapter, *in extenso* [L.], from out to out, from Dan to Beersheba, from hell to breakfast [slang, U.S.], from clew to earing, from the word go [coll.], from the ground up, down to the ground [coll.], from top to bottom, *de fond en comble* [F.], from top to toe, from head to foot, *a capite ad calcem* [L.], cap-a-pie, from soup to nuts [slang], *ab ovo usque ad mala* [L.]; **through** and through, through thick and thin; heart and soul, root and branch.

up to the brim, up to the crop, up to the hilt, up to the handle [coll., U.S.], up to the knocker [slang], up to the hub [U.S.], up to the ears, up to the eyes; head and shoulders, neck and heels *or* crop [coll.], over head and ears, hide and hair, body and breeches [slang]; every inch, every whit, every bit; in every respect, in all respects, *sous tous les rapports* [F.], on all counts, at all points, to all intents and purposes, effectually, for good and all, by and large.

53. Incompleteness
(See 52. Completeness; also 730. Noncompletion)

1. *n.* incompleteness, deficientness etc. *adj.,* deficience [rare], deficiency; short measure *or* weight; half weight; scantness, scantiness, scantity, scant sufficiency [coll.]; shortcoming etc. 304; insufficiency etc. 640; imperfection etc. 651; immaturity etc. (nonpreparation) 674; noncompletion etc. 730.

2. *n.* (part wanting) deficiency, deficience etc. *above,* want, lack, need, deficit, defect, shortage, short [coll.], wantage, ullage; defalcation, omission; caret; missing link; interval etc. 198; break etc. (discontinuity) 70; noncompletion etc. 730; insufficiency etc. 640.

3. *v.* be incomplete etc. *adj.;* fall short etc. 304.2; lack etc. (be insufficient) 640.6.

4. *adj.* incomplete, deficient, defective, inadequate, wanting, failing; immature, half-baked [coll.]; in default, in arrear *or* arrears; short, short of, shy *or* shy on [slang]; cut short, bobtailed; meager, scarce, slight, sketchy, scanty, skimp *or* skimpy [coll.], poor, lame, perfunctory; half-and-half; void, jejune, hollow; imperfect etc. 651.4; uncompleted, unfinished etc. (*see* complete, finish etc 729.2); crude etc. (unprepared) 674.7, 8; fractional etc. (partial) 51.8; insufficient etc. 640.8.

5. *adj.* mutilated, garbled, hashed, mangled, butchered, docked, lopped, truncated.

---

53. That quality of being—albeit marvellously—always incomplete.—PROUST. Artistry's haunting curse, the Incomplete.—BROWNING. Sans teeth, sans eyes, sans taste, sans everything.—SHAKESPEARE.

6. *adv.* incompletely etc. *adj.*, by halves, by *or* in half measures, with divided effort; partly etc. 51.9.

54. Composition
(See also 48. Combination)

1. *n.* composition, constitution, construction, formation, embodiment, make, make-up, getup [coll.], setup [coll.], confection [rare], synthesis, compaction [rare]; temperament, nature, character, crasis; synizesis, synaeresis; combination, compound etc. (mixture) 41.4; admission, comprehension etc. (inclusion) 76.

2. *n.* authorship, origination, production, compilation, composition, *recueil* [F.], inditement, conflation, invention, concoction; musical composition, instrumentation; hymnology, hymnody; opus, aria etc. (music) 415.2, 3; designing, painting etc. (graphic arts) 556; modeling, relief etc. (sculpture) 557; writing etc. 590.2; printing etc. 591.

3. *v.* be composed of, be made of, be made up of, be formed of, consist of, be resolved into.

4. *v.* compose, constitute, form, make, make up, fabricate, weave; recompose, precompose; compile, redact, collate, dash off, address, indite, score, draw, draw up, draft; set up etc. (print) 591.14; construct, build etc. (produce) 161.8; compose music etc. 415.26; enter into the composition of etc. (be a component) 56.2; comprise etc. (include) 76.3.

55. Exclusion
(See 76. Inclusion)

1. *n.* exclusion, noninclusion, nonadmission; omission, exception, preclusion, lockout; debarment, debarrance [rare]; rejection, rejectment [rare]; repudiation; prohibition; removal, withdrawal, relegation, elimination, eradication; expulsion, banishment etc. (ejection) 297.1–5.

2. *n.* segregation, separation, isolation, seposition [obs.]; cofferdam.

3. *v.* exclude, bar, bar out, count out [chiefly coll.], reject, repudiate, omit, elide, cut out [coll. and slang], pass over, throw over *or* overboard [coll.], strike off *or* out, leave *or* shut out, eliminate, eradicate, relegate, remove, weed out; ostracize etc. (banish) 297.11.

4. *v.* segregate, separate, isolate; set aside *or* apart, lay aside *or* apart, put aside *or* apart, keep aside *or* apart; sort *or* pick out, weed, winnow, sift, garble [rare]; part, divide etc. (disjoin) 44.7–10.

5. *adj.* excluded etc. *v.*, unrecounted, left *or* shut out, left out in the cold [slang], not included in . . ., not in it, not in the picture [coll.]; extraneous etc. 57.4.

6. *adj.* exclusive, exclusory; preclusive, exceptional, inadmissible, prohibitive, preventive.

7. *prep. etc.* exclusive of, excluding etc. *v.*, barring, bar, except, excepting, with the exception of, save, saving, save and except, bating [rare], beside, besides, unless, without, let alone; notwithstanding etc. 30.8.

56. Component

1. *n.* component, integrant, component part, integrant *or* integral part, ingredient, element, factor, constituent, constituent part *or* portion, part and parcel; leaven; appurtenance, adjunct; feature, aspect; contents, makings [coll.], fixings [coll., U.S.]; personnel, personal; member etc. (part) 51.

2. *v.* be a component etc. *n.*, be *or* form a part etc. 51, enter into, enter into the composition of, combine *or* unite in, merge *or* be merged in, be implicated in, inhere in, belong *or* appertain to; share in etc. (participate) 778.5; constitute, form etc. (compose) 54.4.

3. *adj.* component, constituent, integrant, integral; inherent, essential etc. (intrinsic) 5.6; forming etc. (*see* form etc. 54.4, 5); inclusive etc. 76.5.

57. Extraneousness
(See also 6. Extrinsicality)

1. *n.* extraneousness, alienage, alienism; extrinsicality etc. 6; exteriority etc. 220.

---

54. Little drops of water, / Little grains of sand, / Make the mighty ocean / And the pleasant land.—J. F. CARNEY.
55. He drew a circle that shut me out.—E. MARKHAM.   Beats at our own clay-shuttered doors.—F THOMPSON.
57. They were strangers and pilgrims on the earth.—BIBLE.   I have been a stranger in a strange land —BIBLE.

57.2 – 59.1

2. *n.* foreign body, ~ substance *or* element.

3. *n.* alien, stranger, newcomer, Johnny Newcomer [slang, U.S.], Johnny-come-lately [slang, U.S.], *novus homo* [L.], new chum [coll., Austral.], tenderfoot, maverick [slang, West. U.S.], shorthorn [slang, West. U.S.], jackaroo [coll., Austral.], griffin [Anglo-Ind.]; recruit, rookie [slang]; foreigner, furriner [dial.], outsider, outlander [arch.], barbarian, extern [rare], tramontane [rare], ultramontane; emigrant, *émigré* [F.]; immigrant, immigrator [rare]; settler, colonist, colonizer, metic [Gr. Ant.].

guinea [slang, U.S.], wop [slang, U.S.], dago [slang, U.S. and Can.], bohunk [slang, U.S.], hunky [slang, U.S.], spick [slang], Tony [slang], Chink [slang], Jap [coll.], kike [slang], shonnacker [slang, U.S.], Izzy [slang], hebe [slang, U.S.], sheeny [slang], squarehead [slang], roundhead [slang], mick [slang], shamrock [slang], greaser [slang, U.S.], nigger [coll.]; Afrikander, creole; Easterner, Westerner, Northerner, Yankee [coll.], Southerner [all U.S.]; intruder etc. 228.4; visitor etc. (incomer) 294.4; outcast etc. 893.5.

4. *adj.* extraneous, exotic, foreign, furrin [dial.], foreignistic [coll.], alien, strange [arch.], ulterior, exterior, external, outside; outlandish, outland; barbaric, barbarian; oversea, overseas; tramontane [rare], ultramontane; excluded, exclusive etc. 55.5, 6; extrinsic etc. 6.2.

5. *adv.* abroad, in foreign parts *or* lands; beyond seas, oversea, overseas; on one's travels.

58. Order

(See 59. Disorder; also 60. Arrangement)

1. *n.* order, regularity, uniformity, symmetry, *lucidus ordo* [L.], harmony; music of the spheres; arrangement etc. 60; condition etc. (state) 7; rule etc. 80.

2. *n.* gradation, graduation, shade, succession, procession, progression; series etc. (continuity) 69; rank, place etc. (term) 71.

3. *n.* method, course, system, disposition, arrangement, array; even tenor, routine, route [rare]; regulation, discipline, subordination; economy.

4. *n.* orderliness, tidiness etc. *adj.*; orderly arrangement, perfect order, apple-pie order [coll.], fine whack [slang].

5. *v.* form, be *or* become orderly etc. *adj.*, take an arrangement, arrange *or* range itself, place itself, fall in, fall into arrangement, fall into place, fall into rank, take order, take one's place, take rank; come together, draw up, rally round.

6. *v.* order, adjust, regulate, organize, methodize, systematize, harmonize; standardize, normalize; time, set the tempo.

7. *adj.* orderly, regular, well-regulated, well-ordered, correct, methodic(al), uniform, systematic(al), harmonious; kempt [arch.], trim, neat, spruce, jimp [Scot. and dial. Eng.], trig [dial.], tidy, ship-shape, businesslike; neat as a bandbox *or* pin [coll.], like a cat in pattens; in order, in its proper place, to rights [coll.], in trim, in apple-pie order [coll.], in kilter *or* kelter [coll. and dial.], in whack *or* fine whack [slang], in good shape [coll.]; in normal *or* fit condition, in shape, normal, habitual, usual, *en règle* [F.]; unconfused etc. (*see* confuse etc. 61.2–5); arranged etc. 60.10; symmetrical etc. 242.4; clean etc. 652.14; classificational etc. 75.6.

8. *adv.* in order, in turn, in its turn; step by step, by regular steps, by regular gradations, by regular stages, by regular intervals, by clockwork, gradatim; in series, *seriatim* [NL.], systematically, methodically etc. *adj.*; at regular intervals etc. (periodically) 138.12.

59. Disorder

(See 58. Order; also 61. Derangement)

1. *n.* disorder, disorderliness, untidiness etc. *adj.*; irregularity, ununiformity, unsymmetry, disharmony, deordination [rare]; dishevelment, slovenry, squalor; disunion, disunity; anarchy, anarchism; derangement etc. 61; anomaly, etc. (unconformity) 83; uncleanness etc. 653; formlessness etc. 241.

---

58. Order is Heaven's first law.—POPE. Let all things be done decently and in order.—BIBLE. Good order is the foundation of all good things.—BURKE. Set thine house in order.—BIBLE. A place for everything, and everything in its place.

59. The devil is the author of confusion.—SWIFT. A work where nothing's just or fit; / One glaring chaos and wild heap of wit.—POPE.

2. *n.* confusion, confusedness etc. *adj.*, chaos, anarchy, disarray, deray [arch. and dial.]; confused mass, imbroglio [rare], farrago, jumble, tumble, topsy-turvy, huddle, litter, lumber, rummage [chiefly dial.], medley, omnium-gatherum [coll.], mix [coll.], mix-up [coll.], mux [dial.], mess, holy mess [slang], muss [coll., U.S.], mash, mishmash, hurrah's nest [coll., U.S.], kettle of fish, muddle, hash, hodgepodge, hotchpotch, hotchpot, chowchow, olla-podrida, what the cat brought in [coll., U.S.], *rudis indigestaque moles* [Ovid]; fortuitous concourse of atoms; scattered parts, *disjecta membra* [L.]; mixture etc. 41.4.

3. *n.* complexity, complexness etc. *adj.*, complexus, complication, implication, involvement, involution, entanglement, perplexity, intricacy, intrication [rare]; webwork, maze, meander, labyrinth, wilderness, jungle, Hyrcynian wood; wheels within wheels, clockworks; tangle, tangled skein, sleave, raveling, knot, Gordian knot, gnarl, knarl [obs.]; twist, kink, coil etc. (convolution) 248; network etc. 219.4; unintelligibility etc. 519; enigma etc. 533.2.

4. *n.* turmoil, turbulence, perturbation, ado, to-do [coll.], stir [coll.], disturbance, row [coll.], rowdydow [coll.], fuss, breeze [coll.], squall [coll.], dust [slang], trouble, bother, pother, pudder [obs. exc. dial.], touse [chiefly dial.], commotion, callithump [U.S.], hubbub, tumult, convulsion, bluster, uproar, racket, riot, shindy [slang], shine [slang], randan *or* rantan [dial. and slang], razzle-dazzle [slang], rumpus [coll.], ruckus [dial. and slang], ruction [chiefly dial.], fracas, fraction [dial.], stour [arch. and dial.], embroilment, melee, scramble, spill and pelt, rough-and-tumble.

pandemonium, bear garden, Babel, saturnalia, Donnybrook Fair, confusion worse confounded, most admired disorder, *concordia discors* [L.] hell *or* Bedlam broke loose; bull in a china shop; all the fat in the fire, *le diable à quatre* [F.], the devil to pay, the devil to pay and no pitch hot [coll.]; pretty kettle of fish, pretty *or* nice piece of work, pretty piece of business; broil etc. 713.4; agitation etc. 315.

5. *n.* slattern, sloven, frump [coll.], drab, dowdy, drabbletail, dragletail [coll.], slammock *or* slummock [dial.], malkin [obs. exc. dial. Eng.], traipse [dial.], slubberer [now chiefly dial.], slubberdegullion [arch. and dial.], slut, trollop, alley cat [slang], bitch; pig, swine, hog [all coll.]; vulgarian etc. 851.4.

6. *v.* be disorderly etc. *adj.*, play at cross-purposes, be at sixes and sevens.

7. *v.* disorder, put out of order; muss up [coll., U.S.], ruffle, rumple etc. (derange) 61.2–5; turn topsy-turvy etc. (invert) 218.4; ravel etc. 219.8.

8. *adj.* disorderly, orderless, in disorder, without order, disorganized, disordered, unarranged etc. (*see* arrange etc. 60.6), dislocated; out of order, out of place, out of gear, out of whack [slang], out of kilter [coll.], out of sorts; irregular, desultory, unmethodical, immethodical, unsystematic, unsymmetric(al), indiscriminate, haphazard, promiscuous, casual, random, undirected, aimless, straggling.

confused, perplexed, chaotic, (all) balled up [slang], bedlamitish [coll.], helter-skelter [coll.], huggermugger, ramble-scramble [slang]; disjointed, out of joint; anarchic(al), anarchal, anarchial; deranged etc. 61.6; topsy-turvy etc. (inverted) 218.6; misplaced etc. 185.5; shapeless etc. 241.5; anomalous etc. (unconformable) 83.9; purposeless etc. 621.21.

9. *adj.* untidy, messy [coll.], messed up [coll.], mussy [coll., U.S.], mussed up [chiefly dial. or coll.]; slovenly, frowzy, unkempt, grubby [coll.], slouchy [coll.], dowdy, sloppy [coll.], drabble-tailed, dragletailed, sluttish, frumpish, slatternly, slammocky *or* slummocky [coll.]; careless, slipshod; tousled, tously, tousy [coll. or dial.]; uncombed; squalid; unclean etc. 653.16, 17; uncouth etc. 851.7.

10. *adj.* complex, complexed, intricate, mazy, complicated, perplexed, involved, raveled, tangled, entangled, tangly, snarled, knotted, gnarled, crabbed, inextricable; daedal, Daedalian *or* Daedalean, Daedalic; labyrinthine, labyrinthian, labyrinthic(al); meandering, meandrous, meandry [obs.]; irreducible, irreductible [rare]; difficult etc. 704.8; tortuous, sinuose etc. (convoluted) 248.4; obscure etc. 519.7; imperspicuous etc. 571.2; enigmatic etc. 533.6.

11. *adj.* troublous, tumultuous, turbu-

lent, turbid, unquiet, agitated; riotous etc. (violent) 173.11, 12.

12. *adv.* irregularly etc. *adj.*, by *or* at intervals, by fits, by fits and starts *or* snatches, by *or* in snatches, in spots [coll.]; every now and then, every once in a while [both coll.]; at haphazard, at random; by chance etc. 156.13.

13. *adv.* in disorder *or* confusion etc. *n.*, higgledy-piggledy, helter-skelter [coll.], huggermugger, ramble-scramble [slang], harum-scarum [coll.], willy-nilly [coll.], all balled up [slang], all anyhow [coll.], which way *or* every which way [coll., U.S.], all over the shop [slang]; in a ferment; at cross-purposes, at six and seven *or* sixes and sevens; upside down, topsy-turvy etc. 218.6.

60. Arrangement
(See 61. Derangement; also 58. Order)

Reduction to Order.—**1.** *n.* arrangement, disposal, disposition, disposure; distribution, collocation, allocation, sorting etc. *v.*, assortment, allotment, apportionment; taxis, syntaxis; graduation, organization, ordination; grouping, groupage; system etc. (order) 58; preparation etc. 673.

2. *n.* classification, taxonomy, biotaxy; analysis, division, systematization, categorization, codification, digestion; class etc. 75.

3. *n.* (result of arrangement) systematic collection, syntagma, catalogue, table, atlas, calendar; filing system, file, letter file, index, card index, pigeonholes; scheme, schema, schematism; organism, architecture, cosmos; form, lay, array; outline etc. (plan) 626; register etc. (record) 551; instrumentation, orchestration, score etc. (music) 415.3, 21; orderliness etc. 58.4; stipulation, settlement etc. (compact) 769.

4. *n.* sorter, sifter, sieve, riddle, screen, bolter, colander; grate, grating.

5. *n.* (act of making neat) cleanup, red-up [dial.]; tidy-up, trim-up, police-up, muck-up [all slang].

6. *v.* arrange, order, put *or* set in order, reduce to order, bring into order, introduce order into, put *or* set to rights *or*

in array; put in *or* into shape, put in trim, clear up, clear the decks, trim, trim up, do up [chiefly coll.], fix up [coll.], police *or* police up [coll.], red up [dial.] side *or* side up [coll.], tidy *or* tidy up [chiefly coll.]; neat, neaten, neatify [rare]; fettle *or* fettle up [dial.], spruce *or* spruce up [coll.], clean up.

dispose, dispose of, fix, place, set out, collocate, allocate, compose, space, range, pack, marshal, rally, array, size, group, rank, align, line up; allot, apportion, parcel out, distribute, deal, deal out, cast *or* assign the parts, assign places to; assort, sort, sift, sieve, screen, riddle; string together, thread; prepare etc. 673.6.

7. *v.* classify, class, divide, segregate, group, rank, grade, graduate; file, list, catalogue, tabulate, index, alphabetize, digest, codify.

8. *v.* methodize, systematize, harmonize, regulate, organize, co-ordinate, brigade, echelon, seriate [rare], settle, fix; orchestrate, score.

9. *v.* disentangle, ravel, unravel, unweave, untwist, feaze [dial.]; comb, card; disembroil, unconfuse [rare]; untie etc. (separate) 44.7; disinvolve etc. (simplify) 42.3.

10. *adj.* arranged, disposed, classified, filed etc. *v.*; on file; tabular, tabulate; in order, systematic etc. (orderly) 58.7, 8.

61. Derangement
(See 60. Arrangement; also 59. Disorder)

Subversion of Order; Bringing into Disorder.—**1.** *n.* derangement, disarrangement, misarrangement; disorganization, deorganization; displacement, misplacement, dislocation; discomposure, disturbance, perturbation, razzle-dazzle [slang]; evection; disorder etc. 59; inversion etc. 218; insanity etc. 503.

2. *v.* derange, disarrange, misarrange; disorder, bring into disorder etc. 59; disorganize, deorganize; muddle, jumble, tumble, huddle, shuffle, hustle, fumble; muss *or* muss up [coll., U.S.], mess *or* mess up [coll.], mux *or* mux up [dial.], mix up, mommick *or* mommix [dial.], ass up [slang], make a hash *or* mess of

---

60. All things have their place, knew we how to place them.—G. HERBERT. Who hath disposed the whole world?—BIBLE.

61. Confusion now hath made his masterpiece. —SHAKESPEARE. Confusion on thy banners wait.—GRAY. So quick bright things come to confusion.—SHAKESPEARE. Confusion worse confounded.—MILTON.

it [slang], pie; drag from under the bed [coll., U.S.]; litter, scatter; dishevel, tousle [coll.], touse [dial.], unform, unshape, ruffle, rumple; turn topsy-turvy etc. (invert) 218.4; dement etc. 503.11.

3. *v.* displace, dislocate, unhinge, disjoint, put out of joint, throw out of gear; misplace, mislay.

4. *v.* discompose, throw into disorder *or* confusion, disconcert, unsettle, upset, disturb, trouble, perturb, agitate, toss, embroil, convulse; rattle [coll.], fluster etc. (confuse the mind) 458.9; change etc. 140.6.

5. *v.* complicate, involve, perplex, confound, confuse, muddle, mix up, ball up [slang], tangle, entangle, embrangle, ravel; bedevil; obscure etc. 528.10.

6. *adj.* deranged, disordered, discomposed etc. *v.*; syncretic, syncretistic; disorderly, untidy etc. 59.8, 9; demented etc. 503.12–13.

62. Precedence
(See 63., 281. Sequence; also 64. Precursor, 280. Precession)

1. *n.* precedence, precedency, predecession [rare], antecedence *or* antecedency, anteriority, anteposition, precession [rare], the lead, *le pas* [F.]; epacme; preference etc. 609.2; superiority etc. 33; importance etc. 642; priority etc. (in time) 116; precedent etc. (precursor) 64.

2. *v.* precede, forerun, forego [arch.], prevene [rare], antecede, come first, come *or* go before, go ahead of, go in advance, head, stand at the head, stand first, lead, take the lead, lead the way, lead the dance, lead the cotillion [U.S.], lead the german [U.S.]; take *or* have precedence, have the *pas* [F.]; rank, outrank; have the start etc. (get before) 280.2; be previous etc. (in time) 116.3.

3. *v.* place before, prefix, preface, premise, prelude, prologize, preamble, introduce.

4. *adj.* preceding etc. *v.*, precedent [rare], antecedent, anterior, prior; precursory, precursive; prodromal, prodromous [rare]; prelusive, prelusory; preludious, preludial; prevenient, preliminary, prefatory, proemial, preparatory, inaugural; former, fore [obs.], foregoing, afore-going; before-mentioned, above-mentioned, afore-mentioned, aforesaid, aforenamed, afore-sighted, aforethought, forenamed, forementioned, before-said [arch.], said, named; previous etc. (in time) 116.4; introductory etc. 296.7; preparatory etc. 673.10.

5. *adv.* before etc. (time) 116, (place) 234, (motion) 280.

63. Sequence
(See 62. Precedence, 280. Precession; also 65. Sequel, 281. Sequence)

1. *n.* sequence, succession, successiveness, following, coming *or* following after; consecution, consecutiveness; going after etc. (motion) 281; pursuit etc. (action) 622; posteriority etc. (time) 117; secondariness, subordinacy etc. (inferiority) 34; sequel etc. 65.

2. *n.* continuation, prolongation, extension; order of succession; mantle of Elijah; continuity, series etc. (unbroken sequence) 69; continuance etc. (in action) 143.

3. *v.* succeed, come *or* go after, come next, come on, follow, ensue; follow *or* move behind etc. 281.3; step into the shoes of etc. (supplant) 147.3.

4. *v.* place after, suffix, append, subjoin.

5. *adj.* succeeding, successive, following, ensuing, sequent, sequential, sequacious, subsequent, consequent, proximate, next; consecutive etc. (continuous) 69.6; alternate etc. (periodic) 138.10; later etc. 117.

6. *adv. etc.* after etc. (time) 117.3, 4, (place) 235.14–17, (motion) 281.5; (pursuit) 622.11.

64. Precursor
(See 65. Sequel; also 62. Precedence)

1. *n.* precursor, forerunner, apparitor [obs.], prodrome [obs.], *prodromos* [Gr. πρόδρομος], prodromus [rare], pioneer, *voortrekker* [Du.], avant-courier, *avant-coureur* or *avant-courrier* [F.]; vancour-

---

62. But many that are first shall be last; and the last shall be first.—BIBLE.   The first in glory as the first in place.—HOMER.   None sure will claim in Hell precedence.—MILTON. First come, first served.

63. And it must follow, as the night the day.—SHAKESPEARE.

64. What's past is prologue.—SHAKESPEARE. It was the lark, the herald of the morn.—SHAKESPEARE.

ier [arch.]; harbinger, herald, outrider [obs.]; scout, scouter; leader, bellwether, bell mare; forelooper [S. Afr.], *voorlooper* [Du.]; dawn; predecessor, precedent, antecedent; vanguard etc. 234.2; messenger etc. 534; groundwork etc. (foundation) 215.3; prefigurement, foretoken etc. (omen) 512; informant etc. 527.5; preparer etc. 673.5.

2. *n.* prelude, preamble, preface, prologue, foreword, *avant-propos* [F.], protasis, proem, proemium, plolusion [rare], prolegomenon (*pl.* prolegomena), exordium, introduction, frontispiece; prefix, prefixture [rare]; preliminary, prelim [slang, U.S.]; overture, voluntary, ritornel, *ritornello* [It.], descant; premise, presupposition, postulate, prolepsis; heading etc. (beginning) 66.

3. *adj.* precursory, prelusive etc. (preceding) 62.4.

65. Sequel
(See 64. Precursor; also 63. Sequence)

1. *n.* sequel, sequela (*pl.* sequelae), sequelant; continuation, continue, supplement, appendix (*pl.* appendixes, appendices), postscript, subscript, postface, postlude, epilogue, conclusion, peroration, codicil, colophon, tag, more last words; outgrowth, consequence etc. (effect) 154; sequence etc. 63.

2. *n.* after part *or* afterpart, afterpiece, aftercome [Scot.]; wake, trail, train, queue; aftermath, afterclap, afterglow, aftertaste; aftergrowth, aftercrop, aftergrass; second crop, rowen; arrish, eddish [both dial., Eng.]; afterbirth, afterburden [obs.], placenta, secundines, afterpain; afterthought, second thought, *arrière-pensée* [F.]; suffix, postfix; hinder part, tail etc. (rear) 235; retinue, *cortège* [F.], suite etc. (attendance) 88.5; follower etc. 281.2; tab etc. 39.2; end etc. 67.

66. Beginning
(See 67. End)

1. *n.* beginning, commencement, start, starting point, opening, outstart, outset, setout, incipience *or* incipiency, inception; inchoation, inchoacy [rare]; *fatiha* [Arab.]; first, first beginning, first rattle out of the box, go-off *or* first go-off, kick-off, jump-off, send-off, start-off, take-off [all coll.]; prime, initial, alpha; infancy, incunabula [*pl.*] (*sing.* incunabulum), cradle; debut, coming out [coll.].

inauguration, installation, unveiling [coll.], embarkment, the first step, *le premier pas* [F.], first stage, rising of the curtain; curtain raiser, maiden speech, opener [coll.]; outbreak, onset; initiative, move, first move; first blush, first glance, first sight, first impression; fresh start, new departure; slight beginning, narrow *or* thin edge of the wedge; front etc. 234; prelude, proem etc. 64.2; dawn etc. (morning) 125.1; first attempt etc. 675.2.

2. *n.* genesis etc. (origin) 153, (birth) 161.3.

3. *n.* heading, head, headline, caption, title; overline, banner, banner head *or* line, flag [U.S.], streamer, screamer [U.S.], scarehead [U.S.], spread, spreadhead, drophead, hanger [all journ. cant]; running head *or* title; title page, imprint.

4. *n.* rudiments, elements, principia, outlines, grammar, alphabet, A B C's.

5. *v.* begin, commence, make a beginning *or* start, gin [arch.], start, start in, enter on *or* upon, enter, embark in, set in, set to *or* about, get to, turn to, fall to, go ahead; pitch in, fire away, get going, take off [all coll.]; initiate, inchoate, handsel, do for the first time, take the first step, lay the first stone, cut the first turf; break ground, break the ice, break cover; open, open up, open the door to.

inaugurate, install, institute, incept [rare], introduce, broach, usher in, ring in [coll.], launch, set up, set on foot, set agoing, set abroach, set *or* put the ball in motion, open the ball [slang], open fire, apply the match to a train; take the initiative, take the lead, lead off, lead the way, head, stand at the head, stand first; take the decisive step, cross *or* pass the Rubicon; make an auspicious beginning,

---

65. Gather the sequel by that went before.—SHAKESPEARE. In every affair consider what precedes and what follows.—EPICTETUS.
66. *Omnium rerum principia parva sunt* [The beginnings of all things are small].—CICERO. My way is to begin with the beginning.—BYRON.

Begin, and then the work will be completed.—GOETHE. The beginning, as the proverb says, is half the whole.—ARISTOTLE. *Dimidium facti qui caepit habet* [He who has begun has the work half done].—HORACE. A bad beginning makes a bad ending.—EURIPIDES.

auspicate, get off to a good start [coll.]; ventilate, air; lay the foundation etc. (prepare) 673.6; undertake etc. 676.2; set out etc. (depart) 293.4.

6. *v.* originate, take *or* have origin, come into existence, come into the world, become, see the light, take birth; rise, arise, take rise, take its rise; burst forth, break out, spring *or* crop up; make one's debut, come out [coll.]; conceive, give a beginning to; give origin to etc. (cause) 153.6.

7. *adj.* beginning etc. *v.*, initial, initiatory, initiative; incipient, introductory, proemial [rare]; inaugural, inauguratory; inchoate, inchoative [rare]; prime, primal, primary, primitive, premier [rare]; primigenial, primigenious *or* primigenous, primogenial; original, aboriginal; embryonic, embryonal, embryonary [rare]; rudimentary, rudimental; natal, nascent; elemental, elementary; primeval etc. 124.7.

8. *adj.* first, foremost, front, head, chief, principal, leading, main; maiden.

9. *adv.* first, firstly, *imprimis* [L.], at first, in the first place, erst [obs.], first and foremost, before everything; at *or* in the beginning etc. *n.*; *in limine* [L.]; in the bud, in embryo, in its infancy; from the beginning etc. *n.*, from its birth *or* inception; from *or* at the first go-off, from the word go, at the drop of the hat *or* handkerchief [all coll.]; *ab initio, ab ovo, ab incunabilis, ab origine* [all L.]; formerly etc. 122.14.

67. End
(See 66. Beginning)

1. *n.* end, ending, termination, determination [arch.], terminus, terminal, term, apodosis, conclusion, close, expiration, expiry, consummation, finis, finale, finality, stoppage, windup [coll.], blow-off [slang, U.S.], payoff [slang, U.S.], thirty [Teleg. and slang], fall of the curtain, curtains [slang, U.S.]; last, what the shoemaker threw at his wife [slang]; period, limit, goal, destination; omega, izzard [slang], Z; *dénouement* [F.], catastrophe; doom, crack of doom, doomsday, Day of Judgment, fate; eschatology; discontinuance etc. (cessation) 142; finish etc. (completion) 729; extinction etc. 162.2; dissolution etc. (death) 360; epilogue, appendix etc. (sequel) 65.

2. *n.* extremity, extreme, tip, point, nib, tail, tail end, butt end, tag end, fag end, bitter end, gable end; stub, butt, tag; bottom dollar [coll.], cases *or* case dough [crim. slang, U.S.]; verge etc. (edge) 231.

3. *n.* closing period, close, declining period, breakup, last stage, beginning of the end, *commencement de la fin* [F.]; homestretch, last lap [coll.]; evening etc. 126.1.

4. *n.* finishing stroke *or* blow, ender, end-all, quietus, stopper, finisher [coll.], deathblow, death stroke, *coup de grâce* [F.], settler [coll.], knockout *or* knockout blow [coll.]; K.O. *or* kayo, flattener, sockdolager [U.S.], kibosh, calker [all slang].

5. *v.* end, terminate, determine, determinate [obs.], close, finish, conclude, over [dial. and slang], wind up [coll.]; stop, discontinue etc. (cease) 142.6.

6. *v.* come to an end etc. *n.*, end etc. *above*, come *or* draw to a close, be all over, expire, become void, run out, run its course, pass away, conk out [slang]; die etc. 360.6; reach completion etc. 729.4.

7. *v.* bring to an end etc. *n.*, terminate etc. *above* 67.5, put an end to, make an end of, get it over, get through with; shut up shop, shut down, knock off [coll.], hang up one's ax [coll.], hang up the fiddle [coll.], drop *or* ring down the curtain [coll.], ring down on [coll.]; knock on *or* in the head, knock out [coll.]; K.O. *or* kayo, kibosh, put the kibosh on, put the finisher *or* settler on,

---

Whatever begins, also ends.—SENECA. Better never begin than never make an end.—G. HERBERT. Well begun is half done. *Aller Anfang ist schwer* [Every beginning is difficult]. *Il n'y a que le premier pas qui coûte* [It is only the first step which costs; the beginning is hardest].
67. Whatsoever thou takest in hand, remember the end, and thou shalt never do amiss.—APOCRYPHA. Great is the art of beginning, but greater the art is of ending.—LONGFELLOW.

Some time an end there is of every deed.—CHAUCER. All's well that ends well.—SHAKESPEARE. 'Tis a consummation / Devoutly to be wished.—SHAKESPEARE. *Ultimus Romanorum* [The last of the Romans]. *En toute chose il faut considérer la fin* [In every affair it is necessary to consider the end]. *Finem respice* [Look to the end].

wash up [all slang]; achieve etc. (complete) 729.2; stop etc. (interrupt) 142.7.

8. *adj.* ending etc. *v.*, final, terminal, terminative [rare], determinative, definitive; conclusive, conclusory, last, eventual, farthest, extreme, ultimate; caudal; approaching an end, drawing to a close, vergent [rare], all over but the shouting [coll.]; conterminous, conterminal, conterminate [obs.], conterminant [obs.]; crowning etc. (completing) 729.5; hindermost etc. (rear) 235.9.

9. *adj.* ended etc. *v.*, at an end, settled, decided, conclusive, over, all off [coll.], all bets off [slang], all up *or* U.P. [slang], done with, done for [coll.], set at rest; played out, pegged *or* petered out [coll.]; finished, fini [slang]; completed etc. 729.6.

10. *adj.* penultimate, last but one, ~ two etc.

11. *adv.* finally, conclusively, in fine; at last, at the last; once for all.

12. *adv.* to the end, to the last extremity, to the bitter end, through thick and thin, to the end of the chapter, until the last cat is hung [slang]; to completion etc. 729.8.

68. Middle
(See also 222. Centrality)

1. *n.* middle, middlement [dial.], midst, mid [rare], midmost, middlemost [rare], mediety [obs.], middle *or* central position, thick; middle term, *mezzo termine* [It.]; medium etc. (mean) 29; midcourse etc. 628; centrality etc. 222.

2. *n.* middle part, central portion, intermediate part; diaphragm, midriff, equator; core, kernel etc. (center) 222.2; interior etc. 221.2.

3. *n.* equidistance, equal distance, half distance, midway [obs.], halfway point *or* place, halfway house; bisection, equal division; interjacence etc. 228.

4. *v.* middle, center, put *or* be in the middle; find the middle of, bisect; fold in the middle, double.

5. *adj.* middle, medial, mediate [rare], mesial, mesian, middling [obs. exc. dial.], medium, mean, mid, midmost, middlemost, midway [rare]; midship; midland, mediterranean; equidistant, equatorial; central etc. 222.4; intermediate etc. (interjacent) 228.11.

6. *adv.* midway, halfway, in the middle, halfway in the middle [coll.], in the midst, in the mean, *in medias res* [L.], plump ~, slap ~, slap-dab ~, smack *or* smack-dab in the middle [all slang]; medially, mediumly etc. *adj.*; midships, amidships; *meden agan* [Gr. μηδὲν ἄγαν].

69. Continuity
(See 70. Discontinuity)

Uninterrupted Sequence.—1. *n.* continuity, continuousness, unbrokenness, consecutiveness etc. *adj.*; consecution, succession, progression, course, gradation, catenation, concatenation; unbroken extent, perpetuity, ceaselessness, constant flow; continuation etc. (sequence) 63, (in action) 143.

2. *n.* series, succession etc. *above*; train, rank, file, line, string, thread, queue, row, range, tier; catena, chain; suite, suit, set, team; round, cycle; scale; colonnade, portico, peristyle.

3. *n.* procession, line, string, column, train, etc. *above*; cavalcade, caravan; parade; funeral, ovation, triumph; skimmington, skimmington ride; rank and file; line of battle; array; retinue, *cortège* [F.] etc. (attendance) 88.5.

4. *v.* form a series, follow a series etc. *n.*; fall in, fall in *or* into line; defile, march in procession etc. (file off) 266.21.

5. *v.* give continuity to, continuate [obs.], graduate; arrange in a series etc. *n.*, string together, string, thread; file, list, tabulate.

6. *adj.* continuous, continued, consecutive, serial, successive, immediate; sequent, sequential; progressive, gradual [rare]; uninterrupted, unbroken, unintermitting, unremitting, incessant, constant, ceaseless, endless, perennial, evergreen; linear, in a line *or* row; continuing etc. 143.4; monotonous etc. 104.7.

7. *adv.* continuously, consecutively etc. *adj.*; in unbroken succession, running, hand running [coll.], at *or* on a stretch; in succession, in turn; in a series, *seriatim* [L.], serially; in a line etc. *n.*, in column, in file; in single file, in Indian file; by gradual series, by gradations, gradually [rare], *gradatim* [L.], step by step.

---

69. In masks outrageous and austere / The years go by in single file.—E. WYLIE. Constant dropping wears the stone. *Natura non facit saltum* [Nature makes no leap].

70. Discontinuity
(See 69. Continuity)

Interrupted Sequence.—1. *n.* discontinuity, discontinuousness, disconnectedness etc. *adj.*; disconnection; solution, solution of continuity, ~ connection etc.; pause, interval, intermission, letup [coll.], interruption, caesura, break, broken thread; parenthesis, episode; rhapsody, patchwork, crazy quilt [coll.]; intermittence, alternation etc. (periodicity) 138.2; interim etc. 108a; discontinuance etc. (cessation) 142.

2. *v.* be discontinuous etc. *adj.*, alternate, intermit.

3. *v.* discontinue, pause, interrupt, stop, cease etc. 142.6, 7; disconnect, dissever etc. (disjoin) 44.7, 8; intervene, interpose etc. 228.8, 10.

4. *adj.* discontinuous, discontinued, unsuccessive, disconnected, unconnected, broken, broken off, interrupted, *décousu* [F.]; discrete, discretive; disjunct [rare], disjunctive; spasmodic, desultory, fitful etc. (irregular) 139.2; intermittent, alternate, recurrent etc. (periodic) 138.10; disjoined etc. 44.12.

5. *adv.* discontinuously etc. *adj.*, at intervals, *longo intervallo* [L.], sporadically, spasmodically, intermittently, by snatches, by jerks, by skips, by catches, by *or* at fits, by fits and starts, skippingly, *per saltum* [L.]; "like angel visits, few and far between" (T. Campbell); occasionally etc. 137.4; irregularly etc. 139.3.

71. Term

Station in a Series.—1. *n.* term, rank, grade, gradation, scale, range, remove, station, status, state, stand, standing, footing, position, place, pitch, point, mark, step, *pas* [F.], link, rung, round, round of the ladder, stair, peg; cut, notch, hole [all coll.].

2. *v.* rank, have ~, hold ~, occupy ~, find etc. a place, ~ grade etc. *n.*, fall into a place etc., find one's hole [coll.].

72. Assemblage
(See 73. Dispersion)

1. *n.* assemblage, gathering, ingathering, forgathering, collection, congregation, concourse, conflux, contesseration [obs.]; rendezvous; mobilization, levy, muster, *attroupement* [F.], collocation, colligation; convergence etc. 290.

2. *n.* assembly, gathering etc. *above*, meeting, meet, get-together [coll.], turnout [coll.], gemot *or* gemote; congress, house, senate, legislature, caucus, convention, conventicle, session, séance, eisteddfod, levee; convocation, aud call [college slang]; conclave etc. (council) 696; reunion etc. (social gathering) 892.5; divine service etc. 990.7.

3. *n.* company, band, Bund [G.], tribe, group, gang, outfit, crew, squad, team, string, troop, troupe, body, corps, force, platoon, covey, bunch [coll.], mob [slang], crowd [coll.]; push, shove, mob, hiram [all crim. slang, U.S.]; posse, *posse comitatus* [L.]; caravan; watch; claque; army, regiment etc. (combatants) 726.6, 7; clique, association etc. (party) 712.1–5; attendance etc. 186.6.

4. *n.* crowd, throng, multitude, horde, host, heap [coll.], legion, body, force, swad [slang, U.S.], array, bevy, galaxy; press, crush, cram [coll.], push [slang, U.S.], shove [crim. slang, U.S.], squeeze [coll.]; mob, rabble, *cohue* [F.], rout; flight, cloud, storm, shower, volley; swarm, hive; shoal, school; bunch, pack, kennel, covey, flock, tribe, herd, drove, drive; *mulada, remuda* [both Sp. and West. U.S.]; roundup [West. U.S.]; large number etc. 102.2; great quantity etc. 31.3.

5. *n.* bunch, group, cluster, Pleiades [Astron.] (*pl.*; *sing.* Pleiadum), clump; set, batch, lot; boodle [U.S.], caboodle, boiling, kit, kit and boiling [all slang]; pack, packet, package, budget, parcel, bundle, bindle [tramp slang, U.S], bale, seroon, *serón* [Sp.], fagot, fascine, wisp, truss, tuft; grove, thicket, plump [arch.]; shock, hattock [dial., Eng.], stook [dial.], mow, rick, fardel [arch. and dial.], stack, sheaf; hayrick, haycock, haymow; swath; fascicle, fascicule, fasciculus.

6. *n.* accumulation, cumulation, amassment, acervation, coacervation [rare], coagmentation [obs.], glomeration, agglomeration, conglomeration, conglomerate, aggregation, aggregate, congeries;

---

70. Begin, and cease, and then again begin.—M. Arnold. Life is made up of interruptions.—Gilbert.

72. Two is company, three is a crowd.—Fuller. A crowd is not company, and faces are but a gallery of pictures.—Bacon. I have a rendezvous with Death.—Seeger.

conglobation, conglobulation [rare]; concentration, congestion; lump, mass, gob [dial. and slang], batch, heap, bing [obs. exc. dial.], pile, pyramid, rouleau, tissue; drift, snowdrift; snowball; gleaning, *spicilegium* [L.]; hoard etc. (store) 636; quantity etc. 31.3.

7. *n.* collection, collectanea; ana, budget, compilation, symposium; chrestomathy; museum, library, menagerie etc. (collections) 636.5.

8. *n.* miscellany, miscellanea; assortment, varied assortment, medley, mob [coll.], omnium-gatherum [coll.], Noah's ark; hodgepodge, olla-podrida etc. (mixture) 41.4.

9. *n.* collector, gatherer; whip, whipper-in.

10. *v.* (be or come together) assemble, collect, muster, congregate, come *or* flock together, gather, forgather, gang up [coll.], round in [slang]; meet, unite, join; cluster, bunch, bunch up, flock, swarm, surge, stream, herd, crowd, throng; pig together, pig it together; associate; conglomerate; concentrate; center round, rendezvous, re-sort; huddle, go into a huddle [slang]; reassemble, reunite, reune [slang], rejoin.

11. *v.* (get or bring together) assemble, gather, muster; bring together, get together, draw together, scrape together, lump together, batch together, bunch together; collect, collocate, colligate; get in, whip in, gather in; hold a meeting, meet, convene; convoke, convocate; rake up, dredge, heap, mass, batch, bunch, bunch up, pile, pile up; pack, truss, cram; acervate [rare], agglomerate, aggregate, put together *or* up, compile; group, aggroup, unite; collect *or* bring into a focus, concentrate; collect in a dragnet; heap Ossa upon Pelion; amass, accumulate etc. (store) 636.7.

12. *adj. etc.* assembled, collected etc. *v.*; fasciculate, fascicled, fasciculated; *acervatim* [L.].

13. *adj.* crowded, packed, closely packed, compact, firm, solid, dense, close, serried, all of a heap [coll.], teeming, swarming, populous; crowded to suffocation, packed like sardines, as thick as hops, ~ flies, ~ hail *or* thieves, swarming like maggots, as full as a tick, ready to burst, fit to bust [slang]; full etc. 52.11; overfull etc. 641.5.

14. *adj.* cumulative, accumulative.

73. Dispersion
(See 72. Assemblage)

1. *n.* dispersion, scattering etc. *v.*, scatterment, scatteration [coll.]; aspersion, dissemination, diffusion, dissipation, distribution, respersion [obs.], spread; circumfusion; interspersion, interfusion; affusion, spargefaction [obs.]; disjunction etc. 44; apportionment etc. 786; divergence etc. 291.

2. *n.* flotsam, flotsam and jetsam, waveson [early Eng. Law], waifs and estrays, *disjecta membra* [L.].

3. *v.* disperse, scatter, broadcast, sow, disseminate, diffuse, radiate, spread, spread out, overspread, dispread, ted, strew, bestrew, strow [arch.], straw [obs.], distribute, resperse [obs.]; set abroach; sow broadcast, scatter to the winds; spread like wildfire; spurtle, sprinkle, spatter, squatter [dial.]; intersperse, intersow, interfuse, intersprinkle; circumfuse, spread *or* diffuse around; disband, disembody, dismember; dispel, drive *or* clear away, cast, cast forth, shed, draft *or* draught off, blow off, let out, turn *or* cast adrift; issue, deal out, retail, utter, dispense; apportion etc. 786.3; diverge etc. 291.2.

4. *adj.* dispersed, disseminated, scattered etc. *v.*; strown, strewn, broadcast, dispread; widespread, sparse, sporadic; adrift, stray; disheveled, unkempt, streaming; diverging etc. 291.3.

5. *adj.* dispersive, scattering etc. *v.*, dissipative, diffusive, dispellent [rare]; resolvent [chiefly Med.], disculient [Med.].

6. *adv.* scatteringly, sparsely etc. *adj.*; *sparsim* [L.], here and there, *passim* [L.], in spots [coll.].

74. Focus

Place of Meeting.—1. *n.* focus, focal *or* central point, point of convergence, ~ concentration etc. 290, center of activity, ~ attraction, ~ attention etc.; corradiation [rare]; issue, venue; center etc. 222.2; focalization etc. (convergence) 290; axis etc. 312.5.

2. *n.* meeting place, gathering place, place of meeting *or* resort, rallying point,

---

73. Far and few, far and few / Are the lands where the Jumblies live.—E. LEAR. Tho' thou wert scattered to the wind.—TENNYSON.

point de réunion [F.], resort, rendezvous, hangout [slang, U.S.], haunt, stamping ground [slang], retreat, habitat; headquarters, home, club, lair, diggings [coll.], dig *or* digs [slang, U.S.], den, cave, hole; tryst, trysting place; place of assignation, assignation house; love nest [coll.]; hideaway, hide-out [coll.]; scatter, drum [both crim. slang, U.S.]; jungle *or* jungles, bo camp [both tramp slang, U.S.]; depot etc. 636.4; assembly room etc. 189.10.

3. *v.* focus, focalize, bring *or* come to a point *or* focus, bring into focus; corradiate [rare]; bring to an issue; center, concentrate etc. 222.3; concur etc. (converge) 290.2.

75. Class

1. *n.* class, classification, division, subdivision, category, grouping, head, order; section, department, province, domain, range, sphere, estate, status, predicament.

2. *n.* kind, sort, type, tap [chiefly coll.], lot [coll.], stamp, brand, number [coll.], designation, variety, species, denomination, manner, style, description, feather, color, stripe [usu. derog.], grain, kidney, kin [obs.], the like *or* likes of [coll.]; connection, order, genus (*pl.* genera), gender [arch.], gens, *genre* [F.], strain, family, race, brood, tribe, caste, sept, phylum, clan, breed; subgenus, subspecies, subgroup, suborder, subfamily; make, cast, form, mold; set, kit [coll.], suit, sect; clique, coterie; character etc. (nature) 5.3.

3. *n.* sex, gender [coll. exc. Gram.], *genre* [F.], sect [misuse].

4. *n.* indication, particularization, selection, specification.

5. *v.* classify etc. 60.7.

6. *adj.* classificational, classific, classificatory, classical [rare]; taxonomic(al); divisional, divisionary, divisive; subdivisional, subdivisive; categoric(al) [Philos.], categorematic(al) [Logic; rare]; departmental; sectional, sectionary [rare]; sectary, sectarian, sectarial; denominative, denominational; sortal,

sorty; typal, typic(al); special, specific, individual, particular, peculiar, unique; tribal, racial, family, clannish; classified etc. (arranged) 60.10; systematic etc. (orderly) 58.7.

7. *adj.* sexual, sexuous [rare], sexlike, sexly [rare], sexy [slang].

76. Inclusion
(See 77. Noninclusion, 55. Exclusion)

Comprehension under, or Reference to, a Class.—1. *n.* inclusion, comprisal, comprehension, incorporation, admission, reception; composition etc. (inclusion in a compound) 54.

2. *v.* be included in etc., come *or* fall under, range under *or* with, belong to, pertain *or* appertain to; enter into, merge in.

3. *v.* include, comprise, comprehend, contain, compose, admit, subsume, receive, enclose, incorporate, cover, embody, encircle, encompass, involve, embrace, hold, take in; reckon among, enumerate *or* number among, place *or* arrange under *or* with; take into account *or* consideration, refer to.

4. *adj.* included, including etc. *v.*; of the same class etc. 75; congenerous etc. (related) 9.6.

5. *adj.* inclusive, unexclusive [rare], inclusory [rare], comprehensive, compendious; wide, sweeping etc. (extensive) 31.7; all-inclusive etc. (universal) 78.11; component etc. 56.3.

77. Noninclusion
(See 76. Inclusion)

1. *n.* noninclusion, expulsion etc. (exclusion) 55; rejection etc. (ejection) 297.

2. *n.* outlaw etc. (outcast) 893.5.

78. Generality
(See 79. Speciality)

1. *n.* generality, universality, worldwideness etc. *adj.*; ecumenicity; catholicity, catholicism; generalization.

2. *n.* prevalence, rifeness etc. *adj.*, run,

3. *n.* (generality or entirety of diversified groups) Pan-Americanism, Pan-Anglicanism, Panhellenism, Pan-Ger-

---

75. All sorts and conditions of men.—Book of Common Pr.   Countless the various species of mankind, / Countless the shades which sep'rate mind from mind.—W. Gifford.   Breathes there a man with hide so tough / Who says two sexes aren't enough?—Hoffenstein.

78. For parlor use the vague generality is a life-saver.—G. Ade.

manism, Pan-Slavism, Pan-Sclavism, Pan-Slavonism, Pan-Asianism, Pan-Asiaticism, Pan-Babylonism, Pan-Buddhism, Pan-Celticism, Pan-Hispanism, Pan-Islamism, Pan-Mongolism, Pan-Moslemism, Pan-Prussianism, Pan-Teutonism, etc.

4. *n.* the generality, run, general ∼, common ∼, average *or* ordinary run, usual *or* normal kind etc. 75.2, average, ruck.

5. *n.* everyone, everybody, each and every one, each and every [dial.], one and all, all hands [coll.], all hands and the cook [slang], every man Jack [coll.], every mother's son [coll.], all the world, *tout le monde* [F.], all the world and his brother *or* wife [humorous], the devil and all [coll.]; every Tom, Dick, and Harry [coll.]; whole boodle *or* caboodle, whole kit, whole kit and caboodle *or* boiling, whole boiling, whole toot and scramble *or* stumble [all slang]; all etc. 50.2.

6. *pron.* whatever, whate'er, whatsoever, whatsoe'er, what so *or* whatso [arch. and dial.], whatsomever [dial.], anything soever which.

7. *v.* be general etc. *adj.,* prevail, be going about, stalk about.

8. *v.* generalize, make *or* render general etc. *adj.,* universalize; reduce to general laws, give a general form to; derive *or* induce a general conception, apply generally, give a general applicability; broaden, spread.

9. *adj.* general, generic, collective; encyclopedic(al); panoramic, bird's-eye.

10. *adj.* prevalent, prevailing, current, rife, rampant, epidemic, besetting; widespread, sweeping etc. (extensive) 31.7; customary, common etc. (habitual) 613.11.

11. *adj.* universal, catholic(al), comprehensive, all-inclusive, all-embracing, world-wide, nation-wide, state-wide, heaven-wide; ecumenic(al); all over [coll.], covered with.

12. *adj.* Pan-African, Pan-Afrikander, Pan-Syrian, Pan-American, Pan-Anglican, Panhellenic, Pan-Germanic, Pan-German, Pan-Arabian, Pan-Asiatic, Pan-Britannic, Pan-British, Pan-Celtic, Pan-Croat, Pan-European, Pan-Gothic, Pan-Slav, Pan-Slavonic, Pan-Slavic, Pan-Sclavic, Pan-Sclavonian, Pan-Slavistic, Pan-Slavonian, Pan-Syrian, Pan-Hispanic, Pan-Latin, Pan-Mongolian, Pan-Pacific, Pan-Russian, Pan-Saxon, Pan-boeotian, Pan-Buddhist, Pan-Christian, Pan-Islam, Pan-Islamic, Pan-Israelitish, etc.

13. *adj. etc.* every, all, every one, each, each one, each and all of, one and all of.

14. *adj.* indefinite, indeterminate, unspecified, impersonal; vague etc. 475.11.

15. *adv.* generally etc. *adj.,* in general, generally speaking, speaking generally, roughly speaking, as a rule, as a matter of course, for the most part, by and large, for better or for worse; in the long run etc. (on an average) 29.5; invariably etc. 16.7; always etc. 112.5; commonly etc. (habitually) 613.13.

79. Speciality
(See 78. Generality)

1. *n.* speciality, *spécialité* [F.], specialty, specificness etc. *adj.*

2. *n.* particularity, singularity, peculiarity, individuality; characteristic, distinctive feature, trait, trick, diagnostic [spec. Med.], physiognomic [rare], lineament, quality, property; idiosyncrasy, idiocrasy; mannerism; *je ne sais quoi* [F.], *nescio quid* [L.]; mark, earmark, distinguishing mark *or* characteristic, differentia (*pl.* differentiae); tendency etc. 176; character etc. (nature) 5.3; identity etc. 13; unity etc. 87.

3. *n.* particulars, details, circumstances, items, counts; minute particulars *or* details, minutiae.

4. *n. etc.* selfhood, selfness [rare]; self, I, I myself, me, myself, oneself, number one [coll.], your Uncle Dudley [slang], yours truly [coll.]; yourself, himself, herself, itself; themselves, theirselves [dial.], theirsens [dial.]; egohood, egoity [rare]; ego, personality, entire self *or* man; *alter, alterum* [both L.], alter ego; subliminal self, subliminal; psyche etc. 994.11; inner man etc. 450.3; world-self etc. 359.3.

5. *v.* specify, designate, mention, determine, denote, indicate, point out, select; differentiate.

6. *v.* specialize, individualize, particularize, give particulars of, give full particulars, detail, give in detail, go into details, itemize; descend to particulars, get

79. Men acquire a particular quality by constantly acting in a particular way.—ARISTOTLE. Who is it that can tell me who I am?—SHAKESPEARE.   Each man . . . is justified in his in-

down to brass tacks [coll.], get down to cases [slang, U.S.], come to the point; make special or specific, specificize [rare].

7. *adj.* special, especial, specific, particular, precise, express, singular, individual; personal, private, intimate, esoteric; respective, several; restricted, limited, confined, fixed, definite, determinate, certain, exclusive, partial; containing particulars, detailed, minute, full, circumstantial; distinguished, noteworthy.

8. *adj.* peculiar, characteristic, typical, representative, distinctive, marked, appropriate, proper, endemic; original; idiosyncratic(al), idiocratic(al); diagnostic; party; unique, uncommon etc. (unusual) 83.10; intrinsic etc. 5.7; characterized etc. 820.3.

9. *adj.* this, this here [dial.], these.

10. *adj.* that, that there [dial.], those; yon, yond, yonder.

11. *adv.* specially, especially etc. *adj.*, in particular, *in propria persona* [L.]; *ad hominem* [L.]; for my ~, your etc. part, as far as regards me, ~ you etc., for all me.

12. *adv.* each, apiece; one by one, severally, respectively, each to each; *seriatim* [NL.], in detail, bit by bit; *pro hac vice* [L.], *pro re nata* [L.].

13. *adv.* namely, nominally, that is to say, *videlicet* [L.], viz., scilicet, scil., sc., to wit.

80. Rule

1. *n.* rule, law, formula (*pl.* formulas, formulae), principle; governing law, prescribed *or* set form, settled *or* established rule, hard and fast rule, standing order *or* dish, Procrustean law, law of the Medes and Persians; regulation, maxim etc. (precept) 697; standard, criterion etc. (prototype) 22; method, system etc. (order) 58; regularity etc. (uniformity) 16; rut, routine etc. (habit) 613.

2. *n.* normality, normalcy, normal state *or* condition, natural *or* ordinary state of affairs.

3. *adj.* regular, constant, steady etc. (uniform) 16.5; methodical, systematic etc. (orderly) 58.7; measured etc.

466.13; customary etc. (habitual) 613.11; according to rule etc. (conformable) 82.8, 9.

81. Multiformity
(See 16. Uniformity)

1. *n.* multiformity, omniformity, multifariousness etc. *adj.*, variety, diversity, variegation, heterogeneity; polymorphism; varied assortment etc. (collection) 72.8, (mixture) 41; irrelation etc. 10; nonuniformity etc. 16a.

2. *adj.* multiform, multifold, multifarious, multigenerous, multiplex, variform [rare], diversiform, amoebiform, manifold, many-sided, omniform, omnigenous, omnifarious, polymorphic, polymorphous, multiphase, metamorphotic, protean, proteiform, heterogeneous, motley, mosaic; epicene; ununiform etc. 16a.2.

3. *adj.* diversified, varied, sorty [coll.], variegated, checked, daedal; indiscriminate, desultory, irregular; divers, various; of various kinds, of sorts [coll.]; all manner of, all sorts *or* kinds of; of all sorts and kinds, of every description, of every color and description; *et hoc genus omne* [L.]; and what not; different etc. 15.7; dissimilar etc. 18.4.

82. Conformity
(See 83. Unconformity; also 23. Agreement)

1. *n.* conformity, conformance, conformation; observance, observation; adaption, adaptation; adjustment, accommodation; line, keeping; reconcilement, reconciliation; custom etc. 613.2; conventionality etc. 852.2; acquiescence, compliance etc. (submission) 725; correspondence, congruity etc. (agreement) 23; uniformity etc. 16; orthodoxy etc. 983a.

2. *n.* example, exemplar, ensample [rare], sample, teaser [trade slang], specimen, representative; exemplification,

---

dividuality.—EMERSON. I celebrate myself and sing myself.—WHITMAN. *Le style est l'homme même* [His style is the man himself]. —BUFFON.
80. Exceptions prove the rule.

81. O Lord, how manifold are thy works!— BIBLE. Variety's the very spice of life.— COWPER. Oh, how various is the scene / Allowed to Man for his demesne!—HOFFENSTEIN. Age cannot wither her, nor custom stale / Her infinite variety.—SHAKESPEARE.
82. They are happy men whose natures sort with their vocations.—BACON. Conform thyself to thy present fortune, and cut thy coat according to thy cloth.—R. BURTON. The

instance, relevant instant, case, case in point, illustration, quotation; object lesson; elucidation, explanation; pattern etc. (prototype) 22.

3. *n.* conformist, conformer, conventionalist, bromide *or* bromidite [slang], formalist, methodologist, precisian, pedant, Philistine.

4. *v.* conform, comply, adapt, adjust, accommodate, meet, suit, fit, shape, correspond; adapt etc. to, agree *or* comply with, tally with, chime *or* fall in with, be guided *or* regulated by; reconcile, settle, compose; rub off corners; harmonize, accord etc. (agree) 23.7; be uniform etc. 16.3.

5. *v.* conform to rule, conventionalize, follow ~, observe ~, go by ~, bend to *or* obey rules *or* precedents, go according to Hoyle [coll.] etc. *adj.,* fall into a custom *or* usage, follow the fashion, follow the crowd *or* multitude, swim *or* go with the stream, ~ tide *or* current, do as others do, *hurler avec les loups* [F.], tread *or* follow the beaten path *or* track; come to time, keep in step, get into line, toe the mark *or* line, walk the chalk, walk the chalk mark *or* line [all coll.]; keep up to standard, pass muster, come up to scratch [coll.]; keep one in countenance; pass current; move in a rut etc. (habit) 613.10; be fashionable etc. 852.6.

6. *v.* exemplify, example, sample, type [rare], instance, produce an instance etc. *n.,* put a case, illustrate, cite, quote; elucidate, explain.

7. *adj.* conformed, adapted etc. *v.;* naturalized etc. (habituated) 613.12.

8. *adj.* conformable, adaptable, adjustable; consistent, harmonious etc. (agreeing) 23.9; compliant etc. (submissive) 725.5.

9. *adj.* conformable to rule, according to rule *or* regulation, according to use *or* custom; according to Cocker, ~ Gunter *or* Hoyle [coll.]; *en règle* [F.], *selon les règles* [F.]; well-regulated etc. (orderly) 58.7; regular etc. (uniform) 16.5; customary, usual etc. (habitual) 613.11; conventional etc. 852.8; preceptive etc. 697.2.

10. *adj.* orthodox, canonical, sound, sound on the goose [coll.], hard-shell [coll., U.S.]; strict, uncompromising etc. (severe) 739.5; faithful, catholic etc. (religion) 983a.7; authentic etc. 494.12.

11. *adj.* exemplary, exemplifying etc. *v.,* illustrative, representative; emblematic, symbolic, typical, prefigurative, figurative.

12. *adv. etc.* conformably etc. *adj.,* in conformity with, in accordance with, in keeping with, uniformly with, consistently with, according to; by rule, by the card; as a rule etc. (generally) 78.15; as usual etc. 613.14.

13. *adv.* for conformity, for the sake of conformity; for form's sake, *pro forma* [L.].

14. *adv.* for example, for instance, as an instance *or* example, *exempli gratia* [L.], e.g., *inter alia* [L.].

83. Unconformity
(See 82. Conformity; also 24. Disagreement)

1. *n.* unconformity, inconsistency, irregularity, deviation, divergence, variety; anomaly, anomalousness etc. *adj.,* anomalism; teratism [Med.]; aberrance *or* aberrancy, aberration; abnormality, abnormity; disagreement etc. 24; nonuniformity etc. 16a; irrelation etc. 10.

2. *n.* nonconformity, nonconformance, disconformity; nonobservance, noncompliance; nonconventionality, unconventionality, originality, informality, Bohemianism; disagreement, dissent; recusance *or* recusancy; infraction ~, breach ~, violation *or* infringement of custom *or* usage; unorthodoxy, sectarianism etc. 984.

3. *n.* unusualness, uniqueness, strangeness; bizarreness etc. *adj.;* bizarrerie [F.], oddity, peculiarity, singularity, rarity, abnormality, exceptionality; idiosyncrasy etc. (eccentricity) 503.6; individuality etc. 79.2.

4. *n.* nonconformist, original, sulphite [slang], Bohemian, eccentric, character

---

virtue in most respects is conformity.—EMERSON.   Examples work more forcibly on the mind than precepts.—FIELDING.   Example is always more efficacious than precept.—AESOP.   Example is a lesson that all men can read.—G. WEST.   When in Rome, do as the Romans do.

83. Whoso would be a man must be a nonconformist.—EMERSON.   All good things which exist are the fruits of originality.—J. S. MILL.   That so few now dare to be eccentric marks the chief danger of the time.—J. S. MILL.   Not conventionally unconventional.—SHAW.   It is a custom / More honored in the breach

[coll.], card [coll.], case [slang]; one in a thousand, one in a way; nondescript, nonesuch [rare].

crank, crackpot, nut, screwball [all slang]; queer chap, queer specimen [coll. or slang]; odd *or* queer fish, bird, queer bird, duck, queer duck, odd stick, geezer, galoot, queer *or* rum customer, rum one, rummy, bird, duck, geezer, [all slang]; codger, duffer [both coll.]; curiosity, oddity, rarity, *rara avis* [L.], exception, abnormality, missing link; radical etc. (reformer) 658.5; recusant etc. (dissenter) 489.3; heretic, sectarian etc. 984.12–14.

5. *n.* hermaphrodite, epicene, androgyne, gynandroid, bisexual, homosexual; Lesbian; pervert, sodomist, sodomite; homo, queer, fairy, pansy, queen, nance, Nancy *or* nancy, Molly *or* molly, Miss Molly, betty, painted Willie, fag, fagot, flute [all slang]; *tertium quid* [L.], neither one thing nor the other.

6. *n.* monstrosity, monster, miscreation, abortion, mooncalf [arch.], cacogenesis [Med.], teratism, teratogeny, teratology; freak, freak of nature, *lucus naturae* [L.]; prodigy, prodigiosity.

7. *n.* (mythical monsters) phoenix, chimera, Hydra, sphinx, manticore *or* manticora, Gorgon, Minotaur, centaur, Sagittary, sea horse, hippocampus, hircocervus, hippocerf, hippogriff *or* hippogryph, hippocentaur, kraken, dipsas, cockatrice, basilisk, wivern, roc, simurgh, dragon, drake [arch.], sea serpent, salamander, griffin, Python, xiphopagus, mermaid, merman, unicorn, ogre, ogress, Cyclops, Cerberus, ant lion; gazook, oink, whangdoodle, gyascutus, prock, sidewinder, wampus, wampus cat, swamp gaboon, whiffle-bird, tree squeak [all humorous]; animal etc. 366.

8. *v.* be unconformable etc. *adj.*, not conform etc. 82.4; abnormalize; leave the beaten path *or* track, get out of line [coll.], infringe ~, break *or* violate a law, ~ habit, ~ usage *or* custom; drive a coach and six through; stretch a point; have no business there; beggar *or* baffle all description.

9. *adj.* unconformable, nonconformable; unconventional, nonobservant; eccentric, irregular, heteroclite, informal, deviative, divergent, aberrant, stray, straying, wandering, wanton, lawless; anomalous, anomalistic; abnormal, abnormous; out of order *or* place, misplaced, out of one's element; out of keeping, out of tune, out of turn [slang], out of line [coll.], out of step; egregious, flagrant, gross; arbitrary, capricious; disagreeing etc. 24.6; unorthodox etc. 984.22.

10. *adj.* unusual, inusitate [rare], unordinary, unnatural, uncustomary, unaccustomed, unwonted, uncommon, unfamiliar, unheard-of, unprecedented, unparalleled, unexampled, undescribed, undescribable, unaccountable, unexpected; unimaginable, inimaginable [obs.], inconceivable, incredible; out of the ordinary, out of the way, out of the common *or* common run, out of *or* off the beaten track, out of the pale; rare, singular, exceptional, extraordinary, unique, *sui generis* [L.], *recherché* [F.], curious, peculiar.

odd, *outré* [F.], quisby [slang], rum [slang], strange, passing strange, queer, funny [coll.], comical [coll.], quaint, nondescript; monstrous, outlandish, exotic [rare], fantastic, fanciful, grotesque, freakish, bizarre, baroque, rococo, weird; teratogenic, teratogenetic, teratoid; remarkable, wonderful, noteworthy, stupendous, marvelous, prodigious; supernatural, preternatural, supernormal; *tombé des nues* [F.]; denaturalized; out [as *out sizes*], off [as *off color*]; newfangled etc. (novel) 123.10; unknown etc. 491.14; superexcellent etc. 648.10.

11. *adj.* original, sulphidic *or* sulphitic [slang], informal, Bohemian, on the free and easy [slang], nonobservant, unconventional, unfashionable, not being done; unimitated etc. 20.3.

12. *adj.* hermaphrodite, hermaphroditic(al); androgynous, androgynal, gynandrous, gynandrian, epicene, bisexual, homosexual, queer [slang], monoclinous, amorphous, heteroclite; adelomorphic, adelomorphous; Lesbian; effeminate; perverted.

13. *int.* what on earth!, what in the world!, what under the sun!, what in hell! [coll.].

---

than the observance.—SHAKESPEARE. If a man does not keep pace with his companions, perhaps it is because he hears a different drummer.—THOREAU. Men whose heads do grow beneath their shoulders.—SHAKESPEARE. Leviathan, that crooked serpent . . . the dragon that is in the sea.—BIBLE.

84. Number
(See also 85. Numeration)

1. *n.* number, numeral, numero, No. *or* no. [abbr.], character, symbol, figure, figger [dial.], cipher, digit, integer; cardinal number; round number; counter; formula (*pl.* formulas, formulae); function; series; figurate numbers, pyramidal numbers, polygonal numbers; quantity etc. 25.

2. *n.* (mathematical sums and elements) complement, subtrahend, multiplicand, multiplier, multiplicator, multiple, submultiple, coefficient, dividend, divisor, factor, quotient, fraction, mixed number, numerator, denominator, decimal, mixed decimal, circulating decimal, repetend, common measure, aliquot part, reciprocal, prime number, totient, quota, quotum [rare], differential, integral, fluxion, fluent, power, root, **radix**, base, exponent, index, logarithm, **antiloga**rithm, modulus.

3. *n.* sum, summation, **difference**, product, count, score, reckoning, tally, tale, the story *or* whole story [coll.], aggregate, amount, gross amount, stick [sporting slang]; total etc. (all) 50.2.

4. *n.* permutation, combination, alternation; election.

5. *n.* variation, variation of a function, variation of an integral, variation of constants *or* parameters.

6. *n.* ratio, proportion; progression, arithmetical progression, geometrical progression, harmonical progression; percentage, per cent *or* percent.

7. *adj.* numeral, numerary, numerative, numerical; figural, figurate, figurative; aliquot, submultiple, reciprocal, prime, fractional, decimal, exponential, logarithmic, logometric, differential, fluxional, integral, totitive; positive, negative; rational, irrational; surd, radical; real, imaginary; possible, impossible.

85. Numeration
(See also 84. Number)

1. *n.* numeration, enumeration, numbering, summation, reckoning, counting, telling [arch.], computation, calculation, calculus [rare], account, estimation, recension, supputation [obs.]; adding, footing, totaling, casting; rhabdology [rare]; dactylonomy; dead reckoning; measurement etc. 466, accountancy etc. 811.4.

2. *n.* mathematics, math [slang], mathematic, mathesis [rare]; pure mathematics, abstract mathematics, applied mathematics, higher mathematics, elementary mathematics; arithmetic, elementary arithmetic, higher arithmetic, political arithmetic, binary arithmetic; algorism, algorithm.

algebra, elementary *or* ordinary algebra, higher algebra, multiple algebra, complex *or* double algebra, vector algebra, quaternian algebra, associative algebra, commutative algebra, nilpotent algebra, noncommutative algebra, subalgebra, proper subalgebra, invariant subalgebra, simple algebra, semisimple algebra, reducible algebra, equivalent algebras, zero algebra, linear algebra, hyperalgebra, n-tuple linear algebra, graphic algebra, Boolian algebra, matrix algebra, division algebra, universal algebra; calculus, differential calculus, integral calculus, infinitesimal calculus, calculus of differences.

geometry, algebraic geometry, analytic geometry, circle geometry, denumerative geometry, descriptive geometry, geodesic geometry, hyperbolic geometry, intuitional geometry, inverse geometry, line geometry, metageometry, natural geometry, projective geometry, speculative geometry, universal geometry, Euclidean geometry, Riemannian geometry; trigonometry, trig [slang], plane trigonometry, spherical trigonometry; analysis; fluxions; geodesy etc. (measurement) 466.8.

3. *n.* statistics, statistology; count, account; recount, recapitulation; census, poll etc. (roll) 86.2; score, tally etc. (sum) 84.3.

4. *n.* (operations) notation, addition, subtraction, multiplication, division, proportion, rule of three, practice, equations, extraction of roots, reduction, involution, evolution, approximation, interpolation,

---

84. *Numero deus impare gaudet* [The god delights in odd numbers].—VERGIL. I've got your number.—HOLMES.
85. And, dear child, mind your arithmetic . . . What would life be without arithmetic, but a scene of horrors?—S. SMITH. The king was in his counting-house / Counting out his money.—NURSERY RHYME. The very hairs of your head are all numbered.—BIBLE.

differentiation, integration, indigitation [rare].

5. *n.* (instruments) calculator, counter; abacus, suan pan [Chin.]; Napier's bones *or* rods; calculating machine, adding machine, arithmometer, arithmograph, comptometer [trade name], difference engine, listing machine; cash register; rule, logometer etc. (measure) 466.4.

6. *n.* mathematician, mathematic [obs.], arithmetician, calculator, abacist; geometer, geometrician; algebraist, trigonometrician, actuary, statistician; geodesist etc. (measure) 466.9.

7. *v.* number, numerate, enumerate, count, tell, tell off, "tell his tale" (Milton), name *or* call over, run over; count up, figure, figure out *or* up, cipher, cipher up, reckon, reckon up [coll.], calculate, compute, supputate [obs.], suppute [obs.], estimate, make *or* furnish an estimate, take an account of, sum, sum up, cast up, score, score up, total, total up, tot up [coll., Eng.]; add, add up; subtract, multiply, divide, extract roots, algebraize; recount, recapitulate; relate, rehearse, recite, detail; call the roll, count noses [coll.], muster, poll, census; keep accounts etc. 811.7.

8. *v.* check, check up, check up on [coll.]; prove, demonstrate; balance, balance the books; audit, overhaul, take stock, inventory, inventorize [rare].

9. *v.* page, paginate, number *or* mark the pages of, affix numbers to, foliate.

10. *v.* amount to, come to, aggregate, come to in its aggregate, total, tot up to [coll., Eng.], be in its totality.

11. *adj.* numerative, numberable, countable, reckonable, computable, calculable; rhabdological [rare]; commensurable, commensurate.

12. *adj.* mathematical, arithmetic(al), algebraic(al), geometric(al), analytic(al), statistic(al).

86. List

1. *n.* list, register, registry, record, inventory, tablet, *tableau* [F.], scroll, screed, brief [obs.]; catalogue, classified catalogue, *catalogue raisonné* [F.]; file, letter file, catalogue file; pamphlet file, pam file [library cant]; index, thumb index, card index; glossary, gloss, vocabulary; table, contents, table of contents; memorandum, memo [coll.]; compendium, synopsis, syllabus, brief, digest; schedule, calendar, calends *or* kalends, docket [U.S.], draft, panel, prospectus, program, line-up [coll.].

bill of fare, menu, carte; invoice, manifest, bill of lading; account, score, tally, terrier; bill of costs, score [slang], damage [slang]; bulletin, bulletin board, score board *or* sheet; totalizator [turf], tote [turf cant]; clergy list, civil service list, army list, navy list, sick list, active list, retired list; ballot, ticket [U.S. polit.], slate [polit. cant]; cadastre *or* cadaster, *cadre* [F.]; chartulary, cartulary; diptych; ledger, journal, memorandum book etc. (record book) 551.3; dictionary etc. 593.4.

2. *n.* roll, roster, rota; check roll, checker roll, bead roll [spec. R.C. Ch.], muster roll *or* book, roll of honor; roll call, muster, capitation [obs.], census, nose count [coll.], poll, returns, census report *or* returns; panel.

3. *v.* list, register, catalogue, record, inscribe, tally, tabulate, enter, enroll, matriculate, post, docket [U.S.], book; manifest; bill, invoice, indent; file, index; inventory, inventorize [rare]; census, poll, count noses [coll.]; schedule, slate [U.S.], line up [coll.], calendar; score, keep score; empanel, impanel.

4. *adj.* listed, catalogued etc. *v.*; inventorial, cadastral.

87. Unity
(See 100. Plurality)

1. *n.* unity, oneness, undividedness, singleness etc. *adj.*; integrality, compaction [rare], compages (*sing.* and *pl.*), consistency, solidarity, coherence, interconnection of parts, organic totality; individuality etc. 79.2; solitude etc. (seclusion) 893.2; isolation etc. (disjunction) 44; unification etc. 48.1; completeness etc. 52; whole etc. 50.

2. *n.* unit, one, ace, monad, monas

---

86. He's got 'em on the list . . . / And they'll none of 'em be missed.—GILBERT.   How index-learning turns no student pale, / Yet holds the eel of science by the tail.—POPE.

87. He travels the fastest who travels alone.—KIPLING.   Liberty and Union, now and forever, one and inseparable.—D. WEBSTER.

[rare] (*pl.* monades); none else, no other, nought beside.

3. *n.* integer, item, individual, entity, point, module.

4. *v.* be one etc. *adj.,* be *or* stand alone.

5. *v.* unify, render one; unite etc. (join) 43.5 (combine) 48.3, 4.

6. *adj.* one, single, singular, individual, sole, *solus* [L.] (*fem. sola*), solitary, lone; sesqui-, one and a half.

7. *adj.* unique, sole, singular, odd, unrepeated, azygous, first and last, only, onliest [dial.], only-begotten, one and only.

8. *adj.* alone, solitary, *solus* [L.] (*fem. sola*), apart, companionless, unaccompanied, unattended; lonely, lonesome; monad, monadic(al); kithless; single-handed, unassisted, unaided; separate, isolated, insular etc. (disjoined) 44.12.

9. *adj.* unific, unitary, unifying, uniting; combinative, combinatory; connectional, connective, connecting; conjunctive, conjunctival; coalescing, coalescent; compact, irresolvable; uniflorous, unilobed, uniglobular, unifoliate, unigenital, uniliteral, unilocular, unimodular; monospermous.

10. *adv.* singly, individually etc. *adj.*; particularly, in the singular; severally, one by one, one at a time; alone, without companions *or* associates, of *or* by itself, all by it's *or* one's lonesome [coll.], *per se* [L.]; apart, in the abstract; solely, simply, exclusively.

87a. Zero

1. *n.* zero, naught *or* nought, cipher, nil, *nichts* [G.]; nix, nixie, goose *or* duck egg [Sport.], duck [Sport.], luke [all slang]; none, scratch etc. (nothing) 2.2; absence etc. 187.

2. *adj.* no, not one, not any, none [arch.].

3. *adv.* none, not at all, in no way, to no extent.

88. Accompaniment

1. *n.* accompaniment, concomitance *or* concomitancy, coexistence, coefficiency; attendant, concomitant, obbligato, coefficient; attribute; context; appendage, accessory, appurtenance etc. (adjunct) 39.

2. *n.* company, association, companionship, fellowship, palship [slang], society; partnership, copartnership.

3. *n.* accompanier, accompanist, accompanyist; attendant, companion, mate, fellow, associate, colleague, *fidus Achates* [L.], consort, spouse; partner, pard [slang, chiefly U.S.], copartner; chum [coll.], comrade etc. (friend) 890; satellite, shadow, hanger-on etc. (follower) 281.2; flunky [coll.], lackey etc. (servant) 746.

4. *n.* escort, conductor; usher, ush [slang]; chaperon, shap [slang], duenna, gooseberry [slang]; retainer, burkundaz [Ind.], bodyguard, safe-conduct, convoy; psychopompos [Gr. Relig.], Hermes, cavalier, squire etc. (lover) 897.6.

5. *n.* attendance, following, *cortège* [F.] *or* cortege, retinue, suite, suit [arch.], rout, trail, train, train of attendants, body of retainers; court; procession etc. 69.3.

6. *v.* accompany, company [arch.], bear *or* keep company, companion, companionize [coll.], attend, hang *or* wait on, hang around with [coll.], associate *or* couple with, consort with, flock together, herd together [coll.], row in the same boat, go with, go hand in hand with; chum, pal, buddy, pal with, chum *or* buddy together, buddy *or* pal up *or* around with [all slang]; take up with [coll.], tie up with [slang]; clique *or* clique with [coll.], gang *or* mob up with [slang]; coexist, concur; follow etc. 281.3.

7. *v.* escort, conduct, usher, convoy, guide, carry [arch. and dial.], tote [coll., U.S.], squire; hustle [U.S.], chase [U.S.], drag [U.S.], flame [all slang]; chaperon, shap [slang], play gooseberry [slang]; precede etc. 280.2; protect etc. 664.3.

8. *adj.* accompanying, accompanimental; concomitant, comitant [rare]; attendant, accessory, obbligato [chiefly

---

Distinct as the billows, yet one as the sea.—J. MONTGOMERY. We are one people and will act as one.—SCHILLER.
88. Two is company, three is a crowd.—FULLER. Every man is like the company he is wont to keep.—EURIPIDES. A merry companion is as good as a wagon.—LYLY. Good company is a good coach.—J. CLARKE. Good company and good discourse are the very sinews of virtue.—I. WALTON. Birds of a feather flock together. *Noscitur a sociis* [A person is known by the company he keeps].

Mus.], associated *or* coupled with; fellow, twin, joint.

9. *adv. etc.* in company with, with, withal [chiefly arch.], together *or* along with, coupled with, in conjunction with; hand in hand *or* glove, side by side, cheek by jowl, arm in arm; therewith, herewith; including, as well as etc. (additionally) 37.8, 9.

10. *adv.* together, in a body, collectively, mutually, in conjunction; conjointly, jointly etc. 43.14.

89. Duality
(See 91. Bisection; also 90. Duplication)

1. *n.* duality, dualism, duplexity, duplicity, biplicity [rare], biformity; polarity.

2. *n.* two, twain [chiefly poetic]; couple, couplet, doublet [Tech., cant, or coll.], brace, pair, match, dyad, duad, twosome [spec. golf], span; twins, pair of twins [coll.], Siamese twins; twin stars, Castor and Pollux, Gemini; deuce, deucer [slang], dace [slang, U.S.; all cards and dice]; snake eyes [slang], crabs, craps [all dice]; jaws, cheeks [as of a vice]; the two, both; yoke, conjugation; distich; dispermy.

3. *v.* pair, unite in pairs, pair off, couple, couple up; bracket, yoke, span [U.S.]; match, mate; conduplicate.

4. *adj.* dual, dualistic; binary, binomial, binate [Bot.], binal [rare]; byadic, duadic; two, twain [chiefly poetic]; twin, biparous; diphyletic; dispermous, dispermic; biduous; conduplicate [chiefly Bot.]; tête-à-tête; duplex, twofold etc. (double) 90.3.

5. *adj.* coupled, paired etc. *v.*; conjugate; bijugate, unijugate [both Bot.].

6. *adj. etc.* both, both the one and the other, the two, not only this but that as well; both two, both twain, all both, all two [all now dial.].

90. Duplication
(See 91. Bisection; also 89. Duality)

1. *n.* duplication, reduplication, reproduction, gemination, ingemination, doubling etc. *v.*; reiteration etc. (repetition) 104; renewal etc. 660.2; duplicate, counterpart etc. (copy) 21.

2. *v.* duplicate, dupe [print. slang], ditto [coll.], double, dub [slang, U.S.], geminate [rare; Tech.]; reduplicate, redouble; repeat etc. 104.4, 5; imitate etc. 19.5–10; renew etc. 660.13.

3. *adj.* duplicate, double, doubled etc. *v.*; bicipital, bicephalous, bidental, bilabiate, bivalve *or* bivalvular, bifold, biform, bilateral, bifarious, bifacial; twofold, two-sided; disomatous; duple [rare], duplex; double-faced, double-headed; twin, biparous; geminous [rare], geminate, ingeminate; second, secondary; dual etc. 89.4.

4. *adv. etc.* doubly etc. *adj.*, to twice as many *or* much, as much again, twofold.

5. *adv.* twice, two times; once more, over again etc. (repeatedly) 104.8.

6. *adv.* secondly, in the second place *or* instance, again, anew, afresh.

91. Bisection
(See 89. Duality, 90. Duplication)

Division into Two Parts.—1. *n.* bisection, bipartition, bifidity, dichotomy, dimidiation [rare], halving etc. *v.*; subdivision, subdichotomy [rare]; division etc. 44.1.

2. *n.* bifurcation, furcation, biforking, forking, branching, ramification, divarication, divergence, separation; fork, crotch, crutch [dial.; as of a tree]; furculum, furcula [both anat.], prong, branch, Y, V.

3. *n.* half, halver *or* halvers [dial. and slang]; moiety, mediety [Law]; hemisphere, semisphere [rare]; fifty percent, fifty per [coll.]; half-and-half, fifty-fifty [slang, U.S.].

4. *v.* bisect, halve, hemisect [rare], cut in two, dimidiate, dichotomize; divide, cleave, split etc. 44.7, 8; go halves, divide with etc. (participate) 778.5.

5. *v.* bifurcate, furcate, fork, branch off *or* out, separate, diverge, divaricate, ramify; angle etc. 244.4.

6. *adj.* bisected, halved etc. *v.*; cloven, cleft; bipartite, dimidiate, biconjugate, bi-

---

89. Two are better than one.—BIBLE.   Two souls with but a single thought, two hearts that beat as one.—BELLINGHAUSEN.

91. Two roads diverged in a yellow wood.—FROST.   Half a loaf is better than none.

geminate, bicuspid, bifid; distichous, distichal; dichotomous, dichotomic, dichotomal; semi-, demi-, hemi-; evenly divided, half-and-half, fifty-fifty [slang, U.S.].

7. *adj.* bifurcate *or* bifurcated, bifurcal [rare], bifurcous [rare]; furcate, furcal, furcular; forked, biforked, two-forked; diverging etc. *v.,* divergent, divaricate; crotched, Y-shaped, V-shaped; angular etc. 244.5.

92. Triality
(See 94. Trisection; also 93. Triplication)

1. *n.* triality, triunity, triplicity, trialism [rare], trilogy, trinity [spec. Theol.]; the Trinity, Trimurti [Hindu] etc. (Deity) 976.3; triplication etc. 93.

2. *n.* three, triad, triplet, ternion, ternary, trine [rare], trio, tercet, terzetto [Mus.], leash [as of hares]; trey [cards and dice], deuce-ace [dice], little trey [dice slang]; trefoil, shamrock, clover; triangle, trident, triennium, trigon [rare], trinomial, trionym, triplopia *or* triplopy, tripod, trireme, triseme, triskelion *or* triskele, trisul *or* trisula, triumvirate; spike team [U.S.], three-up [coll., West. U.S.].

3. *n.* third, tierce; third power, cube.

4. *adj.* trinal, trial [Gram.], trine [rare], triform, trinomial; triarch, triadic(al); three; triune; *tria juncta in uno* [L.]; three in one.

93. Triplication
(See 94. Trisection; also 92. Triality)

1. *n.* triplication, triplicity, trebleness etc. *adj.*; triplicate, second carbon; terza; trine, triality etc. 92.

2. *v.* triplicate, triple, treble, multiply by three, increase threefold, threefold, trinalize [Gram.; rare]; cube.

3. *adj.* triplicate, triple, triplex, treble; threefold, three-ply; tern, ternary; ternate, ternal; trinary [rare], trinal, trine [rare]; trilogic(al), trilogistic(al); triplasic [Gr. and L. Pros.; rare]; third, tertiary.

4. *adv.* triply, trebly, trinely, threefold; thrice, three times.

---

93. A threefold cord is not quickly broken.—BIBLE.

5. *adv.* thirdly, in the third place *or* instance, again and yet again.

94. Trisection
(See 92. Triality, 93. Triplication)

Division into Three Parts.—1. *n.* trisection, tripartition, trichotomy; third, third part, one third.

2. *adj.* trisected, tripartite, triparted, three-parted, trifid, trichotomous, trichotomic, trisculate, ternal; three-sided, trilateral; three-forked, three-pronged, trifurcate *or* trifurcated; trident, tridental, tridentate *or* tridentated, tridentiferous; three-footed, tripodic, tripedal; trifoliolate, trifoliate *or* trifoliated, trifloral, triflorate, triflorous, tripetalous, triadelphous, triarch [all Bot.]; trimerous, 3-merous [coll.; both Bot. and Zool.]; three-cornered, tricornered, tricorn; trigonoid, trigonous, trigonal; triquetrous, triquetral, triquetric; trigrammic, trigrammatic, triliteral; triangular, triangulate; tricuspid; tricapsular, tricapsulate.

95. Quaternity
(See 97. Quadrisection; also 96. Quadruplication)

1. *n.* quaternity, tetralogy, quadrilogy; tetrapody; quatrefoil *or* quadrifoil [Bot.], four-leaf clover; tetragram, tetragrammaton; tetrahedron, tetrahedroid [all Geom.]; tetraphony, four-part diaphony [both Mus.]; square, four-square, quadrilateral, quadrature [obs.], quadrangle, tetragon, tetragram; quadrinomial, biquadrate [both Math.].

2. *n.* four, *delta* [Gr.], tetrad, quaternion, quaternary, quartet *or* quartette, quatre [rare], quadruplet, foursome [esp. golf], Little Joe (from Kokomo) [dice slang].

3. *v.* square, quadrate, reduce to a square.

4. *adj.* quaternary, quaternal [rare], quartile [Tech.], quartic, quadric [Tech.], quadratic, quadrifid, quadriform; quadrinomial, biquadratic [both Math.]; tetract, tetractine, tetractinal, four-rayed [all Zool.]; tetrad, tetradic; quadrivalent, tetravalent; square, four-square, quadrangular, quadrilateral, tetragonal; four.

96. Quadruplication
(See 97. Quadrisection; also 95. Quaternity)

1. *n.* quadruplication, quadruplicature [rare].
2. *v.* quadruplicate, quadruple, quadruplate [obs.], multiply by four, increase fourfold, fourfold, biquadrate [Math.], quadruplex [Teleg.].
3. *adj.* quadruplicate, quadruple, quadruplex, quadrible, quadrable, fourfold, tetraplous [rare], tetraploid, quadrigeminal [Tech.], biquadratic [Math.]; fourth.
4. *adv.* fourthly, in the fourth place *or* instance.

97. Quadrisection
(See 95. Quaternity, 96. Quadruplication)

Division into Four Parts.—1. *n.* quadrisection, quadripartition, quartering etc.
v.
2. *n.* fourth, one fourth, quarter, quartern; quart; farthing.
3. *v.* quadrisect, quarter, divide into four parts.
4. *adj.* quadrisected, quadrifid, quadripartite [rare], quartered, quarter-cut; quadrifoliolate, quadrifoliate; quadrigeminal, quadrigeminous, quadrigeminate; quadripinnate, quadriplanar, quadriserial, quadrivial, quadrifurcate, quadrumanal, quadrumanous.

98. Five
(See 99. Quinquesection)

1. *n.* five, fiver [slang], cinque [spec. cards and dice], quint [cards and dice], quincunx, quintet *or* quintette [spec. Mus.], fivesome [spec. Scot.], quintuple [rare], quintuplet, quinary [rare], pentad; fin, finf, finif, finnif, finnuf, half saw *or* sawbuck, V, vee, one V [all slang, U.S.]; Phoebe, Little Phoebe, fever in the South [all dice slang]; pentagon, pentagram [both Geom.]; pentapody, pentameter, pentastich [all Pros.]; pentarchy, Pentateuch [Bible], pentathlon [Athletics], pentacle, pentalpha; mullet, estoile [both Her.].
2. *n.* six, sixer [slang], sise [rare exc. dice], Captain Hicks [dice slang], half a dozen, sextet [spec. Mus.], sestet [sonnet], sextuplet, hexad; hexagon, hexahedron, hexacosihedroid, hexagram [all Geom.]; hexameter, hexapody, hexastich [all Pros.]; hexavalent [Chem.], hexapod, hexarchy, Hexateuch [Bible], hexastyle [Arch.], hexachord [Mus.], Hexabiblos, hexabromide.
3. *n.* seven, sevener [slang], septenary [rare], heptad; seven-out [dice]; heptagon, heptahedron [both Geom.]; heptameter, heptastich [both Pros.]; heptarchy, Heptateuch [Bible], septet [spec. Mus.], septuor, septennate.
4. *n.* eight, eighter [slang]; Ada Ross the stable hoss, eighter from decatur [both dice slang]; octagon, octahedron [both Geom.]; octave, octavo, octad [spec. Chem.]; octet [Mus.]; ogdoad, octonary; octet [sonnet], octameter [both Pros.]; octastyle [Arch.], utas [Eccl.], Octateuch [Bible], octosyllable.
5. *n.* nine, niner [slang], novenary [rare], ennead, nonary [rare], three times three; quinine (the bitter dose), Carolina nine [both dice slang]; nonage, novena [both Eccl.]; nonagon [Geom.], nonuplet [Mus.], enneastyle [Arch.].
6. *n.* ten, tenner [slang], decad [rare], decade, dicker [spec. of hides]; dews, double fin, saw, sawbuck [all slang, U.S.]; Big Dick, Big Dick from Boston [both dice slang]; decagon, decahedron [both Geom.]; decagram, decigram, decaliter, deciliter, decare, decameter, decimeter, decastere [all metric meas.]; decapod, decastyle [Arch.], decasyllable, decemvir *or* decemvirate [spec. Rom. Antiq.], decennium, decennary, Decalogue [Bible].
7. *n.* (eleven to ninety) eleven, 'leven [dial.]; twelve, dozen, boxcar *or* boxcars [dice slang]; teens; thirteen, long dozen, baker's dozen, devil's dozen; fifteen, quindecima [Mus.], quindene [Ch. Hist.], quindecim [Hist. and Eccl.], quindecennial; twenty, score, double saw *or* sawbuck [crim. slang, U.S.]; twenty-four, four and twenty, two dozen; twenty-five, five and twenty, quarter of a hundred *or* century; forty, twoscore; fifty, half a hundred, half C *or* century [crim. slang, U.S.]; sixty, sexagenary, threescore; seventy, threescore and ten; eighty, fourscore; ninety, fourscore and ten.
8. *n.* hundred, century, one C (crim. slang, U.S.], centred [Hist.], centrev *or* centref [Hist., Welsh]; centennium, centennial, centenary; cental, centigram,

centiliter, centimeter, centiare, **centistere** [all metric meas.]; hundred-weight, cwt.; hecatomb [Gr. Antiq.]; centipede; centumvir [Rom. Antiq.], centumvirate, centurion; bicentenary, bicentennial; tercentenary, tercentennial; one hundred and twenty, great *or* long hundred [coll.]; twelve dozen, one hundred and forty-four, gross.

9. *n.* five hundred, five centuries; five C's, half G *or* grand [both crim. slang, U.S.].

10. *n.* thousand, chiliad, milliad [rare]; millenary [rare], millennium; G, grand, one G *or* grand, thou, yard [all crim. slang, U.S.]; chiliagon, chiliahedron *or* chiliaëdron [both Geom.]; chiliarchia *or* chiliarch [Gr. Antiq.], chiliarchy [obs.]; millepede [Zool.]; milligram, milliliter, millimeter, kilogram, kiloliter, kilometer [all metric meas.]; kilocycle [Radio]; myriad, ten thousand; one hundred thousand, one hundred grand [crim. slang, U.S.], lac *or* lakh [Ind.], plum [obs.].

11. *n.* million; ten million, crore [Ind.].

12. *n.* billion, thousand million, milliard, great *or* long million [coll.].

13. *n.* (trillion etc.) trillion, quadrillion, quintillion, sextillion, septillion, octillion, nonillion, decillion, undecillion, duodecillion, tredecillion, quattuordecillion, quindecillion, sexdecillion, septemdecillion, octodecillion, novemdecillion, vigintillion, zillion [humorous].

14. *v.* multiply by five, ~ six etc.; fivefold, sixfold, etc.; quintuple, quintuplicate; sextuple, sextuplicate; centuple, centuplicate, centuriate [obs.].

15. *adj.* fifth, quinary, quintuple, quintuplicate, fivefold; quincuncial [spec. Bot.], pentastyle [Arch.]; pentad, pentavalent [both Chem.]; quin-, penta-.

16. *adj.* sixth, senary [rare]; sixfold, sextuple, sexpartite; hexagonal, hexahedral, hexangular [all Geom.]; hexad [Chem.], sextuplex [Teleg.], hexastyle [Arch.], sexennial, hexatomic [Chem.]; hexamerous [Bot.]; hex-, hexa-, sex-.

17. *adj.* seventh, septuple, septenary, septimal [rare]; heptagonal, heptahedral, heptangular [all Geom.]; heptamerous [Bot.]; sept-, hept-, hepta-.

18. *adj.* eighth, octuple, octonary; octagonal, octahedral, octan, octangular [all Geom.]; octastyle [Arch.]; oct-, octa-, **octo-**.

19. *adj.* **ninth, ninefold,** novenary [rare], nonary [rare]; enneahedral [Geom.], enneastyle [Arch.]; noven-, nona-, non-, ennea-, enne-.

20. *adj.* tenth, tenfold, decimal, denary, decuple; decagonal, decahedral [both Geom.]; decasyllabic; dec-, deci-, deca-, deka-.

21. *adj.* eleventh, undecennial, undecennary.

22. *adj.* twelfth, duodenary, duodenal; duodecimal.

23. *adj.* thirteenth, fourteenth etc.; 'steenth [coll.]; eleventeenth, umpteenth [both slang]; in one's teens.

24. *adj.* twentieth, vicenary, vicennial, vigesimal, vicesimal.

25. *adj.* sixtieth, sexagesimal, sexagenary.

26. *adj.* seventieth, septuagesimal, septuagenary.

27. *adj.* centuple, centuplicate, centennial, centenary, centurial, hundredfold; secular, hundredth; cent-, centi-, hecto-.

28. *adj.* thousandth, millenary, millennial; kilo-, milli-.

29. *adj.* millionth, billionth etc.

99. Quinquesection
(See 98. Five)

Division into Five or More Parts.—**1.** *n.* quinquesection, quinquepartition, sextipartition etc.; division by five, ~ six etc.; decimation, decimalization; fifth, sixth etc.

2. *v.* divide by five, ~ six etc.; quinquesect; decimate, decimalize.

3. *adj.* divided by five, ~ six etc.; quinquefid, quinqueliteral, quinquepartite; sexpartite, sextipartite; septate, septated; octofid; decimal, tenth, tithe; duodecimal, twelfth; sexagesimal, sexagenary; hundredth, centesimal; millesimal etc.

100. Plurality
(See 87. Unity)

More Than One.—**1.** *n.* plurality, a number, a certain number, one or two, two or three etc., a few, several, indefinite *or* indeterminate number; eleventeen, X-teen, umpteen, umptyum, forty-eleven, jillion [all slang]; multitude etc. (numerousness) 102.2.

2. *n.* majority, plurality, more than

half, greater number, the greatest number; preponderance *or* preponderancy, preponderation; lion's share, Benjamin's mess; excess of votes, plural vote; plurality of causes; superiority etc. 33.

3. *v.* pluralize, plurify, multiply.

4. *adj.* plural, more than one; upwards of, uppards of [dial.]; some, certain; plurative [Logic]; not alone etc. 87.8.

101. Fraction

Less Than One.—1. *n.* fraction, fractional part; half, one half, third, one third, fourth, one fourth etc.; fragment, portion etc. (part) 51.

2. *adj.* fractional, fragmentary, inconsiderable, partial, portional.

102. Numerousness
(See 103. Fewness)

1. *n.* numerousness, multitudinousness etc. *adj.*; numerosity, numerality [obs.], multiplicity; profusion etc. (plenty) 639.2; plurality etc. 100.

2. *n.* multitude, great *or* large number, enormous number, any number, a thousand and one, an abundance, a number, numbers, quantities, scores; array, bevy, galaxy, legion, host, army; all kinds *or* sorts of, quite a shucks [U.S.], dead loads [all slang]; bags, barrels, tons, flock, bunch, good *or* great few, quite a few, no end of, sweet ∼, neat *or* tidy sum [all coll.]; plenty *or* a plenty [chiefly U.S., coll.], passel [dial.]; shoal, swarm, hive, cloud, herd, drove, flight, covey, brood, litter, farrow, fry, nest; "many-headed multitude" (Sidney); all the world and his brother *or* wife [joc.]; mob, crowd etc. (assemblage) 72; sea, batch, power etc. (great quantity) 31.3.

3. *n.* (increase of number) multiplication, multiplying; multiple, multiplier, multiplicator [rare], multiplicand; tables, multiplication table; addition etc. 37.

4. *v.* be numerous etc. *adj.*, teem with, be alive with, creep with, swarm with, swarm like locusts *or* bees; crowd, swarm, come thick upon; multiply; people, populate; outnumber, exceed in number.

5. *adj. etc.* numerous, many, several, sundry, divers, various, not a few, no few; some ten or a dozen, some forty or fifty etc.; half a dozen, half a hundred etc.; twenty or so, fifty or so etc.; twentyish, fiftyish etc.; multitudinous, multitudinal, multitudinary; multifarious, multiferous [rare]; multiple, multiplied, multifold, manifold, myriad, plentiful, plenteous, plenty [chiefly coll.], copious, abundant, abounding, bountiful, bounteous [coll.]; very many, full many, ever so many, quite some [slang], considerable [coll.]; more than one can tell, no end of *or* to [coll.]; a world of, a hundred, a thousand, a myriad, a million, a billion, a quadrillion, a nonillion, a thousand and one.

generous, lavish, profuse, in profusion, prodigal, superabundant, rife, teeming, swarming, alive with, populous, thronged, crowded, studded, thick, thick-coming; thick as hops, ∼ hail, ∼ flies, ∼ thieves etc., "thick as autumnal leaves that strow the brooks in Vallombrosa" (Milton), plenty as blackberries, numerous as the stars in the firmament, numerous as the sands on the seashore, numerous as the hairs on the head, "numerous as glittering gems of morning dew" (Young); and many more, *cum multis aliis* [L.], and what not, and heaven knows what; multinomial [Alg.]; outnumbering; innumerable, endless, etc. (infinite) 105.3.

6. *adv.* numerously, abundantly etc. *adj.*; in abundance, *acervatim* [L.], *en foule* [F.], galore [coll.], without stint, with no sparing hand, no end [coll., U.S.], ever so, ever so much, plenty [coll.]; innumerably, incalculably etc. 105.4.

103. Fewness
(See 102. Numerousness)

1. *n.* fewness, sparseness etc. *adj.*, sparsity, paucity, scarcity, exiguity, rarity; infrequency etc. 137.

---

101. Gives in the long run a net result of zero.—CARLYLE.
102. My name is Legion: for we are many.—BIBLE. Because in the administration it hath respect not to the few but to the multitude, our form of government is called a democracy.—THUCYDIDES. *Defendit numerus* [There is safety in numbers] is the maxim of the foolish; *deperdit numerus* [there is ruin in numbers] of the wise.—C. COLTON. The multitudinous seas.—SHAKESPEARE.
103. It is the minority that have . . . achieved all that is noble in the history of the world.—

2. *n.* a few, small number, only a few, scrimption [dial.]; handful; minority; small quantity etc. 32.2.

3. *adj.* few, not many, hardly *or* scarcely any, precious little [coll.], middling of [dial.], of small number; meager, scant, scanty, sparse, scarce, scrimp, scrimpy [coll.], skimp *or* skimpy [coll.], skimping [chiefly coll.], rare, exiguous; few and far between, thinly scattered, thin, slim; to be counted on one's fingers, to be counted on the fingers of one hand; scarce as hen's teeth [coll.], unrepeated; infrequent etc. 137.2; inconsiderable etc. 32.8.

4. *adj.* fewer, smaller, less, not so much *or* many.

5. *adv.* sparsely etc. *adj.*, scrimp, *sparsim* [L.], here and there, in spots [coll.], dribs-like [dial.]; infrequently etc. 137.3.

104. Repetition

1. *n.* repetition, repeatal [rare], iteration, reiteration, iterance [rare], reiterance [rare], duplication, reduplication, reproduction, recurrence, reappearance, return; succession, run; monotony, harping, monotone; alliteration; *rifacimento* [It.]; renewal etc. (revival) 660.2; periodicity, rhythm etc. 138.2–4; dingdong, drumming etc. (repeated sounds) 407; battology, pleonasm etc. (tautology) 573.2; continuance etc. 143; frequency etc. 136.

2. *n.* repetend, a repetition etc. *above*, repeat, ditto [coll.]; refrain, burden of a song, undersong, chorus, ritornel *or* ritornelle, [Mus.], *ritornello* [It.], bob; bob and wheel, bob wheel; encore, curtain call, curtain [Theat. cant]; recital, rehearsal, recapitulation, summing up, recountal, recounting, restatement, rehash [chiefly coll.]; echo, re-echo; reverberation, repercussion, reflection; chimes, drum, hammer.

3. *n.* retold story, twice-told tale etc. (trite saying) 496.3; Joe Miller etc. (old joke) 842.6.

4. *v.* repeat, iterate, reiterate, reproduce, echo, re-echo, duplicate, dupe [slang], reduplicate, ditto [coll.]; rehearse, do *or* say over again, go over the same ground, go the same round; begin again, resume, return to; recapitulate, reword, recount, retell, tell *or* say over, come again [slang]; cut and come again; ring the changes on; hash up [slang], rehash [chiefly coll.]; conjugate in all its moods, tenses and inflections.

battologize, tautologize; dwell on *or* upon, insist upon, harp upon, harp on one *or* the same string, never hear the last of, sing the same old song *or* tune, mount *or* ride a hobby [coll.]; beat, din, drum, hammer, pound; din *or* drum in the ear; renew etc. (revive) 660.13.

5. *v.* recur, return, reappear, resume; revert, turn *or* go back.

6. *adj.* repeated, repetitional, repetitionary, repetitive, repetitious; iterated, iterative, reiterated, reiterative, reiterate, reiterant; reduplicated, reduplicative, reduplicatory [rare]; recurrent, recurring; re-echoed, re-echoing; ever-recurring, thick-coming, incessant; retold, twice-told; warmed-up *or* -over, *réchauffé* [F.]; tautological etc. 573.8; habitual etc. 613.11; another etc. 15.9; aforesaid etc. 62.4; drumming etc. (sound) 407.11–14; frequent etc. 136.13.

7. *adj.* monotonous, harping, humdrum, singsong, dingdong [coll.], jogtrot; mocking; chiming; worn, worn thin; tedious etc. 841.8; unvaried etc. (uniform) 16.5; constant etc. (continuous) 69.6; habitual etc. 613.

8. *adv.* repeatedly etc. *adj.*, often, again, anew, over again, afresh, once more; ditto, encore, *de novo* [L.], *da capo* [It.], bis; again and again, over and over, over and over again, many times over, time and again, time after time, times without number, year after year, day by day, day after day, "tomorrow and tomorrow and tomorrow" (Shakespeare); many times, several times, a number of times; many a time, full many a time; every now and then, every once in a while [both coll.]; frequently etc. 136.5.

J. B. GOUGH.   Many are called, but few ... chosen.—BIBLE.
104. Like warmed-up cabbage served at each repast, / The repetition kills the wretch at last.—JUVENAL.   Iteration, like friction. is likely to generate heat instead of progress.—G. ELIOT.

Use not vain repetitions.—BIBLE.   *Cantilenam eandem canis* [You are singing the same song; you are giving us the same old stuff].—TERENCE.   *Nullum est jam dictum quod non dictum sit prius* [Nothing is said which has not been said before].—TERENCE.

105. Infinity

1. *n.* infinity, infiniteness, boundlessness etc. *adj.*; infinitude, inexhaustibility, immeasurability, incalculability, illimitability, interminability, incomprehensibility, immensity; eternity etc. (perpetuity) 112; greatness etc. 31.

2. *v.* be infinite etc. *adj.*, have *or* know no limit *or* bounds, have *or* know no end, be without end, go on forever, go on and on, never cease *or* end.

3. *adj.* infinite, illimitable, interminable, interminate, immeasurable, innumerable, incalculable, incomprehensible, unfathomable, unapproachable; without number *or* measure, without bound, without limit *or* end, no end of *or* to; numberless, countless, sumless, measureless; limitless, termless, endless, boundless; untold, unnumbered, unmeasured, unplumbed; unbounded, unlimited, illimited; indefinite, indeterminate; all-embracing, all-covering, all-filling, all-including, all-inclusive, all-comprehensive; fourth-dimensional; exhaustless, inexhaustible; immense; eternal etc. (perpetual) 112.4.

4. *adv.* infinitely, innumerably, incalculably etc. *adj.*, *ad infinitum* [L.]; without end etc. (perpetually) 112.5.

106. Time
(See 107. Timelessness)

1. *n.* time, duration, tenure, term, period, stage, space, tide [arch.], spell, season; Time, Father Time, the enemy [coll.], "Old Time, that greatest and longest established spinner of all" (Dickens), "Old Time, the clock-setter, that bald sexton Time" (Shakespeare), "that old common arbitrator, Time" (ibid.), "that old bald cheater, Time" (Jonson); glass of time, ravages of time, whirligig of time, noiseless foot of Time, scythe of Time; Kronos *or* Cronus [Gr. Myth.]; Saturn [Rom. Myth.]; course etc. 109.

2. *v.* continue, last, endure, dure [arch.], perdure [rare], perennate, go on, run, run on, extend, sustain, stay, remain, abide, stand, subsist, persist, carry on, hold out, stick [coll.]; elapse etc. 109.3; prolong, linger on etc. 110.5–7; tarry etc. 133.7.

3. *v.* pass time, spend *or* while away time, employ *or* use time, fill *or* occupy time, consume time, take *or* take up time, put in time; talk against time; tide over; week-end; Sunday, Monday, Christmas etc. [coll.]; waste time etc. 683.8; procrastinate etc. 133.4–7.

4. *adj.* continuing etc. *v.*, on foot; lasting, permanent etc. (durable) 110.9.

5. *adj.* timely etc. (opportune) 134.7.

6. *adv. etc.* when . . . , at which time, at which moment *or* instant, on which occasion, upon which, whereupon; at what time, on what occasion, whenever *or* when ever [coll.]; at the same time *or* moment that, at the same time as, at that time *or* instant, on that occasion, then; by the time that; *anno Domini* [L.], A.D.; *ante Christum* [L.], A.C., before Christ, B.C.; *anno urbis conditae* [L.], A.U.C.; *anno regni* [L.], A.R.

7. *prep. etc.* during, pending, during the time *or* interval, during the while, in the time *or* course of, in the middle of [coll.], for the period of, over, through, throughout, throughout the continuance *or* course of, until the conclusion of, at a stretch; during pleasure, during good behavior, *quandiu se bene gesserit* [L.].

8. *prep.* until, till, to, up to, up to the time of, as far as, down to, to the time when.

9. *conj. etc.* while, whilst, whiles [arch. and dial.], during the time that, as long as, in the course of, at *or* during which time, in the time of, in the consulship of

---

105. Hold infinity in the palm of your hand.—W. BLAKE.   But how can finite grasp Infinity?—DRYDEN.   As boundless as the sea.—SHAKESPEARE.   A dark / Illimitable ocean, without bound.—MILTON.   Lost in expansion, void and infinite.—BLACKMORE.   Man a.ways sees the infinite shadowed forth in something finite.—CARLYLE.

106. *Tempus edax rerum* [Time the devourer of things].—OVID.   The tooth of time.—SHAKESPEARE.   Time travels in divers paces with divers persons.—SHAKESPEARE.   The time which we have at our disposal every day is elastic.—PROUST.   Time is a great legalizer, even in the field of morals.—H. L. MENCKEN.   Alas, time stays, *we* go.—DOBSON.   Time, you old gipsy man, / Will you not stay, / Put up your caravan / Just for one day?—R. HODGSON.   Time is a sandpile we run our fingers in.—SANDBURG.   The Bird of Time has but a little way to flutter—and the Bird is on the Wing.—OMAR KHAYYÁM—FITZGERALD. *Volat hora per orbem* [Time flies through the world].—LUCRETIUS.   *Tempus fugit* [Time flies].—VERGIL.   Time and tide stayeth for no man.

[joc.]; at the same time that, whileas [arch.], whereas.

10. *phr.* time runs, time runs *or* marches on.

107. Timelessness
(See 106. Time)

1. *n.* timelessness, "neverness" (J. Wilkins), absence *or* want of time, no time, *dies non* [L.]; a time that will never come, *kalendas Graecas* [L.], Greek calends, Tib's *or* St. Tib's Eve, blue moon [slang]; eternity etc. 112.

2. *adj.* timeless, without time, dateless; eternal etc. 112.4.

3. *adv.* never, ne'er [poetic], at no time *or* period, on no occasion, never in all one's born days [coll.], *jamais de ma vie* [F.], never in the world, never on earth, nevermore, *sine die* [L.]; on *or* at the Greek calends, *ad kalendas Graecas* [L.], on St. Tib's Eve, on the 30th of February; not at all.

108. Period
(See 109. Course)

Definite Duration or Portion of Time.—1. *n.* period, point, term, space, stretch, interval, stage, go [slang], span, spell, ghurry [Ind.]; moment, second, minute, hour, day, week; month, moon, moonshine [rare], lunation; semester, quarter; year, twelvemonth; quinquennium, lustrum, luster; decade, decennium, decennary; century; millennium; octave; *novena* [L.], novenary; *annus magnus* [L.], *annus mirabilis* [L.]; season etc. 126a.

2. *n.* era, epoch, age, generation, cycle; aeon; Kalpa, Yuga, Manvantara; epact, monthly *or* menstrual epact; indiction, cycle *or* era of indiction; Stone Age, Bronze Age, Iron Age; Middle Ages, Dark Ages; Mundane Era, Jewish Mundane Era, Chinese Era of Yao, Abraham Era, Nabonassar Era, Olympic Era, Roman *or* Varro Era; Christian Era, Common *or* Vulgar Era; Seleucidan Era, Jalalaean *or* Jalalian Era; Gay Nineties, Golden Age, Jazz Age [all coll.]; Mad Decade [slang, U.S.]; Prohibition Era [U.S.]; Depression Era; Polarian Epoch, Hyperborean Epoch, Lemurian Epoch, Atlantean Epoch, Aryan Epoch.

3. *adj.* epochal etc. (periodical) 138.

109. Course
(See 108. Period)

Indefinite Duration.—1. *n.* course, course of time, progress of time, process of time, succession of time, lapse of time, flow of time, flux of time, stream of time, sweep of time, tract of time, current of time, tide of time, march of time, step of time, flight of time; corridors of time, halls of time; duration etc. 106.

2. *n.* (indefinite time) age, aeon, Kalpa; aorist, aorist tense [Gram.]; blue moon [coll.] etc. 110.3.

3. *v.* elapse, lapse, flow, run, proceed, advance, pass, roll *or* press on, flit, fly, slip, slide, glide; run its course, run out, expire, go *or* pass by; be past etc. 122.6; drag, wear on etc. 110.7; continue etc. 106.2.

4. *adj.* elapsing, passing etc. *v.*; transient etc. 111; progressive etc. 282.3.

5. *adj.* aoristic, aorist, indefinite, undetermined.

6. *adv.* in time, in due time, in due season, in due course, in the course *or* process of time, in the fullness of time.

109a. Interim

Intermediate Period.—1. *n.* interim, intermediate *or* intervening time, time intervening, interval, interlude, intermission, intermittence, recess, rest, pause, interruption, break, pendency; respite, spell, breathing, breathing spell; letup, time out [both coll.]; meantime, meanwhile, while, the while; interregnum, interreign [rare]; snap, cold snap; spare time etc. (leisure) 685.

2. *v.* interlude, intervene, interval, intermit, occur *or* act as an interlude, come *or* separate by an interval, form an interval; let up [coll.]; take time out [coll.].

---

107. Quoth the raven, "Nevermore."—POE.
108. The years like great black oxen tread the world.—YEATS.   And not only a night, an age.—FROST.   Every age, like every human body, has its own distemper.—EMERSON.
109. Tomorrow and tomorrow and tomorrow / Creeps in this petty pace from day to day.—SHAKESPEARE.   *Truditur dies die* [One day makes way for another].—HORACE.   *Eheu! fugaces labuntur anni* [Alas, the fleeting years glide by].—HORACE.   Time rolls his ceaseless course.—SCOTT.

3. *adv.* meanwhile, meantime, whiles [dial. and Scot.], interim, in the meanwhile *or* meantime, in the interim, *ad interim* [L.], in the intervening time, during the interval, for the time being, for a time *or* season; *pendente lite* [L.; Law]; at the same time.

110. Durability
(See 111. Transience)

Long Duration.—1. *n.* durability, durableness, lastingness etc. *adj.*; diuturnity [rare], continuance, constancy, persistence, endurance, permanence, standing; survival, survivance; length of time, distance of time, vista of time; longevity etc. (age) 128; perpetuity etc. 112; slowness etc. 275.

2. *n.* protraction of time, prolongation *or* extension of time; delay etc. 133.2.

3. *n.* long time *or* while, age *or* ages [coll.], aeon, century, eternity, years, years on end, blue moon [coll.], coon's age [coll., U.S.], dog's age [coll.], donkey's years [slang], month *or* week of Sundays [coll.], right smart spell [dial.]; coeternity, sempiternity etc. 112.

4. *n.* lifetime, life-while [rare], life, generation, duration of life, life's duration, period of existence; (all) one's born days, (all) one's natural life [both coll.].

5. *v.* endure, last etc. (continue) 106.2; brave a thousand years.

6. *v.* protract, prolong, extend, lengthen, lengthen *or* draw out, spin out, eke out, perendinate [rare]; temporize, tarry, delay etc. 133.4–7.

7. *v.* be protracted etc. *adj.*, crawl, drag, drag *or* wear on, drag along, drag its slow length along, drag a lengthening chain, linger, linger on.

8. *v.* outlast, outlive, outwear; survive, live to light again.

9. *adj.* durable, endurable [rare], diuturnal [rare], lasting etc. *v.*, lasty [coll. and dial.], of long duration *or* standing, long-standing, long-lasting, long-lived, longeval [rare], longevous, perdurable, perdurant [rare], macrobiotic, evergreen, perennial, sempervirent *or* sempervirid [rare]; lifelong, livelong; abiding, permanent, chronic, fixed, immovable, stable, firm, steadfast, constant, persistent; intransitive, intransient, intransmutable; everlasting, endless etc. (perpetual) 112.4; unchangeable etc. 150.7; continuing etc. 106.4.

10. *adj.* protracted, prolonged, extended, lengthened, spun-out, dragged-out, lingering, long-pending, long-continuing, long-continued, long-drawn, long-drawn-out; long-winded; slow etc. 275.8.

11. *adv.* long, for *or* during a long time, for ever so long, for many a long day, for years on end, for an age [coll.], for ages [coll.], for a coon's *or* dog's age [coll.], for a month *or* week of Sundays [coll.], for ever and a day; *longo intervallo* [L.]; all along, all the year round, all the day long, the livelong day, as the day is long; morning, noon and night; hour after hour, day after day, month after month, year after year; day in day out, month in month out, year in year out; *semper et ubique* [L.], *semper eadem* [L.]; for good, for good and all, for life, till death; permanently, constantly etc. *adj.*; always etc. (perpetually) 112.5; long ago etc. 122.14, 15.

111. Transience
(See 110. Durability)

Short Duration.—1. *n.* transience, transiency, transientness [rare] etc. *adj.*; impermanence *or* impermanency, preterience [rare], ephemerality, evanescence, volatility, fugacity, caducity [rare]; perishability, mortality; velocity etc. 274; instantaneity etc. 113; changeableness etc. 149.

2. *n.* brevity, briefness, shortness etc. *adj.*

3. *n.* short time, little while, brief time, brief *or* limited space of time, small space, span, spurt, bit *or* little bit [coll.], no time, less than no time [coll.]; two shakes, brace of shakes, couple of shakes *or* winks, shake of a lamb's tail [all slang].

4. *n.* transient, transiency, ephemeron (*pl.* ephemera), ephemeral; transient guest *or* boarder, temporary lodger; transient rates; ephemerid [Zool.], shad fly,

---

110. The great use of a life is to spend it for something that outlasts it.—W. JAMES. *Monumentum aere perennius* [A monument more lasting than bronze].—HORACE.

111. The fashion of this world passeth away.—BIBLE. In the presence of eternity, the mountains are as transient as the clouds.—INGERSOLL. It will last about as long as a snowball in hell.—SANDBURG. The stream of time glides

May fly, gnat; nine days' wonder; bubble, smoke.

5. *v.* be transient etc. *adj.*, flit, fly, fleet, gallop, sink, melt, fade, evaporate, vanish, pass away; pass away like a cloud *or* summer cloud, fade like a shadow, vanish like a dream, burst like a bubble, go up in smoke.

6. *adj.* transient, transitory, transitive, transeunt; passing, fleeting, flying etc. *v.*; temporal, temporary; impermanent, preterient [rare], evanescent, volatile, caducous [rare], short-lived, diurnal, cursory; ephemeral, ephemerous [rare]; deciduous, deciduary; perishable, mortal, precarious, shifty, slippery; fugacious, fugitive; provisional, provisory; spasmodic etc. (irregular) 139.2; inconstant etc. 149.6.

7. *adj.* brief, short, quick, brisk, fleet, cometary, meteoric, volatile, summary; hasty, pressed for time etc. 684.5, 6; sudden, momentary etc. (instantaneous) 113.4, 5.

8. *adv.* transiently, temporarily etc. *adj.*; for the moment, *pro tempore* [L.], for a time, awhile; in passing, *en passant* [F.], *in transitu* [L.]; on the point of . . . , *in articulo* [L.].

9. *adv.* briefly, shortly etc. *adj.*; in a short time, at short notice, in no time, in less than no time; in quick order, in nothing flat, before you can say "Jack Robinson" *or* "knife" [all coll.]; in two shakes [all slang]; between cup and lip; instantaneously etc. 113.6; promptly, soon etc. 132.14, 15; to be brief etc. (concisely) 572.4.

112. Perpetuity
(See 113. Instantaneity)

Endless Duration.—**1.** *n.* perpetuity, everlastingness etc. *adj.*, "everness" (J. Wilkins), eternity, infinity, forever, aye, endless time, sempiternity, perenniality [rare], perennity [obs.], perdurability, continuity, continued *or* uninterrupted existence, immortality; athanasy, athanasia; perpetuation; coeternity; timelessness etc. 107; durability etc. 110.

2. *v.* be eternal etc. *adj.*, have no end, have no limits *or* bounds, last *or* endure forever, go on forever, go on and on.

3. *v.* perpetuate, preserve from oblivion, perennialize [rare], eternalize, eternize, immortalize; monumentalize.

4. *adj.* perpetual, eternal, eterne [poetic], everlasting, ever-during, everliving, ever-flowing, eviternal [rare], sempiternal, sempiternous [rare]; dateless, infinite; endless, unending, never-ending, without end, having no end, interminable, boundless, limitless, illimitable; continual, constant, ceaseless, unceasing, incessant, unremitting, unintermitting, uninterrupted, indesinent [obs.]; unfading, never-fading, evergreen, sempervirent *or* sempervirid [rare], amaranthine, perennial; deathless, immortal, undying, never-dying, imperishable, perdurable, perdurant; coeternal; continuing etc. 143.4; permanent etc. (durable) 110.9; timeless etc. 107.2.

5. *adv.* perpetually etc. *adj.*, always, ever, evermore [arch.], ever and anon, aye, for aye, forever, forevermore, forever and ever, forever and aye, forever and amen [coll.], forever and a day [coll.], *ora e sempre* [It.], for good, for good and all, for keeps [coll.].

all along, at all times, for all time, in all ages, throughout the ages, from age to age; endlessly, without end, world without end, time without end; *in saecula saeculorum* [L.]; to the end of time, "to the last syllable of recorded time" (Shakespeare), to the crack of doom, till doomsday; till all is blue [coll.], till hell freezes over [slang]; for all one's natural life, in all one's born days [both coll.], till death, till death do us part; permanently etc. 110.11; incessantly, without ceasing etc. (constantly) 136.6; infinitely etc. 105.4; invariably etc. 16.7; generally etc. 78.15; habitually etc. 613.13.

smoothly on and is past before we know.—Ovid. *Sic transit gloria mundi* [Thus passes the glory of the world]. Here today and gone tomorrow. *Non semper erit aestas* [It will not always be summer].
112. The clock indicates the moment—but what does eternity indicate?—Whitman. Eternity is written in the skies.—Young. Eternity is not something that begins after you are dead, it is going on all the time.—C. P. Gilman. The stiller sea / That stretches everlastingly.

—W. W. Gibson. *Labitur et labetur in omne volubilis aevum* [Gliding on it flows and will flow forever].—Horace. But thou shalt flourish in immortal youth.—Addison. For men may come and men may go but I go on forever.—Tennyson. *Esto perpetuum* [Let it be everlasting].

113. Instantaneity
(See 112. Perpetuity)

Imperceptible Duration.—1. *n.* instantaneity, instantaneousness, immediateness etc. *adj.*; transience etc. 111.

2. *n.* suddenness, abruptness etc. *adj.*; suddenty [chiefly Scot. and Law], sudden [rare], precipitance *or* precipitancy.

3. *n.* instant, moment, second, sec [slang], half a second, minute, trice, twinkling, twinkling *or* twinkle of an eye, twinkling of a bedpost *or* bedstaff [coll.; now rare], twink, wink, bat of an eye [coll.], flash, flash of lightning, breath, crack, jiffy *or* half a jiffy [coll.], jiff [coll.], *coup* [F.], burst, stroke of time, tick, shake *or* half a shake [slang].

4. *adj.* instantaneous, instant, momentary, immediate, quick as thought *or* lightning, rapid as electricity; brief etc. 111.7; punctual etc. 132.9.

5. *adj.* sudden, abrupt, subitaneous [rare]; extempore, extemporaneous; speedy, swift etc. (fast) 274.13; precipitate, headlong, impetuous etc. (hasty) 684.5; unexpected etc. 508.8.

6. *adv.* instantaneously, instantly, instanter, instant [poetic], presto, immediately, *subito* [L. and It.]; in no time, in less than no time, in nothing flat [coll.], in an instant, in a trice, in a jiff *or* jiffy [coll.], in the twinkling of an eye, in the twinkling of a bedpost *or* bedstaff [coll.; now rare], before you can say "Jack Robinson" *or* "knife" [coll.], like a shot, like a shot out of hell [slang], bang-off [slang]; on the instant, on the spot, on the dot [coll.]; at once, right away, without the least delay, *tout à l'heure* [F.]; just then, just now; at the same instant, in the same breath; no sooner said than done; briefly etc. 111.9.

7. *adv.* suddenly, abruptly etc. *adj.*; sudden, on a sudden, of *or* all of a sudden, all at once, in a bang [slang], at a stroke, at one swoop, "at one fell swoop" (Shakespeare), at one jump, *per saltum* [L.], *uno saltu* [L.], *subito* [L. and It.]; pop, plump, plunk, plop, slap, smack [all chiefly coll.]; precipitately, slapdash etc. (hastily) 684.7; unexpectedly etc. 508.11.

---

113. He's sudden if a thing comes in his head.—SHAKESPEARE. The quick of all time is the instant.—D. H. LAWRENCE. Then a soldier . . . / . . . sudden and quick in quarrel.—SHAKESPEARE.

114. Chronometry
(See 115. Anachronism)

Measurement and Record of Time.—1. *n.* chronometry, horometry, chronology, horology, chronography, horography, chronoscopy.

2. *n.* the time, time of day, hour, minute; very time, very minute *or* hour; correct *or* right time, exact time; present time etc. 118.

3. *n.* standard time, civil time, zone time [Naut.]; mean time, solar time, sidereal time, apparent time, Greenwich time; local time, Eastern time, Central time, Mountain time, Pacific time [all U.S. and Can.]; Alaska standard time; Provincial time [formerly], Atlantic time [both Can.]; daylight-saving time, fast time [coll.], summer time [chiefly Eng.].

4. *n.* date, given point of time; month, era, age etc. (period) 108.

5. *n.* (chronological record) chronology, almanac, calendar, calends *or* kalends, style, *fasti* [L., *pl.*], chronogram; chronicle, register, registry, record, annals, journal, diary; astronomical calendar, ~ almanac *or* table, ephemeris [*pl.*]; Ephemeris and Nautical Almanac, Whitaker, Whitaker's Almanack, World Almanac, Poor Richard's Almanac; Julian calendar, Roman calendar, Gregorian calendar, Chinese calendar, Jewish calendar, international fixed calendar, Cotsworth calendar, Swiss plan; perpetual calendar.

6. *n.* timepiece, timekeeper, timer; horologe [Tech.], horologium; chronometer, chronograph, chronoscope; clock, watch; ticker, souper [U.S. crim.], turnip [all slang]; alarm clock, repeater, electric clock, pneumatic clock, program clock, sidereal clock, turret clock, watchman's clock, pendulum clock, pendule, grandfather clock, journeyman, stem-winder [coll.], stop watch, split-second watch, calendar watch, isochronon, metronome; gnomon, dial, sundial; hourglass, sandglass, half-hour glass, half-minute glass, three-minute glass, egg glass; water clock, hydroscope [obs. exc. Hist.], clepsydra, ghurry [Ind.]; pocket chronometer, box chronometer, marine chronometer; time signal, chronopher, time ball.

---

114. If history without chronology is dark and confused, chronology without history is dry and insipid.—HOLMES.

7. *n.* chronographer, chronologist, chronologer, chronicler; horologist, horologer; annalist.

8. *v.* time, fix *or* set the time, mark the time; chronicle, chronologize, calendar; arrange chronologically, make chronological, make a calendar *or* chronological record, reckon chronologically; date, give *or* fix the date; be dated, date at *or* from, bear date; measure time, mark time, keep time, beat time; clock, stop-watch [both coll.]; ring in, ring out; punch in, punch out [both slang].

9. *adj.* chronologic(al), chronometric(al), chronoscopic, chronographic(al), chronogrammatic(al); horologic(al), horometric(al); datal [rare], temporal; metronomic(al); isochronal etc. 138.10, 11.

10. *adv. etc.* o'clock; half past, half after [Eng.], half [Scot.]; half past the corner, half past kissing time [both slang]; a quarter of *or* to; a quarter past *or* after.

115. Anachronism
(See 114. Chronometry)

False Estimation of Time.—1. *n.* anachronism, antichronism [obs.], misdate, parachronism; metachronism; prolepsis, prochronism, anticipation; disregard ∼, neglect *or* oblivion of time; intempestivity etc. (untimeliness) 135.

2. *v.* misdate, mistime, anachronize [rare]; antedate, postdate, overdate, anticipate; take no note of time.

3. *adj.* anachronous, anachronistic; misdated etc. *v.*, undated; overdue; out-of-date *or* season; behind time; untimely etc. 135.6.

116. Priority
(See 117. Posteriority)

1. *n.* priority, previousness etc. *adj.*; antecedence *or* antecedency, anteriority, precedence *or* precedency, precession, pre-existence; the past etc. (preterition) 122.

2. *n.* premise; antecedent, antecedent happening *or* occurrence; precursor etc. 64.

3. *v.* be prior etc. *adj.*, precede, come *or* go before, precurse, be the precursor etc. 64, forerun, forego [arch.], prevene [rare], antecede, pre-exist; dawn; herald, usher in, proclaim, announce; anticipate, forestall etc. (be early) 132.5; presage etc. (portend) 511.9.

4. *adj.* prior, earlier, previous, ci-devant [F.], fore, precedent [rare]; preceding etc. *v.*, anterior, antecedent, pre-existent; former, foregoing etc. (past) 122.8–13; precursory, afore-mentioned etc. 62.4.

5. *adv.* previously etc. *adj.*, in time past, prior to . . . , earlier, before, afore [obs. exc. dial.], beforetime, aforetime, hitherto, heretofore, theretofore, ere, erenow, erewhile *or* erewhiles [arch.], ere then *or* now, before then *or* now, or ever; already, yet; on the eve of . . . ; *ante bellum* [L.]; *ante Christum* [L.], A.C., before Christ, B.C.; then etc. 119.2; formerly etc. 122.14.

6. *adv.* beforehand, aforehand [arch. and dial.], in anticipation *or* advance.

117. Posteriority
(See 116. Priority)

1. *n.* posteriority, subsequence, subsequency, sequence, succession, following, coming after, supervention; continuance, prolongation; remainder, reversion; futurity etc. 121; sequel etc. 65.

2. *v.* be subsequent etc. *adj.*; follow, come *or* go after, succeed, supervene; ensue, attend, emanate [rare], result.

3. *adj.* subsequent, posterior, following, after, later, succeeding, successive, ensuing, consecutive, attendant, postliminary [rare]; sequent, sequential [rare], sequacious [rare]; postdiluvial, postdiluvian; posthumous, after-death; postprandial, after-dinner; future etc. 121.7.

4. *adv.* subsequently etc. *adj.*, after, afterwards, since, later, at a later *or* subsequent period, after a while *or* time; next, in the sequel, close upon . . . , thereafter, eftsoon *or* eftsoons [arch.], from that time *or* moment; whereupon, upon which, whereat, thereupon; hereupon, hereon; *ex post facto* [L.]; in process of time etc. (in future) 121.9, 10.

---

116. *Prior tempore prior jure* [First in time, first in law]. First come first served.

117. I have gone in for posthumous fame.— S. Butler. That which comes after ever conforms to that which has gone before.— Marcus Aurelius.

118. Present Time
(See 119. Different Time, 121. Futurity, 122. Preterition)

1. *n.* present time, the present day *or* time, the present hour *or* moment, the present juncture *or* occasion, the present, this day, this day and age, this hour, now, today; the times, the existing time, the time being; this epoch *or* age, the present age.

2. *adj.* present, actual, instant, current, nonce, latest, existing, that is.

3. *adv.* now, at present, "upon this bank and shoal of time" (Shakespeare), at this time, at this moment etc. 113.3, at the present time etc. *n.,* today, at this time of day, in these days, hereadays, nowadays, nowanights; even now, but now, just now; on the present occasion, for this occasion, *pro hac vice* [L.], for the time being, for the nonce; on the nail, on the spot; on the spur of the moment *or* occasion, prompted by the occasion.

4. *adv.* until now, to this *or* the present day, up to now *or* this time, by this time, up to the present, now *or* then as previously, already, yet, still; formerly etc. 122.14.

119. Different Time
(See 118. Present Time)

Time Different from the Present.—1. *n.* different time, other time, another time; indefinite time etc. 109.

2. *adv.* then, at that time, at that moment *or* instant, on that occasion, in that case *or* instant; again, at another *or* different time, at some other time; once etc. (formerly) 122.14; previously etc. 116.5.

3. *adv. etc.* whenever, whene'er [poetic], whensoever, whensoe'er [poetic], at whatever time, at any time, anywhen [chiefly dial.], any old day or time [coll.], no matter when.

4. *adv.* sometime, someday, some of these days, one of these days, some fine day *or* morning, one fine day *or* morning, some sweet day [coll.], sometime or other, sooner or later; sometimes, at various times, on divers occasions, now and then, at times; in future etc. 121.9.

120. Synchronism

1. *n.* synchronism, synchronization, simultaneousness etc. *adj.,* coincidence, coincident existence, coexistence, coevality, contemporaneity, concurrence, concomitance *or* concomitancy, unity of time; isochronism.

2. *n.* contemporary, coeval, coetanian [obs.].

3. *v.* synchronize, be synchronous etc. *adj.,* concur, contemporize, coincide, coexist; accompany, go hand in hand, keep pace with, keep in step; isochronize; sync *or* sink, be in sync *or* sink [all motion-picture and television cant].

4. *adj.* synchronous, synchronal, synchronic(al), synchronistic(al); coinstantaneous, coetaneous [rare], simultaneous, concomitant, concurrent, collateral; coexistent, coexisting; coeval, coevous [obs.]; contemporary, contemporaneous; coterminous, conterminous; coeternal; isochrone, isochronal, isochronous, isochronic; in sync *or* sink [motion-picture and television cant]; in time, in step, in tempo.

121. Futurity
(See 118. Present Time, 122. Preterition)

Prospective Time.—1. *n.* futurity, future state *or* time, futurition [rare]; prospect, anticipation etc. (expectation) 507, (foresight) 510; posterity etc. 167; posteriority etc. 117.

2. *n.* the future, futurity, hereafter, aftertime, after years, time to come, womb of time, coming *or* subsequent time, ~ age, ~ days, ~ hours, ~ years *or* ages, the morrow, tomorrow, *mañana* [Sp.], the yet [rare]; by-and-by, the sweet by-and-by [coll.], remote *or* distant future; Day of Judgment, doomsday, crack of doom, millennium, millenary, chiliad [rare]; afterlife, afterlifetime [Ins.].

3. *n.* postexistence, future existence, hereafter, future state, next world, afterlife, afterworld, life *or* world to come, life

---

118. The present hour alone is man's.—JOHNSON. One today is worth two tomorrows.—F. QUARLES. Unborn Tomorrow and dead Yesterday.—OMAR KHAYYÁM—FITZGERALD. Tomorrow never comes.

120. It is lucky for the peace of great men that the world seldom finds out contemporaneously who its great men are.—LOWELL. Men resemble their contemporaries even more than their progenitors.—EMERSON. In the human breast / Two master passions cannot coexist.—T. CAMPBELL.

121. *Quid sit futurum cras fuge quaerere* [Do not seek to find out what the morrow will bring].—HORACE. If today will not, tomor-

or world beyond the grave; heaven etc. 981.

4. *n.* approach of time, advent, time drawing on, eventuality; approach etc. 286.

5. *v.* look forward, anticipate etc. (expect) 507.4-6, (foresee) 510.5; forestall etc. (be early) 132.5.

6. *v.* approach, near, come, come on, draw on or near, await, stare one in the face; threaten etc. (impend) 152.2.

7. *adj.* future, hereafter; eventual, ulterior; to-be, to come; coming, near, close at hand etc. (imminent) 152.3; prospective, in prospect etc. (expected) 507.8; after, later etc. (subsequent) 117.3.

8. *adj.* millennial, millenary; chiliadal, chiliadic.

9. *adv.* in future, prospectively etc. *adj.*, hereafter, hereafterward [obs. exc. dial.], in after time, at a later *or* subsequent time, after a time *or* while, anon; in time, in the course *or* process of time, in the fullness of time, in due time, all in good time, eventually, ultimately, in the long run, sometime *or* other, sooner *or* later; tomorrow, *mañana* [Sp.], the day after tomorrow, by and by, in the sweet by-and-by [coll.]; *proximo* [L.], *prox.* [abbr.]; *paulo post futurum* [L.]; one of these days etc. (sometime) 119.4; afterwards, thereafter etc. (subsequently) 117.4; soon etc. 132.15.

10. *adv.* henceforth, henceforwards, thence, thenceforth, thereafter, from this *or* that time, from this *or* that time forward.

11. *prep.* about to, on the eve, ~ point, ~ brink *or* verge of, close upon.

122. Preterition

(See 118. Present Time, 121. Futurity)

Retrospective Time.—1. *n.* preterition, past time; priority etc. 116; retrospection etc. (memory) 505.

2. *n.* the past, heretofore [rare], times *or* days past, time *or* days gone by, bygone times *or* days, former times, foretime [rare]; yesterday, yesteryear; old *or* olden times, old days, the olden time, times *or* days of old *or* yore, yore, yoretime, eld [obs. or poetic], good old times *or* days, long ago, right smart spell ago [dial.], langsyne *or* auld lang syne [chiefly Scot.], wayback [dial. and coll.]; history.

3. *n.* antiquity, antiquary, antiqueness, ancientness, ancient times; time immemorial, remote age *or* time, remote *or* distant past, distance of time; rust *or* cobwebs of antiquity; ancient history, medieval history; antiquities etc. 124.3.

4. *n.* antiquarianism; archaeology; fossilology, fossilogy, palaetiology; paleontology, paleography, paleology, palaeotypography, palaeosophy, paleoanthropography, paleoanthropology, paleobiogeography, paleobiology, paleobotany, paleochorology, paleocosmology, paleoclimatology, paleodendrology, paleogeography, paleography, paleoherpetology, paleohistology, paleohydrography, paleolatry, paleolimnology, paleolithy, paleometeorology, paleopathology, paleophysiography, paleophysiology, paleophytology, paleopotamology, paleopsychology, paleozoology; archaism, medievalism, Pre-Raphaelitism.

5. *n.* antiquary, antiquarian, antiquist [rare]; virtuoso, dryasdust, *laudator temporis acti* [L.]; paleologist, archaeologist, medievalist, Pre-Raphaelite etc. *above*; the Rev. Dr. Dryasdust (Scott), Jonathan Oldbuck (Scott), Herr Teufelsdröckh (Carlyle); Assyriologist, Egyptologist etc.

6. *v.* be past, have expired etc. *adj.*; have run its course, have had its day, pass, pass *or* go by, pass away, blow over; lapse etc. (elapse) 109.3.

7. *v.* retrospect, look back, cast the eyes back; trace back, study the history of, prove the existence *or* occurrence of, examine vestiges *or* remains of; antiquarianize [coll.]; exhume.

8. *adj.* past, gone, gone-by, bygone, foregone [arch.], bypast, ago, agone [arch.], over, passed, passed away, elapsed, lapsed, preterlapsed [rare], ex-

---

row may.—FULLER. I will lend you the wings of the future, for I have them.—R. JEFFERS. I believe the future is only the past again, entered through another gate.—PINERO. Coming events cast their shadow before them. 122. What's past is prologue.—SHAKESPEARE. The eternal landscape of the past.—TENNYSON. The tender grace of a day that is dead / Will never come back to me.—TENNYSON. Lend me the stone strength of the past.—R. JEFFERS. I tell you the past is a bucket of ashes.—SANDBURG. Time does not become sacred to us until we have lived it.—BURROUGHS. *Hoc erat in more majorum* [This was in the manner of our ancestors].

pired, no more, run out, blown over, extinct, never to return, exploded, forgotten, irrecoverable; obsolete etc. (old) 124.6–10.

9. *adj.* (grammar) past, preterit *or* preterite, pluperfect, past perfect.

10. *adj.* former, fore, *ci-devant* [F.], late, whilom [arch.], sometime, quondam, erst [arch.]; previous, antecedent etc. (prior) 116.4; pristine, ancient, ancestral etc. (old) 124.6–9; older etc. 124.10.

11. *adj.* foregoing, afore-going, preceding, last, latter; recent, afore-mentioned etc. 62.4.

12. *adj.* retrospective, retrospect, retroactive, looking back etc. *v.*

13. *adj.* antiquarian, archaeological, paleological etc. *n.*

14. *adv.* formerly, before, afore [obs.], before *or* ere now, erenow, aforetime, hitherto, heretofore; erst, erstwhile, erstwhiles, erewhile, whilom [all arch.]; ago, agone [arch.], apast [obs. exc. dial.], in the past, back.

anciently, of old *or* yore, in days of yore, "in yore agone" (W. Morris), in the olden time etc. *n.,* long ago, long since, a long while *or* time ago, years *or* ages ago, some time ago *or* since, right smart ago [dial.], some time back, a way *or* away back [dial. and coll.], in the memory of man, time out of mind; once, once upon a time, one day, one fine morning, time was; no longer; previously etc. 116.5; already, yet etc. (until now) 118.4; lately etc. 123.13; then etc. 119.2; first etc. 66.9.

15. *adv.* since long ago, long since, from away back [dial. and coll.], since Heck *or* Hector was a pup [slang], since days of yore, since *or* from time immemorial, from time out of mind, since the world was made, since the world was young, since the days of Methuselah, since Adam, since Adam was a boy, since God knows when [slang].

123. Newness
(See 124. Oldness)

1. *n.* newness, recentness etc. *adj.*, recency; novelty, gloss of novelty; newfanglement, newfanglement [slang]; neology etc. 563.7; immaturity etc. (youth) 127; renewal, renovation etc. 660.2; innovation etc. (change) 140; nonimitation etc. 20; dissimilarity etc. 18.1.

2. *n.* a novelty, newfanglement, newfangle [dial. and coll.], newfandanglement [slang], newfandangle [slang], newfangled device, contraption [coll.], newfangled contraption [coll.], new wheeze [slang], new *or* latest wrinkle [slang], the last word [slang], the latest thing, the latest scream [slang], *dernier cri* [F.], spic-and-span novelty.

3. *n.* modernism, modernness, modernity; modernization; futurism, cubism etc. (art) 556.6; the latest fashion etc. 852.

4. *n.* modernist, modernizer, modern, moderner [rare]; neoteric, neoterist, neologist; modern generation; futurist, cubist etc. (artist) 559.1.

5. *n.* upstart, parvenu etc. 876.8.

6. *v.* renew, renovate etc. (restore) 660.8–14.

7. *v.* modernize, render modern etc. *adj.*, adapt to modern persons *or* things; adopt modern ways; futurize [chiefly Art].

8. *adj.* new, recent, late, of yesterday, neoteric(al); fresh, fresh as a rose *or* daisy, fresh as the morning's dew, fresh as paint [coll.]; green, vernal; raw, immature; virgin, virginal; untried, untouched, unhandled, unhandseled, unheard-of, unfamiliar, untrodden, unbeaten; newborn, newfledged; ever-new, evergreen, sempervirent *or* sempervirid [rare]; renewed etc. (restored) 660.17; unused etc. 678.7.

9. *adj.* brand-new, bran-new, new-made, fire-new, span-new, spick-and-span, spick-and-span new; brand spic-and-span new, brand spank-fire new, brand spanking, brand-spanking new, brand splinterfire new, brand splinter new, spanking, spanking new, spank-fire new, splinterfire new, splinternew, split-new [all coll., slang or dial.]; just out [coll.], hot off the fire, hot off [coll.].

10. *adj.* novel, newfangled [contemptuous], newfangle [dial. and coll.]; newfandangled, newfandangle, new-wrinkled [all slang]; unique etc. (unusual) 83.10; dissimilar etc. 18.4; unimitated etc. 20.3.

---

123. Perpetual modernness is the measure of merit in every work of art.—EMERSON. Things are always at their best in the beginning.—PASCAL. *Di novello tutto par bello* [Everything new appears beautiful]. A new broom sweeps clean.

11. *adj.* modern, of recent period, neoteric(al); new-fashioned, new-fashion [dial.], up-to-date, up-to-datish, up-to-the-minute, up-to-dick [slang], up [coll.], on the boat [slang], abreast of the times; ultramodern, ultra-ultra; modernistic, futuristic; modernized.

12. *adv.* newly etc. *adj.*, anew, afresh.

13. *adv.* lately, recently, latterly, of late, not long ago, a short time ago, the other day, only yesterday; just now, right now [chiefly coll.]; formerly etc. 122.14.

124. Oldness
(See 123. Newness)

1. *n.* oldness, age, eld [obs. exc. poetic]; great *or* hoary age, antiquity, rust *or* cobwebs of antiquity, ancientness etc. *adj.*; old age etc. 128.2; senility etc. 499.5; maturity etc. 131.

2. *n.* antiquities, archaisms; ancient relics, relics of the past, reliquiae, remains, organic remains, fossils, petrifications; Egyptian antiquities, Greek antiquities, Roman antiquities, Indian antiquities; Megatheriidae, Theropoda, Saurischia, Sauropoda, Ornithopoda, Ornithischia, Triceratops, Stegosauria, Ceratopsia, Ceratopsidae; prehistoric animal, Megatherium, Megalosaurus, Ceratosaurus, Compsognathus, theropod, sauropod, ornithopod, Dinotherium, dinosaur, mastodon, mammoth, wooly *or* northern mammoth, saber-toothed tiger *or* cat; eolith, paleolith, neolith; aborigine, aboriginal, aboriginary; fossil man, Piltdown man; petrified forest; Babylonian, Assyrian, Sanskrit; antiquarianism etc. 122.4.

3. *n.* tradition, custom, common law, immemorial usage, Sunna [Moham.]; folklore.

4. *v.* be old etc. *adj.*, have had *or* seen its day, have seen its best days, have seen better days [coll.].

5. *v.* render or become old etc. *adj.*, olden [rare], age; obsolesce, become obsolete *or* extinct; antiquate; grow old etc. 128.8; fade, decline etc. (deteriorate) 659.6.

6. *adj.* old, auld [dial. and Scot.], ancient, antique, of yore, of long standing, time-honored, venerable, hoary, vetust [obs.]; olden [chiefly poetic], eldern [arch.]; secondhand; aged etc. (age) 128.9; senile etc. 499.16.

7. *adj.* primitive, prime, primeval; primigenial, primogenial; primigenious, primigenous; primordial, primordiate [rare]; pristine, aboriginal; archaic, archaical [rare]; diluvian, diluvial; antediluvian, antediluvial; Noachian, Noachic(al), arky [slang]; prehistoric, protohistoric, preadamite, antepatriarchal; dateless; fossil, fossilized; paleocrystic, Paleozoic, preglacial, antemundane; Vedic, classic(al), Pre-Raphaelite, medieval; patriarchal, ancestral; beginning etc. 66.7.

8. *adj.* traditional, traditive, traditionary [rare]; prescriptive, customary, unwritten; inveterate, rooted; immemorial, whereof the memory of man runneth not to the contrary.

9. *adj.* antiquated, superannuated, antique, archaic, archaical [rare], of other times, old-world, afterage; old as the hills, old as Methuselah *or* Adam, old as history; out-of-date, out of season, out of fashion, old-fashioned, old-fashion [obs. exc. dial.], old-fashionable [obs.], unfashionable, oldfangled, old-timy [coll.], behind the age *or* times, of the old school, back-number [coll.], black-letter, has-been [coll.], tintype [slang]; stale, fusty, moldy, mildewed, rusty, timeworn, moss-grown, moth-eaten, gone to seed, crumbling, moldering; obsolete, extinct, *passé* [F.], gone out, gone-by, dead, disused, past, run out, outworn.

10. *adv.* older, elder; oldest, eldest, eldermost [dial.]; former etc. 122.10, 11.

125. Morning, Noon
(See 126. Evening, Night)

1. *n.* morning, morn, morningtide [rare or poetic], morning time, morntime, matins [Eccl.], forenoon, foreday; *ante meridiem* [L.], a.m., A.M., Ack Emma [slang, Eng.]; "dewy morn" (Byron), "incense-breathing morn" (Gray), "genial morn" (T. Campbell),

---

124. Age, like distance, lends a double charm.—HOLMES. *Vetera extollimus recentium* [Neglectful of recent events we praise what is old].—TACITUS. There is no new thing under the sun.—BIBLE. *Nullum est jam dictum quod non dictum est prius* [Nothing is said which has not been said before].—TERENCE.

125. Flames in the forehead of the morning sky.—MILTON. Morning roses newly washed with dew.—SHAKESPEARE. For what human ill does not dawn seem to be an allevia-

"grey-eyed morn" (Shakespeare), "rosy-finger'd morn" (Homer), "rich unfolding morn" (Keble), "the opening eyelids of the morn" (Milton); Morning, Aurora, Eos; dawn, the dawn of day, daybreak, dayspring, daylight, dawnlight, day-peep, cockcrow, cocklight, cockcrowing, sunrise, sunup [chiefly dial., Eng.; coll., U.S.]; brightening *or* first brightening [dial.], break *or* peep of day, break *or* crack of dawn, prime, prime of the morning, first blush *or* flush of the morning; aurora, foredawn, the small hours, the wee sma' hours [Scot.], the wee and small [slang].

this morning, this A.M. [coll.]; the morning after, the morning after the night before [both slang]; twilight, crepuscle etc. 126.1; beginning etc. 66.

2. *n.* noon, noonday, noontide, nooning, noontime, midday, meridian, *meridiem* [L.].

3. *adj.* morning, matin, matinal, matutinal, matutinary [rare], antemeridian; twilight, crepuscular etc. 126.5.

4. *adj.* noon, noonday, midday, meridian, meridional [obs.].

5. *adv.* in the morning etc. *n.*, mornings [chiefly dial.]; at sunrise, at the crack of dawn etc. *n.*, with the lark, when the morning dawns.

126. Evening, Night
(See 125. Morning, Noon)

1. *n.* evening, eve [poetic], even [poetic], eventide [arch. and poetic], decline *or* fall of day, close of day, shut of day [dial. and coll.], nightfall, sunset, sunsetting [arch.], sundown, sun-go-down [chiefly dial.], going down of the sun, cockshut [obs. exc. dial.], shank of the afternoon *or* evening [coll.]; vespers, evensong [Eccl. or arch.]; dusk, duskingtide, dusk-down [dial.], dimpsy [dial., Eng.], twilight, twinight [slang], owllight *or* owl's light, crepuscle *or* crepuscule, gloam [poetic], gloaming, glooming [poetic], darkening [Scot. and North. Eng.; dial. U.S.], candlelight, candlelighting, torchlight [rare]; eleventh hour, curfew, bedtime; close etc. 67.3.

2. *n.* afternoon, after [coll.], aft [slang], evening [local Eng. and South U.S.]; *post meridiem* [L.], *p.m.,* P.M., pip emma [slang, Eng.]; this afternoon, this after [coll.], this aft [slang], this P.M. [coll.].

3. *n.* night, nighttime, nighttide, darky [slang], darkmans [crim. slang, Eng.], "sable-vested Night" (Milton), "sable night" (Shakespeare), "dark-eyed night" (Shakespeare), "cowlèd night" (F. Thompson), "dusky night" (Milton), "empress of silence, and the queen of sleep" (Marlowe); darkness of night etc. 421.

4. *n.* midnight, hush *or* dead of night, dead, witching hour *or* time of the night, "the very witching time of night" (Shakespeare), killing time, "noonday night" (Longfellow), "outpost of advancing day" (Longfellow).

5. *adj.* evening, vesper, vespertine; twilight, twilighty; dusk, dusky; crepuscular, crepusculous [rare], crepusculine [rare]; sunsetty.

6. *adj.* nocturnal, night, nightly, nighttime, night-fallen; noctivagant, noctivagous; night-clad etc. (dark) 421.7.

7. *adj.* benighted, benighten [rare], night-overtaken.

8. *adv.* nightly, nights [dial. exc. U.S.], at *or* by night, through the night.

126a. Season

1. *n.* season, period, period *or* division of the year, recurrent *or* annual period; dry ~, rainy *or* cold season, dead *or* off season, strawberry season, theatrical season; social season, the season [Eng.]; big

---

S. Eliot. Black night broods over the deep.—Vergil. Watchman, what of the night?—Bible.
tion?—T. Wilder. Out of the shadows of night / The world rolls into light; / It is daybreak everywhere.—Longfellow. Faster and more fast, / O'er night's brim, day boils at last.—Browning.
126. There sinks the nebulous star we call the sun.—Tennyson. The nightly mercy of the eventide.—Masefield. Through the pale dusk of the impending night.—Longfellow. The evening is spread out against the sky.—T.
126a. Sweet Spring, full of sweet days and roses.—G. Herbert. Spring is a true reconstructionist.—H. Timrod. When the hounds of spring are on winter's traces.—Swinburne. Steep thyself in a bowl of summertime.—Vergil. Come, summer, come, the sweet season and sun!—James I of Scotland. Sumer is icumen in, / Lhude sing cuccu!—Unknown. Summer's lease hath all too short a date.—Shakespeare. I know I am but summer to

season, little season [both U.S.]; Aries, Cancer, Libra, Capricornus; seasonality.

2. *n.* spring, spring season, springtide, springtime, seedtime, grass; vernal equinox.

3. *n.* summer, summer season, summertide, summertime, good old summer time; midsummer; canicular days, dog days.

4. *n.* autumn, fall [U.S.; arch. and dial., Eng.], fall of the year, fall of the leaf, harvest, harvest time; autumnal equinox; Indian summer, St. Martin's summer, St. Luke's summer, little summer of St. Luke, St. Austin's summer, St. Augustine's summer, Allhallow summer [obs.].

5. *n.* winter, winter season, wintertide, wintertime, *hiems* [L.].

6. *adj.* seasonal, in *or* out of season, in season and out of season; summery, autumnal; wintry, wintery; brumous, brumal.

127. Youth
(See 128. Age, 131. Adulthood)

1. *n.* youth, juvenility, juvenescence [rare]; youthhood, youthhead [chiefly Scot.]; youthfulness, youthiness [Scot.], youngness etc. *adj.*; juniority, immaturity, minority, nonage, tender age; teen age, teens; prime of life, flower of life, spring-tide of life, seedtime of life, golden season of life, heyday of youth, "childhood's careless days" (Bryant), "the glad season of life" (Carlyle), age of growing pains [coll.], calf days [coll.], goslings *or* gosling patch [slang], awkward age.

childhood, childage [obs.], childishness; boyhood, boyage [obs.], boyery [obs.], boyishness; girlhood, girlage [obs.], girlery [obs.], girlishness, flapperhood [coll.]; a youth etc. (youngling) 129; newness etc. 123.

2. *n.* adolescence, pubescence, puberty.

3. *n.* infancy, babyhood, incunabula, the cradle, the nursery.

4. *v.* make youthful, youthen, youthify; juvenilify, juvenilize [rare]; rejuvenate, rejuvenesce, reinvigorate.

5. *adj.* youthful, youthy [chiefly Scot.], youthsome [obs. exc. dial.], youthlike; young, youngling; juvenile, juvenescent; immature, raw, green, sappy, unripe, callow, unfledged, newfledged, budding, tender, underage; teen-age, in one's teens, sweet sixteen [slang]; puerile, childlike, childly [rare], childish, kiddish [coll.]; boyish, boylike, beardless; girlish, girllike, maidenly, flapperish [coll.], frying-size [slang].

6. *adj.* adolescent, pubescent, hebetic.

7. *adj.* infant, infantine, infantile; babyish, baby; dollish, doll-like; kittenish, kittenlike; newborn; in the cradle, in swaddling clothes, in long clothes, in arms, in leading strings, at the breast.

8. *adj.* junior, Jr. *or* jr.; younger, puisne [Law].

128. Age
(See 127. Youth; also 131. Adulthood)

1. *n.* age, oldness, elderliness etc. *adj.*, eld [arch.], years, "slow-consuming age" (Gray), longevity; time of life; maturity etc. 131.

2. *n.* old age, senescence, senectitude, senectude; advanced age *or* years, hoary age, ripe age, ripe old age, superannuation, vale of years, declining years, decline of life, the shady side [coll.]; gray hairs, "the sear and yellow leaf" (Shakespeare), "the silver livery of advised age" (Shakespeare), "a crown of glory" (Bible); autumn, winter; three score years and ten; infirm old age, infirmity of age, infirmity, decrepitude; senility etc. 499.5; oldness etc. 124.

3. *n.* climacteric, grand climacteric, change of life, menopause.

4. *n.* seniority, eldership, deanship, primogeniture; senior etc. (elder) 130.

5. *n.* (science of old age) nostology, gerontology, gerocomy.

---

your heart, / And not the full four seasons of the year.—MILLAY. The teeming autumn, big with rich increase.—SHAKESPEARE. Cold autumn, wan with wrath of wind and rain.—SWINBURNE. There is something in the autumn that is native to my blood.—B. CARMAN. Barren winter, with its wrathful nipping cold. —SHAKESPEARE. Winter lingering chills the lap of May.—GOLDSMITH. If Winter comes, can Spring be far behind?—SHELLEY.
127. Youth is wholly experimental.—STEVENSON. He wears the rose of youth upon him.—SHAKESPEARE. But I was one and twenty, / No use to talk to me.—HOUSMAN. My salad days / When I was green in judgement.—SHAKESPEARE. My youth may wear and waste, but it shall never rust in my possession.—CONGREVE. Our most important are our earliest years.—COWPER.
128. Life is most delightful when it is on the downward slope.—SENECA. Grow old along with me! / The best is yet to be.—BROWNING.

6. *v.* be old etc. *adj.*, have had *or* seen one's day, have seen one's best days *or* have seen better days [coll.]; show one's age, look around the clock [coll.].

7. *v.* age, grow old etc. *adj.*, olden [rare], senesce [rare], live to a ripe old age, make old bones [coll.]; wither, wrinkle; decline, wane, fade etc. (deteriorate) 659.6.

8. *adj.* aged, old, elderly, eldern [arch.], grown old, in years, along in years, years old, advanced in life *or* years, past one's prime, on the shady side [coll.], no chicken [coll.]; superannuated, senectuous, antiquated, ancient, old as Methuselah *or* as the hills; patriarchal; gray, gray-headed, gray with age, hoar, hoary; wrinkled, marked with the crow's foot, with crow's feet; ripe, mellow, run to seed, senescent, like the last of pea time; declining, waning, fading, doting, timeworn, moth-eaten [joc.], moss-backed [slang], rusty, effete, decrepit, stricken in years, with one foot in the grave, fossilized [joc.]; gerontic, gerontal; doddering, doddery; senile etc. 499.16.

9. *adj.* senior, Sr., elder, older; eldest, eldermost [dial.], oldest; first-born; primogenitary, primogenous.

129. Youngling
(See 130. Elder)

1. *n.* youngling, youngster [chiefly coll.], younker [coll.], young person, youth, juvenile, minor, immature person, stripling, slip, sprig, sapling, chicken [chiefly coll.], fry *or* young fry [coll.], fledgling, callow [obs.], codling *or* codlin [obs.]; whippersnapper *or* young whippersnapper [chiefly coll.], whipster [rare], whiffet [coll., U.S.], brat, bratling, imp, little monkey, minx; pubescent; hopeful, young hopeful; scion, offspring etc. (descendant) 167.4.

2. *n.* young people, rising generation, younger generation, young fry [coll.], modern crop [coll.]; children, childkind; infantry [obs. exc. joc.].

3. *n.* child, little one, urchin, bairn [Scot.], tot, little tot, tad *or* little tad [U.S.], mite, chit [coll.], scrap, scrap of a child, shaver *or* little shaver [coll. and dial.], little squirt [slang], kid [slang], punk [slang], punk kid [slang], *butcha* [Ind.], imp [derog.], brat [contemptuous], bratling elf, bantling, pickaninny [usu. joc.], chick, chickabiddy, pullet, duckling, kitten, lamb, lambkin, darling, moppet [arch.], cherub, bud, innocent, little innocent; unspanked child, curled darling [both coll.].

4. *n.* boy, lad, laddie, youth, *muchacho* [Sp.], callant *or* callan [Scot. and North. Eng.], hobbledehoy, master, sonny, sonny boy; cub, whelp, colt, pup, puppy [all usu. contemptuous]; bub, bubby, bubby boy [all slang]; schoolboy, cadet; male etc. 373.

5. *n.* girl, girly [coll.], lass, lassie, wench [dial. and slang], miss, missy, little missy, damsel, damoiselle, damosel [arch.], demoiselle, maid, maiden, *muchacha* [Sp.]; colleen, girleen [both Anglo-Ir.]; chicken, flapper, babe, baby, broad [U.S.], curve [U.S.], twist [crim., U.S.], cutie, dame, doll, filly, fluff [U.S.], frail [U.S.], gal, heifer, pussy [all slang]; baggage, bag [slang], hussy, tart

---

Give me a staff of honor for my age.—SHAKESPEARE.   Age is like love; it cannot be hid.—DEKKER.   Old age is an incurable disease.—SENECA.   No man is so old as to think he cannot live one more year.—CICERO.   Everyman desires to live long; but no man would be old.—SWIFT.   No wise man ever wished to be younger.—SWIFT.   To know how to grow old is the master-work of wisdom.—AMIEL. *Peu de gens savent être vieux* [Few people know how to be old].—LA ROCHEFOUCAULD.   Only on the edge of the grave can man conclude anything.—H. ADAMS.   Old age and the wear of time teach many things.—SOPHOCLES.   The older I grow the more I distrust the familiar doctrine that age brings wisdom.—H. L. MENCKEN.   It's no use growing older if you only learn new ways of misbehaving yourself.—SAKI.   A man is as old as he feels, and a woman as old as she looks.
129. Girls have curious minds and fain would know the end of everything.—E. B. BROWNING.

April's amazing meaning doubtless lies / In tall hoarse boys and slips / Of slender girls.—G. DILLON.   For many a rose-lipt maiden / And many a lightfoot lad.—HOUSMAN.   The rosebud garden of girls.—TENNYSON.   Suffer the little children to come unto me, and forbid them not, for such is the kingdom of God.—BIBLE.   A boy's will is the wind's will, / And the thoughts of youth are long, long thoughts.—LONGFELLOW.   First the infant / Mewling and puking in the nurse's arms. / And then the whining school-boy, with his satchel / And shining morning face.—SHAKESPEARE.   Blessings on thee, little man, / Barefoot boy with cheek of tan.—WHITTIER.   Boys are nature's raw material.—SAKI.   Golden lads and girls all must / As chimneysweepers, come to

[slang]; hoyden, tomboy, romp; virgin, herring [crim. slang, U.S.]; schoolgirl, schoolmaid, schoolmiss; female etc. 374.

6. *n.* infant, baby, babe, weanie [Scot.], papoose, *bambino* [It.], baby bunting, babykins [coll.], bouncing baby; nursling, suckling, bottle-boy [dial.]; weanling, yearling, year-old; toddler, toddlekins [slang]; vagitus [Med.].

7. *n.* (animals) younglet, youth [both rare]; birdling, nestling, fledgling; chick, chicky, chickling, pullet, fryer *or* frier; duckling; pup, puppy, whelp; cub; calf, weaner [West. U.S.]; colt, foal; kitten, kit, kitling [dial.], catling; lamb, lambkin, kid; tadpole, polliwog, pollywiggle [obs. exc. dial.], pollyfrog [dial. and slang].

8. *n.* larva, chrysalis, aurelia, cocoon, pupa; nymph, nympha; caterpillar, maggot, grub; worm etc. 366.25.

130. Elder
(See 129. Youngling)

1. *n.* elder, oldster [coll.], old person, old man, old chap, old gentleman, old gent [coll. or vulgar], old codger [coll.], geezer *or* old geezer [slang], old duffer [coll.], old dog [coll.], graybeard, grisard [rare], gaffer [coll. or contemptuous], patriarch, reverend sir; preadamite, antediluvian, Father Time, Methuselah, Nestor, Old Parr; sexagenarian, octogenarian, nonagenarian, centenarian; dotard etc. 501.3; grandfather, forefather etc. (ancestry) 166; veteran etc. 700.3.

2. *n.* antiquated person, antique [joc.], fogy, old fogy, fogram *or* fogrum [coll.], dodo *or* old dodo [coll.], fossil [chiefly coll.], long-hair [slang].

3. *n.* old woman, old lady, granny, old granny, grandam *or* grandame [arch.], dame, gammer [dial., Eng.], trot *or* old trot [arch. and dial.], no chicken [coll.]; old dame, old hen, old heifer, old girl [all slang]; old battle-axe [slang], war horse [coll.], crone, hag, beldam *or* beldame, frump [coll.], old wife; grandmother etc. 166.9.

4. *n.* (classical elderly couples) Darby and Joan, Baucis and Philemon [Gr. and Rom. Myth.].

5. *n.* senior, elder, dean, *doyen* [F.], father; firstling, first-born.

131. Adulthood
(See 127. Youth; also 128. Age)

1. *n.* adulthood, adultness etc. *adj.,* adultism; maturity, majority, full age, full bloom, flower of age, ripe age, age *or* years of discretion; manhood, manhead [arch.], manlihood; womanhood, womanhead [arch.], womanlihood; maturescence; oldness etc. 124.

2. *n.* middle age, *mezzo cammin* [It.], meridian of life, dangerous age [joc.].

3. *n.* adult, grownup [coll.], no chicken [coll.]; man etc. 373.2; woman etc. 374.2.

4. *v.* become adult etc. *adj.,* mature, attain majority, come of age, come to *or* into man's estate, put on long trousers, assume the *toga virilis* [L.], come to *or* into years of discretion, have cut one's eyeteeth [coll.], have sown one's wild oats.

5. *adj.* adult, mature, of age, out of one's teens, of full *or* ripe age, grown-up, full-grown, full-blown, in full bloom, ripe, mellow; marriageable, marriable, nubile; approaching maturity, maturescent; manly etc. (male) 373.4, (virile) 159a.5; womanly etc. (female) 374.11, (effeminate) 160a.5.

6. *adj.* middle-aged, *entre deux âges* [F.], in one's prime.

---

dust.—SHAKESPEARE. The flower of our young manhood.—SOPHOCLES. When I was a child, I spake as a child, I understood as a child, I thought as a child; but when I became a man, I put away childish things.—BIBLE. Young men have a passion for regarding their elders as senile.—H. ADAMS.
130. Venerable men! you have come down to us from a former generation.—D. WEBSTER. Young men think old men are fools; but old men know young men are fools.—G. CHAPMAN. The man of wisdom is the man of years.—YOUNG. The young man who has not wept is a savage, and the old man who will not laugh is a fool.—SANTAYANA. Nobody loves life like an old man.—SOPHOCLES. Few envy the consideration enjoyed by the oldest inhabitant. —EMERSON. Superfluous lags the veteran on the stage.—JOHNSON. The child's toys and the old man's reasons / Are the fruits of the two seasons.—W. BLAKE. *Bis pueri senes* [Old men are twice children].
131. Yet ah, that Spring should vanish with the Rose! / That Youth's sweet-scented manuscript should close!—OMAR KHAYYÁM-FITZGERALD. A fool at forty is a fool indeed.— YOUNG. Only the middle-aged have all their five senses in the keeping of their wits.—H. ALLEN

132. Earliness
(See 133. Lateness)

1. *n.* earliness etc. *adj.*; morning etc. 125.1.

2. *n.* prematurity, immaturity [arch.], prematureness etc. *adj.*, precocity, precipitation, anticipation, prevenience, hastiness, precipitation; a stitch in time; untimeliness etc. 135.

3. *n.* punctuality, promptness etc. *adj.*, promptitude, readiness; expedition, alacrity etc. (quickness) 682.2; haste etc. 684.

4. *n.* (one who is early) early [coll., U.S.], early bird, early riser.

5. *v.* be early etc. *adj.*, be . . . beforehand etc. *adv.*, take time by the forelock; anticipate, foresee, foreglimpse, foretaste, forerun; forestall, obviate; have *or* gain the start, get a head start, steal a march upon; gain time, draw on futurity *or* on the future; bespeak, secure, engage, preengage.

6. *v.* be punctual etc. *adj.*, be on time etc. *adv.*, keep time.

7. *adj.* early, bright and early [coll.], prime, in good season; timely etc. 134.7, 10.

8. *adj.* premature, immature [arch.], precipitate, precocious, prevenient, anticipatory, forward, advanced, rathe [obs. or poetic]; previous, a bit *or* trifle previous [all coll.]; untimely etc. 135.6; unexpected etc. 508.8.

9. *adj.* punctual, Johnny on the spot [slang]; prompt, summary, immediate; ready, expeditious etc. (quick) 682.17; instantaneous etc. 113.4; near-at-hand, impending etc. (imminent) 152.3.

10. *adj.* earlier, previous etc. (prior) 116.4.

11. *adv.* early, betimes, rathe *or* rath [dial. and poetic], in time, in military time, in pudding time [chiefly dial.], in due time.

12. *adv.* beforehand, prematurely etc. *adj.*, too soon, before its *or* one's time; in anticipation; precipitately etc. (hastily) 684.7; unexpectedly etc. 508.11.

13. *adv.* punctually etc. *adj.*, in a punctual manner, precisely; on time, on the minute *or* instant, on *or* to the tick [coll.]; on the dot, on the nose, right on the nail [all slang].

14. *adv.* promptly, prompt [coll.], without delay, without further delay, immediately, immediately if not sooner [joc.], at once, right away, instantly, instanter, on the instant, on the spot, straight, straightway, straightforth, forthwith, forthright, pronto [coll., U.S.], big and pronto [slang, U.S.], incontinently, summarily, quickly, speedily, apace, in no time, in less than no time, before you can say "Jack Robinson" *or* "knife," before the ink is dry; at short notice, extempore, on the spur of the moment *or* occasion, at *or* on sight, *à vue d'œil* [F.], offhand, out of hand; hastily etc. 684.7.

15. *adv.* soon, betimes, almost immediately, presently, directly, *bientôt* [F.], briefly, shortly, in a short time *or* while, right short [dial.], in no long time, ere *or* before long, in a while, after a while, by and by, anon, at the first opportunity, in due time, eftsoon *or* eftsoons [arch.]; speedily, forthwith etc. *above* 132.14; in future etc. 121.9.

133. Lateness
(See 132. Earliness)

1. *n.* lateness, tardiness etc. *adj.*

2. *n.* delay, delayment [obs.], delation [arch.]; tarriance, waiting, moration [rare]; retardation, retardance; prolongation, prorogation, protraction; postponement, deferment, deferral, put-off [chiefly coll.]; adjournment, adjournal; dilatoriness, procrastination, Micawberism, cunctation [rare], Fabian policy; a play for time, stall [slang], standoff [chiefly coll.], hold-off [coll.]; stop, stay, suspension, holdup [coll.].

pause, respite, truce, reprieve, reprieval [rare], moratorium; demurrage, demur, demurral [all rare]; leeway [coll.]; high time; red tape, red-tapery, red-tapism, pink ribbons [slang]; "cir-

---

132. Misers get up early in the morning; and burglars . . . get up the night before.—CHESTERTON. For precocity some great price is always demanded sooner or later in life.—M. FULLER. Early to bed and early to rise, makes a man healthy, wealthy and wise. The early bird catches the worm. First come, first served No sooner said than done

133. Procrastination is the thief of time.—YOUNG. My lord delayeth his coming.—BIBLE. Seven years, my lord, have now passed since I waited in your outward rooms.—JOHNSON. *Nonum prematur in annum* [Let it be kept until the ninth year].—HORACE. *Dum Roma deliberat Saguntum perit* [Even while Rome is deliberating Saguntum is per-

cumlocution office *or* court" (Dickens), chancery suit; *médecine expectante* [F.]; delayage.

3. *v.* be late etc. *adj.*, not be on time etc. 132.13; arrive late, arrive in an armchair [coll.]; keep banker's hours; stand *or* lay over, hang in the balance, hang in the hedge, hang fire.

4. *v.* postpone, delay, stay, put off, shift *or* stave off, wait [coll.], defer, reserve, procrastinate [rare] etc. *below* 133.5, drive [coll.], waive, respite [rare], suspend, hang up [chiefly coll.]; adjourn, prorogue, prorogate; lay *or* set by, lay ∼, set ∼, cast ∼, push *or* put aside, side [coll.], shunt, stand *or* lay over, let the matter stand, table, lay on the table, pigeonhole, shelve, put on the shelf, put on the rack [coll.], put on ice [slang]; consult one's pillow, sleep upon; pretermit etc. 460.7; prolong etc. (protract) 110.6.

5. *v.* procrastinate, be dilatory etc. *adj.*, vacillate, hesitate, hang, hang back, hang fire; dally, dillydally, fiddle-faddle [coll.], dawdle, linger; temporize, gain *or* make time, play for time, stand off [chiefly coll.], hold off [coll.]; stall, stall off, stall for time, stall along *or* around [all slang]; talk against time, filibuster [U.S. polit.], speak for Buncombe [coll., U.S. polit.]; tie up with red tape; not do etc. 681.2.

6. *v.* retard, delay, slacken, slow down, keep back, detain, hold up [coll.]; stop, block etc. (hinder) 706.4.

7. *v.* wait, delay, tarry, stay, bide, bide *or* take one's time, take time, mark time, dally, dillydally, dawdle, linger, loiter; hang around *or* about [coll.], stick around [slang]; hold on [coll.], hold one's horses [slang], keep one's shirt on [slang], sit tight [coll.]; be kept waiting, be stood up [slang], dance attendance, kick *or* cool one's heels [coll.], wait impatiently; *faire antichambre* [F.]; wait *or* stay up, sit up; await etc. (expect) 507.5; continue etc. 106.2.

8. *adj.* late, tardy, slow, behindhand, backward, overdue; moratory; unpunctual, impunctual [rare]; belated, delayed etc. *v.*; in abeyance; untimely etc. 135.6.

9. *adj.* dilatory, delaying, Micawberish; procrastinating, procrastinative, ishing]. Better late than never. *Aufgeschoben ist nicht aufgehoben* [Postponed is not abandoned]. It is too late to shut the stable door when the steed is stolen.

procrastinatory; cunctatious *or* cunctative, cunctatory [all rare]; dillydallying, dillydally [obs. exc. dial.]; indolent etc. 683.13; neglectful etc. 460.8.

10. *adj.* later, postliminary [rare] etc. (subsequent) 117.3.

11. *adv.* late, lateward [obs.], backward, behindhand, behind *or* after time, like a cow's *or* donkey's tail (always behind) [slang]; late in the day, at the eleventh hour, at sunset.

12. *adv.* after delay, at last, at long last, at length, finally, ultimately, eventually; *ex post facto* [L.].

13. *adv.* tardily, slowly, deliberately, leisurely, at one's leisure.

134. Timeliness
(See 135. Untimeliness)

1. *n.* timeliness, opportuneness etc. *adj.*, tempestivity [arch.]; expedience etc. 646; fitness etc. 23.2.

2. *n.* time, occasion, opportunity, chance, show [coll., U.S.], opening, room, scope, space, place, liberty.

3. *n.* suitable occasion, proper occasion, suitable *or* proper time *or* season, high time; good *or* fine opportunity, good *or* some show [coll., U.S.], golden opportunity, well-timed opportunity *or* occasion, favorable opportunity *or* occasion, *mollia tempora* [L.]; clear stage, fair field.

4. *n.* crisis, critical *or* crucial moment, psychological moment, critical point, the scratch [coll.], nick of time, zero hour, moment of crisis; turning point, turn; critical situation, emergency, contingency, exigency, juncture, conjuncture, pass, strait, extremity, push, pinch, squeeze [coll.], rub; predicament etc. 704.2.

5. *v.* be timely etc. *adj.*, suit *or* befit the time, ∼ season *or* occasion; be expedient etc. 646.3.

6. *v.* improve the opportunity *or* occasion, improve the shining hour, seize *or* use an opportunity *or* occasion; turn to account *or* good account, avail oneself of, profit by; strike the iron while it is hot,

134. To seize with power the crisis of a dark decisive hour.—COWPER. There is a tide in the affairs of men / Which, taken at the flood, leads on to fortune.—SHAKESPEARE. Gather ye rosebuds while ye may.—HERRICK. *Carpe diem* [Pluck the day; seize time by the forelock].—HORACE. Opportunity makes a thief.

battre le fer sur l'enclume [F.], make hay while the sun shines, seize the present hour, take time by the forelock, *prendre la balle au bond* [F.].

7. *adj.* timely, timeful [obs.], timeous [rare or Scot.], well-timed, tempestive [arch.], seasonable, opportune, convenient [arch.], expedient, meet, fit, fitting, befitting, suitable, sortable, appropriate, proper, seemly, favorable, propitious, auspicious, lucky, providential, fortunate, happy, felicitous; punctual etc. 132.7, 9.

8. *adj.* critical, crucial, decisive.

9. *adj.* occasional, incidental, casual, accidental; extemporaneous, extemporary; contingent etc. (dependent) 475.15.

10. *adv.* opportunely etc. *adj.,* timely [arch.], in proper time *or* season, in due time *or* course, in the fullness of time, in good time *or* season, all in good time; in the nick of time, just in time, at the eleventh hour; now or never; early etc. 132.11; expediently etc. 646.6.

11. *adv. etc.* by the way, by the by; incidentally, while on the subject, speaking of, *à propos* [F.] *or* apropos of; in passing, *en passant* [F.]; *obiter* [L.], *obiter dictum* [L.]; parenthetically, by way of parenthesis, *par parenthèse* [F.]; for example, *par exemple* [F.]; offhand, extempore, on the spur of the moment *or* occasion; in connection with etc. 9.10.

135. Untimeliness
(See 134. Timeliness)

1. *n.* untimeliness, unseasonableness etc. *adj.,* intempestivity, inopportunity; inexpedience etc. 647; anachronism etc. 115; prematurity etc. 132.2; intrusion etc. 228.3.

2. *n.* unsuitable time *or* occasion, unpropitious ~, unfortunate etc. *adj.* time *or* occasion, evil hour; *contretemps* [F.].

3. *v.* be untimely etc. *adj.,* come amiss; have other fish to fry, be otherwise occupied, be busy *or* engaged; intrude etc. 228.10.

4. *v.* ill time, mistime.

—BACON. Let nothing pass that will advantage you.—CATO. *Nunc aut nunquam* [Now or never]. *Nosce tempus* [Know the time]. A stitch in time saves nine.
135. He tires betimes that spurs too fast betimes.—SHAKESPEARE. Don't cross the bridge till you get to it. After meat mustard, after death the doctor.

5. *v.* lose an opportunity, throw away *or* waste an opportunity, neglect an opportunity, allow *or* suffer the opportunity *or* occasion to pass *or* go by, let slip through the fingers, lock the stable door after the horse *or* steed is stolen; waste time etc. (be inactive) 683.8.

6. *adj.* untimely, untimeous [chiefly Scot.]; unseasonable, ill-timed, ill-seasoned, mistimed, timeless [arch.], intempestive [rare], too late *or* soon, inopportune, inconvenient, untoward, *mal à propos* [F.], unfavorable, inauspicious, unauspicious [rare], unpropitious, unfortunate, unlucky, unhappy; unsuited etc. 24.7; inexpedient etc. 647.3; unpunctual etc. 133.8; premature etc. 132.8; out-of-date etc. 124.9; anachronous etc. 115.3.

136. Frequency
(See 137. Infrequency)

1. *n.* frequency, frequence, oftenness, oftness [rare], commonness, prevalence, quotiety [rare]; repetition etc. 104; continuance etc. 143; constancy, persistence etc. (perseverance) 604a.

2. *v.* do frequently etc. *adv.,* keep on, keep at it, hammer at *or* away, do nothing but; repeat, recur etc. 104.4; continue etc. 143.2; persist etc. (persevere) 604a.2.

3. *adj.* frequent, oftentime, ofttime [rare], often [arch.]; many, many times, not rare, recurrent, thick-coming; frequentative [Gram.]; repeated etc. 104.6, 7; usual etc. (habitual) 613.11; periodic, hourly etc. (regular) 138.9-11.

4. *adj.* constant, continual, steady, steadfast, regular, incessant, unceasing, unintermitting, unremitting, unchanging, unvarying, unstopped, uninterrupted; of daily *or* everyday occurrence, everyday; perpetual etc. 112.4; continuing etc. 143.4.

5. *adv.* frequently etc. *adj.* often, oftens [dial.], oft [arch. or poetic], oftentimes, oftentime [rare], ofttimes, ofttime [arch.], oftentide [obs.], oftly [rare], oftwhiles [rare], often enough; not infrequently, not seldom, unseldom; most often *or* frequently, in many instances, many times, many a time, full many a time, many a time and oft; in quick *or*

136. Nor is he convinced but by length of time and frequency of experiment.—JOHNSON. I'll do and I'll do and I'll do.—SHAKESPEARE.

rapid succession; again and again etc. (repeatedly) 104.8; commonly etc. (habitually) 613.13; periodically etc. 138.12.

6. *adv.* constantly, continually, incessantly etc. *adj.*; without ceasing, at all times, ever and anon; every day, every hour, every moment; daily, hourly etc.; daily and hourly, night and day, day and night; morning, noon and night; hour after hour, day after day, month after month, year after year; day in day out, month in month out, year in year out; perpetually, always etc. 112.5; invariably etc. 16.7.

137. Infrequency
(See 136. Frequency)

1. *n.* infrequency, infrequence, unfrequency; unfrequentness, seldomness etc. *adj.*; seldomcy [rare], rarity; sparseness etc. (fewness) 103.

2. *adj.* infrequent, unfrequent; seldom [arch.], seldseen [arch.], seldom seen; uncommon, rare, almost unheard-of, unprecedented, not within the memory of man *or* the oldest inhabitant, not within one's previous experience; occasional; semioccasional [coll., U.S.]; spasmodic etc. 139.2; scarce etc. (few) 103.3.

3. *adv.* infrequently, unfrequently; seldom, seldomly [rare]; rarely, scarcely, uncommonly, hardly; scarcely *or* hardly ever, seldom ever [now illit.]; not often, unoften; sparsely etc. 103.5.

4. *adv.* occasionally, sometimes, at times, now and then, every now and then [coll.], once and again, once in a while *or* way, every once in a while [coll.], from time to time, there being times when . . . , *toties quoties* [L.]; once in a blue moon [coll.], once in a coon's age [coll., U.S.], once in a dog's age [coll.]; semioccasionally [coll., U.S.]; sporadically etc. 70.5.

5. *adv.* once, on one occasion, just *or* only once, once and for all *or* always, once for all, one time only, for the nonce; *pro hac vice* [L.]; formerly etc. 122.14; then, sometime etc. 119.2–4.

---

137. Like angel visits, few and far between.—T. CAMPBELL. A strain of rareness.—SHAKESPEARE. What is so rare as a day in June?—LOWELL.

138. Regularity of Recurrence
(See 139. Irregularity of Recurrence)

1. *n.* regularity, regularness, steadiness etc. *adj.*; punctuality etc. 132.3.

2. *n.* periodicity, recurrence, regular recurrence, reoccurrence, return, intermittence *or* intermittency; alternation, alternateness, alternacy [rare], alternativeness, alternity [rare]; discontinuity etc. 70; repetition etc. 104; reversion etc. 145.

3. *n.* rhythm, *rhythmus* [L.]; rhyme *or* rime [rare]; cadence *or* cadency, lilt, swing, measure, measured movement; pulsation, beat etc. (oscillation) 314.

4. *n.* round, revolution, periodical revolution, rotation, rota [rare], cycle, circuit, course, series, bout, turn, say; routine etc. 613.4.

5. *n.* anniversary; biennial, triennial, quadrennial, quinquennial, sextennial, septennial, octennial, decennial; tricennial, jubilee, centennial, centenary, bicentennial, bicentenary, tercentenary; fete day; saint's day; birthday, birthright, natal day; Lincoln's Birthday etc. *below*, 138.7.

6. *n.* menses, catamenia etc. 299.7.

7. *n.* (calendarial and sidereal rounds or divisions) days of the week, Sunday etc., Blue Monday [chiefly U.S.]; months of the year, January etc.; festival, feast, fast etc.; Christmas, Christmas Day *or* Eve, Xmas, Merry Christmas, yuletide; New Year's Day, New Year's [coll.]; Twelfth-night, Twelfth-day, Twelfthtide; Ash Wednesday, Maundy Thursday, Good Friday; Easter, Easter Monday; Whitsunday, White Sunday; Whitmonday; Allhallows, Allhallowmas, Hallowmas, Allhallowtide, All Saints' Day, Hallowday [Eng.]; Hallowe'en; All Souls' Day; Candlemas, ground-hog *or* woodchuck day [U.S.]; Dewali, Holi [Ind.]; Bairam, Ramadan, Murharram [all Moham.].

Memorial *or* Decoration Day [U.S.]; Independence Day, Fourth of July [both U.S.]; Empire Day [Eng.]; Dominion Day [Can.]; Labor Day [U.S.]; Columbus Day; Armistice Day, Victory Day; Thanksgiving Day, Thanksgiving [both U.S.]; Lady Day, Annunciation

---

138. The trivial round, the commonplace task.—KEBLE. The punctual coming back, on their due days, of the birds.—EMERSON.

Day; leap year, a woman's year [coll.], bissextile day; St. Swithin's Day; Midsummer Day; May Day; Derby day [Eng.]; Arbor Day; Washington's Birthday; Lincoln's Birthday [both U.S.]; King's Birthday [Eng.]; Orangemen's Day [Ir.]; St. Patrick's Day; Boxing Day [Eng.].

8. *v.* recur, reoccur, recur in regular order *or* succession, reappear, return, revolve, come round, come round again, come *or* occur again, come in its turn; alternate, fluctuate, come and go, intermit; beat, pulsate etc. (oscillate) 314.8–10.

9. *adj.* regular, methodical, systematic(al), punctual, regular as clockwork; steady etc. (constant) 136.4.

10. *adj.* periodic(al), recurrent, recurring etc. *v.*, serial; epochal, seasonal; isochronal, isochronous, isochronic, isochrone; cyclic(al), cyclian; rhythmic(al), rhythmal; pulsative, pulsatile, pulsatory, pulsating, throbbing; intermittent, remittent, alternate, every other; every; frequent etc. 136.3; discontinuous etc. 70.4.

11. *adj.* hourly etc.; daily, diurnal, quotidian [rare]; weekly, tertian, hebdomadal, hebdomadary; biweekly, fortnightly; bimonthly; monthly, menstrual, catamenial; yearly, annual; biennial, triennial, decennial etc. *n.*; centennial, secular; paschal, lenten etc.

12. *adv.* periodically, regularly etc. *adj.*; regular [chiefly dial.], at regular *or* stated intervals, at fixed *or* established periods; from hour to hour, from day to day, *de die in diem* [L.], day by day; frequently etc. 136.5.

13. *adv.* by turns, in turn *or* rotation, alternately, every other day, off and on, ride and tie, hitch and hike, round and round.

139. Irregularity of Recurrence
(See 138. Regularity of Recurrence)

1. *n.* irregularity, uncertainty, unpunctuality; fitfulness etc. *adj.*, intermittence, inconstancy, variability, mutability, changeability, deviation; ecrhythmus; acatastasia [Med.].

2. *adj.* irregular, uncertain, unpunctual; fitful, spasmodic, spastic [Med.], sporadic, intermittent, capricious, erratic, eccentric, desultory, wavering, flickering, unsteady, inconstant, unsettled, uneven, unequal, variable, mutable, changeable, deviative, heteroclite; unmethodical *or* immethodical, unsystematic; rambling, disconnected, broken, rhapsodical [obs.]; ecrhythmic, ecrhythmous; infrequent etc. 137.2; discontinuous etc. 70.4.

3. *adv.* irregularly, fitfully etc. *adj.*, by fits and starts etc. (discontinuously) 70.5.

140. Change
(See 141. Permanence; also 149. Changeableness)

Difference at Different Times.—1. *n.* change, alteration, mutation, permutation, variation, modification; modulation, qualification, inflection; deviation, diversion, shift, turn; break; resolution, conversion etc. (gradual change) 144; revolution etc. (sudden or radical change) 146; eversion etc. (inversion) 218; dislocation etc. 185; changeableness etc. 149; tergiversation etc. (change of mind) 607.

2. *n.* transformation, transfiguration, transfigurement, transmutation, transmogrification [coll.], transubstantiation, mutation, metastasis, metamorphosis; metabolism, metabola *or* metabole [Med. and Zool.]; metathesis, transposition, translocation, elocation [obs.], heterotopia *or* heterotopy [Biol.]; metagenesis; metempsychosis, transanimation, transmigration; metasomatism, metasomatosis [both Geol.]; avatar, deoxidization, deoxidation [both Chem.]; transformism, transmorphism [rare].

3. *n.* innovation, novation [rare], introduction; novelty etc. (newness) 123; neology etc. 563.7.

4. *n.* alterant, alterative, modifier, transformer, transmogrifier [coll.].

5. *v.* change, be changed etc. *adj.*, undergo a change etc. *n.*, assume a new phase, alter, mutate; vary, diversify; wax and wane; modulate, merge into; deviate, turn, shift, veer, jibe, jib, tack, chop,

---

139. Life's fitful fever.—SHAKESPEARE.

140. The ever whirling wheele / Of Change, the which all mortall things doth sway.—SPENSER. We shall all be changed, in a moment, in the twinkling of an eye.—BIBLE. The old order changeth, yielding place to new.—TENNYSON. Let the great world spin forever down

chop and change, swerve, warp, dodge; turn aside, take a turn, turn the corner; tergiversate etc. 607.7–9; shuffle, vacillate etc. (be irresolute) 605.4; blow hot and cold etc. (be capricious) 608.4; be converted etc. 144.8.

6. *v.* work a change, change, alter, mutate, modify; modulate, qualify; vary, diversify, ring the changes; transform, transfigure, transmute, transmogrify [coll.], transubstantiate, transume [obs.], transverse [rare], transshape [rare], convert, resolve, metamorphose; vamp, vamp together *or* up, revamp [chiefly coll.], patch, piece; tamper with; metabolize [Physiol.]; superinduce, superimpose; shuffle the cards, shift the scene, turn over a new leaf; give a turn to, give a color to; influence, sway; turn the scale *or* balance; revolutionize etc. 146.4; invert etc. (reverse) 218.4; convert into etc. 144.6; disturb etc. (discompose) 61.4; differentiate etc. 15.6; render unlike etc. 18.3.

7. *v.* innovate, make innovations, novate, introduce; introduce new blood; neologize, novelize [rare].

8. *adj.* changed, altered etc. *v.*; alterate [obs.]; changeable etc. 149.5, 6; newfangled etc. 123.10.

141. Permanence
(See 140. Change; also 150. Stability)

Absence of Change.—1. *n.* permanence, permanency, changelessness, lastingness, abidingness, durableness etc. *adj.*; durability, duration, persistence *or* persistency, constance *or* constancy, endurance; maintenance, sustentation [rare], preservation, conservation; *status quo* [L.], *status in quo* [L.], static condition, standing; law of the Medes and Persians; standing dish; immutability,

fixity etc. (stability) 150; inertness etc. 172; quiescence etc. 265; obstinacy etc. 606; continuance etc. 143; inaction etc. 681, 683.

2. *n.* conservatism, opposition to change, unprogressivism, standpattism [coll.], standstillism, fogyism, Toryism [Eng.], Hunkerism [U.S.], bitter-enderism *or* bitter-endism [coll.]; laissez-faireism, Fabian policy, let-alone principle, ∼ doctrine *or* policy; *laisser-aller, laisser aller, laissez aller, laissez faire, laisser faire* [all F.]; bigotry etc. 606.2.

3. *n.* conservative, conservatist; unprogressive, unprogressivist; uncompromiser, standpat *or* standpatter [coll.], Hardshell [coll., U.S.], die-hard, bitter-ender [coll.], fogram *or* fogrum [coll.], fogy, old fogy, stick-in-the-mud [coll.], mossback [slang, chiefly U.S.], *laudator temporis acti* [L.], Hunker [U.S.], Bourbon, Tory [Eng.]; reactionary, reactionist; old school, right wing; irreconcilable etc. 606.3.

4. *v.* be permanent etc. *adj.*, not change etc. 140.5; persist, remain, stay, tarry, rest; last, endure, bide, abide, aby [arch.], dwell, maintain, keep, hold, hold on, live, subsist; stand still *or* fast, stay put [chiefly coll.], stand pat [coll.], hold *or* keep one's ground *or* footing; outlive, survive; remain valid, hold good, continue etc. 143.2.

5. *v.* be conservative etc. *adj.*, oppose change, stand on ancient ways, *stare super antiquas vias* [L.], let be, let *or* leave alone, let well enough alone, leave things as they are, *quieta non movera* [L.], let things take their course.

6. *adj.* permanent, enduring etc. *v.*, durable, lasty [chiefly dial.]; changeless, unchanging, unvarying; unchanged, unaltered, intact, inviolate, *qualis ab incepto* [L.]; persistent, constant, monotonous, unchecked, unfailing, unfading; undestroyed, unrepealed, unsuppressed; *pucka* [Ind.]; established, fixed etc. (stable) 150.5; stationary etc. 265.7; unchangeable etc. 150.7.

7. *adj.* conservative, opposed to change, preservative, unprogressive, reactionary, reactionist; uncompromising, standpat

---

the ringing grooves of change.—TENNYSON. Most of the change we think we see in life / Is due to truths being in and out of favor.—FROST.   They are not constant, but are changing still.—SHAKESPEARE.   It is a bad plan that admits of no modification.—PUBLILIUS.   Be ye transformed by the renewing of your minds.—BIBLE.   *Nous avons changé tout cela* [We have changed all that].—MOLIÈRE.
141. The universal human yearning for something permanent, enduring, without shadow of change.—W. CATHER.   What is conservatism? Is it not adherence to the old and tried,

against the new and untried?—LINCOLN.   I take my pleasure without change, and as I lived I live.—W. S. BLUNT.   The absurd man is he who never changes.—BARTHÉLEMY.   The quiet, equable, deadly holder-on.—S. V. BENÉT.

[coll.], standstill, hard-shell [coll., U.S.], die-hard, bitter-end [coll.], fogyish, stick-in-the-mud [coll.].

8. *adv.* permanently etc. *adj.*; *in statu quo* [L.], *uti possidetis* [L., Law], at a stand *or* standstill, without a shadow of turning; for good, for good and all, finally; as usual, as per usual [coll.].

142. Cessation
(See 143. Continuance)

Change from Action to Rest.—1. *n.* cessation, discontinuance, discontinuation; desinence, desistance, surcease [literary], cease [obs. exc. in *without cease*], stopping etc. *v.*, stoppage, stop, quittance [rare], stand, halt, stay, arrest, check; dead stop *or* stand, full stop; end etc. 67; arrival etc. 292; death etc. 360; deadlock, checkmate etc. (hindrance) 706; standstill etc. (quiescence) 265; abandonment etc. 624; disuse etc. 678.

2. *n.* pause, rest, stay, drop, lull, lapse, break, caesura (*pl.* caesuras, caesurae), intermission, intermittance, interval, interregnum, interlude, respite, hesitation, interruption, hitch [chiefly coll.], recess, remission, suspense, suspension, abeyance, letup [coll.]; truce, etc. 723.3; inaction etc. 681; idleness etc. 683.2.

3. *n.* (in debate) closure, cloture, *clôture* [F.].

4. *n.* (in music) interval, rest etc. 413.11–12; stop etc. 417.12.

5. *n.* (punctuation) stop, point; comma, semicolon, colon, period, caesura.

6. *v.* cease, discontinue, stop, stay, halt, hold, belay [Naut. or coll.], stow [slang], quit, leave off, desist, refrain, wind up [coll.]; hold *or* stay one's hand, have done with, drop it [slang], drop everything [slang], give over, surcease [literary], call it a day [coll.], shut up shop, shut down, knock off [coll.], hang up one's ax *or* the fiddle [coll.]; break off, break it off [coll.], break *or* snap the thread, cut off, chop off [slang]; pull up, pull up *or* stop short, bring up with a round turn [coll.], come to a full stop, come to a stand *or* standstill.

stick, stall, hang fire; pause, rest; rest on one's oars, repose on one's laurels; go out, die away, wear off *or* away, pass away; end etc. 67.5, 6; give up etc. (abandon) 624.3; remain etc. (be quiescent) 265.5; relax etc. 687.4; not do etc. 681.2; disuse etc. 678.2.

7. *v.* interrupt, suspend, interpel [obs.], break, intermit, remit; put a stop *or* an end to, put a period to, stop, stay, halt, stall, arrest, stem the tide *or* current, bring to a stand *or* standstill, check, check in full career, pull the check-string, cut short, shut down on *or* upon [coll.]; derail; kill the engine, cut the gun [slang], turn off the juice [slang]; bring to an end etc. 67.7; deadlock, checkmate etc. (thwart) 706.7; intervene etc. (intrude) 228.10.

8. *int.* cease!, stop!, hold!, stay!, desist!, leave off! etc. *v.*; *eheu jam satis!* [L.], *arrêtez!* [F.], halt!, *halte!* [F.], enough!, avast! [Naut.], belay that *or* there! [coll.], have done!, hold on! [coll.], hold hard!, whoa!, a truce to!, soft!, *tenez!* [F.]; cut it out!, can it!, cheese it!, chuck it!, come off!, come off of it!, stow it!, lay off!, let up!, fade away! [all slang]; forbear etc. 623.13; don't etc. 761.6.

143. Continuance
(See 142. Cessation)

Continuance in Action.—1. *n.* continuation, continuity; run; pursuance, maintenance, extension, perpetuation, prolongation; persistence etc. (perseverance) 604a; repetition etc. 104; permanence etc. 141; frequency etc. 136.

2. *v.* continue, be steadfast *or* constant, persist, persevere, endure, keep, keep *or* go on, run *or* jog on, drag on, hold, hold on *or* out, take *or* maintain its course, ride [slang, U.S.]; remain, abide etc. (be permanent) 141.4; do frequently etc. 136.2.

3. *v.* sustain, maintain, prolong, perpetuate, protract, extend; go on, carry *or* keep on, keep going, keep on foot, keep up, keep alive, keep the pot boiling [coll.], keep up the ball [coll.], keep the ball rolling, keep at it, keep driving [coll.], plug at it [slang], plug away *or* along [slang], keep to *or* maintain one's course, hold on

---

142. Let the long contention cease!—M. Arnold. Comes a pause in the day's occupations.—Longfellow. It seemed like the ceasing of exquisite music.—Longfellow. But now thy kingdom shall not continue.—Bible. *Non sum qualis eram* [I am not what I used to be].—Horace.

143. Continual dropping wears away stone.—Lucretius. Continuous as the stars that shine.—Wordsworth.

or pursue the even tenor of one's way.

prosecute to a conclusion, follow up *or* through, see it through [coll.], stay [coll.], stay with it, stay it out, stay the distance [slang, U.S.], stick to, stick [slang], stick it out [slang], sit the bag [slang, U.S.], die in the last ditch, be in at the death; die in harness, die in one's shoes, die at one's post; let it ride [slang, U.S.]; harp upon etc. (repeat) 104.4; uphold etc. (preserve) 670.3, (support) 215.26; stabilize etc. 150.4.

4. *adj.* continuing etc. *v.*, uninterrupted, unintermitting, unremitting, unchanging, unvarying, unvaried, unshifting, unceasing, unstopped, unrevoked, unreversed; persistent, sustained; chronic; inconvertible; continual etc. 136.4; continuous etc. 69.6; undying etc. (perpetual) 112.4.

5. *int.* carry on!, keep it up!, keep at it!, stay with it!, stick with it! [coll.], stand fast!

144. Conversion

Gradual Change to Something Different.—1. *n.* conversion, version [obs.], reduction, resolution, assimilation, assumption; lapse, shift, flux; growth, progress; naturalization; alchemy, chemistry; transmutation etc. (transformation) 140.2; naturalization etc. 184.7; change etc. 140.

2. *n.* regeneration, reformation; proselytization, Catholicization, Protestantization.

3. *n.* transition, transit, transmigration, transportation, passage; phase, stage.

4. *n.* (instruments) melting pot, crucible, alembic, caldron, retort, mortar, potter's wheel, anvil, lathe, blowpipe.

5. *n.* convert, proselyte, neophyte, catechumen, disciple.

6. *v.* convert, convert *or* resolve into, assimilate to, bring *or* reduce to, make, render; mold etc. (form) 240.6; alter etc. (change) 140.6.

7. *v.* regenerate, reform, refound, reorganize, remodel, strike out something new, produce anew; revolutionize etc. 146.4.

---

144. But doth suffer a sea-change / Into something rich and strange.—SHAKESPEARE. Ye compass sea and land to make one proselyte. —BIBLE.

8. *v.* be converted into, come *or* turn to *or* into, run into, fall into, pass into, slide *or* glide into, grow into, merge *or* blend into, melt into, open into, resolve itself into, settle into, come round to, assume the form *or* character of; become, get, wax, grow; mature, mellow, ripen into; melt, blend, merge, lapse, illapse [rare], glide, shift; undergo a change etc. 140.5.

9. *adj.* convertible, conversible [rare], resolvable into, transmutable, transformable, transitional, modifiable.

145. Reversion

1. *n.* reversion, revertal [rare], reverting, retroversion, reverse, reversal, return, returning etc. *v.*, revulsion; reconversion; atavism [Biol.], throwback; escheat [Law]; retrocession, retrogression etc. (regression) 283; relapse etc. 661; recoil etc. 277; inversion etc. 218; restoration etc. 660; alternation etc. (periodicity) 138.2.

2. *n.* turning point, turn, turn of the tide; calm before a storm; critical point etc. (crisis) 134.4.

3. *n.* reversioner, reversionist; pervert, turncoat etc. (apostate) 607.5, 6.

4. *v.* revert, retrovert, reverse, regress, return, come *or* go back; undo, unmake; turn the tide *or* scale; escheat [Law]; relapse etc. 661.3; invert etc. 218.4; recoil etc. 277.3; retreat, turn back etc. 283.5, 6.

5. *adj.* reverted, reversed etc. *adj.*

6. *adj.* reversionary, reversional; regressive, retrogressive, reactionary, revulsionary; retrorse; atavistic [Biol.].

7. *adv.* reversionally etc. *adj.*, on the rebound; against the grain, *à rebours* [F.].

146. Revolution

Sudden or Radical Change.—1. *n.* revolution, striking alteration, organic *or* total change, sweeping change, clean sweep; transilience *or* transiliency [rare]; revulsion; subversion, overthrow, overturn, upset, *bouleversement*

---

145. Till happy chance revert the cruel scene.— PRIOR. Backward, turn backward, O Time, in your flight, / Make me a child again just for tonight!—E. A. ALLEN.
146. Revolutions are not made; they come.— W. PHILLIPS. A revolutionary moment in the world's history is a time for revolutions.—

[F.]; breakup, breakdown; debacle, *débâcle* [F.]; counterrevolution; rebellion, uprising, mutiny etc. (revolt) 742.2.

2. *n.* revolutionism, Bolshevism; sansculottism, *sans-culottisme* [F.], *sansculotterie* [F.].

3. *n.* revolutionist etc. (insurgent) 742.3.

4. *v.* revolutionize, revolute [slang], revolution, render revolutionary, change radically *or* fundamentally, make a clean sweep, break with the past; rebel, insurrect etc. (revolt) 742.5; remodel etc. (regenerate) 144.7.

5. *adj.* revolutionary, revolutional; revulsive, revulsionary; catastrophic, cataclysmic *or* cataclysmal; transilient; radical, red; Bolshevist *or* Bolshevistic, Bolshevik; sans-culottic, sans-culottish; insurrectionary, mutinous, insurgent etc. (rebellious) 742.7.

147. Substitution
(See 148. Interchange)

Change of One Thing for Another.—
1. *n.* substitution, supplanting etc. *v.*, supplantation, replacement, supersession, supersedure, supersedure, commutation, subrogation [Law], surrogation [rare]; metonymy etc. (figure of speech) 521; transfer etc. 783.

2. *n.* substitute, substitution etc. *above,* sub [coll.], succedaneum, proxy, *locum tenens* [L.], warming pan [chiefly coll.], surrogate, alternate, alternative, alternator, supplanter, fill-in, filler-inner [slang], superseder, changeling, *quid pro quo* [L.], equivalent, equal, double, dub [slang, U.S.], dummy, secondary; substituent [Chem.]; ersatz; makeshift, *pis aller* [F.], temporary expedient, stopgap, shift, apology, jury mast; understudy, pinch hitter [coll.], stand-in [motion-picture cant]; ringer, ring-in [both slang]; ghost, ghost writer; scapegoat, goat [slang], fall guy [slang, U.S.]; consideration, exchange value, price, worth, purchase money; representative, deputy etc. 759.

3. *v.* substitute, put in the place of, change for, surrogate [rare], subrogate [Law], suffect [rare], ring in [coll.]; make way for, give place to; serve as a substitute, substitute for, sub for [coll.], supplant, succeed, supersede, replace, cut out [coll.], supply *or* take the place of, swap places with [coll.], step into *or* stand in the shoes of, fill one's shoes, fill in for, spell off [coll.], act for, double for, pinch-hit [coll.].

cover up for, front for, go to the front for, take the rap for, be the goat [all slang]; make a shift with, put up with; borrow of Peter to pay Paul; commute, redeem, compound for; dub in [motion-picture cant]; ghost, ghostwrite; exchange etc. (interchange) 148.3; transfer etc. 783.3.; represent etc. 759.4.

4. *adj.* substituted etc. *v.*, substitutional, **substitutionary, substitutive, alternative; subdititious, supersedable; vicarious, vicarial;** makeshift, make**shifty; temporary, provisional, tentative.**

5. *adv. etc.* instead, in the stead of, in place of, in lieu of, in the room of [obs. exc. dial.], as a substitute etc. *n.*, by proxy; in its stead *or* place, rather than; *faute de mieux* [F.].

148. Interchange
(See 147. Substitution; also 794. Barter)

Double or Mutual Change.—1. *n.* interchange, exchange, counterchange, commutation, permutation, intermutation, alternation; transposition, transposal; shuffle, shuffling; trading, swapping [coll.]; reciprocation, reciprocity, reciprocality; give-and-take, something for something, *quid pro quo* [L.], a Roland for an Oliver, measure for measure, tit for tat, an eye for an eye, an eye for an eye and a tooth for a tooth (Bible); trade, swap [coll.], dicker [chiefly coll., U.S.], switch; blind bargain *or* swap [coll.], pig in a poke *or* bag; cross fire, retort, battledore and shuttlecock; barter etc. 794; retaliation etc. 718; transference etc. 270; transfer etc. 783.

BEVERIDGE. An age of revolution and reformation.—JEFFERSON. The state of mind which creates revolutions.—ARISTOTLE. What country before ever existed a century and a half without a rebellion?—JEFFERSON.
147. Books . . . are a mighty bloodless substitute for life.—STEVENSON. A substitute shines brightly as a king / Until a king be by.—SHAKESPEARE. Outside show is a poor substitute for inner worth.—AESOP.
148. The constant interchange of those thousand little courtesies.—W. IRVING. Exchange is no robbery.—C. H. SPURGEON. Reciprocity exacts her dues.—HORACE.

2. *n.* interchangeableness etc. *adj.*, interchangeability, commutability, permutability.

3. *v.* interchange, exchange, change, counterchange, permute, commute, substitute, transpose, shuffle, switch, trade, swap [coll.], swap horses [coll.], change hands; trade sight unseen *or* unsight unseen; make a blind bargain *or* swap [all coll.]; reciprocate, bandy, give and take, give a Roland for an Oliver etc. *n.*, give as much as one takes, give as good as was sent, return the compliment, pay back, requite, return; play at puss in the corner, play at battledore and shuttlecock; take in another's washing; barter etc. 794.4; retaliate etc. 718.2; transfer etc. 783.3.

4. *adj.* interchangeable, exchangeable, changeable; transmutable, returnable, commutative, fungible [Tech.], substitutive, convertible, mutual, give-and-take, reciprocative, reciprocate [rare]; international, interstate, intertribal, interurban, interscholastic, intercollegiate, interdenominational, intercurrent; reciprocal etc. (correlative) 12.6, 7.

5. *adv.* interchangeably, reciprocally etc. *adj.*; in exchange, as an exchange; conversely, contrariwise; by turns, turn about, turn and turn about, back and forth, backward and forward, backwards and forwards, forward and back, to and fro; each in his *or* its turn, every one in his turn; *mutatis mutandis* [L.]; *vice versa* etc. 14.7.

149. Changeableness
(See 150. Stability; also 140. Change)

1. *n.* changeableness, changefulness etc. *adj.*, mutability, permutability, alterability, modifiability; inconstancy, instability; fluctuation, flux, fluxation [rare] vicissitude; versatility, variability, deviability; mobility, movability, plasticity; vacillation etc. (irresolution) 605; tergiversation etc. 607; capriciousness, fickleness etc. 608.2, 3; alternation etc. (oscillation) 314; transience etc. 111.

2. *n.* (comparisons) moon, Proteus, kaleidoscope, chameleon, quicksilver, shifting sands, rolling stone; weathercock, vane, weather vane, harlequin, Cynthia of the minute, April showers, wheel of fortune; tergiversator, turncoat etc. 607.5, 6.

3. *n.* restlessness etc. *adj.*, disquiet, disquietude, inquietude, unrest, perturbation, fidgets, fidgetiness, dysphoria [Psychol.]; agitation etc. 315.

4. *v.* be changeable etc. *adj.*, fluctuate, vacillate, dacker [Scot. and dial. Eng.], vary, waver, flounder, flicker, flitter [arch.], flit, flutter, quiver, quaver, shake, totter, stagger, tremble, wamble [dial.], wabble, waggle, wiggle, shift, shuffle, swing, sway; alternate, sway *or* shift to and fro, vibrate *or* oscillate between two extremes, blow hot and cold, play *or* play at fast and loose, say one thing and mean another, keep off and on, turn and turn about, ring the changes, have as many phases as the moon.

5. *adj.* changeable, mutable, permutable, alterable, alterative, metagenetic [Biol.], modifiable, eversible; versatile, variable, checkered, ever-changing, many-sided, kaleidoscopic, protean, proteiform; transitional, mobile, movable, plastic.

6. *adj.* inconstant, changeful, changeable, uncertain, unstaid, unsteady, unsteadfast, unreliable, unstable, unfixed, unsettled, unstable as water; vicissitudinous, vicissitudinary, vicissitous [local, U.S.]; fluctuating, alternating, vacillating, wavering, vibratory; restless, uneasy, unquiet, aflutter, fidgety; spasmodic, desultory, fitful; rambling, roving; irregular, unregular; unmethodical *or* immethodical; vagrant, wanton, wayward; volatile, mercurial; afloat, adrift; indecisive etc. (irresolute) 605.5; tergiversating etc. 607.10; capricious, fickle etc. 608.5, 6; erratic etc. (eccentric) 503.17; transient etc. 111.6.

7. *adv.* changeably, inconstantly etc. *adj.*; off and on, in-and-out; to and fro etc. (interchangeably) 148.5; seesaw etc. (alternately) 314.14.

The world's a scene of changes, and to be / Constant, in Nature were inconstancy.—COWLEY. *La donna è mobile* [Woman is fickle]. —PIAVE. *Varium et mutabile semper femina* [Woman is ever a fickle and changeable thing].—VERGIL. A rolling stone gathers no moss. It is a long lane that has no turning.

149. *Plus ça change, plus c'est la même chose* [The more it changes, the more it's the same thing].—A. KARR. There is nothing in this world constant but inconstancy.—SWIFT.

150. Stability
(See 149. Changeableness; also 141. Permanence)

1. *n.* stability, firmness, unchangeableness etc. *adj.*, constancy, establishment, stabilization, stabiliment [rare], stable equilibrium; immutability, immobility, immovability; fixture, fixity, fixidity [rare], fixation, soundness, solidity, stiffness, aplomb or *à plomb* [F.], equilibrium, balance, assurance; vitality, vigor; coherence; permanence etc. 141; inflexibility etc. (hardness) 323; obstinacy etc. 606; resolution etc. 604; quiescence etc. 265; resolution etc. 604.

2. *n.* (comparisons) rock, pillar, tower, foundation; leopard's spots, Ethiopian's skin; law of the Medes and Persians.

3. *v.* be or become stable etc. *adj.*, stabilize [Radio], stand ~, keep *or* remain firm, stick fast, stay put [chiefly coll.], stand pat [coll.], keep *or* hold one's ground *or* footing, weather the storm; build one's house on a rock; establish oneself, settle down etc. 184.14.

4. *v.* stabilize, stabilitate, stabilate, stabilify [rare]; establish, define, fix, set, settle, ground, confirm, make firm etc. *adj.*, stereotype; retain, stet [Print.], keep, keep hold; make good *or* sure; set on its feet, set on its legs [coll.]; float [Com.]; make fast, fasten etc. (attach) 43.6; make permanent etc. (see permanent etc. 141.6); perpetuate etc. (sustain) 143.3.

5. *adj.* stable, stabilized, established, fixed, pat, solid, firm, firm as Gibraltar *or* as a rock, firmly established *or* seated, deep-seated, fast, immovable, irremovable, not to be moved, riveted, rooted, deep-rooted, stated, settled, staple, stereotyped; steady, steadfast; well-grounded, well-founded, on a rock; tethered, moored, anchored, at anchor; confirmed, inveterate; sound, valid, reliable, incontrovertible, indeclinable; fiducial; straight [as in *ten cents straight*]; slang, U.S.]; vested; permanent etc. 141.6; stationary etc. 265.7; inert, etc. 172.3; quiescent etc. 265.7; steadfast in purpose etc. (resolute) 604.7, (persevering) 604a.3, (obstinate) 606.6; uniform etc. 16.5.

6. *adj.* stuck fast, fixed, fast, immovable etc. *above* 150.5; stuck, transfixed, aground, grounded, stranded, high and dry.

7. *adj.* unchangeable, not to be changed, immutable, incommutable, unalterable, unalterative, unmodifiable, standpat [coll.]; invariable, unyielding, undeviating; indefeasible, irretrievable, intransmutable, irresoluble, irrevocable, irreversible, reverseless, inextinguishable, irreducible; indissoluble, indissolvable; indestructible, undying, imperishable, indelible, ineradicable, indeciduous; unsusceptible, insusceptible of change; constant etc. (permanent) 141.6; perennial etc. (durable) 110.9; inflexible etc. (hard) 323.5.

8. *phr.* let it stand, stet [Print.].

151. Eventuality
(See 152. Imminence)

1. *n.* eventuality, eventuation; event, occurrence, go [coll.], go-off [coll.], come-off [coll.], incident, episode, advent, passage [obs.], affair, job [coll.], transaction, proceeding, doing, fact, phenomenon, particular, occasion; experience, adventure; hap, happening, happenstance [coll., U.S.], happen-so [dial. and slang]; contingence [rare], contingency; accident, casualty; matter, concern, business; supervention; emergency, pass etc. (crisis) 134.4; termination etc. (end) 67; consequence, result etc. (effect) 154.

2. *n.* affairs, matters, concerns, circumstances, situation, proceedings, doings, goings on [chiefly coll.], things *or* affairs in general; the world, life, the times; state of affairs, order of the day; course ~, tide ~, stream *or* run of things *or* events, march of events; ups and downs of life, vicissitudes of fortune, chapter of accidents; memorabilia.

3. *v.* eventuate, happen, hap, occur, take place *or* effect, transpire [considered erroneous], come, come off, come about *or* round, come to pass, pass, go off, fall,

---

150. Bright star, would I were stedfast as thou art.—KEATS. With whom is no variableness, neither shadow of turning.—BIBLE. *Caelum non animum mutant qui trans mare currunt* [They who cross the sea change their skies but not their natures].—HORACE. This rock shall fly / From its firm base as soon as I.—SCOTT.

151. One event happeneth to them all.—BIBLE. There is a tide in the affairs of men / Which taken at the flood leads on to fortune.—SHAKESPEARE. Man is not the creature of circum-

151.3 – 153.4

befall, fall in [rare], chance, bechance, betide; arise, start, come into existence, come forth, come *or* draw on, arrive, present itself, show up [coll.], turn up, crop up, spring up, cast up; hold, take its course, run, be on foot; fall *or* turn out, issue, ensue, result, become of; turn out to be, prove; supervene, survene [obs.].

4. *v.* experience, meet with, meet up with [slang], encounter, undergo, suffer, go *or* pass through; fall to the lot of, be one's lot *or* fortune; feel etc. 821.3.

5. *adj.* happening etc. *v.,* going on, doing, current, prevalent, prevailing, in the wind, afloat, on foot, on the carpet *or* tapis; at issue, in question; incidental.

6. *adj.* eventful, stirring, bustling, full of incident; momentous, signal etc. (important) 642.10.

7. *adj.* eventual, coming, final, last, ultimate; contingent.

8. *adv. etc.* eventually, ultimately, finally; in the event of, in case; in the course of things, in the natural *or* ordinary course of things, as things *or* times go, as the world goes *or* wags, as the tree falls, as the cat jumps [coll.], as things turn out, as it may turn out *or* happen in the long run; in the fullness of time etc. (in future) 121.9.

152. Imminence
(See 151. Eventuality)

1. *n.* imminence, imminency, impendence *or* impendency; fate, foredoom etc. (destiny) 601.3; prospect etc. (expectation) 507.

2. *v.* be imminent etc. *adj.,* impend, hang *or* lie over, hang over one's head, hover, threaten, lower *or* lour, menace, loom, await, come *or* draw on, draw near, approach, stare one in the face, be in store for.

3. *adj.* imminent, impending, impendent, overhanging, hanging over one's head, threatening, lowering, menacing, looming, looming in the distance *or* future, looming on the horizon, brewing, preparing, coming, forthcoming, to come,

about to be, about *or* going to happen, near, close, immediate, instant, at hand, near-at-hand, close at hand, in store, in reserve, in the wind, in the womb of time *or* futurity, on the knees *or* lap of the gods, on the cards [coll.]; that will be, that is to be; destined etc. 601.13; in prospect etc. (expected) 507.8; approaching etc. 286.3; future etc. 121.7.

153. Cause
(See 154. Effect)

Constant Antecedent.—1. *n.* cause, origin, source, derivation, genesis, birth, incubation, incunabula [*pl.*] (*sing.* incunabulum), inception, commencement, rise, beginning, prime, principle, element, base; prime mover, *primum mobile* [L.], primordium [rare], *vera causa* [L.], ultimate cause, primary cause, causing cause, *causa causans* [L.], Great First Cause.

author, agent, producer, generator, creator; determinant, determining condition *or* agent, factor, occasion; remote cause; proximate cause; final cause, last straw, last straw that breaks the camel's back, match in the powder barrel; influence, impulse, impulsion, provocation; moment [of force]; parameter [Math.]; variable [Math.]; causative [Gram.]; leaven; reason, ground etc. (motive) 615.1; inducement, provocation etc. (motivation) 615.2; descent etc. (ancestry) 166.

2. *n.* spring, fountain, font, fount, *fons et origo* [L.], fountainhead, springhead, headspring, mainspring, wellspring [arch.], wellhead, well, reservoir.

3. *n.* rudiment, *Anlage* [G.] *or* anlage (*pl. Anlagen,* anlages); egg, germ, nucleus, seed, semen, sperm, milt, roe, spat, spawn; embryo, fetus; bud, gemma, gemmule, gemmula; stem, stock, stirps, trunk; root, radix, radical, radicle, radication [rare]; tap, taproot; etymon [rare exc. Gram.]; groundwork etc. (foundation) 215.3; base etc. 211.

4. *n.* nest, cradle, nursery, nidus, womb, venter [Law], birthplace, breeding place, hotbed, incubator.

---

stances. Circumstances are the creatures of men.—DISRAELI. The blows of circumstance.—TENNYSON.
152. The impending woe sat heavily on his breast.—POPE. In danger imminent.—SPENSER. Destruction sure o'er all your heads impends.—POPE.

153. Things do not happen in this world—they are brought about.—W. HAYS. One always retains the traces of one's origin.—RENAN. *Felix qui potuit rerum cognoscere causas* [Happy is he who has been able to know the reasons for things].—VERGIL. The causes of

5. *n.* causation, causality, causativeness etc. *adj.,* causativity, origination, invention; causativism; production etc. 161.

6. *v.* cause, be the cause etc. *n.,* lie at the root of; causate, originate, invent, give origin *or* rise to, occasion, give occasion to, give birth to, sow the seeds of, produce, make, develop, bring about, bring in its train, bring to pass, set up, set afloat, set on foot; found, broach, institute, install, establish, lay the foundation of; involve, entail; create, generate etc. 161.8–10.

7. *v.* induce, procure, get, obtain, bring, bring on, contrive, effect, draw down, open the door to; superinduce, evoke, provoke, elicit, incite, kindle, suscitate [rare]; work, operate; inspire, persuade etc. (motivate) 615.7–9.

8. *v.* contribute, advance, forward, influence, subserve, redound to, conduce to, lead to; have a hand in, have a finger in the pie [coll.]; determine, decide, turn the scale, have the deciding vote, have the final word; have a common origin.

9. *adj.* causal, causative; etiological, original, primary, primitive, primordial, primeval, aboriginal; protogenic, protogenal; institutive, constitutive; radical, basic, basal, elementary, fundamental; in embryo, embryonic, embryotic, *in ovo* [L.]; germinal, seminal; at the bottom of; connate, with a common origin; originative, formative, creative etc. (productional) 161.11.

10. *adv. etc.* causally etc. *adj.,* behind the scenes; because etc. 155.8.

154. Effect
(See 153. Cause)

Constant Sequent.—**1.** *n.* effect, consequence, consequent; eventuation; result, resultant, resultancy [rare]; upshot, issue, outcome, come-out [slang], outgrowth, fruit, offshoot, offspring, development; derivative, derivation; aftereffect, aftercome [Scot.], aftergrowth, aftercrop, afterclap, aftermath; final issue, *finale* [It.], end, consummation, culmination, conclusion, denouement, catastrophe, pay-off [slang, U.S.]; impression, impress; product etc. 161.6; eventuality etc. 151; sequel etc. 65.

2. *v.* effect, effectuate etc. (complete) 729.2.

3. *v.* be the effect of etc. *n.,* be due to etc. *adj.,* originate in *or* from, derive its origin from, result from, follow *or* accrue from, rise *or* arise from, take its rise from, come from, come out of, come of, spring from, proceed from, grow from, bud from, sprout from, germinate from, issue from, ensue from, flow from, emanate from; depend on, depend *or* hang upon, hinge *or* turn on *or* upon.

4. *v.* take the consequences, reap where one has sown etc. (suffer the penalty) 972.12.

5. *adj.* resulting from etc. *v.,* owing to, due to, caused by, at the bottom of, dependent upon; derived *or* evolved from, derivational, derivative; attributable to etc. 155.4.

6. *adj.* resultant, resultative; consequent, consequential, sequential; eventual, secondary, indirect, contingent.

7. *adv. etc.* consequently etc. *adj.,* as a consequence, in consequence, of consequence [coll.], by consequence [arch.], it follows that, as a natural result, inevitably, naturally, necessarily, of necessity, of course, as a matter of course; therefore etc. (hence) 155.5; accordingly etc. 8.7.

155. Attribution

Assignment of Cause.—**1.** *n.* attribution, assignment, assigning etc. *v.,* assignation; ascription, imputation, arrogation; accounting for, reference to, derivation from etc. *v.;* etiology; palaetiology; theory, hypothesis, assumption; rationale, rational; explanation etc. (interpretation) 522; reason etc. (motive) 615.

2. *n.* filiation, affiliation; paternity etc. (ancestry) 166.

---

events are ever more interesting than the events themselves.—CICERO.   To know truly is to know by causes.—BACON.   There is occasions and causes why and wherefore in all things.—SHAKESPEARE.   Everything is the cause of itself.—EMERSON.
154. Cause and effect are two sides of one fact.—EMERSON.   Whatsoever a man soweth, that shall he also reap.—BIBLE.   Behind the coarse effect is a fine cause.—EMERSON.   Logical consequences are the scare-crows of fools and the beacons of wise men.—HUXLEY.   Thereby hangs a tale.—SHAKESPEARE.   *Cela va sans dire* [That goes without saying].   A tree is known by its fruit.
155. The 'why' is plain as way to parish church.—SHAKESPEARE.   Every why hath a wherefore.—SHAKESPEARE.   *Cherchez la femme* [Look for the woman].

3. *v.* attribute, assign, ascribe, impute, attribute etc. to, lay to, put *or* set down to, refer to, point to, bring home to; account for, assign as the cause of, lay at the door of, father upon; fix the burden of, fix *or* attribute the responsibility for, place the blame *or* responsibility for; place *or* put the blame on, blame, blame for, blame on *or* upon [coll.], saddle on *or* upon, charge on, ground on; point out the reason, find *or* tell the cause of etc. (*see* cause etc. 153.1), tell how it comes, put the saddle on the right horse, find the real culprit; trace to, trace the origin *or* derivation of, derive from; filiate, affiliate, fix the paternity; theorize, hypothesize, assume.

4. *adj.* attributable, assignable, ascribable, imputable, traceable, referable *or* referrible, accountable, explicable; derivable from, derivational, derivative; affiliable, affiliate; putative, putationary; ecbatic [Gram.].

5. *adv.* hence, therefore, wherefore, whence, thence, then, for that *or* this reason, for which reason, by reason of . . . , from *or* for that cause, because of that, on that account, *propter hoc* [L.], on that ground, to that end; ergo, argal [arch.]; thus, thusly [coll.], thuswise; consequently etc. 154.4; accordingly etc. 8.7; logically etc. 476.18–20.

6. *adv.* why, why ever *or* whyever [coll.], whyfor [dial. and arch.], for why [now dial.], forwhy [arch.], wherefore, for which, on what account, on account of what *or* which, for what *or* whatever reason, ~ cause *or* purpose, how; why?, how comes it? etc. (inquiry) 461.28.

7. *adv.* somehow, somehow or other, somehow or another, in one way or another, by some means, in some way, in some such way, somegate [Scot. and North. Eng.].

8. *conj. etc.* since, sith [arch.], as, whereas, inasmuch as, in as much as, for as much as, forasmuch as, in so far as, in view of the fact that, seeing that, seeing as how [dial. and coll.], being as how [dial.], *ex concessio* [L.], considering, in consideration of, taking into account that, by *or* for the cause that, because, because of, for because [rare], for, in that, for the reason that, by reason of, on account of, on the score of, for the sake of, owing to, thanks to; accordingly etc. 8.7.

156. Chance

Absence of Assignable Cause.—**1.** *n.* chance; fortune, luck, joss [Pidgin Eng. and slang], lot; chance *or* unforeseen occurrence, fortuitous *or* casual event, casual [obs.], fortuity, accident, fluke [slang], scratch hit *or* shot [coll.], casualty, adventure, hazard; contingence [rare], contingency; hap, happening, happenstance [coll., U.S.], happen-so [dial. and slang]; Chance, Frank Chance, Fortune, Fortuna, Luck, Lady Luck; break [coll.], the breaks [slang, U.S.]; haphazard, chance-medley, random, random shot, potluck; wheel of fortune *or* chance, Fortune's wheel.

vicissitudes of fortune, ups and downs of life, ins and outs, chapter of accidents; fate etc. (destiny) 601.3; matter of chance, hazard of the die etc. (gamble) 621.2; show [coll.], opportunity etc. (occasion) 134.2; stroke of luck, hit etc. (success) 731; good luck etc. (prosperity) 734; bad luck etc. (adversity) 735; **lucky piece** etc. (talisman) 993.2; absence of design etc. 621.

2. *n.* even chance, equal chance, even break [chiefly coll.], even *or* square odds, six-two-and-even [cant]; half a chance, half a show [coll.]; toss, tossup.

3. *n.* good chance, favorable chance *or* prospect, sporting chance, 1-2-3 chance [slang], good opportunity, good *or* some show [coll.], good possibility, fair shake [slang, U.S.], well-grounded hope, sure bet, good thing [coll.], good thing on ice [slang, U.S.], likely card [slang]; best chance, best bet, chief probability, main chance; inside track [coll.]; likelihood etc. (probability) 472; possibility etc. 470; assurance etc. (certainty) 474.

4. *n.* small chance, little chance, poor chance *or* prospect, poor *or* little opportunity, poor lookout [coll.], poor possibility, poor *or* small show [coll.], scarcely any chance, not half a chance, not half a show [coll.], fighting chance [coll.], Chinaman's *or* dog's chance [slang], ghost of a chance, off *or* outside chance [coll.], poor bet, off bet [coll.]; long

---

156. To a sensible man there is no such thing as chance.—Tieck.   Chance is a word void of sense; nothing can exist without a cause.—Voltaire.   For things said false and never meant, / Do oft prove true by accident.—Butler.   Accidents will occur in the best regu-

odds, long shot [slang], hundred-to-one shot [slang]; unlikelihood etc. (improbability) 473.

5. *n.* no chance, no chance whatever, not a Chinaman's *or* dog's chance [slang], not the ghost of a chance, not a fighting chance [coll.], no show [coll.]; impossibility etc. 471.

6. *n.* fortuitousness, fortuity; adventitiousness, flukiness [slang]; accidentalness, accidentalism, accidentality; indeterminateness, indetermination, indeterminacy.

7. *v.* chance, bechance, come by chance; hap, happen; come, turn up, befall; fall to one's lot, be one's fate etc. 601.3; take a chance, risk etc. 621.17.

8. *v.* chance upon, stumble on, light upon, blunder upon, hit upon, hit.

9. *v.* have a chance *or* an opportunity, stand a chance, have *or* stand a show [coll.] etc. *n.*, admit of; have a chance at, have a fling *or* shot at [slang]; have ~, stand *or* run a good chance etc. *n.*, bid or stand fair to; be possible etc. 470.3; be probable etc. 472.2.

10. *v.* have a small chance, have *or* stand a poor show [coll.] etc. *n.*

11. *v.* have no chance *or* opportunity, have no chance whatever, not have a chance, not have a Chinaman's chance [slang] etc. *n.*; not have *or* stand a snowball's chance in hell [slang], not stand a show [coll.], not be in it [slang], be out of it [slang], be out of the running; be impossible etc. 471.4.

12. *adj.* chance, chanceable [obs.], chanceful [arch.], chancy [coll.]; fortuitous, casual, accidental, fluky [slang], scratch [coll.], adventive, adventitious, incidental, contingent, causeless, uncaused; undetermined, indeterminate; unintentional etc. 621.19–21; haphazard, random etc. (disorderly) 59.8.

13. *adv.* by chance *or* accident, fortuitously, accidentally, casually etc. *adj.*; by a piece of luck, by a fluke [slang], by good fortune; as luck would have it, as it may happen, as it may be, as the case may be, as it may chance, as it may turn up *or* out; at haphazard, at random etc. (irregularly) 59.12; perchance etc. (possibly) 470.7; unintentionally etc. 621.22.

157. Potence
(See 158. Impotence; also 159. Strength)

1. *n.* potence, potency, potentiality, power, powerfulness etc. *adj.*, might, force, vigor, puissance [poetic], dint; powder, soup, steam [all slang]; cogence *or* cogency, validity [rare]; horsepower; force of inertia, vis inertiae; dead force, *vis mortua* [L.]; living force, *vis viva* [L.]; force of life, *vis vitae* [L.]; *vis vitalis* [L.], vital principle, jiva [Hindu]; full force, full blast; potential energy, dynamic energy etc. (energy) 171; strength etc. (degree of power) 159; prepotency, predominance etc. (superiority) 33; sway, control etc. (authority) 737.

2. *n.* ability, ableness, enablement, capability, capableness, capacity, efficiency, efficacy, sufficiency, adequacy, competence; the stuff, the goods, what it takes [all slang]; susceptibility; proficiency, qualification, faculty, endowment etc. (skill) 698.

3. *n.* pulling power, pull, draw, drag, attraction; attraction of gravitation, gravitation, gravity; magnetic *or* electrical attraction, magnetic force, magnetism, magnetization, magnetification [rare]; magnetic field, magnetic curves, magnetic figures, magnetic flux, magnetic dip *or* inclination, magnetic variation *or* declination, magnetic viscosity, magnetic induction; allurement etc. 617.

4. *n.* force of friction, coefficient of friction, starting friction, rolling friction, internal friction, force of viscosity, magnetic friction.

5. *n.* omnipotence *or* omnipotency, almightiness; unlimited power, *carte blanche* [F.].

6. *v.* be able etc. *adj.*, lie *or* be in one's power, can; cut her, cut the mustard, make the grade [all slang].

---

lated families.—DICKENS. Therefore hap good, or hap ill, I will walk on still.—N. BRETON. The happy combination of fortuitous circumstances.—SCOTT. It is more easy to get a favour from Fortune than to keep it.—PUBLILIUS. One eye on heaven and one on the main chance.—THACKERAY. 'Tis more by fortune, lady, than by merit.—SHAKESPEARE. Every dog has his day.

157. They can because they think they can.—VERGIL. No one knows what he can do till he tries.—PUBLILIUS. Man's capacities have never been measured.—THOREAU. Power when wielded by abnormal energy is the most serious of facts.—H. ADAMS. Give me a lever long enough, and a fulcrum strong enough,

7. *v.* empower, give *or* confer power, enable, invest, endue, endow, arm; intensify, give increasing power *or* energy, key up; step up, hop up, jazz up [all slang]; commission etc. 755.4; permit etc. 760.3, 4; strengthen etc. 159.8.

8. *adj.* potent, potential [rare]; powerful, mighty, mightful [arch.], forcible, forceful, dynamic, vigorous, hefty [coll.], puissant; high-powered, high-geared, high-pressure; cogent, valid [rare]; multipotent [rare]; plenipotent [rare], plenipotentiary; omnipotent, almighty; armipotent; strong etc. 159.10–13; energetic etc. 171.9; prepotent, predominant etc. (influential) 175.10; productive etc. 168.7.

9. *adj.* able, able to cut the mustard [slang], capable, equal *or* up to, competent, adequate, effective, effectual, efficient, efficacious; qualified, proficient etc. (skillful) 698.11–15.

10. *adv.* etc. potently etc. *adj.*; by virtue of, by dint of; to the best of one's power, so far as one can, as best one can, *à toute force* [F.].

158. Impotence
(See 157. Potence; also 160. Weakness)

1. *n.* impotence, impotency, powerlessness, unableness etc. *adj.*; inability, disability, disablement, impuissance [rare], caducity, imbecility, incapacity, incapability, incompetence *or* incompetency, inadequacy, insufficiency; inefficience *or* inefficiency, inefficacy, inefficacity [rare], ineffectualness, ineffectuality; ineptitude, inaptitude; unfitness, disqualification, invalidity; indocility; weakness etc. 160; failure etc. 732; unproductiveness etc. 169; uninfluentiality etc. 175a; inutility etc. 645.

2. *n.* helplessness etc. *adj.*; prostration, paralysis, palsy, apoplexy, syncope, sideration [obs.], vincibility, deliquium, collapse, exhaustion, softening of the brain, senility, superannuation, atony, decrepitude, imbecility, neurasthenia, invertebracy, inanition, emasculation, orchotomy.

3. *n.* impotent, incapable, incompetent; *telum imbelle* [L.], *brutum fulmen* [L.], blank cartridge, dud [slang], flash in the pan, *vox et praeterea nihil* [L.], dead letter, bit of waste paper, dummy, Quaker gun; eunuch; cripple etc. 655.20; idiot etc. 501.1; misfit etc. 24.4; weakling etc. 160.4.

4. *v.* be impotent etc. *adj.*, not have a leg to stand on; cannot, cannot do; can't come it *or* cut her, be unable to cut the mustard, not make the grade [all slang]; not be effective, not take [slang]; attempt the impossible, *vouloir rompre l'anguille au genou* [F.] etc. 471.5.

5. *v.* collapse, cave in, break down; faint, swoon, fall into a swoon, drop; end in smoke etc. (fail) 732.5.

6. *v.* render powerless etc. *adj.*, depotentiate [rare], deprive of power, disable, disenable, disarm, incapacitate, disqualify, unfit, invalidate, disinvigorate [rare], unsinew, undermine, deaden, cramp, double up, prostrate, paralyze, muzzle, silence, cripple, becripple, maim, lame, hamstring, hock, hough, handcuff.

tie the hands, hog-tie [coll., U.S.], draw the teeth of, clip the wings of, put *hors de combat* [F.], spike the guns, spike, put a spoke in one's wheels, take the wind out of one's sails, scotch the snake, break the neck *or* back of, unhinge, put out of gear; throttle, strangle, get a strangle hold on, garrote *or* garrotte; kibosh, put the kibosh on [both slang]; ratten [trade-union cant]; weaken etc. 160.8; render useless etc. 645.7; impair etc. 659.8; checkmate etc. 731.10.

7. *v.* unman, unnerve, unbrace, enervate, devitalize; emasculate, evirate [rare]; castrate, geld etc. 38.7; effeminize etc. 160a.4; dishearten etc. 837.8.

8. *adj.* impotent, powerless, forceless, mightless [arch.], unable, incapable, incompetent; inefficient, ineffective, inefficacious; inept, inapt, unapt; unfit, unfitted; unendowed, unqualified, disqualified; disabled, crippled etc. *v.*; disjointed, out of joint, out of gear, unhinged; waterlogged; rudderless; on one's beam-ends, on one's back, prostrate; spent, exhaust-

---

and single-handed I can move the world.—ARCHIMEDES.   *Causa latet vis est notissima* [While the cause is hidden the force is very well known].—OVID.   The powerful grace that lies / In herbs, plants, stones, and their true qualities.—SHAKESPEARE.
158. If wild and weak desires . . . rob the soul of power.—A. NOYES.   The raging impotence of woe.—HOMER.   O most lame and impotent conclusion!—SHAKESPEARE. Young men have a passion for regarding their elders as senile.—H. ADAMS.

ed; done for, done up, done up brown, done brown, done, dead-beat [all coll.]; *hors de combat* [F.], out of the battle, laid on the shelf; decrepit, senile, doddering [coll.], superannuated; weak etc. 160.10–15; harmless etc. 648.13; uninfluential etc. 175a.2; unproductive etc. 169.4; infirm etc. 655.23; insufficient etc. 640.8.

9. *adj.* helpless, defenseless, fenceless [arch.], aidless; indefensible, untenable, without a leg to stand on; pregnable, vulnerable, vincible, conquerable, surmountable; unfriended, friendless, fatherless, guideless; paralytic, paralyzed, palsied, atonic, imbecile; weaponless, unguarded etc. (unprotected) 665.9; graveled [coll.] etc. (in difficulty) 704.11; unaided etc. 160.15.

10. *adj.* unmanned, unnerved, enervated, devitalized, demoralized; nerveless, sinewless, marrowless, pithless, lustless; emasculate, evirate [obs.]; disheartened etc. 837.9.

11. *adj.* nugatory, nugacious; vain, futile, unavailing, bootless, sleeveless [now dial.], empty, inane; fatuous, fatuitous, of no force, inoperative, ineffectual, ineffective, invalid; effete, barren, sterile; invertebrate, invertebral; good-for-nothing, of no use etc. (useless) 645.8; inadequate etc. (insufficient) 640.8; of little consequence, trivial, worthless etc. (unimportant) 643.10–12; unsubstantial etc. 4.5.

158a. Electricity

1. *n.* electricity, electric current, stream of electricity, current, fluid, electric fluid, juice [slang]; conduction current, convection current, displacement current; spark, electric spark; negative electricity, positive electricity; dynamical ∼, voltaic *or* current electricity, voltaism; galvanism, galvanization.

magnetoelectricity, electromagnetism; electromotion; electromotivity, magnetomotivity; electromotive force, electric horsepower; electric field, electrostatic field; electric radiation, electric *or* electromagnetic wave, electric pulse; electric attraction, electric repulsion; electric resistance; magnetism etc. 157.3; telegraphy, telephony, radiophony etc. 532a.1; electric light etc. (luminary) 423.3; illuminant etc. 420.15; fuel etc. 388.

2. *n.* electrification, electricization, electrization.

3. *n.* (science of electricity) electrics, electromechanics, electrotechnics, electrotechnology, electrometry; electrophysiology, electrochemistry, electrobiology, electrobioscopy, electroballistics, electrometallurgy, electropathy, electrotherapeutics, electrotherapy, electrothermics, electrothermancy, magnetology.

4. *n.* circuit, path; complete circuit, loop [cant], closed circuit, live circuit, live wire *or* rail; open *or* broken circuit, break, dead circuit; branch *or* lateral circuit, leg [cant]; multiple circuit *or* connection, multiple series, series multiple *or* parallel; multiplex circuit, mux [cant]; circuital field, vector field.

5. *n.* (electric and magnetic units) amperage, ohmage, voltage, wattage; ampere, amp [cant], coulomb, farad, henry, joule, erg, ohm, volt, watt, kilowatt; megampere, megacoulomb, megafarad, megajoule, megohm, megavolt, megawatt; electron, proton; electron volt, equivalent volt; volt-coulomb; kilocycles, kilos [cant]; megacycles, megs [cant]; ampere turn, ampere-foot, ampere-hour, ampere-minute, ampere-second, kilowatt-hour, watt-hour, ohm-mile.

unit magnetic flux, maxwell, unit flux density, unit intensity of magnetization, gauss, unit magnetic moment, unit magnetic pole, unit magnetic tube of force, unit tube of electric force, unit magnetomotive force, magnetic potential, unit permeability, unit reluctance, oersted, unit reluctivity, unit susceptibility, unit capacity, unit current, unit electromotive force, unit energy, unit power, unit quantity *or* charge, unit capacity, unit inductance, unit resistance, unit dielectric constant, unit difference of potential.

6. *n.* (instruments) electric *or* electricity meter, electrometer, dynometer, electrodynamometer, galvanometer, magnetometer, rheometer, variometer, voltameter, voltammeter, voltmeter, ammeter, amperemeter, wattmeter, watt-hour meter, ohmmeter, ohm-ammeter, megohmmeter, coulomb meter, coulometer, elec-

---

158a. It was Watt who told King George III that he dealt in an article of which kings were said to be fond—Power.—EMERSON. A machine that is like the tools of the Titans put in your hands.—C. FERGUSON. Electricity—greatest servant of man, itself unknown.—C. W. ELIOT.

trostatic voltmeter, multicellular voltmeter; electroscope, galvanoscope, magnetoscope; circuit breaker, air circuit breaker, oil circuit breaker, multiple breaker, reverse circuit breaker, deion circuit breaker; transformer, pot [cant], multiple transformer; step-down transformer, step-up transformer [both cant]; rotary, rotary converter; resistor, choking coil, choker [cant]; resistance box, stove [cant].

photoelectric cell, electric eye; electric clock, electric drill, electric heater, electric furnace, electric organ, electric elevator, electric iron, electric shovel, electric hammer, electric lock, electric refrigerator, electric thermometer, electric pen, electric resonator, electric switch, electropneumatic switch, electropneumatic controller, electric railway, electrophone, electromagnet, electrophorus, electrolyte, electrolytic cell, electrolytic interrupter, electrolytic rectifier.

battery, bat [slang], storage battery, dry cell; voltaic pile, galvanic pile, Volta's pile, electric column; armature, arm [cant]; rotary gap, grinder [cant]; plug, floor plug, pocket [cant]; plugging box, pig [cant]; rheostat, rheo [cant]; safety belt, harness [cant]; climbing irons, spurs [cant], gaffs [cant]; telephone, telegraph, radio etc. 532a.5.

7. *n.* electric motor, electromotor; dynamo, dynamotor; generator, electric generator, motor generator; electric locomotive, trolley car, electromobile; series motor; magnetoelectric machine, magneto, mag [slang].

8. *n.* electric cable *or* wire, conductor, juice string [slang]; telephone wire, buzz wire [slang]; lead, high line [cant]; live wire, hot stuff [slang]; connecting cable *or* wire, jumper.

9. *n.* cable pole, telephone *or* telegraph pole, stick [cant], mast [cant]; dummy pole, dead man *or* deadman [cant]; crossbar, crossarm, mast arm [cant].

10. *n.* electrician, electrifier, electricizer, electrizer, electragist, electrotechnician, circuitman; juicer, juice hand, sparks [all slang]; maintenance man, trouble man, trouble shooter [coll.]; lineman, rigger, pole hiker [cant], groundman, grunt *or* grunter [slang]; radio electrician, radiotrician; electrical engineer; galvanist; electrician *or* linemen crew, juice gang [slang].

11. *v.* electrify, electricize, electrize; electrolyze; magnetize, electromagnetize; galvanize; energize; shock; generate, oscillate [cant]; increase *or* decrease in potential, step up *or* down [cant]; increase the ratio of inductance, stiffen [cant]; apply full voltage, full up [cant]; establish a circuit, plug in, loop in [cant]; switch *or* turn on, turn on the juice [slang], hit it [cant]; switch *or* turn off, turn off *or* pull the juice [slang], kill it [cant]; turn on the light etc. (light) 420.21; turn off the light etc. (extinguish) 421.6.

12. *adj.* electric(al), electriferous, electrifying; electroscopic, electrometric(al), electrostatic(al), electrodynamic, electrokinetic, electroreceptive; electropositive, electronegative, positive, negative; electromagnetic, magnetic, magnetoelectric(al); galvanic, galvanometric, galvanoscopic; electromotive, magnetomotive; dynamoelectric(al); dynamic(al), static, potential; voltametric, voltaic; ohmic; multiplex, diplex, duplex.

159. Strength
(See 160. Weakness; also 157. Potence)

Degree of Power.—1. *n.* strength, strongness [rare], vigor, force, puissance [poetic], might, vitality; physical strength *or* force, main *or* brute force; robustness, stoutness, lustiness, lustihood; muscular strength, muscle, beef [coll.], brawn, brawniness, sinew *or* sinews, thews, thews and sinews, strong arm, robust *or* rugged physique; stamina, guts [slang], nerve, grit, pith, pithiness; spring, elasticity, tension, tone, tonicity; solidity, firmness; power etc. (potence) 157; energy etc. 171; resolution etc. 604.

2. *n.* strengthening etc. *v.*, invigoration, reinvigoration, enlivenment, exhilaration, stimulation, vivification, revivification, refreshment, refocillation [rare].

3. *n.* (science of forces) dynamics, statics.

4. *n.* (comparisons) adamant, steel, iron, oak, heart of oak, iron grip, bone.

5. *n.* feats of strength, athletics, athleticism, gymnastics, acrobatics, acrobat-

---

159. The vigor of his arm was never vain.—DRYDEN.   Inflexible in faith, invincible in arms.—BEATTIE.   God, give me hills to climb / And strength for climbing!—GUITERMAN. *Deos fortioribus adesse* [The gods assist the stronger].—TACITUS.   It is excellent / To

ism, agonistics, calisthenics, palaestra, palaestrics [rare].

6. *n.* strong man, tower of strength; roarer, snorter, muscle man, man mountain, big bruiser, big beef [all slang]; athlete, gymnast, acrobat; wrestler, palaestrian; pancratist, pancratiast; giant, giant refreshed; Goliath, Atlas, Hercules, Antaeus, Samson, Cyclops, Briareus, colossus, Polyphemus, Titan, Brobdingnagian, Tarzan.

7. *v.* be strong etc. *adj.*, have the goods *or* stuff [slang]; not weaken, not let it get one down [slang], take it [slang, U.S.].

8. *v.* strengthen, render strong etc. *adj.*, give strength etc. *n.*, invigorate, vigor [obs. exc. dial.], potentiate [rare], brace, fortify, buttress, sustain, harden, caseharden, steel, gird, gird *or* brace up one's loins; brace up, screw up, wind up, set up, set on one's legs [coll.]; vivify, vivificate [rare], quicken, animate, exhilarate, stimulate; restrengthen, reinforce, reinvigorate, recruit, revive etc. (refresh) 689.2; energize etc. 171.7; empower etc. 157.7.

9. *v.* exert strength etc. *n.*, move by muscular force, muscle [dial.], put plenty of beef into [slang]; use force on, strongarm [coll.].

10. *adj.* strong, strengthy [Scot. and North. Eng.], mighty, vigorous, forcible, puissant, stout, hefty [coll.], rugged, hale, sturdy, stubborn [obs.], husky [coll.], doughty [arch. or joc.], hardy, hard, hard as nails, adamantine, lusty, strapping, stalwart; robust, robustious [joc.]; able-bodied, well-knit, broad-shouldered; muscular, beefy [coll.], brawny; wiry, sinewy, sinewous [rare]; strong as a lion, ~ ox *or* horse, strong as brandy, strong as strong; Herculean, Briarean, Brobdingnagian, Cyclopean, Atlantean, titanic; able, powerful etc. (potent) 157.8, 9.

11. *adj.* athletic, gymnastic, acrobatic, agonistic; palaestral, palaestrian.

12. *adj.* sound, firm, stout, stanch, stable, deep-rooted, valid; sound as a roach, firm as Gibraltar, made of iron; in fine *or* high feather [coll.], like a giant refreshed; proof, weatherproof, rustproof etc.; healthy etc. 654.4.

13. *adj.* unweakened, undiminished, unallayed, unflagging, unfaded, unwithered, unshaken, unworn, unexhausted; in full force *or* swing, going strong [slang]; in the plenitude of power.

14. *adv.* strongly etc. *adj.*; by force, by main *or* brute force, by *or* with the strong arm *or* hand.

159a. Virility
(See 160a. Effeminacy)

1. *n.* virility, virileness, masculinity, ultramasculinity, manliness, manlihood [rare], manhood [arch.], mannishness, manfulness, manlikeness, manly vigor *or* power.

2. *n.* virilizing etc. *v.*, virilization, virification, masculinization.

3. *n.* virile person, virile, masculine, masculine man *or* woman, strongly virile man, he-man [coll.], two-fisted man [coll., U.S.], man with hair on his chest [joc.]; cave man [joc.]; tomboy, hoyden.

4. *v.* make virile etc. *adj.*, virilize, virilify, virify, masculinize, mannify, dewomanize.

5. *adj.* virile, masculine, ultra-masculine, manly, manlike, manful, mannish, he-mannish [coll.], mannified, two-fisted [coll.], broad-shouldered, hairy-chested [joc.], uneffeminate, unfeminine, unwomanly, in the prime of manhood; viripotent; male etc. 373.7; sturdy, lusty etc. (strong) 159.10.

160. Weakness
(See 159. Strength; also 158. Impotence)

1. *n.* weakness, weakliness, feebleness, strengthlessness, unstrength [dial.], debility, debilitation, infirmity, infirmness, decrepitude; frailty, frailness, fragility,

---

have a giant's strength; but it is tyrannous / To use it as a giant.—SHAKESPEARE. *Vires acquirit eundo* [It gains strength as it goes].—VERGIL.   Don't hit at all if it is honorably possible to avoid hitting; but *never* hit soft.—T. ROOSEVELT.   *Caelitus mihi vires* [My strength is of the heaven].

159a. Men of great abilities are generally of a large and vigorous animal nature.—H. TAYLOR.   His limbs were cast in manly mould, / For hardy sports or contest bold.—SCOTT.
160. All hands shall be feeble, and all knees shall be weak as water.—BIBLE.   Weak as a rained-on bee.—TORRENCE.   The weak brother is the worst of mankind.—STEVENSON.   Now in building of chaises, I tell you what, / There is always *somewhere* a weakest spot.—HOLMES.   He knows not how to wink at hu-

flimsiness, gimcrackiness [coll.], unsubstantiality, delicacy; unsteadiness, shakiness etc. *adj.*, weewows [dial.]; lack of vigor, faintness, languor, relaxation, lassitude, dullness, sluggishness; atony, asthenia, adynamia, adynamy [rare], cachexia *or* cachexy [all Med.]; impotence etc. 158; fault etc. 651.2.

2. *n.* weakening etc. *v.*, enfeeblement, enervation, declension ~, loss *or* failure of strength; invalidation.

3. *n.* anemia, bloodlessness, deficiency *or* poverty of blood.

4. *n.* weakling, weak sister [coll.], asthenic, softling [obs.], softy [slang, U.S.], tenderling [rare], jellyfish, invertebrate, weathercock, chicken [coll.], squab, canary [slang], baby, big baby, milksop, namby-pamby, push-over [slang, U.S.], lightweight, poor *or* weak tool [coll.], doormat; mollycoddle etc. 160a.3; impotent etc. 158.3.

5. *n.* (comparisons) reed, thread, rope of sand, hair; house of cards, house built on sand; jerry-built house, jerryism [builders' cant]; baby, kitten, chicken; water, milk and water, gruel, water gruel, cambric tea.

6. *v.* be weak etc. *adj.*, shake, tremble, totter, teeter, dodder; halt, limp; be on one's last legs, have one foot in the grave.

7. *v.* weaken, become weak etc. *adj.*, grow weak *or* weaker, lose strength etc. 159; drop, crumble, give way, fade, languish, decline, flag, fail, go downhill, go on the toboggan [slang, U.S.]; give out, conk out [slang, U.S.], fizzle out [coll.], peg out [slang], peter out [coll.], play out, poop out [slang]; die on the vine [coll.].

8. *v.* render weak etc. *adj.*, deprive of strength etc. 159, unstrengthen, weaken, enfeeble, debilitate, extenuate, invalidate, devitalize, incapacitate, shake, unstring, sap, impair, reduce, impoverish, exhaust, take it out of [coll.]; sprain, strain; blunt, blunt the edge of; decimate; reduce in strength, reduce the strength of; cripple, enervate etc. (render powerless) 158.6, 7; moderate etc. 174.5.

9. *v.* dilute, thin, reduce, attenuate, rarefy, water, add water, irrigate [slang], baptize [slang], cut [coll.], *mettre de l'eau dans son vin* [F.].

10. *adj.* weak, weakly; debilitated, debilitating, debile [obs.]; asthenic [Med.], feeble, unstrong [dial.], strengthless, sapless, marrowless, pithless, nerveless, sinewless, lustless, adynamic [Tech.]; unhardened, soft [spec. coll.], flaccid; faint, faintish; dull, slack, languid, drooping, laid low, spent, effete.

weak as a child *or* baby, weak as a kitten *or* cat, weak as a chicken, weak as a mouse *or* rat, weak as a rag, limp *or* limber as a dishrag, weak as water, weak as milk and water, weak as gruel *or* water gruel, weak as a drink of water, weak as cambric tea, weak as gingerbread; on its *or* one's last legs, with one foot in the grave; weakened, diluted etc. *v.*; impotent, powerless, unnerved etc. 158.8–11; colorless etc. 429.6; effeminate etc. 160a.5.

11. *adj.* frail, slight, delicate, dainty, fragile, frangible, breakable, shattery, crazy [arch.], unsubstantial, unstable, flimsy, slimsy [coll., U.S.], sleazy, gossamery, papery, pasteboardy; gimcrack, gimcracky [coll.]; gingerbread, gingerbready; jerry-built, jerry [builders' cant].

12. *adj.* unsteady, shaky, rickety, ricketish, teetery, tottery, tottering, tottlish [coll.], dotty [coll.], rocky [slang], doddering [coll.], wambly [Scot. and dial. Eng.]; weewow, weewowy [dial.]; cranky, craichy [dial.].

13. *adj.* unsound, unstable, unsubstantial, infirm, decrepit; poor, poorish; wasted, worn etc. (impaired) 659.12.

14. *adj.* wishy-washy, washy, namby-pamby, insipid, watery, milk-and-water, mushy.

15. *adj.* unstrengthened etc. (*see* strengthen etc. 159.8), unsupported, unaided, unassisted; aidless, defenseless etc. (helpless) 158.9.

160a. Effeminacy
(See 159a. Virility)

1. *n.* effeminacy, effeminateness, feminacy, femininity, feminity, femineity, feminality, feminility [rare], muliebrity,

---

man frailty, / Or pardon weakness that he never felt.—ADDISON.   There are two kinds of weakness, that which breaks and that which bends.—LOWELL.   Throughout all past time there has been a ceaseless devouring of the weak by the strong.—SPENCER.
160a. Art thou a man? Thy form cries out thou art; thy tears are womanish.—SHAKESPEARE.

womanity, womanishness, womanliness, unmanliness, sissiness [coll.]; old-womanishness, anility etc. (senility) 499.5.

2. *n.* effeminizing etc. *v.,* effemination, effeminization, feminization, womanization, sissification [coll.].

3. *n.* mollycoddle, effeminate, woman, old wife *or* woman, grandmother, crone [rare], tenderling, sop, milksop, smock-face [arch.], mother's darling, mamma's boy, betty, cotquean [arch.], henhussy, tame cat *or* pussy, Little Lord Fauntleroy [all contemptuous]; sissy, prissy [U.S.], molly, Molly, Miss Molly, Percy, muff, cot betty [U.S.], chicken, goody, goody-goody [all coll.]; cream puff [U.S.], powder puff, ladyfinger, lily, effie [U.S.], panty-waist [U.S.], weak sister [all slang]; soft, softy [both coll.]; weakling etc. 160.4.

4. *v.* make effeminate etc. *adj.,* effeminize, effeminatize, effeminate, feminize, womanize, womanish [obs.], sissify [coll.], demasculinize; unman etc. 158.7.

5. *adj.* effeminate, feminate [obs.], feminine, muliebrous, muliebrile, muliebral [rare], ladylike, womanlike, womanish, womanly, unmanly, smock-faced [arch.], sissy *or* sissyish [coll.], petticoat, soft; female etc. 374.11; old-womanish, puerile etc. (senile) 499.16; weak etc. 160.10.

161. Production
(See 162. Destruction; also 163. Reproduction, 164. Producer, 168. Productiveness)

1. *n.* production, producing etc. *v.,* creation, origination, construction, formation, efformation [rare], conformation, fabrication, manufacture; coinage; diaster [Biol.]; building, architecture, erection, edification [arch.]; constitution, establishment, organization; invention, concoction, composition; creative effort, *nisus formativus* [L.]; workmanship, performance, execution, effectuation; sculpture; causation etc. 153.5; achievement etc. (completion) 729; preparation etc. 673; authorship etc. 54.2, 590.3.

A woman impudent and mannish grown is not more loathed than an effeminate man in time of action.—SHAKESPEARE. Fops at all corners, ladylike in mien.—COWPER.
161. It will not out of the flesh that is bred in the bone.—J. HEYWOOD.   A man is not

2. *n.* generation, genesis, geniture [obs.]; progeneration, procreation, propagation, multiplication, reproduction, begetting, fertilization, gemination, germination, fecundation, fructification [rare], impregnation, breeding; pollinization, pollination; cross-pollination, cross-fertilization, xenogamy; proliferation; spontaneous generation.

archigenesis, archebiosis, abiogenesis, biogenesis, biogeny, blastogenesis, phytogenesis, dysmerogenesis, eumerogenesis, heterogenesis, xenogenesis, oögenesis, merogenesis, metagenesis, monogenesis, pangenesis, parthenogenesis, homogenesis, histogenesis, orthogenesis, isogenesis, epigenesis, digenesis, heterogamy, orthogamy, isogamy, dissogeny, xenogeny, theogony; copulation etc. (coition) 43.2; reproduction etc. 163.

3. *n.* birth, genesis, nativity, childbirth, parturition, delivery, hatching; act of God [joc.], blessed event [slang, U.S.]; incubation; confinement, childbed, *accouchement* [F.]; birth throe, travail, labor; obstetrics, midwifery, tocology, tocogony; stork; Ilithyia [Rom. Myth.], Eileithyia [Gr. Myth.], Juno Lucinia [Rom. Myth.]; pregnancy etc. 168.2; afterbirth etc. (afterpart) 65.2; beginning etc. 66.2.

4. *n.* flowering, blossoming, florescence, efflorescence, inflorescence, unfolding; fruition, fructification.

5. *n.* evolution, development, unfoldment, growth, rise, maturation; entelechy [Philos.], phylogeny *or* phylogenesis, ontogeny *or* ontogenesis, physiogeny *or* physiogenesis, mitosis, vacuolation *or* vacuolization; evolutionism, theory of evolution, Darwinism, Neo-Darwinism, Haeckelism, Lamarckism *or* Lamarckianism, Neo-Lamarckism, Weismannism; Spencerianism.

6. *n.* product, result, production, performance, produce, fruit, flower, blossom, yield, work, *œuvre* [F.], handiwork, creation, creature, offspring, outgrowth; origination, invention, coinage; concoction, composition; opus (*pl.* opera), opuscule; aria etc. (music) 415.2, 3; writing etc. 590.3; book etc. 593; publication etc. 531; work of art etc. 556.8–14; effect etc. 154.

---

completely born until he be dead.—FRANKL Bred amongst the weeds and tares of mine o brain.—T. BROWNE.   That irregular and

7. *n.* structure, construction, building, edifice, erection, fabric; superstructure, superstruction [rare]; pile, tower; compages.

8. *v.* produce, perform, operate, do, bring about, make, create, gar [obs.], form, formulate, construct, compose, evolve, fashion, fabricate, frame, devise, concoct, get up, compound, contrive, manufacture; build, erect, edify [arch.], put together *or* up, set up, run up; raise, rear, grow; establish, found, constitute, institute, install, organize; weave, forge, coin, carve, chisel; roughhew, knock together, knock out [coll.], hammer out, block out, slap up [coll.], do offhand; induce, originate etc. (cause) 153.6, 7; accomplish etc. (complete) 729.2; vivify etc. 359.8; prepare etc. 673.6.

9. *v.* bear, yield, produce, furnish; flower, blossom, sprout, burgeon; fruit, bear fruit, fructify; usher into the world, bring forth; bring forth young, give birth, prolify [rare], teem, yean, ean [dial.], kindle [chiefly dial.], come in [coll., U.S.], find [dial.]; drop, spring, throw [all of animals]; baby [slang], pup, whelp, cub, kitten, foal, calve, lamb, fawn; spawn, spat; miscarry, slink, sling; be born on the wrong side of the blanket, come in through a side door [both slang]; be profitable etc. 775.10.

10. *v.* generate, beget, get, engender, breed, reproduce, procreate, progenerate [rare], propagate, multiply; proliferate; give origin *or* rise to, give being to, bring *or* call into being *or* existence, hatch, breed; fecundate, impregnate etc. (make productive) 168.4; copulate etc. 43.8; reproduce etc. 163.2.

11. *adj.* productional, constructional, creational, formational; manufactural, manufacturing; producible, productible, causable; productive, constructive, creative, formative, fabricative, originative, demiurgic, demiurgeous; generant, generative, genetive, genetic [erroneous usage], genial [rare], genital; gametic, gametal; digenetic, heterogenetic, ontogenetic, xenogenetic etc. *n.*; ectogenous; gamic; hematobious *or* haematobious, hematobic *or* haematobic, sporogenous, sporophorous; fruitful, procreative etc.

168.7, 8; original, causative etc. (causal) 153.9.

12. *adj.* architectural, architectonic(al); structural, constructional, edificial.

13. *adj.* made, fashioned etc. *v.*; country-made, tailor-made, well-made etc.; homemade, homespun, handmade, self-made.

162. Destruction
(See 161. Production; also 165. Destroyer)

1. *n.* destruction, demolition, demolishment, ruin, ruination, wrack [arch. or Scot.], wrack and ruin, perdition, havoc, ravage, devastation, desolation, waste, consumption; blue ruin, ballyhack, ballywack, ballywrack, flinderation [all slang]; dissolution, breakup, breaking up, disruption, disorganization; fall, downfall, *éboulement* [F.], prostration; overthrow, overturn, *bouleversement* [F.], subversion, suppression; biblioclasm; sacrifice; sabotage; destructive incursion, razzia; incendiarism; mutual destruction, a case of dog eat dog [slang]. road to ruin, beginning of the end, *commencement de la fin* [F.]; abrogation etc. 756; impairment, decay, dilapidation etc. (deterioration) 659; waste etc. 638; loss etc. 776.

2. *n.* extinction, extermination, extirpation, elimination, eradication, annihilation, extinguishment, abolishment, abolition, kibosh [slang], washout [slang], curtains [slang, U.S.]; knockout, K.O. [slang], knockout blow; doom, crack of doom; death etc. 360; end etc. 67.

3. *n.* debacle, *débâcle* [F.]; cataclysm, catastrophe; breakup, breakdown, collapse, utter collapse, crash, smash, smash-up, wreck, wrack [arch. or Scot.], shipwreck [fig.], crack-up [coll.]; cave, cave-in [both coll.]; washout; upheaval, eruption etc. (outburst) 173.2.

4. *v.* destroy, deal destruction etc. *n.*, demolish, ruin, ruinate, lay in ruins *or* ashes, lay waste, desolate, devastate, ravage, wreck, shipwreck [fig.]; break *or* cut up, batter, smash, crash, crush, crumple up; laniate [rare], mutilate, shatter, shiver, break ~, tear ~, crush ~, cut

---

timate quality of things made entirely by the human hand.—W. CATHER. 'Tis wise to learn; 'tis God-like to create.—J. SAXE.

162. *Delenda est Carthago* [Carthage must be destroyed].—CATO THE ELDER. To build up cities an age is needed, but an hour destroys

~, shake ~, pull or pick to pieces, flinderate [slang], break (all) to flinderation [slang], break (all) to smithers or smithereens [chiefly coll.], tear to rags or tatters, crush or knock to atoms, make mincemeat of.

exterminate, annihilate, abolish, eradicate, extirpate, deracinate [rare], do or make away with, put an end to, do for [coll.], finish or finish off [chiefly coll.], fix [coll.], cook [slang], kibosh [slang], put the kibosh on [slang], deal a deathblow to, lay out [slang], knock out, K.O. [slang], deal a knock-out blow, seal the doom of, confound [arch.], dish [slang], bring to naught or nought, napoo [slang], put out of existence, wipe out [coll.], wipe up [slang], stamp or trample out, pull or pluck up by the roots, cut up root and branch, strike at the root of, lay the ax to the root of, make short work of, make a clean sweep.

throw overboard, fling or scatter to the winds, throw or cast to the dogs; obliterate, blot out, strike out, erase, cancel, cut short, cut out, take off, expunge, delete, dele, remove, sweep away; extinguish, douse [dial. and coll.], quench, squench [dial.], snuff out, put out, out [dial. and coll.]; nip, nip in the bud or head; cook one's goose or bacon [coll.], settle one's hash [coll.], drive to the dogs; raze, fell, level, level with the ground or dust, pull or tear down, break down, cut down, knock down or over, mow down, blow down, beat down.

undo, unbuild, dismantle, dismast, unrig [chiefly Naut.]; overthrow, overturn, overwhelm, throw down or over, upset, subvert; suppress, quash, squash [chiefly coll.], squelch [coll.], put down, quell, prostrate, lay or trample in the dust, tread or trample underfoot, lay by the heels; dispel, dissipate, dissolve; disrupt, disorganize; sink, scuttle, swamp, engulf or ingulf, submerge; blow up, blast; mine, spring a mine; gut, gut with fire, ravage with fire and sword; devour, swallow up; nullify, annul etc. (abrogate) 756.3; impair etc. 659.8; discard etc. 678.3.

5. v. perish, be destroyed etc. adj., fall, fall to the ground, tumble, topple, totter or topple to its fall, tremble or nod to its fall; break up, crumble, crumble to dust, go or fall to pieces; go to ruin, go to wrack and ruin, go to wreck, go to pot [coll.], go to the dogs, go to perdition, go to glory [coll.], go to smash, go all to smash [coll.], go to shivers, go to shivereens [Scot. and North. Eng.], go to smithers or smithereens [chiefly coll.], go to the wall, go by the board, go up the spout [coll.], go under, be all over with, be done for, be all up with [coll.]; become extinct etc. 2.5; deteriorate etc. 659.6; fail etc. 732.5.

go to the deuce or devil, ~ to hell, ~ to sticks or to sticks and staves, go bung, be all U.P. [all slang].

6. adj. destructive, demolitionary, ruinous; internecine, internecive [rare]; extirpatory, annihilative, deletory [obs.]; subversive, subversionary; incendiary, conflagrative [rare]; catastrophic(al), cataclysmic or cataclysmal; all-destroying, all-devouring, all-engulfing; harmful etc. 649.10; deadly, fatal etc. (mortal) 361.16.

7. adj. destroyed, perished etc. v.; no more, done for [coll.] etc. (extinct) 2.10; lost etc. 776.5.

163. Reproduction
(See also 161. Production, 168. Productiveness)

1. n. reproduction, remaking etc. v., reconstruction, re-establishment, reformation, recreation, regeneration, regenesis, palingenesis; resurgence, resurgency [rare]; procreation, propagation etc. (generation) 161.2; reduplication etc. (repetition) 104, (imitation) 19; reprint, duplicate etc. (copy) 21; revival, reanimation etc. (restoration) 660.1, 2.

2. v. reproduce, remake, make over, re-

---

them.—SENECA. A forest is long in growing, but in a moment is reduced to ashes.—SENECA. One minute gives invention to destroy; / What to rebuild will a whole age employ.—CONGREVE. Havoc, and spoil, and ruin are my gain.—MILTON. A world devote to universal wrack.—MILTON. All men that are ruined are ruined on the side of their natural propensities.—BURKE. While in the progress of their long decay, / Thrones sink to dust, and nations pass away.—F. HOWARD. Round the decay / Of this colossal wreck.—SHELLEY. Prostrate the beauteous ruin lies; and all / That shared its shelter, perish in its fall.—W. PITT.
163. Every generation needs regeneration.—C. H. SPURGEON. When man, with changeless Nature coalescing, / Will undertake regeneration's work.—SHELLEY.

construct, refashion, re-establish, reform, recreate, regenerate; stir the embers; put into the crucible; procreate, propagate etc. (generate) 161.10; repeat etc. 104.4; duplicate etc. 19.5; revive, reanimate etc. (restore) 660.8–14.

3. *adj.* reproductive, reconstructive, reformative, recreative, regenerative, progenitive; renascent, resurgent, reappearing; Hydra-headed; procreative etc. 168.8.

164. Producer
(See 165. Destroyer; also 161. Production, 168. Productiveness)

n. producer, creator, begetter, maker, manufacturer, builder, architect, constructor, artificer, *artifex* [L.], generator, mover; originator, inventor, author, founder, introducer, deviser, prime mover; executor, executrix; carpenter, sailmaker etc. (craftsman) 690.5–9; tailor, haberdasher, shoemaker etc. (clothier) 225.36–40; grower, raiser etc. (agriculturist) 371.2; writer etc. 593.15, 16; artist etc. 559.

165. Destroyer
(See 164. Producer; also 162. Destruction)

n. destroyer, destructor [rare], vandal, Hun; ruiner, exterminator etc. (*see* destroy, ruin, exterminate etc. 162.4); biblioclast; iconoclast, idoloclast; nihilist; moth, worm etc. (blight) 663.2; killer etc. 361.8; executioner etc. 975.5.

166. Ancestry
(See 167. Posterity)

1. *n.* ancestry, parentage, progenitorship [rare]; ancestors, antecedents, fathers, forefathers, foreparents [dial.], forebears, progenitors, primogenitors, grandparents, grandfathers, patriarchs; consanguinity etc. 11.

2. *n.* paternity, paternality, paternalness, paternal parentage, fathership,

fatherhood, fatherhead [obs.]; paternal headship *or* rule; Zeus [Gr. Myth.]; Jupiter, Jove [both Rom. Myth.]; Odin *or* Woden [Norse Myth.]; Dyaus [Hindu Myth.].

3. *n.* maternity, maternality, maternalness, maternal parentage, mothership, motherhood, motherhead [obs.]; Rhea [Gr. Myth.], Cybele [Myth.; Asia Minor, Gr. and Rom.].

4. *n.* extraction, derivation, birth, descent, lineage, line, bloodline, line of ancestors, strain, sept, stirps, stock, breed, progeny [rare], generation [rare]; pedigree, genealogy, genealogical tree, family tree, tree, trunk, stem; filiation, affiliation; side; male line, spear side; female line, distaff *or* spindle side; family, house etc. (race) 11.4; origin etc. 153.

5. *n.* parent, progenitor, genitor [rare], procreator, begetter.

6. *n.* father, sire, paternal ancestor [joc. or affected], pater [coll. or affected], the old man [slang], governor [slang], abba; papa, pa, pap, pappy, pop, pops, dad, daddy, daddums [all affectionate or familiar]; patriarch, paterfamilias; stepfather; foster father; father-in-law.

7. *n.* mother, dam, maternal ancestor [joc. or affected], mater [coll. or affected], the old woman [slang]; mamma, mammy, mam, ma, mom, mommy, mummy, mumsy, motherkin, motherkins [all affectionate or familiar]; progenitress, progenitrix; matriarch, materfamilias; stepmother; foster mother; mother-in-law.

8. *n.* grandfather, grandsire [arch. and dial.], gramfer [dial.], granther [dial.]; gaffer; grandpa, grampa, gramp, grandpapa, grandpap, grandpappy, granddad *or* grandad, granddaddy *or* grandaddy, granddada *or* grandada [all affectionate or familiar]; great-grandfather; old man etc. 130.1.

9. *n.* grandmother, grandam *or* granddam, grandam *or* grandame [of animals], grannam, granam [arch. and dial.], gammer [dial., Eng.], beldam *or* beldame [arch.]; grandmamma; grandma, granma, grandmammy, granny, grammy, gammy [all affectionate or familiar];

---

164. Where every man is his own architect.—BROWNING. The author and finisher of our faith.—BIBLE.
165. The Assyrian came down like the wolf on the fold.—BYRON.
166. He stands for fame on his forefathers' feet.—YOUNG. He who boasts of his descent, praises the deeds of another.—SENECA. The pride of ancestry increases in the ratio of distance.—G. CURTIS. Nothing like blood, sir, in hosses, dawgs, and men.—THACKERAY. Thank God for the iron in the blood of our fathers.—T. ROOSEVELT. You are the bows from which your children as living arrows are sent forth.—GIBRAN.

great-grandmother; old woman etc. 130.3.

10. *adj.* ancestral, parental, patrimonial, patriarchal; family, hereditary, lineal, racial; phyletic, phylogenetic [both Biol.]; paternal, fatherly, fatherlike; maternal, motherly, motherlike.

167. Posterity
(See 166. Ancestry)

1. *n.* posterity, postery [obs.], progeny, progenity [rare], progeniture [rare], issue, offspring, seed, brood, breed, family, generation [obs.], descent; descendants, heirs, sons, children; grandchildren, great-grandchildren; rising generation.

2. *n.* lineage, line, line of descendants, succession, filiation, affiliation, sonship; heredity, heritage, inheritance; primogeniture, postgeniture [rare].

3. *n.* young, brood, litter, farrow, seed, spawn, spat.

4. *n.* descendant, offspring, child, scion, branch [rare], olive branch [fig.]; derived *or* collateral descendant, ramification, offshoot, offset, branch, sprout, sprit, shoot; acrospire, plumule [both Bot.]; son, sonny, male child *or* offspring; daughter, female child *or* offspring; grandchild, grandson, granddaughter; stepchild, stepson, stepdaughter; foster child, foster son *or* daughter; son-in-law, daughter-in-law; heir, heiress; heir apparent, heir presumptive; chip of *or* off the old block; infant, urchin etc. (youngling) 129.

5. *n.* bastard, bantling, illegitimate, illegitimate child, natural child [chiefly dial.], *nullius filius* [L.; Law], the son of nobody.

6. *adj.* filial, sonly, sonlike; daughterly, daughterlike.

7. *adj.* lineal, in a direct line, direct, progenial [rare]; hereditary, inherited; diphyletic [Biol.]; primigenial, primogenial [rare], primogenital, primogenitary, primogenitive [rare].

---

167. Men do not think of sons and daughters when they fall in love.—E. B. Browning. People will not look forward to posterity who never look backward to their ancestors.—Burke.   We are always doing, says he, something for Posterity, but I would fain see Posterity do something for us.—Steele.   The care of posterity is most in them that have no posterity.—Bacon.   From fairest creatures we desire increase.—Shakespeare. Posterity pays every man his honour.—Jonson.   I

168. Productiveness
(See 169. Unproductiveness; also 161. Production, 163. Reproduction, 164. Producer)

1. *n.* productiveness, productivity, fruitfulness etc. *adj.*, fecundity, pregnancy [fig.], luxuriance, uberty [obs.], fructification, pullulation, multiparity, multiplication; fertility, fertilization; proliferation, prolification, prolificity, prolificacy, prolificality; Demeter [Gr. Myth.]; Ceres [Rom. Myth.]; Frey [Norse Myth.]; Isis [Egyptian Myth.]; Baal [Semitic Myth.]; Astarte *or* Ashtoreth [Phoenician Myth.]; propagation, procreation etc. (generation) 161.2; copulation etc. 43.2.

2. *n.* pregnancy, pregnance [obs.]; parturience *or* parturiency, ingravidation [rare], gravidity [rare], gravidness [rare], heaviness, greatness, bigness, awkwardness [dial.], the family way [coll.]; conception; superfetation; birth etc. 161.3.

3. *n.* (comparisons) milk cow, rabbit, Hydra, warren, seed plot, hotbed, rich soil, land flowing with milk and honey, mustard; fertile mind, pregnant idea.

4. *v.* make productive etc. *adj.*, fructify, fertilize, spermatize, impregnate; fecundate, fecundify, fecundize; pollen, pollinate, pollinize, cross-fertilize, cross-pollen, cross-pollinate, cross-pollenize; procreate etc. (generate) 161.10; copulate etc. 43.8.

5. *v.* be productive etc. *adj.*, produce abundantly, multiply, pullulate, teem; proliferate, prolify [rare].

6. *v.* be pregnant etc. *adj.*, teem [rare or dial.], gestate, carry, carry young; conceive, come with child, get in the family way [coll.]; superfetate.

7. *adj.* productive, fertile, pregnant [fig.]; fruitful, fruit bearing; fructiferous, fructuous [rare], fructiparous [rare]; prolific(al), proliferous, proliferant, proliferative; teeming, teemful [dial.]; fecund, uberous, luxuriant, rich, plenteous, copious; creative, originative etc. (productional) 161.11; profitable etc. (useful) 644.5–8; potent etc. 157.8.

---

am the son of the wise, the son of ancient kings.—Bible.   Like father, like son.
168. A virgin shall conceive and bring forth a child.—Bible.   Our women have a proverb, "It is a sad burden to carry a dead man's child."—Fuller.

8. *adj.* procreative, procreant; propagative, propagable; reproductive, generative, progenerative [rare], life-giving, fecundative, spermatic, fertilizing; inceptive; multiparous; omnific.

9. *adj.* pregnant, impregnant [rare], *enceinte* [F.], parturient, teeming [rare or dial.], gravid, heavy, great, big, heavy with, great *or* big with, great *or* big with child *or* young, heavy with child *or* young, with child *or* young, in the family way [coll.], gestant [rare], laden, awkward [dial.]; anticipating, anticipating a blessed event [all slang, U.S.]; lying-in, in the straw [coll.], brought to bed; puerperous, puerperal; superfetate.

169. Unproductiveness
(See 168. Productiveness)

1. *n.* unproductiveness, unfruitfulness, barrenness etc. *adj.*; unproductivity, sterility, infertility, infecundity; otiosity; impotence etc. 158; unprofitableness etc. (inutility) 645.

2. *n.* waste, wasteland, barren *or* barrens, barren land, barren *or* weary waste, "a barren waste, a wild of sand" (Addison), desert, Sahara, karroo *or* karoo, heath; wild, wilderness, howling wilderness; bush, brush; alkali flat; prairie, moor etc. (plain) 344; marsh etc. 345.

3. *v.* be unproductive etc. *adj.*, hang fire, flash in the pan, come to nothing.

4. *adj.* unproductive, unfertile, infertile, unfruitful, unprolific, infecund [rare], infructuose [rare], sterile, otiose, acarpous, barren, arid, addle, jejune; teemless, issueless, fruitless, childless, *sine prole* [L.]; ineffectual, of no effect, null and void; fallow; impotent etc. 158.8; unprofitable etc. (useless) 645.8.

170. Agency

1. *n.* agency, operation, operance *or* operancy, force, working, strain, function, office, maintenance, exercise, work, swing, play; interworking, interaction; procuration, procurement; quickening ~, maintaining *or* sustaining power; home stroke; causation etc. 153; instrumentality etc. 631; mediation etc. 724; influence etc. 175; action etc. (voluntary) 680.

2. *v.* be operative etc. *adj.,* operate, work, act, act on *or* upon, perform, play, support, sustain, strain, maintain, take effect, quicken, strike; have play, have free play.

3. *v.* come *or* bring into operation *or* play, bring to bear upon.

4. *adj.* operative, operating etc. *v.,* operatic [rare], operant [rare]; efficient, efficacious; practical, exertive, conative, effectual, workable; in operation, in force, in action, in play, in exercise; at work, on foot; acted *or* wrought upon; acting etc. 680.7; instrumental etc. 631.4.

5. *prep.* by the agency of etc. *n.*; through etc. (instrumentality) 631.5; by means of etc. 632.4; by the aid of etc. 707.14.

171. Energy
(See 172. Inertness)

1. *n.* energy, physical energy, intensity, force, vigor *or* vigour, vim [coll.], verve, fire, snap [coll.], dash, drive, go [coll.]; punch, kick, pep, pepper, ginger [all slang]; actual *or* kinetic energy, dynamic energy, potential energy, ergal [Phys.]; potence etc. 157; strength etc. 159; exertion etc. 686; life, spirit etc. (voluntary energy) 682.1; mettle, backbone [coll.] etc. (resolution) 604; *vis viva* [L.] etc. (life energy) 359.2.

2. *n.* activity, energetic *or* vigorous action; briskness, quickness etc. *adj.*; hustle [coll.], bustle, stir, agitation, perturbation, splutter; radioactivity, radium emanation; ebullition, ferment etc. (effervescence) 353.3; alacrity etc. (voluntary activity) 682; exertion etc. 686; excitation etc. (mental activity) 824.

3. *n.* acrimony, acridity, acritude

---
169. That small model of the barren earth.—SHAKESPEARE.   This goodly frame, the earth, seems to me a sterile promontory.—SHAKESPEARE.   I pity the man who can travel from Dan to Beersheba, and cry, "'Tis all barren!"—STERNE.   That fruitless and unprofitable art, / Good unto none.—JONSON.   For me it will be enough that a marble stone should declare that a queen having reigned such a time, lived and died a virgin.—QUEEN ELIZABETH.   It is well to lie fallow for a while.—TUPPER.
170. The tools of working our salvation / By mere mechanic operation.—BUTLER.   I myself must mix with action.—TENNYSON.   The day is always his who works in it with serenity and great aims.—EMERSON.   When you are an anvil, hold you still; when you are a hammer, strike your fill.—G. HERBERT.
171. Such a release and increase of human energy as to open a new phase in human his-

[obs.], acrity [obs.]; causticity, virulence, kick [slang], poignancy, harshness etc. *adj.*, severity, edge, point; pungency etc. 392.

4. *n.* energizer, energist; activator, active agent *or* force; excitant, excitator; stimulant, stimulus, stimulator; bracer, pick-me-up [coll.]; aphrodisiac, philter, love potion, cantharis (*pl.* cantharides), Spanish fly, blister beetle.

5. *n.* (comparisons) human dynamo; quicksilver; caffeine, coffee, tea, alcohol; niter, saltpeter; ammonia, carbonate of ammonia, sal ammoniac *or* sal-ammoniac, smelling salts; seasoning etc. (condiment) 393.

6. *n.* (units of energy) energid, erg, dinamode.

7. *v.* energize, give *or* impart energy to etc. *n.*, make energetic etc. *adj.*, stimulate, kindle, enkindle, fire, arouse, rouse, awaken, excite, stir, exert, quicken, animate, enliven, pep up [slang], stir up, set astir, activate [rare], potentialize [rare], invigorate, dynamize, double-shot; intensify, sharpen, whet, key up; step up, hop up, jazz up [all slang]; strengthen etc. 159.8.

8. *v.* strike, hit, impress, make an impression, strike into, strike hard, strike home, hit the mark [coll.]; smite etc. 276.8.

9. *adj.* energetic, energic [rare], energetistic, energico [Mus.]; forceful, forcible; strong, dynamic, vigorous, strenuous, intense, acute, keen, vivid, incisive, trenchant; active, lively, animated, quick, brisk, brisk as a lark *or* bee, stirring etc. *v.*; snappy, peppy, full of pep etc. *n.* [all slang]; radioactive; go-ahead [coll.], enterprising, industrious etc. 682.18, 19; potent etc. 157.8.

10. *adj.* acrid, acridulous, virulent, poignant, caustic, escharotic [Med.], mordant, sharp, keen, cutting, biting, severe, harsh, stringent, drastic; double-edged, double-shotted, double-distilled; racy etc. (pungent) 392.5.

11. *adj.* energizing, rousing, exciting etc. *v.*; excitant, excitative, excitatory.

12. *adj.* aphrodisiac(al), aphroditous.

13. *adv.* energetically, vigorously, forcibly etc. *adj.*; *fortiter in re* [L.]; effectively, with telling effect.

---

tory.—H. G. WELLS.   Energy is Eternal Delight.—W. BLAKE.   The race by vigor not by vaunts is won.—POPE.

172. Inertness
(See 171. Energy)

1. *n.* inertness, inertion [rare], physical inertness, inertia; passiveness etc. *adj.*, passivity; inactivity, inaction; faineance, dormance *or* dormancy, suspense, abeyance *or* abeyancy, torpor, languor; stagnation, stagnancy; vegetation; power of inertia, *vis inertiae* [L.]; fixity, immobility etc. (stability) 150; permanence etc. 141; idleness, apathy etc. 683; rest, calm etc. (quiescence) 265.

2. *v.* be inert etc. *adj.*, hang fire, smolder, sleep, slumber, stagnate, vegetate.

3. *adj.* inert, inactive, static, passive, dormant, latent, suspended, abeyant, in suspense *or* abeyance, sleeping, slumbering, smoldering, unexerted, *fainéant* [F.], stagnant, lifeless, dead, torpid, logy [U.S.], sluggish, leaded, heavy, dull, flat, slack, tame, blunt, fixed, motionless etc. (quiescent) 265.7; immovable etc. (stable) 150.5; idle, apathetic etc. 683.12–16.

173. Violence
(See 174. Moderation)

1. *n.* violence, forcible *or* vehement action, vehemence, force, might, rigor, impetuosity, inclemency, severity, intensity, acuteness, sharpness; fierceness, ferociousness; furiousness, furiosity [rare]; fury, furor, *furore* [It.]; rage, frenzy; exasperation, exacerbation [spec. Med.], irritation; brute force, main force; malignity, outrage etc. (malevolence) 907; uproar, rumpus [coll.], turbulence etc. (turmoil) 59.4; spasm etc. 315.7; hysterics, passion etc. (state of excitability) 825.4.

2. *n.* outbreak, outburst, eruption, upheaval, convulsion, cataclysm; violent passion, orgasm, aphrodisia; burst, bounce, dissiliency; rush, torrent, stream, strain [all spec. of speech]; volcano, volcan, vulcan [obs.]; earthquake, quake, shake [coll.], tremor, temblor.

3. *n.* explosion, displosion [obs.], discharge, bounce [obs.], blowout, blowup; detonation, fulmination, blast, burst; flash, flare, fulguration; bang, boom,

---

172. The immense unwieldiness, sluggishness, inertia, permanence of matter.—T. MANN. *Inertiae dulcedo* [The sweetness of being idle].—TACITUS.
173. Where Life becomes a spasm.—CARROLL. Blown with restless violence round about the

thunder etc. (report) 406.2-4; shot etc. 284.4; gunfire etc. 716.2.

4. *n.* concussion, shock, shog [rare]; jolt, jar etc. (shake) 315.4.

5. *n.* storm, rough weather, tempest; windstorm, sandstorm, thunderstorm, cyclone etc. (wind) 349.11-14; rainstorm etc. 348.11; thunderburst etc. (thunder) 406.4; snowstorm etc. 383.6.

6. *n.* (violent person) violent, berserk *or* berserker, demon, fiend, shaitan *or* sheitan [coll.], hellhound, hellcat, hellion [coll.], beast, wild beast, tiger, dragon, roarer *or* hell-roarer [slang], ringtail roarer [slang, U.S.], holy terror [slang], fire-eater [coll.], spitfire, hotspur, madcap, ugly customer [slang], fury [spec. female]; virago, vixen, termagant, beldam, she-wolf, tigress, witch [all female]; Tisiphone, Megaera, Alecto, Erinys, Fury; the Furies, Dirae, Erinyes, Eumenides; ruffian etc. 913.2.

7. *v.* be violent etc. *adj.,* romp, rampage, rage, roar, riot, storm, fume; rush, tear, rush headlong *or* headforemost; come in like a lion; bear down, ride roughshod; create a disturbance, make a riot, raise a storm, run riot *or* amuck, run wild, cut loose, go on a rampage.

make *or* kick up a row, raise a breeze *or* squall, kick up *or* raise a dust, kick up a shindy, raise the devil, raise the deuce *or* dickens, raise Cain *or* Ned, raise hell *or* Hail Columbia, raise sand, carry on, cut a shine, cut up, cut up rough, roughhouse, raise the roof, whoop it *or* her up, hell around, tear up jack [all slang].

8. *v.* render violent etc. *adj.,* stir up, rouse, arouse, inflame, kindle, enkindle, suscitate [obs.], sharpen, whet, quicken, accelerate, excite, incite, urge, lash, stimulate, foment, exasperate, exacerbate, irritate, madden, infuriate, lash into fury; fan the flame, add fuel to the flame, pour oil on the fire, *oleum addere camino* [L.].

9. *v.* explode, displode [obs.], go off, bark, detonate, detonize, fulminate; let off, discharge, fire, shoot; blow out, blow up, blast; burst, bust [dial. and inelegant]; flash, flare, fulgurate, deflagrate [Chem.]; backfire; crack, bang etc. (make an explosive sound) 406.7-9; shoot etc. 284.13.

10. *v.* break open, force open, prize *or* pry open; break *or* burst out, fly out.

11. *adj.* violent, vehement, severe, furious, fierce, intense, rigorous *or* rigourous, sharp, acute, cutting, piercing, incisive, keen, caustic, vivid, extreme, extravagant, great; rough, tough [coll.]; malevolent etc. 907.6.

12. *adj.* turbulent, turbulous [obs.]; tumultuous, tumultuary; raging, stormy, tempestuous, restless, unquiet, disturbed, troublous, frenzied, furious, infuriate, mad, ravening, frantic; blustering, blustery, blusterous; riotous, rampageous; rambunctious [U.S.], rumbustious *or* rambustious, rumbustical, rumbumptious [all slang]; rampacious [coll.]; uproarious, boisterous, wild, unruly, harum-scarum [coll.], reckless, rampant; orgastic, orgasmic; volcanic; meteoric; agitated etc. 315.13.

13. *adj.* fiery, inflamed, flaming, scorching, hot, red-hot, ardent, hotheaded.

14. *adj.* savage, savagerous [slang, U.S.]; ferocious, fierce, fierce as a tiger *or* bear, vicious; brutish, brutal, bestial; feral, ferine; wild, untamed, tameless, ungentle; barbarous, uncivilized; rude, bluff, brusque, abrupt, waspish; cruel etc. 907.9.

15. *adj.* unmitigated, unsoftened, unquelled, unquenched, unextinguished, unrepressed, unsuppressed, unbridled.

16. *adj.* unmitigable etc. *above* 173.15, insuppressible, irrepressible; ungovernable, uncontrollable etc. (obstinate) 606.6.

17. *adj.* explosive, detonating etc. *v.*; explodable, explosible.

18. *adv.* violently etc. *adj.,* by violence, by storm, by force, by main *or* brute force, forcibly, amain, with might and main, with a high hand, tooth and nail, by force of arms, *vi et armis* [L.], at the point of the sword *or* bayonet; at one fell swoop; through thick and thin; in desperation, with a vengeance; all to pieces, ~ smash *or* smithereens, galley-west and crooked, like blazes [all slang]; *à outrance* [F.], *à toute outrance* [F.]; headlong, headfirst, headforemost.

---

pendent world.—SHAKESPEARE.   These violent delights have violent ends.—SHAKESPEARE.

Do violence to no man.—BIBLE.   Like a bull in a china shop.

174. Moderation
(See 173. Violence)

1. *n.* moderation, moderateness, temperateness etc. *adj.*; temperance, measure, passability, sobriety; medium, happy medium; golden mean, *juste-milieu* [F.], *meden agan* [Gr. μηδὲν ἄγαν], *ariston metron* [Gr. ἄριστον μέτρον], *aurea mediocritas* [L.]; anaphrodisia; lenity etc. 740; even temper, mental calmness etc. (inexcitability) 826; restraint etc. 751; mediocrity etc. 736.

2. *n.* modulation, abatement, falling off, diminution, relaxation, remission, mitigation, assuagement, allayment, alleviation, contemperation [obs.], pacification, tranquilization, quieting, mollification, subduement; reduction etc. (decrease) 36.

3. *n.* moderator, modulator, temperer, mitigator, mollifier; assuager, assuasive; alleviator, alleviative; calmative, sedative etc. (palliative) 662.6; opiate etc. (narcotic) 662.7; arbitrator etc. (mediator) 724.2.

4. *v.* be moderate etc. *adj.,* strike a balance, keep a happy medium, keep the golden mean, steer *or* preserve an even course, keep within bounds *or* compass; keep the peace; sober down, settle down; remit, relent; take in sail; go out like a lamb.

5. *v.* moderate, render moderate, make temperate etc. *adj.*; temper, attemper, soften, modulate, mitigate, lenify [rare], dulcify, deaden, dull, take off the edge, blunt, obtund, sheathe, subdue, chasten, mollify, tranquilize, assuage, swage [dial.], appease, lull, soothe, compose, still, calm, cool, quiet, hush, quell, sober, pacify, tame, lay, allay, abate, rebate [arch.], palliate, slake, slacken, smooth, smooth over, alleviate, smother.

damp, dampen; throw cold water on, throw a wet blanket on; sober down, tone *or* tune down, smooth down, slow down; pour water on the waves *or* troubled waters, pour balm into; weaken etc. 160.8; lessen etc. (decrease) 36.4; check, curb etc. (restrain) 751.6; inactivate etc. 683.11.

6. *adj.* moderate, moderato [Mus.], tempered etc. *v.,* temperate, modulate; gentle, tame, soft, bland, mild; equable, even; mild as milk *or* mother's milk, mild as milk and water, gentle as a lamb; calm, cool, unruffled, untroubled, smooth, slow, quiet, tranquil, still, sober, peaceful, peaceable, pacific, halcyon; reasonable [as in price]; limited, not extreme; not violent, ~ intense etc. 173.11; unexciting, unirritating etc. (*see* excite, irritate etc. 173.8); lenient etc. 740.4; restrained etc. 751.10; mediocre etc. 736.3.

7. *adj.* moderative, modulative, assuasive, lenitive, calmative, calmant, sedative, assuaging etc. *v.,* demulcent, anodyne; antiorgastic, anaphrodisiac; sleep-inducing etc. 683.17.

8. *adv.* moderately etc. *adj.,* in moderation, in reason, within bounds *or* compass; under easy sail, at half speed; gingerly.

175. Influence
(See 175a. Noninfluence)

1. *n.* influence, influentiality, sway, reign, play, swing; power, potence *or* potency; pressure, weight, moment, consequence, prestige, importance; favor, special favor, bias, interest; pull, drag, in, stand-in [all slang]; inside track [coll.]; protection, auspices etc. (patronage) 707.2; incitement, persuasion etc. 615.2, 4; instrumentality etc. 631.

2. *n.* mastery, control etc. (authority) 737.

3. *n.* leverage, pry, prize [dial.], purchase, hold, fulcrumage, *point d' appui* [F.], *pou sto* [Gr. ποῦ στῶ]; fulcrum, foothold etc. (support) 215.4, 5; vantage ground etc. (advantage) 33.2; lever etc. 307.4.

4. *n.* hidden influences, network of secret influences, intrigues; wires, strings, ropes [all coll.]; wirepulling [coll.], lobbyism; hidden *or* latent influence, invisible government.

---

174. Moderation is a fatal thing. Nothing succeeds like excess.—WILDE.   The great mind knows the power of gentleness.—BROWNING. In everything, I wot, there lieth measure.—CHAUCER.   The golden rule in life is moderation in all things.—TERENCE.   *Est modus in rebus* [There is a mean in all things].—HORACE.   A soft answer turneth away wrath.

175. A cock has great influence on his own dunghill.—PUBLILIUS.   They'll take suggestion as a cat laps milk.—SHAKESPEARE.   The salutary influence of example.—JOHNSON.

5. *n.* influential person, influence, influencer; wirepuller [coll.], power behind the throne, friend at *or* in court, kingmaker; tower of strength, host in himself; patron etc. 711.4.

6. *v.* influence, exercise *or* exert influence etc. *n.*, use one's influence, make one's influence felt, affect, weigh with, sway, bias, incline, dispose, determine; move one to, move by influence *or* persuasion; draw, draw on, magnetize; bring influence *or* pressure to bear upon, turn *or* throw one's weight into the scale, act *or* work on *or* upon, bear upon; pull the strings, ~ wires *or* ropes, wirepull [coll.]; lobby [chiefly U.S.]; move, prompt etc. (motivate) 615.7; bring round, persuade etc. (induce) 615.9; be instrumental etc. 631.3.

7. *v.* have influence etc. *n.*, be influential etc. *adj.*, carry weight, weigh, tell, count, draw water [slang, U.S.]; have the *or* an in [slang, U.S.], have the inside track [coll.]; have full play.

8. *v.* have influence over, have the pull over [slang], have it all over [coll.], come it all over [slang], come over [coll.], come it over [slang]; lead, lead by the nose, wind *or* turn around one's little finger, bend to one's will, keep under one's thumb, carry with a high hand; dominate, control etc. 737.11, 12.

9. *v.* gain influence etc. *n.*, gain a footing, take hold, take root, strike root in; gain a hearing, make one's voice heard, be listened to, be recognized; get the mastery of, get control of, gain a hold upon; change the preponderance, turn the scale *or* balance, turn the tables; gain the upper hand etc. (advantage) 33.2.

10. *adj.* influential, influencive [rare]; effective, effectual [rare], efficacious; telling, weighty, potent, prevalent [rare], authoritative, dominant, predominant, preponderant, prepotent, prepollent, regnant; ascendant, in the ascendant, in ascendancy; important etc. 642.10; persuasive etc. 615.11; authoritative etc. 737.15.

11. *adv.* effectively etc. *adj.*, with telling effect, to good account, with a vengeance.

Blessed influence of one true loving human soul on another.—G. Eliot.   Every life is a

175a. Noninfluence
(See 175. Influence)

1. *n.* noninfluence, uninfluentiality, ineffectuality, ineffectiveness, inefficacy, inefficacity [rare], inefficaciousness; unconductivity, nonconductivity, nonconductibility, nonconduciveness, unconduciveness; impotence, powerlessness etc. (impotence) 158; inertness etc. 172.

2. *adj.* uninfluential, uninfluencive [rare], uninfluencing; ineffective, ineffectual, inefficacious; nonconductive, unconductive, nonconducive, unconducive, unconducing [rare]; forceless, powerless etc. 158.8.

176. Tendency

1. *n.* tendency, tendence [rare]; aptness, aptitude; propensity, propenseness, propensitude [rare], propension [now rare], propendency [obs.]; proclivity, predilection, predisposition, proneness, readiness, penchant, bent, turn, bias, warp, twist, leaning, inclination; gravity, gravitation; course, trend, tenor, tone, drift, set; cast, vein, grain, humor, mood; idiocrasy, idiosyncrasy; conduciveness, conducement; conatus, conation [Psychol.], nisus; liability etc. 177; disposition etc. (character) 5.3; intention etc. 620.

2. *v.* tend, have a tendency etc. *n.*, contribute, conduce, serve, head, lead, point, dispose, look, lean, incline, verge, bend to, warp, turn, work *or* gravitate towards, trend, affect, carry; redound to, bid *or* stand fair to; be liable etc. 177.2.

3. *adj.* tending to etc. *v.*, conducive to, conducent to [obs.]; inclined towards, inclining *or* leaning towards, working towards; in a fair way to, likely to, calculated to, minded to, apt to, inclined to, prone to, disposed to, predisposed to, liable to, propense to [arch.]; idiocratic(al), idiosyncratic(al); subservient etc. (instrumental) 631.4; useful etc. 644.5; subsidiary etc. (helping) 707.12.

---

profession of faith, and exercises an inevitable and silent influence.—Amiel.
176. All men that are ruined are ruined on the side of their natural propensities.—Burke. Each man has an aptitude born with him.—Emerson.

177. Liability

1. *n.* liability, liableness etc. *adj.*, likelihood, aptitude, possibility, probability, chance, contingence *or* contingency; susceptivity, susceptibility; tendency etc. 176; obligation etc. (duty) 926.

2. *v.* be liable etc. *adj.*, incur, lay oneself open to, expose oneself to, open the door to, be subjected to, lie under; run the chance, stand a chance; admit of, be in the way of, bid *or* stand fair to; tend etc. 176.2.

3. *adj.* liable to, subject to, susceptive to, open to, exposed to, obnoxious to [rare], in danger of; dependent on, incident to; likely to, apt to etc. (tending to) 176.3; unprotected etc. 665.9.

4. *adj.* contingent, incidental, dependent, possible, on the cards, within range of, at the mercy of.

178. Concurrence
(See 179. Counteraction)

1. *n.* concurrence, concurrency, coagency, coaction, coworking, coadunation, synergy, conjunction, union, combination, alliance, concert, collusion, consilience; concomitance *or* concomitancy, concomitation [obs.]; union in action, combined action *or* agency, combination of power *or* influence, mutual assistance; collaboration, coadjument etc. (co-operation) 709; partnership etc. 712.5; conformity, concordance etc. (agreement) 23; acquiescence, consent etc. (assent) 488.

2. *v.* concur, conduce, conspire, contribute; coact, coadunate, synergize, combine, unite, hitch horses [coll.]; pull together etc. (co-operate) 709.4; help etc. (aid) 707.6; harmonize, jibe [coll., U.S.] etc. (agree) 23.7; acquiesce etc. (assent) 488.6, 7.

3. *v.* go with, go along with, go hand in hand with, be hand in glove with etc. *adj.*; keep pace with, run parallel to.

4. *adj.* concurring etc. *v.*, concurrent; coactive, correspondent [rare], joint, concomitant, coincident, consentaneous [arch.], consilient, co-ordinate; coadunate, coadunative; synergetic, synergistic; in alliance with, banded together; of one mind, of the same mind, at one with, hand in hand with, hand in glove with; coadjuvant, collaborative etc. (co-operative) 709.7; conformable, concordant etc. (agreeing) 23.9; acquiescent, agreed, like-minded etc. (assenting) 488.11, 12.

5. *adv.* concurrently etc. *adj.*, with one voice *or* accord, as one man, shoulder to shoulder.

179. Counteraction
(See 178. Concurrence)

1. *n.* counteraction, opposition, opposure; polarity, contradiction, antagonism, repugnance, antipathy, clashing etc. *v.*, collision, conflict, interference, resistance, renitence *or* renitency, friction; oppugnacy [rare], oppugnance *or* oppugnancy, oppugnation [rare]; contrariety etc. 14; reaction, retroaction etc. (recoil) 277; voluntary opposition etc. 708; voluntary resistance etc. 719; repression etc. (restraint) 751; neutralization etc. (compensation) 30.

2. *n.* counteractant, counteractive, counteragent, oppositionist; obstructive, obstructionist; oppugner, oppugnant [rare]; neutralizer, offset; antidote, remedy, preventative, preventive, prophylactic; vaccine, serum; vaccination, injection, shot [slang]; cross fire, crosscurrent, undercurrent, head wind; counterbalance, counterpoise; counterblast; the opposition.

3. *v.* counteract, counterwork, countervail, run counter, be *or* play at crosspurposes, clash, jostle, cross, contravene, contradict, conflict, interfere *or* conflict with, come in conflict with, go ~, run ~, beat *or* militate against, oppugn; traverse; stultify; antagonize etc. (oppose) 708.2; withstand etc. (resist) 719.3; impede etc. (hinder) 706.4-7; repress etc. (restrain) 751.6; react etc. (recoil) 277.3.

4. *v.* neutralize, compensate, undo, offset, cancel, nullify, annul, frustrate, vitiate; counterbalance, counterpoise; overbalance, overpoise.

5. *adj.* counteractive, counteractant; conflicting, clashing etc. *v.*; oppositive, oppositionary, oppositious; antagonistic, oppugnant, repugnant, retroactive, reni-

---

178. Right and victory do not always concur.—SELDEN.   I shall know that your good is mine; ye shall know that my strength is yours. —KIPLING.   A certain concurrence of circumstances.—CHESTERFIELD.

tent, reactionary; contrary etc. 14.5; oppositional etc. 708.4.

6. *adv. etc.* counteractively etc. *adj.*; contrarily etc. 14.7; in opposition to etc. (against) 708.5; in spite of etc. (notwithstanding) 30.8.

180. Space
(See 180a. Inextension; also 181. Region, 183. The Country)

Indefinite Space.—1. *n.* space, extension, extent, extensiveness etc. *adj.*; expanse, expansion; stretch, sweep, swing, spread, scope, reach, range, latitude, compass, field, way, sphere, arena; room, roomage [rare], roomstead [rare].

2. *n.* spare room, room to spare, elbowroom, margin, leeway; seaway, headway.

3. *n.* open space, free space; opening [U.S.], clearing; open country, wide open spaces; prairie, moor etc. (plain) 344; desert, wilderness etc. (waste) 169.2; rural district etc. (country) 183; vacancy, void etc. (absence) 187.

4. *n.* (unlimited space) infinity, illimitability, interminability, boundlessness etc. *adj.*; universe, creation, all creation, world, wide world, whole wide world, length and breadth of the land, "world without end" (Bible); plenum; heavens, firmament, sky, ether, air; interplanetary ~, interstellar *or* intercosmic space.

5. *n.* proportions, dimensions; breadth, width, span; acreage, acres; acres, roods and perches; square inches, ~ yards etc. (*see* inch, yard etc. 200.6); ares, arpents.

6. *adj.* spacious, roomy, extensive, expansive, capacious, ample, vast, vasty [rare], immense, wide, widespread, far-flung; extended; sizable etc. 192.11.

7. *adj.* unlimited, unending, uncircumscribed, unbounded; illimitable, immeasureable, unmeasured; limitless, endless, boundless, termless, shoreless; without measure, without bound, without limit *or* end, "as boundless as the sea" (Shakespeare), far as the eye can see, infinite; universal, world-wide; beyond the verge.

8. *adv.* extensively etc. *adj.*, right-and-left; far and wide etc. 196.10.

9. *adv.* everywhere, everywheres [dial. and coll.]; here, there and everywhere; all over, all over hell [slang], all over the world, all over the map [coll.], all the world over, throughout the world, throughout the length and breadth of the land, in every place *or* quarter, in all quarters *or* lands; from end to end, from pole to pole, "from China to Peru" (Johnson), "from Indus to the pole" (Pope), from Dan to Beersheba, from hell to breakfast [slang, U.S.], from here out [slang]; on earth, under the sun, in the world, in the wide world, on the face of the earth *or* waters.

everywhence, "from the four corners of the earth" (Shakespeare), from all points of the compass; everywhither, to the four winds, to the uttermost parts of the earth, to hell and back again [slang]; high and low, upstairs and downstairs, inside and out, in every hole and corner.

180a. Inextension
(See 180. Space)

1. *n.* inextension, inextensity, nonextension, nonexpansion, nonexpanse [rare]; point, vanishing point, dot, jot, speck, flyspeck, spot, pinpoint, pinprick, tittle, hair; atom etc. (smallness) 32; cubbyhole etc. 184.4.

2. *adj.* inextensive, inextensional, inextensible, inextensile; nonexpansive, nonexpansional.

181. Region
(See also 180. Space, 182. Country)

Definite Space.—1. *n.* region, area, zone, territory, terrain, ground, soil, land, country; quarter, part, section, district, department, compartment, division; purlieus, vicinage, vicinity, neighborhood; sphere, hemisphere, realm, demesne, domain, dominion, circuit, compass, orb, orbit, ambit, circle, range, province, precinct, premises, confines [arch.], field, pale; location etc. 184.

2. *n.* (territorial divisions) canton,

---

180. The Promised Land always lies on the other side of a wilderness.—H. ELLIS. The question whether space is real apart from space-filling objects . . . dates from early times.—W. T. HARRIS. All places are in one continuous space, an ultimate environment.—W. T. HARRIS. Space is the stature of God.—JOUBERT.
181. To be parochial is to turn away from the great and look at the little.—T. HIGGINSON. He looked, and saw wide territory spread / Before him—towns, and rural works between.—MILTON.

county, shire, province, precinct, *arrondissement* [F.], mofussil [Ind.], parish, diocese, township, commune, ward, wapentake [Hist.], hundred, riding, lathe [Kent, Eng.], soke [Hist.], tithing, bailiwick, state; colony, settlement; principality, kingdom etc. (country) 182; town, village etc. 189.16, 17.

3. *n.* plot, plot of ground *or* land, plat, patch, tract, field, arena; enclosure *or* inclosure, closure [obs.], close, enclave, *enceinte* [F.], croft [Eng.], garth [arch. and dial.]; court, yard etc. (enclosure) 232; square etc. 189.

4. *n.* beat, round, circuit, walk, march.

5. *n.* latitude, clime [poetic], climate, zone, meridian; longitude.

6. *adj.* regional, regionalistic, regionary; sectional, local, topical, parochial, insular, provincial, territorial; topographical, topographic; locational etc. 184.18.

182. Country
(See also 181. Region)

1. *n.* country, nation, state, republic, commonwealth, land, realm; dominion, domain; polity, body politic; empire, empery; *imperium in imperio* [L.]; principality, archduchy, duchy, dukedom, earldom, palatinate; chiefdom, chieftainry, chieftaincy, chieftainship; kingdom, kingship; seneschalty, seneschalsy, seneschalship; protectorate, protectorship; colony, settlement; toparchy, *toparchia* [L.]; power; monarchy, democracy etc. (government) 737.4; territory etc. 181.2.

2. *n.* fatherland, *Vaterland* [G.], motherland, native land *or* soil, home, homeland, God's country, God's own country, the old country [Europe].

3. *n.* (nicknames) Columbia, America the Beautiful, Land of Liberty, Land of the Free and Home of the Brave, melting pot, States, Yankeeland, Uncle Sam, U.S. [United States]; Seward's Folly, Uncle Sam's Attic *or* Icebox [Alaska]; Land of the Cornstalk [Australia]; Cockpit of Europe [Belgium]; Celestial Empire [China]; Sugarbowl of the World [Cuba]; Land of Bondage [Egypt]; Blighty, Sovereign of the Seas, Tight Little Island, Limeyland, John Bull, Land of the Rose [England]; Land of the Thousand Lakes [Finland]; Jean Crapaud [France]; Vaterland [Germany]; Land of Regrets [India]; Bogland, Emerald Isle, Green Island, Land of the Shamrock [Ireland]; Land of the Rising Sun, Land of the Cherryblossoms [Japan]; Mañanaland [Mexico]; Land of the Midnight Sun [Norway]; Crossroads of the World [Panama]; Land of the Thistle, Land of *or* o' Cakes, Auld Sod [Scotland]; Land of the White Elephant [Siam].

183. The Country

1. *n.* the country, rural district, rustic region, province *or* provinces, hinterland, back country, upcountry [coll.], the soil [chiefly poetic], the field [arch.], the bush, yokeldom; hickdom, hoosierdom, hoosier belt, the sticks, the clods [all slang]; countryside, rural neighborhood; cotton belt, tobacco belt, corn belt, wheat belt, citrus belt; dust bowl; wild West, wide open spaces; woods, woodlands, backwoods, forests, timbers, brush; uplands, highlands; lowlands; plain etc. 344; rustic, yokel etc. (peasant) 876.5.

2. *v.* countrify, ruralize, rusticate.

3. *adj.* countrified, country, provincial, rustic, rural, rurigenous [rare], agrarian, agrestic, inurbane, upcountry [coll.], hinterland, back, back-country, backwood *or* backwoods, landward [Scot.], bucolic, Arcadian [poetic], pastoral; hick, hoosier, hayseed, rube [all slang]; yokel, yokelish, farmerish, boorish, clownish, loutish, clodhopping, cloddish, churlish, hobnailed, carlish [literary], borrel [arch.], swainish [rare], woolen [rare], uncultivated; upland, uplandish; wood-

---

182. My country is the world; my countrymen are mankind.—W. L. GARRISON. I have but one life to lose for my country.—N. HALE. They love their land because it is their own, / And scorn to give aught other reason why.—HALLECK. The more I see of other countries the more I love my own.—MME. DE STAËL. Breathes there a man, with soul so dead, / Who never to himself hath said, / This is my own, my native Land?—SCOTT. What bosom beats not in his country's cause?—POPE. Who is here so vile that will not love his country?—SHAKESPEARE.

183. He likes the country, but in truth must own, / Most likes it when he studies it in town.—COWPER. How blessed is he who leads a country life.—DRYDEN. God made the country, and man made the town.—COWPER. Anybody can be good in the country; there are no temptations there.—WILDE. I have no relish for the country; it is a kind of healthy

land, silvan; agricultural etc. 371.9; plebeian etc. 876.11; uncouth etc. 851.7.

184. Location
(See 185. Dislocation)

1. *n.* location, situation, place, position, locality, locale, local, *locus* [L.] (*pl. loci*), site, situs, stead [dial.], habitat, spot, point, hole [slang]; where, whereness, whereabouts *or* whereabout; station, status, stand, standing, standpoint, footing, seat, post, ground, venue; diggings [coll.], digs [slang, Eng.]; bearings, latitude and longitude; region etc. 181; vicinity, environment etc. (surroundings) 227.2.

2. *n.* posture, pose, set, attitude, bearing, carriage, port, air, aspect.

3. *n.* stead, place, lieu, room [obs. exc. dial.].

4. *n.* small place, snug *or* confined place, limited *or* cramped space; tight spot, tight squeeze, pinch [all coll.]; hole in the wall; cubby, cubbyhole; cubbyhouse, dollhouse, playhouse, doghouse; hole, pigeonhole, glory hole [coll.]; village etc. 189.17; closet, attic etc. (room) 191.15, 19; niche, cranny etc. (nook) 191.3; point, dot etc. (inextension) 180a.

5. *n.* localization, locating etc. *v.,* location, situation, placement, emplacement, lodgment, fixation, disposition; collocation, allocation; deposition, reposition, stowage, packing, lading; insertion etc. 300.

6. *n.* establishment, foundation, installation; settlement, colonization.

7. *n.* naturalization, domestication; denization, denizenation, endenization [obs.]; acclimatization etc. (habituation) 613.5.

8. *n.* topography, geography, chorography; map etc. (outline) 626.2.

9. *v.* be located etc. *adj.*, lie, lie in, have its seat in.

10. *v.* locate, situate, place, put, set, seat, park, station, post; deposit, put down, lay down, set down; plump down, plank down [coll., chiefly U.S.], plunk down [chiefly coll.], plop down, slap down; localize, fix in, assign *or* consign to a place *or* locality; reposit, lay away etc. (store) 636.7; put aside, shelve etc. (put away) 678.4; put back, replace etc. (restore) 660.8.

11. *v.* establish, fix, found, install; plant, implant; bed, imbed *or* embed.

12. *v.* lodge, quarter, billet, harbor, shelter, house, room [U.S.], bed; put to bed, tuck in, cradle; lodge on, quarter on, billet on, saddle with.

13. *v.* load, lade, freight, ship, stevedore, place on *or* in, place a load on; pocket, bag; stow, pack etc. (store) 636.7; fill etc. 52.7.

14. *v.* settle, settle down, sit down, locate [coll., U.S.], establish, establish *or* locate oneself, park [slang, U.S.], take up one's abode *or* quarters, take residence at, residence [coll.], put up at, put up one's horses at, hang up one's hat [slang]; take *or* strike root, plant oneself, get a footing; anchor, cast anchor, come to anchor, moor; squat, perch, roost; nest, hive, burrow; domesticate, set up housekeeping, keep house, set up in business, hang up one's shingle [coll.]; reside etc. (inhabit) 186.10; remain, stay etc. 265.5.

15. *v.* camp, encamp, pitch, pitch camp, pitch one's tent, drive stakes [coll.]; bivouac.

16. *v.* naturalize, domesticate; denizen, endenizen, denizenize; adopt, admit; acclimatize etc. (habituate) 613.8.

17. *adj.* located etc. *v.*, situate, posited, ensconced, embedded, embosomed, implanted, rooted; in its element; moored, at anchor; vested in; unremoved; present etc. 186.13.

18. *adj.* locational, locable, positional, situal; environal, environic, environmental; topographical etc. (regional) 181.6.

19. *adj.* naturalized etc. *v.*, domesticated etc. (domestic) 188.12.

20. *adv.* in place *or* position, *in situ* [L.], *in loco* [L.]; here, there etc. (where) 186.18–23.

185. Dislocation
(See 184. Location)

1. *n.* dislocation, displacement, dislodgment, elocation [obs.], deposition;

---

grave.—S. SMITH.   There is nothing good to be had in the country, or, if there be, they will not let you have it.—HAZLITT.
184. Sit in your place, and none can make you rise.—G. HERBERT.   All things have their place, knew we how to place them.—G. HERBERT.   It is not the places that grace men, but men the places.—AGESILAUS.   A place for everything and everything in its place.

unplacement, unshipment [both rare]; heterotopia, heterotopy; misplacement; removal, moving etc. *v.*, shift; metastasis, metathesis; translocation, transplacement, transposition, transplantation; transshipment *or* transhipment, transship; transference etc. 270; ejection etc. 297; change etc. 140.

2. *v.* dislocate, displace, displant [obs.], dislodge, disniche; unplace, unlocate [rare], unseat; translocate [rare], transplace, transplant; move, remove; set ~, lay *or* put aside, put *or* set to one side, side; take away, cart away; take off, draft *or* draught off; disjoint, put out of joint, throw out of gear, unhinge, luxate; transfer etc. 270.6–10; transpose etc. (interchange) 148.3; rout out, banish, empty, unload etc. (eject) 297.8–21; disarrange, disorder etc. (derange) 61.2–5; dispel etc. (disperse) 73.3.

3. *adj.* dislocated etc. *adj.*, dislocate [arch.], dislocatory; heterotopic, heterotopous; metathetic(al); out of joint, out of gear.

4. *adj.* unplaced etc. *v.*, unhoused, unharbored, unestablished, unsettled; houseless, homeless, harborless [arch.].

5. *adj.* misplaced etc. *v.*, out of place, out of its element, out of a situation; in the wrong place, in the wrong box *or* pew [coll.], disorderly etc. 59.8, 9.

186. Presence
(See 187. Absence)

1. *n.* presence, presentness etc. *adj.*; existence etc. 1.

2. *n.* habitation, habitancy, inhabitance *or* inhabitancy, occupance *or* occupancy, occupation, residence, resiance *or* resiancy [obs.]; cohabitation, abode etc. 189.

3. *n.* whereness, ubication [rare], ubiety; whereabouts etc. (location) 184.

4. *n.* omnipresence, ubiquity, ubiquitariness.

5. *n.* permeation, pervasion, penetration; diffusion etc. (dispersion) 73.

6. *n.* attendance, attendancy [obs.]; frequence; turnout [coll.], draw [Theat. slang, U.S.]; standing room only, S.R.O. [Theat.]; assembly etc. 72.3.

7. *n.* attender, attendant, attendee [coll.]; patron, frequenter, *habitué* [F.];

spectator etc. 444; audience etc. 418.7, 8; theatergoer etc. 599.23.

8. *v.* be present etc. *adj.*, occur in a place, lie, stand, remain; fall in the way of; exist in space; exist etc. 1.4.

9. *v.* attend, be present at, present oneself at, find oneself at, appear, show up [coll.], show one's face *or* head; witness, look on, *assister* [F.]; visit, take in, do [coll.]; catch an act [Theat. cant]; watch etc. (look) 441.11; be a spectator etc. 444.3.

10. *v.* inhabit, habitate [rare]; occupy, dwell, reside, stay, remain, hang out [slang], sojourn, keep [coll., U.S.], live, abide, lodge, tenant; bunk, room; perch, roost [dial. or coll.]; nest, nestle [rare]; people, populate; cohabit; take up one's abode etc. (settle) 184.14.

11. *v.* frequent, resort to, haunt, hang around *or* about at, hang out at [slang], revisit.

12. *v.* pervade, permeate, penetrate, diffuse, be diffused *or* disseminated, overspread, overrun, run through, fill, meet one at every turn; interpenetrate etc. 228.9; imbue etc. 41.8.

13. *adj.* present, at hand, within reach, ~ sight *or* call; situate etc. 184.17; existent etc. 1.7.

14. *adj.* inhabited etc. *v.*, resident, resiant [obs.], residential, residentiary; domiciled.

15. *adj.* peopled, populated, populous, full of people.

16. *adv.* in the presence ~, in the face ~, under the eyes *or* under the nose of someone; *vis-à-vis* [F.] etc. (before) 234.9.

17. *adv.* in person, in the flesh [slang], *in propria persona* [L.].

18. *adv.* where, whither, whereabouts, whereabout [rare], whereaway [chiefly Scot.], wheresome [obs.], to what *or* which place.

19. *adv.* wherever, where'er [poetic], wheresoever, wheresoe'er [poetic], wherever it may be.

20. *adv.* here, in this place, on the spot; hereabout *or* hereabouts, in this vicinity; somewhere about *or* near, somewheres about [dial.], somewhere abouts [dial.]; aboard, on board; at home; hither, to this place.

21. *adv.* there, in that place; in *or* amidst such and such surroundings etc. 227.2; back home, down home [both

---

186. In thy presence joy entire.—MILTON.

coll.]; thereabout *or* thereabouts, in that vicinity; thither, to that place.
22. *adv.* here and there, in various places, *passim* [L.]; here, there and everywhere etc. (everywhere) 180.9.
23. *adv.* somewhere, somewheres [dial.], someplace, someplace or other, in some place.

187. Absence
(See 186. Presence)

1. *n.* absence, absency [obs.], nonpresence, awayness [rare]; withdrawal etc. (departure) 293.
2. *n.* nowhereness; nullibicity, nullibiety, nullibility [all rare]; nonexistence etc. 2.
3. *n.* emptiness, voidness [rare] etc. *adj.*; vacuity [rare], vacancy; nonoccupance, nonoccupation, noninhabitance, nonresidence; depletion, exhaustion.
4. *n.* void, vacuum, blank; *tabula rasa* [L.], clean slate.
5. *n.* absentation, nonattendance, nonappearance; truancy, truantcy [rare], truantry; hooky, French leave, cut [coll.]; absence without leave, A.W.O.L. [Mil.]; absenteeism, truantism; shirking etc. (avoidance) 623.
6. *n.* absentee, truant; shirk etc. 623.4.
7. *n.* nobody, no one, no man, nix [slang], not a soul, never a one, ne'er a one [poetic], nary one [dial.], nobody on earth *or* under the sun, nobody present.
8. *v.* be absent etc. *adj.*, not be present etc. (*see* present etc. 186.13), not show up [coll.], absent oneself, make oneself scarce [coll.], keep *or* stay away, keep out of the way; play truant, play hooky, absent oneself without leave, go A.W.O.L. [Mil. slang], take French leave, *filer à l'anglaise* [F.], mooch [now dial. and slang], jump, skip [slang], cut [coll.]; slip off *or* away, slip out; keep *or* hold aloof; withdraw, vacate etc. (depart) 293.4; shirk etc. 623.8.
9. *v.* empty, deplete etc. (evacuate) 297.14.
10. *adj.* absent, not present, nonattendant, away, gone; out of sight; missing, wanting, lacking, minus [coll.], omitted, nowhere to be found; nonresident, from home, away from home; truant, absent without leave, A.W.O.L. [Mil.]; abroad, oversea; on vacation, on tour, on the road; nonexistent etc. 2.7.
11. *adj.* empty, vacant, bare, jejune, void, null, null and void, devoid, hollow, blank, clear; vacuous; unoccupied, uninhabited, untenanted, tenantless, occupantless; deprived of, free from, in default of, in want of; desert, deserted, abandoned, forsaken, Godforsaken [coll.], desolate; dry, drained; unpossessed etc. 777a.3.
12. *adj.* uninhabitable, unhabitable.
13. *adj.* exempt from, not having.
14. *adv.* nowhere, nowheres [dial., U.S.], neither here nor there; nowhither, nowhence [rare].
15. *adv.* elsewhere, elsewhither, somewhere else, not here.
16. *prep.* without, withouten [dial.]; sans, with the lack of, wanting, lacking, less, minus.

188. Inhabitant

1. *n.* inhabitant, inhabiter, habitant, resident, residencer, residenter [chiefly Scot. and dial., U.S.], residentiary, resider, commorant, dweller, indweller, inmate, occupier, occupant, tenant, intern [spec. Med.]; denizen, citizen, sojourner, incumbent, *locum tenens* [L.]; addressee.
2. *n.* townsman, towny *or* townee [slang], towner [slang], villager, oppidan, cockney [obs.], gillie [circus slang, U.S.]; city man, cityite [coll.], cit [coll., derog.], city slicker [slang, U.S.]; burgher, burgess; villein [Hist.]; townswoman, villageress; lake dweller etc. 343a.2; islander etc. 346.2.
3. *n.* householder, housekeeper [arch.]; domiciliary; cottager, cotter, cottier [Eng. and Ir.]; villein, bordar, collibert [all feudal]; innholder etc. (proprietor) 779.2.
4. *n.* lodger, roomer [U.S.], paying guest; boarder, board-and-roomer

---

187. Absence is to love what wind is to a fire; it puts out the little, it kindles the great.—DE BUSSY-RABUTIN.   'Tis ever common / That men are merriest when they are from home.—SHAKESPEARE.   The Lord watch between me and thee, when we are absent one from another.—BIBLE.   Absent in body, but present in spirit.—BIBLE.   A beggarly account of empty boxes.—SHAKESPEARE. "Presents," I often say, "endear absents."—LAMB.   When the cat's away, the mice will play.   Out of sight, out of mind.   Absence makes the heart grow fonder.
188. Americans have a sort of permanent intoxication from within, a sort of invisible

[U.S.]; transient, transient guest *or* boarder; renter, lessee, underlessee.

5. *n.* settler, metic [Gr. Antiq.], habitant [Can. and Louisiana]; colonist, colonizer, colonial; planter; homesteader; squatter, nester [West. U.S.]; sooner [slang, West. U.S.].

6. *n.* backsettler, backwoodsman, hinterlander [slang]; mountaineer, hillbilly [coll.], ridge-runner [slang]; desert rat [West. U.S.].

7. *n.* fellow citizen *or* countryman, compatriot; fellow townsman, townie [slang], home towner [slang], homester.

8. *n.* native, indigene *or* indigena, original, aboriginal, aborigine, aboriginary [rare], binghi [slang, Australia], autochthon (*pl.* autochthones), primitive; old-timer [coll.], sourdough [coll., West. U.S., Can. and Alaska], longhorn [slang, West. U.S.]; shorthorn [coll., West. U.S.].

9. *n.* (nationalities) American, Brother Jonathan, Yankee, Yank [slang], Sammy [slang], Uncle Sam; Australian, Aussie [slang], digger [slang]; Canadian, Canuck [slang], Jean Baptiste [coll.]; Chinaman, Chinese, Chinee *or* heathen Chinee [slang], Chink [slang], Celestial, Sinaean, Sinaic *or* Sinic [rare]; Czech, Bootchkey [slang]; Dutchman, Dutcher [rare], butterbox [slang], Mynheer Closh [slang], Nic Frog; Englishman, Briton, Britisher, John Bull, limey *or* lime-juicer [slang, U.S.], tommy [slang]; Filipino, Philippino [erroneous], gugu [slang]; Frenchman, Frenchy [slang], frog *or* Froggy [slang], Jean [coll.], Jean *or* Johnny Crapaud [coll.], Parleyvoo [slang]; German, Dutchman [careless or slang], Fritz *or* Fritzie [slang], Heinie *or* Heine [slang], Jerry [slang], Hun, Boche *or* Bosche; Hungarian, Hun, hunky [slang]; Irishman, Irisher, Hibernian, Paddywhack [coll.], Paddy [coll.], mick [slang], Teague [coll.], Greek *or* Grecian [slang], Bogtrotter [slang]; Italian, dago [coll.], wop [slang]; Japanese, Jap [coll.], skibby [derog., local U.S.], son of Nippon, Nip [slang], cherry blossom; Jew, Hebrew, Hebe [slang], Israelite, Son of Israel, Izzy [derog.], sheeny [derog.], kike [**derog.**], shonnacker [derog., U.S.], Yiddisher [**slang**], Yid [derog.]; Mexican, Mex [slang], greaser [slang]; Nova Scotian, down-Easter [coll.]; Portuguese, Portagee [coll. or dial.]; Russian, Ivan Ivanovitch [coll.], Red [slang], Bear [coll.]; Scandinavian, Scandinoovian [slang], squarehead [slang]; Scot, Scotchman, Scotsman, Caledonian, Jock [slang], Sandy [slang], Sawney [slang]; Slav, bohunk [slang]; Spaniard, Spanisher [coll.]; Swede, roundhead [slang], Olaf [slang]; Swiss, Colin Tampon [coll.]; Welshman, Cambrian, Taffy [coll.]; Negro etc. 431.4; Caucasian etc. (race) 11.4.

10. *n.* population, habitancy, inhabitancy; inhabitants, people, folk, public; commonweal *or* common weal [arch.], commonwealth; nation, state, realm; community, mir [Russia]; colony, settlement; plantation; household, domestic establishment, family; garrison, crew.

11. *adj.* native, natal; indigenous, indigenal; autochthonal, autochtonous; original, aboriginal, primitive, vernacular; endemic, endemial [rare]; American; Australian; British, English; Canadian; Chinese, Celestial, Sinaean, Sinaic *or* Sinic [rare], Chink [slang], Chinee [slang]; Dutch; Filipino; French, Gallic; German, Germanic; Hungarian; Irish, Hibernian; Italian, woppish [slang]; Jewish, Hebrew, Yiddish; Mexican; Portuguese; Russian; Scandinavian, Scandinoovian [slang]; Scotch, Scottish; Slavonic; Spanish; Swedish; Swiss; Welsh, Cambrian; Negro etc. 431.7; Caucasian, Mongolian etc. (racial) 11.8.

12. *adj.* domestic, domiciliary; native, familiar, family, home, homely [rare], household, domal [rare]; domesticated, domiciliated, domiciled; home-bred; naturalized etc. (*see* naturalize etc. 184.16).

13. *adj.* occupied by, in the occupation of; garrisoned by.

189. Abode

Place of Habitation or Resort.—1. *n.* abode, habitation, habitance [obs.], inhabitance [rare], dwelling, dwelling

---

champagne.—CHESTERTON. But in spite of all temptations / To belong to other nations, / He remains an Englishman.—GILBERT. Sweet tenants of this grove.—COWPER.

189. Foxes have holes and birds of the air have nests.—BIBLE. Home is home, be it never so homely.—DICKENS. Be it ever so humble,

189.1 – 189.12

place, lodgment *or* lodgement, lodging place, lodging *or* lodgings, diggings [coll.], digs [slang, Eng.], domicile, *domus* [L.], residence, resiance *or* resiancy [obs.], *gîte* [F.], place; address, housing, quarters, headquarters, cantonment, tabernacle, berth, seat, lap, perch, roost, nest; joint, dump [both slang and contemptuous]; sojourn [rare], stopping place, stopover; private residence, private [crim. slang, U.S.].

2. *n.* home, abode etc. *above,* home sweet home, homestead, homestall [Eng.], fireside, hearth, hearthstone, chimney corner, ingleside, inglenook *or* ingle nook, roof, home roof, household, domestic household, ménage *or* menage, paternal domicile, the ancestral halls, place where one hangs his hat [joc.]; teacherage; Hestia [Gr. Myth.], Vesta [Rom. Myth.], *lares,* penates [both Rom. Myth.]; native land etc. (fatherland) 182.2, parsonage etc. 1000.5.

3. *n.* house, dwelling etc. *above* 189.1, *casa* [Sp., Pg. and It.], building, structure, edifice, erection, shebang [slang, U.S.], hole [dial., Eng.]; mansion, villa, cottage, chalet, box, lodge, rotunda, tower, *château* [F.], castle, pavilion, hotel, court, manor house, hall, messuage, palace, *palais* [F.], *palazzo* [It.], kiosk, bungalow, chummery [spec. Anglo-Ind.], farmhouse, farm, grange, country house, countryseat, summerhouse, town house, *rus in urbe* [L.].

brownstone house, duplex, frame house, shingle house, brick house, stucco house, twodecker, three-decker etc., skyscraper, apartment house, flat house, tenement, rent [obs. exc. coll., U.S.], monitor building [U.S.], jerry-building, penthouse.

4. *n.* hut, hutch, hovel, dump [slang], sty, pigsty, cabin, cot, cote [dial.], cottage, shanty, shack [coll.], shed, skipper [old slang], bothy *or* boothy [Scot.]; booth, stall; hogan, wigwam, wickiup, tepee, tupek *or* tupik, igloo, jacal [Southwest. U.S.]; dugout, *abri,* [F.]; lean-to, linter [dial., U.S.]; log cabin *or* house, blockhouse; adobe house, adobe, dobe [dial., West. U.S.], sod house; lake *or* lacustrine dwelling, pile house *or* dwelling; bunkhouse, flophouse [slang, U.S.]; hooden [West. U.S.], rancho [Sp. Amer.].

5. *n.* barn, bawn [obs.], stable; cow barn, cowhouse, cowshed, cow byre, byre, shippen *or* shippon [Scot. and dial. Eng.]; henhouse etc. 370.3; sheepfold, pigsty etc. (enclosure) 232; storehouse etc. 636.4.

6. *n.* kennel, doghouse, doghole, dogwam [joc.]; pound, dog pound.

7. *n.* cote, cot; bell cot *or* cote; dovecote, dovecot, pigeon house, columbary *or* columbarium; aviary, birdhouse, bird cage; coop, pen etc. (enclosure) 232.

8. *n.* inn, hostel [arch.], hostelry [arch.], hotel, lodginghouse, rooming house, tavern, cabaret [originally], resthouse [chiefly Ind. and Ceylon], caravansary *or* caravanserai, xenodochium [medieval], dak bungalow [Ind.], khan [Near East], hospital [Hist.], hospice, *posada* [Sp.]; flophouse, crummy [both tramp slang, U.S.]; public house, public [coll., Eng.], pub [slang, Eng.]; alehouse, saloon [U.S.] etc. (barroom) 959.13; coffeehouse, café etc. (restaurant) 298.42.

9. *n.* low resort, dive [chiefly U.S.]; hole [U.S.], dump, joint, place [all slang]; scatter, drum [both crim. slang, U.S.].

10. *n.* assembly hall *or* room, assembly [U.S.]; auditorium, aud [college slang, U.S.]; audience hall, hall of audience, durbar [Ind.]; concert hall; armory; gymnasium, gym [coll.]; theater etc. (drama) 599.10, 11; meetinghouse, church etc. (temple) 1000; meeting place etc. 74.2; parliament etc. (council) 696.

11. *n.* poorhouse, almshouse, townhouse [U.S.], home, farm [coll.].

12. *n.* house and grounds, house and lot [U.S.], messuage, holdings, demesne, estate, manor, ham, tenement, hacienda [Sp. Amer.], homestead, outfit [coll., U.S.], shebang [slang, U.S.], barton [Eng.], toft [Scot. and dial. Eng.; formerly *toft and croft*]; pen [Jamaica], mains [Scot.]; homecroft [Eng.]; cote [Eng. Hist.]; quarters [South. U.S.]; farmstead, ranchería [Sp. Amer. and Southw. U.S.] etc. (farm) 371.4.

---

there's no place like home.—J. H. Payne.
But what on earth is half so dear— / So longed for—as the hearth of home?—E. Brontë.

A man travels the world over in search of what he needs and returns home to find it.—G. Moore.
Heaven is not built of country seats, / But little

13. *n.* retreat, seclusion, resort, haunt, purlieu, hangout [slang, U.S.], stamping ground [slang]; lair, den, cave, hole, covert, mew; cell, adytum, sanctum sanctorum; study, library; aerie, eyrie; hermitage, hermitary [rare], cloister, anchorage; nest, nidus; arbor, bower; breeding place, rookery; sanctuary, asylum etc. (refuge) 666.3, 4; hideaway etc. (hiding place) 530.2.

14. *n.* health resort *or* retreat, sanatorium, spa etc. (hospital) 662.17.

15. *n.* camp, encampment, laager [South Africa], leaguer [Hist.]; bivouac, cantonment; barrack *or* barracks, quarters, casemate, casern *or* caserne; tourist camp, motel [slang, U.S.]; castrametation; tent etc. 223.5.

16. *n.* town, township, metropolis, capital [obs.], municipality, municipium [Rom. Antiq.], city, borough, burgh [Scot.], burg [coll., U.S.]; county town, county seat, courthouse [local U.S.]; suburb; ghetto.

17. *n.* village, hamlet, ham [arch. exc. in compounds], bustee [Ind.], thorp *or* thorpe [now chiefly in compounds], wick [rare exc. in compounds], dorp [Dutch], kraal [South Africa], rancho [Sp. Amer.], clachan [Scot.], pueblo [Amer. Indian], crossroads, jerkwater town [slang, U.S.], jumping-off-place [slang], one-horse town [coll.], tank town *or* station [slang, U.S.]; provincial *or* country town, hick town [slang], oppidum [Rom. Antiq.].

18. *n.* block, block of buildings, square, city block.

19. *n.* square, quadrangle, quad [coll.], plaza, *place* [F.], court, courtyard, wynd [chiefly dial.], close, piazza (*pl. piazze* [It.] *or* piazzas), forum [Rom. Antiq.]; polygon [Mil.]; *piazzetta* [It.], *campo* [It.] (*pl. campi*); colonnade, peristyle, cloister; market place, market, agora [Gr. Antiq.] (*pl.* agorae); yard etc. (enclosure) 232.

20. *n.* circle, circus [Eng.]; crescent.

21. *n.* park, garden, pleasure garden *or* grounds, paradise [spec. an Oriental park], pleasance, plaisance [arch.], common *or* commons.

22. *adj.* urban, oppidan, metropolitan, municipal, burghal, civic; citified; suburban; cosmopolitan.

23. *adj.* palatial, palatian [rare].

190. Contents
(See 191. Receptacle)

1. *n.* contents, insides, filling, stuffing *or* stuffings, wadding, padding, packing; lading, load, cargo, freight, bale, burden, burthen [chiefly arch.], lug [coll.], jag [chiefly dial.]; shipload, carload, cartload, wagonload etc.; cupful, basketful, cup of, basket of etc. (receptacle) 191; lining etc. 224; interior etc. 221.2.

2. *v.* load etc. (fill) 52.7, (place on *or* in) 184.13, (weight) 319.9; overload etc. 641.4.

191. Receptacle
(See 190. Contents)

1. *n.* receptacle, container, vessel, utensil; recipient, receiver, reservatory [obs.]; hopper, hamper; hod, scuttle; brazier; cuspidor, spittoon, spit bucket [joc.]; enclosure etc. 232.

2. compartment, apartment [obs.]; cell, cellule; follicle; crypt, vault, hold; booth, stall, manger; pew, box; hole, cavity, hollow; pigeonhole; cubby, cubbyhole; glory hole [coll.].

3. *n.* nook, corner, cranny, niche, hole [chiefly dial., Eng.], recess, oriel [obs.]; cove, alcove; coin, coign etc. (angle) 244.2; chimney corner etc. (fireplace) 386.2.

4. *n.* bag, sack, sac [rare], poke [arch. *or* dial.], pocket, pouch, pod, budget [dial.], scrip [arch.]; housewife, huswife, hussy [dial.]; nose bag, morral [Sp. Amer.]; sleeping bag, flea bag [army slang]; saddlebag; net; fob; purse etc. 802.2.

5. *n.* handbag, traveling bag, go-away bag [dial., U.S.], satchel, grip *or* gripsack [coll., U.S.], valise, portmanteau [chiefly Eng.]; (*pl.* portmanteaus, portmanteaux); *sac de nuit* [F.], keester *or* keister, peter [both crim. slang, U.S.]; carpetbag [chiefly U.S.], Boston bag [U.S.], Gladstone *or* Gladstone bag, suitcase; kit, knapsack, war bag *or* sack

---

queer suburban streets.—C. MORLEY.   A village is a hive of glass, / Where nothing unobserved can pass.—C. H. SPURGEON.   East or West, home is best.   A man's house is his castle.   A great city, a great solitude.

190. With a cargo of ivory, / And apes and peacocks.—MASEFIELD.
191. Blessed shall be thy basket and thy store. —BIBLE.   It is a difficult matter to argue with

[army slang], rucksack, haversack, tucker bag [Austral.], duffel bag, yannigan bag [slang, U.S.], turkey [slang, U.S. and Can.], sea bag [sea slang]; ditty bag or box, holdall, grab-all [coll.], boodle bag [slang], grouch bag [slang, U.S.]; brief case or bag; school bag; reticule; purse etc. 802.2.

6. *n.* (botany, anatomy, zoology) sac, saccule, sacculus (*pl.* sacculi), cyst, pocket, vesicle, vesica, vasculum, bladder, sound, blister, bleb, bursa, musk bag, utricle, venter, ventricle, sinus (*pl.* sinus), pericarp, udder, capsule, silique, follicle, pod, legume, calyx (*pl.* calyxes, calyces), cancelli, theca (*pl.* thecae); cell, loculus (*pl.* loculi).

7. *n.* stomach, belly, abdomen, venter, wame [Scot. and dial.], ingluvies [Zool.], crop [dial. exc. Zool.], gorge [arch. and dial.], craw, maw, gizzard [coll. and joc. exc. Zool.], tummy [childish]; breadbasket, kitchen, little Mary, the inner man [all slang]; paunch, pod [orig. dial.], tun, bay window [slang], corporation [slang], potbelly, pot [slang], swagbelly [now chiefly dial.]; first stomach, rumen; second stomach, reticulum (*pl.* reticula), honeycomb stomach; third stomach, psalterium (*pl.* psalteria), omasum (*pl.* omasa), manyplies; fourth stomach, abomasum or abomasus, rennet bag; vitals etc. 221.4.

8. *n.* case, incasement, casing; box, chest, kit [chiefly Scot. and dial. Eng.]; crate; carton; coffer, caddie, casket, pyx [rare exc. Eccl.]; monstrance [Eccl.], reliquary, shrine; canister; bin, bunker [Scot.], rack, crib; bandoleer, powder case, caisson, ammunition box, ammo box [mil. slang]; luggage case, imperial [rare]; trunk, box [Eng.], keester or keister [crim. slang, U.S.]; Saratoga trunk; *vache* [F.]; handbox; hatbox; skippet; *vasculum*; hope chest; cedar chest; cage; folio, portfolio; cardcase, file, letter file, filing box or case; sheath; scabbard, socket, quiver, boot.

9. *n.* basket, wisket or whisket [dial., Eng.], skippet [dial.], kit [Eng.]; corbeil, *corbeille* [F.]; crate; pannier, dosser; canister [rare]; crane [Scot.]; bushel, bushel basket; bassinet, cradle, crib; hamper, maund or maun [Scot. and dial.]; clothesbasket, clothes hamper or bin, buck basket; flower basket, fruit basket; wicker basket, reed basket, rush basket, wooden basket, wire basket.

10. *n.* vase, pot, urn; flowerpot, jardiniere, patella, amphora; pottery etc. (ceramics) 384.14.

11. *n.* (spec. for liquids) tank, vat; barrel, keg, cask, kit [chiefly Scot. and dial. Eng.], tun, butt; firkin, kilderkin, puncheon, rundlet, harness cask or tub [sea]; bottle, jar, decanter, ewer, cruse, carafe, flagon, flask, flasket; pocket flask, pocket pistol [slang]; stoup, carboy, canteen, lota [Ind.], mussuk [Ind.]; marine or dead marine [slang], empty; jug, demijohn; pitcher.

vial, phial; cruet, caster; *tazza* [It.]; patera; pot, urn, *urceus* [L.; Rom. Antiq.]; coffee urn, coffeepot, percolator, biggin, tea urn, teapot, samovar; gallipot; bucket, pail, skeel [obs. exc. dial.]; growler [slang, U.S.]; tub, washtub, bathtub; piggin [chiefly dial.], pipkin; cup, mug, noggin, goblet, chalice, tankard, beaker, tig [chiefly dial., Eng.], stein, schooner, scuttle [slang, U.S.], nipperkin [arch.], toby, rummer, horn; glass, tumbler; receiver, retort, alembic, crucible; matrass [Chem.], bolthead; capsule, capsula, scorifier.

bowl, basin, jorum [coll.], punch bowl; tureen, terrine; catch basin or drain; can, tin [Eng.], canister; billy or billycan [orig. Austral.]; cannikin or canakin; kettle, caldron, boiler, G.I. can [army slang]; earthen pot, chatty [Ind.], crock, pan, saucepan, posnet [arch. and dial.]; frying pan, skillet, spider; chamber pot, chamber, jordan [obs. exc. Scot. and dial. Eng.], thunder mug [old slang], can [slang], potty [child's word].

12. *n.* plate, platter, dish; trencher, calabash, porringer, potager [obs.]; saucer, patera [L.] (*pl.* paterae); tray, waiter, salver.

13. *n.* tableware, dining or table utensils; silverware, silver; glassware, chinaware, crockery etc. (ceramics) 384.14.

14. *n.* ladle, dipper, bail, scoop; simpulum [Rom.], cyathus (*pl.* cyathi) or kyathos (*pl.* kyathoi) [both classical Archaeol.]; spoon, tablespoon, teaspoon; labis [Eccl.], *éprouvette* [F.]; shovel, spade, muck stick [slang]; scoop shovel, coal shovel, banjo [slang, U.S.]; loy [Ir.

---

the belly, since it has no ears.—CATO THE ELDER. Let the guts be full, for it's they that carry the legs.—CERVANTES. Whose God is their belly.—BIBLE.

and U.S.], slick; spud, stump spud; trowel, spatula.

15. *n.* cupboard, closet, cabinet; commode, cellaret, chiffonier *or* chiffonnier, *chiffonière* [F.], chifforobe [U.S.], locker, safe, bin, bunker, buffet, press, clothespress, sideboard, bureau, chest, chest of drawers, escritoire, desk, secretary, *secrétaire* [F.], davenport, kitchen cabinet, Canterbury, *étagère* [F.], vargueno, vitrine; drawer, shelf; bookcase etc. 593.13.

16. *n.* room, roomstead [rare], chamber, apartment, cabin [obs. exc. Naut.]; parlor, living room, sitting room, reception room, drawing room, front room, best room [coll.], keeping room [dial., Eng.]; stateroom; presence chamber *or* room; palace, bedroom, boudoir, dormitory; kip, doss [both crim. slang, U.S.]; private chamber, sanctum, sanctum sanctorum, holy of holies, adytum, den; byroom, cubicle, roomlet; library, study, studio, office; dining room *or* hall, refectory, *salle à manger* [F.], mess hall [Mil.].

nursery, schoolroom; playroom, rumpus room [slang, U.S.], billiard room; kitchen, scullery, cookroom, cookhouse, cookery, bakehouse, crumb castle [joc.]; galley, caboose *or* camboose [both Naut.]; pantry, buttery, larder, spence [chiefly Scot.], stillroom [Eng.], cannery; cabinet, cubby, cubbyhole; dairy, dairy house *or* room; garage, coach house; lavatory etc. 652.4; water closet etc. 653.9; lumber room, storeroom etc. (depository) 636.4; smoking room etc. 392a.13.

17. *n.* vestibule, portal, portico, entry, entrance, entrance hall *or* court, entranceway, threshold, court, lobby; narthex, galilee [both Eccl.], corridor, gallery, propylaeum, atrium, tablinum [both Rom. Antiq.], loggia [Arch.], stoa [Gr. Arch.]; hall, hallway; passage, passageway; anteroom, antechamber; waiting room, reception hall *or* room, lounge, swing room [slang, U.S.]; porch, stoop [U.S.], veranda, verandah [chiefly U.S.], piazza [U.S.], levee [South. and West. U.S.], side-kicker [dial., West. U.S.]; sun porch *or* parlor, sleeping porch.

18. *n.* floor, level, story *or* storey; lower floor *or* story, upper floor *or* story; first floor *or* story, ground *or* street floor, *rez-de-chaussée* [F.]; mezzanine, mezzanine floor, *entre-sol* [F.]; clerestory *or* clearstory; second floor *or* story, third story etc.

19. *n.* attic, attic room, loft, garret, sky parlor, cockloft.

20. *n.* cellar, underground room, underground [Eng.], basement, serdab [Archaeol. and Near East]; subbasement; wine cellar; buttery; potato cellar, spud hole [dial. or slang, U.S.]; storm cellar, cyclone cellar, fraid hole [slang, U.S.], funk hole [slang, chiefly Eng.]; hold, hole [both Naut.]; cave etc. 252.3.

21. *n.* suite, suite *or* set of rooms; apartment, flat, tenement; walk-up, walkback [both coll., U.S.].

22. *n.* bower, arbor, pergola, kiosk, pandal [South. Ind.], cabinet; alcove, grotto; conservatory, greenhouse etc. (garden) 371.6.

23. *adj.* vascular, vesicular; capsular, capsulate; saccular, sacculated; ventricular, cystic, cellular, camerated, locular; multilocular, polygastric; gastric, gasteral [rare], stomachic; marsupial, marsupian; siliquose, siliquous.

192. Size
(See **193. Littleness**; also **31. Greatness**)

1. *n.* size, dimensions, proportions, measurement, measure, scantling [obs.], expanse, expansion, extent, scope, range, spread, area; magnitude, amplitude, mass, bulk, volume; largeness, bigness etc. *adj.*; greatness etc. (of quantity or degree) 31; quantity etc. 25.

2. *n.* capacity, content, accommodation, limit; room, roomage [rare], roomstead [now rare]; poundage, tonnage *or* tunnage, cordage; stowage, tankage; caliber etc. (diameter) 202.3.

3. *n.* hugeness etc. *adj.,* enormity, immensity; monstrosity.

4. *n.* corpulence, corporosity [joc., U.S.], bodily bulk, obesity, *embonpoint* [F.], pinguitude [rare], flesh and blood, lustihood [arch.]; plumpness, paunchiness, fatness etc. *adj.*; adiposis, adiposity; corporation [coll.] etc. (stomach) 191.7; rotundity etc. 249.

5. *n.* lump, bulk, block, loaf, mass, swad [slang, U.S.], gob [chiefly dial. and

---

192. I think no virtue goes with size.—EMERSON. He doth bestride the narrow world like a colossus —SHAKESPEARE. Obesity is the

slang], batch, wad, hunk [coll.], hank [dial.], chunk [coll.], whang [Scot. and dial.], clod, nugget.

6. *n.* (something large) slapper [dial.]; whopper *or* whapper, whacker, bumper [all coll.]; thumper, spanker, strapper, banger, lolloper, whaler, whale [all slang]; jumbo [chiefly coll.]; mountain etc. (height) 206.2.

7. *n.* corpulent person, whopper [coll.] etc. *above* 192.6, corporosity [joc., U.S.], lump [coll.], heavyweight, heavy [slang], human *or* man mountain [slang]; fat man, fatty [slang and dial.], humpty-dumpty, tubby [slang], squab, dumpling [coll.], grampus [coll.], porpoise [coll.], pudge [coll.], pudgy [slang], blimp [slang], potbelly.

8. *n.* giant, giantess [*fem.*], gigant [obs.], colossus, titan, Brobdingnagian, Antaeus, Goliath, Polyphemus, Titan, Titaness, Briareus, Norn, Hercules, Cyclops, Gargantua, Aegir, Hler, Gymir, Ran, Fafnir, Fenrir, Gerth, Grendel, Hymir, Loki, Mimir, Wade, Ymir; Jotunn; Gog and Magog; monster, behemoth, leviathan; whale, cachalot, porpoise; hippopotamus, (*pl.* hippopotamuses, hippopotami), hippo [coll.], hippomonstrosity [joc.], river horse, sea cow [rare]; elephant, jumbo [chiefly coll.]; mammoth, dinosaur, dinosaurian, Megalosaurus, megalosaur, megalosaurian, Ceratosaurus, Megatherium, Dinotherium.

9. *n.* full-size, full growth; life-size.

10. *v.* size, adjust, grade, gauge, range, graduate, group, sort, match; arrange etc. 60.6–8.

11. *adj.* sizable, sizely [coll.]; large, big, great, grand, tall [slang, U.S.], considerable, goodly, bulky, substantial, tidy [coll.], voluminous, ample, capacious, comprehensive; massive, massy; bull; spacious etc. 180.6, 7; long etc. 200.12; broad, thick etc. 202.6, 7; high etc. 206.13, 14.

12. *adj.* stout, corpulent, fat, obese, fleshy; plump, full, rotund, tubby [coll.], pudgy; lusty, strapping [coll.], chopping, bouncing; stalwart, brawny, burly; portly, imposing; well-fed, corn-fed, grain-fed; chubby-faced, club-faced [obs.], round-faced, moonfaced; plump as a dumpling *or* partridge, fat as a quail, fat as a pig *or* hog, "fat as a pork hog" (Malory), "fat as a porpoise" (Swift), "fat as a fool" (Lyly), "fat as butter" (Shakespeare), fat as brawn *or* bacon [coll.]; paunchy etc. (big-bellied) 194.11; thickset, chubby etc. (stubby) 201.6; rotund etc. 249.6.

13. *adj.* hulky, hulking, bulky, ponderous, lumpish, lubberly, loutish, overgrown; unwieldy, unwieldly, cumbrous, cumbersome, hippopotamic; puffy, swollen etc. (expanded) 194.10.

14. *adj.* full-sized, full-grown, full-formed, full-blown; life-sized, large as life, large as life and twice as natural [joc.].

15. *adj.* huge, hugeous [joc. or coll.]; immense, enormous, great big [redundant], mammoth, mighty, titanic, colossal, monumental, towering, prodigious, stupendous; monster, monstrous; vast, vasty [arch.]; gigantic, gigantean, gigantine [obs.], gigantal [obs. exc. slang]; giant, giantlike; Cyclopean, Brobdingnagian, Gargantuan, Herculean, Atlantean, Patagonian [obs.]; elephantine, jumbo [chiefly coll.]; megatherian, megatherine; dinosaurian, dinotherian; whopping, whacking, bumping, thumping, thundering, banging, slapping [all coll.]; whaling, spanking, lolloping [all slang].

193. Littleness
(See 192. Size; also 32. Smallness)

1. *n.* littleness, diminutiveness etc. *adj.,* exiguity, inextension; parvitude [rare], parvity [obs.]; smallness etc. (of quantity or degree) 32; narrowness, thinness etc. 203; shortness etc. 201.

2. *n.* (minute object) minute [obs.], minutia (*pl.* minutiae), diminutive, minikin [obs.], minim; point, vanishing point, mathematical point, point of a pin, pin point, pinprick, dot, speck, flyspeck, jot, tittle, mote; atom, atomy, molecule, monad, ion, magneton, micron, electron; mite [chiefly coll.], midge, insect, gnat, fly; runt, shrimp, small fry [chiefly coll.]; particle, scrap, snip, snippet, slip, scratch;

---

mother of abstinence.—Cynic's Calendar. The fat man knoweth not what the lean thinketh.—G. Herbert

193. For who hath despised the day of small things?—Bible. For the proverb saith that many small maken a great.—Chaucer. The

peewee, jitney [both slang]; bantam, banty [coll.]; pony; minnow, minny [coll.].

worm, maggot, grub, larva; mouse, tit, titmouse, tomtit; seed, millet seed, mustard seed, barleycorn; pebble, grain of sand; nubbin, peanut, button, crumb, hair, wart [slang], molehill; fragment, stitch etc. (small part) 51.3; powder etc. 330.3.

3. *n.* miniature, minny [slang]; microcosm, microcosmos; doll, puppet; Elzevir, Elzevir edition; duodecimo, twelvemo [coll.]; brief, abridgment etc. (compendium) 596.

4. *n.* microbe, microorganism; germ, bacterium (*pl.* bacteria), bacillus (*pl.* bacilli), microphyte, microzyme, micrococcus (*pl.* micrococci), zoogloea, schizomycete, diatom.

microspore, zygospore, zygote, arthrospore, zoospore, zoogonidium (*pl.* zoogonidia), gonidium (*pl.* gonidia); animalcule, animalculum (*pl.* animalcula), microzoon (*pl.* microzoa), microzoan; protozoon (*pl.* protozoa), Phytozoaria, rhizopod, foraminifer, mastigopod, mastigophoran, amoeba (*pl.* amoebae), infusorium [rare] (*pl.* infusoria), infusorian, phytozoon (*pl.* Phytozoa), phytozoan, rotifer, entozoon (*pl.* entozoa), entozoan, paramecium (*pl.* paramecia), radiolarian, gregarine, gregarinid; moner, moneron; proton, rudiment, primordium (*pl.* primordia); monad, dyad, triad, tetrad, pentad, hexad, heptad, octad.

5. *n.* dwarf, dwarfling, pygmy, Lilliputian, midget, midge, manikin, chit, fingerling [rare], pigwidgeon [now rare], Pigwiggen, urchin, elf, mite [coll.], atomy, dandiprat [arch.], micromorph [Zool.], homunculus, dapperling, Tom Thumb, hop-o'-my-thumb, runt, shrimp, small fry [chiefly coll.], wart [slang]; Negrito, Negrillo; Alberich, Alviss, Andvari *or* Andwari, Reginn *or* Regin.

6. *n.* (study of microscopic objects) micrology, micrography; microscopy, microscopics; microcosmography, microcosmology, microphysics; microphotography, photomicroscopy, photomicrography.

7. *n.* (instruments) microscope, mike [slang]; micrometer, vernier, interferometer.

8. *adj.* little, small, diminutive, slight, tiny, teeny [coll.], teeny-weeny [coll.], wee [coll.], peewee [slang], little-bitsy [dial. or slang], dinky [slang], pony, miniature, minikin, minute, fine, exiguous; petty [now rare], petite; dapper; baby, baby-sized; bantam, banty [coll.]; one-horse, two-by-four [both coll.]; half-pint, pint-sized; pocket, pocket-sized; portable, portative; limited, cramped; duodecimo, twelvemo [coll.]; breviped, brevipennate; thin, lean etc. (narrow) 203.9–11; dumpy, squat etc. (short) 201.5, 6; inconsiderable etc. (quantity) 32.6–11.

9. *adj.* dwarf, dwarfed, dwarfish; nanoid, pygmy, elfin, Lilliputian, Tom Thumb, Negritic; undersized, stunted; puny, runty [U.S.]; scrubby, scraggy; pollard, pollarded; weazened etc. (shrunk) 195.6.

10. *adj.* infinitesimal, microscopic, inappreciable; intangible, impalpable, evanescent; imperceptible, invisible; atomic, molecular; microbic, microbial, microbious, microorganic; animalcular, amoebic, amoeboid, diatomaceous, diatomic, microzoic, microzoal, microzoan, corpuscular, vestigial, embryonic; rudimentary, rudimental.

11. *adv.* little, small, slightly etc. *adj.*, on a small scale, in a small compass, in a nutshell, *in nuce* [L.], in miniature.

194. Expansion
(See 195. Contraction; also 35. Increase)

1. *n.* expansion, dispansion [obs.], increase of size, enlargement, aggrandizement, amplification, ampliation; heightening, enhancement, accretion, increment; spread, deployment [chiefly Mil.]; stretching, distention *or* distension, inflation, sufflation, tympany; dilation, dilatation, dilatancy; swelling, swellage; turgescence *or* turgescency, turgidness, turgidity; tumidity, tumidness; tumefaction, tumescence, intumescence; puffing, puffiness; dropsicalness, dropsy, edema; pandiculation; rarefaction, rarefication;

---

ant finds kingdoms in a foot of ground.—S. V. BENÉT. A little body often harbors a great soul. A lion may come to be beholden to a mouse.

194. Thine's a tympany of sense.—DRYDEN. So high as heaved the tumid hills.—MILTON. His belly was upblown with luxury, / And eke with fatness swollen were his eyne.—SPENSER.

194.1 – 195.5

magnification etc. (exaggeration) 549; expanse etc. (size) 192; thickness etc. 202.2; extension, augmentation etc. (increase) 35.1.

2. *n.* a swelling etc. *above,* 194.1, swell, rising; diastole; tympanites, tympany; tumor, tumefaction etc. *above,* 194.1; pimple, boil etc. (sore) 655.16; bulge, bulb etc. (convexity) 250.2; knoll, dune etc. (height) 206.2; billow, surge etc. (wave) 348.10.

3. *n.* growth, development, upgrowth; pullulation, gemmation, germination; budding, sprouting etc. *v.*

4. *n.* overexpansion, overdistention, overgrowth, overdevelopment etc.; hypertrophy [Med. and Biol.]; overfulness etc. (redundancy) 641.

5. *v.* become larger etc. (*see* large etc. 192.12), enlarge, expand, widen, broaden, extend; stretch, distend, dilate, swell, fill out; incrassate; spread, spread out, deploy [chiefly Mil.]; mantle; spread like wildfire; overrun, overgrow.

6. *v.* grow, develop, wax, increase, gather; grow up, spring up, shoot up, sprout up; shoot, sprout, bud, burgeon, put forth, germinate, pullulate, vegetate; open, burst forth; grow out, outgrow.

7. *v.* fatten, pinguefy, gain *or* gather flesh, gain weight, take *or* put on weight.

8. *v.* render larger etc. (*see* large etc. 192.11, 12), enlarge, largify [dial.], expand, widen, broaden, extend, greaten [arch.], biggen [chiefly dial., Eng.], aggrandize, amplify, increase, augment, develop; spread out, deploy [chiefly Mil.]; stretch, distend, dilate, swell, inflate, sufflate [rare], huff, puff, puff *or* blow up, bloat; pump, pump up; pack, stuff, pad, cram; rarefy; magnify etc. (exaggerate) 549.2.

9. *adj.* expansive, expansional, expansile.

10. *adj.* expanded etc. *v.*, larger etc. (*see* large etc. 192.11, 12), spread, spread *or* stretched out; fan-shaped, fan-shape, flabelliform, rhipidate; widely extended, widespread, widespreaded [rare]; wide-open; overgrown, overrun; patulous, patulent [rare]; dilatant, distensive; swollen, bloated, turgid, tumid, plethoric; puffy, pursy, blowzy; dropsical, hydropic(al), edematous, edematose, tumorous, tumefacient, tumescent, tumefying; hypertrophied, hypertropic(al) [Med. and Biol.]; enchymatous [Biol.]; bulging, bulbous etc. (convex) 250.9; overfull etc. 641.6.

11. *adj.* big-bellied, abdominous, paunchy, paunched, potbellied, swagbellied [now chiefly dial.]; thick-bodied, thick-girthed; corpulent, obese etc. (stout) 192.12.

195. Contraction
(See 194. Expansion; also 36. Decrease)

1. *n.* contraction, decrease of size, reduction; lessening etc. *v.*, curtailment, defalcation, decrement; compression, compaction [rare], coarctation [obs.], condensation, concentration, constraint; astriction, constriction; constringency, astringency, shrinking etc. *v.*; strangulation, stranglement; corrugation; wasting, consumption, emaciation, marasmus [Med.], attenuation, tabefaction [rare]; tabes [Med.]; atrophy, atrophia [NL.]; systole [Physiol. and Pros.]; haplology, syncope, syncopation [all Gram.]; collapse, prostration; decrease etc. 36; shortening etc. 201.2; narrowing etc. 203.2; closure etc. 261; conciseness etc. 572; compendium etc. 596.3; diminution, diminishment etc. (decrease) 36.1.

2. *n.* contractibility, contractibleness, contractility; compressibility, compressibleness etc.

3. *n.* contractor, astringent, astringer, constringent [rare], constrictor.

4. *v.* contract, compress, cramp, compact, concentrate; coarct [obs.], coarctate [rare]; draw in *or* together, narrow; constrict, constringe; shrink, shrivel, wither, sear, dry up; wizen, wizzen [obs. exc. dial.], weazen; waste, waste away, tabefy [rare]; purse, pucker, purse *or* pucker up; cockle, warp, knit, wrinkle, corrugate; crumple, crumple up; squeeze, tighten, crush, pinch; strangle, strangulate; shrink *or* fall together, collapse; syncopate [Gram.]; decrease, reduce etc. 36.3, 4; shorten etc. 201.4; become thin etc. 203.7, 8.

5. *v.* be smaller than, fall short of, not come up to etc. (be inferior) 34.4.

A full belly makes a dull brain.—FRANKLIN. The more waist the less speed.—CYNIC'S CALENDAR. Her waist is ampler than her life, / For life is but a span.—HOLMES.

195. Years contracting to a moment.—WORDSWORTH. Thou didst contract and purse thy brow.—SHAKESPEARE.

6. *adj.* contractive, contractional, contractile, contractible; contracted, shriveled, withered etc. *v.*; astringent, constringent; tabid, tabescent, tabetic; marantic, marasmic, marasmous, marasmoid [all Med.]; shrunk, shrunken, dried *or* shriveled up, corky, sear; wizened, wizen, wizzen [obs. exc. dial.], weazened, weazen [obs. exc. dial.], weazeny; wizen-faced, weazen-faced; unexpanded etc. (*see* expanded etc. 194.10); smaller etc. (*see* small etc. 193.8); narrow etc. 203.9.

196. Distance
(See 197. Nearness)

1. *n.* distance, distancy [rare], remoteness etc. *adj.*, incontiguity [obs.], longinquity [rare], elongation, longitude [now joc.], length, reach, extent, stretch, range, compass, spread, span, stride; way, ways; chance [dial., U.S.], spell [coll.]; drift; easting, westing, southing, northing; perspective; measurement etc. 466.

2. *n.* great distance, long *or* good way *or* ways, long chalk [coll.], right smart chance *or* spell [dial.], long step, tidy step [coll.], giant's stride, far cry, long range.

3. *n.* distant point *or* region, remote region, jumping-off-place [coll.], Godforsaken place [coll.], the back of beyond [slang]; outpost, outskirt; background; *ultima Thule* [L.], *ne plus ultra* [L.]; antipodes, antipodal points [Math.]; aphelion [Astron.], sky line, offing etc. (horizon) 213.4.

4. *v.* be distant etc. *adj.*, extend to, stretch to, stretch away to, reach to, spread to, lead to, go to, get to; range, have a range; extend out, stretch out, reach out; outreach, outstretch, outlie; remain at a distance, keep one's distance, keep *or* stand away *or* off, keep *or* stand clear of, keep *or* stand aloof.

5. *adj.* distant, distal, remote, removed, far, far-off, faraway, right smart off [dial.], incontiguous [obs.]; yon, yonder, yond [obs. exc. dial.]; ulterior; transmarine, transpontine, transatlantic, transalpine; tramontane; ultramontane, ultramundane; hyperborean, hyperboreal [rare]; antipodean; out-of-the-way, Godforsaken [coll.]; inaccessible, unapproachable; apart, asunder; long etc. 200.12.

6. *adv.* at a distance etc. *n.*, off, away, aloof; distantly etc. *adj.*, distad [Anat.], far, far off *or* away, afar, afar off, a long ~, ~ great *or* good way off, a long cry to, wide away, "over the hills and far away" (Gay), back of beyond [slang].

7. *adv.* yonder, yander [dial.], yon [now dial.], yond [arch. and dial.].

8. *adv. etc.* beyond, yond [arch. and dial.], yonder *or* yonder of [dial.]; farther, further, farther *or* further away; beyond the bounds, beyond range, out of range, beyond reach, out of reach, out of sight, *à perte de vue* [F.], out of hearing, out of the way, out of the sphere of, over the border.

9. *adv. etc.* wide of, clear of; wide of the mark, abroad, all abroad, astray, afield, far afield.

10. *adv.* far and wide, far and near, distantly and broadly, widely, broadly, abroad; to the uttermost parts of the earth, from pole to pole etc. (extensively) 180.8, 9.

11. *adv.* apart, aside, asunder [obs.]; wide apart *or* asunder, "as wide asunder as pole and pole" (Froude), "as far as the east is from the west" (Bible), *longo intervallo* [L.]; at arm's length.

197. Nearness
(See 196. Distance)

1. *n.* nearness, closeness etc. *adj.*, proximity, approximation, propinquity, appropinquity [rare], vicinity, vicinage, precinct, neighborhood, contiguity, adjacence *or* adjacency, apposition, juxtaposition; convergence etc. (near approach) 290; nearing etc. (approach) 286.

2. *n.* short distance, short way *or* ways, short step, brief span, piece [obs. exc. dial.], spell [coll.], a few ways [dial., U.S.]; close quarters *or* range, stone's

---

196. 'Tis distance lends enchantment to the view.—CAMPBELL.   Sweetest melodies / Are those that are by distance made more sweet.—WORDSWORTH.   To the vulgar eye, few things are wonderful that are not distant.—CARLYLE.

Memory, no less than hope, owes its charm to "the far away."—BULWER-LYTTON.   Over the hills and far away.—J. GAY.   There's a magic in the distance, where the sea-line meets the sky.—A. NOYES.
197. A man's best things are nearest him.—R. M. MILNES.   Never from thy side henceforth to stray.—MILTON.   Closer is He than breathing, / Nearer than hands or feet.—TENNYSON.   What is nearest touches us most.—

throw, spitting distance [joc.], bowshot, gunshot, pistol shot; earshot, earreach, mouth shot [dial.]; whoop, whoop *or* two whoops and a holler *or* hello [all slang]; ace, bit [coll.], crack, spot [slang], hair, hairbreadth *or* hairsbreadth, inch, span, step; short course *or* passage, short cut, beeline.

3. *n.* purlieus, neighborhood, environs etc. (surroundings) 227.2; confines, bounds etc. (edge) 231.

4. *n.* neighbor, neighborer; bystander; borderer; perihelion; abutter etc. 199.2.

5. *v.* be near etc. *adj.,* adjoin, join [coll.], abut, neighbor, trench on, border, border on *or* upon, verge upon, stand by, approximate; cling to, clasp, hug, huddle [chiefly dial.]; hug the shore *or* land; follow close upon, tread on the heels of; hang about, hang upon the skirts of, hover over; be warm *or* hot, burn [all coll.].

6. *v.* near, draw near etc. (approach) 286.2; approach near *or* together etc. (converge) 290.2.

7. *v.* bring or place near, place side by side etc. *adv.,* juxtapose, juxtaposit, join, adjoin, abut, neighbor.

8. *adj.* near, nigh, close, intimate, vicinal, contiguous, adjacent, adjoining; neighboring, neighbor; propinquant, propinquous [rare], propinque [rare]; bordering, bordering upon; proximate, proximal; juxtapositional, juxtapositive; in the vicinity of, in the neighborhood; around, about [both coll.]; near-by, close by, at hand, close at hand, near-at-hand, handy; warm, hot, burning [all coll.]; near the mark; near run, near the wind, close to the wind, close-hauled.

9. *adj.* nearer, closer etc. *above,* near [obs. exc. dial.].

10. *adj.* nearest, closest etc. *above* 197.8, nearmost [chiefly dial.].

11. *adv. etc.* near, nigh, hard, hard *or* fast by, close to, close *or* hard upon, at close quarters; near by, nearabout *or* nearabouts [now dial.], nigh about [dial.]; about, around [coll., U.S.], close about; not far from, at no great distance, but a step; in an inch of, within an ace of; within reach *or* range, within call *or* hearing, within earshot *or* earreach, within a whoop *or* two whoops and a holler *or* hello [slang], within a stone's throw, in spitting distance [joc.]; bordering upon, verging to *or* on, on the confines of, at the threshold of, on the brink *or* verge of, on the point of, on the skirts of, on the heels of.

in the environs of, in the vicinity of (*see* vicinity etc. 227.2); next door to, at one's door, at one's feet *or* elbow, at one's finger's end *or* tip, under one's nose; in sight of, in the presence of; fornent, fernint, fornenst, ferninst [all dial.]; in juxtaposition etc. *n.*; side by side etc. (beside) 236.

12. *adv.* nearly etc. *adj.,* near, near by [Scot.], nigh by [dial.], nearaway *or* nearaways [rare]; almost, about, around [coll., U.S.], all but, as good as, wellnigh; barely, scarcely, hardly; thereabout *or* thereabouts, hereabout *or* hereabouts; roughly, roundly, in round numbers, generally; approximately, approximatively.

198. Interval
(See 199. Contiguity)

1. *n.* interval, interspace, intervening space, space, interstice, intersection; interruption, interregnum; hiatus, hiation [rare], caesura, lacuna (*pl.* lacunae, lacunas) break, gap, gulf etc. *below,* 198.2, 3; separation etc. 44.1; omission etc. 53.2.

2. *n.* cleft, chasm, crevice, crack, cranny, creek [obs. exc. dial.], chink, chap, gap, fissure, scissure, incision, cut, gash, slit, split, rift, rent, rime, breach, break, fracture, rupture, fault, flaw; leak; hole etc. (opening) 260; cavity etc. 252.2; trench etc. 259.2.

3. *n.* (geographic) gorge, gap, notch [U.S.], cut, ravine, close [U.S.], nullah [Anglo-Ind.], cañon; gulch [U.S.], gully, *barranca* [Sp.]; defile, pass, passage; clough, cleuch *or* cleugh [Scot.]; chasm, abyss, abysm, gulf; yawning chasm, ~ abyss *or* gulf; crevasse; *couloir* [F.], chimney; inlet, outlet; frith, firth; strait; cove, *abra* [Sp. Amer.]; narrow etc. 203.3; valley etc. 252.5.

4. *v.* interval, set at intervals, space, in-

JOHNSON. He only says, "Good fences make good neighbors."—R. FROST. All is well with him who is beloved of his neighbors.—G. HERBERT. He who enjoys a good neighbor has a precious possession.—HESIOD.

198. Between us and you there is a great gulf fixed.—BIBLE. So huge the chasm between the false and true.—BROWNING. 'Twixt host and host but narrow space was left, / A dreadful interval.—MILTON.

terspace, separate, part, dispart, set *or* keep apart, hiate [rare], remove; gape etc. (open) 260.11–14.

5. *adj.* intervallic, with an interval, far between; intervaled *or* intervalled, spaced, interspaced etc. *v.*; gaping, chinky, breachy, dehiscent, cloven; rimose *or* rimous, rimulose [Bot. and Zool.]; fissury, fissural.

6. *adv.* at intervals, *longo intervallo* etc. (discontinuously) 70.5.

199. Contiguity
(See 198. Interval)

Actual Contact.—1. *n.* contiguity, contiguousness etc. *adj.*, contingence, contact, taction, touch, connection, apposition, juxtaposition; abuttal, abutment; osculation [Geom.]; touching, meeting etc. *v.*; tangency, tangence [rare]; appulse, appulsion [Tech.]; recounter, rencounter, rencontre; syzygy [Tech.]; union, junction, conjunction, conjugation; coincidence, coexistence; proximity etc. (nearness) 197; adhesion etc. (coherence) 46.

2. *n.* abutter, joiner; tangent; borderer etc. (neighbor) 197.4.

3. *v.* be contiguous etc. *adj.*, touch, meet, contact, come in contact, join [coll.], adjoin, conjoin, connect, append, abut, abut on *or* upon, neighbor, border; osculate [Geom.]; go with, march with; coincide, coexist; graze, rub, brush, scrape, skim; adhere etc. 46.5.

4. *adj.* contiguous, touching etc. *v.*, in contact etc. *n.*, contactual [rare], contingent, conterminous, adjacent; juxtapositional, juxtapositive; osculatory [Geom.]: pertinent [obs.]; tangent, tangential; end to end, hand to hand; close to etc. (near) 197.8, 11; with no interval etc. 198.8, 11.

200. Length
(See 201. Shortness)

1. *n.* length, longness etc. *adj.*, longitude [chiefly Tech. or joc.]; mileage, footage etc. (*see* foot etc. *below* 200.6); extent, span etc. (distance) 196; measurement etc. 466.

2. *n.* oblongness, oblongitude.

3. *n.* a length, piece, coil, roll, run.

4. *n.* line, strip, stripe, streak, band, bar, rule [obs.]; radius, spoke.

5. *n.* lengthening etc. *v.*, prolongation, elongation, production, protraction, extension; stretch, tension.

6. *n.* linear measure, lineal measure, measurement of length; line, nail, inch, hand, handbreadth, palm, foot, cubit, yard, ell, fathom, rod, pole, furlong, mile, chain, arpent [Can.], kos [Ind.], vara [Sp. and Pg.]; nautical measure, knot, fathom, cable's length, nautical mile, statute mile, league; meter, kilometer, centimeter etc. 466.3.

7. *n.* rule, yardstick etc. (measuring instruments) 466.4.

8. *v.* be long etc. *adj.*, outstretch, stretch out, extend out, reach out; "drag its slow length along" (Pope), drag a lengthening chain; sprawl; extend to etc. (be distant) 196.4.

9. *v.* lengthen, render long etc. *adj.*, elongate, prolong, extend, produce [now rare exc. Geom.], protract, stretch; lengthen out, let out, draw out, spin out; drawl.

10. *v.* look along, view in perspective.

11. *v.* enfilade, rake [both Mil.].

12. *adj.* long, longsome [arch. and dial.], longish, lengthy; lengthened, elongated, elongate [rare], outstretched, extended, protracted, prolonged; far-reaching, extensive; interminable, without end, no end of [coll.]; as long as my arm, as long as today and tomorrow, a mile long; sesquepedalian, sesquepedal, jawbreaking [slang], crackjaw; unshortened etc. (*see* shorten etc. 201.4); tall etc. (high) 206.13; large etc. 192.11; distant etc. 196.5.

13. *adj.* long-legged, long-limbed, leggy, lath-legged [coll.], lathy [coll.], spindle-legged, spindle-shanked, gangle-shanked [slang]; lanky etc. (thin) 203.10, 11; lengthy [coll.], tall etc. (high) 206.13.

14. *adj.* oblong, oblongated, oblongitudinal; prolonged, elongated etc. *above* 200.12; rectangular, elliptical.

15. *adv.* lengthwise, lengthways, at length, longitudinally, along; endwise, endways, endlong; tandem; in a line etc. (continuously) 69.7.

16. *adv.* from end to end, from one end to the other, from beginning to end, from

---

200. What! will the line stretch out to the crack of doom?—SHAKESPEARE.   You shall not know the length of my foot.—LYLY.   The letter is too long by half a mile.—SHAKESPEARE.

out to out, from cover to cover; from stem to stern, fore and aft; from top to bottom, *de fond en comble* [F.], from head to foot, *a capite ad calcem* [L.], from top to toe, from the crown of the head to the sole of the foot; over all, all over.

201. Shortness
(See 200. Length)

1. *n.* shortness, briefness etc. *adj.*, brevity; conciseness etc. 572; littleness etc. 193; lowness etc. 207; inch, span etc. (short distance) 197.2.

2. *n.* shortening etc. *v.*, abbreviation, abbreviature [obs.]; abridgment, *abrégé* [F.]; concision, retrenchment, curtailment, decurtation [obs.], epitomization, truncation, obtruncation [rare], condensation; elision, ellipsis, syncope; reduction etc. (decrease) 36; deduction etc. 38; compression etc. (contraction) 195; epitome etc. (compendium) 596.

3. *n.* abridger, epitomizer, epitomist; truncator, obtruncator [obs.].

4. *v.* shorten, render short etc. *adj.*, abbreviate, curtail, abridge, epitomize, condense, abstract, take in, boil down, retrench; cut short, cut off short; stunt, check the growth of; snub, nip; pollard; foreshorten [Drawing]; compress etc. (contract) 195.4; clip, truncate etc. (deduct) 38.4-6; reduce etc. 36.4.

5. *adj.* short, brief, abbreviatory, summary, elliptic(al), succinct, "short and sweet" (T. Lodge); curt, curtate, curtal [arch.], decurtate; compendious, compendiary; compact, compacted; synoptic(al); terse, laconic etc. (concise) 572.3; little etc. 193.8, 9; low etc. 207.7.

6. *adj.* stubby, stubbed, stumpy [coll.], thickset, stocky, stodgy, stuggy [dial., Eng.], chubby, chumpy [coll.], chunky [coll.], squat, squattish, squatty, squidgy [rare], dumpy, squab, squabbish, squabby, punchy [coll.], pudgy, tubby [coll.], spuddy [dial. and coll.]; scrubby, scrub; pug, pugged; snub, snubbed, snubby;

pug-nosed, snub-nosed; *retroussé* [F.], turned-up; obese etc. (stout) 192.12; rotund etc. 249.6.

7. *adv.* shortly etc. *adj.*; in short etc. (concisely) 572.4.

8. *adv.* short [as *to stop short*], abruptly, suddenly, all of a sudden.

202. Breadth, Thickness
(See 203. Narrowness, Thinness)

1. *n.* breadth, broadness etc. *adj.*, width, latitude [now rare], amplitude, span, expanse, spread; beam [Naut.].

2. *n.* thickness etc. *adj.*, crassitude [obs.]; solidity etc. (density) 321; corpulence etc. (size) 192; dilation etc. (expansion) 194.

3. *n.* diameter, bore, caliber *or* calibre, scantling [obs.], radius (*pl.* radii, radiuses), module [Numis.].

4. *v.* broaden, grow *or* make broad etc. *adj.*, widen, spread, spread out, outspread, outstretch; expand etc. 194.5–8.

5. *v.* thicken, thick; inspissate etc. (solidify) 321.7.

6. *adj.* broad, wide, ample, roomy, spacious, expansive, extensive; extended, outspread, outstretched; wide-wayed, wide-spaced, wide-spanned; "broad as the world" (Lowell), "wide as a church-door" (Shakespeare); beamy [Naut.]; broad-gauge, broad-gauged; discoid, discoidal, discous [Bot.]; fanlike, fan-shaped, fan-shape, flabelliform, rhipidate.

latifoliate, latifolious [both rare; bot.]; broad-leaved, broad-leafed; laticostate, broad-ribbed, wide-ribbed; latidentate, broad-toothed, wide-toothed; broad-headed, broad-faced, broad-shouldered, broad-brimmed, broad-tailed; wide-arched, wide-armed, wide-banked; wide-branched, wide-breasted, wide-brimmed, wide-winged, wide-eared, wide-elbowed, wide-rimmed *or* -brimmed; wide-faced, wide-framed, wide-hipped, wide-lipped, wide-nosed, wide-ribbed, wide-tracked, wide-streeted; large etc. 192.11.

7. *adj.* thick, thick as a rope; thick-footed, thick-ankled, thick-wristed, thick-fingered, thick-toed, thick-toothed, thick-eared, thick-barred, thick-coated, thick-walled, thick-barked, thick-bodied, thick-girthed, thick-necked, thick-ribbed, thick-

---

201. *Est brevitate opus, ut currat sententia* [Terseness is needed that the thought may run free].—HORACE. Both short and sweet some say is best.—MIDDLETON. This is the short and the long of it.—SHAKESPEARE. An abridgment of all that was pleasant in man.—GOLDSMITH. Not that the story need be long, but it will take a long while to make it short.—THOREAU.

202. Wide is the gate, and broad is the way, that leadeth to destruction.—BIBLE. No wider than the heart is wide.—MILLAY.

stalked, thick-stemmed, thick-tailed; solid etc. (dense) 321.8; thickset etc. (stubby) 201.6.

8. *adv.* broadwise, broadways, broadside foremost.

203. Narrowness, Thinness
(See 202. Breadth, Thickness)

1. *n.* narrowness etc. *adj.,* exility; hair, hairbreadth *or* hairsbreadth, finger's breadth; exiguity etc. (littleness) 193.

2. *n.* narrowing etc. *v.,* angustation [rare]; stricture, organic stricture, constriction, coarctation [all Med.]; compression etc. (contraction) 195.

3. *n.* narrow, narrows, strait; neck, isthmus; channel, canal; pass, ghat [Ind.]; defile, ravine etc. 198.3.

4. *n.* thinness etc. *adj.,* slimth [dial.]; tenuity, attenuation, extenuation; emaciation, marcor [obs.], macilence *or* macilency [rare].

5. *n.* (comparisons) paper, wafer, lath, slat, rail, rake, splinter, slip, shaving, streak, vein; shadow, mere shadow; Banbury cheese, whipping post; skeleton, anatomy, atomy [obs. exc. joc.]; skin and bones, mere skin and bones; lantern jaws, hatchet face.

6. *n.* (thin person) lank [rare], lanky [slang], skinny [slang], slim [slang], scrag, shadow, skeleton, walking skeleton, study in anatomy, corpse, barebone, bag *or* stack of bones, rackabones [coll., U.S.], rattlebones [coll.], spareribs [coll.], slab-sides [dial. and slang], thingut [obs.], spindleshanks [coll.], spindlelegs [coll.], gangleshanks [slang], lathlegs [slang], bean pole, beanstalk, broomstick, clothes pole [all joc. or contemptuous]; tall person etc. 206.6.

7. *v.* narrow, become *or* render narrow etc. *adj.,* taper; draw in etc. (contract) 195.4.

8. *v.* thin, become *or* render thin etc. *adj.,* thin away, ~ down, ~ off *or* out, thinnen [dial.], leanen [dial.], gaunt down [dial.], slim, slim down, slenderize, meager, reduce; reduce weight, lose flesh;

bantingize, bant [coll.]; attenuate, extenuate, rarefy; dilute etc. 160.9.

9. *adj.* narrow, slender, slim, strait [arch.], not broad etc. 202.6; close, tight, confined, restricted, limited, coarctate, incapacious; scant, scanty; taper, tapered, tapering; angustate [rare], angust [obs.]; angustifoliate, angustirostrate, angustiseptal, angustisellate; contracted etc. 195.6; unexpanded etc. (*see* expanded etc. 194.10); little etc. 193.8.

10. *adj.* thin, slender, slim, slimmer [Scot.], slimmish; fine, finespun; gracile, graciliscent; slight, slight-made, delicate; flimsy, slimsy [coll., U.S.]; tenuous, rare, rarefied, subtle, subtile [arch.], unsubstantial, imponderable; threadlike etc. (filamentous) 205.7.

11. *adj.* lean, fleshless, spare, meager, lank, lanky, gaunt, gaunted, gaunty, gawky, gawkward [slang, U.S.], skinny, scrawny [U.S.], scraggy, weedy [coll.], slinky [dial.], spindling, spindly [coll.], lathy [coll.], flat-sided [coll.], slab-sided [slang, U.S.], slap-sided [dial. and slang, U.S.], ribby [coll.], rawboned, rattle-boned [slang], bony, skeletal, herringgutted [coll.], gangling [coll.], gangly [coll. and dial.]; lath-legged [coll.], spindle-legged, spindle-shanked, gangle-shanked [slang]; attenuated, attenuate, extenuated, extenuate [obs.].

starved, starveling; shriveled, withered, marcid [obs.], pinched, poor, peaked [coll.], haggard; wizened, wizen, wizzen [obs. exc. dial.], weazened, weazen [obs. exc. dial.], weazeny; macilent [rare], emaciated; tabic, tabetic, tabid, marantic, marasmic, marasmous, marasmoid [all Med.]; worn to a shadow, "worn to the bones" (Shakespeare); "lean as a rake" (Chaucer), slender as a thread, thin *or* skinny as a lath, ~ rail, ~ whipping post, ~ wafer etc. *n.*; lean-faced, hatchet-faced, lantern-jawed; wizen-faced, weazen-faced; long-legged etc. 200.13; tall etc. 206.13.

204. Layer

1. *n.* layer, stratum (*pl.* strata), bed, couch, *couche* [F.]; substratum, floor; scarp, escarpment; post, measure, magma [all Geol.]; stage, course, coping [Arch.], zone, level, story, tier; dess [Scot. and North. Eng.].

2. *n.* lamina (*pl.* laminae, laminas),

---

203. Pinch, a hungry, lean-faced villain, a mere anatomy.—SHAKESPEARE. And he is lean and lank and brown as is the ribbed sea-sand.—WORDSWORTH. Meager were his looks; / Sharp misery had worn him to the bones.—SHAKESPEARE. His dominions were very narrow and scanty.—LOCKE.

lamella (*pl.* lamellae, lamellas), leaf, sheet, foil; flake, scale; wafer, disk; plate, platter; coat, coating, veneer, film, membrane, pellicle, peel, skin; cut, slice, rasher, shive, shaving; table, tablet, slab; flag, flagstone; pane, panel; board, plank; fold, lap, flap, ply, plait; eschar [Med.]; overlay, integument etc. (covering) 223.

3. *n.* stratification, lamination, lamellation, foliation; delamination, desquamation [Med.], exfoliation; squamosity, squamousness, scaliness etc. *v.*

4. *v.* form in layers etc. *n.*, stratify, laminate; delaminate, desquamate [Med.], exfoliate; flake, scale; slice, cut, shave, skive, peel, pare; plate, coat, veneer; overlay etc. (cover) 223.22.

5. *adj.* laminated *or* laminate, laminous, laminose [rare], laminiferous; lamellar, lamellated *or* lamellate, lamelliferous, lamelliform; stratified, stratiform; scaly, flaky, scabby, scurfy; squamous, squamose, squamosal, squamoid, squamate, squamiferous; micaceous, micacious; filmy, filmlike; membranous, membranaceous; foliated, foliate [rare], foliaceous; tabular, tabloid; discoid, discoidal; spathic, spathose.

205. Filament

1. *n.* filament, filamentule; fiber; fibril, fibrilla (*pl.* fibrillae); capillament [obs. exc. bot.]; capillary, vein; veinlet, veinule, veinulet, venule, venula; cilium (*pl.* cilia), ciliolum (*pl.* ciliola); tendril, cirrus (*pl.* cirri); gossamer, web, cobweb, spider *or* spider's web; barbel, barbule; hair etc. 256.3–7.

2. *n.* thread, threadlet; packthread, sewing thread, darning cotton; yarn, harl, flax, cotton, silk, near-silk [chiefly coll.], rayon, nylon, Celanese [trade name], linen, wool.

3. *n.* cord, line, string, strand; cable, wire; strap, strop; twist, braid, inkle, oxreim [S. Afr.]; thong, whang [Scot. and dial.], boondoggle [slang, U.S.], brail [falconry]; rope, hemp, oakum, jute, sennit, pepper-and-salt rope [coll.], wire rope, clothesline, towline; whipcord; stay, fast, guy, guy rope; painter, lanyard etc. (ship's ropes) 273.10; lasso, halter etc. (fastening) 45.2; tendon, funicle etc. (ligament) 45.4.

4. *n.* cordage, cording, ropework, roping; tackle, tack, gear, service *or* serving [Naut.]; rigging etc. (ship) 273.9.

5. *n.* strip, shred, slip, spill, list, taenia, band, fillet, fascia; tape, tapeline; ribbon, ribband *or* riband [arch.]; lath, slat; splinter, sliver, shiver, shaving; ligule, ligula.

6. *v.* filament, shred, make threads of.

7. *adj.* filamented etc. *v.*, filamentar, filamentary, filamentous, filamentose, filamentoid, filamentiferous, filaceous [rare], filiform; fibrous, fibrilous, fibrilliferous, fibry, fibrilliform; fibrovascular; threadlike, thready; stringy, ropy, wiry; capillary, capillaceous, capilliform; cirrose, cirrous; funicular, funiculate; anguilliform; flagelliform; taeniate, taeniform, taenoid; venose, venous, veinous, veinal [rare]; ligulate, ligular; finespun, wiredrawn, attenuate; hairy etc. 256.13, 14.

206. Height
(See 207. Lowness)

1. *n.* height, hight [obs. exc. dial.], heighth [obs. exc. dial.], perpendicular distance, altitude, elevation, exaltation, sublimity [arch.], eminence, prominence, celsitude [obs.], pitch, loftiness etc. *adj.*; stature, procerity [rare]; stratosphere, ionosphere.

2. *n.* a height, elevation, eminence, tower [now rare], *alto* [Sp. Amer.], rise, uprise, rising ground, vantage point *or* ground; mount, mountain, alp; hill, knap, down, moor [dial., Eng.], brae [Scot. and dial. Eng.], kop [S. Afr.], fell [Scot. and North. Eng.; now only in proper names]; hillock, monticle, monticule, hummock, mound, barrow [now only in proper names], knoll, tump [dial., Eng.], kopje [S. Afr.]; dune, sand dune; ridge, *arête* [F.], chine, spine, kame [Scot. and North. Eng.], comb [Scot. and dial.], esker; horseback, hogback, hog's-back;

206. I will lift up mine eyes unto the hills.—BIBLE. Behold the height of the stars, how high they are!—BIBLE. Mountains are earth's undying monuments.—HAWTHORNE. Uprose the mystic mountain range.—TENNYSON. Man can climb to the highest summits, but he cannot dwell there long.—SHAW. Bare steeps where desolation stalks.—WORDSWORTH. Every hill hath his dale.—B. MELBANCKE.

plateau, table, tableland; table mountain, butte [U.S.], *picacho* [Sp.; Southwest. U.S.], loma [Southwest. U.S.].

promontory, mull [Scot.], point; crag, craig [Scot. and North. Eng.]; ledge, shelf; pinnacle, peak, pike [chiefly North. Eng.], crest, tor; range, mountain range, chain, watershed, divide; heights, uplands, highlands; soaring *or* towering heights, dizzy height; oread [Gr. Myth.]; utmost height etc. (summit) 210; steep, cliff etc. (precipice) 212.3; headland etc. 250.5.

3. *n.* tower; turret, *tourelle* [F.]; campanile, belfry, bell tower; cupola; dome; martello, martello tower; barbican; windmill tower, observation tower, fire tower; steeple, spire, *flèche* [F.]; minaret; stupe, tope, pagoda, pyramid; pylon; sikhara, vimana, gopura [all Ind.]; mole [Rom. Antiq.]; shaft, thill; pillar, column, post [obs.]; pilaster; obelisk; monument; colossus; skyscraper.

4. *n.* pole, pile [obs.], stick, post, shaft, staff, stave; telegraph pole *or* post, telephone pole *or* post; tent pole; flagpole, flagstaff; pikestaff; Maypole; totem pole *or* post; pile, spile, spiling, forepole [Min.]; mast etc. 273.12; beam, bar etc. (support) 215.12–16.

5. *n.* high water, high tide, flood tide, spring tide.

6. *n.* (tall person) longlegs, longshanks, daddy longlegs, granddaddy longlegs, high-pockets, lengthy, long drink of water [all slang or joc.]; six-footer, seven-footer etc. [coll.]; bean pole, gangleshanks [slang] etc. (tall, thin person) 203.6; giant etc. 192.8.

7. *n.* giraffe (*pl.* giraffe *or* giraffes), dromedary [S. Afr.], cameleopard, giraffe camel; Giraffidae, Alticamelus; Camelidae, Cameloidea, Tylopoda, okapi, Samotherium, Sivatherium.

8. *n.* (measurement of altitude) hypsography, hypsometry, altimetry; hypsometer, altimeter.

9. *v.* be high etc. *adj.*, tower, soar, hover, rear, uprise, rise, ascend, mount, spire; bestride, ride, perch; stand on tiptoe.

10. *v.* rise above, tower above, exceed in height etc. *n.*, surmount, top, overtop,

o'ertop; overlook, command; beetle *or* jut over etc. (overhang) 214.5; overlie etc. 223.27.

11. *v.* become high etc. *adj.*, grow, grow high *or* taller, upgrow, uprise, rise up; ascend etc. 305.4–6.

12. *v.* heighten, height [now Scot. and dial. Eng.], render high etc. *adj.*; raise etc. (elevate) 307.5.

13. *adj.* high, high-reaching, elevated, eminent, sublime [arch.], exalted, prominent, lofty, steep, supernal, tall, lengthy [coll.]; monumental, colossal; aerial; high-set, high-pitched; towering, soaring etc. *v.*; high *or* tall as a maypole, ~ poplar *or* steeple, higher than a cat's back [slang]; perching, incessorial; breast-high, knee-high etc.; long-legged etc. (long) 200.12, 13; lanky etc. (lean) 203.11; large etc. 192.11, 15.

14. *adj.* skyscraping, sky-high, heaven-kissing, cloud-touching; cloud-topped, cloud-capped.

15. *adj.* higher, superior, greater; over, above etc. *adv.*; upper, uppermost; highest etc. (topmost) 210.6.

16. *adj.* overhanging etc. 214.8; overlying etc. 223.30.

17. *adj.* upland, highland; hilly, knobby [U.S.]; mountained, mountainous; alpine, alpen, alpestrine, alpigene; subalpine; monticoline, monticolous, montigeneous, montiform; hill-dwelling, mountain-dwelling.

18. *adj.* hypsographic(al), hypsometric(al), altimetric(al).

19. *adv.* on high, high up; aloft, aloof; up, upward *or* upwards; above, over, o'er [poetic], overhead; above one's head, over head and ears; airward, skyward; in the air, in the clouds; upstairs, abovestairs; tiptoe, on tiptoe; on stilts; on the shoulders of . . .

207. Lowness
(See 206. Height)

1. *n.* lowness, lowlihood [arch.]; debasement, abasement [arch.]; subjacency; shortness etc. 201; prostration etc.

Hills peep o'er hills, and alps on alps arise.—POPE.   Yon towers, whose wanton tops do buss the clouds.—SHAKESPEARE.   The higher the hill the lower the grass.—FULLER.   As high as Heaven and as deep as Hell.—BEAUMONT AND FLETCHER.   A lofty pleasure-dome.—COLERIDGE.   They came to the Delectable Mountains.—BUNYAN.

207. Low though I am, I have not fallen so low that I am beneath you too, for beneath you there can be nothing.—OVID.   Lay him low, lay

(horizontality) 213; depression etc. (concavity) 252; depth etc. 208; lower story, basement etc. 191.18, 20; base etc. 211.
2. *n.* low water, low tide, ebb tide, neap tide, neap.
3. *n.* lowland, downland [rare].
4. *n.* (comparisons) feet, heels, molehill, blade of grass, grasshopper, duck, jack rabbit, chaw of tobacco [dial.].
5. *v.* be low etc. *adj.,* lie low; crouch, squat, slouch; cower, wallow, grovel, welter; lie under, underlie; lie flat etc. (horizontal) 213.5.
6. *v.* lower, render low etc. *adj.*; debase etc. (depress) 308.4.
7. *adj.* low, low-lying, lying low, unelevated, not high etc. 206.13; base [arch.], debased; neap; crouched, squat; knee-high to a grasshopper, ~ duck *or* jack rabbit [slang], knee-high to a chaw of tobacco [dial.]; short etc. 201.5, 6; flat, prostrate etc. (horizontal) 213.8, 9; depressed etc. (concave) 252.10; deep etc. 208.8–13.
8. *adj.* low-necked, low-cut, décolleté.
9. *adj.* lower, inferior, under, nether, subjacent; less advanced [Biol.]; earlier etc. [Geol.].
10. *adj.* lowest, lowermost, undermost, nethermost; bottom, rock-bottom.
11. *adv.* under, underneath, beneath, aneath [Scot. and dial. Eng.], 'neath [poetic and dial.]; below, alow [now chiefly Naut.]; underfoot; underground; down, adown, downwards; downstairs, belowstairs, below deck [Naut.]; at the foot of, at the base of; at a low ebb; below par, below the mark.

208. Depth
(See 209. Shallowness)

1. *n.* depth, deepness etc. *adj.,* profundity; depression etc. (concavity) 252; lowness etc. 207.
2. *n.* pit, shaft, hole, hollow, cavity, well, depth, deep, abyss, abysm, chasm, gulf, yawning abyss, ~ chasm *or* gulf; bowels; crater; crevasse; bowels of the earth; bottomless pit *or* gulf, infernal pit, hell; dark depths, unknown depths, unfathomed deeps; pitfall etc. 667.2.
3. *n.* ocean depths, deep sea, deep, deeps, depths, Bassalia [Biogeog.] abyss, abyssal zone; bathyal zone, pelagic zone; bottom of the sea, "bosom of the Deep" (Milton), sea *or* ocean bottom, bottom waters, floor, bed, benthos, benthon, Davy Jones's locker [coll.].
4. *n.* sounding *or* soundings [Naut.], depth sounding, depth of water, water; echo depth sounding; bathometry, bathymetry; bathometer, bathymeter; fathomer, sounding lead, ~ rod, ~ bottle *or* line, sound, plumb line, plumb, plummet, bob, plumb bob, lead, dipsey *or* deep-sea line *or* lead; sounding machine, Kelvin machine, Tanner-Blish machine; fathometer; probe [Surg.].
5. *n.* draft *or* draught [Naut.], submergence, submersion, sinkage, displacement.
6. *v.* deepen, render deep etc. *adj.,* sink, lower; dig, excavate etc. 252.9.
7. *v.* sound, take soundings, make a sounding, heave ~, cast *or* sling the lead, fathom, plumb, plumb-line, plumb the depths.
8. *adj.* deep, profound; deep-seated, deep-rooted; sunk, sunken; knee-deep, ankle-deep; down-reaching etc. 306.7; low etc. 207.7.
9. *adj.* abysmal, abyssal, yawning; bottomless, soundless, plumbless, fathomless, unfathomed, unfathomable; deep as a well, deep as the sea.
10. *adj.* subterranean, subterraneous, subterrene [obs.], underground; buried.
11. *adj.* subaqueous, underwater; submarine, undersea; submerged etc. (*see* submerge etc. 310.5).
12. *adj.* deep-sea, dipsey [Naut.]; Bassalian [Biogeog.] abyssal; bathyal, bathyorographical, bathysmal, bathybic [Biol.]; bathymetric, bathymetrical; benthal, benthonic; benthopelagic, bathypelagic.
13. *adj.* deep-bosomed, bathycolpic, bathycolopian, bathycolpian.
14. *adv.* out of one's depth, beyond one's depth; over one's head, over head and ears.

---

him low, / In the clover or the snow!—G. H. BOKER. To lowest pitch of abject fortune.—MILTON.
208. Deep calleth unto deep.—BIBLE. The dark and backward abysm of time.—SHAKESPEARE. Under every deep a lower deep opens.—EMERSON. The profound seas hide in unknown shadows.—SHAKESPEARE. Under the whelming tide / Visit'st the bottom of the monstrous world.—MILTON. The profundities of hip pockets.—A. BENNETT. Still waters run deep.

209. Shallowness
(See 208. Depth)

1. *n.* shallowness, depthlessness etc. *adj.,* want of depth etc. (*see* depth etc. 208) superficiality; veneer, mere scratch, pinprick.
2. *n.* shallow, shallow place, shoal, shallow *or* shoal water, flat; bank, reef, bar, sand bar, sandbank.
3. *v.* shallow, become *or* make shallow *or* shallower etc. *adj.*; decrease in depth etc. (*see* depth etc. 208), shoal; fill in *or* up, silt up.
4. *adj.* shallow, depthless, fleet [chiefly dial., Eng.]; slight, superficial, trivial, cursory; skin-deep, ankle-deep, knee-deep; just enough to wet one's feet.
5. *adj.* shoal, shoaly.

210. Summit
(See 211. Base)

1. *n.* summit, summity [arch.], upper end *or* extremity, highest point *or* position, utmost *or* maximum height, maximum, *ne plus ultra* [L.], height, top, tiptop, tip-crowning point, pinnacle, spire, peak, *pico* [Sp.], knoll [obs. exc. dial.], head, headpiece, *caput* [L.] (*pl. capita*), brow, edge, crest, cap, crown, culmination, culminating *or* crowning point, point, tip, nib, pitch [obs.], vertex (*pl.* vertexes, vertices), vertical [obs.], apex (*pl.* apexes, apices), culmen [rare or Zool.], zenith, acme, climax, meridian. topgallant, capsheaf [both also fig.]; crisis, turning point, turn of the tide; climatic climax, edaphic climax [both Phytogeog.]; pole, North Pole, South Pole; topgallant mast, skyscraper; crow's-nest; watershed, water parting; fountainhead; supremacy etc. 33.3; perfection etc. 650.
2. *n.* top side, upper side *or* surface, uppermost part, upside, upward [obs.], top, topside [Naut.]; upper story, top floor; upper deck etc. (deck) 273.8.
3. *n.* head [Anat.], headpiece, pate [now joc. or derogatory], poll [dial. or joc.], top [as in *from top to toe*]; sconce, noddle [both coll.]; noodle, knob, nob, bean, dome, attic, loft, garret, upper story, belfry, bun, cocoa, conk, crumpet, nut, noggin [all slang]; skull, cranium (*pl.* craniums, crania); pericranium, epicranium; brainpan, brain box, brain case; think tank, phrenology box [both slang].
4. *n.* (architecture) architrave, frieze, cornice, corona, coping, coping stone, zoophorus (*pl.* zoophori), capital, headpiece, headboard, lintel, capstone; headmold, head molding, hoodmold; fastigium, drip, larmier, epistyle, sconce, pediment, entablature, tympanum, housetop, gable end, clerestory *or* clearstory; attic etc. 191.19; roof etc. 223.6.
5. *v.* top, crown, cap, crest, head, tip, peak, surmount; culminate, consummate, climax; overtop etc. (rise above) 206.10.
6. *adj.* top, tiptop, tip-crowning, topmost, uppermost, overmost, highest etc. (*see* high etc. 206.13), topgallant [also fig.]; maximum, maximal; culminating etc. *v.,* culminal [rare], culminant [rare]; summital, apical, vertical, zenithal; acmic, acmatic; meridian, meridional; capital, head, chief, paramount, pre-eminent, superior, supreme; polar, polaric.
7. *adv.* atop, in the topmost position, at *or* on the top, on top of, topside [coll.]; at the top of the tree *or* ladder, on top of the roost; *en flûte* [F.].

211. Base
(See 210. Summit)

1. *n.* base, basal *or* lowest part *or* position, basement, bottom, foot, sole, nadir; lowest level, rock bottom, bedrock, hardpan [chiefly U.S.]; hold, hole [Naut.]; bilge; keel, keelson *or* kelson; centerboard; patten, bottom plate *or* sill; plinth; dado; wainscot; baseboard, mopboard [U.S.]; cullet, collet; basis, groundwork etc. (foundation) 215.3; root etc. (rudiment) 153.3; lowness etc. 207.
2. *n.* ground part, ground, earth, *terra firma* [L.]; floor, flooring; deck; parquet; pavement, pave [chiefly U.S.], paving; flag, flagging; carpet; ground floor etc. 191.18; platform etc. 215.21.
3. *n.* bed [of water], bottom, floor,

---

209. Shallow brooks that flowed so clear / The bottom did the top appear.—DRYDEN.
210. Now in the summit of Love's topmost peak.—A. AUSTIN.   The rocky summits, split and rent, formed turret, dome, or battlement.—SCOTT.   The very acme and pitch of life.—POPE.
211. Bedrock matters of fact.—GALSWORTHY. The bottom is out of the Universe!—KIPLING.

basin, channel, coulee [U.S.]; ocean bottom etc. (ocean depths) 208.3.

4. *n.* foot [Anat.], sole [chiefly poetic], extremity [affected or joc.], hoof [joc. or slang exc. Zool.], pes (*pl.* pedes), pedal [affected or joc.], *pied* [F.], hand [as of an ape or hawk], trotter [joc. exc. Zool.]; pedal extremity, dog [U.S.], beetle-crusher, dew-beater, kick, kicker, tootsy [all slang or joc.]; paw, pad, *patte* [F.; Her.], pat [slang], pud [coll.]; forefoot, hind foot; harefoot, splayfoot, clubfoot; toe, tootsy [slang]; heel; sole.

5. *adj.* basal, basic, fundamental, radical, essential, elementary, primary, primitive, original; bottom, bottommost, undermost, nethermost, lowermost, lowest; rock-bottom, bedrock [coll.]; nadiral; based on, founded on, grounded on, built on; supporting etc. 215.28.

212. Verticality
(See 213. Horizontality)

1. *n.* verticality, erectness etc. *adj.,* perpendicularity, *aplomb* [F.]; orthogonality, right-angledness, right-angularity, rectangularity; post etc. (support) 215.16; straightness etc. 246.

2. *n.* vertical, upright, perpendicular, plumb, normal [Geom.]; orthodiagonal; right angle; rectangle, square; vertical circle, azimuth circle; upright brace.

3. *n.* precipice, cliff, steep, *peña* [Sp., Southw. U.S.], bluff, wall, scar, krans [S. Afr.], crag, craig [Scot. and North. Eng.]; scarp, escarpment; palisade, palisades; incline etc. 217.2.

4. *n.* erecting etc. *v.,* erection, elevation.

5. *n.* (instruments) square, T square, try square, carpenter's square; plumb, plumb line *or* bob, plummet, bob, lead.

6. *v.* be vertical etc. *adj.,* stand up, stand erect *or* upright, stand on end, stick *or* cock up.

7. *v.* render vertical etc. *adj.,* set *or* raise up, stick *or* cock up, erect, elevate, rear, raise, pitch; uprear, upraise, uplift, upheave; upend, stand on end; raise on its legs, set on its feet; plumb, plumb-line, set *à plomb* [F.]; square.

8. *adj.* vertical, upright, bolt upright, upended etc. *v.,* erect, unrecumbent [rare], stand-up, standing up etc. *v.*; perpendicular, sheer, plumb, straight-up, straight-up-and-down, up-and-down; rampant [Her.]; precipitous, bluff etc. (steep) 217.12; right-angle, orthogonal, rectangular etc. (angular) 244.5; straight etc. 246.5.

9. *adv.* vertically etc. *adj.,* upright, up; on end, up *or* right on end, endwise, endways; perpendicular [obs. or careless], plumb, *à plomb* [F.]; at right angles, square; on one's feet *or* legs.

213. Horizontality
(See 212. Verticality)

1. *n.* horizontality, horizontalness etc. *adj.,* horizontalism, horizontalization [rare]; lowness etc. 207.

2. *n.* recumbency, recumbence [now rare], recubation [obs.], procumbency *or* procumbence [rare], decumbency *or* decumbence, discumbency *or* discumbence [obs.], accumbency *or* accumbence [rare], accubation, prostration, reclination, couchancy [rare], proneness etc. *adj.*; supination, resupination.

3. *n.* horizontal, plane, platform [obs.], level, flat, homaloid [Math.], dead level *or* flat; horizontal plane, level plane; horizontal line, level line; horizontal projection; horizontal parallax; horizontal axis; horizontal pendulum; horizontal bar; horizontal fault; water level, sea level, mean sea level; terrace, terracette; parterre; esplanade; ground, earth, floor; bowling green, cricket ground, croquet ground *or* lawn; table, billiard table; stratum etc. (layer) 204; prairie, plateau etc. (plain) 344; estrade, dais etc. (platform) 215.21.

4. *n.* horizon, horizon's rim, sky line; sea line, coast line, offing; apparent ∼, local *or* visible horizon, sensible horizon, celestial ∼, rational ∼, geometrical *or* true horizon, artificial *or* false horizon; azimuth.

5. *v.* be horizontal etc. *adj.,* lie, recline, repose, accumb [obs.], couch; lie down, lie flat *or* prostrate, lie on its face *or* back, lie on a level; sprawl, loll; sit down etc. 308.6.

---

212. Down some monstrous precipice.—Keats. Bare steeps, where desolation stalks.—Wordsworth. Plumb down he falls.—Milton.

213. Which, as the wind, / Blew where it listeth, laying all things prone.—Byron. The plains and the prairies where pools are far apart.—S. Teasdale. As flat as a pancake.

6. *v.* render horizontal etc. *adj.*, horizontalize [rare], level, flatten, smooth, even, equalize, align *or* aline; lay, lay down, lay out, lay level, lay level with the ground, raze *or* rase.

7. *v.* prostrate, supinate, prone [South. U.S.], fell, drop, bring down, sink; knock down, floor, ground, grass [slang], gravel [coll.], bowl over *or* down [coll.]; squelch, squash [both coll.]; cut *or* hew down, whack down [coll.], mow down.

8. *adj.* horizontal, horizontic(al) [rare]; homaloidal, level, flat, smooth, even, plane, plain, flush; level as a floor, ~ a plain etc. *n.,* flat as a billiard table, ~ a bowling green etc. *n.,* flat as a pancake, ~ a fluke, ~ a flounder, ~ a board, ~ my hand etc., smooth as glass; calm, calm as a mill pond; alluvial.

9. *adj.* recumbent, recubant [rare], recubate [rare], procumbent, accumbent, decumbent, discumbent [obs.], lying etc. *v.,* prone, couchant, *couché* [F.], jacent [now rare], prostrate; supine, resupine; resupinate, resupinated [both Bot.]; downthrown etc. 308.9.

10. *adv.* horizontally, level etc. *adj.*; on a level; at water level, *à fleur d'eau* [F.], at sea level; on one's back *or* face; on all fours; on its beam ends; flat etc. 251.6.

214. Pendency
(See 215. Support)

1. *n.* pendency, pendulosity, pensility, dependence *or* dependency, suspension, suspensation [rare], hanging etc. *v.*; hang, droop, dangle; overhang, overhanging; pendanting [Arch.], support etc. 215.

2. *n.* pendant, pendule [rare], pendle [obs. exc. dial.], pendicle, penduline [Zool.]; hanger, hanging, hanging appendage, drop; eardrop, earring, lavaliere, *pendeloque* [F.]; tippet, tassel; lobe, ear lobe; tail, tailpiece; train, queue, pigtail; flap, skirt, pendulum, hangnail, pendant post, pendant switch, pendant tackle; chandelier etc. 423.10.

3. *n.* suspender, support, supporter, hanger; suspenders, pair of suspenders, braces [Eng.], gallowses [chiefly dial.], galluses [dial.]; sock supporter, garter; knob, stud, spar, horse, tenterhook; peg, nail etc. (pin) 45.5; button, hook, ring etc. (fastening) 45.2.

4. *v.* be pendent etc. *adj.,* pend, depend, hang, swing, dangle, lower, droop; swag [dial.]; flap; draggle, daggle, trail, flow.

5. *v.* overhang, hang over, impend; project, beetle, jut, beetle *or* jut over; rise above etc. 206.10; overlie etc. 223.27.

6. *v.* suspend, hang, sling; fasten to, etc. (attach) 43.6.

7. *adj.* pendent, pendulous, pendulant, pendular, penduline [Zool.], pensile, dependent; pending, hanging, suspended etc. *v.*; loose, flowing; weeping [as a willow], nodding, cernuous [as a flower].

8. *adj.* overhanging, pendulous etc. *above,* impending; beetle; beetling, jutting, beetling *or* jutting over, projecting; incumbent, superincumbent; overlapping etc. (overlying) 223.30.

9. *adj.* pendanted, having a pendant etc. *n.*; caudate, caudated, tailed.

215. Support
(See 214. Pendency)

1. *n.* support, supportance [now rare], supportal [obs.], supporture [obs.], supportation [obs.], supportment [obs.]; upholding etc. *v.,* upkeep, maintenance, sustainment [rare], sustenance, sustentation [now rare], subvention; suspension etc. (pendency) 214.

2. *n.* supporter, support, upholder, sustainer, maintainer, prop, post [fig., obs.], staff [fig.], stave [fig.], staddle [obs.], crutch [fig.], stay, mainstay, brace, bracer, buttress [fig.], shoulder [fig.], arm [fig.], strengthener; reinforce, reinforcement; strut, shore, raker; guy, shroud, ratline, skid, rib, splint, bandage, lap, anvil, cue rest, jigger [slang], monkey [builders' cant], hod, block, stirrup, stilts, shoe, sole, heel; suspender etc. (pendant) 214.2, 3; peg etc. (pin) 45.5; clasp, buckle etc. (fastening) 45.2; rope etc. (cord) 205.3, 4.

3. *n.* foundation, *fond* [F.], base, basis, platform [fig., rare], rest, ground, *terra firma* [L.], groundwork, substratum, substructure, substruction, subvention, understructure, understruction, underbuilding, underpinning; solid rock *or* bot-

---

214. This pendulous round earth.—MILTON. The pendent world.—SHAKESPEARE.

215. The Lord is my rock and my fortress.—BIBLE. Give me a lever long enough, and a fulcrum strong enough, and single-handed I can move the world.—ARCHIMEDES. The strong

tom, bedrock, rock bottom; riprap [U.S.]; stand, standard; pediment, pedestal; plinth, subbase; sill [also fig.], doorsill, window sill; socle; first stone, foundation stone, cornerstone, headstone; rudiment etc. 153.3; floor, foot etc. 211; backbone etc. 235.4; scaffold etc. *below* 215.8; preparation etc. 673.

4. *n.* footing, foothold, hold, purchase; stance, stand, standing, standing place, *locus standi* [L.], *pou sto* [Gr. ποῦ στῶ], basis for operations, stable position; vantage ground, ∼ point *or* post, advantage ground [rare], vantage; footrest, step, stair, round, rung.

5. *n.* fulcrum (*pl.* fulcra), fulciment [obs.], bait [U.S.], bearing, point of support, *point d'appui* [F.], resting point *or* place, rest; thole, tholepin; rowlock, oarlock; grimmal, gimbal; fulcrummage etc. (leverage) 175.3; lever etc. 307.4.

6. *n.* axle etc. (axis) 312.5.

7. *n.* handle, hold, grasp, hilt, haft, helve, shaft, shank, stalk, handstaff; snath, crop, snead [chiefly Scot. and dial.], brake, spindle, loom, lug, bow, bail, tiller, rudder, helm, knocker, handle bar, withe, sally, tote, tale [rare], rounce, pull, crank, trigger.

8. *n.* frame, framework, framing, skeleton; sash, casement; case, rack, crib, curb; lattice, latticework; arbor; scaffold, scaffolding, *échafaudage* [F.]; stage; yoke; supportasse [obs.]; braced frame or framing.

9. *n.* trestle, trestle legs [rare], trest [now Scot. and dial.]; horse, sawhorse, sawbuck, buck; clotheshorse; trestle board *or* table, trestle and table; trestle bridge; trestle legs, trestle post; trestle tree [Naut.]; trestlework, trestling.

10. *n.* buttress, buttressing; flying buttress, *arc-boutant* [F.]; hanging buttress; pier buttress, buttress pier; pier, sea wall, breakwater; abutment, shoulder.

11. *n.* bracket, brace; bracket capital, corbel, consol, modillion; cantilever, gusset, shoulder, cheek, *cul-de-lampe* [F.] (*pl. culs-de-lampe*).

12. *n.* beam, timber, caber, pole, spar [obs. exc. dial.]; I beam, H beam; wooden beam, iron beam, steel beam; tie, tie beam; girder, plate girder, box girder, lattice girder; iron girder, steel girder, wooden girder; truss, truss beam; ridgepole, ridge strut; stud, studding; summer, breastsummer, bressomer [arch.], summertree; rafter, angle-rafter, hiprafter; crossbeam, crosstie; trave, traverse, travis [dial., Eng.], trevis [Scot.]; joist, strut, lintel, balk, batten, scantling, transom, stringpiece, sleeper, corbel.

13. *n.* shaft, pole, pile [obs.], bar, rod, stick; wagon shaft *or* pole, tongue, wagon tongue, thill, nib [dial., Eng.], neap [U.S.], disselboom [S. Afr.]; reach, wagon reach, perch; boom, spar, sprit, outrigger; mast etc. 273.12; Maypole etc. (height) 206.4.

14. *n.* stalk, stem, caulis [Bot.], trunk, caudex [Bot.]; pedicle, pedicel, pedicellus *or* pediculus, peduncle [all Bot.]; petiole, petiolus (*pl.* petioli), petiolule [all Bot.]; caulicle [Bot.], cauliculus [Arch.] (*pl.* cauliculi); culm, haulm [both Bot.]; spear, spire, blade; stipe [Bot.] (*pl.* stipes) stipes [Zool.] (*pl.* stipites).

15. *n.* staff, stave, staddle [obs.], stick, rod; walking stick, cane, Malacca cane; pikestaff [now rare], alpenstock; pastoral staff, shepherd's staff, crook; crosier, cross, cross-staff, paterissa; pilgrim's staff, bourdon; crutch, crutchstick [dial., U.S.]; lathee [Anglo-Ind.]; cowlstaff [arch. and dial.]; caduceus; thyrsus [Gr. Rel.]; lituus [Rom. Antiq.]; maulstick; stump [cricket]; baton, wand.

16. *n.* post, standard, upright, upright bar *or* brace, perch [now rare]; column, pillar, pile [obs.], pier; pilaster; colonnette, columella; banister, baluster; balustrade, balustrading; crown post, king post; caryatid (*pl.* caryatids, caryatides), atlas (*pl.* atlantes), telamon (*pl.* telamones); gatepost, doorpost; jamb, doorjamb; stile, mullion; leg, shank, trestle [obs.]; trestle post, trestle leg; stanchion, stanchel [obs. exc. Scot.], stancher [Scot. and North. Eng.]; stake, stob [dial.]; pale, picket, palisade; snubbing post.

17. *n.* capital [Arch.], head, crown, cap; bracket, bracket capital, corbel, console; cymatium, corona, taenia, abacus, echinus, gorgerin, astragal, antefix, mutule, guttae, triglyph, metope, dentil, modillion, bell.

---

base and building of my love / Is as the very centre of the earth.—SHAKESPEARE. With

Atlantean shoulders, fit to bear / The weight of mightiest monarchies.—MILTON. My only strength and stay.—MILTON.

18. *n.* arch, arc, archway, span, vault, concameration, arcade, arcature; dome, cupola; cove, fornix [Anat.] (*pl.* fornices), skewback, ogive, ogee, lancet, apse, concha (*pl.* conchae); fixed arch, primitive arch, segmental arch, round arch, horseshoe arch, flat arch, three-centered *or* basket-handle arch, four-centered *or* Tudor arch, shouldered arch, rowlock arch, trefoil arch, rampant arch; keystone, headstone, voussoir.

19. *n.* shelf, shelve, ledge; mantel, mantelshelf, mantelpiece; retable, superaltar, gradin, *gradino* [It.], predella [all Eccl.]; settle; hob; shoulder.

20. *n.* table, board, stand; dining table, the mahogany [coll.]; coffee table, tea table, teapoy; dressing table, dresser; desk, secretary, *secrétaire* [F.]; tripod, trivet, trivet table; console, console table; turntable; dais [arch.]; counter; easel; table top, slab.

21. *n.* platform, flatform [dial.]; floor, estrade, dais, pulpit [arch. or spec.], stage; landing stage *or* place, landing; rostrum, soapbox [chiefly coll.], stump [chiefly coll., U.S.]; suggestum [Rom. Antiq.], emplacement [Fort.], perron, catafalque, drop, roundtop [Naut.].

22. *n.* seat, chair, bench, sill; easy chair, armchair, *fauteuil* [F.], rocking chair, elbowchair; wing chair, draft chair; rocker; morris chair; long chair, long-sleeve chair [Anglo-Ind.]; stool, footstool, milking stool, foldstool, folding stool, camp stool, kneeling stool, *prie-dieu* [F.], cricket, hassock, taboret; tripod, trivet; form, school form *or* bench; pew; settle, settee, dais [Scot.], sofa, lounge, *chaise longue* [F.], davenport, divan, ottoman, squab, couch, day bed; love seat, spoon holder [local, U.S.], *causeuse* [F.], *tête-à-tête* [F.]; musnud [Oriental]; back seat, rumble seat, rumble; throne etc. 747.

23. *n.* saddle, cack *or* kack [slang, U.S.]; montura, hull, leather, wood, pine [all West. U.S.]; riding saddle, bridal saddle, English riding saddle, English cavalry saddle, U.S. cavalry saddle, cowboy saddle, cow *or* stock saddle, sidesaddle; packsaddle, aparejo, basto [West. U.S.], kyack [West. U.S.]; panel, pillion; pommel, horn; apple, biscuit, nubbin [all slang]; saddle skirts, bastos [West. U.S.]; saddlebag, alforja, *alforge* [Pg.; West. U.S.]; girth, girt; cinch, latigo [West. U.S.]; stirrup; cantle; jockey.

24. *n.* bed, couch, bunk, kip [dial. and slang]; doss, hay [U.S.], crummy [U.S., tramp slang], downy, the feathers, flop [U.S.], roost [all slang]; berth, cot, pallet, day bed, tester bed, feather bed, French bed, four-poster, crib, cradle, bedstead; shakedown, breakdown [slang, U.S.]; trundle bed, truckle bed; hammock, swing; litter, stretcher; bedding; under-bed, under-bedding, mattress, paillasse, pallet; pillow, cushion, bolster; mat, rug; coverlet etc. (covering) 223.9.

25. *n.* Atlas, Hercules *or* Herakles; tortoise that supports the earth.

26. *v.* support, bear, carry, hold, sustain, maintain, shoulder; keep up, back up, bolster up, shore up, bear up, hold up; uphold, upbear; brace, prop, buttress, stay; mainstay; underbrace, underprop, underpin, underset; bottom, found, base, ground, bed; embed; cradle, pillow; give ~, furnish ~, afford ~, supply *or* lend support; riprap; aid etc. 707.6–8.

27. *v.* be supported etc. *adj.*, lie on, recline on, repose on, lean on, rest on, stand on, sit on, bear on, abut on, be based on etc. *adj.*; have at one's back; bestride, bestraddle.

28. *adj.* supporting, supported etc. *v.*; sustentative, sustentational, sustentacular [Anat.]; Atlantean; based on, fundamental etc. (basal) 211.5.

29. *adj.* columnar, columned, columnated; columelliform, columellar *or* columellate [Bot. and Zool.]; cylindrical etc. 249.8.

30. *adj.* pedicled, pedunculate *or* pedunculated, pedicellate *or* pedicellated.

31. *adv.* astride, astraddle, straddle, straddleback, straddle-legged.

216. Parallelism
(See 217. Obliquity)

1. *n.* parallelism, parallelization, coextension, equidistance, concentricity; collineation, collimation; parallelotropism.

2. *n.* parallel, paralleler, parallel line, ~ curve *or* surface; parallelogram; parallelepipedon, parallelopipedon, parallel-

---

216. This life . . . / Henceforth is parallel with Thine.—E. JUDSON. When honor runs parallel with the laws of God.—ADDISON. My young remembrance cannot parallel a fellow to it.—SHAKESPEARE.

epiped, parallelopiped [all Geom.] ; parallelograph, parallelometer ; parallel rule *or* ruler, parallel bar, parallel columns, parallel rods, parallel file, parallel trench [Mil.], parallel dash, parallel vice.

3. *v.* parallel, be parallel etc. *adj.*, equal, coextend; extend *or* run in a direction parallel to.

4. *v.* parallelize, render parallel etc. *adj.*, place parallel to, bring into parallelism with, collimate, collineate, equidistance ; furnish with a parallel, match.

5. *adj.* parallel, parallelistic, coextensive, equidistant, collateral, concentric, concurrent; alongside, abreast; aligned, equal, even; parallelogrammatic(al), parallelogrammic(al) ; parallelotropic; parallelodrome, parallelodromous [both Bot.] ; parallelinervate, parallelinerved, parallelinervous [all Bot.] ; parallelepipedal, parallelepipedonal, parallelepipedous, parallelepipedic [all Geom.].

6. *adv.* alongside etc. (beside) 236.9.

217. Obliquity
(See 216. Parallelism)

1. *n.* obliquity, obliquation [now rare], obliqueness, crookedness etc. *adj.*; deviation, divergence, digression, excursion, declination, deflection, deflexure, swerve, sheer, skew, turn, twist, warp, bent, bend, bias; leaning etc. *v.*, inclination, incline [rare], slope, slopeness, slant, tilt, pitch, list, cant; sag, swag, sway, lurch; bevel, bezel; diagonality; angularity etc. 244; curvature etc. 245; distortion etc. 243; oblique motion etc. 279.2; circuit etc. 629.

2. *n.* incline, inclined surface *or* plane, slope, tilt, bent, grade, gradient [chiefly Eng.], pitch, ramp, bank [obs. or dial. exc. spec.] ; acclivity, upward slope, ascent, ascension [arch.], climb, rise, rising, rising ground *or* grade, uprise, uprising, upgrade, upgo, upclimb, uplift, upway [rare], upwith [chiefly Scot.], uphill.

declivity, downward slope, devexity [obs.], descent, dip, drop, fall, decline, downgrade, downgate [obs. exc. Scot.], downhill; gentle *or* easy slope, easy ascent *or* descent, glacis; rapid *or* steep slope, stiff ascent *or* climb; hillside, side; shelving beach; talus; *montagne russe*

[F.] ; tower of Pisa ; hill, mound etc. (height) 206.2 ; cliff etc. (precipice) 212.3.

3. *n.* diagonal, diagonal line *or* plane, catercorner [rare] etc. *adj.*

4. *n.* zigzag, zig, zag; zigzaggery, flexuosity [Bot.] ; chevron [spec. Arch.].

5. *v.* oblique, obliquate [now rare], be *or* render oblique etc. *adj.*; deviate, diverge, deflect, bear off, angle, angle off, swerve, veer, sheer, slue, skew, turn, twist, bend, bias, crump [obs. exc. dial.] ; crook, crooken; distort etc. 243.3 ; curve etc. 245.3.

6. *v.* incline, slope, slant, shelve, list, pitch, tilt, cant, careen, keel; sidle ; sag, swag, sway, lurch; ascend, rise, uprise, go uphill; descend, decline, fall, go downhill; slope backwards, retreat [Aeronaut.].

7. *v.* be diagonal etc. *adj.*, catercorner etc. *adj.*, cater [dial.].

8. *v.* zigzag, zig, zag, stagger, crankle, wind in and out.

9. *adj.* oblique, tilted, sloping etc. *v.*, aslope, inclined, clinal, slant, aslant, recumbent, recubant [rare] ; kimbo [obs.], akimbo ; bevel, beveled ; loxic, loxotic, loxodromic [all Med.] ; out of the perpendicular *or* horizontal, not straight *or* true, not upright *or* prone; antiparallel ; plagihedral [Cryst.] ; backhand, backhanded; curved etc. 245.4; indirect etc. (deviative) 279.8, (circuitous) 311.6; angular etc. 244.5.

10. *adj.* sloping upward, uphill, rising, uprising, ascending, acclivous, acclivitous, acclive [obs.], acclinate.

11. *adj.* sloping downward, downhill, falling, descending ; declining, declinate, declined, declivous, declivitous, declivate, declive; proclive, proclivous [both rare] ; synclinal, anticlinal ; hanging [as *hanging gardens*].

12. *adj.* steep, steepy [rare] ; precipitous, precipitate [obs.] ; bluff, abrupt, bold, sheer, sharp, rapid, headlong, breakneck, stiff, arduous, heavy ; straight-up etc. (vertical) 212.8.

13. *adj.* crooked, bent, crump [obs. exc. dial.], askew, skew, skewed, awry, wry, bias, thraw *or* thrawn [chiefly Scot.], thrawart [Scot.] ; skew-jawed, skew-gee, askewgee, agee *or* ajee, agee-

---

217. Straight down the Crooked Lane.—Hood. By the surer mode of zigzag.—Burke. Why should I strive to set the crooked straight?—W. Morris.

jawed, wamper-jawed, antigodlin *or* antigoglin [U.S.], catawampous, catawamptious, catabiased, weewow, weewaw [U.S.], yaw-ways [all dial. or slang]; cockeyed [U.S.], screwy [U.S.], galley-west, galley-west and crooked, skywest, skywest and crooked [all slang]; crooked as a ram's horn, crooked as a dog's hind leg, crooked as a Virginia fence [U.S.]; distorted etc. 243.5; circuitous etc. 311.6.

14. *adj.* transverse, transversal; across etc. 219.9–12.

15. *adj.* diagonal, diagonic [rare], diagonial [obs.]; bendwise [Her.]; cater-corner *or* catercornered, catacorner *or* catacornered, catercornerways, catacornerways, kittycorner *or* kittycornered [U.S.], capercorner *or* capercornered [dial. U.S.], catabiased; catawampous [dial.] etc. *above* 217.13.

16. *adj.* zigzag, zigzagged, zigzaggy, zigzagwise, zigzagways; flexuous [Bot.], staggered, crankled; chevrony, chevronwise, chevronways [all spec. Arch.].

17. *adv.* obliquely, etc. *adj.*, on *or* to one side, all on one side, by a side wind, at an angle; askew, awry etc. *adj.*; slopewise, slopeways, slantwise, slantways, aslant, aslantwise; sidewise, askance etc. (laterally) 236.8; deviatively etc. 279.9.

18. *adv.* transversely, transverse; athwart, across etc. 219.12.

19. *adv.* diagonally, diagonially, diagonalwise, cater [dial.]; catercorner etc. *adj.*

218. Inversion

1. *n.* inversion, introversion, introversal [rare]; eversion, ectropion [Med.]; reverse, reversal, reversion, revulsion; retroversion, retroflexion *or* retroflection; transposition, transposal; subversion, subversal; overturn, overthrow, upset, *culbute* [F.]; capsize, capsizal, capsizement; somersault, somerset; cart wheel, pirouette; topsy-turvification, topsy-turvyhood, topsy-turvyism, topsy-turvydom; invagination, intussusception, introsusception [all Med.]; pronation and supination; contrariety etc. 14; contraposition etc. 237; derangement etc. 61; turn of the tide etc. (turning point) 145.2.

2. *n.* (grammar and rhetorics) metastasis, metathesis; anastrophy, anastrophe; hyperbaton, hypallage, hysteron proteron, palindrome, synchysis, tmesis, parenthesis; chiasm, chiasmus (*pl.* chiasmi).

3. *n.* inverse, reverse; opposite etc. 237.2; antithesis etc. (the contrary) 14.2; counterpart etc. (analogue) 17.5.

4. *v.* invert, inverse [rare], introvert, retrovert; reverse, transpose, put the cart before the horse, turn the tables, turn the scale *or* balance, turn the cat in the pan [obs.]; subvert, evert [arch.], overturn, overthrow, *culbuter* [F.], upset, overset, upturn; turn topsy-turvy etc. *adj.*, topsy-turvy, topsy-turvify, topsy-turvyize, topsyturn [now rare]; invaginate, intussuscept, introsuscept [all Med.]; revert etc. 145.4.

5. *v.* be inverted etc. *adj.*, turn ~, go *or* wheel round *or* about, turn to the right-about [coll.]; turn ~, tilt *or* topple over, overturn, upturn, turn turtle, upset, capsize, keel over.

6. *adj.* inverted, reversed etc. *v.*, wrong side out, inside out; wrong side up, upside down, on one's head, bottom *or* keel upwards, *sens dessus dessous* [F.]; topsy-turvy, topsy-turvied, topsyturned [now rare]; topside-turfway, topside-totherway, topside-the-other-way [all slang]; ectropic; hyperbatic [Gram.]; palindromic(al) [Gram.]; reverse etc. (contrary) 14.5; opposite etc. 237.6.

7. *adj.* top-heavy, topsided [dial.], lopsided; unbalanced, overbalanced; unstable, unsteady.

8. *adv.* inversely etc. *adj.*, by inversion; heels over head, head over heels; topsy-turvy etc. *adj.*, hirdie-girdie; vice versa etc. (contrarily) 14.7.

219. Crossing

1. *n.* crossing, intersecting etc. *v.*, intersection, transversion, decussation, chiasm *or* chiasma [Anat. and Biol.].

2. *n.* crossway, crossing, crosswalk, crossroad, crosspoint [Eng.], *carrefour* [F.], intersection, intercrossing; level crossing [Eng.], grade crossing [U.S.];

---

218. That inverted bowl they call the sky.—OMAR KHAYYÁM—FITZGERALD. *Delphinum appingit sylvis in fluctibus aprum* [He portrays a dolphin in the forest, a wild boar in the waves].—HORACE. Motives by excess reverse their very nature.—COLERIDGE.
219. Weave. weave the sunlight in your hair.—T. S. ELIOT. Teased by the crisscross of the

railway crossing; overcrossing, undercrossing.

3. *n.* interlacing etc. *v.,* interlacement, interlacery; interweavement, intertexture, interdigitation, interconnection, interjoinder; reticulation, cancellation; inosculation, anastomosis; rivulation.

4. *n.* network, webwork, meshwork, tissue, reticulum; net, netting, mesh, moke [dial., Eng.], web, weave; lace, lacery, lacing; screen, screening; sieve, sifter, riddle; rocker, cradle; Hippocrates' sleeve; wicker, wickerwork; mat, matting; lattice, latticework; trellis, wattle; grate, grating; grillwork, grill, grille; gridiron, grid; tracery, fretwork, fret, filigree; plexus, plexure; reticle, reticule [Optics]; wreath, braid, plait, plat [now dial.]; chain [spec. Radio], catena; intertwist, twist; entanglement etc. (complexity) 59.3; knot etc. 45.3.

5. *n.* textile, texture, tissue, fabric, textile fabric, woven fabric, cloth, rag, material, goods, dry goods; homespun, Jacquard weave *or* fabric, Jacquard *or* jacquard, broadloom; herringbone, pepper-and-salt, thunder and lightning; linen, fine linen, damask; linene, linenette; muslin, *mousseline* [F.], *mousseline de soie* [F.], satin, silk, China silk, oil silk, near-silk, rayon, nylon, Celanese [trade name], sheers, gossamer, chiffon, faille, crepe de Chine, crepe, crape, Shantung, taffeta, taffety, velvet, velours, brocade; cotton, cambric, cotton cambric, cambric muslin, twill, *toile* [F.], drilling, drill, drugget, lisle, crash, poplin, piqué, terry cloth, seersucker, denim, monk's cloth, burlap, chintz, percale, gingham, corduroy, voile, dimity, lawn, calico, crinoline, marquisette, organdy, organza, cheesecloth, broadcloth, chenille.

mohair, flannel, jersey, worsted, stamin, stammel, felt, wool, cashmere, gabardine, serge, tweed, mantua, say, tabaret, mackintosh, mackinaw, castor, radium, linsey-woolsey, frieze, fustian, byssus, byssin, haircloth, murrey; lace, point, needle point, Greek *or* Roman lace *or* point, reticella *or* reticello, tapestry, net, netting, mosquito netting, sacking, hopsacking, corseting, veiling, ticking; Axminster, chenille Axminster; plaid, mantua, manta, canvas, tarpaulin, oilcloth, linoleum; clothes etc. 225.1.

6. *n.* cross, crux [spec. Her.], X, cruciform; crucifix, rood; christcross, crisscross; T, tau; crossbar.

7. *v.* cross, crucify [rare], crucifix [obs.], intersect, intercross, decussate, crisscross, crossbar.

8. *v.* interlace, intertwine, interweave, interknit, intertex [obs.], interthread, intertissue, interleave *or* interleaf, intertie, intertwist, interdigitate, interconnect, interjoin; twine, entwine; weave, inweave; intort, raddle, knit, twist, wreath; net; plait, pleat, plat, braid; felt, twill; tangle, entangle, mat, ravel, knot; link, interlink; lock, interlock; dovetail, mortise; splice; inosculate, anastomose; mix etc. 41.6; convolve etc. 248.3.

9. *adj.* cross, crossing, crossed etc. *v.*; decussate, decussated; chiasmal, chiasmic; secant; fretted; transverse, across etc. *adv.*; oblique etc. 217.9–15.

10. *adj.* crucial, cruciate, cruciferous, crucigerous [rare], cruciform, cross-shaped, crosslike, x-shaped, cross, crossed.

11. *adj.* netlike, retiform, reticular, reticulate, reticulated, reticuled [rare], reticulose; aerolar, aerolate, aerolated; cancellate, cancellated, cancellous; latticed, grated, barred, crossbarred, streaked; woven, textile; plexal, plexiform; anastomotic, anastomosed; inosculate, inosculated; web-footed, palmiped.

12. *adv.* crosswise, crossway, crossways; cross, across; thwart, thwartly, thwartwise [rare], athwart, athwartwise, overthwart; transverse, transversely, athwartship, athwartships; contrariwise; cross-grained; at grade [U.S.]; obliquely etc. 217.17–19; sidewise etc. (laterally) 236.8.

220. Exteriority
(See 221. Interiority)

1. *n.* exteriority, externality, externity [rare], extraneity [rare], outwardness etc. *adj.*; exteriorization, externalization; extraterritoriality, extrality [coll.]; eccentricity; extrinsicality etc. 6; extraneousness etc. 57; circumjacence etc. 227.

2. *n.* exterior, external, extern [obs.],

outside; surface, superficies; disk [Bot.]; superstratum; face, facet; extrados [Arch.]; skin etc. (covering) 223; side etc. 236.

3. *n.* outsider, extern [rare] etc. (alien) 57.3.

4. *v.* be exterior etc. *adj.*; lie around etc. 227.3.

5. *v.* place externally etc. *adv.*; put *or* turn out.

6. *v.* exteriorize, externalize, objectify, objectize [rare], actualize; visualize, envisage.

7. *adj.* exterior, external, extern [rare], extraneous, outward, outer, outermost, outside, outlying, outstanding; outdoor; alfresco, *al fresco* [It.]; surface, superficial; discal, discoid [Bot.]; extralateral; extramural, *extra muros* [L.]; extraprovincial; extraliminal, extraliminary [rare]; extramundane, extraterrene, extraterrestrial, exterrestrial, extraterritorial, exterritorial; extraembryonic; extraenteric, perivisceral [both Zool.]; extramorainic, extramorainal; extragalactic [Astron.]; extramarginal [Psychol.], subconscious; extramatrical [Biol.]; extramolecular [Chem.]; extrapolar; extrasolar; extratribal; extratubal; extratympanic, extrauterine, extraplacental, extramedullary, extraserous, extratarsal, extraventricular [all Med.]; exomorphic [Geol.]; ecdemic [Med.]; eccentric(al); extrinsic etc. 6.2; round about etc. 227.4, 5.

8. *adv.* externally, outwardly etc. *adj.*; outwards, out, without, outside, *ab extra* [L.].

9. *adv.* outdoors, out of doors; in the open, in the open air, *sub Jove* [L.], *sub die* [L.], *à la belle étoile* [F.], alfresco.

221. Interiority
(See 220. Exteriority)

1. *n.* interiority, internality, inwardness etc. *adj.*; internalization; intrinsicality etc. 5; interjacence etc. 228.

2. *n.* interior, inside, internal *or* inner part, inner, interne *or* intern [poetic]; innermost, innermost part, inmost being, recesses, innermost recesses; penetralia

---

Thy soul's immensity.—WORDSWORTH. Reared upon the base of outward things.—WORDSWORTH.
221. This is not good for the insides of human beings.—KIPLING. Though our out-

[*pl.*] penetral [*sing.*; rare]; interspace; subsoil, substratum; intrados [Arch.]; bosom, breast; substance, inner reality etc. (essence) 5.2; middle etc. 68.2; heart, pith etc. (center) 222.2; insides etc. (contents) 190.

3. *n.* inland, inlands, interior, incountry [Scot.], upcountry [coll.], hinterland, midland, midlands; backwoods, the sticks etc. (the country) 183.

4. *n.* vitals, vital organs, viscera, entrails, tripes [obs. exc. dial.], intestines, bowels, guts [vulg. or Tech.], gizzard [joc. and coll.], chitterlings [of animals], internals, inners [coll. and dial.], insides [coll.], inwards [coll.], inner man [joc.], stuffings [slang]; blind gut, caecum; fore-gut, hind-gut; mid-gut, mesogaster; ilium, duodenum, jejunum; rectum, anus; heart, ticker [slang]; lungs, brain, liver, kidneys; abdomen, abdominal organs; stomach etc. 191.7.

5. *n.* gland, glandule [rare]; gland cell; suprarenal, suprarenal gland, ~ body *or* capsule, pituitary, pituitary gland *or* body, gonad, prostate, thyroid, thyroid gland *or* body, pancreas, sebaceous glands, salivary glands, simple *or* compound glands; tubular *or* saccular glands; lymphatic glands; sweat glands; lymphatic etc. 350.4.

6. *n.* enterology, enterography, enterotomy, enteropathy, enteritis, splanchnology; peristalsis, vermiculation; endocrinology.

7. *n.* inmate, intern etc. (inhabitant) 188.

8. *v.* intern, internalize, make internal etc. *adj.,* place *or* keep within; imprison etc. (confine) 751.8; inclose etc. (circumscribe) 229.2; embed etc. (insert) 300.5.

9. *adj.* interior, internal, intern [arch.], inner, inside, inward, intraneous [rare], intimate; inmost, innermost; intraregarding; indoor; deep-rooted; intracanal, intracellular, intralobular, intramarginal, intramolecular, intramundane, intraocular, intraseptal, intratelluric, intra-uterine, intravascular, intravenous, intraventricular; intramural, *intra muros* [L.]; intrinsic etc. 5–6; subjective etc. 317.7; interjacent etc. 228.11.

10. *adj.* inland, upcountry; midland, mediterranean.

---

ward man perish, yet the inward man is renewed day by day.—BIBLE.

11. *adj.* visceral, splanchnic; intestine, intestinal; duodenal; rectal; abdominal, stomachic; coeliac, coelian.

12. *adv.* internally etc. *adj.*, in, inly, inside, within, withinside [obs. exc. Scot.], withinward, withinwards, withinforth [obs.], ben [Scot.]; herein, therein, wherein; from within, *ab intra* [L.]; indoors *or* indoor, withindoors; at home, to home [dial.], in the bosom of one's family.

13. *prep.* within, inside of, enclosed *or* inclosed by; not beyond *or* exceeding, in the reach *or* limits of.

222. Centrality
(See also 68. Middle)

1. *n.* centrality, centralness etc. *adj.*, centricality; centralization, concentralization, centralism; focalization, concentration etc. (convergence) 290.

2. *n.* center, central point *or* position, centry, centrum, centroid; nucleus, nucleolus; core, kernel, heart, gist, jet, pith, marrow; navel, nave [rare], umbilicus, omphalos; bull's-eye; central body, centriole, centrosome, centrosphere; center of gravity, ∼ pressure, ∼ percussion, ∼ oscillation, ∼ buoyancy etc.; metacenter; metropolis; middle etc. 68; focus etc. 74; axis etc. 312.5; backbone etc. 235.4; interior etc. 221.2.

3. *v.* centralize, render central etc. *adj.*, center, middle; concentralize, concenter, concentrate; bring to a focus etc. 74.3; converge etc. 290.2.

4. *adj.* central, centric(al); concentric; centroidal; middlemost, midmost; nuclear, nucleate; axial, pivotal, focal; navel, umbilical; centrosymmetric; centrolineal; centripetal; homocentric(al); metropolitan; middle etc. 68.5; convergent etc. 290.3.

5. *adv. etc.* centrally etc. *adj.*, in the center *or* middle of, at the midmost point, at the heart of etc. *n.*

223. Covering
(See 224. Lining)

1. *n.* covering, overlaying etc. *v.*, obduction [obs.]; superposition, superimposition; imbrication; lorication; incasement *or* encasement, enchasement.

2. *n.* cover, kiver [dial.], covering, coverlet [obs.], coverage, covert, coverture, shelter, screen, shroud, shield, veil, mantle, coat, cloak, guise, investment; canopy, awning, tent, pavilion, blanket [all also fig.]; integument, tegument, tegmen (*pl.* tegmina), tegmentum (*pl.* tegmenta); protective covering, cortex [fig.], thick skin; overlay, overlayer; tablecloth, cloth; altar cloth *or* carpet, cerecloth, chrismal [Eccl.]; clothing etc. 225; headdress, mask etc. (clothing) 225; concealment etc. 530; disguise etc. 545.5; sunshade, eye shade, lamp shade etc. (shade) 424; safeguard etc. 666; exterior etc. 220.2; layer etc. 204.2.

3. *n.* canopy, tilt [obs.], pavilion, tester, awning, shamianah [Ind.]; baldachin; marquee, marquise; tarpaulin, tarp [slang], tarpolian [obs. exc. dial.].

4. *n.* umbrella, 'brella [dial.], brolly [slang, Eng.]; bumbershoot [slang], sunshade, *en-tout-cas* [F.], mush *or* mushroom [slang, Eng.], chatta [Ind.], gingham [coll.]; gamp; parasol, bumbersoll [slang].

5. *n.* tent, pavilion, canvas, canvas *or* rag bungalow [U.S.]; top, whitetop, round top, big top [all circus slang]; A tent, bell tent, fly tent, Sibley tent, wall tent, lean-to tent, canoe tent, kibitka [Russian], praetorium [Rom. Antiq.]; shelter tent, *tente d'abri* [F.], pup *or* dog tent [slang]; wigwam, tepee, tupek; booth, stall; tentage, canvas [both collective].

6. *n.* roof, roofing, top, housetop; shingle, shingling; slate, slating; tile, tiling; pantile, thatch, lead; mansard roof, M roof, hip roof, hip-and-valley roof, Jerkinhead roof, pyramidal roof, curb roof, gable roof, lean-to *or* shed roof, penthouse roof, French roof, gambrel roof, flat roof, deck, barrack roof [local, U.S.], bulkhead [Eng.], dome, cupola; ceiling, *plafond* [F.], planchment [local, U.S.].

7. *n.* lid, led [dial.], top, cover, covercle [obs.], cap; operculum [Bot. and Zool.]; bulkhead [U.S.]; stopper, cork, bottle cap.

---

222. Boston State house is the hub of the solar system.—HOLMES.   I hear it in the deep heart's core.—YEATS.   The abysmal dark

Of the unfathomed center.—H. COLERIDGE. Concentering all their precious beams.—MILTON.

223. All that beauty hath doth cover thee.—SHAKESPEARE.   Cover thy head . . . nay,

8. *n.* rug, carpet; namda [Ind.], nammad [Persia]; Oriental rug, Persian rug, Turkish rug, Caucasian rug, Turkoman rug, Chinese rug, Indian rug, East Indian rug; Brussels carpet, body Brussels, imperial Brussels, tapestry Brussels; camel's hair rug, mohair rug; scatter rug, throw rug; steamer rug, automobile rug; linoleum, Congoleum [trade name].

9. *n.* coverlet, coverlid [chiefly dial.], cover, spread, robe, blanket, rug [Eng.]; bedcover, bedspread; counterpane, counterpin [dial.]; quilt, comfort *or* comforter *or* comfortable [all U.S.], comfy [slang], eiderdown, eiderdown quilt, parker [local, U.S.], patchwork quilt, rildy [local, U.S.]; sheet, sheeting, linen, muslin, percale; tidy, antimacassar; lap robe, buffalo robe [U.S.]; pillowcase, pillow slip, case, slip; bedcovers, bedclothes, bedding.

10. *n.* horsecloth, horse blanket, caparison, housing; saddle blanket, saddlecloth, apishamore [Northwest. U.S.], tilpah [Southwest. U.S.]; namda [Ind.] etc. *above* 223.8.

11. *n.* wrapper, wrapping; casing, case; sheathing, sheath; jacket, envelope, capsule; involucrum, involucre; sac, vesicle; cyst, cystis (*pl.* cystides); bandage, plaster, lint, dossil, pledget, fingerstall; enclosure etc. 232.

12. *n.* skin, integument etc. *above* 223.2, cuticle, cuticula, rind [as of bacon]; hide, leather, pelt, bark, jacket [all joc. of persons]; pelt, peltry [collective], hide, coat, jacket, fell, fur [all of animals]; epidermis, scarfskin, ecderon, ectoderm; dermis, derma, derm [rare], corium, cutis, *cutis vera* [L.]; epithelium, pavement epithelium, endothelium; pellicle, membrane, membrana; enderon; bare skin; the buff [coll.], birthday suit [joc.], the raw [slang] etc. (nudity) 226.2.

fleece, lambskin, sable, golden sable, red sable, Tartar sable, Alaska sable, black sable, kolinsky, mink, brook mink, water mink, marmink, marmot, muskrat, muskutrine, beaver, beaverskin, beaverette, electric beaver, seal, sealskin, electric seal, Hudson Bay seal, polar seal, New Zealand seal, Australian seal, Roman seal, coast seal, marten, black marten, skunk, chinchilla, chinchillette, fox,

fox hair, black fox, red fox, white fox, rabbit, rabbitskin, leopard, leopardskin, Baltic leopard, Coney leopard, tiger, Baltic tiger, cat, catskin, mole, moleskin, Coney mole, electric mole, ermine, ermelin *or* ermilin [arch.], erminette, molin, miniver, shagreen, genet; leather; leatherette, near-leather [chiefly coll.]; chamois.

13. *n.* castoff skin, cast skin, cast, slough, desquamation, exuviae [*pl.*].

14. *n.* hull, pericarp, husk, shuck, shell, shale [obs.], pod, cod [chiefly dial.]; testa, episperm; cornhusk, corn shuck [U.S.]; legume, legumen; peasecod, pea pod; slique, follicle; spore case, capsule, theca, bur *or* burr; glume, gluma; lemma; chaff, bran, palea, flight [dial., Eng.]; nutshell etc. *below* 223.16.

15. *n.* peel, peeling, rind, skin, epicarp, slough [obs. exc. dial.], bark; cortex, cortical tissue, periderm, peridium; dermatogen.

16. *n.* incrustation, incrustment [rare], crust, coating, shell; eggshell; sea shell, marine shell, cockleshell, oyster shell, clam shell, snail shell, conch, conch shell, winkle, winkle shell; carapace, turtle shell, armadillo shell; nutshell, cocoa shell; pastry shell, piecrust; efflorescence [Chem.]; scale, lamina (*pl.* laminae, laminas), shale [now dial.]; scab, eschar [Med.].

17. *n.* wing cover, elytron, elytrum, elytrin.

18. *n.* coating, coat, veneer, facing, sheathing; pellicle, film, scum; sheathing board, weatherboard, clapboard, shingle; pavement, paving, pave [chiefly U.S.]; engobe; varnish, enamel etc. (paint) 428.5; ointment etc. (oil) 356.

19. *n.* plaster, stucco, grout, mortar; chinking, daubing; clay, adobe; composition, compo; cerement; cement, concrete; scagliola; roughcast; plasterwork, stuccowork, cementwork.

20. *n.* dermatology, dermatography, dermatopathy, dermatoplasty, dermoplasty.

21. *n.* malacology, conchology, conchometry, testaceology [rare], testaceography.

22. *v.* cover, superpose, superimpose, overlay, lay over, overspread; tip, cap, top; roof; dome, endome; bulkhead, bulkhead in; clothe etc. 225.41; screen, shroud etc. (conceal) 528.10.

---

prithee, be covered.—SHAKESPEARE. Blessed is he whose sin is covered.—BIBLE. The blanket of the dark.—SHAKESPEARE.

23. *v.* wrap, enwrap *or* inwrap, wrap up; case, incase *or* encase, enchase; sheathe *or* sheath, envelop; bind, tie up.

24. *v.* coat, cloak, mantle; veneer, face; loricate; enamel, gild, gloss; plate, electroplate; parget; weatherboard, clapboard, shingle; pave; paper; tar; dab, daub, bedaub, smear, besmear; lay it on thick; do over; varnish, lacquer etc. (paint) 428.10; anoint etc. (lubricate) 332.4.

25. *v.* incrust *or* encrust, crust.

26. *v.* plaster, stucco, cement, mortar; roughcast; daub etc. *above* 223.24.

27. *v.* overlie, lie over, cover; overlap, imbricate; overarch, arch over; overhang etc. 214.5; overtop etc. 206.10.

28. *adj.* covered etc. *v.*, covert, under cover; hooded, cowled; culcullate, culcullated; loricate, loricated; armored, encuirassed, armor-plated, ironclad; screened etc. (*see* screen etc. 528.10); scaly etc. (laminated) 204.5.

29. *adj.* covering etc. *v.*, vaginant, vaginate, vaginal; screening etc. (*see* screen etc. 528.10).

30. *adj.* overlying, overlapping etc. *v.*; imbricate, imbricated; incumbent, superincumbent, supernatant, superimposed; lapstreak, clinker-built, shingled, equitant [Bot.]; overhanging etc. 214.8; above etc. 206.15, 19.

31. *adj.* integumentary, integumental; tegumentary, tegumental, tegmental.

32. *adj.* cutaneous, cuticular; endermic, endermatic; skinlike, skinny; epidermal, epidermic, epidermoid *or* epidermoidal; dermal, dermic, dermoid, dermatoid; hypodermal, hypodermic, subcutaneous; cortical; epicarpal; testaceous; dermatological, dermatopathic, dermatoplastic, dermoplastic, dermatophytic.

33. *adj.* rooflike, tectiform.

224. Lining
(See 223. Covering)

1. *n.* lining, inner coating *or* covering, interlining; inlayer, inlay, inlaying; facing; sheathing; doubling, doublure; bush, bouche, bushing; wainscoting, wainscot; wall, paries [Biol.] (*pl.* parietes); brattice, brattish; incrustation, stalactite, stalagmite; filling, stuffing etc. (contents) 190; ceiling etc. (roof) 223.6.

2. *v.* line, interline, inlay; face; sheathe; incrust; ceil, ceiling; wainscot; bush, bouche, fill, stuff etc. 52.7.

225. Investment
(See 226. Divestment)

1. *n.* investment, investure [obs.], investiture, vestment, vestiment [rare], vesture, vestiture [obs.]; clothes, clothing, apparel, wear, wearing apparel, gear, habiliment, habit, dress, dressing, raiment, garments, garmenture [rare], rags [derog.], robes, robing, shroud, garb, attire, tire [arch.], drapery, costume, costumery [rare], array, fig [coll.], feathers, guise, toilet *or* toilette, trim, bedizenment, dizenment [rare], linen; wearables, toggery, togs, duds [all coll.]; covering etc. 223; cloth etc. (textile) 219.5; canonicals etc. 999.

2. *n.* wardrobe, apparel etc. *above*, things, outfit, livery, harness, turnout, layout [slang], caparison, make-up, rigging, rig [coll.], rig-out [slang], trappings, traps [coll.], duds [coll.]; trousseau; accouterments, fittings etc. (equipment) 634.

3. *n.* garment, article of clothing, piece of wearing apparel, raiment, robe, frock, gown, habit, tog [coll.], dud [coll.], wearable [coll.], rag [derog.], shroud [obs.], fig leaf [slang].

4. *n.* ready-made clothes, ready-mades, store clothes [dial.], slops, confections [Gallicism], hand-me-downs [slang].

5. *n.* rags, tatters, old clothes, duds [chiefly dial.].

6. *n.* mourning clothes, mourning, weeds, weepers.

7. *n.* suit, suit of clothes, frock, dress, rig [coll.], costume, habit, bib and tucker [coll.]; one-piece *or* two-piece suit.

8. *n.* uniform, livery, harness [crim. slang, U.S.]; regimentals, khaki, olive-drab; blouse [U.S.]; continentals [Amer. Hist.]; blues, whites; policeman's uniform, brass buttons [slang]; sailor suit, nauticals; square rig, fore-and-aft rig [both coll., Eng.]; prison uniform, stripes, pinchback [crim. slang, U.S.].

---

224. Always wear them inside out / To show the lining.—E. T. FOWLER.   There's a silver lining / Through the dark cloud shining.—L. G. FORD.   Every cloud has a silver lining.

225. The soul of this man is his clothes.—SHAKESPEARE.   Through tattered clothes small vices do appear; / Robes and furred gowns hide all.—SHAKESPEARE.   I have no

9. *n.* civilian dress, civvies [slang], cits [slang], mufti [coll., chiefly Eng.], plain clothes; shore clothes, long togs [Naut. slang].

10. *n.* costume, character dress; masquerade dress, masquerade; theatrical costume, theatricals, scenery [Theat. slang]; clown's costume, dots [circus slang]; medieval court costume, hawbuck harness [Theat. slang]; tights.

11. *n.* mask, masque, visor, vizard [arch.], false face; domino, domino mask; burglar's mask, alibi rag [crim. slang]; masquerade etc. (disguise) 545.5; screen etc. (cover) 223.2; concealment etc. 528.

12. *n.* veil, veiling, veiler; yashmak, purdah [Ind.], shade; muffler, scarf; fall; netting, gauze.

13. *n.* finery, frippery, gaudery, flashery [slang], flash [slang], showy clothes, war paint [coll.], fofarrow [slang], lugs [coll., U.S.]; best clothes, best, best bib and tucker [coll.], Sunday best *or* black [coll.], Sunday clothes [joc. or slang], Sunday-go-to-meeting clothes *or* Sunday-go-to-meetings [both joc. or slang], fine *or* full feather, glad rags [slang, U.S.], new clothes, dress-ups [slang]; gaudiness etc. 851.2; ostentation etc. 882.

14. *n.* dress clothes *or* suit, formal dress, formals, full dress, fair winds [slang], soup-and-fish [slang]; evening dress *or* gown, dinner clothes; dress coat, frock coat, tail coat, tails [slang], swallowtail [coll.], swallowtail *or* swallow-tailed coat [chiefly coll.], pigeontail *or* pigeon-tailed coat [slang], spiketail *or* spiketail coat [slang, U.S.], claw hammer, claw-hammer *or* claw-hammered coat [coll.]; Tuxedo, Tuxedo coat *or* jacket, Tux [coll.]; Prince Albert coat, Prince Albert; cutaway [coll.], cutaway coat; dinner coat *or* jacket; mess jacket, shell jacket [both Mil.].

15. *n.* cloak, outer garment, overdress, outer dress, mantle, manteel [obs.], mantevil [Hist.], frock, robe, pelisse, housing, wrap, wrapper, wrap-up, wrap-around, wrap-round; mantua [Hist.], manta, mantellone [Eccl.]; mantelet, mantelletta [Eccl.]; jubbah, jupon [obs.]; gipon, pourpoint.

cape, pelerine, sagum, haik [N. Afr.], caftan, huke [obs.], plaid [Scot.], mantilla; smock, smock coat *or* frock; gabardine, cardinal, talma, tabard, paletot, frock, blouse, burnoose *or* burnous [N. Afr.], poncho [Sp. Amer.]; shawl, cashmere *or* Cashmere shawl; veil; chuddar, [Anglo-Ind.]; tunic, *tunica* [NL.], kirtle [arch.], chlamys [Gr. Antiq.], houppelande [Hist.]; roquelaure [now chiefly dial.], rokelay [dial.].

16. *n.* coat, jacket, jupe [Scot.]; ben, tog [both chiefly thieves' slang]; spencer, jerkin [Hist. or dial.], coatee, *chaqueta* [Sp.], doublet, jumper, frock coat, sack coat, swagger coat [coll.], monkey jacket [chiefly coll.], Mackinaw *or* Mackinaw coat [local, U.S.], cardigan *or* cardigan jacket, sports coat *or* jacket, shooting jacket, dressing jacket, smoking jacket; peacoat, pea jacket, pilot jacket.

shadbelly, shad-bellied coat [both coll.]; patched coat, joseph [tramp slang]; knit jacket, knittie [slang, U.S.]; woolen jacket, woolly *or* wollies [slang, U.S.]; sweater, blazer, sweat shirt; waistcoat, weskit [dial.], vest, benjy [crim. slang], petticoat [dial., Eng.]; sleeve waistcoat; dinner coat *or* jacket etc. *above* 225.14.

17. *n.* overcoat, greatcoat, surcoat, surtout, paletot; benjamin, benny [both thieves' slang]; ulster; wraprascal, wrap-around, wrap-round; dreadnought *or* dreadnaught, fearnought *or* fearnaught; raincoat, waterproof, waterproof coat, wet feathers [coll.], oilskins, slicker [U.S.], mackintosh; tarpaulin, tarp [coll.].

18. *n.* waist, shirt, shirtwaist, intimate [slang], sark [arch. or dial.], shift [dial.], jupe [Scot.]; bodice, body [now chiefly dial.], corsage; blouse, blou [slang, Eng.]; middy, middy blouse; hickory shirt; O.D. *or* olive-drab shirt; dress shirt, blaze-faced shirt [slang], biled rag [dial.].

19. *n.* dress, frock, gown; shirt, overskirt, kirtle [arch. and dial.], jupon, jupe [chiefly Scot.], petticoat; hoop skirt, farthingale, crinoline; kilt, filibeg *or* philabeg; pannier; underskirt etc. *below* 225.25; evening gown etc. *above* 225.14.

---

more doublets than backs, no more stockings than legs, nor no more shoes than feet.—SHAKESPEARE. The hood makes not the monk, nor the apparel the man.—R. GREENE. Eat to please yourself, but dress to please others. FRANKLIN. There is not so variable a thing

20. n. apron, *tablier* [F.]; pinafore, gabardine [local, Eng.], tier [local, U.S.]; bib; smock, smock coat *or* frock.

21. n. trousers, pair of trousers, trouse [arch.], trews [arch. exc. Scot.], breeches, britches [dial.], pantaloons, pants [coll.], jeans [chiefly U.S.], galigaskins [now joc.], kicks [slang], kickseys *or* kicksies [slang, Eng.], sit-upons [coll.], strides [slang]; unmentionables, unutterables, inexpressibles, indescribables, innominables [all slang or joc.; now rare].

corduroy trousers, corduroys, cords [coll.]; tweeds; bell-bottoms; peg-top trousers, pegtops; bags, sacks; slacks; knee breeches, smallclothes *or* smalls [arch.], trouserettes, pantalets, shorts; knickerbockers, knickers [coll.], plus fours; bloomers, rompers; high-water pants [slang]; overalls, blue jeans [chiefly U.S.]; drawers, shintiyan [Moslem]; waterproof trousers; ducks, whites.

22. n. breechcloth, waistcloth, loincloth, G string, dhoti [Ind.], moocha [S. Afr.], *gagne* [F.]; diaper, dydee [coll.], hipping *or* hippen [Scot. and dial. Eng.].

23. n. dishabille, *déshabillé* [F.], undress; negligee, *négligé* [F.]; morning dress, tea gown, dressing gown; *peignoir* [F.], wrapper, robe-de-chambre [F.], kimono; dressing sack *or* jacket, smoking jacket; lounging robe, bathrobe; pajamas *or* pyjamas, P.J.'s [slang], lounging pyjamas.

24. n. night clothes, nightgown, nightie [coll.], bedgown, nightshirt, *sac de nuit* [F.]; pyjamas.

25. n. undergarments, underclothing, underclothes, undies [slang], underwear, U-wear [slang], winter *or* summer underwear, drawers, intimates [slang], body clothes, lingerie, smallclothes, smalls [coll.]; woolen underwear, woolly *or* woollies [slang, U.S.].

union suit, combination, B.V.D.'s [trade name]; undershirt, skivvie shirt [slang, U.S.], sark [arch. and dial.], wrapper; undervest, underwaistcoat; underskirt, petticoat, coat [now dial.], camisole, slip, shift; chemise, shimmy *or* shimmey [dial. and coll.]; Balmoral; underpants [coll.], panties [coll.], step-ins,

shorts, bloomers; brassière, bra [slang], bandeau; girdle, stomacher; corset, stays, jupes [Scot.]; corselet, combination, corset cover, underbody [dial., U.S.]; bustle, bishop, *tournure* [F.], pannier.

26. n. headdress, headgear, headclothes, head, coiffure, haberdashery, millinery; headpiece, cap, hat, chapeau, castor, bonnet; lid, dicer, tile, benny, skimmer, katy [all slang]; silk hat, top hat, topper [slang], plug hat *or* plug [slang, chiefly U.S.], stovepipe hat *or* stovepipe [coll., U.S.], opera hat; felt hat, wide-awake *or* wide-awake hat, billycock *or* billycock hat [coll.]; bowler [Eng.], derby [U.S.], hard-boiled hat [joc.], kelly [slang, U.S.]; crush hat, crushable; sombrero, ten-gallon hat [coll., U.S.]; picture hat.

sun hat, sunbonnet, sundown; sun helmet, pith hat *or* helmet; topee [Ind.]; puggree [Ind.]; cocked hat, scraper [slang]; fore-and-after, fore-and-aft [both coll.; Naut.]; sou'wester, fantail [Eng.]; straw hat, straw basher [slang, U.S.]; Panama hat *or* panama, leghorn; bearskin; beaver, cock-and-pinch [slang]; tam, tam-o'-shanter; skullcap, nightcap; mobcap, boudoir cap, Dutch cap; hood, coif, capote, calash; Salvation-Army bonnet; rumal [Ind.], turban, fez, tarboosh, shako, busby; kepi, forage cap, campaign hat, overseas cap; kerchief, coverchief, headkerchief [rare], ear muff, kaffiyeh [Arab.], wimple; snood; chignon, rat [coll., U.S.]; helmet etc. 717.2; wig etc. 256.4.

27. n. footwear, footgear, *chaussure* [F.]; shoes, boots; dogs, kicks, clodhoppers [all slang]; veld schoen [S. Afr.]; bootees, bootikins; pumps; buskins; Oxfords, Oxford shoes *or* ties; slippers, sandals, moccasins; gums, gumshoes; sneakers, sneaks, creepers [all slang]; gymnasium shoes, tennis shoes, overshoes, galoshes, arctics, rubbers; brogues, brogans, stogies; clogs, wooden shoes, pattens; high-topped shoes, high-lows, half boots; bluchers, Blucher boots *or* shoes; top boots, jack boots *or* jackboots, hip boots; hessians, Hessian boots; wellingtons, Wellington boots; lace shoes, button shoes; riding boots; snowshoes, pattens [rare], ski [also *sing.*] *or* skis.

28. *n.* leggings, gaiters, galligaskins [dial.], gambados, antigropelos, *chivarras* or *chivarros* [Sp.; Southw. U.S.]; gamashes [arch. exc. Scot. and North. Eng.], *gamache* [F.]; spats, spatterdashes; *chaparajos* or *chaparejos* or *chaparreras* [Sp. Amer.], chaps [coll.], shaps [West. U.S.]; puttee, putt [slang]; leg armor, greaves.

29. *n.* stockings, hosiery, hose, gaskins [obs. exc. dial.]; half hose, socks; trunk hose.

30. *n.* gloves; gauntlets, gantlets; mousquetaires, mousquetaire gloves; kids, kid gloves, suède gloves; mittens, mitts; muff.

31. *n.* sleeve; armlet; cuff, wristband.

32. *n.* children's clothes, short clothes, smallclothes, smalls [coll.]; rompers, jumpers, creepers; baby linen, layette, swaddling clothes; diaper etc. *above* 225.22.

33. *n.* neckwear; neckpiece, neckcloth, neckband; choke [slang], choker [chiefly slang]; necktie, tie, cravat, stock; collar, ruff, boa; celluloid collar, spit-and-rub [joc.]; chemisette, guimpe, tucker; *rabat* [F.], rabato; scarf; tippet; kerchief, neckerchief, neckercher [now dial]; muffler, comforter.

34. *n.* waistband, waist belt, waistcloth, bellyband, sash, girdle, girth, girt, band, belt, cummerbund [Ind.], cestus [Gr. and Rom. Antiq.], baldric, fascia.

35. *n.* garment making, tailoring; dressmaking; haberdashery, millinery; shoemaking, cobbling.

36. *n.* clothier, clother [obs.], mercer [Eng.], outfitter, costumer, costumier; glover; hosier; draper, linen draper.

37. *n.* tailor, tailoress [*fem.*], *tailleur* [F.], sartor [joc.], stitch [joc.], snip [slang], habit maker; whipcat [dial.]; whip louse [contemptuous, old slang], darzee [Ind.]; busheler, bushelman, bushelwoman [both U.S.].

38. *n.* dressmaker, modiste, *couturière* [*fem.*, F.], *couturier* [*masc.*, F.], mantuamaker [arch.], seamstress *or* sempstress; needlewoman, needleworker.

39. *n.* haberdasher, hatter, milliner.

40. *n.* shoemaker, cordwainer [arch.], Crispin, cobbler, snob [Scot. and dial.], souter [Scot. and dial.], bootmaker.

41. *v.* invest, vest [rare], clothe, enclothe, garb, dud [slang], dress, dress up, attire, tire [arch.], array, dight *or* bedight [arch.], robe, enrobe, apparel, mantle, habilitate [rare], costume, deck, bedeck, drape, harness, endue *or* indue [fig.], dizen, bedizen, deck out, trick up *or* out, fig out; wrap, enwrap *or* inwrap, wrap up, wrap round, circumvest [obs.], muffle up, envelop, sheathe, shroud, swathe, swaddle; breech, coat, jacket, gown; cover etc. 223.22–24.

42. *v.* outfit, equip, accouter, caparison, rig, rig out *or* up, fit, fit out, turn out, costume, habit.

43. *v.* don, put on, huddle on, slip on, get on, rag out *or* up [slang, U.S.], dress in, dress etc. *above* 225.41.

44. *v.* primp, spruce up [coll.] etc. (ornament) 847.11.

45. *v.* wear, carry, bear, have on, be dressed in, use *or* affect . . . in dressing, assume, sport [coll.].

46. *adj.* invested, clothed etc. *v.,* clad, decent [Theat. slang], dight *or* bedight [arch.], *costumé* [F.]; barbed, barded; shod, *chaussé* [F.]; *en grande tenue* [F.] etc. (smart) 847.14.

47. *adj.* in dishabille, *en déshabillé* [F.], in undress, in negligee, décolleté.

48. *adj.* investmental, investmentary, vestmental, vestmented, vestmentary, vestimental [rare], vestimentary [rare]; sartorial, sartorian [rare].

226. Divestment
(See 225. Investment)

1. *n.* divestment, divestiture, divesture; undressing, unclothing etc. *v.*; decortication, excoriation; desquamation, exfoliation; exuviation, ecdysis [both Zool.]; trichosis.

2. *n.* nudity, nudation [rare], denudation, indecency [Theat. slang], bareness etc. *adj.*; the nude, the altogether [coll.], *tout ensemble* [F.], the buff [coll.], the raw [slang], birthday suit [joc.], nature's garb, nature in the raw [joc.], state of nature; not a stitch, not a stitch to one's

---

a plate.—Cynic's Calendar.   Fine feathers make fine birds.   Clothes make the man. An ape's an ape, a varlet's a varlet, / Though they be clad in silk and scarlet.

226. Naked came we into the world, and naked shall we depart from it.—Aesop.   The plain bald pate of Father Time Himself.—Shakespeare.   The nakedness of woman is the

name *or* back [both coll.]; undress etc. (dishabille) 225.23.

3. *n.* hairlessness, baldness, acomia, alopecia; bald-headedness, bald-patedness; beardlessness; depilation; baldhead, baldpate.

4. *v.* divest, divesture [rare]; uncover, expose, lay open, bare, lay bare, denude; strip, strip to the buff [coll.]; undress, unclothe, undrape, ungarment, unapparel, unarray, disrobe, dismantle, put off, take off, cast off, doff, off [rare]; uncoif; unwrap; do a strip-tease [Theat. slang].

5. *v.* peel, pare, skin, flay, excoriate, decorticate, bark; strip, strip from; scalp; husk, hull, pod, shell.

6. *v.* shed, molt, cast, cast the skin, slough, exuviate [Zool.], mew [arch.].

7. *v.* scale, flake, scale *or* flake off, desquamate, exfoliate.

8. *adj.* divested, undressed etc. *v.*; unclad, bare, bald, naked, stark-naked, startnaked [obs. exc. dial.], nude, raw [slang], in a state of nature, in nature's garb, *in puris naturalibus* [L.], in one's birthday suit [joc.], in the buff [coll.], in native buff [coll.], stripped to the buff [coll.], in the raw [slang], in the altogether [coll.], indecent *or* not decent [Theat. slang], sky-clad [joc.], with nothing on, wearing a smile [joc.], leafless [coll. or poetic]; without a stitch, without a stitch to one's name *or* back [coll.]; "naked as a worm" (Chaucer), "naked as my nail" (J. Heywood), bare as the back of one's hand; bareback, barebacked; in dishabille etc. (*see* dishabille etc. 225.23); threadbare etc. (deteriorated) 659.

9. *adj.* barefoot, barefooted, unshod; discalceate, discalced.

10. *adj.* hairless, depilous, acomous, bald, bald as a coot; bald-headed, bald-pated, tonsured; beardless, whiskerless, shaven, clean-shaven, smooth-shaven, smooth-faced; smooth, glabrous, glabrate.

11. *adj.* divestitive, divestive; exuvial, sloughy; flaky, scaly; desquamative, desquamatory; exfoliatory, exfoliative.

work of God.—W. BLAKE.   O fair undress, best dress!—THOMSON.   Beauty when most unclothed is clothed best.—P. FLETCHER. Silk was invented so that women could go naked in clothes.—MAHOMET.   Suddenly a flower cried: / "Oh, let's take off our gowns."—N. CRANE.

227. Circumjacence
(See 228. Interjacence)

1. *n.* circumjacence, circumjacency, circumfluence [rare], circumambience *or* circumambiency, circumposition, encompassment, environment, circumscription [rare], circumference [now rare], surrounding etc. *v.*; encincture, circumcincture; circumambulation; circumduction [rare]; exteriority etc. 220.

2. *n.* surroundings, environs, environment, environage [rare], entourage, circumjacencies, circumambiencies, circumstances, circumferences [obs.], *alentours* [F.]; milieu, purlieus, precincts; neighborhood, vicinity, vicinage; outskirts, outposts, borderlands, suburbs, *faubourgs* [F.], *banlieue* [F.] *or* banlieu, boulevards, periphery; atmosphere, medium (*pl.* media); background, setting, scene [as in *a change of scene*]; bounds, borders etc. (edge) 231.

3. *v.* be circumjacent etc. *adj.*, lie around etc. *adv.*, surround, environ, compass, encompass, compass about, enclose *or* inclose, cincture, encincture, encircle, circle, circumvent, circumpose, circumference [rare], circumfer [obs.], girdle, gird, begird, engird, belt, ring, loop, ensphere, embrace, skirt, hedge; invest, endue; go round, twine round, circumambulate; circumflect, circumflex; beset, hem in etc. (circumscribe) 229.2, 3; round etc. 247.6.

4. *adj.* circumjacent, surrounding etc. *v.*, ambient, circumambient, circumfluent, circumcinct [rare], cinctured; girt, begirt; circumferential, circumferent [obs.]; round [rare], roundabout; suburban, neighboring; circumflect, circumflex; circumaxile, circumaxillary; circumesophagal, circumesophageal; circumocular, circumanal, circumbuccal, circumbulbar, circumcallosal, circumcorneal, circumgenital, circumintestinal, circumtonsillar, circumnuclear, circumrenal, circumorbital, circumpallial, circumumbilical, circumvascular.

5. *adv.* around, round, about; round about; without; all round *or* around, on every side, on all sides, right-and-left;

227. It is your human environment that makes climate.—MARK TWAIN.   It lies around us like a cloud, / A world we do not see.—H. B. STOWE.   It is no friendly environment, this of thine.—CARLYLE.

228. Interjacence
(See 227. Circumjacence)

1. *n.* interjacence, interjacency, intercurrence, intervenience *or* interveniency, interlocation, interposition, interposure; interiority etc. 221; equidistance etc. (middle) 68.

2. *n.* interjection, introduction, interpolation, intercalation; interlineation; interspersion; embolism; interlocution, remark, parenthetical *or* side remark, aside, parenthesis; episode; flyleaf; infiltration, permeation etc. (impregnation) 41.2; injection etc. (insertion) 300; interdigitation etc. (interlacing) 219; addition etc. 37.

3. *n.* intervention, intrusiveness etc. *adj.*, intrusion, intrudance, obtrusion, interposure, interposition, intromission, insinuation, imposition, encroachment, inroad, incursion, invasion, intravasation; interruption; irruption; intermediation etc. (mediation) 724; intermeddling etc. 682.8; untimeliness etc. 135.

4. *n.* intruder, obtruder, interloper, loper [slang], interferer, interrupter, imposer, trespasser, buttinsky [slang], chiseler [slang, U.S.]; crasher, gate crasher [both slang, U.S.]; intermeddler, Paul Pry etc. (meddler) 682.11; alien etc. 57.3.

5. *n.* intermediary, intermedium, mediary, medium; link, connecting link, connection, go-between; mediator etc. 724.2; deputy etc. 759.

6. *n.* partition, *cloison* [F.], septum, interseptum, septulum, dissepiment; diaphragm, midriff; mediastinum, mediastine [rare]; wall, panel; brattice, brattish; bulkhead; perpend, perpend wall; dividing line, midrib [fig.], party line *or* wall.

7. *v.* be interjacent etc. *adj.*, lie between, come *or* get between etc. (*see* between etc. *below* 228.13), intervene, interpose.

8. *v.* interject, put between etc. (*see* between etc. *below* 228.13), sandwich, interpose, intercalate, interpolate, interjaculate, interlard; introduce in, insert in, insinuate in, inject in, implant in; wedge in, edge in, worm in, smuggle in, throw in, jam in, foist in, run in, work in, drag in, lug in, let in; interleaf, interleave; interweave, interdigitate, dovetail etc. (interlace) 219.8; insinuate, introduce etc. (insert) 300.5; add etc. 37.3.

9. *v.* interpenetrate, interfuse, intersperse, permeate, pervade; infiltrate, infuse etc. (imbue) 41.8.

10. *v.* intrude, intruse [obs.], obtrude, interfere, interrupt, interlope, interpose, intervene, insinuate, invade, impose, encroach, trespass; break in upon, break in, bust in [slang or dial.], barge in [coll.], cut in, thrust in, press in, put in, drive in, pop in, drop in; butt in, horn in, chisel in, muscle in [all slang]; nose in [coll.], poke ~, stick *or* thrust one's nose in, put in an oar, put *or* shove in one's oar, foist oneself upon, foist in, worm *or* work in, wedge in, edge in, introduce the thin edge of the wedge; crash, crash in, crash the gates [all slang, U.S.]; have a finger in, have a finger in the pie; clash, conflict, collide, encounter; meddle etc. 682.14.

11. *adj.* interjacent, interposed, intervening etc. *v.*; intervenient, intercalary; intermediate, intermediary, intermedial; medial, mediate [rare], mesial, mesian, mean, medium, mesne [Law], median, middle; septal, embolismal; parenthetical, episodic; mediterranean, midland; embosomed; merged.

intercolumnar, intercostal, intercurrent, interfacial, intergrown, interlineal, interlobular, interlocular, intermaxillary, intermolecular, intermundane, internasal, interneural, internodal, interoceanic, interosseal, interosseous, interpolar, interradial, interrenal, interscapular, interseptal, interstellar, interplanetary, interstitial, intervalvular, intervascular, interventricular, intervertebral.

12. *adj.* intrusive, obtrusive, interfering etc. *v.*, interferent, intervenient, institutive [rare], invasive, epenthetic; interruptive, interruptory, irruptive [rare].

13. *adv. etc.* between, atween [arch.], betwixt, 'twixt, betwixt and between [coll.]; amid, amidst, mid, 'mid, midst, 'midst, in the midst, *in medias res* [L.], among, amongst, 'mongst, in the thick of; sandwichwise; midway etc. 68.6; parenthetically, *obiter dictum* [L.] etc. (by the way) 134.11.

---

228. He has an oar in every man's boat, and a finger in every pie.—CERVANTES. Rued his rash intrusion.—TENNYSON.

229. Circumscription
(See also 230. Outline)

1. *n.* circumscription, enclosure *or* inclosure, confinement, limitation, restriction, restraint; circumvallation; cincture, encincture; an enclosure etc. 232.

2. *v.* circumscribe, enclose *or* inclose, limit, bound, confine, restrict, restrain; mark off, demarcate, delimit, delimitate, define, determine; shut in, hem in, pen in, hedge in, wall in, fence in, rail in, fence *or* hedge etc. round, lap [obs.], picket, corral; encyst; block, blockade; beset, beleaguer, besiege; compass about, surround etc. 227.3; outline etc. 230.3.

3. *v.* infold *or* enfold, envelop, incase *or* encase, enchase, enclasp, enwrap *or* inwrap, enshrine, embosom, embay, involve.

4. *adj.* circumscribed etc. *v.,* circumscript, circumscriptive, circumambient, circumcinct [rare], cinct [rare]; shut in *or* up, mewed up, pent up, lapt [obs.], bound, "cabined, cribbed, confined" (Shakespeare), under restraint etc. *n.*; embedded, buried *or* immersed in, embosomed in, in the bosom of; icebound, wind-bound, weather-bound, landlocked; in a ring fence; begirt, surrounded etc. (*see* surround etc. 227.3); limited etc. 233.3; outlined etc. 230.4.

230. Outline
(See also 229. Circumscription)

1. *n.* outline, contour, delineation, boundary, pale, bounds, lines, lineaments, *galbe* [F.; Art], *tournure* [F.], circumference; perimeter, periphery; skeleton, framework; relief, configuration, profile, silhouette; main features, general principles; draft, sketch, map etc. (plan) 626.2; conspectus, summary etc. (compendium) 596; prospectus, program etc. (schedule) 611.2; coast line, offing etc. (horizon) 213.4; surroundings etc. 237.2.

2. *n.* zone, zonar, zodiac, baldric [poetic], circuit, orb, orbit, ambit, girdle, belt, band, girth, girt, cingle [rare], cingulum [Tech.], cincture, clasp; cordon etc. (enclosure) 232; circle etc. 247.2.

3. *v.* outline, contour, delineate, define, determine; block, block out, mark off, demarcate; draft *or* draught, diagram, trace, sketch, rough in; silhouette, profile; circumscribe etc. 229.2.

4. *adj.* outlinear, delineatory; outlined etc. *v.,* clearly defined; perimetric(al), peripheral; circumferential; circumscribed etc. 229.4.

231. Edge

1. *n.* edge, verge, brink, brim, rim, brow, boundary, boundary line *or* point, bound, bounds, pale, border, bordure, borderland, border line, curb, margin, limit, hedge, confine, confines, skirt, outskirt, outpost, frontier, fringe, hem, side, coast [arch.], ledge; frame, enframement; periphery, perimeter; lip, labium [Tech.] (*pl.* labia), labellum [Bot.] (*pl.* labella), labrum [Zool.] (*pl.* labra); flange, flanch [rare]; featheredge; shore etc. 342.2; threshold etc. (portal) 260.4, (vestibule) 191.17; extremity etc. (end) 67; surroundings etc. 227.2; purlieus etc. 197.3.

2. *n.* (fringelike border) fringe, fimbriation, fimbria [Tech.]; edging, bordering, trimming, skirting; hem, selvage *or* selvedge, list, welt; flounce, frill, furbelow, valance.

3. *v.* edge, border, rim, skirt, fringe, befringe [rare], hem, margin, marginate, coast [arch.], verge [rare], line, bound; purl, cotise, purfle, bind, dado.

4. *adj.* border, bordering etc. *v.*; marginal, marginate; labial, labiated; limbiferous, limbic [Anat.]; coastal, littoral.

5. *adj.* edged, bordered etc. *v.*; fimbriated etc. (fringed) 256.17.

232. Enclosure

1. *n.* enclosure, closure, close; cincture, encincture; pen, fold, confine, coop, cloister [obs.], garth [arch. and dial.]; yard,

In the great zone of heaven.—MILTON. I'll put a girdle round about the earth / In forty minutes.—SHAKESPEARE.
231. Upon the borders of these solitudes.—BENTHAM. To larger sight the rim of shadow is the line of light.—T. W. PARSONS. The furthest verge that ever was surveyed by English eye.—SHAKESPEARE.
232. I am a temporary enclosure for a temporary purpose.—H. G. WELLS. Within the

229. I am, being woman, hard beset.—E. WYLIE. There's such divinity doth hedge a king.—SHAKESPEARE. Keep within bounds.—CERVANTES.
230. Outlined in Fame's illusive light, / May stalk a silhouette sublime.—J. T. TROWBRIDGE.

court, courtyard, wynd [chiefly dial.]; square, quadrangle, quad [coll.]; curtilage, compound; farmyard, barton [Eng.]; barnyard, stockyard, corral, paddock; pasture, croft [Eng.], wood lot; keddah [Ind.]; pound, dog pound; pinfold, penfold; sheepfold, cattlefold; sty, pigsty, piggery, pigpen; chicken coop, hen coop, hen cote, henyard, chicken yard; booth, stall, manger; *enceinte* [F.], circumvallation, body [Fort.]; cage; kennel, cote, barn etc. (abode) 189; menagerie etc. 370.3; receptacle etc. 191; envelope etc. (wrapper) 223.11; zone, girdle etc. (outline) 230; prison etc. 752.1.

2. *n.* fence, boundary, confine, hay [arch.], dike [Scot. and dial. Eng.]; paling, pale [arch.]; palisade, palisado [rare]; picketing, picket fence; weir; rail, railing; balustrade, balustrading; ring fence, zigzag fence; sunk fence, haha; wall, garden wall, stone wall, dead wall; parapet, rampart, vallation; contravallation, countervallation [both Fort.]; cordon; hedge, hedgerow, quickset hedge; espalier, trellis; barrier, barricade etc. (fortification) 717.3; door, gate etc. (portal) 260.4; obstacle etc. 706.2.

3. *v.* enclose, inclose, pen in etc. (circumscribe) 229.2, 3.

233. Limit

1. *n.* limit, utmost, uttermost, utmost extent, *ne plus ultra* [L.], extreme, outside [coll.], term, termination, terminus, terminal, end, period, pale, march, mark [Hist.], bound, bourn *or* bourne [arch.]; limits, confines, marches, bounds; boundary, boundary line, landmark, high-water mark; line of demarcation *or* circumvallation; Pillars of Hercules; turning point, Rubicon; curbstone, kerbstone [Eng.], edgestone; floodgate, sluice; verge, frontier etc. (edge) 231.

2. *v.* limit, delimit, restrict, restrain, stint, bound, compass, confine; define, demarcate, determine, fix, specify, condition, qualify; circumscribe etc. 229.2.

---

pinfold of his own conceit.—WORDSWORTH. A yard she had, enclosed all about / With sticks, and a dry ditch without.—CHAUCER.
233. Every man takes the limits of his own field of vision for the limits of the world.—SCHOPENHAUER. The undiscovered country from whose bourne / No traveller returns.—SHAKESPEARE.

3. *adj.* limited etc. *v.*, limitary, limitate [rare], limital, limitable, terminal, terminable, conterminal, conterminate [obs.], bound, boundary; definite, determinate, fixed, defined, clear-cut, specific, exact, precise, unequivocal; circumscribed etc. 229.4.

4. *adv.* thus far, thus far and no further, so far, just so far.

234. Front
(See 235. Rear)

1. *n.* front, fore, fore part *or* forepart, forefront, foreside [obs. or Tech.]; head, heading; frontispiece, frontal, frontage; face, façade; facet, *facette* [F.]; facia; disk; foreground, front view *or* position, proscenium; priority, anteriority; obverse [of a medal], head [of a coin]; beginning etc. 66; precession etc. 280.

2. *n.* van, vanguard, advance guard; forerank, front rank, first line, first line of battle; outpost, Cossack post; scout, forerunner etc. (precursor) 64.

3. *n.* prow, prore [poetic], stem, rostrum [Rom. Antiq.] (*pl.* rostra, rostrums); nose, beak; bowsprit, jib boom.

4. *n.* face [Anat.], front, visage, physiognomy [often joc.]; phiz, phizog [both slang], features, lineaments, countenance, favor, mazard [arch. and joc.], façade [joc.], jib [dial. and slang]; mug, mush, pan, index, kisser, lug, map, puss [all slang]; brow, forehead.

5. *n.* chin, mentum [Anat.], whiskers [slang]; point, point of the chin, button [slang], knockout *or* sleep button [boxing slang].

6. *n.* physiognomy, physnomy [obs.], metoposcopy, phrenology; physiognomist, metoposcopist, phrenologist.

7. *v.* front, confront, face, meet; outbrazen, brave, dare, defy, oppose, buck [coll.], buffet, breast; bend forwards; come to the front etc. *n.*, be *or* stand in front etc. *adv.*; go before, go in the van etc. *adv.*; lead, head etc. (precede) 280.2.

8. *adj.* front, frontal; anterior, fore, forward; foremost, headmost; first, chief.

9. *adv. etc.* before, in front, in the lead,

---

234. *Frons est animi janua* [The forehead is the door to the mind].—CICERO. *Auxilium non leve vultus habet* [The face is no little help].—OVID. *Imago animi vultus est* [The countenance is the reflection of the soul].—CICERO. In the faces of men and women I see God.—

in the van, in advance, in the foreground, in the lee of; ahead, right ahead; foremost, headmost; before one's face *or* eyes, under one's nose; face to face, vis-à-vis, *front à front* [F.].

10. *adv.* frontward *or* frontwards, frontad, forward *or* forwards, headward *or* headwards, onward *or* onwards.

235. Rear
(See 234. Front)

1. *n.* rear, rearward [now rare], arrear [arch.], rear end, back, back side, posterior, behind, hind end, hind part, hinder *or* hindmost part, after part *or* afterpart, stern, tail, tail end, tailpiece, heel, heelpiece, afterpiece; background, setting, hinterland; reverse [of a coin], tail [of a coin]; posteriority; back door, postern, postern door; back seat, rumble, rumble seat; hindhead, occiput [Tech.]; nape, scruff, scruff of the neck; suffix, postfix.

2. *n.* rear rank, rear guard, rear, rearward [now rare].

3. *n.* back [Anat.], dorsum (*pl.* dorsa), tergum [Zool.] (*pl.* terga).

4. *n.* backbone, spine, spina [Tech.], spinal *or* vertebral column, vertebra (*pl.* vertebrae), chine [Zool.], rachis, ridgebone [arch.]; ridge; center etc. 222.2; foundation etc. 215.3.

5. *n.* rump, croup, buttocks, butt [vulgar or dial. exc. Zool.], posteriors, posteriority [rare], hips, fundament, bottom [coll.], arse [now vulgar], ass [vulgar], stern [chiefly coll.], seat, rear [vulgar], fud [Scot. and North. Eng.], tail [vulgar], backside [vulgar], hind end [vulgar], behind [vulgar], bum [now vulgar], fanny [slang, U.S.], breech, prat [slang], crupper [of a horse], podex [Zool.]; dorsal region, lumbar region, anal region, gluteal region, hindquarters, loin; haunches, hunkers [Scot. and dial.], hunkies [dial. and slang]; aitchbone, edgebone; hipbone, innominate bone, haunch bone, hench bone [dial.]; anus.

6. *n.* tail, caudal appendage, cauda [Tech.], caudation, flap *or* flapper, pole [sporting slang]; tailpiece, appendage, [both joc.]; bunt [Scot. and Eng.], fud [Scot. and North. Eng.], scut [all of a hare]; single [of a deer; Eng.], brush of a fox], wreath [of a boar; obs.], fantail [of fowls], *empennage* [F., Aeronaut.]; rattail, rat's-tail; dock, stub; queue, cue, pigtail; wake, train etc. (sequel) 65.2.

7. *n.* stern [Naut.], buttocks [rare], heel; poop, counter, tail end, rudder; sternpost, rudderpost; mizzen, mizzenmast.

8. *v.* be behind etc. *adv.*; fall astern; bend backwards; bring up the rear; follow etc. (pursue) 622.6.

9. *adj.* rear, rearward, back, posterior, postern, after, aft [Naut.], hind; hinder, hindmost, hinmost [obs.], hindermost, hindhand, posteriormost, aftermost, aftmost [Naut.], rearmost; last etc. (final) 67.8.

10. *adj.* posterial, dorsal, tergal, neural, lumbar, gluteal.

11. *adj.* caudal, caudate, caudated, tailed; caudiform, taillike.

12. *adj.* spinal, vertebral; rachial, rachidial, rachidian.

13. *adj.* backswept, swept-back [as the wing of an airplane].

14. *adv. etc.* behind, ahind [dial.], aback [arch.], in the rear etc. *n.*; in the rear of, in back of, at the back of etc. *n.*; in the background; behind one's back; back to back.

15. *adv.* after; aft, abaft, abaff, baft, baff, astern [all Naut.].

16. *adv.* rearward *or* rearwards, hindward *or* hindwards, tailward *or* tailwards, backward *or* backwards, back [arch.].

17. *adv.* dorsally etc. *adj.*, dorsad, posterial [Anat. and Zool.].

236. Side
(See 237. Contraposition)

1. *n.* side, flank, pleuron [Zool.], paries [Biol.] (*pl.* parietes), flitch [as of bacon]; hand, arm, wing, leg, temple, profile, loin; thigh, haunch, hip; cheek, jowl; beam; broadside; gable, gable end; laterality [rare]; outside etc. 220.2; inside etc. 221.2; border etc. (edge) 231; east, west

---

WHITMAN. My face I don't mind it / Because I'm behind it.—A. EUWER. I have always considered my face a convenience rather than an ornament.—HOLMES.
235. Where the vanguard camps today, the rear shall rest tomorrow.—G. MASSEY. The back is made for the burden.—CARLYLE. *Ogni medaglia ha il suo rovescio* [Every medal has its reverse].

etc. (direction) 278.2; right etc. 238.2; left etc. 239.2.

2. *n.* lee, lee side, leeward, leeboard [obs.]; quarter; lee wheel, lee helm, lee anchor, lee sheet, lee tack; lee shore; lee tide, leeward tide.

3. *n.* weather, weather side, windward *or* windwards [chiefly coll.], windward side, weatherboard, luff [rare]; weather wheel, weather helm, weather anchor, weather gauge, weather sheet, weather tack, weather rail, weather bow, weather deck; weather roll; windward tide, weather-going tide, windward ebb, windward flood.

4. *v.* side, flank, skirt, border, edge, fringe, befringe, margin, marginate, verge [rare]; be on one side etc. *adv.*; sidetrack etc. (deflect) 279.6, 7.

5. *v.* sidle, side [rare], move *or* direct to the side, lateralize, edge, veer, skew; crabsidle [coll.]; sideslip, skid; deviate etc. 279.4–7.

6. *adj.* side, lateral; flanking etc. *v.*; parietal [Tech.]; sideling, sloping, inclined; sidelong, sidewise etc. *adv.*; collateral.

7. *adj.* sided, flanked etc. *v.*; one-sided, unilateral; two-sided, bilateral, dihedral [Tech.]; bifacial; three-sided, tri-lateral, triquetrous [Tech.]; four-sided, quadrilateral, tetrahedral [Tech.]; many-sided, multilateral, polyhedral *or* polyhedrical [Geom.], polyhedric [rare], polyhedrous [rare].

8. *adv.* laterally etc. *adj.*, laterad [Anat.]; sideways *or* sideway, sidewise, sidewards *or* sideward, sideling, sidling, sidelings *or* sidelins [Scot. and dial. Eng.], sidelong; edgeways *or* edgeway, edgewise; edgelong, edgling [both obs.]; askance *or* askant, asquint; on the other side *or* hand; broadside on; alee, leeward, to leeward, toward the lee etc. *n.*; aweather, windward, to windward, toward the windward etc. *n.*; on her beam ends; right-and-left; obliquely etc. 217.17–19; crosswise etc. 219.12; deviatively etc. 279.9.

9. *adv. etc.* beside, besides [obs.], aside *or* aside of [arch. and dial.], alongside, abreast, on one side, on the side, by, by the side of, sidelong, sidling, sidelings *or* sidelins [Scot. and dial. Eng.], in juxtaposition; fornent, fernint, fornenst, ferninst [all dial.]; side by side, tête à tête, cheek by cheek, cheek to cheek, shoulder to shoulder, yardarm to yardarm; parallel to etc. 216.5; near etc. 197.11.

237. Contraposition
(See 236. Side)

1. *n.* contraposition, counterposition [rare]; anteposition, opposition; polarity; *contrapposto* [It.; Art]; subcontrariety [Logic]; contrariety etc. 14; inversion etc. 218.

2. *n.* opposite side, other side, *alteram partem* [L.]; reverse, inverse; opposite, counterpole etc. (the contrary) 14.2; counterpart etc. (analogue) 17.5.

3. *n.* antipodes etc. (*see* antipode etc. 14.2), opposites, opposite poles, north pole and south pole, north and south, east and west; heads or tails; contrapositives, contraposita [both Logic]; antipodal points, antipoints [both Math.].

4. *v.* contrapose, counterpose [rare], oppose, set over against etc. *prep.*; convert by contraposition, contraposit [Logic].

5. *v.* be opposite etc. *adj.*, oppose, contrast; face, front, confront; subtend.

6. *adj.* contrapositive, opposite, reverse, inverse, diametric(al), antithetic; contra, counter; antipodal, antipodean, antipodic; subcontrary; facing etc. *v.*; converse, diametrically opposite etc. (contrary) 14.5, 6.

7. *prep.* opposite to etc. *adj.*, in opposition to etc. *n.*, against, over against; versus, *vs.*; facing etc. *v.*, face to face, vis-à-vis; as poles asunder.

238. Dextrality
(See 239. Sinistrality)

1. *n.* dextrality, dexterity, dexterousness etc. *adj.*, right-handedness; ambidexterity; dextrocularity, dextroduction, dextroversion; dextrorotation, dextrogyration.

2. *n.* right, right hand *or* side, right-hand side, orthodox side [baseball slang], dexter, off side [of a horse or vehicle], starboard [Naut.]; Epistle side [Eccl.], decanal side [of a choir; Eccl.], recto [of a book], right-hand division [Mil.]; right

---

237. Antipodes of each other in temper and endowment.—LOWELL. In tale or history your beggar is ever the just antipode to your king.—LAMB.

field, dexter meadow [baseball slang]; starboard tack [Naut.].

3. *adj.* dextral, dexterous *or* dextrous, dexterical, dexter; right, right-hand, starboard [Naut.]; dextrorse, dextrorsal [both Bot.]; right-handed, dextromanual; dextrosinistral, sinistrodextral; dextropedal; dextrocardial [Anat.]; dextrocerebral [Neurology]; dextrocular; dextrorotatory, dextrogyrate, dextrogyratory, dextrogyrous, dextrogyre.

4. *adj.* ambidextrous, ambidexterous, ambidextral, ambidexter.

5. *adv.* dextrally etc. *adj.,* dextrad, rightward *or* rightwards, rightwardly; ambidextrously etc. *adj.*

239. Sinistrality
(See 238. Dextrality)

1. *n.* sinistrality, sinistration, leftness, left-handedness; sinistrogyration.

2. *n.* left, left hand *or* side, left-hand side, wrong side [coll.], unorthodox side [baseball slang], near side [of a horse or vehicle], port [Naut.], portside [chiefly slang exc. Naut.], larboard [Naut.]; Gospel side [Eccl.], cantorial side [Eccl.], verso; port tack [Naut.].

3. *n.* left hand, southpaw [slang], portside flinger [baseball slang], wrong hand [coll.], *sinistra* or *sinistra mano* [It.; Mus.].

4. *n.* left-handed person, sinistral, left-hander, lefty [slang], portsider [slang, U.S.].

5. *adj.* sinistral, sinistrous, sinister; left, left-hand; larboard, port [both Naut.]; sinistrorse, sinistrorsal [both Bot.]; left-handed, sinister-handed [obs.], sinistromanual; sinistrodextral, dextrosinistral; sinistrocerebral; sinistrocular; sinistrogyrate, sinistrogyric; ambliveous [rare].

6. *adv.* sinistrally etc. *adj.,* sinistrad, leftward *or* leftwards, leftwardly; larboard, port, aport [all Naut.].

240. Form
(See 241. Formlessness)

1. *n.* form, shape, figure, formity [obs.], formation, efformation [rare], conformation; figuration, configuration; format, constitution, fabric, texture, structure, architecture, construction; make-up [coll.], getup [coll.], setup [coll., U.S.], stack-up [slang]; frame, framework; make, build, *tournure* [F.], set, cut, stamp, type, turn, cast, mold, plasmature [obs.], impression, pattern; style, fashion; anatomy, carcass; contour, *galbe* [F.; Art], profile, silhouette.

2. *n.* feature, outward appearance, cut of one's jib [coll.]; lineaments, aspect etc. (appearance) 448.4, 5.

3. *n.* forming etc. *v.,* formation, efformation [rare], information [now rare], formature, conformation, figuration, plasmation [rare]; sculpture; construction etc. (production) 161.

4. *n.* (science of form and structure) morphology, promorphology, tectology; geomorphology; structural botany; organology, organography, osteology, osteography; histology etc. (science of texture) 329.2.

5. *n.* (similarity of form) isomorphism, isomorph.

6. *v.* form, efform [rare], inform [rare]; shape, figure, fashion, pattern, trim, lick *or* put into shape; work up into, knead; set, fix, arrange; carve, cut, chisel, hew; cast, stamp, mint; model, mold, sculpture; hammer *or* knock out, rough-hew, roughcast; sketch, block out; construct, build etc. (produce) 161.8.

7. *adj.* formative, informative [rare], efformative [obs.]; formal, formational; morphotic, plastic, plasmatical [rare]; formable, fictile etc. (soft) 324.6; creative, constructive etc. 161.11.

8. *adj.* (in biology) plasmatic, plasmic, protoplasmic, plastic, metabolic.

9. *adj.* structural, textural, architectural, formal, organic, anatomic(al), morphologic(al).

10. *adj.* (similar in form) isomorphic, isomorphous.

241. Formlessness
(See 240. Form)

1. *n.* formlessness, shapelessness etc. *adj.,* amorphism, amorphy [rare], amorphia [Med.], informity [rare]; disorder etc. 59.

---

240. This is the shape of the leaf, and this of the flower.—C. AIKEN.   God formed man of the dust of the ground.—BIBLE.   The architecture of grasses, plants, and trees.—TYNDALL.

241. If shape it might be call'd that shape had none.—MILTON.   The earth was without form and void.—BIBLE

2. *n.* confused mass, omnium-gatherum [coll.] etc. (confusion) 59.2.

3. *n.* (person) unlicked cub, rough diamond *or* diamond in the rough [coll.].

4. *v.* destroy form *or* shape; unform, unshape; deform etc. (distort) 243.3; derange etc. 61.2–5.

5. *adj.* formless, shapeless, amorphous *or* amorphic, inform, unformed, unshapen, unfashioned; unhewn, uncut; anomalous; orderless etc. 59.8.

6. *adj.* rough, rude, unlicked etc. (uncouth) 851.7; uneven, roughhewn etc. 256.12–17.

242. Symmetry
(See 243. Distortion)

Regularity of Form.—1. *n.* symmetry, proportion, proportionality, balance, keeping, correspondence, harmony, congruity, conformity, consistence *or* consistency, co-ordination, uniformity, regularity, evenness; parallelism, coextension; shapeliness; finish; eurythmy, eurythmics; dynamic symmetry; bilateral ~, trilateral *or* multilateral symmetry; radiation; peloria, regular *or* irregular peloria [all Bot.]; comeliness etc. (beauty) 845.

2. *n.* arborescence, arborization, treelikeness etc. *adj.,* ramification, branching; arborvitae *or* arbor vitae.

3. *v.* symmetrize, make symmetrical etc. *adj.,* proportionate, regularize, balance, harmonize.

4. *adj.* symmetric(al), proportioned, well-proportioned, balanced, well-balanced, well-set, well-set-up [coll.]; regular, uniform, even, equal; coequal, coordinate; parallel, coextensive; finished; radiate, radiated; orderly etc. 58.7.

5. *adj.* shapely, well-proportioned etc. *above,* well-made, well-formed, well-favored; trim, neat; comely etc. (beautiful) 845.8–13.

6. *adj.* arborescent, arboresque, arboriform, arboreal, arborean, treelike, tree-shaped; dendriform, dendroid *or* dendroidal, dendritic(al); branched, branching; ramiform, ramous, ramose; fernlike, fern-shaped; filiciform, filicoid; subarborescent; papilionaceous.

---

242. What immortal hand or eye / Could frame thy fearful symmetry?—W. BLAKE.

243. Distortion
(See 242. Symmetry)

Irregularity of Form.—1. *n.* distortion, detorsion, contortion, contortuosity [rare], twisting etc. *v.;* deformity, deformation, informity [obs.], malformation, malconformation, monstrosity, misproportion, misshape, want of symmetry etc. (*see* symmetry etc. 242); anamorphosy, anamorphosis; kyphosis [Med.]; mutilation, truncation; disfigurement, defacement; knot, warp, buckle, screw, twist; grimace; talipes [Med.], clubfoot; teratology [Med.]; crookedness etc. (obliquity) 217; ugliness etc. 846; imperfection etc. 651; blemish etc. 848.

2. *n.* perversion, misdirection, misrepresentation, misinterpretation, misconstruction, misconstruing etc. *v.;* misapplication etc. (misuse) 679.1.

3. *v.* distort, contort, turn awry, twist, writhe, warp, buckle, screw, gnarl, knot, wrench, wring, wrest, torture; crook, crooken; deform, misshape; mutilate, truncate; disfigure, deface, blemish, mar; grimace, make faces; uglify etc. 846.5.

4. *v.* pervert, garble, misinterpret, misrender, misconstrue, misrepresent, misdirect; misapply etc. (misuse) 679.2.

5. *adj.* distorted, contorted, warped, twisted etc. *v.;* unsymmetric(al), irregular; anamorphous, anamorphic; bent, crump [obs. exc. dial.]; crooked as a ram's horn, crooked as a dog's hind leg, crooked as a Virginia fence [U.S.]; one-sided, on one side; deformed, inform, malformed, misshapen, misbegotten, misproportioned, ill-proportioned, ill-made, ill-shaped, out of shape, curtailed of one's fair proportions; grotesque, monstrous.

kyphotic [Med.], humpbacked, hunchbacked, bunch-backed, crookbacked, crooked-backed, camel-back; round-shouldered; bandy, bandy-legged, bow-legged; knock-kneed; taliped *or* talipedic, clubfooted, splayfoot; snub-nosed, pug-nosed; scalene; simous; askew, awry etc. (crooked) 217.13; ugly etc. 846.6–9; stumpy [coll.] etc. (stubby) 201.6; gaunt

---

243. That conjunction of the grotesque ... with passionate contortion and horror, so characteristic of Gothic art.—STEVENSON. All the contortions of the sibyl, without the inspiration.—BURKE. Then, since the heav'ns have shap'd my body so, / Let hell make crook'd my mind to answer it.—SHAKESPEARE.

etc. (lean) 203.11; bloated etc. (expanded) 194.10; imperfect etc. 651.4; disfigured, defaced etc. (blemished) 848.3.

6. *adj.* distortive, detortive [rare]; contortive, contortional, contortionate.

244. Angularity
(See 245. Curvature)

1. *n.* angularity, angularness etc. *adj.*, aduncity, aquilinity; bifurcation etc. 91.2; obliquity etc. 217.

2. *n.* angle, corner, coin, quoin, bight; crook, hook, bend, inflection; cusp; fork, furculum, furcula [Anat.], prong, branch, Y, V, crotch, crutch, groin; crane; fluke; elbow, knee, knuckle, ankle; falcation, falx [Med.], falchion, scythe, sickle; zigzag, zig, zag; right angle, acute angle, obtuse angle, salient angle, re-entering angle, spherical angle; triangle, trigon; wedge, cuneus; lozenge, diamond; rhomb, rhombus, rhomboid; cube, die, dice; rectangle, square, quadrangle, quadrilateral, quadrant, quadrate [obs.], quadrature.

polygon, pentagon, hexagon, heptagon, octagon, oxygon, decagon; rhombohedron, tetrahedron, tetrahedroid, pentahedron, hexahedron, octahedron, dodecahedron, icosahedron, trapezohedron; prism, prismoid; pyramid, pyramidion; parallelepiped, parallelepipedon; parallelogram; Platonic bodies; curb roof, gambrel roof etc. (roof) 223.6; niche, recess etc. (nook) 191.3; fold etc. 258; notch etc. 257.

3. *n.* (angular measurement) goniometry; trigonometry, trig [school slang]; altimeter, pantometer, clinometer, graphometer, goniometer; theodolite, transit theodolite, transit; sextant, quadrant.

4. *v.* angle, turn *or* bend at an angle, bend, elbow, hook, crook; angle off *or* away, go off on a tangent; zigzag, zig, zag; form *or* come to a corner *or* angle, corner [U.S.]; crinkle, wrinkle; fork, ramify etc. (bifurcate) 91.5.

5. *adj.* angular, cornered, crooked, bent, akimbo, kimbo [obs.], geniculate *or* geniculated; crotched, Y-shaped, V-shaped; sharp-cornered, sharp, pointed, edgy, abrupt; dovetailed; crinkled, wrinkled; wedge-shaped, cuneiform, cuneate *or* cuneated; triangular, trigonal, trilateral; quadrangular, quadrilateral, quadrate, quadrant [obs.], foursquare, rectangular, square; orthogonal, orthodiagonal, orthometric; right-angled, rightangular, right-angle; multiangular, multilateral.

polygonal, pentagonal etc. *n.*; tetrahedral, pentahedral etc. *n.*; prismed, prismal, prismatic(al), prismatoidal; pyramided, pyramidic(al), pyramidal, pyramidoidal *or* pyramoidal; cubic(al), cubeshaped, cubiform, cubed, diced; rhombic(al), rhomboidal; forked, furcate etc. (bifurcate) 91.7; jagged, serrate etc. (notched) 257.6; zigzag etc. (oblique) 217.9–16; knock-kneed etc. (distorted) 243.5; hooked, aduncous etc. (hookshaped) 245.8; rostrate, hook-nosed etc. (beak-shaped) 245.9; falcate, falciform etc. (sickle-shaped) 245.20.

245. Curvature
(See 246. Straightness, 244. Angularity; also 247. Circularity)

1. *n.* curvature, curvity [rare], curvation, curving; turn, sweep; bend, bending, bendification [slang]; flex, flexure, flection, conflexure [obs.], inflection; incurvature, incurvity [obs.], incurvation; excurvature, excurvity [obs.], excurvation; recurvature [rare], recurvity [obs.], recurvation [rare]; bow, bowing, arcuation; arching, vaulting, concameration; aduncity, aquilinity; circularity etc. 247; sinuosity etc. (convolution) 248; rotundity etc. 249; obliquity etc. 217.

2. *n.* curve, flexion etc. *above*, sinus, bought [obs. exc. dial.]; bow, arc; arch, arcade, vault, concameration; crook, hook; crescent, meniscus, crescent moon, half-moon, lunula, lunule [Zool. and Anat.], lunulet, semicircle, horseshoe; loop; crane neck; parabola, hyperbola; catacaustic, diacaustic; caustic; geanticline, geosyncline; catenarian, catenary, festoon; conchoid, cardioid; tracery; arched roof, ceilinged roof; bay window, bow window; curl, curlicue etc. (coil) 248.2.

3. *v.* curve, be *or* render curved etc.

---

244. We rub each other's angles down.—TENNYSON.   The solid angularity of facts.—EMERSON.   As lines, so loves oblique, may well / Themselves in every angle greet.—A. MARVELL.

245. Flowing curves of beauty.—WHITTIER. Her poor life is like the arch of a crescent.—PINERO.   Curved is the line of Beauty.—W. MACCALL.

adj., bend, bendify [slang], bought [obs.], turn, sweep; crook, hook; incurve, incurvate; excurve, excurvate [both rare]; recurve, recurvate [rare]; deflect, inflect; sag, swag [obs. exc. dial.]; arc [Elec.]; arcuate, bow, embow; arch, vault, concamerate [rare]; re-enter; coil, curl, frizzle etc. (convolve) 248.3; deviate etc. 279.4–7; oblique etc. 217.5; round, circle etc. 227.3; rotund etc. 249.6.

4. *adj.* curved, curvate *or* curvated, curving, curvy, curvatious [slang], curviform, curvilineal *or* curvilinear; bent, bendified [slang]; incurved, incurving, incurvous, incurvate *or* incurvated; recurved, recurving, recurvous, recurvate *or* recurvated; excurved, excurvous, excurvate *or* excurvated [all rare]; geanticlinal, geosynclinal; deviative etc. 279.8; oblique etc. 217.9–16; circular etc. 247.8, 9; convex etc. 250.9; concave etc. 252.10; rotund etc. 249.6–11.

5. *adj.* bow-shaped, bowlike, bowed, embowed; convex, convexed; arcuate *or* arcuated, arcual, arciform, arclike; arched, archy [rare], vaulted; bowlegged etc. (distorted) 243.5.

6. *adj.* crescent-shaped, crescentlike, crescent, crescentiform, crescentic; meniscal, meniscate, meniscoid *or* meniscoidal; convexo-concave; sigmoid, semilunar, semicircular; horned, horny, hornlike; bicorn, bicornute *or* bicornuate, bicornuous [rare], bicorned, bicornous.

7. *adj.* moon-shaped, moonlike; lunar, lunate *or* lunated, luniform, lunular, lunulate *or* lunulated; Cynthian; semilunar, crescent-shaped etc. *above* 245.6.

8. *adj.* hook-shaped, hooklike, hooked, aquiline; unciform, uncate *or* uncated, uncinal, uncinate *or* uncinated; hamulate *or* hamulated, hamate *or* hamated, hamiform, hamose *or* hamous [rare]; aduncate *or* aduncated, aduncous, adunc *or* aduncal; unguiform, unguiculate *or* unguiculated; hook-nosed etc. *below*.

9. *adj.* beak-shaped, beaklike, beaked; bill-shaped, bill-like, billed; rostrate *or* rostrated, rostriform, rostroid, rostulate [Zool.], rhamphoid; aquiline etc. *above*, aquiline-nosed, hook-nosed, Roman-nosed, crooknosed, crookbilled, eaglelike.

10. *adj.* bell-shaped, bell-like; campaniform, campanular, campanulous, campanulate *or* campanulated.

11. *adj.* boat-shaped, boatlike; navicular, naviform; cymbiform, scaphoid.

12. *adj.* heart-shaped, heartlike; cordiform, cardioid, cordate *or* cordated.

13. *adj.* helmet-shaped, helmetlike; galeiform, galeate *or* galeated; cassideous.

14. *adj.* kidney-shaped, kidneylike, reniform.

15. *adj.* lens-shaped, lenticular, lentoid, lentiform; meniscal, meniscoid.

16. *adj.* oar-shaped, remiform [rare].

17. *adj.* pear-shaped, pearlike, pyriform; obconic(al).

18. *adj.* shell-shaped, shell-like; conchate *or* conchated, conchiform, conchylaceous [rare], conchoidal [Min.].

19. *adj.* shield-shaped, shieldlike; scutate *or* scutated, scutiform; peltate *or* peltated; clypeate *or* clypeated, clypeiform.

20. *adj.* sickle-shaped, sicklelike; falcate *or* falcated, falculate *or* falculated [rare], falciform.

21. *adj.* tongue-shaped, tonguelike; linguiform, lingulate, ligulate.

22. *adj.* turnip-shaped, turniplike, napiform.

246. Straightness
(See 245. Curvature)

1. *n.* straightness, rectilinearity, rectilinearness, directness etc. *adj.*; rigidity, inflexibility etc. (hardness) 323; perpendicularity etc. (verticality) 212.

2. *n.* straight line, straight course *or* path, direct line, right line, beeline, air line; short cut; crosscut; straight shot; great-circle track *or* path [Naut.].

3. *v.* be straight etc. *adj.*, have no turning, not incline ∼, ∼ bend ∼, ∼ turn *or* deviate to either side; go straight, steer a straight course etc. 278.6.

4. *v.* straighten, set *or* put straight etc. *adj.*, rectify; unbend, unfold, unwrap; uncurl etc. (*see* curl etc. 248.3), unravel etc. (*see* ravel etc. 219.8).

5. *adj.* straight, straight-lined, rectilinear *or* rectilineal, direct, even, right, true, in a line, linear; unbent etc. *v.*, undeviating, unturned, undistorted, unswerving; virgate, inflexible etc. 323.5; perpendicular etc. (vertical) 212.8.

---

246. Why should I strive to set the crooked straight?—W. Morris. Straight onward to his goal he trod.—Whittier. Straight is the line of Duty.—W. MacCall. Straight down the crooked lane.—Hood.

6. *adv.* straightly etc. *adj.*, straight, on the straight; straight as an arrow etc. (directly) 278.13.

247. Circularity
(See also 248. Convolution, 245. Curvature, 249. Rotundity)

Simple Circularity.—1. *n.* circularity, roundness, annularity, etc. *adj.*; curvature etc. 245; rotundity etc. 249.

2. *n.* circle, round, rondel [arch.], roundel [chiefly dial.], rondelle [rare *or* Tech.], rundle [obs. exc. spec.], roundure *or* rondure [rare], roundabout [rare], disk, radius, O; circlet, roundlet; ring, ringlet; annulus [Tech.], annulet; hoop, hoople [local, U.S.].

bracelet, armlet; eye, eyelet; loop, looplet; noose, lasso; bight; tire; felly, felloe; hub, hubble [U.S.], nave; zone, zonar, zodiac; cycle, circuit; orb, orbit; cordon, cordonnet; band, belt, sash, girdle, cummerbund [Ind.], cestus, cest *or* ceste, cincture, baldric, fillet, fascia; wreath, garland; crown, corona, coronet; chaplet, necklace; collar, collarband, neckband; areola *or* areole, aureole, halo; wheel etc. 312.4; coil etc. 248.2; circuit etc. 629; turn etc. 311.2.

3. *n.* oval, ovule, ovum [Arch.], ovoid; ellipse, ellipsoid, oblate *or* oblong spheroid; sphere etc. 249.2.

4. *n.* cycloid, epicycloid, epicycle.

5. *n.* semicircle, half circle, hemicycle; quadrant, sextant, sector.

6. *v.* round, make round etc. *adj.*; round a corner etc. 311.4; curve etc. 245.3, rotund etc. 249.5.

7. *v.* circle, go round, encircle etc. 227.3; describe a circle etc. (circuit) 311.3.

8. *adj.* circular, round, rounded, annular, ringlike, discoid; fasciate, fasciated; cycloidal etc. *n.*; spherical, orbicular etc. (rotund) 249.6–11; curved etc. 245.4.

9. *adj.* oval, ovate, ovoid, ovoidal [rare], oviform, elliptic(al), egg-shaped; obovate, obovoid [both Bot.]; pear-shaped etc. 245.17.

---

247. I watched the little circles die.—Tennyson.   He drew a circle that shut me out.—W. V. Moody.

248. Convolution
(See also 247. Circularity)

Complex Circularity.—1. *n.* convolution, involution, circumvolution, winding etc. *v.*, windings and turnings; meander, meandering; tortuosity, tortility; sinuosity, sinuation, sinuousness; flexuosity, flexuousness; undulation, wave; anfract [obs.], anfracture [obs.], anfractuosity; ambagiousness, ambages; torsion, intorsion; inosculation; rivulation; reticulation etc. (interlacing) 219; labyrinth, maze etc. (complexity) 59.3; circuity etc. 311; circuitous course etc. (circuit) 629.

2. *n.* coil, quoil [dial.], whorl, roll, rundle [obs.], curl, curlicue; spiral, helix, volute; screw, corkscrew; tendril, cirrus (*pl.* cirri); worm, snake, serpent, viper, eel; scollop *or* scallop, escalop *or* escallop; kink, twist, twirl; buckle; ammonite, snakestone; ringlet, love lock etc. (hair) 256.3.

3. *v.* convolve, be convoluted etc. *adj.*, wind, twine, twirl, twill, twist, turn, twist and turn, meander; serpentine, serpent [rare], worm; screw, corkscrew [coll.]; coil, quoil [dial.], curl, curlicue, crisp, kink; friz *or* frizz, frizzle; wrinkle, crinkle; crimp, crape, indent; scollop *or* scallop, escalop *or* escallop; wring; intort; contort; entwine, wreathe etc. (interlace) 219.8; curve etc. 245.3.

4. *adj.* convoluted, twisted, winding, meandering etc. *v.*; meandrous, meandry [obs.]; tortile, tortive [obs.], tortuous, tortuose; sinuose, sinuous, sinuate; anfractuous; flexuous, flexuose; reclinate [rare]; rivose, rivulose [chiefly Bot.]; sigmoid, sigmoidal; wreathy, wreathlike; frizzed, frizzly, frizzy; ruffled, *crêpé* [F.]; buckled; kinky, curly; ambagious, ambagitory; mazy, labyrinthic etc. (complex) 59.10; roundabout etc. (circuitous) 311.6.

5. *adj.* spiral, spiriferous, spiroid; helical, helicoid *or* helicoidal; anfractuose; screw-shaped, screwy, corkscrew, corkscrewy; cochlear, cochleate, cochleous [rare]; turbinated, turbinoid, turbinal, turbiniform.

6. *adj.* snakelike, snaky, snake-shaped; serpentine, serpentile, serpentoid, serpentinoid, serpentinous, serpentiform;

---

248. Lingering rivers in meanders glide.—Blackmore.   The lowing herd winds slowly o'er the lea.—Gray.

anguiform, anguine, anguineous, anguineal; eellike, eel-shaped; anguilliform, anguilloid, anguillous; wormlike, vermiform, vermicular; lumbriciform, lumbricine; scolecoid, scolecid [both Zool.]; peristaltic [Physiol.].

7. *adj.* wavy, undulatory, undulating, undulate *or* undulated, undate *or* undated [Bot.; rare]; billowy, rolling.

8. *adv.* convolutely, windingly etc. *adj.*; in-and-out, round and round.

249. Rotundity
(See also 247. Circularity)

1. *n.* rotundity, rotundness, roundness etc. *adj.*; sphericality, sphericity, spherosity [rare], spheroidicity, spheroidity [rare], spheroidism; globosity, globularity; orbicularity, orbiculation; orotundity; cylindricality, cylindricity; annularity etc. (circularity) 247; corpulence etc. 192.4.

2. *n.* sphere, spheroid, ball, orb, globe, globoid; spherule, globule, globelet, orblet; spherulite [Min.]; geoid; drop, vesicle, bulb, pellet, clew, pill, marble, pea, orange, apple, billiard ball, cannon ball, knob, pommel, horn, knot, boulder, pebble; oblate *or* oblong spheroid, ellipsoid etc. (oval) 247.3.

3. *n.* cylinder, cylindroid; barrel, drum; roll, rouleau, roller, rolling pin; round, rung, rundle; column, rod etc. (support) 215.13–16.

4. *n.* cone, conoid, conelet; complex cone, cone of a complex; ice-cream cone, pine cone, volcanic cone, alluvial cone, Seger cone, cone pulley, cone wheel, cone speaker [Radio], cone shell, cone anchor, cone bearing, cone bit, cone brake, cone clutch, cone compass, cone coupling, cone delta, cone gamba, cone joint, cone lathe, cone pepper, cone plate, cone *or* coniferous tree, cone valve, cone wheat; bullet; funnel; pyramid.

5. *v.* rotund, render rotund etc. *adj.*, give rotundity etc. *n.*, round, round out, fill out; sphere, spherify, spheroidize, form into a sphere, ball, roll into a ball.

6. *adj.* rotund, rotundate *or* rotun-dated; round, rounded, rounded out, round as a ball, ~ an apple etc. *n.*; gibbous, gibbose; circular etc. 247.8, 9; bell-shaped, pear-shaped etc. (curved) 245.4–22; bulbous etc. (convex) 250.9; fat, plump etc. (stout) 192.12; chubby etc. (stubby) 201.6.

7. *adj.* spheric(al), spheroid *or* spheroidal, spheroidic(al), spheriform, spherular, sphere, sphery, spherelike; globular, globical [obs.], globous, globose, globoid, globate *or* globated, globelike, globe-shaped; orbic(al), orbicular, orbiculate *or* orbiculated, orbed, orb, orblike, orby; egg-shaped etc. (oval) 247.9.

8. *adj.* cylindric(al), cylindroid *or* cylindroidal; columnar etc. 215.29; snakelike, vermiform etc. 248.6.

9. *adj.* cone-shaped, conelike; coniform [rare], conic(al), conoid *or* conoidal, conoidic(al) [rare], coned, coniferous; spheroconic, spherical conic; funnel-shaped, infundibuliform, infundibular, infundibulate; pyramidal.

10. *adj.* bead-shaped, beadlike; moniliform, monilate, moniloid [all Bot. and Zool.].

11. *adj.* rice-shaped, ricelike, riziform.

250. Convexity
(See 251. Flatness, 252. Concavity)

1. *n.* convexity, convexness, convexedness; excurvature, excurvation, excurvity [obs.]; protuberance *or* protuberancy, protuberosity [rare]; protrusion, protrusiveness; projection, projectment [obs.]; prominence, salience, boldness; camber; gibbosity, gibberosity [rare]; intumescence, tumescence, tumidity, tumefaction; swell, swelling, swellage, swollenness; dilation, dilatation, dilatancy; excrescence, excrescency; fungosity; nodosity, nodulation; tuberosity, tuberousness; carunculation.

2. *n.* a protuberance, convexity, projection etc. *above*; convex, bulge, bilge, bouge [now rare], bow; salient; intumescence, tumescence; swell, swelling, rising, pimple [fig.]; bump, hump, hunch, bunch; thank-you-ma'am [U.S.], cahot [chiefly Can.]; knob, knur, knurl, gnarl, knot; lump, clump; bulb, bulbil [Bot. and

---

249. The thick rotundity o' the world.—SHAKESPEARE. She is spherical, like a globe.—SHAKESPEARE. *In se ipso totus teres atque rotundus* [Complete in himself, polished and well-rounded].—HORACE.

250. The knobbes sittynge on his chekes.—CHAUCER. So high as heaved the tumid hills.—MILTON.

Anat.], bulblet; node, nodule, nodulus, nodulation, nodosity; ridge, rib; button, stud.

lip, flange; withers, shoulders, back, dorsum; elbow, bend; beehive; excrescence, growth, outgrowth, abnormal protrusion *or* growth, morbid development; process, apophysis, condyle [all Anat. and Zool.]; pustule, papule, pimple, boil, gumboil, carbuncle, wen, whelk, pock, proud flesh, sarcoma, corn, mole, wart, verruca, furuncle, polypus, exostosis, bleb, blob [chiefly dial.], blister, bulla, blain; fungus, fungosity; tumor, tumefaction; tubercle, tuberosity; caruncle, caruncula, carunculation; bubo, bubonocele; bubble etc. 353.1; billow, surge etc. (wave) 348.10; cameo etc. (relief) 557.6; belly etc. 191.7; denticle etc. (tooth) 253.3.

3. *n.* breast, bosom, bust, chest, crop [now dial.], thorax; bubby [now vulg.], booby [slang], mamma; papilla, pap [arch. exc. dial.], nipple, teat, tit [now vulgar exc. Zool.], titty [familiar], dug [now derog. exc. Zool.], mammilla, *mamelon* [F.]; mammillation, mamelonation.

4. *n.* nose, nese [Scot.], olfactory organ, snout [chiefly coll. exc. Zool.], snoot [coll.], nozzle [slang exc. Zool.], muzzle [Zool.], proboscis [joc. exc. Zool.], trunk [as of an elephant], antlia [Zool.] (*pl.* antliae); nib, neb [rare exc. Scot.]; beak, bill, pecker [all slang exc. Zool.]; smeller, breather, beezer, bugle, claret jug, conk, snitch [all slang]; nostrils, noseholes [obs. exc. dial. Eng.]; olfactories etc. 398.4.

5. *n.* point of land, point, promontory, foreland, headland, head, mull [Scot.], naze, ness [chiefly in place names], peak [rare], cape, tongue, bill, spur; neck, neck of land; reef, coral reef; breakwater, mole, jetty, jutty; peninsula, chersonese; delta, isthmus; ridge, hill, mound etc. (height) 206.2.

6. *n.* arch, vault etc. 215.18.

7. *v.* be convex etc. *adj.,* convex; excurve, excurvate [both rare]; project, protrude, protuberate; bulge, bilge, bouge, bag, belly, swell, dilate, round, bunch [now rare], pout; belly out, round out etc.; jut out, stand out, stick out, poke out; stick up, bristle up, start up, cock up, shoot up; arcuate, bow, embow, arch, vault, concamerate [rare]; swell over, bend over; jut over etc. (overhang) 214.5.

8. *v.* render convex etc. *adj.,* convex, protuberate [rare] etc. *above*; boss, emboss, chase, raise; nodulate, nodulize.

9. *adj.* convex, convexed; excurved, excurvous, excurvate *or* excurvated [all rare]; protuberant, protuberous [rare], protuberantial; protrusive, protrusile; prominent, salient, bold; projecting, bulging, swelling etc. *v.*; bellied, bowed, arched etc. *v.*; bumpy, bumped; gibbous, gibbose, gibberose [rare]; hemisphered, hemispheric(al).

bulbous, bulbose; noded, nodose, nodiform, nodiferous; noduled, nodulated, nodular, nodulose *or* nodulous; torose, knobbed, knobby, knotty, gnarled; hubby, hubbly [both U.S.]; clavate, clavated, claviform; subclavate etc.; caruncular, carunculous, carunculate *or* carunculated; furuncular, furunculous, furunculoid; mammalian, mammiferous, mammillary, mammiform; papulous, papulose; papillose, papillous [rare], papillate, papillar, papillary, papillulate.

tuberous, tuberculous; tumorous, tumefacient, tumescent, tumefying; fungiform, fungilliform [rare]; cornute; odontoid; lentiform, lenticular; club-shaped; saddle-shaped, selliform; ventricose; warty, verrucated, verrucose; excrescential; tumid, swollen etc. (expanded) 194.10.

10. *adj.* in relief, raised, *repoussé* [F.]; chased, bossed, embossed, bossy.

251. Flatness
(See 250. Convexity, 252. Concavity)

1. *n.* flatness, planeness etc. *adj.,* complanation; smoothness etc. 255.1.

2. *n.* flat, homaloid [Math.], plane, level etc. (horizontal) 213.3; flats, prairie etc. (plain) 344.

3. *n.* (comparisons) floor; plate, platter; table, tablet, slab; flag, flagstone; board, plank.

4. *v.* flatten, render flat etc. *adj.,* complanate [obs.]; squelch, squash [both coll.]; level, fell etc. 213.6, 7; plane, even etc. (smooth) 255.4.

---

251. He has crushed his nose . . . as flat as a pancake.—STERNE.   Beat all your feathers as flat as pancakes.—MIDDLETON.   His nose as flat as a cake beaten to his face.—ERASMUS.

5. *adj.* flat, flattened, flattish; complanate, homaloidal [Math.], plane, plain, even, flush, level; flat as a pancake, ∼ a fluke, ∼ a flounder, ∼ a board, ∼ my hand etc.; discoid *or* discoidal; horizontal etc. 213.8; smooth etc. 255.5.

6. *adv.* flat, flatly [rare], flatways, flatwise; lengthways, lengthwise, at full length; on a level etc. (horizontally) 213.10.

252. Concavity
(See 250. Convexity, 251. Flatness)

1. *n.* concavity, concavation [rare], indentation, hollowness etc. *adj.*; incurvature, incurvation, incurvity [obs.].

2. *n.* cavity, concavity, concave, depression, dip, hollow, hole, sink; indentation, dent, dint; dimple; impression, impress, imprint, print; alveolus (*pl.* alveoli), alveole, alveolation; antrum (*pl.* antra), sinus (*pl.* sinus, sinuses); lacuna (*pl.* lacunae, lacunas), lacune [rare]; sinkhole, pothole, thank-you-ma'am, breaker, water butt, cradle, pitchhole, chuckhole, cahot, wash, Yankee bump, love-hole, dips-and-ducks [all dial.]; vug *or* vugg, vugh, [all Min.]; follicle, follicule; cup, basin, bowl.

crater, crump hole [army slang]; pit, excavation, grave [chiefly dial. exc. as tomb], well, shaft, groove [now dial.], mine, colliery; caisson, fougasse, countermine; socket; honeycomb; trench, trough etc. (furrow) 259; gully, gulch etc. (cleft) 198.2, 3; chasm, abyss etc. 208.2; notch etc. 257.

3. *n.* cave, cavern, cove [Scot. and North. Eng.], antre [arch.], dugout, subterrane; subway, tube, underground [Eng.]; hole, burrow, tunnel; den, kennel [obs.], lair, covert, cellar etc. 191.20.

4. *n.* recess, alcove, cove etc. (nook) 191.3; cubbyhole, pigeonhole etc. (compartment) 191.2; cul-de-sac etc. (closure) 261; inlet, bay etc. 343.

5. *n.* valley, vale [poetic], dale, dell, dingle, coomb, bottom, slade [obs.], strath [Scot.], gill, ghyll [Scot. and dial. Eng.], glade, glen, donga [S. Afr.], nullah [Ind.], grove [obs. exc. dial.], park [U.S.]; gorge, ravine etc. 198.3.

6. *n.* intaglio etc. (engraving) 558.3.

7. *n.* excavator, digger, sapper, miner; driller; tunneler, sand hog [cant.]; spade, shovel, steam shovel; dredge, dredger, dredging machine.

8. *v.* be concave etc. *adj.*, retreat, retire, cave in.

9. *v.* render concave etc. *adj.*, concave, hollow, hollow out, dish, dish out, depress, dent, indent, dint, pit; excavate, scoop, scoop out, gouge, gouge out, dig, dig out, delve [arch.], grave [arch. and dial.]; mine, sap, drive, sink, lower; burrow, tunnel; cave in, stave in; deepen etc. 208.6.

10. *adj.* concave, hollow, hollowed, hollowed out; depressed, dented, indented; sunk, sunken; retreating, retiring; incurved, incurving, incurvous, incurvate *or* incurvated; cavernous; caved in, stove in; alveolate, alveolar, alveoliform; dished, dishing; cupped, cup-shaped, calathiform; favaginous, faveolate, favose; scyphose, scyphiform; funnel-shaped, infundibuliform, infundibular, infundibulate; capsular, capsulate *or* capsulated; cellular; bell-shaped etc. (curved) 245.4-22; cone-shaped etc. 249.9; honeycombed, porous etc. (open) 260.15, 17.

253. Sharpness
(See 254. Bluntness)

1. *n.* sharpness, keenness etc. *adj.*, acuity, acumination; mucronation, spinosity.

2. *n.* point, spike, spikelet, spine, pile [obs.], prong, tine, tang [Scot. and dial. Eng.]; nib, neb; spicule, spiculum; pin, needle, nail, tack; pine, pine needle; prick, prickle; spur, rowel; barb, barblet, barbule; spit, cusp; horn, antler; snag, snaggle; tag; quill; arista, awn; brush, beard [both Bot.].

thorn, bramble, brier, nettle, bur *or* burr, sticker [coll.]; thistle, thistle sage, thistle poppy; catchweed, cleavers, goose grass; hairif [dial. Eng.]; beggar's-lice *or* beggar-lice, beggar-ticks *or* beggar's-ticks; yucca, Adam's-needle *or* Adam's-needle-and-thread, bear grass [U.S.]; porcupine, hedgehog; cheval-de-frise (*pl.* chevaux-de-frise); comb, fine-tooth comb, flax comb; harrow, peg-tooth har-

---

252. With hollow eye and wrinkled brow.— SHAKESPEARE.

253. How sharper than a serpent's tooth!— SHAKESPEARE. Like a lean knife between the ribs of Time.—A. B. DOUGLAS.

row, spring-tooth harrow; barbwire, barbed wire; hair, bristle etc. 256.3, 7.

3. *n.* tooth, pearl, ivory [slang], dental [joc.], poose [childish]; fang, tang [now dial.]; snag, snaggletooth, peg; bucktooth, gagtooth *or* gang tooth [obs. exc. dial.]; dogtooth *or* dog tooth, canine tooth, eyetooth; molar, grinder, premolar; bicuspid; incisor, cutter, fore tooth; tusk, tush [chiefly arch. *or* dial.]; scrivello; teeth, game [Scot.], picket fence [slang]; false teeth, uppers and lowers, bridgework, dental bridge; projection, dent [Tech.], jag; denticle, denticulation, dentil *or* dentel [all Arch., furniture etc.]; cog, sprocket, ratchet; saw tooth.

4. *n.* spire, steeple, *flèche* [F.], pinnacle; peak etc. (summit) 210; crag, tower etc. (height) 206.2–4.

5. *n.* cutting edge, knife-edge; sharp edge, keen edge, featheredge, razoredge.

6. *n.* edge tools, cutlery; blade, knife, cutter, whittle [obs. exc. Scot. and dial. Eng.]; jackknife, pigsticker, toad stabber *or* sticker [all slang]; steel, cold steel, naked steel; penknife, pocketknife, paring knife, bread knife, butcher knife, case knife; bowie knife, belduque [Southwest. U.S.], Arkansas toothpick [slang, U.S.], Kansas neck blister [slang, U.S.]; drawing knife *or* drawknife, drawshave; razor, safety razor, safety [coll.], electric razor; surgical knife, scalpel, bistoury, lancet.

ax *or* axe, hatchet; tomahawk, tommyax [Austral.]; adz *or* adze, carpenter's adz, cooper's adz, canoe *or* spout adz; pick, pickax, mattock, bill [obs.]; billhook, bill, black bill, brown bill; bushwhacker [U.S.]; gaff, harpoon, eelspear; oxgoad, elephant goad, ankus [Ind.]; cleave, cleaver; scythe, sickle; scissors, shears; wedge; plowshare, colter; sword, spear, battle-ax etc. (arms) 727.3–6; bodkin, awl etc. (perforator) 262; saw etc. 257.3.

7. *n.* sharpener, sharper; hone, grindstone, whetstone, whetrock [dial.], rubstone, oilstone; emery, emery wheel; carborundum, novaculite; steel; strop, strap; file etc. 255.3.

8. *v.* be sharp etc. *adj.*, come *or* taper to a point, end in a point, acuminate; bristle with.

9. *v.* sharpen, render sharp etc. *adj.*, edge, acuminate, cuspidate; file, grind, whet, strop; set, reset; point, sharpen to a point, spiculate [rare]; barb, barbate [rare].

10. *v.* cut etc. (sunder) 44.

11. *adj.* sharp, keen, edged, acute, cutting, poignant [obs. exc. fig.]; sharp-edged, keen-edged, razoredged, knife-edged, featheredged; sharp *or* keen as a razor, sharp as a needle, "sharp as a two-edged sword" (Bible), sharpened etc. *v.*, set; aculeate *or* aculeated, acuminate *or* acuminated; pointed, spiculate *or* spiculated; needlelike, needle-shaped; acicular, aciculate *or* aciculated [Bot. and Zool.], aciform.

tapered, tapering; subulate *or* subulated, awl-shaped; mucronate *or* mucronated, mucronulate; spiked, spiky; cusped, cuspidate *or* cuspidated; prickly, pricky [now dial.]; muricate *or* muricated, muriculate *or* muriculated; echinate *or* echinated, echinulate *or* echinulated [Bot. and Zool.]; acanaceous, acanthopodous; spiny, spinous, spinulose, spinulescent, spinuliferous; apiculate *or* apiculated; thorny, brambly, briery, thistly; pectinate *or* pectinated, comblike; awned, awny, aristate; setarious, setaceous; studded; snaggy, snagged, snaggled; digitate *or* digitated; double-edged, two-edged; tetrahedral [Cryst.].

12. *adj.* barbed, barbate *or* barbated; barbellate [Bot.]; glochidious, glochidiate [both Bot.]; bristly etc. 256.14.

13. *adj.* arrow-shaped, arrowlike, arrowy, arrowheaded; sagittal, sagittate *or* sagittated, sagittiform.

14. *adj.* spear-shaped, spearlike, hastate, hastiform [rare]; lance-shaped, lancelike, lanceolate, lanciform.

15. *adj.* sword-shaped, swordlike, gladiate, ensate, ensiform, xiphoid.

16. *adj.* scimitar-shaped, acinaciform.

17. *adj.* spindle-shaped, fusiform.

18. *adj.* reed-shaped, reedlike, reedy; calamiform [rare], arundinaceous.

19. *adj.* horn-shaped, hornlike; corniform, cornute *or* cornuted; horned, horny; corniculate *or* corniculated, cornified, cornigerous, cornific; crescent-shaped etc. 245.6.

20. *adj.* tooth-shaped, toothlike; dentiform, dentoid, odontoid.

21. *adj.* star-shaped, starlike, starry; stellate *or* stellated, stellular, stelliform.

254. Bluntness
(See 253. Sharpness)

1. *n.* bluntness, dullness etc. *adj.,* obtundity.

2. *v.* blunt, become *or* render blunt etc. *adj.,* dull, obtund, take off the point *or* edge, unedge [rare], turn; impair in force, ~ keenness *or* susceptibility, repress, weaken.

3. *adj.* blunt, dull, dullish, obtuse, lacking sharpness etc. (*see* sharpness etc. 253.1), unsharpened, unedged, unpointed, pointless, bluff; edentate, toothless.

255. Smoothness
(See 256. Roughness)

1. *n.* smoothness, sleekness etc. *adj.,* polish, gloss, glaze, shine, levigation; lubricity etc. (lubrication) 332.

2. *n.* smooth surface, smooth, plane, level, flat, dead level *or* flat; ice, macadam, asphalt, marble, alabaster, ivory; down, satin, silk, velvet, velveteen, velumen, slide; bowling green etc. (horizontal) 213.3.

3. *n.* smoother, smooth; sleeker, slicker; planer, plane, smoothing *or* smooth plane, jointer, fore plane, jack plane, bench plane, scrub plane, block plane, rabbet plane, circular plane, routing plane, core-box plane, bullnose, combination plane, grooving plane, head, toothing plane, thumb plane, reed plane, match plane, scraper plane, dado plane, filletster plane, chamfer plane, edge plane, beading plane, sash plane, dovetail plane; trowel, curbing trowel, corner trowel, guttering trowel, pointing trowel, brick trowel, plastering trowel, circle *or* cove trowel, radius trowel.

press, presser, mangle, calender; iron, flatiron, sadiron, electric iron; roller, steam roller, rolling pin; harrow, drag; sandpaper, emery paper, emery board; file, nail file, flat file, square file, knife file, half-round file, round *or* rattail file, triangular *or* three-square file, hand file,

cross file, slitting file, cant, mill file, pillar file; burnish, burnisher; pumice, pumice stone, pummy *or* pummy-stone [dial.]; chamois; varnish, wax, turpentine and beeswax.

4. *v.* smooth, smoothen [rare], levigate, plane, planish, flatten, level, even, equalize; rub, scour, buff, polish, shine [coll.], burnish, furbish, sleek, slick [coll.], gloss, glaze, glance [metal work], luster; varnish, wax; grind, file, sand, sandpaper, emery, pumice; mow, shave; pave, macadamize, asphalt; roll, harrow, drag; press, hot-press, iron, mangle, calender; lubricate etc. 332.4.

5. *adj.* smooth, devoid of roughness etc. (*see* roughness etc. 256.1), with even surface, even, level, plane, flat, regular, uniform; unroughened, unwrinkled etc. (*see* rough etc. 256.12); polished etc. *v.,* sleek, slick [coll.], glossy, *glacé* [F.], glassy; smooth as glass, ~ ice etc. *n.*; slippery, slithery [chiefly dial.], sliddery [now dial.], slippery as an eel; glabrous, glabrate, glabrescent; leiodermatous, leiocephalous, leiophyllous; velvety, velutinous; silky, silken, sericeous [Tech.]; woolly, lanate etc. (nappy) 256.15; lubricous etc. 332.5; oily etc. (unctuous) 355.3.

256. Roughness
(See 255. Smoothness)

1. *n.* roughness, unsmoothness, ruggedness etc. *adj.,* rugosity, salebrosity, asperity, irregularity; corrugation; nodosity, nodulation; pubescence *or* pubescency, pilosity, villosity, hispidity [all Tech.]; arborescence etc. 242.2; nonuniformity etc. 16a; texture etc. 329.

2. *n.* rough surface, rough, broken ground, bent [arch.]; ripple, corrugation, washboard; washboard road, corduroy road; corduroy, burlap, monk's cloth, sacking, homespun, linsey-woolsey; tooth, grain, grit; bur *or* burr, cocklebur; grater, nutmeg grater.

3. *n.* hair, hairlet; filament, filamentule; pubescence, pubes [both Bot. and

---

254. Thy sythe is dull; whet it for shame.—G. HERBERT.　　Blunting all other sensibilities.—G. ELIOT.
255. Smooth as monumental alabaster.—SHAKESPEARE.　　A smooth spot of glassy quiet 'mid those battling tides.—SHELLEY. And thou, son of man, take thee a sharp knife,

take thee a barber's razor, and cause it to pass upon thine head, and upon thy beard.—BIBLE. Smooth and sleek with ease and home-keeping habits.—PLUTARCH.
256. Flesh like slag in a furnace, knobbed and withered and grey.—KIPLING.　　Then wel-

Zool.]; villus [Tech.] (*pl.* villi); capillament [Bot.]; cilium (*pl.* cilia), ciliolum (*pl.* ciliola); fleece, wool, fur, fell, pelt, coat; head of hair, crine, crop, crop of hair, mat, thatch [joc.], mop, shock, shag, mane; tuft, knot, topknot; chignon, waterfall [coll.]; gray hair, grizzle; red hair, carrottop [slang]; black ~, white ~, blond etc. hair; artificial blonde, peroxide blonde.

tress, lock, curl, ringlet; beaucatcher [coll.], lovelock, heartbreaker [coll.], kiss curl *or* kiss-me-quick [coll.], spit curl [coll.], drop curl, swing curl; elflocks, scolding locks [coll.], follow-me-lads [slang]; bang; fringe, fimbria [Bot.] (*pl.* fimbriae), cilia [Bot.]; frizz, frizzle; puberal hair, pubes; hair-do [coll.], haircut; permanent wave, permanent; pompadour; braid, plait, band; switch, cue, queue, pigtail, rat's-tail *or* rattail [joc.], tail; roach [coll., U.S.]; bun, rat's nest [joc.]; hair mat, rat [coll., U.S.]; curl paper, papillote.

4. *n.* wig, toupee, scalp doily [joc.]; periwig, jasey [coll. and joc.], peruke, Ramillie, frizz, front, Gregorian, Brutus, *Chedreux* [F.], grizzle.

5. *n.* beard, barb [obs.], whiskers; Charley, muff, ticker, wind tormentors [all slang]; side whiskers, sideburns [U.S.], burnsides [coll., U.S.]; muttonchop beard *or* mutton chops [slang]; chin whiskers, imperial, Vandyke, goatee, Galways [slang, U.S.]; brush [Bot.]; barbel, barbule [both Zool.]; mustache, soup-strainer [joc.]; handle bars, handlebar mustache [both slang].

6. *n.* eyelashes, lashes, cilia (*sing.* cilium), blinkers [slang].

7. *n.* bristle, seta [Tech.] (*pl.* setae), setula *or* setule [Tech.], striga [Bot.] (*pl.* strigae), pappus [Bot.], barb [Bot.]; feeler, vibrissa (*pl.* vibrissae); pile, arista (*pl.* aristae), awn [all Bot.]; beard, brush [both Bot.]; point etc. 253.2.

8. *n.* feather, plume; plumule, filoplume, down feather, quill, scapular, covert, beam *or* beam feather, pinion, remex (*pl.* remiges); crest, tuft, topknot, panache [spec. of a helmet].

9. *n.* plumage, plumosity, feather [chiefly in *pl.*], feathering; down, fluff,

---

come each rebuff / That turns earth's smoothness rough.—BROWNING. Rough-hew them how we will.—SHAKESPEARE.

breast feathers, mail [spec. of a hawk] mantle, hackle, mirror, speculum (*pl.* specula).

10. *n.* nap, pile, shag; fleece, wool, velvet, plush, byssus; fluff, flue, down, fur, moss.

11. *v.* roughen, render rough etc. *adj.*, rough, rough up, engrail [arch.]; crinkle, crankle [obs.], wrinkle, crisp, ruffle, crumple, rumple, knurl; corrugate; rough out, roughcast, roughhew; stroke the wrong way, rub the fur the wrong way, go the wrong way of the goods, go against the grain, set on edge.

12. *adj.* rough, rough as a bear, ~ nutmeg grater etc. *n.*; unsmooth, unpolished, uneven, ununiform, unkempt, unlevel, irregular, inequal, broken, coarse; rugged, rugose, rugous, rugulose; jagged, ragged; craggy, cragged; scraggly, scragged, scraggy; bumpy, rocky; corrugate *or* corrugated, washboardy; wrinkled, crinkled etc. *v.*; wrinkly, crinkly, crankling [obs.]; choppy, ruffled.

nodose, nodular, nodulated; knotted, knotty; gnarled, gnarly; knurled, knurly; rough-grained, coarse-grained, cross-grained; homespun, linsey-woolsey; scabrous [Bot.], scabby, scurfy, scaly, flaky, asperous [Bot.]; leafy, laminate; wooded, well-wooded; roughhewn, roughcast; arborescent etc. 242.6; angular etc. 244.5; notched etc. 257.6; furrowed etc. 259.4; sharp etc. 253.11, 12.

13. *adj.* hairy, hirsute, pubescent [Bot.]; pappous, pappose; pileous, pilous, pilose; trichogenous, trichoid; ciliate, ciliated; cirrose, cirrous, cirrate, cirrated [all Zool.]; filamentous, filamentose, filamentar *or* filamentary, filamentiferous, filaceous [rare], filiform; crinose, crinite; barbate *or* barbated, barbigerous; bearded, whiskered, bewhiskered; unshorn, unshaven; woolly-headed; bushy, shaggy, shagged; tufted, crested; hispid etc. *below*.

14. *adj.* bristly, bristling, bristlelike, hirsute, "like quills upon the fretful porcupine" (Shakespeare); setal, setose, setous [rare], setaceous, setarious, setiferous, setigerous, setiform; hispid, hispidulous, hispidulate; strigal, strigose, strigate, strigillose [all Bot.]; barbed, barbate *or* barbated [Bot.]; barbellate, barbulate [both Bot.]; glochideous, glochidiate [both Bot.]; spiked, prickly etc. (sharp) 253.11, 12.

15. *adj.* nappy, pily, shaggy; downy, fluffy, fluey [rare]; velvety, velutinous; woolly, flocculent, floccose [spec. Bot.]; lanate *or* lanated, lanuginous, lanuginose; tomentose [Tech.].

16. *adj.* feathery, plumose, plumous [rare], plumate, plumigerous; hirsute.

17. *adj.* fringed, befringed, fringelike; fimbriate *or* fimbriated, fimbricate *or* fimbricated; laciniate *or* laciniated, laciniform, laciniose; edged etc. 231.5.

18. *adv.* roughly etc. *adj.*, in the rough.

19. *adv.* against the grain, the wrong way, the wrong way of the goods.

257. Notch

1. *n.* notch, nick, nitch [obs. exc. dial.], cut, cleft, gash, blaze, scotch, score, nock [as of an arrow], jag, depression, dimple; dint, dent, indent, indentation, indention; crena, crenel.

2. *n.* serration, serrature, serrate margin; dentil band [Arch.]; dentil, dentel, dentile, denticle [all chiefly Arch.]; denticule [Arch.]; denticulation, dentilation [rare], dentification; crenulation, crenelation, crenula (*pl.* crenulae), crenation, crenature, crenel [spec. Bot.]; scallop *or* scollop, escalop *or* escallop; rickrack, picot edge, vandyke; teeth, saw teeth; comb.

3. *n.* saw, handsaw, crosscut saw, ripsaw, keyhole saw, dovetail saw, double-cut saw, circular saw, concave circular saw, buzz saw, band saw, vertical saw, mill *or* milling saw, lightning *or* M saw, electric saw, lumberman's saw, two-handed saw, bucksaw, kitchen saw, stairbuilder's saw, butcher's saw, hack saw, surgeon's saw, helicoidal saw, jig saw, wood saw, saw knife, saw machine, pit saw, splitsaw, whipsaw.

4. *n.* embrasure, battlement, castellation, machicolation.

5. *v.* notch, nick, nitch [obs. exc. dial.], cut, gash, scotch, score, blaze, jag, scarify, crimp; dint, dent, indent; scallop *or* scollop, escalop *or* escallop; tooth, serrate, pink, mill [as coins]; Vandyke; crenelate, crenulate.

6. *adj.* notched, nicked etc. *v.*; crenate *or* crenated, crenelate *or* crenelated, cren-

ulate *or* crenulated; dentate *or* dentated, dentelated; toothed, saw-toothed, saw-like; palmate *or* palmated; serrate *or* serrated, serratic, serratile [rare], serrulate *or* serrulated, serriform; scalloped *or* scolloped, escaloped *or* escalloped; jagged, jaggy; angular etc. 244.5; rough etc. 256.12.

258. Fold

1. *n.* fold, double, doubling, duplicature; plica, plicature, plication; pleat, plait, plat [now dial.], ply; knife plait *or* pleat, box plait *or* box pleat, accordion pleat *or* plait; crease, creasing; tuck, gather; flection, flexure; joint, elbow, hinge; wrinkle, rimple, crinkle, crankle, crumple, rumple, rivel [arch.], ruck, ruffle, pucker, cockle, corrugation; flounce, frounce [obs.]; lapel; dog's-ear, dog-ear; crow's-feet; furrow etc. 259.

2. *n.* folding etc. *v.*, foldure [rare], infoldment *or* enfoldment; plication, plicature.

3. *v.* fold, make a fold in, double, fold ~, double *or* turn over *or* under, infold *or* enfold; plicate, pleat, plait, plat [now dial.], ply, crease; wrinkle, rimple, crinkle, crankle [arch.], crumple, rumple, rivel [arch.], ruck, ruffle, pucker, cockle, cocker [dial.], corrugate; curl, curl up *or* under; frizz, frizzle; flounce, frounce [arch.]; tuck, gather; shirr, smock; twill, quill, flute; hem; dog-ear, dog's-ear.

4. *adj.* folded, doubled, wrinkly, puckery etc. *v.*; enfolden [poetic]; plicate, plicatulate, pliciferous, pliciform; corrugate *or* corrugated; foldable, plicatile.

259. Furrow

1. *n.* furrow, groove, rut, ruck [dial., Eng.], sulcus, scratch, streak, stria (*pl.* striae), crack, cranny, chink, score, cut, gash, incision, slit; chamfer, fluting; cradle etc. (thank-you-ma'am) 252.1; corduroy road etc. (rough surface) 256.2; wrinkle etc. (fold) 258.

2. *n.* trench, entrenchment *or* intrenchment, sap [Mil.], grave [chiefly dial.], ditch, dike, fosse, trough, dugout, cut,

---

257. Silent hills indenting / The orange band of eve.—HOUSMAN. A dint in a character.—S. WILBERFORCE.

258. Wind and sun puckers made him look hawklike.—MASEFIELD. Not tricked and frounced as she was wont.—MILTON.
259. Thou canst help time to furrow me with age.—SHAKESPEARE.

coupure [Fort.], canal; graff [Hist.], grip [Hunt. or dial.], moat [Fort.], gallery [Fort.]; scarp, escarp, counterscarp; levee; ha-ha; channel, aqueduct etc. (conduit) 350; ravine etc. (cleft) 198.2, 3.

3. *v.* furrow, groove, scratch, streak, crack, score, cut, carve, chisel, gash, slit, incise, channel, chamfer, flute; grave, engrave, etch, enchase, bite in; hatch, crosshatch; mezzotint, demitint; plow; corrugate.

4. *adj.* furrowed etc. *v.*, ribbed, striated, sulcate *or* sulcated; canaliculate *or* canaliculated, canaliferous; unisulcous, unisulcate *or* unisulcated; bisulcous, bisulcate *or* bisulcated; trisulcous, trisulcate *or* trisulcated; corduroy, corduroyed; corrugate, corrugated; costate, rimiform [rare]; rough etc. 256.12.

260. Opening
(See 261. Closure)

1. *n.* opening, aperture, apertness [arch.], hole, slot, orifice; outlet, inlet; hiatus, hiation [rare]; gape, gap; foramen, foraminule, fenestra; perforation, terebration, pertusion [obs.], puncture; acupuncture, acupunctuation, acupuncturation; sieve pit [Bot.]; fontanel *or* fontanelle; transforation; pinhole, keyhole, loophole, porthole, peephole, mousehole, pigeonhole; placket, placket hole; manhole; vent, venthole; blowhole, air hole, spiracle; pore; eye, eyelet, eye of a needle; vomitory [Rom. Arch.]; crevice, crack, etc. (cleft) 198.2, 3; chasm, abyss etc. 208.2; tunnel, pit, cave etc. (cavity) 252.2, 3; passage etc. 302.

2. *n.* mouth, mouthpiece [joc.], gob [dial. *or* vulgar], gab [Scot.], muzzle [joc. exc. Zool.], maxilla [Zool.]; bazoo, kisser, mug, mush, trap, yap [all slang]; jaws, mandibles.

3. *n.* embouchure, *embouchement* [F.], debouchment [rare]; ostiary [obs.]; mouth, *bouche* [F.]; jaws; muzzle, nozzle; crater; mouthpiece.

4. *n.* portal, postern, threshold; door, doorway; entrance, entry, entryway, entranceway; passage, passageway, way; gate, gateway; lich gate [arch.]; barway; trap, trap door; hatch, hatchway, heck [dial.]; cellarway; storm door, dingle [North. U.S.]; front door, back door, side door; carriage entrance, portecochere; doorpost, durn [now dial.]; lobby, porch etc. (vestibule) 191.17; inlet etc. 294.5; outlet etc. 295.5; edge etc. 231.

5. *n.* window, casement [poetic]; casement window; port, porthole; light, skylight; fanlight, fan window; bull's-eye, *œil-de-bœuf* [F.]; grilled *or* grated window, wicket, lattice; bay window, window bay, bow window, oriel, dormer; lantern; windore [obs. exc. dial.] fenestration; embrasure, *abat-jour* [F.] splay; pane, windowpane, window glass; window shade, blind, Venetian blind; window shutter, windowshut [obs. exc. dial. Eng.]; window case, window back, window bar, window board, window box, window frame, window head, window stop, window sash, window sill, window stile, window screen.

6. *n.* tube, tubulation, pipe, fistula, duct, canal, vessel; pipette, tubulet, tubule, tubulus [rare], tubulure [Chem.]; main; water pipe, waste pipe, organ pipe, flue pipe, reed pipe, standpipe; flume; gut; pipe line; hose, rubber hose, garden hose; siphon, tap; catheter [Med.]; adjutage; ostium; smokestack, stovepipe, chimney, flue, funnel; nozzle, nose; stem, straw, reed; thunder tube, fulgurite; bore, caliber; gullet, intestines etc. (conduit) 350; air pipe etc. 351; tobacco pipe etc. 392a.6.

7. *n.* porousness, porosity, sievelikeness, cribriformity; sieve, strainer, sifter, filter, colander, riddle, screen, cribble; cribellum [Zool.]; honeycomb; net, seine.

8. *n.* (act of opening) opening, piercing etc. *v.*; penetration, perforation, apertion [arch.], pertusion [obs.], terebration; impalement; acupuncture, acupunctuation, acupuncturation.

9. *n.* gaping, yawning, hiation [rare], oscitance *or* oscitancy, dehiscence, pandiculation.

10. *n.* opener, opening device; can opener, tin opener [Eng.]; bottle opener, corkscrew; key, screw [thieves' slang],

---

260. The windows of heaven.—BIBLE. I am the door; by me if any man enter in, he shall be saved.—BIBLE.   The gates wide open stood.—MILTON.   Magic casements, opening on the foam / Of perilous seas, in faery lands forlorn.—KEATS.   All paradise could, by the simple opening of a door, let itself in upon him. —WORDSWORTH.

clavis; latchkey, front-door key; master key, skeleton key, passkey, *passe-partout* [F.]; passport; pass, safe-conduct, open-sesame, password; medium etc. 631.2.

11. *v.* open, ope [poetic]; fly open, spring open; tap; cleave, crack, cut, split, slit, incise, lance; rent, tear, rip; crack open, cut open, tear open etc.; lay open, throw open; stave in, cave in, break *or* burst in, bust in [dial. and inelegant]; part, dispart, separate, divaricate, spread out; cut a passage through; make way *or* room for.

12. *v.* unclose, uncover, uncase, unsheathe, unseal, uncork, unwrap, unfold, undo, unstop, unlock, unclog, deobstruct [rare]; unclutch, unclench; unveil, undrape, uncurtain; disclose, expose, reveal, bare.

13. *v.* gape, gap, yawn, hiate [rare], dehisce.

14. *v.* perforate, pierce, empierce [obs.], penetrate, puncture, stick, prick, punch, pink, stab; spike, spear, lance; gore; bore, auger, drill; ream, rime [Eng.]; gouge, gouge out; transpierce, transfix; enfilade; impale, spit; trepan, trephine [both Surg.]; riddle, honeycomb; tunnel, mine etc. 252.9; insert etc. 300.5.

15. *adj.* open, unclosed, perforated etc. *v.*; perforate; dehiscent, ringent, oscitant, yawning, gaping; agape, ajar; patulous, expanded, extended, distended; wide-open, unrestricted; patent, bare, exposed, unconcealed; hollow etc. 252.10.

16. *adj.* tubular, tubed, tubate, tubiform; tubulose *or* tubulous, tubulate *or* tubulated; tube-shaped, tubelike; pipe-shaped, pipelike, piped; cannular, cannulate *or* cannulated; fistulous *or* fistulose, fistulatous [rare], fistular, fistuliform; vesicular, vesiculate, vascular.

17. *adj.* porous, sievelike, cribriform, honeycombed, riddled; spongy, spongious *or* spongiose.

18. *adj.* foraminous, foraminose [obs.], foraminiferous; foraminulate, foraminulous *or* foraminulose.

19. *adj.* follicular, folliculate *or* folliculated, folliculous *or* folliculose.

20. *adj.* openable, penetrable etc. *v.*; pervious, permeable, accessible.

21. *adj.* opening etc. *v.*, aperient.

22. *int.* open up!, Open sesame!, gangway!, passageway!, make way!

261. Closure
(See 260. Opening)

1. *n.* closure, closing etc. *v.*, occlusion, stoppage, blockage, blockade; embolism, embolus; infarct, infarction; constipation, obstipation; blind alley *or* corner, *cul-de-sac* [F.], dead end, dead-end street; blind gut, caecum; appendix, vermiform process *or* appendix; imperforation, impermeability, imperviousness etc. adj.; operculum; barrier, obstruction etc. (obstacle) 706.2; stopper etc. 263; contraction etc. 195; recess etc. 252.4; keddah [Ind.] etc. (enclosure) 232.1.

2. *v.* close, occlude, shut, stop, cover, block, blockade, dam, plug, cork, bung; stanch, staunch, stench [obs. exc. Scot.]; fill, stuff; wrap, sheathe; stop up, shut up etc.; fasten, secure; lock, lock up, bolt, bar; button, zip up; seal, seal up, plumb; choke, throttle; trap; shut *or* close the door; slam, clap, snap; hinder etc. 706.4; cicatrize etc. (heal) 660.16.

3. *adj.* closed etc. *v.*, shut, unopened etc. (*see* open etc. 260.11, 15); blank; operculate *or* operculated, opercled, opercular, operculiferous, operculigerous, operculigenous, operculiform; caecal.

4. *adj.* unpierced, pierceless, unperforated etc. (*see* perforate etc. 260.14), imperforate, infarcted; untrodden, pathless, wayless, trackless, invious [obs.].

5. *adj.* unpierceable, unperforable, impermeable etc.; impervious; impassable, unpassable.

6. *adj.* close, fast, shut fast, tight, snug, compact, stanch, firm; watertight, airtight, unventilated, hermetically sealed.

262. Perforator

n., perforator, piercer, puncturer, puncher, punch; puncheon, punch pliers, borer, auger, drill, chisel, gimlet, wimble, awl, bradawl, gouge, scoop, corkscrew, dibble, trocar, probe, bodkin, needle, pin, broach, spike bit; reamer, rimer [Eng.]; lance, lancet; stylet, stiletto; trepan, trephine; punching machine, punching press; punch, die *or* matrix, single-action ~, double-action *or* triple-action die,

---

261. Now stir the fire, and close the shutters fast.—Cowper. What deep wounds ever closed without a scar.—Byron.
262. When he himself might his quietus make / With a bare bodkin.—Shakespeare.

solid die, chaser; spear etc. (weapon) 727.3–6; knife etc. 253.6.

263. Stopper

1. *n.* stopper, stop, stopple, stopgap, plug; cork, bung, spike, spill, spile, tap, spigot, peg, pin; ram, rammer, ramrod; piston, can [slang]; stopping, wadding, stuffing, padding, packing; dossil, tent, pledget, sponge, tampon, tampion *or* tompion [all Surg.]; tourniquet; lock, padlock; key etc. 260.10; closure etc. 261; obstacle etc. 706.2; cap etc. (lid) 223.7.

2. *n.* valve, valvule, valvula [Anat.]; gate, head gate; slide valve; faucet, spigot [U.S.], tap [chiefly Eng.], dossil [obs. exc. dial. Eng.], cock, stopcock; outlet etc. 295.5.

264. Motion
(See 265. Quiescence)

1. *n.* motion, moving etc. *v.*, movement, move, stir; motivity, motive power, motility, movableness; motorium; mobilization; conduction; countermotion, evolution; activity etc. 682.

2. *n.* locomotion, progress etc. (progressive motion) 282; travel etc. 266; navigation etc. 267; transference etc. 270; velocity etc. 274.

3. *n.* course, career, set, passage, flow, flux, flight, stream, run, rush, onrush, ongoing; drift, driftage.

4. *n.* kinetics [Phys.], kinematics [Phys.], kinesis [Philos.]; metakinesis [Philos.], telekinesis [psychical research], kinesiatrics [Med.], chemokinesis [Chem.], karyokinesis [Biol.], photokinesis [Physiol.]; dynamics etc. (mechanics) 276.5.

5. *v.* motion, gesture etc. (signal) 550.20.

6. *v.* move, go, hie, gang [Scot. and dial. Eng.], wend [obs.], locomote [coll.], sashay [slang, U.S.], budge, stir, pass; roll, roll on; flow, stream, run, drift, course, slide, glide, flit, sweep along; move on *or* along, shove on *or* along [coll.], mog [dial.]; move over, mooch over [slang]; shift, change, shift *or* change place; dodge, duck [coll.]; keep going *or* moving, be on the go etc. *adv.*; walk etc. (travel) 266.12–22; advance etc. (progress) 282.2.

7. *v.* set in motion, put in motion, move; render movable, mobilize; motivate etc. 615.7; impel etc. 276.7; propel etc. 284.10–14.

8. *adj.* moving etc. *v.*, in motion; transitional, metabatic [Phys.]; motor, motorial, motary [rare], motive, motile, motiferous, motific [rare]; mercurial, quicksilver; traveling etc. 266.23–27; restless, unquiet etc. (inconstant) 149.6; progressive etc. 282.3.

9. *adj.* kinetic(al) [Phys.], kinematic(al) [Phys.]; metakinetic [Philos.], telekinetic [psychical research], kinesiatric [Med.], kinesodic [Physiol.], kinesthetic, kinetogenic [Biol.], kinetoscopic, chemokinetic [Chem.], karyokinetic [Biol.], photokinetic [Physiol.].

10. *adv.* under way, under sail; on the move *or* go, on the wing *or* fly, on the tramp *or* march; on the run, on the jump [coll.], on the hop [slang]; on *or* upon the gad [coll.], on the drift [slang, U.S.].

265. Quiescence
(See 264. Motion)

1. *n.* quiescence, quiescency, stillness, quietness etc. *adj.*; quiet, quietude, rest, repose, tranquillity, serenity, placidity, indisturbance [rare], imperturbation [rare], peace, composure, calm; dead calm, deathlike calm; up-and-down wind, Irishman's hurricane, soldier's wind [all joc., Naut.]; anticyclone; silken repose, statuelike repose; inertia; fixity, immobility etc. (stability) 150; permanence etc. 141; sleep etc. (inactivity) 683; stagnation etc. (inertness) 172; silence etc. 403.

2. *n.* pause, lull etc. (cessation) 142.

3. *n.* standstill, stillstand, stand; dead stand, dead stop, full stop; lock, deadlock, dead set; fix; embargo; stop etc. (cessation) 142.

4. *n.* resting place, lodging place, *gîte*

---

264. No motion but the moving tide, a breeze, / Or merely silent Nature's breathing life.—WORDSWORTH.   The lazy foam, forever in motion, and never moved away.—WORDSWORTH. Our nature is movement; absolute stillness is death.—PASCAL.   *Eppur si muove* [Nevertheless it does move].—GALILEO.   Πάντα ῥεῖ [Everything flows].—HERACLITUS.

265. The stilly hour when storms are gone.—T. MOORE.   Deeds will be done,—while he boasts his quiescence.—A. BENNETT.   The noonday quiet holds the hill.—TENNYSON.   I had not power to stir or strive.—BYRON.

[F.]; last home, cemetery etc. (grave) 363.13, 14; haven etc. (refuge) 666.3, 4; retreat, home, bivouac etc. (abode) 189; pillow, bed etc. (support) 215; goal etc. (destination) 292.6.

5. *v.* be quiescent etc. *adj.,* keep quiet, rest, repose, remain, stay, tarry, mark time, stick, stand, be at a standstill etc. *n.*; remain motionless, freeze [coll.], stand *or* lie still, stand *or* stick fast, stand firm, keep *or* remain firm, stay put [chiefly coll.]; stand like a post, stand like a stuck pig [coll.]; not stir, not stir a step, not stir a peg [coll.]; not breathe, hold one's breath; stay in place, stay in one place, remain *in situ* [L.].

stay at home, keep within doors, go to bed, live the life of a clam; vegetate, stagnate; rest one's bonnet on a chair [dial., U.S.], rest one's face and hands [dial. or slang, U.S.]; let alone, let well enough alone; abide, abide one's time, rest and be thankful; stop, pause etc. (cease) 142.6; stay at, dwell etc. (inhabit) 186.10; establish etc. (settle) 184.14, (stabilize) 150.4; not do etc. 681.2; heave to, cast anchor etc. (be inactive) 683.8.

6. *v.* quiet, quell, calm, becalm, hush, still, stay, allay, pacify, tranquilize, compose, settle, soothe, lull, put at rest; put *or* lull to sleep; lay an embargo on; stop etc. (interrupt) 142.7.

7. *adj.* quiescent, quiet, still, stilly [poetic], calm, placid, tranquil, hushed etc. *v.,* hush [arch.], at rest; reposing, resting etc. *v.*; restful, peaceful, reposeful; unmoved, undisturbed, unruffled; unstirring, not a leaf stirring; not a breath of air, becalmed; nothing doing [slang]; immobile, immotile, immotive, immotioned [rare], unmoving, moveless, motionless, fixed, stationary, statuelike; standing still etc. *v.,* not moving etc. 264.8; dead-still, stock-still, perfectly still.

still as a statue, ~ post, ~ stove *or* mouse, still *or* calm as death; at anchor, riding at anchor; sedentary, untraveled, stay-at-home; cataleptic [Tech.]; immovable etc. (stable) 150.5; permanent etc. 141.6; dormant, stagnant etc. (inert) 172.3; sleeping etc. (inactive) 683.12, 16; silent etc. 403.6, 7.

8. *adv.* at a standstill etc. *n.,* at the halt, at rest, *re infecta* [L.].

9. *int.* stop! etc. (cease!) 142.8.

266. Travel
(See also 268. Traveler)

1. *n.* travel, traveling etc *v.,* locomotion, passage, course; peregrination, peregrinity; itinerancy, itineracy, itineration [rare]; travels, journeyings, peripatetics [joc.]; world travel, globe-trotting [coll.]; movement etc. (motion) 264; parade, caravan etc. (procession) 69.3; wanderer etc. (traveler) 268.

2. *n.* wandering, roving etc. *v.*; pererration [obs.], peregrination, peregrinity; nomadism, nomadization; vagabondism, vagabondage, vagabondry [rare]; vagrancy, hoboism [U.S.]; gadding, gad [coll.]; wanderlust; tourism, touristry; Alpine Club.

3. *n.* migration, transmigration, passage, trek; emigration, immigration, demigration [obs.], intermigration, migrant etc. 268.3.

4. *n.* walking etc. *v.,* ambulation, perambulation, pedestrianism; footwork, legwork [both coll.]; walk, ramble, hike [coll.], march, tramp, mush [Northw. Amer.]; stroll, saunter, promenade, *pasear* [Sp. Amer. and coll. U.S.], airing, jaunt, constitutional [coll.], stretch; turn, whirl [coll.]; peripatetic journey *or* exercise, peripatetication, peripateticization, peripateticism; hitchhike [slang, U.S.]; exercise etc. 686.2.

5. *n.* gait, pace, step, stride, footfall; port, portance [arch.], carriage, bearing, poise, *tournure* [F.]; saunter; shuffle, shamble; hobble, limp, claudication [obs.], hitch; totter, stagger; toddle, paddle; slouch, droop; stride, straddle; mincing gait, scuttle, prance, flounce, stalk, strut, swagger; swing, roll; amble, pace, single-foot [U.S.], piaffer; hop, jump; goose step; tiptoe; march, double march, quick *or* quickstep march, military march; run, trot etc. (velocity) 274.3; walk, jog, dogtrot etc. (slowness) 275.2.

There is not wind enough to twirl / The one red leaf.—COLERIDGE.. A maiden never bold; / Of spirit so still ... her motion / Blush'd at itself.—SHAKESPEARE. The wind ceased, and there was a great calm.—BIBLE.

266. The fool wanders, the wise man travels.—FULLER. Fools are aye fond o' flittin', and wise men o' sittin'.—J. RAY. A gentleman ought to travel abroad, but dwell at home.—

6. *n.* nightwalking, noctambulation, noctambulism; night-wandering, noctivagation; sleepwalking, somnambulation, somnambulism; sleepwalk; nightwalker etc. 268.7.

7. *n.* riding, motoring etc. *v.*; motorism; equitation, horsemanship; manège *or* manege, manage [arch.]; ride, drive; spin, whirl [both coll.]; skimmington, skimmington ride [now rare, Eng.]; joy ride [coll.]; straw-ride [coll., U.S.]; lift [coll.], pickup [slang]; ride and tie; rider etc. 268.8.

8. *n.* journey, *jornada* [Sp. and Southw. U.S.], trip, tour, turn [obs.], excursion, discursion [obs.], expedition, trek; peregrination, ramble [spec. on foot], gait [Scot. and dial.]; voyage, passage [both now rare, exc. by water]; course, run; pilgrimage, hadj [Arab.]; campaign; turn, whirl [coll.]; circuit, round trip; grand tour, extended journey, *Wanderjahr* [G.] (*pl. Wanderjahre*), wanderyear; ride, drive etc. *above*; walk etc. *above* 266.4, promenade, jaunt; outing, airing, junket [coll., U.S.]; sight-seeing trip, rubberneck tour [slang, U.S.]; jump [chiefly coll.], hop [slang]; leg [coll.]; voyage etc. (navigation) 267.6.

9. *n.* itinerary, route, circuit, round, beat; course, road etc. (path) 627.2; seaway etc. 267.8; airway etc. 267a.20; Baedeker etc. (guidebook) 694.7.

10. *n.* stopping place, stop, stop-off, stopover, layover; terminus, terminal [U.S.]; station, railway *or* railroad station, station house, depot [U.S.], *gare* [F.]; quarantine; encampment etc. (camp) 189.15.

11. *n.* legs, leglets, limbs, shanks, nethers [rare], hind legs [joc. exc. Zool.], podites [Zool.]; stumps, pegs, pins [all coll.]; stems, props, trotters, ponies, shanks' mares, ~ mules *or* horses, underpins *or* underpinnings, locomotives, propellers, gams [all slang]; gamb *or* gambe, jamb [sing.; all esp. Her.]; bowlegs, baker's legs, scissor-legs; bayonet legs; gangleshanks, longshanks, spindlelegs, spindleshanks, lath legs [all slang]; shin, ankle, hock; thigh, hock [dial.], popliteal space, ham, drumstick [of a fowl]; gigot [as of lamb]; foot etc. 211.4.

12. *v.* travel, betake oneself, direct one's course, bend one's steps *or* course, hit [now rare], wend; journey, trip [now rare], take a journey *or* trip, go a journey, go on a journey, wayfare, trek, peragrate [rare], peregrinate, tour, tourist [coll.], itinerate [rare]; hit the trail [slang], take the road, go on the road [Theat.]; flit, take wing; pilgrim, pilgrimage, go on *or* make a pilgrimage; travel extensively, globe-trot [coll.]; travel over, traverse, course, patrol; traverse *or* scour the country; campaign; go on a sightseeing trip, sight-see; stump, take the stump [both coll., U.S.]; move etc. 264.6.

13. *v.* go for an outing *or* airing, take the air, *pasear* [Sp. Amer. and coll. U.S.]; go out for a walk, take one's constitutional [coll.]; take a turn *or* whirl; have a run; promenade, make a promenade.

14. *v.* wander, roam, rove, range, gad *or* gad about, go on the gad [coll.], traipse *or* trapes [dial.], gallivant, haze, haze around *or* about [coll.], knock around *or* about [coll.], bat around *or* about [slang], mooch [now dial. and slang], expatiate [rare], nomadize, prowl, stray, straggle, meander, jaunt, ramble, stroll, saunter, peregrinate, go *or* run about, go one's *or* the rounds; become a vagabond, vagabond, vagabondize, vag it [tramps' slang, U.S.], hobo [U.S.], tramp; hover.

15. *v.* migrate, transmigrate, trek; emigrate, immigrate, demigrate [obs.], intermigrate.

16. *v.* walk, travel *or* go on foot *or* afoot, pedestrianize, ambulate, peripateticate, step, tread, pace, track, pad, foot, foot it, leg, leg it; hoof it, beat *or* pad the hoof, ankle, go on the heel and toe [U.S.], go on the marrowbone stage, ride shanks' mare, ~ mules *or* horses, take *or* ride the shoe-leather *or* hobnail express, mope, stump it, stir one's stumps, walk the chalks [all slang]; peg ~, jog ~, wag *or* shuffle on *or* along; march, mush [Northw. Amer.], footslog [slang], tramp, hike [coll.]; hitchhike [coll.], hitch rides [slang, U.S.].

stroll, saunter; traipse *or* trapes

FULLER. How much a dunce, that has been sent to roam, / Excels a dunce that has been kept at home.—COWPER. I should like to spend the whole of my life traveling, if I could anywhere borrow another life to spend at home. —HAZLITT. Travel teaches toleration.—

[dial.]; shuffle, shamble; plod, peg, trudge, drag one's freight [slang, U.S.], stump [coll.], lumber, barge, lunge; hobble, limp, claudicate [obs.], hitch; totter, stagger; toddle, paddle; slouch; stride, straddle; stalk, strut, swagger; mince, sashay [slang, U.S.], scuttle, prance, flounce; swing, roll; trip, skip, foot; hop, jump; jog, jolt; amble, bundle, bowl along; pace; single-foot [U.S.]; piaffe, piaffer.

goose-step [coll.], do the goose step; do the lock step, do the one-two [crim. slang]; creep, pussyfoot [slang]; tiptoe, go on tiptoe; stamp, stomp [dial.]; *pasear* [Sp. Amer. and coll. U.S.]; go for or take a walk etc. *n.*, stretch the legs, take a stretch, take one's constitutional [coll.]; promenade, make a promenade; perambulate, circumambulate; hit the road *or* trail, pound the pavement, fan the highway [all tramp slang]; walk the tracks, count ties [tramp slang].

17. *v.* nightwalk, noctambulate; sleepwalk, walk in one's sleep, somnambulate.

18. *v.* ride, drive, go for a ride *or* drive; spin, take *or* go for a spin *or* whirl [all coll.]; ride in *or* on a vehicle, vehiculate [rare]; go by car, automobile, auto [coll.]; taxicab, taxi *or* taxy; motorcycle, bicycle, cycle [coll.], wheel [coll.]; go by train *or* rail, railroad [U.S.]; go by trolley, ~ streetcar etc., trolley [coll.], tram [Eng.]; joy-ride, take a joy ride [both coll.]; navigate etc. 267.10; fly etc. 267a.30; burn up the road, step on the gas [slang] etc. (speed) 274.9, 10.

19. *v.* ride or drive a horse, take horse, go on horseback; ride bareback, ride in the slick [West. U.S.]; ride across country, lark [coll.]; prance, frisk, fisk [obs.]; caracole; trot, gallop etc. (speed) 274.9.

20. *v.* glide, slide, glissade, coast, skim, skate, sweep; ski, toboggan, sled; bellywhop [dial.].

21. *v.* file off, defile, march in procession, go in a column etc. (procession) 69.3; parade, go on parade.

22. *v.* go to, repair to, resort to, hie to, direct one's course to, bend one's steps to, betake oneself to, visit.

23. *adj.* traveling etc. *v.*, itinerant, itinerary, itinerarian; peripatetic(al); ambuling, ambulant, ambulatory, ambulatorial, ambulative; perambulating, perambulant [rare], perambulatory; pedestrian; touristic(al), touristy [coll.]; moving etc. 264.8.

24. *adj.* wandering etc. *v.*, discursive, vagrant, vagabond, landlouping; nomad, nomadic; circumforaneous, circumforanean [obs.]; mundivagant; foot-loose, foot-loose and fancy-free; migratory, migrational.

25. *adj.* nightwalking, noctambulous, noctambulant, noctambulistic; nightwandering, noctivagous, noctivagant [rare]; sleepwalking, somnambulant, somnambular, somnambulistic.

26. *adj.* wayworn, way-weary, travelworn, travel-stained.

27. *adj.* self-moving, self-propelling, self-propellent, self-acting, automatic *or* automatical; automobile, automotive; locomobile, locomotive.

28. *adv.* on foot, afoot, footback [obs. exc. dial.], on footback; on the heel and toe [U.S.], on the marrowbone stage, on shanks' mares, mules *or* horses, on the shoe-leather *or* hobnail express [all slang].

29. *int. bon voyage!* [F.] etc. (farewell) 293.14.

267. Navigation
(See also 269. Mariner, 273. Ship)

1. *n.* navigation, navigating, seafaring, seafare [rare], voyaging, sailing, cruising, shipping [obs.]; boating, yachting; plane ~, traverse ~, spherical ~, parallel ~, middle ~, latitude ~, Mercator ~, great-circle *or* composite sailing; seamanship; pilotship, pilotage, helmage [rare], steerage; proper piloting; circumnavigation, periplus; celestial navigation; coastal navigation, dog-barking navigation [derog.]; aquatics; volatility, buoyancy; sea legs; ship etc 273; mariner etc. 269; navy etc. 726.10; lee, windward etc. (side) 236.2, 3; soundings, draft etc. (depth) 208.4, 5.

2. *n.* embarkment, embarkation etc. (departure) 293.1.

3. *n.* disembarkment, disembarkation, debarkation etc. (landing) 292.1.

DISRAELI. I dislike feeling at home when I am abroad.—SHAW. Strong and content I travel the open road.—WHITMAN.

267. A ship without ballast is unstable and will not go straight.—SCHOPENHAUER. Well then,—our course is chosen, spread the sail.—

4. *n.* maneuvers, tactical maneuvers, tactics; formation cruising; fleet work.

5. *n.* (submarines) submergence, dive; stationary dive, running dive, crash dive; immersion, submersion etc. (plunge) 310.1, 2.

6. *n.* voyage, sail, cruise, course, passage; journey etc. 266.8.

7. *n.* way, progress, motion through the water; steerageway, headway, sternway, leeway, driftway.

8. *n.* seaway, waterway, fairway, ocean *or* sea lane, ocean traffic lane, ship route, steamer track; sea etc. 341; canal etc. 350.

9. *n.* swimming, bathing, natation, balneation; diving, floating; fin, flipper, fish's tail; bathing suit, trunks; swimming pool etc. (bath) 652.4; dive etc. (plunge) 310.1.

10. *v.* navigate, sail, cruise, seafare, voyage, journey by water, go in a vessel, go by ship, ship [obs.], go on *or* take a voyage etc. *n.*; ride the sea *or* waves, walk the waters, plow the waves, ∼ deep, ∼ main *or* ocean; steam, steamer, steamboat; boat, yacht; bear *or* carry sail; cross, traverse; sail through, pernavigate [rare]; sail round, circumnavigate; cross the ocean, hop the drink [slang]. run a blockade, run the gantlet; lay, lay aloft, lay forward etc.; traverse a yard, brace a yard fore and aft; heave, haul, bouse [cant]; kedge; warp; boom; heave round; heave short; heave apeak; heave the log; haul down, board; spar down; ratline down, clap on ratlines; unlash, cut *or* cast loose; clear hawse; shift the rudder, keep her so etc. *below* 267.69–71.

11. *v.* pilot, helm, coxswain, steer, guide, direct, manage, handle, run, operate; conn *or* cond, be at the conn; shape *or* chart a course; uphelm, ease the helm etc. *below* 267.70.

12. *v.* anchor, come to anchor, lay anchor, let go the anchor, cast anchor, heave the hook [Naut. slang]; carry out the anchor; approach anchorage; moor, run out a warp *or* rope; lash, lash and tie; snub the chain; foul the anchor; back an anchor; disembark etc. (land) 292.9.

13. *v.* ride at anchor, ride, lie, rest; ride easy, ride hard [obs.]; ride aportoise *or* aportlast [obs.]; ride hawse full; lie athwart.

14. *v.* lay *or* lie to, lay *or* lie by; lie near *or* close to the wind, head to wind *or* windward, be under the sea; lie off, lie off the land *or* shore; lay *or* lie up.

15. *v.* weigh anchor, bring the anchor home, break ground, loose the anchor [obs.], loose for sea; raise the dead, heave and raise the dead [both Naut. slang]; unmoor, cast off, ∼ loose *or* away; embark etc. 293.6.

16. *v.* get under way, under weigh [erroneous], put *or* have way upon, put *or* shove off; hoist the blue Peter; go to sea, put (out) to sea; set sail, hoist sail, unfurl *or* spread sail, heave out a sail, make sail, trim sail, deck [cant]; hang out the washing, give her muslin [both Naut. slang]; clap ∼, crack *or* pack on sail, put on (more) sail; clap on, crack on, pack on; crowd sail, give her beans [Naut. slang]; keep them rap-full; bagpipe a sail, bagpipe the mizzen [both cant]; sneer (a ship), make all sneer again [both cant]; gather way, freshen the way [cant]; go full speed ahead *or* astern.

17. *v.* run, run *or* sail before the wind, sail bunt fair [cant], run *or* sail with the wind, run *or* sail down the wind, sail off the wind, sail free, sail with the wind aft, sail with the wind abaft the beam; run *or* sail with the wind quartering.

18. *v.* sail against the wind, sail on the wind, sail in *or* into the wind, sail up the wind, sail by the wind, sail to windward, head to wind *or* windward; sail in *or* into the wind's eye, sail in the teeth of the wind [both cant].

19. *v.* sail near the wind, sail close to the wind, lie near *or* close to the wind, hold a close wind, sail close-hauled, closehaul; work ∼, beat *or* eat to windward, beat, ply, luff; sail too close to the wind, sail fine [rare], touch the wind, pinch, luff and lie *or* touch her [cant]; lay (a ship) down, careen etc. *below* 267.34.

20. *v.* gain to windward of, eat to windward of, eat the wind out of; have the wind of, be to windward of.

21. *v.* make way, gather way, make headway *or* sternway; make leeway etc. *below* 267.23.

W. FALCONER.   She starts,—she moves,—she seems to feel / The thrill of life along her keel. —LONGFELLOW.   She comes majestic with her swelling sails.—SOUTHEY.   See the shaking funnels roar, / With the Peter at the fore.—

22. *v.* course, take *or* follow a course; shape a course for, lay *or* lie a course for, lay *or* lie up for; keep *or* hold the course *or* a course, hold on the course *or* a course, stand on *or* upon a course, stand on a straight course, maintain *or* keep the bearing, keep pointed, cape [cant]; keep *or* put the rudder amidships.

23. *v.* drift off the course, discourse, yaw, yaw off, bear off etc. *below* 267.24, drift, sag, bag on a bowline [cant]; sag ~, bear ~, ride *or* drive to leeward, make leeway, drive; drift with the current, fall down.

24. *v.* alter the course, change the bearing, bear off *or* away [spec. to leeward], bear to starboard *or* port, tack, busk, cast, jib, break, yaw, veer, wear, sheer, shift, turn, heel, cant, cant round *or* across, haul, haul off *or* to; bring ~, put ~, cast ~, throw ~, fetch *or* go about, bring ~, swing *or* heave round, luff round [rare]; about ship, turn *or* put back, turn on her heel, wind; miss stays; jibe; tack down wind, stand off and on, back and fill; put the rudder hard left *or* right, put the rudder *or* helm hard over, put the rudder amidships, ease the rudder *or* helm, give her more rudder etc. *below* 267.70.

bring *or* heave to, heave to on starboard *or* port tack; starboard, port; bear *or* head to windward, haul the wind *or* one's wind, bring by *or* on the wind, bring in *or* into the wind, uphelm, put the helm up; close-haul, sail near the wind etc. *above* 267.19; bring off the wind, bear off *or* away, put the helm to leeward, bear *or* head to leeward; pay off the head (of a vessel); swing the stern; box off; veer *or* wear short, bring by the lee, broach to, build a chapel [cant]; double *or* round a point; deviate etc. 279.4.

25. *v.* back water, go astern, go full speed astern, make sternway.

26. *v.* sail for, make for *or* toward, make at, run *or* stand for, head *or* steer toward, lay for, lay a course *or* one's course for, bear up for; bear up to, bear down on *or* upon, run *or* bear in with, close with; close with the land, run *or* bear in with the land; heave *or* go alongside, lay (a ship) aboard, go board and board; lay *or* lie in; put in *or* into, put into port, approach anchorage.

27. *v.* sail away from, run *or* stand from, stand off *or* bear off from, head *or* steer away from, lay away *or* off from; put off, shove off; stand off and on.

28. *v.* clear the land, bear off the land, lay *or* settle the land, make sea room.

29. *v.* make land, reach land, close with the land etc. *above* 267.26; sight land.

30. *v.* coast, range the coast, lie along the shore, hug the shore *or* land, keep hold of the land [cant], make free with the land [Naut. slang].

31. *v.* ride out, ride; ride out *or* ride a storm, ride out a gale *or* breeze, weather the storm, make heavy *or* bad weather.

32. *v.* run down, run foul *or* afoul of, sail into, run in *or* into, collide, fall aboard; nose *or* head into, run prow ~, end *or* head on, run head and head; run broadside on.

33. *v.* shipwreck, wreck, be sewed up; go aground, ground, beach, strand, run on the rocks, pile up [coll.], cast away; ground hard and fast.

34. *v.* careen, list, heave *or* lay down, lie along, heel, keel; broach to etc. *above* 267.24; sail too close to the wind etc. *above* 267.19.

35. *v.* capsize, upset, overset, overturn, turn over, upset etc. the boat, keel *or* heel over; sink, founder, go down, go to the bottom, go to Davy Jones's locker [slang]; scuttle.

36. *v.* go overboard, go by the board, go over the board *or* side.

37. *v.* trim, trim up, trim ship, trim the dish [Naut. slang]; trim by the head *or* stern, put in proper fore-and-aft trim, give greater draft fore and aft, put on an even keel; shift ballast, wing up ballast; break out ballast, break bulk, shoot ballast; clear the decks, clear for action; trim sail etc. *above* 267.16.

38. *v.* reduce sail, shorten *or* take in sail, snug down [cant], reef, reef one's sails; double-reef; lower sail, dowse sail [cant]; run under bare poles.

39. *v.* take bearings, cast a traverse; correct distance and maintain the bearings; run down the latitude; take a sight, shoot Charley Noble [Naut. slang], shoot the sun [cant], bring down the sun; box the compass.

40. *v.* take soundings etc. (depth) 208.7.

KIPLING. Running all over the sea trying to get behind the weather.—CONRAD. All I ask is a tall ship and a star to steer her by.—MASEFIELD.

41. *v.* signal, speak, hail and speak; cheer ship; unfurl *or* hoist a banner, unfurl an ensign, break out a flag; hoist the blue Peter; show one's colors, exchange colors; salute, dip; make her number; jibber the kibber [cant].

42. *v.* (battleships) maneuver, execute a maneuver; heave in together, cruise *or* maneuver in formation, keep in formation, maintain position, keep station, keep pointed, steam in line, steam in line of bearing; convoy.

43. *v.* (submarines) surface, bring *or* come to the surface, break water; submerge, go below, dive; rig for diving etc. *below* 267.72.

44. *v.* float, ride; scud, run, shoot; skim, *effleurer* [F.], walk the water.

45. *v.* pitch, toss, tumble, toss and tumble, pitch and toss, plunge, rear, roll, rock, reel, swing, sway, lurch, flounder, wallow, welter; buffet the waves, bruise the sea [Naut. slang].

46. *v.* row, paddle, ply the oar, pull, scull, punt; give way, row away; catch *or* cut a crab *or* lobster [coll.]; feather, feather an oar; sky an oar [coll.]; row dry [coll., Eng.]; pace, shoot; ship oars etc. *below* 267.69.

47. *v.* swim, bathe, go in swimming *or* bathing; float, float on one's back; wade, go in wading; dive, plunge.

48. *adj.* nautical, marine, maritime, naval, seafaring, seagoing, ocean-going; oceanic etc. 341.5.

49. *adj.* navigable, boatable; seaworthy etc. 273.15.

50. *adj.* sailing etc. *v.*; floating, afloat, watching [of a buoy]; fluking, afluking, all afluking [all coll.]; close-hauled.

51. *adj.* trim, trimmed, well-trimmed, apoise.

52. *adj.* aquatic, natatory, natatorial, natational; grallatorial, grallatory [both Zool.].

53. *adv.* on board, on ship board, on board ship, aboard, all aboard, afloat; on deck, topside; in sail; before the mast; across the bow, athwart the hawse, athwarthawse.

54. *adv.* under way, under weigh [erroneous], with way on; at sea, on the sea, on a voyage; under sail *or* canvas, with sails spread; under press of sail, ~ canvas *or* steam; under steam; under bare poles; on *or* off the bearing or course; in soundings; homeward bound; hard aport etc. *below* 267.70.

55. *adv.* before the wind, with the wind, down the wind, off the wind, with the wind aft, with the wind abaft the beam, bunt fair [cant]; running free; wing and wing, wung-out [cant]; under the wind, under the lee.

56. *adv.* against the wind, on the wind, in *or* into the wind, up the wind, by the wind, head to wind; in *or* into the wind's eye, in the teeth of the wind [both cant].

57. *adv.* near the wind, close to the wind, close-hauled, on a bowline, ahold [obs.].

58. *adv.* leeward, alee, to leeward etc. (*see* lee etc. 236.2); on the lee beam.

59. *adv.* windward, aweather, to windward etc. (*see* windward etc. 236.3).

60. *adv.* larboard etc. (left) 239.2, 5; starboard etc. (right) 238.2, 3.

61. *adv.* at water line, on the water line.

62. *adv.* alongside, board and board, yardarm to yardarm.

63. *adv.* at anchor, at road [obs.], riding at anchor; lying to.

64. *adv.* afoul, in collision; head and head, head ~, end *or* prow on; broadside on.

65. *adv.* aground, on the rocks; hard and fast.

66. *adv.* overboard, over the board *or* side, by the board, aft the fantail [joc.].

67. *adv.* shipshape, Bristol fashion *or* style, ataunt, all-a-taunto [cant], bung-up and bilge-free [cant]; trim, in trim; in proper fore-and-aft trim, on even keel.

68. *adv.* aft, abaft, abaff, baft, baff, astern, at *or* in poop [obs.]; fore and aft.

69. *int.* (orders, calls) ahoy!, ahoy there!, ship ahoy!; avast!, hold fast!; belay!, belay that *or* there!; aye, aye!, aye, aye, sir!; heave!, heave ho!, heave and awash!; lend a hand!, lend us your pound! [slang]; stand by!, stand by to weigh anchor!, stand by the main sheet! etc.; aloft!, aloft there!; keep one hand for yourself and one for the ship!; turn out!, show a leg!, rise and shine!; man overboard!; aboard!, all aboard!, take ship!; up oars!, give way!, row away!, way enough!, ship oars!

70. *int.* (orders to the helm) up helm!, down helm!, port!, larboard!, starboard!, helm aport!, helm astarboard!, helm alee!, helm aweather!, hard aport!, hard alee!, hard astarboard!, hard aweather!, hard over!, put the helm *or* rudder hard over!, right!, left!, right *or* left rudder!, right *or* left standard rudder!, right *or* left five (ten *etc*.) degrees rudder!, right *or* left half rudder!, right or left full rudder!, right *or* left handsomely!

give her more rudder!, shift the rudder!, meet her!, ease the helm *or* rudder!, rudder amidships!, nothing to the right *or* left!, nothing to the north'ard, ~ east'ard, ~ south'ard *or* west'ard!, no nearer!, how is your rudder?, how does she head?, keep her so!, steady!, steady so!, steady as you go!; about ship! etc. *above* 267.24.

71. *int*. (orders to the engine room) starboard *or* port engine!, all engines!, ahead!, back!, astern!, all engines ~, starboard *or* port engine ahead!, ~ back!, ~ ahead one-third!, ~ ahead two-thirds!, ~ ahead standard!, ~ ahead full!, ~ back one-third!, ~ back two-thirds!, ~ back full!, ~ full speed ahead!, ~ full speed astern!, ~ slow ahead! *or* slow astern!

72. *int*. (submarine orders) rig for diving!, ventilate inboard!, shift the control!, stations for diving!, secure the engines!, secure the main induction!, close the conning tower hatch!, ahead both motors!, flood the tank!, blow the tank!, flood main ballast!, close main vents!, flood 2000 etc. pounds in after trim!

267a. Aeronautics
(See also 269a. Aeronaut)

1. *n*. aeronautics, aerial navigation, aviation, avigation, aerodromics, volation *or* volitation, airplaning, planing [coll.], skyriding, flying, flight; aviatoriality, aeronautism; aerodonetics; airmanship, pilotship, pilotage, air pilotage; hydroplaning, volplaning etc. *v*.; ballooning, balloonation, balloonery; blind *or* instrument flying, blind soaring; barnstorming [coll.]; heavy ~ *or* ironhanded flying [cant]; sky writing; celestial navigation; aeropathy, aerophobia; airsickness; air legs; air line; air service etc. 726.9; aeronaut etc. 269a; aircraft etc. 273a; position light etc. (lights) 428.6.

2. *n*. (allied sciences) aerotechnics, aerodynamics, aerography, aeromechanics, aerostatics, aerostation, aerometry, pneumatics, aeronautical engineering, aeroscopy, aerophysics, hydrostatics, aerology, climatology, meteorology, micrometry, photometry, aerophotography, aerocartography, kinematics, kinetics.

3. *n*. (technical terminology) propulsive efficiency, tail force, margin of power, positive direction of roll, sweepback, slip, skin friction, direction of relative wind, resultant force, bearing, amplitude, aerocurve, aerodynamic *or* air volume, airplane heading, aspect ratio, effective aspect ratio, beam direction, camber, *décalage* [F.], equivalent monoplane, fineness ratio, flight path, righting *or* restoring moment, stagger.

4. *n*. (angle) aileron angle, blade angle, coning angle, dihedral angle, longitudinal dihedral angle, downwash angle, drift angle, effective helix angle, elevator angle, flapping angle, flight path angle, gliding angle, minimum gliding angle, landing angle, rudder angle, trim angle, zero-lift angle, angle of dead rise, angle of heel, angle of incidence *or* wing setting, angle of pitch, angle of roll *or* bank, angle of sideslip, angle of stabilizer setting, angle of yaw, angle of attack, absolute ~; critical ~, effective *or* induced angle of attack.

5. *n*. (center) aerodynamic center, elastic center, center of buoyancy, center of gravity, center of mass, center of pressure, center-of-pressure coefficiency.

6. *n*. (axes) horizontal *or* longitudinal axis, fore-and-aft axis, X axis; lateral axis, Y axis; normal axis, Z axis; elastic axis, wing axis, drag axis, positive lift axis; yawing, yaw, positive direction of yaw.

7. *n*. (stability) automatic stability, directional stability, lateral stability, longitudinal stability, inherent stability, dynamic stability, static stability.

8. *n*. (load) basic load, design load, full load, normal load, pay load, ultimate load, useful load; power loading, span loading, unsymmetrical loading, wing loading.

9. *n*. (pressure) altitude *or* height pressure, dynamic pressure, impact pres-

---

267a. For I dipt into the future . . . / Saw the heavens fill with commerce, argosies of magic sails.—TENNYSON.   Birds can fly, and why can't I?—J. T. TROWBRIDGE.   Heard the heavens fill with shouting, and there rained a ghastly dew / From the nations' airy navies

sure, manometer pressure, center of pressure, center of pressure coefficiency, superpressure; stress, working stress, breathing stresses; torsion, torsional stress, torque, propeller torque; structural fatigue.

10. *n.* thrust, propeller thrust, effective propeller thrust, static propeller thrust, line of thrust *or* flight.

11. *n.* pitch, pitch ratio, effective pitch, geometrical pitch, zero-thrust pitch, aerodynamic pitch; angle of pitch, positive direction of pitch.

12. *n.* lift, lift ratio, lift force *or* component, aerostatic lift, dynamic lift, gross lift, useful lift, lift direction, margin of lift.

13. *n.* drag, resistance; drag ratio, drag force *or* component, induced drag, wing drag *or* resistance, parasite *or* structural drag *or* resistance, profile drag, effective profile drag, head resistance, drag direction, cross-wind force.

14. *n* drift, drift angle; lateral drift, leeway.

15. *n.* flow, air flow, laminar flow, streamlike flow, turbulent flow.

16. *n.* wash, wake; backwash, slipstream, propeller race, race of the propeller; down-wash; prop-wash [cant].

17. *n.* (speed) air speed, operating *or* flying speed, minimum flying speed, sinking speed, get-away *or* take-off speed, hump speed, landing speed, terminal speed, ground speed, pitch speed, peripheral speed.

18. *n.* revolutions, revs [cant]; revolutions per minute, R.P.M.

19. *n.* (air, atmosphere) airspace, navigable airspace; stratosphere, substratosphere, tropopause, troposphere; ceiling, ballonet ceiling, service ceiling, static ceiling, absolute ceiling, ceiling zero; visibility, visibility zero; fog, soup [slang]; high-pressure area, low-pressure area; trough, trough line; air pocket *or* hole, air bump, pocket, hole, bump; head wind, tail wind.

20. *n.* airway, air route, air line; compass course, true course; track, course etc. (path) 627.2, 3.

21. *n.* (altitude) altitude of flight, sextant altitude, absolute altitude, critical altitude, density altitude, pressure altitude; clearance; ground elevation.

22. *n.* (horizon) rational *or* true horizon, sensible horizon, apparent *or* visible horizon, artificial *or* false horizon.

23. *n.* flight, volitation, volation; hop, jump, air jump [all slang]; solo, solo flight, solo hop [slang]; blind *or* instrument flight; formation flight; inverted flight; pay hop [Mil. slang]; test flight, test hop [slang]; observation flight; radius of action, navigation radius.

24. *n.* (maneuvers) acrobatic *or* tactical evolutions or maneuvers, acrobatics, aerobatics; hedgehopping, roadhopping, carhopping [all slang, U.S.]; rolling, crabbing, banking etc. *v.*; fishtailing; zoom, chandelle; dive, nose dive, power dive; autorotation, spin, flat spin, inverted spin, normal spin, power spin, uncontrolled spin, tail spin, falling leaf.

loop, spiral loop, ground loop, normal loop, outside loop, inverted normal *or* outside loop, dead-stick loop [cant], wing-over, looping the loop; roll, barrel roll, aileron roll, outside roll, snap roll; flipper turns, Immelmann turn, reverse turn, reversement; stall, whip stall; spiral, split "S", sideslip, push-down, pull-up, pull-out, glide, volplane.

25. *n.* take-off, hopoff [slang]; take-off run, taxiing *or* taxying; daisy-clipping, grass-cutting [both slang]; ground loop; level-off; take-off distance.

26. *n.* landing, perch [slang], arrival; landing run; ballooning in, parachute approach; blind *or* instrument landing, glide landing, stall landing, dead-stick landing [cant], fishtail landing, sideslip landing, emergency landing, level *or* two-point landing, normal *or* three-point landing, Chinese landing [slang], Chinese three-point landing [slang], crash landing, nose-over, nose-up, tail-high landing, tail-low landing, pancake landing, thumped-in landing [slang].

27. *n.* crash, crack-up, crock-up [Eng.]; washout [slang]; nose-over, crash landing etc. *above*.

28. *n.* airdrome, aerodrome, drome [coll.], airport, airfield, air harbor [Can.], air base, nest [slang], aviation field, landing field, landing, field, airship station; emergency landing field; landing strip, taxiway, runway; fairway, launching way; apron; transition strip;

---

grappling in the central blue.—TENNYSON. Darius was clearly of the opinion / That the air is also man's dominion.—J. T. TROWBRIDGE.

housing, hangar, dock, shed, airship shed; mooring mast; pylon.

29. *n.* (aeronautical instruments) tachometer, tac [slang]; altimeter, aneroid altimeter, electrical capacity altimeter, optical altimeter, sound-ranging altimeter; recording altimeter, altigraph, air log [cant]; aerograph, meteorograph; anemometer, recording anemometer, anemograph; turnmeter, turn indicator, turn-and-bank indicator, bank *or* banking indicator; compass, card compass, card magnetic compass, earth inductor *or* earth induction compass, induction compass, sun compass; hygrometer, recording hygrometer, hygrograph; Pitot tube, Pitot-static tube, Pitot-Venturi tube, Venturi tube; wind cone *or* sock, sock.

autosyn, accelerometer, aeroscope, ammeter, climatometer, fuel quantity indicator, radio, bearing plate, ceiling-height indicator, directional gyro, hub dynamometer, flight recorder, gyro horizon, inclinometer, manifold pressure gauge, octant, ozonometer, nephoscope, photometer, polymeter, potentiometer, spirit level, sting, terrain clearance indicator, transit instrument, wind indicator, thermostat, viscosimeter.

aerometer, air-speed head, anemoscope, engine gauge, fuel flow indicator, position indicator, barometer, Bourdon tube, calorimeter, drift meter, evaporimeter, galvanometer, hypsometer, intervalometer, micrometer, pitch *or* pitching indicator, pluviometer, pyrometer, rate-of-climb indicator, static tube, thermograph, yawmeter, variometer, instrument board *or* panel.

30. *v.* fly, flit, wing, take wing, make wing, wing one's way, take a flight, ride the skies, take to the air, take the air, take to the airways, go by air, lindy [slang], volitate, be wafted, navigate the air, avigate, aviate, airplane, aeroplane, aero, plane [coll.], go by plane [coll.]; soar, drift, hover; hydroplane, volplane, balloon etc. (*see* aircraft etc. 273a).

31. *v.* pilot, control, be at the controls, manipulate, drive; fly, aviate etc. *above*; do the stickwork, herd, push a crate [all slang]; fly blind, fly by instruments, fly by the seat of one's pants [slang]; follow the beam, ride the beam [cant]; barnstorm [coll.]; stunt [coll.], perform aerobatics; crab, crab the wind; fishtail, kick her tail around [slang]; zoom, hoick [cant], chandelle.

ascend, climb, mount; dive, nose-dive, make a nose dive, pique; spin, go into a tail spin etc. *n.*; loop, loop the loop; roll, wing-over, spiral, undulate, porpoise, feather, yaw, sideslip, bank, skid, dip, nose down, nose up, pull up, push down, pull out, glide, stall, fly in formation, mush through, taxi *or* taxy, plow, fight the controls [slang]; hedgehop, roadhop, carhop [all slang, U.S.].

32. *v.* accelerate, gun the motor [slang], boost, step on the gas [slang]; rev, rev up [cant].

33. *v.* take off, hop *or* hop off [slang], take to the air, go *or* fly aloft.

34. *v.* land, set her down [cant]; alight, light; descend, fly down; level off, flatten out; up-wind, down-wind; overshoot, undershoot; pancake, pancake a landing; make a dead-stick landing [cant] etc. *n.*; settle down, balloon in; fishtail down; nose up, nose over.

35. *v.* crash, crack up, crock up [Eng.]; spin in, fail to pull out.

36. *v.* bail out, parachute, make a parachute jump, make a brolly-hop [slang, Eng.].

37. *adj.* aeronautic(al), aeropleustic, aerial; aviatic, aviatorial, aviatory; aerodonetic, aerotechnical, aerostatic(al), aeromechanic(al), aerodynamic(al), aerophysical, aeromarine; volant, volatic [now rare], volitant, volatile [now rare], volitational; airworthy; air-minded, air-conscious; air-wise; airsick.

38. *int.* switch off!, contact!, let her go!

268. Traveler
(See also 266. Travel)

1. *n.* traveler, journeyer, wayfarer, trekker, tripper [coll.], goer; cruiser, voyager, *voyageur* [F.], sailor; globe-girdler, globe-trotter [coll.]; tourist, tourer, dude [slang, West. U.S.]; transient, transient guest *or* boarder; excursionist, sight-seer, rubberneck *or* rubbernecker [slang, U.S.]; commuter, straphanger [coll.]; explorer; adventurer; mountaineer, mountain climber; touristry

---

268. But there are wanderers o'er Eternity / Whose bark drives on and on, and anchored ne'er shall be.—BYRON. I will sing, I will go, and never ask me why / I was born a rover and a passer-by.—TORRENCE.   "Is there any-

etc. (travel) 266.2; traveling salesman etc. (traveler) 758.5.

2. *n.* wanderer, rover, roamer, rambler, straggler, gad *or* gadabout [coll.], gadling [obs.], runabout, go-about [chiefly dial.], mover, peregrinator [rare], itinerant, itinerarian [rare], itinerary [rare], passer-by, peripatetic [joc.], bird of passage, nomad; Wandering Jew, Ahasuerus, Ancient Mariner, Flying Dutchman.
drifter [coll.], floater [coll.], scattering [arch.]; vagabond, vagabondager [rare], vag [slang, U.S.], vagrant, landlouper, tramp, turnpiker, hobo [U.S.], bo [slang, U.S.], stiff *or* bindle stiff [slang, U.S.], knight of the road [joc.], bum *or* bummer [slang, U.S.], swagman *or* swagsman [Austral.], sundowner [coll., Austral.], prog *or* progger [dial., U.S.], loafer, wastrel, stray, waifs and strays; gypsy, Romany, *zingaro* [It.] (*pl. zingari*); Arab, street Arab; beachcomber; camper; runagate, runaway, fugitive, refugee; pilgrim, palmer, hadji [Arab.]; booly [Irish Hist.]; comers and goers.

3. *n.* migrant, migrator, trekker; immigrant; emigrant, emigree, *émigré* [F.]; evacuee, *évacué* [F.] (*fem. évacuée*), vackie [slang, Eng.].

4. *n.* runagate etc. (fugitive) 623.4, (apostate) 607.5.

5. *n.* courier, runner etc. (messenger) 534.

6. *n.* pedestrian, walker, walkist, foot traveler, foot passenger, hoofer [slang], peregrinator [rare], peripatetic [joc.], tramp, tramper, hiker [coll.]; hitchhiker [slang]; jaywalker [coll.].

7. *n.* nightwalker, noctambulist, noctambule, noctivagator [obs.]; sleepwalker, somnambulist, somnambulator, somnambule.

8. *n.* rider, horseman, horsewoman, horseback rider, horsebacker, equestrian, equestrienne [*fem.*]; trainer, breaker, broncobuster [slang, U.S.], buckaroo, [Southwest. U.S.]; cowboy, cowgirl, puncher *or* cowpuncher [coll., U.S.], *vaquero* [Sp. Amer.]; whip, huntsman; postilion, postboy; cavalier; roughrider; jockey, jock [slang].

9. *n.* driver, reinsman [rare], whip, Jehu [joc.], charioteer; coachman, coachy [coll.], *cocher* [F.], *cochero* [Sp.], *voiturier* [F.], *vetturino* [It.], gharry-wallah [Ind.]; stage coachman; dragoman; cabman, cabdriver, cabby [coll.], hackman, hacky [coll.], jarvey [slang, Eng.]; wagoner, drayman, truckman; carter, cartman, carman; teamster, four-up driver [West. U.S.]; mule driver, muleteer; oxen driver, bullwhacker [U.S.]; elephant driver, mahout; camel driver, cameleer; syc [Ind.].

10. *n.* automobile driver, automobilist, autoist [coll.], motorist; chauffeur, *chauffeuse* [F. *fem.*], James [slang]; truck driver, truckman; speed demon *or* maniac [coll.], speeder, scorcher [slang], racer; road hog [slang], Sunday driver [joc.]; joy-rider [coll.]; hit-and-run driver; back-seat driver [joc.]; bus driver; taxi *or* taxicab driver; jitney driver, jitneur, jitneuse [*fem.*]; cabdriver etc. *above.*

11. *n.* engine driver [Eng.], engineman, engineer [U.S.]; hogger, hoghead, boiler head, lokey man [all slang, U.S.]; motorman; Casey Jones.

12. *n.* railroad man, railroader [U.S.], rail [slang, U.S.; chiefly in *old rail*]; conductor, guard [Eng.]; brakeman, guard [U.S.]; brakie, shack, fielder, stringer [all slang, U.S.]; fireman, stoker; smoke agent, bakehead [both slang, U.S.].

269. Mariner
(See also 267. Navigation)

1. *n.* mariner, navigator, sailor, sailorman, seaman, seafarer, seafaring man, sea dog [coll.], waterman [obs.], water dog [coll.], shipman [obs. or poetic], windjammer [on sailing vessel; coll.], *matelot* [F.], Jack, jacky, Jack afloat, jack-tar, tar, tarpaulin [now rare], lobscouser [slang], salt [coll.]; limey *or* lime-juicer (English sailor) [slang, U.S.]; man-of-war's man, bluejacket, gob [slang, U.S.], galiongee [Turk.]; marine, devil dog [slang, U.S.], jolly [slang, Eng.], leatherneck [slang]; horse marine.

---

body there?" said the Traveller, / Knocking on the moonlit door.—DE LA MARE. Nature makes us vagabonds, the world makes us respectable.—A. SMITH. Hallelujah, I'm a bum, hallelujah, bum again.—SONG, ANON. A rolling stone gathers no moss.

269. The keen, eye-puckered, hard-case seaman.—MASEFIELD. Round the world and home again / That's the sailor's way.—W. ALLINGHAM. Your seamen are like your element, always tempestuous.—FARQUHAR. The wonder is always new that any sane man

common *or* ordinary seaman, O.D.; able seaman, A.B. *or* a.b.; old salt [coll.], old sea dog [coll.], shellback [slang], barnacle-back [slang]; deep-sea man, blue-water sailor; fresh-water sailor, fair-weather sailor, lubber, landlubber, landsman [all derog.]; pirate, sea rat [rare]; Ancient Mariner, Flying Dutchman; Jonah; navy etc. 726.10; naval officers etc. 745.12.

2. *n.* boatman, boater, waterman; oar, oarsman, rower; ferryman, ferryboat man; bargeman, barger, bargee [Eng.], bargemaster; lighterman; gondolier, *gondoliere* [It.].

3. *n.* (ship's crew) hand, deck hand, deckie [Eng.]; stoker, bakehead [slang]; stokehold crew, black gang [slang]; cabin boy, drudge [slang]; yeoman, ship's writer; purser, nipcheese [obs. slang]; ship's carpenter, chips [slang]; ship's cooper, bungs *or* Jimmy Bungs [slang]; ship's tailor, snip *or* snips [slang]; steward, stewardess; afterguard.

4. *n.* (ship's officers) captain, commander, sailing master, master mariner, skipper, old man [coll.], *patron* [F.]; navarch [Gr. Antiq.]; mate, first *or* chief mate, second ~, third ~ etc. mate, boatswain's mate; boatswain, bos'n, pipes [slang]; naval officers etc. 745.12.

5. *n.* steersman, helmsman, pilot, coxswain, cox [coll.], wheelman, boatsetter.

6. *n.* (malingering sailor) sham Abram *or* Abraham, galley stoker, lead swinger, soldier *or* sojer [all slang or derog.].

7. *n.* longshoreman, loader, stevedore, wharf *or* dock hand, docker, dock-walloper [slang], roustabout [U.S.].

8. *n.* landsman, landlubber etc. 342.7.

269a. Aeronaut
(See also 267a. **Aeronautics**)

1. *n.* aeronaut, aviator, aeroplaner, airplaner, aeroplanist, airplanist, airman, bird [coll.], birdman [coll.], man-bird [coll.], flier *or* flyer, avigator, navigator, aerial navigator, aerialist, pilot, stickpusher [slang]; airwoman, birdwoman [coll.], aviatress, aviatrix, aviatrice; ace, wizard of the air, flying fool [slang]; monoplanist, balloonist etc. (*see* monoplane, balloon etc. 273a); observer, spotter [Mil. cant], scout; war bird [coll.], eagle *or* American eagle [slang, U.S.], devil dog of the air [coll., U.S.], hell-diver [slang]; bomber, cuckoo [slang]; gimper [slang]; kiwi, penguin [both cant]; barnstormer [coll.]; stunt man, stunter, stunt flier [all coll.]; flying circus; Icarus, Daedalus.

2. *n.* parachutist, chutist *or* chuter [coll.], parachute jumper; paratrooper.

3. *n.* (personnel) landing *or* ground crew; ground tester, flight tester; aircraftsman, aeromechanic, aeronautical engineer; rigger, parachute rigger; stewardess; ground school.

270. Transference
(See also **271. Carrier**)

1. *n.* transference, transfer, transferal [rare], transplantation, transmittal, transmission, transumption [rare], transposal, transposition, translation, translocation, elocation [obs.], delocalization, displacement, dislodgment, removal, removement, movement, moving etc. *v.*, remotion; amotion; shift; transit, transition, passage; metastasis, metathesis; delivery, deliverance; transfusion; infection, contagion; portamento [Mus.]; transfer etc. (of property) 783; change etc. 140; interchange etc. 148; dispersion etc. 73; dislocation etc. 185.

2. *n.* transportation, transportal [rare], transportance [rare], transportment [obs.], transference etc. *above*, transvection [rare], convection, conveyance, conduction, carriage, carry [U.S. and Can.], carrying etc. *v.*, gestation [obs.], portage, porterage, haulage, waftage; cartage, truckage; ferriage; telpherage; freightage, freight; shipment, transshipment; asportation; deportation, extradition etc. (banishment) 297.3; traction etc. 285.

3. *n.* (thing transferred) drift, silt, diluvium [Geol.], alluvium, alluvion, sinter [Geol.], loess [Geol.], debris *or* débris, detritus, deposit, moraine; sublimate, [Chem.], sediment, precipitation; deed,

bequest, legacy, lease; quitclaim; present etc. (gift) 784.3.

4. *n.* freight, shipment, goods [Eng.], cargo, lading, load, jag [chiefly dial.], lug [coll.], haul, tote [coll.], portage [arch.]; baggage [chiefly U.S. and Can.], luggage [chiefly Eng.]; mail etc. 592.4.

5. *n.* transferee, grantee, donee, legatee, devisee, indorsee; assignee etc. (consignee) 758.1.

6. *v.* transfer, translocate, transplace [rare], transplant, transmit, transpose, translate, transume [rare], elocate [obs.], delocalize, displace, dislocate, dislodge, move, remove, shift, change; shunt; transfuse; decant, draft *or* draught off; propel etc. 284.10; pull etc. 285.4.

7. *v.* transfer to, deliver, pass, pass over, forward, reach, hand, hand over, put in the hands of, turn over to, make over to; give etc. 784.8–13.

8. *v.* transport, transfer etc. *above* 270.6, port [obs.], convey, carry, bear, pack [chiefly West. U.S.], tote [coll., U.S.], lug [coll.], buck, jag [chiefly dial.], take, bring, fetch, fetch and carry; shoulder, back [coll.], hump [slang, Austral.], ride [coll.]; conduct, convoy; carry off *or* away, asport [rare]; haul, vehicle, vehiculate [rare], cart, wagon, truck, coach, sled [chiefly U.S.], sledge, boat, ferry, ship, raft, float, chair, horse etc.; waft, whisk, wing; deport, extradite, etc. (banish) 297.11.

9. *v.* send, dispatch; depute, commission, delegate, relegate, consign, commit; ship, freight, embark, express [chiefly U.S.]; post, mail, air-mail.

10. *v.* ladle, lade, bail, bucket, dip, scoop; shovel, spade.

11. *adj.* transferable, transmittable, transmissible, transumptive [rare]; movable, removable; conveyable, portable, portative; transportive, transportable, transportative; assignable, devisable, bequeathable, negotiable; conductive, conductional; contagious, catching, infectious, communicable; metastatic(al), metathetic(al); mailable.

12. *adv.* transferably etc. *adj.*; from hand to hand, from pillar to post; by transfer [U.S.], by freight, by rail, by trolley, by steamer, by airplane; by express, by mail, by special delivery.

13. *adv.* on the way, on the road, *en route* [F.], *in transitu* [L.], in transit, *chemin faisant* [F.], on the wing; as one goes, by the way; in passing, *en passant* [F.]; in mid-progress.

271. Carrier
(See also 270. Transference)

1. *n.* carrier, conveyer, transporter, transferrer, tranter [obs.], *voiturier* [F.], bearer, porter; redcap [U.S.], boy; *cargador* [P.I.], freighter; express, expressman; stevedore; coolie; conductor; pigeon post, *Taubenpost* [G.]; carrier pigeon, homing pigeon; bus boy, omnibus; water carrier etc. 348.16; teamster, chauffeur, truck driver etc. (driver) 268.9–11; vehicle etc. 272; ship etc. 273; aircraft etc. 273a; letter carrier etc. 534.2.

2. *n.* beast of burden, pack animal, pack horse, ~ mule etc., sumpter, sumpter horse, ~ mule etc., beast, cattle [obs.]; camel, ship of the desert, dromedary, llama, oont [Anglo-Ind.]; elephant, Jumbo, *hathi* [Hind.]; ox, buffalo; reindeer; sledge dog, husky.

3. *n.* horse, hoss [dial.], equine, steed, prad [slang, Eng.]; garran, nag [derog.], naggy; prancer [slang exc. spec.], pranker [obs.], dobbin, neigher [rare], quad [slang, Eng.], goer [usu. qualified]; charger, courser [poetic]; pony, Shetland *or* Shetland pony, shelty, Indian pony, Welsh pony, tatt *or* tattoo [Ind.], tit [chiefly dial.], polo pony, cow pony; range horse, mustang, broomtail, cayuse [all chiefly West. U.S.]; bronco, bronc [slang]; bucking broncho, buckjumper, sunfisher [slang].

hunter, stalking-horse; road horse, roadster; saddle horse, saddler, riding horse, rider, rouncy [arch.], palfrey, mount, remount; cavalry horse, cavalry [collective]; driving horse, carriage horse, cart horse, gigster, dray horse, draft horse, work horse, plow horse; shaft horse, thill horse, thiller, fill horse *or* filler [obs. exc. dial.]; wheel horse, wheeler; lead, leader; hack, hackney; pack horse, sumpter, sumpter horse, bidet [Mil.]; post horse; runner, clipper; galloper, trotter, ambler, single-footer, clicker; pacer, side-wheeler, sidewinder [slang]; stepper, high-stepper, prancer;

---

271. I was not made a horse; / And yet I bear a burthen like an ass.—SHAKESPEARE. The seat on a horse makes gentlemen of some and grooms of others.—CERVANTES. O for a

pad, padnag; boneshaker [slang], racker; daisy cutter [slang]; post horse.

thoroughbred, blood horse, hot-blooded horse [turf cant], number horse [turf cant]; foal, colt, filly [*fem.*]; mare, girl [dial., U.S.]; brood mare, stock horse; stallion, stud [U.S.], studhorse, top horse [dial., U.S.], entire horse, entire; gelding, horse [spec.]; horseflesh [collective].

4. *n.* (breeds of horses) Turk, Arab, Barb *or* barb, Belgian, American Standardbred, Galloway, Clydesdale, Shire horse, tarpan, Morgan, jennet, Narragansett, Waler, Percheron *or* Percheron Norman, Thoroughbred, Hambletonian, Houyhnhnm, punch *or* Suffolk punch, Suffolk; Shetland pony etc. *above*.

5. *n.* (colored horses) pinto [West. U.S.], roan, chestnut, sorrel, gray, black, white, ginger, grizzle, dun; bay, bayard; piebald, skewbald, calico pony [coll., U.S.], painted pony [coll., U.S.].

6. *n.* (inferior horse) crock, scalawag *or* scallawag, weed [slang or cant], stiff [turf slang], screw [coll.], goat [turf slang], jade [derog.], rip [coll or slang], skate [slang], dog [turf slang], plug [coll. or slang], Rosinante, planter [derog.], buzzard *or* crowbait [slang], snide [slang]; runt; balky horse, balker, dweller; roarer, whistler; cribber [cant]; rogue, outlaw [local, U.S.], ladino [Southeast. U.S.].

7. *n.* (scrawny horse) bone yard [slang], rackabones [coll., U.S.], scrag, hatrack [slang], stack of bones, Rosinante.

8. *n.* race horse, racer, gee-gee [coll.], bangtail, pony [slang], pelt *or* hide [slang, U.S.], racing machine [slang]; entry, starter, nomination in the race [turf cant]; stake horse, staker; plate horse, plater; mudder, mud lark [both turf cant]; slater [turf cant]; pot [turf cant], favorite *or* betting favorite; goat [slang] etc. *above* 271.6.

9. *n.* (famous horses) Pegasus (winged horse of Greek fable), Grani (Sigurd's magic steed), Bucephalus (Alexander the Great's war horse), Alborak (Mohammed's winged horse of ascension), Sleipnir (Odin's eight-legged steed), Incitatus (the steed of Caligula, the Roman Emperor), Rosinante (Don Quixote's bony steed), Vegliantino *or* Veillantif (Orlando's steed), Roan Barbary (favorite horse of Richard II), White Surrey (favorite horse of Richard III), Marengo (Napoleon's white horse), Black Saladin (Warwick's horse), Copenhagen (Wellington's charger at Waterloo), Black Bess (Dick Turpin's fleet mare), Bayard (Rinaldo's bay steed), kelpie *or* kelpy (equine water sprite of Gaelic mythology).

10. *n.* ass, donkey, jackass, jack, burro, dickey, cuddy [Scot. and dial. Eng.], moke [slang], longear [coll.], neddy *or* Neddy [slang]; Jerusalem pony, Arcadian nightingale, Missouri hummingbird, mountain *or* Rocky Mountain canary [all joc.]; jenny, jenny ass, jennet; wild ass, onager, kiang, chigetai.

11. *n.* mule, maud *or* Maud [slang]; hinny; sumpter mule, sumpter.

12. *adj.* equine, equestrian, equestral [rare]; horsy.

13. *adj.* asinine, mulish.

272. Vehicle
(See also **273. Ship**)

1. *n.* vehicle, conveyance, carriage, bus [slang], chariot [joc. exc. spec.].

2. *n.* wagon, wain [arch.]; dump wagon, dumpcart, spring wagon, sloven [East. Can. and Newfoundland].

3. *n.* van, caravan; covered wagon, prairie schooner [U.S.], Conestoga wagon *or* wain.

4. *n.* carriage, *voiture* [F.], voiturette, four-wheeler, buggy, gharry [Ind.]; coach, chariotee, chariot, phaeton, mail phaeton, dearborn [U.S.], break, tallyho *or* tallyho coach, four-in-hand coach, drag, curricle, whisky [obs.], landau, barouche, kittereen [W. Ind.], victoria, brougham, Concord buggy, wagonette, rockaway, britska, ekka [Ind.], araba, kibitka, berlin, sulky, desobligeant, *dormeuse* [F.].

runabout, glass coach, fly [Eng.], droshky; chaise, post chaise [Hist.]; clarence, growler [slang, Eng.]; calash, *calèche* [F.]; sociable *or* sociable coach, vis-à-vis; cabriolet, cabriole [erron.];

---

horse with wings!—SHAKESPEARE. A horse! a horse! my kingdom for a horse!—SHAKESPEARE. All lay the load on the willing horse.—FULLER.

272. I can't afford a carriage, / But you'll look sweet upon the seat / Of a bicycle built for

hackney, hackney coach, hack; fiacre, *vettura* [It.]; cariole, carryall [U.S.], charabanc *or* char-à-banc (*pl.* charabancs, char-à-bancs).

5. *n.* two-wheeler, two-wheeled cart *or* carriage, cart; tumbrel *or* tumbril, dray, Whitechapel cart, Cape cart [S. Afr.], *charrette* [F.], curricle, gig, tonga [Ind.], jigger, cabriolet, tilbury, dogcart, trap [coll.], cariole, road cart, shandrydan [Scot., Ir. and dial.].

bullock cart, hackery [Ind.]; dumpcart, tip cart, coup-cart [chiefly Scot.], coup *or* coop [obs. exc. dial.]; chaise, chay [corruption], shay [dial.], "one hoss shay" (Holmes); *calèche* [F.; Quebec], calash; jaunting *or* jaunty car, sidecar [Ir.], inside *or* outside jaunting car; hansom, hansom cab; jinrikisha [Jap.], ricksha [coll.]; handcart etc. *below* 272.11.

6. *n.* (public vehicles) stage, stagecoach, stage wagon [obs.], *diligence* [F.]; mail coach; omnibus, bus, kitereeen [Southw. Eng.]; motorbus, taxicab etc. *below* 272.15; hackney etc. *above* 272.4; hansom etc. *above*; train etc. *below* 272.18, 19; streetcar etc. *below* 272.20.

7. *n.* patrol wagon, wagon, police van, Black Maria [coll., U.S.].

8. *n.* equipage, rig, turnout [coll.], team, coach-and-four.

9. *n.* team, pair, span; tandem, randem; spike team, spike [U.S.], unicorn; three-in-hand, four-in-hand etc.; threeup, four-up etc. [U.S.]; coach-and-four.

10. *n.* truck, hand truck, warehouse *or* railroad truck, stake truck, wagon truck, tongue truck, dump truck, lorry, dolly; van, autotruck etc. *below* 272.15.

11. *n.* handcart, handbarrow; manumotor; pushcart, push car; barrow, wheelbarrow; baby carriage, wagon [coll.], perambulator, pram [chiefly Eng.], gocart; wheel chair, Bath chair; jinrikisha etc. *above* 272.5.

12. *n.* litter, portable couch; stretcher, palanquin, sedan *or* sedan chair, tonjon [Ceylon], norimon [Jap.], lectica [Rom. Antiq.], horse litter, camel litter, *cacolet* [F.], brancard, handbarrow; polki, muncheel, doolie, dandy, jampan, kajawah [all Ind.].

13. *n.* sled, sledge, sleigh; bob, bobsled *or* bobsleigh [U.S.]; double-ripper, double-runner [U.S.]; belly-bumper, belly-buster *or* belly-whopper [slang], pigsticker [slang], scoot [logging cant], drag, dray, skid, hurdle [Hist.], cutter, jumper [U.S. and Can.], toboggan, cariole [Can.], pung [U.S.]; ski (*pl.* ski *or* skis), snowshoes, skates; bob skate, bob [U.S.].

14. *n.* cycle, wheel [coll.], machine [coll.]; monocycle, quadricycle; hydrocycle; tricycle, trike [slang]; bicycle, bike [slang], jigger, boneshaker [slang]; push bicycle, push bike [coll., Eng.]; tandem bicycle, tandem; safety bicycle, safety [coll.]; motorcycle, motocycle, motorbike [slang]; velocipede; dandy horse, draisine, hobby; scooter.

15. *n.* automobile, autocar, motorcar, motocar; auto, motor, machine, car [all coll.]; bus, heap [U.S.], crate [U.S.], flivver, boat, petrol pram [Eng.], tub [all slang]; coupé, coup *or* coop [slang]; convertible coupé, touring coupé, coupelet; roadster, runabout, touring car, sedan, convertible sedan, sedan limousine, limousine, brougham, electric brougham, berline *or* berlin, coach, landaulet, berline-landaulet, phaeton, cabriolet, torpedo, racer, autobolide.

tractor, locomobile, steamer; electromobile, electric [coll.]; truck, autotruck, auto carrier [Eng.]; dump truck; lorry; van, moving van, transfer [local, U.S.]; taxicab, cab, taxi [coll.], autocab; nighthawk [slang, U.S.]; omnibus, bus, autobus, motorbus, jitney [coll.]; ambulance, hearse.

16. *n.* (allied automobile terms) tonneau, chassis, radiator, fender, running board, rumble seat; ignition, generator, distributor, self-starter, crank, flywheel, gear, gearbox, differential, piston, cylinder, cylinder head, manifold, intake *or* intake manifold, exhaust *or* exhaust pipe; carburetor *or* carburettor, ammeter, speedometer, oil gauge, brake, clutch, gear shifter, steering wheel, universal joint, crankshaft, transmission, overdrive, shock absorber, radius rod, cam, camshaft; spark plug, sparking plug [Eng.]; magneto, mag [slang]; safety gear, safety [coll.]; connecting rod, conrod [slang]; valve, gate [slang]; primer, choke, automatic choke; accelerator, gun [slang].

---

two.—H. DACRE. I've been workin' on the railroad, / All the livelong day.—UNKNOWN. In hacks and gilded chariots.—POPE.

engine, motor; top, turret top, convertible top; hood [U.S.], bonnet [Eng.]; windshield [U.S.], windscreen [Eng.]; tire, pneumatic tire, pneumatic; balloon tire, balloon; rebuild, retread; flat tire, flat; tube, inner tube; rim; gasoline, gas [coll.], petrol [Eng.]; trailer; garage.

17. *n.* tractor, traction engine; caterpillar tractor, caterpillar, cat [slang]; tank [Mil.], caterpillar tank; go-devil.

18. *n.* train; choo-choo, choo-choo train [both childish]; accommodation train; parliamentary train; passenger train; local, local train; special, special train; limited, limited train; express, express train; lightning express, cannon ball *or* cannon-ball express [slang], manifest [Railroad cant]; freight train [U.S. and Can.], freighter, goods train [Eng.], rattler [tramp slang, U.S.]; baggage train [U.S. and Can.], luggage train [Eng.]; electric train, electric [coll.]; subway [U.S.], underground [Eng.]; tube [coll.]; streamliner; 1st ∼, 2nd *or* 3rd class train; rolling stock; railway etc. (roadway) 627.5; trolley etc. (streetcar) *below* 272.20.

19. *n.* railway car, car, coach, carriage [Eng.]; passenger car, chair car, drawing-room car, palace car, parlor car, Pullman car; sleeping car, sleeper; freight car [U.S. and Can.], goods waggon [Eng.], rattler [tramp slang, U.S.]; boxcar [U.S.], box *or* covered waggon [Eng.]; flatcar, flat, truck [Eng.]; gondola *or* gondola car [U.S.], open waggon [Eng.]; baggage car [U.S. and Can.], luggage van [Eng.], van [Eng.]; stock car; dinghy; mail car, mail van [Eng.]; dining car *or* compartment, diner; smoking car *or* compartment, smoker; caboose, buggy [U.S.]; coal car; refrigerator car, reefer [tramp slang, U.S.]; tank car, tank; way car; rubble car, truck car; 1st-class ∼, 2nd-class *or* 3rd-class carriage *or* compartment, caravan [Eng.].

20. *n.* streetcar [U.S.], trolley car [U.S. and Can.], tram *or* tramcar [Eng.]; electric car, electric [coll.]; trolley bus, trackless trolley; surface car; subway car [U.S.], underground car [Eng.]; horsecar [U.S.], horse box [Eng.], jigger [cant, U.S.]; Jim Crow *or* Jim Crow car [coll., South. U.S.].

21. *n.* handcar, pushcart, push car, go-devil, trolley.

22. *adj.* vehicular, vehiculatory [rare]; curricular.

273. Ship
(See also 267. Navigation, 269. Mariner)

1. *n.* ship, watercraft, craft, vessel, bottom, bark, embarkation [arch.], boat, bus [slang], hulk, timber [poetic], tub [slang], bucket [slang], packet, hooker [derog.]; transport, transport ship *or* vessel; liner, ocean liner, ocean greyhound [coll.], floating hotel *or* palace; merchant ship *or* steamer, merchantman; freight steamer, freighter; packet, packet boat *or* ship.

steamer, steamship, steamboat; excursion steamer, hurrah boat [slang]; paddle boat *or* steamer, inside walkee [pidgin Eng.]; side-wheeler [coll.], side-kicker [slang, U.S.], sidewinder [slang, U.S.]; stern-wheeler [coll., U.S.], stem-winder [slang], kickup [slang, U.S.]; turbine steamer, screw steamer, mail steamer etc.; rotor ship, rotor; coaler, collier; spar-deck vessel, spar-decker; ark, tender, storeship, whaler, slaver, coaster, fishing boat *or* vessel, trawler, coast guard *or* revenue cutter [U.S.], caravel, argosy; derelict; man-o-war, submarine etc. (combatant) 726.11.

2. *n.* sailing vessel, sailboat, sail, sailer, windjammer [coll.], barge [obs.], galleon; fore-and-aft schooner, fore-and-aft *or* fore-and-after [coll.]; three-masted ∼, four-masted etc. schooner; three-master, four-master etc.; three-sticker, four-sticker etc. [coll.]; baggala, snow, brig, hermaphrodite brig, brigantine, barkentine, bark, four-masted bark, schooner, topsail schooner, bastard schooner, scooter, *chasse-marée* [F.].

sloop, cutter, yacht, yawl, dandy, ketch, smack, lugger, corvette *or* corvet, clipper, galleon [Hist.], galiot, galleass, polacre *or* polacca, shallop [now rare], catboat, cat, buss, pinnace [Hist. *or* poetic], frigate, bully [Newfoundland], square-rigger, outrigger, keelboat, proa [Malaysia], praam, caravel, felucca, bilander, dogger, hooker, carrack [Hist.], corsair, piragua, pirogue, tartan, junk, lorcha [Pg.], saic, xebec, dhow.

---

273. Whither, O splendid ship, thy white sails crowding, / Leaning across the bosom of the urgent West.—BRIDGES.   All the marvelous beauty of their bows.—MASEFIELD.   Those

3. *n.* galley, pentaconter, bireme, trireme, quadrireme, quinquereme, foist, galley foist [all Hist.]; galleas etc. *above.*

4. *n.* boat, bateau [chiefly Can. and Louisiana] (*pl.* bateaux), catboat, cat; tugboat, tug; dispatch boat, advice boat [arch.]; pilot boat, pilot; ferry boat, ferry; jolly boat, jolly; ark, broadhorn [West. U.S.]; cockle, cockleboat, cockleshell, cockboat, cock [obs.], cog; shell, racing shell; motorboat, outboard motorboat, speedboat; hydroplane, gliding boat, hydroglider; iceboat, ice canoe, ice yacht; pair-oar, four-oar, eight-oar etc.; rowboat *or* rowing boat.

barge, lighter, hoy, catamaran, pinnace, launch, lifeboat, flyboat, canalboat, flatboat, shallop, gig, funny [Eng.], skiff, scow, dinghy, wherry, coble, punt [chiefly Eng.], lerret [Eng.], randan, coracle, houseboat, dahabeah [Egypt], wanigan [U.S.], nuggar [Egypt], praam, gondola, caïque, kayak, bungo, canoe, log canoe, dugout, piragua, pirogue, bunder boat [Ind.], sampan; sailboat etc. *above* 273.2.

5. *n.* float, raft, pontoon.

6. *n.* marine, "wooden walls" (Themistocles); mercantile *or* merchant marine; argosy, fleet, flotilla; whaling fleet, fishing fleet etc.; rum row [coll., U.S.]; navy etc. 726.10.

7. *n.* (parts of ships) sick bay, faker's palace [slang]; rail, monkey rail; strake, garboard strake; keel, false keel, bilge keel; keelson, sister *or* side keelson, bilge keelson; back, keel and keelson; conning tower; crow's-nest; foretop, maintop, mizzentop; helm, lee helm, weather helm, stearing gear, hand gear, electrohydraulic steering gear, telemotor, tiller, rudder, rudderstook, rudderpost; post, sternpost; sheets, foresheets, stern sheets; hawsepiece, hawse timber.

topside; below, brig, hold, stokehold; hatch, heck [dial.], hatchway; conning tower hatch; companionway, companion, companion ladder; gangway, gangplank; galley, stateroom, roundhouse, head, scuttle butt, stanchion, futtock, cutwater, bow, beam, counter, poop, heel, water line, waterway, bulwarks, sail loft, entrance, run, hawsehole, limber hole, porthole, bull's-eye; sheave hole, foresheet *or* mainsheet sheave hole; lee side, weather side etc. (side) 236.2, 3; prow etc. (front) 234.3; stern etc. (rear) 235.7.

8. *n.* deck, floor; main deck, lower deck, orlop deck, bridge deck, protective deck, promenade deck, boat deck, second ∼, third etc. deck, berth deck [now rare], gun deck, watertight deck, splinter deck, superstructure deck, half deck, partial hold deck; upper *or* top deck, weather deck, hurricane deck, shelter deck, spar deck; poop, poop deck, poop royal [obs.]; forecastle *or* fo'c'sle, forecastle deck; anchor deck, monkey deck *or* forecastle; platform deck, platform, first ∼, second ∼ etc. platform; forward deck, after deck, middle deck, forward ∼, after *or* middle protective section; inclined protective deck, inclined splinter deck; between-decks, 'tween-decks.

9. *n.* rigging, rig, tackling, tackle, gear, service *or* serving, ropework, roping, hempen bridle [slang]; standing rigging, running rigging; forerigging, fore-topmast rigging; cordage etc. 205.4.

10. *n.* (ropes) fast, bow-head ∼, quarter ∼, breast *or* stern fast; forerunner, foreganger; hawser, halser [obs.]; earing, head earing, reef earing; guess-rope, guess-warp; guest rope, grab rope [U.S. navy], boat line [U.S.]; roband *or* ropeband, robbin; stay, fore-skysail stay, foreroyal stay, flying-jib stay, fore-topgallant stay, jibstay, fore-topmast stay, fore-topmast staysail-stay, forestay, main-skysail stay, main-royal stay, main-topgallant stay, main-topmast stay, mainstay, mizzen-skysail stay, mizzen-royal stay, mizzen-topgallant stay, mizzen-topmast stay, mizzen stay, bobstay; backstay, fore-topmast backstay, fore-topgallant backstay, foreroyal backstay, fore-skysail backstay.

brace, fore-skysail brace, fore-royal brace, fore-topgallant brace, upper *or* lower fore-topsail brace, forebrace, main-skysail brace, main-royal brace, main-topgallant brace, upper *or* lower main-topsail brace, main brace, mizzen-skysail brace, mizzen-royal brace, mizzen-topgallant brace, upper *or* lower mizzen-topgallant brace, upper *or* lower mizzen-topsail brace, crossjack brace; lift, fore-

---

proud ones swaying home / With mainyards backed and bows a cream of foam.—MASEFIELD. Oh, the little cargo-boats, that sail the wet seas roun', / They're just the same as you an' me a-plyin' up an' down!—KIPLING. That packet of assorted miseries which we call a

skysail lift, foreroyal lift, fore-topgallant lift, fore-topsail lift, fore lift, main-skysail lift, main lift, main-royal lift, main-topgallant lift, main-topsail lift, mizzen-skysail lift, mizzen-royal lift, mizzen-topgallant lift, mizzen-topsail lift, crossjack lift, lower-boom topping lift.

halyard, foretrysail peak halyard, maintrysail peak halyard, spanker peak halyard; tack, foretack, lee tack, starboard *or* port tack; guy, jib guy, flying jib guy; martingale, jib martingale, flying jib martingale; shroud, bowsprit shroud, fore-topgallant shroud, foreroyal shroud, fore-skysail shroud, futtock shroud, after shroud; vang, fore-trysail vang, maintrysail vang, spanker vang; sheet, spanker sheet, foresheet, mainsheet, lee sheet, weather sheet; gasket, sea gasket, harbor gasket; footropes, Flemish horses, Jacob's ladder, ratline *or* ratlin, life line, whisker jumper, stirrup, backropes, swifter, lanyard, mooring pendant, painter, timenoguy, boltrope, brail, span, downhaul, messenger, buntline, spring, bowline; bowline knot, hawser bend etc. (knot) 45.3.

11. *n.* tackle, purchase; foretackle, runner and tackle, runner, single tackle, double *or* twofold tackle, threefold ~, fourfold etc. tackle, stay tackle, deck tackle, hatch tackle, yard tackle, fore-and-aft tackle, single-whip tackle, gun tackle, luff tackle, single *or* double Spanish burton, Bell's tackle *or* purchase.

12. *n.* spars, timber; mast, pole, stick [coll.], tree [coll.]; bare poles, soldier's masts [coll.]; foremast, mainmast, mizzenmast, topmast, fore-topmast, main-topmast, mizzen-topmast, topgallant mast, fore-topgallant mast, main-topgallant mast, mizzen-topgallant mast, foreroyal mast, main-royal mast, mizzen-royal mast, skysail mast, fore-skysail mast, main-skysail mast, mizzen-skysail mast; yard, foreyard, main yard, crossjack yard, fore-topsail yard, lower *or* upper fore-topsail yard, main-topsail yard, lower *or* upper main-topsail yard, mizzen-topsail yard, lower mizzen-topsail yard, topgallant yard, fore-topgallant yard, main-topgallant yard, mizzen-topgallant yard.

foreroyal yard, main-royal yard, mizzen-royal yard, skysail yard, fore-skysail yard, main-skysail yard, mizzen-skysail yard; sprit, bowsprit; boom, jib boom, flying jib boom, spanker boom, lower boom, fore-topmast-studding-sail boom, main-topmast-studding-sail boom, fore-topgallant-studding-sail boom, main-topgallant-studding-sail boom, foreroyal-studding-sail boom, main-royal-studding-sail boom, martingale *or* dolphin striker boom, whisker boom; gaff, trysail gaff, foretrysail gaff, main-trysail gaff, spanker gaff; bumpkin *or* bumkin *or* boomkin, tack bumpkin, brace bumpkin, mainbrace bumpkin; crosstree; yardarm; jack, fore jack; doubling of the masts; sheer pole.

13. *n.* sail, canvas, muslin, cloth, rag [coll.]; balloon sail, ballooner; mainsail; mizzen sail, crossjack; jib, inner jib, outer jib, flying jib; staysail, fore-topmast staysail, main staysail, main-topmast staysail, main-topgallant staysail, main-royal staysail, mizzen staysail, mizzen-topmast staysail, mizzen-topgallant staysail, mizzen-royal staysail; stern staysail, jimbo [cant]; topsail, fore-topsail, lower *or* upper fore-topsail, lower *or* upper main topsail, lower *or* upper mizzen topsail, fore gaff-topsail, main gaff-topsail, baby jib topsail.

topgallant sail, fore-topgallant sail, main topgallant sail, mizzen topgallant sail; royal, foreroyal, main royal, mizzen royal; skysail, sky-gazer [rare], skyscraper [coll.], cloud cleaner [slang]; main skysail, mizzen skysail, fore-skysail; moonsail, moonraker, stargazer [rare], jolly jumper; studding sail, lower studding sail, fore-topmast studding sail, fore-topgallant studding sail, foreroyal studding sail, main-topmast studding sail, main-topgallant studding sail, main-royal studding sail; spanker; lugsail, lug, dipping lug, standing lug, balance *or* French lug; fly-by-night; kites, flying kites, lady's pocket handkerchief [slang], sail teaser [slang]; crowd of sail.

14. *n.* (equipment) hawse bag, jackass; calking iron, hawsing iron [rare]; anchor, hook *or* mud hook [slang]; Dunn anchor, Baldt anchor, bower anchor,

---

ship.—KIPLING. The ship, a fragment detached from the earth.—CONRAD. Some frail bark in winter's midnight roar.—SHELLEY.

A great ship asks deep waters.—G. HERBERT. Your argosies with portly sail . . . / Do overpeer the petty traffickers.—SHAKESPEARE.

sheet anchor, stream anchor, stern anchor, center anchor, starboard *or* port anchor; belaying pin; toggle; kevel; bollard; windlass, horizontal windlass, vertical windlass, capstan, nigger [U.S.]; mooring swivel *or* shackle; buoy, life buoy; pump, bilge pump; holystone; bible, prayer book, ecclesiastical brick [all slang]; hawse hook; hawsepipe; hawser clamp; oar, paddle, scull, sweep, pole; barometer, barograph, thermograph, hygrograph, anemoscope, anemometer, compass; dipsy lead, fathometer etc. (sounding) 208.4.

15. *adj.* seaworthy, sea-kindly, snug, bold; watertight, waterproof, drop-dry [cant]; A 1, A one, A 1 at Lloyd's; navigable etc. 267.49.

16. *adj.* rigged, decked, trimmed; monkey-rigged [rare]; bald-headed [slang]; shipshape etc. 267.67.

273a. Aircraft
(See also **267a.** Aeronautics, **269a.** Aeronaut)

1. *n.* aircraft, aerocraft, aeroplane, airplane, plane [coll.], aero [coll.], aeronef, ship, *avion* [F.], machine, flying machine; bus, crate, boat, jalopy, job, heap [all slang]; landplane; monoplane, single-decker [coll.]; high-wing *or* low-wing monoplane, midwing monoplane; parasol monoplane, parasol; biplane, double-decker [coll.]; triplane, tripe [slang], triple-decker [coll.]; quadruplane, quad [coll.], four-decker [coll.]; multiplane; sesquiplane; single-seater, *monoplace* [F.]; two-seater, *biplace* [F.].

sport plane, flyabout [coll.]; executive *or* club plane; pusher, pusher plane *or* airplane; canard; tractor, tractor plane *or* airplane; *monocoque* [F.], monocoupe; shipplane, shipboard plane; tailless airplane; tandem, tandem plane *or* airplane; rotor, rotor plane; gyroplane; Autogiro *or* autogiro, giro, windmill *or* windmill plane [slang]; taxiplane, taxi; helicopter; ornithopter, orthopter, wind flapper [cant], mechanical bird; transport, transport plane, aerobus [coll.]; air liner; cruiser, air crusier; feeder; cargo plane; mailplane; stratoliner; trainer; penguin; truss etc. (parts) *below*

273a. I wouldn't be surprised to see a railroad in the air, / Or a Yankee in a flyin' ship a goin' most anywhere.—J. H. YATES.

273a.10; kite; rocket ship *or* plane, robot plane; construction model, dog ship [cant].

2. *n.* battleplane, warplane, combat plane, fighting plane, fighter; *avion-canon* [F.]; attack plane, attack bomber; bombing plane, bomber, cuckoo [slang]; torpedo bomber; diving *or* dive bomber, hornet [slang]; patrol plane, patrol bomber; scout plane, scout; pursuit plane, pursuit, army *or* navy pursuit, peashooter [slang]; observation plane; utility plane; Spitfire etc. (makes) *below* 273a.4.

3. *n.* seaplane, waterplane, hydroplane, hydro-airplane, hydro-aeroplane, aerohydroplane, aeroboat, duck [slang]; clipper, flying boat, boat seaplane; amphibian *or* amphibion, amphibian transport.

4. *n.* (airplane makes) Bell P-39, Airocobra, Boeing B-17E, Flying Fortress, Boeing XPBB-1, Sea Ranger, Brewster F2A-1, Buffalo, Consolidated B-24D, Liberator, Consolidated PBY-5, Cataline, Consolidated PB2Y-3, Coronado, Curtiss-Wright CW-21, Curtiss SB2C-1, Helldiver, Curtiss P-40, Hawk, Tomahawk, Warhawk, Kittyhawk, Curtiss C-46, Commando, Curtiss C-76, Caravan, Douglas A-20A, Havoc *or* Boston, Douglas SBD-3, Dauntless, Douglas C-47, Sky Train, Grumman TBF-1, Avenger, Grumman F4F-3, Wildcat, Lockheed A-29, Hudson, Lockheed B-34, Ventura, Lockheed P-38, Lightning, Martin B-26, Marauder, North American B-25, Mitchell, North American P-51, Mustang, Republic P-47B, Thunderbolt, Vought-Sikorsky SB2U-3, Vindicator, Vought-Sikorsky F4U-1, Corsair, Vultee P-66, Vanguard, Vultee A-35, Vengeance, Aeronca L-3, Defender, Piper L-4B-4, Taylorcraft L-2A, flivver plane [slang], flying jeep, grasshopper [both slang], Curtiss J.N., Jenny [slang], Curtiss N.C., Nancy [slang], Douglas B-19 (all U.S.).

Armstrong-Whitworth Whitley, Avro Manchester, Avro Lancaster, Avro Anson, Blackburn Skua, Blackburn Roc, Boulton-Paul Defiant, Bristol Blenheim, Bristol Beaufort, Bristol Beaufighter, Bristol Bombay, De Havilland Mosquito, Fairey Swordfish, Fairey Albacore, Fairey Seafox, Gloster Gladiator, Handley-Page Hampden, Handley-Page Halifax, Hawker Hurricane, Short Stirling, Short Sunderland, Supermarine Spitfire,

Spits [slang], Vickers Wellington, West- and Whirlwind, Westland Lysander (all British).
IL-2, Stormovik, I-15, Chato, YAK-4, I-53, Chica, MIG-3, YAK-1, ARK-3, KOR-1 (all Russian); Amiot, Bloch, Breguet, Breguet 462 B-4, Vultur, Dewoitine, Farman, Hanriot, Latecoere, Leo, Loire, Morane-Saulnier, Nieuport, Potez (all French); Fokker, Koolhaven (both Dutch); Arado, Blohm and Voss, Dornier, Fieseler Storch, Focke-Wulf Focke-Wulf FW-200, Kurier, Heinkel, Henschel, Junkers, Junkers Ju-87B, Stuka, Messerschmitt (all German); Breda, Caproni, Caproni Reggiane, Caproni Vizzola, Fiat, Macchi, Meridionali, Piaggio, Savoia-Marchetti, Savoia-Marchetti SM.82, Canguru (all Italian); Mitsubishi, Mitsubishi B-27, Darai, Kawasaki, Aichi, Kawanishi, Nakajima, Showa, Mitsubishi S-00, Zero, Hiro, Mitsubishi H-96 (all Japanese).

5. *n.* aerostat, lighter-than-air craft; aeronat, airship, ship, dirigible, blimp [coll.]; rigid ~, nonrigid ~, semirigid *or* flexible airship *or* dirigible; Zeppelin *or* zeppelin, zepp [coll.], Graf Zeppelin; balloon, dirigible balloon, captive balloon, free balloon, pilot balloon, barrage balloon, sounding balloon, ceiling balloon, stratosphere balloon; kite balloon; kite sausage, sausage balloon, sausage [all slang]; observation balloon, obbo [slang, Eng.]; fire balloon, montgolfier; envelope etc. (parts) *below* 273a.12.

6. *n.* glider, gliding machine, aerodone; sailplane; aviette; student glider.

7. *n.* parachute, chute [coll.], umbrella [slang], brolly [slang, Eng.]; pilot parachute; shroud lines, harness, pack, vent, rip cord, safety loop; parachute jump, brolly-hop [slang, Eng.].

8. *n.* kite, box kite, Hargrave *or* cellular kite, Eddy kite, tetrahedral kite, observation *or* war kite [now rare].

9. *n.* carrier, carrier ship, aircraft *or* airplane carrier, shipplane carrier, seaplane carrier.

10. *n.* (airplane parts) truss, wing truss; stringers; stay, jackstay; strut, drag strut *or* compression rib; oleo leg; drag wire, drift wire, stagger *or* incidence wire, brace wire, lift wire, control wires, antidrag wire, antilift *or* landing wire, safety wire; patch, channel patch, finger patch, suspension patch; gusset; gore;

propeller, prop [cant], airscrew [Eng.], stick [cant], dead stick [cant]; controllable propeller, adjustable propeller; gyroscope, windmill [slang]; propeller root; spinner; nose, snout [cant], bow; *cabane* [F.]; fuselage, body, *monocoque* [F.]; nacelle; *longéron* [F.].

hood, bonnet; gas-shaft hood, maneuvering valve hood; cowling, cowl; cockpit cowling, engine cowling, ring cowling, cowling former, cowling pan; turtleback; wing, *aile* [F.]; wing rib, former *or* false rib; loom; deck; walking beam; washin, washout; leading edge, entering edge, trailing edge; spray strip; cat strip; cockpit, office [slang], cabin, hatch, booby hatch [slang]; tail unit, ~ assembly *or* group, tail, empennage; tail boom; instrument board *or* panel; controls; control stick *or* lever, Joyce stick, joy stick [slang], stick [cant]; horn; automatic pilot, gyropilot, robot pilot, mechanical pilot, macaviator.

throttle, gun [slang]; quadrant, control quadrant; carburetor altitude control, altitude mixture control, automatic boost control; rudder bar, rudder pedals; rudder, diving rudder; elevating rudder, elevator, flipper [slang]; control surface, air control, airfoil *or* aerofoil; aileron, external aileron, Frise aileron, slotted aileron, upper-surface aileron; flap, split flap; tab, trimming tab; slat; pilot plane; air scoop; stabilizer, tail plane, stub-wing stabilizer; fin, tail fin, vertical fin, offset fin, fin carrier; spoiler, interceptor.

landing gear, undercarriage, beaching gear; retractable landing gear; emergency landing gear, flotation gear; oleo gear; tail wheel; tail skid, wing skid, jury skid, skid fin; runners [for snow or ice]; bumper bag; arresting hook; wheel cowlings, pants *or* wheel pants [slang], tin drawers [slang]; float, pontoon; stabilizing *or* side float, inboard *or* outboard stabilizing float, single *or* central float; keel; port *or* portside, starboard *or* starboard side; gun mount; bomb rack, bomb sight, bomb release; tachometer etc. (aeronautical instruments) 267a. 29.

11. *n.* aeromotor, mill [slang], power plant; cam engine, radial engine, double-row radial engine, compression-ignition engine, vertical engine, inverted engine, right-hand *or* left-hand engine, rotary, supercharged engine, axial-type, V-type,

W-type, X-type; motor mount; fuel tank, belly tank; tank baffle; fuel dope.

12. *n.* (aerostat parts) envelope, gas chamber *or* cell; ballonet *or* ballonette, balloonet [erron.]; ballonet diaphragm; rip panel; manhole appendix; gland; pressure flap; deflation *or* inflation sleeve; antiflutter wire, chord wire, diametral wire, radial wire, fairing wire, main *or* secondary shear wire, netting wire; axial cable, control cable, mooring cable; cone, axial cone, danger cone, mooring cone; drag ∼, trail *or* guide rope; control line, handling line, landing *or* mooring line, yaw line, mast yaw line, sandbag line, suspension line.

mooring harness; tail drag; girder, box girder, cruciform girder; walkway girder; longitudinal, main longitudinal, intermediate longitudinal; transverse, main transverse, intermediate transverse; catwalk; gondola, car; side *or* wing car, subcloud car, observation car; observation platform; basket; basket suspension, suspension bar *or* ring, winch suspension; free-balloon net, gas-cell net, inflation net.

274. Velocity
(See 275. Slowness)

1. *n.* velocity, swiftness, quickness etc. *adj.*; speed, celerity, pernicity [obs.], rapidity, haste, hurry, dispatch; rate, rate of motion, bat [coll.], pace, tread, step, stride, gait, clip [coll.], progress, lick [coll.], legs [slang, chiefly Naut.]; eagle speed, lightning speed; smart ∼, lively ∼, rattling ∼ [coll.], spanking ∼ [slang], strapping ∼ [slang], swift etc. *adj.* rate *or* pace, round pace, tall stepping [slang]; flying, flight; expedition etc. (activity) 682.2; haste etc. (voluntary action) 684; transience etc. 111.

2. *n.* acceleration; pickup, speed-up [both coll.].

3. *n.* run, race [obs. or Scot.], cursitation [rare]; dash, rush, scurry, scamper, scud, scuddle [obs. or Scot.], scuttle, scour, scorch [coll.], sprint; spurt *or* spirt, spurtle, burst, burst of speed, flutter [coll.]; canter; gallop, lope, high lope, hand gallop, full gallop; dead run; trot, round trot; dogtrot etc. 275.2; quickstep march etc. (gait) 266.5.

4. *n.* race, career, course; automobile race, horse race, foot race, marathon *or* marathon race, boat race, torpids [Oxford Univ.], relay *or* relay race, go-as-you-please [coll.], Derby, sweepstakes, handicap *or* handicap race, steeplechase, hurdle race, broose [Scot. and North. Eng.], lampadedromy [Gr. Antiq.], regatta.

5. *n.* speeder, scorcher [slang], clipper [coll.], flier, goer, stepper, hot-shot [slang, U.S.], hummer [slang], hustler [coll.], sizzler [slang], speed demon *or* maniac [coll.]; racer, foot racer, automobile racer etc.

6. *n.* (comparisons) lightning, greased lightning [slang], thunderbolt, streak of lightning, streak, blue streak [coll.], light, electricity, wireless, telegraph, wind, shot, cannon ball, rocket, arrow, dart, hydrargyrum, quicksilver, mercury, express train, torrent, bat, bat out of hell [slang], eagle, antelope, courser, race horse, barb, gazelle, greyhound, hare, doe, squirrel, camel bird, swallow, swallow flight, chickaree, chipmunk, hackee [U.S.], ostrich.

7. *n.* Mercury, Ariel, Puck, Camilla, Harlequin.

8. *n.* velocimeter, speedometer; log, patent log, log line.

9. *v.* speed, move quickly etc. *adv.*, trip, fisk [obs.], hie [arch. or poetic], hasten, haste [literary], make haste, hurry, sprint, post, spank, scud, scuddle [obs. or Scot.], scuttle, scurry, scamper, skedaddle [slang], scoot, scour, go it, come it [coll.], ball the jack [slang, U.S.], run, run like mad [coll.], run along, cut along [coll.], bowl along, bolt, dart, fly, flit, wing one's way, fly on the wings of the wind, outstrip the wind, breeze *or* breeze along [slang], hit *or* burn the breeze [slang], split the breeze *or* wind [slang].

make time, race, shoot, tear, tear along, hop *or* hop along [slang], zip, whiz, whisk, sweep, skim, brush, barrel [slang, U.S.], boom, bound, spring, scorch [coll.], sizzle [slang], dash on, clip [coll.], chase [coll.], cover ground, get over the ground; dig, get out and dig [both slang], get [slang, U.S.], git [dial., U.S.], get up *or* out and get *or* git [slang, U.S.], bundle, bundle on *or* along, hump *or* hump it [slang, U.S.], go like lightning, ~ a shot etc. *n.*, go like a bat out of hell [slang] etc. *adv.*, go hell-bent for election [slang, U.S.] etc. *adv.*, powder [coll.], pour it on [slang, U.S.], ride hard, clap spurs to one's horse, railroad [slang, U.S.].

step *or* step along [coll.], step lively [coll.], step on it [slang], step on the gas [slang], do some tall stepping [slang], make strides *or* rapid strides, make the best of one's way, put one's best leg *or* foot foremost, stir one's stumps [slang], peg [coll.]; gallop, lope, trot, canter; carry sail, crowd sail, give her beans [Naut. slang], crack *or* pack on sail, put on sail [all Naut. or fig.]; go all out [Sport. slang], go *or* run wide open, go at full blast [coll.] etc. *adv.*; march in quick *or* double-quick time, make a forced march [Mil.]; race, run a race, boat-race, horse-race etc. *above* 274.4; act with haste 684.3; cut and run [coll.] etc. (depart quickly) 293.5.

10. *v.* accelerate, put on, put on more speed, crack on, speed up, hurry up [coll.], quicken, quicken *or* mend one's pace, gain ground, pick up speed; give her the gas, step on her tail; urge, spur etc. (hasten) 684.2.

11. *v.* spurt, make a spurt, make a dash, dash ahead *or* along, put on *or* make a burst of speed.

12. *v.* keep up with, keep pace with, run neck and neck.

13. *adj.* fast, speedy, swift, rapid, quick, fleet, expeditious, snappy [slang]; agile, nimble, nimble-footed, light-footed, light-legged, light of heel; winged, eagle-winged; mercurial, electric, telegraphic; swift as an arrow etc. *n.*, quick as lightning etc. *n.*, quick as thought; hasty etc. 684.5; sudden etc. 113.5.

14. *adv.* swiftly, quickly etc. *adj.*; fast, quick, double-quick, in double-quick time, on the double *or* double-quick [coll.], apace, with speed etc. *n.*, at a great rate, at railway speed, on eagle's wings, at a good bat *or* clip [coll.], with great *or*

all haste, posthaste, P.D.Q. [slang], headlong, hell-bent [slang, U.S.], hell-bent for election *or* leather [slang, U.S.], tantivy [arch.], alive [coll.], hand over hand *or* fist.

lickety-split, lickety-cut, lickety-brindle [all slang, U.S.]; trippingly, by leaps and bounds, whip and spur, *velis et remis* [L.], *ventre à terre* [F.]; like a shot, like a bat out of hell [slang], like lightning, like greased lightning [coll.] etc. *n.*; like sixty [coll., U.S.], like all forty [slang], like all possessed [coll., U.S.], like mad [coll.], like sin [slang]; to beat the band, ~ the Dutch, ~ the deuce, ~ the devil etc. [slang]; with rapid strides, with giant strides, *à pas de géant* [F.], in seven-league boots; in high, in high gear *or* speed; under press of sail, ~ canvas, ~ sail and steam [Naut.]; with haste etc. (hastily) 684.7; *allegro* [It.] etc. (music) 415.32.

15. *adv.* at full speed, with all speed, in full sail, at full drive, at the top of one's speed, for all one is worth [coll.], as fast as one's legs *or* heels will carry one, as fast as one can lay feet to the ground, all out [Sport. slang], wide open; at full blast, ~ bat, ~ butt, ~ chisel, ~ drive *or* pelt [all chiefly coll.].

275. Slowness
(See 274. Velocity)

1. *n.* slowness, leisureliness, sluggishness etc. *adj.*; drawl; lentitude, lentor [rare]; languor etc. 683.4; durability etc. 110.

2. *n.* slow motion, leisurely gait *or* pace, walk; creep, crawl; snail's *or* tortoise's pace, snail's trot; strolling gait, saunter, stroll; dead *or* funeral march, slow march, slow time; mincing steps; dog trot, jog trot; jog, rack; amble, pace etc. (gait) 266.5.

3. *n.* retardation, retardment, retard; slackening, slowing down etc. *v.*; slow-down, slow-up, letup, ease-off, ease-up [all coll.]; deceleration, negative *or* minus acceleration [all Mech.]; drag, lag; delay etc. 133.2.

4. *n.* slow goer, slow-foot, slow coach [coll.], slowpoke [coll.], poke [slang,

---

in vain.—JOHNSON.   To thy speed add wings. —MILTON.   I'll put a girdle round about the earth / In forty minutes.—SHAKESPEARE.

275. When left to herself, Nature is in no particular hurry.—VAN LOON.   He is easy-paced; this snail.—DONNE.   I will thitherward hie

U.S.], lingerer, loiterer, dawdler, dawdle, laggard, stiff [slang], stick-in-the-mud [coll.], drone, slug, sluggard, slugabed [arch.], Weary Willie [coll.], dead one or 'un [slang]; tortoise, snail; idler etc. 683.7.

5. *v.* move slowly etc. *adv.*, slug [dial.], lag, drag, drag one's freight [slang], drawl [now rare], trail, linger, loiter, dawdle, dally, dillydally, take one's time, take one's own sweet time [coll.], get no place fast [slang], inch, inch along, steal along, go at a snail's pace; walk, traipse *or* trapes [dial.], mosey [slang, U.S.], poke; saunter, stroll; toddle, waddle, wabble, wobble, wamble; slouch, shuffle, shamble; flag, falter, halt, hobble; limp, claudicate [obs.]; totter, stagger; plod, plug [slang], trudge, stump, lumber; plod along, poke along etc.; rub on, jog on; jog-trot, dogtrot; mince, step short; march in slow time, march in funeral procession; hang back, procrastinate etc. (be late) 133.3–7; be leisurely etc. (*see* leisurely etc. 685.4).

6. *v.* creep, crawl, go on hands and knees, grovel; worm, worm along, worm one's way.

7. *v.* retard, delay, decelerate [Mech.], slow down *or* up, let up, ease up, slacken, slacken speed, slacken one's pace, reduce the speed, relax, moderate, check, curb, rein in, throttle down, lose ground; put on the drag, brake, apply the brake, put on the brakes; reef, shorten *or* take in sail [Naut.]; back water, backpedal; clip the wings.

8. *adj.* slow, slack, leisurely, lingering etc. *v.*; dillydallying, dillydally [obs. exc. dial.]; moderate, gentle, easy, deliberate, gradual; imperceptible, insensible; slow-going, slow-moving, slow-creeping, slow-crawling, slow-running, slow-sailing; slow-foot, slow-footed, slow-legged, slow-gaited, slow-paced, slow-stepped, slow-winged; snaillike, turtlelike, tortoiselike; poking, poky, slow-poky [coll]; dilatory, tardy etc. (late) 133.8, 9; indolent, languid etc. 683.13, 14; protracted etc. 110.10.

9. *adj.* creeping, crawling etc. *v.*; reptatorial *or* reptatory, reptant, repent.

10. *adv.* slowly etc. *adj.*, leisurely, slow, dead slow [coll.], slow as slow, slower than death, ~ cold molasses [coll.], ~ a funeral *or* the seven-year itch [coll.], too slow to grow fast [slang]; at a snail's *or* turtle's pace, at a funeral pace; with mincing steps, with faltering *or* halting steps; at slow *or* half speed, under easy sail [Naut.], in low gear *or* speed; in slow tempo, in march time; *largo* [It.] etc. (music) 415.31.

11. *adv.* gradually etc. *adj.*, gradatim; step by step, bit by bit, little by little, by little and little, inch by inch, an inch at a time, by inches, by degrees, by slow degrees; consecutively, *seriatim* [L.].

276. Impulse
(See 277. Recoil)

1. *n.* impulse, impulsion, impelling force, impetus; momentum, moment [Tech.]; push, pulsion, thrust, shove, boost [coll., U.S.], boom; jog, jolt, jostle; butt, bunt; discharge etc. (explosion) 173.3; throw etc. (propulsion) 284; instigation etc. (motivation) 615.2.

2. *n.* clash, collision, colliding etc. *v.*, cannon, occursion [obs.], encounter, meeting, bump, crash, impact; appulsion, appulse; shock, shog [rare], brunt; *élan* [F.]; percussion, concussion; smash, smashup, crack-up [all coll.]; charge etc. (attack) 716.

3. *n.* blow, dint, stroke, hit, knock, bat [now coll.], slam, bang, crack [coll.], plunk [coll.], whack, smack, thwack, rap, wipe [dial. and slang], box, cuff, buffet, fillip, belt [slang], clout [coll.], squash, douse [now dial. and slang], whop [now dial.], swap [obs.], swat [slang], punch, punce [obs.], poke, dig, brunt [obs.], thump, pelt, yerk [obs. exc. dial.], jab, plug [slang], cut, chop, clip [coll.], lick [coll.], peg [dial. and coll.], soak [slang], sock [slang]

tap, rap, pat, dab; slap, flap; spank, whip, stripe; thrust, pass, swing, lunge, foin [arch.]; side *or* glancing blow, side-

---

276. The first blow is half the battle.—GOLDSMITH. The first blow is as much as two.—G. HERBERT. A hit, a very palpable hit.—SHAKESPEARE.

winder [slang]; sideswipe or sideswiper [coll.]; backhand, backhander; haymaker, roundhouse, Long Melford [all boxing cant]; carom, double carom [both billiards], cannon [billiards, chiefly Eng.]; kick, boot, *ruade* [F.], calcitration; beating etc. (punishment) 972.3.

4. *n.* hammer, sledge hammer, claw hammer, tack hammer, steam hammer; mall, maul [arch.], mallet; flail, frail [dial.]; ram, rammer, ramrod, battering-ram; monkey; tamp, tamper, tamping iron; pile driver, pile-driving engine; tap, tapper; punch, puncher; bat; cant hook [U.S. and dial. Eng.]; cudgel etc. (club) 727.7; ax etc. 253.6; pulverizer etc. 330.4; pulper etc. 354.3; mortar etc. 144.4.

5. *n.* (science of mechanical forces) mechanics; dynamics, dynometry; kinetics, kinematics etc. (motion) 264.4.

6. *n.* (instruments) dynamometer, dynamograph; seismometer, seismograph.

7. *v.* impel, give an impetus etc. *n.*, set going or agoing, put or set in motion, move, animate, actuate, forward, drive, thrust, push, shove, boost [coll., U.S.], boom; goad, prod, poke, jog, jolt, jostle, hustle, hurtle; elbow, shoulder; bunt, butt, put [dial., Eng.], run ∼, bump or butt against, knock or run one's head against; cant; throw, start etc. (propel) 284.10–14; urge, prompt, instigate etc. (motivate) 615.7.

8. *v.* strike, hit, smite, knock, box, cuff, thump, belt [slang], bat [now coll.], bang, slam [now chiefly dial.], dash, poke, punch, pink, thwack, smack, bang, crack [coll.], wipe [dial. and slang], whack, whop [now dial.], clip [slang], plunk [coll.], swat [slang], swap [obs.], peg [dial. and coll.], wallop [Scot., dial. Eng., coll. U.S.], douse [now dial. and slang], yerk [obs. exc. dial.], jab, plug [slang], thump, soak [slang], sock [slang], tamp, baste, paste [slang], lambaste [slang], clout [dial. and coll.], larrup [coll.], pelt.

patter, batter, beat, buffet, pummel, belabor, lay on; fetch a blow, hit a clip [coll.] etc. *n.*; tap, rap, pat, dab; slap, flap; lunge, foin [arch.]; graze, strike with a glancing blow, sideswipe [coll.]; carom [billiards], cannon [billiards, chiefly Eng.]; kick, fetch a kick, boot, calcitrate; strike out, fan out, fan [Sport.]; strike at etc. (attack) 716.5; come to blows etc. 720.8; whip etc. (punish) 972.6.

9. *v.* collide, come or enter into collision, clash, foul, fall or run foul of, meet, encounter, impringe, bump, run or bump into; hurt, hurtle; crash, smash, smash up, crack up.

10. *adj.* impulsive, impellent, impelling etc. *v.*, pulsive; dynamic(al), dynamistic; kinetic, kinematic(al); propulsive etc. 284.15.

277. Recoil
(See 276. Impulse)

1. *n.* recoil, recoilment [rare], reaction, retroaction, return, revulsion, rebound, ricochet, backlash, repercussion, recalcitration, kick, *contrecoup* [F.]; rebuff, repulse; reflection, reflex, reflux; springing back, drawing or shrinking back etc. *v.*; spring, boomerang; ducks and drakes; recession etc. 287; elasticity etc. 325; echo etc. (reverberation) 408.2; counteraction etc. 179; reversion etc. 145; retaliation etc. 718.

2. *n.* reactionary, reactionist, recalcitrant.

3. *v.* recoil, react, rebound, resile, ricochet, repercuss [rare], recalcitrate, kick, kick ∼, spring ∼, fly or bound back; draw or shrink back, shrink, flinch, wince, blink, blench, shy, jib, start aside, dodge, duck [coll.]; reverberate, re-echo etc. 408.7; counteract etc. 179.3; revert etc. 145.4; recede, return etc. 283.5; be elastic etc. 325.3, 5.

4. *adj.* recoiling etc. *v.*, refluent, repercussive, recalcitrant, revulsive; reactionary, reactive; retroactionary, retroactive; regressive etc. 283.7.

5. *adv.* on the recoil, ∼ rebound or return.

278. Direction
(See 279. Deviation)

1. *n.* direction, bearing, course, set, trend, trending etc. *v.*, run, drift, tenor, inclination, bent, aim, tack, dip; steering, steerage; collimation, collineation; orientation; tendency etc. 176; leeward, wind-

---

277. Which has been indulged to excess almost always produces a violent reaction.—PLATO.
278. I may wander from east to occident.—SHAKESPEARE. Westward the course of empire takes its way.—G. BERKELEY. The wan

ward, weather side etc. (side) 236.2, 3; right etc. 238.2; left etc. 239.2.

2. *n.* points of the compass, cardinal points; rhumb; north, south; east, sunrise, orient, Levant [obs. exc. Mediterranean]; west, sunset, occident; azimuth, magnetic azimuth.

3. *n.* line, range, quarter; line of march; alignment; collimation line, line of collimation [Astron.]; track, course etc. (path) 627.2; beeline etc. (straight line) 246.2.

4. *v.* direct, point, turn, bend, trend, verge, incline, dip, determine; direct ~, tend ~, bend ~, point etc. towards, point to *or* at, aim *or* level at, take aim; conduct to.

5. *v.* go towards *or* to, steer for *or* towards, make for *or* towards, be bound for, bend one's steps toward, direct ~, steer ~, bend *or* shape one's course, align one's march; west, wester, western; east, easter etc.

6. *v.* go directly, go straight, go straight to the point, march on a point, make a beeline, take the air line, steer a straight course, follow a course, keep *or* hold one's course, not deviate etc. (*see* deviate etc. 279.4-7).

7. *v.* orient, orientate, ascertain *or* get the bearings etc. *n.*; see which way the wind blows, see which way the cat jumps [coll.]; box the compass.

8. *adj.* direct, straightforward, straightaway; undeviating, unswerving etc. (straight) 246.5.

9. *adj.* directable, directive, steerable, leadable, dirigible, guidable, aimable, determinable.

10. *adj.* directional, directive; north, norther, northern, northerly, northly [obs.]; south, souther [obs.]; southern, southerly, southly [obs.]; east, easter [obs. exc. dial.], eastern, easterly, easternly [rare], eastly [obs.], oriental, orient [now poetic]; west, wester [Scot. and dial. Eng.], western, westerly, westernly, westly [obs.], occidental, occident [obs.]; northeast, northeasterly; northwest, southeast etc.; northeast by east, northeast by north etc.; N by E, NNE, NE, NE by N etc.; northward, south-

ward etc. *adv.*; easternmost, easternmost, westernmost etc.

11. *adv.* directionally etc. *adj.*; northward *or* northwards, north'ard [chiefly Naut.], norward [poetic], northwardly; southward, eastward etc.; easterly etc. *adj.*; eastabout, westabout etc. [Naut.]; northeastward, northeastwardly etc.; in the west etc. *n.*

12. *adv.* hither, thither, whither; *en avant* [F.] etc. (forward) 282.5.

13. *adv. etc.* directly, direct, straightly, straight, straightforward *or* straightforwards, straightways *or* straightwise [obs.], straightway *or* straightaway [obs.], straight as an arrow, in a beeline, in a direct *or* straight line, in line *or* a line with, as the crow flies, full tilt at, point-blank.

14. *adv.* windward, leeward etc. (side) 236.8 (navigation) 267.55-59.

15. *adv.* in all directions, in every direction, in all manner of ways, every which way [coll., U.S.], everywhither, every-way, everywhere, everywheres [dial. and coll.], on every side, *quaquaversum* [L.], to every place; from every quarter, everywhence; from *or* to the four winds, from *or* to the four corners of the earth.

16. *prep.* through, by, by the way of, by way of, via, by a route passing through.

17. *prep.* toward *or* towards, to *or* in the direction of, to, on the way to, on the road *or* high road to; versus.

279. Deviation
(See 278. Direction)

1. *n.* deviation, desultory motion, wandering, swerving etc. *v.*; diversion, divergence, divarication, digression, divagation, evagation [obs.], declination, aberration, variation, exorbitation; flection; deflection, deflexure; refraction; drift, swerve, sheer, turn, bend, obliquation [now rare]; sweep; vagrancy; disorientation.

2. *n.* motion sideways, oblique motion, sidling etc. *v.*; tack, yaw [both Naut.]; right *or* left passage [riding]; echelon [Mil.], knight's move [chess]; zigzag etc. (obliquity) 217.

3. *n.* devious way, deviation etc. *above* 279.1, byway, by-pass, side road, byroad, bypath, bypaths and crooked ways; detour etc. (circuit) 629.

---

sun westers.—W. E. HENLEY. Follow thy nose, and thou wilt be there presently.—J. HEYWOOD. He wanders east. He wanders west. / Where will he ever come to rest?—G. DILLON.

4. *v.* deviate, alter one's course, change he bearing, depart from, vary, diverge, livaricate, tralineate [obs.], shift, turn, rend, swerve, veer, sheer, heel, bear off, ousk; tack, jibe, yaw etc. (navigation) 267.24; bend etc. (curve) 245.3; go out of one's way etc. (circuit) 311.3.

5. *v.* stray, go astray, straggle, digress, wander, divagate, drift, go adrift, ramble, rove; meander, wind, twist; twist and turn; lose one's way.

6. *v.* deflect, deviate, cause to deviate, divert from its course, change the course or direction of, shift, turn, bend; crook, twist, skew, bias, warp; put on a new scent; shunt [Eng.], switch [U.S.].

7. *v.* turn aside *or* to the side, draw aside, side, sidetrack; step *or* move aside or to the side, bear off *or* to the side, turn away from, steer clear of, make way for, get out of the way of; go off, ease off, edge, edge off *or* away; fly off, go *or* fly off at a tangent; glance, glance off; echelon [Mil.]; sidle, crabsidle [coll.] etc. 236.5; angle off etc. (oblique) 217.5–8; start aside, shy, dodge etc. (recoil) 277.3.

8. *adj.* deviative, deviatory, deviant [rare], deviating etc. *v.*; aberrant, errant; excursive, discursive; devious, desultory, loose, rambling, roving, wandering, vagrant, stray, erratic, undirected, indirect; roundabout etc. (circuitous) 311.6; crooked, zigzag etc. (oblique) 217.9–16; curved etc. 245.4.

9. *adv. etc.* deviatively etc. *adj.*, astray from, round about, wide of the mark; every which way [coll., U.S.] etc. (in all directions) 278.15; circuitously etc. 311.7; obliquely etc. 217.17–19; sideling etc. (laterally) 236.8.

280. Precession

(See 63., 281. Sequence; also 62. Precedence)

Going Before.—1. *n.* precession, leading, heading etc. *v.*; anteposition, the lead, le pas [F.]; precedence etc. 62; priority etc. 116; van etc. (front) 234; precursor etc. 64.

2. *v.* precede, go before, go ahead, go in the van, go in advance, forego [arch.], forerun, head, stand at the head, stand first, front [obs.], lead, take the lead, go in the lead, lead the way; lead the dance, lead the cotillion [U.S.], lead the german [U.S.]; usher in, introduce, herald, proclaim; get before, get ahead *or* in front of, come to the front, get *or* have the start, get a head start, steal a march upon; outstrip etc. 303.4; take precedence etc. (first in order) 62.2; conduct, guide etc. (escort) 88.7.

3. *adj.* preceding, leading etc. *v.*; precessional; precedent, precedentary [rare], precedaneous [obs.]; first, foremost, headmost.

4. *adv.* in advance, ahead of time, in the lead, in the van, in front, before, ahead, first, foremost, headmost; in anticipation etc. (beforehand) 116.6.

281. Sequence

(See 62. Precedence, 280. Precession; also 63. Sequence)

Going After.—1. *n.* sequence, following etc. *v.*, succession, run [cards]; coming after etc. (order) 63, (time) 117; pursuit etc. 622; sequel etc. 65.

2. *n.* follower, heeler [slang], successor, tagtail, tail [slang], shadow; attendant, satellite, hanger-on, dangler, adherent; sectary *or* sectator [rare], partisan; trainbearer; pursuer etc. 622.4; sycophant etc. 886.2; disciple etc. 541.2; accompanier, following etc. 88.3–5.

3. *v.* follow, follow *or* move behind, pursue, go after, fly after, tag *or* tag after [coll.], heel, tread *or* follow on the heels *or* in the steps of, tread close upon, go *or* follow in the wake *or* rear of, come up in the rear, trail, trail after *or* behind, follow in the trail of, camp on the trail of, shadow, follow as a shadow, tail [coll.], hang on the skirts of; dog, bedog, hound; dodge; chase etc. 622.6, 7; track, trace etc. (seek) 461.16; accompany etc. 88.6, 7; succeed etc. 63.3.

4. *v.* lag, lag behind, loiter, linger, loiter *or* linger behind, get behind.

5. *adv. etc.* behind, in the train *or* wake of; after etc. (order) 63.5, 6, (time) 117.3, 4, (place) 235.14–17, (pursuit) 622.11.

---

280. Whoever is foremost, leads the herd.—SCHILLER.

281. Flee it, and it will flee thee, / Follow it, and it will follow thee.—T. HOWELL.   No! I am not Prince Hamlet, nor was meant to be; / Am an attendant lord.—T. S. ELIOT.   Men, like cattle, follow him who leads.—BYRON.

282. Progression
(See 283. Regression)

Motion Forwards, Progressive Movement.—1. *n.* progression, progress, progressiveness etc. *adj.*; advancing etc. *v.*, advance, advancement; ongoing, on-go, onward course; furtherance, further [obs. exc. dial.]; way, headway; flood tide, flood; locomotion etc. (motion) 264.2, (travel) 266; improvement etc. 658; success etc. 731.

2. *v.* progress, advance, proceed, go, go *or* move forward etc. *adv.*; step forward, pass on *or* along; jog on, rub on, wag on [obs.], roll on; forge ahead, drive on *or* ahead, push *or* press on *or* onward, push *or* press forward; make one's way, work one's way, carve one's way, push *or* force one's way, edge one's way, elbow *or* shoulder one's way; go with the stream, drift along; shoot ahead, go full steam ahead; make progress, ∼ headway etc. *n.*, make strides, ∼ rapid strides etc. (speed) 274.9, get ahead, get over the ground, gain ground; make up leeway, make up for lost time; keep *or* hold one's course; move etc. 264.6; succeed etc. 731.5.

3. *adj.* progressive, profluent, advancing etc. *v.*, ongoing, forward-looking, go-ahead [coll.]; moving etc. 264.8.

4. *adv.* progressively etc. *adj.*, in progress, in mid-progress.

5. *adv. etc.* forward *or* forwards, onward *or* onwards; forth, on, along, ahead; under way, under sail; *en avant* [F.]; en route for, on one's *or* the way to, on the road *or* high road; *in transitu* [L.] etc. (on the way) 270.13.

283. Regression
(See 282. Progression)

Motion Backwards.—1. *n.* regression, regress, regressiveness etc. *adj.*; retrocession, retrogression, retrogradation, retroaction; reverse, reversal, reversion, *volte-face* [F.], retreat, *reculade* [F.]; withdrawal, retirement; remigration; recidivism *or* recidivity, recidivatio [Criminol.]; backsliding etc. (relapse) 661; recession etc. (motion from) 287.

2. *n.* reflux, refluence, regurgitation return; resilience, resiliency; backwater ebb tide, ebb; reflection etc. (recoil) 277.

3. *n.* countermotion, countermovement; countermarching, countermarch.

4. *n.* turning point etc. (reversion 145.

5. *v.* regress, recede, return, revert retrocede, retrograde, retrogress; retreat sound *or* beat a retreat, withdraw, retire regrade [rare]; back, back up, back ou *or* down [coll.], back water, crawfisl [coll., U.S.], crawl [slang, U.S.]; go ∼ come ∼, hark ∼, fall ∼, break ∼, ge *or* run back, take the back track, retrace one's steps, dance the back step; countermarch; remigrate; surge back, ebb, regurgitate; draw back, shy etc. (recoil) 277.3; backslide etc. (relapse) 661.3.

6. *v.* turn back, put back [chiefly Naut.], turn round *or* around, veer, swivel, veer ∼, swivel *or* swing round, pivot pivot about, turn a pirouette, wheel, wheel about, turn upon one's heel, double, double back, turn one's back upon; face about, about-face, right-about-face, do *or* execute an about-face *or* a rightaboutface, turn *or* face to the rightabout, do a turn to the rightabout, volte-face, perform a *volte face*; box the compass; put about [Naut.] etc. (alter the course) 267.24, 25.

7. *adj.* regressive, receding etc. *v.*, recessive, refluent, reflex, recidivous, resilient; retrogressive, retrograde; crablike; reactionary etc. 277.4; relapsing etc. 661.4.

8. *adv.* backward *or* backwards, back, hindward *or* hindwards, rearward *or* rearwards, arear, astern [Naut.]; *à reculons* [F.], *à rebours* [F.]; counter-clockwise, contraclockwise.

284. Propulsion
(See 285. Traction)

Motion Given to an Object Situated in Front.—1. *n.* propulsion, propulsity

---

282. Onward, Christian soldiers, / Marching as to war.—S. BARING-GOULD. We now move forward in a great and gallant company.—W. CHURCHILL. Not to go back is somewhat to advance.—POPE.
283. One must draw back to leap the better.—MONTAIGNE. All that is human must retrograde if it do not advance.—GIBBON. Back-ward, turn backward, O Time, in your flight.—E. A. ALLEN. He who moves not forward goes backward! A capital saying!—GOETHE. Let us make an honourable retreat.—SHAKE-SPEARE. To retire is not to flee.—CERVANTES. A bad penny always comes back.
284. If any have a stone to shy, / Let him be

rare], propelling etc. *v.*, propelment, *vis tergo* [L.]; push etc. (impulse) 276.

2. *n.* projection, trajection, jaculation; jaculation etc. (ejection) 297.

3. *n.* throw, fling, sling, cast, hurl, huck, chunk [chiefly U.S.], heave, shy, pitch, peg [coll.].

4. *n.* shot, shoot [rare], discharge; salvo, volley, spray; bowshot, gunshot, stoneshot, potshot; inner; carton; bull's-eye; detonation, fulmination etc. (explosion) 173.3; bullet, shrapnel etc. (missile) 727.14; gunfire etc. 716.2; bark, crack etc. (report) 406.2-4.

5. *n.* projectile, trajectile; discus, quoit; ball, baseball, soft ball, tennis ball, golf ball etc.; missile etc. 727.14.

6. *n.* propeller, propellant, propellent, propulsor, driver; screw, twin screws; turbine; prop [cant] etc. (aircraft) 273a.10.

7. *n.* thrower, hurler, flinger, chucker, jaculator [rare], pitcher; shot-putter, javelin thrower, discus thrower, discobolus.

8. *n.* shooter, shot, shotress [*fem.*; obs.]; gunner, gun, gunman; rifleman, musketeer, carbineer; archer, toxophilite, bowman; marksman, markswoman, sharpshooter; good shot, dead shot, crack shot; artilleryman etc. (soldier) 726.4; Nimrod, hunter etc. (pursuer) 622.4.

9. *n.* (science of propulsion) ballistics, gunnery, archery.

10. *v.* propel, propulse [obs.], drive, drive *or* impel forward *or* onward; give motive power; move etc. 264.7; motivate etc. 615.7; push etc. (impel) 276.7.

11. *v.* project, traject, jaculate [rare]; ejaculate, expel etc. (eject) 297.8.

12. *v.* throw, fling, sling, cast, chuck, chunk [chiefly U.S.], toss, shy, hurl, heave, pitch, pelt, peg [coll.], let fly, launch, dash, bung; flirt, fillip; cant, jerk; dart, lance, tilt; put, put the shot; lapidate, stone, rock [coll., U.S.]; bowl, trundle; pitchfork.

13. *v.* shoot, fire, fire off, let off, let fly, discharge; gun [coll.], rifle [rare], pistol; catapult; strike, hit, plug [slang]; snipe, pot, hull, flight, pelt, riddle; potshot, take a potshot; go off, bark etc. (explode) 173.9; shoot at etc. 716.6.

14. *v.* start, start off, give a start *or* impulse to, put *or* set in motion, set going *or* agoing; send, send off *or* forth; bundle, bundle off; launch, launch forth *or* out; trundle etc. (set in rotation) 312.7.

15. *adj.* propulsive, propulsory, propulsatory [rare], pulsive; propellent, propelling etc. *v.*; impellent etc. (impulsive) 276.10.

16. *adj.* projectile, trajectile; jaculative [rare], jaculatorial [rare], jaculatory; ejaculative, ejaculatory; ballistic.

285. Traction
(See 284. Propulsion)

Motion Given to an Object Situated Behind.—1. *n.* traction, drawing, hauling etc. *v.*, haulage, towage; *vis a fronte* [L.]; transportation etc. 270.2.

2. *n.* pull, draw, draft *or* draught, haul, lug [coll.], tug, strain; rake; "a long pull, a strong pull, and a pull altogether" (Dickens).

3. *n.* jerk, yank [coll., U.S.], twitch etc. *v.*; shake etc. 315.4.

4. *v.* draw, pull, haul, trek [S. Afr.], lug, tug, tow, take in tow; trail, train; drag, draggle, snake [coll., U.S.]; rake; troll, trawl.

5. *v.* jerk, yerk [obs. exc. dial.], yank [coll., U.S.]; twitch, tweak, twang, pluck, snatch, wrench, bob, flip, flick, flirt, flounce, hitch, perk, jet; jig, jiggle, jigget [coll.]; jog, joggle; shake etc. 315.8.

6. *adj.* tractional, tractive, tractile; drawing, pulling etc. *v.*

286. Approach
(See 287. Recession)

Motion Towards.—1. *n.* approach, approachment [now rare], proach [obs.]; approaching, nearing etc. *v.*; proximation, approximation, appropinquation [arch.]; access; appulse, appulsion; afflux, affluxion; advent etc. (approach of time) 121.4; nearness etc. 197.

2. *v.* approach, proach [obs.]; proximate, approximate, appropinquate [arch.]; near, anear [arch.], nigh [rare], draw near *or* nigh, go *or* come near, advance near *or* nearer, come to close quarters; advance, accede [rare]; move

---

David and not I.—E. Wylie. Fling but a stone, the giant dies.—M. Green. Stormed at with shot and shell.—Tennyson. I shot an arrow into the air.—Longfellow.

286. Wherefore approached ye so nigh unto the city?—Bible.

towards, set in towards, make towards *or* for, make up to, lay for [Naut.], hit for, steer for; follow close upon, tread on the heels of, gain upon, bear down on *or* upon; bear up; make land, close with the land, run in with the land [all Naut.]; hug the shore *or* land, keep hold of the land [Naut. cant], make free with the land [Naut. slang]; come etc. (approach of time) 121.6; impend etc. 152.2; approach near *or* together etc. (converge) 290.2.

3. *adj.* approaching, nearing etc. *v.*; approximate, approximative; affluent; connivent; impending etc. (imminent) 152.3; converging etc. 290.3.

4. *adj.* approachable, accessible, get-at-able [coll.], come-at-able [coll.], attainable.

5. *adv.* on the way, on the road *or* high road.

6. *int.* approach!, come!, come near!, come on!, come here!, come hither!, here!, forward!, advance!

287. Recession
(See 286. Approach)

Motion From.—1. *n.* recession, recess [obs.], recedence, retrocedence; retirement, withdrawal, retreat; regress, retrogradation, retrocession etc. (regression) 283; departure etc. 293; recoil etc. 277; flight etc. (avoidance) 623.

2. *v.* recede, retrocede; go, go *or* move back, fall *or* stand back, move from *or* away from, retreat, retire, withdraw; go *or* move away, get away, drift away; move off, stand off, sheer off, swerve off; ebb, decline, wane, sink; go out with the tide; retrograde, retrogress etc. (regress) 283.5, 6; shrink etc. (avoid) 623.6–10.

3. *adj.* recessive, recedent, retrocedent, receding etc. *v.*; retrogressive etc. (regressive) 283.7.

288. Attraction
(See 289. Repulsion)

Motion Towards, Actively.—1. *n.* attraction, attractiveness, attractivity; pull, draw, drag; pulling ~, drawing *or* dragging to *or* towards; adduction; magnet-

ism, gravity etc. (pulling power) 157.; allurement etc. 617.

2. *n.* attractor, attractant, attrahent magnet, artificial magnet, bar magne horseshoe magnet, electromagnet; mag netite, magnetic iron *or* iron ore, load stone, lodestar, polestar, lode [arch. siderite; decoy etc. (lure) 617.2.

3. *v.* attract, pull, draw, drag, pull ~ draw *or* drag towards; magnetize, mag net; adduce, adduct [Physiol.]; charn decoy etc. (lure) 617.4.

4. *adj.* attracting, drawing etc. *v.*; at tractive, attrahent; adducent, adductive seductive, tempting etc. (alluring) 617.

5. *int.* go away etc. (begone) 297.23.

289. Repulsion
(See 288. Attraction)

Motion From, Actively.—1. *n.* repul sion, repulse, repellence *or* repellency, re pelling etc. *v.*; retrusion, retraction; ab duction.

2. *v.* repulse, repel, retrude [rare] drive ~, push *or* thrust back *or* from chase, chase *or* drive away, dispel; sen off *or* away, send about one's business send packing, pack off, send off *or* awa with a flea in one's ear [coll.], send t the rightabout; ward off, hold off, kee at arm's length; turn one's back upon give the cold shoulder, snub; abduct, ab duce [obs.]; repercuss.

3. *adj.* repulsive, repellent, repelling etc. *v.*; abducent, abductive; repercussive

290. Convergence
(See 291. Divergence)

Approach Near or Together.—1. *n.* convergence, convergency, confluence concourse, conflux; congress, concur rence, meeting; concentration, concen tralization, focalization; corradiation [rare]; appulse, appulsion; asymptote [Math.]; point of convergence etc. (fo cus) 74; centrality etc. 222.

2. *v.* converge, approach near *or* to gether, concur [rare]; come *or* run to gether, unite, meet, fall in with, clos

---

288. Of our language he was the lodestar.—LYDGATE.

289. Take no repulse, whatever she doth say.—SHAKESPEARE. Home-made dishes tha drive one from home.—HOOD.
290. Colours mingle, features join, / And line converge.—AKENSIDE. The mountains con verge into a single ridge.—JEFFERSON.

with, close in upon; enter in, pour in; centralize, center, come to a center, center round *or* in; concentralize, concentricate [obs.], concenter, concentrate; bring *or* come to a point etc. (focus) 74.3; near etc. (approach) 286.2.

3. *adj.* converging etc. *v.*, convergent, concurrent, confluent, confluxible [rare]; focal, confocal [Math.]; asymptotic(al) [Math.]; centripetal; centrical etc. 222.4; approaching etc. 286.3.

291. Divergence
(See 290. Convergence)

Recession from Each Other.—1. *n.* divergence, divergency, divarication; aberration; declination; radiation; ramification, branching etc. *v.*; forking, furcation etc. (bifurcation) 91.2; separation, division etc. (disjunction) 44; dispersion etc. 73; deviation etc. 279.

2. *v.* diverge, divaricate, aberrate; go off *or* away, glance off, file off, fly off, fly *or* go off at a tangent; radiate; ramify, ramificate [rare], branch, branch off *or* out; fork, furcate, bifurcate etc. 91.5; recede etc. 287.2; deviate etc. 279.4-7; divide, part, separate etc. 44.7; spread, scatter etc. (disperse) 73.3.

3. *adj.* diverging etc. *v.*, divergent, divaricate; aberrant, aberrational; radiant, radial; centrifugal, centrifuge; forked, furcate etc. (bifurcate) 91.7; dispread etc. (dispersed) 73.4.

292. Arrival
(See 293. Departure)

1. *n.* arrival, coming, reaching etc. *v.*; advent, access [rare], approach, subvention [rare], attainment; cessation etc. 142; completion etc. 729.

2. *n.* landing, landage [obs.]; debarkation, disembarkation, disembarkment.

3. *n.* return, recursion [obs.]; remigration; re-entry, re-entrance; homecoming, home-come [rare].

4. *n.* meeting, joining, encounter, rencounter, rencontre; re-encounter, rejoining.

5. *n.* reception, welcome etc. (hospitality) 892.4.

6. *n.* destination, goal, bourn *or* bourne, journey's end; terminal point, terminal, terminus, last stop; arrivage [obs.], halting place *or* ground, landing place *or* stage, resting place; home; haven, port etc. 666.4.

7. *v.* arrive, arrive at, come, get, come *or* get to, come at, come to hand, reach, hit, strike [coll.], approach, attain, gain, make, fetch, fetch up; come *or* get to one's journey's end, reach one's destination etc. *n.*; subvene [rare]; come up with *or* to, overtake; pitch one's tent, set up camp; reach completion etc. 729.4; make one's appearance etc. (appear) 446.2; come in etc. (enter) 294.6; drop in etc. (visit) 892.10.

8. *v.* alight, light; dismount, unhorse, light and rest one's saddle [South. U.S.]; detrain, debus [slang], disemplane.

9. *v.* land, come to land, set foot on dry land, reach land; make land, close with the land, run in with the land [all Naut.]; put in *or* into, put in *or* into harbor; go ashore, debark, disbark [rare], disembark, unboat; cast anchor etc. (anchor) 267.12; land [Aeronaut.] etc. 267a.34.

10. *v.* meet, encounter, rencounter [rare], come in contact with, come across, hit, hit up with [coll.], bump into [coll.], come *or* light upon, burst upon, pitch upon; pop upon, bounce upon, plump upon [all coll.]; join, rejoin.

11. *adj.* arriving etc. *v.*; terminal.

12. *adv.* hither, here, to this place, homeward bound.

13. *int.* welcome!, *bienvenu!* [F.]; hail!, all hail!; greetings!, good day!, good morrow!, good morning!, good afternoon!, good evening!; come in and rest your bonnet on a chair!, light and rest your saddle! [both South. U.S.].

293. Departure
(See 292. Arrival)

1. *n.* departure, departition [rare], department [obs.], depart [arch.]; going,

---

291. Two roads diverged in a yellow wood.—FROST.   Our paths in the world diverged so wide.—BROWNING.
292. Journeys end in lovers meeting.—SHAKESPEARE.   When men are arrived at the goal, they should not turn back.—PLUTARCH.   Our watchmen from the towers, with longing eyes / Expect his swift arrival.—DRYDEN.
293. Stand not upon the order of your going, / But go at once.—SHAKESPEARE.   Boot! sad-

leaving etc. *v.*; leave-taking, leave, *congé* [F.], decession [now rare], withdrawal, retreat, removal, absquatulation [chiefly coll., U.S.]; go-off [coll.], setoff, setout [coll.], outset, start; quittance [rare], vacation [now rare], evacuation, abandonment; debouchment, debouch, *débouché* [F.]; decampment, discampment [obs.]; embarkment, embarkation; take-off [Aeronaut.], hop *or* hopoff [Aeronaut., slang]; exit etc. (egress) 295; flight etc. 623.2; recession etc. 287; disappearance etc. 449; absence etc. 187.

2. *n.* leave-taking, adieu (*pl.* adieus, adieux), farewell, good-by *or* good-bye, Godspeed, send-off [coll.], valediction; valedictory, valedictory address; valedictorian.

3. *n.* point of departure, starting point *or* post, take-off; port of embarkation.

4. *v.* depart, part [arch.], take one's departure *or* leave, leave, farewell [Naut.], go, up and go [dial. and coll.], go off *or* away, go one's way, go *or* get along, be getting along [coll.], get off *or* away, gang along [Scot. and dial.], set out *or* off, set forward, be off, be gone, make off, move off *or* away, march off *or* away, take oneself off *or* away, push off, start out *or* off, start, boun [arch.].

set forth, go forth, sally forth, sally, issue, issue forth, debouch; wag, clear out, pike [all coll.]; hit the trail, make oneself scarce, pipe off, shove on *or* off, toddle along [all slang]; sashay, sashay off *or* along, mosey, mosey off *or* along [all slang, U.S.]; quit, vacate, evacuate, abandon; retreat, retire, withdraw, remove; break *or* tear oneself away; check out [chiefly U.S.]; take off [Aeronaut.], hop *or* hop off [Aeronaut., slang]; make one's exit, go off the stage; leave home, go from home; decamp, break camp, strike camp *or* tent, pull up stakes; emerge etc. 295.6; absent oneself etc. 187.8; disappear etc. 449.2.

5. *v.* depart quickly, ∼ hastily etc. (*see* quickly etc. 274.14), leave *or* depart in a hurry, hurry away, hasten off, make off, take off *or* out, take flight, take to flight, take wing, fly, flit, flee, fly *or* flit away, wing one's flight, decamp, pack, pack off *or* away, spring, spring off *or* away, whip off *or* away, scamper off, dash off, set off at a score, go off like a shot, beat a retreat, tear off *or* out, strike out, run off *or* away, run for one's life, take to one's heels.

leg it, stump it, walk one's chalks, pull foot, beat it [U.S.], *vamos* [Sp.], vamoose [U.S.], mizzle, blow [U.S.], slope, cut one's stick, cut stick, guy [Eng.], light out [U.S.], dig out [U.S.], dust, get up *or* out and get *or* git, lam, take it on the lam [U.S.], skin out [all slang]; cut, cut away, cut off, cut and run, absquatulate [U.S.], scoot, put, go on the double *or* double-quick, shin out [U.S.], skelter off *or* away, skip, skip out *or* away [all coll.]; light a shuck [dial.], scaddle [dial.], hook it [slang and dial.], get *or* git [slang and dial., U.S.]; run away from etc. (avoid) 623.10.

6. *v.* embark, go aboard, go on board; go on ship board, take ship, take shipping [arch.]; entrain, emplane, embus; break ground etc. (weigh anchor), put off, put *or* go to sea etc. (get under way) 267.15, 16.

7. *v.* take leave, say *or* bid good-by etc. *n.*, farewell.

8. *adj.* departing, leaving etc. *v.*; on the lam [slang, U.S.]; valedictory.

9. *adj.* departed etc. *v.*, gone, gone off *or* away, left.

10. *adv.* hence, thence, whence; away, from here; outward-bound; on the wing, on the move; with a foot in the stirrup.

11. *int.* begone! etc. (ejection) 297.23.

12. *int.* all aboard!, aboard!, 'board!

13. *int.* to horse!, boot!, saddle!

14. *int.* farewell!, fare you *or* ye well!, adieu!, good-day!, good-by *or* good-bye!, bye-bye! [coll.], so long! [slang], be good! [slang], au revoir!, *vale!* [L.], good luck!, *pax vobiscum!* [L.], all good go with you!, God bless you!, Godspeed!, *auf Wiedersehen!* [G.], come again!, *au plaisir de vous revoir!* [F.], *vive valeque!* [L.]; *glückliche Reise!* [G.], pleasant journey!, *bon voyage!* [F.], happy landing!; good night!; good morning, good day etc. (welcome) 292.13.

294. Ingress
(See 295. Egress)

1. *n.* ingress, ingression, introgression; entrance, entrancement, entry, entree,

dle! to horse and away!—BROWNING. Take this and hook it.—A. BENNETT. Always leave them laughing when you say good-bye.—G. COHAN.

entrée [F.]; ingoing, incoming, income; penetration, interpenetration; influx, influxion, inflow, indraft *or* indraught, inpour, inrun, inrush, illapse [rare]; infiltration; insinuation, interjection etc. (interjacence) 228.2, 3; insertion etc. 300; impregnation etc. 41.2; inroad, intrusion, invasion, irruption etc. (intervention) 228.3; access, admission etc. (reception) 296.

2. *n.* immigration, incoming population, foreign influx.

3. *n.* import, importation.

4. *n.* incomer, comeling [arch.], comer, entrant; visitor *or* visiter, visitant, guest; immigrant, immigrator [rare]; settler, colonist, colonizer, metic [Gr. Antiq.]; newcomer etc. (alien) 57.3; buttinsky [slang] etc. (intruder) 228.4.

5. *n.* inlet, ingress, entrance, entranceway, entryway, entry, adit, approach, access, means of access, ingate [North. Eng.], in [slang, U.S.], way in; introit [obs.], introitus [Anat.]; orifice, mouth, portal, door etc. (opening) 260; entrance hall, lobby etc. (vestibule) 191.17; conduit etc. 350; gulf etc. 343; passage, avenue etc. (path) 627.2.

6. *v.* enter, ingress [rare], go *or* come in *or* into, find one's way into, set foot in *or* on, put in *or* into [chiefly Naut.]; gain *or* have the entree; penetrate, interpenetrate; flow *or* pour in, inflow, inpour, inrush; filter in *or* into, infiltrate; slip *or* creep in, wriggle *or* worm oneself into, insinuate oneself; pop in, break *or* burst in, bust in [dial. and inelegant], come busting in [dial. and slang], barge in [coll.], thrust in, push *or* press in; butt in [slang], trespass etc. (intrude) 228.10; insert etc. 300.5; arrive etc. 292.7.

7. *v.* give entrance etc. (receive) 296.

8. *adj.* ingressive, entering etc. *v.*, entrant [rare], incoming, ingoing, inbound, inceptive [Gram.]; in, inward.

295. Egress
(See 294. Ingress)

1. *n.* egress, egression, exit, exodus, emersion, emanation; issue, issuance; emergence, emergency [now rare]; outgoing, outgo; outcoming, outcome; exudation; transudation; effusion, extravasion; exfiltration, filtration; percolation; lixiviation, leaching; leakage, leaking, leak;. seepage, seep; oozing, ooze; drainage, drain; distillation, distillage [rare]; outbreak, outburst, eruption, proruption [rare]; outpour, outpouring; outflow, outflowing; effluence, effusion; efflux, effluxion, defluxion; flowoff, runoff; gush etc. (jet) 348.5; evacuation, discharge etc. (ejection) 297; perspiration etc. (excrement) 299.2–7; departure etc. 293; escape etc. 671; disappearance etc. 449; extraction etc. 301.

2. *n.* emigration, demigration [obs.]; remigration; departure etc. 293; deportation, expatriation etc. (banishment) 297.3.

3. *n.* export, exportation; shipment.

4. *n.* outgoer, goer, leaver; departer etc. (*see* depart etc. 293.4); emigrant, *émigré* [F.], migrant; redemptioner [Hist., U.S.]; colonist etc. 294.4.

5. *n.* outlet, egress, exit, outgo, outcome, outcast [rare], outgate [Scot. and North. Eng.], out [slang, U.S.], way out; vent, ventage, venthole; debouch [Mil.], *débouché* [F.]; outgate, sally port [Mil. and Naut.]; vomitory [Rom. Arch.]; emunctory, pore; mouth, door etc. (opening) 260; spout, sluice etc. (conduit) 350; blowhole etc. (air passage) 351; head gate, tap etc. (valve) 263.2; passage, avenue etc. (path) 627.2; loophole etc. 671.4.

6. *v.* egress, emerge, emanate, issue, go ~, come ~, move *or* pass out, pass off, come *or* issue forth; exit, make an exit, make one's exit; depart etc. 293.4.

7. *v.* exude, exudate, transude; emit, discharge, debouch, disembogue, effuse, extravasate; find vent, run out *or* through; leak, leak out; drip, dribble, drop, trickle, trill, distill *or* distil; exfiltrate, filtrate, filter; percolate; lixiviate, leach; drain, seep, ooze; perspire, wet [chiefly dial.], sweat, be *or* get in a muck of sweat [coll.]; strain, transcolate [obs.]; flow *or* pour out, well out, gush *or* spout out; flow, pour, well, surge, gush, jet, spout; vomit forth, egorgitate [rare]; break *or* burst forth, ~ out *or* through; escape etc. 671.6; give vent to, let out etc. (eject) 297.13; excrete etc. 297.13.

8. *v.* emigrate, demigrate [obs.]; remigrate.

---

295. They have their exits and their entrances. —SHAKESPEARE. The outgoings of the morning.—BIBLE.

295.9 — 297.8

9. *adj.* egressive, emergent, emerging etc. *v.*; outgoing, outbound, outward-bound; emanant, emanational, emanative; exudative, exudatory [rare]; transudative, transudatory; percolative, porous, pervious, leaky; eliminative, emunctory, depurative; eruptive, erumpent; effluent, effusive; sweaty etc. 299.10, 11; ejective etc. 297.22.

296. Reception
(See 297. Ejection)

Motion Into, Actively.—1. *n.* reception, admission, admittance; immission, intromission; entrance, entry, entree, *entrée* [F.]; access, accessibility; introduction, introducement [now joc.]; initiation, inition [obs.]; ingestion, imbibition; absorption, absorbition [obs.]; reabsorption, resorbence; engorgement, ingurgitation; inhalation, inhalement, inspiration; suction, sucking; eating, drinking etc. 298; insertion etc. 300; interjection etc. 228.2; importation etc. (ingress) 294.

2. *v.* receive, admit, immit, immiss [obs.], intromit [rare], let *or* take in, give entrance *or* admittance to, give an entree, open the door to, throw . . . open to; ingest, imbibe; absorb, adsorb; inhale, inspire, breathe *or* draw in; suck, suck in *or* up; snuff, snuff in *or* up.

3. *v.* swallow, ingurgitate; engulf, engorge; gulp, gulp down; eat, drink etc. 298.44-47.

4. *v.* readmit, reabsorb, resorb.

5. *v.* introduce, introduct [obs. exc. joc.]; induct, bring in, import; immit, immiss [obs.]; instill, implant, infiltrate; inject etc. (insert) 300.5; interject etc. 228.8.

6. *adj.* receptive, receptual, recipient, introceptive; admitting etc. *v.*, admissive, admissory, admissible; intromissive, intromittent; ingestive, imbibitory; absorbent, resorbent.

7. *adj.* introductory, introductive, introducible; initiatory, initiary [rare]; preliminary etc. (preceding) 62.4.

---

296. To give admittance to a thought of fear.—SHAKESPEARE.   He desired admittance to the king.—DRYDEN.

297. Ejection
(See 296. Reception)

Motion Out Of, Actively.—1. *n.* ejection, ejectment, expulsion, ejaculation [now chiefly Physiol.], ousting etc. *v.*; the chuck [slang, Eng.] etc. *below* 297.4; rejection, rejectment [rare]; emission; extrusion, detrusion; expedition, dispatch; deposal, deposition; exudation etc. (egress) 295; removal etc. (displacement) 185; extraction etc. 301.

2. *n.* eviction, dislodgment, dispossession; ouster [Law]; depopulation; rogue's march.

3. *n.* banishment, relegation, exclusion, excommunication, disfellowship, proscription [chiefly Hist.], expatriation; exile, exilement; ostracism, ostracization; deportation, transportation, extradition; rustication.

4. *n.* dismissal, discharge, *congé* [F.]; the bounce *or* the grand bounce [U.S.], the chuck [Eng.], order of the boot, the gate, the sack, the can, yellow cover [all slang]; walking papers *or* ticket, mittimus [all coll.]; dishonorable discharge, bobtail [Mil. slang]; deposal etc. 756.2.

5. *n.* evacuation, vacation [now rare], voidance; egestion [Physiol.], ejaculation [Physiol.], disemboguement, dejection [Physiol.], disgorgement, elimination, removal; clearance, clearage; excretion, secretion, secernment; defecation; eruption, eruptiveness, eruptivity; belch, ructation, eructation; vomition, vomiting, egurgitation [rare], emesis [Med.]; emetic; tapping, drainage; effusion, extravasation, paracentesis; bloodletting, venesection, phlebotomy; excrement etc. 299; salivation etc. (saliva) 299.5.

6. *n.* ejector, expeller, ouster, evictor; bouncer [U.S.], chucker, chucker-out, boot-giver [all slang].

7. *n.* outcast etc. 893.5.

8. *v.* eject, expel, extrude, ejaculate [now chiefly Physiol.], cast, oust, relegate, remove, exclude, reject, throw over *or* overboard, throw to the dogs, throw *or* cast out, ∼ off *or* aside, turn out; turn out neck and heels, ∼ neck and crop *or* head and shoulders, rout out [all coll.], bundle off *or* out, send ∼, turn *or* cast

---

297. Have you not learned great lessons from those who reject you?—WHITMAN.   From mine own earldom foully ousted me.—TENNYSON.

adrift, turn off *or* away, sweep ~, brush *or* whisk off *or* away, send away.

send packing, send about one's business, send to the rightabout, send away with a flea in the ear [coll.], send to Jericho [coll.], send to the showers [Sport. slang, U.S.], bow out, show the door *or* gate; drive *or* chase out, drum out; kick [U.S.], bounce [U.S.], give the bounce *or* grand bounce [U.S.], give the chuck [Eng.], give the air, give the order of the boot, throw out on one's ear [all slang]; throw away etc. (discard) 678.3; displace etc. 185.2; extract etc. 301.5.

9. *v.* evict, oust etc. *above*, dislodge, dispossess, turn out of doors, turn out of house and home, turn *or* put out bag and baggage; unhouse, unkennel.

10. *v.* depopulate, dispeople, unpeople.

11. *v.* banish, relegate, exile, ostracize, exclude, disfellowship, drum out, excommunicate, expatriate, send to Coventry; deport, transport, extradite, extradition [rare], lag [slang], ablegate [obs.]; ban, proscribe, outlaw; rusticate.

12. *v.* dismiss, discharge, cashier, displace, let off *or* out, strike off the rolls, kick downstairs; kick [U.S.], fire, fire out, bounce [U.S.], sack, give the sack, dejob, give the ax, can, give the can, give the chuck [Eng.], give the gate [all slang]; give one his mittimus, give one his walking papers *or* ticket [all coll.]; break, bust [slang]; disbar, deprive of office etc. (depose) 756.5.

13. *v.* let out, give vent *or* exit to, give out *or* off, emit, discharge, debouch, pour out *or* forth, excern [obs.], egest [Physiol.], disgorge; embogue [obs.], disembogue; send out *or* forth, dispatch; extrude, detrude; spend, expend; excrete, secrete, secern; defecate; broach, tap, draw off; suck, suck up *or* out; extravasate; let blood, venesect, phlebotomize; spout, squirt, spurt *or* spirt; spill, slop, splash; open the sluices *or* floodgates, turn on the tap; let one's breath out, exhale, expire, breathe *or* blow out; perspire etc. (exude) 295.7; breathe, blow etc. (wind) 349.22, 23.

14. *v.* evacuate, void; empty, empty out, deplete, exhaust; drain, drain to the dregs; purge, clean out, clear off, ~ out *or* away, sweep out, make a clean sweep, clear the decks.

15. *v.* urinate, stale [obs. exc. dial.],
 micturate [erron.], make water, piss [now vulg.], wet.

16. *v.* disembowel, disbowel [rare], embowel [rare], eviscerate, gut, exenterate [rare], stool, have a bowel movement.

17. *v.* root out *or* up, uproot, unearth, averruncate [obs.], get out, weed out, eliminate, eradicate, extirpate, deracinate, exterminate, get rid of, do away with, shake off.

18. *v.* vomit, spew, egurgitate [rare], puke [vulg.], disgorge, cast [now chiefly dial.], cast *or* heave the gorge, bring *or* cast up, throw up [coll.], unswallow [slang]; retch, keck, heave; be seasick, feed the fish [joc.].

19. *v.* salivate, ptyalize; drivel, drool, slobber, slabber, slaver; sputter, splutter; expectorate, spit, spew; clear the throat, hawk.

20. *v.* belch, berp [slang, U.S.]; eruct, eructate.

21. *v.* unpack, unlade, unload, disburden, dump [chiefly U.S.]; unship, break bulk [Naut.].

22. *adj.* ejective, emissive, extrusive; egestive; salivant; eliminative, eliminant; vomitive, vomitory; emitting, emitted etc. *v.*; excretory etc. 299.10, 11; exudative etc. (egressive) 295.9.

23. *int.* begone!, get you gone!, get *or* go along! *or* along with you!, get *or* go away!, go your way!, away!, away *or* off with you!, go about your business!, be off!, avaunt!, aroint! [arch.], *allez-vous-en!* [F.], *va-t'en!* [F.], shoo!, "get thee behind me, Satan!" (Bible); skiddoo!, cheese it!, make yourself scarce!, walk your chalks! [all slang]; beat it!, vamoose!, scram!, skedaddle! [all slang, U.S.]; get *or* git! [slang and dial., U.S.]; go! etc. (depart) 293.4, 5.

298. Eating

1. *n.* eating, feeding etc. *v.*, ingestion, consumption, devourment, deglutition; discussion [coll.]; chewing, mastication, manducation, rumination; feasting, epulation; epicurism, gastronomy, gastrology; omnivorousness, pantophagy; carnivorism, carnivorousness; hippophagism, hippophagy; vegetarianism, lacto-

298. In the land of Egypt . . . we sat by the fleshpots, and did eat bread to the full.—BIBLE.
Now good digestion wait on appetite, and

298.1 – 298.12

vegetarianism; herbivority [rare], phytophagy; gluttony etc. 957; appetite etc. 865.3; appetizer, sauce etc. (condiment) 293.

2. *n.* bite, morsel; mouthful; cud, quid; bolus; gob [dial. and slang], gobbet [arch.]; lunch *or* luncheon [obs. exc. dial.]; chew, chaw [dial.]; nibble, nip; munch, crunch, craunch, scrunch, champ, snap, gnash.

3. *n.* drinking etc. *v.*, potation; compotation, symposium [Gr. Antiq.]; drunkenness etc. 959; thirst etc. 865.3.

4. *n.* drink, potion, potation, libation [joc.]; dram, draft *or* draught, drench, guzzle [vulg.], swig [coll.], swill [slang], sip, sup, suck, pull [coll.], lap, gulp; nip, peg; beverage, drinkable [coll.], liquor, liquid, liquid food, potable; nonalcoholic beverage, soft drink [coll., U.S.].

milk, cream; buttermilk, sourdook [Scot.]; chocolate, cocoa; coffee, tea, iced tea, maté *or* mate; ade, lemonade, limeade, orangeade etc.; milk shake, malted milk, malt [coll.]; water, ice water; carbonated water, soda water, soda, pop [slang], ice-cream soda, root beer, Coca Cola [trade name]; phosphate, orange ~, lemon etc. phosphate; cider, punch; gin etc. (alcoholic drinks) 959.4–10; nectar, ambrosia etc. (sweets) 396.5; broth etc. *below* 298.16; water etc. 337.

5. *n.* food, foodstuff, feed, eatables, edibles, comestibles, victuals, viands, *bouche* [F.], ingesta, cates [obs.], fare, cheer, creature comfort, creature, tucker [chiefly Austral.]; grub, grubbery, chuck, chow, prog, peck, scoff, eats, belly timber, belly cheer *or* entertainment [all slang]; pabulum, pabulation [rare]; nutriment, nourishment, nurture, refection, provision, provender [now joc.], keep, subsistence, sustenance, sustentation; meat [fig.], bread [fig.], daily bread, staff of life; board, table; condiment etc. 393.

6. *n.* provisions, provender, supplies, food supply; rations, tommy [Mil. slang, Eng.], viaticum, commons, tucker [chiefly Austral.], allowance, allotment; contents of the larder; garrison ~, travel ~, field ~, reserve *or* Filipino rations [Mil.]; short commons; emergency rations, iron rations [Mil. cant]; groceries, grocery; commissariat etc. (provision) 637.1; provision shop, grocery store etc. (mart) 799.

7. *n.* fodder, feed, provender; forage, pasturage, pasture [rare]; grain, corn, oats, barley, meal; hay, straw; ensilage; forage grass etc. (grass) 367.9.

8. *n.* diet, dietary; regimen; liquid diet, spoon food *or* meat, spoon victual *or* victuals [inelegant and dial.].

9. *n.* delicacy, dainty, goody [coll.], kickshaw, marchpane, marzipan, luxury, regale [now rare], *bonne bouche* [F.], morsel, choice bit; titbit, tidbit [U.S.]; *pièce de résistance* [F.]; savory; ambrosia, nectar, sweetmeat, tuck [slang] etc. (sweets) 396.2, 5.

10. *n.* fleshpots, fat of the land, good *or* high living, good cheer.

11. *n.* breadstuff; bread, *pain* [F.], punk [tramp slang, U.S.], staff of life; loaf of bread, tommy [Scot. and dial. Eng.]; white bread, dark bread, wholewheat bread, rye bread, pumpernickel, pumpernickel bread, graham bread.

corn bread, corn pone [South. U.S.], corn tash [South. U.S.], johnnycake [South. U.S.]; corn dodger, corn dab [both South. U.S.]; ashcake, hoecake [South. U.S.]; damper [Austral.]; sourbread, sourcake [dial. Eng.]; unleavened bread, matzoth [Jewish]; biscuit; hardtack, hard tommy [Mil. slang, Eng.], pantile [Naut. slang], sea biscuit, ship biscuit, pilot biscuit; cracker, soda cracker, graham cracker; bun; muffin; dumpling, doughboy [coll.]; scone; rusk, zwieback, Brussels biscuit.

12. *n.* (pastries, cakes and desserts) pastry, patisserie, French pastry, *petits fours* [F.], Danish pastry, pasty; patty, patty-cake; *bouche* [F.], patty shell, *vol-au-vent* [F.]; pie, *pâté* [F.], mince ~ apple ~, custard ~, pumpkin etc. pie; shortbread; tart, fruit ~, jelly ~, custard etc. tart; apple dumpling, apple slump *or* grunt [dial.]; dowdy, pandowdy [U.S.], apple dowdy [U.S.]; cake, *gâteau* [F.]; shortcake, devil's food cake, angel's food cake, chocolate cake etc.; pancake, griddlecake, hot cake, flapcake, flapjack [U.S. or dial.]; chapatty [Ind.];

---

health on both.—SHAKESPEARE.   Sit down and feed and welcome to our table.—SHAKESPEARE.   Bachelor's fare: bread and cheese and kisses.—SWIFT.   My dinner was noble and enough.—PEPYS.   Life, withindoors, has few pleasanter prospects than a neatly arranged

waffle; fritter, flitter [dial.], *beignet* [F.]; apple fritter, *beignet de pommes* [F.]; doughnut; friedcake, cruller, twister, boil cake, jumble, bismarck, fasnacht [all dial., U.S.]; sinker [slang, U.S.]; cooky [U.S.], biscuit [Eng.]; macaroon, *macaron* [F.].

pudding, cornstarch pudding, plum pudding, apple pudding etc.; stewed fruit, compote; stewed apples, stewed prunes etc.; puff, cream puff; whipped cream; turnover; charlotte, charlotte russe; meringue; sweetmeat etc. (sweets) 396.2.

13. *n.* frozen dessert, ice; water ice [chiefly Eng.], sherbet [U.S.]; ice cream, *crème glacée* [F.]; vanilla ~, strawberry ~, chocolate etc. ice cream; sundae *or* ice-cream sundae [U.S.], college ice; ice-cream soda, banana split, banana royal, ice-cream cone, frappé; frozen pudding.

14. *n.* jelly, jam etc. (preserve) 396.3.

15. *n.* cereal, breakfast food; porridge, barley ~, pease etc. porridge; mush, hasty pudding, supawn [local, U.S.]; hominy [U.S.], oatmeal, gruel, crowdy [Scot. and dial. Eng.], *atole* [Sp. Amer.], samp [U.S.], frumenty.

16. *n.* soup, pottage, *potage* [F.]; turtle ~, oxtail ~, tomato ~, vegetable etc. soup; julienne, vermicelli soup; okra soup, gumbo; broth, *bouillon* [F.]; gravy soup, consommé; stock; bisque; chowder, clam chowder, oyster chowder, fish chowder; mulligatawny.

17. *n.* stew, oyster ~, beef etc. stew; meat stew, *etuvée* [F.]; mulligan stew *or* mulligan [slang, U.S.]; provençal stew, bouillabaisse; ragout, salmi; Irish stew, fricassee, salmagundi, goulash, Hungarian goulash, curry; chow mein, chop suey [U.S.].

18. *n.* fish, *poisson* [F.]; salmon; sole; fillet of sole, filet de sole, fried sole, *sole frite* [F.]; whiting, *merlan* [F.]; trout, *truite* [F.]; mackerel, *maquereau* [F.]; herring, *hareng* [F.]; kipper, kippered salmon *or* herring; cod, codfish, *morue* [F.]; sturgeon, Albany beef [slang]; haddock, finnan haddie *or* haddock; lobster, *homard* [F.]; lobster à la king; lobster Newburg; shrimp, *crevette* [F.]; prawn; oyster, *huître* [F.]; pickled oysters, *huîtres marinées* [F.]; oysters on *or* in the half shell, *huîtres à l'écaille* [F.]; sea slug, *bêche de mer* [F.], trepang; eel, *anguille* [F.]; crab, crab meat, soft-shell crab; crawfish *or* crayfish, *écrevisse* [F.]; shad, plaice, bluefish, swordfish, sardine, scrod [U.S.], sturgeon, tarpan, tuna, pike, periwinkle, blue point, clam; fish eggs, roe, caviar *or* caviare.

19. *n.* meat, flesh; butcher's meat; roast meat, roast, *rôti* [F.]; broiled ~, boiled ~, braised ~, stewed etc. meat, *bouilli* [F.]; barbecue; saddle, hind saddle, fore-saddle, knuckle, shank, plate, joint, loin, mincemeat, mince, forcemeat, meat balls, fricandeau, fricando, fricandels, fricandelles; hash; croquettes, haggis [Scot.], meat loaf, meat pie, pilau [Ind.], scrapple, ponhaus [dial.]; meat jelly, aspic.

20. *n.* beef, *bœuf* [F.]; roast beef, *rosbif* [F.], chuck roast, pot roast; beefsteak, *bifteck* [F.]; round steak, rump steak, club steak, flank steak, porterhouse steak, sirloin steak; Hamburg steak, Hamburger, hamburg; corned beef, corned Willie [slang], Admiralty ham [Naut. slang]; corned beef and cabbage; beef and cabbage, bubble and squeak; canned beef, bully *or* bully beef; boiled beef; rump, chuck, beef à la mode, chipped beef, salt beef; beef extract, beef juice, beef tea.

21. *n.* veal, *veau* [F.]; calf's head, *tête de veau* [F.]; calf's liver, *foie de veau* [F.]; sweetbread, *ris de veau* [F.]; veal cutlet etc. below 298.27.

22. *n.* mutton, *mouton* [F.]; lamb, *agneau* [F.]; saddle of mutton; leg of lamb, leg of mutton; baked sheep's head, jimmy; lamb fries, mountain oysters [joc.]; mutton chop etc. below 298.27.

23. *n.* pork, *porc* [F.]; ham, *jambon* [F.]; small ham, *jambonneau* [F.]; bacon, Canadian bacon; salt pork *or* bacon, sow-belly [coll.], side meat [South. U.S.]; sucking pig, *cochon de lait* [F.]; pigs' knuckles, pigs' feet, trotters, *pieds de cochon* [F.]; pork chop etc. below 298.27.

24. *n.* sausage, *saucisson* [F.]; frankfurt *or* frankfurter, weiner, weinee [slang], hot dog [slang, U.S.]; liverwurst, *salame or salami* [It.], Bologna sausage, boloney [dial.]; sausage meat, country sausage, *Bratwurst* [G.] (*pl. Bratwürste*).

25. *n.* poultry, *volaille* [F.], fowl; chicken, *poulet* [F.], hen, pullet, poulard; capon, duck, *canard* [F.], Long Island duck, duckling; roast duck, *canard rôti* [F.]; goose, turkey; guinea fowl; broiler, fryer, roaster; wing, leg, wishbone, drumstick, breast, white meat; pheasant etc. *below*.

26. *n.* game, venison, rabbit, *lapin* [F.], hare, *lièvre* [F.], jugged *or* stewed hare, *civet* [F.]; pheasant, *faisan* [F.], partridge, *perdrix* [F.], snipe, quail, wild duck, *canard sauvage* [F.], mallard, [F.], canvasback, teal duck *or* teal, grouse, ricebird, pigeon, squab.

27. *n.* chop, cutlet, *côtelette* [F.]; *côtelette au naturel* [F.]; mutton chop, *côtelette de mouton* [F.]; pork chop, *côtelette de porc frais* [F.]; veal cutlet, *côtelette de veau* [F.]; *côtelette à la maître d'hôtel* [F.], *côtelette à la jardinière* [F.] etc. *adv*.

28. *n.* eggs, *œufs* [F.]; boiled eggs, *œufs à la coque* [F.]; fried eggs, *œufs sur le plat* [F.]; poached eggs, *œufs pochés* [F.]; scrambled eggs, *œufs brouillés* [F.]; fresh eggs; dropped eggs; shirred eggs; stuffed eggs; deviled eggs; omelet, omelette; soufflé; fish eggs etc. *above* 298.18.

29. *n.* cheese, *fromage* [F.]; cheesecake, *talmouse* [F.]; cheesemold, *moule à fromage* [F.]; cheese fondue, cheese straws; Welsh rabbit, Welsh rarebit [erron.]; golden buck; cream cheese, cottage cheese, smearcase [dial.], pot cheese [dial.], Dutch cheese; schweizerkäse *or* schweizer; Neufchâtel, Gruyère, Swiss, Emmental *or* Emmentaler, Gorgonzola, Parmesan, Cheddar, Cheshire, Wisconsin, New York, Roquefort, American, Camembert, Brie, Munster, Edam, Gouda, Limburg *or* Limburger, Liederkranz, Wensleydale; Neufchâtel cheese, Gruyère cheese, etc.; process cheese; grated cheese.

30. *n.* vegetables, *légumes* [F.]; greens; asparagus, *asperges* [F.]; peas, *pois* [F.]; green peas, *petits pois* [F.];
artichoke, *artichaut* [F.]; cabbage, *chou* [F.]; Brussels sprouts, *choux de Bruxelles* [F.]; cauliflower, *chou-fleur* [F.] (*pl. choux-fleurs*); lettuce, *laitue* [F.], romaine, Cos lettuce, beans, *haricots* [F.], frijoles; lima beans; string beans; French beans, *haricot verts* [F.]; kidney beans; scarlet runners; potatoes, *pommes de terre* [F.]; Idaho potatoes, spuds [dial.], Irish potatoes, bog apples [slang]; yams, sweet potatoes, *patates* [F.].

spinach, *épinards* [F.]; succory, endive, *chicorée* [F.]; sauerkraut, kraut, choucroute [F.]; salsify, *salsifis* [F.], oyster plant; tomato, *tomate* [F.], love apple; celery, *céleri* [F.]; cress, *cresson* [F.]; water cress, *cresson de fontaine* [F.]; beets, beetroots [Eng.], *betteraves* [F.]; parsnips, turnips, *navets* [F.]; radish, *radis* or *rave* [F.]; horse radish, *raifort* [F.]; onion, *oignon* [F.]; scallion; shallot, *échalote* [F.]; cucumber, *concombre* [F.]; mushrooms, *champignons* [F.]; pumpkin; squash, summer squash, acorn squash, Hubbard squash; eggplant, *mélongène* [F.], mad apple; rhubarb, *rhubarbe* [F.]; truffle, *truffe* [F.]; slaw, coleslaw; succotash [U.S.].

31. *n.* fruit; figs, *figues* [F.]; cherries, *cerises* [F.]; apple, *pomme* [F.]; pear, *poire* [F.]; alligator pear, avocado; apricot, *abricot* [F.]; peach, *pêche* [F.]; pineapple, ananas; plantain, banana; breadfruit, grapefruit, orange, lemon, lime, mango, mangosteen, grapes, raisins, currants, prunes; berries, cranberries, loganberries, blueberries, blackberries, gooseberries, whortleberries, huckleberries, raspberries, strawberries; stewed fruit etc. *above* 298.12.

32. *n.* melon, watermelon, muskmelon, cantaloupe, nutmeg melon, Persian melon, honeydew melon.

33. *n.* nuts, *noisettes* [F.], mast; nutlet; kernel, meat; peanut, goober pea *or* goober [South. U.S.], pinder [dial.], ground-pea [dial.]; walnut, black walnut, *noix* [F.]; chestnut, *châtaigne* [F.]. Brazil nut, niggertoe [chiefly U.S.]; almond, *amande* [F.]; burnt almond, *amande pralinée* [F.]; bitter almond,

---

My soul is dark with stormy riot, / Directly traceable to diet.—HOFFENSTEIN. The apple grows so bright and high, / And ends its days in apple pie.—HOFFENSTEIN. The insipid and depressing beverage . . . tea.—M. ARNOLD.

amande amère [F.]; sweet almond, *amande douce* [F.]; shelled almonds, *amandes cassées* [F.]; almond paste, *pâte d'amande* [F.]; almond soup, *savon d'amande* [F.]; coconut, hazelnut, filbert, pecan nut, pistachio nut, cashew nut.

34. *n.* meal, repast, feed [now coll.], scoff [slang], spread [coll.], mess, table, board, collation; refreshment, refection, regalement, entertainment; breakfast, *petit déjeuner* [F.], *déjeuner* [F.], déjeuné *or* dejeune; *chota hazri* [Anglo-Ind.]; meat breakfast, *déjeuner à la fourchette* [F.]; brunch [coll.]; lunch, luncheon, tiffin [Anglo-Ind.]; hot luncheon, dinette [Eng.]; dinner, *diner* or *diné* [F.]; supper, *souper* or *soupé* [F.]; picnic, junket [U.S.].

35. *n.* light repast *or* refreshment, luncheon, lunch, light lunch, spot of lunch [slang], bever [chiefly dial.], snack [coll.], bait [obs. exc. dial.], bite *or* bite to eat [coll.], piece [dial., U.S.], a lick and a smell [slang].

36. *n.* hearty meal, healthy meal [coll.], full *or* substantial meal, square meal [coll.], square [slang; chiefly in *three squares*], man-sized meal, large order, full-course dinner.

37. *n.* feast, *festa* [It.], festal board, banquet, spread [coll.], tuck [slang], tuck-in *or* tuck-out [slang], blowout [slang], junket, feed *or* big feed [coll.], regale [now rare].

38. *n.* serving, service; helping, second helping; course; dish, plate; side dish, hors d'oeuvre; appetizer, whet; antepast; entree, *entrée*, entremets; *relevé* [F.]; remove [Eng.]; dessert.

39. *n.* (manner of service or cooking) service, counter service, self-service, table service; *cuisine* [F.]; table d'hôte, ordinary; à la carte; cover, *couvert* [F.]; cover charge; American plan, European plan.

40. *n.* menu, bill of fare, carte.

41. *n.* eater, consumer, devourer, diner, luncher; mouth, hungry mouth; diner-out; boarder, board-and-roomer; omnivore, pantophagist; flesh eater, meat eater, carnivore, omophagist, predacean; man-eater, cannibal; vegetarian, lacto-vegetarian; plant-eater, herbivore, phytivore [rare], phytophagan; grass-eater, graminivore; grain-eater, granivore; glutton, epicure etc. 957.2.

42. *n.* restaurant, eating house *or* room, dining room *or* hall, lunch room, cookshop; eat house, eatery, beanery, lunchery, luncheonette, lunch counter, hashery, hash house, place [all slang]; café, *caffe* [It.]; chophouse; coffeehouse, coffee-room, coffee shop, *estaminet* [F.]; buffet, lunch counter *or* stand, quick-lunch counter; hot-dog stand [slang, U.S.]; snack bar, *bistro* [coll., Fr.]; grill, grill-room; cafeteria [U.S.], luncheteria [slang, U.S.]; automat; cabaret, café chantant, café dansant; mess hall; canteen; sutler's shop, sutlerage [rare], sutlery; cookhouse, cookshack [slang, U.S.]; lunch counter, drugstore; lunch wagon, diner, chuck wagon [slang, West. U.S.]; tavern etc. (inn) 189.8.

43. *v.* feed, dine; nourish, nurture, foster, sustain, strengthen; satisfy, gratify; regale; bread, meat; breakfast, lunch, dinner, supper; cater, victual, provision, provender, purvey, mess, forage; pasture, put out to pasture, graze; supply etc. (provide) 637.4.

44. *v.* eat, feed, dine, fare, bite [now dial.], devour, ingest, swallow, consume, take *or* get down, take, take *or* lay in, dispatch, down, put away [coll.], discuss [coll.], break bread; refresh *or* entertain the inner man, appease *or* feed the animal, feed one's tapeworm [all joc.]; feed one's face, tuck in, scoff, chuck [U.S.], chuck up [U.S.], grub [U.S.], grub up [U.S.], grease the gills, line the jacket, surround [all slang].

breakfast, break one's fast; lunch, luncheon; dine, dinner; sup, supper; mess, go to mess; fall to, pitch in [coll.]; lick, pick, peck [coll.], nibble, eat like a bird; snack, piece [coll.]; eat heartily, eat a hearty meal etc. *n.*, eat like a horse, eat one's head off [coll.], do oneself proud [coll.], do justice to, play a good knife and fork [dial., Eng.]; eat someone out of house and home; feast, banquet, regale; gobble, gulp, bolt, gobble ~, gulp *or* bolt down; gorge, gormandize etc. (be gluttonous) 957.3; lick one's chops [coll.], make one's mouth water etc. (desire) 865.12, 14.

45. *v.* chew, chaw [dial.]; masticate, manducate; ruminate, chew the cud; champ, munch, craunch, crunch, scrunch; nibble, gnaw; mumble.

46. *v.* feed on *or* upon, feast upon, batten upon, fatten upon; browse, graze, crop.

47. *v.* drink, drink in *or* up, wet one's clay, ~ whistle *or* swallow [coll. or joc.]; quaff, sip, sup, bib, swig [coll.], swill [coll.], guzzle [vulg.]; suck, suck in *or* up; lap, lap up; toss off *or* down, toss one's glass *or* drink; drink one's fill; empty one's glass, drain the cup; wash down; tipple, carouse etc. 959. 15–17.

48. *adj.* eating etc. *v.,* pabulatory [rare], vorant [now Her.]; omnivorous, pantophagous; flesh-eating, meat-eating, carnivorous, omophagous *or* omophagic, zoophagous [rare], predaceous *or* predacious; man-eating, cannibal, cannibalic; vegetable-eating, vegetarian, lactovegetarian; plant-eating, herbivorous, phytivorous, phytophagous *or* phytophagic *or* phytophagan; grass-eating, graminivorous; grain-eating, granivorous.

49. *adj.* eatable, edible, esculent, comestible, gustable, alimentary; nutritive, nutritious; dietetic; culinary; gastric; succulent; cereal, cibarious [rare].

50. *adj.* done, well-done, well-cooked, *bien cuit* [F.]; overcooked, overdone, high [of game], ripe [of cheese]; undercooked, not done, underdone, rare, *saignant* [F.].

51. *adj.* drinkable, potable, potulent [obs.]; bibulous.

52. *adv.* (manner of cooking or serving) *à la béarnaise, à la bonne femme, à la bordelaise, à la bourgeoise,* à la carte, table d'hôte, à la casserole, en casserole, *à la Chateaubriand, à la cocotte, à la coque, à la Crécy, à la créole, à la Croissy, à la dauphine, à la dauphinoise, à la diable, à la florentine, à la française, à la godiveau, à la jardinière, à la julienne,* à la king, *à l'allemande, à la lyonnaise, à la macédoine, à la Maintenon, à la maître d'hôtel,* à la Marengo, à la Maryland, *à la matelote, à l'américaine, à la milanaise,* alamode, à la mode, *à la mode de Caen, à la napolitaine,* à la Newburg, *à l'anglaise, à la normande, à la parisienne, à la Périgord, à la polonaise, à la printanière, à la ravigote, à la reine, à la russe, à la serviette, à la Soubise, à la suisse, à la tartare, à l'aurore, à la vinaigrette, à l'espagnole, à l'estragon, à l'italienne, au beurre fondu, au beurre roux, au fromage,* au gratin, *au gras, au jus, au kirsch, au maigre, au naturel, aux fines herbes, au vert pré, au vin blanc, aux petits pois* [all F. or quasi F.].

299. Excretion

That Which is Excreted or Ejected.—
1. *n.* excretion, excrement, eccrisis [Med.], discharge, emanation, evacuation, ejection; dejection, dejecture; exudation, exudate; transudation, transudate; secretion, secernment; effusion, flux; extravasation, extravasate; ecchymosis, ecchymoma; leucorrhea, the whites; carbon dioxide; excreting etc. (evacuation) 297.5.

2. *n.* excrements, excreta, excretes, secreta, egesta, ejecta, ejectamenta, dejecta, exuviae; feces, feculence, defecation; diarrhea; lientery, lienteria [both Med.]; dysentery; coeliac flux *or* passion [Med.]; peccant humor, pus, matter; ordure etc. (dung) 653.7; offal etc. 653.6.

3. *n.* urine, water [euphemistic], piss [now vulg.], lant [obs.], stale [now only Zool.], micturition.

4. *n.* perspiration, sweat, diaphoresis [Med.], water, *sudor* [L.], sudation [rare]; profuse perspiration, swelter, sudoresis [NL.], muck of sweat [coll.]; sweating room, sudatorium, sudarium, sudatory; sweat bath etc. 382.6.

5. *n.* saliva, spittle, sputum (*pl.* sputa), spit, rheum; salivation, ptyalism, spitting, expuition *or* exspuition [rare]; catarrh, hay fever, cold.

6. *n.* hemorrhage, hemorrhea, bleeding, bloody flux.

7. *n.* menses, menstrual discharge, ~ flow *or* flux, catamenial discharge, catamenia, monthlies, courses, period(s).

8. *n.* (study of excretions) eccrinology.

9. *v.* excrete, urinate, salivate etc. (eject) 297.13, 14, 15, 19; sweat etc. (exude) 295.7.

10. *adj.* excretory, excretive, excretionary; secretory, secretive, secretionary, secretitious [rare]; fecal, feculent; eliminative etc. (ejective) 297.22; exudative etc. (egressive) 295.9.

11. *adj.* sweaty, perspiry [coll.], sticky [coll.]; in a sweat *or* perspiration, in a muck of sweat [coll.], in a heat; sudatory, sudorous [rare], sudoric, sudorific,

---

299. He spat on the ground and made clay of the spittle.—BIBLE.

sudoriferous, sudoriparous; moist etc. 339.7; hot etc. 382.16.

300. Insertion
(See 301. Extraction)

Forcible Ingress.—1. *n.* insertion, introduction, insinuation, importation, infixion, injection, inoculation; impregnation, infusion, instillation, imbuement; implantation, planting etc. *v.*; interjection, intervention etc. 228.2, 3; entrance etc. (ingress) 294; addition etc. 37; reception etc. 296.

2. *n.* burial etc. (interment) 363; immersion etc. (submergence) 310.2.

3. *n.* insert, insertion etc. *above* 300.1; inset, inlay, embedment; addition etc. 39.

4. *n.* enema, clyster, glyster, lavage, lavement.

5. *v.* insert, introduce, insinuate, enter, import, infix, inject, inoculate; implant, plant; impregnate, infuse, instill, imbue, imbrue; inset, inlay, imbed *or* embed, bed, bed in; put in, thrust in, stick in, ram in, stuff in, tuck in, press in, drive in, pop in, drop in, whip in; pack in, impack; interject, intrude etc. 228.8, 10; introduce irrelevantly etc. 109.4; plunge *in medias res* [L.] etc. (speak plainly) 576.2; inweave, dovetail etc. (interlace) 219.9; pierce etc. (perforate) 260.14; add etc. 37.3.

6. *v.* ingraft *or* engraft, graft; bud; inarch.

7. *v.* bury etc. (inter) 363; immerse, dip etc. (plunge) 310.4, 5.

301. Extraction
(See 300. Insertion)

Forcible Egress.—1. *n.* extraction, withdrawal, removal, elimination, eradication, evulsion, extirpation, extermination; extrication, evolvement; ejection etc. 297; export etc. (egress) 295.

2. *n.* avulsion, forcible separation, wrench.

3. *n.* expression, squeezing etc. *v.*; distillation.

4. *n.* extractor, corkscrew, can opener, forceps, pliers.

5. *v.* extract, withdraw, draw, draw out, take out, pull out, tear out, pluck out, pick out, get out, weed out, grub up *or* out, rake out; pull *or* pluck up, pull *or* pluck up by the roots, unroot, uproot, root up *or* out, averruncate [obs.]; remove, eradicate, extirpate, exterminate, eliminate; extricate, evolve; excavate, dig out *or* up, dredge; eviscerate etc. (eject) 297.8–21.

6. *v.* elicit, extract etc. *above*, exact, extort, draw *or* bring out *or* forth, wring *or* wrest from.

7. *v.* express, squeeze *or* press out, wring, wring out; distill *or* distil.

8. *adj.* extracted etc. *v.*

302. Passage

Motion Through.—1. *n.* passage, passing etc. *v.*, transcursion [obs.]; transilience, transiliency [rare]; penetration, interpenetration; permeation, pervasion; transudation; infiltration; exosmosis, exosmose; osmosis, osmose; endosmosis, endosmose; intercurrence, intervention; ingress etc. 294; egress etc. 295; path etc. 627.2; pass, defile etc. 198.2; conduit etc. 350; opening etc. 260; journey etc. 266.8; voyage etc. 267.6; transmission etc. (transference) 270.

2. *v.* pass, go; work ~, make ~, force ~, worm ~, thread etc. one's way, make *or* force a passage, cut one's way through, make way; pass *or* go through, penetrate, interpenetrate; permeate, pervade; pass *or* go over, traverse, go over the ground; pass *or* go across, cross, ford, cut across; thread, thrid [arch. or dial.]; file, enfile [obs.], enfilade; repass, pass and repass; find an opening, ~ one's way, ~ a vent etc. (*see* opening etc. 260); pass by etc. (outstrip) 303.4; hand, transmit etc. (transfer) 270.6, 7; pierce etc. (perforate) 260.14.

3. *adj.* passing etc. *v.*; transilient; intercurrent; endosmosic, endosmotic; exosmic, exosmotic; osmotic.

4. *adv.* in passing, *en passant* [F.]; by the way etc. 134.11; on the way etc. 270.13.

---

301. I live by squeezing from a stone / The little nourishment I get.—E. WYLIE.   Pluck out the heart of my mystery.—SHAKESPEARE. Extracted from many objects.—SHAKESPEARE.

302. You may not pass, you must return.—SHAKESPEARE.   Thou shalt not pass.—BIBLE. *Ils ne passeront pas* [They shall not pass].—PÉTAIN.

303. Overrunning
(See 304. Shortcoming)

Motion Beyond.—1. *n.* overrunning, overrun, overpass, overpassing etc. *v.*; overstep [rare], transgression, trespass, trespassage [rare], inroad, advancement, incursion, intrusion, encroachment, infraction, infringement, entrenchment *or* intrenchment; transcendence etc. (superiority) 33; redundance etc. 641.

2. *v.* overrun, overgo, overpass, overreach, overstep, overstride; run ~, go ~, pass ~, reach etc. beyond; overshoot, overshoot the mark, overshoot the field [Aeronaut.]; overleap, overjump, leap *or* jump over; overskip, skip over; overlap, override, lap *or* ride over; overtake, pass, go *or* pass by.

3. *v.* run over, overrun etc. *above*; overspread, spread over; overgrow, grow over, infest; overflow, flow over; deluge, inundate.

4. *v.* outstrip, outrun, overrun etc. *above* 303.2, outstep, outrival, outdo, outgo; outride, override; outleap, overleap, outjump, overjump; outmarch; distance, leave in the lurch *or* rear, throw into the shade; get *or* shoot ahead of, steal a march upon; show in front, come to the front; beat, surpass etc. (exceed) 33.5; lead etc. (precede) 280.2.

5. *v.* overstep, transgress, trespass, intrude, encroach, accroach [rare], infringe, invade, advance upon, trench on, entrench *or* intrench on; strain, stretch, strain *or* stretch a point; pass *or* cross the Rubicon.

6. *adv.* ahead, in advance, to the front, beyond the mark.

304. Shortcoming
(See 303. Overrunning)

Motion Short Of.—1. *n.* shortcoming, falling short etc. *v.*, shortfall, fall-shortage [coll.], shortage; delinquency; default, defalcation; leeway; labor in vain, fizzle [coll.], dud [slang], flash in the pan, flivver [slang], washout [slang], no go [coll.]; decline, slump; inadequacy, want, lack etc. (insufficiency) 640; deficiency etc. (incompleteness) 53; noncompletion etc. 730; imperfection etc. 651; failure etc. 732; inferiority etc. 34.

2. *v.* fall short, fall short of, come short, come short of, stop short, stop short of; not reach, fail to reach, ~ arrive at *or* attain; want, lack, be found wanting *or* lacking, be deficient etc. *adj.*, kick the beam; miscarry, miss the mark, miss stays [Naut.], miss one's mooring; fall through, fall down [coll.], fall to the ground, fall flat, flat out [coll., U.S.], collapse, come to nothing, end *or* go up in smoke, fizzle out [coll.]; decline, lose ground, slump; be insufficient etc. 640.6; be imperfect etc. 651.3; fail etc. 732.5; not complete etc. 730.2.

3. *adj.* short, short of, deficient, inadequate, lacking, wanting, minus; unreached; perfunctory etc. (neglectful) 460.8; incomplete etc. 53.4.

4. *adv.* behind, behindhand, in arrear *or* arrears.

5. *adv.* amiss, astray, beside the mark, far from it, to no purpose, *re infecta* [L.]; within the mark, within compass *or* bounds.

305. Ascent
(See 306. Descent)

Motion Upwards.—1. *n.* ascent, ascension, ascendance *or* ascendence, mounting ~, passage *or* motion upwards, rising etc. *v.*, rise, uprise, uprisal, upgo, upgang [now dial.], upcome [Scot.]; climb, upclimb, escalade; upgrowth, updraft, upsurgence, upswing; upleap, upspring etc. (leap) 309; upheaval etc. (elevation) 307; upgrade, acclivity etc. (incline) 217.2; increase etc. 35; improvement etc. 658.

2. *n.* stairs, stair, stairway, staircase, *escalier* [F.], steps, flight of steps *or* stairs; spiral stairs, winding staircase; ladder, scale, Jacob [slang], scaling ladder, stepladder, Jacob's ladder [Naut.]; stile; companion ladder, companionway, companion, accommodation ladder, side ladder, gangway ladder, quarter ladder,

---
303. Your zeal outruns my wishes.—Scott. Shoot not beyond the mark, as the proverb says.—Terence.
304. Thou art weighed in the balances, and art found wanting.—Bible. Fell a trifle short of the . . . expectation.—Dickens.
305. And the souls mounting up to God / Went by her like thin flames.—D. G. Rossetti. Shall shine the traffic of Jacob's ladder / Pitched betwixt heaven and Charing Cross.—F. Thompson. Men do not heed the rungs by which they climb.—Masefield. Slowly

stern ladder [all Naut.]; back stairs, *escalier dérobé* [F.]; perron, landing; fire escape; escalator etc. (elevator) 307.3.

3. *n.* (comparisons) rocket, skyrocket; lark, skylark; climber, mountain climber.

4. *v.* ascend, mount, rise, arise, uprise, upheave, upgo, upcome, go up, get up, come up, rise up, work one's way up; start up, spring up, shoot up, upstart, upspring, upshoot, upspear [as grass]; upturn, turn upwards; upstream, upsurge, surge, stream *or* surge upwards; upspin, spin upwards; upwind, wind *or* curl upwards; upgrow, grow up; aspire, aim high; upleap etc. (leap) 309.4; float etc. (be light) 320.5; increase etc. 35.4; improve etc. 658.6.

5. *v.* climb, climb up, upclimb, clamber, clamber up, scramble *or* scrabble up, shin *or* shin up [coll.], ramp [arch. and dial.]; swarm, swarm up, upswarm; escalade, scale, scale the heights; climb over, surmount; overtop, o'ertop [poetic].

6. *v.* tower, spire; soar, plane, go *or* fly aloft, hover, float, float in the air.

7. *adj.* ascendant *or* ascendent, ascensional; ascending, uprising etc. *v.*; upward etc. *adv.*; scandent, scansorial [Zool.]; excelsior; uphill, acclivous etc. (sloping upward) 217.10, 12; upturned, upcast etc. (elevated) 307.8; buoyant, supernatant etc. (light) 320.7.

8. *adv.* up, upward *or* upwards, uppard *or* uppards [obs. exc. dial.], upwith [Scot.]; skyward, heavenward, toward the empyrean; uplong, upalong; upstream, upstreamward; uphill, uphillward; upstairs, upstair; up attic, up garret, up steps [all dial.]; uptown [coll.]; up north.

306. Descent
(See 305. Ascent)

Motion Downwards.—1. *n.* descent, descension [rare], downcome, comedown; falling etc. *v.*, fall, downfall, drop, slump; sink [rare], sinkage, decline, subsidence, lapse, cadence; decurrence *or* decurrency, decursion [obs.]; tilt, inclination, declension, declination; droop, sag, swag; dip etc. (plunge) 310; lowering, downcast etc. (depression) 308; declivity, downgrade etc. (incline) 217.2.

2. *n.* tumble, fall, *culbute* [F.], cropper [coll.], mucker [slang], flop [slang], spill [coll.]; headlong fall, header [coll.]; fate of Lucifer, ~ Icarus *or* Phaëthon; stumble, trip.

3. *n.* slide, slidder [Scot. and dial. Eng.]; slip, slippage, glissade [on snow], glissando [Mus.]; landslide [U.S.], landslip [Eng.]; snowslide [U.S.], snowslip [Eng.]; avalanche; debacle, *débâcle* [F.].

4. *v.* descend, avale [obs.], go *or* come down; fall, drop, fall *or* drop down, pitch *or* plunge downward; gravitate; sink, decline, subside, lapse, droop, sag, swag; set, settle; slump, slump down, flump, flump down, flop, flop down [coll.]; slip *or* slide down, slip, slide, slidder [now dial.], glissade, [on snow]; come down a peg [coll.]; dip etc. (plunge) 310.4; throw down, let fall etc. 308.4, 5; decrease etc. 36.3.

5. *v.* get down, alight, light; perch; dismount, unhorse, light and rest one's saddle [South. U.S.]; land [Aeronaut.] etc. 267a.34; crouch, stoop etc. 308.7.

6. *v.* tumble, fall, tumble *or* fall down, come ~, fall *or* get a cropper [coll.], come a mucker [slang], take a fall *or* tumble, take a flop [slang], take a spill [coll.], precipitate oneself; sprawl, spread-eagle [coll.], measure one's length, fall prostrate *or* headlong, take a header [coll.]; plump, plop, plump *or* plop down; topple down *or* over, nod to its fall; topple, titubate [rare], lurch, pitch; stumble, trip.

7. *adj.* descending etc. *v.,* descendent; down, down-reaching, downcast; decursive, decurrent [Bot.]; labent [rare], deciduous; sloping downward, declivitous, steep etc. 217.11, 12; deep etc. 208.8–13.

8. *adv.* down, downward *or* downwards, downwith [Scot.]; downhill, downgrade [coll.]; downstreet; down-

---

climb the moon-touched mountains up their stairway to the sky.—S. Hageman.   They climbed the steep ascent of heaven.—Heber. The spiral of its steep ascent.—E. Underhill. 'Tis common proof / That lowliness is young ambition's ladder / Whereto the climber-upward turns his face.—Shakespeare.
306. The rest of the way will be only going down.—S. Teasdale.   And so never ending,

but always descending.—Southey.   From morn to noon he fell, from noon to dewy eve. —Milton.   Some falls are means the happier to arise.—Shakespeare.   One may sooner fall than rise.—J. Ray.   All things that rise will fall.—Sallust.   Every slip is not a fall.—Fuller.

line [Railroad]; downstream, downstreamward [rare]; downstairs, downstair; downtown [coll.]; down south.

307 Elevation
(See 308. Depression)

1. *n.* elevation, raising etc. *v.*, sublevation, erection, lift; upheaval, upthrow, upcast, upthrust; sublimation, exaltation, eminence; hill, mountain etc. (height) 206; improvement etc. 658; ascent etc. 305.

2. *n.* lifter, erector *or* erecter; crane, derrick; windlass, capstan, winch, tiller; pulley, cone pulley, tackle, gun, luff, runner; dredge, dredger, dredging machine, elevator dredge; jack, jackscrew.

3. *n.* elevator, *ascenseur* [F.], lift [chiefly Eng.]; escalator, moving staircase *or* stairway; dumb-waiter.

4. *n.* lever, pry, prize [now dial.]; bar, prying bar, crowbar, crow, iron crow, gavelock [arch. and dial.]; jemmy, jimmy; handspike, marlinespike; revolving lever; arm, limb, wing; leverage etc. 175.3; fulcrum etc. 215.5.

5. *v.* elevate, sublevate, raise, rear, erect, lift, boost [coll., U.S.], hoist, heave; raise ~, lift etc. up, set up, stick up; upraise, uplift, uprear, uphoist, upheave; upthrow, upcast; heighten, height [now Scot. and dial. Eng.], render high etc. (*see* high etc. 206.13); perk up, perch up [obs.]; hold *or* bear up *or* aloft, uphold, upbear; buoy, buoy up; mount, give a leg up [coll.], give a lift; exalt, sublimate, place *or* set on a pedestal; improve etc. 658.6.

6. *v.* pick up, take up, gather up, draw up, drag up, fish up; dredge, dredge up *or* out.

7. *v.* stand up, rise up, get up; jump up, spring to one's feet; stand erect, hold oneself up *or* erect, hold one's head up, draw oneself up to his full height.

8. *adj.* elevated etc. v.; upturned, *retroussé*, turned up; upthrown, upcast; erect, upright, uplifted; stilted; attollent; rampant; eminent, lofty etc. (high) 206.13, 14; ascendant etc. 305.7.

9. *adj.* elevating etc. *v.*, elevatory; erective, erectile.

10. *adv.* elevatedly, erectly etc. *adj.*; on the shoulders of . . . ; on stilts; on one's legs, on one's hind legs [coll.]; on high etc. 206.19.

308. Depression
(See 307. Elevation)

1. *n.* depression, lowering etc. *v.*, abasement [arch.], debasement; detrusion; diminution, reduction; dent, dip etc. (cavity) 252.2; descent etc. 306.

2. *n.* overthrow, overset, overturn; upset, upturn, turnover, spill [coll.]; downthrow, downcast; precipitation, prostration; subversion, subversal.

3. *n.* bow, nod etc. (obeisance) 928.2.

4. *v.* depress, lower, let *or* take down, take down a peg [coll.], abase [arch.], debase, sink, bring low, reduce, couch; bear down, downbear; thrust ~, press *or* push down, detrude; drop, let drop *or* fall; dent, hollow etc. (render concave) 252.9.

5. *v.* overthrow, overturn, overset, upset, upturn, turn over, spill [coll.]; subvert, level, lay level, fell, raze, raze to the ground, down [arch. *or* coll.], bring ~, take *or* pull down, knock down; cut *or* hew down, whack down [coll.], mow down; throw ~, cast ~, fling *or* dash down, bowl down *or* over [coll.], drop, floor, ground, gravel [coll.], grass [slang], precipitate, prostrate, throw prostrate, prone [South. U.S.], supinate; throw *or* pitch headlong, spread-eagle [coll.]; trample in the dust, pull about one's ears; pull off one's high horse, take off one's perch [both slang].

6. *v.* sit, sit down, seat oneself; squat, get down on one's hunkers [Scot. and dial.]; perch, roost; couch, recline etc. 213.5.

7. *v.* crouch, stoop, bend, cower, get down.

8. *v.* bow, nod. etc. (make obeisance) 928.6.

9. *adj.* depressed etc. *v.*, at low ebb, at a low ebb; detrusive; downcast, downthrown; overthrown, upset; prostrate etc. (recumbent) 213.9.

---

307. Like a lily lifted high and white.—C. ROSSETTI.   But from this earth, this grave, this dust, / My God shall raise me up, I trust!— RALEIGH.

309. Leap
(See 310. Plunge)

1. *n.* leap, jump, hop, spring, bound, saltation [rare]; upleap, upspring; standing ~, running *or* flying jump; broad jump, standing *or* running broad jump; high jump, standing *or* running high jump; hurdle, hurdle race, the hurdles, timber topping [slang], steeplechase; vault, pole vault, demivolt, pounce.

2. *n.* caper, dido [coll., U.S.], antic, capriole, gambol, frisk, curvet, cavort [U.S.]; prance, prank [obs. exc. dial.]; caracole *or* caracol; *gambade* [F.], gambado; buck, buckjump, leapfrogging; falcade; hop, skip and jump; frolic, dance etc. (amusement) 840.3, 6.

3. *n.* jumper, leaper, hopper etc. *v.*, saltatory [rare]; broad jumper, high jumper; hurdler, hurdle racer, timber topper [slang]; vaulter, pole vaulter; bucking bronco, buckjumper, sunfisher [slang]; kangaroo, wallaby, jerboa kangaroo, bettong *or* bettonga; flying fish; jumping rodent *or* rat, jerboa, jerboa mouse, kangaroo rat; chamois, goat; frog, toad; grasshopper, hoppergrass [dial., U.S.]; flea, flea beetle, flea bug, flea hopper, flea louse; skipper, skipjack, jumping jack; jumping bean.

4. *v.* leap, jump, hop, leapfrog, spring, bound, vault, saltate [rare]; leap ~, jump etc. up, upleap, upspring; dive upwards, updive; leap ~, jump etc. over, hurdle, clear, negotiate [cant]; start, start up, start aside; pounce, pounce on *or* upon.

5. *v.* caper, cut capers [coll.], cut a dido [coll., U.S.], antic, capriole, curvet, cavort [U.S.], gambol, gambado, frisk, leap and frisk, jump about, bob, bounce, flounce, trip, skip; romp, ramp [now dial.]; prance, prank [obs. exc. dial.]; caracole *or* caracol; buck, buckjump; frolic, dance etc. (amusement) 840.21.

6. *adj.* leaping, capering, etc. *v.*; saltatorial, saltatoric, saltatory; frisky, lively, capersome, rompish, skittish.

---

309. Leaping and flashing / From morn till night.—Lowell.   Leaps the live thunder.—Byron.   And make whole cities caper in the air.—Marlowe.   One must draw back to leap the better.—Montaigne.

310. Plunge
(See 309. Leap)

1. *n.* plunge, dip; drop, fall, header [coll.]; nose dive, power dive [both Aeronaut.]; crash dive, stationary dive, running dive [all submarine]; swoop, pounce; dive, swan dive, gainer, jackknife, fancy diving; belly-buster, belly-whopping [both dial.].

2. *n.* submergence, submersion, immersion, immergence, engulfment, inundation, baptism, ducking etc. *v.*; insertion etc. 300.2; burial etc. (interment) 363.

3. *n.* diver, deep-sea diver, plunger etc. *v.*; diving bird, loon, auk, penguin, grebe, sea gull, sea duck etc.; diving boat, diving bell, diving helmet, diving hood, diving suit *or* dress.

4. *v.* plunge, dip, duck; dive, souse; drop, fall, pitch; swoop, swoop down; pounce, pounce on *or* upon; nose-dive, make a nose dive, pique [all Aeronaut.]; plump, plunk, plop; take *or* make a plunge, take a header [coll.], pitch headlong, plunge *or* dive headfirst; pitch and plunge etc. (be agitated) 315.9; descend etc. 306.4.

5. *v.* submerge, submerse, immerse, immerge, merge, sink, bury, engulf, inundate, deluge, douse, souse, plunge in water, drown; dip, duck etc. *above*; baptize; scuttle [Naut.], send to the bottom, send to Davy Jones's locker [slang], feed the fish; founder, go down, go to the bottom, go down like a stone, get out of one's depth; mire, mire down; wallow etc. 311.5; bathe etc. 652.9; insert etc. 300.7.

6. *adj.* submergible, submersible; soundable.

311. Circuity

Curvilinear Motion.—1. *n.* circuity, circuitousness, circuition [arch.], circulation; circumvention, circumambulation, circumambience *or* circumambiency, circumflexion, circumfluence [rare], cir-

---

310. Two points in the adventure of a diver, / One—when, a beggar, he prepares to plunge, / One—when, a prince, he rises with his pearl. / Festus, I plunge!—Browning.   Like foundered galleons sucked down.—D. Marquis.
311. I may wallow in the lily beds.—Shakespeare.   The common vicissitude and wheel of things.—Southey.   Throws his steep flight in many an aery wheel.—Milton.

311.1 – 312.7

cumnavigation, circummigration, circumvolation [rare]; excursion; compass [arch.], encompassment [obs.]; volutation; Northwest Passage; circuit etc. 629; ambit etc. (region) 181; rotation etc. 312; convolution etc. 248; evolution etc. 313.

2. *n.* turn, bend, curvet; volution, evolution; anteversion, antroversion; retroversion, retortion [rare]; twist, wrench; twirl, spiral etc. (coil) 248.2; circuit etc. 629; circle etc. 247.2.

3. *v.* circuit, circuiteer, make *or* perform a circuit, make *or* describe a circle *or* complete circle, move in a circle, circulate; circle, encircle; compass, encompass; go round *or* around, go about *or* round about; go out of one's way; detour, make a detour; go the round, make the round of, circumambulate, circumvent, circumvolate [rare], circumflex, circummigrate; circumnavigate, "put a girdle round about the earth" (Shakespeare); go *or* pass through 180° *or* 360°.

4. *v.* turn, bend, curve; wheel, heel, swivel, swing, pivot, double; round, turn *or* round a corner, double a point [Naut.]; roll, cock, cast, goggle, troll; turn around etc. (turn back) 283.6; put about [Naut.] etc. (alter the course) 267.24; turn aside etc. (deviate) 279.4-7; wind, meander etc. (convolve) 248.3.

5. *v.* wallow, welter, flounder, roll about, volutate.

6. *adj.* circuitous, going round, roundabout; ambagious, ambagitory; circumambient, circumambulatory, circumfluent, circumfluous, circumvolant, circumforaneous; circumflex, circumflect; circumnavigatory, circumnavigable; indirect, undirect; backhand, backhanded; devious etc. (deviative) 279.8; sinuous, tortuous etc. (convoluted) 248.4-6; crooked, zigzag etc. 217.13, 16; circumlocutory etc. 573.9.

7. *adv.* circuitously etc. *adj.*, round about, about it and about, in a roundabout way, by an indirect course, by a side door, by a side wind; from pillar to post; deviatively etc. 279.9.

312. Rotation

1. *n.* rotation, revolution, rolling etc. *v.*, roll, gyration, circulation, circination

[obs.], turbination; circumrotation, circumvolution [rare], circumgyration; circumfusion; surge; circuity etc. 311.

2. *n.* whirl, whirlabout, whirligig, wheel, reel, spin, swivel, turn, pirouette, gyre, gurge, eddy, swirl, twirl; convolution, convolute; whir, whirry [Scot.], vortex; whirlpool etc. 348.8; whirlwind etc. 349.13; somersault, cart wheel etc. (inversion) 218.1.

3. *n.* vertiginousness, verticity [obs.]; vertigo, dizzy round.

4. *n.* (comparisons) rundle, rundel [dial.]; flywheel, spur wheel, balance wheel, potter's wheel, spinning wheel, paddle wheel, mill wheel, contrate wheel, crown wheel, vortex wheel; cogwheel, gearwheel, gear, gearing, bevel bearing, spur gearing; wheel of fortune, Fortune's wheel; Ixion's wheel; wheels within wheels; roller, roller bearing; propeller, prop [Aeronaut.], airscrew [Aeronaut., Eng.], stick [Aeronaut. cant; chiefly in *dead stick*]; whirligig, whirly, whirlabout, carrousel, merry-go-round; top, teetotum; jack, smokejack [Hist.], spit; revolving door; gyro [coll.], gyroplane, gyroscope, gyrocompass, gyrostat, gyrometer, gyrowheel, gyrocar; screw, turbine, windmill, treadmill, whirl drill, whirling table, revolving lever, rolling stone; ball etc. (sphere) 249.2.

5. *n.* axis, axle, pivot, gudgeon, trunnion, swivel, spindle, arbor, pin, pole, radiant; axle spindle, axle shaft, axle bar, axletree; axle box, journal box, journal, jewel; hotbox; hub, hubble [U.S.], nave; gimmal, gimbal; bobbin, spool, reel, mandrel; hinge, hingle [obs. exc. dial.]; rowlock, oarlock; center etc. 222.2; focus etc. 74.

6. *n.* (science of rotation) trochilics, gyrostatics.

7. *v.* rotate, revolve, roll, turn, round, turn round, spin, spin like a top *or* teetotum, rev [Aeronaut. cant], turbinate [rare], gyrate, gyre, wheel, reel, whirl, whirligig, twirl, swivel, pirouette, swirl, gurge; eddy, whirlpool; circle, circulate; circumrotate, circumvolve [rare], circumvolute, circumgyrate [rare], circumgyre [obs.]; circumfuse; whirl dizzily, vertiginate [rare]; roll along, trundle,

---

312. The slithy toves / Did gyre and gimble in the wabes.—CARROLL. White mist circumvolves about her.—A. LOWELL. The silent swirl of bats.—E. B. BROWNING. Some vertiginous whirl of fortune.—DE QUINCEY. The whirligig of time.—SHAKESPEARE.

troll, bowl; surge, billow; roll up, furl; box the compass.

8. *adj.* rotating etc. *v.*, rotatory, rotary, rotational, rotative; trochilic, vertiginous; circumrotatory, circumvolutory, circumgyratory; gyral, gyratory, gyrational; whirly, swirly, gulfy; whirlabout, whirligig; vortical, vorticose; whirlwindy, whirlwindish; gyrostatic, gyroscopic.

9. *adv.* rotatively etc. *adj.*, round and round, round about, in a circle around, in circles, like a horse in a mill; in a spin etc. *n.*; head over heels, heels over head; clockwise, counterclockwise.

313. Evolution

1. *n.* evolution, unrolling, unfolding etc. *v.*; unfoldment, evolvement; development, Darwinism etc. (production) 161.5; eversion etc. (inversion) 218.

2. *v.* evolve, evolute [coll.]; unroll, unfold, unfurl, unwind, uncoil, untwist, untwine, unravel; open, expand, develop, become open, ~ disclosed *or* developed.

3. *adj.* evolutional, evolutionary, evolutionist, evolutionistic, evolutive; ontogenic [Biol.] etc. (producible) 161.11.

314. Oscillation

Reciprocating Motion, Motion To and Fro.—1. *n.* oscillation, vibration, vibratility, libration; vibratiunculation, vibratiuncle [both rare]; wave motion, pendulation, motion of a pendulum; nutation, circumnutation; fluctuation, fluctuosity [rare]; undulation, undulatance; vacillation, vacillancy [rare]; winding etc. 248.1; roller, swell etc. (wave) 348.10.

2. *n.* pulsation, pulse, beat, throb; palpitation, pitapat, pitapatation [joc.]; ticktock, drumming etc. (sound) 407; flutter etc. 315.5; rhythm etc. 138.3.

3. *n.* alternation, reciprocation; coming and going etc. *v.*, to-and-fro, ebb and flow, flux and reflux, systole and diastole; libration of the moon, libration in latitude; ups and downs; crossruff [card playing]; seesaw, teeter, teeter-totter, wigwag; changeableness etc. 149.

4. *n.* seismicity, seismism; seismology, seismography, seismometry.

5. *n.* swing, sway, swag, rock, lurch; wag, waggle; wave, waver; lilt, rhythm.

6. *n.* oscillator, vibrator; pendulum, pendulum wheel; seesaw, teeter [U.S.], teeter-totter, teeterboard, teetery-bender; shuttle; rocking stone, logan *or* loggan stone.

7. *n.* (instruments) oscilloscope, oscillograph, oscillometer; vibroscope, vibrograph; seismoscope, seismograph, seismometer.

8. *v.* oscillate, vibrate, librate, nutate, fluctuate, pendulate; undulate, wave, waver; swing, sway, swag, dangle, reel, rock, lurch, roll, toss, pitch; wag, waggle; wobble *or* wabble, wamble [dial.]; bobble, bob, move *or* bob up and down; dance, shake, quiver etc. (agitation) 315.9–11.

9. *v.* pulsate, pulse, beat, throb, pant, palpitate, go *or* beat pitapat; drum, tick etc. (sound) 407.8, 9; flutter etc. 315.10.

10. *v.* alternate, reciprocate, go to and fro etc. *adv.*, to-and-fro, come and go, pass and repass, ebb and flow, ride and tie, hitch and hike, back and fill; seesaw, teeter, teeter-totter; shuttle, shuttlecock; wigwag, wibble-wabble [coll.], zigzag.

11. *v.* wave, brandish etc. (agitate) 315.8.

12. *adj.* oscillating etc. *v.*, oscillatory, oscillative [rare]; vibratory, vibrative, vibratile, libratory; pulsatory, pulsative, pulsatile; palpitant, pitapat; vacillatory, vacillant [now rare]; undulatory, undulant; reciprocal, reciprocative, reciprocate [rare]; alternate, to-and-fro, shuttlewise; pendulous.

13. *adj.* seismic(al), seismological, seismographic, seismometric.

14. *adv.* alternately etc. *adj.*, up and down, to and fro, back and forth, backward and forward, backwards and forwards, in-and-out, from side to side, from pillar to post, off and on, ride and tie, hitch and hike, round and round; seesaw, zigzag, wibble-wabble [coll.]; like buckets in a well.

---

313. Unfolds both heaven and earth.—SHAKESPEARE. Unfold the passion of my love.—SHAKESPEARE.
314. The old unquiet breast . . . fluctuates to and fro.—M. ARNOLD. The ripe corn under the undulating air undulates like an ocean.—SHELLEY.

315. Agitation

Irregular Motion.—1. *n.* agitation, perturbation, perturbance *or* perturbancy [rare], trepidation, trepidity, unrest, restlessness, stir, disquiet, disquietude, inquietude, disturbance, turmoil, turbulence, tumult, tumultuation [obs.], hubbub, commotion, fomentation, rout, fuss, fluster, flurry, bustle, hurly-burly, racket; excitation etc. 824; excitement etc. 825.2-5; fear etc. 860; storm etc. (violence) 173.

2. *n.* ferment, ebullition etc. (effervescence) 353.3.

3. *n.* shaking etc. *v.,* jactation, vibration, vibratory oscillation, quassation [rare], succussion *or* succussation; jactitation *or* jactation [Med.]; shakes [dial., U.S.], shivers *or* cold shivers [coll.], ague.

4. *n.* shake, quake, quiver, quaver, tremor, tremble, shiver, twitter, didder; ripple, riffle [U.S.]; rock, lurch, sway; shift, shuffle; bob, bobble [coll.]; jog, joggle; jig, jiggle, jigget [coll.]; jostle, jolt, jar, bounce, jounce, bump; cahot [chiefly Can.], thank-you-ma'am [U.S.]; shock, shog [rare]; jerk etc. 285.3; earthquake etc. (outbreak) 173.2.

5. *n.* flutter, flitter [arch.], flicker, dance; shake, quiver etc. *above*; sputter, splutter; flap, flop [coll.]; palpitation, pitapatation [joc.], pitapat, pitter-patter; throb etc. (pulsation) 314.2.

6. *n.* twitching etc. *v.,* vellication; fidgets, fidgetiness; floccillation, tilmus [both Med.]; fits, convulsions; epilepsy, falling sickness; chorea, the jerks, St. Vitus's dance; megrims, staggers, blind staggers, mad staggers, stomach staggers [all Vet.]; subsultus [Med.]; tarantism *or* tarantulism [Med.].

7. *n.* spasm, throe, paroxysm, epitasis [Med.], convulsion, convulse [poetic], eclampsia [Med.]; seizure, grip, stroke, attack, fit, ictus [Med.]; tonic spasm, entasia [Med.], tetanus, holotony, laryngismus [Med.]; clonic spasm; cramp, Charley horse [coll., U.S.]; the bends, caisson disease; orgasm, frenzy etc. (state of excitability) 825.4.

8. *v.* agitate, perturb, perturbate, disturb, disquiet, discompose, trouble, stir, ruffle, rouse, excite, foment, flurry, convulse; churn, whip, whisk, beat; stir, shake etc. *below,* stir up, shake up, churn up, whip *or* beat up; set vibrating *or* quaking, cause to quiver *or* totter, vibrate, rock, sway, swing, wave; wag, waggle; flap, flutter; brandish, flourish, bandy, wield; jog, joggle; jig, jiggle, jigget [coll.]; jostle, hustle, jolt, jar, jounce, bounce, buffet, bump; hitch etc. (jerk) 285.5.

9. *v.* be agitated etc. *adj.,* shake, vibrate, tremble, quiver, quaver, quake, shiver, twitter, didder, jactitate [rare], trepidate [rare]; bob, bobble [coll.], bob up and down; jump, pitch, plunge, pitch and plunge, jump ~, pitch etc. about, toss, tumble, jump like a parched pea; flounder, stumble, stagger, totter, sway, lurch, rock, roll, reel, reel like a drunken man; wabble *or* wobble; wag, waggle; wiggle, wriggle; writhe, squirm, twire [obs.], twist and turn; shift, shuffle; bustle, buskle [obs.]; shake *or* tremble like an aspen leaf; be the sport of winds and waves, be driven from pillar to post *or* from post to pillar, keep between hawk and buzzard.

10. *v.* flutter, flitter [arch.], flicker, flick, bicker, waver, dance; shake, quiver etc. *above*; sputter, splutter; flap, flop [coll.]; palpitate, go pitapat, pitter-patter; throb etc. (pulsate) 314.9.

11. *v.* twitch, jerk, vellicate, move jerkily, ~ convulsively *or* spasmodically; fidget, have the fidgets etc. *n.*

12. *v.* ferment, effervesce etc. (bubble) 353.8; ebullate [rare], wallop [Scot. and dial.]; bubble, bubble up; simmer.

13. *adj.* agitated, shaking etc. *v.*; tremulous, quassative [rare], successive; desultory, subsultory [obs.]; saltant, saltatorial, saltatoric, saltatory; shaky, jerky, jerkish [rare]; convulsive, vellicative; twitchy *or* twitchety [coll.], fidgety, restless, unquiet, troublous, all of a twitter [coll.], all of a flutter; effervescent, effervescive; disturbed, frenzied etc. (turbulent) 173.12; excited etc. 824.9-11.

14. *adv.* agitatedly etc. *adj.,* by fits and starts, *per saltum* [L.]; hop, skip and jump; in convulsions, in fits, in a flutter,

---

315. With pulses that beat double.—E. B. Browning.   A tumultuous privacy of storm.—Emerson.   This age / Shakes like a reed in the unheeding storm.—Shelley.   Right as an aspes leaf she gan to quake.—Chaucer. Accept, if the choice be forced upon you, commotion before stagnation.—Tyndall.   A storm in a teacup.   A tempest in a teapot.

in a twitter [coll.]; "with many a flirt and flutter" (Pope).

316. Materiality
(See 317. Immateriality)

1. *n.* materiality, materialness, corporealness etc. *adj.*; corporeity, corporality, corporeality, substantiality; physical condition, flesh and blood, corporeal nature, material ~, corporeal etc. *adj.* existence; plenum (*pl.* plenums, plena).

2. *n.* matter, brute matter, materiality etc. *above,* material, stuff, hyle [Philos.], substance, material *or* corporeal substance; body, corpus (*pl.* corpora); element, principle, hypostasis, substratum (*pl.* substrata), groundwork, essential substance, physical basis; chemical; parenchyma [Tech.]; pabulum; frame; materials etc. 635; protoplasm etc. (organic matter) 357; inorganic matter etc. 358.

3. *n.* object, article, contrivance, device; thing, something; gadget; thingum, thingumadoodle, thingumabob, thingemajig, dinkus, jigger, hickey, dojigger, dohickey, dohickus, dohinkus, dohinkey, doodad, dodab, dofunny, whatchy, hootnanny [all dial., coll. or slang]; *je ne sais quoi* [F.]; what's-its-name [coll.] etc. 565.4.

4. *n.* materialization, corporealization, substantialization; insubstantiation [rare], embodiment; incarnation, reincarnation.

5. *n.* (science of matter) physics, natural *or* physical science, natural philosophy; *philosphie positive* [F.], positive philosophy, positivism; materialism, physicism, substantialism; somatology, somatics, somatism; hylism, hylicism, hylology [rare]; hylotheism.

6. *n.* materialist, physicist, corporealist [rare], substantialist; somatist, somatologist; hylicist, hylist [rare]; hylotheist; irreligionist etc. 989.4.

7. *v.* materialize, materiate [rare]; corporealize, make corporeal etc. *adj.*; substantialize, substantify, substantiate; insubstantiate [rare], incorporate, corporify, body, embody, personify; incarnate, incarn [rare]; reincarnate; externalize, exteriorize.

8. *adj.* material, materiate; corporeal, corporeous, corporal; physical, unspiritual etc. (*see* spiritual etc. 317.6); bodily, fleshly, somatic(al), hylic, substantial, tangible, ponderable, palpable, sensible; embodied etc. *v.,* incarnate; parenchymatous, parenchymatic, parenchymal; real etc. 1.8.

9. *adj.* materialistic(al), somatologic(al), hylotheistic(al); heterodox etc. 984.22.

10. *adj.* objective, external, impersonal, nonsubjective.

317. Immateriality
(See 316. Materiality)

1. *n.* immateriality, immaterialness; incorporeity, incorporality, incorporeality; insubstantiality, unsubstantiality, unsubstantialness, unsubstantiation; inextension, nonextension; nonexteriority, nonexternality; spirituality, spiritualness, spirituosity, spirituousness; spiritual world *or* realm, astral plane.

2. *n.* incorporeal being *or* entity, incorporeal, incorporeity, immateriality, unsubstantiality; spirit etc. (specter) 980a (psyche) 994.11; astral body etc. 994.12.

3. *n.* immaterialism [Philos.], idealism, Berkeleianism; Platonism, Platonic Idea *or* Ideal; psychism, panpsychism; hylozoism; animism; spiritualism etc. 994.4.

4. *n.* immaterialist, idealist; Berkeleian, Platonist; psychist, panpsychist, hylozoist; animist; spiritualist etc. 994.14.

5. *v.* immaterialize, dematerialize, unsubstantialize; disembody, discarnate; spiritualize, spiritize.

6. *adj.* immaterial, immateriate [obs.]; incorporeal, incorporal, incorporate, incorporeous; insubstantial *or* unsubstantial; intangible, impalpable, asomatous, unembodied, bodiless; unfleshly etc. (*see* fleshly etc. 316.8); unsolid [rare]; disembodied, discarnate, decarnate *or* decarnated; animistic, animative; Platonic, Platonistic etc. *n.*; unearthly, unworldly, extramundane; superphysical, hyper-

---

316. The immense unwieldiness, sluggishness, inertia, permanence of matter.—T. Mann. All Matter is indifferent to Form.—K. Digby. What is mind? No matter. What is matter? Never mind.—T. H. Key. And the Word was made flesh and dwelt among us.—Bible.

317. It lies around us like a cloud, / A world we do not see.—H. B. Stowe. This bodiless creation.—Shakespeare. There is a natural body, and there is a spiritual body.—Bible.

physical; spiritual etc. (spectral) 980a.4, (psychical) 994.22; supersensual etc. (supernatural) 976.14; imponderable etc. (light) 320.7.

7. *adj.* subjective, nonobjective; personal, individual; inherent etc. (intrinsic) 5.6; internal etc. 221.9.

318. World

1. *n.* world, creation, all creation, universe, nature, cosmos; plenum [L.] (*pl.* plenums, plena); macrocosm, macrocosmos, megacosm; earth, *terra* [L.], terrene [rare], sphere, globe, terrestrial globe, terrestrial [rare], "the pendent world" (Shakespeare); vale, vale of tears; wide world, whole wide world, four corners of the earth, the length and breadth of the land; Rhea, Gaea [both Gr. Myth.], Persephone, Persephassa, Proserpina, Kore *or* Core, Despoina [Gr. and Rom. Myth.], Cybele [Myth.; Asia Minor, Gr. and Rom.], Tellus *or* Tellus Mater [Rom. Myth.].

2. *n.* heavens, heaven, sky, welkin [arch.], empyrean, firmament, *caelum* [L.], lift *or* lifts [now chiefly dial.], hyaline, azure, cerulean, blue, blue sky, the blue serene, air, ether, "starry cope" (Shelley), starry heaven *or* heavens, vault, vault *or* canopy of heaven, "this majestical roof fretted with golden fire" (Shakespeare), "infinite meadows of heaven" (Longfellow), aerial region, celestial spaces; Atlas [Gr. Myth.]; Tyr, Frigg [both Norse Myth.], Varuna [Hindu Myth.]; paradise etc. (heaven) 981.

3. *n.* heavenly body, celestial body *or* sphere, luminary, star, orb, sphere; starry host, "these blessed candles of the night" (Shakespeare), "the burning tapers of the sky" (Shakespeare), "golden fruit upon a tree / All out of reach" (G. Eliot), "the forget-me-nots of the angels" (Longfellow), "the pale populace of Heaven" (Browning).

fixed star, variable star; planet, terrestrial planet, inferior planet, superior planet, secondary planet, major planet; minor planet, planetoid, asteroid; Mercury, Venus, Earth, Mars, Jupiter, Saturn, Uranus, Neptune, Pluto; evening star, Vesper, Hesper, Hesperus; morning star, daystar, Lucifer, Phosphor, Phosphoros *or* Phosphorus; Dog Star, Canicula, Sirius; North Star, polestar, polar star, Polaris, Cynosure; Bull's Eye, Aldebaran.

comet, blazing star [obs.]; falling *or* shooting star, meteor, meteoroid; meteorite, meteorolite, aerolite, uranolite, uranolith [rare]; nebulae, planetary $\sim$, diffuse $\sim$, spiral *or* dark nebula; coalsack, Coalsack *or* Black Magellanic Cloud; nebulous stars; solar system; music *or* harmony of the spheres.

4. *n.* sun, orb of day, daystar [poetic]; Helios, Hyperion; Titan, Phaëthon, Phoebus, Phoebus Apollo, Apollo [all Gr. Myth.]; Sol, Saturn [both Rom. Myth.]; Ra *or* Amen-Ra [Egyptian Myth.]; Shamash [Semitic Myth.]; Surya, Savitar [both Hindu Myth.]; photosphere, chromosphere; sunlight etc. (daylight) 420.8; parhelion etc. (nebulous light) 420.12.

"the glorious lamp of Heav'n, the radiant sun" (Dryden), "of this great world both eye and soul" (Milton), "centre and sire of light" (P. J. Bailey), "that orbed continent, the fire / That severs day from night" (Shakespeare).

5. *n.* moon, parish lantern [dial. Eng.], piece of green cheese [joc.], orb of night, queen of heaven, queen of night, silverfooted queen; Diana, Phoebe, Cynthia, Artemis, Hecate *or* Hekate, Selene [all Gr. and Rom. Myth.]; Luna [Rom. Myth.]; Astarte [Phoenician Myth.]; silvery moon, wan moon; crimson moon, blood-red moon; new moon, wet moon; crescent moon, crescent, waxing *or* increasing moon; increscent moon, increscent; decrescent moon, decrescent, waning *or* decreasing moon; half-moon, demilune, first *or* last quarter; full moon, plenilune [poetic], harvest moon, hunter's moon; the man in the moon; moonlight etc. 420.9; paraselene etc. (nebulous light) 420.12.

"sovereign mistress of true melancholy" (Shakespeare), "Queen and huntress, chaste and fair" (Jonson), "that huntress of the silver bow" (Hood), "that

---

318. World without end.—BIBLE. The created world is but a small parenthesis in eternity.—T. BROWNE. To see the world in a grain of sand.—W. BLAKE. Our Copernican globe is a great factory or shop of power, with its rotating constellations, times, and tides.

orbed maiden with white fire laden" (Shelley), "the wandering Moon" (Milton), "bright wanderer, fair coquette of Heaven" (Shelley), "a ghostly galleon tossed upon cloudy seas" (A. Noyes), "the wat'ry star" (Shakespeare), "the governess of floods" (Shakespeare), "Maker of sweet poets" (Keats).

6. *n.* constellation, configuration, asterism; zodiac, signs of the zodiac; the Chained Lady, Andromeda; the Eagle, Aquila; the Wagoner, the Charioteer, Auriga; the Herdsman, Boötes; the Giraffe, Camelopardalis, Camelopardiis, Camellus; the Hunting Dogs, Canes Venatici; the Lady in the Chair, Cassiopeia, Cassiope, Cassiopeia's Chair; the Lizard, Lacerta; the Lesser Lion, Leo Minor; the Lynx, Lynx; the Lyre, Lyra; the Serpent Bearer, Ophiuchus, Serpentarius; the Winged Horse, Pegasus; the Rescuer, the Champion, Perseus; the Arrow, Sagitta; the Monarch, Cepheus; Berenice's Hair, Coma Berenices; the Northern Crown, Corona Borealis, Corona; the Swan, Cygnus; the Dolphin, Delphinus; the Dragon, Draco; the Foal, Equuleus; Hercules; the Shield of Sobieski, Scutum Sobieskii, Scutum; the Serpent, Serpens; the Northern Triangle, the Triangle, Triangulum; the Great Bear, the Dipper, the Big Dipper, Charles's Wain, Ursa Major, Ursa; the Lesser Bear, the Little Bear, Ursa Minor; the Little Fox, Vulpecula.

the Ram, Aries; the Bull, Taurus; the Hyades *or* Hyads; the Pleiades, the Atlantides; the Twins, Gemini; the Crab, Cancer; the Lion, Leo; the Virgin, Virgo; the Balance, Libra; the Scorpion, Scorpio; the Archer, Sagittarius; the Goat, Capricorn, Capricornus; the Water Bearer, Aquarius; the Fishes, Pisces.

the Air Pump, Antlia, Antlia Pneumatica; the Bird of Paradise, Apus; the Altar, Ara; the Ship Argo, Argo, Argo Navis; the Keel ~, Carina ~, the Mast ~, Malus ~, the Poop ~, Puppis ~, the Sails ~, Vela of Argo; Carina, the Keel; Malus, the Mast; Puppis, the Poop; Vela, the Sculptor's Tool, Caelum; the Dog, Canis Major, Canis, Orion's Hound; the Lesser Dog, Canis Minor; the Centaur, Centaurus; the Sea Monster, Cetus; Chameleon, Chamaeleon; the Compasses, Circinus; Noah's Dove, Columba, Columba Noae; the Wreath, Corona Australis, Corolla; the Crow, Corvus; the Cup, Crater; the Cross, the Southern Cross, Crux; the Goldfish, the Swordfish, Dorado; the River Eridanus, Eridanus; the Furnace, Fornax; the Crane, Grus; the Clock, Horologium; the Sea Serpent, Hydra; the Water Snake, Hydrus; the Indian, Indus; the Hare, Lepus; the Wolf, Lupus; the Table Mountain, Mensa, Mons Mensae; the Microscope, Microscopium; the Unicorn, Monoceros; the Fly, Musca; the Rule, Norma; the Octant, Octans; the Giant Hunter, Orion, Orion's Belt, Orion's Sword, the Peacock, Pavo; the Phoenix, Phoenix; the Painter's Easel, Pictor; the Southern Fish, Piscis Australis *or* Austrinus, Piscis; the Net, Reticulum; the Sculptor's Workshop, Sculptor; the Sextant, Sextans; the Telescope, Telescopium; the Triangle, the Southern Triangle, Triangulum Australe; the Toucan, Tucana; the Flying Fish, Volans, Piscis Volans.

7. *n.* galaxy, Milky Way, galactic circle, *Via Lactea* [L.].

8. *n.* meridian, celestial meridian; colures, equinoctial *or* solstitial colure; equator, celestial equator, equinoctial circle; equinox, vernal *or* autumnal equinox; longitude, celestial longitude, geocentric longitude, heliocentric longitude, galactic longitude, astronomical longitude, geographic *or* geodetic longitude; ecliptic, orbit; houses [Astrol.]; signs, signs of the zodiac.

9. *n.* cosmology, cosmography, cosmogony; cosmism, cosmic philosophy, cosmic evolution; geodesy, geodaesia, geodetics, geodetic engineering, geodynamics.

10. *n.* (science of heavenly bodies) astronomy, astrology, stargazing; uranography, uranology, uranometry; astrognosy, astrography, astrochemistry, astrophysics, astrophotography, astrophotometry; eidouranion; planetarium, orrery; observatory; astromancy etc. 511.4.

—EMERSON. The universe, as far as we can observe it, is a wonderful and immense engine. —SANTAYANA. O brave new world.— SHAKESPEARE. This majestical roof fretted with golden fire.—SHAKESPEARE. This gorgeous arch with golden worlds inlay'd.—YOUNG. Slowly, silently, now the moon / Walks the night in her silver shoon.—DE LA MARE.

11. *n.* cosmologist, cosmogonist, cosmogoner; cosmographer, cosmographist; geodesist, geodete, geodetic engineer; geographer.

12. *n.* astronomer, astrologer, stargazer; uranologist, uranographer, uranographist; astrophysicist, astrochemist, astrophotographer.

13. *n.* astrologer, astrologian, astrologaster [derog.], astromancer, stargazer, Chaldean, figure caster *or* flinger [obs.]; seer etc. 513.2.

14. *adj.* worldly, earthly, earthy, mundane, terrestrial, terrestrious [obs.], terrene, terreous [obs.], telluric; terraqueous; subastral, sublunar *or* sublunary, under the sun; temporal; fluvioterrestrial; geodesic(al), geodetic(al).

15. *adj.* cosmic(al), universal; cosmogonal, cosmogonic(al); cosmographic(al); extraterrene, extraterrestrial.

16. *adj.* celestial, heavenly, empyrean, empyreal, uranic, astral, astronomic(al), starry, stellar, stellary, sphery; sidereal, sideral [spec. Astrol.]; astrologic(al), astrologistic, astrologous; planetary, planetarian, planetal; planetesimal, planetoidal, asteroidal; nebular, nebulous, nebulose; solar, heliacal *or* heliac; lunar, lunular, lunate, lunulate, lunary, Cynthian [poetic]; semilunar, semilunary; interstellar, intersidereal; star-spangled, starry, star-studded.

17. *adv.* on earth, on the face of the earth *or* globe; here below, under the sun, *sub Jove* [L.], *sub dio* [L.], under the stars, *à la belle étoile* [F.], beneath the sky, under heaven; in all creation, throughout the length and breadth of the land, to *or* from the four corners of the earth.

319. Gravity
(See 320. Levity)

1. *n.* gravity, gravitation, weight, heaviness etc. *adj.,* heft [coll.]; ponderance [rare], ponderosity, ponderation [rare]; pressure; specific gravity, relative density *or* weight; poundage, tonnage; mass, lump; burden, burthen [chiefly arch.], load, lading, freight, bale, cumber, cumbrance, encumbrance *or* incumbrance, incubus, incumbency, superincumbency; counterweight, counterpoise, counterbalance; ballast, ballasting.

2. *n.* (comparisons) lead, millstone, plumb, plummet, sinker, bob; mountain; Ossa upon Pelion.

3. *n.* weighing etc. *v.,* ponderation, trutination [obs.].

4. *n.* weight, unit of weight *or* mass; avoirdupois weight, troy weight, apothecaries' weight; grain, gr., dram, dr., ounce, oz., pound, lb., hundredweight, cwt., ton, tn., long hundredweight, l. cwt., long ton, l. tn.; pennyweight, dwt.; scruple, s.; stone, carat, metric carat, carat grain; metric ton, millier, tonneau, quintal, myriagram, kilogram, kilo, kg., hectogram, hg., decagram, gram, gr., decigram, dg., centigram, cgm., milligram, mgrm.

5. *n.* (weighing instruments) weighing machine, balance, balance of precision, precision balance, long-arm balance, short-arm balance, analytical balance, assay balance, bullion balance, alloy balance, Danish balance, Roman balance, steelyard, weigh beam, scalebeam, beam, weighbridge, Nicholson's balance, spiral balance, spring balance, scales, weighing scales, scale of precision, precision scale, counter scale, automatic-indicating scale, cylinder drum scale, barrel scale, fan scale, flexure plate scale, plate fulcrum scale, spring scale.

6. *n.* science of gravity, statics.

7. *v.* gravitate, descend, drop, plunge, sink, settle, subside, precipitate; be attracted, incline, tend, point, head, lead, lean.

8. *v.* weigh, weight [coll.], scale [rare], poise, balance, trutinate [obs.], heft [coll.]; counterweigh, counterbalance, counterpoise, equiponderate; be heavy etc. *adj.,* have weight etc. *n.,* ponderate [now rare]; weigh ~, rest ~, bear heavily ~, press *or* press hard on *or* upon, oppress, weigh down, burden etc. *below.*

9. *v.* weight, make heavy etc. *adj.,* weigh down, attach weights to, ingravidate [now rare and chiefly fig.], load, lade [arch.], cumber, encumber *or* incumber, burden, burthen [chiefly arch.], freight, tax, hamper, saddle; pile, stuff, wad, pack, pad; pile Ossa upon Pelion; overburden, overweight etc. (overload) 641.4.

10. *v.* outweigh, overweigh, overweight, overbalance, outbalance, outpoise, overpoise [both chiefly fig.], downweigh [rare], weigh down *or* out.

---
319. Weighed in the balances and found wanting.—BIBLE.

11. *adj.* gravitative, gravitational.
12. *adj.* weighty, heavy, hefty [coll.], ponderous, ponderable, onerous, oppressive, burdensome, cumbersome, cumbrous, unwieldy, massive, lumpish, lumpy; incumbent, superincumbent; static(al).

320. Levity
(See 319. Gravity)

1. *n.* levity, lightness etc. *adj.*, buoyancy, volatility, imponderability; imponderables [Tech.]; imponderabilia [NL.]; rarity etc. 322.
2. *n.* (comparisons) feather, dust, mote, down, thistledown, flue, fluff, cobweb, gossamer, straw, chaff, cork, bubble; float, buoy; ether, air.
3. *n.* leaven, leavening; ferment, barm, yeast, zyme, enzyme, pepsin, diastase.
4. *v.* lighten, render light etc. *adj.*, levitate, make buoyant, buoy up, uplift, upraise; disburden, unburden, unload.
5. *v.* be light etc. *adj.*, be buoyed up, rise, soar, hover, float, swim, plane.
6. *v.* leaven, ferment, work, raise, pepsinate [Tech.], effervesce.
7. *adj.* light, weightless, levitative, imponderable, imponderous, subtile, subtle, airy, ethereal, gossamery, feathery, corky [coll.], buoyant, volatile, floaty; superfluent, superfluitant, supernatant; foamy, frothy; light as air, ∼ thistledown, ∼ a feather etc. *n.*; sublimate, sublimated; suberose, suberous, subereous; portable, carriable etc.; rare etc. 322.4.
8. *adj.* leavening, fermenting etc. *v.*; fermentative, yeasty, barmy; frothy, foamy; enzymic, enzymatic [rare], zymic, zymotic, zymogenic, zymologic(al), zymolytic; diastatic; peptic(al).

321. Density
(See 322. Rarity)

1. *n.* density, solidity, solidness, denseness etc. *adj.*; consistence *or* consistency, spissitude, crassitude; impenetrability, impermeability, imporosity; incompressibility; costiveness, constipation; specific gravity, relative density; cohesion etc. (coherence) 46; thickness etc. 202.2.
2. *n.* indivisibility, indivisibleness etc. *adj.*; inseparability, impartibility, infrangibility, indiscerptibility; indissolubility, indissolvability [rare], insolubility; infusibility; sessility [Tech.].
3. *n.* densification, thickening etc. *v.*, condensation, compression, consolidation; solidification, setting, concretion, crystallization; inspissation, incrassation, coagulation; gelatination, gelatinization, jellification; caseation; precipitation; precipitate, sediment etc. (dregs) 40.2.
4. *n.* solid body, solid, body, mass, lump, gob [now chiefly dial. and slang], block, cake, knot; concrete, concretion; conglomerate, conglomeration; stone, rock; bone, gristle, cartilage.
5. *n.* clot, clod [obs.], grume, coagulum; crassament [obs.], crassamentum; casein, caseinogen, paracasein; legumin; curd, lopper [obs. exc. Scot.], clabber, bonnyclabber, clotted cream, Devonshire cream; sour milk etc. 397.2.
6. *n.* (instruments), aerometer, densimeter, densitometer; hydrometer, lactometer, urinometer.
7. *v.* densify, densen; thick, thicken; condense, compress, squeeze, ram down, compact, consolidate, press together, crowd, cram, constipate [rare]; inspissate, spissate [rare]; incrassate, coagulate, clot, congeal; gelatinize, gelatinate, jellify, jelly, jell [coll., U.S.]; curd, curdle, cruddle [dial.], clabber, lopper [now dial.]; precipitate, deposit; solidify, solidate [now rare]; concrete, cement, fix, set, take a set, cake, crystallize; granulate, corn [obs.]; kern [chiefly dial.], candy; petrify etc. (harden) 323.4; conglomerate etc. (cohere) 46.5-8.
8. *adj.* dense, solid, solidified etc. *v.*, pucka [Anglo-Ind.], compact, close, serried, thick, thickset, crass, spiss [obs.], stuffy; substantial, firm; massive, lumpish; impenetrable, impermeable, imporous; incompressible; constipated, costive; clotted, grumose, grumous; caseous; knotted, knotty, gnarled; crystallitic, crystalline, crystallizable; cohesive etc. (coherent) 46.9.
9. *adj.* undissolved, unmelted, unliquefied, unthawed.
10. *adj.* indivisible, individable, undividable, inseparable, impartible, infrangi-

---

320. No more than a light leaf / Or a snowflake in spring.—E. WYLIE.   The thoughts of others / Were light and fleeting.—HOUSMAN.   Steps with a tender foot, light as on air.—TENNYSON.   The grass stoops not, she treads on it so light.—SHAKESPEARE.   Trifles light as air.—SHAKESPEARE.
321. O, that this too too solid flesh would melt. —SHAKESPEARE.

ble, indiscerptible; undissolvable, indissolvable [rare], indissoluble, insoluble; infusible; sessile [Tech.].

322. Rarity
(See 321. Density)

1. *n.* rarity, rareness etc. *adj.*, tenuity, ethereality; subtlety, subtility, subtilty; compressibility; lightness etc. 320; ether etc. (gas) 334.2.

2. *n.* rarefaction, rarefication [rare]; attenuation, subtilization, refinement; dilatation, inflation etc. (wind) 349.

3. *v.* rarefy, attenuate, thin, subtilize, refine; dilate, inflate etc. (blow up) 349.24; gasify etc. 334.6.

4. *adj.* rare, rarefied etc. *v.*; subtile [now rare], subtle; thin, fine, tenuous, flimsy, slight, unsubstantial, spongy [derog.]; ethereal etc. (light) 320.7; uncompact, uncompressed etc. (*see* compact etc. 321.8).

5. *adj.* rarefiable, rarefactive, rarefactional.

323. Hardness
(See 324. Softness)

1. *n.* hardness, rigidness etc. *adj.*, rigidity, rigor; durity, induration, renitence *or* renitency, callosity; temper, razor ~, saw-file ~, tool ~, spindle ~, chisel ~, set *or* die temper; inflexibility, unflexibility, impliability [rare], unpliability, immalleability [rare], unmalleability, intractability, unalterability, immutability; inextensibility, unextensibility, unextendibility; inelasticity etc. 326; severity etc. 739; toughness etc. 327.

2. *n.* hardening etc. *v.*, induration; petrification, petrifaction, petrescence *or* petrescency; lapidification, lapidity, lapidescence [obs.]; fossilization, fossilification, fossilation; lithification; cornification, hornification; chondrification, cartilaginification; glaciation; vitrification, vitrifaction, vitrescence; ossification; crystallization.

3. *n.* (comparisons) stone, rock, flint, marble, crystal, quartz, granite, adamant; bone, fossil, cartilage; calculus (*pl.* calculi, calculuses); hardware; oak, heart of oak; board, hardwood; block, brick; steel, iron, nails; concrete, cement; osmiridium, iridosmine *or* iridosmium.

4. *v.* harden, become *or* render hard etc. *adj.*, stiffen, callous, indurate, temper; petrify, lapidify; fossilize, fossilify; lithify [Geol.]; vitrify, vitrificate [obs.]; glacify; ossify; cornify, hornify; crystallize, granulate etc. (solidify) 321.7; mineralize etc. 358.3.

5. *adj.* hard, rigid, rigorous, indurate *or* indurated, stark, tense, firm, tough, renitent, stubborn; inflexible, unflexible, impliable [rare], unpliable, unpliant, immalleable [rare], unmalleable, intractable, untractable, intractile, inelastic, unalterable, immutable, unyielding, unbending, unlimber; stiff, stiff as a poker, stiff as buckram; virgate, rodlike; ramroddy, pokerish [both coll.]; inextensile, inextensible, unextensible, unextendible; impenetrable, impregnable, proof.

hard as nails, ~ a rock etc. *n.*; adamantine, adamantean; lapideous, lapidose [rare], lapidary, lapidific(al); stony, rocky, stonelike, rocklike, lithoid *or* lithoidal, concrete, cement, cemental; vitreous, vitrescent, vitrescible, vitrifiable; horny, cornified, corneous, callous; bony, osseous, ossific, ossified; cartilaginous, chondric; petrified, petrific [rare], petrifactive; lapidified, fossilized; crystallized, crystalloid *or* crystalloidal; gritty; starch, starched, starchy; inelastic etc. 326.3; tough etc. 327.5; resistant etc. 719.5; severe etc. 739.5.

324. Softness
(See 323. Hardness)

1. *n.* softness, pliableness etc. *adj.*, pliability, pliancy, plasticity, flexibility, sequacity, malleability, ductility, ductibility, tractability, tractility, facility, flaccidity, elasticity; extensibility, extendibility; laxity, laxation; flocculence *or* flocculency.

2. *n.* softening etc. *v.*, mollification, mollescence, dulcification, demulsion, assuagement; laxation, relaxation.

3. *n.* (comparisons) clay, alumina, argil; wax, putty, butter, dough, pudding; cushion, pillow, feather bed; pad-

---

322. Plain truths lose much of their weight when rarefied into subtleties.—CUDWORTH. Melted into air, thin air.—SHAKESPEARE.
323. His heart is as firm as a stone; yea, as hard as a piece of the nether millstone.—BIBLE

324. From softness only softness comes.—GOGARTY.   Straight, but as lissome as a hazel wand.—TENNYSON.   I will knead him; I will make him supple.—SHAKESPEARE.   Thou

ding, wadding; velvet, satin, silk; wool, fleece; down, eider down.

4. *v.* soften, render soft etc. *adj.*, mollify, dulcify, demulce *or* demulceate [now rare], leniate [obs.], assuage, mellow, milden, tender [rare], gentle [rare]; dissolve; relax, lax [obs. exc. dial. and slang], laxate; mash, smash, squash [coll.]; knead, massage; melt, thaw etc. (liquefy) 335.4.

5. *v.* be pliant etc. *adj.*, yield, give, relent, relax, bend, unbend.

6. *adj.* soft, not hard etc. (*see* hard etc. 323.5), tender, delicate; mellow, mellowy; yielding etc. *v.*, supple, pliant, pliable, flexible, flexile, flexuous, plastic, ductile, ductible [rare], fictile, tractile, tractable, malleable, moldable, sequacious, elastic, facile, dough-faced [coll.], impressible, impressionable, susceptible, responsive, receptive, sensitive; formable, formative; bendable, bendsome; lithe, lithesome, lissome, limber; extensile, extensible; lax, relaxed; flaccid, flabby, limp, flimsy.

doughy, pasty; aluminose, aluminous; loamy, clayey; argillaceous, argilliferous [both Min.]; squashy, squishy [dial.], squelchy; soft as butter, ~ silk etc. *n.*, "soft as woman's love" (Hammond), "soft as sinews of the new-born babe" (Shakespeare), tender as a chicken, yielding as wax, ~ dough etc. *n.*; boggy etc. (marshy) 345.3; muddy etc. 352.9; pulpy etc. 354.5.

7. *adj.* downy, fluffy, fluey [rare], feathery, fleecy, woolly; lanate *or* lanated, lanuginose *or* lanuginous; flocculent, floccose, flocculose, flocky; villose, villous.

8. *adj.* velvety, velvetlike, velutinous; satiny, satinlike; silky, silklike, silken, sericeous.

9. *adj.* spongy, edematous, medullar *or* medullary [Tech.], pithy.

10. *adj.* softening, mollifying etc. *v.*; mollient, emollient, remollient [obs.], mollescent, mollitious; demulcent, assuasive, lenitive, lenient.

325. Elasticity
(See 326. Inelasticity)

1. *n.* elasticity, elasticness, springiness etc. *adj.*; spring, resilience *or* resiliency,

buoyance *or* buoyancy [fig.], renitence *or* renitency; tensibility, tensility; extensibility, extendibility; ductility, ductibility [rare]; stretch, stretchability; flexibility, adaptability; rebound, reflex etc. (recoil) 277.

2. *n.* (comparisons) rubber, Indiarubber *or* indiarubber, caoutchouc; elastic, gum elastic; whalebone, baleen; turf, moss; balloon, blimp [coll.]; racket, battledore.

3. *v.* be elastic etc. *adj.*, bear extension, stretch; expand, extend etc. (enlarge) 194.5; spring back etc. (recoil) 277.3; give, yield etc. (be pliant) 324.5.

4. *v.* render *or* make elastic etc. *adj.*, elasticize.

5. *adj.* elastic, springy, resilient, buoyant [fig.], renitent; extensible, extensile, extendible, tensile, tensible, ductile, stretchable, stretchy [coll.]; flexible, flexile; adaptable, responsive.

326. Inelasticity
(See 325. Elasticity)

1. *n.* inelasticity, irresilience *or* irresiliency; inflexibility etc. (hardness) 323; want of elasticity etc. 325.

2. *v.* render *or* make inelastic etc. *adj.*, inelasticate.

3. *adj.* inelastic, irresilient; inflexible etc. (hard) 323.5.

327. Toughness
(See 328. Brittleness)

1. *n.* toughness, strength, resistance; tenacity, cohesiveness etc. (coherence) 46; gumminess, glutinousness, viscidity etc. (semiliquidity) 352; hardness etc. 323.

2. *n.* (comparisons) leather, white leather *or* whitleather, tawed leather, shoe leather; gristle, cartilage.

3. *v.* be tough etc. *adj.*, resist fracture.

4. *v.* toughen, render tough etc. *adj.*

5. *adj.* tough, strong, resistant, resisting; leathery, leatherlike, coriaceous; tough as leather, ~ whitleather etc. *n.*; gristly, cartilaginous; stringy, ropy,

---

canst mould him into any shape like soft clay. —HORACE.
325. He was elastic in body and youthful.—

HERGESHEIMER. The common resiliency of the mind from one extreme to another.—JOHNSON. His spirit, too, was of astonishing elasticity.—M. ARNOLD.
327. The old are tenacious.—HAZLITT.

fibrous; tenacious, cohesive etc. (coherent) 46.9; gummy, glutinous etc. (viscid) 352.8; hard etc. 323.5; stubborn etc. (obstinate) 606.6.

328. Brittleness
(See 327. Toughness)

1. *n.* brittleness, breakableness, frangibleness etc. *adj.*; frangibility, fragility, frailty; fissility; friability etc. (pulverulence) 330.
2. *n.* (comparisons) eggshell *or* egg shell; glass, spun glass, glass rod; glasshouse, house of cards; celery.
3. *v.* be brittle etc. *adj.*, break, burst, bust [dial.], crack, snap, split, fracture, tear, rive, rend, rupture, give way, fly apart, fall to pieces, crash, crush, shatter, shiver, splinter; crumble etc. (be pulverized) 330.7.
4. *adj.* brittle, brash [U.S.], crisp, crushable, breakable, lacerable, frangible, fragile, frail, delicate, shattery [rare], shatterable, shivery, splintery; fissile; gimcrack, gimcracky [coll.]; short, cold-short, hot-short, redshort [all Metal.]; brittle as glass, crisp as celery; friable, crumbly etc. (pulverable) 330.9.

329. Texture

1. *n.* texture, contexture, intertexture, fabric; surface, tissue, grit [of stone], grain, fineness *or* coarseness of grain, ingrain, fiber, nap, pile, shag, tooth, warp and woof *or* weft; structure, build, constitution etc. (form) 240; roughness etc. 256; web, textile etc. 219.4, 5.
2. *n.* (science of texture) histology, myology, myography, splanchnology, splanchnography, neurology, neurography, angiology, angiography, adenology, adenography; organology etc. (science of form) 240.4.
3. *adj.* textural, textile, textorial [rare], textrine [rare]; splanchnic, splanchnological, adenological etc. *n.*; fine, fine-grained, delicate, subtile, subtle, gossamer, gossamery, filmy; coarse, coarse-grained; homespun, linsey-woolsey; ingrain, ingrained; nappy etc. (rough) 256.12, 15; structural etc. 240.9.

---

329. That wonderful contexture of all created beings.—DRYDEN.

330. Pulverulence

1. *n.* pulverulence, pulverableness, powderiness etc. *adj.*; friability, arenosity, sabulosity; granularity, granulation; efflorescence [Chem.]; brittleness etc. 328.
2. *n.* pulverization, comminution, trituration, tripsis [Med.], contusion, levigation, abrasion, attrition, detrition, multure, limation, filing etc. *v.*; granulation, granulization, granulitization; attenuation, erosion, corrosion etc. (decay) 659.2.
3. *n.* powder, dust, attritus; cosmetic powder, face powder; efflorescence [Chem.]; crumb, crumble; grain, granule, granulet; grit, sand, gravel, shingle; meal, bran, flour, farina, rice, paddy; spore, sporule; limature [obs.], filings, raspings, scobs, shavings, parings, sawdust; detritus, debris *or* débris; scurf, scale, flake, floccule, flocculus (*pl.* flocculi); soot, smut, smoke; cloud *or* puff of smoke, cloud of dust *or* sand; dust storm, sandstorm etc. (wind) 349.12; particle etc. (smallness) 32.2.
4. *n.* pulverizer, mill, arrastra *or* arrastre, gristmill; grater, nutmeg grater; rasp, file; pestle, pestle and mortar; grinder, ball grinder, pebble grinder, grindstone, grinding stone; masher; kern [dial.], quern, quernstone, millstone; roller, steam roller, corrugated roller.
5. *n.* koniology, konimeter, koniscope.
6. *v.* pulverize, powder, reduce *or* grind to powder, comminute, triturate, contriturate, levigate, bray, crumble, crumb, disintegrate; granulate, granulize, granulitize; scrape, file, rasp, abrade, rub down, grind, grate; beat, pound, thrash *or* thresh; bruise, contuse, contund [rare]; mash, smash, crush, crunch, craunch, scranch [now chiefly dial.], scrunch [coll. and dial.]; attenuate.
7. *v.* be reduced to powder etc. *n.*, powder, come *or* fall to dust, crumble, crumble to *or* into dust, disintegrate, be disintegrated etc. *adj.*, fall to pieces, break up; granulate.
8. *adj.* pulverulent, pulverant [rare], pulverous, pulvereous, pulveraceous, pul-

---

330. Yielding to nothing, not even the rose, / The dust has its reasons wherever it goes.— N. CRANE.   Though the mills of God grind slowly, yet they grind exceeding small.—LONGFELLOW.   This dust was once the man.—

verized; powdery, dusty, comminute, triturate; fine, impalpable; chalky, chalklike; mealy, floury, farinaceous; branny, scurfy, furfuraceous, lentiginous, lepidote [Bot.], flocculent, flaky; granular, granulate *or* granulated; sandy, gritty, sabulose *or* sabulous, sabuline, arenose, arenarious, arenaceous, psammous; sporous, sporaceous; efflorescent [Chem.]; disintegrated, detrited, detrital; attrite [obs.], attrited; gone to dust, reduced to powder, in pieces, smashed to smithereens *or* smithers.

9. *adj.* pulverable, pulverizable, pulverulent; friable, crimp, short, crisp, crumbly, chalky, shivery; brittle etc. 328.4.

331. Friction
(See 332. Lubrication)

1. *n.* friction, frication, affrication, confrication, abrasion, limation, rub, rubbing etc. *v.*, elbow grease [joc.]; massage, massaging; facial [coll.], facial massage; anatripsis, anatripsology [both Med.]; erasure; force of friction etc. (potence) 157.4.

2. *n.* massager, massagist, masseur, masseuse [*fem.*], massageuse [*fem.*], masser, rubber.

3. *v.* rub, friction [rare], frictionize, affricate, abrase, abrade, fray, scrub, scour, burnish, polish, shine [coll.], rub up *or* off; rosin, wax; graze, raze; scratch, scrape, file, rasp, grind, grate; gnash, gnaw; crunch, craunch, scranch [now chiefly dial.], scrunch [coll. and dial.]; knead, massage; rub down, curry, comb; rub out, erase, raze; chafe, fret, gall; grate on, set the teeth on edge etc. 410.6, 7.

4. *adj.* frictional, fricative [Phonet.]; abrasive, abradant; arrosive; attrite [rare], attritive, anatriptic [Med.].

332. Lubrication
(See 331. Friction)

Freedom from Friction; Prevention of Friction.—1. *n.* lubrication, lubrification

[rare], lubricity, unction, anointment, oiling etc. *v.*; unctuousness etc. 355; smoothness etc. 255.

2. *n.* lubricant, lubricator; ointment, anointment [obs.], salve, balm, unguent, unguentum [Pharm.], unction; lenitive, lenient [obs.], emollient [all Med.]; mucus; synovia [Anat.], synovial fluid; saliva, spit, spittle, sputum; graphite, plumbago, black lead; grease, glycerin etc. (oil) 356.1.

3. *n.* lubritorium, lubritory; grease rack, grease pit.

4. *v.* lubricate, lubricitate [obs.], lubrify [rare]; oil, grease, anoint, salve [arch.], smear, daub, dress, liquor, dope [slang], pinguefy; lard; glycerin *or* glycerine, glycerinate, glycerolate, glycerize, glycerinize; pomade; wax, beeswax; slick, slick on [both co'l.]; smooth the way, grease the wheels [coll.], soap the ways [slang]; smooth etc. 255.4.

5. *adj.* lubricant, lubricating etc. *v.*, lubric [rare], lubricous, lubricative, lubricatory; lenitive, emollient [both Med.]; mucous, mucose [rare], muculent; synovial; salivary, salivous; oily etc. (unctuous) 355.3; slippery etc. (smooth) 255.5.

333. Fluidity
(See also 335. Liquefaction, 337. Water)

1. *n.* fluidity, liquidity, liquefaction, liquidness etc. *adj.*; chylifaction, chylification [both Physiol.]; serosity; gaseity etc. 334; solubility etc. 335.2.

2. *n.* fluid, liquid, liquor; juice, sap; latex [Bot.], milk; serous fluid, serum, lymph, humor, rheum, ichor, sanies, chyle, mucus, pus; beverage etc. 298.4; intoxicating liquor etc. 959.4–10; water etc. 337; semiliquid etc. 352.3–5; gas etc. 334.2.

3. *n.* blood, gore, claret [slang], ichor [Gr. Myth.], cruor, humor; grume.

4. *n.* (science of liquids at rest) hydrology, hydrostatics, hydrodynamics, hydrometry, hydrokinetics.

5. *n.* (instruments) fluidometer, hydrometer, hydrophone, hydrostat.

6. *n.* pump, force pump, lift *or* lifting pump, displacement pump, air lift, suction pump, bucket pump, jet pump,

---

WHITMAN. Grind their bones to powder.—SHAKESPEARE. Golden lads and girls all must / As chimney sweepers, come to dust.—SHAKESPEARE. For dust thou art, and unto dust shalt thou return.—BIBLE.
331. We rub each other's angles down.—TENNYSON. Elbow grease gives the best polish.

333. And sure, the reverent eye must see / A purpose in Liquidity.—R. BROOKE.

rotary pump, centrifugal pump, piston pump, shell pump; sand pump; air pump; hydraulic ram; plunger, forcer, air chamber; blower etc. 349.20.

7. *adj.* fluid, fluidal, fluible [obs.]; liquid, liquidy, liquiform [rare]; sappy, juicy, succulent; serous, sanious [Med.], lymphatic, rheumy, ichorous; chylifactive, chylifactory, chylificatory, chylific, chyliferous, chyliform [all Physiol.]; bloody etc. (red) 434.9; watery etc. 337.6; fluent etc. 348.26; semiliquid etc. 352:7–9; liquefied etc. 335.7.

8. *adj.* hydrologic(al), hydrostatic(al), hydrodynamic(al), hydrometric(al).

334. Gaseity
(See also 336. Vaporization, 338. Air)

1. *n.* gaseity, gaseousness etc. *adj.*, gaseosity [rare]; vaporosity, vaporescence; flatulence *or* flatulency, flatuosity [obs.]; etherealism, ethereality; volatility; gasification, aeration etc. (vaporization) 336.

2. *n.* gas, aeriform ~, elastic *or* compressible fluid, volatile, vapor; air, ozone [coll.], ether; fume, reek, effluvium, flatus, miasm *or* miasma, mephitis, mephitic air; natural gas, coal gas, oil gas, air gas, carbureted water gas; illuminating gas, sewer gas; acetylene, chlorine; hydrogen, parahydrogen, carbon monoxide, nitrogen, oxygen, ozone; rare ~, noble *or* inert gas, helium, neon, argon; methane, marsh gas; carbon dioxide, carbonic-acid gas; ammonia, ammoniacal gas, ammonium carbonate, volatile alkali [old Chem.].

war gas, poison gas, asphyxiating *or* lethal gas, vesicatory gas; mustard gas, yellow-cross liquid; lachrymatory gas, lachrymator, tear gas; sneeze gas, diphenylchloroarsine, adamsite; laughing gas, nitrous oxide; damp, chokedamp, blackdamp, firedamp, afterdamp [all Min.]; steam, water vapor; cloud etc. 353.5.

3. *n.* (science of elastic fluids) pneumatics, pneumatology, pneumatonomy, pneumatostatics.

4. *n.* (instruments) pneumatoscope, pneumatometer; gasometer, gas meter; aerometer etc. 338.8.

5. *n.* bladder, air bladder, swim *or* swimming bladder, sound.

6. *v.* gasify, render gaseous etc. *adj.*; aerify, etc. (air) 338.10; vaporize etc. 336.5; rarefy etc. 321.3.

7. *adj.* gaseous, gasiform, gassy, gaslike; aeriferous, airiferous, aeriform, aerial, aeric(al), aery, airy, airish, airlike; ethereal, etheric(al), etheriform, ethereous, etherous; volatile, volatilous [obs.]; vaporous, vaporose, vaporish, vaporific, vaporiferous, vaporlike, vapory; flatulent, flatuous [obs.].

8. *adj.* pneumatic, pneumatical [now rare], pneumatolytic *or* pneumatolitic, pneumatologic(al); aerostatic(al), aerodynamic, aeromechanic(al), aeroscopic, aerographic(al).

335. Liquefaction
(See also 333. Fluidity, 337. Water)

1. *n.* liquefaction, liquidization, liquidation [obs.], liquation [obs.], liquescence *or* liquescency; fluidification, fluidization; solubilization; dissolution; melting etc. *v.*, deliquescence, deliquation *or* deliquiation [obs.], deliquium [obs.]; colliquation [obs. exc. Med.], colliquefaction [obs.]; thaw; lixiviation; fusion, flux.

2. *n.* solubility, solubleness; dissolvability, dissolvableness; dissolubility, dissolubleness.

3. *n.* solution, dissolution; decoction, apozem [rare], cremor [rare]; lixivium, flux; mixture, infusion etc. 41.1–4.

4. *n.* solvent, dissolvent, dissolver, dissolving agent, resolvent, resolutive, diluent, liquefier, liquefacient, menstruum; universal solvent, alkahest.

5. *v.* liquefy, render *or* become liquid etc. (*see* liquid etc. 333.7), liquidize, liquidate [obs.], liquate [obs.], liquesce; fluidify, fluidize; melt, run, flow [obs.], colliquate [obs. exc. Med.]; deliquesce, deliquate *or* deliquiate [obs.]; thaw, thaw out, unfreeze; solve, dissolve, resolve, solubilize, hold in solution; chylify [Physiol.]; gasify etc. 334.6; fuse etc. (heat) 384.21.

6. *v.* leach, lixiviate, percolate.

7. *adj.* liquefied, melted etc. *v.*; molten; liquid etc. (fluid) 333.7.

8. *adj.* liquefactive, liquescent, deliquescent, colliquative [obs. exc. Med.], melting etc. *v.*; dissolutive, dissolutional; dissoluble, dissolvable, soluble, liquefiable, liquidable, meltable; leachy, porous,

9. *adj.* solvent, dissolvent, resolvent, resolutive, diluent, alkahestic(al).

336. Vaporization
(See also 334. Gaseity, 338. Air)

1. *n.* vaporization, vaporation [obs.], evaporation, volatilization, gasification, atomization, sublimation, distillation; cupellation, cohobation [now rare]; aeration, aerification; etherealization, etherification; exhalation, exhaustion; fumigation; smoking, steaming etc. *v.*

2. *n.* vaporability, vaporizability, evaporability, volatility; vaporosity, vaporousness etc. (gaseity) 334.

3. *n.* vaporizer, evaporator, atomizer, spray, cohobator, still, fine-still, retort.

4. *n.* vaporarium, vapor bath, vaporium, vaporary [obs.].

5. *v.* vaporize, render *or* become vaporous etc. *adj.*, vaporate [obs.], evaporate; volatize, volatilize; gasify, atomize, sublime, sublimate; distill, finestill; cohobate [now rare]; aerify, aerate; etherealize [rare], etherify; emit vapor, exhale, exhaust, reek, smoke, steam; fume, fumigate, perfume; spray.

6. *adj.* vaporized, volatilized etc. *v.*

7. *adj.* volatile, volatilous [obs.], volatilizable; vaporous, vaporose, vaporish, vapory, vaporific, vaporiferous, vaporescent, vaporative [obs.], vaporable, vaporizable; vaporing, reeking etc. *v.*; evaporable, evaporative; fumy, fumous [rare]; steamy, smoky; vaporlike etc. (gaseous) 334.7.

337. Water
(See also 333. Fluidity, 335. Liquefaction)

1. *n.* water, *aqua* [L.], *agua* [Sp.], *eau* [F.], lymph [poetic], Adam's ale *or* wine [joc.], crystal [poetic], burn [Scot. and dial.], *aqua pura* [L.], H_2O; watery element, flood [poetic or rhetorical]; drinking water, rain water, spring water; limewater, mineral water, waters; heavy water, hydrol, dihydrol, trihydrol [all Chem.]; water vapor, steam; diluent, fluid etc. 333.2; ocean etc. 341; lake etc. 343a; marsh etc. 345; stream, deluge, tide etc. (water in motion) 348; hot water etc. 382.5; urine etc. 299.3.

2. *n.* watering, wetting etc. *v.*; madefaction [now rare], humectation [rare], spargefaction [obs.], affusion, baptism, irrigation, seepage [U.S., Scot. and dial. Eng.], infiltration, maceration, saturation, dilution; aspersion, aspergation, Asperges [Eccl.]; immersion etc. (submergence) 310.2; ablution, balneation, bath etc. (cleaning) 652.2, 3.

3. *n.* sprinkler, sparger, sparge, sprayer, spray, atomizer; aspergill *or* aspergil, *aspergillum* [Eccl.]; shower, shower bath, needle bath; syringe, fountain syringe, douche, enema; sprinkling *or* watering can, watering pot, watering cart; nozzle, rose, rosehead.

4. *v.* be watery etc. *adj.*, reek, ooze, leak.

5. *v.* water, add water, wet, moist [obs. exc. dial.], moisten, damp, dampen, madefy [obs.], humect *or* humectate [rare]; sprinkle, besprinkle, bedew, spray, sparge, asperge, asperse [now rare]; splash, swash, splatter, spatter, bespatter; dabble, paddle; slop, slobber; pour on, affuse [rare]; soak, seethe, steep, macerate, souse, drench, drouk [chiefly Scot. and North. Eng.], sop, sodden, saturate; irrigate; inundate, deluge, flood; impregnate, inject, imbue, imbrue; infiltrate, percolate, seep [chiefly Scot. and U.S.]; gargle; syringe, douche; sponge; dip, immerse, plunge etc. (submerge) 310.5; wash, bathe etc. (clean) 652.9; dilute etc. 160.9.

6. *adj.* watery, waterish; aqueous, aquatic; hydrous, lymphatic; balneal; diluent, solvent, hydrotic(al); infiltrative, seepy, oozy; drenching etc. *v.*; wet etc. (moist) 339.7; liquid etc. 333.7; diluted, weak etc. 160.10, 14.

338. Air
(See also 334. Gaseity, 336. Vaporization)

1. *n.* air, ether, ozone [coll.], atmosphere, aerosphere [rare], sphere [poetic], welkin [arch.], lift [now chiefly dial.]; sky etc. (heavens) 318.2; hot air etc. 382.4.

2. *n.* atmospheric strata, layers; strato-

---

337. We never know the worth of water till the well is dry.—FULLER.   Honest water, which ne'er left man i' the mire.—SHAKESPEARE

Fish within their watery residence.—DRYDEN. Men really know not what good water's worth. —BYRON.   Dirty water does not wash clean. —J. RAY.
338. Heaven's sweetest air.—SHAKESPEARE. But soft! methinks I scent the morning air.—

sphere, isothermal region; substratosphere, tropopause, troposphere; ozone layer *or* blanket; Heaviside layer *or* region, ionosphere; airspace, ceiling etc. (aeronautics) 267a.19.

3. *n.* open air, open, outdoors, out-of-doors, great out-of-doors.

4. *n.* weather, climate, clime; rise and fall of the barometer *or* mercury; stormy weather etc. (windiness) 349.14; rainy weather etc. (rain) 348.11; hot weather etc. 382.3; cold weather etc. 383.3.

5. *n.* isobar, isopiestic, isopiestic line; isoplere, isometric, isometric line [all Thermodynamics].

6. *n.* ventilation, perflation, aerage, airing etc. *v.*; oxygenation, oxygenization; exposure to the air; ventilator, aerator [rare], ventilating *or* cooling system, air conditioner, air filter; fan etc. (blower) 349.20, 21; ventiduct, louver etc. (air passage) 351; cooler etc. 387.

7. *n.* (science of air) aerology, aerometry, aeroscopy, aerography, aerophysics, aerotechnics, aerodynamics, aeromechanics, aerostatics, aerostation, aerocartography; atmospherology; barometry, barometrography; meteorology, climatology; eudiometry; pneumatics etc. 334.3; aerodromics etc. (aeronautics) 267a.

8. *n.* (instruments) barometer, baroscope, aneroid, weatherglass, weather prophet, weather gauge; barograph, barometrograph; vacuometer, eudiometer; aerometer, airometer, air meter; aeroscope.

9. *n.* weather vane, weathercock, vane, cock, wind vane, wind gauge *or* indicator; wind cone, sock [both Aeronaut.].

10. *v.* air, aerate, aerify, wind, ventilate, perflate [rare]; pneumatize, oxygenate, oxygenize; fan, winnow; arterialize [Physiol.]; deodorize etc. 399.5.

11. *adj.* airy, aery, airish, aeric(al), airiferous, aeriferous, aerial, aeriform, airlike; atmospheric(al); ethereal, ethereous, etherous, etheric(al), etheriform; pneumatic, pneumatical [now rare]; flatulent; effervescent; alfresco; exposed, lofty [as a room], roomy, light; breezy etc. (windy) 349.25.

12. *adj.* aerologic(al), aerometric, aeroscopic, aerographic(al), aerotechnical, aerodynamic(al), aeromechanic(al), aerostatic(al), aeronautic(al); meteorologic(al); eudiometric(al); barometric(al), barographic, baroscopic(al); isobaric, isopiestic; isometric; pneumatologic(al).

13. *adv.* in the open air, in the open, alfresco; out of doors, outdoors; beneath the sky, under the sun, *à la belle étoile* [F.], under the stars, *sub Jove* [L.], *sub dio* [L.].

14. *adv.* out of the blue, out of a clear sky, like a bolt from the blue.

339. Moisture
(See 340. Dryness)

1. *n.* moisture, moistness, dampness etc. *adj.*; damp, wet, humidity, humectation; humidification; exudation, exhalation; mist, haze etc. (cloud) 353.5; marsh etc. 345.

2. *n.* dew, dewdrops, "dew-beads" (G. Eliot), "the tears which stars weep" (P. J. Bailey), "tears of the sky for the loss of the sun" (Chesterfield), "the gems of morning, but the tears of mournful eve" (Coleridge), "gems of earth and sky begotten" (G. Eliot); night dew, evening damp, *serein* [F.]; fog drip; false dew.

3. *n.* (science of humidity) hygrology, hygrometry, psychrometry, hygroscopy [rare], hygrostatics.

4. *n.* (instruments) hygrometer, hygrograph, hygrodeik, hygroscope, hygrothermograph; psychrometer; humidor; hygrostat.

5. *v.* moisten, moist [obs. exc. dial.]; render humid etc. *adj.*, humidify, humify, humidate [obs.]; dampen, wet etc. (water) 337.5.

6. *v.* be moist etc. *adj.*, not have a dry thread; reek, drip; perspire etc. (exude) 295.7.

7. *adj.* moist, moisty; damp, dampish; wet, wettish, madid [now rare], humid, dank, muggy, sticky [coll.]; juicy; watery etc. 337.6; vaporous etc. 336.7; misty etc. (cloudy) 353.11; rainy etc. 348.27; sweaty etc. 299.11.

8. *adj.* soaked, saturated, wringing-wet, wet to the skin, soaking, soaking wet, reeking, dripping, dripping wet; sodden, soppy, soggy, sloppy, swashy

---

SHAKESPEARE. My sisters, the birds, ye are greatly beholden to God for the element of the air.—ST. FRANCIS OF ASSISI.

339. I must go seek some dewdrops here / And hang a pearl in every cowslip's ear.—SHAKESPEARE. I am aware of the damp souls

[Eng.], squashy, plashy, soft; well-watered, irriguous; muddy etc. 352.9; swampy etc. (marshy) 345.3.

9. *adj.* dewy, roric, roral [rare], rorulent, roriferous [rare], rorifluent [rare], rorid [obs.], roscid [rare].

10. *adj.* hygric, hygrometric, hygroscopic, hygrophanous, hygrophilous, hygrothermal.

340. Dryness
(See 339. Moisture)

1. *n.* dryness, aridness etc. *adj.*, aridity, siccity [rare], drought *or* drouth.

2. *n.* drying etc. *v.*, siccation, desiccation, exsiccation [rare]; dehydration, anhydration; anhydromyelia [Med.]; evaporation, vaporation [obs.]; arefaction [rare], insolation, infumation [rare], dephlegmation, drainage; mummification.

3. *n.* drier, siccative, desiccative, desiccator, exsiccative, exsiccator; evaporator, evaporizer [rare]; dehydrator, dehydrant.

4. *n.* (comparisons) dust, bone, stick, mummy, biscuit, cracker; desert etc. (waste) 169.2.

5. *v.* dry, become *or* render dry etc. *adj.*, dry up; air-dry; siccate [rare], desiccate, exsiccate; dehydrate, anhydrate; arefact [rare], arefy [obs.]; evaporate, subject to evaporation, evaporize [rare], evapor [obs.], vaporate [obs.]; insolate, sun, sun-dry; infumate [rare], smoke, smoke-dry; torrefy *or* torrify, burn, kiln, bake, parch, scorch, sear, wither, shrivel, rivel [arch.]; mummify; soak up, sponge, swab, wipe; drain, draw off, exhaust, empty.

6. *v.* be dry etc. *adj.*, thirst.

7. *adj.* dry, dry as dust etc. *n.*, arid, arescent, waterless, unwatered, undamped, anhydrous, bone-dry, droughty; siccific, siccant [rare], siccate [obs.], siccaneous [rare]; dephlegmatory; juiceless, sapless; corky; husky; thirsty, thirsting.

8. *adj.* rainless, without rain, fine, fair, bright and fair, pleasant.

9. *adj.* dried, dried up, withered, parched etc. *v.*; sear or sere, burnt, adust; siccate [obs.], siccated, desiccate *or* desiccated, exsiccate [obs.], exsiccated; evaporate [rare], evaporated.

10. *adj.* drying etc. *v.*, siccative, siccant, siccaneous [rare]; exsiccative, exsiccant; desiccative, desiccatory, desiccant; evaporative.

11. *adj.* waterproof, watertight, moistureproof, dampproof, leakproof, dripproof, stormproof, storm-tight, rainproof, raintight, floodproof.

341. Ocean
(See 342. Land)

1. *n.* ocean, sea, great sea, main *or* ocean main [poetic], mere [arch.], tide [chiefly poetic], salt water, the brine, "the whelming brine" (Cowper), the briny [slang], the briny deep, the vast deep, "the vasty deep" (Shakespeare), the deep, the deep sea, the deep blue sea, holm [arch.], Davy Jones's locker [coll.]; pond, herring pond, fishpond, millpond [all joc.]; drink *or* big drink [slang, U.S.]; hyaline [poetic], the seven seas; high seas; wave, tide etc. 348.9, 10; seaway etc. (navigation) 267.8; ocean basin etc. (depths) 208.3.

"great Neptune's ocean" (Shakespeare), "the loud resounding sea" (Homer), "the farspooming Ocean" (Keats), "the always wind-obeying deep" (Shakespeare), "the treacherous sea" (Hood), "the desert of the sea" (Bible), "the wavy waste" (Hood), the watery waste, "old ocean's gray and melancholy waste" (Bryant), "the rising world of waters dark and deep" (Milton), "the bitter sea" (W. Morris), "Neptune's salt wash" (Shakespeare), "salt flood" (Shakespeare), "salt wave" (Shakespeare), "the great naked sea shouldering a load of salt" (Sandburg), "unpath'd waters" (Shakespeare), "the world of waters wild" (Thomson), "the glad, indomitable sea" (B. Carman), "the majestic main" (Thomson).

---

of housemaids.—T. S. ELIOT. My lips were wet, my throat was cold, / My garments all were dank.—COLERIDGE. The world globes itself in a drop of dew.—EMERSON.
340. With throats unslaked, with black lips baked.—COLERIDGE. In a drought the thirsty creatures cry.—DRYDEN. The sear, the yellow leaf.—SHAKESPEARE.

341. I must go down to the seas again, to the lonely sea and the sky.—MASEFIELD. All the rivers run into the sea; yet the sea is not full. —BIBLE. I have a profound respect for the sea as a moral teacher.—AGUECHEEK. The sea never changes and its works, for all the talk of men, are wrapped in mystery.—CONRAD. To me the sea is a continual miracle.—WHIT-

341.2 – 342.6

2. *n.* spirit of the sea, "the old man of the sea" (Homer), sea devil, Davy, Davy Jones; god of the sea, Varuna [Hindu Myth.], Neptune, Poseidon, Oceanus, Triton [all Gr. and Rom. Myth.]; Oceanid, Nereid, Thetis [all Gr. Myth.], mermaid, siren, merman, seaman *or* sea man; water spirit etc. 979.10.

3. *n.* oceanography, hydrography, bathymetry.

4. *n.* oceanographer, hydrographer.

5. *adj.* oceanic, marine, maritime; pelagic, pelagian [rare], pelagious [obs.]; oceanographic(al), hydrographic(al); bathymetric(al), bathyorographical, bathysophic(al), bathybic [Biol.]; benthonic [Biol.]; cotidal; seagoing etc. (Naut.) 267.48; seaworthy etc. 273.15.

6. *adv.* at sea, on the sea; afloat etc. (aboard) 267.53, 54.

7. *adv.* oversea *or* overseas, transmarine, across the sea, over the drink [slang, U.S.]; abroad [U.S.].

8. *adv.* oceanward *or* oceanwards, seaward *or* seawards; by sea.

342. Land
(See 341. Ocean)

1. *n.* land, earth, ground, carpet [Aeronaut. slang], soil, terra firma, terrene, terrain [obs. exc. spec.], clay, marl [poetic], loam [arch.], mold [arch. and dial.]; dry land; continent; mainland, main; midland, inland *or* inlands, interior; island etc. 346; plain etc. 344; highland etc. (height) 206.2; cliff etc. (precipice) 212.3; delta, peninsula etc. (point of land) 250.5; district, tract etc. (region) 181; acre etc. (proportions) 180.5; realty, real estate etc. (property) 780.4; fatherland etc. (country) 182.

2. *n.* shore, coast, strand, *playa* [Sp.], beach, waterside, foreshore; bank, embankment; seashore, seacoast, seaside, seaboard, seabeach, sea bank, sea margin; coastland, coastal region, littoral; rock-bound coast, iron-bound coast; scar, scaur [Scot. and Ir.]; loom of the land;

derelict; innings; reclamation, made land; alluvium, alluvion; border etc. (edge) 231.

3. *n.* soil, sod, glebe [poetic]; clay, cledge [local, Eng.], argil; potter's clay, china clay, porcelain clay; kaolin, kaolinite; residual clay, sedimentary clay; boulder clay, till; indurated clay, metal, clunch, shale, cloam [dial., Eng.], wacke; chalk; marl, shell marl, greensand marl; loam, loamy soil; gumbo, gumbo soil; humus, mold, leaf mold; subsoil; clod, clot [obs. exc. dial.].

4. *n.* rock, stone; boulder, river boulder, shore boulder, glacial boulder; sarsen, sarsen stone, druid stone; crag; marble, flint, slate, porphyry, granite, adamant, crystal, clint, dolomite, basalt, tufa; buhrstone *or* burrstone, burr *or* buhr; traprock, trap; limestone, mudstone, quarrystone, rottenstone, sandstone, freestone, braystone, quartz, cairngorm, aventurine, goldstone, smokestone, soapstone, steatite, brownstone, brimstone, pumice, chalkstone, clinkstone, phonolite, crowstone, dripstone, stalagmite, stalactite, greenstone, fieldstone, floatstone, ironstone, sand, grain of sand, gravel; chesil [Eng.], grit [now rare], gritstone, gritrock, grail [arch. or poetic], shingle [chiefly Eng.], beach [Eng.]; fingerstone, pebble, pebblestone, checkstone, jackstone, drakestone; chuckie [Scot.]; peckle, pecket [rare].

pavestone, tilestone, slabstone, flagstone, flag; cobblestone, cobble, coggle [obs. exc. dial.]; curbstone, kerbstone [Eng.], edgestone; doorstone, footstone, copestone, coping stone, coping, cornerstone, bondstone; bakestone, lapstone; precious stones etc. (gems) 847.8; monolith etc. (monument) 363.15.

5. *n.* (science of land) geography, geographics; geodesy, geognosy, geogony; *Geopolitik* [G.], geopolitics, geophysics; agronomics, geoponics etc. (agriculture) 371; geology etc. (mineralogy) 358.2.

6. *n.* (scientist) geographer, geodesist, geologist, geognost; agriculturist etc. 371.2.

MAN. There is nothing so desperately monotonous as the sea, and I no longer wonder at the cruelty of pirates.—LOWELL. Roll on, thou deep and dark-blue Ocean, roll!—BYRON. Sea, that breakest for ever, that breakest and never art broken.—W. WATSON.
342. And God said, Let . . . the dry land appear.—BIBLE. Of the earth, earthy.—BIBLE. The earth produces all things, and receives all again.—FULLER. The richest soil, if uncultivated, produces the rankest weeds.—PLUTARCH. Their soil was barren and their hearts were hard.—VERGIL. Where soil is, men grow, / Whether to weeds or flowers.—KEATS. Yea, the quiet and cool sod / Bears in her breast the dream of God.—J. H. WHEELOCK.

7. *n.* landsman, landman, landlubber [Naut.; derog.]; horse marine, freshwater sailor etc. (mariner) 269.
8. *v.* land, disembark etc. (arrive) 292.9.
9. *adj.* terrestrial, terrestrious [obs.], terrene, terreous [obs.]; earthy, earthly; telluric, tellurian; terraqueous; continental; midland, inland, mediterranean; alluvial; geophilous.
10. *adj.* coastal, littoral, seaside; riparian, riparial [Zool.], riparious, ripicolous, Ripuarian, riverain, riverine.
11. *adj.* landed, predial etc. (propertied) 780.8.
12. *adj.* territorial etc. (regional) 181.6.
13. *adj.* geographic(al), geodesic(al), geodetic(al), geognostic(al), geologic(al); geoponic etc. (agricultural) 371.9.
14. *adv.* on land, on dry land, on terra firma; on shore, ashore; by land.

343. Inlet, Gulf

1. *n.* inlet, indraft *or* indraught [obs.]; cove, creek; bay, bight; gulf; arm of the sea, arm, armlet, reach, loch [Scot.], mere [arch. and dial.]; fiord; mouth, estuary [obs.], firth *or* frith, kyle [Scot.], bayou [U.S.]; lagoon, *laguna* [It. and Sp.]; harbor, natural harbor; road *or* roads, roadstead; strait *or* straits, narrow *or* narrows, narrow seas; euripus (*pl.* euripi), belt, gut, sound; canal etc. (conduit) 350.1; entrance etc. 294.5.
2. *adj.* gulfy, gulflike; gulfed, bayed etc. *n.*

343a. Lake, Pool

1. *n.* lake, loch [Scot.], lough [Ir.], mere; tarn, terne [obs.]; lakelet, pond, pondlet, pool, linn [Scot.], tank [U.S. and dial. Eng.]; water hole, water pocket, *alberca* [Sp.]; fishpond; millpond, millpool; salt pond, salina; puddle, plash, sump [chiefly dial.], slab [now chiefly dial.]; wallow, hog wallow, buffalo wallow; broad [local, Eng.], fen; lagoon,

---

343. I see in you the estuary that enlarges and spreads itself grandly as it pours into the great sea.—WHITMAN.
343a. Far north, far north are the sources of the great river, / The headwaters, the cold lakes.—S. V. BENÉT.

laguna [Sp. and It.]; well, artesian well; cistern, tank, reservoir; dam, dike; standing *or* sheet of water, dead water; swimming pool etc. (bath) 652.4.
2. *n.* lake dweller, laker, lacustrian, lacustrine dweller *or* inhabitant; pile dweller *or* builder.
3. *adj.* lakish, laky, lakelike; lacustral, lacustrine, lacustrian; pondy, pondlike, lacuscular.

344. Plain

1. *n.* plain, plains, flat, flats, level, level land, open country, wide open spaces, champaign country, champaign, campagna [obs.]; reach, stretch, expanse; prairie, shaking *or* trembling prairie, lone prairie; steppe [Russ.], pampas [S. Amer.], *pampa* [Sp.], savanna [South. U.S.], tundra [arctic], vega [S. Amer.], campo [S. Amer.], sebkha [N. Afr.], common, wold, weald, veld [S. Afr.]; moor, moorland, down *or* downs, fell [Eng.], heath; basin, *playa* [Sp.], salt pan *or* saltpan; salt marsh; alkali flat; desert, barren *or* barrens, waste, barren *or* weary waste; wild *or* wilds, wilderness; bush, brush; plat, plot; plateau, tableland, table; mesa, mesilla [U.S.]; desert, wilderness etc. (waste) 169.2; meadow etc. (grassland) 367.11.
2. *adj.* champaign; campestral, campestral [obs.], campestrian, campestrine; plain etc. (horizontal) 213.8.
3. *adj.* alluvial, fluvio-marine.

345. Marsh

1. *n.* marsh, marshland, swamp, swampland, fen, fenland, moor, moorland, morass, marish [arch.], moss [chiefly Scot. and North. Eng.], bog, peat bog, mire, quagmire, slough, sump [chiefly dial.], wash, baygall [South. U.S.], *ciénaga* [Sp.], jheel [Ind.], vlei [S. Afr.]; bottom *or* bottoms, holm [Eng.]; innings; salt marsh; quicksand,

---

344. The plains are everlasting as the hills.—P. J. BAILEY. Turn away forever / To the plains and the prairies where pools are far apart.—S. TEASDALE. And we are here as on a darkling plain.—M. ARNOLD. A barren waste, a wild of sand.—ADDISON.
345. The funny things that live in woodland, marsh, or bog.—ANON. In the marsh beneath the moon.—W. R. BENÉT. Like to the greatness of God is the greatness within / The

cricksand [dial., U.S.]; mud, mud puddle etc. 352.5.

2. *v.* mire, sink *or* stick in mire, bog, mire *or* bog down, stodge.

3. *adj.* marshy, swampy, swampish, moory, moorish, fenny, marish [arch.]; boggy, boggish, miry; plashy, splashy, spouty [coll.], poachy, oozy, quaggy, squashy, squelchy, sloppy, sposhy [dial. U.S.], uliginose *or* uliginous, lutose, spongy, soft; paludal; quicksandy; muddy etc. 352.9.

346. Island

1. *n.* island, isle [chiefly poetic]; islet, holm, eyot *or* ait [Eng., chiefly dial.]; calf; bar, key, cay [W. Ind.], *caye* [Sp.], reef, atoll; archipelago.

2. *n.* islander, islandman [rare], islandress [rare], islesman, isleman [rare], insular, insulary [rare].

3. *v.* insulate, isolate, island, isle [rare], enisle [rare].

4. *adj.* insular, insulary [rare], insulated, isolated; island, islandic [rare], islandy; seagirt, surrounded by water; archipelagic, archipelagian.

347. Flow

Fluid in Motion.—1. *n.* flow; stream etc. (of water) 348, (of air) 349.

2. *v.* flow etc. 348; blow etc. 349.

348. Stream

Running Water.—1. *n.* stream, watercourse, *arroyo* [Sp.], river; creek [chiefly U.S.], crick [dial.]; brook, branch [U.S.]; run, race, beck [Eng.], gill, bourn *or* bourne, burn [chiefly Scot. and dial.], sike [chiefly Scot. and North. Eng.], lake [obs. exc. dial.], rindle [now chiefly dial.], rundle [dial.], runnel, runlet, streamlet, brooklet, rivulet; rill, rillet; fresh, freshet; tributary, feeder, branch, fork, prong [dial. U.S.], pup [slang, Alaska]; affluent, effluent; anabranch; reach; King of Rivers, Amazon; Father of Waters, Mississippi; channel etc. (conduit) 350.

2. *n.* flow, flowing etc. *v.*, flux, profluence, stream, current, tide [chiefly poetic], sluice, surge, gush, course, onward course, rush, onrush, run, race, career; drift, driftage; copious flow, large stream, river, torrent, niagara, flood, deluge; millrace, mill run; undercurrent, undertow; confluence, corrivation [obs.]; defluxion, downflow, downpour; regurgitation, backflow; outflow, effluence etc. (egress) 295; inflow, indraft *or* indraught etc. (ingress) 294.

3. *n.* overflow, overflowing etc. *v.*, alluvion, alluvium, inundation, exundation [rare], flood, waterflood, deluge, the Flood, cataclysm, debacle; freshet; washout.

4. *n.* trickle, trill, dribble, drip, drop, plash, spurtle; distillation, distillage [rare]; percolation, percolating etc. *v.*; eavesdrop *or* eavedrop, eavesdrip [now rare], stillicide, stillicidium; exfiltration, seepage etc. (egress) 295.

5. *n.* jet, spout, spouting etc. *v.*, spurt, spurtle, squirt, spray, splash, rush, gush, swash, flush; *jet d'eau* [F.], fountain, fount, font; natural fountain, spring; mineral springs, sulphur springs, hot springs; geyser; Old Faithful, Old Frightful [joc.]; fountainhead etc. (source) 153.2.

6. *n.* rapid *or* rapids, ripple *or* riffle [U.S.], riff [local, U.S.], ripraps [local, U.S.]; chute, shoot.

7. *n.* waterfall, fall *or* falls, Niagara, niagara, cataract, catadupe [obs.], cascade, force *or* foss [Scot. and North. Eng.], linn [chiefly Scot.], sault [U.S. and Can.], spout [rare].

8. *n.* eddy, gurge, surge, swirl, twirl, whirl; whirlpool, vortex, gulf, gurglet [rare], maelstrom; Maelstrom, Charybdis, Galofaro; countercurrent, counterflow, counterflux.

9. *n.* tide, tidal current *or* stream, tidal

---

range of the marshes, the liberal marshes of Glynn.—LANIER. Ye marshes, how candid and simple and nothing-withholding and free.—LANIER.
346. Past the setting of the sun / To wizard islands, of august surprise.—V. LINDSAY. Oh, it's a snug little island! /A right little, tight little island.—T. DIBDIN. The isles of Greece, the isles of Greece! / Where burning Sappho loved and sung.—BYRON. This royal throne of kings, this sceptred isle.—SHAKESPEARE.
348. Rivers are moving roads.—PASCAL. He smote the rocks and the waters gushed out. —BIBLE. I will cause it to rain upon the earth forty days.—BIBLE. When it rains, it rains on all alike.—J. RAY. It never rains but it pours.

flow *or* flood, tiderace; bore etc. *below*; tideway, tide gate; riptide; direct tide, opposite tide; spring tide; high tide, high water, full tide; low tide, low water; neap, neap tide; flood tide, ebb tide; ebb, reflux, refluence; ebb and flow, flux and reflux.

10. *n.* wave, billow, surge, swell, heave; sea, heavy swell; long sea, short sea; roll, roller; ground swell; tidal wave, bore, tidal bore, eagre; comber, beachcomber [U.S.]; surf, breakers; wavelet, ripple, riffle [U.S.]; feather [submarine]; whitecaps, white horses, ladies' fingers [Naut. slang], skipper's daughters [Naut. slang]; rough *or* heavy sea, rough water, dirty water *or* sea, pecky sea [coll.], choppy *or* chopping sea, chop, choppiness. "the circling wave" (Vergil), "the swelling tide" (Scott), "billows wild" (H. B. Stowe), "the furrow'd sea" (Shakespeare), "the lofty surge" (Shakespeare), "the billows' rage" (Byron), "roaring seas" (J. Gay), "the hell of waters" (Byron), "the many-twinkling smile of ocean" (Keble).

11. *n.* rain, rainfall, fall, precipitation, wet; rainstorm, shower, sudden shower, scud [chiefly Scot. and dial. Eng.], brash [Scot. and dial.]; sprinkle, drizzle, mizzle [now dial.], drisk [U.S.], drizzling rain *or* mist; mist, evening mist, *serein* [F.]; heavy rain, plash [chiefly dial.], pouring rain, pour, downpour, downflow, downfall, deluge, flood, cloudburst, spout, waterspout, rainspout, driving rain, drenching *or* soaking rain, drencher, soaker; goose drownder, fence lifter, gully washer, root searcher [all local, U.S.].
"tremulous skeins of rain" (T. Aldrich); rainy *or* wet weather, falling weather [coll.], dirty weather, dirt [coll., Naut.], greasy weather [Naut.], cat-and-dog weather [coll.], spell of rain, wet; rains, rainy season, monsoon; predominance of Aquarius, reign of St. Swithin; rain water; Indra [Hindu Myth.], Jupiter Pluvius [Rom. Myth.], the Rain Giver; thundersquall, thunder-gust, thundershower, thunderplump [rare exc. Scot. and dial. Eng.]; thunder etc. 406.4.

12. *n.* rain gauge *or* gage, pluviometer, pluvioscope, pluviograph; ombrometer; udometer, udomograph; hyetometer, hyetometrograph, hyetograph.

13. *n.* (gauge for measuring tides and heights of rivers) fluviograph, fluviometer; marigraph, Nilometer, hydrometrograph, hydrodynamometer.

14. *n.* (science of fluids in motion) hydraulics, hydrodynamics, hydrostatics, hydrokinetics, hydromechanics; pegology; fluviology.

15. *n.* (science of rain, snow, etc.) hyetology, hyetography; pluviography, pluviometry.

16. *n.* water carrier *or* bearer, water boy, bheesty [Ind.]; the Water-Bearer, Aquarius.

17. *v.* flow, issue, stream, pour, surge, run, course, rush, gush, flood; flow ∼, surge etc. back, regurgitate; flow out etc. (egress) 295.6, 7; flow in etc. (enter) 294.6; wind, meander etc. (convolve) 248.3.

18. *v.* overflow, flow over, exundate [rare], inundate, flood, deluge; spill, slop, slosh, spill etc. out *or* over.

19. *v.* trickle, dribble, dripple, drip, drop, spurtle, percolate, distill *or* distil; ripple, rumble, gurgle, guggle, burble, bubble, babble, murmur, purl, trill, lap, plash, splash, swash, slosh, wash; ooze, seep etc. (exude) 295.7.

20. *v.* jet, spout, spurt, spurtle, gush, well, surge; vomit, vomit out *or* forth, exgurgitate [rare].

21. *v.* eddy, gurge, surge, swirl, whirl, reel, spin.

22. *v.* billow, surge, swell, heave, toss, roll, undulate; rise and fall, ebb and flow.

23. *v.* (cause a flow) pour out, spill etc. (discharge) 297.13; irrigate, drench etc. (water) 337.5.

24. *v.* (stop a flow) stanch, stench [obs. exc. Scot.]; dam etc. (close) 261.2; obstruct etc. 706.4.

25. *v.* rain, precipitate, fall, wet [chiefly dial.], weep [poetic]; shower, shower down; sprinkle, spit [coll.], drizzle, mizzle [now dial.]; rain hard, rain *or* come down in torrents, rain cats and dogs [coll.], rain pitchforks [coll.], "rain daggers with their points downward" (R. Burton), rain tadpoles *or* bullfrogs [slang, U.S.], rain blue blazes [slang], pour, pour with rain; set in.

26. *adj.* flowing, streaming etc. *v.*; fluent, profluent, affluent; flowing down, defluent, decurrent; diffluent, deliquescent; fluvial, fluviatile, fluviatic; streamy, streamful, streamlike; tidal; choppy, pecky [coll.]; gulfy, vortical; stillatitious

[rare], stillicidious [obs.]; hydragogue [Med.]; meandering, flexuous etc. (convoluted) 248.4; billowy, undulating etc. (wavy) 248.7.

27. *adj.* rainy, showery; pluvious, pluviose [rare], pluvial; drizzly, drizzling, mizzly [now dial.], drippy; cat-and-doggish [coll.]; wet, wettish etc. (moist) 339.7.

349. Wind

Air Flow.—**1.** *n.* wind, draft *or* draught, air, stream, air stream, flow, air flow, movement of air, flatus, current, air current; undercurrent; "wind, that grand old harper" (A. Smith), "wings of wind" (Pope); afflation, afflatus; sufflation, inflation, dilation, dilatation, expansion; insufflation, inspiration, inflow, inrush; efflation, exsufflation, expiration, expulsion; emanation, aura [Tech.]; perflation etc. (ventilation) 338.6.

2. *n.* Aeolus [Gr. and Rom. Myth.], Vayu [Hindu Myth.], god of the winds; Boreas [north], Eurus [east]; Zephyr *or* Zephyrus, Favonius [west]; Notus [south], Caurus [northwest]; Afer [southwest] (Milton); Wabun [east], Kabibonokka [north], Shawondasee [south], Mudjekeewis [west] (all Longfellow).

3. *n.* (slang terms) blower; snow eater, thawer; sneeze; noser, dead muzzler; howler, rattler, roarer, screamer, sneezer, snifter, twister; duster, sander, black roller.

4. *n.* puff, puff of air *or* wind, capful of wind [Naut.], whiff, whiffet.

5. *n.* breeze, light *or* gentle wind, soft-blowing wind, zephyr, gale [poetic], air [chiefly poetic], breath, breath *or* stir of air; light *or* gentle breeze, moderate breeze, lady's wind [Naut. slang]; fresh breeze; cool breeze, doctor [coll.]; sea breeze, ocean air.

6. *n.* gust, guest [Naut. slang], blast, flaw, flurry, scud [chiefly Scot. and dial. Eng.]; keen *or* violent blast, squall; thick squall, black squall, white squall.

7. *n.* wintry wind, raw wind, sharp *or* piercing wind, cold *or* icy wind, biting wind, nipping *or* nippy wind, "a nipping and eager air" (Shakespeare), icy blasts.

8. *n.* hot wind etc. (hot air) 382.4.

9. *n.* (individual winds) mistral, foehn, bise [F.], *vendaval* [Sp.], *solano* [Sp.], *tramontana* [It.], tramontane; Euroclydon, gregale; sirocco; khamsin, samiel, harmattan; levant *or* levanter; chinook; trade *or* trade wind, monsoon, antitrades; simoom, typhoon.

10. *n.* (head and beam winds) head *or* head-on wind, dead wind, muzzler, dead muzzler, noser *or* nose-ender [slang]; beam wind, favorable wind, soldier's wind [coll.].

11. *n.* windstorm, wind, big *or* great wind, high wind, ill wind, storm, stormy winds, tempest, tempestuous wind, "tempestuous rage" (Shakespeare), tornado, blizzard, wuther [dial.], blow, violent *or* heavy blow, stiff *or* strong wind, gale; half a gale, whole gale; hurricane, harrycane [dial.]; norther, *bise* [F.]; northeaster, nor'easter; northwester, nor'wester, chocolate gale [Naut. slang; W. Ind.]; southeaster, sou'easter; southwester, sou'wester; easter, easterly; wester, westerly; souther; thundersquall, thunder-gust.

12. *n.* dust storm, sandstorm, shaitan [Ind.], khamsin [Egypt], devil [coll., Ind.], black blizzard *or* roller [dial.], duster, sander, dancing devil [all slang].

13. *n.* whirlwind, whirlblast, whirlicane, wind eddy, cyclone, twister [U.S.], tornado, willy-willy [Austral.], typhoon [tropics], *baguio* [Sp.], rotary storm; waterspout, rainspout.

14. *n.* windiness etc. *adj.*, ventosity [obs.]; windy weather, stormy weather, rough weather, dirty *or* foul weather, dirt [coll., Naut.], ugly *or* wicked weather, stress of weather; dirty sky etc. (cloudiness) 353.4.

15. *n.* calm, dead calm, not a breath *or* stir of air; up-and-down wind, Irishman's hurricane [both joc., Naut.].

16. *n.* (science of wind) anemology, anemography, anemometry; pneumatics; aerology, aerometry, aerography, aerodynamics.

17. *n.* (instruments) wind gauge *or* gage, anemometer, anemoscope, anemograph, anemometrograph; weather vane etc. 338.9.

---

349. Enclosed in a tumultuous privacy of storm.—EMERSON. While mocking winds are piping loud.—MILTON. The storm is up and all is on the hazard.—SHAKESPEARE. Blow, winds, and crack your cheeks! rage! blow!—SHAKESPEARE. He that will use all

18. *n.* respiration, breathing etc. *v.*; inspiration, inhalation; expiration, exhalation, suspiration, sigh; normal respiration, eupnea [Med.]; difficult *or* labored respiration, dyspnea [Med.]; sneeze, sternutation; sternutator, sternutative, errhine [Med.]; hiccough *or* hiccup; belch etc. 297.5.

19. *n.* lungs, bellows, lights [now beasts]; ctenidia [Zool.] (*sing.* ctenidium), branchiae [Zool.] (*sing.* branchia); gills.

20. *n.* blower, bellows; centrifugal blower, rotary blower; respirator, respiratory apparatus, inspirator, lungmotor, pulmotor [trade name]; blowpipe, blowtube, blowgun; air pump etc. (pump) 333.6; ventilator etc. 338.6.

21. *n.* fan, punkah [Ind.], flabellum [Eccl.], thermantidote [Ind.], electric fan; ventilator etc. 338.6; ventiduct etc. (air passage) 351; cooler etc. 387.

22. *v.* blow, waft, float, flow, stream, move, issue; puff, huff [arch. and dial.]; whiff, whiffle; breeze, breeze up, freshen; gather, brew; set in, blow up a storm; bluster, wuther [dial.], flaw [rare], squall; blow hard *or* furiously, blow great guns, blow a hurricane, rage, storm; blow lightly, zephyr [rare]; whisper, murmur, sough, sigh, sob, moan, groan, growl, snarl, wail, howl, scream, roar, whistle, pipe, sing, sing in the shrouds; ventilate, fan etc. (air) 338.10.

23. *v.* respire, breathe; inhale, inspire; exhale, expire; suspire, sigh; blow, puff, pant, gasp, wheeze; sniff, sniffle, snuff, snuffle; sneeze, cough; hiccup *or* hiccough; belch etc. 297.20.

24. *v.* blow up, inflate, sufflate [rare], aerate, huff, puff, puff up, bloat, dilate, stretch, distend, swell, expand; pump, pump up.

25. *adj.* windy, airy, breezy, blowy; gusty, blasty, flawy, squally; blustery, blusterous, blustering; wind-swept, bleak, raw, exposed; windwayward [poetic]; boreal, borean; favonian; aeolian.

26. *adj.* stormy, tempestuous; dirty, foul; cyclonic, typhoonish; raging, boisterous etc. (turbulent) 173.12; rainy etc. 348.27; cloudy etc. 353.11.

27. *adj.* blown up, inflated etc. *v.*, inflate [rare].

28. *adj.* anemological, anemographic, anemometric(al); aerologic(al), aerographic(al), aerodynamic.

29. *adj.* pulmonic, pulmonary, pulmonate.

30. *adj.* nasal, nasalized; sternutative, sternutatory, errhine [Med.].

31. *adj.* flatulent, flatuous [obs.]; windy, ventose; gassy etc. 334.7.

350. Conduit

1. *n.* conduit, channel, duct, way, passage, passageway, adit, course; watercourse, waterway, aqueduct; canal, ditch, dike, moat, trench, entrenchment *or* intrenchment, *tranchée* [F.], flume [U.S.]; chute, shoot; ha-ha; *acequia, acequia madre* [both Sp.]; main, water main; race, headrace, tailrace; gap, water gap, arroyo, *caño* [Sp.], canyon, *cañoncito* [Sp.], gorge, flume [U.S.], chasm, ravine, gulch [U.S.]; coulee [West. U.S.], *coulée* [F.]; gully, gullet [rare], gullyhole [chiefly dial.].

drain, sough [Eng.], scupper; sewer, cloaca, headchute [Naut.]; piscina *or* piscine [Eccl.]; gutter, kennel; gutter tile, pantile; culvert, culbert [dial.]; trough, troughway, troughing; pentrough, penstock [U.S.]; spout, waterspout, gargoyle, waterworks; pipe, hose, funnel etc. (tube) 260.6; tunnel etc. (cave) 252.3; vent etc. (outlet) 295.5; entryway etc. (inlet) 294.5; seaway etc. 267.8; stream etc. 348.

2. *n.* floodgate, flood-hatch, gate, valve, penstock, sluice, sluice gate, water gate, dock gate, lock, lock gate, head gate; tide gate; *aboideau, aboiteau, abito* [all F.; Can.]; weir, weir box, lock weir.

3. *n.* (for metal) ingate, runner, tedge.

4. *n.* (anatomy) vessel, blood vessel, artery, vein, *vena* [L.]; aorta; lymphatic, lymphatic vessel; emunctory; pore; intestines, guts [now vulg.], puddings [now dial. and vulg.], bowels, entrails; hind-gut, fore-gut; blind gut, caecum; small intestine, duodenum, jejunum, ileum; large intestine, colon, rectum; gullet, esophagus *or* oesophagus, throat, gorge, hals *or* halse [obs. exc. dial.], weasand, wizen [Scot. and dial. Eng.];

---

winds, must shift his sail.—J. Fletcher. For they have sown the wind, and they shall reap the whirlwind.—Bible. The wind bloweth where it listeth.—Bible. You can't catch the wind in a net. An ill wind that bloweth no man good.

fauces, isthmus of the fauces; windpipe etc. 351.3; pancreas etc. (gland) 221.5.

5. *adj.* vascular etc. (tubular) 260.16.
6. *adj.* excretory etc. (egressive) 295.9.

351. Air Passage

1. *n.* air passage, air duct, airway, air shaft, shaft; air pipe, air tube; air hole, blowhole, breathing hole, spiracle, touchhole, spilehole; vent hole, vent, ventage; ventiduct, ventilator; transom, louver, louverwork; bung, bunghole; smokeshaft, smokestack, flue, chimney, funnel; pipe etc. (tube) 260.6; blowpipe etc. (blower) 349.20; ventilator etc. 338.5.

2. *n.* nostril, nosehole [obs. exc. dial. Eng.].

3. *n.* windpipe, trachea (*pl.* tracheae), weasand, wizen [Scot. and dial. Eng.]; larynx, voice box; bronchus (*pl.* bronchi), bronchial tube.

352. Semiliquidity

1. *n.* semiliquidity, semifluidity; viscidity, viscosity; viscousness, stickiness, mucidness etc. *adj.*; mucosity, gummosis, gummosity [rare], glutinosity [rare], gelatinity, spissitude, crassitude, lentor [now rare]; colloidality [Tech.]; succulence *or* succulency; lactescence; pulpiness etc. 354.

2. *n.* viscidization, glutinization; emulsification, emulsionization; lactation; inspissation, thickening etc. (densification) 321.3.

3. *n.* semiliquid, semifluid; goo [slang, U.S.], gluten, paste, pap, gum, mucilage; coagulum, crassamentum, clot, grume; gelatin, jelly, jam; dough, batter; isinglass, ichthyocol *or* ichthyocolla; mucus, pus, phlegm, pituite; lava; albumen, albuminoid; glair, egg white; starch, starch paste; cream; lactarene *or* lactarine, casein; curd, clabber, bonnyclabber, clotted cream, Devonshire cream; emulsion, emulsoid.

protein, protean, proteide, nucleoprotein, glycoprotein, phosphoprotein, lecithoprotein, metaprotein, lactoprotein *or* lactoproteid, coagulated protein; rob, sirup, molasses, treacle [chiefly Eng.]; size, sizing; mastic, mastic gum; poultice; gruel, porridge, loblolly; *purée* [F.], soup, gumbo, gravy; pudding; glue etc. (cement) 45.6; pulp etc. 354.2; butter etc. (oil) 356; varnish etc. (resin) 356a.

4. *n.* mud, muck, clay, slush, slosh, sludge, sposh [dial. U.S.], squash, slime, slab [now chiefly dial.], slop, ooze; gumbo, gumbo soil; alluvium, alluvion, silt.

5. *n.* mud puddle, mudhole, puddle, loblolly [dial. U.S.], slab [now chiefly dial.], slop; mire etc. (marsh) 345.

6. *v.* viscidize, glutinize; emulsify, emulsionize; churn, beat up; inspissate, thicken etc. (densify) 321.7; mash etc. (pulp) 354.4.

7. *adj.* semiliquid, semifluid, semifluidic; half-melted, half-frozen; milky, lacteal, lactean [rare], lacteous, lactescent, lactiferous; emulsive, emulsifying, emulsifiable; succulent; pulpy etc. 354.5.

8. *adj.* viscid, viscous, viscose, viscidulous, viscoid *or* viscoidal; mucid, muculent, mucous; gluey, gluelike, gaumy, gummy, gumlike, gummous, gummose; sticky, tacky, tenacious, tough; ropy, stringy; clammy, sammy [chiefly dial.]; gelatinous, gelatinoid; gelatose; glutinous, glutinose, glutenous, glutose; doughy, pasty; buttery; thick, turbid, crass, grumous, stodgy; gooey [slang, U.S.], squashy etc. *below*; slab [arch. and dial.], slabby; lentous [obs.], pituitous; tremelloid, tremellose; amylaceous, starchy; cohesive etc. (coherent) 46.9.

9. *adj.* muddy, mucky, mucksy [dial.], sossly *or* sozzly, slushy, sloshy, sludgy, sposhy [dial. U.S.], sloppy, slabby, slab [arch. and dial.], splashy, plashy, squashy, squdgy [dial.], squushy *or* squshy [dial.], squishy, squelchy, oozy, uliginose *or* uliginous, lutose; gumbo; miry etc. (marshy) 345.3; dirty etc. 653.16.

353. Bubble, Cloud

Mixture of Liquid and Air.—1. *n.* bubble, bleb, blob [chiefly dial.], globule, vesicle, bulla [Med.], blister, bladder; air bubble, soap bubble.

2. *n.* foam, froth, spume, fume, scud [coll.]; spray, surf, spoondrift *or* spindrift, "stinging, ringing spindrift" (Kip-

---

353. The bubble winked at me and said, "You'll miss me, brother, when you're dead."—O. HERFORD. The earth hath bubbles, as the water has.—SHAKESPEARE. One cloud is enough

ling); suds, lather; fizz *or* fiz; head, scum, cream, collar [slang].

3. *n.* effervescence *or* effervescency, bubbling etc. *v.*; ferment, fermentation; ebullition, ebullience *or* ebulliency; evaporation, exhalation, emanation; aeration.

4. *n.* cloudiness etc. *adj.*, nebulosity, nubilation, obnubilation [rare]; dirty sky.

5. *n.* cloud, vapor, steam, haze, film; mist, drisk [U.S.]; fog, soup [slang]; smog [U.S.], frost smoke; pea soup, peasoup fog [both coll.]; nebule; cumulus, nimbus, meteor, woolpack, curl cloud, goat's-hair [coll.], messengers [dial., Eng.]; scud, rack; storm cloud, squall cloud; rain cloud, water carrier; thundercloud, thunderhead; fleecy cloud, billowy cloud; cirrus; stratus, cirro-stratus, cumulo-stratus; cirro-cumulus, mackerel sky; mare's-tail, colt's-tail, cat's-tail, cocktail; shade etc. 424; nebula etc. (heavenly body) 318.3.

6. *n.* (science of clouds) nephology, nephelology [rare], nephelognosy; meteorology.

7. *n.* (instruments) nephoscope; nephelometer, nephograph.

8. *v.* bubble, bubble up, burble; froth, foam, spume; effervesce, ferment, work; ebullate *or* ebulliate [rare], boil; bleb [dial.], blob, blub, blubber [obs. exc. dial.], plop, wallop [Scot. and dial.]; fizz *or* fiz, fizzle; spark, sparkle; snap, pop; simmer; guggle, gurgle; scum, mantle; aerate; bubble over, boil over.

9. *v.* cloud, becloud, cloud over, overcloud, overcast, overshadow, shadow, shade, darken over, adumbrate; nubilate; smoke, oversmoke; fog, befog; mist, haze.

10. *adj.* bubbling etc. *v.*, bubbly, frothy, foamy, nappy [obs.], effervescent, effervescive, sparkling, *mousseux* [F.], fizzy; sudsy, soapy; heady, with a head on, with a collar on [slang], up [coll.].

11. *adj.* cloudy, overclouded etc. *v.*, overcast; vaporous, hazy, misty, dirty; foggy, soupy [slang], pea-soup [coll.]; cirrous, cirrose; nebulous, nebulose; nubilous, nubiferous; cumulous, thunderheaded; stratus, nimbose; moist etc. 339.7.

12. *adj.* nephological, nepheloscopic, nephelometric; meteorologic(al).

354. Pulpiness

1. *n.* pulpiness, pastiness etc. *adj.*; pulpification, pulpefaction [Med.], maceration; pulpitis, pulpalgia, pulpectomy, pulpotomy [all Dent.]; semiliquidity etc. 352.

2. *n.* pulp, pap, paste, dough, mash, mush, smash, squash, crush; sauce, butter; apple sauce, apple butter, peanut butter etc.; anchovy paste, mashed potatoes; paper pulp, wood pulp; pulpboard, pasteboard; pulp lead, white lead; dental pulp, pulp cavity, pulp chamber, pulp canal [all Dent.]; grume, batter etc. (semiliquid) 352.3-5.

3. *n.* pulper, pulpifier, macerater *or* macerator, pulp machine *or* engine; smasher, masher, potato masher.

4. *v.* pulp, pulpify; mash, smash, squash, crush; masticate, macerate; jellify etc. 321.7.

5. *adj.* pulpy, pulpous, pulpal, pulpaceous [rare], pulplike; fleshy, succulent, soft and flabby; pasty, doughy; pithy, spongy; baccate; grumous, muddy etc. (semiliquid) 352.7-9; soft etc. 324.6.

355. Unctuousness
(See also 356. Oil)

1. *n.* unctuousness, unctiousness etc. *adj.*, unctuosity, lubricity; pinguefaction, pinguescence [rare]; saponacity [joc.]; adiposis, adiposity; ointment, anointment etc. (lubrication) 332; suavity etc. 894.2.

2. *v.* oil etc. (lubricate) 332.4; pinguefy etc. (fatten) 194.7.

3. *adj.* unctuous, unctious, unctional; unguent, unguentary, unguentous, unguentiferous, unguinous; oleaginous, oleic [Chem.], oily, greasy; fat, fatty, adipose, sebaceous; pinguid, pinguedinous; lardy, lardaceous, lardiform; buttery, butyraceous; soapy, saponaceous, saponary [obs.]; cerate, waxy; smooth, slick, sleek, slippery, slithery [chiefly dial.], sliddery [now dial.]; suave etc. 894.13; lubricant etc. 332.5.

356. Oil
(See also 355. Unctuousness)

1. *n.* oil, *oleum* [L.], mineral ~, vegetable *or* animal oil etc. *below* 356.2-4;

---

to eclipse all the sun.—FULLER. If there were no clouds, we should not enjoy the sun.—J. RAY. Every cloud has a silver lining.
354. The tasteless dough of existence.—O. HENRY. My cake is dough.—SHAKESPEARE.
356. With odorous oil thy head and hair are sleek.—PERSIUS.

356.1 – 357.4

fixed ~, fatty ~, volatile *or* essential oil; drying ~, semidrying *or* nondrying oil; grease, fat; pomade, pomatum; stearin, stearine, tristearine; elain *or* elaine, olein, oleine, triolein; palmitin, palmitine, tripalmitin; glycerin *or* glycerine, glycerol, glycerole, glycerite; glycerogel, glycerogelatin, glycerin jelly; salve etc. (lubricant) 332.2.

    2. *n.* (mineral oils) rock oil, fossil oil, petroleum, mineral ~, rock *or* natural petroleum; Seneca oil [U.S.]; benzine, petroleum benzine; naphtha, naphthalene, shale naphtha, shale spirit, shale oil; gasoline *or* gasolene, gas [coll.], petrol [chiefly Eng.]; kerosene, coal oil, fuel oil, furnace oil; mineral colza ~, mineral seal *or* mineral sperm oil; Barbados tar; petroleum jelly, petrolatum, vaseline; paraffin *or* paraffine.

    3. *n.* (vegetable oils) sweet *or* edible oil, castor *or* ricinus oil, cottonseed oil, linseed oil, croton oil, bay *or* bayberry oil, Macassar oil, palm oil, nut oil; fusel oil *or* fusel, grain oil; kekuna ~, kekune *or* candlenut oil, Spanish-walnut oil; corn oil; colza *or* rape oil; olive oil, peanut ~, groundnut *or* arachis oil; coconut oil *or* butter, cocoa *or* cacao butter; pine oil, pine-needle oil, pine-tar oil; turpentine, oil *or* spirits of turpentine, gum spirit, wood turpentine, turps [coll.]; copaiba; oleoresin etc. 356a.1.

    4. *n.* (animal oils and fats) porpoise oil, seal oil, shark *or* shark-liver oil, whale, neat's-foot oil; cod *or* cod-liver oil; halibut-liver oil, haliver oil [trade name]; doegling oil, arctic sperm oil, bottlenose oil; menhaden oil, sperm oil, spermaceti; cream, top milk; butter, butter fat, dairy butter; margarine, oleomargarine, oleo oil, oleo; ghee [Ind.]; fat, adipose tissue, blubber, tallow, suet; lard, lard oil, shortening; dripping *or* drippings, exunge [obs.]; adipocere.

    5. *n.* soap, bath soap, toilet soap, laundry soap, saddle soap, Castile soap, marine soap, glycerin soap, tar soap, soap powder, powdered soap, washing powder, wash ball, soap flakes, granulated soap; brown soap, green soap; solid *or* hard soap, soft *or* semifluid soap, liquid soap; lead *or* metallic soap; amole; suds, lather.

    6. *n.* cerate, wax, beeswax, sealing wax, floor wax, vegetable wax, mineral wax, fossil wax, ader wax, ozocerite, **ceresin** *or* **ceresine**.

356a. Resin

    1. *n.* resin *or* resina; rosin, colophony *or* colophonium; gum, gum resin, gum rosin; resin oil, oleoresin; synthetic resin, resinoid; resinate, colophonate; wood rosin, pine resin, fossil resin, vegetable resin, resin *or* rosin spirit; bitumen, pitch, mineral pitch, tar, asphalt *or* asphaltum; camphor; mastic; amber, ambergris; Bakelite [trade name]; lacquer etc. (paint) 428.5.

    2. *v.* resin, resinize, resinate, resinify, rosin; varnish, lacquer etc. (paint) 428.10.

    3. *adj.* resinous, resiniferous, resinaceous [rare], resinogenous, resinic, resinoid, resiny; rosinous [rare], rosiny; tarry, pitchy; gummy, gummous, gummose, gumlike; mastic, masticic; bituminous, bitumenoid; asphaltic, asphaltite; varnished, lacquered etc. *v.*

357. Organic Matter
(See 358. Inorganic Matter)

    1. *n.* organic ~, animate *or* living matter, living nature, organized matter, organic *or* organized world; organization, organism, organity [all rare]; animal and vegetable kingdom, plant and animal life, fauna and flora, biota.

    2. *n.* organism, organity [rare], organic being, living being *or* thing, individual; bion, physiological individual; morphon, morphological individual.

    3. *n.* protoplasm *or* protoplasma, plasm *or* plasma; cytoplasm, metaplasm, karyoplasm, bioplasm, trophoplasm, idioplasm, endoplasm, ectoplasm; cell; proteid, protein; albumen, albumin, albuminoid; chromatin; centrosome, nucleolus, karyosome, vacuole, chromosome, idant; protoplast, protozoan, amoeba; karyaster, erythroblast, dysmeromorph, antherozoid.

    4. *n.* germ, germinal matter, germ plasm *or* plasma, germ cell, embryo; ovum, egg cell, egg; oösperm, zygote, oösphere, oöcyte, oœcium, ovicell, oögonium; oöphyte, oöspore; oögamy, gamete, gametophore, gametophyte, sporophyte, sporocyte, sporocyst, sporocarp,

---

357. Great is this organism of mud and fire.—SANTAYANA.   And what if all of animated nature / Be but organic harps diversely fram'd, / That tremble into thought?—COLERIDGE.

cystocarp, sporogonium, sporozoite, gametangium, antherid *or* antheridium; macrospore, megasporangium; microspore, microsporangium.

biophore *or* biophor, biogen, bioblast, pangen, plasome; blastoderm, mesoblast, mesoplast; holoblast; zoogloea; zooid; zoon (*pl.* zoa); sperm, sperm cell, spermatozoon (*pl.* spermatozoa), spermatozoid *or* spermatozooid, spermatocyte, spermatophore, spermatium (*pl.* spermatia), zoospore, swarm spore; macrogamete, microgamete; seed, semen, milt, roe; spermogonium, spermary, sperm gland, testis, testicle; ovary.

5. *n.* (science of organisms) biology; botany etc. 369; zoology etc. 368; physiology etc. 359.5; anatomy etc. 329.2; morphology etc. 240.4; genetics, cytology; natural history, natural science; cell *or* cellular theory; biotaxy, taxonomy; ecology, ontogeny, phylogeny, organic chemistry; Darwinism etc. (evolution) 161.5; generation etc. 161.2.

6. *n.* paleontology etc. (antiquarianism) 122.4; fossils etc. (antiquities) 124.2; fossilization etc. (hardening) 323.2; mummification etc. (interment) 363.

7. *n.* naturalist, natural scientist; biologist, bacteriologist, embryologist; zoologist etc. 368.2; botanist etc. 369.9; paleontologist etc. (antiquary) 122.5.

8. *adj.* organic, organized; biotic, zooid *or* zooidal; animate etc. (living) 359.10.

9. *adj.* protoplasmic, protoplastic, plasmic *or* plasmatic; cytoplasmic, metaplasmic, karyoplasmic, bioplasmic, trophoplasmic, idioplasmic; cellular, cellulous; proteinaceous; albuminous *or* albuminose, albuminoidal; nuclear, nucleate, nucleolar, nucleolate *or* nucleolated; vacuolar, protozoan; amoebic, amoeboid.

10. *adj.* germinal, germal [rare], embryonic; ovarian, oviferous, ovicular, oviparous; oöphytic, oösporic, oösporous; oögamous, heterogamous, autogamous, isogamous; gamic, sporogenous; spermatic, spermatogenetic, spermatoid, spermatophoral, spermatozoal; blastodermic, mesoblastic, holoblastic, biogenetic; zoogloeic, zoogloeal; unsegmented, dioecious, monoecious.

11. *adj.* biological, physiological etc. *n.*

12. *adj.* paleological etc. (antiquarian) 122.13; fossilized etc. (hard) 323.5.

358. Inorganic Matter
(See 357. Organic Matter)

1. *n.* inorganic *or* unorganic matter, inanimate *or* lifeless matter, brute matter, inorganized *or* unorganized matter, inorganization [rare], mineral kingdom *or* world; mineral etc. 635.6.

2. *n.* mineralogy, geology, geognosy, geoscopy, metallurgy, metallography, petrology; inorganic chemistry; oryctics, oryctology, oryctognosy, oryctography [all obs.].

3. *v.* mineralize, mineralogize; petrify, lithify etc. (harden) 323.4.

4. *adj.* inorganic *or* unorganic, inorganized *or* unorganized, inanimate, azoic, mineral; lithoid etc. (hard) 323.5.

359. Life
(See 360. Death)

1. *n.* life; living etc. *v.*, vitality, vividity [obs.], animation, animate existence; viability, viableness; being etc. (existence) 1; vivacity etc. 682.1.

"one dem'd horrid grind" (Dickens), "one long process of getting tired" (Butler), "a bridge of groans across a stream of tears" (P. J. Bailey), "a beauty chased by tragic laughter" (Masefield), "a tumble-about thing of ups and downs" (Disraeli), "a ladder infinite-stepped" (R. Burton), "a perpetual instruction in cause and effect" (Emerson), "a flame that is always burning itself out" (Shaw), "a long lesson in humility" (Barrie), "a document to be interpreted" (Amiel), "a fiction . . . made up of contradiction" (Blake).

2. *n.* life force *or* energy, force of life, living force; *vis viva, vis vitae* or *vitalis* [all L.]; vital force *or* energy, "*élan vital*" [F.] (Bergson), impulse of life, vital principle, vital spark *or* flame; Prometheus, Deucalion and Pyrrha; Promethean spark, spark of life, divine spark, breath, life breath, breath of life, breath of one's nostrils, divine breath, vital air, essence of life, life principle, tuck [coll., U.S.], vital spirit, vital fluid, anima,

---

359. *Mon métier et mon art, c'est vivre* [My business and my art is to live].—MONTAIGNE. *La vida es sueño* [Life is a dream].—CALDERON. We live not as we wish, but as we can.—MENANDER. Life . . . is a tale / Told by an idiot. full of sound and fury, / Signifying noth-

anima divina [L.], divine soul, *anima bruta* [L.], *divina particula aurae* [L.]; pneuma, prana [Vedic and Hindu]; jivatma, atman jiva [all Hindu]; blood, lifeblood, heartblood *or* heart's blood; growth energy *or* bathmism; spirit, soul etc. (psyche) 994.11.

3. *n.* universal life force, world spirit *or* soul, *anima mundi* [L.], oversoul, logos *or* Logos, archeus, world principle, world-self, universal ego *or* self, infinite spirit, supreme soul *or* principle, nous; Atman, Brahma [both Hindu], the Absolute, God, Nature; Mind, Divine Mind, Soul, Life, Principle, Truth, Love [all Christian Science]; mahat [Theosophy].

4. *n.* vivification, vivifying etc. *v.*, vitalization, animation; revivification etc. (revival) 660.2.

5. *n.* (science of life) physiology, biology etc. 357.5; biochemistry, etiology, embryology, animal economy.

6. *v.* live, be alive etc. *adj.*, have life etc. *n.*; breathe, live and breathe, fetch *or* draw breath, draw the breath of life, breathe the vital air; walk the earth; be, subsist etc. (exist) 1.4.

7. *v.* come to life, become alive etc. *adj.*, come into existence *or* being, come into the world, see the light, be born; quicken, revive, come to, show signs of life.

8. *v.* vivify, vivificate [rare], vitalize, energize, animate, quicken, make alive etc. *adj.*, imbue *or* endow with life, put life into, bring to life, bring *or* call into existence *or* being, give life to; beget, give birth to etc. (produce) 161.8–10; revive, reanimate etc. (restore) 660.13.

9. *v.* keep alive, keep body and soul together, keep the wolf from the door, be spared, have nine lives like a cat; support life.

10. *adj.* living, alive, alive and kicking [coll.], born, breathing, quick, animate, animated, vital *or* vitalic, zoetic, imbued *or* endowed with life, in life, in the flesh, in the land of the living, on this side of the grave, aboveground; tenacious of life; existing etc. 1.7.

11. *adj.* vivifying etc. *v.*, vivific (al) [rare], vivificative [rare], vivifican [obs.]; animative; animating etc. *v.*; life-giving, Promethean.

12. *adj.* viable, vital [obs.], livable *or* liveable, capable of living, likely to survive; fit to live *or* survive.

360. Death
(See 359. Life; also 361. Killing, 362. Corpse)

1. *n.* death, dying etc. *v.*, decease, demise, obit [obs.], dissolution, departure, passing away, passing of the soul, release, taking off [coll.], ebb of life, quietus, fall; end etc. 67 of life, cessation etc. 142 of life, loss etc. 776 of life, extinction etc. 162 of life; the end; last roundup [slang, West. U.S.], last rattler [tramp slang, U.S.]; rest, eternal rest *or* sleep, the last sleep; the debt of nature, last debt, summons of death, final summons; last muster, last curtain call [both coll.]; curtains [slang, U.S.]; jaws of death, hand *or* finger of death; shades of death; bridge of death, river of death, Styx etc. 982.3; Jordan, Jordan's bank, Stygian shore; the grisly terror.

euthanasia, euthanasy [now rare]; happy release, *bona mors* [L.]; natural death *or* decay, breakup of the system; sudden death, untimely end; stroke of death, death stroke; death struggle, last breath *or* gasp, dying breath, death rattle, agony, death agonies; deathbed, deathwatch; dying day, day of death, deathday, "the supreme day and the inevitable hour" (Vergil); bereavement, loss; heart failure; drowning, *noyade* [F.], watery grave; smotheration; mortification, gangrene; mortality, death rate; doom etc. (destiny) 601.3; fatal disease etc. 655; deathblow etc. 67.4.

---

ing.—SHAKESPEARE. One life;—a little gleam of Time between two eternities.—CARLYLE. How good is man's life, the mere living!—BROWNING. Life is real! Life is earnest! And the grave is not its goal.—LONGFELLOW. Brief and powerless is man's life; on him and all his race the slow, sure doom falls pitiless and dark.—B. RUSSELL. Life is a jest and all things show it: / I thought so once and now I know it.—J. GAY. Life is far too important a thing ever to talk seriously about.—WILDE. Life . . . is a predicament.—SANTAYANA. Is life worth living? It depends on the liver.—ANON. Life is a fatal complaint, and an eminently contagious one.—HOLMES. Life's perhaps the only riddle / That we shrink from giving up.—GILBERT. *Ars est longa, vita brevis* [Art is long, life is short].

360. All victory ends in the defeat of death . . . But does defeat end in the victory of death? —E. O'NEILL. And Death is beautiful as feet of friend / Coming with welcome at our

"the latter end" (Bible); "the journey's end" (Shakespeare); "that dreamless sleep" (Byron); "a debt we all must pay" (Euripides); "the debt which cancels all others" (C. Colton); "the tribute due unto nature" (Sterne); "a knell / That summons thee to heaven or to hell" (Shakespeare); "kind Nature's signal of retreat" (Johnson); "valley of the shadow of death" (Bible); "crossing of the bar" (Tennyson); "the way of all flesh" (Butler); "the downward path" (Horace); "the crown of life" (Young).

2. *n.* (personification of death) Death, "Black Death" (Ovid), "Pale Death" (Horace), "the pale priest of the mute people" (Browning), "that grim ferryman" (Shakespeare), "Hell's grim Tyrant" (Pope), "the king of terrors" (Bible), the Reaper, the Grim Reaper, Old Floorer [slang], "the Pilot of the Galilean lake" (Milton); the angel of death, death's bright angel, Azrael; scythe *or* sickle of Death.

3. *n.* necrology, obituary, obit, obituary notice, register of deaths, roll of the dead, mortuary roll, bill of mortality.

4. *n.* death song, dirge etc. (mourning) 839.3.

5. *n.* swan song, *chant du cygne* [F.].

6. *v.* die, expire, perish, cease to live, depart, quit this world, make one's exit, pass on, pass away, meet one's death *or* end, end one's life *or* days, end one's *or* this earthly career, depart this life, shuffle off this mortal coil, lose one's life, lay down one's life, relinquish *or* surrender one's life, resign one's life *or* being, give up the ghost, yield the ghost, yield one's breath, breathe one's last, go out like the snuff of a candle, fall asleep, close one's eyes, take one's last sleep, awake to life immortal, "put on immortality" (Bible), put off mortality.

go to glory, go to kingdom come [slang], go home, go home feet first [slang], go to one's last home, go to one's long account, pay the debt of nature, go over to *or* join the majority, ~ great majority *or* greatest number, join one's ancestors, be gathered to one's fathers, join the choir invisible, give an obolus to Charon, cross the Stygian ferry, pass over, pass over Jordan, "put out to sea" (Tennyson), go out with the ebb, "walk through the valley of the shadow of death" (Bible), go to the happy hunting grounds, "go the way of all earth" (Bible).

return to dust *or* the earth, come *or* turn to dust, drop *or* sink into the grave; go west, go up, go off, drop off [all coll.]; pop off, step off, step off the deep end, go *or* pop off the hooks, fly off the handle, knock off, pipe off, kick off, kick the bucket, hop the twig, shove off, kick up one's heels *or* toes, turn *or* cock up one's toes, turn up one's toes to the daisies, hand *or* pass in one's checks *or* chips, peg out, slip one's breath *or* wind, slip one's cable, coil up one's cable *or* rope, take the last count, croak [all slang]; die *or* lay down one's life for one's country, make the supreme sacrifice, do one's bit; fire one's last shot, lose the number of one's mess [both Mil. slang].

fall *or* drop down dead, bite the dust *or* ground [coll.]; come to an untimely end, die all at once [joc.]; die in harness, die in one's boots *or* shoes, die with one's boots *or* shoes on; die a natural death, die in bed; die game *or* valiantly, die fighting, die in the last ditch; die lying down; catch one's death [chiefly coll.], catch one's death of cold; smother; receive one's death warrant, receive notice to quit [slang], be put on the spot [Crim. slang, U.S.]; come to end etc. 67.6; cease to exist etc. 2.5; die a violent death etc. 361.13.

7. *v.* drown, go to Davy Jones's locker [coll.], go to a watery grave, make a hole in the water [slang].

8. *adj.* dead, lifeless, without life, deceased, demised, defunct, croaked [slang], departed, departed this life, gone, gone the way of all flesh, gone west [coll.], dead and gone, dead and done for [coll.], done for [coll.], no more, finished [coll.], taken off *or* away, released, bereft of life, out of the world, called home, launched into eternity, born into a better world,

---

journey's end.—LOWELL.   Death hath a thousand doors to let out life. / I shall find one.—MASSINGER.   A man can die but once; we owe God a death.—SHAKESPEARE.   Golden lads and girls all must / As chimney-sweepers come to dust.—SHAKESPEARE.   For dust thou art, and unto dust shalt thou return.—BIBLE.   O death, where is thy sting?   O grave, where is thy victory?—BIBLE.   And I looked, and behold a pale horse: and his name that sat on him was Death.—BIBLE.   I will die in the last ditch.—WILLIAM III, PRINCE OF

gone to a better land, gone to glory, gone to kingdom come [slang], "gathered to his fathers" (Bible), numbered with the dead, with the saints, dead in the Lord, asleep in Jesus, asleep, sleeping, reposing, at rest, resting easy [coll.], out of one's misery.

stone-dead, dead as a doornail or doorpost, dead as a herring, dead as mutton, dead as nits [all coll. or slang]; cold [slang, U.S.], "as cold as any stone" (Shakespeare), stiff [slang]; death-struck, death-stricken, smitten with death; late, late lamented; asleep in the deep, in a watery grave, under hatches [Naut. slang]; inanimate, exanimate [rare], azoic; stillborn; extinct etc. 2.10.

9. *adj.* dying etc. *v.,* moribund, morient [obs.], near death, near one's end, at the end of one's rope [coll.], at the point of death, at death's door, at the portals of death, in the jaws of death, on one's last legs [coll.], tottering on the brink of the grave, with one foot in the grave, going, going off *or* out, done for [coll.], booked [slang], on the spot [crim. slang, U.S.], under sailing orders [Naut. slang], on one's deathbed, in the agony of death, at the last gasp; *in articulo* [L.], *in extremis* [L.], *aux abois* [F.].

10. *adj.* deathlike, deathly, mortuous [rare]; mortuary.

11. *adj.* post-mortem, postmortuary, postmundane, post-obit, postobituary, posthumous.

12. *adv.* after death, *post obit* or *post obitum* [L.], post mortem [L.].

13. *phr.* death impends, life hangs by a thread, one's days are numbered, one's hour is come, one's race is run, one's doom is sealed, Death knocks at the door, Death stares one in the face, the sands of life are running out.

361. Killing
(See also 360. Death)

Destruction of Life; Violent Death.—
1. *n.* killing, slaying etc. *v.,* slaughter, trucidation, occision [obs.], bloodshed, foul play; homicide, manslaughter, murder, bloody *or* blue murder [slang], assassination; carnage, butchery, internecion [rare], massacre, pogrom, saturnalia of blood, flow *or* effusion of blood; blood, gore; fusillade; thuggism, thuggee, thuggery; martyrdom; lapidation; mass murder; drowning etc. (death) 360; organized murder etc. (warfare) 722; immolation, holocaust etc. (oblation) 990.6; execution, hanging etc. (capital punishment) 972.4; gallows etc. 975.4.

2. *n.* (words in *-cide,* referring to both doer or agent and deed) regicide, matricide, fratricide, homicide, suicide, infanticide, uxoricide, vaticide, insecticide; aborticide; parricide, patricide.

3. *n.* suicide, self-murder, self-destruction, *felo-de-se* [Anglo-L.] (*pl. felones-de-se*); disembowelment, hara-kiri [Jap.], seppuku [Jap.], happy dispatch [joc.]; suttee, sutteeism [both Ind.]; car of Jagannath *or* Juggernaut.

4. *n.* suffocation, stuffocation [joc.], smotheration, asphyxiation; strangulation, strangling etc. *v.,* garrote *or* garrotte.

5. *n.* fatality, fatal accident, violent death, casualty, disaster, calamity.

6. *n.* deathblow, death stroke, *coup de grâce* [F.], quietus etc. (finishing stroke) 67.4.

7. *n.* (destruction of animals) slaughter, slaughtering, butchering, butchery; hunting, shooting etc. (chase) 622.2.

8. *n.* killer, slayer, slaughterer, butcher, croaker [slang], bloodshedder; murderer, manslayer, Cain, assassin; cutthroat, bravo, thug, gorilla [slang, U.S.], apache, gunman [chiefly U.S.]; gun, trigger man, rod, rodman, torpedo [all crim. slang, U.S.]; garroter *or* garrotter, strangler; burker, burkite; hatchet man, highbinder [U.S.]; poisoner; lapidator [rare]; head-hunter; cannibal, maneater; matador; suicide; fratricide etc. *above* 361.2; executioner etc. 975.5; huntsman etc. (pursuer) 622.4.

9. *n.* place of slaughter, field of blood *or* bloodshed, field of slaughter, Aceldama *or* aceldama, potter's field; shambles,

---

ORANGE. *De mortuis nil nisi bonum* [(Say) nothing but good of the dead]. *Omnia mors aequat* [Death levels all things].—CLAUDIAN. *Memento mori* [Remember you must die]. Dead men tell no tales.
361. The King's argument was that anything that had a head could be beheaded.—CARROLL. Assassination has never changed the history of the world.—DISRAELI. Pity it is to slay the meanest thing.—HOOD. Murderers walk the earth beneath the curse of Cain.—HOOD. I come fairly to kill him honestly.—BEAUMONT

abattoir, slaughterhouse, stockyard; battlefield etc. 728.2.

10. *v.* kill, slay, put to death, deathify, deprive of life, take one's life away, make away with, put out of the way, put an end to, get rid of, dispatch, do to death, finish [chiefly coll.], finish off, victimize; murder, commit murder etc. *n.*, assassinate; launch into eternity, send to glory, send to kingdom come [slang], send to one's last account; send west, fix, settle, do for [all coll.]; do in, croak, corpse, bump off, polish off, kick into the beyond, lay out, take care of, put one easy, put one out of his misery, give the business *or* works, put the kibosh on, blot out, erase, wipe out [all slang].

shed blood, spill blood, bloody one's hands with, dye *or* imbrue one's hands in blood, pour out blood like water, wade knee-deep in blood; slaughter, butcher, massacre, decimate; give *or* deal a deathblow, give the quietus etc. *n.*, silence [slang]; cut off, nip in the bud; sign one's death warrant, strike the death knell of; give no quarter; fell, bring down, drop, drop *or* stop in one's tracks; shoot, shoot down, saw off [crim. slang, U.S.]; riddle, pump full of lead [slang]; blow ~, knock *or* dash one's brains out, brain; knock in *or* on the head; blackjack, club; stone, rock [coll., U.S.], lapidate; poison; hang, electrocute etc. (execute) 972.8.

11. *v.* strangle, garrote *or* garrotte, throttle, choke, burke; stop the breath, stifle, suffocate, smother, stuffocate [joc.], asphyxiate; drown.

12. *v.* cut down, put to the sword *or* the edge of the sword, sword, knife, bayonet, saber, run through, stab, pierce; cut the throat, jugulate; hack, cut to pieces.

13. *v.* be killed etc. *v.*, die a violent death, die violently, come to a violent death, meet with foul play, get one's everlasting [slang], welter in one's blood.

14. *v.* commit suicide etc. *n.*, suicide [coll.], take one's own life, kill oneself, do away with *or* put an end to oneself; dash *or* blow one's brains out.

15. *adj.* murderous, slaughterous, killing etc. *v.*; bloodthirsty, bloody-minded; sanguinary, sanguine, sanguinolent, sanguineous; bloody, bloodstained, gory, ensanguined; red-handed; homicidal etc. *n.*; cruel etc. 907.9.

16. *adj.* mortal, mortuous [rare], fatal, lethal; deadly, deathly, deathful [rare]; mortiferous [obs.], lethiferous; internecine, internecinal [rare], internective [rare], interneciary [rare]; destructive etc. 162.6.

17. *int.* let him have it!, give it to him!, thumbs down!

362. Corpse

1. *n.* corpse, corps [obs.], corse [arch.], body, dead body, lich [Scot. and dial. Eng.], the dead, the defunct, the deceased, the departed, carcass, cadaver, ghost [obs.], food for worms *or* fish, remains, mortal remains, relics [now poetic], reliquiae; stiff, deader [both slang]; dust, ashes, earth, clay, tenement of clay, "this mortal coil" (Shakespeare); bones, dry bones, skeleton; carrion, crowbait; long pig; mummy, mummified body, mummification; organic remains, fossils etc. (antiquities) 124.2.

2. *adj.* corpselike, deathlike; cadaverous, cadaveric.

363. Interment

1. *n.* interment, burial, burying etc. *v.*; sepulture, entombment, humation [obs.], inhumation; earth bath, ground sweat [both slang or joc.].

2. *n.* cremation, incremation [rare], incineration, burning, reduction to ashes; pyre, funeral pile.

3. *n.* embalmment, embalming etc. *v.*; mummification.

4. *n.* funeral, funeral solemnity, funeral rites *or* ceremonies, funeration [obs.], burial etc. *above* 363.1, burying [dial.], burial ceremonies, last duty *or* service, last *or* final rites, exequies, obsequies, obit [obs.]; wake; funeral procession, dead march, exequy [rare], muffled drum; funeral oration *or* sermon, funeral [obs. exc. dial.]; elegy; dirge, etc. (mourning) 839.3, 4.

---

362. He'd make a lovely corpse.—DICKENS. Scooped from the sacred earth where his dear relics lie.—WORDSWORTH. Many a nobleman lies stark and stiff.—SHAKESPEARE.
363. Let the dead bury their dead.—BIBLE. Like one that wraps the drapery of his couch /

5. *n.* knell, passing bell, death bell *or* signal, funeral ring, tolling, tolling of the knell.

6. *n.* undertaker, mortician, funeral director; embalmer.

7. *n.* mourner, griever, lamenter, keener [Ir.]; mute, professional mourner; pallbearer, bearer.

8. *n.* graveclothes, shroud, winding sheet, cerecloth, cerements; pall.

9. *n.* hearse; dead wagon [slang].

10. *n.* coffin, casket [chiefly U.S.], box, kist [Scot.], pall [fig.], hearse [arch.]; crate, bone box *or* house, six-foot bungalow, wooden kimono *or* overcoat [all slang]; shell, sarcophagus.

11. *n.* urn, cinerary urn, funeral urn, mortuary urn *or* vessel, bone pot, ossuary.

12. *n.* bier, litter.

13. *n.* grave, burial place, place of interment *or* sepulture, sepulcher, bier [obs.], hearse [arch.], tomb, pit, resting place, "the lone couch of his everlasting sleep" (Shelley), last home, long home, narrow house, house of death, low house, low green tent, deep six [slang]; vault, crypt, burial chamber; ossuary, ossuarium; charnel house, bone house, shrine; mausoleum (*pl.* mausoleums, mausolea); catacombs; mastaba [Archaeol.]; shaft grave tomb [Archaeol.]; dokhma [Persia], tower of silence; catafalque; mound, tumulus, barrow.

14. *n.* graveyard, burial ground, cemetery, bone yard [slang, U.S.], necropolis, polyandrium [Gr. Antiq.], golgotha, memorial park, city *or* village of the dead, marble city [slang]; churchyard, God's acre; potter's field; Golgotha, Calvary; lich gate.

15. *n.* monument, marker, memento; hearse [arch.], shrine; memoria, memorial; stone, gravestone, tombstone, headstone, footstone; slab, slat [dial.], tablet, obelisk, pillar, column, shaft, monolith; cross; cenotaph; cairn *or* carn; cromlech, dolmen, megalith, cyclolith [all Archaeol.]; tope, stupa [both Buddhist]; pyramid.

16. *n.* epitaph, inscription, *hic jacet* [L.].

17. *n.* deadhouse, morgue, mortuary, lich-house, funeral home *or* parlor, undertaker's establishment; crematory, crematorium, burning ghat [Ind.].

18. *n.* autopsy, necropsy, necroscopy, post-mortem, post-mortem examination.

19. *n.* disinterment, exhumation, disinhumation [rare], disentombment, unearthing etc. *v.*

20. *v.* inter, inhume, inhumate [rare], bury, lay in the grave, consign to the grave *or* tomb, grave [arch.], tomb, entomb, ensepulcher [rare], inearth, plant [coll., now chiefly U.S.], sepulture [rare], hearse; put six feet under, [slang]; shrine [obs.], enshrine; urn [rare], inurn; hold *or* conduct a funeral, funeralize [South. U.S.], funerate [obs.]; deliver a funeral oration *or* sermon, preach a funeral [dial.].

21. *v.* cremate, incremate, incinerate, burn, reduce to ashes.

22. *v.* lay out, prepare for burial; balm [arch.], embalm; mummify; lie in state.

23. *v.* be buried etc. *adj.*, lay one's bones; count daisies, push up daisies, turn *or* cock up the toes to the daisies, become a landowner, take an earth bath *or* ground sweat [all joc.].

24. *v.* disinter, exhume, disinhume [rare], disentomb, unbury, unearth.

25. *adj.* funereal, funeral, funerary, *funèbre* [F.], funebrial [now rare]; mortuary, mortuarian; exequial, obsequial, feral, burial, sepulchral; cinerary; necroscopic(al); elegiac, plaintive, dirgelike etc. (mournful) 839.13–15; gloomy, sorrowful etc. (sad) 837.9–11.

26. *adj.* buried etc. *v.*, returned to dust *or* earth, "in the dark union of insensate dust" (Byron).

27. *adv.* in memory, *in memoriam* [L.].

28. *adv.* beneath the sod, under the sod *or* ground, underground; six feet under, [slang]; at rest, resting in peace.

29. *phr.* R.I.P., *requiescat* or *requiescant in pace* [L.]; rest in peace; *hic jacet* [L.], *ci-gît* [F.], here lies.

364. Animality

(See 365. Vegetation; also 366. Animal)

1. *n.* animality, animalism, animalness [rare], animal nature, animal life *or* existence; physique; flesh, flesh and blood; corporeal nature etc. (materiality) 316.

2. *n.* animalization, carnalization, sensualization; animation.

3. *v.* animalize, reduce to animalism,

About him, and lies down to pleasant dreams.—BRYANT.   Warriors carry the warrior's pall.—TENNYSON.   To whom life is heavy, the earth will be light.—SIENKIEWICZ.

carnalize, sensualize; incarnate etc. (materialize) 316.7.

4. *adj.* fleshly, in the flesh, physical, carnal, bodily, corporeal, corporal; human etc. 372.5.

365. Vegetation
(See 364. Animality; also 367. Vegetable)

1. *n.* vegetation, vegetality [rare], vegetism, vegetativeness, vegetability [obs.], vegetable life *or* existence; herbage, flowerage.

2. *v.* vegetate, grow, shoot up; grow out, outgrow; germinate, pullulate, sprout, put forth, bud, burgeon; blossom, bloom, flower; flourish, luxuriate, grow rank *or* lush, grow like a weed; overgrow, overrun; fungate; make vegetate etc. 367.12.

3. *adj.* vegetative, vegetal; vegetable etc. 367.14–17.

4. *adj.* luxuriant, flourishing etc. *v.*, rank, dense, lush; wild, growing wild; jungly, jungled; overgrown, overrun.

366. Animal
(See 367. Vegetable; also 364. Animality)

1. *n.* animal life, animal kingdom, kingdom Animalia, brute creation, fauna; birds, beasts and fish; fowls of the air, beasts of the field, fish of the sea, denizens of the day; domestic animals, livestock, cattle; wild animals *or* beasts, *ferae naturae* [L.], game; branch, subkingdom, phylum, class, order, family, genus (*pl.* genera), species, subspecies, variety; Zoophyta, zoophytes; bipeds, quadrupeds; male animal etc. 373.6; female animal etc. 374.8; mammals, vertebrates, invertebrates etc. 368.3–10; mythical monsters etc. 83.7.

2. *n.* animal, creature, critter [dial.], created being, living being *or* thing, creeping thing; dumb animal *or* creature, dumb friend, brute, beast; horse, ass, elephant, camel etc. (beast of burden) 271.2–11; giraffe etc. 206.7; zebra etc. 440.2; mule, zebrass etc. (hybrid) 41.5; mammoth, dinosaur etc. (antiquities) 124.3; kangaroo etc. (jumper) 309.3; zoon, zooid etc. (germ) 357.4; animalcule etc. (microbe)

193.4; hippopotamus etc. (giant) 192.8.

3. *n.* Felidae [Zool.], Felinae [Zool.], cats, cat family, felines; skunk, polecat, European polecat, fitchew, foumart, foulmart [Scot. and dial. Eng.]; stink cat, zoril; catamount [U.S.], catamountain, cougar, mountain lion, deer tiger; lion, king of beasts, Leo; tiger, leopard, panther, hyena, lynx, wildcat, bobcat, jaguar, puma; cheetah.

4. *n.* cat, domestic cat, house cat, feline, puss, pussy, pussy cat, grimalkin, gib, mouser; tom, tomcat; kitten, kit, kitty, kitling [dial.], catling; Angora, Angora *or* Persian cat, Maltese cat, tortoise-shell cat, tabby, coon cat, Manx cat; Cheshire cat, Chessycat [coll.].

5. *n.* Canidae [Zool.], canines; fox, reynard *or* Reynard, Reinecke Fuchs, Reynard the Fox; prairie fox, kit fox, gray fox, red fox, arctic *or* white fox; coyote, dingo, brush wolf, medicine wolf [West. U.S.], prairie wolf, wolf; timber wolf, lobo [West. U.S.]; jackal.

6. *n.* dog, canine, hound, hound-dog [South. U.S.], tyke *or* tike, bowwow, snarleyyow [joc.]; bone-crusher, bone-polisher, tail-wagger, pooch [all slang]; whelp, pup, puppy; mongrel, cur, mutt [slang]; pariah dog, pye-dog [both Ind.]; bitch, gyp [U.S.], slut, lady; brach, brachet [both arch.]; house dog, watchdog; stock dog, sheep dog, sheepherd *or* shepherd's dog, collie; fancy dog, show dog; toy dog, lap dog.

poodle, poodle dog, Japanese poodle, toy poodle; bulldog, English bulldog, French bulldog, Boston bull *or* terrier, bull terrier; bloodhound, greyhound, staghound, foxhound, boarhound, Russian *or* Siberian wolfhound, otterhound; deerhound, deerdog; husky, Eskimo dog; Pomeranian, pom [coll.]; spitz, spitz dog; hunting *or* sporting dog, gun dog, bird dog; harrier, beagle, pointer; setter, gun dog, English setter, Gordon setter, Irish setter; retriever; water dog, water spaniel; spaniel, cocker spaniel, King Charles spaniel, toy spaniel; terrier, fox terrier, Yorkshore terrier, Irish terrier, Skye terrier, toy terrier, Dandie Dinmont terrier, Airedale terrier, Airedale; dachshund, dachshound; badger dog; chow,

---

366. I think I could turn and live with the animals, they are so placid and self-contained.— WHITMAN. Animals are such agreeable friends—they ask no questions, they pass no criticisms.—G. ELIOT. Those who'll play with cats must expect to be scratched.—CER-

chowchow; mastiff, police dog, coach dog, bandog, lurcher, St. Bernard, Newfoundland, pug, turnspit.

7. *n.* swine, pig, hog, porker; hogget [obs. exc. dial.], hoggerel; shoat *or* shote, piggy; boar, sow; razorback; Berkshire, Cheshire, Chester White, Duroc-Jersey, Hampshire, Poland China, Tamworth, Yorkshire; wild boar, babirusa; wart hog, peccary.

8. *n.* sheep, mutton [joc.]; lamb, lambkin; ewe, ewe lamb; ram, tup, wether; bellwether; tag, teg; Corriedale, Cheviot, Cotswold, Dorset Horn, Hampshire Down, Leicester, Lincoln, Merino, Oxford Down, Romney, Southdown, Shropshire, Suffolk; wild sheep, argali, mouflon, mountain sheep, urial, Thian Shan *or* Marco Polo's sheep.

9. *n.* goat; he-goat, billy goat *or* billy [coll.]; she-goat, nanny goat *or* nanny [coll.]; kid, kiddy; Angora goat, Cashmere goat; wild goat, mountain goat, Rocky Mountain goat, bezoar goat, ibex, markhor, goat antelope; gnu goat, takin.

10. *n.* antelope, eland, addax, nilgai, oryx, steinbok, steenbok, chamois, kudu; American antelope, pronghorn antelope *or* pronghorn; sable antelope, black buck; addax; harnessed antelope, guib; hartebeest, kaama; gazelle, springbok *or* springbuck; gnu, wildebeest; white-tailed gnu, black wildebeest; brindled gnu, blue wildebeest; gnu goat etc. *above.*

11. *n.* deer, deerlet; stag, hart; doe, hind, roe; elk, American elk, wapiti; roe, roe deer, roebuck; mouse deer, musk deer, chevrotain; caribou, moose, reindeer, sambar, black-tailed *or* mule deer, white-tailed *or* Virginia deer, fallow deer, red deer.

12. *n.* cattle, kine; dairy cattle *or* cows, beef cattle; bovine, bovine animal *or* creature, beef (*pl.* beeves *or* beefs); cow, milch *or* milk cow, milcher, dairy cow, bossy [U.S.], cush *or* cusha [dial.]; Alderney, Jersey, Guernsey, Galloway, belted Galloway, Angus, Aberdeen Angus, Holstein; bull, bullock, top cow [dial.]; gelding, castrate; steer, stot [obs. exc. Scot. and dial. Eng.]; ox; calf, slow elk [slang, U.S.], heifer, yearling; dogie, leppy [both West. U.S.]; maverick [West. U.S.]; shorthorn, longhorn; butthead, muley head, muley cow [all dial.]; redpolls, Red Polled; zebu, Brahmany bull.

13. *n.* wild ox, yak, musk ox; buffalo, bison, American bison, cow of the plains, Indian buffalo, gaur, aurochs, urus, water buffalo *or* ox, Cape buffalo; cattalo.

14. *n.* armadillo, peba, poyou, peludo, giant armadillo; tatou, tatou peba, tatouay.

15. *n.* bear, bar [dial.]; polar bear, grizzly bear, brown bear, European brown bear, American black bear, cinnamon bear, Syrian bear, sloth bear, polar bear, ice bear.

16. *n.* monkey, monk [coll. or joc.]; ape, anthropoid ape, orangutan *or* orang, gorilla, chimpanzee; baboon, drill, mandrill, chacma; marmoset; lemur.

17. *n.* Rodentia [Zool.], gnawers, rodents; vermin, varment *or* varmint [dial.]; chipmunk, squirrel, ground squirrel, antelope chipmunk *or* squirrel [U.S.]; American red squirrel, chickaree; flying squirrel, flying phalanger; gopher, pocket gopher, pouched rat; prairie dog; mongoose; raccoon, coon; ferret, monk [coll., U.S. and Can.]; weasel, mousehound [local, Eng.]; ermine, stoat; hare, rabbit, jack rabbit, bunny, Easter bunny, cottontail, Belgian hare; cavy, guinea pig; hedgehog, porcupine, quill pig [slang], brush-tailed porcupine; marmot, flying marmot; woodchuck, ground hog, whistler, whistle-pig [local, U.S.]; beaver; bandicoot, rabbit bandicoot; rat, mouse; bat, flying mouse; flying fox; flying lemur, lugo.

18. *n.* Reptilia [Zool.], reptiles; Amphibia [Zool.], amphibians; Batrachia [Zool.], batrachians; lizard, saurian, iguana, eft, newt, chameleon, gecko, Gila monster, beaded lizard, salamander, dragon; horned toad, horned lizard; crocodile, crocodilian, mugger [Ind.], gavial [Ind.], cayman, American crocodile; alligator, gator [slang, U.S.]; dinosaur etc. (antiquities) 124; basilisk, cockatrice etc. (mythical monsters) 83.7.

19. *n.* serpent, snake, viper, ophidian; asp, adder, coral *or* harlequin snake, copperhead; krait [Ind.], cobra, cobra de capello, king cobra; rattlesnake, rattler; constrictor, boa constrictor, boa, ana-

---

VANTES. Some crush-nosed, human-hearted dog.—BROWNING. It is time, Postumus, to say something about my three goats.—MARTIAL.

Exit, pursued by a bear.—SHAKESPEARE. The little foxes, that spoil the vines.—BIBLE. The foxes have holes, and the birds of the air

conda; python; dipsas, cockatrice etc. (mythical monsters) 83.7.

20. *n.* frog, croaker, paddock [obs. exc. Scot. and dial. Eng.], pad [obs. exc. dial.]; toad, tree toad *or* frog; bullfrog; tadpole, polliwog, pollyfrog [dial. U.S.], pollywiggle [dial. *or* slang].

21. *n.* (marine creatures; aquatic animals) Pisces [Zool.], fish *or* fishes; seal, sea lion, walrus, fur seal, elephant seal; octopus (*pl.* octopuses, octopi, octopodes), octopod, devilfish; crayfish [usu. Eng.], crawfish [usu. U.S. and Ir.], crawdad [local, U.S.], anklebone [coll.]; sea horse, hippocampus; dolphin, dolphinoid, porpoise, sea pig, beluga, killer, narwhal; whale, cete [rare], sperm whale, baleen whale, finback, rorqual, sulphurbottom, right whale, whalebone whale.

humpback, blackfish, grampus, zeuglodont; shark, carchariid *or* charcharioid [Zool.], man-eater, tiger of the sea, blue shark, hammerhead, shovelhead, porbeagle, basking shark, dogfish; ray, batoid [Zool.], sting ray, sawfish, skate, barndoor skate; sunfish, sun [coll.]; flying fish, flying gurnard; game and food fish, lobsters etc. (sea food) 298.18; starfish etc. (echinodermata) 368.5; shellfish etc. (mollusca) 368.6, 7; crustaceans etc. (Arthropoda) 368.8.

22. *n.* Aves [Zool.], birds, feathered tribe, fowl *or* fowls; wild fowl, waterfowl, sea fowl; songbird, singing bird, feathered songster, warbler; dickey, dickeybird [both coll.]; lark, meadow lark; finch, goldfinch, zebra finch; titmouse, chickadee; thrush, hermit thrush, missel bird *or* thrush, veery, mavis; pigeon, squab, dove; ringdove, cushat, wood pigeon; swan, cygnet, goose, gander; duck, drake, wild duck, mallard, canvasback, teal duck, wood duck; ruddy duck, fool duck; ouzel, ring ouzel, water ouzel; blackbird, red-winged blackbird; flycatcher, fly-catching warbler.

woodpecker, peckerwood [dial., U.S.], woodpeck [rare]; red-headed woodpecker, golden-winged woodpecker, flicker, red-shafted flicker; sparrow, song sparrow, chipping sparrow, vesper sparrow; martin, sand martin; bird of paradise, parrot, parakeet; gull, sea gull; albatross, wandering albatross, sooty albatross,
short-tailed albatross, black-footed albatross, yellow-nosed albatross; petrel, black petrel, fork-tailed petrel, black-capped petrel; stormy petrel, Mother Carey's chicken; fulmar, Mother Carey's goose; blue jay, jay bird [dial.]; owl, bird of Minerva, bird of night, hoot owl, screech owl, wood owl.

bird of prey, hawk, falcon, vulture; buzzard, turkey buzzard; eagle, eaglet, *aquila* [L.], bird of freedom, bird of Jove, bald eagle, ringtail, harpy eagle, sea eagle, erne *or* ern; grouse, ruffed grouse; black grouse, black game, blackcock; crane, heron, bittern, egret, flamingo, stork; blackcap, hummingbird, Blackburnian warbler, canary, vireo, linnet, brown thrasher, siskin, crossbill, aberdevine, chewink, peewee, lapwing [Scot.], nightingale, magpie, cuckoo, mockingbird, catbird, laughing jackass, starling, myna, mina, bobolink, reedbird, ricebird, cardinal bird, cowbird, crow, rook, jackdaw, raven, kingfisher, sandpiper, lyrebird, robin, kingbird, swallow, swift, oriole, bluebird.

23. *n.* poultry, fowl *or* fowls; barnyard fowl, barn-door fowl, dunghill fowl; domestic fowl, chicken, chick, chicky, chickabiddy; cock, cock-a-doodle-doo *or* cock-a-doodle [joc.], rooster [U.S.], chanticleer [poetic]; cockerel, spring chicken, broiler, fryer; hen, Partlet, biddy [coll.]; setting hen, skrock hen [dial., U.S.]; Bantam, banty [coll.], Ancona, Andalusian, Black Spanish, Brahma, Campine, Cochin, Cornish, Dorking, Hamburg, Houdan, Langshan, Leghorn, Minorca, Orpington, Plymouth Rock, Rhode Island Red, Sussex, Wyandotte; guinea fowl, guinea cock, guinea hen; peafowl, peacock, peahen; turkey, brush turkey, gobbler.

24. *n.* Insecta [Zool.], insects; bug, harlequin cabbage bug, potato bug, buffalo bug, rose bug, squash bug, water bug, Croton bug, sow bug, chinch bug; beetle, bee beetle, buffalo carpet beetle, cucumber flea beetle, striped cucumber beetle, elm-tree beetle, fruit-tree barb beetle, snout beetle, Colorado beetle; Japanese beetle; billbeetle, billbug; weevil, curculio, plum curculio, nut weevil, grain weevil, boll weevil, flour weevil, pea weevil, rice

---

have nests.—BIBLE. My sisters, the birds, ye are greatly beholden to God for the element of the air.—ST. FRANCIS OF ASSISI(?). Hark!

hark! the lark at heaven's gate sings.—SHAKESPEARE. Master, I marvel how the fishes live in the sea.—SHAKESPEARE.

weevil, weed weevil; roach, cockroach. locust, cicala, cicada, dog-day cicada, grasshopper, cricket; borer, peach-tree borer, peach-twig borer, apple-tree borer, hickory borer, squash *or* squash-vine borer; scorpion, *alacrán* [Sp.]; ant, emmet [arch. and dial.]; pismire, pissant [obs. exc. dial.], antymire [dial.]; agricultural ant, carpenter ant, slave ant, house ant, black ant, red ant; white ant, termite; bee, honeybee, queen bee, drone, worker, bumblebee; wasp, hornet, yellow jacket; fly, housefly, horsefly, horn fly, gadfly, sawfly, dragonfly, caddis fly, bee fly; robber fly, hornet fly, June fly; May fly, ephemerid; butterfly, moth; punkie fly, nosee-um [coll.]; hellgrammite, dobson.

bedbug, B-flat [joc.], chinch; vermin, varmint *or* varment [dial.]; flea, sand flea, dog flea, cat flea; chigoe, chigger, jigger, jigger flea; louse, wood louse, plant louse; body louse, grayback *or* greyback; cootie, crumb [U.S.], seam squirrel, active citizen, bosom chum [all slang]; nit, mite, midge, gnat; mosquito, skeeter [dial.]; springtail, podura, Lepisma, silverfish, firebrat, ant lion, earwig; firefly etc. 423.13.

25. *n.* Vermes [Zool.], worms, cotton worm, bollworm, ear *or* corn-ear worm, cankerworm, cutworm, fall webworm, tobacco worm, tomato worm, army worm, wireworm, silkworm; earthworm, angleworm, fishworm; glowworm, fireworm; shipworm, spileworm; flatworm, platyhelminth [Zool.] etc. (invertebrata) 368.5; caterpillar etc. (larva) 129.8.

26. *adj.* animal, animalic [rare], animalian, animalistic; zoic, zooid *or* zooidal, zoologic(al); mammalian; equine; bovine, vaccine; canine, caninal [rare]; feline, feliform; fishy, piscatory, piscatorial, piscine, piscinal, pisciform; gallinaceous, rasorial, solidungulate, soliped; planktonic, nekteric, benthonic; molluscous, vermicular etc. [Zool.] 368.11–19.

27. *adj.* reptile, reptilian, reptiliary, reptilious [rare], reptiliferous, reptiligerous, reptiloid, reptiliform, reptilelike; snakish, snaky, snakelike; serpentine, serpentile, serpenticide *or* serpenticidal, serpentiferous, serpentivorous, serpentoid, serpentiform, serpentlike; viperish, vipery, viperine, viperan, viperian, viperoid, viperiform, viperlike; anguine, colu-

brine; ophic [rare], ophidian, ophiologic, ophiomorphous.

367. Vegetable
(See 366. Animal; also 365. Vegetation)

1. *n.* vegetable *or* plant life, vegetable kingdom, vegetation, flora, plants; Flora, Pomona [Rom. Myth.]; herbage, herbs, herbaceous vegetation; growth, stand, crop; plantation; phylum, division, class etc. 366.1.

2. *n.* vegetable, vegetal [rare]; plant, herb, wort; seed plant, seedling, plantlet; exotic, annual etc. *adj.*; weed; legumes, pulse; asparagus, peas etc. (food) 298.30; fungus, moss etc. 369.4–8.

3. *n.* seaweed, alga (*pl.* algae), fucus, fucoid, conferva (*pl.* confervae), confervoid, wrack, dulse *or* delisk, kelp, rockweed, sea lettuce; sea lentil, gulfweed, sargasso, sargassum; plankton, benthos.

4. *n.* foliage, foliation, leafage, verdure, frondescence [rare]; praefoliation, vernation; spray; ramage; stalk, leafstalk, petiole, petiolule; seed stalk, stipule, funicule; limb, branch, bush, bough, stem, twig, sprig, rice [obs. exc. dial.], switch; shoot, offshoot, burgeon, sprout; runner, sarmentum (*pl.* sarmenta), tendril, bine; tigella, tigelle, tigellum, tigellus; leaf, frond; leaflet, foliole; blade, lamina; flag; needle, pine needle; pad [U.S.]; bract, bractlet, bracteole; petal; seed leaf, cotyledon; calyx leaf, sepal.

5. *n.* flower, blossom, bloom; bud, burgeon; blow, blowth [rare]; floweret, floret, floscule; flower stalk, peduncle, pedicel *or* pedicle; flowering plant; flowerage, flowering, florescence, inflorescence, florification; full bloom, anthesis.

6. *n.* tree, timber [chiefly U.S.]; sapling, seedling; pollard; timber tree; oak, elm, beech, birch, pine, palm, spruce, fir, hemlock, yew, larch, cedar, savin *or* savine, juniper, maple, alder, ash, myrtle, magnolia, olive, poplar, willow, linden, lime, banyan, teak, acacia, deodar, pipal, eucalyptus, gum, redwood, mahogany, ebony; apple tree etc. (*see* apple etc. 298.31); walnut tree etc. (*see* walnut etc. 298.33); lumber etc. (wood) 635.3.

---

367. What is a weed? A plant whose virtues have not yet been discovered.—EMERSON. To me the meanest flower that blows can give / Thoughts that do often lie too deep for tears. —WORDSWORTH. The groves were God's

7. *n.* wood *or* woods, woodland, timberland, timber, forest, forest land, forestry; wold, weald [both obs.]; primeval forest *or* forest primeval; virgin forest, old growth; woodlet, grove, coppice, copse, copsewood, holt [arch. and dial.], hurst, spinney [Eng.], spinet [obs.], frith [now dial. Eng.], clump of trees, tope [Ind.], thicket, covert, bosk, bosket, boscage, *bocage* [F.], brake, shaw [arch. and dial.]; motte [local, U.S.], chamisal [Calif.], chaparral, hanger, orchard; park, paradise, chase [Eng.]; bush, bosch, brush; jungle *or* jungles; wild, wildwood, wilderness, howling wilderness; boschveld, bushveld.

Pan [Gr. Myth.], Faunus [Rom. Myth.], Vitharr [Norse Myth.], the goat god; faun, satyr, silenus, panisc *or* panisk; wood nymph, nymphid, dryad, hamadryad; sylvan deity.

8. *n.* undergrowth, underwood, undershrubs, underbrush, brushwood, brush, copsewood, copse, coppice, frith [now dial. Eng.], boscage, *bocage* [F.], brake; heath, heather, fern, bracken, furze, gorse, whin, broom, genista, sedge, rush, bulrush, bamboo; shrub, bush, scrub, coppet; creeper, vine.

9. *n.* grass, green herbage, greenery, greens, verdure; grassland etc. *below*; forage grass, lawn grass, ornamental grass; aftergrass, second growth *or* crop; fog, fog grass [dial.], foggage [Scot. and North. Eng.]; timothy, timothy grass, ribbon grass, meadow grass, spear grass, wire grass, bluejoint, crab grass, bunch grass, meadow fescue, tall fescue, meadow foxtail, sheep's fescue, grama *or* mesquite grass, gama *or* sesame grass; bent *or* bent grass; redtop, English grass; switch grass, black bent *or* black bent grass; bluegrass, Kentucky bluegrass; pin grass, alfilaria; clover, alfalfa, lucerne *or* lucern, purple medic; cereal, wheat, rye, barley, buckwheat, oats, rice; maize, Indian corn; forage, hay etc. (fodder) 298.7.

10. *n.* turf, greensward, green, sward, sod.

11. *n.* grassland, grass, meadow land, meadow, mead, pasture, pasturage, pasture land, haugh [Scot. and dial. Eng.], lea, pen [Jamaica], field, park [Eng.], *agostadero* [Sp.], maidan [Ind.]; meadow nymph, limoniad; grassplot *or* grassplat, green, greenyard, lawn; campus [U.S.]; park, common, village green; putting green [Golf]; prairie, pampas etc. (plain) 344.1.

12. *v.* raise, make vegetate, vegetate [rare], cause growth in, grow; plant, cultivate etc. 371.8; sprout, grow etc. (vegetate) 365.2.

13. *v.* timber, retimber; coppice, copse; bush.

14. *adj.* vegetable, vegetal, vegetive [obs.], vegetative, vegetarian; herbose *or* herbous, herby, herbal, herbaceous; leguminous *or* leguminose, leguminiform; grassy, grasslike; verdant, verdurous; turfy, turflike; mossy, moss-grown; fungous, fungiform, fungoid; floral, floreal [rare]; tigellate; radiculose, radicular, radicated, radiciform; radiciflorous, rhizanthous; endogenous, exogenous; deciduous, dicidary [rare]; evergreen; botanical etc. 369.11.

15. *adj.* arborary, arboreous, arboral, arboreal, arborical [obs.], arborescent; wooden, woody, wooded; silvan *or* sylvan, sylvestrian [rare]; treelike, treeful; dendritic(al), dendroid, dendriform; ligneous, lignose *or* lignous [rare], lignescent; bosky, cespitose, copsy.

16. *adj.* algal, fucoid, confervoid; planktonic, benthonic.

17. *adj.* native, domestic, garden, indigenous; native-grown, home-grown; naturalized, acclimated *or* acclimatized; exotic, tropical; annual, perennial, hardy; biennial, triennial; wild.

368. Zoology
(See 369. Botany; also 366. Animal)

1. *n.* zoology, zoonomy, zoography, zootomy; anthropology, anthropotomy; ornithology, ornithotomy; ichthyology, ichthyotomy; herpetology, herpetotomy; morphology, promorphology; anatomy, histology, cytology, embryology, genetics, physiology; animal physiology; mammalogy, mastology, ophiology, malacology; taxonomy, ecology, bionomics, eth-

---

first temples.—BRYANT. This is the forest primeval.—LONGFELLOW. *Nous n'irons plus au bois, les lauriers sont coupés.*—T. DE BANVILLE. [We'll to the woods no more, / The laurels all are cut.—HOUSMAN.] A triangular slope of turf, which the indulgent might call a lawn.—SAKI.

ology; helminthology; paleontology; entomology, entomotomy; protozoology; vermeology; taxidermy; comparative anatomy etc.

2. *n.* zoologist, zoographer, zoographist, zootomist; morphologist, promorphologist; anthropologist, anthropotomist; ornithologist, ornithotomist; ichthyologist, ichthyotomist; herpetologist, herpetotomist; entomologist, entomotomist; anatomist, histologist, cytologist, physiologist; mammalogist, mastologist; ecologist, ethologist; protozoologist; ophiologist, malacologist, helminthologist, paleontologist; vermeologist, taxonomist, taxidermist.

3. *n.* Protozoa (unicellular animals *as against* Metazoa, multicellular animals): Sarcodina; Actinopoda; Rhizopoda, rhizopods; Foraminifera, foraminifers; Radiolaria, radiolarians; Mastigophora, mastigophorans; Flagellata, Sporozoa, sporozoans; Gregarinida, Gregarinae, Gregarinaria, gregarines; Infusoria, infusorians.

4. *n.* Porifera (sponges), poriferans; Spongiae, Spongiozoa; Calcarea; Hexactinellida; Demospongiae; Coelenterata *or* Coelentera (polyps, jellyfishes): Cnidaria; Hydrozoa (jellyfishes, medusae, polyps), hydrozoans; Scyphozoa; Anthozoa (corals, polyps), anthozoans; Ctenophora: Tentaculata; Nuda.

5. *n.* (Vermes, worms) Platyhelminthes (flatworms), platyhelminths: Turbellaria; Trematoda; Cestoda; Nemertinea; Nemathelminthes (roundworms), nemathelminths: Nematoda; Acanthocephala; Chaetognatha; Trochelminthes (wheel animalcules): Rotifera, rotifers; Gastrotricha; Annelida (segmented worms), annelids, annelidans, anneloids: Archiannelida; Chaetopoda; Hirudinea; Gephyrea, gephyreans, gephyeoids.

6. *n.* Molluscoida (bryozoans, lamp shells): Bryozoa, Polyzoa (sea mosses); Phoronidea; Brachiopoda (lamp shells), brachiopods.

7. *n.* Echinodermata (starfishes, sea urchins): Pelmatozoa; Asterozoa; Ophiuroidea (brittle stars), ophiurids, ophiuroideans, ophiuroids, ophiurans; Asteroidea; Asteriidae, asteridians; Echinozoa; Echinoidea (sea urchins), echinoids; Holothurioidea (sea cucumbers), holothurians, holothures; Pelmatozoa; Crinoidea (stone lilies), crinoids, crinoideans; Cystoidea *or* Cystidea, cystideans, cystids; Blastoidea, blastoids; Edrioasteroida.

8. *n.* Arthropoda (crustaceans, insects): Myriapoda (centipedes, galleyworms, millepedes), myriapods; Branchiata; Tracheata; Crustacea, crustaceans; Trilobita, trilobites; Limuloidea; Xiphosura (king crabs); Entomostraca (barnacles), entomostracans; Malacostraca (lobsters, crabs), malacostracans; Onychophora; Pauropoda; Diplopoda; Chilopoda; Symphyla; Insecta, insects; Arachnida *or* Arachnoidea (spiders, scorpions, mites, ticks), arachnids, arachnidans; Merostomata.

9. *n.* Mollusca (mollusks): Amphineura (chitons); Gastropoda (slugs, snails), gastropods, univalves; Scaphopoda (tooth shells, tusk shells), scaphopods; Lamellibranchia, lamellibranches, bivalves; Pelecypoda; Cephalopoda (cuttlefish, squid, octopus, nautilus) cephalopods.

10. *n.* Chordata: Hemichorda; Urochorda; Tunicata; Cephalochorda; Acrania; Vertebrata (*as against* Invertebrata, invertebrates); Craniata; Ostracodermi; Cyclostomata (lampreys), cyclostomes; Elasmobranchii; Pisces, fishes; Selachii (sharks, rays), selachians; Holocephali *or* Holocephala (chimaeras, spooks), holocephalans *or* holocephalians; Teleostomi (ganoids, bony fishes), teleosts, teleosteans; Crossopterygii; Dipnoi (lungfishes), dipnoans; Amphibia, amphibians; Batrachia, batrachians; Reptilia, reptiles; Aves, birds; Mammalia, mammals, mammalians; Prototheria; Monotremata, monotremes; Allotheria; Eutheria; Marsupialia, marsupials, marsupians, marsupialians; Placentalia, placentals; Monodelphia.

11. *adj.* zoologic(al), zoographic(al) etc. *n.*; animal etc. 366.26.

12. *adj.* protozoan, protozoal, protozoic; rhizopodous; foraminiferous, foraminous, foraminated; radiolarian; flagellate; infusorial, infusory; gregarine etc. *n.*

13. *adj.* coelenterate, poriferan; spongiose *or* spongious, spongoid, spongiform; anthozoan, anthozoid; corallaceous, coralliferous, coralliform, coralligenous,

coralligerous, coralloid or coralloidal; polyparous, polypean; hydrozoal, hydroid; medusiform, medusoid etc. *n*.

14. *adj*. echinodermatous, echinodermal; pelmatozoan; crinoidean, crinoid or crinoidal; ophiuran, ophiuroid; asteridian; echinoid, holothurian etc. *n*.

15. *adj*. vermicious, vermicular, vermiculate, vermiculose or vermiculous, vermiform; gephyrean, gephyreoid; annelid, annelidan, annelidous etc. *n*.

16. *adj*. molluscan, molluscous; lamellibranch, lamellibranchiate; bivalvular, bivalvous, bivalved; gastropod, gastropodous; univalve, univalved, univalvular; cephalopodic, cephalopodous; nautiloid, nautiloidean etc. *n*.

17. *adj*. molluscoid, molluscoidal; bryozoan; brachiopod etc. *n*.

18. *adj*. arthropodal, articulate; branchial, branchiate, branchiferous; tracheate; crustacean, crustaceous; arachnoid or arachnoidal, arachnidan, arachnidial; insectile, insected etc. *n*.

19. *adj*. vertebrate, vertebrated, vertebral; cyclostome, cyclostomous; amphibian, amphibial [rare], amphibious; batrachian, batrachoid; avicular; mammalian, mammiferous etc. *n*.; reptilian, piscatorial etc. (animal) 366.26.

369. Botany
(See 368. Zoology; also 367. Vegetable)

1. *n*. botany, physiological botany, structural botany, systematic botany; phytography, phytology, phytotomy, phytonomy, phytobiology, phytopathology; phytochemistry, phytochimy [obsoles.], vegetable chemistry; pomology; vegetable physiology, herborization; dendrology; mycology, fungology; algology.

2. *n*. herbarium, herbal [obs.], herbary [rare], *hortus siccus* [L.]; botanic garden etc. (garden) 371.6.

3. *n*. phyton, phytomer, phytomeron.

4. *n*. Thallophyta (thallus plants), thallogens, thallophytes: Algae, algae; Cyanophyceae (blue-green algae); Chlorophyceae (green algae); Phaeophyceae (brown algae); Rhodophyceae (red algae); Fungi, fungi; Schizomycetes (fission fungi, bacteria); Myxomycetes (slime molds); Phycomycetes (algal fungi, water molds); Ascomycetes (sac fungi, lichen, lichen fungi); Basidiomycetes (basidium fungi, rusts, smuts, puffballs, mushrooms, toadstools).

5. *n*. bryophyta (moss plants), bryophytes: Hepaticae (liverworts); Musci (mosses); Iceland moss, Reindeer moss, rock moss.

6. *n*. pteridophyta (fern plants), pteridophytes; Lycopodiales (ground pines, club mosses, quill worts); Lycopodiaceae (club mosses); Selaginellaceae; Sigillaria, Stigmaria; Equisetaceae, Equisetales (horsetails), equisetum; Calamites, calamite; Filicales, Filices (ferns), filicoids; Cycadofilicales, Cycadofilices (cycad ferns), cycadofilicales.

7. *n*. lepidodendraceae (fossil trees): Lepidodendron, lepidodendroids, lepidodendrids.

8. *n*. spermatophyta (seed plants), spermatophytes: Gymnospermae (naked-seeded plants), gymnosperms; Cycadales, cycads; Gnetales, gnetums; Ginkgoales, ginkgoes; Pinales or Coniferae (cone-bearing evergreens), conifers; Angiospermae (covered-seeded plants), angiosperms; Monocotyledones, Endogenae (cereals, palms, lilies, orchids, bananas, pineapples); monocotyledons, endogens; Dicotyledones (oaks, apples, sunflowers, peas), dicotyledons.

9. *n*. botanist, botanologer [obs.]; phytologist, phytotomist, phytobiologist, phytopathologist; dendrologist; mycologist, fungologist; algologist; herbalist, herbist, herborist, herbarist [arch.], herbarian; pomologist; horticulturist etc. (agriculturist) 371.2.

10. *v*. botanize, herborize, herbarize [arch.], herbalize.

11. *adj*. botanic(al), botanological [obs.]; phytologic(al), phytobiological, phytochemical, phytogenous or phytogenetic; dendroid or dendroidal, dendritic(al), dendrologous, dendriform; fungous, fungoid, fungiform; mycologic(al), mycetoid; pomological; thalloid, thalline; muscoid, musciform; equisetaceous, equisetiform; filicoid, filiciform; angiospermous, angiospermatous; hepatic, lycopodiaceous, lepidodendroid, gymnospermous, cycadaceous, coniferous, monocotyledonous, endogenous, dicotyledonous etc. *n*.; horticultural etc. (agricultural) 371.9; herbal etc. (vegetable) 367.14–17.

370. Animal Culture

1. *n.* animal culture, animal husbandry; breeding, stockbreeding; horsemanship, horse training, manège; veterinarianism, veterinary art, farriery [obsoles.]; pisciculture, fish culture; apiculture, beekeeping.

2. *n.* taming etc. *v.*, cicuration [obs.], domestication, domesticization [rare].

3. *n.* (animal enclosure) menagerie, *Tiergarten* [G.]; zoological garden, zoo [coll.]; bear pit; apiary, alvearium, alveary, beehive, hive; vivarium; aquarium, fishery, fishpond; hatchery, fish hatchery; swan pond, duck pond; aviary, birdhouse, bird cage; hen coop, chicken coop, hen house, hen cote, chicken house, chicken yard, hen yard; incubator; coop, corral, pound, sty, cage etc. (enclosure) 232; barn, kennel, cote etc. (abode) 189.5-7.

4. *n.* animal husbandman, stockman [Austral. and U.S.], stockholder [now rare], stockkeeper [Austral.], keeper; gamekeeper; cowkeeper, cowboy, cowgirl, cowpuncher [U.S.], *vaquero* [Sp. Amer.]; drover, herder, herdsman, herdboy; oxherd, cowherd, neatherd, grazier; shepherd, shepherdess, sheepherder [chiefly U.S.]; goatherd, goatherdess; gooseherd, gooseboy, goosegirl; swineherd, pigman; stableman, stableboy, groom, tiger [old slang], hostler *or* ostler, equerry; breeder, trainer; horse trainer, breaker, broncobuster [slang, U.S.]; horseshoer, farrier; apiarist, apiarian [rare], apiculturist, beekeeper; bullwhacker [U.S.] etc. (driver) 268.9; veterinarian etc. (doctor) 662.19.

5. *v.* breed, train, take in hand, raise, rear, bring up, bring up by hand.

6. *v.* tame, cicurate [obs.], gentle; domesticate, domesticize [rare]; break, break in, break to harness; cage etc. (confine) 751.8.

7. *v.* tend stock, groom, rub down, brush, currycomb; water, feed, fodder; bed, bed down, litter; drench, embrocate; milk, milch [obs.]; shear; herd, drive, guide; spur, prick, lash, goad, whip; corral, round up; yoke, harness, harness up [coll.], hitch, hitch up [coll.], bridle, saddle, cinch [U.S.].

8. *v.* incubate, hatch; sit, brood, cover.

9. *v.* swarm, hive.

10. *adj.* domesticated etc. *v.*, domestic; tame, broken, gentle, docile.

371. Agriculture

1. *n.* agriculture, husbandry, farming, cultivation, culture; tillage, tilth; agrology, agronomy *or* agronomics, agrogeology; georgics, geoponics, geopony [rare]; horticulture, gardening, landscape gardening; truck gardening, olericulture; flower gardening, floriculture; viniculture, viticulture; arboriculture, silviculture, forestry.

2. *n.* agriculturist, agricultor [rare], agronomist, husbandman, farmer, granger [U.S.], yeoman, cultivator, tiller, tiller of the soil; grower, raiser; plowman, plowboy; reaper, sower; nurseryman, horticulturist, gardener, landscape gardener, truck gardener; florist, floriculturist; vine culturist, vinegrower, viniculturist, viticulturist, vintager, *vigneron* [F.]; arboriculturist, silviculturist, forester; woodsman, backwoodsman; woodcutter, wood chopper; logger, lumberman [U.S. and Can.], lumberjack [U.S. and Can.]; rustic etc. (peasant) 876.5; botanist etc. 369.9.

3. *n.* (gods of agriculture) vegetation spirit, corn god, Ceres, Dionysus *or* Dionysos, Gaea *or* Gaia, Triptolemus *or* Triptolemos; Demeter, Thesmophoros; Persephone *or* Proserpina *or* Proserpine *or* Persephassa, Kore *or* Cora.

4. *n.* farm, farmstead, plantation, grange, ranch, rancho [Southwest. U.S.], rancheria [Southwest. U.S.], location [Austral.], mains [Scot.], pen [Jamaica]; demesne farm, homestead, toft [Scot. and dial. Eng.], barton [Eng.], hacienda [Sp. Amer.]; homecroft [Eng.]; cote [Eng., Hist.]; chicken ranch, cattle ranch; messuage etc. 189.12.

5. *n.* field, tract, plat, plot, patch, piece *or* parcel of land, cultivated land, croft [Eng.]; lot [U.S.]; cleared land, clear-

---

370. Prayers / For tamed and shabby tigers / And dancing dogs and bears.—R. HODGSON. *Etiam fera animalia, si clausa teneas, virtutis obliviscuntur* [Even savage animals, if kept shut up, forget their courage].—TACITUS.

371. The first farmer was the first man, and all historic nobility rests on possession and use of land.—EMERSON. He that by the Plough would thrive, / Himself must either hold or drive.—FRANKLIN. Farming is not really a business; it is an occupation.—W. WOODWARD.

ing; wheat field, corn field etc.; meadow etc. (grassland) 367.11.

6. *n.* garden, garden patch, nursery, plantation; kitchen garden, market *or* truck garden, flower garden, botanic(al) garden, *Jardin des Plantes* [F.], sunken garden; conservatory, cabinet, summerhouse, glasshouse, greenhouse, hothouse, stovehouse [Eng.], forcing house, coolhouse; forcing pit, force bed, hotbed, cold frame; bed, flower bed; border, avenue, hedge; grassplot *or* grassplat, lawn, green, greenyard; shrubbery; arboretum, orchard; pinery, pinetum; vineyard, vinery; orangery, peachery etc.; park etc. 189.21; arbor etc. (bower) 191.22; herbarium etc. 369.2.

7. *n.* crop, harvest etc. 636.3.

8. *v.* farm, ranch, raise crops; cultivate, till, till the soil; garden; plant, implant, set, sow, seed, seed down; transplant, reset; grow, raise; reap, mow, cut, harvest, crop, gather, pick, pluck; crop herbs, herb [coll., U.S.], herbalize; herborize *or* herbarize [arch.]; manure, fertilize, dress the ground; turf, sod, sod down *or* over; dig, spade, delve, dibble, plow, harrow, rake, hoe, weed, lop and top; backset [U.S.]; prune, cut, thin out; graft, engraft *or* ingraft; force; bed, bed up.

9. *adj.* agricultural, agrarian, agrestic, agrestian; agronomic(al), agronomial; geoponic(al), georgic(al); praedial, landed; vinicultural, viticultural; horticultural, olericultural; arboricultural, silvicultural; rural, rustic etc. (countrified) 183.3; botanical etc. 369.11.

372. Mankind

1. *n.* mankind, humankind, human species, human race, race of man, humanity, mortality, flesh, generation of man; mortals, "the plumeless genus of bipeds" (Plato); lord of creation; homo, homo sapiens, anthropos, Man.

2. *n.* people, persons, folk *or* folks, people in general, public, general public, community, world, world *or* community at large, society; state, realm, commonweal *or* common weal [arch.], commonwealth, body politic, republic, nation, nationality; ourselves, yourselves; million etc. (commonalty) 876; population etc. (inhabitants) 188.10.

3. *n.* human being, human, person, personage, man, homo (*pl.* homines), anthropos; fellow [chiefly coll.], member of the human race, individual, creature, fellow creature *or* man, mortal, soul, living soul, body, somebody, one, some one *or* someone, *quidam* [L.]; member, customer, scout [all coll.]; party [slang], wallah [coll., Anglo-Ind.], duck [slang], wight [joc. or arch.], guy [derog. *or* slang]; earthling, worldling; head, hand, nose; God's image.

"the aristocrat amongst the animals" (Heine), "the most intelligent of animals —and the most silly" (Diogenes), "a tool-using animal" (Carlyle), "a tool-making animal" (Franklin), "a god in ruins" (Emerson), "an intelligence served by organs" (Emerson), "Nature's sole mistake" (Gilbert), "that unfeather'd two-legged thing" (Dryden), "but breath and shadow, nothing more" (Sophocles), "political animal" (Aristotle).

4. *n.* anthropology, anthropogeny, anthropography, anthropotomy, androtomy; ethnology, ethnography; anthroposophy, humanism; sociology, social science etc. (public welfare) 906.3.

5. *adj.* human, humanistic, hominine [rare], mortal; personal, individual; manlike, anthropoid; fleshly etc. 364.4.

6. *adj.* public, general, common, communal, societal, social; national, state, provincial; civic, civil; cosmopolitan, international; universal etc. 78.9–11.

---

372. So God created man in his own image, in the image of God created he him.—BIBLE. Thou hast made him a little lower than the angels.—BIBLE. Man is a reasoning animal.—SENECA. Man is a reed, but he is a thinking reed.—PASCAL. Man . . . an extract or compendious image of the world.—BACON. The proper study of mankind is man.—POPE. The still, sad music of humanity.—WORDSWORTH. Man is Creation's masterpiece. But who says so?—Man!—GAVARNI. After all there is but one race—humanity.—G. MOORE. The old, proud pageant of man.—MASEFIELD. Man consists of body, mind, and imagination. —MASEFIELD. Nations are the citizens of humanity, as individuals are the citizens of the nation.—MAZZINI. Our true nationality is mankind.—H. G. WELLS. *Homo homini aut deus aut lupus* [Man is to man either a god or a wolf].—ERASMUS. Man is a name of honor for a king.—CHAPMAN. Every man is as God made him, ay, and often worse.— CERVANTES. A man's a man for a' that!— BURNS. Man is a military animal, / Glories in gunpowder, and loves parade.—P. J. BAILEY.

373. Male
(See 374. Female)

1. *n.* male, male being, masculine, he, him.

2. *n.* man, male etc. *above,* male person, homo (*pl.* homines), *hombre* [Sp.], sire, fellow, feller [dial. and vulg.]; lad; chap, chappie, guy, Jack, scout [all coll.]; bloke, John, Johnny, duck, cove, jigger, joker [all slang]; gill, swipe [both slang, Eng.]; jasper, mug [both slang, U.S.]; wallah [coll., Anglo-Ind.], horse [joc.]; gentleman, gent [vulg. or joc.], don, sahib [Ind.]; goodman [arch.]; boy etc. (youth) 129.4; old man etc. (elder) 130; father, grandfather etc. 166.6, 8; husband etc. 903.7; bachelor etc. 904.2; adult etc. 131.3.

3. *n.* mister, Mr., Master, monsieur *or* M. (*pl.* messieurs *or* MM.), Messieurs *or* Messrs. [*pl.*], *Herr* [G.] (*pl. Herren*), *signor or signore* [It.] (*pl. signori*), signior *or* seignior, *signorino* [It.] (*pl. signorini*), *señor* [Sp.] (*pl. señores*), *senhor* [Pg.]; sir, sire, sirrah [arch. and dial.]; Dan [arch.], Don, *mein Herr* [G.], Mynheer; huzoor, mirza etc. 877.2; dom, pater etc. 877.4.

4. *n.* mankind, man, men, world *or* realm of men, manhood, menfolk *or* menfolks [coll.], male sex; male variety [joc.]; human kind etc. 372.

5. *n.* manhood etc. (adulthood) 131; manliness etc. (virility) 159a.

6. *n.* male animal, male etc. *above* 373.1; cock, rooster [U.S.], chanticleer, cock-a-doodle-doo   *or*   cock-a-doodle [joc.]; cockerel; drake; gander; peacock; gobbler, turkey gobbler; dog; boar; stag, hart, buck; entire horse, entire, stallion, studhorse, stud [U.S.], top horse [dial. U.S.]; tom, tomcat, gib [rare]; hegoat etc.; billy goat *or* billy [coll.]; ram, tup, wether, bull, bullock, top cow [dial.]; steer, stot [obs. exc. Scot. and dial. Eng.]; ox; male brute, cow brute, cow critter [all dial.]; gelding, castrate; gellion [dial.].

7. *adj.* male, masculine, he-; manly, manlike; gentlemanly, gentlemanlike; mannish, unwomanly etc. (virile) 159a.5; boyish etc. (youthful) 127.5.

---

373. A man is as good as he has to be, and a woman as bad as she dares.—E. HUBBARD.

374. Female
(See 373. Male)

1. *n.* female, female being, feminine [now coll.], she, her.

2. *n.* woman, womanbody [Scot. and North. Eng.], female etc. *above,* female person, *femme* [F.], feme [obs.], maness [rare], womanfolk [dial.], weaker vessel [joc.], fair [arch. exc. slang], slut [arch.]; dame, hen, petticoat, skirt [all slang or derog.]; Jane, broad, calico, curve, fem, frail, moll [all U.S. slang or derog.]; squaw.

frow, *Frau* [G.], *vrouw* [Du.]; belle; mistress, mastress [obs.], madam [vulg., U.S.]; Sahibah [Ind.], *mem-sahib* [Hind.], bibi [Ind.]; lady, milady, gentlewoman, *donna* [It.], *doña* [Sp.], *dona* [Pg.], *domina* [L.] (*pl. dominae*); matron, dame, dowager, gammer [dial. Eng.]; good woman, goodwife [arch.], goody; girl etc. 129.5; old woman etc. (elder) 130.3; mother, grandmother etc. 166.7, 9; wife etc. 903.8; bachelor girl, spinster etc. 904.3; mollycoddle etc. (effeminate person) 160a.3; adult etc. 131.3.

3. *n.* mistress, Mrs., missis *or* missus [illit.], madam, madame *or* Mme. (*pl.* mesdames), ma'am *or* mam [coll.], marm [dial.], *Frau* [G.], *vrouw* [Du.], *signora* [It.], *señora* [Sp.], *senhora* [Pg.]; Sahibah [Ind.], *mem-sahib* [Hind.], bibi [Ind.]; *Dona* [Pg.], *Doña* [Sp.], *Donna* [It.], dame.

4. *n.* miss, *mademoiselle* [F.] (*pl.* mesdemoiselles), *Fräulein* [G.], *signorina* [It.], *señorita* [Sp.], *senhorita* [Pg.].

5. *n.* womankind, woman, women, world *or* realm of women, womanhood, feminie [arch.], femininity, feminity, feminality, femality, womenfolk *or* womenfolks [coll.], calico [joc., U.S.]; the distaff, the sex, the fair, fair sex, softer sex, weaker sex, "the lesser man" (Tennyson), female sex; female variety [joc.], the eternal feminine, *das Ewig-*

---

374. *Varium et mutabile semper femina* [Woman is ever a fickle and changeable thing].—VERGIL.   Frailty, thy name is woman.—SHAKESPEARE.   Women's beauty, like men's wit, is generally fatal to the owners.—CHESTERFIELD.   Women are silver dishes into which we put golden apples.—GOETHE.   Earth's noblest thing, a woman perfected.—LOWELL. The female of the species is more deadly than the male.—KIPLING.   A woman's guess is

Weibliche [G.]; matronage, matronhood, matronship.

6. *n.* womanhood etc. (adulthood) 131; effeminacy etc. 160a.

7. *n.* harem, gynaeceum (*pl.* gynaecea), seraglio (*pl.* seragli, seraglios), serai [erron.], zenana [Ind.], purdah [Ind.].

8. *n.* female animal, female etc. above 374.1; hen, Partlet, biddy [coll.]; guinea hen; peahen; bitch, slut, gyp [U.S.], brach *or* brachet [arch.]; sow; ewe, ewe lamb; she-goat, nanny goat *or* nanny [coll.]; doe, hind, roe; mare, girl [dial., U.S.]; brood mare, stock horse; filly; cow, bossy [U.S.], cush *or* cusha [dial.]; heifer; lioness; tigress; vixen; she-bear, she-lion etc.

9. *n.* feminism, womanism, woman's *or* women's rights, rights of women; woman *or* female suffrage, suffragettism; emancipation of women.

10. *n.* feminist, womanist, suffragist, woman-suffragist, suffragette.

11. *adj.* female, feminine, gynecic, she-; womanly, womanlike; ladylike, gentlewomanlike, gentlewomanly; matronly, matronal, matronlike; womanish, unmanly etc. (effeminate) 160a.5; girlish etc. (youthful) 127.5.

375. Physical Sensibility
(See 376. Physical Insensibility)

1. *n.* sensibility, physical sensibility, sensitiveness etc. *adj.*, feeling, impressibility, affectibility, perceptivity, susceptivity, susceptibility; aesthetics; moral sensibility etc. 822.

2. *n.* sensation, sense, impression, feeling; consciousness etc. (knowledge) 490.

3. *v.* be sensible of etc. *adj.*, sense, sensate, feel, perceive, apprehend; feel keenly *or* exquisitely.

4. *v.* render sensible etc. *adj.*, sensitize, sharpen, refine, excite, stimulate, stir, cultivate; aestheticize.

5. *v.* cause sensation, impress, excite *or* produce an impression.

6. *adj.* sensible, sensitive, sensuous, sentient; perceptive, susceptive, susceptible, impressive, impressionable, impressible, responsive, alive, alive to impressions, answering quickly to, quick in response, easily affected; thin-skinned, tender; oversensitive, oversensible; aesthetic; conscious, aware etc. (knowing) 490.12, 13.

7. *adj.* acute, sharp, keen, vivid, intense, lively.

8. *adv.* to the quick, on the raw.

376. Physical Insensibility
(See 375. Physical Sensibility)

1. *n.* insensibility, physical insensibility, insensibleness etc. *adj.*, insentience, insusceptibility, unimpressibility, induration, unfeeling, unconsciousness; palsy, paralysis; hemiplegia, motor paralysis; anesthesia, narcosis, narcotization, hypnosis, stupor, sopor, coma; twilight sleep, *Dämmerschlaf* [G.]; sleep etc. (inactivity) 683; moral insensibility etc. 823; numbness etc. 381.

2. *n.* anesthetic, anesthetic agent; local *or* general anesthetic; hypnotic, soporific; ether, chloroform, chloral; gas, ethylene; laughing gas, nitrous oxide; exhilarating gas, protoxide of nitrogen; refrigeration, freezing; opiate, novocain etc. (narcotic) 662.7; sedative etc. (palliative) 662.6.

3. *v.* be insensible etc. *adj.*, have a thick skin, have a hide like a rhinoceros.

4. *v.* render insensible etc. *adj.*, blunt, dull, deaden, obtund, numb, benumb, stupefy, stun; freeze, refrigerate; paralyze, palsy; anesthetize, chloroform, put under the influence of chloroform etc. *n.*, put to sleep, sopite [now rare], hypnotize, mesmerize, magnetize, narcotize, drug, dope [slang]; soothe, allay etc. (moderate) 174.5.

5. *adj.* insensible, insensate, insentient, insensitive, unsensitive, senseless, unfeeling, unconscious; impercipient, imperceptive; numb, dead, deadened etc. *v.*, unfelt; callous, thick-skinned, pachydermatous; hard, hardened, casehardened, inured; proof, impervious; obtuse, dull,

---

much more accurate than a man's certainty.—KIPLING.   Women are wiser than men because they know less and understand more.—J. STEPHENS.   I expect that woman will be the last thing civilized by man.—MEREDITH. Something feminine—not effeminate, mind—is discoverable in the countenances of all men of genius.—COLERIDGE.   A woman's work is never done.

376. Like dull narcotics numbing pain.—TENNYSON.   A drowsy numbness pains / My sense, as though of hemlock I had drunk.—KEATS.   Hers the silence and the calm of mute insensate things.—WORDSWORTH.

anesthetic; paralytic, palsied, palsy-stricken.

377. Physical Pleasure
(See 378. Physical Pain)

1. *n.* pleasure, physical pleasure, sensual *or* sensuous pleasure, bodily enjoyment, gratification, animal gratification, satisfaction, delight, sensual delight, carnal pleasure; sensuality, sensuosity, sensuousness etc. *adj.*; dissipation, round of pleasure; gusto, relish, zest, titillation; hedonism; happiness, felicity etc. (mental enjoyment) 827.

2. *n.* comfort, well-being, ease, self-ease [rare], heart's ease, cosiness, snugness, restfulness, peace, peacefulness; creature comforts; luxuriousness, luxury, lap of luxury, bed of down *or* roses, bed of ease, flowery beds of ease, velvet, clover, purple and fine linen; contentment etc. 831.

3. *n.* treat etc. (source of pleasure) 829.3.

4. *v.* enjoy, pleasure [rare], feel pleasure *or* gratification, experience *or* receive pleasure, relish, appreciate; luxuriate in, revel in, riot in, bask in, swim in, wallow in; feast on, gloat over *or* on; smack the lips, roll under the tongue.

5. *v.* live in comfort etc. *adv.,* live on the fat of the land, bask in the sunshine, *faire ses choux gras* [F.], be in clover [chiefly coll.] etc. *adv.*

6. *v.* please, give pleasure etc. 829.4.

7. *adj.* pleasing, gratifying etc. *v.*; affording pleasure etc. *n.,* satisfactory, grateful, refreshing, comforting, cordial, genial, titillative; sensuous, sensual; voluptuous, voluptuary [now rare]; hedonic, hedonistic; agreeable etc. (pleasurable) 829.7, 8; lovely etc. (beautiful) 845.8–13; palatable etc. (savory) 394.7; sweet etc. 396.8; fragrant etc. 400.10; melodious etc. 413.27.

8. *adj.* comfortable, easeful, easy, restful, peaceful, cosy, snug, snug as a bug in a rug; roomy; convenient; at home, homely [arch. and dial.]; luxurious.

---

377. *Voluptates comendat rarior usus* [A more rare indulgence in pleasures enhances them].—JUVENAL.   Sweet is pleasure after pain.—DRYDEN.   When you are sincerely pleased, you are nourished.—EMERSON.   The man who finds most pleasure for himself is often the man who least hunts for it.—CHESTERTON.   Bankrupt of life yet prodigal of ease.—DRYDEN.

9. *adv.* in comfort, at ease, at one's ease, in clover [chiefly coll.], on velvet [slang], on a bed of roses etc. *n.*; without care *or* worry, *sans souci* [F.].

378. Physical Pain
(See 377. Physical Pleasure)

1. *n.* pain, physical pain, bodily pain *or* suffering, suffering, sufferance [rare], hurt, misery [dial.], dolor [obs.], malaise, discomfort, distress; nip, pinch, pang, twinge, twitch; crick, kink, stitch; smart, tingle; shoot, shooting, shooting pain, sharp ~, piercing *or* stabbing pain; palpitation, throb, throbbing, throbbing pain; gnawing *or* grinding pain, gnawing of the bowels; burn, burning pain; sore, soreness; cut, laceration; ache, aching etc. *v.*

headache, head, cephalalgy, cephalalgia, misery in the head [dial.]; sick headache, hemicrania, migraine, megrim; backache, crick in the back, misery in the back [dial.]; earache, otalgia; toothache, odontalgia; stomach-ache, bellyache [vulg.], colic; gripe *or* gripes, tormina; cramp *or* cramps, Charley horse [coll., U.S.]; the bends [coll.], caisson disease; neuritis, neuralgia; ischialgia, sciatica; face ague, trigeminal neuralgia, *tic douloureux* [F.]; rheumatism, rheumatiz [dial.], rheumatics [dial.]; lumbago; arthritis, gout, podagra; stiff neck, torticollis; convulsion, throe etc. (spasm) 315.7; mental suffering etc. 828.8.

2. *n.* torment, torture, painful trial, agony, anguish, lancination, rack, cruciation, crucifixion, martyrdom, hell upon earth.

3. *n.* sufferer, martyr etc. 828.8.

4. *v.* pain, give *or* inflict pain etc. *n.,* hurt, wound, afflict; burn, sting; bite, nip, tweak, pinch; pierce, prick, stab, cut, lancinate; gnaw, grind, gripe; gall, fret, chafe, rasp, grate; torment, torture, rack, agonize, harrow, lacerate, crucify, cruciate [obs.], excruciate, wring, convulse; martyr, martyrize; prolong the agony,

---

378. I'll rack thee with old cramps, / Fill all thy bones with aches, make thee roar.—SHAKESPEARE.   Pain pays the income of each precious thing.—SHAKESPEARE.   He has seen but half the Universe who never has been shewn the house of Pain.—EMERSON.   Pain is no evil, / Unless it conquer us.—KINGSLEY.   Pain with a thousand teeth.—W. WATSON.   No pains, no gains.

kill by inches; flog etc. (punish) 972.5–9; grate upon the ear etc. 410.7.

5. *v.* suffer, feel ~, experience ~, undergo ~, bear ~, endure ~, sustain ~, suffer etc. pain etc. *n.*; hurt, ache; smart, tingle, shoot, twinge, twitch; agonize, bleed [fig.], writhe, wince, make a wry face; sit on thorns *or* pins and needles.

6. *adj.* pained, afflicted etc. *v.*; in pain etc. *n.*, in a state of pain, hurt; hurting, suffering etc. *v.*; on the rack, under the harrow; torminous, torminal; gouty, podagric.

7. *adj.* painful, hurtful, baleful [rare], afflictive, hurting, aching; sore, raw; with exposed nerves; grave, harsh, hard, acute, poignant, pungent, sharp, piercing, biting, severe, cruel, caustic, consuming, corroding, excruciating, racking, agonizing, torturous; tormenting, tormentive *or* tormentative [rare].

379. Touch

1. *n.* touch, contact, tact [now rare], taction, tactility, impact, attaint [arch.], trait [arch.]; tangence [rare], tangency; feel, feeling, handling; light touch, lambency; graze, glance, brush; kiss, osculation; lick, licking; caress, rub, kneading, massage; palpation, palpability; contrectation [rare]; stereognosis [Tech.].

2. *n.* (organ of touch) tactile organ, feeler, antenna (*pl.* antennae); palp, palpus (*pl.* palpi); tongue, red rag [slang, Eng.]; finger, digit, forefinger, thumb; palm, hand etc. 781.3.

3. *v.* touch, feel, feel of, palpate, handle, palm, paw, finger, pass *or* run the fingers over, thumb; caress, stroke, rub, massage, knead; manipulate, wield; fumble, grope, grabble; twiddle, tweedle [obs. exc. dial.]; throw out a feeler; touch lightly, brush, graze, glance, lick, sweep; kiss, osculate; contact [Tech.], come into contact, join, adjoin, border, neighbor, meet, hit, impinge, lap.

4. *adj.* touching etc. *v.*, tangent, stereognostic [Tech.], adjacent, abutting, contiguous; touching lightly, lambent.

5. *adj.* touchable, tangible, palpable, tactile, tactual [Tech.], contactual [rare].

379. Touch with thrilling fingers.—Meredith. O for the touch of a vanished hand!—Tennyson. *Noli me tangere* [Touch me not].—Vulgate.

380. Sensations of Touch
(See 381. Numbness; also 379. Touch)

1. *n.* tingling etc. *v.*, tingle, thrill; formication, paresthesia [both Med.]; creeps, cold creeps [both coll.]; sting, prickle *or* prickles, prickling *or* pricking sensation; aura [Med.].

2. *n.* tickle, tickling, titillation, vellication.

3. *n.* itch, itching etc. *v.*; mange, scab, scabies; psora, pruritus, prurigo [all Med.].

4. *v.* tingle, thrill; itch, have the itch etc. *n.*; creep, have the creeps etc. *n.*; prick, prickle, sting.

5. *v.* tickle, titillate, vellicate, kittle [Scot. and dial. Eng.]; goose [U.S.].

6. *adj.* tingly, tinglish, tingling etc. *v.*; itchy, scabious, mangy; psoric, psoroid [both Med.]; formicative [Med.], creepy, crawly; prurient.

7. *adj.* ticklish, tickling etc. *v.*, tickly, titillative, vellicative, kittle, kittlish [Scot. and dial. Eng.]; goosy [U.S.].

381. Numbness
(See 380. Sensations of Touch)

Insensibility to Touch.—1. *n.* numbness, benumbedness etc. *adj.*, unfeeling; pins and needles; anesthesia, narcosis etc. (insensibility) 376.

2. *v.* numb, benumb; fall asleep; deaden, paralyze, stupefy etc. (render insensible) 376.4.

3. *adj.* numb, numbed, benumbed etc. *v.*; unfeeling, unfelt; dead, deadened; asleep; anesthetic, narcotic; dazed, dazy [rare]; insensible etc. 376.5.

382. Heat
(See 383. Cold; also 384. Calefaction, 386. Heater, 389. Thermometer)

1. *n.* heat, hotness, warmness etc. *adj.*; warmth, hot [now dial.], temperature, torridity, calidity [obs.], caloric, caloricity [Physiol.]; fervor, fervency, fervidity,

380. I would thou didst itch from head to toot and I had the scratching of thee.—Shakespeare. 'Tis better than riches to scratch when it itches.—J. Ray. Itch . . . also is pleasing.—Bacon.
382. If you light your fire at both ends, the middle will shift for itself.—Addison. Whirlwinds of tempestuous fire.—Milton. Fear no more the heat o' the sun.—Shake-

ardor; heat wave; blood heat, body heat; steam heat, gas heat, electricity; incandescence *or* incandescency; incalescence *or* incalescency [rare]; recalescence, decalescence; diathermancy *or* diathermance, diathermaneity; adiathermancy, athermancy; transcalency; phlogiston [old Chem.], phlogisis; thermogenesis; liquation; insolation; warming etc. 384.

2. *n.* intense heat, torrid heat etc. *adj.*, red heat, white heat, tropical heat, Afric heat, Indian heat, Bengal heat, summer heat; sweltering heat, swelter.

3. *n.* hot weather, sunny *or* sunshiny weather; summer, midsummer; dog days, canicular days, canicule [rare]; summer day, hot day, roaster [coll.]; broiling sun, midday sun, sun at noon; heat wave, hot wave, monkeys [slang]; vertical rays; sun etc. 318.4.

4. *n.* hot air, superheated air; hot wind; volcanic wind; khamsin, harmattan, *solano* [Sp.], sirocco, samiel, simoom.

5. *n.* hot water, boiling water etc. *adj.*; steam, vapor; superheated steam; volcanic water; hot *or* warm springs, thermae; geyser; Old Faithful, Old Frightful [joc.].

6. *n.* hot *or* warm bath, hot *or* warm tub [coll.]; therm, thermae; steam bath, vapor bath, sweat bath, Turkish bath, Russian bath, Finnish bath; hot shower; hot-air bath; sudatorium etc. (bathhouse) 386.6; electric bath etc. 652.3.

7. *n.* flush, glow, blush, bloom, redness, whiteness; rubicundity; hectic, hectic flush *or* fever; febricity, pyrexia etc. (fever) 655.4.

8. *n.* fire, flame, glim [slang], blaze, ingle, devouring element; conflagration, combustion, ignition; flash, scintilla, scintillation, spark; coal, live coal; sheet of fire; wavering *or* flickering flame, "lambent flame" (Dryden); sea of flames; gas flame, carbon flame etc.; gas jet, pilot light *or* burner; cheerful fire; bonfire, bonner [slang, Eng.], tandle [Scot.]; balefire, needfire [rare], signal fire, beacon, signal beacon, beacon fire, watch fire; fiery cross; alarm fire, two-alarm ⁓, three-alarm etc. fire; wildfire, prairie fire, forest fire; open fire; campfire; smudge fire, smudge [both U.S.]; death fire, pyre,

funeral pile; volcano, active volcano, vulcan [obs.], burning mountain; fire god, Hephaestus [Gr. Myth.], Vulcan [Rom. Myth.], Agni [Hindu Myth.]; light etc. 420.

9. *n.* firework *or* fireworks, pyrotechnics, pyrotechny; cracker, firecracker, cannon cracker, cracker bonbon, ladyfinger, torpedo, bomb, candlebomb, squib, cap, sparkler, girandole, fizgig, whiz-bang *or* whizz-bang, flowerpot; rocket, skyrocket, Roman candle; flare, flare-up, snake, serpent; pin wheel *or* pinwheel, Catherine wheel; noisemaker etc. 404.4.

10. *n.* thermal unit, British thermal unit, Board of Trade unit; calorie, small calorie, great calorie; therm.

11. *n.* (fire and light worship) fire worship, pyrolatry; fire worshiper, pyrolater; sun worship, heliolatry; sun worshiper, heliolater; star worship, Sabaism, Sabaeanism [erron.]; star worshiper, Sabaist, Sabaean [erron.]; Parsiism, Zoroastrianism; Parsi, Zoroastrian.

12. *n.* (science of heat) thermology, thermotics, thermodynamics; volcanology; pyrology, pyrognostics, pyrotechnics *or* pyrotechny.

13. *v.* be hot etc. *adj.*, burn, singe, scorch, parch, scald, grill, broil, simmer, stew, toast, roast, swelter; boil, bile [dial.], seethe, ebullate *or* ebulliate [rare]; blaze, flame, glow, flush; reek, fume, smolder, smoke, funk [slang]; steam; pant, gasp; incandesce; recalesce; sweat etc. 295.7.

14. *v.* heat, burn etc. 384.16–21.

15. *adj.* warm, calid, mild, genial; sunny, sunshiny; summery, estival, canicular; tepid, luke, lukewarm; toasty [coll.], warm as toast; blood-warm, blood-hot; unfrozen; calefactive etc. 384.22.

16. *adj.* hot, fiery etc. *below*; calorific, torrid, tropical, burning, sweltering, sweltry, swelty [dial.], baking, roasting, toasting, parching, scorching, scalding, broiling, simmering; boiling, seething, ebullient; burning-hot, scalding-hot, roasting-hot, scorching-hot, smoking-hot, piping-hot, sizzling-hot, red-hot, white-hot; hot as fire, hot as pepper *or* red pepper, hot as hell *or* blazes [vulg.], hot enough to roast an ox, like a furnace *or* oven; fervid, fervent, ardent; thermal, thermic, thermotic(al), thermogenic, thermogenetic, thermogenous; hot-blooded, warm-blooded; recalescent, decales-

---

SPEARE. Better a little fire that warms than a big one than burns.—J. RAY. The nearer the fire, the hotter.—CHAUCER.

cent; molten etc. (heated) 384.23, 24; sweaty etc. 299.11.

17. *adj.* fiery, igneous; ignited, burning, blazing, ablaze, flaming, aflame, afire, on fire, in flames, in a blaze, alight, glowing, aglow, in a glow, live, incandescent; candent, incandent [rare]; flickering, aflicker; unquenched, unextinguished; smoldering, fuming, reeking, smoking; inflamed, phlogotic, phlogistic; pyrognomic.

18. *adj.* sultry, stifling, suffocating, stuffy, close, oppressive.

19. *adj.* feverish, fevered, feverous, in a fever, hectic; febrile, febricose [rare], febrific, febrifacient; pyretic, pyrexic [rare]; inflamed, burning etc. *above* 382.16, 17.

20. *adj.* pyrological, pyrognostic; pyrotechnic(al); pyrogenic, pyrogenous.

21. *adj.* diathermic, diathermal, diathermanous.

22. *adj.* adiathermic, adiathermal, adiathermanous, athermanous.

23. *adj.* volcanic, volcanian [rare], plutonic; volcanological.

24. *adj.* isothermal, isothermic(al).

383. Cold
(See 382. Heat; also 385. Refrigeration, 387. Cooler)

1. *n.* cold, coldness, coolness etc. *adj.*; coolth [dial. or joc.]; frigidity, gelidity, algidity, severity, inclemency, rigor; "a hard, dull bitterness of cold" (Whittier).

2. *n.* (sensation of cold) chilliness etc. *adj.*, chill; shivering etc. *v.*, shivers, cold shivers, didders, dithers [chiefly dial.], chattering of the teeth; creeps, cold creeps [both coll.]; goose flesh *or* skin, goose pimples, goose *or* duck bumps [dial.], horripilation; *arrector pili* [NL.] (*pl. arrectores pilorum*); rigor; ache, aching; frostbite, chilblains.

3. *n.* cold weather, bleak weather, freezing ~, wintry ~ etc. *adj.* weather; zero weather; cold wave, snap, cold snap; winter, depth of winter, hard winter; wintry wind etc. 349.7.

4. *n.* (cold place) Siberia, Nova Zembla, Alaska, Iceland, Greenland, Greenland's icy mountains; arctic, North Pole; antarctic, South Pole; Frigid Zones, Arctic Circle, Antarctic Circle; polar front, cold front, wind-shift line, squall line [all Meteorol.].

5. *n.* ice, snow ice; sleet, glaze, glazed frost; hail, hailstone; soft hail, graupel [Meteorol.]; hailstorm, ice storm [Meteorol.]; frost, Jack Frost, hoarfrost, hoar, rime, rime frost, white frost, *pruina* [L.]; black frost; hard frost, sharp frost; frost smoke; ice needle *or* crystal; lolly, slush, slosh; sludge, slob; icicle, iceshockle *or* iceshogle [Scot. and dial. Eng.]; thick-ribbed ice.

iceberg, berg, floa, ice floa *or* float, ice raft, ice pack, ice field, jokul [Iceland]; calf; snowberg, snow mountain; glacier, glacieret, glaciation, "motionless torrents, silent cataracts" (Coleridge); firm, névé, granular snow; icecap; Piedmont glacier; ground ice, anchor ice, frazil [Can. and North. U.S.]; icequake; ice age, glacial epoch; ice cubes, dry ice; refrigeration etc. 385.

6. *n.* snow, driven snow; snowfall, fall of snow, snowstorm, snow blast, flurry, blizzard; snowflake, flake, crystal; snow dust; snowdrift, snowbank, snow wreath [Eng.], snow roller; snow blanket, snow bed, snow field, snowcap; snowball; snowslide, snowslip, avalanche, snow avalanche.

7. *v.* be cold etc. *adj.*, shiver, quiver, quake, shake, tremble, shudder, didder, dither [chiefly dial.]; chill, become chilled, have a chill, have the cold shivers etc. *n.*; freeze, freeze to death, perish with cold, starve [now dial.]; horripilate.

8. *adj.* cold, bleak, raw, bitter, biting, cutting, nipping, nippy, snappy [coll.], piercing, pinching, fresh, keen, inclement, severe, rigorous; gelid, algid, froren [obs.], frore *or* frory [arch.]; icy etc. *below*; frigid, freezing, freezing cold, numbing; wintry, winterlike, hiemal *or* hyemal, brumal, hibernal; arctic, Siberian, boreal; hyperborean, hyperboreal [rare]; cold as ice, cold as marble, ~ a stone, ~ lead, ~ iron etc., cold as a frog, cold as charity, cold as Christmas, cold enough to freeze the tail off a brass monkey [joc.]; shivering etc. *v.*, shivery, shaky, dithery [chiefly dial.], aguish; frozen, frozen to death,

---
383. Poor Tom's a-cold.—SHAKESPEARE. An hour's cold will suck out seven years' heat. —J. DENHAM. Trust not one night's ice.— G. HERBERT. He dwelleth i' the cold o' the moon.—BROWNING. St. Agnes' Eve—Ah, bitter chill it was! / The owl, for all his feathers, was a-cold.—KEATS. The pity of the snow that hides all scars.—E. MARKHAM.

starved [now dial.], *transi de froid* [F.]; frostbitten, frost-nipped.

9. *adj.* icy, icelike, ice-cold, cold as ice etc. *above,* glacial; ice-built; frosty, frosted, frost-beaded, frost-chequered, hoary, hoarfrosted, rime-frosted; frost-riven, frost-rent; frosty-faced, frosty-whiskered; frozen out, icebound, snowbound; frost-bound, frost-fettered; frozen etc. 385.7.

10. *adj.* cool, coolish; chill, chilly; cool as a cucumber, cool as custard; lacking in warmth etc. 382; lukewarm, tepid etc. (warm) 382.15.

11. *adj.* unwarmed, unheated; unthawed, unmelted.

12. *adj.* isocheimal, isocheimenal, isocheimic.

13. *adv.* coldly etc. *adj.*; *à pierre fendre* [F.]; with chattering teeth.

384. Calefaction
(See 385. Refrigeration; also 382. Heat, 386. Heater)

1. *n.* calefaction, tepefaction, torrefaction, increase of temperature; warming, heating etc. *v.*
2. *n.* melting etc. *v.,* fusion; thaw; liquefaction etc. 335.
3. *n.* burning etc. *v.,* cineration, incineration; combustion; oxidation; adustion [obs.]; flagration [obs.], conflagration; deflagration [Chem.]; incension [obs.], accension [arch.]; cremation, concremation; the stake, burning at the stake, auto-da-fé (*pl.* autos-da-fé), *auto de fe* [Sp.] (*pl. autos de fe*), auto; scorification; cautery, cauterization; ustulation [rare]; calcination; carbonization; cupellation.
4. *n.* ignition, inflammation; lighting, kindling etc. *v.*
5. *n.* incendiarism, arson; pyromania.
6. *n.* incendiary, arsonist, arsonite, conflagrator [rare], firer [rare]; pyromaniac, firebug [coll., U.S.]; *pétroleur* [F.], *pétroleuse* [F.; *fem.*].
7. *n.* boiling etc. *v.,* coction, ebullition, ebullience *or* ebulliency, estuation [obs.]; elixation [obs.]; decoction; ebullioscope, ebulliometer.
8. *n.* burn, ambustion [rare]; singe, scorch, scald etc. *v.*; sunburn, sunscald.
9. *n.* sunstroke, sun [coll.], siriasis [Med.], insolation [Med.], *coup de soleil* [F.].

10. *n.* inflammability, combustibility etc. *adj.*
11. *n.* cauterant, cauterizer, cauter, cautery; hot iron, brand, branding iron; caustic, escharotic, corrosive; decoction, apozem *or* apozema; moxa; acid, chlorous acid, hypochlorous acid, perchloric acid, nitrochlorohydric acid, nitromuriatic acid etc.; nitric acid, hydrogen nitrate; sulphuric acid, hydrogen sulphate; lunar caustic, silver nitrate; arsonic acid, arsonate; radium, uranium.
12. *n.* incinerator, cremator, crematory, crematorium, burning ghat [Ind.], burner, calcinatory; cupel; furnace etc. 386.1.
13. *n.* wrap, coverlet etc. (covering) 223.9–11; muffler, muff, mittens, ear muffs etc. (clothing) 225.
14. *n.* ceramics, ceramic ware; pottery, crockery, porcelain, Satsuma ware, gombroon, faience, majolica, crouch ware, salt-glazed ware, Rockingham ware, Staffordshire ware, Lowestoft ware, Leeds pottery, Mexican pottery, Crown Derby, spode, jasper ware, Wedgewood ware, Toft ware, queen's ware, Castleford ware; Worcester ware, old Worcester; china, chinaware; Sèvres, Sèvres ware; delft, delftware; Palissy ware, Limoges ware; Meissen ware, Dresden china, Berlin ware.

eggshell porcelain, luster pottery, lusterware *or* lustreware; crackle, Chinese crackle, Bohemian crackle; bisque, biscuit; whiteware, white pottery; blackware, basalt; earthenware, stoneware, ironstone ware *or* china, cottage china; printed wares, portrait pieces, Allervale pottery; enamel, enamelware, cloisonné *or* cloisonné enamel, champlevé *or* champlevé enamel; terra cotta, clay, fire clay, clayware; crock, pot, vase, urn, mug, jug, bowl; tile; mosaic; brick, firebrick, silica brick, refractory brick, chrome brick, salmon brick, unburnt brick; adobe; china stone, kaolin; clay, china clay, porcelain clay.

glass, glassware, glasswork, vitrics; crown glass, flint glass, uranium glass, Venetian glassware, Swedish glass, Lalique glass, Steuben glass, Fostoria, hobnail glass, milk glass, pressed glass, blown glass, cut glass, etched glass, wire *or* wired glass, Sandwich glass, ornamental glass; porcelain glass, cryolite glass; sheet glass, plate glass, plate, pane, windowpane; looking glass etc. (mirror) 445.4.

15. *n.* (products of combustion) scoria (*pl.* scoriae), dross, slag, ash *or* ashes, embers, cinder *or* cinders, clinker, coal, coke, carbon, charcoal, lava; soot, smut, coom *or* coomb [Scot. and dial. Eng.], culm; smoke, smudge, oxide.

16. *v.* heat, hot [now dial.], make hot etc. (*see* hot etc. 382.16), warm, chafe, calefy [obs.], tepefy, mull [as wine], digest [Chem.], foment, incandesce; superheat, overheat.

17. *v.* ignite, fire, set fire to, set on fire, build a fire, kindle, enkindle, inflame, illuminate [rare], light, light up, strike a light, apply the match *or* torch to, conflagrate; rekindle, relight, relume; fan the flame, feed, feed the fire, add fuel to the flame, poke *or* stir up the fire, blow up the fire; make a bonfire, build a campfire etc. (*see* fire etc. 382.8); catch on fire, burst into flame, take, take fire, blaze up; feed, stoke etc. (fuel) 388.8.

18. *v.* burn, torrefy, blister, scorch, parch; singe, swinge [obs. exc. dial.]; sear, bake etc. *below*; cauterize, brand, burn in; oxidize, oxidate, corrode, char, carbonize; calcine, calcinate [rare]; deflagrate [Chem.]; cupel, cupellate [rare]; smelt, scorify; incinerate, combust [arch.], comburate, cremate, burn up, consume, burn *or* reduce to ashes, burn to a cinder; burn off, nigger off [local U.S. and Can.]; commit *or* consign to the flames, throw in the fire; blaze, flame etc. 382.13.

19. *v.* cook, prepare; boil, bile [dial.], ebullate *or* ebulliate [rare], stew, seethe, simmer, parboil, brew; fricassee; steam; sear, braze, barbecue; fry, griddle, pan; frizz, frizzle; grill, grid [rare], broil, pan-broil; devil; curry; bake, oven-bake; roast; toast; baste, jipper [Naut. slang]; do to a turn, do to rags [coll.]; recook, reheat, warm over.

20. *v.* insolate, sun; bask, bask in the sun, sun oneself; sun-dry.

21. *v.* melt, run, flow [obs.], colliquate [obs. exc. Med.], fuse, flux; thaw, thaw out; liquefy etc. 335.5.

22. *adj.* calefactive, calefactory, calefacient; heating, warming, burning etc. *v.*; conflagrant, conflagrative, comburent; inflammable, burnable, accendible, combustible; deflagrable [Chem.]; inflammatory, inflammative, kindling etc. *v.*; slow-burning, free-burning etc.; cauterant, calcinatory; estuous [rare]; scoriaceous, apozemical; transcalent; radioactive; salamandrine; warm, hot etc. 382.15–24.

23. *adj.* heated etc. *v.*, het *or* het up [dial.]; burnt, adust; ustulate; sun-burned *or* sunburnt; sodden, sad [obs. exc. dial.]; reheated, recooked, warmed-over, *réchauffé* [F.]; hot etc. 382.16–19.

24. *adj.* molten, melted etc. *v.*; liquefied etc. 335.7.

385. Refrigeration
(See 384. Calefaction; also 383. Cold, 387. Cooler)

1. *n.* refrigeration, infrigidation, reduction of temperature; cooling, freezing etc. *v.*; glacification, glaciation, conglaciation [obs.], congelation; refreezing, regelation; electric refrigeration, gas refrigeration; solidification, crystallization etc. (condensation) 321.3; ice etc. 383.5; refrigerator etc. 387.

2. *n.* incombustibility, incombustibleness etc. *adj.*

3. *n.* fire extinguisher *or* annihilator, extinguisher, *extincteur* [F.]; fire engine; asbestos, amianth *or* amianthus; earth flax, mountain flax; fire fighter, fireman; fire brigade, fire engine, fire department.

4. *v.* refrigerate, frigorify [rare], infrigidate; render cold etc. (*see* cold etc. 383.8), cool; refresh, freshen; fan, ventilate, air; chill, chill to the bone *or* marrow, make one's teeth chatter, make one shiver etc. (be cold) 383.7; nip, cut, pierce, bite; numb, benumb, petrify; freeze, ice, glacify, glaciate, conglaciate [obs.], congeal; freeze to death, starve [now dial.]; refreeze, regelate.

5. *v.* extinguish, quench, out, douse [coll. and dial.], snuff, snuff out, dout [obs. exc. dial. Eng.], blow out, put out, stamp out, annihilate; damp, choke, smother, stifle, slack; become extinguished, go out, burn out, die, die out *or* away; fizzle, fizzle out [both coll.].

6. *adj.* refrigerative, refrigeratory, refrigerant, infrigidative [rare], frigoric, frigorific(al), frigiferous, algific; cooling, chilling, freezing etc. *v.*; freezable, glaciable.

7. *adj.* cooled, chilled etc. *v.*; frozen, gelid, froren [obs.], frore *or* frory [arch.]; frozen out etc. (icy) 383.9.

8. *adj.* incombustible, uninflammable, unflammable; asbestine, asbestic; amianthine, amianthoid *or* amianthoidal; fireproof, flameproof.

386. Heater
(See 387. Cooler; also 382. Heat, 384. Calefaction)

1. *n.* heater, fireless heater *or* cooker, electric heater, gas heater, steam heater, water heater, ingot heater, bloom heater, iron heater, rivet heater, plate heater, tire heater; calefactor, calefactory, warming house [Eccl.]; stove, gas stove, oil stove, electric stove, air-tight stove, Franklin stove, Dutch stove; cookstove, range, kitchener [Eng.]; salamander, salamander stove; furnace, fiery furnace, volcano [fig.], blast furnace, electric furnace; reverberatory, reverberatory furnace *or* kiln; athanor; forge; tuyère, tewel; hypocaust [Hist., Arch.]; oven, Dutch oven, tin oven, brick oven; stovehouse; kiln, brickkiln, limekiln, acid kiln, enamel kiln; radiator, register.

foot stove, foot warmer; warming pad, warming pan; firebox, tinderbox; cooker, pressure cooker, cookery; boiler, superheater, kitchen boiler, double boiler, pan boiler; caldron, *caldera* [Sp.], seething caldron; pot, urn, kettle, stewpan, broiler; skillet, griddle, frying pan, spider; chafer, chafing dish *or* pan; brazier; retort, crucible, alembic; still, distiller; coil; waffle iron; iron, flatiron, sadiron; curler, curling iron *or* tongs; toaster, toasting fork, electric toaster; blast lamp, blowtorch, acetylene torch *or* welder, blowpipe, welding blowpipe; incinerator etc. 384.12.

2. *n.* fireplace, hearth, ingle; fireside, ingleside, inglenook *or* ingle nook, ingle cheek [Scot. and Ir.], chimney corner, hearthstone; hob, hub; fireguard, fireboard, fire screen, fender.

3. *n.* fire irons; andiron, firedog; tongs, pair of tongs, fire tongs, coal tongs; poker, stove poker, salamander [chiefly dial. Eng.], fire hook; lifter, stove lifter;

pothook, crook, crane, chain; trivet, tripod; spit, turnspit; grate, grating, grid, gridiron, griddle [obs. exc. dial.], stovehouse [Eng.]; shovel, coal shovel, banjo [slang, U.S.]; damper; coal scuttle *or* hod.

4. *n.* cookroom, cookery, kitchen, scullery, cookhouse, crumb castle [joc.]; galley, caboose *or* camboose; bakehouse, bakery.

5. *n.* hothouse, conservatory, hotbed etc. (garden) 371.6.

6. *n.* (bathhouse) hot bath, thermae [*pl.*]; *caldarium* [L.], tepidarium, vaporarium; sudatory, sudatorium, sudarium; sweat room, sweating room; hot shower, sweat bath etc. 382.6; bathroom etc. (lavatory) 652.4.

387. Cooler
(See 386. Heater; also 383. Cold, 385. Refrigeration)

1. *n.* cooler, refrigerator, refrigeratory, refrigerated box *or* room, frigidarium, icebox, ice chest, Frigidaire [trade name]; frigidaire, electric refrigerator, gas refrigerator; refrigerator car, reefer [tramp slang, U.S.]; refrigerating plant, ice plant, icehouse; cold storage; coolhouse; refrigerating machine *or* engine, ice machine, freezing machine, freezer, ice-cream freezer; ice pail, wine cooler; ice bag, ice pack, cold pack; ventilator etc. 338.6; fan etc. 349.21.

2. *n.* cooling agent, coolant; refrigerant, refrigerative [rare]; ice, dry ice, ice cubes; freezing mixture, liquid air, ammonia, carbon dioxide, ether; cold cream etc. (oil) 356; lemonade, cold drink etc. 396.5.

388. Fuel

1. *n.* fuel, firing, combustible; dope, fuel dope; fire barrel; fireball; briquette; carbon, gas carbon; peat, turf; petroleum, gasoline etc. (oil) 356; gas etc. 334.2; electricity etc. 158a; illuminant etc. 420.15.

2. *n.* coal, stove coal; soft *or* bituminous coal; hard *or* anthracite coal, blind coal, glance coal; lignite, brown coal; candel coal, cannel, cannel coal; steam-

---

386. Sighing like furnace.—SHAKESPEARE. Heat not a furnace for your foe so hot / That it do singe yourself.—SHAKESPEARE. Shadrach, Meshach, and Abed-nego fell down bound into the midst of the burning fiery furnace.—BIBLE. A fair fire makes a room gay.—J. RAY.

388. Coal is a portable climate.—EMERSON. Adding fuel to the flame.—MILTON.

boat ~, broken *or* grate ~, egg ~, nut ~, chestnut ~, stove ~, pea ~, buckwheat ~, flaxseed *or* mustard-seed coal; slack, coal dust, culm, coom *or* comb; coke; charcoal; cinders, embers etc. (products of combustion) 384.15.

3. *n.* firewood, stovewood, wood; kindling wood, kindling *or* kindlings; brush, brushwood; bavin [Eng.], fagot, log, backlog, yule log *or* clog.

4. *n.* lighter, light *or* lights; igniter, sparker; pocket lighter, cigar *or* cigarette lighter; torch, flaming torch, flambeau, mussal [Ind.], taper, spill; brand, firebrand; wick, candlewick, lampwick; portfire; flint, flint and steel; fuse, squib [chiefly Min.]; chemical ~, concussion ~, percussion ~, electric ~, friction ~, time ~, base *or* point fuse; detonating fuse, detonator, cap, blasting cap, exploder, electric exploder.

5. *n.* match, lucifer; lights [chiefly Eng.]; friction match, locofoco [obs. U.S.]; safety match, vesuvian, vesta, fusee; Congreve, Congreve match; linstock [obs. exc. Hist.].

6. *n.* tinder, touchwood; punk, spunk, German tinder, amadou; tinder fungus; pyrotechnic sponge; tinderbox.

7. *n.* fumigator, incense, joss stick; disinfectant; sulphur, brimstone.

8. *v.* fuel, supply with fuel, add fuel to the flame, feed, coal, stoke; light, fire etc. (ignite) 384.17.

9. *adj.* combustible, inflammable etc. (calefactive) 384.22.

10. *adj.* carbonaceous, carboniferous, carbonigenous [rare]; coaly.

389. Thermometer
(See also 382. Heat)

n. thermometer, mercury, glass; clinical thermometer, dry-bulb *or* wet-bulb thermometer, black-bulb thermometer, gas thermometer, electric thermometer, thermoelectrometer, thermometrograph, register *or* self-registering thermometer, telethermometer, resistance thermometer, galvanothermometer, metallic thermometer, platinum thermometer, thermostat, thermophile, thermoregulator, pyrometer, calorimeter.

390. The full flavor, the whole relish of delight.—H. W. BEECHER. We catch flavors,

390. Taste
(See 391. Insipidity; also 393. Condiment)

1. *n.* taste, flavor, savor, sapor [obs.], sapidity; sip, sup, bite; taster, sample, specimen; soupçon, touch, trace, hint, suggestion, tinge, spice, dash, bit, scrap, snap [now dial.]; smack, smatch [dial., Eng.]; tang, twang [dial., Eng.]; aftertaste, farewell [obs. exc. dial.]; palate, tongue, tooth, stomach; gusto, zest etc. (relish) 394.2; refinement etc. (taste) 850; pepper, salt etc. (condiment) 393.

2. *n.* tasting etc. *v.*, gustation, degustation, discussion [coll.].

3. *v.* taste, tasten [rare]; flavor [rare], try the flavor of, savor, sip, sup, sample, discuss [coll.], roll on the tongue; degust, degustate [both rare]; smack, smatch [dial., Eng.]; relish, tickle the palate etc. 394.5, 6.

4. *adj.* gustatory, gustative; gustable, tastable; flavored, flavorous, flavorsome, flavory, flavorful; gustful [arch.], gusty [chiefly Scot.]; sapid, saporous, saporific; spiced, strong etc. (pungent) 392.5; palatable etc. (savory) 394.7.

391. Insipidity
(See 390. Taste, 392. Pungency)

1. *n.* insipidity, tastelessness etc. *adj.*, untaste, vapidity, jejunity.

2. *adj.* insipid, void of taste etc. (*see* taste etc. 390), tasteless, gustless [obs.], unflavored, flavorless, savorless, unsavory, jejune, ingustible [obs.]; weak, thin, milk-and-water, wishy-washy, mild, vapid, *fade* [F.], flat, stale, indifferent, neither one thing nor the other; untasted.

392. Pungency
(See 391. Insipidity)

1. *n.* pungency, pungence, piquance [rare], piquancy, poignance, poignancy,

---

and roll them on our tongues.—T. E. BROWN. Your lordship . . . hath yet some smack of age in you, some relish of the saltness of time.— SHAKESPEARE. Come, give us a taste of your quality.—SHAKESPEARE.
391. Insipid as the queen upon a card.—TENNYSON.
392. The wood-fire pungence of smoked ham.— UNTERMEYER. Sugar and spice and all things nice.—SOUTHEY. The acidity of the

haut goût [F.], high relish *or* flavor, high seasoning, strong taste, strength, tang, twang [dial., Eng.], race, nip; guts, kick [both slang]; punch, smack, snap, zip, ginger [all coll.]; sharpness etc. *adj.*, edge, causticity, astringency, austerity, severity; acridity, acrity [obs.], acritude [obs.], acrimony; acerbity, acerbitude [obs.]; mordancy, mordacity; tartness, acidity etc. (sourness) 397; bitterness etc. (unsavoriness) 395.

2. *n.* (pungent articles) niter, saltpeter; brine; ammonia, carbonate of ammonia; sal ammoniac *or* sal-ammoniac, *sal volatile* [NL.]; smelling salts; hartshorn; mint, peppermint; cordial, peppermint cordial, pousse-café; seasoning, mustard, cayenne etc. (condiment) 393; gall etc. 395.3; acid, vinegar etc. 397.2; bracer etc. (tonic) 662.5; (liquor) 959.10.

3. *v.* be pungent etc. *adj.*, nip, bite, bite the tongue, sting.

4. *v.* render pungent, season, flavor, savor, spice, bespice, salt, pepper, pickle, brine, devil, curry.

5. *adj.* pungent, piquant, poignant, racy, zippy [coll.], nippy, snappy [coll.], with a kick [slang] etc. *n.*; sharp, keen, piercing, stinging, biting, acrid, acrimonious, mordant, mordacious, astringent, harsh, rough, severe, austere, caustic, escharotic [Med.]; acerb, acerbic, acerbate; strong, gamy, high, strong-flavored, high-flavored, full-flavored, high-tasted, high-seasoned; seasoned, spiced etc. *v.*; spicy, nutty [slang]; peppery, hot, hot as pepper; vellicative, vellicating; tart etc. (sour) 397.6; unsavory, bitter etc. 395.5-7; exciting etc. 824.12.

6. *adj.* salt, salty, salted, saltish, saline, briny, brackish, salt as brine, salty as a herring, like Lot's wife.

392a. Tobacco

1. *n.* tobacco, *tabac* [F.], Lady Nicotine, nicotia [poetic], nicotian, snout [slang], the weed [coll.], fragrant *or* divine weed, Indian weed *or* drug, filthy weed, "dirty weed" (G. Hemminger), "pernicious weed" (Cowper), "that tawney weed" (Jonson), "sublime tobacco" (Byron), "divine tobacco" (Spenser); terbacker, tobacker, baccer, backy [all dial.]; funked *or* funky tobacco; tabacum [Pharm.]; tabacin [Chem.].

Broadleaf, Connecticut Broadleaf, Havana, Havana seed, Cuban, Latakia, Turkish tobacco, Virginia; green tobacco; cut tobacco, canaster, shag, bird's-eye; roll *or* twist tobacco, pigtail tobacco; cake *or* plug tobacco, cavendish; leaf, seconds, lug; Congo tobacco etc. (poisonous plants) 663.6; hashish etc. (narcotic) 662.7.

2. *n.* smoking tobacco, smokings *or* smokin's [dial. or slang], smoke *or* smokes [slang], jack [slang, U.S.]; pipeful, pipe; tobacco jar, humidor; bird's-eye etc. *above.*

3. *n.* cigar, weed [coll.]; segar, seegar [both dial.]; rope, woodbine, stinker [all slang]; stogie, toby [slang, U.S.], colorado cigar, cheroot; trichinopoly, trichi [coll.].

4. *n.* cigarette, gasper [slang, Eng.]; cig, fag, coffin nail *or* tack, pill [all slang]; cigarette papers.

5. *n.* butt, stub; old soldier, corpse, hobo's delight, dinch, dobe, scag, snipe [all slang].

6. *n.* pipe, tobacco pipe; corncob pipe *or* corncob; clay pipe, clay [coll.], TD [coll., U.S.]; meerschaum, hookah, narghile *or* nargileh; brier, *bruyère* [F.].

7. *n.* chewing tobacco, chewings *or* chewin's [dial. or slang], eating tobacco [dial.], spit-and-run [joc.]; navy, cavendish, niggerhead *or* negrohead; twist, pigtail; plug, cake; quid, cud [slang], fid [dial.], chew, chaw [dial.]; tobacco juice, ambeer [dial.].

8. *n.* snuff, snoose [coll., West. U.S.]; rappee; pinch of snuff, rear of snoose

---

lemon will very aptly figure pungency of raillery.—JOHNSON. From the spicy shore / Of Araby the Blest.—MILTON. Then to the spicy nut-brown ale.—MILTON. The spice and salt that season a man.—SHAKESPEARE.
392a. Heaven's last, best gift, my ever new delight.—MILTON. Thou weed, who art so lovely fair and smell'st so sweet.—SHAKESPEARE. A lone man's companion, a bachelor's friend, a hungry man's food, a sad man's cordial, a wakeful man's sleep, and a chilly man's fire.—KINGSLEY. Tobacco hic, / If a man be well it will make him sick.—J. RAY. A good cigar is as great a comfort to a man as a good cry to a woman.—BULWER-LYTTON. Hold on with a bulldog grip, and chew and smoke as much as possible.—LINCOLN. A woman is only a woman, but a good Cigar is a Smoke.—KIPLING. What this country really needs is a good five-cent cigar.—T. R. MARSHALL.

[slang, West. U.S.]; snuff bottle, snuffbox, snuff mill *or* mull [Scot.]; snuff stick *or* swab, snuff brush [So. U.S.], dip.

9. *n.* nicotine, nicotina [obs.], nicotia; Nicotiana; nicotianin [Chem.], tobacco camphor; tabacin.

10. *n.* smoking, using, chewing etc. *v.*; smoke, chew; puff, drag [slang]; tabacosis, tobaccoism, nicotinism, nicotism [rare].

11. *n.* smoker, chewer etc. *v.*; tobacco user, tobacconalian [joc.], tobacchian [obs.], tobaccophile, tobaccoite, nicotian; snuffer, snuff dipper.

12. *n.* tobacconist, tobacconer [obs.], tobaccoman [rare]; tobacco store, cigar store; snuffman; tobacco bar.

13. *n.* smoking room, smoke room [chiefly Eng.], smoker [coll.], smokery, fumistery [rare]; *tabagie* [F.].

14. *v.* smoke, use tobacco, funk [slang], drink [obs.]; inhale, puff, draw, drag [coll.], pull; "smoke like a furnace" (Gilbert), "smoke like a chimney" (Barham); chew, chaw [dial.], quid [now dial.]; take snuff, dip *or* inhale snuff.

15. *adj.* tobacco, tobaccolike, tobaccoy, tobaccofied [rare]; nicotinian *or* nicotinean, nicotinic; smoking etc. *v.*; colorado; funked, funky; mellow, rich, ripe; snuffy; blended, mixed.

393. Condiment

1. *n.* condiment, relish, achar [Ind.], appetizer, flavoring, seasoning, spice; cinnamon, nutmeg, mace, allspice, ginger, clove, pot herbs; thyme, sage, marjoram, parsley, shallot, *fines herbes* [F.]; mint, peppermint; dill, dillseed *or* dill seeds; salt; pepper, black pepper, white pepper, green *or* bell pepper; red *or* cayenne pepper, cayenne; capsicum, capsician; paprika; pimpernel.

sauce, sass [dial.]; applesauce, cranberry sauce etc.; *sauce piquante, sauce tartare, sauce relevée, sauce douce* [all F.]; tabasco, tabasco sauce; catchup; chili, chili sauce, chili pepper, chili vinegar; pimento; mustard, French *or* German mustard; cubeb; radish, horseradish; leek, onion, wild onion, garlic; hedge garlic, sauce-alone; chutney; vinegar, pickle etc. 397.2; vanilla etc. (*see* vanilla ice cream etc. 298.13.).

2. *v.* season etc. (render pungent) 392.4.
3. *adj.* pungent etc. 392.5.

394. Savoriness
(See 395. Unsavoriness)

1. *n.* savoriness, palatableness etc. *adj.*, palatability, delectability.

2. *n.* savor, relish, zest, gust [arch.], gusto, *goût* [F.], gratification; smack, tang etc. (taste) 390.1.

3. *n.* savory, titbit etc. (delicacy) 298.9; sweetmeat etc. (sweets) 396.2.

4. *n.* appetizer, *apéritif* [F.], *hors d'œuvre* [F.].

5. *v.* be savory etc. *adj.*, tempt the appetite, taste good, taste like more [joc.], tickle *or* flatter the palate.

6. *v.* savor, relish, like, enjoy, delight in, appreciate, smack the lips; degust, degustate [both rare]; savor of, taste of, smack of; taste etc. 390.3.

7. *adj.* savory, palatable, to one's taste, tasty [now coll.], tasteful [now rare], good-tasting, toothful [obs.], toothsome, toothy [coll.], delicious, delectable, gustful [arch.], gusty [chiefly Scot.], good, nice, exquisite, elegant [vulg.], fit for a king, distinctive; larruping, larruping-good, scrumptious, scrumtedelicious, yummy [all slang]; flavorful, flavorous, flavory, flavorsome; appetizing, tempting, lickerish *or* liquorish [obs.], mouth-watering; rich, rich-flavored; luscious, deluscious [slang]; ambrosial, ambrosian; delicate, dainty; piquant; sapid, saporous, saporific; nectareous etc. (sweet) 396.8; desirable etc. 865.21; pleasing etc. 377.7; 829.7.

395. Unsavoriness
(See 394. Savoriness)

1. *n.* unsavoriness, unpalatableness etc. *adj.*, unpalatability, undelectability.

2. *n.* bitterness, acridness etc. *adj.*; acridity, acritude [obs.], acrimony; amarity, amaritude [both rare]; acerbity, acerbitude [obs.]; austerity, severity etc. (pungency) 392; acidity etc. (sourness) 397.

3. *n.* gall, gall and wormwood; bitters,

---

393. 'Tis the sour sauce to the sweet meat.—DRYDEN.

394. A delicacy beyond the China luxury.—LAMB.   The poetry of the table.—UNTERMEYER.

395. It's a strong stomach that has no turning.—CYNIC'S CALENDAR.

astringent bitters; angostura, angostura bark; rue, quassia, aloes, asafetida, hemlock, myrrh; Mara, Marah [both Bible]; sickener, nauseant; bitter pill.

 4. *v.* be unsavory etc. *adj.*; sicken, disgust, nauseate etc. (repel) 830.7; pall, turn the stomach; not have the stomach for.

 5. *adj.* unsavory, unpalatable, unappetizing, untasty [now coll.], untasteful, distasteful, undelicious, undelectable, inesculent [rare], uninviting, unpleasant, unpleasing, displeasing, disagreeable; uneatable, inedible; ill-flavored, ill-tasted; unsweet, unsweetened; dry; dislikable etc. 867.9; insipid etc. 391.2.

 6. *adj.* bitter; bitter as gall etc. *n.*; acrid, acrimonious; acerb, acerbic, acerbate; hard, harsh, rough, austere etc. (pungent) 392.5; acidulous etc. (sour) 397.6.

 7. *adj.* nasty, offensive, repulsive, odious, disgusting, revolting, loathsome, fulsome, noisome, noxious, obnoxious, bad, foul, vile; sickening, nauseating, nauseous, nauseant; rank, strong [coll.], strong-tasting; high; rancid, stale etc. (putrid) 653.17; fetid etc. 401.4.

396. Sweetness
(See 397. Sourness)

 1. *n.* sweetness, sugariness etc. *adj.*, saccharinity, dulcity [obs.], dulcitude [rare]; sugar-coating.

 2. *n.* sweets, sweet stuff, sweetmeats, confections, confectionery, tuck [slang]; candy, sugar candy, taffy, butterscotch, chocolate, caramel, fondant, bonbon, sugarplum, mint, peppermint, toffee, toffy, Scotch kisses, peanut brittle, honey crisp, fudge, nougat, glacé, licorice, candied cherries, ∼ cranberries etc. (*see* cherries, cranberries etc. 298.31); lollipop, lolly [coll.]; honey; manna; cake, pie, ice cream etc. (pastries and desserts) 298.12, 13.

 3. *n.* preserve, conserve, confiture, comfiture [rare], comfit; jam, jelly, *gelée* [F.], apple ∼, grape etc. jelly *or* jam (*see* apple, grapes etc. 298.31), jujube; Barle-Duc; gelatin, Jello [trade name]; marmalade, squish [slang]; apple ∼, peach etc. butter (*see* apple, peach etc. 298.31); applesauce, cranberry sauce etc. (*see* apple, cranberry etc. 298.31).

 4. *n.* sweetening, sweetener; short sweetening [dial., U.S.], sugar; maple sugar, cane sugar, corn sugar, beet sugar, granulated sugar, powdered sugar, loaf *or* lump sugar; raw sugar, brown sugar, saccharin; long sweetening [dial., U.S.], molasses, treacle; sirup, maple sirup, corn sirup, cane sirup; sorghum; sweet ∼, sugar *or* saccharine sorghum, sorgo.

 saccharide, monosaccharide, disaccharide, glucose, grape sugar, fructose, fruit sugar, sucrose, saccharose, dextrose, invert sugar, lactose, milk sugar, maltose, malt sugar, galactose, Dulcin [trade name], dulcitol [all Chem.].

 5. *n.* (sweet beverages) nectar, ambrosia; hydromel, mead, metheglin, liqueur, cordial, sweet wine, punch; sugar-water, *eau sucrée* [F.]; julep, mint julep [U.S.]; orangeade, lemonade, limeade, cold drink, soda, pop, ginger pop; ginger ale, root beer, Coca Cola [trade name], coke [coll.]; ice-cream soda etc. (frozen dessert) 298.13.

 6. *n.* saccharization, saccharification, dulcification [obs.], dulcoration [obs.], edulcoration, sweetening etc. *v.*

 7. *v.* sweeten, render sweet etc. *adj.*; sugar, honey; saccharize, saccharify; dulcify [rare], dulcorate [obs.], edulcorate; candy, candify; sugar-coat; mull; sugar off [local, U.S. and Can.].

 8. *adj.* sweet, sweetened, sweetful [now dial.], dulcet [arch.], sugary, sugared, honied, candied; sugarsweet, honeysweet, sweet as sugar *or* honey; saccharine, saccharinish, saccharous, sacchariferous, saccharoid *or* saccharoidal; nectareous, nectarious [rare], nectareal, nectarean, nectarian; oversweet, cloying, rich, luscious; sugar-coated etc. *v.*; bittersweet, sour-sweet; melliferous; mellifluent, mellifluous, dulcifluous [rare]; pleasing etc. 377.7.

RILEY.   Sweets to the sweet.—SHAKESPEARE. Take the sweet with the sour.—J. HEYWOOD. Sweet meat must have sour sauce.—JONSON. Ah that such sweet things should be fleet, / Such fleet things sweet.—SWINBURNE. The little sweet doth kill much bitterness.—KEATS.

---

396. Every white will have its blacke, / And every sweet its soure.—T. PERCY.   Put not your trust in vinegar—Molasses catches flies!—

397. Sourness
(See 396. Sweetness)

1. *n.* sourness, tartness etc. *adj.,* acidity, acetosity, acescence *or* acescency, acerbity, acerbitude [obs.], verjuice; subacidity; bitterness etc. 395.2; pungency etc. 392.2.

2. *n.* (sour articles) vinegar, *vinaigre* [F.], pickle, souring [dial. Eng.]; sour pickle, sweet pickle, dill pickle, bread-and-butter pickle, cucumber pickle, gherkin, acid, acetum, acetic acid; tartar, tartaric acid, cream of tartar; sauerkraut, *choucroute* [F.]; verjuice, lemon juice, grape juice etc.; lemon, lime, sour *or* bitter orange, sour grapes, green fruit, sour cherry, chokecherry, chokeberry, choke pear; crab, crab apple, choke apple; emu apple, sour plum; sourberry, cranberry; sour clover [West. U.S.], bitter clover; sourbread, sourcake [dial. Eng.]; buttermilk, sourdook [Scot.]; sour milk *or* cream, clabbered milk; bonnyclabber etc. 321.5.

3. *n.* souring etc. *v.,* acidification, acidulation, acetification, acetization [rare], acetic *or* acetous fermentation, acescence.

4. *v.* sour, souren [Scot. and North. Eng.], render *or* turn sour etc. *adj.;* acidify, acidulate, acetify, acetize [rare]; tartarize; ferment.

5. *v.* be sour etc. *adj.,* set the teeth on edge, pucker the mouth.

6. *adj.* sour, soured, sourish, soury [rare]; acid, acidulous, acidulent, acidulated; acetic, acetous, acetose, acescent; acerb, acerbic, acerbate; tart, tartish; crab, crabbed; vinegarish, vinegary, sour as vinegar etc. *n.*; subacid, subacidulous; green, unripe, hard; astringent, styptic; bitter etc. 395.6; pungent etc. 392.5.

398. Odor
(See 399. Inodorousness)

1. *n.* odor, odorament [obs.], smell, scent, spice, snuff [rare], savor, essence, redolence, effluvium (*pl.* effluvia), emanation, exhalation, breath, whiff, fume, trail, nidor [obs.]; odorousness etc. *adj.;* pungence *or* pungency; perfume etc. (fragrance) 400; fetor etc. 401.

2. *n.* smelling etc. *v.,* olfaction.

3. *n.* sense of smell, power of smelling, scent, olfaction, olfactory.

4. *n.* olfactories, olfactory organs; olfactory nerves, olfactory pit; nostrils, noseholes [obs. exc. dial. Eng.]; nose etc. 250.4.

5. *v.* have an odor etc. *n.,* smell, smell of; scent, scent of [both now rare]; emit ~, emanate *or* give out a smell, yield an odor etc. *n.;* breathe, exhale, effluviate [rare]; smell strong of, reek; stink etc. 401.3.

6. *v.* make odorous etc. *adj.,* stink up etc. 401.3; odorize [rare], scent, perfume etc. 400.9.

7. *v.* smell, scent, sniff, snuff, nose, inhale, breathe, breathe in.

8. *adj.* odorous, odorant [rare], odorate [now rare], odoriferant, odoriferous, odorific [rare], nidorulent [rare]; smelling, smellful, smellsome, smelly, whiffy [slang], nosy [coll.]; effluvious, redolent; strong-smelling, strong-scented, strong, heady, pungent, penetrating, piercing, sharp, keen; reeking, reeky; fragrant etc. 400.10; malodorous etc. 401.4.

9. *adj.* olfactory, olfactive, olfactible *or* olfactable; quick-scented.

399. Inodorousness
(See 398. Odor)

1. *n.* inodorousness, absence *or* want of smell etc. (*see* smell etc. 398).

2. *n.* deodorization, fumigation; deodorizer, deodorant; lime, chlorine; fumigant, fumigator.

3. *v.* be inodorous etc. *adj.,* not smell etc. (*see* smell etc. 398.5).

4. *v.* deodorize, fumigate; ventilate etc. (air) 338.10.

5. *adj.* inodorous, inodorate [obs.], scentless, unscented, without smell etc. (*see* smell etc. 398).

6. *adj.* deodorant, deodorizing; deodorized.

400. Fragrance
(See 401. Fetor)

1. *n.* fragrance *or* fragrancy, aroma, perfume, *parfum* [F.], bouquet, incense,

---

398. There is nothing like an odour to stir memories.—W. McFee.   Smells are surer than sounds or sights / To make your heart-strings crack.—Kipling.
400. So perfumed that the winds were love-sick.

sweet smell *or* odor, savory smell, aromatic perfume, nosegay; scent, essence, redolence etc. (odor) 398.

2. *n.* perfumery, *parfumerie* [F.], per**fumes, scents,** aromatics, attar, atar; aromatic water, essential *or* volatile oil; perfumes of Arabia; ambrosia, ambrose [rare]; pastille, incense; joss stick, lozenge, troche; smelling salts, balm, bal**sam,** potpourri, pulvil [obs.]; fragrance of flowers, florescence; pomade, pomatum, pomander; toilet water etc. *below.*

3. *n.* tuberose, hyacinth, heliotrope, rose, jasmine, lavender lily, lily of the valley, violet, arbutus, carnation, sweet pea, lilac; champaca oil, oil of myrcia; rose water, rose oil; Florida Water [trade name]; cologne, cologne water, Eau de Cologne; frankincense, olibanum; incense, myrrh; bergamot; civet, musk.

incense wood, incense cedar, incense juniper, incense shrub; agalloch *or* agallochum, agalwood *or* agalawood, eaglewood, calambac *or* calambour, aloes, aloeswood, lignaloes, linaloa; sandal, sandalwood; cedar, cedarwood; champac; frankincense pine; loblolly pine; bayberry, Jamaica bayberry, bay leaf; balsam, fir balsam; clove, cinnamon, horehound, mint; civet cat, muskrat; musk root; bay rum; naphtha water; sweet grass, new-mown hay.

4. *n.* bouquet, nosegay, posy, boughpot; boutonniere, buttonhole [coll.]; spray, wreath, garland, chaplet.

5. *n.* scent bottle, smelling bottle, vinaigrette; perfumer, perfumizer, fumigator, scenter, odorator, odorizer; atomizer, spray; censer *or* censor, incenser [obs.], incense burner, incensory, incensorium; thurible, thuribulum [rare]; perfuming dish, *parfumoir* [F.]; scent bag, sachet.

6. *n.* perfumer, *parfumeur* [F.]; perfumeress, *parfumeuse* [F.]; thurifer, thuribuler [rare]; censer bearer, altar boy.

7. *n.* perfuming etc. *v.*; incensation, thurification [both rare]; enfleurage.

8. *v.* be fragrant etc. *adj.,* have a perfume etc. *n.,* smell sweet, stink good [joc.].

9. *v.* perfume, fumigate, scent, cense, incense, essence, thurify, thurificate [rare], odorize [rare], aromatize; pastille.

10. *adj.* fragrant, agreeable in smell, aromatic, olent [rare], redolent, scented, essenced, perfumed, perfumy, sweet, sweet-smelling, sweet-scented, fragrant *or* sweet as a rose, ∼ new-mown hay etc. *n.,* savory, balmy, spicy, heady; ambrosial, ambrosian; perfumatory [rare]; odoriferous etc. (odorous) 398.8; pleasing etc. 377.7.

401. Fetor
(See 400. Fragrance)

1. *n.* fetor, foetor, fetidness etc. *adj.,* offensive odor, bad smell, malodor, nidorosity [rare], stench, stink, mephitis, miasm *or* miasma, graveolence *or* graveolency [rare]; stale *or* musty odor, fust [dial., Eng.], frowst; empyreuma; body *or* perspiration odor, B.O. [coll.]; bad *or* offensive breath, halitosis; putridity etc. 653.4; decay etc. 659.2.

2. *n.* (comparisons) skunk, polecat, stink cat, zoril; European polecat, fitchew, foumart, foulmart [Scot. and dial. Eng.]; stoat, ermine; peccary; asafetida; fungus (*pl.* fungi); garlic, onion, leek, skunk cabbage; stinker, stinkpot, stinkball, stinkhorn, stinkbush, stinkweed, stinkwood, stinkstone; stink bomb; dung, garbage etc. (filth) 653.4-7; rot etc. (decay) 659.2.

3. *v.* stink, be malodorous etc. *adj.,* have a bad *or* offensive smell etc. *n.,* smell, smell bad *or* badly, smell to heaven *or* high heaven, offend the nostrils, stink in the nostrils, stench [obs.], reek, funk [slang], smell strong etc. *adj.*; smell *or* stink up; stink out.

4. *adj.* fetid, malodorous, nidorous [rare], odorous, unpleasantly odorous, stinking, smelling, ill-smelling, smellsome, smellful, smelly, stenchy, whiffy

---

—SHAKESPEARE.　Fragrant the fertile earth after soft showers.—MILTON.　The sweetest essences are always confined in the smallest glasses.—DRYDEN.　And all Arabia breathes from yonder box.—POPE.　He thought her penny scent a sweeter thing / Than precious ointment out of alabaster.—MASEFIELD

401. The rankest compound of villainous smell that ever offended nostril.—SHAKESPEARE. Foul breath is noisome.—SHAKESPEARE.　All the perfumes of Arabia will not sweeten these little hands.—SHAKESPEARE.　Most putrefactions . . . smell either fetid or moldy.—BACON.　I counted two-and-seventy stenches, / All well defined, and several stinks.—COLERIDGE.

[slang], nosy [coll.], graveolent [rare], mephitic(al); olid, olidous [obs.]; rank, strong [coll.], strong-smelling, high; tainted, off; reeking, reeky; suffocating, unbearable, empyreumatic(al); repulsive, fulsome, noisome etc. (nasty) 395.7; rancid, putrid etc. (foul) 653.17.

402. Sound
(See 403. Silence)

1. *n.* sound, noise, sonant; sonance *or* sonancy, sonorescence; sonority etc. (resonance) 408; audibility etc. (hearing) 418.

2. *n.* tone, tune [rare], sound; speech sound, transition sound *or* glide, breath sound; vowel, front ~, central *or* back vowel, low ~, mid *or* high vowel; monophthong, diphthong, triphthong; consonant; vowellike, semivowel; labial, labiodental, labiovelar; tongue-blade *or* tongue-front consonant; palatal, dental, alveolar; stop, voiced *or* voiceless stop, mute, check, occlusive; continuant, fricative, spirant, nasal, affricate; tonic, phthongal, sonant, vocal; nonsonant, nonvocal, surd; liquid, guttural etc. *adj.*; guna, vriddhi, svarabhakti; phoneme.

sound *or* tonal quality, tonality, tonation, intonation, pitch, key, note, pervading note, burden, strain, tenor, vein; inflection, modulation, modification, cadence, number, expression; accent, accentuation; emphasis, stress; timbre, color, coloring, tone color, clang, *Klang* [G.], clang color *or* tint, *Klangfarbe* [G.]; tongue, voice, *voce* [It.], tone of voice, intonation *or* inflection of voice, speech tune *or* melody; *voce di petto, voce di testa, voce mista, voce velata* [all It.]; overtone, undertone; demitone, semitone; fundamental tone, fundamental; inherent *or* semantic tone; low tone etc. 408.6; high tone etc. 410.2; melody etc. 413.4.

3. *n.* sounding etc. *v.*, sonation, sonification, sondation [chiefly Archaeol.], phonation; utterance etc. 580.3.

4. *n.* (sound symbol) phonogram, phonograph; phonetic; ideophone; ideograph etc. (letter) 561.1; phonetic symbol, phonetic alphabet, alphabet of the International Phonetic Association *or* IPA; notation etc. (music) 415.23.

5. *n.* acoustics, phonics, phonetics, phonology; sound *or* phonetic law; Grimm's law, sound shifting *or* shift, *Lautverschiebung* [G.]; Verner's law; phonography; diacoustics, diaphonics; catacoustics, cataphonics; polycoustics; telephony, radiophony, photophony; polyphony, polyphonism; homophony, monophony; ideophonetics, phonetism.

6. *n.* acoustician, phonetist, phoneticist, phonetician; phonographer, phonographist.

7. *v.* sound, make a sound *or* noise, produce sound, give out *or* emit sound, give forth, noise, phonate; re-sound; resound etc. 408.7.

8. *v.* phoneticize, phonetize, represent phonetically, transcribe, respell phonetically.

9. *adj.* sounding, soniferous, sonorific [rare], sonorescent; sonant, sonantal, sonantic; sonorous etc. (resonant) 408.9.

10. *adj.* audible, hearable, distinct, clear, plain, definite, articulate.

11. *adj.* phonetic(al), phonic; tonic, phthongal, pretonic, posttonic; sounded; sonantized etc. *n.*; vocal etc. *n.*; voiced; intonated; voiceless, unvoiced; dentilingual, linguadental, cerebral, velar, uvular, guttural; close, open, rounded, tense *or* narrow, wide *or* lax; mouillé; liquid, lateral; mixed; sharp, strong, hard; flat, weak, soft.

12. *adj.* acoustic(al), phonic, phonetic(al); diacoustic, polycoustic; homophonic, homophonous, monophonic, monophonous, monodic; ideophonous; phonocamptic [rare]; auditory etc. (hearing) 418.13.

403. Silence
(See 402. Sound)

1. *n.* silence, silentness, soundlessness, stillness etc. *adj.*; quiet, q.t. [slang], quietude; still, peace, whist [Ir.], hush, shush, lull, rest [Mus.]; quiescence *or* quiescency; *silentium, silentium altum*

---

402. Not many sounds in life, and I include all urban and rural sounds, exceed in interest a knock at the door.—LAMB.   Sound loves to revel in a summer night.—POE.   Beauty born of murmuring sound.—WORDSWORTH.   And learn, my sons, the wondrous power of Noise.—POPE.
403. The silence surged softly backward / When the plunging hoofs were gone.—DE LA MARE.   Silence, like a poultice, comes / To heal the blows of sound.—HOLMES.   Three

[both L.], intense hush, solemn ~, awful ~, dead or deathlike silence, silence of the grave or tomb; golden silence; inaudibility; hush or dead of night, dead; mutescence; muteness etc. (taciturnity) 585, (aphonia) 581.

2. *n.* silencer etc. (muffler) 408a.4.

3. *v.* be silent etc. *adj.*, keep silence, keep still or quiet; hold one's tongue etc. (not speak) 585.3.

4. *v.* become silent etc. *adj.*, silence [rare], hush, shush, quiet, quieten [chiefly Eng.], quiet down, pipe down [coll.], sound off [slang exc. spec.], lay off [slang]; soft-pedal, put on the soft pedal [both slang]; quiesce.

5. *v.* silence, render silent etc. *adj.*, put to silence, still, hush, shush, quiet, quieten [chiefly Eng.], clamor, whist [arch. and dial.]; soft-pedal, put on the soft pedal [both slang]; stifle, muffle, smother, suppress, stop; squash, squelch [coll.]; kibosh, put the kibosh on [both slang], put the lid on, shut down on or upon [both coll.]; muzzle, gag, stop one's mouth etc. (render mute) 581.5.

6. *adj.* silent, still, stilly [poetic], quiet, quietsome [obs. exc. dial.], calm, hush [arch.], hushed etc. *v.*, whist [arch. and dial.], soundless, toneless, noiseless, echoless, inaudible; quiet or still as a mouse, silent as a post or stone, "noiseless as fear in a wide wilderness" (Keats), so quiet etc. that one might hear a feather or pin drop; silent as the grave or tomb, still as death, "hush as death" (Shakespeare), deathlike, awful, solemn; tacit; mute etc. (speech) 581.7, 585.4; soft etc. (faint) 405.9.

7. *adj.* unsounded, not sounded, voiceless etc. 402.11, toneless; unvocalized, unvocal, nonsonant, nonintoned, surd, atonic, aphonic, aphonous, quiescent, mute, silent, unpronounced, unuttered, unarticulated.

8. *adv.* silently, quietly etc. *adj.*; quietlike, easy [both coll.]; *sub silentio* [L.],

in silence, in dead or perfect silence.

9. *int.* silence! *silentium!* [L.], hush!, shush!, tush!, sh!, hist!, chut!, tut!, pax! *tais-toi!* [F.], be quiet!, be silent!, be still!, keep still!, keep quiet!, quiet!, quiet please!, *tace!* [L.], soft!, whisht! [Ir. and dial.], whist! [now chiefly dial.], hold your whist! [Ir.], pipe down! [coll.], belay that! or there! [Naut., coll.]; lay off!, sound off!, stow it!, can it!, cheese it! [all slang]; mum!, hold your tongue!, shut up! [coll.] etc. (speech) 585.6.

404. Loudness
(See 405. Faintness)

1. *n.* loudness, noisiness, vociferousness etc. *adj.*; vociferance, vociferosity; intensity ~, vehemence ~, force ~, power etc. of sound etc.; sonority, sonorosity [obs.], sonorousness; swell, swelling; surge, surge of sound.

2. *n.* noise, loud noise, mere noise, racket, din, clamor, song [coll.], gaff [coll.], vociferation, roar, uproar, tintamarre [arch.], tumult, hubbub, hullabaloo, ballyhoo [coll.], bobbery, pandemonium, Bedlam, hell or Bedlam let loose, hell broke loose [slang], brawl, fracas, rumpus [coll.], ruckus [dial. and slang], ruction [chiefly dial.], rowdydow [coll.]; alarm or alarum, larum [all arch.]; clang, clangor; charivari, shivaree [dial. U.S.], serenade [coll.]; outcry etc. 411.2; clatter etc. (rattle) 407.5, discord etc. 414.

3. *n.* blare, bray, blast, toot, tootle, honk; trumpet blast or blare, trumpet call, sound or flourish of trumpets, fanfare, tantara or tantarara, tarantara, tattoo [Mil.].

4. *n.* noisemaker, razzle-dazzle, horse fiddle [coll., U.S.], ticktack, bull-roarer, bull fiddle, catcall; whizzer, whizgig, whiz-bang or whizz-bang; clack, clacker; snapper, clapper; cracker, cracker bonbon; rattle, rattlebox, watchman's rattle; popgun; horn, automobile horn, Klaxon or klaxon [trade name]; siren, steam siren; whistle, steam whistle; calliope, calliophone; megaphone; stentor or Sten-

---

things are ever silent . . . Thought, Destiny, and the Grave.—BULWER-LYTTON. Give me my scallop-shell of quiet.—RALEIGH. *Tacent satis laudant* [Their silence is praise enough]. —TERENCE. Our noisy years seem moments in the being / Of the eternal Silence.—WORDSWORTH. The hush of night.—BYRON. Silence which doth follow talk.—SHELLEY. Silence gives consent.

404. With blare of bugle, clamor of men.— TENNYSON. The trumpet's loud clangor excites us to arms.—DRYDEN.

tor; lungs; boiler room *or* factory; firearm, explosive, bomb etc. 727.10–14; firecracker etc. (fireworks) 382.9; detonator etc. 388.4; alarm etc. 669.

5. *v.* be loud etc. *adj.*, rend the air *or* skies, fill the air; din, din ~, ring *or* thunder in the ear, pierce ~, split *or* rend the ears *or* head; deafen, stun; make one's windows shake *or* rattle; awake *or* startle the echoes, resound, resound in the ears; swell, surge; boom, thunder etc. 406.7–9.

6. *v.* be noisy etc. *adj.*, make a noise etc. *n.*, noise, uproar [rare], hullabaloo [rare], brawl, racket; kick up a dust *or* racket, kick up *or* raise a hullabaloo, raise the roof, raise Cain *or* Ned, raise the devil *or* the devil's delight, raise hell *or* hell's delight, raise Hail Columbia, make *or* let hell pop, whoop it up [all slang]; *faire le diable à quatre* [F.]; clang, clangor; ballyhoo [coll.]; shout, vociferate etc. (cry) 411.5–7; bellow etc. (animal cry) 412.2; fulminate etc. (detonate) 406.8, 9; clatter etc. (rattle) 407.10.

7. *v.* blare, bray, blast, toot, tootle, sound; honk, honk ~, sound *or* blow the horn, klaxon; tattoo [rare], sound a tattoo [both Mil.].

8. *adj.* loud, sonorous, tonant, deep, full, powerful, vehement, emphatic; loud-sounding, high-sounding, big-sounding; big-voiced, clarion-voiced, loud-voiced; stentorian, stentorophonic [obs.]; trumpet-tongued, trumpet-voiced; enough to wake the dead, enough to wake seven sleepers; deafening, ear-deafening, ear-splitting, ear-rending, ear-piercing; piercing etc. (shrill) 410.10; booming, thundering etc. 406.11.

9. *adj.* noisy, rackety, uproarious, clangorous, obstreperous, blustering, turbulent, blatant, tonant; clamant, clamorous, clamorsome [Scot. and North. Eng.]; clattering, clattery; vociferous, etc. 411.8.

10. *adj.* multisonous, multisonant.

11. *adv.* loudly etc. *adj.*, aloud, loud, lustily; with a loud voice, at the top of one's voice *or* lungs, at the pitch of one's breath, in full cry, with one wild yell, with a whoop and a hurrah; like a ton ~, load *or* thousand of bricks [coll.]; that one can't hear oneself think; like hell let loose etc. *n.*

405. Faintness
(See 404. Loudness)

1. *n.* faintness, lowness, dimness etc. *adj.*

2. *n.* faint sound, whispering sound etc. *adj.*; whispering etc. *v.*, whisperation, whisper, soft whisper, breath, "still small voice" (Bible); veiled voice, *voce velata* [It.]; undertone, underbreath; murmur, murmuration [now rare]; sigh, faint sigh; susurration, susurrus; bombilation, bombination; hum, rustle etc. *v.*; pinfall; muffled tone etc. (nonresonance) 408a.

3. *n.* muffler, mute etc. 408a.4.

4. *v.* be faint etc. *adj.*, scarcely be heard, steal *or* waft on the ear, melt in the air, float in the air.

5. *v.* murmur, mutter; susurrate, susurr [rare]; rustle, whistle [obs. exc. dial.], brustle [dial.], brush, stir, swish, whisk, sweep; ripple, rumble, babble, purl, trill, flow; gurgle, guggle; trickle, dribble, dripple; lap, plash, splash, swash, slosh, wash; sough, moan, sigh, sob, whine, wail, "wail with feeble moan" (Baillie), "waft a sigh from Indus to the pole" (Pope).

6. *v.* hum, thrum, bum, drone, boom, bombilate, bombinate, buzz, whiz *or* whizz, whir, purr.

7. *v.* bubble, burble, blubber [obs. exc. dial.], blub, blob, plop, wallop [Scot. and dial.].

8. *v.* muffle, mute etc. 408a.5.

9. *adj.* faint, low, soft, gentle, dim, feeble, weak; faint-sounding, low-sounding etc.; faint-voiced, low-voiced etc.; indistinct, unclear, scarcely ~, barely etc. audible, just audible; inaudible; dull, stifled, muffled, dampened, muted, softened, subdued; murmured, whispered etc. *v.*; soothing, soothful, restful; dulcet etc. (melodious) 413.27; quiet etc. (silent) 403.6.

10. *adj.* murmuring, whispering etc. *v.*; murmurous, murmurish; whisper, whispery, whisperous; rustly [rare]; susurrous, susurrant.

11. *adv.* faintly etc. *adj.*, low, faint; su-

---

405. Whisper cannot give a tone.—BACON. The mingled notes came softened from below. —GOLDSMITH. A little noiseless noise among the leaves, / Born of the very sigh that silence heaves.—KEATS. Beauty born of murmuring sound.—WORDSWORTH.

surringly [rare], in a whisper, with bated breath, with the finger on the lips, under one's breath, *sotto voce* [It.], in a low tone, in an undertone, between the teeth; aside, in an aside; *sordamente* [It.], *sordo* [It.], *à la sourdine* [F.]; *piano, pianissimo* [both It.; Mus.]; out of earshot.

406. Snap

Sudden and Violent Sounds.—1. *n.* snap, crack, crackle etc. *v.*; snapping, crackling etc. *v.*; crepitation, decrepitation.

2. *n.* report, explosive noise *or* sound, explosion, displosion [obs.], discharge, detonation, fulmination, bounce [obs.], eruption, blowup, blowout, burst, blast, crash, clap, bang, bingo, pop, crack, shot, bark, firing; gunshot, gunfire, salvo, volley, spray, fireworks, trigger talk [slang]; percussion, repercussion.

3. *n.* boom, booming etc. *v.,* bomb [now rare], bombination, bombilation, cannonade, rumble, roll, roar, hollow roar, peal, reel [Scot.]; drumfire etc. 407.3; hum etc. 405.2.

4. *n.* thunder, thundering etc. *v.,* peal, clap, crash, peal ~, clap *or* crash of thunder, thunderpeal, thunderclap, thundercrack, thunderblast, thunderburst, thunderthump [obs.], thunderstroke; Jupiter Tonans [Rom. Myth.], Thor *or* Donar [Norse Myth.], Indra [Hindu Myth.]; thunderbolt etc. (lightning) 420.6; thundercloud etc. (cloud) 353.5; thundersquall etc. (rain) 348.11.

5. *n.* snapper, cracker, clapper.

6. *n.* detonator etc. (lighter) 388.4; gun etc. (firearm) 727.10–12; explosive etc. (ammunition) 727.13; firecracker etc. (fireworks) 382.9.

7. *v.* snap, crack, clack, clap, rap, tap, knock, bounce, smack, slam, bang, crash, clash, whack, whop *or* whap [now dial.], swap [now dial.], crump [coll., Eng.], bump; slap, flap; slam-bang, slap-bang [both coll.]; click, tick; crackle, crepitate; decrepitate; fizzle, sizzle etc. 409.3.

8. *v.* detonate, detonize; make an explosive sound etc. *n.,* explode, displode [obs.], go off, fire [rare], fulminate, blow up, blow out, blast, crash, clap, bang, pop, crack, bark; percuss, repercuss [now rare]; burst on the ear, blast the ear.

9. *v.* boom, bombilate, bombinate, thunder, peal, rumble, roar, bell; hum etc. 405.6.

10. *adj.* snapping etc. *v.,* crepitant; fulminant, fulminatory, explosive.

11. *adj.* thundering, thunderous *or* thundrous, thundery, thunderlike; tonant, fulminating, tonitruous; loud etc. 404.8.

12. *adv.* bang, slap-bang, slam-bang [all coll.]; kerbang, kerbam, cachuck, cachunk [all slang].

13. *int.* bang!, crash! etc. *v.*; bam!, bingo!, bowie!, powie!, smacko!, socko! [all slang].

407. Roll

Repeated and Protracted Sounds.—1. *n.* roll, rolling etc. *v.,* rumble, rumblement [rare], roar, bell; reel [Scot.], peal, peal of bells, ~ thunder etc.; dingdong, singsong, ding-a-ling; water roll, bell roll, bass roll; tintinnabulation etc. 408.1; bombilation etc. (boom) 406.3, 4, (hum) 405.2; reverberation, toll etc. 408; repetition etc. 104; pulsation etc. 314.2.

2. *n.* trill, trillo [Mus.]; trillet, *trilletto* [It.; Mus.]; tremolo, tremolant, tremolando [all Mus.], tremulant *or* tremolo note; *Nachschlag* [G.]; tremble, quaver, quiver, flutter, shake; *Bebung* [G.] (*pl. Bebungen*), vibrato [both Mus.]; murmur etc. 405.1.

3. *n.* drum, drumming etc. *v.,* thrum, drum music, drumbeat; drumfire, barrage, cannonade; ruff, ruffle [both Mil.]; *berloque* [F.; Mil.]; rattle, rub-a-dub, rataplan, rattan [rare], rantan *or* rantan [coll.], rat-tat, rat-tat-tat, rat-a-tat, rattattoo, rat-tattle, tat-tat, tat-tat-tat; tattoo, devil's tattoo; patter, pitter-patter, pitapat, pitapatation [joc.], palpitation, throb, pound, beat; footfall, tread, hoofbeat; pulsation etc. 314.2; boom etc. 406.3.

4. *n.* tick, ticktick, ticktock, ticktack.

---

406. The thunderlike percussion of thy sounds.—SHAKESPEARE.

407. The tintinnabulation that so musically wells / From the bells.—POE. The double double double beat of the thundering drum.—DRYDEN. A thousand trills and quivering sounds.—ADDISON. No rest for Niagara, but perpetual ran-tan on those limestone rocks.—THOREAU. Blue Walden rolls in cannonade.—EMERSON.

5. *n.* rattle, rattling etc. *v.*, brattle [Scot. and North. Eng.], ruckle [Scot. and dial. Eng.], rattlety-bang; clatter, clutter, clitter [dial. Eng.], clitterclatter, chatter, clack, clacket [dial.]; racket; clamor, noise etc. 404.2.

6. *v.* roll, rumble, roar, bell, peal; sound a roll upon; bombilate etc. (boom) 406.9, (hum) 405.6; toll, reverberate, re-echo etc. (resonate) 408.7, 8.

7. *v.* trill, tremolo, tremble, quaver, quiver, flutter, shake.

8. *v.* drum, thrum, beat, pound, thump, throb, palpitate, go *or* beat pitapat, patter, pitter-patter; rub-a-dub, rataplan etc. *n.*; tattoo [rare], drum ~, beat *or* sound a tattoo, beat *or* drum a devil's tattoo; ruffle, beat a ruffle [both Mil.]; drum *or* din in the ear; pulsate etc. 314.9.

9. *v.* tick etc. *n.*

10. *v.* rattle, brattle [Scot. and North. Eng.], ruckle [Scot. and dial. Eng.]; clatter, clutter, clitter [dial., Eng.], chatter, clack; be noisy etc. 404.6.

11. *adj.* rolling, rumbling, drumming etc. *v.*; palpitant; dingdong [coll.], singsong etc. (repeated) 104.6, 7; resonant etc. 408.9, 10.

12. *adj.* tremulant, tremulous, tremolant; *trillando, tremoloso* [both It.], tremolando [all Mus.].

13. *adj.* humming, droning etc. (*see* hum etc. 405.6); like a bee in a bottle.

14. *adj.* rattling etc. *v.*, rattly, rattlesome; clattery.

408. Resonance
(See 408a. Nonresonance)

1. *n.* resonance, resonancy; sonorousness etc. *adj.*, sonority, sonorosity [obs.]; vibration, vibrating etc. *v.*; vocal resonance; timbre, clang color etc. (tone) 402.2; ventriloquism etc. 580.6.

2. *n.* reverberation, reverberating etc. *v.*; reflection, repercussion, rebound, resound, echo, re-echo.

3. *n.* resonant sound, resonant, sonority.

4. *n.* ringing etc. *v.*, tintinnabulation; ring, jingle, jinglejangle, tinkle, toll etc. *v.*; bell note *or* tone, bell chime, bell roll.

5. *n.* bell, tintinnabulum (*pl.* tintinnabula), jingle bell, gong; chimes etc. 417.13; dinner bell, ~ gong *or* chimes; cymbals, *Becken* [G.].

6. *n.* low note *or* tone, deep note, grave note, base *or* bass, base *or* bass note; basso; deep bass, basso profundo; baritone *or* barytone; contralto; chest voice, *voce di petto* [It.]; pedal point, organ point.

7. *v.* be resonant etc. *adj.*, resonate; reverb, reverberate, reverbrate [arch.], repercuss [now rare]; sound, resound; echo, re-echo; rebound, surrebound [rare], reply, be repeated, continue; reflect, send back, return; quaver, throb etc. (roll) 407.6–10; gurgle etc. (murmur) 405.5.

8. *v.* ring, tintinnabulate, peal, toll, sound, chime; ding, ding-a-ling, ding-dong, dingle, jingle, tingle, tinkle; tink, ting, chink, clink; clank, clang, clangor; gong; ring in the ear, ring on the air.

9. *adj.* resonant, vibrant, repercussive; resounding, reverberating etc. *v.*; reverberant, reverberative, reverberatory, reverbatory, reverberate [obs.], reverbrate [arch.]; sonorous, sonorant, sonoric; mellow, mellifluous; rich, full; deep, deep-toned, deep-pitched, deep-set, deep-sounding, deepmouthed, deep-echoing; hollow, sepulchral.

10. *adj.* ringing etc. *v.*, bell ringing, tinnient [obs.]; tintinnabulant, tintinnabular *or* tintinnabulary, tintinnabulate, tintinnabulous.

408a. Nonresonance
(See 408. Resonance)

1. *n.* nonresonance, nonresonancy; mutescence; muffled tone, muffled drums; muted trumpet, *tromba sorda* [It.]; cracked bell; faintness etc. 405.2.

2. *n.* dead sound, thud, dull thud; thump, flump, crump [coll., Eng.], clump, clunk, plunk, plump, bump; pad, pat.

3. *n.* muffler, silencer, mute; soft pedal, damper pedal; sordine, sourdine, *sordino* [It.]; hushcloth, silence cloth; gag, bandage, muzzle.

4. *v.* muffle, mute, dull, deaden, soften,

---

408. Resonant with the fall of statued fountains.—DISRAELI. His arms resounded as the boaster fell.—POPE. Every fateful / Echo bears his amorous speech.—HEINE. The vales his voice rebound.—DRYDEN. Blow bugle; answer, echoes, dying, dying, dying.—TENNYSON. Ere the last echo dies within our ears.—L. W. REESE. As when hollow rocks retain / The sound of blustering winds.—MILTON.

damp, dampen, drown, smother, stifle, throttle, subdue, repress, hush, quiet, damp ~, deaden etc. the sound *or* reverberations; soft-pedal, apply *or* put on the soft pedal.

5. *v.* thud, thump etc. *n.*

6. *adj.* nonresonant, dead, mute; muted, muffled etc. *v.*; *sordo* [It.] (*fem. sorda*), sordine, sourdine; dull, flat, toneless.

409. Sibilation

Hissing Sounds.—1. *n.* sibilation, sibilance *or* sibilancy; hiss, hissing etc. *v.*; sternutation.

2. *n.* (comparisons) goose; serpent, snake, viper.

3. *v.* sibilate, hiss, buzz, whiz *or* whizz, wheeze, whistle, sneeze, sputter, squash, zip, swish; snore, snork [dial.], snort; fizz, fizzle; sizz [coll.], sizzle; sniff, sniffle; snuff, snuffle; aspirate; lisp.

4. *adj.* sibilant, sibilous, sibilatory; hissing etc. *v.*; wheezy; sternutative.

410. Stridor

Harsh and High Sounds.—1. *n.* stridor, stridence *or* stridency, stridulation; stridulousness, harshness, raucousness etc. *adj.*; raucity, raucidity [rare]; cacophony etc. (discord) 414.

2. *n.* high note *or* tone, acute note; high voice, head voice *or* tone, *voce di testa* [It.]; soprano, treble, tenor, alto, falsetto; whistle, shriek etc. *v.*

3. *n.* twang, twangle [rare], nasal twang etc. (imperfect speech) 583.1.

4. *n.* whistle, penny whistle, willow whistle; penny trumpet, piccolo, fife; pipes, bagpipe *or* bagpipes, *Dudelsack* [G.], doodlesack [Scot.]; Panpipes, Pandean pipes, syrinx; steam whistle, siren etc. 404.4.

5. *v.* stridulate, crick, creak, chirk [obs. exc. Scot.]; screak, squeak, squawk, shriek, screech, scream, shrill, squeal; whine, wail; caterwaul.

6. *v.* be harsh etc. *adj.*, sound harshly,

grate, scrape, scratch, rasp, grind; crunch, craunch, scranch [now chiefly dial.], scrunch [coll. and dial.], crump, crush; burr, saw, snore, buzz, whiz *or* whizz; growl, snarl, grumble, groan; croak, caw; bray; clash, jar, jangle; clank, clink; twang, twangle [rare], twank [chiefly dial., Eng.]; be discordant etc. 414.3.

7. *v.* grate upon the ear, jar upon the ear, offend the ear, pierce ~, split *or* rend the ears *or* head, grate on, set the teeth on edge, *écorcher les oreilles* [F.]; get on one's nerves, jangle the nerves.

8. *v.* whistle, toot, tootle, tweedle, tweedledee, pipe, bugle, sound, peal, wind, blow.

9. *adj.* strident, strident-voiced, stridulant, stridulent, stridulous, stridulatory; stridulating, grating, jarring etc. *v.*; harsh, harsh-sounding, jangly [rare], coarse, hoarse, horrisonant [obs.], husky, rude, rough, gruff, grum; raucous, raucid [rare]; squeaky, squawky; dry; cracked; stertorous, stertorious; cacophonous etc. (discordant) 414.4.

10. *adj.* shrill, sharp, acute, high; high-sounding, high-pitched, high-toned; trumpet-toned, trumpet-tongued, trumpet-voiced; piercing, ear-piercing; loud etc. 404.8.

411. Cry

1. *n.* cry, call, shout, yell etc. *v.*; view halloo, yoicks [both Hunt.]; crying, screaming etc. *v.*; caterwaul, bark etc. (animal cry) 412; hurrah, tiger [coll.] etc. (cheer) 838.4.

2. *n.* outcry, vociferation, clamor, gaff; exclaim [arch.], exclamation, ejaculation, ecphonesis; chorus; hue [obs. exc. dial.], hue and cry; hubbub, hullabaloo etc. (noise) 404.2.

3. *n.* plaint, wail etc. (lamentation) 839.

4. *n.* vociferousness etc. *adj.*, vociferosity.

5. *v.* cry, call, shout, yell, hoot; halloo, hollo, yo-ho, yoick; whoop, hoop [rare]; howl, yowl, yawl [now dial.]; bawl,

---

409. The people shall hiss at thee.—BIBLE. A dismal universal hiss, the sound of public scorn.—MILTON. Leaves got up in a coil and hissed.—FROST.

410. With clamor of voices dissonant and loud.—LONGFELLOW. The vile squeaking of the wry-necked fife.—SHAKESPEARE. With impetuous recoil and jarring sound.—MILTON.

411. And with no language but a cry.—TENNYSON. I sound my barbaric yawp over the roofs of the world.—WHITMAN. An atmosphere of shrieks and moans; prayers vociferated like blasphemies and whispered curses.—CONRAD.

brawl, bellow, roar, roar *or* bellow like a bull; pipe, scream, screech, screak, shriek, shrill, squeak, squeal, squall; yelp, yap, yawp; huzza, hurrah etc. (cheer) 838.8; weep etc. 839.8; caterwaul etc. (animal sounds) 412.2.

6. *v.* wail, whine, sob etc. (lament) 839.6–10.

7. *v.* vociferate, vociferize [rare]; cry out, call out, yell out, shout out, sing out; make an outcry etc. *n.*; ejaculate, exclaim, give an exclamation; give tongue, give cry, hue [obs. exc. dial.], raise *or* lift up the voice, utter with a loud voice; shout ∼, cry *or* thunder at the top of one's voice etc. *adv.*; split the throat *or* lungs, strain the voice *or* throat; rend the air, make the welkin ring; clamor, utter with clamor, make a clamor, be clamorous etc. *adj.*

8. *adj.* vociferous, vociferant, vociferative [rare]; clamant, clamorous, clamorsome [Scot. and North. Eng.]; crying etc. *v.*; loud-voiced, loudmouthed, full-mouthed, openmouthed; stentorian etc. (loud) 404.8, 9.

9. *adv.* at the top of one's voice *or* lungs etc. (loudly) 404.11.

412. Ululation

Animal Sounds.—1. *n.* ululation, howling, barking etc. *v.*; latration, belling, challenge; stridulation; ululu; call, cry, howl, caterwaul, bark etc. *v.*; birdcall, note, wood-note, clang.

2. *v.* ululate, cry, call; howl, yowl, yawl [now dial.]; wail, whine, pule; troat; roar, bell, bellow, rebellow, blare, bawl; moo, low; bleat, blate, blat [coll.], blatter; bray; whinny, neigh, nicker [chiefly dial.]; bay, bay the moon; bark, latrate, give tongue; yelp, yap, yawp; growl, snarl, yarr [Scot. and dial. Eng.]; grunt, gruntle; snort, snork [dial.]; squeal, squall; squawk; squeak, screak, screech, scream; crick, creak, chirk [obs. exc. Scot.], stridulate.

purr, thrum [Scot. and dial. Eng.]; mew, mewl, miaow, caterwaul; quack, honk; cronk, crunk; croak, chirk [obs. exc. Scot.], plunk, caw; crow, cock-a-doodle, cock-a-doodle-doo; cackle, gaggle, guggle; cluck, clack, chuck, chuckle; chirrup, chirp, chirk [obs.], cheep, peep, pule [now rare], yap [dial.]; chatter, chitter; tweet, twit [Scot. and dial. Eng.], twitter, sing, warble, carol, pipe, whistle; trill, roll; gobble, gabble; hoot, hoo, whoo [obs.]; coo; cuckoo; hum, boom, buzz; hiss, whistle.

3. *adj.* ululant, ululative [rare], ululatory; crying, howling etc. *v.*; blatant; latrant; mugient, remugient [obs.]; reboant [rare]; deep-mouthed, full-mouthed.

413. Concord
(See 414. Discord)

Harmony; Melody; Rhythm.—1. *n.* concord, harmony, concordance, concert, consonance *or* consonancy, accord, accordance, harmonious accordance, monochord, concent [arch.], concentus, diapason, agreement of sounds; symphony, symphonia; synchronism, synchronization; tune, attune, attunement; euphony; chime, chiming etc. *v.*; unison, unisonance; homophony, monophony, monody; light *or* heavy harmony; three-part harmony etc.; harmony *or* music of the spheres; music etc. 415; harmonics etc. (science of music) 415.24.

2. *n.* polyphony, polyphonism, polyphonium, polyphonic composition; contrapuntal composition, counterpoint, contrapunto; strict *or* plain counterpoint, free counterpoint, single ∼, double *or* triple counterpoint; *faux-bourdon* [F.], faburden [Hist.]; descant etc. (contrapuntal music) 415.4.

3. *n.* orchestration, instrumentation, harmonization; arrangement, adaptation; phrasing, modulation, intonation, preparation, suspension, solution, resolution, tone painting.

4. *n.* melody, musical quality, music, musicality; musicalness, melodiousness, tunefulness etc. *adj.*; tune, attune, tone, tuneful *or* musical sound, pleasing *or*

---

412. And smale fowles maken melodye.—Chaucer. Then nightly sings the staring owl, / Tu-whit; / Tu-who, a merry note.—Shakespeare. I had rather be a dog, and bay the moon.—Shakespeare. The jay makes answer, as the magpie chatters.—Wordsworth. With bark and whoop and wild halloo.—Scott. A robin . . . piping a few querulous notes.—W. Irving.
413. Concord of sweet sounds.—Shakespeare. Lulled with sound of sweetest melody.—Shakespeare. The hidden soul of harmony.—Milton. Heard melodies are sweet, but those

sweet sound *or* tone; musical *or* rhythmical succession of sounds, succession of musical tones; dulcetness, mellifluence; melodism; melodic curve; melodics etc. (science of music) 415.24; song, strain etc. (air) 415.2.

5. *n.* tonality, timbre, clang color etc. (tonal quality) 402.2.

6. *n.* note, musical note, notes of a scale; sharp, flat, natural; incidental, incidental note; whole note, semibreve; double whole note, breve; half note, minim; quarter note, crochet; eighth note, quaver; sixteenth note, semiquaver; thirty-second note, demisemiquaver; tercet, triplet; sustained note, drone; bourdon, burden; dominant, dominant note; enharmonic, enharmonic note; staccato, spiccato; responding note, report; shaped note, patent note; tone etc. 402.2; high note etc. 410.2; low note etc. 408.6; grace note etc. (ornament) *below* 413.10; notation etc. 415.23.

7. *n.* key; keynote *or* key note, leading *or* fundamental note; tonic, tonic key; major *or* minor key, tonic major *or* minor; supertonic, mediant, submediant, dominant, subdominant, subtonic; pedal point, organ point.

8. *n.* harmonic, harmonic tone, overtone, upper partial tone; flageolet tone.

9. *n.* chord; common chord, triad; harmonic triad, major *or* minor triad, diminished triad, augmented triad, perfect *or* imperfect triad, inverted triad; seventh ∼, ninth etc. chord, major *or* minor chord, tonic chord, dominant chord; consonant chord, concord; enharmonic chord, enharmonic; broken chord, arpeggio; unbroken chord, *concento* [It.].

10. *n.* ornament, grace, arabesque, embellishment, *fioritura* [It.], *agrémens* [*pl.*; F.]; division, florid phrase *or* passage; incidental, incidental note; grace note, birdy [slang], appoggiatura; short appoggiatura, *acciaccatura* [It.]; mordent, single mordent, double *or* long mordent; inverted mordent, pralltriller; turn, back *or* inverted turn; cadence, cadenza; roulade, flourish, flight, run, passage; trill, trillo etc. 407.2.

11. *n.* interval, degree, step, note, tone; prime *or* unison interval, second ∼, third etc. interval, major *or* minor interval, harmonic *or* melodic interval, enharmonic interval, diatonic interval; diatessaron [Hist.]; whole step, major second; half step, half tone, semitone, minor second; diatonic semitone, chromatic semitone, less semitone, quarter semitone, tempered *or* mean semitone; quarter step, enharmonic diesis.

12. *n.* rest, pause, bar, measure; whole rest, semibreve; half rest, minim; quarter rest; crochet etc. (note) *above* 413.6.

13. *n.* pitch, musical pitch, tune, tone, key, note; height, depth; relative pitch, absolute pitch; classic(al) pitch, concert *or* high pitch, diapason ∼, normal ∼, French ∼, international *or* low pitch, Stuttgart *or* Scheibler's pitch, philharmonic pitch, philosophical pitch.

14. *n.* voice, *voce* [It.]; *voce di petto, voce di testa, voce mista, voce velata,* [all It.]; base, bass, basso; deep bass, basso profundo; *basso buffo* [It.]; *basso cantante* [It.], lyric bass; drone, drone bass, bourdon, burden; baritone *or* barytone; tenor, lyric tenor; soprano, mezzo-soprano, alto, contralto, coloratura, treble, falsetto; descant, *bassus* [L.] etc. (part) 415.13.

15. *n.* register, compass, range, diapason, scale; chest *or* thick register, head *or* thin register.

16. *n.* scale, gamut, sol-fa etc. *below*; diatonic scale, chromatic scale, enharmonic scale, major *or* minor scale, harmonic *or* melodic minor, whole-tone scale.

17. *n.* sol-fa, tonic sol-fa, sol-fa *or* tonic sol-fa syllables *or* notation, do-re-mi; do, re, mi, fa, sol, la, ti, do; fixed-do system, movable-do system; Aretinian syllables, ut, re, mi, fa, sol, la; solmization etc. 415.18.

18. *n.* (diatonic series) tetrachord, chromatic tetrachord, enharmonic tetrachord, Dorian *or* Doric tetrachord; hexachord, pentachord.

19. *n.* octave, *ottava* [It.]; *ottava alta, ottava bassa* [both It.]; small octave, great octave; contraoctave, subcontraoctave, double contraoctave.

20. *n.* mode, octave species; Greek mode, Dorian ∼, Doric ∼, Phrygian ∼, Lydian ∼, mixolydian ∼, hypodorian ∼, hypophrygian ∼, hypolydian ∼, hypomixolydian ~, Aeolian ~, Locrian ~, hypoaeolian *or* hypolocrian mode; ecclesiastical ~, Gregorian *or* medieval mode, authentic *or* plagal mode; major *or* minor mode.

21. *n.* rhythm, *rhythmus* [L.], rhythmical flow, rhyme *or* rime [rare], meter, measure, cadence *or* cadency, number *or* numbers, lilt, swing; authentic cadence, plagal cadence, mixed cadence, perfect *or* imperfect cadence, half cadence; deceptive *or* false cadence, interrupted *or* suspended cadence; rhythmicality, rhythmicity; rhythmic etc. (science of music) 415.24.

22. *n.* tempo, time, time pattern; simple time *or* measure, compound time *or* measure; two-part *or* duple time, simple duple time; three-part *or* triple time; four-part *or* quadruple time, compound duple time; five-part *or* quintuple time, six-part *or* sextuple time, seven-part *or* septuple time, nine-part *or* nontuple time; two-four ~, six-eight etc. time; mixed times; rallentando, ritardando; syncopation, syncope, syncopated time *or* rhythm; ragtime, rag [coll.]; dance time; waltz time, andante tempo etc. (*see* waltz, andante etc. 415.6–8).

23. *n.* accent, accentuation, rhythmical accent *or* accentuation, ictus, emphasis, stress; grammatical accent, rhetorical accent; tone ~, musical ~, pitch *or* stress accent, intonation; rising *or* falling accentuation; beat, throb, pulse, pulsation; accented *or* unaccented beat, strong *or* weak beat; downbeat, upbeat, offbeat; bar beat.

24. *v.* harmonize, chord, concord [obs.], accord, consonate, concert [rare], symphonize, chime, blend, be harmonious etc. *adj.*, sound together in harmony, synchronize; tune, tune up, attune, atone, chord [poetic], put in tune; voice, string; tone down, tone up; orchestrate; assonate.

25. *v.* melodize, make melody etc. (play) 416.18; compose melodies, set to melody etc. (compose) 415.26.

26. *adj.* harmonious, harmonizing etc. *v.*, harmoniacal [obs.], harmonic(al), harmonistic, *armonioso* [It.]; agreeing in sound, concordant, consonant; concentual, concentuous, concentive [all rare]; symphonious, symphonic [rare]; unisonant, in unison; in chorus, in concord etc. *n.*; in tune, in tone [obs. exc. dial.]; attune, attuned; synchronous, synchronal, synchronic(al), synchronistic(al), in sync *or* sink [slang, U.S.]; orchestral, orchestric; isotonic; homophone [rare], homophonous, homophonic; monophonic, monophonous, monodic; assonant, assonantal, assonantic.

27. *adj.* melodious, melodial, melodic, melodical [obs.]; musical, musiclike, music-tongued, music-flowing; tuneful, tuny [coll.], tunable; pleasant *or* agreeable in sound, pleasant-sounding, agreeable-sounding; lyric(al), melic; songful, songish [rare], songy [rare], songlike.

dulcet, sweet, sweet to the ear, sweet-sounding, sweet-flowing, dulcifluous [rare]; mellifluent, mellifluous, mellisonant; mellow, mellowy, mellow-sounding, mellow-toned; soft, soft-sounding, soft-toned; euphonious, euphonous [rare], euphonic(al), euphonistic [rare]; euphoniously sonorous, canorous; clear, clear-sounding, clear-toned, clear as a bell; silvery, silver-toned; fine-toned, full-toned, deep-toned; ariose; pleasant, agreeable etc. (pleasurable) 829.7, 8.

28. *adj.* tonal, tonalitive, tonic, chromatic, enharmonic; semitonal, semitonic; demitonal, demitonic.

29. *adj.* rhythmic(al), rhythmal, rhythmed; cadent, measured, metric(al); in rhythm, in rhyme [rare], in numbers; pulsative, pulsatile, pulsatory, pulsating; rhythmizable.

30. *adv.* in time *or* tempo, *a tempo* [It.], in the groove [slang, U.S.]; *al rigore di tempo, a rigore del tempo* [both It.]; *all' ottava, coll' ottava* [both It.]; adagio, allegro etc. (musical directions) 415.30–32.

414. Discord
(See 413. Concord)

1. *n.* discord, discordance *or* discordancy, discordantness etc. *adj.*, dissonance *or* dissonancy, diaphony, diaphonia, cacophony, want of harmony etc. 413; atonality, atonalism; *concordia discors* [L.]; percussion; consecutive fifths; harshness etc. (stridor) 410.

---

414. Above the pitch, out of tune, and off the hinges.—RABELAIS. So discord oft in music makes the sweeter lay.—SPENSER. Take but degree away, untune that string, / And hark

2. *n.* (discordant or confused sounds) discord, discordant note, sour note [coll.] etc. *adj.*; Babel, babble, pandemonium, confusion worse confounded, hell broke loose, hell *or* Bedlam let loose; Dutch concert, cat's concert, marrowbones and cleavers [all coll.]; charivari, shivaree [dial., U.S.], serenade [coll.]; jangle, clangor; racket, clamor etc. (noise) 404.2.

3. *v.* be discordant etc. *adj.*, discord, cacophonize [rare]; grate, jar etc. (sound harshly) 410.5-7.

4. *adj.* discordant, dissonant, dissonate [obs.], dissonous [rare], diaphonic(al); absonant, absonous [obs.]; inharmonious, unharmonious; immelodious, unmelodious; unmusical, untuneful, untunable, untuned, tuneless, atonal; out of tune, out of tone [obs. exc. dial.]; off-key, off-tone, off-pitch; flat, sharp; sour [coll.], unsweet [rare]; cacophonous, cacophonic(al); harsh, jarring, raucous etc. (strident) 410.9, 10.

415. Music
(See also 416. Musician, 417. Musical Instruments)

1. *n.* music, *musica* [L.], musical [obs.]; "the speech of angels" (Carlyle), "the only universal tongue" (S. Rogers), "the universal language of mankind" (Longfellow), "the poor man's Parnassus" (Emerson), "the brandy of the damned" (Shaw); melody, harmony etc. (concord) 413.

2. *n.* air, aria, tune, tone [dial.], melody, melodia, note, song, lay, descant, strain, measure [poetic], dump [arch.]; canto, cantus; popular air *or* tune; song etc. *below* 415.10.

3. *n.* piece, musical piece *or* composition, piece of music; opus (*pl.* opera), composition, production, work; arrangement, adaptation, orchestration, harmonization; *morceau* [F.], bagatelle, arioso, cavatina, monody, arabesque, suite, pianologue, incidental music, chamber music, program music, swan song; rondo, rondeau, rondino, rondoletto; pastoral, pastorale (*pl.* pastorali, pastorales); toccata, *toccatina* [It.]; caprice, capriccio, capriccetto, humoresque; rhapsody; fugue, *aria fugata* [It.]; canon, perpetual *or* circular canon; potpourri, medley; fantasia, fantasie; *Fantasiestück* [G.], *divertissement* [F.].

serenade, serenata (*pl.* serenatas, serenate); *aubade* [F.], morning song *or* serenade; evening *or* night music, evening song; *Abendmusik, Nachtmusik* [both G.]; nocturne; barcarole *or* barcarolle, boat song; *Zigeunerlied* [G.], gypsy song; cantabile, *aria cantabile* [It.]; sonata, sonatina (*pl.* sonatinas, sonatine); concert music *or* piece, concerted piece, concertstück; concerto, *concertino, concerto grosso, concertante* [all It.]; symphony, symphonic music; symphonic ode *or* poem, tone poem *or* poetry; *étude* [F.]; variation, descant, *air varié* [F.]; curtain tune, curtain raiser *or* lifter; chaser [slang]; recorded music, canned music [slang]; set, minstrelsy.

4. *n.* contrapuntal music, counterpoint; prick song, descant, *cantus figuratus* [ML.]; plain song, plain singing [rare], *cantus planus* [ML.], *cantus firmus* [ML.], Gregorian chant *or* melody; polyphony etc. 413.2.

5. *n.* mensurable music, *musica mensurata* [L.]; measured music, *cantus mensurabilis* [ML.]; musical *or* harmonic proportion; alteration, prolation, augmentation, diminution.

6. *n.* lively music, fast *or* spirited music, lilt; syncopated music, syncopation; ragtime, rag [both coll.]; jazz; hot jazz, swing, jive [slang, U.S.]; scherzo, allegro, allegretto, presto.

7. *n.* dance music *or* rhythm, foot music [coll.], ballad; *allemande* [F.], *passamezzo* [It.], passemeasure, ziganka, saltarello, bolero, habanera, fandango, *bourrée* [F.], courante, *furlana* [It.], *forlane* [F.], galliard, cinquepace, juba [U.S.], mazurka *or* mazourka, boutade, branle, gavotte *or* gavot, rigadoon, strathspey, reel, jig, hornpipe, polka, one-step, two-step, fox trot; saraband; tarantella, *tarantelle* [F.]; waltz, *valse* [F.], concert

---

what discord follows!—SHAKESPEARE. I never heard / So musical a discord, such sweet thunder.—SHAKESPEARE. Like sweet bells jangled, out of tune and harsh.—SHAKESPEARE. **415.** I am never merry when I hear sweet music.—SHAKESPEARE. Music hath charms to soothe the savage breast.—CONGREVE. Such sweet compulsion doth in music lie.—MILTON. Of all noises I think music the least disagreeable.—JOHNSON. The music arose with its voluptuous swell.—BYRON. Music's golden tongue.—KEATS. Music, when soft voices

waltz; minuet; chacona, *chaconne* [F.], chaccon, *passacaglia* [It.]; ragtime, jazz etc. *above*.

8. *n.* slow music, slow movement, Lydian measures; adagio, adagietto, andante, andantino, largo, larghetto; march, martial music, dead march; pibroch; coronach [Scot. and Ir.], dirge etc. (lament) 839.

9. *n.* soft music, siren strains; piano, pianissimo; lullaby, cradlesong, *berceuse* [F.], *Schlummerlied* [G.].

10. *n.* vocal music, vocalism, vocalization; song, lay, lied (*pl.* lieder), canticle, carol, ditty; ballad, ballade, ballata (*pl.* ballate); choral ballad; canzon [arch.], *canzone* [It.]; canzonet, *canzonetta* [It.]; chant, chaunt [arch.]; *Kunstlied* [G.] (*pl. Kunstlieder*), art song; drinking song, *brindisi* [It.]; war song; sea song; love song, torch song [coll.]. folk song, popular song, *Volkslied* [G.] (*pl. Volkslieder*), song hit, blues *or* blues song, theme song; *serena, alba* [both Pr.]; recitative, recitativo (*pl.* recitativi, recitativos); aria, arietta, ariette; *aria parlante, aria d'imitazione, aria d'agilità, aria da chiesa, aria da capo, aria buffa* [all It.]; bravura, *aria di bravura* [It.]; colorature, coloratura, *aria di coloratura* [It.]; cantabile, *aria cantabile* [It.]; anthem, national anthem; wedding song, bridal hymn, *Brautlied* [G.]; croon, croon song; pastoral, barcarole, serenade, *aubade* [F.] etc. *above* 415.3; choral, cantata etc. *below* 415.12; choral service, opera etc. *below* 415.17.

11. *n.* sacred music, sacred song *or* tune, psalm, hymn, hymn-tune, choral *or* chorale, anthem; motet; paean, doxology; Passion music *or* oratorio; spiritual *or* Negro spiritual, psalmody, hymnody, hymnology; responsory, offertory etc. *below* 415.14; *Te Deum* [L.] etc. (glorification) 990.2.

12. *n.* part music, concerted *or* harmonized music; part song, part singing; glee; descant; chorus, choral *or* chorale, choral composition, choral ballad; catch, troll, round, rondeau, rondo; madrigal, madrigaletto; cantata, lyric cantata; serenata (*pl.* serenatas, serenate), serenade; oratorio, Passion music *or* ora-

torio; solo, arioso; duet, duo (*pl.* duos, dui), *duettino* [It.]; trio, terzet, terzetto; quartet *or* quartette; quintet *or* quintette; sextet *or* sextette, sestet; septet *or* septette, septuor; octet *or* octette; opera etc. *below* 415.17.

13. *n.* part, melody *or* voice part, voice, instrument; real part, auxiliary *or* additional part; tonic section; descant, canto, cantus, soprano, tenor, treble; second, alto; bassus, bass; baritone etc. (voice) 413.14; passage etc. *below* 415.15.

14. *n.* response, responsory *or* responsary [Eccl.], report, answer; antiphon, antiphony, antiphonal chanting *or* singing; offertory, offertory sentence *or* hymn [Eccl.].

15. *n.* passage, phrase, strain, part, movement; division, roulade; period, musical sentence; section; measure; *alla breve*; verse, stanza; chorus, burden, bourdon, refrain, response; cadence, cadenza, harmonic close; overture, prelude, *Vorspiel* [G.], introduction, voluntary, descant, vamp; concert overture, choral prelude etc.; coda, tailpiece; ritornel *or* ritornelle, ritornello, symphony; interlude, intermezzo (*pl.* intermezzi, intermezzos); bass passage, ground bass, *basso ostinato* [It.]; arpeggio passage; tutti, tutti passage; bridge, bridge passage; rallentando, ritardando; piano, pianissimo; staccato, spiccato, fortissimo, diminuendo, legato; andante, adagio etc. (slow music) *above* 415.8.

16. *n.* impromptu, extempore, improvisation, interpolation, vamp; lick, hot lick, riff [all slang, U.S.].

17. *n.* musical performance, musicale, musical [coll.]; choral service, service of song, sing [coll.], singing [South. U.S.], community singing, singfest [slang], singsong [coll.], sing-sing [derog.]; concert, symphony concert, chamber concert; Philharmonic concert, philharmonic; popular concert, pop *or* pop concert [coll.]; popular [coll.]; promenade concert, prom [coll.]; open-air concert, serenade, *aubade* [F.]; Dutch concert, cat's concert [both coll.]; recital; *Sängerfest* [G.], eisteddfod [Welsh].

---

die, / Vibrates in the memory.—SHELLEY. Music must take rank as the highest of the fine arts.—SPENCER. Music that gentlier on the spirit lies than tired eyelids upon tired eyes.—TENNYSON. I hear America singing, the varied carols I hear.—WHITMAN. Like the

Singspiel [G.], song-play, music *or* lyric drama; opera, operetta, *opéra ballet* [F.]; ballet, *ballet d'action, ballet divertissement* [both F.], musical comedy, minstrel show, chorus show, song-and-dance act; oratorio; farewell performance, swan song; audition [coll.], hearing; choral symphony etc. (choir) 416.12.

18. *n.* solmization, solfeggio, sol-fa, sol-fa exercise; vocal exercise, vocalise, vocalization; rehearsal; sight singing *or* reading; tonic sol-fa, sol-fa notation etc. 413.17.

19. *n.* theme, motive, motif; leitmotiv, leitmotif.

20. *n.* (style) performance, execution, touch, expression; song *or* lied form, primary form; sonata form, sonata allegro; intonation; repercussion; pizzicato, staccato, spiccato, parlando; legato effect, slur; glissando (*pl.* glissandi), gliss [slang], smear [slang]; trill etc. (ornament) 413.10.

21. *n.* score, musical score *or* copy, music, copy, draft, transcript, arrangement; part; full *or* orchestral score, compressed *or* short score, piano score, vocal score, instrumental score; opera score, opera; *libretto* [It.] (*pl.* librettos, libretti); sheet music; songbook, songster; hymnbook, hymnal; music paper, music demy; music roll.

22. *n.* staff, stave [chiefly Eng.]; line, ledger line; bar, bar line; space, degree; brace.

23. *n.* notation, character, mark, symbol, signature, sign, *segno* [It.]; dot; custos, direct; cancel; clef, G ~, F *or* C clef, soprano ~, alto *or* tenor clef; measure *or* time signature, tempo mark, metronome *or* metronomic mark; pause; repeat mark, *presa* [It.] (*pl. prese*), *da capo* [It.]; slur, tie, enharmonic tie, vinculum; staccato mark, nonlegato mark; swell; accent, accent mark; note etc. 413.6.

24. *n.* (science of music) music, musicology, musicography; harmony, harmonics; melodies; rhythmic; hymnology, hymnography.

25. *n.* musicomania, musicophobia; music lover etc. 416.15.

26. *v.* compose, write, arrange, score, set, set to music *or* melody, fit with music, music, musicalize, musicate [rare], melodize, harmonize, orchestrate, instrumentate, instrument; rhythmize, rhythmicize; adapt, make an adaptation, adapt to music; transpose; concert [rare]; counterpoint; fugue, ballad etc. *n.*

27. *v.* play, sing etc. 416.18–23.

28. *adj.* musical, musiclike; musicological; musicoartistic, musicodramatic, musicopoetic, musicophilosophical, musicomechanical; instrumental, pianistic(al), violinistic etc.; vocal, vocalistic; choral, choric; operatic; orchestral, orchestric; symphonic, symphonetic; concert, concerted; harmonic, harmonistic; enharmonic(al); philharmonic; music-loving, music-mad; melic, lyric(al); songlike, songish, songy [both rare], songful; pure, tempered; contrapuntal, polyphonic, polyphonical [rare]; modal, classic, modern; program, imitative, falsetto, *sonata-allegro* [It.]; minuetic, minuetish; melodious, harmonious etc. 413.26–29.

29. *adj.* syncopated; ragtime, ragtimey [coll.]; jazz; jazzy, jazzed, jazzed up [all slang]; hot, swingy [both slang].

30. *adv.* (style) *a ballata, alla polacca, alla tedesca, alla zingara, alla zoppa* [all It.]; fortissimo, *tutta forza* [It.]; *abbandono* [It.]; *appassionato, appassionatamente* [It.]; *agitato, con agitazione* [both It.]; *brillante* [It.], crescendo, *accrescendo* [It.]; diminuendo, *morendo* [It.]; piano, pianissimo; *sordo* [It.]; *agilmente, con agilità* [both It.]; *leggiero* [It.]; *amabile* [It.]; affettuoso; *con amore* [It.], amoroso; legato, arioso; *dolce* [It.]; scherzoso; *capriccioso, a capriccio* [both It.]; staccato; *lamentabile* [It.]; *a cappella, alla cappella* [both It.]; parlando; *con alcuna licenza* [It.].

31. *adv.* (slowly) largo, larghetto; *allargando* [It.]; adagio, adagietto, andante, andantino, andante moderato; *calando* [It.]; *a poco* [It.]; lento; ritardando, rallentando.

32. *adv.* (fast) allegro, allegretto; accelerando; *veloce* [It.]; *affrettando* [It.]; *vivace, vivacissimo, con brio, con anima* [all It.]; presto, prestissimo; *desto* [It.].

---

faint, exquisite music of a dream.—T. MOORE.
Music is feeling then, not sound.—W. STEVENS.
Music I heard with you was more than music.
—C. AIKEN.   Music my rampart, and my only one.—MILLAY.

33. *adv.* al segno, dal segno [both It.] ; da capo, D.C., da capo al fine, da capo al segno [all It.].

416. Musician
(See also 415. Music)

1. *n.* musician, musicianer [coll.], musiker [chiefly dial.], musico, music maker, minstrel [poetic], player, performer, tunester, harmonist; artiste, virtuoso (*pl.* virtuosos, virtuosi), virtuoso [*fem.*] (*pl.* virtuose); maestro (*pl.* maestros, maestri); instrumentalist, instrumentist; band musician, bandman *or* bandsman [slang]; symphony musician, symphonist; concert musician, concertist; recitalist; syncopator, ragtimer [coll.]; jazz musician, jazzer [slang]; swing musician, swingster [slang]; accompanist, accompanyist; soloist, duettist etc. (*see* solo, duet etc. 415.12); musicologist, musicographer; minstrelsy, tin-pan alley.

2. *n.* wind musician, wind-instrumentalist, windjammer [slang], horn player, hornist, horner, piper, tooter; clarinetist *or* clarionetist, saxophonist, trombonist, bugler, fifer, piccoloist, oboist, bassoonist, cornettist *or* cornetist; trumpeter, trumpet major [Mil.]; flutist, flautist; lutist, lutanist; accordionist, concertinist.

3. *n.* string musician, strummer, thrummer, twanger; lyrist, luter, theorbist, citharist, zitherist, guitarist, banjoist, mandolinist; violinist, fiddle [Scot.], fiddler [coll. or derog.], tweedledee [derog.], catgut scraper [slang]; bass violinist, contrabassist; violoncellist, cellist *or* 'cellist [coll.], celloist [coll.]; violist, viola; harpist, harper.

4. *n.* pianist, pianiste, pianofortist, piano player, ivory tickler *or* thumper [slang]; pianolist; harpsichordist, clavichordist, monochordist.

5. *n.* organist, organer, organ player.

6. *n.* hurdy-gurdist *or* hurdy-gurdyist, hurdy-gurdy man; organ-grinder.

7. *n.* drummer, drum [Mil.; rare], drums [slang], *tambourgi* [Turk.], tympanist; kettledrummer, timpanist; taborer; tambourine, tambo [coll.]; drum corps.

8. *n.* cymbalist, cymbaler, cymbaleer.

9. *n.* orchestra, Kapelle [G.] (*pl.* Kapellen); string orchestra, string band; symphony orchestra, symphony; band, brass band, military band, German band, concert band, ragtime band, jazz band, swing band; street band, street musicians, waits [Hist.]; ensemble; strings, woodwind *or* woodwinds, brass *or* brasses, string ~, woodwind *or* brass section.

10. *n.* vocalist, vocalizer, singer, songster, songbird, warbler, voice, melodist, cantor, caroler; songstress, singstress, *cantatrice* [F. and It.] (*pl. cantatrices, cantatrici*); chanter, chaunter [arch.]; chantress, chauntress [arch.]; prima donna (*pl.* prima donnas, prime donne); improvisator, *improvvisatore* [It.], *improvvisatrice* [It.; *fem.*]; minstrel, minstrelless [rare]; wandering *or* itinerant minstrel, gleeman [arch.], gleemaiden [arch.], jongleur, troubadour, ballad singer, balladier [obs.], bard, runer [Gothic], rhapsodist, street singer, wait [Hist.], serenader; negro minstrel, blackface; end man, bones; blues singer, torch singer [coll.]; crooner.

chorist, chorister *or* choirister, chorus singer, choralist, choirman, choirboy; chorus girl, chorine [slang], singsong girl [pidgin Eng.]; psalm singer, hymner; Meistersinger, *Minnesänger* [G.], minnesinger; sol-faist, tonic sol-faist; bassist, bass, basso (*pl.* bassos, bassi), base; *buffo, basso buffo* [both It.]; tenor, alto etc. (voice) 413.14.

11. *n.* songbird, singing bird, songster, feathered songster, warbler; nightingale, philomel [poetic]; lark, ringdove, bulbul, cuckoo, thrush, song thrush, mavis, canary, song sparrow, mockingbird, oriole.

12. *n.* choir, quire [arch.], Kapelle [G.], chorus, voices, ensemble; *Liedertafel, Liederkranz* [both G.], choral *or* singing club *or* society; *a cappella* choir; festival chorus; choral symphony, sing band [slang]; quartet etc. 415.12.

13. *n.* conductor, leader, music director *or* supervisor, *Kapellmeister* [G.]; orchestra leader, bandmaster, band major, drum major [Mil.]; concertmaster, concertmeister, *Konzertmeister* [G.]; choirmaster, chorister *or* choir-

---

416. Set thy own songs, and sing them to thy lute.—DRYDEN.   He was a fiddler, and consequently a rogue.—SWIFT.   Blows out his brains upon the flute.—BROWNING.   Gaily the troubadour / Touched his guitar.—T. H. BAYLY.   We are the music-makers / And we

416.13 – 417.3

ister [U.S.], *maestro di cappella* [It.]; song leader, choir chaplain [Eccl.], precentor, cantor.

14. *n.* composer, scorer, arranger; melodist, melodizer; harmonist, harmonizer; orchestrater *or* orchestrator; instrumentalist [rare]; symphonist; tone poet; ballad maker *or* writer, ballader, balladmonger; madrigalist, madrigaler; lyric writer, lyrist; hymnist, hymnographer, hymnologist; contrapuntist.

15. *n.* music lover, philharmonic, music fan [slang], musicofanatic; hepcat, jitterbug [both slang, U.S.]; musicmonger; concertgoer, operagoer; tonalist.

16. *n.* (patrons) Orpheus; Apollo, Apollo Musagetes; Siren; the Muses, the Nine, sacred Nine, tuneful Nine, tuneful quire [arch.], Pierides; Erato, Euterpe, Polymnia *or* Polyhymnia, Terpsichore.

17. *n.* musicianship; performance, execution, touch, expression; fiddlery.

18. *v.* play, perform, execute, render, music, musicalize, melodize, make music *or* melody, utter musically, produce tunes, tune [poetic], tweedle; rhythmize, rhythmicize; syncopate, jazz *or* jazz up [slang], rag [coll.]; accompany, play *or* sing a second; concert [rare], concertize; symphonize; chord, octave; transpose.

twang, twank [dial., Eng.], pluck, plunk, pick, strum, thrum; sweep, sweep the strings *or* chords; strike the lyre, touch the guitar etc. (*see* guitar etc. 417); violin, fiddle [coll. or derog.], scrape [derog.], saw [coll. or derog.], bow; pound ~, tickle ~ *or* paw the ivories; organ, grind the organ; blow ~, sound *or* wind the horn, blow, wind, toot, tootle, pipe, whistle, bugle, sound; bagpipe, doodle [Scot. and dial. Eng.]; play the fife, ~ timbrel etc. (*see* fife, timbrel etc. 417).

19. *v.* beat time, beat the drum, drum, thrum, beat, pound, thump; pat, pat juba [chiefly dial., U.S.]; tattoo [rare], beat *or* sound a tattoo; ruffle, beat a ruffle [both Mil.]; kettledrum, tambourin etc. (*see* percussion instruments 417.10).

20. *v.* sing, vocalize, carol [poetic], cantillate [rare], descant, lilt, troll; chirp, chirrup; twit [Scot. and dial. Eng.], twitter; warble, trill, tremolo, quaver; roulade; chant, chaunt [arch.]; intone, intonate, tone [rare]; hum, croon; yodel, warble [U.S.]; pipe, whistle, tweedledee; chorus, sing in chorus, choral [rare]; minstrel; ballad; serenade; solmizate, sol-fa, do-re-mi.

21. *v.* begin to play *or* sing, break into song, strike up, strike up a tune, strike up the band, tune up [coll.], pipe up, pipe up a song, yerk out.

22. *v.* conduct, direct, lead, wield the baton.

23. *v.* be musical etc. *adj.* 415.27, have an ear for music, have a musical ear, have a correct ear, have absolute pitch.

24. *adj.* musicianly, musical; virtuose [rare], virtuosic; lyric, dramatic; coloratura, florid, brilliant; choral, choric, choristic [rare]; orchestral, orchestric.

417. Musical Instruments

1. *n.* musical instruments, music [now rare]; concert; band, orchestra; string band, brass-wind band etc.; tweedledee, tweedledum; musical glasses, harmonica; musical stones; jew's-harp *or* jews'-harp.

2. *n.* string instruments, strings; harp, *arpa* [It.]; lyre, lute, archlute *or* archilute, theorbo, bell harp, claviharp, cither, cithara, cittern *or* cithern, gittern, zither, aeolian harp *or* lyre, crowd [Celtic], psaltery, dulcimer, langspiel, euphonon, tamboura, hexachord, polychord, harmonichord, melodicon, melodion, samisen.

banjo, banjo-zither, banjorine; ukulele, uke [coll.]; banjo-ukulele, banjo-uke [coll.], banjuke, banjulele; guitar, Spanish guitar; *bandurria* [Sp.], bandore, pandore, pandora; pandura, mandolin, mandola, mandore, mando-bass, mandocello, mandolute; vina [Ind.]; trumpet marine, tromba marina.

3. *n.* viol, vielle; violette; tenor, tenor viol, viol *or* viola d'amore, viol *or* viola da braccio, viol *or* viola da spalla; bass, bass *or* base viol, bass violin, bass fiddle [coll.], violoncello, cello *or* 'cello [coll.], viol *or* viola da gamba, viol *or* viola di bordone, viol *or* viola di fagotto, viol *or* viola bastarda; violoncello piccolo; bull fiddle [coll.], doghouse [slang, U.S.], contrabass, contrabasso, double bass *or* base, double-bass viol; *basso da camera* [It.].

violin, *violino* [It.], fiddle [coll.], crowd [dial., Eng.]; Stradivarius, Stradivari, Strad [coll.]; Cremona, Guarnerius *or* Guarnieri *or* guarneri; violinette, violino piccolo; kit, kit violin; tenor violin, violotta, *Bratsche* [G.]; viola, viola alta, viola pomposa [obs.]; troubadour fiddle; rebec *or* rebeck.

4. *n.* wind instruments, winds; wood *or* wood-wind instruments, wood winds, woods; brass *or* brass-wind instruments, brass winds, brasses, *Blechinstrumente* [G.]; reed instruments; horn, *corno* [It.] (*pl. corni*), pipe [poetic or arch.], tooter; flute, *flauto* [It.]; bass flute, alto flute; fipple flute *or* pipe, flageolet; pipe, tabor pipe; fife; piccolo, *flauto piccolo* [It.]; oboe, hautboy; *oboe d'amore* [It.]; tenor oboe, tenoroon, *oboe di caccia* [It.]; bass *or* basset oboe, heckelphone; musette; harmoniphon [obs.]; bassoon; *basson quinte* [F.; obs.]; double bassoon, contra bassoon, contrafagotto.

clarinet *or* clarionet, bass clarinet; tenor clarinet, basset horn, *corno di bassetto* [It.]; English horn, *cor anglais* [F.], *corno Inglese* [It.]; bugle, bugle horn; trumpet, tromba (*pl.* trombe), clarion; lituus (*pl.* litui), conch [now chiefly art], lure; cornet, cornet-à-pistons, cornopean; trombone, *tromba da tirarsi* [It.]; slide trombone, sliphorn [slang], sackbut [arch.]; saxophone, sax [coll.]; saxhorn, saxtuba, saxcornet, *Flügelhorn* [G.]; alto saxhorn, althorn *or* alt horn, ballad horn; mellophone; bass horn *or* saxhorn, *basson russe* [It.], tuba; tenor tuba, euphonium; baritone *or* barytone; bombardon, pommer; ophicleide.

French horn, orchestral horn, *corno di caccia* [It.]; serpent; post horn; hornpipe; pipes, bagpipe *or* bagpipes, union pipes, doodlesack [Scot.], *Dudelsack* [G.]; musette, sordellina, chanter,

drones; Panpipe *or* Panpipes, Pandean pipes, syrinx; mouth organ *or* harp, harp, French harp [dial.], harmonica, harmonicon, harmoniphon [obs.]; ocarina, sweet potato [coll.]; whistle, willow whistle, penny whistle; calliope, calliophone; accordion, dago's piano [joc.]; concertina, squiffer [slang, Eng.]; bandonion; humming top.

5. *n.* organ, pipe organ, reed organ, cabinet organ, tracker action organ, tubular-pneumatic organ, electro-pneumatic organ, hydraulic organ, swell organ, choir organ, solo *or* orchestral organ, echo organ, antiphonal organ, pedal organ, church organ, altar *or* chancel organ, gallery organ, floating organ, American organ; melodica, melodeon, harmonium, symphonion, vocalion, choralcelo, seraphine *or* seraphina; barrel organ, hand organ, grind organ, street organ, hurdy-gurdy, vielle.

6. *n.* piano, pianoforte; pianette, pianino; grand piano, grand; concert-grand piano, concert grand; baby-grand piano, baby grand; square piano, upright piano; harpsichord, clavier, *Klavier* [G.], clavicymbal, clavicembalo (*pl.* clavicembali), cembalo; clavichord, clarichord, monochord, manichord *or* manichordon; clavicithern, clavicytherium; spinet, couched harp, virginal, pair of virginals; lyrichord, harmonichord; violin piano, piano-violin; mechanical piano, player piano, piano player, player, Pianola [trade name]; street piano.

7. *n.* hurdy-gurdy, vielle; hand organ etc. (organ) *above* 417.5.

8. *n.* music box, musical box; orchestrion, orchestrina; juke box [slang, U.S.].

9. *n.* phonograph, graphophone, gramophone, record player, Victrola [trade name]; recorder, reproducer; Dictaphone; phonograph record, disk, wax [cant].

10. *n.* percussion instruments, percussions, percussives; battery [coll.]; drum, *caisse* [F.], tympan, tympanum, tympanon, tympany; kettledrum, kettle [coll.], timpano (*pl.* timpani); snare drum, side drum, *caisse roulante* [F.]; bass drum, *caisse grosse* [F.]; tom-tom,

tam-tam; timbrel, tambourine, tambourin, *tambour de basque* [F.], tabor; taboret, tabret, tambouret [rare]; cymbals, potlids [slang], *Becken* [G.]; triangle; gong, tonitruone; bells, tintinnabula, chimes; orchestral bells, glockenspiel, carillon; vibraphone, vibes [slang]; xylophone, marimba; celesta; clappers, snappers, castanets, bones, rattle, rattlebones.

11. *n.* mute, sourdine, sordine, sordino; sordet, sourdet; damper pedal, soft pedal; hat, derby.

12. *n.* stop, register; foundation stop, mutation stop; flue pipe, reed pipe; principal, Principal, Dulciana Principal, melodia, diapason, open diapason, stopped diapason, cromorne, cromorna, cremona, tuba, celesta, flageolet, *fagotto* [It.]; flute, trombone, dolcan, dulciana, gemshorn, serpent.

13. *n.* (parts; equipment) string, music wire, piano wire, fiddlestring, catgut, snare; bow, violin *or* fiddle bow, fiddlestick; plectrum, plectron, pick; reed; mouthpiece; keys, piano keys, ivories [slang]; soundboard, sounding board, *abatvoix* [F.]; resonance box; drumhead, drumskin; drumstick, jazz stick; timpani drumstick, tymp stick; metronome, rhythmometer; tone measurer, monochord, sonometer; tuning fork, pitchfork [obs. exc. joc.], diapason; pipe, pitch pipe; music rack, music lyre; music case; music roll, piano player roll.

418. Hearing
(See 419. Deafness)

1. *n.* hearing, audition, auscultation, sense of hearing, sense *or* perception of sound, ear; audibleness, audibility; earful [slang].

2. *n.* a hearing, audition [coll.], tryout [coll., U.S.], audience, interview, conference, admittance, attention; trial etc. (examination) 461.3.

3. *n.* good hearing, acute ~, nice ~, delicate ~, quick ~, sharp *or* correct ear; musical ear, ear for music, nice ear for music.

4. *n.* earshot, earreach, hearing, range, reach, carrying distance, sound.

5. *n.* ear, "the hearing ear" (Bible), listener [slang], lug [now chiefly Scot. and dial.], acoustic organ, auditory apparatus; shell, concha [Tech.], conch; auricle, pinna, atrium; lobule, lobe; labyrinth, vestibule, cochlea; auditory canal, acoustic *or* auditory meatus; auditory *or* Eustachian tube; eardrum, tympanum; malleus, hammer; incus, anvil; stapes, stirrup, auditory nerve; auditory ganglion, acoustic tubercle; cauliflower ear, crop-ear etc. *adj.*

6. *n.* (instruments) ear trumpet, speaking trumpet, auriphone; auriscope, otoscope; headphone, earphone [coll.]; receiver, telephone receiver; phone [coll.], detectaphone, dyophone, electrophone, magnetophone, Geophone *or* geophone, hydrophone, kinetophone, lithophone, vitaphone, tracheophone, topophone, techniphone, radiophone, photophone, osteophone, optophone, odophone, motophone, megaphone; stethophone, stethoscope, auscultator; microphone, mike [slang]; speaker, loud-speaker; dictaphone [trade name], Dictograph *or* dictograph *or* dictagraph [trade name]; telephone etc. 532a.5; phonograph etc. 417.9.

7. *n.* hearer, listener, auditor, audient [rare], hearkener; eavesdropper, listener-in [coll.]; auscultator [Med.].

8. *n.* audience, auditory, house, congregation, theater, gallery; gods [coll.], gallery gods [coll.], celestials [slang]; orchestra, pit [chiefly Eng.], pittites [Eng., Theat.].

9. *n.* (science of hearing) otology, otoscopy, auriscopy; otopathy, otography, otoplasty, otorhinolaryngology; acoustics etc. 402.5.

10. *n.* (scientist) otologist, aurist; otorhinolaryngologist.

11. *v.* hear, overhear, catch, get [slang], take in, perceive by the ear; list [arch.], listen, hark [now rare], hearken [now chiefly poetic], heed, attend, give attention, give ear, give ~, lend *or* bend an ear; listen to, attend to, give a hearing to, give audience *or* attention to; hang upon the lips of, be all ear *or* ears [coll.], listen with both ears, strain one's ears, prick up the ears,

---

418. The hearing ear is always found close to the speaking tongue.—EMERSON. I was all ear.—MILTON. Walls have ears.—J. SHIRLEY. Give every man thy ear, but few thy voice.—SHAKESPEARE. Friends, Romans, countrymen, lend me your ears.—SHAKESPEARE

keep one's ears open; eavesdrop, listen in [coll.]; auscultate [Med.]; hear out; hear tell of [now coll. and dial.], hear say [coll.]; get an earful [slang].

12. *v.* be heard, become audible, meet ~, catch *or* reach the ear, fall upon the ear; ring in the ear.

13. *adj.* hearing etc. *v.,* auditory, auditive, auditual, aural, auricular, otic [Tech.], acoustic(al), phonic; audible etc. 402.10.

14. *adj.* eared, auricled, auriculate; big-eared, long-eared, dog-eared, mouse-eared, close-eared, crop-eared, droop-eared, flap-eared, flop-eared, lop-eared, prick-eared, cauliflower-eared, open-eared, sharp-eared.

15. *adv.* listening attentively, all ears [coll.]; *arrectis auribus* [L.], with ears pricked up.

16. *int.* hark!, hark ye!, hearken!, hear!, hear ye!, hear ye, hear he!, list!, listen!, oyez!, attend!, attention!.

419. Deafness
(See 418. Hearing)

1. *n.* deafness, hardness *or* dullness of hearing, surdity [rare], deaf ears; deaf-dumbness, deaf-muteness, deaf-mutism, deaf-and-dumbness, surdimutism.

2. *n.* inaudibility, inaudibleness.

3. *n.* deaf-mute, surdomute, deaf-and-dumb person.

4. *n.* (comparisons) adder, beetle, slowworm, blindworm, stone, post, door, doornail, trunkmaker.

5. *n.* dactylology, deaf-and-dumb alphabet, manual alphabet, one-hand *or* two-hand alphabet; lip reading, oral method.

6. *v.* be deaf etc. *adj.,* have no ear; shut ~, stop *or* close one's ears, turn a deaf ear.

7. *v.* deafen, deaf [arch. and dial.],

When the ear heard me, then it blessed me.—BIBLE. He that hath ears to hear, let him hear.—BIBLE. We have two ears and one mouth that we may listen the more and talk the less.—ZENO. Ears are eyes to the blind.—SOPHOCLES.
419. Music . . . is neither good nor bad to the deaf.—SPINOZA. Our deafness each one laughs about.—BÉRANGER. None so deaf as those that will not hear.—M. HENRY. Who is so deaf or so blind as he / That wilfully will neither hear nor see?—J. HEYWOOD. Trouble deaf heaven.—SHAKESPEARE.

---

render deaf, stun, split the ears *or* eardrum.

8. *adj.* deaf, hard ~, dull *or* thick of hearing, deaf-eared, dull-eared, earless, unhearing, surd; stone-deaf, deaf as a stone, ~ a trunkmaker etc. *n.,* "like the deaf adder that stoppeth her ear" (Bible); deafened, stunned; deaf and dumb, deaf-dumb, deaf-mute; inattentive etc. 458.10.

9. *adj.* inaudible, unhearable, out of earshot, ~ hearing etc. (*see* earshot, hearing etc. 418.4); silent etc. 403.6, 7.

420. Light
(See 421. Darkness; also 423. Luminary)

1. *n.* light, radiant *or* luminous energy [Phys.], radiation, radiance *or* radiancy, irradiance *or* irradiancy, irradiation, illumination, emanation, incandescence, glow, gleam, glim [slang], glint, luster, shine, nitency [rare]; effulgence, refulgence *or* refulgency, fulgor *or* fulgour, fulgidity [rare]; "God's first creature" (Bacon), "God's eldest daughter" (Fuller), "the prime work of God" (Milton).

brightness etc. *adj.,* brilliance *or* brilliancy, splendor, lucence *or* lucency, lucidity; radiant splendor, resplendence *or* resplendency, transplendency [rare], dazzlement, dazzling brilliance, blare, glare, glaring light; sheen, gloss; streaming light, flood of light; starlight; afterglow, sunset glow; side light; candle power, bougie decimale, Hefner candle, lumen, lux, foot-candle; lamp etc. (luminary) 423; fire, firework, fire and light worship etc. 382.8, 9, 11; chiaroscuro etc. 421.1.

2. *n.* luminosity, luminousness etc. *adj.*

3. *n.* ray, beam, gleam, leam [obs. exc. Scot. and North. Eng.], stream, streak, pencil, glade, patch, ray ~, beam etc. of light; sunbeam, sun spark; moonbeam, cone of light; cathode ray, alpha ray, beta ray, gamma ray, ultraviolet ray, infrared ray; Roentgen *or* Röntgen ray, roentgen *or* röntgen ray, X ray; X-ray radiation, X radiation; actinic ray *or* light, actinism.

4. *n.* flash, blaze, flame, coruscation, fulguration [now rare], gleam, glint, glance; flash ~, gleam etc. of light,

---

420. And God said, Let there be light: and there was light.—BIBLE. Truly the light is sweet, and a pleasant thing it is for the eyes

420.4 – 420.18

flashlight; facula [Astron.] (*pl.* faculae).

5. *n.* glitter, glitterance [rare], glittering etc. *v.*; glimmer, shimmer, flicker, flutter, twinkle, blink; sparkle, spark; scintilla, scintillation; glisten, glister; wavering *or* flickering light, "lambent flame" (Dryden).

6. *n.* lightning, lighten [obs.], flash *or* stroke of lightning, fulguration [now rare], fulmination, fulminant [rare], levin [arch. and dial.], levining [obs.], levin bolt *or* brand, bolt, bolt from the blue, bolt of lightning, firebolt, thunderbolt, thunderball, thunderstroke, thunderlight [arch.]; fork *or* forked lightning, chain lightning, globular *or* ball lightning, summer *or* heat lightning, sheet lightning, dark lightning [Meteorol.]; Jupiter Fulgur *or* Fulminator [Rom. Myth.].

7. *n.* (artificial illumination) candlelight, candleshine, rushlight; gas, gaslight; lamplight, lantern light, torchlight, firelight; midnight oil; spotlight, limelight, footlights; incandescent light, electric light, fluorescent light, zircon light etc. (lamp) 423.2–6.

8. *n.* daylight, dayshine, broad daylight, light of day; day, daytime, daytide [poetic]; sunlight, sunshine, shine; glare of the sun, glaring sunlight; midday sun, noonday *or* noontide light; sunburst; sunbeam, sun spark, ray of sunlight; dawn etc. (morning) 125; twilight, sunset etc. (evening) 126.1; sun etc. 318.4.

9. *n.* moonlight, moonshine, moonglow; moonbeam, moonglade [poetic]; moon etc. 318.5.

10. *n.* reflection, reflectance; refraction, refractivity; dispersion, diffusion; blink, iceblink, snowblink, water blink.

11. *n.* luminescence, autoluminescence, chemiluminescence *or* chemicoluminescence, triboluminescence, electroluminescence, cathode luminescence, crystalloluminescence, thermoluminescence, photoluminescence, fluorescence; bioluminescence, noctilucence; phosphorescence, tribophosphorescence; phosphorescent substance *or* body; *ignis fatuus* [L.], will-o'-the-wisp *or* will-with-the-wisp, jack-o'-lantern, friar's lantern, firedrake [obs.]; fata morgana; St. Elmo's light *or* fire, Helena [obs.], corposant; double corposant, Castor and Pollux [Naut.], ectoplasm, exteriorized protoplasm; firefly etc. 423.13.

12. *n.* nebulous light, luminous vapor, nimbus; nebula (*pl.* nebulae, nebulas), nebule [rare]; galactic nebula, anagalactic nebula, planetary nebula, diffuse nebula, spiral nebula, dark nebula; nebula of Andromeda, ~ Lyra *or* Orion; coalsack; zodiacal light, Gegenschein, counterglow; polar lights, aurora; northern lights, aurora borealis; southern lights, aurora australis; parhelion (*pl.* parhelia), parhelic circle *or* ring, mock sun, sun dog; anthelion (*pl.* anthelia), antisun, countersun; paraselene (*pl.* paraselenae), mock moon, moon dog; photometeor.

13. *n.* halo, nimbus, aura, aureole, aureola, gloriole [rare], glory, *vesica piscis* [L.; Eccl. Art]; corona, aurora.

14. *n.* lighting etc. *v.*, enlightenment, illumination; radiation, irradiation; gaslighting, electric lighting, incandescent lighting, arc lighting etc. (*see* gaslight, electric light etc. 423.2–8); direct lighting, indirect lighting; decorative lighting, stage lighting, floodlighting, overhead lighting.

15. *n.* illuminant, luminant; gas etc. 334.2; petroleum, gasoline etc. (oil) 356; electricity etc. 158a; fuel etc. 388; luminary etc. 423.

16. *n.* photics, photology, photometry; optics; dioptrics, catoptrics; actinology, actinometry; radiology, radiometry, radioscopy; photography, photolithography, photomicrography; phototelegraphy; phototherapy, heliotherapy; radiotherapy, ray therapy; heliology, heliometry, heliography; heliometer, radiometer, refractometer; photometer etc. 445.

17. *v.* shine, shine forth, give light etc. *n.*, glow, gloze, beam, gleam, glint, glance; flare, blaze, flash, fulgurate; radiate, effulge [rare], spread light, shoot out beams; be bright etc. *adj.*, shine brightly, glare; daze, dazzle, bedazzle.

18. *v.* glitter, glimmer, shimmer, twinkle, blink, flicker, flutter, waver, dance, coruscate; spark, sparkle, scintillate; glisten, glister, glisk [chiefly Scot.].

---

to behold the sun.—BIBLE. Every light has its shadow.—J. RAY. Where there is much light, the shadows are deepest.—GOETHE. The two noblest things, which are sweetness and light.—SWIFT. Light is the first of painters.—EMERSON. Medicinal as light.—LOWELL.

19. *v.* luminesce, phosphoresce, glow *or* gleam in the dark.

20. *v.* illuminate, illumine, illume [poetic], luminate, lumine [now rare]; lighten, enlighten, light, light up, supply with light, brighten, irradiate; shed light *or* shine upon, cast *or* throw light upon, overshine; floodlight.

21. *v.* light, strike a light, turn *or* switch on the light; relight, reillumine, relume; kindle etc. (ignite) 384.17.

22. *adj.* luminous, luminant, luminarious [rare], luminiferous, luminificent, luminative; illuminant, illuminate [arch.], illuminated; irradiate, irradiated; light, lightsome, lightish, alight; lucid, lucent, luculent, lucific [rare], luciferous [rare], relucent; nitid [rare], nitidous; gleaming, shining etc. *v.*; shiny, beamy, lamping, lustrous, bright, bright as silver; radiant, lambent, orient; glaring, glary; brilliant, vivid, splendid, splendrous *or* splendorous, splendent, resplendent, transplendent [rare], garish; fulgid, fulgorous, fulgurant, fulgent, effulgent, refulgent; rutilant, rutilous.

blazing, in a blaze, ablaze; glowing, aglow; glossy, glassy; sheen [dial. or poetic], sheeny; burnished, polished, shined; spangled, bespangled, studded; sunny, sunshiny, light as day, bright as noonday *or* the noonday sun; starbright, starlit, starlike; clear, serene, transparent [poetic], pellucid, unobscured; cloudless, unclouded; meteoric; luminary etc. 423.14; star-studded etc. (celestial) 318.16.

23. *adj.* sparkling, scintillating etc. *v.*; scintillant, scintillose *or* scintillous [rare], scintillescent; glittery, glimmery, glimmerous, shimmery, fluttery, flickery, flicky [coll.], twinkly, blinky.

24. *adj.* (scientific) radiological, actinic; optic(al); photic, photologic(al), photographic, photometric(al), photogenic; heliological, heliographic, heliophobous; catoptric(al).

421. Darkness
(See 420. Light; also 422. Dimness, 424. Shade)

1. *n.* darkness, dark, lightlessness etc. *adj.*; obscurity, obscure; tenebrity, tenebrosity; intense darkness, pitch-darkness, Cimmerian darkness, Stygian darkness, Egyptian darkness, darkness invisible, "obscure darkness" (Bible), "the palpable obscure" (Milton), "the suit of night" (Shakespeare); chiaroscuro, chiaro-oscuro, clair-obscure [all Art]; night, dead of night etc. 126.3, 4; blackness etc. (dark color) 431; dimness etc. 422.

2. *n.* gloom, gloomth, gloominess etc. *adj.;* somber, murk [now chiefly dial.]; shadow etc. (semidarkness) 422.2, 3.

3. *n.* obscuration, adumbration, obumbration [now rare], obtenebration [rare], caligation [obs.], offuscation [obs.]; black-out, dim-out; obfuscation, obfuscity [rare]; extinguishment, extinction; eclipse, total eclipse; shadowing etc. (*see* shadow etc. 422.6), overshadowment; gathering of the clouds.

4. *v.* be dark etc. *adj.,* be in darkness etc. *n.*

5. *v.* darken, bedarken, dark [arch.]; obscure, obfuscate, offuscate [obs.], adumbrate, obumbrate [now rare], obtenebrate [rare], eclipse; gloom, cast a gloom over, somber, murk *or* mirk; grow dark, darkle, lower *or* lour; shade, cloud etc. (dim) 422.6, 7.

6. *v.* extinguish, quench etc. 385.5; turn *or* switch off the light, kill the light [motion-picture cant].

7. *adj.* dark, black, darksome, darkling, darkful [rare]; lightless, without light etc. (*see* light etc. 420); unlighted, unilluminated etc. (*see* illuminated etc. 423.14); obscure, caliginous, clothed *or* shroud in darkness; tenebrous, tenebrose, tenebrious; pitch-dark, pitch-black, pitchy, "dark as a wolf's mouth" (Scott); night-dark, night-black, dark *or* black as night, nocturnal; night-clad, night-cloaked, night-enshrouded, night-mantled, night-veiled, night-hid, night-filled; sunless, moonless, starless; shorn **of its** beams; black etc. (color) 431.7; dim, shady etc. 422.8, 9; opaque etc. 426.4.

8. *adj.* gloomy, gloomful, dark and gloomy; somber, sombrous; murk [now

---

421. And darkness was upon the face of the deep.—BIBLE. Men loved darkness rather than light, because their deeds were evil.— BIBLE. It is sure to be dark if you shut your eyes.—J. RAY. O dark, dark, dark, amid the blaze of noon.—MILTON. Dark with excessive bright.—MILTON. And all around was darkness like a wall.—W. MORRIS. Blemishes are hid by night and every fault forgiven;

poetic and dial.], murky, murkish, murksome [rare]; swart [poetic], dusk, dusky, dismal, dreary, funereal, melancholy, uncheerful, lurid, lowering *or* louring; Stygian, Stygial [rare]; shadowy etc. 422.9.

9. *adj.* darkening, obscuring etc. *v.*; obscurant, obscurantic.

10. *adv.* darkly etc. *adj.*, darkling, darklings [rare]; in the dark, in the night *or* the dark of night, at *or* by night, through the night; dimly etc. 422.10.

11. *adv.* as pitch, as a *or* the pit, that one cannot see one's hand, as Erebus.

422. Dimness
(See 420. Light; also 421. Darkness)

1. *n.* dimness, indistinctness etc. *adj.*, obscurity, fuliginosity; dimout; darkness etc. 421; paleness etc. (light color) 429.

2. *n.* semidarkness, semidark, partial darkness, half-light, *demi-jour* [F.], dusk, duskiness etc. *adj.*; "the shadow of a shade" (Aeschylus); partial eclipse, partial shadow; aurora; lackluster, lacklusterness; starlight, firelight, candlelight, rushlight; moonlight etc. 420.9; glimmer etc. (glitter) 420.5; gloom etc. 421.2; twilight, crepuscule etc. (morning) 125.1, (evening) 126.1.

3. *n.* shadow, shadowing, shade, shading, shadiness; shady spot, dark place; umbra, umbrage [obs.]; gloom, gloomth; "shadows numberless" (Keats); penumbra; moonshade.

4. *n.* skiagram, skiagraph; shadowgram, shadowgraph; radiogram, radiograph; silhouette; skiagraphy, shadowgraphy.

5. *n.* nebulousness etc. *adj.*, nebulosity; nubilation, obnubilation [rare].

6. *v.* dim, bedim, render dim etc. *adj.*, obscure, obfuscate; blur, blear; mist, enmist, bemist; fog, befog; cloud, becloud, encloud, cloud over, overcloud, nubilate; shadow, shade, cast *or* spread a shadow *or* shade, encompass with shadow; overshadow, overshade, overcast, darken over, adumbrate; oversmoke; darken etc. 421.5.

7. *v.* grow dim etc. *adj.*, cloud over etc. *above*; dusk, dusken [rare]; gloom, gloam [chiefly Scot.], loom, lower *or* lour; fade, pale; darkle etc. (darken) 421.5; flicker, glimmer etc. (glitter) 420.18.

8. *adj.* dim, dimmish, dimmy, dimpsy [dial. Eng.]; obscure, indistinct, vague, faint, pale, shadowed forth; filmy, hazy, misty, foggy, cloudy, clouded etc. *v.*; nebulous, nebulose, nubilous, nubilose, nubiferous, nubilated, obnubilated [rare], obnubilous [obs.]; semidark, darkish, darksome; dusk, dusky; lackluster, lacklustrous, shorn of its beams; dull, leaden, somber, dun, glassy; blurred, blurry, bleared, bleary, blear; dingy, grimy, smoky, sooty, muddy, dirty, fuliginous; smeared, besmeared; smirched, besmirched; twilight, crepuscular etc. (evening) 126.5; dark etc. 421.7, 8.

9. *adj.* shadowy, shady, shaded; overshadowed, overshaded, overcast, umbrageous; gloomy etc. 421.8.

10. *adv.* dimly etc. *adj.*, shadowy, as a shadow, in the shadow *or* shade; darkly etc. 421.10.

423. Luminary
(See also 420. Light)

Source of Light.—1. *n.* luminary, luminant, illuminant, light, glim [slang]; luster; lamp, lantern, candle, taper, torch [all fig.]; illumination etc. 420; flame, fireworks etc. (fire) 382.8, 9; match etc. (lighter) 388.4-6; star, sun, moon etc. 318.3-7.

2. *n.* lamp, lamplet; gas lamp, gaslight; oil lamp, Carcel lamp, flame lamp, Argand lamp, petanne lamp, sun *or* sunlight burner, Hefner lamp, moderator lamp, aphlogistic *or* glow lamp; table lamp, floor lamp, bridge lamp; miner's lamp, safety lamp, lampion; night lamp *or* light, *veilleuse* [F.]; lantern, lanthorn

---

darkness makes any woman fair.—OVID.   A good many things go around in the dark besides Santa Claus.—H. HOOVER.   All cats are grey in the dark.
422. The lengthening shadows wait.—HOLMES. Within the green glooms of the shadowy oak.— LOWELL.   Fade away into the forest dim.— KEATS.   Now fades the glimmering landscape on the sight.—GRAY.   Draw the gradual dusky veil.—COLLINS.   The shades of night were falling fast.—LONGFELLOW.
423. My candle burns at both ends / . . . It gives a lovely light!—MILLAY.   A candle lights others and consumes itself.—H. BOHN.

[arch.]; barn lantern, searchlight lantern, railroad lantern, magic lantern; dark lantern, darky [slang], bull's-eye, police lantern; Chinese lantern, Japanese lantern; jack-o'-lantern, jack-o'-lanthorn [now rare], lamplight, lantern light etc. (light) 420.7.

3. *n.* electric *or* incandescent light *or* lamp, filament lamp, glow *or* carbon light *or* lamp, vacuum tube, tungsten ~, tantalum *or* quartz lamp, zircon ~, calcium ~, klieg *or* kleig light, shunt ~, daylight ~, Sheringham daylight ~, osmium *or* Nernst lamp, Moore light, ~ lamp *or* tube, flashlight, flashing light, flashing lamp, focus ~, projector ~, vapor *or* uviol lamp, neon lamp *or* tube, Finsen light *or* lamp; mercury ~, mercury-vapor *or* mercury-arc lamp; arc lamp, arc [coll.]; electric arc, flaming arc; magnetite arc ~, open arc *or* enclosed arc lamp.

spotlight, spot [coll.], limelight [Eng.]; pickle, rifle [both motion-picture cant]; baby *or* junior spotlight; sun lamp, sun spot, sun arc, sun [coll.]; floodlight, flood lamp, flood [coll.]; broadside, broad [motion-picture cant]; searchlight, searchlight lantern, search lamp; battery lamp, electric torch; flashlight, flash, flasher.

4. *n.* (vehicle lamps) headlight, head lamp; antidazzle lamp; side light, side lamp; taillight, tail lamp; stop light, stop lamp.

5. *n.* signal light *or* lamp, beacon; rocket, signal rocket, skyrocket, Roman candle; candlebomb; flare, flare-up; lighthouse; traffic lights, stop-and-go lights, stop *or* red light, green light; pilot light *or* lamp, bull's-eye indicator; flashlight etc. *above* 423.3; beacon fire, balefire etc. (fire) 382.8.

6. *n.* (aviation) beacon, landmark ~, airport ~, airway ~, code ~, radiomarker *or* radio-range beacon; identification ~, navigation ~, position *or* course light; approach ~, landing *or* landing-direction light; boundary ~, obstruction ~, anchor ~, fixed ~, blinker *or* flashing light; ceiling light *or* projector.

7. *n.* candle, taper; dip, farthing dip, tallow dip [coll.]; tallow candle, tallow; wax candle, wax, bougie; bayberry candle; rush candle, rushlight; corpse candle, death light; candlelight etc. (light) 420.7.

8. *n.* torch, flaming torch *or* light, flambeau, brand [poetic], mussal [Ind.], link; torchlight.

9. *n.* light holder, lamp holder, lampstand; torch holder, torch staff; candleholder, candlestick, candlestand, candelabrum (*pl.* candelabra, candelabrums), candelabra lamp holder, girandole, sconce; light socket.

10. *n.* chandelier, gaselier, gasoliery, electrolier, lustre *or* luster; corona, corona lucis, crown, circlet.

11. *n.* burner, gas burner, Argand burner, Bunsen burner, fishtail burner; moderator; mantle, gas mantle, incandescent mantle, Welsback mantle; jet, gas jet; bulb, electric bulb; filament, carbon filament, tungsten filament; globe, light globe; tube, vacuum tube, vacuum discharge tube, Braun tube, Crookes tube, Geissler tube, focus tube; lamp shade etc. 424.5.

12. *n.* wick, taper; candle wick, lampwick; fuse, squib [chiefly Min.].

13. *n.* firefly, fire beetle, glowfly, lampfly; glowworm, fireworm; candle fly, lantern fly, will-o'-the-wisp etc. 420.11.

14. *adj.* luminary; illuminated, lighted, lit, alight, ablaze, aglow; gaslit, candlelit, lamplit, lamplighted etc. *n.*; lampful [poetic]; starlit, moonlit, sunlit; self-luminous, self-illuminated; luminous etc. 420.22–24.

424. Shade
(See also 421. Darkness)

1. *n.* shade, shelter, shield, mantle etc. (cover) 223.2–6; shadow etc. 422.3; cloud, mist etc. 353.5; covert etc. (hiding place) 530.2.

2. *n.* sunshade, sun shield; canopy, umbrella, tent, roof etc. (covering) 223.1–6; hat, sun hat, sunbonnet etc. (headdress) 225.26.

3. *n.* screen, curtain, veil, purdah

Girt with tapers' holy shine.—MILTON.   A lamp unto my feet, and a light unto my path.—BIBLE.   Let there be lights in the firmament of the heaven to divide the day from the night.—BIBLE.

424. Close up his eyes and draw the curtain close.—SHAKESPEARE.   Welcome, ye shades! ye bowery thickets, hail!—THOMSON.   The Lord is thy shade upon thy right hand.—BIBLE.

[Ind.]; window curtain, window shade; sash, sash curtain; portiere, *portière* [F.]; blind, Venetian blind *or* shutter, *jalousie* [F.]; shutter, window shutter, windowshut [obs. exc. dial. Eng.]; bamboo shade *or* screen, chick [Anglo-Ind.]; window screen, screen door, screen gate; smoke screen [Mil.]; occulter, occulting screen; concealment etc. 528, 530.

4. *n.* eyeshade, eyeshield, opaque; blinkers, blinds, blinders; goggles, colored spectacles, smoked glasses, sunglasses.

5. *n.* light shield, lamp shade; moonshade; fin, blinker, ear, gobo, nigger [all motion-picture cant]; light filter, diffusing screen; butterfly, silk, gauze [all motion-picture cant]; gelatin filter, jelly [motion-picture cant]; celluloid filter, cello [motion-picture cant]; frosted lens, frost [motion-picture cant].

6. *v.* shade, screen, veil etc. *n.*; draw a curtain, put up *or* close the shutters; cast a shadow etc. (dim) 422.6; darken etc. 421.5.

7. *adj.* shady etc. (shadowy) 422.9.

425. Transparency
(See 426. Opacity; also 427. Semitransparency)

1. *n.* transparency, transparence, transparentness etc. *adj.*, translucence *or* translucency, lucence *or* lucency, lucidity, pellucidity, transpicuity [rare], diaphaneity, hyalescence, clarity, limpidity; crystallinity, vitreosity; fluorescence; translumination, transillumination.

2. *n.* transparent medium, translucent substance, hyaline; water, lymph; crystal, glass; window, windowpane; crystal glass, flint glass; diamond, hyalite, citrine, beryl, chrysolite, moonstone, quartz, rose quartz, chalcedony; diaphane; gossamer, silk, oil silk, chiffon, sheers; lace, lacery; veil, veiling; tissue, tissue paper, oilpaper, Cellophane *or* cellophane [trade name]; onionskin, onionpeel.

3. *v.* be transparent etc. *adj.*; transmit light.

4. *adj.* transparent, translucent, lucid, pellucid, lucent, tralucent [obs.], transpicuous [rare], pervious [rare]; clear, limpid, serene; hyaline, hyaloid [rare];

425. Translucent, flickering wings between the sun and me.—STEVENSON.

hyalescent; hyalinocrystalline [Min.]; crystal, crystalline, crystal-clear, clear as crystal; glassy, glasslike; vitreous, vitreal, vitrean, vitriform; diaphanous, diaphane; sheer, thin; gossamer, gossamery, gossamered.

426. Opacity
(See 425. Transparency)

1. *n.* opacity, opaqueness etc. *adj.*, intransparency, nontransparency, nontranslucency; fuliginosity; nubilation, obnubilation [rare]; obfuscation, obfuscity [rare].

2. *n.* film, cloud etc. 353.5.

3. *v.* opaque, render opaque etc. *adj.*; obfuscate, offuscate [obs.]; becloud etc. (dim) 422.6; darken etc. 421.5.

4. *adj.* opaque, opacous [now rare], intransparent, nontransparent, nontranslucent, adiaphanous, impervious to light; obfuscated, obfuscous; murky, murkish, murksome [rare], murk [now poetic and dial.]; fuliginous, turbid, thick, muddy, dirty; foggy, cloudy, misty; nubilous, nubilose, nubiferous, obnubilous [obs.]; smoky, fumid [obs.]; dark etc. 421.7.

427. Semitransparency
(See 426. Opacity; also 425. Transparency)

1. *n.* semitransparency, semipellucidity, semidiaphaneity; iridescence, opalescence, milkiness, pearliness etc. *adj.*

2. *n.* (comparisons) gauze, muslin, cypress *or* cyprus [Hist.], bombyx; film; mica, mother-of-pearl, nacre; opal glass, opaline; frosted glass, glass bricks; mist etc. (cloud) 353.5.

3. *v.* become opalescent etc. *adj.*, opalesce, opalize; cloud, cloud over; frost, frost over.

4. *adj.* semitransparent, semipellucid, semidiaphanous; semiopaque, semiopacous [obs.]; opalescent, iridescent, opaline, opaloid; pearly, milky; frosty, frosted; nacreous, nacrous, nacry; hazy, misty.

428. Color
(See 429. Colorlessness)

1. *n.* color, hue, tint, tinct [poetic], tincture [poetic], tinge, shade, tone, cast,

426. The opaque substance of his animal being.—HAWTHORNE
428. Mocking the air with colours idly spread.—SHAKESPEARE.   Colors seen by candle-

complexion; blush, flush, glow; dye, stain; half tint, demitint; bright color, loud *or* screaming color [coll.] etc. *adj.*; pure *or* full color, warmth of color; fresh *or* high color; glow; positive color, complimentary color, broken color, local color, undercolor; primary color *or* primary; primitive color, secondary color, tertiary color; chromatic color, achromatic *or* neutral color; hue cycle, color cycle *or* gamut; red, green etc. 430–439; painting etc. (graphic arts) 556.2, 9; variegation etc. 440.

2. *n.* color quality *or* value, colorimetric quality, coloration, coloring, keeping, tincture; tone, key, note; chroma, chromaticity; chromism, chromatism.

3. *n.* coloring matter, color, coloring, colorant, tinction, tincture, pigment, stain; dye, dyestuff; opaque color, transparent color; chromogen; *gouache* [F.]; medium, vehicle; distemper, tempera; yellow ochre, red lead etc. (pigments and dyes) 430–439.

4. *n.* (dyes) basic ~, fast ~, wool fast ~, direct cotton ~, mordant ~, vat *or* developing dye; lake, mineral pigment; natural dye *or* dyestuff, artificial *or* synthetic dye; acid color *or* dye, aniline *or* aniline dye, alizarin, alizarin dye *or* color; sulphoncyanine, naphthol; azo dye; anthracene, crocein, methylene; madder, madder bloom, refined madder, madder extract, *garanceux* [F.] garance, pincoffin.

5. *n.* paint, painting [now rare]; oils, oil paints *or* colors; water colors, dry water colors, moist *or* wet water colors; water glass; lacquer, synthetic lacquer, Chinese lacquer, clear lacquer; lac, shellac; varnish, megilp *or* megilph, japan; copal, copalite, copaline; elemi, animé; enamel, glaze; engobe, calcimine, coat, coating, coat of paint; undercoat, undercoating, priming, primer, prime coat, ground, flat coat, dead-color; wash, wash coat, flat wash; fresco; make-up, cosmetics; drier, thinner; turpentine, turps [coll.]; whitewash etc. 430; zinc white, red ochre etc. (paints and pigments) 430–439.

6. *n.* coloring, painting etc. *v.*; coloration, tinction, pigmentation.

7. *n.* science of colors, colorifics, chromatics, chromatology, chromatography, chromatoscopy; spectrum analysis, spectrology.

8. *n.* (instruments) chromatoscope, chromoscope; chromatometer, chromometer, colorimeter; chromatrope, chromotrope; chromatograph; prism, spectroscope, kaleidoscope.

9. *v.* color, colorize [rare], apply color etc. *n.*, adorn *or* beautify with color; tinge, tint, tinct [poetic], tincture, hue, tone, complexion, stain, dye, pigment; imbue, imbrue; illuminate, emblazon; deep-dye, fast-dye; grain, ingrain; redden, brown etc. 430–440.

10. *v.* paint, sling paint [slang]; coat, cover, face; dab, daub, bedaub, smear, besmear; slick, slick on [both coll.]; slapdash [coll.], slap-dab [slang]; enamel, gloss, glaze; gild, parget; varnish, japan, lacquer, shellac; undercoat, deadcolor, flat, prime; turpentine, turp [slang]; shade, shadow; distemper; stipple; fresco; calcimine; wash; make up, apply cosmetics; whitewash etc. 430.7; limn, depict etc. (represent) 554.7; decorate etc. (ornament) 847.11.

11. *v.* be unharmonious etc. *adj.*, clash, collide [coll.], swear at [slang]; be too prominent, cut [Art].

12. *adj.* colorific, colorative, tinctorial, tingent [obs.]; colorable, tingible; chromatic, prismatic, polychromatic; chromatogenous; chromatophoric, chromatophorous.

13. *adj.* colored, tinted etc. *v.*; tinct [poetic], hued; complexioned, complected [dial., U.S.]; full, full-colored; deep, deep-colored, deep-dyed, of the deepest color *or* hue; double-dyed, fast-dyed; ingrain; wash-colored; slapdash [coll.], slap-dab [slang].

14. *adj.* colorful, colory [coll.]; bright, vivid, intense, rich, gorgeous, gay; bright-colored, rich-colored, gay-colored, high-colored; many-colored, parti-colored etc. (variegated) 440.5.

15. *adj.* gaudy, florid, garish, showy, flaunting, flashy, ostentatious, loud

---

light / Will not look the same by day.—E. B. BROWNING. Like flame, like wine . . . / The colors of the sunset stream.—W. R. BENÉT. We weave with colors all our own.—WHITTIER. They have many pleasant colours and lustres /
To recommend them.—A. LOWELL. Thy woods, this autumn day, that ache and sag / And all but cry with color.—MILLAY. Every gaudy color / Is a bit of truth.—N. CRANE.

[coll.], screaming [coll.], glaring, flaring; raw, crude.

16. *adj.* inharmonious, discordant, incongruous, clashing, colliding [coll.]; off-color, off-tone.

17. *adj.* soft-colored, soft, softened, subdued, mellow, delicate, tender, sweet, pearly.

18. *adj.* harmonious, congruous, consonant, accordant, pleasing.

19. *adj.* dull, dull-colored; sad, sad-colored, sober, somber, grave, gloomy, dismal, dreary, drab, dead, deadened, lifeless, leaden, flat; plain, plain-colored; **dark etc. 421.7; gray etc. 432.4.**

429. Colorlessness
(See 428. Color)

1. *n.* colorlessness, achromatism, achromaticity; paleness etc. *adj.*, pallor, pallidity; etiolation; achroma, achromasia [both Med.]; anemia [Med.]; neutral tint, monochrome, black and white; achroite, achroacyte, achroglobin, achromacyte; dimness etc. 422.

2. *n.* decoloration, decolorization, achromatization; discoloration, discolorization, discolorment, bleaching, fading etc. *v.,* etiolation; whitening etc. 430.2.

3. *n.* decolorant, decolorizer; bleach, bleacher; bleaching powder, bleaching clay *or* earth, bleach liquor, *eau de Javelle* [F.], Javelle water, chlorine, chlorine water, peroxide, sulphuric acid, hydrochloric acid, lime, gray sour.

4. *v.* lose color etc. (*see* color etc. 428), become colorless etc. *adj.,* fade, fade out, pale, turn pale, bleach, bleach out, whiten, wan, vanish, fly, go.

5. *v.* deprive of color, decolor, decolorize; discolor, discolorate; etiolate, etiolize [rare]; achromatize, whiten, fade, pale, wash out, tone down, dim, dull, tarnish; blanch, bleach, peroxide.

6. *adj.* colorless, hueless etc. (*see* color, hue etc. 428.1); uncolored etc. (*see* colored etc. 428.13) decolorate; etiolated, washed-out etc. *v.*; achromatic, achromatinic, achromic [Med.]; dim, weak, faint, pale, pallid, wan, sallow; pale as death, ~ ashes, ~ witch, ~ a ghost, ~ a corpse etc., "pale as his shirt" (Shakespeare); anemic, bloodless; pale-faced, tallow-faced; lurid, ghastly, cadaverous, haggard, sickly; ashy, ashen; dull, dead, lifeless, drab, cold, leaden, glassy; lackluster, lacklustrous.

7. *adj.* light-colored, light-hued, light, fair; blond, towheaded etc. (whitish) 430.9; gray etc. 432.4.

430. Whiteness
(See 431. Blackness)

1. *n.* whiteness, whitishness etc. *adj.*; albescence; white, silver etc. *adj.*; hoariness, canescence; milkiness, lactescence; albinism, albinoism; leucoderma *or* leucodermia [Med.], leucopathy.

2. *n.* whitening etc. *v.*; albification, albication, dealbation; etiolation; etiolization [rare]; bleaching etc. (decoloration) 429.2.

3. *n.* (comparisons) snow, driven snow; sheet, paper, milk, fleece, lily, ivory; marble, alabaster; flour; moon; chalk, creta; silver, albata, German silver, white metal, pewter, britannia, platinum; eburine, eburite; white man, Caucasian, Caucasian race, Xanthochroi; paleface; white trash, buckra [dial., U.S.]; bright skin, fay, kelt, pink, whitie [all slang or dial.].

4. *n.* (paints and pigments) white lead, *blanc d'argent* [F.], carbonate of lead, Paris white, zinc white, zinc oxide, zinc sulphide, flake white, Chinese white, Dutch white, pearl white; permanent white, blanc fixe, baryta white, barium sulphate; *blanc de fard* [F.] blanc d'Espagne; indigo white.

5. *n.* whitewash, whiting, whitening, calcimine.

6. *v.* whiten, white, render *or* become white etc. *adj.,* white out [printing]; albify [rare], dealbate [rare]; etiolate, etiolize [rare]; bleach, blanch; grizzle, besnow, frost, silver.

7. *v.* whitewash, white, calcimine; gloze, gloss, gloss over [all fig.].

8. *adj.* white, pure white; shining white, pure shining white, bright, shin-

---

429. Pallor that lovers ever prize.—CLAUDIAN. Of ashy semblance, meager, pale, and bloodless. —SHAKESPEARE. Why so pale and wan, fond lover? / Prithee, why so pale?—SUCKLING. The pale ports o' the moon.—F. THOMPSON.

430. Everye white will have its blacke.—T. PERCY. The white radiance of eternity.— SHELLEY. Whiter than new snow on a raven's back.—SHAKESPEARE. Whited sepulchers, which indeed appear beautiful outward. —BIBLE.

ing; snow-white, snowy, white as snow, "white as driven snow" (Shakespeare), niveous; candent, candid [arch.]; frosty, frosted; hoar, hoary; grizzled, grizzly, canescent; silver, silvery; argent, argenteous, argentine; chalky, cretaceous; lint-white, milk-white etc. *n.*, milky, lactescent; marmoreal, marmorean; albificative, albicant, albescent, albinistic; white as a sheet, ~ chalk etc. *n.*, like snow etc. *n.*; lily-white, white as a lily, "white as the whitest lily on a stream" (Longfellow).

9. *adj.* whitish, whity, light, fair, high in tone; cream, creamy; pearl, pearly, pearl-white; ivory, ivory-white, like ivory etc. *n.*; gray-white, dun-white; blond *or* blonde, ash-blond, platinum blond; artificial blond, peroxide blond, drugstore blond [joc.]; blond-headed, blond-haired; towheaded, tow-haired; light-colored etc. 429.7; ashen, cinereal etc. (gray) 432.4.

431. Blackness
(See 430. Whiteness)

1. *n.* blackness, darkness etc. *adj.*, dark color *or* tone; black, sable etc. *adj.*; nigritude, nigrescence; nigrities [Med.]; swarth, swarthiness, swartness; lividness, lividity; Black Monday, Black Friday.

2. *n.* blackening, darkening etc. *v.*; nigrification [rare], denigration, infuscation [rare].

3. *n.* (comparisons) jet, ink, sloe, pitch, coal, tar, charcoal; smoke, soot; smut, smutch, smudge, smirch; ebony, ebon [now poetic]; devil, smith; raven, crow; night; ace of spades.

4. *n.* Negro (person), nigger [coll. and derog.], colored person, black, blackamoor; dingy [dial. and derog., U.S.]; darky, blacky, Sambo, Quashee *or* quashee, Quashie *or* quashie, ebony [all derog.]; "the image of God . . . cut in ebony" (Fuller); coon, crow, Jim Crow, shine, dinge, jig, jigaboo, moke [all derog., U.S.]; colored man, man of color; buck, buck Negro *or* nigger [all derog., chiefly U.S.]; uncle [derog., South. U.S.]; colored woman; Negress, wench [both derog., local, U.S.]; mammy, auntie [both derog., South. U.S.]; pickaninny, nigger baby, niggerling [all derog.].

Afric, African; Ethiopian, Ethiop *or* Ethiope, "swarthy Ethiope" (Shakespeare); Negroid, Mandingo, Senegambian, Sudanese, Papuan, Bushman, Melanesian, Hottentot; Pygmy, Negrillo, Negrito; blackfellow; Geechee, Gullah [both South. U.S.]; sambo, zambo; Afro-American, Afro-European, Afro-Asiatic; mulatto etc. (mongrel, crossbreed) 41.5.

5. *n.* (pigments and dyes) lampblack, ivory black, blue black, ink black; Brunswick black, japan; black ink, writing ink, printing *or* printer's ink, India *or* Indian ink, China *or* Chinese ink; soot, soot black; nigrosine; blackface, blackface make-up; alizarin cyanine, aniline black, anthracite black, cachou de Laval, diphenyl black, direct deep black, immedial black, naphthol black, naphthylamine black, sulphur black.

6. *v.* blacken, black, render black etc. *adj.*, infuscate [rare]; denigrate, nigrify; negroize; darken, bedarken, dark [arch.]; somber, murk; shade, shadow; blot, blotch, smut, smudge, smutch, smirch; soot, smoke.

7. *adj.* black, sable, dhu; Negro *or* negro, Negroid; nigrous, nigrine, nigricant, Negritic, nigritudinous; ebony, "black as ebony" (Shakespeare); deep black, of the deepest dye; pitch-black, pitch-dark, pitchy, black *or* dark as pitch; night-black, night-dark, black *or* dark as night, black as midnight; inky, inky-black, ink-black, black as ink; jetty, jet-black; coaly, coal-black, black as coal; sloe-black, sloe-colored; raven, raven-black, black as my hat, ~ a shoe, ~ a tinker's pot, ~ November; black as the ace of spades, ~ a Negro etc. *n.*, "black as hell" (Shakespeare); black-and-blue, livid.

432. Grayness

1. *n.* grayness, grayishness etc. *adj.*, gray color *or* tone, neutral tint *or* shade;

---

431. Black as the Pit from pole to pole.—W. E. HENLEY.   More black than ash-buds in the front of March.—TENNYSON.   I am black, but O my soul is white!—W. BLAKE.   Cyprus black as e'er was crow.—SHAKESPEARE.

432. From the winter's gray despair.—W. E. HENLEY.   'Tis gone and all is gray.—BYRON. All cats are grey in the dark.

gray, silver etc. *adj.*; field gray, dove gray *or* color; crystal *or* cinder gray, cadet gray, French gray; Quaker gray, Quaker drab, acier; pepper and salt; grisaille [Art].

2. *n.* (pigments and dyes) Payne's gray, zinc gray, gray induline; diaminogen; black etc. 431.

3. *v.* gray *or* grey, render *or* become gray, grizzle, silver, dapple.

4. *adj.* gray *or* grey, grayish, gray-colored, gray-toned, gray-hued, gray-tinted; dun, drab, dingy, dull, leaden, livid; somber, sober, sad, dreary; cool, cold; iron-gray, steel-gray, French-gray; Quaker-gray, Quaker-drab, quaker-colored; dove-gray, dove-colored; pearl-gray, pearl, pearly; silver-gray, silver, silvery, silvered; grizzly, grizzled; ash-colored, ashen, ashy, favillous [rare]; cinerous, cineritious, cinereal; limy, calcareous; dapple-gray, dappled-gray, dappled; gray-spotted, gray-speckled; gray-white, gray-black, gray-blue, gray-brown, gray-green etc.; slate-colored, stone-colored, mouse-gray *or* mouse-colored; whitish etc. 430.9; light-colored etc. 429.7.

433. Brownness

1. *n.* brownness, brownishness etc. *adj.*, brown color *or* tone; brown, cinnamon etc. *adj.*; tan, tenné, tawny, adust; sun tan, Merida; Vandyke brown, Cologne brown, Verona brown; otter brown, pickaninny; *feuille-morte* [F.], autumn leaf, dead leaf, philamot, foliage brown; mummy brown, snuff color; cocoa, cocoa brown, sienna brown; burnt almond, coconut brown; coffee, coffee brown; acorn, meadow lark; madder brown, brown madder; Mars brown, Argos brown; Castilian brown, old cedar, Tanagra; alesan, café au lait, café noir, French nude.

2. *n.* (pigments and dyes) bister, brown ocher, mummy, sepia, Vandyke brown; umber, terra umbra, burnt *or* calcined umber, raw umber, Cyprus earth *or* umber, partridge, Roman umber, Sicilian umber, Turkey umber; sienna, burnt sienna, raw sienna, terra sienna; acid brown, aurin, azoflavine, Bismarck brown, Bordeaux, chrysamine, direct brown, Manchester brown, resorcin brown, sulphoncyanine.

3. *v.* brown, embrown, render *or* become brown etc. *adj.*; tan, bronze; suntan, sunburn.

4. *adj.* brown, brownish; cinnamon, hazel, puce, ecru, fuscous, brunet *or* brunette; tan, adust [rare], tawny; tan-faced, tan-skinned, sun-tanned; khaki, khaki-colored; musteline, musteloid; chocolate, chocolate-colored, chocolate-brown; cocoa, cocoa-colored, cocoa-brown; coffee, coffee-colored, coffee-brown; toast-brown, nut-brown, mahogany-brown, seal-brown; yellowish-brown, brownish-yellow; reddish-brown etc. *below*; fawn, fawn-colored; snuff-colored, mummy-brown; umber, umber-colored, umber-brown; olive, olive-brown; brown as a berry, ∼ mahogany, ∼ oak leaves, ∼ coffee etc.

5. *adj.* reddish-brown, brownish-red; sepia, roan, sorrel, henna, mahogany, terra-cotta, rufous, foxy; livid-brown, lurid; auburn, titian *or* Titian; russet, russety, russetish; rust, rust-colored, rusty, rust-red; ferruginous, ferrugineous [rare], ferruginean [now rare]; rubiginous, rubiginose; liver-brown, liver-colored; bronze, bronze-colored, bronzed; coppery, copperish, copper-colored; chestnut, chestnut-colored, chestnut-brown, castaneous; bay, bay-colored, bayard; sunburned *or* sunburnt.

434. Redness

1. *n.* redness, reddishness etc. *adj.*, rubescence, erubescence, rubicundity, rubricity; ruddiness, rud [obs. exc. dial.], color.

2. *n.* red, rouge [rare], rubelle, gules [Her.], scarlet, vermilion, crimson, maroon, magenta, ruby, damask, stammel, murrey, cerise, tile red, Pompeian red, hellebore red, Vandyke red; cardinal, cardinal red; carnation, carnation red; Turkey red, Adrianople red; Indian red, Persian red, Persian earth, iron red, Chinese red, Japanese red, Majolica

---

433. Know then, that I consider brown for ladies' eyes, the only color.—C. Morley. How bronze the gold grows in the chestnut wood!—Van de Woestyne.

434. The red, red grass a thousand miles.—W. Cather. Red for valor.—C. Sumner. Red as a rose is she.—Coleridge. Oh, my

earth, Naples red, Prussian red, scarlet ocher.

carminette, carmine, lake, carmine lake; burnt lake, burnt crimson lake, burnt carmine; madder carmine, madder red; madder scarlet, scarlet madder; madder crimson, crimson madder; solferino, solferino red; chrome red, chrome scarlet; poppy red, coquelicot; cherry, cherry red; copper, copper red, carnelian.

3. *n.* pink, cameo pink, mallow pink, opera pink, livid pink; rose, *couleur de rose* [F.]; carnation rose, tea rose, primrose, chrome primrose; burnt rose, Pompeii; rose madder, madder lake *or* pink; flesh, flesh color *or* tint, flesh red *or* pink, incarnadine, moonlight; Dutch pink, English pink, Italian pink, madder yellow, yellow madder, stil-de-grain yellow; salmon, salmon pink, annatto; apricot, peach.

4. *n.* reddening etc. *v.*, rubefaction, rubification, rubrication, rubescence, erubescence; blush, flush, glow, bloom; hectic, hectic flush *or* fever.

5. *n.* (comparisons) garnet, ruby, ruby spinel, bloodstone, jasper, fire opal, carbuncle, carnelian, sardonyx, morganite, kunzite; rose opal, rose quartz, rose topaz, rose tourmaline; rust, iron mold; rose, primrose, cardinal flower, lobelia, carnation; cherry, cranberry; apricot, peach; cardinal, cardinal bird, cardinal grosbeak, redbreast, redstart; lobster, turkey cock; Indian, redskin; Injun, buck, chief, Sitting Bull [all slang]; Algonquin, Algonquian, Athapascan, Athabasca, Chipewyan, Yellowknife, Copper Indian, Ojibway, Iroquois, Iroquoian, Mohawk, Oneida, Onondaga, Cayuga, Seneca, Mahican, Mohican, Creek, Choctaw, Chickasaw, Seminole, Sioux, Dakota, Hopi, Pueblo Indian, Araucanian, Arawak, Inca, Maya, Mayan, Aztec.

6. *n.* (red pigments and dyes) redding, cinnabar, cochineal, stammel, fuchsin *or* fuchsine, vermilion, vermilionette, madder, alizarin *or* alizarine, rubiate, annatto, realgar, minium, red lead, Vandyke red, palladium red, light red, red pink; red ocher, terra rosa, ruddle, rud [chiefly dial., Eng.]; rubine *or* rubin, Congo rubine; Venetian red, Siena; In-

---

luve is like a red, red rose.—BURNS. And Marian's nose looks red and raw.—SHAKESPEARE.

dian red, Persian red; amidonaphthol red, azogrenadine, cresol red, ponceau, roccellin, rose bengale, toluidine red; rouge, lip rouge, lipstick.

7. *v.* redden, red [arch. and dial.], render red etc. *adj.,* rouge, ruddy [rare], ruddle, rud [obs. exc. dial]; rubify [rare], rubricate, rubricize; crimson, encrimson [rare]; vermilion, scarlet [rare]; incarnadine, pinkify, pinken [rare]; red-ink; lipstick; rust; carmine, madder etc. *n.*; bloodstain etc. (discolor) 440a.2.

8. *v.* become red etc. *adj.,* redden, blush, flush, color, color up, mantle, glow.

9. *adj.* red, scarlet etc. *n.*; red-colored, red-hued, red-dyed, red-looking; reddish, reddish-colored; ruddy, ruddied; ruby-colored, ruby-red, rubiate, rubineous, rubious [rare], rubric(al), rubricate, rubricose, rubicund; rufous, rufulous.

sanguine, sanguineous, bloody, bloody-red, blood-red, blood-colored, red as blood, gory; wine-colored, wine-red, claret-colored, vinaceous; cherry-colored, cherry-red; fiery, flaming, flame-colored, flame-red, fire-red, red as fire, red as a hot *or* live coal; warm, hot, glowing; brick-colored, brick-red, bricky, lateritious; carmine, incarmined; lake-colored, laky; red as a lobster, ~ a turkey cock etc. *n.*; reddish-amber, reddish-gray etc.; reddish-brown etc. 433.5; bloodstained etc. (discolored) 440a.3.

10. *adj.* pink, pink-colored, pinkish, pinky; incarnadine, rose etc. *n.*; rosy, rose-colored, rose-hued, rose-red, roseate; flesh-color *or* flesh-colored, flesh-tinted, flesh-pink; coral, coral-colored, coralline, coral-red; salmon, salmon-colored, salmon-pink; peach-colored, apricot-colored.

11. *adj.* red-complexioned, ruddy-complexioned, warm-complexioned, red-fleshed, red-faced, red, florid, rubicund, ruddy, sanguine, glowing, blooming, rosy, hectic, flushed, inflamed; blushing, reddened etc. *v.*; blowzed, blowzy; burnt, sunburned *or* sunburnt.

12. *adj.* redheaded, red-haired, red-crested, red-crowned, red-polled, red-tufted; sandy, carroty, brick-red, chestnut, auburn; Titian *or* titian, Titian-red.

13. *adj.* reddening etc. *v.*, rubescent, erubescent, rubificative, rubrific.

435. Greenness

1. *n.* greenness, greenishness etc. *adj.,* greenhood, green color *or* tone, verdancy, verdure, viridescence, viridity.

2. *n.* green, verte [Her.], blue and yellow; chrysolite green, apple green, chrysoprase green, variscite green, turquoise green, duck green, Egyptian green, beryl green, glaucous green, grass green, leek green, serpentine green, cobalt green, zinc green, yew green, pea green, cucumber green, leaf green, Brunswick green, mignonette, celadon, corbeau, bice; chrome *or* chromium green, milori green, viridine green, viridian, emeraude, Veronese green; emerald, emerald green, Mitis green, Schweinfurt green, Vienna green; terre-verte, *terra verde* [It.].

moss, moss green; myrtle, myrtle green; fir, fir green; olive, olive green; shamrock, shamrock green, Irish green, Kelly green; bottle green, meadow brook; Nile, Nile green; aquagreen, sea *or* sea-water green, marine green; aquamarine *or* aqua marina; reseda; Guignet's green, Mittler's green; verdigris, verdigris green, verdet, verditer green; Montpellier green, Spanish green.

3. *n.* (comparisons) grass, clover, shamrock, moss, myrtle; emerald, malachite, chrysoprase, demantoid, peridot, jasper, chrysolite, olivine, beryl; verd antique, *verde antico* [It.] verdigris, aquamarine; reseda, mignonette, absinthe, crème de menthe.

4. *n.* (pigments and dyes) Brunswick green, viridian, bice, verditer, glauconite, green ocher, malachite green, sap green, zinc green, cobalt green; Paris green, emerald green, Guignet's green; terre-verte, *terra verde* [It.]; celadon, celadonite; chrome *or* chromium green, chrome oxide green, transparent chromium oxide, chromic oxide; acid fuchsine, benzoyl green, chrysoidine, gallein, galloflavine, Guinea green, Janus green, methyl green, phenosafranine.

5. *v.* green, render *or* become green etc. *adj.,* verdigris [rare].

6. *adj.* green, verdant, verdurous; greenish, virent [rare], virescent, viridescent [rare], verdigrisy; grass-green, grass-colored, green as grass; chlorine, chlorochrous; citrine, citrinous; olive, olive-green, olivaceous; beryl-green, berylline; leek-green, porraceous; emerald, emerald-green, smaragdine; blue-green, bluish-green, greenish-blue; yellow-green, yellowish-green, greenish-yellow; glaucous, glaucous-green; apple-green, pea-green etc. *n.*

436. Yellowness

1. *n.* yellowness, yellowishness etc. *adj., yellow etc. adj.,* yellow color *or* tone, or [Her.]; jonquil yellow, citron yellow, sulphur yellow, cadmium yellow, pyrethrum yellow, golden pheasant; chrome, chrome yellow; lemon chrome, chrome lemon; madder yellow, yellow madder, stil-de-grain yellow; lemon yellow, golden yellow etc. *adj.*

2. *n.* (medical) xanthochroia, xanthosis, xanthoderma, xanthocyanopia *or* xanthocyanopsia, xanthochromia; jaundice, yellow jaundice, icterus.

3. *n.* (comparisons) crocus, saffron, jonquil, buttercup, dandelion, goldflower, goldenrod, primrose; flax, straw; sand, sulphur, canary; lemon, citron, apricot, peach, quince; topaz; gold, gilt, gilding; gold piece, guinea; butter, yolk; London fog; Chinese, Japanese etc. 188.9; yellow race, yellow peril.

4. *n.* (pigments and dyes) gamboge, justic, massicot, cadmium yellow, yellow ocher, Claude tint, aureolin; chrome, chrome yellow; Paris yellow, Cassel yellow; Indian yellow, euxanthin, purree; king's yellow, orpiment; lemon yellow, barium chrome *or* chromate, barium yellow, baryta yellow, permanent yellow; xanthin, xanthein, xanthophyll; acid yellow; auramine, aurin, butter yellow, canarin, chrysophenin, fast yellow, immedial yellow, metanil yellow, mikado yellow, naphthol yellow, phosphine, tartrazine.

5. *v.* yellow, render *or* become yellow etc. *adj.*; gild, begild, engild, golden [rare], deaurate [now rare]; jaundice; chrome etc. *n.*

6. *adj.* yellow, yellowish; aureate, gold, gold-colored, golden, golden-yellow, gilt, gilded; canary, canary-yellow; cit-

---

435. Everything I look on seemeth green.— SHAKESPEARE.   He maketh me to lie down in green pastures.—BIBLE.

436. The golden apples of the sun.—YEATS. The yellow shine of daffodils.—L. ABERCROMBIE. Come unto these yellow sands.—SHAKESPEARE.

ron; citron-colored, citron-yellow, citrine, citreous; lemon, lemon-colored, lemon-yellow; sulphur-colored, sulphur-hued, sulphur-tinted, sulphur-yellow; pale, pale-yellow, fallow, sallow; lutescent, luteous, luteolous; fulvous, fulvescent, fulvid [rare].

tawny or tawney, tenné; cream, cream-colored, creamy; sand-colored, sandy; ocherous or ochreous, ochery or ochry; flaxen, flaxen-colored, flax-colored; straw, straw-colored; buff, buff-colored, buff-yellow; beige, ecru; saffron, saffron-colored, saffron-hued, saffron-yellow; apricot, apricot-colored; peach, peach-colored; xanthic, xanthous; xanthochroid; yellow-faced, yellow-complexioned, yellow-cheeked; jaundiced, icterine, icterous or icterious, icteroid; golden-haired, flaxen-haired, blond or blonde, auricomous; xanthocarpous, xanthopous [Bot.; rare]; yellow as saffron, ∼ a quince etc. *n.*, yellow as a crow's foot.

437. Purpleness

1. *n.* purpleness, purplishness etc. *adj.*, purple etc. *adj.*, purple color *or* tone, purpure [Her.], blue and red; bishop's purple, gridelin, amethyst, damson, heliotrope, mallow, mallow purple, pansy violet, madder violet, Mars violet, fluorite violet, plum, raisin, raisin black, Burgundy, livid purple *or* violet.

2. *n.* lividness, lividity.

3. *v.* purple, empurple, render purple etc. *adj.*

4. *adj.* purple, purpie [Scot.], purple-colored; purplish, purplescent, purpurate [arch.]; lavender, lavender-blue, lilac, violet, violaceous, magenta, mulberry, puce, mauve, hyacinthine, amethystine, solferino; plum-colored, raisin-colored; livid.

438. Blueness

1. *n.* blueness, bluishness etc. *adj.*, blue color *or* tone; bloom.

2. *n.* blue; calamine blue, Persian blue, lavender blue, *émail, bleu Louise* [both F.]; Italian blue, Dresden blue, wisteria blue, hyacinth, dahlia, jouvence blue, madder blue, peacock blue, sea blue, French blue, midnight blue, cadet blue, robin's-egg blue, baby blue, watchet [arch.]; azure, azure blue; cerulean, cerulean blue; sky, sky blue, sky color; *bleu de Lyon* [F.], national blue; navy, navy blue, marine, marine blue.

bice, bice blue, azurite blue; ultramarine, ultramarine blue; cyan, cyan blue; cyanine blue, Leitch's blue; aquamarine *or* aqua marina; electric, electric blue; steel, steel blue; sapphire, sapphire blue; beryl, beryl blue; Prussian blue; milori blue, Brunswick blue; turquoise, turquoise blue, blue turquoise; old blue, *bleu passé* [F.].

3. *n.* (comparisons) lapis lazuli, azure stone, lazulite; sapphire, beryl, turquoise, aquamarine, indicolite; sky, blue eyes, sea; wisteria, hyacinth, cornflower, dahlia, bluebell, blue myrtle, lavender, blue daisy; bluegrass, blue-eyed grass; bluebird, blue jay, blue goose, bluebreast.

4. *n.* (pigments and dyes) bluing, ultramarine, smalt, *bleu d'azur, bleu de Saxe* [both F.], bice, cobalt, cyanogen, cyanin *or* cyanine, leucocyan, azure, indigo, zaffer, Brunswick blue, Prussian blue, French blue, new blue, syenite blue; ceruleum, *bleu céleste* [F.]; aniline blue, azo blue, benzoazurine, bleu lumière, ciba blue, direct *or* trypan blue, Indanthrene *or* indanthrene blue, isamine blue, lacmoid, methyl *or* methylene blue, water blue.

5. *v.* blue, render blue etc. *adj.*, azure etc. *n.*

6. *adj.* blue, blue-colored; navy-blue, sky-blue etc. *n.*; sky-colored, sky-dyed; cerulean, ceruleous; cyanic, cyaneous, cyanean; azure, azurine, azurean, azurous, azured, azure-blue, azure-colored, azure-tinted; atmospheric (al); garter-blue; peacock-blue, pavonine, pavonian; beryl-blue, berylline; bluish, azury, cerulescent; light-blue, lightish-blue, light-bluish, pale-blue, watchet [arch.]; retiring; cool, cold; black-and-blue, livid.

439. Orange

1. *n.* orange, orange color *or* tone, red and yellow, tangerine; burnt orange, Mars orange; henna; old gold; chrome orange, orange chrome yellow; cadmium

---

437. I never saw a purple cow.—G. Burgess. His cohorts were gleaming in purple and gold.—Byron.
438. Blue color is everlastingly appointed by the Deity to be a source of delight.—Ruskin. Blue, darkly, deeply, beautifully blue.—Southey.

orange, cadmium yellow, **marigold yellow**; orange madder, madder orange; orange vermilion.

2. *n.* (comparisons) orange, tangerine, mandarin, apricot; orangeberry, orange creeper, orange daisy, orange lily, orange hawkweed, marigold; orangebird, orange-crowned warbler.

3. *n.* (pigments and dyes) ocher; orange ocher, burnt Roman ocher, Spanish ocher, Tangier; cadmium, cadmium orange, cadmium yellow; helianthin, methyl orange; orange lead, orange mineral *or* minium; chrome orange, orange chrome yellow; zinc orange; henna; orange shellac.

4. *v.* render orange etc. *adj.,* warm; gild etc. 436.5.

5. *adj.* orange etc. *n.,* orangey [coll.], orange-colored, orange-hued, reddish-yellow; ocherous *or* ochreous, ochery *or* ochry; gold-colored, old-gold etc. *n.*; apricot, apricot-colored; brass-colored, brass, brassy; warm, hot, glowing; flame-colored, flaming; orange-red, orange-yellow, reddish-orange, yellowish-orange.

440. Variegation

1. *n.* variegation, motley, multicolor, parti-color *or* party-color, polychrome; dichroism, trichroism; iridescence *or* iridescency, iridization, irisation; play of colors; maculation, spottiness; striation, striature, striae; mixture etc. 41.4.

2. *n.* (comparisons) spectrum, rainbow, iris, tulip, peacock, chameleon, butterfly, zebra, leopard, jaguar, panther, cheetah, ocelot, ophite, nacre, mother-of-pearl, tortoise shell, opal, cymophane, marble, mackerel, mackerel sky, harlequin, plaid, Joseph's coat; tricolor.

3. *n.* check, plaid, tartan, patchwork; marquetry, parquet, parquetry, mosaic, tesserae, tessellation, checkerwork; chessboard, checkerboard, checkers.

4. *v.* variegate, vary, diversify; polychrome, polychromize; stripe, streak, striate; iris, iridize, iridesce; check, checker; fleck, speck, speckle, bespeckle; sprinkle, besprinkle; mottle, stipple, dap-

ple, spot, bespot, maculate; tattoo, stigmatize; inlay, tessellate; damascene; embroider, braid, quilt; marble, marbelize; mix etc. 41.6.

5. *adj.* variegated, divers-colored, many-colored, many-hued; multicolor, multicolored, multicolorous; versicolor, versicolored, versicolorate, versicolorous; parti-color *or* party-color, parti-colored *or* party-colored; colorful, colory [coll.]; of all manner of colors, of all the colors of the rainbow, daedal, kaleidoscopic(al); polychrome, polychromic, polychromatic; dichromic, dichromatic; trichromic, trichromatic; bicolor, bicolored; tricolor, tricolored; nevoid; mixed etc. 41.9.

6. *adj.* iridescent, iridal, iridial, iridian, iridine [rare]; irised, irisated; opalescent, opaline, opaloid; pearly, pearlish; tortoise-shell; prismatic(al), prismal; nacreous, nacrous, nacry; shot; pavonine, pavonian; chatoyant; chameleonic, chameleonlike.

7. *adj.* mottled, motley; pied, piebald, skewbald, pinto; dapple, dappled; marbled, pepper-and-salt, paned, clouded, cymophanous.

8. *adj.* checkered, mosaic, tessellated, plaid.

9. *adj.* spotted, spotty; blotched, blotchy; punctate, punctated; specked, speckled, speckledy, speckly, specky; flecker, fleckered; maculate, maculated, maculose, maculiferous, macular; freckled, freckly; flea-bitten; studded; discolored etc. 440a.3.

10. *adj.* striate, striated, striatal, strial [rare]; streaked, streaky; barred, veined; brinded, brindle, brindled; tabby; watered; strigose, strigillose, strigate, striolate; listed.

440a. Discoloration

1. *n.* discoloration, discolorization, discolorment, discolor; maculation, macule, macula; taint, tainture [obs.]; spot, stain, blemish etc. *v.*; stigma (*pl* stig-

---

440. Glory be to God for dappled things— / For skies as couple-coloured as a brindled cow. —G. M. HOPKINS. Iris all hues, roses and jessamin.—MILTON. I do set my bow in the cloud, and it shall be for a token of a covenant between me and the earth.—BIBLE. To paint the rainbow's varying hues.—SCOTT. My heart leaps up when I behold / A rainbow in the sky.—WORDSWORTH. Motley's the only wear.—SHAKESPEARE. They stripped Joseph out of his coat, his coat of many colors.—BIBLE.
440a. One mask of brooses both blue and green. —DICKENS. The birth marks / Of the but-

mata, stigmas), stigmatism; freckle, lentigo, mole; birthmark, nevus; bruise, black-and-blue mark; black eye, mouse [slang], shanty [slang, U.S.]; anemia etc. (colorlessness) 429.1; jaundice, xanthosis [Med.] etc. (yellowness) 436.2; mark etc. 550.7.

2. *v.* discolor, discolorate [rare], stain, distain [arch.], tinge, taint, attaint, maculate, soil, defile, sully, grime, begrime, dinge [coll. and dial. Eng.], murk [now rare], tarnish, dim, slubber [now chiefly dial.], stigmatize, blemish, mar, deface, blot, blotch, smudge, smut, smutch, smirch, besmirch, smear, besmear, blur, slur [now chiefly dial.], slurry [obs. exc. dial. Eng.]; spot, bespot, speck, speckle, bespeckle, spatter, bespatter; smoke, soot; bloodstain, blood [arch.], bloody, ensanguine; bruise, batter, dinge [chiefly Eng.], give a black eye; blacken etc. 431.6; scorch, blister etc. (burn) 384.18; fade etc. (decolor) 429.5; mark etc. 550.19.

3. *adj.* discolored etc. *v.*, discolorate [rare]; maculate, maculated, macular, maculose, maculiferous; blotchy, blurred, blurry, dingy, grimy, smudgy, smutty, smutchy; smoky, sooty; murky, murkish, murksome [rare]; stigmatic(al), stigmatal, stigmal, stigmatiferous; livid, black-and-blue; spotted, blotched etc. 440.9; jaundiced, icterine etc. (yellow) 436.6; bloodstained, gory etc. 361.15.

441. Vision

(See 442. Blindness, 443. Defective Vision; also 445. Optical Instruments)

1. *n.* vision, seeing etc. *v.*, visual sense, sight, eyesight, eye, light [poetic], speculation [arch.], conspectuity [obs.]; perception, discernment, ken; perspicacity, perspicuity [erron.]; acute sight, sharp *or* quick sight; clear sight, unobstructed vision; far-sight, farsightedness; optics etc. 445.7; television etc. 532a.

2. *n.* look, sight, see [rare], looksee [slang, U.S.], eye, view, regard, aspect [now rare], espial; observance, observation; glance, glance of the eye, glimpse, glint [Scot. and dial.], eyeshot, peep, peek, flash [slang], glim [Scot. and slang U.S.], slant [coll.], half an eye, quick *or* cursory look, cast, quick cast of the eyes, coup d'œil, flicker *or* twinkle of an eye.

gaze, stare; glare, glower, glaring *or* glowering look, scowling *or* lowering look; sidelong look, glime [dial.]; leer, leering look; sly look *or* glance; scrutiny, survey, inspection, ocular inspection *or* examination, conspection [obs.], examination, perlustration, contemplation, speculation; once-over, double-O [both slang, U.S.]; reconnoissance, reconnaissance; espionage; watch, lookout; look-through, look-in; introspection; autopsy; sharp ~, piercing *or* penetrating look *or* glance; eyeful [coll., U.S.].

3. *n.* sight-seeing, rubberneck tour [slang, U.S.], excursion, globe-trotting [coll.].

4. *n.* viewpoint, standpoint, point of view; angle, light etc. (aspect) 448.4.

5. *n.* observatory, observation post, post of observation; lookout, watchtower, tower, beacon, pharos, lighthouse; belvedere, gazebo, crow's-nest [Naut.]; peephole, sighthole, loophole; ringside, ringside seat; grandstand, bleachers [U.S.], gallery, top gallery; nigger heaven, paradise, peanut gallery [all slang].

6. *n.* field of view *or* observation, field of vision *or* regard [Psychol.], range of vision *or* sight, visibility, eyereach, eyesight, eyeshot, sight-shot [rare], ken; sight, vista, view, horizon, prospect, perspective, outlook; theater, amphitheater, arena; bird's-eye view, panoramic view.

7. *n.* eye, oculus (*pl.* oculi), ocular [joc.], optic [now usu. joc.], orb [poetic], peeper [coll.]; window [rare or poetic], mince pie [Austral. and U.S. underworld slang], winker [coll.]; blinker, glim, lamp, ogle, goggle [all slang]; visual organ, organ of vision; naked eye, unassisted *or* unaided eye; sharp ~, piercing *or* penetrating eye, gimlet eye, eagle eye; eagle glance, eye of an eagle, ~ hawk *or* lynx; peeled eye [coll.], weather eye [coll. or joc.]; sights

---

terflies.—N. CRANE.   Out, damned spot! out, I say!—SHAKESPEARE.   We shall your tawny ground with your red blood discolor.—SHAKESPEARE.
441. The sense of sight is indeed the highest bodily privilege, the purest physical pleasure, which man has derived from his Creator.—

S. SMITH.   Every man takes the limits of his own field of vision for the limits of the world.—SCHOPENHAUER.   The eyes have one language everywhere.—G. HERBERT.   The heart's letter is read in the eyes.—G. HERBERT.

[dial. Eng. and slang], daylights [slang].

clear eyes, bright eyes, starry orbs; seductive eyes, bedroom eyes [slang, U.S.], come-hither look [coll.]; goggle-eyes, bugging eyes [slang]; saucer eyes, saucers [slang]; corner of the eye, tail [coll.]; eyelids, eyelashes, winkers [coll.], blinkers [slang]; pupil, sight of the eye [dial.]; eyeball, retina (*pl.* retinas, retinae), lens, cornea, optic nerve; cockeyes, walleyes etc. (defective eyes) 443.4.

8. *n.* evil eye, blighting glance, malign eye *or* look; basilisk, cockatrice.

9. *n.* (comparisons) eagle, hawk, bird, cat, lynx, weasel; Argus.

10. *v.* see, behold, observe, view, discern, perceive, descry, sight, have in sight, make out, spot [coll.], twig [coll.], discover, distinguish, recognize, spy, espy, ken [arch. and dial.], witness, notice, command a view of, get ~, have *or* catch sight of, get a load of [slang, U.S.], take in, cast the eyes on *or* upon, set *or* lay eyes on, clap eyes on [coll.], look on *or* upon etc. *below,* see with one's own eyes; hang an eye on, pipe, lamp, nail, peg [all slang]; glimpse, get *or* catch a glimpse of, glint; see at a glance, see with half an eye, pipe off [underworld slang, U.S.]; see the back *or* heels of.

11. *v.* look, look at, take a look at, take a gander at [slang, U.S.], have a looksee [slang, U.S.], look on *or* upon, gaze at *or* upon, turn *or* bend the eye to *or* on, turn *or* bend the looks upon, direct the eyes upon, cast the eyes on *or* upon etc. *above,* give the eye [coll.], watch, pipe [slang], view, survey, scan, regard, ken [arch.]; keep in sight *or* view, hold in view; look about *or* round, glance round; reconnoiter, case [underworld slang, U.S.], spy out, peep out, tout [slang]; get an eyeful [coll., U.S.]; lift up the eyes, open the eyes; take in the sights etc. (be a spectator) 444.3; keep watch etc. (be vigilant) 459.4; watch for etc. (expect) 507.4.

12. *v.* scrutinize, scrutinate; look closely at, eye, ogle, perlustrate, inspect, scan, examine, study, review, pass under review, view in all its phases, take stock of, contemplate, overhaul, give the once-over *or* double-O [slang, U.S.]; take one's measure [slang], size *or* size up [coll.]; look over *or* through, pore over, run over, run *or* pass the eye over *or* through.

13. *v.* gaze, fix ~, fasten *or* rivet the eyes upon, keep the eyes upon, look hard *or* intently at; eye, ogle; stare, look [coll.], gape, gawk [coll.], gaup *or* gaw [dial.], goggle; crane, crane the neck; rubber, rubberneck [both slang, U.S.]; peer, pry, peep, peek, take a peep *or* peek; play at bopeep *or* peekaboo; look full in the face, look straight in the eye, hold one's eye *or* gaze; glare, glower; gloat, gloat on *or* over, gaze with satisfaction, gaze with malignant *or* unhallowed satisfaction; strain the eyes.

14. *v.* glance, glint, cast a glance, glance at *or* upon, take a glance at, take a slant *or* squint at [slang], give a quick *or* cursory look etc. *n.,* take a cursory view of; examine cursorily, glance over, run *or* pass the eyes over, run over, skim, skip over *or* through, dip into.

15. *v.* look *or* gaze askance *or* askant, look obliquely, give a sidelong look etc. *n.,* glime [dial.], cut one's eye [slang]; squint, squinch [dial.], squint the eye, look asquint; cock the eye; look down one's nose at [coll.].

16. *v.* leer, leer the eye, look leeringly, give a leering look.

17. *v.* look away, turn one's look away, turn away the eyes, look another way, avert the eyes, break one's eyes away, stop looking; turn away from, turn the attention from, turn the back upon; drop one's eyes *or* gaze, cast one's eyes down; avoid one's gaze, cut eyes [coll.]; not look etc. 442.5.

18. *adj.* visual, ocular, optic(al), ophthalmic, scopic; seeing, looking etc. *n.*; visible etc. 446.4.

19. *adj.* televisual, televisional, televisionary.

20. *adj.* clear-sighted, clear-eyed; sharp-sighted, keen-sighted; farsighted, farseeing; gimlet-eyed, ferret-eyed; lynx-eyed etc. *n.*

21. *adv. etc.* in sight of etc. (visibly) 446.6.

22. *adv.* with open eyes, with one's

What the eye sees not, the heart rues not.—
J. HEYWOOD.   One's eyes are what one is.—
GALSWORTHY.   Hundreds of people can talk

for one who can think, but thousands can think for one who can see.—RUSKIN.

eyes open, with a weather eye open [coll.], with one's eyes peeled [coll.].

23. *adv.* at sight, as seen, at a glance; at first sight *or* view, at the first blush; *prima facie* [L.; Law], upon presentation.

24. *int.* look! etc. (attention) 457.10.

442. Blindness
(See 441. Vision; also 443. Defective Vision)

1. *n.* blindness, sightlessness, benightedness etc. *adj.*; anopsia *or* anopsy [Med.], cecity [rare], excecation [obs.], ablepsia, ablepsy [obs.]; amaurosis [Med.], *gutta serena* [L.], drop serene, teichopsia [Med.]; cataract; blind side, blind spot; snow blindness etc. (dim-sightedness) 443.2.

2. *n.* (aids for the blind) Braille, braille, Braille type, English *or* American Braille, New York point, Gall's serrated type, Boston type, Howe's American type, Moon *or* Moon's type, Alston's Glasgow type, Lucas's type, Frere's type; line letter, string alphabet, writing stamps; noctograph, writing frame; visagraph.

3. *v.* blind, render blind etc. *adj.*, excecate [obs.]; snow-blind; darken, benight, obscure, eclipse; blind the eyes, blindfold, hoodwink; throw dust in one's eyes; put one's eyes out, gouge; screen from sight etc. (conceal) 528.10; dazzle etc. 443.13.

4. *v.* be blind etc. *adj.*, not see, not see for looking [joc.], not see hair nor hide of [slang, U.S.]; grope in the dark, walk in darkness; lose sight of; be blindfolded, have the eyes bandaged.

5. *v.* not look, close *or* shut the eyes; shut the eyes to, be blind to; wink *or* blink at; avert the eyes, look away etc. 441.17.

6. *adj.* blind, eyeless, sightless, visionless, unseeing, unobserving, undiscerning, unperceiving, amaurotic [Med.], dark, benighted, rayless; stone-blind, stark-blind, sand-blind [arch.]; blind as a bat, blind as a mole, blind as an owl; blindfold, blindfolded; blinded etc. *v.*; snow-blind, snow-blinded; blind-alley, closed at one end, impassable; dead, dead-end; hidden, concealed, obscure; dim-sighted etc. 443.15.

443. Defective Vision
(See also 442. Blindness)

1. *n.* defective vision, imperfect vision, faulty eyesight, defect of sight, anopsia *or* anopsy [Med.], anopia [Med.]; cast in the eye, strabismus [Med.]; cross-eye, cross-eyedness, convergent strabismus [Med.], esotropia [Med.]; upward strabismus, anoöpsia [both Med.]; myopia [Med.], nearsightedness, shortsightedness, near-sight, short sight; presbyopia [Med.], farsightedness, long-sightedness, long sight; astigmatism, astigmism, astigmia, astigmatic sight; myopic astigmatism; confusion of vision, double sight; one-eyedness, monocularity.

color blindness, dichromatism, red-green blindness, Daltonism, deuteranopia, green blindness, protanopia, red blindness, blue-yellow blindness, tritanopia, achromatopsia, monochromatism, xanthocyanopia, xanthocyanopsia, xanthocyanopsy [all Med.]; ophthalmia, cirsophthalmia, psorophthalmia, ophthalmia neonatorium [all Med.]; nystagmus [Med.].

2. *n.* dim-sightedness, purblindness etc. *adj.*; dim *or* dull sight, half sight, failing sight; blearedness, lippitude, lippitudo [Med.]; day blindness, hemeralopia [Med.]; night blindness, moon blindness, moon-blind, moonblink, day sight, nyctalopia [Med.]; snow blindness, niphablepsia [Med.]; cataract; albinism; blindness etc. 442.

3. *n.* squint, squinch [dial.], strabism *or* strabismus [Med.], heterotropia [Med.].

4. *n.* (defective eyes) cross eyes, swiveleyes [slang], cockeyes, goggle eyes, gooseberry eyes, klieg eyes [motion picture cant]; saucer eyes, saucers [slang]; squint eyes, gimlet eyes [coll.]; walleyes, eyes of wall [rare].

5. *n.* black eye, bruised eye; bunged-

---

442. Can the blind lead the blind? shall they not both fall into the ditch?—BIBLE. A pebble and a diamond are alike to a blind man.—FULLER. He that is stricken blind cannot forget / The precious treasure of his eyesight lost.—SHAKESPEARE. O dark, dark, dark, amid the blaze of noon.—MILTON. There is none so blind as they that won't see.—SWIFT. In the kingdom of blind men, the one-eyed is king.

443. Night after night / He sat and bleared his

up eye, eye in mourning, goog, mouse, shiner, shanty [all slang].

6. *n.* winking, blinking, nictation, nictitation; winker, blinkard.

7. *n.* dizziness, swimming, scotomy *or* scotoma [Med.].

8. *n.* (limitation of vision) screen, blinker, blinder etc. (shade) 424.

9. *n.* optical illusion, illusion, delusion, trick, trick of eyesight, fallacy *or* deception of vision, false light, hallucination, vision, specious appearance, seeming, *faux air* [F.]; refraction, distortion, distorted image, anamorphosis; virtual image, virtual focus; phasm, phasma [obs.], phantasmagoria *or* phantasmagory, phantasm, phantasma, phantom, phantom of the imagination, vision, apparition, appearance, show, presence, shape, ghostly form, hue [obs.]; mirage, fata morgana, looming; aftermirage, spectrum, ocular spectrum; *ignis fatuus* [L.] etc. (luminescence) 420.11; imagining etc. 515.4; specter etc. 980a.1.

10. *v.* have faulty eyesight etc. *n.,* be dim-sighted etc. *adj.,* see indistinctly, see through a prism, "see through a glass, darkly" (Bible), "see men as trees walking" (Bible); have a mote in the eye, have a mist before the eyes, have a film over the eyes; see double.

11. *v.* wink, blink; nictate, nictitate, bat the eyes [coll.].

12. *v.* squint, squinch [dial.], squint the eye, look asquint, look askance *or* askant, screw up the eyes, goggle, glime [dial.], look forty ways for Sunday [slang, U.S.]; cock the eye.

13. *v.* dazzle, bedazzle, daze, confuse, glare, blind, blind the eyes, dim.

14. *adj.* poor-sighted; astigmatic(al); nystagmic [Med.]; blinking, blinky, blink-eyed; squinting, squinty, asquint, squint-eyed, squinch-eyed [dial.], strabismal *or* strabismic(al) [Med.]; cross-eyed, cockeyed, glare-eyed, goggle-eyed, bug-eyed [slang], red-eyed, yellow-eyed, gooseberry-eyed, saucer-eyed, moon-eyed, swiveleyed [slang], walleyed, boss-eyed [dial. Eng.]; farsighted, longsighted, presbyopic [Med.]; nearsighted, shortsighted, myopic(al) [Med.], mope-eyed; one-eyed, monocular, monoculate, monoculous, blind of one eye; color-blind; dichroic.

15. *adj.* dim-sighted, dull-sighted, dim-eyed, weak-eyed, feeble-eyed, mole-eyed; purblind, half-blind; blear-eyed, bleary-eyed; film-eyed, filmy-eyed; snow-blind, snow-blinded; hemeralopic, nyctalopic; blind etc. 442.6.

444. Spectator

1. *n.* spectator, beholder, observer, looker, looker-on, onlooker, watcher, viewer, seer, gazer, witness, eyewitness, bystander, passer-by; scrutator, scrutineer, scrutinizer; sharp-sighted observer, oculist [rare]; sight-seer, excursionist, rubberneck *or* rubbernecker [slang, U.S.], globe-trotter [coll.]; inlooker, inspector; watchman, lookout etc. (warner) 668.4, (guard) 717.6; spy etc. (secret agent) 528.8; attender etc. 186.7; theatergoer etc. 599.23.

2. *n.* spectators, lookers-on etc. (*see* spectator, looker-on etc. *above*); gallery, grandstand, bleachers [U.S.]; house, gallery gods [coll.] etc. (audience) 418.8.

3. *v.* be a spectator etc. *n.,* spectate [obs. exc. slang]; rubber, rubberneck [both slang, U.S.]; sight-see, see the sights, take in the sights, see the elephant [coll.]; witness, behold etc. (see) 441.10, 11; look on, take in etc. (attend) 186.9.

445. Optical Instruments

1. *n.* optical instrument; lens, converging lens, diverging lens, concave lens, convex lens, meniscus, periscopic lens, hand lens; magnifying glass, magnifier; reading glass, reader [coll.]; burning glass, sunglass; prism; scope, stereoscope, pseudoscope, polyscope, abdominoscope, gastroscope, helioscope, polariscope, polemoscope, periscope; microscope; simple *or* single microscope, compound microscope, projecting micro-

---

eyes with books.—LONGFELLOW. I am a watcher whose eyes have grown dim.—BROWNING.

444. Though the most be players, some must be spectators.—JONSON.
445. Where the telescope ends, the microscope begins. Which of the two has the grander view? —HUGO. Men seldom make passes / At girls who wear glasses.—D. PARKER.

scope, ultramicroscope; kaleidoscope; kaleidophon *or* kaleidophone; spectroscope, spectrometer; chromatrope, thaumatrope; photometer, optometer, eriometer, actinometer, lucimeter, radiometer.

2. *n.* telescope, glass; dumb telescope, elbow telescope, zenith telescope, water telescope, vernier telescope, terrestrial telescope, inverting telescope, panoramic telescope, refracting telescope, reflecting telescope, mercurial telescope; prism telescope, teinoscope; binocular, prism binocular; spyglass, field glass, opera glass, lorgnette.

3. *n.* spectacles, specs [coll.], glasses, eyeglasses, pair of glasses *or* spectacles, barnacles [coll., Eng.], glims [slang], windows [slang], sights [dial. Eng. and slang], gig lamps [slang]; reading glasses, readers [coll.]; horn-rimmed glasses; pince-nez, nippers [slang], *lorgnon* [F.]; colored glasses, preserves, sunglasses; goggles, blinkers, lorgnette; monocle, quizzing glass; eyeglass, glass, eyepiece, ocular, lens.

4. *n.* mirror, reflector, speculum, glass, looking glass, seeing glass [now dial.]; cheval glass, psyche [now rare]; hand mirror, magic mirror, window mirror, rear-view mirror, pier glass.

5. *n.* camera, Kodak *or* kodak [trade name]; hand camera; camera lucida, camera obscura; motion-picture camera, cinematograph *or* kinematograph; candid camera; photographic telescope, photomicroscope; photography etc. 556.4.

6. *n.* magic lantern, projector; motion-picture projector, vitascope, Kinetoscope *or* kinetoscope [trade name], cinematograph *or* kinematograph [chiefly Eng.], Biograph *or* biograph [trade name]; stereopticon, megascope.

7. *n.* optics, optometry; abdominoscopy, gastroscopy, microscopy etc. (*see* abdominoscope, gastroscope, microscope etc. *above* 445.1, 2).

8. *n.* optician, optometrist, oculist, ocularist; microscopist, telescopist etc. (*see* microscope, telescope etc. *above* 445.1, 2).

9. *adj.* scopic, gastroscopic, microscopic etc. *n.*

10. *adj.* spectacled, bespectacled; oculate, oculated; goggled; monocled, monocular [joc.].

446. Visibility
(See 447. Invisibility)

1. *n.* visibility, perceptibility, perceivability, discernibility; ocular proof, ~ evidence *or* demonstration; distinctness, conspicuousness etc. *adj.*; conspicuity [rare]; high *or* low visibility, visibility zero [Aeronaut.]; exposure; outcrop, outcropping, basset [Geol.]; appearance etc. 448.1; manifestation etc. 525; field of view etc. 441.6.

2. *v.* become *or* be visible etc. *adj.*, appear, peer [arch.], make its appearance, appear to one's eyes, meet ~, catch *or* strike the eye, come in sight *or* view, heave in sight [Naut. or coll.], show, show itself, show its face, show up [coll.], turn up, present itself, present itself to the view, open to the view.

manifest itself, become manifest, reveal itself, become revealed, discover itself, expose *or* betray itself, produce itself, materialize, rise, arise, rear its head, loom, appear on the horizon, emerge, issue, issue forth, come forth, come out, come forward, come to hand, come upon the stage; float before the eyes; look forth, peep *or* peer out; crop out, outcrop, basset [Geol.]; see the light, see the light of day; break through the clouds; burst upon the view *or* sight, break *or* burst forth, spring forth, spring up, pop up, start up; loom large, stand forth, stand out, glare; reappear; live in a glass house; attract the attention etc. (*see* attention etc. 457); arrive etc. 292.7; be disclosed etc. 529.6.

3. *v.* render visible etc. *adj.*, visibilize; expose to view etc. (manifest) 525.2.

4. *adj.* visible, visual, perceptible, perceivable, discernible, seeable, beholdable, observable, noticeable; in sight, in view, in full view, exposed to view; in evidence; manifest, apparent, evident, open, revealed, unhidden, unconcealed, unclouded, unshaded.

5. *adj.* distinct, plain, clear, definite, well-defined, well-marked, recognizable, obvious, evident, palpable, patent, autoptic(al); unmistakable, not to be mistaken; clear as day *or* daylight, plain as the sun at noon, plain as a pikestaff

---

446. All is clear from east to west.—EMERSON. This is as plain as a nose in a man's face.—RABELAIS.

[coll.], plain as the way to parish church [coll.], plain as plain can be; glaring, staring, stark-staring, conspicuous, prominent, pronounced, in bold ~, strong or high relief.

6. *adv. etc.* visibly, distinctly, clearly etc. *adj.*; in sight of, *à vue d'œil* [F.], in one's eye, before one, before *or* under one's eyes, under one's very eyes, under one's nose [coll.]; *oculis subjecta fidelibus* [L.]; *veluti in speculum* [L.]; apparently etc. 448.8.

447. Invisibility
(See 446. Visibility)

1. *n.* invisibility, invisibleness etc. *adj.*, imperceptibility, nonappearance; concealment etc. 528; delitescence etc. (latency) 526.

2. *v.* be invisible etc. *adj.*, not be seen, blush unseen, escape notice; lie hid etc. (be concealed) 528.16; lurk etc. (be latent) 526.3.

3. *v.* render invisible etc. *adj.*, conceal etc. 528.10.

4. *adj.* invisible, unvisible, not visible etc. (*see* visible etc. 446.4), unperceivable, imperceptible, unperceptible [rare], indiscernible, undiscernible *or* undiscernable, unseeable, unbeholdable; unapparent, nonapparent; not in sight, out of sight, behind the curtain *or* scenes; eclipsed, in eclipse, under an eclipse; viewless [rare], sightless, sightproof; unconspicuous, inconspicuous; unseen, unbeheld etc. (*see* see, behold etc. 441.10); covert, hidden etc. (concealed) 528.17, 18; delitescent etc. (latent) 526.6.

5. *adj.* indistinct, indistinguishable, unrecognizable, unclear, indefinite, undefined, ill-defined, ill-marked, vague, mysterious, faint, pale, dim, dark, darkish, shadowy, obscure, uncertain, confused, out of focus; blurred, blurry, bleared, bleary, blear; misty, hazy, fuzzy; screened, veiled etc. (*see* screen, veil etc. 424.6).

6. *adv.* invisibly etc. *adj.*; out of sight, behind the curtain *or* scenes, *à perte de vue* [F.]; under an eclipse.

---

447. I sent my Soul through the Invisible.—OMAR KHAYYÁM—FITZGERALD.   O world invisible, we view thee.—F. THOMPSON.

448. Appearance
(See 449. Disappearance)

1. *n.* appearance, appearing, materializing etc. (*see* appear, materialize etc. 446.2); materialization, occurrence, manifestation, revelation, disclosure, exposure, exposition, exhibition, presentation, display, opening, unfolding, unfoldment, rising of the curtain; emergence, issuance; showup [coll.], turnup; visibility etc. 446.1.

2. *n.* phenomenon (*pl.* phenomena), sight, spectacle, scene, view; outlook, prospect, vista, lookout, perspective; bird's-eye view; scenery, scenic view, scape, landscape, seascape, riverscape, waterscape, airscape, skyscape, cloudscape, cityscape, townscape; picture, tableau, representation; exhibit, exhibition, exposition, display, show; pageant, pageantry; stage, stage setting, stage-set, *mise en scène* [F.]; stage effect, stage trick; phantasmagoria *or* phantasmagory; panorama, diorama, cosmorama, georama; ostentatious display etc. 882.

3. *n.* apparition, phantasm, phantom etc. (optical illusion) 443.9.

4. *n.* aspect, appearance, look, looks, sight, view [obs. exc. dial.], feature etc. *below,* favor, guise, ostent, mien, complexion, color, image, cast, turn, air, carriage, bearing, port, demeanor, presence, expression; seeming, semblance, effect, impression, apparent character, show, outward show, front, outward *or* external appearance; angle, slant [coll.], twist [slang], phase, phasis, side; respect, light; shape, figure, fashion etc. (form) 240; standpoint etc. 441.4.

5. *n.* lineaments, features, traits, lines, outline, contour, silhouette, profile; face, countenance, favor, visage, physiognomy, physnomy [obs.]; phiz, phizog [both slang], cast of countenance, cut of one's jib [coll.], *tournure* [F.]; outside, exterior.

6. *v.* appear, seem, look, exhibit, present, evidence, show, have ~, present ~, exhibit ~, wear ~, carry ~, bear ~,

---

448. *Nimium ne crede colori* [Don't trust too much in appearance].—VERGIL.   *Fronti nulla fides* [No faith is to be put in outward appearances].—JUVENAL.   Appearances are very deceitful.—LE SAGE.   After all, you can't expect men not to judge by appearances.—E. GLASGOW.

ake ~, take on *or* assume the appearance *or* semblance of, look like; appear to one's eyes, present itself to the view; figure, cut a figure; manifest, be manifest etc. 525.3; make its appearance etc. (become visible) 446.2.

7. *adj.* apparent, appearing, seeming, ostensible; appearanced [coll., U.S.]; open to view; distinct, clear etc. (visible) 446.5, 6, (manifest) 525.4.

8. *adv.* apparently, seemingly etc. *adj.*; to all appearance *or* appearances, to all seeming, as it seems; on the face of it, *prima facie* [L.]; to the eye; at first sight *or* view, at the first blush; manifestly etc. 525.7; distinctly, clearly etc. (visibly) 446.6.

449. Disappearance
(See 448. Appearance)

1. *n.* disappearance, disappearing, vanishing etc. *v.*; vanishment, dissolution, fade-out, fadeaway; evanescence, evanescency [rare]; eclipse, occultation; vanishing point; dissolving view, dissolve [motion-picture cant]; departure etc. 293; exit etc. (egress) 295.

2. *v.* disappear, disappear *or* vanish into thin air, vanish, vanish from sight, do the vanishing act [slang, U.S.], evaporate, fade, fade out *or* away, do a fade-out [slang, U.S.], dissolve, melt, melt away, sink, sink away, die, die out *or* away, go, go away, fly, fleet [arch.], pass, pass out *or* away, pass out of sight, pass out of the picture [coll.], retire from sight, become lost to sight *or* view, be seen no longer, be gone etc. *adj.*, leave no trace, "leave not a rack behind" (Shakespeare); eclipse [poetic], suffer *or* undergo eclipse, occultate; lose sight of, see no longer; depart etc. 293.4; take French leave etc. (flee) 623.10.

3. *v.* cause to disappear etc., vanish [rare]; efface etc. 552.2.

4. *adj.* disappearing etc. *v.*, evanescent.

5. *adj.* disappeared etc. *v.*, missing, lost, lost to sight *or* view, gone.

450. Intellect
(See 450a. Absence of Intellect)

1. *n.* intellect, *intellectus* [L.; Philos.]; active *or* passive intellect *or* reason; *intellectus agens, intellectus possibilis* [both L.]; active *or* agent intellect, possible intellect; dividing *or* combining intellect; mind, reason, *Verstand* [G.]; intelligence, intelligency [rare], understanding, *Vernunft* [G.], nous, psyche; mentality, brain *or* brains, brain-stuff [coll.], gray matter [coll.], head.

intellection [obs.], intellectuality, rationality, thinking principle; intellectual ~, reasoning etc. *adj.* faculties *or* powers, cogitative faculties, mentals; wits, parts, faculties, senses; consciousness; wit, capacity, genius; percipience *or* percipiency, perception, apperception, conception, judgment; wisdom etc. 498; instinct etc. (intuition) 477a.

2. *n.* brain, seat of thought *or* the intellect, organ of thought, encephalon, head, headpiece, pate [now joc. or derog.]; sconce, noddle [both coll.]; noodle, noggin, bean, upper story [all slang]; sensory, sensorium; prosencephalon, forebrain; telencephalon, endbrain; diencephalon, betweenbrain, 'tweenbrain, 'twixtbrain; mesencephalon, midbrain; rhombencephalon, hindbrain; metencephalon, cerebellum, little brain; cerebrum; myelencephalon, afterbrain, medulla; medulla oblongata; pons; arbor vitae, *arbor vitae cerebelli* [NL.], tree of life; gray matter, white matter; brain pan etc. (head) 210.3.

3. *n.* inmost mind, inner recesses of the mind, *penetralia mentis* [L.], inner man, inmost *or* essential nature, inmost heart *or* soul, true being, vital principle, seat *or* center of life; heart, heart's core, heart of hearts, secret *or* inner recesses of the heart, cockles of the heart; breast, bosom; subconscious mind, the subconscious, the subliminal; soul, spirit etc. (psyche) 994.11; ego etc. 79.4.

4. *n.* (science of the mind) psychology, psychologics [rare]; faculty ~, rational ~, existential ~, functional ~,

---

449. *Deficit omne quod nascitur* [Everything which is born passes away].—QUINTILIAN.
450. *Teloque animus praestantior omni* [A mind is more excellent than every weapon].—OVID. Man is a reasoning animal.—SENECA. Every man's reason must be his guide.—CHESTERTON. In nature there's no blemish but the mind.—SHAKESPEARE. My mind is my kingdom.—T. CAMPBELL. How fleet is a glance of the mind.—COWPER. That mind and soul, according well, may make one music.—TENNYSON.

structural ∼, dynamic ∼, physiological ∼, abnormal ∼, differential ∼, genetic ∼, applied ∼, academic *or* popular psychology; motor psychology, behaviorism, self psychology, Gestalt psychology.

psychonomics, psychography; psychophysics, psychonomics, psychography; psychophysics, psychophysiology; psychobiology, psychobiochemistry; psychotechnology; psychogenesis, psychogenetics; psychotherapy, psychotherapeutics; psychopathy, psychopathology, alienism, psychiatry; psychoanalysis *or* psychanalysis, Freudianism, Freudian theory, psychodiagnostics; psychometry, psychoasthenics, psychodynamics, psychostatics; mental *or* moral philosophy, philosophy of the mind; noology, nooscopics; ideology; phrenology, craniology, cranioscopy; psychics etc. 994.2, 3; philosophy etc. 451.4–23.

5. *n.* (scientist) psychologist, psychologue; psychotechnician; psychopath, psychopathist, psychopathologist, psychiatrist, alienist; psychographer, psychographist; psychophysiologist, psychophysicist; psychotherapist, psychotherapeutist; psychoanalyst, psychoanalyzer; psychometer, psychometrist, psychist etc. 994.13–16.

6. *v.* intellectualize, intelligize [rare], rationalize, reason etc. (think) 451.27.

7. *v.* note, notice, take notice *or* cognizance of, mark, realize, perceive, observe, regard, heed, see, be aware *or* conscious of; appreciate.

8. *adj.* intellectual, mental, rational, reasoning etc. *v.*, psychic(al), psychologic(al), spiritual; endowed with intellect *or* reason, brainy [coll.]; cognitive; cerebral; percipient, appercipient; noological, nooscopic; subjective; scholarly etc. (studious) 539.6, (learned) 490.15, 16; intelligent etc. 498.9.

9. *adj.* conscious, cognizant etc. (aware) 490.12, 13; sensible etc. 375.6.

10. *adj.* subconscious, subliminal, superconscious, supraliminal; coconscious, extramarginal.

450a. Absence of Intellect
(See 450. Intellect)

1. *n.* absence ∼, want *or* poverty of intellect etc. (*see* intellect etc. 450.1), unintellectuality, brainlessness etc. *adj.*, vacancy, vacuity, vacancy *or* emptiness o mind, empty head, empty-headedness mindlessness etc. *adj.*; vacant attic, un furnished garret, space to let, nobody home, nobody home in the upper story [all slang]; brutality, brute instinct, brute force; unintelligence etc. 499; incogitancy etc. 452.

2. *adj.* mindless, brainless, witless, rea sonless, void of reason, unendowed with intellect, empty-headed; unintelligent etc 499.11–17; thoughtless etc. (incogitant) 452.3.

451. Thought
(See 452. Incogitance; also 453. Idea)

1. *n.* thought, thinking etc. *v.*, exercise *or* exercitation of the intellect, intellection, cogitation, excogitation, cerebration, mentation, reflection, consideration contemplation, meditation, rumination study, lucubration, speculation, deliberation, ponderation [now rare], mental la bor, headwork, brainwork, workings o the mind; self-communing, self-counsel self-consultation.

thoughtfulness, pensiveness etc. *adj.* thoughts, inmost thoughts, secre thoughts; current *or* flow of thought o ideas, train of thought; association o ideas; deep thought *or* reflection, heavy thinking, tall headwork [slang], straigh thinking; close study, application etc. (at tention) 457; idea etc. 453.

2. *n.* mature thought, ripe idea; after thought, second thought *or* thoughts, re flection, reconsideration, re-examination review; retrospection, recollection etc (memory) 505.

3. *n.* reverie etc. (abstraction) 458.3.

4. *n.* philosophy, love of wisdom, *an cilla theologiae* [L.], handmaid of theol ogy; philosophical opinions *or* principles philosophical system *or* school, school o thought; natural philosophy etc. (nat ural science) 316.5; mental *or* mora philosophy etc. (psychology) 450.4 (ethics) 926.4.

metaphysics, metaphysic, transphysica science, *philosophia prima* [L.]; theory of knowledge, epistemology; logic, logis tic, doctrine of terms, doctrine of the judgment, doctrine of inference; tradi

---

451. It is a great advantage for a system o philosophy to be substantially true.—SANTA YANA. To him whose elastic and vigorou

ional *or* Aristotelian logic, modern *or* epistemological logic, pragmatic ~, instrumental *or* experimental logic, psychological logic *or* psychologism, symbolic *or* mathematical logic; ethics etc. 926.4; social philosophy; psychology etc. 450.4; esthetics, aesthetic; theory of value; sophistry etc. 477; ethicism, deism, theism etc. 984.4.

5. *n.* (Hindu philosophy) Hinduism etc. 984.11, Mimamsa, Uttara *or* Purva Mimamsa, Sankhya, Nyaya; Saiva Sidhanta.

6. *n.* (Greek and Greco-Roman philosophy) Ionian *or* Ionic school; Heraclitenism; Eleatic school, Eleaticism; atomism; Sophistic philosophy, Sophism; pre-Socratic philosophy; Pythagorean school, Pythagoreanism *or* Pythagoism; Neo-Pythagoreanism; Pyrrhonism, Pyrrhonian *or* Pyrrhonic philosophy.

7. *n.* Socratic philosophy *or* school, Socratism, Socratic method *or* induction; Megarian *or* Megaric school, Eristic school, Megarianism; Elian *or* Elean school, Eretrian school; Cynic philosophy, Cynicism; hedonistic school, hedonism; Cyrenaic school, Cyrenaic hedonism, Cyrenaicism; Platonic philosophy, Platonism, philosophy of the Academy; Neoplatonism; Aristotelian philosophy, Aristotelianism, philosophy of the Lyceum; eudaemonism; Peripatetic school.

8. *n.* Stoic philosophy *or* school, Stoicism, philosophy of the Porch; Epicureanism, philosophy of the Garden.

9. *n.* patristic philosophy, patristicism; Gnosticism, Manichaeism *or* Manicheism, Augustinianism; African school, Alexandrian school, eclecticism; philosophy of the ante-Nicene Fathers, philosophy of the post-Nicene Fathers.

10. *n.* scholastic *or* Scholastic philosophy, Scholasticism; Thomism, Scotism; realism, nominalism; Averroism; Neo-Scholasticism.

11. *n.* (modern philosophy) post-Reformation philosophy; humanism, rationalism, sensationalism, empiricism, moralism, voluntarism, Cartesianism, Spinozism, Leibnitzianism *or* Leibnizianism, panphenomenalism, political philosophy; egoistic hedonism, psychological hedonism, universalistic hedonism.

12. *n.* (modern German philosophy) Kantianism, critical philosophy, Fichteanism, Hegelianism, Herbartianism, Schellingism *or* Schellingianism, Schopenhauerism, neocriticism; Einstein theory, relativism, theory of relativity.

13. *n.* (modern French philosophy) traditionalism, Positivism *or* positivism, Comtism, Bergsonism, sociological school.

14. *n.* (modern English philosophy) associated psychology, utilitarianism, Spencerian philosophy, Neo-Hegelianism.

15. *n.* (modern Italian philosophy) Vicoism, sensism, empiricism, criticism, ontologism.

16. *n.* (modern American philosophy) pragmatism, new ethical movement; Neo-Hegelianism, Neo-Hegelian movement.

17. *n.* idealism, idealistic philosophy; metaphysical idealism, epistemological idealism, critical idealism, subjective idealism, objective idealism; absolute idealism, philosophy of the Absolute; immaterialism; transcendentalism; Berkeleian philosophy, Berkeleianism *or* Berkeleyism; transcendentalism, transcendental idealism; Platonism etc. *above* 451.7.

18. *n.* skepticism *or* scepticism, zetetic philosophy; Pyrrhonism, Pyrrhonian *or* Pyrrhonic philosophy; agnosticism; relativity of knowledge.

19. *n.* monism, philosophical unitarianism, mind-stuff theory; pantheism.

20. *n.* pluralism; dualism, mind-matter theory.

21. *n.* evolutionism, Darwinism etc. (evolution) 161.5.

22. *n.* cosmology (*see* cosmologer etc. 318.11), ontology.

23. *n.* mysticism etc. (esoteric sciences) 994.

24. *n.* philosopheme, philosophical

---

thought keeps pace with the sun, the day is a perpetual morning.—THOREAU. Thoughts are seeds of future deeds.—H. ROMAINE. The highest possible stage in moral culture is when we recognize that we ought to control our thoughts.—DARWIN. Thought is the soul of act.—BROWNING. To think is to act.—EMERSON. Thinking is the function; living is the functionary.—EMERSON. Go speed the stars of Thought.—EMERSON. The power of Thought is the magic of the Mind.—BYRON.

proposition etc. (argument) 476.3; hypothesis etc. (premise) 476.3, 4.

25. *n.* philosopher etc. 476.9.

26. *n.* thought transference etc. (telepathy) 994.8.

27. *v.* think, bethink [arch.], cogitate, excogitate, cerebrate, mentalize [rare], reason, rationalize, intellectualize, intelligize [rare], reflect, deliberate, speculate, contemplate, meditate, ponder, revolve, study, muse, ruminate, chew the cud [coll.], digest, discuss; concentrate upon, meditate upon, think over, ponder over, brood over, con over, muse on *or* upon, muse over, mouse over [U.S.], mull over [coll., U.S.], ruminate over, deliberate upon, reflect over, revolve *or* turn over in the mind, run over in one's thoughts; weigh, perpend [arch. or joc.].

think about, bestow thought *or* consideration upon, occupy the mind *or* thoughts with, give *or* apply the mind to, put one's mind to, apply oneself to, bend *or* turn the mind *or* thoughts to, direct the mind upon, give thought to, exercise the mind, set the brain *or* wits to work, use one's head, trouble one's head about, put on one's thinking *or* considering cap [coll.]; dream etc. (abstract oneself) 458.6; trow [arch.], fancy etc. (believe) 484.8, (suppose) 514.6.

28. *v.* think hard, think one's head off [joc.], rack *or* ransack the brains, crack the brains [coll.], beat *or* cudgel the brains, work one's head to the bone [joc.], sweat over [coll.], stew over [slang], hammer *or* hammer away at, hammer out, do some tall head work [slang] etc. *n.*

29. *v.* consider, take under *or* into consideration, take counsel, take under advisement, think it over; commune with oneself, bethink oneself; sleep upon, advise with *or* take counsel of one's pillow; reconsider, re-examine, review.

30. *v.* occupy the mind *or* the thoughts, fix *or* engage the thoughts; have in *or* on one's mind, have on the brain [coll.], have constantly in one's thoughts, run in the head; occupy, absorb ~, enwrap *or* engross the thoughts; come uppermost, be uppermost in the mind.

31. *v.* harbor ~, cherish ~, entertain ~, foster ~, nurse *or* nurture an idea bear in mind, have in mind.

32. *v.* suggest itself, present itself, present itself to the mind *or* the thoughts strike one, strike the mind; occur, occur to one's mind, come into one's head, pass through one's head *or* mind, enter one's mind, pass in the mind *or* the thoughts cross one's mind, flash on *or* across the mind, flit across the view, fasten itself on the mind.

33. *v.* make an impression, sink on penetrate into the mind, sink in [coll.] catch the thoughts, wake *or* awaken the mind, arrest the thoughts.

34. *v.* philosophize, philosophate [obs.], philosophy [obs.], interpret or explain philosophically, assign rational causes; Socratize, Pythagorize *or* Pythagoreanize, Pyrrhonize etc. *n.*; syllogize.

35. *adj.* thoughtful, pensive, meditative, reflective, cogitative, excogitative contemplative, speculative, deliberative studious [rare], museful; musing, thinking etc. *v.*; wistful; sober; considerate etc. (careful) 459.7.

36. *adj.* absorbed, engrossed, rapt wrapped in thought, lost in thought, occupied, preoccupied.

37. *adj.* dreamy, in a reverie etc. (abstracted) 458.11.

38. *adj.* philosophical, philosophistic(al); Pyrrhonic, Pyrrhonian; Ionic Ionian; Pythagoric(al), Pythagorean hedonic(al), hedonist, hedonistic; Platonic(al), Socratic(al), sophistic(al) Stoic(al) etc. *n.*; philosophicohistorical philosophicolegal, philosophicojuristic philosophicopsychological, philosophicoreligious, philosophicotheological; calm unruffled, imperturbable etc. (inexcitable) 826.9; rational, wise etc. 498.9–11.

39. *adv.* thoughtfully, pensively etc. *adj.*; all things considered, taking everything into consideration *or* account.

452. Incogitance
(See 451. Thought)

Want of Thought.—1. *n.* incogitance *or* incogitancy [rare], absence of mind, absent-mindedness, vacancy, vacancy *or* emptiness of mind, vacuity, fatuity, inanity, thoughtlessness etc. *adj.*; poverty of intellect etc. 499; unintellectuality etc. 450a.

Those that think must govern those that toil.—
GOLDSMITH. Man holds an inward talk with himself alone, which it behoves him to regulate well.—PASCAL.

2. *v.* not think etc. (*see* think etc. 51.27), not think of, make the mind a blank, let the mind lie fallow; dismiss from the mind *or* thoughts, put away thought, divert the mind *or* thoughts, relax *or* unbend the mind; be absent-minded etc. (be inattentive) 458.5, 6.

3. *adj.* incogitant, incogitative, thoughtless, senseless, unideaed, unideal [obs.], unthinking, unreasoning, inconsiderate; inane, vacant, vacuous, blank, empty, empty-headed, unoccupied; mindless etc. 450a.2; unintellectual, nonunderstanding etc. (unintelligent) 499.11, 2.

4. *adj.* unthought of, undreamt of, unconsidered; off one's mind; incogitable, inconceivable, not to be thought of.

453. Idea

Object of Thought.—**1.** *n.* idea, idee [obs. exc. dial.], *Idee* [G.], notion, concept, conception, conceit [arch.], thought, apprehension, impression, perception, image, image in the mind, eidolon, sentiment, reflection, observation, consideration.

abstract idea; archetype, formative notion, guiding *or* organizing conception, regulative principle; main idea, where the hen scratches [slang, U.S.], big idea [chiefly coll.]; not a bad idea, bright thought, bright *or* brilliant idea, brain storm [coll.], inspiration; gag, wheeze, wrinkle, wrinkle in one's horn [all slang]; novel idea, new *or* latest wrinkle [slang], new slant [coll.], new twist [slang]; absurd idea, fool notion [coll.]; fixed idea, *idée fixe* [F.]; idée-force [Philos.]; *ideatum* [ML.], ideate [both Philos.]; Platonic idea; view, opinion etc. (conviction) 484.2; theory etc. (supposition) 514; whim, fancy etc. (caprice) 608.

2. *adj.* ideaed *or* idead; ideagenous; ideation, ideational.

454. Topic

1. *n.* topic, subject, subject of thought, matter, subject matter, what it is about, motif, theme, text, commonplace [now rare], locus [rare], business, affair, matter in hand, material for thought; food for thought, mental *or* intellectual pabulum; point, point at issue, point in question; item on the agenda; gist, pith, nub [coll., U.S.]; thesis, statement, proposition, maxim, theorem; resolution, motion; motive, leitmotiv *or* leitmotif [Mus.]; head, chapter; problem, issue etc. (question) 461.10.

2. *adj.* topical, thematic(al); thought-challenging, thought-giving, thought-inspiring, thought-involving, thought-moving, thought-provoking, thought-working; subjective, nominal [Gram.].

3. *adv. etc.* under consideration *or* advisement, in contemplation etc. (in question) 461.26; relative to etc. 9.5.

4. *adv.* in the thoughts *or* mind, on the mind, on the brain [coll.], uppermost in the mind *or* thoughts; *in petto* [It.], in the heart, in one's inmost thoughts.

455. Curiosity
(See 456. Incuriosity)

1. *n.* curiosity, curiousness, inquisitiveness, interest, interestedness, thirst for knowledge, mental acquisitiveness, inquiring mind; prying etc. *v.*, officious *or* meddling inquisitiveness, nosiness [coll.]; meddlesomeness etc. 682.8; newsmongery etc. 532.3; questioning etc. (inquiry) 461.

2. *n.* inquisitive, inquisitive *or* curious person, quidnunc, questioner, inquirer, querier, querist, quiz, question box [slang], walking interrogation point *or* question mark [joc.], curiosity shop [slang], nosy [coll.], nosy Parker [slang], busybody, busy [slang], pry, Paul Pry, snoop *or* snooper [U.S.], Peeping Tom, eavesdropper, rubberneck *or* rubbernecker [slang, U.S.]; Lot's

---

with it.—J. AUSTEN. An Idea isn't responsible for the people who believe in it.—D. MARQUIS.
454. That favourite subject, Myself.—BOSWELL. Do you keep to the old topics?—BARRIE. They would talk of nothing but fashionable topics.—GOLDSMITH.
455. This disease of curiosity.—ST. AUGUSTINE. Most people want to know only in order to talk.—PASCAL. Too much curiosity lost Paradise.—A. BEHN. Curiosity is one of the most permanent and certain characteristics of a vigorous intellect.—JOHNSON. One is never entirely without the instinct of

---

453. The idea exists only by virtue of the form.—PATER. All thoughts of a turtle are turtles, and of a rabbit, rabbits.—EMERSON. One never does form a just idea of anybody beforehand; one takes up a notion and runs away

wife; gossip etc. (newsmonger) 532.5; sight-seer etc. 444.1.

3. *v.* be curious etc. *adj.,* take an interest in, prick up the ears; stare, gape; rubber, rubberneck [both slang, U.S.]; lionize.

4. *v.* pry, Paul-Pry, snoop [U.S.], nose, poke ~, stick *or* thrust one's nose in; peer, peep; search, ferret out, nose out; meddle etc. 682.14.

5. *adj.* curious, inquisitive, quizzical, quizzish [rare], quizzy [rare], burning with curiosity, curious as a cat; overcurious, supercurious; prying etc. *v.*, nosy [coll.], snoopy [coll., U.S.]; rubberneck, rubbernecked [both slang, U.S.]; agape, agog, all agog; open-mouthed, open-eyed; inquisitorial etc. (inquiring) 461.24; meddlesome etc. 682.22.

456. Incuriosity
(See 455. Curiosity)

1. *n.* incuriosity, incuriousness etc. *adj.*; intellectual inertia; unconcern, insouciance etc. (indifference) 866; apathy etc. (insensibility) 823.

2. *v.* be incurious etc. *adj.,* have no curiosity etc. (*see* curiosity etc. 455.1); mind one's own business, pursue the even tenor of one's way, glance neither to the right hand nor to the left; take no interest in etc. 823.3.

3. *adj.* incurious, not curious etc. (*see* curious etc. 455.5), uninquisitive, uninquiring; uninterested, unconcerned etc. (indifferent) 866.4; bored etc. 841.9; impassive, apathetic etc. 823.5, 6; inattentive etc. 458.10.

457. Attention
(See 458. Inattention)

1. *n.* attention, attentiveness, mindfulness, heedfulness etc. *adj.*, heed, ear, consideration, thought, mind [dial.]; observance, observation; note, notice, advertence *or* advertency, regard, respect.

2. *n.* close attention, active ~, intense ~, diligent ~, deliberate *or* exclusive thought *or* attention, close study *o* scrutiny, deep study, deep *or* profoun thought *or* attention, labored attentior absorbed attention *or* interest, absorp tion, concentration, application, close ap plication, fixed regard; intentness, ir tentiveness [rare], special consideratior pains, diligence, diligent attention, de votion, care, observant care, circumspec tion; study, scrutiny etc. (examination 461.3; reflection, deliberation etc (thought) 451.

3. *n.* minute attention, minutenes: meticulous minuteness, meticulousness meticulosity, exactness, exactitude, nice ty, preciseness, precision, circumstantial ity, particularity, attention to detail pedantry, pedantism *or* pedanticism finicalness, finicality, finicism, finicking ness, finickiness; care etc. 459; discrim nation etc. 465.

4. *v.* be attentive etc. *adj.,* attend, ten [obs. exc. dial.], heed, mind, observe look, see, view, mark, remark, animac vert, notice, take notice, note, make *o* take note of; advert to, attend to, giv *or* pay attention *or* heed to, direct *o* give the mind *or* attention to, turn *o* bend the mind *or* attention to, devot oneself to, devote the mind *or* thought to, fix *or* rivet the mind *or* thoughts or trouble one's head about, give a though to, apply the mind *or* attention to, occup oneself with.

look at, ~ to, ~ into, ~ after *or* ove see to, give the eye to, turn *or* bene the eye on *or* upon, fix *or* rivet the ey on; incline one's ear, incline *or* lend ar ear to, hearken to, hark, list [arch.] listen, give ear to, prick up the ears, b all ears etc. *adj.*; have an eye to, have in one's eye, bear in mind, entertain, take into consideration *or* account, keep ir sight *or* view, hold in view, have regar to, take cognizance of, recognize; appl oneself, occupy oneself.

attend to *or* mind one's business, tenc to one's business [obs. exc. dial.]; lool out, watch out [coll., U.S.], mind ou [dial.]; look lively *or* alive, look sharp look slick *or* slippy, sit up and take no tice, keep one's eye on the ball, not miss a trick, not overlook a bet [all coll.] contemplate, consider etc. (think of)

---

looking around.—WHITMAN. The curiosity of a simian is as excessive as the toil of an ant. —C. DAY. He that pryeth into every cloud may be struck with a thunderbolt.—J. RAY. Curiosity killed the cat.
457. My son, attend to my words.—BIBLE. Attend to the voice of my supplication.—BIBLE.

Attention is the first and fundamental thing ir volition.—W. JAMES.

51.27; inspect, scrutinize etc. (examine) 461.17–21; watch etc. (be careful) 59.3–6.

5. *v.* revert to, hark back to, return to, recur to.

6. *v.* meet with attention, fall under one's notice *or* observation, catch the attention, catch ~, meet *or* strike the eye, attract notice *or* attention, arrest *or* engage attention, arrest the thoughts, fix *or* rivet one's attention, wake *or* awaken the mind *or* thoughts, excite notice, invite *or* solicit attention, claim attention, claim one's thoughts, absorb *or* engross the mind *or* thoughts, engage the mind *or* thoughts, be present to the mind, be uppermost in the mind; be under consideration etc. (*see* under consideration etc. 454.3).

7. *v.* call *or* direct attention to, bring under *or* to one's notice, call *or* bring to notice, point out, point at *or* to, instigate [obs.]; put *or* lay the finger on, indicate, designate, specify, mark, tick off [slang], pipe off [slang, U.S.]; show etc. (make manifest) 525.2; inform etc. 527.7.

8. *v.* call *or* bring to attention; come to attention, stand at attention [all Mil.].

9. *adj. etc.* attentive, tentful [obs. exc. dial.], mindful, heedful, regardful, regarding with attention *or* care, advertent, circumspect; observing etc. *v.,* observant, watchful, on the watch *or* lookout, vigilant, agog, openmouthed, open-eared, open-eyed, all eyes, all ears, all eyes and ears, wakeful, awake, broad *or* wide awake, fly [slang], live [chiefly U.S.], alive, alert, on the alert, on the *qui vive* [F.].

on one's toes, on the job [coll.], Jerry on the job [slang], Johnny on the spot [slang], there with the goods [coll.], all there [coll.], ready, smart, bright, sharp; slick, slippy [both coll.]; intent, attentive [rare]; intent on, taken up with, occupied with, engaged in, engrossed in, absorbed with *or* by, wrapped in, rapt, undistracted, upon the stretch; ever head and ears in, head over heels in [coll.]; preoccupied etc. (abstracted) 458.11; steadfast etc. (persevering) 604a.3; careful etc. 459.7.

10. *int.* attention!, 'tention! [Mil., coll.]; attend!, see!, observe!, look!, look you!, look here!, look to it!, lo!, behold!, lo and behold!, witness!, hark!, hark ye!, list! [arch.], listen!, mind!, mind you!, mark!, mark you!, mark my words!, I'd have you to know!, notice!, note!; *nota!, nota bene* [both L.], N.B., n.b.; hail!, ahoy!, hello!, hollo!, hallo!, halloo!, halloa!, yo-ho!, yoo-hoo!, soho!, ho!, hey!, hi!, hist!, *ecco!* [It.]; hello etc. there!; oyez!; look out!, watch out!, [coll., U.S.], mind out! [dial.]; look lively! *or* alive!, look sharp!, look slick! *or* slippy! [all coll.]; watch your step! etc. (be careful!) 459.10.

458. Inattention
(See 457. Attention)

1. *n.* inattention, inattentiveness, heedlessness, thoughtlessness, inconsiderateness etc. *adj.;* inconsideration, want of consideration, ~ of thought etc. (*see* consideration, thought etc. 457.1), *étourderie* [F.], failure to pay attention, inadvertence *or* inadvertency; disregardance, disregard; overlooking, oversight; nonobservance, inobservance, unobservance; negligence etc. (neglect) 460; indolence, supineness etc. (inactivity) 683; insouciance etc. (indifference) 866.

2. *n.* flightiness, giddiness etc. *adj.*

3. *n.* abstraction, abstract thought *or* musing, fit of abstraction, distraction, distracted thought *or* attention, detachment, detachment *or* absence of mind, absent-mindedness, vague thoughts, blind contemplation, profound meditation *or* abstraction, depth of thought, bemusement, absorption, absorption of mind, mental absorption, engrossment, preoccupation.

musing, deep *or* somber musing, muse, trance, reverie, study, brown study, woolgathering, moonraking [dial., Eng.], dreaming, daydreaming, pipe dreaming [coll.], castle-building; dream, daydream, pipe dream [coll.], pipe [slang]; air castle, castle in the air, castle in Spain, *château en Espagne* [F.]; fancy, idle fancy, vagary.

4. *n.* confusion, distraction, disconcertion, discomposure, perplexity, confoundment, bewilderment, fluster, flusteration *or* flustration [coll.], flurry, rattle [slang], jingle [slang, U.S.], muddle,

---
458. With patient inattention hear him prate.—MEREDITH. The disease of not listening, the malady of not marking.—SHAKESPEARE. Had it been a bear it would have bitten you.

muddlement, fuddle [coll.], fuddlement [coll.], befuddlement, daze, dazzle, razzle-dazzle [slang], unsettlement, disturbance, perturbation, pother, bother, botheration [coll.], stew [coll.], pucker [coll.]; haze, fog.

5. *v.* be inattentive etc. *adj.*, not heed etc. (*see* heed etc. 457.4), give no heed, pay no attention, pay no mind [dial.], think little of, take no note *or* notice of, take no thought *or* account of, pay no regard to, disregard, overlook, pass over *or* by, close *or* shut one's eyes to; forget oneself; dismiss ~, discard *or* discharge from one's thoughts *or* mind, put out of one's head, ~ mind *or* thoughts, wean one's thoughts from, think no more of, drop the subject, set ~, put ~, lay *or* turn aside, turn away from, turn one's attention from, turn a deaf ear to, turn one's back upon, cast behind one's back; wander from the subject, let one's attention wander, get off the track [coll.]; possum [coll., U.S.], play *or* act possum; not think etc. 452.2; neglect etc. 460.4–7; be insensible etc. 823.3.

6. *v.* abstract oneself, muse, moon [coll.], dream, daydream, pipe-dream [coll.], let one's attention wander, let one's mind run on other things, dream of *or* muse on other things, be somewhere else, be absent, be woolgathering etc. *n.,* let one's wits go bird's nesting *or* a woolgathering, indulge in reverie etc. *n.,* be absent-minded etc. *adj.*

7. *v.* escape notice *or* attention, escape one, not fall *or* come under one's notice *or* observation, pass one by, not enter into one's head, come in one ear and go out at the other; forget etc. 506.4.

8. *v.* distract, distract the attention, ~ mind *or* thoughts, divert attention, divert the mind *or* thoughts, draw off the attention.

9. *v.* confuse, throw into confusion, disconcert, discompose, put out, distract, perplex, ball up [slang, U.S.], confound, bewilder, moider [dial., Eng.], fluster, flusterate *or* flustrate [coll.], fuss *or* fuss up [slang], flurry, rattle [coll.], jingle [slang, U.S.], muddle, fuddle [coll.], befuddle, becloud, addle the wits, make one's head swim, dizzy, daze, dazzle, bedazzle, razzle-dazzle [slang], upset, unsettle, disturb, perturb, bother, faze [coll., U.S.], feeze [obs. exc. dial.], flummox [slang].

10. *adj.* inattentive, not attentive etc (*see* attentive etc. 457.9); inobservant unobservant, nonobservant; unheeding heedless; regardless, disregardful, disregardant; respectless, undiscerning, unreflecting, unmindful, mindless, thoughtless, inconsiderate, inadvertent, not on the job [coll.]; blind, deaf; cursory, percursory [rare], offhand; negligent etc (neglectful) 460.8, 9; reckless etc 863.7; clumsy etc. 699.12; listless etc (indifferent) 866.4; incurious etc. 456.3 forgetful etc. 506.8; insensible etc. 823.5

11. *adj. etc.* abstracted, distracted, distraught, distrait, detached, absent, absent-minded, faraway, elsewhere, somewhere else, not all there, with one's thoughts elsewhere, lost, lost in thought preoccupied, engrossed, absorbed, engrossed *or* absorbed in thought, wrapped in thought, rapt.

bemused, dreaming, dreamy, napping daydreaming, daydreamy, pipedreaming [coll.], dreaming of *or* musing on other things, moony [coll.], in a reverie etc *n.,* woolgathering, a woolgathering moonraking [dial., Eng.], castle-building, in the clouds; sleeping, asleep, asleep at the base [slang, U.S.], asleep on the job [slang], not on the job [coll.], dead to the world, unconscious; rambling wandering; caught napping, off one's guard etc. (inexpectant) 508.7.

12. *adj. etc.* confused, bewildered, rattled [coll.] etc. *v.*; in a rattle [slang] in a razzle-dazzle [slang], in a pucker [coll.], in a stew [coll.], in a pother, all hot and bothered [slang], flustery, distracted, muzzy [coll.], mazed, muddleheaded, fuddlebrained [coll.]; fogged, foggy, hazy; dazed, dazy, in a daze; dizzy, giddy, woozy [slang], vertiginous, swimming, turned around, going around in circles, like a chicken with its head cut off [coll.]; punch-drunk, slap-happy [both slang, U.S.]; brainsick; foggy, addlepated etc. 499.12.

13. *adj.* scatterbrained [coll.], shatterbrained, shatterpated, rattlebrained, rattleheaded, rattlepated, scramblebrained [slang], shuttle-witted [Scot.], bird-witted, hen-headed [coll.], cocklebrained, harebrain, harebrained, giddy, giddybrained, giddy-headed, giddy-pated, giddy-witted, giddy as a goose, flighty, volatile, barmy, barmybrained, featherbrained, jingle-brained [slang], ga-ga

[slang, U.S.]; empty-headed, empty-pated, empty-noddled, empty-skulled; thoughtless, witless, brainless.

14. *adv.* inattentively, inadvertently etc. *adj.*; *per incuriam* [L.].

15. *int.* at ease!, stand at ease!, stand easy!

459. Care
(See 460. Neglect)

1. *n.* care, carefulness, heedfulness etc. *adj.*; heed, concern, regard, reck [arch. or poetic], solicitude, anxiety, pains, serious attention; prudence, circumspection etc. (caution) 864; forethought etc. 510.2; precaution etc. (preparation) 673; orderliness etc. 58.4; accuracy etc. 494.3; meticulousness etc. (minute attention) 457.3; conscientiousness etc. 939.2.

2. *n.* vigilance, watchfulness etc. *adj.*, surveillance, watch, vigil, lookout, tout [slang], watch and ward; watching, invigilation; watchful eye, weather eye [coll.], sharp eye, open eyes, eyes of a lynx, eyes of Argus; espionage etc. (reconnoitering) 461.8.

3. *v.* be careful etc. *adj.*, take care *or* good care, take heed, have a care, mind, mind what one is doing *or* about, mind one's business, mind one's P's and Q's [coll.], cut one's coat according to the cloth, speak by the card; watch one's step [slang], pick one's steps, put the right foot forward; think twice, be cautious, take precautions etc. 864.3, 4; pay attention to etc. 457.4.

4. *v.* be vigilant etc. *adj.*, keep watch, keep watch and ward, keep vigil, keep tout [slang], watch, vigil, be on the watch *or* lookout, keep a good *or* sharp lookout, look sharp, look about one, look with one's own eyes, be on one's guard, have all one's eyes *or* wits about one, keep one's eyes open, have the eyes open, keep one's eyes peeled [slang], keep a weather eye open [coll.], keep the ears on *or* to the ground; stop, look and listen; sleep with one eye open; look out, watch out [coll., U.S.], mind out [dial.]; mind one's eye, look lively *or* alive, look slick *or* slippy [all coll.];

watch for etc. (expect) 507.4, 5; be alert etc. 682.15.

5. *v.* care, heed, reck [arch. or poetic], mind, notice, think, consider, take care, ~ heed *or* thought of, feel care *or* solicitude, have *or* feel concern *or* interest.

6. *v.* care for, take care of, look *or* see to, look after, look *or* watch out for [coll.], keep tab on [coll.], take about [Scot.], attend to, keep an eye on *or* upon, keep a sharp eye on *or* upon, keep in sight *or* view, watch over, keep watch over, watch, mind, exercise oversight, ride herd on [slang, West. U.S.], foster; chaperon, matronize, play gooseberry; protect etc. 664.6; minister to etc. 746.8; defend etc. 717.7.

7. *adj.* careful, regardful, heedful, advertent, thoughtful, mindful, considerate, solicitous, taking care etc. *v.*, marked with care, done with care; painstaking, painful [arch.]; sure-footed; prudent, wary etc. (cautious) 864.6; scrupulous etc. (conscientious) 939.8; tidy etc. (orderly) 58.7; exact, meticulous etc. (accurate) 494.11; *cavendo tutus* [L.] etc. (safe) 664.10.

8. *adj. etc.* vigilant, watchful, on the lookout, *aux aguets* [F.], observant, guarded, guardful [rare], on guard, on one's guard, alert, on the alert, on the *qui vive* [F.], on the job [coll.], wakeful, awake, broad *or* wide awake, all eyes, agog, with open eyes, with one's eyes open, open-eyed, Argus-eyed, lynx-eyed; sleepless, unsleeping; attentive etc. 457.9; on the watch for etc. (expectant) 507.7.

9. *adv.* carefully etc. *adj.*, with care, easy [coll.]; gingerly etc. (cautiously) 864.8.

10. *int.* be careful!, careful!, careful now!; watch out!, beware!, beware of the dog!; take care!, take it easy!; look out! etc. (attention!) 457.10.

460. Neglect
(See 459. Care)

1. *n.* neglect, neglectfulness, carelessness etc. *adj.*; negligence *or* negligency,

---

459. Be sober and keep vigil.—NEALE. Not only watchful at night, but alert in the drowsy afternoon.—PATER. The five watchful senses. —MILTON. *Quis custodiet istos custodes* [Who will guard the guards?]—JUVENAL. Be sober, be vigilant; because your adversary the Devil . . . walketh about.—BIBLE. Care will kill a cat.—WITHER. The incessant care and labor of his mind.—SHAKESPEARE.
460. Whose most tender mercy is neglect.— CRABBE. His noble negligences teach / What

culpa [Law], laches, laxity, laxness, remissness; inadvertence *or* inadvertency; disregard, disregardance; slight, oversight, omission, default, abandon; *laisser-aller, laisser aller, laissez aller, laissez faire, laisser faire* [all F.]; conspiracy of silence; paraleipsis *or* paralepsis *or* paralipsis [Rhetoric]; the go-by [slang], the run-around [slang, U.S.].

inattention etc. 458; nonobservance etc. 773; indolence, supineness etc. (inactivity) 683; nonchalance etc. (insensibility) 823; imprudence, recklessness etc. (rashness) 863; slovenry etc. 59.1; inexactness etc. (inaccuracy) 495.4; improvidence etc. (nonpreparation) 674; noncompletion etc. 730; procrastination, deferment etc. (delay) 133.2; cut, cold shoulder [both coll.] etc. (snub) 930.4; dereliction etc. 927.

2. *n.* careless work, hasty work, slovenly performance, bad job, sad work, neglect of execution; neglect of duty; slapdash, a lick and a promise [both coll.]; neglected work, holiday [slang, chiefly Naut.]; bungling etc. 699.3, 4.

3. *n.* neglector *or* neglecter, negligent, negligent person, slapdash [North. Eng., dial.], ignorer, disregarder, trifler, waiter on Providence, Micawber, procrastinator, drifter [coll.], dead one [slang], stiff [slang]; slacker [coll.] etc. (shirker) 623.4; waster, wastrel etc. (prodigal) 818.2; bum [slang, U.S.], loafer etc. (idler) 683.7; tramp, hobo [U.S.] etc. (wanderer) 268.2; bungler etc. 701.

4. *v.* be negligent etc. *adj.*, neglect, take no care of, not take care of etc. (*see* take care of etc. 459.6); overlook, disregard, forget, slight, pass over *or* by, pass up [slang, U.S.], let pass, blink *or* wink at, connive at, gloss over, take no note *or* notice of, take no thought *or* account of, leave out of one's calculation, pay no attention *or* regard to, leave in *or* out in the cold [coll.], lose sight of.

let slip, let slide [coll.], let go, leave go [dial.], let it ride [slang, U.S.], let take its course, let the grass grow under one's feet; forget oneself; not think *or* consider, not give a thought to; be inattentive etc. 458.5, 6; be caught napping etc. (not expect) 508.4; be rash etc. 863.5; not do etc. 681.2; not observe etc. 773.3.

5. *v.* ignore, refuse to notice, close *or* shut one's eyes to, not see for looking [joc.]; refuse to hear, turn a deaf ear to, let come in one ear and go out at the other; not trouble oneself with, not trouble one's head with *or* about, have no truck with [coll. and dial.]; let well enough alone, turn one's back upon; keep *or* leave out of sight, sink, throw into the background.

dismiss from one's thoughts *or* mind, forget about it, forget, let it go [coll.], think no more of, drop the subject, put ~, set ~, cast *or* lay aside, push *or* thrust aside *or* to one side; laugh off *or* away, dismiss with a laugh; slight, make light of, treat with indifference *or* disdain, turn up one's nose at, sneeze at, toss the head; give the go-by [slang], give the run-around [slang, U.S.]; cut, turn the cold shoulder to [both coll.] etc. (snub) 930.7.

6. *v.* do carelessly *or* superficially, do by halves, do in a slipshod fashion, do anyhow *or* all anyhow, do in any old way [coll.] etc. *adv.*; perfunctorize, perfunctorate [both rare]; perstringe [now rare], scamp, skimp [coll.], trifle, fribble, trifle with, play with, slight, slight over [now rare], pass over, pass over lightly *or* superficially, slip *or* skip over, slur, slur over, skim, skim over, skim the surface, touch upon, touch upon lightly *or* in passing, touch lightly, hit the high spots [slang], give a lick and a promise [coll.].

toss off *or* out, knock off *or* out [coll.], hammer *or* pound out, bat out [slang], slap out [coll.], slapdash [coll.]; toss *or* throw together; go off half-cocked *or* at half cock [coll.]; do slap-bang [coll.] etc. 863.8; botch etc. 699.9; not complete etc. 730.2.

7. *v.* pretermit, leave undone, fail to perform, forbear, skip, jump, miss, omit, cut [coll.], let be *or* alone, let a-be [Scot. and dial. Eng.], pass over, pass up [slang, U.S.], abandon; leave a loose thread, leave at loose ends; procrastinate, delay, shelve etc. (postpone) 133.4.

8. *adj.* neglectful, neglective, negligent, neglecting etc. *v.*; careless, heed-

---

others' toils despair to reach.—PRIOR.   Such sweet neglect more taketh me / Than all th' adulteries of art.—JONSON.   Procrastination is the thief of time.—YOUNG.   A carelessness of life and beauty marks the glutton, the idler and the fool in their deadly path across history. —MASEFIELD.

less, unheeding, disregardful, **disregardant**, regardless, respectless, thoughtless, unthinking, inconsiderate, mindless, unmindful, forgetful, culpose [Law], inadvertent, unsolicitous; lax, loose, slack, remiss; perfunctory, perfunctionary, perfunctorious; cursory, percursory [rare], offhand; imprudent, reckless etc. 863.6, 7; clumsy etc. 699.12; inattentive etc. 458.10; indolent etc. 683.13; insouciant etc. (indifferent) 823.5; slovenly etc. (disorderly) 59.8, 9; improvident etc. (shiftless) 674.11; procrastinating etc. (dilatory) 133.9; nonobservant etc. 773.5.

9. *adj.* unwary, unwatchful, unvigilant; unobservant, inobservant, nonobservant; unguarded, off one's guard; incircumspect [rare], uncircumspect; absent, absent-minded; sleeping, asleep; asleep at the base, asleep on the job, not on the job [all slang, U.S.]; off one's guard etc. (inexpectant) 508.7.

10. *adj.* neglected, unattended to, uncared-for, unthought-of, unheeded, unperceived, unseen, unobserved, unnoticed, unmarked, unremarked, unregarded, disregarded, overlooked, missed, passed over, passed up [slang, U.S.], ignored, slighted; abandoned, left undone; out in the cold, left out in the cold [both coll.]; buried in a napkin, hid under a bushel; postponed, shelved etc. (*see* postpone, shelve etc. 133.4).

11. *adj.* unexamined, unstudied, unsearched, unscanned, unweighed, unsifted, unexplored.

12. *adv.* neglectfully, negligently, carelessly etc. *adj.*; anyhow, in any old way [coll.], any which way *or* anywhichway [slang], helter-skelter [coll.], ramble-scramble [slang], hand over head [now rare], happen what may; *per incuriam* [L.], through carelessness; slap-bang [coll.] etc. (recklessly) 863.8; in an unguarded moment etc. (unexpectedly) 508.11.

13. *int.* never mind!, no matter!, think no more of it!, do not give it another thought!, let it pass!, let it go! [coll.], ignore it!, forget it! [coll.], skip it! [slang], drop it! [slang]; it will be all the same a hundred years hence!, it will all come out in the wash! [coll.]; what's the difference!, what's the diff! [slang], what do I care!; what matter! etc. 643.14.

461. Inquiry
(See 462. Answer)

1. *n.* inquiry, enquiry, inquiring etc. *v.*, inquiration [dial.], inquirendo, inquisition, inquest, percontation [rare]; zetetic.

2. *n.* search, research, quest, hunt, hue and cry, shag [slang], looksee [slang, U.S.]; frisk, frisking, fan, fanning [all underworld slang, U.S.]; rummage, ransack [arch.]; still hunt [U.S.]; chase etc. (pursuit) 622.

3. *n.* examination, examen, exam [coll.], ex [slang], quiz [U.S.], go [Eng., Univ. cant], test; inspection, scrutiny, survey, perusal, review, investigation, indagation; probe, probation [now rare]; search, research etc. *above*; exploration, explore [coll.], explorement [rare], exploratory examination; check, check-up; critical examination, criticism, critique; analysis, analyzation; assay, docimasy, titration [Chem. and Physiol.], dissection, anatomy, resolution, sifting etc. *v.*

autopsy, post-mortem examination, post-mortem ex post facto examination; trial, assize, inquest, inquisition, inquisitional examination; oral examination, oral [coll.]; written examination, written [coll.]; previous examination, little go [Cambridge Univ. cant], responsions *or* smalls [Oxford Univ. cant]; first public examination, moderations *or* mods [Oxford Univ. cant]; midyear examination, midyear *or* midyears [coll.]; final examination, final *or* finals [coll.], greats *or* great go [Oxford Univ. cant]; honors [Eng. Univ. cant], tripos [Cambridge Univ. cant]; intelligence test, Binet test, alpha *or* beta test, aussage test; hearing, audition [coll.]; cross-examination etc. *below* 461.9; study, consideration etc. (thought) 451.

4. *n.* close inquiry, ~ examination etc. (*see* inquiry, examination etc. *above*), strict inquiry, searching investigation, strict *or* rigorous examination, careful *or* thorough search, exhaustive study; perquisition, perscrutation, pervestigation [obs.]; deep study etc. (close attention) 457.2.

---

461. Gently scan your fellow man.—BURNS.
To seek your hero in a distant soil!—GRAY.
Examine well your own thoughts.—CHAUCER.
He that questioneth much shall learn much.—

461.5 – 461.16

5. *n.* introspection, introspectiveness, inlook *or* inlooking [rare], self-examination; introspectionism.

6. *n.* re-examination, reinquiry, recheck, review, revision, rebeholding; research etc. (*see* search etc. *above* 461.3).

7. *n.* pre-examination, preliminary *or* previous examination, presurvey, preview, presearch.

8. *n.* reconnoitering etc. *v.*, reconnoiter, reconnaissance *or* reconnoissance, exploitation, advance *or* preliminary examination *or* survey; espionage, espial; domiciliary visit [Law]; look behind the scenes, peep behind the curtain; lantern of Diogenes.

9. *n.* questioning etc. *v.*, interrogation, interrogatory; quizzery [rare], quizzism, quizzification [rare]; quiz, examination etc. *above* 461.3; cross-examination, cross-interrogation, cross-questioning; grilling, roasting [coll.], third degree [coll., U.S.], *question extraordinaire* [F.]; interpellation; catechism, catechesis, catechization; catechetical method, Socratic method *or* induction; zetetic philosophy, Pyrrhonism, skepticism; challenge, dispute; inquisitiveness etc. (curiosity) 455; discussion etc. (reasoning) 476.

10. *n.* question, query, *quaere* [L.] inquiry *or* enquiry; problem, case *or* point in question, subject of dispute, issue, question *or* point at issue, point to be solved, point *or* matter in dispute, disputed point, moot point *or* case; proposition [Logic], porism [Geom.]; argument [obs.], *quodlibet* [L.]; questionnaire, questionary; catch question; feeler, leading question; puzzling *or* baffling question *or* problem, poser etc. (enigma) 533.2; vexed question, knotty point etc. (dilemma) 704.4; bone of contention etc. 713.5; subject etc. (topic) 454.

11. *n.* interrogation point, question mark, question stop [rare], ?.

12. *n.* inquirer *or* enquirer, querier, querist, questioner, questionist, interrogator, interrogatrix [*fem.*], poser [Hist.], quizzer, quiz, catechist; inquisitor, inquisitionist; cross-questioner, cross-interrogator, cross-examiner; interlocutor, interlocutress *or* interlocutrice *or* interlocutrix [*fem.*]; zetetic, seeker,

BACON. It is the modest, not the presumptuous inquirer, who makes a real and safe progress.—ST. JOHN.

searcher, search [rare], perquisitor; quidnunc etc. (inquisitive) 455.2.

13. *n.* examiner, examinant, investigator, indagator, inspector, inlooker, probator [obs.]; analyzer, analyst; scrutator, scrutinizer, scrutineer, perscrutator; reconnoiterer, spy, detective etc. (secret agent) 528.

14. *v.* inquire *or* enquire, make inquiry etc. *n.*, take up ∼, institute ∼, pursue ∼, follow up ∼, conduct *or* carry on an inquiry, bring in question, ask about, ask questions, put queries, seek to know by questioning, make examination *or* inquiry respecting; question, query, ask, demand, ask a question, propose *or* propound a question; inquisite, inquisition, make inquisition; ask for one's hand etc. 765.4.

15. *v.* interrogate, question, questionmark, put to the question, require an answer, inquire of, query, quiz [U.S.], quizzify [rare], pose [obs.], buzz [underworld slang, U.S.], catechize, examine, examine *or* try by questions; pump, pump for information, worm out of; probe, sound, sound out, feel, feel out, feel the pulse, pick *or* suck the brain of; interpellate; cross-question, cross-interrogate, cross-examine; roast [coll.], grill, put on the grill [coll.], sweat [slang], third-degree [slang, U.S.], put through the third degree [coll., U.S.], put the pressure on [coll.], put the screws to [slang, U.S.], go over [slang, U.S.]; try etc. 969.11.

16. *v.* seek, search, seek *or* search for, go in search for, look, pry, peer, look round *or* around, look for, look around *or* about for, look out for, see after, try to find, hunt, hunt for *or* after, scout for [coll.], fish for, dig *or* delve for, prowl after, mouse, pursue, quest, follow, follow up, clue *or* clew, seek *or* follow a clue *or* clew, trail, follow the trail *or* scent of, track, track down, ∼ in [rare], ∼ out *or* up, trace, trace down *or* up, nose, nose out, smell *or* sniff out, hunt out, search out, ferret out, fish out, pry out, scout out [coll.]; hunt up, look up.

rake, scour, rummage, ransack, look ∼, peer *or* pry into every hole and corner, look high and low, look upstairs and downstairs, look all over hell [vulg.], leave no stone unturned, turn everything upside down *or* inside out, visit *or* look behind the scenes; rifle, forage; gun for, go gunning for; still-hunt [U.S.]; frisk, fan, give a frisking *or* fanning [all underworld slang, U.S.]; feel for etc. (experiment) 463.8, 9.

17. *v.* examine, examinate [rare], subject to examination etc. *n.,* take stock of, look *or* peer at, look *or* search through, go over *or* through, look over, overlook, overhaul, scrutinize, scan, peruse; study, consider, contemplate, give *or* bend the mind to, devote oneself to, devote the mind *or* attention to, fix *or* rivet the mind *or* thoughts on; review, pass under review; search, search through, explore, investigate, pervestigate [rare], indagate, inspect, inlook, look *or* peer into, search into, pry into, dive *or* delve into, probe, sound, fathom; introspect, examine introspectively; discuss, canvass, agitate.

test, analyze, make an analysis, assay, titrate [Chem. and Physiol.]; anatomize, dissect, break down, separate, reduce, parse, resolve, sift, winnow, thrash out; check, check over *or* through, check up on [coll.], audit, make sure of; size *or* size up [coll.], take one's measure [slang]; post-mortem, autopsy; put to the proof etc. (experiment) 463.8; feel, touch etc. (grope) 463.9; take into consideration, think over etc. (think) 451.27–29; discuss etc. (reason) 476.10, 11.

18. *v.* examine thoroughly, make a thorough examination *or* study, examine *or* study closely *or* intently, make a close study of, look closely at, scrutinize etc. *above,* subject to close scrutiny *or* investigation, view *or* try in all its phases, examine point by point, go over step by step, go deep into, probe to the bottom *or* quick; perscrutate, pervestigate; study absorbedly, pore over, mouse over [U.S.].

19. *v.* examine cursorily, take a cursory view of, give a quick *or* cursory look, glance at *or* over, take a glance at, cast *or* pass the eyes over, give the once-over [slang, U.S.], run over, run the eye over, scan [coll.], pass over, pass over lightly *or* superficially, slip *or* skip over *or* through, skim, skim over *or* through, slur, slur over, touch upon, touch upon lightly *or* in passing, perstringe [now rare], dip into; turn over the leaves, flip through the pages.

20. *v.* re-examine, recheck, reinquire, reconsider, review, rebehold; retrace, retrace one's steps, go back over; research etc. (*see* search etc. *above* 461.16).

21. *v.* pre-examine, presurvey, preview, presearch.

22. *v.* reconnoiter, make a reconnaissance etc. *n.,* case [underworld slang, U.S.], spy, spy out, play the spy, peep out, scout, scout out [coll.], tout [slang], pry.

23. *v.* be in question etc. *adv.,* undergo examination.

24. *adj.* inquiring, questioning etc. *v.*; inquirent [rare], interrogative, percontatorial [rare], zetetic; inquisitory [rare], inquisitorial, inquisitorious [rare], inquisiturient, inquisitional; catechetic(al), catechistic(al); indagative, indagatory [rare]; investigative, investigatory, investigational; explorative, exploratory, explorational; analytic(al); in search *or* quest of, on the lookout for, loaded *or* out for bear [slang, U.S.], in the market for; all-searching; inquisitive etc. (curious) 455.5.

25. *adj.* doubtful, questionable, undetermined, undecided etc. (uncertain) 475.9, 10; disputed etc. (*see* dispute etc. 485.6).

26. *adv. etc.* in question *or* dispute, in *or* at issue, in course of inquiry, in contemplation, *ad referendum* [L.], under consideration, ~ investigation etc. *n.,* under advisement, *sub judice* [L.], up *or* open for discussion, before the house, on foot, on the docket, on the table, on the floor, on the carpet, on the tapis, *sur le tapis* [F.]; on the agenda.

27. *adv. etc.* what?, what on earth?, what in all the world?, what the hell? [slang]; in what respect?; what is the matter?, what's in the wind?, what's in the air?, what's afoot?, what's up?; who?, which?

28. *adv. etc.* why?, wherefore?, why ever? *or* whyever? [coll.], why for? *or* whyfor? [dial. and arch.], for why? [now dial.]; *pourquoi?* [F.], *warum?* [G.], how?, how come? [coll.], how comes it?, how does it come to pass?, how does it happen?, how is it?, how so?, how ever? [coll.], on what account?, from what cause?, for what cause *or* reason?, what is the reason?, what is it

all about?; why the heck? *or* hell? [vulg.].

29. *adv. etc.* when?, at what time?, in what period?, on what occasion?, how long ago?, how soon?, when ever? [coll.].

30. *adv. etc.* where?, whereabouts?, whereabout? [now rare], whence?, whither?, where away? [chiefly dial.], whereaway? [chiefly Scot.], whereto?, whereunto? [arch.], wheretill? [now Scot.], whereuntil? [rare], to what *or* which place?

31. *adv. etc.* ain't? [now coll.], *n'est-ce pas?* [F.], *nicht wahr?* [G.], *verdad?* [Sp.].

32. *int.* really?, indeed?, is that so?; I wonder!; you don't say!; *quaere* [L.].

462. Answer
(See 461. Inquiry)

1. *n.* answer, response, responsal [obs. exc. Hist.], respond [rare], respondence *or* respondency, reply, replication, riposte *or* ripost, rejoinder, retort, return, comeback [slang]; rise [slang]; subjoinder; acknowledgment, receipt; rescript, rescription [arch.]; repartee, clever ~, ready *or* witty reply *or* retort, snappy comeback [slang]; password, high sign [slang, U.S.]; *risposta* [It.; Mus.]; echo, re-echo, reverberation; counterstatement, counterblast, countercharge, contraremonstrance; contradiction, rebuttal; yes-and-no answer, evasive reply; back answer, fling etc. (gibe) 930.3; confutation etc. 479; oracle etc. 513.

2. *n.* (legal) surrejoinder, surrebutter, surrebuttal, rebutter, counterstatement, answer, rebuttal, reply, rejoinder, replication, plea etc. (defense) 937.2.

3. *n.* explanation, solution etc. (interpretation) 522; discovery etc. 481a.1, reason, rationale etc. (motive) 615.

4. *n.* answerer, replier, responder, respondent, responser; defender, defendant, respondent, claimant [all Law].

5. *v.* answer, make *or* give answer etc. *n.*, respond, reply, replicate [rare], say,

riposte *or* ripost, rejoin, retort, return, return for answer, flash back; come back, come back at, come right back at [all slang]; acknowledge, make acknowledgment, receipt [U.S., rare]; rebut, make a rebuttal; repartee [rare]; echo, re-echo; answer back; parry etc. (confute) 479.2.

6. *v.* (legal) surrebut, surrejoin, rebut, reply, counterclaim; plead etc. (defend) 937.6.

7. *v.* explain etc. (interpret) 522; determine, fathom, solve etc. (discover) 481a.3–5.

8. *v.* answer to, answer, respond to, respond [U.S., rare], respond to satisfactorily, act in response; correspond etc. (be related) 9.3.

9. *v.* answer the purpose, serve etc. (suffice) 639.3, (be useful) 644.2.

10. *v.* get an answer etc. *n.*, provoke response, get a rise out of [slang].

11. *adj.* answering etc. *v.*, responsive, respondent, responsorial [rare]; antiphonal, antiphonic; oracular, Oedipean; conclusive.

12. *adj.* answerable, accountable, responsible, liable, amenable, unexempt from.

13. *adv. etc.* for this reason, because etc. (since) 155.8.

14. *int.* eureka! etc. 480a.9.

463. Experiment

1. *n.* experiment, experimentation, trial, tryout [coll.], workout [slang], test, docimasy, probation [now rare], tentative method, experimental use *or* application; essay, assay; proof, verification, criterion, diagnostic; decisive trial *or* criterion, crucial test, *experimentum crucis* [L.]; severe trial *or* test, ordeal; trial and error; audition [coll.], hearing; trial flight, test hop [slang, Aeronaut.]; experimentalism; docimology; analysis, investigation etc. (examination) 461.3; attempt etc. 675.

2. *n.* empiricism, rule of thumb.

3. *n.* speculation, venture, random

---

462. Will your answer serve fit to all questions?—SHAKESPEARE. A soft answer turneth away wrath.—BIBLE. I called him, but he gave me no answer.—BIBLE. It is not every question that deserves an answer.—PUBLILIUS.

463. It is as foolish to make experiments upon the constancy of a friend as upon the chastity of a wife.—JOHNSON. In the full tide of successful experiment.—JEFFERSON. The man who makes the experiment deservedly claims the honour and the reward.—HORACE. The proof of the pudding is in the eating.

shot, leap in the dark etc. (gamble) 621.2, 6.

4. *n.* feeler; pilot *or* messenger balloon, trial balloon, *ballon d'essai* [F.]; pilot engine; scout; straw to show the wind; weathervane etc. 338.9.

5. *n.* reagent, crucible, check, touchstone; pyx, pyx chest, trial of the pyx [all Eng.]; curcuma paper, turmeric paper, litmus paper.

6. *n.* experimenter, experimentist, experimentalist, experimentator, experimentarian [now rare]; tester, tryer-out; experimental engineer; assayer, essayer, essayist; analyst, analyzer; chemist; prospector; forty-niner, Argonaut, Argonaut of '49 [all U.S.]; speculator, venturer etc. (gambler) 621.15.

7. *n.* experimentee, testee, subject, object, guinea pig.

8. *v.* experiment, experimentize, experimentalize; make an experiment etc. *n.*, experiment *or* practice upon, test, try, test *or* try out [coll.], give a tryout [coll.], give a workout [slang], make a trial of, give a trial to, subject to trial, operate by test *or* trial; try it on [slang], try it on the dog [Theat. cant]; essay, assay; put ∼, bring *or* submit to the test *or* proof, prove, verify; try one's strength; audition [coll.], give an audition [coll.], give a hearing; attempt etc. 675.3.

9. *v.* grope, feel *or* grope for, feel ∼, grope *or* pick one's way, fumble; feel, touch; put *or* throw out a feeler, send up a trial balloon *or* pilot balloon, see how the land lies *or* the wind blows, consult the barometer, feel the pulse; fish for, bob for, angle; cast *or* beat about for, beat the bushes; search, probe, explore etc. 461.16, 17.

10. *v.* speculate, venture, etc. (chance) 621.17, (attempt) 675.3.

11. *v.* stand the test *or* proof, stand up, pass, pass an examination, pass muster, satisfy, be satisfactory etc. 831.7.

12. *adj.* experimental, experimentative, experimentarian [now rare]; probative, probatory, probationary; analytic(al); docimastic(al), docimological; speculative, tentative, provisional; empirical; trial-and-error.

13. *adj.* tried, tested; proved, proven.

14. *adv.* experimentally etc. *adj.*, by rule of thumb, by trial and error; on trial, under examination, on *or* under probation, under suspicion, on approval.

464. Comparison

1. *n.* comparison, comparing, likening etc. *v.*; collation, comparative *or* relative estimate, comparative relation, comparability; comparableness, comparativeness etc. *adj.*; ratio, proportion; parallelism, parallelization; identification; balance, contrast, opposition; confrontment, confrontation; simile, similitude; metaphor, allegory etc. (figure of speech) 521; relation etc. 9; similarity etc. 17; difference etc. 15, 18.

2. *v.* compare, bring into comparison, make *or* institute a comparison etc. *n.*, liken, like [now dial.], compare *or* liken to *or* with, collate, match; similize, similitude, similitudinize, simile [rare]; set side by side, put alongside, place by the side of; place in juxtaposition, juxtapose, juxtaposit; parallel, parallelize, draw a parallel; contrast, oppose, set over against, set over against one another, set in opposition, confront, set *or* pit against one another; balance, weigh; connect, bring into relation with etc. (relate) 9.4; differentiate etc. 15.6; allegorize etc. (figure) 521.2.

3. *v.* compare notes, exchange views *or* observations, match dope [slang, U.S.].

4. *v.* be comparable etc. *adj.*, compare, compare to *or* with, admit *or* be worthy of comparison, parallel; vie, vie with; be like, resemble etc. 17.7.

5. *adj.* comparative, comparatival [Gram.], collative [rare], contrastive, connective, parallelistic; relative etc. 9.5; metaphorical etc. 521.3.

6. *adj.* comparable, equiparable [obs.]; proportionable, proportional, proportionate; approximative etc. 9.7; like, analogous etc. (similar) 17.10–16.

7. *adv. etc.* comparatively etc. *adj.*, as compared with etc. *v.*; relatively etc. 9.9.

---

464. Compare dead happiness with living woe. —SHAKESPEARE. Shall pack horses... compare with Caesars?—SHAKESPEARE. Comparisons are odorous.—SHAKESPEARE. Comparisons are odious.

465. Discrimination
(See 465a. Indiscrimination)

1. *n.* discrimination, distinguishment, distinction, differentiation, diorism, perception *or* appreciation of differences; diagnosis, diagnostication; criticism; critique; judgment, discernment, flair, acuteness, acumen, insight, penetration, perspicacity; discretion, discreetness etc. *adj.*; tact, finesse; taste, discriminating taste, aesthetic *or* artistic judgment, appreciation, critical judgment *or* appreciation.

sensitivity, sensibility; nice *or* subtle distinction, refined discrimination, delicacy of perception, critical niceness, nicety, refinement, delicacy, subtlety; hair-splitting, overnice *or* oversubtle distinction; meticulousness etc. 457.3; precision, exactness etc. (accuracy) 494.3; estimation, appraisal etc. (measurement) 466; good judgment etc. (wisdom) 498.3; good taste etc. 850; bad taste etc. 851; fastidiousness etc. 868; choice etc. 609.

2. *v.* discriminate, distinguish, exercise discretion *or* discrimination, use discernment etc. *n.*, take into account *or* consideration; separate, segregate, sever, severalize, divide, set apart, separate the sheep from the goats, separate the wheat from the tares, separate *or* winnow the chaff from the wheat, sift; draw the *or* a line, fix *or* set a limit; balance, weigh, give *or* allow due weight to, weigh carefully; pick and choose; exercise critical judgment, criticize; diagnose, diagnosticate; split hairs, make a nice *or* subtle distinction etc. *n.*; differentiate etc. 15.6; display taste etc. 850.4; be fastidious etc. 868.3.

3. *v.* discriminate *or* distinguish between, make a distinction, draw distinctions, recognize *or* perceive differences; know which is which, know what's what [coll.], "know a hawk from a handsaw" (Shakespeare); select etc. 609.7.

4. *adj.* discriminating etc. *v.*, discriminative; discretional, discretionary; distinctive [rare], dioristic(al) [obs.]; critical, diacritic(al); diagnostic; tactful, discreet; perceptive, perspicacious, keen, acute, astute; nice, subtle, fine, delicate; differentiative etc. 15.8; tasteful etc. 850.5; finical etc. (fastidious) 868.4; selective etc. 609.15.

465a. Indiscrimination
(See 465. Discrimination)

1. *n.* indiscrimination, indiscriminateness, indistinctness [rare], indistinction, want of distinction etc. 465, lack of discernment, inability to discriminate; uncriticalness; promiscuousness, promiscuity.

2. *v.* be indiscriminate etc. *adj.*, not discriminate etc. (*see* discriminate etc. 465.2), overlook etc. (460.4) a distinction; confound, confuse, muddle, tumble, jumble, jumble together, heap indiscriminatingly; swallow whole, judge in a lump; use loosely.

3. *adj.* indiscriminate, indiscriminated, indiscriminative, indiscriminating, undiscriminating, not discriminating etc. (*see* discriminating etc. 465.4); indistinguished, indistinguishable, undistinguished, undistinguishable, indistinct [rare], lacking distinction; imprudent, injudicious, ill-judged, ill-advised, ill-imagined, ill-devised, inconsistent; indiscreet, indiscretionary; tactless, untactful; uncritical, uncriticizing; unmeasured; promiscuous, haphazard etc. (disorderly) 59.8, 13; purposeless etc. 621.21.

466. Measurement

1. *n.* measurement, measure, measuration, admeasurement, mensuration, metage, survey, valuation, appreciation, assessment; assize, assizement; appraisal, appraisement; estimate, estimation; measuring, gauging etc. *v.*; dead reckoning [Naut.]; reckoning, calculation, computation etc. (numeration) 85; extent etc. (size) 192, (distance) 196, (length) 200, (quantity) 25; discrimination etc. 465.

2. *n.* measure, gauge, rule, yardstick [fig.], standard, pattern, model, type, scale, canon, criterion, test, check; norm, norma.

---

465. *Ne e quovis ligno Mercurius fiat* [Let Mercury not be carved from every stick].—ERASMUS. There is a lot of difference in pioneering for gold and pioneering for spinach. —W. ROGERS. He could distinguish, and divide / A hair 'twixt south and south-west side. —BUTLER. *Il y a fagots et fagots* [There are fagots and fagots].

466. With what measure ye mete, it shall be measured to you again.—BIBLE.

466.3 – 466.12

3. *n.* (measures) linear measure etc. 200.6, cubic ~, liquid ~, dry ~, square *or* circular measure, chain measure, apothecaries' fluid measure, surveyor's area measure, metric system, weight etc. 319.4.

millimeter, centimeter, decimeter, meter, decameter, hectometer, kilometer, myriameter; square foot, square yard etc. (*see* foot, yard etc. 200.6), square millimeter etc., acre, township, centiare, are, hectare; cubic foot, cubic yard etc. (*see* foot, yard etc. 200.6), cubic millimeter etc.; link, chain; square link, square pole, square rod, square chain, acre.

gill, pint, quart, gallon, barrel, hogshead, milliliter, centiliter, deciliter, liter, decaliter, hectoliter, kiloliter, stere; minim, dram; peck, bushel; second, minute, quadrant, circle *or* circumference; ampere, volt etc. (electrical units) 158a.5.

4. *n.* (measuring instruments) meter, measure, measurer; rule, ruler, straightedge; foot rule, two-foot rule, yardstick; slide *or* sliding rule, slip stick [slang]; size stick; tape, measuring tape, tape measure, graduated tape, steel [coll.]; square, steel square, set square, T square, try square; compass, dial; dividers, calipers; gauge, standard gauge, broad *or* wide gauge, narrow gauge; measuring machine; level, spirit level; plumb, plumb rule, plumb line, plummet, bob, plumb bob, lead; dipsey, dipsey *or* deep-sea line *or* lead [Naut.]; log, log line, patent log, taffrail log, harpoon log, ground log [all Naut.]; logometer; line, chain, engineer's ~, Gunter's *or* surveyor's chain, rod; scale, graduation, graduated scale; nonius; quadrant, theodolite; transit, transit theodolite; viagraph.

steelyard, balance etc. (weighing instruments) 319.5; vernier etc. (minuteness) 193.7; adding machine etc. (numeration) 85.5; anemometer etc. (wind) 349.17; barometer etc. (air) 338.8; bathometer etc. (depth) 208.4; dynamometer etc. (force) 276.6; galvanometer etc. (electricity) 157a.6; goniometer etc. (angle) 244.3; photometer etc. (optical instruments) 445; radiometer etc. (light) 420.16; stethoscope etc. (medical) 662.22; thermometer etc. 389; chromatometer etc. (color) 428.8; nephelometer (cloud) 353.7; pneumatometer etc. (gas) 334.4; speedometer etc. (velocity) 274.8; oscillometer etc. (oscillation) 314.7; hydrometer etc. (fluid) 333.5; hygrometer etc. (moisture) 339.4; hyetometer, fluviometer etc. (rain) 348.12, 13; clock etc. (timepiece) 114.6.

5. *n.* watermark, water line *or* waterline; light water line, load water line, load-line mark, Plimsoll mark *or* line [all Naut.]; floodmark, tidemark, high-water mark.

6. *n.* landmark etc. (limit) 233.

7. *n.* co-ordinates, ordinate and abscissa, polar co-ordinates, latitude and longitude, declination and right ascension, altitude and azimuth.

8. *n.* (science of measurement) stereometry, planimetry, altimetry, topography, cartography; chorometry, chorography; hypsometry, hypsography; surveying, land surveying; geodesy, geodetics, geodaesia; orthometry [rare]; cadastre, cadastral survey, cadastration; metrology, science of weights and measures; geometry etc. (mathematics) 85.2; goniometry etc. (angular measurement) 244.3.

9. *n.* measurer; surveyor, land surveyor; geodesist, geodete; chorographer, topographer, cartographer; geometer etc. (mathematician) 85.6.

10. *v.* measure, mensurate [rare], mete, meter, gauge; value, valuate, place *or* set a value on; assess, rate, appraise; estimate, form an estimate, make *or* furnish an estimation; appreciate, prize; size, size up [both coll.]; measure out, mark the bounds *or* limits of; span, pace, step, inch; caliper, divide, apply the compass etc. *n.*, dial.

weigh, balance, strike a balance, poise, hold the scales, place in the beam; kick the beam; plumb, probe, sound, fathom, heave the log *or* lead [Naut.]; survey, plot, block in *or* out, rule, draw to scale; graduate, calibrate; quantify etc. 25.5; take the average etc. 29.2; reckon, calculate, compute etc. (numerate) 85.7; quantify etc. 25.5.

11. *adj.* measuring etc. *v.,* metric(al); mensurational, mensurative, mensural; geodetic(al), geodesic(al); cadastral, hypsographic(al), hypsometric(al), chorographic(al), topographic(al), cartographic(al).

12. *adj.* measurable, mensural, mensurable, gaugeable, fathomable, estimable, determinable, computable, assess-

467. Evidence
(See 468. Counterevidence)

1. *n.* evidence, proof, medium of proof; promise *or* premiss, data (*sing.* datum), praecognitum (*pl.* praecognita); facts, grounds; evidence in chief, primary *or* secondary evidence, external *or* extrinsic evidence, internal *or* intrinsic evidence, direct *or* indirect evidence; documentary evidence, collateral evidence etc. *adj.*; presumptive *or* circumstantial evidence; presumption; hearsay evidence, hearsay [coll.]; conclusive evidence etc. (demonstration, proof) 478; sign etc. (indication) 550; trace etc. 551.5.

2. *n.* testimony, testament [erron.], testification, attest, attestation, witness; testimonial, testimonium; declaration, affirmation, averment, allegation, statement, admission, word; deposition, *procès-verbal* [F.]; affidavit, affidavy [dial.]; compurgation, wager of law [Hist.].

3. *n.* confirmation, affirmation, affirmance, corroboration, support, ratification, authentication, verification.

4. *n.* authority, warrant, credential, diploma, voucher, certificate, docket, document, *pièce justificative* [F.]; testamur [Eng., Univ.]; visa, visé; exhibit; citation, reference, quotation; record etc. 551; muniments, deed, warranty etc. (security) 771; signature, seal etc. (identification) 550.11.

5. *n.* writ, summons etc. (lawsuit) 969.2, 3, 6.

6. *n.* witness, indicator, eyewitness, earwitness, bystander; deponent, testifier, attestant, attester *or* attestor, attestator; cojuror, compurgator, oath helper [Hist.]; sponsor.

7. *v.* evidence, evince, show, shew [chiefly Eng.]; demonstrate, exhibit; manifest, display, betoken, set forth; express, represent, denote, imply, involve; argue, tell; breathe, bespeak, speak for itself, speak volumes; connote, connotate; have *or* carry weight, weigh; rest upon, depend on *or* upon, repose upon; give indication of etc. (indicate) 550.18.

8. *v.* testify, testate [rare], attest, give evidence etc. *n.*, witness, give *or* bear witness, warrant, depose, vouch, avouch, swear, certify, acknowledge, give one's word, deliver as one's act and deed.

9. *v.* confirm, affirm, corroborate, bear out, support, uphold, sustain, fortify, warrant, ratify, indorse *or* endorse, validate; have *or* make out a case, establish, authenticate, circumstantiate, substantiate, make good, verify, show, prove, quote chapter and verse; bring home to, bring to book, bring off; visa, countersign etc. 488.10.

10. *v.* adduce, evidence, attest, cite; quote, name, present, advance, assign, instance, allege, plead; refer to, appeal to; call, call to witness, bring forward, bring on, bring into court, produce *or* confront witnesses; collect ~, bring together *or* rake up evidence.

11. *adj.* evidential, evidentiary, evidencive [rare]; testatory, testificatory, testimonial [rare]; grounded on, founded on, based on; verificative, verifiable, veridical; confirmatory, corroborative, collateral, supportive, ratificatory; significant, weighty, overwhelming, damning; firsthand, authentic; conclusive; final, decisive, determinative; cumulative, oral, documentary, hearsay, ex parte, presumptive, constructive, circumstantial, nuncupative; deducible etc. (demonstrative) 478.3–5; indicative etc. 550.21.

12. *adj.* evident etc. (manifest) 525.4, 5.

13. *adv. etc.* evidentially etc. *adj.*, by inference; according to, witness, a fortiori; still more, still less; in corroboration of etc. *n.*; *valeat quantum valere potest* [L.]; under seal, under one's hand and seal; at first hand, at second hand.

---

467. Where are the evidence that do accuse me?—SHAKESPEARE. He who furnishes a voucher for his statements argues himself unknown.—SENECA. The attest of eyes and ears.—SHAKESPEARE. Some circumstantial evidence is very strong, as when you find a trout in the milk.—THOREAU. Compassed about with so great a cloud of witnesses.—BIBLE.

468. Counterevidence
(See 467. Evidence)

1. *n.* counterevidence, evidence on the other hand *or* side, other side *or* reverse of the shield, conflicting evidence, opposition; disproof, disproval; *reductio ad absurdum* [L.]; counterprotest; denial, contradiction etc. (negation) 536; plea, alibi, excuse etc. (vindication) 937.

2. *v.* countervail, run counter to, contravene, oppose, conflict; tell another story, turn the scale, alter the case, turn the tables, cut both ways, prove a negative; check, weaken; disprove, rebut etc. (confute) 479.2; contradict etc. (deny) 536.2; upset, subvert etc. (destroy) 162.4.

3. *adj.* countervailing etc. *v.,* counter, contradictory, contrary, negatory; refutative etc. (confutative) 479.3.

4. *adj.* unattested, unauthenticated, unsupported, unsupported by evidence; supposititious, unfounded etc. (untrue) 546.6.

5. *adv. etc.* conversely, contra, contrarily, contrariwise, on *or* to the contrary, *per contra* [L.], on the other hand *or* side, as an offset, in opposition, oppositely; in rebuttal; *tu quoque* [L.].

469. Qualification

1. *n.* qualification, limitation, restriction, modification, coloring; allowance, grains of allowance, grant, consideration, extenuating circumstances; cession, concession; mitigation, abatement, deduction.

2. *n.* condition, provision, proviso, stipulation, specification, arrangement, situation, circumstance, case; requisite, prerequisite; exception, exemption, reservation; saving clause etc. (conditions) 770.1.

3. *v.* qualify, limit, modify, narrow, restrict, restrain; affect, give a color to, take color from; adjust to, regulate by; leaven, temper, soften, modulate, moderate, assuage, mitigate, lenify [now rare], abate, reduce, diminish.

4. *v.* allow for, make allowance for, take into account, admit exceptions, admit, grant, concede, acknowledge.

5. *v.* take exceptions, file exceptions, except, object, raise objections, rise to a point of order.

6. *adj.* qualifying etc. *v.,* qualificatory, qualificative; modificatory, conditional, contingent; provisional, provisory; extenuating, extenuatory; restrictive, limitative; mitigative, mitigatory; palliative, palliatory; assuasive, lenitive; exceptional, exceptionable.

7. *adv.* conditionally etc. *adj.,* admittedly, allowedly, by allowance, with grains of allowance, with a grain of salt, *cum grano salis* [L.], with a reservation *or* exception, *exceptis excipiendis* [L.]; notwithstanding, notwithstanding that, regardless of that, be that as it may, such being the case, although such be the case, yet, rather, nevertheless, however, but; if possible, wind and weather permitting etc. 470.8.

8. *conj. etc.* provided, provided that, provided always, providing, with this proviso etc. *n.,* it being provided etc. *v.;* in case, in case that, in the event of, on condition, on condition that, with the stipulation etc. *n.,* with the understanding, in consideration of, according as, subject to; if, if that [arch.], if only, if so be, if it be true that, if case be [arch. and dial.], gif [Scot. and dial. Eng.], gin [Scot.], an *or* an if [arch.], namely if.

so, so that, so as, so *or* as long as; but, however, still, nevertheless, yet, even, though, although, for all that, after all, at all events, in any event *or* case, in either case; whether, whether or not; unless, unless that; if not, were it not that; admitting, granting, allowing etc. *v.;* admitting that, allowing that etc.; supposing that, on the supposition that etc. 514.13.

470. Possibility
(See 471. Impossibility)

1. *n.* possibility, possibleness etc. *adj.,* conceivability, likelihood, show [coll.]; potentiality, potency; what may be, what is possible; *possibile* [L.; Philos.] (*pl. possibilia*), the possible, the attainable

---

468. There are two sides to every question.—PROTAGORAS.   *Audire alteram partem* [To listen to the other side].
469. The exception proves the rule.
470. Nothing is impossible.—LA ROCHEFOUCAULD.   To believe only possibilities is not Faith, but mere Philosophy.—T. BROWNE.

etc. *adj.*; mere *or* remote possibility, perhaps; compossibility; compatibility etc. (agreement) 23; reasonability etc. 476.7; credibility etc. 484.5; contingency, good possibility, even chance, good chance etc. 156.2, 3.

2. *n.* practicability, practicableness etc. *adj.*, feasibility, workability, negotiability [coll.]; attainability, accessibility, superability.

3. *v.* be possible etc. *adj.*, have *or* stand a chance *or* good chance, have *or* stand a show [coll.], bid *or* stand fair to; have a leg to stand on, admit of, bear.

4. *v.* render possible etc. *adj.*, possibilitate [rare]; put in the way of, bring to bear, bring together.

5. *adj.* possible, *in posse* [L.], within the bounds of possibility, conceivably possible, conceivable, imaginable, thinkable, cogitable, likely; contingent, potential, on the cards *or* dice; compossible; compatible etc. 23.9; plausible etc. 472.6; admissible etc. (logical) 476.16; credible etc. 484.15.

6. *adj.* practicable, feasible, workable, performable, negotiable [coll.], doable, actable, achievable; within reach *or* measurable distance, accessible; attainable, obtainable; surmountable, superable.

7. *adv.* possibly etc. *adj.*, in a possible manner, by a possible means, by any possibility, *in posse* [L.]; on the bare possibility, on the off chance [coll.], by merest chance; perchance, perhaps, perhazard [arch.], peradventure; maybe, it may be, as it may be, as the case may be, mayhap [arch.], haply, for all *or* aught one knows; supposedly etc. 514.12.

8. *adv.* if possible, wind and weather permitting; God willing, *Deo volente* [L.], D.V.; as luck may have it, as it may chance, as it may turn up *or* out; everything being equal, all things considered; conditionally etc. 469.7.

471. Impossibility
(See 470. Possibility)

1. *n.* impossibility, unpossibility [now dial.], impossibleness etc. *adj.*; what cannot be, what can never be; sour grapes; hopelessness etc. 859; discrepancy etc. (disparity) 24.2; not a chance etc. (*see* chance etc. 156).

2. *n.* impracticability *or* unpracticability, impracticableness etc. *adj.*, infeasibility *or* unfeasibility, unworkability; unattainability, inaccessibility *or* unaccessibility, sour grapes; insuperability *or* unsuperability.

3. *n.* (comparisons) Canute commanding the tide, Dame Partington and her mop, Sisyphus.

4. *v.* be impossible etc. *adj.*, be an impossibility etc. *n.*, be a waste of time; have no chance whatever etc. 156.11.

5. *v.* attempt impossibilities, attempt the impossible, seek *or* strive after impossibilities; try to square the circle, ~ find the elixir of life, ~ discover the philosopher's stone, ~ discover the grand panacea, ~ find the fountain of youth, ~ discover the secret of perpetual motion, ~ wash a blackamoor white, ~ change the leopard's spots, ~ skin a flint, ~ make a silk purse out of a sow's ear, ~ make bricks without straw, ~ weave a rope of sand, ~ extract sunbeams from cucumbers, ~ get figs from thistles, ~ milk the ram *or* milk a he-goat into a sieve.

look for a needle in a haystack *or* in a bottle of hay; try to catch a weasel asleep, ~ be in two places at once, ~ gather grapes from thorns, ~ fetch water in a sieve, ~ catch wind in cabbage nets, ~ fling eels by the tail *or* make cheese of chalk; have nothing to go upon; labor in vain etc. 645.6.

6. *adj.* impossible, unpossible [now dial.], not possible etc. (*see* possible etc. 470.5), beyond the bounds of possibility *or* reason, contrary to reason *or* fact, at variance with the facts, self-contradictory; implausible, inconceivable, unthinkable, not to be thought of, absurd; unimaginable, inimaginable [obs.]; incompatible etc. 24.6; hopeless etc. 859.7.

7. *adj.* impracticable *or* unpracticable, infeasible *or* unfeasible, unachievable, unworkable; insuperable *or* unsuperable, insurmountable *or* unsurmountable; unattainable, not attainable etc. (*see* attainable etc. 470.6); unobtainable, in-

---

The glories of the Possible are ours.—B. TAYLOR.   A thousand possibilities sprang to life in his pullulating brain.—LYTTON STRACHEY.
471. When once you have taken the Impossible into your calculations, its possibilities become practically limitless.—SAKI.   Few things are impossible in themselves.—LA ROCHEFOUCAULD. *Il a la mer à boire* [He has the sea to drink up].

obtainable [rare]; beyond reach, out of reach, out of the question, not to be had, not to be had for love or money, beyond control, beyond or out of one's power, ~ depth, ~ reach or grasp, too much for one, *ultra crepidam* [L.]; inaccessible or unaccessible, un-come-at-able [coll.], impassable or unpassable, impervious, innavigable or unnavigable; inextricable, unsolvable.

472. Probability
(See 473. Improbability)

1. *n.* probability, likeliness etc. *adj.,* likelihood, liability, aptitude; verisimilitude, appearance of truth; plausibility, ostensibility; presumption, presumptive or circumstantial evidence; chance, prospect, reasonable or fair chance or prospect, well-grounded hope; theory of probability, probability curve or curve of probability; probabilism; probable cause [Law]; even chance, good chance etc. 156.2, 3; credibility etc. 484.5; reasonability etc. 476.7.

2. *v.* be probable etc. *adj.,* be a probability etc. *n.,* give or lend color to, imply, indicate, point to, bid or stand fair to, promise, make fair promise, lead one to expect; seem likely, like to [coll.], offer a good prospect; have a good chance etc. 156.9.

3. *v.* presume, infer, gather, venture, advance, suppose; take for granted, conclude, deduce, think likely, dare say; flatter oneself; expect etc. 507.4; count upon etc. (believe) 484.7–9.

4. *v.* make probable etc. *adj.,* give probability to etc. *n.,* probabilize, put in the way of.

5. *adj.* probable, likely, like [now coll.], liable, apt, hopeful, promising, fair, in a fair way, on the cards or dice; presumable, presumptive; verisimilar, verisimilous [rare].

6. *adj.* plausible, specious, ostensible, apparent, colorable; well-founded, well-grounded, well-invented, *ben trovato* [It.]; credible etc. (believable) 484.15; reasonable etc. (logical) 476.16; possible etc. 470.5.

7. *adv.* probably, presumably etc. *adj.*;

in all probability or likelihood, likely, very or most likely, like [rare], very like, belike [arch.], like enough, as like as not [coll.], according to every expectation; apparently, seemingly, to all seeming, to all appearance or appearances; on the face of it, *prima facie* [L.]; ten ~, a hundred etc. to one, dollars to doughnuts [U.S.], all Lombard Street to a China orange; everything being equal, all things considered.

8. *phr.* there is a probability, the chances or odds are, appearances or chances are in favor of, there is reason to believe, ~ think or expect, I dare say or daresay.

473. Improbability
(See 472. Probability)

1. *n.* improbability, unlikeliness etc. *adj.,* unlikelihood, bare possibility, poor ~, small or unfavorable prospect; ghost of a chance, long odds etc. (small chance) 156.4; incredibility, doubtfulness etc. 485.3.

2. *v.* be improbable etc. *adj.,* be an improbability etc. *n.,* violate or stretch the probabilities, strain one's credulity, be a stretch on the imagination, go beyond reason, go beyond the bounds of reason or probability, run counter to the laws of nature; have or stand a small chance, have or stand a poor show [coll.] etc. 156.4.

3. *adj.* improbable, unlikely, unheard-of, contrary to all reasonable expectation, contrary to fact or experience, at variance with the facts, fishy [coll.]; more than doubtful, implausible, inconceivable; unimaginable, inimaginable [obs.]; doubtful etc. 475.9; incredible etc. (unbelievable) 485.11; unreasonable etc. (illogical) 477.10.

4. *int.* not likely!, no fear!; I ask you! [slang].

474. Certainty
(See 475. Uncertainty)

1. *n.* certainty, certitude, confidence, surety, assurance; assuredness, sureness

---

472. Almost all human life depends on probabilities.—VOLTAIRE.   Lest men suspect your tale untrue / Keep probability in view.—GRAY.   Fate laughs at probabilities.—BULWER-LYTTON.

473. At times truth may not seem probable.—BOILEAU.   If this were played upon a stage now, I could condemn it as an improbable fiction.—SHAKESPEARE.
474. The only certainty is that nothing is certain.—PLINY THE ELDER.   Facts are stubborn

etc. *adj.*; dead ∼, moral *or* absolute certainty; sure thing, sure bet, sure card, cinch, lead-pipe cinch, open-and-shut case [all slang]; conviction, convincement; unqualification, unquestionability, undeniability, indisputability, incontestability, incontrovertibility, irrefutability, irrefragability, unimpeachability, infallibility, reliability; inevitability, ineluctability; fact etc. (actuality) 1.2; truth etc. 494; proof etc. (demonstration) 478; good chance etc. 156.3.

2. *n.* certification, verification, ascertainment, confirmation, assurance; reassurance, reassessment; attest, attestation.

3. *n.* dogmatism, dogmatization; positivism, positiveness; infallibilism; fanaticism etc. (craze) 503.7; bigotry etc. 606.2; hyperorthodoxy etc. 983a.5.

4. *n.* dogmatist, dogmatizer, dogmatic theorist; doctrinaire, positivist, infallibilist, Sir Oracle; bigot, opinionist etc. (obstinate person) 606.3; zealot etc. (fanatic) 504.2.

5. *v.* be certain etc. *adj.,* be *or* rest assured, feel sure; bet on, gamble on, go bail on, bet one's bottom dollar on [all coll.]; stand to reason; know, know for certain, doubt not, have *or* make no doubt.

6. *v.* make certain etc. *adj.,* certify, attest, insure *or* ensure, assure, clinch, cinch [slang], cinch the deal [slang], determine, ascertain, decide, settle, fix, confirm, find out, find out once for all *or* for certain; make sure, see to it; set at rest, verify, "make assurance double sure" (Shakespeare); make sure of, make oneself easy about *or* on that score, assure *or* satisfy oneself; remove *or* dismiss all doubt, admit of no doubt, make no doubt; reassure.

7. *v.* dogmatize, lay down the law.

8. *adj.* certain, sure, sure-enough [dial., U.S.], sure-fire [slang, U.S.]; positive, absolute, unqualified, determinate, definite, unequivocal, categorical, unmistakable; decided, decisive, apodictic *or* apodeictic, apodictal *or* apodeictal; cocksure [coll.]; dead sure, sure as death, sure as death and taxes, sure as fate, sure as a gun *or* as a gun is iron [coll.], sure as eggs is eggs *or* X is X [coll.], sure as God made little green apples [slang], sure as hell *or* the devil etc. [vulg.], as sure as I live and breathe [slang], sure as preaching [slang, U.S.]; evident, clear, apparent etc. (manifest) 525.4; undoubting etc. 484.12; true etc. 494.10–14.

9. *adj.* assured, made sure, convinced, confident, bound; determined, predetermined; decided, ascertained, authenticated, fixed, settled, in the bag *or* sack [slang], on ice [slang, U.S.], open-and-shut [coll., U.S.]; well-founded, well-grounded; solid, firm, secure, stable, established; proved etc. (demonstrated) 478.4.

10. *adj.* conclusive, ultimate, final, determinative, decisive, convincing; undeniable, unquestionable, indubitable *or* undubitable, undoubtable [now rare], indisputable, incontestable, incontrovertible, irrefutable, irrefragable, unanswerable, inappealable, unimpeachable; demonstrative etc. 478.3.

11. *adj.* inevitable, unavoidable etc. (necessary) 601.11.

12. *adj.* indubious, indubitable etc. *above* 474.10, undoubted, uncontested, undisputed, unquestioned, unquestionate; questionless, doubtless; without *or* beyond a doubt *or* question, without *or* beyond a shade *or* shadow of doubt, past dispute, beyond all dispute *or* question.

13. *adj.* authoritative, authentic, orthodox, catholic, canonical, doctrinal, standard, received; cathedral, *ex cathedra* [L.].

14. *adj.* infallible, inerrable, inerrant, unerring, unfailing, to be depended upon, dependable, trustworthy, reliable, sound; unchangeable etc. 150.7.

15. *adj.* dogmatic(al), positive, positivistic; opinioned, opinionated, opinionate, opinionative, opiniative [now rare], *opiniâtre* [F.], wedded to an opinion; self-opinioned, self-opinionated; pragmatic(al), categoric(al), oracular, absolute, arbitrary, dictatorial, magisterial; doctrinary, doctrinaire; bigoted etc. 606.7; prejudiced etc. 481.10; unreasonable etc. 477.10; zealotic etc. (fanatical) 503.18; hyperorthodox etc. 983a.8.

16. *adv.* certainly, certes [arch.], surely, assuredly, positively, absolutely, definitely, precisely, exactly, admittedly, un-

---

things.—SMOLLETT. Dogmatism is puppyism come to its full growth.—JERROLD. Better be sure than sorry. Nothing is certain but death and the taxes. God's mill grinds slow but sure.

mistakably, decidedly, decisively, undeniably, unquestionably, indisputably, incontestably, incontrovertibly, irrefutably, irrefragably, unequivocally, unconditionally; undoubtedly, undoubtably [obs. exc. dial.]; indubitably *or* undubitably, indubitatively [rare]; *à coup sûr* [F.], for certain, for ~, of *or* to a certainty, for fair [slang]; sure, to be sure, sure enough; sure thing, surest thing you know, sure Mike [all slang, U.S.]; indeed, indeedy [coll., U.S.]; doubtless, no doubt, beyond doubt *or* question, without doubt etc. *adj.*, questionless [rare]; of course, as a matter of course.

at any rate, at all events; without fail, whatever may happen, happen *or* come what may *or* will, if the worst comes to the worst; cost what it may, *coûte que coûte* [F.]; rain or shine, live or die, sink or swim; and no mistake [coll.], nothing else but [slang], no two ways about it, no buts about it [coll.]; no ifs, ands or buts; in truth, in fact etc. (truly) 494.15; yes etc. 488.14; actually etc. 1.9.

17. *phr.* it is certain, there is no question, there is not a shadow of doubt, that goes without saying, *cela va sans dire* [F.], *ipse dixit* [L.], that is a matter of course, that leaps to the eye, *cela saute aux yeux* [F.], that is evident; the die is cast etc. (necessity) 601.16.

475. Uncertainty
(See 474. Certainty)

1. *n.* uncertainty, uncertainness, uncertitude *or* incertitude, unsureness; doubt, doubtfulness, dubiousness, dubiety, dubiosity, dubitancy [now rare], dubitation; indetermination, undetermination [rare], indecision; vacillation, vacillancy [rare], fluctuation, wavering etc. *v.*; hesitation, hesitancy; suspense, state of suspense; insecurity, precariousness; equivocality, equivocacy, ambiguity; aporia, diaporesis; timidity, want of confidence etc. (fear) 860; irresolution etc. 605; gamble etc. 621.

2. *n.* perplexity, quandary, dilemma, horns of a dilemma, Morton's fork [Hist.], confoundment, bewilderment, disconcertion, embarrassment, fix [coll.], hobble [coll.], pucker [coll.], confusion; muddle, muddlement; puzzle, puzzlement; baffle, bafflement; bother, botheration [coll.], botherment [coll.]; nonplus, nonplusation *or* nonplussation.

3. *n.* vagueness, indefiniteness etc. *adj.*; obscurity, obscuration; haze, fog; unintelligibility etc. 519.

4. *n.* fallibility, unreliability; unreliableness, untrustworthiness etc. *adj.*; errability, errancy.

5. *n.* an uncertainty etc. *above* 475.1, something or other, open question, undecided *or* unsettled matter; contingency, double contingency, possibility upon a possibility; blind bargain, pig in a poke, leap in the dark; needle in a haystack *or* bottle of hay; roving commission; gamble etc. 621.

6. *v.* be uncertain etc. *adj.*, doubt, have one's doubts, dubitate [rare], question, puzzle over; wonder, wonder whether; hesitate, demur, pause, falter, hang back, hang fire, hang in doubt, stop to consider; waver, vacillate, swing from one thing to another, back and fill, toss and turn, wander aimlessly; stumble, stagger, boggle, flounder, beat about; miss one's way, lose oneself, lose the clew *or* clue, lose the scent; not know which way to turn, not know where one stands, not know whether one stands on one's head or one's heels; lose one's head, muddle one's brains; not know what to make of, not be able to make head or tail of; be at sea, float in a sea of doubt.

7. *v.* depend, be dependent, pend, hang, hang on *or* upon, hang around, hang in suspense, rest, hinge, turn upon, revolve around.

8. *v.* perplex, confound, bewilder, baffle, mystify, bamboozle [coll.], puzzle, pose, put out, disconcert, embarrass, dismay, disturb, bother, moider [dial.], flummox [slang]; confuse, muddle, ball up [slang], addle the wits, make one's head swim, daze, fog; nonplus, stick [coll.], tree [coll.], stump [coll., chiefly U.S.], put up a tree *or* stump [slang], floor [coll.], gravel [coll.], throw [slang], throw on one's beam ends, get [chiefly coll.], get one down [coll.], beat [coll.], lick [slang], put to it, put to one's

---

475. *Dum in dubio est animus paulo memento huc illus impellitur* [While the mind is in doubt it is driven this way and that by a slight impulse].—TERENCE.   Doubts are more cruel than the worst of truths.—MOLIÈRE.   A strong dilemma in a desperate case.—SWIFT.

wit's end, keep one guessing, keep in suspense; throw off the scent, put off the track.

9. *adj.* uncertain, unsure; doubtful, doubtsome [Scot. and dial. Eng.], doubtable; in doubt, *in dubio* [L.]; dubitable, dubitative, dubious; questionable, disputable, debatable, contestable, controvertible, refutable, unsustainable, deniable; open, open to question *or* doubt; moot, mooted; casual, random, aimless; equivocal, ambiguous; speculative; improbable etc. 473.3; untenable etc. 485.11.

10. *adj.* undecided, undetermined, unascertained, undemonstrated, unsustained, unconfirmed, unsettled, unfixed, yet to be decided, not finally determined; untold, uncounted; unconvinced, unconfident; untried, speculative, experimental, tentative; irresolute etc. 605.5.

11. *adj.* vague, indefinite, indeterminate, indeterminable, undefinable, undefined, indistinct, indistinguishable, confused, unclear, indecisive, obscure, shadowed forth, veiled, mysterious, cryptic, oracular.

12. *adj.* perplexing, puzzling, bewildering etc. *v.*; apocryphal, hypothetical; paradoxal, paradoxical; problematic etc. (enigmatic) 533.6; embarrassing etc. 704.9; labyrinthian, involved etc. (complex) 59.10.

13. *adj.* unauthoritative, unauthentic, unauthenticated, unorthodox, unofficial.

14. *adj.* fallible, errable, undemonstrable, untrustworthy, unreliable; slippery, ticklish, precarious, insecure, unstable, unsubstantial *or* insubstantial, chancy [coll.], speculative.

15. *adj.* dependent, pending etc. *v.*, contingent, contingent on, dependent on, dependent *or* depending on circumstances, subject to, incidental to, incidental, occasional, conditional; provisional, provisionary [now rare], provisory; in suspense, in a state of suspense, up in the air.

16. *adj.* in a state of uncertainty, in a dilemma etc. *n.*, on the horns of a dilemma; on tenterhooks; perplexed, bewildered, nonplused etc. *v.*; at a nonplus, at a loss, on one's beam ends, put-out, up in the air, in the wind; at one's wit's end, *au bout de son latin* [F.], at the end of one's rope *or* tether; hard put, hard put to it, beat, stuck, floored, graveled, treed, stumped [all coll.], up a tree *or* stump, up against it, thrown, sunk [all slang]; distracted, distraught; lost, abroad, astray, adrift, at sea, off the track, out of one's reckoning, out of one's bearings, bushed; fogged, foggy, hazy, in a cloud, ~ fog *or* haze; mazed, mazeful, in a maze.

muddled, in a muddle; all balled up, all hot and bothered [both slang, U.S.]; turned around, going around in circles, like a chicken with its head cut off [coll.]; in a pucker, in a hobble, in a fix [all coll.]; wavering etc. *v.*, inconstant, changeable, changeful, variable, unsettled, unsteady, fitful, capricious, fickle; on the fence [coll.]; irresolute etc. 605.5.

17. *adv.* uncertainly, doubtfully etc. *adj.*; at random; until things straighten out, while things are so uncertain, in this state of suspense; *pendente lite* [L.]; *sub spe rati* [L.].

18. *phr.* who can tell?, who knows?, who shall decide when doctors disagree?; Heaven knows!; you never can tell!, don't be too sure!

476. Reasoning
(See 477. Sophistry, 477a. Intuition)

1. *n.* reasoning, rationalizing etc. *v.*, rationalization; rationality, rationalism, ratiocination; logic etc. (philosophy) 451.4; logicalization; process of reasoning, train *or* chain of reasoning *or* thought; dialectics, dialecticism; syllogism, syllogistic reasoning, syllogistic, syllogistics [rare], syllogization; deduction, deductive reasoning, argument by deduction; induction, inductive reasoning, argument by induction, epagoge; philosophical induction, inductive *or* Baconian method; hypothesis and verification; inference, inferentialism; generalization, particularization; a fortiori reasoning, a priori reasoning, a posteriori reasoning; discursive reasoning, discourse; synthesis, analysis.

2. *n.* argumentation, argument, argification [dial.]; debate, discussion, com-

---

He is no wise man who will quit a certainty for an uncertainty.—JOHNSON. The world uncertain comes and goes.—EMERSON.

476. Man is a reasoning animal.—SENECA. Logic is mainly valuable wherewith to exterminate logicians.—CHESTERTON. Wrong

ment, ventilation; controversy, controversion; dispute, disputation; polemics, disceptation, litigation, pilpul, contention, wrangling, set-to [coll.]; argy-bargy [chiefly Scot. and dial. Eng.]; logomachy, war of words, verbal engagement *or* contest, passage of words; tonguefence, wordfence [both rare]; paper war, *guerre de plume* [F.]; dingdong argument [coll.]; polemic(al), polemic argument *or* controversy; sophistical reasoning *or* argumentation, ergotism [rare]; conversation etc. (interlocution) 588; contest etc. 720.2; lawsuit etc. 969; disquisition etc. (dissertation) 595; quarrel etc. 713.3.

3. *n.* argument, *argumentum* [L.]; case, plea, *plaidoyer* [F.]; proposition, *propositio* [L.], statement; philosophical proposition, philosopheme; pure proposition, *propositio de in esse* [L.]; necessary *or* apodictic proposition, *propositio de necessario* [L.]; universal proposition, *propositio de omni* [L.]; *propositio in sensu composito* [L.], *propositio in sensu diviso* [L.]; empirical proposition, empeirema *or* empirema [rare]; pros, cons, pros and cons.

4. *n.* premise *or* premiss, term, lemma, position, proposition, assumed position, sumption, assumption, supposal, presupposition, hypothesis, thesis, theorem, starting point, basis, ground, foundation; postulate, postulation [rare], postulatum; hypothesis ad hoc; data (*sing.* datum); major premise, minor premise; a priori principle, apriorism, apriority; principle etc. (axiom) 496.2; philosopheme etc. 451.24.

5. *n.* syllogism, logical scheme *or* analysis, prosyllogism; mode; first ~, second ~, third *or* fourth figure; pseudosyllogism, sophistic syllogism, paralogism; sorites, progressive *or* Aristotelian sorites, regressive *or* Goclenian sorites; enthymeme; dilemma, horns of a dilemma.

6. *n.* good reasoning, logical sequence; logical etc. *adj.* argument *or* reasoning, correct ~, just ~, sound ~, valid ~, strong ~, forcible *or* persuasive reasoning; cogent argument, cogency; conclusive argument, comprehensive argument; good case, strong argument, knockdown argument, strong point; force of argument; *reductio ad absurdum* [L.].

7. *n.* reasonableness etc. *adj.*, reasonability, rationality; logicality, logicity; sense, common sense; credibility etc. (believability) 484.5; possibility etc. 470; plausibility etc. (probability) 472.

8. *n.* reason etc. (motive) 615.

9. *n.* reasoner, ratiocinator; rationalizer, rationalist; logician, logistician, logicalist, logicaster [derog.]; controverter, controvertist, controversialist; arguer, argufier [coll.]; debater, wrangler, disputant, mooter, disceptator, pilpulist, eristic; polemic, polemist, polemicist, polemician; logomach, logomacher, logomachist; tonguefencer, wordfencer [both rare]; dialectic, dialectician; syllogist, syllogizer; casuist.

philosopher, philosoph *or* philosophe, philosophist [now rare], philosophister [rare], philosophizer, philomath; philosopheress, philosophess, sophist etc. 477.6; Plato, Socrates; Platonist, Socratist etc. (*see* Platonism, Socratism etc. 451.4–23).

10. *v.* reason, exercise the reason, rationalize, rationate, ratiocinate [now usu. joc.]; logicize [rare], logicalize; intelligize [rare], intellectualize; try conclusions; philosophize; syllogize; generalize, particularize; think etc. 451.27–29; examine etc. 461.17; deduce, infer etc. (judge) 480.6.

11. *v.* argue, argy [dial.], argufy [coll. and dial.], argify [dial.]; reason, discuss, canvass, debate, dispute, discept, polemize [rare], logomachize, wrangle, spar [coll.], contend, contest, contest in words, bandy words *or* arguments, chew the rag [slang], chop logic, hold *or* carry on an argument, join issue, stir ~, agitate ~, ventilate *or* torture a question; argue sophistically, ergotize [rare].

take up a side *or* case, take one's stand upon, put up an argument [coll.], insist, maintain, emphasize, underline, lay stress on; open a discussion *or* case, propose, bring up, moot; come to the

---

reasoning sometimes lands poor mortals in right conclusions.—G. ELIOT. In arguing, answer your opponent's earnest with jest, and his jest with earnest.—ARISTOTLE. The only way to get the best of an argument is to avoid it.— D. CARNEGIE. To him who looks upon the world rationally, the world in its turn presents a rational aspect.—HEGEL. *Troppo disputare la verità fa errare* [Too much arguing makes truth stray away].

point; comment upon, moralize upon; pettifog [coll.]; argue to no purpose, whistle down the wind [coll.]; converse etc. 588.9; quarrel etc. 713.7; litigate etc. 969.10.

12. *v.* be reasonable etc. *adj.,* be logically evident, stand to reason; hold good, hold water [coll.], have a leg to stand on; be common sense, speak sense.

13. *adj.* reasoning etc. *v.,* rational, rationalistical; ratiocinant, ratiocinative, ratiocinatory [rare]; analytic(al).

14. *adj.* argumentative, argumental; controversial, disputatious, eristic(al), polemic(al), logomachic(al), pilpulistic, dialectic(al); discursive, discursory; litigious etc. 969.13.

15. *adj.* debatable, controvertible etc. (uncertain) 475.9.

16. *adj.* logical, logic, logistic(al); reasonable, reasonal [obs.]; rational, rationable [obs.]; sensible, sane, sound, legitimate, just, justifiable, admissible; as it should be, as it ought to be; well-founded, well-grounded; inferential, inferrible *or* inferable; credible etc. (believable) 484.15; possible etc. 470.5, 6; probable, plausible etc. 472.5, 6.

17. *adj.* (logic) syllogistic(al), soritical, epagogic, inductive, deductive, synthetic(al), dialectic(al), enthymematic(al), categorical, hypothetical, conditional, Aristotelian.

18. *adv.* logically etc. *adj.*; a fortiori, a priori, a posteriori; pro and con.

19. *adv.* therefore etc. (hence) 155.5; consequently etc. 154.7.

20. *adv.* finally, lastly, in fine, in conclusion; after all, *au bout du compte* [F.], on the whole, taking one thing with another, taking everything into consideration.

21. *conj.* for, because etc. (since) 155.8.

477. Sophistry
(See 476. Reasoning)

1. *n.* sophistry, sophisticism, sophism; philosophastry, philosophastering, philosophism; illogicalness, speciousness etc. *adj.*; speciosity, illogical ∼, specious etc. *adj.* reasoning, false *or* vicious reasoning, sophistical *or* misleading argumentation, special pleading, casuistry; Jesuitry, jesuitism *or* Jesuitism; paralogy, paralogism; perversion, distortion; chicane, chicanery; mystification; meshes *or* cobwebs of sophistry; misjudgment etc. 481; false teaching etc. 538; fallacy etc. (error) 495; quackery etc. 544.2; affectation of knowledge etc. 491.4.

2. *n.* a sophism, sophistry, philosophism, solecism, elench; *elenchus* [L.] (*pl. elenchi*), *ignoratio elenchi* [L.]; inconsistency, antilogy; claptrap, moonshine, mere *or* empty words; bad case, weak point, flaw in an argument, "lame and impotent conclusion"(Shakespeare); paralogism, pseudosyllogism, sophistic syllogism; fallacy etc. (error) 495.

3. *n.* quibble, quiblet [obs. exc. U.S.], quirk, cavil, shift, shuffle, dodge, jesuitism, *quodlibet* [L.], quillet [arch.]; quiddit [arch.], quiddity; ambiguousness, ambiguity; ambages [now rare] etc. (circumlocution) 573.3.

4. *n.* quibbling etc. *v.,* quibble [rare], prevarication, cavil, quiddity [now rare]; equivocation, equivoque *or* equivoke [rare]; evasion, subterfuge; subtlety, hairsplitting, overrefinement; begging of the question, *petitio principii* [L.]; mental reservation, *arrière-pensée* [F.]; tergiversation etc. 607.

5. *n.* unreasonableness etc. *adj.,* illogicality, irrationality, alogy [obs.]; foolishness etc. 499.6; absurdity etc. 497.

6. *n.* sophist, sophister, sophistress [*fem.*]; paralogist, paralogician; philosophaster, philosophister [rare], philosophist, philosoph *or* philosophe, philosophling, philosophuncule *or* philosophunculist [rare]; casuist, casuistess [*fem.*]; quibbler, caviler, equivocator, shuffler; waverer etc. 605.3; tergiversator etc. 607.4; affecter etc. 853.4.

7. *v.* sophisticate, paralogize, reason ill, reason illogically etc. *adv.,* reason in a circle, prove that black is white and white black, travel out of the record, put oneself out of court, not have a leg to stand on; pervert, distort, misapply; mystify; varnish, gloss over; elenchize; misjudge etc. 481.5; mislead etc. 495.11; misinterpret etc. 523.2; misrepresent etc. 555.4; falsify etc. 544.3.

8. *v.* quibble, resort to quibble *or* quibbles, cavil, equivocate, prevaricate, trifle, palter, cog [arch.], fence, parry, shuffle, shift, dodge, shy, evade, elude, *répondre*

---

477. My dear Madam, nonsense can only be defended by nonsense.—JOHNSON. *Non sequitur* [It does not follow].

en Normand [F.], beg the question, beat about the bush, cut blocks with a razor, play at *or* play fast and loose, blow hot and cold; pettifog [coll.]; refine, subtilize, split hairs, make a nice *or* subtle distinction; be circumlocutory etc. 573.5.

9. *adj.* sophistic(al), philosophistic(al), casuistic(al); jesuitic(al), jesuitish, jesuitist; specious, hollow, plausible, *ad captandum, ad captandum vulgus* [L.], captious; deceptive, misleading; illusive, illusory.

10. *adj.* illogical, unreasonable, without reason, without rhyme or reason, irrational, unsound, unsubstantial *or* insubstantial, invalid, faulty, unscientific, unphilosophical, untenable, inconclusive, unproved *or* unproven, unwarranted, not following; incongruous, inconsistent, unconnected; self-contradictory, self-annulling; inconsequent, inconsequential; ungrounded, groundless; paralogistic, paralogical.

absonous [obs.], absonant; ill-judged, ill-advised, ill-devised, ill-imagined; fallacious, fallible; unsustained, unsustainable; unauthentic, unauthenticated; questionable, controvertible, disputable, debatable, contestable; weak, feeble, poor, flimsy, loose; vague, obscure, abstruse; irrelevant etc. 10.6; false, incorrect etc. (erroneous) 495.12–14; nonsensical etc. (foolish) 499.15, (absurd) 497.4; improbable etc. 473.3; prejudiced etc. 481.10; bigoted etc. 606.7.

11. *adj.* quibbling, caviling etc. *v.,* pettifogging [coll.], captious, frivolous, evasive; hairsplitting, oversubtle, overrefined, finespun.

477a. Intuition
(See 476. Reasoning)

1. *n.* intuition, intuitiveness etc. *adj.,* intuitivism, intuicity, intuitive reason *or* knowledge, sensitive knowledge, intuitive *or* subconscious perception, immediate knowledge *or* cognition, direct perception, immediate apprehension, innate *or* instinctive knowledge, instinct, innate *or* inborn proclivity, native *or* natural tendency, blind *or* unreasoning impulse, sixth sense; second sight, insight; ready *or* quick insight *or* apprehension, perceptivity, discernment; intuitive preconception, a priori knowledge, anticipation; presentiment, inspiration; association, rule of thumb; divination etc. 511.2; clairvoyance etc. 994.7; imagination etc. 515.

2. *n.* intuitionism, intuitionalism, intuitivism.

3. *v.* intuit, know *or* apprehend by intuition, sense, feel, feel it in one's bones [coll.], judge intuitively etc. *adv.*; hazard a proposition; talk at random.

4. *adj.* intuitive, intuitional, intuent, intuitable, knowing *or* perceiving by intuition; independent of *or* anterior to reason, involuntary, automatic, spontaneous, impulsive; instinctive, natural, inherent, innate, inspirational; divinatory etc. 511.11; clairvoyant etc. 994.22.

5. *adv.* intuitively, instinctively etc. *adj.*; by intuition.

478. Demonstration
(See 479. Confutation)

1. *n.* demonstration, proof, probation, comprobation [obs.], confirmation, corroboration, verification, substantiation, authentication, establishment, rigorous *or* absolute demonstration *or* establishment, apodixis *or* apodeixis, conclusive evidence, conclusiveness etc. *adj.*; medium of proof etc. (evidence) 467; *experimentum crucis* [L.] etc. (test) 463.1; argument etc. 476; undeniability, irrefragability etc. (certainty) 474.

2. *v.* demonstrate, prove, prove true, show, make out, establish, confirm, verify, corroborate, substantiate, circumstantiate, bear out, support, uphold, sustain, make good, authenticate; hold good, hold water [coll.]; settle, settle the question, set the question at rest, reduce to demonstration, prove one's point, have

---

477a. Instinct is untaught ability.—Bain. Instinct is intelligence incapable of self-consciousness.—J. Sterling. Sagacity and a nameless something more—let us call it intuition.—Hawthorne. Faith become a passionate intuition.—Wordsworth. A moment's insight is sometimes worth a life's experience.—Holmes.

478. *Exitus acta probat* [The outcome justifies the act].—Ovid. For now the field is not far off / Where we must give the world a proof / Of deeds, not words.—Butler. What is now proved was once only imagined.—W. Blake. For nothing worthy proving can be proven, / Nor yet disproven.—Tennyson. A thing that nobody believes cannot be proved too often.

the best of the argument; follow, follow from, follow as a matter of course; evince, manifest etc. (evidence) 467.7; stand to reason etc. (be reasonable) 476.12.

3. *adj.* demonstrative, demonstrating etc. *v.,* demonstrational; demonstrable, demonstratable; apodictic *or* apodeictic, apodictal *or* apodeictal; probative, probationary; convincing, irresistible, categorical, explicit, crucial; determinative, undeniable etc. (conclusive) 474.10; evidential etc. 467.11.

4. *adj.* demonstrated, proved etc. *v.*; proven [arch. and dial.]; unconfuted, unanswered, unrefuted, undenied; evident etc. (manifest) 525.4; ascertained etc. (assured) 474.9.

5. *adj.* deducible, derivable, sequential, consequential, consectary [obs.], inferrible *or* inferable, inferential, deductive, illative, following.

6. *adv.* of course, as a matter of course etc. (consequently) 154.7.

7. *phr.* it is proven, *probatum est* [L.], there is nothing more to be said, it must follow; *quod erat demonstrandum* [L.], Q.E.D.

479. Confutation
(See 478. Demonstration)

1. *n.* confutation, refutation, refutal; disproof, disproval, disprovement [rare], proof of error *or* falsehood; conviction, redargution [now rare], invalidation; exposure, exposition, *exposé* [F.]; rebutment, rebuttal; answer, complete answer, retort, effective retort; unanswerable *or* conclusive argument, knockdown argument, floorer, sockdolager [slang, U.S.], corker [slang]; clincher, crusher, settler, finisher, squelcher [all coll.]; *reductio ad absurdum* [L.]; denial etc. (negation) 536.

2. *v.* confute, refute, redargue [obs. exc. Scot.], disprove, invalidate, negative, rebut, answer, answer conclusively; expose, bewray [arch.], show up, expose *or* show one's weak point, show *or* prove the fallacy of, convince; dismiss; explode, scatter to the winds; defeat, confound [arch.], overwhelm, overthrow, overturn, down, floor, gravel [coll.], settle, finish [now chiefly coll.], dispose of.

squash [chiefly coll.], squelch [chiefly coll.], crush, smash all opposition; parry, silence, put *or* reduce to silence, shut up, stop the mouth of; clinch an argument *or* a question, knock the bottom out of an argument [coll.], cut the ground from under one's feet, not leave a leg to stand on; have, have on the hip, have the better of; oppose etc. (countervail) 468.2; dispute etc. (deny) 536.2.

3. *adj.* confutative, refutative, refutatory; confuting, confuted etc. *v.*; condemned on one's own showing, condemned out of one's own mouth, "hoist with his own petard" (Shakespeare), contradictory etc. (countervailing) 468.3, (negatory) 536.3.

4. *adj.* confutable, refutable, disprovable, defeasible.

5. *phr.* it is not proven, it does not follow, it does not hold water, the argument falls to the ground, *cadit quaestio* [L.], the case is dismissed.

480. Judgment
(See 481. Misjudgment)

1. *n.* judgment, adjudgment, judicature, judication [rare], adjudication, dijudication; conclusion, result, upshot; decision, determination, verdict, finding, deduction, inference, ergotism [obs.], illation; corollary, porism; moral; award, sentence, report, decree; precedent; *res adjudicata, res judicata* [both L.]; opinion, conviction etc. (belief) 484; good judgment etc. (wisdom) 498.3; critical judgment, discretion etc. (discrimination) 465; choice etc. 609.

2. *n.* estimate, estimation; appraisement, appraisal; valuation, valorization,

---

Shaw. We must never assume that which is incapable of proof.—G. H. Lewes. The proof of the pudding is in the eating.
479. *Suo sibi gladio hunc jugulo* [I cut this man's throat with his own sword].—Terence. You have not converted a man because you have silenced him.—J. Morley. It is certainly not the least charm of a theory that it is refutable.—Nietzsche. Satan stood—confuted and convinced / Of his weak arguing and fallacious drift.—Milton. Confutation is my name, the friend of truth and frankness.—Menander.
480. The Lord judge between me and thee.—Bible. God shall judge the righteous and the wicked.—Bible. A Daniel come to judgment.—Shakespeare. Forbear to judge, for we are sinners all.—Shakespeare. O most

appreciation, consideration, assessment, ponderation [rare].

3. *n.* criticism, critique; review, notice, report, comment; censure etc. 932.2.

4. *n.* judge, umpire etc. 967.

5. *n.* critic, criticizer, criticaster, criticule, critikin; censor, censurer; connoisseur, *conoscente* [It.]; reviewer, revieweress; commenter, commentator.

6. *v.* judge, judicate [rare], exercise the judgment; adjudge, adjudicate, dijudicate; conclude, draw ⁓, come to *or* arrive at a conclusion; make a decision, decide, find, determine, make up one's mind, resolve, ascertain, settle; arbitrate; distinguish, perceive, discern; deduce, derive, gather, collect, glean, infer, draw an inference, reckon [coll.], calculate [coll., U.S.], suppose, presume, surmise, think, allow [dial.], regard, consider, deem, esteem, imagine, fancy, weet [obs.], ween [arch.], trow [arch.]; opine, opinion [obs. exc. dial.], give *or* pass an opinion, form an opinion; set at rest etc. (make certain) 474.6.

7. *v.* estimate, form an estimate; gauge, appreciate, prize, value, appraise, assess, rate, rank, count, account; size, size up [both coll.].

8. *v.* sit in judgment, hold the scales; judge, try, examine *or* investigate judicially, hear, try a cause, hear a cause *or* case, conduct a trial.

9. *v.* pronounce judgment, give ⁓, deliver *or* pass judgment, judge, pronounce, decree, order, ordain, award, assign, report, rule, bring in a verdict; sentence, pass sentence; doom etc. (condemn) 971.2; acquit etc. 970.3.

10. *v.* criticize, critique; comment upon, review; pass under review, investigate etc. (examine) 461.17; censure etc. 932.7.

11. *adj.* judicial, judiciary, judgmatic(al) [coll.]; judicative, judicatory, judicatorial; juridic(al), juristic(al);

---

lame and impotent conclusion.—SHAKESPEARE. In a case of dissension, never dare to judge till you've heard the other side.—EURIPIDES. We shall be judged, not by what we might have been, but what we have been.—SEWELL. *La critique est aisée et l'art est difficile* [Criticism is easy and art is difficult].—DESTOUCHES. Criticism comes easier than craftsmanship.—ZEUXIS. And stand a critic, hated yet caress'd.—BYRON. For I am nothing if not critical.—SHAKESPEARE. It is easier to be critical than to be correct.—DISRAELI.

confirmatory; determinative, decisive etc. (conclusive) 474.10.

12. *adj.* judicious etc. (wise) 498.11.

13. *adj.* critical, censorious etc. (disapprobatory) 932.11.

14. *adv.* on the whole, all things considered, taking one thing with another, taking all this into consideration, everything being equal, other things being equal, this being so, *quae cum ita sint* [L.]; therefore, wherefore.

481. Misjudgment
(See 480. Judgment)

1. *n.* misjudgment, obliquity of judgment, warped judgment, poor judgment; miscalculation, miscomputation, misreckoning, misestimation, misconjecture; mistake, misconception etc. (error) 495; misconstruction etc. (misinterpretation) 523; overestimation etc. 482; underestimation etc. 483; inexpectation etc. 508; sophistry etc. 477.

2. *n.* prejudgment, prejudication [rare], forejudgment, preconception, preconceived judgment *or* opinion, prejudice, prenotion, prenotice, prevention, predilection, prepossession, predisposition, preapprehension, presumption, presupposition, foregone conclusion; fixed idea, *idée fixe* [F.]; *mentis gratissimus error* [L.], fool's paradise; forethought etc. 510.2; presentiment etc. (foreboding) 511.6.

3. *n.* bias, warp, twist, quirk, waywardness; infatuation, obsession; prepossession, prejudice etc. *above*; partiality, one-sidedness, partial ⁓, one-sided ⁓, narrow ⁓, confined *or* superficial idea etc. (*see* idea etc. 453); narrow-mindedness; shortsightedness, purblindness etc. *adj.*; blind side, blind spot, mote in the eye; pedantism, pedantry; hypercriticism; bigotry etc. 606.2; bent, inclination etc. (tendency) 176; whim, crotchet etc. (caprice) 608.

4. *n.* class *or* race prejudice; cliquism,

---

481. Stiff in opinions, always in the wrong.—DRYDEN. The quirks of blazoning pens.—SHAKESPEARE. All prejudices may be tracked back to the intestines.—NIETZSCHE. Trifles unconsciously bias us for or against a person from the very beginning.—SCHOPENHAUER. The partisan, when he is engaged in a dispute, cares nothing about the rights of the question.—SOCRATES.

cliquishness; parochialism, provincialism; jingoism etc. 884.2.

5. *v.* misjudge, misestimate, miscalculate, misreckon, miscompute, misdeem, misesteem, misthink, misconjecture, misconstrue, fly in the face of facts, reckon without one's host; misconceive, get the wrong sow by the ear etc. (err) 495.7, 8; misunderstand etc. (misinterpret) 523.2; overestimate etc. 482.3; underestimate etc. 483.3; reason ill etc. 477.7.

6. *v.* prejudge, forejudge, prejudicate [rare], preconceive, presuppose, presume; jump *or* rush to a conclusion, come to a hasty conclusion, go off half-cocked *or* at half cock [coll.]; foresee etc. 510.5.

7. *v.* be prejudiced etc. *adj.*, have a bias etc. *n.*, have only one idea, run away with the notion, not see beyond one's nose *or* an inch beyond one's nose, see but one side of the question, look only at one side of the shield, view with jaundiced eye, view through distorting spectacles; dogmatize.

8. *v.* prejudice, prepossess, influence, bias, warp, twist, give a bias etc. *n.*; color by prejudice, jaundice.

9. *adj.* misjudging etc. *v.*, ill-judging, wrongheaded.

10. *adj.* prejudiced, prepossessed, biased etc. *v.*; prejudicious [rare], partial, one-sided, ex parte, superficial; intolerant, narrow-minded etc. (bigoted) 606.7; unreasonable etc. 477.10; positive etc. (dogmatic) 474.15; infatuated, besotted etc. (fanatical) 503.18.

481a. Discovery

Result of Search or Inquiry.—1. *n.* discovery, detection, finding etc. *v.*, find, disclosure, exposure, espial, revelation, ascertainment, determination; trover etc. 775.2.

2. *n.* solution, resolution, unriddling etc. *v.*, denouement; explanation, answer etc. (interpretation) 522.

3. *v.* discover, find, find out, find up [dial., Eng.], detect, spot [coll.], espy, descry, discern, determine, ascertain, make out; come across, meet with, come upon, fix upon, hit upon, fall upon, light upon, pitch upon, stumble on *or* upon, lay one's finger *or* hands upon, fall in with; educe, elicit, bring *or* drag out, evolve; smoke, smoke out; catch, catch tripping; trace, trace down *or* out, hunt down *or* out, fish out, worm out, ferret out, pry out, spy out, scout out [coll.]; root out *or* up, dig out *or* up, grub up, unearth, disinter, uncover, bring to light; reveal, expose etc. (disclose) 529.3, 4; see etc. 441.10; learn etc. 539.3.

4. *v.* solve, resolve, unriddle, decipher, decode, find the solution, clear up, set at rest, crack, do, work, work out; find out, make out, determine etc. *above*; unravel, ravel, ravel out; untangle, disentangle; unlock, pick *or* open the lock; find the key of, find a clew *or* clue to; puzzle out, figure out, dope out [slang]; get at, get *or* arrive at the truth etc. (*see* truth etc. 494.1), get to the bottom of, fathom; have it, hit it; hit the right nail on the head, put the saddle on the right horse; explain etc. (interpret) 522.6.

5. *v.* see through, penetrate, see daylight, see through a millstone [coll.], see in its true colors, see the cloven hoof, open the eyes to.

6. *v.* recognize, realize, know, identify, distinguish, discern, perceive, see, notice, make out, make [slang], spot [coll.], nail [coll.], peg [slang], get a line on [slang, U.S.]; know again, recover *or* recall knowledge of, reidentify.

7. *v.* scent, sniff, smell; sniff *or* smell out, nose out; smell a rat [coll.]; be near the truth, be warm [coll.] etc. adj., burn [coll.].

8. *adj.* near a discovery *or* solution, on the right scent, on the trail of; hot, warm [both coll.].

9. *int.* eureka!, I have it!, at long last!, finally!, *thalassa!* or *thalatta* [Gr.].

482. Overestimation
(See 483. Underestimation)

1. *n.* overestimation, overestimate, overvaluation, overrating etc. *v.*; much cry and little wool, much ado about nothing, storm *or* tempest in a teapot; fine talking *or* writing; overpraise, megalomania; optimism; exaggeration etc. 549; rodomontade, hot air [slang] etc. (boast-

---

481a. It is a profound mistake to think that everything has been discovered; as well think the horizon the boundary of the world.—LEMIERRE.   Canst thou by searching find out God?—BIBLE.   Finding's keeping.

482. All his geese are swans.

ing) 884; conceit etc. (vanity) 880; eulogy etc. (commendation) 931.2; flattery etc. 933; redundance etc. 461.

2. *n.* eulogist etc. 935; boaster etc. 884.3; egoist etc. 880.3.

3. *v.* overestimate, set too high an estimate *or* a value upon, overvalue, overrate, overprize, overweigh, overmeasure, overcount, overreckon, outreckon, overpraise, overesteem, overstrain, strain, stretch, estimate too highly, think *or* make too much of, attach too much importance to, make mountains of molehills, catch at straws, make the most, ∼ best *or* worst of, make two bites of a cherry; magnify etc. (exaggerate) 549.2; overdo etc. 641.3; have too high an opinion of oneself etc. 880.4; eulogize, extol to the skies etc. (commend) 931.6; flatter etc. 933.2; misjudge etc. 481.5.

4. *adj.* overestimated, overrated etc. *v.*; pretentious etc. (ostentatious) 882.8, (vain) 880.6, (boastful) 884.7; exaggerated etc. 549.3.

483. Underestimation
(See 482. Overestimation)

1. *n.* underestimation, underestimate, undervaluation, underrating etc. *v.*; pessimism; self-detraction, self-depreciation; depreciation etc. (detraction) 934; modesty etc. 881.

2. *n.* depreciator etc. 936.

3. *v.* underestimate, set too low an estimate *or* a value upon, undervalue, underrate, underreckon; misprize, disprize; minimize, think *or* make too little of, attach too little importance to, not do justice to, make *or* think nothing of, set at nought, set no store by, make little *or* light of; shake off like water from a duck's back, shake off as dewdrops from the lion's mane; pessimize; belittle, depreciate etc. (detract) 934.3; misjudge etc. 481.5.

4. *adj.* underestimated etc. *v.*, unvalued, unprized.

484. Belief
(See 485. Unbelief, Doubt; also 486. Credulity)

1. *n.* belief, credence, credit, assurance, faith, trust, troth, confidence, affiance, reliance; dependence on, reliance on *or* in etc.; stock [slang], store [coll.]; sanguine expectation etc. (hope) 858; credulity etc. 486; orthodoxy etc. 983a; piety etc. 987.

2. *n.* conviction, persuasion, convincement, plerophory [rare]; self-conviction, self-persuasion; firm ∼, implicit ∼, settled ∼, fixed ∼, rooted ∼, deep-rooted ∼, staunch ∼, well-founded ∼, unshaken ∼, steadfast ∼, inveterate ∼, dispassionate *or* impartial belief; *uberrima fides* [L.]; opinion, mind, conception, view, thought, think [slang], thinking; assumption, presumption; impression etc. (idea) 453; surmise etc. (supposition) 514; conclusion etc. (judgment) 480.

3. *n.* a belief, tenet, dogma, precept, principle, article, principle *or* article of faith, maxim, rule, canon; position, view, way of thinking, theory; doctrine, teaching, system of belief *or* opinions; school, cult; ism; creed, credo, credenda; articles of religion, doctrinal statements; gospel, gospel truth; catechism; popular belief *or* opinion, public opinion, *vox populi* [L.]; religion etc. (sect) 984.3.

4. *n.* profession, confession, declaration, profession ∼, confession *or* declaration of faith.

5. *n.* believability, believableness etc. *adj.*, credibility, plausibility [coll.], conceivability; possibility etc. 470; probability etc. 472; reasonability etc. 476.7.

6. *n.* believer, truster, accepter, receiver; true believer, orthodox; the faithful, the believing; Christian, convert etc. 987.4.

7. *v.* believe, believe in, exercise belief in, admit, accept, receive, credit, accredit, give credit *or* credence to, give faith to, pin one's faith to, have faith in, have *or* repose confidence in, confide ∼, hope *or* trust in, put trust in, trust, trust to *or* unto, place reliance in *or* on, allow *or* attach some weight to, lay one's account for.

---

483. If she undervalue me, / What care I how fair she be?—RALEIGH.

484. *Tarde quae credita laedunt credimus* [We are slow to believe what hurts when believed.—OVID. They can because they think they can.—VERGIL. Faith is the assent to any proposition, on the credit of the proposer.—LOCKE. A belief is not true because it is useful.—AMIEL. *Quot homines tot sententiae* [As many opinions as men].—TERENCE. To one fixed trust my spirit clings.—WHITTIER. Nothing is so firmly believed as that we least know.—MONTAIGNE. The brute necessity of believing

depend ~, rely ~, lean *or* rest on *or* upon, count ~, calculate *or* reckon on *or* upon, build upon, bank on *or* upon [coll.], allot on *or* upon [dial., U.S. and Can.]; take stock in [slang], set store by [coll.]; swear by, take one's oath upon; bet on, gamble on, go bail on, bet one's bottom dollar on [all coll.]; take for granted, take *or* accept for gospel, take on trust *or* credit; take one's word for, take at one's word; be wedded to; swallow [coll.] etc. (be credulous) 486.3; be pious etc. 987.6.

8. *v.* think, opine, be of the opinion, trust, consider, deem, esteem, weet [obs.], ween [arch.], trow [arch.], regard, be afraid [coll.], allow [dial.], reckon [coll.], calculate [coll., U.S.], estimate, guess, suppose, assume, presume, judge, surmise, suspect, expect [chiefly coll.], imagine, fancy, wis [arch.], daresay *or* dare say; conceive, apprehend, realize, see; hold, hold as, account as, set down as *or* for, view as, look upon, have it, take, take it, take for; have ~, hold ~, possess ~, entertain ~, adopt ~, imbibe ~, embrace ~, foster ~, nurture *or* cherish a belief *or* an opinion, hazard an opinion.

9. *v.* doubt not, have *or* make no doubt; be *or* rest assured, be *or* feel sure etc. *adj.*; know, know for certain.

10. *v.* convince, convict, convert, wean, bring round, bring *or* win over, bring to reason, bring to one's senses, persuade, satisfy, assure, bring *or* drive home to; cram down the throat; have the ear of, gain the confidence of; produce *or* carry conviction, be convincing; persuade ~, assure *or* satisfy oneself, make oneself easy about *or* on that score, make sure of, make up one's mind.

11. *v.* find credence, go down, be swallowed [coll.] etc. (*see* swallow etc. 486.3), be received etc. *v.*; be current etc. *adj.*, pass current; possess the mind,

take hold *or* possession of the mind.

12. *adj.* believing etc. *v.*, undoubting, unquestioning, unhesitating; indubious, undoubtful, doubtless, questionless; under the impression, impressed with; positive, confident; convinced, satisfied, assured etc. *v.*; sure, cocksure [coll.] etc. (certain) 474.8; pious etc. 987.10–12.

13. *adj.* confiding, trustful, suspectless [obs.], unsuspecting, unsuspicious, void of suspicion; credulous etc. 486.5.

14. *adj.* believed, accredited, trusted etc. *v.*; unsuspected, undoubted, unquestioned, undisputed, uncontested; putative, putationary.

15. *adj.* believable, credible, tenable, conceivable, plausible [coll.], confidential, reliable, trustworthy, dependable, to be depended upon; downable, swallowable [both coll.]; satisfying, satisfactory; fiducial, fiduciary; persuasive, impressive; possible etc. 470.5; probable etc. 472.5, 6; reasonable etc. (logical) 476.16; indubitable, unquestionable etc. 474.10.

16. *adj.* doctrinal, creedal; canonical, orthodox etc. (authoritative) 474.13.

17. *phr.* I believe, I do believe, I think etc. *v.*, methinks [arch. or poetic], meseems [arch.], it seems to me, to the best of my belief, according to my belief, to my eyes, in my opinion, in my judgment, *me judice* [L.], I dare say, I doubt not, I have no doubt, I am sure etc. *adj.*, I am convinced etc. *v.*; believe me!, take my word for it!; depend *or* rely upon it!, be *or* rest assured!, I'll warrant you! etc. (affirmation) 535.8.

485. Unbelief, Doubt
(See 484. Belief; also 487. Incredulity)

1. *n.* unbelief, disbelief, want of belief *or* faith; misbelief, miscreance *or* miscreancy [arch.]; minimifidianism; freethinking, free thought; incredulity etc. 487; heresy etc. (heterodoxy) 984.1; infidelity, atheism, agnosticism etc. (irreligion) 989; dissent etc. 489; change of mind, retraction etc. (tergiversation) 607.

---

something so long as life lasts.—SANTAYANA. The believing man is the original man.—CARLYLE. Youth is confident, manhood wary, and old age confident again.—TUPPER. *Credite posteri* [Let posterity believe it]!—HORACE. *Credimus ut cognoscamus* [We believe in order to know].—ST. AUGUSTINE. *Crede experto* [Believe an experienced person]! *Vide et crede* [See and believe]. Seeing's believing. *Crede quod habes, et habes* [Believe that you have it, and you have it]. Many men, many minds. *Credo quia impossibile* [I believe because it is impossible].

485. How prone to doubt, how cautious are the wise!—HOMER. Lord, I believe; help thou mine unbelief.—BIBLE. They could not enter in because of unbelief.—BIBLE. Stands not within the prospect of belief.—SHAKESPEARE. I will listen to anyone's convictions,

2. *n.* doubt, doubtfulness, dubiousness, dubiety, dubiosity, dubitancy [now rare], dubitation; discredit, discredence; skepticism, Pyrrhonism; misdoubt, mistrust, distrust, diffidence [arch.], misgiving, demur, suspicion, jealousy, scruple, boggle, qualm; hesitation, indecision etc. (uncertainty) 475; suspiciousness etc. 487.2; fearfulness etc. 860.2.

3. *n.* unbelievability, unbelievableness etc. *adj.*, incredibility, implausibility [coll.], inconceivability; doubtfulness etc. *above*; improbability etc. 473.

4. *n.* unbeliever, disbeliever, atheist, infidel etc. 989.4; pagan, heathen etc. 984.20; backslider etc. (apostate) 607.5; heretic etc. 984.12.

5. *v.* disbelieve, unbelieve, misbelieve, not believe etc. (*see* believe etc. 484.7); reject, refuse to believe etc. (incredulity) 487.3; refuse to admit etc. (dissent) 489.4; be irreligious etc. 989.5.

6. *v.* doubt, dubitate [rare], doubt the truth of, have ∼, harbor *or* entertain doubts *or* suspicions, have one's doubts, be doubtful, ∼ skeptical etc. *adj.*, skepticize; take with a grain of salt; mistrust, distrust, diffide [obs.]; suspect, suspicion [now dial.], smell a rat [coll.]; discredit, give no credit *or* credence to; question, challenge, dispute, bring *or* call in question, raise a question, throw doubt upon, cause ∼, raise ∼, start ∼, suggest *or* awake a doubt *or* suspicion; doubt one's word, give one the lie in one's throat; deny etc. 536.2; disagree etc. 489.4; fear etc. 860.2.

7. *v.* demur, scruple, boggle, qualm [rare], hesitate, pause, stick at, hang back, hang in doubt *or* suspense, falter, waver, shy at; take exception, protest, object, raise objections; carp, cavil, wrangle, ergotize [rare].

8. *v.* be unbelievable etc. *adj.*, strain one's credulity, shake *or* stagger one's faith *or* belief, shake, stagger, startle; perplex, fill with doubt; go beyond the bounds of reason *or* probability etc. (be improbable) 473.2.

9. *adj.* unbelieving etc. *v.*, unbelieffull; faithless, lacking faith etc. (*see* faith etc. 484); nullifidian, minimifidian; miscreant [arch.], heretic(al), heterodox; incredulous etc. 487.4.

10. *adj.* doubting etc. *v.*, doubtful, doubtsome [Scot. and dial. Eng.], in doubt; dubious, dubitative; from Missouri [slang, U.S.]; skeptic(al); Pyrrhonic, Pyrrhonian; infidel, infidelic(al) [both rare]; mistrustful, distrustful; suspicious, suspectful [rare]; scrupulous, qualmish; undetermined, uncertain etc. 475.9-16.

11. *adj.* unbelievable, untenable, incredible, implausible [coll.], inconceivable, not to be believed, hard to believe, hard of belief, unworthy *or* undeserving of belief etc. (*see* belief etc. 484), open to doubt *or* suspicion, doubtful, doubtable, dubitable, questionable, problematic(al); suspicious, suspect [arch.]; staggering, staggering to one's belief *or* faith; disputable, controvertible etc. (uncertain) 475.9, (illogical) 477.10; unreliable, undemonstrable etc. (fallible) 475.14; improbable etc. 473.3.

12. *adv.* with a grain of salt, *cum grano salis* [L.]; with some reservation *or* allowance, with caution.

486. Credulity
(See 487. Incredulity; also 484. Belief)

1. *n.* credulity, credulousness etc. *adj.*, gullibility, cullibility [obs.], dupability, deceivability; blind faith, unquestioning belief; gross credulity, infatuation; self-delusion, self-deception; superstition, *Aberglaube* [G.]; one's blind side; belief etc. 484.

2. *n.* credulous person etc. (dupe) 547.

3. *v.* be credulous etc. *adj.*, accept unquestioningly, follow implicitly, take on trust, take for granted *or* gospel, take on faith; run away with a notion *or* an idea, jump *or* rush to a conclusion; down, gulp down, swallow, swallow

---

but pray keep your doubts to yourself.—Goethe. Belief consists in accepting the affirmations of the soul; unbelief, in denying them.—Emerson. There lives more faith in honest doubt, / Believe me, than in half the creeds.—Tennyson. Faith and unfaith can ne'er be equal powers; / Unfaith in aught is want of faith in all.—Tennyson. The faculty of doubting is rare among men.—A. France. *Timeo Danaos et dona ferentes* [I fear the Greeks bringing gifts].—Vergil.

486. The sanguine credulity of youth.—Bible. Your noblest natures are most credulous.—Chapman. Credulity is the man's weakness, but the child's strength.—Lamb. A little credulity helps one on through life very smoothly.—E. Gaskell. Let any man speak long enough, he will get believers.—Stevenson.

whole [all coll.]; swallow hook, line and sinker [slang]; eat up, devour, gobble up *or* down [all slang]; bite, nibble, rise to the fly, take the bait [all slang]; go for, fall for [both slang]; think the moon is made of green cheese, take *or* grasp the shadow for the substance, catch at straws; believe etc. 484.7.

4. *v.* practice on one's credulity, impose upon etc. (deceive) 545.7, 10.

5. *adj.* credulous, gullible, pigeonable [slang], dupable, stuffable [slang], easily deceived etc. (*see* deceive etc. 545.7), easily convinced etc. (*see* convince etc. 484.10), easy [coll.], easy to stuff [slang], ready *or* inclined to believe; simple, green, naïve *or* naïf, childish, silly, stupid, soft; overcredulous, overconfident, overtrustful; infatuated; superstitious; trustful, unsuspecting etc. (confiding) 484.13; deceivable etc. 545.14.

487. Incredulity
(See also 486. Credulity; also 484. Unbelief, Doubt)

1. *n.* incredulity, incredulousness etc. *adj.*, withholding of belief, refusal to believe, inconvincibility *or* unconvincibility; skepticism, disbelief etc. (unbelief) 485, (irreligion) 989.

2. *n.* suspiciousness etc. *adj.*, suspicion, scrupulosity, qualmishness; distrust etc. (doubt) 485.2.

3. *v.* be incredulous etc. *adj.*, refuse to believe etc. (*see* believe etc. 484.7), refuse to admit *or* accept, not swallow [coll.] etc. (*see* swallow etc. 486.3), shut one's eyes to, shut *or* stop one's ears to, turn a deaf ear to, hold oneself aloof, reject, ignore, "*nullius jurare in verba magistri*" (Horace); distrust, skepticize etc. (doubt) 485.6.

4. *adj.* incredulous, not credulous etc. (*see* credulous etc. 486.5), hard *or* shy of belief, disposed to doubt, indisposed to believe, unwilling to admit *or* accept, inconvincible *or* unconvincible; undeceivable, hoaxproof; doubtful, skeptical, suspicious etc. (unbelieving) 485.9, 10.

488. Assent
(See 489. Dissent)

1. *n.* assent, assentment [arch.], assentation, accession, acquiescence, agreement; yes, yea etc. *adv.*; nod, nod of assent; consent etc. 762; concurrence etc. 178; affirmation etc. 535; willingness etc. 602; approval etc. (approbation) 931.

2. *n.* acknowledgment, recognition, recognizance [rare].

3. *n.* unanimity, unanimousness etc. *adj.*, unanimity of opinion *or* assent, joint assent, common assent *or* consent, consensus, consensus of opinion, *consensus omnium* [L.], consension [rare], consentaneity, consentaneousness, consentience, consent [arch.], acclamation, agreement, general agreement, agreement of all; like-mindedness, meeting of minds; unison, chorus, concert, one voice; accord, accordance; concord, concordance; concurrence, concurrency, sympathy, understanding, mutual understanding; popular *or* current belief *or* opinion, public opinion, *vox populi* [L.]; co-operation etc. 709.

4. *n.* ratification, confirmation, authentication, certification, endorsement *or* indorsement, approval, acceptance, verification, validation, O.K. [slang]; affirmance, affirmation; subscription, signature, sign manual, John Hancock [coll.]; mark, cross, stamp, stamp of approval, seal, sigil, signet; visa, visé; corroboration etc. 467.3.

5. *n.* assenter, assentant [obs.]; affirmant, confirmist, consenter, covenantor, subscriber, endorser *or* indorser, professor, professant [obs.].

6. *v.* assent, give *or* yield assent etc. *n.*, acquiesce, agree, agree to *or* with, hold with, accede, accept, receive; lend oneself to, subscribe to; yes etc. *adv.*, say yes etc. *adv.* to; vote for, give one's voice for; consent etc. 762.2; be willing etc. 602.6; approve etc. 931.5.

7. *v.* concur, accord, consent, coincide, agree, agree with, agree in opinion, gee [dial. and slang], enter into one's views, enter into the ideas *or* feelings of, con

---

487. I'm from Missouri; you've got to show me.—W. D. VANDIVER.   Incredulity robs us of many pleasures, and gives us nothing in return.—LOWELL.   Knowledge of divine things for the most part, as Heraclitus says, is lost to us by incredulity.—PLUTARCH.

488. He who lightly assents will seldom keep his word.—LAO-TSZE.   To assent to (a proposition) is to acquiesce in it as true.—NEWMAN.   His silence answers yes.—EURIPIDES.   The public mind is the creation of the Master Writers.—DISRAELI.   Public opinion alway

form to, be at one with etc. *adj.*, go with, go along with, fall ~, chime *or* strike in with, close with, meet; reciprocate, echo, ditto [coll.], say ditto to; join in the chorus, go ~, float *or* swim with the stream *or* current, get on the band wagon [coll.], *hurler avec les loups* [F.].

8. *v.* come to an agreement *or* understanding, arrive at an agreement, come to terms, get together [coll.], shake on it [slang], call it square [coll.], call it a go [coll.], be a go [coll.], be a bargain, be on [slang]; strike a bargain etc. 794.6.

9. *v.* acknowledge, own, admit, allow, avow, aver [arch.], grant, warrant, concede, yield, consent [obs.], accept, testify, confess; recognize, agnize [arch.], respect, yield *or* submit to, defer to; come round to, abide by.

10. *v.* ratify, confirm, affirm [obs. exc. Law], endorse *or* indorse, certify, verify, validate, accept, O.K. [slang], approve, sanction; amen, say amen to; visa, visé; sign, countersign, undersign, underwrite, subscribe to; seal, sign and seal, set one's hand seal to; corroborate etc. 467.9; guarantee etc. 771.6.

11. *adj.* assenting etc *v.*, assentive, assentant [obs.], assentaneous, assentatious; acquiescent, concurrent, agreed, content; consenting etc. 762.3; willing etc. 602.8; affirmative etc. 535.6.

12. *adj.* unanimous, solid [Polit. cant, U.S.]; with one consent *or* voice, consentient, consentaneous, concentive [rare], consentual, consensual; concurrent, concordant, of one accord; likeminded, of one mind, of the same mind, of a piece; at one, at one with, on all fours with; agreed on all hands, agreed *or* carried *nemine contradicente* or *nem. con.* [L.] etc. *adv.*, carried by acclamation.

13. *adj.* uncontradicted, unchallenged, unquestioned, uncontroverted.

14. *adv. etc.* yes, yea [now chiefly coll.], aye *or* ay, ugh [Amer. Indian]; yep, yeah, uh-huh [all coll.]; yes sir, yes ma'am; yes sirree [coll., U.S.], yes sirree Bob [slang, U.S.]; indeed, indeedy [coll., U.S.], yes indeed, yes indeedy [coll., U.S.]; sure [now slang], surely, assuredly, to be sure; sure thing, sure Mike [both slang, U.S.]; certainly, certes [arch.]; good, well and good, very well; granted, conceded, *ex concesso* [L.], of course, even so, just so, as you say, you said it, that's it, that's just it; really, truly, absolutely, positively, exactly, precisely; unquestionably, no doubt, doubtless; you bet [slang], forsooth.

15. *adv. etc.* be it so, so be it, so mote it be, so shall it be, so is it, so it is; amen; by all means, by all manner of means.

16. *adv.* affirmatively, in the affirmative.

17. *adv.* unanimously etc. *adj.*, by common consent, with one consent *or* accord, with one voice, *una voce* [L.], in chorus, to a man, as one man, one and all, on all hands; without contradiction, *nemine contradicente* or *nem. con.*, *nemine dissentiente* or *nem. dis.* [both L.], without a dissentient voice; concordantly etc. 714.5.

489. Dissent
(See 488. Assent)

1. *n.* dissent, dissentment, dissentience, dissidence; nonassent, nonassentation, nonconsent [rare], nonconcurrence, nonagreement, disagreement, difference, difference *or* diversity of opinion, refusal *or* unwillingness of assent; recusance *or* recusancy, recusation; disaffection; dissension, discordance, schism etc. (discord) 713; discontent etc. 832; noncompliance etc. (refusal) 764; nonconformity etc. (unconformity) 83, (sectarianism) 984.2; unwillingness etc. 603; secession etc. (abandonment) 624; apostasy, recantation etc. 607.2, 3; disapproval etc. (disapprobation) 932.

2. *n.* protest, protestation, kick [coll.]; objection, objectation [rare]; remonstrance, expostulation; dispute, challenge; scruple, demur, boggle; exception, rejection, drawback; protestantism; contradiction, denial etc. (negation) 536.

3. *n.* dissenter, dissentient; noncontent, noncon [coll.]; nonconformist, re-

---

is in advance of the Law.—GALSWORTHY. That mysterious independent variable of political calculation, Public Opinion.—HUXLEY. Silence gives consent.

489. And protest, only a bubble in the molten mass, pops and sighs out, and the mass hardens. —R. JEFFERS. All Protestantism, even the

cusant; nonjuror, nonjurant; sectary, sectarist [rare], sectarian; protestant, protester, protestator [rare]; separatist, seceder etc. (apostate) 607.5; rebel etc. (insurgent) 742.3; heretic etc. 984.12, 13.

4. *v.* dissent, differ in opinion, differ, disagree, disagree with, agree to differ *or* disagree [joc.]; beg to differ, beg leave to disagree; differ *toto caelo* [L.], differ diametrically; not agree to etc. (*see* agree etc. 488.6-10), refuse assent *or* consent, nonconsent [rare].

say no etc. (*see* no etc. 536.4), not hear to [coll.], not countenance, view with disfavor, look black upon, look askance *or* askant at; revolt at, revolt from the idea; have no notion of, not have the least idea of; shake the head, shrug the shoulders; not admit, refuse to admit *or* accept, repudiate; take exception, demur, scruple, boggle, kick [coll.], protest, object, raise objections, raise one's voice against; quibble, cavil, wrangle, ergotize [rare]; challenge, call in question etc. (doubt) 485.6; contradict etc. (deny) 536.2; recant etc. 607.9; secede etc. (abandon) 624.3; be unwilling etc. 603.4; disapprove etc. 932.5; refuse etc. 764.2.

5. *adj.* dissenting etc. *v.*, dissentient, dissentious, dissident; protestant, recusant; nonjuring, nonjurant; unconvinced, unconverted; intolerant; negative etc. 536.3; unconsenting etc. (refusing) 764.5; unwilling etc. 603.5; disagreeing etc. 24.6; discontented etc. 832.5; schismatic etc. (sectarian) 984.23; discontented etc. 832.5; discordant etc. 713.9.

6. *adj.* unavowed, unacknowledged; out of the question.

7. *adv.* dissentingly etc. *adj.*; at variance *or* odds with, at issue with; under protest.

8. *adv.* no etc. 536.4.

9. *int.* God forbid!, not for the world!, not on your life! [coll.], I'll be hanged if . . . ! [coll.], not another word!, no sirree! [coll., U.S.], not if I know it!, by no means!, never tell me!, your humble servant! [arch]; pardon me!, I beg your pardon!

most cold and passive, is a sort of dissent.—BURKE. A general union of total dissent.—LOWELL.

490. Knowledge
(See 491. Ignorance)

1. *n.* knowledge, cognizance, cognition, cognoscence [obs.]; ken, know [coll.], acquaintance, familiarity, privity savvy, sabe [both slang, U.S.]; comprehension, apprehension; recognition, recognizance [now rare]; appreciation, appreciativeness; conscience, consciousness; awareness, sensibility; perception apperception; knowledge of acquaintance, abstractive knowledge, intellective knowledge, representative knowledge information etc. 527; intelligence, wisdom etc. 498; worldly knowledge etc 698.4; intuitive knowledge, insight etc (intuition) 477a; precognition etc. (foreknowledge) 510.3; skill etc. 698; theory of knowledge etc. (philosophy) 451.4.

2. *n.* learning, enlightenment, acquired knowledge, acquirements, mental acquirements *or* acquisitions, attainments, accomplishments; information info [slang, U.S.]; store of knowledge treasury of information; body of knowledge, lore; scholarship, schoolcraft [arch.], schoolery [rare]; erudition reading, letters; literature [rare], book knowledge *or* learning, booklore, bibliology; bookishness, bookiness; pedantry pedantism; book madness, bibliomania bibliomanianism, bibliomanism; love *or* worship of books, bibliophilism, bibliolatry.

culture, *Kultur* [G.], cultivation, menticulture; liberal education, higher education; proficiency, experience, experimental knowledge, practical knowledge technical *or* professional knowledge; acquisition of knowledge etc. 539; education etc. (teaching) 537.

3. *n.* profound knowledge, deep ~ solid etc. *adj.* knowledge, acroatic *or* acroamatic knowledge, wide ~, vast *or* extensive knowledge, encyclopedic(al)

---

490. Knowledge is power.—BACON. Knowledge is a treasure, but practice is the key to it —FULLER. Through knowledge we behold the world's creation.—SPENSER. An investment in knowledge pays the best interest.—FRANKLIN. The desire of knowledge, like the thirst of riches, increases ever with the acquisition of it.—STERNE. Knowledge and timber shouldn't be much used till they are seasoned.—HOLMES. *Empta dolore docet experientia* [Experience bought by pain teaches] Experience is the surest standard by which to

knowledge; pansophy, pansophism; pantology; infinite *or* universal knowledge *or* wisdom, all-knowingness, omniscience *or* omnisciency.

4. *n.* slight knowledge, smattering of knowledge etc. 491.3.

5. *n.* progressive knowledge, advance *or* progress of knowledge, ~ learning *or* science, march of intellect.

6. *n.* tree of knowledge, tree of knowledge of good and evil; forbidden fruit.

7. *n.* (system or body of knowledge) science, ology [chiefly joc.], branch *or* department of knowledge, discipline [arch.]; acroama, acroamatics, acroamatic teaching *or* doctrine; etiology, science *or* doctrine of causes; doctrine, body of doctrine; pandect; cyclopedia, encyclopedia, circle of knowledge *or* sciences.

8. *n.* (cross references) philosophy etc. 451.4–23; sophistry etc. 477; republic of letters etc. (literature) 560.8; school, doctrine etc. (belief) 484.3; physics etc. 49.2; mathematics etc. 38.3, 85.2, 466.8; chronometry etc. 114; evolutionism, abiogenesis etc. 161.2; micrology etc. 193.6; enterology etc. 221.6; dermatology, malacology etc. 223.20, 21; kinetics etc. 264.4, 276.5; eccrinology etc. 299.8; astronomy etc. 318.10; koniology etc. 330.5; oceanography etc. 341.3; zoology etc. 368; botany etc. 369; acoustics etc. 402.5, 418.9; skiagraphy etc. 422.4; logic etc. 476; navigation etc. 267; aeronautics etc. 267a.

science of existence etc. 1.3; science of quantity etc. 25.3; science of measurement etc. 466.8; science of organisms 357.5; science of old age etc. 128.5; science of electricity etc. 158a.3; science of forces etc. 159.3; science of form and structure etc. 240.4; science of mechanical forces etc. 276.5; science of propulsion etc. 284.9; science of rotation etc. 312.6; science of matter etc. 316.5; science of texture etc. 329.2; science of liquids at rest etc. 333.4; science of fluids in motion etc. 348.14; science of elastic fluids etc. 334.3; science of rain, snow etc. 348.15; science of air etc. 338.6; science of humidity etc. 339.3; science of land etc. 342.5; science of clouds etc. 353.6; science of minerals etc. 358.2; science of life etc. 359.5; science of heat etc. 382.12; science of music etc. 415.23; science of colors etc. 428.7; science of the mind etc. 450.4.

9. *v.* know, have knowledge of etc. *n.*, be cognizant of etc. *adj.*, ken [now chiefly Scot.], con [obs.], perceive, apprehend, scan [now rare], cognize, recognize, discern, see, get a sight of, understand, fathom, make out, comprehend, conceive, realize, appreciate; savvy, sabe [both slang, U.S.]; have, possess; wit, weet, ween, trow [all arch.]; perceive *or* apprehend as true, recognize as valid *or* as a fact, have mental certitude in regard to, perceive with understanding and conviction; have immediate experience, be conversant with etc. *adj.*, have practical knowledge of; be apprized of, have information about.

10. *v.* know well, know full well, have a good *or* thorough knowledge of, have dead to rights [slang], have down pat [coll.], have down cold [slang, U.S.], be well-informed etc. *adj.*; have in one's head, have at one's fingers' ends *or* tips, know by heart *or* rote, be master of, know like a book, know inside out, know backwards, know down to the ground [coll.], *connaître le dessous des cartes* [F.]; know one's stuff [slang, U.S.], know one's onions [slang, chiefly U.S.], know the ropes; know what's what [coll.] etc. 698.8.

11. *v.* learn, acquire knowledge etc. 539; come to one's knowledge etc. (become informed) 527.11; discover etc. 480a.3–7.

12. *adj.* knowing etc. *v.*, knowledgeable [coll.], conscious, aware, sensible, cognitive, cognizant, jerry [slang], gnostic [joc. or slang], understanding, intelligent, hep [slang, U.S.], fly [slang]; percipient, perceptive, apperceptive, appercipient; shrewd, wise etc. 498.10, 11; cunning etc. 702.6.

---

rest.—WASHINGTON. All experience is an arch, to build upon.—H. ADAMS. Experience is the name everyone gives to his mistakes.—WILDE. Familiarity breeds contempt.—AESOP. Only so much do I know as I have lived.—EMERSON. Wearing all the weight /

Of learning lightly like a flower.—TENNYSON. He who has imagination without learning has wings and no feet.—JOUBERT. All I know is just what I read in the papers.—W. ROGERS. Experience is the mother of wisdom.

13. *adj.* aware of, cognizant of, conscious of; acquainted with, made acquainted with; privy to, no stranger to; *au fait, au courant* [both F.]; in the secret, in the know [slang], let into, behind the scenes *or* curtain; up to [coll.], alive to, awake to, wise to [coll.], up to snuff [slang]; apprized of, informed of; undeceived.

14. *adj.* versed in, read *or* well-read in, forward in, strong in, at home in; conversant with, familiar with; proficient in etc. (skilled) 698.14.

15. *adj.* informed, educated, instructed, enlightened, taught; full of information *or* learning, erudite, learned, lettered; posted, posted up, well-posted [all coll.]; well-informed, well-conned, well-educated, well-grounded, well-versed, well-read, deep-read, widely read; book-read, book-learned, book-taught, book-fed, book-wise, bookful [rare]; solid, deep, profound, abstruse; acroatic, acroamatic; omniscient, all-knowing; autodidactic, self-taught, self-educated, self-made; *savant* [F.] etc. (wise) 498.11.

16. *adj.* bookish, booky, book-minded; book-loving, bibliophilic, bibliophilist *or* bibliophilistic; bibliophagic; scholastic, scholarly; blue [coll.], bluestocking; high-brow, high-browed, high-browish [all slang]; book-learned etc. *above*; studious etc. 539.6; intellectual etc. 450.8.

17. *adj.* known etc. *v.*, ascertained, recognized, received; pat, down pat [both coll.]; well-known, well-kenned; widely *or* commonly known, universally recognized, known by every schoolboy, familiar, familiar as household words, household, common, commonplace, popular, current, proverbial; notorious, noted; general, prevalent, universal etc. 78.9–11; trite etc. 843.6.

18. *adj.* knowable, knowledgeable [obs.], cognizable, cognoscible, ascertainable, discoverable, discernible, perceptible, distinguishable, understandable, comprehensible.

19. *adj.* scientific, etiological, pansophic(al), pantologic(al); encyclopedic, philosophical etc. *n.*

20. *adv.* to one's knowledge, to the best of one's knowledge, as every schoolboy knows.

491. Ignorance
(See 490. Knowledge)

1. *n.* ignorance, ignorantness, want of knowledge etc. (*see* knowledge etc. 490); nescience, unscience [rare *or* obs.], inscience [rare]; incognizance, unconsciousness, incomprehension, unacquaintance; unlearnedness, inerudition ineducation [rare]; illiteracy, illiterateness, illiterature [rare]; dark, darkness benightment, unenlightenment, blindness; greenness, greenhornism, green in the eye; inexperience, simplicity; crass ignorance; "the mother of impudence" (C. H. Spurgeon), "the mother of admiration" (G. Chapman), "blind and naked Ignorance" (Tennyson); ignorantism, obscurantism; unintelligence etc 499; inexperience etc. (unskillfulness) 699.

2. *n.* matter of ignorance, sealed book *terra incognita* [L.], unknown *or* unexplored ground, virgin soil, Dark Continent; unknown quantity, x, y, z; dark horse; enigma etc. 533.2.

3. *n.* imperfect knowledge, slight knowledge, vague notion; smattering smattering of knowledge; half-learning superficiality, shallowness, sciolism dilettantism, dilettantship; incapacity glimmering, inkling etc. (hint) 527.6 bewilderment etc. (perplexity) 475.2.

4. *n.* (affectation of knowledge) pedantry, pedantism; bookishness, bookiness; Philistinism, Philistinishness; empiricism, empiricalness; sophistry etc 477; charlatanry, quackery etc. (dissembling) 544.2.

5. *n.* Dark Ages, Middle Age *or* Ages; Dark-Ageism, Middle-Ageism medievalism; Gothicism, barbarism etc 851.1.

6. *v.* be ignorant etc. *adj.*, ignore [arch.]; not know etc. (*see* know etc 490.9), know not, know not what, know nothing of, know from nothing [slang U.S.]; have no idea, ~ notion *or* con-

491. *Quantum animis erroris inest* [How much error there is in human minds]!—OVID *Nec scire fas est omnia* [It is not permitted to know all things].—HORACE. There is no darkness but ignorance.—SHAKESPEARE. Ignorance never settles a question.—DISRAELI Ignorance is not innocence, but sin.—BROWNING. Ignorance is the mother of prejudice —J. BRIGHT. A little learning is a dangerous

ception, not have the least *or* remotest idea; not know chalk from cheese, not know B from a bull's foot, ~ a battledore *or* a broomstick, not know beans, not know beans when the bag is open, not know up from down, not know straight up; be blind to, "see through a glass, darkly" (Bible), have a film over the eyes; grope in the dark, walk in darkness; have green in the eye; wonder, wonder whether; not pretend to say, not take upon oneself to say; not know what to make of etc. (not understand) 519.5.

7. *v.* keep in ignorance etc. (keep secret) 528.11.

8. *adj.* ignorant, nescient, inscient [rare]; incognizant, incognitive; unknowing, unaware, unconscious, unacquainted, unapprized, unconversant, uninformed, unenlightened, unversed, uninitiated, a stranger to; green, green as grass *or* a gourd, verdant [coll.], unripe, raw; simple, dumb [coll., U.S.], stupid, umpish, dense, crass; empty, emptyheaded; witless, weetless [obs.]; unwitting, unweeting [obs.]; inexperienced etc. 699.14; unintelligent etc. 499.11; unaccustomed etc. 614.3.

9. *adj.* unlearned, inerudite *or* unerulite, uneducated, unschooled, uninstructed, untaught, untutored, unread, unlettered, unguided, borrel [arch.], gramnarless, illiterate, lay [obs.]; bookless, unbooked, unbooklearned, unbookish; uncultivated, uncultured, unrefined, rude; low-brow, low-browed, low-browish [all coll.]; Philistine, Philistinian, Philistinic, Philistinish; unskilled etc. 599.13; immature etc. 674.8.

10. *adj.* in the dark, in darkness, dark; benighted, belated [arch.]; blinded, blindfold, blindfolded, hoodwinked; misinformed, at fault; at sea etc. (uncertain) 475.16.

11. *adj.* behindhand, behind, behind the age *or* times, backward.

12. *adj.* sciolistic, sciolous [now rare]; half-learned, half-baked [coll.]; shallow, superficial; dilettante, dilettantish.

13. *adj.* empiric(al); quack, quackish; charlatan, charlatanic(al), charlatanish, charlatanistic; pedantic(al); wise in one's own conceit.

14. *adj.* unknown, unapprehended, unexplained, unascertained, uninvestigated, unexplored, unheard-of, unsuspected, unapparent, unperceived, undisclosed, unrevealed, undivulged, undiscovered, unexposed, sealed; incognito, incognita [*fem.*], incog [coll.]; concealed etc. 528.17, 18; unfamiliar, strange etc. (unusual) 83.10.

15. *adj.* unknowable, incognizable, incognoscible, unascertainable, undiscoverable, indiscernible, imperceptible, indistinguishable, incomprehensible.

16. *adv.* ignorantly, unknowingly etc. *adj.*; unawares; for anything *or* aught one knows, not that one knows.

17. *int.* God knows!, God only knows!, the Lord knows!, Heaven knows!, dear knows! [dial.], land knows! [coll.], nobody knows!, damned if I know! [vulg.], I give up!; you've got me!, ask me another!, search me! [all slang]; how should I know?; *je ne sais pas!* [F.], who knows?

18. *phr.* ignoramus, no bill, no true bill, ignored [all Law]; not found.

492. Scholar
(See 493. Ignoramus)

1. *n.* scholar, scholarian [rare], scholastic, a gentleman and a scholar; learned man, man of learning, ~ letters *or* education, literary man, *homo multarum literarum* [L.]; *savant* [F.], *savante* [F.; *fem.*]; pundit [Ind.], moolvi [Moham.], munshi [Ind.], mullah [Moham.], guru [Ind.], clerk [arch.]; bookman, bibliosoph, bibliognost.

schoolman, professor, academician, doctor, fellow, don [Eng. Univ. cant]; wrangler, optime [both Cambridge Univ.]; intellectual; intelligentsia; connoisseur, *connaisseur* [F.]; scholiast, commentator, annotator; classicist, classicalist; littérateur *or* litterateur; literati

---

thing.—POPE. Better know nothing than half-know many things.—NIETZSCHE. It is better to understand little than to misunderstand a lot.—A. FRANCE. Where ignorance is bliss, 'tis folly to be wise.—GRAY. Jack of all trades and master of none.

492. Hell is paved with the skulls of great scholars.—G. FIRMIN. This man decided not to Live but Know.—BROWNING. I offer perpetual congratulation to the scholar; he has drawn the white lot in life.—EMERSON. And what the actor could effect, / The scholar could

[*pl.*], literatus; illuminate, illuminati [*pl.*]; bachelor, master etc. (academic degrees and titles) 877.3; student etc. (learner) 541.

2. *n.* giant of learning, colossus of knowledge, mine of information, walking encyclopedia; pantologist; prodigy, intellectual prodigy, genius, mental genius, man of genius, wizard [chiefly coll.], mastermind, masterhead; *uomo universale* [It.]; Admirable Crichton, Mezzofanti, learned Theban, Dominie Sampson; Socrates, Plato, Solomon; sage etc. 500.

3. *n.* bookworm, bookmonger, *helluo librorum* [L.]; grind, greasy grind, dig [all college slang, U.S.]; booklover, bibliophile, bibliophilist; book worshiper, bibliolater, bibliolatrist; bibliomaniac, bibliomane, bibliomanian.

4. *n.* pedant, pedantess; pedagogue, pedagogist; Gamaliel, Dr. Pangloss; bluestocking [coll.], blue [coll.], *bas bleu* [F.]; high-brow [slang]; doctrinaire, doctrinarian [rare]; instructor etc. 540; affecter etc. 853.4.

5. *n.* scientist, scientician [rare], scient [rare], man of science, scientific investigator.

6. *n.* (cross references) mathematician etc. 85.6; chronographer etc. 114.7; archaeologist etc. (antiquary) 122.5; somatologist, physicist etc. 316.6; cosmologist, astronomer, astrologist etc. 318.11-13; oceanographer etc. 341.4; geographer, geodesist etc. 342.6; biologist etc. (naturalist) 357.7; zoologist etc. 368.2; botanist etc. 369.9; phonetician etc. 402.6; otologist etc. 418.10; psychologist etc. 450.5; cartographer, surveyor etc. 466.9; philosopher etc. 476.9; paralogist etc. (sophist) 477.6; philologist etc. 560.7; oceanographer, koniologist, logician, student of the science of heat etc. (*see* oceanography, koniology, logic, science of heat etc. 489.8).

493. Ignoramus
(See 492. Scholar)

1. *n.* ignoramus, ignorant, ignatz [slang, U.S.], dunce, duffer, wooden spoon [Cambridge Univ. cant], greenhead [obs.], greenhorn, greeny [coll.], greener [slang], no scholar, low-brow [slang], moron, illiterate; illiterati [joc.], unintelligentsia; bonehead [slang], numskull [coll.] etc. (stupid person) 501; tenderfoot, tyro etc. (novice) 541.6; lubber etc. (bungler) 701; dupe etc. 547.

2. *n.* sciolist, smatterer, dabbler, trifler, dilettante, half scholar; wiseacre, wise guy [slang, U.S.]; charlatan, quack etc. (impostor) 548.3.

494. Truth
(See 495. Error)

1. *n.* truth, trueness etc. *adj.*, troth [arch.], sooth [arch.], verity, right, conformity to fact *or* reality; plain ~, honest ~, sober ~, unalloyed ~, unqualified ~, stern *or* exact truth; the naked truth, *"nuda veritas"* (Horace); unvarnished truth, unvarnished tale; the straight truth, the straight of it [slang]; the truth, the whole truth and nothing but the truth; gospel, gospel truth, scripture Bible, Bible truth, honest-to-God truth [slang]; realism; fact, actuality etc. (reality) 1.2; intrinsic truth, inner reality, true being etc. (essence) 5.2; truthfulness etc. (veracity) 543; probity etc. 939.

2. *n.* authenticity, validity, genuineness etc. *adj.*; orthodoxy etc. 983a.

3. *n.* accuracy, exactitude; exactness preciseness etc. *adj.*; precision, mathematical precision, scientific exactness nicety, delicacy, subtlety, refinement rigor, rigidity; fidelity, constancy, conformity to rule; the very words, *ipsissima verba* [L.]; orthology; clockwork precision etc. (regularity) 16.2; discrimination etc. 465; meticulousness etc. (minute attention) 457.3; care etc. 459 scrupulousness etc. (fastidiousness) 868

4. *n.* the right *or* real thing, what is right, what's what [coll.], the proper thing, just the thing, the very thing, genuine article, the article [slang], the good [slang, U.S.], the case, the ticket [coll.] the card [slang or coll.], the cheese *or* real cheese [slang], the McCoy *or* the

---

presage.—T. CAMPBELL. Showed him the gentleman an' scholar.—BURNS. He was a scholar, and a ripe and good one.—SHAKE-SPEARE. The scholar who cherishes the lov of comfort is not fit to be deemed a scholar.—CONFUCIUS.
494. *Nihil est veritatis luce dulcius* [Nothing is sweeter than the light of truth].—CICERO

real McCoy [slang, U.S.], the real Simon Pure, not an illusion etc. (*see* illusion etc. 495.5); reality etc. 1.2.

5. *v.* be true etc. *adj.*, be the case etc. *n.*; stand the test, stand *or* hold up, stand *or* hold up in the wash [slang], hold good *or* true, hold water [coll.], hold together [coll.]; ring true, have the true ring; be truthful etc. 543.2.

6. *v.* be accurate etc. *adj.*; dot the i's and cross the t's.

7. *v.* render true etc. *adj.*, true, adjust, regulate, fix, set, square; readjust, reset.

8. *v.* prove true etc. *adj.*; substantiate etc. (demonstrate) 478.2.

9. *v.* get at the truth etc. (solve) 480a.4.

10. *adj.* true, not erroneous etc. (*see* erroneous etc. 495.12–17), unerroneous; veritable, sooth [arch.], sure-enough [dial. and slang, U.S.], real, actual, factual, true to the facts; true as gospel *or* the gospel, true as steel, true as touch *or* touchstone; unrefuted, unconfuted; substantially true, categorically true; realistic; truthful etc. (veracious) 543.3; undoubted, unimpeachable, undeniable etc. (certain) 474.8–14.

11. *adj.* accurate, exact, precise, correct, right, all right *or* alright [coll.], just, just right, dead right, dead to rights [slang, U.S.]; faithful, constant, unerring; definite, positive, absolute, absolutely ~, definitely *or* positively right.

strict, stern, severe; rigid, rigorous; well-defined, clean-cut, clear-cut; even, square, straight, straight-up-and-down; mathematically exact, mathematical; scientifically exact, scientific; religious, religiously exact, meticulous, curious, particular, nice, delicate, fine; punctual, punctilious; orthological, literal; careful etc. 459.7; literal etc. 516.9; scrupulous etc. (fastidious) 868.4, (conscientious) 939.8.

12. *adj.* authentic, genuine, real, good, bona fide, legitimate, rightful; sterling, eighteen-carat, blown in the glass [slang, U.S.], all wool and a yard wide [coll.]; authoritative, trustworthy, reliable, straight [slang], dependable, sure, sound etc. (valid) *below*, honest-to-God [slang]; veridical, veridicous [rare]; official, ex officio; orthodox etc. 82.10, 983a.7; unimitated etc. 20.3.

13. *adj.* pure, simon-pure, natural, naked, unadulterated, unsophisticated, unalloyed, unmixed, uncorrupted, undefiled, unqualified, unvarnished; uncolored, in its true colors, true-blue.

14. *adj.* valid, well-grounded, well-founded, sound, solid, substantial, pucka [Ind.], tangible; undistorted, undisguised, unaffected, unexaggerated, unromantic, unflattering; unideal, unimagined.

15. *adv.* truly, really etc. *adj.*; really-truly [coll.], verily, pardie [arch.], sooth [arch.], soothfast [arch.], forsooth, in sooth [arch.], in truth, in good *or* very truth, in good *or* very sooth [arch.], in reality, in fact, in point of fact, as a matter of fact, to state the fact *or* truth, to tell the truth, sooth to say [arch.], of a truth, with truth; indeed, indeedy [coll., U.S.]; no buts about it [coll.], nothing else but [slang].

beyond question *or* doubt, undoubtedly etc. (certainly) 474.16; truthfully etc. 543.4; honor bright [coll.] etc. (affirmation) 535.8; actually etc. 1.9; in effect etc. (intrinsically) 5.8.

16. *adv.* accurately, exactly, precisely etc. *adj.*; straight [coll.], square, right [now chiefly coll.], to-rights [coll. and dial.], just, just right, just so [coll.]; to *or* within an inch, to a hair, ~ tittle, ~ turn, ~ T *or* nicety; ad unguem [L.]; neither more nor less; in every respect, in all respects; strictly speaking, to be exact etc. *adj.*; chapter and verse; word for word, to the letter, verbatim etc. (literally) 19.14.

Veritas nunquam perit [Truth never dies].—SENECA. *Magna est veritas et praevalet* [Great is the truth and it prevails].—VULGATE. *Veritatis simplex oratio est* [The language of truth is simple].—SENECA. Pure truth hath no man seen nor e'er shall know.—XENOPHANES. Truth is the highest thing that man may keep.—CHAUCER. Time dissipates to shining ether the solid angularity of facts.—EMERSON. Truth is the object of philosophy, but not always of philosophers.—J. C. COLLINS. Truth crushed to earth shall rise again, / The eternal years of God are hers.—BRYANT. There is nothing so powerful as truth,—and often nothing so strange.—D. WEBSTER. Man's primary allegiance is to his vision of truth, / And he is under obligation to affirm it.—J. ADDAMS. Analogy is milk for babes, but abstract truths are strong meat.—TUPPER. Truth may be blamed, but cannot be shamed. Fact is stranger than fiction.

495. Error
(See 494. Truth)

1. *n.* error, erroneousness, untrueness etc. *adj.*; untruth, wrong, fallacy, falsity; aberration, aberrance *or* aberrancy; anachronism, metachronism, parachronism, prochronism; mumpsimus; misrepresentation etc. 555; misconstruction etc. (misinterpretation) 523; miscomputation etc. (misjudgment) 481; false reasoning etc. (sophistry) 477; falsehood etc. (untruthfulness) 544, (untruth) 546; heterodoxy etc. 984.

2. *n.* mistake, miss; fault, *faute* [F.]; error, erratum (*pl.* errata), corrigendum (*pl.* corrigenda); misconception, misapprehension, misunderstanding; cross-purposes; misstatement, misreport; inadvertence *or* inadvertency, oversight, omission, loose thread; misprint, typographical error; flaw, blot.

3. *n.* blunder, bevue; bloomer, bobble, bone, boner, bonehead, miscue [all slang]; break *or* bad break, fool mistake, dumb trick, fault-slip, slip-up [all coll.]; *lapsus* [L.]; slip, trip, stumble, misstep, false *or* wrong step; *faux pas* [F.], fox paw [joc.].

slip of the pen, *lapsus calami* [L.], clerical *or* typographical error etc. *above*; blunder in speech, verbal *or* grammatical blunder, solecism, slipslap [coll.], slip of the tongue, *lapsus linguae* [L.]; bull, Irish bull, Irishism, Hibernianism, Hibernicism; mispronouncement, mispronunciation; ridiculous blunder, funny mistake, scream, screamer, howler [slang]; malapropism, malaprop; spoonerism, Partingtonism, Leiterism; botch, *étourderie* [F.] etc. (bungle) 699.4; act of folly, absurdity, indiscretion etc. (foolish act) 499.7; failure etc. 732.

4. *n.* inaccuracy *or* unaccuracy, inexactitude, inexactness etc. *adj.*; neglect etc. 460.

5. *n.* delusion, illusion, misconception etc. *above* 495.2, trick, bubble, fool's paradise; phantasm [arch.], phantom [obs.];
false impression, warped *or* distorted impression *or* idea; self-deceit, self-deception; misbelief, heresy etc. (heterodoxy) 984; hallucination etc. 503.5; false light, fallacy of vision etc. (optical illusion) 443.9; fantasy, figment of the imagination, dream etc. (imagination) 515; fata morgana etc. 420.11.

6. *v.* be erroneous etc. *adj.*; not hold water [coll.], not ring true etc. (*see* true etc. 494.5).

7. *v.* err, be in error, be wrong, ~ mistaken etc. *adj.*, have another guess coming [coll.]; receive a false impression, lie *or* labor under a false impression etc. *n.*, take the shadow for the substance; deceive oneself, be deceived etc. (*see* deceive etc. 545.7); fall into error, miss the truth, deviate, wander, stray, go astray, deviate ~, wander etc. from the truth.

be in the wrong, be in the wrong box; bark up the wrong tree, back the wrong horse, aim at a pigeon and kill a crow, take *or* get the wrong sow by the ear, ~ the wrong pig by the tail *or* the wrong bull by the horns, put the saddle on the wrong horse, count one's chickens before they are hatched, reckon without one's host; misbelieve, sin; misreckon, miscalculate etc. (misjudge) 481.5; misconstrue etc. (misinterpret) 523.2.

8. *v.* mistake, make a mistake etc. *n.*; misidentify, err *or* mistake in recognizing *or* identifying; be *or* play at cross-purposes.

9. *v.* blunder, make a blunder etc. *n.*, commit an absurdity, pull a bloomer, ~ boner etc. *n.*, slip, slip up, trip, stumble, miscue [slang], bull [slang, U.S.], put one's foot in it [coll.]; put one's foot in one's mouth [slang], misspeak oneself [dial. or slang]; blunder into, bonehead into [slang]; botch, boggle etc. (bungle) 699.9.

10. *v.* admit a mistake, confess a fault, acknowledge the corn [coll.].

11. *v.* mislead, misguide, misdirect, lead astray, lead into error; put on a false scent, throw off the scent, drag *or*

---

495. What is the use of running when you are on the wrong road.—J. RAY. *Mentis gratissimus error* [A most pleasant misapprehension]. —HORACE. One goes to the right, the other to the left; both err, but in different ways.— HORACE. Who errs and mends, to God himself commends.—CERVANTES. To err is human, to forgive divine.—POPE. Error is worse than ignorance.—P. J. BAILEY. Error is not a fault of our knowledge, but a mistake of our judgment.—LOCKE. Error is a hardy plant! it flourisheth in every soil.—TUPPER. Love truth, but pardon error.—VOLTAIRE. No man prospers so suddenly as by others' errors.—BACON. So the last error shall be worse than the first.—BIBLE. A miss is as good as a mile. *Errare humanum est* [To err is human].

draw a red herring across the trail, ~ track *or* path; pervert, misstate etc. (falsify) 544.3; misinform etc. (misteach) 538.2; misinterpret etc. 523.2; misrepresent etc. 555.4; fool etc. (deceive) 545.7, 10; sophisticate etc. 477.7.

12. *adj.* erroneous, not true etc. (*see* true etc. 494.9), untrue, void *or* devoid of truth etc. (*see* truth etc. 494.1), erring etc. *v.,* false, fallacious, defective, faulty, faultful, at fault, wrong, peccant; wide, wide of the mark; out, all out [coll.]; errant, aberrant, straying etc. *v.,* astray, abroad, all abroad; adrift, at sea; remote *or* removed from the fact, off; apocryphal, unreal; perverted, distorted; heretical etc. (heterodox) 984.22; imperfect etc. 651.4; abortive etc. 732.8.

13. *adj. etc.* mistaken, in error, under an error etc. *n.*; at fault, wrong etc. *above*; in the wrong, all in the wrong, all wet [slang, U.S.]; in the wrong box; off *or* out in one's reckoning, off the track; on a false scent, on the wrong scent *or* trail, up the wrong tree; at cross-purposes.

14. *adj.* inaccurate *or* unaccurate, incorrect *or* uncorrect, inexact *or* unexact, unprecise.

15. *adj.* delusive, delusory, deluding etc. *v.*; illusive, illusory; hallucinational, hallucinative, hallucinatory; imaginary etc. 515.12–14; deceptive etc. 545.12, 13.

16. *adj.* unauthentic, unauthenticated; untrustworthy, unreliable, undependable; unsound, unsubstantial *or* insubstantial, without foundation, baseless; groundless, ungrounded; unsustained, unsustainable, controvertible etc. (uncertain) 475.9–14; illogical etc. 477.10; spurious etc. 545.13.

17. *adj.* exploded, refuted, discarded, dismissed, rejected, discredited; obsolete, outworn, passé, passée [*fem.*].

496. Maxim

1. *n.* maxim, aphorism, apothegm, dictum (*pl.* dictums, dicta), adage, proverb, epigram, gnome, saying, saw, sentence, phrase, word, byword, mot, motto, moral, phylactery; proverbial ~, epigrammatic ~, pithy ~, sententious etc. *adj.* expression *or* saying; common *or* current saying; witticism etc. 842.4.

2. *n.* axiom, theorem, scholium; soothsay [rare], truth, truism, self-evident truth, general *or* universal truth, universally accepted truth, received ~, admitted *or* recognized maxim; wise *or* sage maxim *or* truth, wise expression *or* saying, oracle, wisdom [now rare]; proposition, *propositio* [L.], protasis [rare]; principle, principium, principia [*pl.*]; settled principle, dogmatic principle *or* precept; formula, formulary; precept, preception [obs.]; prescript, prescription; recipe, receipt; law, rule, authoritative rule *or* maxim; dictate, dictum (*pl.* dicta, dictums); golden rule; postulate etc. (premise) 476.4; doctrine etc. (belief) 484.3; conclusion etc. (judgment) 480.

3. *n.* trite saying, commonplace ~, hackneyed *or* stereotyped saying *or* expression, commonplace, banality, triviality [arch.], bromide *or* bromidium [slang], cliché, platitude, *fadaise* [F.], chestnut [slang], familiar tune, old song [coll.], old saw, old hat [slang], old story [coll.]; retold story, twice-told tale, warmed-over cabbage [coll.], *réchauffé* [F.], prose, prosaism, prosaicism; old joke etc. 842.6; triteness etc. 843.2; repetition etc. 104.

4. *v.* make maxims etc. *n.,* aphorize, apothegmatize, epigrammatize.

5. *adj.* aphoristic, aphorismic, aphorismatic; apothegmatic [rare], proverbial, phylacteric, axiomatic(al), gnomic(al); sententious, pithy, piquant, terse.

6. *adv.* aphoristically, proverbially etc. *adj.*; as the saying is, as they say, as the fellow says [dial. or coll.], as it has been said, as it was said of old.

497. Absurdity

1. *n.* absurdity, absurdness, foolishness etc. *adj.*; foolery, imbecility, asininity, inanity, fatuity; sciamachy; stupidity,

---

496. An obvious moral is indeed a heavy protuberance.—LANDOR. They should be realizing their high maxims in the concrete.—NEWMAN. Proverbs are short sentences drawn from long experience.—CERVANTES. For I am proverb'd with a grandsire phrase.—SHAKESPEARE. Full of wise saws and modern instances.—SHAKESPEARE.
497. No one is exempt from talking nonsense; the misfortune is to do it solemnly.—MONTAIGNE. For daring nonsense seldom fails to hit, / Like scattered shot, and pass with some for wit.—BUTLER. A little nonsense now and then / Is relished by the wisest men.—ANON.

piece of stupidity, *bêtise* [F.]; nonsense, nonsensicality; stuff, stuff and nonsense; inconsistency, obvious inconsistency, ridiculous incongruity, self-contradiction, logical contradiction, paradox; stultification, stultiloquy [rare], stultiloquence [rare]; futility, nugacity, ineptitude; *absurdum* [L.]; bathos, anticlimax, comedown.

ludicrousness, comicality etc. (ridiculousness) 855; moonshine, fiddle-faddle [coll.] etc. 517.2; sophism, unreasonableness, irrationality etc. 477.1, 2; extravagance etc. (exaggeration) 549; travesty, parody etc. (burlesque) 856.3; tomfoolery etc. (buffoonery) 842.3; howler [slang], bull etc. (blunder) 495.3.

2. *v.* be absurd etc. *adj.,* commit an absurdity, employ absurdity etc. *n.,* pass from the sublime to the ridiculous; rhapsodize, romance; be ridiculous etc. 855.3; play the fool etc. 499.9; talk nonsense etc. 517.6; blunder etc. 495.9; joke, play practical jokes etc. 842.8.

3. *v.* render absurd etc. *adj.,* stultify; make a fool of, burlesque etc. 856.4-6.

4. *adj.* absurd, nonsensical, senseless, insensate; foolish, stupid, silly, poppycockish [coll.], asinine, imbecile, crazy, screwy [slang, U.S.], inane; inept, inapt; fatuous, fatuitous; fantastic(al), monstrous, preposterous, egregious, flagrant, gross, *outré* [F.], extravagant, bombastic, inflated, high-flown, rhapsodic(al), bizarre; inconsistent, incongruous, paradoxical; self-contradictory, self-annulling; stultitious [obs.], stulty [obs.], stultiloquent [rare]; amphigoric; ludicrous, farcical etc. (ridiculous) 855.5; odd, grotesque etc. (unusual) 83.10; sophistical, irrational, unreasonable etc. 477.9, 10; meaningless etc. 517.8, 9; trifling etc. 643.11.

5. *int.* that's absurd! etc. *adj.,* nonsense!, stuff!, stuff and nonsense!, fiddledeedee!, fiddle-faddle! [coll.], fiddlesticks! [coll.]; fudge!, applesauce!, baloney!, razzberries! [all slang, U.S.]; pish!, pish-pash!, poo!, phoo!, pho!, phoh! [rare], pooh!, pooh-pooh!, phooey! [coll.], poof!, pugh!, pshaw!, bah!, bosh! [coll.], balderdash!, hooey! [slang], humbug!, poppycock! [coll.], rubbish!, rats! [slang], twaddle!, in your hat! [slang], my eye! [coll.]; come off!, come off of it! [both slang]; tell it to the marines! [coll.]; it is to laugh!,

that's a laugh!, that slays *or* kills me! [all slang].

498. Intelligence, Wisdom
(See 499. Unintelligence, Folly)

1. *n.* intelligence, intelligency [now rare]; capacity, mental capacity, capacity of the mind, capacity to know *or* apprehend, reach *or* compass of mind, caliber; power of conceiving, ~ judging *or* reasoning, intellectual power, faculty of understanding, understanding, *Verstand* [G.], comprehension, apprehension, grasp of intellect; sabe, savvy [slang, U.S.]; docity [dial.], docility [now rare]; intellectual gifts *or* talents, parts, wits; wit, mother wit, natural *or* native wit *or* understanding; sense, senses; intelligence quotient, I.Q., mental ratio, mental age; mind, brains etc. (intellect) 450; knowledge etc. 490; information etc. 527.

2. *n.* sagacity, sagaciousness, shrewdness, acuteness etc. *adj.*; mental acuteness, acuteness of mind, quickness *or* acuteness of sense, keenness of discernment *or* penetration, keenness in intellectual *or* practical matters, sharpness of wit *or* intelligence, acute discernment, keen mental vision *or* penetration, penetration in perception, ~ discernment *or* discrimination, native cleverness, ready wit.

acumen, gumption [coll. and dial.]; perspicacity, perspicuity [erron.], perspicacy [obs.]; percipience *or* percipiency, perception, apperception; penetration, discernment; farsightedness, long-sightedness; subtility, subtilty, subtlety; good mental capacity, bright intelligence, *esprit* [F.], clear *or* quick thinking, quick parts; cunning etc. 702; refinement etc. (taste) 850; eagle eye etc. (eyes) 441.7.

3. *n.* wisdom, wiseness, sageness etc. *adj.*; sapience, sagacity etc. *above,* good *or* sound understanding; rationality, reasonableness; sense, good ~, common *or* plain sense, horse sense [coll., U.S.], due sense of; judgment, good *or* sound judgment, sound perception *or* reasoning, soundness of judgment, judicious-

---

498. He is truly wise who gains wisdom from another's mishap.—Publilius. They call him the wisest man to whose mind that which is required at once occurs.—Cicero. Who knows useful things, not many things, is wise.

ness; long head [coll.], longheadedness; solidity, depth, profundity; enlargement of mind, enlarged views.

"the conqueror of fortune" (Juvenal), "the only liberty" (Seneca); Athena [Gr. Myth.], Minerva [Rom. Myth.], Apollo [Gr. Myth.], Odin [Norse Myth.], the Sphinx, Thoth [both Egyptian Myth.]; critical judgment, discretion etc. (discrimination) 465; worldly wisdom, tact etc. 698.4; profound knowledge etc. 490; prudence etc. (caution) 864; foresight etc. 510.

4. *n.* mental poise, aplomb, balance, ballast, self-possession, presence of mind, *sang-froid* [F.] *or* sangfroid, sobriety; level head [coll.], levelheadedness, well-balanced *or* well-regulated mind.

5. *n.* genius, lambent flame of intellect, fire of genius, heaven-born genius; *Geist* [G.], spirit, soul; inspiration, afflatus, divine afflatus; unusual mental power, extraordinary mental superiority; talent, aptitude etc. (skill) 698.

6. *n.* bright idea, inspiration etc. 453.

7. *v.* be intelligent etc. *adj.*, be an intelligent being, possess intelligence etc. *n.*, have all one's wits about one, have all one's marbles [slang], have something on one's head besides one's hat [slang], have use of the intellectual faculties, have power of comprehension *or* understanding, have a head on one's shoulders [slang]; be reasonable, listen to reason; be discerning, have *or* show perspicacity etc. *n.*, see into *or* through a millstone; understand etc. 518.4; discern etc. (see) 441.10; discriminate etc. 465.2; know what's what [coll.] etc. 698.8.

8. *v.* be brilliant etc. *adj.*, scintillate, coruscate, shine [chiefly coll.].

9. *adj.* intelligent, knowing, understanding, reasonable, rational, sensible, bright; not so dumb [coll., U.S.], *pas si bête* [F.]; strong-minded, strongheaded; in one's right mind etc. (sane) 502.5; intellectual etc. 450.8.

10. *adj.* sagacious, quick of apprehension, of keen penetration, with acute mental vision etc. *n.*; keen, cute [coll.], acute, sharp, quick, shrewd, argute, astute, subtle, canny [arch. or dial.], sly [now dial.], pawky [Scot. and dial. Eng.]; quick-witted, nimble-witted, keen-witted, sharp-witted, needle-witted, sharp as a needle; clear-witted, clearheaded; hardheaded, longheaded.

alive, alert, fly [slang]; awake, broad *or* wide awake; smart, smart as a whip *or* steel trap, brainy [coll.]; bright, brilliant; nobody's fool, no dumbbell, not born yesterday [all slang]; perspicacious, perspicuous [erron.]; perceptive, percipient, apperceptive, appercipient; discerning, penetrating, piercing; alive to, aware etc. (knowing) 490.12–15; clever etc. 698.11; cunning etc. 702.6; farsighted etc. 510.6.

11. *adj.* wise, sage, sagacious etc. *above,* sapient, *savant* [F.], knowing, gnostic [joc. or slang]; wise as a serpent *or* an owl, wise as Solomon, ~ Solon etc. (*see* Solomon, Solon etc. 500); wise in one's generation, wise beyond one's years, in advance of one's age.

judicious, judicial, judgmatic(al) [coll.]; discreet, discriminative, discriminating; sound, sensible, reasonable, rational; philosophical; levelheaded, coolheaded, cool; well-advised, well-judged; prudent, politic, considerate, circumspect, calculating, thoughtful, reflecting; sober, sober-minded; staid, solid, profound, deep, abstruse; acroatic, acroamatic; authoritative, oracular; expedient etc. 646.4; erudite, learned, enlightened etc. (informed) 490.15; experienced etc. 698.15.

12. *adj.* unprejudiced, unbiased, unwarped, unswayed, unbigoted, unprepossessed, unjaundiced, undazzled, unperplexed, uninfluenced, impartial, dispassionate, disinterested, of unwarped judgment; broad, broad-minded, wide-minded; tolerant, lenient, indulgent, liberal, ecumenic(al), catholic, latitudinarian.

unprovincial, unhidebound, unsettled, unrooted, unpositive, undogmatic, unpragmatic(al); unopinioned, unopinionate, unopinionative, unopiniative [rare], unwedded to an opinion; unbesotted, uninfatuated, unfanatical; open, open-

---

—AESCHYLUS.   Genius, in truth, means little more than the faculty of perceiving in an unhabitual way.—W. JAMES.   With the ancient is wisdom; and in length of days understanding.—BIBLE.   Wisdom is never dear, provided the article be genuine.—H. GREELEY.

Wisdom is the abstract of the past.—HOLMES. Wisdom is the principal thing; therefore, get wisdom; and with all thy getting get understanding.—BIBLE.   To perceive things in the germ is intelligence.—LAO-TSZE.

minded, accessible, responsive, amenable; persuadable, persuasible; forbearing, forbearant; freethinking, libertine [derog.]; unrestricted, unlimited etc. (unconstrained) 748.13, 15; equitable, fair etc. (just) 941.3.

499. Unintelligence, Folly
(See 498. Intelligence, Wisdom)

1. *n.* unintelligence, unwisdom, unintellectuality, want of intelligence etc. (*see* intelligence etc. 498), want of intellect etc. (*see* intellect etc. 450); incapacity, meanest capacity; low I.Q. *or* intelligence quotient; ignorance etc. 491.

2. *n.* stupidity, obtuseness etc. *adj.*, obtusity [rare], density, insulsity [rare], stolidity, hebetude, oafdom, jobbernowlism [coll., Eng.], dullardism, dull understanding, clouded perception; numskulledness etc. *adj.*, numskullery, numskullism [all coll.]; poor head, blockhead, bonehead [slang], chucklehead [coll.], numskull [coll.] etc. *adj.*; unskillfulness etc. 699.

3. *n.* mental deficiency, poverty of intellect; feeble-mindedness etc. *adj.*, weakness of mind, weakness in the upper story [coll.]; amentia, imbecility, morosis, simplicity; moronity, moroncy, moronism, moronry; idiocy, idiotism [rare], driveling idiocy; insanity etc. 503.

4. *n.* empty-headedness etc. 450a.1.

5. *n.* senility, senilism, senile weakness, senile dementia, caducity, decrepitude; puerility, childishness, second childishness, second childhood, babyhood; old-womanishness, anility; dotardism, dotage, "talking age" (Goldsmith); old age etc. 128.2.

6. *n.* folly, foolery; foolishness, silliness etc. *adj.*; want of good sense, ninnyism, ninnyship, simpletonianism, *niaiserie* [F.], morology, sottage [rare], ineptitude, nugacity, fatuity, futility, inanity; frivolity, levity of mind; inconsistency; lip wisdom, conceit; infatuation; tomfoolery etc. (buffoonery) 842.3; thoughtlessness, giddiness etc. (inattention) 458; nonsense etc. (absurdity) 497, (unmeaningness) 517.2, 3; irrationality etc. 477.5; indiscretion, imprudence etc. (rashness) 863.

7. *n.* foolish act, act of folly, foolish *or* stupid thing, foolish thing to do, trick, fool's trick, fool trick [coll.], folly, stupidity, absurdity, sottery [obs.], *sottise* [F.]; imprudence, indiscretion, indiscreet act, imprudent *or* unwise step, foolish procedure; blunder etc. 495.3; bungle etc. 699.4.

8. *v.* be unintelligent etc. *adj.*, lack intelligence etc. (*see* intelligence etc. 498), have space to let [slang] etc. *n.*, have a block for a head, have cobwebs in the attic [slang], have fat in the head, have a head full of blubber; not see an inch beyond one's nose, not have enough sense to come in out of the rain.

9. *v.* behave unintelligently *or* foolishly, fool, fool around, tomfool [coll.], play *or* act the fool etc. (*see* fool etc. 501), make a fool of oneself, stultify oneself, put oneself out of court; be the fool, be the goat [coll.]; trifle, frivol [coll.], get funny [slang]; lose one's head *or* senses, take leave of one's senses; begin at the wrong end, put the cart before the horse, put a square peg in a round hole, make two bites of a cherry, strain at a gnat and swallow a camel, reckon without one's host.

10. *v.* dote, drivel etc. (talk nonsense) 517.6.

11. *adj.* unintelligent, unintellectual, unreasoning, irrational, unwise; without intelligence, not bright etc. (*see* bright etc. 498.9), unendowed with intellect etc. (*see* intellect etc. 450), ungifted; senseless, insensate; mindless, witless, reasonless, brainless; lack-brained, lackwitted, lean-minded, lean-witted, short-witted; unenlightened etc. (ignorant) 491.8, 9; incogitant etc. 452.3.

12. *adj.* stupid, doltish, dumb [coll., U.S.], insulse [rare], obtuse, dull, dullard, dense, blunt, stolid, crass, heavy, sluggish, sottish, blockish, chumpish [coll.], lumpish, oafish, bovine, thick [coll.], slow, slow of comprehension; hebetudinous, hebetate, hebete [rare]; Boeotian, Boeotic; inapprehensible, undiscerning, nonunderstanding; stupid-headed, dull-headed, dull-pated, dull-

---

499. The alluring yet ineluctable problem of human folly.—W. McFee. The visionless officialized fatuity.—S. Sassoon. Men are so necessarily foolish that not to be a fool is merely a varied freak of folly.—Pascal.

Beauty and folly are old companions.—Franklin. The folly of one man is the fortune of another.—Bacon. If you think that to grow a beard is to acquire wisdom, then a goat is

brained, dull-witted, blunt-witted, thickheaded, thick-pated, thickskulled, thickbrained, thick-witted, dumbheaded [slang, U.S.], blunderheaded, jolterheaded, joltheaded, chowderheaded, chuckleheaded [coll.], pigheaded, muttonheaded [coll.], beetleheaded, buffleheaded [obs.], cabbageheaded [coll.], pumpkin-headed, gross-headed, sapheaded [coll.], lunkheaded [coll., U.S.], beefheaded, beefbrained, beef-witted, fatheaded [coll.], fat-witted, dough-headed [slang, U.S.], boneheaded [slang], numskulled [coll.], clodpated, muddybrained, muddleheaded, blunderheaded, addleheaded, addlepated, addlebrained, puzzleheaded, puzzlepated.

dead from the neck up, dead above or between the ears, muscle-bound between the ears [all slang]; dizzy [now coll. and dial.], dopey [slang], groggy [coll.], punch-drunk [slang]; foggy, foggy in the crumpet or upper story [slang]; unteachable, unlearnable; dim-sighted, shortsighted, nearsighted, purblind, blind, blind as a bat; prosaic etc. 843.5; clumsy etc. 699.12.

13. *adj.* mentally deficient, wanting [dial.], not all there [coll.]; half-witted, half-baked [coll.]; simple, simpletonian, simple-witted, simple-minded; feebleminded, weak-minded, weak, feeble, weak in the upper story [coll.]; imbecile, idiotic, moronic, nitwitted [slang]; driveling, babbling; nutty, batty, balmy, balmy in the crumpet; loony, ga-ga [all slang]; crazy etc. 503.12.

14. *adj.* empty-headed, empty-minded, empty-noddled, empty-pated, emptyskulled; rattlebrained, rattleheaded; empty, vacant, vacuous; thoughtless, giddy etc. (scatterbrained) 458.13; incogitant etc. 452.3.

15. *adj.* foolish, fool [now coll.], silly, sappy, dizzy [now coll. and dial.], barmy, barmybrained, goosy, asinine, inane, blandly inane; fatuous, fatuitous; dotard, dotardy; senseless, insensate, nonsensical; foolheaded, foolheady; soft [coll.]; spoony [slang], maudlin; apish, simian, simious; unwise, injudicious, unreasonable, ill-judged, ill-imagined, ill-advised, ill-devised; improper, unseemly; inconsistent, incongruous, penny-wise and pound-foolish; inane etc. (absurd) 497.4; irrational, without reason etc. (unreasonable) 477.10; useless etc. 645.8; inexpedient etc. 647.3; frivolous etc. (trivial) 643.11; meaningless etc. 517.8.

16. *adj.* senile, anile, decrepit, oldwomanish, grannified [coll.]; puerile, childish, childlike, in one's second childhood etc. *n.*; infantile, infantine; babyish, babish; doting, doted [obs.], doited [chiefly Scot.]; dotard, dotardy; doddering, doddery; old etc. 124.6; aged etc. 128.9.

17. *adj.* shallow, shallow-witted, shallow-headed, shallowpated, shallowbrained, shallow-minded, not deep or profound intellectually, superficial; *borné* [F.], limited, narrow; narrow-minded etc. (prejudiced) 481.10, (bigoted) 606.7.

500. Sage
(See 501. Fool)

1. *n.* sage, sapient, wise man *or* wiseman, wisehead, wizard [obs.]; master, mastermind, master spirit of the age; mahatma, adept; longhead, thinker; authority, oracle, mentor; luminary, shining light; Magian, Magus (*pl.* Magi); *magnus Apollo* [L.], Solomon, Buddha, Confucius, Socrates, Plato, Mentor, Nestor; savant, pundit, philosopher etc. (scholar) 492.

2. *n.* wiseacre [iron.], wisenheimer [slang, U.S.], wise guy [slang], wiseling, witling; wise fool, Scottish Solomon; Gothamite, wise man of Gotham; fool etc. 501.1.

3. *n.* the wise, the Magi; Wise Men of Egypt, Three Wise Men, Three Kings of Cologne; Gaspar, Melchior, Balthasar; the Wise Men, Seven Wise Men of Greece, Seven Wise Masters, Seven Sages, Philosophical Pleiad; Solon, Chilon, Pittacus, Bias, Periander, Epimenides, Cleobulus, Thales.

---

500. If a little knowledge is dangerous, where is the man who has so much as to be out of danger?—HUXLEY. A wise man, like the moon, only shows his bright side to the world.—J. C. COLLINS. And still they gazed, and still the wonder grew / That one small head could carry all he knew.—GOLDSMITH. Nothing in human life is more to be lamented, than that a wise man should have so little influence.—HERODOTUS. *Les fous font les festins et les sages les mangent* [Fools give banquets and wise men eat them].

---

at once a complete Plato.—LUCIAN. *Misce stultitiam consiliis brevem* [Mix some small folly with your wisdom].—HORACE.

4. *adj.* sage, sagacious etc. (wise) 498.10, 11; learned, erudite etc. (informed) 490.15; venerable etc. 928.9.

501. Fool
(See 500. Sage)

1. *n.* fool, tomfool, precious fool [coll.], ninny, ninnyhammer, mutt [slang], boob [slang], booby, chump [coll.], sap [slang], prize sap [slang], saphead [slang], loony [slang], looby, hoddy-doddy [obs.], noddy, tomnoddy, tommy noddy, nonny [dial.], noodle, doodle [obs.], nizy [obs.], gabby [coll.], dizzard [now chiefly dial.], jobbernowl [coll., Eng.], nincompoop [coll.], witling, *badaud* [F.], jerk [slang, U.S.], zany [chiefly Eng.], daw [arch.], flat [slang], put, stick [coll.], stock, sop, numps [obs.], tony [obs.], spoony [slang], goose, buzzard [obs.], owl, donkey, ass, asshead.

colt, calf [coll.], mooncalf, bull calf [coll.]; sill [slang], silly [coll.], silly ass [slang]; soft [coll.], softy [coll.], softhead; sot [obs. exc. Scot.]; stupid, stupidhead, dolt, dunce, duffer [coll.], doit [Scot. and North. Eng.], *niais* [F.], dummy *or* dumby; dumbhead, dumbbell, dumb-bunny [all slang, U.S.].

dullard, dully [coll.], dullhead, dunderpate, dunderhead, block, blockhead, woodenhead [coll.], squarehead [slang], bonehead, solid ivory, numskull [coll.], thickhead [coll.], thickskull, thickwit, lunkhead [coll., U.S.], chucklehead [coll.], chowderhead, jolthead, jolterhead, muttonhead [coll.], loggerhead, beetlehead, grosshead [obs.], noodlehead, cabbagehead [coll.], pumpkin head, fathead [coll.], blubberhead [slang], doughhead [slang, U.S.], bakehead [slang, U.S.], bullhead, blunderhead.

clod, clodpole *or* clotpole, clodpoll *or* clotpoll, clodpate *or* clotpate; oaf, lout, loon, lown [obs. exc. dial. and Scot.], lubber, swab [dial. and slang], sawney [dial., Eng.], galoot [slang], gowk, gawk, gawky, lummox [dial. and slang], rube [slang], yokel, clodhopper; shallowbrain, shallowpate; simp [slang], simpleton, Simple Simon, idiot, driveling idiot, imbecile, moron, changeling [arch.], nitwit [slang], dimwit [slang], half-wit, lackwit, lack-brain; natural, natural idiot, born fool, natural-born fool.

no conjurer, no Solomon etc. (*see* Solomon etc. 500); Boeotian, Gothamite; men of Boeotia, wise men of Gotham; wiseacre etc. 500.2; greenhorn etc. (ignoramus) 493, (dupe) 547; madman etc. 504; buffoon etc. 599.20; bungler 699.5.

2. *n.* scatterbrain *or* scatterbrains [coll.], shatterbrain, shatterpate, rattlebrain, rattlehead, rattlepate; harebrain, featherbrain; giddybrain, giddyhead, giddypate; addlebrain, addlehead, addlepate; dizzy, dizzy dame [both slang, U.S.].

3. *n.* dotard, "the sickly dotard" (Prior), dote [obs.]; driveler, babbler, *radoteur* [F.]; senile, old fogy [coll.], old wife *or* woman, crone [rare], grandmother, henhussy, cotquean [arch.], betty [derog.], cot betty [slang, U.S.].

4. *n.* childish person, child, mere child, baby, infant, innocent.

5. *phr.* (he) will not set the Thames on fire, ~ does not exactly scintillate, ~ *n'a pas inventé la poudre* [F.].

502. Sanity
(See 503. Insanity, Eccentricity)

1. *n.* sanity, saneness, soundness etc. *adj.*; soundness of mind, rationality, normalcy, normality, balance, sobriety, lucidity; lucid interval [Med.]; senses, sober senses; sound mind, *mens sana* [L.].

2. *v.* be sane etc. *adj.*, be in possession of all one's senses, retain one's senses *or* reason.

3. *v.* become sane etc. *adj.*, come to

---

501. *Stultorum plena sunt omnia* [Fools everywhere].—CICERO.   A fool's bolt is soon shot.—SHAKESPEARE.   I had rather have a fool to make me merry than experience to make me sad.—SHAKESPEARE.   Fools rush in where angels fear to tread.—POPE.   Fools grow without watering.—FULLER.   You may lead an ass to knowledge, but you cannot make him think.—CYNIC'S CALENDAR.   Nobody can describe a fool to the life, without much patient self-inspection.—F. COLBY.   *Barbae tenus sapientus* [Men wise as far as their beards].   *Fortuna favet fatuis* [Fortune favors fools].
502. It's fitter being sane than mad.—BROWNING.   Good sense, which only is the gift of Heaven, / And though no science, fairly worth the seven.—POPE.   Sanity is a madness put to good uses.—SANTAYANA.   *Qui poterit sanum fingere, sanus erit* [He who can simulate sanity will be sane].—OVID.   *Mens sana in corpore sano* [A sound mind in a sound body].—JUVENAL.

one's senses, sober down, cool down *or* off; get things into proportion, see things in proper perspective.

4. *v.* render sane etc. *adj.,* bring to one's senses, bring to reason, bring round *or* around [coll.], restore, sober.

5. *adj.* sane, sane-minded, sane in mind, not deranged (*see* deranged etc. 503.12); compos, compos mentis [both Law]; rational, reasonable, lucid, normal, wholesome, sound, mentally sound, of sound mind, sound-minded, right, right-minded, in one's right mind, in possession of one's faculties *or* senses, all there [slang]; in one's sober senses, sober, sober-minded; intelligent etc. 498.9.

6. *adv.* sanely etc. *adj.*; in reason, within reason, within the bounds *or* limits of reason, within bounds; according to the dictates of reason *or* common sense, in the name of common sense.

503. Insanity, Eccentricity
(See 502. Sanity; also 504. Madman, Eccentric)

Mental Derangement or Aberration.—
1. *n.* insanity, unsanity; insaneness, craziness etc. *adj.*; dementia, demency [rare], dementation [rare]; lunacy, bedlam, mania, furor, mental alienation, aberration, aberration of mind, derangement, mental derangement *or* disorder, disordered mind *or* reason, shattered mind, diseased *or* unsound mind, unsoundness of mind, psychopathic condition, pixilation [dial.].
rabies, hydrophobia, canine madness; furious rabies, dumb rabies *or* madness; pathomania, moral insanity; dipsomania, oenomania *or* oinomania; amuck, murderous insanity *or* frenzy; corybantiasm, corybantic insanity *or* frenzy; amentia, monomania, paranoia, paranomia, lycanthropy, fugue, kleptomania, psychokinesia, dementia praecox, dementia paralytica, pathological lying; morosis, idiocy etc. (mental deficiency) 499.3; alienism, psychiatry, psychiatrist etc. (science of mind) 450.4, 5; amnesia etc. 506.3.

2. *n.* psychosis, psychopathy, psychopathia; psychoneurosis, neurosis, neurasthenia, neurotic *or* psychoneurotic condition; pathoneurosis, pathopsychosis; anxiety neurosis, compulsion neurosis; emotional instability, emotionalism; psychasthenia; psycholepsy; shellshock; hysteria, hysterics; manic-depressive insanity; hypochondria, hypochondry, hypochondriasm [rare], hypochondriasis, hyp *or* hip [coll.], hyps *or* hips [coll.], melancholia, megrims, "moping melancholy and moonstruck madness" (Milton), schizophrenia, functional disintegration, mental dissociation, dissociation of personality, split personality, alternating ∼, double *or* dual personality, multiple personality.

3. *n.* delirium, deliriousness, deliracy [rare], delirament [now rare]; phrenitis, phrenesia [rare], phrenesis [rare]; brain fever, brain storm, calenture of the brain; raving, rage, fury, furor, frenzy, fever; fit, paroxysm; incoherence, wandering, distraction; vertigo, dizziness, giddiness, swimming, lightheadedness; delirium tremens, pathological drunkenness etc. (alcoholism) 959.2.

4. *n.* sunstroke, heatstroke, *coup de soleil* [F.], siriasis [Med.], calenture, thermic fever.

5. *n.* hallucinosis, hallucination, pathological *or* abnormal illusion; fantastic vision, fantod [slang], blue devils [coll.], blue Johnnies [slang, Austral.], pink spiders [slang], snakes; nightmare, daymare [rare], incubus, bad dream; illusion, delusion etc. 495.5; imagining etc. 515.4.

6. *n.* eccentricity, idiosyncrasy, idiocrasy, idiocrasis; erraticism, queerness etc. *adj.,* oddity, peculiarity, peculiarity of disposition *or* character; twist, mental twist, kink, kink in one's horn [slang, U.S.], crank, quirk, quip, crotchet, conceit, freak, maggot, maggot in the brain, bee in the bonnet *or* head [coll.]; capriciousness etc. 608.2.

7. *n.* craze, mania, fanaticism, infatuation, obsession, delirament [now rare], crazy fancy, fascination, enthusiasm, passion; zealotism, zealotry; monomania, paranoia; ruling passion, fixed idea, *idée fixe* [F.]; faddishness, faddiness [coll.], faddism, fadmongery; fad, whim etc. (caprice) 608; phobia etc. 860.4; fervor etc. 821.2; hyperorthodoxy etc. 983a.5.

8. *n.* insane asylum, asylum, lunatic

---

503. No excellent soul is exempt from a mixture of madness.—ARISTOTLE. Whom the gods would destroy they first make mad.—LONGFELLOW. Though this be madness, yet there is method in't.—SHAKESPEARE. O, that way madness lies; let me shun that—

asylum, asylum for the insane, madhouse, bedlam, bethlehem [rare], home, college; bathouse, bughouse, nuthouse, booby hatch [all slang]; psychopathic hospital *or* ward; sanitarium etc. (hospital) 662.17.

9. *v.* be insane etc. *adj.*, have a demon *or* devil; have a loose screw, have a screw ~, tile *or* slate loose, have bats in the belfry, ~ a leak *or* bubbles in the thinktank, ~ wheels in the head, ~ rats in the upper story, ~ a button missing, ~ a guest in the attic, ~ a hole in one's wig, ~ apartments, ~ rooms *or* space to let [all slang]; have water topside [pidgin Eng.]; ramble, wander; rave, rage, rant, fume; foam *or* froth at the mouth, drivel, drool, slaver; babble, dote.

10. *v.* go mad etc. *adj.*, lose one's senses *or* reason, take leave of one's senses, lose one's head, go off one's head [coll.]; go off one's nut *or* chump, go off one's base *or* rocker, go off the track *or* trolley, blow one's top, lose one's taffy [all slang]; run amuck.

11. *v.* drive insane etc. *adj.*, insanify [rare], madden, dement, dementate [rare], craze, loco [coll., U.S.], shatter, derange, unhinge, unbalance, turn one's brain *or* head, addle the wits, send one out of his head [coll.], befool, infatuate, obsess, possess, pixilate [dial.].

12. *adj.* insane, unsane, not sane etc. (*see* sane etc. 502.5), mad, maddened, crazy, crazed, lunatic, moon-struck, maniac(al), *aliéné* [F.], unsound, of unsound mind etc. *n.*, not of sound mind, non compos [Law], *non compos mentis* [L.; Law], dement [rare], demented, dementate, deranged, unhinged, unbalanced, unsettled, unsettled in one's mind, daft, loco *or* locoed [coll., U.S.], touched, touched in the head, teched [dial.], off, off one's head, out of one's mind, ~ head, ~ senses *or* wits, senseless, insensate, reasonless, bereft of reason, not all there [coll.], far-gone, cracked [coll.], crackbrained, shatterbrained, shatterpated, madbrained, brainsick; possessed, all-possessed, possessed with a demon *or* devil, pixilated [dial.].

not right, not right in one's head, not right in the upper story [coll.], not in one's right mind, wrong in one's head; mad as a hatter *or* March hare, "mad as Ajax" (Chapman), mad as a weaver, crazier than a bedbug, ~ coot *or* loon; stark-mad, stark-staring mad; nuts, nutty, screwy, daffy, dippy, dotty, goofy, wacky, loony *or* luny, batty, bats, balmy, balmy in the crumpet, beany, buggy, bughouse, cuckoo, off one's nut *or* chump, off in the upper story, off one's base *or* rocker, off the track *or* trolley, off the hinges, with bats in the belfry [all slang]; psychopathic, psychopathologic(al), psychotic; monomaniac(al); lycanthropic, lycanthropous; kleptomaniac; imbecile, idiotic etc. (mentally deficient) 499.13.

13. *adj.* rabid, rabic; maniac(al), raving mad, raving, raging, ranting, wild, furious, violent, frantic, beside oneself, frenzied, frenetic(al); amuck; foaming *or* frothing at the mouth; haggard, wild-eyed, wild-looking; fitful, fittyfied [dial.]: Corybantic, dithyrambic.

14. *adj.* delirious, phrenetic, raving etc. *above*; wandering, rambling, doting, incoherent, flighty; off, off one's head, out of one's head *or* mind; lightheaded, giddy, dizzy, vertiginous; mazed, distracted, distraught etc. (bewildered) 475.16.

15. *adj.* psychoneurotic, neurotic, neurasthenic, manic-depressive; hysteric(al); psychasthenic; shell-shocked.

16. *adj.* hypochondriac, hyppish [rare], hippish [coll.], hipped *or* hypped [coll.].

17. *adj.* eccentric, idiocratic(al), idiosyncratic(al); erratic, particular [obs.], queer [coll.], queer in the head [coll.], odd, peculiar, strange, outlandish, unnatural; twisted, kinky [U.S.], screwy [slang], crotchety; maggoty, maggotpated [obs.]; capricious etc. 608.5; irregular etc. (inconstant) 149.6.

18. *adj.* fanatic(al), infatuated, obsessed, prepossessed, besotted, excessively enthusiastic, overzealous, zealotic(al); faddish, faddy [coll.], fadmongering; dogmatic etc. 474.15; prejudiced etc. 481.10; overrighteous etc. 988.12; hyperorthodox etc. 983a.8; unreasonable etc.

SHAKESPEARE. Great wits are sure to madness near allied.—DRYDEN. I think for my part one-half of the nation is mad—and the other not very sound.—SMOLLETT. Who knows of madness whether it is divine or whether it be of the pit?—DUNSANY. Insanity is often the logic of an accurate mind overtaxed.—HOLMES. *Quos Deus vult perdere prius dementat* [Whom God wishes to destroy he first deprives of reason].

477.10; extravagant etc. (inordinate) 31.9; opinionated etc. (bigoted) 606.7.

504. Madman, Eccentric
(See also 503. Insanity, Eccentricity)

1. *n.* madman, crazy etc. 503.12 person, lunatic, dement, crackbrain, crackskull [rare], cracked wit, bedlam, bedlamite, candidate for bedlam, Tom o' Bedlam, phrenetic, noncompos, psychopath, psychopathic case; demoniac, energumen; loon, loony, nut, bat, coot, goof, crackpot, screwball [all slang]; maniac, raving lunatic; madcap; monomaniac, crank [coll.]; kleptomaniac, kleptomanist; phobiac [rare], phobic, phobe; automaniac; dipsomaniac; paranoiac; hypochondriac etc. 837.5; idiot, imbecile etc. (fool) 501.

2. *n.* fanatic, fan [slang], energumen, infatuate, devotee, bug [slang], nut [slang], enthusiast, rhapsodist, seer, highflier *or* highflyer; zealot, zealotist; faddist, fadmonger; dogmatist etc. 474.4; opinionist etc. 606.3.

3. *n.* eccentric, erratic, maggot-pate [obs.]; freak, character, crank [all coll.]; crackpot, nut, screwball, queer bird, odd *or* queer card, queer case, odd *or* queer fish, rum customer, queer potato [all slang].

505. Memory
(See 506. Oblivion)

1. *n.* memory, memoria, memento [joc.], remembrance, rememorance [rare], recollection, recall [rare], mental reproduction *or* recurrence; recognition, recognizance [now rare], reidentification; mirror of the mind, mind's eye, eye of the mind; tablets of the memory, Memory's halls *or* pictures; corner *or* recess of the memory, inmost recesses of the memory.

"that inward eye" (Wordsworth), "the warder of the brain" (Shakespeare), "the treasury and guardian of all things" (Cicero), "storehouse of the mind, garner of facts and fancies" (Tupper); commemoration etc. (celebration) 883.

2. *n.* retentivity, retentiveness, retention; retentive memory etc. *below.*

3. *n.* good memory, faithful *or* trustworthy memory, exact *or* correct memory, ready *or* prompt memory, retentive memory, tenacious memory, capacious memory; memory for faces, camera eye.

4. *n.* remembering, recalling etc. *v.*; recalling to the memory, rememoration [obs.], recollection, reminiscence, retrospect, retrospection, looking back, looking back on things past, review, review *or* contemplation of the past, reconsideration, reflection; afterthought etc. (mature thought) 451.2.

5. *n.* reminder, remindal; remembrance, remembrancer; jogger [coll.], flapper; prompt, prompter, prompting; mnemonic device, mnemonic, mnemonicon; token of remembrance, memento, token, souvenir, keepsake, relic; word to the wise, suggestion etc. (hint, tip) 527.3, 4.

6. *n.* memorandum (*pl.* memoranda), memo [coll.], memoir, memorial [obs. exc. Law], commonplace; memorandum book, memo book [coll.], notebook, pocketbook, engagement book, promptbook, commonplace book, adversaria; memory book [U.S.], scrapbook, album; birthday book, address book.

7. *n.* memorial, testimonial etc. (monument) 551.4.

8. *n.* memories, memorabilia, memoranda, memoirs, memorials.

9. *n.* mnemonics, mnemotechny, mnemotechnics, mnemonization; art of memory improvement, artificial memory; Mnemosyne [Gr. Myth.].

10. *v.* remember, rememorate [obs.], member [obs. exc. dial.], mem [slang], recollect, recomember [dial. U.S.], recall, call *or* recall to mind *or* remembrance, call ∽, summon *or* conjure up, mind, remind [obs.], think back, carry one's thoughts back, look back *or* backwards, look back upon, look back upon

---

504. Who is yonder poor maniac?—SOUTHEY. There is a pleasure, sure, / In being mad, which none but madmen know.—DRYDEN. 'Tis the times' plague, when madmen lead the blind.—SHAKESPEARE. Every madman thinks all other men mad.—PUBLILIUS.

505. Memory is the diary that we all carry about with us.—WILDE. O call back yesterday, bid time return.—SHAKESPEARE. Fresh and lasting ... in remembrance.—SHAKESPEARE. Beasts and babies remember, that is, recognize: man alone recollects.—COLERIDGE. A man of great memory without learning hath a rock and a spindle and no staff to spin.—G. HERBERT. Lay it where childhood's dreams are twined / In Memory's mystic band.—CARROLL. Music, when soft voices die, / Vibrates in the memory.—SHELLEY. *Parsque est me-*

things past, review in retrospect, review, pass in review, rake up the past, redeem from oblivion, revive, renew; reminisce, reminiscence [rare], indulge in *or* give oneself up to reminiscences; bethink oneself, think upon; recover *or* recall knowledge of, recognize, reidentify, place, spot [coll.]; commemorate, memorialize etc. (celebrate) 883.3.

11. *v.* keep in memory, keep ∼, hold *or* bear in mind, keep in view, have ∼, hold ∼, bear ∼, carry ∼, keep *or* retain in the thoughts, ∼ mind *or* memory; retain memory *or* remembrance of, keep in recollection of; keep, retain, treasure; not be able to forget *or* get out of one's head, be deeply impressed with, sink in the mind; keep up the memory of, keep the memory alive *or* green; keep the wound green; brood over, dwell on *or* upon.

12. *v.* be remembered etc. (*see* remember etc. *above* 505.10), recur, recur to the mind; flash on the mind, flash across the memory; be in one's thoughts *or* mind, live *or* dwell in one's memory, remain in one's memory, remain indelibly impressed on the memory, haunt one's thoughts, run in the head; rankle, rankle in the breast, get under one's skin [slang].

13. *v.* memorize, rememorize, commit to memory; con, con over; fix ∼, rivet ∼, imprint ∼, impress ∼, stamp ∼, grave ∼, engrave ∼, store ∼, treasure up ∼, bottle up ∼, embalm ∼, bury *or* enshrine in the memory *or* mind; load ∼, store ∼, stuff *or* burden the memory *or* mind with; get into one's head, drive *or* hammer into one's head; get *or* learn by heart *or* rote, learn word for word; have *or* know by heart *or* rote, have at one's fingers' ends *or* tips; repeat by heart *or* rote, give word for word, repeat, repeat like a parrot, say one's lesson; learn etc. 539.3.

14. *v.* renew *or* refresh the memory, rub up the memory, rub up, polish up [coll.], brush up, get up on [slang]; try to recall, tax *or* task the memory, rack *or* ransack the brains, beat *or* cudgel the brains, crack the brains [coll.].

15. *v.* remind, mind [now chiefly dial.], put in mind, remember, remembrance [rare], cause to remember, put in remembrance, bring back to the memory, bring to recollection, renew *or* refresh the memory of, awake *or* awaken the memory, jog *or* flap the memory, pull by the sleeve; prompt, give the cue; suggest to, call the attention to; suggest etc. (hint) 527.8.

16. *v.* memorandize, write memoranda, memorandum [rare], make a memorandum, make a note of etc. (record) 551.8.

17. *adj.* recollective, rememorative [obs.], rememorant [rare], memorious [obs.], memoried; reminiscent, reminiscential, reminiscitory; mindful, remindful, suggestive, mnemonic; retentive.

18. *adj.* remembered, recollected etc. *v.*; recalled to the memory, retained in the memory, pent up in the memory, present to the mind, unforgotten; vivid, fresh, green, alive; still vivid etc.; vivid etc. in the memory *or* in remembrance, alive etc. in memory; enduring, enduring in the memory; uppermost in one's thoughts.

19. *adj.* memorable, rememberable, recollectable *or* recollectible, memorial [obs.]; *beatae memoriae* [L.], of blessed memory; worthy of being remembered etc. (important) 642.10.

20. *adj.* unforgettable, not *or* never to be forgotten, never to be erased from the mind, indelible, indelibly impressed on the mind *or* memory.

21. *adj.* memorial, commemorative, kept in remembrance.

22. *adv.* by heart, *par cœur* [F.], by rote, by *or* from memory, *memoriter* [L.], without book.

23. *adv. etc.* in memory of, to the memory of, in remembrance *or* commemoration, *in memoriam* [L.]; *memoria in aeterna* [L.].

506. Oblivion
(See 505. Memory)

1. *n.* oblivion, obliviousness, forgetfulness etc. *adj.*; forgetness [rare], oblivis-

---

minisse doloris [It is part of grief to remember].—OVID.   *Mendacem memorem esse oportet* [A liar must have a good memory].—QUINTILIAN.   *Forsan et haec olim meminisse juvabit* [And perhaps sometime it will be pleasant to recall these things].—VERGIL.

506. The tooth of time / And razure of Oblivion.—SHAKESPEARE.   A slow and silent stream, / Lethe the River of Oblivion.—MILTON.   We may with advantage at times forget what we know.—PUBLILIUS.   Forget that I remember, / And dream that I forget.—

cence [rare]; amnesty; obliteration etc. 552.1 of the past, insensibility etc. 823.1 to the past; forget [coll.]; Lethe, waters of Lethe *or* oblivion, draft of oblivion; misremembrance.

2. *n.* defective memory, short ~, loose ~, treacherous ~, untrustworthy *or* failing memory, mind *or* memory like a sieve.

3. *n.* amnesia, decaying memory, failure *or* loss of memory, lapse of memory, gap in the memory; anterograde amnesia, retrograde amnesia, infantile amnesia, systematic amnesia, verbal amnesia; lethologica.

4. *v.* forget, clean forget; disrecollect, disremember [both dial. and coll.], forget to remember [joc.], have no remembrance etc. 505.1; lose, lose sight of; fall *or* sink into oblivion, escape one, slip *or* escape the memory, fade *or* die away from the memory, be forgotten etc. *adj*.

5. *v.* be forgetful etc. *adj.*, have a short memory etc. *n.*, have no head; have on the tip of the tongue; misremember.

6. *v.* efface ~, erase ~, dismiss ~, discard *or* discharge from the memory *or* thoughts, put out of one's mind *or* head, consign to oblivion, consign to the tomb of Capulets; cast behind one's back, wean one's thoughts from, think no more of etc. (turn the attention from) 458.5; let bygones be bygones etc. (forgive) 918.3.

7. *adj.* forgotten etc. *v.*, clean forgotten, unremembered, unrecollected, past recollection, bygone, out of the mind, lost, gone, gone out of one's head *or* recollection, consigned to oblivion, buried *or* sunk in oblivion.

8. *adj.* forgetful, forgetting, oblivious, memoryless, mindless, unmindful, Lethean, with a mind *or* memory like a sieve, insensible to the past; amnesic, amnestic, amnemonic; heedless etc. (inattentive) 458.10, (neglectful) 460.8.

507. Expectation
(See 508. Inexpectation)

1. *n.* expectation, expectance *or* expectancy, anticipation; prospect, prospection; contingency, contingence [rare], contingent; reckoning, calculation, contemplation; foresight etc. 510; imminence etc. 152; unastonishment etc. 871.

2. *n.* sanguine expectation, assurance, confidence, reliance, trust, faith, conviction, confident ~, firm ~, fixed *or* implicit expectation; assumption, presumption; good prospect etc. (good chance) 156.3; probability etc. 472; certainty etc. 474; hope etc. 858.

3. *n.* anxious ~, ardent ~, eager *or* breathless expectation; suspense, waiting, abeyance; anxiety, anxietude, anxiousness; apprehension, apprehensiveness; torment of Tantalus.

4. *v.* expect, be expectant etc. *adj.*, anticipate, have in prospect, have *or* keep in view, contemplate, have in contemplation, promise oneself; look with expectation, look forward to, look for, watch for, look out for, watch out for [coll., U.S.], keep a good *or* sharp lookout for; make one's mouth water; hope etc. 858.6; hope for etc. (desire) 865.11; foresee etc. 510.5; think likely etc. (presume) 472.3; lead one to expect etc. (promise) 511.10; be unastonished etc. 871.2.

5. *v.* await, wait, wait for, wait on *or* upon [coll.], lie in wait for, stay *or* tarry for; watch, watch and wait *or* pray; bide, abide, bide one's time, mark time; stand at attention, hold one's breath; be in store for etc. (be imminent) 152.2.

6. *v.* plan on *or* upon, count on *or* upon, calculate *or* reckon on *or* upon, allot on *or* upon [dial., U.S. and Can.], bank on *or* upon [coll.], bargain for, lay one's account for; prepare for etc. 673.7.

7. *adj.* expectant, expecting etc. *v.*, in expectation etc. *n.*; anticipant, anticipative, anticipatory; looking forward to, on the watch *or* lookout for, *aux aguets* [F.]; open-eyed, openmouthed; gaping, agape, agog, all agog; in suspense, on tenterhooks, on tiptoe, on the tiptoe of expectation, on edge [coll.], on the rack; ready, eager, hopeful etc. 858.9.

8. *adj.* expected etc *v.*, foreseen; looked for, hoped for; in prospect etc. *n.*, prospective; future, forward [Com.], coming; in one's eye, in view, on the horizon; impending etc. (imminent) 152.3.

9. *adv. etc.* expectantly etc. *adj.*; in the

SWINBURNE. A retentive memory is a good thing, but the ability to forget is the true token of greatness.—E. HUBBARD. Out of sight, out of mind.
507. Suspense in news is torture.—MILTON. What we anticipate seldom occurs; what we least expected generally happens.—DISRAELI. I suppose, to use our national motto, "something will turn up."—DISRAELI. A watched pot is long in boiling.

event of, as a possible contingency; with breathless expectation etc. *n.*, with bated breath, with eyes *or* ears strained, with muscles tense; with ears pricked up, *arrectis auribus* [L.].

508. Inexpectation
(See 507. Expectation)

1. *n.* inexpectation, nonexpectation, unexpectation [obs.], inexpectance *or* inexpectancy; inexpectedness, unexpectedness etc. *adj.*; unanticipation, nonanticipation; unforeseen contingency, the unforeseen; false expectation etc. (disappointment) 508; miscalculation etc. (misjudgment) 481; nonpreparation etc. 674.

2. *n.* surprise, surprisal, surprisement [rare], surpriser; sudden burst, thunderclap, thunderbolt, bolt out of *or* from the blue; blow, staggerer [coll.], rouser [coll.], eye opener; surprise party [U.S.]; astonishment, amazement etc. (wonder) 870.

3. *n.* start, shock, jar [coll.], jolt [slang], turn [coll.], twitch [slang].

4. *v.* not expect etc. (*see* expect etc. 507.4), be caught napping etc. *adj.*, be taken by surprise etc. *adv.*; start, be given a start etc. *n.*; not bargain for, come *or* fall upon.

5. *v.* be unexpected etc. *adj.*, come unawares etc. *adv.*, appear unexpectedly etc. *adv.*, turn up, pop up [chiefly coll.], drop from the clouds, appear like a bolt out of the blue, come *or* burst like a thunderclap *or* thunderbolt, burst *or* flash upon one, steal *or* creep upon; take *or* catch unawares, catch napping *or* off one's guard, catch with one's pants down [slang].

6. *v.* surprise, take by surprise, spring a surprise [coll.], catch *or* take unawares etc. *above*, come upon unexpectedly *or* without warning, pounce ~, bounce *or* spring upon, spring a mine upon; pay a surprise visit, drop in upon [coll.], give a surprise party; startle, start [obs. exc. Scot.], jump [rare], jar [coll.], jolt [slang], take aback [coll.], shock, electrify, stun, stupefy, petrify, paralyze, stagger, take away one's breath, throw on one's beam ends, throw off one's guard,

give a turn [coll.], bowl down *or* over [coll.], strike all of a heap [coll.], upset, unsettle; astound etc. (astonish) 870.3; catch unprepared etc. 674.6.

7. *adj.* inexpectant, nonexpectant, unexpectant, unexpecting; unanticipative, nonanticipative; unsuspecting, unaware, unwarned, unadvised, unadmonished; napping, off one's guard, caught napping *or* off one's guard; inattentive etc. 458.10, 11; unprepared etc. 674.7; unwary etc. 460.9.

8. *adj.* unexpected, inexpected, unanticipated, unlooked for, unhoped for, unforeseen; contrary to *or* against expectation, beyond *or* past expectation, out of one's reckoning; dropped from the clouds, out of the blue; unheard-of etc. (unusual) 83.10; sudden etc. 113.5; premature etc. 132.8.

9. *adj.* surprising, surprisable [rare], startling etc. *v.*; astonishing etc. 870.7.

10. *adj.* surprised etc. *v.*, struck with surprise; wonder-struck etc. (astonished) 870.6.

11. *adv.* unexpectedly etc. *adj.*, unawares, *à l'improviste* [F.], without notice *or* warning; by surprise, in an unguarded moment, like a thief in the night, like a thunderbolt *or* thunderclap, like a bolt from the blue, like a lightning flash; abruptly, pop etc. (suddenly) 113.7; prematurely etc. (beforehand) 132.12; unpreparedly etc. 674.12.

12. *phr.* little would one expect *or* think, nobody would ever expect, ~ suppose *or* think, who would have thought, it beats the Dutch!, can such things be?; do tell! [coll., U.S.] etc. (wonder) 870.11.

509. Disappointment

1. *n.* disappointment, sad *or* bitter disappointment, failure of expectation *or* hope, blighted hope, dashed hopes, hope deferred, nonfulfillment of one's hopes *or* expectations, abortive attempt, slip 'twixt cup and lip, trick of fortune; afterclap; much cry and little wool, much ado about nothing, much noise and slight result, labor in vain; false *or* vain expectation, forlorn hope; buffet, blow; frustration,

---

508. The flash of a mighty surprise.—W. WATSON.   Blessed is he who expects nothing, for he shall never be disappointed.—POPE.   The unexpected always happens.

509. As for disappointing them, I should not so much mind; but I can't abide to disappoint myself.—GOLDSMITH.   Man must be disappointed with the lesser things of life before he

check, balk, foil, bafflement; comedown, letdown [coll.]; fallen countenance; disillusionment etc. (undeception) 545a; miscalculation etc. (misjudgment) 481; failure etc. 732; discontent etc. 832; regret etc. 833; hopelessness etc. 859.

2. *v.* disappoint, disappoint one's expectations, defeat expectation *or* hope; balk, bilk, frustrate, thwart, foil, cross, baffle; balk ~, frustrate etc. one's expectations *or* hopes, crush ~, dash *or* blight one's hope, come *or* fall short of expectation; disconcert, put out; dumfound *or* dumbfound, dumfounder *or* dumbfounder; disillusion etc. (undeceive) 545a.2; disgruntle etc. (dissatisfy) 832.4.

3. *v.* be disappointed, not realize one's hopes *or* expectations; look blank, look blue, look *or* stand aghast *or* agog; laugh on the wrong side of one's mouth, laugh out of the other corner of the mouth [both coll.].

4. *adj.* disappointed, bitterly disappointed, put-out; balked, thwarted etc. *v.*; defeated of expectation *or* hope, out of one's reckoning; disgruntled etc. (discontented) 832.5; regretful etc. 833.3.

5. *adj.* disappointing, unsatisfactory etc. 832.6; short of expectations, not up to ~, below *or* under par.

510. Foresight
(See also 511. Prediction)

1. *n.* foresight, prospicience, prevision; forecast, foreglimpse, foreglance, foregleam; prospect, prospection; anticipation; farseeingness, farsightedness, longsightedness; long head [coll.], longheadedness; sagacity, wisdom etc. 498.2, 3; expectation etc. 507; second sight etc. (clairvoyance) 994.7.

2. *n.* forethought, predeliberation, presurmise; foregone conclusion etc. (prejudgment) 481.2; providence etc. (preparation) 673; care etc. 459; prudence etc. (caution) 864.

3. *n.* foreknowledge, forewisdom, precognition, prescience, presage; preconceived notion, prenotion [rare], preapprehension; presentiment, premonition [coll.]; prognosis etc. (prediction) 511; prejudice etc. 481.2.

4. *n.* foretaste, antepast, prelibation.

5. *v.* foresee, see beforehand, foreglimpse, foretaste, forecast, divine, anticipate, contemplate, look forward to, look ahead, look beyond, look ~, pry *or* peep into the future; have an eye to the future, have an eye to the main chance; see one's way; see how the land lies *or* the wind blows, see how the cat jumps [coll.]; foreknow, know beforehand, precognize; scent from afar, feel it in one's bones [coll.]; have *or* exercise foresight etc. *n.*; predict etc. 511.7; expect etc. 507.4; forejudge etc. 481.6; forestall etc. (be beforehand) 132.5; forewarn etc. 668.7; forearm etc. 864.4.

6. *adj.* foreseeing etc. *v.*, foresighted, foresightful [rare]; precognitive, precognizant; prescient, presciental [obs.], prescious [obs.]; farseeing, farsighted, longsighted; longheaded etc. (sagacious) 498.10; anticipatory, prospective etc. 507.7, 8; provident etc. (preparatory) 673.10; predictive etc. 511.1.

7. *adv. etc.* foreseeingly etc. *adj.*, with foresight etc. *n.*; against the time when . . . , for a rainy day.

511. Prediction

1. *n.* prediction, predication [erron.], foretelling etc. *v.*, forecast, prophecy, vaticination, ariolation [obs.], premonstration [obs.]; presage, presagement; prognostication, prognosis, prognostic prophasis [Med.]; proclamation, announcement, preannouncement, prepublication; prefigurement, prefiguration; auspice etc. (omen) 512.1; oracle, prophet etc. 513; foreknowledge etc. (foresight) 510.

2. *n.* divination, divining, pythonism, mantology [rare]; augury, auguration [obs.]; soothsay, soothsaying, hariolation; intuition etc. 477a; fortunetelling,

---

can comprehend the greater.—BULWER-LYTTON. For of all sad words of tongue or pen, / The saddest are these: "It might have been!"— WHITTIER. *Dis aliter visum* [To the gods it has seemed otherwise].—VERGIL. The mountain brought forth a mouse.
510. A prudent man foreseeth the evil.—BIBLE. Till all that it foresees it finds.—LONGFELLOW.

Who would the miseries of man foreknow?— DRYDEN. *Mihi cura futuri* [I shall take care of the future].
511. And these does she apply for warnings, and portents / And evils imminent.—SHAKESPEARE. Thus in the beginning the world was so made that certain signs come before certain events.—CICERO. I know of no way

necromancy etc. (sorcery) 992; spiritualism etc. 994.4; clairvoyance etc. 994.7.

3. *n.* (forms of divination) aeromancy, alectoromancy, alectryomancy, aleuromancy, alphitomancy, anthropomancy, anthroposcopy, arithmancy, astromancy etc. *below,* austromancy, axinomancy, belomancy, bibliomancy, bletonism, botanomancy, capnomancy, ceromancy, chirognomy, chirology, chiromancy, cleromancy, coscinomancy, crithomancy, crystallomancy, dactyliomancy, dactylomancy [erron.], extispicy, gastromancy, geloscopy, genethliacs, genethlialogy, geomancy, gyromancy, halomancy, haruspicy, hieromancy, hieroscopy, hydromancy, ichthyomancy, lithomancy, meteoromancy, molybdomancy, myomancy, necromancy, nomancy, oenomancy, omoplatoscopy, oneiromancy, onomancy, onychomancy, ophiomancy, orniscopy, ornithomancy, palmistry, pegomancy, pessomancy, psephomancy, psychomancy, pyromancy, rhabdomancy, scapulimancy, scapulomancy, sciomancy, sideromancy, sortilege, stichomancy, theomancy.

4. *n.* astrology, astromancy, horoscopy; genethlialogy, genethliacs, genethliac astrology, judicial *or* mundane astrology; horoscope, nativity; constellation, house etc. 318.6, 8; astrologer etc. 318.13.

5. *n.* (means of divination) tea leaves, shadows, dice, cards, ghosts, stars, meteors, winds, entrails, snakes, herbs, arrows, pebbles, stones, rings, numbers, letters, books; oracle, crystal, Bible, fire, wand, dough, salt, wax, water; crystal ball; Halloween nuts, Halloween mirror; divining rod *or* stick, wand, witch hazel; hand of glory, wax image, teraphim; charm etc. (talisman) 993.2-5.

6. *n.* foreboding, forebodement, boding; forebode, bode, abode, abodement, aboding [all obs.]; presentiment, preapprehension, premonition, premonishment [rare], omination [obs.], augury, auguration [obs.]; presage, presagement [obs.]; portent, portention *or* portension [rare], portentment [rare], portendance [rare]; prenotice, prenotation, prenotion [rare]; forewarning etc. 668.2; apprehension, misgiving etc. (fearfulness) 860.2; threatening etc. 909.

7. *v.* predict, make a prediction etc. *n.,* predicate [erron.], foretell, forecast, dope *or* dope out [slang], prognosticate, prognose [Med.], prophesy, vaticinate, divine, ariolate [obs.], presage, forebode, bode [arch. and dial.], portend [now rare], omen, soothsay; augur, augurate [obs.]; tell *or* declare beforehand, judge the future, calculate in advance; fortunetell, tell fortunes; haruspicate; hariolate, hariolize [obs.]; cast a horoscope *or* nativity; foresee etc. 510.5.

8. *v.* herald, usher in, precurse, be the precursor etc. (*see* precursor etc. 64.1); premise; proclaim, announce, preannounce, prepublish.

9. *v.* portend, forebode, bode, abode [obs.], presage, divine, omen, ominate [obs.], croak, prognosticate; augur, augurate [obs.]; auspicate, foreshow, preshow, foretoken, betoken, preindicate, presignify, premonstrate [obs.]; foreshadow, shadow forth, typify, pretypify; prefigure, prefigurate [rare], figure [obs.]; signify, point to etc. (indicate) 550.18; lower (threaten) 909.2; forewarn etc. 668.7; forerun, herald etc. 116.3.

10. *v.* promise, foretoken etc. *above,* give ground for expecting, lead one to expect, hold out ~, raise *or* excite expectation *or* hope, bid fair, stand fair to.

11. *adj.* predictive, predictory, predictional; prophetic(al), fatidic(al), fatiloquent [rare], presageful, oracular, divinatory, haruspical; prognostic, prognosticatory; vaticinal, vaticinant [rare]; vaticinatory; sibylline, sibyllic *or* sibylic; pythonic(al) [rare]; precursive, precursory, precursal, precurrent; ominous, ominative [obs.].

portentous, portentive [obs.], portending; foreboding, boding, bodeful; augural, augurial, augurous [rare]; premonitory, premonitive; monitory, monitorial; presentient, presentimental [rare]; extispicious; weather-wise; auspicious, inauspicious etc. 512.3-5; prescient etc. (foreseeing) 510.6; forewarning etc. 668.10; indicative etc. 550.21.

12. *adj.* predictable, divinable etc. *v.*

13. *adj.* predicted etc. *v.,* predicate, an-

---

of judging the future but by the past.—P. HENRY.   Coming events cast their shadows before.—T. CAMPBELL.   Ancestral voices prophesying war.—COLERIDGE.   Yet Caesar shall go forth; for these predictions / Are to the world in general as to Caesar.—SHAKESPEARE. *Auspicium melioris aevi* [Omen of a better age].

nunciate [obs.], foretold, forecast, foreshown, foreseen, foreglimpsed, foreknown; indicated etc. 550.22.

512. Omen
(See also 513. Oracle)

1. *n.* omen (*pl.* omens, omina), indication of the future, premonitory sign, premonitor, foretoken, augury, auspice, bode [obs.], abode [obs.], divination, soothsay; presage, presager, presagement [obs.]; prognostic, prognostication; prefigurement, prefiguration; sign of the times, *auspicium melioris aevi* [L.]; sign, token etc. (indication) 550; harbinger etc. (precursor) 64; prediction etc. 511; warning sign etc. 668.3.

2. *n.* (omens) bird of ill omen, storm petrel, Mother Carey's chicken; halcyon birds; black cat; gathering clouds, clouds on the horizon, messengers [dial., Eng.]; thundercloud, thunderhead; thunder, lightning; rainbow; comet, shooting star.

3. *adj.* ominous, foreboding etc. (predictive) 511.11.

4. *adj.* auspicious, auspicial; of good omen, favorable, propitious; rosy, promising, happy, lucky, fortunate, prosperous; halcyon, halcyonic, halcyonian.

5. *adj.* inauspicious, unauspicious [rare]; inominous [rare], ill-omened, ill-boding, ill-fated, ill-starred, evil-starred, unfavorable, unpropitious, unpromising, unfortunate, unlucky; sinister, sinistral [obs.]; threatening, lowering; doomed, planet-struck, planet-stricken; ominous etc. *above* 512.3; bad etc. 649.8; hopeless etc. 859.7; fearful etc. 860.15.

513. Oracle
(See also 512. Omen)

1. *n.* oracle, oraculum (*pl.* oracula); Delphian *or* Delphic oracle, Pythian oracle; Delphic tripod, tripod of the Pythia; Dodona, oracle *or* oak of Dodona; adytum; cave of the Cumaean sibyl; Sibylline Books *or* Oracles, Sibylline leaves; interpreter etc. 524; adviser etc. 695.3.

2. *n.* prophet, predictor, forecaster; *vates, vates sacer* [both L.], druid, seer, soothsayer, augur, sibyl, mantologist

[rare]; divine [obs.], diviner, divinator; fortune teller, crystal-gazer, palmist; geomancer, geomant [rare]; haruspice, haruspex, extispex; dopester, tipster [both slang], tout *or* touter [slang, U.S.]; python, pythoness; prophetess, valicinatress [rare], divineress; Pythia, Pythian, Delphian sibyl; Cumaean sibyl, sibyl of Cumae; Babylonian *or* Persian sibyl, Libyan sibyl, Cimmerian sibyl, Erythraean sibyl, Samian sibyl, Hellespontine *or* Trojan sibyl, Phrygian sibyl, Tiburtine sibyl; sphinx, Tiresias, Cassandra, Oedipus [all Gr. Myth.].

Joseph, Joshua, Samuel, Isaiah, Jeremiah, Ezekiel, Hosea, Joel, Amos, Obadiah, Jonah, Micah, Nahum, Habakkuk, Zephaniah, Haggai, Zechariah, Malachi, Daniel; Mohammed, Joseph Smith [Mormon]; astrologer etc. 318.13; psychic etc. 994.14; sorcerer etc. 992.2, 3; interpreter etc. 524.

3. *n.* weather prophet, weather caster *or* forecaster, weather spy [rare], weather sharp [slang], weathermaker, weatherman [coll.], weather wizard [obs.], weatherwiser [obs.], meteorologist; Old Probabilities *or* Old Prob, Clerk of the Weather [both joc., U.S.]; Old Moore, Zadkiel; weather bureau, weather station; weather vane etc. 338.9.

514. Supposition

1. *n.* supposition, suppose, supposal, suppositum, supposing etc. *v.*; putation, speculation, divination; presupposition, presupposal; presumption, assumption, surmise, inference, conjecture, guess, guesswork, hypothesis; theory, theoretic, theoric [arch.]; theorem, theorum [Marxian]; thesis, thesicle [rare]; proposal, proposition, *propositio* [L.]; postulate, postulation [rare], postulatum; position, assumed position; condition, conditional; datum, data.

2. *n.* vague supposition, suggestion, bare suggestion, suspicion, inkling, hint, intimation, impression, idea, notion; rough guess, shot [coll.].

3. *n.* supposititiousness, supposable-

---

512. In this omen the anger of Heaven they read.—BULWER-LYTTON.
513. All the augurs turned pale at the sight.—BULWER-LYTTON. What say the augurers?—SHAKESPEARE. A prophet is not without honour, save in his own country, and in his own house.—BIBLE.
514. To trust the soul's invincible surmise / Was all his science and his only art.—SANTA-

ness [rare] etc. *adj.*; suppositality [obs.], conjecturality [rare].

4. *n.* theoretics, theorics.

5. *n.* supposer, surmiser, assumer; conjecturer, conjecturalist [rare]; guesser, guessworker; theorist, theorizer, theoretic, theoretician, theorician; speculator, speculatist [rare]; notionalist, notionist [rare]; hypothesist, hypothetist [rare]; doctrinaire, doctrinarian.

6. *v.* suppose, presume, assume, surmise, expect [chiefly coll.], suspect, suspicion [now dial.], conjecture, guess, infer [coll.], understand, gather, conclude, deduce, judge, consider, reckon [coll. or dial.], calculate [coll., U.S.], allow [dial.], divine, imagine [coll.], fancy, dream, conceive, believe, trow [arch.], deem, wis [arch.], ween [arch.], feel, think, be inclined to think, opine [now chiefly joc.]; say, dare say, be afraid [coll.]; take, take it, take it into one's head, take for granted; give a guess, hazard *or* venture a guess *or* conjecture; presuppose, presurmise; theorize, hypothesize.

7. *v.* propound, propose, submit, start, broach, bring forward, set before the mind, put *or* set forth, throw out *or* put forward a suggestion *or* supposition, put a case, open up a question *or* subject; move, make a motion; postulate, predicate, posit [Logic].

8. *v.* suggest, allude to etc. (hint) 527.8; suggest itself etc. 451.32.

9. *adj.* supposed etc. *v.*, suppositional, suppositionary, suppositive, suppository, supposititious; conjectural, presumptive, assumptive, hypothetic(al), theoretical, academical; speculative, speculatory; putative, putationary; postulational, postulatory [now rare]; gratuitous, given, mooted; imaginary etc. 515.12–14; unreal etc. 2.8.

10. *adj.* supposable [rare], presumable, conjecturable etc. *v.*; imaginable etc. 515.15.

11. *adj.* suggestive, allusive, referential; stimulative, stimulating.

12. *adv. etc.* supposedly, theoretically etc. *adj.*; seeming, seemingly, seemly [arch.]; quasi, as if, as though, as it were; in a sense, in a certain sense *or* degree; in a manner, in a manner of speaking; according to the hypothesis, *ex hypothesi* [L.]; perhaps, for all *or* aught one knows etc. (possibly) 470.7.

13. *conj.* supposing that, assuming that etc. *v.*; supposing [coll.], on the supposition that etc. *n.*; if by way of hypothesis, according to the hypothesis, *ex hypothesi* [L.]; allowing that, in case that, if etc. (provided) 469.8.

515. Imagination

1. *n.* imagination, imagining etc. *v.*, imaginativeness etc. *adj.*, imagery; fancy, active fancy, flight of fancy, fumes of fancy, fantasy, phantasy, fantastic representation, fanciful *or* visionary thinking, conceit; "such stuff as dreams are made on" (Shakespeare); productive $\sim$, constructive *or* creative imagination, creative thought, mental creation *or* invention, originality, conception, excogitation, inspiration, poetic imagination; reproductive imagination; mythification, mythogenesis; imaginative power etc. 597.9; intuition etc. 477a.

2. *n.* idealization, ideality, idealism; romanticism, utopianism; quixotism, quixotry; castle-building, dreaming, daydreaming etc. *v.*

3. *n.* lively imagination *or* fancy, vivid imagination, fertile *or* pregnant imagination, warm $\sim$, heated $\sim$, excited $\sim$, sanguine $\sim$, ardent $\sim$, fiery $\sim$, boiling $\sim$, wild $\sim$, uncontrolled $\sim$, playful $\sim$, bold *or* daring imagination; vivacity of imagination, verve.

4. *n.* imaginative conception, imagining, imaginary, product of the imagination, creation *or* coinage of the brain, creature of the imagination, figment, figment of the imagination, mental representation *or* presentation, *Vorstellung* [G.], image, mental image, fictive creation, fiction, myth, fancy, idle fancy, fantasy, phantasy, fantasque [rare], phantasm *or* phantasma, vagary, rhapsody, romance, gest, shadow, chimera, vapor, bubble.

idealization, idealized creation; conceit, maggot, whim, whimwham, whimsey; imagery, dreamery, "thick-coming fan-

---

YANA. Veneer'd with sanctimonious theory.—TENNYSON. Supposition is greater than truth.—BACON.

515. Imagination is not a talent of some men but is the health of every man.—EMERSON. Imagination rules the world.—NAPOLEON.

cies" (Shakespeare); extravaganza, phantasmagoria; fantasia; pipe dream [coll.] etc. (dream) *below,* air castle, castle in the air, castle in Spain, *château en Espagne* [F.], pleasure dome of Kubla Khan; *le pot au lait* [F.], pot of gold at the foot of the rainbow; man in the moon, Flying Dutchman, great sea serpent.

illusion, delusion etc. 495.5; phantom etc. (optical illusion) 443.9; fata morgana etc. (luminescence) 420.11; fantastic vision etc. (hallucination) 503.5; stretch of the imagination etc. (exaggeration) 549; work of fiction etc. (narrative) 594.2; poetry etc. 597; play etc. (drama) 599; sonata etc. (music) 415.3.

5. *n.* dream, reverie, muse, trance; daydream, pipe dream [coll.], pipe [slang], golden dream, vision; dream of Alnaschar; nightmare, daymare [rare], incubus [Med.], bad dream; brown study etc. (abstraction) 458.3.

6. *n.* utopia, paradise, heaven, heaven on earth, Heavenly City, Celestial City, Land of Beulah, New Jerusalem; Atlantis, Arcadia, Agapemone, Eden, "Happy Valley" (Johnson), fairyland, land of Prester John, Kingdom of Micomicon, "Estotiland *or* Estotilandia" (Milton), Laputa, Shangri-la; Cockaigne, Lubberland; Dixie, Dixie Land, Dixie's Land; millennium, kingdom come; Land of Promise, land of behest [arch.], Promised Land, land flowing with milk and honey; cloudland, dreamland.

7. *n.* imaginer, imaginist [rare], imaginator [rare]; visionary, idealist, seer, mopus [slang], dreamer, daydreamer, castle-builder, fancymonger, fanciful projector; romantic, romanticist, romancer; Quixote, Don Quixote; utopian, utopianist, utopist [rare], utopianizer, utopographer; fantasist *or* phantasist, fantast *or* phantast; phantasmagorist, phantasmagorian; rhapsodist, enthusiast, highflier *or* highflyer; mythmaker, mythographer; creative artist.

8. *v.* imagine, imagine of [arch.], imaginate [rare], exercise the imagination *or* fancy, image, fancy, conceive, form a conception *or* mental image of, produce by the imagination, represent to the mental vision, picture, picture ~, represent ~, fancy *or* figure to oneself; conjure up, call *or* summon up, call to mind.

give play *or* the reins to the imagination *or* fancy, give free rein to the imagination, let one's imagination run wild, allow one's imagination to run away with one; indulge in fantasy etc. *n.*, phantasize, fantasticate [rare]; build castles in the air; idealize, utopianize, quixotize, rhapsodize; romance, romanticize; tilt at windmills.

9. *v.* dream, dream of, daydream, pipedream [coll.], indulge in revery etc. *n.*, "see visions and dream dreams" (Bible), conjure up a vision.

10. *v.* create, originate, devise, contrive, invent, make up, coin, fabricate, hatch, hatch up, concoct, frame; improvise, improvisate; excogitate, think out, think up [U.S.], dream up [slang, U.S.]; set one's wits to work, strain *or* crack one's invention.

11. *adj.* imaginative, imaginous [obs.], imagining etc. *v.*; original, inventive, creative, fertile, productive, ingenious; visionary etc. *below.*

12. *adj.* imaginary, imagined etc. *v.*, imaginal, imaginational, imagerial; fanciful, fancical [obs. exc. dial.], fancy, fancy-bred, fancy-born, fancy-built, fancy-framed, fancy-formed, fancy-woven, fancy-wrought; visionary, viewy [coll.], Utopian *or* utopian, quixotic (al); notional, whimsical, maggoty; figmental, figmentary [rare]; castle-built, air-built, air-drawn, airy, made of empty air; vaporous, vapory; cloud-built, cloud-born, cloud-woven; in the clouds, *in nubibus* [L.].

ideal, idealistic(al); romantic(al), romanticist, romanticistic; fantastic(al), fantasque [rare], high-fantastical, fantasied; phantasmic(al), phantasmal, phantomatic, phantomic(al), phantom; phantasmagoric(al), phantasmagorial; fabulous, fictitious, legendary; mythic(al), mythological; fairy, fairylike; ben

---

That inward eye / Which is the bliss of solitude.—WORDSWORTH. Tell me where is fancy bred, / Or in the heart or in the head?—SHAKESPEARE. Sweetest Shakespeare, Fancy's child.—MILTON. Your old men shall dream dreams; your young men shall see visions.—BIBLE. The centre of every man's existence is a dream.—CHESTERTON. He is a dreamer; let us leave him: pass.—SHAKESPEARE. We are the music-makers, / And we are the dreamers of dreams.—O'SHAUGHNESSY. We are such stuff / As dreams are made on.—SHAKESPEARE. *Tous songes sont mensonges* [All dreams are lies].

trovato [It.]; chimerical etc. (unsubstantial) 4.5, 6; unreal etc. 2.8; illusory etc. 495.15; theoretical, hypothetical etc. (suppositional) 514.9.

13. *adj.* extravagant, high-flown, flighty, preposterous; rhapsodic(al), ecstatic(al), fanatic(al), enthusiastic.

14. *adj.* dreamy, dreamlike, dreaming, dreamful; dream-born, dream-built, dream-created, dreamlit; dreamy-eyed, dreamy-minded, dreamy-souled; dream-beset, dream-ridden, dream-haunted; daydreamy, daydreaming, pipe-dreaming [coll.], castle-building; tranced, entranced, in a trance.

15. *adj.* imaginable, imaginal, fanciable, conceivable; presumable etc. 514.10.

516. Meaning
(See 517. Unmeaningness)

1. *n.* meaning, meaningness; significantness etc. *adj.*; significance, signification, significature; sense, expression, import, purport, implication, connotation, denotation; drift, tenor, spirit, bearing, coloring; force, effect; intent, intention; purpose, aim, object, design, scheme, scope [arch.]; accepted meaning, acceptance, acception, acceptation.

common ∼, ordinary ∼, regular ∼, usual ∼, conventional ∼, standard ∼, popular ∼, colloquial ∼, natural ∼, unstrained ∼, obvious ∼, manifest ∼, evident ∼, apparent ∼, prima-facie ∼, ostensible ∼, plain ∼, simple ∼, patent ∼, express ∼, explicit ∼, primary ∼, primitive ∼, original ∼, initial ∼, fundamental ∼, essential ∼, substantial ∼, material ∼, pertinent ∼, relevant ∼, broad *or* general meaning; hidden meaning etc. (latency) 526; allusion, suggestion etc. (hint) 527.4; explanation, definition etc. (interpretation) 522.

2. *n.* literality, literalism, literalness etc. *adj.*, literal ∼, strict *or* real meaning, ∼ sense *or* interpretation, true *or* exact etc. meaning, the letter.

3. *n.* equivalence *or* equivalency, equivalent meaning; synonymy, antonymy; synonymity, synonymousness etc. *adj.*; synonym, antonym; poecilonym, polyonym [rare]; homonym, metonym, heteronym; analogue, analogon (*pl.* analoga); equivalent etc. (equal) 27.5; simile, metaphor etc. (figure of speech) 521; synonymicon [rare] etc. (dictionary) 593.4.

4. *n.* (thing signified) matter, subject, subject matter; significant, significative; argument, text; substance, sum and substance; gist, pith etc. (essence) 5.2.

5. *v.* mean, signify, connote, denote, express, import, purport, convey, imply, implicate, involve, infer, suggest, intimate, allude to, argue, breathe, bespeak, betoken, indicate, point to; represent, symbolize, typify; bear a meaning, have a significance etc. *n.*; have in mind, intend, purpose, resolve, destine, aim, direct, drive at; declare.

6. *v.* synonymize, express by a synonym etc. *n.,* use synonyms, give the synonym of, provide with synonyms, consignify.

7. *v.* understand, grasp the meaning etc. 518.4; understand by etc. (interpret) 522.6.

8. *adj.* meaning etc. *v.,* expressive, suggestive, allusive, indicative; significant, significative, significatory; meaningful, full of *or* pregnant with meaning, pregnant, eloquent, pithy; express, explicit etc. (manifest) 525.4, 5; graphic etc. (intelligible) 518.5, 6.

9. *adj.* literal, real, verbal; metaphrastic(al); strict, exact etc. (accurate) 494.11.

10. *adj.* meant etc. (implied) 526.7.

11. *adj.* synonymous, antonymous, synonymic(al), synonymatic; poecilonymic, polyonymal [rare], polyonymic [rare]; consignificant, consignificative [rare]; equivalent etc. (equal) 27.8, 9.

12. *adv.* meaningly, significantly etc. *adj.*; true to the fact; to that effect, that is to say etc. (in explanation) 522.9; evidently etc. 525.7; apparently etc. 448.8.

13. *adv.* literally, verbatim etc. 19.14.

517. Unmeaningness
(See 516. Meaning)

1. *n.* unmeaningness, meaninglessness, senselessness etc. *adj.*; unsignificancy, in-

---

516. Who found no substitute for sense.—T. S. ELIOT.   Take care of the sense and the sounds will take care of themselves.—CARROLL.   Our Playwright may show / In some fifth act what this wild Drama means.—TENNYSON.   A meaning suited to his mind.—TENNYSON.   A deep meaning often lies in old customs.—SCHILLER.   In every object there is inexhaustible meaning.—CARLYLE.   For the letter killeth, but the spirit giveth life.—BIBLE.
517. No one is exempt from talking nonsense: the misfortune is to do it solemnly.—MON-

significance *or* insignificancy; empty sound, *vox et praeterea nihil* [L.], "sounding brass and a tinkling cymbal" (Bible), "a tale told by an idiot, full of sound and fury, signifying nothing" (Shakespeare); "weasel words" (T. Roosevelt); dead letter; unintelligibility etc. 519.

2. *n.* nonsense, stuff, stuff and nonsense, pack of nonsense, balderdash, *niaiserie* [F.], flummery, trumpery, flapdoodle [coll.], twaddlement [rare], twaddle, twattle, twaddy [rare], twiddletwaddle, fudge, rubbish, trash, trash and nonsense, truck [coll.], poppycock [coll., U.S.], bosh [coll.], blatherskite [coll.], moonshine, fiddledeedee, fiddle-faddle [coll.]; buncombe *or* bunkum [coll., orig. U.S.], flumdiddle *or* flummadiddle [coll.], humbug, hocus-pocus; nonsensification.

piffle, applesauce, baloney [both U.S.], rot, tommyrot, hogwash, tosh [chiefly Eng.], kibosh, blah [U.S.], hooey, horsefeathers [U.S.], bushwa *or* bushwah, bunk, hokum [all slang]; foolishness, inanity etc. (absurdity) 497, (folly) 499.6.

3. *n.* nonsensical talk, voluble nonsense, foolish speech, unmeaning words, mere words, twaddle etc. *above,* blather, babble, babblement, bibble-babble, gabble, gibblegabble, blabber, jabber, gibber, gibberish, patter, prate, prattle, prattlement [rare], rattle, palaver, jargon, *bavardage* [F.], *baragouin* [F.], guff [slang], gash [Scot.], clack, gas [slang], hot air [slang], bull [slang, U.S.], blah *or* blahblah [slang, U.S.], gammon [coll.], skimble-scamble, slipslap [coll.], wishwash; rigmarole, rigmarolery; amphigory; fustian, bombast, rant, rodomontade, claptrap; doting etc. *v.,* dotage; dribble, drivel, drool, slaver.

4. *n.* scribbling etc. *v.,* scribble, scrabble, scribble-scrabble, scrawl, daub, pothookery, pothooks, hangers, pothooks and hangers.

5. *v.* mean nothing, be unmeaning etc. *adj.*; render nonsensical etc. *adj.,* nonsensify.

6. *v.* talk nonsense etc. *n.,* twattle, twaddle, twaddleize, babble, bibble-babble, gabble, gibblegabble, jabber, gibber, jibber [rare], patter, prate, prattle, fiddlefaddle [coll.], rattle, palaver, clack, gas [slang], bull [slang, U.S.], rodomontade, rant; dote, drivel, drool, slaver, utter drivel.

7. *v.* scribble, scrabble, scribble-scrabble, scrawl, scratch, daub.

8. *adj.* unmeaning, meaningless, senseless, without sense etc. (*see* sense etc. 516), nonsensical; not significant etc. 516.8, unsignificant, insignificant, unsignificative, insignificative [obs.]; trivial, trifling; inexpressive, unexpressive, expressionless; vacant, blank; inane etc. (absurd) 497.4, (foolish) 499.15.

9. *adj.* twaddly, twaddling, twattling [rare], rubbishy, trashy, washy, wishywashy [coll.], trumpery, fiddle-faddle [coll.], skimble-scamble, poppycockish [coll.].

10. *adj.* unmeant, unsignified, unimplied, unsuggested, unintimated, unindicated, unintended; tacit, unexpressed etc. 526.8.

11. *adj.* inexpressible, undefinable, ineffable, unutterable, unspeakable, unwhisperable, incommunicable, unmentionable, unhintable.

12. *int.* nonsense! etc. 497.5.

518. Intelligibility
(See 519. Unintelligibility)

1. *n.* intelligibility, intelligibleness, comprehensibleness etc. *adj.*; comprehensibility, apprehensibility, understandability, knowability, cognizability, explicability, conceivability, penetrability; distinguishability, recognizability; perspicuity, transpicuity, lucidity, limpidity, clarity, clearness; legibility, decipherability; definition, precision; plain speech *or* speaking, plain words, plain English.

2. *v.* be intelligible etc. *adj.,* lie on the surface, tell its own tale, speak for itself, speak volumes.

3. *v.* render intelligible etc. *adj.,* sim-

TAIGNE. It is a tale / Told by an idiot, full of sound and fury, / Signifying nothing.— SHAKESPEARE. Never deviates into sense.— DRYDEN. Alas! / Our dried voices, when / We whisper together / Are quiet and meaningless.—T. S. ELIOT. A little nonsense now and then / Is relished by the wisest men.

518. Unless one is a genius, it is best to aim at being intelligible.—A. HOPE. Understand a plain man in his plain meaning.— SHAKESPEARE. The more we understand individual objects the more we understand God. —SPINOZA. I want, by understanding myself, to understand others.—K. MANSFIELD

518.3 – 519.6

plify, clarify, clear, clear up, shed *or* throw light upon, illuminate, elucidate; popularize; explain etc. (interpret) 522.6.

4. *v.* understand, comprehend, apprehend, conceive, realize, ken |now chiefly Scot.], savvy [slang, U.S.], sense [chiefly coll., U.S.], take, take in, get [slang], get into *or* through one's head *or* thick head [coll. or slang], catch, catch on [coll.], catch *or* get the drift [slang], grasp, seize, apprehend ~, grasp *or* seize the meaning; collect; fathom, follow, blow wise to [slang, U.S.].

make, make out, make out clearly, see, discern, perceive; see daylight [coll.], see the light; penetrate, see through, see far into, see into *or* through a millstone; see at a glance, see with half an eye; catch *or* take in, get the idea [slang]; master; understand by etc. (interpret) 522.6; be intelligent etc. 498.7.

5. *adj.* intelligible, comprehensible, apprehensible, discoverable, knowable, cognizable, explicable, accountable, conceivable, penetrable; understandable, easily understood, easy to understand etc. *v.*; clear, clear as crystal, clear as day *or* daylight, clear as noonday *or* the sun at noonday; lucid, pellucid, limpid, perspicuous, transpicuous, transparent, translucent, luminous; plain, distinct, clear-cut, definite, precise, explicit, unequivocal, unambiguous, unmistakable, unconfused; legible, decipherable; distinguishable, recognizable; intelligible to the meanest capacity, for the million, popularized; exoteric(al); obvious, evident etc. (manifest) 525.4, 5.

6. *adj.* graphic, telling, vivid; expressive etc. (meaning) 516.8; illustrative etc. (interpretive) 522.8.

7. *adv.* intelligibly, understandably etc. *adj.*; in plain terms *or* words, in plain English.

519. Unintelligibility
(See 518. Intelligibility)

1. *n.* unintelligibility, unintelligibleness, incomprehensibleness etc. *adj.*; incomprehensibility, inapprehensibility, ununderstandability *or* inunderstandability, inconceivability, inexplicability, unknow-

ability, incognizability, inscrutability, undiscoverability, unrecognizability; undecipherability, illegibility; obscurity, obscuration; unclarity, imperspicuity; darkness of meaning; doubtful meaning; transcendentalism; unmeaningness etc. 517; ambiguity etc. 520; perplexity etc. (complexity) 59.3, (uncertainty) 475.2, 3; mystification etc. (concealment) 528; latency etc. 526.

2. *n.* (something unintelligible) Dutch, double Dutch, High Dutch [slang], Greek, Hebrew, Choctaw; sealed book; *dignus vindice nodus* [L.]; puzzle, riddle etc. (enigma) 533.2; knotty point, paradox etc. (dilemma) 704.4; gibberish etc. (unmeaning) 517, (jargon) 563.4; cryptograph etc. 528.5.

3. *v.* be unintelligible etc. *adj.*, be all Greek etc. *n.* to one, have a doubtful meaning, pass comprehension *or* understanding, require explanation etc. (*see* explanation etc. 522.1).

4. *v.* render unintelligible etc. *adj.*; obscure etc. (conceal) 528.10, (darken) 421.5; perplex, confuse etc. (complicate) 61.5, (bewilder) 475.8.

5. *v.* not understand etc. (*see* understand etc. 518.4), not understand all one knows [joc.]; not know what to make of, make nothing of, make neither head nor tail of, not be able to make head or tail of, not be able to account for, not have the first idea, not see for looking [joc.]; give up, pass [coll.]; miss, lose, lose the clue *or* clew; be at sea etc. (*see* at sea etc. 475.16), wonder etc. 870.2; "see through a glass, darkly" (Bible) etc. (be ignorant) 491.6; misunderstand etc. (misinterpret) 523.2.

6. *adj.* unintelligible, ununderstandable *or* inunderstandable, not understandable etc. (*see* understandable etc. 518.5), incomprehensible, inapprehensible, incognizable, unknowable, unfathomable, undiscoverable, indistinguishable, unrecognizable, unaccountable, inexplicable, inscrutable, impenetrable; insolvable, insoluble; inconceivable, inconceptible [obs.]; undecipherable *or* indecipherable, illegible; above ~, beyond *or* past comprehension *or* understanding, beyond one's depth, above one's head, above one's

---

Once one understands, action is easy.—SUN YAT-SEN.
519. God hath not made a creature that can comprehend him.—T. BROWNE. What we

do not understand we do not possess.—GOETHE. A perfect nonplus and baffle to all human understanding.—SOUTHEY.

bend [coll.], as Greek etc. *n.* to one; paradoxal, paradoxical; puzzling etc. (enigmatic) 533.6.

7. *adj.* obscure, imperspicuous, vague, indefinite, indeterminate, indistinct, ambiguous; unclear, clear as mud [joc.], muddy; dim, dark, clothed *or* shrouded in darkness, caliginous; shadowy, shadowed forth; clouded, cloudy, foggy, hazy, misty, seen through a mist; nebulous, nebulose; shrouded in mystery, mysterious, mystic(al) ; recondite, abstruse, profound, deep, steep [coll.], tough [coll.], heavy [coll.], acroamatic(al), esoteric, occult; metempiric(al) ; transcendental; hidden etc. 528.17, 18; latent etc. 526.6; crabbed, perplexed etc. (complex) 59.10; equivocal etc. 520.5.

8. *adj.* inexpressible etc. 517.11.

520. Equivocalness

1. *n.* equivocalness, equivocacy, equivocality, equivoque *or* equivoke; ambiguousness etc. *adj.*, ambiguity, ambiguity of meaning; duplexity in meaning, double meaning; homonymy; amphibology, amphilogy, amphilogism; ambilogy, ambiloquy [obs.] ; anagrammatism; sphinx, Delphic oracle; equivocation etc. (quibbling) 477.4, (falsehood) 544.

2. *n.* equivocal, equivocality, equivoque *or* equivoke; ambiguity, equivocal *or* ambiguous word *or* expression; *mot à double entente, double entente, double-entendre* [all F.] ; quibble, verbal quibble; paronomasia; paragram [rare], anagram, acrostic; homonym; amphibole [obs.], amphiboly, amphibologism; pun etc. (wordplay) 842.5; conundrum, riddle etc. (enigma) 533.2.

3. *v.* equivocate, use equivocal *or* ambiguous language, indulge in ambiguity etc. *n.*; prevaricate etc. (quibble) 477.8, (falsify) 544.5.

4. *v.* be equivocal etc. *adj.*, have two meanings etc. (*see* meaning etc. 516.1), admit of different interpretations.

5. *adj.* equivocal, equivocatory, equivoque *or* equivoke [obs.] ; ambiguous, ambifarious [obs.] ; double, duplex; amphibolous, amphibolic, amphibological; ambiloquent, ambiloquous [both obs.] ; homonymic, homonymous; doubtful, indeterminate etc. (uncertain) 475.9-15, obscure etc. 519.7; double-tongued etc. (dissembling) 544.8.

521. Figure of Speech

1. *n.* figure of speech, *façon de parler* [F.], figure, turn of expression, way of speaking; image, imagery; metaphor, metaphorical expression; tralatition, tralation [obs.] ; trope, metonymy, enallage, catachresis, synecdoche, antonomasia, antithesis, metathesis, metalepsis, apostrophe, litotes; onomatopoeia, onomatopoësis, onomatopoesy [rare]; simile, similitude; satire, irony; personification, prosopopoeia; apologue, parable, fable; allegory, allegorization; euphemism, euphuism; climax, anticlimax; hyperbole etc. (exaggeration) 549; exclamation etc. 580.5; interrogation etc. 461.10; expression etc. (phrase) 566; ornament etc. 577.

2. *v.* figure, symbolize, typify, exemplify, represent *or* express by metaphor etc. *n.*, metaphorize [rare], allegorize, fable, personify; simile [rare], similize, similitude, similitudinize; represent etc. 554.7.

3. *adj.* figurative, symbolic, typical, translative [rare] ; metaphorical, tropical, tralatitious, catachrestic(al), antonomastic(al), antithetic(al) ; parabolic(al), allegoric(al) ; allusive, referential; euphemistic(al), euphuistic(al) ; ironic(al), satiric(al) ; flowery, florid etc. (ornate) 577.6; comparative etc. 464.5.

4. *adv.* figuratively, metaphorically etc. *adj.*; figuratively speaking, so to say *or* speak, in a manner of speaking [coll.], as it were.

522. Interpretation
(See 523. Misinterpretation; also 524. Interpreter)

1. *n.* interpretation, definition, definement; explanation, explication; elucida-

---

520. A double meaning shows double sense.—Hood.   The sentences, . . . being strong on both sides, are equivocal.—Shakespeare.

521. When I can't talk sense, I talk metaphor.—J. Curran.   All slang is metaphor, and all metaphor is poetry.—Chesterton.   A tired metaphor.—Byron.   Language . . . what is it all but Metaphors?—Carlyle.

522. Explanations explanatory of things explained.—Lincoln.   A great interpreter of life ought not himself to need interpretation.—J Morley.   I hate definitions.—Disraeli.   He that can define . . . is the best man.—Em-

tion, dilucidation [obs.]; *éclaircissement* [F.], enucleation; exegesis, exposition, expounding; solution, resolution, answer, finding, key, clew *or* clue; light; diagnosis, prognosis, prophasis [Med.]; sense etc. (meaning) 516; deduction, inference etc. (judgment) 480; description etc. 594; dictionary etc. 593.4; reason, rationale etc. (motive) 615.

2. *n.* rendering, rendition, reddition; version, reading, lection; construction, construe [Gram.]; translation, translate [obs.]; paraphrase, rewording etc. *v.*, free translation; amplified rendering, amplification; metaphrase, literal ~, verbal *or* word-for-word translation; interlinear, interlineary, interlinear ~, interlineary *or* interlineal translation; gloss, key, clavis (*pl.* claves, clavises), Bohn; bone, pony [U.S.], horse [Eng.], trot [U.S.], cab [Eng.], crib [all school slang]; Targum, Chaldee Paraphrase.

3. *n.* accepted interpretation *or* meaning, conventional *or* usual interpretation, acception, acceptation, acceptance.

4. *n.* comment, commentary, commentation; note, annotation, note of explanation, explanatory note *or* comment; marginal [rare], marginal annotation; scholium (*pl.* scholia, scholiums), scholion; gloss, glossary; exegesis; exemplification, illustration; critique, review etc. (criticism) 480.3, (dissertation) 595.

5. *n.* (science of interpretation) exegetics, exegetic [rare]; hermeneutics, hermeneutic; symptomatology, semeiology, semeiotics [all Med.]; diagnostics, prognostics; physiognomics, physiognomy; metoposcopy; oneirology, oneirocritics, oneirocriticism; astrology, chiromancy, palmistry etc. (divination) 511.3, 4; paleography etc. (linguistics) 560.6.

6. *v.* interpret, explain, define, enucleate; expound, exposit; construe, put a construction on; infer, draw an inference; understand, understand by, be given to understand, gather from, take ~, receive *or* accept to mean; comment upon, commentate [rare], make explanatory comments; exemplify, illustrate; render, translate, transcribe, do ~, put *or* turn into, transfuse the sense of; read, spell out; read between the lines; discover the meaning of, make out, decipher, unravel etc. (solve) 481a.4; account for, assign as the cause of etc. (attribute to) 155.3; elucidate etc. (render intelligible) 518.3; tell, enlighten etc. (inform) 527.7; show, demonstrate etc. (manifest) 525.2.

7. *v.* paraphrase, rephrase, reword, restate, state differently, rehash; express broadly, give a free translation; Targum, Targumize.

8. *adj.* interpretative, interpretive; hermeneutic(al), explanatory, exegetic(al), elucidative; expositive, expository; explicative, explicatory; definitional, definitive; construable, inferential; illustrative, illustrational; exemplificative, exemplificational; translational, translative; translatory; commentatorial, commentarial; annotative, scholiastic; symptomatological, semeiological; diagnostic, prognostic; paraphrastic, metaphrastic; Targumic(al); informative etc. 527.13; descriptive etc. 594.7.

9. *adv.* in explanation etc. *n.*, to explain etc. *v.*, that is to say, *id est* [L.], i.e., that is, *videlicet* [L.], viz., *scilicet* [L.], scil., to wit, namely, in other words, in words to that effect, to that effect; strictly speaking; in plain words etc. 518.7.

523. Misinterpretation
(See 522. Interpretation)

1. *n.* misinterpretation, misapprehension, misunderstanding, misconception, misacceptation [obs.], misapplication, misrendering, mistranslation; misexplanation, misexplication; misconstruction, bad ~, wrong ~, erroneous *or* false construction, false coloring; perversion, distortion; eisegesis; abuse of terms, misuse of words, catachresis; misreading, misspelling; cross-reading; misjudgment etc. 481; mistake etc. (error) 495; misrepresentation etc. 555.

2. *v.* misinterpret, misapprehend, misunderstand, misconceive, misdeem, misapply, misrender, mistranslate; misconstrue, put a false construction on etc. *n.*, give a false coloring, give a false impression *or* idea; misexplain, explain wrongly; explain away; misspell, misread, mis-

---

ERSON. I wish he would explain his explanation.—BYRON. Live to explain thy doctrine by thy life.—PRIOR. If you wish to converse with me, define your terms.—VOLTAIRE.

523. To be great is to be misunderstood.—EMERSON. Great men are too often unknown, or, what is worse, misknown.—CARLYLE. Blunders round about a meaning.—POPE.

quote, mis-cite; garble, pervert, distort, detort [obs.], twist ~, wrench ~, wring ~, wrest ~, stretch or strain the sense or meaning; look through dark or rose-colored glasses; be out, be off or away off [slang]; misjudge etc. 481.5; mistake etc. (err) 495.7, 8; misrepresent etc. 555.4; not understand etc. 519.5.

3. *adj.* misinterpreted, misunderstood etc. *v.*, eisegetical, catachrestic(al); confused, perplexed, balled up [slang] etc. 59.8, 10.

4. *adv.* wrongly etc. (*see* wrong etc. 495.12–17); *à tort et à travers* [F.].

524. Interpreter
(See also 522. Interpretation)

1. *n.* interpreter, interpretator [obs.], interpretress [*fem.*]; expositor, expounder, exponent, explainer, explicator, exegete, definer, demonstrator; dragoman, drogman [obs.]; hermeneut, hermeneutist [both rare]; linguist [obs. exc. local], linguister or lingster [obs. exc. dial. U.S.]; interlocutor, interlocutress or interlocutrice or interlocutrix [*fem.*]; translator or translater, translatress or translatrix [*fem.*]; metaphrast, paraphrast; Oedipus, Joseph; oneirocritic; prophet etc. (oracle) etc. 513; go-between etc. (mediator) 724.2; spokesman etc. (deputy) 759; guide etc. 694.6; informant etc. 527.5; teacher etc. 540.

2. *n.* commentator, scholiast, annotator; glossarist, glossograph, glossographer; reviewer etc. (critic) 480.5; (dissertator) 595.3.

525. Manifestation
(See 526. Latency)

1. *n.* manifestation, manifestness etc. *adj.*; showing etc. *v.*, show, demonstration, presentation, exhibition, exposition, display, production, materialization, unfoldment; show-off [coll.], showup [coll.], showdown; expression, evincement, indication, evidence; *épanchement* [F.]; conspicuousness etc. *adj.*, conspicuity [rare]; salience or saliency, prominence, flagrance or flagrancy, revelation, divulgence etc. (disclosure) 529; publication etc. 531; exhibit etc. (spectacle) 448.2; perspicuity etc. (intelligibility) 518; visibility etc. 446.

2. *v.* manifest, show, shew [chiefly, Eng.], exhibit, demonstrate, display, materialize, present, set forth, produce, draw or bring out, trot out [coll.], bring forth, bring forward or to the front, bring to or into view, hold up to view, visibilize, hold up the mirror to, show up, expose, expose to view, make visible, show forth, bring to light, bring or call into notice, lay open, bare, make no mystery or secret of; uncover, unscreen, uncloak, undrape, unshroud, uncurtain, unveil, unmask, unfold, unroll, unfurl; make plain etc. *adj.*, bring out in bold, ~ strong or high relief.

set or place before one, lay before one's eyes, tell to one's face; manifest oneself, show one's face, show one's colors or true colors, wear one's heart upon one's sleeve, speak out; reveal, divulge etc. (disclose) 529.3, 4; proclaim etc. (publish) 531.7, 8; elicit etc. (discover) 481a.3; indicate, evince etc. (evidence) 467.7; translate, explain etc. (interpret) 522.6; decipher, decode etc. (solve) 481a.4.

3. *v.* be manifest etc. *adj.*, speak for itself, stand to reason, go without saying, be self-evident etc. *adj.*; leap to the eye, stare one in the face, loom large; appear on the horizon, rear its head; look, seem etc. (appear) 448.6.

4. *adj.* manifest, apparent, evident, obvious, plain, perspicuous, clear, defined, definite, distinct, palpable, patent, ostensible, avowed, express, explicit, autoptic(al), exoteric(al); visible, perceptible, perceivable, discernible, seeable, observable, noticeable; self-evident, self-evidential, self-evidencing; open, open-and-shut [coll., U.S.], open as day, overt; naked, bare, barefaced [arch.].

revealed, disclosed, not obscure or hidden, unobscure, unhidden, unconcealed, undisguised, unclouded, unshaded, uncovered, unveiled, unscreened, uncloaked, undraped, unshrouded, uncurtained, un-

---

524. I traversed a dominion / Whose spokesman spake out strong.—HARDY. Oh, . . . give me commentators plain, / Who with no deep researches vex the brain.—CRABBE. Every man's reason must be his guide.—CHESTERTON.

525. What makes all doctrines plain and clear? / About two hundred pounds a year.—BUTLER.

Thus manifest to sight the god appeared.—DRYDEN. For this thing was not done in a corner.—BIBLE. *Fari quae sentiat* [To say what one feels].—HORACE..

masked; unmistakable, not to be mistaken; manifestative, manifestive [rare]; demonstrative, demonstrational; clear or plain as day or daylight, clear or plain as noonday or the sun at noonday; plain as a pikestaff, plain as the nose on one's face, plain as the way to parish church [all coll.]; manifested etc. *v.*; conclusive, indubitable etc. (certain) 474.8–12; intelligible etc. 518.5.

5. *adj.* conspicuous, noticeable, notable, pronounced, salient, striking, prominent, in the foreground; bold, in bold ~, strong or high relief; notorious [obs.], flagrant, arrant, glaring, staring, stark-staring; showy, flaunting, daring etc. (ostentatious) 882.8, 9; loud [coll.], garish etc. (gaudy) 851.8.

6. *adj.* manifestable, capable of being shown, disclosable, producible; unconcealable, unhidable.

7. *adv.* manifestly, evidently, openly etc. *adj.*; before one's eyes or very eyes, under one's nose [coll.], to one's face, face to face; in the open, in open court or streets, in plain sight, in broad or open daylight, in the face of day or heaven, on the stage; in market overt, in the market place, at the cross-roads; aboveboard, on the table; cards on the table, *cartes sur table* [F.]; prima facie; at the first blush, at first sight; in set terms, without reserve; to all appearances etc. (apparently) 448.8.

8. *phr.* that is apparent etc. *adj.*; that goes without saying, it speaks for itself etc. *v.*; *res ipsa loquitur* [L.], *cela va sans dire* [F.], that is a matter of course, that is understood, the meaning lies on the surface, *cela saute aux yeux* [F.], that leaps to the eye, you can see it with half an eye, it needs no ghost to tell us.

526. Latency
(See 525. Manifestation)

1. *n.* latency, latence, latentness etc. *adj.*, latitancy [rare]; delitescence or delitescency, dormancy, quiescence, abeyance, inactivity, passivity, inertia; potentiality, possibility; inexpression; imperceptibility, darkness, adumbration; obscurity, obscuration; obscure factor, concealed being or nature, hidden or occult meaning, more than meets the eye or ear; nigger in the woodpile [coll.], snake in the grass; undercurrent; Delphic oracle; concealment etc. 528; secret etc. 533; invisibility etc. 447; silence etc. (taciturnity) 585; latent influence etc. 175.4.

2. *n.* implication, allusion, insinuation etc. (hint) 527.4.

3. *v.* be latent etc. *adj.*, lurk, couch, smolder, underlie, make no sign, escape observation, ~ detection, ~ notice, ~ recognition etc.; lie hid etc. (be concealed) 528.16.

4. *v.* imply, implicate; insinuate etc. (hint) 527.8; involve, connote etc. (mean) 516.5.

5. *v.* render latent etc. *adj.* latentize; mysticize [rare], symbolize; laugh in one's sleeve; keep back etc. (conceal) 528.10, 11.

6. *adj.* latent, latitant [rare]; lurking etc. *v.*, dormant, quiescent, inert, inactive; suspended, abeyant, in suspense or abeyance; potential, possible; delitescent, lying hid; hidden, secret, cryptic, occult etc. (concealed) 528.17–21; invisible etc. 447.4; obscure etc. 519.7.

7. *adj.* implied, implicated, meant, inferred, intimated, insinuated, hinted, suggested; implicit, tacit, understood; implicative, implicatory, implicational; inferential, by inference or implication; insinuant [rare], insinuative, insinuatory; allusive, allusory [obs.]; constructive, construed; suggestive, indicative; indirect, involved.

8. *adj.* unexpressed, not expressed, unmentioned, unpronounced, unsaid, unbreathed, untalked-of, untold, unsung, unproclaimed, unpublished, unwritten; unexposed etc. (unrevealed) 528.18; unsignified etc. (unmeant) 517.10.

9. *adv.* latently etc. *adj.*, on the tip of one's tongue, between the lines, below the surface; secretly etc. 528.24.

527. Information
(See 528. Concealment; also 532. News)

1. *n.* information, enlightenment, light

---

526. *Tacitum vivit sub pectore vulnus* [The wound unuttered lives deep within the breast]. —VERGIL.   Nothing is secret, that shall not be made manifest.—BIBLE.   A man without passion is only a latent force.—AMIEL.   The apple already lies potentially in the blossom.— LOWELL.   Latencies of violence.—HUXLEY.
527. To give me information is thy office.— EURIPIDES.   I only ask for information.— DICKENS.   Benignant information is hi hobby.—GUITERMAN.   I'll tell the world.

527.1 – 527.11

or lights, acquaintance, intelligence, knowledge; know, dope, goods, info [all slang]; communication, intercommunication; telling etc. *v.*, account, declaration, statement, word, report, mention, specification; notice, notification; intimation, monition; presentment, representation; indirect *or* incidental information, side light; instruction etc. (teaching) 537; disclosure etc. 529; description etc. 594; announcement, publicity etc. (publication) 531; message etc. (news) 532; betrayal etc. 940.4.

2. *n.* inside information *or* facts, actual facts, private *or* confidential information; inside, inside dope, low-down, real know, hot tip [all slang].

3. *n.* tip, tip-off, point, pointer [all coll.]; steer, office [both slang]; whisper, passing word, word in the ear, flea in the ear [coll.]; word to the wise, *verbum sapienti* [L.]; advice, aviso, advisement [arch.]; warning etc. 668.

4. *n.* hint, intimation, indication, suggestion, suspicion, inkling; glimmer, glimmering; cue, clue *or* clew, scent; implication, inference, allusion, insinuation, innuendo; subaudition, subauditur; telltale; gentle hint, broad hint; reminder etc. 505.5.

5. *n.* informant, teller, apprizer, intelligencer [now rare], enlightener, annunciator, reporter, notifier, adviser etc. *v.*; mouthpiece, spokesman; communicator, communicant; authority, witness; tipper, tipster [coll.], tout *or* touter [slang]; *amicus curiae* [L.]; newsmonger etc. 532.5; harbinger, herald etc. (messenger) 534, (precursor) 64; exponent, explainer etc. (interpreter) 524; guide etc. 594.6.

6. *n.* informer, snitch [slang], snitcher [chiefly slang], tattler, tattletale [coll.], telltale, talebearer, blab, blabber, blabberer [obs. exc. dial.], blab-mouth [slang], betrayer, delator, squealer [coll.], squeaker [slang], peacher [slang]; stool pigeon [coll.], stoolie [slang]; nark [slang], *mouchard* [F.], spy, police spy, undercover man, spotter [cant, U.S.]; eavesdropper, peeper, Peeping Tom; complainant etc. (accuser) 938.2; traitor etc. 949.3.

7. *v.* inform, give by way of information, tell, acquaint, impart, communicate, divulge [rare], convey the knowledge of, make known, apprize *or* apprise, advise, enlighten, inform *or* tell of, acquaint with, impart *or* communicate to, mention, let fall, express, represent, present, put *or* set forth, set ~, lay *or* put before, let one know, have one to know, give one to understand, put in *or* into one's head, put one in possession of; notify, give notice *or* notification, bring ~, send ~, leave *or* write word; report, give a report of, report progress.

instruct etc. (teach) 537.9–11; explain etc. (interpret) 522.6; disclose etc. 529.3, 4; announce, annunciate etc. (publish) 531.7, 8, (affirm) 535.3; retell, give an account of etc. (describe) 594.5; specify, point out etc. (direct attention to) 457.7; speak etc. 582.6.

8. *v.* hint, intimate, indicate, signify, suggest, insinuate, give ~, drop *or* throw out a hint, give an inkling of; imply, implicate; infer, leave an inference; allude to, make an allusion to, hint at, glance at; prompt, give the cue; remind etc. 505.15.

9. *v.* tip, tip off, give one a tip [all coll.] etc. *n.*; tip the wink, give the office [both slang], give a pointer to [coll., U.S.], give points to [coll.]; let in on [slang], let *or* put next to [slang, U.S.], put on to [slang, U.S.], give confidential information etc. *n.*, mention privately *or* confidentially; breathe, whisper, whisper in the ear, put a flea in one's ear [coll.]; make a sign etc. (signal) 550.20; warn etc. 668.6.

10. *v.* inform on *or* against, tell on [coll.] betray, tattle, blab; squeal, peach, split, put the finger on [U.S.], blow, blow the gaff [Naut.], cross up [U.S.], doublecross, sell out, nark, rat, stool, blow ~, squeal etc. on [all slang]; act as a talebearer, turn informer etc. *n.*; turn king's *or* queen's evidence [Eng.], turn state's evidence [U.S.]; divulge etc. (disclose) 529.3, 4; accuse etc. 938.4; testify against etc. 969.10.

11. *v.* become *or* be informed of, get wise to [slang] etc. 490.13–15; become alive *or* awake to, awaken to, open one's eyes to; come to one's knowledge, come to *or* reach one's ears; hear, overhear; get scent of etc. *n.*; learn etc. 539.3; know etc. 490.9, 10; understand, gather from

---

SHAKESPEARE. Whoever you are, to you endless announcements!—WHITMAN. A little bird told me. *Scire facias* [Let it be known].

etc. (interpret) 522.6; be disclosed etc. 529.6.

12. *adj.* informed etc. 490.15; informed of, in the know [slang], wise to [slang] etc. (aware of) 490.13.

13. *adj.* informative, informing etc. *v.*, informatory, informational; communicative, communicatory; intelligential, intelligentiary [obs.]; advisory, advisatory; monitory, monitorial; nuncupative, nuncupatory [obs.]; instructive etc. (educational) 537.12; revelatory etc. (disclosive) 529.8; expository etc. (interpretative) 522.8; annunciatory, proclamatory etc. (promulgatory) 531.11.

14. *adj.* hinted, insinuated etc. (implied) 526.7.

15. *adv.* from information received, according to reports *or* rumor, from notice given, as a matter of general information, by common report, according to *or* from what one can gather; in the air, by the underground route; as they say etc. 532.10.

528. Concealment
(See 529. Disclosure; also 533. Secret)

1. *n.* concealment, hiding etc. *v.*, secretion, burial, occultation, mystification; invisibility etc. 447; seclusion etc. 893.2; ambush, hiding place etc. 530; screen etc. 424.3; mask etc. 225.11; disguise etc. 545.5; pretext etc. 619; dissimulation etc. 544.2; latency etc. 526.

2. *n.* secrecy, secretiveness, closeness etc. *adj.*; reticence *or* reticency, reserve, reservation; mental reservation, *arrière-pensée* [F.]; privacy, privity [obs.]; huggermugger [arch.], huggermuggery; suppression, repression; evasion, subterfuge; misprision, negative *or* positive misprision, misprision of felony [Law]; dark, underhand secrecy, underhand dealing; seal of secrecy; Freemasonry, Freemasonism; aside; silence etc. (taciturnity) 585; secret etc. 533; white lie etc. (half-truth) 546.3.

3. *n.* stealth, furtiveness etc. *adj.*; stalking, still hunt [U.S.]; slyness etc. (cunning) 702.

4. *n.* mysticism, occultism etc. (esoteric sciences) 994.

5. *n.* cryptography, cryptology, steganography; symbolism; cryptograph, cryptogram, steganogram; cipher, code, cable code; secret ~, invisible *or* sympathetic ink; palimpsest, *codex rescriptus* [L.].

6. *n.* (something concealed) nigger in the woodpile [coll.], bug under the chip [coll., U.S.]; snake in the grass, *anguis in herba* [L.]; stowaway, blind baggage [slang]; masked battery; sealed book; enigma etc. (secret) 533; rocks, reefs etc. (hidden danger) 667.

7. *n.* masquerader, masker, masquer [rare], mask, domino; mummer, mime, mimer, mimester [rare], mimic; disguiser, guiser [Scot. and dial. Eng.], guisard [Scot.]; incognito, incognita [*fem.*]; wolf in sheep's clothing etc. (impostor) 548.3.

8. *n.* secret agent, emissary, undercover man; spy, espier, spial [obs.]; spotter [cant, U.S.]; scout, tout [slang], reconnoiterer.

9. *n.* detective, investigator, sleuth [U.S.], man hunter, Sherlock Holmes; hawkshaw, sleuthhound, beagle [all coll.]; tec, dick [U.S.], gumshoe, gumshoe man, flatfoot, busy, nose [all slang]; police detective *or* spy, *mouchard* [F.], plain-clothes man [coll.], bull *or* fly bull [slang, U.S.]; spotter [cant, U.S.]; hotel detective, dick, house dick [slang, U.S.]; arson investigator; federal agent, G-man [coll., U.S.]; Federal Bureau of Investigation, F.B.I. [U.S.]; constable etc. 745.10.

10. *v.* conceal, hide, secrete, cache, stash [crim. slang, U.S.], plant [slang], ensconce, cover, cover up, screen, cloak, shroud, veil, curtain, blind; bury, sink; render invisible; put *or* keep out of sight *or* view, screen from sight *or* observation, throw a veil over, draw the veil, draw *or* close the curtain; mask, bemask, disguise, camouflage, dissemble, counterfeit.

obscure, cloud, becloud, befog, shade, keep in *or* throw into the shade, keep in the background; eclipse, occult, occul-

---

528. How cunningly nature hides every wrinkle of her inconceivable antiquity under roses and violets and morning dew!—EMERSON. It is more difficult to disguise feelings which one has than to feign those which one has not.—LA ROCHEFOUCAULD. Hide their ignominious heads.—HOMER. False face must hide what the false heart doth know.—SHAKESPEARE. Seal up your lips and give no words but mum: / The business asketh silent secrecy.—SHAKESPEARE. But let concealment, like a worm i'

tate; seal, lock, seal up, lock up, bottle up; cover up one's tracks, hide one's trail; hide one's light under a bushel, bury one's talent in a napkin; fence with a question; latentize etc. 526.5; shut one's eyes to etc. (ignore) 460.5.

11. *v.* keep secret, keep dark; keep it a deep, dark secret [coll.]; keep close *or* snug, keep back, keep to oneself, keep from, withhold, reserve, not let it go further, not tell, not breathe a word *or* syllable about, not give away [coll.] etc. 529.3, 4, "tell it not in Gath" (Bible), keep one's own counsel, make no sign, not let the right hand know what the left is doing; suppress, stifle, smother, muffle, hush up, huggermugger; keep *or* leave in the dark, keep in ignorance; hold one's tongue etc. (not speak) 585.3.

12. *v.* speak covertly, speak in privacy, mention privately; say under the breath, breathe, whisper, whisper in the ear.

13. *v.* hoodwink, blindfold etc. (blind) 442.3; bamboozle [coll.] etc. (deceive) 545.7, 10.

14. *v.* mystify, puzzle etc. (perplex) 475.8.

15. *v.* code, codify, use a code *or* cipher.

16. *v.* be concealed etc. *adj.,* not be seen; eclipse, suffer an eclipse, go into an eclipse; occult, occultate; retire from sight, hide oneself, hide out [coll.], go *or* stay in hiding, lie hid *or* hidden, lie in ambush, lie perdu, lie snug *or* close, lie low [coll.]; play at bopeep *or* hide and seek, hide in holes and corners; couch, lurk, sneak, skulk, slink, prowl, steal, gumshoe [slang, U.S.]; seclude oneself etc. 893.6.

17. *adj.* concealed etc. *v.,* hid, hidden, perdu; buried, underground; recondite, dark, abstruse, obscure, cryptic(al), mystic(al); mysterious, occult, esoteric, anagogic(al); arcane, arcanal; cabalic, cabalistic(al); clouded, wrapped in clouds, in a cloud, ∼ fog, ∼ mist *or* haze; in darkness, in the shade *or* dark; behind a screen etc. 424.3; under an eclipse, in eclipse; latent etc. 526.6; secluded etc. 893.10; invisible, indistinct etc. 447.4, 5.

18. *adj.* unrevealed, undisclosed, undivulged, unexposed, unapparent, unvisible *or* invisible, unseen, unperceived, unspied, undiscovered, unexplored, untraced, untracked, unexplained, unsolved; untold etc. (unexpressed) 526.8; unknown etc. 491.14.

19. *adj.* in hiding etc. *n.,* in ambush, in a dark corner, under cover, lying hid etc. *v.,* latitant [rare].

20. *adj.* disguised etc. *v.,* in disguise; incognito (*fem.* incognita), incog [coll.]; counterfeit etc. (spurious) 545.13.

21. *adj.* secret, covert, clandestine, huggermugger, surreptitious, undercover, underground, hole-and-corner [coll.], furtive, obreptitious, stealthy, feline, sly, skulking etc. *v.*; underhand, underhanded; private, privy; auricular, confidential; inviolate, inviolable; irrevealable, unrevealable; mysterious, arcane etc. above 528.17.

22. *adj.* secretive, reticent, reserved, evasive; close-mouthed, uncommunicative etc. (taciturn) 585.4.

23. *adj.* cryptogrammic, cryptogrammatic(al); cryptographal, cryptographic(al); steganographic(al).

24. *adv. etc.* secretly, surreptitiously etc. *adj.*; in secret, *in petto* [L.], *en tapinois* [F.], in *or* up one's sleeve, under the cloak of, nobody the wiser; in private, in privy, *in camera* [L.]; aside, *sotto voce* [It.], under the breath, with bated breath, in a whisper; in silence, *sub silentio* [L.]; behind the scenes, behind the curtain, ∼ a screen etc. (*see* curtain, screen etc. 424.2), in the dark etc. *adj.,* in a corner, in the background; behind the veil, behind the veil of secrecy.

behind *or* with closed doors, *januis clausis* [L.], *à huis clos* [F.], in secret session; under the rose, *sub rosa* [L.]; underground, underboard, under the table; under cover, *à couvert* [F.]; underhand, underhandedly; by stealth, on the sly [coll.], *à la dérobée* [F.], like a thief in the night, behind one's back; by a side door, by a side wind; in holes and corners, in a hole-and-corner way [both coll.]; huggermugger, in huggermugger [arch.].

into the eternal secret, into the realms supersensible, into the supreme mystery; beyond the veil, beyond mortal ken, hid from mortal vision; incognito etc. *adj.*; latently etc. 526.9.

25. *adv.* confidentially etc. *adj.,* in confidence, in strict confidence, under the seal of secrecy, off the record [slang, U.S.];

529. Disclosure
(See 528. Concealment)

1. *n.* disclosure, revealing etc. *v.*, revealment, revelation; divulgence, divulgement, divulgation, evulgation; exposition, exposure, exposé; discovery, retection [obs.], deterration [obs.]; showup, showdown; denouement, catastrophe; telling etc. (information) 527; manifestation etc. 525; publication etc. 531; disillusionment etc. (undeception) 545a.

2. *n.* confession, shrift, acknowledgment, admission, allowance [now rare], concession; avowal, avowance; confession from the heart, *épanchement de cœur* [F.]; confessional, confessionary; repentance etc. 950; apology etc. 952.2.

3. *v.* disclose, reveal, discover, unconceal, unhide, uncover, unveil, unscreen, uncloak, undrape, unshroud, uncurtain, unfold, unroll, unkennel, draw ~, draw aside ~, lift ~, raise ~, remove *or* tear the veil *or* curtain, remove the cover *or* screen, open, open up, lay open, bare, lay bare, expose, show up, bring to light; unmask, dismask, raise ~, lift ~, drop ~, remove *or* throw off the mask; unseal, remove *or* break the seal; make evident *or* manifest, evidence, evince; show, shew [chiefly Eng.]; inform etc. 527.7; manifest etc. 525.2; open the eyes of, disabuse etc. (undeceive) 545a.2.

4. *v.* divulge, divulgate, evulgate; reveal, make known, tell, breathe, whisper, utter, give utterance to, vent, give vent to, out with [coll.], come out with, come out with it [coll.], come it [slang], let fall *or* drop, let on [coll.], let slip, blurt out, let out, let the cat out of the bag [coll.], spill, spill the beans [slang], leak [slang], blab, tattle.

betray, peach [slang], beef [slang], split [slang], let into the secret, let in on, betray *or* reveal a secret *or* confidence, give away [coll.], give away the racket [slang], give the show away [slang], blow the gaff [Naut. slang], tell tales, tell tales out of school, talk out of turn [crim slang, U.S.]; inform on etc. 527.10; break the news, make public etc. (publish) 531.7, 8; talk etc. 582.6.

5. *v.* confess, break down and confess [slang], 'fess up [slang], acknowledge, admit, allow, avow, concede, grant, own, own up [coll.], "own the soft impeachment" (Sheridan), cough up [slang], acknowledge the corn [slang, U.S.], throw off all disguise, turn inside out.

make a clean breast, make a clean breast of it, unbosom oneself, get it out of one's chest [slang], get it out of one's system [slang], out with it [coll.], spit it out [coll.], open up [coll.], open on, lay bare one's mind, unburden *or* disburden one's mind, ~ conscience *or* heart, say *or* speak the truth, talk [coll.], sing [slang, U.S.], squeak [slang], squawl [slang, U.S.], come clean [slang, U.S.], show one's hand *or* cards, lay ~, place on, put one's cards on the table; tell the truth etc. 543.2; repent etc. 950.3.

6. *v.* be disclosed etc. *adj.*, transpire, become known, discover itself, come to light, out, come ~, leak ~, ooze ~, creep ~, peep *or* crop out, ~ forth *or* up, break forth, break through the clouds, show its face, show its colors *or* true colors, flash on the mind; appear, come in sight etc. (become visible) 446.2; reach the ear etc. (become informed of) 527.11.

7. *adj.* disclosed, revealed, unconcealed, unhidden etc. *v.*; not concealed etc. 528.15; open etc. (manifest) 525.4.

8. *adj.* disclosive [rare], divulgatory, revealing etc. *v.*, revelative, revelatory, revelational; expositive, expository; confessional, confessionary, confessory; informative etc. 527.13.

530. Ambush, Hiding
(See also 528. Concealment)

Place or Means of Concealment.—1. *n.* ambush, ambushment, ambuscade, ambuscado [arch.], *guet-apens* [F.]; lurk, lurking hole *or* place; blind, stalking horse; pitfall etc. (snare) 545.4, 667.2.

2. *n.* hiding place, hiding, hidlings o

---

529. Confession of our faults is the next thing to innocency.—Publilius. To say: "I am Lazarus, come from the dead, / Come back to tell you all, I shall tell you all."—T. S. Eliot. Mordre wol out, certein, it wol nat faille.—Chaucer. Confession is good for the soul. A fault confessed is half redressed.

530. In masks outrageous and austere.—1 Wylie. Who may, in the ambush of m name, strike home.—Shakespeare.

hidlins [Scot., Ir., and dial. Eng.], hideaway, hide-out [coll.], concealment, subterfuge, cover, secret place, recess, corner, dark corner, hole, hidie-hole [Scot.], holes and corners; covert, coverture, undercovert; cache, stash [crim. slang, U.S.]; cubby, cubbyhole; closet, abditory [rare], *oubliette* [F.], crypt, vault; fraid hole [slang, U.S.], funk hole [slang]; retreat etc. (refuge) 666.3, (resort) 189.13; safe, strongbox etc. (treasury) 802.

3. *n.* screen, veil etc. (cover) 223.2, (shelter) 424; cloud etc. 353.5; mask etc. 225.11; disguise etc. 545.5.

4. *n.* covert way, secret passage, backway, back door, sally port, side door; back stairs, *escalier dérobé* [F.]; underground route, underground railroad, grapevine, grapevine telegraph.

5. *v.* ambush, ambuscade, lie in ambush etc. 528.16; lie in wait for, lurk, waylay; set a trap for etc. (ensnare) 545.9.

531. Publication

1. *n.* publication, publishing etc. *v.*, publishment; propagation, promulgation, evulgation, ventilation, dissemination, diffusion, circulation, broadcasting etc. *v.*; issue, issuance; proclamation, proclaim [rare]; pronouncement, pronunciamento, *pronunciamiento* [Sp.]; announcement, annunciation, enunciation; declaration, indiction [rare], manifesto; notice, notification; report, reportage; public announcement, general notice etc.; divulgation etc. (disclosure) 529; edict etc. (decree) 741.3.

2. *n.* edition, issue, number; impression, imprint, print; printing etc. 591; book, newspaper, magazine etc. (a publication) 593.

3. *n.* publicity, publicness, notoriety, limelight [coll.], spotlight [coll.], *réclame* [F.], currency, flagrancy, cry, hue and cry, bruit [arch.], report; *vox populi* [L.]; publicity story, press notice *or* report, write-up [slang], blurb [coll.], puff [chiefly coll.], plug [slang, U.S.], ballyhoo [slang].

4. *n.* advertisement, ad [coll.]; notice, public notice; reader, reading notice; want ad [coll.], for-want advertisement; teaser [slang, U.S.]; advertising matter, literature [coll.]; bill, *affiché* [F.], placard, poster, banner [cant]; sheet, six ~, twenty-four etc. sheet; leaf, leaflet, handbill, dodger, flyer *or* flier, folder; broadside, broadsheet; circular, circular letter; encyclical, encyclical letter; program, programma; spread, double-page spread; agony column [coll.]; sky advertising, skywriting.

5. *n.* publisher, publisheress [*fem.*]; promulgator *or* promulgater, disseminator; propagator, propagatress *or* propagatrix [*fem.*]; proclaimer, proclaimant, proclamator; announcer, annunciator, enunciator, nunciate; reporter etc. (journalist) 593.16.

6. *n.* publicizer, publicist, publicity man *or* agent, press agent; advertiser, adman, adsmith [joc.], ad writer [coll.], copy writer; blurbist [coll.], plugger [slang, U.S.], booster [slang, U.S.]; ballyhoo, ballyhooer, ballyhoo man [all slang]; skywriter; billposter, bannerman [cant]; sandwich boy *or* man; adcraft [coll.].

7. *v.* publish, publish abroad, air, vent, ventilate, blow propagate, promulgate, circulate, spread, spread about *or* abroad, broadcast, diffuse, disseminate, noise abroad, bruit, bruit about, put about, bandy about, hawk about, whisper *or* buzz about, rumor, rumor about, cry about *or* abroad; divulge, divulgate, evulgate; make known, make public, bring ~, lay *or* drag before the public, bring *or* drag into the open, give out, give to the world.

put forth *or* forward, put ~, give *or* send forth, get out, issue, emit, broach, utter, tell, declare, voice, speak *or* talk of, give tongue; announce, annunciate, enunciate; proclaim, proclaim from the housetops, proclaim at the crossroads *or* market cross, proclaim at Charing Cross; herald, heraldize [rare]; blaze *or* blazon, blaze *or* blazon about *or* abroad; sound a trumpet, trumpet *or* thunder forth, announce with flourish of trumpets *or* beat of drum; cry out, raise a cry *or* hue and cry; report, cover [cant]; give tidings

---

531. Thou god of our Idolatry, the Press.—COWPER.   A chiel's amang ye takin' notes / And, faith, he'll prent it!—BURNS.   All I know is just what I read in the papers.—W.

ROGERS.   Report me and my cause aright / To the unsatisfied.—SHAKESPEARE.   *Semel emissum volat irrevocabile verbum* [A word once spoken flies away never to be called back]. —HORACE.

of, break the news, set news afloat, raise a report.

8. *v.* publicize, give publicity etc. *n.*, advertise, blurb [coll.], plug [slang, U.S.], boost [slang], ballyhoo [slang]; bring *or* drag into the limelight, throw the spotlight on [both coll.]; press-agent [coll.], act as press agent etc. *n.*; post, post up, post bills etc. *n.*, poster, placard; circularize; skywrite.

9. *v.* be published etc., be *or* become public etc. *adj.*, break [cant], divulge, come out, issue, go forth, find vent, take air, see the light; go ~, fly ~, buzz *or* blow about, get about *or* abroad, get afloat, acquire currency, pass current, go the rounds, go through the length and breadth of the land, pass from mouth to mouth, spread, circulate; run *or* spread like wildfire.

10. *adj.* published etc. *v.*, public, made public; notorious, flagrant, arrant; in circulation, current etc. (reported) 532.8; open etc. (manifest) 525.4.

11. *adj.* promulgatory, propagatory; proclamatory, annunciatory, annunciative [rare], enunciatory, enunciative, nunciative [rare]; declaratory, declarative; circular, encyclic(al).

12. *adv.* publicly etc. *adj.*, in public, in open court, with open doors; in the limelight *or* spotlight [coll.]; for publication.

532. News
(See also 527. Information)

1. *n.* news, tidings, intelligence, information, word; advice, advisement [arch.], aviso; news item, piece *or* budget of news; article, news article, story, copy [cant]; beat, scoop [both cant]; print, newsprint, letterpress; good news, glad tidings, gospel, evangel; fresh news, latest information, spot news [slang]; old *or* stale news, old story, retold story, warmed-over cabbage [coll.], *réchauffé* [F.], chestnut [coll.]; war news etc. 722.8; newspaper etc. 593.6.

2. *n.* message, dispatch, word, communication, communiqué, errand [arch.], intermessage; bulletin, newsbill [Eng.]; express; embassy, embassage, ambassade *or* embassade [arch.]; pneumatogram; letter, note etc. (correspondence) 592; telegram, telephone call etc. 532a.2, 3; messenger etc. 534.

3. *n.* report, reportage [rare], rumor, flying rumor, hearsay, on-dit, gossip, piece of gossip, buzz, whisper, cry, bruit [arch.], talk, by-talk, gup [Anglo-Ind.], common talk *or* gossip, village *or* town talk, talk of the village *or* town, table *or* tea talk, topic of the day, idea afloat, news stirring; babble, babblement; tattle, tittle-tattle; chat, chitchat; canard, extravagant *or* absurd report, hoax; gossipry, gossipred, newsmongery; grapevine, grapevine telegraph, underground route.

4. *n.* scandal, malicious gossip, dirt [slang]; scandalmongery, scandalmongering, scandalmonging; *scandalum magnatum* [L.]; slander, defamation etc. (detraction) 934.

5. *n.* newsmonger, scandalmonger, gossip, quidnunc, busybody, busy [slang], tabby [coll.], granny [derog.], talebearer, telltale, tattletale [coll.], tattler, tittle-tattler, babbler, blab, blabber, blabberer [obs. exc. dial.], chatterer; Paul Pry etc. (inquisitive) 455.2; meddler etc. 682.11; muckraker, slanderer etc. 936.1.

6. *v.* report, rumor etc. (publish) 531.7, 8.

7. *v.* gossip, tattle, tittle [now chiefly dial.], tittle-tattle, prate, prattle, babble, chat, chatter, clatter, talk, tell idle tales, tell tales out of school; whisper about etc. (publish) 531.7.

8. *adj.* reported, rumored etc. (*see* report, rumor etc. 531.7); publicly reported, currently rumored, current, rife, afloat, floating, going about, in circulation, in every one's mouth, all over the town; many-tongued; published etc. 531.10.

9. *adj.* with news value, newsy [coll.], snappy [slang].

10. *adv.* as they say, as it is said, as the story goes *or* runs, as the fellow says [coll., U.S.], it is said; by common report etc. 527.15.

---

532. *Spargere voces in vulgum ambiguas* [To spread deceptive reports among the people].— VERGIL.   As cold waters to a thirsty soul, so is good news from a far country.—BIBLE. This news is old enough, yet it is every day's news.—SHAKESPEARE.   Some tell, some hear, some judge of news, some make it.—DRYDEN. When a dog bites a man that is not news, but when a man bites a dog that is news.—J. BOGART [?].   Foul whisperings are abroad.

532a. Telephone and Wireless Communication

1. *n.* telephony, telephonic transmission; telegraphy, telegraphic transmission; wireless, wireless telephony, wireless telegraphy; radiophony, radiotelephony; radiotelegraphy; television; electricity etc. 158a.

2. *n.* telephone call, phone call [coll.], call, telepheme [rare], telephone message.

3. *n.* telegram, telegraph, telegrapheme, telegraphic dispatch etc. 532.2; wireless telegram, wireless [coll.], wire [coll.]; cablegram, cable; radiotelegram, radiogram, radio [coll.], marconigram; lettergram, letter telegram, night letter; heliogram; Morse code etc. (code) 550.15.

4. *n.* radiobroadcast, radiocast, broadcast, broadcasting etc. *v.*; television broadcast, telecast; electrical transcription.

5. *n.* (instruments) telephone, phone [coll.]; magnetotelephone, microtelephone, monotelephone, pantelephone, radiotelephone, thermotelephone; dial telephone; telegraph, telegraph instrument, wireless telegraph, wireless; semaphore ~, electric *or* Morse telegraph; dial telegraph, disk telegraph, needle telegraph, writing telegraph, multiple telegraph, indicator telegraph, field telegraph, typotelegraph, autotelegraph, pantelegraph, magnetotelegraph; telegraphone, telephonograph; heliograph.

radio, wireless [chiefly Eng.]; radiophone, radiotelephone, wireless telephone; radiotelegraph; line radio, wired radio, wired wireless [chiefly Eng.]; set, receiving set, receiver, radio receiver; transmitting set, transmitter, radio transmitter; transmitting station, radio station; microphone, mike [slang]; phone, headphone, earphone [coll.]; receiver, telephone receiver; telegraph pole, telephone wires etc. (electricity) 158a.8.

6. *n.* telephoner, phoner [coll.]; telegrapher, telegraph operator, telegraph clerk, sparks [slang]; amateur telegrapher, ham [slang]; broadcaster, radiobroadcaster, radiocaster; radio electrician, radiotrician; volume engineer; announcer; radio listener, listener-in [slang]; radiobserver, looker-in [slang]; televisor.

7. *v.* telephone, phone [coll.], call, call up, put in *or* make a telephone call etc. *n.*

8. *v.* telegraph, telegram, wireless, [coll.], wire [coll.]; cable; radio, radiotelegraph, radiograph, radiogram.

9. *v.* broadcast, radiobroadcast, radiocast, wireless [chiefly Eng.], transmit, send, put *or* go on the air [coll.]; telecast, televise.

10. *adj.* telephonic, telegraphic, wireless, radiophonic, radiotelephonic, radiotelegraphic; televisional, televisual.

533. Secret
(See also 528. Concealment)

1. *n.* secret, secrecy [rare], privacy [rare], privity [obs.], private [obs.], private *or* personal matter, secret *or* private communication, confidential *or* privileged communication [Law], confidence, reservation [obs.]; dead secret, deep *or* profound secret; deep, dark secret [coll.]; sealed book; secrets of the prison house; skeleton in the closet, ~ cupboard *or* house; secretiveness etc. 528.2.

2. *n.* enigma, mystery, arcanum (*pl.* arcana), puzzle, crossword, crossword *or* jigsaw puzzle; problem, puzzling *or* baffling problem, why, question, enigmatic question, point to be solved, poser, sticker [slang], grueler [slang, Eng.]; graveler, floorer, stumper, staggerer, enough to puzzle a Philadelphia lawyer [U.S.], tough proposition [all coll.]; nut to crack, hard nut to crack; riddle, conundrum, charade, rebus; mystery of mysteries, *arcanum arcanorum* [L.]; Asian mystery; the Sphinx, riddle of the Sphinx; *crux criticorum* [L.]; knotty point, vexed question etc. (dilemma) 704.4; *terra incognita* [L.] etc. (ignorance) 491.2; intricacy, labyrinth etc. (complexity) 59.3; inexplicability etc. (unintelligibility) 519; anagram etc. 561.5.

3. *v.* keep secret etc. (conceal) 528.10, 11.

532a. This is a marvel of the universe: / To fling a thought across a stretch of sky.—J. PEABODY.   What hath God wrought!—MORSE.

533. There are no secrets better kept than the secrets that everybody guesses.—SHAW. Every human creature is constituted to be that profound secret and mystery to every other.—DICKENS.   Mum, it is a secret.—BOSWELL-JOHNSON.   The secret things belong unto the Lord our God.—BIBLE.

4. *v.* mystify, puzzle etc. (perplex) 475.8.
5. *adj.* secret, hidden etc. 528.17–23.
6. *adj.* enigmatical, puzzling etc. (*see* puzzle etc. 475.8), riddling, problematic(al), cryptic(al); mystic(al) [now rare], mysterious, shrouded in mystery; arcane, arcanal; logographic, logogrammatic; anagrammatic(al), monogrammatic(al); inexplicable, inscrutable etc. (unintelligible) 519.6, 7; labyrinthian, involved etc. (complex) 59.10; perplexing etc. 475.12.

534. Messenger

1. *n.* messenger, intermessenger [rare], angel [rare exc. Rel.], intelligencer [now rare], commissionaire; nuncio [now rare], *nuntius* [L.], nunciate, enunciator, annunciator, announcer; proclaimer, proclamator, proclaimant; dispatch bearer *or* rider, carrier, courier, runner, express, post [chiefly Hist.], poster, postrider, postilion [obs.], chiaus [Turkey]; dak, hircarra, peon, chuprassy [all Ind.]; estafette.
postboy, errand boy, chore boy; bellboy, bellhop [slang, U.S.]; newsboy, news vendor, newsy [coll., U.S.]; king's messenger, state messenger, pursuivant [obs.]; crier, trumpeter, bellman; bearer of glad tidings, evangel; Gabriel; Hermes, Iris [both Gr. Myth.]; Mercury [Rom. Myth.]; Ariel; Paul Revere; herald, harbinger, forerunner etc. (precursor) 64; internuncio, envoy, emissary etc. (deputy) 759; informant etc. 527.5.
2. *n.* mail, mail carrier [U.S.], mailman, postman, postboy, post [arch. and dial.], letter carrier; postmaster, postmistress; postal clerk; mailer, mail boat, packet boat, post boat; mail train, mail car, post car, post-office car; mailplane; mail coach, post coach, postcart; poster, post horse; carrier, carrier pigeon, homing pigeon; pigeon post, *Taubenpost*

---

534. Not snow, nor rain, nor heat, nor gloom of night stays these couriers from the swift completion of their appointed rounds.—HERODOTUS. I will send my messenger, and he shall prepare the way before me.—BIBLE.   Tell him there's a post come from my master, with his horn full of good news.—SHAKESPEARE.   None love the messenger who brings bad news.—SOPHOCLES.   How beautiful upon the mountains are the feet of him that bringeth good tidings, that publisheth peace.—BIBLE.

[G.]; post, post office etc. (correspondence) 592.4.

535. Affirmation
(See 536. Negation)

1. *n.* affirmation, affirmance, assertion, asseveration, averment, declaration, allegation, position, deposition, profession, statement, say, word; predication, predicate [Philos.]; attest, attestation; protest, protestation; pronouncement, pronunciation [obs.]; announcement, annunciation, enunciation; dictum, saying, ipse dixit; positive declaration *or* statement, positiveness etc. *adj.*, emphasis, stress; acknowledgment, confirmation etc. (assent) 488; remark, observation etc. (remark) 582.4; testimony, confirmation etc. (evidence) 467.2, 3.
2. *n.* swearing etc. *v.*, swear [coll.], adjuration, oath, vow, pledge, word, assurance, guarantee, warrant, solemn declaration etc. (*see* declaration etc. *above*); avow, avowal, avowance; avouch [rare], avouchment; affidavit, affidavy [dial.].
3. *v.* affirm, assert, make an assertion etc. *n.*, assever, asseverate, aver, declare, say, have one's say, state, allege, profess, protest, predicate, pronounce; announce, annunciate, enunciate; advance, propose, propound, present, offer, put *or* set forth, put forward, broach, pretend [now rare]; hold out, maintain, contend; confirm etc. 467.9; acknowledge etc. (assent) 488.6–10.
4. *v.* depose, make deposition etc. *n.*, depone, avow, avouch, vouch, warrant, certify, guarantee, assure; give *or* bear witness, attest, testify, testate [rare]; vow, swear, rap [arch. slang], swear the truth, speak *or* assert under *or* on oath, make *or* take one's oath, take one's Bible oath, make ∼, swear *or* put in an affidavit, call heaven to witness; swear by bell, book and candle; swear till one is black *or* blue in the face, swear till all's blue [both coll.]; swear by etc. (believe) 484.7; adjure etc. (promise) 768.3, 5.
5. *v.* insist upon, emphasize, stress, lay emphasis *or* stress upon, take one's stand

---

535. Assertion, unsupported by fact, is nugatory.—JUNIUS.   Oaths are but words, and words but wind.—BUTLER.   It is not the oath that makes us believe the man, but the man the oath.—AESCHYLUS.   These things I will that thou affirm constantly.—BIBLE.

upon, assert roundly *or* positively, dogmatize, lay down, lay down the law, raise one's voice, have the last word; rap out; reaffirm, reassert, repeat.

6. *adj.* affirmative, affirmant, affirming etc. *v.*; assertive, assertative, assertional, assertorial; declarative, declaratory; predicative, predicatory, predicational; pronunciative, pronunciatory; insistent, confident, trenchant, dogmatic, definitive, formal, solemn, categorical, peremptory, positive, absolute, emphatic, flat, broad, round, pointed, marked, clear, unmistakable, decided; ex-cathedra; certain etc. 474.8–15; express, explicit etc. (manifest) 525.4; assentive etc. 488.11.

7. *adv.* affirmatively etc. *adj.*, in the affirmative; with emphasis, ex cathedra, without fear of contradiction.

8. *phr., int.* I must say, give me leave to say, let me tell you, you can take it from me! [coll.], I'd have you to know, you may be sure, you may rest assured, I assure you, I hope to tell you [slang], I'll warrant you, I'll warrant, I'll say [slang], I'll venture to say, I'll engage to say, I'll tell the world [slang], I'll answer for it!, I'll be bound; I'll take my oath, upon oath, upon my word!, upon my honor!, on my word of honor!, honor bright [coll.], by my troth, by my sooth [arch.], believe me [coll.], honest Injun [joc.], honest to God [coll.], so help me God!; egad, by jingo!, by Jove!, by George! [all coll.].

seriously, sadly, in sober sadness, in all soberness *or* seriousness, in all conscience, all joking aside *or* apart, not to mince the matter *or* words, in fact, indeed, i' faith, marry [arch. and dial.], why, *dixi!* [L.]; you bet!, you bet you!, you bet your life!, you bet your boots! [all slang]; right!, righto! [coll.], all right! [coll.], alrighty! [slang], darn right! [slang]; O.K.! *or* okay! [coll.]; and how!, and I don't mean maybe! [both slang, U.S.]; not half! [coll., Eng.] yes etc. 488.14; certainly etc. 474.16; forsooth, in truth etc. (truly) 494.15.

536. Negation
(See 535. Affirmation)

1. *n.* negation, abnegation, *démenti* [F.], denial, disavowal, disaffirmation, disownment; disclamation, disclaimer; abjuration, abjurement, forswearing etc. *v.*; contradiction, contravention, controversion, traversal, gainsay [rare]; recusance *or* recusancy, recusation; nonagreement, protest etc. (dissent) 489; refusal etc. 764; prohibition etc. 761; repudiation etc. (rejection) 610; retraction etc. (recantation) 607.3; rebuttal, refutation etc. (confutation) 479; disproof etc. (counterevidence) 468.

2. *v.* deny, give denial to etc. *n.*, shake the head; no, say no etc. *adv.*; negate, negative; contradict, contravene, controvert, traverse, oppose, gainsay, dispute, impugn, join issue upon; belie, give the lie to, give one the lie in one's throat; disclaim, disown, disaffirm, disavow, disallow, abjure, forswear, abnegate, renounce; not hear to [coll.], protest etc. (dissent) 489.4; refuse etc. 764.2–4; prohibit etc. 761.2; repudiate etc. (reject) 610.2; rebut, refute etc. (confute) 479.2; bring *or* call in question etc. (doubt) 485.6; retract etc. (recant) 607.9; revoke etc. (abrogate) 756.3, 4; set aside etc. (ignore) 460.5.

3. *adj.* negative, negatory; denying, denied etc. *v.*; abnegative, abjuratory, revocatory, contradictory, contrary, repugnant, recusant, at issue; dissentient etc. 489.5; confutative etc. 479.3.

4. *adv.* no, nope [coll.], no sirree [coll., U.S.], nay, nix [slang]; nowise, noway *or* noways; not, not a bit, ~ whit *or* jot, not at all, not in the least, not so; not a bit of it, not much, not if one can help it, not for the world, not on your life, not by a long chalk *or* by long chalks, not by a long shot *or* sight [all coll.]; no such thing, nothing of the kind *or* sort; to the contrary, *tout au contraire* [F.], quite the contrary; far from it; on no account, in no respect; by no means, by no manner of means; negatively etc. *adj.*; God forbid etc. (dissent) 489.9.

537. Teaching
(See 538. Misteaching, 539. Learning; also 540. Teacher)

1. *n.* teaching, schooling etc. *v.*, schoolery [rare], schoolcraft [arch.]; instruction, education, edification, enlighten-

---

536. Do not strike him dead with a denial.—ADDISON.   Thou thrice denied, yet thrice beloved.—KEBLE.

537. It made me gladsome to be getting some education, it being like a big window opening.—M. WEBB.   To prepare us for complete liv-

ment, tuition; tutelage, tutorage, tutorship; direction, guidance; indoctrination, inculcation, inoculation; initiation; preinstruction; pedagogy, pedagogics, didactics; opsimathy [rare]; explanation etc. (interpretation) 522; learning etc. (knowledge) 490; information etc. 527.

2. *n.* training etc. *v.*, discipline, preparation, cultivation, qualification, development; exercise, exercitation, drill, practice.

3. *n.* persuasion, proselytism, conversion, conviction; propagandism, propaganda.

4. *n.* kindergarten, elementary ∼, primary ∼, grammar-school ∼, common-school ∼, secondary ∼, high-school ∼, higher ∼, college ∼, collegiate ∼, university ∼, academic ∼, liberal ∼, classical ∼, religious ∼, denominational ∼, secular ∼, technical *or* military education; normal *or* vocational training; propaedeutics, moral tuition *or* education; humanities, humanism, humane studies; coeducation.

5. *n.* physical education, physical drill, gymnastics, calisthenics, eurythmics; sloyd.

6. *n.* lesson, lecture, harangue, discourse, disquisition, talk, prelection; sermon, preachment; apologue, parable; chalk talk [coll.]; recital, recitation; exercise, task, assignment, imposition.

7. *n.* study, branch of learning; curriculum, course, course of study, class [arch.]; school [Oxford Univ.]; three R's, A B C's; physics, mathematics etc. (system or body of knowledge) 490.8.

8. *n.* chautauqua, Chautauqua system *or* course, lyceum [U.S.].

9. *v.* teach, give instruction etc. *n.*, instruct, learn [now illit. or vulg.], edify, educate, school; pupilize, tutor, coach; prime, cram [coll.], grind [coll.]; direct, guide; inculcate, indoctrinate, inoculate, infuse, instill, infix, imbue, impregnate, implant, engraft *or* ingraft, graft; impress upon the mind *or* memory, beat into, beat into the head; sow the seeds of, disseminate, propagate; show, bring forward, show how; give an idea of, put up to [slang], put in the way of.

put in the right, set right; sharpen the wits, enlarge the mind, open the eyes; give new ideas, teach an old dog new tricks [coll.]; teach a cock to crow, teach a dog to bark, teach a fish to bite, teach a hen to cluck, teach a serpent to hiss, teach iron to swim [all coll.]; preinstruct; initiate, instruct in the rudiments *or* principles; enlighten etc. (inform) 527.7; improve etc. 658.8; convince etc. 484.10.

10. *v.* train, drill, exercise, practice; discipline, take in hand; form, ground, qualify; breed, rear, bring up, fetch up [dial.], develop, cultivate, foster, nurture; dry-nurse, put to nurse, put through a course of sprouts [all coll., U.S.], lick into shape [coll.]; break, break in, tame; familiarize with, inure etc. (habituate) 613.8; prepare etc. 673.6.

11. *v.* expound, exposit; set forth, state, present; lecture, discourse, harangue, prelect, hold forth, give *or* read a lesson etc. *n.*; preach, sermon [now rare], sermonize; moralize, point a moral.

12. *adj.* educational, educationary [rare]; edifying, teaching etc. *v.*; instructive, instructional; scholastic, academic, doctrinal, hortatory, homiletic(al), didactic, propaedeutic(al), propagative; disciplinal, disciplinary; cultural, culturine; humanistic, humane; coeducational; informative etc. 527.13; pedagogic etc. 540.7; scholarly etc. 541.9; schoolish etc. 542.9.

13. *adj.* educated, taught etc. (informed) 490.15.

538. Misteaching
(See 537. Teaching)

1. *n.* misteaching, misinstruction, miseducation [rare], misinformation, misintelligence, mispersuasion [arch.], misdirection, misguidance, misleading etc. *v.*, false *or* dangerous teaching; perversion, distortion; the blind leading the blind; college of Laputa; sophistry etc. 477; misrepresentation etc. 555.

2. *v.* misteach, misinstruct, miseducate,

---

ing is the function which education has to discharge.—SPENCER. Train up a child in the way he should go: and when he is old, he will not depart from it.—BIBLE. They who educate children well are more to be honoured than they who produce them.—ARISTOTLE. Practice is the best of all instructors.—PUBLILIUS. *Adeo in teneris consuescere multum est* [Thus training is of great importance in the early years].—VERGIL. Practice makes perfect. 538. A man of vast and varied misinformation. —W. GAYNOR

misinform, misdescribe, miscorrect, misdirect, misguide; pervert, distort, detort [obs.]; unteach; mislead etc. 495.11; misrepresent etc. 555.4; deceive etc. 545.7; lie etc. 544.4.

3. *adj.* mistaught, misinformed etc. *v.*

4. *adj.* misteaching etc. *v.*, misinstructive, miseducative, unedifying.

539. Learning
(See 537. Teaching)

1. *n.* learning, acquisition of knowledge etc. (*see* knowledge etc. 490) *or* skill etc. (*see* skill etc. 698); acquirement, attainment, mental cultivation, edification; self-instruction, self-education; study, reading, perusal; wide reading; grind, cram [both coll.]; lore, erudition, scholarship etc. (acquired knowledge) 490.2; inquiry etc. 461; education etc. (teaching) 537; docility etc. (willingness) 602; aptitude etc. (talent) 698.2.

2. *n.* pupilage, tutelage; novitiate, novitiation; apprenticeship, prenticeship [arch. and dial.].

3. *v.* learn, get, acquire ~, gain ~, obtain ~, receive ~, take in ~, drink in ~, imbibe ~, pick up ~, gather ~, collect *or* glean knowledge *or* learning; acquaint oneself with, make oneself acquainted with; master, make oneself master of; learn by heart *or* rote, commit to memory etc. (memorize) 505.13; come to one's knowledge etc. (become informed) 527.11; be educated etc. (*see* educate etc. 537.9, 10); discover etc. 481a.3-7.

4. *v.* study, regard studiously, read, spell, peruse, con, pore over, thumb over, run over *or* through, wade through, glance *or* run the eye over *or* through, scan [coll.], turn over the leaves, dip into, plunge into; consume *or* burn the midnight oil, mind one's book, bury oneself in, grind [slang], cram *or* cram up [coll.], get up, coach up [coll.]; school [rare], go to *or* attend school, undergo schooling etc. (*see* schooling etc. 537); serve one's *or* an apprenticeship, serve one's time.

5. *adj.* learned, erudite etc. (informed) 490.15.

6. *adj.* studious, devoted to the acquisition of knowledge etc. *n.*; scholastic, scholarly etc. (bookish) 490.16; intellectual etc. 450.8; diligent, assiduous, sedulous etc. (industrious) 682.19; contemplative etc. (thoughtful) 451.35.

7. *adj.* teachable, instructable *or* instructible etc. (*see* teach etc. 537.9); docile etc. (willing) 602.8, 9; apt etc. 698.11.

540. Teacher
(See 541. Learner; also 537. Teaching)

1. *n.* teacher, instructor, educator, institutor [obs.], preceptor, trainer, guru [Ind.], khoja [Moham.], munshi [Anglo-Ind.], pundit [Ind.], mullah [Moham.], dominie [chiefly Scot.]; master, *maestro* [Sp.]; schoolmaster, schoolman, schoolteacher, schoolkeeper; professor, prof [slang]; pedagogue, pedagogist; tutor, tutorer; coach, coacher; *Privatdocent* or *Privatdozent* [G.], docent; governor [obs.], don [coll., Eng.], pupilmonger [obs.], dry nurse [slang], bear leader [joc.]; crammer [coll.], grinder [college slang, Eng.].

athletic coach *or* trainer, paedotribe [Gr. Antiq.]; underteacher, usher [Eng.]; precentor, coryphaeus [Oxford Univ.]; abecedarian; kindergarten teacher, kindergartner *or* kindergartener; pupil teacher; disciplinarian; expositor etc. (interpreter) 524; pedant etc. 492.4; preparer etc. 673.5; adviser etc. 695.3.

2. *n.* instructress, teacheress [rare],

---

539. When I am dead, I hope it may be said: / "His sins were scarlet, but his books were read."—BELLOC. With just enough of learning to misquote.—BYRON. The more a man looks at a thing, the less he can see it, and the more a man learns a thing the less he knows it.—CHESTERTON. Learning without thought is labor lost; thought without learning is perilous.—CONFUCIUS. Whoso neglects learning in his youth, loses the past and is dead for the future.—EURIPIDES. Talking makes a ready man, but reading a full man.—BACON. From contemplation one may become wise, but knowledge comes only from study.—E. A. NEWTON.

540. Those having torches will pass them on to others.—PLATO. The master loseth his time to learn / When the disciple will not hear.—CHAUCER. He is wise who can instruct us and assist us in the business of daily virtuous living.—CARLYLE. The man who can make a hard thing easy is the educator.—EMERSON. A teacher affects eternity; he can never tell where his influence stops.—H. ADAMS. It is the supreme art of the teacher to awaken joy in creative expression and knowledge.—EINSTEIN. He is either dead or teaching school. —ZENOBIUS. He who can, does; he who cannot, teaches.—SHAW. *Qui docet discit* [He who teaches, learns].

540.2 – 542.1

educatress, preceptress, tutoress, dame [rare], mistress, pundita [Ind.]; schoolmistress, schoolma'am or schoolmarm [U.S.], schooldame; governess, duenna; pedantess etc. 492.4.

3. *n.* lecturer, lector [Hist. and Eccl.], lectress [*fem.*; rare], reader, prelector, prolocutor, preacher; chalk talker [coll.].

4. *n.* guide, director, regulator; pioneer, apostle, missionary, propagandist; pilot etc. 694.6; monitor, mentor etc. (adviser) 695.3; example etc. (prototype) 22.

5. *n.* faculty, faculty members, professorate, teaching staff.

6. *n.* instructorship, professorship, professorhood, professorate, professoriate; tutorship, tutorhood, tutorism [rare], tutory [obs. exc. Law], tutorage, tutelage; schoolmastery, schoolmasterism; lectureship, readership; chair.

7. *adj.* pedagogic(al), professorial, preceptoral, preceptorial, tutorial; tuitional, tuitionary; teacherish, teachery, teacherly, teacherlike; schoolteacherish, schoolteachery, schoolteacherly, schoolteacherlike; schoolmasterish, schoolmastery, schoolmasterly, schoolmasterlike, schoolmastering; schoolmistressy, schoolma'amish; scholastic etc. (educational) 537.12, (schoolish) 542.9, (scholarly) 541.9.

541. Learner

(See 540. Teacher; also 539. Learning)

1. *n.* learner, scholar, scholarian [rare], scholastic; educatee, student, pupil, *élève* [F.], school child, schoolboy; schoolgirl, schoolmaid, schoolmiss; classman, schoolman; alumnus [*masc.*] (*pl.* alumni), alumna [*fem.*] (*pl.* alumnae); questionist, questioner, inquirer; monitor, prefect.

2. *n.* disciple, chela [Ind.], follower, apostle, proselyte.

3. *n.* college student, colleger, collegian, collegianer [Scot.], collegiate, academician [rare], varsity student [coll.]; college boy *or* girl; coed *or* co-ed [U.S.].

4. *n.* undergraduate, undergrad [coll.]; freshman, fresh *or* freshie [slang], plebe *or* pleb [West Point and Annapolis cant]; sophomore, soph [coll.]; junior;

senior; sophister, junior *or* senior sophister [all Eng.]; commoner [Oxford Univ.], pensioner [Cambridge Univ.], sizar [Cambridge and Dublin], servitor [Oxford Univ.], exhibitioner, scholar, fellow commoner [Eng. Univ.]; demy [Magdalen Coll., Oxford]; questionist [Cambridge and Harvard]; honor man, class man [Oxford Univ.]; wrangler, optime [both Cambridge Univ.]; passman.

5. *n.* graduate student, graduate, grad [coll.], alumnus etc. *above* 541.1; postgraduate student, postgraduate, postgrad [coll.]; inceptor [Cambridge Univ.]; Bachelor of Arts, Master of Arts etc. 877.3.

6. *n.* novice, novitiate, tyro, beginner, entrant, newcomer, tenderfoot, puny [obs.], inceptor [obs.], initiate, neophyte, catechumen, chela [Ind.]; *blanc-bec* [F.], greenhorn, greenhead [obs.], greeny [coll.], greener [slang], gosling [coll.]; debutant, debutante [*fem.*], deb [slang]; recruit, raw recruit, rooky [slang]; probationer, probationist; apprentice *or* 'prentice [arch.], articled clerk; abecedarian, alphabetarian; ignoramus etc. 493; bungler etc. 701.

7. *n.* schoolmate, school companion, schoolfellow, classmate, classfellow, fellow student *or* pupil, condisciple [rare], *condiscipulus* [L.].

8. *n.* class, form, school [Eng.], grade, room, division, remove [Eng.]; seminar, seminary.

9. *adj.* scholarly, scholarlike, scholastic; pupillary, *in statu pupillari* [L.], in leading strings; monitorial, Lancasterian [Hist.]; collegiate, collegial, collegebred; sophomoric(al), sophomoral; abecedarian, rudimentary; probational, probationary, probatory; prentice *or* 'prentice; learned, bookish etc. 490.15, 16; studious etc. 539.6; academic etc. (educational) 537.12, (schoolish) 542.9.

542. School

1. *n.* school, educational institution, institution of learning, institute, academy,

---

541. And then the whining schoolboy, with his satchel / And shining morning face.—SHAKESPEARE.   A dillar a dollar, a ten o'clock scholar, / Why do you come so soon?—NURSERY

RHYME.   The scholar is the student of the world.—EMERSON.   This man decided not to Live but Know.—BROWNING.   Self-education is fine when the pupil is a born educator.—J. A. SHEDD.
542. Thou hast most traitorously corrupted the youth of the realm in erecting a grammar

seminary, phrontistery; schoolhouse, school building; private ~, public ~, free ~, endowed ~, state-aided ~, grant-in-aid ~, day ~, night *or* boarding school, board school [obs.]; *pensionnat* [F.]; elementary ~, common *or* grammar school [U.S.]; grade school [U.S.], grades [U.S.]; infant school, kindergarten, nursery, nursery school, day nursery, crèche.

primary school, primary; secondary school; *Gymnasium, Realgymnasium, Realschule* [all G.], real school; preparatory school, prep school [coll., U.S.]; lyceum, *lycée* [F.]; junior high school, junior high [coll.], intermediate school; high school, high [coll.]; college, Alma Mater, fresh-water college [coll., U.S.], junior college; university, varsity [coll.]; graduate school, post-graduate school.

teachers' training college, normal school, normal; coeducational school, dual school [chiefly Eng.]; language school, grammar school [Eng.], Latin school; correspondence school, extension course, university extension; technical school, technological school *or* institute; polytechnic school, polytechnic; vocational ~, occupational *or* trade school, school of arts and crafts; conservatory, conservatoire, conservatorio, conservatorium; art school, school of art; music school, college *or* academy of music; commercial ~, business *or* secretarial school; riding ~, fencing *or* wrestling school, gymnasium, palaestra [Antiq.], dancing school.

religious school; Sunday *or* Sabbath school, Bible school, theological seminary, divinity ~, missionary ~, parish ~, parochial *or* convent school; charity school, reform school, reformatory; private ~, district ~, denominational ~, continuation ~, library ~, summer *or* vacation school; ground school [Aeronaut.], law school, medical school.

2. *n.* (British) dame *or* dame's school [chiefly Hist.]; voluntary ~, nonprovided ~, government ~, board ~, mission ~, higher grade ~, middle ~, middle-class ~, collegiate, modern ~, upper ~,

lower ~, municipal secondary ~, municipal technical ~, national ~, council *or* provided school.

Friends' School, King Henry VIII's School, King Edward's School, Queen Elizabeth's School, Queen Mary's School, Blue-Coat School; Christ's Hospital; public school, Eton, Harrow, Rugby; Merchant Taylors' School; College of Preceptors, Royal Academy ~, London College *or* Trinity College of Music, Royal College of Organists.

3. *n.* military school *or* academy; United States Military Academy, West Point; Royal Military Academy, Woolwich [Eng.]; Royal Military College, Sandhurst [Eng.]; naval school *or* academy; United States Naval Academy, Annapolis, Royal Naval College [Eng.]; training ship for the royal navy [Eng.], training ship for the merchant *or* mercantile marine.

4. *n.* denomination, sect, school, school of thought, persuasion, ism, order, communion, church; disciples, followers, adherents, imitators; class etc. 75; party etc. 712.

5. *n.* schoolroom, classroom, recitation room, lecture room *or* hall, theater, amphitheater.

6. *n.* school desk, desk, school seat; school table, reading table; ambo, lectern, pulpit, forum, stage, rostrum, platform, hustings, tribune, dais.

7. *n.* schoolbook etc. 593.5.

8. *n.* directorate, board, syndicate; Council of Education, School Board, College Board, Board of Regents, Board of Education, Board *or* Prefect of Studies, Textbook Committee.

9. *adj.* schoolish, scholastic, academic, institutional; collegiate, collegial; palaestral, palaestrian; gymnasial, gymnastic [rare]; cultural etc. (educational) 537.12; pedagogic etc. 540.7; scholarly etc. 541.9.

543. Veracity
(See 544. Falsehood)

1. *n.* veracity, veraciousness, truthfulness etc. *adj.*; truthtelling, truth-speaking

---

school.—SHAKESPEARE.   Creeping like snail / Unwillingly to school.—SHAKESPEARE.   A university should be a place of light, of liberty, and of learning.—DISRAELI.   The Common School is the greatest discovery ever made by man.—H. MANN.   Still sits the school-house by the road, / A ragged beggar sleeping.—WHITTIER.

543. Wherefore putting away lying, speak every man truth with his neighbour.—BIBLE. Tell truth and shame the devil.—SHAKESPEARE. This above all: to thine own self be true, / . . . Thou canst not then be false to any man.—

etc. *adj.*; veridity, veridicality; sincerity, candor, honesty, fidelity, *bonne foi* [F.]; plain dealing, plain speaking; truth-loving, love of truth; truth, sooth [arch.], troth [arch.]; light of truth; honest *or* unvarnished truth etc. 494; *bona fides* [L.] etc. (probity) 939; ingenuousness etc. (artlessness) 703.

2. *v.* be truthful etc. *adj.,* speak *or* tell the truth, speak *or* tell true; tell the truth and shame the devil, tell the truth, the whole truth and nothing but the truth; speak without equivocation *or* mental reservation, speak by the card; paint in its true colors, show one's true colors; swear the truth, speak on oath etc. (depose) 535.4; make a clean breast etc. (confess) 529.5; speak one's mind etc. 703.3; not lie etc. (*see* lie etc. 544.4); not deceive etc. (*see* deceive etc. 545.7); undeceive etc. 545a.2.

3. *adj.* veracious, truthful, trothful [arch.], truthy [chiefly dial.], true, soothfast [arch.], truthtelling, truth-speaking, truth-declaring, truth-passing, truth-bearing, truth-guarding, truth-seeking, truth-desiring, truth-loving, truth-filled; truehearted, true-souled, true-spirited, true-tongued, true-dealing, true-devoted, true-disposing, true-meaning, true-speaking; veridical, veridicous [rare].

honest, reliable, dependable, trusty, trustworthy, straight [slang], true-blue, as good as one's word; sincere, candid, frank, open, straightforward, unreserved; aboveboard, open and aboveboard; openhearted, frankhearted, simplehearted; undissembling, undissimulating, unassuming, unpretending, unfeigning, undisguising; guileless, pure; unfeigned, unpretended, undisguised, unaffected, unassumed, undissimulated, undissembled, undistorted, unexaggerated, bona fide; unperjured; scrupulous etc.

SHAKESPEARE. I had rather seal my lips, than, to my peril, / Speak that which is not.—SHAKESPEARE. Dare to be true; nothing can need a lie.—G. HERBERT. Too much honesty did never man harm.—J. CLARKE. Truth can never be told so as to be understood, and not be believed.—W. BLAKE. Speaking truth is like writing fair, and only comes by practice.—RUSKIN. Nothing astonishes men so much as common sense and plain dealing.—EMERSON. A truth that's told with bad intent / Beats all the lies you can invent.—W. BLAKE. When in doubt, tell the truth.—MARK TWAIN. Honesty is the best policy. *Esto quod esse videris* [Be what you seem to be].

(upright) 939.7–10; outspoken, ingenuous etc. (artless) 703.4.

4. *adv.* veraciously, truthfully etc. *adj.*; to tell the truth, to speak truthfully, with truth, of a truth, in truth, in good *or* very truth; in sooth, in good *or* very sooth, sooth to say, soothfast [all arch.]; in earnest, in good earnest; in *or* with good faith, bona fide, with no nonsense, without equivocation, *in foro conscientiae* [L.], from the bottom of one's heart; as the dial to the sun, as the needle to the pole; truly etc. 494.15; by my troth, honor bright [coll.] etc. (affirmation) 535.8.

544. Falsehood
(See 543. Veracity; also 545. Deception, 546. Untruth)

1. *n.* falsehood, falseness, untruthfulness etc. *adj.*; untruth, untroth [arch.]; falsity, falsification, false coloring *or* construction; falsifying, lying etc. *v.*; fibbery, mendacity, pseudology; pseudologia phantastica, pathological lying, mythomania; misstatement, misconstruction, perversion, distortion, perversion *or* distortion of the truth; subreption; prevarication, equivocation; weasel words; invention, fabrication; forgery, counterfeiting, plagiarism, perjury, false swearing; casuistry, Jesuitry, jesuitism.

a falsehood, lie etc. 546; fraud, deceit, guile etc. (deception) 545; dishonesty, unfairness etc. (improbity) 940; artfulness etc. (cunning) 702; misrepresentation etc. 555; exaggeration etc. 549; error etc. 495.

2. *n.* dissembling etc. *v.*, dissemblance, dissimulation, simulation, pretense, pretension, false pretense *or* pretension, sham, make-believe, put-on [dial. and slang]; acting, play-acting [coll.]; fake, fakement, fakery [all coll.]; humbug, humbuggery, bosh [coll.], *blague* [F.], gammon [coll.], bunk [slang], buncombe [coll., orig. U.S.], flam, flimflam, bam [slang]; quackery, quackism, quackishness; charlatanry, charlatanism, charla-

---

544. No one means all he says, and yet very few say all they mean.—H. ADAMS. No man speaks the truth or lives a true life two minutes together.—EMERSON. *Mendacem memorem esse oportet* [A liar must have a good memory].—QUINTILIAN. False words are not only evil in themselves, but they infect the soul with evil.—SOCRATES. I said in my haste, All men are liars.—BIBLE. A liar will not

tanship; four flush, four-flushing [both chiefly slang]; bluff, bluffery [rare]; hypocrisy, hypocrisis; insincerity or unsincerity, cant.

Machiavellism, Machiavellianism; hollowness, mockery, empty or hollow mockery; show, mere show, empty show, moonshine; appearance, semblance, mere outside, front or false front [coll.]; hypocritical sorrow, crocodile tears; lip homage or service, mouth honor, mealy-mouthedness, cajolery, flattery; duplicity, doubleness of heart or speech, double-dealing, two-facedness etc. *adj.*

Judas kiss; pretext etc. 619; lip homage, cajolery etc. (flattery) 933; bad faith, perfidy etc. (improbity) 940; mystification etc. (concealment) 528; disguise etc. 545.5; sophistry etc. 477; flattery etc. 933; pedantry etc. 491.4; pharisaism etc. (sanctimony) 988.2.

3. *v.* falsify, misstate, misquote, miscite, misreport, belie, sophisticate, pervert, distort, detort [obs.], garble; put a false construction or appearance upon, give a false coloring, give a color to, color, varnish, gloss over, put a gloss upon, dress up, disguise; embroider; cook or cook up, doctor or doctor up, deacon, hocus, fake or fake up [all coll.]; fabricate, invent, trump up, get up, spin, hatch, concoct, coin; counterfeit, forge, plagiarize; cry wolf; mislead etc. 495.11; be dishonest etc. 940.6; misrepresent etc. 555.4.

4. *v.* lie, falsify etc. *above,* prevaricate etc. *below,* fib, tarradiddle [coll.], bull [slang, U.S.], story [coll.], fishify [slang], cog [now rare], throw the bull [slang, U.S.], be a liar etc. (*see* liar etc. 548.5), utter a falsehood etc. *n.,* tell a lie etc. (*see* lie etc. 546), speak falsely etc. *adv.,* be untruthful etc. *adj.,* deviate from the truth; swear falsely, forswear, perjure oneself, bear false witness; lie flatly, lie in one's throat, lie like a trooper or conjurer; stretch the truth, draw the longbow etc. (exaggerate) 549.2; romance etc. (imagine) 515.8; misinform etc. 538.2.

5. *v.* prevaricate, equivocate, equivocate on, weasel [coll.], palter, trifle with the truth, mince the truth, say one thing and mean another, play or play at fast and loose, blow hot and cold; shuffle, fence, beat about the bush etc. (quibble) 477.8.

6. *v.* dissemble, dissimulate, simulate, feign, assume, put on, pretend, counterfeit, sham, fake [coll.], gammon [coll.], make believe, make out like [coll.], put on an act [slang, U.S.], act, play-act [coll.], act or play a part, make a show of, affect, profess, pass off for, sail under false colors, four-flush [slang]; sham Abram or Abraham, malinger, act the old soldier [coll.]; possum [coll., U.S.], play or act possum; play false, play a double game; cry sour grapes.

mask, bemask; disguise, conceal the real facts, hide under false appearance or by false pretense, put on the mask, put on a front or false front [coll.]; cant, practice hypocrisy etc. *n.,* act hypocritically, act or play the hypocrite etc. *v.,* hypocrize [rare]; clean the outside of the platter; be deceptive etc. (deceive) 545.7–10; make a pretext of etc. 619.2.

7. *adj.* false, unveracious, mendacious, lying etc. *v.,* untruthful, truthless, trothless [arch.]; unfair, uncandid; subreptitious; uningenuous, disingenuous; jesuitic(al), jesuitist, casuistic(al); falsified, forsworn etc. *v.;* untrue etc. 546.6; erroneous etc. 495.12–17; sham, counterfeit etc. (spurious) 545.13; dishonest, perfidious, treacherous, faithless etc. 940.8–12; deceitful etc. (deceptive) 545.12; artful etc. (cunning) 702.6.

8. *adj.* dissembling, canting etc. *v.;* insincere, unsincere; hypocrite, hypocritic(al), hypocrital [rare]; tartufian or tartuffian, tartufish or tartuffish; Machiavellic, Machiavellian; double, double-dealing, double-tongued, doublehanded, double-minded, doublehearted, double-faced, two-faced, Janus-faced; smooth-faced, smooth-tongued, smooth-spoken, bland, mealymouthed; plausible; affected etc. 853.6; pharisaic etc. (sanctimonious) 988.11.

9. *adv.* falsely etc. *adj., à la Tartufe* [F.], with a double tongue, under false pretense or pretension; slyly etc. (cunning) 702.7.

---

be believed, even when he speaks the truth.—AESOP.   O, what a goodly outside falsehood hath!—SHAKESPEARE.   The best liar is he who makes the smallest amount of lying go the longest way.—BUTLER.   A Hair perhaps divides the False and True.—OMAR KHAYYÁM —FITZGERALD.   But all was false and hollow; though his tongue / Dropped manna.—MILTON.   *Falsus in uno falsus in omnibus* [False in one thing, false in everything].

545. Deception

(See 545a. Undeception; also 544. Falsehood)

1. *n.* deception, deceptivity, deceiving etc. *v.*; deceptiveness, deceitfulness etc. *adj.*; deceit, guile, covin [arch.]; flimflam, flimflammery [coll.]; subtlety, subtilty, subtility [rare]; fraud, fraudulence *or* fraudulency; imposition, imposture; bluff, bluffery [rare]; spoof, spoofery [both slang]; humbug, humbuggery, humbuggism; gammon [coll.], bunk [slang], buncombe [coll., orig. U.S.], hokum [slang]; bamboozle, bamboozlement [both coll.].

jockeyism, jockeyship; chicane, chicanery; trickery, *espièglerie* [F.], sophistry [now rare], coggery [obs.], pettifoggery, sharp practice, underhand practice *or* dealing, superchery, cozenage, circumvention, ingannation [obs.]; collusion, connivance; straw bail, straw bond [both coll.]; straw bid [coll., U.S.]; ballot-box stuffing [U.S.]; dishonesty, treachery, foul play etc. (improbity) 940; craft, knavery etc. (cunning) 702; misrepresentation etc. 555; falsification, duplicity, dissimulation etc. (falsehood) 544; untruth etc. 546.

2. *n.* delusion, deluding etc. *v.*; gull, gullery [both arch.]; jugglery, jugglement [rare]; *escamotage* [F.]; sleight of hand, legerdemain; hocus-pocus, hokey-pokey [coll.], hanky-panky [coll.]; prestidigitation, prestigiation [obs.]; conjuration, magic etc. (sorcery) 992.

3. *n.* trick, device, cheating device, wile, wily device, wheeze [slang], *ficelle* [F.], cog, dodge, shift. blind, feint, plant [slang], bubble [arch.], fetch, catch [dial.], chouse [coll.], bite [obs., coll.], trepan, *espièglerie* [F.], hoax, *blague* [F.], bam [slang], barney [slang], flam, flimflam, spoof [slang], gull [arch.], deceit, deception, cheat, fraud, dishonesty, swindle, ramp [slang, Eng.], gyp [slang], sell [coll.], have [slang], piece of sharp practice etc. *above* 545.1; fake, fakement [both coll.]; chicane [now rare], chicanery [usu. pl.].

hocus [arch.], hocus-pocus; legerdemain, juggle, juggler's trick, sleight-of-hand trick, trick of sleight of hand; thimblerig, thimblerigging; cardsharping; bunko, bunko game; confidence game *or* trick, con game [slang]; brace game, drop game, gum game, panel game, shell game, skin game [all slang]; bag of tricks, tricks of the trade, tricks upon travelers; stratagem, artful dodge etc. (artifice) 702.3; practical joke etc. (prank) 842.7.

4. *n.* snare, trap, gin, springe, trepan, hook, sniggle, noose; pitfall, trapfall, deadfall, *trou-de-loup* [F.] (*pl.* trous-de-*loup*), pit; flytrap, mousetrap, rattrap, bear trap, mantrap, deathtrap, firetrap; Dionaea, Venus's flytrap; trap door, sliding panel, false bottom; springtrap, spring net; spring gun, set gun; mine; cobweb, net, meshes, toils; lime, birdlime; baited trap, *guet-apens* [F.], tub to the whale; ambush etc. 530.1; decoy, bait etc. (lure) 617.2.

5. *n.* disguise, disguisal, disguisement, guise [obs. exc. dial.]; mummery, borrowed plumes, front *or* false front [slang], false colors, camouflage; maskery [obs.], masquerade, masquerade dress; visor, vizard; incognito, incognita [*fem.*]; masked battery; concealment etc. 528, 530; mask etc. 225.11; cloak, screen, veil etc. (cover) 223.2; dissemblance etc. 544.2; pretext etc. 619.

6. *n.* spurious article, *spuria* [NL. *pl.*], sham, make-believe, mock, counterfeit, "counterfeit presentment" (Shakespeare), forgery, fraud, bastard, bam [slang], duffer [slang, Eng.], phony [slang], snide [slang], chouse [coll.], fake, fakement [both coll.]; mockery, empty *or* hollow mockery, whited *or* painted sepulcher; tinsel, paste, false jewelry, scagliola, ormolu, mosaic gold, brummagem, German silver, albata, paktong, white metal, britannia metal, paint; near-silk, near-leather, near-antique [all coll., U.S.]; ape-ware [slang, U.S.]; gold brick [coll., U.S.]; green goods [U.S.]; jerry-building, jerryism [builders' cant]; man of straw; imitation etc. 19; copy etc. 21.

7. *v.* deceive, beguile, Machiavellize, take in, victimize, trick, hoax, cheat, cozen, cog, sharp, let in, come over [coll.], come it over [slang], hocus, hocus-pocus [coll.], do [coll.], chouse [coll.], bite [chiefly coll.], bilk, jilt [obs.], bubble

---

545. You may fool all the people some of the time; you can even fool some of the people all the time; but you can't fool all of the people all the time.—LINCOLN [?]. O, what a tangled web, we weave / When first we practice to deceive.—SCOTT. The first and worst of

[arch.], flam, flimflam [coll.], bamboozle [coll.], hum [slang or coll.], humbug, gum [slang, U.S.], gammon [coll.], sell [slang], nab [slang], pluck [rare], jockey, bilk [coll.], nick [slang and dial.], gouge [coll., U.S.], fob *or* fub, nuzzle [rare], nousle [obs.], diddle [dial. and slang], daddle [coll.], bob [obs., slang], bucket [slang], gudgeon, mump [now chiefly dial.], lurch [arch.], abuse [arch.].

impose on *or* upon, put on *or* upon, practice upon, play upon; betray, play one false; delude, deludher [Anglo-Ir.]; hoodwink, blindfold, blind, blind one's eyes, throw dust into the eyes; play at hide-and-seek; bluff, bluff off, four-flush [slang]; gild the pill, put a good face upon, make things pleasant, divert; pass by trickery, play off, palm off, foist off, fob off [arch.]; palm upon, foist upon; be deceptive etc. *adj.*; practice deception etc. *n.*, live by one's wits.

bunko, sell gold bricks [coll., U.S.]; cog a die, cog the dice; cheat at cards, play with marked cards; thimblerig; conjure, juggle; jerry-build; snatch a verdict; mislead etc. 495.11; misrepresent etc. 555.4; misinform etc. 538.2; lie, dissemble etc. (falsify) 544.3–6; swindle, defraud etc. 791.12; be cunning etc. 702.5.

8. *v.* circumvent, overreach, outreach, outwit, outmaneuver, steal a march upon, give the go-by [coll.], give the run-around [slang, U.S.], leave in the lurch.

9. *v.* ensnare *or* insnare, snare, trap, entrap, catch in a trap, springe [rare], pitfall [rare], trepan, sniggle, hook, hook in, illaqueate [rare]; entangle, enmesh; trip, trip up; set *or* lay a trap *or* snare for, bait the hook, forelay [obs.], spread the toils, throw a tub to a whale; lime, birdlime; catch etc. (seize) 789.9; decoy, lure, inveigle etc. (lure) 617.4; ambush etc. 530.5.

10. *v.* fool, befool, sot [rare], dupe, gull, cully [obs.], practice on one's credulity, take in, let in, fool to the top of one's bent, make a fool etc. (*see* fool etc. 501) of, trifle with [now rare]; stuff, stuff up, spoof [all slang]; play upon, play a trick or practical joke upon, send on a fool's errand; cajole, flatter; make game of etc. (ridicule) 856.4, 5.

11. *v.* counterfeit, sham etc. (dissemble) 544.6.

12. *adj.* deceptive, deceptious, deceptitious, deceptory [obs.], deceiving etc. *v.*, deceitful, deceivable [arch.]; trickish, tricky, tricksy [rare]; covinous [Law], hollowhearted, guileful, insidious; flam, flimflam; delusive, delusory; illusive, illusory; elusive, elusory; collusive, collusory [obs.]; conniving, connivant, connivent [obs.]; misleading etc. (*see* mislead etc. 495.11); artful, crafty etc. (cunning) 702.6; perfidious, treacherous etc. (dishonest) 940.8–12; false etc. 544.7.

13. *adj.* spurious, counterfeit, bogus [chiefly coll.], snide [slang], false, sham, specious, make-believe, fake [coll.], phony [slang, U.S.], brummagem [slang, Eng.], queer [crim. slang, U.S.], shoddy, colorable, so-called, pretended, feigned, simulated, trumped-up, scamped, forged, fraudulent, tricky, fictive, fictitious, factitious, artificial, bastard, illegitimate.

mock, pseudo, quasi, trick [slang], near- [coll., U.S.], ape- [slang, U.S.]; not genuine, not what it is cracked up to be [slang]; flash, tinsel, tawdry, meretricious, pinchbeck, plated, alloyed; catchpenny; smooth, glossy; adulterated, sophisticated, cooked [coll.], doctored [coll.]; unsound, unsubstantial *or* insubstantial, rotten at the core; jerry-built, jerry [builders' cant]; surreptitious; untrue etc. 546.6; unauthentic etc. 495.16; disguised etc. 528.20; imitation etc. 19.12; affected etc. 853.6; illegal etc. 964.5.

14. *adj.* deceivable, gullible etc. (credulous) 486.5.

15. *adv.* deceptively, spuriously etc. *adj.*; under false colors, under cover of, under the garb of; over the left [slang].

545a. Undeception
(See 545. Deception)

1. *n.* undeception, undeceiving etc. *v.*, unbeguilement [rare], disabusal, disen-

---

all frauds is to cheat / Oneself.—P. J. Bailey. A quicksand of deceit.—Shakespeare. O serpent heart, hid with a flowering face!—Shakespeare. Ah that deceit should steal such gentle shapes.—Shakespeare. *Decipimur specie recti* [We are deceived by an appearance of right].—Horace. *Fraus est celare fraudem* [It is a fraud to conceal a fraud]. All is not gold that glitters.
545a. With all our most holy illusions knocked higher than Gilderoy's kite, / We have had a jolly good lesson, and serves us jolly well right! —Kipling.

chantment; disillusion, disillusionment, liberation from *or* deprivation of illusion etc. (*see* illusion etc. 495.5); debunkment [slang, U.S.]; disclosure etc. 529; disappointment etc. 509.

2. *v.* undeceive, unbeguile [rare], disabuse, set right, put straight, correct, unblindfold, open the eyes *or* clear the mind of, set free, disenchant; disillusion, disillusionize, disillude, free from *or* deprive of illusion etc. (*see* illusion etc. 495.5); burst the bubble, puncture one's balloon [coll.]; unfool, unbefool [rare]; debunk [slang, U.S.]; unmask etc. (disclose) 529.3; disappoint etc. 509.2; tell the truth etc. 543.2.

3. *adj.* undeceptive, undeceiving, undeceitful; unbeguiling, unbeguileful; disillusioning, disillusive, disenchanting.

546. Untruth
(See also 544. Falsehood)

1. *n.* untruth, untroth [arch.], untruism, falsehood, falsification, lie, prevarication, mendacity, fib, flam, tarradiddle [coll.], *blague* [F.], fabrication, forgery, invention, concoction, trumped-up ~, false etc. *adj.* story *or* statement, story [coll.], yarn [coll.], romance, fiction, myth, fable, incredible *or* farfetched story, tall story [coll.], cock-and-bull story, fish story [coll.], piscatorial prevarication [joc.], bedtime story [coll.], nursery tale, traveler's tale, Canterbury tale, fairy tale, press-agent's yarn [coll.], galley *or* cook's galley yarn [Naut. slang].

ghost story, gooseberry [slang], canard, shave [slang, Eng.], sell [coll.], hoax, hum [slang], fake [coll.], bosh [coll.], bunk [slang], bull [slang, U.S.], hot air [slang], claptrap, moonshine, all my eye *or* all my eye and Betty Martin [coll.], mare's-nest, farce; misstatement, misrepresentation, perversion, distortion, perversion *or* distortion of the truth, twister [slang]; *suggestio falsi* [L.], false interpretation, deceiving explanation, gloss; falseness, untruthfulness etc.

546. The cruellest lies are often told in silence.—STEVENSON. Sin has many tools, but a lie is the handle which fits them all.—HOLMES. A lie in time saves nine.—CYNIC'S CALENDAR. A very honest woman, but something given to lie.—SHAKESPEARE. *Se non è vero è ben trovato* [If it is not true it is very well invented].—BRUNO.

544; deception etc. 545; false plea etc. (pretext) 619; error etc. 495.

2. *n.* monstrous lie, consummate lie, rapping lie [slang], rapper [dial. and slang], whopper *or* whapper [coll.], bounce, bouncer [coll.]; cram, crammer, banger, howler, stretcher, large *or* tall order [all slang]; gross ~, flagrant *or* shameless falsehood, barefaced lie, dirty lie [coll. or slang]; exaggeration etc. 549.

3. *n.* half-truth, white lie, pious fraud; mental reservation etc. (secrecy) 528.2.

4. *v.* ring untrue etc. *adj.,* be an untruth etc. *n.,* have a false meaning *or* appearance, have a hidden meaning.

5. *v.* falsify, lie etc. 544.3–6.

6. *adj.* untrue, not true etc. (*see* true etc. 494.9), void *or* devoid of truth etc. (*see* truth etc. 494), truthless, trothless [arch.], contrary to fact, false, fallacious, false as dicers' oaths; without foundation, unfounded; *ben trovato* [It.], trumped-up, invented, fabricated, forged, fraudulent; fictive, fictitious, factitious, supposititious; illusory, elusory; erroneous etc. 495.12–17; spurious etc. 545.13; faithless etc. 940.10; fishy [coll.] etc. (improbable) 473.3; unattested etc. 468.4.

7. *adj.* untruthful, unveracious etc. 544.7.

547. Dupe
(See 548. Deceiver)

1. *n.* dupe, credulous *or* gullible person, gull, gudgeon, *gobe-mouche* [F.], cully [now rare], fish [coll.], April fool, bubble [arch.], easy mark [coll.], hoaxee, victim [chiefly coll.]; jay, sucker, pigeon, cull, cinch [all slang]; push-over, come-on [both slang, U.S.]; mark, mooch [both crim. slang, U.S.]; greenhorn, greeny [coll.], greener [slang]; puppet, cat's-paw; Simple Simon, boob [slang], chump [coll.], flat etc. (fool) 501; ignoramus etc. 493; laughingstock etc. 857.

2. *v.* dupe, fool etc. (deceive) 545.7, 10.

3. *v.* be deceived, ~ duped etc. (*see* deceive, dupe etc. 545.7, 10), be the dupe of; go for, fall for [both slang]; be trapped, fall into a trap; nibble at *or* swal-

547. One begins by being a dupe and ends by being a rascal.—DESCAMPS. One dupe is as impossible as one twin.—J. STERLING. You believe him your dupe; but if he is pretending to be so, who is the greater dupe, he or you?—LA BRUYÈRE.

low the bait; bite, nibble, rise to the fly, take the bait [all slang]; down, swallow, swallow whole [all coll.]; swallow hook, line and sinker [slang].

4. *adj.* credulous etc. 486.5.

548. Deceiver
(See 547. Dupe)

1. *n.* deceiver, beguiler, deluder, hoaxer, trepan; humbug, humbugger; tricker, trickster; serpent, snake, snake in the grass, cockatrice, double-dealer, Janus, Judas; dissembler, dissimulator; Machiavel, Machiavelli, Machiavelist; intriguer, intrigant; Jesuit, casuist; sophist, sophister; jilt, jilter; shuffler, equivocator, quibbler; Indian giver [coll., U.S.], rogue, rascal, traitor etc. (bad person) 949.

2. *n.* cheat, cheater; cozener, bilker [coll.], flimflammer [coll.], diddler [coll. or slang], bamboozler [coll.], gull [slang], jockey, juggler; sharp [slang], sharper; cardsharp, cardsharper; confidence man, con man [cant]; spieler [coll.]; crimp, crimper; bunko steerer, capper, come-on man [all slang, U.S.]; decoy duck, stool pigeon; straw bidder [coll., U.S.]; ringer, coin ringer [both slang]; horse trader, horse coper [Eng.]; carpetbagger [slang, U.S.]; jobber; swindler etc. 792.8.

3. *n.* impostor, pretender, humbug, precious humbug, fraud [coll.], gull [slang], fourflusher [slang], quack, quacksalver, charlatan, empiric, mountebank, saltimbank *or* saltimbanco [arch.] *or* saltimbanque, *blagueur* [F.]; fake, faker [both slang]; bluff, bluffer; medicaster; Cagliostro, Fernam Mendez Pinto; wolf in sheep's clothing, ass in lion's skin, jackdaw in peacock's feathers; malingerer, sham Abram *or* Abraham [Naut. cant]; adventurer, adventuress; masquerader etc. 528.7; affecter etc. 853.4; actor etc. 599.19; sciolist etc. 493.2; attitudinarian etc. 882.5; boaster etc. 884.3; usurper etc. 925.4.

4. *n.* hypocrite, canter, pharisee, tartufe *or* tartuffe, Tartufe *or* Tartuffe, Mawworm, Pecksniff, Joseph Surface, "saint abroad and a devil at home" (Bunyan).

5. *n.* liar, untruther, falsifier, pseudologist [obs. exc. joc.], story-teller [coll.],

storier [coll.], prevaricator, equivocator, fabricator, romancer, fabulist, spinner of yarns; fibber, fibster; taradiddle, tara-diddler [both coll.]; Ananias, Tom Pepper [Naut. slang], Scapin; consummate liar, "liar of the first magnitude" (Congreve), *menteur à triple étage* [F.], crammer [slang], bouncer [coll.], dirty liar [coll. or slang]; pathological liar, pseudologue, mythomaniac; perjurer, false witness.

6. *n.* legerdemainist, juggler, sleight-of-hand performer; tricker, trickster, performer of tricks; prestidigitator, prestigiator [rare]; magician, conjuror etc. (sorcerer) 992.2, 3.

549. Exaggeration

1. *n.* exaggeration, exaggerating etc. *v.*, magnification, overstatement, tall talk [coll.], hyperbole, strain, stretch, stretch of the imagination *or* truth; coloring, high coloring, embroidery, fringe; extravagance *or* extravagancy, extravagation [obs.]; extremity, extremism [rare]; excess, excessiveness etc. *adj.*; immoderation, immoderacy; exorbitance *or* exorbitancy, inordinacy, intemperance.

overpraise, overcommendation, overlaudation; gooseberry, giant gooseberry [both slang]; caricature, caricatura [now rare]; overpatriotism, chauvinism, jingoism, spread-eagleism [coll., U.S.]; Munchausenism, Baron Munchausen; men in buckram; enlargement, amplification etc. (expansion) 194; storm *or* tempest in a teapot *or* teacup, much ado about nothing etc. (overestimation) 482; ostentation etc. 882; flattery etc. 933; puffery etc. (boasting) 884; rant, bombast etc. (grandiloquence) 577.2; false coloring etc. (falsehood) 544; misrepresentation etc. 555; aggravation etc. 835; flight of fancy etc. (imagination) 515; stretcher [slang], whopper [coll.], fish story [coll.] etc. (lie) 546; absurdity etc. 497; redundance etc. 641.

2. *v.* exaggerate, magnify, pile up, aggravate, heighten, enhance, enlarge be-

---

548. It is a double pleasure to deceive the deceiver.—LA FONTAINE. I am falser than vows made in wine.—SHAKESPEARE.

549. *Excitabat enim fluctus in simpulo* [For he made waves in a ladle].—CICERO. Exaggeration is to paint a snake and add legs.—CHINESE PROVERB. They make of a fly an elephant, and of a molehill a mountain.—BECON. An exaggeration is a truth that has lost its

yond bounds, enlarge *or* increase beyond the normal, stretch [coll.], strain, stretch *or* strain a point, ~ the sense, ~ the meaning *or* the truth, overstate the truth, overstate, overspeak [rare], overtell [rare], overlay, overcharge, overpicture [rare], overdraw; overshoot the mark, draw ~, pull ~, use *or* shoot a *or* the longbow, spin a long yarn [coll.], make exaggerated statements, hyperbolize, deal in the marvelous, out-Herod Herod, run riot, talk at random.

color, overcolor, color highly *or* too highly; embroider; extravagate, delineate extravagantly; maximate, maximize; make much of, make the most of; make a mountain of a molehill; overpraise, overcommend, overlaud; indulge in jingoism etc. *n.*, spread-eagle [coll., U.S.], make the eagle scream [U.S.]; enlarge, amplify etc. (expand) 194.8; overdo etc. 641.3; overestimate etc. 482.3; puff etc. (boast) 884.5; lie, give a false coloring etc. (falsify) 544.3, 4; misrepresent etc. 555.4; talk big [coll.] etc. (be bombastic) 577.5; flatter etc. 933.2.

3. *adj.* exaggerated etc. *v.*, hyperbolic(al), overdone, overwrought, overgreat, overlarge, overmuch, extravagant, excessive, immoderate, extreme, fabulous, intemperate, exorbitant, undue, unreasonable, preposterous, outrageous, egregious, *outré* [F.]; highflying, high-flown, highfalutin *or* highfaluten *or* highfaluting [coll.]; stilted, on stilts; large, tall [both coll.]; overpatriotic, spread-eagle [coll., U.S.], jingoistic, chauvinistic; overestimated etc. 482.4; redundant etc. 641.5; grandiloquent etc. 577.7; ostentatious etc. 882.8.

550. Indication

1. *n.* indication, signification, denotation, connotation, implication, hint, suggestion, inference; symptom, mark, sign, evidence, manifestation, telltale; designation, specification, particularization; proof, demonstration; symbolism, symbolization; symptomatology, semeiology, semeiotics; pathognomy; sign of the times; prefigurement etc. (omen) 512, (prediction) 511; trace etc. (record) 551; warning etc. 668; alarm etc. 669.

2. *n.* sign, ensign, symbol, emblem, token, tessera, mark, badge, note, signal, signum (*pl.* signa), device, cipher, figure, type; index (*pl.* indexes, indices), indice [obs.], indicia (*sing.* indicium); indication, indicant, indicator; point, pointer; cue, clew *or* clue, key; testimony, testimonial; reference, reference mark; dollar mark; warning sign etc. 668.3; emblem of authority, scepter etc. 747; trophy etc. 733; gauge etc. (measure) 466.4.

3. *n.* gesture, gesticulation; motion, movement; wink, glance, leer; nod, shrug, beck; touch, nudge; byplay, dumb show, pantomime, chironomy; sign language, dactylology, dactylography; deaf-and-dumb alphabet, one-hand *or* two-hand alphabet.

4. *n.* track, trail, path, mark, wake, spoor, scent; vestige, trace; print, footprint, footmark, footstep, step, pad, pug [Ind.], *piste* [F.]; ichnite, ichnolite; fingerprint, thumbprint.

5. *n.* motto, epigraph, epitaph, posy [arch.].

6. *n.* earmark, mark of identification *or* distinction, characteristic *or* distinguishing mark, indication of character, character, characteristic, diagnostic, physiognomic [rare], trait, feature, distinctive feature, peculiarity, lineament, quality, type, property, criterion [obs.], cast, trick; badge, mark etc. *above* 550.2; brand etc. *below* 550.11; stamp, impress, impression; cloven hoof.

7. *n.* mark, marking; lineation, delineation; line, stroke, dash, stripe, streak; scratch, scar, score; dot, spot, point; speck, speckle, freckle; jot, jotting; tick, ticking; stigma (*pl.* stigmata, stigmas), stigmatism; mark of disgrace, brand, mark of Cain, stripes, broad arrow; sublineation, underline, underlining, underscore, underscoring; note, annotation;

---

temper.—GIBRAN. A friend exaggerates a man's virtues.—ADDISON. There is no one who does not exaggerate.—EMERSON. Make all the little fishes talk like big whales.—GOLDSMITH. The reports of my death are greatly exaggerated.—MARK TWAIN.
550. Your gesture cries it out.—SHAKESPEARE. The weary sun . . . / Gives signal of a goodly day tomorrow.—SHAKESPEARE. Let us raise a standard to which the wise and honest can repair.—WASHINGTON. *Ecce signum* [Behold the sign]. *Ex pede Herculem* [From the foot (one may judge) Hercules; the part is an index to the whole].

print, imprint, impress, impression; dint, dent, indent, indentation, indention; stamp, seal; fingerprint, thumbprint, thumb mark; dactylogram, dactylograph; footprint etc. *above* 550.4; engraving etc. 558; nick, blaze etc. (notch) 257; stain, blemish etc. (discoloration) 440a.

8. *n.* punctuation, punctuation marks; dash, hyphen; parenthesis, brackets, crotchets; quotation marks, quotes [coll.]; interrogation, interrogation *or* question point *or* mark; exclamation, exclamation point *or* mark; period, dot, point; comma, colon, semicolon; accent, acute *or* grave accent; long, macron; short, breve; asterisk, star; dagger, obelisk, double dagger; crowfoot, diaeresis, caret, brace, ellipsis, leaders, section, parallels, paragraph, index, asterism, cedilla, guillemets [rare], tilde, circumflex, apostrophe.

9. *n.* (map drawing) hachure, contour line; isobar, isobaric *or* isopiestic line; isotherm, isothermal line; isobase, isobath, isobathic line; latitude, longitude, meridian, equator.

10. *n.* landmark, seamark; cairn *or* carn, menhir, catstone; Pillars of Hercules; lighthouse, watchtower, pharos; post, staff; milepost, milestone; signpost, guidepost, directing post; blaze; finger post, handpost; sign, signboard, guideboard; pointer, hand, direction, guide, cynosure; guiding star, lodestar, polestar, Polaris, *l'Etoile du Nord* [F.], North Star.

11. *n.* identification, identification badge *or* bracelet; sign, high sign [slang], *mot de passe* [F.], password, pass, *mot d'ordre* [F.], watchword; countersign, open-sesame; tessera; grip; countersignature, countermark, counterstamp, counterfoil; stub, duplicate, tally; seal, sigil, signet, cachet; brand, paraph, stamp, label; ticket, bill, billet, letter; check, chop [Orient]; broad arrow; government mark; trade-mark *or* trademark, hallmark; totem; card, address card, visiting card, *carte de visite* [F.], press card, membership card.

voucher, witness, credential, diploma, attestation; signature, sign manual; autograph, autography, hand, handwriting; cipher, monogram; superscription; endorsement *or* indorsement, indorsation [Scot.]; title, heading, docket; tonsure;

scalp lock; mortarboard [coll.], cap and gown, hood; caste mark, tilaka [Hindu]; catchword, shibboleth.

12. *n.* insignia, ensign, badge, symbol, emblem; figurehead, eagle; heraldry, heraldic symbol; crest, shield; arms, coat of arms, armorial bearings, supporters, hatchment, achievement, scutcheon, escutcheon; cockade; brassard; royal ~, ecclesiastical and military insignia etc. (insignia of authority) 747; garland, medal etc. (trophy) 733.

13. *n.* flag, pennant, pennon, bunting, standard, ensign, colors, streamer; banner, banneret; banderole, bandrol, bannerol; vexillum, labarum [both Rom. Antiq.]; oriflamme; whip, coachwhip; red flag, green flag etc.; white ~, blue *or* red ensign [Eng.]; Old Glory [coll.], Stars and Stripes, Star-spangled banner; red, white and blue; tricolor, *drapeau tricolor* [F.]; flag at half mast, half-masted flag, union down; burgee, blue peter, jack, ancient [arch.], gonfalon, union jack, guidon, signal flag.

14. *n.* signal, sign; beacon, signal beacon; signal siren *or* whistle, signal bell *or* gong; signal gun, signal shot; watchman's rattle, police whistle; fog signal *or* alarm, fog bell, foghorn; bell signal, bell [Naut.]; signal post, signal mast; traffic signal, traffic lights, stop-and-go lights, red *or* stop light, green *or* go light; semaphore, semaphore signal; telegraph, telegraphy; wigwag; heliograph, heliogram; calumet, peace pipe, pipe of peace, rocket, code beacon etc. (signal light) 423.5; beacon fire, balefire etc. (fire) 382.8; fire alarm, burglar alarm etc. (alarm) 669.

15. *n.* code, Morse code, cable code, telegraphic alphabet; dot, dash; telegraphy etc. 532a.

16. *n.* call, summons, word of command; crow ~, duck ~, goose ~, hawk *or* moose call; bugle call, trumpet call; reveille, taps, last post [Eng.]; alarm, alarum; battle cry, rallying cry; sacring bell [obs.], Angelus, Angelus bell; cry etc. 411.

17. *n.* symbology; dactylography, Bertillon system; chiromancy, palmistry, crystallomancy, anthropomancy etc. (divination) 511.3; astrology etc. 511.4; physiognomics etc. (science of interpretation) 522.5; graphology etc. (writing) 590.1; phrenology etc. 450.4.

18. *v.* indicate, index, be indicative etc. *adj.*, be the sign of etc. *n.*, give token, sign *or* indication of, signify, betoken, denote; connote, connotate; imply, involve, argue, bespeak, testify, attest, evince, evidence, manifest, declare, discover, reveal, display, disclose, set forth, present, exhibit, register, show, read; speak for itself, speak volumes; point to, point out; prove, demonstrate; represent, stand for, typify, symbolize; designate, specify etc. (direct attention to) 457.7; make known, intimate etc. (inform) 527.7, 8; preindicate, prefigure etc. (portend) 511.9.

19. *v.* mark, put a mark etc. *n.* on, mark out *or* off, note, tick, earmark, dot, spot, score, dash, trace, chalk; label, tag, ticket, docket; seal, sign and seal, set one's hand and seal; sign, countersign, undersign; underline, underscore; print etc. (engrave) 558.5; nick, blaze etc. (notch) 257.5; blemish, spot etc. (discolor) 440a.2.

20. *v.* signal, signalize, give a signal etc. *n.*, sign, make a sign etc. *n.*; beck [arch.], beckon; motion, nod, nudge, shrug, raise *or* hold up the finger *or* hand, saw the air; wink, glance, leer; give the high sign, tip the wink, give the office [all slang]; gesture, gesticulate; wave, wave the hand; wave $\sim$, unfurl $\sim$, hoist *or* hang out a banner etc. *n.*, break out a flag; show one's colors, exchange colors; speak, hail and speak [Naut.]; salute, dip; jibber the kibber [Naut. cant]; give *or* sound an alarm, raise a cry; beat the drum, sound the trumpet; give the cue, tip off [coll.] etc. 527.8, 9; warn etc. 668.6.

21. *adj.* indicative, indicatory, indicant, indicating etc. *v.*; connotative, denotative; significant, significative, significatory; implicative, implicatory, implicational; inferential, suggestive; demonstrative, demonstrational; exhibitive, exponential [rare]; pointing out, bringing to notice; distinctive, distinguishing, diacritical; characteristic, representative, typical, emblematic, symbolic(al); diagnostic; symptomatic, semeiotic, sematic, pathognomonic(al); ominous etc. (predictive) 511.11; evidential etc. 467.11.

22. *adj.* indicated, marked etc. *v.*; pertinent, pointed; known by. recognizable by.

23. *adv.* symbolically etc. *adj.*, in token of; in dumb show, in pantomime.

551. Record

(See 552. Obliteration; also 553. Recorder)

1. *n.* record, recordation, recording; register, registry; chronicle, annals; memorabilia (*sing.* memorabile), memoirs, memorials; factum; adversaria, miscellanea, miscellany *or* miscellanies; chartulary, cartulary; diptych.

certificate, docket, voucher, diploma, credential, warrant; affidavit, affidavy [dial.]; deposition, *procès-verbal* [F.]; memorandum (*pl.* memoranda), memo [coll.], memoir, memorial [obs. exc. Law], commonplace; note, notes, notation, jottings; minute, minutes; entry, item; inscript, inscription, scription [obs.]; endorsement *or* indorsement, indorsation [Scot.]; signature, sign manual, autograph; copy, duplicate, carbon, carbon copy; bulletin, bulletin board, scoreboard *or* score sheet; totalizator, tote [turf cant]; excerpt, *excerpta* [L.], extract; muniments, deed etc. (security) 771; file, card index etc. (list) 86; paper, document etc. (writing) 590.3.

2. *n.* archive *or* archives, public record, official memorandum *or* copy, state paper, government publication; almanac, gazetteer, geographical dictionary, atlas; Nautical Almanac, World Almanac, Almanach de Gotha, Whitaker's Almanack, Poor Richard's Almanack; Statesman's Yearbook, Lloyd's Register, Who's Who; Red Book, Blue Book; red book, blue book *or* bluebook, green $\sim$, white *or* yellow book, *livre jaune* [F.]; Congressional Records, Hansard [Eng.]; returns, report, *compte rendu* [F.], account, minutes, proceedings; census, census report *or* returns; legend, history, biography etc. (narrative) 594.2.

3. *n.* record book, notebook, pocketbook, blankbook, pad; memorandum book, memo book [coll.], promptbook, engagement book, commonplace book, adversaria; scrapbook, memory book [U.S.], album; calendar, tablet, catalogue; classified catalogue, *catalogue rai-*

---

551. The best witness is a written paper.—SANDBURG.   Among the giant fossils of my past.—E. B. BROWNING.   Records that defy the tooth of time.—YOUNG.   *Exegi monumentum aere perennius* [I have reared a monument more enduring than bronze].—HORACE.

sonné [F.]; journal, ephemeris (*pl.* ephemerides) [obs.], diary; log, logbook; account book, ledger, daybook; cashbook, petty cashbook; yearbook, annual; Domesday book, Domesday; magazine, newspaper etc. (book) 593.

4. *n.* monument, monumental record, memorial, memento, remembrance, testimonial, token, souvenir; slab, tablet, obelisk, pillar, column, monolith, hoarstone [Eng.]; shrine, reliquary, memoria; hatchment, achievement; scutcheon, escutcheon; commemoration etc. (celebration) 883; gravestone etc. 363.15; statue etc. 554; trophy, medal etc. 733.

5. *n.* trace, vestige, relic, remains, mark left behind, sign *or* evidence of something once present; scar, cicatrix (*pl.* cicatrices); mark, footmark etc. (track) 550.4; evidence etc. 467.

6. *n.* phonograph record, record, cylinder, disk, wax [cant]; piano-player roll; ticker, ticker tape.

7. *n.* recording etc. *v.*, recordation, reduction to writing; registry, registration; enrollment *or* enrolment, tabulation; entry, booking, insertion; journalism.

8. *v.* record, put *or* place upon record, register, list, docket, inscribe, inscroll, enroll, catalogue, chronicle, calendar; write, write out, write down, jot down, mark down, put down, set down, commit *or* reduce to writing, put in writing, set down in writing, put in black and white, put on paper; make an entry, enter, book, insert; post, post up; note, note down, make a note; minute, take a minute, write minutes; memorandize, memorandum [rare], make a memorandum; summarize, reduce to a summary; return, make a return; mark off, tick off; report etc. (inform) 527.7; sign etc. (mark) 550.19, (ratify) 488.10.

9. *adj.* recording etc. *v.*, recordant [rare], recordatory, recordative; autographic, self-recording.

10. *adv.* on record, on file, in one's good *or* bad books.

552. Obliteration
(See 551. Record)

1. *n.* obliteration, erasure, rasure [rare]; cancel, cancellation; circumduction [rare], deletion, blot, effacement, extinction; *tabula rasa* [L.].

2. *v.* obliterate, erase, raze [rare], efface, expunge, cancel, dele, blot, blot ~, rub ~, wipe ~, strike ~, scratch *or* sponge out, ~ off *or* away, draw the pen through, rule out, apply the sponge; cause to disappear, vanish [rare]; deface, render illegible.

3. *adj.* obliterated etc. *v.*, leaving no trace.

4. *adj.* unrecorded, unregistered, unwritten; printless, out of print; intestate.

553. Recorder
(See also 551. Record)

1. *n.* recorder, recordist, record-maker; register, registrar, registrary [obs.]; clerk, baboo [Ind.], bookkeeper, *Custos Rotulorum* [ML., Eng. Law], Master of the Rolls; notary, prothonotary; scribe, secretary, stenographer etc. (writer) 590.11, 12; author, journalist etc. 593.15, 16.

2. *n.* annalist, chronicler, chronographer, historian, historiographer; biographer, biographist; autobiographer, autobiographist; memorialist; antiquary etc. 122.5.

3. *n.* recording instrument *or* apparatus, mechanical recorder, recorder; Dictaphone; autograph, autographic recorder; seismograph, seismometer; speed recorder, speedometer; log, patent log, taffrail log, harpoon log, ground log; pedometer, passometer; ticker, ticker tape; time recorder, time clock; cash recorder, cash register; turnstile; votograph; receiver, telephone *or* telegraph receiver, siphon receiver; telegraphone, telegraphophone, telephonograph; phonograph etc. 417.9; anemometer, adding machine etc. (measuring instruments) 466.4.

554. Representation
(See 555. Misrepresentation)

1. *n.* representation, representment [rare], illustration, delineation; depict-

---

552. *Delenda est Carthago* [Carthage must be destroyed].—Cato the Elder.
553. An angel writing in a book of gold.—L. Hunt.   The journalists are now the true kings and clergy.—Carlyle.   The newspaper-man is, more than most men, a double personality.—H. Adams.
554. Art is life seen through a temperament.—Zola.   Art is the perfection of nature.—T.

554.1 – 556.1

ment, depiction, depicture; picture, picturization; portraiture, portrayal, portrayment [rare]; imagery, iconography; design, designing; art, fine arts, graphic arts, arts of design, ornamental art; painting, drawing etc. (graphic arts) 556; sculpture etc. 557; engraving etc. 558; imitation etc. 19; likeness etc. (copy) 21; description etc. 594.

2. *n.* personation, personification, impersonation; drama etc. 599.

3. *n.* a representation etc. *above* 554.1; facsimile, facsimile impression, squeeze [cant]; image, likeness etc. (copy) 21; perfect likeness etc. 17.6; portrait, photograph etc. (picture) 556.9–14.

4. *n.* figure, figurine, icon, puppet, doll, marionette, manikin *or* mannequin, lay figure, model; image, effigy, *effigies* [L.]; fantocine, fantoccini; wax, wax figure, waxwork; bust, busto [obs.]; sculpture, piece *or* article of sculpture; statue, statuette, statuary; monument; figurehead; cameo etc. (relief) 557.6; graven image etc. (idol) 991.4.

5. *n.* map, chart etc. (outline) 626.2.

6. *n.* delineator, depicter *or* depictor; picturer, portrayer, limner; draftsman, designer etc. (artist) 559.

7. *v.* represent, delineate, depict, depicture, picture, picturize, draw *or* paint a picture, portray, set forth, limn; convey an impression of, register [slang]; take *or* catch a likeness, hit off; shadow forth *or* out, adumbrate; embody, body forth, figure; illustrate, elucidate; trace, copy; describe etc. 594.5; symbolize etc. 521.2; paint, etc. 428.10; draw etc. 556.17; carve, model etc. 557.9; engrave etc. 558.5.

8. *v.* personate, personify, impersonate; dress up [coll.], pose as, act, enact, act a part, take the part of, act out, characterize, assume a character, hold the mirror up to nature; play etc. (drama) 599.26; mimic etc. (imitate) 19.5–10.

9. *adj.* representative, representing etc. *v.*; illustrative, illustratory; depictive, delineatory, picaresque; figurative, emblematic(al), typical, symbolic(al); iconic(al), iconological; Renaissance, trecento, quattrocento, cinquecento, Directoire; imitative etc. 19.12; like etc. 17.10–16; graphic etc. (descriptive) 594.7.

555. Misrepresentation
(See 554. Representation)

1. *n.* misrepresentation, misrepresentment [rare], misrepresenting etc. *v.*; misstatement, misreport; perversion, distortion, false coloring; falsification etc. 544; deception etc. 545; misteaching etc. 538; misinterpretation etc. 523; exaggeration etc. 549; error etc. 495.

2. *n.* bad likeness, daub, scratch; distorted image, distortion, anamorphosis; anamorphoscope; convex *or* concave mirror, Claude Lorraine mirror.

3. *n.* burlesque, travesty etc. (caricature) 21.3.

4. *v.* misrepresent, pervert, distort, detort [obs.], anamorphose, garble, twist, twist ~, wring ~, wrench *or* wrest the sense *or* meaning; give a false coloring, put a false construction *or* appearance upon; misstate, misquote, mis-cite, misreport; understate, underdraw; overstate, overdraw, stretch, strain; daub, scratch; falsify, lie etc. 544.3–6; deceive etc. 545.7; be dishonest etc. 940.6; misteach etc. 538.2; mislead etc. 495.11; misinterpret etc. 523.2; exaggerate etc. 549.2; sophisticate etc. 477.7.

5. *v.* burlesque, travesty etc. (caricature) 19.8.

6. *adj.* misrepresented etc. *v.*, blue-sky [coll., U.S.].

556. Graphic Arts
(See also 559. Artist)

1. *n.* graphic arts, art, fine arts, *beaux-arts* [F.], arts of design; design, designing; portraiture, portrait [rare]; limnery

---

BROWNE. Every genuine work of art has as much reason for being as the earth and the sun.—EMERSON. All art constantly aspires towards the condition of music.—PATER. Art is nothing more than the shadow of humanity. H. JAMES. A work . . . of art should carry its justification in every line.—CONRAD. Great art is an instant arrested in eternity.—HUNEKER. Architecture, sculpture, painting, music and poetry, may truly be called the efflorescence of civilized life.—SPENCER. A map they could all understand.—CARROLL.

555. Parodies and caricatures are the most penetrating of criticisms.—A. HUXLEY. If the man who paints only the . . . surface he sees before him were an artist, the king of artists would be the photographer.—WHISTLER. 556. The canvas glow'd beyond ev'n nature warm.—GOLDSMITH. Nothing so resembles a daub as a masterpiece.—GAUGUIN. What

[rare]; architecture, "frozen music" (Schelling); scenography, ichnography, orthographic projection; artistic quality, virtu; ornamental art, decoration etc. (ornament) 847; sculpture etc. 557; engraving etc. 558; artist etc. 559.

2. *n.* painting etc. *v.*, the brush; historical ~, portrait ~, marine ~, flower ~, interior ~, genre ~, scene *or* landscape painting, oil *or* water coloring *or* painting; encaustic, encaustic painting, cerography; grisaille; a painting etc. *below* 556.9.

3. *n.* black and white, chiaroscuro *or* chiaro-oscuro; drawing etc. *v.*; charcoal, pencil, chalk; pen and ink; a drawing etc. *below* 556.9.

4. *n.* photography, kodakry; motion-picture photography, cinematography; radiography, X-ray photography, skiagraphy; spectroheliography, photospectroheliography; photogravure, rotogravure; color photography, heliochromy; sculptography; camera etc. 445.5; photographer etc. 559.7.

5. *n.* composition, treatment, technique, arrangement, values, atmosphere, tone; shadow, shading; line; grouping; balance; perspective.

6. *n.* style, artistry, lines; school; the grand style, high art; classicism, neoclassicism, romanticism; realism, naturalism, genre; ornamentalism, ornamental art; idealism, symbolism, impressionism, neoimpressionism, pointillism, expressionism, Dadaism, modernism, futurism, cubism, vorticism, surrealism.

7. *n.* (schools) eclectic, Barbizon, plein-air; Italian, Lombard, Tuscon, Sienese, Bolognese, Florentine, Milanese, Modenese, Neapolitan, Paduan, Roman, Umbrian, Venetian; British, Scottish, Pre-Raphaelite; Dutch; Flemish; French; German; Spanish; Mexican; American; school of Raphael etc. (*see* Raphael etc. 559.3).

8. *n.* work of art, object of art, *objet d'art* [F.], art, piece, work, study, masterpiece, masterwork; composition, brain child; virtu, article *or* piece of virtu; curio, conversation piece, bric-a-brac; artware; inlaid work, *fleur-de-lis* [F.] etc. (ornamentation) 847.3–9; statue etc.

(figure) 554.4; creation etc. (production) 161.6; representation etc. 554.

9. *n.* picture, picturization, tableau, canvas, study; mural, mural painting; drawing, draft *or* draught, sketch; rough draft *or* draught, rough, *brouillon* [F.], *ébauche* [F.], outline; pencil drawing, charcoal drawing, water-color drawing etc.; painting, painture [obs.].

oil painting, oil [coll.]; water-color painting, water color; *gouache* [F.]; tempera; fresco, fresco painting; still life, study in still life, still [coll.]; *pasticcio* [It.], pastiche; portrait, portraiture; whole *or* full-length portrait, half-length portrait, three-quarters portrait; head; profile; miniature; silhouette, shadow figure; mosaic; stained glass, stained glass window; tapestry, batik; trace, tracing; cartoon, caricature, comic [coll.], funnies [slang, U.S.]; image, likeness etc. (representation) 554, (copy) 21; ideogram etc. 590.9.

10. *n.* scene, view, prospect, scape; landscape, landskip [arch.]; waterscape, riverscape; seascape, seapiece; airscape, skyscape, cloudscape; cityscape, townscape; perspective representation, scenograph, bird's-eye view; panorama, diorama; exterior, interior.

11. *n.* photograph, photographic [rare], photo [coll.]; snapshot, snap [coll.]; shot [coll.]; daguerreotype, calotype, talbotype, collotype; tintype, ferrotype; heliotype, heliograph; heliochrome, heliochromtype; ping-pong [cant]; close-up; still photograph, still; rotograph, rotogravure, roto; sculptograph; film, negative, positive, print; exposure; motion picture etc. 599.9.

12. *n.* radiograph, radiogram, scotograph; X-ray photograph, X ray.

13. *n.* shadowgraph, shadowgram; skiagraph, skiagram, skiograph, skiogram.

14. *n.* spectrograph, spectrogram; spectroheliogram, photospectroheliogram.

15. *n.* studio, *atelier* [F.]; gallery, museum, picture gallery, art gallery *or* museum; pinakotheke, glyptotheca.

16. *n.* (art materials) palette *or* pallet; easel; palette knife, spatula; brush, paintbrush; pencil, lead pencil, black lead; crayon, charcoal, chalk, pastel; stump;

---

garlic is to salad, insanity is to art.—SAINT-GAUDENS.   Art is limitation; the essence of every picture is the frame.—CHESTERTON. Great art is as irrational as great music. It is mad with its own loneliness.—G. J. NATHAN. *Mutum est pictura poema* [A picture is a silent poem].   *Fecit, delineavit* [He made it, he drew it].

painter's cream; pigment, paint etc. (coloring matter) 428.3–5; yellow ochre, red lead etc. (specific pigments and dyes) 430–439.

17. *v.* limn, design, draw, sketch, pencil, chalk, scratch, hatch, dash off; draw in pencil, paint in oils etc. *n.*; chalk out, square up; stencil; pastiche; depict, portray etc. (represent) 554.7; color, paint etc. 428.9, 10; decorate etc. (ornament) 847.11.

18. *v.* photograph, photographize [rare], photo [coll.], kodak, take a photograph etc. *n.*, take one's picture, shoot [slang, U.S.]; snap, snapshot; daguerreotype, talbotype, calotype.

19. *adj.* graphic(al), pictorial, pictury, picturesque; artistic(al), arty [coll.]; painted etc. *v.*; photographic; monochrome, polychrome; scenographic; genre; impressionist, neoimpressionist; symbolist, expressionist, futurist, cubist, modernist, Dadaist, vorticist, surrealist; in the grand style; painty, pastose.

20. *adv.* graphically etc. *adj.*, in pencil etc. *n.*

557. Sculpture

1. *n.* sculpture, sculpturing, modeling, carving etc. *v.*; wood carving, xyloglyphy; statuary; wax modeling, ceroplastics; anaglyphy, anaglyptics, anaglyptography; glyptotheca; sculptor etc. 559.4, 5.

2. *n.* monumental sculpture (*see* monument etc. 551.4); architectural sculpture; decorative sculpture; garden sculpture; portrait sculpture; bust, statuette etc. (figure) 554.4.

3. *n.* sculpturation, sculpturing, sculptured marking.

4. *n.* statue etc. (figure) 554.4; cast etc. (copy) 21.

5. *n.* (statues) Apollo Belvedere, Venus of Milo *or* Melos, Cnidian Aphrodite, Venus de' Medici, Dying Gaul, Farnese Hercules, Laocoön, Niobe, Silenus and Infant Bacchus, Theseus, Centaur and Eros, The Wrestlers, David (Michelangelo), Mercury Taking Flight, The Thinker (Rodin); Nike, Winged Victory *or* Nike of Samothrace.

6. *n.* relief, relievo; low relief, bas-relief, basso-relievo, *basso-rilievo* [It.] (*pl. bassi-rilievi*); high relief, alto-relievo, *alto-rilievo* [It.]; half relief, mezzo-relievo, *mezzo-rilievo* [It.]; glyph, anaglyph, coelanaglyphic sculpture; intaglio (*pl.* intaglios, intagli), *intaglio rilievo or rilevato* [It.]; chased *or* embossed relief, boss, embossment; medal, medallion; cameo, plaque; sculptured glass, cameo glass.

7. *n.* ceramics, ceramic ware etc. 384.14.

8. *n.* (tools, materials) chisel, stonecutters' chisel, tooth chisel, wire chisel, turning chisel, wood-working chisel; point, nine-point, twelve-point; knife, wood carver's knife; mallet; modeling tool, spatula; terra cotta, clay, modeling clay, plasticine [trade-mark name], plastic, wax; stone, marble, bronze.

9. *v.* sculpture, sculp *or* sculpt [joc.], insculpture, insculp [now rare]; carve, cut, chisel; model, mold *or* mould; cast.

10. *adj.* sculptural, sculptitory, sculpturesque; statuary, statuesque, statuelike; monumental, monumentary; glyphic, glyptic(al); anaglyphic, anaglyptic; anastatic; ceroplast, ceroplastic; ceramic.

11. *adj.* sculptured etc. *v.*, sculpt, sculptile; in relief, in high *or* low relief.

558. Engraving

1. *n.* engraving, engravement; chasing, chiseling, etching etc. *v.*; etch; line engraving, stipple engraving, chalk engraving, steel engraving, process engraving, half-tone engraving, painter etching *or* engraving; dry point; stone *or* gem engraving, lithography, lithogravure, chromolithography, photolithography; glyptics, glyptography; wood engraving, lignography, xylography; wax process, wax engraving *or* etching, cerography; plate engraving.

chalcography, glyphography, zincography; autotypy, autotypography; photoengraving, photogravure, photomechanical process, rotogravure; helioengraving, heliogravure; heliotypy, heliotypography; *criblé* [F.], *la manière criblée* [F.]; illustration, illumination; half tone; vig-

---

557. The more the marble wastes, / The more the statue grows.—MICHELANGELO.   A sculptor wields / The chisel, and the stricken marble grows / To beauty.—BRYANT.   The statue is then beautiful when it begins to be incomprehensible.—EMERSON.

558. Like . . . a signet shalt thou engrave the two stones with the names of the children of Israel.—BIBLE.   All that I own is a print, / An etching, a mezzotint.—BROWNING.

nette; *cul-de-lampe* [F.]; headpiece, tailpiece; marking, line, stipple, burr.

2. *n.* printing etc. *v.*, plate printing, copperplate printing, anastatic printing, lithographic printing; block printing, xylography, xylotypography; linoleum-block printing, rubber-block printing; color printing, three-color process; type printing etc. 591.

3. *n.* impression, impress, imprint, print; engraving, engravement; intaglio (*pl.* intaglios, intagli), intagliation; etching, etched plate; plate, steel plate, glyphograph; copperplate, chalcograph; zinc plate, zincograph; stereotype, electrotype, autotype; aquatint, mezzotint, lithotint; stone *or* gem engraving, glyptograph; lithograph, chromolithograph, photolithograph; photoengraving, photointaglio; rotograph, rotogravure; helioengraving, heliograph, heliotype; wax engraving, cerograph, encaustic; chalk engraving, graphotype; wood engraving *or* print, lignograph, xylograph; block, block print, linoleum-block print, rubber-block print; cut, woodcut; proof, artist's proof.

4. *n.* (tools, materials) graver, burin, etching point, dry point, style, needle; die, punch, stamp, intaglio, last, mint, seal; plate, stone, block, negative; etching ground *or* varnish, etching ball; chemical agent, nitric acid, hydrofluoric acid.

5. *v.* engrave, grave; insculpture, insculp [now rare]; tool, character, chase, enchase, emboss, incise, inscribe, cut, carve, chisel, stipple, scrape, etch; bite, bite in; impress, imprint, print; stamp, enstamp; stereotype, electrotype, lithograph etc. *n.*; prove, pull; reprint; mark etc. 550.19.

6. *adj.* engraved, insculptured etc. *v.*; "insculp'd upon" (Shakespeare); glyphic, glyptic(al), glyptographic; lapidary, lapidarian, lapideous; lithographic(al) etc. *n.*

559. Artist

1. *n.* artist, *artiste* [F.], limner, depicter *or* depictor, portrayer, picturer; drawer, sketcher, draftsman *or* draughtsman; designer, costume designer, dress designer, color designer; architect, architectress; cartoonist, caricaturist; scenograph, scenographer; ornamentist, ornamentalist; pastelist; copyist; impressionist, neoimpressionist; modernist, futurist, cubist, vorticist, surrealist; dabbler, dauber, daubster, dilettante; Royal Academician, R.A.

2. *n.* painter, paintress [*fem.*], painter stainer, brush, brother of the brush, colorist; oil painter, oil-colorist; water-color painter, water-colorist; landscape painter, landscapist; portrait painter, portraitist; miniature painter, miniaturist; scene painter, scenist, scenewright; historical painter, marine painter, flower painter, still-life painter, genre painter, pleinairist; enameler, enamelist.

3. *n.* (painters) Masaccio, Fra Angelico, Filippo Lippi, Boticelli, Michelangelo, da Vinci, Raphael, del Sarto, Correggio, Titian, Tintoretto, van Eyck, Dürer, Rubens, Vandyke, Rembrandt, Hals, de Hooch, Hobbema, El Greco, Velasquez, Murillo, Goya, Poussin, Boucher, Watteau, Fragonard, Greuze, David, LeBrun, Ingres, Hogarth, Reynolds, Gainsborough, Turner, Blake, Delacroix, Rossetti, Courbet, Corot, Millet, Rousseau, Daumier, Monet, Manet, Degas, Renoir, Seurat, Cézanne, van Gogh, Picasso, Braque, Matisse, Rivera, Kandinski, Klee, Copley, Gilbert Stuart, Homer, Ryder, Whistler, Bellows, Rockwell Kent, Thomas Benton, Grant Wood.

4. *n.* sculptor, sculptress [*fem.*], sculpturer; statuary; figurer, *figuriste* [F.]; graver, carver, chiseler; modeler, molder *or* moulder.

5. *n.* (sculptors) Phidias, Praxiteles, Cellini, Pisano, Ghiberti, Donatello, della Robbia, Michelangelo, Rodin, Brancusi, Maillol, Saint-Gaudens, Epstein.

6. *n.* engraver, graver; chaser, embosser, inscriber, carver, etcher; glyptician [rare], lapidary, lapidist [rare], lapicide; chalcographer, chalcographist; lithographer, chromolithographer, photolithog-

---

559. Dead he is not, but departed,—for the artist never dies.—LONGFELLOW. It came to pass that after a time the artist was forgotten, but the work lived.—O. SCHREINER. An artist is a dreamer consenting to dream of the actual world.—SANTAYANA. Artists must be sacrificed to their art. Like bees, they must put their lives into the sting they give.—EMERSON. Nature sings her exquisite song to the artist alone, her son and her master.—WHISTLER. Nothing can come out of an artist that is not in the man.—H. L. MENCKEN. The great artists of the world are never Puritans, and seldom even ordinarily respectable.—H. L. MENCKEN.

rapher; lignographer, xylographer, glyptographer, cerographer, zincographer, photoengraver, painter etcher *or* engraver, line engraver.

7. *n.* photographer, photographist, kodaker, cameraman; cinematographer, cinematographist; candid-camera photographer; snapshotter, snap shooter; daguerreotypist, calotypist, talbotypist; radiographer, X-ray photographer, skiagrapher.

560. Language

1. *n.* language, speech, tongue, talk, idiom, idiotism [obs.]; lingua; lingo, patter [both usu. joc. or derog.]; vocabulary, phraseology etc. (diction) 569; dialect, jargon, patois etc. 563.4-6.

2. *n.* vernacular, vernacular language; vulgate, vulgar [rare], vulgar tongue; native *or* mother tongue, language of one's fathers; *langue du pays* [F.], *Landessprache* [G.]; koine etc. *below* 560.5; colloquialism etc. 563.3.

3. *n.* conventional *or* accepted speech; literary language; correct *or* good English, Standard English, the king's *or* queen's English; classicism, classicalism.

4. *n.* inflectional ~, isolating ~, polytonic ~, monosyllabic *or* agglutinative languages; synthetic *or* analytic languages; Austroasiatic ~, Austronesian ~, Bantu ~, Dravidian *or* Dravido-Munda languages; Hamitic ~, Indian *or* American Indian languages; Indo-Chinese ~, Sino-Tibetan ~, Tibeto-Burman *or* Tibeto-Chinese languages; Indo-European ~, Indo-Germanic *or* Aryan languages; Ural-Altaic ~, Ugro-Altaic ~, Finno-Tatar ~, Turanian ~, Ugrian ~, Ugro-Finnic ~, Finno-Ugric ~, Finnic *or* Uralian languages; Semitic languages.

Achinese, Afghan, Aka, Albanian, Algonquin, Amharic, Annamese, Arabic, Aramaic, Araucan, Armenian, Assamese, Austral, Avestan, Aymara, Balinese, Baluchi, Bashkir, Batan, Battak, Bengali, Bihari, Bikol, Brahui, Breton, Bugi, Bulgarian, Buriat, Burmese, Caroline, Castilian, Catalan, Cham, Chamorro, Cheremiss, Chibcha, Chin, Chinese, Chuvash, Coman, Coptic, Czechoslovak, Dafla, Danish, Dutch, Dyak, Egyptian, English, Eskimo, Estonian, Ethiopian, Fiji, Finnish, Flemish, Formosan, French, Frisian, Gadaba, Gaelic, Galcha, Garo, German, Gilbertese, Gold, Gondi, Greek, Gujarati, Gypsy, Hawaiian, Hebrew, Hindustani, Ho, Ibanag, Icelandic, Igorot, Ilokano, Irish, Italian, Jagatai, Jakun, Japanese, Javanese, Juang, Kabyle, Kachin, Kafiri, Kalmuck, Kamasin, Kanarese, Kara-Kalpak, Karen, Kashmiri, Kasubian, Kavi, Kazan Tatar, Kharia, Khasi, Khmer, Khond, Khowar, Kiranti, Kirghiz, Kodagu, Kohistani, Koibal, Kongoese, Korwa, Kuki, Kumyk, Kurdish, Kurukh, Lahnda, Lampong, Lamut, *langue d'oc* [F.], *langue d'oïl* [F.], Lapp, Latin, Lettish, Limbu, Lithuanian, Livonian, Low German, Madurese, Magyar, Makassar, Malagasy, Malay, Malayalam, Maltese, Malto, Manchu, Mangar, Manobo, Manx, Maori, Marathi, Marquesan, Marshall, Maya, Meithei, Mishmi, Mon, Mongolian, Montes, Mordvinian, Moro, Mru, Muong, Murmi, Muskogee, Naga, Newari, Niasese, Nicobarese, Niue, Nogai, Norwegian, Oraon, Oriya, Osmanli, Ossetic, Ostyak, Pahari, Palau, Palaung, Pali, Pampango, Pangasinan, Panjabi, Permian, Persian, Phrygian, Plattdeutsch, Polish, Portuguese, Prakrit, Provençal, Quechuan, Rajasthani, Rejang, Rhaeto-Romanic, Romany, Ronga, Rumanian, Russian, Sakai, Samoan, Sanskrit, Santali, Sassak, Savara, Selung, Semang, Serbo-Croatian, Shan, Shilha, Shina, Siamese, Sindhi, Singhalese, Slovenian, Sorbian, Soyot, Spanish, Sundanese, Swahili, Swedish, Syriac, Syryenian, Tagalog, Tahitian, Tamashek, Tamil, Tavghi, Teleut, Telugu, Tibetan, Tigré, Tigriña, Tino, Tipura, Toda, Tongan, Tuamotuan, Tulu, Tungus, Tupi, Turkoman, Uigur, Ukrainian, Uzbek, Veps, Visayan, Vote, Wa, Welsh, Yenisei, Yurak, Zenaga, Zulu-Kaffir.

5. *n.* international auxiliary language, international ~, universal ~, world *or* auxiliary language, interlingua, pasilaly; lingua franca; Koine *or* koine Sabir, Chinook, Chinook *or* Oregon Jargon, pidgin English, pidgin Malay, *bêche-de-mer*

---

560. A classic is something that everybody wants to have read and nobody wants to read. —MARK TWAIN. In science, read, by preference, the newest works, in literature, the oldest. The classic literature is always modern. —BULWER-LYTTON. Language is the archives of history ... language is fossil poetry. —SWIFT. Languages are the pedigrees of nations.—JOHNSON.

[F.], beach-la-mar, beche-le-mar, Hindustani, kitchen Kaffir, Swahili, Hausa, Kiswahili; pasigraphy; Solresol, Lingualumina, Blaia Zimondal, Ro; Volapük, Esperanto, lingua internaciona, Ido, Antido, Lingvo Kosmopolita, Esperantido, Nov-Esperanto, Latinesce, Nov-Latin, Monario, Occidental, Europan, Optez, Romanal, Latino *or* Latino sine flexione, Idiom Neutral, Novial, Arulo.

6. *n.* linguistics, linguistry [rare], linguistic science, science of language, philology, speechcraft, speechlore [rare]; glossology, glottology; semantics, semasiology; paleography; linguipotence [rare]; etymology etc. (lexicology) 562.4; grammar etc. 567; phonetics etc. 402.5.

7. *n.* linguistic student *or* scholar, linguist, linguistician [rare], linguister *or* lingster [obs. exc. dial. U.S.]; philologist, philologer, philologian, philologue [rare], philologaster [derog.]; grammarian, grammatist, grammaticaster [derog.]; polyglot, polyglottonist; etymologist, etymologer; eponymist; lexicologist, lexicographer, lexicographist [rare], lexiconist, glossologist, glossographer, glossarist, glossarian; glottologist; vocabulist, vocabularian; phonologist, phonologer [rare], orthoëpist; dialectician, dialectologist, dialector; Hebraist, Hellenist, Sanskritist; Sinologist, Sinologer, Sinologue; colloquialist, neologist etc. 563.11, 12.

8. *n.* literature, letters, polite literature, belles-lettres, Muses, humanities, *litterae humaniores* [L.]; republic of letters, field of literature; dead languages; learned *or* classical languages, classics; scholarship etc. (learning) 490.2.

9. *adj.* linguistic(al), lingual; philologic(al), philologistic [rare]; glossologic(al), glottologic(al); semantic, semasiological; bilingual, diglot *or* diglottic; hexaglot; polyglot, polyglottic, polyglottal, polyglottous, polyglottonic; English, French, German etc. *n.*; vernacular, dialectal etc. (colloquial) 563.16; lexicological, etymological etc. 562.8, 9.

10. *adv.* in English, *Anglice* [ML.]; in French, in German etc. *n.*

561. Letter

1. *n.* letter, character, sign, symbol, written character, alphabetic *or* phonetic character; initial, initial letter; majuscule, uncial, capital, cap [coll.], upper case [Print.]; minuscule, lower case [Print.]; digraph, trigraph; ideogram, ideographic, ideograph; rune; hieroglyphic writing etc. (writing) 590.1; type etc. (printing) 591.6; vowel, consonant etc. (sound) 402.2; phonogram, phonetic symbol etc. 402.4.

2. *n.* alphabet, letters, letters of the alphabet, ABC *or* A B C's, abecedary; christcross *or* crisscross, christcross-row *or* crisscross-row [all arch. and dial. Eng.]; Latin *or* Roman alphabet, Russian *or* Cyrillic alphabet; Hebrew alphabet; Arabic alphabet; Greek alphabet; German alphabet; Sanskrit alphabet, Devanagari, Nagari, Brahmi; runic alphabet, futhorc *or* futharc; ogam; alphabetics, alphabetism; string alphabet etc. (aids for the blind) 442.2; written character etc. 590.9.

3. *n.* syllable, phone, single utterance, unit of pronunciation; monosyllable, dissyllable, polysyllable; affix, prefix, suffix.

4. *n.* spelling, orthography; phonetic spelling, phonetics, phonography; metagram, metagrammatism; glossic, glossotype, palaeotype; spelling match *or* bee, spelldown *or* spellingdown.

5. *n.* cipher, code, device; monogram, monograph [erron.]; anagram, anagrammatism; acrostic, double *or* triple acrostic; cryptography, cryptograph, cryptogram; logogram, logograph, logogriph.

6. *v.* letter, initial, inscribe, character, sign, mark, stamp; alphabet, alphabetize, arrange alphabetically.

7. *v.* cipher, write in cipher, use ciphers, invent ciphers, code; decipher, decode; transliterate, translate; make *or* construct acrostics, design monograms, play anagrams.

8. *v.* spell, spell out, orthographize, form words, separate letters, trace out; spell backward; spell down [dial. U.S.], hold a spelldown etc. *n.*; gunate.

9. *adj.* literal, lettered etc. *v.*; alphabetic(al), abecedarian; syllabic, monosyllabic, dissyllabic, polysyllabic; acrostic *or* acrostichic; majuscular, uncial, capital, upper-case [Print.]; minuscular, lower-case [Print.]; hieroglyphic etc. (written) 590.15.

---

561. Syllables govern the world.—SELDEN. *Vox audita perit littera scripta manet* [The spoken word dies, the written letter remains].

562. Word

(See also 563. Barbarism, Colloquialism)

1. *n.* word, term, vocable, expression, locution, utterance, unit of speech *or* discourse, articulate sound, articulation; syllable, monosyllable; root, etymon, primitive; derivative; ideophone; sememe, morpheme; synonym, antonym; poecilonym; polyonym [rare]; homonym, metonym, heteronym; analogue, *analogon* [Gr.]; ghost word *or* name, phantomnation; name etc. 564.2–4; parts of speech etc. 567.2; long word, sesquipedalian etc. (grandiloquence) 577.2; portmanteau word, neologism, colloquialism etc. 563.

2. *n.* onomatopoeia, onomatopoësis, onomatopoesy [rare]; bowwow theory, pooh-pooh theory; onomatopoeic word, onomatopoeian, onomatope, onomatoplasm.

3. *n.* verbiage, vocabulary, phraseology etc. (diction) 569; verbosity, wordiness etc. (diffuseness) 573; loquacity etc. 584.

4. *n.* lexicology, lexicography, lexigraphy; glossology, glossography; etymology, derivation, origin, genesis, glottogony; eponymy, eponymism; terminology, orismology; translation; pronunciation, orthoëpy, phonology; philology etc. (linguistics) 560.6; lexicon etc. (dictionary) 593.4.

5. *n.* lexicologist, glossologist, etymologist etc. (linguistic student) 560.7.

6. *v.* word, express etc. (phrase) 566.3.

7. *v.* philologize; etymologize, derive, trace, deduce; eponymize; translate.

8. *adj.* verbal, literal; vocabular, vocabularian; lexic(al), lexicologic(al), lexigraphic(al), lexicographic(al), lexicographian; glossologic(al), glossographic(al); titular, nominal etc. 564.8; oral, unwritten etc. (spoken) 582.10; philological etc. (linguistic) 560.9.

9. *adj.* etymologic(al), derivative, glottogonic; conjugate, paronymous.

10. *adj.* verbose, wordy etc. (diffuse) 573.7; loquacious etc. 584.5.

11. *adv.* verbally etc. *adj.*, verbatim etc. (literally) 19.14.

---

562. In the beginning was the Word.—Bible. Longer than deeds liveth the word.—Pindar. Words once spoke can never be recalled.—Horace. I was never so bethump'd with words.—Shakespeare. Words are but the signs of ideas.—Johnson. The artillery of words.—Swift. Words, like Nature, half

563. Barbarism, Colloquialism

1. *n.* barbarism, caconym, impropriety, vulgarism; corruption, abuse of language *or* terms, missaying, antiphrasis, pseudology; foreignism; vulgarity etc. (inelegance) 579; malapropism etc. 565.2; solecism etc. (ungrammaticism) 568.

2. *n.* unconventional language, unaccepted speech, substandard words, underworld of speech.

3. *n.* colloquialism, colloquial expression, colloquial *or* unrefined speech, spoken language, vulgate; vulgar tongue etc. (vernacular) 560.1.

4. *n.* jargon, lingo, lingua, patois, cant, argot, bat [Anglo-Ind.]; flash, flash tongue; slang, slanguage [joc.], slangism; St. Giles's Greek, thieves' Latin, peddler's French, billingsgate; back slang, rhyming slang; pig Latin, dog Latin; gibberish, gibber, jabber, patter, *baragouin* [F.]; Dutch, double Dutch, High Dutch [slang], Greek, Hebrew, Choctaw; confusion of tongues, Babel.

5. *n.* dialect, patois, idiom, provincialism, localism, regionalism, regional speech, isogloss; dialectal accent *or* pronunciation, accent, brogue, twang; Anglicism, Briticism; Gallicism, Scotticism, Americanism; Hibernicism, Irishism; ogam; Pennsylvania Dutch; baboo English, *chee-chee* [both Anglo-Ind.]; cockney, cockneyese; dialect dictionary, idioticon; talk, tongue etc. (language) 560.1.

6. *n.* lingua franca, Esperanto, Volapük etc. 560.5.

7. *n.* neology, neologism, neoterism, newfangled nomenclature, new word *or* term; coined *or* manufactured word, coinage; nonce word; vogue word; newness etc. 123; innovation etc. 140.3.

8. *n.* hybridism, hybrid, hybrid word *or* derivative; macaronic, macaronicism; contamination, crossbreeding.

9. *n.* portmanteau word, portmanteau, portmantologism; telescope word, blendword.

10. *n.* archaism, archaicism, antiquated word *or* expression; obsolescence; obsoletism; monkish Latin, dead language

---

reveal and half conceal the soul within.—Tennyson. Words pay no debts.—Shakespeare.
563. Slang is language that takes off its coat, spits on its hands, and goes to work.—Sandburg.

11. *n.* colloquialist, colloquializer; jargonist, jargoner, jargonizer; slangster, slang-whanger [slang]; dialectician, dialectologist, dialector.

12. *n.* neologist, word-coiner, coiner of words, neoterist, innovator.

13. *v.* colloquialize, make colloquial, use colloquialisms etc. *n.*; jargon, jargonize; cant, sling the bat [slang, Anglo-Ind.]; slang, slang-whang [slang]; dialectalize; Americanize, Anglicize, Galicize.

14. *v.* neologize, neoterize, coin words.

15. *adj.* barbarous, barbaric, barbarian; unconventional, unaccepted, substandard; vulgar, unrefined etc. (inelegant) 579.3.

16. *adj.* colloquial, vernacular, unliterary, undignified, informal; slang, slangy, slangish, slangous [rare], slanguar [joc.]; cant, flash, argotic; jargonic, jargonish, jargonal; dialect, dialectal, dialectic(al).

17. *adj.* neologic(al), neologistic(al); neoteric(al), neoteristic(al).

18. *adj.* archaic, archaical [rare], archaistic; obsolescent; obsolete, dead.

564. Nomenclature
(See 565. Misnomer, Anonymity)

1. *n.* nomenclature, naming etc. *v.*, nuncupation, nomination [rare], denomination, appellation, compellation, designation; christening, baptism; cognomination; terminology, phraseology, orismology, glossology, toponymy, technology; antonomasia.

2. *n.* name, *nomen* [L.], nomination [obs.], denomination, moniker *or* moncker [slang], handle [slang], designation, style, compellation; appellative; title, titulus, handle to one's name [coll.]; head, heading, caption; address.

proper name; first name, Christian name, given name [coll.], baptismal name; last name, family name, patronymic, surname; cognomen, cognomination; praenomen, agnomen [both Rom. Antiq.]; eponym; *nomen conservandum* [L.], *nomen novum* [L., Bot. and Zool.], *nomen nudum* [L., Biol.]; byname, epithet; trade-mark *or* trademark, trade name, trade-mark name; signature, sign manual; autograph, autography; synonym; antonym; empty title *or* name; namesake, cognominal [obs.]; nickname etc. 565.3.

3. *n.* term, expression, locution; catchword, byword, byname; technical term, technicalism, technicality; cant etc. (jargon) 563.4–6; word etc. 562.

4. *n.* noun, pronoun, proper noun, common noun, adherent noun, adverbial noun, verbal noun, noun substantive, noun adjective, quotation noun.

5. *n.* namer etc. *v.*, nomenclator, nomenclaturist.

6. *v.* name, nomenclature, nominate [now rare], denominate, appellate [rare], designate, call, clepe [arch.], term, style, dub, characterize, define, describe, specify, distinguish by the name of; label, tag; title, titule [now rare]; entitle, intitule; christen, baptize; cognomen [rare], cognominate; nickname etc. 565.6.

7. *v.* be called etc. *adj.*, hight [arch.], go *or* be known by the name of, go *or* pass under the name of, bear the name of, rejoice in the name of.

8. *adj.* named, called etc. *v.*; y-clept *or* y-cleped [arch.], appellatived, known as, known by the name of; nominal, so-called; nuncupatory, nuncupative [both obs.]; titular; cognominal.

9. *adj.* terminological, phraseologic(al), orismological, glossological, technologic(al).

10. *phr.* what one may well ~, fairly ~, properly *or* fitly call.

565. Misnomer, Anonymity
(See 564. Nomenclature)

1. *n.* misnomer, misnaming etc. *v.*, wrong name, incorrect term *or* designation.

2. *n.* malapropism, malapropoism, malaprop, slipslap [coll.]; Mrs. Malaprop

---

564. There is no stone without its name.—LUCAN. What's in a name? That which we call a rose / By any other name would smell as sweet.—SHAKESPEARE. He said true things, but called them by wrong names.—BROWNING. I find it very interesting to know the signification of names.—M. ARNOLD. In a very plain sense the proverb says, Call one a thief and he will steal.—CARLYLE. These are a few of their princely names, these are a few of their great, proud, glittering names.—T. WOLFE.

565. A nickname is the heaviest stone that the devil can throw at a man.—HAZLITT. Nicknames and whippings, when they are once laid

(Sheridan), Mrs. Slipslop (Fielding); grammatical blunder etc. 495.3; ungrammaticism etc. 568.

3. *n.* nickname, byname, byword, cognomen, moniker [slang] etc. 564.2; sobriquet *or* soubriquet; alias, another name, assumed name *or* title, fictitious name, pseudonym, anonym, *nom de guerre* [F.]; pen name, nom de plume; stage name, *nom de théâtre* [F.]; pet name, little name, babyism; pseudonymity, pseudonymousness etc. *adj.*

4. *n.* what's-its-name, what's-his-name, what's-her-name, what-you-may-call-it, what-you-may-call-'em, what-you-may-call-him, what-you-may-call-her, whatcha-ma-call-'em, what-d'ye-call-'em, what-d'ye-call-it [all coll.]; *je ne sais quoi* [F.]; such-and-such, such a *or* an one [now rare], so-and-so, Mr. *or* Mrs. So-and-So, "Sergeant What-is-name" (Kipling); thingamabob [coll.] etc. (object) 316.3.

5. *n.* anonymity, anonymousness etc. *adj.*, anonym.

6. *v.* misname, misnomer, miscall, misterm, call out of one's name [coll.], nickname; assume a name *or* alias, take an assumed name *or* alias.

7. *adj.* misnamed etc. *v.*, misnomed; pseudonymous, pseudonymal, pseudonymic; so-called, quasi, would-be, *soi-disant* [F.]; self-called, self-styled, self-christened.

8. *adj.* malapropian, malapropish, malapropos.

9. *adj.* anonymous, anonymal [obs.], anon.; nameless, unnamed, unspecified, undesignated, unacknowledged, undefined, innominate, without a name, having no name.

10. *adv.* by whatever name, under any name.

566. Phrase

1. *n.* phrase, expression, locution, utterance; clause, sentence, paragraph; idiom, idiotism; turn of expression, idiomatic turn of speech, peculiar expression; set phrase *or* term; phraseogram, phraseograph; euphemism etc. (figure of speech) 521; paraphrase etc. (rendering) 522.2; periphrase etc. (circumlocution) 573.3; saying, motto etc. (maxim) 496; figure of speech etc. 521; phraseology etc. (nomenclature) 564, (diction) 569.

2. *n.* phraser, phrasemaker, phrasemonger, phraseman.

3. *v.* phrase, express, give expression *or* words to, word, word it, put into words, clothe in words, couch in terms, express by *or* in words, find words to express; voice, vocalize; put, present; speak by the book *or* card; style, designate, describe etc. (name) 564.6; talk, say etc. (speak) 582.6.

4. *adj.* phrased etc. *v.*, phrasy [coll.], phraseologic(al); idiomatic.

5. *adv.* in set phrases *or* terms, in good set terms, in round terms.

567. Grammar
(See 568. Ungrammaticism)

1. *n.* grammar, accidence, syntax, analysis, praxis, paradigm, syllepsis, synopsis inflection, case, declension, conjugation jussive; nunnation, mimmation; syllabification, syllabication; *jus et norma loquendi* [L.]; diction etc. 569; Lindley Murray etc. (textbook) 593.5; philology etc (linguistics) 560.6.

2. *n.* parts of speech, adjective, verb adverb, preposition, conjunction, interjection; noun, pronoun etc. 564.4.

3. *n.* punctuation, punctuation marks quotation marks, comma etc. (mark) 550.8.

4. *n.* grammarian, philologist etc. (linguistic student) 560.7.

5. *v.* grammaticize, grammar [rare] parse, analyze; inflect, conjugate, decline; punctuate, use punctuation mark etc. 550.8; syllabify, syllabize, syllabicate

6. *adj.* grammatic(al), syntactic(al) inflectional, synoptic; punctuate, punctuative, punctuational [rare].

568. Ungrammaticism
(See 567. Grammar)

1. *n.* ungrammaticism, ungrammar, un grammaticalness etc. *adj.*; solecism, ba *or* faulty grammar, deviation from th idiom *or* the rules of syntax; corruptio of speech, talkee-talkee; impropriety; ca

---

on, no one has discovered how to take off.—LANDOR. What is so nameless as beauty, / Which poets, who give it a name, / Are only unnaming forever?—W. BYNNER.
566. A world of thought in one translucent phrase.—H. B. CARPENTER.

cology, cacography etc. (inelegance) 579; barbarism etc. 563; malapropism etc. 565.2; grammatical blunder, bull etc. (blunder) 495.3.

2. *v.* be ungrammatical etc. *adj.,* use bad *or* faulty grammar, murder the language, murder the king's *or* queen's English, speak *or* write out of the idiom, infringe *or* violate the rules of grammar, break Priscian's head; solecize, use solecisms, commit a solecism.

3. *adj.* ungrammatic(al), solecistic(al), incorrect, inaccurate, faulty, improper, unseemly, incongruous; slipslap; malapropian etc. 565.8; inelegant etc. 579.2.

569. Diction

1. *n.* diction, phraseology, phrase, phrasing, wording, verbiage, vocabulation [rare], vocabulary, speech, talk [coll.], language, dialect, parlance, locution, expression, rhetoric, grammar; style, manner, mode, strain, vein, manner of speaking *or* writing, mode *or* style of expression, manner of expressing thought in language, mode *or* form of speech, use of words, selection *or* choice of words, expression of ideas.

distinctive *or* characteristic mode of presentation, peculiar *or* particular manner of expression, peculiarity *or* particularity of phrasing; idiom, idiologism; composition; literary power, authorship, artistry; ready pen, the pen of a ready writer; the grand style *or* manner, *la morgue littéraire* [F.]; command of words, elocution etc. 582.3; manner of speaking, enunciation etc. (utterance) 580.3.

2. *v.* style, word etc. (phrase) 566.3.

570. Perspicuity
(See 571. Imperspicuity)

1. *n.* perspicuity, clearness, lucidity, plain speaking etc. (intelligibility) 518; exactness etc. (accuracy) 494.3.

2. *adj.* perspicuous, clear, explicit etc. (intelligible) 518.5, 6, (manifest) 525.4, 5; exact etc. (accurate) 494.10.

571. Imperspicuity
(See 570. Perspicuity)

1. *n.* imperspicuity, obscurity, darkness of meaning etc. (unintelligibility) 519; involution, complexity, confusion etc. (disorder) 59; ambiguity etc. (equivocalness) 520; inexactness etc. (inaccuracy) 495.4.

2. *adj.* imperspicuous, obscure, vague etc. (unintelligible) 519.6, 7; involved, confused etc. (disorderly) 59.8, 10; inexact etc. (inaccurate) 495.14.

572. Conciseness
(See 573. Diffuseness)

1. *n.* conciseness, briefness etc. *adj.,* brevity, economy of speech *or* language; laconics, laconism, laconicism; ellipsis, syncope; monostich; abbreviation etc. (shortening) 201.2; compression etc. (contraction) 195; epitome etc. (compendium) 596; portmanteau word etc. 563.9.

2. *v.* be concise etc. *adj.,* come to the point, make a long story short, cut the matter short, laconize; telescope; abridge, condense etc. (shorten) 201.4, (abstract) 596.4.

3. *adj.* concise, brief, short, "short and sweet" (T. Lodge), terse, laconic, pithy, succinct, crisp, trenchant, summary, neat, close, compact, compressed, condensed, epigrammatic(al), sententious, elliptic(al); curt, curtal [arch.], curtate, decurtate; pointed, to the point; pregnant; compendious etc. 596.5.

4. *adv.,* concisely, briefly etc. *adj.*; in brief, in short, in epitome, in a word, in a few words, in substance, for the sake of brevity, for shortness' sake, to be brief, to come to the point, to cut the matter short, to make a long story short.

---

569. Style is the dress of thoughts.—CHESTERFIELD. Style: a certain absolute and unique manner of expressing a thing, in all its intensity and color.—PATER. His diction blazes up into a sudden explosion of prophetic grandeur.—DE QUINCEY. *Le style c'est de l'homme* [A man's style is a part of him].—BUFFON.

570. Clear conception leads naturally to clear and correct expression.—BOILEAU.

571. Now we see through a glass, darkly.—BIBLE. *Brevis esse laboro, obscurus fio* [I strive to be brief, I become obscure].—HORACE. 572. Since brevity is the soul of wit, / And tediousness the limbs and outward flourishes, / I will be brief.—SHAKESPEARE. Whatever advice you give, be brief.—HORACE. As man is now constituted, to be brief is almost a condition of being inspired.—SANTAYANA.

5. *phr.* it comes to this, the long and short of it is, the gist is.

573. Diffuseness
(See 572. Conciseness)

1. *n.* diffuseness, profuseness etc. *adj.*, exuberance, prolixity; wordiness, verbosity, verbiage, cloud of words, *copia verborum* [L.]; longiloquence, largiloquence [obs.]; drivel, twaddle, drool; rant, rodomontade, harangue, peroration; effusion, flow of words etc. (loquacity) 584; grandiloquence etc. 577.2.

2. *n.* tautology, tautologism, tautophony; battology, perissology [obs.], pleonasm, macrology, dilogy; expletive, padding; superfluity etc. (redundance) 641; repetition etc. 104.

3. *n.* circumlocution, ambages [now rare], circumambages [rare], indirect *or* roundabout way of speaking, roundabout phrases; periphrase, periphrasis; digression, episode, excursus; ambiguity, equivocation etc. (quibble) 477.3, 4.

4. *n.* expatiation, amplification, enlargement, expanding etc. *v.*; dilation, dilatation [both now rare].

5. *v.* be diffuse etc. *adj.*, expatiate, descant, dilate, amplify, expand, enlarge, enlarge upon, relate at large, tell in detail, extend, protract, spin *or* draw out, spin a long yarn, run out on, launch out, branch out; pad, fill out; speak at length, perorate, harangue, rant, rodomontade; drivel, twaddle, drool; digress, maunder, ramble; be circumlocutory etc. *adj.*, circumlocute [joc.]; equivocate, beat about the bush etc. (quibble) 477.8; be loquacious etc. 584.4.

6. *v.* tautologize, battologize; iterate, dwell on *or* upon, harp upon etc. (repeat) 104.4.

7. *adj.* diffuse, diffusive; profuse, profusive; prolix, copious, exuberant, extravagant; wordy, verbose; longiloquent, largiloquent [obs.]; lengthy, long, longsome, long-winded, long-spun, long-drawn-out, spun-out, protracted; rambling, maundering, roving, desultory, discursive, digressive; padded, episodic, flatulent, bombastic etc. (grandiloquent) 577.7; loquacious etc. 584.5.

8. *adj.* tautologic(al), tautologous, tautophonic(al); battological; pleonastic(al) [rare]; superfluous etc. (redundant) 641.5; repetitional etc. 104.6, 7.

9. *adj.* circumlocutory, periphrastic, ambagious, ambagitory; roundabout etc. (circuitous) 311.16.

10. *adv.* diffusely etc. *adj.*, at large, at length, *in extenso* [L.]; about it and about.

574. Vigor
(See 575. Feebleness)

1. *n.* vigor, vigorousness etc. *adj.*, power, strength, force, intellectual force, strong language; gravity, weight.

2. *n.* spirit, punch [slang], pep [slang], point, pungence *or* pungency, piquance *or* piquancy, poignance *or* poignancy.

3. *n.* vehemence, passion, verve, ardor, enthusiasm, glow, fire, warmth.

4. *n.* loftiness, elevation, sublimity, grandeur; eloquence etc. (oratory) 582.3.

5. *adj.* vigorous, strong, powerful, forceful, forcible, mordant, biting, trenchant, incisive, graphic, impressive, nervous; sensational.

6. *adj.* spirited, lively, sparkling, racy, bold, slashing, crushing; pungent, piquant, poignant; peppy, full of pep *or* punch [all slang]; pointed, full of point, pithy, sententious.

7. *adj.* vehement, passionate, impassioned, burning, glowing, warm.

8. *adj.* lofty, elevated, sublime, grand, poetic, eloquent.

9. *adj.* weighty, ponderous, heavy, deep, profound.

10. *adv.* vigorously, vehemently etc. *adj.*; in set *or* good set terms, in no measured terms; in glowing terms, with heart on fire.

575. Feebleness
(See 574. Vigor)

1. *n.* feebleness, weakness etc. *adj.*, enervation, jejunity, flaccidity, vapidity, poverty, frigidity.

---

573. One of the worst plagues of society is this thoughtless, inexhaustible verbosity.—Mrs. H. Ward.   He draweth out the thread of his verbosity finer than the staple of his argument.—Shakespeare.

574. His talk was like a charge of horse.—Masefield.   Thoughts that breathe and words that burn.—Gray.

575. This is the way the world ends / Not with a bang but a whimper.—T. S. Eliot.

2. *adj.* feeble, weak, bald, meager, slight, poor, colorless, tame, jejune, insipid, vapid, watery, washy, wishy-washy [coll.], languid; nerveless, enervated; cold, frigid; dull, dry, monotonous, unvaried; prosing, prosy, prosaic; careless, slovenly, loose, lax, sloppy, slipslap, slipshod, disjointed, disconnected, sketchy; inexact; puerile, childish; flatulent, frothy.

576. Plainness
(See 577. Ornament; also 849. Simplicity)

1. *n.* plainness, simpleness etc. *adj.*, simplicity, *simplex munditiis* (Horace), lack of ornamentation, severity; plain words *or* terms, plain English, common parlance; Saxon English; household words.

2. *v.* speak plainly, waste no words, call a spade a spade, plunge *in medias res* [L.], come to the point, not beat about the bush.

3. *adj.* plain, simple, unornamented, unadorned, unvarnished, homely, homespun, neat, severe, chaste, pure, Saxon, commonplace, matter-of-fact, natural, prosaic, sober, unimaginative; dry, unvaried, monotonous etc. 575.2.

4. *adv.* plainly etc. *adj.*, in plain words *or* terms, in plain English, in common parlance; point-blank, to the point.

577. Ornament
(See 576. Plainness; also 847. Ornamentation)

1. *n.* ornament, ornamentation, adornment, embellishment, embroidery, frills; ornateness, rhetoricalness etc. *adj.*; flourish, flourish of rhetoric; floridity, flowers of speech *or* rhetoric; fine writing, purple passages *or* patches; preciousness, preciosity; Minerva press; rhetoric, declamation; euphuism; euphemism; alliteration; inversion, anastrophe; antithesis, trope etc. (figure of speech) 521.

2. *n.* grandiloquence, magniloquence, magniloquy [rare], altiloquence, altiloquy [obs.]; turgidity, turgescence *or* turgescency; pretentious language, pretentiousness etc. *adj.*, pretension; affectation, teratology [obs.], grandiosity, orotundity, pomposity, inflation; bombast, bombastry; rant, fustian, rodomontade, buncombe *or* bunkum [coll.], bunk [slang], balderdash, Barnumism, highfalutin *or* highfaluting [coll.], high-flown diction, big *or* tall talk [coll.].

big-sounding *or* high-sounding words, lexiphanicism; sesquipedalianism, sesquipedalism, sesquipedality; *sesquipedalia* [L.], sesquipedalian words, *sesquipedalia verba* [L.]; sesquipedalian, big *or* long word, jawbreaker [slang]; prose run mad; phrasemongering, phrasemongery; tautology etc. (diffuseness) 573; exaggeration etc. 549; boasting etc. 884; redundance etc. 641.

3. *n.* rhetorician, rhetor; phrasemonger, euphuist, euphemist.

4. *v.* ornament, ornamentalize; decorate, adorn, embellish, embroider, enrich, varnish, overlay with ornament, overcharge, overload; euphemize, euphuize.

5. *v.* be bombastic etc. *adj.*, bounce, Barnumize; buncomize, talk big, lay *or* pile it on, talk highfalutin [all coll.]; smell of the lamp; exaggerate etc. 549.2.

6. *adj.* ornate, ornamented etc. *v.*, figured, flamboyant, frothy, flashy, rich; flowery, florid; rhetorical; euphuistic(al), euphemistic(al); alliterative; figurative etc. 521.3.

7. *adj.* grandiloquent, grandiloquous, magniloquent, altiloquent, altiloquious [obs.]; gassy, windy [both coll.]; grandiose, bombastic, fustian, mouthy, orotund, ostentatious, showy, flaunting, swelling, pompous, flatulent, inflated, tumid; turgid, turgent [now rare], turgescent; lofty, tall [coll.], imposing, sonorous, lexiphanic, Johnsonian; highflying, high-flown, high-flowing, highfalutin *or* highfaluting [coll.]; high-sounding, big-sounding, great-sounding; grandisonant, grandisonous; sesquipedal, sesquipedalian; jawbreaking [slang], crackjaw; pedantic, pedantical [rare]; stilted, on stilts; declamatory, pretentiously rhetorical, sententious; redundant etc. 641.5; exaggerated etc. 549.3; diffuse etc. 573.7; affected etc. 853.6; boastful etc. 884.7.

8. *adv.* ornately, grandiloquently etc. *adj.*; *ore rotundo* [L.], with well-rounded speech, with rounded phrase.

---

576. An honest tale speeds best being plainly told.—SHAKESPEARE.

577. To gild refined gold, to paint the lily, to throw a perfume on the violet.—SHAKESPEARE.

578. Elegance
(See 579. Inelegance)

1. *n.* elegance, elegancy, gracefulness etc. *adj.*, grace, refined gracefulness *or* propriety, propriety, refinement, discrimination, restraint; taste, good *or* fastidious taste; polish, finish; distinction, clarity, purity; felicity, ease; simplicity, harmonious simplicity; balance, rhythm, symmetry, proportion, harmony; concinnity, concinnation [rare]; euphony, euphonia [rare], euphonism; euphemism; euphuism; Atticism, Attic salt; classicism, classicalism; well-rounded *or* well-turned periods, flowing periods; the right word in the right place.

2. *n.* purist, classicist, stylist.

3. *v.* display elegance etc. *n.*, discriminate nicely; flow smoothly *or* with ease; point an antithesis, round a period.

4. *adj.* elegant, proper, correct, appropriate, seemly, comely, tasteful, refined, restrained, polished, simple, chaste, pure, artistic(al), Attic, Ciceronian, Saxon, academic(al); classic(al), classicistic; concinnate, concinnous [rare]; graceful, easy, readable, fluent, flowing, tripping; unaffected, natural, unlabored; mellifluous, mellifluent, mellisonant; euphonious, euphonic(al), euphonistic [rare]; euphemistic(al), euphuistic(al); felicitous, happy, neat, well *or* neatly put *or* expressed.

579. Inelegance
(See 578. Elegance)

1. *n.* inelegance, inelegancy, want of elegance etc. 578; tastelessness etc. *adj.*, poor *or* bad taste; vulgarity, vulgarism, vulgar speech *or* writing; barbarism, Gothicism, impropriety, impurity; cacology, cacoëpy, mispronunciation; poor diction, bad speaking *or* pronunciation, poor choice of words; cacography, incorrect *or* bad writing, loose *or* slipshod construction, ill-balanced sentences; cacophony, uncouth *or* disagreeable words, words that break the teeth *or* dislocate the jaw affected elegance, euphuism, Marinism Gongorism; solecism etc. (ungrammaticism) 568; caconym, slang etc. 563; fustian etc. (grandiloquence) 577.2; mannerism etc. (affectation) 853.

2. *n.* inelegant speaker *or* writer, vulgarian, barbarian; cacographer; euphuist Marinist, Gongorist.

3. *adj.* inelegant, tasteless, in bad taste offensive to ears polite, uncouth, low, vulgar, indecorous, gross, unseemly, rude crude, coarse, unpolished, uncourtly, undignified, unrefined, impure, outlandish grotesque; barbarous, barbaric, barbarian; unclassical; doggerel, mongrel; incorrect, improper, cacographic(al) graceless, ungraceful; harsh, abrupt; dry ponderous, labored, forced, cramped stiff, formal, *guindé* [F.], affected, mannered, artificial, awkward, halting; Gongorist *or* gongoristic, Gongoresque; solecistic etc. (ungrammatical) 568.3; slangy etc. (barbarous) 563.15, 16; turgid etc (grandiloquent) 577.7; malapropian etc 565.8.

580. Voice
(See 581. Aphonia)

1. *n.* voice, *vox* [L.], *voce* [It.]; vocality, vocal, vocal sound; good voice loud *or* powerful voice (*see* loud, powerful etc. 404.8), musical etc. voice (*see* musical etc. 413.27), unmusical etc. voice (*see* unmusical etc. 414.4), harsh etc voice (*see* harsh etc. 410.9, 10); intonation, tone of voice etc. (tone) 402.2.

2. *n.* vocal organs, organs of speech vocal cavities; glottis, vocal chink; voice box, larynx; syrinx; vocal sac; vocal cords *or* bands, vocal lips, vocal processes vocal folds; lungs etc. 349.19.

3. *n.* utterance *or* utterancy, vocal utterance *or* expression, vocalization, locution, expression, voice, tongue, prolation [obs.], phonation, articulation, articulate sound; enunciation, pronunciation, orthoëpy; mode of utterance *or* pronunciation, mode of speech, style of vocal expression, manner of speaking, delivery attack; distinctness *or* clearness of articulation; diction etc. 569; speech, remark etc. 582.

---

578. Let your speech be always with grace, seasoned with salt.—BIBLE. I would advise those who do not speak elegantly, not to speak at all.—CHESTERFIELD. Elegant as simplicity.—COWPER. True ease in writing comes from art, not chance.—POPE.
579. Though I be rude in speech.—BIBLE. Rude am I in my speech / And little bless'd with the soft phrase of peace.—SHAKESPEARE. To speak and to offend, with some people, are but one and the same thing.—LA BRUYÈRE.

580. Out of the abundance of the heart the mouth speaketh.—BIBLE. How sweetly sounds the voice of a good woman.—MASSIN-

4. *n.* accent, accentuation; emphasis, stress; rhythmical stress, ictus; broad accent, strong accent, pure accent, native accent, foreign accent; brogue, twang.

5. *n.* exclamation, exclaim [arch.], ejaculation, expletive, ecphonesis; vociferation etc. (cry) 411.

6. *n.* ventriloquism, ventriloquy, ventrilocution; gastriloquism, gastriloquy [both rare]; ventriloquist, ventriloque [rare], gastriloquist [rare].

7. *n.* phonology etc. (sound) 402.5.

8. *v.* voice, give voice, ~ utterance, ~ tongue *or* expression, vocalize, prolate [obs.], utter, sound, express, articulate, enunciate, pronounce, deliver, emit; accent, accentuate, emphasize, stress; talk, say etc. (speak) 582.6; phrase etc. 566.3.

9. *v.* exclaim, ejaculate, rap out; cry, vociferate etc. 411.5, 7.

10. *v.* ventriloquize, gastriloquize [rare].

11. *adj.* vocal, voiceful [poetic]; phonic, phonetic; enunciated, enunciative, enunciatory; articulate, articulated; accentual, accentuate, accentuated; subvocal, subtonic; pretonic, posttonic; oral etc. (spoken) 582.10.

12. *adj.* (phonetics) voiced, vocalized etc. (sounded) 402.11.

13. *adj.* ventriloquous, ventriloqual, ventriloquial, ventriloquistic, ventriloque [rare]; gastriloquous, gastriloquial [both rare].

581. Aphonia
(See 580. Voice)

1. *n.* aphonia, aphony, absence *or* want of voice; voicelessness, dumbness, muteness etc. *adj.*; mutism, mutescence, obmutescence [rare]; dysphonia *or* dysphony; deaf-mutism, deaf-muteness, deaf-dumbness, deaf-and-dumbness, surdimutism; silence etc. 403, (taciturnity) 585.

2. *n.* mute, dummy; deaf-mute, deaf-and-dumb person, surdomute.

3. *n.* muted voice, muffled tones, soft *or* low voice, small *or* little voice; veiled voice, *voce velata* [It.]; undertone, underbreath, bated breath; murmur, murmuration [now rare]; whisper, whispering etc. *v.*, whisperation, breath; stage whisper.

4. *v.* be mute etc. *adj.*, stick in the throat; hold one's tongue, keep silence etc. (not speak) 585.3.

5. *v.* render mute etc. *adj.*, mute, mum [obs.], muzzle, gag, throttle, choke off, stop one's mouth, cut one short, drown the voice, muffle, smother, stifle, deafen, suppress, stop; strike dumb, dumfound, dumfounder; put to silence, hush etc. (silence) 403.5.

6. *v.* speak softly *or* low, murmur, mutter; whisper, whisper in the ear, breathe; aspirate.

7. *adj.* aphonous, aphonic; nonvocal, unvocal; voiceless, tongueless, speechless, wordless, breathless; tacit, mum, dumb, mute, obmutescent [rare], tongue-tied, inarticulate; mute as a fish, ~ stockfish *or* mackerel; deaf and dumb, deaf-dumb, deaf-mute; silent etc. (taciturn) 585.4, (still) 403.6.

8. *adj.* (phonetics) unvoiced, surd etc. (unsounded) 403.7.

9. *adv.* voicelessly etc. *adj.*; with bated breath, *sotto voce* [It.] etc. (faintly) 405.11.

582. Speech
(See 583. Imperfect Speech)

1. *n.* speech, talk, talking etc. *v.*, locution, parole, palaver, prattle, gab [coll.], gaff [slang], lip [slang], chin music [joc., U.S.], prolation [obs.], utterance, discourse, elocution [now rare], spoken language, verbal intercourse, oral communication, word of mouth; words, accents; faculty of speech, power of speaking; conversation etc. (interlocution) 588; chatter etc. 584.2.

2. *n.* a speech, speechment [rare], speechification [joc.], speeching, talk, spiel [slang, U.S.], say; address, public address, formal speech; discourse, lecture, prelection, declamation, harangue, tirade, screed, diatribe, exhortation; sermon, sermonet; preachment, preaching,

---

ER. Her voice was ever soft, gentle, and low; an excellent thing in woman.—SHAKEPEARE. Speak clearly, if you speak at all; / Carve every word before you let it fall.—HOLMES. Thy voice is a celestial melody.—LONGFELLOW.

81. You have not converted a man because you have silenced him.—J. MORLEY. *Vox faucibus haesit* [His voice stuck in his throat].—VERGIL.

582. Speech is the image of life.—DEMOCRITUS. Let thy speech be short, comprehending much in a few words.—APOCRYPHA. It is easy for men to talk one thing and think another.—

preachification [coll.], preach [coll.], religious discourse; monologue; recitation, recital, recitement [rare]; rhetorical discourse *or* address, oration, peroration [now rare], elocution; salutatory [U.S.]; valediction, valedictory, valedictory address *or* oration; travelogue; allocution etc. 586; soliloquy etc. 589; dissertation etc. 595.

3. *n.* oratory, elocution, eloquence, facundity [obs.], rhetoric; speechcraft, wordcraft; speaking, public speaking; declamation, delivery, enunciation, expression; command of language *or* words, power of speech, gift of the gab [coll.], *usus loquendi* [L.]; recitationalism [rare]; multiloquence, fluency etc. (loquacity) 584; loftiness etc. 574.4.

4. *n.* remark, spoken remark, uttered words, statement, word, say, saying, utterance, expression, allegation, assertion, pronouncement, dictum, dict [arch.], position, observation, comment, mention; declaration, dick [slang]; sentence, phrase.

5. *n.* speaker, talker, utterer etc. *v.*; spokester, spokesman, spokeswoman; prolocutor, prolocutress *or* prolocutrix [*fem.*]; mouthpiece; public speaker, speechmaker, speecher, speechifier [joc.], speakeress [*fem.*], jawsmith [slang, U.S.], demagogue; rhetor, rhetorician; elecutioner, elocutionist; orator, oratress *or* oratrix [*fem.*].

Hermes; Demosthenes, Cicero; soapbox orator, soapboxer; stump orator, spellbinder [U.S.]; lecturer, prelector, reciter, reader; preacher, preacheress [*fem.*]; sermonizer, sermonist, sermoner, sermoneer [rare]; expositor, expounder; chalk talker [coll.]; patterer, patterist; monologist, monologuist; improvisator, *improvvisatore* [It.], *improvvisatrice* [It., *fem.*]; chatterer etc. 584.3; gossip etc. 532.5; conversationalist etc. (interlocutor) 588.5; soliloquist etc. 589.2.

6. *v.* speak, talk, patter [chiefly slang], wag the tongue [coll.], mouth, word [arch. or dial.], gab [coll.], spiel [slang, U.S.], parley [now chiefly joc.]; say, breathe, utter, present, deliver, emit, let out [coll.], come out with, mention, let fall, put *or* set forth, pour forth, voice,

give tongue *or* voice, give utterance, expression *or* words to, articulate, enunciate, pronounce, state, assert, aver, allege, declare, tell, communicate, convey, relate, recite, comment, remark, observe.

rap out, blurt out; have *or* say one's say, speak one's mind, speak up *or* out, outspeak, open one's lips *or* mouth, lift *or* raise one's voice, break silence; put in a word, put in a word or two, come or break in with; have on one's lips, have at the end *or* tip of one's tongue; express etc. (phrase) 566.3; impart, make known etc. (inform) 527.7; divulge etc. 529.6, announce, proclaim etc. (publish) 531.7, chatter etc. (be loquacious) 584.4; speak to etc. (address) 586.2; talk together etc (converse) 588.7; soliloquize etc. 589.3, talk big [coll.] etc. (be bombastic) 577.5, argue etc. 476.11; **gossip etc.** 532.7; ex claim etc. 580.9.

7. *v.* declaim, make *or* deliver a speech etc. *n.*, speechify [joc.], speechmake [rare], demagogue [coll., U.S.], address hold forth, be on one's legs, discourse spiel [slang, U.S.], mouth, harangue perorate, flourish, spout [coll.], rant elocute [derog.], elocutionize; recite oration, orate, oratorize [all coll.]; stump [coll., U.S.], go on *or* take the stump platform, soapbox; lecture, prelect preach, preachify [coll.]; sermon [now rare], sermonize, read a sermon; spell bind.

8. *v.* be eloquent etc. *adj.*, have a tongue in one's head, have the gift of gab [coll.] etc. *n.*

9. *v.* be said etc., pass one's lips, escape one's lips, fall from the lips *or* mouth.

10. *adj.* spoken, vocal, oral, unwritten not written, nuncupative, parol, acro amatic(al); phonic, phonetic(al); out spoken; verbal etc. 562.8; conversationa etc. (interlocutory) 588.10.

11. *adj.* speaking etc. *v.*, well-speak ing, well-spoken, true-speaking, clean speaking, clean-spoken, plain-speaking plain-spoken, free-speaking, free-spoken loud-speaking, loud-spoken, soft-speak ing, soft-spoken, English-speaking etc (*see* English etc. 560.4).

12. *adj.* eloquent, facund [arch.], ora torical, rhetorical, elocutionary, declama

PUBLILIUS. An honest man, sir, is able to speak for himself.—SHAKESPEARE. She speaks poignards and every word stabs.—

SHAKESPEARE. Pour the full tide of elo quence along.—POPE. Speech is but broke light upon the depth of the unspoken.—G. ELIO

tory; Demosthenean *or* Demosthenian, Ciceronian, Tullian; fluent, multiloquent etc. 584.5.

13. *adv.* orally etc. *adj.*, by word of mouth, *viva voce* [L.], from the lips of, from his own mouth.

14. *phr.* quoth he [arch.], said he etc. *v.*, sez I [coll. and slang].

583. Imperfect Speech
(See 582. Speech)

1. *n.* imperfect speech, defective speech *or* utterance, speech defect, impediment in one's speech, bone in the neck *or* throat; inarticulateness etc. *adj.*, inarticulacy, inarticulation; stammering, stuttering etc. *v.*; hesitation, traulism; titubancy, titubation; betacism, betacismus; mytacism; stutter, lisp, drawl etc. *v.*; tardiloquence [obs.]; nasal tone *or* accent, twang, twangle [rare], nasal twang; falsetto, childish treble, false *or* artificial voice; cracked *or* broken voice, broken tones *or* accents, broken speech, talkee-talkee; mispronunciation, mispronouncement; cacology, cacoëpy.

foreign accent, brogue etc. (accent) 580.4; harshness, raucity etc. (stridor) 410; solecism etc. (ungrammaticism) 568; slip of the tongue etc. (blunder) 495.3.

2. *v.* speak imperfectly, talk incoherently, be inarticulate etc. *adj.*, be unable to put two words together; have an impediment in one's speech, have a bone in one's neck *or* throat; mumble, mutter, maund [obs.], maunder, mouth; muffle, mump, speak thickly; jabber, gibber, gabble; splutter, sputter; drawl, drag; lisp; shake, quaver; mince, clip one's words; croak, crow; nasalize, nose, speak through one's nose, snuffle.

3. *v.* stammer, stutter, titubate [now rare], hesitate, falter, halt, hammer [obs. *or* dial. Eng.], stumble; balbutiate, balbucinate [both obs.]; haw, hum *or* hem and haw.

4. *v.* mispronounce, misspeak, missay [rare]; murder the language, murder the king's *or* queen's English.

5. *adj.* imperfectly spoken *or* pronounced; inarticulate, inarticulated, indistinctly articulated; lisping, stammering etc. *v.*; titubant; tremulous, shaky; tardiloquent, tardiloquous [both obs.]; drawly; throaty, guttural, thick; nasal, twangy; cacoëpistic, mispronounced etc. *v.*; affected; indistinct etc. (unintelligible) 519.6, 7; hoarse, husky, stertorous etc. (strident) 410.9, 10; cacophonous etc. (discordant) 414.4; ungrammatical etc. 568.3.

584. Loquacity
(See 585. Taciturnity)

1. *n.* loquacity, loquaciousness, talkativeness etc. *adj.*; much speaking, multiloquence, garrulity, polylogy [rare]; volubility, fluency, voluble *or* fluent tongue, loose tongue; flow of words, *flux de bouche, ~ mots* or *paroles* [F.]; effusion, gush, slush; *cacoëthes loquendi* [L.], *furor loquendi* [L.]; verbosity etc. (diffuseness) 573; eloquence, gift of gab [coll.] etc. (oratory) 582.3.

2. *n.* chatter, jabber, gibber, babble, babblement, prate, prattle, prattlement [rare], gabble, gab [coll.], blab, blabber, blather *or* blether, clack, cackle, *caquet* [F.], *caqueterie* [F.], mag [coll.], palaver, jaw [slang], *bavardage* [F.], twattle, twaddle, twaddy [rare], twiddle-twaddle, gibblegabble, bibble-babble, chitter-chatter, prittle-prattle, mere talk, idle chatter; talky-talk, talkee-talkee [all coll.]; guff, gas, hot air, blah, blah-blah [all slang]; rigmarole, rigmarolery; amphigory, amphigouri; small talk etc. (chat) 588.2; nonsensical talk etc. 517.3; talk etc. (speech) 582.

3. *n.* chatterer, chatterbox, chatterbag [dial.], chatterbasket [dial.], babbler etc. *v.*, blab, rattle, "agreeable rattle" (Goldsmith), blather, blatherskite [coll., U.S.], driveler, mag [coll.], chattermag, magpie, jay, parrot, *moulin à paroles* [F.], idle chatterer, talkative person, big *or* great talker [coll.], spendthrift of one's tongue, word-slinger [derog.]; jaw-box, gasbag, windbag, windjammer, hot-air artist, rattletrap [all slang]; ranter; gossip etc. (newsmonger) 532.5; talker etc. 582.5.

---

583. His pale lips faintly stammered out a "No."—DICKENS. Inarticulate with rage and grief.—W. MORRIS.

584. Much talk, much foolishness.—TALMUD. A fool can noght be stille.—CHAUCER. The empty vessel giveth a greater sound than a full barrel.—LYLY. What a spendthrift is he of his tongue!—SHAKESPEARE. Who think too little, and who talk too much.—DRYDEN. The light effusions of a heedless boy.—BYRON.

4. *v.* be loquacious etc. *adj.*, chatter, patter, prate, prattle, palaver, babble, gabble, gibblegabble, jabber, jibber [rare], gibber, blab, blatter [now chiefly dial.], blather *or* blether, twaddle, twattle, rattle, rattle on, clack, clack like a hen, mag [coll.], jaw [slang], shoot off one's mouth *or* face [slang], gas [slang], spout [coll.], pour forth, gush.

talk *or* run on like a mill race, talk oneself out of breath, talk oneself hoarse, be hoarse with talking; screed, screed off *or* away; talk one to death, talk one's head off, talk one deaf and dumb, talk one into a fever, talk the hind leg off a mule, ~ jackass, ~ cow etc.; talk at random, ramble, maunder; outtalk; speak at length, expatiate, rant etc. (be diffuse) 573.5; din in the ears etc. (repeat) 104.4; talk nonsense etc. 517.6.

5. *adj.* loquacious, talkative, talky, babblative, garrulous, linguacious [obs.], polyloquent [rare]; multiloquent, multiloquous; chattering etc. *v.*, chatty; gabby, gassy, windy [all coll.]; jawy [slang]; gimbaljawed [slang, U.S.]; voluble, fluent, glib; flip [now coll.], flippant [obs.]; effusive, gushy, slushy; long-winded, verbose etc. (diffuse) 573.7; eloquent etc. 582.12.

6. *adv.* loquaciously, fluently etc. *adj.*; trippingly on the tongue, the tongue running on, with tongue running fast *or* loose.

585. Taciturnity
(See 584. Loquacity)

1. *n.* taciturnity, silence, habitual silence, muteness, obmutescence [rare]; reserve, reservation, reserve in speaking; reticence *or* reticency, disinclination to speak, forbearance from speech, uncommunicativeness; laconism, laconicism; economy of language *or* expression, brevity in speech, pauciloquy, curtness, conciseness; secrecy etc. 528.2.

2. *n.* taciturn person, taciturnist, laconic, man of few words, person of silence, clam [coll., U.S.]; Spartan, Laconian.

3. *v.* not speak etc. 582.6, be silent etc. *adj.*, keep silence, keep still *or* quiet, hold one's peace, say nothing, save one's breath [coll.], hold one's breath, not breathe a word, not let out a peep [coll.], not say boo, remain mum, lay *or* place the finger on the lips, not let a word escape one, make no sign, keep to oneself.

hold one's tongue, keep one's tongue between one's teeth, bite the tongue, put a bridle on one's tongue, put a padlock on one's mouth, seal one's lips *or* mouth, shut *or* close one's mouth, keep one's mouth shut, shut up [coll.]; keep one's trap shut, button up one's lip, clam up, dummy up [all slang]; not have a word to say, have not a word to throw at a dog; have a bone in the neck *or* throat, stick in one's throat; keep secret etc. 528.11.

4. *adj.* taciturn, not loquacious etc. 584.5, indisposed to talk, disinclined to speak, not given to conversation, unconversable, uncommunicative, word-bound, costive [obs.], reticent, reserved; close, close as wax, close-mouthed, close-tongued; laconic, pauciloquent, curt, concise, brief, sententious, sparing of words; silent, habitually silent, mum, mute, obmutescent [rare]; silent as the grave, ~ a post etc. (still) 403.6; speechless, tongue-tied, dumb etc. (aphonous) 581.7; secretive etc. 528.22.

5. *adv.* taciturnly, laconically etc. *adj.*; in *or* with few words, *paucis verbis* [L.].

6. *int.* silence!, hold your tongue!, shut up! [coll.], shut your mouth! [coll.], pipe down [coll.], ring off [slang], not another word!, mum!, mum's the word!; hush!, tush! etc. (sound) 403.9.

The hare-brained chatter of irresponsible frivolity.—DISRAELI. To varnish nonsense with the charms of sound.—C. CHURCHILL. A loose tongue is just as unfortunate an accompaniment for a nation as for an individual.—T. ROOSEVELT.
585. It is a point of wisdom to be silent when occasion requires.—PLUTARCH. Let a fool hold his tongue and he will pass for a sage.—PUBLILIUS. I have often regretted my speech, never my silence.—PUBLILIUS. Much that well may be thought cannot wisely be said. —ANON. It is easier not to speak a word at all than to speak more words than we should. THOMAS À KEMPIS. Well-timed silence hath more eloquence than speech.—TUPPER. The power of holding one's tongue, which is reticence.—JOWETT. Blessed is the man who, having nothing to say, abstains from giving in words evidence of the fact.—G. ELIOT. My one claim to originality among Irishmen is that I have never made a speech.—G. MOORE. Silence is the most perfect expression of scorn.— SHAW. *Cave quid dicis quando et cui* [Take care what you say and to whom].

586. Allocution
(See 587. Response)

1. *n.* allocution, alloquy [obs.], talk, address, hortatory *or* authoritative address; smoke talk, chalk talk [both coll.]; apostrophe, interpellation, appeal, invocation; salutation, salutatory [U.S.]; word in the ear; lecture etc. (speech) 582.2.

2. *v.* address, parley, speak to, approach, make up to [coll.], apostrophize, appeal to, invoke; take aside, talk to in private; take by the button, buttonhole, buttonhold; accost, call to, halloo, hail, greet, salute; lecture, preach etc. (declaim) 582.7.

3. *int.* halloo!, soho!, hey! etc. (attention) 457.10.

587. Response
(See 586. Allocution)

n. response etc. (answer) 462.

588. Interlocution
(See 589. Soliloquy)

1. *n.* interlocution, collocution, colloquy; conversation, *conversazione* [It.], converse; confabulation, confab [coll.]; talk, talkfest [slang], chinfest [slang], tell [dial.], say [dial.], speech, palaver, word, intercourse, verbal intercourse, oral communication, communion, commerce, interchange of speech, discourse, "the sweeter banquet of the mind" (Pope), "the feast of reason and the flow of soul" (Pope); dialogue, duologue, dialogism; trialogue; *"mollissima fandi tempora"* (Vergil).

2. *n.* chat, chitchat, tattle, tittle-tattle, prattle, prittle-prattle, babble, babblement, cackle, small talk, idle talk; familiar talk *or* conversation, causerie, collogue [dial.], friendly chat, coze; intimate *or* private conversation, tête-à-tête; town talk, gossip etc. (report) 532.3; chatter etc. 584.4; visit etc. 892.3.

3. *n.* conference, parley, palaver, confabulation [rare], colloque [obs.], powwow [U.S.], huddle [slang], *pourparler* [F.], indaba [South Afr.], discussion, interchange of views; council, council fire [North Am. Ind.]; consultation, interview, congress, audience, audition [coll.], hearing, reception; conclave, convention etc. (assembly) 696.2–6; audience hall etc. 189.10.

4. *n.* debate, controversy etc. (argumentation) 476.2.

5. *n.* interlocutor, interlocutress *or* interlocutrice *or* interlocutrix [*fem.*]; converser, conversationist, conversationalist; collocutor, colloquist, colloquialist; confabulator, discourser etc. *v.*; dialogist, dialoguer; talker, spokesman etc. (speaker) 582.5, (deputy) 759; go-between etc. (mediator) 724.2; interpreter etc. 524; questioner etc. (inquirer) 461.12; arguer etc. (reasoner) 476.9.

6. *n.* gossip etc. (newsmonger) 532.5.

7. *v.* converse, hold ~, carry on ~, join in *or* engage in a conversation etc. *n.*, talk together, talk *or* speak with, converse with, discourse with, commune with, commerce with, have a talk with, have a word with, bandy words, parley, palaver, chin [slang], chin-chin [pidgin Eng.], chat, chew the rag [slang]; prittle-prattle, tittle-tattle; confabulate, confab [coll.]; colloque, colloquize; have a friendly chat, coze; be closeted with, talk with one in private, talk with tête-à-tête, have a private *or* intimate conversation; dialogue, dialogize; put in a word, put in a word or two, come *or* break in with; shine in conversation; talk etc. (speak) 582.6; gossip etc. 532.7.

8. *v.* confer, hold conference etc. *n.*, parley, palaver, powwow [U.S.], go into a huddle [slang], lay *or* put heads together, consult, counsel, advise, confer with, consult with, advise with, discuss with, take up with, reason with, discuss, talk over.

9. *v.* debate, dispute etc. (argue) 476.11.

10. *adj.* interlocutory, interlocutive [rare]; conversable, conversational; confabular, confabulatory; collocutory

---

588. With thee conversing I forget all time.—MILTON.   Many can argue, not many converse.—A. B. ALCOTT.   Conversation is an art in which a man has all mankind for his competitors.—EMERSON.   A sort of chit-chat, or small talk, which is the general run of conversation . . . in most mixed companies.—CHESTERFIELD.   "The time has come," the Walrus said, / "To talk of many things."—CARROLL.   Inject a few raisins of conversation into the tasteless dough of existence.—O. HENRY.

[rare], colloquial, discoursive [obs.]; chatty, chitchatty, cozy *or* cosy [Eng.], tête-à-tête; conferential.

589. Soliloquy
(See 588. Interlocution)

1. *n.* soliloquy, monology, monologue; apostrophe.

2. *n.* soliloquist, soliloquizer; monologist *or* monologuist, monologian; Dr. Johnson, Coleridge; Hamlet.

3. *v.* soliloquize, monologize, monologue; say ~, talk *or* speak to oneself, think out loud *or* aloud; address an imaginary audience, address the four walls, rehearse a speech; apostrophize, say aside.

4. *adj.* soliloquizing etc. *v.,* soliloquacious [rare]; monologic(al); apostrophic, apostrophal [rare].

590. Writing

1. *n.* writing, chirography, calligraphy, autography, handwriting, hand, fist [coll.]; manuscript, script, scripture [arch.], scription; penscript, penmanship, pencraft, quill driving [derog. or joc.], inkslinging, ink spilling [both slang], pen *or* pencil driving *or* pushing [slang], pen and ink; scrive [chiefly Scot.], scrivening, scrivenery.

typing [coll.], typewriting; macrography, micrography; cuneiform writing, cuneiform; hieroglyphic writing, hieratic writing, demotic writing; uncial writing, ogam, lexigraphy, cerography, stylography, stelography [rare], monography, opisthography; stroke *or* dash of the pen, *coup de plume* [F.]; graphology, graphiology.

2. *n.* authorship, authorcraft, writership, pencraft, writing; composition, preparation, production, origination, inditement; lucubration; journalism; *cacoëthes scribendi* [L.], graphomania, scribblemania *or* scribbleomania, writer's itch, itch for writing.

3. *n.* a writing, written matter, piece of writing, piece, copy, scroll, paper, document, composition, work, opus [*pl.* opera], brain child, production, tracing; scrip, script, scripture [arch.], *litterae scriptae* [L.], scrive [chiefly Scot.]; inscript, inscription, scription [obs.]; engrossment; jottings, dottings; draft *or* draught, rough draft *or* copy, rough, outline; manuscript, MS., Ms., ms. (*pl.* MSS., Mss., mss.); flimsy; penscript; typescript, typoscript; original, author's copy; matter, live matter, dead matter, standing matter [all Print.].

ancient manuscript, codex (*pl.* codices); *codex rescriptus* [L.], palimpsest; Rosetta stone; opisthograph; paper, article, screed, essay, theme, thesis, treatise, monograph; *morceau* [F.]; potboiler; rescript, rewriting, rewrite, revise, revision; chirograph, handwriting etc. *above* 590.1; autograph, autography; signature, sign manual; holograph; macrograph, micrograph; cerograph, encaustic; line; write-up [slang].

register, chronicle etc. (record) 551; pamphlet, magazine etc. (book) 593; novel, history etc. (narrative) 594.2; poem etc. 597.2; advertising matter, broadsheet etc. (advertisement) 531.4; musical composition, score etc. (music) 415.3, 21; transcription, carbon copy etc. (duplicate) 21; superscription etc. (indication) 550.11.

4. *n.* (style of handwriting) hand, fist [coll.]; Italian writing, Spencerian writing, bold hand, round hand, slanting hand, perpendicular hand, letter hand, longhand.

5. *n.* calligraphy, good *or* fine writing *or* hand, good fist [coll.], legible writing, copybook hand, elegant penmanship, running ~, flowing *or* cursive hand; calligraph, fine specimen of handwriting.

6. *n.* cacography, bad writing *or* hand, poor fist [coll.], cramped *or* crabbed hand, illegible handwriting, *griffonage* [F.], *barbouillage* [F.]; scribblement, scribblage; scribbling, scribble etc. *v.;* *pattes de mouche* [F.], fly tracks; ill-formed letters, illegible characters; pothookery, pothooks, hangers, pothooks and hangers.

---

589. As I walk'd by myself, I talk'd to myself, / And myself replied to me.—B. BARTON.
590. *Scribendi recte sapere et principium et fons* [Accurate thinking is the beginning and the fountain of writing].—HORACE. Written with a pen of iron, and with the point of a diamond.—BIBLE. If you wish to be a good writer, write.—EPICTETUS. Look in thy heart and write.—SIDNEY. Composition is, for the most part, an effort of slow diligence and steady perseverance.—JOHNSON. No man but a blockhead ever wrote except for

7. *n.* shorthand, short writing, speed writing, stenography, phonography, brachygraphy, tachygraphy; pasigraphy, polygraphy, logography, stenotypy; contraction.

8. *n.* cryptography, steganography, secret writing; cipher, code.

9. *n.* (written characters) script, scripture [arch.]; cursive character, cursive; cuneiform character, cuneiform, arrowhead; rune, futhorc *or* futharc; ideogram, ideograph; hieroglyph *or* hieroglyphic, hieratic *or* demotic style; character, symbol etc. (letter) 561.1; alphabet etc. 561.2; Braille etc. (aids for the blind) 442.2.

10. *n.* writing materials, stationery; paper, writing paper, copy *or* copying paper, letter paper, cap, foolscap, parchment, vellum, flimsy, scroll; demy, papyrus, biblus *or* biblos; quire, ream; pad, writing pad; tablet, table, block, stone, marble, pillar; slate, blackboard; pencil, automatic pencil; pen, fountain pen; reed, plume, quill, goose quill; style, stylograph; stylographic pen; ink, writing ink *or* fluid, copying ink, printing ink, indelible ink; secret ~, invisible *or* sympathetic ink; ink bottle, inkhorn, inkpot, inkwell, inkstand; typewriter; writing case *or* cabinet, writing desk *or* table; blankbook, notebook etc. (record book) 551.3.

11. *n.* writer, penman, pen, penner, pen *or* pencil driver *or* pusher [slang], quill driver [joc.], inkslinger, ink spiller [slang], knight of the plume, ~ pen *or* quill [joc.], scribbler [derog.]; writeress, penwoman; scribe, scrivener, amanuensis, secretary, recording secretary, clerk, baboo [Ind.]; copyist, copier, transcriber; typewriter, typer [coll.], typist; chirographer; calligrapher, calligraphist; cacographer; cerographist; monographist; graphologist, graphiologist, graphomaniac; author, journalist etc. 593.15, 16; recorder etc. 553.

12. *n.* stenographer, stenographist; shorthand writer, shorthander [coll.]; brachygrapher, brachygraphist; tachygrapher, tachygraphist, tachygraph; phonographer, phonographist; stenotypist; logographer.

13. *v.* write, pen, pencil, drive *or* push the pen *or* pencil [slang]; stain *or* spoil paper, shed *or* spill ink [both joc.]; take pen in hand, take up the pen; scribble, scrabble, scribble-scrabble, scratch, scrawl; scribe, scrive [chiefly Scot.], scriven [arch.]; inscribe, engross; scroll, inscroll; trace, copy, transcribe; manifold; shorthand, write *or* take down in shorthand; write *or* take down in longhand; typewrite, type [coll.]; enface; rewrite, revise; put in writing, write down etc. (record) 551.8; sign etc. (mark) 550.19, (ratify) 488.10.

14. *v.* author, compose, formulate, produce, prepare, originate, indite; draw up, draft; dash off, knock off *or* out [coll.], throw on paper; ghost, ghostwrite; edit, editorialize [cant]; novelize, historize etc. (describe) 594.5; write poetry etc. 597.12; scenarioize etc. (dramatize) 599.25.

15. *adj.* written, manuscript, inscribed etc. *v.,* in writing, in black and white; under one's hand; scriptory; scriptorial, scriptural; literal; scribbly, scribblative [rare], scribblatory; uncial, runic, cuneiform, hieroglyphic(al), hieratic, demotic; longhand, in longhand.

16. *adj.* shorthand, in shorthand; stenographic(al), phonographic(al), brachygraphic(al) [obs. exc. Hist.], tachygraphic(al); pasigraphic(al), polygraphic(al), logographic(al).

17. *adj.* cryptographic(al), steganographic(al).

18. *adv.* pen in hand, with pen in hand; with the pen of a ready writer, *currente calamo* [L.].

591. Printing

1. *n.* printing, type printing, typography, *ars artium omnium conservatrix* [L.]; palaeotypography; chromotypography, chromotypy; chromoxylography; autotypography, autotypy; stereotypography, stereotypy, stereotypery; phototypography, phototypy; composing etc. *v.,* composition, typesetting, presswork; sheetwork; publishing, publication; plate printing etc. (engraving) 558.2; the press etc. 593.17.

2. *n.* print, imprint, impress, impression, letterpress; newsprint; typescript,

---

BYRON. Damn the age; I will write for antiquity.—LAMB. All writing comes by the grace of God.—EMERSON.
591. Though an angel should write, still 'tis *devils* must print.—T. MOORE. The printing-
money.—JOHNSON. As though I lived to write and wrote to live.—S. ROGERS. Nature's noblest gift—my gray goose quill.—

copy, printed page, type page; matter, printed matter, type matter; live matter, dead matter, standing matter; text, context; dummy; page, column, section; note; catchword; signature; justification; folio; reprint, reissue; macule, mackle; offprint; offcut; offset, setoff; bookplate, book stamp, colophon; chromolithograph etc. (engraving) 558.3.

3. *n.* proof, proof sheet, pull, slip, trial impression; galley, galley proof; page proof, foundry proof, plate proof, press proof, author's proof; revise, press revise; advance sheets.

4. *n.* headline, banner, running head etc. (heading) 66.3.

5. *n.* (equipment) measure, type measure; scale, type scale; type metal, type casting, type mold; type foundry, letter foundry; stick, composing stick, foot stick, gutter stick; composing rule, composing frame, composing stand; chase, form, galley, case, boxes; gauge, gauge pin, feed gauge; guide, dabber, gutter; brayer, boss, batter, bank; bearer, guard; bed, blanket, tympan, turtle, platen, bevel, burr, frame, frisket, gripper; quoin, slur, ratchet, reglet; guillotine, rounce, cylinder; overlay, underlay.

6. *n.* type, impressed form, stamp, print, letter; linotype, monotype, stereotype, electrotype, autotype, albertype, ambrotype, chromotype, zincotype, stenotype, lithotype; logotype, ligature; lowercase, minuscule; upper case, majuscule, capital, cap [coll.]; small capital, small cap [coll.]; bastard type, bottle-assed type, fat-faced type; strike, matrix; jet, sprue; body, type body; face, type face; shoulder, counter, serif, nick, groove, feet; stem, shank; beard, neck; font, fount [Eng.], pie; Braille type etc. (aids for the blind) 442.2.

7. *n.* (type sizes, point system) 3-point, excelsior; 3½-point, brilliant; 4½-point, diamond; 5-point, pearl; 5½-point, agate, ruby; 6-point, nonpareil; 7-point, minion; 8-point, brevier; 9-point, bourgeois; 10-point, long primer; 11-point, small pica; 12-point, pica; 14-point, English; 16-point, Columbian; 18-point, great primer.

8. *n.* (type styles) Old English, Gothic, German text, antique, clarendon, French, Elzevir, old style, Caslon, Caslon old style, Ionic, chapel text, typewriter, black letter, roman, italic, cursive, script, standard, lightface; boldface, fullface; extraboldface, extrabold.

9. *n.* space, patent space, justifying space; quadrat, quad; em quad, em; en quad, en; 3-em, thick space; 4-em, 5-em, thin space; 6-em, hair space; bar, slug, type bar *or* slug.

10. *n.* press, printing press *or* machine; cylinder press, rotary press, web press, Linotype press, electrotype press, letter press, platen press, perfecting press *or* machine, proof press.

11. *n.* pressroom, composing room, city room, local room, make-up room, proofroom; filing room, library, morgue [slang].

12. *n.* printer, pressman; compositor, typesetter; typographer, typographist [rare]; proofer; devil, printer's devil; stereotypist, stereotyper; linotypist, linotyper etc. *v.*; job printer, book printer etc.

13. *n.* proofreader, proof corrector, reader, typerighter [joc.]; copyreader, copyholder.

14. *v.* print, imprint, impress, stamp, enstamp, strike off; publish, issue, get *or* bring out; autotype, linotype, monotype, stereotype etc. *n.*; macule, mackle; offset; compose, set, set in print, set up, stick [cant], make up; impose, justify, overrun, rout, mortise; put to press, put to bed [cant], see through the press; prove, pull; reprint, reissue; engrave etc. 558.5.

15. *v.* distribute; pie, pie a form.

16. *v.* be printed etc., go to press, pass through the press, come out, appear in print.

17. *v.* proofread, proof-correct, read, read *or* correct copy.

18. *adj.* typographic(al), autotypographic(al), stereotypic(al) etc. *n.*; printed etc. *v.*, in print *or* type, typeset; solid in galleys; kerned; boldface; boldfaced, full-faced; light-faced; upper-case, lower-case; pied.

592. Correspondence

1. *n.* correspondence, epistolary intercourse, written communication, letter writing; *furor scribendi* [L.].

592. A letter does not blush.—CICERO. More than kisses, letters mingle souls; / For, thus friends absent speak.—DONNE. As keys do

press is either the greatest blessing or the greatest curse of modern times.—BARRIE.

2. *n.* epistle, letter, billet, missive, dispatch, communication, message; letteret [rare], note, line, chit *or* chitty [Ind.]; love letter, *billet-doux* [F.], billy-do [joc.], mash note [slang]; fan letter [Theat. slang]; business letter; reply, answer, acknowledgment, favor; rescript, rescription [arch.]; these presents [Law]; drop letter; form letter.

circular, circular letter; encyclical, encyclical letter; round robin; bulletin; bull, apostolic *or* papal brief; monitory, monitory letter; pastoral, pastoral epistle; letter of credence [Law]; letter of credit, letter of delegation, letter of license, letter of indication [all Com.]; postal order, postal note, post-office order, money order; postscript; lettergram, night letter etc. (telegram) 532a.3.

3. *n.* card, post card *or* postcard, postal card, postal [coll., U.S.]; letter card [Eng.]; picture postcard.

4. *n.* mail, post, letters, mailbag [fig.]; air *or* aerial mail; fan mail [Theat. slang]; parcel post, parcels post; letter post, printed paper *or* half-penny post, newspaper post, book post [all Eng.]; special delivery, express [Eng.]; first-class ∼ second-class ∼, third-class *or* fourth-class mail; postage; mailbag, letter bag; mailbox, letter box, postbox, post-office box; drop, letter drop; post office, post [Eng.]; post day [Eng.]; postmark; mailman, mailplane etc. 534.2.

5. *n.* correspondent, writer, letter writer, epistolarian [rare], communicator; contributor; foreign correspondent etc. (journalist) 593.16.

6. *v.* correspond, correspond with, communicate by letter *or* writing, write to, write *or* send a letter to, letter [rare], epistolize [rare], dispatch, let one know by mail *or* post; send a note, drop a line to [coll.]; keep up a correspondence, deluge with letters, bombard; acknowledge, answer, reply, reply by return mail; postcard; circularize; mail, post; air-mail.

7. *adj.* epistolary, epistolarian; post, postal, mail.

593. Book

1. *n.* book, writing, bible [obs.], tome, work, production, brain child, volume,

copy, sheet [rare], publication, opus (*pl.* opera); magnum opus, *opus magnum* [L.]; folio; opuscle, opuscule, opusculum; potboiler; booklet, brochure, chapbook, pamphlet, tract, leaflet, folder, circular; handbook, manual, enchiridion, vade mecum; pocketbook, pocket manual; copybook; manuscript book, codex (*pl.* codices).

rare book, first edition, early edition, Elzevir, Elzevir book *or* edition, Aldus, Aldine, Aldine book *or* edition; incunabulum (*pl.* incunabula), cradle book, Fifteener; novel, history etc. (narrative) 594.2; libretto, songbook etc. (musical score) 415.21; chronicle, annals etc. (record) 551; notebook, memorandum book etc. (record book) 551.3; guidebook etc. 694.7; playbook etc. 599.16; syllabus etc. (compendium) 596; treatise etc. (dissertation) 595; broadsheet etc. (advertisement) 531.4; issue, number etc. (edition) 531.2.

2. *n.* compilation, ana, symposium; collection, collectanea, collectarium [Eccl.]; miscellany, miscellanea; delectus, book of extracts *or* selected passages; quotation book, book of quotations; anthology, spicilege [rare], posy [rare], garland; album, photograph album; book of verse etc. 597.4; analecta etc. (excerpts) 596.2.

3. *n.* reference book *or* work, work of reference; encyclopedia, cyclopedia; concordance; catalogue, cat [slang]; classified catalogue, *catalogue raisonné* [F.]; directory, city directory, telephone book; bibliography; atlas, almanac, Blue Book etc. (archive) 551.2.

4. *n.* dictionary, wordbook, lexicon, vocabulary, index; glossary, gloss; thesaurus (*pl.* thesauri), storehouse *or* treasury of words, synonymicon [rare]; onomasticon, idioticon, gradus, polyglot, rhyming dictionary; geographical dictionary, atlas etc. (archive) 551.2; list etc. 86; definition etc. (interpretation) 522.

5. *n.* textbook, text, schoolbook, manual, manual of instruction; hornbook, battledore [obs.], primer; abecedary [rare], abecedarium; grammar; copybook; Lind-

---

open chests, / So letters open breasts.—J. HOWELL. Letter-writing, that most delightful way of wasting time.—J. MORLEY.

593. A room without books is a body without a soul.—CICERO. I can study my books at any time, for they are always disengaged.— CICERO. Books have led some to learning and others to madness.—PETRARCH. Volumes that I prize above my dukedom.—SHAKE-

ley Murray, Cocker, New England Primer.

6. *n.* journal, gazette, periodical, serial, ephemeris (*pl.* ephemerides); magazine; newspaper, news, paper, sheet [slang], tabloid, tab [cant]; daily, weekly, monthly, quarterly; annual, yearbook; diary, daybook etc. (record book) 551.3.

7. *n.* make-up; part, division, section, book, number; serial, *livraison* [F.]; chapter, verse, paragraph, passage, clause, phrase, column; page, leaf, folio; fly leaf; recto, verso *or* reverso; title, title page, bastard title, binder's title, subtitle; imprint, printer's imprint; dedication; contents, table of contents, table, list of plates *or* illustrations, index (*pl.* indexes, indices); errata; text; article; frontispiece, foreword etc. (prelude) 64.2; supplement, appendix etc. (sequel) 65; head, caption etc. (heading) 66.3.

8. *n.* (sizes) quarto, 4vo; octavo, 8vo; cap 8vo, demy 8vo, imperial 8vo, medium 8vo, royal 8vo, post 8vo, pott 8vo, crown 8vo, foolscap 8vo; duodecimo, twelvemo *or* 12mo; sextodecimo, sixteenmo *or* 16mo; octodecimo, eighteenmo *or* 18mo.

9. *n.* bookbinding, bibliopegy; folding; stitching, wire stitching; tooling, blind tooling, gold tooling; binding, case, cover, jacket; quarter ∼, half *or* three-quarter binding; full leather; Aldine ∼, Arabesque ∼, Byzantine ∼, Etruscan ∼, Fanfare ∼, Grolier ∼, Harleian ∼, Jansenist ∼, Maioli *or* Roxburgh binding.

10. *n.* (binding materials) paper, paper boards, bookboard, binder's board, cardboard, buckram, linen, cloth, book cloth, skiver, leather, roan, pigskin, Russia, Turkey morocco, Levant morocco, seal, parchment, vellum.

11. *n.* library, *bibliothèque* [F.], bibliothec, bibliotheca, bibliotheke [obs.], bibliothecary [arch.], athenaeum *or* atheneum, bookroom, bookery; public library, lending library, circulating library, book club; Vatican Library, Bibliothèque Nationale, Library of Congress, British Museum, Bodleian Library, Deutsche Bücherei; American Library Association, A.L.A.

12. *n.* bookstore, bookshop, bookseller's shop, *librairie* [F.]; bookstall, bookstand.

13. *n.* bookholder, bookrest, book support, book end; bookcase, bookpress [rare], bookrack, bookstand, bookshelf; stack, bookstack; book table, book tray, book wagon *or* truck; folio, portfolio.

14. *n.* bookman, bibliologist, bibliographer; publisher, bookmaker, bookwright, book printer; bookbinder, bibliopegist; book-folder; bookdealer, bookseller, book salesman, ∼ agent, ∼ canvasser *or* solicitor; bibliopole, bibliopolist; book collector; librarian, bibliothec, bibliothecary, *bibliothécaire* [F.]; curator; bibliognost, bibliosoph; bibliophile, bookworm etc. (scholar) 492.

15. *n.* author, writer, *littérateur* [F.], scribe [joc. *or* derog.], adjective jerker [slang], word painter, word-seller; authoress, writeress, penwoman; bookman, bookwright; hack writer, hack, literary hack, grubstreet writer, penny-a-liner, creeper [slang], scribbler, potboiler [coll.]; free lance [coll.]; ghostwriter, ghost; magazine writer, magaziner, magazinist; novel writer, novelist; bibliographer; compiler; the scribbling race. inkslinger [slang], penman etc. 590.11; story writer etc. (narrator) 594.4; biographer, annalist, historian etc. (recorder) 553; poet etc. 597.10; playwright etc. (dramatist) 599.22; prose writer etc. 598.2; essayist, reviewer etc. (dissertator) 595.3; lexicographer etc. (linguist) 560.7; originator etc. (producer) 164.

16. *n.* journalist, newspaperman, newsman, writer for the press, gentleman *or* representative of the press, pressman [cant. chiefly Eng.]; reporter, leg man [slang], interviewer; newspaperwoman, reporteress; correspondent, foreign correspondent, war correspondent, special

---

SPEARE. Books are ships which pass through the vast seas of time.—BACON. Books are the shrine where the saint is, or is believed to be.—BACON. Books, the children of the brain.—SWIFT. Books without the knowledge of life are useless.—JOHNSON. The true University of these days is a Collection of Books.—CARLYLE. Many a quaint and curious volume of forgotten lore.—POE. Books are good enough in their own way, but they are a mighty bloodless substitute for life.—STEVENSON. There are books which take rank in our life with parents and lovers and passionate experiences.—EMERSON. Some books leave us free, and some books make us free.—EMERSON. Books are the treasured wealth of the world, the fit inheritance of generations and nations.—THOREAU. Life is too short for reading inferior books.—RUSKIN. There is no Past so long as Books shall live.

correspondent, own correspondent; publicist; rewriter, rewrite man [U.S.]; reviser, diaskeuast; editor, subeditor, news editor; copy editor [U.S.], copyman; editorial writer, leader writer [Eng.]; columnist, paragrapher, paragraphist; reader, literary adviser; publisher etc. 531.5.

17. *n.* the press, public press, fourth estate; Fleet Street [Eng.]; journalism.

18. *n.* bibliology, bibliography; bookcraft; bookselling, bibliopolism, bibliopoly, bibliopolery; bibliogenesis, bibliogony; bibliophobia, biblioclasm, bibliomancy, bibliokleptomania; book learning, booklore etc. (learning) 490.2.

19. *v.* write, author etc. 590.13, 14; compile, collect etc. (assemble) 72.11; publish etc. 531.7, 8.

20. *adj.* bibliological, bibliographic(al); bibliothecal, bibliothecary, bibliothecarial; bibliothetic, bibliopolar, bibliopolic(al), bibliopolistic; bibliopegic, bibliopegistic(al); booklearned, bibliophilic etc. (informed) 490.15, 16.

594. Description

1. *n.* description, account, statement, report, narration, relation, recital, rehearsal; storytelling; sketch, word painting *or* picture, graphic account; pastel, vignette, monograph; minute *or* detailed account, particular *or* circumstantial account, full and particular account, specifications, particulars, full particulars; recital *or* summary of facts, summary, résumé, review, retelling, recapitulation; exposition, exposé [now rare]; delineation, depiction, picturization etc. (representation) 554; explanation, definition etc. (interpretation) 522.

2. *n.* narrative, story, tale, yarn, account, legend, chronicle; history, historiette, annals, ancient ∼, medieval *or* modern history; epic, saga; memoirs, memorials, memorabilia (*sing.* memorabile); factum; personal narrative, journal, letters, biography, autobiography, life, adventures, fortunes, experiences, confessions; obituary, necrology; anecdote, ana; fiction, work of fiction; romance, love story; adventure story, thriller [coll.], detective story *or* yarn, "grue" (Stevenson); western story, western, westerner; fairy tale, nursery tale; fable, parable, apologue, allegory; short story, storiette; novel, novelette *or* novelet, *nouvelle* [F.], *novella* [It.], *novela* [Sp.]; dime novel, dreadful, penny *or* shilling dreadful, shilling shocker [slang]; book etc. 593.

3. *n.* historiography, chronography; historic Muse, Clio.

4. *n.* narrator, relator *or* relater etc. *v.*; *raconteur* [F.], anecdotist; storier, storyteller, teller of tales, spinner of yarns, word painter; story writer, short-story writer; fabulist, fableist, fabler; romancer, romancist, romancealist [rare]; novelist, novelettist *or* novelletter; sagaman; chronographer, historian, biographer etc. (annalist) 553.2; writer etc. 593.15, 16.

5. *v.* describe, set forth, characterize, analyze, give words to, tell, narrate, relate, recount, give *or* render an account of; report, give a report of, make a report, draw up a statement; retell, review, sum up, run over, recapitulate, rehearse, fight one's battles over again; storify, tell a story, unfold a tale, romance, novelize; historize, historicize; stick to the facts, show life as it is; throw into essay form, ∼ story form *or* book form; picture, portray etc. (represent) 554.7.

6. *v.* detail, particularize, itemize, specify, tell in detail, enter into *or* descend to details *or* particulars, give a full and particular account etc. *n.*

7. *adj.* descriptive, graphic, suggestive, well-drawn; narrative, storied, anecdotic; epic(al), Homeric; historic(al), historiographic(al), chronographic(al); biographic(al), autobiographic(al); traditive, traditional, traditionary; legendary, mythical, fabulous; romantic, idealistic; realistic, true to life, lifelike; depictive, delineatory etc. (representative) 554.9; explanatory, expository etc. (interpretative) 522.8.

Bulwer-Lytton. Of all the needs a book has, the chief need is, that it be readable.—Trollope. All the sweet serenity of books.—Longfellow. There is no frigate like a book / To take us lands away.—E. Dickinson. Shut not your doors to me, proud libraries.—Whitman.
594. To hold, as 'twere, the mirror up to nature.—Shakespeare. Biography is the only true history.—Carlyle. A well-written life is almost as rare as a well-spent one.—Carlyle. There is properly no History; only Biography.—Emerson. A good storyteller is a person who has a good memory and hopes other people haven't.—I. Cobb.

595. Dissertation

1. *n.* dissertation, treatise, essay, thesis, theme, paper, discourse, disquisition, descant, memoir, homily, pandect, digest, excursus, monograph; tract [now rare], tractate, tractation [obs.]; exposition, expounding; discussion etc. (reasoning) 476; study, consideration etc. (thought) 451; investigation etc. (inquiry) 461; lecture, sermon etc. (speech) 582.2.

2. *n.* commentary, commentation; critical discussion, criticism, critique; review, report, notice, write-up [coll.]; article; leader [chiefly Eng.], leading article, editorial; running commentary.

3. *n.* dissertator, dissertationist; discourser, descanter *or* descantist, expositor, essayist, pamphleteer, publicist; monographer, monographist; commentator *or* commentater, commenter; critic, criticizer; criticaster, critickin, criticule; reviewer, revieweress; editor, leader writer; annotator, scholiast.

4. *v.* dissertate, dissert, give a dissertation etc. *n.*; discourse, discuss, descant, take up, treat of, deal with, handle, go into, canvass, ventilate, write upon, touch upon; comment, comment upon, commentate; criticize, critique, review.

5. *adj.* dissertative, dissertational; disquisitive, disquisitional, disquisitionary [rare]; discursive, discoursive; expository, expositorial; commentarial, commentatorial; critical.

596. Compendium

1. *n.* compendium, compend, abstract, précis, epitome, brief, abridgment, *abrégé* [F.], condensation, abbreviature, pandect, digest, sum and substance, *multum in parvo* [L.], analysis, *aperçu* [F.], synopsis, syllabus, conspectus; outline, topical outline, skeleton; outlines, contents, heads; prospectus; summary, résumé, review, recapitulation; excerpt, extract; passage, selected passage; minute, note; draft, sketch etc. (outline) 626.2; miniature etc. 193.3.

2. *n.* excerpts, *excerpta* [L.]; extracts, ana, fragments, cuttings, clippings, *spicilegium* [L.], literary gleanings, flowers, fugitive pieces *or* writings; analects, analecta; miscellany, miscellanea; collection, collectanea; compilation, anthology etc. 593.2–4.

3. *n.* abbreviation etc. (shortening) 201.2; compression etc. (contraction) 195; conciseness etc. 572.

4. *v.* abridge, abstract, epitomize, synopsize, make ~, prepare ~, draw *or* compile an abstract etc. *n.*; edit; condense etc. (shorten) 201.4.

5. *adj.* compendious, compendiary; abridged etc. *v.*, *abrégé* [F.]; synoptic(al); analectic; analytic(al); variorum; abbreviatory, compact etc. (short) 201.5; concise etc. 572.3.

6. *adv.* in epitome, in short etc. (briefly) 572.4.

597. Poetry
(See 598. Prose)

1. *n.* poetry, poetics, poesy, minstrelsy [arch.], rhyme *or* rime, verse, song, "musical thought" (Carlyle), "the rhythmical creation of beauty" (Poe), "the language of the gods" (S. Rogers), "emotion recollected in tranquillity" (Wordsworth), "*vinum daemonum*" (St. Augustine); blank verse; free verse, vers libre; runic verse, runes; epic poetry *or* verse, epopee, epopoeia; elegiac poetry *or* verse, elegiac *or* elegiacs; satirical poetry, satire; heroic verse, mock-heroic verse; lyric poetry, ballad poetry, narrative poetry, alliterative poetry; Leonine verse (*see* Leonine etc. *adj.*); light verse, society verse, *vers de societé* [F.].

2. *n.* poem, poetical *or* metrical composition, poesy [now rare], verse, rhyme *or* rime, song, lay; verselet, versicle, versicule [rare], *versiculus* [L.]; lyric, lyric poem; epic, epic poem, epos, epopee, epopoeia; pastoral poem, pastoral, bucolic, georgic; rondeau, rondel, roundel, rondelet [rare], roundelay; rhapsody; idyl *or* idyll, *idyllium* or *idyllion* [L.]; dithyramb, dithyrambus; palinode, palinody [arch.]; ode, epode, eclogue, Anacreontic, sonnet, triolet, sestina, virelay,

---

595. Oh, you chorus of indolent reviewers!— TENNYSON.   You know who the critics are? —the men who have failed in literature and art. —DISRAELI.   Whatever shall we do in that remote spot? Well, we will write our memoirs. —NAPOLEON.   He who would write and can't write, can surely review.—LOWELL.
596. Infinite riches in a little room.—MARLOWE.

597. He coulde songes make and well indite.— CHAUCER.   A poem round and perfect as a star.—A. SMITH.   Every poem should be made up of lines that are poems.—EMERSON. The song that nerves a nation's heart is in it-

ballade, cento, gazel, madrigal, monody, elegy, amoebaeum, satire, nursery rhyme, jingle, limerick; opera, libretto.

3. *n.* (bad poetry) doggerel, doggerel verse, crambo clink *or* jingle [Scot.], Hudibrastic verse; macaronics, macaronic verse; lame verses, limping meters, halting rhyme.

4. *n.* book of verse, anthology, posy [arch.], garland; miscellany, *"disjecta membra poetae"* (Horace); poetic works, poesy; compilation etc. 593.2.

5. *n.* versification, poetization, prosody, orthometry [rare]; poetics, poeticism; poetcraft, versecraft, versemaking; rhyming etc. *v.*, rhymery *or* rimery [derog.]; versemongering, versemongery; poetastering, poetastery, poetastry, poetasterism; scansion, scanning; *furor poeticus* [L.]; poetic license, *licentia vatum* [L.].

6. *n.* metrical structure *or* pattern, verse form, verse, versification; rhythm, rhyme *or* rime [rare], cadence, meter, measure, numbers; metrical unit, foot; ictus, beat, accent, accentuation, rhythmical accent *or* accentuation; iambus, iambic, iamb; trochee, dactyl, anapaest, spondee, mora, trisème, tretrasème; caesura, diaeresis; dimeter, trimeter, tetrameter, catalexis; pentameter, hexameter, heptameter; Alexandrine; anacrusis; antispast; elegiac, elegiac meter.

7. *n.* (poetic division) measure, strain; verse, stanza, stave, strophe; antistrophe; line, line of poetry; canto; couplet, distich; triplet, tercet, tristich; quatrain, tetrastich; pentastich, hexastich, heptastich, octastich; octave, *ottava rima* [It.]; sextet *or* sextette, sestet; refrain, chorus, burden, envoy, *l'envoi* [F.].

8. *n.* rhyme *or* rime, rhyme word *or* syllable, rhyming verse *or* poetry, jingle, crambo [derog.]; alliteration, assonance; masculine *or* feminine rhyme, perfect *or* imperfect rhyme, initial rhyme, end *or* tail rhyme, rhyme royal, *bout-rimé* [F.]; rhyme scheme; rhyming dictionary.

9. *n.* muse, tuneful Nine, Apollo, Apollo Musagetes, Calliope, Parnassus, Helicon, Pierides [all Gr. Myth.]; Bragi [Norse Myth.]; poetic inspiration *or* genius, creative imagination, poesy [poetic], creative *or* imaginative power, fire of genius, coal from off the altar, Pierian spring; creative imagination etc. (imagination) 515.

10. *n.* poet, poetess [*fem.*], bard, muse, Parnassian, scop [Hist.], maker [arch.], creator, composer, songsmith, "painter of the soul" [D'Israeli]; rhymer *or* rimer, rhymester *or* rimester; versemaker, versesmith, versewright [rare], verseman, verser [rare], versifier, versificator [rare], versificatrix [*fem.*, rare], versicler [rare], versemonger, versifiaster; poetaster, poetastress [*fem.*], poetito [rare], poeticule, poetizer, poetling; minor poet, major poet; laureate, poet laureate; minstrel, jongleur; troubadour, *trovatore* [It.], trouveur, trouvère; *Meistersinger, Minnesänger* [both G.], minnesinger; improvisator, *improvvisatore* [It.], *improvvisatrice* [It., *fem.*].

ballad maker *or* writer, ballader, balladmonger; runer, runesmith; pastoral poet, bucolic, bucoliast; epic poet, epic [obs.], epopoeist; rhapsodist, rhapsode [Gr. Antiq.]; lyrist, scald, idylist *or* idyllist, sonneteer, dithyrambic, satirist, elegiast, palinodist, vers librist, *vers libriste* [F.], librettist.

poet-artist, poet-dramatist, poet-playwright, poet-painter, poet-musician, poet-historian, poet-novelist, poet-satirist, poet-thinker, poet-seer, poet-priest, poet-saint, poet-plowman, poet-farmer, poet-humorist, poet-king, poet-princess, poet-pilgrim, poet-patriot, poet-warrior; Bard of Avon, Shakespeare; Bard of Rydal Mount, Wordsworth; Bard of Ayrshire, Burns, Poets' Poet, Spenser; *"genus irritabile vatum"* (Horace).

11. *n.* poethood, poetship; poet-laureateship.

12. *v.* poetize, poeticize, poesy, write *or* compose poetry, build the stately rime, sing deathless songs, make immortal verse, sing, "lisp in numbers" (Pope); versify, make verses, string verses together; rhyme *or* rime, alliterate; cap verses *or* rhymes; scan.

13. *adj.* poetic(al), poetly [rare], poetesque [rare], poetastric(al) [derog.]; poetlike, poetwise; lyric(al), tuneful;

self a deed.—TENNYSON. The true poem is the poet's mind.—EMERSON. I sound my barbaric yawp over the roofs of the world.—WHITMAN. I do but sing because I must.—TENNYSON. Unlock my heart with a sonnet-key.—BROWNING. I learnt life from the poets.—DE STAËL. Who writes poetry imbibes honey from the poisoned lips of life.—W. R. BENÉT. A poem should not mean, but be. —A. MACLEISH.

metric(al), rhythmic(al); iambic, dactylic, spondaic(al), trochaic, anapaestic, antispastic.

dramatic, lyrico-dramatic; epic, epopoean, lyrico-epic, Homeric(al); heroic; mock-heroic, Hudibrastic; pastoral, bucolic(al); elegiac(al), amoebaeic, scaldic, dithyrambic, rhapsodic(al), idyllic(al); georgic, Anacreontic, runic; Melibean, Ionic, Sapphic, Alcaic, Pindaric, Pierian, Leonine; poetico-philosophic, poetico-mystical, poetico-mythological; rhyming *or* riming, rhymic *or* rimic, rhymy *or* rimy [rare]; assonant, assonantal, assonantic; alliterative.

598. Prose
(See 597. Poetry)

1. *n.* prose, prosaism, prosaicism [rare], prosaicness; poetic prose; history etc. (narrative) 594.2; essay etc. (dissertation) 595.

2. *n.* prose writer, essayist, monographer etc. (dissertator) 595.3; novelist, story writer etc. (narrator) 594.4; historian etc. (annalist) 553.2.

3. *v.* prose, write prose *or* in prose.

4. *adj.* prosaic, prosy, prosing, prosal [obs.], unpoetic(al); rhymeless *or* rimeless, unrhymed *or* unrimed; matter-of-fact etc. (dull) 843.5, 6.

599. Drama

1. *n.* drama, the drama, the stage, the theater, the play, the footlights, the boards, the scene [arch.]; show business; stagedom, stageland, playland, land of make-believe; patron god of drama, Dionysus, Muse of tragedy, Melpomene, Muse of comedy, Thalia [all Gr. Myth.]; Thespis; theatromania, theatrophobia.

2. *n.* dramatics, dramaturgy, dramaticism, dramatism; theatrics, theatricism, theatricalism, theatricals, theatricality [rare], theatricalness etc. *adj.*; histrionics, histrionicism, histrionism; dramatic ~, histrionic *or* Thespian art, acting, play-acting [coll.]; melodramatics, melodramatism; theatercraft, stagecraft, stagery, scenecraft; *mise en scène,* stage setting.

3. *n.* play, stage play, piece, vehicle; drama, dramaticule [rare]; legitimate, legitimate drama, legit [slang, U.S.]; melodrama, *mélodrame* [F.], melodram, sensation drama; tragedy, *tragédie* [F.], tragedietta; buskin, cothurnus; tragicomedy, *drame* [F.]; mystery, miracle play, morality, morality play; mask, masque; pantomime, dumb show; charade, proverb, *proverbe* [F.].

spectacle, pageant, extravaganza, drama de tramoya; dramalogue; monodrama, monodram, monologue; duologue, dialogue; trialogue; vaudeville; review, musical review; ballet; opera, operetta, lyric drama, *dramma per musica* [It.]; comic opera etc. *below;* photoplay etc. *below* 599.9.

4. *n.* comedy, *comedia* [Sp.], *comédie* [F.]; *comedia de figuron, comedia de santo, comedia devota, comedia heroica* [all Sp.]; comedy of character; comedy of manners; comedy drama; musical comedy, comic opera, comedy ballet; masked comedy; sentimental comedy, *comédie larmoyante* [F.]; light comedy, comedietta; genteel comedy; low comedy, broad *or* raw comedy, *comédie rosse* [F.]; slapstick comedy, slapstick; farce, farcetta [rare], farce comedy, exode [Rom. Antiq.]; harlequinade, *arlequinade* [F.]; travesty, *travesti* [F.]; burlesque, burletta, *comédie bouffe* [F.]; tragicomedy etc. *above* 599.3; sock, cap and bells, motley.

5. *n.* act, scene, stanza [slang], turn, number; curtain raiser *or* lifter, *lever de rideau* [F.]; introduction, induction [arch.]; expository, expository scene; prologue, epilogue; interlude, *divertissement* [F.]; finale, stet finale [cant]; afterpiece; exode, exodus, exodos; chaser [slang]; curtain, curtain call; tableau, *tableau vivant* [F.]; hokum *or* hoke act [slang]; blackface act, black-and-tan [slang]; song and dance, song-and-dance act.

6. *n.* acting, play-acting [coll.], performing etc. *v.*; performance, playwork; ham *or* hammy acting [slang]; business, stage business *or* trick, acting device, bag

---

598. Prose,—words in their best order.—COLERIDGE.
599. *Fere totus mundus exercet histrionem* [Almost the entire world plays a part].—PETRONIUS.   All the world's a stage, / And all the men and women merely players.—SHAKESPEARE.   The play's the thing.—SHAKESPEARE.   Come, sit down, every mother's son, and rehearse your parts.—SHAKESPEARE.   The play, I remember, pleased not the million; 'twas caviare to the general.—SHAKESPEARE.

of tricks; *jeu de théâtre* [F.], *coup de théâtre* [F.]; stunt, gag [both coll.]; hokum, hoke [both slang]; buffoonery, slapstick, patter; make-believe, pretense etc. (dissembling) 544.2; personation etc. (representation) 554; gesture etc. 550.3; stagecraft etc. *above* 599.2.

7. *n.* role, part, piece, cue, lines, cast, pageant [now rare]; character, characterization; repertoire, repertory; stock [cant]; leading role, lead; minor role, bit; feeder, straight part [cant]; walking part, walk-on, walk-through; relief, comic relief; heavy [cant].

8. *n.* theatrical performance, theatricality [rare], show [coll.], pitch [slang, U.S.], presentation, stage presentation *or* performance, production, entertainment; exhibit, exhibition; benefit performance; amateur performance; variety performance, variety [cant]; premier performance, *première* [F.]; debut, bow; farewell performance, swan song, tenor's farewell [joc.]; audition [coll.], hearing.

personal appearance, flesh show [slang, U.S.]; chorus show, leg show [slang]; hootchy-kootchy show, cooch *or* coochie show [slang]; repertory show, rep show [slang]; minstrel show, minstrel; circus, the big top, carnival, side show; puppet show, fantoccini, Punch-and-Judy show; peep show, raree show; galanty show; shadow show, *ombres chinoises* [F.]; engagement, playing engagement; stand, one-night stand [cant].

9. *n.* motion picture, moving picture [coll.], movie [coll.], picture show [coll.], motion-picture show, moving-picture show [coll.], movie show [coll.], film, cinema [chiefly Eng.]; photoplay, photodrama; sound motion picture, talking picture, talkie [coll.], talk *or* talking film [coll.], gabbie [slang], squawkie [slang]; cinemelodrama; the films [coll.], the movies [coll.], the cinema, the screen, the silver screen; movieland, moviedom [both coll.]; motion-picture theater etc. *below*; motion-picture camera, magic lantern etc. 445.5, 6.

10. *n.* theater, theatron [Gr. Antiq.], odeum, house, playhouse; opera, opera house; music hall, concert hall; amphitheater, hippodrome, Coliseum *or* Colosseum, stadium, bowl; circus, big top; legitimate theater, legit [slang, U.S.]; repertory theater; vaudeville theater; burlesque theater; motion-picture theater, moving-picture theater [coll.], movie theater [coll.], movie show [coll.], picture house [coll.], cinema [chiefly Eng.], cinema theater [Eng.], cinematograph *or* kinematograph [chiefly Eng.], little theater, community theater; Greek theater; assembly room etc. 189.10.

11. *n.* auditorium, auditory [rare]; house, front [cant]; bald-headed row [slang]; orchestra seats, orchestra, pit [chiefly Eng.], parquet; orchestra circle *or* parterre, parquet circle; dress circle, horseshoe *or* diamond horseshoe [slang]; box, *baignoire* [F.], stall [chiefly Eng.]; stage boxes, proscenium boxes; parterre, parterre boxes; balcony, gallery; peanut gallery, nigger heaven, paradise [all slang]; mezzanine, mezzanine floor.

12. *n.* stage, the boards, theatron [Hist.]; proscenium; movable stage, revolving stage; dead stage, live stage [both cant]; right stage, R.; left stage, L.; down left, D.L.; down right, D.R.; up left, U.L.; up right, U.R.; orchestra, orchestra pit; trap, trap door; coulisse, wings; dressing rooms, greenroom; flies, loft; grid [coll.], gridiron; dock; platform etc. 215.21.

13. *n.* stage requisites, properties, props [cant]; breakaway [cant]; practicable, practical, practical piece *or* prop [all cant]; theatrical costume; make-up, grease paint, clown white.

14. *n.* lights, floats, footlights, foots [slang]; limelight, spotlight, spot [slang].

15. *n.* scenery, scene; screen, flat; side scene, coulisse, wing, border; tormentor, tormentor wing; teaser, teaser curtain; wingcut, woodcut; transformation, transformation scene; flipper; curtain, cloth, rag [slang], hanging; drop, drop scene, drop curtain; backdrop, back cloth, back scene; act drop *or* curtain, oleo [cant]; tab; fire curtain, asbestos curtain, asbestos; set, stage-set, stage setting.

16. *n.* playbook, promptbook, script, dialogue, libretto, opera, score, text; lines,

---

A perfect Tragedy is the noblest production of human nature.—ADDISON. "The world's a stage,"—as Shakespeare said one day; / The stage a world—was what he meant to say.—

HOLMES. Come, children, let us shut up the box and the puppets, for our play is played out.—THACKERAY. The theatre . . . is a place for diverting representation.—H. L. MENCKEN.

actor's lines, side [slang]; plot, scene plot.

17. *n.* stageman; stagehand, flunky [derog.]; sceneman, sceneshifter, grip [cant, U.S.]; flyman; carpenter, chips [slang]; electrician, juicer [slang]; chief *or* head electrician, gaffer [slang, U.S.]; machinist; scenist, scene painter, scenewright; costumer, costumier, costumière, wigmaker; make-up man *or* artist; prompter, pit man; callboy; playreader; master of ceremonies, M.C. [slang]; ballyhoo man, spieler, barker [all slang].

ticket seller, scalper *or* ticket scalper; ticket collector, gate man; usher, usherer, usher-in; usheress, usherette; agent, actor's agent, playbroker, ten-percenter [slang, U.S.]; advance agent, booking agent; publicity man *or* agent; manager, actor-manager, acting manager; stage manager, stage director; *entrepreneur* [F.], impresario; backer, angel [slang], patron, patroness; producer, theatrician.

18. *n.* cast, *dramatis personae* [L.], persons in the play; company, troupe; repertory company, rep show [slang]; stock company, stock [cant].

19. *n.* actor, performer, player, stage player *or* performer, stager [arch.], playactor [coll.], Thespian, Roscius, artiste, mummer, theaterian [obs.], theatrical [coll.], trouper, histrio; actress, playactress [coll.], playwoman [rare]; dramatizer, dramatic actor, legitimate actor; old stager, old stage hand; ham, ham actor, ham chewer, hamfatter [all slang]; star, headliner, headline *or* feature attraction; lead, leading man *or* lady, protagonist; *diva* [It.], prima donna, *prima buffa* [It.]; first tragedian, heavy lead [cant]; juvenile lead; hero, heroine.

masker, masquer [rare], mask, masque [obs.]; pantomimist, pantomimic; strolling player, barnstormer [coll.]; tragedian, *tragédien* [F.], tragedienne [*fem.*], heavy [cant]; villain, dirty heavy [slang], menace, Simon Legree; character actor, character man *or* woman, character; juvenile, *jeune premier* [F.], ingénue, soubrette; debutant, debutante [*fem.*]; matinee idol [slang]; foil, feeder, straight man [cant], stooge [slang, U.S.]; utility man, utility, general utility; protean [slang]; study [cant.].

mute, figurant *or* figurante; walking gentleman *or* lady, walk-on; supernumerary, super [cant], supe [cant]; extra, bit player [both coll., motion pictures]; understudy, stand-by, substitute; photoplayer, motion-picture actor, movie actor [coll.], movie star [coll.]; vaudevillist, vaudevillian; blackface actor, blackface; end man, bones; tambo, tambourine; chorus girl, chorus singer; ballet girl, danseuse etc. (dancer) 840.9; pretender etc. 548.3.

20. *n.* comedian, *comédien* [F.], comedienne [*fem.*], comic, funnyman; farcist, farcer, *farceur* [F.], *farceuse* [F., *fem.*]; buffoon, *buffo* [It.]; clown, fool, jester, zany, merry-andrew, wearer of the cap and bells, jackpudding [arch.], pickleherring; mummer, mime, mimer, mimester [rare], mimic, mimologist; guiser [Eng. and Scot.], guisard [Scot.], gysart [obs.].

harlequin, harlequina [*fem.*]; motley fool, wearer of the motley; Punch, Punchinello, Pulcinella; Polichinelle; grimacer, grimacier; pantaloon, Columbine, mountebank, Scaramouch; light comedian, genteel comedian, low comedian, slapstick comedian, hokum *or* hoke comic [slang]; Jack Pudding, Hanswurst, *Pickelhering* [G.], Punch and Judy; humorist etc. 844.

21. *n.* acrobat, tumbler, posture master, contortionist, juggler; ropedancer, ropewalker, funambulist.

22. *n.* dramatist, dramatizer, playcraftsman, stagewright, playwright, playwrightess [*fem.*], playwriter, dramatic author *or* writer; dramaturgist, *dramaturge* [F.]; mimographer, mimist [obs.]; monodramatist; melodramatist; tragic dramatist, tragedian, tragedist [rare]; comedian, comedist; *farceur* [F.], *farceuse* [F., *fem.*], farcer, farcist; librettist; photoplaywright, scenario writer, scenarist, scenarioist, motion-picture writer; dramatic critics, crix [slang, U.S.].

23. *n.* theatergoer, playgoer; moviegoer [coll.], motion-picture fan [slang]; first-nighter; standee [coll.]; *claqueur* [F.], claquer, clapper, hired applauder; pass holder, deadhead [coll.]; waiting line, queue, cue, tail; attender etc. 186.7; spectator etc. 444.

24. *n.* attendance etc. 186.6; audience etc. 418.8.

25. *v.* dramatize, represent dramatically, make into a drama, convert into a play; theatrize, theatricalize; melodramatize; movieize [coll.]; scenarize, scena-

rioize; present, stage, produce, put on [coll.], put on the stage, put on a show [coll.]; star, feature [coll., U.S.], headline; set, set the stage; paper the house [slang].

26. *v.* act, perform, play, play-act [coll.], tread the stage *or* boards, strut the boards, strut one's stuff [slang, U.S.]; act out, enact; act ~, play *or* perform a part; take a part, sustain a part, act *or* play the part of; act like a trouper; troupe, barnstorm [coll.]; gag, patter [both slang]; spout, rant; overact, chew up the scenery [joc.], act all over the stage; milk a scene [cant]; go through one's part, read one's lines, rehearse; register emotion, ~ grief *or* joy [slang]; emote [joc.], emotionalize.

make one's debut *or* bow, come out; open a show, open a show cold [cant]; ring up *or* down, ring up *or* down the curtain; enter, exit, make one's entrance *or* exit; act as foil *or* feeder, stooge [slang, U.S.], play straight for [cant]; star, have one's name in lights; supe [slang], sketch, double in brass [cant], slapstick, try it on the dog [slang]; represent, personate etc. 554.7, 8; mimic etc. (imitate) 19.5–10; make believe, pretend etc. (dissemble) 544.6; monologize etc. (soliloquize) 589.3.

27. *v.* attend etc. 186.9.

28. *adj.* dramatic(al), dramaturgic(al); theatric [rare], theatrical, theatral, theaterlike, theaterwise; stagy, stagelike; histrionic(al), Thespian, make-believe, scenic(al); spectacular, vivid, impressive, striking; tragic(al), tragicodramatic, tragedical [rare]; buskined, cothurned; monodramatic(al), melodramatic(al), comic, tragicomic, farcical, operatic, legitimate, vaudevillian, heavy [cant], protean [slang]; slapstick, slapsticky; cinematic(al), cinematographic(al); ham, hammy [both slang]; stellar, all-star [cant]; backstage, upstage; theatricable, stageworthy; stagestruck; movie-minded [coll.].

29. *adv.* on the stage *or* boards, before an audience, before the curtain, before the footlights *or* floats, in the limelight *or* spotlight; behind the scenes.

600. Will
(See 601. Necessity)

1. *n.* will, volition, volitiency, velleity; conative power, conation [Psychol.], conatus; voluntarism [chiefly Philos.], voluntaryism, voluntarity [rare], voluntariness; spontaneity, spontaneousness, self-activity, self-determination; originality; wish, desire, mind, pleasure, will and pleasure, one's own sweet will; free will, *liberum arbitrium* [L.]; freedom etc. 748; intent, purpose etc. (intention) 620; will power, determination etc. (resolution) 604; option etc. (choice) 609; discretion etc. (discrimination) 465.

2. *v.* will, volitionate, exercise volition etc. *n.*; list [arch.], see *or* think fit; use *or* exercise one's discretion, take upon oneself, take one's own course, take the law into one's own hands, do of one's own accord, do upon one's own authority *or* responsibility, take the responsibility, take the bit between one's teeth, paddle one's own canoe, stand on one's own legs, stand on one's rights, have one's will, have a will of one's own, have one's own way, have it all one's way; do what one chooses etc. (be free) 748.8; choose etc. 609.7; decide, determine etc. (resolve) 604.6, (judge) 480.6.

3. *adj.* willed [chiefly in composition, as *strong-willed, self-willed* etc.]; minded, disposed, inclined etc. (willing) 602.8, (intended) 620.4.

4. *adj.* volitional, volitionary, volitive, volitient, voluntary; willing; willful; conative, conational; optional, optionary [rare]; discretional, discretionary; unforced etc. (free) 748.12–17.

5. *adv.* volitionally, voluntarily etc. *adj.*; at will, at choice, at pleasure, *al piacere* [It.], at one's pleasure, *a beneplacito* [It.], at one's will and pleasure, at one's own sweet will, at one's discretion, *à discrétion* [F.], *ad libitum* [L.], *ad arbitrium* [L.]; as one wishes, as it pleases *or* suits oneself, as one thinks best *or* proper, as it seems good *or* best, as far as one desires, according to one's purpose.

of one's own accord *or* free will, on one's own [coll.], of *or* on one's own initiative, on one's own account *or* responsibility, out of one's own head; *motu proprio, proprio motu, suo motu, ex mero*

---

600. With will one can do anything.—SMILES. No one can rob us of our free will.—EPICTETUS. Sir, we know the will is free, and there's an end on't.—JOHNSON. Will and intellect are one and the same thing.—SPINOZA. Where there's a will there's a way.

motu [all L.]; by choice etc. (optionally) 609.17, 18; purposely etc. (intentionally) 620.5; willingly etc. 602; freely etc. 748.21.

601. Necessity
(See 600. Will)

1. *n.* necessity, necessitude, necessitation; obligation, obligement; inevitability, inevitableness, unavoidableness etc. *adj.*; *anagke* [Gr. ἀνάγκη], what must be, spur of necessity; stern ∼, hard ∼, iron ∼, dire ∼, imperious ∼, inexorable etc. necessity; need etc. (requirement) 630; compulsion etc. 744; Hobson's choice etc. (choicelessness) 609a.

2. *n.* involuntariness etc. *adj.*, blind impulse, natural impulse, natural *or* unreasoning prompting, instinct, native *or* natural tendency, inborn *or* innate proclivity.

3. *n.* destiny, destination; doom, foredoom, crack of doom; fatality, fate, kismet, fortune, lot, cup [Biblical], portion, dispensation; God's will, will of Heaven, Heaven; handwriting on the wall, book of fate; Fortune's wheel, wheel of fortune *or* chance; ides of March; astral influence, stars, planets; predestination etc. (predetermination) 611; imminence etc. 152.

4. *n.* fates, *Fata* [L.], Sisters three, Weird Sisters (Macbeth), Parcae [Rom.], Moirai [Gr.], Norns [Teut.]; Clotho, Lachesis, Atropos [Gr. Fates]; Ananke; Nona, Decuma, Morta [Rom. Fates]; Urth, Verthandi, Skuld [Norse Fates].

5. *n.* last shift, last resort *or* resource, *dernier ressort* [F.]; a shot in the locker [coll.], a card up one's sleeve; makeshift, *pis aller* [F.] etc. (expedient) 646.2.

6. *n.* necessitarianism, necessarianism, necessism; determinism, destinism [rare], fatalism.

7. *n.* necessitarian, necessarian, necessist; determinist, destinist [rare], fatalist; automaton, pawn.

8. *v.* necessitate, render necessary etc. *n.*; require etc. 630.2; oblige etc. (compel) 744.2.

9. *v.* destine, destinate; ordain, devote, appoint, have in store for; doom, foredoom; predestine etc. (predetermine) 611.3.

10. *v.* lie under a necessity etc. *n.*, have no choice *or* alternative, be one's fate etc. *n.*; be necessary, be destined etc. *adj.*; be in for, be under the necessity of, be obliged, be forced *or* driven, be swept on, be drawn irresistibly; be pushed to the wall, be driven into a corner; "make a virtue of necessity" (Shakespeare).

11. *adj.* necessary, necessitous, necessitative; inevitable, inescapable, inevasible, irrevocable, inexorable, unpreventable, uncontrollable, ineluctable, indefeasible; unavoidable, avoidless; irresistible, resistless; binding etc. (compulsory) 744.3; needful etc. (requisite) 630.3; choiceless etc. 609a.3.

12. *adj.* necessitarian, necessarian; deterministic, fatalistic.

13. *adj.* destined, fated, ordained, written, set apart, devoted, elect; kismetic; doomed, foredoomed; fateful, big with fate; predestined etc. (predetermined) 611.5; imminent etc. 152.3.

14. *adj.* involuntary, instinctive, automatic, spontaneous, blind, mechanical; unconscious, unwitting, unthinking; unintentional etc. (accidental) 621.20; unpremeditated etc. (impulsive) 612.4; reluctant etc. (unwilling) 603.5.

15. *adv. etc.* necessarily etc. *adj.*, of *or* from necessity, of course, as a matter of course, *ex necessitate rei* [L.], by stress of, by force *or* stress of circumstances, perforce, needs must, without choice; *nolens volens* [L.], willy-nilly, will he, nill he; will I, nill I; will ye, nill ye; whether one will or not, willing or unwilling, *bon gré mal gré* [F.]; cost what it may, *coûte que coûte* [F.]; *coûte qu'il coûte* [F.]; for lack of something better, *faute de mieux* [F.]; if necessary, if need be, whatever may happen, happen *or* come what may *or* will, let come what may, *vogue la galère* [F.], if the worst comes to the worst, rain or shine; by force etc. (compulsorily) 744.4; unwillingly etc. 603.6.

---

601. Necessity has no law.—RABELAIS. *Fata viam invenient* [The Fates will find the way].—VERGIL. Fate leads the willing, drags the unwilling.—CLEANTHES. We are what we must / And not what we would be.—MEREDITH. 'Tis vain to quarrel with our destiny.—MIDDLETON. *Quisque suos patimur manes* [We each suffer our own destinies].—VERGIL. Destiny has more resources than the most imaginative composer of fiction.—F. MOORE. There's a divinity that shapes our ends, / Rough-hew them how we will.—SHAKESPEARE. What doctrine call ye this, *Che sera, sera:* / What will be, shall be?—MARLOWE. He that is born to be hanged shall never be drowned.

16. *phr.* it is necessary etc. *adj.,* it must be, it needs must be, it must needs be, it will be, it must have its way, it cannot be helped, there is no helping it *or* help for it; it is in the cards *or* books, it is written.

602. Willingness
(See 603. Unwillingness)

1. *n.* willingness, willinghood [rare], readiness, promptness etc. *adj.*; willing mind *or* heart, willing ear; good will *or* goodwill, cheerful consent, geniality, cordiality; assent etc. 488; compliance etc. (consent) 762; pleasure etc. (will) 600; alacrity, eagerness etc. 682.2, 3.

2. *n.* propensity, propendency [obs.], propension [now rare], propensitude [rare]; proneness etc. *adj.*, proclivity, favorable disposition, inclination, animus, leaning, tendency, bias, bent, turn; *penchant* [F.], liking etc. (desire) 865; frame of mind, humor etc. (disposition) 820; aptitude etc. (talent) 698.2.

3. *n.* docility, docibleness [rare], docibility [rare]; persuadability, persuasibility, persuadableness, persuasibleness; tractability, pliability etc. (softness) 324; susceptibility etc. 615.5.

4. *n.* voluntary labor, voluntary; labor of love, self-appointed task, unrewarded effort, unpaid *or* gratuitous service; social service, welfare work.

5. *n.* volunteer, voluntary [rare]; unpaid worker, free-will worker; social worker, welfare worker.

6. *v.* be willing etc. *adj.,* have a willing mind etc. *n.,* lend ~, give *or* turn a willing ear; be of favorable disposition etc. *n.,* incline, lean to *or* towards, propend [now rare]; think good *or* proper, see *or* think fit; had *or* would as lief, had *or* would as leave [now dial.], would as lief as not, would as leave as not [now dial.], not care if one does [coll.]; have a mind to, have half a mind to, have a good *or* great mind to, feel like [coll.].

hold *or* cling to; enter with a will, go into heart and soul etc. *adv.*; go in for, go in at, have a go at [all coll.]; take up, plunge into, jump at, catch at; gorge the hook, swallow the bait, swallow bait and all; swallow bait, hook and sinker; swallow hook, line and sinker; have *or* make no scruple of, make no bones of [coll.]; meet halfway; acquiesce etc. (assent) 488.6, 7; comply etc. (consent) 762.2.

7. *v.* volunteer, proffer etc. (offer) 763.2, 3.

8. *adj.* willing, willinghearted, minded, willed, inclined, disposed, predisposed, prone, propense [arch.], favorably minded, ~ inclined *or* disposed, well-disposed, favorable, agreeable, compliant, fain, lief [arch.], nothing loth, game [coll.], on [slang]; in the mood, ~ vein, ~ humor *or* mind, in a good mood etc.; genial, cordial, gracious, cheerful, delighted; ready, prompt, forward; eager, enthusiastic etc. (fervent) 821.6; content etc. (assenting) 488.11; consenting etc. 762.3.

9. *adj.* docile, suasible, persuasible, persuadable, easily persuaded; easygoing; tractable, pliant, facile etc. 324.6; teachable etc. 539.7; manageable etc. 705.6.

10. *adj.* voluntary, volunteer, gratuitous, spontaneous; unsought, unbesought; unasked etc. (*see* ask etc. 765.4); unbidden etc. (*see* bid etc. 741.4); unforced etc. (free) 748.12–17; elective etc. (optional) 609.14.

11. *adv.* willingly etc. *adj.,* with willingness etc. *n.,* with a will, with good will, with right good will, *de bonne volonté* [F.], gladly, with pleasure, with all one's heart, heart and soul, heart in hand, heartily, to one's heart's content *ex animo* [L.], *con amore* [It.], with willingness and zeal, with delight, with open arms, at the drop of a hat [coll.]; graciously, with good grace, *de bonne grâce* [F.]; nothing loath, without reluctance *or* demur, of one's own accord, freely, fain; as lief, as lief as not; by all means, of course etc. (assent) 488.14, 15; permissibly etc. 760.7; voluntarily etc. 600.5.

603. Unwillingness
(See 602. Willingness)

1. *n.* unwillingness, indisposedness etc. *adj.,* indisposition, disinclination, nill [arch.], renitence *or* renitency, reluctance; aversion, aversation [arch.]; nol-

602. Nothing is troublesome that we do willingly.—JEFFERSON.   A willing heart adds feather to the heel.—BAILLIE.   Where your will is ready, your feet are light.—G. HERBERT. Barkis is willin'.—DICKENS.

603. My feet reluctant linger at the gate.—LONGFELLOW.   When in the dark, / Unwilling, alone we embark.—BRIDGES.   He who

leity, nolition [both rare]; indocility etc. (obstinacy) 606; slowness etc. 275; dissent etc. 489; refusal etc. 764.

2. *n.* scrupulousness, scrupulosity; qualm *or* twinge of conscience, misgiving, scruple, qualm, shrinking, recoil, demur; hesitation, hesitance *or* hesitancy; delicacy etc. (fastidiousness) 868.

3. *n.* unwilling service, forced labor; slavery, peonage; compulsion etc. 744; shirker etc. 623.4.

4. *v.* be unwilling etc. *adj.*, nill [arch.], would rather not, not care to, not feel like [coll.], not find it in one's heart to, not have the heart *or* stomach to; grudge, begrudge; demur, scruple, stick at, stickle, shy, fight shy of, duck [slang], dodge, blink, blench, swerve, recoil, shrink, pull *or* hang back, hesitate, hang fire; avoid, shirk etc. 623.6-9; refuse etc. 764.2-4; oppose etc. 708.2; dissent etc. 489.4.

5. *adj.* unwilling, disinclined, indisposed, averse, adverse, renitent, reluctant, grudging, demurring, shrinking, shy of; loath *or* loth, loathful [obs. exc. Scot.]; not in the mood *or* vein, not content; laggard, backward, remiss, slack, slow to; involuntary, forced; restive, restiff [obs.]; irreconcilable; scrupulous, squeamish etc. (fastidious) 868.4; dissenting etc. 489.5; opposed etc. 708.4; unconsenting etc. (refusing) 764.5.

6. *adv.* unwillingly, loathly [now rare], grudgingly etc. *adj.*; with a heavy heart, with a bad *or* an ill grace, under protest, against *or* sore against one's wishes *or* will, against the grain, *à contre-cœur* [F.], "*invita Minerva*" (Horace); in spite of one's teeth, in spite of oneself, *malgré soi* [F.], *malgré lui* [F.]; unwilling to hear of, deaf to; not if one can help it, not for the world etc. (no) 536.4; *nolens volens* [L.] etc. (necessarily) 601.15; perforce etc. (compulsion) 744.4.

7. *phr.* I will not!, far be it from me! etc. (I refuse!) 764.8; not at any price!, not on your life!, nothing doing!

604. Resolution
(See 605. Irresolution)

1. *n.* resolution, resoluteness etc. *adj.*, determination, decision, resolve, will, firmness of mind *or* spirit, backbone [coll.], mettle, pluck, spunk [coll.], game, grit, clear grit, sand [slang], stamina, guts [slang], pith, bottom; fixed ~, set *or* settled purpose, unswerving determination, unyielding resolution; devotion, devotedness; doggedness, dogged resolution; intransigence *or* intransigency, *intransigeance* [F.], intransigentism; tenacity etc. (perseverance) 604a; obstinacy etc. 606; constancy, firmness etc. (stability) 150; inflexibility etc. (hardness) 323; vigor etc. (strength) 159, (energy) 171; courage etc. 861; zeal etc. (eagerness) 682.3; intention etc. 620.

2. *n.* will power, strength *or* force of will, strength of mind, iron will, will of iron, indomitable ~, unconquerable etc. will, will *or* mind of one's own, moral courage, ~ fiber *or* strength.

3. *n.* self-control, self-command, self-possession, self-reliance, self-government, self-restraint, self-conquest, self-denial, self-mastery, mastery etc. over self, *aplomb* [F.]; temperance etc. 953.

4. *n.* (comparisons) fighting cock, gamecock; bulldog; British lion; intransigent, bitter-ender [coll.] etc. (conservative) 141.3.

5. *v.* be resolute etc. *adj.*, have determination etc. *n.*; have a mind of one's own, know one's own mind; stick at nothing, not stick at trifles; mean business, have blood in one's eyes [both coll.]; persist etc. (persevere) 604a.2; not yield an inch etc. (be obstinate) 606.5.

6. *v.* resolve, will, determine, decide, purpose, make up one's mind, form a resolution *or* resolve, come to a determination *or* conclusion, conclude, fix, seal, settle, determine once for all, bring to a crisis, drive matters to an extremity; assume a resolute attitude, steel oneself, grit one's teeth, set one's teeth *or* jaw, take the bit in one's mouth *or* teeth, nail one's colors to the mast, set one's back against the wall, take one's stand, stand firm, stand pat [coll.], keep *or* hold one's ground *or* footing, hold fast, adhere resolutely, stick, stick fast, stick to one's guns, put one's foot down, stand no nonsense,

---

hath no stomach to this fight.—SHAKESPEARE. Nothing is so easy but it becomes difficult when done with reluctance.—TERENCE.
604. The dauntless spirit of resolution.—SHAKESPEARE. How terrible is constant resolution.—SHAKESPEARE. He only is a well-made man who has a good determination.—EMERSON. Prudent, cautious self-control / Is wisdom's root.—BURNS. Than self-restraint there is nothing better.—LAO-TSZE. I am the master of my fate: / I am the captain

not listen to the voice of the charmer, insist upon, make a point of, set one's mind *or* heart upon.

burn one's bridges, kick down the ladder, throw away the scabbard; give oneself up to, go in for [coll.], devote oneself to, put one's heart into, buckle to, buckle oneself, put ~, lay *or* set one's shoulder to the wheel, take the bull by the horns, rush *or* plunge *in medias res* [L.], make a dash at; take a decisive step etc. (choose) 609.7, 8; take upon oneself etc. (undertake) 676.2.

7. *adj.* resolved, determined etc. *v.*; bound [coll., U.S.], resolute, earnest, serious, decided, definite, peremptory, unhesitating, unfaltering, unswerving, unflinching, unshrinking, steadfast in purpose, set [now dial.], settled, fixed, firm, firm as Gibraltar, grim, stern, solid, stanch, indomitable, inexorable, relentless, not to be shaken *or* put down; iron, cast-iron; irrevocable, irreversible; undeflectable, not to be deflected; pat, standpat [coll.]; intransigent, uncompromising; steeled to *or* against, proof against; *in utrumque paratus* [L.].

strong-willed, strong-minded; self-possessed, self-reliant; plucky, game, gritty [coll.], mettlesome, game to the backbone, game to the last *or* end; inflexible, unyielding etc. (hard) 323.5; unchangeable etc. (stable) 150.5-7; tenacious etc. (obstinate) 606.6, (persevering) 604a.3.

8. *adj.* resolved upon, determined upon, decided upon, set upon [now dial.], bent upon, intent upon, fixed upon; bent on etc.

9. *adv.* resolutely, seriously, earnestly etc. *adj.*; dingdong [coll.], in earnest, in good earnest; with all one's heart, heart and soul, tooth and nail, hammer and tongs; on one's mettle; manfully, like a man; with high heart *or* courage, with a high soul.

at all risks *or* hazards, at all events, in any event, at any rate, at any risk *or* hazard, at any price, ~ cost *or* sacrifice, whatever the cost, cost what it may, *coûte que coûte* [F.], *coûte qu'il coûte* [F.]; survive or perish, live or die, sink or swim, rain or shine, neck or nothing;
whatever may happen, happen *or* come what may *or* will, let come what may, *vogue la galère* [F.], if the worst comes to the worst, once for all, in some way or another, *à bis ou à blanc* [F.], as though life depended upon it; perseveringly etc. 604a.4.

604a. Perseverance

1. *n.* perseverance, singleness *or* tenacity of purpose, persistence *or* persistency, steadiness etc. *adj.*, constancy, application, plodding, dogged perseverance, pertinacity, tenacity, bulldog tenacity, stick-to-itiveness [coll.], staying power, stay [chiefly coll.], endurance, indefatigability; patience, patiency [rare]; sedulity etc. (industry) 682.5; continuance etc. 143; stamina, grit etc. (resolution) 604; obstinacy etc. 606.

2. *v.* persevere, persist, endure, stay [coll.], stick, stick *or* stay with it, stick to, stick to one's last, ~ knitting *or* mutton [coll.], stick to one's guns, hang on, hang on for dear life [coll.], cling *or* adhere to, hold fast, hold on, carry on, keep on, keep to *or* maintain one's course, keep at, keep perseveringly at, keep at it, keep going, keep driving [coll.], keep the pot boiling [coll.], keep the ball rolling, keep up the ball, keep up, bear up, hold up, hold out, stick out, stick it out [slang], stay it out, never say die, not give up, not give up the ship [coll.], go the whole length, go all lengths, go the limit [slang], go the whole hog [slang], follow *or* prosecute to a conclusion, follow out *or* up, see it through [coll.].

be in at the death, die in the last ditch, die in harness, die in one's shoes, die at one's post, die game, go down with flying colors; keep doggedly at, plod, peg, peg away *or* along; plug, plug at it, plug away *or* along [all slang]; move heaven and earth, leave no stone unturned; go through fire and water, "ride with the whirlwind and direct the storm" (Addison); continue etc. 143.2; be resolute etc. 604.5; take no denial etc. (be obstinate) 606.5; do thoroughly etc. 729.3.

604a. The Will which says ... "Hold on!"—KIPLING. The secret of success is constancy to purpose.—DISRAELI. To persevere in one's duty and be silent.—WASHINGTON. God is with those who persevere.—KORAN. If at first you don't succeed, / Try, try, try again.

---

of my soul.—W. E. HENLEY. Free peoples can escape being mastered by others only by being able to master themselves.—T. ROOSEVELT.

3. *adj.* persevering, perseverant; persisting, persistent; pertinacious, dogged, tenacious, stick-to-itive [coll.]; frequent, constant, steady, steadfast, *tenax propositi* [L.], steady as time, unremitting, unintermitting, undeviating, unwavering, unfaltering, unswerving, unflinching, unsleeping, unflagging, undrooping, untiring, never-tiring, unwearied, indefatigable, indomitable, relentless, game to the last *or* end, undaunted, patient; enduring, endurant; uninterrupted; sedulous, plodding etc. (industrious) 682.19; unchangeable etc. (stable) 150.5–7; resolute etc. 604.7.

4. *adv.* perseveringly etc. *adj.*, through thick and thin, through fire and water, through evil report and good report, *per fas et nefas* [L.], *vogue la galère* [F.], rain *or* shine, fair or foul, in sickness and in health; sink or swim etc. (resolutely) 604.9.

605. Irresolution
(See 604. Resolution)

1. *n.* irresolution, indetermination, undetermination [rare]; infirmity of purpose, indecision, instability, inconstancy, unsettlement; vacillation, vacillancy [rare]; fluctuation, fluctuation of mind, oscillation, pendulation, alternation, shilly-shally, wobble *or* wabble; variableness, variability, variation; hesitating etc. *v.*, hesitation, hesitance *or* hesitancy; demur, demurrage, demurral; suspense, state of suspense; halfheartedness, lukewarmness, Laodiceanism; half measures; uncertainty etc. 475; changeableness etc. 149; capriciousness, fickleness etc. 608.2, 3; tergiversation etc. 607; choicelessness etc. 609a; fearfulness etc. 860.2.

2. *n.* weak will, weakness etc. *adj.*; loss of will power, abulia, abulomania; pliancy etc. (softness) 324; timidity, want of confidence etc. (fear) 860; cowardice etc. 862.

3. *n.* waverer, shuffler, trimmer, wobbler *or* wabbler, shilly-shally, shilly-shallyer, dillydallier; ass between two bundles of hay; shuttlecock, feather, piece of thistledown, butterfly, chameleon, weathercock, shifting sand, house built on sand; doughface [coll.], opportunist, Dite Deuchars, Laodicean; tergiversator, turncoat etc. 607.4, 5; equivocator etc. 477.6.

4. *v.* be irresolute etc. *adj.*, show indecision etc. *n.*, not know one's own mind, not know where one stands, not know whether one stands on one's head or one's heels; hesitate, pause, falter, demur, hang back, hang in doubt, keep *or* hang in suspense, hang fire, hover, wait to see how the cat jumps *or* the wind blows, stop to consider, debate, balance, weigh one thing against another, consider both sides of the question, think twice about, leave *ad referendum* [L.]; dally with, coquet with; have two minds, be of two minds.

waver, vacillate, fluctuate, alternate, pendulate, oscillate, vary, trim, shift, shuffle, palter, swing from one thing to another, waver between two extremes, go around in circles, wabble *or* wobble, shilly-shally, dillydally, seesaw, teeter-totter, back and fill, keep off and on, toss and turn, hum *or* hem and haw, will and will not, "let 'I dare not' wait upon 'I would'" (Shakespeare); be thrown off one's balance, stagger, flounder, stumble, boggle, toss, pitch, stagger like a drunken man; change etc. 140.5; blow hot and cold etc. (be capricious) 608.4; tergiversate etc. 607.7; sit on the fence, straddle [both coll.] etc. 628.2; be afraid etc. 860.8; dawdle etc. 683.8.

5. *adj.* irresolute, irresolved, unresolved; undetermined, unsettled, undecided, indecisive, infirm of purpose; double-minded, of two minds; hesitating etc. *v.*, hesitant; fidgety, tremulous; wavering, vacillating etc. *v.*; vacillant [now rare], vacillatory; oscillative [rare], oscillatory; shilly-shally, wabbly *or* wobbly, palsied, off one's balance; going around in circles, like a chicken with its head cut off [coll.]; halfhearted, doublehearted; lukewarm, neither hot nor cold, Laodicean; easygoing; variable, inconstant, unstable etc. (changeable) 149.5, 6; capricious, fickle etc. 608.5, 6; unsure, doubtful, at a loss etc. (uncertain) 475.9, 10, 16; tergiversating etc. 607.10; choiceless etc. 609a.3.

---

605. Through indecision opportunity is often lost.—Publilius. How long halt ye between two opinions?—Bible. Was ever feather so lightly blown to and fro as this multitude?—Shakespeare. At war 'twixt will and will not.—Shakespeare. There is no more miserable human being than one in whom nothing is habitual but indecision.—W. James. Weak and irresolute is man.—Cowper.

6. *adj.* weak-willed, feeble-minded, weak, frail, without a will of one's own, unable to say "no"; abulic; dough-faced [coll.], pliable etc. (soft) 324.6; timid etc. (cowardly) 862.4.

7. *adv.* irresolutely, irresolvedly etc. *adj.*; in an irresolute *or* undecided manner, in faltering accents; shilly-shally, shill-I-shall-I; on the sands; off and on, from pillar to post etc. (alternately) 314.14.

606. Obstinacy
(See 607. Tergiversation)

1. *n.* obstinacy, obstinance *or* obstinancy [rare], obstinateness, doggedness, stubbornness etc. *adj.*; self-will, tough will, mind *or* will of one's own; pertinacity, tenacity, "tough tenacity of purpose" (Symonds), dogged resolution; perversity, *perversité* [F.]; cussedness, pure cussedness [both coll., U.S.]; contumacy, contumacity; obduracy, obduration [rare]; indocility, impersuasibility, intractability, incorrigibility; immovability etc. (stability) 150; inflexibility etc. (hardness) 323; resolution etc. 604; perseverance etc. 604a; unwillingness etc. 603.

2. *n.* bigotry, intolerance, illiberality, narrow-mindedness, stiff neck; opinionatedness, opinionativeness, opiniativeness [rare], opiniatry [obs.]; shortsightedness, purblindness; blind side, blind spot, mote in the eye; pedantry, pedantism; positivism etc. (dogmatism) 474.3; monomania, fanaticism etc. (craze) 503.7; standpattism [coll.] etc. (conservatism) 141.2; prejudice etc. (bias) 481.3; prudery etc. 853.2; hyperorthodoxy etc. 983a.5; sanctimony etc. 988.2.

3. *n.* obstinate person, mule [coll.], donkey, ass, perverse fool, bullhead, bullethead [coll., U.S.], pighead, hard *or* tough case [slang], irreconcilable; intransigent, intransigentist, *intransigeant* [F.]; bigot, stickler; opinionist, opinionatist [obs.], opiniator [obs.], opiniaster [rare]; positivist etc. (dogmatist) 474.4; zealot, enthusiast etc. (fanatic) 504.2;

standpatter, bitterender [both coll.] etc. (conservative) 141.3; affector etc. 853.4.

4. *n.* (comparisons) bulldog, turtle, bull, mule, donkey, ass.

5. *v.* be obstinate etc. *adj.*, stickle, hold out, stand out; take no denial, not take "no" for an answer; have one's own way, have it all one's way, have one's will, have *or* insist on having the last word, not yield an inch; die hard, die fighting, fight to the last ditch, fight against, fly in the face of facts; opinionate [rare], be wedded to an opinion, hug a belief; persist etc. (persevere) 604a.2; stand pat [coll.], hold one's ground etc. (be resolute) 604.5, 6; refuse etc. 764.2.

6. *adj.* obstinate, obstinacious [rare]; willful *or* wilful, self-willed, strong-willed; dogged, bulldogged, tenacious, pertinacious; stubborn, *entêté* [F.], heady, headstrong, bullheaded, bulletheaded [coll., U.S.], pigheaded, mulish, obstinate *or* stubborn as a mule; contrary, contrarious [now rare]; perverse, snivy *or* snivey [dial.], wayward, froward, untoward, cross-grained, contumacious; obdurate, tough, casehardened, hard-set, hardmouthed, hard-bitten *or* hard-bitted.

firm, immovable, not to be moved, intractable *or* untractable, impracticable, indocile; obstreperous, incorrigible, pervicacious [now rare], refractory, recalcitrant, unruly, ungovernable, unmanageable, uncontrollable *or* incontrollable, unsubmissive; irrepressible *or* unrepressible, insuppressible *or* unsuppressible; restive, resty [obs. exc. dial.]; balky, balking; sullen, sulky, stuffy [coll.]; unmoved, uninfluenced, unaffected; unyielding, inflexible etc. (hard) 323.5; unchangeable etc. 150.7; determined, inexorable etc. (resolute) 604.7; resistant etc. 719.5.

7. *adj.* bigoted, bigotish; hidebound, creed-bound; stiff, stiff-backed, stiff-necked, stiffhearted; set, set in one's ways [both now dial.]; settled, rooted; firm, immovable etc. *above*; uncompromising, intransigent, irreconcilable; opinioned, opinionated, opinionate, opinionative, opiniative [now rare], *opiniâtre* [F.],

---

606. Obstinacy in a bad cause is but constancy in a good.—T. BROWNE.   Let it be virtuous to be obstinate.—SHAKESPEARE.   A stubborn heart shall fare evil at the last.—BIBLE.   The gods that unrelenting breast have steel'd, / And curs'd thee with a mind that cannot yield.—HOMER.   I know the stubborn temper of the man; / He may be broken, but can ne'er be bent.—SENECA.   It is only an error of judgment to make a mistake, but it argues an infirmity of character to adhere to it when discovered.—C. N. BOVEE.

opiniaster [rare], wedded to an opinion; self-opinioned, self-opinionated; conceited, egotistical; positive, positivistic.

impervious, impervious to reason; impersuasible, impersuadable, unpersuadable; deaf, deaf to advice *or* reason; shortsighted, nearsighted, purblind; intolerant, illiberal; provincial, insular, parochial, confined; small, little; narrow, narrow-minded, narrow-souled, narrow-spirited, mean-spirited; strait [arch.], strait-laced; prejudiced etc. 481.10; infatuated, obsessed etc. (fanatical) 503.18; unreasonable etc. 477.10; positive etc. (dogmatic) 474.15; strict etc. 739.5; prudish etc. 853.7; hyperorthodox etc. 983a.8.

8. *adv.* obstinately etc. *adj.*, with set jaw, with sullen mouth, with a stiff neck.

607. Tergiversation
(See 606. Obstinacy)

1. *n.* tergiversation, tergiversating etc. *v.,* change of mind *or* purpose; reverse, reversal; about-face, *volte-face* [F.], rightabout-face, rightabout, a turn to the rightabout; change etc. 140; changeableness etc. 149; vacillation etc. (irresolution) 605; capriciousness, fickleness etc. 608.2, 3; equivocation etc. (quibbling) 477.4.

2. *n.* apostasy, recreancy, reactionaryism, reactionism; perversion, diversion; defection, desertion, secession etc. (abandonment) 624; backsliding, recidivism etc. (relapse) 661; infidelity etc. 940.2.

3. *n.* recantation, forswearing etc. *v.,* repudiation, disavowal, withdrawal; retraction, retractation; renunciation, renunciance [rare], renouncement; revokement, revocation; abjurement, abjuration; palinode, palinody [arch.]; disclaimer, disclamation; rejection etc. 610; resignation etc. 757; relinquishment etc. (abandonment) 624; dissent etc. 489; denial etc. (negation) 536; abrogation etc. 756; repentance etc. 950.

4. *n.* tergiversator, tergiversant; timeserver, timepleaser, timist [obs.]; ambidexter, double-dealer, Janus; coquet, flirt; trimmer, shuffler, weathercock etc.

(waverer) 605.3; equivocator etc. 477.6.

5. *n.* apostate, recreant, crawfish [slang, U.S.], bolter, mugwump [polit. cant, U.S.], deserter, rat [slang], Vicar of Bray; renegade, runagate, runaway; turncoat, turntippet [obs.], turntail, turnback; come-outer [coll., U.S.], separatist; schismatic, schismatist [rare]; seceder, secessionist, secessioner; secesh, secesher [both coll., U.S.]; pervert, backslider, recidivist; reversioner, reversionist; reactionary, reactionist; traitor etc. 949.3; dissenter etc. 489.3; rebel etc. (insurgent) 742.3; heretic, sectarian etc. 984.12, 13.

6. *n.* rat [slang], scab, knobstick [Eng.], snob [Eng.], blackleg [all trade-union cant].

7. *v.* tergiversate, change one's mind *or* intention, change one's song, ~ tune *or* note, shift one's ground, go upon another tack; come round, come over *or* round to an opinion; go ~, pass ~, change *or* skip from one side to another, swing from one thing to another; shift, deviate etc. (change) 140.5; shuffle, vacillate etc. (be irresolute) 605.4; blow hot and cold etc. (be capricious) 608.4; sit on the fence, straddle [both coll.] etc. (be neutral) 628.2; veer round, aboutface etc. (turn back) 283.6.

8. *v.* apostatize, go over, change sides, turn one's coat, turn cloak, *tourner casaque* [F.]; desert, forsake, secede etc. (abandon) 624.3; be faithless etc. 940.7.

9. *v.* recant, retract, revoke, repudiate, renounce, abjure, forswear, disavow, disown, deny, disclaim, unsay, recall, take back, withdraw, back down *or* out [coll.], back water, retrace one's steps, crawfish [coll., U.S.], crawl [slang, U.S.], draw in one's horns; eat one's words, eat crow, eat humble pie; think better of it, be of another mind; return *or* come back to one's first love; reform etc. (repent) 950.3, 4; relinquish, wash one's hands of etc. (abandon) 624.3; rescind etc. (abrogate) 756.3; dissent etc. 489.4; resign etc. 757.2; apologize etc. 952.5.

10. *adj.* tergiversating etc. *v.,* tergiversant; slippery as an eel, trimming, ambidextrous, timeserving, unreliable;

---

607. Renegadoes, who ne'er turn by halves.—DRYDEN. That mild apostate from poetic rule.—BYRON. He ... felt toward those whom he had deserted that peculiar malignity

... characteristic of apostates.—MACAULAY. Straight they changed their minds, flew off, and into strange vagaries fell.—MILTON. How soon ... ease would recant / Vows made in pain, as violent and void!—MILTON.

changeful etc. 149.6; irresolute etc. 605.5; capricious, fickle etc. 608.5, 6.

11. *adj.* apostate, apostatic *or* apostatical; recreant, renegade, false, unfaithful; reactionary, reactionist; revulsive, revulsionary; backsliding, recidivistic etc. 661.4.

12. *adj.* recanting etc. *v.*, abjuratory, revocatory; renunciative, renunciatory; repudiative, repudiatory.

608. Caprice

1. *n.* caprice, whim, whimsey *or* whimsy, whimwham; *capriccio* [It.], boutade, flimflam, freak, fad, vagary, fancy, notion, fantastic notion, quip, conceit, crotchet, quirk, crank, kink, kink in one's horn [slang, U.S.], maggot, maggot in the brain, bee in the bonnet *or* head [coll.], humor, fit; prank, fantastic trick, escapade; craze etc. 503.7.

2. *n.* capriciousness, whimsicalness etc. *adj.*; caprice, whimsicality, fantasticality, freakery, freak; coquetry, flirtation; faddishness, faddiness [coll.], faddism, fadmongery; erraticism etc. (eccentricity) 503.6.

3. *n.* fickleness etc. *adj.*, levity, *légèreté* [F.]; variability, inconstancy etc. (changeableness) 149, (irresolution) 605; tergiversation etc. 607.

4. *v.* be capricious etc. *adj.*, blow hot and cold, play *or* play at fast and loose, keep off and on, turn and turn about, say one thing and do *or* mean another, have as many phases as the moon; strain at a gnat and swallow a camel; have a maggot in the brain etc. *n.*; take it into one's head, conceive as a sudden notion; coquet *or* coquette, flirt; vacillate, fluctuate etc. (be changeable) 149.4, (be irresolute) 605.4; tergiversate etc. 607.7.

5. *adj.* capricious, full of whims etc. *n.*, whimsical, crotchety, kinky [U.S.], humorsome, skittish, fitful, fanciful, fantastic, freakish; maggoty, maggot-pated [obs.]; faddish, faddy [coll.], fadmongering; vagrant, wanton, wayward, unrestrained, undisciplined, uncontrolled, fast

and loose; hysterical; contrary, captious; unreasonable, not amenable to reason, penny-wise and pound-foolish; arbitrary; erratic etc. (eccentric) 503.17; unconformable etc. 83.9.

6. *adj.* fickle, frivolous, giddy, light, light-minded, lightsome, feathery [rare], frothy, volatile, mercurial, without ballast; irresponsible, sleeveless [now dial.], unreliable, undependable, not to be relied *or* depended upon; coquettish, flirtatious; variable, inconstant, unstable etc. (changeable) 149.5, 6; tergiversating etc. 607.10; irresolute etc. 605.5.

7. *adv.* capriciously etc. *adj.*, at one's own sweet will [coll.]; by fits, by fits and starts; without rhyme *or* reason, without counting the cost.

609. Choice
(See 609a. Choicelessness, 610. Rejection)

1. *n.* choice, choosing etc. *v.*, choose [dial.], election, pick, optation [rare]; co-optation, co-option; selection, excerption, excerpt, *excerpta* [L.; *pl.*], extraction, extract; option, optionality; alternate choice, alternative, alternativity; *embarras de choix* [F.], dilemma; adoption, acceptance, espousal, embracement; novation [Law]; eclectism, eclecticism, electicism [rare]; determination, decision etc. (resolution) 604, (judgment) 480; discretion etc. (discrimination) 465; the pick etc. (best) 648.4.

2. *n.* preference, preferability, preferment [rare]; prelation [rare], predilection, prepossession, predisposition, prejudice, partiality; rather, drather, druther [all dial.]; first choice, preoption; precedence etc. 62; liking etc. 865.1.

3. *n.* election, voting etc. *v.*; vote, voice, poll; plumper, fagot vote [Eng.], straw vote; ballot, ticket [U.S.], straight ticket, Australian ballot; voting sign, show of hands, uplifted hands; *viva voce* [L.], aye *or* ay, nay; primary election, primary, direct primary; general election; suffrage, adult suffrage, manhood suffrage, woman suffrage, universal suffrage; suffragism, suffragettism; popular vote *or* decision, *vox populi* [L.]; plebiscite, plebiscitum; referendum (*pl.* referen-

---

508. The only difference between a caprice and a life-long passion is that the caprice lasts a little longer.—WILDE.   Peggy has a whim of iron.—O. HERFORD.   Fancy . . . is as capricious as the accidents of things.—WORDSWORTH. Follow this way or that, as the freak takes you. —STEVENSON.

609. The difficulty in life is the choice.—G. MOORE.   Many are called but few are chosen. —BIBLE.   I have chosen thee in the furnace of affliction.—BIBLE.   Of harmes two the less

dums, referenda); proportional representation, cumulative vote *or* system of voting, single vote, Hare system, list system; division; elective franchise; electioneering; ballot box, polls.

4. *n.* voter, elector, balloter, constituent; suffragist, suffragette; floater, repeater [both U.S.]; fagot voter [Eng.], straw voter; electorate, constituency.

5. *n.* appointment, assignment, consignment, designation, allotment, allocation; post, position, office.

6. *n.* (comparisons) apple of discord, choice of Hercules, Scylla and Charybdis, good and evil, wheat and chaff *or* tares, sheep and goats.

7. *v.* choose, elect, select, pick, opt, optate [rare], use *or* exercise one's option, make *or* take one's choice etc. *n.*, make choice of, fix upon, pitch upon, single out, pick out, choose out, make a selection, take by selection, decide *or* settle upon, decide between, draw the line; excerpt, extract; separate, segregate, divide, set apart, cull, glean, winnow, sift; separate *or* winnow the chaff from the wheat, separate the wheat from the tares, separate the sheep from the goats, decide between the good and the bad; pick one's way; balance, weigh.

adopt, accept, take up, embrace, espouse, go in for [coll.]; indulge one's fancy; co-opt, co-optate; pick and choose; discriminate between, exercise discretion etc. (discriminate) 465.2, 3; will etc. 600.2; do what one chooses etc. (be free) 748.8.

8. *v.* make a decision, make up one's mind, take a decided *or* decisive step, commit oneself to a course, pass *or* cross the Rubicon, cast in one's lot with, take for better *or* for worse; decide, determine etc. (resolve) 604.6, (judge) 480.2.

9. *v.* prefer, have preference etc. *n.*, take *or* decide by way of preference, prefer to, ~ before *or* above, set before *or* above, regard *or* honor before, favor, hold in greater favor, like better; rather, have one's rathers, ~ drathers *or* druthers [dial.], choose rather, had *or* have rather; had *or* would as lief, had *or* would as leave [now dial.]; think proper, see *or* think fit *or* best, please, list [arch.], incline *or* lean to *or* towards; fancy etc. (desire) 865.11.

10. *v.* vote, poll, ballot, give a *or* the voting sign, vote by ballot, ~ show of hands *or viva voce* [L.], hold up one's hand; plump; divide.

11. *v.* appoint, elect, assign, consign, designate, allot, allocate, detail; co-opt, co-optate etc. *above* 609.7; place in office, choose for a post *or* position; draft *or* draught, detach, enlist; reserve, set apart, set one's seal upon, mark out for.

12. *v.* put to choice, offer for one's choice, set before, hold out ~, present *or* offer the alternative; put to the vote, have a show of hands.

13. *adj.* choice etc. (best) 648.9.

14. *adj.* optional, optionary [rare]; co-optive, co-optative; elective, electoral [rare]; voluntary etc. 602.10.

15. *adj.* choosing etc. *v.*, optant, selective, elective, eclectic(al); preferable, preferential; choiceful, choicy [coll., U.S.], choosy [U.S.], picky [slang], fickle in choosing; finical etc. (fastidious) 868.4; discretional etc. (discriminating) 465.4.

16. *adj.* chosen, selected etc. *v.*, elect, select.

17. *adv. etc.* optionally etc. *adj.*, at the option of, at choice, at one's will; on approval, if one wishes, whether or not; either, or, either the one or the other; once for all; at pleasure etc. (voluntarily) 600.5.

18. *adv.* by choice *or* preference, in preference, preferably; first, sooner, rather, before.

609a. Choicelessness
(See 609. Choice)

1. *n.* choicelessness, absence of choice etc. (*see* choice etc. 609.1), no choice *or* alternative, Hobson's choice, not a pin to choose, six of one and half a dozen of the other, distinction without a difference; any, the first that comes, first come first served, that or nothing; necessity etc. 601; neutrality etc. 628.1; irresolution etc. 605.

2. *v.* have no choice *or* alternative, be

---

is for to choose.—CHAUCER. Of two evils, choose neither.—C. H. SPURGEON. A man should choose with careful eye / The things to be remembered by.—R. P. T. COFFIN.

609a. There's small choice in rotten apples.—SHAKESPEARE. Where to elect there is but one, / 'Tis Hobson's choice,—take that or none.—T. WARD. Hanging and wiving goes by destiny.—SHAKESPEARE.

without preference etc. 609.2; have that or nothing, take it or leave it [coll.]; waive, not vote, abstain *or* refrain from voting, leave undecided; lie under a necessity etc. 601; be neutral etc. 628.2.

3. *adj.* choiceless, without choice; necessary etc. 601.11; neutral etc. 628.3; irresolute etc. 605.5.

610. Rejection
(See 609. Choice)

1. *n.* rejection, rejectment [rare], repudiation, exclusion, withdrawal; declension, declination, declinature; refusal etc. 764; denial etc. (negation) 536; recantation etc. 607.

2. *v.* reject, repudiate, disclaim, disown, renounce, abjure, refuse to have anything to do with, set at nought; exclude, except; repel, repulse; reject with contempt *or* disdain, scorn to receive *or* accept, spurn, scout; decline etc. (refuse) 764.2; deny etc. 536.2; retract etc. (recant) 607.9; discard, lay aside etc. (disuse) 678.2–5.

3. *adj.* rejected etc. *v.,* reject [arch.]; not chosen etc. (*see* chosen etc. 609.16), not to be thought of, out of the question, declined with thanks; rejective, declinatory.

4. *adv.* neither, neither the one nor the other; *non haec in foedera* [L.].

611. Predetermination
(See 612. Impulse)

1. *n.* predetermination, premeditation, predeliberation, foregone conclusion, preconceived opinion, *parti pris* [F.]; preconcert, prearrangement, put-up job [coll.], setup [slang], open-and-shut case [coll., U.S.]; preordination, foreordination; predestination, foredestiny; doom, foredoom; predestinarianism, Calvinism; fate etc. (destiny) 601.3; intention etc. 620.

2. *n.* schedule, things to be done, prospectus, program *or* programme, bill, card, order of the day, line-up [coll.], book, calendar, docket [U.S.], slate [U.S.], protocol; agenda, list of agenda; register, roster, panel, poll, muster, cadre; bill of fare, menu; outline, sketch etc. (plan) 626.2; policy etc. 692.2.

3. *v.* predetermine, premeditate, preresolve, resolve beforehand; preconcert, precontrive, predesign, pre-establish, prearrange, arrange etc. beforehand; stack the cards, pack the deal [both slang]; predestine, predestinate; foreordain, foreordinate, preordain, preorder, order beforehand; doom, foredoom; destine etc. 601.9; plan etc. 626.9; intend etc. 620.3.

4. *v.* schedule, book, program, bill, line up [coll.], calendar, slate [U.S.], docket [U.S.], register, poll, impanel, empanel, draft *or* draught.

5. *adj.* predetermined, premeditated, predestined etc. *v.*; aforethought, prepense, advised, studied, designed, calculated; cut and dried *or* dry, open-and-shut [coll., U.S.], stacked [slang], put-up [coll.]; foregone, forehand; destined etc. 601.3; intended etc. 620.4.

6. *adj.* well-laid, well-devised, well-weighed, maturely considered, cunning.

7. *adv.* premeditatedly etc. *adj.,* with premeditation etc. *n.*; advisedly, deliberately etc. (intentionally) 620.5.

612. Impulse
(See 611. Predetermination)

1. *n.* impulse, mental impetus; natural impulse, blind impulse; sudden thought, inspiration, flash, spurt; impromptu, extempore, extemporization, improvisation; impulsion, incitement etc. (motivation) 615.2.

2. *n.* impulsive person, creature of impulse; improviser *or* improvisor, improvisator, *improvvisatore* or *improvisatore* [It.], *improvvisatrice* or *improvisatrice* [It.; *fem.*], extemporizer.

3. *v.* be impulsive etc. *adj.,* act on the spur of the moment, rise to the occasion, say what comes uppermost, say what comes first into one's head; improvise, extemporize, do offhand, cook up; flash on the mind.

4. *adj.* impulsive, unpremeditated, un-

---

610. Let your left hand turn away what your right hand attracts.—TALMUD.
611. With Earth's first Clay / They did the Last Man knead.—OMAR KHAYYÁM—FITZGERALD. Intimates are predestined.—H. ADAMS. The best laid schemes o' mice and men.—BURNS

612. A thing of impulse and a child of song.—BYRON. What is now reason was formerly impulse.—OVID. A quotation, like a pun, should come unsought.—R. CHAPMAN. To its own impulse every creature stirs.—M. ARNOLD.

meditated, unprompted, unguided, unguarded, indeliberate [rare], rash, natural, snap; extemporaneous, improvised etc. *v.*, improvisate, improvisatory, improvisatorial, improviso, *improvisé* [F.]; spontaneous, instinctive etc. (involuntary) 601.14; accidental etc. 621.20; unprepared etc. 674.7.

5. *adv.* impulsively, extemporaneously etc. *adj.*; extempore, *à l'improviste* [F.], impromptu, offhand, on the spur of the moment *or* occasion, without premeditation; unpreparedly etc. 674.12.

613. Habit
(See 614. Want of Habit)

1. *n.* habit, habituality [rare], habitualness etc. *adj.*; habitude, habitual attitude *or* state of mind, settled disposition *or* tendency, habitual course *or* practice, long-continued practice, force of habit, one's old way, second nature; *"veteris vestigia flammae"* (Vergil); characteristic behavior *or* tendency, characteristic, trait, trick.

2. *n.* custom, use, usage, way, practice, dastur [Ind.], prescription, observance, institution; wont, wonting; consuetude, *consuetudo* [L.]; prevalence, run; social habit *or* custom, conventional usage etc. (fashion) 852; conformity etc. 82.

3. *n.* rule, usual course *or* procedure, regular course, matter of course, uniform *or* established course of things, common *or* ordinary run of things, general state of things, common practice, systematic method *or* practice, settled *or* established rule, prescribed *or* set form, standing order.

4. *n.* routine, route [rare], run, usual run of things, fixed practice *or* procedure, jog, trot, goose step; grind, daily grind [both coll.]; rut, groove, track, round, beat, beaten path, ~ track *or* ground; red tape, red-tapery, red-tapism; regularity etc. 16.2.

5. *n.* habituation, assuefaction [obs.], assuetude [obs. exc. med.], inurement, hardening, radication [obs.], seasoning, familiarization, naturalization, domestication; acclimation, acclimatization; orientation.

6. *n.* addiction, addictedness, confirmed *or* inveterate habit, indulged inclination; bad habit *or* custom, cacoëthes; Circean cup.

7. *n.* creature of habit, habitual [coll.]; habitué, frequenter; addict, fiend [coll.]; case, hard case, the limit [all slang]; drug *or* narcotic addict, dope fiend [slang], dope [slang]; drunkard etc. 959.11; conventionalist etc. (conformist) 82.3.

8. *v.* habituate, inure, accustom, wont, familiarize, adapt, season, naturalize, domesticate; acclimatize, acclimate; harden, caseharden; addict; train etc. 537.10.

9. *v.* become habitual etc. *adj.*, become a habit, come into use, take root, gain *or* grow upon one.

10. *v.* be wont etc. *adj.*, wont; get in a rut, move *or* travel in a groove *or* rut, run on in a groove, tread *or* follow the beaten path *or* track, go round like a horse in a mill, go on in the old jog-trot way, *stare super antiquas vias* [L.]; get wound up in red tape; take to, accustom oneself to, acquire ~, contract *or* fall into a habit, addict oneself to, cling *or* adhere to; keep in practice, keep one's hand in; fall into a custom etc. (conform to rule) 82.5.

11. *adj.* habitual, habituary [obs.], according to habit, repeated *or* established by force of habit; customary, accustomary; prescriptive, wonted, normal, usual, common, commonplace, ordinary, familiar, household, vernacular, popular, current, frequent, regular, besetting, set, stock, everyday, of daily *or* everyday occurrence, well-trodden, jog-trot; consuetudinary, consuetudinal; general, prevalent, universal etc. 78.9–11; repeated etc. 104.6, 7; conventional etc. 852.8; conformable to rule etc. 82.9.

12. *adj.* habituated, *habitué* [F.]; accustomed, inured, naturalized, adapted, seasoned etc. *v.*; used to, attuned to, at home in, conversant with, familiar with; wont, wonted; in the habit of, given to, addicted to, wedded to, devoted to, permeated with, imbued with, soaked in, never free from; confirmed, inveterate, established, fixed, permanent, radicated [rare], rooted, deep-rooted, ingrafted *or* engrafted, ingrained.

13. *adv.* habitually, commonly etc. *adj.*;

---

613. *Consuetudo quasi altera natura* [Habit is almost a second nature].—CICERO. *Magna est vis consuetudinis* [Mighty is the force of habit].—CICERO. *Abeunt studia in mores*

[Practices become habits].—OVID. Habit is a cable; we weave a thread of it every day, and at last we cannot break it.—H. MANN. How use doth breed a habit in a man.—SHAKE-

according to habit etc. *n.*, from habit, by *or* from force of habit; in the natural order of things, in the order of the day; most often *or* frequently; as a rule, for the most part etc. (generally) 78.15; frequently, constantly etc. 136.5, 6; invariably etc. 16.7; always etc. 112.5.

14. *adv.* as usual, as per usual [coll.], in the usual manner, as is one's wont, as things go, as the world goes, as the sparks fly upwards; *more solito* [L.], *more suo* [L.], *more majorum* [L.], *ex more* [L.]; *ad instar* [L.], *instar omnium* [L.]; as you were [Mil.].

614. Want of Habit
(See 613. Habit)

1. *n.* want of habit, unaccustomedness etc. *adj.*, newness to; nonprevalence, unprevalence; inusitation [rare]; disusage, desuetude etc. (disuse) 678; infraction of usage etc. (nonconformity) 83.2; inexperience etc. 699.

2. *v.* discontinue a custom *or* habit, break a habit, cure oneself of, wean oneself from, break one's chains *or* fetters; do old things in a new way, give a new dress to old ideas, give an original touch; wear off; disuse etc. 678.2–5; infringe a custom *or* usage etc. (not conform) 83.8.

3. *adj.* unaccustomed, unused, unfamiliar, uninured, unseasoned, unhabituated, unwonted, not in the habit of, ungiven to, unwedded to, undevoted to, new to; unconversant, green etc. (unskilled) 699.13–16, (ignorant) 491.8; uncustomary etc. (unusual) 83.10; new etc. 123.8; unconventional, nonobservant etc. (unconformable) 83.9.

4. *adv.* unaccustomedly etc. *adj.* contrary to custom, ~ usage *or* convention; for once, just once, just this once.

615. Motive

1. *n.* motive, reason, rational, rationale, rational ground, reason why, wherefore [coll.], the why and the wherefore [coll.]; pro and con; consideration, account; ground, basis, occasion, call, principle, key, keystone, root, spring, mainspring, springs of action; prime mover, *primum mobile* [L.], primordium [rare]; secret motive, ulterior motive; mental reservation, *arrière-pensée* [F.]; intention etc. 620; cause etc. 153; explanation etc. 522.

2. *n.* motivation, inducement, prompting etc. *v.*, instigation, provocation, stimulation, actuation, abetment, insistence, instance, urge, press, dictate, inspiration, encouragement, advocacy; incitement, incitation; impulse, impulsion; influence etc. 175; allurement etc. 617; excitement etc. 824.

3. *n.* incentive, provocative, stimulus, spur, prick, fillip, whip, lash, goad, ankus [Ind.], rowel, whet, dram.

4. *n.* persuasion, suasion, persuasive, persuasiveness; hortation, exhortation; advice etc. 695; solicitation etc. (request) 765.

5. *n.* susceptibility, impressibility, attractability; persuadability etc. (docility) 602.3; tractability etc. (softness) 324.

6. *n.* instigator, prompter, abettor, *agent provocateur* [F.], suggester, agitator; incendiary, firebrand; coaxer, wheedler; lobbyist.

7. *v.* motivate, motive, move, propel, impel, give an impulse to etc. *n.*, prompt, call up, evoke, provoke, animate, stimulate, actuate, forward, instigate, put up to [slang], incite, urge, spur, prick, goad, prod, lash, whip, egg on [coll.], urge on *or* forward, hound on, set on, hurry on, push, press; bear upon, bring pressure to bear upon, turn *or* throw one's weight into, throw one's weight into the scale; inspire, inspirit, spirit, spirit up; rouse, arouse; act ~, work *or* operate on *or* upon; encourage, give encouragement, pat *or* clap on the back *or* shoulder; exhort, call on *or* upon; advocate, recommend; force, enforce; keep in countenance, back up; excite etc. 824.2.

8. *v.* sway, affect, bias, incline etc. (influence) 175.6.

9. *v.* induce, persuade, prevail with, ~

SPEARE. It is a custom / More honoured in the breach than the observance.—SHAKESPEARE. Man is a pliable animal, a being who gets accustomed to everything!—DOSTOEVSKI. The miller fails to notice the clack of his mill. —G. F. STOUT.
615. *Le cœur a ses raisons que la raison connoit pas* [The heart has its reasons, which reason does not know].—PASCAL. Strong reasons make strong actions.—SHAKESPEARE. There is occasions and causes why and wherefore in all things.—SHAKESPEARE. No man does anything from a single motive.—COLERIDGE. 'Tis the motive exalts the action.— M. J. PRESTON. Never ascribe to an opponent motives meaner than your own.—BARRIE.

on *or* upon, draw ~, win *or* talk over, overcome, carry, bring round, bring over, conciliate, bring to reason, bring to one's senses; lead, lead one to; hook *or* hook in [slang], land [coll.]; sell, sell one on [both coll., U.S.]; move, move one to, move by influence *or* persuasion; turn, turn one's head, turn the scale; determine, dispose; enlist, procure, engage; coax; wheedle, cajole; convince etc. 484.10.

10. *v.* be induced, follow advice, follow the bent *or* dictates of, obey a call; act on principle; yield to temptation etc. 617.1; persuade oneself, make oneself easy about, make sure of, make up one's mind; come over, go *or* come round [both coll.], yield, concede etc. (consent) 762.2.

11. *adj.* inductive, inductional, inducive [rare]; persuasive, persuasory [rare], suasive, suasory [obs.]; hortative, hortatory; influential etc. 175.10; provocative etc. (exciting) 824.12, (tempting) 617.6.

12. *adj.* persuadable etc. (docile) 602.9.

13. *adv., conj.* because, therefore etc. (attribution) 155.5–8.

616. Dissuasion

1. *n.* dissuasion, determent, deterrence, deterrent; disinclining etc. *v.*, discouragement; damper, wet blanket, cold water; contraindicant, contraindication; dehortation, dehortative [both rare]; monition, admonition; remonstrance, expostulation etc. (deprecation) 766; advice etc. 695; constraint etc. (restraint) 751; curb etc. 752.2; disinclination etc. (unwillingness) 603.

2. *v.* dissuade, dehort [rare], contraindicate, advise *or* exhort against, cry out against, warn; remonstrate, expostulate etc. (deprecate) 766.2.

3. *v.* disincline, render averse etc. 603.5, indispose, discourage, dishearten, dispirit, disenchant, disaffect, deter, divert, wean from, repel; shake, stagger; throw cold water on, throw *or* lay a wet blanket on, damp, cool, chill, blunt, calm, quiet, quench; hold back etc. (restrain) 751.6; turn aside etc. (deviate) 279.4–7, (avert) 706.5.

A man's acts are usually right, but his reasons seldom are.—E. HUBBARD.   A man always has two reasons for doing anything—a good reason and the real reason.—J. P. MORGAN.
616. I do not give you to posterity as a pattern to imitate, but as an example to deter.—JUNIUS.

4. *adj.* dissuasive, dissuasory [rare], dissuading etc. *v.*; dehortative, dehortatory [both rare]; expostulative, expostulatory; admonitory, monitory, monitorial, monitive [obs.].

5. *adj.* dissuaded etc. *v.*; uninduced etc. (*see* induce etc. 615.9); disinclined etc. (unwilling) 603.5.

617. Allurement

Attractive Inducement.—1. *n.* allurement, enticement, allectation [obs.], *agacerie* [F.], temptation, tantalization, fascination, captivation, enchantment, charm, attraction, attractiveness etc. *adj.*, winning ways; draw, pull [both slang]; seducement, seduction; witchery, bewitchery, bewitchment; hypnotism, mesmerism; blandishment, cajolery, soft *or* honeyed words, song of the Sirens, voice of the tempter; forbidden fruit, golden apple; spell etc. 993; magnetism etc. 157.3; loadstone, magnet etc. 288.2; inducement etc. (motivation) 615.2.

2. *n.* lure, charm, come-on [slang, U.S.], drawing card; decoy, decoy duck, stool pigeon; bait, ground bait, baited trap, silver hook; red herring, trail of a red herring; attractor etc. 288.2; bribe etc. 618.2; trap etc. (snare) 545.4.

3. *n.* tempter, seducer, seductor; temptress, enchantress, seductress, siren; Siren, Circe, Lorelei *or* Lurlei; vampire, vamp [slang].

4. *v.* lure, allure, entice, attract, charm, becharm, fascinate, captivate, enrapture, bewitch, carry away, seduce, vamp [slang], inveigle, decoy, lead on, beckon; draw, draw on; bait, offer bait to, bait the hook, bait *or* angle with a silver hook; hold out temptation *or* allurement, tempt, tantalize, titillate; appetize, whet the appetite, make one's mouth water, *faire venir l'eau à la bouche* [F.]; court, invite; make things pleasant, gild the pill; hypnotize, mesmerize; ensnare etc. 545.9.

5. *adj.* alluring, seducing, etc. *v.*; attractive, seductive, enchanting, entranc-

617. Yet have they many baits and guileful spells to inveigle and invite the unwary sense.—MILTON.   Allurements and baits of superstition.—T. BROWNE.   It is good to be without vices, but it is not good to be without temptations.—W. BAGEHOT.   To beguile many and be beguiled by one.—SHAKESPEARE.   Beauty draws us by a single hair.—POPE.   Bait the hook well: this fish will bite.—SHAKESPEARE.

ing, enravishing, prepossessing, engaging, winning, winsome, taking, tantalizing, exciting, killing [coll.], heart-robbing, interesting, inviting; provocative, *provoquant* [F.]; appetizing, mouth-watering; delightful etc. 829.8; lovely etc. (beautiful) 845.8–13; likable etc. 897.17; inductive etc. 615.11.

618. Bribery

Corrupt Inducement.—1. *n.* bribery, graft [coll.], subornation, bribery and corruption; purchase etc. 795.

2. *n.* bribe, sop, sop to Cerberus, sop in the pan; palm oil, oil of palms [both joc.]; grease [slang], soap [slang, U.S.], *douceur* [F.], bonus [coll.], tip, baksheesh *or* bakshish [Near East], boodle [coll.]; hush money; payment etc. 973.2; gift etc. 784.3; lure etc. 617.2.

3. *v.* bribe, grease, oil, anoint, grease *or* oil the palm *or* hand, tickle the palm *or* in the palm, fix [all coll.]; palm, reach, square, sugar [all slang]; tip, subsidize, purchase, buy, buy off, hire, throw a sop to, put a sop into the pan, angle with a silver hook, approach, suborn, tamper with, corrupt; give etc. 784.8.

619. Pretext

Ostensible Motive.—1. *n.* pretext, mere pretext, pretense, pretension, false pretense *or* pretension; ostensible motive, ~ ground *or* reason, alleged motive *or* purpose, professed purpose *or* intention, allegation, profession, claim; mere *or* empty words, claptrap, moonshine;

---

618. Shall we now / Contaminate our fingers with base bribes?—Shakespeare. He refuseth the bribe, but putteth forth his hand.—Fuller. Honesty stands at the gate and knocks, and bribery enters in.—B. Rich. Few men have virtue to withstand the highest bidder.—Washington. Turn from the glitt'ring bribe thy scornful eye, / Nor sell for gold what gold could never buy.—Johnson. Bribes, believe me, buy both gods and men.—Ovid. All those men have their price.—R. Walpole. Just for a handful of silver he left us, / Just for a riband to stick in his coat. —Browning.

619. Pretexts are not wanting when one wishes to use them.—Goldoni. Any excuse will serve a tyrant.—Aesop. The slightest approach to a false pretence / Was never among my crimes.—Carroll.

advocation, advocacy; false plea, lame excuse, sour grapes; shift, makeshift; handle, peg to hang on; feint, subterfuge, putoff, dust thrown in the eye, tub to a whale, blind, guise, mask, cover, cloak; gloss, varnish, color, false color; stalking-horse; appearance, semblance, show, empty show; excuse, plea etc. (vindication) 937.2; apology etc. 952.2; white lie etc. 546.3; special pleading etc. (sophistry) 477; concealment etc. 528; disguise etc. 545.5; sham etc. (dissimulation) 544.2; lip homage etc. (flattery) 933; loophole etc. 671.4; evasion etc. 623.

2. *v.* pretext, make a pretext of, use *or* allege as a pretext etc. *n.*, pretex [obs.], allege, claim, profess, plead, shelter oneself under the plea of, take one's stand upon, make capital of; furnish a handle etc. *n.*, provide a loophole (*see* loophole etc. 671.4); cry sour grapes, say the grapes are sour; tell a white lie; color, lend a color to, gloss over, gloze [rare], varnish, slur, whitewash, put a good face upon; throw a tub to a whale, throw dust in the eyes; find a loophole (*see* loophole etc. 671.4); crawl *or* creep out of; offer an excuse etc. (justify) 937.6; pretend etc. (dissemble) 544.6; cover, cloak; disguise etc. (conceal) 528.10.

3. *adj.* pretexed, alleged etc. *v.*; pretextuous [rare], used *or* serving as a pretext etc. *n.*; pretended etc. (spurious) 545.13; apologetic, excusing etc. (vindicative) 937.9; ostensible etc. (manifest) 525.4.

4. *adv.* ostensibly, under the pretext of . . . etc. *n.*, as an excuse etc. 937.2.

620. Intention
(See 621. Chance)

1. *n.* intention, intent, intentionality; purpose, plan, design, ambition, project, prospect, proposal, contemplation, mind, animus, will, eye, view, purview [Law], lookout; fixed intention, set *or* settled purpose, resolution, resolve, determination, decision, ultimatum; teleology; motive etc. 615; undertaking etc. 676; inclination, drift etc. (tendency) 176; wish

---

620. Hell is paved with good intentions.—Johnson. "He means well" is useless unless he does well.—Plautus. You must take the will for the deed.—Swift. 'Tis not what man Does which exalts him, but what man Would do!—Browning. Life has a value

etc. (desire) 865; predetermination etc. 611.

2. *n.* object, objective, aim, end, object in mind, end in view, goal, destination, mark, point, butt, target, bull's-eye, quintain; game, quarry, prey; final cause, *raison d'être* [F.], "the be-all and the end-all" (Shakespeare); by-end, by-purpose.

3. *v.* intend, purpose, plan [coll.], design, mean, mind [obs. exc. dial.], aim, expect, propose, purpose to oneself, harbor a design etc. *n.,* have in view *or* contemplation, have in mind, have *in petto* [It.], have in one's eye, have an eye to, have a mind to, have half a mind to, have a good *or* great mind to, aspire to *or* after, endeavor, bid for, labor for, be at *or* after, determine upon, set before oneself, study to.

contemplate, meditate, take into one's head, think of, dream of, talk of; plan on, figure on, calculate on [all coll.]; allot on *or* upon, reckon on [both dial.]; aim at, drive at, point at, level at, take aim; destine, destinate; take upon oneself etc. (undertake) 676.2; pursue etc. 622.6; premeditate etc. 611.3.

4. *adj.* intentional, intended, intending etc. *v.*; advised, express, determinate; disposed, inclined, willed, minded; bound for; in view, in prospect, in the breast of, *in petto* [It.]; at stake, on the anvil, on the carpet *or* tapis; teleological; bent upon etc. (resolved) 604.8; prepense etc. (predetermined) 611.5.

5. *adv.* intentionally, advisedly etc. *adj.*; wittingly, knowingly, studiously, pointedly, designedly, purposely, on purpose, by design, deliberately, with intent etc. *n.*, with one's eyes open, with malice aforethought, in cold blood; to all intents, to all intents and purposes; *quo animo* [L.]; *cui bono* [L.]; with premeditation etc. 611.7; voluntarily etc. 600.5.

6. *prep. etc.* for, to; for the purpose of, with the view of, with a view to, with an eye to, in order to *or* that, to the end that, with the intent that, in contemplation of; in pursuance of, pursuant to; on account of, for the sake of.

---

only when it has something as its object.—HEGEL.   Who keeps one end in view makes all things serve.—BROWNING.   With affection beaming in one eye, and calculation shining out of the other.—DICKENS.

621. Chance
(See 620. Intention)

Absence of Design.—**1.** *n.* chance, fortune, lot, luck etc. (absence of assignable cause) 156; fortune etc. (destiny) 601.3; opportunity, occasion etc. (time) 134.2, (expedience) 646; stroke of luck etc. 731.2; good luck etc. 734.2; bad luck etc. 735.2; rabbit's foot, swastika etc. (talisman) 993.2.

2. *n.* gamble, matter of chance, gambling chance, chance at odds, potluck, blind bargain, pig in a poke, leap in the dark, turn *or* roll of the wheel, turn of the table *or* cards, fall of the cards, hazard of the die, cast *or* throw of the dice, flip of the coin, heads or tails; toss, toss-up; speculation, risk, die, hazard, jeopardy, venture; flutter, flier *or* flyer [both slang]; reckless *or* hazardous speculation, plunge [slang]; fluke [slang]; lot, draw; uncertainty etc. 475; rashness etc. 863.

3. *n.* wager, bet, stake, lay [obs.], shot [slang], play, hazard; ante, blind [poker]; coppered bet [cant, U.S.], heeled bet [cant], open bet, sleeper [faro]; reckless bet, random shot, potshot, shot in the dark [slang]; pyramid; flat play [cant].

4. *n.* pot, jack pot, pool, stakes, kitty [chiefly slang], *cave* [F.]; bank, tiger [faro].

5. *n.* odds, price; overlay [cant]; equivalent odds; even *or* square odds, even break [chiefly coll.], six-two-and-even [cant]; short odds, ten-to-one shot [slang]; long odds, long shot [slang], hundred-to-one shot [slang]; even chance, good chance, small chance, no chance etc. 156.2–5.

6. *n.* gambling, gaming, sporting, betting etc. *v.*; speculation, play; cardsharping; lots, *sortes* [L.]; *sortes Vergilianae* [L.]; drawing *or* casting lots, sortition; sortilegy; futures.

7. *n.* (games of chance) hazard, roulette, fan-tan [Chin.], cross and pile [arch.], cup tossing, chuck farthing, pitch *or* chuck and toss, chuck-a-luck *or* chuckluck; crack-loo, crackaloo [both slang, U.S.]; horse racing, the turf, sport of kings; sweepstake *or* sweepstakes, sweep *or* sweeps; pari mutuel (*pl.* paris mu-

---

621. Death and the dice level all distinctions.—S. FOOTE.   Gambling is a principle inherent in human nature.—BURKE.   For most men (till by losing rendered sager) / Will back

tuels); *rouge et noir* [F.], faro etc. (card games) 840.12; brace game etc. (trick) 545.3.

8. *n.* dice (*pl.*; *sing.* die), bones [coll.], cubes, ivories, devil's bones *or* teeth [all slang]; craps, crap shooting, crap game [all chiefly coll.]; elbow shaking [slang]; indoor golf, Negro golf, African dominoes, Mississippi marbles, Memphis dominoes, animated dominoes *or* ivories [all joc.]; poker dice; cheating dice, false *or* crooked dice, loaded dice, doctors [old slang]; flats, goads, tats [all slang]; dice box, devil's box [slang], bird cage.

9. *n.* throw of dice, throw, cast, roll, shot, hazard of the die; losing throw, crap *or* craps; natural, nick [both cant]; two, deuce etc. 89.2, snake eyes [slang]; three, deuce-ace, trey, little trey [slang] etc. 92.2; four, Little Joe (from Kokomo) [slang] etc. 95.2; five, cinque, quint, Phoebe *or* Little Phoebe [slang], fever in the South [slang] etc. 98.1; six, size *or* sise *or* sice [cant], Captain Hicks [slang] etc. 98.2; seven, seven-out [cant] etc. 98.3; eight, eighter (from Decatur) [slang], Ada Ross the stable hoss [slang] etc. 98.4; nine, quinine (the bitter dose) [slang], Carolina nine [slang] etc. 98.5; ten, Big Dick (from Boston) [slang] etc. 98.6; twelve, boxcar *or* boxcars [slang] etc. 98.7.

10. *n.* lottery, raffle, draw [slang, U.S.]; turkey draw [slang, U.S.]; Genoese *or* number lottery, lotto; Dutch *or* class lottery, interest lottery, tombola; grab bag, ~ barrel *or* box [coll., U.S.].

11. *n.* gambling wheel, wheel, wheel of chance *or* fortune, Fortune's wheel; roulette wheel; raffle wheel.

12. *n.* pari-mutuel *or* pari-mutuels, pari-mutuel machine; totalizer, totalizator.

13. *n.* counter, check, chip, fish [slang], bone.

14. *n.* gambling establishment, gambling *or* gaming house, gambling den, betting house, hell, gambling hell, Domdaniel, *tripot* [F., slang], casino; joint, flat, crib [all slang]; pool room; bucket shop; stock exchange etc. (exchange) 799.3.

---

their own opinions by a wager.—BYRON.
The gambling passion lurks . . . at the bottom of every heart.—BALZAC. Nothing venture, nothing win.

15. *n.* gambler, gamester, gamestress [*fem.*], player, operator [stock exchange], hazarder, venturer, adventurer, sporting man *or* woman, sportsman, sport [coll.], better *or* bettor, wagerer, punter; speculator, speculatist; heavy *or* reckless better, plunger [slang]; petty gambler, piker [slang, U.S.]; tinhorn, tinhorn gambler [both slang]; oraler [chiefly turf slang]; sharpshooter [slang], sharper, sharp [slang], cardsharp *or* cardsharper; pool shark [coll.]; dicer, crap shooter [coll.], elbow shaker [slang], knight of the elbow [joc.]; man of the turf, turf player; bookmaker, bookie [coll.]; betting ring.

16. *n.* mascot, *mascotte* [F.].

17. *v.* chance, risk, hazard, jeopard, stake; venture, adventure, venture upon; speculate, gamble, game, sport, play, try one's luck *or* fortune; chance it, chance one's luck *or* hand [coll.], take one's chance, take a chance, take the chances of, try the chance, leave *or* trust to chance *or* luck, trust to the chapter of accidents, rely on fortune, gamble on, take *or* run the risk, tempt fortune, set at hazard, stand the hazard of the die; go it blind [slang], take a leap in the dark, buy a pig in a poke, take potluck.

cast *or* draw lots, set on a cast, cut the cards *or* deck; toss up, toss *or* flip the coin, call heads or tails, call the coin; play at dice, shoot craps [chiefly coll.]; play the ponies [slang]; put into a lottery, raffle; shuffle the cards; bechance, happen etc. 156.7; have a chance etc. 156.9; be rash etc. 863.5.

18. *v.* bet, wager, make a bet, punt, stake, lay, lay a wager, post [slang]; bet on *or* upon, back; bet *or* play against, copper [cant, U.S.], buck *or* fight the tiger [faro]; take a flyer [slang]; bet heavily *or* recklessly, plunge [slang]; make modest bets, pike [slang, U.S.]; ante, ante up; double the blind, straddle [both poker]; meet a bet, see, call, cover, fade [dice], see one's blind [poker]; pass; stand pat.

19. *adj.* speculative, uncertain etc. 475.9; chancy [coll.], hazardous, risky etc. (dangerous) 665.7.

20. *adj.* accidental, unintended, unintentional, undesigned, unpurposed, not meant, never thought of; unexpected, unforeseen; unthinking, unwitting; unpremeditated etc. 612.4; involuntary etc.

601.14; casual, fortuitous etc. (chance) 156.12.

21. *adj.* purposeless, without purpose etc. 620.1, designless, causeless, driftless, aimless, undirected; indiscriminate etc. 465a.3; unmethodical, promiscuous, haphazard etc. (disorderly) 59.8.

22. *adv.* accidentally, unintentionally, unwittingly etc. *adj.*; fortuitously, casually etc. (by chance) 156.13.

622. Pursuit
(See 623. Avoidance)

Purpose in Action.—**1.** *n.* pursuit, pursuance, pursuing etc. *v.*, prosecution; game; scramble, struggle; business etc. 625; enterprise etc. (undertaking) 676; endeavor etc. (essay) 675; quest etc. (search) 461.2; sequence etc. (order) 63, (motion) 281.

2. *n.* chase, hunt, *battue* [F.], race, chevy *or* chivy [Eng.], shag [slang], shikar [Ind.]; hunting, coursing etc. *v.*; venery, venation [now rare]; sport, sporting; steeplechase, fox hunting *or* chase, shooting, hawking, still hunt [U.S.]; hue and cry; Artemis [Gr. Myth.], Diana [Rom. Myth.], Ull [Norse Myth.].

3. *n.* fishing, fishery, angling, piscation [rare]; piscatology, halieutics.

4. *n.* pursuer, pursuant; hunter, huntsman; sportsman, Nimrod, shikari *or* shikaree [Ind.], stalker, courser; huntress [*fem.*], sportswoman; trapper, trappist; follower etc. 281.2; shooter etc. 284.8; hound etc. 366.6.

5. *n.* fisher, fisherman, angler, wormer [coll.], peterman [Hist.]; piscator, piscatorian, piscatorialist; Waltonian, "the compleat angler" (I. Walton); dibber, dibbler; troller, trawler; jacker [U.S.]; drifter.

6. *v.* pursue, prosecute, follow, follow up, take to, go in for; run, run in pursuit of; run after, make after, prowl after; direct *or* bend one's steps, take *or* adopt a course, steer *or* shape one's course, hold a course, tread a path, pursue the even tenor of one's way; be absorbed in; carry on etc. (practice) 625.6, (do) 680.6; take up, engage in etc. (undertake) 676.2; set about etc. (begin) 66.5; endeavor etc. (essay) 675.3; aim at etc. (intend) 620.3; shadow, tail [coll.]; etc. 281.3; trail, track etc. (seek) 461.16.

7. *v.* chase, give chase, shag [slang], hunt, go hunting etc. *n.*, stalk, shikar [Ind.], course, sport; hound, dog; still-hunt [U.S.]; start game; hunt for etc. (seek) 461.16.

8. *v.* fish, go fishing etc. *n.*, angle, bob for, cast one's hook *or* net; bait the hook; dap, dib, dibble; trawl, troll; guddle [chiefly Scot.], torch, spin, whiff, spoon, shrimp, drive, grig, gig, fly-fish.

9. *v.* rush upon, rush headlong at, ride at, run full tilt at, jump at, make a leap at, snatch at; run down.

10. *adj.* pursuing etc. *v.*, pursuant, in pursuit, in hot pursuit, in full cry; on the track *or* trail, on the scent; in quest of etc. (inquiring) 461.24.

11. *prep.* after, following the course of, in pursuit *or* pursuance of; after (sequence) 281.5, (order) 63.6, (time) 117.4, (place) 235.14–17.

12. *int.* (huntsmen's halloo) halloo!, yoicks!, soho!; tallyho!, tallyho over!, tallyho back!

623. Avoidance
(See 622. Pursuit)

1. *n.* avoidance, avoidment, evasion, elusion, avolation [now rare], shunning etc. *v.*; go-by [slang], run-around [slang, U.S.], the slip; subterfuge, shift, shuffle; dodge, side step; shirking etc. *v.*, malingery; retreat etc. (recession) 287; seclusion etc. 893.2; quibble, equivocation etc. 477.3, 4; pretext etc. 619; truancy, hooky etc. (nonattendance) 187.5; nonpayment etc. 808; nonobservance etc. 773, idleness etc. 683.2; dereliction etc. 927.

2. *n.* flight, fleet, wing, decampment, absquatulation [joc.], elopement, abscondence [rare]; powder, runout powder, runout [all slang, U.S.]; leg bail, leg bail and land security [both slang]; escape etc. 671; departure etc. 293.

3. *n.* abstention etc. (abstinence) 953.2.

---

622. Seek thee out some other chase, / For I myself must hunt this deer to death.—Shakespeare.   Don't think to hunt two hares with one dog.—Franklin.   You pursue. I fly; you fly, I pursue: such is my mind.—Martial. What follows I flee; what flees I ever pursue.—Ovid.

623. Evasion is unworthy of us and is always the intimate of equivocation.—Balzac.   He who flees from trial confesses his guilt.—Pub-

4. *n.* shirker, slacker [coll.], shirk, quitter [U.S.], dodger, piker [slang], soldier *or* old soldier [orig. Naut. slang], sojer *or* soger [slang], eyeservant, eyeserver, malingerer, sham Abram *or* Abraham [Naut. cant]; funker [coll.], flunker [coll., U.S.]; welsher [slang]; truant; idler etc. 683.7 neglector etc. 460.3; absentee etc. 187.6; coward etc. 862.2.

5. *n.* fugitive, runaway, runagate, renegade, absconder, eloper, levanter, skedaddler [coll., U.S.], refugee; maroon; deserter etc. (apostate) 607.5.

6. *v.* avoid, shun, fight shy of, keep one's distance, keep at a respectful distance, keep away from, keep clear of, steer clear of [coll.], keep *or* get out of the way of, dodge etc. *below* 623.9, evade, elude, circumvent, double, get around [coll.], steal a march upon, give the slip, give the go-by [slang], give the runaround [slang, U.S.], pass up [slang, U.S.], ditch [slang, U.S.], shuffle off, throw off the scent, play at hide and seek.

turn away from, turn one's back upon, turn on one's heel, set one's face against, slam the door in one's face; keep from, have nothing to do with, have no hand in, take no part in, keep ~, stand *or* hold aloof; let alone, let well enough alone; make way for, give place to; lead one a chase *or* merry chase, lead one a dance *or* pretty dance; parry, shift *or* put off; jump, skip [slang]; skip bail [slang]; beat about the bush, equivocate etc. (quibble) 477.8; escape etc. 671.6; not observe etc. 773.3; not pay etc. 808.5; be unwilling etc. 603.4.

7. *v.* abstain, refrain, forbear etc. 953.5; not attempt etc. 681.2.

8. *v.* shirk, slack, pike [slang]; lie down on, lie down on the job [both slang]; lie *or* rest upon one's oars, not pull fair, be a passenger in the boat, be a dead weight; malinger, sham Abram *or* Abraham, soldier, soger *or* sojer [slang], act *or* come the old soldier [coll.]; funk [coll.], flunk [coll., U.S.]; shirk out of [coll.]; get out of, sneak *or* slip out of; welsh [slang]; play truant, take French leave etc. (be absent) 187.8; be inactive etc. 683.8.

9. *v.* shrink, recoil, shy, flinch, wince, blink, blench, quail; shrink back, pull ~, draw *or* hang back; dodge, duck [slang], swerve, sheer off; retire etc. (recede) 287.2; be afraid etc. 860.8; be cowardly etc. 862.3.

10. *v.* flee, fly, take flight, take to flight, take wing, turn tail, run, cut and run [coll.], run off *or* away, run away from, run for one's life, beat a retreat, slip the cable, absquatulate [joc.], leg it, take to one's heels, turn on one's heel, show the heels, show a clean *or* light pair of heels, turn one's back upon, decamp, elope, avolate [now rare], abscond, take French leave; make a break for it, clear out, skedaddle, skip, skip out *or* up [all coll.]; slip ~, slink *or* steal off *or* away, shirk off *or* away [coll.], sneak *or* slip out of; maroon; escape etc. 671.6; desert etc. (abandon) 624.3.

slope, mizzle, dust, duck out, duck and run, walk one's chalks, pull foot, skin out, mooch *or* mouch off, cut stick, cut one's stick, make oneself scarce, take to the tall timber, fly the coop, give leg bail [all slang]; beat it, blow, scram, lam, take it on the lam, take a powder *or* runout powder [all slang, U.S.]; levant, guy, bunk [all slang, Eng.].

11. *adj.* avoidable, escapable, eludible; evadable, evasible; preventable *or* preventible; avoided etc. *v.*, unsought, unattempted.

12. *adj.* evasive, evasional; elusive, elusory; fugitive, runaway; shy, shrinking etc. 862.4, shifty, sly etc. (cunning) 702.6; nonobservant etc. 773.5.

13. *int.* forbear!, keep off!, hands off!, *sauve qui peut!* [F.], devil take the hindmost!; cease! etc. 142.8.

624. Abandonment

1. *n.* abandonment, quittance [rare], withdrawal, defection, desertion, secession; relinquishment, surrender; vacation [now rare], evacuation; *nolle prosequi* [L.]; cave of Abdullam; discontinuance etc. (cessation) 142; apostasy, recantation etc. (tergiversation) 607; re-

---

624. Unto each man comes a day when his favorite sins all forsake him.—J. HAY.   I only have relinquished one delight.—WORDSWORTH.   I did renounce the world, its pride and greed.—E. B. BROWNING.   Rats desert a sinking ship.

volt etc. 742.2; abrogation etc. 756; resignation etc. 757; desuetude etc. (disuse) 678; cession etc. (relinquishment of property) 782.

2. *n.* deserter, seceder etc. (apostate) 607.5.

3. *v.* abandon, forsake, leave in the lurch, go back on [coll.], turn one's back upon, depart from, withdraw, quit, leave, leave behind, take leave of, bid a long farewell; vacate, evacuate; desert, rat [slang]; secede, pull out [coll.], withdraw one's support, bolt [U.S.].

relinquish, give up, throw up, throw over *or* overboard [coll.], surrender, yield, waive, forgo, have done with, wash one's hands of, drop, drop all idea of, drop like a hot potato, turn up [now slang], hold *or* stay one's hand, quit one's hold, give over, shut up shop, throw up the game *or* cards, give up the point *or* argument; pass to the order of the day, move the previous question, table the motion, table; nol-pros [Law]; renege, renig [coll.]; leave off, desist, stop etc. (cease) 142.6; change sides etc. (apostatize) 607.8; back out [coll.], abjure etc. (recant) 607.9; resign etc. 757.2; cede, let go etc. (relinquish property) 782.3; discard etc. (disuse) 678.2, 3; revolt etc. 742.5; flee etc. 623.10.

4. *adj.* abandoned, forsaken, relinquished etc. *v.*; castoff, derelict; unpursued.

625. Business

1. *n.* business, occupation, employment, employ [arch.], work, pursuit, activity, racket [slang], affair, concern, lookout [coll.], matter, case, what one is doing *or* about; means of support, living, livelihood; venture, enterprise etc. (undertaking) 676; commerce, trade etc. (barter) 794; businessman etc. (merchant) 797; office, shop etc. 691.

2. *n.* task, matter in hand, thing to do, agendum (*pl.* agenda), work, job, chore [U.S.], stint, errand, commission, mission, assignment, charge, care, duty, exercise; things to do, irons in the fire, fish to fry; labor etc. 686.3; press of business etc. 682.7.

3. *n.* function, part, role, cue; province, department, capacity, sphere, orb, realm, compass, scope, field; walk, walk of life; beat, round, routine; career, life, course, race.

4. *n.* office, place, post, chargeship, incumbency, job [coll.], situation, position, station, berth, billet, appointment, engagement, service, employ [arch.].

5. *n.* vocation, calling, occupation, business, work, line, line of business *or* work, métier *or* metier, way [coll.], profession, cloth, faculty [arch.], trade, industry, practice, mystery [arch.], art; craft, handicraft; industrial arts; avocation, hobby, side line.

6. *v.* busy, occupy, engage, concern, employ, spend, devote, practice, carry on, exercise; pass ∼, employ *or* spend the time, occupy etc. one's time, busy etc. oneself; prosecute etc. (pursue) 622.6; be busy etc. 682.13; work etc. (labor) 686.6.

7. *v.* busy oneself with *or* in, occupy *or* engage oneself with, pass ∼, employ *or* spend one's time in, engage in, devote oneself to, employ oneself in *or* upon, concern oneself with, make it one's business etc. *n.*; be about, be doing, be engaged *or* employed in, be occupied with, be at work on; have one's hands in, have in hand, have on one's hands *or* shoulders, bear the burden; turn one's hand to etc. (undertake) 676.2; have one's hands full etc. (be busy) 682.13; have to do with etc. 680.6.

8. *v.* ply one's trade *or* task, labor in one's vocation, carry on a business *or* trade, drive a trade, do *or* transact business, keep a shop; pursue a course, pursue the even tenor of one's way; attend to business, attend to one's work; enter a profession, set up in business, hang out one's shingle [joc. and coll., U.S.].

9. *v.* officiate, serve, act, act *or* play one's part, do duty, discharge *or* perform the office, ∼ duties *or* functions of, serve in the office *or* capacity of, hold *or* fill an office etc. *n.*, hold down a job [slang]; conduct etc. 692.4.

---

625. *Par negotiis neque supra* [Equal to his business and not above it].—TACITUS. The playthings of our elders are called business.—ST. AUGUSTINE. Drive thy business or it will drive thee.—FRANKLIN. Never fear the want of business. A man who qualifies himself for his calling never fails of employment.—JEFFERSON. A business with an income at its heels.—COWPER. There is no better ballast for keeping the mind steady on its keel . . . than business.—LOWELL. *Les affaires sont les affaires* [Business is business].—MIRBEAU. Why not have a bit of romance in business when it costs nothing?—SHAW.

10. *v.* be in the hands of, be on the anvil *or* stocks, be in the fire, pass through one's hands.

11. *adj.* businesslike, practical, efficient, thorough, prompt; occupational, professional, vocational; avocational, hobbyhorsical [joc.]; official, functional; workday, workaday, prosaic; systematic, methodical etc. (orderly) 58.7.

12. *adj.* busy, industrious etc. 682.19, 20.

13. *adj.* in hand, in the fire etc. (in preparation) 673.13.

14. *adv.* professionally etc. *adj.,* in the course of business, all in the day's work.

626. Plan

1. *n.* plan, scheme, schema, device, design; project, projection; proposal, proposition; presentation, suggestion; resolution, motion; game, little game; well-laid etc. 611.6 plan; base of operations; intention etc. 620; method, system etc. (way) 627; organization etc. (arrangement) 60; policy etc. 692.2; undertaking 676.

2. *n.* outline, delineation, sketch, draft *or* draught, drawing, diagram, skeleton, design, pattern, plan *or* plans, layout [coll.], plot, protocol, copy; rough, rough *or* roughcast draft *or* copy, *brouillon* [F.], *ébauche* [F.]; proof, revise; figure, fig.; chart, map, *carte du pays* [F.]; outline map; relief map; road map, ground plan, projection, elevation; ichnography, cartography; conspectus, summary etc. (compendium) 596; model etc. 22.1; specifications etc. (description) 594; schedule etc. 611.2; roadbook, Baedeker etc. (guidebook) 694.7.

3. *n.* program, bill, prospectus etc. (schedule) 611.2.

4. *n.* platform, plank, slate [U.S.], ticket [U.S.]; policy etc. 692.2.

5. *n.* contrivance, invention, receipt, nostrum, device; alternative, loophole; stratagem etc. (artifice) 702.3; trick etc. 545.3; shift etc. (expedient) 646.2; gadget [slang] etc. (object) 316.3.

6. *n.* plot, intrigue, conspiracy, complot, cabal, machination; underplot, counterplot; mine, countermine; pipelaying [slang, U.S.], wirepulling [coll.].

7. *n.* measure, step, action, course, procedure; stroke, stroke of policy; master stroke, trump, trump card, court card; *cheval de bataille* [F.], great gun; *coup* [F.], *coup d'état* [F.]; good *or* clever move, bold stroke, good hit; bright thought *or* idea, great idea.

8. *n.* planner, projector, designer, plotter, promoter, contriver; organizer, founder, author, artist, builder; schemer, schemist, schematist [obs.]; strategist, machinator, maneuverer *or* manoeuvrer, tactician; conspirer, conspirator; Machiavel, Machiavelli, Machiavellian, Machiavellist, intrigant, intriguer.

9. *v.* plan, design, frame, contrive, arrange, devise, concoct, concert; hatch, hatch up; project, forecast, plan ahead, contrive *or* plan beforehand, lay down a plan, shape *or* mark out a course; outline, delineate, sketch, draft *or* draught, diagram, chart, map, draw up, draw up a plan; lay out, map out, strike out, cut out, chalk out; cast, recast; take steps *or* measures; prepare etc. 673.6; intend etc. 620.3; predesign, preconcert etc. (predetermine) 611.3.

10. *v.* plot, hatch a plot, scheme, conspire, complot, cabal, intrigue, maneuver *or* manoeuvre, machinate; counterplot, countermine; lay a train.

11. *adj.* planned, arranged, devised etc. *v.*; on the carpet *or* tapis, *sur le tapis* [F.], on the table, under consideration, under advisement; in preparation etc. 673.13.

12. *adj.* planning, scheming etc. *v.*; schemy [coll.], schemeful; artful etc. (cunning) 702.6.

627. Way

1. *n.* way, method, manner, means, system, wise [rare], gait, form, mode, fashion, style, cut, tone, guise; *modus operandi* [L.], mode of procedure; ways and means; policy, procedure etc. (line of conduct) 692; scheme, device etc. (plan) 626.

---

626. It is a bad plan that admits of no modification.—PUBLILIUS. His mind teeming with schemes.—SCOTT. A mighty maze! but not without a plan.—POPE. The best laid schemes o' mice and men / Gang aft a-gley.—BURNS. All human plans and projects come to naught.—BROWNING.

627. Though this be madness, yet there is method in 't.—SHAKESPEARE. The wrong way always seems the more reasonable.—G. MOORE. There's no road has not a star above it.—

2. *n.* path, track, trail, road, run, route, way, course, career, march, tack, line, line of way *or* road, trajectory, orbit, beat, corridor, aisle, alley, lane, avenue, artery, channel; pass, passage, passageway; approach, access, means of access; covered way, cloister, arcade, colonnade, gallery; ambulatory, *ambulatorium* [ML.]; pathway, footpath, walk, sidewalk, *trottoir* [F.], foot pavement [Eng.], board walk; public walk, promenade, esplanade, alameda [Southwest. U.S.], parade, *prado* [Sp.], mall; towpath, towing path; berm *or* berme; bridle track *or* path, horse path *or* road; bypath, byway, bypaths and crooked ways; byroad, by-pass; overpass, underpass; beaten track *or* path, rut, groove; backway, back stairs *or* door.

itinerary etc. 266.9; mid-course etc. 628; short cut, beeline etc. 246.2; detour etc. (circuit) 629; secret passage etc. (covert way) 530.4; gateway, doorway etc. (portal) 260.4; entranceway etc. (inlet) 294.5, (vestibule) 191.17; exit etc. (outlet) 295.5; stairway etc. 305.2; canal etc. (conduit) 350; tunnel etc. (cave) 252.3.

3. *n.* roadway, thoroughfare, road, street, highway, highroad, driveway, avenue, parkway, boulevard, turnpike, coach road; main road, state highway, King's *or* Queen's highway, royal road, broad highway; place, row; lane, vennel [Scot. and dial. Eng.]; alley, alleyway; blind alley or corner, cul-de-sac, dead end, dead-end street; back street; causeway, causey; embankment, terrace; private driveway; speedway, speed road; highways and byways; seaway etc. 267.8; airway etc. 267a.20; crossroad, intersection etc. (crossway) 219.2.

4. *n.* pavement, pave [chiefly U.S.], *pavé* [F.], paving; macadam, asphalt, cement, tar, concrete, tile, bricks, stone, pavestones, tilestones; flags, flagstones, flagging; cobblestones, cobbles, coggles [obs. exc. dial.]; curbstone, kerbstone [Eng.].

5. *n.* railway, railroad, rail; tram [Eng.], tramline [Eng.], tramway, tramroad; trolley track, streetcar line, street railway, electric railway; elevated railway, elevated [coll.], el *or* L [coll.]; subway [U.S.], underground [Eng.], tube; horse railway *or* railroad, light railroad, by-line, junction, branch, switchback; cable railway etc. *below* 627.6.

6. *n.* ropeway, cableway, wireway, wire road *or* ropeway, cable *or* rope railway; telpher, telpherway, telpher ropeway, telpher line *or* railway.

7. *n.* bridge, span, viaduct; footbridge; stepstone, steppingstone; overbridge, overpass; drawbridge, bascule bridge; floating bridge, bateau bridge, pontoon; plank; gangplank, gangboard, gangway; pass, ford, ferry; Bifrost [Myth.].

8. *adv.* how, in what way *or* manner, by what mode *or* means, to what extent, in what condition, for what reason, by what name, to what effect, at what price; after this fashion, in this way, thus, so, thus and so.

9. *adv.* anyhow, anyway, in any way, anywise, by any means, by any manner of means, in any event, at any rate, in any case, nevertheless, however.

10. *adv.* somehow, somegate [Scot. and North. Eng.], by some means, somehow or other *or* another, in one way or another, *per fas et nefas* [L.], by fair means or foul, by hook or by crook.

628. Mid-course

1. *n.* mid-course, middle course *or* way, midway [obs.], middle state, middle ground, middle of the road, fence [coll.], neutrality; half measures, half-and-half measures; middle etc. 68; golden mean etc. (mean) 29, (moderation) 174; compromise etc. 774; mediocrity etc. 736.

2. *v.* steer a middle course, keep *or* preserve a middle course, maintain a middle position, keep the golden mean, keep a happy medium, avoid both Scylla and Charybdis; be *or* remain neutral etc. *adj.*, stand neuter, keep in the middle of the road, sit on the fence [coll.], straddle [coll.], go halfway, strike *or* preserve a balance, trim; compromise etc. 774.2; steer a straight course etc. 278.6; be of

---

EMERSON. Any road leads to the end of the world.—FITZGERALD. They kept the noiseless tenor of their way.—GRAY. I will find a way or make one.—HANNIBAL.

628. He knows to live who keeps the middle state, / And neither leans on this side nor on that.—POPE. To find the medium asks some share of wit, / And therefore 'tis a mark fools never hit.—COWPER. Providence never stands neuter.—SOUTHEY. Beware the middle mind / That purrs and never shows a tooth. —E. WYLIE. *Medium tenuere beati* [Happy are they who have held to the middle course].

two minds, wait to see how the cat jumps etc. (be irresolute) 605.4; be mediocre etc. 736.2.

3. *adj.* neutral, neuter [arch.]; in the middle of the road, on the fence [coll.], impartial; neither one thing nor the other, neither hot nor cold; even, evenly balanced; half-and-half, fifty-fifty [slang, U.S.]; indifferent etc. 866.4; without choice etc. 609a.3; intermediate etc. 29.3.

4. *adv.* midway etc. 68.6; in the mean etc. 29.4; in moderation etc. 174.8.

629. Circuit

1. *n.* circuit, circuitous course *or* path, indirect road, roundabout way, roundabout, digression, excursion, detour, circumbendibus [joc.]; circumambience *or* circumambiency, circumambulation, ambages, ambit, round, compass [arch.], tour, turn, cycle, orbit, lap, loop; devious way etc. 279.3; winding etc. (convolution) 248; twist, zigzag etc. (obliquity) 217.1, 4; circle etc. 247.2; circuity etc. 311.

2. *v.* go round about, go out of one's way, detour, make a detour, circumambulate, make *or* perform a circuit etc. 311.3; meander etc. 279.5; beat about the bush etc. 477.8.

3. *adj.* circuitous, roundabout etc. 311.6; wandering etc. (deviative) 279.8; crooked, zigzag etc. 217.13, 16.

4. *adv.* in a roundabout way etc. (circuitously) 311.7.

630. Requirement

1. *n.* requirement, need, necessity, necessary, essential, want, requisite, demand *or* call for; prerequirement, prerequisite, prerequisition [rare]; desideratum, desideration; essentiality, indispensability; exigency, urgency, stress, pinch, "necessity's sharp pinch" (Shakespeare); matter of necessity, case of need, needfulness etc. *adj.,* case of life or death, matter of life and death, *sine qua non* [L.], the least one can do *or* require; the necessaries *or* necessities, the necessaries *or* necessities of life; lack etc. 640.3; desire etc. 865; requisition etc. (request) 765, (demand) 741.2; obligation etc. 601 744; compulsion etc. 744.

2. *v.* require, need, want, feel the want of, have occasion for, stand in need of, not be able to dispense with *or* do without; render necessary etc. *adj.,* necessitate, create a necessity for, call for, put in requisition; prerequire; desiderate; oblige etc. (compel) 744.2; lie under a necessity etc. 601.10; lack etc. 640.6; desire etc. 865.11; make requisition etc. (prescribe) 741.5.

3. *adj.* requisite, required etc. *v.,* needful, imperative, essential, indispensable; necessary, necessitous, necessitative; called for, in demand *or* request, in want of; prerequisite; inevitable, unavoidable etc. 601.11; exigent, pressing etc. (urgent) 642.13; compulsory etc. 744.3; obligatory, obliged etc. 926.9, 10.

4. *adv.* of necessity etc. (necessarily) 601.15.

631. Instrumentality

1. *n.* instrumentality, subservience *or* subserviency; mediation, intermediation, intermediacy; means etc. 632; agency etc. 170; influence etc. 175; aid etc. 707; intervention etc. 724.

2. *n.* medium, intermedium, intermediary, intermediate, intermediate agency *or* instrument, interagent, agent, means, tool, instrument, vehicle, cat's-paw, hand; minister, handmaid, maid, servant, slave, valet; midwife, *accoucheur* [F.], *accoucheuse* [F., *fem.*], obstetrician; steppingstone, stepstone; go-between etc. (mediator) 724.2; key etc. (opener) 260.10; expedient etc. 646.2.

3. *v.* be instrumental etc. *adj.,* serve, subserve, promote, minister, officiate, pander to, tend; mediate, intermediate, come *or* go between; intervene, interpose etc. 724.3; use one's influence etc. 175.6; be useful etc. 644.2.

4. *adj.* instrumental, serviceable, subservient, ministerial; mediatorial, intermedial, intermediary, intermediate; conducive, conducent [obs.]; operative etc.

---

629. Digressions, incontestably . . . are the life, the soul of reading.—STERNE. The longest way round is the shortest way home.
630. Make yourself necessary to somebody.—EMERSON. *Necessitas non habet legem* [Necessity has no law]. Needs must when the devil drives.

631. Man is thy most awful instrument / In working out a pure intent.—WORDSWORTH. I thank God and thee; he was the author, thou the instrument.—SHAKESPEARE. The bold are but the instrument of the wise.—DRYDEN.

631.4 – 633.4

170.4; useful etc. 644.5; mechanical etc. 633.5.

5. *prep., adv.* through, by, per, by dint of, by *or* in virtue of, by way of, through the medium of etc. *n.,* along with, on the shoulders of; whereby, thereby, hereby; by the agency of etc. 170.5; by means of etc. 632.4; by the aid of etc. 707.14.

632. Means

1. *n.* means, wherewith, wherewithal; resources, ways, ways and means, means to an end, conveniences, appliances, means and appliances; expedients, devices, measures, steps; cards to play, two strings to one's bow; method etc. (way) 627; resort, shift etc. (expedient) 646.2; provision etc. 637; aid etc. 707; instrumentality etc. 631; instrument etc. 633, (medium) 631.2; stock in trade, capital etc. (fund) 636.2; last resource etc. 601.5.

2. *v.* have the means, have *or* possess means etc. *n.,* have something to draw on, have something laid by, have something laid by for a rainy day; have powerful friends, have friends at court.

3. *v.* find means etc. *n.,* provide the wherewithal; get by hook or by crook, obtain by fair means or foul; beg, borrow, or steal.

4. *adv., prep.* by means of, with, herewith, therewith, wherewith, wherewithal; by all means, by every means; by dint of etc. (through) 631.5; by the agency of etc. 170.5; by the aid of etc. 707.14; by what means etc. (how) 627.8; by any means etc. (anyhow) 627.9; by some means etc. (somehow) 627.10.

633. Instrument

1. *n.* instrument, tool, implement, apparatus, device, contrivance, appliance, convenience, organ, utensil, vehicle; agent, cat's-paw etc. (medium) 631.2; means etc. 632.

2. *n.* machine, mechanism, mechanical contrivance *or* tool; engine, gin, mill, motor; machinery, enginery; movements, mechanical movements; wheelworks, clockworks, wheel and axle, wheels within wheels, epicyclic train; power plant; engineering.

3. *n.* (types of engines) steam, electric, gas, oil, air, caloric *or* heat, Diesel, internal-combustion, turbine, external-combustion, piston-valve, side-valve, Corliss, double-acting *or* -action, single-acting *or* -action, direct-acting *or* -action, triple-expansion, oscillation, oscillation-cylinder, reciprocating, rotary, condensing, noncondensing, compound, beam, radial, trunk, stationary, portable, vertical, horizontal, diagonal, inclined, locomotive, marine, fire, rose, pumping, refrigerating, ruling, hoisting, blowing etc.; traction engine etc. 272.17; automobile engine etc. 272.16; aeromotor etc. 273a.11; dynamo, generator etc. 158a.7.

4. *n.* (cross references) measuring instruments 466.4 etc.; weighing instruments etc. 319.5; optical instruments etc. 445; musical instruments etc. 417; nautical instruments etc. 273.9–14; aeronautical instruments etc. 267a.29; automobile mechanism etc. 272.16; recording instruments etc. 553.3.

vise, tongs etc. 781.2; suspender etc. 214.3; supporter, trestle etc. 215; wheel etc. 312.4; crane, windlass, elevator, lever etc. 307.2–4; dredge etc. 252.7; buckle, chain, nail etc. 45; adding machine etc. 85.5; clock etc. 114.6; vaporizer etc. 336.3; sprinkler etc. 337.3; weathervane etc. 338.9; pump etc. 333.6; bellows, fan etc. 349.20, 21; stove etc. 386; lamp etc. 423; lighter etc. 388.4–6; detonator etc. 406; fire extinguisher etc. 385.3; refrigerator etc. 387; receptacle etc. 191; tube, pipe etc. 260.6; valve, faucet etc. 263.2; floodgate etc. 350.2; key etc. 260.10; extractor etc. 301.4; square, plumb line etc. 212.5; knife, ax etc. 253.6; saw etc. 257.3; bodkin, awl etc. 262; arms etc. 727; hammer etc. 276.4; graver, style etc. 558.4; die etc. 22.3; modeling tool, chisel etc. 557.8; pencil, typewriter etc. 590.10; printing press etc. 591.10; hone, grindstone etc. 253.7; plane, trowel etc. 255.3;

---

632. My extremest means / Lie all unlock'd to your occasions.—SHAKESPEARE. You take my life, / When you do take the means whereby I live.—SHAKESPEARE. With all appliances and means to boot.—SHAKESPEARE. For what are riches, empire, pow'r, / But larger means to gratify the will?—CONGREVE. Increased means and increased leisure are the two civilisers of man.—DISRAELI.
633. The tools to him that can handle them.—CARLYLE. There is no jesting with edge tools.—BEAUMONT AND FLETCHER. A good workman is known by his tools.

pulverizer, mill etc. 330.4; pulper etc. 354.3; crucible, mortar etc. 144.4; sieve etc. 60.4; bell etc. 408.5; horn etc. 404.4; whistle etc. 410.4; ear trumpet, headphone etc. 418.6; thermometer etc. 389; stethoscope etc. 662.22; microscope etc. 193.7.

5. *adj.* mechanical, machinal [rare], machinelike; engineering; power-driven, motor-driven; locomotive, locomotor; propulsive, driving, hoisting, elevating, lifting etc.; electric, steam etc.; instrumental etc. 631.4.

634. Equipment

1. *n.* equipment, equipage, gear, outfit, harness [arch.], caparison, apparatus, tackle, tackling [now rare], rig, rigging, trappings, traps [coll.], fittings, appointments, appliances, accouterments, appurtenances, things, impedimenta, *matériel* [F.], paraphernalia, furniture, furnishing, furnishings, fixtures, supplies, provisions; plant; upholstery; munitions, armament; implement, tool etc. (instrument) 633; goods, effects etc. (property) 780; wardrobe etc. 225.2; provision etc. 637; preparation etc. 673; rations etc. 298.6.

2. *v.* equip, furnish, rig, rig up *or* out, appoint, fit, fit up *or* out, accouter *or* accoutre, heel [slang, U.S.], outfit, gear, harness [arch.], array, dress, deck, fettle [dial., Eng.]; arm, man, munition; supply, provision etc. (provide) 637.4; prepare etc. 673.6.

3. *adj.* equipped, furnished, fitted etc. *v.*; well-equipped, well-fitted, well-stocked, well-supplied, well-provided, well-heeled [slang, U.S.]; ready, in harness etc. (prepared) 673.11; provided etc. 637.6.

635. Materials

1. *n.* materials, stuff, substances; raw material, staple, stock; material etc. (matter) 316.2; writing materials etc. 590.10; bookbinding materials etc. 593.10; art materials etc. 556.16, 557.8, 558.4.

2. *n.* (building materials) sticks and stones, lath and plaster, bricks and mortar; brick, tile etc. (ceramics) 384.14; mortar, cement etc. (plaster) 223.19; girder, rafter etc. (beam) 215.12; roofing etc. 223.6; varnish, enamel etc. (paint) 428.5.

3. *n.* wood, timber, lumber; hardwood, softwood; oak, maple, walnut, mahogany, Philippine mahogany, burl, ash, birch, cedar, pine, knotty pine, spruce, fir, hemlock, ebony, juniper, alder, myrtle, olive, linden, eucalyptus, pipal, deodar, acacia, magnolia, yew, palm, fruit wood, gumwood, rosewood, teakwood, zebrawood, beechwood, redwood, tulipwood; driftwood; stick, stick of wood, stave; board, plank; two-by-four, three-by-four etc.; slab, puncheon; clapboard, wallboard, siding; lath, single *or* double lath, lath and half lath; shingle, shake; log, clog [now Scot. and N. of Eng.]; beam, post etc. 215.12, 16; pole etc. 206.4; tree, wood etc. 367.6, 7; firewood etc. 388.3; incense wood etc. 400.3.

4. *n.* paper, *papier* [F.]; cap, foolscap; paper board, cardboard, pasteboard, pulpboard, strawboard, millboard, binder's board; carton; *papier-mâché* [F.]; sheet, leaf, page; quire, ream; parchment, vellum, papyrus etc. (writing paper) 590.10; newspaper etc. 593.6.

5. *n.* fabrics, cloth etc. (textile) 219.5.

6. *n.* mineral, element, metal; manganese, marl, mercury, mica, molybdenum, graphite, magnesium, barite, bauxite, bromine, chromite, gypsum, lime, lithium, magnesite, phosphate, potassium, pyrite, salt, silica, sulphur, tantalum, diatomite, emery, titanium, tungsten, uranium, feldspar, fluorite, fluor spar, garnet, gold, silver, aluminum, copper, zinc, tin, lead; iron, steel, pig iron, cast iron, wrought iron, decarbonized iron; bullion, gate, regulus, ingot, sow, pig, mine pig; ore, ironstone; coal, coke etc. (fuel) 388.2; petroleum etc. (oil) 356.2; asphalt, mineral pitch etc. (resin) 356a.

7. *n.* stone etc. 342.4; precious stone etc. (gem) 847.8.

---

634. And all trades, their gear and tackle and trim.—G. M. HOPKINS.   Accoutred as I was, I plunged in.—SHAKESPEARE.

635. The material always comes before the work. The hills are full of marble before the world blooms with statues.—P. BROOKS.   All the means of action— / The shapeless masses, the materials— / Lie everywhere about us.—LONGFELLOW.

636. Store

1. *n.* store, budget, hoard, treasure; stores, supplies, provisions; lumber; abundance etc. (great quantity) 31.3, (plenty) 639.2; mass, heap, collection etc. (accumulation) 72.6, 7; department store etc. (mart) 799; merchandise etc. 798.

2. *n.* fund, supply, stock; stock in trade, supply on hand; capital, capital stock, accumulated stock *or* supplies, capital goods; reserve, reserves, reservoir, something in reserve, reserve source *or* supply, fresh *or* additional stock *or* store, extra supply, *corps de réserve* [F.], reserve fund, nest egg, savings, *bonne bouche* [F.], backlog [coll.], a shot in the locker [coll.], ace in the hole [slang], a card up one's sleeve; relay; resource, resources, available means; source, source of supply, staple; rich source, abundant store, mine, bonanza [U.S.], vein, lode, quarry; spring, fount, fountain, well, wellspring [obs. exc. fig.]; orchard, garden, farm; milch cow, hen; sinking fund; plenty etc. 639.2; funds etc. 800.2.

3. *n.* crop, harvest, vintage, yield, produce, product, gleaning.

4. *n.* storehouse, storeroom, store closet, store, storage, depository, repository, conservatory, reservoir, depot, staple, promptuary [obs.], magazine, lumber room, stock room; repertory, repertorium [rare]; warehouse, wareroom, *entrepôt* [F.], godown [Oriental]; treasure house, treasury; cache, stash [criminal slang, U.S.]; glory hole [coll.]; pantry, buttery, larder, spence [chiefly Scot.], stillroom [Eng.], cannery; cellar; dairy, dairy house *or* room; garner, granary, grain elevator, silo; mow, rick, haymow, hayloft, hayrick; armory, arsenal; dock; freight yard, power station, carbarn, train shed, roundhouse.

coffer, closet, cupboard etc. 191.8, 15, 16; safe-deposit vault, bank etc. 802; file, card index etc. 86; archive etc. 551.2; pond, tank etc. (pool) 343a; stable, byre etc. (barn) 189.5; piggery, dog pound etc. (enclosure) 232; henhouse etc. 370.3; thesaurus, encyclopedia etc. 593.3, 4; memory etc. 505.

636. Laying up in store for themselves a good foundation against the time to come.—BIBLE. Lay not up for yourself treasure upon earth.—BOOK OF COMMON PRAYER. Once more the liberal year laughs out / O'er richer stores than gems of gold.—WHITTIER.

5. *n.* (collections) museum, gallery; picture gallery, art gallery *or* museum; pinakotheke *or* pinacotheca, glyptotheca; Metropolitan Museum, National Museum, British Museum, Louvre; Madame Tussaud's; library etc. 593.11; aquarium, menagerie, zoological garden etc. 370.3; conservatory, greenhouse etc. (garden) 371.6.

6. *n.* storing etc. *v.*, storage; cold storage, dry storage; conservation etc. (preservation) 670.

7. *v.* store, lay in store etc. *adj.*, store *or* stow away, put *or* lay away, stow down, salt down *or* away [coll.], store up, lay up, put up, hoard up, treasure up, heap up, garner up, save up, collect a reserve supply, accumulate, amass, hoard, garner, fund, stock, gather into barns; lay in, lay in a supply, ∼ stock *or* store; pile, heap, stack; deposit, reposit, stow, bank; cache, stash [criminal slang, U.S.]; warehouse, reservoir; file, file away; pack, pack away; collect etc. (assemble) 72.11; supply, furnish etc. (provide) 637.4; load etc. 184.13; acquire etc. 775.6.

8. *v.* reserve, save, retain, keep, keep in reserve etc. *adj.*, keep by one, keep *or* hold back; set *or* lay apart *or* aside, put ∼, lay *or* set by; husband, husband one's resources; save up, save to fall back upon, keep as a nest egg, save ∼, put by *or* provide for *or* against a rainy day, feather one's nest, look after the main chance [coll.]; preserve etc. 670.3, 4; have in store *or* reserve etc. (be provided) 637.5; be economical etc. 817.3.

9. *adj.* stored etc. *v.*, in store, in stock, on hand, in the store, in reserve, in ordinary; supernumerary, spare, to spare.

637. Provision
(See 638. Waste)

1. *n.* provision, providence [now rare], providance [now Scot.], providing etc. *v.*; supply, supplyment [obs.]; grist, grist to the mill; purveyance; replenishment, reinforcement; commissariat; provisions, supplies etc. (equipment) 634, (stores) 636; provender, groceries etc. (food) 298.6; resources etc. (means) 632, (fund) 636.2; subvention, reinforce-

637. Soul, thou hast much goods laid up for many years.—BIBLE. Have good grist at hand to grind.—T. D. ENGLISH. Providence for war is the best prevention of it.—BACON.

ments etc. (aid) 707.3, 5; preparation etc. 673.

2. *n.* provider, supplier, caterer, commissary, quartermaster, steward, khansamah [Ind.], purser, manciple, feeder, victualer *or* victualler, batman, comprador *or* compradore [China]; purveyor, purveyancer; grocer, fishmonger etc. 797.11; landlord, host etc. (proprietor) 779.2.

3. *n.* provision shop, grocery store etc. (mart) 799.

4. *v.* provide, supply, furnish, give, afford, present, contribute, yield; stock, store; fund; provide for, make provision *or* due provision for; find, find one in; provision, provender, purvey, cater, victual, forage; replenish, replete [rare], reinforce; recruit, beat up for; fill, fill up; supply a defect, make good, make up; lay in a supply etc. 636.7; provide against a rainy day etc. 636.8; arm, fit out etc. (equip) 634.2; make ready etc. (prepare) 673.6–8; feed etc. 298.43.

5. *v.* be provided etc. *adj.,* have in store *or* reserve, have to fall back upon; keep by one etc. (reserve) 636.8; be prepared etc. 673.9.

6. *adj.* provided, supplied etc. *v.*; prepared etc. 673.11; equipped etc. 634.3.

7. *adj.* provisional, provisionary, provisory; conditional etc. (dependent) 475.15, (circumstantial) 8.5; temporary etc. 111.6; tentative etc. 463.12; preparatory etc. 673.10.

638. Waste
(See 637. Provision)

1. *n.* waste, wastage, wasting etc. *v.*; needless destruction, useless consumption *or* expenditure; consumption, consumpt [chiefly Scot.]; exhaustion, depletion, expenditure, dissipation, decrement; wear, wear and tear; loss etc. 776; diminution, shrinkage, ebb etc. (decrease) 36; decomposition etc. 49; deterioration etc. 659; loss etc. 776; leakage etc. (egress) 295; wastefulness etc. (prodigality) 818; misuse etc. 679; devastation etc. (destruction) 162; uselessness etc. (inutil-

ity) 645; desert etc. 168.2; rubbish etc. 645.4.

2. *v.* waste, consume, spend, expend, use, use up, dissipate, exhaust, deplete, impoverish, swallow up; drain, drain of resources; spill; waste away, wear out *or* away; cast ∼, throw *or* fling away, fool ∼, muddle *or* fritter away, scatter to the winds, sow broadcast; "waste its sweetness on the desert air" (Gray); cast pearls before swine, waste powder and shot, pour water into a sieve, burn the candle at both ends, carry coals to Newcastle, kill the goose that lays the golden egg, *manger son blé en herbe* [F.]; labor in vain etc. 645.6; squander etc. 818.3; lay waste, desolate etc. (destroy) 162.4.

3. *v.* run to waste, go to waste, run *or* go to seed, fall "into the sere, the yellow leaf" (Shakespeare); run dry, dry up; ebb, melt away etc. (diminish) 36.3; leak etc. (run out) 295.7; deteriorate etc. 659.6, 7.

4. *adj.* wasted, gone to waste, run to seed, dried up, at a low ebb, thrown away; useless etc. 645.8.

5. *adj.* wasteful etc. (prodigal) 818.

639. Sufficiency
(See 640. Insufficiency)

1. *n.* sufficiency, sufficientness etc. *adj.,* slight sufficiency [joc.], "an elegant sufficiency" (Thomson), *quantum sufficit* [L.], adequacy, enough, no less, competence *or* competency, satisfactory amount, satisfaction.

2. *n.* plenty, plenitude; plenteousness, copiousness etc. *adj.*; amplitude, abundance, galore [coll.], prolixity, profusion, prodigality, lavishment, exuberance, exuberant plenty, great abundance, lavish supply, overflowing fullness *or* supply, overflow, affluence, opulence *or* opulency, great plenty, ample supply *or* sufficiency, enough and to spare; fullness *or* fulness, full; cornucopia, horn of plenty, horn of Amalthaea *or* Amalthea; fat of the land, "a land flowing with milk and honey" (Bible); goddess of plenty, Abundantia; full measure, bellyful [vulg.] etc. (fill) 52.3; repletion etc. (redundance) 641;

---

638. Wilful waste brings woeful want.—FULLER.   Time wasted is existence, used is life.—YOUNG.   Waste its sweetness on the desert air.—GRAY.   Getting and spending we lay waste our powers.—WORDSWORTH.   It is only what is good in Man / That wastes and withers there.—WILDE.

639. Unto every one that hath shall be given, and he shall have abundance.—BIBLE.   Here is God's plenty.—DRYDEN.   Sufficient unto the day is the evil thereof.—BIBLE.   Enough is as good as a feast.

satiety etc. 869; great quantity etc. 31.3; abundant store, mine etc. (fund) 636.2; wealth etc. 803; numerousness etc. 102.

3. *v.* be sufficient etc. *adj.,* suffice, do, just do, serve, avail, answer, answer *or* serve the purpose, pass muster, fill the bill [coll.], meet requirements, satisfy; have enough etc. *n.,* eat ∼, drink *or* have one's fill, get a bellyful [vulg.] etc. 52.3.

4. *v.* be plentiful etc. *adj.,* abound, exuberate, teem, flow, stream, rain, shower down, pour, pour in, swarm, creep with, bristle with; superabound etc. 641.2.

5. *v.* render sufficient etc. *adj.,* replenish, fill etc. 52.7.

6. *adj.* sufficient, sufficing etc. *v.,* enough, adequate, satisfactory, equal, commensurate, proportionate, correspondent, competent, suitable, valid, tangible; sufficient for, ∼ to *or* unto, equal to, equal to all demands; up to the mark, up to the handle *or* knocker [coll., U.S.]; effectual etc. 644.7.

7. *adj.* plenty, plenteous, plentiful, "plenty as blackberries" (Shakespeare); ample, abundant, abounding etc. *v.,* copious, copiously supplied, provided fully *or* abundantly, richly charged, impregnated *or* imbued, replete, flush, affluent, rich, liberal, bountiful, bounteous, prevalent, prevailing, rife, rampant, epidemic, besetting, lavish, prodigal, prolix, copious, exuberant, extravagant, luxuriant, teeming, enough and to spare; diffuse, diffusive; profuse, profusive; stintless, unstinting, unstinted, without stint; unmeasured, unsparing, unwasted; unexhausted, exhaustless, inexhaustible; wantless, without want; wholesale, widespread etc. (extensive) 31.7; well-provided etc. (equipped) 634.3; full etc. 52.11; redundant etc. 641.5.

8. *adv.* sufficiently, plentifully, amply, fully, abundantly etc. *adj.*; plenty [coll.], in abundance etc. *n.,* galore [coll.], no end [coll., U.S.], with no sparing hand, without stint, to one's heart's content, *ad libitum* [L.]; full, to the full, in full measure; to the good.

9. *int.* enough!, hold!, *eheu jam satis!* [L.] etc. (cease) 142.8.

640. Insufficiency
(See 639. Sufficiency)

1. *n.* insufficiency, insufficience [rare], inadequacy, inadequateness etc. *adj.,* none to spare; low water, ebb tide; bare subsistence; deficiency etc. (incompleteness) 53; shortcoming etc. 304; imperfection etc. 651; incompetence etc. (impotence) 158; inutility etc. 645; insolvency etc. 808.2.

2. *n.* scarcity, scarceness etc. *adj.,* dearth, paucity, stint; scantiness, scantness, scantity, scant sufficiency [coll.]; shortage, short [coll.].

3. *n.* want, wantage; lack, need, destitution, deprivation; exigence *or* exigency; inanition, starvation, famine, drought *or* drouth; indigence etc. (poverty) 804; bankruptcy etc. 808.2; imperfection etc. 651; requirement etc. 630.

4. *n.* depletion, exhaustion; vacancy etc. (emptiness) 187.3.

5. *n.* pittance, dole, scrimption [dial.], drop in the bucket, cheeseparings and candle ends; short allowance, short-commons, half rations, pinchgut money *or* pay [sea slang]; fast day, banyan day, Lent; mite, bit etc. (small quantity) 32.2.

6. *v.* be insufficient etc. *adj.,* not suffice etc. 639.3, kick the beam, be found wanting *or* lacking; want, lack, need, miss, require; be on short allowance *or* short commons; fall short etc. 304.2; be in want etc. (poor) 804.7.

7. *v.* render insufficient etc. *adj.*; deplete, exhaust etc. (consume) 638.2, (empty) 297.14; stint etc. (be parsimonious) 819.3.

8. *adj.* insufficient, inadequate, too little, not enough etc. 639.6, unequal to; slack, at a low ebb, at low-water mark; deficient etc. (incomplete) 53.4; inefficient, incompetent etc. (impotent) 158.8; ineffective etc. 732.8; useless etc. 645.8; imperfect etc. 651.4.

9. *adj.* meager, poor, thin, lean, puny, slender, slim, slight; spare, sparing; stunted, stinted; starved, starveling, half-starved; undernourished, underfed, famine-stricken, famished; emaciate, emaciated.

10. *adj.* scarce, sparse; scant, scanty; scrimp, scrimpy [coll.]; skimp, skimpy [coll.], skimping [chiefly coll.]; not to

640. But from him that hath not shall be taken away even that which he hath.—BIBLE. *Fortuna multis dat nimium, nulli satis* [Fortune gives many too much, no one enough].—MARTIAL. How can we say "enough" on earth—/ "Enough" with such a craving heart?—C. ROSSETTI. Thou art weighed in the balances, and art found wanting.—BIBLE.

be had, not to be had for love or money, not to be had at any price; scarce *or* scarcer than hen's teeth.

11. *adj.* wanting, lacking etc. *v.*; found wanting; short, short of; shy, shy of *or* on [both slang]; out of, destitute of, devoid of, bereft of, denuded of, minus [coll.], without, jejune; out of pocket, at the end of one's rope *or* tether; in want etc. (poor) 804.7; without resources etc. 632.1; vacant, bare etc. (empty) 187.11; imperfect etc. 651.4.

12. *adj.* insufficiently provided, ill-provided, ill-furnished, ill-stored, ill off; unprovided, unsupplied, unstored, untreasured, unreplenished, unfed; empty-handed, shorthanded.

13. *adv. etc.* insufficiently, inadequately etc. *adj.*; in default of, for want of; failing.

641. Redundance

1. *n.* redundance, redundancy, redundant; superabundance, superfluity, nimiety [rare], exorbitance *or* exorbitancy, inordinacy, excess, surplus, surplusage, superplus [obs. exc. Scot.], overplus, overage, overset, overmeasure, oversupply, overfullness etc. *adj.*, pleonasm, plethora, surfeit, glut, engorgement, congestion, repletion, enough in all conscience, *satis superque* [L.], enough and to spare, more than enough, much of a muchness [coll.]; too much, too many; too much of a good thing, *toujours perdrix* [F.].

overload, overburden, surcharge, supersaturation; overdose, sickener; overrun, overrunning, overflow, deluge, flood; drug, drug on *or* in the market; expletive, padding, embroidery, frills *or* frillery [coll.]; supererogation, work of supererogation; bonus, premium; epact, annual epact, menstrual *or* monthly epact; margin; lion's share, Benjamin's mess; too many irons in the fire; luxury, extravagance; *embarras de richesses* [F.], embarrassment of riches, money to burn [coll.]; overpraise, overcommendation, overlaudation; verbosity, tautology, circumlocution etc. (diffuseness of speech) 573; grandiloquence etc. 577.2; satiety etc. 869; bellyful [vulg.] etc. (fill) 52.3; overexpansion etc. 194.4; exuberance, prodigality, profusion etc. (plenty)

639.2; intemperance etc. 954; exaggeration etc. 549; overestimation etc. 482; remainder etc. 40.

2. *v.* superabound, overabound, know no bounds; overwhelm, overswarm, overgrow, overrun, run riot, meet one at every turn; overflow, overbrim, run ~, flow ~, well *or* brim over; remain on one's hands, hang heavy on hand; swarm, bristle with etc. (abound) 639.4.

3. *v.* overdo, overgo, overreach, override, overjump, overfly; overshoot, overshoot the mark; overact, overplay, overspeak, overinform, overstudy, oversow, overproduce, overissue, overexpose, overdye, overdress, overdevelop, overcut, overdare, overcrop, overcorrect, overlift, overcertify, overbuy, overlay, overcharge, overburn, overbuild, overspend, overpay, overcolor, overset; overreckon, overmeasure, overcount; overweigh, overbalance, overbear; overcarry, carry too far; overdraw, overexpand, overstretch, overstrain, stretch, strain; overlaud, overcommend, overpraise; overwork, overlabor.

carry coals to Newcastle *or* salt to Dysart, bring owls to Athens, bear pots to Samos isle *or* crocodiles to Nile, carry timber to a wood; *pisces natare docere* [L.], teach fishes to swim, teach one's grandmother to suck eggs; kill the slain, butter one's bread on both sides, put butter upon bacon, "to gild refined gold, to paint the lily, to throw a perfume on a violet" (Shakespeare), employ a steam engine to crack a nut, burn the candle at both ends, have too many irons in the fire; exaggerate etc. 549.2; overestimate etc. 482.3; lavish, squander etc. (be prodigal) 818.3.

4. *v.* overload, overlade, overburden, overweight, overweigh, overfill, fill to overflowing, surcharge, supersaturate, glut, gorge, surfeit; hepatize; choke, suffocate; overstock, oversupply; whelm, overwhelm; engulf, inundate, deluge, flood, drench; drug, drug the market; overdose, overfeed; pile up, pile it on; lay it on, lay it on thick, lay it on with a trowel; load, saturate etc. (fill) 52.7; cloy, satiate etc. 869.4.

5. *adj.* redundant, superfluous, *de trop* [F.], unnecessary, needless, unneeded, uncalled-for, surplus, overplus, super-

641. My cup runneth over.—BIBLE. Why then, can one desire too much of a good thing?—SHAKESPEARE. Enough, with over-measure.—SHAKESPEARE. My candle burns at both ends, / It will not last the night.—MILLAY. It never rains but it pours.

abundant, overmuch, inordinate, exorbitant, fancy, extravagant, immoderate, undue, unwarranted, overgreat, overdone, overwrought, overweening, out of bounds *or* all bounds; excess, excessive, in excess; steep, stiff, unchristian [all coll.]; too much, too many; overgrown, overblown; expletive, expletory; supernumerary, spare, to spare, enough and to spare; on one's hands, heavy on hand; intemperate etc. 954.4; lavish, profuse, prodigal etc. (plenty) 639.7; exaggerated etc. 549.3; verbose, pleonastic, circumlocutory etc. (diffuse) 573.7-9; grandiloquent etc. 577.7; supplemental, adscititious etc. (additional) 37.7; useless etc. 645.8.

6. *adj.* overfull, overcharged, overloaded etc. *v.*; overladen, supersaturated, drenched; plethoric, plethorical [rare]; gorged, stuffed, smothered, ready to burst; overflowing, cram-full, crammed *or* filled to overflowing, running over; replete, brimful, saturated etc. (full) 52.11; packed etc. (crowded) 72.13; dropsical, turgid etc. (swollen) 194.9; satiated etc. 869.6.

7. *adv.* redundantly etc. *adj.*, overmuch, too much, too far; too, over, overly; without measure, out of measure, beyond measure *or* all measure; extra, overplus, more than enough, beyond need, beyond the mark; over one's head, over head and ears, up to one's eyes *or* ears; over and above etc. (in addition) 37.8.

642. Importance
(See 643. Unimportance)

1. *n.* importance, consequence, prominence, eminence *or* eminency, notability, significance, salience, consideration, concern, import, mark, moment, weight, interest, note; materialness etc. *adj.*, materiality; distinction, prestige, nobility, splendor, sublimity, grandeur, majesty, dignity; figure, name; pre-eminence, supereminence; greatness etc. 31; superiority etc. 33; primacy, paramountcy etc. (supremacy) 33.3; precedence etc. 62; fame etc. (repute) 873; value etc. (goodness) 648.

2. *n.* gravity, seriousness, solemnity; no joke, no laughing matter; matter of life and death, case of life or death; urgence *or* urgency, insistence *or* insistency, pressure, stress, exigency, pinch.

3. *n.* notabilia, memorabilia, great doings; red-letter day.

4. *n.* salient point, cardinal point, outstanding *or* distinctive feature, important ~, principal ~, prominent ~, essential etc. part, essential matter, essential, gravamen, *sine qua non* [L.], great point, main thing, main chance, precise thing, thing of interest, matter of concern, object of note; key, keynote; keystone, cornerstone; cream, salt; sum and substance, "the be-all and the end-all" (Shakespeare), head and front; essentials, fundamentals, basics, basic *or* essential facts, brass tacks [coll.], cases [slang, U.S.], turkey [coll., U.S. and Can.]; half the battle; substance, gist etc. (essence) 5.2; trump card etc. (measure) 626.7.

5. *n.* person of importance *or* consequence, personage, great personage, personage of distinction, man of mark, great man, notable, notability, somebody, something, figure, bigwig, great card, nabob, mogul, big ~, great *or* grand mogul, panjandrum, "the Grand Panjandrum himself" (S. Foote), worthy, pasha *or* bashaw [Turk.], sachem, magnate, the only pebble on the beach [U.S.], *rara avis* [L.], pillar of the state, ~ church *or* community, "pillars of society" (Ibsen); "the choice and master spirits of the age" (Shakespeare); celebrity etc. 873.9; grandee, magnifico etc. (noble) 875.4-8. big shot [U.S.], big bug, ~ gun *or* cheese, high-muck-a-muck [U.S.], it *or* It, big it *or* It, nob, gilded rooster [all slang]; big man, great gun, mugwump, heavyweight [all coll.]; his nabs *or* nibs, his importance [all joc.].

6. *n.* chief, principal, paramount, top sawyer [coll.], first fiddle, *primus inter pares* [L.], biggest frog in the pond [slang, U.S.]; prima donna, star; director etc. 694; master etc. 745.

7. *v.* be important etc. *adj.*, be something, be somebody, be an object, be worthy of consideration, deserve *or* merit

---

642. *Non numero haec judicantur sed pondere* [These things are judged by weight, not by number].—CICERO. Thy own importance know.—POPE. With grave / Aspect he rose, and in his rising seem'd / A pillar of state.—MILTON. Enterprises of great pith and moment.—SHAKESPEARE. *Amoto quaeramus seria ludo* [Let us put joking aside and treat of serious things].—HORACE.

notice *or* regard; import, signify, matter, count, tell, weigh, carry weight, draw water [slang, U.S.]; play first fiddle etc. (be superior) 33.5; cut a figure etc. 873.10.

8. *v.* give importance to, attach *or* ascribe importance to, value, rate highly, care for, set store by *or* upon, treasure, prize, appreciate; make much of, make a fuss *or* stir about, make an ado *or* much ado about.

9. *v.* emphasize, stress, lay emphasis *or* stress upon, place emphasis on, give emphasis to, accent, accentuate, punctuate, feature [coll., U.S.]; mark, mark with a white stone; underline, underscore; put in italics; ∼ capitals etc., write in letters of gold.

10. *adj.* important, of importance etc. *n.*, material, to the point, salient, signal, momentous, consequential, marked etc. *v.*, notable, noteworthy, remarkable, worthy of remark *or* notice, not to be overlooked *or* despised; memorable, rememberable, worthy of being remembered; unforgettable, never to be forgotten, never to be erased from the mind; considerable, substantial, great, grand, big, noble, august, eminent, prominent, outstanding, conspicuous, distinguished; big-league, major-league, bigwigged; striking, impressive, commanding, imposing; outstanding, extraordinary, exceptional, rare; particular, special; stirring, eventful.

big-time [slang]; not to be sneezed at, heavyweight [both coll.]; egregious [now joc.]; noble etc. 875.10.

11. *adj.* significant, telling, trenchant, emphatic, decided, positive, forceful, pregnant; *tanti* [L.].

12. *adj.* weighty, of weighty import, heavy, ponderous, grave, serious, solemn, earnest.

13. *adj.* urgent, pressing, crying, clamorous, absorbing, exigent, insistent, instant, importunate; critical, crucial; requisite etc. 630.3.

14. *adj.* paramount, essential, fundamental, radical, vital, of vital etc. importance; prime, primary; at the head of, at the top of the tree, to the front, in the front rank, in the zenith; main, principal, chief etc. (supreme) 33.8; first-rate, A 1 [coll.] etc. (best) 648.9.

15. *adv.* mainly, in the main, above all etc. 33.10.

643. Unimportance
(See 642. Importance)

1. *n.* unimportance, insignificance *or* insignificancy, irrelevance *or* irrelevancy, inconsequentiality, immateriality, ineffectuality, nugacity; nothingness, paltriness etc. *adj.*; inconsequence, inconsequentiality.

2. *n.* triviality, trivialism; fribble, fribblery [rare]; inanity, frivolity, levity; much ado about nothing, tempest *or* storm in a teapot *or* teacup, *tempête dans un verre d'eau* [F.], much cry and little wool; smallness etc. 32.

3. *n.* trifle, triviality, insignificant, insignificancy, thing of little value *or* importance, trivial *or* paltry affair, small *or* trifling matter, no great matter, matter of indifference, *peu de chose* [F.], a little thing, hardly *or* scarcely anything, matter of no importance *or* consequence, no object, nothing, mere nothing, nothing in particular, nothing to signify, nothing to speak of *or* worth speaking of, nothing to boast of, nothing to write home about, nought *or* naught, thing of naught, nullity, nihility, obscurity, bagatelle, fribble, gimcrack, gewgaw, bauble, trinket, kickshaw, knickknack, whimwham; fiddlestick, fiddle-faddle [coll.], fidfad [coll.], fingle-fangle [obs.], duffer [slang].

hair, straw, pin, button, rush, feather, bubble, peppercorn, fig, fico [arch.], prune, peanut, bean, hill of beans [coll.], row of pins [coll.], pinch of snuff, molehill, shucks [slang], flivver [slang], hoot [slang], rap, iota, jot, mote, mite, doit, duit, continental [U.S.], curse, rap, picayune [coll.], tinker's dam *or* damn, tinker's curse *or* cuss, halfpenny, bawbee [Scot.], farthing, brass farthing, cent, two cents, red cent [coll., U.S.], mill, pistareen; pai, pice [both Ind.]; song, old song; drop in the ocean *or* bucket, dust in the balance, feather in the scale, fleabite, pinprick, snap of the fingers *or* of one's thumb; joke, jest, farce, mere joke *or* farce, child's play.

4. *n.* trivia, trifles etc., *nugae* [L.], minutiae; details, minor details.

---

643. *Magno conatu magnas nugas* [Great trifles at great effort].—Terence. These little things are great to little men.—Goldsmith. Hear you this Triton of the minnows?—Shakespeare. *Dare pondus idonea fumo* [Fit to give importance to smoke, to

5. *n.* trumpery, frippery, stuff, trash, truck [coll.], rubbish, chaff; gimcrackiness [coll.], gimcrackery; "trifles light as air" (Shakespeare), froth, foam, bubble, smoke, cobweb; small beer, small fry; moonshine, fudge etc. (nonsense) 517.2; refuse etc. 645.4.

6. *n.* unimportant person, nobody, nonentity, nullity, nihility, obscurity, nothing, nought *or* naught, cipher, "an O without a figure" (Shakespeare), insignificant, insignificancy, no one knows who, nobody one knows, no great shakes *or* catch [coll.], lightweight [coll.], tinhorn [slang], whiffet [coll.], whippersnapper, two-spot [slang], scrub, runt [contemptuous], little fellow, man in the street; mediocrity, mediocre [rare]; man of straw, jackstraw; lay figure, puppet, dummy; *vox et praeterea nihil* [L.]; nine days' wonder; small beer, small fry; Mr. and Mrs. Nobody, John Doe and Richard *or* Mary Roe; Tom, Dick, and Harry; Brown, Jones, and Robinson; commonalty etc. 876; underling, second fiddle etc. (inferior) 34.3.

7. *v.* be unimportant etc. *adj.*, be of no importance etc. 642, not matter, not count [coll.], cut no ice [coll.], signify nothing, go for nothing, little matter, matter *or* signify little, not matter a straw etc. *n.*, not amount to anything, not amount to a hill of beans [coll.] etc. *n.*; feel insignificant, feel like two cents [coll.].

8. *v.* attach little importance to, consider unimportant, make little of, make light of, make *or* think nothing of, set at nought, set no store by, not care a straw about etc. *n.*

9. *v.* trifle, fribble, frivol [coll.], faddle [dial., Eng.], fiddle-faddle [coll.], fiddle with trifles, fool around, spend *or* waste in trifling *or* on trifles, concern oneself with trifles, fuss over trifles; make much ado about nothing, make mountains out of molehills, make a great commotion about a matter of small importance, have a storm *or* tempest in a teacup *or* teapot; tumble *or* stumble over one's shadow; dally, potter etc. (idle) 683.8.

10. *adj.* unimportant, of little *or* small importance, of no importance *or* account, of no great importance, no great shakes [coll.], of little *or* no consequence, inconsequential, insignificant, immaterial, unessential *or* nonessential, not vital, irrelevant, inappreciable, inconsiderable, ineffectual; small, little, minute; no skin off one's nose *or* elbow [coll.]; ordinary, common, commonplace; uneventful; inferior etc. 34.5; indifferent, soso etc. (mediocre) 736.3; vain etc. (useless) 645.8; humble, common etc. (ignoble) 876.11.

11. *adj.* trifling, trivial, idle, petty, puny, niggling, peddling, piddling, mincing, fribbling, fribble; fidfad, fiddlefaddle [both coll.]; picayune, picayunish [U.S.]; poking [rare], pokey *or* poky; finicking *or* finiking, finikin, finical, finicky; nugatory, nugacious; slight, slender, flimsy, superficial, shallow, light, airy, frothy, frivolous, inane, unworthy of serious consideration; ridiculous etc. 855.5; foolish etc. (absurd) 497.4.

12. *adj.* paltry, poor, mean, meager *or* meagre, measly [slang], sorry, pitiful, contemptible, beneath contempt, shabby, miserable, wretched, vile, scrubby, scrannel [arch.], weedy, trashy, trumpery, scurvy, beggarly, niggardly, cheap, catchpenny, twopenny-halfpenny, two-for-a-cent *or* -penny, dime-a-dozen, two-by-four [coll.], one-horse [coll.], small-fry; tinhorn, tin-pot, tin-potty [all slang]; gimcrack, gimcracky [coll.]; second-rate, third-rate, fourth-rate; unworthy of regard *or* consideration, beneath notice; worthless, not worth the pains, not worth the powder and shot, not worth-while, not worth mentioning *or* speaking of, not worth a thought, not worth a rap, ~ a straw etc. *n.*; bad etc. 649.8.

13. *phr.* it does not matter, it matters not, it does not signify, it is of no consequence *or* importance, it makes no difference, it cannot be helped, it is all the same; for aught one cares.

14. *int.* no matter!, never mind!, *n'importe!* [F.], what matter!, what boots it!, what of that!, what of it!, what's the odds!, a fig for!, what's the difference!, what's the diff! [slang]; stuff!, tut! etc. (nonsense) 497.5; think no more of it! etc. 460.13.

---

trifles].—PERSIUS. A mistake of no very great moment—in fine, a mere slip.—BARHAM. No matter how important you are, you may get the measles.—SANDBURG. *Le jeu ne vaut pas la chandelle* [The game is not worth the candle].

644. Utility
(See 645. Inutility)

1. *n.* utility, usefulness etc. *adj.*, usability, serviceability, profitability, adaptability, applicability, availability; efficacy, efficiency, adequacy; service, use, stead, avail, boot [arch.], benefit, advantage, behalf; value, worth, money's worth; step in the right direction; help etc. (aid) 707; commonweal etc. (public welfare) 906.3; subservience etc. (instrumentality) 631; function etc. 625.3; expedience etc. 646; productiveness etc. 168; utilization etc. 677.3; utilitarianism etc. 906.3.

2. *v.* be useful etc. *adj.*, be of use etc. *n.*, avail, serve, do, suffice, answer, answer *or* serve a purpose, serve one's turn, fill the bill [coll.]; bestead, stand one in good stead; profit, remunerate, bear fruit, reap the benefit of, find one's account *or* advantage in; be the making of, make a man of; benefit, do good etc. (be beneficial) 648.6; subserve etc. (be instrumental) 631.3; contribute, conduce etc. (tend) 176.2.

3. *v.* render a service, render yeoman's service, perform *or* discharge a function, act a part, bear *or* lend a hand, pull an oar; help etc. 707.6–11.

4. *v.* utilize; render useful etc. (*see* useful etc. 677.8).

5. *adj.* useful, of use etc. *n.*, serving etc. *v.*, serviceable, good for; of general utility, utilitarian, practical, practicable, pragmatic(al); subservient etc. (instrumental) 631.4; helpful etc. 707.12; advantageous etc. (beneficial) 648.12; salubrious etc. 656.5; conducive etc. (tending) 176.3.

6. *adj.* valuable, of value, profitable, gainful, remunerative, worth-while, worth one's salt; invaluable, beyond price; fruitful etc. (productive) 168.7.

7. *adj.* effectual, effective, efficient, efficacious; capable, competent; adequate etc. (sufficient) 639.6.

8. *adj.* usable, applicable, available, ready, handy, at hand; on hand, on tab, on deck [coll.]; commodious, adaptable; all-round [coll.], of all work.

9. *adv.* usefully etc. *adj.*, in a useful manner; for use, for service; in the public service, for the good of the people *or* public, *pro bono publico* [L.].

645. Inutility
(See 644. Utility)

1. *n.* inutility, uselessness, unprofitableness etc. *adj.*; unprofitability, unserviceability; inefficacy, inefficacity [rare]; ineptitude, inaptitude; inadequacy etc. (insufficiency) 640; incompetence, inefficiency etc. (impotence) 158; unskillfulness etc. 699; unfruitfulness etc. (unproductiveness) 169; inexpedience etc. 647; waste etc. 638.

2. *n.* worthlessness etc. *adj.*, vanity, *vanitas vanitatum* [L.], inanity, nugacity, futility.

3. *n.* labor in vain, labor lost, labor of Sisyphus, lost trouble *or* labor, bootless errand, sleeveless errand [now dial.]; wild-goose chase, goose chase; work of Penelope, Penelope's web; flash in the pan, *brutum fulmen* [L.]; failure etc. 732.

4. *n.* rubbish, rubbishry; rubble, junk [coll.], trash, refuse, lumber, truck [coll.], dust [Eng.], debris *or* débris, *rudera* [L.], litter, clamjamfry [chiefly Scot.], rummage [chiefly dial.], tripe [slang], crap [slang], stuff, shoddy; odds and ends, oddments, orts, leavings, sweepings; offal, offaling; waste, wastage, wastements; raff [dial.], riffraff; chaff, stubble; weeds, tares; gurry [now chiefly U.S.], broken meat; castoffs, castoff clothes; rags, bones, waste paper *or* wastepaper; rubbish heap, trash pile, junk heap [coll.], dust hole [Eng.], glory hole [coll.], wasteyard, dump; wastepaper basket, wastebasket, waste bin [Eng.]; dross, slag etc. (dregs) 40.2; garbage, offscourings etc. (filthy refuse) 653.6.

5. *v.* be useless etc. *adj.*; fail etc. 732.5.

6. *v.* labor in vain, use vain efforts, roll the stone of Sisyphus, beat the air, lash the waves, fish in the air, milk the ram, milk a he-goat into a sieve, drop a bucket into an empty well, pour water into a sieve, sow the sand, bay the moon, preach

---

644. *Sua cuique utilitas* [To everything its use]. —Tacitus. Usefulness and baseness cannot exist in the same thing.—Cicero. Sensible people find nothing useless.—La Fontaine. Everything in the world is good for something. —Dryden. Life, like every other blessing, derives its value from its use alone.—Johnson. Nothing can have value without being an object of utility.—K. Marx.

645. If [a thing] be useless, the labor contained in it is useless.—K. Marx. Useless as a candle in a skull.—Cowper.

or speak to the winds, whistle jigs to a milestone, kick against the pricks, tilt at windmills, hold a farthing candle to the sun, look for a needle in a haystack *or* bottle of hay, lock the stable door after the horse *or* steed is stolen, cast pearls before swine, go on a bootless errand *or* wild-goose chase; try to make bricks without straw, try to wash a blackamoor white etc. (attempt the impossible) 471.5; carry coals to Newcastle etc. (redundance) 641.3; fail etc. 732.5; mismanage etc. 699.6, 7.

7. *v.* render useless etc. *adj.,* dismantle, dismast, dismount, disarm, unrig [chiefly Naut.]; throw a wrench in the machinery, throw a monkey wrench into the works; cripple, disable, disqualify, put out of gear etc. (render powerless) 158.6; disuse etc. 678.2; render unfit etc. 674.5.

8. *adj.* useless, inutile, inefficacious, unavailing, of no use, ~ avail etc. 644, bootless, sleeveless [now dial.], fruitless, gainless, profitless, unprofitable, unremunerative, unserviceable; worthless, valueless, unsalable, good-for-nothing *or* -naught, no-good [coll.], no-account [dial., U.S.], dear at any price, not worth having, not worth the powder and shot, not worth one's salt; not worth a straw etc. 643.12, of no earthly use, fit for the dust hole *or* wastepaper basket; nugatory, nugacious; vain, futile, idle, empty, inane; fatuous, fatuitous; effete, barren, sterile; ill-spent; dispensable.

inept, ineffective, inoperative etc. (impotent) 158.8–11; incompetent etc. 699.15; unfit etc. (inexpedient) 647.3; inadequate etc. (insufficient) 640.8; unproductive etc. 169.4; superfluous etc. (redundant) 641.5; worn-out etc. (impaired) 659.12; thrown away etc. (wasted) 638.4; unimportant etc. 643.10; abortive etc. 732.8.

9. *adv.* uselessly etc. *adj.,* to little purpose, to no purpose, to little or no purpose.

10. *int.* what's the use!, what's the good!, *cui bono?* [L.], *quo animo?* [L.], of what use *or* good is it?, for what good?

---

646. Expediency is the science of exigencies.—KOSSUTH. As much an expedient as lighting by gas.—GLADSTONE. Too fond of the Right to pursue the Expedient.—GOLDSMITH. Though peace be made, yet it is interest that keeps peace.—CROMWELL. Principle is ever my motto, not expediency.—DISRAELI.

646. Expedience
(See 647. Inexpedience)

1. *n.* expedience, expediency, desirableness etc. *adj.,* desirability, advisability; fitness etc., suitability, propriety; advantage, opportunity; opportunism; pragmatism, pragmaticism; adaptation to an end; timeliness etc. 134; utility etc. 644; right etc. 922; dueness etc. 924.

2. *n.* expedient, expediency, means to an end, means to further an end, avail, resort, resource, shift, dodge [coll.], kink, ruffle, working proposition; temporary expedient, makeshift, *pis aller* [F.], stopgap, subterfuge; device etc. (contrivance) 626.5; means etc. 632; last resort etc. 601.5.

3. *v.* be expedient etc. *adj.,* produce the goods [coll.]; suit, befit etc. (agree) 23.7; suit *or* befit the time, ~ season *or* occasion etc. (be timely) 134.5.

4. *adj.* expedient, expediential; desirable, advisable, commendable, recommendable, advantageous, meet, fit, fitting, befitting, becoming, due, right, proper, seemly, decorous, appropriate, acceptable, eligible, suitable, sortable, politic, convenient, *in loco* [L.], apt and suitable to the end in view; profitable, worth-while; seasonable, opportune etc. (timely) 134.7; wise etc. 498.11; just etc. 941.3; ethical etc. 926.12; good etc. 648.8; right etc. 922.5.

5. *adj.* practical, practicable, effective, pragmatic(al).

6. *adv.* expediently, conveniently etc. *adj.*; in the right place; at a critical moment, ~ period *or* point; in the nick of time etc. (opportunely) 134.10.

647. Inexpedience
(See 646. Expedience)

1. *n.* inexpedience, inexpediency, undesirableness etc. *adj.,* undesirability, unadvisability *or* inadvisability; unfitness, unsuitability, impropriety, infelicity, inaptitude; discommodity, incommodity, inconvenience, disadvantage, drawback; inopportunity etc. (untimeliness) 135; inutility etc. 645; wrong etc. 923; undueness etc. 925.

2. *v.* be inexpedient etc. *adj.,* be put to inconvenience; be untimely etc. 135.3.

---

647. Impropriety is the soul of wit.—MAUGHAM.

3. *adj.* inexpedient *or* unexpedient, undesirable, unadvisable *or* inadvisable, unsuitable, dissuitable [rare], inappropriate, unappropriate [rare], unfit, unfitting, unbefitting, unbecoming, misbecoming, untoward, unworthy, unseemly, improper, undue, wrong; infelicitous, unhappy, unfortunate; unapt, inapt, inept; ineligible, inadmissible, objectionable; impolitic, indiscreet, injudicious, unwise, imprudent, ill-advised, ill-contrived; inconvenient, incommodious, discommodious, disadvantageous, troublesome, unsatisfactory; dedecorous [rare], indecorous, *contra bonos mores* [L.]; out of place, out of character *or* keeping, in the wrong place; unmeet; unprofitable etc. (useless) 645.8; unseasonable, inopportune etc. (untimely) 135.6; unjust etc. 941a.3; bad etc. 649.8; foolish etc. 499.15; wrong etc. 923.4.

4. *phr.* it is inexpedient, I wouldn't do it if I were you, it is very unwise, it will never do, it doesn't pay, it's not worth the trouble, the game is not worth the candle, *le jeu ne vaut pas la chandelle* [F.].

648. Goodness
(See 649. Badness)

1. *n.* goodness, excellence, merit, virtue, desert, worth, value, price, credit; virtuousness etc. 944; beneficence etc. 906; pleasure giving etc. 829; betterment etc. (improvement) 658.

2. *n.* good, weal [arch.], welfare, well-being, interest, advantage, "consummation devoutly to be wished" (Shakespeare); behoof, behalf; benefit, benison [arch.], benefaction, blessing, boon, favor, service, good turn; profit, avail, boot [arch.], gain, godsend, prize, windfall, harvest, treasure-trove; greatest good, *summum bonum* [L.], main chance, world of good; commonweal etc. 906.3; prosperity etc. 734.1; right etc. 922.

3. *n.* superexcellence, superbness etc. *adj.*, supereminence, quintessence; superiority etc. 33; perfection etc. 650.

4. *n.* (something excellent) good thing, gem, jewel, diamond, pearl, tidbit, treasure, pure gold, all wool; choice, pick, select, elect, elite, best, very best, prize, flower, cream, prime, nonesuch, *nonpareil* [F.], *crème de la crème* [F.], gem of the first water, flower of the flock, cock of the walk, ~ loft *or* roost, salt of the earth, *rara avis* [L.], champion, prodigy, wonder; one in a thousand, one in a way; masterpiece etc. 698.5; pink etc. (paragon) 650.2; good person etc. 948.

best ever, first-rater, top-notcher, oner, caution, find, beat [all coll.]; trump, pip, brick, pippin, peach, lulu, knockout, crackajack, corker, calker *or* caulker, daisy, dandy *or* the dandy, jim-dandy, darb, humdinger, winner, honey, dazzler, the cheese, the nuts [all slang].

5. *v.* be good etc. *adj.,* be all wool etc. *n.*, be the real thing; look good to [coll.]; stand the proof *or* test, pass muster; excel, transcend etc. (be superior) 33.5.

6. *v.* be beneficial etc. *adj.,* benefit, advantage, serve, help, contribute, boot [arch.], avail, profit, good [obs.], produce *or* do good, do good to, produce a good effect, do a world of good; be the making of, make a man of; do no harm, break no bones; confer a benefit, do a good turn; better etc. (improve) 658.8.

7. *v.* vie, outvie, challenge comparison, emulate, rival.

8. *adj.* good, excellent, fine, nice, *bueno* [Sp.], *bon* [F.], bonzer [slang, Austral.], *très bon* [F.], gallows [slang and dial.], clever [now chiefly dial.], above par [coll.]; dandy, swell, rum, keen, bully, crackajack, great, grand [all slang]; admirable, estimable etc. (praiseworthy) 931.11; pleasing etc. 829.7–9; virtuous etc. 944.3; genuine etc. (authentic) 494.12; better etc. (superior) 33.7; expedient etc. 646.4.

9. *adj.* best, very best, choice, select, picked, elect, prime, capital, of the first water, first-rate, first-class, first-chop [Anglo-Ind. and coll.], top-hole [slang, chiefly Eng.], bang-up [slang]; tiptop, top-notch, A 1, A one *or* A number 1,

---

648. Who does not befriend himself / By doing good?—SOPHOCLES.   Hold fast that which is good.—BIBLE.   Good and evil ben two contraries.—CHAUCER.   So shines a good deed in a naughty world.—SHAKESPEARE.   I have always believed that good is only beauty put into practice.—ROUSSEAU.   From seeming evil still educing good.—THOMSON.   Goodness is the only investment that never fails.—THOREAU.   Be good, sweet maid, and let who will be clever.—KINGSLEY.   It is not enough to do good; one must do it the right way.—J. MORLEY.   A good heart is better than all the heads in the world.—BULWER-LYTTON.

crack, gilt-edge *or* gilt-edged [all coll.]; matchless, peerless, unparalleled etc. (supreme) 33.8; paramount etc. 642.14.

10. *adj.* superexcellent, superlatively etc. 33.10; good, superb, super [chiefly slang], superfine, exquisite, highwrought; precious, of great price, worth its weight in gold, worth a king's ransom, precious as the apple of the eye, good as gold; priceless, beyond price, invaluable, inestimable; rare, exceptional, extraordinary etc. (unusual) 83.10; perfect etc. 650.5.

11. *adj.* tolerable, moderately good, fair, tidy [coll.], decent, good enough, well enough, pretty good, pretty well, not amiss, not bad, better than nothing; presentable; bearable, passable, acceptable, admissible, satisfactory, unobjectionable, unexceptionable; up to the mark, up to par [both coll.]; middling, soso etc. (mediocre) 736.3; imperfect etc. 651.4.

12. *adj.* beneficial, salutary, favorable, advantageous, edifying; serviceable etc. (useful) 644.5; profitable etc. (valuable) 644.6; helpful etc. 707.12; healthful etc. (salubrious) 656.5.

13. *adj.* harmless, hurtless, uninjurious, unobnoxious, innocuous, innoxious, innocent, inoffensive, unoffending; impotent etc. 158.8.

14. *adv.* excellently etc. *adj.*, well, aright, not amiss, all for the best; commendably etc. 931.12.

15. *adv.* beneficially etc. *adj.*, for one's benefit, in one's favor, ∼ interest etc. *n.*, to one's advantage etc. *n.*

16. *int.* good! etc. (bravo!) 931.13.

649. Badness
(See 648. Goodness)

1. *n.* badness, hurtfulness etc. *adj.*, peccancy, peccability, virulence *or* virulency; malignance *or* malignancy, malignity; damnability, damnification; machinations of the devil; tender mercies [iron.]; wickedness, depravity etc. (vice) 945; guilt etc. 947; malevolence etc. 907; painfulness etc. 830.

2. *n.* evil, bad, wrong, ill, harm, hurt, injury, scath *or* scathe [arch. and dial.], woe, mischief, abomination; prejudice;

nuisance, annoyance, vexation, grievance, crying evil; *amari aliquid* [L.], gall and wormwood, thorn, thorn in the flesh *or* side, fly in the ointment, worm in the apple *or* rose, skeleton in the closet, snake in the grass, "something rotten in the state of Denmark" (Shakespeare); ills that flesh is heir to, "all ills that men endure" (Cowley); Pandora's box; bane etc. 663; pestilence, visitation etc. (disease) 655.2, 3; damage etc. (impairment) 659.3, misfortune etc. (adversity) 735; Satan etc. 978; evil spirit etc. 980.

3. *n.* bad influence, ill wind, evil star, evil genius, frowns of fortune; hoodoo [coll.], jinx [slang], Jonah, jadu [Hind.]; evil spirit etc. 980.

4. *n.* ill-treatment, maltreatment, illuse, ill-usage, misusage, abuse, molestation, oppression, persecution, outrage, atrocity, ravage, torture; disservice, ill service, ill turn, bad turn; foul play; brutality, cruelty etc. (malevolence) 907.

5. *n.* bad person etc. 949; evildoer etc. 913.

6. *v.* harm, hurt, bane, injure, wound, scathe *or* scath [arch. and dial.], damnify, inflict harm *or* injury, do evil, do an ill office to, do a mischief etc. *n.*; disserve, do disservice to; wrong, aggrieve, grind, oppress, persecute, trample *or* tread upon, bear hard upon, run hard, put upon, weigh down, weigh heavy on, overburden; victimize; bring *or* lead into trouble, get into trouble; damage etc. (impair) 659.8, 9; ruin etc. (destroy) 162.4; pain, molest etc. (physically) 378.4, (mentally) 830.3–6.

7. *v.* maltreat, ill-treat, ill-use, misuse, abuse, outrage, do violence, torture, agonize, crucify, break on the wheel, rack, put on *or* to the rack, wreak one's malice on, turn and rend one, do one's worst, dip *or* imbrue one's hands in blood; buffet, batter, bruise, scratch, maul; whip etc. (punish) 972.5–7; be severe etc. 739.4; be malevolent etc. 907.5.

8. *adj.* bad, evil, ill, wrong, arrant, untoward, cheesy [slang], punk [slang, U.S.], lousy [slang]; as bad as bad can

---

649. Sufficient unto the day is the evil thereof. —BIBLE. Woe unto them that call evil good and good evil.—BIBLE. For the good that I would I do not; but the evil which I would not, that I do.—BIBLE. Of harmes two the less is for to choose.—CHAUCER. There is some soul of goodness in things evil, / Would

be, as bad as they make 'em [coll.]; dire, terrible, dreadful, atrocious [coll.], horrid, horrible, deplorable, wretched, awful [coll.], sad, grievous, lamentable, regrettable, pitiful, pitiable, woeful, dismal, grave, black, gross, shocking, flagrant, flagitious, villainous, heinous, scandalous, shameful, infamous, nefarious, ghastly, vile, abominable, base, odious, obnoxious, execrable, detestable, despicable, contemptible, hateful, rank, peccant, scurvy, foul, fulsome, noisome, putrid [slang], rotten [slang].

cursed, accursed; damned, damnable, damnatory, damnific [rare]; bloody [vulg.], beastly [coll.], confounded, infernal, hellish, devilish, diabolic(al), ungodly [coll.], sinister; evil-fashioned, evil-shaped, evil-qualitied, evil-looking, evil-favored, evil-hued, evil-faced, evil-headed, evil-eyed, evil-thewed, evil-savored, evil-affected, evil-gotten; ill-contrived, ill-disposed, ill-conditioned, poor, mean etc. (paltry) 643.12; inferior etc. 34.5; unfortunate etc. (adverse) 735.8,9; wicked, sinful etc. 945.11; reprehensible etc. (blameworthy) 932.14; malignant etc. (malevolent) 907.6; inadvisable etc. (inexpedient) 647.3; unprofitable etc. (useless) 645.8; irremediable etc. (hopeless) 859.7; imperfect etc. 651.4.

9. *adj.* intolerable, unbearable, unacceptable, inadmissible, objectionable, exceptionable, unsuitable, unsatisfactory.

10. *adj.* harmful, hurtful, scatheful *or* scathful [now dial.], baneful, baleful, injurious, deleterious, detrimental, pernicious, noxious, nocent [now rare], noisome, malefic *or* malefical, malignant, prejudicial, disserviceable, disadvantageous, wide-wasting, disastrous; mischievous, full of mischief, mischief-making; damaging, corrupting etc. (*see* damage, corrupt etc. 659.8, 9); corrosive, corroding; virulent etc. (insalubrious) 657.3, (malevolent) 907.6-9; ruinous etc. (destructive) 162.6; deadly etc. (mortal) 361.16; painful etc. 830.9.

11. *adv.* badly etc. *adj.*, bad [coll.], ill, wrong, evil, in an evil manner, with malignity etc. *n.*, to one's cost; awful, awfully, dreadful [both dial. and coll.]; amiss, awry, out of joint.

12. *int.* that's too bad! etc. 932.16.

650. Perfection
(See 651. Imperfection)

1. *n.* perfection, perfectness, faultlessness etc. *adj.*; indefectibility, impeccability, impeccancy; pink, pink *or* acme of perfection; quintessence, *ne plus ultra* [L.]; acme, height etc. (summit) 210; best etc. 648.4; superexcellence etc. 648.3; transcendence etc. (superiority) 33; Utopia etc. 515.6.

2. *n.* paragon, *beau idéal* [F.] *or* beau ideal, good example, "the observed of all observers" (Shakespeare), *chevalier sans peur et sans reproche* [F.]; standard, pattern, mirror etc. (prototype) 22.

3. *n.* (comparisons) phoenix, philosophers' stone, Koh-i-noor; corker, trump [both slang]; black tulip; *cygne noir* [F.], black swan; Admirable Crichton, Bayard, Roland, Sidney; choice, best etc. 648.4; masterpiece etc. 698.5.

4. *v.* perfect, bring to perfection etc. *n.*; ripe, ripen; mature, maturate; consummate, crown etc. (complete) 729.2, 3.

5. *adj.* perfect, free from imperfection etc. 651; faultless, spotless, unspotted, stainless, unblemished, unmarred, untainted, immaculate, impeccable; indefectible, indefective [rare], indeficient [rare]; whole, entire, intact, sound, sound as a roach, right as a trivet, in perfect condition, harmless, unharmed, uninjured, unimpaired, undamaged, unhurt, unspoiled, undeformed, undefaced; unscathed, scatheless, scathless [now dial.]; complete in itself, well-rounded; unimpeachable, beyond all praise, *sans peur et sans reproche* [F.]; inimitable, unparagoned etc. (supreme) 33.8; consum-

650. *In se ipso totus teres atque torundus* [Complete in himself, polished and well-rounded].—HORACE. That ye may be perfect and entire, wanting nothing.—BIBLE. Let us go on into perfection.—BIBLE. Be ye therefore perfect, even as your Father which is in heaven is perfect.—BIBLE. Trifles make perfection, and perfection is no trifle.—MICHELANGELO. Every thing that grows / Holds in perfection but a little moment.—SHAKESPEARE. In this broad earth of ours, / ... Nestles the seed Perfection.—WHITMAN. What's come to perfection perishes.—BROWNING.

---

men observingly distil it out.—SHAKESPEARE. The belief in a supernatural source of evil is not necessary; men alone are quite capable of every wickedness.—CONRAD. Blindness we may forgive, but baseness we will smite.—W. V. MOODY.

650.5 — 652.4

mate etc. (complete) 52.9, 10, (completed) 729.6; acmic, summital etc. (top) 210.6; best, superexcellent etc. 648.9, 10; perfected etc. (completed) 729.6.

6. *adv.* perfectly etc. *adj.*, to perfection, *ad unguem* [L.], with a finish, to the limit; clean, clean as a whistle; completely etc. 52.13–15.

651. Imperfection
(See 650. Perfection)

1. *n.* imperfection, imperfectness, faultiness etc. *adj.*; deficience [rare], deficiency, defection [obs.]; inadequacy etc. (insufficiency) 640; incompleteness etc. 53; noncompletion etc. 730; immaturity etc. 674.2, 3; mediocrity etc. 736; shortcoming etc. 304.

2. *n.* fault, defect, flaw, breach, "little rift within the lute" (Tennyson), weak point, hole, hole in one's coat, screw loose, seamy side; catch [coll.], snag, drawback; *mésalliance* [F.], bar sinister [Her.]; taint, attainder; drop of black blood, touch of the tar brush [coll.]; blemish etc. (disfiguration) 848, (discoloration) 440a; shortcoming etc. 304; weakness etc. 160; error etc. (mistake) 495.2.

3. *v.* be imperfect etc. *adj.*, have a defect etc. *n.*, lie under a disadvantage, bear within it the seeds of decay, rot before it ripens, spring a leak, not pass muster, kick the beam; fall short etc. 304.2.

4. *adj.* imperfect, not perfect etc. 650.5; faulty, at fault, in default; defective, unsound, tainted, out of tune; deficient, short of, wanting, found wanting, weighed in the balance and found wanting, below its full strength *or* complement, below standard; below par, below the mark [both coll.]; not up to sample *or* specification, not up to scratch [coll.], not up to snuff [slang]; second-rate, third-rate, fourth-rate.

---

651. But thou art no such perfect thing: / Rejoice that thou art not.—WORDSWORTH. He censures God who quarrels with the imperfections of men.—BURKE. It is only imperfection that complains of what is imperfect.—FÉNELON. No perfection is so absolute / That some impurity doth not pollute.—SHAKESPEARE. A goodly apple rotten at the heart.—SHAKESPEARE. Faultless to a fault.—BROWNING. 'Tis true, perfection none must hope to find / In all the world, much less in womankind.—POPE.

inferior etc. 34.5; inadequate etc. (insufficient) 640.8; incomplete etc. 53.4, 5; partial etc. 51.8; immature etc. (unprepared) 674.7, 8; impaired etc. 659.12; blemished etc. 848.3; stigmatic etc. (discolored) 440a.3; specked, blotched etc. (spotted) 440.9; warped, deformed etc. (distorted) 243.5; peccant etc. (bad) 649.8, (erroneous) 495.12; moderately good etc. (tolerable) 648.11; indifferent, soso etc. (mediocre) 736.3.

5. *adv.* imperfectly etc. *adj.*; to a limited extent, pretty, rather, tolerably etc. 32.14; almost etc. 32.15.

652. Cleanness
(See 653. Uncleanness)

1. *n.* cleanness, cleanliness, immaculateness etc. *adj.*; immaculance, immaculacy; purity, freedom from foulness *or* dirt; purity of heart etc. 960; innocence etc. 946.

2. *n.* cleaning, cleansing, washing, bathing etc. *v.*; purification, epuration [rare], defecation, purgation, expurgation, abstersion, detersion, lavage, lavation, lustration, ablution, lotion [obs.], wash-up, elution [Chem.], elutriation, clarification, lixiviation, edulcoration, washout; natation, balneation; colature [rare]; despumation; lavatory, lavabo [both Eccl.]; washwork; dry cleaning, steam cleaning; sanitation, disinfection, fumigation, ventilation, deodorization; drainage, sewerage; washday; irrigation, aspersion etc. (watering) 337.2; immersion etc. (submergence) 310.2.

3. *n.* bath, bathe [chiefly Eng.], tub [coll.]; shower, shower bath, needle bath, hot *or* cold shower; sponge bath, sponge; hip bath, sitz bath; electric bath, radium bath, sulphur bath, acid bath; sweat bath etc. (hot bath) 382.6.

4. *n.* lavatory, *lavatorium* [L.]; washery, washroom, washhouse, washshed; laundry, laundry room; toilet [U.S.], toilet room; bath, bathroom, bathhouse, bathing place, balneary, *balnearium* [L.], *balneum* [L.] (*pl. balneae, balnea*); shower, shower bath; swimming pool *or* bath, natatorium, natatory [now rare],

---

652. Wash me and I shall be whiter than snow.—BIBLE. Empty, swept, and garnished.—BIBLE. I'll purge and leave sack and live cleanly.—SHAKESPEARE. Above all things,

pool, plunge, swimming hole; public bath, baths; thermae, sudatory, *caldarium* [L.] etc. (hot bath) 386.6; water closet etc. 653.9.

5. *n.* washbasin, washbowl, washdish, basin, trough; tub, washtub, bathtub; sink, kitchen sink; piscina, lavabo [both Eccl.]; washpot, washing pot; wash boiler, wash barrel, wash pitcher, washing maid, dishpan, finger bowl, *lavadero* [Sp.].

6. *n.* cleaner, cleaner-up, cleaner-off, cleaner-out, cleaning woman; washer, washerwoman, washwoman, washerwife [Scot.], washmaid, washing maid, *lavandera* [Sp.], laundress; washerman, washman, *lavandero* [Sp.], dhobi [Ind.], laundryman; dry cleaner; dishwasher, dish cleaner, washpot [now rare], pot-walloper [slang], scullion, dishwiper; sweep, sweeper, mehtar [Ind.] (*fem.* mehtrani), street sweeper, crossing sweeper, white wings [local, U.S.], dustman [Eng.], scavenger, mud lark [slang]; chimney sweep *or* sweeper, flue cleaner.

7. *n.* (cleaning devices) brush, wash brush; broom, besom, whisk, whisk broom; duster, feather duster; dustcloth; carpet cleaner *or* sweeper, vacuum cleaner, vacuum; mop, swab; hose; washer, washing machine, washing engine, dishwasher; scrubber, scrubbing board, washboard; washcloth, washrag, facecloth, dish mop; towel, bath towel, hand towel, face towel, dish towel; napkin, serviette, cloth, doily, bib; handkerchief, kerchief; sudary [arch.], sudarium; mat, doormat, rug, drugget; refiner, refinery; sieve, riddle, screen, filter, strainer; colature [rare], colatorium; blotter, sponge; scrape, scraper; comb, rake.

8. *n.* cleansing agent, cleanser, cleaner, wash, lotion; abstergent, detergent; solvent, cleaning solvent; lixiviator, lixivial solution, lixivium; benzene, benzine, benzol, benzolin; washing soda, sodium carbonate; lye, chloride of lime, buck [dial.]; purifier etc. *v.,* purificator, mundatory [Eccl.]; disinfectant, disinfector; fumigant, fumigator; deodorant, deodorizer;

soap etc. 356.5; antiseptic, cathartic etc. (medicine) 662.8, 9.

9. *v.* clean, cleanse, purify, purge, expurgate, expurge [now rare], absterge [rare], deterge, depurate, epurate [rare], defecate, elutriate, edulorate, decrassify; clarify, clear; clear out, rout out, sweep out, clean house, make a clean sweep, spruce up [coll.]; lave, wash, bathe, tub, launder, buck [now dial.], wash out, elute; rinse, scrub, swab, scour, full, flush, wipe, mop, wring, sponge, soap, shampoo; leach, lixiviate; despumate, skim; steam-clean, dry-clean *or* -cleanse; manicure, pedicure.

10. *v.* refine, separate, rack, strain, drain; filter, filtrate, percolate; sift, winnow, sieve, bolt, screen, riddle; pick, weed; eliminate etc. 42.4.

11. *v.* comb, rake, heckle, hackle, hatchel, card; scrape, rasp.

12. *v.* sweep, brush, brush up, whisk, broom; vacuum-clean, vacuum [coll.].

13. *v.* disinfect, fumigate, ventilate, deodorize, whitewash.

14. *adj.* clean, cleanly, cleaned etc. *v.*; pure, expurgate, immaculate, undefiled, spotless, taintless, stainless, unstained, unspotted, unsoiled, unsullied, unblemished, untarnished, untainted, uninfected; clean as a new penny, clean as a whistle, like a cat in pattens; neat, tidy etc. (orderly) 58.7; uncorrupted etc. 944.4; innocent etc. 946.5, 6; pure in heart etc. 960.2.

15. *adj.* cleansing, purifying etc. *v.*; purificative, purificatory; expurgative, expurgatory, expurgatorial; abstergent, detergent, abstersive [rare], depurative; purgative, cathartic; lavatory, lavational; balneatory, balneal.

653. Uncleanness
(See 652. Cleanness)

1. *n.* uncleanness, uncleanliness etc. *adj.,* impurity; immundity, immundicity [obs.]; squalor; obscenity etc. (impurity of mind) 961; untidiness, slovenry etc. (disorder) 59.

2. *n.* defilement, filthiness etc. *adj.,* pollution, befoulment, corruption, contamination, maculation, abomination; fetor etc. 401.

---

keep clean. It is not necessary to be a pig in order to raise one.—INGERSOLL. Cleanliness is not next to godliness nowadays, for cleanliness is made an essential and godliness is regarded as an offense.—CHESTERTON. Cleanliness is next to Godliness.

653. They that touch pitch will be defiled.—SHAKESPEARE. If dirt was trumps, what hands you would hold!—LAMB. To dig and delve in nice clean dirt / Can do a mortal little

3. *n.* soil, soilure, soilage; taint, tainture [obs.]; stain, blot, blotch, daub, blur, smear, smudge, smutch, smirch, smot [Scot.], spot, speck, speckle.

4. *n.* putrescence, putridity, putrefaction; rot etc. (decay) 659.2; fetor etc. 401.

5. *n.* dirt, filth, dust, grime, smudge, smut; soot, smoke; flue, lint; slime, slop, sossle [dial.], slubber [chiefly dial.], sludge, slush, slosh, sposh [U.S.], slab [now chiefly dial.], muck; mud etc. 352.4; mire etc. (marsh) 345.

6. *n.* offal, offaling; slough, draff, carrion; garbage, swill, hogwash [coll.], dishwater, bilge water, ditch water; rinsings, scourings, offscourings, outscourings; scum, offscum, scum of the earth; scurf, furfur, dandruff; tartar, fur; refuse, waste etc. (rubbish) 645.4; dross, slag etc. (dregs) 40.2; exuviae, pus, urine, perspiration etc. (excrements) 299.2-4.

7. *n.* dung, ordure, stercoration [now rare], argol [Mongol.], lientery, lienteria, stool, feculence, feces *or* faeces, droppings, jakes [dial. Eng.]; movement, bowel movement; sewage, sewerage; manure, fertilizer, muck, guano, compost; coprolite, coprolith; excrement, excreta etc. 299.1, 2.

8. *n.* (receptacle of filth) sink, sink of corruption, sump [Scot. and dial. Eng.], sough [dial. Eng.], cesspool; sewer, drain, common sewer, cloaca, cloaca maxima (*pl.* cloacae maximae); dunghill, manure pile *or* heap, midden [chiefly dial.], mixen [arch. or dial. Eng.], colluvies; dust hole [Eng.] etc. (rubbish) 645.4.

9. *n.* water closet, w.c., toilet [U.S.], cloaca, *cabinet d'aisance* [F.], latrine, privy [now local], necessary [now dial.], jakes [arch. exc. slang]; outhouse, backhouse, backy [dial.]; Mrs. Jones, can, johnny, locus [all slang]; head, roundhouse [both Naut.]; comfort station, rest room.

10. *n.* sty, pigsty, pigpen; stable, Augean stable; dump, hole [both slang]; slum, rookery.

11. *n.* vermin, lice etc. (insects) 366.24.

12. *n.* lousiness, pediculosis, pediculation, phthiriasis [Med.].

13. *n.* sloven, pig [coll.], dowdy etc. (slattern) 59.5.

14. *v.* be *or* become unclean etc. *adj.*, wallow in the mire; corrupt etc. (decay) 659.7; smell to high heaven, reek etc. (stink) 401.3.

15. *v.* render unclean etc. *adj.*, unclean, uncleanse; dirt, dirty, cover with dirt etc. *n.*; soil, foul, befoul, nasty [obs. exc. dial.], sully, filthify, pollute, defile, maculate, contaminate, corrupt, leaven; stain, bestain, distain [arch.]; taint, tarnish, blemish, spot, blot, blotch, daub, slubber [now chiefly dial.], blur, smear, smudge, smutch, smirch, besmirch, besmutch, besmudge, besmut, besmear, bemire, beslime, begrime, bespot, begrease; speck, speckle, bespeck, bespeckle; spatter, splatter, splash, bespatter, besplatter, besplash; drabble, dabble, daggle, drabble in the mud; smoke, besmoke; roil, rile [coll., chiefly U.S.].

16. *adj.* unclean, uncleanly; soiled, dirtied etc. *v.*; dirty, grimy, dusty, snuffy, mussy [coll., U.S.]; smutty, sooty, smoky; unwashed, unscoured, unswept, unwiped, unstrained; unpurified, impure; not to be handled without gloves, not to be handled with kid gloves; dreggy; bloody, gory; squalid; slovenly, slatternly etc. (untidy) 59.9; mucky, sossly, sloppy etc. (muddy) 352.9; gross etc. (impure in mind) 961.9.

17. *adj.* foul, filthy, defiled etc. *v.*, defiled with filth etc. *n.*, disgustingly dirty, offensive, repulsive, repellent, disgusting, revolting, coarse, odious, loathsome, fulsome, noisome, noxious, obnoxious, vile, nasty, beastly, abominable; sickening, nauseating, nauseous, nauseant; rank, strong [coll.], high; putrid, putrefactive, putrescent, putrefied; rotting etc. *v.*, rotten, flyblown, saprogenic *or* saprogenous, carious, rotten as a pear *or* cheese.

tainted, touched, off, stale, rancid, decayed, maggoty, gone bad, bad, peccant, corrupt; reasy *or* reasty [obs. exc. dial.], reechy [dial. Eng.], reeky; stagnant, stagnatory; moldy, mildewed, musty, fusty, frowy, frowzy, frowsty [dial. Eng. and coll.]; scurfy, lentiginous *or* lentiginose; impetiginous, purulent; feculent, fecal; slimy, mucid; dungy, excrementitious; stercoraceous, stercoral, stercorous, stercoricolous; fimetarious, fimicolous; polluting etc. *v.*; fetid etc. 401.4.

18. *adj.* lousy, pedicular, pediculous.

---

hurt.—J. K. BANGS.   Dirt is not dirt, but only something in the wrong place.—LORD PALMERSTON.

654. Health
(See 655. Disease; also 656. Salubrity)

1. *n.* health, healthiness, soundness etc. *adj.*; sanity [now rare], soundness of body, healthy state of body, good state of health, clean bill of health, good ~, rude ~, robust etc. health, well-being, fine fettle, fine whack [slang], fine *or* high feather [coll.]; bloom, full bloom; strength, vigor; incorruption, incorruptibility; eupepsia *or* eupepsy, euphoria *or* euphory; convalescence, pickup [slang, U.S.], upgrade; Hygeia [Gr.], Aesculapius [Rom.].

2. *v.* be in health etc. *adj.*, be bursting with health *or* vigor, be full of pep [slang], never feel better, bloom, flourish, enjoy good health *or* a good state of health, have a clean bill of health; keep body and soul together, keep on one's legs.

3. *v.* return to health, take a new *or* fresh lease on life, add years to one's life, recruit; convalesce, be convalescent; get better etc. (improve) 658.6; recuperate etc. 689.3; recover etc. 660.15; restore to health etc. (cure) 660.12.

4. *adj.* healthy, healthful, in health etc. *n.*; well, sound, whole, hearty, hardy, hale, stanch *or* staunch, vigorous, strong, brave; robust, robustious [joc.]; fresh, green, blooming, florid, flush; sound of wind and limb, sound as a roach *or* bell, hearty as a buck, in good health, in good case.

fresh as a daisy *or* rose, fresh as April, in fine fettle, in fine *or* high feather [coll.], in the pink [coll.], in the pink of condition, fine [coll.], in fine whack [slang], fit, fit as a fiddle [coll.], fit and fine [coll.], bobbish [slang], chipper [coll., U.S.], bursting with health *or* vigor, full of life and vigor, in full bloom, walking on air; tolerably well, tolerable [dial.], fairly well, as well as can be expected, on one's legs; uninjured etc. (preserved) 670.6.

655. Disease
(See 654. Health)

1. *n.* disease, illness, sickness etc. *adj.*; sick [rare], ailing etc. *v.*, *morbus* [L.], morbidity, infirmity, indisposition, ailment, ail, malady, disorder, complaint, affection, affliction, distemperature [arch.], disability, loss of health, alteration, defect; debility, debilitation, decrepitude; delicacy, delicate health; valetudinariness, valetudinarianism; invalidity, invalidism, invalescence [rare]; contagious *or* infectious disease, febrile disease, sporadic disease, endemic, endemic disease; dangerous illness, fatal disease; prostration, breakdown, collapse; breakup of the system, general breaking up; impairment, decline, decay etc. (deterioration) 659; weakliness etc. 160; physical pain etc. 378.

2. *n.* infection, contagion, miasma *or* miasm, pollution, contamination, corruption, taint, virus; poisoning, intoxation, intoxication, venenation [Med.]; septic poisoning, septicity; blood poisoning, septicemia, toxemia, pyemia; epidemic, pandemia, pestilence, pest, plague; bubonic plague, white plague, Black Death; plague spot, pesthole; poison etc. 663.4.

3. *n.* seizure, grip, visitation, attack, stroke, fit, ictus; spasm, throe, paroxysm, convulsion, epitasis, eclampsia, frenzy; epilepsy, falling sickness, grand mal, petit mal, psychic epilepsy, Jacksonian epilepsy; apoplexy, bloodstroke; tonic spasm, entasia, tetanus; holotony, laryngismus; clonic spasm, clonus; cramp, Charley horse [coll., U.S.]; caisson disease, the bends; stroke of paralysis etc. *below* 655.15.

4. *n.* fever, feverishness etc. *adj.*, calenture, febrility, febricity, pyrexia; pernicious fever, congestive fever; intermittent fever, intermittent; remittent fever, remittent; hectic fever *or* flush, hectic; febrile diseases etc. *below* 655.15; delirium etc. 503.3; flush etc. 382.7.

5. *n.* (diseases, ailments) goiter, bron-

---

654. Health and good estate of body are above all gold, and a strong body above infinite wealth.—BIBLE.   A healthy body is the guest-chamber of the soul; a sick, its prison.—BACON.   Health and cheerfulness mutually beget each other.—ADDISON.   Give me health and a day, and I will make the pomp of emperors ridiculous.—EMERSON.   Joy and Temperance and Repose / Slam the door on the doctor's nose.—LONGFELLOW.   I enjoy convalescence. It is the part that makes the illness worth while.—SHAW.   *Mens sana in corpore sano* [A sound mind in a sound body].—JUVENAL.

655. While the sick man has life there is hope.—CICERO.   The whole head is sick, and the whole heart faint.—BIBLE.   This sickness

chocele, struma, tracheocele; lockjaw, tetanus, trismus; bloody flux, hemorrhage, flux, issue; diarrhea, dysentery; jaundice, icterus; asphyxiation; apnea, rickets, rachitis; appendicitis; gallstones, biliary calculus, stone; hernia, rupture; varicosis, varicose veins; arteriosclerosis, hardening of the arteries; rheumatism, rheumatiz [dial.], rheumatics [dial.]; lumbago, arthritis; gout, podagra; dropsy, edema; elephantiasis, elephantiasis Graecorum; beriberi; paresis, softening of the brain; Riggs' disease, pyorrhea; stiff neck, torticollis; anthrax, woolsorter's disease; colic, gripe *or* gripes; tormina; malnutrition, cachexia *or* cachexy; anemia, bloodlessness.

headache, stomach-ache, earache, toothache etc. (pain) 378; mental disease etc. (insanity) 503, (idiocy) 499.3; delirium etc. 503.3; delirium tremens, pathological drunkenness etc. (alcoholism) 959.2; sunstroke etc. 503.4.

6. *n.* (febrile and infectious diseases) ague, malaria, malarial fever, dengue, dandy fever, breakbone fever; yellow fever, yellow jack; typhoid fever, typhoid, enteric fever; typhus; eruptive fever; scarlet fever, scarlatina; smallpox, variola, varioloid; cow pox, vaccinia; chicken pox, varicella; measles, rubeola; diphtheria, diphtheritis; cholera, cholera morbus, sporadic cholera, Asiatic cholera, cholera infantum, summer complaint; sleeping *or* sleepy sickness, African lethargy, encephalitis lethargica; leprosy.

7. *n.* venereal disease, French disease, Gallic disease, *morbus gallicus* [L.], pox, syphilis; clap *or* claps, dose of claps, dose [all slang]; gonorrhea, blennorrhea, blennorrhagia.

8. *n.* (eye diseases) trachoma, conjunctivitis, pinkeye; cataract, caligo, pin and web, amaurosis, gutta serena.

9. *n.* (respiratory diseases) laryngitis, tonsillitis, quinsy, cynanche, bronchitis, croup, angina, thrush; catarrh, rheum; cold, common cold; influenza, flu [coll.], grippe, *la grippe* [F.]; pneumonia, phthisi-pneumonia, lobar pneumonia, bronchopneumonia, bronchial ~, catarrhal *or* lobular pneumonia; hay fever, rose cold; asthma, bronchial asthma, cardiac asthma; whooping cough, pertussis; cough.

10. *n.* tuberculosis, t.b. [coll.], white plague, phthisis; pulmonary phthisis *or* tuberculosis, consumption; galloping consumption; scrofulotuberculosis, scrofula, tuberculous lymphadenitis, king's evil; miliary tuberculosis, paratuberculosis, nephrotuberculosis, fibrotuberculosis, pseudotuberculosis.

11. *n.* wasting disease, marasmus, emaciation, atrophy; chlorosis, greensickness; anemia, leukemia, leucocythemia; consumption etc. *above*.

12. *n.* heart disease, carditis, myocarditis, pericarditis, pyopericarditis, endocarditis, valvular lesion; hypertrophy of the heart, dilatation of the heart, atrophy of the heart, fatty degeneration of the heart; angina pectoris, palpitation of the heart, palpitation; heart failure.

13. *n.* indigestion, poor digestion, dyspepsia; pyrosis, water qualm; heartburn, cardialgia; seasickness, *mal de mer* [F.], airsickness; nausea, nauseation; qualm, qualmishness; giddiness, vertigo; constipation, autointoxication.

14. *n.* nervous disorder, neurosis, case of nerves; compulsion neurosis, anxiety neurosis, myoneurosis, acroneurosis, neuritis, neuroticism, neurasthenia; ischialgia, sciatica; face ague, trigeminal neuralgia, *tic douloureux* [F.]; fidgets, floccillation, tilmus; chorea, the jerks, St. Vitus's dance; locomotor ataxia, *tabes dorsalis* [NL.]; subsultus; tarantism *or* tarentism; paresthesia; hysterics, hysteria; shock, mental shock, trauma, nociassociation; shellshock; nervous prostration *or* breakdown; epilepsy etc. *above* 655.3; psychosis, psychoneurosis etc. 503.2.

15. *n.* paralysis, palsy; stroke of paralysis, shock [coll.]; motor paralysis, sensory paralysis; general paralysis *or* paresis; incomplete paralysis, paresis; hemiplegia, paraplegia *or* paraplegy, diplegia; shaking palsy, *paralysis agitans* [L.], Parkinson's disease; infantile paralysis, acute anterior poliomyelitis; neuroparalysis.

16. *n.* sore, inflammation, fester; rising, swelling; boil, gumboil, pimple, pap-

---

doth infect / The very lifeblood of the enterprise.—SHAKESPEARE. Diseases desperate grown / By desperate appliance are relieved, / Or not at all.—SHAKESPEARE. That dire disease, whose ruthless power / Withers the beauty's transient flower.—GOLDSMITH. All ills that men endure.—COWLEY. They do certainly give very strange and new-fangled names to diseases.—PLATO.

ule, pustule, carbuncle, wen, whelk, pock, corn, mole, wart, verruca, furuncle, polyp, exostosis, bleb, blob [chiefly dial.], bulla, blister, blain, chancre, scab; bubo, bubonocele; canker, canker sore, noma, water canker, canker of the mouth; cancer, carcinoma; ulcer, ulceration; tubercle, tuberosity; tumor, tumefaction, tumescence, intumescence; hemorrhoids, piles; gathering, abscess, imposthume [rare], aposteme; excrescence, growth, morbid *or* malignant growth, proud flesh; sarcoma; mortification, sphacelus, sphacelation; enanthema *or* enanthem, gangrene; slough, caries, necrosis; peccant humor, pus, corruption [now dial.]; wound etc. 659.4.

17. *n.* eruption, rash, brash, breaking-out; canker rash; dartre, exanthema *or* exanthem; scabies, itch, psora; pox, eczema, tetter, psoriasis; lichen, papular rash; lichen tropicus, prickly heat; impetigo; erythema; erysipelas, St. Anthony's fire; urticaria, hives, nettle rash; herpes; herpes zoster, shingles; herpes circinatus, ringworm; miliaria, pemphigus, rupia.

18. *n.* (veterinary) anthrax, splenic fever, charbon, milzbrand, malignant pustule, quarter evil *or* ill, Texas fever, blackwater, murrain, bighead, hog cholera, epizootic, heaves, croup, distemper; blackleg, black quarter; cattle plague, rinderpest, steppe murrain, glanders, milk sickness; foot-and-mouth disease, aphthous fever; rot, sheep rot; scabies, mange; megrims, staggers, blind staggers, mad staggers, stomach staggers.

19. *n.* (science of disease) pathology, pathogeny, etiology; nosology, nosography, nosogeny; bacteriology, immunology, parasitology, protozoology; semeiology, semeiography; symptomatology, diagnostics; diagnosis, prognosis, prognostic, prognostication; therapeutics, medicine etc. (healing art) 662.16.

20. *n.* sick person, sickling, sufferer; valetudinary [rare], valetudinarian, *valétudinaire* [F.], valetudinarist; invalid, martyr to disease; patient, case, victim; inpatient, outpatient; clinic [now rare]; cripple, lame, halt; impotent, incapable; sick, infirm, "the halt, the lame, and the blind" (Bible).

21. *v.* ail, be *or* feel ill etc. *adj.*, suffer, labor under, be affected with, complain of; sicken, take sick *or* ill, take ~, catch ~, fall a victim to *or* be stricken by a disease, ~ an infection etc. *n.*; break out, break out in a rash; fail, weaken, lose strength, lose one's grip, waste away, dwindle, droop, flag, wilt, languish, pine, peak, halt, gasp; drop down in one's track, be laid by the heels; keep one's bed, lay up *or* by, lie helpless, lie on one's back; malinger etc. (dissemble) 544.6.

22. *v.* afflict, disorder, derange; sicken, sickly; infect, taint, contaminate, disease, afflict with disease etc. *n.*; enfeeble, weaken, debilitate, extenuate, devitalize, invalidate, incapacitate, reduce; shake, unstring, unnerve; poison, empoison, venenate [rare], envenom; injure, cripple, wound etc. (impair) 659.8; pain etc. 378.4.

23. *adj.* ailing etc. *v.*, ill, unwell, sick, sickish, indisposed, poorly [chiefly coll.], seedy [coll.], out of health, out of sorts [coll.], under the weather [U.S.], on the sick list, affected *or* afflicted with illness, taken ill, in a bad way, in danger, at a low ebb, laid low; queasy, squeamish, qualmish, qualmy, qualm-sick, nauseated; prostrate, on one's back, laid up, confined, bedridden, invalided, in hospital; on one's last legs [coll.], with one foot in the grave etc. (moribund) 360.9; hurt, suffering etc. (pained) 378.6; feverish etc. 382.19; delirious etc. 503.14.

24. *adj.* infirm, unsound, unbraced, sickly, cranky [dial.]; valetudinary, valetudinarian; unhealthy, healthless, in poor health, in declining health, on the wane *or* decline, languid, drooping, flagging; poor, poorly [chiefly coll.], poorlyish [chiefly coll.]; reduced, reduced in health, reduced to a skeleton; pale, anemic, bloodless, chlorotic; faint, faintish, feeling faint; crippled, lame, halt, halting, spavined; touched in the wind, broken-winded, gasping; injured, decrepit etc. (impaired) 659.12; weakly, feeble, unsteady etc. (weak) 160.10–15; incurable etc. (hopeless) 859.7; helpless, *hors de combat* [F.] etc. (impotent) 158.8, 9.

25. *adj.* diseased, morbid, tainted, contaminated, vitiated, peccant, corrupt; cankered, ulcerated, gangrened, mortified, sphacelate, carious; poisoned, septic(al); tabid, tabetic, tabescent; syntectic(al); leprous; mangy; palsied, paralytic; syphilitic, luetic; pneumonic, pulmonic, phthisic(al), consumptive, rachitic; tubercular, tuberculous; dropsical, hydropic(al); edematous, edematose;

tumorous, tumefacient, tumescent; gouty, podagric; dyspeptic; varicose; contagious etc. 657.5.

656. Salubrity
(See 657. Insalubrity; also 655. Health)

1. *n.* salubrity, salubriousness, wholesomeness, healthfulness etc. *adj.*
2. *n.* hygiene, hygienics, hygiantics [rare], hygiastics [rare], hygiology, hygeology [rare], hygeiolatry [rare]; hygienization, sanitation; pure air, wholesome food, nourishment, exercise, tonic; immunity.
3. *n.* hygienist, hygieist *or* hygeist, hygiologist; sanitarian, sanitarist; valetudinarianist.
4. *v.* be salubrious etc. *adj.,* make for health, conduce to health, be good for, agree with.
5. *adj.* salubrious, salutary, salutiferous [rare], wholesome, healthful, healthy, beneficial, benign, good, good for; tonic, bracing, invigorating, roborant, corroborant; nutritious, nutritive; sanitary, prophylactic; hygienic, hygienal [rare], hygiantic [rare], hygiastic [rare], hygiestic [rare]; Hygeian; sanative etc. (remedial) 662.25; restorative etc. 660.18; useful etc. 644.5.
6. *adj.* innoxious etc. (harmless) 648.13.

657. Insalubrity
(See 656. Salubrity)

1. *n.* insalubrity, insalubriousness, unwholesomeness, unhealthfulness etc. *adj.*; plague spot, pesthole; death in the pot; poisonousness, toxicity; poison etc. 663.4–6; contagion etc. (infection) 655.2.
2. *v.* be insalubrious etc. *adj.,* not be good for etc. 656.4, disagree with; shorten one's days.
3. *adj.* insalubrious, unhealthful, unhealthy, unhealthsome, unwholesome, noxious, noisome, deleterious, bad; morbific(al), morbiferous; septic; virulent, venomous, envenomed, poisonous, mephitic(al); toxic, toxicant, toxiferous; narcotic(al), narcotinic; septic, putrefactive, putrefacient; baneful etc. 663.7; harmful etc. (bad) 649.8–11; deadly etc. (mortal) 361.16.
4. *adj.* innutritious, unnutritious [rare]; indigestible, undigestible [rare]; ungenial, uncongenial.
5. *adj.* contagious, infectious, catching, taking, communicable, inoculable, zymotic; pestilent [now rare], pestilential, pestiferous; epidemic, epizootic, pandemic; endemic(al), endemial [rare]; sporadic, sporadial [rare].

658. Improvement
(See 659. Deterioration)

1. *n.* improvement, melioration, amelioration, betterment; mend, amendment, emendation, mending etc. *v.*; advance, advancement; progress, progression, headway; promotion, perfection, preferment, furtherance, enrichment, enhancement, development, up [coll.]; rise etc. (ascent) 305; lift etc. (elevation) 307; increase etc. 35; revival, recovery, repair etc. (restoration) 660; purification etc. 652.2.
2. *n.* cultivation, culture, *Kultur* [G.], refinement, polish; menticulture [rare], mind culture, cultivation of the mind, march of intellect; race culture, civilization, acculturation; euthenics, eugenics; culture zone.
3. *n.* revision, revisal, revise, revised edition *or* version, new edition *or* issue; correction, rectification, emendation, amendment; re-examination, review, reconsideration, second thoughts; *limae labor* [L.].
4. *n.* reform, reformation; reformism; progressivism, progressism; radical reform, radicalism, revolutionary socialism, Bolshevism; reformandum; new leaf; reformatory, reform school; regeneration etc. (revival) 660.2.
5. *n.* reformer, reformist, reformado;

---

656. Early to bed and early to rise, / Makes a man healthy, wealthy and wise.—FRANKLIN. The preservation of health is a duty. Few seem conscious that there is such a thing as physical morality.—SPENCER. Hygiene is the only useful part of medicine.—ROUSSEAU. An apple a day keeps the doctor away.
657. The contagion of a sick mind affects the body.—OVID. The contagion of crime is like that of the plague.—NAPOLEON. Sickness is catching.—SHAKESPEARE. What's one man's poison, signior, / Is another's meat or drink.—BEAUMONT AND FLETCHER.
658. Human improvement is from within outwards.—FROUDE. Culture would not be culture if it were not an acquired taste.—J. C. POWYS. The longing to be primitive is a dis-

progressive, progressivist, progressionist, progressist [now rare]; radical, red; Bolshevik, Bolshevist, Bolshie [coll.].

6. *v.* improve, become *or* get better; meliorate, ameliorate; mend, amend; look up [coll.], advance, progress, make progress, ∼ headway etc. *n.,* get *or* go ahead, make strides *or* rapid strides, make up for lost time, run *or* shoot up; mature, develop, ripen, fructify; pick up, come about *or* round, rally, take a favorable turn, take a turn for the better, turn over a new leaf, turn the corner, raise one's head, gain strength; have sown one's wild oats; rise, climb etc. (ascend) 305.4, 5; lift, uplift etc. (elevate) 307.5; increase etc. 35.3; recuperate etc. 689; recover etc. 660.15; return to health etc. 654.3.

7. *v.* profit by, be better for, be improved by, reap the benefit of, make capital out of, make good use of, make the most of, turn to right *or* good account, place to good account, set off to advantage, improve the occasion.

8. *v.* render better etc. *adj.,* better; meliorate, ameliorate; improve, make an improvement etc. *n.,* improve upon, refine upon, refine, elaborate, develop, perfect, promote, cultivate, advance, forward, bring forward, bring on, enhance, fatten, enrich, mellow; mend, amend, emend, emendate; rectify, correct; lift, uplift, inspire; civilize; repair, remedy, cure etc. (restore) 660.8–14; purify etc. 652.9; benefit, help etc. 648.6.

9. *v.* refresh, revive etc. (resuscitate) 660.13, (reinvigorate) 689.2.

10. *v.* touch up, brush up, furbish up, vamp up, warm up; rub up, brighten up, polish, shine [coll.]; put in order etc. (arrange) 60.6.

11. *v.* revise, redact, edit, digest, review, correct, make corrections, make improvements etc. *n.*; amend, emend, emendate; revise one's thoughts, reconsider, view in a new light, think better of.

12. *v.* reform, reclaim, reorganize, remodel etc. (restore) 660.8–14.

13. *v.* palliate, mitigate etc. (relieve) 834.4.

14. *adj.* improved, bettered etc. *v.*;

better, preferable, better off, better for, all the better for; better-advised.

15. *adj.* improving, advancing etc. *v.*; progressive, ongoing, forward-looking, go-ahead [coll.]; on the mend, on the upgrade; reformatory, reformative, reformational, reformationary [rare]; cultural, accultural; emendatory, corrective etc. (remedial) 662.25; reparatory etc. (restorative) 660.18.

16. *adj.* improvable, corrigible, correctable, amendable, remediable, curable, sanable [rare], restorable, recoverable, retrievable.

17. *adv.* on reconsideration, on second thoughts, on better advice, *ad melius inquirendum* [L.].

659. Deterioration
(See 658. Improvement)

1. *n.* deterioration, debasement, decadence *or* decadency, devolution, degradation; retrogradation, retrogression, retrocession; degeneration, degeneracy, degenerateness; depravation, depravement [rare], depravedness, demoralization; decline, declination, declension, falling off etc. *v.,* wane, ebb; recidivism, recidivity, perversion, diversion; recidivation; backsliding etc. (relapse) 661; decrease etc. 36; waste etc. 638; decrepitude, caducity etc. (senility) 499.5; depravity etc. (vice) 945; disease etc. 655.

2. *n.* decay, decomposition, disintegration, dissolution, resolution, catalysis [rare], breakup, disorganization, corruption, dilapidation, ravages of time, wear, wear and tear, erosion, corrosion, consumption, waste, attenuation, marcescence, marasmus, atrophy; putrefaction, putrescence, putridity; rot, rottenness; caries [Med.], cariosity; necrosis; mold, moldiness, blue mold, black mold; mucor [rare], must, mildew, dry rot; canker, rust, "moth and rust" (Bible); worm, moth etc. (blight) 663.2; fetor etc. 401; abrasion etc. (pulverization) 330.2.

3. *n.* impairment, damage, *damnum* [L.], injury, harm, hurt, hurting, scath *or* scathe [arch. and dial.], labefaction *or* labefactation, loss, detriment; outrage, havoc, inroad, ravage, devastation, deso-

---

ease of culture.—SANTAYANA. Progress is / The law of life.—BROWNING. Acorns were good until bread was found.—BACON. Every day, in every way, I am getting better and better.—COUÉ.

659. What a falling off was there!—SHAKESPEARE. Whoever degrades another degrades me.—WHITMAN. All that is human must retrograde if it does not advance.—GIBBON.

lation; poisoning, blood poisoning, venenation [rare], ptomaine poisoning; corruption, vitiation, pollution, contamination, defedation [now rare], defilement; adulteration, sophistication, alloy; perversion, prostitution; breakdown, collapse; destruction etc. 162.

4. *n.* wound, trauma; incision, cut, scratch, gash; puncture, stab; laceration, mutilation; abrasion, scuff, scuff-burn, mat-burn, floor-burn; bruise, discoloration, black-and-blue mark, black eye; burn, first ~, second *or* third degree burn; mortal wound, *immedicabile vulnus* [L.]; scab; scar, cicatrice, blemish, pock; sore etc. 655.16.

5. *n.* wreck, mere wreck, wreck of one's former self, jade, rackabones [U.S.], skate [U.S.], tacky *or* tackey [South. U.S.], plug [slang or coll., U.S.].

6. *v.* deteriorate, become *or* grow worse etc. *adj.,* impair [now rare], degenerate, fall off, go off [coll.], retrograde, retrogress, decline, wane, ebb, subside, droop, lapse, sink, go down, go downhill; run to waste, run to seed; go to the bad, go to pot [coll.], go to the dogs, go to the deuce *or* devil [slang], go to glory [coll.], go to perdition, go to smash, go all to smash [coll.], go to sticks *or* sticks and staves [slang]; go from bad to worse, go farther and fare worse, jump out of the frying pan into the fire, avoid Scylla and fall into Charybdis.

fade, wither, shrivel, dry up, sear, fall "into the sere, the yellow leaf" (Shakespeare); wizen, wizzen [obs. exc. dial.]; break, bust [dial.], burst, spring a leak, crack, craze, start; break down, collapse, cave in, totter, topple, topple down *or* over, topple *or* totter to its fall, tremble *or* nod to its fall; be the worse for, be the worse for wear, have seen better days; backslide etc. (relapse) 661.3; perish etc. 162.5; die etc. 360.6; age etc. 128.8; afflict etc. 655.22.

7. *v.* decay, go *or* fall into decay, cause to decay, decompose, disintegrate, undergo dissolution, go *or* fall to pieces, break up, crumble, crumble into dust, erode, corrode, rust, oxidize, wear, wear out *or* away, waste, waste away, consume away; gnaw, eat, eat away, gnaw at the root of;

canker, cankereat; rot, putrefy, putresce, corrupt, spoil, go bad, fester, rankle, mortify, sphacelate, gangrene; mold, molder, mildew.

8. *v.* impair, make worse etc. *adj.,* put back, deteriorate, damage, endamage, injure, harm, hurt, scath *or* scathe [arch. and dial.], shend, spoil, mar; labefy, labefact [both rare]; play the deuce, ~ devil *or* mischief with [coll.], play havoc *or* sad havoc with, play the very devil with [coll.]; cripple, becripple, maim, lame, hock, hough, hamstring, hog-tie [coll., U.S.], tie hand and foot, handcuff, scotch, cramp; wound, stab, pierce, scratch, lacerate, mangle, mutilate, disfigure, bruise, blemish, deface, scar; deal a blow to, buffet, maul, batter, hit between wind and water; sprain, strain; blight, blast; sap, mine, undermine, shake, sap the foundations of.

break, bust [dial.], burst; crack, craze; break up, break ~, tear etc. to pieces, laniate [rare], break (all) to flinderation [slang], break (all) to smithers *or* smithereens [chiefly coll.], shatter, shiver, smash, crush, make mincemeat of; ravage, despoil, devastate, desolate, dilapidate; waste, lay waste; decimate; disorganize, dismantle, dismast; blunt, blunt the edge of; weaken etc. 160.8; disable etc. 158.6; destroy etc. 162.4; afflict etc. 655.22.

9. *v.* corrupt, debase, degrade, deprave, debauch, deflower, defile, contaminate, pollute, vitiate, infect, taint, canker, ulcerate; denaturalize, leaven, alloy, adulterate, sophisticate, tamper with, doctor [coll.], prejudice; pervert, warp, prostitute; demoralize, brutalize etc. (render vicious) 945.10; stain etc. (dirty) 653.15.

10. *v.* poison, empoison, venenate [rare], envenom.

11. *adj.* deteriorating, crumbling, declining etc. *v.*; retrogressive, retrograde, degenerate, decadent; *fin de siècle* [F.]; on the wane, on the decline, on the downgrade, on the downward track; tottering, nodding to its fall; injurious etc. (harmful) 649.10.

12. *adj.* impaired, deteriorated, hurt, injured etc. *v.*; altered for the worst, worse, the worse for, all the worse for, the worse for wear, worn, shopworn, shelfworn, worn to a shadow *or* thread, worn to rags, worn to the stump, timeworn, passé, shabby, seedy [coll.], tacky [coll.,

---

Where one man advances, hundreds retrograde; and the balance is always in favor of universal deterioration.—PEACOCK. A general flavor of mild decay.—HOLMES.

U.S.], threadbare, ragged, frayed, weathered, weather-beaten, battered, dilapidated, ramshackle, tumble-down, broken-down; secondhand, hand-me-down, reach-me-down [both slang]; faded, washed-out, run-down, laid low, at a low ebb, in a bad way, far-gone, on one's last legs; reduced, reduced to a skeleton.

wasted, wilted, withered, marcescent; deciduous; tabid, tabetic, tabescent; broken, out of repair, ~ order *or* condition, out of commission [coll.], out of whack [slang], out of tune, sprung, shaken; decrepit, worn-out, used up [coll.], fit for the dust hole *or* wastepaper basket; done, done up, done for [all coll.]; effete, spent, exhausted; crippled, lame etc. (infirm) 655.24; feeble, unsteady, unsound etc. (weak) 160.10–13; imperfect etc. 651.4; beyond hope, past cure etc. (hopeless) 859.7; useless etc. 645.8.

13. *adj.* decayed, decomposed, putrified etc. *v.*; putrid, putrefactive, putrescent; rotten, corrupt, peccant, bad, gone bad, carious, cankered, mortified, sphacelate, gangrened, rotten as a pear *or* cheese, rotten at *or* to the core; saprogenic, saprogenous, saprophilous, saprophytic; blighted, flyblown, maggoty, moth-eaten, worm-eaten; moldy *or* mouldy, moldering *or* mouldering, moss-grown, mildewed; musty, fusty, frowy, frowzy, frowsty [dial. Eng. and coll.]; stale, rancid, reasy *or* reasty [obs. exc. dial.], reechy [dial., Eng.], tainted, touched, off; rusty, rust-eaten, rust-worn, rust-cankered.

660. Restoration
(See 661. Relapse)

1. *n.* restoration, restoral [rare], restorance [obs.]; *rifacimento* [It.], restitution, reinstatement, reinvestment, replacement, rehabilitation, re-establishment, reconstitution, readjustment, reorganization, redintegration; reclamation, retrieval, recuperation, redemption, salvation, salvage; recovery, comeback [coll.], return; improvement etc. 658; relief etc. 834.

2. *n.* revival, revivement [rare], reviviscence *or* revivescence; renovation, renewal; resuscitation, reanimation, revivification, reversion, reconversion, resurrection; renaissance, renascence; rebirth, new birth; rejuvenation, rejuvenescence, second youth; regeneration, regeneracy, regenerateness, regenesis, palingenesis; resurgence, resurgency [rare]; resumption, *résumption* [F.]; refreshment etc. 689; reproduction etc. 163; recurrence etc. (repetition) 104; reform etc. 658.4; vivification etc. 359.4.

3. *n.* reconstruction, remaking etc. *v.*, recreation, remodelment; re-formation, reformation.

4. *n.* reparation, repair; repairing, mending, tinkering etc. *v.*; trouble shooting [coll.]; rectification, correction, redress, making right etc. *v.*, satisfaction, compensation.

5. *n.* cure, recure [obs.], sanation [obs.]; curing, healing etc. *v.*; partial ~, attempted ~, radical ~, perfect ~, certain etc. cure; instauration; cicatrization; disinfection; convalescence, recuperation; recruital, recruiting etc. *v.*, recruitment; sanativeness etc. *adj.*; corrective, restorative, panacea etc. (remedy) 662.

6. *n.* curableness, restorableness etc. *adj.*; curability, reparability, retrievability, recoverability.

7. *n.* mender, fixer, doctor [coll.], repairer, repairman; trouble man, trouble shooter [coll.]; renovator *or* renovater, revivor [obs.], reviver, renewer; carpenter, plumber, mechanic, tinker etc. (craftsman) 690.5–10; cobbler etc. 225.40; physician etc. 662.19.

8. *v.* restore, put back, replace, reinstate, re-establish, re-estate, reinstall, rehabilitate, reconstitute, reorganize, readjust, place *in statu quo* [L.]; convert, reconvert; reintegrate, make whole; refit, recruit, fill up, fill up the ranks, reinforce; return, recoup etc. 790.3.

9. *v.* redeem, reclaim, recover, retrieve, ransom; rescue etc. (deliver) 672.2.

10. *v.* remedy, rectify, correct, redress, make good *or* right, make all square, put *or* set right *or* to rights, put *or* set straight, set up; right etc. 922.3; better etc. (improve) 658.8.

11. *v.* repair, mend, fix, fix up [coll.],

---

660. It is part of the cure to wish to be cured.—SENECA. And his hand was restored whole as the other.—BIBLE. For of the most high cometh healing.—BIBLE. Physician, heal thyself.—BIBLE. The first was called Dr. Diet, the second Dr. Quiet, the third Dr. Merryman.—W. BULLEIN. With the help of a surgeon, he might yet recover.—SHAKESPEARE.

doctor [coll.], remedy etc. *above* 660.10, put in repair, put in shape *or* condition, retouch, botch, do up, patch up, plaster up, service, overhaul; vamp, vamp up, revamp; tinker, tinker up; cobble; splice, bandage, bind up wounds, dress; stanch, calk, careen; darn, fine-draw, heelpiece.

12. *v.* cure, recure, work a cure, kill or cure, heal, restore to health, remedy etc. *above* 660.10, relieve, stay, break of, bring round, set on one's feet *or* legs, snatch from the jaws of death; set, knit.

13. *v.* revive, revivify, resuscitate, reanimate, recall to life, recondition, regenerate, rejuvenate, put *or* infuse new blood *or* life into; renew; renovate, renovize; rewarm, warm up *or* over, rekindle, reheat the ashes, stir the embers; reinvigorate etc. (refresh) 689.2; vivify 359.8; repeat etc. 104.4.

14. *v.* reconstruct, reform, recreate, refashion, remake, make over, rebuild, build afresh *or* anew; remodel, new-model.

15. *v.* recover, rally, revive, return, come round, pull through, weather the storm, be oneself again, get well, get round, get the better of, get up, get about, get over; survive, live to light again; come to, come to oneself, come to life again, rise from the grave *or* one's ashes, resurrect [rare], rise again, live again; resurge, resume, reappear; recuperate etc. 689.3; improve etc. 658.6.

16. *v.* heal, heal over, skin over, cicatrize, heal *or* right itself.

17. *adj.* restored, renewed, remedied etc. *v.*; redivivus, renascent; convalescent, in a fair way, none the worse.

18. *adj.* restorative, restoratory [rare], restoring etc. *v.*; restitutive, restitutory; analeptic(al); reparative, reparatory; recuperative, recuperatory; revivatory, reviviscible [rare], reviviscent; sanative, sanatory; curative etc. (remedial) 662.25; relieving etc. 834.7; salubrious etc. 656.5; improving etc. 658.15; refreshing etc. 689.4.

19. *adj.* restorable, recoverable, remediable etc. (improvable) 658.16.

661. Relapse
(See 660. Restoration)

1. *n.* relapse, lapse, falling back etc. *v.*; backsliding, backslide; fall, fall from grace; recidivation, recidivism, recidivity; recrudescence *or* recrudescency, re-crudency; perversion, declension, reversion etc. 145; retrogression, retrogradation etc. (regression) 283; deterioration etc. 659; apostasy etc. 607.2.

2. *n.* backslider, recidivist, pervert etc. (apostate) 607.5.

3. *v.* relapse, lapse, backslide, slide back, slip back, sink back, fall back, have a relapse, be overcome, be overtaken, yield again to, fall again into, return; recidive, recidivate [rare]; fall, fall from grace; retrograde etc. (regress) 283.5; retrovert etc. 145.4; deteriorate etc. 659.6, 7.

4. *adj.* relapsing, backsliding etc. *v.*; recidivous, recidivistic, recrudescent; retrograde etc. (regressive) 283.7; apostate etc. 607.11.

662. Remedy
(See 663. Bane)

1. *n.* remedy, cure, corrective, relief, help, aid, assistance, redress [obs.]; restorative, analeptic; specific, specific remedy; alterant, alterative; sovereign remedy; curing, healing etc. 660.5.

2. *n.* nostrum, recipe, receipt, prescription; patent medicine, quack remedy.

3. *n.* panacea, universal remedy, cure-all, heal-all, allheal [obs.], catholicon, panchreston [obs.], panpharmacon *or* pampharmacon [rare], panace [rare], panax [rare], polychrest, elixir, *elixir vitae* [ML.], elixir of life, philosophers' stone.

4. *n.* medicine, medicinal, medicament; physic, drug, pharmacon, potion; elixir, balsam, balm, cordial, tisane *or* ptisan; dose, draft *or* draught; pill, bolus; electuary, confection, conserve; lincture, linctus; simple; pharmacopoeia, dispensatory.

5. *n.* tonic, stimulant, bracer, reviver [slang], roborant, pick-me-up [coll.]; smelling salts, aromatic spirits of ammonia, coffee, tea, alcohol.

6. *n.* palliative, alleviative, sedative, lenitive, calmative, anodyne, paregoric, demulcent, emollient, balm; assuasive, as-

---

661. To what relapse / Unlook'd for are we fallen!—MILTON.   No man, having put his hand to the plow, and looking back, is fit for the kingdom of God.—BIBLE.
662. *Temporis ars medicina fere est* [The art of medicine is usually a matter of time].—OVID. Extreme remedies are very appropriate for ex-

suager; abirritant, embrocation, lotion, liniment, salve, ointment, anointment [obs.], unguent, unguentum, oil; olive oil; petroleum jelly, petrolatum, vaseline; cerate, gum arabic; arnica; glycerin or glycerine, glycerol, glycerole; glycerogel, glycerogelatin, glycerin jelly; traumatic, harquebusade, vulnerary; fomentation; collyrium, eyesalve, eyewater, eyewash; soothing sirup, cough sirup; anaphrodisiac; chloroform etc. (anesthetic) 376.2; sleep-inducer etc. 683.6; poultice etc. *below* 662.14; moderator etc. 174.3.

7. *n.* narcotic, opiate, drug, dope [slang]; opium, hop *or* hops [low, U.S.], gow *or* ghow [cant, U.S.]; hemp, Indian hemp, bhang [Ind.], ganja [Ind.], canabis, hashish; morphine, cocaine, novocain, Heroin, snow [slang, U.S.], nepenthe *or* nepenthes, laudanum, atropine, stramonium, hyoscyamus, marijuana *or* marihuana; knockout drops, mickey finn [both slang, U.S.].

8. *n.* prophylactic, preventive, preventative, protective; antiseptic, germicide, bactericide, disinfectant; dentifrice, tooth paste *or* powder; mouthwash, gargle; fumigant, fumigator; iodine, Mercurochrome [trade name], benzoic acid, peroxide, alcohol, boric acid.

9. *n.* cathartic, physic, purgative, apeient, deobstruent, laxative; carminative; calomel, salts; Epsom salts, castor oil, mineral oil, mineral water.

10. *n.* emetic, vomitive, vomit; nauseant.

11. *n.* vermifuge, anthelmintic, helminthic, helminthagogue.

12. *n.* counteractive, counteractant, counteragent; antidote, antipoison, mithidate [old Pharm.], alexipharmic, alexteric, theriaca *or* theriac, counterpoison, antivenin *or* antivenene; serum, antierum, antibody; antifebrile, febrifuge; antispasmodic; counterirritant, sinapism, vesicatory etc. *below* 662.14.

13. *n.* suppurative, suppurant; maturtive, maturant; vesicatory etc. *below*.

14. *n.* dressing, bandaging; plaster, *emplastrum* [L.], court plaster; compress, pledget, poultice, cataplasm, epithem, sinapism, stupe, dossil, tent; tampon, tampion *or* tompion; vesicatory, vesicant; fingerstall; bandage, band, binder, cravat, brace, roller, fillet, tourniquet; sling, splint; tape, adhesive tape; lint, cotton, absorbent cotton, gauze, sponge.

15. *n.* treatment, medical treatment; regimen, regime; diet, dietary, dietetics; *vis medicatrix* [L.], *vis medicatrix naturae* [L.], *vis naturae* [L.]; *médecine expectante* [F.]; first aid; bloodletting, bleeding, venesection, phlebotomy, cupping, sanguisuge, leeches; operation, surgical operation, the knife [coll.], major *or* minor operation; electrolysis, electrolyzation.

16. *n.* healing art, leechcraft [arch.], acology; medicine, materia medica; therapeutics, therapy, vocational therapy; pharmacy, pharmacology, pharmaceutics; posology, dosology; gynecology, gyniatrics, gynecological therapeutics; surgery, chirurgery [arch.]; orthopedics, orthopedia, orthopraxy, orthopraxis, orthopedic surgery; constitutional therapy, organotherapy, sarcology [rare].

naturopathy; hydrotherapy, hydropathy, cold-water cure; psychotherapy, psychotherapeutics, psychopathology; psychiasis, faith healing *or* cure, mind cure; Christian Science, theotherapy, divine healing; radiotherapy, heliotherapy; serotherapy, serum therapy; aerotherapy, pneumatotherapy; dentistry, surgical dentistry; obstetrics, tocology, tocogony, midwifery; chiropody, chiropodistry; chiropractics, chiropraxis; osteopathy, chiroplasty, allopathy, homeopathy, eclecticism, heteropathy, pediatrics; pathology, nosology etc. 655.19; hygiene etc. 656.2.

17. *n.* hospital, *hôpital* [F.], infirmary, sick berth *or* bay [Naut.]; valetudinary [rare], valetudinarium [chiefly Rom. Antiq.]; clinic, *clinique* [F.], polyclinic; general hospital, *hôtel-Dieu* [F.]; special hospital, ward; cancer ∼, children's ∼, dental ∼, fever ∼, maternity ∼ *or* lying-in ∼, ophthalmic etc. hospital *or* ward; psychopathic hospital *or* ward, psychiatry; pesthouse, lazar house, lazaretto, lazaret; lock hospital [Eng.]; *maison de santé* [F.], *hôtel des invalides* [F.]; sanitarium, sanatorium; health resort, spa, watering place, baths, springs, mineral

---

reme diseases.—HIPPOCRATES. The fruit thereof [tree] shall be for meat, and the leaf thereof for medicine.—BIBLE. Throw physic to the dogs, I'll none of it.—SHAKE-SPEARE. You rub the sore, / When you should bring the plaster.—SHAKESPEARE. The cure is worse than the disease.—MASSINGER. Learn from the beasts the physic of

662.17 – 662.27

springs, warm *or* hot springs, thermae, pump room, well; hospice, *hospitium* [L.] (*pl. hospitia*), asylum, home; Red Cross; sickroom; sickbed; ambulance; insane asylum etc. 503.8.

18. *n.* pharmacy, dispensary, dispensatory, druggery, chemist's shop [Eng.], apothecary's shop; drugstore etc. (restaurant) 298.42.

19. *n.* doctor, doc [coll.], physician, physicianer, physicker [coll.], leech [arch.], medical practitioner, medical man, medic, medical [coll.], medico [coll.], mediciner [now rare], med [slang], croaker [slang, U.S.], disciple of Aesculapius; medicine man, medicine; general practitioner, g. p. *or* G. P. [coll., Eng.], specialist.

internist, gynecologist, orthopedist, chiropodist, anesthetist, hydropathist, dermatologist, consultant, medical attendant, dresser, bonesetter; surgeon, chirugeon [arch.], sawbones [slang, U.S.]; plastic surgeon; operator, operative surgeon *or* dentist; aurist, otologist; oculist, ophthalmologist, optometrist; dentist, toothdrawer; dental surgeon; osteopath, osteopathist; chiropractor, **chiropractic; psychiatrist,** neurologist; Mind-healer, Christian Science practitioner; obstetrician, *accoucheur* [*masc.*, F.], *accoucheuse* [*fem.*, F.], midwife, granny [South. U.S.], gamp [coll.]; mental healer, faith curer, faith-curist, faith healer.

medical examiner, coroner; horse doctor, horse leech [arch.], farrier [obs.], veterinary, veterinarian, vet [coll.]; medicaster, medicine monger, horse doctor [derog.], *médecin tant pis* [F.], quack, quacksalver, medical charlatan; medical student, medic [coll.], medico [coll.]; intern, resident; Hippocrates, Aesculapius, Galen; masseur etc. 331.2.

20. *n.* nurse, sister, nursing sister, granny [South. U.S.]; trained nurse, graduate nurse; practical nurse, district nurse, monthly nurse; probe [slang], probationist, probationer; nursemaid etc. (guardian) 664.3.

21. *n.* pharmacist, pharmaceutist, pharmacopolist, druggist, chemist [Eng.], chemist and druggist [Eng.], pharmaceutical chemist, apothecary, dispenser, posologist.

22. *n.* (instruments) stethoscope, stethometer, stethograph; spirometer, respirometer, pneumeter, pneumatometer, spirograph, pneumatograph; sphygmometer, sphygmograph; pulmotor, lungmotor; thermometer etc. 389.

23. *v.* remedy, cure, repair etc. (restore) 660.8–13.

24. *v.* apply a remedy etc. *n.*, remedy, doctor [coll.], minister to, attend, treat, nurse; medicate, physic, drug, dope [slang], dose, drench with physic; dress the wounds, bandage, poultice, plaster, strap, splint; bleed, cup, leech; let blood, transfuse; fill, extract; manicure, pedicure; massage, rub; consult, specialize, operate, anesthetize, straighten, mold, deliver, electrolyze; palliate etc. (relieve) 834.4; prevent etc. (avert) 706.5.

25. *adj.* remedial, curative, healing, corrective, emendatory, analeptic(al), alterative; sanative, sanatory; medical, medicinal, therapeutic; therial, theriacal; surgical, chirurgical [arch.]; antidotal, alexiteric, alexipharmic(al); febrifugal, antifebrile; antiluetic, antisyphilitic; vermifugal, anthelmintic, helminthic; prophylactic, preventive, protective; aseptic, antiseptic, germicidal, bactericidal, disinfectant; detersive, detergent, abstersive, abstergent.

purifying, cleansing; depurative, depuratory; cathartic, laxative, aperient, purgative, deobstruent; carminative; emetic, vomitive, vomitory; neurotic; tonic, bracing, invigorating, roborant, corroborant; palliative, lenitive, paregoric(al), abirritative, anodyne, assuasive, balsamic, demulcent, emollient, sedative, calmative, calmant, narcotic; hypnotic, soporific, soporiferous, soporose *or* soporous; traumatic, vulnerary; allopathic, homeopathic, eclectic, hydropathic, heteropathic, electrolytic(al); restorative etc. 660.18; improving etc. 658.15; salutary etc. (salubrious) 656.5; relieving etc. 834.7.

26. *adj.* dietetic(al), dietary; alimentary, alimental; nutritious, nutritive; digestive, digestible, peptic(al).

27. *adj.* remediable, curable etc. (improvable) 658.16.

---

the field.—Pope. God heals, and the Doctor takes the fee.—Franklin. It is the sick who need medicine and not the well.—Jefferson.

Many dishes, many diseases; many medicines, few cures.—Franklin.

663. Bane
(See 662. Remedy)

1. *n.* bane, curse, cause of harm, torment, thorn in the flesh *or* side, pea in the shoe, pest, pestilence, afflictive evil, affliction, infliction, plague, scourge; infestation, infestment; cross, burden, burthen [arch.]; hereditary evil, *damnosa hereditas* [L.]; bête noire, bugbear, white elephant, skeleton in the closet, snake in the grass; *amari aliquid* [L.], gall, gall of bitterness, gall and wormwood; mischief, woe etc. (evil) 649.2; nuisance, vexation etc. 830.2; disease etc. 655; thorn, nettle etc. (point) 253.2; viper, demon etc. (evildoer) 913; adversity etc. 735.

2. *n.* blight, blast; rust, smut, fungus (*pl.* fungi), bacteria, moth, "moth and rust" (Bible), worm, worm in the apple *or* rose, worm at the heart of the rose, canker, cancer; locust, cankerworm etc. (insects) 366.23, 24; mildew, dry rot etc. (decay) 659.2.

3. *n.* sting, stinger; fang, tang [now dial.]; bee sting, snake bite.

4. *n.* poison, leaven, virus, venom, venin, toxic, toxicant, intoxicant [now rare]; deliriant, delirifacient; poisonousness, toxicity; toxicology; poisoning etc. (infection) 655.2.

5. *n.* (poisons) arsenic, prussic acid, antimony, tartar emetic, strychnine, nicotine, azote [rare], aconite, arsenious oxide, arsenious acid, bichloride of mercury, carbonic acid, cyanide of potassium, carbolic acid, corrosive sublimate, nitrogen; hydrocyanide, hydrocyanic acid; tannin, tannic acid; chlorine, chlorine dioxide *or* peroxide; rat poison, ratsbane; mephitic air *or* gas, carbonic gas, carbon monoxide, carbon dioxide; malaria, miasm *or* miasma, effluvium, mephitis; poison gas, coal gas, chokedamp etc. (gas) 334.2.

6. *n.* (poisonous plants) nux vomica, hellebore, upas, henbane, mescal, foxglove, death camass, monkshood, sheep laurel, May apple, opium poppy, poison sumac, castor-oil plant, Jimson weed, pokeweed, locoweed, poison ivy, Gastrolobium, Swainsona, greyana; hemlock, poison hemlock, water hemlock; nightshade, black nightshade, deadly nightshade, belladonna, banewort; Congo tobacco, hemp, Indian hemp, Albany hemp; bhang [Ind.], opium etc. (narcotic) 662.7.

7. *adj.* baneful etc. (harmful) 649.10; poisonous etc. (insalubrious) 657.3.

664. Safety
(See 665. Danger; also 666. Safeguard, Refuge)

1. *n.* safety, safeness etc. *adj.*, security, surety; danger past *or* over, storm blown over, clear coast; assurance, confidence etc. (sense of security) 858.

2. *n.* protection, safekeeping, safeguard [arch.]; protectorship, guardianship, guardiancy [rare], tutelage, guidance, patronage, custody, auspices, care, heed, keep [arch.], keeping, charge; ward, wardage [rare], wardship, wardenship, watch and ward; safe-conduct, warrant of security, pass, passport, *passe-partout* [F.]; preservation etc. 670; defense etc. 717; precaution etc. (preparation) 673, (warning) 668.

3. *n.* protector, protectress, *protectrix* [ML.]; guardian, governor [slang], patron, warden, warder, custodian, custodier [now chiefly Scot.], *custos* [L.], keeper, caretaker, curator; gamekeeper; ranger, rangeman, range rider [chiefly West. U.S.]; castellan; safe-conduct, escort, convoy, bodyguard, retainer, burkundaz [Ind.]; chaperon, shap [slang], gooseberry [slang], third person; duenna, governess; nurse, nursemaid, nurserymaid, nursegirl, *bonne* [F.], amah [Oriental], ayah [Ind.], mammy [U.S.], granny [South. U.S.], dry nurse, wet nurse; lifesaver [coll.], lifeguard; guardian angel, tutelary god etc. (familiar spirit) 979.10; defender, guard etc. 717.5, 6; national guard, militia etc. (army) 726.6; jailer etc. 753; tutor etc. (teacher) 540; constable etc. 745.10; safeguard etc. 666.1, 2.

4. *v.* be safe etc. *adj.*, keep one's head

---

663. My bane and my antidote are both before me.—ADDISON.   Loathsome canker lives in sweetest bud.—SHAKESPEARE.   One drop of poison infecteth the whole tun of wine.—LYLY.   Venom destroys venom.—LANGLAND.   Then, venom, to thy work.—SHAKESPEARE.

664. Out of this nettle, danger, we pluck this flower, safety.—SHAKESPEARE.   I would give all my fame for a pot of ale and safety.—SHAKESPEARE.   Early and provident fear is the mother of safety.—BURKE.   He who fights and runs away / May live to fight another

above water, ride out *or* weather the storm, tide over, save one's bacon [coll.], light upon one's feet; bear a charmed life, possess nine lives; escape etc. 671.6.

5. *v.* save etc. (preserve) 670.3, (deliver) 672.2, (economize) 817.3.

6. *v.* protect, render safe etc. *adj.*, guard, safeguard, ward [arch.], shield, shelter, screen, cover, shroud, cloak, panoply; harbor, ensconce, house, nestle; flank; watch over, keep watch over; support, take charge of, foster, nurse, ride herd on [slang, West. U.S.]; garrison, man the garrison; intrench *or* entrench, dig in; mine, countermine; take care of etc. 459.6; defend etc. 717.7, 8; fence round etc. (circumscribe) 229.2; secure etc. (bind) 751.7; preserve etc. 670.3, 4; convoy, chaperon etc. (escort) 88.7.

7. *v.* watch, tout [slang], keep watch, keep watch and ward, keep vigil, keep guard, keep tout [slang]; mount guard, perform sentry go, go on one's beat, patrol; be on one's guard etc. (be vigilant) 459.4.

8. *v.* seek safety etc. *n.*, take shelter, seek refuge etc. 666.3, break for the woods, break for the tall timber [U.S.], fly to, run into port; find refuge etc. 666.5.

9. *v.* take precautions, look before one leaps etc. (be cautious) 864.4; prepare for etc. 673.7.

10. *adj.* safe, free from danger etc. 665, safe and sound, sure [now rare], secure, in safety *or* security, in shelter, in harbor *or* port, at anchor, in the shadow of a rock, on sure ground, on terra firma, high and dry, above water, on the safe side, out of danger, out of the meshes, out of harm's reach *or* way; under cover, under lock and key; *cavendo tutus* [L.]; unthreatened, unmolested, unhazarded; not dangerous (*see* dangerous etc. 665.7), unhazardous, unperilous, sound, reliable, trustworthy, dependable, unprecarious, steady, stable, firm, "founded upon a rock" (Bible); airworthy; seaworthy, sea-kindly, snug; uninjured etc. (preserved) 670.6.

11. *adj.* protected, sheltered etc. *v.*; defended etc. (*see* defend etc. 717.7); under the protection of, under the shield of, under the wing of, under the shadow of one's wing; invulnerable, impregnable, inexpugnable, unattackable, unassailable; proof, proof against; bulletproof, ballproof, shellproof, bombproof; fireproof, fire-resisting; waterproof, watertight, drop-dry [Naut. cant]; weatherproof, weather-tight; defensible etc. 717.10; armored etc. 717.9; armed etc. 722.12.

12. *adj.* protecting etc. *v.*, protective, protectory [rare]; prophylactic; guardian, tutelary; preservative etc. 670.5; defensive etc. 717.9.

13. *adv.* safely, securely etc. *adj.*; with safety etc. *n.*, with impunity, *ex abundante cautela* [L.].

14. *int.* all's well!, all clear!, all serene!; at rest!, at ease!

665. Danger
(See **664.** Safety; also **667.** Source of Danger)

1. *n.* danger, peril, jeopardy, hazard, risk; insecurity, instability; dangerousness, precariousness etc. *adj.*; endangerment, imperilment; cause for alarm, rocks *or* breakers ahead, storm brewing, clouds gathering, clouds on the horizon; apprehension etc. (sense of danger) 860; source of danger etc. 667; warning etc. 668; alarm etc. 669.

2. *n.* exposure, openness to danger, liability, susceptibility, susceptivity, vulnerability; vulnerable point, heel of Achilles.

3. *n.* dangerous course, road to ruin, "*facilis descensus Averni*" (Vergil); dangerous practice, ticklish business [coll.]; rashness etc. 863; narrow escape etc. 671.2.

4. *v.* endanger, expose to danger etc. *n.*, put in danger, bring into danger *or* peril, bring about the danger of, peril, imperil, risk, expose, threaten danger; jeopard, jeopardize, jeopardy, put in jeopardy; compromise; hazard, put to hazard, set at hazard; venture, adventure; lay a trap for etc. (ensnare) 545.9; threaten etc. 909.2.

---

day.—GOLDSMITH. He who goes the lowest builds the safest.—P. J. BAILEY. 'Tis sweet to hear the watchdog's honest bark.—BYRON. He is safe from danger who is on guard even when safe.—PUBLILIUS. The way to be safe is never to be secure.—FULLER. 'Tis man's perdition to be safe.—EMERSON. No one can build his security upon the nobleness of another person.—W. CATHER.
665. Danger, the spur of all great minds.—G. CHAPMAN. Without danger the game grows cold.—G. CHAPMAN. As soon as there is life there is danger.—EMERSON.

5. *v.* expose oneself to danger etc. *n.*, risk etc. *above,* lay oneself open to, open the door to, run the chance *or* risk, undertake the risk of, engage in a forlorn hope; tempt Providence, defy danger, lean *or* trust to a broken reed, stand *or* sleep on a volcano, sit on a barrel of gunpowder, live in a glass house, beard the lion in his den, put one's head in the lion's mouth, march up to the cannon's mouth, play with fire, go through fire and water, go out of one's depth, go to sea in a sieve, carry too much sail, sail too near the wind, run the gantlet.

6. *v.* be in danger etc. *adj.,* have one's name on the danger list, have the chances *or* odds against one, be exposed to danger etc. *n.,* run into *or* encounter danger, incur danger; hang by a thread, tremble on the verge, totter on the brink, feel the ground sliding from under one, have to run for it; be despaired of, be overdue [Naut.]; be proscribed, be under sentence of death.

7. *adj.* dangerous, dangersome [obs. exc. dial.], attended ~, beset *or* fraught with danger, full of risk, risky, chancy [coll.], hazardous, perilous, parlous [arch.], unsafe, unhealthy [coll.]; unsure, uncertain, doubtful, dubious, in question; insecure, unreliable, untrustworthy, unsound, infirm, built upon sand, unstable, unsteady, shaky, tottery; precarious, critical, ticklish, slippery, slippy, on slippery ground, hanging by a thread etc. *v.,* trembling in the balance; threatening etc. 909.3; ominous, ill-omened etc. 511.11, 512.3, 5; rash etc. 863.6, 7; fearful etc. 860.15.

8. *adj.* in danger etc. *n.,* exposed to danger, endangered etc. *v.,* in a bad way; at the last extremity, reduced to the last extremity; with a halter round one's neck, between the hammer and the anvil, between Scylla and Charybdis, between two fires, on the edge, ~ brink *or* verge of a precipice, ~ volcano etc., in the lion's den, under fire, not out of the wood, on a lee shore, on the rocks, on the wrong side of the wall, in the condemned cell, under sentence of death; at bay, *aux abois* [F.], with one's back to the wall; in danger of etc. (liable to) 177.3.

9. *adj.* unprotected, unshielded, unscreened, unsheltered, uncovered, unguarded, undefended, unfortified, unarmored, unarmed, weaponless, guardless, defenseless, fenceless [arch.], harborless, exposed, open, vulnerable, expugnable, pregnable; open to etc. (liable) 177.3; helpless etc. 158.9.

10. *int.* danger!, beware! etc. (caution) 864.9.

666. Safeguard, Refuge
(See 667. Source of Danger)

Means of Safety.—1. *n.* safeguard, refuge, palladium, safety device, safety appliance, safety [coll.]; safety cage, safety hoist *or* lift, safety switch, safety stop, safety razor, safety pin, safety match, safety catch, safety lock, safety chain, safety link, safety lamp, safety hanger [Railroad], safety glass, safety bolt, safety dog, safety curtain [Theat.], safety gear, safety bicycle, safety belt; safety valve, blow valve, snifting valve.

lightning rod, lightning conductor; safety rail, guardrail, handrail, handrailing; life preserver, safety buoy, life buoy, buoy, swimming belt, cork jacket, breeches buoy, water wings; lifeboat, life raft; parachute, chute [coll.]; steppingstone, plank; bulkhead, watertight compartment; quarantine, *cordon sanitaire* [F.]; protector etc. 664.3; guard, fender, bulwark etc. (protective device) 717.2–4; shield, screen etc. (cover) 223.2; safe, safety-deposit box etc. (treasury) 802.

2. *n.* anchor, hook [slang], mud hook [slang]; sea anchor, sheet anchor, sacred anchor [Gr. and Rom. Antiq.], Trotman's anchor, Martin's anchor, mushroom anchor, drag anchor, mooring drag [Aeronaut.], floating anchor, killick, bower; kedge anchor, kedge; grapnel, grappling iron; ballast; moorings; guy, guy rope; mooring buoy, mooring mast *or* tower; check, brake etc. (hindrance) 706; bolt, hasp etc. (fastening) 45.2; mainstay etc. (support) 215.2.

Pleased with the danger, . . . / He sought the storms.—DRYDEN.   Great things through greatest hazards are attained.—J. FLETCHER. Perils commonly ask to be paid in pleasures.—BACON.   Yet have I something in me dangerous.—SHAKESPEARE.

666. *Ein' feste Burg ist unser Gott* [A mighty fortress is our God].—LUTHER.   A tabernacle . . . for a covert from storm.—BIBLE. Earth has no other asylum for them than in its own cold bosom.—SOUTHEY.   Eternity, be thou / My refuge!—M. ARNOLD.

3. *n.* refuge, place of security, refuge in the time of need, haven etc. *below,* safehold, sanctuary, mew, cover, covert, coverture, shelter, *abri* [F.], retreat, subterfuge, recess, recourse, resort, resource; sanctum, sanctum sanctorum, adytum, cell; dugout, storm cellar, cyclone cellar, air-raid shelter, bombproof dugout, funk hole [slang, chiefly Eng.], fraid hole [slang, U.S.]; asylum, ward, ark, home, farm [coll.], refuge for the destitute, almshouse, poorhouse, townhouse [U.S.]; hermitage, cloister; safety zone, safety isle *or* island; rock, pillar, tower; last resort *or* resource, *dernier ressort* [F.]; hiding place etc. 530.2; fasthold etc. (stronghold) 717.4; loophole etc. (means of escape) 671.3, 4.

4. *n.* anchorage, moorings, port, seaport, haven, harbor, harbor of refuge; roadstead, road *or* roads; bund, bunder [both Oriental]; dock, basin; landing, landing place, pier, wharf, dock, jetty, jutty, quay *or* key; mole, breakwater, embankment; water wing [Arch.]; destination etc. 292.6.

5. *v.* find refuge etc. *n.,* take *or* find shelter, take refuge, claim sanctuary, throw oneself into the arms of, reach shelter, reach home, reach running water, reach in time, run into port, make port, make the harbor, anchor in the roadstead, crouch in the lee of; seek safety etc. 664.8.

6. *v.* bar the gate, lock *or* bolt the door, let the portcullis down, raise the drawbridge.

667. Source of Danger
(See 666. Safeguard, Refuge)

1. *n.* source of danger, hidden danger, rocks, reefs, coral reef, sunken rocks, snags, bank, shelf, shoals, shallows, flat, lee shore, rock-bound *or* ironbound coast, breakers, breakers *or* rocks ahead; sands, sand bar, sandbank, sandy foundation, Goodwin sands; quicksands, syrt *or* syrtis [rare]; slippery ground; derelict; undertow, undercurrent; mine, masked battery; spring gun, set gun; hornet's nest, death in the cup *or* pot, sword of Damocles, wolf at the door; snake in one's bosom, snake in the grass; rapids etc. 348.6;

whirlpool etc. 348.8; tidal wave etc. 348.9; ambush etc. 530.

2. *n.* pitfall, trapfall, deadfall, *trou-de-loup* [F.], pit; trap door; trap etc. (snare) 545.4; abyss etc. 208.2.

668. Warning
(See also 669. Alarm)

1. *n.* warning, warn [rare], caution, caveat; advice, aviso, advisement, [arch.]; word to the wise, *verbum sapienti* [L.], word in the ear, flea in the ear [coll.]; notification, admonitory notification; monition, admonition; dehortation, contraindication; lesson, example, ensample [arch.], deterrent example; alarm etc. 669; threat etc. 909; notice, tip [coll.] etc. (information) 527; danger etc. 665.1.

2. *n.* forewarning, prewarning, premonition, premonishment [rare], precaution; prenotification, prenotice, prenotion [rare]; portent, portention [rare], portendment [rare], portendance [rare]; foreboding etc. 511.6; tip [coll.] etc. 527.3.

3. *n.* warning sign, cautionary sign, monitor, premonitor, premonitory sign, sign of the times, warning piece, warning voice; handwriting on the wall, *mene, mene, tekel, upharsin* [Heb.]; black cat; birds of ill omen, stormy petrels, Mother Carey's chickens; gathering clouds, clouds on the horizon, messengers [dial., Eng.]; thundercloud, thunderhead; red light, red flag; yellow flag, quarantine flag, yellow jack; symptom, premonitory symptom; premonitory apparition, death light, ~ fire *or* flame; ominous dreams; Cassandra; omen etc. 512; sign, token, signal etc. (indication) 550.1, 2, 14; foghorn etc. (alarm) 669.

4. *n.* warner, jiggerman *or* jiggers man [slang, U.S.]; lookout, lookout man; watchman, watcher, watch, watch and ward; sentinel, sentry; signaler, signalist; flagman, flags [slang]; lighthouseman.

5. *n.* watchtower, lookout etc. (observatory) 441.5.

---

668. Beware the ides of March.—SHAKESPEARE.   Ah! what a warning for a thoughtless man.—WORDSWORTH.   Forewarned is forearmed.   *Verbum sat sapienti* [A word to the wise is sufficient].   *Un averti en vaut deux* [A person warned is equal to two].

6. *v.* warn, warnish [obs. exc. Scot.], give notice *or* warning, caution, advise, admonish, put on one's guard; sound the alarm etc. 669.3; tip the wink [slang] etc. (signal) 550.20, (give a tip) 527.9.

7. *v.* forewarn, prewarn, premonish [rare], precaution, prenotify; forebode, omen etc. (portend) 511.9; threaten etc. 909.2; foresee etc. 570.5.

8. *v.* beware etc. (be cautious) 864.3.

9. *adj.* warning etc. *v.*, cautionary; monitory, monitorial; admonitory, admonitive [rare]; symptomatic, sematic [Biol.]; alarming.

10. *adj.* forewarning etc. *v.*, premonitive, premonitory; ominous, foreboding etc. (predictive) 511.11; threatening etc. 909.3.

11. *int.* jiggers!, cheese it! [both slang]; beware etc. 864.9.

669. Alarm
(See also 668. Warning)

Indication of Danger.—1. *n.* alarm, alarum, larum [arch.], note of alarm, alarm signal, warning sound; beat of drum, sound of trumpet, hue and cry; war cry, war whoop, call to arms; general alarm, general [now rare], *générale* [F.]; alert, *alerte* [F.], air-raid alarm; tocsin, alarm bell; signal of distress, SOS, flag at half-mast *or* half-staff; blue lights; fire cross, fiery cross; danger signal, red light, red flag; fog signal *or* alarm, fog bell, foghorn; burglar alarm; fire alarm, fire bell, fire flag, still alarm; siren, whistle, steam siren *or* whistle; horn, automobile horn, klaxon [trade name]; hooter, buzzer; police whistle, watchman's rattle; alarm clock; alarm gauge, alarm valve; yellow flag etc. (warning) 668.3; apprehension, terror etc. (fear) 860; danger etc. 665; alarmist etc. 860.6.

2. *n.* false alarm, cry of wolf; bugbear, bugaboo, bogy, hoax; flash in the pan, blank cartridge, dud.

3. *v.* alarm, give ~, raise ~, sound ~, turn in *or* beat an alarm, ring the tocsin; sound a general alarm, beat the general [now rare], *battre la générale* [F.]; cry wolf; half-mast; warn etc. 668.6; frighten etc. 860.10.

4. *adj.* alarmed, aroused, agitated, disturbed, excited, startled; warned (*see* warn etc. 668.6); fearful etc. 860.14.

5. *adj.* alarming, warning etc. 668.9; frightful etc. 860.15.

670. Preservation

1. *n.* preservation, preserval, conservation, saving, salvation, keeping, safekeeping, maintenance, support, sustentation [rare]; *vis conservatrix* [L.]; economy etc. 817; protection etc. 664.2; defense etc. 717.1; conservatism etc. (permanence) 141.

2. *n.* (means of preservation) preservative, preserver; dehydration, anhydration, evaporation; drying, canning, pickling etc. *v.*; refrigeration, freezing; mummification; prophylaxis; *cordon sanitaire* [F.]; hygiene etc. 656.2.

3. *v.* preserve, keep, keep safe, ~ sound *or* intact, secure, maintain, sustain, uphold, support, keep up, keep alive, not willingly let die, keep in existence, save, reserve [now rare], spare; conserve, conservate [rare]; nurse; guard etc. (protect) 646.6, (defend) 717.7; take care of etc. 459.6; hold one's ground etc. (persist) 141.4; be conservative etc. 141.5; sustain etc. 143.3.

4. *v.* preserve from decay, save from decomposition, preservatize; embalm, mummify; cure, dry, season, salt, brine, pickle, kipper, corn, marinate *or* marinade; smoke, smoke-cure, smoke-dry, infumate [rare]; freeze, refrigerate; bottle, pot, can, tin [chiefly Eng.]; dehydrate, anhydrate, evaporate.

5. *adj.* preserving etc. *v.*, preservative, preservatory; conservative, conservatory; prophylactic; protective etc. 664.12; defensive etc. 717.9.

6. *adj.* preserved, kept etc. *v.*; intact, sound, sound as a roach *or* bell, safe, safe and sound, with a whole skin, without a scratch, unscratched, unimpaired, unbroken, uninjured, unhurt, unharmed, unscathed, unmaimed, unsinged, unmarred, unblemished, untainted, unspoiled, in perfect condition; harmless, scatheless, scathless [now dial.].

---

669. Sound an alarm in my holy mountains.— BIBLE   The trumpet's loud clangor / Excites us to arms.—DRYDEN   Confused alarms of struggle and flight.—M. ARNOLD.

670. O Lord, thou preservest man and beast.— BIBLE.   Behold, I am with thee, and will keep thee.—BIBLE

671. Escape

1. *n.* escape, scape [now dial.], 'scape, escapement [rare]; avolation [now rare], elopement; getaway [coll.], come-off [coll.], impunity; riddance; jail-break; elusion, flight etc. (avoidance) 623; deliverance etc. 672; liberation etc. 750; emergence, leakage etc. (egress) 295.

2. *n.* narrow escape, hairbreadth escape, close call [coll.], near *or* close shave [coll.], near squeak [slang, Eng.], squeeze [slang], tight squeeze [slang].

3. *n.* (means of escape) fire escape; ladder, rope ladder, hook and ladder; fire net, life net; lifeboat, life raft; life-saving mortar *or* gun; life car; life line; parachute, chute [coll.]; drawbridge; sally port, postern door *or* gate, back door; life buoy, safety valve etc. (safeguard) 666.1; secret passage etc. (covert way) 530.4; refuge etc. 666.3; hiding place etc. 530.2.

4. *n.* loophole, starting hole [obs.], hole to creep out of, come-off [coll.], way out, way of escape; vent etc. (opening) 260, (outlet) 295.5; pretext etc. 619; alibi [coll.], extenuating circumstances etc. 937.2, 3; extenuation etc. 937.3.

5. *n.* escaper, escapee, escapist; refugee etc. (fugitive) 623.5.

6. *v.* escape, 'scape, scape [now dial.], avolate [now rare], make *or* effect one's escape, make good one's escape, break loose, break away, get away, make a getaway [coll.], get off, get clear of, get well out of, *échapper belle* [F.], wriggle ~, slip *or* sneak out of, slip away, give one the slip, slip through the hands *or* fingers of; slip the collar, shake off the yoke, break one's bonds; save one's bacon [coll.], escape with a whole skin; jump, skip [both coll.]; escape prison, break jail, fly the coop [slang]; escape without penalty, go scot free; have a narrow escape etc. *n.*, escape with *or* by the skin of one's teeth; elude etc. (avoid) 623.6; flee etc. 623.10; find vent, issue forth etc. (egress) 295.6, 7; weather the storm etc. (be safe) 664.4; go free etc. 750.4.

7. *adj.* escaped etc. *v.*, fled, clear, away, out of, well out of, scot-free; loose, at large etc. (free) 748.12.

---

671. I am escaped with the skin of my teeth.—BIBLE. An inch in a miss is as good as an ell.—CAMDEN. Adventure must start with running away from home.—BOLITHO.

672. Deliverance

1. *n.* deliverance, rescue, ransom, liberation, extrication, release, emancipation, riddance; salvation, redemption; exemption, immunity; reprieve, reprieval [rare]; escape etc. 671; deliverer etc. (savior) 912.2.

2. *v.* deliver, rescue, come to the rescue, save, free, render free, liberate, set free, extricate, release, emancipate, redeem, ransom, bring off *or* through; rid, get rid of; *tirer d'affaire* [F.], get the wheel out of the rut, snatch from the jaws of death; retrieve etc. (restore) 660.8, 9.

3. *adj.* deliverable, extricable, redeemable, rescuable.

4. *int.* to the rescue!, help!, man overboard!; a rescue!, saved!

673. Preparation
(See 674. Nonpreparation)

1. *n.* preparation, preparing, making ready etc. *v.*; ready, readying [both coll.]; provision, providence [now rare]; equipment, furnishing, furnishment, accouterment, armament, arrayal; prearrangement, previous arrangement *or* adaptation, precaution, preconcertedness, preconcertion [rare], predisposition; elaboration, perfection, maturation, evolution; gestation, hatching, incubation, sitting; practice, rehearsal; preparative, preparatory, preparatory act *or* measure, note of preparation; education, training etc. (teaching) 537; anticipation, forethought etc. (foresight) 510; inurement etc. (habitation) 613.5; manufacture, concoction etc. (production) 161; arrangement etc. 60; adjustment etc. (adaptation) 23.3; groundwork etc. (foundation) 215.3.

2. *n.* (preparation of food) cooking, cookery, culinary art, cuisine; magirology, magiric [both rare]; brewing.

3. *n.* (preparation of the soil) cultiva-

---

672. He that taketh warning shall deliver his soul.—BIBLE. It is a deliverance which does not deliver.—EMERSON. He . . . swore, with sobs, that he would labor my delivery.—SHAKESPEARE. In the course of justice, none of us / Should see salvation: we do pray for mercy.—SHAKESPEARE. He hath sent me . . . to preach deliverance to the captives.—BIBLE.
673. In all things, success depends upon previous preparation, and without such preparation there is sure to be failure.—CONFUCIUS.

tion, tilling, plowing etc. *v.*; sowing, semination.

4. *n.* preparedness, readiness, fitness; ripeness, mellowness, maturity.

5. *n.* preparer, *preparateur* [F.], preparator [Tech.], preparationist; paver, pavior, paver of the way, pathfinder, trail blazer; forerunner etc. (precursor) 64; trainer etc. (teacher) 540.

6. *v.* prepare, ready [coll.], make *or* get ready, make preparations *or* arrangements, fix [chiefly South. U.S.], get up, settle preliminaries, sound the note of preparation; prepare *or* pave the way, break the ice, smooth the path *or* road, clear the way, make all clear for, open the way, open the door to; prepare the ground *or* soil, till *or* cultivate the soil, plow the ground, dress the ground, sow the seed; lay a train, dig a mine; dig the foundations etc. (*see* foundation etc. 215.3), lay the first stone, erect the scaffolding; prime, prime and load.

fit, adapt, adjust, qualify, set, attune, put in tune, ~ trim, ~ train, ~ gear *or* working order; wind up, screw up; steam up, get up steam; harness, put in harness; elaborate, develop, refine, perfect; mature, maturate, bring to maturity; ripen, mellow, season; temper, anneal, smelt; equip etc. 634.2; provide etc. 637.4; coach, train etc. (teach) 537.9, 10; inure etc. (habituate) 613.8; compound, form etc. (produce) 161.8; cook etc. 384.19; cure, dry etc. (preserve) 670.4; put in order etc. (arrange) 60.6; map out etc. (plan) 626.9; begin etc. 66.5.

7. *v.* prepare for, make provision *or* due provision for, fix for *or* to [dial.], take steps *or* measures, take precautions, look out for in advance, procure beforehand, provide for *or* against, guard against, make sure against, forearm, prepare for the evil day, provide for *or* against a rainy day, feather one's nest, lay in provisions, keep as a nest egg, save to fall back upon, have a rod in pickle, lay by, husband one's resources, make investments; set one's house in order, make all snug, clear the decks, clear for action; close one's ranks; shuffle the cards; plan on etc. 507.6.

8. *v.* prepare oneself, get ready, get set [coll.], lay oneself out for, get into harness, gird up one's loins, buckle on one's armor, shoulder arms; trim one's tackle *or* foils, sharpen one's tools, whet the knife *or* sword; practice, rehearse; undergo schooling etc. (study) 539.4.

9. *v.* be prepared, be ready etc. *adj.*, hold oneself in readiness, watch and pray *or* wait, keep one's powder dry, *venienti occurrere morbo* [L.]; anticipate etc. (foresee) 510.5.

10. *adj.* preparatory, preparative, preparing etc. *v.*; afoot etc. *adv.*, brewing, brooding, forthcoming; in store for, in reserve; precautious, precautionary, precautional; provident, provisional; inchoate; preliminary etc. (preceding) 62.4.

11. *adj.* prepared etc. *v.*, ready, in readiness, all ready, prepared and ready, well-prepared, primed, loaded for bear [slang, U.S.]; good and ready, set, all set, on the mark [all coll.]; *semper paratus* [L.], *"in utrumque paratus"* (Vergil); ready for use, ready to one's hand, handy, at one's elbow, on the table; prepared for, equal to, up to; in gear, in working order, in practice, running smoothly; snug; in *or* at harness, in the saddle, booted and spurred; in war paint, in full feather [coll.]; in arms, up in arms, in battle array, sword-in-hand; well-armed, well-heeled [slang, U.S.], armed at all points, armed to the teeth, armed cap-a-pie; mature, ripe, mellow; elaborate, labored, high-wrought; on the alert etc. (vigilant) 459.8; practiced etc. (skilled) 698.13, 14; provided etc. 637.6; equipped etc. 634.3.

12. *adj.* ready-prepared, ready-made, ready-shapen, ready-formed, ready-mixed, ready-furnished, ready-dressed, ready-cooked; ready-to-wear, ready-for-wear; ready-cut, cut and dried *or* dry.

13. *adv.* in preparation, undergoing preparation, in course of preparation, under construction, going on, in progress *or* process, in agitation, in embryo, in hand, in train, on the stocks, on the anvil, in the fire, on foot, afoot, afloat, astir, abroad, abroach; in anticipation; under revision; under consideration etc. (planned) 626.11.

Forewarned, forearmed; to be prepared is half the victory.—CERVANTES. Put your trust in God; but mind to keep your powder dry.—[ASCRIBED TO CROMWELL.] To be prepared for war is one of the most effectual means of preserving peace.—WASHINGTON. Be ye also ready; for in such an hour as ye think not, the Son of man cometh.—BIBLE.

674. Nonpreparation
(See 673. Preparation)

1. *n.* nonpreparation, unpreparation, want of preparation etc. (*see* preparation etc. 673); unpreparedness, unreadiness, unfitness etc. *adj.*; unqualification, disqualification; unprovision, improvidence; improvisation, extemporization, impromptu, extempore; neglect etc. 460; inexpectation etc. 508.

2. *n.* immaturity *or* unmaturity, undevelopment, crudity, rawness etc. *adj.*; unculture *or* inculture, uncultivation *or* incultivation; abortion; precocity, prevenience etc. (prematurity) 132.2; incompleteness etc. 53; imperfection etc. 651.

3. *n.* undeveloped condition, original *or* untouched condition, natural state, nature, state of nature; virgin soil, unweeded garden; rough diamond, diamond in the rough; unlicked cub; rough copy etc. (outline) 626.2; raw material etc. 635.1; germ, embryo etc. (rudiment) 153.3.

4. *v.* be unprepared etc. *adj.,* want preparation etc. 673, lie fallow, *s'embarquer sans biscuit* [F.], live from hand to mouth, go off half-cocked *or* at half cock [coll.], be caught napping; leave undone etc. (pretermit) 460.7; extemporize etc. 612.3.

5. *v.* unprepare, render unfit etc. *adj.*; dismantle etc. (render useless) 645.7, (divest) 226.4.

6. *v.* catch unprepared, take *or* catch unawares, come upon unexpectedly etc. (surprise) 508.6.

7. *adj.* unprepared, without preparation etc. (*see* preparation etc. 673); unready, unbegun, unorganized, unarranged, unfurnished, unprovided, unequipped, untrimmed; unfit, unfitted; unqualified, disqualified; out of order, out of kilter *or* kelter [coll.], out of gear; unconcocted, uncooked, unboiled; off one's guard etc. (inexpectant) 508.7, 8; unpremeditated etc. (impulsive) 612.4.

8. *adj.* immature *or* unmature, not mature, callow, unfledged, unhatched, unnurtured, *kutcha* [Ind.], unripe, raw, green, rude, crude, coarse, unrefined, unlicked; uncultivated, uncultured; rough, roughcast, roughhewn, in the rough, unpolished, uncut; rough-edged, deckle-edged; undeveloped, unfinished, undone, unhewn, unformed, unfashioned, unwrought, unlabored, unblown; undigested *or* indigested, ill-digested; unmellowed, unseasoned, unleavened; half-baked [coll.], half-cocked [coll., U.S.]; rudimental, rudimentary; embryonic, embryotic, in embryo, *in ovo* [L.]; abortive, abortional; precocious, prevenient etc. (premature) 132.8; incomplete etc. 53.4; imperfect etc. 651.4; uninformed, untaught (ignorant) 491.9, 10.

9. *adj.* natural, in a state of nature, *in puris naturalibus* [L.]; artless, inartificial; virginal, untouched, unsullied; undressed etc. 226.8.

10. *adj.* fallow, untilled, uncultivated, unsown.

11. *adj.* shiftless, improvident, inadvertent, slack, lax, loose, remiss, thoughtless, heedless, happy-go-lucky, unguarded; thriftless, unthrifty; negligent etc. 460.8.

12. *adv.* unpreparedly etc. *adj.,* at half cock [coll.]; without premeditation etc. 612.5; by surprise etc. (unexpectedly) 508.11.

675. Essay

1. *n.* essay, trial, attempt, endeavor, aim, effort, exertion, struggle, move; try, go, fist, fling, shot [all coll.]; crack, whack, slap, dab, stab, lick, jab, stagger, whirl, shy [all slang]; venture, adventure; experiment etc. 463.

2. *n.* first attempt, first move, first rattle out of the box [slang], *coup d'essai* [F.]; debut etc. (beginning) 66.

3. *v.* essay, try, tempt [arch.], attempt, make an attempt, ~ effort etc. *n.,* strive, endeavor, use one's endeavor, try one's hand, go to market [coll.]; lift a finger, lift the hand; try to, try and [coll.], aim at; give it a whirl [slang], have a go at [coll.], take a shy at [slang] etc. *n.*; venture, adventure, venture at, ~ on *or* upon, dare to engage in, take one's chance with,

---

674. Unforeseen, they say, is unprepared.—DRYDEN.   He who is not prepared today, will be less so tomorrow.—OVID.   'Tis a vile thing to die, my gracious lord, / When men are unprepared and look not for it.—SHAKESPEARE.

675. No one knows what he can do till he tries.—PUBLILIUS.   Admire those who attempt great things, even though they fail.—SENECA.   The attempt and not the deed / Confounds us.—SHAKESPEARE.   Nothing is achieved before it be thoroughly attempted.—SIDNEY.   Some-

speculate, try one's luck *or* fortune, tempt fortune; try anything once; try for, endeavor to attain; undertake etc. 676.2; experiment etc. 463.8; feel one's way etc. (grope) 463.9.

4. *v.* try hard, push, make a bold push, try until one is black in the face, break an arm *or* blood vessel, do *or* break a leg, file a strong bid [coll.], move heaven and earth; struggle etc. (exert oneself) 686.5, 6.

5. *v.* try one's best *or* utmost, use *or* exert one's best *or* utmost endeavor, do one's best *or* level best, do one's utmost, do the best one can, do all one can, do all in one's power, do as much as in one lies, do what lies in one's power, play one's best card, put one's best *or* right foot foremost, put one's whole soul in one's work, put all one's strength into, strain every nerve, spare no efforts *or* pains, take pains, go the whole length, go all lengths, go through fire and water, move heaven and earth, leave no stone unturned, do *or* work wonders.

6. *adj.* tentative, empirical etc. (experimental) 463.12.

676. Undertaking

1. *n.* undertaking, enterprise, emprise *or* emprize [arch.], adventure, venture, engagement; large undertaking, tall order [slang]; occupation, matter in hand etc. (business) 625.1, 2; project etc. (plan) 626; attempt, move etc. (essay) 675; pursuit etc. 622; promise etc. 768; intention 620.

2. *v.* undertake, enterprise [arch.], engage in, enter on *or* upon, embark in *or* upon, venture upon, devote oneself to, give oneself up to, go in *or* out for [coll.]; assume, take up, betake oneself to, take on, take upon oneself, take upon one's shoulders, take in hand, put *or* turn one's hand to, tackle [coll.], go about, set about, set to, buckle to, fall to, plunge into, launch into *or* upon, launch forth, put in hand, put in *or* into execution, set forward, go to do; put *or* lay one's shoulder to the wheel, put one's hand to the plow, take the bull by the horns; have too many irons in the fire, bite off more than one can chew [coll.].

attempt etc. (essay) 675.3; begin etc. 66.5; have in hand etc. (occupy oneself with) 625.7; have many irons in the fire etc. (be busy) 682.13; engage etc. (promise) 768.3; intend etc. 620.3; pursue etc. 622.6.

3. *adj.* undertaken etc. *v.*, on the anvil etc. (in preparation) 673.13.

4. *int.* here goes!, shoot! [coll.].

677. Use
(See 678. Disuse, 679. Misuse)

1. *n.* use, employment, employ; exercise, exercitation; application, appliance, adhibition, administration; disposition, disposal; service, wear; recourse, resort; usufruct, enjoyment of property, right of using, user [all Law]; consumption, usance [both Econ.]; usefulness, benefit etc. (utility) 644.

2. *n.* usage, function, particular service; mode of using *or* treating, treatment, practice, conduct, wont, procedure, mode of procedure, manner of working *or* operating, *modus operandi* [L.]; method etc. (way) 627; custom etc. 613.2.

3. *n.* utilization, conversion to use, employment, employing etc. *v.*

4. *n.* user, employer, operator, manipulator; enjoyer, consumer, absorber; purchaser, buyer; purchasing public, market, demand, public *or* popular demand.

5. *v.* use, utilize, make use of, put to use, put in practice *or* operation, set in motion, set to work, employ, ply, work, wield, handle, manipulate, exercise, exert, practice; play, play off; resort to, have recourse to, recur to, fall back upon, take to [coll.], betake oneself to, take up with, lay one's hand to, avail oneself of, take advantage of, make the most of, profit by, exploit, turn to account, convert to one's service, convert *or* turn to use, put into requisition, press *or* enlist into serv-

---

thing attempted, something done, / Has earned a night's repose.—LONGFELLOW. If at first you don't succeed, / Try, try, try again.
676. My ventures are not in one bottom trusted / Nor to one place.—SHAKESPEARE. The long-lost ventures of the heart.—LONGFELLOW. So many worlds, so much to do!—TENNYSON. In every affair consider what precedes and what follows, and then undertake it.—EPICTETUS.

677. The use of things is all, and not the store.—JONSON. Time wasted is existence, used is life.—YOUNG. 'Tis use alone that sanctifies expense.—POPE. In all human action those faculties will be strong which are used.—EMERSON. The used key is always bright.—FRANKLIN.

ice, put into operation, call *or* bring into play, call *or* draw forth.

dispose of, assign to a use, dedicate, devote, consecrate; task, tax, put to task; apply, administer, adhibit; bring to bear upon; make a handle of, make a cat's-paw of; make a shift with, make the best *or* most of; take advantage of, find one's account *or* advantage in, reap the benefit of.

6. *v.* use up, devour, swallow up, absorb, consume, spend, expend, dissipate, exhaust, deplete, impoverish; drain, drain of resources.

7. *adj.* used, employed etc. *v.*; in use, in practice etc. *n.*; secondhand, worn etc. (impaired) 659.12.

8. *adj.* useful etc. 644.5; subservient etc. (instrumental) 631.4; helpful etc. 707.12; conducive etc. (tending) 176.3.

678. Disuse
(See 677. Use)

1. *n.* disuse, desuetude, disusage, disusance [rare], inusitation [rare]; obsolescence, obsoleteness, obsoletion [rare], obsoletism; nonprevalence, unprevalence; abstinence, abstention, forbearance; discontinuance etc. (cessation) 142; relinquishment etc. 782.

2. *v.* disuse, disutilize, cease to use, discontinue the use *or* practice of, have done with, abandon, drop, give up, leave off; supersede; obsolete [now rare], obsolesce; discontinue etc. (cease) 142.6; relinquish etc. 782.3; dismantle (render useless) 645.7.

3. *v.* discard, fling ~, throw ~, cast etc. off *or* away, throw out, throw over, throw *or* heave overboard, throw *or* cast to the dogs, throw *or* scatter to the winds, sweep ~, brush *or* whisk off *or* away, get rid *or* quit of, rid oneself of, wash one's hands of, cast off, jettison, relegate, remove, eliminate, reject, part with, give away, cast behind; discard as useless, trash, wastebasket; extirpate etc. (excise) 38.5; make away with etc. (destroy) 162.4; eject etc. 297.8.

4. *v.* put away, lay up, lay up in a napkin, lay ~, set ~, cast ~, push *or* put aside, side [coll.], lay *or* set by, shunt, shelve, put *or* lay on the shelf, put on the rack [coll.], table, lay on the table, pigeonhole.

5. *v.* not use, do without, dispense with, let alone, not touch, forbear, abstain, spare, waive, neglect; keep back, reserve.

6. *adj.* disused etc. *v.*, out of use, done with; run down, worn-out, not worth saving; obsolete, obsolescent.

7. *adj.* unused, not used etc. *v.*, inusitate [rare]; unemployed, unapplied, unexercised, unessayed, untouched, untrodden, unculled, ungathered; undisposed of, unspent; uncalled-for, unrequired; nonprevalent, unprevalent, unprevailing; unaccustomed etc. 614.3; new etc. 123.8, 9.

8. *int.* no use!, what's the use!, of what use?

679. Misuse
(See 677. Use)

1. *n.* misuse, misusage, misemployment, misapplication, misappropriation, misdirection, perversion; ill-use, ill-usage, abuse, prostitution, profanation, desecration; outrage, atrocity; maltreatment etc. 649.4; waste etc. 638.

2. *v.* misuse, misemploy, misapply, misappropriate, misdirect, pervert; employ a steam engine to crack a nut, cut blocks with a razor; ill-use, abuse, prostitute, profane, desecrate; maltreat etc. 649.7; overtask etc. (task) 686.8.

680. Action
(See 681. Inaction; also 682. Activity)

1. *n.* action, acting, doing etc. *v.*; movement, employment, praxis, operation, performance, transaction, execution, manipulation, perpetration, effectuation, dispatch *or* despatch; exercise, exercitation; swing, play; evolution; interaction,

---

678. Is a candle brought to be put under a bushel, or under a bed? and not to be set on a candlestick?—BIBLE.   That one talent which is death to hide / Lodged with me useless.—MILTON.

679. The more ancient the abuse, the more sacred it is.—VOLTAIRE.   Who first misuse, then cast their toys away.—COWPER.   O, she misused me past the endurance of a block.—SHAKESPEARE.

680. 'Tis deeds must win the prize.—SHAKESPEARE.   The great end of life is not knowledge, but action.—T. HUXLEY.   I myself must mix with action, lest I wither by despair.—TENNYSON.   The only things in life in which we can be said to have any property, are our actions.—C. COLTON.   We live in deeds not years.—P. J. BAILEY.   To live is not merely to breathe, it is to act.—ROUSSEAU.

interworking; activeness etc. (activity) 682; work etc. (business) 625, (labor) 686.3; procedure etc. (conduct) 692.

2. *n.* act, action, deed, do [coll.], gest *or* geste, performance, feat, stunt [coll.], exploit, effort, adventure, transaction, job, proceeding, measure, step, maneuver, bout, passage, move, stroke, blow, touch, go [coll.]; acta, doings, dealings; coup, *coup de main, coup d'état* [all F.]; overt act [Law]; achievement etc. (completion) 729.

3. *n.* handiwork, handicraft, craftsmanship, workmanship, manufacture; product etc. 161.6.

4. *n.* actor, doer etc. (agent) 690.

5. *v.* act, operate, function, work, play, move, proceed, go it [coll.]; take action, take steps, put in action *or* motion, put in *or* into practice, strike a blow, lift a finger, stretch forth one's hand; act on *or* upon; take in hand etc. (undertake) 676.2.

6. *v.* do, up and do [dial. and coll.], perform, exercise, execute, prosecute, pursue, carry on, transact, enact, discharge, dispatch *or* despatch, produce, effect, put into effect *or* practice, carry into effect, carry out, carry through, work out, bring about, get through, achieve, make, render; pull [slang], pull off [coll.]; commit, perpetrate, inflict.

practice, serve, work, play [coll.], employ oneself, ply one's task, be at work, pursue a course, run in a race; have to do with, have a hand in, have a finger in the pie, be a party to, be a participator in, participate in, take part in, act ∼, play *or* perform a part in, bear a hand, pull an oar; do one's do [coll.], do one's stuff [slang], do the needful [slang]; have in hand etc. (business) 625.7; labor etc. 686.5, 6; accomplish, carry into execution etc. (complete) 729.2, 3.

7. *adj.* acting, performing etc. *v.*; in action, in play, in exercise, in harness, in the midst of things; active etc. 682.16-24; in operation etc. (operative) 170.4; at work etc. (busy) 682.20.

8. *adv.* in the act, in the very act, *in flagrante delicto* [L.], while one is at it, while one's hand is in, red-handed.

681. Inaction

(See 680. Action; also 683. Inactivity)

1. *n.* inaction, stagnation, stagnancy, vegetation; passiveness, passivity, passivism; *laisser-aller, laisser aller, laissez aller, laissez faire, laisser faire* [all F.]; do-nothingness, do-nothingism, do-nothing policy, Fabian policy, *laissez-faire* etc. policy, laissez-faireism, standstillism, standpattism [coll.], noninterference, nonresistance; watching and waiting, watchful waiting; idleness, apathy etc. (inactivity) 683; quiescence etc. 265; repose etc. 687; dormancy etc. (inertness) 172; fixity, immobility etc. (stability) 150; static condition etc. (permanence) 141; rest, interregnum etc. (pause) 142.2; procrastination, deferment etc. (delay) 133.2; neglect etc. 460.

2. *v.* not do, not act etc. (*see* do, act etc. 680.5, 6); not attempt etc. (*see* attempt etc. 675.3), hold, spare, forbear, refrain, abstain, abstain *or* keep from doing, do nothing, not stir, not lift a finger *or* hand, not move a foot, fold one's arms, twiddle one's thumbs, pass the time, fill up the time, beguile the time, while away the time, while away the tedious hours, bide one's time, take time, mark time, kick *or* cool one's heels [coll.], watch and wait, lie in wait, hang fire, stand *or* hold aloof, rest and be thankful, remit *or* relax one's efforts; lie *or* rest upon one's oars, repose on one's laurels; take no part in, have nothing to do with, have no hand in.

let pass, let slip, let slide [coll.], let go, leave go [illit. and dial.], let it ride [slang, U.S.]; leave *or* let alone, leave *or* let well alone, leave *or* let well enough alone, let be, let things take their course,

---

So much to do; so little done.—C. RHODES. Act, act in the living present!—LONGFELLOW. Action is the proper fruit of knowledge.—FULLER. Execute every act of thy life as though it were thy last.—MARCUS AURELIUS. The materials of action are variable, but the use we make of them should be constant.—EPICTETUS. Suit the action to the word, the word to the action.—SHAKESPEARE. Action is eloquence.—SHAKESPEARE. Handsome is as handsome does. Actions speak louder than words.

681. It is, no doubt, an immense advantage, to have done nothing, but one should not abuse it.—RIVAROL. To do nothing is in every man's power.—JOHNSON. To do nothing is the way to be nothing.—N. HOWE. Did nothing in particular, / And did it very well.—GILBERT. That indolent but delightful condition of doing nothing.—PLINY THE YOUNGER. Heaven ne'er helps the men who will not act.—SOPHOCLES. Inaction is cowardice.—EMERSON.

let it have its way, leave things as they are, *quieta non movere* [L.], *stare super antiquas vias* [L.], live and let live; *laisser faire,* ~ *passer* or *aller* [F.], idle etc. (be inactive) 683.8; procrastinate, wait etc. 133.5, 7; remain motionless, repose, stagnate etc. (be quiescent) 265.5; smolder, slumber etc. (be inert) 172.2; stand still etc. (be permanent) 141.4; stop, pause etc. (cease) 142.6; disregard etc. (neglect) 460.4.

3. *adj.* inactive, not doing etc. *v.,* do-nothing; *laissez-faire* or *laisser-faire* [F.], *laissez-aller* or *laisser-aller* [F.]; unoccupied, idle etc. 683.12; motionless etc. (quiescent) 265.7; passive, dormant, stagnant etc. (inert) 172.3.

4. *adv.* doing nothing, with nothing to do, with the hands in the pockets, with the hands behind one's back, with folded arms, *les bras croisés* [F.]; *pour passer le temps* [F.]; at a stand *or* standstill, at the halt, *re infecta* [L.].

682. Activity
(See 683. Inactivity; also 680. Action)

1. *n.* activity, action, activeness, briskness, liveliness etc. *adj.*; animation, vivacity, energy, life, spirit, verve, dash, drive; pep, pepper, ginger, kick [all slang]; snap, vim, punch, go [all coll.]; vigor etc. (physical energy) 171; motion etc. 264.

2. *n.* quickness, smartness, alertness, readiness, nimbleness etc. *adj.*; rapidity, agility, alacrity, promptitude, dispatch *or* despatch, expedition; velocity etc. 274; haste etc. 684; punctuality etc. 132.3; skill etc. 698.

3. *n.* eagerness, avidity, enthusiasm, zeal, ardor, passion, fire, *perfervidum ingenium* [L.], *empressement* [F.]; fervor, fervency; *furore* [It.], furor; earnestness, intentness; willingness etc. 602; devotion etc. (resolution) 604.

4. *n.* enterprise, initiative, aggressive energy; go-getterism, the get-there [both slang]; push, drive, getup, get-up-and-get *or* -go, go, go-ahead, go-to-itiveness, up-and-comingness, gumption, spunk [all coll.].

5. *n.* industry, industriousness, laboriousness, assiduousness etc. *adj.*; assiduity, sedulity [rare], painstaking, diligence, indefatigability, application; businesslike habits, habits of business; perseverance etc. 604a; drudgery etc. (labor) 686.3; business etc. 625.

6. *n.* bustle, hustle [coll.], movement, stir, fuss, flurry, flutter, splutter, fluster, sputter, ferment, stew [coll.], hubbub, ado, bother; restlessness, fidgets, fidgetiness.

7. *n.* press of business, no sinecure, plenty to do, a great deal doing [coll.], a lot going on [coll.], many irons in the fire, great doings, busy hum of men, the madding crowd, the thick of things, thick of the action, battle of life.

8. *n.* meddling, intermeddling etc. *v.*; meddlesomeness, officiousness, intrusiveness etc. *adj.*; intrusion, obtrusion, interference; interposition etc. (intervention) 228.3; officious inquisitiveness etc. (curiosity) 455.

9. *n.* wakefulness, pervigilium, *insomnium* [L.], insomnia, restlessness, sleeplessness.

10. *n.* man of action, busy bee, hummer [slang], humdinger [slang, U.S.], hustler [coll.], rustler [slang, U.S.], go-getter [slang], go-ahead [coll.], live man [U.S.], live wire [coll.], human dynamo [coll.]; sharp fellow, blade; new broom; enthusiast, zealot etc. (fanatic) 504.2.

11. *n.* meddler, intermeddler, busybody, busy [slang], pick-thank [arch.], buttinsky [slang]; pry, Paul Pry, snoop *or* snooper [U.S.]; intruder etc. 228.4; gossip etc. (newsmonger) 532.5; hinderer etc. 706.3.

12. *v.* be active etc. *adj.*, stir, stir about, bestir oneself, stir one's stumps [coll.], make a stir, bustle, hustle [coll.], rustle [slang, U.S.], fuss, make a fuss, kick up *or* raise a dust, flutter, scramble, be about, step lively [coll.], go it, lay about one, peg away, keep moving, keep on, carry on, keep at it, keep going, keep driving [coll.], keep the pot boiling [coll.], keep the ball rolling, keep up the ball; push, push *or* press forward, push *or* press on *or* onward, drive on *or* ahead, go ahead, forge ahead, fight *or* elbow one's way, make ~, work *or* carve one's way, shoot ahead, go full steam ahead.

682. Pray to God and ply the hammer.—CERVANTES.   Diligence is the mother of good fortune.—CERVANTES.   Industry is the soul of business and the keystone of prosperity.—DICKENS.   Industry is a loadstone to draw all good things.—R. BURTON.   Nothing great was

not suffer the grass to grow under one's feet, make the most of one's time, improve the shining hour, make hay while the sun shines, get up early, catch a weasel asleep, steal a march, kill two birds with one stone, seize the opportunity, lose no time, not lose a moment, make short work of, dash off, do *or* work wonders; go all lengths, move heaven and earth, leave no stone unturned; have one's fling, run the round of, run riot; make haste etc. 684.2–4; make progress etc. 282.2.

13. *v.* be busy etc. *adj.*, have many irons in the fire, have one's hands full, have much on one's hands, have other things to do, have other fish to fry, not have a moment to spare, not have a moment that one can call one's own; get busy etc. (set to work) 686.7; busy oneself etc. 625.6–8; work etc. (labor) 686.6.

14. *v.* meddle, busybody, tamper with, mix oneself up with, busy oneself with, concern oneself officiously *or* impertinently with, mind others' business, not mind one's own business, intermeddle, interfere, intrude, obtrude, butt *or* horn in [slang], poke ~, stick *or* thrust one's nose in, put *or* shove in one's oar, insinuate one's attentions; have a finger *or* hand in, have a finger in the pie; interpose etc. 228.10; pry etc. 455.4.

15. *v.* be alert etc. *adj.*, be full of pep [slang], have a lot of kick [coll.]; have all one's wits about one, look sharp, look slick *or* slippy [coll.], look lively *or* alive [coll.], keep one's eyes open etc. (be vigilant) 459.4.

16. *adj.* active, brisk, brisk as a lark *or* bee; lively, animated, energetic, vivacious, spirited, full of life, live [chiefly U.S.], alive, alive and kicking [coll.], frisky, breezy; peppy, full of pep, feeling one's oats [all slang]; full of go, snappy, corky [all coll.]; chirk, chipper [both coll., U.S.]; in action etc. 680.7.

17. *adj.* quick, expeditious, prompt, yare [arch.], instant, ready, spry [coll. and dial.], sharp, smart, smart as a whip *or* steel trap, quick as a lamplighter; alert, fly [slang], on the alert, on one's toes, on the job [coll.], on the *qui vive* [F.];
awake, broad *or* wide awake; nimble, fleet, sprightly, agile, light-footed, nimble-footed, nimble as a squirrel; swift etc. (fast) 274.13.

18. *adj.* forward, eager, avid, ardent, zealous, keen, enterprising, pushing, aggressive; up-and-coming, go-ahead [both coll.]; adventurous, venturous, venturesome; earnest, in earnest; resolute etc. 604.7.

19. *adj.* industrious, assiduous, diligent, sedulous, notable [obs.]; painstaking, painful [arch.], hard-working, plodding etc. (*see* plod etc. 686.6), energetic, strenuous, never idle; indefatigable, untiring, never-tiring, unwearied, never weary, never tired; sleepless, unsleeping; businesslike; unflagging etc. (persevering) 604a.3; intent etc. (attentive) 457.9; studious etc. 539.6.

20. *adj.* busy, full of business, busy as a bee *or* housewife, busy as a hen with one chicken [coll.], hard at work, hard at it, up to one's ears; occupied, engaged, employed, working etc. (*see* work etc. 686.6), at work, on duty, in harness, up in arms, on one's legs *or* feet, up-and-doing *or* -stirring [coll.]; on the move, on the hop *or* jump [coll.], on one's toes, on the run; laboring etc. 686.9.

21. *adj.* bustling, hustling [coll.] etc. *v.*; restless, restless as a hyena; unquiet, agitated, fussy, fidgety.

22. *adj.* meddling etc. *v.*, meddlesome, officious, overofficious, busy, busybody, pushing, forward, intrusive, obtrusive; prying etc. (curious) 455.5.

23. *adj.* astir, stirring, agoing, afoot, on foot; in full swing; eventful.

24. *adj.* sleepless, slumberless, wakeful; insomnolent, insomnious [both rare].

25. *adv.* actively etc. *adj.*, featly [arch.], with life and spirit, with wings, full tilt; *in mediis rebus* [L.], in the midst of things; with might and main etc. 686.11; with haste etc. 684.7.

26. *int.* keep going!, keep moving!, move on!, push on!, go ahead!; *age quod agis!* [L.]; step lively! etc. (make haste!) 684.8.

683. Inactivity
(See 682. Activity; also 681. Inaction)

1. *n.* inactivity, unactivity, inaction, inactiveness etc. *adj.*; inanimation [rare],

---

ever achieved without enthusiasm.—EMERSON. The world belongs to the enthusiast who keeps cool.—W. MCFEE. The doctrine of the strenuous life.—T. ROOSEVELT. For aye as busy as bees / Been they.—CHAUCER. Busy people are never busybodies.—CYNIC'S CALENDAR. Elbow grease gives the best polish.

683. Who more busy than he that hath least to do?—T. DRAXE. A life of dignified otios-

suspended animation; stagnation, passivity etc. 681; inertness etc. 172; quiescence etc. 265; repose etc. 687; immobility etc. (stability) 150; permanence etc. 141; delay etc. 133.2.

2. *n.* idleness, idlehood, idlety [Scot. and North. Eng.], idleset [Scot. and Ir.], idlesse [arch.], *dolce far niente* [It.], want of occupation, inoccupation, unemployment, idle hands, idle hours, time hanging on one's hands; loafing, loaf [coll.]; idling, pottering, dawdling etc. *v.*; shirking, malingery etc. (avoidance) 623; idle spell, respite, rest etc. (pause) 142.2; leisure etc. 685.

3. *n.* indolence, remissness, do-nothingness, dilatoriness, laziness etc. *adj.*; laze [coll.], do-nothingism, faineance *or* faineancy, indiligence [rare], sloth, inexertion, inertia, procrastination, ergophobia, otiosity; hoboism, vagrancy; spring fever [joc.]; Castle of Indolence.

4. *n.* languor, supineness, dullness, sluggishness etc. *adj.*; lassitude, lethargy, apathy, kef, phlegm; hebetude, hebetation; lentitude, lentor [rare]; torpor, torpidity, torpitude [now rare], torpescence; stupor, stupefaction; statuvolence, statuvolism; drowsiness, sleepiness etc. *adj.*; somnolence *or* somnolency, somnolescence; oscitance *or* oscitancy, oscitation; pandiculation; sand in the eyes, heavy eyelids; anesthesia; fatigue etc. 688; slowness etc. 275; weariness etc. 841.

5. *n.* sleep, sleepry [Scot.], slumber, balmy sleep, the arms of Morpheus; balmy, doss [Eng.], shut-eye [all slang]; land of Nod, sleepland, slumberland, dreamland; nap, doze, drowse, snooze [coll.], snoozle [chiefly dial.], spot of sleep [slang, Eng.], wink, wink of sleep, forty winks [coll.], noddins and bobbins [coll.], calk [Naut. slang], cat nap, siesta, beauty sleep [coll.].

profound ~, deep ~, sound *or* heavy sleep, swoon, coma, trance, sopor, ecstasis, lethargic sleep; catalepsy, cataplexy; somnolism, somnipathy; mesmerism, mesmeric *or* hypnotic sleep, hypnotic somnolence, hypnosis, hypnotism, hypnology; peaceful sleep, sleep of the just; sleeping *or* sleepy sickness, lethargus [Med.], African lethargy, encephalitis lethargica [Med.]; hibernation, estivation; Somnus, Morpheus, sandman, dustman; repose etc. 687; dream etc. 515.5.

6. *n.* sleep-inducer, sleep-producer, sleep-provoker, sleep-bringer, sleep-stuff, sleeping draught, somnifacient; soporific, hypnotic; sedative, opiate etc. 662.6, 7; lullaby etc. 415.9.

7. *n.* idler, idleman [rare], his idleship [joc.], loafer, lounger, do-little, do-nothing, fainéant, indolent, afternoon farmer, drone, slug, sluggard, slugabed [arch.], laggard, dawdle, dawdler, dallier, dilly-dallier, mope, moper, loller, lingerer, waiter on Providence, clock watcher, eye-servant, stick-in-the-mud [coll.], good-for-nothing, Weary Willie [coll.], lazzarone (*pl.* lazzaroni), moocher [now dial. and slang], lubber, lubbard [rare].

bum, bummer, stiff, dead beat, pike, piker, soldier *or* sojer, bench warmer, lounge lizard [U.S.], dead one *or* 'un [all slang]; lazybone *or* lazybones, lazylegs, lazyboots [coll.]; sleeping partner, dummy; sleepy [coll.], sleepyhead, somnivolent, lie-abed, sleeper, slumberer, sleeping beauty; opium eater, lotus-eater; dormouse, marmot; the Fat Boy in Pickwick, Mr. Micawber [both Dickens]; tramp, hobo etc. (wanderer) 268.2, beggar etc. 767.2; malingerer etc. (shirker) 623.4; slow coach [coll.] etc. 275.4; neglector etc. 460.3.

8. *v.* be inactive etc. *adj.*, idle, do nothing, laze, lazy [coll.], loaf, lounge, loll, lollop [coll., Eng.], dally, dillydally, trifle, piddle, peddle, potter, putter [U.S.], dabble, faddle [dial. Eng.], fribble, fiddle-faddle [coll.], slug [obs.], loiter, linger, dawdle, lag, slouch, poke, take one's time, take it easy, take things as they come, drift, drift with the current, swim with the stream, lead an easy life, loll in the lap of indolence *or* luxury, eat the bread of idleness.

idle ~, trifle ~, fritter *or* fool away

---

ity.—THACKERAY. Sloth is the tempter that beguiles, and expels from paradise.—A. B. ALCOTT. Sloth, like rust, consumes faster than labor wears.—FRANKLIN. The sad fatigue of idleness.—M. GREEN. Go to the ant, thou sluggard; consider her ways and be wise.—BIBLE. For sluggard's brow the laurel never grows; / Renown is not the Child of indolent repose.—THOMSON. It is well to lie fallow for a while.—TUPPER. I loaf and invite my soul.—WHITMAN. And duller should'st thou be than the fat weed / That roots itself in ease on Lethe wharf.—SHAKESPEARE. For Satan finds some mischief still / For idle

time, while away the time, pass the time, waste *or* consume time, procrastinate, kill time, kick *or* cool one's heels [coll.], whistle for want of thought, twiddle one's thumbs, fold one's arms, not lift a finger *or* hand, let the grass grow under one's feet, lose time, waste the precious hours, burn daylight; bum [U.S.], bum around [U.S.], haze, haze about *or* around, swing the lead [Eng.], swing the bat, whip the cat, soldier *or* sojer [all slang]; mooch, mooch around [both now dial. or slang].

lie idle, lie fallow, lie around, lie *or* lay off, lie up, lie on the shelf, lay *or* lie by [Naut.], lay *or* lie to [Naut.], bring to, heave to; anchor, cast anchor, come to anchor, ride at anchor; lie *or* rest upon one's oars, rest *or* repose on one's laurels, lie back on one's record; sleep at one's post, go to sleep over; have nothing to do, have nothing on [slang]; idle at one's expense, loaf on [coll.], lay *or* lie down on [slang]; malinger etc. (shirk) 623.8; stagnate, remain motionless etc. (be quiescent) 265.5; smolder, slumber etc. (be inert) 172.2; repose etc. 687.3; move slowly etc. 275.5.

9. *v.* sleep, be asleep etc. *adj.*, slumber, rest in the arms of Morpheus, pound the ear [slang, U.S.]; snooze [coll.], snoozle [chiefly dial.], doze, drowse, nap, take a nap etc. *n.*; sleep soundly *or* heavily, sleep like a top, ~ log *or* dormouse; get sleepy, nod; weigh down the eyelids; yawn, oscitate, gape, gap [dial.]; go to bed, turn in [coll.], hit the hay [slang]; go to sleep, settle to sleep, go off to sleep, fall *or* drop asleep, drop off [coll.], calk off [Naut. slang], close the eyes, seal up the eyes; hibernate, estivate; oversleep; snore; repose etc. 687.3; dream etc. 515.9.

10. *v.* languish, expend itself, droop, sink, decline, flag, pine, hang fire; relax.

11. *v.* inactivate, unactivate, unactive [rare]; sluggardize; somnify [rare]; mitigate etc. (moderate) 174.5.

12. *adj.* inactive, unactive; idle, idlish, idleset [Scot. and Ir.]; idling, loafing etc. *v.*; désœuvré [F.], leisured, unoccupied, unemployed, disengaged, out-of-work, out of a job *or* employ; rusty; fallow etc. 674.10; not doing etc. 681.3; motionless etc. (quiescent) 265.7; dormant, stagnant etc. (inert) 172.3; reposing etc. 687.6.

13. *adj.* indolent, lazy, do-nothing, fainéant, slothful, remiss, slack, lax, shiftless, laggard, lackadaisical, maudlin, lazy as Ludlam's dog; dilatory etc. 133.9; negligent etc. 460.8; indifferent etc. 823.5.

14. *adj.* languid, supine, lentitudinous, sluggish, phlegmatic, lymphatic, otiose, heavy, dull, hebetudinous, dopey [slang], leaden, lumpish, dead, lethargic(al), apathetic, listless, lifeless, soulless, exanimate, inert; torpid, torpescent, torpedinous [rare], torporific; drony, dronish; slow etc. 275.8; weary etc. 841.9.

15. *adj.* sleepy, sleepful, sleep-filled, full of sleep, sleep-desiring, slumbery, slumberous, dozy, snoozy [coll.], drowsy, oscitant, nappy, yawny, stretchy [coll.], dreamy, lethargic(al), comatose, heavy, heavy with sleep, sleep-swollen, sleep-drowned, sleep-drunk; somnific, somniferous, somnial [rare], somniative [rare], somnolent, somnolescent; half asleep, with half-shut eyes; Morphean.

16. *adj.* sleeping etc. *v.*, asleep, in the arms *or* lap of Morpheus; in dreams, in dreamland; fast ~, dead *or* sound asleep, in a sound sleep, sound as a top, dormant, comatose, unconscious, dead, dead to the world; unwakened, unawakened; reposing etc. 687.6.

17. *adj.* sleep-inducing, sleep-producing, sleep-bringing, sleep-causing, sleep-compelling, sleep-inviting, sleep-provoking, sleep-tempting, sleep-soothing, balmy; somnifacient, somniferous, somnific, somnolent; soporose *or* soporous [obs.], soporific, soporiferous; hypnotic, mesmeric(al), sedative etc. 174.7.

684. Haste
(See 685. Leisure)

1. *n.* haste, hurry, scurry, rush, scuttle, scamper, dash, drive, scramble, hustle [coll.], bustle, fuss, flurry, flutter, sputter, splutter, fidget; urgency [arch.], no

---

hands to do.—I. WATTS. Sing we for love and idleness, / Naught else is worth the having. —E. POUND. Sleep that knits up the ravel'd sleave of care.—SHAKESPEARE. The mystery of folded sleep.—TENNYSON. Thou driftest gently down the tides of sleep.—LONGFELLOW Slumber lay so deep / Even her hands upon her lap / Seemed saturate with sleep.—DE LA MARE. Idleness is the root of all evil. Idle folks have the least leisure.

684. Hasty climbers have sudden falls.—J. RAY. There is no workman, what-so-ever he be, / That may both worken well and hastily.

time to be lost; acceleration, dispatch *or* despatch, expedition; precipitance *or* precipitancy, precipitation, precipitousness etc. *adj.*; impetuosity, *brusquerie* [F.]; celerity, speed etc. (velocity) 274; promptness etc. (punctuality) 132.3.

2. *v.* hasten, haste [now literary and dial.], hasty [obs. exc. Scot.]; hurry, hurry up [coll.], hustle [coll.], rush, accelerate, speed, quicken, expedite, precipitate, forward; urge, whip, lash, flog, spur, goad, prod, prick, push, press, drive ~, urge etc. forward, hurry etc. on, whip on, hound on, egg on, set on; express, railroad [coll., U.S.]; speed up etc. 274.10.

3. *v.* make haste, hasten etc. *above* 684.2, act with haste, hurry, hurry up [coll.], rush, scurry, scuttle, scamper, scramble, hustle [coll.], bustle, fuss, flutter, splutter, fidget; hurry etc. about, dart to and fro; hurry etc. on, dash on, press *or* push on, press forward, scuttle along, bundle on; bestir oneself, stir one's stumps [coll.]; lose no time, not lose a moment; make short work of, make the best of one's time *or* way; move quickly, run etc. (speed) 274.9.

4. *v.* be in haste, be in a hurry etc. *n.*; have no time to lose *or* spare, have not a moment to lose *or* spare; work against time, work under pressure; be precipitate etc. *adj.*, plunge, plunge headlong, jump at.

5. *adj.* hasty, hastish, hasteful; hurried, expeditious; scrambling, pushing, pressing etc. *v.*; impetuous, impulsive, precipitate, headlong, breakneck, furious, boisterous, feverish; brusque, abrupt, blunt; cursory, passing, superficial; urgent [arch.]; speedy, swift etc. (fast) 274.13; sudden etc. 113.5.

6. *adj.* in haste, in a hurry etc. *n.*, in hot haste, in all haste; pressed for time, hard pressed, ~ pushed *or* run, breathless; impatient etc. 825.8.

7. *adv.* hastily, hurriedly, precipitately

etc. *adj.*; helter-skelter, hurry-scurry, holus-bolus, slapdash, slap-bang [coll.]; hop, skip, and jump; hotfoot, full tilt, full-drive, pell-mell, headlong, headforemost, *à corps perdu* [F.], head over heels, heels over head, head and shoulders, hand over head [now rare], hand over hand *or* fist; in haste etc. *adj.*, with haste, with great *or* all haste, with breathless speed, posthaste, amain.

by cable, by telegraph, by wireless [coll.], by air mail, by return mail, by airplane, by steam [coll.], by forced marches; quickly, apace etc. (swiftly) 274.14; beforehand etc. 132.12; all at once etc. (suddenly) 113.7; without delay, immediately etc. (promptly) 132.14; actively etc. 682.25.

8. *int.* make haste!, hurry!, hurry up! [coll.], rush!, immediate!, urgent!; get a move on! [coll.], get a wiggle on! [slang], stir your stumps! [coll.], step lively!; look lively *or* alive! [coll.], look slick *or* slippy! [coll.], look sharp!, sharp is the word!; quickmarch!, double!, charge! [all Mil.].

685. Leisure
(See 684. Haste)

1. *n.* leisure, ease, convenience, freedom; free *or* spare time, spare hours *or* moments, odd moments, dodge times [slang], time to spare, time to burn [slang, U.S.], time on one's hands, time hanging heavy on one's hands, time at one's disposal *or* command, time; *otium cum dignitate* (Cicero); vacation etc. 687.2; interim etc. 108a; idleness etc. 683.2.

2. *v.* have leisure etc. *n.*, be master of one's time, take one's leisure, ~ time *or* ease, do at one's leisure *or* convenience; *desipere in loco* (Horace); while away the time etc. (inaction) 681.2; take one's time etc. (move slowly) 275.5; repose etc. 687.3–5.

—Chaucer. Too swift arrives as tardy as too slow.—Shakespeare. There is nothing more requisite in business than despatch.—Addison. Business dispatched is business well done, but business hurried is business ill done.—Bulwer-Lytton. Never lose your presence of mind, and never get hurried.—Emerson. Though I am always in haste I am never in a hurry.—Wesley. The more haste the less speed. Haste makes waste. Make haste slowly.

685. *Deus nobis haec otia fecit* [A god has conferred this leisure upon us].—Vergil. The wisdom of a learned man cometh by opportunity of leisure; and he that hath little business shall become wise.—Apocrypha. Retired Leisure / That in trim gardens takes his pleasure.—Milton. A life of leisure and a life of laziness are two things.—Franklin. Employ thy time well if thou meanest to gain leisure.—Franklin. Leisure is the time for doing something useful.—N. Howe.

3. *adj.* leisured, unoccupied etc. (inactive) 683.12–14.
4. *adj.* leisurely, unhurried, hasteless, easy, deliberate; at one's leisure, at one's convenience, at one's own sweet time; slow etc. 275.8.

686. Exertion
(See 687. Repose)

1. *n.* exertion, effort, struggle, stretch, strain, stress, stress and strain, heft [obs. exc. dial.], tug, pull, throw; great effort, dead lift, hard ~, strong *or* long pull, "a long pull, a strong pull, and a pull all together" (Dickens), uphill work, hard work; ado, great ado; trouble, pains; attempt, endeavor etc. (essay) 675; energy etc. 171.

2. *n.* exercise, exercitation; practice, drill; sport, play; athletic exercise, athletics, gymnastics, palaestrics [rare], calisthenics, eurythmics *or* eurhythmics; racing, running, jumping, riding etc.; violent exercise, breather [coll.]; constitutional [coll.] etc. (walk) 266.4.

3. *n.* labor, work, employment, industry, toil, moil, swink [arch. and dial.], travail [rare], fatigue, sweat [arch.], sweat of one's brow, grind, drudgery, slavery; plodding, hammering etc. *v.*; fag [coll., Eng.], faggery, fagging; hard work *or* labor, hard [cant], warm work, hard *or* tough grind [coll.], toil and trouble, uphill work etc. *above* 686.1; manual labor, handiwork, elbow grease [joc.]; *limae labor* [L.]; laboriousness, operoseness etc. *adj.*, operosity; stroke *or* stitch of work, stroke, lick [coll.], spell, stretch, spurt *or* spirt; task, occupation etc. (business) 625; difficult task etc. (difficulty) 704; easy work etc. 705.2.

4. *n.* laborer etc. (worker) 690.2.

5. *v.* exert oneself, exert *or* tax one's energies, use exertion etc. *n.*, put forth one's strength, put forth a strong arm, huff and puff, strive, strain, struggle, pull, tug, ply; ply the oar, tug at the oar, take the laboring oar; take trouble *or* pains, trouble oneself; make *or* stretch a long arm; try etc. (essay) 675.3–5.

6. *v.* labor, struggle etc. *above*, work, toil, moil, toil and moil, slave, fag, swink [arch.], drudge, grind, dig [coll.], grub, plod, hammer, peg, peg away *or* along, work ~, drudge etc. away; plug, plug at it, plug away *or* along [all slang]; work hard, work one's head off [coll.], work one's fingers to the bone, work like a horse *or* cart horse, work like a dog, work like a slave *or* galley slave, work like a coal heaver, work like a nigger [coll.], work like a Briton; sweat [coll.], sweat and slave [coll.], sweat like a nigger at election [slang, U.S.].

work *or* fight one's way, lay about one, hammer at, wade through, drag a lengthened chain; redouble one's efforts, do double duty, work double hours *or* double tides, work day and night, sit up, burn the midnight oil, burn the candle at both ends; overwork, overlabor, overdo; be busy etc. 682.13; busy oneself, ply one's trade etc. 625.6–8; take in hand etc. (undertake) 676.2; hustle [coll.], bestir oneself etc. (be active) 682.12; try hard etc. 675.4, 5; stick to etc. (persevere) 604a.2.

7. *v.* set to work, fall to work, get busy, fall to, buckle to, turn to, set to *or* about, enter on *or* upon, start in, launch into *or* upon, wade into, plunge into; pitch in *or* into, fire away, tackle, tackle down *or* to, knuckle to *or* down to, get going [all coll.]; light into, hop *or* jump to it [all slang]; put *or* lay one's shoulder to the wheel, put one's hand to the plow, take the bull by the horns, bend the bow.

8. *v.* task, tax, work, busy, keep busy, impose a task upon, lay a burden upon, burden, oppress with great labor, fag, sweat [coll.], drive, strain; overtask, overtax, overwork, overburden, overdrive, overstrain; fatigue etc. 688.5.

9. *adj.* laboring, working etc. *v.*; workday, workaday, prosaic; hard at work etc. (busy) 682.20; hard-working etc. (industrious) 682.19.

10. *adj.* laborious, arduous, toilsome, burdensome, onerous, heavy [coll.], hefty

---

686. Come unto me, all ye that labour and are heavy laden.—BIBLE. There is nothing truly valuable which can be purchased without pains and labour.—ADDISON. Work and acquire, and thou hast chained the wheel of Chance.—EMERSON. The nobility of labor—the long pedigree of toil.—LONGFELLOW. *Labor omnia vincit* [Hard work conquers all things].—VERGIL. Before virtue the immortal gods have put the sweat of man's brow.—HESIOD. He who strives / Will find his gods strive for him equally.—EURIPIDES. In the sweat of thy face shalt thou eat bread.—BIBLE. If any would not work, neither should he eat.—BIBLE. What profit hath a man of all his labour which he taketh under the sun?—BIBLE. All work and no play makes Jack a dull boy.

[coll., U.S.], tough [coll.], elaborate [arch.], operose, strenuous, strained, troublesome, uphill, Herculean; hard-fought, hard-earned; painful [arch.], painstaking; exercising, gymnastic, athletic, calisthenic(al); palaestric, palaestral, palaestrian; difficult etc. 704.8; wearisome etc. (fatiguing) 688.8.

11. *adv.* laboriously, arduously etc. *adj.,* lustily, with much ado, with might and main, with all one's might, *totis viribus* [L.], *manibus pedibusque* [L.], *pugnis et calcibus* [L.], *vi et armis* [L.], with a strong hand, with sledge hammer, tooth and nail, *unguibus et rostro* [L.], hammer and tongs, heart and soul, to the best of one's ability; by the sweat of one's brow, *suo Marte* [L.]; uphill, upstream, against the stream; through thick and thin etc. (perseveringly) 604a.4; with difficulty etc. 704.12.

687. Repose
(See 686. Exertion)

1. *n.* repose, silken repose, rest, ease, relaxation; inactivity, sleep etc. 683.1–5; quiet, stillness etc. (quiescence) 265.

2. *n.* vacation, recess, respite, breathing time *or* spell, breathing, spell, pause, halt, stay, lull, intermission; letup, time out [both coll.]; day of rest, *dies non* [L.]; Sabbath, Sunday, Lord's Day, First day; holiday etc. 840.5; Christmas etc. 138.7; spare time etc. (leisure) 685.

3. *v.* repose, rest, rest and be thankful, take rest, take one's ease, take it easy [coll.]; go to rest, lie down, recline, couch, settle to rest; sprawl, loll; recline on a bed of down, recline on an easy chair; go to bed, ~ sleep etc. 683.9; lie idle etc. 683.8; lie still etc. (be quiescent) 265.5.

4. *v.* relax, unbend, unbrace, slacken; lie *or* rest upon one's oars, repose on one's laurels; take breath etc. 689.3; stay one's hand, pause etc. (cease) 142.6.

5. *v.* vacation, holiday, take a holiday etc. *n.,* take time out [coll.], shut up shop; Sunday, Christmas etc. [coll.].

6. *adj.* reposing, reposed etc. *v.*; reposeful, restful, peaceful; inactive, sleeping etc. 683.12, 16; quiescent etc. 265.7.

7. *adj.* vacational, holiday, ferial, festal; sabbatic *or* sabbatical.

8. *adv.* at rest, at ease, at one's ease.

688. Fatigue
(See 689. Refreshment)

1. *n.* fatigue, tiredness, weariness etc. *adj.*; tire [chiefly dial.], tucker [coll., U.S.]; fatiguing task, fag [coll., Eng.]; lassitude, drowsiness etc. (languor) 683.4.

2. *n.* shortness of breath, anhelation [rare], dyspnea, panting, labored breathing.

3. *n.* faintness, fainting, deliquium [arch.], goneness, exhaustion, collapse, prostration; nociassociation [Med.]; faint, swoon, coma, syncope, lipothymy *or* lypothymia, sopor, stupor.

4. *v.* be fatigued, become weary etc. *adj.*; tire etc. *below,* jade, irk [obs. exc. dial.], fag [now rare], droop, sink, flag, wilt, peg out [slang]; lose breath *or* wind, gasp, pant, puff, blow; faint, swoon, drop, fall in a faint etc. *n.,* succumb; get sleepy, yawn etc. 683.9.

5. *v.* fatigue, tire, weary, flag, exhaust, jade, harass, knock up [coll., Eng.], fag, tucker [coll., U.S.], take the tuck out of [coll., U.S.], tire ~, weary ~, fag etc. out, wear out, poop out [slang], weary *or* tire to death, do up [coll.], use up [coll.], frazzle [chiefly U.S.], bleed white, prostrate; bore etc. 841.5; tax etc. 686.8.

6. *adj.* fatigued, tired, exhausted etc. *v.*; weary, wearíful, full of weariness etc. *n.,* drooping etc. *v.,* enfeebled, spent, played out, tired out, fagged out, tuckered out [coll., U.S.], worn out, bushed [slang

---

687. Repose is a good thing, but boredom is its brother.—VOLTAIRE.   The best of men have ever loved repose.—THOMSON.   The end and the reward of toil is rest.—BEATTIE. Too much rest itself becomes a pain.—HOMER. Take rest; a field that has rested gives a bountiful crop.—OVID.   Rest a mile and run a mile.—PALSGRAVE.   To repair our nature with comforting repose.—SHAKESPEARE.   In quiet she reposes: / Ah! would that I did too.—M. ARNOLD.   He maketh me to lie down in green pastures.—BIBLE.

---

688. Art thou pale for weariness?—SHELLEY. I care not for my spirits if my legs were not weary.—SHAKESPEARE.   I 'gin to be aweary of the sun.—SHAKESPEARE.   Even the weariest river / Winds somewhere safe to sea.—SWINBURNE.   My body is weary to death of my mischievous brain; / I am weary forever and ever of being brave.—E. WYLIE.

or dial., U.S.], knocked up [coll., Eng.], dog-weary, dog-tired, dead-tired, tired to death, weary unto death, dead-alive, more dead than alive, ready to drop, on one's last legs.

tired-armed, tired-winged, weary-winged; weary-laden, "tired and weary-laden" (Bible); dead, dead-beat, done, done up, used up [all coll.]; all in, beat, pooped out, pegged out [all slang]; faint, faintish, feeling faint; tired-looking, weary-looking, tired-eyed, tired-faced, haggard, seedy [coll.]; worn, worn to a frazzle or shadow, weary-worn, toilworn, wayworn, way-weary; weary-footed, foot-weary, footsore; prostrate, hors de combat [F.]; overfatigued, overtired, overwearied, overspent; unrefreshed, unrestored; drowsy etc. 683.15.

7. *adj.* breathless, windless, winded, pumped [slang], blown, out of breath, short of breath or wind, short-breathed, short-winded, broken-winded, touched in the wind, anhelose or anhelous [rare], panting etc. *v.*, puffing and blowing; dyspneal, dyspneic; asthmatic.

8. *adj.* fatiguing, wearing, wearying, tiring etc. *v.*; fatiguesome, tiresome, wearisome, wearyful, mortal [coll.], yawny [coll.]; tedious, boring etc. 841.8; laborious etc. 686.10.

689. Refreshment
(See **688. Fatigue**)

1. *n.* refreshment, refreshing, bracing etc. *v.*; recovery of strength, refection, invigoration, vivification, reinvigoration, revivification, refocillation [rare], enlivement, exhilaration, stimulation; recuperation, recuperance; regale, regalement; revival, repair etc. (restoration) 660; relief etc. 834.

2. *v.* refresh, freshen, freshen up, fresh up [chiefly dial.], refect [arch.], revivify, revive, reinvigorate, reanimate, re-enliven, brace, brace up, set up, set on one's legs or feet [coll.], exhilarate, stimulate, fortify, animate, quicken, put or infuse new life or blood into; vivify, vivificate [rare]; brisk, brisken; regale, cheer, give or take refreshment, refresh the inner man; cool, air, fan; restore, renew etc.

660.8, 13; relieve etc. 834.4; strengthen etc. 159.8.

3. *v.* recuperate, recruit, recover ∼, recruit ∼, regain or renew one's strength, get better, raise one's head, rally, revive, perk up, come to, come to oneself, feel like a giant refreshed; take a favorable turn, take a turn for the better; regain or recover breath, gather ∼, take or draw breath, take a long breath, drink in the ozone; recover etc. 660.15.

4. *adj.* refreshing, bracing etc. *v.*, refreshful; recuperative, revivatory etc. (restorative) 660.18.

5. *adj.* refreshed etc. *v.*, fresh, fit, untired, unwearied.

690. Agent

1. *n.* agent, doer, actor, performer, practitioner, perpetrator; operator, operative; executor, executrix; mediary, medium, interagent, reagent; factor, steward; minister etc. (instrument) 631.2; representative etc. (deputy) 759; servant etc. 746.

2. *n.* worker, workman, workingman, laboring man, laborer, day laborer, navvy [Eng.], hand, workhand, man; workwoman, workingwoman, workgirl; toiler, moiler, drudge, hack, plodder, fag, fagger, slave, work horse, beast of burden; hewers of wood and drawers of water; employee or employé or employe, hireling, hired man or hand, wageworker, help [local, U.S.]; menial, flunky [derog.], mere tool; roustabout [U.S.], lumper, stevedore; apprentice, prentice [coll. or dial.]; bee, ant, termite; hustler [coll.] etc. (man of action) 682.10.

3. *n.* factotum, general servant [Eng.], general [coll.], do-all [coll.], servant of all work, man of all work; maid of all work, general housework maid [U.S.].

4. *n.* co-worker, fellow worker, associate, colleague etc. (auxiliary) 711; personnel [F.] etc. (staff) 746.7; dramatis personae [L.] etc. 599.18.

5. *n.* craftsman, handicraftsman, craftworker, artisan, artificer, *artifex* [L.], artist, skilled laborer, journeyman; mechanic, mechanician, machinist; engineer, civil engineer, structural engineer, elec-

---

689. There's refreshment even in toil.—KEATS. They that wait upon the Lord shall renew their strength.—BIBLE. For they have refreshed my spirit and yours.—BIBLE.

690. *Faber est quisque fortunae suae* [Each one is the maker of his own fortune].—SALLUST. The labourer is worthy of his hire.—BIBLE. A workman that needeth not to be ashamed.—

trical engineer, mining engineer, military engineer, sanitary engineer; plumber, gas fitter; carpenter, chips [slang], woodworker, cabinetmaker; builder, architect, mason, bricklayer, puddler, tinker, contractor.

6. *n.* smith, smither [Eng.], smithier [arch.], smithy; forger, Vulcan [Rom. Myth.], Hephaestus [Gr. Myth.]; goldsmith, silversmith, bronzesmith, coppersmith, brass-smith, platinumsmith, tinsmith, ironsmith, blacksmith, toolsmith, boltsmith, scissors-smith, bladesmith, gunsmith, stonesmith, hammersmith, clocksmith, swordsmith, tiresmith, wiresmith, axlesmith, hedgesmith, knifesmith, locksmith, anvilsmith, picksmith, sawsmith, scythesmith, boilersmith, coachsmith, carriagesmith; metalworker etc. *below* 690.9.

7. *n.* wright, boatwright, shipwright, cartwright, coachwright, wagonwright, wainwright, wheelwright, timberwright, tilewright, housewright, millwright, plowwright, bookwright, gatewright, pitwright, butterwright, candlewright, millwright.

8. *n.* maker, manufacturer etc. (producer) 164; anvil maker, arrow maker, axmaker *or* axemaker, bagmaker, balance maker, barrelmaker, basketmaker, bedmaker, beermaker, bellmaker, bellowsmaker, beltmaker, blanketmaker, blockmaker, board maker, bobbin maker, bodymaker, boilermaker, boltmaker, bookmaker, bootmaker etc. 225.40, bottlemaker, bowmaker, boxmaker, brakemaker, breadmaker, brickmaker, bridgemaker, broommaker, brushmaker, bucketmaker, bulletmaker, bushmaker, buttermaker, button maker, cabinetmaker, cakemaker, candlemaker, candymaker, canvas maker, capmaker, carpetmaker, cartmaker, casemaker, cementmaker, chainmaker, chairmaker, cheese maker, cider maker, cigarette maker, cigar maker, cloakmaker, clockmaker, clogmaker, clothmaker, coachmaker, coffinmaker, collar maker, colormaker, combmaker, coremaker, couchmaker, cradlemaker, cratemaker, cupmaker, diemaker, dishmaker, dollmaker, doormaker, dressmaker etc. 225.38, fanmaker, feather maker, feltmaker, fiddle maker, glassmaker, glovemaker, gluemaker, gunmaker, harness maker, hatmaker, hookmaker, ice maker, inkmaker, ironmaker, kettlemaker, lacemaker, lampmaker, leathermaker, lens maker, lockmaker, map maker, modelmaker, nail maker, needlemaker, netmaker, papermaker, patternmaker, penmaker, pie maker, porcelain maker, potmaker, road maker, ropemaker, rugmaker, sackmaker, saddle maker, safemaker, sailmaker, saltmaker, sausage maker, sawmaker, scale maker, scarf maker, screw maker, scythe maker, shoemaker etc. 225.40, soapmaker, steelmaker, sugar maker, tentmaker, tilemaker, watchmaker, wigmaker, wine maker.

9. *n.* (workers) metalworker, goldworker, ironworker, brassworker, wireworker, woodworker, waxworker, sawworker, clothworker, flintworker, garmentworker, glassworker, butterworker, chalkworker, fieldworker, needleworker, pieceworker, saltworker, shellworker.

10. *n.* (cross references) domestic, lackey, maid etc. (servant) 746; laundress etc. 652.6; miner, tunneler etc. (excavator) 252.7; printer, proofreader etc. 591.12, 13; bookmaker etc. 593.14; tailor, haberdasher, etc. 225.36–40; repairman etc. (mender) 660.7; electrician etc. 157a.10; porter etc. (carrier) 271; water carrier etc. 348.16; coachman, chauffeur, engineman, railroader etc. (traveler) 268.8–12; mariner etc. 269; aviator etc. 269a; painter, sculptor, engraver, photographer etc. (artist) 559; writer, journalist etc. 593.15–17; stagehand etc. 599.17; actor etc. 599.18–21; scientist etc. 492.5; teacher etc. 540; lexicographer etc. 560.7; lawyer etc. 968; doctor, nurse, pharmacist etc. 662.19–21; optician etc. 445.8; masseur etc. 331.2; undertaker etc. 363.6; merchant etc. 797; clerk, secretary, stenographer etc. 590.11, 12; farmer etc. (agriculturist) 371.2; cowboy, herdsman etc. (stockman) 370.4; mailman etc. 534.2.

691. Workshop

n. workshop, workhouse, shop, plant, office; sweatshop; hive, hive of indus-

---

BIBLE. By the work one knows the workman.—LA FONTAINE. A carpenter's known by his chips.—SHAKESPEARE. He was an honest man and a good bricklayer.—SHAKESPEARE.

691. The Continent will not suffer England to be the workshop of the world.—DISRAELI. America is God's crucible, the great Melting

try, beehive, alveary, *alvearium* [L.]; laboratory, lab [coll.]; factory, manufactory, *usine* [F.]; works, steelworks, ironworks, copperworks, brassworks, wireworks, boilerworks, gasworks, scrapworks, saltworks, printworks, glassworks, tryworks, bleachworks etc.; nailery; bindery; mill, rolling mill, powder mill, sawmill, flour mill, coffee mill, cotton mill etc.; armory, arsenal; mint; foundry *or* foundery, forge, furnace; cabinet, bureau; dock *or* docks, dockyard, shipyard, yard, slip, wharf; roundhouse; laundry etc. 652.4; cookroom etc. 386.4; studio etc. 556.15; farm, garden etc. 371.4–6.

692. Conduct

1. *n.* conduct, behavior, havior [arch. and dial.]; deportment, comportment, carriage, *maintien* [F.], address, demeanor, mien, guise, bearing, manner, air, presence, *prestance* [F.], observance, moral action; practice, praxis; manner of conducting *or* carrying oneself, *modus operandi* [L.], line *or* course of conduct, line of action, proceeding, procedure, process; way, ways; acts, actions, goings on; correct deportment, good behavior, manners, good manners; behaviorism, behavior psychology; management etc. (direction) 693; transaction, execution etc. (action) 680; method etc. (way) 627; usage etc. 677.2.

2. *n.* policy, polity; game, little game; tactics, devices, expedients; strategy, strategics; plan etc. 626; program etc. (schedule) 611.2; platform etc. 626.4.

3. *n.* career, life, course, race, walk, province, line, role; path etc. 627.2; function etc. 625.3.

4. *v.* conduct, carry on, advance, forward, help forward, maintain, proceed with, prosecute, administer, execute, enact, transact, discharge, dispatch *or* despatch; deal with, have to do with, treat, handle; take action, take steps *or* measures; manage etc. (direct) 693.4, 5; officiate etc. 625.9.

Pot where all the races of Europe are melting and re-forming!—I. ZANGWILL.
692. As the occasion, so the behaviour.—CERVANTES. We give advice, but we cannot give conduct.—LA ROCHEFOUCAULD. Behavior is a mirror in which everyone shows his image.—GOETHE. Conduct is three-fourths of our life and its largest concern.—M. ARNOLD.

5. *v.* conduct oneself, behave oneself, comport oneself, demean oneself, bear oneself, carry oneself, acquit oneself, behave, behave etc. well *or* ill; take *or* adopt a course, steer *or* shape one's course, run a race, lead a life, play a game, play one's part, play one's cards; shift for oneself, paddle one's own canoe; bail one's own boat.

6. *adj.* conducting etc. *v.*; directing etc. 693.6.

7. *adj.* behavioral, behaviorist, behavioristic, behaviorized.

693. Direction
(See also 694. Director)

1. *n.* direction, directing, managing etc. *v.*; management, government, gubernation [obs.], conduct, regulation, guidance, steerage, pilotage; bossism [slang, U.S.]; legislation, legislature; reins, reins of government, helm, rudder; *régime* [F.], regime, regimen; monarchy, oligarchy etc. (governments) 737.4–6; advice etc. 695.

2. *n.* supervision, superintendence, surveillance, oversight, eye of the master; ministry, ministration, administration; jurisdiction, judicature, judicatory; control, controlment; charge, care, auspices, patronage, protection; board of control etc. (council) 696; command etc. (dominion) 737.2, 3.

3. *n.* managership, directorship, administratorship, generalship, governorship, leadership, stewardship, proctorship; statesmanship, statecraft, kingcraft, queencraft, premiership, senatorship; husbandry, ménage *or* menage, domestic management, housekeeping, housewifery; economy, economics, political economy; portfolio; mastership etc. 737.3.

4. *v.* direct, manage, govern, regulate, conduct, carry on, handle, run [coll., U.S.]; order, prescribe, cut out work for; head, lead, lead *or* show the way, take the lead, lead on, guide, steer, pilot, take the helm, be at the helm, handle ~, hold *or* take the reins, crack the whip, drive, tool [slang].

---

693. What government is best? That which teaches us to govern ourselves.—GOETHE. He that would govern others, first should be / The master of himself.—MASSINGER. No man ever saw a government.—W. WILSON. The world is governed too much.—UNKNOWN.

5. *v.* superintend, supervise, boss [coll.], overlook, oversee, look after, see to; administer, administrate; control, keep in order, pull the strings *or* wires, be the guiding force, pull the stroke oar; patronize, matronize; have the care *or* charge of, have *or* take the direction of; be in the seat of authority, take *or* occupy the chair, have the portfolio, have ~, hold *or* fill an office; preside, preside at the board; straw-boss [coll.]; command etc. (rule) 737.11.

6. *adj.* directing etc. *v.*, directive, regulative, executive, administrative, supervisory, boss [coll.]; governmental, gubernatorial, gubernative [now rare]; jurisdictional, jurisdictive; official, ex officio, ex-official; hegemonic(al); dictatorial, bossy [coll.]; ruling, predominant etc. (authoritative) 737.15, 16.

7. *adv.* in charge, in control, at the head, at the helm; in the seat of authority, in the saddle [coll.], on the throne; under the auspices *or* guidance of, in the hands of, in one's power, under one's control, at one's command, at one's nod.

694. Director
(See also 693. Direction)

1. *n.* director, manager, governor, executive, rector, dictator, controller, comptroller, husband [arch.], administrator, *entrepreneur* [F.]; intendant, superintendent, super [slang], supervisor, overseer, overlooker, overman, foreman, *caporal* [Sp. Amer.], boss [coll.], baas [Du.], gaffer [Eng.], taskmaster, ganger; subforeman, straw boss [coll.]; aedile [Rom. Hist.]; inspector, surveyor, visitor, ranger; enterpriser, projector, organizer; monitor; supercargo, husband, ship's husband; impresario; leader, coryphaeus, precentor, bellwether, file leader; fugleman, flugelman; ringleader, agitator, demagogue; choragus *or* choregus; collector; chairman, chair, speaker.

2. *n.* head, chief, captain, king, president etc. (master) 745.1–12.

3. *n.* officer, official, officiant; functionary, *fonctionnaire* [F.]; executive officer, executive, magistrate; minister; officeholder, office-bearer, Jack-in-office, factotum; bureaucrat; red-tapist; government and military officers etc. 745.2–12.

4. *n.* statesman, statist [rare], politician, legislator, politico, lawgiver, statemonger [derog.]; officer of state, Secretary of State, Reis Effendi [Turk.]; political dictator, boss [slang, U.S.], power behind the throne, kingmaker, wirepuller, strategist; Minos, Draco; congressman etc. 696.8.

5. *n.* steward, factor, bailiff, seneschal, major-domo; housekeeper, matron; proctor, procurator, curator, librarian; clerk of works; landreeve; croupier; agent etc. (deputy) 759.

6. *n.* guide, guider; director, directory; conductor, leader, shepherd, cicerone, *valet de place* [F.], courier, dragoman, pilot; helmsman, steersman; postilion *or* postillion, postboy; guiding star, lodestar *or* loadstar, polestar, Polaris, North Star, *l'Etoile du Nord* [F.], cynosure; guideboard, guidepost, signpost; finger post, handpost; pointer, finger, hand; needle, compass; adviser etc. 695.3; interpreter etc. 524; informant etc. 527.5.

7. *n.* guidebook, handbook, instruction book, manual, *vade mecum* [L.], directory, itinerary, road map, roadbook; Baedeker, Bradshaw, Murray; map, chart etc. (plan) 626.2.

695. Advice

1. *n.* advice, advisement [arch.], aviso, counsel, piece of advice, word to the wise, *verbum sapienti* [L.], word in the ear, flea in the ear [coll.], tip [coll.], suggestion, recommendation, advocacy; hortation, exhortation etc. (persuasion) 615.4; dehortation [rare], admonition, expostulation, remonstrance etc. (deprecation) 766; instruction, injunction etc. (precept) 697; guidance etc. (direction) 693; advisability etc. (expedience) 646.

2. *n.* consultation, parley etc. (conference) 588.3; conclave, convention etc. (assembly) 696.2.

---

694. To be a leader of men one must turn one's back on men.—H. ELLIS.   They that govern the most make the least noise.—SELDEN. Either I am the foremost horse in the team, or I am none.—FLETCHER.

695. Many receive advice, few profit by it.— PUBLILIUS.   Advice when most needed is least heeded.—J. RAY.   He that will not be counselled cannot be helped.—FULLER.   Nobody can give you wiser advice than yourself.— CICERO.   One gives nothing so liberally as advice.—LA ROCHEFOUCAULD.   Beware lest clamor be taken for counsel.—ERASMUS.

3. *n.* adviser *or* advisor, prompter, counsel, counselor, admonisher, admonitor, monitor, mentor, Nestor; sage etc. 500; oracle etc. 513; teacher etc. 540; guide etc. 694.6.

4. *v.* advise, counsel, give a piece of advice etc. *n.*, suggest, recommend, prescribe, advocate; admonish, exhort, prompt, urge, move; expostulate, remonstrate.

5. *v.* enjoin, enforce, charge, instruct; call, call upon; dictate.

6. *v.* advise with, confer with, discuss with, take up with, consult together, lay *or* put heads together, deliberate, discuss, talk over; exchange observations *or* views, compare notes; consult, refer to, call in; hold conference etc. (confer) 588.8.

7. *v.* take advice *or* counsel, follow advice, follow, follow implicitly; be advised by, have at one's elbow, take one's cue from.

8. *adj.* advisory, commendatory, recommendatory; expostulative, expostulatory; admonitory; monitory, monitorial; hortative, hortatory; dehortative, dehortatory [both rare]; consultative, consultatory; dictatory, dictatorial; didactic.

9. *v.* advisable, desirable, commendable etc. (expedient) 646.4.

696. Council

1. *n.* council, deliberative *or* advisory body; committee, subcommittee, comitia [Rom. Hist.], court, chamber, cabinet, bench, staff; board, board of control, ~ works, ~ overseers etc.; junta, divan, musnud, Sanhedrin [Jewish Antiq.], amphictyonic council [Gr. Hist.]; syndicate; privy council, common council, county council, parish council, city council; zemstvo [Russ.]; tribunal etc. 966.

When all is done, the help of good counsel is that which setteth business straight.—BACON. To profit from advice requires more wisdom than to give it.—COLLINS. We ask advice but we mean approbation.—C. COLTON. Good but rarely came from good advice.—BYRON. It is always a silly thing to give advice, but to give good advice is absolutely fatal. —WILDE. One can advise comfortably from a safe port.—SCHILLER. He had only one vanity; he thought he could give advice better than any other person.—MARK TWAIN.
696. The Parliament of Man, the Federation of the world.—TENNYSON. A Parliament is

2. *n.* assembly, assemblage, *assemblée* [F.]; meeting, gathering, congregation, congress, concourse, synod, muster, sitting, séance, camarilla, conclave, convention, convocation, conference, consultation, audience, hearing, session, durbar [Ind.], palaver, *pourparler* [F.], powwow [U.S.]; council fire [N. Amer. Ind.]; plenum, caucus, quorum.

3. *n.* (ecclesiastical) parochial council *or* court, parochial church council, diocesan ~, provincial ~, primatial ~, national ~, plenary ~, general ~, universal *or* ecumenical council; convocation, synod, congregation, church, chapter, directory, vestry, consistory, conventicle, conclave, convention, classis, conference, session, presbytery.

4. *n.* legislature, legislative body, senate, General Assembly, parliament, congress, national council, States-General, diet, *Congreso Nacional* [Sp.], *Congresso Nacional* [Pg.]; soviet (Russia), Duma (Russia), Storting *or* Storthing (Norway), Bundesversammlung (Austria, Switzerland), Rigsdag (Denmark), Riksdag (Sweden), Oirechtas (Eire), Cortes (Spain), Cortes Geraes (Portugal); witan, witenagemot *or* witenagemote [Anglo-Saxon Hist.].

5. *n.* upper house, upper chamber, First Chamber, senate, *senatus* [Rom. Hist.], *Sénat* [F.], *Senado* [Sp. and Pg.], *Senato* [It.], legislative council, House of Lords, House of Peers; Bundesrat (Austria), Landsting (Denmark), Eduskunta (Finland), Reichsrat (Germany), Felsöház (Hungary), Seanad Eireann (Eire), Lagting (Norway), Första Kammaren (Sweden), Ständerat (Switzerland), Cámara de Senadores (Chile, Mexico).

6. *n.* lower house, lower chamber, Second Chamber, House of Representatives, House of Commons, The House, Legislative Assembly, Chamber of Deputies, *Chambre des Députés* [F.], *Cámara de Diputados* [Sp.], *Câmara dos Deputados* [Pg.], *Camera dei Deputati* [It.]; Nationalrat (Austria, Switzerland), Folketing (Denmark), Reichstag (Germany), Képviselöház (Hungary), Dail Eireann (Eire), Odelsting (Norway), Andra Kammaren (Sweden).

---

nothing less than a big meeting of more or less idle people.—W. BAGEHOT. Synods are mystical Bear-gardens.—BUTLER.

7. *n.* councilor *or* councillor, counselor *or* counsellor, councilman, councilwoman.

8. *n.* congressman, congresswoman, congressist, congressionist, Member of Congress, M.C.; Member of Parliament, M.P.; representative, representative of the people; senator, senatress, senatrix; assemblyman, assembler; legislator, legislatress; statesman etc. 694.4.

9. *adj.* council, curule; congressional, senatorial, parliamentary; synodic(al), synodal.

697. Precept

1. *n.* precept, instruction, direction, stage direction, charge, injunction; dictate, dictum; prescript, prescription; recipe, receipt; principle, principia; settled principle, dogmatic precept *or* principle; rule, canon, law, code, convention, rule of conduct, working rule, golden rule, maxim; regulation, *règlement* [F.]; norm, norma (*pl.* normae); standard, model; form, formula, formulary; written law, *lex scripta* [L.]; unwritten law, *lex non scripta* [L.]; code *or* body of laws, code, *corpus juris* [L.], digest, capitulary; technicality, nice *or* fine point, punctilio; order etc. (command) 741; advice etc. 695.

2. *adj.* preceptive, mandatory, didactic, instructive; prescript, prescriptive; according to rule etc. 82.9; customary etc. (habitual) 613.11.

698. Skill
(See 699. Unskillfulness)

1. *n.* skill, skillfulness, adroitness, expertness, cleverness, dexterousness *or* dextrousness etc. *adj.*; dexterity, facility, address, finesse, proficiency, efficiency, sufficiency, efficacy, adequacy, competence, callidity [rare], craft, panurgy [rare]; ingenuity, ingeniosity [now rare]; ambidexterity, versatility; mastery, mastership; seamanship, airmanship, marksmanship, horsemanship etc.; ropewalking, ropedancing; readiness etc.

(quickness) 682.2; craftiness etc. (cunning) 702; knowledge etc. 490.

2. *n.* talent, gift, endowment, natural endowment etc., genius, faculty, ability, capability, capacity, qualification, habilitation, forte, turn, bent; aptness, aptitude; knack, art, hang, trick, sleight; felicity, *curiosa felicitas* [L.]; turn for, capacity for, genius for etc.; talents, parts; the goods, the stuff, what it takes [all slang]; intellectual talents, mother wit etc. (intelligence) 498; propensity etc. 602.2.

3. *n.* accomplishment, acquirement, attainment; art, science; finish, finished execution; technique, technic, practical *or* technical knowledge, technology.

4. *n.* experience, worldly wisdom *or* knowledge, knowledge of the world, *l'usage du monde* [F.], sophistication; *savoir-faire* [F.], experienced cleverness, management, wit, address; tact, tactfulness; diplomacy, diplomatics, diplomatism; sagacity, wisdom, poise etc. (intelligence) 498; discretion etc. (caution) 864.

5. *n.* masterpiece, masterwork, master stroke, *coup de maître* [F.], chef d'œuvre, *tour de force* [F.]; trump, trump card.

6. *n.* proficient, adept etc. 700.

7. *v.* be skillful etc. *adj.*, possess ability etc. *n.*, excel in, shine in *or* at [chiefly coll.], be master of, be there at [slang], be up to [coll.], have it in one [coll.], have a turn for etc. *n.*, have a good head for, be at home in.

8. *v.* know what's what, know a thing or two, know what's o'clock, know what o'clock it is, know the time of day, have been through the mill, have cut one's wisdom teeth *or* eyeteeth [all coll.]; know the ropes, know one's stuff *or* onions [slang, U.S.], know all the ins and outs, know all the answers [slang, U.S.], "know a hawk from a handsaw" (Shakespeare).

know on which side one's bread is buttered, know what one is about, know one's way about, know the ways of the world, have been around [slang], be worldly-wise etc. *adj.*, have *savoir-faire*

---

697. No arts are without their precepts.—Dryden.   No rule is so general, which admits not some exceptions.—R. Burton.   Ascend above the restrictions and conventions of the world, but not so high as to lose sight of them.—R. Garnett.
698. Skill is stronger than strength.—Fuller. Skill to do comes of doing.—Emerson.   The perfection of art is to conceal art.—Quintilian. Skill and confidence are an unconquered army.—G. Herbert.   Natural abilities are like natural plants, that need pruning by study.—Bacon.   'Tis God gives skill, / But not with-

[F.] etc. *n.*; have all one's wits about one, see into *or* through a millstone, see one's way, see which way the wind blows, see where the wind lies; see how the land lies; know well etc. 490.10; be intelligent etc. 498.7.

9. *v.* exercise skill etc. *n.*, demonstrate one's ability, strut one's stuff [slang, U.S.]; exercise one's discretion, look after the main chance, make a virtue of necessity, cut one's coat according to one's cloth, live by one's wits, feather the oar, sail near the wind, play one's cards well, hit the right nail on the head, put the saddle on the right horse.

10. *v.* take advantage of, make the most profit by etc. (use) 677.5; make hay while the sun shines etc. (improve the occasion) 134.6.

11. *adj.* skillful, expert, proficient, dexterous *or* dextrous, adroit, deft, adept, apt, handy, quick, ready, clever, cute [coll.], slick [slang]; masterly, masterful; crack [coll.], crackajack [slang]; ingenious, Daedalian, resourceful; ambidextrous, versatile, generally capable, all-round [coll.]; neat-handed, fine-fingered, nimble-fingered, sure-footed; shrewd, sharp, smart etc. (sagacious) 498.10; cunning etc. 702.6.

12. *adj.* competent, capable, able, adequate, efficient, qualified, fitted, fit *or* fitted for, cut out for [coll.], equal to, up to, up to the mark [coll.], up to snuff [slang], *au fait* [F.].

13. *adj.* skilled, accomplished, practiced, trained, initiated, prepared, primed, finished; talented, gifted, endowed; thoroughly trained *or* skilled, thoroughbred [now rare]; educated etc. 490.15.

14. *adj.* skilled in, proficient in, strong in, good at, a good hand at, master of, at home in, up in, well up in, up on one's stuff [slang, U.S.]; familiar with, conversant with, versed *or* well-versed in, conversant, well-versed, well-grounded; acquainted with etc. (aware of) 490.13.

15. *adj.* experienced, grown old in experience, seasoned, veteran; worldly-wise, world-wise, wise in the ways of the world, sophisticated, hard-boiled [coll.], *blasé* [F.]; wise etc. 498.11.

16. *adv.* skillfully etc. *adj.*, with skill etc. *n.*, with consummate skill, with fine technique, like a machine; artistically, *secundum artem* [L.]; well etc. 648.14; to the best of one's ability etc. (exertion) 686.11.

699. Unskillfulness
(See 698. Skill)

1. *n.* unskillfulness, unskill [arch.] want of skill etc. 698; inexpertness, uncleverness etc. *adj.*; unproficiency, indexterity [rare], unfacility, inaptitude, incompetence *or* incompetency, inability, incapability, incapacity, inefficiency, unsufficiency, inadequacy, infelicity; inexperience, unexperience, lack of experience *or* experimental knowledge; unaccustomedness; unqualification, disqualification; ignorance etc. 491; stupidity, folly etc. 499.2, 6; indiscretion etc. (rashness) 683; thoughtlessness etc. (inattention) 458; carelessness etc. (neglect) 460; inutility etc. 645.

2. *n.* mismanagement, mismanage [rare]; misconduct, misdirection, misguidance, misgovernment, misrule, misapplication; misadministration, maladministration; inexpedience *or* inexpediency; bad policy, impolicy; misfeasance, malfeasance; absence of rule, rule of thumb.

3. *n.* bungling etc. *adj.*, botchery; awkwardness, clumsiness etc. *adj.*; butterfingers [coll.], handful of thumbs [joc.]; too many cooks, sprat sent out to catch a whale.

4. *n.* bungle, botch, botchery, *étourderie* [F.], *gaucherie* [F.], *balourdise* [F.], boggle, boggle-de-botch *or* boggle-dy-botch [coll.], bobble [slang], foozle [coll.], blunder, bevue, barney [slang, Eng.], slip, trip, stumble, fudge, fumble, muff, clumsy performance, poor fist [coll.], bad job, sad work, hash [coll.], mess [coll.]; *faux pas* [F.] etc. 495.3; act of folly etc. 499.7; careless work etc. 460.2.

5. *n.* bungler etc. 701; fool etc. 501.

6. *v.* be unskillful etc. *adj.*, not have the knack etc. 698.2, not be up to [coll.],

---

out men's hands.—G. Eliot. Doing easily what others find difficult is talent; doing what is impossible *for talent* is genius.—Amiel. The gods help them that help themselves.—Aesop. Luck is infatuated with the efficient.

699. *Non omnia possumus omnes* [Not all of us can do all things].—Vergil. What he doth, he doth by rule of thumb, and not by art. —W. Hope.

not have it in one [coll.]; have green in the eye etc. (be ignorant) 491.6.

7. *v.* not know what one is about, not see an inch beyond one's nose, stand in one's own light, not know one's interest, not know on which side one's bread is buttered, quarrel with one's bread and butter, throw a stone in one's own garden, kill the goose that lays the golden egg, put oneself out of court, pay dearly for one's whistle, cut one's own throat, burn one's fingers, play with fire, jump out of the frying pan into the fire, kick against the pricks.

run ~, knock *or* dash one's head against a stone wall, split upon a rock, break one's back, bring the house about one's ears, sow the wind and reap the whirlwind, make two bites of a cherry, cut blocks with a razor, fight with a shadow, grasp at a shadow, catch at straws, lean on a broken reed, lock the stable door after the horse *or* steed is stolen, reckon without one's host, count one's chickens before they are hatched, buy a pig in a poke, go on a wild-goose chase, go on a fool's errand, go further and fare worse, take the dirty end of the stick [coll.].

begin at the wrong end, put the cart before the horse, bark up the wrong tree, back the wrong horse, be in the wrong box, aim at a pigeon and kill a crow, get the wrong bull by the horns, get the wrong pig by the tail *or* sow by the ear [coll.], put the saddle on the wrong horse, put a square peg into a round hole, put new wine into old bottles, play at cross-purposes, say one thing and do another, strain at a gnat and swallow a camel, lose *or* miss one's way, take a wrong turn, overshoot the mark, fall into a trap, catch a Tartar, have too many irons in the fire, have too many eggs in one basket.

do by halves etc. (not complete) 730.2; make bricks without straw etc. (attempt the impossible) 471.5; hold a farthing candle to the sun etc. (labor in vain) 645.6; carry coals to Newcastle etc. (redundance) 641.3; take the shadow for the substance etc. (credulity) 486.3; carry too much sail etc. (be rash) 863.5; behave foolishly etc. 499.9; fail etc. 732.5, 6.

8. *v.* mismanage, manage improperly, misrule, misconduct, misguide, misdirect, misapply; misadminister, maladminister.

9. *v.* bungle, blunder, boggle, bobble [coll.], bull [slang, U.S.], foozle [coll.], muff, fumble, have a handful of thumbs [joc.], flounder, lumber, hobble, stumble, trip, slip, slip up, stub one's toe, miss one's footing; botch, bitch [vulg.], slubber [now chiefly dial.], mar, spoil, make sad work of; bosh, hash, hash up, mess up, make a mess *or* hash of, make a poor fist at *or* of, put one's foot in it [all coll.]; bugger, bugger up, gum up the works [all slang, U.S.]; blunder on *or* upon, blunder into, barge in *or* into [coll.], bonehead into [slang]; blunder away; make a *faux pas* [F.] etc. 495.9; do carelessly etc. 460.6; fail etc. 732.5.

10. *v.* become inefficient etc. *adj.*, get out of practice, go *or* run to seed [coll.], become rusty, slip, slip up, lose one's cunning.

11. *adj.* unskillful, inexpert, unproficient, inefficient, unclever, unfacile, undexterous *or* undextrous, undeft, inadept; unapt, inapt.

12. *adj.* clumsy, bungling etc. *v.*, awkward, lubberly, oafish, lumpish, blockish, blunderheaded, fudgy [U.S.], *gauche* [F.], maladroit, unhandy, left-handed, heavy-handed, clumsy-fisted, butterfingered [coll.]; all thumbs, with a handful of thumbs [both joc.]; gawky, gawkish, gawkhammer [dial., Eng.]; ungainly, uncouth, ungraceful, graceless, inelegant; slovenly, slatternly; bulky, hulky, unwieldy, unmanageable; cumbrous, cumbersome; careless etc. (neglectful) 460.8; thoughtless etc. (inattentive) 458.10; reckless etc. 863.7; stupid etc. 499.12.

13. *adj.* unskilled, unaccomplished, unpracticed, untrained, uninitiated, unprepared, unprimed, unfinished; untalented, ungifted, unendowed; uneducated etc. 491.9.

14. *adj.* inexperienced, unexperienced, unseasoned, untried, amateurish, raw, green, green as grass *or* a gourd, verdant [coll.], unripe, not dry behind the ears [joc.], half-baked [coll.]; unskilled in, unpracticed in, unconversant with, unaccustomed *or* unused to, unfamiliar *or* unacquainted with, new to, a stranger to, uninitiated; unaccustomed etc. 614.3; ignorant etc. 491.8; naïve etc. (artless) 703.4.

15. *adj.* incompetent, incapable, unable, inadequate, unqualified, disqualified, ill-qualified, unfit, unfitted, unadapted, not equal *or* up to, not cut out for [coll.]; un-

adjusted, maladjusted; useless etc. 645.8.

16. *adj.* out of practice, soft [coll.], rusty, not what one used to be [coll.].

17. *adj.* ill-managed, ill-conducted, ill-contrived, ill-devised, ill-imagined, ill-judged; ill-advised, misadvised, unadvised; misconducted, misguided, unguided; unwise, injudicious etc. (foolish) 499.15.

700. Proficient
(See 701. Bungler)

1. *n.* proficient, expert, adept, dab [coll.], dabster [coll. or dial.], darb [slang], graduate, master, past master, master hand, skilled *or* practiced hand, nice ~, good *or* clean hand, no slouch [slang, U.S.], crack [coll.], crackajack [slang], ace [chiefly coll.], shark [slang], sharp [slang], bear [slang, U.S.], caution [coll.]; genius, man of genius, prodigy, wizard [chiefly coll.], mastermind, master head; mahatma; Admirable Crichton; connoisseur, *connaisseur* [F.]; topnotcher [coll.], top sawyer, first fiddle. *chef de cuisine* [F.]; protagonist, prima donna, *première danseuse* [F.], star; Jack-of-all-trades *or* Jack-of-all-works, handy man; marksman, good ~, dead *or* crack shot, practiced *or* experienced eye; ropedancer, ropewalker, funambulist; savant, intellectual prodigy etc. (scholar) 492.1, 2; juggler, cardsharp etc. (deceiver) 548; pickpocket, swindler etc. (thief) 792.

2. *n.* picked man, medalist *or* medallist, prizeman; champion, champ [slang].

3. *n.* veteran, vet [coll.]; old hand, old-timer [coll.], old file, old stager, old soldier, old campaigner, war horse [coll.], longhorn [coll., West. U.S.]; salt *or* old salt [coll.], old sea dog [coll.], shellback [slang], barnacle-back [slang]; man of experience, sophisticate, man of the world; elder etc. 130.

4. *n.* tactician, strategist etc. (person of cunning) 702.4.

701. Bungler
(See 700. Proficient)

n. bungler, blunderer, blunderbuss, blunderhead, bullhead, clumsy [coll.], fumbler, fumble-fist [coll.], butterfingers [coll.], muff [coll.], muffer [coll.], boggler, botcher, bosher [coll.], hash [chiefly Scot.], slubberer [now chiefly dial.], marplot, bull in a china shop, hen with its head cut off [coll.]; stick, poor stick, odd stick [all coll.]; lubber, looby, swab [slang], lout, oaf, clown, duffer [coll.], loon, lown [obs. exc. Scot. and dial.], lobster [slang], donkey, galoot [slang], lummox [dial. and slang], bohunk [slang, U.S.], chucklehead [coll.], lunkhead [coll., U.S.], doit [Scot. and North. Eng.], slouch, slob [derog.], lump [coll.], clod, clodhopper, clodpoll *or* clodpole, yokel, rube [slang], sawney [dial. Eng.]; gawk, gowk, gawky, gawkhammer [dial. Eng.]; colt, calf [both coll.].

no conjuror, one who will not set the Thames on fire; fish out of water, ass in lion's skin, jackdaw in peacock's feathers; Lord of Misrule, Abbot of Unreason [both Hist.]; Mrs. Malaprop, Mrs. Partington; awkward squad [Mil.]; landlubber etc. (mariner) 269; sloven etc. (slattern) 59.5; greenhorn etc. (novice) 541.6; ignoramus etc. 493; neglector etc. 460.3.

702. Cunning
(See 703. Artlessness)

1. *n.* cunning, cunningness, slyness, artfulness, craftiness etc. *adj.*; craft, "the ape of wisdom" (Locke); satanic cunning, the cunning of the serpent; finesse, subtlety, subtilty, subtility [rare]; chicane, chicanery; crafty *or* deceitful cunning, fraudulent skill *or* dexterity, guile, sharp practice, knavery, pettifoggery, dodgery, trickery; jugglery, jugglement [rare]; hocus-pocus, hokeypokey [coll.], hanky-panky [coll.]; maneuvering, intriguing etc. *v.*; intrigue, intriguery; wirepulling [coll.], backstairs influence; temporization; cleverness etc. (skill) 698; deceit etc. 545; duplicity etc. (dissembling) 544.2; treachery, rascality etc.

---

700. An expert is a person who avoids the small errors as he sweeps on to the grand fallacy.—B. STOLBERG. *Experto credite* [Believe one who has proved it; believe an expert]. —VERGIL. An expert is only a damned fool a long ways from home.—SANDBURG.
701. You have been a boggler ever.—SHAKESPEARE. Your blunderer is as sturdy as a rock.—COWPER.
702. We take cunning for a sinister or crooked wisdom.—BACON. Cunning is the dark sanctuary of incapacity.—CHESTERFIELD

(improbity) 940; stealth etc. (concealment) 528; sagacity etc. 498.2.

2. *n.* Machiavellianism, Machiavellism; political cunning, politics; diplomacy, diplomatics; jobbery, graft [coll.], pipelaying [U.S.]; gerrymandering, gerrymander [both polit. cant, U.S.].

3. *n.* artifice, art, wile, device, wily device, machination, maneuver, stratagem, policy [now rare], trick, juggle, dodge, artful dodge, shift, *espièglerie* [F.], ruse, *ruse de guerre* [F.]; game, little game; sleight, feint, blind, subterfuge, evasion, circumvention, dust thrown in the eye; fake, fakement [both coll.]; bag of tricks, tricks of the trade, tricks upon travelers; cheating device, deception etc. 545.3; trap etc. (snare) 545.4; contrivance, plot etc. 626.5, 6.

4. *n.* cunning person, person of cunning, slyboot *or* slyboots [joc.], fox, reynard, sly dog [coll.], sly old fish [coll.], coon [coll., chiefly U.S.], dodger, Artful Dodger, file [slang], crafty rascal, smooth *or* slick citizen [coll.], slicker [slang], trickster, juggler, jockey, keener [West. U.S.], Philadelphia lawyer [coll., U.S.]; horse trader, horse coper [Eng.]; Indian giver [coll., U.S.].

schemer, schemist, schematist [obs.]; intriguer, intrigant; strategist, machinator, maneuverer, tactician; Machiavel, Machiavelli, Machiavellian, Machiavellist; diplomat, diplomatist, diplomatic(al) [rare]; politician, politico, politicaster; jobber, grafter [coll.], carpetbagger [slang, U.S.], pipelayer [U.S.], wirepuller [coll.], repeater [U.S.], floater [U.S.], gerrymanderer [polit. cant, U.S.].

5. *v.* be cunning etc. *adj.,* live by one's wits, finesse, use artifice *or* stratagem, maneuver, machinate, manipulate, gerrymander, Machiavellize; intrigue, beguile, trick, play tricks with, play a deep game; stoop to conquer, introduce the thin end of the wedge, undermine, waylay, throw off one's guard, temporize; be too much for, be too deep for, get the better of, snatch a thing from under one's nose,

snatch a verdict; scheme, conspire etc. (plot) 626.10; deceive etc. 545.7–10; steal a march upon, overreach etc. (circumvent) 545.8.

6. *adj.* cunning, crafty, artful, wily, sly, slim [S. Afr.], slick [slang], slippery, feline, vulpine, insidious, shifty, cagey [slang], leery [slang], canny, pawky [Scot. and dial. Eng.], politic, diplomatic, arch, shrewd, acute, sharp, sharp as a needle, astute, knowing, up to snuff [slang]; subtle, subtile.

cunning as a fox *or* serpent, too clever by half, slippery as an eel, not to be caught with chaff; tricky, tricksy [rare], trickish; Machiavellian, Machiavellic, Machiavellist, Machiavellistic; scheming, schemy [coll.], schemeful; designing, contriving, intriguing; conniving, connivant, connivent [obs.]; timeserving, temporizing; deep, deep-laid, profound; clever etc. (skillful) 698.11; false etc. 544.7; deceptive etc. 545.12; rascally, treacherous etc. 940.8–12; stealthy, underhand etc. (secret) 528.21; sagacious etc. 498.10; evasive etc. 623.12.

7. *adv.* cunningly, slyly etc. *adj.*; on the sly [coll.], by a side wind *or* door, *à la dérobée* [F.], like a thief in the night.

703. Artlessness
(See **702. Cunning**)

1. *n.* artlessness, ingenuousness, naïveness etc. *adj.*; naïveté, unsophistication, inartificiality, simplicity, nature; singleness of heart *or* purpose, candor, sincerity, plain speaking, abandon, *bonhomie* [F.]; veracity etc. 543; honesty etc. (probity) 939; innocence etc. 946.

2. *n.* unsophisticate, naïve *or* naïf, ingénue, innocent, child, mere child, lamb, dove, gosling [coll.], tenderfoot; greenhorn, greeny [coll.], greener [slang], *blanc-bec* [F.]; debutant, debutante, deb [slang]; rough diamond, diamond in the rough; *enfant terrible* [F.].

3. *v.* be artless etc. *adj.,* wear one's heart on one's sleeve; be free with one, be round with one, look one in the face;

The weak in courage is strong in cunning.—W. BLAKE.   Machination is worth more than force.—RABELAIS.   So art lies hid by its own artifice.—OVID.   Many foxes grow grey, but few grow good.—FRANKLIN.   The devil knew not what he did when he made man politic; he crossed himself by 't.—SHAKESPEARE.   Practical politics consists in ignoring facts.—H. ADAMS.

703. What is true, simple and sincere is most congenial to man's nature.—CICERO.   Simplicity of character is no hindrance to subtlety of intellect.—J. MORLEY.   In love the artless catch the game, / And they scarce miss who never aim.—M. GREEN.   As frank as rain on cherryblossoms.—E. B. BROWNING.

call a spade a spade, speak plainly, speak out, speak one's mind.

4. *adj.* artless, simple, simplehearted, simple-minded, naïve *or* naïf, *ingénu* [F.], childlike, inartificial *or* unartificial, natural, plain, pure, native, unsophisticated, untutored, unaffected, unassuming, unpretending, unfeigning, undissimulating, undissembling, undesigning, guileless; trustful, unsuspicious, confiding.

ingenuous, frank, frankhearted, openhearted, open, open as day, aboveboard, open and aboveboard, sincere, candid, straightforward, forthright, whole-footed [coll.], flat-footed [slang, U.S.], unreserved, free-spoken, free-tongued, plainspoken, outspoken, blunt, downright, direct, untrimmed, unvarnished, unflattering, unpoetical, matter-of-fact; singlehearted, single-minded; Arcadian; veracious etc. 543.3; honest etc. 939.7; innocent etc. 946.5; inexperienced etc. 699.14.

5. *adv.* frankly, sincerely etc. *adj.*; in all soberness *or* seriousness, in all conscience, in plain words *or* English, without equivocation, with no nonsense, all joking aside *or* apart, without mincing the matter, not to mince the matter.

704. Difficulty
(See 705. Facility)

1. *n.* difficulty, difficultness, arduousness, hardness etc. *adj.*; difficult task, task of Sisyphus, Sisyphean labor, Herculean task, Augean task, man-sized job, tough job [coll.], tough proposition [coll.], large *or* tall order [slang], teaser [coll.], rasper [slang], uphill work *or* going, heavy sledding, hard road to travel; hard row to hoe, hard row of stumps [both coll., U.S.]; dead weight, dead lift; hardship etc. (adversity) 735; stumbling block etc. (obstacle) 706.2; hard work etc. (exertion) 686.1, 3.

2. *n.* predicament, difficult situation, position of difficulty, unpleasant situation, trying condition *or* position, nice *or* pretty predicament, plight, sorry plight, pickle *or* pretty pickle [chiefly coll.], pass, pretty pass, strait, plunge [now dial.], troublesome situation, trouble, matter, trial, rattle [slang], scrape, jam [coll., U.S.].

peck *or* sea of troubles, hornet's nest, ado; to-do, how-do-you-do, how-d'ye-do, how-de-do, nice *or* pretty how-do-you-do etc., fix, hobble, go, pretty *or* nice go, pretty kettle of fish, hot water, hole [all coll.]; embarrassment, embarrassment of affairs, embarrassing position *or* situation; complicated state of things, complication, imbroglio, mess, holy mess [coll.], muddle, mix [coll.], scramble, stew [coll.]; slough, quagmire; tight place *or* spot, tight squeeze [all coll.]; critical situation, pinch etc. (crisis) 134.4; misfortune etc. 735.3.

3. *n.* impasse, position of unavoidable difficulty, unescapable predicament; cul-de-sac, blind alley; corner, hole [coll.], tree, end of one's rope *or* tether, wit's end, extremity; deadlock, dead set, stand, standstill, halt, stop; nonplus, nonplusation *or* nonplussation; obstacle etc. 706.2.

4. *n.* dilemma, horns of a dilemma, difficult *or* perplexing alternative; vexed question, *vexata quaestio* [L.]; nut to crack, hard nut to crack; knot, node, nodus, Gordian knot, knotty point, *dignus vindice nodus* [L.]; paradox; asses' bridge, *pons asinorum* [L.]; crux, hitch, brunt, stress, rub, squeeze [coll.], pinch, where the shoe pinches; nice ~, subtle *or* delicate point, delicacy, delicate ground, thin ice, ticklish card to play; problem, poser etc. (enigma) 533.2; quandary etc. (perplexity) 475.2; entanglement, involvement, intricacy etc. (complexity) 59.3.

5. *v.* be difficult etc. *adj.*, run one hard, go hard with one, go against the grain, try one, try one's patience, put one out, be put to one's shifts *or* wit's end; nonplus, pose etc. (perplex) 475.8; be impossible etc. 471.4.

6. *v.* be in difficulty etc. *n.*, meet with difficulties, struggle ~, grapple *or* contend with difficulties, labor under difficulties, have a hard time of it, have much ado with, be put to one's shifts, labor under a disadvantage, bear the brunt, come to the pinch *or* push, fish in troubled waters, buffet the waves, swim against the

---

704. He who accounts all things easy will have many difficulties.—LAO-TSZE.   The greater the difficulty, the greater the glory.—CICERO.   What is worth while must needs be difficult.—OVID.   It is too hard a knot for me t' untie.—SHAKESPEARE.   Ay, there's the rub.—SHAKESPEARE.   All things are difficult before they are easy.—FULLER.   A difficulty raiseth the spirits of a great man.—SAVILE.   These are the times that try men's souls.—T.

current *or* stream, scud under bare poles, walk on eggshells *or* hot coals, dance on a hot griddle, hold the wolf by the ears.

get *or* plunge into difficulties, get into a scrape etc. *n.*, bring a hornet's nest about one's ears, stir up a hornet's nest, go off *or* in at the deep end [coll.], put one's foot in it [coll.], let oneself in for; stick fast, stick in the mud, come to a stand *or* deadlock; get all tangled, ~ snarled *or* wound up, get all balled up [slang], weave a tangled web; flounder, boggle, struggle, beat about; grope in the dark, lose one's way; not know which way to turn etc. (be uncertain) 475.6.

7. *v.* place in difficulty etc. *n.*, put in a position of difficulty, put one in a hole [coll.] etc. *n.*; involve, enmesh, entangle; corner, run *or* drive into a corner, chase up a tree [coll.] *or* stump [slang, U.S.], tree [coll.], drive to the wall, put one's back to the wall, have on the ropes; embarrass, bother, pother, moider [dial.], put out, disconcert, disturb; lead a wild-goose chase, lead a pretty dance.

8. *adj.* difficult, difficile; not easy etc. 705.5, uneasy [rare], uneath [arch.]; hard, tough [coll.], wicked [coll.], troublesome, toilsome, irksome, painful, operose, laborious, steep [coll.], uphill, arduous, strenuous, onerous, burdensome, heavy [coll.], hefty [coll., U.S.], Herculean, formidable, ill-conditioned, crabbed, rugged; hard-fought, hard-earned; full of difficulties, entangled by difficulties, encompassed with difficulties, surrounded by difficulties, beset with difficulties; set with thorns, thorny, spiny; knotted, knotty; sooner *or* more easily said than done, not to be made with rose water, not to be handled with kid gloves; delicate, ticklish, risky, critical, nice, exacting; complicated, intricate, entangled etc. (complex) 59.10.

9. *adj.* embarrassing, disconcerting, awkward, inconvenient, plaguy [coll.], trying; perplexing etc. 475.12.

10. *adj.* unmanageable, difficult to manage, difficult *or* hard to deal with, not easily managed *or* dealt with, intractable *or* untractable, uncontrollable *or* incontrollable, ungovernable, unruly, unyielding, unbending, untoward, perverse, refractory; unwieldy, awkward, clumsy, bulky, ponderous; stubborn etc. (obstinate) 626.6; inflexible, unpliable etc. (hard) 323.5.

11. *adj.* in difficulty, under a difficulty, laboring under a difficulty, in trouble, in a predicament, in a scrape, in a jam [coll., U.S.], in the soup [slang], in a mess *or* muddle, in a cleft stick, in deep water, out of one's depth, surrounded by shoals *or* breakers; in hot water, in the suds, in a fix, in a hobble, in a hole, in a box, in a pickle, in a nice *or* pretty pickle [all coll.]; at an impasse, cornered, in a corner, driven into a corner, driven to the wall, with one's back to the wall, treed [coll.], up a tree [coll.], up a stump [slang, U.S.], *in extremis* [L.], driven to extremity, at the end of one's rope *or* tether, at one's wit's end, on one's beam ends, *au bout de son Latin* [F.], at a stand *or* standstill, at a nonplus, nonplused *or* nonplussed.

floored, graveled [both coll.]; stranded, aground, grounded, on the rocks, high and dry; stuck, stuck *or* set fast; straitened, reduced to straits, in desperate straits, sorely pressed, hard pressed, hard-set, hard run, run hard, hard up [slang], pinched, up against it [slang], hard put [coll.], put to it, hard put to it [coll.], put to one's shifts, driven from post to pillar *or* pillar to post; put out, thrown out; at bay, *aux abois* [F.]; in a dilemma, on the horns of a dilemma, between two stools, between Scylla and Charybdis, between the Devil and the deep blue sea; at cross-purposes; at a loss etc. (uncertain) 475.16; unfortunate etc. 735.9.

12. *adv.* with difficulty, with much ado; hardly, arduously etc. *adj.*; uphill, upstream, against the stream, against the grain, *à* or *au rebours* [F.]; in spite of difficulties, *invita Minerva* [L.], in the teeth of; at a pinch, upon a pinch; laboriously etc. 686.11.

705. Facility
(See 704. Difficulty)

1. *n.* facility, ease, easiness etc. *adj.*; disencumbrance, disentanglement; plane *or* plain sailing, smooth *or* straight sail-

---

705. For easy things, that may be got at will, / Most sorts of men do set but little store.— SPENSER.   What is easy is seldom excellent. —JOHNSON.   Easy come, easy go.

ing, smooth road, royal road, clear course, clear coast, clear stage, free play; Easy Street [coll.], velvet [slang]; facilities, advantages, opportunities; dexterity, address etc. (skill) 698; feasibility etc. (practicability) 470.2; pliancy etc. (softness) 324; freedom etc. 748.

2. *n.* easy task *or* work, sinecure, holiday task, mere child's play, simple twist of the wrist; cinch, snap, soft snap, soft thing, pipe, picnic, pie, gravy [all slang]; shore duty.

3. *v.* be easy etc. *adj.*, go easily, run *or* work smoothly, work well, work like a machine, hit on all four etc. cylinders [coll.], go *or* run on all fours [coll.], obey the helm; take it easy, flow ~, swim *or* drift with the stream *or* current, go with the tide; make little, ~ light *or* nothing of, think nothing of; see one's way, have it all one's own way, have the game in one's own hands, walk over the course, win at a walk *or* canter, win hands down [coll.]; be at home in etc. (be skillful) 698.7.

4. *v.* facilitate, render easy etc. *adj.*, ease, smooth, make smooth, smooth *or* pave the way, grease *or* soap the way [slang], prepare the way, clear the way, make all clear for, make way for, open the way, open the door to; leave a loophole, leave a hole to creep out of; grease the wheels [coll.], lubricate, pour oil on; give the reins to, give full play, allow full swing; lighten, lighten the labor; disburden, disencumber, disembarrass, disentangle, disengage, deobstruct, unclog, extricate, unravel, unknot, untie *or* cut the knot, free, clear, exonerate, emancipate; popularize; help, promote etc. (aid) 707.6.

5. *adj.* easy, not difficult etc. 704.8, easily accomplished, facile, soft [coll.], cushy [slang], simple, simple as ABC [coll.], easy as pie [slang], easy as falling off a log [coll.], nothing to it [coll.]; light, unburdensome; easygoing, easy-flowing, easy-running, easy-osey [Scot.]; at ease, in a state of ease, at home, quite at home, in one's element, in smooth water; on Easy Street [coll.], on velvet [slang]; easy of access, accessible, approachable, within reach, open to, for the million.

6. *adj.* manageable, easily managed, not difficult to move *or* influence, wieldy [rare], toward, towardly, submissive, compliant; yielding, ductile, pliant etc. (soft) 324.6; docile etc. 602.9.

7. *adj.* unburdened, disburdened; unencumbered, disencumbered; unembarrassed, disembarrassed; exonerated, unloaded, unhampered, unhindered, unobstructed, untrammeled; unrestrained etc (free) 748.12, 13.

8. *adv.* easily etc. *adj.*, easy [illit. or coll.], without difficulty etc. 704, with no effort, readily, smoothly, swimmingly, on easy terms, singlehanded, with one hand tied behind one's back, hands down [coll.], like nothing [slang]; on wheels, on friction wheels.

706. Hindrance
(See 707. Aid)

1. *n.* hindrance, hinderance, hampering etc. *v.*, obstruction, impediment, embarrassment, stoppage, estoppel [Law], deadlock, arrest, check, checkmate, interruption, interception, interference, obtrusion, preclusion, counteraction, prevention, detention, determent, inhibition, setback; retardment, retardation; restraint, constraint; blockage, blockade; stricture, striction, constriction, restriction, coarctation; infarct, infarction; checkmate etc. (defeat) 732.3; opposition etc. 708; prohibition etc. 761.

2. *n.* obstacle, hinderer, obstructer etc. *v.*; obstruction, obstructive, obstructant; barrier, impediment, hamper, handicap, hindrance, difficulty, let [arch.], curb, holdback, stay, stop, hitch, catch, knot, spoke, remora, drag, clog, skid, brake; screw loose, spoke in one's wheel, grit in the oil, lion in the path, trail of a red herring; stumbling block, stumbling stone; snag, snags and sawyers [U.S.], sawyer [U.S.], planter [local, U.S.]; encumbrance, incumbrance [now rare], burden, burthen, onus, cross, millstone round one's neck, impedimenta, lumber, pack, load; weight, dead weight *or* lift, drag weight; drag sail, drag sheet, drift sail; check, countercheck.

checkrein, bearing rein; bit, curb bit, snaffle; block, blockade; barrier, bar, portcullis, rampart, bulwark, bulkhead, buffer; stile, turnstile, turnpike; bank,

---

706. All impediments in fancy's course / Are motives of more fancy.—SHAKESPEARE. Let me not to the marriage of true minds / Admit

embankment, mound, mole; dam, weir, boom, beaver dam; clot, embolus, embolism; ill wind, head wind; drawback, objection, disadvantage; stopper etc. 263; barricade etc. (fortification) 717.3; wall etc. (fence) 232.2; gate etc. (portal) 260.4; shackle, fetter etc. (restraint) 752.2, 3; anchor etc. 666.2; preventive etc. (prophylactic) 662.8; closure etc. 261; impasse etc. 704.3.

3. *n.* hinderer, frustrater etc. *v.*; obstructive, obstructionist; addleplot, marplot; spoilsport, damper, wet blanket, kill-joy, crapehanger [slang], dog in the manger [coll.]; filibuster, filibusterer [both U.S.]; oppositionist etc. 710.2; buttinsky [slang] etc. (intruder) 228.4, (meddler) 682.11.

4. *v.* hinder, impede, embarrass, let [arch.], restrict, inhibit, interfere, interrupt, intercept, obstruct, clog, hamper, cramp, trammel, entrammel, snub, curb, constrain, keep from, hold *or* keep back, hold up [coll.], keep *or* hold in check, hold in leash; check, countercheck; put on the brakes, clog *or* scotch the wheels; retard, slacken, delay, detain; stop, estop, stay, put a stop *or* end to, bring to a stop, deadlock; block, blockade, block up, block *or* stop the way; bar, barricade, bolt, lock; hedge in, hedge round; choke, choke off, cut off; preclude, debar, foreclose; discommode, incommode, put to inconvenience; filibuster [U.S.]; shackle etc. (restrain) 751.6, 7; dam etc. (close) 261.2; prohibit etc. 761.2.

5. *v.* avert, keep off, stave off, ward off, fend off, fend, forfend [arch.], deflect, repel, obviate, turn aside, sidetrack, draw off, prevent, nip in the bud; disincline etc. 616.3.

6. *v.* encumber *or* incumber, cumber, burden, lumber, hamper, handicap, weigh down, saddle with, load with; overburden, overload, overlay, overwhelm.

7. *v.* thwart, frustrate, scotch, balk, foil, checkmate, counteract, counterwork, countermine, contravene, traverse, circumvent, overthwart, override, upset; confound, flummox [slang], nonplus, discountenance, disconcert, baffle; faze [coll., U.S.], feeze *or* feaze [obs. exc. dial]; spoil, mar; throw a wrench in the machinery, throw a monkey wrench into the works [both coll.]; scotch the wheel, put a spoke in one's wheel, spike one's guns, clip the wings of, tie one's hands, put one's nose out of joint [coll.]; take the wind out of one's sails, steal one's thunder, cut the ground from under one, undermine; damp, throw *or* lay a wet blanket on, throw cold water on, put an extinguisher on, spoil sport; stand in the way of, act as a drag, hang like a millstone round one's neck; defeat etc. 731.9, 10; oppose etc. 708.2; resist etc. 719.3.

8. *adj.* hindering etc. *v.*, hindersome [dial.]; preventive, preventative, prophylactic [Med.], preclusive, deterrent; inhibitive, inhibitory; obstructive, obstruent; impeditive, impedient, impedimentary, impedimental; onerous, burdensome; cumbersome, cumbrous; intrusive, obtrusive, in the way; unfavorable; restrictive etc. 751.13.

9. *adj.* hindered, encumbered etc. *v.*; wind-bound, waterlogged, heavy-laden; hard-pressed etc. 704.11.

10. *adj.* unassisted, unaided, unseconded etc. (*see* assist, second etc. 707.6-11); singlehanded, alone.

11. *adv.* under handicap etc. *n.*, with everything against one, with one's wheels clogged, through all obstacles, with *or* under many difficulties.

707. Aid
(See 706. Hindrance)

1. *n.* aid, aidance, assistance, help, cast [arch.], succor, boot [arch.], service, accommodation, subvention [now rare]; support, supportance [now rare]; maintenance, keep, upkeep; provision, providence [now rare], providance [now Scot.]; ministry, ministration; advance, advancement; furtherance, promotion, boost [slang, U.S.], lift, conducement; hand, helping hand; turn, good turn; benevolence etc. 906; helper etc. (auxiliary) 711, (benefactor) 912; coadjuvancy etc. (co-operation) 709; instrumentality etc. 631; means etc. 632; use, benefit etc. (utility) 644; charity etc. (benevolence) 906.

2. *n.* patronage, fosterage, auspices,

---

impediments.—SHAKESPEARE. Help refused / Is hindrance sought and found.—BROWNING. Something between a hindrance and a help.—WORDSWORTH.

707. *Haud ignara mali miseris succurrere disco* [Not inexperienced in misfortune, I have learned to aid the wretched].—VERGIL. One thing asks the help of another.—HORACE.

protection, care, guidance, championship, countenance, favor, interest, advocacy, encouragement, backing.

3. *n.* sustenance, sustentation [rare]; means of support, maintenance, subsistence, alimentation, nurture, nourishment, nutrition; eutrophy [Med.]; manna in the wilderness; subsidy, bounty, subvention; food, provisions etc. 298.5, 6; means etc. 632; provisions, supplies etc. (equipment) 634, (stores) 636.

4. *n.* relief, mitigation, alleviation; comfort, ease, easement; rescue, deliverance; help at a dead lift, help in time of need, aid in time of danger *or* difficulty; remedy, redress, indemnification; supernatural aid, *deus ex machina* [L.].

5. *n.* reinforcements, additional force, auxiliaries, succors, contingents, recruits.

6. *v.* aid, assist, help, succor, befriend, come to the aid of, bring ~, give ~, furnish ~, afford *or* supply aid etc. *n.*, lend one's aid, give ~, lend *or* bear a hand *or* helping hand, stretch *or* stretch forth a helping hand, hold out a helping hand, take by the hand, take in tow, give one a lift, boost [slang], give a leg *or* shoulder, give a leg up, give one a cast [arch.], give a turn, do a good turn, help a lame dog over a stile; minister *or* administer to, tender to, pander to; relieve, rescue, free, deliver; set up, set agoing, set on one's legs, put on one's feet; contribute, subscribe to, chip in [coll.]; give new life to, be the making of; reinforce, recruit; set ~, put *or* push forward, give a shove *or* impulse to, promote, further, forward, advance, speed, expedite, quicken, hasten, lend wings to; put forth; render a service etc. 644.3; facilitate etc. 705.4; be benevolent etc. 906.5.

7. *v.* support, give ~, furnish ~, afford ~, supply *or* lend support, sustain, maintain, keep, upkeep, bear, upbear, uphold, hold up, shoulder, prop, bolster, bolster up.

8. *v.* second, stand by, stick by, stand behind *or* back of, get behind [slang], back, back up, endorse, abet, work for, make interest for, go to bat for [slang], stick up for [coll.], take up the cudgels for, take the part of, take up ~, adopt *or* espouse the cause of, advocate, hold a brief for [coll.], give moral support to, countenance, keep in countenance, lend oneself to, lend one's countenance to, lend one's favor *or* support to, lend one's name to, give one's support *or* countenance to, subscribe to, patronize, take up, smile upon, shine upon, favor, befriend; enlist under the banners of etc. (side with) 709.5.

9. *v.* nourish, nurture, foster, cherish, cultivate; nurse, dry-nurse, wet-nurse, suckle, put out to nurse, cradle; foment, feed *or* fan the flame.

10. *v.* serve, do service to etc. 746.9; take care of etc. 459.6; subserve etc. (be instrumental) 631.3; be of use to etc. 644.2; benefit etc. 648.6; conduce etc. (tend) 176.2.

11. *v.* oblige, accommodate, consult the wishes of; humor, cheer, encourage.

12. *adj.* aiding, helping etc. *v.*; aidful, helpful, helpsome [dial.], helply [obs. exc. dial.]; furthersome [chiefly Scot.], contributory, ministrant, assistant, auxiliary, adjuvant, subservient, subsidiary, ancillary; accessary, accessory; at one's beck, at one's beck and call; co-operative etc. 709.7; salutary etc. (beneficial) 648.12; serviceable etc. (useful) 644.5; conducive etc. 176.3; serving etc. 746.9.

13. *adj.* favorable, propitious, favorably inclined, well-disposed, well-affected, well-intentioned, well-meant, well-meaning; amicable etc. (friendly) 888.4; obliging etc. (benevolent) 906.6.

14. *prep.* by the aid of, with the assistance of etc. *n.*; helped by; by the agency of etc. 170.5; by means of etc. 632.4; through etc. 631.5.

15. *prep.* in aid of, in the service of, in favor of, in the name of, in futherance of, on account of, on ~ *or* in behalf of, on the part of, for the sake of.

16. *int.* help!, save us!, to the rescue!, this way!, *au secours!* [F.], *à moi!* [F.].

708. Opposition
(See 709. Co-operation)

1. *n.* opposition, opposure, contradiction, contravention, hostility, antagonism,

---

Bear ye one another's burdens.—BIBLE. Help the lame dog over the stile.—FULLER. God befriend us as our cause is just.—SHAKESPEARE.   God helps those who help themselves.—SIDNEY.   Sweet the help / Of one we have helped!—E. B. BROWNING.

708. *Notor in adversum* [I strive against opposition].—OVID.   Opposition is the surest persuasion.—CYNIC'S CALENDAR.   The Duty

repugnance *or* repugnancy, antipathy, clashing, collision, conflict; oppugnance *or* oppugnancy, oppugnacy [rare], oppugnation [rare]; impugnation, impugnment; contrariness, contrariousness [rare], contrariety; cross fire, crosscurrent, undercurrent, head wind; counterplot; counteraction etc. 179; resistance etc. 719; restraint etc. 751; hindrance etc. 706; competition etc. (contention) 720; disagreement etc. (discord) 713; unwillingness etc. 603.

2. *v.* oppose, be hostile to etc. *adj.*, repugnate [rare], antagonize, counteract, counterwork, go *or* act in opposition to, run counter to, fly in the face of, kick against, cross, fall out with, set *or* pit against, contend against, go against, go dead against, run against, beat against, militate against, make a stand against, take one's stand against, make a dead set against, set oneself against, set one's face against, turn one's back upon, set at nought, slap in the face, slam the door in one's face; raise one's voice against, vote against, protest against, object, kick [now coll.]; discountenance, disfavor, withhold *or* withdraw one's favor.

contradict, contravene, oppugn, belie, gainsay, take issue with, assert the contrary of; be contrary to, be *or* play at cross-purposes, come in conflict with; withstand etc. (resist) 719.3; hinder, thwart etc. 706.4, 7; restrain etc. 751.6; be unwilling etc. 603.4.

3. *v.* encounter, meet, confront, face, come face to face with, cross the path of, run *or* fall foul of; breast, stem, breast *or* stem the tide, ~ current *or* flood, breast the wave, buffet the waves, beat up against, make head against; compete with, contend with etc. 720.8, 9.

4. *adj.* oppositional, opposing, opposed etc. *v.*; anti [coll.], adverse, overthwart, cross, contradictory, conflicting, oppugnant, repugnant, antagonistic(al), hostile, unfriendly, inimical, at cross-purposes, at variance, at odds, at issue, at war with, in controversy with, in opposition, in hostile array, with crossed bayonets, at daggers drawn, up in arms; unfavorable, unpropitious; contrary etc. 14.5; resistant etc. 719.5; contentious, competitive etc. 720.12, 13; unwilling etc. 603.5; counteractive etc. 179.5.

5. *prep., adv.* against, agin [dial.], dead against, versus, adverse to, opposed to, in opposition to, counter to, in conflict with, at cross-purposes, cross, contrariwise, against the grain; against the current, ~ stream *or* tide, against the wind, with a head wind, with the wind ahead, with the wind in one's teeth.

6. *prep.* in defiance of, in the face *or* teeth of; in spite of etc. (notwithstanding) 30.8.

709. Co-operation
(See 708. Opposition)

1. *n.* co-operation, coadjuvancy, coadjument, coadjutement [rare], coadjutorship; joint operation, mutual assistance, collective action, union in action, concurrent effort *or* labor, concurrence *or* concurrency, coaction, coagency, co-working, collaboration, participation; collusion, collusiveness; complicity, conspiracy, confederacy; concerted effort, concert; coefficiency, coefficacy; coadministration; synergy, synergism; "a long pull, a strong pull, and a pull altogether" (Dickens); logrolling [chiefly U.S.]; *quid pro quo* [L.].

2. *n.* association, alliance, affiliation, cahoot *or* cahoots [slang], league, federation, confederation, confederacy, coalition, combination, union, unification, fusion, conjunction, conjuncture, conjugation, consolidation, incorporation; hookup, tie-up, tie-in [all coll.]; partnership, copartnership; fraternity, confraternity, fraternization; sodality, fellowship, colleagueship, comradeship, Freemasonry; party spirit, *esprit de corps* [F.]; partisanship, clanship; joint stock, pool; society, company etc. 712.

3. *n.* agreement, general agreement, agreement of all; concord etc. 23, 714; unanimity etc. 488.2; compact etc. 769.

4. *v.* co-operate, coadjute [now rare], coadjuvate, concur, conspire, collude, coact, co-work, collaborate, work *or* labor together, act *or* operate jointly with, act together, pull together, hold *or* hang together, cling to one another, keep to-

---

of an Opposition is to oppose.—G. TIERNEY. Take arms against a sea of troubles, / And by opposing end them.—SHAKESPEARE.

709. All for one, one for all.—DUMAS. United we stand, divided we fall!—G. P. MORRIS. All your strength is in your union.—LONGFELLOW. We must all hang together,

gether, league ~, band or club together, be banded together, be in league with, fraternize, hunt in couples, lay one's heads together, stand shoulder to shoulder, unite one's efforts, concur or work to one end, concert, act or work in concert, act in harmony, play ball [coll.], pool, pool one's interests; join forces, confederate etc. (league) 48.4; be concordant etc. 714.2.

5. *v.* side with, take sides with, join, join with, join up with [slang], unite with, strike in with, throw in with [slang], swing in with [coll.], line up with [coll.], cast in one's lot with, join hands with, go hand in hand with, go along with, make common cause with, mix oneself up with, take part with, take the part of, enter into ~, go in or join partnership with, go or go in cahoots with [slang], enlist under the banner of; rally round, flock to; be ~, row or sail in the same boat, sail on the same tack; come to, pass over to, come into the views of; espouse the cause of etc. (second) 707.8.

6. *v.* participate, be a participator in, be a party to, lend oneself to, join in, sit in [coll.], chip in [coll.], take or bear part in, take ~, act ~, play or perform a part in, have to do with, have a hand in, have a finger in the pie; bear a hand, pull an oar; share in etc. 778.5.

7. *adj.* co-operative, co-operating etc. *v.*, in co-operation etc. *n.*; coadjuvant, coadjutant, coadjutive; coactive, coalitional, collaborative, hand in glove with, in cahoots [slang]; synergetic, synergistic; in league etc. (leagued) 48.6; communistic etc. 778.8; helpful 707.12; concurrent etc. 178.4.

8. *adv.* co-operatively etc. *adj.*, in co-operation with, together, in the same boat, in concert with, en masse; side by side, hand in hand, hand in glove, shoulder to shoulder; as one man etc. (unanimously) 488.17; concordantly etc. 714.5.

710. Opponent
(See 711. Auxiliary)

1. *n.* opponent, adversary, antagonist, oppugnant [rare], opposite [arch.], adverse or opposite party; the opposition; enemy etc. 891; assailant etc. 716.4; combatant etc. 726; gamester etc. (player) 840.17.

2. *n.* oppositionist, opposer; obstructive, obstructionist; disputant, brawler, wrangler, brangler [rare], filibusterer [U.S. polit.]; extremist, bitter-ender [U.S.]; irreconcilable, die-hard or diehard; hinderer etc. 706.3.

3. *n.* malcontent, reactionary, agitator etc. 832.2; rebel, revolutionist etc. (insurgent) 742.3.

4. *n.* rival, corrival, competitor, contestant, contender, emulator, entrant; the field.

711. Auxiliary
(See 710. Opponent)

1. *n.* auxiliary, adjunct, ally, confederate, associate, consociate, colleague, companion, attendant, consort, confrere, mate, teammate, partner, pard or pardner [slang, chiefly U.S.], comate, copartner, side-partner, side-kick or sidekicker [slang, U.S.]; adjuvant, adjutant, *avudante* [Sp. Amer.]; assistant, aid, aider, help, helper, helpmate, helpmeet, helping hand, arm of flesh, dry nurse [slang], man Friday; right hand, right-hand man; *aide-de-camp* [F.]; cohelper, coaid, co-worker, fellow worker or laborer, workfellow, collaborator, co-operator; coadjuvant, coadjutant, coadjutor, coadjutator [rare]; coadjutress, coadjutrix; nominal ~, holding-out or quasi partner, special partner, general partner, silent partner; secret partner, dormant or sleeping partner; confidant, comrade etc. (friend) 890; handmaid etc. (servant) 746.

2. *n.* puppet, cat's paw, creature, tool, instrument, hand, jackal, *âme damnée* [F.]; jackstraw, man of straw; satellite etc. (follower) 281.2, (sycophant) 886.2; servant etc. 746.

3. *n.* accomplice, complice [arch.], confederate, fellow conspirator; accessory, accessory after the fact; partner or ac-

---

710. He that wrestles with us strengthens our nerves and sharpens our skill. Our antagonist is our helper.—BURKE. Treating your adversary with respect is giving him an advantage to which he is not entitled.—JOHNSON.

711. I took my man Friday with me.—DEFOE. Patron: Commonly a wretch who supports with insolence, and is paid with flattery.—JOHNSON.

---

or assuredly we shall all hang separately.—FRANKLIN. I shall know that your good is mine; ye shall know that my strength is yours.—KIPLING. Two heads are better than one.

complice in crime, *particeps criminis* [L.], *socius criminis* [L.].

4. *n.* upholder, candleholder, bottleholder [coll.], abettor, seconder, backer, angel [slang], supporter, advocate, partisan, champion, patron, Maecenas, friend at *or* in court, favorer, fautor [rare], well-wisher, sympathizer, sectary, votary.

712. Party

1. *n.* party, body of partisans, side, division, interest; faction; class, sect, caste, school, order, denomination, communion, church; crew, team, squad, string, band, troop; detachment, posse; phalanx; family, clan etc. (race) 11.4.

2. *n.* clique, coterie, set, knot, circle, ring, junto, cabal, camarilla, club, group, push [slang], mob [slang]; crowd, bunch, outfit, constituency [all coll.]; gang etc. (company) 72.3.

3. *n.* community, body, group, fellowship, sodality; brotherhood, fraternity, confraternity, fraternal order; sisterhood, sorority; familistery, *familistère* [F.].

4. *n.* society, association, union, league, alliance, coalition; combination, combine [coll., U.S.]; federation, confederation, confederacy; institute, institution; *Bund*, *Verein* [both G.]; bund [slang, U.S.], plunderbund [coll., U.S.]; gang, tong [Chin.], ring, machine; trade-union *or* trades-union; customs union, *Zollverein* [G.]; social circle etc. 892.7.

5. *n.* company, guild, establishment, firm, concern, house; partnership, copartnership; corporation, corporate body, body corporate; joint concern, joint-stock company; trust, syndicate, monopoly, cartel, pool; merger, consolidating company; holding company; stock company.

6. *n.* (political parties) Republicans, Democrats, Conservatives, Liberals, Radicals, Socialists, Progressives, Federalists, Confederates, Tories, Whigs; Fascisti, Fasci, Black Shirts [all It.]; National Socialist party, NSDAP, Nazis [all G.]; Bolsheviki, Mensheviki, Minimalists, Maximalists [all Russ.]; Bourbon, Tory etc. (conservative) 141.3; radical, progressive etc. (reformer) 658.5.

7. *v.* form a party etc. *n.*, found a firm, ~ house etc. *n.*; form an alliance, incorporate, league etc. (combine) 48.3, 4.

8. *v.* become a member, take up membership, join, join up [slang], enlist, enroll, enter, become connected with, associate *or* league oneself with; unite with, throw in with [slang] etc. (side with) 709.5.

9. *adj.* partisan, sectional, sectionary [rare]; sectary, sectarian, sectarial; denominational; cliquish, cliquy; clubbable *or* clubable [coll.].

10. *adj.* in league, confederated, incorporated etc. (leagued) 48.6; co-operative etc. 709.7.

713. Discord
(See also 714. Concord)

1. *n.* discord, discordance *or* discordancy, disaccord, dissonance, dissidence, conflict, faction, friction; jarring, clashing etc. *v.*; jar, clash, shock; a screw loose; cat-and-dog life; Kilkenny cats; contentiousness etc. 722.6; enmity etc. 889; hate etc. 898; opposition etc. 708.

2. *n.* variance, difference, disparity, disagreement, dissension, dissent, misunderstanding, cross-purposes, odds, *brouillerie* [F.]; falling out, breach of friendship, breach, rupture, break, schism, split, rift, disruption, division, division in the camp, house divided against itself, "rift within the lute" (Tennyson); open rupture, breaking off of negotiations, recall of ambassadors, declaration of war.

3. *n.* quarrel, dispute, tiff, miff [dial. and slang], huff, bicker, *tracasserie* [F.], litigation, contention, strife, feud, set-to [coll.], run-in [slang, U.S.], squabble, altercation, barney [slang], scrap [slang], *démêlé* [F.], snarl, wrangle, brabble [arch.], brabblement [arch.], cample [dial., Eng.], jangle, tow-row [Scot. and dial. Eng.], snip-snap [rare], spat [coll. and dial.], words, high words, cross questions and crooked answers; bickering, wrangling etc. *v.*; family jars; controversy etc. (argument) 476.2; fight etc. (contest) 720.2; disputant etc. 710.2.

4. *n.* broil, brawl, embroilment, embranglement, imbroglio, scramble, row

---

712. When great questions end, little parties begin.—W. BAGEHOT.   Hail! Hail! the gang's all here.—D. A. ESTROM.

713. *Discordia fit carior concordia* [Discord makes concord more precious].—PUBLILIUS. If a house be divided against itself, that house cannot stand.—BIBLE.   All your danger is in

[coll.], fracas, fraction [dial.], rumpus [coll.], ruckus [dial. and slang], ruction [chiefly dial.], stramash [chiefly Scot.], breeze [coll.], squall [coll.], shindy [slang], touse [chiefly dial.], riot; disturbance, commotion etc. (turmoil) 59.4; scuffle, fray etc. (contest) 720.2; warfare etc. 722.

5. *n.* subject of dispute, disputed point, bone of contention, bone to pick, crow to pluck, apple *or* brand of discord, *casus belli* [L.], ground of quarrel, battleground; question at issue etc. (subject of inquiry) 461.10.

6. *v.* disaccord, disagree, differ, differ in opinion, hold discordant views, refuse to agree, be at variance, pull different ways, have no measures with, misunderstand one another, conflict, clash, jostle, jar; live like cat and dog, live a cat-and-dog life; have a bone to pick with, have a crow to pluck with.

7. *v.* quarrel, dispute, litigate, altercate, squabble, tiff, spat [coll. or dial.], scrap [slang], huff, row [coll.], brabble, wrangle, jangle, brangle, cample [dial., Eng.], cangle [Scot.], nag, bicker, have words with, fray [arch.], fratch [chiefly dial.], spar [coll.], set to, make the fur fly, lock horns, fall foul of, join *or* put in issue; pluck a crow with, pick a bone with; brawl, broil, turn the house out of window; make *or* kick up a row, kick up *or* raise a dust, raise a breeze *or* squall [all slang]; pick a quarrel, fasten a quarrel on; fall out, have a falling-out; split, break with, break squares with, part company with; declare war, throw in *or* fling down the gauntlet; argue etc. 476.11; fight etc. (contend) 720.8.

8. *v.* sow dissension, stir up dissension etc. *n.*; set at odds, set *or* pit against, sick on *or* at, set by the ears; embroil, entangle; disunite, widen the breach; rub one's fur the wrong way, go against the grain; get one all het up [dial.], get one hot under the collar [coll.].

9. *adj.* discordant, dissident etc. (disagreeing) 24.6; dissentient etc. 489.5; quarrelsome etc. 901.9.

10. *adj.* at variance, on bad terms, at odds, at crosspurposes, at sixes and sevens, at war, at strife, at feud, at high words, at loggerheads, at daggers drawn, up in arms, embroiled, by the ears; torn, disunited.

714. Concord
(See 713. Discord)

1. *n.* concord, concordance, accord, harmony, symphony, rapport, affinity, agreement, correspondence, response, like-mindedness; congeniality, compatibility; understanding, good *or* cordial understanding, *entente cordiale* [F.]; union, unison, unity; bonds of harmony, cement of friendship; happy family; amity etc. (friendship) 888; sympathy etc. (love) 897; peace etc. 721; unanimity etc. 488.3; co-operation etc. 709; reconciliation etc. (pacification) 723.

2. *v.* be concordant etc. *adj.*, accord, agree, respond, correspond, understand one another, reciprocate, enter into one's views, enter into the ideas *or* feelings of, sympathize with, gee [slang and dial.], cotton [coll.], get along with, hit it off with [coll.], harmonize with, be in harmony with, fall *or* chime in with, blend in with, go hand in hand with, be at one with, sing in chorus, put up one's horses together, hitch horses [coll.], fraternize, hold fellowship, have brotherly feelings; keep the peace, remain at peace; pull together etc. (co-operate) 709.4.

3. *v.* render concordant etc. *adj.*, accord etc. 23.8; reconcile etc. (pacify) 723.4, 5; mediate etc. 724.3.

4. *adj.* concordant, accordant, according, agreeing etc. *v.*, agreeable, congenial, compatible, reconcilable, harmonious, in accord etc. *n.*; in rapport, *en rapport* [F.]; like-minded, of the same mind, of one mind, at one; cemented, united, allied; fraternal; friendly etc. 888.4; at peace etc. (pacific) 721.4; conciliatory etc. (pacificatory) 723.6.

5. *adv.* concordantly etc. *adj.*, in concert; with one accord etc. (unanimously) 488.17; hand in hand etc. (co-operatively) 709.8.

---

discord.—LONGFELLOW. A very pretty quarrel as it stands.—SHERIDAN. It takes two to make a quarrel. *Lis litem generat* [One quarrel begets another].

714. *Nam concordia parvae res crescunt, discordia maximae dilabuntur* [Concord makes small things grow; discord makes great things decay.]—SALLUST. *Concordia discors* [A discordant concord].—HORACE. All concord's born of contraries.—JONSON. The sweet milk of concord.—SHAKESPEARE. Where all was harmony, and calm and quiet.—BYRON. Birds in their little nests agree.—I. WATTS.

715. Defiance

1. *n.* defiance, defial, defy *or* defi [now slang]; daring etc. *v.*, dare, double-dare; challenge, stump [coll., U.S.], cartel; gage, gauntlet, glove, slap of the glove; war cry, war whoop; threat etc. 909.

2. *v.* defy, bid defiance to, hurl defiance at, set at defiance, set at nought, laugh to scorn, affront; beard, "beard the lion in his den" (Scott); bite the thumb at, thumb one's nose at, snap the fingers at; dare, double-dare; challenge, call out, stump [coll., U.S.], throw *or* fling down the gauntlet, ∼ glove *or* gage; throw *or* toss one's hat in the ring [coll.]; show fight, show one's teeth, show *or* put up a bold front, bluster, look big, stand with arms akimbo, double *or* shake the fist, dance the war dance; accept a challenge, call a bluff *or* one's bluff [coll.]; threaten etc. 909.2; brave etc. (courage) 861.5.

3. *adj.* defiant, defying, daring etc. *v.*; with arms akimbo, with fists doubled, with teeth bared; bold, audacious, insolent, contemptuous, greatly daring, regardless of consequences; reckless etc. 863.7; rebellious etc. (disobedient) 742.6, 7; bellicose etc. (warlike) 722.13; threatening etc. 909.3.

4. *adv.* defiantly etc. *adj.*, in defiance of, in the teeth of, under one's very nose; in open rebellion.

5. *int.* I defy you!, I dare *or* double-dare you!, come on!, come if you dare!, marry come up! [arch. or dial.], do your worst!, hoity-toity!

716. Attack
(See 717. Defense)

1. *n.* attack, assault, assault and battery; onset, onslaught, charge, push [slang], dead set at, run at *or* against; offense, aggression; incursion, inroad, invasion, irruption; dragonnade *or* dragoonade; raid, air raid; foray, razzia; sally, sortie; storm, storming; siege, beleaguerment, investment, encompassment; bombardment, cannonade, strafe [slang], hate [slang]; blitzkrieg, blitz [coll.]; surprisal, sudden *or* surprise attack, *ruade* [F.], *coup de main* [F.], camisado *or* camisade [arch.]; escalade, boarding; zero hour; point of attack, base of operations; echelon; open order; close formation; encounter, conflict etc. (contest) 720.2; warfare etc. 722.

2. *n.* fire, firing etc. *v.*, gunfire, fireworks, trigger talk [slang], discharge; barrage, volley, salvo, spray, fusillade, drumfire, broadside, *feu d'enfer* [F.]; bombardment etc. *above*; direct fire, ricochet fire, plunging fire, rolling fire, horizontal fire, vertical fire, platoon fire, file firing, file fire, raking fire, cross fire, time fire, percussion fire, fire of demolition; shot etc. 284.4; explosion etc. 173.3.

3. *n.* thrust, pass, lunge, swing, foin [arch.], cut, coup, stab, jab [coll.], stoccado *or* stoccata [arch.]; carte *or* quarte and tierce; bayonet; home thrust; blow etc. (impulse) 276.3.

4. *n.* attacker, assailant, assailer, assaulter, aggressor, invader; fusilier *or* fusileer, dragoon, uhlan; opponent etc. 710; combatant etc. 726.

5. *v.* attack, assault, assail, assume *or* take the offensive, be *or* become the aggressor; strike the first blow, throw the first stone, fire the first shot; lift a hand against, draw the sword against, take up the cudgels; have at, make a set *or* dead set at, set *or* fall upon, pounce upon, pitch into [coll.], light into [slang, U.S.], sail into [chiefly coll.], head into [slang], wade into [chiefly coll.], lay into [slang], lay at, crack down on [slang], go for [coll.], launch out against, advance against *or* upon, march upon *or* against, bear down upon; charge, run a tilt at, ride full tilt against, make a dash *or* rush at, dash at, rush at, tilt at, run at, fly at, hawk at; let out at, let fly at, let drive at, make a thrust *or* pass at, aim *or* deal a blow at, strike ∼, thrust ∼, poke etc. at, take a shot, ∼ fling *or* shy at.

cut and thrust, saber, bayonet, give one the bayonet, put to the sword, stab; attack tooth and nail, lay about one, harry, drive *or* press one hard, be hard upon;

---

715. He breathed defiance to my ears.—Shakespeare. And dar'st thou then / To beard the lion in his den?—Scott. I do defy him, and I spit at him.—Shakespeare.
716. Better pointed bullets than pointed speeches.—Bismarck. "Charge, Chester, charge! On, Stanley, on!" / Were the last words of Marmion.—Scott. Charge once more, then, and be dumb.—M. Arnold. The Assyrian came down like the wolf on the fold.—Byron. Attack is the best defense.

beset, beleaguer, besiege, lay siege to, set upon on all sides, invest, encompass; storm, take by storm; escalade, scale the walls, board, go over the top [coll.]; raid, invade, inroad, make an inroad, make an irruption into; run down, bring to bay, close with, break a lance with; strike home, strike at the root of; plant a battery, sap, mine; war etc. 722.9; fight etc. (contend) 720.8; strike etc. 276.8; resist etc. 719.3.

6. *v.* fire upon, fire at, fire a shot at, shoot at, pop at, let off a gun at, let loose the dogs of war [coll.]; open fire, open up on [slang]; draw a bead on [U.S.], level at; snipe, snipe at; bombard, strafe [slang], shell, cannonade, barrage, blitz [slang], pepper, fusillade, fire a volley, pour a broadside into; bomb; torpedo, submarine [coll.]; spring a mine.

7. *v.* stone, rock [coll., U.S.], throw a stone, throw stones at, lapidate, pelt, hurl at, hurl against, hurl at the head of; brickbat [coll.].

8. *adj.* attacking etc. *v.*, aggressive, offensive, combative; incursive, invasive, irruptive; obsidional, obsidionary.

9. *adv.* on the offensive, on the warpath, up in arms, at bay.

10. *int.* attack!, advance!, charge!, "Charge, Chester, charge! On, Stanley, on!" (Scott), over the top!, up and at them!, give 'em hell! [coll.]; fire!, open fire!; to arms! etc. 722.15.

717. Defense
(See 716. Attack; also 719. Resistance)

1. *n.* defense, defence, guard, ward, watch and ward; self-defense, self-protection, self-preservation; protection etc. 664.2; preservation etc. 670; resistance etc. 719.

2. *n.* safeguard, guard, shield, screen, buffer, fender; armor, mail, coat of mail, panoply, buckler, scutum [Rom. Antiq.], target, aegis, breastplate, cuirass, backplate, habergeon, brigandine, hauberk, gauntlet, lorica, helm [arch.], armet, basinet, sallet *or* salade, camail, vambrace, rerebrace, cubitiere, greaves, jamb, heaume, morion, cabasset, beaver, visor, face guard, sollerets, *pédieux* [F., *pl.*]; headpiece, siege cap, casque, casquetel, helmet, steel helmet, tin hat [soldiers' cant.]; spiked helmet, *Pickelhaube* [G.]; caparison, housings; bard *or* barde, chamfron; carapace, shell; spines, needles; smoke screen, occulting screen; protective *or* safety device etc. 666; weapons etc. 727.

3. *n.* fortification, muniment; bulwark, rampart, vallum [Rom. Antiq.], vallation, contravallation *or* countervallation, circumvallation; fosse, vanfoss, trench, mine, countermine, dugout, moat, ditch, entrenchment *or* intrenchment; scarp, escarp, counterscarp; parapet, bank, embankment, dike, mole, mound; earthwork, fieldwork; fence, wall; sunk fence, ha-ha; palisade, stockade, laager [S. Afr.], sangar [Ind.]; barrier, barricade; boom; portcullis, chevaux de frise [*pl.*]; abatis; entanglement, barbed-wire entanglement.

battlement, merlon; glacis; casemate; buttress, abutment; breastwork, banquette, mantelet *or* mantlet, tenaille *or* tenail, ravelin, curtain; demilune, halfmoon; bastion, demibastion, redan; vauntmure [rare], faussebraie *or* faussebraye, advanced work, hornwork, lunette, outwork; barbican, redoubt, sconce, fortalice; lines; machicolation, bartizan, loophole, balistraria; postern gate, sally port.

4. *n.* stronghold, hold, safehold, fasthold, fastness, keep, ward, donjon, citadel, capitol, castle, tower, tower of strength, fort, fortress, fortification, acropolis, garrison [now rare], propugnaculum, kila [Ind.], pa [New Zealand]; barracoon, barrack; peel, peel tower, peelhouse; rath [Ir. Antiq.]; martello tower, martello; blockhouse, wooden walls; haven, sanctuary etc. (refuge) 666.3, 4; prison etc. 752.1.

5. *n.* defender, champion, advocate, vindicator; Defender of the Faith, *Fidei Defensor* [L.]; paladin, knight-errant; protector etc. 664.3.

6. *n.* guard, warden, warder; watch, watcher, watchman, watchkeeper, lookout, sentinel, sentry, vedette, picket; advanced guard, vanguard, van; rear guard; patrol, patrolman, patroller; night watchman, Charley [Eng.]; doorkeeper, gatekeeper, porter, concierge, chokidar [Anglo-Ind.], durwaun [Anglo-Ind.],

---

717. Stand in your own defence; / Or hide your heads like cowards, and fly hence.—SHAKESPEARE. Love your neighbor as yourself but don't take down your fence.—SANDBURG. Millions for defense but not a cent for tribute.—R. HARPER.

ostiary, usher, tiler *or* tyler; yeoman of the guard *or* royal guard, beefeater [both Eng.]; hayward; railway *or* train guard, flagman; lifeguard, lifesaver [coll.]; bodyguard, retainer, burkundaz [Ind.]; safe-conduct, escort, convoy; watchdog, bandog, house dog, Cerberus; coast guard; body of guards, ward [arch.], garrison; guardian etc. (protector) 664.3; jailer etc. 753; policeman etc. 745.10; national guard, militia etc. (army) 726.6.

7. *v.* defend, fend [arch.], forfend [arch.], secure, ward [arch.], guard, safeguard, shield, screen, shelter, shroud, cover, cloak, guard etc. against, bear one harmless; fortify, battle, embattle, fence, entrench *or* intrench, blockade, barricade; garrison, engarrison, man; arm, harness [arch.], accouter; protect etc. 664.6; take care of etc. 459.6; keep watch etc. (be vigilant) 459.4; preserve etc. 670.3.

8. *v.* repel, repulse, drive back, put to flight, give a warm reception to [iron.]; parry, fend off, ward off, beat off, keep off; hold *or* keep at bay, hold at arm's length; resist invasion, stand siege; be *or* act on the defensive, show fight; maintain *or* stand one's ground, hold one's own, hold ~, bear *or* stand the brunt, fall back upon, stand in the gap, stand by.

9. *adj.* defensive, shielding etc. *v.*; fortified, battled, embattled; armed, in arms, well-armed, heavy-armed, full-armed, bristling with arms, armed cap-a-pie, armed at all points, armed to the teeth; armored, panoplied, mailed, mail-clad, accoutered, harnessed [arch.], "in complete steel" (Shakespeare); iron-plated, ironclad; loopholed, castellated, machicolated, casemated; under arms etc. (warring) 722.12; protective etc. 664.12.

10. *adj.* defensible, tenable; invulnerable, proof against etc. (protected) 664.11.

11. *adv.* defensively, on the defensive; in defense, in self-defense; at bay, *pro aris et focis* [L.].

12. *int.* no surrender!, *ils ne passeront pas!* [F.], they shall not pass!

718. Retaliation

1. *n.* retaliation, talion, reprisal, requital, retribution, reciprocation, retort, exchange; counter, counterstroke, counterblast, counterproject; return of evil for evil, *quid pro quo* [L.], like for like, measure for measure, tit for tat, blow for blow, a Roland for an Oliver, an eye for an eye, a tooth for a tooth, give-and-take, diamond cut diamond, a game at which two can play; boomerang, the biter bit; reproof valiant, retort courteous; *lex talionis* [L.]; revenge etc. 919; recrimination etc. (accusation) 938; compensation etc. 30; reaction etc. (recoil) 277; punishment etc. 972; reparation etc. (reward) 973; due reward *or* punishment, comeuppance [coll., U.S.] etc. (deserts) 924.2; interchange etc. 148.

2. *v.* retaliate, retort, requite, make requital, ~ reprisal *or* retribution, pay, repay, pay back, pay off, pay off old scores, pay out [coll.], pay home, pay back in full measure, pay one in his own coin, pay in the same coin, repay *or* requite in kind, give one a dose of his own medicine [coll.], put *or* inflict in return, return the like, return the compliment, return evil for evil, return like for like, give one tit for tat etc. *n.*, give and take, give as much as one takes, give as good as was sent, give in kind, cap, match, reciprocate, give in exchange, exchange blows.

hit back at [coll.], get back at [slang], come back at [coll.], turn upon, turn the tables upon, serve one out [coll.], settle *or* square accounts, settle the score [coll.], get even with [coll.], even the score, be *or* make quits, fix [coll.]; give one his deserts, give one his comeuppance *or* comeuppings [coll., U.S.]; take revenge etc. 919.4; punish etc. 972.5; reward etc. 973.3; recriminate etc. 938.4; interchange etc. 148.3.

3. *v.* get one's deserts etc. 973.4.

4. *adj.* retaliatory, retaliative, retaliating etc. *v.*; retributive, recriminatory, reciprocal, talionic; revengeful etc. 919.6.

5. *adv.* in retaliation, *en revanche* [F.], in revenge, in requital, in reprisal etc. *n.*

719. Resistance
(See also 717. Defense)

1. *n.* resistance, stand, front; repulse, repulsion; rebuff, reaction, countertend-

---

718. He that strikes with the sword shall be beaten with the scabbard.—J. HEYWOOD. Vice received her retribution due.—COWPER. She pays him in his own coin.—SWIFT. Eye for eye, tooth for tooth, hand for hand, foot for foot.—BIBLE.
719. This choice is left you, to resist or die.—

ency, withstanding etc. *v.*, renitence *or* renitency, repugnance *or* repugnancy; oppugnance *or* oppugnancy; oppugnacy [rare], oppugnation [rare]; reluctance [arch.], reluctation [rare]; recalcitrance *or* recalcitrancy, recalcitration; opposition etc. 708; defense etc. 717.

2. *n.* strike, labor strike, tie-up [U.S.], lockout, walkout [coll., U.S.], turnout [coll., chiefly Eng.], barring out, hartal [Ind.]; sit-down strike; boycott, boycottage; rebellion etc. (revolt) 742.2.

3. *v.* resist, offer resistance etc. *n.*, not submit etc. 725.4; withstand, make a stand against, take one's stand against, stand up against, stand, take one's stand, make a stand, make a resolute stand, put *or* set one's foot down [coll.], stand fast *or* firm, stand *or* hold one's ground, hold one's own, hold out, stick it out [coll.], bear up against, be proof against; put up a front, present a front, confront, face; set one's face against, fly in the face of, struggle ~, fight *or* strive against, grapple with, exert force in opposition, make a determined resistance.

reluct, reluctate [rare]; recalcitrate, kick against, kick against the pricks; resist to the end, fight to the last ditch, never say die, sell one's life dearly, die hard; breast *or* stem the tide, ~ current, ~ stream *or* flood, breast the wave, buffet the waves; repel, repulse, keep at bay; oppose etc. 708.2; lift the hand against etc. (attack) 716.5; hinder, thwart etc. 706.4, 7; counteract etc. 179.3.

4. *v.* strike, go on strike, walk out, turn out, lock out, bar out; boycott; picket, go on *or* do picket duty; rebel etc. (revolt) 742.5.

5. *adj.* resistant, resistive, resisting etc. *v.*; renitent, repellent, repulsive, repugnant, oppugnant, recalcitrant, up in arms; unsubmissive, unresigned; oppositional etc. 708.4; rebellious etc. 742.7; indomitable etc. (resolute) 604.7, (persevering) 604a.3; stubborn, immovable etc. (obstinate) 606.6; unyielding etc. (hard) 323.5; proof against etc. 644.11.

6. *int.* hands off!, keep off!

7. *int.* never say die!, stick it! [coll.], show what you're made of!

HOMER. Unfold to us some warlike resistance—SHAKESPEARE.

720. Contention

1. *n.* contention, contest, contestation; conflict, struggle, strife, digladiation [rare], altercation, litigation; competition, emulation, *concours* [F.], rivalry; corrivalry, corrivalship; quarreling etc. (*see* quarrel etc. 713.7); controversy etc. (argument) 476.2; dissension etc. (variance) 713.2; opposition etc. 708; warfare etc. 722; quarrelsomeness etc. (ill-humor) 901; contentiousness etc. (warlikeness) 722.6; bone of contention etc. 713.5.

2. *n.* a contest, conflict, fray, affray, battle, combat, fight, scrap [slang], set-to [coll.], run-in [slang, U.S.], barney [slang, Eng.], bout, match, game, go [coll.], affair, event, action, engagement, encounter, rencounter, *rencontre* [F.], collision, clash, clash of arms, brush, tilt, joust, skirmish, tussle, scuffle, struggle, scramble, mix-up [coll.], embroilment, melee, *mêlée* [F.], dogfight, scrimmage, brabble; tournament, tourney; *passage d'armes* [F.], passage at *or* of arms; feud, blood feud, vendetta; free fight, free-for-all [cant].

battle royal, pitched battle, sham fight *or* battle, hand-to-hand fight, stand-up fight [coll.], running fight *or* engagement, tug of war; aerial battle, dogfight; bullfight, tauromachy; gladiatorial contest, gladiatorism; hard-fought contest, run, run for one's money, sharp contest; death struggle, struggle for life *or* death, fight to the death, fight to the last ditch, war to the death *or* knife, *guerre à mort* *or* *outrance* [F.], Armageddon; quarrel, brawl etc. 713.3, 4; argument etc. 476.2; sports and games etc. 840.11, 12; foray etc. (attack) 716.

3. *n.* duel, duello [rare], single combat, monomachy, *monomachia* [L.], satisfaction, affair of honor; triangular duel; appeal to arms etc. (warfare) 722.

4. *n.* naval engagement, naumachia *or* naumachy, sea fight.

5. *n.* race, run, heat; dash, hundred-yard dash etc.; torch race, lampadedromy, lampadephoria [both Gr. Antiq.]; broose [Scot. and N. of Eng.], go-as-

---

720. A man of strife and a man of contention.—BIBLE. And of their vain contest appeared no end.—MILTON. A contentious man will never lack words.—J. JEWEL. Let the long contention cease.—M. ARNOLD.

you-please [coll.], match race, relay race, cross-country race, point-to-point race; foot race, automobile race, motorcycle race, bicycle race, dog race; boat race, rowing or sailing race, yacht race, Torpids [Oxford Univ.], regatta.

horse race, harness race, invitational race, claiming race, plate race, stake race, purse race; handicap race, handicap; chase, steeplechase, hurdle race; sweepstake or sweepstakes, sweep or sweeps [coll.]; Derby, Kentucky Derby; horse racing, the turf, the sport of kings; Derby Day, field day; gymkhana [orig. Anglo-Ind.].

6. n. pugilism, boxing, fisticuffs, the fights [coll.], prize fighting; boxing match, prize fight, spar, mill [cant], set-to [coll.], bout, round.

7. n. wrestling, rassling or rastling [dial. U.S.], samo [Jap.], kushti [Hind.]; catch-as-catch-can, Greco-Roman, Cornish, Westmorland, Cumberland [all styles of wrestling]; jujitsu.

8. v. contend, contest, combat, fight, scrap [slang], put up a scrap [slang], battle, strive, struggle, scramble, tussle, scuffle, skirmish; reluct, reluctate; tourney, joust, jostle, tilt, run a tilt or a tilt at, couch one's lance, break a lance with; encounter, clash, collide, fall or run foul of, meet or fight hand to hand, bring to bay, close with, come to close quarters, engage, take on [slang], join issue, contend etc. with, grapple with, tilt with, engage with, bandy with, try conclusions with, have a brush with, cross swords, measure swords with, fall or go to loggerheads, lock horns, tangle with [slang], pitch into [coll.], lay into [slang], light into [slang, U.S.], sail into [chiefly coll.], set to, fight it out, fight like devils.

come to blows, exchange blows or fisticuffs, box, mill [slang], spar; fence, thrust and parry; wrestle, rassle or rastle [dial. U.S.], go to the mat with; duel, fight a duel, give satisfaction; pull a gun [slang], draw the trigger, exchange shots; lift one's hand against, draw the sword against, take up the cudgels, take up the glove or gauntlet, accept the challenge, enter the lists, come to the scratch; square, square up or off [both coll.]; war etc. 722.9; wrangle etc. (quarrel) 713.7; argue etc. 476.11; oppose etc. 708.2, 3; attack etc. 716.5.

9. v. compete with, vie with, cope with, contend in rivalry, come into rivalry, rival, outvie, emulate, seek or strive for the same thing; race with, run a race.

10. v. contend for, fight etc. for, stipulate for, stickle for, insist upon, make a point of.

11. adj. contending etc. v., at loggerheads, at war, at issue; oppositional etc. 708.4.

12. adj. contentious, combative, belligerent etc. (warlike) 722.13; quarrelsome etc. 901.9.

13. adj. competitive, competitory; emulous, rival, in competition or rivalry, in friendly rivalry; cutthroat.

721. Peace

(See 722. Warfare; also 723. Pacification)

1. n. peace, *pax* [L.], peacefulness etc. adj., freedom from war, exemption from hostilities, public tranquillity, quiet life, piping time of peace; the storm blown over; pacifism, pacificism; neutrality; Pax Britannica, Pax Dei, Pax Ecclesiae, Pax Romana; amity etc. (friendship) 888; good will etc. (benevolence) 906; harmony etc. (concord) 714; tranquillity etc. (quiescence) 265; truce etc. 723.3.

2. n. pacifist, pacificist, peace man, peace lover, peacemonger [derog.]; conscientious objector, conchie [slang]; noncombatant; peacemaker etc. (mediator) 724.2.

3. v. be at peace, keep the peace, remain at peace, be a pacifist; be in harmony with etc. (concord) 714.2; become reconciled etc. 723.5; pacify etc. 723.4.

4. adj. pacific, pacificatory; peaceable, peaceful, peacelike; calm, tranquil, untroubled, halcyon; unpugnacious, unbellicose, unbelligerent, uncontentious, noncombative; pacifistic, neutral; at peace; bloodless; concordant etc. 714.4.

---

721. *Paritur pax bello* [Peace is the offspring of war].—NEPOS.   Peace is liberty in tranquillity.—CICERO.   Seek peace and pursue it. —BIBLE.   My argument is that War makes rattling good history; but Peace is poor reading.—HARDY.   Peace is always beautiful.— WHITMAN.   The peace of fact is not the peace of principle.—AMIEL.   There never was a good war or a bad peace.—FRANKLIN. Peace hath her victories no less renowned than war.—MILTON.   The first and fundamental law of Nature, which is, to seek peace and follow it.—HOBBES.

5. *int.* peace be to you!, peace be with you!, *pax vobiscum!* [L.], "peace be to this house!" (Bible), go in peace!, *"vade in pace!"* (Vulgate).

722. Warfare
(See 721. Peace; also 726. Combatant)

1. *n.* warfare, war, combat, fighting etc. *v.*, military operations, the war game, state of war, hostilities, declared *or* open hostilities, bloodshed, arms, the sword, arbitrament of the sword, force *or* might of arms, *ultima ratio regum* [L.], ordeal of battle, grim-visaged war, *horrida bella* [L.]; *guerre à mort* or *à outrance* [F.], war to the death *or* knife, war to the finish *or* end, fight to the last ditch, fight to the death, Armageddon; war to end war.

civil war, revolutionary war, revolution, religious war; desert warfare, guerrilla warfare, mobile warfare, mountain warfare, naval warfare, offensive warfare, open war *or* warfare, war of movement, partisan warfare, position warfare, war of position, stabilized warfare, trench warfare, aerial warfare, bacteriological warfare, chemical warfare, economic warfare, land warfare, mine warfare, psychological warfare, war of nerves, siege warfare, underground warfare, war of attrition, total war *or* warfare; irregular warfare, internecine war, bushfighting.

Titanomachy, gigantomachy [Gr. Myth.], angelomachy, logomachy, Batrachomyomachy *or* Batrachomyomachia; battle array, order of battle; operations, active operations, combined operations, co-ordinated operations, fluid operations, major *or* minor operations, night operations, overseas operations, joint operatins, amphibious operations, flying operations; service, active service; contention etc. 720; battlefield etc. 728.2; warrior, militarist etc. (combatant) 726.

2. *n.* warcraft, war, art *or* rules of war, military evolutions; strategy, defensive strategy, grand strategy, offensive strategy; tactics, aerial tactics, applied tactics, barrier tactics, blitzkrieg *or* blitzkrieg tactics, cavalry tactics, fire tactics, grand tactics, infantry tactics, linear tactics, maneuver tactics, mobile tactics, shock tactics, columnar tactics, mob tactics; maneuvering, kriegspiel, *Kriegsspiel* [G.], siegecraft, castrametation; generalship, soldiership; chivalry, knightly skill, knighthood, knight-errantry; ballistics, gunnery; fleet work etc. (maneuvers) 267.4.

3. *n.* call to arms, appeal to arms *or* the sword, wager of battle, declaration of war; mobilization, recruiting, service call, rally; rallying cry *or* signal, war cry, war whoop, battle cry *or* call; slogan, watchword, password, word of command; war song, battle song *or* hymn, martial music, national anthem; *rappel* [F.], drum call to arms, beat of drum, tom-tom; battle horn, clarion, trumpet, bugle, pibroch; fiery cross, bloody shirt, black flag, battle flag; war hatchet, tomahawk.

4. *n.* campaign, war, expedition, hostile expedition, military campaign *or* expedition, crusade, jihad [Moham.]; invasion, raid etc. (attack) 716.

Boer War, Civil War, Crimean War, Crusades, Franco-Prussian War, Gallic Wars, Hundred Years' War, Napoleonic Wars, Peloponnesian War, Punic Wars, American Revolution, French Revolution, Russo-Japanese War, Spanish-American War, Thirty Years' War, Wars of the Roses, World War.

5. *n.* battle, conflict, fight, *passage d'armes* [F.] etc. (contest) 720.2; naval engagement etc. 720.4; foray, sally etc. (attack) 716; broil etc. 713.4.

(important battles) Actium, Agincourt, Antietam, Spanish Armada, Belleau Wood, Blenheim, Bull Run, Bunker Hill, Chateau Thierry, Gettysburg, Hastings, Jutland, Marne, Mukden, Philippi, Salamis, Sedan, Tannenberg, Thermopylae, Trafalgar, Verdun, Waterloo, Yorktown, Ypres.

6. *n.* warlikeness, combativeness, contentiousness etc. *adj.*; belligerence *or* bel-

---

722. War should never be entered upon until every agency of peace has failed.—McKinley. To measure manhood by the sword.—Spenser. Man is a military animal, / Glories in gunpowder, and loves parade.—P. J. Bailey. We made war to the end—to the very end of the end.—Clemenceau. I have not yet begun to fight.—J. P. Jones. I am tired and sick of war. Its glory is all moonshine.—W. Sherman. War is cruel and you cannot refine it.—W. Sherman. War is hell.—W. Sherman. Nothing except a battle lost can be half so melancholy as a battle won.—Wellington. He that is truly dedicate to war /

ligerency, pugnacity, bellicosity, bellicism, martiality, militancy, militarism, militaryism, waving of the bloody shirt; hostility, antagonism; warpath; quarrelsomeness etc. (ill-humor) 901; chauvinism etc. 884.2.

7. *n.* war-god, Mars [Rom. Myth.], Ares [Gr. Myth.], Odin *or* Woden [Norse Myth.], Tyr [Hindu Myth.]; war-goddess, Bellona, Juno Curitis *or* Quiritis [both Rom. Myth.].

8. *n.* war news, war bulletin, war extra; war correspondent etc. (journalist) 593.16.

9. *v.* war, warfare, make war, go to war *or* battle, go on the warpath, carry on war *or* hostilities, engage in hostilities, wage war, "let slip the dogs of war" (Shakespeare), battle, do *or* give battle, join *or* engage in battle, take the field, take the law into one's own hands, raise up in arms, take up arms, take up the cudgels *or* sword, fly to the sword, appeal to the sword, draw *or* unsheathe the sword, wield the sword, flesh one's sword, throw away the scabbard, shoulder a musket, be under fire, smell powder, fight the good fight.

keep the field, hold one's ground; spill blood, imbrue the hands in blood; give one's life for one's country, sell one's life dearly; fight one's way, cut one's way out *or* through; campaign, make an expedition, go on a crusade; declare war, dig up the tomahawk *or* hatchet; fight, combat, cross words etc. (contend) 720.8; go over the top [coll.] etc. (attack) 716.5, 6.

10. *v.* call to arms, mobilize, recruit, rally; give the battle cry etc. *n.*, cry havoc; kindle *or* light the torch of war, send round the fiery cross; wave the bloody shirt; raise one's banner, hoist the battle flag *or* black flag; arm etc. (equip) 634.2.

11. *v.* serve, see *or* be on service *or* active service; enlist, enroll, join up [slang] etc. (become a member) 712.8.

12. *adj.* warring, battling etc. *v.*; bearing arms, in arms, under arms, up in arms, in open arms, sword-in-hand; battled, embattled, in battle array.

13. *adj.* warlike, warful [rare]; fighting etc. *v.*; fightin', fightin'est, fighty [all dial.]; martial, military, militant, militaristic; soldierly, soldierlike; chivalric, chivalrous; combative, contentious, gladiatorial, belligerent, bellicose, pugnacious, armigerous, aggressive, offensive; fierce, savage; unpacific, unpeaceful, unpeacable [rare]; hostile, antagonistic, inimical; quarrelsome etc. 901.9; chauvinistic etc. 884.8; defiant etc. 715.3; courageous etc. 861.8.

14. *adv.* at war, in the field, in battle array, up in arms etc. *above* 722.12; *flagrante bello* [L.], in the midst of battle, in the thick of the fray; in the cannon's mouth, at the point of the gun; at swords' points, at the point of the bayonet *or* sword.

15. *int.* to arms!, *aux armes!* [F.], to your tents!, O Israel!, *c'est la guerre!* [F.], *"vae victis!"* (Plautus); attack! etc. 716.10.

723. Pacification
(See also 721. Peace)

1. *n.* pacification, conciliation, reconciliation, reconcilement, *rapprochement* [F.], shaking of hands; reunion, reunition [rare]; propitiation, placation, appeasement; adjustment, accommodation, arrangement, settlement, arbitration; terms, compromise; mollification etc. (modulation) 174.2; mediation etc. 724; peacemaker etc. (mediator) 724.2.

2. *n.* peace offering, propitiatory gift, pacifics [*pl.*], placation, olive branch; calumet, peace pipe *or* pipe of peace; overture, preliminaries of peace; parley etc. (mediation) 724.

3. *n.* truce, armistice, pacification, peace, treaty of peace, suspension of hostilities *or* arms, breathing spell *or* time; truce of God, *Treuga Dei* or *Domini* [ML.]; convention; *modus vivendi* [L.]; hollow truce, *pax in bello* [L.]; truce flag, flag of truce *or* peace, white flag; cartel; cartel ship, *un vaisseau parlementaire* [F.].

4. *v.* pacify, reconcile, appease, placate, propitiate, conciliate, make peace, make to be at peace, bring to terms, restore to

---

Hath no self-love.—SHAKESPEARE. Pride, pomp, and circumstance of glorious war.—SHAKESPEARE. He saith among the trumpets, Ha, ha; and he smelleth the battle afar off, the thunder of the captains, and the shouting.—BIBLE.

723. Thou hast touched me and I have been translated into thy peace.—ST. AUGUSTINE.

friendship, restore harmony, bring back to harmony *or* agreement, put in tune, bring together, reunite, heal the breach, bridge over, settle differences, arrange matters, accommodate, adjust, settle, set straight, fix up [coll.], mend, patch, patch up, patch up a friendship *or* quarrel; pour oil on the troubled waters, pour balm into; make a peace offering, hold out the olive branch, hoist ~, show *or* wave the white flag; negotiate a peace, dictate peace; mollify, tranquilize etc. (moderate) 174.5; harmonize etc. (accord) 23.8; mediate etc. 724.3.

5. *v.* become reconciled etc., make up a quarrel *or* difference, make up, kiss and make up [coll.], make it up, make matters up, settle one's differences, meet halfway, *tantas componere lites* [L.], mend one's fences [polit. slang, U.S.], let the wound heal, come round, come together, come to an understanding, come to terms, shake hands, smoke the calumet *or* pipe of peace, make peace, cease hostilities, raise a siege, bury the hatchet, put up *or* sheathe the sword, lay down one's arms, turn swords into plowshares; keep the peace etc. 721.3; forgive etc. 918.3.

6. *adj.* pacificatory, conciliatory, reconciliatory, accommodative, pacific; pacifying, propitiating etc. *v.*; propitiatory, propitiative, propitial [rare] ; placatory, placative; mediatory etc. 724.4; concordant etc. 714.4.

7. *adj.* pacifiable, placable, appeasable, forgiving.

724. Mediation

1. *n.* mediation, mediatization, mediatorialism, mediatorship; intermediation, intervention, interposition, interference, intercession, interagency, umpirage, negotiation, good offices; arbitrament, arbitration; diplomacy, diplomatics, diplomatism, diplomatology; parley; conciliation etc. (pacification) 723; agency etc. 170; instrumentality etc. 631.

2. *n.* mediator, intermediator, intermediate agent, intermediate, intermedium, intermediary, interagent, intercessor, interceder, intervener, internuncio, interpleader [Law], go-between, medium, middleman, connection [chiefly crim. slang, U.S.], front *or* front man [crim. slang, U.S.]; moderator, arbiter, arbitrator; negotiator, negotiant, negotiatress

or negotiatrix [*fem.*]; umpire, referee, referendary [now rare]; interlocutor, interlocutress *or* interlocutrice *or* interlocutrix [*fem.*]; peacemaker, make-peace, pacificator, propitiator, reconciler; *parlementaire* [F.], parliamentary, parliamentary agent; spokesman, diplomatic agent etc. (deputy) 759; judge etc. 967; lawyer etc. 968.

3. *v.* mediate, mediatize [rare], intermediate, intercede, intervene, interpose, interfere, step in, moderate, negotiate, propitiate, patch up, arrange, straighten out, adjust, adjust differences, meet halfway, bring to terms *or* an understanding; arbitrate, agree to arbitration, abide by arbitration, submit; umpire, referee; *componere lites* [L.]; harmonize etc. (accord) 23.8; conciliate etc. (pacify) 723.4.

4. *adj.* mediatory, mediatorial, mediating etc. *v.*; intermediatory, intermediary, intermedial; intercessory, interventional, negotiable; propitiatory, propitiative, propitial [rare]; interlocutory, interlocutive [rare]; diplomatic(al), diplomatial [erron.]; pacificatory etc. 723.6.

725. Submission

1. *n.* submission, submittal, submissiveness etc. *adj.*; yielding etc. *v.*, acquiescence, compliance, deference, resignation, passivity, nonresistance; obedience etc. 743; humility etc. 879; subjection etc. 749; conformity etc. 82; forbearance etc. (sufferance) 826.4.

2. *n.* surrender, cession, capitulation, renunciation, abandonment, relinquishment, backdown [coll.]; recession, recedence.

3. *v.* submit, yield, yield *or* defer to, comply, acquiesce, accede, relent, give way, succumb, resign, resign oneself, yield resignedly, be submissive etc. *adj.*; stoop, bend, bend the neck, bow, bow submission, bend *or* bow to, knuckle to [coll.], bend *or* bow to one's will, bend *or* bow before the storm, bend to one's yoke, knuckle down *or* under; knock under, knock under board *or* table; kneel to, bend the knee to, fall on one's knees before, crouch before, fall at one's feet,

---

725. O calm, dishonourable, vile submission!—SHAKESPEARE. Taught to submit, / A harder lesson that than to command.—THOMSON. Ye ben submitted through your free assent.—CHAUCER.

throw oneself at the feet of, prostrate oneself before.

yield *or* bend obsequiously to, truckle to, cringe to, kowtow [Chin.], bow and scrape; yield under humiliating circumstances, humble oneself, demean oneself [coll.], eat humble pie, eat crow, eat *or* swallow the leek, swallow the pill, eat dirt, lick the dust, kiss the rod, turn the other cheek; *avaler les couleuvres* [F.], swallow an insult, pocket the affront, take, pocket, swallow, eat, stomach, digest; submit with a good grace, grin and abide, grin and bear it, shrug the shoulders, make the best of it, make a virtue of necessity; obey etc. 743.2; be subject etc. 749.3.

4. *v.* surrender, cede, capitulate, give up, give way, give ground, give in, cave in [coll.], acknowledge defeat, cry quits, throw ~, toss *or* chuck up *or* in the sponge [coll.], throw in the towel, hoist ~, show *or* wave the white flag, lower ~, haul down *or* strike one's flag *or* colors, lay down *or* deliver up one's arms, hand over one's sword, deliver up the keys, yield the palm, draw in one's horns [coll.], cease opposition, come to terms; suffer judgment by default; be defeated etc. 732.6.

5. *adj.* submissive, submitting, yielding etc. *v.*; compliant, acquiescent, resigned, deferential, complaisant, obeisant, subservient, unassertive, passive; unresisting, nonresisting; docile, tractable; crouching, prostrate, on one's marrowbones [joc. or slang], on one's knees, on bended knee; meek etc. (forbearant) 826.10, (humble) 879.4, 5; obsequious etc. (servile) 886.4; obedient etc. 743.3; pliant etc. (soft) 324.6; subject etc. 749.6; conformable etc. 82.8; dutiful etc. 926.8.

726. Combatant
(See also 722. Warfare)

1. *n.* combatant, fighter, battler, scrapper [slang], disputant, wrangler, litigant, belligerent, contender, contestant, competitor, player, struggler, tussler, scuffler, jouster, gladiator; duelist, fencer, swordsman, *sabreur* [F.], *beau sabreur* [F.]; bullfighter, toreador, *torero* [Sp.]; wrestler, rassler *or* rastler [dial., U.S.]; fighting cock, gamecock; champion, champ [slang], paladin; controversialist etc. (reasoner) 476.9; assailant etc. (attacker) 716.4; opponent etc. 710.

2. *n.* pugilist, pug [slang], boxer, fighting man, prize fighter, bruiser, miller [slang or cant], sparrer.

3. *n.* militarist, militant, war dog *or* hound [chiefly U.S.]; Rajput [Hind.]; chauvinist etc. 884.4.

4. *n.* soldier, warrior, warfarer, brave, fighting man, man-at-arms, militant [rare], military man, militaster [derog.], serviceman, food for powder, fodder for cannon, cannon fodder, *Kanonenfutter* [G.]; warrioress, Amazon; redcoat, Tommy Atkins, tommy, Johnny (English soldier); doughboy, G.I., Sammy, Yank (U.S.); poilu (French soldier); Fritz, Jerry, Heinie, Hun, Boche (German soldier); Janizary *or* Janissary (Turkish soldier); bing boy (Canadian soldier); Aussie, digger (Australian soldier); Jock, lady of *or* from hell (Scottish soldier); veteran, vet [coll.], campaigner *or* old campaigner, war horse [coll.]; common soldier, private, buck private [slang, U.S.], peon, sepoy [Ind.].

infantry soldier, infantryman, foot soldier, footman [rare], footslogger [slang]; light infantryman, chasseur, Zouave; artilleryman, artillerist, gunner, cannoneer, musketeer, rifleman, jäger, sniper; sharpshooter, *bersagliere* [It.]; machine gunner, *mitrailleur* [F.]; carabineer, *carabinier* [F.], *carabinière* [It.], *carabinero* [Sp.]; fusilier *or* fusileer; bomber, bomb thrower, bombardier; torpedoer, torpedoist; grenadier; cavalry soldier, cavalryman, mounted infantryman, trooper, sowar [Ind.]; dragoon, light *or* heavy dragoon; cuirassier, hussar, lancer; engineer; sapper, sapper and miner.

guardsman, *gendarme* [F.]; yeoman, yeoman of the guard, beefeater [Eng.]; spearman, pikeman, halberdier; archer, bowman; knight, esquire, armiger, companion; *légionnaire* [F.], legionary; par-

726. An army, like a serpent, travels on its belly.—FREDERICK THE GREAT. I love a brave soldier who has undergone the baptism of fire.—NAPOLEON. The backbone of the Army is the Non-Commissioned Man.—KIPLING. Soldiers are citizens of death's grey land, / Drawing no dividend from time's tomorrows.—S. SASSOON.

tisan soldier, *franc-tireur* [F.]; skirmisher, *tirailleur* [F.]; mercenary, *condottiere* [It.], Hessian; irregular, irregular soldier, Croat [Hist.], free lance, freebooter, mosstrooper, marauder, guerrilla; bushwhacker [U.S.], bushfighter; Myrmidon [Gr. Myth.], Mameluke [Hist.], spahi, bashi-bazouk [Turk], Cossack; standard-bearer, ensign; officer etc. (military authorities) 745.11.

5. *n.* recruit, rookie [slang, U.S.], raw recruit, tenderfoot, conscript, drafted man, draftee; recruits, levy, draft, boot (Navy); awkward squad, raw levies *or* recruits; Landsturm, Landwehr.

6. *n.* army, armed force, fighting machine, this man's army [slang], soldiery, military, troops, forces, Sabaoth, host, array, rank and file; the line, troops of the line; line of defense, first ~, second etc. line of defense; regular *or* active army, regulars; irregular troops; standing army, militia, organized militia, national militia, mobile militia, territorial militia, reserve militia; National Guard, *garde nationale* or *royale* [F.], state guard [U.S.].

auxiliary *or* reserve forces, reserves, auxiliaries, army reserves, home reserves, territorial reserves, territorial *or* home defense army, supplementary reserves, organized reserves, second ~, third etc. line of defense, Landwehr, Landsturm, trainband [Eng., Hist.], minutemen [U.S., Hist.], fencibles [arch.]; volunteers, volunteer navy, volunteer militia; yeomanry.

7. *n.* corps, corps troops, army corps, *corps d'armée* [F.]; division, subdivision, section, unit, outfit [slang], troop, sotnia [Russ.], wing, detachment, garrison, brigade, regiment, battalion, company, battery, platoon, legion, phalanx, cohort; squad, squadron; maniple, manipulus [Rom., Hist.]; column, flying column; rank, file; posse, *posse comitatus* [L.].

engineer corps, corps of engineers; Women's Army Auxiliary Corps, Waacs *or* Wacs [coll.], Women's Army Corps, Wacs [coll.]; New Zealand Army Corps, Anzacs [coll.]; drum and bugle corps; Army Service Corps, Quartermaster Corps, Service of Supplies, service company, ~ battery *or* troop; train, military train, combat train, field train; guard, guards, yeomen of the guard, beefeaters [Eng.], household troops, Horse Guards, Foot Guards, Swiss Guards; picket, outlying *or* inlying picket.

8. *n.* horse and foot, cavalry and infantry; cavalry, horse, light horse, mounted infantry *or* rifles; infantry, foot, light infantry, rifles; artillery, gunners, horse artillery, field artillery, light artillery, heavy artillery.

9. *n.* air service, aviation service, air force, flying corps, air arm [Eng.], fourth arm [coll.]; strategic air force, tactical air force; Air Force, U.S. Air Force, Navy Air [all U.S.]; Royal Air Force [Eng.], R.A.F.; parachute troops, paratroops [coll.]; squadron, group, flight [U.S.], wing; aviation etc. 267a; aeronaut etc. 269a; battleplane etc. 273a.2.

10. *n.* navy, naval forces, first line of defense; fleet, flotilla, argosy, armada, squadron, *escadrille* [F.], division; mosquito fleet; naval militia, naval brigade; naval reserve, Royal Naval Reserve [Eng.]; marine, mercantile *or* merchant marine; Marine Corps, marines, the first to fight, leathernecks [slang], devil dogs [slang, U.S.], jollies [slang, Eng.]; Women Accepted for Volunteer Emergency Service [U.S.], Waves [coll.], Women's Royal Naval Corps [Eng.], Wrens [coll.]; man-of-war's man etc. (mariner) 269; naval officers etc. 745.12; navigation etc. 267.

11. *n.* man-of-war *or* man-o'-war, ship of war, battleship, warship, war vessel, war castle, armored vessel, ironclad, caravel; His Majesty's Ship, H.M.S. [Eng.], United States Ship, U.S.S.; line-of-battle ship, ship of the line; dreadnought, superdreadnought; cruiser, battle cruiser, scout cruiser, light cruiser, heavy cruiser, armored *or* protected cruiser; destroyer, destroyer leader; second-line destroyer, second-line battleship; torpedo-boat destroyer *or* catcher, torpedo catcher [rare]; submarine chaser, subchaser, eagle boat [U.S.], E-boat [coll.]; mine ship, mine layer; sweeper, mine sweeper; submarine, submersible, sub [coll.], U-boat, *U-boot, Unterseeboot* [both G.]; gunboat, river gunboat, torpedo boat.

flagship, turret ship, ram, monitor, floating battery, frigate, sloop of war, corvette *or* corvet, mosquito boat, bomb ketch *or* vessel [Hist.], privateer, first-rate; carrier, carrier ship, **aircraft *or* air-**

726.11 – 727.11

plane carrier, shipplane carrier, seaplane carrier; patrol boat *or* vessel, scout, submarine patrol boat; cutter, coast guard cutter [both U.S.]; naval auxiliary, depot ship, tender, destroyer tender, submarine tender, aircraft tender, storeship, tanker, fuel ship, ammunition ship, repair ship, fireboat, hospital ship; troopship, transport, transport ship *or* vessel; guard ship *or* boat, convoy; ship etc. 273.

12. *n.* war horse, charger, destrier [arch.], cavalry horse, trooper.

727. Arms

1. *n.* arms, weapons, deadly weapons, *apparatus belli* [L.], munitions, armament, armature; panoply, stand of arms; armory, arsenal; armor etc. (safeguard) 717.2.

2. *n.* ballistics, gunnery, archery.

3. *n.* side arms, *armes blanches* [F.]; steel, cold steel, blade, brand [arch.]; sword, good *or* trusty sword, naked sword *or* steel; broadsword, machete, bolo [P.I.], kukri [Ind.], Toledo, Ferara, claymore, glaive [arch.]; saber, cutlass, hanger, bilbo, falchion, scimitar, rapier, tuck [Hist.], foil, yataghan; dagger, poniard, baselard, dirk, stiletto, katar [Ind.], creese *or* kris; dudgeon [arch.], dudgeon dagger; skean, skean dhu [Scot.]; bayonet, sword bayonet, sword stick, pigsticker [slang], toadstabber [slang]; bowie knife, belduque [Southwest. U.S.], Arkansas toothpick [slang, U.S.], Kansas neck blister [slang, U.S.]; knife etc. (edge tools) 253.6.

4. *n.* ax, battle-ax, Lochaber ax, adaga, poleax *or* poleaxe, halberd *or* halbert, partisan, gisarme; bill, black bill, brown bill; tomahawk, tommy-ax [Austral.]; hatchet etc. (edge tools) 253.6.

5. *n.* spear, lance, pike, spontoon, assagai, javelin, jereed, jerrid, dart, shaft, bolt, reed; harpoon, gaff, eelspear; weet-weet, womera, throwing *or* throw stick, boomerang; oxgoad, ankus.

6. *n.* arrow, missile, shaft, dart, bolt; quarrel [Hist.], vire, chested arrow, footed arrow, bobtailed arrow, self arrow, cloth-yard shaft; arrowhead, barb; flight, volley.

7. *n.* club, war club, waddy [Austral.], mace, truncheon, bludgeon, cudgel, shillelagh, bat, billy; staff, handstaff, quarterstaff, cane, stick, walking stick; life preserver, blackjack, sandbag; ram, battering-ram; rod etc. 975.2.

8. *n.* knuckle-duster, brass knuckles, knucks *or* brass knucks [coll.].

9. *n.* sling, slingshot, beany [slang]; bow, longbow, self bow, carriage bow, bow and arrow, crossbow; catapult, arbalest, ballista, trebuchet *or* trebucket, mortar.

10. *n.* firearm, *armes à feu* [F.; *pl.*], gun, shooter [coll.], shooting iron [slang, U.S.], piece; iron, rod, gat [all crim. slang, U.S.]; small arms, musketry; musket, firelock, fowling piece, rifle, bone-crusher [slang], fusil [Hist.], escopette *or* escopet, carbine, blunderbuss, musketoon, Brown Bess, matchlock, harquebus, caliver, hackbut *or* hagbut, shotgun, petronel [Hist.], small-bore, magazine gun; twenty-two, forty-five etc.; needle gun, Dreyse rifle; muzzleloader, breechloader, chassepot; air gun, wind gun; automatic gun *or* pistol, automatic, revolver, repeater; six-shooter, six gun [both coll.]; pistol, barker [slang]; gunflint; gunlock.

11. *n.* artillery, cannon, dogs of war [coll.], ordnance; park, park of artillery; battery, gun battery; siege artillery, battering *or* siege train, field artillery, heavy field artillery, mountain artillery, coast artillery; field gun, fieldpiece; cannon, gun of position, heavy gun, mountain gun, siege gun, Big Bertha [slang], seacoast gun, howitzer, carronade, culverin, falconet, jingal, pedrero; *bouche à feu* [F.], smoothbore, rifled cannon, ten-pounder; swivel, swivel gun; machine gun, *mitrailleuse* [F.], auto-rifle, submachine gun, machine cannon, pom-pom, Gatling gun, Maxim gun, Lewis gun; antiaircraft gun, aerogun, Archibald *or* Archie [slang]; *Minenwerfer* [G.], minnie [slang]; mine thrower, mortar, trench gun *or* mortar; flame thrower *or* projector, Flammen-

---

727. *Arma virumque cano* [Arms and the man I sing].—Vergil.   The cannons have their bowels full of wrath.—Shakespeare.   The cannons . . . spit forth their iron indignation. —Shakespeare.   I have no words, / My voice is in my sword.—Shakespeare.   Good sword has often been in poor scabbard.—G Herbert.   There are no manifestoes like cannon and musketry.—Wellington.   To Man the weapon; to Heaven the victory.— Shaw.

werfer [G.], *lance-flamme* [F.]; robot.

12. *n.* (gun makes) Springfield, Luger, Enfield, Flobert, Westley Richards, Snider, Martini-Henry, Lee-Metford, Lee-Enfield, Mauser, Mannlicher, Minié; Vickers, Vickers-Maxim, Garling, Benet-Mercie, Armstrong, Lancaster, Paixhans, Whitworth, Parrott, Krupp, Maxim, Gatling, Lewis.

13. *n.* ammunition, munition, powder and shot; explosive, high explosive; powder, gunpowder, "villanous saltpetre" (Shakespeare); guncotton, pyroxylin, dynamite, melinite, cordite, gelignite, lyddite, nitroglycerin, trinitrotoluene, trinitrotolunine, TNT *or* T.N.T.; cartridge, cartouche *or* cartouch, ball cartridge; fulgurite; detonator etc. 388.4.

14. *n.* missile, projectile, trajectile; bolt, ball; shot, canister shot, bar shot, cannon shot, langrage *or* langrel shot, round shot, chain shot, slung shot; grapeshot, grape, *mitraille* [F.]; bullet, manstopping bullet, dumdum bullet, explosive bullet, expanding bullet; shell, high-explosive shell, *obus explosif* [F.]; shrapnel; infernal machine, bomb, smoke bomb, gas bomb, fire bomb; depth bomb, ash can [slang]; torpedo, spar torpedo, submarine torpedo, aerial torpedo; fireball; grenade, hand grenade, rifle grenade; petard; carcass; rocket, congreve rocket; slug, stone, rock, brickbat.

15. *n.* war gas, poison gas etc. (gas) 334.2.

728. Arena

1. *n.* arena, field, scene, scene of action, theater, walk, course, hustings, platform, stage, sphere, lists; amphitheater, circus, hippodrome, coliseum, Colosseum, stadium, bowl; racecourse, *corso* [It.], turf; gymnasium, palaestra; tiltyard, tilting ground; cockpit; bear garden; ring, prize ring, bull ring; *Campus Martius* [L.], *Champ de Mars* [F.]; campus [U.S.], playing field, playground; playhouse etc. 599.10–12.

2. *n.* battlefield, battleground, theater *or* seat of war, field of battle, field *or* ground of conflict, field of slaughter, field of blood *or* bloodshed, aceldama *or* akeldama, the front; battle line, line of battle; over there [U.S.], out there [Eng.]; no man's land; camp, encampment, tented field.

729. Completion

(See 730. Noncompletion; also 52. Completeness)

1. *n.* completion, accomplishment, achievement, effectuation, fulfillment *or* fulfilment, realization, attainment, performance, production, execution, discharge, dispatch *or* despatch, consummation, culmination, conclusion, finish, winding-up, work done, *fait accompli* [F.]; elaboration, perfection; *finale* [It.], denouement, catastrophe; final touches, final ~, last ~, crowning *or* finishing touch *or* stroke, *coup de grâce* [F.], finisher [coll.], crowning of the edifice; coping stone, copestone, keystone; termination, close etc. (end) 67; arrival etc. 292; completeness etc. 52; success etc. 731.

2. *v.* complete, render complete etc. *adj.*, accomplish, achieve, effect, effectuate, compass, consummate, do, execute, enact, make, produce, go *or* get through, work out, hammer out, bring about, bring through, bring to pass, bring to a head, dispatch *or* despatch, knock off [coll.], polish off, dispose of, make short work of, set at rest, perform, discharge, fulfill *or* fulfil, realize, attain, put in practice *or* force, put into effect *or* practice, carry into execution *or* effect, carry through, carry out.

follow *or* prosecute to a conclusion, finish off *or* up, wind up [coll.], give the final touch to etc. *n.*, culminate, round out, bring to a happy issue; elaborate, perfect, bring to perfection; ripe, ripen; mature, maturate, bring to maturity; crown, crown all, cap; clinch, clench; stamp, seal, set the seal on, put the seal to; make good, be as good as one's word; bring to an end etc. 67.7; succeed etc. 731.5.

3. *v.* do thoroughly, do up brown [slang], do to a turn, do to a frazzle [slang], do down to the ground [coll.], not do by halves, do oneself proud [coll.], drive home, deliver the goods [coll., U.S.], fill the bill [coll., U.S.]; go the

---

729. Achievement has come to be the only real patent of nobility.—W. WILSON. How my achievements mock me!—SHAKESPEARE. Is there anything in life so disenchanting as attainment?—STEVENSON. The reward of a thing well done is to have done it.—EMERSON. My race being run, I love to watch the race.—MASEFIELD. All over but the shouting.

limit [slang], go the whole length *or* way, go all lengths, go to all lengths, go the whole hog [slang], go the whole figure [slang], go all out [slang]; leave no stone unturned etc. (persevere) 604a.2.

4. *v.* reach completion etc. *n.*, culminate, come about, come to pass, come to a head *or* crisis, come to its end, run its course, run one's race, touch ~, reach *or* attain the goal, go into effect *or* practice, finish, wind up [coll.]; ripe, ripen; mature, maturate, reach maturity; die a natural death, die of old age; reach etc. (arrive) 292.7; end etc. 67.5, 6.

5. *adj.* completing, finishing, concluding, crowning etc. *v.*; completive, completory; conclusive, conclusory; final etc. (ending) 67.8.

6. *adj.* completed, perfected, finished etc. *v.*; complete, perfect, consummate, exhaustive, fully realized, brought to a finish etc. *n.*, sped; mature, ripe; wrought, wrought out; done, done for [coll.], done up brown [slang], done to a turn, done to a frazzle [slang]; ended etc. 67.9.

7. *adv.* completely etc. (thoroughly) 52.13-15.

8. *adv.* to completion etc. *n.*, with absolute finish, with *or* to perfection, to a turn, to a frazzle [slang]; to crown all, as a last stroke, as a fitting climax; to the end etc. 67.12.

730. Noncompletion
(See 729. Completion; also 53. Incompleteness)

1. *n.* noncompletion, nonaccomplishment, nonachievement, nonfulfillment *or* nonfulfilment, unfulfillment *or* unfulfilment, nonexecution *or* inexecution, nonperformance; work of Penelope, Sisyphean labor, ~ toil *or* task; incompleteness etc. 53; shortcoming etc. 304; imperfection etc. 651; neglect etc. 460.

2. *v.* not complete etc. 729.2, leave undone, leave unfinished etc. *adj.*, fail to perform, do by halves, scotch the snake not kill it, let alone, lose sight of, hang fire, be slow to, go off half-cocked *or* at half cock [coll.]; let slip, let slide [coll.];

neglect etc. 460.4; scamp, slight etc. (do superficially) 460.6; fail to attain, stop short etc. (fall short) 304.2.

3. *adj.* uncompleted, not completed etc. *v.*, unfinished, unaccomplished, unfulfilled, unperformed, unexecuted, undone; sketchy; half-baked, half-cocked [both coll.]; incomplete etc. 53.4; frustrated etc. 732.9.

4. *adv.* with the matter unfinished, *re infecta* [L.], without the final touches *or* finishing stroke; incompletely etc. 53.6.

731. Success
(See 732. Failure)

1. *n.* success, successfulness etc. *adj.*, favorable *or* prosperous issue *or* outcome, fortunate outcome, prosperity in an undertaking, speed [arch.]; time well spent; half the battle; continued success, success all along the way; run of luck, streak of luck [coll.]; luck etc. (prosperity) 734; profit etc. (gain) 775.2; advance etc. (progress) 282; accomplishment, achievement etc. (completion) 729.

2. *n.* stroke of success, ~ luck *or* fortune, piece of good luck *or* fortune, lucky *or* fortunate stroke *or* hit, lucky strike [slang, U.S.], stroke, good *or* bold stroke, *coup* [F.], feat, go, hit; master stroke, *coup de maître* [F.], trump card; great *or* extraordinary stroke of luck, big *or* smash hit [slang], smash [slang], tenstrike [coll.], fluke [slang], great ~, striking *or* sensational success, howling *or* roaring success [slang], killing [coll.].

3. *n.* victory, triumph, conquest, a feather in one's cap [coll.]; winning, win [coll.]; knockout, K.O. [slang]; easy victory, walkover [coll.]; winning streak [coll., U.S.]; subdual etc. (defeat) 732.3; subjugation etc. (subjection) 749; mastery etc. (dominion) 737.2, 3; ascendancy etc. (advantage) 33.1, 2.

4. *n.* victor, winner, conqueror, defeater, triumpher, vanquisher, subduer, subjugator, master, master of the situation *or* position; victress, victrix [rare]; champion, champ [slang]; conquistador [Sp., Hist.], pancratiast [Gr. Antiq.].

731. *Veni vidi vici* [I came, I saw, I conquered].—CAESAR.   Success is a rare paint, hides all the ugliness.—SUCKLING.   Beware of rashness, but with energy and sleepless vigilance go forward and give us victories.—

5. *v.* succeed, be successful etc. *adj.*, have success etc. *n.*, crown with success, meet with success, click [slang], go over [coll.], come off well *or* successfully, turn out well, pan out [coll.], speed [arch.], fare well, work well, do *or* work wonders; score a success, make a hit, make a lucky strike [slang, U.S.], strike oil [slang U.S.], turn up trumps, ring the bell; win through, achieve one's purpose, gain one's end *or* ends, gain ~, attain ~, carry ~, secure *or* win a point *or* object; find one's account in, turn to account *or* good account, strive to some purpose.

manage, contrive; come it, make a go of it, negotiate [all coll.]; make the grade, cut the mustard, turn the trick, deliver the goods, get there [all slang]; win ~, make ~, work *or* find one's way, make good, make one's mark, make a noise in the world [coll.], cut a swath, set the world, ~ river *or* Thames on fire; reap *or* gather the fruits *or* benefit of harvest, get in the harvest; hit the mark, hit the right nail on the head, hit it, nick it; turn the corner *or* a corner; accomplish, achieve etc. (complete) 729.2; make progress etc. 282.2; prosper etc. 734.5; make profit etc. 775.7.

6. *v.* triumph, be victorious etc. *adj.*, gain *or* obtain a victory, chain victory to one's car, prevail; win, win out [coll.], win ~, carry *or* gain the day, win the battle, finish in front, make a killing [coll.]; win the prize, ~ palm *or* laurels, bear the palm, bear away the bell, bring home the bacon [coll., U.S.], take the cake [slang, U.S.], win one's spurs; come off with flying colors, walk over [coll.], walk over the course, win in a canter *or* walk [slang], win hands down [coll.], walk off with the game [slang], take *or* carry by storm, carry all before one, make short work of, remain in possession of the field; have the game in one's own hands, have the ball at one's feet; fluke, win by a fluke [both slang]; break the record, reach a new high [coll.].

7. *v.* surmount, overcome a difficulty *or* an obstacle, overcome, get over, rise above, *se tirer d'affaire* [F.], make head against, stem the torrent, ~ tide *or* current, weather the storm, keep one's head above water, tide over.

8. *v.* gain the ascendancy, triumph over, gain *or* obtain the advantage, get *or* gain the upper *or* whip hand, get a pull over [slang], get the edge on, ~ bulge on, ~ deadwood on, ~ jump on *or* drop on [all slang], get the better *or* best of, get the start of, get a strangle hold on; have the advantage etc. 33.6; distance, surpass etc. (be superior) 33.5.

9. *v.* defeat, conquer, vanquish, worst, get the better *or* best of, make the enemy bite the dust, break the neck *or* back of, skin [slang], beat, drub, euchre [slang], floor, undo; overcome, overwhelm, overthrow, overturn, overpower, overmaster, overmatch, override, overreach, overset; upset, trip up, trip the heels of, lay by the heels.

outdo, outwit, outflank, outmaneuver, outgeneral; lick, whip, thrash, trim, fix, settle, settle one's hash, cook one's goose, put one's nose out of joint, gravel, do for [all coll.]; lick to a frazzle [coll., U.S.], beat hollow *or* all hollow [coll.]; shut out, whitewash [coll.]; discomfit, rout, put to the rout, put to flight, put out of court; master, subdue, quell, put down, suppress, crush, squelch [coll.], quash, reduce, roll *or* trample in the dust, tread *or* trample underfoot; subjugate 749.5; circumvent, elude etc. (avoid) 623.6.

10. *v.* checkmate, check, stick [coll.], deadlock, stalemate, trump, nonsuit, nonplus, confound, flummox [slang], stump [coll., chiefly U.S.]; corner, run *or* drive into a corner, drive to the wall, put one's back to the wall, chase up a tree [coll.] *or* stump [slang, U.S.], tree [coll.]; put *hors de combat* [F.], put the kibosh on [slang], put an extinguisher upon, calk [Naut., slang], silence; bring to a standstill, stop etc. (interrupt) 142.7; hinder, thwart etc. 706.4, 7; spike, put a spoke in one's wheels etc. (render powerless) 158.6.

11. *adj.* successful, succeeding etc. *v.*; victorious, triumphant, flushed *or* crowned with success, set up [coll.]; undefeated, unbeaten etc. *v.*; ascendant, in the ascendant, in ascendancy; well-spent; in full swing; prosperous, fortunate etc. 734.7, 8.

12. *adv.* successfully etc. *adj.*, swimmingly, *à merveille* [F.], to one's heart's content; beyond all expectation **or hope,**

LINCOLN.   The success of any great moral enterprise does not depend upon numbers.—
GARRISON.   You've done yourselves proud.—
MARK TWAIN.   *Rien ne réussit comme le succès* [Nothing succeeds like success].

beyond one's fondest dreams, beyond the dreams of avarice, beyond one's deserts; to some purpose, to good purpose; in triumph, with flying colors.

732. Failure
(See 731. Success)

1. *n.* failure, unsuccessfulness etc. *adj.,* unsuccess, nonsuccess, ill success; nonfulfillment *or* nonfulfilment, unfullfillment *or* unfulfilment; flop [slang, U.S.], frost [slang], flivver [slang], fizzle [coll.], flunk [coll., U.S.], mull [coll., Eng.], poor fist [coll.], no go [coll.], "lame and impotent conclusion" (Shakespeare); complete ~, utter ~, dead *or* flat failure, fiasco, washout [slang]; frustrated attempt, frustration; abortive attempt, abortion, miscarriage, misfire, flash in the pan, *brutum fulmen* [L.], dud [slang]; explosion, bursting of the bubble.

collapse, crash, smash; slip, slip-up [coll.], slip 'twixt cup and lip; miss, oversight, omission; vain *or* ineffectual attempt *or* effort, inefficacy, inefficacity [rare]; goose chase, wild-goose chase; losing game; comedown, letdown [coll.]; failure of expectation etc. (disappointment) 509; labor in vain etc. 645.3; shortcoming etc. 304; misfortune etc. (adversity) 735; bankruptcy etc. (insolvency) 808.2; impotence etc. 158.

2. *n.* clumsy failure, *faux pas* [F.] etc. (blunder) 495.3; botch etc. (bungle) 699.4.

3. *n.* defeat, vanquishment, conquerment, beating, drubbing, licking [coll.], undoing, overthrow, overturn, discomfiture, rout, repulse, rebuff; fall, downfall, collapse, smash; ruin, perdition, *affaire flambée* [F.]; utter defeat *or* overthrow, whitewash [coll.], complete check, checkmate, stalemate, fool's mate, nonsuit, deadlock, quietus, deathblow; subdual, subduement [rare]; subjugation etc. (subjection) 749; victory etc. 731.3; hindrance etc. 706.

4. *n.* unsuccessful person, failure, flop [slang, U.S.], also-ran; false alarm [slang], flash in the pan, dud [slang];

flunker [coll., **U.S.**], flunky [slang, U.S.]; goner [slang], gone coon, ~ goose *or* gosling [slang]; victim, prey; bankrupt etc. 808.4; misfit etc. 24.4.

5. *v.* fail, not succeed etc. (*see* succeed etc. 731.5), be unsuccessful etc. *adj.,* be a failure etc. *n.,* flop [slang, U.S.], flummox [slang], fizzle *or* fizzle out [coll.], peg out [slang], peter out [slang], go up [coll.], not get to first base [slang, U.S.], get left [slang, U.S.], fall, fall down [slang], fall down on the job [coll.], fall through, fall to the ground, fall between two stools, fall dead, fall stillborn, fall flat, flat out [coll.], collapse, crash, explode, end *or* go up in smoke, go up like a rocket and come down like the stick, flash in the pan, come to nothing, be all over *or* up with, fail ignominiously.

bring to naught *or* nought, make nothing of, take nothing by one's motion, lose one's labor, do in vain, make vain efforts etc. *n.*; slip, slip up [coll.], make a slip, stumble, trip; miss, miss one's aim, miss one's footing, miss the mark, miss *or* lose one's way, miss stays [Naut.]; miss fire, misfire; miscarry, abort, go amiss *or* astray, go wrong, go cross, go hard with, come off ill, turn out ill, take an ugly turn, take a wrong turn, go on a wrong tack.

go from bad to worse, jump out of the frying pan into the fire, sow the wind and reap the whirlwind; go to the dogs, go to pot [coll.], go to the wall; come to grief, stick in the mud, run aground, split upon a rock, run *or* dash one's head against a stone wall, break one's back, break down; sink, drown, founder, have the ground cut from under one; strike out, fan *or* fan out [slang]; flunk *or* flunk out [coll., U.S.], pluck [orig. Eng. Univ. slang], plough [Eng. Univ. slang]; labor in vain etc. 645.6; fall short etc. 304.2; dash one's hope etc. (disappoint) 509.2; go to ruin etc. (perish) 162.5; make a blunder etc. 495.9; bungle etc. 699.9; go bankrupt etc. 808.6.

6. *v.* be defeated etc. *adj.,* fall, succumb, lose, lose out [coll.], lose the day, come off second best, get *or* have the worst of it, bite *or* lick the dust, fall a

---

732. There is not a fiercer hell than the failure in a great object.—KEATS.   There is the greatest practical benefit in making a few failures early in life.—HUXLEY.   They fail and they alone, who have not striven.—T. ALDRICH.

To fail at all is to fail utterly.—LOWELL. Success is counted sweetest / By those who ne'er succeed.—E. DICKINSON.   The game is up.—SHAKESPEARE.   Thou art weighed in the balances, and art found wanting.—BIBLE.

prey to, not have a leg to stand on; acknowledge defeat etc. (surrender) 725.4.

7. *adj.* unsuccessful, successless, not successful etc. 731.11, meeting with *or* resulting in failure, failing etc. *v.,* stickit [Scot.], at fault; unfortunate etc. 735.9.

8. *adj.* abortive, abortional; miscarrying, miscarried; stillborn, sterile, addle, fruitless, bootless, lame, ineffectual, ineffective, inefficacious, of no effect, coming to naught; unavailing etc. (useless) 645.8; insufficient etc. 640.8; inefficient etc. (impotent) 158.8; wide of the mark etc. (erroneous) 495.12.

9. *adj.* frustrated, thwarted, crossed, foiled, scotched, balked, dashed, dished [coll.], flummoxed [slang], disconcerted; thrown on one's beam ends, thrown off one's balance, thrown on one's back, unhorsed; unhinged, *décousu* [F.]; stultified, befooled, victimized, hoist with *or* on one's own petard; unaccomplished etc. (uncompleted) 730.3.

10. *adj.* stranded, aground, grounded, on the rocks, high and dry, castaway, swamped, foundered, capsized; wrecked, shipwrecked; stuck, stuck *or* set fast.

11. *adj.* failed etc. *v.,* flunked [coll., U.S.], plucked [orig. Eng. Univ. slang], ploughed [Eng. Univ. slang]; lost, unwon.

12. *adj.* defeated, vanquished, conquered, worsted, beat, licked [coll.], whipped [coll.], trimmed [coll.], skinned [slang], euchred [slang], settled [coll.], graveled [coll.], floored, discomfited; overcome, overthrown, overpowered, overmatched, overborne, overridden; outdone, outwitted, outflanked, outmaneuvered; checkmated, nonsuited etc. *v.*; shut out, whitewashed [coll.]; subdued, quelled, suppressed, crushed, reduced; all up with, done up, done for [all coll.]; undone, ruined, desolate, hard-hit, broken, knocked on the head, ruined root and branch, *hors de combat* [F.].

13. *adv.* unsuccessfully etc. *adj.,* to little *or* no purpose, in vain, *re infecta* [L.].

733. Trophy

1. *n.* trophy, prize, reward, award, palm, laurel *or* laurels, bays, crown, chaplet, wreath, garland, feather in one's cap [coll.]; honor, badge *or* mark of honor, "blushing honors" (Shakespeare); decoration, decoration of honor, ornament, *fourragère* [F.]; ribbon, riband, blue ribbon, *cordon bleu* [F.], red ribbon, red ribbon of the Legion of Honor; cordon, grand cordon; civic crown; cup, loving cup, pot [slang]; garter; star, gold star; favor, token, love knot; Nobel Prize, Pulitzer Prize; citation, eulogy; flying colors; triumphal arch; first, second etc. prize, booby prize, consolation prize; insignia etc. 550.12.

2. *n.* medal, medallion; Carnegie medal; war medal, service medal, soldier's medal, military medal; Distinguished Service Medal (Navy), Distinguished Service Cross, Navy Cross, Distinguished Flying Cross, Silver Star Medal (Army), Order of the Purple Heart, Distinguished Service Medal (Army), Medal of Honor (Navy), Medal of Honor (Army), Congressional medal (all U.S.); Military Cross, Distinguished Conduct Medal, Victoria Cross, Distinguished Service Order, Military medal, Distinguished Flying Cross (all British); Croix de guerre, Médaille Militaire (both French); Iron Cross, Pour le mérite (both German); Medal for Valor, Cross of Merit (both Italian).

Civil War Campaign medal, Indian Campaign medal, Spanish Campaign medal, Spanish War Service medal, Army of Cuban Occupation medal, Army of Puerto Rican Occupation medal, Philippine Campaign medal, Philippines Congressional medal, China Campaign medal, Army of Cuban Pacification medal, Mexican Service medal, Mexican Border Service medal, Victory medal (all U.S. Army, Hist.).

734. Prosperity
(See 735. Adversity)

1. *n.* prosperity, weal [arch.], welfare, well-being; thrift [obs.], thriving condition; roaring trade, land-office business [coll., U.S.]; prosperous condition, clo-

---

733. Now are our brows bound with victorious wreaths.—SHAKESPEARE.   The laurel, meed of mighty conquerors.—SPENSER.

734. The lines are fallen unto me in pleasant places; yea, I have a goodly heritage.—BIBLE. A comfortable career of prosperity, if it does not make people honest, at least keeps them so.—THACKERAY.   Reverse cannot befall that fine Prosperity / Whose sources are in-

ver, velvet [slang], good ~, comfortable *or* easy circumstances, ease, life of ease, bed of roses; fat of the land, milk and honey, loaves and fishes, fleshpots of Egypt; favorable conditions, prosperous influence; fair wind, fair wind and no favor; tide, flood, high tide; success etc. 731; affluence etc. (wealth) 803; blessing, godsend etc. (good) 648.2.

2. *n.* good fortune *or* luck, fortune, luck, smiles of fortune; run of luck, streak of luck [coll.]; piece of good luck *or* fortune, fluke [slang]; stroke of luck etc. 731.2; lucky piece etc. (talisman) 993.2.

3. *n.* prosperous times, good *or* piping times, bright ~, palmy *or* halcyon days; sunshine, bright clouds, fair weather; golden age, golden time, Saturnian age, *Saturnis regna* [L.], millennium.

4. *n.* man of substance, made man; fortunate, lucky dog [coll.]; *enfant gâté* [F.], spoiled child of fortune; man of wealth etc. 803.2.

5. *v.* prosper, fare well, speed [arch.], thrive, flourish, go on well, ~ smoothly *or* swimmingly, run smooth *or* smoothly, run on all fours [coll.], sail before the wind, swim with the tide, keep afloat, keep *or* hold one's head above water; drive a roaring trade, do a land-office business [coll., U.S.]; be prosperous etc. *adj.,* rise *or* get on in the world, make a noise in the world [coll.], make good, make one's mark, make *or* work one's way, feather one's nest, make one's fortune, make one's pile [slang], grow rich; have a good *or* fine time of it, live on the fat of the land, live in clover, live on velvet [slang], live a life of ease, bask in the sunshine; grow fat, fatten, batten; blossom, bloom, blow, flower, fructify, bear fruit; improve, look up [coll.]; succeed etc. 731.5.

6. *v.* be fortunate etc. *adj.,* have good fortune etc. *n.,* have a run of luck, have a stroke of luck etc. 731.2, take a favorable turn, turn up trumps [coll.], drop into a good thing; light *or* fall on one's feet *or* legs, bear a charmed life.

7. *adj.* prosperous, flourishing, thriving etc. *v.*; in a fair way, in good case, in full *or* high feather; well off, well-to-do, well to do in the world, well-to-live [arch.], set up [coll.]; in clover, on velvet [slang], on a bed of roses, comfortable, at one's ease; successful etc. 731.11; wealthy etc. 803.8.

8. *adj.* fortunate, lucky, providential; in luck, in a good way [slang]; born under a lucky star, born with a silver spoon in one's mouth, born on the sunny side of the hedge; propitious, halcyon etc. (auspicious) 512.4.

9. *adv.* prosperously etc. *adj.,* swimmingly; beyond all expectation *or* hope, beyond one's fondest dreams, beyond the dreams of avarice, beyond one's deserts; luckily etc. *adj.,* as luck *or* good luck would have it.

735. Adversity
(See 734. Prosperity)

1. *n.* adversity, adverse circumstances, hardship, hard lines, hard case, hard life; trouble, matter, rattle [slang], embarrassment; bother, botherment, botheration [both coll.]; affliction, infliction, visitation, scourge, trial, care, cross, load; burden, burthen [arch.]; pressure, stress, pinch, rub; peck *or* sea of troubles, ups and downs of life, miseries of human life, "the thousand natural shocks that flesh is heir to" (Shakespeare); purgatory, hell, hell upon earth; ordeal, fiery ordeal; bitter cup, bitter draft, bitter pill; distress, misery etc. (pain) 828; evil etc. 649; curse, blight etc. (bane) 663.1, 2; difficulty etc. 704; failure etc. 732.

2. *n.* bad fortune *or* luck, evil fortune, ill luck, tough luck [coll.], hard luck, hard *or* unhappy lot; frowns of fortune, evil dispensation, ill wind; turn of fortune against one, a horse on one [slang]; broken fortunes; the sport of fortune; evil star etc. (bad influence) 649.3.

3. *n.* misfortune, misventure [arch.], misadventure, mishap, mischance, con-

---

terior.—E. DICKINSON. *Felix se nescit amari* [The prosperous man does not know whether he is loved or not].—LUCAN. *Donec eris felix multos numerabis amicos* [As long as you are fortunate you will number many friends].—OVID. When good luck comes to thee, take it in.—CERVANTES. Good fortune is not known until it is lost.—CERVANTES. It is better to be lucky than wise.—J. RAY. When fortune favours, none but fools will dally. —DRYDEN. Lucky at cards, unlucky at love.

735. Calamity is man's true touchstone.—BEAUMONT AND FLETCHER. Bad luck often brings good luck.—FULLER. In every adversity of fortune, to have been happy is the most unhappy kind of misfortune.—BOETHIUS. Fortune is not satisfied with inflicting one calamity.—

tretemps [F.], casualty, accident, grief, disaster, calamity, catastrophe; shock, blow, hard *or* nasty blow; collision, crash; wreck, shipwreck, smash [coll.], smash-up, crack-up [coll.]; cave, cave-in [both coll.]; fatal mischief, tragedy; reverse, check, backset, setback, comedown; plight, strait etc. (predicament) 704.2; failure etc. 732; evil etc. 649.2.

4. *n.* hard times, bad times, sad times, time out of joint; iron age; evil day, rainy day; cloud, dark cloud, gathering clouds.

5. *v.* suffer adversity etc. *n.*, have trouble, meet with *or* encounter hardship, be up against it [coll.], have a hard time of it, run one hard, go hard with, go against the grain, try one, put one out, be put to one's shifts *or* wit's end, not know which way to turn.

6. *v.* suffer misfortune etc. *n.*, be unfortunate etc. *adj.*, fall on evil days, go on ill, not prosper etc. 734.5; come to grief, bring a wasp's *or* hornet's nest about one's ears; go downhill, fall from one's high estate, go down in the world, go to the dogs, go to pot [coll.], deteriorate, decay, sink, decline, have seen better days; go to rack and ruin etc. (perish) 162.5.

7. *v.* bring bad luck, hoodoo [coll., U.S.]; Jonah, jinx, put the jinx on [all slang].

8. *adj.* adverse, untoward, sinister, conflicting, contrary; opposed, opposing, opposite, in opposition; disastrous, calamitous, ruinous, dire, deplorable; evil etc. 649.8-11.

9. *adj.* unfortunate, unlucky, unblest, unprosperous, unhappy, hapless, fortuneless, luckless, in ill luck, out of luck, down on one's luck [coll.], badly *or* ill off, behindhand, down in the world; in adverse circumstances, adversely circumstanced; clouded, under a cloud; on the road to ruin, on the wane, on its last legs; hoodooed [coll., U.S.], Jonahed [slang], jinxed [slang]; ill-starred, evil-starred, born under an evil star, born with a wooden ladle in one's mouth; ominous, inauspicious etc. 512.3, 5; in trouble etc. 704.11; poor etc. 804.7; unsuccessful etc. 732.7.

10. *adv.* adversely, unfortunately etc. *adj.*; as ill luck would have it; if the worst comes to the worst; from bad to worse, out of the frying pan into the fire.

736. Mediocrity

1. *n.* mediocrity, mediocreness etc. *adj.*, *aurea mediocritas* [L.], matter of indifference, average capacity, moderate *or* average circumstances, normality, respectability; peanut politics, peanut policy; mediocre [rare], mediocrist [rare], common or garden variety [coll.]; middle classes, *bourgeoisie* [F.]; golden mean etc. (mean) 29, (moderation) 174; mid-course etc. 628; imperfection etc. 651.

2. *v.* be mediocre etc. *adj.*, barely pass muster, get by [slang], get along [coll.], get on tolerably, go fairly, jog on; keep the golden mean etc. (be moderate) 174.4, (steer a middle course) 628.2.

3. *adj.* mediocre, middling, tolerable, passable, fair, fairish, fair to middling [coll.], no great shakes [coll.], indifferent, ordinary, common, commonplace, common or garden [coll.], average, medium, betwixt and between [coll.], soso, sosoish [chiefly coll.], *couci-couci* [F.], *comme ci comme ça* [F.], mere; of a sort, of sorts [both coll.]; bearable, admissible, unobjectionable, unexceptionable; not much to boast of, nothing to brag about; one-horse, two-by-four [both coll.]; secondary, second-best, second-rate; third-rate, fourth-rate etc.; insipid, milk-and-water, wishy-washy [coll.], namby-pamby; middle-class, *bourgeois* [F.]; moderate etc. 174.6; moderately good etc. 648.11; imperfect etc. 651.4; trivial, petty, paltry etc. (unimportant) 643.10-12.

4. *adv.* moderately, tolerably etc. (in some degree) 32.14.

PUBLILIUS. Sweet are the uses of adversity.—SHAKESPEARE. Affliction is enamor'd of thy parts, / And thou art wedded to calamity.—SHAKESPEARE. Adversity is the first path to truth.—BYRON. Misfortunes come on wings and depart on foot.—BOHN. There is something in the misfortunes of even our best friends that does not wholly displease us!—GREENSLET.

736. The universal subjugator, the commonplace.—GOETHE. Not below mediocrity, nor above it.—JOHNSON. Mediocre minds generally condemn everything which passes their understanding.—LA ROCHEFOUCAULD. No characteristic trait had he / Of any distinctive kind.—GILBERT. To mediocrity genius is unforgivable.—E. HUBBARD.

737. Authority
(See 738. Laxity)

1. *n.* authority, authoritativeness etc. *adj.*, legal *or* rightful power, right to command *or* act, power *or* right to exercise authority, right of control, right, power, potence *or* potency, authorization, prerogative; divine right, dynastic rights; *jus divinum* [L.], *jus nocendi* [L.]; despotism etc. (arbitrary power) 739.2; commission etc. 755; permission etc. 760; scepter etc. (insignia of authority) 747; influence etc. 175.

2. *n.* dominion, dominance *or* dominancy, domination; supremacy, primacy, suzerainty; sovereignty *or* sovranty, dynasty [now rare], royalty, regality, regalia, majesty, imperiality; kingship, kinghood; the throne, the crown; empire, empery; command, rule, sway, reign; *régime* [F.], regime, regimen; dictation, dictature; jurisdiction, judicature, judicatory; control, controlment; hold, grasp, grip, gripe, reach; clutches, talons, fangs; overruling influence *or* power, influence, pressure, weight, moment, consequence; ascendance *or* ascendancy, upper *or* whip hand; prestige, preponderance, prepotence *or* prepotency, prepollence *or* prepollency; predominance *or* predominancy, predomination; government, administration etc. (direction) 693.

3. *n.* mastership, masterhood, masterdom, mastery; lordship, leadership, headship, directorship, superintendence *or* superintendency, hegemony; seigniory *or* seignory *or* seigneury, seignoralty; chieftainship, chieftaincy, chieftainry, chiefery *or* chiefry; kingship, kinghood; presidentship, presidency; premiership; prefectship, prefecture; protectorship, protectorate; seneschalship, seneschalsy, seneschalty; caliphship, caliphate; pashaship, pashadom, pashalik; magistrateship, magistrature, magistracy; consulship, proconsulship; patriarchship, patriarchy, patriarchate; dictatorship, dictature; electorate.

4. *n.* (governments) monarchy, limited *or* constitutional monarchy; aristarchy, aristocracy; oligarchy, democracy, demagogy; representative *or* constitutional government, republic; heteronomy; thearchy, theocracy; autocracy, monocracy; diarchy, duarchy, duumvirate; triarchy, triumvirate; dominion rule, colonial government; autonomy, self-government, home rule; republicanism, federalism; pantisocracy; stratocracy, military government, militarism, martial law, rule of the sword; absolutism, imperialism, czarism, Caesarism, kaiserism; Nazism, Fascism; feodality, feudality, feodatory, feudatory, feudal system, feudalism; patriarchy, patriarchate; municipal *or* city government, municipality, bailiwick, shrievalty; constabulary, constablewick.

5. *n.* gynocracy, gynecocracy, gynarchy, petticoat government; matriarchy, matriarchate, metrocracy.

6. *n.* socialism, social democracy, collectivism, nationalism, communism, communalism, Marxism, Bolshevism, sovietism.

7. *n.* officialism, bureaucracy; beadledom, Bumbledom; red-tapism, red-tapery, red-tapedom.

8. *n.* state, body politic etc. (country) 182.

9. *n.* acquisition of authority, accession; usurpation, arrogation etc. (assumption) 925.3; installation etc. (commission) 755.

10. *v.* authorize, warrant etc. (grant) 760.4; order etc. (command) 741.4.

11. *v.* rule, sway, command, control, govern, boss [coll.], preside over, head, lead, be master etc. 745, have the portfolio, be at the head of etc. *adj.*; have ~, hold *or* possess authority, exercise ~, exert *or* wield authority etc. *n.*; administer, administrate; occupy the chair, be in the seat of authority etc. 747.5; reign, be seated on the throne, possess *or* occupy the throne, wield the scepter, wear the crown; hold office, be in office, fill an office, hold *or* occupy a post; manage, superintend etc. (direct) 693.4, 5.

12. *v.* dominate, predominate, preponderate, prevail, have superiority over, have the ascendancy, have the upper *or* whip hand, have control of, control, master, have the mastery of, have on the hip; gain a hold upon, take the lead, play first

---

737. *Regibus esse manus an nescis longas* [Am I not aware that kings have long arms?]—Ovid. A dog's obeyed in office.—Shakespeare. Drest in a little brief authority.—Shakespeare. Authority intoxicates / And makes mere sots of magistrates.—Butler. Authority forgets a dying king.—Tennyson. I go for all sharing the privileges of the government who assist

fiddle; overrule, override, overawe, overbear; rule the roast, wear the breeches [coll.], lord it over, hold in hand, keep under, make a puppet of, lead by the nose, turn around one's little finger, keep under one's thumb, carry with a high hand, bend to one's will; give the law to, lay down the law; be master of the situation, hold one's own, have the ball at one's feet, have it all one's own way, have the game in one's own hands; change the preponderance, turn the scale *or* balance, turn the tables; rule with a rod of iron etc. (domineer) 739.4; have influence over etc. 175.8.

13. *v.* assume authority, take *or* assume command, take the command, assume the reins of government, take the reins into one's hand, ascend or mount the throne; grasp ~, seize *or* wrest authority etc. *n.*, usurp, arrogate, seize, assume, usurp etc. power, wrest the law to one's advantage; usurp *or* seize the throne, usurp the prerogatives of the crown.

14. *v.* be governed by, be in the power of, be under the rule *or* dominion of.

15. *adj.* authoritative, possessing authority etc. *n.*, clothed with authority; commanding, ruling etc. *v.*; regnant, regnal; at the head, dominant, predominant, preponderant, prepotent, prepollent, prevalent, hegemonic(al), chief, paramount, supreme; ascendant, in the ascendant, in ascendancy; gubernative [now rare], gubernatorial, governmental; governing; executive, administrative; official, ex officio; bureaucratic(al), departmental; dictatorial, bossy [coll., U.S.]; imperious, imperative, imperatorial; peremptory, overruling, autocratic(al), absolute, positive, arbitrary; potent, powerful, puissant, mighty; compulsory etc. 744.3; stringent, despotic etc. (severe) 739.5; influential etc. 175.10; commanding etc. 741.8; authorized etc. (due) 924.10; executive etc. (directing) 693.6.

16. *adj.* sovereign, suzerain; regal, royal, dynastic(al); kinglike, kingly, "every inch a king" (Shakespeare); majestic, majestious; royalist, royalistic; monarchic(al), monarchial; imperial, imperialistic; princely, princelike; queenly, queenlike; feudal; oligarchic(al), autocratic(al) etc. *n.*

17. *adv. etc.* by authority of, in the name of, in *or* by virtue of, under the auspices of, in the hands of; at one's command, at one's nod, at one's pleasure, *ex mero motu* [L.]; by lifting one's finger, by a dash *or* stroke of the pen; *de par le Roi* [F.], by order of the king; *ex cathedra* [L.].

738. Laxity
(See 737. Authority)

Absence of Authority.—1. *n.* laxity, laxness, looseness, slackness; remission, relaxation; interregnum; negligence etc. 460; toleration etc. (lenity) 740; freedom etc. 748.

2. *n.* anarchy, anarchism; lawlessness, misrule, disorder, disorganization, chaos; license, licentiousness; mob rule *or* law, mobocracy, ochlocracy; nihilism, terrorism, violence, reign of terror *or* violence, brute force, lynch ~, Lydford ~, martial *or* club law, *argumentum baculinum* [L.], *le droit du plus fort* [F.]; anarch, anarchist; insubordination, insurgence etc. (disobedience) 742; revolt etc. 742.2.

3. *n.* deprivation of power, dethronement, disenthronement, discrownment, deposal, deposition, impeachment; abdication; usurpation, arrogation etc. (assumption) 925.3.

4. *v.* be lax etc. *adj., laisser faire* [F.], *laisser aller* [F.]; hold a loose rein, give the reins to, give rope enough, give a free course to, give free rein to; tolerate; relax; misrule; act without authority, act on one's own responsibility, go beyond the length of one's tether; have one's swing *or* fling.

5. *v.* deprive of authority, usurp authority, undermine the authority of; depose, dethrone, unthrone, disenthrone, discrown, uncrown.

6. *v.* abdicate, resign, demit, relinquish, renounce, give up, surrender.

7. *adj.* lax, loose, slack, licensed, weak, unexacting; adespotic, undespotic; not imperious (*see* imperious etc. 737.15); remiss etc. (neglectful) 460.8; unbridled, reinless etc. (unconstrained) 748.13; lenient etc. 740.4.

---

in bearing its burden.—LINCOLN. Government of the people, by the people, for the people.—LINCOLN.

738. Pleasant it is for the little tin gods / When great Jove nods.—KIPLING. When the cat's away the mice will play.

8. *adj.* anarchic(al), lawless, ungoverned, unruly, licentious, disorderly, disorganized, chaotic; nihilistic, terroristic; revolutionary etc. (rebellious) 742.7.

739. Severity
(See 740. Lenity)

1. *n.* severity, strictness, harshness etc. *adj.*; rigor, rigidity, stringency, austerity, hard lines *or* measures, tender mercies [iron.]; precisianism, formalism; inclemency etc. (pitilessness) 914a; inflexibility etc. (hardness) 323; arrogance etc. 885.

2. *n.* arbitrary power, absolutism, despotism, dictatorship, autocracy, tyranny, domineering, domination, oppression, reign of terror; right of the strongest, *le droit du plus fort* [F.]; strong ∼, heavy *or* high hand, iron hand, ∼ rule *or* sway, iron heel *or* boot; brute force, coercion etc. (compulsion) 744.

3. *n.* tyrant, despot, bashaw, the Grand Panjandrum himself, hard master, Draco, oppressor, inquisitor; disciplinarian, martinet, stickler, precisian; usurper etc. 925.4.

4. *v.* be severe etc. *adj.*, domineer, tyrannize, grind, oppress, override, trample *or* tread upon, trample *or* tread down, trample *or* tread under foot, crush under an iron heel, ride roughshod over, hold *or* keep a tight hand upon, rule with a rod of iron, put on the screw, come down on *or* upon [coll.], bear hard upon, bear *or* lay a heavy hand on, deal hardly *or* harshly with, deal hard measure to, force down the throat, chastise with scorpions, dye with blood, rivet the yoke; inflict, wreak, impose; bully etc. (intimidate) 860.12; coerce etc. (compel) 744.2; give no quarter etc. (be pitiless) 914a.2; ill-treat etc. 649.7.

5. *adj.* severe, strict, stringent, harsh, dour [Scot.], rigorous, rigid, stiff, stern, stubborn, firm, uncompromising, exacting, exigent, *exigeant* [F.], inexorable, obdurate, austere, hardheaded, hardboiled [coll.], hard-shell [coll., U.S.], relentless, Spartan, Draconian, searching, unsparing, ironhanded, peremptory, absolute, positive, Procrustean, arbitrary, autocratic(al); imperative, imperious, imperatorial; tyrannical, despotic(al), dictatorial, highhanded, domineering, overbearing, grinding, withering, pressing, oppressive, extortionate, inquisitorial; precisian, precise, formal, punctilious.

inflexible etc. (hard) 323.5; arrogant etc. 885.8; coercive etc. (compulsory) 744.3; heartless, cruel etc. 907.8–9; inclement, ruthless etc. (pitiless) 914a.3.

6. *adv.* severely, harshly, tyrannically etc. *adj.*; with a high, ∼ strong, ∼ tight *or* heavy hand, at the point of the bayonet *or* sword.

740. Lenity
(See 739. Severity)

1. *n.* lenity, lenitence *or* leniency, lenitude [rare], lenience *or* leniency; mildness, gentleness etc. *v.*; tolerance, toleration; indulgence, indulgency [rare]; humanity, mercy, clemency, forbearance, quarter, favor; moderation etc. 174; compassion etc. 914; laxity etc. 738.

2. *v.* be lenient etc. *adj.*, tolerate, bear with; *parcere subjectis* [L.], spare the vanquished, give quarter.

3. *v.* indulge, let one have his own way, allow one to go his own gait, gratify, humor, spoil.

4. *adj.* lenient, mild, mild as milk *or* mother's milk, gentle, soft, moderate, easy; tolerant, indulgent, long-suffering; forbearing, forbearant; complaisant, unconcerned, easygoing; lax etc. 738.7; clement, compassionate etc. (pitying) 914.6.

741. Command

1. *n.* command, commandment, order, ordinance, *hukm* [Hind.], bidding, dictum, do [coll.], say-so [coll.], hest, behest, word, word of command, *mot d'or-*

---

739. Severity breedeth fear, but roughness breedeth hate.—BACON. Severity is allowable where gentleness is in vain.—CORNEILLE. A state has no worse foe than a tyrant.—EURIPIDES. Fear not the tyrants shall rule forever.—SHELLEY. The tyranny of a multitude is a multiplied tyranny.—BURKE.

740. And what makes robbers bold but too much lenity?—SHAKESPEARE. Sweet mercy is nobility's true badge.—SHAKESPEARE. Nothing emboldens sin so much as mercy.—SHAKESPEARE. And earthly power doth then show likest God's / When mercy seasons justice. —SHAKESPEARE. The quality of mercy is not strained, / It droppeth as the gentle rain from heaven.—SHAKESPEARE. Spare the rod and spoil the child.
741. *Sic volo sic jubeo* [Thus I will, thus I command].—JUVENAL. Who hath not served

dre [F.], call, beck, nod; direction, injunction, charge, instruction, precept; prescript, prescription; appointment, fixture.

2. *n.* demand, exaction, imposition, requisition, requirement, claim; reclamation, revendication [rare]; ultimatum; request etc. 765.

3. *n.* decree, decreement, decrete [Rom. Law], decreet [Scot.], *decretum* [L.], decretal [Eccl.]; decree law, *décret loi* [F.]; dictate, dictation; edict, *edictum* [L.]; authoritative decision; imperative, imperative rule, act, fiat; mandate, caveat, rescript, writ, mittimus, mandamus, ordination, bull, dispensation, brevet, ukase, firman; placet, *placitum* [L.]; *hatti-sherif, hatti-humayun* [both Turk., Hist.]; proclamation, proclaim [rare]; pronouncement, pronunciamento *or pronunciamiento* [Sp.]; declaration, indiction [rare], manifesto; notice, notification; order of the day; warrant, passport; summons, writ of summons, subpoena, citation; *nisi prius* [L.]; *senatus consultum* [L.]; plebiscite, plebicitum; enactment etc. (law) 963.2.

4. *v.* command, order, ordain, dictate, direct, instruct, bid, enjoin, charge, call on *or* upon; decree, enact, make *or* issue a decree, make a requisition, give an order, issue a command, give the word *or* word of command; give *or* lay down the law, put *or* set one's foot down [coll.]; call to order; remand; rule etc. 737.11, 12; legalize etc. 963.4.

5. *v.* prescribe, set, appoint, mark out; make *or* put in requisition, require, require at the hands of; demand, make a demand; exact, inflict, lay, lay upon, impose, tax, task; prescribe ~, set *or* impose a task, set to work.

6. *v.* claim, lay claim to; reclaim, revendicate [rare]; request etc. 765.4.

7. *v.* cite, summon, advoke, call *or* send for, subpoena.

8. *adj.* commanding etc. *v.*, mandatory, obligatory, imperative; decretive, decretal, decretory; jussive, jussory [rare]; prescript, prescriptive, preceptive, instructive; decisive, final, conclusive, irrevocable, without appeal; authoritative etc. 737.15.

cannot command.—FLORIO. He that most courteously commandeth, to him men most obey.—CHAUCER. For some must follow and some command.—LONGFELLOW.

9. *adv.* commandingly etc. *adj.*, in a commanding tone; by order *or* command, by order *or* decree of, by a dash *or* stroke of the pen, at the word of command, as ordered, ~ commanded, ~ required *or* requested, to order.

742. Disobedience
(See 743. Obedience)

1. *n.* disobedience, unruliness, mutinousness etc. *adj.*; insubordination, insubmission [rare], noncompliance, contumacy, obstinacy; infraction, infringement, violation, breach, trespass, transgression; nonobservance etc. 773; violation of law etc. 964.2.

2. *n.* revolt, insurgence, insurrection, rebellion, mutiny, mutineering, outbreak, rising, uprising, *émeute* [F.], *levée en masse* [F.], *Jacquerie* [F.], riot; sedition; treason, petty treason, misprision of treason; high treason, *lèse-majesté* [F.], lese majesty; revolution, convulsion, overthrow, overturn, upset, *coup d'état* [F.]; counterrevolution; revolutionism, Bolshevism *or* Bolshevikism; sans-culottism, *sans-culottisme* [F.], *sans-culotterie* [F.]; *sabotage* [F.]; strike etc. 719.2; defection, secession etc. (abandonment) 624; anarchy etc. 738.2.

3. *n.* insurgent, mutineer, rebel, rebeller [now rare], rioter, brawler; malcontent, noncontent [rare], *frondeur* [F.], agitator, demagogue *or* demagog; revolter, revolutionary, revolutionist, revolutioner; sans-culotte, sans-culottist; Bolshevik, Bolshevist, Bolshie [coll.]; anarchist, anarch; Red, *bonnet rouge* [F.], Red Republican, Jacobin, Carbonaro [It.]; Fenian, Sinn Feiner; Spartacus, Masaniello, Wat Tyler, Jack Cade; secessionist, separatist, renegade etc. (apostate) 607.5; dissenter etc. 489.3.

4. *v.* disobey, violate, break, infringe, transgress, trespass, trench on, trample on *or* upon, trample under foot, drive a coach and four *or* six through, set au-

---

742. Of Man's first disobedience, and the fruit / Of that forbidden tree.—MILTON. Let not another's disobedience to Nature become an ill to you.—EPICTETUS. There is little hope of equity where rebellion reigns.—SIDNEY. Revolutions have never lightened the burden of tyranny: they have only shifted it to another shoulder.—SHAW. It is not the insurrections of ignorance that are dangerous, but the revolts of intelligence.—LOWELL.

thority at nought, take the law into one's own hands; shirk, slide out of, slack; disregard etc. 773.3.

5. *v.* revolt, rebel, mutiny, mutineer, insurrect, riot, run riot, kick over the traces, fly in the face of, refuse to support, bolt [U.S., Polit.]; rise, rise up, rise up in arms; revolutionize, overthrow, overturn, upset; strike etc. 719.4; secede etc. (abandon) 624.3; set at defiance etc. (defy) 715.2.

6. *adj.* disobedient, disobeying etc. *v.*; uncomplying, uncompliant; unsubmissive, unruly, ungovernable, intractable, breachy, insubordinate, impatient of control, restive, refractory, contumacious, recalcitrant; wayward, lawless, transgressive; nonobservant etc. 773.5.

7. *adj.* rebellious, rebelly [coll.]; mutinous, mutineering etc. *v.*; riotous, seditious, insurgent, insurrectionary, revolutionary, Jacobinic, "agin the government"; sans-culottic, sans-culottish; radical, red; Bolshevik, Bolshevist *or* Bolshevistic; anarchic etc. 738.8; resisting etc. 719.5; defiant etc. 715.3.

743. Obedience
(See 742. Disobedience)

1. *n.* obedience, obediency, compliance, acquiescence, deference, resignation, complaisance, submissiveness; passiveness, passivity; unresistance, nonresistance; observance etc. 772; ductility etc. (softness) 324; submission etc. 725; subjection etc. 749; obsequiousness etc. (servility) 886.

2. *v.* be obedient etc. *adj.*, obey, bear obedience to, comply, answer the helm, do one's bidding, do what one is told, come at one's call, do suit and service, attend to orders; serve faithfully, ~ loyally *or* devotedly, give faithful, ~ loyal *or* devoted service, serve without question; follow the lead of, follow to the world's end, play second fiddle; resign oneself to,
be resigned *or* submissive to; submit etc. 725.3; serve etc. 746.8; observe etc. 772.3, 4.

3. *adj.* obedient, obediental [rare]; complying etc. *v.*, compliant, acquiescent; law-abiding; loyal, faithful, devoted; at one's command *or* orders, at one's call *or* beck and call, under beck and call, under control; restrainable; resigned, passive, complaisant, deferential; unresisting, nonresisting; henpecked, tied to one's apron strings, in leading strings; ductile, pliant etc. (soft) 324.6; submissive etc. 725.5; subject etc. 749.6; obsequious etc. (servile) 886.4; observant etc. 772.5; dutiful etc. 926.8; serving etc. 746.9.

4. *adv.* obediently etc. *adj.*, as you please, if you please; in compliance with, in obedience to; obediently yours, at your service, ~ command *or* orders.

744. Compulsion

1. *n.* compulsion, obligation, obligement; press, pressure; enforcement, duress, constraint, coaction; coercion, coercive force *or* methods, high-pressure methods, violence, the strong arm [coll.]; force, *ultima ratio* [L.], main force, physical force, brute force *or* strength, *brutum fulmen* [L.], the sword, the big stick, the club, *argumentum baculinum* [L.], club ~, lynch ~, mob *or* martial law, the force of might *or* right, *le droit du plus fort* [F.], *force majeure* [F.]; impressment into service, press, conscription, draft; eminent domain; necessity etc. 601; requirement etc. 630; Hobson's choice etc. 609a; restraint etc. 751.

2. *v.* compel, force, make, constrain, drive, press, bear upon, bear down upon [coll.], bring pressure to bear upon, enforce, necessitate, require, oblige, say it must be done, make a point of, insist upon, take no denial; use force upon, employ violent measures, strong-arm [slang], dragoon, coerce, use coercion; force upon, cram ~, thrust *or* force down

---

743. Obedience, bane of all genius, virtue, freedom, truth.—SHELLEY. Obedience is the mother of success.—AESCHYLUS. Give obedience where 'tis truly owed.—SHAKESPEARE. Obedience alone gives the right to command.—EMERSON. Obedience is the courtesy due to kings.—TENNYSON. Let them obey that know not how to rule.—SHAKESPEARE. One so small / Who knowing nothing knows but to obey.—TENNYSON. Theirs not to make reply, theirs not to reason why.—TENNYSON

744. Force is not a remedy.—J. BRIGHT. Force is of brutes.—DRYDEN. Tries force because persuasion fails.—BROWNING. I would give no man a reason upon compulsion. —SHAKESPEARE. Pressed into service means pressed out of shape.—FROST. There is a homely old adage which runs: "Speak softly and carry a big stick; you will go far."—T. ROOSEVELT.

the throat; force from, wrest, exact, extort, wring from, squeeze, screw, put the screw *or* screws on, put *or* turn on the screw; take by force, seize, commandeer; draft, conscript, press, impress; bind, bind over; bear *or* press down, pin *or* tie down; drag into; restrain etc. 751.6

3. *adj.* compulsory, compulsatory, compulsive, compelling etc. *v.*; coactive, obligatory, imperative, importunate, peremptory, binding, required, unavoidable, forcible, high-pressure, not to be trifled with; coercive, coercitive, strong-arm [coll.]; necessary etc. 601.11; requisite etc. 630.3; restraining etc. 751.13; authoritative etc. 737.15; severe etc. 739.5.

4. *adv.* compulsorily, forcibly etc. *adj.*; on compulsion, by force etc. *n.*, by force of arms, *vi et armis* [L.], under the lash, at the point of the sword *or* bayonet, by a strong arm; *de rigueur* [F.]; perforce, by force *or* stress of circumstances, by stress of, under press of; of necessity etc. 601.15; under protest etc. (unwillingly) 603.6.

745. Master
(See 746. Servant)

1. *n.* master, person in authority, *padrone* [It.], *patron* [F.], lord, lord and master, seigneur, seignior, controller, comptroller, governor, rector, ruler, dictator, captain, commander, commandant, overman, overlord, headman, head, senior, superior, dean, principal, paramount, top sawyer [coll.], first fiddle, kingpin [coll.]; lord of the ascendant, cock of the walk, ~ loft *or* roost, cock of the midden [arch.], biggest frog in the pond [slang, U.S.]; chief, big chief [slang, U.S.]; sachem, Grand Sachem; boss [coll.], baas [Du.]; employer; paterfamilias, patriarch; mistress, gray mare [slang]; rectoress *or* rectress, rectrix [now rare]; mother superior; foreman, leader etc. (director) 694; proprietor etc. 779.2; sahib [Ind.] etc. 373.3.

2. *n.* potentate, sovereign, suzerain, monarch, ruler, crowned head, emperor, imperator, king, anointed king, the anointed, majesty, his majesty, royal person, royal, royalty; paramount, lord paramount, overlord, overking; liege, liege lord; chief, chieftain; autocrat, despot, tyrant, oligarch, dictator; usurper, arrogator; prince, duke etc. (nobility) 875.5–8.

3. *n.* Caesar, Kaiser, czar, czarevitch; pendragon; voivode *or* waywode, hospodar; doge; sheik; lama; Tenno, mikado, tycoon, shogun; werowance, sagamore, sachem, cacique, Inca; Sophy, Mogul, Great *or* Grand Mogul, shah, padishah.

4. *n.* raja *or* rajah, maharaja *or* maharajah, rana, maharana, maharao etc., rawal, rawat, rao, rai, raikwar, raikbar, raikat, raja bahadur, maharaja bahadur, rai *or* rao bahadur, Gaekwar, thakur, Nizam, nawab, Jam, mirza, dewan, sirdar [all Ind.].

5. *n.* Sultan, Grand Turk, Grand Seignior, caliph, Imam, sayid, hakim, khan, Nizam, nawab, wali *or* vali, amir, emir, mir, mirza, mian, dewan [all Moham.].

6. *n.* empress, queen, sultana, czarina; rani, maharani, begum; princess etc. 875.8.

7. *n.* regent, protector, viceroy, exarch, palatine, khedive, dey, bey *or* beg, beglerbeg *or* beylerbey, pasha *or* bashaw, one-tailed ~, two-tailed *or* three-tailed pasha *or* bashaw, sherif, tetrarch, satrap, mandarin, woon, nabob; burgrave, commissioner, deputy commissioner, collector.

8. *n.* the authorities, the powers that be, "them above" (Eliot), the government, sircar [Ind.], Sublime Porte [Turk.]; staff, *État Major* [F.].

9. *n.* official, officiant, officer, public official, public servant; executive officer, executive, magistrate, dewan [Ind.]; functionary, *fonctionnaire* [F.]; commissioner, commissionaire; chief executive officer, president, prime minister, premier, eparch [Gr.]; vizier, grand vizier [both Turk.]; collector [Ind.], deputy commissioner; governor, lieutenant governor, stadholder *or* stadtholder; city manager, mayor, *maire* [F.], Lord Mayor.

lord lieutenant [Brit.], prefect, chancellor, councilor, selectman, archon [Gr.], provost, syndic, burgomaster, *corregidor* [Sp.], seneschal, alderman, bailie [Scot.], warden, constable, lictor [Rom. Antiq.], mace-bearer; reeve, portreeve; alcalde,

---

745. He that is a master must serve.—G. Herbert.   Uneasy lies the head that wears a crown.—Shakespeare.   He is master and lord of his brothers / Who is worthier and wiser than they.—Swinburne.   Lord of thy presence and no land beside.—Shakespeare.

alcaide; bailiff, bumbailiff [Eng., derog.], bound bailiff [Eng. Law], tipstaff, catchpole *or* catchpoll; tithingman, exciseman [Eng.], gauger; customhouse officer, customs official, *douanier* [F.]; municipality, bailiwick; bureau, office, cutcherry [Ind.], department, portfolio, secretariat; statesman etc. 694.4; congressman etc. 696.8.

10. *n.* constable, police constable, policeman, police, officer [coll.], police officer, sheriff, shrieve, bluecoat [coll.], roundsman [U.S.], gendarme, beagle [coll.], marshal, peace officer, law enforcement agent, arm of the law; bobby, peeler [both coll., Eng.]; cop, copper, gumshoe, gumshoe man, dick, bull, harness bull, flatfoot [all slang]; policewoman, constabless [rare], sheriffess, police matron; patrolman [chiefly U.S.]; bailiff etc. *above*; deputy sheriff, deputy; police sergeant, police captain, police inspector, police commissioner; police force, police, constabulary, constablery, shrievalty, sheriffalty, sheriffry, sheriffdom, policedom; constablewick, sheriffwick; sheriffship, sheriffhood, constableship; plain-clothes man [coll.] etc. (detective) 528.9; guard etc. 717.6.

11. *n.* (military authorities) officer, commissioned officer, noncommissioned officer, petty officer, warrant officer, staff officer; orderly officer, officer of the day; chief officer, commander, commandant, aga [Moham.]; commander in chief, generalissimo, captain general, seraskier [Turk.], hetman [Russ.], sirdar; marshal, *maréchal* [F.], field marshal.

general, lieutenant general, major general, brigadier general, colonel, lieutenant colonel, major, captain, brigadier; subahdar [Ind.], centurion; ressaldar, ressaidar [both Ind.]; subaltern officer, subaltern; lieutenant, jemadar [Ind.], first lieutenant, second lieutenant, sublieutenant; sergeant, havildar [Ind.], sergeant major, master sergeant, technical sergeant, staff sergeant; top sergeant [coll.], top kick [slang, U.S.]; corporal, naik [Ind.], lance corporal, acting corporal; drum major; color sergeant, ensign, cornet, standard-bearer; adjutant, aide-de-camp, brigade major, quartermaster; cadet.

12. *n.* (naval authorities) admiral, vice-admiral, rear admiral, commodore, captain, commander, navarch [Gr. Antiq.], lieutenant commander, lieutenant, lieutenant junior gradè, ensign, mate, quartermaster; skipper, master; warrant officer, petty officer etc. *above*.

746. Servant
(See 745. Master)

1. *n.* servant, servitor, retainer, follower, assistant, help [local, U.S.], henchman, menial, slavey [coll.], yeoman [Hist.], gillie; employee *or* employé *or* employe, hireling, mercenary, pensionary; man, boy, *garçon* [F.], man Friday; attendant, servant in attendance, waiter, usher, squire; khidmatgar, bearer, hamal, chokra [all Ind.]; office boy; page, buttons [coll.], footboy; trainbearer, cupbearer; bellboy, bellhop [slang, U.S.]; caddie; bootblack, boots; steward, house steward, khansamah [Ind.]; bailiff, castellan, seneschal, major-domo; chamberlain, groom of the chambers; livery *or* liveried servant, butler, major-domo [joc.], lackey, flunky; footman, *valet de pied* [F.]; valet, *valet de chambre* [F.]; college servant, gyp [Cambridge Univ.], scout [Oxford Univ.], cad [Eng. Univ. cant.]; orderly; domestic, household assistant, domestic *or* house servant.

kitchenman, scullion, dishwasher, potwalloper [slang]; cook, chef, *chef de cuisine* [F.]; tapster, barman [Eng.]; bartender, barkeeper, barkeep [U.S.]; stableman, stableboy, hostler *or* ostler, equerry; groom, groomsman, tiger [old slang]; hired man, servant of all work, man *or* maid of all work, do-all [coll.], general servant [Eng.], general [coll.], factotum; apprentice, prentice; attaché; official; underling etc. (inferior) 34.3; agent etc. 690; deputy etc. 759; puppet etc. 711.2; auxiliary etc. 711; errand boy etc. (messenger) 534; secretary, clerk etc. (writer) 590.11; herdsman etc. 370.4.

---

746. He that is greatest among you shall be your servant.—BIBLE.   No man can serve two masters.—BIBLE.   Art thou less a slave because thy master loves and caresses thee?—PASCAL.   A faithful and good servant is a real godsend, but truly 'tis a rare bird in the land.—LUTHER.   We may live without friends; we may live without books; / But civilized man can not live without cooks.—BULWER-LYTTON.   A servant and a cock should be kept but a year.—FULLER.

2. *n.* maid, maidservant, servitrix, servantess, girl, servant girl, lady help [Brit.], biddy [coll., U.S.], amah [Oriental]; handmaid, handmaiden; lady's maid, lady's waiting maid, waiting maid *or* woman, lady in waiting, abigail, soubrette, *bonne* [F.], ayah [Ind.]; housemaid, parlormaid, kitchenmaid, scullery maid, Cinderella; chambermaid, *femme or fille de chambre* [F.], bedmaker; barmaid, tapstress; milkmaid, milkeress [rare]; maid of all work, *bonne pour tout faire* [F.], slavey [coll.], general housework maid [U.S.], general [coll.]; charwoman; nursemaid etc. (guardian) 664.3; washerwoman etc. (cleaner) 652.6.

3. *n.* dependent, client, *protégé* [F.], ward; pensioner, pensionary, beadsman, beadswoman [both arch.], sizar [Cambridge and Dublin Univs.]; hanger-on, parasite etc. (sycophant) 886.2.

4. *n.* serf, vassal, slave, thrall, helot, *âme damnée* [F.]; bondslave, bondman, bondsman; bondwoman, bondswoman, bondmaid, odalisque *or* odalisk; negro, nigger [coll.]; villein *or* villain [Hist.], churl *or* ceorl [Hist.], ryot [Ind.], *adscriptus glebae* [L.]; peasant etc. 876.5.

5. *n.* subject, liege, liege man, liege subject, people.

6. *n.* retinue, body of retainers etc. (attendance) 88.5.

7. *n.* staff, personnel, employees, the help [esp. U.S.], servantry, associates, associate workers, force, crew, gang; office force, clerical staff.

8. *v.* serve, do service to, work in the service of, work for, be useful to, minister *or* administer to, pander to, tend, attend, wait *or* attend on *or* upon, dance attendance upon, do for [coll.], fag; pin *or* fasten oneself upon, hang on the sleeve of; servant, valet, maid; chore, do the chores [both U.S.]; char, do chars [both Eng.]; officiate, act; wait on hand and foot, help etc. (aid) 707.6–11; take care of etc. 459.6; subserve etc. (be instrumental) 631.3; be of use to etc. 644.2; benefit etc. 648.6; be obedient etc. 743.2.

9. *adj.* serving, ministering, waiting, attending, in the train of, in one's pay *or* employ; at one's call etc. (obedient) 743.3; in subjection etc. 749.6; serviceable etc. (useful) 644.5; helpful etc. 707.12.

10. *adj.* servile etc. 886.4.

747. Insignia of Authority

1. *n.* insignia of authority, ensign ~, emblem *or* badge of authority, scepter, staff *or* rod of office *or* authority, rod, staff, baton, wand, mace, truncheon, fasces [Roman]; caduceus, Mercury's staff, ~ rod *or* wand, Hermes' staff; toga, mantle; portfolio; gavel; badge, ensign etc. (insignia) 550.12.

2. *n.* (royal insignia) regalia; royal scepter, rod of empire; orb; robe of state *or* royalty, purple, ermine; purple pall; crown, royal crown, coronet, tiara, diadem; cap of maintenance, ~ dignity *or* estate, triple plume, Prince of Wales's feathers, uraeus [Egyptian]; signet, seal, privy seal *or* signet [British].

3. *n.* (ecclesiastical insignia) tiara, triple crown; ring, keys; miter, crosier, crook, staff; cardinal's hat, bishop's shovel hat, ~ apron, ~ sleeves, ~ lawn *or* gaiters; fillet.

4. *n.* (military insignia) epaulet *or* epaulette, star, bar, eagle, crown [British], oak leaf; chevron, stripe [slang]; Sam Browne belt; stripe, service stripe; medal etc. 733.2.

5. *n.* seat of authority, saddle [coll.], chair, bench, seat, seat of state; throne, royal seat, stall [obs.], Peacock throne [Chinese], musnud [Oriental]; gaddi, raj-gaddi [both Ind.]; divan, leewan; woolsack [British].

6. *n.* helm, rudder, reins, reins of government.

748. Freedom
(See 749. Subjection)

1. *n.* freedom, liberty, independence, license, loose, unconstraint, self-determination; immunity, exemption, exception, franchise, privilege, prerogative, right; franchise, enfranchisement, affranchisement; free speech, freedom of speech; own initiative, own hook *or* sayso [coll.]; run, the run of . . . [both coll.]; liberalism; eleutherism [rare], eleuthero-

---

747. Scepter and Crown / Must tumble down, / And in the dust be equal made / With the poor crooked scythe and spade.—J. SHIRLEY.   1 give this heavy weight from off my head, / And this unwieldy sceptre from my hand, / The pride of kingly sway from out my heart.—SHAKESPEARE.

748. Where liberty dwells, there is my country.—FRANKLIN.   The God who gave us life

mania; permission etc. 760; emancipation etc. (liberation) 750; exoneration, absolution etc. (acquittal) 970; facility etc. 705; laxity etc. 738.

2. *n.* scope, range, latitude, room, reach, swing, play, full swing, free play, full *or* free scope, free course *or* vent, free field and no favor, elbowroom, margin, leeway [coll.], wide berth; rope, rope enough to hang oneself; liberty hall.

3. *n.* political independence, self-determination; autonomy, self-government, home rule; free trade.

4. *n.* noninterference, nonintervention, let-alone principle, ~ doctrine *or* policy; *laisser-aller, laisser aller, laissez aller, laissez faire, laisser faire* [all F.]; laissez-faireism; Monroe Doctrine [U.S.].

5. *n.* free land, freehold; alod, alodium; frankalmoign [Eng. Law], tenure in *or* by free alms [Eng. Law]; dead hand, mortmain [Law].

6. *n.* freeman, liveryman [Eng.]; burgher, burgess; citizen, denizen; freedman, dedititian [Rom.].

7. *n.* independent, free lance, freethinker, free trader *or* freetrader, freebooter, nonpartisan, isolationist.

8. *v.* be free etc. *adj.*, have one's own way, have it all one's way, have a will of one's own, do what one likes, ~ wishes, ~ pleases *or* chooses, please oneself [coll.], go as one pleases, go one's own way, go at large, have one's fling, paddle one's own canoe [coll.], stand on one's own legs, stand on one's rights, shift for oneself, do on one's own hook *or* sayso [coll.]; have free scope etc. *n.*, have the run of [coll.]; make oneself quite at home, feel at home.

9. *v.* take a liberty, make free with, use a freedom, presume, venture; take leave, take French leave, go A.W.O.L. [coll.].

10. *v.* allow freedom etc. *n.*, give one liberty *or* license, let one go at will *or* unchecked, give one leeway [coll.] etc. *n.*, give *or* let one have rope [coll.], give the reins to, give one his head, give full play, allow full swing, let go one's own way; open the way, open the door to, leave the door open; make free of, give the freedom of; give the franchise, enfranchise, affranchise; free, exempt, immunize, excuse, release, discharge, let off [coll.], pass over, spare, save the necessity; dispense with, give dispensation; remise, remiss [rare], remit; liberate etc. 750.2, 3; permit etc. 760.3; exonerate, absolve etc. (acquit) 970.3.

11. *v.* not interfere etc. 706.4, leave *or* let alone, let it take its course, *laisser faire* [F.], *laissez aller* [F.], live and let live, leave to oneself, mind one's own business.

12. *adj.* free, scot-free, independent, go-as-you-please, loose, foot-loose, foot-loose and fancy-free, at large, at liberty, disengaged, clear, out of harness; free as air, free as a bird; free-acting, free-going, free-moving, free-working, free-spirited; free-speaking, free-tongued; freeborn, free-bred; freehold, alodial, alodian; Eleutherian; liberal, liberalistic; free-thinking, libertine [derog.]; liberated etc. 750.5; escaped etc. 671.7.

13. *adj.* unconstrained, unrestrained, unchecked, unprevented, unhampered, unhindered, unobstructed, unrestricted, unconfined, uncontrolled, untrammeled, uncaught, unbuttoned, unbound, unchained, unshackled, unfettered, unbridled, uncurbed, unmuzzled, unreined, reinless; libertine [now rare]; unforced, uncompelled, uncoerced; irrepressible; unburdened etc. 705.7; lax etc. 738.7; incontinent etc. 961.10; intemperate etc. 954.4.

14. *adj.* unsubject, ungoverned, unenslaved, unenthralled, unvanquished.

15. *adj.* unlimited, limitless, illimitable, with unlimited power *or* opportunity; unconditioned, unconditional; unqualified, unrestricted, unbounded, absolute, arbitrary, full, plenary.

16. *adj.* unbiased, uninfluenced, impartial, etc. (unprejudiced) 498.12; equitable, fair etc. (just) 941.3.

17. *adj.* self-determined, independent, self-reliant, self-directing, self-governing, self-governed, autonomous, sovereign; discretionary etc. (volitional) 600.4;

---

gave us liberty at the same time.—JEFFERSON. God grants liberty only to those who love it, and are always ready to guard and defend it.—D. WEBSTER. Give me liberty, or give me death!—P. HENRY. Give me liberty to know, to utter, and to argue freely according to conscience, above all liberties.—MILTON. For what avail the plough or sail, / Or land or life, if freedom fail?—EMERSON. The lovers of freedom will be free.—BURKE. Οὐδεὶς ἐλεύθερος ἑαυτοῦ μὴ κρατῶν [No man is free who is not master of himself].—EPICTETUS.

spontaneous etc. (voluntary) 602.10.

18. *adj.* exempt, immune, clear; exempted, released, excused, excepted, let off [coll.], spared; privileged, licensed, favored; irresponsible, unaccountable, unanswerable, unliable, not liable, unsubject, not subject; freed etc. 750.5.

19. *adj.* gratuitous etc. 815.10.

20. *adj.* at ease, at one's ease, *dégagé* [F.], at home, quite at home, in one's element.

21. *adv.* freely etc. *adj.*, without restraint etc. 751; *ad libitum* [L.] etc. (at will) 600.5; permissibly etc. 760.7.

749. Subjection
(See 748. Freedom)

1. *n.* subjection, subjugation, bondage; *servitus* [L.], servitude, involuntary servitude; thrall, thralldom, enthrallment; slavery, enslavement; servage [rare], serfage, serfdom, serfhood, serfism; vassalage, vassalism, vassality; villenage, villeinhood; feudalism, feudality; dependence *or* dependency, slavish dependence; subordination, subordinacy; oppression, repression; conquest; badge of slavery; submission etc. 725; obedience etc. 743; subdual etc. (defeat) 732.3; constraint etc. 751; bonds, yoke etc. (means of restraint) 752.2.

2. *n.* service, servitude, servitorship; employment, employ; tendance, tutelage, clientship.

3. *v.* be subject etc. *adj.*, be *or* lie at the mercy of, depend on, depend ~, lean *or* hang upon, play second fiddle, be a mere machine, ~ puppet, ~ doormat *or* football, not dare to say one's soul is his own, drag a chain; fall a prey to, fall under; submit etc. 725.3; obey etc. 743.2.

4. *v.* serve etc. 746.8.

5. *v.* subjugate, subject, reduce to subjection *or* slavery, slave [now rare], enslave; enthrall, inthrall, bethrall; take captive, lead captive *or* into captivity; hold in bondage, hold captive, hold in leash *or* leading strings, hold in swaddling clothes, have at one's apron strings, hold or keep at one's beck and call; tame, gentle [coll. and dial.], break in; subdue, master, quell, suppress, crush, quash, put down, tread *or* trample under foot, roll *or* trample in the dust, drag at one's chariot wheel; make a puppet, ~ sport *or* plaything of, use as a doormat, treat like dirt under one's feet; oppress, weigh down; rule etc. 737.11, 12; defeat etc. 731.9.

6. *adj. etc.* subject, subjected, enslaved etc. *v.*; in subjection etc. *n.*, dependent, subordinate, servitorial [rare], thrall [arch.], in bonds, in harness, under control, under the lash, on the hip; led by the nose, in leading strings, tied to one's apron strings, henpecked; in one's control, in one's pocket, under one's command *or* orders, at one's beck and call, under one's thumb, at one's mercy, in one's power, in one's hands *or* clutches, at one's feet; the puppet, ~ sport *or* plaything of, a slave to; used as a doormat, treated like dirt under one's feet; downtrodden, downtrod; feudal, feudatory; stipendiary; constrained etc. 751.10; slavish etc. (servile) 886.4; submissive etc. 725.5; obedient etc. 743.3; serving etc. 746.9.

7. *prep., adv.* under, below, beneath, underneath, in a subordinate position, at the feet of, under the heel of; under orders *or* command, at one's orders; with no mind, ~ will *or* soul of one's own.

750. Liberation
(See 751. Restraint)

1. *n.* liberation, disengagement, release, enlargement [arch.], emancipation, disenthrallment, manumission; affranchisement, enfranchisement; discharge, dismissal; quitclaim, deed of release; deliverance etc. 672; escape etc. 671; acquittal etc. 970; freedom etc. 748; liberator etc. (savior) 912.2.

2. *v.* liberate, free, render free, set free, set at liberty, emancipate, manumit, enlarge [arch.], set at large, release, let go, let loose, let out, cast *or* turn adrift; disenthrall, disinthrall; affranchise, enfran-

---

749. Servitude that hugs her chain.—GRAY. Once fully enslaved, no nation, state, city of this earth, ever afterward resumes its liberty. —WHITMAN. There is no freedom on earth or in any star for those who deny freedom to others.—E. HUBBARD. I believe this government cannot endure permanently half slave and half free.—LINCOLN.

750. Proclaim liberty throughout all the land unto all the inhabitants thereof.—BIBLE. We are not to expect to be translated from despotism to liberty in a feather bed.—JEFFERSON. In giving freedom to the slave we assume freedom to the free.—LINCOLN. *Adoro, imploro, ut liberes me* [I adore, and implore that thou liberate me]!—MARY QUEEN OF SCOTS.

chise; discharge, dismiss; demobilize, demob [slang], disband; reprieve; deliver etc. 672.2; absolve etc. (acquit) 970.3.

3. *v.* loose, loosen, unloose, unloosen; unfetter, unshackle, unchain, untie, unfasten, unbind, unbandage, unharness, unbridle, unpinion, unmanacle, unhandcuff, untie one's hands, unhobble, unstrap, unlash, unleash, untether, untruss, unyoke, unhook, unpin; disengage, disentangle, extricate, clear; unhand; unlock, unlatch, unbolt, unbar; unimprison, uncage, uncoop; unclose, uncork, unclog; unmuzzle, ungag.

4. *v.* become free, go free *or* scot free, gain one's liberty etc. 748, get rid *or* clear of, deliver oneself from, shake off the yoke, slip the collar, tear asunder one's bonds, cast off trammels, break loose, break prison; escape etc. 671.6.

5. *adj. etc.* liberated, freed etc. *adj.*; breathing free air again, one's own master again; loose, at large etc. (free) 748.12.

6. *int.* unhand me!, unhand me, villain!; let go!, let me go!, reprieve!

7. *int.* go in peace! etc. 721.5.

751. Restraint
(See 750. Liberation)

1. *n.* restraint, constraint, constrainment [rare]; cohibition, inhibition; check, curb, control, repression, discipline, limitation; restriction, striction, stricture, constriction; hindrance etc. 706; opposition etc. 708; prohibition etc. 761; coercion etc. (compulsion) 744; subjection etc. 749; dissuasion etc. 616; counteraction etc. 179; shackle etc. (means of restraint) 752.2; composure, self-restraint etc. (inexcitability) 826; moderation etc. 174.

2. *n.* confinement, imprisonment, incarceration, internment, impoundment, entombment; committal, commitment; detention, captivity, quarantine; thrall, enthrallment; duress, durance; limbo.

3. *n.* arrest, arrestment, arrestation [rare], pinch [slang]; capture, caption, apprehension, seizure.

4. *n.* custody, keep, care, protection, charge, ward.

5. *n.* restrictionist, repressionist, monopolist, protectionist.

6. *v.* restrain, put *or* lay under restraint, constrain, restrict, restringe [rare], check, curb, control, withhold, hold *or* keep back, hold in check, hold in leash *or* leading strings, keep within bounds, keep from, pull *or* rein in, keep, hold, hold fast, keep a tight hand on; repress, suppress, keep under, smother; inhibit, cohibit; prohibit etc. 761.2; hinder etc. 706.4-7; oppose etc. 708.2; compel etc. 744.2; disincline etc. 616.3; counteract etc. 179.3; moderate etc. 174.5.

7. *v.* bind, bind fast, tie, tie up, string, strap, lash, leash, pinion, tie ~, pin *or* peg down, fasten, make fast, secure; trammel, entrammel; chain, enchain; put in irons, fetter, shackle, manacle, handcuff; tie one's hands; bind *or* tie hand and foot, forefoot [slang, West. U.S.], hog-tie [coll., U.S.]; swathe, swaddle; hopple, hobble; tether, moor, picket, peg *or* stake out; bridle, muzzle, gag; forge fetters.

8. *v.* confine, imprison, jail [U.S.], gaol [Eng.], jug [slang], incarcerate, intern, impound, immure, entomb, pen, coop, cloister; cage, encage; clap *or* lay under hatches, throw *or* cast in prison, put into bilboes, close the door upon; shut up, clap up, coop up, box up, mew up, bottle up, cork up, seal up, button up; shut in, pen in, hem in, bolt in, wall in, rail in; lock up *or* in, keep under lock and key; enthrall, inthrall, bethrall, hold in thrall.

9. *v.* arrest, make an arrest, put under arrest, take *or* make prisoner *or* captive, take up, pick up [coll.], take charge of, take into custody, give *or* put in charge *or* custody; [rare], cohibit [rare]; pinch, make a pinch, nab, lag, run in [all slang]; apprehend, capture, captivate [rare], seize, collar [coll.], lay by the heels, lead captive, lead into captivity; commit, consign, send *or* commit to prison; subjugate etc. 749.5.

10. *adj.* restrained, constrained etc. *v.*; under restraint, under discipline *or* control, under prohibition; moderate etc. 174.6.

11. *adj.* bound, shackled etc. *v.*; in bonds, in irons *or* chains; weather-bound, wind-bound, icebound; hidebound, barkbound.

---

751. Restraint from ill is freedom to the wise.
—DEFOE.   To be captived in endless durance.
—SPENSER.   In durance vile here must I wake and weep.—BURNS.   Checked like a bondman.—SHAKESPEARE.

12. *adj.* imprisoned, confined, pent up, locked up etc. *v.*; in prison etc. 752.1, in confinement, in captivity, behind bars, under lock and key, under hatches, in the guardhouse, in lob's pound, in durance vile, in custody *or* charge, "cabined, cribbed, confined" (Shakespeare), doing *or* serving time [coll. or slang]; under arrest; on parole.

13. *adj.* restraining etc. *v.*, constrictive, restrictive, restrictionary [rare]; limitative, limitary; cohibitive, inhibitive, inhibitory; repressive, repressory, repressionary; hindering etc. 706.8; coactive etc. (compulsory) 744.3.

752. Prison, Shackle

Means of Restraint.—1. *n.* prison, prisonhouse, jail [U.S.], gaol [Eng.], penal institution *or* settlement, keep, bastille *or* bastile, *oubliette* [F.], tolbooth [Scot.], lockup, bridewell [Eng.], limbo *or* limbus, calaboose [local, U.S.], chauki [Ind.], hell, pound, pinfold *or* penfold; police station, station house, watchhouse, roundhouse [arch.], thana [Ind.]; penitentiary, state prison; guardhouse, guardroom [both Mil.]; brig [Naut.]; cage, coop, den, cell; donjon, dungeon, black hole; house of correction, reformatory, reform school; sponging house, debtor's prison; house of detention; detention camp, quarantine station, workhouse [U.S.], panopticon; enclosure etc. 232; stronghold etc. 717.4.

choky [Eng.], jug, college, cooler, quod, booby hatch, can [U.S.], hoosegow [U.S.], stir [U.S.], big house [U.S.], rattle [Naut.], pen [all slang]; clink, station [both coll.]; Batille, Tower, Newgate, Fleet, Marshalsea, King's *or* Queen's Bench, Sing Sing.

2. *n.* (restraining devices) shackle, fetter, trammel, manacle, gyve, bond, bonds, irons, chains, pinion; check, curb; hopples, hobbles; handcuffs, cuffs; stocks, bilboes; strait jacket, strait-waistcoat; collar; yoke, poke [local, U.S.]; harness, bridle, halter, freno [West. U.S.], headstall, cavesson, hackamore [West. U.S.], jaquima [Southwest.

U.S.]; rein, reins, bearing rein, checkrein, martingale; leading strings; lines [U.S. and dial., Eng.], ribbons [coll.]; bit, snaffle; muzzle, gag; tether, picket; guy, guy rope; rope, chain etc. (fastening) 45.2–4, (cord) 205.3; brake, drag etc. (obstacle) 706.2.

3. *n.* lock, bolt, bar, padlock.

753. Jailer
(See 754. Prisoner)

n. jailer, gaoler [Eng.], keeper, warder, turnkey, screw [slang]; custodian, custodier [now chiefly Scot.], *custos* [L.]; warden, principal keeper; guard etc. 717.6; protector etc. 664.3.

754. Prisoner
(See 753. Jailer)

1. *n.* prisoner, convict, con [slang], captive, *détenu* [F.], collegian [slang, Eng.], stir bird [slang, U.S.], cageling, lag [slang], lagger [slang], culprit; jailbird [coll., U.S.], gaolbird [coll., Eng.]; ex-convict; parolist, parolee, ticket-of-leave man *or* ticket-of-leaver [Eng.].

2. *v.* be imprisoned etc. 751.12, stand committed, do *or* serve time [coll.].

755. Commission
(See 756. Abrogation)

Vicarious Authority.—1. *n.* commission, delegation, deputation, legation, mission, embassy; authority, authorization; warrant, charge, trust, brevet, diploma, exequatur; proxy, power of attorney, procuration; mandate, agency of mandate; consignment, assignment, errand, task, office; agency, agentship; clerkship.

---

752. Stone walls do not a prison make / Nor iron bars a cage.—LOVELACE. No man loveth his fetters, be they made of gold.—J. HEYWOOD. Prisons are built with stones of Law.—W. BLAKE. The black flower of civilized society,
a prison.—HAWTHORNE. The vilest deeds like poison-weeds / Bloom well in prison air.—WILDE. Whilst we have prisons it matters little which of us occupies the cells.—SHAW. Self is the only prison that can ever bind the soul.—VAN DYKE.
753. Am I my brother's keeper?—BIBLE. Pale Anguish keeps the heavy gate / And the Warder is Despair.—WILDE.
754. Come, let's away to prison: / We two alone will sing like birds i' the cage.—SHAKESPEARE. Then, when I am thy captive, talk of chains.—MILTON. All that we know who lie in gaol / Is that the wall is strong.—WILDE.
755. There is no man deputed of the king to hear thee.—BIBLE.

2. *n.* appointment, nomination; return; charter; ordination; installation, inauguration, investiture; accession, coronation, enthronement.

3. *n.* regency, regentship; vice-regency, vice-regentship.

4. *v.* commission, delegate, depute, deputize; consign, assign, charge, intrust *or* entrust, commit, commit to the hands of, set *or* place over, convey, authorize, empower, accredit, engage, employ, hire, bespeak, appoint, name, nominate, ordain, send out; return; install, instate, induct, inaugurate, invest, chair; crown, throne, enthrone, enthronize; enroll, enlist; give power of attorney to; license etc. (grant) 760.4.

5. *v.* be commissioned, represent etc. 759.4.

6. *adv. etc.* instead of, in lieu of, in place of, in behalf of, in one's stead, in one's place, in one's shoes, by proxy, as proxy for, as a substitute for, as representing, as an alternative, *per procurationem* [L.], *in loco parentis* [L.].

756. Abrogation
(See 755. Commission)

1. *n.* abrogation, repeal, rescission, defeasance; revocation, revokement; renege, renig [coll.]; countermand, counterorder; annulment, nullification; *vacatur* [L.]; *nolle prosequi* [L., Law]; canceling etc. *v.,* cancellation, cancel; abolishment, abolition; dissolution; repudiation, retractation etc. (recantation) 607.3; abandonment etc. 624; destruction etc. 162.

2. *n.* deposal, deposition; deprivation, displacement, disestablishment, disendowment; dethronement, disenthronement, discrownment; secularization, deconsecration, discannonization; dismissal etc. 297.4.

3. *v.* abrogate, revoke, renege, renig [coll.], repeal, rescind, reverse, retract, recall; countermand, counterorder; overrule, override; cancel, cancellate [rare]; annul, abolish, disannul, dissolve, quash, nullify, nol-pros [Law], make void, declare null and void, invalidate, sweep *or* brush away, throw over *or* overboard, throw to the dogs, cast behind, set aside;

do away with, put an end to etc. (destroy) 162.4.

4. *v.* disclaim, disown, divest oneself, break off; renounce, repudiate etc. (recant) 607.9.

5. *v.* depose, divest *or* deprive of office, remove from office, displace, disestablish, disendow, cashier, break, unfrock, oust, strike off the rolls; unseat, unsaddle; uncrown, discrown, unthrone, dethrone, disenthrone; disbar, disbench; secularize, deconsecrate, discannonize; dismiss etc. 297.12.

6. *adj.* abrogated etc. *v.,* invalid, void, null and void; *functus officio* [L.].

757. Resignation

1. *n.* resignation, resignment, [now rare], demission, vacation [now rare]; retirement, retiral; withdrawal, withdrawment; abdication; relinquishment etc. (abandonment) 624, (renunciation) 782; retraction, disclamation etc. (recantation) 607.3.

2. *v.* resign, tender ~, pass in *or* hand in one's resignation, demit [chiefly Scot.], retire, retire *or* withdraw from office, vacate, vacate one's seat, relinquish one's office, give up one's post; abdicate, renounce the throne, give up the crown; accept the stewardship of the Chiltern Hundreds [Eng.]; give up, relinquish, wash one's hands of etc. (abandon) 624.3; abjure, renounce, disclaim etc. (recant) 607.9.

3. *adj.* resigning etc. *v.,* resignful [rare]; renunciative, renunciatory, renunciant [rare]; abjuratory, disclamatory [rare]; repudiative, repudiatory; abdicative, abdicant.

758. Consignee

1. *n.* consignee, assignee, trustee, nominee; assignee in fact [Law]; garnishee; committee.

2. *n.* functionary, placeman, curator;

---

756. The end of life cancels all bands.—SHAKESPEARE.

757. Though a king may abdicate for his own person, he cannot abdicate for the monarchy.—BURKE.   Let him give up his place like a guest well filled.—HORACE.   General Washington set the example of voluntary retirement after eight years.—JEFFERSON.

758. It is fortunate that diplomats generally have long noses, since usually they cannot see beyond them.—P. CLAUDEL.   Diplomacy: lying in state.—CYNIC'S CALENDAR.

treasurer etc. 801; agent, factor, reeve [Eng. Hist.], steward, gomashta [Ind.], bailiff, clerk, secretary, attorney, solicitor, proctor, broker, dalal [Ind.], dubash [Ind.]; insurer, underwriter, commission agent, auctioneer, one's man of business; factotum etc. (director) 694; caretaker; underagent, employee *or* employé *or* employe; servant etc. 746.

3. *n.* negotiator, go-between; middleman; walking delegate.

4. *n.* delegate; commissary, commissioner; emissary, envoy, commissionaire; messenger etc. 534.

5. *n.* salesman, traveler, bagman, *commis voyageur* [F.], traveling salesman, commercial traveler, drummer [U.S.], traveling man; touter [coll.], barker [coll.]; agent etc. (seller) 797.2.

6. *n.* reporter, correspondent etc. (journalist) 593.16.

759. Deputy

1. *n.* deputy, proxy, *alter ego* [L.], *locum tenens* [L.], *badli* [Hind.], vicar, lieutenant, surrogate, secondary, representative, delegate, minister, broker, negotiator, connection [chiefly crim. slang, U.S.], front *or* front man [crim. slang, U.S.], agent, instrument, tool, factor, steward, proctor, gomashta [Ind.], dubash [Ind.], one's man of business; commission agent, commissary, commissioner, commissionaire; friend at *or* in court, next friend [Law], *amicus curiae* [L.], prochein ami *or* amy [Law].

exponent, advocate, champion, patron; spokesman, spokeswoman, spokester, speaker, mouthpiece; prolocutor, prolocutress *or* prolocutrice *or* prolocutrix [*fem.*]; interlocutor, interlocutress *or* interlocutrice *or* interlocutrix [*fem.*]; *parlementaire* [F.], parliamentary, parliamentary agent; apparitor; attorney, solicitor; clerk, secretary; walking delegate; substitute etc. 147.2; go-between, middleman etc. (mediator) 724.2; lawyer etc. 968; servant etc. 746; messenger etc. 534; secret agent etc. 528.8, 9; interpreter etc. 524.

2. *n.* diplomatist, diplomat, diplomatic agent, diplomatic; plenipotentiary, plenipotent [rare], minister plenipotentiary;

ambassador, envoy, emissary, minister, chargé d'affaires, attaché; legate, vice-legate; nuncio, internuncio, consul, proconsul [Rom. Antiq.]; resident, minister resident; diplomatic staff, *corps diplomatique* [F.], embassy.

3. *n.* vice-agent, vice [coll.]; vice-president, vice-chairman, vice-governor, vice-director, vice-master, vice-dean, vice-dictator, vice-warden, vice-burgomaster, vice-provost, vice-admiral, vice-general; regent, vice-regent, viceroy, vicegerent, vicar, vice-emperor, vice-king, vice-sultan, vice-caliph; vice-queen, vicereine; vice-priest, vice-pope, vice-bishop, vice-abbot, vice-prefect, vice-prior, vice-rector.

4. *v.* be deputy etc. *n.*, represent, stand for, appear for, hold a brief for, answer for, act in the place of, act for, stand *or* walk in the shoes of, fill one's shoes, stand in the stead of, serve in one's stead; front for, go to the front for [both slang]; substitute for etc. 147.3.

5. *v.* deputize, depute; delegate etc. (commission) 755.4.

6. *adj.* deputy, deputative; acting, representative, vice; vicegerent, viceregal; viceregal, viceroyal; plenipotentiary, plenipotent [rare]; consular, proconsular.

7. *adv. etc.* in behalf of, by proxy etc. (instead of) 755.6.

760. Permission
(See 761. Prohibition)

1. *n.* permission, leave, sanction, allowance, vouchsafement, sufferance; tolerance, toleration; indulgence, indulgency [rare]; liberty, law, license, concession, grace, dispensation; favor, special favor; exemption, release; connivance; authorization, warranty, accordance, admission; consent etc. 762; right etc. (privilege) 922.2.

2. *n.* permit, warrant, license, sanction, grant, authority, brevet, precept, firman, *hukm* [Hind.], imprimatur, purwannah [Anglo-Ind.], charter; *carte blanche* [F.]; pass, passport, safeconduct, safe-

---

759. The deputy elected by the Lord.—SHAKESPEARE. The Few assume to be the *deputies,* but they are often only the *despoilers* of the *many.*—HEGEL.

760. Suffer the little children to come unto me, and forbid them not; for of such is the kingdom of God.—BIBLE. He to whom much is permitted should take least advantage of it.—SENECA. Who has no will but by her high permission.—BURNS.

guard; furlough, ticket of leave [Eng.]; patent, certificate of invention, *brevet d'invention* [F.], copyright.

3. *v.* permit, give permission etc. *n.*, let, leave [dial.], allow, admit, recognize, accord, vouchsafe, favor, humor, gratify, indulge; suffer, bear with, tolerate; stretch a point, wink at, connive at, shut one's eyes to; give power *or* full power, give *carte blanche* [F.]; leave alone, leave it to one; leave the door open, open the door to, open the floodgates; give the reins to etc. (allow freedom) 748.10; consent etc. 762.2.

4. *v.* grant, empower, enable, charter, enfranchise, privilege, confer a privilege, license, authorize, warrant, entitle, sanction, sanctify, entitle, prescribe, ordain, allot, patent [rare], facultate [rare]; intrust etc. (commission) 755.4.

5. *v.* ask permission *or* leave, beg ~, crave *or* request permission *or* leave.

6. *adj.* permissive, permitting etc. *v.*; admissive, admissory; permissible, admissible, allowable; permitted etc. *v.*, permissioned; unprohibited, unforbid [arch.], unforbidden; lawful, legitimate, legal, licit; patent; faculative, optional; lenient, tolerant, indulgent; forbearing, forbearant; unconditional; consenting etc. 762.3; authorized, warranted etc. 924.10.

7. *adv.* permissibly, licitly etc. *adj.*; *avec permission* [F.], with permission, by ~, with *or* on leave etc. *n.*, *pace* [L.]; *speciali gratia* [L.], by special favor, under favor of; freely etc. 748.21; *ad libitum* [L.] etc. (at will) 600.5; yes, by all means etc. (assent) 488.14, 15; willingly etc. 602.11.

761. Prohibition
(See 760. Permission)

1. *n.* prohibition, forbiddance, forbiddal; inhibition, veto, disallowance, denial, injunction, embargo, ban, taboo *or* tabu, proscription; interdict, interdiction; restriction, cohibition; forbidden fruit; *Index Expurgatorius* [L.], *Index Libro-*

rum Prohibitorum [L.]; Maine law, Volstead Act, Eighteenth Amendment [all U.S.]; restraint etc. 751; hindrance etc. 706; illegality etc. 964.

2. *v.* prohibit, inhibit, forbid, disallow, deny, bar, debar, preclude, forfend [arch.], interdict, put under an interdiction, embargo, taboo *or* tabu, ban, put under the ban, veto, put one's veto upon, proscribe, exclude, shut out, shut *or* bolt the door, show the door, warn off, dash the cup from one's lips; forbid the banns; cohibit, restrict, keep in *or* within bounds, withhold, limit, circumscribe; restrain etc. 751.6; hinder etc. 706.4.

3. *adj.* prohibitive, prohibitory, prohibitionary; prohibiting, forbidding etc. *v.*; inhibitive, inhibitory; proscriptive, restrictive, exclusive.

4. *adj.* prohibited etc. *v.*, not permitted etc. 760.6, unallowed, unlicensed, unauthorized, contraband, under the ban, taboo *or* tabu, not to be thought of; illegal etc. 964.5.

5. *adv.* on no account etc. (no) 536.4.

6. *int.* don't!, don't do that!, enough!, no more of that!, that will never do!, leave off!; hands off!, keep off!, keep off the grass!; hold!, stop! etc. (cease) 142.8; God forbid! etc. 766.5.

762. Consent
(See 764. Refusal; also 488. Assent)

1. *n.* consent, acquiescence, compliance, agreement, concession, accession, acknowledgment, acceptance; yielding etc. *v.*, yieldance [now rare], yieldingness; assent etc. 488; approval etc. 931; willingness etc. 602; permission etc. 760; promise etc. 768.

2. *v.* consent, give consent, yield assent, admit, allow, concede, grant, yield, come over *or* round, give in, acknowledge, agnize [arch.], comply with, acquiesce, agree to, fall in with, accede, embrace an offer, close with, take at one's word, have no objection, not refuse etc. 764.2; satisfy, meet one's wishes; deign, vouchsafe; vote for, give one's voice for,

---

761. Touch not; taste not; handle not.—BIBLE. Forbid us thing, that thing desyren we.—CHAUCER.   Forbidden wares sell twice as dear.—J. DENHAM.   Vicious actions are not hurtful because they are forbidden, but forbidden because they are hurtful.—FRANKLIN. Forbidden fruit is sweet.

762. Silence gives consent.—GOLDSMITH. And whispering, "I will ne'er consent,"—consented.—BYRON.   Barkis is willin'.—DICKENS.   The concessions of the weak are the concessions of fear.—BURKE.   Life cannot subsist in society but by reciprocal concessions. —JOHNSON.

lend one's support to; assent, concur etc. 488.6–9; approve etc. 931.5; turn a willing ear etc. (be willing) 602.6; be induced etc. 615.10; promise etc. 768.3; permit etc. 760.3, 4.

3. *adj.* consenting etc. *v.*, consentant, consentient, consentive, consentful; acquiescent, compliant, agreeable [coll.], content, accordant; assenting etc. 488.11; willing etc. 602.8; permissive etc. 760.6.

4. *adv.* consentingly etc. *adj.*; willingly etc. 602.11; yes, be it so etc. 488.14, 15.

763. Offer
(See 765. Request)

1. *n.* offer, proffer, presentation, tender, kid, overture, advance, submission; proposal, proposition; motion; invitation; ultimatum; candidature, candidacy; offering etc. (gift) 784.3.

2. *v.* offer, proffer, overture, make an overture etc. *n.*, present, tender, propose, submit, invite, hold out, put forward, place in one's way, lay at one's feet, put *or* place at one's disposal, put in one's power, make possible; advance, make advances; move, make a motion; bid, bid for, make a bid; put forth; give etc. 784.8; offer for sale etc. 796.5; press etc. (entreat) 765.5.

3. *v.* volunteer, come forward, be a candidate, candidate [coll.], offer *or* present oneself, stand *or* bid for, seek, be at one's service.

4. *adj.* offering, offered etc. *v.*; in the market, for sale, to let, for *or* on hire, at one's disposal.

764. Refusal
(See 762. Consent)

1. *n.* refusal, refusing, declining etc. *v.*; declination, declension, declinature; noncompliance, incompliance; nonconsent [rare], nonacceptance, rejection, denial, negation, abnegation, protest; disclamation, disclaimer; recusance *or* recusancy, recusation [Law]; renouncement, renunciation; discountenance, disapproval, disapprobation; peremptory ~, flat *or* point-blank refusal; repulse, rebuff; dissent etc. 489; unwillingness etc. 603.

2. *v.* refuse, not consent etc. 762.2, nonconsent [rare], reject, forswear, decline, deny, disallow, nill [arch.], turn down [slang], abnegate, negate, negative, say no to, refuse *or* withhold one's assent *or* consent, shake the head, close the hand *or* purse; grudge, begrudge; pass [card-playing]; disclaim, protest; refuse point blank, put *or* set one's foot down [coll.]; not yield an inch etc. 606.5; dissent etc. 489.4; be unwilling etc. 603.4.

3. *v.* discountenance, not countenance, disapprove of, refuse to look with favor upon, view with disfavor, look black upon, look askance *or* askant at, stand aloof, not hear of *or* to, turn a deaf ear to, turn one's back upon, set one's face against, have nothing to do with, wash one's hands of, set aside, cast behind one.

4. *v.* repel, repulse, rebuff, shut *or* slam the door in one's face, send to the right-about, send away with a flea in the ear [coll.]; refuse to receive, deny oneself to, not be at home to; resist, cross.

5. *adj.* refusing etc. *v.*, declinatory, rejective, disclamatory [rare], protestant, negatory, inacquiescent, uncomplaisant; recusant, recusative [rare]; unconsenting, nonconsenting; uncomplying, noncompliant, incompliant; not willing to hear of, deaf to; restive, restiff [now rare]; unwilling etc. 603.5; dissenting etc. 489.5.

6. *adj.* refused etc. *v.*, ungranted, out of the question, not to be thought of, impossible.

7. *adv.* on no account, by no means, by no manner of means, nothing doing [slang], not for the world; not on your life, not by a long chalk *or* by long chalks, not by a long shot *or* sight [all coll.]; no etc. 536.4.

8. *phr.* I refuse!, by no manner of means!, I will not!, far be it from me!, not if I can help it!, I won't!, I'll be hanged if I will!, like fun I will!, count me out!, you have another guess coming!, catch me! [all coll.].

---

763. Their offers should not charm us.—C. ROSSETTI.   Man proposes, but God disposes.—THOMAS À KEMPIS.   Take the goods the gods provide thee.—DRYDEN.
764. One refusal no rebuff.—BYRON.   'Tis fine to see them scattering refusals.—BYRON.

That he may know how to refuse the evil.—BIBLE.   He could refuse more gracefully than other people could grant.—CHESTERTON.   I have other fish to fry.

765. Request
(See 763. Offer; also 767. Petitioner)

1. *n.* request, requisition, petition, suit, prayer, postulation, solicitation, application, canvass, address, invitation; invocatory plea *or* prayer, solemn entreaty, invocation; rogative [rare], rogation [Eccl.]; touch [slang]; begging letter, round robin; mendicity, mendicancy, mendication [rare], beggary; orison etc. (worship) 990.3; incantation etc. (sorcery) 992; claim etc. (demand) 741.2.

2. *n.* entreaty, beseechment, appeal, imprecation, importunity, imploration, impetration, supplication, obsecration, obtestation; adjuration, conjuration [arch.].

3. *n.* proposal, proposition, overture, motion, submission, advancement, suggestion, offer, instance.

4. *v.* request, make a request etc. *n.*, ask, beg, crave, sue, pray, petition, prefer a petition, solicit, invite, make bold to ask, beg leave, make application, apply to, put to, call on *or* upon; ask for, trouble one for, whistle for [coll.]; bespeak, canvass, tout [cant, Eng.], make interest, court, seek; ask for one's hand, pop the question [coll.]; offer up prayers etc. (worship) 990.11; bid for etc. (offer) 763.2; demand, claim etc. 741.5, 6.

5. *v.* entreat, implore, beseech, plead, supplicate, beg hard, appeal, invoke, invocate [rare], evoke, impetrate, imprecate, ply, press, urge, beset, besiege, importune, dun, tax; adjure, conjure; obsecrate, obtest [both rare]; clamor for, cry to, cry aloud, cry for help; kneel to, fall on one's knees, throw oneself at the feet of, get *or* come down on one's marrowbones [joc. or slang]; ask for pity etc. 914.5.

6. *v.* go a-begging, beg, mendicate [rare], mump, mooch [slang], cadge [coll.], bum [slang, U.S.], panhandle [slang], beg one's bread, beg from door to door, pass the hat [slang]; beg a boon, hit up [slang, U.S.]; touch, make a touch [both slang].

7. *adj.* requesting etc. *v.*, precatory, imprecatory, invitatory, imploratory [rare], rogatory, solicitous, cap in hand; suppliant, supplicant, supplicative [rare], supplicatory; petitional [rare], petitionary; invocative, invocatory; postulant, postulatory [rare]; obsecrationary, obsecratory [both rare]; begging, mendicant; on one's knees *or* bended knees, on one's marrowbones [joc. or slang].

8. *adj.* importunate, insistent etc. (urgent) 642.13.

9. *int.* please, prithee [arch.], I pray thee [arch.], pray, do, pray do, be so good as, be good enough, have the goodness, vouchsafe [arch.], will you, please you [arch.], may it please you, if it please you, if you please; for God's, ~ goodness, ~ heaven's *or* mercy's sake!

766. Deprecation

1. *n.* deprecation, remonstrance, expostulation, protest; dehortation, dehortative [both rare]; advice etc. 695; dissuasion etc. 616.

2. *v.* deprecate, remonstrate, expostulate, protest, enter a protest, dehort [rare], pray against, cry out against; dissuade etc. 616.2, 3.

3. *adj.* deprecatory, deprecative; remonstratory, remonstrative, remonstrant; expostulatory, expostulative; dehortatory, dehortative [both rare].

4. *adj.* unsought, unbesought; unasked, unrequested, unsolicited.

5. *int.* God forbid!, Heaven forbid!, Heaven forfend!, forbid it Heaven!, cry you mercy!, far be it from!; don't! etc. 761.6.

767. Petitioner
(See also 765. Request)

1. *n.* petitioner, applicant, supplicant, suppliant, suitor, candidate, claimant, postulant, aspirant, competitor, bidder; solicitor, canvasser; tout [slang], touter

---

765. Their pleas were diff'rent, their request the same.—POPE.   He did entreat me, past all saying nay.—SHAKESPEARE.   Ask, and it shall be given you.—BIBLE.   When I come to ask for my good, I quake in fear lest my prayer be granted.—TAGORE.   When the gods wish to punish us they answer our prayers.—WILDE.   He who begs timidly courts a refusal.—SENECA   Who fears to ask, doth teach to be deny'd.—HERRICK.
766. The lady doth protest too much, methinks.—SHAKESPEARE.
767. The real beggar is indeed the true and only king.—LESSING.   Set a beggar on horseback, and he will ride a gallop.—R. BURTON.   A beggar through the world am I.—LOWELL.   Speak with me, pity me, open the door: / A beggar begs that never begg'd before.—SHAKESPEARE.   Beggars should be no choosers.

[coll.], runner [U.S.]; barker [coll.], spieler [slang, U.S.]; ballyhooer, ballyhoo man [both slang]; pothunter, prizer [arch.].

2. *n.* beggar, mendicant, mumper, cadger [slang], panhandler [slang], moocher [slang], fakir [Ind.], schnorrer [Yiddish], sannyasi [Ind.], sturdy beggar; bum, bummer [both slang, U.S.]; tramp etc. (wanderer) 268.2; idler etc. 683.7; vagabond etc. 876.9; sponger etc. (sycophant) 886.2; pauper etc. 804.3.

768. Promise

1. *n.* promise, undertaking, word, troth, plight, pledge, parole, word of honor, solemn declaration *or* word, vow, oath, profession, assurance, guarantee, insurance, obligation, stipulation; warrant, warranty; avow, avowal, avowance; avouch [rare], avouchment; affidavit, affidavy [dial.]; contract, covenant etc. (compact) 769; consent etc. 762.

2. *n.* engagement, pre-engagement; affiance, troth [arch.], betrothal, betrothment, trothplight [arch.], marriage contract *or* vow, plighted faith *or* love, *gage d'amour* [F.], handfast, handfasting [both arch.].

3. *v.* promise, give a promise etc. *n.*, pledge, plight, hold out an expectation, undertake; engage, make *or* form an engagement, enter into *or* on an engagement; answer for, be answerable for; contract an obligation, become bound to, become sponsor for; give one's word *or* word of honor, pledge *or* plight one's honor, vow, avow, avouch, vouch, warrant, certify, guarantee, assure; give *or* bear witness, attest, testify, testate [rare]; swear etc. (depose) 535.4; covenant etc. (contract) 769.5; consent etc. 762.2.

4. *v.* affiance, affy, betroth, contract [now rare], plight faith, pledge one's faith to, plight one's troth *or* faith, troth-plight [arch.], handfast [arch.], take the vows *or* marriage vows, engage *or* promise in marriage, become engaged etc. *adj.*

5. *v.* adjure, administer an oath, put to one's oath, swear a witness, swear in.

6. *adj.* promising etc. *v.*, promissory; votive; under *or* upon oath, under hand and seal, upon the Book, on *or* upon affirmation.

7. *adj.* promised, pledged etc. *v.*; bound, committed, compromised, in for it [coll.]; engaged, affianced, betrothed, trothplight [arch.], intended [coll.], beholden etc. (obliged) 926.10.

8. *phr.* I promise, I'll warrant, I'll warrant you, I assure you, you may be sure, you may rest assured, I'll engage to say, I'll answer for it, I'll be bound, I'll take my oath, upon my oath, upon my word *or* honor, on my word of honor, honor bright [coll.], by my troth, by my sooth [arch.], in all soberness, I call God to witness, so help me God, believe me [coll.], you can take it from me [coll.], my word for it, my head upon it, as true as I live *or* live and breathe.

769. Compact

1. *n.* compact, contract, bundobust [Ind.], deal [coll.], agreement, understanding, bargain, dicker [chiefly coll., U.S.], go [coll.], whiz *or* whizz [slang, U.S.], affidation [rare], pact, paction [chiefly Scot.], bond, covenant; indenture [Law]; contract by deed, specialty, stipulation, convention, cartel; gentleman's agreement, *entente cordiale* [F.]; negotiation; engagement etc. (promise) 768; transaction etc. 794.3.

2. *n.* treaty, protocol, concordat, *Zollverein* [G.], *Sonderbund* [G.], charter, pragmatic sanction; Magna Charta *or* Carta.

3. *n.* settlement, arrangement, adjustment; execution, completion, conclusion; compromise etc. 774.

4. *n.* confirmation, ratification etc. 488.4.

5. *v.* contract, covenant, agree for; indent; engage etc. (promise) 768.3.

---

768. Never promise more than you can perform.—PUBLILIUS.   An honest man's word is as good as his bond.—CERVANTES.   Promise is debt.—CHAUCER.   Promise is most given when the least is said.—G. CHAPMAN.   A man apt to promise is apt to forget.—FULLER.   Who never promiseth but he means to pay.—SHAKESPEARE.   Some persons make promises for the pleasure of breaking them.—HAZLITT.   If we've promised them aught, let us keep our promise!—BROWNING.

769. 'Tis not in the bond.—SHAKESPEARE.   There never was a better bargain driven.—SIDNEY.   Open covenants of peace openly arrived at.—W. WILSON.   Make every bargain clear and plain, / That none may afterwards complain.

769.6 — 771.11

6. *v.* negotiate, treat, stipulate, make terms; bargain etc. 794.5.

7. *v.* make a compact etc. *n.*, strike a bargain etc. 794.6; come to terms etc. (come to an agreement) 488.8.

8. *v.* settle, fix by agreement, arrange, adjust, straighten out, set at rest; execute, make; conclude, close, close with, complete, clinch *or* clench; compromise etc. 774.2.

9. *v.* confirm, ratify etc. 488.10.

10. *adj.* contractual, agreed etc. *v.*, conventional; under hand and seal, signed, sealed; signed, sealed and delivered.

11. *adv.* as agreed upon, as promised, as contracted for, according to the contract, ∼ bargain *or* agreement.

770. Conditions

1. *n.* conditions, terms, stipulations, conditional stipulations, qualifications, strings [coll.], provisions, specifications, obligations, circumstances, grounds, memoranda; requisites, prerequisites; article of agreement, article, clause; saving clause, salvo [rare]; ultimatum; *sine qua non* [L.]; *casus foederis* [L.]; proviso etc. (condition) 469.2.

2. *v.* condition, make it a condition, stipulate, insist upon, make a point of; bind, tie up, fence *or* hedge in; have a string to it [coll.].

3. *adj.* conditional, qualificatory, stipulatory, contingent; provisional, provisory; guarded, fenced, hedged in.

4. *adv.* conditionally, provisionally etc. *adj.*; with qualifications, with a reservation *or* exception, *exceptis excipiendis* [L.], with a string to it [coll.]; *pro re nata* [L.]; on condition, with the stipulation etc. (provided) 469.8.

771. Security

1. *n.* security, guaranty, guarantee; warranty, warrant, assurance, insurance, surety, gage, pledge, plight [rare], *pignus* [L.], pignoration, vadium [Law]; bond, tie; deposit, stake, bail, replevin, pawn,

---

771. What are fantastically termed securities.— S. W. MITCHELL. Where there's a will there's a lawsuit.—CYNIC'S CALENDAR. I crave the law, / The penalty and forfeit of my bond.—SHAKESPEARE.

534

earnest, handsel; caution money, caution; collateral security *or* warranty, collateral; muniments, title deeds and papers; paper, parchment; instrument, certificate, docket, note, voucher; deed, deed poll, deed of arrangement, deed of assumption; debenture, debenture bond, naked debenture, floating debenture, mortgage debenture.

vadium vivum [L.], living pledge; *vadium mortuum* [L.], dead pledge, mortgage, monkey [slang, Eng.]; hypothec [Law], *hypotheca* [L.], hypothecation; bottomry bond, bottomry; real security, security on property, lien; bill, bill of exchange, bill of sale; promissory note, I O U; covenant, contract, indenture; contract by deed, specialty; deed *or* covenant of indemnity, recognizance; probate, attested copy; settlement, will, testament, last will and testament; codicil; *pignus legale* [L.], *pignus judiciale* [L.]; personal security, specific security, shifting *or* floating security, security for costs; parole etc. (promise) 768; loan etc. 787; credit etc. 805; payment etc. 807; credential etc. (authority) 467.4.

2. *n.* guarantor, guarantee, warrantee, sponsor, surety, bail, hostage; mainpernor, mainprise [Law]; godchild, godfather, godmother; sponsion, sponsorship.

3. *n.* acceptance, endorsement, authentication etc. (ratification) 488.4.

4. *n.* acquittance, quittance; discharge, release; receipt.

5. *v.* give security etc. *n.*, go bail, pledge, handsel, impignorate, mortgage, hypothecate, bottomry; pawn, put in pawn; spout, put up the spout, hock [all slang]; borrow etc. 788.2.

6. *v.* guarantee, warrant, assure, insure, certify; accept; promise etc. 768.3; indorse, underwrite etc. (ratify) 488.10.

7. *v.* execute, make, complete etc. (settle) 769.8.

8. *v.* hold as security etc. *n.* take *or* hold a lease, hold in pledge; grant a lease etc. (let) 787.6.

9. *adj.* pledged, pawned etc. *v.*; in pawn, up the spout [slang], in hock [slang]; at stake, on deposit, as earnest; impignorate, pignorate, pignorative [rare], pignoratitious; secure.

10. *adj.* let, leased, held in pledge.

11. *adj.* sponsorial, sponsional [rare], as sponsor etc. *n.*

772. Observance
(See 773. Nonobservance)

1. *n.* observance, observation, performance, fulfillment *or* fulfilment, satisfaction, discharge; acquittance, acquittal; compliance, acquiescence, concurrence; acknowledgment; obedience etc. 743.

2. *n.* adhesion, adherence, constancy, continued observance, steady attachment, unswerving fidelity, exact observance; fidelity etc. 939.4.

3. *v.* observe, comply with, respect, acknowledge, abide by, be faithful to, act up to, cling *or* adhere to, keep, meet, fulfill *or* fulfil, satisfy, discharge, carry out, carry into execution, execute, perform, do one's office; obey etc. 743.2.

4. *v.* keep faith with, perform ~, fulfill *or* discharge an obligation, keep *or* make good one's word *or* promise, acquit oneself, make good, redeem one's pledge, stand to one's engagement.

5. *adj.* observant, faithful, true, loyal, constant, as good as one's word; true as the dial to the sun, true as the needle to the pole; punctual, punctilious, scrupulous, meticulous; obedient etc. 743.3; honorable etc. 939.7; literal etc. (exact) 494.10.

6. *adv.* faithfully etc. *adj.*; to the letter etc. (literally) 19.14.

773. Nonobservance
(See 772. Observance)

1. *n.* nonobservance, inobservance, unobservance; nonfulfillment *or* nonfulfilment, nonperformance, noncompliance; disregard, disregardance; failure, omission, default, slight, oversight; laches, laxity, laxness, slackness, casualness, informality; inattention etc. 458; neglect etc. 460; evasion etc. 623; disobedience etc. 742.

2. *n.* infringement, infraction etc. (disobedience) 742; bad faith etc. 940.2.

3. *v.* not observe etc. 772.3, disregard, overlook, slight, fail, omit, pass over *or* by, pass up [slang, U.S.], let pass, blink *or* wink at, connive at, take no note *or* notice of, take no thought *or* account of, leave out of one's calculation, pay no attention to, shut *or* close one's eyes to, set aside; neglect, ignore etc. 460.4, 5; evade, elude etc. (avoid) 623.6.

4. *v.* not keep faith with, not keep one's word etc. 772.4, go from one's word; go back on, go back on one's word *or* promise [both coll.]; palter, stretch *or* strain a point; infringe, violate etc. (disobey) 742.4.

5. *adj.* nonobservant, inobservant, unobservant; unfaithful, untrue, unloyal, inconstant; remiss, slack, lax, loose, casual; disregardful etc. (negligent) 460.8; evasive etc. 623.12; lawless, transgressive etc. (disobedient) 742.6.

774. Compromise

1. *n.* compromise, composition, commutation, mutual *or* reciprocal concession, abatement of differences, reciprocal abatement; adjustment etc. (settlement) 769.3; compensation etc. 30; middle ground etc. (mean) 29, (mid-course) 628.

2. *v.* compromise, make *or* reach a compromise, adjust *or* settle differences, make mutual concessions, compound, commute, take the mean, strike a balance, meet halfway, split the difference, go fifty-fifty [slang, U.S.], give and take; arbitrate, agree to arbitrate, submit to arbitration, abide by arbitration; patch up, bridge over; make the best *or* most of, make a virtue of necessity; take the will for the deed; come to terms etc. (come to an agreement) 488.8; adjust etc. (settle) 769.8; steer a middle course etc. 628.2.

775. Acquisition
(See 776. Loss)

1. *n.* acquisition, gaining etc. *v.*, acquirement, obtainment, attainment, lucre [arch.]; procuration, procurement; collection, cumulation, accumulation, amassment; money-making, moneygrubbing; recipience etc. (receiving) 785; appro-

---

772. A strict observance of the written laws.—Jefferson.   The iron force of adhesion to the old routine.—M. Arnold.
773. More honoured in the breach than the observance.—Shakespeare.
774. A lean compromise is better than a fat lawsuit.—G. Herbert.   Every compromise was surrender and invited new demands.—Emerson.   All government . . . is founded on compromise and barter.—Burke.
775. They well deserve to have / That know the strong'st and surest way to get.—Shake-

775.1 – 776.2

priation etc. (taking) 789; purchase etc. 795.

2. *n.* gain, profit, pelf, lucre, filthy lucre, boot [arch.], perquisite; profits, earnings, winnings, innings, pickings, returns, avails, receipts, take; proceeds, produce, product; outcome, output; fruit, crop, harvest; second crop, aftermath; godsend, windfall; loaves and fishes, fleshpots of Egypt; net *or* gross profit; find, finding, trove, trover, *trouvaille* [F.], foundling; benefit etc. (good) 648.2; income etc. (receipt) 810; remuneration, emolument, prize etc. (reward) 973; gift etc. 784.3–6; booty etc. 793; success etc. 731.

3. *n.* recovery, retrieval, repossession, revendication [rare]; replevin, replevy; redemption, salvage, trover; resumption etc. 789.3.

4. *n.* inheritance, heritance, heritage, inheritage [rare], patrimony, birthright, descent, reversion; heirdom, heirship; primogeniture, ultimogeniture; coheirship, coparcenary *or* coparceny, jointure; thirds; appanage; hereditament, corporeal *or* incorporeal hereditament; heritable, movable, heirship movable [Scot.], heirloom; legacy, dowry etc. (bequest) 784.6; fee etc. (estate) 780.2; heir etc. 779.5.

5. *n.* (fraudulent acquisition) subreption, obreption; stealing etc. 791.

6. *v.* acquire, get, gain, obtain, secure, procure, win, earn, pick, pick up, glean, gather, collect, get *or* gather in, get together, scrape up *or* together, rake up, dig up; net, bag, sack; take possession, come *or* enter into possession, come by, come in for; get hold of, get between one's finger and thumb, get into one's hand, get one's fingers *or* hands on, lay hands on, get at; harvest, get in the harvest, crop, reap, reap and carry; find, come at, ~ across *or* upon, light *or* pitch upon, scare up [slang]; derive, draw; accumulate, treasure up etc. (store) 636.7; receive etc. 785.3; take, appropriate etc. 789.7–12.

7. *v.* profit, make *or* draw profit, turn to profit *or* account, make capital out of, capitalize on, make money by, obtain a return, reap *or* gain an advantage, turn a penny *or* an honest penny, make the pot boil, bring grist to the mill, make *or* coin money; realize, clear; make a fortune etc. (*see* fortune etc. 803.1); succeed etc. 731.5.

8. *v.* inherit, receive an inheritance etc. *n.*, come by, come in for, step into a fortune, step into the shoes of, succeed to.

9. *v.* recover, get back, regain, retrieve, revendicate [rare], redeem, repossess, retake, resume, reoccupy, come by one's own; replevin, replevy.

10. *v.* be profitable etc. *adj.*, pay, answer; accrue etc. (be received) 785.4; yield, produce etc. (bear) 161.9.

11. *adj.* acquisitive, acquiring etc. *v.*

12. *adj.* gainful, remunerative, productive, profitable, advantageous, paying, well-paying, lucrative.

13. *adv.* profitably etc. *adj.*, in the way of gain, for money, *lucri causa* [L.]; at interest.

776. Loss
(See 775. Acquisition)

1. *n.* loss, privation, bereavement; perdition, deperdition [arch.]; forfeiture, lapse; consumption, exhaustion, depletion, expenditure, dissipation, decrement; damage; riddance; total loss; distressing *or* painful loss, funeral [slang]; losing streak [coll., U.S.]; deprivation etc. (dispossession) 789.2; disentitlement etc. 925.2; decrease etc. 36; waste etc. 638; squandering etc. (prodigality) 818; leakage etc. (egress) 295; destruction etc. 162.

2. *v.* lose, incur *or* experience loss, meet with a loss, miss, mislay, let slip, allow to slip through the fingers, be deprived of, forfeit; drop, kiss good-by [both slang]; lose out, come out at the

---

SPEARE. There is no gathering the rose without being pricked by the thorns.—PILPAY. Everything goes to him who wants nothing.—J. RAY. Light gains make heavy purses.—BACON. Resolved to take Fate by the throat and shake a living out of her.—L. ALCOTT. Take care to get what you like or you will be forced to like what you get.—SHAW.

776. The loss which is unknown is no loss at all.—PUBLILIUS. There are occasions when it is undoubtedly better to incur loss than to make gain.—PLAUTUS. What's lost today may be won tomorrow.—CERVANTES. For better is a little loss than a long sorrow.—LANGLAND. No man can lose what he never had.—I. WALTON. A wise man loses nothing, if he but save himself.—MONTAIGNE. Farewell! thou art too dear for my possessing.—SHAKESPEARE.

little *or* small end of the horn [both coll.]; fail etc. 732.5, 6.

3. *v.* squander, dissipate etc. (be prodigal) 818.3; waste etc. 638.2.

4. *v.* be lost etc. *adj.,* lapse.

5. *adj.* lost, forfeit, forfeited, gone out of one's possession; dissipated; abandoned, reprobate; long-lost; showing a loss, in the red [slang, U.S.], to the bad [coll.]; irretrievable etc. 859.7; destroyed etc. 162.7.

6. *adj.* deprived of, shorn of, parted with, deperdite [rare], denuded, bereaved, bereft, divested, cut off, rid of, quit of, out of pocket, off one's hands; minus [coll. exc. Math.], lacking, wanting; disinherited, cut off without a cent; dispossessed etc. 789.16.

7. *int.* farewell to . . . !, adieu to . . . !, good-by to . . . !, good riddance!

777. Possession

(See 777a. Nonpossession; also 779. Possessor)

1. *n.* possession, possessing etc. *v.*, seizin *or* seisin; nine points of the law; occupancy, occupation; hold, holding; tenancy, tenure; apronstring tenure [coll.]; gavelkind; villenage, villeinhold; socage, chivalry, knight service; dependency; *métayage* [F.], métayer system; prepossession, preoccupancy; chose in possession, bird in hand; *uti possidetis* [L.]; retention etc. 781; property etc. 780.

2. *n.* exclusive possession, monopoly, corner; engrossment, forestallment, regratement [both Hist.]; usucapion *or* usucaption [Rom. Law], prescription; impropriation, appropriation.

3. *n.* possessorship, ownership, proprietorship, lordship; seigniory, seigneury [F. and Can., Hist.], seignioralty.

4. *v.* possess, have, hold, maintain, occupy, fill, enjoy; own, have for one's own *or* very own; be possessed of, be the possessor of etc. 779, be one's property etc. 780, have in hand etc. *adj.*; have a firm hold of etc. (retain) 781.4.

5. *v.* monopolize, hog [slang], have all to oneself; engross, forestall, regrate [both Hist.]; corner, get a corner on; usucapt [Rom. Law]; impropriate, appropriate.

6. *v.* belong to, pertain to, appertain to; vest in.

7. *adj.* possessing etc. *v.*, in possession of, possessed of, seized of, master of; endowed with, blest with, instinct with, fraught with, laden with, charged with; worth.

8. *adj.* possessed, owned etc. *v.*; own, one's own, one's very own; on hand, in hand, in one's hands *or* grasp, in one's possession, by one, at one's command *or* disposal; in store, in stock; unsold, unshared.

777a. Nonpossession

(See 777. Possession)

1. *n.* nonpossession; absence etc. 187; exemption etc. (freedom) 748.

2. *v.* not have etc. 777.4, be without etc. *adj.*

3. *adj.* unpossessed of, not possessing etc. 777.7, unblest with, out of, without, lacking, wanting, minus [coll.]; unobtained, unacquired etc. (*see* obtain, acquire etc. 775.6); untenanted etc. (vacant) 187.11; deprived of etc. 776.6; dispossessed etc. 789.16; exempt etc. 748.18.

778. Participation

Joint Possession.—1. *n.* participation, partaking, sharing etc. *v.*; possession ~, occupancy *or* tenancy in common, joint possession *or* tenancy, cotenancy; partnership, copartnership; snacks, snips [old slang], cahoot *or* cahoots [slang], whacks [slang]; coheirship, coparcenary *or* coparceny, jointure; gavelkind; joint *or* common stock; co-operation etc. 709; share etc. (portion) 786.2.

2. *n.* communion, community of possessions *or* goods; communization, com-

---

777. Possession is eleven points in the law.—CIBBER.   As having nothing, and yet possessing all things.—BIBLE.   As much as thou hast, so much art thou worth.—CERVANTES.   Bliss in possession will not last.—J. MONTGOMERY.   Possession means to sit astride of the world, / Instead of having it astride of you.—KINGSLEY.   It is preoccupation with possession . . . that prevents men from living freely and nobly.—B. RUSSELL.   You can lead a horse to water, if you've got the horse.—SANDBURG.   The greatest possession is self-possession.—CYNIC'S CALENDAR.   A bird in the hand is worth two in the bush.   Finding's keeping.

778. Friends share all things in common.—DIOGENES.   What's mine is yours and what is yours is mine.—SHAKESPEARE.   Not what we give, but what we share.—LOWELL.

munalization; communism, communalism, collectivism, socialism.

3. *n.* participator, participant, partaker, sharer; partner, copartner; shareholder; cotenant, joint tenant, tenants in common; coheir, coparcener.

4. *n.* communist, communitarian, communalist, collectivist, socialist.

5. *v.* participate, partake, share, share in, come in for a share, go shares, go snacks, go snips [old slang], go cahoots [slang]; share and share alike, divide with, divvy up [slang], halve, go halves, go halvers [coll.], go fifty-fifty [slang, U.S.], split the difference; apportion etc. 783.3; join in, have a hand in etc. (co-operate) 709.6; apportion etc. 786.3; enter into etc. 56.2.

6. *v.* communize, communalize, possess in common, possess as joint tenants etc. *n.*

7. *adj.* participative, participatory, participating etc. *v.*

8. *adj.* communistic, communalistic, socialistic; profit-sharing; co-operative etc. 709.7.

9. *adv.* in common, on shares, share and share alike.

779. Possessor
(See also 777. Possession)

1. *n.* possessor, holder, person in possession; occupant, occupier; tenant, intern, lodger, renter, lessee, underlessee; tenant on sufferance, tenant at will; tenant from year to year, tenant for years, tenant for life; mortgagor, mortgage holder.

2. *n.* proprietor, proprietary, owner; proprietress, proprietrix; impropriator, impropriatrix; master, mistress; lord, laird [Scot.]; landlord, landlady, landholder, landowner, zamindar [Ind.]; lord of the manor, lord of the paramount; vavasor *or* vavasour [Feud. Law]; mesne lord, mesne; planter; host, hostess; mine host; innholder, innkeeper, restaurateur, hotelkeeper, *hôtelier* [F.]; householder etc. 188.3.

3. *n.* landed gentry, landed interest.

4. *n.* trustee, holder of the legal estate, cestui que trust *or* qui trust [Law]; mortgagee; in trust.

5. *n.* heir, heritor, inheritor; heiress, inheritress, inheritrix; legatee, legetary [now rare]; coheir, coparcener; heir portioner [Scot.]; heir expectant; heir apparent, heir presumptive; heir general, heir whatsoever [Scot.], heir at law; heir of inventory [Scot.], beneficiary heir; heir of provision, heir by destination; heir of the body; reversioner, reversionary [rare]; remainderman; beneficiary etc. 785.2.

780. Property

1. *n.* property, properties, possessions, holdings, belongings, goods, chattels, effects, estate and effects; *meum et tuum* [L.]; burdensome possession, white elephant [coll.]; seizin, tenure etc. (possession) 777; ownership etc. 777.3.

2. *n.* estate, interest, stake, right, title, claim, demand, holding; absolute interest, vested interest, contingent interest, beneficial interest, equitable interest; use, trust, benefit; easement, right of common, right of user; particular estate, legal estate, equitable estate, paramount estate, estate at sufferance, estate at will, estate for years; estate for life; estate pur autre vie [Law]; feudal estate, feud *or* feod, fief, fee, fee tail, fee simple; estate in fee, estate tail *or* in tail, estate in tail male, ~ female *or* general; alodium; freehold, estate of freehold; copyhold; lease, leasehold; remainder; reversion; expectancy; estate in expectancy; term, limitation; settlement, strict settlement.

3. *n.* dower, legacy etc. (bequest) 784.6; inheritance etc. 775.4.

4. *n.* realty, real property, real estate, chattels real, tenements; landed property, land, lands, grounds, acres; hereditaments, corporeal *or* incorporeal hereditament; acquest; messuage, mesestead [arch.], toft [Scot. and dial. Eng.], hacienda [Sp. Amer.], manor, honor [feudal Law, Eng.], domain, demesne, zamindari [Ind.], arado [Southwest. U.S.]; plant, fixtures; ground, 342; ranch, plantation etc. (farm) 371.4; freehold etc. 748.5.

5. *n.* personalty, personal property, ~ estate *or* effects, chattels personal, be-

---

779. All heiresses are beautiful.—DRYDEN. The owner should bring honor to the house, not the house to its owner.—CICERO.

780. I carry all my possessions with me.—BIAS. All the possessions of mortals are mortal.—METRODORUS. Few rich men own their own property. The property owns them.—INGERSOLL. Is it not lawful for me to do what I will with mine own?—BIBLE.

longings, things, duds [slang], traps [coll.], trappings, rattletraps, paraphernalia, appointments, appurtenances, movables; parcels [Eng.]; equipage etc. 634.

6. *n.* impedimenta, luggage, baggage, bag and baggage; cargo, lading.

7. *n.* assets, means, ways and means, resources, circumstances; stock, stock in trade, what one is worth, what one will cut up for [coll.]; wealth etc. 803; money etc. 800; income etc. (receipts) 810.

8. *adj.* propertied, landed, praedial, manorial, alodial, seignioral, seigneurial; freehold, copyhold, leasehold; feudal, feodal; hereditary, entailed; real, personal.

9. *adv.* to one's credit, to one's account, to the good; to his heirs, to one and his heirs for ever, to the heirs of his body, to his heirs and assigns, to his executors, ~ administrators and assigns; *suum cuique* [L.].

781. Retention
(See 782. Relinquishment)

1. *n.* retention, retainment, prehension [chiefly Zool.], keeping, keep [arch.], detention, custody; hold, grip, gripe, clutch, clutches, grasp, clasp; iron grip, firm hold; retentivity, prehensility; tenacity etc. 46.2; seizure etc. (taking) 789; possession etc. 777.

2. *n.* (gripping instruments) grip, clinch, clamp, clasp, holdfast, vise; pincers *or* pinchers, *pincette* [F.], nippers, tweezers, tongs, forceps, pliers; wrench, Stillson wrench, monkey wrench; clip, grapnel etc. (fastener) 45.2.

3. *n.* (prehensile organs) clutches, claws, talons, ungues (*sing.* unguis), ungulae (*sing.* ungula), pounces; nails, fingernails; manus (*sing.* manus), chelae (*sing.* chela), nippers, pincers; tentacles, tentacula (*sing.* tentaculum); fingers, digits, hooks [slang]; hand, fist, nieve *or* neif [arch. and dial.], paw, palm; fangs etc. (teeth) 253.3.

4. *v.* retain, keep, maintain, hold; grasp, gripe, grip, clutch, clinch, clench, clasp; hug, embrace; hold fast *or* tight, keep a firm hold upon, have a firm hold of, have an iron grip on; hold one's own,

hold one's ground; secure, withhold, detain, hold *or* keep back; keep close; entail, tie up; possess etc. 777.4.

5. *adj.* retentive, retaining etc. *v.*; tenacious, stick-to-itive [coll.]; prehensile, prehensive, prehensory, prehensorial.

6. *adj.* unforfeited, undeprived, undisposed, uncommunicated.

7. *adj.* incommunicable, inalienable; in mortmain; in strict settlement.

782. Relinquishment
(See 781. Retention)

1. *n.* relinquishment, renunciation, expropriation, dereliction, cession, surrender, release, dispensation, riddance; abandonment etc. (of a course) 624; resignation etc. 757; disuse etc. 678.

2. *n.* derelict, castoff, cast-by, castaway; jettison, jetsam, flotsam and jetsam; abandoned farm [U.S.]; waif, foundling.

3. *v.* relinquish, release, quit one's hold, let go, let slip, give up, surrender, yield, cede, spare, drop, resign, forgo, have done with, waive, yield, renounce, abandon, throw up, throw over *or* overboard, dismiss, expropriate, give away, part with, dispose of, wash one's hands of; maroon; discard, lay aside etc (disuse) 678.3, 4.

4. *adj.* relinquished, surrendered etc. *v.*; castoff, cast-by, castaway, derelict; unowned, disowned; unappropriated.

783. Transfer

1. *n.* transfer, transference, transferal [rare]; transmission, transmittal; conveyance, conveyancing; assignment, assignation; consignment, consignation; alienation, abalienation; demise, limitation; delivery, deliverance; enfeoffment; bargain and sale, lease and release; translocation etc. 270; exchange etc. (interchange) 148; barter etc. 794; substitution etc. 147.

2. *n.* succession, reversion; shifting use, shifting trust; devolution.

3. *v.* transfer, convey, transmit, assign, consign, make over, hand over, hand down, turn over, hand, pass, pass over, transmit, deliver, negotiate; alien, alienate, abalienate; enfeoff; confer,

---

781. Keep what you have got; the known evil is best.—PLAUTUS. Keep all you have and try for all you can.—BULWER-LYTTON. They should take who have the power, / And they should keep who can.—WORDSWORTH.

782. Forgo this vantage, Greek.—SHAKESPEARE. I only have relinquished one delight.—WORDSWORTH.

grant etc. (give) 784.8, 9; exchange etc. (interchange) 148.3; substitute etc. 147.3; translocate etc. 270.6-9.

4. *v.* change hands, change from one to another; devolve, succeed; come into possession etc. (acquire) 775.6.

5. *adj.* transferable, transmissive, alienable, negotiable, reversional; heritable, inheritable.

6. *adv.* by transfer etc. *n.*, on lease.

784. Giving

(See 785. Receiving, 789. Taking; also 790. Restitution)

1. *n.* giving, bestowal, bestowment; presentation, presentment; donation, accordance, consignment, dispensation, communication, dotation, endowment, investment; conferment, conferral; cession, concession; delivery, deliverance; donation party [dial., U.S.], shower.

2. *n.* charity, almsgiving; philanthropy etc. (benevolence) 906; liberality etc. 816.

3. *n.* gift, donation, donative, present, *cadeau* [F.], fairing, boon [arch.], grant, vouchsafement, offer [now rare], offering; gratuity, vail [arch.], largess, bounty, sportula, tip, fee, *douceur* [F.], *pourboire* [F.], *Trinkgeld* [G.], baksheesh [Near East], cumshaw, dash *or* dashee [Africa]; premium, bonus, boot [now dial.], lagniappe [Louisiana], pilon [Southwest. U.S.]; handsel; consideration, compensation; honorarium; alms, dole, handout [slang, U.S.]; alms fee, Peter *or* Peter's pence *or* penny; Christmas gift, Easter offering; peace offering; Indian gift [coll., U.S.]; white elephant [coll.]; offertory, collection; oblation etc. 990.6; reward etc. 973; bribe etc. 618.2.

4. *n.* grace, act of grace; benefit, benison [arch.], benefaction; blessing, kindness, act of kindness, boon, favor, service, turn, good turn, good *or* kind deed, labor of love; help, assistance etc. (aid) 707; kindness etc. 906.2.

---

784. It is more blessed to give than to receive.—BIBLE.   Give, and it shall be given unto you.—BIBLE.   *Res est ingeniosa dare* [To give is a thing that requires genius].—OVID.   One gift well given recovereth many losses.—FULLER.   Rich gifts wax poor when givers prove unkind.—SHAKESPEARE.   Apter to give than thou wilt be to ask.—BEAUMONT AND FLETCHER.   Behold I do not give lectures or a little char-

5. *n.* allowance, contribution, subscription, subsidy, subvention, tribute; pin money, pittance; alimony; pension, annuity, tontine.

6. *n.* bequest, legacy; devise, will, testament, last will and testament; dower, dowry, endowment, dot, dotation; thirds; appanage; amortization, amortizement; alimony; inheritance etc. 775.4.

7. *n.* giver, donor, donator, grantor, vouchsafer, presenter, bestower, conferrer, fairy godmother; almoner, almsgiver, almsman [rare]; testator, testatrix; settlor [Law]; feoffor; investor, subscriber, contributor; Indian giver [coll., U.S.]; philanthropist etc. 911; benefactor etc. 912.

8. *v.* give, present, donate [chiefly U.S.], dotate [rare], bestow, confer, grant, vouchsafe, allow, accord, award, tip [slang], slip [slang], let have; dispense, dispose of, give away, give out, deal *or* dole out, mete out; fork out, shell out [both slang]; make a present, give a gift etc. *n.*; contribute, chip in [coll.], kick in [slang, U.S.], subscribe; render, impart, communicate; offer etc. 763.2; pay etc. 807.6; bribe etc. 618.3; be benevolent etc. 906.5; reward etc. 973.3.

9. *v.* deliver, put into the hands of, hand, pass, hand over, deliver over, fork over [slang], pass over, turn over, make over, come across with [slang].

10. *v.* furnish, supply, provide, afford; provide for, make provision *or* due provision for; accommodate with, indulge with, favor with; shower down upon, lavish, pour on; thrust upon.

11. *v.* give up to, part with, yield; cede, concede; spare; sacrifice.

12. *v.* intrust *or* entrust, commit, consign, assign, confide, relegate; invest, vest in.

13. *v.* endow, dower, assign dower, settle upon, bequeath, bequest, leave, devise, will to; dot, dotate [both rare]; endow with, bless with.

14. *adj.* given, allowed etc. *v.*; allowable, concessional, communicable; dona-

---

ity, / When I give I give myself.—WHITMAN.   Freely ye have received; freely give.—BIBLE.   To him who gives is given.—MASEFIELD.   One must be poor to know the luxury of giving.—G. ELIOT.   'Tis Heaven alone that is given away, / 'Tis only God may be had for the asking.—LOWELL.   The gift without the giver is bare.—LOWELL.

tive, contributory, tributary; gratuitous etc. 815.10.

15. *adj.* charitable, philanthropic, almsgiving etc. (benevolent) 906.6–8; unselfish, magnanimous etc. 942.5, 6; generous etc. (liberal) 816.4.

16. *adv.* as a gift etc. *n.*, in charity, toward the endowment fund.

17. *adv.* don't mention it!, think no more of it!, forget it! [coll.], not another word!, glad to do it!, you are welcome!

785. Receiving
(See 784. Giving)

1. *n.* receiving etc. *v.*, receival, reception, recipience *or* recipiency, receipt, susception [rare], assumption, acceptance; admission, admittance; acquisition etc. 775.

2. *n.* recipient, receiver, accipient; donee, grantee, assignee, devisee; beneficiary, *bénéficiaire* [F.]; legatee, legatary; feoffee; lessee, relessee; stipendiary; almsman, almswoman; pensioner, pensionary; heir etc. 779.5.

3. *v.* receive, be in receipt of, get, obtain, gain, secure, come by, come in for, take in, take off one's hands; pocket, put into one's pocket; admit, accept; have coming in, have an income of, draw *or* derive from; have in prospect; acquire etc. 775.6; take etc. 789.7–9.

4. *v.* be received, come in, come to hand, pass *or* fall into one's hand, go into one's pocket, fall to one's share *or* lot, come *or* fall to one, accrue; yield etc. 810.4.

5. *adj.* receiving etc. *v.*, receptive, recipient; stipendiary, stipendarian; pensionary.

786. Apportionment

1. *n.* apportionment, portioning, sharing etc. *v.*; allotment, consignment, assignment, allocation, appointment, appropriation, dispensation, dispersion, distribution, division, deal, partition, repartition, administration.

2. *n.* portion, share, part, piece, cut [slang, U.S.], whack [slang], snip [old slang], snack, lot, allotment, allowance, end [coll.], divvy [slang], dividend, percentage, commission, rake-off [slang, U.S.], contingent, measure, dose, dole, meed, pittance, modicum, *quantum* [L.], ration, ratio [now rare], proportion, quota, mess; equal share, half, halver [coll.]; lion's share, Benjamin's mess, big end [slang].

3. *v.* apportion, portion, parcel, partition, divide, divvy *or* divvy up [slang], distribute, disperse, dispense, billet, allot, allocate, assign, appropriate, appoint, detail, administer, cast, share, mete, dole, deal, carve, whack up [coll.], split, split up, portion ~, dole etc. out; cut a melon [slang, U.S.]; divide with; come in for a share etc. (participate) 778.5.

4. *adj.* apportioned etc. *v.*, respective.

5. *adv.* respectively, each to each, by lot, in equal shares.

787. Lending
(See 788. Borrowing)

1. *n.* lending, loan, advance, accommodation; investment, sinking fund; Liberty Loan, War Loan; mortgage etc. (security) 771; credit etc. 805.

2. *n.* lender, loaner; moneylender, moneymonger, money broker, moneyer [obs.], banker; usurer, Shylock; lessor; mortgagee; pawnbroker, pawn [coll.], lumberer [slang], my uncle [slang]; financier etc. 797.6–8; creditor etc. 805.3.

3. *n.* pawnshop, pawnbrokery, pawn [coll.], hock shop [slang], spout [slang], *mont de piété* [F.], my uncle's [slang]; sign of the three balls.

4. *v.* lend, loan, advance, accommodate with, come across *or* down with the needful [slang]; give credit etc. 805.4.

5. *v.* invest, entrust *or* intrust, embark, place *or* put out to interest, place, put, risk, venture, sink, fund.

6. *v.* let, lease, grant a lease, demise,

---

785. We receive but what we give.—Coleridge.　To receive honestly is the best thanks for a good thing.—G. Macdonald.　It is better to deserve without receiving, than to receive without deserving.—Ingersoll.
786. Our portion is not large, indeed; / But then how little do we need.—N. Cotton.　I carry off the chief share because I am called the Lion!—Phaedrus.

787. A good man sheweth favour, and lendeth.—Bible.　Lend only what you can afford to lose.—G. Herbert.　Lend, and the chances are that you lose your friend if ever you get back your money.—Bulwer-Lytton.　God bless pawnbrokers! They are quiet men.—M. Wilkinson.

set [Scot., Law], hire, rent, rent etc. out; sublease, sublet, underlet, subrent.

7. *adj.* loaned etc. *v.*, lent, let.

8. *adv.* on loan, on security; in advance.

788. Borrowing
(See 787. Lending)

1. *n.* borrowing etc. *v.*, pledging, pawning, hocking [slang]; borrowed plumes; plagiarism etc. (theft) 791; debt etc. 806; borrower etc. (debtor) 806.4.

2. *v.* borrow, borrow the loan of [joc.], take up [coll.], get the needful [slang]; raise money, raise the wind [slang], fly a kite [slang]; borrow of Peter to pay Paul; pawn etc. (give security) 771.5; run into debt etc. 806.6; charge etc. 805.5; appropriate etc. 789.8.

3. *v.* hire, rent, lease, take a lease *or* demise, hire *or* take by the hour, ~ mile, ~ year etc.; sublease, subrent; purchase etc. 795.3.

789. Taking
(See 784. Giving)

1. *n.* taking, appropriating etc. *v.*, appropriation, impropriation, annexation [slang]; capture, caption; apprehension, prehension [chiefly Zool.], seizure; abduction, ablation; abstraction, ademption; androlepsia *or* androlepsy; acquisition etc. 775; theft etc. 791; reception etc. (taking in) 785; clutch, grip etc. (retention) 781.

2. *n.* dispossession, disseizin *or* disseisin [Law], bereavement, divestment; privation, deprivation, deprivement; distraint, distress; attachment, execution; sequestration, confiscation; disinheritance, disherison; disentitlement etc. 925.2; eviction etc. 297.2, 3; loss etc. 776.

3. *n.* resumption, reoccupation; reprises [Law], reprisal; recovery etc. 775.3.

4. *n.* rapacity, rapaciousness etc. *adj.*, predacity; extortion, bloodsucking, vampirism.

5. *n.* take, catch, capture, seizure, haul.

6. *n.* taker, captor, capturer; extortioner, extortionist, bloodsucker, vampire, harpy, vulture, bird of prey; dispossessor, disseizor *or* disseisor; usurper, arrogator; raptor [obs.], plunderer, ravisher, robber, despoiler.

7. *v.* take, receive etc. 785.3; take possession etc. (acquire) 775.6.

8. *v.* appropriate, impropriate [Eng., Eccl. Law], annex [slang], adopt, apply, assume, usurp, arrogate, possess oneself of, take possession of, obtain *or* take for oneself, arrogate to oneself, commandeer [coll.], help oneself to, make use of, make free with, dip one's hands into, lay under contribution; abstract; imitate; plagiarize, pirate, lift [coll.], cabbage, convey; steal etc. 791.9; borrow etc. 788.2.

9. *v.* seize, wrest, lay ~, take ~, catch *or* get hold of, lay *or* clap hands on [coll.], get one's fingers *or* hands on, get between one's finger and thumb, fasten upon, grapple, grip, gripe, grasp, clasp, grab, clutch, claw, clinch, clench; hug, embrace; prehend, apprehend; catch, capture, collar [coll.], hook, nab [slang], grab [coll.], nip, snatch, snag, snare, lay by the heels, take prisoner; bag, sack, pocket; snap up, nip up, whip up, catch up; pluck, pick, crop; lay fast hold of, take firm hold of *or* upon; take by assault *or* storm, reave [arch.], ravish, rape, lay violent hands on; take by the throat, throttle; intercept; levy, distrain, replevy; ensnare etc. 545.9; abduct etc. 791.11.

10. *v.* take away, carry off etc. (abduct) 791.11; deduct etc. 38.4; reduce etc. 36.4; curtail etc. 201.4.

11. *v.* dispossess, disseize *or* disseise [Law], take from *or* away from, deprive of, ease one of, snatch from one's grasp, deprive, bereave, divest, confiscate, attach, accroach, wrest, usurp, sequester, sequestrate; disinherit, cut out of one's will, cut off, cut off with a shilling, cut off without a cent; disown, unown; force from, tear from *or* away from, wrench ~, wrest *or* wring from, squeeze, sponge, ex-

---

788. Be not made a beggar by banqueting upon borrowing.—APOCRYPHA.   Neither a borrower nor a lender be.—SHAKESPEARE.   Borrowing is not much better than begging.—LESSING.   The borrower runs in his own debt.—EMERSON.   Let us all be happy, and live within our means, even if we have to borrow the money to do it.—A. WARD.   Who goes a borrowing, goes a sorrowing.   Money borrowed is soon sorrowed.
789. Let him take who take can.—RABELAIS.   Take, I give it willingly.—UHLAND.   Take the good the gods provide thee.—DRYDEN.   Let us take it as it comes.—GILBERT.   Give him an inch and he'll take an ell.

tort; disentitle etc. 925.7; evict, oust etc. (eject) 297.8–12.

12. *v.* strip, shear, fleece, skin [slang], displume, pluck, despoil, impoverish, eat out of house and home, drain to the dregs, gut, dry, exhaust, swallow up, absorb; suck dry, suck like a leach, suck the blood of, bleed [coll.].

13. *v.* catch at, jump at, make a grab at, snap at, snatch at; spring *or* pounce upon, swoop down upon; reach, stretch forth one's hand, make a long arm [coll.]; scramble for.

14. *v.* retake, resume, reoccupy etc. (recover) 775.9.

15. *adj.* taking, grasping, catching etc. *v.*; privative, deprivative; prehensile, prehensive, prehensory, prehensorial; predacious, predatory; wolfish, lupine, rapacious, raptorial; ravening, ravenous; parasitic; all-devouring, all-engulfing; thieving etc. 791.14.

16. *adj.* taken, dispossessed etc. *v.*; bereft etc. 776.6.

17. *adv.* at one swoop, at one fell swoop.

790. Restitution
(See 784. Giving)

1. *n.* restitution, return, reinstatement, reinvestment, recuperation; restoration, restoral [rare]; rendition, reddition; reparation, atonement; compensation, indemnification; rehabilitation etc. 660.

2. *n.* recovery, release, redemption; replevin, replevy; reversion; remitter; retrieval etc. 775.3.

3. *v.* restore, restitute [rare], make restitution etc. *n.*, return, give *or* bring back, give *or* render up, let go, release, unclutch; disgorge, regorge, regurgitate; remit, reimburse, recoup, compensate, indemnify; revest, reinvest; reinstate, reestate; replace, repair etc. 660.8–14.

4. *v.* recover, take back again, redeem, reclaim, retrieve, ransom; replevy, replevin; get back etc. 775.9.

5. *adj.* restitutive, restitutory; restoring etc. *v.*, restorative, restoratory [rare]; compensatory, indemnificatory; reversionary, redemptive, revertible; recuperative etc. 660.18.

6. *adv.* in restitution etc. *n.*, in full restitution; as partial compensation; to atone for.

791. Theft
(See also 792. Thief)

1. *n.* theft, stealing etc. *v.*, stealage, stealth [arch.], thievery, theftdom [Scot.], robbery, priggism [cant]; larceny, petit *or* petty larceny, grand larceny, simple larceny, mixed ~, compound *or* aggravated larceny; burglary, burgle [coll.], housebreaking, second-story work; safecracking, safebreaking, safeblowing; bank robbery; highway robbery, holdup [slang, U.S.], stick-up [slang]; pilfering, pilferage, pilfer; shoplifting.

chicken stealing; sneak thievery; abstraction; abaction, cattle stealing, cattle lifting [coll.]; pocket picking, pickpocketing, pickpocketry, pickpocketism; embezzlement, peculation; abduction, kidnaping; plagiary [rare], plagiarism, autoplagiarism; appropriation etc. (taking) 789; dishonesty etc. (improbity) 940.

2. *n.* pillage, spoliation, direption [Hist.], plunder, sack, sackage [rare], rapine, depredation, brigandage, latrocinium [Rom. Hist.]; rape, ravishment; raid, foray, razzia; filibustering, filibusterism; piracy, piratism [rare], piratery [rare], privateering, buccaneering.

3. *n.* extortion, squeezing etc. *v.*, shakedown [slang]; blackmail, badger game [cant]; Black Hand [U.S.], Camorra [It.].

4. *n.* a theft, steal, grab, filch, take, haul; annexation, pinch, lift, shakedown [all slang]; job, clout [both cant, U.S.]; pilfer, burglary etc. *above* 791.1.

5. *n.* swindle, fraud, cheat, ramp [slang, Eng.], gyp [slang], confidence game etc. (deception) 545.1, 3.

6. *n.* thievishness etc. *adj.*, furacity [rare], rapacity, predacity; kleptomania.

7. *n.* license to plunder, letter of marque.

8. *n.* den of thieves, den of Cacus; Alsatia, Whitefriars.

9. *v.* steal, thieve, rob, commit robbery etc. *n.*, purloin, take, borrow [joc.], lurch [arch.], manavel *or* manarvel [Naut. slang], snatch, snaffle [chiefly dial.,

---

790. Oh, bring back my Bonnie to me.—ANON. Each loss has its compensation.—H. BUTTERWORTH.

791. If from my thousand pecks you steal but one, / My loss is small, but you're by sin undone.—HORACE. Flat burglary as ever was

Eng.], palm, bag, cabbage, make off with etc. *below* 791.11, disregard the distinction between *meum* and *tuum;* crib, lift, hook [all coll.]; prig, nip [both cant]; cop, annex, snitch, ramp [Eng.], swipe [U.S.], pinch, mooch, nick, snare [all slang]; pilfer, filch; abstract; burglarize [coll.], burgle [coll.], commit burglary; pickpocket, pick one's pockets; hold up [coll.], stick up [slang], bail up [slang, Austral.]; highjack *or* hijack [slang, U.S.].

poach; pirate, plagiarize, convey; smuggle, run; peculate, embezzle; rob Peter to pay Paul; set a thief to catch a thief; appropriate etc. 789.8.

10. *v.* plunder, pillage, rifle, sack, ransack, loot, spoil, spoliate, despoil, deprecate, strip, fleece, sweep, gut, forage, maraud, filibuster; pirate, buccaneer, privateer.

11. *v.* abduct, carry *or* convey away, take ∼, carry *or* bear off, make *or* run off *or* away with, hurry off with, take away, spirit away; kidnap, crimp, shanghai; impress, press [rare]; seize etc. 789.9.

12. *v.* swindle, defraud, practice fraud upon, cheat, cozen, victimize, trepan *or* trapan, bite [chiefly coll.], gull, cully [obs.], mulct, bilk, bubble [arch.], jockey, pluck [now slang], fleece, shave, nick [slang and dial.], rook [coll. or slang], gudgeon, lurch [arch.], flam, flimflam, diddle [dial. and slang]; do, chouse, bamboozle, gouge, daddle [all coll.]; gyp [U.S.], ramp [Eng.], nab, pigeon, bucket [all slang]; bamboozle [coll.], flimflam etc. out of, beguile of *or* out of, obtain under false pretenses, live by one's wits; bunko, play a bunko game etc. 545.3, sell gold bricks [coll., U.S.]; thimblerig; cheat at cards, play with marked cards; cog a die, cog the dice; deceive etc. 545.7–10; not pay etc. 808.5.

13. *v.* extort, sponge, screw, squeeze, wring from, shake down [slang]; blackmail, levy blackmail, badger [cant].

14. *adj.* thieving etc. *v.,* thievish, thefterous [rare]; larcenous, larcenish, larcenic [rare]; stealy, priggish [cant], furtive [rare], furacious [rare], light-fingered, sticky-fingered [joc.]; looting, committed.—SHAKESPEARE. How great his theft who robs himself.—N. COTTON. What a liberal confounding of those pedantic distinctins of *meum* and *tuum!*—LAMB.

plundering, spoliative; piratic(al), piraty, piratelike; predaceous, predatory, raptorial, rapacious etc. (taking) 789.15; dishonest etc. 940.8.

792. Thief
(See also 791. Theft)

1. *n.* thief, robber, stealer, purloiner, *homo trium literarum* (Plautus), *chor* [Gypsy]; lifter, prig, prigger, crook, gun [all slang]; larcenist, larcener; pilferer, rifler, filcher; spoiler, depredator, pillager, plunderer, marauder; harpy, falcon, hawk; land pirate, land rat; plagiarist, pirate, literary pirate; poacher; sneak thief, prowler; shoplifter; chicken thief; cattle thief, abactor, abigeus, duffer [slang, Austral.], rustler [slang, U.S.]; smuggler, contrabandist.

2. *n.* burglar, yegg *or* yeggman [slang], cracksman [slang], housebreaker, second-story thief *or* worker; safecracker, safeblower, safebreaker, peteman *or* peterman [slang, U.S.]; bank robber.

3. *n.* brigand, bandit, freebooter, dacoit [Ind.], rover, ranger, picaroon, filibuster, rapparee [Ir.]; bushranger, mosstrooper [Hist.], Bedouin; thug, desperado, hoodlum [coll.], hood [slang, U.S.], highbinder [slang], gorilla [slang, U.S.], strongarm man [U.S.], sandbagger; wrecker.

4. *n.* highwayman, highway robber, hightoby [slang, Eng.], footpad, knight of the road; holdup, holdup man [both slang, U.S.]; stick-up, sticker-up, stick-up man [all slang]; highjacker *or* hijacker, [slang, U.S.].

5. *n.* pirate, corsair, viking, sea king, buccaneer, privateer; Paul Jones, Captain Kidd, Long John Silver.

6. *n.* pickpocket, pickpurse [rare], cutpurse; fingersmith, dip, ganef, file, wire [all slang]; purse snatcher; swell mob,

792. Always set a thief to catch a thief.—FULLER. A plague upon it when thieves cannot be true one to another!—SHAKESPEARE. Thieves are never rogues among themselves.—CERVANTES. He that is once a thief is ever more in danger.—LANGLAND. Hang a thief when he is young and he'll no steal when he is old.—J. RAY. One thief knoweth another.—T. DRAXE. The thief steals from himself.—EMERSON. There is honour among thieves.—SCOTT. Thieves respect property. They merely wish the property to become their property.—CHESTERTON.

swellmobsmen [both slang]; light-fingered gentry.

7. *n.* abductor, kidnaper; shanghaier; crimp, crimper.

8. *n.* swindler, sharper, shark, spieler [coll., U.S. and Australasia], cozener, diddler [coll. or slang], jockey, Greek, *chevalier d'industrie* [F.], bunkoman; defrauder, fraud [coll.]; cheat, cheater; gypper, gypster [both slang, U.S.]; humbug, humbugger; sharp, magsman, skin, rook, gull [all slang]; bilker, flimflammer, bamboozler, gammoner [all coll.]; blackleg [coll.], jackleg [slang, U.S.], leg [slang, Eng.]; tricker, trickster; thimblerigger.

ringer, coin ringer [both slang]; money clipper; cardsharp, cardsharper; confidence man, con man [slang]; land shark, land pirate; mortgage shark; badger, badger worker [both cant]; horse trader, horse coper [Eng.]; carpetbagger [slang, U.S.]; peculator, embezzler; defaulter, welsher [slang]; Artful Dodger, Jeremy Diddler; counterfeiter etc. (coiner) 800.18.

9. *n.* fence, receiver of stolen goods; swagman *or* swagsman, smasher, lock [all slang].

10. *n.* (famous thieves) Bill Sikes, Jack Sheppard, Dick Turpin, Claude Duval, Jonathan Wild, Macheath, Nevison, Autolycus, Robert Macaire, Thief of Bagdad, Robin Hood, Jesse James.

793. Booty

1. *n.* booty, spoil *or* spoils, plunder, prize, loot, swag [slang], pillage, seizure, haul, take, grab, pickings, prey, stolen goods, steal, stealings, stealage, lift [slang], filch; perquisite, boodle [Polit., cant], graft [coll.], pork barrel [Polit., cant, U.S.]; blackmail; *spolia opima* [L.]; gain etc. 775.2.

2. *adj.* looting etc. (thieving) 791.14.

794. Barter
(See also 148. Interchange)

1. *n.* barter, bartering, trading etc. *v.*; exchange, traffic, truck, trade, commerce;

---

793. A case of Booty and the Beast.—D. MARQUIS.   To protect the booty when it is too late.—PLAUTUS.   To the victor belong the spoils.
794. It is easy to escape from business, if you will only despise the rewards of business.—

god of commerce, Mercury; intercourse, dealing *or* dealings, business, business intercourse, merchantry, mercantile business, buying and selling; bargain and sale, lease and release; mercantilism, commercialism; custom; commutation; composition; free trade; truck system; transfer etc. 783; *quid pro quo* [L.], a Roland for an Oliver etc. (interchange) 148; reciprocation etc. 12.2; sale etc. 796.

2. *n.* speculation, speculative buying and selling, agiotage, jobbing, stockjobbing, stockbroking, brokery, brokerage.

3. *n.* transaction, business transaction, negotiation, engagement, bargain, deal [coll.], dicker [chiefly coll., U.S.]; trade, swap [coll.], switch; blind bargain *or* swap [coll.], pig in a poke *or* bag; agreement etc. (compact) 769.

4. *v.* barter, traffic, deal, truck, buy and sell, give and take, trade, exchange, change, give in exchange, swap [coll. and dial.], swap horses [coll.], switch; trade sight-unseen *or* unsight-unseen, make a blind bargain *or* swap [all coll.]; interchange etc. 148.3; sell etc. 796.5.

5. *v.* bargain, drive a bargain, negotiate, bid for, dicker [chiefly coll., U.S.], haggle, higgle, chaffer, huckster, stickle, cheapen, beat down; underbid, outbid; ask, charge.

6. *v.* strike a bargain, make a bargain, make a dicker [chiefly coll., U.S.], put through a deal; come to terms etc. (come to an agreement) 488.8.

7. *v.* drive a trade, carry on *or* ply a trade, carry on a business, traffic as a business, be in business, be in the city, keep a shop; deal in, employ one's capital in.

8. *v.* trade with, deal with, have dealings with, have truck with, do *or* transact business with, frequent as a customer, patronize [coll.]; open an account with, have *or* keep an account with.

9. *v.* speculate, give *or* bait with a sprat to catch a herring *or* mackerel; buy low

---

SENECA.   A business with an income at its heels.—COWPER.   Traffic's thy god; and thy god confound thee!—SHAKESPEARE.   Trade which, like blood, should circularly flow.—DRYDEN.   The craft of the merchant is this bringing a thing from where it abounds, to where it is costly.—EMERSON.   Commerce is the great civilizer. We exchange ideas when we exchange fabrics.—INGERSOLL.   The propensity to truck, barter, and exchange one thing for another . . . is common to all men.—A. SMITH.

and sell high, buy in the cheapest and sell in the dearest market; stag the market [London Stock Exchange], rig the market [Exchange cant].

10. *adj.* commercial, trading etc. *v.*; mercantile, mercatorial [rare]; wholesale, retail; exchangeable, interchangeable; marketable etc. (salable) 796.7.

11. *adv.* on the market etc. (for sale) 796.9.

795. Purchase
(See 796. Sale)

1. *n.* purchase, buying, purchasing etc. *v.*; buy; emption, *emptio* [L., Law]; preemption, refusal, right of emption *or* sole emption, prior right of purchase, preemption right, right of pre-emption; coemption; repurchase; slave trade; bribery etc. 618; bargain etc. 815.2; acquisition etc. 775; expenditure etc. 809.

2. *n.* buyer, purchaser, emptor [Law], vendee; shopper, marketer; windowshopper; client, customer; patron, patronizer [both coll.]; coemptor, coemptionator; by-bidder, capper [slang], Peter Funk [U.S.]; clientele, clientry, clientage, patronage [coll.], custom; merchant etc. 797.

3. *v.* purchase, buy, procure, make *or* complete a purchase, make a buy, blow oneself to [slang]; buy up, take up [coll.]; invest in, put one's money in; buy in, buy into, buy off, buy out; repurchase, buy back *or* again; regrate [obs. exc. Hist.]; pay for etc. 807.6; rent etc. (hire) 788.3; spend etc. 809.3; bribe etc. 618.3.

4. *v.* shop, market, go shopping *or* a-shopping; window-shop.

5. *adj.* purchasing, buying etc. *v.*; emptional, emptorial; coemptional, coemptive; cliental.

796. Sale
(See 795. Purchase)

1. *n.* sale, selling etc. *v.*, vent [rare], vend [Eng.], disposal; closing-out sale, sellout [slang]; fire sale; wholesale, retail; market, demand; agreement of sale; salesmanship; custom etc. (barter) 794; salesman etc. (merchant) 797.

2. *n.* auction, auction sale, roup [Scot. and North. Eng.], vendue, public sale, subhastation [rare], cant [chiefly Ir.], outcry, sale by outcry, sale at *or* by auction, sale to the highest bidder; Dutch auction; bid, bidding; straw bid [coll., U.S.]; by-bid, cap [slang]; by-bidding, capping [slang]; auction stand, block, sale block; auctioneer etc. 797.5; by-bidder etc. (buyer) 795.2.

3. *n.* sales talk, spiel [slang, U.S.], ballyhoo [slang]; sales resistance.

4. *n.* salableness etc. *adj.*, salability, marketability, vendibility.

5. *v.* sell, vend, hawk, peddle, dispense; offer for sale, put up for sale; market, bring to market; make *or* effect a sale, turn into money, realize, dispose of, sell off; sell out, sell up; regrate, retail, sell *or* dispense by retail; wholesale, sell *or* dispense by wholesale; dump, unload, place; sell over the counter; sell forward, sell for future delivery; undersell; trade, bargain, deal in etc. (barter) 794.4–6.

6. *v.* auction, auction off, auctioneer, sell at auction [esp. U.S.], sell by auction [esp. Eng.], put up to *or* at auction, put on the block, sell at the spear, roup [Scot. and North. Eng.], cant [chiefly Ir.], outcry, bring to *or* under the hammer, knock down, assign to a bidder, sell to the highest bidder; bid, make a bid, offer; by-bid, cap [slang].

7. *adj.* salable, marketable, vendible, **merchantable, staple; in** demand, **popular**.

8. *adj.* unsalable, unmarketable etc.; on the shelves, shelved, on one's hands, unbought, unsold.

9. *adv.* for sale, to sell, in *or* on the market, in the marts of trade, in the way of trade; on 'change; over *or* across the counter; at *or* by auction, at the spear, on the block, under the hammer; at a bargain, marked down.

797. Merchant

1. *n.* merchant, trader, trafficker, dealer, chapman [arch.], monger, chandler;

---

795. Buy not what you want, but what you need.—CATO.   The timely buyer / Hath cheaper his fire.—T. TUSSER.   'Tis pleasant purchasing our fellow creatures; / And all are to be sold.—BYRON.   *Caveat emptor* [Let the buyer look out for himself].
796. Go and sell that thou hast.—BIBLE.   Everyone lives by selling something.—STEVEN-SON.   The time to sell is when you have a customer.—SANDBURG.
797. A merchant of great traffic through this world.—SHAKESPEARE.   The merchant has

tradesman, tradesperson [rare], tradeswoman; businessman, businesswoman; shopman, shopkeeper, storekeeper; tallyman, tallywoman; roupingwife [Scot.]; retail merchant, retailer, regrater; wholesale merchant, wholesaler; buyer etc. 795.2; caterer, purveyor etc. (provider) 637.2.

2. *n.* seller, salesman, salesperson, salesclerk; saleswoman, saleslady; clerk, counterjumper [coll.]; agent, selling agent, sales agent, *institor* [L.]; traveling salesman, traveler, commercial traveler, traveling agent, traveling man *or* woman, *commis-voyageur* [F.], bagman, drummer [U.S.], runner [coll.], solicitor etc. below 797.4; bookseller, book salesman, ~ agent, ~ canvasser *or* solicitor; sales manager; salespeople, sales force.

3. *n.* vendor *or* vender, peddler *or* pedlar, huckster, hawker, higgler, colporteur, monger, chapman [Eng.], cadger; cheap-Jack, cheap-John [both coll.]; camelot [F.], faker [slang], sutler, *vivandier* [F.] (*fem. vivandière*); costerman, costermonger [both chiefly Eng.].

4. *n.* solicitor *or* soliciter, canvasser, runner [U.S.], tout [slang], touter [coll.]; barker [coll.], spieler [slang, U.S.]; ballyhooer, ballyhoo man [both slang].

5. *n.* auctioneer, rouper [Scot. and North. Eng.], Peter Duff [slang, U.S.].

6. *n.* financier, moneyer [rare], capitalist, investor; banker; moneylender etc. 787.2.

7. *n.* broker, stockbroker, exchange broker, mortgage broker, insurance broker, cotton broker, bill broker, hotel broker; money broker, money changer, changer [arch.]; cambist; agent etc. (deputy) 759; pawnbroker etc. (lender) 787.2.

8. *n.* jobber, stockjobber; bear, bull [both Stock Exchange].

9. *n.* merchantry, tradesmen, tradesfolk, tradespeople.

10. *n.* firm, house, corporation etc. (company) 712.5.

11. *n.* provision merchant, grocer, groceryman, greengrocer, butcher, fishmonger, fishwife; jeweler; confectioner; florist; druggist, chemist etc. (pharmacist) 662.21; bookdealer etc. (bookman) 593.14; perfumer etc. 400.6; tobacconist etc. 392a.12; haberdasher etc. 225.39; wine merchant etc. (liquor dealer) 959.12.

798. Merchandise

1. *n.* merchandise, commodities, wares, good, effects, vendibles, articles, articles of merchandise, goods for sale, stock, produce; staple commodities; supplies, stock in trade etc. (stores) 636.1, 2; cargo etc. (contents) 190.

2. *n.* merchandising, marketing, retailing etc. (*see* market, retail etc. 796.5).

3. *n.* dry goods, soft goods [Eng. and Austral.], white goods; sheet etc. (coverlet) 223.9; towel etc. (cleaning devices) 652.7; hardware, household goods, housewares, kitchen goods, kitchenware; china etc. (ceramics) 384.14; glassware, dishes; plate etc. 191.12; silverware etc. (tableware) 191.13; cutlery; linens, furniture, furnishings; toilet goods, toilet articles, toiletries, cosmetics; orthopedic supplies; drugs etc. 662.2–14; men's and boys' clothing, men's wear, men's furnishings, haberdashery, girls' and women's clothing, ladies' fashions, children's wear, infants' wear; furs; headwear, millinery; neckwear; lingerie, underwear, hosiery, nightwear; footwear, shoes.

clothing, wearing apparel etc. (investment) 225; yard goods; material, fabric etc. 219.5; notions; sportswear, sporting goods; toy etc. 840.16; costume jewelry; jewelry etc. 847.7; leather goods; portmanteau etc. (handbag) 191.5; stationery; book etc. 593.1–5; flowers; groceries, food etc. 298.5, 6, 11–15; candy etc. (sweets) 396.2; liquor etc. 959.4–7; tobacco etc. 392a.1–8; optical instruments etc. 445; photographic goods *or* instruments; camera etc. 445.5, 6; radio goods *or* instruments; receiver, transmitter etc. 532a.5; electrical goods *or* appliances; electrical instruments etc. 158.6, 7; refrigerator etc. 387; stove etc. 386.

---

no country.—JEFFERSON. Merchant and pirate were for a long period one and the same person. Even today mercantile morality is really nothing but a refinement of piratical morality.—NIETZSCHE.

798. *Proba mers facile emptorem reperit* [Good merchandise finds a ready buyer].—PLAUTUS. Ill ware is never cheap. Pleasing ware is half sold.—G. HERBERT. To things of sale a seller's praise belongs.—SHAKESPEARE.

799. Mart

1. *n.* mart, market, market place, place of trade, gunge [Ind.], cheap [arch.], rialto, *boutique* [F.], store, shop, *magasin* [F.], emporium, staple, *entrepôt* [F.], wareroom, warehouse [chiefly Eng.], establishment; bazaar, fair, exposition; open market, market overt; general store, department store, mail-order house, chain store; stall, booth; shopboard, counter; countinghouse; office etc. (workshop) 691.

2. *n.* hall, guildhall, market hall, tolbooth [chiefly Scot.], tollhouse [now local, Eng.], town hall.

3. *n.* exchange, stock exchange, 'change, bourse, Bourse, the street [cant], Wall Street [U.S.], Lombard Street [Eng.], curb, curb market; pit, provision pit, wheat pit [all U.S.].

4. *n.* grocery, grocery shop *or* store [U.S.], provision shop *or* store, groceteria [cant], dairy, greengrocery, vegetable store *or* market, meat shop *or* market, butcher shop, fish store, delicatessen, bakery, bakeshop; tobacco store, cigar store; candy store, confectionery; drugstore, chemist's shop [Eng.]; antique shop *or* store, second-hand shop *or* store; finding store [U.S.], grindery warehouse [Eng.], sutler's shop, sutlery, sutlerage [rare]; canteen, Post Exchange [U.S.], P.X. [slang]; horse market, Tattersall's; bookstore etc. 593.12; hardware etc. shop *or* store (*see* hardware etc. 798.3).

800. Money

1. *n.* money, legal tender, medium of exchange, circulating medium, currency, cash, money in hand, ready money, money of account; coinage, mintage, coin of the realm, sterling [Eng.], dollars, almighty dollar, wherewithal *or* wherewith, lucre, filthy lucre [coll.], pelf, muck [derog.], root of all evil, mammon; fractional currency, postal currency; finance, money matters.

(slang terms) the actual, the needful, kale, rhino, brass, blunt, dust, sugar, salt, mopus, tin, chink, dough, jack, gingerbread, oof, ooftish, spondulics *or* spondulix, ballast, boodle, bunce, gilt, corn, corn in Egypt, *dinero* [Sp.], gelt [joc.], mazuma, pony, possibles, remedy, salve, grease, ointment, oil of palms, moss, rocks, dibs, simoleons, shekels, berries, bones, bucks, iron men, bullets, horse nails, plunks, clinkers, beans, chips, wampum, shinplasters.

2. *n.* funds, moneys, finances, exchequer, purse, budget, pocket, treasure, substance, assets, resources, pecuniary resources, commands, command of money, means, ways and means, stock, capital; principal, corpus (*pl.* corpora); bottom dollar [coll.]; supplies, reserves etc. (fund) 636.2; riches etc. (wealth) 803.1; income, revenue etc. (receipt) 810.1.

3. *n.* wampum, wampumpeag, peag, sewan, roanoke, cowrie, amole.

4. *n.* specie, hard money, hard cash, coin, piece; chip, chinker, clinker, jingler, banger, shiner, brad, button, holy stone, mint drop, nail, rock [all slang]; roll of coins, rouleau.

5. *n.* gold piece, slug [Hist.], yellow boy [slang, Eng.]; gold money, ochre [slang, Eng.], gilt [now chiefly slang]; ten-dollar gold piece, ned [slang], eagle [all U.S.]; five-dollar gold piece, half ned [slang], half eagle [all U.S.]; twenty-dollar gold piece, double eagle [both U.S.]; twenty-franc gold piece, napoleon [F.]; guinea, sovereign, pound sovereign, crown, half crown [all Eng.]; ducat, louis d'or, moidore, mohur.

6. *n.* paper money, note, legal-tender note, bank note, bill; Federal reserve note, national-bank note; long green, folding money, mint leaves, lettuce, rags [all slang]; greenback [U.S.], frogskin [slang, U.S.]; gold certificate, yellow boy [slang]; blueback [U.S.], shinplaster [slang, U.S.]; *assignat* [F.].

7. *n.* negotiable instrument *or* paper, commercial paper, paper; bill of exchange, hundi [Ind.], bill, note, certificate, voucher, warrant, debenture, order, draft *or* draught; check, cheque

---

799. The market is a place set apart where men may deceive each other.—ANACHARSIS. The market is the best garden.—G. HERBERT. Keep thy shop, and thy shop will keep thee.—G. CHAPMAN.
800. Money brings honor, friends, conquest, and realms.—MILTON. Money never cometh out of season.—T. DRAXE. Money begets money.—J. RAY. If money go before, all ways do lie open.—SHAKESPEARE. Beauty is potent, but money is omnipotent.—J. RAY. Money makes the man.—BECON. *Nervi belli pecuniam infinitam* [Plenty of money is the sinews

[Eng.]; exchequer bill, treasury bill [both Eng.]; bond, debenture bond; stocks and bonds, stocks, bonds; government bond, Liberty bond, Defense bond, War bond, Defense stamp; money order, postal order, post-office order; Federal reserve bank note; note of hand, promissory note, I O U; due bill; scrip, coupon, token, slug, counter, chip, dib; credit instrument etc. 805.2.

8. *n.* (denominations) mill, cent, ¢, penny [coll.], copper, red cent [coll.], five cents, nickel [coll.], jitney [slang], ten cents, dime, bit [dial.], short bit [dial.], long bit [dial.], twenty-five cents, quarter, two bits [coll.], fifty cents, half dollar, four bits [coll.], dollar, $; buck, boffo, bean, berry, bone, smacker, iron man, cart wheel [all slang, U.S.]; dollar bill, silver dollar, two-dollar ~, five-dollar ~, ten-dollar ~, twenty-dollar etc. bill.

farthing, halfpenny, mag *or* meg [slang, Eng.], penny, d., copper, twopence, threepence, threepenny bit, fourpence, groat, sixpence, teston, shilling, s., bob [slang, Eng.], florin, half crown, crown, ten shilling note, ten bob note [slang, Eng.], pound, £, quid [slang, Eng.], pound ~, five-pound ~, ten-pound etc. note, guinea.

anna, rupee (India), belga (Belgium), cent (China, Netherlands etc.), centavo (Portugal, Argentina etc.), escudo (Portugal), peso (Argentina, Mexico etc.), centesimo, soldo, lira (Italy), centime, franc (France, Belgium, Switzerland), sou (France), dinar (Iraq etc.), dollar (China, Mexico etc.), drachma (Greece), stiver, gulden (Netherlands), kopeck, ruble (Russia), krone (Denmark, Norway), mark, reichsmark, pfennig (Germany), milreis, reis (Brazil), centimo, peseta (Spain), sen, yen (Japan).

doit, duit, mite, rap, farthing etc. (trifle) 643.3.

9. *n.* counterfeit, counterfeit money, false *or* bad money, queer [slang], bogus, bogus money *or* certificate, snide [slang], base coin, flash note; forgery, forged *or* fictitious check, bad check, rubber check [slang]; kite [slang]; fancy stocks.

10. *n.* sum, amount; aggregate, sum total; round *or* lump sum; balance, balance sheet; proceeds etc. (receipts) 810.

11. *n.* large sum, good sum, mint, pot [coll. and slang], great wealth, thousands, millions, cool million, ~ hundred etc.; tidy sum, money to burn, power ~, mint ~, barrel *or* raft of money [all coll.]; barrel, pile, wad [all slang].

12. *n.* bank roll, package of money; roll, wad [both slang, U.S.].

13. *n.* ready money, the ready [coll.], cash, *argent comptant* [F.], money in hand.

14. *n.* petty cash, pocket money, pin money, spending money, change, small change, small coins.

15. *n.* precious metals; gold, ochre [slang, Eng.], gilt [now chiefly slang], ridge [old slang]; nugget, gold nugget, slug; bullion, ingot, bar; silver; coin gold *or* silver, bronze, copper, nickel, aluminum.

16. *n.* (science of coins) numismatics, numismatology, chrysology.

17. *n.* solvency, responsibility, reliability, solidity, soundness etc. *adj.*

18. *n.* coiner, coin stamper, minter, mintman, moneyer; counterfeiter, forger, smasher [slang], duffer [slang, Eng.].

19. *v.* monetize, issue, utter, circulate; fiscalize [rare]; remonetize, reissue; demonetize.

20. *v.* coin, mint; counterfeit, forge, circulate bad money, shove the queer [slang].

21. *adj.* monetary, pecuniary, crumenal [obs.], fiscal, financial, sumptuary, numismatic(al); sterling; nummary; nummiform, coin-shaped.

22. *adj.* solvent, sound, substantial, good, reliable, responsible, solid, with a good rating; able to pay, able to pay 20 shillings to the pound [Eng.] *or* 100 cents to the dollar [U.S.]; unindebted etc. 807.10.

801. Treasurer
(See also 802. Treasury)

n. treasurer, bursar, purser, purse bearer, cashkeeper, banker, depositary, quaestor [Hist.], steward, trustee; receiver, liquidator; accountant, expert accountant, Accountant General; paymaster,

---

of war].—CICERO.   Money is like manure—good only when spread around.—SANDBURG.   Solvency is entirely a matter of temperament and not of income.—L. P. SMITH.   This bank-note world.—HALLECK.   *Argent fait le jeu* [Money talks].

801. Be it better or be it worse, / Please you the man that bears the purse.—DELONEY.

cashier, teller; almoner; cambist; Chancellor of the Exchequer, Secretary of the Treasury, Minister of Finance.

802. Treasury
(See also 801. Treasurer)

1. *n.* treasury, treasure house, bank, exchequer, fisc, *fiscus* [L.], hanaper, cutcherry [Ind.], bursary, hold, stronghold, strongbox, strong room, coffer, locker, safe, chest, cupboard, crypt, vault, safe-deposit *or* safety-deposit box *or* vault, moneybox, cash box, cash register; till, tiller; almonry; depository etc. (storehouse) 636.4, 5.

2. *n.* purse, wallet, pocketbook, portemonnaie, pouch [arch.], scrip [arch.], poke [dial. and thieves' slang]; skin, leather, poge, kick [all thieves' slang]; bag, handbag, moneybag, purse strings; pocket.

803. Wealth
(See 804. Poverty)

1. *n.* wealth, riches, moneybags [coll.], fortune, handsome fortune, opulence *or* opulency, affluence, independence; *embarras de richesses* [F.]; long purse, full purse, well-lined purse, heavy purse, purse of Fortunatus; loaves and fishes, fleshpots of Egypt; mine of wealth, bonanza, El Dorado, Pactolus, Golconda, Potosi, philosophers' stone; the golden touch; mint of money [coll.] etc. (large sum) 800.11; great abundance etc. (plenty) 639.2; prosperity etc. 734; capital, means etc. (funds) 800.2; assets etc. 780.7; property etc. 780; lucre, pelf etc. (money) 800.1.

2. *n.* rich man, wealthy man, moneyed man, warm man [old slang], man of wealth, ~ means *or* substance, have [coll.], richling, moneybags [coll.], jack-full-of-money [slang], nabob, tippybob [slang], capitalist, plutocrat; millionaire, billionaire; Croesus, Midas, Plutus, Dives, Timon of Athens, Danaë; butter-and-egg man, butter-and-egger [both slang, U.S.]; timocracy, plutocracy.

3. *n.* parvenu, *nouveau riche* [F.] etc. (upstart) 876.8.

4. *v.* be rich etc. *adj.,* have wealth etc. *n.,* have money to burn [coll.], roll *or* wallow in wealth *or* riches; worship Mammon, worship the golden calf.

5. *v.* afford, well afford; command money *or* a sum; make both ends meet, hold one's head above water.

6. *v.* become rich etc. *adj.,* fill one's pockets, feather one's nest, make *or* coin money, make a fortune, make one's pile [slang], strike it rich, come into money; have the golden touch.

7. *v.* enrich, richen, imburse [rare].

8. *adj.* wealthy, rich, warm [old slang], pecunious, affluent, opulent, moneyed, worth a great deal, well-to-do, well to do in the world, well-to-live [arch.], well off, set up [coll.], in funds *or* cash, in the money [coll. or slang], provided for, well provided for, with a power of money etc. (large sum) 800.11, rolling *or* wallowing in wealth *or* riches, made of money, rich as Croesus, flush, flush with *or* of money, fat, abounding in riches, in full feather; oofy, tinny, well-heeled, lousy-rich, filthy-rich [all slang]; prosperous etc. 734.7.

804. Poverty
(See 803. Wealth)

1. *n.* poverty, impecuniosity, indigence, penury, pauperism, destitution, want, need, neediness etc. *adj.,* lack, necessity, privation, distress, difficulties, straits, bad ~, poor ~, needy ~, embarrassed ~, reduced *or* straitened circumstances, slender *or* narrow means, hand-to-mouth existence, *res angusta domi* [L.], low water [slang, U.S.], light purse, empty

---

802. Light purse, heavy heart.—FRANKLIN. The purse of the people is the real seat of sensibility.—JEFFERSON. Who steals my purse steals trash.—SHAKESPEARE. Mind your till and till your mind.—C. H. SPURGEON.
803. He has not acquired a fortune; the fortune has acquired him.—BION. *Dummodo sit dives Barbarus ipse placet* [So long as he is rich even a barbarian is attractive].—OVID. He heapeth up riches, and knoweth not who shall gather them.—BIBLE. He that maketh haste to be rich shall not be innocent.—BIBLE. No man's fortune can be an end and worthy of his being.—BACON. Knowledge makes one laugh, but wealth makes one dance.—G. HERBERT. Excess of wealth is cause of covetousness.—MARLOWE. It is better to live rich than to die rich.—JOHNSON. It is plain madness to live in want that you may die rich.—JUVENAL. The man who dies rich dies disgraced.—CARNEGIE. He was born with a silver spoon in his mouth.
804. Poverty is the parent of revolution and crime.—ARISTOTLE. Blessed be ye poor: for

purse *or* pocket, "a beggarly account of empty boxes" (Shakespeare), broken fortune, loss of fortune, Queer Street, wolf at the door; bankruptcy etc. 808.2.

2. *n.* mendicity, mendicancy, mendication [rare], beggary.

3. *n.* poor man, poorling, have-not [coll.], pauper, starveling, *pauvre diable* [F.], down-and-out, down-and-outer; the poor; bankrupt etc. 808.4; beggar etc. 767.2.

4. *v.* be poor etc. *adj.*, have little *or* nothing, want, lack, starve, live from hand to mouth, live on Queer Street, have seen better days, find it hard going, *tirer le diable par la queue* [F.], not have a penny etc. (*see* penny, sou etc. 800.8), not have a shot in the locker; run into debt etc. 806.6.

5. *v.* become poor etc. *adj.*, go down in the world, go to the dogs, go to rack and ruin; go on the parish, go to the poorhouse *or* almshouse.

6. *v.* render poor etc. *adj.*, impoverish, reduce, reduce to poverty, pauperize, fleece, bring on the parish; bankrupt, ruin, break.

7. *adj.* poor, poverty-stricken, badly ~, poorly *or* ill off, hard up [coll.], down-and-out, indigent, reduced, embarrassed, under hatches, on one's uppers, on Queer Street, in want etc. *n.*, needy, necessitous, distressed, pinched, straitened, put to one's shifts *or* last shifts, at the end of one's rope, on the edge *or* ragged edge [coll.], unable to keep the wolf from the door, unable to make both ends meet, down to bedrock.

impecunious, impecuniary; moneyless, penniless, fortuneless, dowerless, unportioned, unmoneyed, short of money, out of funds, without *or* not worth a rap etc. (*see* rap, penny etc. 800.8), *qui n'a pas le sou* [F.], without a penny to bless oneself with, without a shot in the locker, out of pocket, destitute, impoverished, pauperized, fleeced, stripped, bereft, be-

reaved; oofless, beanless, broke, flat, flat broke, stone-broke, stony, strapped, beat [all slang]; poor as a church mouse, poor as a rat, poor as a coot [coll.], poor as Job, poor as Job's turkey [coll.]; out at elbows *or* heels, seedy [coll.], in rags, barefooted; beggarly, beggared; involved etc. (in debt) 806.7; bankrupt etc. 808.10; unprosperous etc. (unfortunate) 735.9.

8. *adv. in forma pauperis* [L.].

805. Credit
(See 806. Debt)

1. *n.* credit, trust, tick [coll.], strap [slang, Eng.], score, tally; account, credit account; *crédit mobilier* [F.]; loan etc. 787.1.

2. *n.* credit instrument, paper credit, letter of credit, *lettre de créance* [F.], circular note; duplicate; credit slip [Eng.], deposit slip; debenture, mortgage, lien etc. (security) 771; draft etc. (negotiable instrument) 800.7.

3. *n.* creditor, credit man; creditress, creditrix [rare]; dun, dunner; debtee; mortgagee, lessor etc. (lender) 787.2.

4. *v.* credit, accredit, entrust *or* intrust, give *or* extend credit, place to one's credit *or* account, charge, charge to one's account, tick [coll.], sell on credit; lend etc. 787.4.

5. *v.* receive credit, take credit, charge, charge to one's account, keep an account with; have one's credit good for; run up an account etc. (get into debt) 806.6; fly a kite [slang] etc. (borrow) 788.2.

6. *adj.* accredited, credited, of good credit, of unlimited credit, well-rated.

7. *adv.* on credit, on tick [slang], on trust, on account, *à compte* [F.], to the credit *or* account of.

806. Debt
(See 805. Credit)

1. *n.* debt, indebtment, obligation, liability, debit, due *or* dues, score; floating debt; borrowing etc. 788.

---

yours is the kingdom of God.—BIBLE. Steep'd in poverty to the very lips.—SHAKESPEARE. I am as poor as Job, my lord, but not so patient.—SHAKESPEARE. Poverty is no vice, but an inconvenience.—FLORIO. The short and simple annals of the poor.—GRAY. Poverty demoralizes.—EMERSON. Poverty makes strange bedfellows.—BULWER-LYTTON. The forgotten man at the bottom of the economic pyramid.—F. D. ROOSEVELT. As poor as a church mouse. Beggars can't be choosers.

805. A poor man has no credit.—AUSONIUS. He that has no credit owes no debts.—MIDDLETON. Creditors have better memories than debtors.—FRANKLIN.
806. Debt is the worst poverty.—FULLER. Knowing how the debt grows, I will pay it.—MIDDLETON. Debt is a prolific mother of folly and of crime.—DISRAELI.

806.2 — 807.11

2. *n.* arrears, arrear, arrearage; deferred payment, deficit, default; insolvency etc. (nonpayment) 808.

3. *n.* interest, premium, price, rate, price *or* rate of premium; excessive *or* exorbitant interest, usury, *usura* [L.], *usurae usurarum* [L.]; simple interest, compound interest, compensatory interest, net interest, gross interest.

4. *n.* debtor, borrower, mortgagor; defaulter etc. 808.3.

5. *v.* be in debt etc. *adj.*, owe, be over head and ears in debt, be in difficulties.

6. *v.* get into debt, go in debt, incur *or* contract a debt etc. *n.*, run into debt, outrun *or* overrun the constable [coll.], run up a bill, ~ a score *or* an account, go on tick [coll.]; borrow etc. 788.2; charge to one's account etc. 805.5.

7. *adj.* indebted, in debt, plunged in debt, over head and ears in debt, deep in debt, involved *or* deeply involved in debt, involved, deeply involved, tied up, encumbered *or* incumbered, in embarrassed circumstances, in difficulties; defaultant, insolvent etc. 808.9, 10; poor etc. 804.7.

8. *adj.* chargeable, liable, answerable for.

9. *adj.* unpaid, unrequited, unremunerated, unrewarded; owing, due, in arrear *or* arrears, outstanding; gratis etc. 815.10.

807. Payment
(See 808. Nonpayment)

1. *n.* payment, defrayment, discharge, settlement, clearance, liquidation, satisfaction, reckoning, arrangement; quittance, acquittance.

2. *n.* pay, pay-off [slang], remittance, consideration, installment, stake; fee, footing, garnish [obs.]; subsidy; tribute; contingent, quota; expenditure etc. 809; remuneration, allowance etc. (reward) 973; cash etc. (ready money) 800.13; deposit, earnest etc. (security) 771.

3. *n.* repayment, reimbursement, return, retribution, reparation, redress, amends, atonement; compensation etc. 30.

4. *n.* acknowledgment, release, voucher, receipt, receipt in full, receipt in full of all demands.

5. *n.* payer, defrayer; paymaster, liquidator etc. (treasurer) 801.

6. *v.* pay, make payment etc. *n.*, defray, honor a bill, acknowledge, redeem; pay over, hand over, stump up [coll. Eng.], ante *or* ante up; pay out, hand out; put down, lay down, lay one's money down; pay for, pay the costs; foot the bill, pay the piper, pay sauce for all [all coll.]; pay one's way, pay one's shot, pay one's footing; pay one's share, chip in [coll.], go Dutch [slang]; pay to the tune of [coll.]; give etc. 784.8, 9; pay out etc. (expend) 809.3; pay exorbitantly etc. 814.4; purchase etc. 795.3.

(slang terms) kick in, shell *or* fork out, fork over, pony up [U.S.], cough up, come across, come through with, come down with, come down with the needful, plank down, decorate the palm *or* counter, tickle *or* grease the palm, post.

7. *v.* discharge, settle, quit [arch.], acquit oneself of, square *or* settle accounts, make accounts square, pay up, pay off, pay in full, satisfy, clear, liquidate, strike a balance; account with, reckon with, settle with, settle ~, balance *or* square accounts with, pay out [coll.], quit scores [arch.], get even *or* quits with, even up the score [slang], wipe *or* clear off old scores, pay old debts.

8. *v.* pay cash, make a cash payment, pay ready money, pay spot cash, pay cash down, pay down on the nail [slang], put one's money on the line [slang], pay cash on delivery, pay C.O.D., pay at sight, pay in advance, pay as you go; cash.

9. *v.* repay, refund, reimburse, make repayment, disgorge; pay in kind, pay one in his own coin, give tit for tat; compensate etc. 30.4, 5; reward etc. 973.3; get even with [coll.] etc. (retaliate) 718.2.

10. *adj.* paid etc. *v.*, paid in full; spent, expended; unindebted, unowed, owing nothing, out of debt, above water, clear of debt, clear, all clear, all straight; solvent etc. 800.22.

11. *adv.* money down, cash down, cash on delivery, C.O.D., on the nail [slang].

---

807. Pay me that thou owest.—BIBLE. Always pay; for first or last you must pay your entire debt.—EMERSON. Every man must pay his scot.—EMERSON. He that pays last payeth but once.—J. HOWELL. Let us pay with our bodies for our souls' desire.—T. ROOSEVELT. He who pays the piper can call the tune.

808. Nonpayment
(See 807. Payment)

1. *n.* nonpayment, default, defaulture [rare], defalcation [now rare], delinquence *or* delinquency; protest, repudiation; whitewash, whitewashing [both coll., Eng.]; dishonored *or* protested bill, wastepaper bond; evasion etc. 623.

2. *n.* insolvency, bankruptcy, failure, collapse, crash; run upon a bank; overdrawn account, insufficient funds; insufficiency etc. 640; poverty etc. 804; failure etc. 732.

3. *n.* defaulter, defaultant, defalcator, delinquent; welsher [slang]; absconder, lavanter, eloper, skedaddler [coll., U.S.]; debtor etc. 806.4.

4. *n.* insolvent, insolvent debtor, bankrupt, lame duck [slang], man of straw; poor man etc. 803.3; failure etc. 732.4.

5. *v.* not pay etc. 807.6–8, pay over the left shoulder [coll.], protest, dishonor, repudiate, nullify, stop payment; default, defalcate; avoid payment, shirk out of [coll.], welsh [slang]; pay under protest, button up one's pockets, draw the purse strings; have one's check dishonored *or* protested; swindle etc. 791.12; evade etc. 623.6.

6. *v.* go bankrupt, go broke [slang], become insolvent *or* bankrupt, fail, break, crash, collapse, be ruined, go to ruin, go on the rocks, go to the wall, go to pot [coll.], go to the dogs, go up [coll.], be gazetted.

7. *v.* bankrupt, ruin, break etc. (impoverish) 804.6.

8. *v.* absolve of bankruptcy, clear of indebtedness, whitewash [coll., Eng.], cancel, sponge, apply the sponge, wipe the slate clean.

9. *adj.* defaulting etc. *v.*, defaultant, delinquent, behindhand, in arrear *or* arrears; in debt etc. 806.7.

10. *adj.* insolvent, bankrupt, broke [slang], ruined, gazetted, in the gazette, on the rocks; penniless etc. (poor) 804.7.

11. *adj.* unpaid etc. 806.9; gratis etc. 815.10.

---

808. A pound of care pays not a dram of debt.—DEKKER.   Great is bankruptcy: the great, bottomless gulf.—CARLYLE.   Bankrupt in fortune and reputation.—SHERIDAN.   Bankrupt of life, yet prodigal of ease.—DRYDEN.

809. Expenditure
(See 810. Receipt)

1. *n.* expenditure, money going out, spendings, outgoings, outlay, disbursement, circulation; expenses; prime cost etc. (price) 812; purchase etc. 795.

2. *n.* (money paid) payment, pay etc. 607.1, 2; remuneration, stipend etc. (reward) 973; bribe etc. 618.2; gift etc. 784.3–6; deposit, earnest etc. (security) 771.

3. *v.* expend, spend, disburse, pay out, lay out, fork *or* shell out [slang]; go ~, run *or* get through; open the purse, loose *or* untie the purse strings; make up a sum; invest etc. 787.5; pay etc. 807.6–9.

810. Receipt
(See 809. Expenditure)

1. *n.* receipt, receipts, money coming in, income, incomings [rare], revenue, returns, proceeds, avails, take; value received; gross receipts, net profit; assets etc. 780.7; earnings etc. (gain) 775.2; remuneration, wages etc. (reward) 973; premium, bonus etc. (gift) 784.3; pension etc. (allowance) 784.5; dower etc. (bequest) 784.6; inheritance etc. 775.4.

2. *n.* rent, rental, rentage [rare], rent-roll, gavel [obs. exc. Hist.]; rack rent *or* rackrent; dues etc. 812.2.

3. *v.* receive etc. 785.3; acquire etc. 775.6; take etc. 789.7.

4. *v.* yield, bring in, afford, pay, return; produce etc. (bear) 161.9; accrue etc. (be received) 785.4.

811. Accounts

1. *n.* accounts, accompts [arch.]; outstanding accounts, uncollected *or* unpaid

---

809. Know when to spend and when to spare, / And you need not be busy; you'll never be bare.—FULLER.   Never spend your money before you have it.—JEFFERSON.   It is not a custom with me to keep money to look at.—WASHINGTON.   He who spends all he gets is on his way to beggary.—S. SMILES.   Riches are for spending.—BACON.
810. *Vectigalia nervos esse rei publicae* [Revenues are the sinews of the state].—CICERO.   If you put nothing into your purse, you can take nothing out.—FULLER.   I think I could be a good woman if I had five thousand a year.—THACKERAY.
811. Annual income twenty pounds, annual expenditure nineteen nineteen six, result happiness.—DICKENS.

accounts, accounts receivable, assets, receipts; accounts payable, expenditures, liabilities; charge account, cash account; open *or* running account, account current; debtor and creditor account; profit and loss account; *compte rendu* [F.], account rendered; account stated; account, reckoning, tally, terrier [Law], score; balance.

2. *n.* entry, item, minute, note, notation; single entry, double entry; credit, debit.

3. *n.* statement, account, bill, bill of accounts *or* costs, score [slang], damage [slang]; invoice, manifest, bill of lading, budget.

4. *n.* accountancy, accounting, bookkeeping; business ∼, commercial *or* monetary arithmetic; audit; computation, calculation etc. (numeration) 85.

5. *n.* account book, ledger, journal, daybook, register, registry, record book, books; cashbook, petty cashbook; log, logbook *or* log book; purchase ledger, accounts payable ledger; sales ledger, accounts receivable ledger; bankbook, passbook; balance sheet.

6. *n.* accountant, bookkeeper, calculator, reckoner, actuary, registrar, recorder, clerk; chartered accountant, C.A. [Eng.]; certified public accountant, C.P.A. [U.S.]; auditor, bank examiner; accounting party.

7. *v.* keep accounts, make up *or* cast up accounts; make an entry, enter, post, post up, book, docket [U.S.], note, minute; credit, debit; carry over; balance, balance accounts *or* the books; wind up accounts; bill, invoice, indent; compute, sum up etc. (number) 85.7; settle accounts etc. (discharge) 807.7.

8. *v.* take account of, take stock, overhaul; inventory, inventorize [rare]; audit, examine the books.

9. *v.* falsify, falsify *or* garble accounts, cook *or* doctor accounts [coll.], salt, surcharge.

10. *adj.* accounting, bookkeeping; statistical etc. (mathematical) 85.12.

812. Price

1. *n.* price, amount, cost, expense, prime cost, charge, figure, quotation, demand, damage [slang], score [slang], fare, hire; shot, scot, scot and lot; market price, price current, current quotation.

2. *n.* dues, duty, toll, tax, taxation, impost, tariff, cess, assessment, fee, commission, tallage [Eng. Law, Hist.], levy, avania [Turkey], *octroi* [F.], gavel [Hist.], custom, excise, benevolence [Hist.], exactment, exaction; gabelle, salt tax; capitation, capitation tax, poll tax, poll, pollage [rare]; state tax, provincial tax, likin [Chin.]; tithe, tenths [Hist.]; liquor tax, abkari [Ind.]; doomage [U.S.], assessment on default; brokerage, wharfage, freightage, salvage, towage; poundage, tonnage, tonnage and poundage [Hist.]; rent etc. 810.2; fine etc. (penalty) 974.2.

3. *n.* worth, rate, value, par value; valuation, estimation, appraisement; money's worth, pennyworth etc.

4. *v.* price, set a price on, fix the price of, place a value on, value, valuate, evaluate, appraise, rate.

5. *v.* charge, demand, ask, require, exact, assess, levy, impose, impost [rare, U.S.], tax, assess a tax upon, lay *or* put a duty on etc. *n.,* doom [U.S.]; fine, levy a distress etc. (penalize) 974.3.

6. *v.* cost, fetch, sell for, yield, afford, bring, bring in; put *or* set one back [slang], stand one in [coll.]; come to, amount to, mount up to.

7. *adj.* priced, appraised, rated; to the tune of [coll.]; *ad valorem* [L.].

8. *adj.* chargeable, taxable, assessable, dutiable, leviable; tithable.

813. Discount

1. *n.* discount, cut, deduction, rebate, abatement, concession, reduction, depreciation, allowance, qualification, set-off, drawback; rebatement; percentage; poundage; agio; backwardization, backwardation [both Eng.]; contango [Eng.]; salvage; tare, tare and tret.

2. *v.* discount, bate, rebate, abate, deduct, cut, strike off, mark down, reduce, take off, give, allow, make allowance; depreciate.

3. *adj.* discounting etc. *v.,* concessional, depreciative.

4. *adv.* at a discount, at a bargain, marked down, below par.

---

812. I know my price.—SHAKESPEARE. No mortal thing can bear so high a price, / But that with mortal thing it may be bought.—RALEIGH. The worth of a thing is what it will bring. Every man has his price.

814. Dearness
(See 815. Cheapness)

1. *n.* dearness, expensiveness, costliness etc. *adj.*, high ~, fancy *or* famine price, pretty penny [coll.], heavy pull upon the purse; extravagance, excessive charge, overcharge, exorbitance, extortion.
2. *v.* be dear etc. *adj.*, cost much, cost a pretty penny [coll.]; rise in price, look up.
3. *v.* overcharge, make pay through the nose [coll.], hold up [coll.], soak [slang], bleed [coll.], skin [slang], fleece, extort.
4. *v.* pay exorbitantly *or* excessively, pay too much, pay size, pay big [slang], pay dearly, pay dearly *or* too dear for one's whistle, pay through the nose [coll.], pay the devil.
5. *adj.* dear, expensive, costly, high, high-priced, precious, valuable, of great price, above *or* beyond price; worth a pretty penny [coll.], worth its weight in gold, worth a king's ransom; priceless, of priceless value, invaluable, inestimable.
6. *adj.* exorbitant, excessive, extravagant, unreasonable, extortionate; dear-bought.
7. *adv.* dear, dearly etc. *adj.*; at great cost, at heavy cost, at a high price, *à grands frais* [F.], at a premium.

815. Cheapness
(See 814. Dearness)

1. *n.* cheapness, inexpensiveness, reasonableness etc. *adj.*; low price, nominal price; nominal rent, peppercorn rent; drug on *or* in the market.
2. *n.* bargain, advantageous purchase, buy *or* good buy [coll.], *bon marché* [F.]; pickup, snap, steal [all slang]; pennyworth, good pennyworth.
3. *n.* cheapening etc. *v.*, depreciation, decline, slump, sag [slang].
4. *n.* gratuitousness etc. *adj.*, gratuity; absence of charge, no charge; labor of love; free admission, free seats, free quarters, free ticket, pass; gift etc. 784.3.
5. *n.* pass holder, deadhead [coll.].
6. *v.* be cheap etc. *adj.*, cost little, buy for a mere nothing, buy dirt-cheap, buy for a song *or* old song, buy at a bargain, get a good pennyworth, get one's money's worth.
7. *v.* cheapen, lower, reduce, mark down, beat down; cut, shave, pare, trim, slash; come down *or* fall in price, depreciate, decline, sag, run off, slump; reach a new low [coll.].
8. *adj.* cheap, inexpensive *or* unexpensive, low, low-priced, moderate, nominal, reasonable; worth the money, well worth the money, worth the whistle; *bon marché* [F.]; cheap *or* good at the price, cheap at half the price [joc.]; dog-cheap, dirt-cheap, cheap as dirt, cheap and nasty [coll.], dime-a-dozen [coll.]; peppercorn; catchpenny.
9. *adj.* reduced, depreciated, marked down etc. *v.*; half-price.
10. *adj.* gratuitous, gratis, free, free as air, for nothing, for love, costless, expenseless, without charge, not charged, untaxed, scot-free, shot-free, rent-free, free of cost *or* expense, complimentary, honorary, unbought, unpaid-for; giftlike, gifty [coll.]; unpaid etc. 806.9; given etc. 784.14.
11. *adv.* cheaply etc. *adj.*, on *or* upon the cheap [coll., Eng.]; at a bargain, *bon marché* or *à bon marché* [F.], for a song *or* mere song; at a reduction; at cost *or* cost price, at prime cost.

816. Liberality
(See 817. Economy; also 818. Prodigality)

1. *n.* liberality, liberalness, unselfishness etc. *adj.*; generosity, munificence, bounty; hospitality; open *or* free hand, open ~, large *or* free heart; enough and to spare; giving etc. 784; beneficence etc. (charitableness) 906.2; magnanimity etc. 942.2.
2. *n.* cheerful giver, free giver etc. *adj.*; giver etc. 784.7; philanthropist etc. 911; patron etc. 711.4; benefactor etc. 912.

---

814. The things are most dear to us which have cost us most.—MONTAIGNE.   He has paid dear, very dear, for his whistle.—FRANKLIN.   What we obtain too cheaply we esteem too lightly; it is dearness only which gives everything its value.—T. PAINE.   You cannot make a cheap palace.—EMERSON.
815. Ill ware is never cheap.—G. HERBERT. What costs little is valued less.—CERVANTES.
Things of greatest profit are set forth with least price.—LYLY.   Never buy what you do not want because it is cheap; it will be dear to you.—JEFFERSON.   A glutted market makes provision cheap.—POPE.   Not how cheap, but how good.—W. MORRIS.
816. It snewed in his hous of mete and drynke. —CHAUCER.   For his bounty. / There was

816.3 – 819.1

3. *v.* be liberal etc., give *or* spend freely, give cheerfully, give carte blanche, give with both hands, give the coat off one's back, shower down upon, spare no expense; open the purse, loose *or* untie the purse strings; be hospitable, keep open house, fill one's house with guests.

4. *adj.* liberal, free, free with one's money, generous, munificent, princely, unselfish, ungrudging, unsparing, unstinting; bounteous, bountiful; handsome, ample, sumptuary, lavish, copious, profuse; openhanded, freehanded; openhearted, largehearted, bighearted, greathearted, freehearted; hospitable; beneficent etc. (charitable) 906.7; prodigal etc. 818.4; magnanimous etc. 942.6.

5. *adv.* liberally, ungrudgingly etc. *adj.*; with an unsparing hand, with open hands, with both hands.

817. Economy
(See 816. Liberality; also 819. Parsimony)

1. *n.* economy, savingness, thriftiness etc. *adj.*; saving, thrift, frugality, prevention of waste, care; husbandry, good housewifery; retrenchment; economist, save-all; parsimony etc. 819.

2. *n.* savings, nest egg, reserve fund etc. (fund) 636.2.

3. *v.* be economical etc. *adj.*, practice economy, economize, save, make both ends meet, keep within compass, keep within one's means *or* budget, cut one's coat according to one's cloth; keep one's head above water, meet one's expenses, pay one's way, look after the main chance [coll.]; retrench, cut down expenses; invest money, put out to interest; save up, provide against a rainy day etc. (reserve) 636.8.

4. *adj.* economical, frugal, careful, thrifty, saving, chary, spare, sparing; sufficient; plain; parsimonious etc. 819.4.

---

no winter in't.—Shakespeare.   Liberality consists less in giving a great deal than in gifts well-timed.—La Bruyère.   The glory of the house is hospitality.
817. *Magnum est vectigal parsimonia* [Thrift is a great revenue].—Cicero.   Frugality is a handsome income.—Erasmus.   Penny and penny laid up will be many.—J. Ray.   Economy, the poor man's mint.—Tupper.   Though on pleasure she was bent, / She had a frugal mind.—Cowper.   Economy is the art of making the most of life. The love of economy is the root of all virtue.—Shaw.

5. *adv.* sparingly etc. *adj.*, with a sparing hand, *ne quid nimis* [L.].

818. Prodigality
(See 819. Parsimony; also 816. Liberality)

1. *n.* prodigality, wastefulness, unthriftiness etc. *adj.*; wastry [Scot.], waste, extravagance, profusion, dissipation, squandering etc. *v.*; pound-foolishness, pound-folly, penny wisdom; money burning one's pocket; intemperance etc. 954.

2. *n.* prodigal, wastrel, waster, wastethrift, losel [arch. exc. dial.], spendthrift, high roller [slang, U.S.], squanderer, spender, spend-all, scattergood [arch.]; locust; prodigal son.

3. *v.* be prodigal etc. *adj.*, squander, lavish, blow in [slang], run through, throw one's money away, fool ~, potter ~, muddle *or* fritter away, cast ~, throw *or* fling away, sow broadcast, scatter to the winds.

make ducks and drakes of one's money, squander one's substance in riotous living, burn the candle at both ends, spend money like water, pour water into a sieve, cast pearls before swine, kill the goose that lays the golden eggs, *manger son blé en herbe* [F.]; spend more than one has, overdraw, outrun *or* overrun the constable [coll.]; waste, dissipate, use, use up, spend, consume, exhaust, spill, drain, eat out of house and home; misspend, throw good money after bad, throw the helve after the hatchet; overdo etc. 641.3; overindulge etc. (be intemperate) 954.3.

4. *adj.* prodigal, thriftless, unthrifty, improvident, wasteful, losel [arch. exc. dial.], overliberal, extravagant, lavish, profuse; dissipative, dissipated; poundfoolish, penny-wise and pound-foolish; intemperate etc. 954.4.

5. *int.* keep the change!; easy come, easy go!; hang expense!

819. Parsimony
(See 818. Prodigality; also 817. Economy)

1. *n.* parsimony, parsimoniousness, stinginess etc. *adj.*; pinching, scrimping

---

818. Spendthrift alike of money and of wit.—Cowper.   Squandering wealth was his particular art.—Dryden.   The prodigal robs his heir, the miser himself.—Fuller.   His money burns a hole in his pocket.
819. *Desunt inopiae multa avaritiae omnia* [Many things are wanting to poverty, every-

etc. *v.*; ungenerosity, illiberality, penury [now rare], avarice, *auri sacra fames* [L.], tenacity, avidity, rapacity, extortion, malversation, venality, cupidity; stint *or* stent; miserly economizing, cheeseparing, cheeseparings and candle ends; pinchgut money *or* pay [Naut. slang]; selfishness etc. 943; economy etc. 817.

2. *n.* miser, niggard, churl, screw, tightwad [slang, U.S.], skinflint, skin [slang], codger [dial., Eng.], save-all [dial.], moneygrub, moneygrubber, muckworm, scrimp [coll.], pinchfist, pinchgut [vulg.], pinchpenny [now rare], lickpenny, hunks [coll.], curmudgeon, harpy, Hessian [U.S.]; Harpagon, Euclio, Silas Marner, Daniel Dancer.

3. *v.* be parsimonious etc. *adj.,* stint, pinch, gripe, scrimp, skimp [coll.], screw, skin a flint [coll.], pinch a sixpence till it squeaks; starve, famish, live upon nothing; grudge, begrudge; hold back, withhold; dole out; have an itching palm, grasp, grab; stop one hole in a sieve; drive a bargain etc. 794.5.

4. *adj.* parsimonious, penurious, stingy, miserly, save-all, moneygrubbing, mean, shabby, peddling, penny-wise, niggardly, tight [coll.], near, near as the bark on a tree, close, closehanded, closefisted, hardfisted, hardhanded [obs.], straithanded [obs.], tightfisted, pinching, gripping, stinting, scrimping, skimp [coll.] skimping [coll.], skimpy [coll.], cheeseparing, sparing, chary, grudging, illiberal, ungenerous, churlish, hidebound, sordid, mercenary, venal, covetous, usurious, avaricious, greedy, extortionate, rapacious; economical etc. 817.4; selfish etc. 943.4.

820. Affection

1. *n.* affection, disposition, character, nature; temper, temperament, temper *or* temperament of mind; idiosyncrasy, idiocrasy, idiocrasis; bent *or* turn of mind, bent, turn, bias, warp, twist, leaning, inclination, tendency, animus, propensity, propensitude [rare], propendency [obs.], propension [now rare], propenseness, proneness, proclivity, predilection, predisposition, diathesis; frame *or* habit of mind, humor, mood, tone, frame, vein, grain, streak, stripe, cast, cue, attitude, heart, spirit, mettle; qualities, characteristics, peculiarities, traits; emotion etc. (feeling) 821; love etc. 987.

2. *n.* (seat of affections) soul etc. (psyche) 994.11; heart, bosom etc. (inner man) 450.3.

3. *adj.* characterized, affected, formed, molded, cast, framed; tempered, attempered; characteristic etc. (peculiar) 79.8.

4. *adj.* disposed, dispositioned, dispositional; predisposed, prone, propense [arch.], inclined, bent, minded, in the vein, ~ humor *or* mood; disposed to etc. (tending to) 176.3.

5. *adj.* inborn, inherent etc. (intrinsic) 5.6.

821. Feeling

1. *n.* feeling, emotion, passion, affection, sentiment, deep sense; sentience *or* sentiency, sensation, impression, experience, response; inspiration; emotional nature, heart, soul; ruling *or* master passion, pervading spirit; tender feeling, ~ emotion *or* passion, tenderness, softness, sympathy, pathos, pity, tender sorrow; tender susceptibility etc. (sensibility) 822; love etc. 897; thrill etc. (state of excitement) 825.2.

2. *n.* fervor, fervency, warmth of feeling, warmth, heat, fire, passion, ardor, zeal, *empressement* [F.], unction, enthusiasm, verve, furor, *furore* [It.], gush [coll.], gusto, vehemence, heartiness, cordiality, earnestness, eagerness; spirit, heart; fullness of the heart, heyday of the blood, flow of the soul; glow, blush, suf-

---

and capricious behavior of the passions.—FIELDING. 'Tis sweet to feel by what fine-spun threads our affections are drawn together.—STERNE. Every soul is a circus.—V. LINDSAY. Character is an historical fruit, and the result of a man's biography.—AMIEL. Our characters are the result of our conduct.—ARISTOTLE. Character,—a reserved force which acts directly by presence and without means.—EMERSON.
821. My affection hath an unknown bottom, like the bay of Portugal.—SHAKESPEARE. Seeing is believing, but feeling's the naked truth.—J. RAY. Feeling hath no fellow.—J.

thing to avarice].—PUBLILIUS. The love of money is the root of all evil.—BIBLE. The devil lies brooding in the miser's chest.—FULLER. The unsunn'd heaps of miser's treasures.—MILTON. A crusty old fellow, as close as a vise.—HAWTHORNE.
820. The mainspring of life is in the heart.—AMIEL. Man is only truly great when he acts from the passions.—DISRAELI. The fantastic

fusion, flush; hectic, hectic flush; fever etc. (state of excitement) 825.2; ecstasy etc. 827.2; fanaticism etc. (craze) 503.7.

3. *v.* feel, receive an impression etc. *n.,* be impressed with etc. *adj.,* entertain ∼, harbor *or* cherish a feeling etc. *n.*; remark; experience, taste, prove [arch.], suffer, undergo, go *or* pass through; labor under, smart under; respond, catch the flame *or* infection, enter into the spirit of; thrill etc. (be excited) 824.7.

4. *adj.* feeling etc. *v.,* of *or* with feeling etc. *n.,* sentient, affectional; sensuous, sensory, sensorial; emotive, emotional.

5. *adj.* lively, quick, smart, strong, sharp, acute, cutting, piercing, incisive, keen, trenchant, pungent, racy, piquant, poignant, caustic.

6. *adj.* fervent, fervid, warm, passionate, impassioned, warmhearted, glowing, ardent, burning, hot, red-hot, fiery, flaming, hearty, devout, cordial, sincere, zealous, enthusiastic, earnest, eager, wistful, breathless, avid, keen, gushing [coll.], boiling over; delirious, feverish, febrile, flushed; rabid, fanatical, overzealous.

7. *adj.* impressed, moved, touched, affected, impressed etc. with *or* by, penetrated with, seized with, imbued with, devoured by.

8. *adj.* deep-felt, homefelt, heartfelt; deep, profound, indelible; pervading, absorbing; impressive, soul-stirring etc. (exciting) 824.12; piercing etc. (penetrating) 824.13.

9. *adv.* heartily, heart and soul, from the bottom of one's heart, *ab imo pectore* [L.], *de profundis* [L.], at heart, *con amore* [It.], devoutly.

822. Sensibility
(See 823. Insensibility)

1. *n.* sensibility, moral sensibility, acuteness of feeling; sensibleness, sensitiveness, susceptibleness etc. *adj.*; susceptibility, susceptivity; impressibility, affectibility; perceptibility, perceptivity; expressibility, mobility; sensitive plant; physical sensibility etc. 375; excitability etc. 825; fastidiousness etc. 868; feeling etc. 821.

2. *n.* tender susceptibility, tenderness, softness etc. *adj.*; sentiment, sentimentality, sentimentalism; tender ∼, sensitive *or* warm heart.

3. *n.* sore point, ∼ place *or* spot, quick, raw, where the shoe pinches.

4. *v.* be sensible etc. *adj.,* have a tender heart etc. *n.,* be all heart; take to heart, treasure up in the heart; shrink, wince, blench, quiver.

5. *v.* touch a sore spot *or* place, touch to the quick, touch on the raw, flick one on the raw.

6. *adj.* sensible, sensitive, sentient; emotionable, emotional, emotionally sensitive, impressible, impressionable; susceptive, susceptible; perceptive, alive to; impassionable; expressive, mobile, tremblingly alive; unduly sensible, oversensitive, thin-skinned, without skin; fastidious etc. 868.4; excitable etc. 825.8; irascible etc. 901.7.

7. *adj.* tender, soft, maudlin, sentimental, romantic; tenderhearted, softhearted, warmhearted.

8. *adv.* sensibly, sensitively etc. *adj.*; to the quick, on the raw, to the core *or* inmost core.

823. Insensibility
(See 822. Sensibility)

1. *n.* insensibility, moral insensibility, want of sensibility etc. 822, insensibleness, insensitiveness, insentience, unfeeling, unfeelingness, unconsciousness, induration, inappetence *or* inappetency, insusceptibility; unimpressionableness, unimpressibility; impassiveness, impassibility, impassivity, stoicism; analgesia, analgesis; obtundity, dullness, numbness,

---

RAY. Affection, like melancholy, magnifies trifles.—L. HUNT. There are some feelings time cannot benumb.—BYRON. Some feelings are to mortals given / With less of earth in them than heaven.—SCOTT. Sensations sweet, / Felt in the blood and felt along the heart.—WORDSWORTH. You cannot demonstrate an emotion or prove an aspiration.—J. MORLEY. The advantage of the emotions is that they lead us astray.—WILDE.
822. Nothing is little to him that feels it with great sensibility.—JOHNSON. *La tendresse est le repos de la passion* [Tenderness is the re-

pose of passion].—JOUBERT. Sentimentality is the error of supposing that quarter can be given or taken in moral conflicts.—SHAW. If she could weep, they said, / She could love, they said.—DUNSANY. A Sensitive Plant in a garden grew.—SHELLEY. Every form of human life is romantic.—T. HIGGINSON.
823. Moral indifference is the malady of the cultivated classes.—AMIEL. Afflictions induce callosities.—T. BROWNE. We are cold

deadness; hebetude, hebetation; torpor, torpidity, torpitude [now rare], torpescence; stupor, stupefaction.

apathy, lethargy, phlegm, supineness, dispassion, insouciance, unconcern, indifference, lukewarmness, nonchalance; *sang-froid* [F.], coolness, coldness, frigidity; callousness, callosity, hardness, hardness of heart, obduracy; hard heart, heart of stone *or* marble, cold heart *or* blood, blood and iron, stock and stone; dry eyes; thick skin, rhinoceros hide; physical insensibility etc. 376; imperturbation etc. (inexcitability) 826; indifference etc. 866; incuriosity etc. 456.

2. *n.* stoic, man of iron, Indian, Spartan; pococurante, pococurantist.

3. *v.* be insensible etc. *adj.*, show insensibility etc. *n.*, have a thick skin, ~ a heart of stone etc. *n.*, not care *or* mind, not be affected by, have ~, feel *or* take no interest in, *nil admirare* [L.]; have no desire etc. 866.3; disregard etc. 460.4; set at nought etc. 483.3; turn a deaf ear to etc. (inattention) 458.5; have no curiosity etc. 456.2.

4. *v.* render insensible etc. *adj.,* callous, blunt, dull, obtund, numb, benumb, paralyze, deaden, hebetate, stun, stupefy; inure, harden, harden the heart, caseharden, steel, sear; brutify, brutalize.

5. *adj.* insensible, insensitive, unsensitive, unconscious, unfeeling, unemotional, dispassionate, passionless, spiritless, heartless, soulless, unmoral; unimpressible, unimpressionable; insusceptible, unsusceptible; impassive, impassible; frigid, cold, coldhearted, cold-blooded, cold as charity; indifferent, unconcerned, uninterested, insouciant, halfhearted, tame, lukewarm, Laodicean, careless, regardless, disregardful, disregardant, mindless, unmindful, *sans souci* [F.], nonchalant; pococurante, pococurantic, pococurantish, pococurantist.

blind to, deaf to, dead to; dull, obtuse, obtundent, flat; apathetic, phlegmatic, supine, sluggish, languid, lethargic, comatose, stupefied; numb, numbed, benumbed; torpid, torpescent, torpedinous [rare], torporific; imperturbable etc. (inexcitable) 826.9; inattentive etc. 458.10;
incurious etc. 456.3; indolent etc. 683.13; indifferent etc. 866.4.

6. *adj.* unaffected, unimpressed, uninspired, unexcited, unmoved, unanimated, unstirred, untouched, unruffled, unshocked, unstruck; unblushing etc. (brazen) 885.10.

7. *adj.* callous, thick-skinned, pachydermatous, impervious, hard, hardhearted, hardened, casehardened, inured, steeled against, proof against; unfelt.

8. *adv.* insensibly etc. *adj.,* without being moved, ~ touched *or* impressed; in cold blood; with dry eyes; *aequo animo* [L.] etc. 826.12.

824. Excitation
(See also 825. Excitability)

1. *n.* excitation, excitation of feeling, excitement, mental excitement, galvanism, high pressure, stimulation, piquancy, provocation, inspiration, calling forth, infection, animation, electrification, agitation, perturbation; fascination, intoxication, ravishment, enravishment, entrancement; unction; emotional appeal, heart interest [slang]; sensationalism, yellow journalism, melodrama; irritation etc. (resentment) 900; passion, thrill etc. (state of excitability) 825.2–5.

2. *v.* excite, affect, touch, strike, smite, impress, interest, move, animate, stimulate, actuate, infect, impassion; inspirit, spirit up; inspire, call forth, evoke, provoke, summon up, call up, work up, blow up, get up, get up the steam; rake up, rip up; act ~, work *or* operate on *or* upon; stir, set astir, stir up, stir the blood; stir the feelings, play on the feelings; quicken, sharpen, whet; fillip, give a fillip; raise, raise up; rouse, arouse; wake, waken, awake, awaken, wake up.

kindle, enkindle, light up; illumine, illuminate; fire, set on fire, inflame, apply the torch, fire *or* warm the blood; heat, warm, foment; fan, fan into a flame, fan the fire *or* flame, blow the coals, stir the embers, feed the fire, add fuel to the flame *or* fire, foster, raise to a fever heat; keep

---

824. The Powers / That stir men's spirits, waking or asleep.—MASEFIELD. My senses swooned in ecstasy.—TAGORE. Inanimate things cannot stir our affections.—NEWMAN. Astir with delicious excitation.—A. REPPLIER. A blush is no language, only a dubious flag-signal.—G. ELIOT.

up, keep the pot boiling; rekindle, revive; infuse life into, give new life to, bring *or* introduce new blood; thrill, intoxicate, fascinate; enrapture etc. (delight) 829.5; incite etc. (motivate) 615.7.

3. *v.* agitate, disturb, perturb, perturbate, disquiet, discompose, stir, ruffle, fluster, flutter, flurry, shake, jolt, jar, startle, stagger, shock, give one a shock *or* turn; strike dumb, strike all of a heap [coll.], stun, astound, electrify, galvanize, petrify; upset, turn one's head.

4. *v.* penetrate, pierce, go through one, come home to the feelings, touch a string *or* chord, touch the heart *or* soul, go to one's heart, sink into the mind *or* heart, possess ~, pervade ~, imbue ~, penetrate ~, affect *or* disturb the soul, prey on the mind; touch a sore spot *or* place, touch to the quick, touch *or* flick one on the raw; open the wound, turn the knife in the wound.

5. *v.* irritate, sting, cut, sting *or* cut to the heart *or* quick, wound, chafe, exasperate, aggravate [coll.], provoke, pique, try one's temper, infuriate, madden, stir the blood, make one's blood boil, lash into a fury.

6. *v.* become excited etc. *adj.,* flare up, flash up, flame up, fire up, take fire, burst into a flame, break out, explode, go *or* fly off, go *or* fly off at a tangent, fly off the handle [slang], fly into a passion, go into hysterics; catch the infection, work oneself up; run mad etc. (rage) 825.7; lose one's temper etc. 900.9.

7. *v.* be excited etc. *adj.,* thrill, tingle, tingle with excitement; swell, swell with emotion, be full of emotion; draw a deep breath, heave, pant; throb, palpitate, go pitapat; tremble, shiver, quiver, quaver, quake, flutter, twitter, vibrate, shake, shake like an aspen leaf; fidget, have the fidgets; pitch, toss, tumble, toss and turn, toss on one's pillow, not have a wink of sleep; wiggle, wriggle, writhe, squirm, twist and turn; twitch, jerk.

8. *v.* change color, turn color, mantle; whiten, pale, turn pale; darken, turn black in the face, look black *or* blue; turn red, blush, flush, crimson, glow, warm.

9. *adj.* excited, agitated etc. *v.*; wrought-up, *éperdu* [F.], astir, sparkling, swelling, on the *qui vive,* in a quiver etc. *n.,* all in a pucker [coll.], all of a flutter *or* twitter, with quivering, ~ trembling *or* twitching lips, with tears in one's eyes; hot, red-hot, warm, burning, glowing, fervent, fervid, flushed, burning etc. with excitement; feverish, febrile; black *or* blue in the face; white, pale.

10. *adj.* overwrought, high-wrought; overcome, overwhelmed, overpowered, overmastered; upset, *bouleversé* [F.], struck all of a heap [coll.]; on one's high ropes, on one's high horse; fuming, seething, ebullient, boiling over, ready to burst; flaming, burning, fiery; frenzied, raging, raving, ranting, foaming at the mouth; wild, frantic, delirious, mad, rabid, demoniac(al), violent, fierce, furious, carried away, distracted, beside oneself, out of one's wits, amuck; hysteric(al), in hysterics; wild-eyed, wild-looking, haggard, harrowed; lost, tempest-tossed, ready to sink.

11. *adj.* rampant, clamorous, uproarious, turbulent, tempestuous, tumultuary, boisterous; vehement etc. 825.10.

12. *adj.* exciting, thrilling etc. *v.*; swelling, heart-swelling, heart-expanding, heart-thrilling, heart-stirring, spirit-stirring, soul-stirring, soul-subduing; impressive, imposing, telling; provocative, *provoquant* [F.]; stimulating, stimulative; electric, galvanic; sensational, yellow, melodramatic; overcoming, overwhelming, overpowering, overmastering, more than flesh and blood can bear; spicy, piquant etc. (pungent) 392.5; tantalizing etc. (alluring) 617.5; irritating, agonizing etc. (painful) 830.9–18.

13. *adj.* penetrating, piercing, cutting, stinging, biting, sharp, keen, caustic, astringent, harsh, rough, severe; deep-felt etc. 821.8.

14. *adv.* excitedly, thrillingly etc. *adj.*; with plenty of pep, with punch [both slang]; with beating *or* leaping heart, with heart beating high, with heart going pitapat *or* pitter-patter, with one's heart leaping into one's mouth; with the blood up, with one's blood boiling; with glistening eyes; under a strain; till one is black *or* blue in the face.

825. Excitability

(See 826. Inexcitability; also 824. Excitation)

1. *n.* excitability, excitableness etc. *adj.,* impetuosity; impatience, intoler-

---

825. When passion entereth at the fore-gate, wisdom goeth out the postern.—FULLER.

ance, nonendurance; irritability, irascibility etc. (ill-humor) 901; itching etc. (desire) 865.

2. *n.* state of excitement *or* excitability, excitement; fever, fever of excitement, heat, fever-heat, fire, flame; turn, shock; thrill, tingling; transport, intoxication; agony; desperation, distraction; fervor etc. 821.2.

3. *n.* trepidation, trepidity; perturbation, perturbance *or* perturbancy [rare]; agitation, fluster, flutter, ruffle, fuss, flurry, pother, bother, stew [coll.], turmoil, tumult, turbulence, commotion, to-do [coll.], ado, bustle, stir, whirl, hurry, hurry-scurry *or* hurry-skurry, hurly-burly; ferment, effervescence, ebullition, fume, blood boiling; disquiet, disquietude, inquietude.

unrest, restlessness; fidgets, fidgetiness; nervousness, jitters [slang], stage fright, buck fever [coll.]; quivering, quavering, quaking, shaking; quiver, quaver, shiver, didder, dither, twitter, tremor, tremble, flutter; pulsation, palpitation, pitapatation [joc.], pitapat, pitter-patter; throb, throbbing; panting, heaving.

4. *n.* fury, furor, *furore* [It.]; fierceness, ferociousness, furiousness, furiosity [rare]; violent emotion, vehemence, tempestuousness, boisterousness, turbulence; passion, rage, raging *or* tearing passion, towering rage *or* passion, frenzy, madness, delirium; raving, raging, ranting; hysterics, fit, paroxysm etc. (spasm) 315.7; violence etc. 173; anger etc. 900.3.

5. *n.* outburst, outbreak, breaking out, burst, explosion, eruption, upheaval, convulsion; whiff, gust, storm, tempest, scene.

6. *v.* be impatient etc. *adj.,* be out of all patience, not be able to bear etc. 826.6, bear ill, chafe, champ the bit; fuss, fret, worry; fidget etc. (be excited) 824.7.

7. *v.* rage, rave, rant, storm, tear; fume, foam, seethe, boil, boil over, simmer, burn, stew [coll.], be in a stew [coll.]; run *or* go wild, run mad, run *or* go amuck, run riot; *faire le diable à quatre* [F.], play the deuce *or* devil [slang], raise Cain, ~ Ned, ~ hell, ~ sand, ~ the devil *or* the mischief [all slang]; flare up, explode etc. (become excited) 824.6; lose one's temper etc. 900.8, 9.

8. *adj.* excitable, easily excited, in an excitable state; mettlesome, high-mettled, high-strung; startlish, skittish; impatient, intolerant; irritable, irascible etc. (ill-humored) 901.7; excited, exciting etc. 824.9–13.

9. *adj.* unquiet, mercurial, restless, nervous, fidgety, fussy, chafing etc. *v.*; hasty, hurried; electric, galvanic; feverish, febrile, delirious.

10. *adj.* vehement, violent, demonstrative, wild, furious, fierce, fiery, passionate, hotheaded, madcap; turbulent, tumultuary etc. (rampant) 824.11.

11. *adj.* impulsive, impetuous, hasty, overhasty, quick, sudden; uncontrolled, ungoverned, uncontrollable, ungovernable, irrepressible, inextinguishable, stanchless; burning, simmering; volcanic, ready to burst forth.

12. *adv.* excitably etc. *adj.,* in trepidation etc. *n.*; in confusion, pell-mell.

826. Inexcitability
(See 825. Excitability)

1. *n.* inexcitability, inexcitableness etc. *adj.,* imperturbability, inirritability, even temper, dispassion, lack of nerves; unastonishment etc. 871; insensibility etc. 823.

2. *n.* calmness etc. *adj.,* mental calmness *or* serenity, unruffled calm, peace of mind, tranquil mind, composure, placidity, indisturbance, imperturbation, tranquillity, serenity; quiet, quietude, quietism; coolness, *sang-froid* [F.], nonchalance; content etc. 831.

3. *n.* equanimity, poise, *aplomb* [F.], balance, ballast; levelheadedness, level head [coll.], well-balanced *or* well-regulated mind; command of temper, self-command, self-possession, self-control, self-restraint, restraint, presence of mind; staidness etc. *adj.,* gravity, sobriety; demureness, demurity; Quakerism; philosophicalness, philosophy.

4. *n.* sufferance, endurance, forbearance, nonresistance, fortitude, stoicism,

---

The . . . fiery vehemence of youth.—SCOTT. Quiet to quick bosoms is a hell.—BYRON. Fill'd with fury, rapt, inspired.—COLLINS. Sudden alarms, rushing to and fro, trepidations of . . . fugitives.—DE QUINCEY.

826. *Mens aequa in arduis* [An even mind in adversities].—HORACE. An undisturbed mind is the best sauce for adversity.—PLAUTUS. Have patience and endure.—OVID. Ye have heard of the patience of Job.—BIBLE. Endur-

suppression *or* subjugation of feeling; longanimity, long-suffering, long-sufferance [arch.]; tolerance, toleration; patience, patience of Job, "patience on a monument" (Shakespeare); passiveness, passivity; impassiveness, impassibility, impassivity; resignation etc. (submission) 725.

5. *v.* be composed etc. *adj.*, take it easy, take things easily, take things as they come, rub on [coll.], live and let live; *laisser faire* [F.], *laisser aller* [F.]; take easily *or* coolly, take in good part; preserve one's equanimity, *aequam servare mentem* [L.].

6. *v.* endure, bear, forbear [now dial.], support, sustain, stand, suffer, tolerate, bide, abide, aby, brave, brook, thole [obs. exc. dial.], disregard; bear with, put up with, take up with, abide with, bear the brunt, bear well; carry on, carry through; make light of, make the best of; submit to, resign *or* reconcile oneself to, shrug the shoulders; submit with a good grace, grin and bear it, grin and abide; keep one's countenance, put a good face on; swallow an insult, pocket the affront, turn the other cheek, take, pocket, swallow, stomach, eat, digest; be borne etc., go down; be content etc. 831.3.

7. *v.* compose, calm, cool, tranquilize etc. (moderate) 174.5; repress etc. (restrain) 751.6; render insensible etc. 823.4.

8. *v.* compose oneself, overcome ~, repress *or* allay one's excitability etc. (*see* excitability etc. 825), master one's feelings, make oneself easy, make one's mind easy, set one's mind at ease *or* rest; calm down, cool down *or* off, grow cool, thaw.

9. *adj.* inexcitable, imperturbable, undisturbable; unirritable, inirritable; dispassionate, unpassionate, coldblooded; composed, collected, recollected, calm, peaceful, placid, unruffled etc. *below* 826.11, quiet, quiet as a mouse, tranquil, serene, poised, nonchalant; *dégagé* [F.], easy, easygoing; unconstrained, unembarrassed; self-possessed, self-controlled, self-restrained; cool, coolheaded, levelheaded, cool as a cucumber [coll.], cool as custard [coll.]; steady, steady-handed, steady-nerved; unnervous, nerveless; staid, sober, sober-minded, grave, sober as a judge, sedate, demure; philosophic(al), Platonic; undemonstrative; unsusceptible etc. (insensible) 823.5.

10. *adj.* meek, tolerant, unresisting, enduring etc. *v.*, forbearant, long-suffering, longanimous, passive, stoic(al), resigned, chastened, subdued, content; patient, armed with patience, patient as Job; tame, gentle, gentle as a lamb, lamblike, *suaviter in modo* [L.]; clement, mild, mild as milk *or* mother's milk, mild as milk and water; soft, soft as peppermint; pacific, peaceful, peaceable; yielding etc. (submissive) 725.5; humble etc. 879.4.

11. *adj.* unexcited, unstirred, unruffled, untroubled, undisturbed, unperturbed, unimpassioned; composed, cool etc. *above* 826.9.

12. *adv.* inexcitably, calmly etc. *adj.*; "like patience on a monument smiling at grief" (Shakespeare); more in sorrow than in anger; *aequo animo* [L.].

827. Pleasure
(See 828. Pain; also 829. Pleasurableness)

1. *n.* pleasure, gratification, enjoyment, great satisfaction, fruition; pleasurable excitement, thrill, kick [slang]; hedonics, hedonism; relish, well-being etc. (physical pleasure) 377; pleasurableness etc. 829; satisfaction etc. (content) 831; amusement etc. 840.

2. *n.* happiness, gladness, delight, delectation, oblectation [rare], glee, cheer, sunshine; joy, joyance, joyancy [rare]; felicity, blessedness, bliss; beatitude, beatification; enchantment, transport, rapture, ravishment, ecstasy, unalloyed happiness etc.; paradise, heaven, third *or* seventh heaven; cheerfulness etc. 836; fullness of the heart etc. (fervor) 821.2.

3. *n.* pleasant time, palmy *or* halcyon days; golden age, *Saturnia regna* [L.]; honeymoon.

4. *n.* land of pleasure, Eden, Arcadia etc. (Utopia) 515.6.

5. *v.* be pleased etc. *adj.*, feel *or* ex-

---

ance is nobler than strength, and patience than beauty.—RUSKIN. Sorrow and silence are strong, and patient endurance is godlike.—LONGFELLOW. Beware the fury of a patient man.—DRYDEN. What can't be cured, must be endured. As if butter would not melt in his mouth.

827. In life there is nothing more unexpected and surprising than the arrivals and departures of pleasure.—A. SMITH. There is a pleasure that is born of pain.—O. MEREDITH. I wish you all the joy that you can wish.—SHAKESPEARE. Joy ruled the day and love the night.—DRYDEN. Joy rises in me like a summer's

perience pleasure etc. *n.*, joy, delight, delectate, oblectate [rare], enjoy oneself, hug oneself, be in heaven etc. *n.*, tread on enchanted ground, fall *or* go into raptures; be in clover [chiefly coll.], bask in the sunshine; feel at home, breathe freely.

6. *v.* enjoy, joy [arch.], pleasure [rare], be pleased with, receive *or* derive pleasure from, get a kick out of [slang], delight in, rejoice in, indulge in, luxuriate in, revel in, riot in, bask in, wallow in, gloat over *or* on; take to, take a fancy to; appreciate, like, have a liking for; relish, roll under the tongue, smack the lips; enter into the spirit of; take in good part; treat oneself to, solace oneself with.

7. *v.* please etc. 829.4–6.

8. *adj.* pleased, not sorry, gratified, proud [now chiefly dial.], delighted; glad, gladsome; charmed, intrigued [coll.]; pleased as Punch, pleased as a child with a new toy; pleased with, favorably impressed with, sold on [slang]; satisfied etc. (content) 831.6; amused etc. 840.24.

9. *adj.* happy, happy as a king, happy as a lark, happy as a clam at high water [U.S.], happy as the day is long, thrice happy, *ter quaterque beatus* [L.]; joyful, joyous, joyant [rare]; blest, blessed, blissful, "throned on highest bliss" (Milton); beatific(al), beatified; with sparkling eyes, with joyful face; unalloyed, without alloy, cloudless, painless; cheerful etc. 836.7–9.

10. *adj.* overjoyed, rapturous, raptured, enraptured, entranced, enchanted, imparadised, enravished, ravished, ecstatic, rapt, in raptures, in ecstasies, in paradise etc. *n.*, in a transport of delight, transported, carried away, beside oneself, beside oneself with joy, all over oneself [slang]; tickled, tickled to death [slang], tickled silly *or* pink [slang]; elate, elated; exulting, jubilant.

11. *adj.* hedonic(al), hedonistic.

---

morn.—COLERIDGE. It is comely fashion to be glad,— / Joy is the grace we say to God.—INGELOW. The first fine careless rapture.—BROWNING. Happiness consists in the multiplicity of agreeable consciousness.—JOHNSON. No man can enjoy happiness without thinking that he enjoys it.—JOHNSON. To fill the hour—that is happiness.—EMERSON. We have no more right to consume happiness without producing it than to consume wealth without producing it.—SHAW. Those who bring sunshine to the lives of others cannot keep it from themselves.—BARRIE. What one relish-

12. *adj.* pleasing etc. 829.7–9.
13. *adv.* happily etc. *adj.*, with pleasure etc. *n.*; willingly etc. 602.11.

828. Pain
(See 827. Pleasure; also 830. Painfulness)

Displeasure; Mental Suffering.—**1.** *n.* pain, suffering etc. *v.*, sufferance [rare], mental suffering; passion, ache, pang, dolor [poetic], distress, bale, woe; affliction, infliction; trial, tribulation, trials and tribulations; ordeal, fiery ordeal; the iron entering the soul; smart etc. (physical pain) 378; source of pain etc. (painfulness) 830.

2. *n.* displeasure, dissatisfaction, discomfort, malaise, discomposure, disquiet, inquietude, uneasiness, vexation of spirit; taking [coll.]; anhedonia, analgesia; discontent etc. 832; disgust etc. (dislike) 867; resentment etc. 900.

3. *n.* wretchedness, bitterness, infelicity, misery, anguish, agony, desolation; heartache, aching heart, heavy heart, bleeding heart, broken heart; prostration, prostration of soul; extremity, depth of misery, "Slough of Despond" (Bunyan); miseries of human life, "the thousand natural shocks that flesh is heir to" (Shakespeare); unhappiness, grief etc. (sadness) 837; despair etc. 859.1.

4. *n.* annoyance, aggravation [coll.], irritation, fret, vexation, mortification, chagrin; pother, bother, botherment [coll.], botheration [coll.]; trouble, troublement [coll. and dial.], peck of troubles, "sea of troubles" (Shakespeare); worry, worriment [coll.]; bore; thorn in the side etc. (source of annoyance) 830.2.

5. *n.* care, troubled thought, anxiety, solicitude, concern, cark [arch.], anxious *or* corroding care, cankerworm of care, carking cares [arch.].

6. *n.* torture, torment, cruciation, crucifixion, martyrdom, passion, rack, laceration, lancination; vivisection; purgatory, hell, hell upon earth; cruelty etc. 907.3.

---

es, nourishes.—FRANKLIN. *Sua cuique voluptas* [Each to his own pleasures].
828. Momentary joy breeds months of pain.—SHAKESPEARE. For ever the latter end of joy is woe.—CHAUCER. Our sincerest laughter / With some pain is fraught.—SHELLEY. Grief, that's beauty's canker.—SHAKESPEARE. Sorrows our portion are: ere hence we go, /

828.7 — 829.4   564

7. *n.* nightmare, ephialtes, incubus.

8. *n.* sufferer, victim, prey, martyr, object of compassion, wretch, shorn lamb.

9. *v.* suffer, suffer ~, feel ~, experience ~, undergo ~, bear *or* endure pain etc. *n.*, pain, ail, hurt, ache, bleed, labor under afflictions, have a bad time of it, go hard with, be troubled in mind, take to heart; take up the cross, bear the cross, stagger under the cross; quaff the bitter cup, drain the cup of misery to the dregs; be on pins and needles, sit on thorns; agonize, writhe, wince, make a wry face; come to grief; be the victim of, fall a sacrifice to; smart, tingle etc. (physical pain) 378.5; suffer adversity etc. 735.5, 6.

10. *v.* fret, chafe, stew [coll.], fret and fume, take on [coll.], be in a taking [coll.], cark [arch. exc. dial.]; worry, worry oneself, worry oneself sick; complain etc. 839.10.

11. *v.* grieve, sorrow, pine etc. (be sad) 837.6; mourn etc. (lament) 839.6-12; despair etc. 859.5.

12. *v.* pain etc. 830.3.

13. *adj.* pained, in pain, in a state of pain, full of pain etc. *n.*; suffering, aching, hurting etc. *v.*; hurt, wounded, distressed, afflicted; injured, injured in spirit; grieved, aggrieved; harrowed, tortured, racked, crucified, lancinated, lacerated, convulsed, agonized, under the harrow, on the rack, in limbo, between hawk and buzzard; mortified, chagrined; shocked, appalled; horrified, horror-stricken; in physical pain etc. 378.6.

14. *adj.* displeased, discomposed, discomforted, disturbed, perturbed, troubled, disquieted, uneasy, uncomfortable, ill at ease; fazed [coll., U.S.], feezed *or* feazed [obs. exc. dial.]; in a taking, in a way [both coll.]; offended, disgusted, sickened, sick of, nauseated, queasy; abhorrent etc. 898.5; discontented etc. 832.5; out of humor etc. 901.7; weary etc. 841.9; resentful etc. 900.12, 13.

15. *adj.* annoyed, irritated, provoked, bothered, troubled, disturbed, ruffled, piqued, irked, vexed, plagued, tormented, worried, galled, chafed, nettled; roiled, riled [coll. and dial.].

16. *adj.* wretched, miserable, infelicitous, poor, sorry, steeped to the lips in misery; woeful, woebegone; crushed, stricken, cut up [coll.], cut to the heart; heart-stricken, heartscalded [dial. Eng.], heartbroken, brokenhearted; careworn, heavy-laden; unhappy, sorrowful etc. (sad) 837.9-13; in tears etc. (lamenting) 839.13, 14; in despair etc. 859.7.

829. Pleasurableness
(See 830. Painfulness; also 827. Pleasure)

Capability of Giving Pleasure.—1. *n.* pleasurableness, pleasantness, agreeableness etc. *adj.*; pleasure-giving, jucundity [rare], jocundity, delectability; manna in the wilderness, land flowing with milk and honey, "the shadow of a great rock in a weary land" (Bible); flowery beds of ease; fair weather; sunny side, bright side; pleasure etc. 827; amusement etc. 840.

2. *n.* delightfulness etc. *adj.*, ravishment, enravishment, enchantment, entrancement, bewitchment, fascination, captivation; attraction etc. (allurement) 617.

3. *n.* treat, refreshment, feast, banquet, feast *or* banquet of the soul; regale, regalement; source of pleasure *or* gratification, cause of delight *or* enjoyment; a sight for sore eyes [coll.]; dainty etc. (delicacy) 298.9; sweetmeat etc. (sweets) 396.2.

4. *v.* please, cause ~, produce ~, create ~, give ~, afford ~, offer ~, present *or* yield pleasure etc. 827, take ~, tickle *or* hit one's fancy, meet one's wishes; satisfy, gratify, slake, satiate, quench; indulge, humor, flatter; treat, regale, refresh; interest; amuse etc. 840.20.

Crosses we must have; or, hereafter, woe.—HERRICK.   Remembering mine affliction and my misery, the wormwood and the gall.—BIBLE. Pain is the price that God putteth upon all things.—J. HOWELL.   Pain is no evil, / Unless it conquer us.—KINGSLEY.   Affliction is not sent in vain, young man, / From that good God who chastens whom he loves.—SOUTHEY   Misery makes strange bedfellows.

829. Please all, and you will please none.—AESOP.   *Decies repetita placebit* [It will please though ten times repeated].—HORACE. I would rather please one good man than many bad.—PITTACUS.   Charms strike the sight but merit wins the soul.—POPE.   He more had pleased us had he pleased us less.—ADDISON.   The art of pleasing is to seem pleased. HAZLITT.   The man who gives pleasure is as charitable as he who relieves suffering.—G. MOORE.   Satisfy a few; to please many is bad.—SCHILLER.   Men may be convinced, but they cannot be pleased, against their will.—JOHNSON.

5. *v.* delight, tickle, titillate, carry away, transport, imparadise, enrapture, entrance, enchant, fascinate, captivate, bewitch, take; charm, becharm; ravish, enravish; win ~, gladden *or* rejoice the heart, warm the cockles of the heart, do one's heart good; bless, beatify; gladden etc. (cheer) 836.6; attract etc. (allure) 617.4.

6. *v.* make things pleasant, make everyone feel happy, popularize, gild the pill, sweeten; smooth the troubled waters, pour oil upon the troubled waters.

7. *adj.* pleasurable, giving pleasure etc. *v.*, pleasure-giving, pleasing, pleasant, amiable, agreeable, grateful, gratifying, acceptable, likable, to one's liking, ~ mind *or* taste; welcome, welcome as the roses in May; comforting, comfortable; luxurious, voluptuous; refreshing, regaling etc. *v.*; cordial, genial; glad, gladsome; sweet, delectable, nice, dainty, delicate, delicious, dulcet; luscious etc. 396.8; palatable etc. 394.7; satisfactory etc. 831.7; cheering etc. 836.12; good etc. 648.8; amusing etc. 840.22; desirable etc. 865.21.

8. *adj.* delightful, felicitous, exquisite, lovely, charming, prepossessing, engaging, winning, winsome, taking, fascinating, captivating, killing [coll.], bewitching, enchanting, entrancing, ravishing, enravishing, heart-robbing, heartfelt, rapturous, thrilling, ecstatic, beatific(al), seraphic; empyrean, paradisaic(al), Elysian, heavenly; attractive, inviting etc. (alluring) 617.5.

9. *adj.* palmy, sunny, halcyon, Saturnian.

10. *adv.* pleasurably, delightfully etc. *adj.*; to one's delight, to one's heart's content; in utter satisfaction, in clover; from a full heart.

830. Painfulness

(See **829. Pleasurableness**; also **828. Pain**)

Capability of Giving Pain.—**1.** *n.* painfulness, unpleasantness, disagreeableness etc. *adj.*; disagreeability, *désagrément* [F.], unpalatability, undesirability, unacceptability; deplorability, pitiability, lamentability; pain, displeasure etc. 828.

2. *n.* (source or cause of pain) affliction, infliction, curse, woe, visitation, scourge, plague, pestilence, infestation, molestation; provocation, offense, "head and front of one's offending" (Shakespeare); stroke, shock, blow; cut, the iron entering the soul, "unkindest cut of all" (Shakespeare); trouble, troublement [coll. and dial.], "sea of troubles" (Shakespeare); hot water, hornet's nest; pother, bother, botherment [coll.], botheration [coll.]; annoyance, aggravation [coll.], grievance, nuisance, pest, vexation, mortification, worry, fret, gall.

sting, thorn, thorn in the side, crown of thorns; oppression, cross, load, burden, burthen [arch.]; cares, carking cares [arch.], canker worm of care; trial, tribulation, trials and tribulations; bitter pill, bitter draft *or* draught, bitter cup, cup *or* waters of bitterness; gall, gall and wormwood; sickener, nauseant; wound, injury, hurt; sore subject, skeleton in the closet, pea in the shoe, where the shoe pinches, rub, fly in the ointment, worm in the apple *or* rose, crumpled rose leaf; cancer, ulcer; canker, blight etc. (bane) 663.1, 2; sorrow etc. 837.3, 4.

3. *v.* pain, cause ~, occasion ~, give ~, bring ~, induce ~, produce ~, create *or* inflict pain etc. 828; hurt, wound, hurt *or* wound the feelings, scathe or scath [arch. and dial.], afflict, distress, displease, discompose, discommode, incommode, put out; faze [coll., U.S.], feeze *or* feaze [obs. exc. dial.]; pierce, prick, stab, lancinate, cut, cut up [coll.], cut to the heart, wound ~, sting *or* cut to the quick; bite, snap at, assail; bite the hand that feeds one; gripe etc. (physical pain) 378.4; smite etc. (punish) 972.5–9.

4. *v.* grieve, make unhappy etc. (sadden) 837.8.

5. *v.* annoy, torment, pester, plague, molest, worry, harass, harry, badger, heckle, bait, tease, tantalize, bullyrag, persecute, beset, infest, tweak the nose; pother, bother, trouble, fash [chiefly Scot. and North. Eng.], disquiet, disturb, agitate; irk, vex, mortify, irritate, provoke, sting, nettle, gall, fret, chafe, grate, grate *or* jar upon the feelings, go against the grain, get on one's nerves, give one a pain [slang], gripe, get [slang], get one's

---

830. Nothing gives pleasure but that which gives pain.—Montaigne. I must be cruel only to be kind.—Shakespeare. What deep wounds ever closed without a scar?—Byron.

Mighty men shall be mightily tormented.—Apocrypha. Every despot must have one disloyal subject to keep him sane.—Shaw.

goat [slang], burn up [slang], aggravate [coll.], exasperate, try the patience, pique; roil, rile [coll. and dial.]; aggrieve, affront, enrage, ruffle, sour the temper; give offense etc. 900.10.

6. *v.* torture, torment [now rare], agonize, harrow, rack, scarify, crucify, cruciate [obs.], excruciate, lacerate, convulse, wring; martyr, martyrize; put on *or* to the rack, break on the wheel, tar and feather, ride on a rail, masthead, keelhaul; barb the dart; plant a dagger in the breast, put a thorn in one's side; buffet, batter, beat up [slang], bruise, beat black and blue, beat to a mummy *or* jelly; prolong the agony, kill by inches.

7. *v.* repel, revolt, offend, shock; sicken, disgust, nauseate, stink in the nostrils, go against the stomach, turn the stomach, make one sick; stick in one's throat, stick in one's gizzard [coll.]; go against the grain, set the teeth on edge, grate on the ear; rankle, gnaw, corrode; horrify, appall; freeze the blood, make the flesh creep, make the hair stand on end, make the blood curdle *or* run cold, make one shudder; be unsavory etc. 395.4; be hateful etc. 898.4.

8. *v.* haunt, haunt the memory, obsess, beset, besiege, harass, weigh *or* prey on the heart, ~ mind *or* spirits, leave an aching void.

9. *adj.* painful, causing pain etc. 828, hurting etc. *v.*; dolorific(al), dolorous; sore, raw etc. (physical pain) 378.7.

10. *adj.* unpleasant, unpleasing, displeasing, disagreeable; unlikable, dislikable; distasteful, untasteful, untasty [now coll.], unpalatable, unsavory, unappetizing, undelicious, undelectable, uneatable, inedible, inesculent [rare]; sour, bitter; unattractive, uninviting, unalluring; undesired, undesirable; unwelcome, unwished, uncared-for, unvalued, unacceptable, unpopular, thankless.

11. *adj.* distressing, distressful; afflicting, afflictive; grievous, piteous, woeful, rueful, mournful, deplorable, pitiable, lamentable, sad, affecting, touching, pathetic; depressing, depressive; disheartening, dreary, melancholy, joyless, cheerless, dismal; comfortless, uncomfortable.

12. *adj.* annoying, irritating, provoking, aggravating [coll.], exasperating, mortifying, stinging, galling, unaccommodating, invidious, vexatious, tiresome, irksome, wearisome, troublesome, awkward; plaguing, plaguesome, plaguy [coll.]; importune, importunate; teasing, pestering, bothering, harassing, worrying, tormenting, carking [arch.].

13. *adj.* shocking, terrific, grim, appalling, crushing; dreadful, fearful, frightful; thrilling; tremendous, dire; heartbreaking, heart-rending, heart-wounding, heart-corroding, heartsickening; harrowing, rending; vulgar etc. 851.6, 7.

14. *adj.* odious, execrable, repulsive, repellent, repugnant, revolting, forbidding, frightful, abhorrent, offensive, disgusting, sickening, vile, foul, nasty, noisome, fulsome, noxious, obnoxious, abominable, hateful, contemptible, despicable, beastly, hideous; loathsome, loathful; nauseous, nauseating; horrid, horrible, horrific, horrifying; ugly etc. 846.6–8.

15. *adj.* acute, sharp, sore, severe, grave, hard, harsh, cruel, biting, caustic, cutting, corroding, consuming, racking, excruciating, searching, searing, grinding, grating, agonizing.

16. *adj.* cumbrous, cumbersome, burdensome, onerous, oppressive, weighty, heavy.

17. *adj.* desolating, withering, tragical, disastrous, calamitous, ruinous.

18. *adj.* insufferable, intolerable, insupportable, unendurable, unbearable, past bearing, not to be borne *or* endured, more than flesh and blood can bear, enough to drive one mad, enough to provoke a saint, enough to make a parson swear [coll.], enough to try the patience of Job.

19. *adv.* painfully etc. *adj.*, with pain etc. 828; deuced *or* deucedly [slang]; under torture, in agony; out of the depths.

831. Content
(See 832. Discontent)

1. *n.* content, contentment, contentedness etc. *adj.*; satisfaction, entire satisfaction; complacence *or* complacency, self-complacence *or* -complacency; ease, peace of mind; quietism; moderation; serenity etc. 826.2; cheerfulness etc. 836; comfort

---

831. Shut up in measureless content.—SHAKESPEARE. Contentment is the smother of invention.—CYNIC'S CALENDAR. Sweet are the thoughts that savor of content.—R. GREENE. Too grateful for the blessing lent / Of simple tastes and mind content!—HOLMES.

etc. 377.2; patience etc. (sufferance) 826.4; resignation etc. (submission) 725.

2. *n.* contented person, waiter on Providence; quietist.

3. *v.* be content etc. *adj.,* rest satisfied, rest and be thankful, take the good the gods provide, let well enough alone, feel oneself at home, hug oneself; take up with, take in good part; be reconciled to, make one's peace with; get over it; take heart, take comfort; put up with etc. (endure) 826.6.

4. *v.* render content etc. *adj.,* content, satisfy, comfort; put *or* set at ease, set one's heart *or* mind at ease *or* rest; speak peace, conciliate, reconcile, win over, propitiate, disarm, beguile; gratify etc. (please) 829.4; tranquilize etc. 174.5.

5. *v.* be tolerated etc. 826.6, go down, go down with [coll.], do.

6. *adj.* content, contented, satisfied etc. *v.*; with the mind at ease, at ease, at one's ease, *sans souci* [F.], without care, easygoing, not particular; comfortable, of good comfort, at home, at rest, in one's element, snug; imperturbable, not easily perturbed; unafflicted, unvexed, unmolested, unplagued; unrepining; cheerful etc. 836.7; patient, resigned etc. (meek) 826.10; pleased etc. 827.8.

7. *adj.* satisfactory, satisfying; adequate, commensurate, sufficient, ample, equal to; bearable, passable, acceptable, admissible, agreeable, unobjectionable, unexceptionable; desirable etc. 865.21.

8. *adv.* contentedly etc. *adj.,* to one's heart's content; all for the best.

9. *int.* content!, very well!, good!, well and good!, good for you!, all the better!, so much the better!, better and better!, it will do!, that will do!, done!; shake!, put it there! [both slang]; amen! etc. (assent) 488.14, 15.

832. Discontent
(See 831. Content)

1. *n.* discontent, discontentment, discontentedness etc. *adj.*; dissatisfaction, unsatisfaction; "the winter of our discontent" (Shakespeare); mortification, vexation of spirit, soreness; heartburning, heartgrief; cold comfort; inquietude; hypercriticism; indignation meeting; cave of Adullam; displeasure etc. 828.2; sadness etc. 837; dissent etc. 489; complaint etc. (lamentation) 839; disappointment etc. 509; regret etc. 833.

2. *n.* malcontent, noncontent [rare]; grumbler, growler, grouser [slang], murmurer, croaker, complainer, faultfinder, censurer, *laudator temporis acti* [L.]; kicker, grouch, crank [all coll.]; fussbudget, crab, bellyacher [all slang, U.S.]; rebeller [now rare], *frondeur* [F.], agitator, demagogue; reactionary, reactionist; seditionary, seditionist; irreconcilable, die-hard, bitter-ender [U.S.]; pessimist etc. (sad person) 837.5; rebel, revolutionist etc. (insurgent) 742.3; antagonist, opposer etc. (opponent) 710; lamenter etc. 839.5.

3. *v.* be discontented etc. *adj.,* feel discontent etc. *n.*; quarrel with one's bread and butter; repine, wish one to Jericho, wish one at the bottom of the Red Sea; shrug the shoulders; make a wry face, pull a long face; knit one's brows; look blue, look black, look black as thunder, look blank, look glum; take ill, take in bad part, take to heart; take on [coll.], fret, chafe, make a piece of work [coll.]; grumble etc. (complain) 839.10.

4. *v.* cause discontent etc. *n.,* make dissatisfied etc. *adj.,* dissatisfy, displease, disappoint, disgruntle, mortify, put out [coll.], disconcert, cut up [coll.], dishearten.

5. *adj.* discontented, disgruntled, dissatisfied etc. *v.*; unsatisfied, ungratified; malcontent, malcontented; out of humor *or* temper, in bad humor, in high dudgeon, in a fume; sore, sore as a crab [both coll.]; grouchy [coll.], fuss-budgety [slang, U.S.]; exigent, exacting, critical, hypercritical; glum etc. (sad) 837.9; regretful etc. 833.3; disappointed etc. 509.4; displeased etc. 828.14; dissentient etc. 489.5.

6. *adj.* unsatisfactory, dissatisfactory, unsatisfying, ungratifying; displeasing, disappointing, disheartening, disconcert-

---

832. Admiring others' lots, our own we hate.—HORACE. *Curtae nescio quid semper abest rei* [Something is always lacking to one's fortune].—HORACE. Content you in my discontent.—SHAKESPEARE. Let thy discontents be thy secrets.—FRANKLIN. Discontent is the want of self-reliance: it is infirmity of will.—EMERSON. One thing only has been lent / To youth and age in common—discontent.—M. ARNOLD. Discontent is the first step in the progress of a man or a nation.—WILDE.

ing, mortifying; inadequate, incommensurate, insufficient.

7. *int.* so much the worse!, *tant pis!* [F.], that's bad!, it couldn't be worse!, worse and worse!

833. Regret

1. *n.* regret, regretfulness etc. *adj.,* repining etc. *v.;* nostalgia, homesickness, *Heimweh* [G.], *mal du pays* [F.], *maladie du pays* [F.]; bitterness, heartburning; remorse, compunction etc. (penitence) 950; lamentation etc. 839; disappointment etc. 509; discontent etc. 832.

2. *v.* regret, deplore, repine, be sorry for; be nostalgic etc. *adj.,* cast a longing lingering look behind; rue, rue the day; *infandum renovare dolorem* [L.]; repent etc. 950.3; bewail etc. (lament) 839.6; express regret etc. (apologize) 952.5; prey on the mind etc. (haunt) 830.8.

3. *adj.* regretting etc. *v.,* regretful; nostalgic, homesick; remorseful etc. (penitent) 950.5; lamenting etc. 839.13; disappointed etc. 509.4; discontented etc. 832.5.

4. *adj.* regretted etc. *v.,* much to be regretted, regrettable; lamentable etc. (bad) 649.8.

5. *int.* what a pity!, too bad!, that's too bad!; hang it!, hang it all! [both coll.].

834. Relief
(See 835. Aggravation)

1. *n.* relief, deliverance, easement, softening, alleviation, mitigation, palliation, abirritation [Med.], mollification, assuagement, allayment, subduement, soothing etc. *v.;* sense *or* feeling of relief, sigh of relief; lullaby, cradlesong, *berceuse* [F.], *Schlummerlied* [G.]; refreshment etc. 689.

2. *n.* solace, consolation, encouragement, comfort, crumb of comfort, balm in Gilead.

---

833. Wild with all regret.—TENNYSON. Make the most of your regrets . . . To regret deeply is to live afresh.—THOREAU. I am homesick for my mountains.—B. CARMAN. When, sick for home, she stood in tears amid the alien corn.—KEATS.
834. Thy rod and thy staff they comfort me.—BIBLE. Be comfort to my age.—SHAKESPEARE. The gentle relief of another's care.—W. BLAKE. Whence comes solace? . . . in cleaving to the Dream.—HARDY.

3. *n.* lenitive, alleviative etc. (palliative) 662.6.

4. *v.* relieve, ease, alleviate, mitigate, palliate, abirritate [Med.], soothe, swage [dial.], assuage, lay, allay, soften, soften down, mollify, appease, subdue, pacify; salve, pour balm into, pour oil on; foment, poultice, stupe; dull, deaden, dull *or* deaden the pain; slake, slacken; smooth the ruffled brow of care, temper the wind to the shorn lamb, lay the flattering unction to one's soul; take the load off one's mind, take off a load of care; disburden, lighten etc. (facilitate) 705.4; remedy, cure etc. (restore) 660.8-13; refresh etc. 689.2; improve etc. 658.8.

5. *v.* solace, console, comfort, give comfort, bear up, pat on the back, encourage, set at ease; cheer etc. 836.6.

6. *v.* be relieved, feel relief, have a feeling of relief, breathe more freely, draw *or* heave a sigh of relief, draw a long breath; be comforted, take comfort; dry the eyes *or* tears, wipe away the tears; pull oneself together.

7. *adj.* relieving, easing, soothing etc. *v.;* lenitive, assuasive, palliative, anodyne, demulcent, emollient, balmy, balsamic, abirritative [Med.], paregoric(al), sedative, narcotic; calmative, calmant; consolatory, comforting; curative etc. (remedial) 662.25; restorative etc. 660.18.

835. Aggravation
(See 834. Relief)

1. *n.* aggravation, exasperation, exacerbation, heightening etc. *v.;* exaggeration etc. 549; irritation etc. (annoyance) 828.4.

2. *v.* aggravate, render worse, heighten, exasperate, exacerbate, acerbate, embitter, sour, enrage, envenom, provoke; fan the flame etc. (excite) 824.2; irritate etc. 824.5; annoy etc. 830.5.

3. *v.* become aggravated etc. *adj.;* go from bad to worse etc. (deteriorate) 659.6.

4. *adj.* aggravated etc. *v.,* worse, unrelieved.

5. *adj.* aggravating etc. *v.,* aggravative,

---

835. When sorrows come, they come not single spies, / But in battalions.—SHAKESPEARE. One woe doth tread upon another's heels, / So fast they follow.—SHAKESPEARE. It never rains but it pours.

exasperative, exacerbescent, irritative; annoying etc. 830.12.

6. *adv.* worse and worse, from bad to worse, out of the frying pan into the fire.

836. Cheerfulness
(See 837. Sadness; also 838. Rejoicing)

1. *n.* cheerfulness, cheeriness, blitheness etc. *adj.*; cheer, geniality, gaiety *or* gayety, gaiety of heart, *gaieté de cœur* [F.], sunshine of the mind *or* breast, light heart; good humor, ~ nature *or* temper, *bon naturel* [F.]; spirits, high spirits, animal spirits, flow of spirits; glee, high glee; Euphrosyne; *l'allegro* [It.]; hedonics, hedonism; gladness, joy etc. (happiness) 827.2; optimism etc. (hopefulness) 858.2; content etc. 831.

2. *n.* vivacity, liveliness etc. *adj.*, life, alacrity, animation, *allégresse* [F.].

3. *n.* merriment, mirth, jocundity, joviality, jollity, hilarity, levity, exhilaration; laughter etc. (rejoicing) 838; merrymaking etc. (amusement) 840; jocularity etc. (wit) 842.

4. *v.* be cheerful etc. *adj.*, have the mind at ease; keep up one's spirits, keep a stiff upper lip [slang], bear up; put a good face upon, view the bright side of the picture, view things *en couleur de rose* [F.], look through rose-colored spectacles; *ridentem dicere verum* [L.]; become cheerful, cheer up, brighten up, light up, perk up, take heart; cast away care, drive dull care away.

5. *v.* rejoice, sing, laugh, smile etc. 838.5–8.

6. *v.* cheer, make cheerful etc. *adj.*, cheerfulize, gladden, enliven, elate, exhilarate, invigorate, animate, inspire, inspirit, raise the spirits, put in good humor, rejoice, give joy to, cheer *or* rejoice the heart; delight etc. 829.5; amuse etc. 840.20; solace 834.5.

7. *adj.* cheerful, cheerfulsome [dial.], cheery, cheerly [arch.], of good cheer; blithe, blithesome; gay, gay as a lark; in

spirits, in good *or* high spirits, in high feather; light, lightsome, lighthearted; smiling, laughing; breezy, bully [slang], chipper [coll., U.S.], jaunty, debonair *or* debonaire, free and easy, carefree, airy, buoyant, bright, sunny, palmy, riant, sparkling; canty [Scot. and dial. Eng.], "crouse an' canty" (Burns); spirited, spiritful [rare], full of spirit; sprightly, sprightful, spry; lively, animated, vivacious, all alive; brisk, brisk as a bee; *allegro* [It.]; glad, happy etc. 827.8, 9; contented etc. 831.6; optimistic etc. (hopeful) 858.9.

8. *adj.* merry, merry as a cricket *or* grig, "as merry as the day is long" (Shakespeare); mirthful, hilarious; joyous, joyful, joyant [rare]; gleeful, gleesome; jolly, jolly as a thrush *or* sandboy; jovial, jocund, jocose, jocular; mirth-loving, laughter-loving; Abderian.

9. *adj.* elate, elated; jubilant, exulting, cock-a-hoop, flushed.

10. *adj.* playful, full of play, playsome, playful as a kitten; sportive, *folâtre* [F.], frolicsome, gamesome, frisky, tricksy, waggish; rollicking, rollicksome, rollicky [coll.].

11. *adj.* winsome, bonny, hearty, buxom.

12. *adj.* cheering, inspiriting, exhilarating etc. *v.*; pleasing etc. 829.7.

13. *adv.* cheerfully, cheerily etc. *adj.*; with good cheer, with a cheerful heart, with relish, with zest; on the crest of the wave.

14. *int.* cheer up!, come!, never say die!, "hence, loathed Melancholy!" (Milton), away with melancholy!, begone dull care!

837. Sadness
(See 836. Cheerfulness; also 839. Lamentation)

1. *n.* sadness, unhappiness, dejectedness etc. *adj.*; dejection, depression, lowness *or* depression of spirits, low ~, drooping *or* depressed spirits, heaviness *or* failure of heart, sinking heart, jawfall [rare], infestivity, gloom; despondence *or* despondency, black despondency, "Slough of Despond" (Bunyan); melan-

---

836. Be of good cheer.—BIBLE. The best of healers is good cheer.—PINDAR. A merry heart goes all the day.—SHAKESPEARE. A cheerful look makes a dish a feast.—G. HERBERT. A cheerful temper joined with innocence will make beauty attractive, knowledge delightful, and wit good-natured.—ADDISON. Cheerful without mirth.—BYRON. Good humour may be said to be one of the very best articles of dress one can wear in society.—THACKERAY.

837. A plague of sighing and grief.—SHAKESPEARE. Down, thou climbing sorrow.—SHAKESPEARE. And such a want-wit sadness makes of me, / That I have much ado to

choly, melancholia; dismals, blues [coll.], blue devils [coll.], mopes, lachrymals, mumps, dumps *or* doleful dumps [coll.], dolefuls [coll.], doldrums, vapors [arch.], megrims, horrors.

hypochondria, hypochondry, hypochondriasm [rare], hypochondriasis, hyps [coll.], *la maladie sans maladie* [F.]; pessimism, cynicism; *taedium vitae* [L.], disgust of life; anhedonia, analgesia; discontent etc. 832; weariness etc. 841; despair etc. 859.1; *mal du pays* [F.] etc. (regret) 833; sullenness etc. 901.2.

2. *n.* gravity, demureness etc. *adj.,* solemnity; long face, grave face; sullen looks etc. 901.3.

3. *n.* sorrow, grief, woe [arch.], dole [arch. and dial.], gnawing grief; heartfelt grief, heartgrief, heartache, aching heart, heavy heart, bleeding heart, broken heart; prostration, prostration of soul; misery etc. (wretchedness) 828.3.

4. *n.* (cause of dejection) damp, weight, oppression, weight ∼, depression *or* damp of the spirits; skeleton at the feast, death's-head, *memento mori* [L.]; sorry sight; affliction etc. 830.2.

5. *n.* sad person, seek-sorrow, self-tormenter *or* self-tormentor, *Heauton Timoroumenos* [Gr. ἑαυτὸν τιμωρούμενος], *il penseroso* [Old It.], mope, sourbelly [joc.], sourpuss [slang], dog in the manger [coll.], Job's comforter, spoilsport, damper, wet blanket [coll.], kill-joy, crapehanger [slang]; pessimist, cynic; hypochondriac, hypochondriast, *malade imaginaire* [F.]; grumbler etc. (malcontent) 832.2.

6. *v.* be sad etc. *adj.,* look downcast, lower *or* lour, hang down the head, pull *or* make a long face, laugh on the wrong side of the mouth, grin a ghastly smile, look blue, look like a drowned man; lay *or* take to heart; give way, lose heart, despond, droop, sink, languish, break one's heart; yearn, pine, repine, pine away; brood over, mope, fret, take on [coll.]; grieve, sorrow; mourn etc. (lament) 839.6–12, despair etc. 859.5; sulk, frown etc. (be sullen) 901.6; ache, bleed etc. (suffer) 828.9.

7. *v.* keep from laughing, refrain from laughter, repress a smile, keep one's countenance, keep a straight face.

8. *v.* sadden, make unhappy etc. *adj.,* hyp [coll.], deject, depress, depress the spirits, discourage, dishearten, dispirit, dull, lower, sink, damp, dampen, damp *or* dampen the spirits, damp ∼, dash *or* wither one's hopes, dash, knock down, cast a gloom *or* shade on; look black upon, frown upon; grieve, sorrow, plunge into sorrow, cut up [coll.], wring ∼, pierce ∼, lacerate *or* rend the heart, break one's heart, tear *or* rend the heartstrings, pull at the heartstrings, make the heart bleed; wring tears from, draw tears; prostrate, unman; weigh *or* lie heavy on the mind *or* spirits, prey on the mind, haunt the memory; pessimize [rare].

9. *adj.* sad, unhappy, out of humor *or* sorts, in bad humor, dejected, dispirited, downcast, downhearted, heavy-hearted, low-spirited, in low spirits, despondent, tristful, doleful; woeful, woebegone; uncheerful, uncheery, cheerless, joyless, spiritless; melancholy, melancholic, a prey to melancholy, down in the mouth [coll.], in the dumps *or* doleful dumps, in the suds [coll.], in the doldrums *or* depths, sullen, mumpish, dumpish, glum; moody, moodish; mopish, mopy [coll.], moping; pensive, *penseroso* [It.]; chapfallen *or* chopfallen, jawfallen [rare], crestfallen; discouraged, disheartened; prostrated, unmanned; grievous, lamentable; sulky etc. 901.8; discontented etc. 832.5; funereal etc. 363.25.

10. *adj.* dismal, gloomy, somber, *triste* [F.], dark, clouded, murky, lowering, glowering, frowning, lugubrious, saturnine, funereal; drear, dreary, drearisome; weary, weariful, wearisome; flat, dull, dull as dishwater, dull as a beetle.

11. *adj.* sorrowful, sorrowing etc. *v.,* sorrow-struck, sorrow-stricken, sorrow-wounded, sorrow-torn, sorrow-worn, sorrow-wasted, sorrow-beaten, sorrow-blinded, sorrow-clouded, sorrow-shot, sorrow-burdened, sorrow-laden, sorrow-sighing, sorrow-sobbing, sorrow-sick; mournful, mournsome; grieved, aggrieved, in grief etc. *n.,* plunged in grief; plaintful, tearful etc. 839.13, 14; steeped to the lips in misery etc. (wretched) 828.16.

12. *adj.* disconsolate, inconsolable, forlorn, comfortless; desolate, *désolé* [F.];

---

know myself.—SHAKESPEARE. 'Tis impious in a good man to be sad.—YOUNG. Sorrow's crown of sorrow is remembering happier things. —TENNYSON. Melancholy is the pleasure of being sad.—HUGO.

sick at heart, heartsick, soul-sick; lost; in despair etc. 859.7.

13. *adj.* overcome, broken-down, borne-down, bowed-down, downfallen, sunk, crushed, dashed, stricken, cut up [coll.]; heart-struck, heart-stricken, heartscalded [dial. Eng.]; heartbroken, brokenhearted; undone, unnerved, unmanned.

14. *adj.* hypochondriac(al), hypochondrial, hypped [coll.], hyppish [rare].

15. *adj.* pessimistic, pessimist, cynical; hopeless etc. 859.7.

16. *adj.* serious, sedate, staid, demure, earnest, sober, solemn, rueful, wan; grave, grave as an undertaker *or* judge, grave as a mustard pot [coll.]; grim, grim-visaged, grim-faced, long-faced.

17. *adv.* sadly etc. *adj.*, with a long face, with tears in one's eyes.

838. Rejoicing
(See 839. Lamentation; also 836. Cheerfulness)

1. *n.* rejoicing, exultation, triumph, jubilation; reveling etc. *v.*, revelry, revelment; heydey; merrymaking etc. (amusement) 840; merriment etc. 836.3; jubilee etc. (celebration) 883; paean, *Te Deum* [L.] etc. (glorification) 990.2.

2. *n.* smile, smiling etc. *v.*; grin, broad grin; sardonic grin, smirk, simper.

3. *n.* laughter, laughing etc. *v.*, laugh; giggle, titter, snicker, snigger, chuckle, cackle, crow; shout, shriek; burst *or* outburst of laughter, fit ∼, shout ∼, roar *or* peal of laughter; Homeric laughter, hearty laugh; horselaugh, guffaw; cachinnation; risibility, risibilities, risibles.

4. *n.* cheer, huzza, hurrah, hurray [coll.], cry, shout, yell [U.S. and Can.], tiger [coll.]; hosanna, hallelujah *or* halleluiah, alleluia *or* alleluiah *or* alleluja; applause etc. 931.4.

5. *v.* rejoice, jubilate, exult, joy, delight, glory, bless *or* thank one's stars, congratulate oneself, hug oneself, rub one's hands, clap hands, smack the lips, throw *or* fling up one's cap; dance *or* skip for joy, dance, skip, frisk, rollic, revel; sing, carol, chirp, chirrup, lilt, cry for joy; sing a *Te Deum*, sing a paean of triumph; exult, triumph; hold jubilee etc. (celebrate) 883.3; make merry etc. 840.21; gladden etc. (cheer) 836.6.

6. *v.* smile, have a smile, look with a smile; grin, grin like a Cheshire cat [coll.]; simper, smirk.

7. *v.* laugh, laugh outright, burst out, burst out laughing, burst into a roar *or* fit of laughter; shout, give a shout of laughter, shriek, roar, roar with laughter; be convulsed with laughter, shake with laughter, shake like jelly; burst *or* split with laughter, split [coll.], split one's sides, hold both one's sides, die *or* nearly die with laughing; giggle, titter, snicker, snigger, smicker [obs.], chuckle, cackle, crow; guffaw, horselaugh, mock, laugh in one's sleeve.

8. *v.* cheer, give a cheer etc. *n.*, huzza, hurrah, hurray [coll.], cry, shout, yell, yell oneself hoarse; applaud etc. 931.6.

9. *adj.* rejoicing etc. *v.*, jubilant, exultant, flushed; elate, elated; celebrating etc. 883.5.

10. *adj.* laughing etc. *v.*, ready to burst *or* die with laughter, convulsed with laughter, shaking like a jelly; risible; laughable etc. (ludicrous) 855.5.

11. *adv.* laughingly, with a roar of laughter etc. *n.*, in fits of laughter, amid peals of laughter; on *or* with a broad grin; in mockery.

12. *int.* hurrah!, hurray! [coll.], huzza!, *hoch!* [G.], one cheer more!, three cheers!, hip, hip, hurrah!, aha!, hail!, all hail!, tra-la-la!, hallelujah *or* halleluiah!, alleluia *or* alleluiah *or* alleluja!, hosanna!, praise be!, praise the Lord!, Heaven be praised!, glory be!, glory be to God!, glory to God!, glory to God in the highest!, *tant mieux* [F.]; bravo! etc. 931.13.

839. Lamentation
(See 838. Rejoicing; also 837. Sadness)

1. *n.* lamentation, lamenting, mourning etc. *v.*; lament, plaint, complaint, murmur, mutter, grumble, groan, moan, whine, whimper, sob; wail, wail of woe;

---

838. *Ride si sapis* [Laugh if you are wise].—MARTIAL. Rejoice with them that do rejoice, and weep with them that weep.—BIBLE. They laugh that win.—SHAKESPEARE. Laughter holding both his sides.—MILTON. Laugh and the world laughs with you, / Weep and you weep alone.—E. W. WILCOX. He laughs best who laughs last. Laugh and be fat.
839. Oh that my head were waters, and mine eyes a fountain of tears.—BIBLE. If you have

839.1 — 839.18

ululu, ululation; cry, outcry, scream, howl, bawl; jeremiad, dolorous tirade; sigh, suspiration, deep sigh; regret etc. 833; repentance etc. (penitence) 950; discontent etc. 832.

2. *n.* weeping, crying etc. *v.*; "weeping and gnashing of teeth" (Bible), lachrymation, lachrymals, tears, flood of tears, fit of crying, melting mood; cry, good cry [both coll.]; tearful eyes, swimming ∼, brimming *or* overflowing eyes; tear, teardrop, lachryma (*pl.* lachrymas, lachrymae); lachrymatory, tear bottle.

3. *n.* dirge, funeral *or* death song, funeral *or* dead march, dump [arch.], coronach [Scot. and Ir.], keen [Ir.], nenia [rare], requiem, elegy, epicedium, threne [rare], monody, threnody; funeral, knell etc. 363.4, 5.

4. *n.* mourning, mourning garments, weeds, widow's weeds, crape, black, deep mourning, sackcloth and ashes; cypress, cypress lawn, funereal cypress; emblem of sorrow, badge of black, willow, mourning band, mourning ring.

5. *n.* lamenter, mourner etc. 363.7; grumbler etc. (malcontent) 832.2; Niobe, Heraclitus, Jeremiah, Mrs. Gummidge.

6. *v.* lament, mourn, keen [Ir.], grieve, sorrow, weep over, bewail, bemoan, deplore, give sorrow words; *infandum renovare dolorem* (Vergil); regret etc. 833.2; repent etc. 950.3.

7. *v.* sigh, give ∼, breathe ∼, draw ∼, heave *or* fetch a sigh, sigh "like furnace" (Shakespeare).

8. *v.* weep, cry, sob, greet [arch. and dial.], blubber, snivel, bibber, whimper, yammer [dial.], pule, drop *or* shed tears *or* a tear, give way to tears, melt *or* burst into tears, dissolve in tears, *fondre en larmes* [F.]; pipe, pipe the eye [both slang]; cry one's eyes out, cry oneself blind.

9. *v.* wail, moan, groan, whine, yelp, howl, yowl, yawl [now dial.], squall, cry, yell, ululate, roar, bellow, roar *or* bellow like a bull, bawl; cry out lustily, rend the air, scream; vociferate etc. 411.5-7; mew etc. (animal sounds) 412.2.

10. *v.* complain, kick [coll.], grumble, murmur, mutter, growl, grouch [coll.], clamor, croak, grunt, fret, fuss, make a fuss about, take on [coll.], fret and fume; bellyache, crab, gripe, grouse [all slang]; complain without cause, cry out before one is hurt; criticize etc. (censure) 932.7; be discontented etc. 832.3.

11. *v.* show signs of grief, make a wry face, gnash one's teeth, wring one's hands, tear one's hair, beat one's breast, roll on the ground.

12. *v.* go into mourning, wear mourning, put on mourning, wear the willow etc. *n.*

13. *adj.* lamenting, mourning etc. *v.*; mournful, plaintful, plaintive; ululant, clamorous, crying to high heaven; complaining etc. *v.*, querulous, querimonious; in mourning, in sackcloth and ashes etc. *v.*; regretting etc. 833.3; sorrowful etc. 837.11; wretched etc. 828.16.

14. *adj.* tearful, tear-falling; lachrymal, lachrymose, lachrymatory; in the melting mood, on the edge of tears, ready to cry; in tears, with tears in one's eyes, with tearful *or* watery eyes, with swimming, ∼ brimming *or* overflowing eyes, with eyes suffused, bathed *or* dissolved in tears, "like Niobe, all tears" (Shakespeare).

15. *adj.* dirgelike, dirgeful; elegiac *or* elegiacal, epicedial, threnetic(al); funereal etc. 363.25.

16. *adj.* lamentable etc. (bad) 649.6.

17. *adv.* lamentingly, tearfully etc. *adj.*; *les larmes aux yeux* [F.]; *de profundis* [L.].

18. *int.* alas!, alack!, O dear!, heigh-ho!, ah me!, woe's me!, wellaway!, welladay!, lackaday!, alackaday!, alas the day!, lackadaisy!, that I had ever been born!, *O tempora, O mores!* [L.], what a pity!, *hinc illae lacrimae!* (Terence), *miserabile dictu!* [L.], too true!

---

tears prepare to shed them now.—SHAKESPEARE. The small orb of one particular tear.—SHAKESPEARE. Tears are the noble language of the eye.—HERRICK. Tears such as angels weep.—MILTON. The agony of reluctant tears.—BYRON. Heaven knows we need never be ashamed of our tears.—DICKENS.

Tears, idle tears, I know not what they mean.—TENNYSON. Only human eyes can weep.—MARVELL. And weep the more because I weep in vain.—GRAY. Light sufferings give us leisure to complain.—DRYDEN. I mourn'd and yet shall mourn with ever-returning spring —WHITMAN.

840. Amusement
(See 841. Weariness)

1. *n.* amusement, entertainment, diversion, pleasurable diversion, divertisement, *divertissement* [F.], relaxation, fun, play, sport, game; regale [rare], regalement, treat; joviality, pleasantry; pastime, *passe-temps* [F.]; avocation, hobby, hobbyhorse; labor of love; pleasure etc. 827; laughter etc. 838.3; wit etc. 842.

2. *n.* festivity, merrymaking, skylarking, merriment, jollity, jollification [coll.], joviality, conviviality, revelry, revelment, reveling, revels; festive occasion, festival, *fiesta* [Sp.], fete *or* fête, gala, blowout [slang], jamboree [slang], high jinks [coll.]; Holi, Dewali [both Hind.]; Bariram, Muharram [both Moham.]; rural festival, *fête champêtre* [F.].
  regatta, field day, *Turnerfest* [G.], gymkhana; picnic, junket [U.S.], squantum [local, U.S.]; clambake, fish fry, beefsteak fry, barbecue [U.S.]; wayzgoose; beanfeast [Eng.]; kettledrum [coll.]; drum, drum major, rout, hurricane, tempest [all arch.]; symposium; fair, *feria* [Sp.], carnival; Mardi gras; saturnalia; heyday; rejoicing etc. 838.1; jubilee etc. (celebration) 883; party etc. (social gathering) 892.5; feast etc. 298.37; concert etc. (music) 415.17.

3. *n.* frolic, gambol, romp, frisk, caper, rig, *fredaine* [F.]; revel, lark [coll.], high old time [coll.], escapade, *échappée* [F.], fling, spree, bout, randy [Scot. and dial. Eng.], randan [dial. and slang]; rantan *or* ran-tan [slang], bust, tear, beano [all slang]; bender, hellbender, toot, bat, bum [all slang, U.S.], carouse, carousal; orgy, debauch etc. (dissipation) 954.2, (drinking bout) 959.3; prank etc. 842.7.

4. *n.* round of pleasure, a short life and a merry one, racketing, holiday-making; debauchery etc. (dissipation) 954.2.

5. *n.* holiday, red-letter day, gala day, play day, fete *or* fete day, festival day, day of festivities, feria (*pl.* feriae); high holiday, bank holiday [Eng.], legal holiday [U.S.]; high days and holidays; Christmas, Mayday etc. 138.5, 7; day of rest etc. (vacation) 687.2.

6. *n.* dance, hop [coll.], shindig, [slang, U.S.], promenade, prom, ball, *bal* [F.], cantico [local U.S.]; masquerade; masquerade ball, *bal masqué* [F.], *bal costumé* [F.]; cornwallis [U.S.]; stag dance; nautch [Ind.]; dancing etc. *v.*, terpsichore.

7. *n.* (dances) polka, minuet, one-step, two-step, fox trot, turkey trot, mazurka, galop, gallopade, fandango, bolero, boutade, gavotte *or* gavot, *allemande* [F.], rigadoon, *passamezzo* [F.], ziganka, *ballo* [It.], *saltarello* [It.], *habanera* [Sp.], *malaguena* [Sp.], *bourrée* [F.], *courante* [F.], *furlana* [It.], galliard, *gopak* or *hopak* [Russ.], *branle* [F.], cakewalk, breakdown, step dance, tap dance, sand dance, *pas seul* [F.], skirt dance, folk dance, interpretative dance, morris dance, mistletoe-bough dance, sword dance, snake dance, Portland fancy.
  waltz, valse; saraband; tarantella, *tarantelle* [F.]; country-dance, *contre-danse* [F.], longways dance; schottische, strathspey, jig, hornpipe; fling, Highland fling; reel, Scotch reel, Virginia reel, Sir Roger de Coverley; square dance, quadrille, lancers, German; cotillion; dance of death, *danse macabre* [F.]; cantico, kantikoy; *chonchina* [Jap.], cancan, *danse du ventre* [F.], shimmy, hula; ballet, concert dance; ragtime, jazz etc. (music) 415.6, 7.

8. *n.* (dance steps) *gambade* [F.], gambado; *pas* [F.], chassé, coupe; shuffle, double shuffle; pigeonwing, heel-and-toe, buck and wing, grapevine.

9. *n.* dancer, *danseur* [F.], terpsichore, terpsichorean [coll.]; danseuse; geisha, geisha girl [both Jap.]; nautch girl, bayadere [both Ind.]; skirt dancer; step dancer, clog dancer, tap dancer, heel-and-toe dancer, buck-and-wing dancer; morris dancer; figure dancer, figurant, figurante; jitterbug [slang, U.S.]; hula dancer, hula girl; ballet dancer, ballet girl; *première danseuse* [F.], coryphée.

10. *n.* sports, games; athletic sports, athletics; gymnastics; track events; tournament; game, contest, pugilism, wrestling etc. (contention) 720; swimming etc. 267.9; sporting etc. (gambling) 621.6.

---

840. *Dulce est desipere in loco* [It is pleasant to act foolishly in the right place].—HORACE. If you would rule the world quietly, you must keep it amused.—EMERSON. Work consists of whatever a body is obliged to do, and Play consists of whatever a body is not obliged to do.

11. *n.* (sports and games) skating, ice skating, roller skating; tobogganing, sledding; **tennis, lawn tennis; rackets,** Ping-pong, squash, pallone, fives, trap bat and ball, badminton, battledore and shuttlecock, pall-mall, croquet, golf, curling, hockey, shinny; ball, cricket, rounders, baseball, basketball, pushball, captain ball, lacrosse; football, Rugby, Rugger [coll.]; association football, soccer; tilting, tilting at the ring, tent pegging, quintain; knur and spell [Eng.], quoits, discus, hammer throwing, horseshoe throwing, putting the weight *or* shot; hurdling, leapfrog; French and English, tug-of-war; race, sack race, potato race, obstacle race, three-legged race; hop skip and jump; horse racing, the turf, the sport of kings; sweepstake *or* sweepstakes, sweep *or* sweeps, polo, water polo; shooting, archery, rifle shooting.

blindman's buff, hunt the slipper, hide-and-seek, kiss in the ring; snapdragon; cross questions and crooked answers, twenty questions, what's my thought?, charades, crambo, dumb crambo, crisscross, proverbs, *bouts rimés* [F.]; hopscotch; jacks, jackstones; mumble-the-peg *or* mumblety-peg; tiddlywinks; cat, tipcat; bowling, **bowls;** billiards, pool, pyramids, bagatelle, **skittles,** ninepins, tenpins [U.S.], tivoli; chess, draughts, checkers *or* chequers, Chinese checkers, gobang, go, **shogi,** backgammon, dominoes, halma; merels, fox and geese, "the royal game of goose" (Goldsmith); chuck-a-luck, dice etc. (games of chance) 621.7.

12. *n.* (card games) cards; loo, cribbage, *bésique* [F.], drole, *écarté* [F.], picquet, all fours, quadrille, omber *or* ombre, reverse, Pope Joan, commit, boston, twenty-one, *vingt-et-un* [F.], *rouge et noir* [F.], faro, quinze, thirty-one, put, speculation, connections, brag, cassino, lottery, commerce, snipsnapsnorum, lift smoke, blind hookey, Polish bank, Earl of Coventry, banker [Eng.], monte, reversi, squeezers, old maid, fright, beggar-my-neighbor, goat, hearts, patience, solitaire, pairs; poker, stud poker, blind poker, draw poker, penny ante; straight poker, bluff; **bridge, contract bridge,** contract, auction bridge, auction, whist, five hundred; rum, rummy, gin rummy; euchre, cutthroat euchre, railroad euchre; Russian bank; napoleon, nap [coll.]; lotto, keno; rubber, round; jack pot, bank.

13. *n.* (playing cards) picture cards, face cards, court cards; ace, king, queen, joker; jack, knave; bower, right *or* left bower, best bower; diamonds, hearts, clubs, spades; hand; dummy; royal flush, flush, full house, straight, three of a kind, pair; trump; pack, deck.

14. *n.* (place of amusement) ballroom, dance hall, dance palace; gymnasium, gym [coll.]; billiard room, pool room; shooting gallery; pleasure garden *or* ground, pleasance, plaisance [arch.], park, paradise, common *or* commons; athletic field, playground, cricket ground, archery ground, polo ground, croquet ground *or* lawn, golf links; court, racket court, tennis court, squash court, badminton court; bowling alley, bowling green; rink, glaciarium, ice rink, skating rink; racecourse, track; stadium, hippodrome, concert hall etc. (theater) 599.10; casino etc. 621.14; swimming pool etc. 652.4.

Vauxhall, Ranelagh, Hurlingham, Lord's, Epsom, Newmarket, Doncaster, Sandown Park, Henley, Cowes, Mortlake [all Eng.]; Coney Island, Brooklands, Sheepshead Bay, Belmont Park, Saratoga, New London, Forest Hills, Longwood [all U.S.]; Monte Carlo; Longchamps.

15. *n.* (amusement devices) merry-go-round, carrousel, roundabout, flying horses; ferris wheel; seesaw, teeter-totter; swing; *montagne Russe* [F.]; aerial railway, scenic railway; roller coaster, chutes; peep show, puppet show, raree show, galanty show, Punch-and-Judy show, marionettes.

16. *n.* toy, plaything, bauble, knickknack, gimcrack, gewgaw, kickshaw, whimwham, trinket; doll, baby doll, paper doll, rag doll, puppet, marionette; dollhouse, doll carriage, doll furniture; teetotum, top; popgun, air gun *or* rifle,

---

—MARK TWAIN. Old boys have their playthings as well as young ones; the difference is only in the price.—FRANKLIN. A man cannot spend all this life in frolic.—JOHNSON. In Xanadu did Kubla Khan / A lofty pleasure-

dome decree.—COLERIDGE. He capers, he dances, he has the eyes of youth.—SHAKESPEARE. Foot it featly here and there.—SHAKESPEARE. That vague kind of penitence which holidays awaken next morning.—DICKENS.

water pistol; ball, bat, racket; toy soldiers, lead soldiers; blocks, alphabet blocks; educational toys, mechanical toys.

17. *n.* player, reveler, frolicker, frisker, gamboler, carouser, skylarker, pleasurer, pleasurist, pleasure seeker, playboy [slang, U.S.]; sportsman, sporting man [now rare], sport, gamester; sportswoman, gamestress; archer, toxophilite; ballplayer, cricketer, footballer etc.; contestant etc. (opponent) 710, (combatant) 726; wrestler, pugilist etc. (combatant) 726.1, 2; jumper etc. 309.3; huntsman, fisherman etc. 622.4, 5; gambler etc. 621.15.

18. *n.* master of the revels, master of ceremonies, *arbiter elegantiarum* [L.], *arbiter bibendi* [L.], toastmaster.

19. *n.* devotee, follower, votary, zealot, enthusiast, energumen; fan, bug, nut [all slang]; rooter [slang, U.S.]; turfman.

20. *v.* amuse, entertain, divert, enliven; tickle, tickle the fancy, titillate, raise a smile *or* laugh, put in good humor; cause ~, create ~, occasion ~, raise ~, excite *or* produce laughter, convulse with laughter, set the table in a roar, be the death of one; recreate; interest; treat, regale; gladden etc. (cheer) 836.6; please, delight etc. 829.4–6.

21. *v.* amuse oneself, give oneself over to pleasure, be on pleasure bent, make merry, drown care, drive dull care away, play, game [now dial.], sport, disport, revel, frolic; gambol, frisk, romp, ramp [now dial.], caper, cut capers [coll.], antic, curvet, cavort [U.S.], flounce, trip, skip; dance, trip the light fantastic, trip it on the light fantastic toe; junket, feast, banquet, "eat, drink, and be merry" (Bible); carouse, spree, go on a spree etc. *n.*, wanton, run a rig, sow one's wild oats, have one's fling, take one's pleasure, paint the town red [slang], see life, *desipere in loco* (Horace); make *or* keep holiday, go a-Maying; toy, dally, while away the time, beguile the time, kill time; wassail etc. 959.16; celebrate etc. 883.3.

22. *adj.* amusing, entertaining, diverting etc. *v.*; recreative, recreational, lusory; festive, festal; jovial, jolly, jocund; pleasing etc. (pleasurable) 829.7, 8; humorous etc. (witty) 842.9; laughable etc. (ludicrous) 855.5.

23. *adj.* playful, playful as a kitten, sportive, waggish, roguish, rompish; prankish, pranky.

24. *adj.* amused etc. *v.*, "pleased with a rattle, tickled with a straw" (Pope); pleased etc. 827.8.

25. *adv.* playfully etc. *adj.*, at play, in sport.

841. Weariness
(See 840. Amusement)

1. *n.* weariness, tiredness etc. *adj.*, ennui, boredom; fatigue etc. 688; lassitude, drowsiness etc. (languor) 683.4; dullness etc. 843; sadness etc. 837.

2. *n.* disgust of life, *taedium vitae* [L.]; disgust etc. (repugnance) 867.2; satiety etc. 869.

3. *n.* tedium, monotony, humdrum, irk; wearisomeness, tediousness etc. *adj.*; sameness, sameliness, samesomeness [dial.], wearisome sameness *or* uniformity; undeviation, unvariation, invariability; drearihood, drearihead [arch.]; dull work; heavy hours, time on one's hands, time hanging heavily on one's hands; regularity etc. (uniformity) 16; twice-told tale etc. 496.3.

4. *n.* bore, proser, twaddler, dryasdust, pest, nuisance, buttonholer; fossil, stick, wet blanket [all coll.]; flat tire, drip, droop, pill, stiff, pain in the neck [all slang].

5. *v.* weary, tire, jade, weary *or* tire to death, bore, irk, bore to death, ~ tears *or* distraction, bore stiff [slang], bore out of one's life, bore out of all patience, set *or* send to sleep; buttonhole; harp upon, dwell on *or* upon, harp upon one *or* the same string, sing the same old song *or* tune, mount *or* ride a hobby [coll.]; fatigue etc. 688.5.

6. *v.* disgust, nauseate etc. (repel) 830.7; pall, cloy etc. (sate) 869.4.

7. *v.* be weary etc. *adj.*, be tired of *or* with, be bored by, yawn, die with ennui.

8. *adj.* wearying etc. *v.*, wearing, weariful, wearisome; boring, boresome; tiresome, irksome, mortal [coll.], "weary,

---

841. We often pardon those who bore us, but never those whom we bore.—LA ROCHEFOUCAULD.   The secret of being a bore is to tell everything.—VOLTAIRE.   A bore is a man who, when you ask him how he is, tells you.—B. L. TAYLOR.   A man who lets himself be bored is even more contemptible than the bore.—BUTLER.   Weary of myself and sick of asking / What am I and what I ought to be.—M. ARNOLD.   Even the weariest river / Winds somewhere safe to sea.—SWINBURNE.

stale, flat, and unprofitable" (Shakespeare); tedious, monotonous, humdrum, singsong, dingdong [coll.], jog-trot, wearsomely uniform, too much with us [coll.]; drear [rare], dreary, drearisome; prosy, prosing, prosaic; dry-as-dust; harping, prolix, long-winded; dry, uninteresting etc. (dull) 843.5, 6; fatiguing etc. 688.8; repetitional etc. 104.6, 7; regular etc. (uniform) 16.5.

9. *adj.* weary, weariful, tired etc. *v.*; tired to death, weary unto death; flagging, spiritless; *blasé* [F.], life-weary, weary of life; bored, irk [obs. exc. dial.], uninterested, bored stiff [slang]; disgusted, sick of; fatigued etc. 688.6; languid, sleepy etc. 683.14, 15.

10. *adv.* wearily etc. *adj.*, *usque ad nauseam* [L.].

842. Wit
(See 843. Dullness; also 844. Humorist)

1. *n.* wit, wittiness etc. *adj.*, humor, drollery, pleasantry, *esprit* [F.], salt; Attic wit, Attic salt, Atticism; ready wit; fancy, whim; comedy etc. 855.2.

2. *n.* jocularity, jocosity, jocoseness, facetiousness, whimsicality, whimsicalness; waggishness, waggery; comicality etc. 855.1; merriment etc. 836.3.

3. *n.* buffoonery, buffoonism; fooling, foolery, tomfoolery; trickery, waggish trickery, harlequinade, horseplay; shenanigans, monkeyshines [both slang, U.S.]; ridiculousness etc. 855.

4. *n.* witticism, jest, joke, capital joke, wisecrack [slang], gag [slang], play of wit, *jeu d'esprit* [F.], quip, quirk, quiz, crank, conceit, *concetto* [It.], quiddity [rare], *plaisanterie* [F.], mot, bright *or* happy thought, bright *or* brilliant idea, *mot pour rire* [F.], smart saying, bon mot; story, yarn, funny story, good story; flash of wit, scintillation; repartee, persiflage, badinage, banter; retort, sally, clever ~, ready *or* witty reply *or* retort, snappy comeback [slang], *quid pro quo* [L.]; facetiae, quips and cranks; *canorae nugae* [L.]; cream of the jest, point, *quodlibet* [L.]; jestbook; epigram etc. (maxim) 496; bad joke etc. 851.3.

5. *n.* wordplay, play upon words, *jeu de mots* [F.], missaying, corruption, abuse of terms, paronomasia, clinch [now rare], *calembour* [F.]; pun, punning; equivoque, equivocality, *équivoque* [F.], double-entendre [F.], *double entente* [F.], *mot à double entente* [F.]; quibble, verbal quibble; anagram, paragram [rare], acrostic, double acrostic; amphiboly, amphibologism; palindrome; idle conceit; riddle etc. 533.2; parody etc. 856.3.

6. *n.* old joke, trite joke, hoary-headed joke, joke with whiskers [joc.], chestnut, old chestnut [both slang]; Joe Miller, Joe Millerism; twice-told tale, retold story, warmed-over cabbage [coll.], *réchauffé* [F.]; bromide [slang] etc. (trite saying) 496.3; triteness etc. 843.2; repetition etc. 104.

7. *n.* prank, trick, roguish *or* waggish trick, *espièglerie* [F.], practical joke, quiz, *boutade* [F.], antic, caper, frolic, rig [obs. exc. dial.], vagary, monkey trick; monkeyshine, shenanigan [both slang, U.S.].

8. *v.* joke, jest, wisecrack [slang], crack a joke, cut jokes, get off a joke, tell a good story; pun; make fun of, make merry with, joke at one's expense; perpetrate a joke, play tricks *or* pranks, play a practical joke, trick; bandy *or* exchange jokes, repartee [rare], retort, flash back, come back, come back at, come right back at [all slang]; flash, sparkle, scintillate; *ridentem dicere verum* [L.]; banter etc. (ridicule) 856.4; set the table in a roar etc. (amuse) 840.20.

9. *adj.* witty, humorous, funny, jocular, jocose, facetious, whimsical, merry and wise, *spirituel* [F.], pleasant [arch.]; droll, drollish; smart, clever, brilliant, scintillating, sparkling, keen, cute [coll.], pungent, sprightly; keen-witted, quick-witted, nimble-witted; Attic; full of

---

842. *Adhibenda est in jocando moderatio* [One should be moderate in his jests].—CICERO. This keen encounter of our wits.—SHAKESPEARE. A witty woman is a treasure; a witty beauty is a power.—MEREDITH. Impropriety is the soul of wit.—MAUGHAM. The delectable form which intelligence takes in its moments of surplus power—the form of wit. —S. P. SHERMAN. For the love of laughter, hinder not the humour of his design.—SHAKESPEARE. Humour is the mistress of tears.— THACKERAY. Humor is gravity concealed behind the jest.—J. WEISS. Nothing spoils a romance so much as a sense of humour in the woman.—WILDE. Everything is funny as long as it is happening to somebody else.— W. ROGERS. I never dare to write / As funny as I can.—HOLMES.

point, *ben trovato* [It.]; waggish, roguish; prankish, pranky; playful etc. 840.23; comic etc. 855.5; amusing etc. 840.22.

10. *adv.* in fun, *pour rire* [F.], in sport, in play, in joke, in jest, for the jest's sake.

843. Dullness
(See 842. Wit)

1. *n.* dullness, flatness etc. *v.*; dullery [rare], infestivity, jejunity; want of originality, dearth of ideas; prosaism, prosaicism; prose, matter of fact; heavy book *or* story, *conte à dormir debout* [F.]; stupidity etc. 499.2; monotony etc. (weariness) 841.

2. *n.* triteness, commonplaceness etc. *adj.*; banality, triviality [arch.]; platitude, commonplace etc. (trite saying) 496.3; old joke etc. 842.6.

3. *v.* be dull etc. *adj.,* fall flat, fall flat upon the ear; hang fire; prose, platitudinize; take *au sérieux* [F.].

4. *v.* render dull etc. *adj.,* damp, depress, throw cold water on, lay a wet blanket on.

5. *adj.* dull, dullsome [rare], dull as dish water; devoid of interest, uninteresting, unentertaining, unlively, slow, dry, dry-as-dust, arid, bald, pointless, jejune, flat, insipid, vapid, tasteless, insulse [rare], "weary, stale, flat, and unprofitable" (Shakespeare); drear [rare], dreary, drearisome; prosaic, prosy, prosing; heavy, ponderous, elephantine; boring, monotonous etc. (wearying) 841.8; stupid etc. 499.12.

6. *adj.* trite, trivial [arch.], stereotyped, stock, set, banal, common, commonplace, familiar, everyday, household, matter-of-fact, platitudinous, bromidic [slang], corny [slang, U.S.], threadbare, worn thin, moth-eaten, stale, warmed-over; hackney, hackneyed; well-known etc. 490.17.

---

843. Gentle dullness ever loves a joke.—POPE. We are growing serious and, let me tell you, that's the very next step to being dull.—ADDISON. Learn'd, without sense, and venerably dull.—C. CHURCHILL. Fill a dull man to the brim with knowledge and he will not become less dull.—BALFOUR. Dull as an alderman at church, or a fat lapdog after dinner.—HOLCROFT. Commonplace people dislike tragedy because they dare not suffer and cannot exult.—MASEFIELD.

844. Humorist
(See also 842. Wit)

n. humorist, wit, witling, *bel-esprit* [F.], joker, jester, wisecracker [slang], wag, wagwit, *drôle de corps* [F.], life of the party, galliard [arch.], spark, *bon diable* [F.], "agreeable rattle" (Goldsmith); *persifleur* [F.], banterer, reparteeist; punster, punner; epigrammatist; zany, madcap; caricaturist, parodist, burlesquer; jack-a-dandy; Jack-in-the-green; Joe Miller; funnyman, clown etc. (comedian) 599.20; laughingstock etc. 857.

845. Beauty
(See 846. Ugliness)

1. *n.* beauty, beautifulness, loveliness, comeliness etc. *adj.*; pulchritude, elegance, grace, *belle tournure* [F.], concinnity, delicacy, refinement, charm, *je ne sais quoi* [F.], *nescio quid* [L.]; good looks, good effect; bloom, glow; polish, gloss; the beautiful, τὸ καλόν or *to kalon* [Gr.]; beauty unadorned; the flower of, the pink of; symmetry etc. 242; pleasurableness etc. 829.

2. *n.* brilliance *or* brilliancy, radiance, luster, splendor, gorgeousness etc. *adj.,* magnificence, grandeur, glory, sublimity.

3. *n.* a beauty, charmer, *charmeuse* [F.], fascinator, enchantress, eyeful [coll., U.S.], picture [coll.], "the face that launch'd a thousand ships" (Marlow); beaut, dream, looker, good *or* swell looker, sight *or* treat for sore eyes, stunner, dazzler, fetcher, peach, bear, knockout, raving beauty [all slang]; belle, reigning beauty; *beau idéal* [F.] *or* beau ideal, paragon; Venus [Rom. Myth.], Venus of Milo; Aphrodite, Hebe [both

---

844. Jesters do oft prove prophets.—SHAKESPEARE. A jest loses its point when the jester laughs himself.—SCHILLER. He must not laugh at his own wheeze; / A snuff-box has no right to sneeze.—K. PRESTON. The saddest ones are those that wear / The jester's motley garb.—D. MARQUIS.

845. Everything has its beauty but not everyone sees it.—CONFUCIUS. He hath made everything beautiful in his time.—BIBLE. A thing of beauty is a joy forever.—KEATS. "Beauty is truth, truth beauty,"—that is all / Ye know on earth, and all ye need to know.—KEATS. What a strange illusion it is to suppose that beauty is goodness.—TOLSTOY. Beauty is its own excuse for being.—EMERSON. Beauty is the virtue of the body, as virtue is the beauty of the soul.—EMERSON. Euclid alone / Has

Gr. Myth.]; Apollo, Apollo Belvedere, Hyperion, Adonis, Antinoüs, Narcissus [all Gr. and Rom. Myth.]; Astarte [Phoenician Myth.]; Balder, Freya [both Norse Myth.]; Helen of Troy, Cleopatra; the Graces, peri, houri.

4. *n.* (comparisons) butterfly; garden; flower, wild flower, rose, violet, orchid, anemone, asphodel, buttercup, daffodil, lily, lily of the valley, rhododendron, windflower; cameo; bijou, jewel etc. (ornament) 847; work of art etc. 556.8, 9; statue etc. 554.4; melody etc. 413.4.

5. *n.* beautifying etc. *v.*, beautification; calisthenics, physical culture; make-up, cosmetics, powder, rouge, lip rouge, lipstick, eye shadow, mascara, eyebrow pencil, cold cream, vanishing cream, foundation cream, hand cream *or* lotion; landscape gardening; decoration etc. 847.

6. *v.* be beautiful etc. *adj.*, shine, beam, bloom; look fit to kill, knock one's eyes out [both slang].

7. *v.* beautify, render beautiful etc. *adj.*; become one, set off, grace, suit, fit; *se faire une beauté* [F.]; powder, rouge, make-up, apply cosmetics etc. (*see* cosmetics etc. *above* 845.5); decorate etc. (ornament) 847.11.

8. *adj.* beautiful, beauteous, endowed with beauty; pulchritudinous, handsome, pretty, pretty as a picture, lovely, graceful, elegant, exquisite, flowerlike, delicate, dainty, refined; easy on the eyes, not hard to look at, long on looks, looking fit to kill, nifty [all slang]; harmonious etc. (music) 413.26, (color) 428.18.

9. *adj.* attractive, charming, fetching [coll.], catching, fascinating, alluring, enchanting, engaging, enravishing, entrancing, bewitching, captivating, intriguing; provocative, *provoquant* [F.].

10. *adj.* comely, goodly, personable, agreeable, pleasing, seemly [obs. exc. dial.], sightly, fair, decent [arch.], proper [arch. and dial.], likely [chiefly dial.], bonny, becoming, good-looking, well-favored, well-informed, well-made, well-proportioned, shapely; symmetrical etc. 242.4, 5.

11. *adj.* trim, tidy, neat, trig, natty [coll.], dapper, spruce, smart, classy [slang], jimp [Scot. and dial. Eng.], jaunty, quaint [arch.], tricksy, tight [now chiefly dial.]; glossy, sleek.

12. *adj.* blooming, in full bloom; rosy, ruddy; rosy-cheeked, cherry-cheeked; bright, bright-eyed.

13. *adj.* brilliant, shining, beaming, sparkling, glowing, radiant, splendorous *or* splendrous, splendid, resplendent, resplendently beautiful, dazzling, rich, gorgeous, ravishing, superb, magnificent, grand, fine, glorious, heavenly, divine, sublime; devastating, stunning, killing, raving [all slang].

14. *adj.* perfect etc. 650.5.

15. *adj.* presentable, passable etc. (tolerable) 648.11.

16. *adj.* artistic(al), arty [coll.], of consummate art; esthetic; picturesque, pictorial, pictury; paintable, *fait à peindre* [F.]; well-composed, well-grouped, well-arranged, well-varied; curious; ornamental etc. 847.12; tasteful etc. 850.5.

846. Ugliness
(See 845. Beauty)

1. *n.* ugliness, homeliness, unseemliness etc. *adj.*; inelegance, want of symmetry, inconcinnity [rare]; uglification; deformity etc. (distortion) 243; disfigurement etc. (blemish) 848; imperfection etc. 651; squalor etc. (uncleanness) 653; baldness etc. (hairlessness) 226.3.

2. *n.* forbidding countenance, vinegar aspect, hanging look, wry face, face that would stop a clock [coll.].

3. *n.* eyesore, object, figure, ugly duckling, sight [coll.], fright; scarecrow; hag, harridan, strumpet, witch; specter; monster, *"monstrum horrendum informe ingens"* (Vergil); satyr; Aesop, Caliban; blemish etc. 848.

---

looked on Beauty bare.—MILLAY. The fatal gift of beauty.—BYRON. Personal beauty is a greater recommendation than any letter of introduction.—ARISTOTLE. A fair exterior is a silent recommendation.—PUBLILIUS. Beauty without grace is the hook without the bait.—EMERSON. Was this the face that launch'd a thousand ships / And burnt the topless towers of Ilium?—MARLOWE. It is a misfortune to be too handsome a man.—PLAUTUS. Handsome is that handsome does.—GOLDSMITH. The perception of beauty is amoral.—THOREAU. It is in rare and scattered instants that beauty smiles even on her adorers.—SANTAYANA.

846. Over-great homeliness engendereth dispraising.—CHAUCER. No one blames a man for being ugly.—ARISTOTLE. Oh gracious, why wasn't I born old and ugly?—DICKENS. Beauty's only skin deep, but ugly goes to the bone.—A. B. EVANS.

(comparisons) sin, the wrath of God, hell; a mud fence; a toad, a crow, an octopus, a baboon, a monkey.

4. *v.* be ugly etc. *adj.*, look ill, look a sight *or* fright [coll.]; make faces, grimace.

5. *v.* render ugly etc. *adj.*, uglify; deform etc. (distort) 243.3; disfigure, blemish etc. (impair) 659.8; soil etc. 653.15.

6. *adj.* ugly, homely, uncomely, unsightly, unshapely, unlovely, unseemly, not fit to be seen; unbeautiful, unbeauteous, beautiless; inartistic, unornamental; plain, ordinary; ugly as sin, ugly as a toad etc. *n.*; forbidding, frightful, hideous, uncanny; horrid, horrible, horrific, horrifying; grotesque, monstrous.

7. *adj.* misshapen, misproportioned etc. (distorted) 243.5; crooked etc. 217.13; shapeless etc. (formless) 241.5; gaunt etc. (lean) 203.11; dumpy etc. (stubby) 201.6; obese etc. (stout) 192.12, 13; bloated etc. 194.10.

8. *adj.* unprepossessing, ill-favored, hard-favored, evil-favored; ill-looking, evil-looking; hard-featured, hard-visaged; grim, grim-faced, grim-visaged; grisly, ghastly, gruesome, macabre; ghostlike, deathlike, cadaverous; haggard; squalid; blowzy; graceless, ungraceful; inelegant, uncouth, ungainly, stiff, rugged, rough, awkward, clumsy, slouching, rickety, gawky, lumpish, lumping, lumbering, hulking, hulky, bulky, unwieldy; coarse, gross etc. (vulgar) 851.6, 7.

9. *adj.* repellent, repulsive etc. (odious) 830.14; displeasing etc. (unpleasant) 830.10.

847. Ornamentation
(See **848. Blemish, 849. Simplicity;** also **577. Ornament**)

1. *n.* ornamentation, ornament, ornamental art, ornature [rare], ornation [rare]; ornateness etc. *adj.*, elegance; adornment, decoration, embellishment, elaboration, embroidery; garnish, garnishment; architecture, frozen music (Schopenhauer); illustration, illumination; purple patches, flowers of rhetoric etc. 577; design, arts of design etc. 554;

art etc. 556; painting etc. 556.2; engraving etc. 558; beautification etc. 845.5.

2. *n.* frippery, finery, gaudery, trickery, trappings, superfluity; frills, frilling, frillery, frilliness; gingerbread; spangle, spanglet [rare]; paste; tinsel, clinquant, pinchbeck; gilt, gilding; tawdriness etc. 851.2; ostentation etc. 882; showy clothes etc. 225.13.

3. *n.* (ornamentations) fretwork, tracery, filigree, arabesque, foliation, imbrication, strapwork, interlacing, checkering, cuspidation, reeding; Moresque, Morisco; vermiculated work, vermiculation; scroll, spiral, wave, flourish, running scroll, guilloche, zigzag; diaper, diapering; striping, lining, banding; spotting, powdering; frostwork, frosting; tooling, figure work, niello; inlaid work, parquetry; beaten work, *repoussé* [F.], *repoussage* [F.]; metalwork, wrought-iron work, bent-iron work; panelwork, paneling; stenciling, batik; graffito; vignette, *fleuron* [F.]; appliqué, appliqué work.

headpiece, tailpiece; *cul-de-lampe* [F.]; bow, knot; shoulder knot, epaulet *or* epaulette; aglet, aigulet [rare]; frog; star, rosette; feather, plume, panache, egret, aigrette; fillet, snood; make-up, cosmetics etc. 845.5; intaglio etc. (relief) 557.6; engraving etc. 558.3; enamel, varnish etc. (paint) 428.5.

4. *n.* (architectural) molding *or* moulding, listel, fillet, fascia, torus, billet, ovolo, astragal, reed, cavetto, scotia, *congé* [F.], patera, apophyge, ogee, beak, splay, volute, scrollhead, cornice, frieze, cartouche, finial, terminal, boss, cusp, acanthus, fret; foil, trefoil, quatrefoil, cinquefoil; bead, beading; cyma, *cyma recta* [L.]; egg and tongue, egg and dart, egg and anchor; pilaster, column, caryatid (*pl.* caryatides), atlantes (*sing.* atlas), telamon (*pl.* telamones).

5. *n.* (floral) wreath, festoon, garland, chaplet, crown, bays, laurel; bouquet, spray, nosegay, posy [arch. or coll.], corsage, boutonniere, flower.

6. *n.* needlework, fancywork; embroidery, broidery [arch.]; lace, duchesse lace, pillow lace; point lace, point, needle point, needle-point lace; tatting, crochet, guipure, insertion, Valenciennes, Mechlin *or* Mechlin lace; brocade, brocatel;

---

847. It is not only fine feathers that make fine birds.—Aesop.   Ornament is but the guiled shore / To a most dangerous sea.—Shakespeare.   Hide with ornaments their want of Art.—Pope.   The first spiritual want of a barbarous man is Decoration.—Carlyle.   Ornamentation is the principal part of archi-

trimming, edging, binding, galloon, fringe, border, motif; frill, frilling, frillery; bugles, beads; drapery, over-drapery; tapestry, hanging, arras; tassel; *drap d'or* [F.]; millinery.

7. *n.* jewelry, bijouterie; jewel, bijou; tiara, crown, coronet, diadem; ring, bracelet, bangle, armlet, anklet, earring, nose ring, carcanet [arch.]; chain, necklace, torque, locket; brooch, chatelaine.

8. *n.* gem, precious stone, stone; diamond, brilliant; pearl, pearlet; sapphire, lapis lazuli, ruby; emerald, beryl, aquamarine, alexandrite; opal, fire opal, girasol *or* girasole; garnet, carbuncle; jade, jadestone; tourmaline; amethyst, plasma; turquoise; topaz; coral; chalcedony, agate, onyx, sard, sardonyx, chrysoprase, carnelian, cat's-eye, jasper; heliotrope, bloodstone; hyacinth, jacinth, zircon, jargon *or* jargoon; chrysolite, peridot; spinel, spinel ruby; moonstone, sunstone; oriental opal, ~ emerald etc., occidental opal, ~ emerald etc. [now rare]; gem of the first water; birthstone.

9. *n.* trinket, trinklet; gewgaw, knickknack, gimcrack, kickshaw, whimwham, bauble, fribble; gaud; bric-a-brac; trifle etc. 643.3.

10. *n.* virtu, article of virtu etc. (work of art) 556.8.

11. *v.* ornament, ornamentalize; decorate, trim, adorn, beautify, dandify, adonize [rare], embellish, enrich, garnish, set out; dress, dress up; deck, bedeck; dizen, bedizen; dight, bedight [both arch.]; primp, prink, prank, primp ~, prink *or* prank up, trick up *or* out, fig out, array, titivate *or* tittivate, spruce up [coll.]; smarten, smarten up; spangle, bespangle; bead; embroider, work, fret; grain, engrain; blazon, emblazon; illuminate, illustrate; furbish, burnish, polish; make up, apply cosmetics etc. (beautify) 845.7; gild, enamel etc. (paint) 428.10; tool, emboss etc. (engrave) 558.5.

12. *adj.* ornamental, ornamentary [rare], decorative; beautifying, embellishing, adorning etc. *v.*; becoming, artistic etc. (beautiful) 845.8–16.

13. *adj.* ornamented, adorned, beautified etc. *v.*; ornate, rich, elegant, fancy; flowery, flashing, glittering; gorgeous, splendid; splendacious, splendiferous [both joc.]; fine, fine as a Mayday queen; festooned; spangled, bespangled, new-spangled; gilt, begilt, new-gilt; tessellated, inlaid; champlevé, cloisonné, topiary [rare]; showy etc. (gaudy) 851.8, (ostentatious) 882.8.

14. *adj.* smart, chic, gay, dashing, spruce, dapper, classy [slang], jaunty, tricksy [rare]; tricked out, pranked out, dressed up etc. *v.*; bedight [arch.], dressed to advantage, well-groomed; in one's best bib and tucker [coll.], in Sunday best, *endimanché* [F.]; *en grande tenue* or *toilette* [F.], in full dress, in evening dress *or* clothes, in court dress; fashionable etc. 852.7.

848. Blemish
(See 847. Ornamentation)

1. *n.* blemish, disfigurement, disfiguration, defacement; maculation, macule, macula; stain, tarnish, spot, blot, blotch, speck, speckle, patch, smirch, smutch, smudge, smot [Scot.], blur, daub, smear; stigma (*pl.* stigmas, stigmata), stigmatism; scar, scab, pock, blister; blobber *or* blubber lip, harelip; adactylism, adactylia; freckle, birthmark, bruise etc. (discoloration) 440a; blain, wart, mole etc. (protuberance) 250.2; flaw, defect etc. (fault) 651.2; soil, dirt etc. 653.3, 5; deformity etc. (distortion) 243; injury etc. (impairment) 659.3, 4; eyesore etc. 846.3.

2. *v.* blemish, stain, stigmatize etc. (discolor) 440a.2; soil etc. 653.15; disfigure, deface etc. (injure) 659.8; deform etc. (distort) 243.3; uglify etc. 846.5.

3. *adj.* blemished, disfigured, defaced; maculate, stigmatic etc. (discolored) 440a.3; speckled, blotched etc. (spotted) 440.9; soiled etc. (unclean) 653.16; deformed etc. (distorted) 243.5; injured etc. (impaired) 659.12; imperfect etc. 651.4.

---

tecture.—RUSKIN.   Inestimable stones, unvalued jewels, / All scattered in the bottom of the sea.—SHAKESPEARE.

848. Let a blemish, which perhaps is small, be undisguised. A fault which is hidden is deemed greater than it is.—MARTIAL.   Read not my blemishes in the world's report.—SHAKESPEARE.   The birth marks / Of the butterflies.—N. CRANE.

849. Simplicity
(See 847. Ornamentation; also 576. Plainness)

1. *n.* simplicity, simpleness, plainness, chasteness etc. *adj.*; chastity, purity, restraint, severity; unornamentation, unadornment, unembellishment; beauty unadorned, undress, nudity; common or garden variety; artlessness etc. 703.

2. *v.* simplify, render simple etc. *adj.*, reduce to simplicity etc. *n.*, strip of ornament, chasten, restrain; commonplace.

3. *adj.* simple, plain, homespun, ordinary, common, commonplace, matter-of-fact, everyday, workday, garden, household, workaday, plebeian, Philistine; homely, homish, homelike; prosy, prosaic, unpoetical; inartificial *or* unartificial, unpretending, unassuming, unfeigning, unflattering, unaffected, free from affectation, natural, native; informal, *sans façon* [F.]; *simplex munditiis* (Horace); simple-minded, unsophisticated etc. (artless) 703.4; tasteful etc. 850.5.

4. *adj.* inornate, chaste, pure, restrained, severe; free from ornament etc. 847; unornate, unornamented, unadorned, undecorated, ungarnished, unembellished, unenriched, unvarnished, unarranged, untrimmed, undecked, unarrayed, undressed, naked, nude, bare, bald, blank; unfurbished, unpolished.

850. Taste
(See 851. Vulgarity)

1. *n.* taste, good ~, refined *or* cultivated taste; tastefulness etc. *adj.*; fine feeling, refinement, delicacy, nicety, subtlety, tact, finesse, flair; gust, gusto; *to prepon* [Gr. τὸ πρέπον], polish, elegance, grace, culture, cultivation; aesthetics; "caviare to the general" (Shakespeare);

---

849. Beauty of style and harmony and grace and good rhythm depend on simplicity.—PLATO. Elegant as simplicity.—COWPER. What a power has white simplicity.—KEATS. Nothing is more simple than greatness; indeed, to be simple is to be great.—EMERSON. Simplicity of character is no hindrance to subtlety of intellect.—J. MORLEY. No architecture is so haughty as that which is simple.—RUSKIN.
850. It is one of the greatest blessings that so many women are so full of tact.—OSLER. The life of man is stronger than good taste.—MASEFIELD. The wild vicissitudes of taste.—JOHNSON. Taste is the literary conscience

discretion etc. (discrimination) 465; fastidiousness etc. 868.

2. *n.* virtuosity, virtu, artistic taste, connoisseurship, dilettantism, dilettanteism, fine art of living; *friandise* [F.], epicurism; fine art etc. 556.

3. *n.* man of taste, epicure, epicurean; gourmet, gourmand, *bon vivant* [F.], connoisseur, *cognoscente* [It.]; virtuoso, judge, critic; *arbiter elegantiae* or *elegantiarum* [L.]; dilettante, amateur; euphemist, purist, precisian; Aristarchus, Corinthian, Aristotle, Stagirite, Petronius.

4. *v.* exercise *or* display taste etc. *n.*, appreciate, judge, criticize; exercise discrimination etc. 465.2; be fastidious etc. 868.3.

5. *adj.* tasteful, in good taste, tasty [coll.]; *comme il faut* [F.]; refined, cultivated; classical, Attic; *tiré à quatre épingles* [F.]; nice, subtle, fine, delicate, *délicat* [F.], dainty; precise; formal; euphemistic, proper, seemly, chaste etc. (elegant) 578.2; unaffected etc. (simple) 849.3, 4; attractive, charming etc. (beautiful) 845.8, 9; aesthetic etc. (artistic) 845.16; discriminative etc. 465.4; fastidious etc. 868.4.

6. *adj.* to one's taste, to one's mind, after one's fancy.

7. *adv.* tastefully etc. *adj.*, with taste etc. *n.*, with quiet elegance, with elegant simplicity, without ostentation.

851. Vulgarity
(See 850. Taste)

Bad Taste.—1. *n.* vulgarity, vulgarness, coarseness etc. *adj.*; vulgarism, Gothicism, *grossièreté* [F.], unrefinement, indelicacy, inelegance *or* inelegancy, impropriety, indecorum, *brusquerie* [F.], incivility, *gaucherie* [F.]; barbarism, barbarity; bad taste, *mauvais goût* [F.], *mauvais ton* [F.]; rusticity, inurbanity; parvenuism, parvenudom; loud

---

of the soul.—JOUBERT. Love of beauty is Taste.—EMERSON. *De gustibus non est disputandum* [Concerning tastes there is no disputing]. Every man to his taste.
851. Vulgarity is an inadequate conception of the art of living.—CREIGHTON. It is considered more withering to accuse a man of bad taste than of bad ethics.—CHESTERFIELD. A thing is not vulgar merely because it is common.—HAZLITT. Not all the pumice of the

behavior [coll.], misbehavior, misconduct, conduct unbecoming a gentleman; rowdyism, ruffianism, blackguardism, vandalism; brutality, brutishness, brutification; savagery, savagism; ribaldry; ill breeding etc. (discourtesy) 895; vulgar speech etc. 579; obscenity etc. (impurity) 961.

2. *n.* gaudiness, gaudery, tawdriness etc. *adj.*; cheap jewelry, tinsel, paste; showy clothes etc. (finery) 225.13; frippery etc. 847.2; ostentation etc. 882.

3. *n.* bad joke, *mauvaise plaisanterie* [F.], poor joke, joke in bad taste; obscene *or* risqué story, équivoque, *double-entendre* [F.], *doubleentente* [F.], *mot à double entente* [F.]; trite joke etc. 842.6; practical joke etc. (prank) 842.7.

4. *n.* vulgarian, vulgar ∼, coarse ∼, rude *or* unrefined person, low *or* vulgar fellow, *épicier* [F.]; rough, roughneck [slang]; rough diamond, diamond in the rough; cub, unlicked cub; tomboy, hoyden; snob, cad [coll.], bounder [coll.], gent [joc. or vulg.]; vulgarist, ribald; boor, clown, barbarian etc. (commonalty) 876.5-7; slut, trollop etc. (slattern) 59.5; knave etc. 949; sensualist etc. 954a; libertine etc. 962.

5. *v.* be vulgar etc. *adj.*, be a vulgarian etc. *n.*, show a want of tact *or* consideration; talk shop, smell of the shop; misbehave, cut up [slang], roughhouse.

6. *adj.* vulgar, unrefined, inelegant, indelicate, coarse, crass [now rare], rude, ribald, low-minded, gross, indecorous, improper, unseemly, unbeseeming, unpresentable, *contra bonos mores* [L.]; untasteful, tasteless, in bad taste; ungenteel, shabby-genteel; ungentlemanly, ungentlemanlike; unladylike, unfeminine; homely, homespun, homebred; doggerel, mongrel; extravagant, monstrous, horrid; low, base, ignoble, vile, scurvy, sorry, scrubby, beggarly; uncivil, ill-mannered etc. (discourteous) 895.6; obscene, foul-mouthed etc. (impure) 961.9; shocking etc. 830.13.

7. *adj.* uncouth, unpolished, uncultivated, uncultured, unkempt, uncombed, untamed, unlicked, incondite [rare], rough, rude, crude, crass, raw, woolen [rare]; graceless, ungraceful; lubberly, cloddish, lumpish, boorish, borrel [arch.], clownish, loutish, churlish, carlish; wild, wild as a hawk, wild as an unbacked colt; rowdy, rowdyish; blackguard, blackguardly; uncivil, uncivilized; savage, savagerous [slang, U.S.]; brutish, brutified; barbarous, barbaric, barbarian, barbaresque, Gothic *or* gothic; heathenish, heathen; outlandish, tramontane; Bohemian, unconventional; unclassical; rustic, provincial etc. (countrified) 183.3; plebeian etc. 876.11; slovenly, slatternly etc. (untidy) 59.9.

8. *adj.* gaudy, tawdry, showy, flashy, garish, loud [coll.], screaming [coll.], jazzy [slang], sporty [coll.], meretricious, brummagem [slang], obtrusive, flaunting, flaring, glaring, flaming, glittering; florid, flowery; ostentatious etc. 882.8; affected etc. 853.6; ornate etc. 847.13; conspicuous etc. 525.5.

852. Fashion

1. *n.* fashion, fashionableness etc. *adj.*, fashionability; style, *ton* [F.], mode, vogue, bon ton, prevailing taste, the rage, the go [coll.], *dernier cri* [F.], the last word [slang], the latest fashion, the latest thing, the latest scream [slang]; height of fashion, star of fashion, glass of fashion, "the glass of fashion and the mould of form" (Shakespeare); form etc. 240; demeanor, appearance etc. (aspect) 448.4; method, manner etc. (way) 627; modernism etc. 123.3.

2. *n.* convention, conventionalism, *convenance* [F.], conventionality, conventional usage *or* practice, prevailing conventional usage, prevailing form *or* usage, social usage, ∼ form, ∼ habit *or* custom, order of the day, conventions of society, conventionals [coll.], dictates of society, the proprieties; dictates of Mrs. Grundy, Grundyism, Mrs. Grundy; propriety, *bienséance* [F.], decorum; form, good form, formality; etiquette, point of etiquette; punctilio, punctiliousness; practice, observance etc. (custom) 613.2; conformity etc. 82.

---

polish'd town / Can smooth the roughness of the barnyard clown.—HOLMES. On with the dance! Let joy be unrefined!—CYNIC'S CALENDAR. Glitter—and in that one word how much of all that is detestable do we express!—POE.

852. So many lands, so many fashions.—G. CHAPMAN. The fashion / Doth wear out more apparel than the man.—SHAKESPEARE. Fine clothes wear soonest out of fashion.—FULLER. Fashion is gentility running away

3. *n.* gentility, polish, refinement etc. (courtesy) 894; nobility etc. 875.

4. *n.* society, fashionable ~, polite *or* high society, *bon ton* [F.], high life, fashionable life, *beau monde* [F.], town [arch.], *monde* [F.], world, fashionable world; Vanity Fair, Mayfair; court, drawing room; persons of fashion, social group, smart set [coll.], the four hundred [U.S.], upper ten [coll.], upper ten thousand, upper crust [coll.], upper cut [coll.], cream of society; elite, aristocracy etc. (nobility) 875.2.

5. *n.* fashionable person, fashionable, person of fashion, man *or* woman of the world, leader of fashion; society person, socialite [coll.]; clubman, clubwoman; *arbiter elegantiae* or *elegantiarum* [L.] etc. 850.3.

6. *v.* be fashionable etc. *adj.*, be the rage etc. *n.*, have a run, pass current; follow *or* keep up with the fashion, conform to *or* fall in with the fashion, be *or* get on the band wagon [slang], be *or* get in the swim [coll.], swim *or* go with the stream, ~ tide *or* current, follow the crowd, do as others do, keep in step, keep up appearances, behave oneself.

give a tone to society, cut a figure in society [coll.], be a member of the best clubs, brush shoulders with the nobility; appear at court, be presented at court; set the fashion, bring into fashion; conventionalize etc. (conform) 82.4, 5.

7. *adj.* fashionable, stylish, modish, swell [slang], *recherché* [F.], in fashion etc. *n.*, alamode, *comme il faut* [F.], all the rage, all the go [coll.]; admitted *or* admissible in society etc. *n.*, presentable, being done; up-to-date, up-to-datish, up-to-the-minute, up-to-dick [slang], up [coll.], abreast of the times, on the boat [slang]; new-fashioned, new-fashion [dial.]; *à la française, à la parisienne, à l'anglaise, à l'américaine* [all F.]; chic, spruce etc. (smart) 847.14.

8. *adj.* conventional, according to use *or* custom, prescriptive, wonted, established, fixed, stipulated, cut and dried *or* dry [coll.], understood, admitted, recognized, acknowledged, received, approved, orthodox, correct, right, proper, decorous; customary, accustomary [arch.]; prevalent, prevailing; current, popular; traditional, traditive, traditionary [rare]; habitual etc. 613.11; conformable to rule etc. 82.9.

9. *adj.* genteel, gentlemanly etc. (courteous) 894.12, (noble) 875.10.

10. *adj.* unfashionable, old-fashioned, out-of-date etc. (antiquated) 124.9.

11. *adv.* fashionably etc. *adj.*, for fashion's sake, according to the dictates of society *or* Mrs. Grundy, in the latest style *or* mode.

853. Affectation

1. *n.* affectation, affectedness etc. *adj.*; *minauderie* [F.], pretension, pretense, airs, put-on [dial. and slang], *simagrée* [F.], show, mere *or* false show, mere outside, front *or* false front [coll.]; mannerism, trick of behavior; stiffness, formality, buckram; purism; precisianism; pedantry, pedantism; prunes and prisms; euphuism; euphemism; charlatanism, charlatanry, charlatanship; quackery, quackism, quackishness; hypocritical sorrow, crocodile tears; grimace; false pretension etc. (dissembling) 544.2; pomposity etc. (grandiloquence) 577.2; (ostentation) 882; boasting etc. 884; sanctimony etc. 988.2.

2. *n.* prudery, prudity [rare]; prudishness, priggishness etc. *adj.*; false *or* mock modesty, *mauvaise honte* [F.], false shame; bigotry etc. 606.2; fastidiousness etc. 868.

3. *n.* foppery, dandyism, coxcombry, coquetry, puppyism, conceit.

4. *n.* affecter, lump of affectation, mannerist, pretender, actor, play-actor [coll.], performer; grimacer, grimacier [rare]; *précieuse* [F.], *précieuse ridicule* [F.]; purist; poetaster; euphuist; euphemist; *bas bleu* [F.], bluestocking [coll.], blue [coll.]; prig, prude, prudist, puritan; precisian, formalist; attitudinarian etc. 882.5; fop etc. 854; pedant etc. 492.4; sophist etc. 477.6; charlatan, hypocrite etc. (deceiver) 548.1-4; flatterer etc. 935.2; bigot etc. 606.3; pietist etc. 988.6.

853. They are the affectation of affectation.—FIELDING.   Any affectation whatsoever in dress implies . . . a flaw in the understanding.—CHESTERFIELD.   Conceit in weakest bodies strongest works.—SHAKESPEARE.   The foolish, fashionable air / Of knowing all and feeling nought.—PATMORE.

from vulgarity, and afraid of being overtaken.—HAZLITT.   Fashion, the arbiter and rule of right.—STEELE.   The tyranny of Mrs. Grundy is worse than any other tyranny we suffer under.—SPENCER.

5. *v.* affect, assume, put on, simulate, register [slang], pretend, counterfeit, sham, fake [coll.], feign, make believe, make out like [coll.], make a show of, profess, pass off for, act *or* play a part, act, play-act [coll.]; mince, mince it, prink [dial. Eng.]; coquet, flirt a fan; simper, smirk, bridle; languish; euphuize; euphemize; overact, overdo; pose, give oneself airs etc. (be ostentatious) 882.6; boast etc. 884.5.

6. *adj.* affected, full of affectation, pretentious, flashy; high-sounding, big-sounding; mannered, *maniéré* [F.]; unnatural, artificial, stagy, theatrical; insincere, unsincere; conceited, coxcomical, foppish, dandified; simpering; sentimental, namby-pamby; languishing; euphuistic(al), euphemistic(al); overwrought, overdone, overacted; canting, hypocritical etc. (dissembling) 544.8; make-believe etc. (spurious) 545.13; pompous etc. (grandiloquent) 577.7, (ostentatious) 882.8; sanctimonious etc. 988.11.

7. *adj.* prudish, priggish, prim, smug, demure, *tiré à quatre épingles* [F.], mincing, affectedly nice, Quakerish, puritanical, precise [now rare], narrow, straitlaced, stiff-necked, hidebound, barkbound; stilted, stiff, formal, in buckram; starch, starched; pedantic(al); pragmatic(al); overmodest; bigoted etc. 606.7; finical etc. (fastidious) 868.4.

854. Fop

1. *n.* fop, fine gentleman, dandy, swell [coll.], exquisite, coxcomb, dude [coll.], beau, ladies' man, macaroni [Hist.], blade, blood, buck [arch.], spark, carpet knight, popinjay, puppy [derog.], *petit maître* [F.], jackanapes, jack-a-dandy, bantam cock [coll.], man about town, fribble; prig, prude; masher; affecter etc. 853.4; attitudinarian etc. 882.5.

2. *n.* fine lady, *grande dame* [F.]; belle, toast; flirt, coquette etc. (flirt) 902.6.

855. Ridiculousness
(See also **856.** Ridicule, **857.** Laughingstock)

1. *n.* ridiculousness, ludicrousness etc. *adj.,* ridiculosity, farcicality, comicality, drollery; amphigory *or* amphigouri, nonsense verse, doggerel verse *or* doggerel; malaprop, malapropism; spoonerism, Partingtonism, Leiterism; bathos, anticlimax; foolishness etc. (absurdity) 497; buffoonery etc. 842.3; howler [slang], Hibernicism etc. (blunder) 495.3; laughing stock etc. 857.

2. *n.* farce, mere farce; comedy, *comédie* [F.], *comedia* [Sp.]; broad humor, broad *or* raw comedy, *comédie rosse* [F.], low comedy; slapstick comedy, slapstick; *vis comica* [L.]; burlesque etc. 856.3; musical comedy etc. (drama) 599.4.

3. *v.* be ridiculous etc. *adj.,* commit an absurdity, play *or* act the fool, make a fool of oneself, play *or* ride the goat [coll.], stultify oneself, put oneself out of court; pass from the sublime to the ridiculous; raise a laugh etc. (amuse) 840.20.

4. *v.* make ridiculous etc. 856.5.

5. *adj.* ridiculous, ludicrous, comic(al), farcical, funny, humorous, amusing, quizzical, laughable, risible, rich, screaming, killing [coll.], too funny *or* killing for words [coll.], too funny for anything *or* any use [coll.]; droll, drollish; whimsical, whimsical as a dancing bear; tragicomic(al), seriocomic(al), mock-heroic; doggerel; nonsensical etc. (absurd) 497.4; odd, grotesque etc. (unusual) 83.10; burlesque etc. 856.7; trivial etc. 643.11.

6. *int.* that's ridiculous!, that's a laugh! [slang] etc. (that's absurd) 497.5.

856. Ridicule
(See also **855.** Ridiculousness, **857.** Laughingstock)

1. *n.* ridicule, derision, irrision [rare], raillery, mockery, banter, persiflage, badi-

---

854. Of all the fools that pride can boast, / A Coxcomb claims distinction most.—J. Gay. True fops help nature's work, and go to school / To file and finish God Almighty's fool.—Dryden. A six-foot column of fop, a lighthouse without any light atop.—Hood. Where none are beaux, 'tis vain to be a belle.—Lyttleton.

855. *Du sublime au ridicule il n'y a qu'un pas* [From the sublime to the ridiculous it is but a step].—Napoleon. They that are serious in ridiculous things will be ridiculous in serious affairs.—Cato the Elder.

856. Ridicule often decides matters of importance more effectually, and in a better manner, than severity.—Horace. Ridicule is the test of truth.—J. Ray. I defy the wisest man in the world to turn a truly good action into ridi-

nage, twit, chaff; quiz, quizzing etc. *v.*; joke, jest; asteism; irony, sarcasm; sardonic grin *or* smile, snicker *or* snigger, smirk, grin, leer, fleer; scoffing etc. 930.2; disparagement etc. (detraction) 934.

2. *n.* squib, lampoon etc. (personality) 934.2.

3. *n.* burlesque, parody, satire; travesty, *travestie* [F.]; caricature, *caricatura* [It.]; macaronic, macaronic composition; farce etc. 855.2; absurdity etc. 497.

4. *v.* ridicule, laugh at, grin at, smile at, snicker *or* snigger, te-hee, laugh in one's sleeve; make fun *or* game of, poke fun at, deride, mock, banter, rally, chaff, joke, jest, twit, roast [slang], guy [coll., U.S.], jolly [coll.], rag [slang, Eng.], smoke [now rare], haze [U.S.], rally; taunt, laugh to scorn etc. (scoff) 930.6; disparage etc. 934.3.

5. *v.* make ridiculous etc. 855.5, make a fool *or* April fool of, make a goat of [coll.], make merry with, show up [coll.], turn into ridicule, stultify, get the laugh on [slang]; fool etc. 545.10.

6. *v.* burlesque, satirize, parody, caricature, travesty.

7. *adj.* derisive, derisory; bantering etc. *v.*, quizzical, mock; ironical, sarcastic, cynical, Rabelaisian; burlesque, macaronic(al), caricatural; mock-heroic, Hudibrastic; scurrilous etc. 929.5; contemptuous etc. 930.8; disparaging etc. 934.4.

8. *adv.* in ridicule etc. *n.*, in jest, as a joke, to raise a laugh.

857. Laughingstock

n. laughingstock, jestingstock, gazingstock, jest, joke, butt, game, fair game, figure of fun [coll.], byword, derision, quiz, victim, monkey; April fool etc. (dupe) 547; buffoon etc. 599.20.

858. Hope

(See 859. Hopelessness, 860. Fear)

1. *n.* hope, hopes, fond *or* fervent hope, sanguine *or* happy expectation, trust, confidence, conviction, reliance, faith, affiance; assurance, reassurance; secureness, security; assumption, presumption; well-grounded hope, promise, good omen *or* auspices, good *or* bright prospect, clear sky; cheer, cheerful prospect; desire etc. 865.

2. *n.* hopefulness etc. *adj.*, buoyancy, optimism, enthusiasm, heart of grace, aspiration; anticipation etc. (expectation) 507; cheerfulness etc. 836.

3. *n.* ray of hope, beam ∼, gleam ∼, glimmer *or* flash of hope, star of hope, dawn of hope, bit of blue sky, silver lining of the cloud, bottom of Pandora's box, balm in Gilead.

4. *n.* airy hopes, unfounded expectations, fool's paradise, bubble; *le pot au lait* [F.], pot of gold at the foot of the rainbow; idle fancy, dream etc. (imagination) 515.4–6; illusion etc. 495.5; mirage etc. (optical illusion) 443.9.

5. *n.* optimist; hoper, hopeful etc. *adj.*, person; ray of sunshine, little ray of sunshine [both slang]; utopian etc. (imaginer) 515.7.

6. *v.* hope, be *or* live in hopes, feel ∼, entertain ∼, harbor ∼, indulge ∼, cherish ∼, feed ∼, foster ∼, nourish *or* encourage hope, cling to the hope, feel confident, rest assured, presume, trust, confide, rely on, put one's trust in, lean upon, pin one's hope upon; pin one's faith upon etc. (believe) 484.7; anticipate, promise oneself etc. (expect) 507.4; hope for etc. (desire) 865.11.

7. *v.* be hopeful etc. *adj.*, look on the bright side of, view on the sunny side, *voir en couleur de rose* [F.], put a good *or* bold face upon, put the best face upon; keep one's spirits up, take heart, take heart of grace, be of good heart *or* cheer;

---

cule.—Fielding.   He who laughs and is himself ridiculous, bears a double share of ridicule.—Shaftesbury.   Mockery is the fume of little hearts.—Tennyson.   There are very few who would not rather be hated than laughed at.—S. Smith.   Surely there must be some meaning beneath all this terrible irony.—Shaw. 857. Let us not be laughing-stocks to other men's humours.—Shakespeare.   Building castles in the air, and making yourself a laughing-stock.—Cervantes.
858. *Nil desperandum* [Never despair].—Horace.   *Ego spem pretio non emo* [I do not purchase hope for a price].—Terence.   Hope to the end.—Bible.   The miserable have no other medicine / But only hope.—Shakespeare. Better a good hope than a bad holding.—Cervantes.   Hope is a better companion than fear.—Tupper.   Hope is cheap as despair.—Fuller.   Our hopes must center in ourselves alone.—Dryden.   When there is no hope, there can be no endeavour.—Johnson. Hope is the second soul of the unhappy.—Goethe.   The mighty hopes that make us men.—Tennyson.   The Promised Land always lies on the other side of a wilderness.—H. Ellis.   Where there's life there's hope.

flatter oneself, "lay the flattering unction to one's soul" (Shakespeare); hope for the best, make the best of it, hope against hope, catch at a straw, count one's chickens before they are hatched.

8. *v.* give hope, inspire ~, raise *or* hold out hope, raise expectations, encourage, pat on the back, hearten, cheer, inspirit, assure, reassure, buoy up, keep in countenance; promise, bid fair, augur well, be in a fair way, look up; embolden etc. 861.7.

9. *adj.* hopeful, hoping etc. *v.*, inclined to hope, in hopes etc. *n.*, full of hope, confident, assured, sanguine, optimistic(al), with agreeable expectation, happily expectant, in good heart, heartsome [chiefly Scot.], buoyed up, buoyant, elate, elated, flushed, exultant, enthusiastic; utopian; expectant etc. 507.7; cheerful etc. 836.7.

10. *adj.* fearless, free *or* exempt from fear, ~ suspicion, ~ distrust *or* despair, unsuspecting, unsuspicious, undespairing; dauntless etc. (courageous) 861.8.

11. *adj.* propitious, auspicious, favorable; promising, of promise, full of promise; looking up, probable, on the high road to, within sight of shore *or* land; reassuring, encouraging, inspiriting, cheering, bright; roseate, rosy, rose-colored, *couleur de rose* [F.]; of good omen, *de bon augure* [F.].

12. *int.* God speed!, good luck!

859. Hopelessness
(See 858. Hope)

1. *n.* hopelessness, absence *or* want of hope, loss *or* failure of hope, blighted hope, dashed hopes, hope deferred, vain *or* faint hope, false *or* vain expectation; futility, vanity; pessimism, cynicism; desperation, despair, cave of despair, cave of Trophonius, "Slough of Despond" (Bunyan); despondency etc. (sadness) 837; wretchedness etc. 828.3; disappointment etc. 509; airy hopes etc. 858.4; impossibility etc. 471.

---

859. *Lasciate ogni speranza, voi ch'entrate* [All hope abandon, ye who enter here].—DANTE.   Our hap is loss, our hope but sad despair.—SHAKESPEARE.   My ending is despair.—SHAKESPEARE.   To eate thy heart through comfortless despaires.—SPENSER. No change, no pause, no hope, yet I endure.—SHELLEY.   Tears from the depth of some divine despair.—TENNYSON.   Hope deferred maketh the heart sick.

2. *n.* gloomy outlook, dark future, dark *or* black clouds, clouds on the horizon, black spots in the horizon.

3. *n.* forlorn hope, *enfants perdus* [F.]; goner [slang], gone case *or* coon [slang, U.S.]; desperate case *or* enterprise, hopeless undertaking.

4. *n.* pessimist, cynic, Job's comforter, bird of bad *or* ill omen, crapehanger [slang] etc. (sad person) 837.5; faultfinder etc. (detractor) 936.

5. *v.* despair, yield to despair, lose ~, give up ~, abandon *or* relinquish hope *or* all hope, give up, ~ over *or* way, lose heart, despond, falter; be sad etc. 837.6.

6. *v.* shatter one's hopes, destroy ~, dash ~, crush *or* blight one's hope, dash the cup from one's lips, undermine one's foundation, take away one's last hope, drive to despair etc. *n.*; disconcert, put out.

7. *adj.* hopeless, desperate, despairing etc. *v.*, in despair, *au désespoir* [F.]; forlorn, given up *or* over, gone; past *or* beyond hope, beyond recall, irrecoverable, irretrievable, irreclaimable, irredeemable, irrevocable, irreversible; incorrigible, irreformable; past cure *or* mending, beyond remedy, remediless, irremediable, cureless, incurable, immedicable, irreparable, immitigable; ruined, undone; futile, vain; out of the question, not to be thought of etc. (impossible) 471.6, 7; inconsolable etc. (disconsolate) 837.12; pessimistic etc. 837.15; wretched etc. 828.16; lost etc. 776.5, 6.

8. *adj.* unpropitious, unpromising etc. (inauspicious) 512.5.

860. Fear
(See 858. Hope)

1. *n.* fear, fright, affright [arch.], affrightment [arch.]; scare, boof [local U.S.], alarm, dread, awe, terror, horror, dismay, consternation, abject fear; panic, panic fear *or* terror; funk, mortal *or* blue funk [all coll.]; stampede, chute [West. U.S.]; cowardice etc. 862.

2. *n.* fearfulness, apprehensiveness etc. *adj.*; want of confidence etc. 861, timidity, timor [rare]; anxious concern, solicitude, anxiety, care; diffidence, apprehen-

---

860. *Degeneres animos timor arguit* [Fear betrays ignoble souls].—VERGIL.   Fear came upon me, and trembling; . . . the hair of my flesh stood up.—BIBLE.   Our fears do make

sion, misgiving, suspension, scruple, boggle, qualm; demur, demurral, demurrage, demurity; mistrust etc. (doubt) 485.2; hesitation etc. (irresolution) 605; foreboding etc. 511.6; uncertainty etc. 475.

3. *n.* trepidation, trepidity, fear and trembling; perturbation, perturbance *or* perturbancy [rare]; inquietude, disquietude; jitters [slang, U.S.], nervousness, restlessness etc. *adj.*; stage fright, buck fever [coll.]; throbbing heart, palpitation, pitapatation [joc.], heartquake, heart-sinking; shakes [dial. U.S.], shivers *or* cold shivers [coll.], creeps *or* cold creeps [coll.]; sweat, cold sweat; feeze [coll., U.S.]; shaking, etc. (agitation) 315.3; shake, shiver etc. 315.4.

4. *n.* phobia, claustrophobia, agoraphobia, batophobia, hypsophobia, demonophobia, doraphobia, dysmorphophobia, heresyphobia; hypsophobia, lyssophobia, neophobia, airphobia, photophobia, pyrophobia, sitiophobia, thanatophobia, zoophobia, bacteriophobia, toxicophobia, syphilophobia, pharmacophobia, dermatophobia, phobophobia; Germanophobia, Russophobia, Francophobia, Anglophobia, Gallophobia etc.; aversion etc. (dislike) 867, (hatred) 898; craze etc. 503.7.

5. *n.* intimidation, frightening etc. *v.*, scaremongering, terrorism, reign of terror; threat etc. 909.

6. *n.* alarmist, terrorist, scaremonger; sheep in wolf's clothing.

7. *n.* frightener, scarer etc. *v.*; scarecrow, scare-bird; scarebabe, scare-sinner; nightmare, incubus; ogre, ogress; Gorgon, Hurlothrumbo, fee-faw-fum, *bête noire* [F.]; goblin etc. (bugbear) 980; ghost etc. (specter) 980a.

8. *v.* fear, be afraid etc. *adj.*, have qualms etc. *n.*, stand in awe of, stand aghast, dread, apprehend, eye askance; sit upon thorns, be on pins and needles; take fright *or* alarm, funk [coll.], quail, cower, crouch; start, shy, fight shy; pale, grow *or* turn pale; be in a daze; not dare to say one's soul is one's own; skulk etc. (cowardice) 862.3; flinch, wince etc. (shrink) 623.9; flee etc. 623.10; falter,

hesitate etc. (be irresolute) 605.4; falter, distrust etc. (doubt) 485.6.

9. *v.* tremble, tremble in one's boots *or* shoes, tremble like an aspen leaf, tremble *or* shake all over; shake, shiver, quaver etc. (be agitated) 315.9.

10. *v.* frighten, fright, affright; inspire *or* excite fear etc. *n.*, put in fear, raise apprehensions, scare, funk [coll.], startle, disquiet, give a turn; awe, strike awe into; astound, appall; terrify, strike terror into; frighten from one's propriety, frighten out of one's wits *or* senses, strike dumb, strike all of a heap [coll.], unman, horrify, harrow up the soul; stun, stupefy, petrify; make one's flesh creep, make one's hair stand on end, make one's blood run cold, make one's teeth chatter, make one tremble, take away *or* stop one's breath; give ~, raise *or* sound an alarm, cry wolf; alarm etc. 669.3.

11. *v.* daunt, dismay, disconcert, abash; awe, overawe; faze [coll. or dial.], feeze *or* feaze [dial. Eng. and coll. U.S.]; deter, dishearten, discourage.

12. *v.* intimidate, cow, browbeat, bully, bulldoze [coll., U.S.], buffalo [slang, U.S.], huff, hector, harass, dragoon; terrorize, put in bodily fear; bluster, bluster out of *or* into; threaten etc. 909.2; lord it over etc. (domineer) 885.5.

13. *v.* obsess, haunt etc. 830.8.

14. *adj.* afraid, afeard *or* afeared [arch. and dial.], fearful, fearing etc. *v.*, in fear, fear-struck, fear-stricken, haunted with fear etc. *n.*, afraid of one's shadow; scared, ascared [dial.], ascare; diffident, anxious, apprehensive; nervous, tremulous, jittery [slang, U.S.], shaky, skittish, restive, restless, fidgety; frightened, in a fright etc. *n.*; alarmed, startled, disquieted.

terrified, terror-struck, terror-stricken, terror-smitten, terror-shaken, terror-troubled, terror-riven, terror-ridden, terror-driven, terror-crazed; in a panic, panic-struck, panic-stricken; horrified, horror-struck, horror-stricken; awed, awe-struck, awe-stricken; dismayed, astounded, appalled, aghast; frightened to death, frightened out of one's wits, unmanned; petrified, stupefied, stunned; white as a sheet, pale as ashes, ~ death

---

us traitors.—SHAKESPEARE. Early and provident fear is the mother of safety.—BURKE. Fear always springs from ignorance.—EMERSON. Entertaining hope means recognising fear.—BROWNING. Fear is the parent of cruelty.—FROUDE. Keep your fears to yourself but share your courage.—STEVENSON. To him who is in fear everything rustles.—SOPHOCLES. The only thing we have to fear is fear itself.—F. D. ROOSEVELT.

or a ghost; hysterical, in hysterics; more frightened than hurt; timid, shy etc. (cowardly) 862.4.

15. *adj.* frightening, frightful, frightsome [Scot.]; fear-inspiring, fearful, fearsome; scaring, scareful [dial.], scaresome [dial.]; alarming, startling, disquieting, dismaying, astounding, appalling.

terrifying, terrorful, terrorsome, terrorific, terror-striking, terror-inspiring, terror-bringing, terror-giving, terror-breeding, terror-breathing, terror-bearing, terror-fraught, terror-haunted; terrible, terrific; horrid, horrible, horrific; awe-inspiring, awful; dire, direful; fell, formidable, redoubtable, tremendous, dreadful, ghastly, shocking; Gorgonian, Gorgonlike; petrifying, stunning, stupefying; creepy; perilous etc. (dangerous) 665.7; portentous etc. 511.11.

16. *adv.* in fear, in terror etc. *n.*, *in terrorem* [L.], in fear of one's life, with fear and trembling; in a funk, in a mortal *or* blue funk [all coll.].

861. Courage
(See 862. Cowardice)

1. *n.* courage, resoluteness, fearlessness, boldness etc. *adj.*; bravery, valor, spirit, dash, daring, derring-do, audacity, gallantry, intrepidity, prowess, chivalry, *courage sans peur* [F.], contempt *or* defiance of danger; heroism; confidence, self-confidence, self-reliance; manhood, manliness; nerve, pluck, grit, clear grit, sand [slang], mettle, backbone [coll.], spunk [coll.], stamina, guts [slang], bottom, pith, game, hardihood, fortitude, virtue, bulldog courage; heart, stout heart, heart of oak; resolution etc. 604; rashness etc. 863; defiance etc. 715.

2. *n.* exploit, feat, deed, act, achievement, enterprise, emprise, heroic act *or* deed, bold stroke.

3. *n.* brave person, brave, *chevalier sans peur et sans reproche* [F.], man of courage *or* mettle, a man; hero, demigod, paladin; heroine, demigoddess; Hercules, Theseus, Perseus, Achilles, Hector; knight-errant, Don Quixote, Lancelot, Sir Galahad; Amazon, Penthesilea, Joan of Arc; the brave; daredevil etc. 863.2.

4. *n.* (comparison) lion, tiger, panther, bulldog; gamecock, fighting cock.

5. *v.* be courageous etc. *adj.*, dare, venture, make bold, brave; face ∼, front ∼, affront *or* confront danger, look in the face, look danger in the face, look full in the face, confront, face, meet, meet in front, put a bold face upon, show *or* present a bold front, face the music; beard, "beard the lion in his den" (Scott); defy ∼, despise *or* mock danger, put one's head in the lion's mouth, bell the cat, take the bull by the horns, march up to the cannon's mouth, go through fire and water, run the gantlet; stand, stand to one's guns, stand fire, stand up against; take a dare; defy etc. 715.2.

6. *v.* nerve oneself, get up nerve, muster ∼, summon up *or* pluck up courage, take courage *or* heart, screw up one's nerve *or* courage, "screw your courage to the stickingplace" (Shakespeare); come to *or* up to scratch; hold up one's head; bear up, bear up against.

7. *v.* embolden, encourage, give ∼, infuse *or* inspire courage, nerve, put upon one's mettle, rally, keep in countenance, make a man of; hearten, cheer etc. (give hope) 858.8.

8. *adj.* courageous, brave, valiant, valorous, gallant, intrepid, plucky, gritty [coll.], mettlesome, resolute, doughty, hardy, stout, stouthearted, ironhearted, lionhearted; game, game to the backbone, game to the last *or* end; spirited, spiritful, high-spirited, high-mettled; manly, manful; bold, bold-spirited, bold as a lion, bold as brass [coll.].

daring, audacious, fearless, dauntless, awless *or* aweless, dreadless; undaunted, unappalled, undismayed, unawed, unblenched, unabashed, unalarmed, unflinching, unshrinking, unblenching, un-

---

861. It is easy to be brave from a safe distance.—AESOP.   *Fortes fortuna adjuvat* [Fortune favors the brave.].—TERENCE.   *Gratior ac pulchro veniens in corpore virtus* [Valor displayed by a handsome body is the more pleasing].—VERGIL.   If all the world were just, there would be no need of valor.—PLUTARCH.   Be strong, and quit yourselves like men.—BIBLE.   The valiant never taste of death but once.—SHAKESPEARE.   I dare do all that may become a man.—SHAKESPEARE.   None but the brave deserves the fair.—DRYDEN.   Self-trust is the essence of heroism.—EMERSON.   Our hoard is little, but our hearts are great.—TENNYSON.   The bravest are the tenderest.—B. TAYLOR.   No coward soul is mine.—E. BRONTË.   The greatest test of courage on the earth is to bear defeat without losing heart.—INGERSOLL.   Every dog is a lion at home.

apprehensive; confident, assured, self-reliant; heroic, heroistic [rare], herolike; chivalrous, chivalric; soldierly etc. (warlike) 722.13.

9. *adj.* enterprising, adventurous, venturous, venturesome.

862. Cowardice
(See 861. Courage)

Excess of Fear.—1. *n.* cowardice, cowardness [rare], cowardliness etc. *adj.*; pusillanimity, Dutch courage [coll.], abject fear, faintheart, cold feet [slang, U.S.]; poltroonery, poltroonism; dastardy, dastardice [both arch.]; funk, mortal *or* blue funk [all coll.]; yellow streak [slang], white feather; timidity etc. (fear) 860; irresolution etc. 605.

2. *n.* coward, poltroon, dastard, arrant coward, craven, caitiff, sneak, slink [Scot. and dial. Eng.], cur [derog.], recreant, coistrel *or* coistril [arch.], white feather, white liver [coll.], chicken, rabbit, baby *or* big baby [coll.], one that cannot say "bo" to a goose; fraid-cat, fraidy-cat, scaredy-cat [all slang]; funk, funker, flunker [all coll.]; shy cock, dunghill cock; Bob Acres, Jerry sneak; shirker etc. 623.4; weakling etc. 160.4; milksop, sissy etc. (mollycoddle) 160a.3.

3. *v.* be cowardly etc. *adj.*, be a coward etc. *n.*, be unable to say "bo" to a goose, have a yellow streak [slang]; get cold feet [slang, U.S.], funk [coll.], flunk [coll., U.S.], show the white feather; quail, cower, skulk, slink, sneak; be afraid etc. 860.8; shy, flinch etc. (shrink) 623.9; turn tail etc. (flee) 623.10.

4. *adj.* cowardly, cowardy [dial.], coward; uncourageous, unvaliant, unvalorous, unheroic, ungallant, unintrepid, undaring, spunkless [coll.], unable to say "bo" to a goose, pusillanimous, fearful, afraid of one's shadow; weakhearted, fainthearted, chickenhearted, henhearted, pigeonhearted; white-livered, lily-livered, milk-livered; yellow, with a yellow streak [both coll.]; funking, funky [both coll.]; spiritless, poor-spirited; timid, timorous, timorsome [obs. exc. dial.]; shy, coy, bashful, skittish, shrinking; unmanly, unmanful; unwarlike, unsoldierlike; afraid etc. 860.14, infirm of purpose etc. 605.5, 6; soft etc. (effeminate) 160a.5.

5. *adj.* dastard, dastardly; pusillanimous, poltroon, base, craven, recreant, caitiff, dunghill; cowering, sneaking, skulking.

6. *adv.* uncourageously etc. *adj.*; in a blue funk [coll.] etc. (in fear) 860.16.

863. Rashness
(See 864. Caution)

1. *n.* rashness, recklessness, incautiousness etc. *adj.*; want of caution etc. 864, temerity, imprudence, indiscretion, overconfidence, presumption, audacity, foolhardihood; precipitance *or* precipitancy, precipitation; impetuosity, *brusquerie* [F.]; levity; desperation; Quixotism, knight-errantry; fire-eating; too many eggs in one basket; heedlessness, thoughtlessness etc. (inattention) 458; carelessness etc. (neglect) 460; gambling etc. 621.6; blind bargain, leap in the dark etc. (gamble) 621.2; folly etc. 499.6, 7; an indiscretion etc. (foolish act) 499.7.

2. *n.* daredevil, rashling [obs.], madcap, madbrain, hotspur, adventurer, harum-scarum [coll.], rantipole, hellcat, fireeater [coll.]; Icarus, Daedalus.

3. *n.* bravo, daring villain, desperado, hector, bully, bucko, scapegrace; dynamiter, dynamitard.

4. *n.* gambler etc. 621.15.

5. *v.* be rash etc. *adj.*, stick at nothing, play a desperate game, defy ∼, mock *or* despise danger, tempt Providence, *donner tête baissée* [F.], run into danger etc. 665, rush on destruction, go on a forlorn hope; *jeter le manche après la cognée* [F.]; play with fire *or* edged tools, march up to the cannon's mouth, put one's head

---

862. To see what is right and not to do it is want of courage.—CONFUCIUS.   For all men would be cowards if they durst.—J. WILMOT.   Cowards die many times before their deaths.—SHAKESPEARE.   The coward only threatens when he is safe.—GOETHE.   There grows / No herb of help to heal a coward heart.—SWINBURNE.   The coward stands aside, / Doubting in his abject spirit, till his Lord is crucified.—LOWELL.   Cowards do not count in battle; They are there, but not in it.—EURIPIDES.

863. *Non semper temeritas est felix* [Rashness is not always fortunate].—LIVY.   *Paucis temeritas est bono multis malo* [Rashness is good for a few, bad for many].—PHAEDRUS.   *Après nous le déluge* [After us the deluge].—LOUIS XV.   And though he stumbles in a full career, / Yet rashness is a better fault than fear.—DRYDEN.   Reckless youth makes rueful age.

in the lion's mouth, beard the lion in his den, take the bull by the horns, go through fire and water, sleep *or* stand on a volcano, sit on a barrel of gunpowder, live in a glass house.

carry too much sail, sail too near the wind, ride at single anchor, go out of one's depth, go to sea in a sieve, take a leap in the dark, buy a pig in a poke, bet against a dead certainty, count one's chickens before they are hatched, reckon without one's host, catch at straws, trust to *or* lean on a broken reed, have too many eggs in one basket, knock *or* run one's head against a stone wall, kick against the pricks; be thoughtless etc. (*see* thoughtless etc. 458.10); be careless etc. (*see* careless etc. 460.8); gamble etc. 621.17.

6. *adj.* rash, incautious, indiscreet, injudicious, imprudent, improvident, temerarious, temerous, temeritous, uncalculating; overconfident, overweening; thoughtless, careless etc. (negligent) 460.8; giddy etc. (inattentive) 458.10, 13.

7. *adj.* reckless, wanton, wild, desperate, madcap, madbrain *or* madbrained, devil-may-care, daring, death-defying, foolhardy, harebrained; harum-scarum [coll.], rantum-scantum [obs.], rantipole; hotheaded, hot-brained, hot-blooded; impetuous, impulsive, precipitate, headlong, breakneck, furious, boisterous, feverish; venturesome, venturous, adventurous, Quixotic; fire-eating; heedless etc. 458.10; clumsy etc. 699.12.

8. *adv.* recklessly, carelessly, precipitately etc. *adj.*; *à corps perdu* [F.], *tête baissée* [F.], headlong, headforemost, heels over head, head over heels, hand over head [now rare]; holus-bolus, hurry-scurry, helter-skelter, ramble-scramble [coll.]; slapdash, slapbang [coll.], slam-bang [coll.]; hell-bent, hell-bent for election *or* leather [all slang, U.S.]; full-drive, full tilt; happen what may.

864. Caution
(See 863. Rashness)

1. *n.* caution, cautiousness etc. *adj.*, discretion, prudence, care, heed, solici-

---

864. The cautious seldom err.—Confucius. Let every man look before he leaps.—Cervantes. *Timeo Danaos et dona ferentes* [I fear the Greeks bringing gifts].—Vergil.

tude, circumspection, calculation, deliberation; Fabian policy, Fabianism; safety first; vigilance etc. (carefulness) 459.2; precaution etc. (preparation) 673, (warning) 668; forethought etc. 510.2; wisdom etc. 498.3.

2. *n.* coolness, self-possession etc. (inexcitability) 826.2, 3.

3. *v.* be cautious etc. *adj.*, have a care, take care *or* good care, take heed, take heed at one's peril, take it easy [coll.]; beware, ware [dial.]; mind, mind what one is doing *or* about, mind one's eye [coll.], mind one's P's and Q's [coll.]; be on one's guard, be on the watch *or* lookout, keep a good *or* sharp lookout, look sharp, look slick *or* slippy [coll.], look lively *or* alive [coll.], look about one, have all one's eyes *or* wits about one, keep one's eyes open, keep a weather eye open [coll.], keep one's eye peeled [slang], keep the ears on *or* to the ground.

stop, look and listen; look out, watch out [coll. U.S.], mind out [dial.]; watch one's step [slang], pick one's steps, put the right foot forward, move warily, feel one's ground *or* way, pussyfoot; make haste slowly, *festina lente* [L.]; keep out of harm's way, keep out of troubled waters, keep at a respectful distance, stand aloof; let well enough alone, *ne pas reveiller le chat qui dort* [F.], let sleeping dogs lie; bridle one's tongue.

4. *v.* take precautions, take steps *or* measures, forearm, guard against, make sure against, make sure, "make assurance double sure" (Shakespeare); play safe [coll.], keep *or* be on the safe side; look after the main chance, cut one's coat according to one's cloth; think twice, give it a second thought; look before one leaps.

see how the land lies *or* the wind blows, see how the cat jumps [coll.]; prepare for the evil day, provide for *or* against a rainy day, feather one's nest, keep as a

---

Be not the first by whom the new is tried, / Nor yet the last to lay the old aside.—Pope. Beware of rashness, but with energy and sleepless vigilance go forward and give us victories. —Lincoln. Discretion is the better part of valor. He that fights and runs away, may live to fight another day. An ounce of discretion is worth a pound of wit. *Ante victoriam ne canas triumphum* [Do not celebrate the victory before you have conquered]. *Noli irritare leones* [Do not stir up lions]. *No firmes carta que no leas / no bebas aqua que no veas* [Sign no paper without reading it and drink no water before seeing it].

nest egg, have a rod in pickle, save to fall back upon, lay by, husband one's resources; make all snug, clear the decks, clear for action, reef, take in a reef, double-reef topsails, have an anchor to windward [all Naut.]; anticipate etc. (foresee) 510.5.

5. *v.* caution etc. (warn) 668.6, 7.

6. *adj.* cautious, wary, gingerly, circumspect, prudent, canny [Scot.], discreet, politic, noncommittal; precautious, precautionary, precautional; guarded, guardful [rare], on guard, on one's guard; suspicious, leery [slang], chary, shy of; stealthy; safe, on the safe side; *cavendo tutus* [L.]; *in medio tutissimus* [L.]; unenterprising, unadventurous; overcautious, overcareful; careful, vigilant etc. 459.7, 8.

7. *adj.* cool, self-possessed etc. (inexcitable) 826.9.

8. *adv.* cautiously etc. *adj.*, gingerly, easy [coll.]; carefully etc. 459.9.

9. *int.* beware!, ware!, be careful!, take care!, have a care!, look out!, watch out! [coll., U.S.], mind out! [dial.], mind!, mind your eye! [coll.], mind your business!, mind *or* take care what you are about!, watch your step! [slang], keep your eyes open!, look sharp!, look slick *or* slippy! [coll.], look lively *or* alive! [coll.], stop! look! listen!, be on your guard!, *prenez garde!* [F.], *cave canem!* [L.], take it easy! [coll.], safety first!, danger!, below there!, jiggers! [slang].

865. Desire
(See 866. Indifference, 867. Dislike, 869. Satiety)

1. *n.* desire, wish, want, fancy, fantasy [arch.]; desideration, *desiderium* [L.]; like, liking, love, fondness, relish; *penchant* [F.], *béguin* [F.], partiality, inclination, leaning, proclivity, weakness, bent, turn, mind, animus; propensity, prependency [obs.], propension [now rare], propensitude [rare]; insatiable desire, cacoëthes; prurience *or* pruriency, itch, itching, itching palm; predilection etc. (preference) 609.2; need, exigency etc. (requirement) 630; hope etc. 858.

2. *n.* longing, hankering, yearning, yen [slang], craving, coveting, concupiscence [now rare], aspiration; ambition, vaulting ambition; eagerness, zeal, ardor, *empressement* [F.], breathless impatience, solicitude, anxiety, overanxiety; longing *or* wistful eyes, sheep's eyes.

3. *n.* appetite, appetition, appetence *or* appetency; hunger, stomach, twist [slang, Eng.], mouth-watering, torment of Tantalus; sharp appetite, keenness; thirst, thirstiness, polydipsia [Med.], drought *or* drouth [now chiefly dial.]; edge of appetite *or* hunger; sweet tooth [coll.].

4. *n.* greed, greediness, covetousness, ravenousness etc. *adj.*; extreme *or* inordinate desire, lust, avarice, avidity, voracity, rapacity, cupidity, grasping, canine appetite; gluttony etc. 957.

5. *n.* passion, mania, monomania etc. (craze) 503.7; dipsomania etc. (insanity) 503.1.

6. *n.* concupiscence, sensuous desire etc. (carnality) 961.3.

7. *n.* desirer, wisher etc. *v.*; desiderant [rare], esurient; votary, devotee, fan [slang], zealot, enthusiast; amateur, dilettante (*pl.* dilettantes, dilettanti); solicitant, aspirant, candidate; cormorant etc. 957.2; lover etc. 897.6.

8. *n.* (object of desire) desire, desired; desideratum, desideration; optative [rare], something to be desired, "a consummation devoutly to be wish'd" (Shakespeare), height of one's ambition; idol; love, sweetheart etc. 897.7; favorite etc. 899; want etc. (requirement) 630; attraction etc. (allurement) 617; whim etc. (caprice) 608.

9. *n.* wish-bringer, Fortunatus's cap, wishing cap, wishing stone, wishing well; wishbone, wishing bone.

10. *n.* love potion, aphrodisiac, philter, cantharis (*pl.* cantharides), blister beetle, Spanish fly.

11. *v.* desire, be desirous etc. *adj.*, have a longing etc. *n.*, desiderate, list [arch.],

---

865. The sea hath bounds but deep desire hath none.—SHAKESPEARE. Desire hath no rest.—R. BURTON. The desire of the moth for the star.—SHELLEY. There are two tragedies in life. One is not to get your heart's desire. The other is to get it.—SHAW. Ah, but a man's reach should exceed his grasp / Or what's a heaven for?—BROWNING. Ambition destroys its possessor.—TALMUD. Ambition has its disappointments to sour us, but never the good fortune to satisfy us.—FRANKLIN. If thou rise with an appetite, thou art sure never to sit down without one.—W. PENN. Life is a progress from want to want, not from enjoyment to enjoyment.—JOHNSON. The

wish, want, would fain do *or* have, would be glad of; want to, wish to, burn to; fancy, take to, take a fancy to, have a fancy for; have a mind to, have an eye to, take into one's head, have at heart, be bent upon, set one's eyes upon, set one's heart *or* mind upon, set one's cap at *or* for [coll.]; cast sheep's eyes upon, look sweet upon [coll.].

covet, hunger after, thirst after, crave after, lust after, itch after, hanker after, aspire after, run mad after; wish for, hope for, yearn for, yen for [slang, U.S.], raven for, long for, pine for, languish for, sigh for, cry for, gape for, gasp for, pant for, die for; catch at, grasp at, jump at; find in one's heart; hope etc. 858.6; like, care for etc. (love) 897; prefer etc. 609.9; be willing etc. 602.6.

12. *v.* hunger, hunger for *or* after, be hungry etc. *adj.*, have a good appetite, play a good knife and fork [coll.], lick one's chops [coll.]; thirst, thirst for *or* after.

13. *v.* woo, court, solicit, fish for, whistle for, put up for [slang]; make love etc. 902.7.

14. *v.* excite desire, cause ~, create ~, raise *or* provoke desire, hold out temptation, tempt, tantalize, titillate, take one's fancy; appetize, whet the appetite, make one's mouth water, *faire venir l'eau à la bouche* [F.]; attract etc. (lure) 617.4.

15. *v.* gratify desire, meet one's wishes etc. (please) 829.4.

16. *adj.* desirous, desiring etc. *v.*; desiderative, desiderant; orectic, orective; appetitive, appetitious [obs.], appetitional, appetent; optative; wishful, wistful, longing; anxious, curious, at a loss for, sedulous, solicitous; itching, with itching fingers; partial to [coll.]; fain [arch.]; inclined etc. (willing) 602.8; lustful etc. (carnal) 961.11.

17. *adj.* eager, overeager, avid, keen, burning, fervent, fervid, ardent, agog, all agog, breathless, impatient, enthusiastic, bent ~, intent *or* set on *or* upon, mad after, *enragé* [F.], rabid, dying for, devoured by desire.

18. *adj.* aspiring, ambitious, vaulting, skyaspiring, high-reaching.

19. *adj.* craving, ravening, hungering etc. *v.*; hungry, sharp-set, peckish [coll.], esurient, lickerish *or* liquorish, the mouth watering, with an empty stomach, pinched *or* perishing with hunger, starved, famished, hungry as a hunter, ~ hawk, ~ horse *or* church mouse; half-starved, half-famished; thirsty, athirst, parched with thirst, dry, droughty *or* drouthy [now chiefly dial.].

20. *adj.* greedy, voracious, rapacious, openmouthed, covetous, grasping, extortionate, exacting, sordid, *aliene appetens* [L.]; ravening, ravenous, ravenous as a wolf; piggish, hoggish, swinish, greedy as a hog; omnivorous, all-devouring; insatiable, insatiate; unquenchable, quenchless.

21. *adj.* desirable, optable [rare]; desired *v.*, much to be desired; in demand, popular; appetizing, appetitive, appetible, mouth-watering; provocative, tantalizing; pleasurable etc. 829.7; luscious etc. 396.8; palatable etc. 394.7; satisfactory etc. 831.7.

22. *adv.* desirously, wistfully etc. *adj.*; fain; with eager appetite.

23. *int.* would that!, would it were!, O for!, if only!.

866. Indifference

1. *n.* indifference, indifferentness, coldness, lukewarmness etc. *adj.*; Laodiceanism; neutrality; want of interest, unconcern, insouciance, nonchalance; anorexia *or* anorexy, inappetence *or* inappetency; anaphrodisia; apathy etc. (insensibility) 823; disdain etc. 930; carelessness etc. 460; inattention etc. 458; incuriosity etc. 456; irreligion etc. 989.

2. *n.* anaphrodisiac *or* antaphrodisiac, lust-quencher, passion-queller.

3. *v.* be indifferent etc. *adj.*, stand neuter *or* neutral, have ~, feel *or* take no interest in, not care *or* mind, *nil admirari* [L.]; have no desire, ~ taste *or* relish for, care nothing for *or* about, not care for, not care a straw for *or* about; set at nought etc. (make light of) 483.3; spurn etc. (disdain) 930.5.

4. *adj.* indifferent, cold, frigid, cool,

---

only way to get rid of a temptation is to yield to it.—WILDE. The wish is father to the thought. If wishes were horses, beggars would ride.

866. I know thy works, that thou art neither cold nor hot: I would thou wert cold or hot.—BIBLE. We are cold to others only when we are dull in ourselves.—HAZLITT. Moral indifference is the malady of the cultivated classes.—AMIEL. Happy are the men whom nature has buttressed with indifference and cased

cool as a cucumber, lukewarm, Laodicean; neither hot nor cold, neither one thing nor the other; neuter, neutral; unconcerned, uninterested, insouciant, nonchalant, blasé; pococurante, pococurantish, pococurantic, pococurantist; careless, regardless, mindless, unmindful, *sans souci* [F.], listless, lackadaisical, easygoing, devil-may-care, dispassionate, halfhearted, unambitious, unaspiring, undesirous, unsolicitous, unattracted, inappetent, all one to; blind to, deaf to, dead to; impassive, impassible; apathetic etc. (insensible) 823.5; inattentive etc. 458.10; incurious etc. 456.3; irreligious etc. 989.6.

5. *adj.* undesirable, unattractive etc. (unpleasant) 830.10; insipid etc. 391.2.

6. *adv.* indifferently etc. *adj.*, with utter indifference; for aught one cares.

7. *int.* never mind!, who cares!, it's all one to me!

867. Dislike
(See 865. Desire)

1. *n.* dislike, distaste, disrelish, displacency [rare]; disaffection, disfavor; disinclination, reluctance etc. (unwillingness) 603; displeasure etc. 828.2; hate etc. 898; enmity etc. 889; phobia etc. 860.4; disapproval etc. 932; resentment etc. 900.

2. *n.* repugnance, disgust, abomination, execration, antipathy, abhorrence, horror, mortal horror *or* antipathy, hatred, detestation; loathing, loathfulness [rare]; aversion, averseness, aversation [arch.]; nausea, queasiness, sickness, pall [rare], qualm; *taedium vitae* [L.], disgust of life; shuddering, cold sweat.

3. *n.* sickener, nauseant; gall and wormwood etc. 395.3; 830.2.

4. *v.* dislike, mislike, disrelish, disfavor, have ~, entertain ~, conceive *or* take a dislike *or* an aversion to, not care for, have no use for, have no taste *or* stomach for, not be able to bear, ~ endure *or* abide; mind; object to, would rather not; shrug the shoulders at, shudder at, turn up the nose at, look askant *or* askance at; make a mouth, ~ wry face *or* grimace, make faces, grimace; eschew, have nothing to do with; shun etc. (avoid) 623.6; shrink from etc. 623.9; loathe, detest etc. (hate) 898.3; take amiss etc. (resent) 900.6; disapprove etc. 932.5.

5. *v.* feel disgust etc. *n.*, be nauseated, sicken at; have enough of etc. (be satiated) 869.5.

6. *v.* cause dislike etc. *n.*, disincline, displease; excite hatred etc. 898.4; disgust, nauseate, sicken etc. (repel) 830; pall etc. (sate) 869.4.

7. *adj.* disliking etc. *v.*, averse to, loath, adverse, shy of, out of conceit with, disinclined; sick of, heartsick, dog-sick; nauseated, queasy etc. (displeased) 828.14; resenting etc. 900.12; unfriendly etc. 889.3; abhorrent etc. (hating) 898.5.

8. *adj.* disliked etc. *v.*, uncared-for, unvalued, unpopular, out of favor; unloved (hated) etc. 898.6.

9. *adj.* dislikable, unlikable; disagreeable etc. (unpleasant) 830.10; repulsive, repugnant, loathsome etc. (odious) 830.14; unappetizing, inedible etc. (unsavory) 395.5; insufferable etc. 830.18.

10. *adv.* to one's displeasure, to one's disgust etc. *n., usque ad nauseam* [L.].

11. *int.* faugh!, foh!, pah!, ugh!

868. Fastidiousness

1. *n.* fastidiousness, fastidiosity; fastidium, squeamishness, circumstantiality, particularity, difficulty in being pleased; finicalness, finickingness, finickiness, finicism, finicality; scrupulousness, scrupulosity; punctiliousness, punctilio, punctiliosity [rare]; punctuality [now rare]; meticulousness, meticulosity; preciseness, precision; exactness, exactitude; nicety, delicacy, subtlety, refinement; overscrupulousness, overparticularity, overnicety, oversubtlety; overcriticalness, hypercriticism, hairsplitting.

conscientiousness etc. 939.2; discrimination etc. 465; epicurism etc. (taste)

---

in stoicism.—DE MAUPASSANT. Let the world slide, let the world go; / A fig for care, and a fig for woe!—J. HEYWOOD. I care for nobody, no, not I, / If no one cares for me.—BICKERSTAFF. The tragedy of love is indifference.—MAUGHAM.
867. I do desire we may be better strangers.—SHAKESPEARE. I do not love thee, Dr. Fell; / The reason why I cannot tell.—T. BROWNE. The strong antipathy of good to bad.—POPE.

868. *Noli me tangere* [Touch me not].—VULGATE. The fastidious are unfortunate: nothing can satisfy them.—LA FONTAINE. In language one should be nice but not difficult.—LOWELL.

850; prudery etc. 853.2; scruple etc. 603.2.

2. *n*. epicure, gourmet, connoisseur etc. (man of taste) 850.3.

3. *v*. be fastidious etc. *adj*., have exquisite taste, have nice discrimination; split hairs, make a nice *or* subtle distinction; hunt for the crumpled rose-leaf; mince, mince it, mince the matter; look a gift horse in the mouth, see spots on the sun, see the mote in one's brother's eye; exercise discrimination etc. 465.2; turn up one's nose at etc. (disdain) 930.5.

4. *adj*. fastidious, squeamish, scrupulous, punctilious, punctual, particular, queasy, thin-skinned, querulous, difficult, hard *or* difficult to please, meticulous, exacting, precise, strict; finical, finicking *or* finicky *or* finikin; nice, subtle, fine, refined, delicate, *délicat* [F.], dainty; picky [slang], choosy *or* choosey [slang, U.S.], choicy [coll., U.S.]; overscrupulous, overconscientious, overparticular, oversubtle, overnice; overcritical, hypercritical, hairsplitting; censorious etc. 932.11; conscientious etc. 939.8; discriminative etc. 465.4; prudish etc. 853.7; oversensitive etc. 822.6; tasteful 850.5.

869. Satiety
(See 865. Desire)

1. *n*. satiety, satiation, cloyedness etc. *adj*., surfeit, glut, plethora, repletion, engorgement, saturation, satisfaction, enough in all conscience, *satis superque* [L.], more than enough, too much of a good thing, *toujours perdrix* [F.]; fill, full [coll.], bellyful [vulg.], skinful [coll.]; plenty etc. 639.2; superfluity etc. (redundance) 641; weariness etc. 841.

2. *n*. cloyer, surfeiter, overdose, sickener, nauseant; a diet of cake, *"crambe repetita"* (Juvenal).

3. *n*. spoiled child, *enfant gâté* [F.].

4. *v*. sate, satiate; cloy, accloy; glut, gorge, pall, jade, surfeit, satisfy; overgorge, overdose, overfeed; spoil; saturate etc. (fill) 52.7; overload etc. 641.4; bore etc. (weary) 841.5.

5. *v*. be satiated etc. *adj*., have enough, have quite enough, have one's fill, have too much, have too much of a good thing, have a bellyful [vulg.] etc. *n*.; feel disgust etc. 867.5.

6. *adj*. satiated, satiate, sated; surfeited, satisfied, cloyed, jaded, glutted, gorged, surfeit-gorged, gorged with plenty, with a bellyful [vulg.] etc. *n*.; surfeit-swelled, surfeit-swollen; fed-up, fed to the gills *or* neck [all slang]; overgorged, overfed; sick of, heartsick; used up [coll.]; *blasé* [F.]; saturated etc. (full) 52.11; overfull etc. 641.6.

7. *adj*. cloying etc. *v*., cloysome.

8. *int*. enough!, hold!, *eheu jam satis!* [L.] etc. (cease) 142.8.

870. Wonder
(See 871. Unastonishment; also 872. Prodigy)

1. *n*. wonder, wonderment, astonishment, astoundment, confoundment, bewilderment, flabbergastation [coll.], marvel, admiration, awe, fascination; amazedness etc. *adj*., amazement, mazement [rare], amaze; surprise, surprisal, surprisement [rare]; stupor, stupefaction; sensation; note of admiration; thaumaturgy etc. (sorcery) 992.

2. *v*. wonder, marvel, admire, be surprised etc. *adj*., stare, open one's eye, rub one's eyes, turn up one's eyes, gape, open one's mouth, hold one's breath, look *or* stand aghast *or* agog, look blank, not be able to account for, not know what to make of, not make head or tail of, not know whether one stands on one's head or one's heels, not believe one's eyes, ∼ ears *or* senses; *tomber des nues* [F.]; not understand etc. 519.5.

3. *v*. astonish, amaze, astound, overwhelm, surprise, startle, stagger, bewilder, confound, flabbergast [coll.], fascinate, take one's breath away, turn the head, make one's head swim, make one's hair stand on end, make one's tongue cleave to the roof of one's mouth, make one stare; awe, awe-strike, strike with wonder *or* awe; strike all of a heap, throw on one's beam ends, bowl down *or* over [all coll.]; dazzle, bedazzle, daze; dum-

---

869. Satiety is a neighbor to continued pleasures.—QUINTILIAN. In everything satiety closely follows the greatest pleasures.—CICERO. They are as sick that surfeit with too much, / As they that starve with nothing.—SHAKESPEARE. The ennui of a crushing satiety.—SHAW. Satisfaction is death.—SHAW.

870. Wonder—which is the seed of knowledge. —BACON. Wonder is the daughter of ignorance.—FLORIO. All wonder is the effect of novelty upon ignorance.—JOHNSON.

found, dumfounder, strike dumb; electrify, shock, paralyze, stupefy, stun, petrify.

4. *v.* take by surprise etc. 508.6.

5. *v.* be wonderful etc. *adj.*, beggar *or* baffle description, stagger belief.

6. *adj.* astonished, amazed, surprised etc. *v.*; aghast, agape, agog, all agog, openmouthed, breathless, spellbound, lost in wonder, ~ amazement *or* astonishment, unable to believe one's senses; struck all of a heap [coll.], struck with wonder *or* surprise, wonder-struck, wonder-stricken, awe-struck, thunderstruck; spellbound; like a duck in a fit, like a duck in thunder [both coll.].

7. *adj.* wonderful, wondrous; astonishing, surprising etc. *v.*; marvelous, prodigious, stupendous, extraordinary, striking, remarkable, noteworthy, miraculous, monstrous, fearful, inconceivable, incredible, unimaginable, unheard-of, overwhelming; passing strange, "wondrous strange" (Shakespeare); wonder-working; unusual etc. 83.10.

8. *adj.* indescribable, inexpressible, ineffable, unutterable, unspeakable.

9. *adv.* wonderfully etc. *adj.*, for a wonder, in the name of wonder; strange to say; *mirabile dictu* [L.], *mirabile visu* [L.]; to one's great surprise.

10. *adv.* with wonder etc. *n.*, with gaping mouth, with open eyes, with upturned eyes, with the eyes starting out of one's head.

11. *int.* (of wonder or surprise) lo!, lo and behold!, O!, heyday!, halloo!, what!, indeed!, really!, surely!, humph!, hem!, good heavens!, good lack!, good gracious!, gad so!, welladay!, dear me!, only think!, lackadaisy!, my stars!, my goodness!, goodness gracious!, gracious goodness!, mercy on us!, heavens and earth!, God bless me!, bless us!, bless my heart!, adzooks!, odzookens!, O Gemini!

hoity-toity!, strong!, Heaven save *or* bless the mark!, can such things be?, it beats the Dutch!, zounds!, 'sdeath!, what on earth!, what in the world!, who would have thought it!, you don't say so!, what do you say to that!, how now!, where am I?, fancy!, do tell! [coll., U.S.], *Ciel!* [F.], well, I'll be jiggered! [coll.]; what do you know!, what do you know about that!

Wonder is involuntary praise.—YOUNG. The world will never starve for want of wonders, but only for want of wonder.—CHESTERTON.

871. Unastonishment
(See 870. Wonder)

1. *n.* unastonishment, unamazement, awlessness etc. *adj.*; expectation etc. 507; imperturbability etc. (inexcitability) 826.

2. *v.* be unastonished etc. *adj.*, not be astonished etc. 870.6, *nil admirare* [L.], make nothing of, take it coolly, display imperturbability etc. 826; expect etc. 507.4.

3. *adj.* unastonished, unsurprised, unamazed, unastounded, undumfounded, unbewildered, astonished at nothing; undazzled, undazed; awless *or* aweless, wonderless; blasé etc. 841.9; expecting, expected etc. 507.7, 8.

4. *adj.* imperturbable, calm, cool etc. (inexcitable) 826.9.

5. *int.* no wonder!, of course!, why not?

872. Prodigy
(See also 870. Wonder)

1. *n.* prodigy, prodigiosity, phenomenon, wonder, wonderment, marvel, miracle, amazement, astonishment, sensation, nonesuch [rare], stunner [slang], what no words can paint; rarity, *rara avis* [L.], exception, one in a thousand, one in a way; curiosity, gazingstock, sight, spectacle; lion, social lion; infant prodigy; sign; *annus mirabilis* [L.]; wonders of the world; freak etc. (monstrosity) 83.6.

2. *adj.* prodigious etc. (wonderful) 870.7.

873. Repute
(See also 874. Disrepute)

1. *n.* repute, reputation, "the bubble reputation" (Shakespeare); distinction, mark, name, figure; note, notability, notoriety; fame, famousness etc. *adj.*, renown, kudos [coll.], report, glory, éclat, celebrity; popularity, *aura popularis* [L.], popular repute *or* favor, talk of the

---

872. That indeed a notable miracle hath been done . . . is manifest.—BIBLE. A mouse is miracle enough to stagger sextillions of infidels.—WHITMAN. Here is a wonder, if you talk of a wonder.—SHAKESPEARE. Wonders will never cease.—GARRICK.

873. A good name is better than riches.—PUBLILIUS. All is ephemeral,—fame and the famous as well.—MARCUS AURELIUS. But many that are first shall be last; and the last shall be first.—BIBLE. Who shines in the sec-

town; reputability, good *or* high repute, good odor, good report, esteem, honor, account, regard, respect, credit, *succès d'estime* [F.]; good *or* fair name, name to conjure with; respectability etc. (probity) 939; approbation etc. 931.

2. *n.* illustriousness etc. *adj.*, luster, brilliance *or* brilliancy, radiance, splendor *or* splendour, resplendence *or* resplendency, glory, halo *or* blaze of glory; halo etc. 420.13.

3. *n.* eminence *or* eminency, greatness etc. *adj.*, high mightiness, prominence, elevation, exaltation, distinction, consequence, significance, dignity, prestige, notability, nobility, majesty, grandeur, sublimity; top of the ladder *or* tree; importance etc. 642; pre-eminence etc. (superiority) 33.

4. *n.* rank, position in society, position, standing, footing, *pas* [F.], station, place, status, *locus standi* [L.], order, sphere, degree, grade, class, caste, precedence, condition; notch, cut, hole [all coll.]; brevet rank.

5. *n.* posthumous fame, memory, remembrance; lasting fame, immortality, niche in the temple *or* hall of fame; immortal name, ghost of a great name, "*magni nominis umbra*" (Lucan); commemoration etc. (celebration) 883.

6. *n.* glorification, canonization, dignification, exaltation, elevation, aggrandizement; consecration, dedication; enthronement, enthronization; immortalization, enshrinement; deification, apotheosis; lionization.

7. *n.* an honor, "blushing honor" (Shakespeare); mark of honor, feather in one's cap [coll.] etc. (trophy) 733.

8. *n.* (scholastic honor) *cum laude* [L.] etc. *adv.*, honors, distinction; honorary degree, Doctor Honoris Causa; first; honor society, Phi Beta Kappa, Phi Kappa Phi; scholarship, fellowship; academic degrees etc. 877.3.

9. *n.* celebrity, man of mark *or* note, notable, notability, great man, worthy, great card, name, figure, somebody, *rara avis* [L.], "the observed of all observers" (Shakespeare); cynosure, pillar of the church *or* state; lion, social lion; hero, heroine; the great, "the choice and master spirits of this age" (Shakespeare); elite; galaxy, constellation; person of importance etc. 642.5; paragon etc. (perfection) 650.2; man of rank etc. (nobleman) 875.4.

10. *v.* be distinguished etc. *adj.*, be somebody etc. *n.*; shine, shine forth, glitter, gleam, glow; figure, make *or* cut a figure, cut a dash [coll.], make a splash [coll.], make a noise in the world, make some noise, exalt one's horn, leave one's mark, have a run, live, flourish; be run after, be lionized; be important etc. 642.7.

11. *v.* surpass, outrival etc. (be superior) 33.5.

12. *v.* gain *or* acquire honor etc. *n.*, come to the front, come into vogue, raise one's head; gain *or* win one's laurels *or* spurs, bear the palm, bear away the bell, take the cake [slang, U.S.], bring home the bacon [coll., U.S.]; graduate, take one's degree, pass one's examination, win a scholarship *or* fellowship; star.

13. *v.* honor, show honor toward, do ~, give ~, confer ~, pay *or* render honor to, pay regard to, bestow honor upon, glorify, dignify, ennoble, nobilitate [arch.], aggrandize, elevate, raise, exalt, exalt to the skies; distinguish, confer distinction on, signalize; throne, enthrone, enthronize; crown, crown with laurel; immortalize, hand one's name down to posterity, deify, enshrine; blazon, blow the trumpet; run after, lionize; consecrate, dedicate to, devote to; grace; esteem, hold in esteem, look up to; admire; sing praises to etc. (commend) 931.6; commemorate etc. (celebrate) 883.3.

14. *v.* reflect honor on, shed a luster on, redound to one's honor.

15. *adj.* reputable, estimable, honorable, noble, worthy, creditable; respectable, highly respectable; in good odor, in favor, in high favor; honorific(al).

16. *adj.* distinguished, distingué marked, noted, of note etc. *n.*, notable,

---

ond rank is eclipsed in the first.—VOLTAIRE. Fame's but a hollow echo.—RALEIGH. A great reputation is a great noise: the more there is made, the farther off it is heard.—NAPOLEON. Fame is the thirst of youth.—BYRON. Fame is nothing but an empty name.—C. CHURCHILL. I awoke one morning and found myself famous. —BYRON. The vainest are those who like to be thought respectable.—PINERO. No race can prosper till it learns there is as much dignity in tilling a field as in writing a poem.— B. T. WASHINGTON. *Fax mentis incendium gloriae* [The fire of glory is the torch of the mind]. A prophet is not without honor save in his own country.

noteworthy, notorious, famous, famed, honored, renowned, celebrated, popular, well-known, in everyone's mouth, on everyone's tongue *or* lips, talked-of, talked-about, conspicuous, outstanding, to the front; far-famed, far-heard; consequential, remarkable etc. (important) 642.10.

17. *adj.* illustrious, lustrous, glorious, brilliant, radiant, splendid, splendorous *or* splendrous, splendent, resplendent, bright, shining.

18. *adj.* eminent, prominent, high, elevated, exalted, lofty, great, big [coll.], grand, august, egregious [now joc.], sublime; in the zenith, at the head of the tree, at the top of the tree, of the first water, *sans peur et sans reproche* [F.]; mighty, high and mighty; dignified, proud, stately, imposing; noble, worshipful, lordly, princely, majestic, heaven-born; peerless, pre-eminent etc. (superior) 33.7, 8.

19. *adj.* imperishable, deathless, immortal, fadeless, never-fading, *aere perennius* [L.], time-honored.

20. *adv.* with honor, with distinction, *cum laude* [L.], *magna cum laude* [L.], *summa cum laude* [L.], *insigne cum laude* [L.], *honoris causa* [L.].

874. Disrepute
(See 873. Repute)

1. *n.* disrepute, disreputableness, ingloriousness etc. *adj.*; disreputation, disreputability, ill *or* bad repute, bad name *or* report, bad odor, odium, obloquy, opprobrium, disesteem, discredit, dishonor, disgrace, scandal, humiliation, infamy, "a long farewell to all my greatness" (Shakespeare); disfavor, ill favor; ignominy, ignomy [arch.]; shame, crying *or* burning shame; abasement, debasement; derogation, degradation, unrespectability; disapprobation etc. 932; sense of shame etc. 879.

2. *n.* stigma (*pl.* stigmas, stigmata), stigmatism; brand, reproach, imputation, slur, stain, taint, tarnish, blur, smirch, smutch, smudge, spot, blot, blot in one's escutcheon, badge of infamy; bend *or* bar sinister, baton [both Her.]; champain, point champain [Her.]; scandal, *scandalum magnatum* [L.].

3. *n.* byword, byword of reproach, occasion of contempt, object of scorn, derision, hissing [arch.]; Ichabod.

4. *v.* be in disrepute etc. *adj.*, have a bad name; cut a poor *or* sorry figure, look foolish *or* like a fool, laugh on the wrong side of the mouth [coll.], make a sorry face; go away with a flea in one's ear [coll.], slink away; play second fiddle; wear a halter round one's neck; be conscious of shame etc. (humility) 879.2; keep in the background etc. (modesty) 881.3.

5. *v.* incur disgrace etc. *n.,* disgrace ∼, dishonor ∼, lower *or* degrade oneself, demean oneself [coll.], act beneath one's rank *or* character, derogate, stoop; earn a bad name, forfeit one's good opinion, seal one's infamy; fall from one's high estate, lose caste, recede into the shade.

6. *v.* disgrace, blow upon, bring into discredit etc. *n.,* dishonor, reflect ∼, throw ∼, cast *or* fling dishonor upon, be a reproach to, derogate from; shame, ashame [rare], put to shame, impute shame to, hold up to shame, cry shame upon, bring shame upon, humiliate etc. 879.3.

7. *v.* stigmatize, set a mark of disgrace on, brand, stain, tarnish, blot, taint, sully, bespatter, blacken, defile; slur, cast a slur upon; give a bad name, give a dog a bad name, put in the black book; defame, discredit, vilify, vilipend, malign, tread *or* trample under foot, drag through the mire, heap dirt upon; degrade, debase, bring low, put *or* take down; take down a peg, take down a peg or two [both coll.]; expose, expose to infamy, gibbet; boycott, black-list, blackball, draw up *or* sign a round robin; disbench [Eng.], disbar, unfrock; post.

8. *adj.* disreputable, discreditable, disgraceful, shameful, dishonorable, ignoble, ignominious, inglorious, infamous; base, low, mean, little, petty, paltry, shabby, scrubby, scabby, dirty, beggarly, pitiful, abject, wretched, despicable, contemptible, deplorable, vile, foul, odious, obnox-

---

874. Who can see worse days than he that yet living doth follow at the funeral of his own reputation?—BACON.   Take away my good name and take away my life.—FULLER.   In vain thou strivest to cover shame with shame.—MILTON.   Bankrupt in fortune and reputation.—SHERIDAN.   'Tis better never to be named than to be ill spoken of.—S. CENTLIVRE.   There is no odor so bad as that which arises from goodness tainted.—THOREAU.

ious, execrable, rank, peccant, fulsome, gross, nefarious, heinous, atrocious, arrant, notorious, outrageous, shocking, scandalous, opprobrious, unmentionable, too bad; derogatory, degrading, humiliating; unrespectable; unworthy etc. 940.9.

9. *adj.* in disrepute etc. *n.*, out of repute, ~ favor *or* countenance, at a discount; shorn of one's glory, "shorn of its beams" (Milton); under a cloud, under an eclipse, in the shade, in the background; down in the world, down on one's uppers [coll.], down and out, out at elbows *or* heels, downtrodden; disgraced etc. *v.*, loaded with shame etc. *n.*, unable to show one's face.

10. *adj.* renownless, inglorious, nameless, obscure, unheard-of, unknown, unknown to fame, unnoticed, unnoted, unhonored, unglorified; ignoble etc. 876.11.

11. *adv.* disreputably, shamefully etc. *adj.*; to one's shame, to one's shame be it spoken.

12. *int.* shame!, for shame!, fie!, fie for shame!, fie upon!, fie upon it!, ough!, *pro pudor!* [L.], *O tempora! O mores!* [L.], *sic transit gloria mundi!* [L.].

875. Nobility
(See 876. Commonalty)

1. *n.* nobility, nobleness, aristocraticalness etc. *adj.*; aristocracy, optimacy [rare], noblesse, "caste of Vere de Vere" (Tennyson), *gentilhommerie* [F.], gentility, quality; birth, high *or* noble birth, high descent; blood, blue blood, blue blood of Castile, "all the blood of all the Howards" (Pope); rank, distinction; *ancien régime* [F.]; royalty etc. (dominion) 737.2.

2. *n.* the nobility, *noblesse* [F.], aristocracy, elite, optimates, noble ~, aristocratic *or* patrician class, the classes, upper classes *or* circles, upper cut [coll.], upper crust [coll.], upper ten [coll.], upper ten thousand, the four hundred [U.S.], high life, *haut monde* [F.]; great folks, notables, notabilities; First Families of Virginia, F.F.V.s [U.S.]; peerage, baronage; House of Lords, House of Peers; lords, lords temporal and spiritual; knightage; royalty; high society etc. 852.4.

3. *n.* gentry, gentlefolk *or* gentlefolks, gentlepeople; lesser nobility, *petite noblesse* [F.], samurai [Jap.], better sort, squirarchy *or* squirearchy, landed proprietors, magnates.

4. *n.* noble, nobleman; peer, grandee, magnifico, hidalgo [Sp.], daimio [Jap.], shizoku [Jap.], don [Sp.], blue blood, thoroughbred, patrician, aristocrat, upper-cruster [slang, U.S.], nob [slang], swell [coll.]; pasha *or* bashaw [Turk.], one-tailed ~, two-tailed *or* three-tailed pasha *or* bashaw [Turk.]; lord, laird [Scot.], lording [arch.], lordling; squire, squireen [joc., Eng.]; gentleman, *gentilhomme* [F.]; signor [It.], signior, seignior, señor [Sp.], senhor [Pg.]; noblewoman, peeress, gentlewoman; notable, notability etc. (person of importance) 642.5, (celebrity) 873.9.

5. *n.* duke, grand duke, archduke, marquis, earl, count, viscount, baron, baronet, thane [Hist.]; boyar *or* boyard [Russ.]; knight, cavalier, chevalier, *Ritter* [G.], *caballero* [Sp.]; banneret, knight banneret; vavasor *or* vavasour [Hist.]; esquire, armiger; palsgrave, waldgrave, margrave, landgrave.

6. *n.* duchess, marchioness, viscountess, countess, margravine; lady, dame [Hist.], khanum [Orient.]; *doña* [Sp.], dona [Pg.]; signora [It.] etc. 374.3; empress etc. 745.6.

7. *n.* prince, atheling [Hist.], *Prinz* [G.], *Fürst* [G.], knez [Russ.], mirza [Per.], sheik *or* sheikh, sherif [Moham.], khan [Orient.], emir [Turk. and Moham.]; shahzada [Ind.]; princelet, princling; king etc. (potentate) 745.2, 3; rajah, rana etc. (Hindu ruling princes) 745.4; mawab, wali etc. (Mohammedan ruling princes) 745.5.

8. *n.* princess, *princesse* [F.], infanta [Sp. and Pg.], czarevna *or* tsarevna

---

875. Who is well-born? He who is by nature well fitted for virtue.—SENECA.   This was the noblest Roman of them all.—SHAKESPEARE. The more noble, the more humble.—J. RAY. True nobility is exempt from fear.—SHAKESPEARE.   The nobleman is he whose noble mind / Is filled with inborn worth, unborrowed from his kind.—DRYDEN.   Title and ancestry render a good man more illustrious, but an ill one more contemptible.—ADDISON.   Here all were noble, save Nobility.—BYRON.   Noble by birth, yet nobler by great deeds.—LONGFELLOW.   Noble blood is an accident of fortune; noble actions characterize the great.—GOLDONI.   *Noblesse oblige* [Rank imposes obligations].

[Russ.]; rani, maharani, begum, shahzadi, kumari *or* kunwari, raj-kumari, malikzadi [all Ind.]; empress etc. 745.6.

9. *n.* (rank or office) kingship, kinghood; viscountship, viscountcy, viscounty; dukedom, marquisate, earldom, lordship, baronetcy, knighthood, donship; seigniory *or* seigneury, seignioralty; pashaship, pashadom, pashalik.

10. *adj.* noble, of rank etc. *n.*, high, exalted; patrician, aristocratic(al), highborn, wellborn, well-bred, thoroughbred, blue-blooded, pure-blooded, *pur sang* [F.], of gentle blood, genteel, *comme il faut* [F.]; princely, princelike, "every inch a king" (Shakespeare); gentlemanly, gentlemanlike, ladylike; distinguished, distingué; titled; kingly, queenly etc. (sovereign) 737.16; highly respectable etc. (reputable) 873.15.

876. Commonalty
(See 875. Nobility)

1. *n.* commonalty, commonality, commonage, commons, common people, common run [coll.], salt of the earth, *bourgeoisie* [F.], proletariat, lower *or* humbler classes *or* orders, lower cut [coll.], low life *or* society, rank and file, herd of common people, vulgar *or* common herd, *profanum* or *ignobile vulgus* [L.], "the multitude of the gross people" (Erasmus), *hoc genus omne* [L.], mass of the people *or* of society, the masses, the multitude, the million, "the four million" (O. Henry), the many, the general [arch.], the people.

the populace, the crowd, the horde, the mob, the mobility [joc.], King Mob, the other half, *demos* [Gr. δῆμος], the peasantry, *hoi polloi* [Gr. οἱ πολλοί], great unwashed *or* unnumbered; rabble, rout, the ruck, common ruck, canaille, roughscuff [coll., U.S.], ragabash *or* ragabrash [Scot. and dial. Eng.], ragtag [coll.], "the tag-rag people" (Shakespeare), rag-tag and bobtail; rag, tag and bobtail; "the beast with many heads" (Shakespeare), "the blunt monster with uncounted heads, the still-discordant wavering multitude" (Shakespeare), Brown, Jones, and Robinson; Tom, Dick, and Harry; democracy.

2. *n.* riffraff, raff, chaff, trash, rubbish, dregs, sordes, offscourings, offscum, scum, scum of the earth, dregs ~, scum ~, offscum *or* offscourings of society, *faex populi* [L.], swinish multitude, vermin.

3. *n.* commoner, one of the people, man in the street, *roturier* [F.], bourgeois; plebeian, pleb [slang]; proletarian, proletary, proletaire; democrat, republican; John Smith, Mr. Snooks, Mr. *or* Mrs. Brown *or* Smith; cockney; grisette; demimonde, demimondaine; underling.

4. *n.* obscurity, nobody etc. (unimportant person) 643.6.

5. *n.* peasant, countryman, son of the soil, *terrae filius* [L.], tiller *or* cultivator of the soil, ryot [Ind.], fellah [Ar.] (*pl.* fellahin *or* fellaheen *or* fellahs), tyke *or* tike [arch. exc. Scot. and dial.], hind [Eng.], rustic, hick [slang], hayseed [slang], hoosier [coll., U.S.], clod, clodhopper [coll.], hobnail, joskin [slang], jake [coll., U.S.], yokel, rube *or* reub [slang, U.S.], hodge [coll.], bumpkin, country bumpkin, lumpkin, Tony Lumpkin (Goldsmith), chawbacon [slang], boor, clown, carl [arch. exc. dial.], churl, kern [now rare], loon [arch.], looby, lout, chuff, put, swain.

plowman, plowboy; gaffer; hewers of wood and drawers of water, sons of Martha; farmer etc. (agriculturist) 371.2; villein etc. (serf) 746.4.

6. *n.* rough, roughneck [slang] etc. (vulgarian) 851.4, (ruffian) 887; boor etc. *above* 876.5.

7. *n.* barbarian, Goth, vandal, Philistine, Boeotian, Yahoo, savage, Hottentot, Zulu.

8. *n.* upstart, start-up [rare], parvenu, skipjack, *novus homo* [L.], mushroom, sprout [slang], jack-in-the-pulpit, would-be, *Bourgeois Gentilhomme* [F.], adventurer, "an upstart crow decked in our feathers" (Peele); *nouveau riche* [F.; *pl.* *nouveaux riches*], newly-rich, codfish aristocrat [U.S], pig in clover [slang]; *hesterni quirites* [L.], codfish aristocracy [U.S.].

---

876. Trust not the populace; the crowd is many-minded.—PHOCYLIDES. The mob has many heads but no brains.—FULLER. The play, I remember, pleased not the million; 'twas caviare to the general.—SHAKESPEARE. It rather occurs to me that it's the commonplace people who *do* things.—LEACOCK. I am a member of the rabble in good standing.—W. PEGLER. When Adam dolve, and Eve span, Who was then the gentleman?

876.9 — 878.1

9. *n.* vagabond, vagabondager [rare], vag [slang, U.S.], vagrant; pariah, one despised of society, wastrel, losel [arch. exc. dial.], caitiff, bezonian (Shakespeare), beggarly fellow, wretch, poor creature, pilgarlic, gaberlunzie [Scot.]; ragamuffin, ragabash *or* ragabrash [Scot. and dial. Eng.], tatterdemalion, *sans-culotte* [F.]; Arab, street Arab, gamin, mud lark; waif, stray, waifs and strays; foundling; ragman, ragpicker; sweep, sweeper; outcast of society etc. 893.5; tramp etc. (wanderer) 268.2; beggar etc. 767.2.

10. *v.* be ignoble etc. *adj.*, be of *or* belong to the common herd etc. *n.*, be nobody etc. 643.6.

11. *adj.* ignoble, common, plebeian, proletarian, humble, of low *or* mean parentage, ~ origin *or* extraction, lowbred, lowborn, baseborn, earthborn; dunghill, dunghilly; homely, homespun, parvenu, mushroom, risen from the ranks; cockney, born within sound of Bow bells; untitled; uncouth, barbarian etc. (vulgar) 851.6, 7; low, mean etc. (disreputable) 874.8; lowly etc. (humble) 879.4; no great shakes [coll.] etc. (unimportant) 643.10; obscure, unknown etc. (renownless) 874.10.

12. *adj.* rustic, provincial, boorish etc. (countrified) 183.3.

13. *adv.* below the salt.

877. Title

1. *n.* title, honorific, honor, title of honor, appellation of dignity, ~ distinction *or* respect; handle, handle to one's name [both slang].

2. *n.* (honorifics) Excellency, Grace, Worship, Reverence, Honor, Your ~, His *or* Her Excellency, ~ Honor etc.; Lord, My Lord, milord, Lordship, Your *or* His lordship; Lady, My Lady, milady, Ladyship, Your *or* Her Ladyship; *mem-sahib* [Ind.]; Highness, Royal Highness, Serene Highness, Your ~, His *or* Her Highness; Your Royal Highness, Your ~, His *or* Her Majesty, ~ Most Gracious Majesty *or* Most Excellent Majesty; *mein Herr* [G.]; sir, sire, sirrah [arch. and dial.]; Esquire; master.

mirza [Per.], effendi [Turk.], sirdar [Orient], emir [Moham.], mian [Ind.], malik [Hind.], huzoor [Ind.], khan [Orient], Mir [Ind.], sahib [Ind.], *burra* or *burra sahib* [Ind.], nawab [Ind.], *bahadur* [Hind.]; *signor* [It.] etc. (Mister) 373.3; madame etc. (Mistress) 374.3; baron, prince, princess etc. 875.5–8; king, empress etc. 745.2–6.

3. *n.* (academic rank and titles) bachelor, baccalaureate, Bachelor of Arts, *Baccalaureus Artium* [L.], B.A., Bachelor of Agriculture, B. Ag. *or* B. Agr., Bachelor of Architecture, B.Ar. *or* B. Arch., Bachelor of Business Administration, B.B.A., Bachelor of Divinity, B.D., Bachelor of Education, B.Ed., Bachelor of Laws, LL.B., Bachelor of Theology, *Scientiae Theologicae Baccalaureus* [L.], S.T.B., Bachelor of Literature, B.Litt., Bachelor of Music, Mus. B., Bachelor of Science, B.S.; master, Master of Arts, *Magister Artium* [L.], M.A., Master of Engineering, *Magister in Arte Ingeniaria* [L.], M.I.A.

doctor, doctorate, Doctor of Philosophy, ~ Philology *or* Pharmacy, Ph.D., Doctor of Dental Surgery, D.D.S., Doctor of Dental Science, D.D.Sc., Doctor of Laws, LL.D., Doctor of Literature, D.Litt.; Doctor of Medicine, Medicinae Doctor [L.], M.D.; license, licentiate; Assistant Professor, Associate Professor, Professor, Professor Emeritus; Doctor Honoris Causa etc. (scholastic honor) 873.8; teacher etc. 540.

4. *n.* (ecclesiastical titles) Holiness, Monsignor; dom, friar, brother, sister, frater, pater, father, mother, mother superior; clergy etc. 996.

5. *adj.* noble, most noble; Honorable, the Honorable, the Most Honorable, the Right Honorable; reverend, the Reverend, the Very Reverend, the Right Reverend, the Most Reverend.

878. Pride
(See 879. Humility)

1. *n.* pride, proudness etc. *adj.*; self-esteem, self-respect, self-confidence, self-

877. Oh! a Baronet's rank is exceedingly nice, / But the title's uncommonly dear at the price! —GILBERT.   A prince can mak a belted knight, / A marquis, duke, and a' that.—BURNS. *Perchè non i titoli illustrano gli uomini, ma gli uomini i titoli* [For titles do not reflect honor on men, but rather men on their titles]. —MACHIAVELLI.   The King is dead, long live the King.
878. Pride goeth before destruction, and a haughty spirit before a fall.—BIBLE.   Pride

importance; high notions, crest, dignity, *mens sibi conscia recti* (Vergil); condescension, condescendence; vanity etc. 880; haughtiness etc. (arrogance) 885; airs etc. (ostentation) 882; boasting etc. 884.

2. *n.* proud person, proudling [derog.], proud-belly [slang], swell-head [slang], *un homme haut* [F.], highflier *or* highflyer, swanker [coll.], beggar on horseback; fine gentleman *or* lady, *grande dame* [F.]; bloated aristocrat; the proud; egoist etc. 880.3; boaster etc. 884.3; swaggerer etc. (blusterer) 887.2; upstart etc. 876.8.

3. *v.* be proud etc. *adj.*, act proudly etc. *adv.*, deign, condescend; stoop, stoop to conquer; rear ~, lift up *or* hold up one's head, hold one's head high, hold one's nose in the air, look down one's nose, toss the head, bridle, assume a lofty manner *or* bearing, give oneself airs, put on airs, put on side [slang], put on big looks, look big, act the *grand seigneur;* swell, swell it.

climb *or* get on the high ropes, mount *or* get on one's high horse, ride the high horse [all coll.]; perk, perk it, perk up, perk oneself up; peacock, strut, swagger, stalk, stalk abroad; take the wall, "bear like the Turk no rival near the throne" (Pope), carry with a high hand, set one's back up; put a good face on; look one in the face; be arrogant *or* insolent etc. 885.4-7; be vain etc. 880.4; show off [coll.] etc. (be ostentatious) 882.6; boast etc. 884.5.

4. *v.* be proud of, pride oneself on *or* in, take pride in, glory in, pique oneself on *or* upon; congratulate oneself, hug oneself; not hide one's light under a bushel, not put one's talent in a napkin.

5. *v.* make proud etc. *adj.*, give pride etc. *n.*, do proud [coll.], elate, gratify.

6. *adj.* proud, proudful [now dial.], proudish [rare], proudhearted, proud-minded, proud-spirited, proud-stomached, proud-blooded, proud-crested, proud-looking, proud-glancing, proud-exulting, proud-paced, proud-prancing; self-confident, self-respecting, self-esteeming; swollen *or* bloated with pride, swollen, puffed up, blown, high-swelling, swelled-headed; flushed, flushed with pride; elate [arch.], elated.

elevated, lofty, high, high-toned, mighty, high and mighty, in one's altitudes [coll.]; condescending, condescensive; lofty-minded, high-minded, high-souled, high-mettled, high-plumed, high-headed, high-nosed [coll.], high-toned [coll.]; high-flown, highfalutin *or* highfaluting [coll.]; toplofty, toploftical [rare]; stuck-up, stuck-uppish [both coll.]; perk, perky, perked up; proud as a peacock, proud as Lucifer, as proud as Punch; purse-proud; haughty etc. (arrogant) 885.8; vain etc. 880.6; pretentious etc. (ostentatious) 882.8; boastful etc. 884.7.

7. *adj.* dignified, stately, lordly, baronial, noble, majestic, grand, impressive, imposing; stiff, stiff-necked; stilted, formal, in buckram; starch, starched.

8. *adv.* proudly etc. *adj.*, with pride etc. *n.*, with head erect, with head held high, with nose in air, with nose turned up; *de haut en bas* [F.]; like a lord, *en grand seigneur* [F.].

879. Humility
(See 878. Pride)

1. *n.* humility, humbleness, meekness, lowliness etc. *adj.*; humbleness of spirit, lowliness of mind, lowlihood; abasement, self-abasement; humiliation, mortification, letdown, setdown, humbled pride; shame, disgrace, sense of shame *or* disgrace; modesty etc. 881; resignation etc. (submission) 725; servility etc. 886.

2. *v.* be humble etc. *adj.*, feel small, look foolish; show humility etc. *n.*, humble oneself, demean oneself [coll.], lower

---

and poverty are ill met, yet often seen together. —FULLER. There is none worse / Than a proud heart and a beggar's purse.—COPLAND. Pride that dines on vanity sups on contempt.— H. G. BOHN. Pride and conceit were the original sin of man.—LE SAGE. Proud with the proud, yet courteously proud.—BYRON. The proud will sooner lose than ask their way —C. CHURCHILL. One should die proudly when it is no longer possible to live proudly.— NIETZSCHE. Those in fear they may cast pearls before swine are often lacking in pearls. —SANDBURG. Pride goeth before a fall.

879. *Parvum parva decent* [Humble things befit a humble person].—HORACE. Whosoever shall smite thee on thy right cheek, turn to him the other also.—BIBLE. I thank my God for my humility.—SHAKESPEARE. Humility is a virtue all preach, none practice.—SELDEN. True humility is contentment.—AMIEL. Humble hearts have humble desires.—G. HERBERT. He that is humble, ever shall Have God to be his guide.—BUNYAN. Lowliness is the base of every virtue.—P. J. BAILEY.

one's note *or* tone, sing small [coll.], draw in one's horns [coll.], sober down, hang one's head, hide one's diminished head, hide one's face, not dare to show one's face, not have a word to say for oneself; feel shame *or* disgrace, take shame to oneself, be conscious of shame; be humiliated, get a setdown, be put out of countenance, be shamed, be put to the blush; eat humble pie, eat crow, eat dirt, lick the dust, carry *or* bear coals, drink the cup of humiliation to the dregs; keep in the background etc. (be modest) 881.3; submit etc. 725.3.

3. *v.* humiliate, humble, meeken [now rare], mortify, crush, abash, abase, disgrace, degrade, reduce, lower, bring low, let ~, set *or* take down; take down a peg, take down a peg or two [both coll.]; put out, put out of countenance, put one's nose out of joint [coll.], take the shine out of [coll.], make one sing small [coll.], teach one his distance; leave *or* put in the background, push into a corner, cast *or* throw into the shade; shame, ashame [rare], put to shame, put to the blush; send away with a flea in one's ear [coll.].

4. *adj.* humble, humble *or* poor in spirit, humble-spirited, humble-minded, humblehearted; meek, meek-spirited, meek-minded, meekhearted; lowly, low [now rare]; humble-looking, humble-visaged; meek-looking, meek-browed, meek-eyed; humble-mannered, meek-mannered; modest etc. 881.5, 6; servile etc. 886.4; submissive etc. 725.5; resigned etc. 826.10; lowborn etc. (ignoble) 876.11.

5. *adj.* humbled etc. *v.*, in the dust, humbled in the dust; bowed-down, resigned; down on one's knees, down on one's marrowbones [coll.]; shamed, ashamed; chapfallen, crestfallen; abashed, dashed, out of countenance; shorn of one's glory etc. (in disrepute) 874.9.

6. *adj.* humiliating etc. *v.*, humiliative, humiliatory, humilient [rare], humilific.

7. *adv.* humbly, meekly etc. *adj.*; with due deference, with downcast eyes, with bated breath, on bended knee, on all fours, with one's tail between one's legs.

880. Vanity
(See 881. Modesty)

1. *n.* vanity, conceitedness etc. *adj.*, conceit, self-conceit; self-importance, self-interest, self-complacency, self-content, self-satisfaction, self-sufficiency, self-confidence, self-respect, self-esteem, self-approbation, self-praise, self-glorification, self-laudation, self-gratulation, self-applause, self-admiration, self-worship, self-endearment, self-love, *amour-propre* [F.]; self-exultation, elation; "the sixth insatiable sense" (Carlyle); vainglory, overweening pride, swelled head; egoism, egotism; priggism, priggery; foppery, coxcombry; peacockery, peacockishness; pride etc. 878; arrogance etc. 885; ostentation etc. 882; selfishness etc. 943; overestimation etc. 482; boasting etc. 884; airs etc. 882.2.

2. *n.* vain pretensions, lugs [coll., U.S.], airs etc. (ostentation) 882.2; haughty airs etc. (arrogance) 885.

3. *n.* egoist, egotist; it *or* It [coll.], big it *or* It [slang], the only pebble on the beach [U.S.], know-it-all, Sir Oracle, *vox et praeterea nihil* [L.]; peacock, bantam cock [coll.]; strutter, swaggerer; prig, prude; self-seeker etc. 943.2; swellhead [slang] etc. 878.2; coxcomb etc. (fop) 854; boaster etc. 884.3.

4. *v.* be vain etc. *adj.*, have too high *or* an overweening opinion of oneself, think one is it [slang], be blinded by one's own glory, be stuck on oneself [slang], know it all, lay the flattering unction to one's soul, put oneself forward, fish for compliments; give oneself airs etc. (be ostentatious) 882.6; be proud etc. 878.3, 4; boast etc. 884.5.

5. *v.* render vain etc. *adj.*, inspire with vanity etc. *n.*, inflate, puff up, turn one's head.

6. *adj.* vain, vainglorious, conceited, overproud, overweening, pert, cocky [coll.], forward, high-flown, pretentious, priggish; egotistic(al), egoistic(al); peacockish, peacocky, vain as a peacock; coxcomical, foppish, dandified; wise in one's own conceit, overwise, know-it-all, pragmatical [rare]; puffed up, swell-headed etc. (proud) 878.6; arrogant etc. 885.8;

---

880. An ounce of vanity spoils a hundred weight of merit.—G. HERBERT. No man sympathizes with the sorrows of vanity.—JOHNSON. Pampered vanity is a better thing perhaps than starved pride.—BAILLIE. Vanity plays lurid tricks with our memory.—CONRAD. Vanity is the cause of a great deal of virtue in men.—PINERO. The fuming vanities of earth.—WORDSWORTH. Vain? Let it be so! Nature was her teacher.—HOLMES.

ostentatious etc. 882.8; boastful etc. 884.7; selfish etc. 943.4.

self-glorious, self-important, self-interested, self-opinionated, self-satisfied, self-complacent, self-content, self-sufficient, self-confident, self-respecting, self-esteeming, self-lauding, self-flattering, self-applauding, self-praising, self-admiring, self-worshiping, self-loving, self-endeared.

881. Modesty
(See 880. Vanity)

1. *n.* modesty, unobtrusiveness, bashfulness, timidness etc. *adj.*; timidity, diffidence, retiring disposition, *mauvaise honte* [F.]; reserve, constraint; blush, blushing, flush, suffusion; "blushing honors" (Shakespeare); meekness etc. (humility) 879; false modesty etc. (prudery) 853.2; underestimation etc. 483.

2. *n.* violet, modest violet.

3. *v.* be modest etc. *adj.*, retire, reserve oneself, keep one's distance, keep in the background, remain in the shade, take a back seat [coll.], give way to, not show one's face, hide one's face, hide one's light under a bushel, pursue the noiseless tenor of one's way, "do good by stealth and blush to find it fame" (Pope); cast sheep's eyes; be humble etc. 879.2.

4. *v.* blush, flush, redden, crimson, mantle, change color, color up, blush up to the eyes.

5. *adj.* modest, reserved, constrained, diffident, shrinking, bashful, shy, skittish, coy, demure; timid, timorous, timorsome [obs. exc. dial.]; blushing, blushful; shamefaced, sheepish; meek etc. (humble) 879.4; over-modest etc. (prudish) 853.7.

6. *adj.* unpretentious, unpretending, unassuming, unobtrusive, unostentatious, unboastful, unaspiring; deprecative, deprecatory.

7. *adv.* modestly etc. *adj.*, quietly, privately; without ceremony, without beat of drum, *sans façon* [F.].

---

881. Not stepping o'er the bounds of modesty.—Shakespeare. Thy modesty's a candle to thy merit.—Fielding. Modesty is the only sure bait when you angle for praise.—Chesterfield. Modesty does not long survive innocence.—Burke. Ever with the best desert goes diffidence.—Browning. So sweet the blush of bashfulness, / E'en pity scarce can wish it less.—Byron.

882. Ostentation

1. *n.* ostentation, ostentatiousness, pretentiousness etc. *adj.*; pretense, pretension; display, ostentatious display, show, *étalage* [F.], parade, fanfaronade, flourish, fuss, glitter; impressive effect, figure; shine, dash, splash, splurge [all coll.]; pomp, magnificence, splendor, state, solemnity; pomposity, inflation, orotundity; front [slang], veneer, gloss; ostent; affectation etc. 853; arrogance etc. 885; pride etc. 878; vanity etc. 880; exaggeration etc. 549; frillery etc. (frippery) 847.2; gaudery etc. 851.2; showy clothes etc. 225.13.

2. *n.* pretensions, airs, lugs [coll., U.S.], dog [coll.], side [slang], swank [coll.], showing-off, pretentious showing-off, vainglorious *or* pretentious display *or* parade, vain pretensions, vain *or* arrogant behavior, artificial ~, affected *or* swaggering manner; bounce, strut, swagger; peacockishness, peacockery; pose, posing; attitudinarianism; haughty airs etc. (arrogance) 885.

3. *n.* demonstration, spectacle, exhibit, exhibition, exposition, show; pageant, pageantry, "insubstantial pageant" (Shakespeare); turnout, setout [both coll.]; procession, review, march past, promenade, parade; grand function *or* doings, fete *or* fête, gala, field day; array, arrayal; flying colors, flourish of trumpets etc. (celebration) 883.

4. *n.* ceremony, ritual etc. (rite) 998.

5. *n.* attitudinarian, posture maker, posturer, posturist, poser, show-off [coll.], no modest violet; grandstander, grandstand player [both slang, U.S.]; affecter etc. 853.4; fop etc. 854; hypocrite etc. (pretender) 548.3, 4.

6. *v.* be ostentatious etc. *adj.*, make a show *or* display, show off [coll.], show *or* go through one's paces, strut one's stuff [slang, U.S.], exhibit *or* parade one's wares [slang, U.S.], figure, cut *or* make a figure, cut a shine [coll.], cut *or* make a dash, ~ splash *or* splurge [all coll.], splurge [coll.], splash [slang], glit-

---

882. Hell is paved with big pretensions.—Cynic's Calendar. Lo, all our pomp of yesterday / Is one with Nineveh and Tyre.—Kipling. *Parturient montes, nascetur ridiculus mus* [The mountains are in labor; a ridiculous mouse will be born].—Horace. The ostentatious simplicity of their dress.—Macaulay.

ter, attract attention; put oneself forward, come forward; put up a front [slang], give oneself airs, put on airs, put on [slang], put on side [slang], put on lugs [coll., U.S.], put on dog *or* the dog [coll.], put on big looks, look *or* talk big, blow one's own trumpet *or* horn, have no false modesty, ritz it [slang], act the grand seigneur.

swell, swell it; grandstand [slang, U.S.], play to the gallery *or* galleries [coll.]; attitudinize, pose; peacock, strut, swagger; mince, mince it, prink [dial. Eng.]; parade, promenade, march past; emblazon, blazon forth; set off, set off to good advantage, put a good *or* smiling face upon; mount, have framed and glazed; pretend etc. (affect) 853.5; bluster etc. 887.3.

7. *v.* flaunt, show off [coll.], sport [coll.], display, exhibit, put forward, put forth, hold up, trot out [slang], hand out; dangle, dangle before the eyes; brandish, wave.

8. *adj.* ostentatious, pretentious, showy, airy [now coll.], lofty, tall [coll.], high-toned, ritzy [slang], fandangle [coll.]; high-falutin *or* highfaluting [coll.], high-flown, highflying; imposing, stately, majestic, grand, splendid, magnificent, sumptuous, palatial; splendacious, splendiferous [both joc.]; pompous, inflated, gassy [coll.], swelling; flaunting, flaunty; splurging, splurgy [both coll.]; swank, swanking, swanky [all coll.].

flashing, flashy; splashy [slang], sporty [coll.], jazzy [slang], fancy, glittering, flaming, flamboyant, flaring, glaring, daring, dashing, jaunty, gay, frilly [coll.], frothy; flowery, florid; rory-tory, rory-cum-tory [both dial.]; peacocky, peacockish; affected etc. 853.6; overwrought, overdone etc. (exaggerated) 549.3; high-sounding etc. (grandiloquent) 577.7; ornate etc. 847.13; loud [coll.], garish etc. (gaudy) 851.8; *en grande tenue* [F.] etc. (smart) 847.14; vain etc. 880.6; proud etc. 878.6, 7.

9. *adj.* theatric(al), stagy; dramatic, dramaturgic(al); scenic(al); spectacular.

10. *adj.* ceremonial, ritualistic etc. 998.15.

11. *adv.* ostentatiously, showily etc. *adj.*; with flourish of trumpet, with beat of drum, with flying colors, with a brass band; at the head of the procession; with no false modesty; *ad captandum vulgus* [L.].

883. Celebration

1. *n.* celebration, celebrating etc. *v.*, solemnization, observance; commemoration, memorialization, remembrance, memory; jubilee; ovation, triumph; presentation at court, debut, coming out [coll.]; *feu de joie* [F.], bonfire, illuminations; salute, salvo, salvo of artillery; flourish of trumpets, fanfare, fanfaron [rare], fanfaronade; flying colors; triumphal arch; laudation etc. (commendation) 931.2; jubilation etc. (rejoicing) 838; paean, hallelujah etc. (glorification) 990.2; festival, fete etc. (festivity) 840.2; inauguration, coronation etc. 755.2.

2. *n.* red-letter day, fete day etc. (holiday) 840.5; anniversary, Christmas, Independence Day etc. 138.5, 7.

3. *v.* celebrate, commemorate, memorialize; signalize, solemnize, keep, hallow, keep holiday etc. 840.5, mark with a red letter; hold jubilee, jubilize, jubilate; maffick [coll., Eng.], kill the fatted calf, roast an ox, serve up the Thanksgiving turkey *or* Christmas goose; sound a fanfare, blow the trumpet, beat the drum, fire a salute; do honor to etc. 873.13; laud, sound the praises of etc. 931.6; rejoice etc. 838.5; exult etc. 884.6; paint the town red (slang) etc. (make merry) 840.21.

4. *v.* pledge, drink to, drink a toast to, toast; hobnob, hob-and-nob, drink hob-and-nob *or* hob-a-nob.

5. *adj.* celebrating etc. *v.*, commemorative, memorial, kept in remembrance; solemn; jubilant etc. 838.9.

6. *adv.* in celebration of, in honor of, in commemoration of, in memory *or* remembrance of, to the memory of, *in memoriam* [L.]; as a toast.

7. *int.* hail!, all hail!, *ave!* [L.], *vive!* [F.], long life to!, glory be to!, honor be to!, see the conquering hero comes!; hallelujah! etc. (hurrah) 838.12.

---

883. The yearly course that brings this day about / Shall never see it but a holiday.—SHAKESPEARE. They are ever forward / In celebration of this day.—Shakespeare. I drink to the general joy of the whole table. —SHAKESPEARE.

884. Boasting

1. *n.* boasting, bragging etc. *v.,* braggadocio, braggadocianism, braggartism *or* braggardism, braggartry; boast, brag, vaunt, *blague* [F.], gasconade, highfalutin *or* highfaluting [coll.], bluff, bluster, swagger, bounce, bravado, rant, rodomontade, bombast, gas [slang], hot air [slang], bunk [slang], buncombe *or* bunkum [coll.], bosh [coll.], fine talking, tall talk [coll.]; tall story [coll.], fish story [joc.].

puff [coll.], puffery, self-puffery; jactation, jactitation, jactancy; pretense, pretensions; fanfaronade, fanfaronading; overpraise, overcommendation, overlaudation; much ado about nothing, much cry and little wool; heroics; exultation, gloating etc. *v.*; self-glorification etc. (vanity) 880; exaggeration etc. 549; overestimation etc. 482; magniloquence etc. 577.2.

2. *n.* jingoism, chauvinism, vaingloriousness patriotism, overpatriotism; spread eagle, spread-eagleism [both U.S.]; militarism etc. 722.6; patriotism etc. 906.4.

3. *n.* boaster, brag, braggart, braggadocio, blatherskite [coll.], fanfaron, trumpeter, blower of his own trumpet, bouncer [coll.], bluffer, pretender, *vox et praeterea nihil* [L.]; blowhard, blower, hot-air artist, gasbag, windbag, big bag of wind, windjammer, windy [all slang]; Fourth-of-July orator; Braggadocio, Rodomont, Thraso, Gascon; blusterer etc. 887.2; egoist etc. 880.3; charlatan etc. (impostor) 548.3; puppy etc. (fop) 854.

4. *n.* jingo, jingoist; chauvin, chauvinist; spread eagle, spread-eaglist [both U.S.]; fire-eater [coll., U.S.]; militarist etc. 726.3.

5. *v.* boast, make a boast of, brag, vaunt, flourish, crack, puff, trumpet, glorify [rare], gasconade, vapor, blow [slang], talk big, draw the longbow, speak for Buncombe [U.S.]; brag *or* boast about oneself, brag oneself up [slang], blow one's own trumpet, toot one's own horn, *faire claquer son fouet* [F.], congratulate oneself, hug oneself, pat oneself on the back, take merit to oneself, *se faire valoir* [F.]; bluster, roister, swagger; bluff, four-flush [slang]; overpraise, overcommand, overlaud; indulge in jingoism etc. *n.,* spread-eagle [coll., U.S.], make the eagle scream [U.S.], sing "Rule Britannia" [Eng.]; show off [coll.] etc. (be proud) 878.3; exaggerate etc. 549.2.

6. *v.* exult, triumph, glory, delight, joy, jubilate; crow, crow over [both coll.]; chuckle, cackle, neigh; gloat, gloat over, rejoice, cheer etc. 838.5-8; hold jubilee etc. (celebrate) 883.3.

7. *adj.* boastful, bragging etc. *v.,* braggart, gassy [coll.], windy [coll.], bombastic, inflated, swollen, highfalutin *or* highfaluting [coll.], high-flown, pretentious, extravagant, tall [coll.], flaming, gasconading; fanfaron, fanfaronading; thrasonic(al) [rare]; proud etc. 878.6; vainglorious etc. (conceited) 880.6; magniloquent etc. 577.7.

8. *adj.* jingo, jingoish, jingoist, jingoistic; chauvin, chauvinist, chauvinistic; overpatriotic, spread-eagle [coll., U.S.]; militaristic etc. 722.13; patriotic etc. 906.8.

9. *adj.* exultant, exulting etc. *v.*; elate, elated; jubilant, triumphant, in high feather; flushed, flushed with victory; cock-a-hoop, cock-a-hoopish.

10. *adv.* boastfully, exultantly etc. *adj.*; in triumph; with a blare of trumpets.

885. Arrogance, Insolence
(See 886. Servility)

1. *n.* arrogance, toploftiness [coll.], haughtiness etc. *adj.*; hauteur, pomposity, lofty manner *or* bearing, unwarrantable pretentiousness, inordinate pride *or* confidence, haughty indifference *or* insolence; assumption, presumption; haughty airs, cornstarchy airs [coll.], air of haughty assumption; high horse, high *or* tight ropes, altitudes [all coll.]; snobbery, snobbism *or* snobism; overbearance, domineering etc. *v.*; pride etc. 878; van-

---

884. A vaunter and a liar, all is one.—CHAUCER. Every braggart shall be found an ass.—SHAKESPEARE. The empty vessel makes the greatest sound.—SHAKESPEARE. Great boast and small roast.—COPLAND. Where boasting ends, there dignity begins.—YOUNG. The race by vigor not by vaunts is won.—POPE.

885. Beggars mounted run their horse to death. —SHAKESPEARE. The word that is overbearing is a spur unto strife.—PINDAR. But your heart / Is crammed with arrogance, spleen, and pride.—SHAKESPEARE.

ity etc. 880; disdain etc. 930; airs etc. (ostentation) 882.

2. *n.* insolence, contumely, impertinence, impudence, audacity, procacity, petulance *or* petulancy [now rare], flippance *or* flippancy, assurance, effrontery, front [now rare], hardened front, hardihood, face of brass; brass, bronze, face, cheek [all coll.]; nerve, gall, crust [all slang]; brazenness, malapertness, sauciness etc. *adj.*; sauce [coll.], sass [dial.]; lip [slang], abuse; discourtesy etc. 895; disrespect etc. 929; snub etc. 930.4.

3. *n.* insolent person, malapert, cheeker [slang], saucebox [coll.]; minx, hussy [joc.]; smarty [slang, U.S.], smart aleck [coll., U.S.], wise guy [slang, U.S.]; boldface, brazenface; snob, snobling [joc.].

4. *v.* be arrogant etc. *adj.*, hold one's nose in the air, get on one's high horse [coll.] etc. (act proudly) 878.3.

5. *v.* be domineering etc. *adj.*, domineer, overbear, lord it over, carry with a high hand, dictate, exact, lay down the law, bear *or* beat down; trample *or* tread down, ~ upon *or* under foot; ride roughshod over; browbeat, bully etc. (intimidate) 860.12.

6. *v.* arrogate, assume a lofty bearing, assume, presume, make bold, make free, take a liberty, give an inch and take an ell; patronize.

7. *v.* be insolent etc. *adj.*, have a *or* one's nerve [slang], have the gall, ~ cheek etc. *n.*; treat with insolence etc. *adj.*, *traiter or regarder de haut en bas* [F.], get fresh, ~ smart etc. *adj.*, put to the blush; sauce [coll.], sass [dial.]; brazen out, outbrazen, outbrave, outface, outlook, outstare, stare out of countenance; teach one's grandmother to suck eggs [coll.]; insult etc. (treat with disrespect) 929.3; snub etc. 930.7.

8. *adj.* arrogant, haughtily contemptuous, presumptuously haughty, disdainfully *or* contemptuously proud, haughty, supercilious, contumelious, cavalier, disdainful, contemptuous; patronizing; snobbish, snobby, stuck-up [coll.], high-headed, high-nosed [coll.], snooty [slang], snotty [slang], sniffy [slang], overweening, assuming, would-be, consequential, pompous, lofty, lordly, imperious, magisterial, dictatorial, arbitrary, highhanded, high and mighty; overbearing, domineering; presumptuous, presumptive [now rare].

high-flown, highfalutin *or* highfaluting [coll.]; high-hat, high-hatted, high-hatty [all slang]; toplofty, toploftical [both coll.]; uppish [coll.], uppity [coll., U.S.]; stilted, on stilts; on one's high horse, on one's tight *or* high ropes, in one's altitudes [all coll.]; puffed up etc. (proud) 878.6, 7; vain etc. 880.6.

9. *adj.* insolent, insulting, audacious, impudent, impertinent, pert, malapert, procacious, flip [now coll.], flippant, cocky [coll.], fresh [slang, U.S.], cheeky [coll.], facy [now dial.], crusty [slang], gally [slang, U.S.], nervy [slang], bumptious, bodacious [dial.], gallows [obs. exc. dial. Eng.], brash, saucy, precocious, forward, obtrusive, familiar; presumptuous, presumptive [now rare]; smart [coll.], smarty [coll.], smart-alecky [coll., U.S.]; discourteous etc. 895.6, 7.

10. *adj.* brazen, brazenfaced, barefaced, brassy [coll.], bold, bold as brass [coll.], bluff, unblushing, unabashed, awless *or* aweless, shameless, dead *or* lost to shame.

11. *adv.* arrogantly, insolently etc. *adj.*; with nose in air, with nose turned up, with head held high; with curling lip, with a sneer; with arms akimbo; *de haut en bas* [F.]; with a high hand; *ex cathedra* [L.]; proudly etc. 878.8; contemptuously etc. 930.10.

886. Servility
(See 885. Arrogance, Insolence)

1. *n.* servility, obsequiousness, slavishness etc. *adj.*; vernility [rare], subservience *or* subserviency, abasement, obeisance, prostration; truckling, fawning, toadeating etc. *v.*; toadyism, sycophancy, fawnery, ingratiation, tufthunting, flunkyism, parasitism; apple-polishing, handshaking [both slang, U.S.]; timeserving; servitude, slavery etc. (subjection) 749; obedience etc. 743; humility etc. 879; adulation etc. (flattery) 933.

2. *n.* sycophant, toad, toady, toadeater,

---

886. Away with slavish weeds and servile thoughts.—SHAKESPEARE.   Supple knees / Feed arrogance and are the proud man's fees.—SHAKESPEARE.   Many kiss the hand they wish cut off.—G. HERBERT.   Always mistrust a subordinate who never finds fault with his superior.—COLLINS.

footlicker, bootlick *or* bootlicker [slang, U.S.], lickspit, lickspittle, smell-feast, pickthank [arch. or dial.], truckler, fawner, back-slapper, back-scratcher, clawback [obs. exc. dial. Eng.], tufthunter, groveler, reptile, spaniel, jackal, flunky, snob; apple-polisher, handshaker, yes man [all slang, U.S.].

parasitical dependent, parasite, sucker [slang], leech, barnacle, hanger-on, dangler, adherent, appendage, dependent, satellite, shadow, tagtail, follower, *cavalier servente* or *cavaliere servente* [It.], led captain, henchman; *âme damnée* [F.]; heeler, ward heeler [both polit. cant, U.S.]; beat, dead beat [both slang]; sponge [coll.], sponger; *homme de cour* [F.], courtier; carpet knight; *Graeculus esuriens* [L.]; timeserver; Sir Pertinax MacSycophant; adulator etc. (flatterer) 935.2; servant etc. 746; tool etc. (puppet) 711.2.

3. *v.* be servile etc. *adj.*, fawn, truckle, toady, toadeat, lickspittle, bootlick [slang, U.S.], lick one's shoes, lick the feet of, lick the dust, kiss the hem of one's garment, make a doormat of oneself; grovel, crawl, creep, cower, cringe, crouch, stoop, kneel, bend the knee, fall on one's knees, prostrate oneself, throw oneself at the feet of, fall at one's feet; kowtow, bow, bow and scrape; ingratiate *or* insinuate oneself, worm oneself, creep into the good graces of, pander to, fawn upon, handshake [slang, U.S.], court *or* curry favor, court, pay court to, dance attendance on, follow at heel, pin *or* fasten oneself upon, hang on the sleeve of.

do service, wait on *or* upon; fetch and carry, do the dirty work of; sponge on [coll.], feed on, fatten on, batten on; be a timeserver, keep time to, go with the stream, follow the crowd, worship the rising sun, hold with the hare and run with the hounds, get on the band wagon; adulate etc. (flatter) 933.2.

4. *adj.* servile, slavish, subservient; sycophantic(al), syncophantish [rare], vernile [rare], obsequious, obeisant, fawning, truckling, ingratiating, toadying, toadeating, footlicking, bootlicking [slang, U.S.], back-scratching, sniveling, groveling, cringing, cowering, crouching, crawling, reptilian; beggarly, abject, base, mean; parasitic(al), leechlike, sponging [coll.]; timeserving; abased, prostrate, on one's knees, on one's marrowbones [slang], on bended knee; adulatory etc. (flattering) 933.3; pliant, dough-faced [coll.] etc. (soft) 324.6; subject etc. 749.6; compliant etc. (obedient) 743.3; submissive etc. 725.5; humble etc. 879.4; dependent etc. (subject) 749.6.

5. *adv.* with servility etc. *n.*, hat-in-hand *or* cap-in-hand, "in a bondman's key" (Shakespeare), "with bated breath and whispering humbleness" (Shakespeare).

6. *int.* as you please!, so please you!, as you wish!, as my lord wills!, don't mind me!

887. Bluster

1. *n.* bluster, blustering etc. *v.*, blusteration [coll.]; swagger, bounce, swashbucklery; sputter, splutter; fuss, fluster, flurry, bustle; bluff.

2. *n.* blusterer, vaporer, roisterer, roarer [obs. slang], swaggerer, swashbuckler, fanfaron; bluff, bluffer; fourflusher [slang], jackdaw in peacock's feathers, ass in lion's skin; ranter, raver, slangwhanger [slang]; braggart etc. (boaster) 884.3; puppy etc. (fop) 854; bully etc. (ruffian) 913.2.

3. *v.* bluster, swagger, swashbuckle, strut, bounce, vapor, roister, rollick, kick up a dust [coll.] sputter, splutter; thunder; storm, rage, rant, rave, slang-whang [slang]; talk big, use big words; bluff, bluster and bluff; give oneself airs etc. (be ostentatious) 882.6; bully etc. (intimidate) 860.12.

4. *adj.* blustering etc. *v.*, blustery, blusterous; noisy, "full of sound and fury" (Shakespeare); boisterous, tumultuous etc. (turbulent) 173.12.

888. Friendship
(See 889. Enmity; also 890. Friend)

1. *n.* friendship, friendliness, neighborliness, brotherliness etc. *adj.*; amity, friendly relations, community of interest, fellowship; brotherhood, fraternity, so-

---

887. Stout once a month they march, a blustering band, / And ever but in times of need at hand.—DRYDEN.   I am Sir Oracle, / And when I ope my lips, let no dog bark!—SHAKESPEARE.
888. *Amicitia semper prodest* [Friendship is always helpful].—SENECA.   *Vulgus amicitias utilitate probat* [The common herd values friendships for their utility].—OVID.   Friendship is to be purchased only by friendship.—

dality, confraternity; sisterhood, sorority, sorosis; cordiality, cordial friendship, *entente cordiale* [F.], good *or* cordial understanding; fellow feeling, sympathy, rapport, *rapprochement* [F.], response.

acquaintance, familiarity, intimacy, intimate *or* familiar friendship; sincere friendship, warm *or* ardent friendship, bosom friendship, firm ∼, stanch ∼, tried ∼, lasting *or* fast friendship; devotion, devoted friendship; partiality, favoritism; comradeship etc. (sociality) 892; affection etc. (love) 897; harmony etc. (concord) 714; peace etc. 721; good will etc. (benevolence) 906.

2. *v.* be friendly etc. *adj.*, be friends etc. 890, have the friendship of, be acquainted with, know, have the ear of; hold communication with, have dealings with, fraternize, sororize [rare]; understand, sympathize with; cotton to, hit it off [both coll.]; have a leaning to; make much of; keep company with; bear good will etc. (be benevolent) 906.5; love etc. 897.11; befriend etc. (aid) 707.6.

3. *v.* become friendly etc. *adj.*, become friends, make friends with, cultivate, cultivate the friendship of, make *or* scrape acquaintance with, pick up an acquaintance with, strike up a friendship, strike up with [coll.], take up with [coll.], gain the friendship of, get into favor, get in the good graces of, get chummy with [coll.], buddy up [slang], get one's horses together; make advances, break the ice, pay addresses to, make up to [coll.], hold out *or* extend the right hand of friendship *or* fellowship, shake *or* strike hands with; embrace, hug, receive with open arms, throw oneself into the arms of.

4. *adj.* friendly, friendlike, friendful [obs. exc. dial]; amicable, amical; brotherly, fraternal; sisterly, sororal [rare]; chummy [coll.], neighborly, sympathetic, cordial, unhostile; well-affected, well-disposed, well intentioned, well-meant, well-meaning; friends with, at home with, on good ∼, friendly ∼, amicable ∼, cordial ∼, familiar *or* intimate terms *or* footing, on speaking *or* visiting terms, on borrowing terms [joc.], in good with [coll.], in one's good graces, in one's good books, on the good *or* right side of [coll.]; acquainted, familiar; intimate, close, near; hand and glove, hand-in-hand; thick, thick as thieves [both coll.]; devoted, ardent, warm, warmhearted, hearty; fast, firm, stanch, tried, tried and true; sociable etc. 892.12; harmonious etc. (concordant) 714.5; benevolent etc. 906.6.

5. *adv.* amicably etc. *adj.*, friendly, friendliwise; with open arms, *à bras ouverts* [F.]; *sans cérémonie* [F.]; hand in hand, arm in arm.

889. Enmity
(See 888. Friendship; also 891. Enemy)

1. *n.* enmity, unfriendliness etc. *adj.*, ill will, hostility, antagonism, repugnance, antipathy, conflict, collision, clashing etc. *v.*; oppugnacy, oppugnation [both rare]; animosity, vindictive animosity, vindictiveness; bitterness, rancor; heartburn, heartburning; alienation, estrangement, irreconciliation; dislike etc. 867; hate etc. 898; dissension, quarrel etc. (discord) 713; malevolence etc. 907; unsociability etc. 893.

2. *v.* be unfriendly etc. *adj.*, be at loggerheads, clash, collide, conflict, come in conflict with, be *or* play at cross-purposes; antagonize, act in antagonism; keep *or* hold at arm's length; harden the heart; fall out; alienate, estrange; take umbrage etc. 900.6; bear malice etc. 907.5.

3. *adj.* unfriendly etc. *adj.*, inimical, hostile, antagonistic, repugnant, oppugnant [rare]; at enmity, at variance, at cross-purposes, at loggerheads, at daggers drawn, at open war with, up in arms against; in bad with [slang, U.S.], in bad odor with, in one's bad books; on bad terms, not on speaking terms; cool, cold, coldhearted; alienated, estranged, disaffected, irreconcilable; unsociable etc. 893.9; hating etc. 898.5; uncharitable etc. 907.7; disliking etc. 867.7.

T. Wilson. Nothing is meritorious but virtue and friendship.—Pope. A mystic bond of brotherhood makes all men one.—Carlyle. Friendship is a disinterested commerce between equals.—Goldsmith. Friendship is the gift of the gods, and the most precious boon to man. —Disraeli. Friendship is a union of spirits, a marriage of hearts, and the bond thereof virtue.—W. Penn.

889. Enmity is anger watching the opportunity for revenge.—Cicero. I will put enmity between thee and the woman.—Bible. To be wroth with one we love / Doth work like madness in the brain.—Coleridge.

890. Friend
(See 891. Enemy; also 888. Friendship)

1. *n.* friend, acquaintance, sympathizer, *persona grata* [L.]; confident, confidant [*masc.*], confidante [*fem.*]; neighbor; *alter ego* [L.], other self; intimate, intimate *or* familiar friend; bosom friend, friend of one's bosom; best friend, firm ~, stanch *or* fast friend, devoted friend, warm *or* ardent friend, faithful friend, trusted *or* trusty friend, *fidus Achates* [L.], "a friend that sticketh closer than a brother" (Bible); *amicus usque ad aras* [L.]; friend in need, friend indeed, jack-at-a-pinch.

2. *n.* favorer, well-wisher, advocate etc. (upholder) 711.4.

3. *n.* companion, fellow, fellow companion, consort, comrade, *camarade* [F.], mate, comate, associate, consociate, compeer, colleague, confrere, partner, pard [slang, U.S.], copartner, side partner, side-kick *or* sidekicker [slang, U.S.], crony, old crony, billy [chiefly dial.], buddy [coll.], pal [slang], chum [coll.]; roommate, chamberfellow, bedfellow, bedmate, bunkie [coll., U.S.]; fellow pupil *or* student, schoolfellow, classfellow, classmate, classman; playfellow, playmate; fellow worker *or* laborer, workfellow, benchfellow, yokefellow, shopmate, fellow servant; shipmate; messmate; groomsman, best man; bridesmaid, maid of honor; fellow sufferer; boon companion etc. 892.8; accompanier etc. 88.3.

4. *n.* friends, two of a kind, birds of a feather, *Arcades embo* [L.], *par nobile fratrum* [L., often iron.].

5. *n.* (famous friendships) Pylades and Orestes, Castor and Pollux, Achilles and Patroclus, Diomedes and Sthenalus, Hercules and Iolaus, Theseus and Pirithoüs, Epaminondas and Pelopidas, Nisus and Euryalus, Damon and Pythias, David and Jonathan, Christ and the beloved disciple; Soldiers Three, The Three Musketeers.

6. *n.* host, hostess, mine host; Amphitryon, Boniface; landlord etc. (proprietor) 779.2.

7. *n.* guest, visitor, frequenter, habitué, protégé.

8. *n.* compatriot etc. (fellow citizen) 188.7.

9. *n.* fellow man, fellow being, fellow creature, fellow mortal.

10. *int.* "thank God for a trusty chum!" (Kipling).

891. Enemy
(See 890. Friend; also 889. Enmity)

1. *n.* enemy, foe, foeman; unfriend [rare], Philistine; bitter enemy; open enemy; secret enemy, backfriend [arch.], snake in the grass; archenemy, devil; antagonist etc. (opponent) 710.

2. *n.* public enemy, enemy to society, public enemy number 1, ~ 2 etc.; anarchist etc. (insurgent) 742.3.

892. Sociality
(See 893. Unsociality)

1. *n.* sociality, sociability, sociableness etc. *adj.*; friendly social relations, association, consociation, intercourse, social intercourse, intercommunion; consortship, companionship, fellowship, comradeship, comradery, camaraderie; fraternization, fraternation [rare], fraternism [rare]; intimacy, familiarity; clubbability *or* clubability [coll.], clubbism; *esprit de corps* [F.]; morale; urbanity

---

890. A constant friend is a thing rare and hard to find.—PLUTARCH. A friend that sticketh closer than a brother.—BIBLE. A man that hath friends must shew himself friendly.—BIBLE. A faithful friend is the medicine of life.—APOCRYPHA. Greater love hath no man than this, that a man lay down his life for his friend.—BIBLE. Prosperity makes friends, adversity tries them.—PUBLILIUS. A friend is a person with whom I may be sincere.—EMERSON. Best friend, my well-spring in the wilderness.—G. ELIOT. To each a man that knows his naked soul.—KIPLING. Friends who make salt sweet and blackness bright.—MASEFIELD. A friend in need is a friend indeed. A friend to everybody is a friend to nobody.

891. If thine enemy hunger, feed him; if he thirst, give him drink: for in so doing thou shalt heap coals of fire on his head.—BIBLE. Rejoice not over thy greatest enemy being dead.—APOCRYPHA. A man hath many enemies when his back is to the wall.—J. CLARKE. Treat your friend as if he might become an enemy.—PUBLILIUS. Love your Enemies, for they tell you your Faults.—FRANKLIN. My nearest and dearest enemy.—MIDDLETON. He makes no friend who never made a foe.—TENNYSON. You shall judge of a man by his foes as well as by his friends.—CONRAD. Better an open enemy than a false friend.

892. Everyman is like the company he is wont to keep.—EURIPIDES. Birds of a feather

etc. (courtesy) 894; friendship etc. 888.

2. *n.* conviviality, good-fellowship; jollity, merrymaking etc. (festivity) 840.2.

3. *n.* visiting etc. *v.*, round of visits; visit, call, social call; engagement, appointment, assignation, tryst; trysting place; chat etc. 588.2.

4. *n.* hospitality, hospitableness etc. *adj.*; reception, cordial ~, hearty or warm reception, welcome, hearty welcome, the glad hand [slang]; embrace, hug; *vin d'honneur* [F.]; greeting etc. 894.4.

5. *n.* social gathering, get-together [coll.], sociable [U.S.], party, entertainment, reception, levee, *conversazione* [It.], soiree; at home *or* at-home; hen party [coll.]; stag, stag party [both coll.]; kettledrum [coll.]; drum, drum major, rout, tempest, hurricane [all arch.]; housewarming, house-raising, hanging of the crane; lawn party, garden party, *fête champêtre* [F.]; smoker, smoking party [both coll.].

reunion, social reunion, family reunion; coming-out party [coll.], debut; afternoon party, matinee; morning party, evening party; bee, quilting bee, raising bee; husking bee, cornhusking, corn shucking, husking [all U.S.]; surprise party, donation party [U.S.], infare [chiefly dial.], *partie carrée* [F.], *ridotto* [It.], Dutch treat [coll., U.S.], wake; gathering etc. (assembly) 72.2; festival etc. (festivity) 840.2; ball etc. (dance) 840.6; tea party etc. *below.*

6. *n.* (social meals) breakfast, wedding breakfast, hunt breakfast; luncheon, lunch; tea, afternoon tea, five-o'clock tea, coming-out tea [coll.], high tea, *thé dansant* [F.]; tea party, tea fight [slang], drum; coffee party, *Kaffee-Klatsch* [G.]; dinner, potluck, hunt dinner; bachelor dinner, stag dinner [coll.]; church supper; banquet etc. (feast) 298.37; picnic, clambake etc. (festivity) 840.2.

7. *n.* social circle, circle of acquaintance, company, society, social group; town, court, drawing room; family circle, hearth, family hearth; fellowship, club,

coterie etc. (party) 712; high society etc. 852.4.

8. *n.* sociable person, good mixer [coll., U.S.]; boon companion, boonfellow; good *or* jolly fellow, *bon enfant* [F.]; crony, *bon vivant* [F.]; pot companion, fellow toper; joiner [coll., U.S.], jiner [dial., U.S.].

9. *v.* be sociable etc. *adj.*, associate with, consociate with [rare], sort with, consort with, mix with, mingle with, have intercourse with, keep company with, walk hand in hand with, eat off the same trencher, club together, bear one company, join; fraternize, fraternate [rare], sororize [rare]; intercommunicate, intercommune [rare]; be friendly etc. 888.2.

10. *v.* visit, exchange *or* interchange visits, make *or* pay a visit, call on *or* upon, drop in, look in, look one up, beat up one's quarters [coll.]; leave one's card; pay one's respects etc. 894.8.

11. *v.* receive hospitably, welcome, make welcome, bid one welcome, receive, receive *or* welcome with open arms, hug, embrace; give a warm reception to, kill the fatted calf; be at home, see one's friends, have the latchstring out [U.S.], keep an open house; entertain, entertain guests, give a party etc. *n.*, preside, do the honors [coll.]; crack a bottle with; take potluck with; greet etc. 894.9.

12. *adj.* sociable, social, social-minded; gregarious, companionable, communicative, affable, chummy [coll.], pally, palsy [both slang], accessible, on speaking *or* visiting terms, on borrowing terms [joc.], on one's visiting list; neighborly, neighborlike [rare]; hospitable, receptive; clubbable *or* clubable [coll.], clubbish; conversable, conversational, cozy *or* cosy, chatty, tête-à-tête; familiar, intimate; free and easy, hail fellow well met *or* hail-fellow-well-met; convivial, convival; festive, festal; jovial, jolly; cosmopolitan, international; friendly etc. 888.4.

13. *adv.* sociably etc. *adj.*, on terms of intimacy; *en famille* [F.], in the family circle; in the social whirl; *sans façon* [F.], *sans cérémonie* [F.]; hand in hand, arm in arm.

---

flock together.—ARISTOTLE. Be not forgetful to entertain strangers: for thereby some have entertained angels unawares.—BIBLE. His worth is warrant for his welcome.—SHAKESPEARE. Nature hath fram'd strange fellows in her time.—SHAKESPEARE. Two is company, three is a crowd.—FULLER. A crowd is not company.—BACON. I live in the crowds of jollity, not so much to enjoy company as to shun myself.—JOHNSON. The painful ceremony of receiving and returning visits.—SMOLLETT.

893. Unsociality
(See 892. Sociality)

1. *n.* unsociality, unsociability, unsociableness etc. *adj.*; dissociality, dissociability; inhospitality, inhospitableness *or* unhospitableness; self-sufficiency; domesticity; unfriendliness etc. 889.

2. *n.* seclusion, reclusion, retirement, recess, retreat, withdrawal, alienation, estrangement; solitude, isolation, splendid isolation; aloneness, loneliness etc. *adj.*, lonelihood [rare]; privacy, privity [obs.]; rustication, *rus in urbe* [L.], ruralism, rurality [rare]; eremitism, anchoritism; hermitism, hermitship, hermitry, hermitage [rare]; depopulation, dispeoplement; desertion, desolation, devastation; concealment etc. 528; hermitage, sanctum sanctorum etc. 189.13; wilderness etc. 169.2; avoidance etc. 623.

3. *n.* exclusion, seclusion [now rare]; Coventry; exclusivism; exile, exilement; boycott, boycottage; blockade, embargo; blackball, black list; ostracism, disfellowship etc. (banishment) 297.3; cut [coll.] etc. (snub) 930.4.

4. *n.* recluse, solitaire, solitary, solitudinarian; hermit, eremite, anchorite *or* anchoret, ascetic; santon, Marabout [both Moham.]; hermitess, anchoress, anchoritess; stylite, pillarist, pillar saint; Hieronymian, Hieronymite; cave man, cave dweller, troglodyte; cynic, closet cynic; disciple of Zimmermann, Timon of Athens, Diogenes, St. Simeon Stylites.

5. *n.* outcast, outcast of society, outcaste [Ind.], pariah, leper, Ishmael, *Cagot* [F.], castaway, derelict, man without a country; outlaw, *proscrit* [F.]; expellee, evict [coll., Eng.]; evacuator, evacuee, *évacué* [F.] (*fem. évacuée*); exile, expatriate; *déclassé* [F.] (*fem. déclassée*); waif, stray, waifs and strays; foundling; street Arab, wastrel etc. (vagabond) 876.9; outsider etc. (alien) 57.3.

6. *v.* be *or* live secluded etc. *adj.*, seclude oneself, deny oneself, keep ~, stand *or* hold oneself aloof, keep in the background, keep snug *or* close, shut oneself up, creep into a corner; retire, live in retirement; retire from the world, abandon *or* forsake the world, dissocialize, rusticate, hermitize; take the veil; sport one's oak [Univ. slang, Eng.]; hide oneself etc. 528.16.

7. *v.* exclude, seclude [now rare], refuse to associate with, have no truck with [coll. and dial.], send to Coventry, turn one's back upon, shut the door upon, look cool *or* coldly upon, keep at arm's length, repel; draw a cordon round, cut off from, isolate, maroon; blackball, black-list, draw up *or* sign a round robin; bar, debar; blockade, embargo; exile, ostracize, outlaw etc. (banish) 297.11; cut [coll.], refuse to recognize etc. (snub) 930.7.

8. *v.* depopulate, dispeople, unpeople; desolate, devastate.

9. *adj.* unsociable, insociable; unsocial, insocial [rare]; dissocial, dissociable; uncompanionable, unclubbable *or* unclubable [coll.], *sauvage* [F.]; eremitic(al), eremitish, eremital [rare]; hermitic(al), hermitish, hermitary [rare]; anchoritic(al), anchoretic(al), anchoritish *or* anchoretish; troglodytic; close, snug; domestic, stay-at-home; inhospitable, unhospitable; unfriendly etc. 889.3.

10. *adj.* secluded, secluse [rare]; sequestered, retired; private, privy; in a backwater, isolated, out-of-the-way, out-of-the-world, "the world forgetting by the world forgot" (Pope); solitary, in solitude, solitudinous; lonely, lonesome, alone; unfrequented, unvisited; unfriended, friendless, kithless, homeless; lorn, forlorn; desolate, abandoned, forsaken, deserted, deserted in one's utmost need, left to shift for oneself; outcast, derelict, outside the gates, estranged; uninvited, unintroduced, unwelcome; under an embargo, under a cloud; concealed etc. 528.17.

894. Courtesy
(See 895. Discourtesy)

1. *n.* courtesy, courteousness, politeness etc. *adj.*; manners, good manners *or*

---

893. *Bene qui latuit bene vixit* [He who has lived a retired life has lived well].—OVID. Solitude is often the best society.—J. RAY. Far from the madding crowd's ignoble strife.—GRAY. I never found the companion that was so companionable as solitude.—THOREAU. Secret, and self-contained, and solitary as an oyster.—DICKENS. There is a society in the deepest solitude.—DISRAELI. Far from the clank of crowds.—WHITMAN. Solitude, the safeguard of mediocrity, is to genius the stern friend.—EMERSON. Other people are quite dreadful. The only possible society is oneself.—WILDE. Solitude is very sad, / Too much company twice as bad.—W. ALLINGHAM. Alone as the last man on earth.—GALSWORTHY. Never less alone than when alone.—S. ROGERS.
894. Manner, not gold, is woman's best adorn-

behavior, graceful *or* considerate behavior, courtly politeness, civility, civilization, cultivation, culture, gentility, mansuetude, *bienséance* [F.], comity, amenity, urbanity, polish, refinement, elegance, presence, compliance [arch.]; complaisance, complacency; good temper *or* humor, easy temper, amiability, affability, soft tongue, *prévenance* [F.]; gallantry, chivalry; breeding, good *or* gentle breeding; *savoir-faire* [F.], *savoir-vivre* [F.]; respect etc. 928.

2. *n.* suavity, suaviloquence [rare], blandiloquence [rare], unctiousness etc. *adj.*; fair *or* soft words, sweet *or* honeyed words, soft *or* honeyed phrases, incense; soft sawder, soft soap, butter [all coll.].

3. *n.* a courtesy, polite *or* courteous act, act of courtesy *or* politeness, civility, amenity, urbanity; presentation, introduction; acknowledgment, recognition; reception, *accueil* [F.], welcome; compliments, respects, regards, *égards* [F.], *devoirs* [F.], duty [arch.], best *or* kind regards; remembrances, kind remembrances; love, best love; token, loving cup, *vin d'honneur* [F.], pledge; love token etc. 902.5; condolence etc. 915.

4. *n.* greeting, mark *or* sign of recognition, salaams, nod, wave; salute, salutation; hail, hello, good day, good morrow, good morning, good afternoon, good night; capping, pulling the forelock; shaking hands etc. *v.*, handshake, handclasp, clasp *or* grip of the hand; accolade, embrace, hug, squeeze; kiss, buss, smack, osculation; smile, smile of recognition; curtsy, bow etc. (obeisance) 928.2; welcome etc. 892.4.

5. *n.* adieu, farewell, valediction etc. (leavetaking) 293.2.

6. *n.* pink of courtesy *or* politeness, "the very pink of courtesy" (Shakespeare), "the very pine-apple of politeness" (Sheridan), "the mirror of all courtesy" (Shakespeare), fine flower of courtesy *or* chivalry, *chevalier sans peur et sans reproche* [F.]; cavalier, knight, knight-errant, "a verray parfit gentil knight" (Chaucer); Sidney, Bayard, Chesterfield, Lancelot, Gawain, Sir Walter Raleigh, Colonel Newcome.

7. *v.* be courteous etc. *adj.*, show courtesy etc. *n.*, behave oneself, mind one's manners, mind one's P's and Q's [coll.]; do pleasing acts, do the amiable [coll.], speak one fair, conciliate; be all things to all men; look as if butter would not melt in one's mouth; take in good part; make way for; mend one's manners.

8. *v.* pay one's respects, give *or* send one's regards etc. *n.*, present oneself, do service, wait on *or* upon, pay attentions to; drink a toast to etc. 883.4; dance attendance on etc. 886.3; pay homage to etc. 928.5; visit etc. 892.10.

9. *v.* greet, hail, bid *or* say hello etc. *n.*; shake hands, press *or* squeeze the hand, hold out the hand, hold out *or* extend the right hand of friendship; kiss hands *or* cheeks; give salutations, salute, present arms; move to [dial. Eng.], nod to; smile upon; uncover, cap, doff the cap, raise *or* lift the hat, touch the hat *or* cap, tip the hat to; pull the forelock; bow, curtsy, salaam etc. (make obeisance) 928.6; embrace, kiss etc. 902.8; welcome etc. 892.11.

10. *v.* bid Godspeed, "speed the parting guest" (Pope); cheer, serenade.

11. *v.* render polite etc. *adj.*, polish, rub off the corners *or* rough edges, cultivate, civilize, humanize.

12. *adj.* courteous, polite, civil, urbane, mannerly, good-mannered, well-mannered, well-behaved, well-spoken, well-brought-up, well-bred, gently bred, of gentle manners *or* breeding, polished, refined, civilized, cultivated, genteel, gallant, courtly; chivalrous, chivalric; gentlemanly, gentlemanlike, ladylike; gentle, mild; good-humored, cordial, amiable, affable, familiar [arch.], gracious, obliging; complaisant, complacent; conciliatory, conciliative; neighborly, neighborlike; tactful, graceful; winsome, winning; on one's good *or* best behavior; respectful etc. 928.8.

---

ment.—MENANDER. Courtesy costs nothing.—G. HERBERT. True politeness consists in being easy one's self, and in making every one about one as easy as one can.—POPE. Politeness . . . is fictitious benevolence. JOHNSON. Minds well implanted with solid and elaborate breeding.—MILTON. The greater man the greater courtesy.—TENNYSON. For manners are not idle, but the fruit of loyal nature and of noble mind.—TENNYSON. Fine manners need the support of fine manners in others.—EMERSON. Life is short, but there is always time for courtesy.—EMERSON. Politeness is to do and say / The kindest thing in the kindest way.—LEWISOHN. An acquaintance that begins with a compliment is sure to develop into a real friendship.—WILDE.

13. *adj.* suave, suave-mannered, suave-spoken; suaviloquent, blandiloquous, blandiloquious [all rare]; unctuous, unctious, unctional; bland, oily, oily-tongued, soapy [coll.], buttery [coll.], fine-spoken, soft-spoken, fair-spoken, mealymouthed, honeymouthed, honey-tongued, smooth-tongued, smooth-spoken, smoothly polite, smooth, ingratiating; false, insincere, specious; obsequious etc. 886.4.

14. *adv.* courteously etc. *adj., suaviter in modo* [L.], with perfect courtesy, with a good grace; with open arms, with outstretched arms, *à bras ouverts* [F.].

15. *int.* hail!, all hail!, *ave!* [L.], good luck!, best wishes!, *pax vobiscum!* [L.], all good go with you!, may your shadow never be less!, long life to!; sweet dreams!; greetings! etc. (welcome) 292.13; Godspeed! etc. (farewell) 293.14; bravo etc. 931.13.

895. Discourtesy
(See 894. Courtesy)

1. *n.* discourtesy, discourteousness, rudeness, unpoliteness etc. *adj.*; lack *or* want of courtesy etc. 894, incivility, illiberality, inurbanity, rusticity, ill breeding, ill ~, bad *or* ungainly manners; misbehavior, misconduct, conduct unbecoming a gentleman; vulgarity etc. 851; disrespect etc. 929; snub etc. 930.4; impudence etc. (insolence) 885.2.

2. *n.* gruffness, tartness etc. *adj.*; austerity, severity, spinosity, virulence, causticity, acrimony, acerbity, asperity, astringency, acridity, mordancy, mordacity; amarity, amaritude [both rare]; perversity; cynicism, sarcasm, irony; contumely, unparliamentary language, hard words, short answer, rebuff, rude reproach, scurrilous remark; irascibility etc. (ill-humor) 901.

3. *n.* discourteous person, malapert, saucebox [coll.] etc. (insolent person) 885.3; bear, crosspatch [coll.] etc. (ill-humored person) 901.4.

4. *v.* be discourteous etc. *adj.*, treat with discourtesy etc. *n.*; stare out of countenance, ogle, point at, put to the blush; keep at a distance, keep at arm's length; show the door to, send away with a flea in the ear [coll.]; look cool *or* coldly upon, look black upon, frown at *or* upon; snap, snarl, growl; treat with insolence etc. 885.7; treat with disrespect etc. 929.3; snub etc. 930.7.

5. *v.* render rude etc. *adj.*, brutalize, brutify.

6. *adj.* discourteous, uncourteous; impolite, unpolite; rude, "rude, and scant of courtesy" (Scott), uncivil, ungracious, unceremonious, uncourtly, unmannerly, unmannered, ill-mannered, ill-behaved, ill-conditioned, ill-bred, unbred, unpolished, uncivilized, ungenteel, ungentle, ungallant, inaffable, uncomplaisant, unaccommodating, unneighborly; ungentlemanly, ungentlemanlike; unladylike, unfeminine; cool, cold; perverse; abusive, vituperative; scurrile, scurrilous; impudent etc. (insolent) 885.9; disrespectful etc. 929.5; vulgar etc. 851.6.

7. *adj.* gruff, bluff, blunt, brash, brusque, curt, cavalier, austere, stern, harsh, drastic, rough, crusty, crabbed, sharp, keen, short, trenchant, biting, stinging, piercing, cutting, caustic, virulent, bitter, tart, sour, acrid, acrimonious, acerbic, mordant, mordacious, stringent, astringent, venomous, grim, cruel, brutal, bearish, churlish; doggish, currish; surly, surly as a bear; bristling, thorny; spinose, spinous; sarcastic(al), ironic(al); irascible etc. (ill-humored) 901.7; malevolent etc. 907.6.

8. *adv.* discourteously etc. *adj.*, with discourtesy etc. *n.*, with bad grace.

896. Congratulation

1. *n.* congratulation, gratulation, felicitation; compliments, compliments of the season; good wishes, best wishes.

2. *v.* congratulate, tender *or* offer one's congratulations, gratulate, felicitate; compliment, send one's compliments; give joy, wish one joy, wish many happy returns of the day, wish a merry Christmas and a happy New Year; congratulate oneself etc. (rejoice) 838.5.

3. *adj.* congratulatory, congratulant, congratulational; gratulatory, gratulant.

---

895. No manners at all—no more breeding than a bum-bailey.—CONGREVE. This rudeness is a sauce to his good wit.—SHAKESPEARE. Fit for the mountains and the barb'rous caves, / Where manners ne'er were preach'd.—SHAKESPEARE.

897. Love
(See 898. Hate)

1. *n.* love, fondness, amorousness etc. *adj.*; *Eros* [Gr. ἔρως], Kama [Hind.], amor, amorosity, like, liking, fancy, shine [slang, U.S.], affection, attachment, devotion, regard, admiration, passion, tender feeling *or* passion, heart, flame, fervor, ardor, adoration; transport of love, rapture, enchantment; idolatry, idolization, idolism; infatuated attachment, infatuation; crush, mash, pash, case [all slang]; puppy love, calf love [both coll.]; faithful love, truelove; gyneolatry; gallantry; sympathy, fellow feeling; popular regard, popularity; free love, freelovism; love tale *or* story, the old story; love feast.

friendship etc. 888; brotherly love etc. (benevolence) 906; penchant, yearning etc. (desire) 865; lust, adultery etc. (impurity) 961; love-making etc. 902.

2. *n.* parental love, natural affection, *storge* [Gr. στοργή], mother *or* maternal love, father *or* paternal love.

3. *n.* love affair, affair, amour, amourette, entanglement, liaison, intrigue.

4. *n.* god of love, love god; Cupid, Amor [both Rom.]; Eros [Gr.], Kama [Hindu]; goddess of love, Freya [Norse], Astarte [Phoenician], Aphrodite [Gr.], Venus [Rom.]; infant cupid, cupidon, amourette; amoretto, *amorino* [It.].

5. *n.* myrtle, turtledove, Cupid's bow, Cupid's-dart; love token etc. 902.5.

6. *n.* lover, sweetheart, paramour, admirer, adorer, amorist, infatuate, suitor, wooer, courter, sparker [dial. and slang, U.S.], pursuer, love-maker; inamorato, beau, swain, man, leman [arch.], captive, gallant, cavalier, squire, esquire; sweetie, follower, young man, boy friend, fellow, flame, spark [all coll.]; spooner, spoon, spoony [all slang], necker [slang], petter [coll.]; *amoroso, cavalier servente, cicisbeo* [all It.]; Lothario, Casanova, Romeo, Strephon; flirt etc. 902.6; libertine etc. 962; escort etc. 88.4.

7. *n.* loved one, love, beloved, well-beloved, beloved object, truelove, dear, dear one, dearly beloved, light of one's eyes *or* life, sweetheart, sweetie [coll.], sweet patootie [slang], idol, darling; inamorata, ladylove, mistress, girl [coll.], girl friend [coll.], best girl [coll.]; *amorosa* [It.]; Dulcinea; angel, goddess; favorite etc. 899; honey etc. (terms of endearment) 902.4; paramour, concubine etc. (mistress) 962.3.

8. *n.* affianced lover, affianced, betrothed, fiancé [*masc.*], fiancée [*fem.*], future, intended [coll.].

9. *n.* pair of lovers, pair of turtledoves, lovebirds, bill-and-cooers; Romeo and Juliet, Strephon and Chloë, Abélard and Héloïse, Antony and Cleopatra; Aucassin and Nicolette.

10. *n.* abode of love, love nest [slang]; Agapemone; bridechamber, nuptial apartment, bridal suite; harem, seraglio, serai, zenana.

11. *v.* love, be in love with, be fond of etc. *adj.*; have ∼, entertain ∼, harbor *or* cherish love for etc. *n.*, hold in affection *or* love, like, list [arch.], fancy, have a fancy for, have eyes for [coll.], care for, take an interest in, bear love to, think worlds *or* the world of; affect [arch.], affection, have affection for; endear, hold dear, prize, treasure, cherish, esteem, admire, regard, revere; burn, adore, idolize, love to distraction, be desperately in love, have it bad [slang], *aimer éperdument* [F.], dote on *or* upon; be infatuated, possess an infatuation, have a crush, ∼ mash *or* case on [all slang]; make much of, much [dial.], kill with kindness; feast one's eyes on, be *or* look sweet upon [coll.]; desire etc. 865.11; prefer etc. 609.9; make love etc. 902.7, 8; be friendly etc. 888.2.

12. *v.* become enamored etc. *adj.*, fall in love, lose one's heart, take to, take a liking *or* fancy to, take a shine to [slang, U.S.]; fall for, go for [both slang]; become attached to, cotton to [coll.], cling to; fall head and ears *or* head over heels in love, be swept off one's feet; set one's

---

897. Love is not love / Which alters when it alteration finds.—SHAKESPEARE. *Le plaisir de l'amour est d'aimer* [The pleasure of love is in loving].—LA ROCHEFOUCAULD. *N'aimer guère en amour est un moyen assuré pour être aimé* [To love but little is in love an infallible means of being beloved].—LA ROCHEFOUCAULD.

We that are true lovers, run into strange capers.—SHAKESPEARE. Love is nothing else but an insatiate thirst of enjoying a greedily desired object.—MONTAIGNE. Love's a malady without a cure.—DRYDEN. Let no one who loves be called altogether unhappy. Even love unreturned has its rainbow.—BARRIE. In the

affections on, set one's cap at *or* for [coll.].

13. *v.* excite love, win ~, gain ~, secure *or* engage the love *or* affections of, take the fancy of, make a hit with [slang], win one's heart, wind round the heart; enamor, endear, attach, infatuate, fascinate, charm, becharm, attract, allure, captivate, bewitch, enrapture, inflame with love, carry away, turn the head; seduce, vamp [slang], draw on, tempt, tantalize; pay one's court to etc. (make love) 902.7.

14. *adj.* loving etc. *v.*, lovering, loverly, loverlike, lovesome; amorous, amatory; erotic; fond, affectionate, tender, sympathetic; devoted, full of devotion; ardent, passionate, impassioned; enraptured, rapturous; uxorious, uxorial [rare]; enamored, fascinated, charmed etc. *v.*; in love; smitten, badly smitten [both coll.], heartsmitten, bitten [coll.]; hard hit [slang], far-gone [coll.]; over head and ears in love, head over heels in love; infatuate, infatuated; lovesick, lovelorn; soft [coll.], spoony [slang]; brotherly etc. (benevolent) 906.6.

15. *adj.* in love with, enamored of, fond of, partial to, attached to, wedded to; taken with, smitten with, struck with, sweet on *or* upon, hipped on, gone on *or* upon, far gone on *or* upon, mad about, crazy over *or* about [all coll.]; stuck on, mashed on, keen about *or* over, wild about [all slang].

16. *adj.* loved etc. *v.*, beloved, well-beloved, dearly beloved, dear, dear as the apple of one's eye, dear to one's heart, nearest to one's heart, precious, darling, pet; favorite; popular; to *or* after one's mind, ~ taste *or* fancy, after one's heart *or* own heart; in one's good graces etc. (friendly) 888.4.

17. *adj.* lovable, likable, adorable, amiable [arch.], admirable, lovesome, lovely, sweet; seraphic(al), angelic, like an angel; attractive, charming, winsome etc. (alluring) 617.5.

898. Hate
(See 897. Love)

1. *n.* hate, hatred, detestation, abhorrence, loathing, execration, abomination, aversion, antipathy, odium; disaffection, disfavor; alienation, estrangement, coolness; ill blood, bad blood; bitterness, bitterness of feeling; vials of hate *or* wrath; repugnance etc. (dislike) 867; hostility, animosity etc. (enmity) 889; umbrage etc. (resentment) 900; malice etc. 907; implacability etc. (revengefulness) 919; Anglophobia etc. 860.4.

2. *n.* object of hatred, an abomination, an aversion, bête noire; enemy etc. 891; bitter pill etc. (annoyance) 830.2.

3. *v.* hate, detest, abominate, abhor, loathe, execrate, utterly detest, hold in abomination, have *or* possess hatred for, have ~, entertain ~, conceive *or* take an aversion to, shudder at, revolt against, view with horror; disrelish etc. (dislike) 867.4; shrink from etc. 623.9; bear malice etc. 907.5.

4. *v.* excite hatred, provoke hatred etc. *n.*, be hateful etc. *adj.*; estrange, alienate, set against, sow dissension, set by the ears, envenom, incense; vex, irritate etc. (annoy) 830.5; disgust, horrify etc. (repel) 830.7; cause dislike etc. 867.6.

5. *adj.* hating etc. *v.*, abhorrent, set against; virulent, bitter; averse to etc. (disliking) 867.7; disgusted etc. 828.14; implacable etc. (revengeful) 919.6; at daggers drawn etc. (unfriendly) 889.3.

6. *adj.* hated etc. *v.*, unloved, unbeloved, unlamented, undeplored, unmourned, uncared-for, unendeared, unvalued, loveless; lovelorn, forsaken, rejected, jilted, crossed in love; disliked etc. 867.8.

---

spring a young man's fancy lightly turns to thoughts of love.—TENNYSON. All mankind love a lover.—EMERSON. Love is a familiar; Love is a devil: there is no evil angel but Love.—SHAKESPEARE. For love is blind all day and may not see.—CHAUCER. Love is the fulfilling of the law.—BIBLE. A god could hardly love and be wise.—PUBLILIUS. *Militiae species amor est* [Love is a kind of warfare].—OVID. *Si vis amari ama* [If you wish to be loved, love].—SENECA. *Omnia vincit amor* [Love conquers all things].—VERGIL. *Amantes amentes* [Lovers are lunatics].—TERENCE. All is fair in love and war.

898. Hate and mistrust are the children of blindness.—W. WATSON. Hatred is the coward's revenge for being intimidated.—SHAW. We can scarcely hate any one that we know.—HAZLITT. I like a good hater.—JOHNSON People hate those who make them feel their own inferiority.—CHESTERFIELD. Hatreds are the cinders of affection.—RALEIGH. There is no love lost between us.—CERVANTES. So I can give no reason, nor I will not, / More than a lodged hate and a certain loathing.—SHAKESPEARE. In time we hate that which we often fear.—SHAKESPEARE. Heaven has no rage like love to hatred turned.—CONGREVE.

899. Favorite

1. *n.* favorite, preference, preferment [rare]; pet, fondling, darling, cosset, minion [rare], idol, jewel, apple of one's eye, man after one's own heart, *persona grata* [L.]; spoiled child *or* darling, *enfant gâté* [F.]; teacher's pet; popular ~, general *or* universal favorite, idol of the people, matinée idol; loved one etc. 897.7.

2. *v.* favor etc. (prefer) 609.9.

900. Resentment

1. *n.* resentment, offense, umbrage, pique; displeasure, vexation, irritation, annoyance, aggravation [coll.], exasperation; indignation, indignant displeasure, righteous *or* wrathful indignation; anger, wrath, ire; temper, dander [coll.], Irish [coll. and dial.], monkey [coll. or slang, Eng.], spunk [coll.]; hot temper, heat, warmth, hot blood.

bitter resentment, bitterness of spirit, bitterness, rancor, virulence, acrimony, acerbity, asperity; gall, bile, choler, spleen; soreness, rankling; animosity, vindictive animosity, vindictiveness; grudge, crow to pick, ~ pluck *or* pull; vials of wrath, grapes of wrath; irascibility etc. (ill-humor) 901; hate etc. 898; revenge etc. 919; dislike etc. 867; displeasure etc. 828.

2. *n.* dudgeon, high *or* deep dudgeon, pique, huff, miff [coll.], tiff, pet, pucker [coll.], taking [coll.]; fit of anger, ~ petulence *or* resentment, fit, tantrum [coll.], duck fit [slang], cat fit [slang], conniption [coll., U.S.], paroxysm, convulsion; fume, ferment, stew [coll.]; gnashing of teeth.

3. *n.* rage, passion, passion of rage, towering rage *or* passion, raging *or* tearing passion, furious rage, overmastering wrath, violent resentment, fit of violent anger, violence, vehemence, *acharnement* [F.]; fury, furor, *furore* [It.], fire and fury; outburst of anger, burst, outburst, flare-up [coll.], explosion; storm, scene, high words.

4. *n.* Furies, Dirae, Erinyes (*sing.* Erinys), Eumenides; Alecto, Megaera, Tisiphone.

5. *n.* (cause of umbrage) provocation, affront, offense, "head and front of one's offending" (Shakespeare); *casus belli* [L.], red rag, last straw, sore subject, ill turn; outrage, atrocity; buffet, blow, slap in the face, box on the ear, rap on the knuckles; indignity etc. 929.2; annoyance etc. 830.2.

6. *v.* resent, feel resentment etc. *n.*, be resentful etc. *adj.*; take offense, take umbrage, take huff, take amiss, take ill, take in bad *or* ill part, take exception, take to heart; not take it as a joke, *ne pas entendre raillerie* [F.]; dislike etc. 867.4.

7. *v.* show resentment, redden, color, flush, mantle; growl, gnarl, snap, snarl, show one's teeth; gnash, gnash *or* grind one's teeth, champ the bit; bite one's thumb; give a dirty look [slang], look daggers; frown, pout etc. (be sullen) 901.6.

8. *v.* be angry etc. *adj.*, rage, storm, rave, rant, bluster, carry *or* take on [coll.], fume, stew [coll.], foam, boil, boil with indignation *or* rage, burst with anger, quiver ~, swell *or* foam with rage, foam at the mouth, breathe fire and fury, breathe revenge, stand on one's hind legs, stamp the foot; chafe, fret; burn, seethe, simmer, sizzle, smoke, smolder; kick up a row, ~ dust *or* shindy, raise Cain, ~ the devil, ~ Ned, ~ the mischief *or* the roof [all slang]; have a conniption [coll., U.S.] etc. *n.*; vent one's rage *or* spleen, open *or* pour out the vials of one's wrath, snap off one's head *or* nose, jump down one's throat.

9. *v.* become angry etc. *adj.*, anger, lose one's temper, forget oneself, let one's angry passions rise, get one's dander up

---

899. You have sae soft a voice and slid a tongue, / You are the darling of baith auld and young. —A. RAMSAY.

900. *Ira furor brevis est* [Wrath is a transient madness].—HORACE. Let not the sun go down upon your wrath.—BIBLE. A soft answer turneth away wrath; but grievous words stir up anger.—BIBLE. Anger makes dull men witty, but it keeps them poor.—BACON. As fire kindled by bellows, so is anger by words. —FULLER. Anger is one of the sinews of the soul; he that wants it hath a maimed mind. —FULLER. A man in a passion rides a mad horse.—FRANKLIN. Beware the fury of a patient man.—DRYDEN. To be angry is to revenge the faults of others upon ourselves.— POPE. When angry, count ten before you

[coll.] etc. *below*, fly ~, fall *or* get into a rage *or* passion, fly off the handle [slang], fly off at a tangent, fly out, flare up, bridle up, bristle up, froth up, fire up, kindle, take fire, boil over, burst into a passion, blow one's top [slang], explode; become excited etc. 824.6.

10. *v.* anger, cause *or* raise anger etc. *n.*, make angry etc. *adj.*, excite to anger, kindle wrath, make one hot under the collar [slang], put out of countenance *or* humor, raise one's gorge *or* choler, raise one's dander [coll.], put *or* get one's dander up [coll.], put *or* get one's monkey up [coll. or slang, Eng.], put *or* get one's Irish up [coll. and dial.], put *or* get one's back up, put *or* get one's wind up [coll.], set by the ears.

incense, inflame, fan into a flame, envenom, embitter, stir up bile, stir one's bile, stir the blood, ruffle, roil, rile [coll., chiefly U.S.], discompose, provoke, huff, pique, vex, exasperate, aggravate [coll.], annoy, irritate, nettle, chafe, fret; wound, sting, sting to the quick, hit ~, rub ~, sting *or* strike on the raw; affront, offend, give offense, give umbrage, outrage, insult, hurt the feelings; add fuel to the flame, widen the breach; stick in one's crop *or* gizzard [coll.].

11. *v.* enrage, infuriate, madden, drive one mad, lash into fury, work up into a passion, throw into a ferment, make one's, blood boil, make the ears tingle.

12. *adj.* resentful, resenting etc. *adj.*, resentive [rare]; set against, indignant, offended, hurt, wounded, injured, stung; bitter, acrimonious, rancorous, virulent; up in arms; vindictive etc. (revengeful) 919.6; provoked etc. (displeased) 828.14, 15; disliking etc. 867.7.

13. *adj.* angry, angered etc. *v.*, wroth, wrothsome [rare], wrathy [chiefly coll.], wrathful, irate, ireful, mad [chiefly coll.], sore [coll.], sore as a crab [coll.], waxy [slang, Eng.], stuffy [coll.], hot [slang], hot under the collar [slang], flushed with anger *or* rage, warm, fiery, wrought-up, worked up; raging, fuming, foaming etc. *v.*; in a passion, ~ rage *or* fury, in a stew [coll.], in a taking [coll.], in a fume, in a pucker [dial. or coll.], in a huff, in a wax [slang], in high *or* deep dudgeon.

infuriated, infuriate; furious, *acharné* [F.], rageful, mad with rage, hopping mad [slang], rabid, foaming at the mouth, convulsed with rage; fierce, wild, savage; mad as hops, ~ a hornet *or* a wet hen, fighting ~, roaring *or* raving mad, good and mad [all coll.]; spleeny, spleenish [now rare], spleenful, splenetic; irascent; Achillean; irascible, cross etc. (ill-humored) 901.7.

14. *adv.* angrily etc. *adj.*, in anger, in the height of passion, in the heat of passion, in the heat of the moment; in an ecstasy of rage.

901. Ill-humor

1. *n.* ill-humor, bad humor, bad *or* ill temper; bad blood, ill blood; churlishness, crossness, crabbedness, quarrelsomeness etc. *adj.*; irascibility, irritability, iracundity, procacity [rare], protervity [rare], perversity, petulance *or* petulancy, ill nature, hot blood, temper, fiery ~, irritable etc. *adj.* temper; querulosity, querulity [both rare]; acerbity, acrimony, asperity; gall, bile, choler, spleen, rancor, dander [coll.]; anger etc. (resentment) 900; pugnacity, contentiousness etc. (warlikeness) 722.6; gruffness etc. 895.2; misanthropy etc. 910; malevolence etc. 907; excitability etc. 825.

2. *n.* sullenness, moodiness, surliness, moroseness etc. *adj.*; morosity, sulky *or* sullen mood, fits of sulks, sullens, sulks, frumps [now dial.], mumps, mopes, dolefuls [coll.], dumps *or* doleful dumps [coll.], doldrums, dismals, vapors [arch.], glooming, *bouderie* [F.], grouch [coll.]; huff etc. (dudgeon) 900.2; sadness etc. 837.

3. *n.* sullen looks, black looks, hangdog look, long *or* grave face; scowl, frown, glout [arch. exc. dial.], gloom [chiefly Scot.], glooming.

4. *n.* ill-humored person, gloom [coll.], grouch *or* old grouch [coll.], crosspatch [coll.], crooked stick [coll.], dragon, brabbler, tartar, spitfire, fire-eater [coll.], hothead, hotspur, fury, ugly cus-

---

901. High-stomach'd are they both, and full of ire, / In rage deaf as the sea, hasty as fire.— SHAKESPEARE.   Nursing her wrath to keep it warm.—BURNS.   He is techy and impatient of contradiction, sore with wounded pride.— HAZLITT.   That splenetic temper, which seems to grudge brightness to the flames of hell.—LANDOR.

---

speak; if very angry, an hundred.—JEFFERSON. When angry, count four; when very angry, swear.—MARK TWAIN

tomer [slang]; bear, bruin, grizzly, grizzly bear; scold, common scold; shrew, vixen, virago, termagant, frump [coll.], beldam *or* beldame, she-wolf, tigress, witch; Xanthippe, Kate the Shrew; Sir Fretful Plagiary; *"genus irritabile vatum"* (Horace).

5. *v.* be irascible etc. *adj.*, have a temper etc. *n.*, have a devil in one, be possessed of the devil, have the temper of a fiend; growl, snarl etc. (show resentment) 900.7; fire up etc. (become angry) 900.9.

6. *v.* be sullen etc. *adj.*, sulk, frump, mope, pout, grumble, fret, grouch [slang], grout [coll., U.S.]; look sullen, have a hangdog look, look black, look black as thunder, knit the brow, frown, scowl, lower, glower, glout [arch. exc. dial.]; be sad etc. 837.6.

7. *adj.* ill-humored, ill-affected, ill-disposed, ill-tempered, bad-tempered, in bad *or* ill humor, in a bad *or* shocking temper *or* humor, out of temper, ~ humor *or* sorts, humorsome; cross, cross as crabs, ~ a bear, ~ a bear with a sore head, ~ a cat, ~ a dog, ~ two sticks *or* the tongs [all coll.]; irascible, irritable, cross-grained, churlish, bearish, crusty, *acariâtre* [F.], testy, touchy, techy *or* tetchy, huffy, peevish, pettish, petulant, querulous, captious, fractious, malignant, ugly [coll., U.S.], cantankerous [coll.], bristling, waspish, snappish; doggish, currish; iracund, iracundulous; grouchy [coll.], grouty [coll., U.S.]; grumbling, growling; crabbed, crabby.

bitter, sour, soured, sour as a crab, acerb, acerbic; cankered, choleric, jaundiced, bilious, atrabilious; spleeny, spleenish [now rare], spleenful, splenetic; shrewish, vixenish, vixenly; nagging, naggy [coll.]; cursed, cussed, curst [all now chiefly dial.]; passionate, peppery, fiery, warm, hot, hot-tempered, hotheaded; hasty, overhasty, quick, "sudden and quick in quarrel" (Shakespeare); like touchwood *or* tinder, like a barrel of gunpowder, volcanic, ready to burst forth; resentful, angry etc. 900.12, 13; vindictive etc. 919.6; gruff etc. 895.7; excitable etc. 825.8–11; perverse, froward etc. (obstinate) 606.6; thin-skinned etc. (sensitive) 822.6; malevolent etc. 907.6; misanthropic etc. 910.3.

8. *adj.* sullen, sulky, in the sulks etc. *n.*, surly, surly as a bear, rusty [obs. exc. dial. Eng.], stuffy [coll.], grumpy, mumpish, dumpish, glum, grim, grum, morose, black-browed; moody, moodish; mopish, mopy [coll.], moping; fretful, on the fret; scowling, glowering etc. *v.*; melancholy, dismal etc. (sad) 837.9, 10.

9. *adj.* quarrelsome, contentious, disputatious, fractious, exceptious [rare], wranglesome [rare], controversial, polemic(al); argumentative, argumental; cat-and-dog, cat-and-doggish; litigious, litigatory, litigant; pugnacious, unpeaceful etc. (warlike) 722.13; discordant, unharmonious etc. (disagreeing) 24.6.

902. Love-making, Endearment

1. *n.* love-making, spooning [slang], billing and cooing etc. *v.*; flirtation, coquetry, philander; amorous glances, ogle, side glance, sheep's eyes, goo-goo eyes [slang U.S.]; adultery etc. 961.6.

2. *n.* courtship, courting, wooing etc. *v.*; suit, love suit, addresses, the soft impeachment; serenade; gallantry; betrothal etc. (engagement) 768.2; marriage etc. 903.

3. *n.* endearment, endearance [rare]; caress, pat; dalliance, caressing, fondling etc. *v.*; artful endearments *or* caresses, soft words, blandishment; embrace, hug; kiss, buss, smack, osculation.

4. *n.* (terms of endearment) sweetheart, sweetie, love, darling, dear, deary, precious, precious heart *or* lamb, jewel, pet, petkins, sweet, sweets, sweetkins, honey, honey bunch, honey child, sugar, duck, duckling, angel, angel lamb, babe, baby, cherub, chick, chickabiddy, buttercup, lamb, snookums; moppet, mopsy [both arch.]; loved one etc. 897.7.

5. *n.* love token, token of love; truelove knot, truelover's knot; love ribbon; ring, engagement *or* wedding ring; locket, heart; posy [arch.]; love letter, billet-doux; valentine; myrtle etc. 897.5.

6. *n.* flirt, coquette, gold digger [slang, U.S.], vampire [coll.], vamp [slang]; male flirt, philanderer, philander; cake-

---

902. She's beautiful and therefore to be woo'd / She is a woman, therefore to be won.—SHAKESPEARE. Blessed is the wooing that is not long a-doing.—R. BURTON. And frame love ditties passing rare, / And sing them to a lady fair.—SCOTT. If I am not worth the wooing, I surely am not worth the winning.—LONGFELLOW. Faint heart never won fair lady.

eater, tea hound, lounge lizard [all slang, U.S.].

7. *v.* make love, bill and coo, spoon [slang], neck [slang], pet [coll.]; toy, dally, trifle, wanton; flirt, coquet, gallivant, philander; cast coquettish glances, eye amorously, ogle, look sweet upon [coll.], cast sheep's eyes upon, make goo-goo eyes at [slang U.S.], *faire les yeux doux* [F.]; court, woo, caterwaul [derog.], address, sue, press one's suit, pay court *or* suit to, pay one's court, ~ addresses *or* attentions to, sweetheart [coll.], squire, spark [coll.]; set one's cap at *or* for [coll.]; serenade; propose, make an offer, ask for one's hand, pop the question [coll.]; plight one's troth etc. (affiance) 768.4.

8. *v.* caress, fondle, pet, pat, dandle, cosset, coddle, cocker, cuddle, cherish [arch.], much [dial.]; pat on the head *or* cheek, chuck under the chin; embrace, hug, clasp, take to one's arms, fold *or* strain in one's arms, fold to the heart, press to the bosom; snuggle, nestle, nuzzle; kiss, buss, smack, blow a kiss.

9. *adj.* caressing etc. *v.,* caressive, cuddlesome, cuddly, snuggly; affectionate, demonstrative; kissable.

10. *adj.* flirtatious, flirty, flirtational; coquettish, coy.

11. *adv.* caressingly, caressively etc. *adj.*

903. Marriage
(See 904. Celibacy, 905. Divorce, Widowhood)

1. *n.* marriage, matrimony, wedlock, holy wedlock, spousehood [arch.], spousage [now rare], union, matrimonial union, match; bond of matrimony, *vinculum matrimonii* [L.], wedding knot, nuptial tie *or* knot; married state *or* status, coverture, cohabitation; bed, marriage bed, bridebed; intermarriage, miscegenation; ill-assorted marriage, *mésalliance* [F.]; marriageability, nubility, concubitancy;

Hera *or* Teleia [Gr. Myth.], Juno Pronuba [Rom. Myth.], Frigg [Norse Myth.]; betrothal etc. (engagement) 768.2.

2. *n.* (kinds of marriage) monogamy, monogyny; bigamy, digamy, deuterogamy; trigamy; polygamy, polygyny; polyandry, polyandria, polyandrianism, polyandrism [rare]; left-handed marriage, morganatic marriage; *mariage de convenance* [F.], marriage of convenience; love match; levirate, leviration; common-law marriage; concubinage; harem etc. 374.7.

3. *n.* wedding, bridal, hymen, hymeneals [rare], hymeneal rites, nuptials, spousals, espousals, espousement; nuptial benediction; nuptial song, wedding song, marriage song, epithalamy, epithalamium, hymen, hymeneal; wedding veil, saffron veil *or* robe; altar, hymeneal altar; nuptial apartment, bridechamber, bridal suite; honeymoon.

4. *n.* wedding attendant, usher; best man, bridesman, groomsman; bridesmaid, bridemaiden, maid *or* matron of honor.

5. *n.* married person, spouse, espousal [arch.], mate, yokemate, partner, consort, better half [joc.], "bone of my bones, and flesh of my flesh" (Bible); miscegenator, miscegenist; monogamist, monogynist; bigamist, digamist, deuterogamist; trigamist; polygamist, polygynist, polyandrist; Mormon, Turk, Bluebeard.

6. *n.* newlywed; groom, bridegroom; bride, plighted bride, blushing bride.

7. *n.* married man, husband, man, benedict, baron [Old Law and Her.], goodman [arch. or dial.], old man [joc.]; common law husband; cuckold.

8. *n.* married woman, wife, wife of one's bosom, wedded wife, rib [dial. and joc.], helpmate, helpmeet, better half, gray mare [slang], goodwife [arch. or dial.], old woman [joc.], feme, feme covert [Law], lady [obs. or uncultivat-

---

903. Wedlock is a padlock.—J. RAY.   Man's best possession is a sympathetic wife.—EURIPIDES.   Marriage is an evil that most men welcome.—MENANDER.   *Si qua voles apte nubere nube pari* [If you wish to marry well, marry an equal].—OVID.   Therefore shall a man leave his father and his mother, and shall cleave unto his wife: and they shall be one flesh.—BIBLE.   Render me worthy of this noble wife.—SHAKESPEARE.   Hanging and wiving goes by destiny.—SHAKESPEARE.   Marriages are made in Heaven.—TENNYSON.   Marriage must be a relation either of sympathy or of conquest.—G. ELIOT.   Well-married, a man is winged: ill-matched, he is shackled.—H. W. BEECHER.   When a man meets his fitting mate society begins.—EMERSON.   Marriage is popular because it combines the maximum of temptation with the maximum of opportunity.—SHAW.   Wives must be had, be they good or bad.

ed], squaw [Indian], matron; common law wife; bachelor's wife, Coeleb's wife; concubine, paramour etc. (mistress) 962.3.

9. *n.* married couple, wedded pair *or* couple, man and wife; newlyweds, bride and groom; Darby and Joan, Baucis and Philemon.

10. *n.* affinity, soul mate, spiritual wife *or* husband.

11. *n.* marriage broker, matchmaker, professional matchmaker, schatchen [Yiddish], matrimonial agent; matrimonial agency *or* bureau.

12. *v.* marry, wed, nuptial, join, splice [coll.], hitch [slang], couple, unite, join in marriage, join *or* unite in holy wedlock, tie the nuptial *or* wedding knot; seal; give away, give in marriage; publish ~, call ~, proclaim *or* bid the banns.

13. *v.* be married, get *or* become married, contract matrimony, marry, wed, espouse, wive, take to wife, take to oneself a wife, get hitched [slang], be spliced [coll.], be made one, go off, pair off, lead to the hymeneal altar, take for better or for worse, give one's hand to, bestow one's hand upon, be asked in church; remarry, rewed; intermarry, interwed, miscegenate; affiance, betroth etc. (promise) 768.4.

14. *adj.* matrimonial, marital, conjugal, connubial, wedded, married, nuptial, hymeneal, spousal; bridal; epithalamic, epithalamial; monogamous, monogamic, monogamian, monogamist *or* monogammistic, monogynous; bigamous, bigamic, bigamistic, digamous; polygamous, polygamist *or* polygamistic, polygynous; polyandrous, polyandric; miscegenetic.

15. *adj.* marriageable, nubile, concubitous.

16. *adj.* married, wedded etc. *v.*; one, one bone and one flesh.

17. *adj.* engaged, affianced etc. (promised) 768.7.

904. Celibacy
(See 903. **Marriage**)

1. *n.* celibacy, singleness, single blessedness; misogamy, misogyny; bachelorhood, bachelorship; spinsterhood, maidhood [rare], maidenhood, maidenhead, virginity, pucelage *or* pucellage [rare]; continence etc. 960; monasticism etc. 995.2.

2. *n.* celibate, *célibataire* [F.], celibatarian, celibatory; bachelor, bach [slang], old bachelor; misogamist, misogynist; monk etc. 996.11.

3. *n.* spinster, spinstress, old maid, maid, maiden, virgin, feme sole [Law], bachelor girl, girl-bachelor; vestal, vestal virgin; Diana, St. Agnes; nun etc. 996.12.

4. *v.* be unmarried etc. *adj.*, live single, enjoy single blessedness, keep bachelor hall, bach *or* bach it [slang].

5. *adj.* celibate, celibatic; unmarried, unwedded, single, spouseless, wifeless, husbandless; bachelorly, bachelorlike, bachelorwise; spinsterly, spinsterish, spinsterlike, spinsterial, spinsterous; old-maidish, old-maidenish, maidenly; virgin, virginal; continent etc. 960.2.

905. Divorce, Widowhood
(See 903. **Marriage**)

1. *n.* divorce, divorcement; separation, judicial separation, separate maintenance, *separatio a mensa et thoro* [L.], *separatio a vinculo matrimonii* [L.]; divorcé, divorcée; divorcee.

2. *n.* widowhood, viduity [rare], viduage, viduation; widowerhood, widowership, widowery [rare]; grasswidowhood; weeds, widow's weeds; viduate [Eccl.].

3. *n.* widowed person, widow, widow woman [now chiefly dial.], relict; dowager, queen dowager, dowager duchess etc.; widower, widowman [dial.]; grass widow, grass widower; widower bewitched [rare].

4. *v.* separate, part, live separate, split up [coll.], divorce, get *or* obtain a divorce, unmarry, disespouse [obs.], put away; come to a parting of the ways; widow, be widowed, leave a widow *or* widower.

---

904. One was never married, and that's his hell; another is, and that's his plague.—R. BURTON.   Marriage has many pains, but celibacy has no pleasures.—JOHNSON.   It is a truth universally acknowledged that a single man in possession of a good fortune must be in want of a wife.—J. AUSTEN.   Celibates replace sentiment by habits.—G. MOORE.   Is the single man therefore blessed? No!—SHAKESPEARE.

905. Divorce is the sacrament of adultery.—GUICHARD.   Divorce, the public brand of shameful life.—T. PARNELL.   You evity think that brevity is the soul of widowhood.—SAKI.

5. *adj.* widowly, widowy [rare], widowish, widowlike; widowed, widowered.

906. Benevolence
(See 907. Malevolence)

1. *n.* benevolence, benevolentness, kindness etc. *adj.*; charity, philanthropy, benignity, amiability, grace, goodness *or* warmth of heart, loving-kindness, milk of human kindness, good *or* kindly feelings, good will, good *or* best wishes; Christian charity *or* love, God's love *or* grace; good *or* kindly nature, bonhomie *or* bonhommie; humanity, humanitarianism, philanthropism; altruism, good will to *or* toward man, devotion to human welfare, love of *or* for mankind, brotherly love, *deliciae humani generis* [L.]; fellow feeling, sympathy; toleration, consideration; chivalry, knight-errantry; eudaemonism; love etc. 897; friendship etc. 888; mercy etc. (pity) 914; welfare etc. (goodness) 648; philanthropist etc. 911; magnanimity etc. (unselfishness) 942.

2. *n.* charitableness etc. *adj.,* beneficence, kindness, good *or* kind treatment, good *or* kind offices, labor of love, "the luxury of doing good" (Goldsmith); alms, almsgiving; good works, benevolences, philanthropies, charities; giving etc. 784; magnanimity etc. 942.2; generosity, bounty etc. (liberality) 816; gift etc. 784.3; good turn, benefit etc. (grace) 784.4; aid etc. 707.

3. *n.* public welfare, ~ good *or* service, common *or* general welfare, commonweal *or* common weal, commonwealth [now rare]; universal benevolence, cosmopolitanism; utility, utilitarianism, Benthamism, "the greatest happiness of the greatest number" (Bentham); socialism, communism; Fourierism, phalansterism *or* phalansterianism, Saint-Simonianism; social science, sociology.

4. *n.* public spirit, patriotism, civism, nationality, love of country, *amor patriae* [L.]; chauvinism etc. 884.2.

5. *v.* be benevolent etc. *adj.,* have one's heart in the right place, bear good will, wish well *or* Godspeed, view *or* regard with an eye of favor, take in good part; take *or* feel an interest in, be *or* feel interested in; have a fellow feeling for, sympathize with, feel for, enter into the feelings of; practice the Golden Rule, do as you would be done by, do unto others as you would have them do unto you, meet halfway; treat well, do good, do a good turn, confer a benefit, render a service, be of use; aid etc. 707.6–11; benefit etc. 648.6; give etc. 784.8; be liberal etc. 816.3; bear love to etc. 897.11; fraternize etc. (be friendly) 888.2.

6. *adj.* benevolent, benign, benignant; kind, kindly; good, amiable, cordial, obliging, accommodating, indulgent, gracious, complacent, tender, considerate; warmhearted, kindhearted, tenderhearted, softhearted; goodhumored, goodnatured, well-natured; sympathizing, sympathetic; kindly meant, well-meant, well-meaning, well-affected, well-disposed, well-intentioned; chivalric, chivalrous; brotherly, fraternal; sisterly, sororal [rare]; fatherly, paternal; motherly, maternal; loving etc. 897.14; friendly etc. 888.4; complaisant etc. (courteous) 894.12; merciful etc. 914.6; helpful etc. 707.12, 13.

7. *adj.* charitable, philanthropic(al), beneficent, altruistic, humane, humanitarian, eleemosynary, almsgiving; bighearted, largehearted, freehearted; helpful etc. 707.12; unselfish, magnanimous etc. 942.5, 6; bounteous, generous etc. (liberal) 816.4.

8. *adv.* public-spirited, patriotic(al), cosmopolitan, utilitarian; chauvinistic etc. 884.8.

9. *adv.* benevolently, charitably etc. *adj.*; with good will, with a good intention, with the best intentions, out of deepest sympathy; in charity, in a burst of generosity; *pro bono publico* [L.], for the public good; *pro aris et focis* (Cicero).

These widows, sir, are the most perverse creatures in the world.—ADDISON. 906. Though I speak with the tongues of men and of angels, and have not charity, I am become as sounding brass or a tinkling cymbal.—BIBLE. And now abideth faith, hope, charity, these three; but the greatest of these is charity.—BIBLE. Charity . . . doth not behave itself unseemly.—BIBLE. For this I think charity, to love God for himself, and our neighbour for God.—T. BROWNE. Charity is a virtue of the heart, and not of the hands.—ADDISON. Kind hearts are more than coronets.—TENNYSON. True charity is the desire to be useful to others without thought of recompense.—SWEDENBORG. If you stop to be kind, you must swerve often from your path.—M. WEBB. One good turn deserves another. Charity begins at home.

907. Malevolence
(See 906. Benevolence)

1. *n.* malevolence, ill-disposedness, maliciousness etc. *adj.*; malice, malice prepense *or* aforethought; malignance *or* malignancy, malignity; maleficence, ill will, bad intent *or* intention, tender mercies [iron.]; spite, despite; evil disposition, ill nature, ill blood, bad blood; virulence, venom, rancor, gall, mordacity, acerbity; hardness of heart, heart of stone, obduracy; evil eye, cloven foot *or* hoof; enmity etc. 889; hate etc. 898; resentment etc. 900; ill-humor etc. 901; revengefulness etc. 919.2; maltreatment etc. 649.4; pitilessness etc. 914a; evildoing etc. 945.6; violence etc. 173; harm etc. (badness) 649.

2. *n.* uncharitableness, unkindness etc. *adj.*; "sharp-toothed unkindness" (Shakespeare); uncharity, unbenevolence, unbenignity, unamiability, incompassion [rare].

3. *n.* cruelty, cruelness etc. *adj.*; brutality, savagery, ferity, ferocity, barbarity, inhumanity, truculence, ruffianism, violence, inclemency, severity; abuse, ill-treatment, ill-usage, persecution; inquisition; bloodthirst, bloodthirstiness, cannibalism; torture etc. 828.6.

4. *n.* malevolent act, malefaction, maleficence, evil action *or* deed, bad *or* ill turn, ill service, disservice, "unkindest cut of all" (Shakespeare), foul play; outrage, atrocity; offense etc. (indignity) 929.2, (misdeed) 947.2.

5. *v.* be malevolent etc. *adj.*, bear *or* harbor malice, bear a grudge, betray *or* show the cloven foot; hate etc. 898.3; wreak one's malice on etc. (maltreat) 649.7; hurt, wound etc. (harm) 649.6, (pain) 830.3; torment, harry etc. (annoy) 830.5; agonize, harrow etc. (torture) 830.6; show no mercy etc. 914a.2.

6. *adj.* malevolent, evil-disposed, ill-disposed, ill-intentioned, ill-natured, ill-conditioned, ill-contrived; malicious, maleficent, malefic, malefical [rare], malefi-cial [rare]; malign, malignant; invidious, hateful; spiteful, despiteful; mordacious, caustic, bitter, acrimonious, virulent, rancorous; envenomed, venomous; grinding, galling; incendiary; harsh etc. (gruff) 895.7; ill-humored etc. 901.7, 9; quarrelsome etc. 901.9; treacherous etc. 940.12; revengeful etc. 919.6; evildoing etc. 945.13; harmful etc. (bad) 649.8–11; violent etc. 173.11–16.

7. *adj.* uncharitable, unphilanthropic(al), unbeneficent, unbenevolent; unbenign, unbenignant; unkind, unkindly; unamiable, uncordial, uncomplacent, ungracious, inconsiderate, unaccommodating, disobliging; unsympathizing, unsympathetic; uncompassionate, incompassionate [rare], uncompassioned; unfriendly etc. 889.3.

8. *adj.* heartless, unfeeling, unnatural, bloodless; cold, cold of heart, coldhearted, cold-blooded; hard, hard of heart, hard-hearted, stonyhearted, marblehearted, flinthearted, callous; unmerciful etc. (pitiless) 914a.3; relentless etc. 919.6.

9. *adj.* cruel, cruel-hearted; brutal, brutish, bestial; savage, savagerous [slang, U.S.], savage as a bear *or* tiger; ferocious, ferine, feral; barbarous, barbaric; truculent, vicious, fierce, fell, atrocious; inhuman *or* unhuman, inhumane; fiendish, fiendlike; demoniac(al), diabolic(al), devilish, satanic, hellish, infernal; Tartarean, Tartareous; bloodthirsty, bloody-minded; "cruel as the grave" (Bible), cruel as death; ruthless etc. (pitiless) 914a.3; murderous etc. 361.15; severe etc. 739.15.

10. *adv.* malevolently etc. *adj.*, with bad intent etc. *adj.*, with the ferocity of a tiger, with malice prepense *or* aforethought.

908. Malediction

1. *n.* malediction, malison, curse, imprecation, denunciation, commination, execration; anathema, anathema maranatha [erron.]; ban, proscription, excommunication, thunders of the Vatican; as-

---

907. People often grudge others what they cannot enjoy themselves.—AESOP. *Mala mens malus animus* [Evil mind, evil spirit].—TERENCE. *Homo homini lupus* [Man is a wolf to man].—PLAUTUS. There are some who bear a grudge even to those that do them good.—PILPAY. Rich gifts wax poor when givers prove unkind.—SHAKESPEARE. Malice never spoke well.—CAMDEN. Cruelty ever proceeds from a vile mind, and often from a cowardly heart.—HARINGTON. As ruthless as a baby with a worm, / As cruel as a school-boy.—TENNYSON.
908. A name to all succeeding ages curst.—DRYDEN. With imprecations thus he fill'd the air, / And angry Neptune heard the unright-

persion, disparagement, vituperation, vilification, abuse, contumely, obloquy, invective, opprobrium, scurrility, blackguardism; calumny, calumniation; diatribe, tirade, jeremiad, philippic; more bark than bite; disapprobation etc. 932; defamation etc. (detraction) 934; threat etc. 909; personality etc. 934.2; insult etc. (indignity) 929.2.

2. *n.* swearing etc *v.*, profanity, profane swearing, foul ~, bad ~, strong *or* unparliamentary language, evilspeaking, language [coll.], billingsgate, ribaldry.

3. *n.* oath, profane oath, swear [coll.], curse, cuss [coll., chiefly U.S.], cuss word [coll., U.S.], swearword [coll.], foul invective, expletive, epithet, dirty name [slang], sailor's blessing [joc.], rapper [now dial.].

4. *v.* maledict, curse, accurse, imprecate, damn, confound, blame [coll.], execrate, imprecate [arch.], call down evil upon, invoke *or* call down curses on the head of, devote to destruction, beshrew [arch.], curse up hill and down dale; curse with bell, book, and candle; anathematize, anathemize [rare]; vilify, vilipend, revile, call names, call by hard *or* ugly names, engage in personalities; fulminate, thunder against; denounce, rail at etc. (censure) 932.7, 8; defile etc. (stigmatize) 874.7; defame etc. 934.3; threaten etc. 909.2.

5. *v.* swear, curse, cuss [coll., chiefly U.S.], curse and swear, execrate, rap out an oath, fall a cursing, use language [coll.], let out religion [joc.]; swear like a trooper, make the air blue, swear till one is black *or* blue in the face; swear at, damn, cuss out [slang].

6. *adj.* maledictory, maledictive, maledict [arch.]; imprecatory, damnatory, abusive, vituperative, contumelious; calumnious, calumniatory; scurrile, scurrilous; foul-spoken, foul-tongued, foul-mouthed; cursed, damned etc. *v.*; defamatory etc. 934.4.

7. *int.* curse!, confound!, damn!, beshrew! [arch.], *ruat caelum!* [L.], woe to!, woe betide!, ill betide!, confusion seize!, devil take!, out with!, a plague upon!, out upon!, aroint! [rare], *parbleu!* [F.].

8. *int.* (euphemistic oaths) darn!, dern!, dang!, dash!, drat!, consarn!, hang!, blast!, blame!, goldarn!, goldang!, golding!, gosh-darn!, plague-gone!, doggone!, dingbust!, dagnab!, dadrot!, daddrat!, dadburn!, dadblast!, dadblame!

909. Threat

1. *n.* threat, menace, denunciation, threatening etc. *v.*, minacity [rare], commination; defiance etc. 715; intimidation etc. 860.5; foreboding etc. 511.6; warning, forewarning etc. 668.1–3; omen etc. 512.

2. *v.* threaten, menace, threat [arch. and dial.], utter *or* use threats *or* menaces, hold out by way of menace *or* warning, promise as a threat, utter threats against, promise punishment *or* reprisal, keep *or* hold *in terrorem* [L.], shake ~, double *or* clench the fist at, look daggers, mutter, growl, snarl, gnarl, bark; thunder, fulminate, talk big, use big words; show threatening signs, lower; warn, forewarn etc. 668.6, 7; forebode etc. (portend) 511.9; be imminent etc. 152.2; intimidate etc. 860.12; defy etc. 715.2; endanger etc. 665.4.

3. *adj.* threatening, menacing, abusive; minatory, minacious; comminative, comminatory; warning, forewarning etc. 668.9, 10; ominous, portentous, lowering etc. (predictive) 511.11, 512.3, 5; impending etc. (imminent) 152.3; defiant etc. 715.3.

4. *int.* (threats) *vae victis!* [L.], at your peril!, do your worst!, look out!

910. Misanthropy

1. *n.* misanthropy, misanthropism, cynicism, antisociality; incivism, unpatriotism; selfishness etc. 943; ill-humor etc. 901.

2. *n.* misanthrope, misanthropist; cyn-

---

eous prayer.—POPE.   Consigned his name to universal execration, now and forever.—SHELLEY.

909. Threats without power are like powder without ball.—P. J. BAILEY.   Many a man threatens while he quakes for fear.—G. HERBERT.   An eye like Mars, to threaten and command.—SHAKESPEARE.   If it is not right to hurt, it is neither right nor wise to menace.—BURKE.   Threatened folks live long.—H. PORTER.
910. What is a cynic? A man who knows the price of everything, and the value of nothing.—WILDE.   The worst thing about cynicism is its truth.—CYNIC'S CALENDAR.

910.2 – 914.1

ic, antisocialist, man-hater; Timon, Diogenes; womanhater, misogamist, misogynist.

3. *adj.* misanthropic(al), cynical, antisocial, man-hating; incivic, unpatriotic; selfish etc. 943.4; ill-humored etc. 901.7–9.

911. Philanthropist

n. philanthropist, benevolist, altruist, humanitarian, friend of *or* to man, "the friend of man, to vice alone a foe" (Burns), "a friend to human race" (Homer), "little friend of all the world" (Kipling), "friend to the friendless, to the sick man health" (Coleridge), "one who loves his fellow-men" (Hunt), *amicus humani generis* [L.], public servant, good Samaritan, sympathizer, favorer, well-wisher, good fellow, *bon enfant* [F.], salt of the earth; knight, knight-errant; Robin Hood; eudaemonist; patriot, patrioteer [coll.]; cosmopolite, citizen of the world; utilitarian, Benthamite; socialist, communist; almsgiver etc. 784.7.

912. Benefactor
(See 913. Evildoer)

1. *n.* benefactor, benefactress, benefiter, doer of good works, ministering angel, good Samaritan, befriender, succorer, helper, aider, help, aid, helpmate, helping hand, assister, assistant, "a very present help in time of trouble" (Bible); friend in need, friend indeed, jack-at-a-pinch; giver etc. 784.7; patron, backer etc. (upholder) 711.4; defender etc. 717.5; protector etc. 664.3; guardian angel etc. (familiar spirit) 979.12.

2. *n.* savior, redeemer, deliverer, liberator, rescuer, freer, emancipator, manumitter.

---

911. He believed that he was born, not for himself, but for the whole world.—LUCAN. Mankind will not be reasoned out of the feelings of humanity.—BLACKSTONE. He who loves not his country, can love nothing.—BYRON. Let our object be, our country, our whole country, and nothing but our country.—D. WEBSTER. I love my country better than my family, but I love human nature better than my country.—FÉNELON. But let me live by the side of the road, / And be a friend to man.—S. W. FOSS.
912. I know that my redeemer liveth.—BIBLE.

913. Evildoer
(See 912. Benefactor)

Maleficent Person.—**1.** *n.* evildoer, evil worker, malfeasant, malfeasor, malefactor, malevolent; mischief-maker, marplot; hellion [coll.], hellcat, terror, holy terror [slang], roarer *or* hell-roarer [slang], ringtail roarer [slang, U.S.], fire-eater [coll.], fury; oppressor, tyrant; firebrand, incendiary, agitator, seditionist; terrorist, anarchist, nihilist; destroyer, vandal, iconoclast; Attila, scourge of the human race; serpent, viper, snake, snake in the grass; wrongdoer etc. 949.2; arsonist etc. 384.6; thief etc. 792.

2. *n.* ruffian, rough, tough [coll., U.S.], ugly customer [slang], bully, bulldozer [coll., U.S.], blusterer, rowdy, bravo, thug, plug-ugly [slang, U.S.], larrikin [Austral. and Eng.], hoodlum [coll.], hooligan [slang], gorilla [slang, U.S.], apache, Mohock [Eng. Hist.], desperado, cutthroat, bludgeon man, gunman; gun, trigger man, rod, rodman, torpedo [all crim. slang, U.S.]; garroter *or* garrotter, strangler; hatchet man, highbinder [U.S.]; murderer etc. 361.8.

3. *n.* savage, brute, beast, tiger, hyena, barbarian, semibarbarian, caitiff; Indian, wild Indian, redskin, Apache, Mohawk; cannibal, man-eater, anthropophagite, anthropophaginian, anthropophagist [rare], anthropophagus (*pl.* anthropophagi); wild beast etc. 366.

4. *n.* monster, demon, fiend, devil, devil incarnate, demon in human shape, hellhound, shaitan [coll.]; vampire, lamia, harpy, ghoul; ogre, ogress; Frankenstein's monster; dragon etc. 83.6, 7.

5. *n.* malevolent woman, hag, hellhag, hellcat, witch, virago, vixen, termagant, Jezebel, beldam *or* beldame, she-wolf, tigress, ogress, siren, fury; jade etc. (bad woman) 949.4; Furies etc. 900.4.

914. Pity
(See 914a. Pitilessness)

1. *n.* pity, compassion, commiseration, sympathy, fellow feeling, humanity, mer-

---

913. Tremble thou wretch, / That hast within thee undivulged crimes.—SHAKESPEARE.
914. No beast so fierce but knows some touch of pity.—SHAKESPEARE. He that pities another remembers himself.—G. HERBERT. A brother's suff'rings claim a brother's pity.—

cy, clemency, bowels, bowels of compassion *or* mercy, ruth, forbearance; longsuffering, long-sufferance [arch.]; exorability; tenderness, softheartedness etc. *adj.*; yearning, melting mood; bleeding heart; *argumentum ad misericordiam* [L.]; quarter, grace; leniency etc. (lenity) 740; charity etc. (benevolence) 906.

2. *n.* sympathizer, well-wisher, advocate, champion etc. (upholder) 711.4; friend etc. 890.

3. *v.* pity, have *or* show pity etc. *n.*, take pity on *or* upon, compassion, compassionate, commiserate, sympathize, feel for, enter into the feelings of, have one's heart bleed for; weep, melt, thaw; forbear, relent; relax, give quarter, *parcere subjectis* [L.]; wipe the tears; give a *coup de grâce* [F.], put out of one's misery; be cruel to be kind; condole etc. 915.2.

4. *v.* raise *or* excite pity etc. *n.*, touch, soften, melt, melt the heart, appeal to one's better feelings; propitiate, disarm.

5. *v.* ask for pity, beg for mercy etc. *n.*, cry for quarter, beg one's life; kneel, fall on one's knees, throw oneself at the feet of, get *or* come down on one's marrowbones [joc.]; supplicate, beseech etc. (entreat) 765.5.

6. *adj.* pitying etc. *v.*, pitiful; compassionate, sympathetic, merciful, clement, ruthful, humane, soft, tender, tenderhearted, softhearted, unhardened; exorable, weak; forbearing, forbearant, longsuffering; touched, touched to the heart; with bleeding heart; lenient etc. 740.4; charitable etc. (benevolent) 906.6, 7.

7. *int.* for pity's sake!, for mercy's sake!; mercy!, have mercy!, cry you mercy!, God help you!, poor thing!, poor dear!, poor fellow!; woe betide!

914a. Pitilessness
(See 914. Pity)

1. *n.* pitilessness, mercilessness, ruthlessness etc. *adj.*; want of pity etc. (*see*

ADDISON.   Taught by that Power that pities me, / I learn to pity them.—GOLDSMITH. Pity makes the world / Soft to the weak and noble for the strong.—E. ARNOLD.   Pity and need make all flesh kin.—E. ARNOLD.   Pity is the deadliest feeling that can be offered to a woman.—V. BAUM.   Compassion will cure more sins than condemnation.—H. W. BEECHER. 914a. Is there no pity sitting in the clouds, / That sees into the bottom of my grief?—SHAKESPEARE.   The wretched have no compassion

pity etc. 914), incompassion [rare], inclemency, inexorability, inflexibility, hardness of heart; severity etc. 739; malevolence etc. 907; relentlessness etc. (revengefulness) 919.2.

2. *v.* be pitiless etc. *adj.*, have *or* show no mercy etc. 914, shut the gates of mercy, turn a deaf ear to, give no quarter, claim one's "pound of flesh" (Shakespeare).

3. *adj.* pitiless, unpitying, unpitiful; merciless, unmerciful; ruthless, bowelless, inclement, inexorable; uncompassionate, incompassionate [rare], uncompassioned; unsympathizing, unsympathetic; grimfaced, grim-visaged; harsh etc. (severe) 739.5; hardhearted, cruel etc. (heartless) 907.8, 9; relentless etc. (revengeful) 919.6.

915. Condolence

1. *n.* condolence, consolation, commiseration, sympathy; lamentation etc. 839.

2. *v.* condole, condole with, console, afford *or* supply consolation etc. *n.*, express *or* testify pity etc. 914, commiserate, send one's condolences, sympathize with, express sympathy for, feel for, feel grief *or* sorrow in common with, share one's sorrow; lament etc. 839.6 with.

916. Gratitude
(See 917. Ingratitude)

1. *n.* gratitude, gratefulness, thankfulness etc. *adj.*, feeling *or* sense of obligation, thankful good will.

2. *n.* thanksgiving, thanks, praise, benediction; grace, prayer of thanks; acknowledgment, recognition; thank offer-

---

—JOHNSON.   Shutteth up his bowels of compassion.—JOHNSON.   As ruthless as a baby with a worm.—TENNYSON.
915. Weep with them that weep.—BIBLE. This grief is crowned with consolation.—SHAKESPEARE.
916. Gratitude is the sign of noble souls.—AESOP.   Gratitude is a burden upon our imperfect nature.—CHESTERFIELD.   Gratitude is a fruit of great cultivation; you do not find it among gross people.—JOHNSON.   In everything give thanks.—BIBLE.   Thanks in old age—thanks ere I go / For health, the midday sun, the impalpable air—for life, mere life.—WHITMAN.   Evermore thanks, the exchequer of the poor.—SHAKESPEARE.   Great cause to give great thanks.—SHAKESPEARE.   They say late thanks are ever best.—BACON. Thanksgiving for a former doth invite God to bestow a second benefit.—HERRICK.   The

916.2 – 918.7

ing; paean, *Te Deum* [L.] etc. (glorification) 990.2.

3. *v.* be grateful etc. *adj.,* feel ~, be *or* lie under an obligation, *savoir gré* [F.], not look a gift horse in the mouth, never forget, overflow with gratitude, thank *or* bless one's stars; show gratitude etc. *n.,* thank, give ~, tender ~, render ~, return *or* offer thanks etc. *n.*; acknowledge, recognize; requite; fall on one's knees, get down on one's marrow bones [joc.].

4. *adj.* grateful, thankful, obliged, beholden, indebted to, under obligation.

5. *int.* thanks!, many thanks!, thank you!, gramercy!, much obliged!; *Deo gratias!* [L.], thank God!, thank Heaven!, Heaven be praised!, thanks be to God!, Glory be to God!

917. Ingratitude
(See 916. Gratitude)

1. *n.* ingratitude, ungratefulness, unthankfulness; oblivion of benefits, "benefits forgot" (Shakespeare); ingrate, thankless *or* ungrateful wretch.

2. *v.* be ungrateful etc. *adj.,* lack gratitude etc. 916, feel no obligation, owe one no thanks, forget benefits, look a gift horse in the mouth.

3. *adj.* ungrateful, ingrate, without gratitude etc. 916, unthankful, thankless, unmindful, insensible of benefits.

4. *adj.* unthanked, unacknowledged, unrequited, unrewarded, forgotten; ill-requited, ill-rewarded.

5. *int.* thank you for nothing!

918. Forgiveness
(See 919. Revenge)

1. *n.* forgiveness, pardon, excuse, condonation, grace, indulgence, oblivion, amnesty; indemnity, bill ~, act ~, covenant *or* deed of indemnity; absolution, remission, remission of sin *or* sins; forbearance, longanimity; long-suffering, long-sufferance [arch.]; exoneration, exculpation etc. (acquittal) 970.

2. *n.* conciliation, propitiation, placation etc. (pacification) 723; mollification etc. (modulation) 174.2; mediation etc. 724.

3. *v.* forgive, give *or* grant forgiveness etc. *n.,* forgive and forget, pardon, excuse, condone, forget an injury, think no more of, not give it another *or* a second thought, disregard, regard with indulgence, blink *or* wink at, connive at, let pass, pass over, overlook, ignore, close *or* shut one's eyes to, dismiss from one's thoughts *or* mind, let it go [coll.], let bygones be bygones, down all unkindness; bear with, endure, pocket the affront.

allow for, make allowances for; amnesty, grant amnesty to; remit, grant remission; absolve, give absolution, blot out one's sins, ~ offenses, ~ transgressions *or* debts, wipe the slate clean; not be hard upon, let one down easily; exonerate, exculpate etc. (acquit) 970.3; shake hands, bury the hatchet etc. (become reconciled) 723.5; forget etc. 506.4, 6.

4. *v.* conciliate, propitiate, placate etc. (pacify) 723.4; mollify etc. (moderate) 174.5; ask forgiveness etc. (apologize) 952.5.

5. *adj.* forgiving, placable, conciliatory; remissive, remissory [both rare]; unresentful, unrevengeful; longanimous, long-suffering; forbearing, forbearant; more in sorrow than in anger.

6. *adj.* forgiven, pardoned, excused etc. *v.*; unresented, unavenged, unrevenged, unpunished, unchastised, uncondemned; recommended to mercy.

7. *int.* forgive me!, excuse me!, pardon me!, I beg your pardon!, have mercy!, cry you mercy!, forgive and forget!

---

gratitude of place-expectants is a lively sense of future favours.—R. WALPOLE. When I'm not thanked at all I'm thanked enough.—FIELDING. Words are but empty thanks.—CIBBER. 917. Ingratitude! thou marble-hearted fiend.—SHAKESPEARE. How sharper than a serpent's tooth it is / To have a thankless child!—SHAKESPEARE. Thou art not so unkind / As man's ingratitude.—SHAKESPEARE. Too great haste to repay an obligation is a kind of ingratitude.—LA ROCHEFOUCAULD. 918. *Tout comprendre c'est tout pardonner* [To understand everything is to pardon everything].—MADAME DE STAËL. *Ignoscito saepe alteri*

---

nunquam tibi [Pardon the other person often, yourself never].—AUSONIUS. Father, forgive them; for they know not what they do.—BIBLE. Forgive us our debts as we forgive our debtors.—BIBLE. I pardon him as God shall pardon me.—SHAKESPEARE. To err is human, to forgive, divine.—POPE. Good, to forgive; / Best, to forget!—BROWNING. They who forgive most shall be the most forgiven.—P. J. BAILEY. It is sweeter to fancy we are forgiven than to think we have not sinned.—BALZAC.

919. Revenge
(See 918. Forgiveness)

1. *n.* revenge, revengement [rare], vengeance, avengement, *vindicta* [L.], sweet revenge; vendetta, blood *or* death feud, blood for blood; day of reckoning; reprisal, an eye for an eye; punishment etc. 972.

2. *n.* revengefulness, relentlessness, vindictiveness etc. *adj.*; vindictivolence, immitigability, implacability; rancor etc. (resentment) 900, (malevolence) 907; ruthlessness etc. (pitilessness) 914a; hatred etc. 898.

3. *n.* avenger, vindicator, Nemesis, Eumenides.

4. *v.* revenge, avenge, have one's revenge, take revenge, wreak one's vengeance *or* anger; fix, settle [both coll.]; give no quarter, take no prisoners; get even with [coll.], give an eye for an eye etc. (retaliate) 718.2; punish etc. 972.5.

5. *v.* be revengeful etc. *adj.*, harbor revenge *or* vindictive feeling, breathe vengeance *or* revenge, bear malice, have accounts to settle, have a crow to pluck *or* pick, have a rod in pickle; nurse one's revenge, keep the wound green, rankle, rankle in the breast, brood over, dwell on *or* upon.

6. *adj.* revengeful, vengeful, avenging etc. *v.*; vindictive, vindicatory; punitive, punitory; grudgeful [rare], Achillean, unforgiving, inexorable, implacable, immitigable, remorseless, rigorous, inflexible; relentless, unrelenting, retaliatory etc. 718.4; rancorous etc. (resentful) 900.12, (malevolent) 907.6-9; ill-disposed etc. 901.7-9; ruthless etc. (pitiless) 914a.3; heartless etc. 907.8, 9.

7. *adj.* rankling, festering, sore, *"aeternum servans sub pectore vulnus"* (Vergil).

920. Jealousy

1. *n.* jealousy, jealousness etc. *adj.*, heartburn, jaundiced eye, green in the eye [coll.]; "green-eyed jealousy," "green-eyed monster," "a monster begot upon itself, born on itself" (all Shakespeare); suspicion, jealous *or* envious suspicion, doubt, misdoubt, mistrust, distrust; envy etc. 921.

2. *v.* be jealous etc. *adj.*, have green in the eye [coll.], view with jealousy, view with a jealous *or* jaundiced eye, jealouse [obs. exc. Scot. and dial. Eng.]; suspect, doubt, misdoubt, mistrust, distrust; envy etc. 921.2.

3. *adj.* jealous, jaundiced, jaundice-eyed, yellow-eyed, green-eyed, yellow, green, green with jealousy, jealous as a Barbary pigeon, beside oneself with jealousy; envious etc. 921.3.

921. Envy

1. *n.* envy, enviousness etc. *adj.*, grudging; rivalry; *jalousie de métier* [F.]; ill will, spite; jealousy etc. 920.

2. *v.* envy, covet, break the tenth commandment, burst with envy, cast envious eyes *or* looks; grudge, begrudge; be jealous etc. 920.2.

3. *adj.* envious, envying etc. *v.*, invidious, covetous, beside oneself *or* bursting with envy; grudging, begrudging; *alieni appetens* [L.]; jealous etc. 920.3.

922. Right
(See 923. Wrong)

1. *n.* right, rightfulness etc. *adj.*, what is proper etc. *adj.*, what should be, what

---

919. Vengeance is mine; I will repay, saith the Lord.—BIBLE. Vengeance is not cured by another vengeance, nor a wrong by another wrong.—CHAUCER. To forget a wrong is the best revenge.—J. RAY. Revenge proves its own executioner.—J. FORD. A man that studieth revenge keeps his own wounds green.—BACON. Revenge is sweet.
920. Jealousy is cruel as the grave.—BIBLE. In jealousy there is more self-love than love.
—LA ROCHEFOUCAULD. O jealousy thou magnifier of trifles!—SCHILLER. Jealousy, at any rate, is one of the consequences of love; you may like it or not, at pleasure; but there it is.—STEVENSON. Anger and jealousy can no more bear to lose sight of their objects than love.—G. ELIOT. Love being jealous makes a good eye look asquint.—J. RAY. The ear of jealousy heareth all things.—APOCRYPHA. What frenzy dictates, jealousy believes.—J. GAY.
921. Envy is a pain of mind that successful men cause their neighbors.—ONASANDER. Sicilian tyrants never invented a greater torment than envy.—HORACE. Envy has no holidays.—BACON. Envy, which is proud weakness, and deserveth to be despised.—BACON. The green sickness.—SHAKESPEARE. Envy is the most corroding of the vices, and also the greatest power in any land.—BARRIE. The envious man shall never want woe.—CAMDEN.
922. One truth is clear, / Whatever is, is right.—POPE. Too fond of the Right to pursue the Expedient.—GOLDSMITH. Let us have faith

922.1 — 924.4

ought to be, the seemly, *to prepon* [Gr. τὸ πρέπον], the thing, the proper thing, the right *or* proper thing to do, propriety, decorum; *summum jus* [L.]; dueness etc. 924; fitness, suitability etc. (expedience) 646; truth etc. 494; good etc. 648.2; morals etc. (ethics) 926.4; probity etc. 939; justice etc. 941; virtue etc. 944; innocence etc. 946; authority etc. 737.

2. *n.* privilege, right, due, prerogative, droit [Law], power, grant, prescription, pretension, interest, title, claim, demand; birthright; vested right *or* interest; franchise, enfranchisement, affranchisement; immunity; license etc. (permission) 760.

3. *v.* right, right a wrong, make right etc. *adj.*, correct, rectify, remedy, redress, adjust, regulate, fix, put *or* set right *or* to rights, put *or* set straight, set up, make all square; restore etc. 660.8-12.

4. *v.* be right etc. *adj.*, stand to reason.

5. *adj.* right, rightful; correct, proper, right and proper, as it ought to *or* should be, good, just *or* quite the thing, up to the mark; right as a trivet, right as rain [coll.]; according to Cocker, ~ Gunter *or* Hoyle [coll.], *en règle* [F.], *selon les règles* [F.]; due etc. 924.9; fit, suitable, becoming etc. (expedient) 646.4; true, accurate etc. 494.9, 10; ethical etc. 926.12; upright etc. 939.7-9; fair etc. (just) 941.3; justifiable etc. (vindicable) 937.10; virtuous etc. 944.3, 4; innocent etc. 946.5; legal etc. 963.5; ethical etc. 926.12.

6. *adj.* absolute, positive, definite, dead to rights [slang, U.S.]; unchallenged, unchallengeable; unexceptionable, indefeasible, unalienable *or* inalienable, imprescriptible, unimpeachable, inviolable, sacrosanct.

7. *adv.* rightly, rightfully etc. *adj.*; as is right, ~ just *or* fitting, by right *or* rights, with good right, *à* or *au bon droit* [F.]; in justice, in equity, in reason; *de jure* [L.], *jure humano* [L.], ex officio; by divine right, *jure divino* [L.], *Dei gratia* [L.], by the grace of God; honor-

ably, justly etc. 939.11; duly etc. 924.12.

8. *int.* right!, all right! [coll.] etc. (affirmation) 535.8.

923. Wrong
(See 922. Right)

1. *n.* wrong, wrongfulness etc. *adj.*, impropriety, what ought not to be, what should not be; abomination, grievance, shame, scandal, disgrace; tort [Law]; *malum in se* [L.], *malum prohibitum* [L.]; undueness etc. 925; unfitness, unsuitability etc. (inexpedience) 647; error etc. 495; bad etc. (evil) 649.2; improbity etc. 940; injustice etc. 941a; vice etc. 945; illegality etc. 964.

2. *v.* wrong etc. (harm) 649.6.

3. *v.* be wrong etc. *adj.*, misbecome, **cry to heaven for vengeance.**

4. *adj.* wrong, wrongful; incorrect, improper, not the thing; tortious [Law]; in the wrong, in wrong *or* bad [slang], in the wrong box; undue etc. 925.8; unsuitable, inappropriate etc. (inexpedient) 647.3; bad etc. 649.8; dishonorable etc. 940.8; unjust, unjustifiable etc. 941a.3, 4; immoral etc. 945.11; reprehensible etc. (blameworthy) 932.14; illegal etc. 964.5.

5. *adv.* wrongly etc. *adj.*, wrong.

6. *int.* that's too bad!, it will not do!

924. Dueness
(See 925. Undueness)

1. *n.* dueness, due, entitlement; right, droit etc. (privilege) 922.2; justice etc. 941; fitness, suitability etc. (expedience) 646.

2. *n.* deserts, just deserts, merits, dues, due reward *or* punishment, comeuppance *or* comeuppings [coll., U.S.], comings [slang, U.S.], one's [slang], all that is coming to one [coll.].

3. *n.* warrant, sanction etc. (permit) 760.2; guaranty, bond etc. (security) 771.

4. *n.* claimant, appellant; plaintiff etc. 938.2.

---

that Right makes Might.—LINCOLN. With firmness in the right, as God gives us to see the right.—LINCOLN. God's in his heaven; / All's right with the world.—BROWNING. Our country, right or wrong, when right, to be kept right; when wrong, to be put right.—SCHURZ. The right is more precious than peace.—W. WILSON. A fool must now and then be right, by chance.—COWPER. None of us has **a patent on being right.**—M. TYDINGS.

923. Some kind of wrongs there are, which flesh and blood / Cannot endure.—BEAUMONT AND FLETCHER. Two wrongs do not make a right.
924. Render therefore unto Caesar the things which are Caesar's; and unto God the things that are God's.—BIBLE. Render therefore to all their dues.—BIBLE. Render unto all men their due, but remember thou art also a man.—TUPPER. Give the devil his due.

5. *v.* be due to etc. *adj.,* be the due of, be entitled to, have a right *or* title to, have a claim upon, have it coming [slang, U.S.]; be worthy of, merit, deserve, richly deserve.

6. *v.* get one's deserts, receive one's comeuppance [coll., U.S.] etc. *n.*; be rewarded etc. 973.4; be punished etc. 972.12.

7. *v.* demand, claim, lay claim to, demand *or* claim as one's due, call on *or* upon one for, come upon one for, appeal to for, require, exact, impose, lay under contribution; assert, vindicate a claim, ~ right *or* title; use a right, insist on *or* upon, make a point of, stand upon one's rights, take one's stand, challenge; enforce, put in force; make out a case; reclaim, revindicate, revendicate [rare]; arrogate etc. (assume) 925.6.

8. *v.* entitle, give *or* confer a right etc. 922.2; warrant, sanction etc. (grant) 760.4; legalize etc. 963.4.

9. *adj.* due, becoming, fit, appropriate etc. (expedient) 646.4; proper etc. (right) 922.5; just etc. 941.3.

10. *adj.* warranted, sanctioned, allowed, licensed, authorized, ordained, prescribed, chartered, enfranchised, constitutional; privileged, having ~, enjoying ~, honored *or* endowed with a privilege etc. 922.2; permissible etc. 760.6.

11. *adj.* due to, entitled to, with a right to, deserving, meriting, worthy of; deserved, richly deserved, merited, condign, coming [slang, U.S.]; owed, owing; attributable, ascribable.

12. *adv.* duly etc. *adj.,* as is one's due *or* dues etc. *n.*; as is right etc. (rightly) 922.7.

925. Undueness
(See 924. Dueness)

1. *n.* undueness, absence of right etc. 922, emptiness *or* invalidity of title; unfitness, unsuitability etc. (inexpedience) 647; wrong etc. 923; injustice etc. 941a; exorbitance, inordinacy etc. (redundance) 641.

2. *n.* loss of right, disentitlement, disfranchisement, disqualification; forfeiture etc. (loss) 776; deprivation etc. (dispossession) 789.2.

3. *n.* assumption, usurpation, arrogation, appropriation, adoption, seizure; encroachment, infringement, infraction, breach, violation; tort [Law]; exaction, imposition; lion's share, Benjamin's mess.

4. *n.* usurper, arrogator; pretender etc. (impostor) 548.3; tyrant etc. 739.3.

5. *v.* be undue etc. *adj.,* not be entitled to, have no right *or* title to, have no claim upon.

6. *v.* assume, usurp, arrogate; get under false pretenses, sail under false colors; encroach, infringe, trench on; violate, do violence to; stretch *or* strain a point, give an inch and take an ell; exact, impose; claim etc. (demand) 924.7; appropriate, seize etc. (take) 789.7-9.

7. *v.* disentitle, disfranchise, disqualify, invalidate; dispossess etc. 789.11.

8. *adj.* undue, unmeet, inappropriate, unsuitable etc. (inexpedient) 647.3; improper etc. (wrong) 923.4; unlawful etc. (illegal) 964.5; unjust, unjustifiable etc. 941a.3, 4; inordinate, excessive etc. (redundant) 641.5.

9. *adj.* unwarranted, unauthorized, unallowed, unsanctioned, unprivileged, unjustified, unentitled, unqualified, unchartered; undeserved, unmerited, unearned; out of the question, not to be thought of, preposterous.

10. *adj.* forfeited, forfeit, disentitled, disfranchised, disqualified; deprived of etc. (lost) 776.5, 6.

926. Duty
(See 927. Dereliction of Duty)

1. *n.* duty, what ought to be done, obligation, moral duty *or* obligation, liability, onus, responsibility, bounden *or* imperative duty, imperative, "stern daughter of the voice of God" (Wordsworth); accountableness etc. *adj.,* accountability, amenability; call of duty; function, calling etc. (business) 625.

2. *n.* performance, discharge ~, fulfillment *or* performance of duty, fulfillment, discharge, observance, acquittal, satisfaction, redemption.

3. *n.* conscience, sense of duty *or* right, grace, inward monitor, still small voice within; tender conscience; conscientiousness etc. 939.2.

4. *n.* ethics, morals, morality, morale;

926. Do the duty that lies nearest thee.—CARLYLE. When Duty whispers low, *Thou Must,* / The youth replies, *I can!*—EMERSON. Simple duty hath no place for fear.—WHITTIER. When stern Duty calls, I must obey.—GILBERT.

standard *or* rule of what is proper *or* fitting, propriety, decorum; standards, principles, moral principles; code, code of morals *or* ethics; Ten Commandments, decalogue; ethical ~, mental *or* moral philosophy, ethology, ethonomics, aretaics, aretology [obs.], deontology, casuistry; ethical *or* moral system, egoistic ~, hedonistic ~, eudaemonistic ~, altruistic ~, Christian ~, absolute ~, relative ~, social *or* professional ethics, comparative ethics, utilitarianism, perfectionism, Stoicism, evolutionism, intuitionism, empiricism; virtue etc. 944; right etc. 922.

5. *v.* be the duty of, be incumbent on, be responsible etc. *adj.*, be ~, stand *or* lie under an obligation etc. *n.*, stand responsible for, have to answer for, be answerable for, be bound to, be sponsor for; owe it to, owe it to oneself; behoove, become, befit, beseem; belong to, pertain to; fall to one's lot, devolve on, lie upon, lie on one's head, lie at one's door, rest with, rest on the shoulders of; incur a responsibility etc. *n.*, become bound to, become sponsor for.

6. *v.* take *or* accept the responsibility etc. *n.*, adhere to an obligation, answer for, answer the call of duty, take upon oneself, enter upon a duty, do duty, perform ~, observe ~, fulfill ~, discharge ~, acquit oneself of *or* satisfy a duty *or* an obligation, do ~, fulfill ~, perform *or* discharge one's duty, do the needful, be at one's post, act one's part, do justice to, acquit oneself, make good, redeem one's pledge.

7. *v.* impose a duty etc. *n.*, enjoin, require, exact, bind, bind over, saddle with, prescribe, assign, call on *or* upon, look to, oblige.

8. *adj.* dutiful, duteous; obedient etc. 743.3; compliant etc. (submissive) 725.5; reverent, deferential etc. (respectful) 928.8.

9. *adj.* obligatory, obligational [rare],

Duty is what one expects from others.—WILDE.
Responsibility prevents crimes.—BURKE.
Responsibility's like a string we can only see the middle of. Both ends are out of sight.—W. McFEE. Thus conscience does make cowards of us all.—SHAKESPEARE. No guilty man is acquitted at the bar of his own conscience.—JUVENAL. That little spark of celestial fire—conscience.—WASHINGTON. E'er you remark another's sin, / Bid your own conscience look within.—FRANKLIN. Whatever creed be taught or land be trod, / Man's conscience is the oracle of God.—BYRON.

obligationary [rare]; behooving etc. *v.*, incumbent on *or* upon, chargeable to; binding, imperative, peremptory; required etc. 630.3; stringent etc. (severe) 739.5.

10. *adj.* obliged etc. *v.*, under obligation, beholden, bounden, bound, duty-bound, in duty bound, saddled with, bound by, tied by, tied down; obliged to, beholden to, bound *or* bounden to, due to, indebted to; compromised etc. (promised) 768.7.

11. *adj.* amenable, liable, accountable, responsible, answerable, unexempt from.

12. *adj.* ethical, ethic [now rare], ethologic(al); moral, moralistic; casuistic(al); meet, befitting etc. (expedient) 646.4; right etc. 922.5; honorable, conscientious etc. (upright) 939.7–10; virtuous etc. 944.3, 4.

13. *adv.* dutifully etc. *adj.*, as in duty bound; on one's own responsibility, at one's own risk *or* peril, *suo periculo* [L.]; *in foro conscientiae* [L.], with one's conscience as judge *or* guide; *quamdiu se bene gesserit* [L.], on good behavior; at one's post.

927. Dereliction of Duty
(See 926. Duty)

1. *n.* dereliction of duty, dereliction, failure, nonobservance, nonperformance, nonfulfillment, non-co-operation; relaxation, laxity, laxness, looseness, slackness; eyeservice; dead letter; neglect etc. 460; evasion etc. 623; truancy, hooky etc. (nonattendance) 187.5; idleness, indolence etc. 683.2, 3; violation etc. (disobedience) 742; sin etc. (vice) 945.

2. *n.* shirker etc. 623.4; neglector etc. 460.3; idler etc. 683.7.

3. *v.* fail to perform, neglect etc. 460.4–7; idle, do nothing etc. 683.8; procrastinate, wait etc. 133.5, 7; avoid, shirk etc. 623.6–8; escape etc. 671.6; renounce etc. (recant) 607.9.

4. *v.* violate etc. (disobey) 742.4.

5. *adj.* undutiful, unduteous.

928. Respect
(See 929. Disrespect)

1. *n.* respect, regard, consideration, attention, deference, deferential *or* rever-

927. He trespasses against his duty who sleeps upon his watch, as well as he that goes over to the enemy.—BURKE.

ential regard, reverence, veneration, duty, homage, honor, esteem, estimation, admiration, awe; courtesy etc. 894; approbation etc. 931; devotion etc. (piety) 987; worship etc. 990.

2. *n.* obeisance, obedience [arch.], reverence, homage; bow, nod, bob, inclination, dip [arch.], curtsy, salaam, kowtow, leg [arch.], scrape, bowing and scraping; genuflection *or* genuflexion, kneeling, bending the knee; prostration; salute, salutation, presenting arms; obsequiousness etc. 886; greeting etc. 894.4; worship etc. 990.

3. *n.* respects, regards, *égards* [F.], duty [arch.], *devoirs* [F.], best *or* kind regards.

4. *v.* respect, entertain *or* bear respect for, regard, revere, reverence, hold in reverence, venerate, honor, esteem, admire, think much of, think well of, think highly of, have *or* hold a high opinion of, look up to, defer to, put on a pedestal; observe due decorum, stand upon ceremony; keep one's distance, make room; worship etc. 990.9; idolize etc. 991.6.

5. *v.* do *or* pay homage to, pay respect to, pay one's respects etc. *n.*, pay tribute to, pay attention to, do *or* render honor to, do the honors; salute, present arms; show courtesy etc. 894.7-10.

6. *v.* make obeisance, salaam, kowtow, make one's bow, bow, bow down, nod, incline ~, bend *or* bow the head, bend the neck, move to [dial. Eng.], bob, bob down, curtsy *or* curtsey, bob a curtsy, dip [arch.], scrape, make a leg [arch.], make a leg scrape, bow and scrape; genuflect, kneel, bow *or* bend the knee, get down on one's knees, get down on one's marrowbones [joc.], throw oneself on one's knees, fall on one's knees, fall down before, fall at the feet of, prostrate oneself, kiss the hem of one's garment.

7. *v.* command respect, inspire respect, impose, awe, overawe, awe-strike, strike with awe *or* admiration, take one's breath away, make one stare; dazzle, bedazzle, daze.

8. *adj.* respecting etc. *v.*, respectful, deferential, dutiful, decorous, attentive, ceremonious; reverent, reverential; venerative, venerant [rare], venerational; bareheaded, cap in hand; obeisant, prostrate, on one's knees, on one's marrowbones [slang], on bended knee; courteous etc. 894.12; obsequious etc. 886.4; worshipful etc. 990.15.

9. *adj.* respected, venerated, reverenced, revered etc. *v.*; in high esteem *or* estimation, estimable, honorable, honored; time-honored, venerable, august, emeritus; popular, well-liked; approved etc. 931.10.

10. *adv. etc.* in deference to, with due respect, with all respect, with the highest respect; with submission; excusing the liberty, saving your grace *or* presence, *salva sit reverentia* [L.]; *pace tanti nominis* [L.].

929. Disrespect
(See 928. Respect)

1. *n.* disrespect, disesteem, disestimation, disfavor, disrepute, dishonor, want of esteem etc. 928, low estimation, irreverence; discourtesy etc. 895; contempt etc. 930; insolence etc. 885.2; disparagement etc. (detraction) 934.

2. *n.* indignity, affront, offense, contumely, insult, uncomplimentary remark, left-handed *or* back-handed compliment, aspersion, brickbat [coll.], *"spretae injuria formae"* (Vergil), scurrility, flout, slap, slap in the face; outrage, atrocity; gibe, snub etc. 930.3, 4; personality etc. 934.2; malediction etc. 908; provocation etc. 900.5.

3. *v.* disrespect, show disrespect, treat with disrespect etc. *n.*, be disrespectful etc. *adj.*, dishonor, desecrate; insult, affront, offend, outrage, huff, hurl a brickbat [coll.], add insult to injury; slap in the face, take *or* pluck by the beard; trifle with, make bold *or* free with, take a

---

928. Nothing is good, I see, without respect.—SHAKESPEARE. Whereby we may serve God acceptably with reverence and godly fear.—BIBLE. Deference is the most complicate, the most indirect, and the most elegant of all compliments.—SHENSTONE. Homage is due to kings; they do what they like.—LOUIS XIV. A prophet is not without honour, save in his own country, and in his own house.—BIBLE. There is an admiration which is the daughter of knowledge.—JOUBERT.

929. The spirits of the wise sit in the clouds and mock us.—SHAKESPEARE. A moral, sensible, and well-bred man / Will not affront me, and no other can.—COWPER. His honor rooted in dishonor stood.—TENNYSON. Nothing is left which I can venerate.—WORDSWORTH. An injury is much sooner forgiven than an insult.—CHESTERTON. This is adding insult to injuries.—E. MOORE.

liberty; humiliate, set down; speak slightingly of, slight, vilipend, vilify, call names, indulge in personalities, take a name in vain; throw *or* fling dirt, throw mud at, drag through the mud, bespatter; make faces, make mouths [arch.]; point at, bite the thumb; laugh in one's sleeve; toss in a blanket, tar and feather, make ride the rail, browbeat; be discourteous etc. 895.4; disparage etc. 934.3; treat with contempt, snub etc. 930.5–7; be insolent etc. 885.7.

4. *v.* hold in disrespect etc. (be contemptuous of) 930.5.

5. *adj.* disrespectful, awless *or* aweless, irreverent; insulting etc. *v.*, insolent, contumelious; backhand, backhanded, left-handed; scurrile, scurrilous; rude etc. (discourteous) 895.6; disdainful etc. (contemptuous) 930.8; disparaging etc. 934.4; derisive etc. 856.7.

6. *adj.* unrespected, unworshiped, unenvied, unsaluted; unregarded, disregarded.

930. Contempt

1. *n.* contempt, disdain, scorn, despect [rare], contumely, sovereign contempt; despisal, despisement [both rare]; despisedness, contemptuousness etc. *adj.*; scornful eye; arrogance, insolence etc. 885; disrespect etc. 929; indifference etc. 866; byword of reproach etc. 874.3.

2. *n.* scoffing etc. *v.*, derision, irrision [rare], ridicule, mockery; sarcasm, satire, irony, cynicism; sibilation, hiss, hissing; contemptuous *or* derisive cry, hoot, catcall; Bronx cheer, raspberry, razz [all slang, U.S.]; pooh, pooh-pooh; smile of contempt, scornful laugh *or* smile, snicker *or* snigger; raillery etc. 856; disparagement etc. (detraction) 934; impiety etc. 988; disapprobation etc. 932.

3. *n.* gibe *or* jibe, scoff, flout, jeer, fleer, sneer, mock, taunt, derisive taunt, quip, fling, twit, wipe [dial. and slang], jab [slang], rap [slang, U.S.], slam [coll.], dig [coll.], cut, cutting remark, verbal thrust; scurrility, scurrilous remark; gibing retort, rude reproach, short answer, back answer, comeback [slang];
insult etc. (indignity) 929.2; personality etc. 934.2; retort etc. (answer) 462.

4. *n.* snub, rebuff, slight, spurn, the go-by [slang]; cut, cut direct, the cold shoulder [all coll.]; insolence etc. 885.2; disregard etc. (neglect) 460.

5. *v.* be contemptuous of etc. *adj.*, disdain, despise, contemn, scorn, view with a scornful eye, feel contempt for, hold in contempt *or* disrespect, hold cheap, look down upon, think nothing of, think small beer of [coll.], make little *or* light of, esteem slightly, esteem of small *or* no account, take no account of, care nothing for, set no store by, not care a straw about, set at nought, snap one's fingers at, sneeze at, spit upon; shrug one's shoulders, toss the head; misprize, disprize, spurn, scout, reject with disdain *or* contempt, scorn to receive *or* accept; treat with contempt *or* disdain, *traiter de haut en bas* [F.]; tread *or* trample upon, tread *or* trample underfoot; treat with disrespect etc. 929.3.

6. *v.* scoff, barrack [dial. Eng. and Austral.], gibe *or* jibe, jeer, mock, mob [dial. Eng.], revile, flout, scout, gird, niggle, twit, taunt, cast in one's teeth, give one a wipe [dial. and slang], have a fling at; deride, have *or* hold in derision, hold up to scorn, point at, point the finger of scorn; ridicule, turn into ridicule, make game *or* fun of, poke fun at, laugh at, laugh in one's sleeve, laugh to scorn, snicker *or* snigger; fleer, grin at, grin in scorn; sneer, curl up one's lip; hiss, hoot, catcall; give the raspberry *or* Bronx cheer, razz [both slang, U.S.], whistle at; pooh, pooh-pooh; banter etc. 856.4; disparage etc. 934.3; blaspheme etc. 988.7.

7. *v.* snub, rebuff, put one in his place [coll.], show one his place; high-hat, high-brow, upstage [all slang]; look cool *or* coldly upon, look down one's nose at, turn up one's nose at; cold-shoulder, turn a cold shoulder upon, give *or* turn the shoulder [all coll.]; spurn, turn one's back upon, turn away from, turn on one's heel, set one's face against, slam the door in one's face, send away with a flea in the

---

930. As the air to a bird or the sea to a fish, so is contempt to the contemptible.—W. BLAKE. Contempt will sooner kill an injury than revenge.—H. G. BOHN. It is easy to despise what you cannot get.—AESOP. A dismal universal hiss, the sound of public scorn.—MILTON.

Scorn tempering wrath, yet anger sharpening scorn.—SOUTHEY. Damn with faint praise, assent with civil leer, / And without sneering, teach the rest to sneer.—POPE. The poorest way to face life is to face it with a sneer.—T. ROOSEVELT. Familiarity breeds contempt.

ear [coll.]; cut [coll.], cut dead [slang].
    refuse to acknowledge *or* recognize, slight, disregard, neglect, ignore, pass by, pass up [slang, U.S.], give the go-by [slang], push aside, overlook, take no note *or* notice of, pay no attention *or* regard to, leave in *or* out in the cold [coll.]; avoid, keep one's distance, steer clear of [coll.], dodge, shun, have no truck with [coll. and dial.]; draw the color line [coll.]; keep at a distance, keep at arm's length; tread *or* trample upon, tread *or* trample underfoot; be insolent etc. 885.7.

8. *adj.* contemptuous, disdainful, scornful, withering, contumelious; sarcastic(al), ironic(al), sardonic(al), satiric(al), cynical; supercilious, haughty etc. (arrogant) 885.8; derisive etc. 856.7; disrespectful etc. 929.5.

9. *adj.* contemptible, despicable etc. (bad) 649.8; pitiful etc. (paltry) 643.12.

10. *adv.* contemptuously etc. *adj.*, in *or* with contempt etc. *n.*, "with scoffs, and scorns, and contumelious taunts" (Shakespeare); with curling lip, with a sneer; arrogantly, insolently etc. 885.11.

11. *int.* bah!, pooh!, poo!, phoo!, pho *or* phoh! [rare], poof!, phoey! [coll.], pooh-pooh!, pish!, pish-pash!, pugh!, pshaw!, tut!, fiddledeedee!, fiddlesticks! [coll.], in your hat! [slang], a fig for!, away with!; come off!, come off of it [both slang].

931. Approbation
(See 932. Disapprobation)

1. *n.* approbation, approval, sanction; nod, nod of approval *or* approbation; good opinion, "golden opinions" (Shakespeare); admiration, appreciation, regard; esteem, estimation; assent etc. 488; consent etc. 762; self-approbation etc. (vanity) 880; love etc. 897; popularity etc. (repute) 873.

2. *n.* commendation, praise, bepraisement; glorification, glory; laud, laudation; good word, tribute *or* meed of praise; encomium, panegyric, blurb [slang]; eulogy, *éloge* [F.], eulogium; honor, homage, hero worship; benediction, invocation, blessing, benison; recommendation, advocacy; flattery etc. 933; overpraise etc. (overestimation) 482; celebration etc. 883; commender etc. 935.

3. *n.* compliment, polite commendation, complimentary *or* flattering remark; bouquet, posy [both coll.]; trade-last, T.L. [both slang]; hollow commendation etc. (flattery) 933.

4. *n.* applause, plaudit; clap, handclap, clapping, hand clapping, clapping of hands; acclaim, acclamation; paean, hosanna, hallelujah, alleluia; shout ∼, chorus ∼, peal *or* thunder of applause; cheer etc. 838.4.

5. *v.* approve, approbate, be in favor of, sanction, countenance, keep in countenance, indorse *or* endorse, O.K. [coll.], accredit, give credit, mark with a white mark *or* stone; uphold, hold up, stand up for, stick up for [coll.]; think good ∼, well ∼, much *or* highly of, appreciate, value, prize, set great store by, esteem, hold in esteem, honor, look up to, admire; hail, hail with satisfaction; clap *or* pat on the back, wish Godspeed; assent etc. 488.6; consent etc. 762.2; like etc. 897.11.

6. *v.* commend, express commendation etc. *n.*, pay tribute; laud, belaud; praise, bepraise; acclaim, acclamate [rare]; compliment, pay a compliment etc. *n.*, give a bouquet *or* posy [coll.]; panegyrize, panygyricize; eulogize, puff, extol, extol to the skies, magnify, glorify, exalt, swell, make much of, do proud [coll.], boost [coll., U.S.], root for [slang, U.S.], cry up, *prôner* [F.]; bless, give a blessing to; have *or* say a good word for, put in a good word for, speak well *or* highly of, speak in high terms of; applaud, clap, clap the hands, encore, cheer *or* applaud to the very echo; sing ∼, chant ∼, sound *or* resound the praises of, sing praises to; recommend, advocate; cheer etc. 838.8; flatter etc. 933.2; overpraise etc. (overestimate) 482.3; celebrate etc. 883.3.

---

931. *Tacent satis laudant* [Their silence is praise enough].—TERENCE.   You can tell the character of every man when you see how he receives praise.—SENECA.   Out of the mouth of babes and sucklings thou hast perfected praise.—BIBLE.   How his silence drinks up this applause!—SHAKESPEARE.   A fool always finds a bigger fool to admire him.—BOILEAU.   Praise like gold and diamonds owes its value only to scarcity.—JOHNSON.   Praise undeserv'd is scandal in disguise.—POPE.   The silence that accepts merit as the most natural thing in the world, is the highest applause.—EMERSON.   We ask advice, but we mean approbation.—C. COLTON.   There's no weapon that slays its victim so surely (if well aimed) as praise.—BULWER-LYTTON.

7. *v.* be praiseworthy etc. *adj.*, deserve praise etc. *n.*, deserve, recommend itself, pass muster; redound to the honor, ∼ praise *or* credit of, do credit to.

8. *v.* be praised etc., receive honorable mention, be in favor *or* high favor with, ring with the praises of, win golden opinions, gain credit, find favor with, stand well in the opinion of; *"laudari a laudato viro"* (Cicero).

9. *adj.* approbatory, approbative; commendatory, complimentary, benedictory, laudatory, panegyrical *or* panegyric, eulogistic(al), encomiastic(al), acclamatory; approving etc. *v.*, in favor of, lost in admiration, lavish of praise; uncritical, uncensorious, unreproachful; flattering etc. 933.3.

10. *adj.* approved etc. *v.*, uncensured, unimpeached; in favor, in good odor, in good *or* right [slang, U.S.], in one's good books; in high favor, in high esteem *or* estimation, popular, well-liked; respected etc. 928.9.

11. *adj.* praiseworthy, worthy of praise *or* estimation etc. *n.*, worthy, commendable, laudable, estimable, admirable, meritorious, creditable, unimpeachable, beyond all praise, *sans peur et sans reproche* [F.]; deserving, desertful [rare]; good etc. 648.8; virtuous etc. 944.3, 4.

12. *adv.* commendably etc. *adj.*, with credit, to admiration, with three times three; well etc. 648.14.

13. *int.* bravo!, *bravissimo!* [It.], hear, hear!, aha!, good!, fine!, bully for you! [slang], good for you!, good enough!, so much the better!, do it again!, well done!, euge! [rare], *macte virtute* [L.], so far so good!, that's right!, quite right!, one cheer more!, *viva!* [It.], *vivat!* [L. and F.], *evviva!* [It.], *valete et plaudite!* [L.], encore!, *bis!* [L. and F.]; hurrah! etc. 838.12; may your shadow never be less! etc. (hail) 894.15.

932. Disapprobation
(See 931. Approbation)

1. *n.* disapprobation, disapproval, disesteem, displacency [rare], discountenance [now rare], opposition; objection, exception, rejection, veto; discommendation, dispraise, disvaluation; dislike etc. 867; disparagement, depreciation etc. (detraction) 934; derision, sneer etc. (contempt) 930; nonassent etc. (dissent) 489; noncompliance etc. (refusal) 764; malediction etc. 908; disrepute etc. 874.

2. *n.* censure, reprehension, blame, faultfinding, criticism, animadversion, stricture, obloquy; knock [slang, U.S.], hit [coll.], slam [coll.], rap [slang], home thrust; reflection, imputation, insinuation, innuendo; reprobation, condemnation; denunciation, denouncement; censorship; boycott, boycottage; black list, blackball; hypercriticism, overcriticalness, hairsplitting; accusation etc. 938; censor etc. (detractor) 936.

3. *n.* reproof, reproval; reprimand, rebuke, reproach, reprehension, increpation [arch.], objurgation, exprobration, rating, berating, scolding, chiding, upbraiding, jawing [slang], nagging, hearing [Scot.], castigation, chastisement [obs. exc. dial.], correction, setdown; admonishment, admonition; lecture, curtain lecture; remonstrance, expostulation.

piece *or* bit of one's mind, jobation, tongue-lashing, blowup, blowingup, trimming, wigging, speaking-to, talking-to, roasting, raking, raking-down, dressing, dressing-down [all coll.]; ragging, grooming, going-over, calling-down, jacking-up, bawling-out, lick with the rough side of the tongue, what-for [all slang]; revilement, abuse, vituperation, invective, contumely, hard ∼, cutting *or* bitter words; diatribe, jeremiad, tirade, philippic; rap on the knuckles etc. (punishment) 972.3.

4. *n.* reproving look, dirty *or* nasty look [slang], black look, frown, scowl.

5. *v.* disapprove, not approve etc. 931.5, object to, take exception to, think ill of, *nil admirari* [L.], view with disfavor, view with dark *or* jaundiced eyes, frown at *or* upon, look black upon, view with an evil eye, look askance *or* askant at, shrug the shoulders, turn up the nose at, set one's face against, frown down; make

---

932. Few are wise enough to prefer useful reproof to treacherous praise.—LA ROCHEFOUCAULD. Who reproves the lame must go upright.—S. DANIEL. Of whom to be disprais'd were no small praise.—MILTON. Compound for sins they are inclined to / By damning those they have no mind to.—R. BUTLER. Censure is the tax a man pays to the public for being eminent.—SWIFT. It is much easier to be critical than to be correct.—DISRAELI. We are not amused.—QUEEN VICTORIA.

a wry face at, make a mouth at [arch.]; not countenance, discountenance; disallow, reject, veto, negative, say no to, shake the head at, not hear to; be scandalized at, revolt at, revolt from the idea; have no notice of, not have the least idea of; object, protest, kick [coll.]; demur, scruple, boggle; not consent etc. (dissent) 489.4, (refuse) 764.2, 3; scoff at etc. 930.6; dislike etc. 867.4.

6. *v.* discommend, dispraise, deprecate, disvalue, not be able to say much for; disparage, depreciate etc. (detract) 934.3.

7. *v.* censure, reprehend, *fronder* [F.], pass censure on, criticize, knock [coll., U.S.], slam [coll.], rap [slang], find fault with, faultfind, cut up, pull *or* pick to pieces, pick a hole in one's coat, "hint a fault and hesitate dislike" (Pope), criticize adversely, animadvert on *or* upon, reflect upon, cast reflection upon, cast a reproach *or* slur upon; blame, lay *or* cast blame upon, reproach, impugn; recriminate.

throw a stone at, cast *or* throw the first stone; reprobate, hold up to reprobation; condemn, damn, "damn with faint praise" (Pope); denounce, denunciate; decry, cry down, exclaim ∼, declaim ∼, protest *or* inveigh against, cry out against, cry shame upon, raise one's voice against, raise a hue and cry against, clamor, be outspoken, make a fuss about; boycott, black-list, blackball, draw up *or* sign a round robin; carp, cavil, quibble, wrangle, peck at, nibble at, accuse etc. 938.4; complain etc. 839.10.

8. *v.* reprove, rebuke, reprimand, reprehend, admonish, chide, upbraid, exprobrate, objurgate, scold, rate, berate, betongue, jaw [slang], lecture, read a lesson *or* lecture to, bring *or* call to account *or* order, bring to book, take to task, tell one plainly *or* once for all, correct, castigate, chastise [obs. exc. dial.], lash, trounce, overhaul, rail at, rail at in good set terms, bark *or* yelp at, rave against, thunder *or* fulminate against, load with reproaches, have words with, pick *or* pluck a crow with, have a fling *or* snap at, snap one up, take up, take down, set down.

remonstrate, expostulate; speak *or* talk to, give a piece *or* bit of one's mind, give one a lick with the rough side of the tongue, tongue-lash, roast, rake *or* haul over the coals, blow up, pull up, give it to, give one fits, trim, strafe, score, lay out [all coll.]; call down, rag, groom, give what-for, give a going-over [all slang]; bawl out, jack up [both slang, U.S.]; revile, abuse, vituperate, clapper-claw [arch. and dial.], speak daggers, abuse like a pickpocket; vilify, execrate etc. (maledict) 908.4; give a rap on the knuckles etc. (punish) 972.6.

9. *v.* incur blame, excite disapprobation, get a bad name, forfeit one's good opinion, be under a cloud, come under the ferule, bring a hornet's nest about one's ears; scandalize, shock, revolt.

10. *v.* take the blame, bear the blame *or* responsibility, hold the bag *or* sack [coll.], take the rap for [crim. slang, U.S.], take *or* accept the responsibility, stand corrected, have to answer for.

11. *adj.* disapprobatory, disapproving etc. *v.*; censorious, critical, "nothing if not critical" (Shakespeare), blameful, faultfinding, carping, caviling, captious, sparing of *or* grudging praise; hypercritical, over-critical, hairsplitting; condemnatory, damnatory, denunciatory, reproachful, objurgatory; abusive, vituperative, satirical, sardonic(al), sarcastic(al), ironic(al), cynical; dry, sharp, cutting, biting, severe, withering, trenchant, hard upon; defamatory etc. (disparaging) 934.4.

12. *adj.* disapproved, unapproved; in bad odor, in one's black books, in disfavor; in bad *or* wrong, in the doghouse [both slang, U.S.]; blown upon, exploded, weighed in the balance and found wanting, unblest, at a discount; unlamented, unpitied.

13. *adj.* unpraiseworthy, illaudable; uncommendable, discommendable; objectionable, exceptionable, not to be thought of; unworthy etc. 940.9.

14. *adj.* blameworthy, blamable, worthy of blame, to blame, reprehensible, culpable, chargeable, impeachable, answerable, imputable, accusable, censurable, reprovable, faulty [now rare]; unjustifiable etc. 941a.4; bad etc. 649.8; vicious etc. 945.11–19; guilty etc. 947.4; wrong etc. 923.4.

15. *adv.* reproachfully etc. *adj.*, with a wry face.

16. *int.* it won't do!, it will never do!, it isn't done!, it is too bad!, that's too bad!, marry come up! [arch. or dial.], Oh, come!, 'sdeath! [arch.], *O tempora!*

O mores! [L.], tell it not in Gath!; forbid it Heaven!, God forbid!, Heaven forbid!; away with!, out on you!, out upon it!, fie upon it!, fie upon!, fie!, tut!, shame!, fie for shame!, it smells to heaven!

933. Flattery
(See 934. Detraction)

1. *n.* flattery, wheedling etc. *v.*, adulation, gloze [rare], cajolery, captation, coquetry, blandiloquence [rare], suaviloquence [rare], incense, fair ∼, sweet *or* honeyed words, soft *or* honeyed phrases, "that flattering unction" (Shakespeare), pretty lies, hollow commendation, empty encomium, flummery; soft sawder, soft soap, sawder, soap, butter, salve, taffy, blarney, buncombe *or* bunkum [all coll.]; bunk, oil, grease, eyewash [all slang]; mouth honor, lip homage *or* service.

voice of the charmer, flattering tongue; unctuousness, mealymouthedness etc. *adj.*; euphemism, euphemy [rare]; fawning, sycophancy etc. (servility) 886; praise, compliment etc. (approbation) 931; overpraise etc. (overestimation) 482; exaggeration etc. 549; insincerity etc. (dissemblance) 544.2; flatterer etc. 935.2.

2. *v.* flatter, lay the flattering unction to one's soul, oil the tongue, adulate, wheedle, cajole, coax, glaver [obs. exc. dial.], gloze [now rare], humor, soothe, pet, coquet, slaver, beslaver, bespatter, beslubber, beplaster, pat on the back, puff, commend lavishly, praise to the skies, fool to the top of one's bent; do one proud, pull one's leg, sawder, soft-sawder, softsoap, butter, honey, jolly, blarney, lay it on, lay it on thick [all coll.]; lay it on with a trowel, string, string along, honeyfogle [U.S.], oil, soap [all slang]; make things pleasant, gild the pill.

---

933. Bring no more vain oblations; incense is an abomination unto me.—BIBLE.   There is no greater bane to friendship than adulation, fawning, and flattery.—CICERO.   But when I tell him he hates flatterers, / He says he does, being then most flattered.—SHAKESPEARE.   Lay not that flattering unction to your soul.—SHAKESPEARE.   He that loves to be flattered is worthy o' the flatterer.—SHAKESPEARE.   Just praise is only a debt, but flattery is a present.—JOHNSON.   We love flattery even though we are not deceived by it.—EMERSON.   What really flatters a man is that you think him worth flattering.—SHAW.

curry favor, fawn upon, truckle to etc. (sycophancy) 886.3; praise, compliment etc. (commend) 931.6; overpraise etc. (overestimate) 482.3; exaggerate etc. 549.2.

3. *adj.* flattering, wheedling etc. *v.*; adulatory, fine-spoken, fair-spoken, specious, plausible, fulsome, honeyed, honey-tongued, honeymouthed, mealymouthed, smooth, smooth-tongued, smooth-spoken, soapy [slang], buttery [coll.], oily, oily-tongued, suaviloquent [rare], bland; blandiloquous, blandiloquious [both rare]; unctuous, unctious, unctional; courtierly, courtierlike; fawning, sycophantic etc. (servile) 886.4; complimentary etc. (approbatory) 931.9; insincere etc. (dissembling) 544.8.

4. *adv.* flatteringly etc. *adj., ad captandum* [L.].

934. Detraction
(See 933. Flattery; also 936. Detractor)

1. *n.* detraction, disparagement, depreciation, derogation, defamation, vilification, obloquy, scurrility, aspersion, slur, traducement [rare], invective, contumely, evilspeaking, envenomed tongue; slander, *scandalum magnatum* [L.]; calumny, calumniation; backbiting; discommendation, criticism etc. (disapprobation) 932; malediction etc. 908; derision etc. (ridicule) 856; sarcasm etc. (scoffing) 930.2; disrespect etc. 929; underestimation etc. 483; accusation etc. 938; scandal etc. 532.4; detractor etc. 936.

2. *n.* personality, personal remark, libel, lampoon, skit [Scot. and dial.], squib, pasquil, pasquinade, *chronique scandaleuse* [F.], roorback [U.S.]; insult etc. (indignity) 929.2; gibe etc. 930.3; malediction etc. 908.

3. *v.* detract, derogate, decry, depreciate, discredit, disparage, run down [coll.], cry down, backcap [U.S.], belittle, traduce, asperse, cast aspersions, slur, cast a slur; blow upon, vilipend, vilify, malign, slander, libel, calumniate, defame, bear

---

934. Ill-will never said well.—SHAKESPEARE.   Scandal has ever been the doom of beauty.—PROPERTIUS.   Hurl your calumnies boldly; something is sure to stick.—BACON.   Cut men's throats with whisperings.—JONSON.   Hear no ill of a friend, nor speak any of an enemy.—FRANKLIN.   The world delights to tarnish shining names.—SCHILLER.   To speak no slander, no, nor listen to it.—TENNYSON.

false witness against, not speak well of, speak slightingly *or* ill of; speak ill of behind one's back, backbite; give a bad name, give a dog a bad name; satirize, lampoon, dip the pen in gall; expose, expose to infamy, gibbet; muckrake, throw mud at, throw *or* fling dirt at, drag through the mud, bespatter; degrade, debase, bring low, put *or* take down; take down a peg, take down a peg or two [both coll.].

blacken etc. (stigmatize) 874.7; anathematize etc. (maledict) 908.4; sneer at etc. (scoff) 930.6; discommend, criticize etc. 932.6, 7; underestimate etc. 483.3; dishonor, insult etc. (be disrespectful) 929.3; deride etc. (ridicule) 856.4.

4. *adj.* detracting, disparaging etc. *v.*; detractory, derogatory, defamatory, damnatory, contumelious, traducent [rare], libelous, slanderous, abusive, vilipenditory; calumnious, calumniatory; scurrile, scurrilous; maledictory etc. 908.6; critical, sarcastic etc. (disapprobatory) 932.11; derisive etc. 856.7; insulting etc. (disrespectful) 929.5.

935. Commender
(See 936. Detractor)

1. *n.* commender, eulogist, eulogizer; lauder, laudator; praiser, extoller, encomiast, panegyrist, booster [coll., U.S.], puffer, *prôneur* [F.] *or* proneur; applauder, claquer, *claqueur* [F.]; tout, touter [both coll.]; optimist etc. 858.5.

2. *n.* flatterer, *flatteur* [F.], flattercap [obs. exc. dial. Eng.], adulator, cajoler, wheedler, slaverer, courtier, backslapper, back-scratcher, clawback [obs. exc. dial.], pickthank [arch. and dial.]; blarneyer, soft-soaper, soft-sawderer [all coll.]; Damocles, Sir Pertinax MacSycophant; fawner, toady etc. (sycophant) 886.2.

936. Detractor
(See 935. Commender; also 934. Detraction)

1. *n.* detractor, depreciator, disparager, derogator, knocker [coll., U.S.], barracker [dial. Eng. and Austral.]; defamer, slanderer, libeler, muckraker, calumniator, traducer; dearest foe, good-natured friend [iron.]; backbiter, Sir Benjamin Backbite; satirist, lampooner, pasquinader; faultfinder, *frondeur* [F.], censor, censurer, cynic, critic, caviler, carper, word-catcher; disapprover, *"laudator temporis acti"* (Horace); Zoilus, Thersites; scandalmonger etc. 532.5; pessimist etc. 859.4.

2. *n.* reprover, rebuker, chider, castigator; scold, common scold; reviler, vituperator; shrew etc. 901.4; reprimander etc. (*see* reprimand etc. 932.8).

937. Vindication
(See 938. Accusation)

1. *n.* vindication, justification, warrant; exculpation, disculpation, exoneration, clearance; acquittal etc. 970.

2. *n.* defense *or* defence, statement of defense, argument; plea, pleading; justification, excuse, alibi [coll.], salvo [now rare]; *tu quoque* argument; *argumentum ad hominem* [L.]; denial, objection, exception; demurrer, general *or* special demurrer [all Law]; faulty defense, false plea, lame excuse; apology etc. 952.2; pretext etc. 619; rebuttal, reply etc. (answer) 462; special pleading etc. (sophistry) 477; recrimination etc. (accusation) 938; counterevidence etc. 468.

3. *n.* extenuation, palliation, softening, mitigation; extenuative, palliative; whitewash, whitewashing; gloss, varnish,

---

935. *Pessimum genus inimicorum laudantes.* [The flatterers are the worst kind of enemies]. TACITUS.   Every flatterer lives at the expense of the person who listens to him.—LA FONTAINE.   When flatterers meet, the devil goes to dinner.—J. RAY.   Flatterers make cream cheese of chalk.—HOOD.   A flatterer can risk everything with great personages.—LE SAGE.
936. An evil-speaker differs from an evil-doer only in opportunity.—QUINTILIAN.   The most dangerous of wild beasts is a slanderer; of tame ones, a flatterer.—H. G. BOHN.   He that praiseth publicly will slander privately.—FULLER.   Who by aspersions throw a stone / At th' head of others, hit their own.—G. HERBERT.   He who blackens others does not whiten himself.—SANDBURG.   Rebuke backbiters, and encourage them not by hearkening to their tales.—S. BAGSTER.
937. Excuses are no better than accusations.—MONTAIGNE.   Never make a defence or apology before you be accused.—KING CHARLES I.   An excuse is a lie guarded.—SWIFT.   Better a bad excuse, than none at all.—CAMDEN.   I do not trouble my spirit to vindicate itself or

color; allowance, qualification; extenuating circumstances; loophole etc. 671.4.

4. *n.* vindicator, justifier, advocate, proponent, defender; apologist, apologizer, apologete; defendant etc. 938.3.

5. *v.* vindicate, justify, warrant, give sufficient grounds *or* good reasons for, serve as *or* provide justification for, be justified by the event, prove *or* show to be just, prove the truth of, prove one's case; furnish a handle, provide a loophole etc. 671.4; excuse, be an excuse for etc. *n.*; exculpate, disculpate, exonerate, clear, clear the skirts of, set right; acquit etc. 970.3.

6. *v.* offer as justification etc. *n.*, justify, present an answer *or* pleading in defense of, defend, offer *or* make a defense, offer *or* say in defense, allege in support *or* vindication, support, uphold, sustain, maintain.

claim [coll.], assert, advocate, champion, espouse, stand up for, stick up for [coll.], speak up for, contend for, speak for, put in a good word for, plead for, make a plea, offer as a plea, plead one's cause, argue for, urge reasons for; excuse, alibi [coll.], offer excuse for, offer *or* give as an excuse; endeavor *or* seek to remove blame from, seek indulgence for, seek to extenuate, seek exemption *or* release; plead ignorance; confess and avoid.

7. *v.* apologize for, make apology for; express regret etc. 952.5.

8. *v.* extenuate, palliate, soften, mince; cover with excuses, conceal *or* disguise the enormity of, slur, varnish, gloze [rare], gloss over, put a gloss upon, put a good face upon, whitewash, color, lend a color to; allow for, make allowance for, take the will for the deed, do justice to, give the Devil his due.

9. *adj.* vindicative, vindicatory, justificatory; vindicating, justifying, excusing etc. *v.*; apologetic(al); exculpatory, disculpatory; extenuating, extenuative, palliative.

10. *adj.* vindicable, justifiable, excusable, pardonable, expiable, remissible, venial; defensible, warrantable, allowable, reasonable, legitimate; unobjectionable, inoffensive; unblamable etc. (inculpable) 946.6; right etc. 922.5.

---

be understood, / I see that the elementary laws never apologize.—WHITMAN. *Qui s'excuse, s'accuse* [He who excuses himself, accuses himself].

938. Accusation
(See 937. Vindication)

1. *n.* accusation, accusal, condemnation, inculpation, blame, charge, imputation, reproach, slur, exprobration [rare], delation, complaint, attack, taxing, challenge; denunciation, denouncement; crimination, incrimination; recrimination, retort, countercharge; impeachment, arraignment, indictment; bill of indictment, true bill; allegation, allegation of fact; trumped-up charge, put-up job [slang], frame *or* frame-up [slang]; gravamen of a charge; censure, reproof etc. 932.2, 3; slander, libel etc. (detraction) 934; lawsuit etc. 969.

2. *n.* accuser, accusant, accusatrix [*fem.*]; suitor, party to a suit, prosecutor, plaintiff, complainant, claimant, appellant, libelant, delator; informant, informer etc. 527.5, 6.

3. *n.* accused, defendant, prisoner, respondent, correspondent, libelee, litigant; panel, parties litigant; defender etc. (vindicator) 937.4.

4. *v.* accuse, bring accusation, lodge a complaint, charge with an offense, prefer charges, charge, challenge, tax, attack, impute, implicate, inculpate, condemn, place to one's account, hang *or* pin something on [slang]; denounce, denunciate; criminate, incriminate; impeach, arraign, indict; blame, place *or* fix the blame *or* responsibility for, blame on *or* upon [coll.], lay the blame on, lay *or* cast blame upon; accuse of, charge with, saddle with, lay to one's door, lay to one's charge, bring home to, cast *or* throw in one's teeth, take to task *or* account.

reproach, twit, taunt with; slur, cast a slur on; cast a stone at, cast the first stone at; have *or* keep a rod in pickle for, have a crow to pluck *or* pick with; recriminate, retort an accusation, countercharge; shift the blame *or* responsibility, pass the buck [coll.]; trump up a charge, put up a job [slang], frame *or* frame up [slang]; censure etc. 932.7; inform on etc. 527.10; prosecute etc. 969.10.

5. *adj.* accusing etc. *v.*, accusatory, accusative; inculpative, inculpatory; crimi-

---

938. The breath of accusation kills an innocent name.—SHELLEY. I do not know the method of drawing up an indictment against an whole people.—BURKE. I own the soft impeachment.—SHERIDAN. Where are the evidence that do accuse me?—SHAKESPEARE.

natory, incriminatory, recriminatory; imputative, denunciatory, condemnatory, damnatory.

6. *adj.* accused, charged etc. *v.*; suspected; under suspicion, under a cloud, under surveillance.

7. *adj.* accusable, imputable, impeachable etc. (blameworthy) 932.14; inexcusable etc. (unjustifiable) 941a.4; vicious etc. 945.11–19; guilty etc. 947.4.

939. Probity
(See 940. Improbity)

1. *n.* probity, uprightness, honorableness etc. *adj.*; integrity, rectitude, honesty, honor; respectability; principles, high principles; court of honor; fairness etc. (justice) 941; truth etc. 494; veracity etc. 543; candor, sincerity etc. (artlessness) 703; right etc. 922; virtue etc. 944; innocence etc. 946; purity etc. 960; reputability etc. 873.

2. *n.* conscientiousness, scrupulousness etc. *adj.*; scrupulosity, punctiliosity [rare], punctuality [now rare]; scruple, qualm, misgiving, demur, shrinking, recoil; hesitation, hesitance *or* hesitancy; point of honor, fine *or* delicate point, point, punctilio, delicacy, nicety, subtlety, refinement; particularity etc. (fastidiousness) 868; care etc. 459; sense of right, grace etc. (conscience) 926.3; twinge of conscience etc. (penitence) 950.

3. *n.* trustworthiness etc. *adj.*, reliability, dependability; incorruption [arch.], incorruptibility, inviolability.

4. *n.* constancy, faithfulness etc. *adj.*, fidelity, loyalty, faith, singleness of heart; good faith, *bona fides* [L.], *bonne foi* [F.]; truth [arch.], troth, true blue; allegiance, fealty, homage, devotion; tie, bond; attachment, adherence, attachment *or* adherence to right.

5. *n.* man of honor, man of his word, gentleman, *gentilhomme* [F.], *fidus Achates* [L.], *preux chevalier* [F.], *galantuomo* [It.], honest man, square *or* straight shooter [coll.], regular fellow [slang, U.S.], brick [slang or coll.], trump [slang], white man [slang, U.S.], trueman [arch.], true-blue, truepenny, true Briton.

6. *v.* be honorable etc. *adj.*, deal honorably, draw a straight furrow, shoot straight [coll.], put one's cards on the table, *"vitam impendere vero"* (Juvenal), make a point of; keep one's word *or* promise, be as good as one's word *or* promise, keep faith with, not fail, redeem one's pledge, acquit oneself, make good; do one's duty etc. 926.6; be fair etc. 941.2; speak the truth etc. (veracity) 543.2; keep on the straight and narrow way etc. (be virtuous) 944.2; redound to one's honor etc. 931.7.

7. *adj.* upright, uprighteous, right; honest, honest as daylight, honest as the day, honest as the day is long; square-shooting, straight-shooting, straight-up-and-down, up-and-up, on the up-and-up, on the level, on the square [all coll.]; straight, white [both slang]; honorable, jealous of honor; reputable, noble, manly, estimable, worthy, creditable, *sans peur et sans reproche* [F.].

respectable, highly respectable; ethical, moral; uncorrupt, uncorrupted; law-abiding, law-honest, lawlike, law-loving, law-revering; truehearted, true-souled, true-spirited, true-dealing; principled, high-principled, high-minded, right-minded; open, openhearted, open as day; aboveboard, open and aboveboard; guileless, ingenuous, frank, candid etc. (artless) 703.4; veracious etc. 543.3; virtuous etc. 944.3, 4; innocent etc. 946.5; pure etc. 960.2; observant etc. 772.5.

8. *adj.* conscientious, tender-conscienced, conscionable [now rare], scrupulous, religious, strict, nice, punctilious, punctual; overconscientious, overscrupulous; particular etc. (fastidious) 868.4; careful etc. 459.7; precise etc. 494.10; fair etc. (just) 941.3.

9. *adj.* trustworthy, trusty, trustful [rare], faithworthy, sure, reliable, dependable, to be depended on, as good as one's word, tried, true, tried and true;

---

939. Honour is not won / Until some honourable deed be done.—MARLOWE. His heart as far from fraud as heaven from earth.—SHAKESPEARE. The measure of life is not length, but honesty.—LYLY. Godlike erect, with native honour clad.—MILTON. Every honest man will suppose honest acts to flow from honest principles.—JEFFERSON. An honest man's the noblest work of God.—POPE. Subtlety may deceive you; integrity never will.—CROMWELL. Principle is ever my motto, not expediency.—DISRAELI. And thus he bore without abuse / The grand old name of gentleman.—TENNYSON. Yours is a thoroughbred heart.—SHAW.

unfalse, unperfidious, untreacherous; inviolable, incorruptible.

10. *adj.* constant, faithful, loyal, stanch, true, true-blue, true-hearted, true to the core, true to one's colors, true as the needle to the pole, true as the dial to the sun, constant as the northern star, "marble-constant" (Shakespeare), single-hearted, steadfast, steady, unerring, unfailing, resolute, firm.

11. *adv.* honorably, honestly etc. *adj.*; in all honor, in *or* with good faith, *bona fide* [L.], *foro conscientiae* [L.], from the bottom of one's heart; on the level, on the square [both coll.]; as the dial to the sun, as the needle to the pole; aboveboard, without concealment *or* deception, with no nonsense, with cards on the table, *cartes sur table* [F.]; in earnest, in good earnest.

12. *int.* on my honor!, honor bright [coll.] etc. (affirmation) 535.8.

940. Improbity
(See 939. Probity)

1. *n.* improbity, deviation from rectitude etc. 939, dishonesty, dishonor, laxity, venality; knavery, roguery, villainy, rascality, scoundrelism, reprobacy [rare]; unrespectability; wrong etc. 923; unfairness etc. (injustice) 941a; turpitude etc. (vice) 945; impurity etc. 961; culpability etc. (guilt) 947; disreputability etc. 874; falsehood etc. 544; deception etc. 545; misrepresentation etc. 555; mouth honor etc. (flattery) 933; bribery etc. 618; cunning etc. 702.

2. *n.* faithlessness etc. *adj.*, infidelity, inconstancy, falsity, disloyalty; divided allegiance, hyphenated allegiance [cant]; bad faith, *mala fides* [L.], Punic faith, *Punica fides* [L.]; violation, breach of promise, ~ trust *or* faith; barratry [Law]; apostasy etc. 607.2; nonobservance etc. 773.

3. *n.* untrustworthiness etc. *adj.*; unreliability, undependability.

4. *n.* treacherousness, perfidiousness etc. *adj.*; treachery, perfidy, double-dealing, duplicity, foul play; Iscariotism, betrayal, Judas kiss, treason, petty treason, misprision of treason; high treason, *lèse-majesté* [F.], lese majesty; sedition; informing against, information; cunning etc. 702.

5. *n.* sharp practice, underhand practice *or* dealing, corruption, jobbery, dodgery, pettifoggery, *supercherie* [F.], *espièglerie* [F.], trickery, heads I win tails you lose; chicane, chicanery; trimming, shuffling; piece of sharp practice, graft [coll.], job, fishy transaction; fraudulence etc. (deception) 545; fraud etc. (trick) 545.3; theft etc. 791.

6. *v.* be dishonest etc. *adj.*, play with marked cards, live by one's wits, sail near the wind; sell oneself, seal one's infamy; disgrace oneself etc. 874.5; lie, dissemble etc. (falsify) 544.3–6; take in, flimflam [coll.] etc. (deceive) 545.7–10; misrepresent etc. 555.4; misinform etc. 538.2; mislead etc. 495.11; steal, swindle etc. 791.9–12; be unfair etc. 941a.2; bribe etc. 618.3.

7. *v.* be faithless etc. *adj.*, not keep faith with, fail, go back on [coll.], play one false, sell out [slang], betray; doublecross [slang], cross up [slang, U.S.], go over to the enemy; break one's word *or* promise, go back on one's word *or* promise [coll.]; jilt; squeal [slang] etc. (inform on) 527.10; apostatize etc. 607.8; desert, forsake etc. (abandon) 624.3.

8. *adj.* dishonest, dishonorable, unconscientious, unconscienced, unconscionable, unscrupulous, unprincipled, knavish, scampish, rascally, villainous, felonious, reprobate, blackguard, corrupt, venal, sinister, lawless, criminal, crooked, tortuous, insidious, Machiavellian, dark, fishy [coll.], questionable, recreant, sneaking, pettifogging; uningenuous, disingenuous; dead to honor, lost to shame; temporizing, timeserving; tricky, tricksy [rare], trickish; scheming, schemy [coll.], schemeful; designing, contriving, intriguing; conniving, connivant.

disreputable etc. 874.8; wicked etc. 945.11–19; deceitful, fraudulent etc. (deceptive) 545.12, 13; untruthful, dissembling etc. (false) 544.7, 8; misleading etc. (*see* mislead etc. 495.12); crafty etc.

---

940. 'Tis my opinion every man cheats in his way, and he is only honest who is not discovered.—S. CENTLIVRE. Crooked counsels and dark politics.—POPE. His honor rooted in dishonor stood / And faith unfaithful kept him falsely true.—TENNYSON. Corruption, the most infallible symptom of constitutional liberty.—GIBBON. Corruption is a tree, whose branches are / Of an unmeasurable length.—BEAUMONT AND FLETCHER.

(cunning) 702.6; unfair etc. (unjust) 941a.3; thieving etc. 791.14.

9. *adj.* unworthy, uncommendable, unhandsome, discreditable, improper, indiscreet, undignified, *infra dignitatem* [L.], beneath one, *contra bonos mores* [L.]; unmanly, ungentlemanly, ungentlemanlike; unchivalric, unknightly; unbecoming, untoward etc. (inexpedient) 647.3; unpraiseworthy etc. 932.13; reprehensible, culpable etc. (blameworthy) 932.14; disreputable etc. 874.8.

10. *adj.* faithless, of bad faith, unfaithful, untrue, disloyal, inconstant, unsteadfast, fickle; false, falsehearted; barratrous [Law].

11. *adj.* untrustworthy, untrusty, untrustful [rare], trustless, trothless [arch.], unfaithworthy, unsure, unreliable, undependable, not to be depended upon.

12. *adj.* treacherous, perfidious, shifty, slippery, slippery as an eel; double, double-dealing, doublehearted, doubleminded, double-tongued, doublehanded, double-faced, two-faced, Janus-faced; traitorous, betraying, Iscariotic(al); treasonish, treasonful, treasonous, treasonable.

13. *adv.* dishonestly etc. *adj., mala fide* [L.], like a thief in the night, by crooked paths; by foul means, by fair means or foul.

941. Justice
(See 941a. Injustice)

1. *n.* justice, justness, fairness etc. *adj.*; equity, impartiality, just *or* plain dealing, fair play, a fair field and no favor; square dealing, square *or* straight shooting [both coll.]; *suum cuique* [L.], measure for measure, give-and-take, *lex talionis* [L.]; the fair *or* right thing, the handsome thing [coll.], square deal [coll.]; scales of Justice; poetic justice; retributive justice, nemesis; Jupiter Fidius, Dius Fidius, Fides, Fides publica *or* populi Romani [all Rom.]; karma; Justitia, Nemesis, Astraea, Themis, Rhadamanthus; honesty etc. (probity) 939; right etc. 922; dueness etc. 924; legality etc. 963.

2. *v.* be fair etc. *adj.*, deal fairly, ~ squarely *or* impartially, see fair play, see one righted, see justice done, do justice to, serve one right, put the saddle on the right horse, hold the scales even, give and take, *audire alteram partem* [L.]; do the handsome thing, shoot straight with, give a square deal [all coll.]; play fair, tote fair [dial. U.S.], play the game [coll.], play cricket [slang], show a proper spirit; pay one's dues, give everyone his due, give the Devil his due; recompense etc. (reward) 973.3; be honorable etc. 939.6.

3. *adj.* just, equitable, equal [arch.], evenhanded, balanced, fair, square, fair and square, candid, proper, good, as it ought to *or* should be; right, rightful; square-dealing, square-shooting, level [all coll.]; impartial, impersonal, dispassionate, disinterested, uninfluenced; unbiased, unwarped etc. (unprejudiced) 498.12; conscientious etc. 939.8; due etc. 924.9; meet, fit etc. (expedient) 646.4; legal etc. 963.5.

4. *adj.* justifiable, reasonable, excusable etc. (vindicable) 937.10.

5. *adv.* justly, fairly etc. *adj.*; in justice, in equity, in reason, as is right, ~ just *or* fitting; in a fair manner, by fair means, upon even terms, without distinction of persons, without regard *or* respect to persons.

941a. Injustice
(See 941. Justice)

1. *n.* injustice, unjustness, unfairness etc. *adj.*; inequity, iniquity; partiality, prejudice, prepossession, bias, warp, leaning, inclination; favoritism, nepotism; partisanism, partisanship; gross injustice; dishonesty etc. (improbity) 940;

---

941. Justice is blind, he knows nobody.—Dryden.   Justice discards party, friendship, kindred, and is therefore always represented as blind.—Addison.   There are in nature certain fountains of justice, whence all civil laws are derived.—Bacon.   Those eternal laws of justice, which are our rule and our birthright.—Burke.   Justice without wisdom is impossible.—Froude.   The administration of justice is the firmest pillar of government.—Washington.   Live and let live is the rule of common justice.—L'Estrange.   The hour of justice does not strike / On the dials of this world.—Maeterlinck.   Whoever fights whoever fails, / Justice conquers evermore.—Emerson.

941a. 'A book,' I observed, 'might be written on the injustice of the just.'—A. Hope.   Delay of justice is injustice.—Landor.   The extremity of justice is extreme injustice.—Grafton.   It is better to suffer injustice than to do it.—Emerson.

wrong etc. 923; undueness etc. 925; exorbitance, inordinacy etc. (redundance) 641.

2. *v.* be unfair etc. *adj.,* do wrong, reap where one has not sown, give an inch and take an ell, rob Peter to pay Paul; favor, lean towards; encroach, impose upon.

3. *adj.* unjust, unfair, inequitable *or* unequitable, unequal [arch.], iniquitous, uncandid, unbalanced, one-sided; wrong, wrongful; partial, biased, warped, prejudiced, prepossessed, jaundiced, interested, influenced; unjustified etc. (undue) 925.8, 9; unmeet etc. (inexpedient) 647.3; inordinate, excessive etc. (redundant) 641.5; unconscientious etc. 940.8.

4. *adj.* unjustifiable, unreasonable, unallowable, unwarrantable, indefensible, objectionable; inexcusable, inexpiable, unpardonable, irremissible; reprehensible etc. (blameworthy) 932.14; wrong etc. 923.4; wicked etc. 945.11–19.

942. Unselfishness
(See 943. Selfishness)

1. *n.* unselfishness, disinterest, disinterestedness etc. *adj.*; self-denial, self-abnegation, self-sacrifice, self-forgetfulness, self-immolation, self-subordination, self-subjection, self-abasement; self-renouncement, self-renunciation; self-devotion, self-devotement [rare]; stoicism, asceticism; martyrdom, suttee, kenosis [Theol.]; self-control etc. (resolution) 604.3.

2. *n.* magnanimity, elevation of spirit *or* purpose, elevation, exaltation, sublimity; chivalry, knight-errantry, heroism; labor of love; altruism etc. (benevolence) 906; generosity etc. (liberality) 816.

3. *n.* (comparisons) Good Shepherd, Good Samaritan, Bishop Bienvenu (Hugo), Sydney Carton (Dickens), Mr. Greatheart (Bunyan).

4. *v.* be unselfish etc. *adj.,* make a sacrifice, lay one's head on the block; put oneself in the place of others, do as one would be done by, do unto others as you would that they should do unto you, observe the Golden Rule.

942. Generosity is the flower of justice.—HAWTHORNE. Many men have been capable of doing a wise thing, more a cunning thing, but very few a generous thing.—POPE. The real drawback to marriage is that it makes one unselfish. Unselfish people are colorless.—WILDE.

5. *adj.* unselfish, self-denying, self-abnegatory, self-sacrificing, self-renouncing, self-abasing, self-forgetful, self-unconscious; self-neglectful, self-neglecting; self-devotional, self-devoted; disinterested, dispassionate, impartial, impersonal; stoic(al), ascetical.

6. *adj.* magnanimous, princely, handsome, great, high, elevated, lofty, exalted, sublime; noble-minded, high-minded; bighearted, greathearted, largehearted; freehearted; chivalrous, heroic; altruistic etc. (benevolent) 906.6–8; generous etc. (liberal) 816.4.

943. Selfishness
(See 942. Unselfishness)

1. *n.* selfishness, meanness, self-interestedness etc. *adj.,* self-interest, self-seeking, self-pleasing, self-indulgence, self-advancement, self-solicitude, self-consideration, self-jealousy, self-sufficiency, self-absorption, self-occupation; nepotism, charity that begins at home; self-worship, egotism etc. (vanity) 880; illiberality etc. (parsimony) 819; misanthropy etc. 910.

2. *n.* self-seeker, self-pleaser, self-advancer; timepleaser, timeserver, temporizer; tufthunter, fortune hunter; nepotist; worldling; monopolist, hog, road hog, end-seat hog [coll.]; dog in the manger, *canis in praesepi* [L.]; egoist etc. 880.3.

3. *v.* be selfish etc. *adj.,* please ~, indulge ~, pamper *or* coddle oneself, consult one's own wishes *or* pleasure, feather one's nest, look after one's own interests, take care of *or* look out for number one [coll.], look to *or* have an eye to the main chance, know on which side one's bread is buttered, give an inch and take an ell.

943. Selfishness is the greatest curse of the human race.—GLADSTONE. Selfishness is the only real atheism.—ZANGWILL. Next to the very young, I suppose the very old are the most selfish.—THACKERAY. Selfishness is calm, a force of nature: you might say the trees were selfish.—STEVENSON. He that lives not somewhat to others, liveth little to himself.—MONTAIGNE. Every man for himself and God for us all.—J. HEYWOOD. Man seeks his own good at the whole world's cost.—BROWNING. He's been true to *one* party, and that is himself.—LOWELL. Other people are quite dreadful. The only possible society is oneself.—WILDE. Every man for himself and the devil take the hindmost. Heads I win, tails you lose.

4. *adj.* selfish, **self-seeking**, self-pleasing, self-advancing, self-indulgent, self-considerative, self-jealous, self-sufficient, self-besot, self-aware, self-centered, self-occupied, self-absorbed, wrapped up *or* centered in oneself; interested, self-interested; self-blind, self-blinded; self-assuming, self-assumed; mean [coll.]; egotistical etc. (vain) 880.6; worldly etc. 989.9; illiberal, ungenerous etc. (parsimonious) 819.4; misanthropic etc. 910.3.

5. *adv.* selfishly etc. *adj.*, for oneself, from selfish *or* interested motives, to gain some private ends.

944. Virtue
(See 945. Vice)

1. *n.* virtue, virtuousness, righteousness, goodness etc. *adj.*; aretaics; *"mens sibi conscia recti"* (Vergil); morality, moral rectitude; merit, worth, excellence, value, credit, desert; cardinal virtues, prudence, fortitude, temperance, justice; well-doing, good behavior, well-spent life; integrity etc. (probity) 939; innocence etc. 946; purity etc. 960; reputability etc. 873; self-denial etc. (temperance) 953; self-control etc. 604.3; courage etc. 861; morals etc. (ethics) 926.4; piety etc. 987.

2. *v.* be virtuous etc. *adj.*, practice virtue etc. *n.*, be on one's good *or* best behavior, act well, acquit oneself well, fight the good fight, mind one's P's and Q's [coll.], set an example *or* a good example, command *or* master one's passions; keep in the right path, keep on the straight and narrow way, walk the straight path; discharge one's duty etc. 926.6.

3. *adj.* virtuous, good, moral, just,

---

944. *Esse quam videri bonus malebat* [He preferred to be rather than to seem good].—SALLUST.   Before virtue the immortal gods have put the sweat of man's brow.—HESIOD.   Virtue is not left to stand alone. He who practices it will have neighbors.—CONFUCIUS.   Virtue is a vivid and separate thing, like pain or a particular smell.—CHESTERFIELD.   Virtue is like a rich stone, best plain set.—BACON.   Seek Virtue; she alone is free.—MILTON.   There is never an instant's truce between virtue and vice.—THOREAU.   Virtue is the performance of pleasant actions.—J. STEPHENS.   Virtue consists, not in abstaining from vice, but in not desiring it.—SHAW.   Virtue is the fount whence honour springs.—MARLOWE.   *Virtutis fortuna comes* [Good fortune is the comrade of virtue].

righteous, right-minded, well-intentioned, nice, excellent, exemplary, creditable, meritorious, meritory [obs.], worthy, sterling, noble, noble-minded, wholesouled; right, correct; holy, holy-minded, heavenly-minded; saintly, saintlike; heaven-born, angelic, seraphic, godlike; unworldly, unearthly; matchless, peerless; admirable, estimable etc. (praiseworthy) 931.11; upright etc. 939.7–9; pious etc. 987.10.

4. *adj.* uncorrupt, uncorrupted, unsinful, unwicked, uniniquitous, undemoralized, undissolute, undebauched, undepraved, undegenerate; innocent etc. 946.5; pure etc. 960.2; untainted, undefiled etc. (clean) 652.14.

5. *adv.* virtuously etc. *adj.*, *a merito* [L.].

945. Vice
(See 944. Virtue)

1. *n.* vice, sinfulness, badness, wickedness etc. *adj.*; sin, "thou scarlet sin" (Shakespeare), "the transgression of the law" (Bible); immorality, peccancy, iniquity, evil, bad, wrong, error, demerit, obliquity, reprobacy, want of principle; obduracy, hardness of heart, heart of stone; evil nature, the Devil within one, Adam, old Adam, offending Adam; cloven foot *or* hoof, horns, evil eye; peccability; deviation from rectitude etc. (improbity) 940; criminality etc. (guilt) 947; infamy etc. (disrepute) 874; obscenity, carnality etc. (impurity) 961; backsliding etc. (relapse) 661; impiety etc. 988.

2. *n.* turpitude, moral turpitude; baseness, depravedness etc. *adj.*; depravement [rare], depravation; degeneracy, degeneration; pravity, depravity, abjection, decadence *or* decadency, debasement, degradation, demoralization, corruption, pollution, abomination, damnability, flagrance *or* flagrancy, profligacy, abandonment, *gusto picaresco* [L.].

3. *n.* delinquency, dereliction, omission,

---

945. *Alitur vitium vivitque tegendo* [Vice is nourished by secrecy].—VERGIL.   *Genus est mortis male vivere* [It is a kind of death to lead an evil life].—OVID.   One man's wickedness may easily become all men's curse.—PUBLILIUS.   Ye have ploughed wickedness, ye have reaped iniquity.—BIBLE.   There is no peace, saith the Lord, unto the wicked.—BIBLE.   How oft is the candle of the wicked put out! and how

neglect, failure, moral failure; laxity, looseness of morals.

 4. *n.* weakness, weakness of the flesh, infirmity, frailty; weak point *or* side, foible; failing, failure.

 5. *n.* defect, deficiency [now rare], deficiency; hole, hole in one's coat; vicety [rare], imperfection, fault, flaw, blemish, blot, blot in one's escutcheon, blotch, spot, smudge, smutch, smirch, smot [Scot.], stigma (*pl.* stigmas, stigmata), taint, stain; soil, soilure, soilage.

 6. *n.* evil conduct, evildoing, wrongdoing, malpractice, misconduct, misbehavior, naughtiness, misdoing, misdemeanor, misfeasance, malfeasance, nonfeasance, malversation, corruption, evil courses, machinations of the devil; misprision, negative *or* positive misprision, misprision of treason *or* felony [Law]; transgression, infraction; impropriety, indecorum; crime, criminality; malignity, cruelty etc. (malevolence) 907; misdeed etc. 947.2.

 7. *n.* reprobate, sinner etc. 949.

 8. *n.* sink, sink *or* den of iniquity *or* corruption, den, Alsatian den, Domdaniel, hell; hole, joint [both slang]; opium den; brothel etc. 961.7; gambling house etc. 621.4.

 9. *v.* be sinful etc. *adj.*, sin, sinner it [joc.], commit sin, offend, do amiss, err, transgress, trespass, misdemean oneself, forget oneself, misconduct oneself, misdo [rare], misbehave; sow one's wild oats; deviate from the path of virtue, leave the straight and narrow, take a wrong course, go astray; fall, lapse, slip, trip; go to the bad, ∼ dogs *or* devil, go to pot [coll.], go to hell, go to hell on a poker [slang]; backslide, fall from grace etc. (relapse) 661.3.

 10. *v.* render vicious etc. *adj.*, vitiate, demoralize, brutalize, drive to the dogs; debase, degrade etc. (corrupt) 659.9.

 11. *adj.* vicious, given to vice etc. *n.*; sinning etc. *v.*, sinful; immoral, unmoral; wicked, bad, evil, naughty [arch.], iniquitous, wrong, recreant, reprobate, un-

righteous, unvirtuous, unsaintly, ungodly, unholy; virtueless, graceless, shameless, heartless; arrant, wayward, wanton, prodigal; defective, faulty, imperfect; evil-qualitied, evil-looking, evil-favored, evil-savored, evil-hued, evil-eyed, evil-affected; evil-disposed, ill-disposed, ill-conditioned; peccable.

 guilty etc. 947.4; reprehensible, culpable etc. (blameworthy) 932.14; unjustifiable etc. 941a.4; unchaste, incontinent etc. (impure) 961.9–11; impious etc. 988.7; knavish etc. (dishonest) 940.8–12.

 12. *adj.* infirm, weak, soft [coll.], frail, spineless, invertebrate, unsound, unstable, unsteady, shaky; lax, slack, loose, loose-moraled, of loose morals, of easy virtue, light.

 13. *adj.* evildoing, wrongdoing, malfeasant, malefactory, misbehaving, naughty, disorderly; scampish, unprincipled etc. (dishonest) 940.8–12; malevolent etc. 907.6–9.

 14. *adj.* evil-minded, evilhearted, baseminded, low-minded, low-thoughted.

 15. *adj.* corrupt, corrupted, vice-corrupted; rotten, peccant, tainted, contaminated, vitiated; warped, perverted; debased, degraded, demoralized, depraved, debauched, dissolute, degenerate, profligate, abandoned, gone to the bad *or* dogs, sunk ∼, lost *or* steeped in iniquity, lost to virtue, rotten at *or* to the core.

 16. *adj.* base, low, vile, foul, abominable, black, grave, gross, felonious, nefarious, scurvy, shameful, disgraceful, scandalous, infamous, villainous, heinous, monstrous, flagrant, flagitious, incarnate, atrocious, rank; cursed, accursed, damnable.

 17. *adj.* diabolic(al), Mephistophelean *or* Mephistophelian, satanic, devilish, demoniac(al); fiendish, fiendlike; hellish, hellborn, infernal, Stygian.

 18. *adj.* hardened, hardened in vice, hardhearted, tough, hard-boiled [coll.], hard, casehardened, obdurate, inured; seared, callous, thick-skinned, pachydermatous, impervious; deep-dyed, of a deep dye.

 19. *adj.* irreclaimable, irreformable, incorrigible, recidivous, hopeless, beyond *or* past hope, beyond correction *or* reclaim, past praying for, lost.

 20. *adv.* wickedly, sinfully etc. *adj.*; wrong, without excuse.

 21. *int.* fie upon!, shame! etc. 874.12.

---

oft cometh their destruction upon them!—BIBLE. All wickedness comes of weakness.—ROUSSEAU. To sanction vice and hunt decorum down.—BYRON. The world loves a spice of wickedness.—LONGFELLOW. Our faith comes in moments; our vice is habitual.—EMERSON. A man must either imitate the vicious or hate them.—MONTAIGNE. Wild oats make a bad autumn crop.—CYNIC'S CALENDAR.

946. Innocence
(See 947. Guilt)

1. *n.* innocence, innocency, freedom from guilt (*see* guilt etc. 947), guiltlessness etc. *adj.,* incorruption [arch.], impeccability, inerrability; clean hands, clean slate, unspotted reputation, clear conscience; purity etc. 960; immaculacy etc. (cleanness) 652; virtue etc. 944; artlessness etc. 703.

2. *n.* innocent, newborn babe, babe unborn, child, mere child, lamb, dove.

3. *v.* be innocent etc. *adj.,* have clean hands etc. *n.,* know no wrong.

4. *v.* exculpate etc. (vindicate) 937.5, (acquit) 970.

5. *adj.* innocent, free from guilt etc. 947, not guilty etc. 947.4, unguilty, guiltless, faultless, blameless, sinless, bloodless, clear, unerring, unfallen, *"integer vitae scelerisque purus"* (Horace), *sans peur et sans reproche* [F.], "without unspotted, innocent within" (Dryden); uncorrupted, unperjured, unbought, unbribed, unpurchased; innocent as a lamb etc. *n.,* lamblike, dovelike, childlike; with clean hands, with a clear conscience etc. *n.*; chaste etc. (pure) 960.2; stainless, undefiled etc. (clean) 652.14; virtuous, uncorrupt etc. 944.3, 4; artless etc. 703.4; harmless etc. 648.13.

6. *adj.* inculpable, unculpable [rare]; *rectus in curia* [L.]; unblamable, unblameworthy; irreproachable, irreprovable [rare], irreprehensible, unexceptionable, unobjectionable, uncensurable, unimpeachable, above suspicion; venial etc. (vindicable) 937.10.

947. Guilt
(See 946. Innocence)

1. *n.* guilt, guiltiness etc. *adj.,* criminality, culpability, chargeability, blamability,

reprehensibility, peccability; deviation from rectitude etc. (improbity) 940; sinfulness etc. (vice) 945; twinge of conscience etc. (penitence) 950.

2. *n.* misdeed, misdoing, evildoing, wrongdoing, misdemeanor, misfeasance, malfeasance, malefaction, wrong, *malum* [L.], evil, peccancy, offense *or* offence, tort [Law]; violation, transgression, trespass, infringement, infraction, breach, break; delict, delictum [both Law]; error, fault, indiscretion, peccadillo, trip, slip, lapse; sin, "deed without a name" (Shakespeare); besetting sin, crying sin; unpardonable ~, deadly *or* mortal sin, sin of commission; sin of omission, nonfeasance, omission, failure, dereliction, delinquency; *malum in se* [L.], *malum prohibitum* [L.]; felony, crime, capital crime; outrage, atrocity, enormity.

3. *n.* corpus delicti [Law], body of the crime.

4. *adj.* guilty, peccant, criminal, to blame, in fault, faulty, weighed in the balance and found wanting; culpable, chargeable etc. (blameworthy) 932.14.

5. *adv.* in the very act, *in flagrante delicto* [L.], red-handed.

948. Good Person
(See 949. Bad Person; also 648. Goodness)

1. *n.* good person, worthy, nature's nobleman, salt of the earth, Christian; white man, brick, trump [all slang]; gem, jewel, diamond, pearl; flower, cream, *crème de la crème* [F.]; one in a thousand *or* ten thousand, a man among men; paragon, *chevalier sans peur et sans reproche* [F.]; good example, exemplar, model, pattern, standard; hero, god, demigod;

---

946. Blessed are the pure in heart; for they shall see God.—BIBLE. What stronger breastplate than a heart untainted?—SHAKESPEARE. Innocence has nothing to dread.—RACINE. He that knows no guilt can know no fear.—MASSINGER. The exactest vigilance and caution can never maintain a single day of unmingled innocence.—JOHNSON. To dread no eye, and to suspect no tongue, is the greatest prerogative of innocence.—JOHNSON. The sweet converse of an innocent mind.—KEATS. The innocent are gay.—COWPER.
947. *Cui prodest scelus is fecit* [The crime was committed by the one whom it would bene-

fit].—SENECA. Men's minds are too ready to excuse guilt in themselves.—LIVY. Guilt is always jealous.—J. RAY. My stronger guilt defeats my strong intent.—SHAKESPEARE. Suspicion always haunts the guilty mind.—SHAKESPEARE.
948. All men are born good.—CONFUCIUS. When you see a good man, think of emulating him; when you see a bad man, examine your own heart.—CONFUCIUS. The wicked flee when no man pursueth: but the righteous are bold as a lion.—BIBLE. My meaning in saying he is a good man, is to have you understand me that he is sufficient.—SHAKESPEARE. A good man should and must / Sit rather down with loss, than rise unjust.—JONSON. Good men are the stars, the planets of the ages wherein they live, and illustrate the times.—JONSON. Only the young die good.—CYNIC'S CALENDAR.

saint, angel, seraph; rough diamond, diamond in the rough; the good, the righteous; Galahad; honest man etc. 939.5; innocent etc. 946.2; philanthropist etc. 911; benefactor etc. 912.

2. *n.* good woman, heaven's noblest gift, "a perfect woman, nobly planned" (Wordsworth), queen; goddess, demigoddess; virgin, vestal, vestal virgin, Madonna; Lucretia; Diana [Rom. Myth.], Artemis, Athena Parthenos [both Gr. Myth.].

949. Bad Person
(See 948. Good Person; also 649. Badness)

1. *n.* bad person, rascal, precious rascal, scoundrel, villain, rogue, knave, blackguard, reprobate, *polisson* [F.], scamp, scalawag [coll.], skeesicks [coll., U.S.], rascalion *or* rascallion, rapscallion, rap [slang], rep, loon, lown [obs. exc. dial. and Scot.], limb [coll.], scapegrace, black sheep, rotter [slang], sad dog [coll.], cullion, bounder [coll.], recreant, miscreant, wrong 'un [slang], budmash [Ind.], caitiff, wretch, mean wretch, ronyon [arch.], varlet [arch.], hyena [coll.], rat [slang], *âme-de-boue* [F.], *drôle* [F.].

"a rascally yeaforsooth knave," "a foul-mouthed and calumnious knave," "poor cuckoldy knave," "a poor, decayed, ingenious, foolish, rascally knave," "an arrant, rascally, beggarly, lousy knave," "a slipper and subtle knave, a finder of occasions," "a whoreson, beetle-headed, flap-ear'd knave," "filthy, worsted-stocking knave; a lily-livered, action-taking knave," "a knave; a rascal; an eater of broken meats; a base, proud, shallow, beggarly, three-suited, hundred-pound, filthy, worsted-stocking knave" (all Shakespeare).

good-for-nothing, good-for-naught, ne'er-do-well, losel [arch. exc. dial.], *mauvais sujet* [F.], *vaurien* [F.]; devil, devil incarnate, demon in human shape; hellbound, rakehell, rakehell, rake, roué, loose fish [coll.], rip [coll.], rounder [slang]; cur, dog, hound, whelp, mongrel; reptile, viper, serpent, snake, snake in the grass; wolf in sheep's clothing, ass in lion's skin, jackdaw in peacock's feathers; sneak, Jerry Sneak; shyster [U.S.]; degenerate, pervert; lost sheep, *âme damnée* [F.], fallen angel, one who has sold himself to the devil; delinquent, defaulter, truant; bad example; Nana Sahib, Lazarillo de Tormes, Scapin.

mischiefmaker, ruffian etc. (evildoer) 913; cheat, impostor, liar etc. (deceiver) 548; thief etc. 792; murderer etc. 361.8; sensualist etc. 954a; renegade, backslider etc. (apostate) 607.5; prodigal etc. 818.2; outcast of society etc. 893.5.

2. *n.* wrongdoer, worker of iniquity, malefactor, sinner, transgressor, delinquent; malfeasor, misfeasor, nonfeasor [all Law]; misdemeanant, misdemeanist; culprit, offender, felon, criminal, crook [coll.]; convict, jailbird [U.S.], gaolbird [Eng.]; ticket-of-leave man, ticket-of-leaver [both Eng]; outlaw, *proscrit* [F.], fugitive; desperate criminal, desperado; gallows bird [coll.], Jack Ketch's pippin [old slang]; evildoer etc. 913; brigand, swindler etc. (thief) 792.

3. *n.* traitor, betrayer, snake in the grass, rat [slang], archtraitor; Judas Iscariot, Benedict Arnold, Quisling, Brutus; treasonist; telltale, squealer [slang] etc. (informer) 527.6; turncoat, renegade etc. (apostate) 607.5; double-dealer etc. (deceiver) 548.

4. *n.* bad woman, jade, Jezebel, quean, wench, slut; hag, witch etc. (malevolent woman) 913.5; adulteress etc. 962.2.

5. *n.* the wicked, the evil, the reprobate etc. 945.11; sons of men, sons of Belial, sons *or* children of the devil, children of darkness; lowest dregs of vice; scum of the earth etc. (riffraff) 876.2.

950. Penitence
(See 951. Impenitence)

1. *n.* penitence, repentance, remorse, sorrow, contrition, compunction; self-re-

---

valiant, great in villainy!—SHAKESPEARE. There never was a bad man that had ability for good service.—BURKE. As there is a use in medicine for poison, so the world cannot move without rogues.—EMERSON. A wicked man is his own hell.
950. Joy shall be in heaven over one sinner that repenteth.—BIBLE. Ye sorrowed to repentance.—BIBLE. I desire rather to feel compunction than to know its definition.—THOMAS

---

949. Honest men and knaves may possibly wear the same cloth.—FULLER. *Et sceleratis sol oritur* [And the sun rises on the wicked too].—SENECA. God bears with the wicked, but not forever.—CERVANTES. Their feet run to evil.—BIBLE. O villain, villain, smiling, damned villain.—SHAKESPEARE. Thou little

proach, self-accusation, self-condemnation, self-conviction, self-humiliation; pangs ~, qualms ~, stings ~, prickings ~, twinge ~, twitch ~, touch *or* voice of conscience; resipiscence; deathbed repentance; *locus poenitentiae* [L.], stool of repentance, cutty stool [Scot.], mourners' bench [local, U.S.]; regret etc. 833; penance, apology etc. (atonement) 952; confession etc. 529.2; lamentation etc. 839; recantation etc. 607.3; redemption etc. 987.3.

2. *n.* penitent, repentant [rare], "a sadder and a wiser man" (Coleridge); prodigal son, returned prodigal; Magdalen.

3. *v.* repent, be penitent etc. *adj.*, think better of; plead guilty, sing *miserere* or *de profundis* [L.], cry *peccavi* [L.], say *culpa mea* [L.], own oneself in the wrong, humble oneself; learn by experience; be sorry for, rue etc. (regret) 833.2; do penance etc. (atone) 952.4; express regret etc. (apologize) 952.5; confess etc. 529.5; bewail etc. (lament) 839.6; recant etc. 607.9; knock under etc. (submit) 725.3.

4. *v.* reform, turn over a new leaf, put on the new man, turn from sin; reclaim, redeem, regenerate, convert, amend, set straight again, make a new man of, restore self-respect.

5. *adj.* penitent, repentant, penitential, penitentiary; remorseful, sorry, contrite, touched; conscience-smitten, conscience-stricken; self-reproachful, self-reproaching, self-accusing, self-condemning, self-humiliating, self-convicting, self-convicted; softened, melted; regretful etc. 833.3.

6. *adv.* penitently etc. *adj., mea culpa* [L.], *de profundis* [L.].

951. Impenitence
(See 950. Penitence)

1. *n.* impenitence, irrepentance, recusance *or* recusancy, uncontriteness etc. *adj.*, lack of contrition etc. 950; hardness of heart, heart of stone, seared conscience, induration, obduracy; deaf ears.

2. *v.* be impenitent etc. *adj.*, steel *or* harden the heart, turn away from the light; die game, die and make no sign.

3. *adj.* impenitent, unrepentant, uncontrite, recusant, remorseless, unremorseful; relentless, unrelenting; obdurate, hard, hardened, seared.

4. *adj.* unrepented, unatoned; graceless, shriftless; unreformed, unreclaimed, lost; irreclaimable etc. 945.19.

952. Atonement

1. *n.* atonement, reparation, amends, satisfaction, compensation, expiation, redemption, reclamation, conciliation, propitiation, redress; quittance, quits [rare]; recompense, recompensation [obs. exc. Scot. Law]; indemnification, indemnity; compromise, composition; sacrifice, peace offering etc. (oblation) 990.6.

2. *n.* apology, apologia, apologetic, abject apology, *amende honorable* [F.]; excuse, justification etc. (vindication) 937.2; acknowledgment, admission etc. (confession) 529.2.

3. *n.* penance, maceration, mortification, flagellation, lustration, shrift [arch.]; purgation, purgatory; sackcloth and ashes; sacrament of penance; penitence etc. 950; fasting etc. 956; penalty etc. 974.

4. *v.* atone, atone for, expiate, propitiate, recompense, compensate, make compensation, make amends, make good, make matters up, give satisfaction, pay the forfeit *or* penalty, wipe off old scores, set one's house in order, reclaim, recoup, redeem, repair, redress, ransom, absolve, purge, shrive; do *or* perform penance, stand in a white sheet, repent in sackcloth and ashes.

5. *v.* apologize, express regret, beg pardon, ask forgiveness, beg indulgence, *faire amende honorable* [F.]; get *or* fall down on one's knees, get *or* fall down on

---

À KEMPIS. To do it no more is the truest repentance.—LUTHER. Indeed, indeed, Repentance oft before I swore.—OMAR KHAYYÁM —FITZGERALD. When all is gone, repentance comes too late.—FULLER. He who is penitent is almost innocent.—SENECA. And wet his grave with my repentant tears.—SHAKESPEARE.
951. No power can the impenitent absolve.—DANTE. I ne'er repented anything yet in my life, / And scorn to begin now.—BEAUMONT AND FLETCHER. The world will not believe a man repents; / And this wise world of ours is mainly right.—TENNYSON. Never to repent and never to reproach others, these are the first steps to wisdom.—DIDEROT.
952. When the scourge / Inexorable, and the torturing hour / Calls us to penance.—MILTON. The hearts of good men admit of atonement.—HOMER. Apologies only account for that which they do not alter.—DISRAELI.

one's marrowbones [joc.]; take back, eat one's words etc. (recant) 607.9; excuse, offer in defense etc. (justify) 937.6, 7.

6. *adj.* atoning etc. *adj.*, propitiatory, expiatory, conciliatory, satisfactional; sacrifice, sacrificial, sacrificatory [rare]; piacular, piaculous [rare]; apologetic(al).

953. Temperance
(See 954. Intemperance)

1. *n.* temperance, moderation, sobriety, frugality, forbearance, abnegation; renouncement, renunciation; denial, self-denial; restraint, self-restraint; self-control etc. 604.3; continence etc. 960; asceticism etc. 955.

2. *n.* abstinence *or* abstinency, abstention, abstainment, abstemiousness; eschewal, eschewance [rare]; total abstinence, teetotalism; nephalism, Rechabitism; encraty [rare], Encratism; Pythagorism, Pythagoreanism; gymnosophy; Stoicism; vegetarianism, fruitarianism; prohibition, prohibitionism; asceticism etc. 955; sobriety etc. 958; avoidance etc. 623.

3. *n.* abstainer, abstinent; teetotaler, teetotalist; nephalist, Rechabite, hydropot, water-drinker; vegetarian, fruitarian; gymnosophist, gymnosoph [rare]; Pythagorean, Pythagorist; Encratite, Apostolic; ascetic etc. 955.2.

4. *n.* prohibitionist, dry [slang], Good Templar; Band of Hope [Eng.], Women's Christian Temperance Union, W.C.T.U.

5. *v.* be temperate etc. *adj.*, refrain from indulgence, refrain, abstain, forbear, spare, withhold, hold back, eschew, keep from, keep ∼, stand *or* hold aloof from, have nothing to do with, take no part in, have no hand in, let alone, let well enough alone, deny oneself, know when one has had enough; exercise self-control, ∼ self-denial *or* self restraint, control oneself, control the carnal man *or* the old Adam, control the fleshly lusts; swear off, renounce, take the pledge, get on the wagon *or* water wagon [slang], "look not upon the wine when it is red" (Bible), drink Adam's ale [coll.]; avoid etc. 623.6.

6. *adj.* temperate, moderate, sober, frugal, restrained, sparing, stinting, measured, within compass; abstinent, abstentious, abstemious; teetotal; sworn off, on the wagon *or* water wagon [slang]; vegetarian, fruitarian; continent etc. 960.2; ascetic etc. 955.3.

954. Intemperance
(See 953. Temperance)

1. *n.* intemperance, intemperateness, inabstinence; indulgence, self-indulgence; excessive indulgence, overindulgence, immoderation, unrestraint, inordinacy, excess, crapulence *or* crapulency; sensualism, sensuality; voluptuousness, voluptuosity, volupty; luxuriousness, sybaritism, luxury, lap of luxury; epicurism, epicureanism; incontinence etc. 961.2; gluttony etc. 957; drunkenness etc. 959; prodigality etc. 818; redundance etc. 641.

2. *n.* dissipation, licentiousness etc. *adj.*; free living, high living [coll.]; debauchery, debauchment; debauch, orgy, saturnalia; revelry etc. (festivity) 840.2; carousal, spree etc. (frolic) 840.3, 4, (drinking bout) 959.3.

3. *v.* be intemperate etc. *adj.*, overdo, overindulge, carry too far, carry to excess, dine not wisely but too well; indulge, indulge one's appetites, give free rein to indulgence etc. *n.*, live well *or* high, live on the fat of the land, "eat, drink, and be merry" (Bible), "look upon the wine when it is red" (Bible); wallow in voluptuousness etc. *n.*, volupt [rare], voluptuate [rare], luxuriate.

---

953. *Appetitus rationi obediant* [Let the passions be amenable to reason].—CICERO. Ask God for temperance; that's the appliance only / Which your disease requires.—SHAKESPEARE. Temperance is the nurse of chastity.—WYCHERLEY. Brevity is the soul of drinking, as of wit.—LAMB. Drink not the third glass which thou canst not tame, / When once it is within thee.—G. HERBERT. Holy dictate of spare Temperance.—MILTON. Eat not to dullness; drink not to elevation.—FRANKLIN. Health, longevity, beauty, are other names for personal purity; and temperance is the regimen for all.—A. B. ALCOTT.

954. *Trahit sua quemque voluptas* [Each one is carried away by his own desires].—VERGIL. Belike we must be incontinent that we may be continent; burning is quenched by fire.—MONTAIGNE. Full of supper and distempering draughts.—SHAKESPEARE. Nothing moderate is pleasing to the crowd.—BACON. The best things carried to excess are wrong.—C. CHURCHILL. Since the creation of the world there has been no tyrant like Intemperance.—GARRISON. 'Tis not the drinking that is to be blamed, but the excess.—SELDEN. If we

dissipate, engage in dissipation, plunge into dissipation, sensualize, debauch, wanton, rake, lead a dissolute life, live hard *or* fast, run riot, squander one's money in riotous living, burn the candle at both ends, have one's fling, sow one's wild oats; carouse, revel etc. (amuse oneself) 840.21, (drink) 959.16; tipple etc. 959.15; squander, lavish etc. (be prodigal) 818.3.

4. *adj.* intemperate, inabstinent; indulgent, self-indulgent; overindulging etc. *v.*, overindulgent; immoderate, inordinate, excessive, in excess; crapulous, crapulent; sensual, sensuous [rare]; voluptuous, voluptuary [now rare]; luxurious, given to luxury, bred *or* nursed in the lap of luxury; epicurean, epicurish; Sybaritic(al), Sybaritish; indulged, pampered; full-fed, high-fed; gluttonous etc. 957.14; drunken etc. 959.23; incontinent etc. 961.10; uncurbed, unbridled etc. (unconstrained) 748.13; prodigal etc. 818.4; redundant etc. 641.5.

5. *adj.* dissipated, licentious, dissolute, debauched; free-living, high-living [coll.]; saturnalian, orgiastic, Corybantic; incontinent, rakish etc. (unchaste) 961.10.

954a. Sensualist

n. sensualist, voluptuary, Sybarite, man of pleasure, *bon vivant* [F.], carpet knight; dissipater *or* dissipator; free liver, hard liver, high liver [coll.]; epicure, epicurean, votary *or* swine of Epicurus; gourmet, gourmand; Sardanapalus, Heliogabalus; hedonist, tragalist [rare]; glutton etc. 957.2; rake, debauchee etc. (libertine) 962.

955. Asceticism

1. *n.* asceticism, austerity, puritanism, anchoritism, Sabbatarianism, cynicism; Yoga; mortification, maceration, flagellation, martyrdom; abstinence etc. 953.2; fasting etc. 956.

2. *n.* ascetic, puritan, Sabbatarian, cynic, *Heauton Timoroumenos* [Gr.]; bhikshu [Ind.], sannyasi [Hind.], yogi *or* yogin; dervish, fakir [both Moham.]; martyr; hermit etc. (recluse) 893.4; abstainer etc. 953.3.

3. *adj.* ascetic, austere, puritanical, anchoritic(al), Sabbatarian; abstinent etc. (temperate) 953.6.

956. Fasting
(See 957. Gluttony)

1. *n.* fasting, starvation [arch.], punishment of Tantalus.

2. *n.* fast, spare *or* meager diet, lenten diet, "lenten entertainment" (Shakespeare), *soupe maigre* [F.], short-commons *or* rations; Barmecide feast; xerophagy, xerophagia; *jour maigre* [F.], fast day, fish day, banyan day; Lent, Quadragesima, Quadragesima Sunday; Ramadan [Moham.].

3. *v.* fast, not eat, starve [arch.], dine with Duke Humphrey, keep the larder lean, make *or* take two bites of a cherry.

4. *adj.* fasting etc. *v.*, lenten, quadragesimal; unfed; starved etc. (hungry) 865.19.

957. Gluttony
(See 956. Fasting)

1. *n.* gluttony, gluttonousness, greediness etc. *adj.*; greed, voracity, edacity, rapacity, gulosity, crapulence *or* crapulency, "swinish gluttony" (Milton); epicurism, epicureanism; gastronomy, gastrology [joc.]; pantophagy; guttling, guzzling etc. *v.*; intemperance etc. 954.

2. *n.* glutton, greedy *or* ravenous eater, hefty *or* husky eater [coll.], belly-god,

---

give more to the flesh than we ought, we nourish an enemy.—St. Gregory.
954a. Serenely full, the epicure would say, / Fate cannot harm me—I have dined to-day.—S. Smith. The sons of Belial, flown with insolence and wine.—Milton.
955. Thou belongest to that hopeless, sallow tribe which no wine of this world will ever warm.—Melville. When asceticism is rational it is a discipline of the mind and body to fit men for the service of an ideal.—W. Lippmann.
956. 'Tis but a three years' fast: / The mind shall banquet, though the body pine.—Shakespeare. Surfeit is the father of much fast.—Shakespeare. Spare Fast, that oft with gods doth diet.—Milton. The fool that eats till he is sick must fast till he is well.—Thornbury. He fasts enough who eats with reason.—A. J. Cronin.
957. His belly was upblown with luxury / And eke with fatness swollen were his eyne.—Spenser. Swinish gluttony / Ne'er looks to Heaven amidst his gorgeous feast.—Milton. He needs no more than birds and beasts to think, / All his occasions are to eat and drink. —Dryden. The eye is bigger than the belly.

greedygut *or* greedyguts [vulg.], gorger, gormandizer, guttler, cormorant, gastronome, Apicius; hog, pig [both coll.]; gourmand, gourmet; epicure, epicurean; pantophagist.

3. *v.* be gluttonous etc. *adj.*, eat greedily, indulge one's appetite, gluttonize, gormandize, gorge, engorge, glut, cram, stuff, guttle, guzzle, devour, devour ravenously, raven, bolt, gobble, gulp, wolf, gobble ~, gulp ~, bolt *or* wolf down, play a good knife and fork [coll.], eat like a horse, eat one's head off [coll.]; eat out of house and home; overeat, overgorge, overindulge, eat one's fill, satiate; have a ravenous appetite, have a capacious maw *or* gorge, have the stomach of an ostrich.

4. *adj.* gluttonous, greedy, gormandizing etc. *v.*, voracious, edacious, rapacious, ravenous, Apician; hoggish, piggish, swinish, greedy as a hog; crapulous, crapulent; pantophagic, pantophagous; omnivorous, all-devouring; insatiable, insatiate; overfed, overgorged, overindulged; intemperate etc. 954.4.

958. Sobriety

(See 959. Drunkenness; also 953. Temperance)

1. *n.* sobriety, soberness, unintoxicatedness etc. *adj.*; nephalism, teetotalism etc. (abstinence) 953.2; nephalist, hydropot etc. (abstainer) 953.3; prohibitionist etc. 953.4.

2. *v.* take the pledge etc. 953.5.

3. *adj.* sober, in one's sober senses *or* right mind, in possession of one's faculties; undrunk, untipsy, unintoxicated; uninebrious, uninebriate, uninebriated; cold sober [slang], sober as a judge; able to walk the chalk, able to walk the chalk mark *or* line [both coll.]; temperate etc. 953.6.

959. Drunkenness

(See 958. Sobriety; also 954. Intemperance)

1. *n.* drunkenness, insobriety, intoxication, befuddlement, temulence *or* temulency [rare]; tipsification, obfuscation, fuddle, fuddlement [all coll.]; inebriety, inebriacy, inebriation; ebriety, ebriosity [both rare]; bibacity, bibulosity; drinking, tippling etc. *v.*; winebibbing, winebibbery; potation, compotation, symposium [Hist.]; pot-valiance *or* pot-valiancy, pot-valor, Dutch courage; crapulence, crapulousness; hang-over [slang, U.S.]; bacchanalianism; Bacchus [Rom. Myth.], Dionysus [Gr. Myth.]; Bacchae, bacchante, maenad; intemperance etc. 954.

2. *n.* alcoholism, dipsomania, oenomania *or* oinomania; pathological drunkenness; *mania* or *dementia a potu* [L.], delirium tremens, D.T.'s, the horrors [both coll.]; jim-jams, blue Johnnies, pink spiders *or* elephants, snakes in the boots, gallon distemper [all slang]; grog blossom, bottle nose [both coll.]; gin drinker's liver, cirrhosis of the liver.

3. *n.* drinking bout, drunken carousal *or* revelry, spree, bout, guzzle [vulg.], potation, wassail, randy [Scot. and dial. Eng.], randan [dial. and slang]; carouse, carousal; booze, fuddle [both coll.]; drunk, soak, binge, bust, tear, skate, rantan *or* ran-tan, bout with John Barleycorn [all slang]; bat, bender, hellbender, jag, toot, bum, souse [all slang, U.S.]; bacchanal, bacchanalia, bacchanalian; debauch, orgy.

4. *n.* liquor, intoxicating liquor, "the luscious liquor" (Milton), hard liquor [U.S.], spirits, ardent spirits, intoxicant, toxicant, inebriant, potable, potation, beverage, drink, strong drink, alcoholic drink, alcohol, the creature [dial. and joc.], grog, tipple, budge [local, U.S.], guzzle [vulg.], Bacchus, nectar of the gods, firewater; booze, bouse, fuddle, tipsifier [all coll.]; rum, the Demon Rum [both U.S.]; the bottle, the cup, the cup that cheers, little brown jug; punch bowl, the flowing bowl; cordial, liqueur; hocus, micky finn [slang, U.S.], knockout drops [slang, U.S.].

(slang terms) lush, hooch, likker, alky, eyewater, fogram *or* fogrum [Naut.], ammunition, corpse reviver, tangle-legs, diddle, ruin, blue ruin, tape, lap, conversation water, gullet wash, neck oil, oil of

---

958. Honest water, which ne'er left man in the mire.—SHAKESPEARE.   A cup of cold Adam from the next purling spring.—T. HUGHES. A Rechabite poor Will must live, / And drink of Adam's ale.—PRIOR.   No woman should marry a teetotaller or a man who does not smoke.—STEVENSON.
959. Woe unto them that rise up early in the morning, that they may follow strong drink.—BIBLE.   But they also have erred through

joy, sorrow drowner, bosom friend, courage, Dutch courage, liquid courage, tonic, medicine, snake medicine.

5. *n.* malt liquors, brew, bub [old slang]; beer, "barmy beer" (Dryden), ale, stout, bitter [Eng.], schnapps [U.S.]; malt, swipes [Eng.], hops, suds, stingo [all slang]; bock ~, lager ~, weiss ~, Munich ~, Pilsener *or* schenk beer, near-beer; small beer, belch [vulg.].

6. *n.* distilled liquors, spirits; brandy, *eau de vie* [F.], *aguardiente* [Sp.], cognac, armagnac; whisky *or* whiskey, Scotch ~, Irish *or* Canadian whisky, bourbon, rye; gin, Hollands, Holland gin, schnapps, Schiedam schnapps, sloe gin, Jamaica gin; rum, Cuban rum, Bacardi, Puerto Rican rum, Jamaica rum, German rum, clean rum; arrack; vodka; applejack; tequila; liqueur, cordial, curaçao, Cointreau, crème de menthe, *crème de cacao* [F.], *crème de moka* [F.], *crème de noyau* [F.], cherry ~, apricot ~, peach *or* blackberry brandy *or* cordial, kirsch, kirschwasser, Danzig brandy *or* goldwater, benedictine, drambuie, absinthe *or* absinth, Pernod, cassis, chartreuse, maraschino, anisette.

7. *n.* wine, *vin* [F.], *vino* [Sp.]; red wine, rosy wine, "the wine that is red" (Bible), *vin rosé* [F.], white wine, vintage wine, dry *or* sweet wine, still *or* sparkling wine, heavy *or* light wine, full *or* thin wine, rough *or* smooth wine, fortified wine; claret, Bordeaux, Medoc, Sauterne; Burgundy, sparkling Burgundy, Chablis; champagne, canary, Madeira, Malaga, muscatel, Tokay; Rhine wine, Moselle, Riesling, hock; sherry, amontillado, manzanilla; port, vintage port, tawny *or* ruby port; Chianti; *vin du pays* [F.], *vin ordinaire* [F.]; dago red [slang, U.S.]; domestic wine, California wine, Ohio wine, New York State wine.

8. *n.* mixed drink, punch, cocktail, highball [coll., U.S.], gin rickey, mint julep [U.S.], bishop, negus, purl, swizzle, flip; wassail, lamb's wool; sling, gin sling [both U.S.]; smash, brandy smash, whisky smash; whisky sour; toddy, hot toddy; fizz, gin fizz.

9. *n.* illicit liquor, hooch, bootleg *or* bootlegged liquor [U.S.], bootleg [U.S.], moonshine, shine [U.S.], moonlight [all slang]; home-brew, bathtub gin *or* liquor [slang, U.S.]; bootlegging [U.S.], moonshining, moonlighting [all slang]; rumrunning [U.S.].

10. *n.* dram, nip, nipper, draft *or* draught, drop, sip, sup, suck, drink, potion, potation, libation [joc.], drench, guzzle [vulg.]; peg, swig, swill, pull, toothful, tickler [all coll.]; drop in the eye, shot, calker *or* caulker, facer, snifter, smile, wet [all slang]; reviver [slang], eye opener [slang, U.S.]; bracer, refresher, pick-me-up [all coll.]; hair of the dog, hair of the dog that bit you [both coll.]; nightcap [coll.]; chaser [coll., U.S.], *pousse-café* [F.]; stirrup cup, parting cup, doch-an-dorrach, ~ -dorroch *or* -dorris [Scot.]; cheering drink *or* cup, cheerer [Scot. and N. of Eng.].

11. *n.* drunkard, sot, toper, tippler, bibber, guzzler, swiller, lovepot, tosspot, dram drinker, tavern haunter, thirsty soul, devotee of *or* to Bacchus, slave of the beast; tun, boozer *or* bouser, fuddler, swigger [all coll.]; winebibber, oenophilist; hard drinker, big drunk [slang]; alcoholic, alcoholist; carouser, reveler, wassailer; bacchanal, bacchanalian; addict etc. 613.7.

(slang terms) drunk, booze, lush, lusher, sponge, soak, soaker, guzzle, hooch hound, boozehound, ginhound, hooch *or* booze guzzler, mug blot, bottle sucker, elbow bender *or* crooker, barfly, swillbelly, swillpot, swilltub, swillbowl, tank, moist-'un, Admiral of the Red; stew, souse, bum, rummy, rum hound, booze fighter [all U.S.].

12. *n.* liquor dealer, rummy [slang, U.S.]; bartender, barkeeper, barkeep [U.S.], barman [Eng.], tapster, publican [Eng.]; barmaid, tapstress; wine seller, wine merchant, vintner; moonshiner, moonlighter [U.S.], bootlegger [all slang]; blind-pigger [slang, U.S.]; rumrunner [U.S.]; distiller, stiller [rare]; brewer, brewster [now Scot. and dial. Eng.], brewmaster; liquorist [rare].

13. *n.* barroom, bar, taproom, tap [coll.], tavern, pothouse, mughouse, ale-

---

wine and through strong drink.—BIBLE. O God, that men should put an enemy in their mouths to steal away their brains!—SHAKESPEARE. He bids the ruddy cup go round, / Till sense and sorrow both are drowned.— SCOTT. For ilka man that's drunk's a lord. —BURNS. Good wine lures back the winebibber.—M. ARNOLD. There are two things that will be believed of any man whatsoever, and one of them is that he has taken to drink.—

house, rumshop [U.S.], grogshop, dramshop, groggery [U.S.], gin mill [slang], gin palace [coll.], exchange [slang, U.S.], boozer [slang, Eng.]; saloon [U.S.], drinking saloon, saloon bar [Eng.]; public house, public [coll., Eng.], pub [slang, Eng.]; cabaret, night club, café dansant; beer parlor, beerhouse, jerry shop [slang, Eng.], beer garden; wine shop, *bistro* [coll., F.], barrel house [slang, U.S.], dive [chiefly U.S.]; speakeasy [slang, U.S.], blind tiger [slang], blind pig [slang, U.S.], shebeen [Ir. and Scot.]; inn etc. 189.8.

14. *n.* distillery, distiller, still; brewery, brewhouse; winery, wine press; bottling works.

15. *v.* tipple, drink, nip, grog, guzzle, swizzle, soak, bib, sot [rare], tun, quaff, sip, sup, lap, lap up, crack a bottle, take a whet, slake one's thirst, cheer *or* refresh the inner man, drown one's sorrows *or* troubles, commune with the spirits [joc.], sacrifice at the shrine of Bacchus; toss off *or* down, toss one's glass *or* drink; drink off *or* up, empty one's glass, drain the cup, drink bottoms-up, leave no heeltaps; drink deep, drink one's fill; drink hard, drink like a fish; take a drop *or* glass too much; drunken, get drunk; take to drink *or* drinking; be intemperate etc. 954.3.

(colloquial terms) tope, booze, bouse, swig, swill, fuddle, moisten *or* wet one's clay, ~ whistle *or* swallow, wet the red lane; take a hair of the dog *or* of the dog that bit you.

(slang terms) liquor, liquor up, booze, boozify, swack, lush, souse, bum, tank up, fire up, prime up, hit the booze *or* bottle, have one's swill, splice the main brace, drown the shamrock, dip the beak, exercise ~, bend ~, crook *or* raise the elbow, take one's elbow exercise, take a drop in the eye.

16. *v.* carouse, spree, go on a spree etc. *n.*, revel, wassail, debauch, "eat, drink, and be merry" (Bible), paint the town red [slang]; dissipate etc. 954.3.

17. *v.* drink to, drink a toast, toast, drink *or* pledge the health of; wet [slang], wet a bargain *or* deal [slang], make a Dutch bargain *or* wet bargain.

18. *v.* inebriate, make drunk etc. *adj.*, intoxicate, addle, fuzzle [obs.], befuddle, bemuse, besot, tipple [now rare], make one see double, get into one's head; fuddle, tipsify, overtake [all coll.]; boozify, swack, stew, souse [U.S.], pollute, plaster [U.S.], pickle, illuminate, disguise, crock [all slang].

19. *v.* be drunk etc. *adj.*, show one's drinks [coll.], see double, have a jag on [slang], have a drop *or* glass too much, have one over the eight [coll.]; stagger, reel; pass out [slang, U.S.].

20. *v.* bootleg [U.S.], moonshine, moonlight [all slang].

21. *adj.* drunk, drunken, in a state of intoxication etc. *n.*, intoxicated, inebrious, inebriate, inebriated, tipsy, bacchic(al), in liquor, in one's cups, *inter pocula* [L.], smelling of the cork, under the influence of liquor, the worse for liquor, having had a drop too much, top-heavy, dizzy, giddy, muddled, addled, flustered, bemused, mellow, merry, jolly, happy, gay, nappy, beery, sodden, besotted, drenched, maudlin, seeing double, reeling, far-gone; temulent, temulentive [both rare]; full [vulg.], fou [Scot.]; pot-valiant, potvalorous, full of Dutch courage; crapulous, crapulent.

(colloquial terms) boozy, bousy, fuddled, obfuscated, muzzy, groggy, ginny, hearty, flush, flushed, glorious, overtaken, with one over the eight; drunk as a piper, ~ a fiddler, ~ a lord, ~ an owl, ~ Chloë *or* David's sow.

(slang terms) lush, lushy, soused [U.S.], soaked, boiled, canned, corned, crocked, crocko, heeled, jingled [U.S.], hiccius-doccius [Eng.], cut, pickled, plastered [U.S.], shellacked [U.S.], fried, fried to the gills, oiled, lubricated, jugbitten, fresh, afflicted, organized, polluted, potted, tanked, loaded, primed, primed to the muzzle, ~ barrel *or* trigger, screwed, raddled, sprung, sewed up, squiffy, swacked, disguised, gilded, balmy, cockeyed, cockeyed drunk, elevated, high, high as a kite, in one's airs *or* altitudes, out of altitudes, lit up, illuminated, glowing, fired up, charged up, hopped up, jagged up, pie-eyed, roaring *or* rip-roaring drunk, stinko, tight; half-seas over, bearing *or* flying the ensign,

---

TARKINGTON. Candy is dandy / But liquor is quicker.—O. NASH. A bumper of good liquor / Will end a contest quicker / Than justice, judge, or vicar.—SHERIDAN. Tonight with wine drown care.—HORACE.

listing to starboard, decks-awash, carrying *or* with too much sail, in the wind *or* wind's eye, three sheets in the wind *or* the wind's eye, with the top gallant sails out [all Naut. slang].

22. *adj.* dead-drunk, blind drunk, blind [coll.], overcome, out [coll.], out cold [slang], passed out [slang, U.S.], blotto [slang], stiff [slang], helpless, under the table.

23. *adj.* bibulous, bibacious, given *or* inclined to drink, addicted to drink *or* the bottle, drunken, sottish, liquorish, liquor-loving, liquor-drinking, winebibbing; drinking, toping etc. *v.*; intemperate etc. 954.4.

24. *adj.* inebriating, intoxicating etc. *v.*; inebriative, inebriant; alcoholic, spirituous, ardent, strong, hard [U.S.].

960. Purity
(See 961. Impurity)

1. *n.* purity, decency, delicacy, decorum, modesty, shame; pudicity, pudicitia; chastity, virtue, honesty [arch. or rare], continence *or* continency; virginity, virgin [rare], pucelage *or* pucellage [rare]; Platonic love, Platonism; innocence etc. 946; immaculacy etc. (cleanness) 652; celibacy etc. 904; temperance etc. 953; virgin etc. (celibate) 904.2, 3.

2. *adj.* pure, pure-hearted, pure in heart; decent, delicate, decorous, modest; chaste, virtuous, honest [arch.], "as chaste as Diana" (Shakespeare), "as chaste as unsunn'd snow" (Shakespeare), "chaste as morning dew" (Young); continent; virgin, virginal; Platonic; faultless, sinless etc. (innocent) 946.5; spotless, immaculate, undefiled etc. (clean) 652.14; holy, uncorrupted etc. 944.3, 4; celibate etc. 904.5.

961. Impurity
(See 960. Purity)

1. *n.* impurity, grossness etc. *adj.*, immodesty, indelicacy, inelegance *or* inelegancy, indecency, impropriety, impudicity, obscenity, vulgarity, scurrility, fescenninity, ribaldry, bawdry, pornography; smut, dirt, filth; *double entente* [F.] etc. 851.3; vice etc. 945.

2. *n.* unchastity, wantonness, licentiousness etc. *adj.*; incontinence, dissipation, rakery [now rare], venery, wenching, fornication; libertinism, libertinage; debauchery, debauchment; intemperance etc. 954.

3. *n.* carnality, animalism, sensuality, flesh; animal *or* carnal nature, the beast, Adam, the Old Adam, the offending Adam; lewdness, lasciviousness etc. *adj.*; concupiscence, lust, passion, carnal passion, fleshly lust, sensuous desire, sexual desire *or* lust, bodily appetite, aphrodisia, salacity, pruriency, lechery, lubricity; nymphomania; satyrism, satyriasis; oestrus, oestrum, oestrous *or* oestrus cycle, heat, rut, must; unnatural desires, incest, sodomy, sadism, masochism; homosexuality, pederasty, Lesbianism, Sapphism; bloodthirst, bloodthirstiness; cannibality, cannibalism; desire etc. 865.

4. *n.* seduction, seducement; violation of chastity, violation, debauchment, defloration, defilement, abuse, stupration, rape; allurement etc. 617.

5. *n.* intrigue, liaison etc. (love affair) 897.3.

6. *n.* social evil, prostitution, harlotry, whoredom, bordel, streetwalking, meretricious traffic, Mrs. Warren's profession; whoremastery, whoremonging; concubinage; adultery, criminal conversation [Law], cuckoldry, cuckoldom; free love, free-lovism.

7. *n.* brothel, house of prostitution, ~ joy *or* ill fame, bagnio, bawdyhouse, whorehouse [vulg.], bordel, Yoshiwara [Jap.], stew, dive, sink of iniquity; cat house, crib, joint [all slang]; panel house *or* den; red-light district, tenderloin, street of fallen women, stews.

8. *v.* be impure etc. *adj.*; defile, seduce, debauch, abuse, violate, rape, stuprate

---

960. A woman's chastity consists, like an onion, of a series of coats.—HAWTHORNE. An unattempted woman cannot boast of her chastity.—MONTAIGNE. She is chaste who was never asked the question.—CONGREVE. The sun-clad power of Chastity.—MILTON. The very ice of chastity is in them.—SHAKESPEARE. Be warm, but pure; be amorous, but chaste.—BYRON. To the pure all things are pure.—SHELLEY. A soul as white as heaven. —BEAUMONT AND FLETCHER. Who can find a virtuous woman? for her price is far above rubies.—BIBLE.

961. To be carnally minded is death.—BIBLE. Wantonness for evermair, / Wantonness has been my ruin.—BURNS. What men call gallantry, and gods adultery, / Is much more common where the climate's sultry.—BYRON.

[rare], deflower, ravish, ruin, force; prostitute; commit adultery etc. *n.*; intrigue; wanton, dissipate etc. (be intemperate) 954.3.

9. *adj.* impure, unpure; immodest, shameless, unblushing, brazenfaced; indecorous, indelicate, inelegant, indecent, Fescennine, scurrilous, low, vulgar, risqué, coarse, gross, broad, ribald, obscene, lewd, bawdy, pornographic, sultry [slang], lurid, smutty, dirty, unclean, foul, filthy, nasty, vile, fulsome, offensive, not to be mentioned to ears polite; foul-mouthed, foul-spoken; improper, unbecoming, unseemly; wicked etc. 945.11–19.

10. *adj.* unchaste, unvirtuous, incontinent, wanton, licentious, Cyprian, adulterous, debauched, dissipated, dissolute, lewd, abandoned, profligate, free, rampant, wild, fast, light, gay, rakish; rakehell, rakehellish, rakehelly; loose, of loose character *or* morals; frail, weak; of easy virtue *or* morals, easy [coll.], no better than she should be; on the loose [coll.], on the town *or* streets, on the *pavé* [F.]; whorish, scarlet, fallen, streetwalking, Paphian, meretricious; prostitute, prostituted; intemperate etc. 954.4, 5; uncurbed, unbridled etc. (unconstrained) 748.13.

11. *adj.* carnal, carnal-minded; fleshly, sensual, voluptuous, animalistic, theroid, brutish, swinish; bestial, beastly, beastlike; concupiscent, lustful, prurient, salacious, lickerish, lewd, lascivious, lecherous, libidinous, goatish, satyric(al), erotic; lubricous, lubricious [rare], lubric(al) [rare]; oestrous, oestrual; ruttish, rutty; must, musty; burning, hot, in heat; incestuous; bloodthirsty, flesh-devouring; cannibal, cannibalic, cannibalistic; desirous etc. 865.16.

962. Libertine

1. *n.* libertine, rake, rakehell [arch.], loose fish [coll.], profligate, rip [coll.], bounder [coll.], cad, rounder [slang]; wolf, woman *or* skirt chaser, love pirate [all slang]; fast man, intrigant, lecher, satyr, goat, old goat, whoremaster, whoremonger, whorehound [slang], *paillard* [F.], adulterer, fornicator, gay dog, gay deceiver, fancy man, gigolo, chartered libertine, *vieux marcheur* [F.]; debauchee, debaucher; seducer, ravisher, defiler, violator, violater, rapist, raper; pederast, sodomite, sodomist, fairy [slang], pansy [slang], homosexual, homo [slang]; Lothario, Don Juan, Bluebeard, Casanova; voluptuary etc. 954a.

2. *n.* adulteress, fornicatress, loose woman, woman of easy virtue *or* morals, strumpet, wench, trollop, trull, baggage, hussy, drab, bitch [vulg.], jade, minx, quean, mopsy [dial. Eng.], slut, harridan, wanton, *Lorette* [F.], *cocotte* [F.], *petite dame* [F.], grisette; pack, naughty pack [both arch.]; demirep, tart, broad [U.S.], chippy [U.S.], piece (all slang).

prostitute, courtesan *or* courtezan, bona roba [arch.], demimondaine, scarlet woman, harlot, whore, punk [obsoles.], fallen woman, erring sister, *fille de joie* [F.], daughter of joy, woman, woman of the town, streetwalker, *poule* [F.], painted woman, Cyprian, Paphian, stew, meretrix, laced mutton [old slang], unfortunate woman; cat, bat, bag [all slang]; white slave; pickup; Sapphist, Lesbian; Jezebel, Messalina, Delilah, Thais, Phryne, Aspasia, Lais, Sadie Thompson, Mrs. Warren; demimonde, frail sisterhood.

3. *n.* mistress, kept woman *or* mistress, concubine, paramour, doxy, *petite amie* [F.], spiritual wife.

4. *n.* procurer, pimp, pander, mackerel [arch.], *maquereau* [F.], runner [slang, U.S.], bawd; procuress, *conciliatrix* [L.], madam [coll.]; white slaver.

963. Legality
(See 964. Illegality)

1. *n.* legality, legitimacy, lawfulness etc. *adj.*; legalization, legitimatization, legiti-

---

The lusts and greeds of the Body scandalize the Soul; but it has to come to heel.—L. P. SMITH. The new lust gives the lecher the new thrill.—MASEFIELD.
962. Lewd fellows of the baser sort.—BIBLE. This is a subtle whore.—SHAKESPEARE. In silk and scarlet walks many a harlot.—W. C. HAZLITT.

963. *Ex facto jus oritur* [From the fact arises the law].—BLACKSTONE. *Corruptissima republica plurimae leges* [In the most corrupt state, the most laws].—TACITUS. The majesty and power of law and justice.—SHAKESPEARE. We must not make a scarecrow of the law.—SHAKESPEARE. The Law, our kingdom's golden chaine.—DEKKER. Who breaks no law is subject to no king.—G. CHAPMAN. The gladsome light of jurisprudence.

mization; legislature, legislation; constitutionality, constitutionalism; codification; legal process; justice etc. 941.

2. *n.* law, *lex* [L.], constitution, statute, rubric, canon, institution; ordinance, ordonnance; act, enactment; rule, ruling; prescript, prescription; regulation, *règlement* [F.]; dictate, dictation, dictum; form, formula, formulary, formality; standing order; bylaw *or* byelaw; habeas corpus; *fieri facias* [L.]; equity; common law; unwritten law, *lex non scripta* [L.]; written *or* statute law, *lex scripta* [L.].
international law, law of nations, *droit des gens* [F.], *jus gentium* [L.]; local law, *lex loci* or *situs* [L.]; law of the land, *lex terrae* [L.]; civil law, *jus civile* [L.]; law of the domicile, *lex domicilii* [L.]; law of general application, *lex generalis* [L.]; law of the forum, *lex fori* [L.]; mercantile law, *lex mercatorum* or *mercatoria* [L.]; criminal law, crown law [Eng.]; canon *or* ecclesiastical law, Corpus Juris Canonici; Corpus Juris Civilis, code *or* body of laws, code, corpus juris, capitulary, pandect, digest; charter; precept etc. 697; edict, rescript etc. (decree) 741.3.

3. *n.* (science of law) jurisprudence, law, nomology; nomography.

4. *v.* legalize, legitimate, legitimize, legitimatize; legislate, make *or* pass a law, enact, ordain, put in force; constitute, constitutionalize; authorize, sanction, prescribe, fix, set, establish; charter; formulate, formalize; regulate, regularize; codify; decree, order etc. (command) 741.4.

5. *adj.* legal, legitimate, lawful, rightful, licit, according to law, accordant with law, conformable to law, within the law; legalized, constituted etc. *v.*; constitutional; vested; statutable, statutory; legislative, legislatorial; judicial, juridic(al); jurisprudent, jurisprudential [rare]; nomistic, nomothetic(al); lawlike; permitted etc. 760.6; lawabiding etc. (upright) 939.7; just etc. 941.3.

6. *adv.* legally etc. *adj.*, by law, *de jure* [L.], in the eye of the law.

964. Illegality
(See 963. Legality)

1. *n.* illegality, unlawfulness, illicitness etc. *adj.*; illegitimacy, illegitimation; bastardy, bastardism; bend *or* bar sinister, baton [both Her.]; unconstitutionality, unauthorization, informality; criminality, criminalism; antinomy; outlawry; prohibition etc. 761.

2. *n.* violation of law, lawbreaking, crime, offense, violation, breach, infraction, infringement, transgression, trespass, contravention; felony, misdemeanor; sin etc. (vice) 945.1; delinquency etc. 945.3; malfeasance etc. (misdeed) 947.2; disobedience etc. 742; unconformity etc. 83.

3. *n.* lawlessness etc. *adj.*, irresponsibility, unaccountability; club law, nihilism etc. (anarchy) 738.2; despotism, tyranny etc. (arbitrary power) 739.2.

4. *v.* violate the law, break the law, transgress, trespass, infringe the law, disobey the law, offend against the law, set the law at defiance, fly in the face of the law, trample the law under foot, ride roughshod over the law, drive a coach and four *or* six through a statute, set the law at naught, make the law a dead letter, disregard the law, take the law into one's own hands, kick over the traces, commit a crime etc. *n.*

5. *adj.* illegal, nonlegal, nonlicit, unlawful, illegitimate, illicit, wrongful, actionable, unallowed, not allowed, against the law; criminal, criminous, criminalistic; unchartered, unconstitutional, unwarranted, unwarrantable, unauthorized; unofficial, informal; injudicial [rare], extrajudicial; contraband; adulterous, adulterine; bastard, misbegot, misbegotten, miscreated; outlaw, outlawed; null and void, a dead letter; prohibited etc. 761.4; forged, fraudulent etc. (spurious) 545.12.

—COKE. Law governs man and reason the law.—FULLER. So many laws argues so many sins.—MILTON. Laws, like houses, lean on one another.—BURKE. Laws too gentle are seldom obeyed; too severe, seldom executed.—FRANKLIN. Laws spring from the instinct of self-preservation.—INGERSOLL. Public opinion always is in advance of the Law.

—GALSWORTHY. *Ignorantia legis neminem excusat* [Ignorance of the law excuses no one]. 964. A law observed is merely law; broken, it is law and executioner.—MENANDER. Laws were made to be broken.—J. WILSON. He who holds no laws in awe, / He must perish by the law.—BYRON. There is no grievance that is a fit object of redress by mob law.—LINCOLN.

6. *adj.* lawless, unrestrained, licentious, unruly, disorderly, disorganized, chaotic; arbitrary, discretionary; irresponsible, unanswerable, unaccountable; anarchic etc. 738.8; unconformable etc. 83.9; transgressive etc. (disobedient) 742.6; criminal etc. (guilty) 947.4.

7. *adv.* illegally etc. *adj.*, in violation of law, *ex delicto* [L.].

965. Jurisdiction

Administration of Justice.—**1.** *n.* jurisdiction, judicature, judicatory, legal authority, ~ right *or* power; soke [Law, Hist.]; original *or* appellate jurisdiction, exclusive *or* concurrent jurisdiction, civil *or* criminal jurisdiction, common-law *or* equitable jurisdiction, in rem *or* in personam jurisdiction; magistracy, magistrature, magistrateship; mayoralty.

administration, government etc. (direction) 693.1–3; dominion, control etc. (authority) 737.1, 2; administrator, official etc. (director) 694; mayor, bailiff, sheriff etc. (civil authorities) 745.9, 10; tribunal etc. 966; judge etc. 967; judgment etc. 480.

2. *n.* bureau, office, department, portfolio, secretariat, cutchery [Ind.]; municipality, bailiwick; constabulary, constablery, sheriffry, sheriffalty, shrievalty; constablewick, sheriffwick.

3. *v.* administer justice, administer, administrate; preside, preside at the board, occupy the chair, have *or* hold jurisdiction over; supervise etc. 693.5; govern etc. 737.11; sit in judgment, try, sentence etc. (judge) 480.6, 8, 9.

4. *adj.* jurisdictional, jurisdictive, juridic(al); judicative, judicatory, judicatorial; judicial, judiciary, judgmatic(al) [coll.]; executive, administrative etc. (directing) 693.6; tribunal etc. 966.7.

5. *adv.* judicially etc. *adj., coram judice* [L.].

966. Tribunal

1. *n.* tribunal, judicature, judicatory, judiciary; court of justice, ~ law *or* arbitration, court, curia, forum, board, durbar [Ind.], divan [Orient.], Areopagus; inquisition; seat of justice, justice ~, judgment *or* mercy seat, bench, woolsack [Eng.]; bar, bar of justice; drumhead; hustings, hustings court; chancery, chancery court, court of chancery, court of conscience; court of equity, equity court; court of probate, probate court.

court of review, appellate court; *cour des aides* [F., Hist.]; court of inquiry [Mil.], court of honor; Permanent Court of International Justice, Permanent Court of Arbitration, Hague Tribunal; court of record, court of wards, court of claims, court of domestic relations, court of requests, divorce court, criminal court, police court, juvenile *or* children's court, circuit court, county court; council etc. 696.

2. *n.* (British courts) sessions, petty ~, quarter ~, special *or* general sessions; assizes, court of assize; High Court, High Court of Justice, High *or* Supreme Court of Judicature, High Court of Appeal, superior courts of Westminster, Court of Queen's *or* King's Bench, court of chancery, Court of Common Pleas, Court of Exchequer, Court of Exchequer Chamber, court of admiralty, court of probate, Court of Divorce and Matrimonial Causes, Court of Appeal, Court of Criminal Appeal, Court of St. James's *or* James, Court of the Duchy of Lancaster, Court of Common Bank, Court of Common Council, Lords Justices' Court, Rolls Court, Vice Chancellor's Court, Stannary Court, Palatine Court, Judicial Committee of the Privy Council; Green Cloth *or* Greencloth, Board of Green Cloth; court of attachments, woodmote; wardmote, wardmote court.

eyre, justices in eyre, Court of High Commission, Star Chamber, burghmoot *or* burghmote, barmote, courtlet, courtbaron, court of piepoudre [all Hist.]; Court of Small Causes [Ind.]; Court of Justiciary [Scot.].

3. *n.* (United States courts) Supreme Court, United States Supreme Court; United States District Court, United States Circuit Court of Appeal, Federal Court of Claims, Court of Private Land Claims, court of sessions, court of errors.

4. *n.* ecclesiastical court, Rota, Sacra Romana Rota, Papal Court, Curia, Court of Arches [Eng.], Court of Peculiars [Eng.], Court of Audience [Eng. Hist.].

5. *n.* court-martial (*pl.* courts-martial), general ~, special *or* summary court-martial, drumhead court-martial.

6. *n.* courthouse, Statehouse [U.S.], townhouse, town hall, court; courtroom; jury box; witness box *or* stand, dock.

7. *adj.* tribunal, tribunitial *or* tribunicial, tribunitian *or* tribunician, tribunitiary, tribunitious [obs.]; appellate; curial; judicative etc. 965.4.

967. Judge

1. *n.* judge, justice, justice of the peace, J. P., judicator, magistrate, alcalde [Sp.], Mr. Justice; his honor, his worship, his lordship; justiciar, justiciary [both Eng. and Scot. Hist.]; arbiter, arbitrator, moderator, umpire, referee, referendary [rare]; jurat; archon, tribune, praetor, ephor, syndic, podesta [It.] [all Hist.]; mollah, ulema, hakim, mufti, cadi [all Moham.]; barmaster [Eng.]; puisne judge *or* justice; lay judge, J.A., judge advocate; P.J., presiding judge, probate judge, police judge, ~ justice *or* magistrate; recorder; judge *or* justice of assize; circuit judge; assessor, legal assessor; receiver, official receiver.

beak [Eng.], his nibs [both Hist.]; mittimus [joc.]; wooden judge [U.S., coll.]; bencher, deemster [both arch.]; Lord Justice, Lord Chancellor, Master of the Rolls, vice-chancellor; Chief Justice, Lord Chief Justice *or* Baron; Baron of the Exchequer; Pontius Pilate, Rhadamanthus, Minos, Solomon; peacemaker, propitiator etc. (mediator) 724.2; critic etc. 480.5; court etc. (tribunal) 966; judgment etc. 480.

2. *n.* jury, twelve men in a box, panel, sessions [Scot.], country; jury of matrons *or* women; inquest, jury of inquest, coroner's jury; jury of the vicinage; grand jury, petty jury.

3. *n.* juror, juryman, jurywoman; talesman; foreman of the jury, jury chancellor [Scot.]; grand-juror, grand-juryman; petty-juror, petty-juryman; recognitor [Eng. Hist.].

4. *v.* judge etc. 480.6–10; administer justice etc. 965.3.

5. *adj.* judicial etc. 480.11.

968. Lawyer

1. *n.* lawyer, barrister, barrister-at-law, attorney, attorney-at-law, solicitor; Solicitor, Supreme Court; S.S.C.; counsel, counselor *or* counsellor, legal adviser, advocate, proctor, procurator, bencher, legist, jurist, jurisconsult, jurisprudent, jurisprudentialist [rare]; pleader, special pleader; private attorney, attorney in fact; prosecuting attorney, prosecutor, public prosecutor; district attorney, D.A.; attorney general, A.G.; civilian; publicist; conveyancer; criminal lawyer, notary, notary public; scrivener, writer.

green bag, shyster [U.S.], ambulance chaser [U.S.], pettifogger [all coll.]; mouthpiece [slang]; pundit, vakil [both Ind.]; law agent, writer to the signet [both Scot.]; King's *or* Queen's counsel, K.C., Q.C., silk, silk gown, silk-gownsman, junior barrister, junior counsel, stuff, stuff gown, stuff-gownsman, leader, sergeant-at-law, tubman, cursitor [all Eng.]; agent, spokesman etc. (deputy) 759; mediator etc. 724.2; judge etc. 967.

2. *n.* bar, legal profession, members of the bar, gentlemen of the long robe; Inns of Court *or* Chancery [Eng.].

3. *v.* practice law, practice at *or* within the bar, lawyer [rare], plead; be called to *or* within the bar, be admitted to the bar, take silk.

4. *v.* disbar, disbench [Eng.], unfrock.

5. *adj.* barristerial, jurisprudent, jurisprudential; forensic, forensal [rare]; at the bar, *banco regis* [L.].

969. Lawsuit

1. *n.* lawsuit, suit, suit in *or* at law, action, proceedings, prosecution, litigation; case, cause; dispute etc. (argument) 476.2, (quarrel) 713.3.

---

967. It is better that a judge should lean on the side of compassion than severity.—CERVANTES. The judge ... decides as he can, and hopes he has done justice.—EMERSON.

968. The first thing we do, let's kill all the lawyers.—SHAKESPEARE. Lawyers' houses are built on the heads of fools.—G. HERBERT. If there were no bad people, there would be no good lawyers.—DICKENS.
969. Discourage litigation. Persuade your neighbors to compromise whenever you can.—LINCOLN. He that goes to law (as the proverb is) holds a wolf by the ears.—R. BURTON.

2. *n.* summons, writ of summons, subpoena, citation; nisi prius; venire, venire facias, venire facias juratores, venire facias de novo, vinire de novo; habeas corpus, writ of habeas corpus; writ of protection; latitat [Eng. Hist.].

3. *n.* arraignment, impeachment, presentment, indictment; bill of indictment, true bill; accusation etc. 938.

4. *n.* arrest, apprehension, imprisonment etc. (restraint) 751.

5. *n.* trial, hearing, inquiry, inquisition, inquest, assize; examination, cross-examination etc. 461.3, 9.

6. *n.* pleadings, arguments at the bar; declaration, claim, deposition, allegation, allegation *or* statement of facts, procès-verbal, bill *or* declaration of rights, information, libel; demurrer, general *or* special demurrer; affidavit, affidavy [dial.]; appeal, writ of error; appeal motion; certiorari, writ of certiorari; plea etc. (defense) 937.2; rebutter, surrejoinder etc. (answer) 462.2; confutation etc. 479; testimony etc. 467.2.

7. *n.* evidence etc. 467; counterevidence etc. 468; corpus delicti etc. 947.3.

8. *n.* verdict, decision, finding, sentence etc. (judgment) 480; innocence etc. 946; acquittal etc. 970; guilt etc. 947; condemnation etc. 971; penalty etc. 974.

9. *n.* litigant, litigator, litigationist; suitor, party to a suit; panel, parties litigant; accessory before *or* after the fact; accusant, defendant etc. 938.2, 3; witness etc. 467.6.

10. *v.* sue, prosecute, litigate, go into litigation, bring suit, sue *or* prosecute at law, go to law, seek in law, seek justice *or* legal redress, appeal to the law, take to court, bring into court, bring a case before the court *or* bar, bring to justice, bring to trial *or* the bar, put on trial, take before the judge, tell it to the judge [joc.], prefer *or* file a claim, prosecute a suit against, bring action against, take *or* institute legal proceedings against, take *or* have the law of *or* on [coll.], law [coll. or dial], lawyer [rare], set down for hearing, implead.

cite, summon, summons, serve with a writ, attach, distrain; arraign, impeach, indict, bring up for investigation, have *or* pull up [coll.]; call, call to witness, bring forward, produce *or* confront witnesses; plead, argue at the bar, challenge the jurors; empanel a jury; hang the jury [coll.].

apprehend, commit etc. (arrest) 751.9; prefer charges etc. (accuse) 938.4; inform on etc. 527.10; give evidence etc. (testify) 467.8; dispute etc. (argue) 476.11, (quarrel) 713.7; defend, plead for etc. (justify) 937.6; affirm etc. 535.3; deny etc. 536.2; confute etc. 479.2; surrebut, surrejoin etc. (answer) 462.6; take oath etc. (depose) 535.4.

11. *v.* try, hear, sit in judgment etc. (judge) 480.6, 8; examine, cross-examine etc. (interrogate) 461.15.

12. *v.* bring in a verdict, pronounce judgment etc. 480.9; acquit etc. 970.3; convict etc. 971.2; penalize etc. 974.3.

13. *adj.* litigious, litigant, litigatory; *coram judice, sub judice* [all L.]; causidical; litigable, actionable; disputatious etc. (argumentative) 476.14, (quarrelsome) 901.9; inquisitorial etc. 461.24.

14. *adv.* at law, in litigation, in court, before the court, ~ bar *or* judge, at bar, at the bar, up for investigation *or* hearing, on trial; *pendente lite* [L.].

970. Acquittal
(See 971. Condemnation)

1. *n.* acquittal, quittance, acquittance; exculpation, disculpation; exoneration, absolution, vindication, remission, compurgation, clearance, quietus; pardon, excuse; respite, reprieve, reprieval [rare]; forgiveness etc. 918; discharge, release etc. (liberation) 750.

2. *n.* impunity, immunity, exemption, indemnity, amnesty.

3. *v.* acquit, exculpate, disculpate [rare], let off [coll.], exonerate, clear, vindicate, absolve, whitewash; assoil [arch.], assoilzie [Scot.]; pardon, excuse; remit, remit the penalty of; reprieve, respite; amnesty, grant amnesty to; forgive etc. 918.3; exempt etc. 748.10; discharge, release etc. (liberate) 750.2.

4. *adj.* acquitted, exonerated etc. *v.,* uncondemned, unpunished, unchastised; recommended to mercy.

---

970. It is safer that a bad man should not be accused, than that he should be acquitted.—LIVY. No guilty man is acquitted at the bar of his own conscience.—JUVENAL.

The worst of law is that one suit breeds twenty. —G. HERBERT. Lawsuits consume time, and money, and rest, and friends.—G. HERBERT.

971. Condemnation
(See 970. Acquittal)

1. *n.* condemnation, conviction, damnation, doom, proscription; attainder, attainture, attaintment; sentence, rap [slang]; death sentence, death warrant; trumped-up charge, put-up job [slang], frame *or* frame-up [slang]; self-condemnation, self-conviction; accusation etc. 938; penalty etc. 974.

2. *v.* condemn, convict, cast [obs. exc. dial.], damn, doom, sentence, pronounce sentence, pass sentence on, prove *or* find guilty, bring home to, attaint, proscribe; nonsuit; give the death sentence, sign the death warrant; convict on a trumped-up charge, put up a job [slang], frame *or* frame up [slang]; pronounce judgment etc. 480.9; penalize etc. 974.3; accuse etc. 938.4; disapprove etc. 932.5–8.

3. *v.* stand condemned, be convicted, be found guilty.

4. *adj.* condemnatory, damnatory; accusatory etc. 938.5.

5. *adj.* condemned, found guilty etc. *v.*; self-condemned, self-convicted.

972. Punishment
(See 973. Reward; also 974. Penalty)

1. *n.* punishment, punition, chastisement, chastening, correction, castigation, discipline, infliction, ferule, trial, whatfor [slang], Jesse [coll., U.S.]; pay, payment; retribution, retributive justice, nemesis; penal retribution, penalty, penalization; providential punishment, judgment; dire *or* harsh punishment, *peine forte et dure* [F.]; Nemesis, Erinys, Eumenides, the Furies; penology; requital etc. (retaliation) 718, (reward) 973; due reward *or* punishment, comeuppance [coll., U.S.] etc. (deserts) 924.2; revenge etc. 919.

2. *n.* (forms of punishment) penal servitude, hard labor, rock pile, galleys; torture, torment, rack, rail-riding, scarpines, picketing, dragonnade, dismemberment; strappado, estrapade; martyrdom; *auto de fe* [Sp.]; *auto-da-fé*, lash, scaffold etc. (instrument of punishment)

975; imprisonment etc. 751.2; transportation, exile etc. (banishment) 297.3.

3. *n.* whipping, beating, cudgeling etc. *v.*; pummel, flagellation, fustigation, bastinado; dressing, dressing-down [both coll.]; strap oil, hazel oil, hickory oil, birch oil, dose of strap oil etc. [all slang]; *argumentum baculinum* [L.], stick law; gantlet; rap on the knuckles, slap in the face, box on the ear; cuff, slap, kick etc. (blow) 276.3.

4. *n.* capital punishment, execution, judicial murder; hanging, floorless jig [slang], the rope *or* noose; lynching, necktie party *or* sociable [slang, U.S.]; impalement, crucifixion; strangling, strangulation, garrote; electrocution, the chair [coll.], the hot seat [slang]; beheading, decapitation, decollation, the guillotine; shooting etc. *v.*; drowning, *noyade* [F.]; disembowelment; hara-kiri, seppuku [both Jap.]; poisoning, hemlock; lethal chamber; killing etc. 361.

5. *v.* punish, inflict punishment etc. *n.*, chastise, chasten, castigate, smite, correct, administer correction, deal retributive justice, bring to retribution, bring *or* call to account *or* order, bring to book, take to task, deal with, settle with, settle *or* square accounts, give one his deserts, serve one right, visit upon, give a lesson to, make an example of, make short work of, make the fur fly; tar and feather, ride on a rail, picket [obs. exc. Hist.], keelhaul, masthead; rack, put on *or* to the rack; penalize etc. 974.3; get even with, get back at [slang] etc. (make requital) 718.2; take revenge etc. 919.4.

(colloquial terms) attend to, give one his comeuppance [U.S.], give one his gruel, fix, get, pay, pay out, take care of, do for, serve one out, settle, settle one's hash, settle the score, give it to, give it one, give one Jesse, take *or* have it out of, dirty one's hands with, come down on *or* upon, jump on *or* upon.

(slang terms) give what-for, give a going-over, climb one's frame [U.S.], clean one's plow, cure, do in, let have it, land on, light into [U.S.], mop *or* wipe up the earth with.

6. *v.* whip, give a whipping etc. *n.*, beat, thrash, thresh, spank, flog, lace, scourge,

---

972. *Culpam poena premit comes* [Punishment presses close upon the fault like a companion]. —Horace.   My punishment is greater than I can bear.—Bible.   Back to thy punishment, / False fugitive.—Milton.   The power of punishment is to silence, not to confute.—Johnson. Eating the bitter bread of banishment.—Shakespeare.   *Nemo bis punitur pro eodem delicto* [No one is punished twice for the same offense].

flagellate, flail, frail [dial.], pummel, swinge, buffet, thump, smite, drub, trounce, baste, bastinado, wipe [dial. or slang], wallop [dial.], cob [dial. Eng.], mill [cant], belabor, lay on, lay about one; lash, administer the lash, horsewhip; strap, belt, cowhide; cudgel, fustigate, birch, cane, switch, give the stick; sandbag, blackjack; cuff, box, slap.

slap the face, box the ears, give a rap on the knuckles etc. *n.*; thrash soundly, blister, batter, beat to a mummy *or* jelly, beat black and blue, bruise, give a black eye; hit, kick etc. (strike) 276.8.

(colloquial terms) lick, larrup, groom, dress, dress down, give a dressing *or* dressing-down, jacket, lace one's jacket, trim, warm, warm one's jacket, comb, whale, welt, tan, tan one's hide, shingle [U.S.], lather, hide, flax [U.S.]; wallop, leather.

(slang terms) ribroast, lambaste, towel [Eng.], belt, fan, anoint, dust one's jacket *or* doublet, take it out of one's hide *or* skin, beat up, beat the sap *or* tar out of; give a dose of birch oil, ~ strap oil, ~ hickory oil *or* hazel oil, rub down with an oaken towel.

7. *v.* pelt, stone, rock [coll., U.S.], lapidate, throw stones at.

8. *v.* execute, inflict capital punishment on, put to death; electrocute, burn [slang]; bring to the gallows, hang, hang by the neck, string up [coll.], gibbet, noose, neck, scrag [coll.], lynch; tuck up, turn off, top off, crap, stretch [all slang]; bring to the block, behead, decapitate, decollate, guillotine; dismember, tear limb from limb; hang, draw and quarter; crucify, impale; shoot; execute by fire, commit to the flames, burn; break on the wheel; strangle, garrote, bowstring; kill etc. 361.10-12.

9. *v.* torture, martyrize etc. 830.6.

10. *v.* transport, extradite, exile etc. (banish) 297.11.

11. *v.* deserve punishment, richly deserve; be heading for a fall, be for it *or* in for it, have it coming [all coll.].

12. *v.* be punished etc., suffer punishment etc. *n.*, suffer, suffer for, suffer the consequences *or* penalty, take one's punishment, take the consequences, take one's medicine, pay the piper, face the music [coll.], take ~, have *or* get one's gruel [coll.], get *or* catch it [coll.], get *or* catch it in the neck [slang]; stand the racket, take the rap [both slang, U.S.]; make one's bed and lie on it, lie *or* sleep on the bed one has made; be hoist on one's own petard, throw a stone in one's own garden; be doubly punished, get it coming and going [slang], sow the wind and reap the whirlwind; get one's deserts etc. 973.4.

13. *v.* be executed etc., die on the scaffold, die with one's boots *or* shoes on, die in one's boots *or* shoes; be hanged, come to the gallows, swing [slang], dance upon nothing [iron.], dance the Tyburn jig [arch.], kick the air, ~ wind *or* clouds [slang].

14. *adj.* punishing etc. *v.*, penalizing, penal, punitive, punitory, inflictive, castigatory.

973. Reward
(See 972. Punishment, 974. Penalty)

1. *n.* reward, recompense, remuneration, compensation, solatium, meed, guerdon, price, consideration, acknowledgment; indemnity, indemnification; quittance, requital, reparation, redress, retribution, satisfaction, reckoning, amends, atonement, return, *quid pro quo* [L.]; award, prize etc. (trophy) 733; due reward, comeuppance [coll.] etc. (deserts) 924.2; punishment etc. 972.

2. *n.* pay, payment; financial reward *or* remuneration, allowance, wages, salary, hire, stipend, emolument, fee, dastur *or* dasturi [Ind.]; shot, scot; tribute, Peter *or* Peter's pence *or* penny; perquisite, perks [slang]; extra pay *or* allowance, batta [Ind.], bonus, bounty, premium, cumshaw [Chin.], largess *or* largesse, vail [arch.]; honorarium, honorary [rare]; dole; solatium, damages, smart money; hush money, blackmail; salvage; mileage; repayment, reimburse-

---

973. *Honor virtutis praemium* [Honor is the reward of valor].—CICERO.   The labourer is worthy of his reward.—BIBLE.   For blessings ever wait on virtuous deeds; / And though a late, a sure reward succeeds.—CONGREVE. The 'wages' of every noble work do yet lie in Heaven or else nowhere.—CARLYLE.   God shall repay: I am safer so.—BROWNING.   The reward of a thing well done is to have done it.—EMERSON.   There are no crown-wearers in heaven who were not cross-bearers here below. —C. H. SPURGEON.   A muezzin from the Tower of Darkness cries, / "Fools, your reward is neither Here nor There."—OMAR KHAYYÁM—FITZGERALD.

ment; earnings, profit etc. (gain) 775.2; income etc. (receipts) 810; gift, gratuity etc. 784.3–6; bribe etc. 618.2.

3. *v.* reward, recompense, remunerate, pay, compensate, guerdon, fee; repay, quit, requite, indemnify, make amends, atone, satisfy, return; award etc. (give) 784.8; make payment etc. 807.6–9.

4. *v.* be rewarded etc., get for one's pains, reap the fruits *or* benefit of, reap where one has sown, sow the wind and reap the whirlwind; get one's deserts, get one's comeuppance *or* comeuppings [coll., U.S.], get one's [slang, U.S.]; serve one right, be rightly served; be hoist on one's own petard etc. (be punished) 972.12.

5. *adj.* rewarding, paying etc. *v.*; remunerative, remuneratory [rare]; compensative, compensatory; retributive, retributory; reparative, reparatory [rare].

6. *adv.* in reward etc. *n.*, as compensation, in consideration of.

974. Penalty
(See 973. Reward; also 972. Punishment)

1. *n.* penalty, penalization, penance [loosely], penal retribution, suffering, pain, pains and penalties, consequent *or* compensating suffering *or* hardship, compensation, price; the devil to pay; wergild *or* weregild, bloodwite [both Hist.]; reparation etc. (atonement) 952; retribution etc. (punishment) 972.

2. *n.* fine, mulct, amercement, sconce, damages; doomage [local U.S.]; forfeit, forfeiture; deodand, praemunire [both Eng. Law, Hist.]; escheat, escheatment; sequestration, confiscation; distress, distraint.

3. *v.* penalize, put ~, impose *or* inflict a penalty on; fine, mulct, amerce, sconce, estreat; levy a distress, distrain; confiscate, sequestrate, sequester; escheat; punish etc. 972.5–10.

4. *adj.* penalizing etc. (punishing) 972.14.

975. Scourge
Instrument of Punishment.—1. *n.* scourge, whip, lash, strap, thong, cowhide, rawhide, knout, *azote* [Sp.], black snake *or* blacksnake, bullwhack [U.S.], kurbash, chabouk [Orient.], quirt, sjambok [S. Afr.], rope's end; cat, cat-o'-nine-tails.

2. *n.* rod, cane, stick, rattan, switch; birch, birch rod; ferule; rod in pickle; cudgel, truncheon etc. (club) 727.7.

3. *n.* pillory, stocks, whipping post, branks, trebuchet, triangle *or* triangles, wooden horse, Iron Maiden of Nuremberg, thumbscrew, rack, wheel, treadmill, crank, galleys, Procrustean bed *or* bed of Procrustes; cucking stool, ducking stool; boot, Oregon boot [U.S.], iron heel, scarpines; prison, shackles etc. 752.

4. *n.* scaffold; block, ax, guillotine, maiden [Scot. Hist.]; stake; cross; gallows, gibbet, tree, drop; hangman's noose, noose, rope, *mecate* [Sp.], halter, hempen collar *or* necktie [slang], bowstring; death chair, electric chair, chair, hot seat [slang].

5. *n.* executioner, executionist, Jack Ketch [Eng.]; hangman, topsman [slang], topping cove [slang, Eng.]; lyncher; headsman, beheader, decapitator; electrocutioner; garroter; killer etc. 361.8.

976. Deity
(See also 979. Mythic and Pagan Deities)

1. *n.* deity, divinity, divineness etc. *adj.*; godship, godhood, godhead *or* Godhead, Fatherhood.

2. *n.* God, Lord, Jehovah, the Deity, the Divinity, Omnipotence, Omniscience, the Omnipotent *or* Omniscient Being, the Omnipotent, the Omniscient, the Infinite Spirit, the Supreme Soul, Providence, the King of Kings, the Lord of Lords, the Almighty, the Supreme Being, the Absolute Being, the First Cause, the Infinite, the Infinite Being, the Eternal, Eternal Being, the All-powerful, the All-wise, the All-knowing, the All-merciful, the All-holy, Demiurge, I Am, the Preserver, the Maker, the Creator, Author *or* Creator of all things.

---

974. I crave the law, / The penalty and forfeit of my bond.—SHAKESPEARE. Some of us will smart for it.—SHAKESPEARE.
975. A rod is for the back of him that is void of understanding.—BIBLE. My father hath chastised you with whips, but I will chastise you with scorpions.—BIBLE. A whip for the horse, a bridle for the ass, and a rod for the fool's back.—BIBLE.
976. I am Alpha and Omega, the beginning and the end, the first and the last.—BIBLE. There are three that bear record in heaven, the Father, the Word, and the Holy Ghost: and these three are one.—BIBLE. The Lord is my

Mind, Spirit, Soul Principle, Life, Truth, Love [all Christian Science].
Deus [L.], *Theos* [Gr. Θεός], *Dieu* or *dieu* [F.], Allah [Moham.], *Khuda* [Hind.], the Great Spirit [N. Amer. Indian], deva [Hind., Buddhism], *kami* [Jap.]; Brahma, the Supreme Soul *or* Essence of the Universe [all Brahmanism or Hinduism]; Buddha, the Blessed One, the Teacher, the Lord Buddha [all Buddhism]; Mazda, Ormazd, Ahura-Mazda, the Lord of Wisdom, the Wise Lord, the Wise One, the King of Light, the Guardian of Mankind [all Zoroastrianism]; Nature; world spirit *or* soul etc. 359.3; god, goddess etc. 979.

(attributes) infinity, infinite goodness, infinite justice, infinite truth, infinite love, infinite mercy; infinite wisdom, omniscience *or* omnisciency; infinite power, omnipotence *or* omnipotency; omnipresence, ubiquity; unity, immutability, holiness, glory, light, majesty, sovereignty; eternity etc. (perpetuity) 112.

3. *n.* the Trinity, the Holy Trinity, the Triune God, Triunity, the Trinity in Unity, Threefold Unity, Three in One and One in Three; Father, Son *or* Word and Holy Ghost; Trimurti, Hindu trinity *or* triad.

4. *n.* God the Father, the Father, the All-father, the Holy Father, Our Father, Our Father which art in Heaven.

(functions) creation, preservation; divine government, theocracy, thearchy; providence, dealings ~, dispensations *or* visitations of providence.

5. *n.* God the Son, Christ, the Christ, Jesus Christ, Jesus of Nazareth, the Nazarene, the Man of Sorrows, the Messiah, the Anointed, the Saviour, the Redeemer, the Mediator, the Intercessor, the Advocate, the Judge, the Son of God, the Son of Man, the Son of David, the Son of Mary, the Only-Begotten, the Lamb of God, the King of Heaven, the King of Glory, the King of Kings, the Lord of Lords, the King of Kings and Lord of Lords, the King of the Jews, the Lord our Righteousness, the Sun of Righteousness, the Prince of Peace, the Good Shepherd, Immanuel, Emmanuel.

the Risen, the Way, the Door, the Truth, the Life, the Bread of Life, the light of the World, the Vine, the True Vine; Logos, the Word, the Word made Flesh, the Incarnation, the Hypostatic Union; the Christ Child, the Infant Jesus.

(functions) salvation, redemption, atonement, propitiation, mediation, intercession, judgment; soteriology.

6. *n.* God the Holy Ghost, the Holy Ghost, the Holy Spirit, the Spirit, the Spirit of God, the Spirit of Truth, Paraclete, the Comforter, the Consoler, the Intercessor, the Dove.

(functions) inspiration, unction, regeneration, sanctification, consolation, grace.

7. *v.* create, fashion, make, form, mold *or* mould.

8. *v.* preserve, uphold, keep, perpetuate, immortalize.

9. *v.* atone, redeem, save, propitiate, expiate; intercede, mediate.

10. *v.* predestinate, predestine, foreordain, preordain; elect, call, ordain.

11. *v.* bless, sanctify, hallow, justify, absolve, glorify.

12. *adj.* almighty, all-powerful, omnipotent; all-wise, all-seeing, all-knowing, omniscient; omnipresent, infinite; ubiquitous, ubiquitary; supreme, preeminent.

13. *adj.* divine, heavenly, celestial; godly, godlike; religious, holy, hallowed, sacred, sacrosanct.

14. *adj.* supernatural, preternatural; supernormal, hypernormal, preternormal; superphysical, hyperphysical; supramundane, extramundane; supersensible, supersensuous, supersensual, pretersensual; superhuman, preterhuman; unearthly, unworldly; spiritual etc. (spectral) 980a.4, (psychical) 994.22; insubstantial etc. (immaterial) 317.6; occult etc. 994.21.

15. *adv.* under God, by God's will *or* help, *Deo volente* [L.], D.V., God willing; *jure divino* [L.], by divine right; in

---

light and my salvation.—BIBLE. God is our refuge and strength, a very present help in trouble.—BIBLE. God shall be my hope, / My stay, my guide and lantern to my feet.—SHAKESPEARE. Thou great First Cause, least understood.—POPE. Naught but God can satisfy the soul.—P. J. BAILEY. Cast all your cares on God; that anchor holds.—TENNYSON. God's in His Heaven—All's right with the world!—BROWNING. If there were no God, it would be necessary to invent him.—VOLTAIRE.

977. Angel
(See 978. Satan)

Beneficent Spirits.—**1.** *n.* angel, celestial, celestial *or* heavenly being, divine messenger, Messenger of God; saint; angel of love, seraph; angel of light, cherub, cherubim, cherubin; principality, archangel; Michael, Gabriel, Raphael, Uriel, Chamuel, Jophiel, Zadkiel, Abdiel; Azrael, angel of death, death's bright angel; heavenly host, host of heaven, choir invisible, Sons of God, ministering spirits, invisible helpers; guardian angel etc. (familiar spirit) 979.12.

2. *n.* (celestial hierarchy of Pseudo-Dionysius) seraphim, cherubim, thrones; dominations *or* dominions, virtues, powers; principalities, archangels, angels.

3. *n.* Madonna, Our Lady, *Notre Dame* [F.], Holy Mary; the Virgin, the Blessed Virgin, the Virgin Mary, the Virgin Mother; *Dei Mater* [L.], Mother of God; *Regina Caeli* [L.], Queen of Heaven; *Regina Angelorum* [L.], Queen of Angels; *Stella Maris* [L.], Star of the Sea; *Redemptoris, Virgo Gloriosa, Virgo Sponsa Dei, Virgo Potens, Virgo Veneranda, Virgo Praedicanda, Virgo Clemens, Virgo Sapientissima, Sancta Virgo Virginum* [all L.].

4. *adj.* angelic, seraphic, cherubic; archangelic; heavenly, celestial; supernatural etc. 976.14.

978. Satan
(See 977. Angel; also 980. Evil Spirits)

Maleficent Spirits.—**1.** *n.* Satan, Satanas, devil *or* Devil, *diable* [F.], *diablo* [Sp.], *Teufel* [G.], *diabolus* [L.], deil [Scot.], Lucifer, Belial, Beelzebub, Eblis, Azazel, Ahriman [Zoroastrianism], Mephistopheles, Mephisto, Shaitan, Sammael, Asmodeus, Abaddon, Apollyon, His Satanic Majesty, the Prince of the Devils, the Prince of Darkness, the Prince of this world, the Prince of the power of the air.

the Wicked One, the Evil One, the Demon, the Fiend, the Foul Fiend, the Tempter, the Adversary, the Evil Spirit, the archenemy, the archfiend, the Devil Incarnate, the Father of Lies, the Author *or* Father of Evil, the serpent, the Old Serpent, the Common Enemy, the angel of the bottomless pit; demon etc. 980.2; Pluto etc. (mythological) 982.4.

(slang terms) the Deuce, the Dickens, the Old Gentleman, Old Nick, Old Scratch, Old Horny, Old Harry, Old Gooseberry, Old Bendy, Old Clootie, Old Ned, Old Poker.

2. *n.* fallen angels, unclean spirits, devils, host of hell, the rulers *or* powers of darkness, inhabitants of Pandemonium; Mammon, Azazel, Belial, Beelzebub.

3. *n.* devilishness etc. *adj.,* devilship, devildom; horns, the cloven hoof, the Devil's pitchfork.

4. *n.* diabolism, devil lore, Satanism, devilry, diablerie, diabolology *or* diabology, demonology, demonography, demonry, demonomy, demonism, demonianism, demonomagy, demonomancy, demon ∼, devil *or* chthonian worship, demonolatry; black magic etc. (sorcery) 992.

5. *n.* diabolist, demonologist, demonologer, demonographer [rare], demonist, demonomist, demoniast; demonolater, chthonian; sorcerer etc. 992.2, 3.

6. *v.* diabolize, demonize; possess, obsess; bewitch, bedevil etc. (sorcery) 992.4.

7. *adj.* satanic, devilish, diabolic(al), hellborn; demoniac etc. 980.9; infernal etc. (hellish) 982.5.

---

977. And flights of angels sing thee to thy rest!—SHAKESPEARE. Angels are bright still, though the brightest fell.—SHAKESPEARE. Look homeward, Angel, now, and melt with ruth.—MILTON. This world has angels all too few, / And heaven is overflowing.—COLERIDGE. Like angel visits, few and far between. —T. CAMPBELL. Be not forgetful to entertain strangers: for thereby some have entertained angels unawares.—BIBLE.
978. Get thee behind me, Satan.—BIBLE. Resist the devil, and he will flee from you.— BIBLE. Talk of the devil and he'll appear.— ERASMUS. 'Tis an easier matter to raise the devil than to lay him.—ERASMUS. 'Tis the eye of childhood / That fears a painted devil.— SHAKESPEARE. The prince of darkness is a gentleman.—SHAKESPEARE. If the devil catch a man idle, he'll set him at work.— FULLER. One devil is like another.—CERVANTES. Every devil has not a cloven foot. —DEFOE. Satan exalted sat, by merit raised / To that bad eminence.—MILTON.

979. Mythic and Pagan Deities

1. *n.* mythic and pagan deities, heathen gods and goddesses; *di majores* [L.], the major deities, the greater gods; *di minores* [L.], the minor deities, the lesser gods; god, *deus* [L.], deity, divinity, heathen *or* pagan deity *or* divinity; goddess, *dea* [L.]; deva, devi [*fem.*], the shining ones; devil-god; godling, godlet, godkin, demigod, hero; demigoddess, heroine; pantheon; theogony.

sun gods etc. 318.4; moon gods etc. 318.5; wind gods etc. 349.2, 3; agricultural gods etc. 371.3; war-god etc. 722.7; god of love etc. 897.4; gods of the lower world etc. 982.4; Fates etc. 601.4; muse etc. 597.9.

2. *n.* (Greek and Latin) Zeus, Jupiter, Jove; Jupiter Fulgur *or* Fulminator, Jupiter Tonans, Jupiter Pluvius, Jupiter Optimus Maximus, Jupiter Fidius; Helios, Hyperion, Phaëthon, Apollon, Apollo, Phoebus, Phoebus Apollo; Ares, Mars; Hermes, Mercury; Poseidon, Neptune; Hephaestus, Vulcan; Dionysus, Bacchus; Pluto, Hades, Dis; Kronos *or* Cronus, Saturn; Eros, Cupid.

(goddesses) Hera *or* Here, Juno; Demeter, Ceres; Persephone, Persephassa, Proserpina, Proserpine, Kore *or* Cora, Despoina; Artemis, Diana; Athena, Minerva; Aphrodite, Venus; Hestia, Vesta; Rhea, Cybele; Gaea *or* Gaia, Tellus.

3. *n.* (Norse) Asa (*pl.* Aesir, Asas), Vanir [*pl.*]; Odin *or* Woden, Thor *or* Donar, Tyr *or* Tiu, Balder, Forseti, Heimdall; Hoenir, Ull, Vitharr, Vali, Bragi; Loki; Njorth, Frey.

(goddesses) Freya, Frigg, Hel, Sif, Nanna, Ithunn, Sigyn.

4. *n.* (Hindu and Brahmanic) Brahma, Vishnu, Siva; Ganesa, Ganpati; Dyaus, Indra, Varuna, Surya, Savitar, Soma, Agni, Vayu, Marut, Hanuman, Yama.

avatars of Vishnu, Matsya, Karma, Varah, Narsinh, Vaman, Parshuram, Rama, Buddha, Kalki, Krishna; Jagannath, Juggernaut.

(goddesses) Ushas, Sarasvati; Lakshmi; Devi, Uma, Gauri, Parvati; Durga, Chandi, Kali.

5. *n.* (Egyptian) Ra *or* Amen-Ra, Neph, Ptah, Min, Khem, Nut, Osiris, Isis, Horus, Nephthys, Set, Anubis, Thoth, Bast, the Sphinx.

6. *n.* (various) Baal, Shamash [both Semitic]; Astarte *or* Ashtoreth (Phoenician); Anu, Bel, Ea (Babylonian); Mumbo Jumbo (African).

7. *n.* elemental, elemental spirit; sylph, gnome, salamander, undine.

8. *n.* nymph, nymphid [rare], dryad, hamadryad, alseid, wood nymph; nymphet, nymphlin [both poetic]; oread, mountain nymph; limoniad, meadow *or* flower nymph; Napaea, glen nymph; Hyades *or* Hyads; Pleiades, Atlantides; water nymph etc. *below* 979.10.

9. *n.* fairy, fairy man *or* woman, fay, sprite, spright [arch.]; fairy queen; banshee *or* banshie, pixy, elf (*pl.* elves), cluricaune, brownie, dwarf, gnome, kobold, nisse, peri; sylph, sylphid; Mab, Oberon, Titania, Ariel; Puck, Robin Goodfellow, hobgoblin; leprechaun; fairyfolk, elfenfolk, shee *or* sidhe (Irish), the little people *or* men, the good folk *or* people [coll.], denizens of the air; fairyland, faërie *or* faëry [arch.]; water sprite etc. *below*; afreet etc. (evil spirit) 980.2, 3.

10. *n.* water spirit, ∼ sprite *or* nymph, nix, nixie [*fem.*], kelpie *or* kelpy, undine; naiad, limniad, fresh-water nymph; Oceanid, ocean nymph, Nereid, sea nymph, sea-maid, sea-maiden, mermaid, siren; Thetis; merman, seaman *or* sea man [rare], man fish; "the old man of the sea" (Homer), Neptune, Poseidon, Oceanus, Triton; Davy, Davy Jones.

11. *n.* sylvan deity, faun, satyr, silenus, panisc *or* panisk, paniscus (*fem.* panisca); Pan, Faunus, Vitharr (Norse), the goat god; wood nymph etc. *above* 979.8.

12. *n.* familiar spirit, familiar, *lar* [L.] (*pl. lares*), *lar familiaris* [L.]; penates, lares and penates; *numen* [L.] (*pl. numena*), genius, good genius, tutelar *or* tutelary genius, ∼ deity, ∼ god *or* spirit, daimon, daemon, demon, special providence, guardian, guide, attendant, godling *or* spirit, invisible helper, ministering angel *or* spirit, angel, guardian angel,

---

979. Where'er he moved, the goddess shone before.—HOMER. Heartly know, / When half-gods go, / The gods arrive.—EMERSON. If we meet no gods, it is because we harbor none.—EMERSON. It is pleasant to die, if there be gods; and sad to live, if there be none.—MARCUS AURELIUS. Great Pan is dead.—PLUTARCH.

good angel, fairy godmother, *genius loci* [L.]; *lares compitales, lares praestites, lares viales, lares permarini* [all L.]; evil genius.

13. *n.* mythology, mythical lore, folklore; fairy lore, fairyism.

14. *adj.* mythic(al), mythological; fabulous, legendary etc. (imaginary) 515.12.

15. *adj.* fairy, faery, fairylike; sylphine, sylphish, sylphlike, sylphidine; elfin, elfish, elflike; nymphic(al), nymphal, nymphean, nymphlike.

980. Evil Spirits
(See also 978. Satan)

1. *n.* evil spirits, demonkind, powers of darkness, host of hell.

2. *n.* demon, fiend, devil, deva, bad ∼, evil *or* unclean spirit; cacodemon, incubus, succubus; jinni *or* jinnee (*pl.* jinn), genie, genius (*pl.* genii), jinniyeh [*fem.*]; evil genius, familiar, familiar spirit; ogre, ogress; afreet, barghest, flibbertigibbet, troll, ghoul, lamia, vampire, Harpy; siren, Parthenope, Lorelei; god of evil, Loki [Norse Myth.], Set [Egyptian Myth.]; Friar Rush; Satan etc. 978.

3. *n.* imp, bad fairy, *diablotin* [F.], sprite, bad peri, pixy, ouphe, urchin [arch.], puck; little *or* young devil, devilkin, deviling.

4. *n.* bugbear, bugaboo, bogy, boggart *or* boggard; boogy, booger, boogerman, boogyman [all dial. U.S.]; MumboJumbo; goblin, hobgoblin, poker [now rare]; fee-faw-fum, bête noire.

5. *n.* fury, avenging spirit; the Furies, the Erinyes, the Eumenides, the Dirae.

6. *n.* changeling, elf child, auf [obs. exc. dial.], oaf.

7. *n.* werefolk, were-animals; werewolf, lycanthrope, *loup-garou* [F.]; werejaguar, uturuncu [S. Amer. Indian]; were-ass, werebear, werecalf, werefox, werehyena, wereleopard, weretiger.

8. *n.* demonology, demonry etc. (diabolism) 978.4.

9. *adj.* demoniac(al), demonic(al), demonial, demonian, demonish, demonlike; fiendish, fiendlike; devilish, devillike; diabolic(al), ghoulish, inhuman; satanic etc. 978.7; hellish etc. 982.5; bewitched etc. 992.7.

980a. Specter

1. *n.* specter, ghost, *Geist* [G.], revenant, spirit, sprite, wraith, spook [now joc.], larva [Rom. Rel.], phantom, phantasm, phantasma, phasm, shade, shadow, *umbra* [L.], apparition, spiritual apparition, appearance, presence, shape, eidolon, idolum, disembodied spirit, soul of the dead; incorporeal being *or* entity, incorporeal, incorporeity, immateriality, unsubstantiality; vision, theophany; astral spirits, astral.

duffy [W. Ind. and U.S.]; haunt *or* hant [dial.]; poltergeist; control, guide [Spiritualism]; banshee; White Lady, the White Ladies of Normandy, the White Lady of Avenel (Scott.); Brocken specter, specter of the Brocken; lemures [Rom. Rel.]; materialization etc. 316.4; *ignis fatuus* [L.] etc. 421.11; apparition etc. (optical illusion) 443.9.

2. *n.* double, etheric double *or* self, cowalker, *Doppelganger* [G.], doubleganger, fetch, wraith; astral body etc. 994.12.

3. *n.* emanation, effluvium, radiation, luminescence, glow, glory, aura; ectoplasm, ectoplasmic manifestation, exteriorized protoplasm; ectoplasy.

4. *adj.* spectral, specterlike; ghostly, ghostish, ghosty, ghostlike; phantom, phantomic(al); spiritual, wraithlike, spooky *or* spookish [coll.], weird, uncanny, eerie, unearthly; disembodied, discarnate, decarnate, decarnated; supernatural etc. 976.14; incorporeal etc. (immaterial) 317.6; psychical etc. 994.22; chimerical etc. (unsubstantial) 4.5, 6.

5. *adj.* haunted, hanted [dial.], spectered [rare], specter-haunted, ghostified [rare].

---

980. For we wrestle not against flesh and blood, but against principalities, against powers, against the rulers of the darkness of this world. —BIBLE. They are neither brute nor human, / They are Ghouls!—POE.

980a. A hunter of shadows, himself a shade.— HOMER. I am thy father's spirit, / Doom'd for a certain term to walk the night.—SHAKESPEARE. Now it is the time of night, / That the graves, all gaping wide, / Every one lets forth his sprite.—SHAKESPEARE. I can call spirits from the vasty deep.—SHAKESPEARE. Of calling shapes, and heck'ning shadows dire. —MILTON. Millions of spiritual creatures walk the earth / Unseen, both when we wake, and when we sleep.—MILTON.

981. Heaven
(See 982. Hell)

1. *n.* heaven, paradise, heavenly kingdom, kingdom of heaven, ~ God *or* glory, God's kingdom, kingdom come [slang], happy land, happy hunting grounds [N. Amer. Indian], Land of the Leal [Scot.], the world above, the next world, eternal home, abode of the blessed, inheritance of the saints in light, nirvana [Buddhist]; heaven of heavens, God's throne, throne of God, the great white throne; God's presence, presence of God; Abraham's bosom; glory, celestial *or* heavenly bliss, eternal *or* unending bliss, never-ending day, eternity; celestial glory, terrestrial glory, telestial glory [all Mormon]; Zion, New Jerusaelm, Holy City, City Celestial, Heavenly *or* Celestial City, Heavenly City of God; Beulah, Beulah Land, Land of Beulah; seventh heaven.
"the treasury of everlasting joy" (Shakespeare), "my Father's house" (Bible), "God's residence" (E. Dickinson), "mansions in the sky" (I. Watts), "that radiant shore" (F. D. Hemans), "the bosom of our rest" (Newman), "heaven's high city" (F. Quarles); Eden, Arcadia etc. (Utopia) 515.6.

2. *n.* (mythological) Olympus, Mount Olympus; Elysium, Elysian fields; Islands *or* Isles of the Blessed, Happy Isles, Fortunate Isles *or* Islands; garden of the Hesperides, Bower of Bliss.

3. *n.* (Norse) Asgard, Valhalla, Glathsheim, Vingolf, Valaskjalf, Hlithskjalf, Thruthvang *or* Thruthheim, Bilskirnir, Ydalir, Sokkvabekk, Sökkvabekkr, Breithablik, Folkvang, Sessrymnir, Noatum, Thrymheim, Glitnir, Himinbjorg, Vithi.

4. *n.* (theosophy) devachan, devaloka, kamavachara, kamaloka, the land of the Gods.

5. *n.* afterlife, hereafter etc. (postexistence) 121.3.

6. *n.* resurrection, translation; apotheosis, deification.

7. *adj.* heavenly, heavenish; paradisaic(al), paradisiac(al); celestial, supernal, unearthly, beatific(al), Edenic, Arcadian, Elysian, Olympian, from on high; divine etc. 976.13.

982. Hell
(See 981. Heaven)

1. *n.* hell, Hades, Sheol, Gehenna, Pandemonium, Tophet, Abaddon, Naraka, avichi *or* avici, *jahannan* [Hind.], the grave, place of departed spirits, abode *or* world of the dead, place of the lost, abode of the damned, habitation of fallen angels, place of torment, world of future punishment, lower world, underworld, nether world, infernal regions, inferno, shades below, the pit, the bottomless pit, the abyss, "a vast, unbottom'd, boundless pit" (Burns); hell-fire, fire and brimstone, lake of fire and brimstone, everlasting fire *or* torment, "the fire that never shall be quenched" (Bible); purgatory, limbo.

2. *n.* (mythological) Hades, Tartarus, Avernus, Acheron, pit of Acheron, "sad Acheron of sorrow, black and deep" (Milton), realms of Pluto [all classical Myth.]; Amenti [Egyptian], Aralu [Babylonian]; Hel, Niflhel, Niflheim *or* Nifelheim, Nastrond *or* Naströnd [all Norse].

3. *n.* (rivers of Hades) Styx, Stygian creek, Acheron, river of woe, Cocytus, river of wailing, Phlegethon, river of fire, Lethe, river of forgetfulness.

4. *n.* god of the lower world, Pluto [Gr. and Rom.], Hades [Gr.], Dis [Rom.]; Rhadamanthus, Erebus, Charon, Cerberus, Minos; Osiris; Persephone, Proserpine, Proserpina, Persephassa, Despoina, Kore *or* Cora [Gr. and Rom.]; Hel, Loki, Frigg [all Norse]; Satan etc. 978.

5. *adj.* hellish, infernal, Hadean [rare], chthonian; Plutonic, Plutonian; Tartarean, Tartareous; Stygian, Stygial [rare], Styxian; Lethean, Acherontic(al), Cocy-

---

981. Heaven means to be one with God.—Confucius.   Lay up for yourselves treasures in heaven.—Bible.   Where imperfection ceaseth, heaven begins.—P. J. Bailey.   I never spoke with God, / Nor visited in heaven; / Yet certain am I of the spot / As if the chart were given.—E. Dickinson.   My hopes in heaven do dwell.—Shakespeare.

982. Hell is a circle about the unbelieving.—Koran.   Hell and Chancery are always open. —Fuller.   Which way I fly is Hell; myself am Hell.—Milton.   Hell itself may be contained within the compass of a spark.—Thoreau.   Hell is the wrath of God—His hate of sin.—P. J. Bailey.   Satan the envious said with a sigh: / Christians know more about their hell than I.—Kreymborg.   Hell is paved with good intentions

tean [rare]; devilish etc. (satanic) 978.7, (demoniac) 980.9.

983. Theology
(See 989. Irreligion; also 996. Laity)

1. *n.* theology, theologics [rare], religion, divinity; theologism; theism, monotheism; doctrinal theology, doctrinism, doctrinalism; dogmatic theology, dogmatics; canonics; hierology, hagiology; hierography, hagiography; Caucasian mystery.

2. *n.* doctrine, dogma, creed, canon, catechism etc. (belief) 484.3; declaration of faith etc. (profession) 484.4; sect etc. 984.3.

3. *n.* theologian, *theologus* [L.], theologizer; theologist, theologer, theologician, theologue [now rare]; theologaster [rare]; divine, scholastic, schoolman, canonist; theist, monotheist; theological *or* divinity student, theological, theologue [coll.]; the Fathers; clergyman etc. 996.

4. *adj.* theologic(al), theologian [rare], religious, divine; canonic(al); doctrinal, doctrinary, doctrinarian [rare]; sectarian etc. 984.23.

983a. Orthodoxy
(See 984. Heterodoxy, Sectarianism)

1. *n.* orthodoxy, orthodoxism, orthodoxality [rare]; soundness of doctrine, soundness, strictness etc. *adj.*; observance, observation; religious truth, true faith, the faith, the Faith, "the faith which was once delivered unto the saints" (Bible); authenticity etc. (truth) 494; steadfast belief etc. (conviction) 484.2; conformity etc. 82.

2. *n.* Christianity, Christianism; Catholicism etc. 984.6.

3. *n.* the Church, Holy Church, the Bride of the Lamb, temple of the Holy Ghost, Church of Christ, body of Christ, collective body of Christians, members

~, disciples *or* followers of Christ; Christendom, Christdom [rare]; church militant, church triumphant, church visible, church invisible; Apostolic Church, Universal Church, the Church Universal; Catholic Church, Roman Catholic Church, Church of Rome, Scarlet Woman [derog.]; Greek Church, Greek Orthodox Church; Established Church, Church of England, Church of Scotland; High Church, Low Church; Broad Church, Free Church; Baptist Church, Methodist Church etc. (*see* Baptist etc. 984.14, 15).

4. *n.* true believer, orthodox Christian, orthodox, orthodoxian [rare], orthodoxist; textualist, textuary; canonist; the orthodox; Christian etc. 987.4.

5. *n.* hyperorthodoxy, precisianism, puritanism; bibliolatry, hagiolatry; Sabbatarianism, sabbatism; intolerance etc. (bigotry) 606.2; positivism etc. (dogmatism) 474.3; zealotry, fanaticism etc. (craze) 503.7.

6. *n.* bigot etc. 606.3; positivist etc. (dogmatist) 474.4; zealot etc. (fanatic) 504.2; puritan etc. (affecter) 853.4.

7. *adj.* orthodox, orthodoxal [rare], orthodoxical; of the faith, of the true faith; firm, sound, sound on the goose [slang], true-blue, faithful, canonical, catholic, Christian, evangelical, divine, scriptural; literal, textual; authoritative, authentic, accepted, received, approved, standard, customary, conventional; correct, right, proper; theistic, monotheistic; unschismatic, schismless; true etc. 494.10–14; conformable etc. 82.8, 9.

8. *adj.* hyperorthodox, overreligious; creed-bound, narrow-minded etc. (bigoted) 606.7; prejudiced etc. 481.10; positive etc. (dogmatic) 474.15; overzealous etc. (fanatical) 503.18; puritanical, strait-laced etc. (prudish) 853.7.

984. Heterodoxy, Sectarianism
(See 983a. Orthodoxy)

1. *n.* heterodoxy, unorthodoxy, heresy, false doctrine, misbelief; unchristianity, anti-Christianity, anti-Christianism; un-Scripturality, anti-Scripturism; iconoclasm; superstition, superstitiousness,

---

983a. The true religion is built upon the rock; the rest are tossed upon the waves of time.—BACON. Christianity is the highest perfection of humanity.—JOHNSON. Whatever makes men good Christians, makes them good citizens.—D. WEBSTER. Prove their doctrine orthodox / By apostolic blows and knocks.—BUTLER. Orthodoxy is the Bourbon of the world of thought; it learns not, neither can it forget.—HUXLEY. Orthodoxy is my doxy; heterodoxy another man's doxy.—WARBURTON.

984. All false religion is in conflict with nature.—ROUSSEAU. The religion of one seems madness to another.—T. BROWNE. Creeds grow so thick along the way / Their boughs

Aberglaube [G.]; fallacy etc. (error) 495; atheism etc. (irreligion) 989; idolatry etc. 991; backsliding etc. (relapse) 661; delusion etc. 495.5.

2. *n.* sectarianism, sectarism, denominationalism, partisanism, the clash of creeds; cultism; secularism; syncretism, eclecticism; schismatism, schismaticalness; recusancy etc. (dissent) 489, apostasy etc. 607.2; nonconformity etc. 83.2.

3. *n.* sect, sectarism, religious order, denomination, persuasion, faction, religion, church, communion, community, affiliation, group, fellowship, order, school, party, society, body, organization; ism, cult; schism, division; belief, faith etc. 484.3.

4. *n.* Protestantism, Calvinism, Quakerism, Methodism, Anabaptism, Mormonism, Arianism, Athanasianism, Jansenism, Stundism, Erastianism, Origenism, Sabellianism, Socinianism, latitudinarianism, Swedenborgianism, Boehmenism, new theology; Adventism, Second Adventism; ethicism, ethical culture; deism, theism; monotheism, Unitarianism; Trinitarianism, Homoousianism, Homoiousianism; tritheism; physicomorphism, anthropomorphism, anthropopathism, anthropopathy; quietism; occultism, psychical research, mysticism etc. (esoteric sciences) 994; skepticism etc. 989.3; materialism etc. 316.5; Neo-Platonism, Gnosticism etc. 451.7, 9.

5. *n.* Anglicanism, Anglo-Catholicism, High-churchism, Puseyism, Tractarianism, Laudism *or* Laudianism, ritualism, Oxford Group movement *or* School.

6. *n.* Catholicism, Catholicity; Roman Catholicism, Romanism; popery, popeism, papism, papistry [all derog.]; Mariology, Mariolatry [derog.]; ultramontanism; Catholic Church etc. 983a.3.

7. *n.* Judaism, Hebraism, Hebrewism, Jewism, Israelitism; rabbinism, Talmudism, Pharisaism, Karaism *or* Karaitism.

8. *n.* Mohammedanism, Islam, Islamism, Moslemism; Wahabiism, Sufism.

9. *n.* psychiasis, spiritual ~, metaphysical *or* mental healing; Christian Science, theotherapy, divine healing; New Thought, Higher Thought, Practical Christianity, Mental Science, Divine Science Church.

10. *n.* paganism, paganry, paganity [now rare], pagandom; heathenism, heathenry, heathenesse [arch.], heathendom; gentilism; pagano-Christianism; mythicism, mythology; animism, animatism; henotheism; polytheism; tritheism; ditheism, dualism; pantheism, theopantism, cosmotheism; idolatry etc. 991.

11. *n.* (Oriental religions) Vedanta, Vedantism; Hinduism, Brahmanism, Brahmoism, Sikhism, Jainism, gymnosophy; yoga, yogism; Buddhism, Lamaism; Confucianism, Taoism; Shinto, Shintoism; Gnosticism, Mandaeism, Sabaeanism; Babi, Babism *or* Babiism, Bahaism, Zoroastrianism *or* Zoroastrism, Magianism; Saivism.

12. *n.* misbeliever, heterodox [obs.], heretic, pervert, miscreant [arch.]; antichrist, antichristian; iconoclast; skeptic etc. (irreligionist) 989.4; backslider etc. (apostate) 607.5.

13. *n.* sectarian, sectary, sectarist [rare], denominationalist, factionist; schismatic, schismatist [rare]; ist, cultist; nonjuror, nonjurant; separatist, come-outer [coll., U.S.] etc. (apostate) 607.5; protestant, recusant etc. (dissenter) 489.3; nonconformist etc. 83.4.

14. *n.* (religious sectaries and cultists) Protestant, Huguenot, Episcopalian, Puritan, Congregationalist, Unitarian, Presbyterian, Lutheran, Calvinist, Methodist, Wesleyan, Baptist, Christian Scientist, Anabaptist, Ubiquitarian, Universalist, Independent, Irvingite, Sandemanian, Glassite, Erastian, Antinomian, Davidist, Familist, Bible Christian, Bryanite, Dunker, Ebionite, Arian, Eusebian, Jovinianist, Quaker, Shaker, quietist, Stundist, Judaist, Boehmenist, Swedenborgian; Trinitarian, Homoousian, Homoiousian; Adventist, Second Adventist; Mormon, Latter-day Saint.

supralapsarian, sublapsarian, infralapsarian; limitarian, orthodox dissenter, restitutionist; monotheist, unipersonalist, latitudinarian, freethinker; occultist, spiritualist etc. (psychist) 994.13–15; materialist etc. 316.6; skeptic etc. 989.4.

15. *n.* Anglican, Anglo-Catholic, High-churchman *or* High-churchist, Tractarian, Puseyite, Laudist *or* Laudian, ritualist.

---

hide God.—L. W. REESE.   The religions we call false were once true.—EMERSON.   A Pagan suckled in some creed outworn.—WORDSWORTH.

16. *n.* Catholic, Roman Catholic, Romanist, papist *or* Papist [derog.]; ultramontane.

17. *n.* Judaist, Judaizer, Hebraist, Hebrew, Jew, Israelite; rabbinist, Talmudist, Sadducee, Karaite; Pharisee.

18. *n.* Mohammedan, Mussulman, Moslem, Islamite; Shiite, Shiah, Sectary; Motazilite, Sunnite, Wahabi, Sufi, dervish, abdal.

19. *n.* faith curer, faith-curist, faith *or* mental healer; New Thoughter *or* Thoughtist, Mental Scientist.

20. *n.* pagan, heathen; non-Christian, non-Mohammedan, non-Jew, gentile, infidel, paynim [arch.], *giaour* [Turk], Kaffir [Moham.]; zendik, zendician, zendikite [all Moham.]; henotheist, pantheist, polytheist; animist; unbeliever etc. (irreligionist) 989.4; idolater etc. 991.5.

21. *n.* (Oriental sectaries) Hindu, Vedantist, Brahman, Gentoo, Sikh, Jain *or* Jaina, gymnosophist; yogi, yogin, yogist; Buddhist, Lamaist *or* Lamaite; Confucianist, Taoist; Shintoist; Gnostic, Mandaean, Sabaean; Babist; Zoroastrian, Parsi, Gheber; Magian, Magus (*pl.* Magi).

22. *adj.* heterodox, heretical, misbelieving, miscreant [arch.], unorthodox, unsound, unscriptural, uncanonical, unchristian, anti-Scriptural, apocryphal; antichristian; iconoclastic; deistic, theistic; nonjuring, nonjurant; fallacious etc. (erroneous) 495.12–16; atheistic, infidelic, skeptical etc. (irreligious) 989.7.8; materialistic etc. 316.9; unconformable etc. 83.9; backsliding etc. 661.4; retrograde etc. 283.7.

23. *adj.* sectarian, sectary, sectarial, denominational; schismatic(al), schismic [rare]; protestant, recusant etc. (dissenting) 489.5; apostate etc. 607.11, 12; Theosophical, Rosicrucian etc. (occult) 994.21.

24. *adj.* Protestant, Methodist, Baptist etc. *n.*

25. *adj.* Catholic(al); Roman Catholic, Roman, Romish [chiefly derog.]; popish, papish, papist *or* Papist, papistic(al) [all derog.]; ultramontane.

26. *adj.* Judaical, Jewish, Hebrew, Hebraic(al), Hebraistic(al), Israelite, Israelitic, Israelitish.

27. *adj.* Mohammedan, Moslem, Islamic, Islamitic, Islamistic.

28. *adj.* pagan, paganish, paganist *or* paganistic, paganic(al); heathen, heathenish; non-Christian, non-Mohammedan, non-Jewish, gentile, paynim [arch.], ethnic(al); pagano-Christian; polytheistic, pantheistic; animist, animistic; Brahmanic, Buddhist etc. *n.*; idolatrous etc. 991.7; infidelic etc. 989.7.

985. Revelation
(See also 986. Sacred Writings)

Biblical Revelation.—**1.** *n.* revelation, inspiration, afflatus, divine inspiration; theopneusty, theopneustia; theophany, theophania.

2. *n.* the Bible, the Book, the Book of Books, the Good Book, the Word, the Word of God, Scripture, the Scriptures, Holy Scriptures, Holy Writ, inspired *or* sacred writings, the Gospel; Vulgate, Authorized Version *or* King James Bible, Douay Bible.

3. *n.* Old Testament, the Law, the Jewish *or* Mosaic Law, Torah; Septuagint, Hexateuch, Octateuch, Pentateuch; the Prophets, major *or* minor Prophets; Hagiographa; Apocrypha.

4. *n.* New Testament, Evangelists, Gospels, the Gospel, Good *or* Glad Tidings; Synoptic Gospels; Epistles, Pauline Epistles, Catholic Epistles, Johannine Epistles; Acts, Acts of the Apostles; Apocalypse, Revelation.

5. *n.* Talmud, Mishnah *or* Mishna, Gemara; Masora *or* Masorah.

6. *n.* inspired writers, the Fathers, the Apostolic Fathers; evangelist, apostle, disciple, saint; Isaiah, Jeremiah etc. (prophet) 513.2.

7. *adj.* scriptural, Biblic(al); holy, sacred; evangelic(al), evangelistic, apostolic(al); revealed, revelational, apocalyptic(al); inspired, theopneustic, theopneusted [rare]; ecclesiastic(al); canonical; textuary, textual; prophetic etc. (predictive) 511.11.

---

985. Thy word is a lamp unto my feet, and a light unto my path.—BIBLE. But the word of the Lord endureth for ever.—BIBLE. A glory gilds the sacred page, / Majestic like the sun, / It gives a light to every age.—COWPER. The word unto the prophet spoken / Was writ on tables yet unbroken.—EMERSON.

8. *adj.* Talmudic(al), Talmudistic(al); Mishnaic, Mishnic(al); Gemaric.

986. Sacred Writings
(See also 985. Revelation)

Non-Biblical Sacred Writings.—1. *n.* Zend-Avesta, Avesta (Zoroastrian); Tripitaka (Buddhist); Granth, Adigranth (Sikh); the Koran *or* Alcoran (Mohammedan), agama (Hindu), Tao Tê Ching (Chinese), the Eddas (Scandinavian), Arcana Caelestia (Swedenborgian), Book of Mormon (**Mormon**); Science and Health with Key to the Scriptures (Christian Science).

2. *n.* (Brahmanic) Veda, Rig-Veda, Yajur-Veda, Sama-Veda, Atharva-Veda; Brahmana, Upanishad, Aranyaka; shastra, sruti, smriti, purana, tantra; Bhagavad-Gita.

3. *n.* (prophets and religious founders), Gautama Buddha (Buddhism), Zoroaster *or* Zarathustra (Zoroastrianism), Confucius (Confucianism), Laotzu (Taoism), Mohammed (Mohammedanism), Nanak (Sikhism), Mahavira, Vardhamana Jnatiputra (Jainism), Mirza Ali Mohammed of Shiraz, the Bab (Babism), Ram Mohan Roy (Brahmo-Samaj), Swedenborg (Swedenborgianism), Joseph Smith (Mormonism), Mary Baker Eddy (Christian Science).

987. Piety
(See 988. Impiety)

1. *n.* piety, piousness, holiness, religiousness etc. *adj.*; religiosity, religionism; religion, theism, devotion; saintship, sainthood; spirituality, spiritual-mindedness; sanctity, sanctitude; odor of sanctity, beauty of holiness; theopathy; theodicy; faith etc. (belief) 484; sanctimony etc. 988.2; veneration, reverence etc. (respect) 928, (worship) 990; virtue etc. 944; humility etc. 879.

2. *n.* sanctification, purification, beatification, edification, inspiration; glorification, exaltation; consecration, canonization, enshrinement; justification; grace; bread of life, body and blood of Christ; unction, baptism etc. 998.4, 5.

3. *n.* redemption, salvation, conversion, regeneration, reformation, adoption; rebirth, new birth; repentance etc. 950.

4. *n.* believer, truster, accepter, receiver, pietist, theist, saint, devotee, devotionalist, devotionist [rare]; religious, religionist, Christian, Nazarene, Nazaritan [rare], Nazarite; churchman, churchite; pillar of the church; convert, proselyte, neophyte, catechumen; disciple; true believer etc. (orthodox) 983a.4.

5. *n.* the believing, the faithful, the good, the righteous, the just, the elect etc. *adj.*; the children of God, the children of light; Christendom, Christdom [rare].

6. *v.* be pious etc. *adj.*, be at one with God, be on God's side, stand up for Jesus, fight the good fight, keep the faith, let one's light shine; have faith etc. (believe) 484.7, 9; venerate, revere etc. (respect) 928.4; worship etc. 990.9.

7. *v.* be converted, get religion [coll., U.S.], receive Christ, experience the divine illumination; repent, reform etc. 950.3, 4.

8. *v.* sanctify, purify, hallow, bless, make *or* pronounce holy, beatify; edify; inspire; glorify, exalt; consecrate, canonize, saint, enshrine; baptize, anoint etc. 998.14.

9. *v.* redeem, regenerate, reform, convert, save, give salvation.

10. *adj.* pious, pietic [rare], pietistic(al); religious, devout, devoted, zealous, godly, spiritual, righteous, just, holy; religious-minded, spiritual-minded, holy-minded, godly-minded, heavenly-minded; pure, pure-hearted, pure in heart; saintly, saintlike; seraphic, angelic; unworldly, unearthly, not of the earth; reverent, reverential, solemn; faithful; Christian, Catholic; believing etc. 484.12; worshipful etc. 990.15; vir-

---

987. *Justitiae soror incorrupta Fides* [Faith uncorrupted, the sister of Justice].—HORACE. Yet have I not seen the righteous forsaken, nor his seed begging bread.—BIBLE. The righteous shall flourish like the palm tree: he shall grow like a cedar of Lebanon.—BIBLE. Faith is the substance of things hoped for, the evidence of things not seen.—BIBLE. His heart is fixed, trusting in the Lord.—BIBLE. A little philosophy inclineth men's minds to atheism, but depth in philosophy bringeth men's minds about to religion.—BACON. To me religion is life before God and in God.—AMIEL. I say the whole earth and all the stars in the sky are for religion's sake.—WHITMAN. See God's world through the rags of this.—MASEFIELD. In the harsh face of life faith can read a bracing Gospel.—STEVENSON.

tuous etc. 944.3; sanctimonious etc. 988.11; overzealous etc. (fanatical) 503.18; bigoted etc. 606.7.

11. *adj.* sanctified, hallowed, consecrated etc. *v.*; holy, sacred, sacrosanct.

12. *adj.* converted, regenerated etc. *v.*; regenerate, reborn.

988. Impiety
(See 987. Piety)

1. *n.* impiety, impiousness, profaneness etc. *adj.*; profanity, profanation, blasphemy, desecration, sacrilege; irreverence, irreverentialism; mockery etc. (scoffing) 930.2; irreligion etc. 989; sin, wickedness etc. (vice) 945.

2. *n.* sanctimony, sanctimoniousness etc. *adj.*; pietism, false piety, pharisaism, cant, mummery, misdevotion; mouth honor, lip worship, lip homage, lip devotion, lip service, lip praise, lip reverence; tartufism *or* tartuffism, tartufery *or* tartuffery; formalism; empty ceremony, solemn mockery; hypocrisy etc. (dissembling) 544.2; affectation etc. 853; bigotry etc. 606.2.

3. *n.* perversion, declension; hardening, hardening of the heart; backsliding, fall from grace etc. (relapse) 661; reversion etc. 145; regression etc. 283; deterioration etc. 659; apostasy etc. 607.2; recusancy etc. (dissent) 489.

4. *n.* worldling, earthling; sacrilegist [rare]; scoffer, blasphemer, Sabbathbreaker; sinner etc. (wrongdoer) 949.2; the wicked etc. 949.5.

5. *n.* pervert, backslider etc. (apostate) 607.5.

6. *n.* religious hypocrite, cant, canter, canting hypocrite, pious fraud, pietist, religionist, tartufe *or* tartuffe, pharisee, Holy Willie (Burns), lip worshiper, lip server, ranter; dissembler, dissimulator; formalist; Tartufe *or* Tartuffe; scribes and Pharisees; puritan etc. (affecter) 853.4; attitudinarian etc. 882.5; bigot etc. 606.3; fanatic etc. 504.2; hypocrite etc. 548.4.

7. *v.* be impious etc. *adj.*, commit sacrilege, profane, desecrate, blaspheme; revile etc. (scoff) 930.6; swear etc. 908.5; sin etc. 945.9.

8. *v.* be sanctimonious etc. *adj.*, cant; snuffle, talk through the nose; hold up the hands in horror, turn up the whites of the eyes; sing psalms for a pretense, make long prayers; dissemble etc. 544.6.

9. *v.* backslide, fall from grace etc. (relapse) 661.3; retrograde etc. 283.5; retrovert etc. 145.4; deteriorate etc. 659.6; apostatize etc. 607.8; forsake etc. (abandon) 624.3.

10. *adj.* impious, profane, irreverent, sacrilegious, blasphemous; unhallowed, unsanctified, unregenerate; perverted, reprobate, hardened; undutiful, disobedient; irreligious etc. 989.6–9; sinful etc. 945.11–19.

11. *adj.* sanctimonious, sanctified; hypocritically devout *or* pious, pietistic(al), pietic [rare], canting, pharisaic(al), unctuous, self-righteous, overrighteous; tartufian *or* tartuffian, tartufish *or* tartuffish; false etc. 544.7, 8; affected etc. 853.6; puritanical, straitlaced etc. (prudish) 853.7; bigoted etc. 606.7; prejudiced etc. 481.10; fanatical etc. 503.18; hypocritical etc. (dissembling) 544.8.

989. Irreligion
(See 983. Theology)

1. *n.* irreligion, irreligionism, indevotion, ungodliness etc. *adj.*; impiety etc. 988; wickedness etc. (vice) 945; apathy etc. (insensibility) 823; indifference etc. 866.

2. *n.* infidelity, infidelism; faithlessness etc. *adj.*, want of faith *or* belief, disbelief, unbelief; atheism; minimifidianism; secularism; paganism etc. 984.10; heresy, anti-Christianity etc. (heterodoxy) 984.1.

3. *n.* skepticism *or* scepticism, doubt, incredulity, nullifidianism, Pyrrhonism, Humism; agnosticism; latitudinarianism, freethinking, free thought; deism; ethical nihilism, nihilism; rationalism; materialism etc. 316.5; incredulity etc. 487.

4. *n.* irreligionist, unbeliever, disbeliever, misbeliever, miscreant [arch.], in-

---

988. He who offers God a second place offers him no place.—RUSKIN.   Impiety—your irreverence toward my deity.—A. BIERCE. Volumes might be written upon the impiety of the pious.—SPENCER.   Thou pure impiety and impious purity!—SHAKESPEARE.

989. The fool hath said in his heart, There is no God.—BIBLE.   Atheism is rather in the lip than in the heart of man.—BACON.   The devil divides the world between atheism and superstition.—G. HERBERT.   Unbelief is blind.—MILTON.   A skeptic is not one who doubts, but

fidel, *giaour* [Turk.]; worldling, earthling; secularist; skeptic *or* sceptic, doubter, dubitant, doubting Thomas, nullifidian, Pyrrhonist, Humist; atheist; agnostic; latitudinarian, freethinker, *esprit fort* [F.]; deist; theophobe *or* theophobiac; antichrist, Antichrist, antichristian, anti-Christian; nihilist; minimifidian; non-Christian, gentile etc. (pagan) 984.20; heretic etc. 984.12; hypocrite etc. 988.6; sinner etc. (wrongdoer) 949.2; backslider etc. (apostate) 607.5; materialist etc. 316.6.

5. *v.* be irreligious etc. *adj.*, lack faith, serve Mammon, contend against the light, deny the truth; dechristianize, anti-Christianize [rare]; disbelieve, doubt etc. 485.5–7; be indifferent etc. 866.3.

6. *adj.* irreligious, unreligious; indevotional, indevout, undevout, devoutless; ungodly, godless, graceless; unholy, unsanctified, unhallowed; impious etc. 988.10; sinful etc. 945.11–19; apathetic, cold, callous etc. 823.5–7; indifferent etc. 866.4.

7. *adj.* infidelic(al), infidelistic, infidel; disbelieving, unbelieving, unconverted, faithless, miscreant [arch.]; unchristian, antichristian, Antichristian, anti-Christian; atheistic; minimifidian; heretical etc. (heterodox) 984.22; pagan etc. 984.28.

8. *adj.* skeptic(al) *or* sceptic(al), doubtful, dubious, dubitative, incredulous, nullifidian, Humean; Pyrrhonic, Pyrrhonian; freethinking, latitudinarian; deistic(al); rationalistic(al); materialistic etc. 316.9.

9. *adj.* worldly, earthly, earthy, terrestrial, mundane, carnal, unspiritual, temporal, profane; secular, secularist *or* secularistic; worldly-minded, earthly-minded, carnal-minded.

990. Worship

1. *n.* worship, adoration, devotion, homage, veneration, reverence; latria,

---

one who examines.—SAINTE-BEUVE. The man that feareth, Lord, to doubt, in that fear doubteth thee.—G. MACDONALD. There lives more faith in honest doubt / Believe me, than in half the creeds.—TENNYSON.
990. Worship is transcendent wonder.—CARLYLE. And learn there may be worship without words.—LOWELL. What greater calamity can fall upon a nation than the loss of worship?—EMERSON. Making their lives a

---

dulia, hyperdulia; genuflection, kneeling, prostration etc. (obeisance) 928.2.

2. *n.* glorification, glory, praise, laudation, exaltation, magnification; hosanna, hallelujah *or* halleluiah, alleluia *or* alleluiah *or* alleluja; laud, paean, doxology, psalm, hymn, anthem, motet, choral *or* chorale, canticle; chant, chaunt [arch.]; Introit, Miserere; Gloria, Gloria in Excelsis Deo, Gloria Patri; *Te Deum* [L.], Agnus Dei, Benedicite, Magnificat, Nunc Dimittis; Sanctus, Tersanctus, Trisagion; response, responsory *or* responsary, report, answer; antiphon, antiphony; offertory, offertory sentence *or* hymn; sacred music etc. 415.11.

3. *n.* prayer, holy breathing, invocation, supplication, rogation, intercession, orison, petition, suit, obtestation, obsecration, imprecation, importunity, imploration, impetration, entreaty, beseechment, appeal; grace, thanks, prayer of thanks, thanksgiving; canonical prayers, breviary; collect, collect of the Mass, collect of the Communion; litany, liturgical prayer; the Lord's Prayer, paternoster *or* Pater Noster; Ave, Ave Maria, Hail Mary; Kyrie eleison; rosary, beads, beadroll; prayer wheel *or* machine; prayer meeting etc. *below* 990.7; prayer book etc. 998.9.

4. *n.* benediction, benedicite, invocation, blessing, benison; sign of the cross.

5. *n.* propitiation, placation, propitiatory gift etc. (pacification) 723; expiation, penance etc. (atonement) 952; fasting etc. 956.

6. *n.* oblation, offering, sacrifice, immolation, incense; libation, drink offering; holocaust, burnt offering; heave offering, thank offering, votive offering, peace offering, sacramental offering, sin *or* piacular offering, whole offering; mactation, human sacrifice, infanticide, hecatomb; idolothyte; self-immolation, sutteeism; scapegoat, suttee; offertory, collection; gift etc. 784.3.

7. *n.* divine service, office, duty, exercises, devotions; praise meeting [local U.S.]; revival, revival meeting, camp meeting, anxious meeting; prayer meeting, prayer *or* prayers; morning devotions, ~ services *or* prayers, matins, lauds; prime, prime song; tierce, under-

---

prayer.—WHITTIER. Religion is not a dogma, nor an emotion, but a service.—R. D. HITCHCOCK.

song; sext; none, nones; evening devotions, ~ services *or* prayers, vesper *or* vespers, vigils, evensong; complin *or* compline, night song *or* prayer; ceremony, Mass etc. (rite) 998; meeting etc. (assembly) 72.2; attendance etc. 186.6; sermon etc. (speech) 582.2.

8. *n.* worshiper, adorer, devotionist [rare], communicant, celebrant; idolizer etc. 991.5; congregation etc. (assemblage) 72.

9. *v.* worship, adore, reverence, venerate, revere, honor, pay divine honors to, lift up the heart, do service, humble oneself, bow down and worship; pay homage etc. 928.5; genuflect, kneel etc. (make obeisance) 928.6; idolize etc. 991.6.

10. *v.* glorify, praise, laud, exalt, extol, magnify, bless, celebrate; praise *or* glorify the Lord, praise God, praise God from whom all blessings flow; praise Father, Son and Holy Ghost; sing praises, sing ~, chant ~, sound *or* resound the praises of, hymn, psalm [rare], doxologize; deacon *or* deacon off [U.S.]; chant, intone etc. (sing) 416.20.

11. *v.* pray, invoke, supplicate, offer *or* put up prayers *or* petitions, commune with God, say one's prayers; tell one's beads, recite the rosary; say grace, give *or* return thanks; petition, beseech etc. (request) 765.4, 5.

12. *v.* bless, give one's blessing, give benediction, confer a blessing upon, invoke benefits upon; make the sign of the cross upon *or* over; hallow etc. (sanctify) 987.8.

13. *v.* propitiate, make propitiation; deny oneself; give alms; offer sacrifice, make sacrifice to, immolate before, offer up an oblation etc. *n.*; vow, offer vows; appease etc. (pacify) 723.4; do penance etc. (atone) 952.4; fast etc. 956.3.

14. *v.* attend service *or* divine service, go to *or* attend church; attend etc. 186.9; assemble etc. 72.10; communicate, attend Mass etc. (ritualize) 998.14.

15. *adj.* worshiping etc. *v.*, worshipful, adorant; devout, devotional; reverent, reverential; venerative, venerant [rare], venerational; solemn; prone *or* prostrate before, in the dust before, at the feet of; pious etc. 987.10; fervent, heartfelt etc. 821.6–8; idolatrous etc. 991.7.

16. *int.* hallelujah *or* halleluiah!, alleluia *or* alleluiah!, hosanna!, praise God!, praise the Lord!, praise ye the Lord!, "praise ye Him . . . all His hosts!" (Bible), Heaven be praised!, glory to God!, glory be to God!, glory be to God in the highest!, bless the Lord!, "bless the Lord, O my soul: and all that is within me, bless His holy name!" (Bible), "hallowed be Thy Name!" (Bible); thank Heaven!, thank God!, thanks be to God!, *Deo gratias!* [L.]; lift up your hearts!, *sursum corda!* [L.].

17. *int.* O Lord!, our Father Who art in heaven!; pray God that!, God grant!, God bless!, God save!, God forbid!, *Domine dirige nos!* [L.].

991. Idolatry

1. *n.* idolatry, idolatrousness etc. *adj.*, idol worship, idololatry, idolomancy, idolism, idolomania, idolodulia; iconolatry, iconoduly; fetishism, hierolatry [rare], ecclesiolatry, bibliolatry; demonism, demonology, demonolatry, chthonian ~, demon *or* devil worship; animal worship; zoolatry; fire worship, pyrolatry, Parsiism, Zoroastrianism; sun worship, heliolatry; star worship, Sabaism; hero worship; paganism etc. 984.10.

2. *n.* idolization, fetishization; deification, apotheosis, canonization [obs.], enshrinement.

3. *n.* sacrifice, immolation, idolothyte etc. (oblation) 990.6.

4. *n.* idol, graven image, golden calf, fetish, eidolon, *thakur* [Hind.], joss [Chin.], lares and penates, god *or* goddess of one's idolatry, devil-god; Baal, Moloch, Dagon, Juggernaut.

5. *n.* idolater, idolatress [*fem.*], idolatrizer, idolizer, idolist, idol worshiper; fetishist, fetisheer *or* fetisher [rare]; ecclesiolater; bibliolater, bibliolatrist; demon *or* devil worshiper, demonolater, chthonian; animal worshiper, zoolater; fire worshiper, pyrolater, Parsi, Zoroastrian; sun worshiper, heliolater; star worshiper, Sabaist, Sabaean [erron.]; pagan etc. 984.20.

6. *v.* idolatrize, idolize, idolify, idol worship, worship idols; worship the golden calf,

---

991. 'Tis mad idolatry / To make the service greater than the god.—SHAKESPEARE. The idol is the measure of the worshipper.—LOWELL. Idolatry is in a man's own thought, not in the opinion of another.—SELDEN.

adorer le veau d'or [F.]; fetish, fetishize; apotheosize, deify, canonize [obs.], enshrine; worship etc. 990.9; put on a pedestal etc. (respect) 928.4; prostrate oneself before etc. (make obeisance) 928.6; make sacrifice to etc. (propitiate) 990.13.

7. *adj.* idolatrous, idolatric(al), idololatric(al), idolistic; fetishic [rare], fetishistic; demonolatrous, chthonian; heliolatrous; bibliolatrous; zoolatrous; idolothyte, idolothytic; worshiping etc. 990.15; pagan etc. 984.28.

992. Sorcery

1. *n.* sorcery, sorcering etc. *v.*, magic; necromancy, psychomancy [rare], theurgy, rune, gramarye [chiefly Hist.], glamour; sympathetic magic; divination; thaumaturgy, thaumaturgia, thaumaturgics, thaumaturgism; conjuration, conjurement; exorcism, exorcisation; exsufflation [Eccl. Hist.]; cantation [rare], incantation; enchantment, entrancement; witchery, witchering [rare], bewitchery, bewitchment, witchwork, witchcraft; white *or* natural magic; black magic, the black art; diablerie, diabolism, demonry, demonology, demonography, demonomancy, demonomagy, demonianism, devilry, bedevilment, Satanism; Black Mass.

sortilege, *sors* [L.], *sortes Homericae* or *Vergilianae* [L.], *sortes Biblicae* or *sacrae* [L.]; hoodoo, voodoo, voodooism, wanga [W. Ind. and South. U.S.]; shamanism; obeah, obeahism; magism, magianism; fetishism; vampirism; ghost dance; magic circle; sabbat, witches' meeting *or* Sabbath; ordeal, ordeal by battle, ~ fire, ~ water *or* lots; divination etc. 511.2–5; hocus-pocus etc. (deception) 545.2, 3; spell etc. 993; delusion etc. 545.2.

2. *n.* sorcerer, miracle-worker, wonder-worker, magician, mage, magus (*pl.* magi), magian, wizard, warlock, necromancer, theurgist, dowser, conjuror, exorcist, incantator [rare]; charmer, enchanter, bewitcher; thaumaturge, thaumaturgist, *thaumaturgus* [ML.]; voodoo, voodooist, wangateur [South. U.S.];

medicine man, medicine; witchman, witch doctor, obeah doctor, hex [local U.S.]; witch-finder, witch-hunter; shaman, shamanist; fetisheer *or* fetisher [both rare]; Faust, Merlin, Comus; Houdin, Houdini; diabolist etc. 978.5; diviner, soothsayer etc. (prophet) 513.2; astrologer etc. 318.13; legerdemainist etc. 548.6.

3. *n.* sorceress, shamaness; witch, witchwoman [dial.], witchwife [Scot., Ir., and North. Eng.], witch doctress; hex [local U.S.], hag, lamia, vampire, ghoul, siren, Harpy; Circe, witch of Endor, Weird Sisters; Gorgon, Medusa, Stheno, Eurale; Vivian, Lady of the Lake.

4. *v.* practice sorcery etc. *n.*, sorcer, magic [coll.], conjure, exorcise, shamanize; spell, cast a spell, spellbind, put obeah on [coll.], witch, bewitch, hex, put a hex on [local U.S.], charm, becharm, enchant, trance, entrance, glamour; be a witch etc. *n.*, ride a broomstick; bedevil, diabolize, demonize; voodoo, hoodoo [coll.]; overlook, look on with the evil eye, cast the evil eye; wave a wand, rub the ring *or* lamp; call up spirits, raise spirits from the dead, raise ghosts, lay ghosts, command jinn *or* genii; hagride; taboo *or* tabu.

5. *adj.* sorcerous [rare], necromantic, magic(al), magian, thaumaturgic(al), cantrip, Circean, weird; incantatory, incantational; witch, witchy, witchlike; hoodoo [coll.], voodoo, voodooistic; shaman, shamanic, shamanist, shamanistic; talismanic(al), telesmatic(al) [arch.], phylacteric(al).

6. *adj.* witching, bewitching, charming, enchanting, entrancing, spellbinding, fascinating, glamorous.

7. *adj.* bewitched, witched, enchanted, charmed etc. *v.*; charm-struck, charmbound; spellbound, spell-caught, spellstruck; witch-charmed, witch-held, witch-struck; witch-ridden, hagridden; possessed, obsessed; haunted, hanted [dial.], ghostified [rare].

993. Spell

1. *n.* spell, magic spell, charm, weird [obs. exc. Scot.], cantrip [chiefly Scot.], wanga [W. Ind. and South. U.S.], glam-

---

992. Midnight hags, / By force of potent spells, . . . / Call fiends and spectres from the yawning deep.—ROWE.   Mumbo-Jumbo will hoodoo you.—V. LINDSAY.

993. The charm dissolves apace.—SHAKESPEARE.   Eye of newt and toe of frog, / Wool

our; witchery, bewitchery, bewitchment, enchantment, entrancement, fascination, captivation; possession, obsession; incantation, conjuration, invocation, exorcism, magic words *or* formula, abracadabra, hocus-pocus, mumbo jumbo, open-sesame; bell, book and candle; runes, Ephesian letters; demonifuge; countercharm; evil eye; sorcery etc. 992; trance etc. 994.6.

2. *n.* talisman, telesm [arch.], charm, amulet, periapt, phylactery, fetish, voodoo, obeah [coll.], Mumbo Jumbo; good-luck charm, lucky piece, rabbit-foot; mascot, *mascotte* [F.]; hoodoo [coll.], jinx [slang]; madstone [U.S.]; love charm, philter; scarab, scarabaeus, scarabee; veronica, sudarium; swastika, fylfot, gammadion.

3. *n.* wand, rod; divining rod *or* stick, witch stick [slang]; Aaron's rod; caduceus, caduce [obs.].

4. *n.* (magic wish-givers) Aladdin's lamp, Aladdin's casket, magic ring, magic belt, magic spectacles, magic carpet, seven-league boots; wishing stone, wishing well; wishing cap, Fortunatus's cap; cap of darkness, Tarnkappe, Tarnhelm; wishbone, merrythought, furculum, furcula.

5. *n.* (fairy lore) fairy ring *or* circle; fern seed; rowan tree, quicken tree [dial. Eng.].

6. *v.* cast a spell etc. (sorcery) 992.4.

7. *adj.* spellbound, enchanted etc. (bewitched) 992.7.

994. Esoteric Sciences

1. *n.* esoteric sciences, esoterics, esotericism, esoterism, esotery; occultism, mysticism, supernaturalism, transcendentalism, hyperphysics; metapsychics, metapsychism, transphysical science, metaphysics, the first philosophy *or* theology, *philosophia prima* [L.]; cabalism, cabala; yoga, yogism, yogeeism; theosophy, reincarnationism, Rosicrucianism; Masonry, Freemasonry, Freemasonism; symbolics, symbolism; anagoge, anagogics; mystery.

2. *n.* psychical research, psychics, psychism, psychicism; psychosophy; psychognosis, psychognosy; psychometry; psychic monism; psychon, monad; psychoplasm; psychology etc. (science of mind) 450.4.

3. *n.* psychophysics, psychophysiology [rare]; double-aspect theory, psychical parallelism, interactionism, epiphenomenonism; epiphenomenon; psychophysical law, Fechner's law; psychosome.

4. *n.* spiritualism, spiritism, psychomancy [rare]; mediumism, mediumistic communication; séance, sitting; divination etc. 511.2, 3; spirit, ghost etc. (specter) 980a; idealism etc. (immaterialism) 317.3.

5. *n.* spirit manifestation *or* communication, psychical ∼, spiritistic ∼, supernormal *or* mediumistic phenomena; spirit rapping, table tipping *or* turning; poltergeist; automatism, automatic ∼, trance *or* spirit writing, psychography; planchette, ouija board; trance speaking; telekinesis; psychorrhagy; ectoplasy; materialization etc. 316.4; ectoplasm etc. (emanation) 980a.3.

6. *n.* trance, ecstasy, ecstasis, rapture, spirit control *or* possession; mesmeric *or* hypnotic trance *or* sleep, hypnosis, hypnoidal state; lethargic hypnosis; cataleptic hypnosis, catalepsy, cataplexy; somnambulistic hypnosis, hypnotic somnolence; self-hypnosis, autohypnosis; mesmerism, hypnotism, hypnology; hypnotic power, animal magnetism, odylic force, odyl *or* odyle, od, biod, elod, magnetod, pantod, hypnotic suggestion, post-hypnotic suggestion, autosuggestion; yoga trance, dharana, dhyana, samadhi; spell etc. 993.

7. *n.* clairvoyance *or* clairvoyancy, clairsentience, clairaudience, crystal vision, psychometry; second sight, insight, sixth sense; intuition etc. 477a; foresight etc. 510; foreboding etc. (prediction) 511; premonition etc. 668.2.

8. *n.* telepathy, mental telepathy, telepathic *or* thought transference *or* transmission, thought reading, mind reading; telepathic dreams, telepathic hallucinations.

---

of bat and tongue of dog.—SHAKESPEARE. They charmed it with smiles and soap.—CARROLL.
994. There rises an unspeakable desire / After the knowledge of our buried life.—M. ARNOLD.

There exists in nature, in myriad activity, a *psychic element* the essential nature of which is still hidden to us.—FLAMMARION. There are more things in heaven and earth, Horatio, / Than are dreamt of in your philosophy.—SHAKESPEARE.

9. *n.* divination etc. 511.2–5; necromancy etc. (sorcery) 992; astrology etc. 511.4; constellations, houses etc. (stars) 318.6–8.

10. *n.* (theosophy) lower *or* mortal nature, higher *or* immortal nature; seven principles; spirit, atman etc. *below*; mind, manas; soul, buddhi; vital force, life principle, prana; astral body, linga sharira etc. *below* 994.12; physical ~, dense *or* gross body, sthula sharira; principle *or* fire of desire, kama.

11. *n.* psyche, spirit, spiritus, soul, ghost [arch.], *Geist* [G.], anima, anima humana, heart, mind, breath, embodied breath; shade, shadow, manes [Rom. Rel.]; vital *or* life principle, vital animal soul *or* spirit, animating principle, psychical *or* spiritual principle, essence *or* substance of life, individual essence, immaterial nature, spiritual being, "the Divinity that stirs within us" (Addison), *anima divina* [L.], *divina particula aurae* [L.], divine spark, vital spark *or* flame.

seat of consciousness, seat *or* center of life, inner man, inmost *or* essential nature, *penetralia mentis* [L.], inmost heart *or* mind, heart of hearts, true being, ego, the self, the I; pneuma, *ousia, skia* [both Gr.]; nephesh, ruach; ba, khu [both Egyptian Rel.]; atman, purusha, jiva, jivatma, prana [all Hinduism]; brute soul, *anima bruta* [L.], crude spirit; vital force etc. (life) 359.2; disembodied spirit etc. (specter) 980a; incorporeal, incorporeal being etc. 317.2.

12. *n.* astral *or* design body, astral, linga sharira, subtle body, vital body, etheric body, bliss body, Buddhic body, spiritual body, soul body; desire *or* kamic body, kamarupa; causal body; mental *or* mind body; aura, auric egg; etheric double etc. 980a.2.

13. *n.* psychist, psychicist; psychophysicist, psychophysiologist [rare]; occultist, esoteric, cabalist, mystic, supernaturalist, transcendentalist, metapsychist; metaphysician, metaphysicist; mahatma, adept; yogi, yogin, yogist; theosophist, reincarnationist, Rosicrucian; Mason, Freemason; mesmerist, hypnotist; psychologist etc. 450.5.

14. *n.* psychic, spiritualist, spiritist, rappist [rare], witch of Endor; medium, spiritualistic medium; ecstatic, ecstatica [rare]; spirit rapper; automatist, psychographist; guide, control; poltergeist.

15. *n.* clairvoyant, clairaudient, psychometer; telepathist, mental-telepathist, thought reader, mind reader.

16. *n.* diviner, seer etc. (prophet) 513.2, 3; astrologer etc. 318.13; necromancer etc. (sorcerer) 992.2, 3.

17. *v.* practice occultism etc. *n.*; cast a horoscope *or* nativity; practice sorcery etc. 992.4; divine, prophesy etc. (predict) 511.7.

18. *v.* practice spiritualism, hold spirit communications, hold a séance *or* sitting, mediumize, call up spirits, raise spirits from the dead, raise ghosts, summon familiar spirits, conjure *or* conjure up spirits; materialize etc. 316.7.

19. *v.* place under control, place in a trance, entrance, subject to suggestion, induce hypnosis, hypnotize, mesmerize, magnetize, psychologize; cast a spell etc. 992.4.

20. *v.* spiritualize, spiritize; etherealize, idealize; immaterialize, dematerialize, unsubstantialize; disembody, disincarnate.

21. *adj.* occult, occultist; esoteric(al), mystic(al), mysterious, anagogic(al), metapsychic(al), metaphysic(al); cabalic, cabalistic(al); supernatural, supernaturalist, supernaturalistic; transcendental, transcendentalist, transcendentalistic; theosophic(al), theosophist; Rosicrucian; Masonic(al), Freemasonic(al).

22. *adj.* psychic(al), psychal [rare]; spiritual, spiritualistic, spiritistic; psychomantic [rare], mediumistic; second-sighted, clairvoyant, clairaudient, clairsentient, telepathic; telekinetic; psychosensory, psychosensorial; automatist, psychometric(al); psychognostic; ghostly etc. (spectral) 980a.4; insubstantial etc. (immaterial) 317.6; hyperphysical etc. (supernatural) 976.14.

23. *adj.* divinatory etc. (predictive) 511.11; astrological etc. (celestial) 318.16.

995. Churchdom

1. *n.* churchdom, church, pale of the church, Christendom, Christdom [rare], Christianity; ministry, apostleship, priesthood; hierarchy, hierocracy; prelacy, episcopacy; clericalism, sacerdotalism, episcopalianism, ultramontanism;

995. So were the churches established in the faith.—BIBLE.

ecclesiology; theocracy; churchcraft, priestcraft; the Church etc. 983a.3; religious sects etc. 984.4–11.

2. *n.* monasticism, monachism, monkery, monkhood, friarhood; celibacy etc. 904.

3. *n.* (ecclesiastical offices and dignities) cardinalate, cardinalship; primacy, archbishopric, archiepiscopate, archiepiscopacy; prelacy, prelature, prelatry [rare], prelateship, prelatehood; bishopric, bishopdom; episcopate, episcopacy; see, diocese, stall; deanery, deanship; canonry, canonicate; prebend, prebendaryship, prebendal stall; benefice, incumbency, glebe, advowson, living; curacy, cure, charge, cure *or* care of souls; rectory, rectorate, rectorship; vicariate, vicarship, vicarage [rare]; priesthood, sacerdotalism; pastorate, pastorship, pastoral charge; deaconry, deaconship; chaplaincy, chaplainship, chaplainry *or* chaplanry [Scot.]; abbacy, abbotcy [rare]; presbytery, presbyterate.

4. *n.* papacy, papality, pontificate, popedom, the Vatican, See of Rome, Apostolic See.

5. *n.* parochial council *or* court, convocation, synod, presbytery etc. (council) 696.3.

6. *n.* orders, holy orders; calling, election, nomination, appointment, preferment, induction, institution, installation, investiture; conferment, presentation; ordination, consecration, canonization, reading in [Eng.]; translation.

7. *v.* call, invite, elect, nominate, appoint, induct, install, invest; confer, present, bestow; ordain, frock, consecrate, canonize, saint; translate.

8. *v.* take orders *or* holy orders, take the veil, take vows, read oneself in [Eng.].

9. *adj.* ecclesiastic(al), ecclesiological; churchly, churchlike, churchish; cleric(al), sacerdotal, priestly, pastoral, ministerial; prelatic(al), prelatial; episcopal, episcopalian; archiepiscopal; hierarchic(al), hierarchal; theocratic(al), theocratist; canonical; capitular, capitulary; monkish, monachal, monastic, monasterial, conventual; abbatial, abbatical; Anglican; Aaronic(al), Levitic(al); pontifical, pontific [rare]; papal, apostolic(al); popish, papish, papist *or* Papist, papistic(al) [all derog.]; ultramontane; priest-ridden.

996. Clergy
(See 997. Laity)

1. *n.* clergy, clerical order, clericals, ministry, priesthood, priestery [derog.], presbytery, the cloth, the pulpit, the desk.

2. *n.* clergyman, divine, ecclesiastic, churchman, cleric, clerical, clerk, clerk in holy orders, minister, minister of the Gospel, parson, pastor, angel, pulpiter, pulpiteer [derog.], *abbé* [F.], curate, servant of God, shepherd, pilot *or* sky pilot [slang], Holy Joe [Naut. slang], devil-dodger [coll.], blackcoat [chiefly coll.], reverend [coll.]; preacher, sermoner, sermoneer [rare], sermonist, sermonizer; chaplain; priest, hierophant, presbyter, cassock, father, father in Christ, padre, abuna; parish priest, curé; confessor, father confessor, spiritual father *or* director, penitentiary; the Reverend, the very *or* right Reverend, his Reverence [chiefly joc.]; Doctor of Divinity; theologian etc. 983.3.

3. *n.* clergywoman, priestess, ministress, preacheress, pastoress, parsoness; nun etc. *below* 996.12.

4. *n.* evangelist, revivalist; missionary, missioner, field preacher, propagandist, colporteur, missionary rector, missionary apostolic; Jesuit etc. *below* 996.11.

5. *n.* (church dignitaries) ecclesiarch, hierarch, patriarch, sacrist, high priest; pope, Holy Father, papa, pontiff, servant of the servants of God; Eminence, reverence; cardinal, cardinal bishop, cardinal priest, cardinal deacon, primate, exarch, metropolitan, archbishop, bishop, angel, prelate, diocesan, suffragan, bishop coadjutor, dean, subdean, archdeacon, prebendary, canon, rural dean, rector, vicar, chaplain, curate; beneficiary, incumbent.

resident, residentiary, residenter [rare]; penitentiary, Grand Penitentiary; clerk, parish clerk, Bible clerk; reader, Bible reader, lay reader, lecturer, lector, anagnost; capitular, capitulary; elder, elderman; deacon, deaconess; churchwarden, churchward [Hist.],

---

996. O most gentle pulpiter! what tedious homily of love have you wearied your parishioners withal!—SHAKESPEARE. To have a thin stipend, and an everlasting parish, Lord, what a torment 'tis!—BEAUMONT AND FLETCHER. A minister, but still a man.—POPE. Priests are extremely like other men, and neither the

churchmaster [dial. Eng.]; questman [Hist.], sidesman; almoner, almsman [rare]; verger, vergeress; beadle, bedral or bedral [Scot.], *suisse* [F.]; sexton, sacristan; acolyte, thurifer, censer bearer; choir chaplain, precentor, succentor; chorister, choirboy; organist.

6. *n.* (Jewish) prophet, priest, high priest, Levite, scribe; rabbi, rabbin.

7. *n.* (Mohammedan) imam, kahin, kasis, sheik, mullah, murshid, mufti, hadji, muezzin, dervish, abdal (*pl.* abdali), fakir, santon.

8. *n.* (Hindu) Brahman, pujari, purohit, pundit, guru, bashara, vairagi *or* bairagi, Ramwat, Ramanandi; sannyasi; yogi, yogin; bhikshu, bhikhari.

9. *n.* (Buddhist) poonghie [Burma], talapoin [Indo-China], bonze, bhikku; lama, Grand Lama *or* Dalai Lama [Tibet].

10. *n.* (pagan) druid, druidess; flamen [Rom. Rel.]; hierophant, hierodule, hieros, daduchus, mystes (*pl.* mystae), epopt (*pl.* epoptae) [all Gr. Rel.].

11. *n.* religious, *religieux* [F.], monastic, monk, cowl [rare]; caloyer, hieromonach; brother, lay brother; cenobite, conventual; pilgrim, palmer; stylite, pillarist, pillar saint; beadsman *or* bedesman; prior, claustral *or* conventual prior, grand prior, general prior; abbot, *abbas* [L.]; lay abbot, *abbas miles* [ML.], abbacomes; mendicant, friar; hermit, anchorite etc. (recluse) 893.4; yogi, dervish etc. (ascetic) 955.2; celibate etc. 904.2.

Franciscan, Gray Friar, Friar Minor, Minorite, Observant, Recollect *or* Recollet, Conventual, Capuchin; Dominican, Black Friar, Friar Preacher, preaching friar *or* brother; Carmelite, White Friar; Augustinian, Augustinian hermit, Austin friar, begging hermit; Benedictine, Black Monk; Jesuit, Loyolite; Crutched Friar, Crossed Friar [obs.]; Templar, Hospitaler; Carthusian, Trappist, Cistercian, Gilbertine, Bonhomme, Cluniac, Premonstratensian, Maturine, Bernardine, Lorettine.

12. *n.* nun, sister, *religieuse* [F.], clergywoman, conventual; abbess, prioress; superioress, mother *or* lady superior, the reverend mother; canoness, regular *or* secular canoness; novice, postulant.

13. *v.* take orders etc. 995.8.

14. *v.* preach, sermonize etc. (declaim) 582.7.

15. *adj.* ministerial, priestly, pastoral etc. (ecclesiastical) 995.8.

16. *adj.* ordained etc. (*see* ordain etc. 995.6), in orders, in holy orders, called to the ministry.

997. Laity
(See 996. Clergy)

1. *n.* laity, laymen, sheep, flock, fold, congregation, assembly, brethren, people; parish, society [U.S.]; class [Methodist Ch.].

2. *n.* layman, laic, secular, churchman, parishioner, catechumen; laywoman, churchwoman.

3. *v.* laicize, secularize.

4. *adj.* lay, laic(al), congregational, popular, civil, nonreligious, nonecclesiastical, nonclerical, nonministerial, nonpastoral; secular, secularist *or* secularistic; temporal, profane etc. (worldly) 989.9.

998. Rite

1. *n.* rite, *ritus* [L.], ritual, rituality, liturgy, ceremony, ceremonial, form, formula, formulary, formality, solemnity, ordinance, observance, function, duty, service, religious ceremony, ∼ service etc.; ministry, ministration; sacrament, sacramental; institution; mystery; symbolism, symbolics; empty ceremony, lip service etc. (sanctimony) 988.2.

2. *n.* (rites) celebration, high celebration; processional; litany, greater *or* lesser litany; invocation, invocation of saints; transfiguration; auricular confession, the confessional, the confessionary; sign of the cross; pax, kiss of peace; reciting the rosary, telling of beads; thurification, incense; Asperges, aspersion, holy water; circumcision; genuflection etc. (obeisance) 928.2; devotions, prayer

998. Do we all holy rites; let there be sung 'Non nobis' and 'Te Deum.'—SHAKESPEARE. The rest . . . will deem in outward rites and specious forms religion satisfied.—MILTON. The occasional exercise of a beautiful form of worship.—W. IRVING. The truth of religion is in its ritual and the truth of dogma is in its poetry.—J. C. POWYS.

---

better or worse for wearing a gown or a surplice.—CHESTERFIELD. God's true priest is always free; / Free, the needed truth to speak, / Right the wronged, and raise the weak.—WHITTIER.

etc. (worship) 990; idolatry etc. 991; incantation, invocation etc. (sorcery) 992; purification, canonization etc. (sanctification) 987.2; absolution etc. (forgiveness) 918; funeral rite etc. 363.4; sermon, exhortation etc. (speech) 582.2.

3. *n.* seven sacraments, mysteries; baptism etc. *below* 998.5; confirmation, imposition *or* laying on of hands; Eucharist etc. *below* 998.6, 7; penance etc. 952.3, repentance etc. 950; extreme unction etc. *below*; holy orders etc. 995.5; matrimony etc. 903.

4. *n.* unction, sacred unction, sacramental anointment, chrism, chrisom, chrismation, chrismatory; extreme unction, last rites, viaticum; ointment; chrismal *or* chrismale, chrismatory.

5. *n.* baptism, baptizement; christening; immersion; sprinkling, aspergation, aspersion; affusion, infusion; baptism for the dead; baptismal regeneration; chrisomloosing; baptistery, font.

6. *n.* Eucharist, Lord's Supper, Last Supper, Communion, Holy Communion, the Sacrament, the Holy Sacrament, housel [arch.]; Postcommunion; intinction; consubstantiation, impanation, subpanation, transubstantiation; real presence; elements, consecrated elements, bread and wine, body and blood of Christ; Eucharistic wafer, loaf, bread, altar bread, consecrated bread, host; Sacrament Sunday; viaticum etc. *above* 998.4; Lord's table, communion cloth etc. 1000.3.

7. *n.* Mass, Mess [now Scot. and dial.], *Missa* [L.], Eucharistic rites; the Liturgy, the Divine Liturgy; High Mass, *Missa solemnis* [L.]; Low Mass, *Missa bassa* [L.]; Rosary Mass, Rosary, Rosary of the Seven Dolors of Mary; Dry Mass, *Missa sicca* [L.]; *Missa publica, Missa privata, Missa cantata* or *media, Missa adventitia* or *manualis, Missa capitularis, Missa legata* [all L.]; *Missa praesanctificatorum* [L.].

Liturgy of the Presanctified; Introit, Kyrie eleison, Gloria, Collect, Epistle, Gradual and Alleluia *or* Tract, Gospel, Credo, Offertory, Lavabo, secreta, Preface, Sanctus, Canon; Memento of the Living, Consecration, Elevation of the Host, Anamnesis, Memento of the Dead; Pater Noster *or* paternoster, Fraction, Agnus Dei, Pax, Communion, Postcommunion, Dismissal, Blessing, Last Gospel.

8. *n.* (sacred and ritualistic articles) relics, sacred relics; reliquary, *reliquaire* [F.], shrine; monstrance; Host; eucharistial, pyx, ciborium; pyx cloth *or* veil; cross, crucifix, rood, holy cross *or* rood, rood tree [now rare], roodstone [rare]; rood cloth; osculatory, pax; Agnus Dei; icon; *Pietà* [It.]; sacramental; holy water; holy-water sprinkler, asperger, asperges, aspergillum; thurible, thuribulum [rare], censer, incensory; cruet; patera; urceus, urceole; rosary, beads, beadroll; prayer wheel *or* machine; candles, seven-branched candlestick; Sanctus bell, sacring bell; Sangraal *or* Sangreal, Holy Grail; altar etc. 1000.3.

9. *n. rituale* [L.], ritual, rite, liturgy, formulary, church book, service book, manual, rubric, canon, ordinal, breviary; missal, Mass book; farse; lectionary, *lectionarium* [L.]; pontifical; Virginal; prayer book, Book of Common Prayer, euchologion *or* euchology, litany.

10. *n.* psalter, psalmbook; hymnbook, hymnal; Psalm Book, Book of Common Order; the Psalms, Book of Psalms, the Psalter, the Psaltery; psalmody, hymnody, hymnology.

11. *n.* ritualism, rituality, ceremonialism, formalism; liturgiology; sacramentalism, sacramentarianism; sabbatism, Sabbatarianism; High-churchism, Anglicanism.

12. *n.* ritualist, ceremonialist, formalist, formulist, formularist; sacramentalist, sacramentarian; sabbatist, Sabbatarian; High-churchman, High-churchist, Anglican.

13. *n.* holyday, hallowday [dial. Eng.], holytide, feast, fast; Sabbath, Sunday, Lord's day; love feast, agape.

Passover, Pentecost; Advent; Christmas, Christmas Day, Christmastide, yuletide; Candlemas, Candlemas Day; Epiphany, Twelfthtide, Twelfth-night, Twelfth-day; Lent, Lententide; Holy Week, Passion Week; Ash Wednesday, Maundy Thursday, Good Friday; Easter, Easter Saturday, ~ Sunday *or* Monday; Eastertide, Easter Time; Ascension Day, Holy Thursday; Whitsuntide, Whitsun, Whitsunday, Whitweek, Whitmonday, Whit-Tuesday, White Sunday; Trinity Sunday, Corpus Christi;

Hallowman, Allhallowmas, Allhallowtide, Allhallows, All Saints, All Saints' Day; All Souls' Day; Lammas, Lammas Day, Lammastide; Michaelmas, Michaelmas Day, Michaelmastide; Martinmas; Annunciation, Annunciation Day, Lady Day.

14. *v.* ritualize, ceremonialize, solemnize, celebrate, observe, keep, perform a rite etc. *n.*, perform service *or* divine service, do duty, minister, officiate; administer the Eucharist, give *or* administer the Sacrament, ∼ Communion etc. *n.*, housel [arch.]; attend *or* celebrate Mass, communicate, attend Communion, receive Communion *or* the Sacrament, partake of the Lord's Supper etc. *n.*; thurify, cense, incense; baptize, christen, dip, immerse; sprinkle, asperge, asperse [now rare]; anoint, chrism; confirm, impose, lay hands on, lay on the hands; administer absolution, absolve, shrive, anele [arch.], give *or* administer extreme unction.

receive absolution, receive extreme unction; confess, make confession; penalize, inflict penance; receive penance, do *or* perform penance, stand in a white sheet, repent in sackcloth and ashes; make the sign of the cross; recite the rosary, tell one's beads; genuflect etc. (make obeisance) 928.6.

15. *adj.* ritual, ritualistic, liturgic(al), solemn; ceremonial, ceremonious; formal, formular, formulary; functional, functionary; sacramental, sacramentarian; Anglican, High-Church; eucharistic(al); paschal; baptismal.

999. Canonicals

1. *n.* canonicals, vestments, vestiments [now rare], vesture, cloth, robes, clericals [coll.], ecclesiastical *or* clerical attire; episcopal vestments, pontificals, pontificalia; liturgical garments, sacramental attire, Eucharistic vestments; robe, gown, cloak, mantle, frock; surplice, cotta, rochet; cassock, soutane; chimer *or* chimere, simar; mantelletta, mantellone, Geneva cloak *or* gown, scapular *or* scapulary, cope, mozzetta *or* mozetta, fanon *or* fano *or* fannel, tippet, stole, alb *or* alba, dalmatic; tunic, tunicle; chasuble, bell chasuble, Gothic chasuble, fiddleback chasuble; pallium, pall [now rare]; hood, cowl, cuculla; capuche, capuchin; amice, almuce, vakass *or* vagas.

biretta, cardinal's hat, shovel hat, miter; tiara, triple crown; skullcap, zucchetto, calotte; Salvation Army bonnet; tonsure; scarf; apron; cincture, cingulum; subcingulum, succinctorium; lawn sleeves; bands, Geneva bands; sandals; buskins; episcopal ring, bishop's ring; pectoral cross, crucifix, rood; staff, pastoral staff, cross staff, crosier *or* crozier, cross, crook, paterissa; costume, clothes etc. (investment) 225.

2. *adj.* vestmental, vestimental [rare], vestmentary, vestimentary [rare].

3. *adj.* vestmented, vested, robed, cowled etc. *n.*

1000. Temple

1. *n.* temple, place of worship, house of God, house of worship *or* prayer, minister, church, kirk [Scot. and dial. Eng.], meetinghouse, bethel, ebenezer [Eng.], conventicle, fane [arch.], sanctuary; basilica, major *or* patriarchal basilica, minor basilica; chapel, chapellany [obs.], chapel of ease, chapel royal; oratory, oratorium; chantry; cathedral, cathedral church, dome [obs.], *duomo* [It.] (*pl. duomi*); synagogue, tabernacle; mosque, masjid [Moham.]; dewal, girja [both Hindu]; pagoda, pagod [arch.]; kiack [Buddhist]; joss house [Pidgin Eng.]; pantheon; sacellum; cella, naos [both Arch.].

2. *n.* shrine, holy place, dagoba [Ind.], naos [Gr. Antiq.], sacrarium, delubrum [both Rom. Antiq.]; tope, stupa [both Buddhist]; reliquary, *reliquaire* [F.]; sepulcher etc. 363.13.

3. *n.* sanctuary, holy of holies, sanctum sanctorum; vestry, sacristy, sacrarium, diaconicon *or* diaconicum; altar, rood altar, altarpiece, altar stole, altar side, altar rail, altar stead, altar mound, altar carpet, altar stair, predella; altar facing *or* front, frontal; altar slab, altar stone, mensal; altar desk, missal stand; Com-

---

999. In sacred vestments mayst thou stand.—POPE.

1000. Mankind was never so happily inspired as when it made a cathedral.—STEVENSON. How the tall temples, as to meet their gods, / Ascend the skies!—YOUNG. What is a church?—Our honest Sexton tells. / ''Tis a tall building with a tower and bells.'—CRABBE. A church is God between four walls.—HUGO.

munion ~, chancel *or* holy table, Lord's table, table of the Lord, God's board, altar; pyx, ciborium; communion *or* sacrament cloth, fanon *or* fannel, corporal *or* corporale, pyx cloth *or* veil; credence; prothesis, table *or* altar of prothesis, chapel of prothesis.

baptistery, font; piscina; stoup, holy-water stoup *or* basin; ambry, aumbry [arch.]; sedilia (*sing.* sedile); reredos; jube, rood screen, chancel screen, rood loft; rood tower, ~ spire *or* steeple, rood stair, rood arch, rood beam, rood cloth; baldachin, baldachino *or* *baldacchino* [It.]; stall, pew, seat, seating; mourners' bench [U.S.], anxious bench *or* seat, penitent form; confessional; pulpit, ambo, lectern, reading desk; chancel, apse, presbytery, nave, triforium, blindstory, aisle, transept, crypt, porch, cloisters; choir; calvary, Easter sepulcher; belfry.

4. *n.* cloister, monastery, convent, nunnery, abbey, priory, friary.

5. *n.* parsonage, pastorage, pastorate, pastorium [South. U.S.], presbytery, rectory, vicarage, manse, deanery, church house, clergy house; glebe; Vatican; bishop's palace; Lambeth.

6. *adj.* churchly, churchlike, churchish; claustral, cloistered, monastic, monasterial, monachal, conventual; ecclesiastic(al) etc. 995.8.

INDEX GUIDE

[See also suggestions and advice on **How to Use the Book,** pp. xxviii f.]

The numbers refer to sections and paragraphs, not to pages. Thus the adjective **Aaronic,** for which the Index gives the reference number 995.9, will be found in section 995, entitled "Churchdom," and within that section in paragraph 9, labeled *adj*.

Note for further ease of reference that the section numbers are given at the top of every page of text.

When several occurrences of a word or phrase entered in the index are to be distinguished, the reference numbers are preceded by an identifying element. Thus the verb **abase** in the somewhat archaic sense of "to lower" will be found in section 308, paragraph 4, and in the more current sense of "to humble" in section 879, paragraph 3.

The identifying element is not always a definition. Often it is merely suggestive of the general sphere of meaning with which a word is connected. Thus the entry **abdication** should not suggest that this word is presented as a synonym of "dethronement" but merely that it occurs, because of its association with the idea of "loss of power on the part of a crowned head of state," in section 738, paragraph 3.

References within parentheses refer to groups of words whose relation to the key word is less direct. Thus the entry **abbreviatory** should be read to mean, not only that this word is listed in section 201, paragraph 5, but also that it is suggested that the related sphere of "compendious" in section 596, paragraph 5, might yield a helpful word or phrase.

Grammatical labels, as *n., v., adj.,* etc., have been used in the index only to distinguish otherwise identical entries. Thus **abandon** *n*. is distinguished from **abandon** *v*., but for the adjective **abandoned** the part of speech has not been indicated.

To keep the Index Guide from becoming unwieldy, a considerable number of words and phrases which could not possibly be expected to serve as starting points for a search of synonyms have not been included. Thus, while the entry **Aladdin's lamp** appears in the Index with a reference to section 993, paragraph 4, where various magic wish-givers are listed, as "magic belt, cap of darkness," etc., these phrases do not figure as special entries in the Index.—In the case of synonyms whose forms are so much alike that they would appear as consecutive entries in the Index, it has often been thought sufficient to list but one form. Thus the reference for **abbatial** must serve also as a reference for "abbatical."

A

A 1 See **A one**
Aaronic 995.9
Aaron's rod 993.3
A.B., a.b. 269.1
abacist 85.6
aback 235.14
abaction 791.1
abactor 792.1
abacus calculator 85.5
   capital 215.17
Abaddon Devil 978.1
   hell 982.1
abaff, abaft
   after 235.15
   astern 267.68
abalienate 783.3
abalienation 783.1
abandon *n*.
   neglect 460.1
   artlessness 703.1
abandon *v*.
   leave 293.4
   pretermit 460.7
   forsake 624.3
   (cease 142.6)

(apostatize 607.8, 9)
(flee 623.10)
(resign 757.2)
(backslide 988.9)
disuse 678.2
relinquish 782.3
~ hope 859.5
~ the world 893.6
abandoned
unoccupied 187.11
neglected 460.10
relinquished 624.4
lost 776.5
forsaken 893.10
wicked 945.15
dissolute 961.10
abandonment
departure 293.1
defection 624
(cessation 142.1)
(apostasy 607.2, 3)
(abrogation 756.1)
(resignation 757.1)
(relinquishment 782.1)
surrender 725.2
turpitude 945.2

abase lower 308.4
   humble 879.3
abased 886.4
abasement
   lowness 207.1
   depression 308.1
   disgrace 874.1
   humility 879.1
   servility 886.1
abash daunt 860.11
   humiliate 879.3
abate
   decrease 36.3, 4
   moderate 174.5
   qualify 469.3
   discount 813.2
abatement
   decrease 36.1
   modulation 174.2
   qualification 469.1
   ~ of differences 774.1
   discount 813.1
abatis, abattis 717.3
abat-jour 260.5
abba 166.6
abbacy 995.3

abbatial 995.9
abbé 996.2
abbess 996.12
abbey 1000.4
abbot 996.11
Abbot of Unreason 701
abbreviate 201.4
   (reduce 36.4)
abbreviation 201.2
   (deduction 38.1)
   (conciseness 572.1)
   (compendium 596.3)
abbreviatory 201.5
   (compendious 596.5)
abbreviature 201.2, 596.1
A B C's
   rudiments 66.4
   studies 537.7
   alphabet 561.2
abdal 984.18; 996.7
Abderian 836.8
abdicant 757.3
abdicate
   ~ the throne 738.6
   resign 757.2

abdication — abrupt

abdication
 dethronement 738.3
 resignation 757.1
Abdiel 977.1
abditory 530.2
abdomen
 stomach 191.7
 vitals 221.4
abdominal 221.11
abducent 289.3
abduct repulse 289.2
 kidnap 791.11
 (seize 789.9, 10)
abduction
 repulsion 289.1
 taking 789.1
 kidnaping 791.1
abductor 792.7
abecedarian *n.*
 teacher 540.1
 novice 541.6
abecedarian *adj.*
 rudimentary 541.9
 alphabetic 561.9
abecedarium 593.5
abecedary
 alphabet 561.2
 textbook 593.2
Abendmusik 415.3
aberdevine, aberdavine 366.22
aberrance
 unconformity 83.1
 error 495.1
aberrant
 unconformable 83.9
 deviative 279.8
 diverging 291.3
 erroneous 495.12
aberrate 291.2
aberration
 unconformity 83.1
 deviation 279.1
 divergence 291.1
 error 495.1
 insanity 503.1
aberrational 291.3
abet 707.8
abetment 615.2
abettor, abetter
 instigator 615.6
 upholder 711.4
abeyance
 nonexistence 2.1
 pause 142.2
 inertness 172.1
 expectation 507.3
 latency 526.1
 in abeyance
 late 133.8
 inert 172.3
 latent 526.6
abeyant
 inert 172.3
 latent 526.6
abhor 898.3
abhorrence
 dislike 867.2
 hate 898.1
abhorrent
 odious 830.14

hating 898.5
 (disgusted 828.14)
 (disliking 867.7)
abide
 continue 106.2
 be permanent 141.4
 (exist 1.4)
 (continue 143.2)
 inhabit 186.10
 ~ one's time 265.5
 await 507.5
 endure 826.6
abide by
 acknowledge 488.9
 observe 772.3
abiding 110.9
abidingness 141.1
abigail 746.2
abigeus 792.1
ability capability 157.2
 skill 698.2
abiogenesis 161.2
abirritant 662.6
abirritate 834.4
abirritation 834.1
abirritative 834.7
abject servile 886.4
 disreputable 874.8
abjection 945.2
abjunctive 44.13
abjuration
 disavowal 536.1
 recantation 607.3
abjuratory
 denying 536.3
 resigning 757.3
 recanting 607.12
abjure
 disavow 536.2
 recant 607.9
 (abandon 624.3)
 (resign 757.2)
 reject 610.2
ablation
 deduction 38.1
 taking 789.1
ablatitious 38.8
ablaze
 burning 382.17
 shining 420.22
 illuminated 382.17
ablepsia 442.1
able capable 157.9
 (strong 159.10)
 competent 698.12
 be able 157.6
able-bodied 159.10
ablution 652.2
 (watering 337.2)
abnegate 536.2
abnegation
 denial 536.1
 refusal 764.1
 temperance 953.1
abnegative 536.3
abnormal 83.9
abnormality 83.1, 3, 4
abnormalize 83.8
abnormal psychology 450.4
abnormity 83.1

aboard here 186.20
 ~ **ship** 267.53
 (at sea 341.6)
 all ~ ! 267.53;
 293.12
 go aboard 293.6
abode
 habitation 189
 (enclosure 232.1)
 (resting place 265.4)
 (menagerie 370.3)
 ~ of the blessed 981.1
 ~ of the damned, ~ of the dead 982.1
 take up one's abode 184.14
 (inhabit 186.10)
aboideau, aboiteau 350.2
abolish destroy 162.4
 abrogate 756.3
abolishment, abolition
 destruction 162.2
 abrogation 756.1
abomasum, abomasus 191.7
abominable
 terrible 649.8
 filthy 653.17
 odious 830.14
 (hateful 898.7)
 base 945.16
abominably 31.23
abominate 898.3
abomination
 evil 649.2
 defilement 653.2
 abhorrence 867.2
 hate 898.1, 2
 wrong 923.1
 turpitude 945.2
aboriginal *n.*
 aborigine 124.2
 native 188.8
aboriginal *adj.*
 original 66.7; 153.9
 primitive 124.7
 native 188.11
aboriginary, aborigine 124.2; 188.8
abort 732.5
aborticide 361.2
abortion
 monstrosity 83.6
 immaturity 674.2
 miscarriage 732.1
abortional 732.8
abortive
 immature 674.8
 miscarrying 732.8
 (useless 645.8)
abound 639.4
 (superabound 641.2)
abounding
 numerous 102.5
 plentiful 639.7
 ~ in riches 803.8
about
 apropos 9.10
 approximately 32.17

near 197.8
 nearly 197.11, 12
 around 227.5
about to
 on the point of 121.11
 ~ ~ be 152.3
be about
 busy oneself with 625.7
 be active 682.12
about-face *n.* 607.1
about-face *v.* 283.6
 (tergiversate 607.7)
about-ship 267.24, 70
above superior 33.7
 higher 206.15
 aloft 206.19
 (overlying 223.30)
abra 198.3
abracadabra 993.1
abrade cut off 38.6
 rub 331.3
 grind 330.6
Abraham's bosom 981.1
abrasion
 deduction 38.1
 pulverization 330.2
 (decay 659.2)
 rubbing 331.1
 wound 659.4
abrasive 331.4
abreast parallel 216.5
 beside 236.9
abrégé
 shortening 201.2
 abridgment 596.1
abri hut 189.4
 refuge 666.3
abridge shorten 201.4
 epitomize 596.4
abridged 596.5
abridger 201.3
abridgment, abridgement
 shortening 201.2
 (decrease 36.1)
 compendium 596.1
 (miniature 193.3)
abroach 673.13
abroad
 in foreign parts 57.5
 absent 187.10
 widely 196.9, 10
 bewildered 475.16
 erroneous 495.12
 afoot 673.13
abrogate 756.3
 (nullify 2.6)
 (destroy 162.4)
 (deny 536.2)
 (recant 607.9)
abrogation 756
 (destruction 162.1)
 (repudiation 607.3)
 (abandonment 624.1)
abrupt sudden 113.5
 savage 173.14
 steep 217.12

abruption — accede

sharp-cornered 244.5
~ style 579.3
impetuous 684.5
abruption 44.2
abruptly short 201.8
  suddenly 113.7
  (unexpectedly 508.11)
abruptness 113.2
abscess 655.16
abscind excise 38.5
  sunder 44.8
abscission
  excision 38.2
  sunderance 44.2
abscond 623.10
abscondence 623.2
absconder
  fugitive 623.5
  defaulter 808.3
absence 187
  (nonexistence 2.1)
  (zero 87a.1)
  (departure 293.1)
  (exemption 777a.1)
absence without leave 187.5
absent v. 187.8
  (depart 293.4)
absent adj.
  absent-minded 458.11
  unwary 460.9
  not present 187.10
  (nonexistent 2.7)
  be absent
  be away 187.8
  muse 458.6
absentation 187.5
absentee 187.6
  (shirker 623.4)
absenteeism 187.5
absent-minded
  preoccupied 458.11
  unwary 460.9
  be absent-minded 458.6
  (not think 452.2)
absent-mindedness
  incogitance 452.1
  abstraction 458.3
absinthe, absinth
  green 435.3
  liqueur 959.6
absolute real 1.8
  downright 31.12
  unqualified 52.10
  certain 474.8, 15
  accurate 494.11
  emphatic 535.6
  authoritative 737.15
  arbitrary 739.5
  unlimited 748.15
  inalienable 922.6
  the Absolute 359.3
absolutely
  positively 31.16
  (utterly 52.14)
  certainly 474.16
  absolutely 488.14
absolution

forgiveness 918.1
  (religion 998.2)
  acquittal 970.1
  (exemption 748.1)
give absolution 918.3
absolutism
  government 737.4
  despotism 739.2
absolve forgive 918.3
  shrive 952.4; 998.14
  acquit 970.3
  (exempt 748.10)
  (release 750.2)
  sanctify 976.11
absonant
  discordant 414.4
  illogical 477.10
absorb combine 48.3
  take in 296.2
  engross 451.30
  ~ the thoughts 457.6
  use up 677.6
  take all 789.12
absorbed
  thoughtful 451.36
  ~ with 457.9
  preoccupied 458.11
absorbent 296.6
absorber 677.4
absorbing
  urgent 642.13
  deep-felt 821.8
absorption
  combination 48.1
  reception 296.1
  close attention 457.2
  preoccupation 458.3
absquatulate
  decamp 293.5
  flee 623.10
abstain not use 678.5
  ~ from doing 680.2
  forbear 953.5
  (avoid 623.7)
abstainer
  abstinent 953.3
  ascetic 955.2
abstainment 953.2
abstemious 953.6
abstemiousness 953.2
abstention
  disuse 678.1
  abstinence 953.2
  (avoidance 623.3)
abstentious 953.6
absterge 652.9
abstergent n. 652.8
abstergent, abstersive adj.
  cleansing 652.15
  antiseptic 662.25
abstinence
  temperance 953.2
  disuse 678.1
  (avoidance 623.3)
  (asceticism 955.1)
  (sobriety 958.1)
abstinent n. 953.3
abstinent adj. 953.6
  (ascetic 955.3)
abstract n. 596.1
in the abstract

separately 44.14
  apart 87.10
abstract adj. 44.12
abstract v. deduct 38.4
  eliminate 42.4
  shorten 201.4
  ~ oneself 458.6
  abridge 596.4
  (be concise 572.2)
  appropriate 789.8
  steal 791.9
abstracted 458.11
abstraction
  deduction 38.1
  disjunction 44.1
  preoccupation 458.3
  (thought 451.3)
  (dream 515.5)
  taking 789.1
  theft 791.1
abstractly 44.14
abstriction 44.2
abstruse
  illogical 477.10
  learned 490.15
  wise 498.11
  obscure 519.7
  hidden 528.17
absurd foolish 497.4
  (illogical 477.10)
  (foolish 499.15)
  (senseless 517.8)
  (trifling 643.11)
  (ridiculous 855.5)
  impossible 471.6
render absurd 497.3
absurdity
  foolishness 497
  (irrationality 477.5)
  (folly 499.6)
  (nonsense 517.2)
  (extravagance 549.1)
  (ridiculousness 855.1)
  (burlesque 856.3)
  foolish act 499.7
  (blunder 495.3)
abulia, abuleia 605.2
abulic 605.6
abulomania 605.2
abuna 996.2
abundance
  quantities 31.3
  (store 636.1)
  multitude 102.2
  plenty 639.2
  (fullness 52.2)
  (wealth 803.1)
in abundance
  abundantly 102.6
  plentifully 639.8
abundant
  numerous 102.5
  plentiful 639.7
  (great 31.6, 7)
Abundantia 639.2
abundantly
  numerously 102.6
  plentifully 639.8
  (fully 31.17)
abuse n.

ill-treatment 649.4
  misuse 679.1
  insolence 885.2
  malevolence 907.3
  malediction 908.1
  berating 932.3
  debauchment 961.4
  abuse of terms
  misinterpretation 523.1
  wordplay 842.5
abuse v.
  deceive 545.7
  maltreat 649.7
  misuse 679.2
  berate 932.8
  debauch 961.8
abusive rude 895.6
  maledictory 908.6
  threatening 909.3
  reproachful 932.11
  slanderous 934.4
abut be near 197.5, 7
  be contiguous 199.3
  be supported 215.27
abutment
  contiguity 199.1
  buttress 215.10
  fortification 717.3
abuttal 199.1
abutter 199.2
  (neighbor 197.4)
abutting 379.4
aby, abye
  be permanent 141.4
  endure 826.6
abysm chasm 198.3
  depth 208.2
abysmal 208.9
abyss chasm 198.3
  depth 208.2, 3
  (cavity 252.2)
  (hole 260.1)
  (pitfall 667.2)
  hell 982.1
abyssal 208.9, 12
abyssal zone 208.3
A.C. 116.5
acacia tree 367.6
  wood 635.3
academic
  theoretical 514.9
  educational 537.12
  (scholarly 541.9)
  scholastic 542.9
  refined 578.4
academic rank 877.3
academician
  scholar 492.1
  student 541.3
academic psychology 450.4
academy 542.1
acanaceous, acanthopodous 253.11
acanthus 847.4
a cappella 415.30
acarpous 169.4
acatastasia 139.1
acaudal 38.9
accede approach 286.2
  assent 488.6

accelerando — account 686

accede (*continued*)
  submit 725.3
  consent 762.2
accelerando 415.32
accelerate
  inflame 173.8
  ~ an airplane 267a.32
  speed up 274.10
  hasten 684.2
acceleration
  velocity 274.2
  haste 684.1
accelerator 272.16
accelerometer 267a.29
accendible 384.22
accension 384.3
accent *n.* tone 402.2
  musical ~ 413.23
  dialectal ~ 563.5
  stress 580.4
  (inarticulation 583.1)
  poetical ~ 597.6
accent *v.*
  accentuate 580.8
  emphasize 642.9
accent mark
  notation 415.23
  typography 550.8
accentuate *adj.* 580.11
accentuate *v.*
  accent 580.8
  emphasize 642.9
accentuation
  tone 402.2
  musical ~ 413.23
  accent 580.4
  poetical 597.6
accept adopt 609.7
  guarantee 771.6
  believe 484.7
  ~ unquestioningly 486.3
  receive 785.3
  assent 488.6, 9, 10
acceptable
  expedient 646.4
  tolerable 648.11
  agreeable 829.7
  satisfactory 831.7
acceptance
  ratification 488.4
  (security 771.3)
  meaning 516.1
  interpretation 522.3
  adoption 609.1
  consent 762.1
  receiving 785.1
acceptation
  meaning 516.1
  interpretation 522.3
accepted 983a.7
accepter 484.6; 987.3
acception
  interpretation 522.3
  meaning 516.1
access
  approach 286.1
  arrival 292.1
  inlet 294.5

reception 296.1
(ingress 294.1)
path 627.2
accessary 707.12
accessibility
  reception 296.1
  practicability 470.2
accessible
  penetrable 260.20
  approachable 286.4
  practicable 470.6
  unprejudiced 498.12
  easy 705.5
  sociable 892.12
accession
  addition 37.1
  (increase 35.1)
  adjunct 39.1
  assent 488.1
  installation 755.2
  consent 762.1
  acquisition of authority 737.9
accessory *n.*
  extrinsicality 6.1
  adjunct 39.1
  (accompaniment 88.1)
  accomplice 711.3
  ~ before the fact,
  ~ after the fact 969.9
accessory *adj.*
  extrinsic 6.2
  additional 37.7
  accompanying 88.8
  assistant 707.12
acciaccatura 413.10
accidence 567.1
accident
  extrinsicality 6.1
  happening 151.1
  fortuity 156.1
  misfortune 735.3
  by accident 156.12, 13
accidental
  extrinsic 6.2
  irrelevant 10.6
  occasional 134.9
  chance 156.12
  undesigned 621.20
  (involuntary 601.14)
  (unpremeditated 612.4)
accidentality 156.6
accidentally
  by chance 156.13
  unintentionally 621.22
acclaim *n.* 931.4
acclaim *v.* 931.6
acclamation
  common consent 488.3
  applause 931.4
acclamatory 931.9
acclimation, acclimatization 613.5
  (naturalization 184.7)
acclimatize
  tame 370.6

habituate 613.8
(naturalize 184.16)
acclinate, acclivitous 217.10
acclivity 217.2
  (ascent 305.1)
acclivous 217.10
  (ascensional 305.7)
accloy 869.4
accolade 894.4
accommodate
  accord 23.8
  equalize 27.7
  conform 82.4
  oblige 707.11
  reconcile 723.4
  favor 784.10
  lend 787.4
accommodating 906.6
accommodation
  adaptation 23.3
  conformity 82.1
  capacity 192.2
  aid 707.1
  reconciliation 723.1
  loan 787.1
accommodation train 272.18
accommodative 723.6
accompanier 88.3
  (follower 281.2)
  (companion 890.3)
accompaniment 88
  (adjunct 39.1)
accompanimental 88.8
accompanist
  attendant 88.3
  musician 416.1
accompany attend 88.6
  (follow 281.3)
  synchronize 120.3
  ~ with music 416.18
accompanying 88.8
accomplice 711.3
accomplish 729.2
  (render complete 52.7)
  (produce 161.8)
  (do 680.6)
  (succeed 731.5)
accomplished 698.13
accomplishment
  learning 490.2
  proficiency 698.3
  completion 729.1
  (success 731.1)
accord *n.*
  agreement 23.1
  concord 413.1
  concurrence 488.3
  concord 714.1
in accord
  agreeing 23.9
  concordant 714.4
of one accord 488.12
of one's own accord
  voluntarily 600.5
  willingly 602.11
with one accord
  concurrently 178.5
  unanimously 488.17

(concordantly 714.5)
accord *v.*
  agree 23.6, 7
  (be uniform 16.3)
  (conform 82.4)
  (render concordant 714.3)
  (pacify 723.4)
  (mediate 724.3)
  attune 413.24
  concur 488.7
  be concordant 714.2
  permit 760.3
  give 784.8
accordance
  uniformity 16.1
  agreement 23.1
  attunement 413.1
  concurrence 488.3
  permission 760.1
  bestowal 784.1
in accordance with
  agreeing with 23.9
  conformably 82.12
accordant
  agreeing 23.9
  color 428.18
  concordant 714.4
  consentant 762.3
  ~ with law 963.5
  be accordant 23.7
according 714.4
according as 469.8
according to
  conformably 82.12
  evidentially 467.13
according to Cocker, according to Hoyle
  conformable 82.9
  right 922.5
accordingly thus 8.7
  (consequently 154.7)
  (hence 155.5)
  (since 155.8)
accordion 417.4
accordionist 416.2
accordion pleat 258.1
accost 586.2
accoucheur
  minister 631.2
  doctor 662.19
account *n.*
  numeration 85.1, 3
  list 86.1
  report 527.1
  record 551.2
  description 594.1, 2
  consideration 615.1
  credit 805.1
  charge ~ 811.1
  statement 811.3
  fame 873.1
give an account of 594.5
  (tell 527.7)
have an account with 794.8
keep an account with 805.5
of no account 643.10

account — acquaintance

on account 805.7
on account of
  since 155.8
  for the purpose of 620.6
  on behalf of 707.15
on no account
  nowise 32.18
  no 536.4
  (prohibited 761.5)
  refusal 764.7
turn to account
  avail oneself of 134.6
  profit by 658.7; 775.7
  utilize 677.5
  succeed 731.5
account v.
  estimate 480.7
  believe 484.8
  ~ with 807.7
account for 155.3
  (interpret 522.6)
account book
  record 551.3
  ledger 811.5
accountable
  attributable 155.4
  answerable 462.12
  intelligible 518.5
  amenable 926.11
accountability 926.1
accountancy 811.4
  (computation 85.1)
accountant
  treasurer 801
  bookkeeper 811.6
accounting 811.4, 10
accounts 811
  keep accounts 811.7
  (compute 85.7)
  square accounts
  retaliate 718.2
  pay 807.7
  punish 972.5
accouplement 43.1
accouter, accoutre
  clothe 225.42
  equip 634.2
  arm 717.7
accouterment, accoutrement 673.1
accouterments, accoutrements 634.1
  (wardrobe 225.2)
accredit believe 484.7
  commission 755.4
  credit 805.4
  approve 931.5
accredited
  believed 484.14
  of good credit 805.6
accretion
  increase 35.1
  coherence 46.1
  expansion 194.1
accroach
  overstep 303.5
  dispossess 789.11
accrue be added 37.6
  result 154.3
  be received 785.4

(yield 810.4)
(be profitable 775.10)
accubation 213.2
accultural 658.15
acculturation 658.2
accumbency 213.2
accumbent 213.9
accumulate
  assemble 72.11
  store up 636.7
  (acquire 775.6)
accumulation
  increase 35.1
  assemblage 72.6
  (quantity 31.3)
  (store 636.1)
  acquisition 775.1
accumulative 72.14
accuracy 494.3
  (care 459.1)
  (discrimination 465.1)
accurate 494.11
  (careful 459.7)
  (literal 516.9)
  (right 922.5)
accurately 494.16
  (literally 19.14)
accurse 908.4
accursed
  execrable 649.8
  wicked 945.16
accusable 932.14
  (imputable 938.7)
accusal 938.1
accusant 938.2
  (litigant 969.9)
accusation 938
  (censure 932.2)
  (detraction 934.1)
  (arraignment 969.3)
  (condemnation 971.1)
accusatory 938.5
  (condemnatory 971.4)
accuse 938.4
  (inform against 527.10)
  (censure 932.7)
  (prosecute 969.10)
  (condemn 971.2)
accused n. 938.3
accused adj. 938.6
accuser 938.2
  (informer 527.6)
accustom 613.8, 10
accustomed 613.12
ace modicum 32.2
  superior 33.4
  unit 87.2
  short way 197.2
  aeronaut 269a.1
  expert 700.1
  playing card 840.13
aceldama, akeldama
  slaughter 361.9
  battlefield 728.2
acerb pungent 392.5
  ill-humored 901.7
acerbate 835.2

acerbic pungent 392.5
  bitter 395.6
  sour 397.6
  gruff 895.7
  ill-humored 901.7
acerbity
  pungency 392.1
  bitterness 395.2
  sourness 397.1
  gruffness 895.2
  resentment 900.1
  irascibility 901.1
  rancor 907.1
acervate 72.11
acervatim
  assembled 72.12
  numerously 102.6
acervation 72.6
acescence 397.1, 3
acescent, acetic 397.6
acetification 397.3
acetify 397.4
acetosity 397.1
acetous 397.6
acetum 397.2
acetylene 334.2
acetylene torch 386.1
achar 393.1
acharné 900.13
acharnement 900.3
ache n. pain 378.1
  coldness 383.2
  mental ~ 828.1
ache v.
  suffer physically 378.4
  suffer mentally 828.9
  (be sad 837.6)
Acheron 982.2, 3
Acherontic 982.5
achievable 470.6
achieve do 680.6
  accomplish 729.2
  (end 67.7)
  (succeed 731.5)
achievement
  insignia 550.12
  hatchment 551.4
  accomplishment 729.1
  (production 161.1)
  (deed 680.2)
Achillean
  wroth 900.13
  revengeful 919.6
Achilles 861.3
Achinese 560.4
aching painful 378.7
  suffering 828.13
achroacyte, achroglobin, achroite, achroma, achromacyte 429.1
achromatic 429.6
achromatism 429.1
achromatization 429.2
achromic 429.6
acicular, aciculate 253.11
acid n.
  cauterant 384.11

sour 397.2
  (pungency 392.2)
  dye 428.4
acid adj. 397.6
acid dye 428.4
acidification 397.3
acidify 397.4
acidity 397.1
  (pungency 392.1)
  (bitterness 395.2)
acidulous 397.6
  (bitter 395.6)
acier 432.1
acinaciform 253.16
acknowledge
  answer 462.5
  testify 467.8
  allow for 469.4
  admit 488.9
  (affirm 535.3)
  confess 529.5
  ~ a letter 592.6
  concede 762.2
  observe 772.3
  pay 807.6
  thank 916.3
acknowledge the corn
  admit a mistake 495.10
  confess 529.5
acknowledged 852.8
acknowledgment, acknowledgement
  answer 462.1
  assent 488.2
  (affirmation 535.1)
  confession 529.2
  (apology 952.2)
  concession 762.1
  observance 772.1
  voucher 807.4
  courtesy 894.3
  reward 973.1
  thanks 916.2
acmatic 210.6
acme limit 52.4
  summit 210.1
  (perfection 650.1)
acmic 210.6
  (perfect 650.5)
acology 662.16
acolyte 996.5
acomia 226.3
acomous 226.10
aconite 663.5
acorn 433.1
acoustic phonic 402.12
  auditory 418.13
acoustician 402.6
acoustic organ 418.5
acoustics 402.5
  (hearing 418.9)
acoustic tubercle 418.5
acquaint inform 527.7
  learn 539.3
acquaintance
  knowledge 490.1
  information 527.1
  friendship 888.1
  friend 890.1

acquainted — adapt 688

acquainted
 aware 490.13
 (proficient 698.14)
 friends 888.2, 4
acquest 780.4
acquiesce assent 488.6
 (concur 178.2)
 (be willing 602.6)
 submit 725.3
 consent 762.2
acquiescence
 assent 488.1
 (concurrence 178.1)
 submission 725.1
 (conformity 82.1)
 obedience 743.1
 consent 762.1
 observance 772.1
acquiescent
 assentive 488.11
 (concurrent 178.4)
 submissive 725.5
 obedient 743.3
 consenting 762.3
acquire 775.6
 (accumulate 636.7)
 (receive 785.3)
 (take 789.7)
acquirement
 knowledge 490.2
 learning 539.1
 accomplishment 698.3
 acquisition 775.1
acquisition 775
 (receiving 785.1)
 (taking 789.1)
 (purchase 795.1)
acquisitive 775.11
acquit 970.3
 (exempt 748.10)
 (release 750.2)
 (forgive 918.3)
 (vindicate 937.6)
acquit oneself
 conduct oneself 692.5
 ~ of an obligation 772.4
 pay 807.7
 do one's duty 926.6
 keep faith with 939.6
 ~ well 944.2
acquittal
 observance 772.1
 performance 926.2
 exculpation 970
 (exemption 748.1)
 (liberation 750.1)
 (forgiveness 918.1)
 (vindication 937.1)
acquittance
 receipt 771.4
 observance 772.1
 payment 807.1
 acquittal 970.1
acre 466.3
acreage 180.5
acres
 proportions 180.5
 realty 780.4

Acres, Bob 862.2
acrid caustic 171.10
 pungent 392.5
 bitter 395.6
 gruff 895.7
acridity
 acrimony 171.3
 pungency 392.1
 bitterness 395.2
 gruffness 895.2
acrimonious
 pungent 392.5
 bitter 395.6
 gruff 895.7
 resentful 900.12
 rancorous 907.11
acrimony
 causticity 171.3
 pungency 392.1
 bitterness 395.2
 gruffness 895.2
 resentment 900.1
 irascibility 901.1
acroama 490.7
acroamatic
 profound 498.11
 oral 582.10
 obscure 519.7
acroamatics 490.7
acrobat athlete 159.6
 performer 599.21
acrobatic 159.11
acrobatics
 athletics 159.5
 aerobatics 267a.24
acropolis 717.4
acrospire 167.4
across 219.12
 (transverse 217.14)
 (obliquely 217.18)
 go across 302.2
acrostic
 ambiguity 520.2
 cipher 561.5
 wordplay 842.5
act *n.* theater 599.5
 deed 680.2
 decree 741.3
 exploit 861.2
 law 963.2
 in the act
 red-handed 680.8
 guilty 947.5
act *v.* operate 170.2
 dissemble 544.6
 personate 554.8
 ~ on the stage 599.26
 (simulate 19.7)
 operate 680.5
 officiate 746.8
 be affected 853.5
 ~ well 944.2
act a part
 dissemble 544.6
 personate 554.8
 act 599.26
 render a service 644.3
 do 680.6
 participate 709.6
 affect 853.5

act for
 substitute 147.3
 represent 759.4
act on, act upon
 operate 170.2
 influence 175.6
 motivate 615.7
 take action 680.5
 ~ ~ the emotions 824.2
act one's part
 officiate 625.9
 do one's duty 926.6
act out
 personate 554.8
 enact 599.26
act the part 19.7
act up to 772.3
 not act 681.2
acta 680.2
actable 470.6
acting *n.*
 dissimulation 544.2
 dramatics 599.2, 6
 doing 680.1
acting *adj.*
 deputy 759.6
 in action 680.7
 (operative 170.4)
actinic 420.24
actinism 420.3
actinology 420.16
actinometer 445.1
actinometry 420.16
action measure 626.7
 act 680.2
 voluntary ~ 680; 682.1
 (conduct 692.1)
 contest 720.2
 lawsuit 969.1
 in action
 operative 170.4
 acting 680.7
 (active 682.16)
 take action act 680.5
 conduct 692.4
actionable
 illegal 964.5
 litigable 969.13
Actium 722.5
activate 171.7
activator 171.4
active
 energetic 171.9
 lively 682.16
 (acting 680.7)
 be active 682.12
 (work 686.6)
 actively 682.25
 (hastily 684.7)
active service 722.1
activity energy 171.2
 business 625.1
 voluntary ~ 682
 (motion 264.1)
act of God 161.2
act of grace 784.4
actor
 stage player 599.19
 (pretender 548.3)
 agent 690.1

 (doer 680.4)
 affecter 853.4
actress 599.19
Acts of the Apostles 985.4
actual *n.* 800.1
actual *adj.* real 1.8
 present 118.2
 true 494.10
actuality 1.2
 (certainty 474.1)
 (truth 494.1)
actualize 220.6
actually 1.9
 (undoubtedly 474.16)
 (truly 494.15)
actuary
 mathematician 85.6
 accountant 811.6
actuate impel 276.6
 motivate 615.7
 excite 824.2
acuity 253.1
aculeate 253.11
acumen
 discrimination 465.1
 sagacity 498.2
acuminate 253.8, 9, 11
acumination 253.1
acupunctuation, acupuncture 260.1, 8
acute forceful 171.9
 violent 173.11
 sharp 253.11
 sensible 375.7
 painful 378.7
 shrill 410.10
 discriminating 465.4
 sagacious 498.10
 cunning 702.6
 intensely felt 821.1
acutely 31.15
acuteness
 violence 173.1
 discrimination 465.1
 sagacity 498.2
 ~ of feeling 822.1
ad 531.2
adactylism 848.1
adage 496.1
adagietto 415.8
adagio *n.* 415.8, 15
adagio *adv.* 415.31
 (tempo 413.30)
Adam sin 945.1
 carnal nature 961.3
adamant
 strength 159.4
 hardness 323.3
 stone 342.4
adamantine
 strong 159.10
 hard 323.5
Adam's ale 337.1
Adam's-needle 253.2
Adam's wine 337.1
adapt accord 23.7, 8
 (adjust 27.7)
 conform 82.4
 ~ to music 415.26
 habituate 613.8

adaptable — admirer

prepare 673.6
become adapted 23.7
adaptable
  conformable 82.8
  elastic 325.5
  available 644.8
adaptability
  elasticity 325.1
  utility 644.1
adaptation
  adjustment 23.3
  conformity 82.1
  orchestration 413.3
  musical ~ 415.3
  ~ to an end 646.1
Ada Ross eight 98.4
  throw of dice 621.9
adcraft 531.6
add affix 37.3
  (increase 35.3)
  (attach 43.6)
  (interject 228.8)
  (insert 300.5)
  compute 37.5
  calculate 85.7
add to increase 35.3
  reinforce 37.4
add up compute 37.5
  ~ ~ to 50.5
addax 366.10
added 37.7
  (increased 35.5)
addendum 39.1
adder 366.19
add fuel to the flame
  increase 35.3
  inflame 173.8
  ignite 384.17
  stoke 388.8
  foment feeling 824.2
  anger 900.10
addict *n.* 613.7
  (drunkard 959.11)
addict *v.* 613.8, 10
addicted
  ~ to 613.12
  ~ to drink 959.23
addiction 613.6
adding
  computation 37.2
  numeration 85.1
adding machine 85.5
additament 39.1
addition accession 37
  (increase 35.1;
  102.3)
  (junction 43.1)
  (interjection 228.2)
  (insertion 300.1)
  adjunct 39.1, 3
  (insertion 300.3)
  mathematics 85.4
in addition
  beyond 33.9
  additionally 37.8,
  10
  (extra 641.7)
additional 37.7
  (increased 35.5)
  (surplus 641.5)
additionally 37.8
  (with 88.9)

addititious, additive 37.7
additory *n.* 37.1
additory *adj.* 37.7
addle *v.* 959.18
addle the wits
  confuse 458.9
  dement 503.11
  perplex 475.8
addle *adj.*
  unproductive 169.4
  abortive 732.8
addlebrain 501.2
addlebrained 499.12
addlehead 501.2
addleheaded 499.12
addlepate 501.2
addlepated 499.12
addleplot 706.3
address *n.* abode 189.1
  name 564.2
  speech 582.2
  allocution 586.1
  conduct 692.1
  skill 698.1, 4
  (facility 705.1)
  petition 765.1
address *v.*
  compose 54.4
  declaim 582.7
  speak to 586.2
  court 902.7
addressee 188.1
addresses 902.2
adduce attract 288.3
  evidence 467.10
adducent 288.4
adduct 288.3
adduction 288.1
adductive 288.4
ade 298.4
adeling See atheling
adelomorphous 83.12
ademption 789.1
adenography 329.2
adenological 329.3
adenology 329.2
adept *n.* sage 500.1
  proficient 700.1
  mahatma 994.13
adept *adj.* 698.11
adequacy ability 157.2
  sufficiency 639.1
  utility 644.1
  competence 698.1
adequate able 157.9
  sufficient 639.6
  (effectual 644.7)
  competent 698.12
  satisfactory 831.7
adhere cohere 46.5
  (adjoin 199.3)
  ~ resolutely 604.6
  persevere 604a.2
  ~ to a habit 613.10
  observe 772.3
  ~ to an obligation
  926.1
adherence
  coherence 46.1
  observance 772.2
  fidelity 939.1

adherent *n.*
  adherer 46.3
  follower 281.2
  hanger-on 886.2
  disciple 542.4
adherent *adj.* 46.9
adherer 46.3
adhesion
  coherence 46.1
  (contiguity 199.1)
  observance 772.2
adhesive *n.*
  cement 45.6
  adherer 46.3
adhesive *adj.* 46.9
adhesiveness 46.2
adhesive plaster 46.3
adhibit 677.5
adhibition 677.1
adiathermancy 382.1
adiathermic 382.21
adieu
  leave-taking 293.2
  farewell 293.14
  loss 776.7
ad infinitum 105.3
ad interim 109a.3
adipocere 356.4
adipose 355.3
adipose tissue 356.4
adiposis, adiposity
  corpulence 192.4
  unctuousness 355.1
adit inlet 294.5
  channel 350.1
adjacency 197.1
adjacent near 197.8
  contiguous 199.4
  touching 379.4
adject 37.3
adjection 37.1
adjective adjunct 39.1
  part of speech 567.2
adjoin add 37.3
  be near 197.5, 7
  be contiguous 199.3
  touch 379.3
adjoining 197.8
adjourn 133.4
adjournment 133.2
adjudge, adjudicate 480.6
adjudication 480.1
adjunct addition 39
  (accompaniment 88.1)
  component 56.1
  auxiliary 711.1
adjuration
  swearing 535.2
  entreaty 765.2
adjure entreat 765.5
  administer an oath 768.5
  (depose 535.4)
adjust equalize 27.7
  (harmonize 23.8)
  order 58.6
  conform 82.4
  size 192.10
  qualify 469.3
  true 494.7

prepare 673.6
reconcile 723.4
settle 769.8
(compromise 774.2)
right 922.3
adjust differences
  mediate 724.3
  compromise 774.2
adjustment
  adaptation 23.2
  (preparation 673.1)
  equalization 27.3
  conformity 82.1
  reconciliation 723.1
  settlement 769.3
  (compromise 774.1)
adjutage, ajutage 260.6
adjutant
  auxiliary 711.1
  staff officer 745.11
adjuvant *n.* 711.1
adjuvant *adj.* 707.12
ad libitum 600.5
  (freely 748.21)
  (permission 760.7)
adman 531.6
admeasurement 466.1
administer apply 677.5
  conduct 692.4
  superintend 693.5
  aid 707.6
  rule 737.11
  serve 746.10
  ~ an oath 768.5
  apportion 786.5
  ~ justice 965.3
  rite 998.14
administration
  use 677.1
  supervision 693.2
  (command 737.2)
  apportionment 786.1
  (jurisdiction 965.1)
administrative
  authoritative 737.15
  directive 693.6
  (jurisdictional 965.4)
administrator 694.1
admirable
  lovable 897.17
  praiseworthy 931.11
  (good 648.8)
  (virtuous 944.4)
Admirable Crichton
  learned man 492.2
  paragon 650.3
  proficient 700.1
admiral 745.12
admiration
  wonder 870.1
  love 897.1
  respect 928.1
  approbation 931.1
admire marvel 870.2
  esteem 873.13
  hold dear 897.11
  respect 928.4
  approve 931.5
admirer 897.6

admissible — adversity

admissible apt 23.10
  admissive 296.6
  logical 476.16
  (possible 470.5)
  tolerable 648.11
  mediocre 736.3
  permissible 760.6
  satisfactory 831.7
  ~ in society 852.7
admissibility 23.2
admission
  inclusion 76.1
  reception 296.1
  (ingress 294.1)
  testimony 467.2
  acknowledgment 488.2
  confession 529.2
  (apology 952.2)
  permission 760.1
  receiving 785.1
admissive
  receptive 296.6
  permissive 760.6
admissory 760.6
admit include 76.3
  naturalize 184.16
  receive 296.2
  allow for 469.4
  believe 484.7
  acknowledge 488.9
  confess 529.5
  allow 760.3
  consent 762.2
  accept 785.3
admit of
  have a chance 156.9
  be liable 177.2
  be possible 470.3
not admit 489.4
admittance
  reception 296.1
  hearing 418.2
  receiving 785.1
admitted 852.7, 8
admittedly
  conditionally 469.7
  certainly 474.16
admixture 41.1, 3, 4
  (solution 335.3)
admonish warn 668.6
  advise 695.4
  reprove 932.8
admonisher 695.3
admonishment 932.3
admonition
  dehortation 616.1
  (advice 695.1)
  warning 668.1
  reproof 932.3
admonitor 695.3
admonitory
  dissuasive 616.4
  warning 668.9
  advisory 695.8
ado turmoil 59.4
  bustle 682.6
  great effort 686.1
  predicament 704.2
  excitement 825.3
  make an ado 642.8
adobe house 189.4

plaster 223.19
  ceramics 384.14
adolescence 127.2
adolescent 127.6
Adonis 845.3
adonize 847.11
adopt
  naturalize 184.16
  choose 609.7
  appropriate 789.8
adoption choice 609.1
  assumption 925.3
  conversion 987.3
adorable 897.17
adorant 990.15
adoration love 897.1
  worship 990.1
adore love 897.11
  worship 990.9
adorer lover 897.6
  worshiper 990.8
adorn
  ~ with color 428.9
  ~ speech 577.4
  ornament 847.11
adornment
  ornate speech 577.1
  ornamentation 847.1
adown 207.11
adrift *adj.*
  irrelative 10.5
  unconnected 44.12
  scattered 73.4
  unstable 149.6
  uncertain 475.16
  erroneous 495.12
  cut adrift 44.7
  go adrift 279.5
adrift *adv.* 44.14
adroit 698.11
adroitness 698.1
adscititious
  extrinsic 6.2
  additional 37.7
  (surplus 641.5)
  completing 52.12
adsmith 531.6
adsorb 296.2
adulate 933.2
  (truckle to 886.3)
adulation 933.1
  (sycophancy 886.1)
adulator 935.2
  (sycophant 886.2)
adulatory 933.3
  (sycophantic 886.4)
adult *n.* 131.3
  (man 373.2)
  (woman 374.2)
adult *adj.* 131.5
  become adult 131.4
adulterate imbue 41.8
  corrupt 659.9
adulterated 545.13
adulteration
  imbuement 41.2
  corruption 659.3
adulterer 962.1
adulteress 962.2
  (bad woman 949.4)
adulterous
  unchaste 961.10

illicit 964.5
adultery 961.6
adulthood 131
adumbrate cloud 353.9
  obscure 421.5
  overshadow 422.6
  represent 554.7
adumbration copy 21.1
  obscuration 421.3
  latency 526.1
aduncity
  angularity 244.1
  curvature 245.1
aduncous 245.8
adust *n.* 433.1
adust *adj.* dried 340.9
  burnt 384.23
  tan 433.4
ad valorem 812.7
advance *n.*
  increase 35.1
  progression 282.1
  (improvement 658.1)
  (success 731.1)
  aid 707.1
  offer 763.1
  loan 787.1
in advance
  beyond 33.9
  beforehand 116.6
  before 234.9
  in front 280.4
  ahead 303.6
  on loan 787.8
make advances
  offer 763.2
  become friendly 888.3
advance *v.*
  increase 35.4
  elapse 109.3
  contribute 153.8
  progress 282.2
  (move 264.6)
  approach 286.2
  ~ upon 303.5
  adduce 467.10
  presume 472.3
  allege 535.3
  improve 658.6, 8
  conduct 692.4
  aid 707.1
  attack 716.5, 10
  offer 763.2
  lend 787.4
advanced
  ~ in years 128.8
  premature 132.8
advanced work 717.3
advance guard 234.2
advancement
  progression 282.1
  overstepping 303.1
  improvement 658.1
  aid 707.1
  proposal 765.3
advantage *n.*
  superiority 33.2
  (leverage 175.3)
  (victory 731.3)
  use 644.1

690

expedience 646.1
  good 648.2
have the advantage
  be unequal 28.2
  be superior 33.6
  (gain the ascendancy 731.8)
advantage *v.* 648.6
advantage ground
  advantage 33.2
  footing 215.4
advantageous
  expedient 646.4
  beneficial 648.12
  (useful 644.5)
  profitable 775.12
advene be added 37.6
  approach 286.2
advent ~ of time 121.4
  (approach 286.1)
  event 151.1
  arrival 292.1
Advent 998.13
Adventism 984.4
Adventist 984.14
adventitious
  extrinsic 6.2
  (circumstantial 8.5)
  chance 156.12
adventitiousness 156.6
adventive 156.12
adventure *n.*
  event 151.1
  fortuity 156.1
  attempt 675.1
  undertaking 676.1
  feat 682.2
adventure *v.*
  hazard 621.17; 665.4
  attempt 675.3
adventurer
  traveler 268.1
  deceiver 548.3
  hazarder 621.15
  rash person 863.2
  upstart 876.8
adventures 594.2
adventure story 594.2
adventurous
  enterprising 682.18
  bold 861.9
  rash 863.7
adverb 567.2
adversaria
  memorandum book 505.6
  record 551.1
  notebook 551.3
adversary 710.1
  the Adversary 978.1
adverse contrary 14.5
  unwilling 603.5
  opposed 708.4, 5
  untoward 735.8
  (evil 649.8)
  disliking 867.7
adverse circumstances 735.1
adversely 735.10
adversity 735
  (bane 663.1)

advert — aery

(evil 649.2)
(difficulty 704.1)
(failure 732.1)
advert 457.4
advertence 457.1
advertent
  attentive 457.9
  careful 459.7
advertise, advertize 531.8
advertisement, advertizement 531.4
  (writing 590.3)
advertiser, advertizer 531.6
advice tip 527.3
  news 532.1
  warning 668.1
  counsel 695
  (persuasion 615.4)
  (admonition 616.1)
  (direction 693.1)
  (injunction 697.1)
  (remonstrance 766.1)
  take advice 695.7
advice boat 273.4
advisability 646.1
advisable 646.4
  (commendable 695.9)
advise inform 527.7
  confer 588.8
  warn 668.6
  counsel 695.4
  advise with
  ~ one's pillow 451.29
  confer 588.8; 695.6
advised
  premeditated 611.5
  intended 620.4
advisedly 620.5
  (premeditatedly 611.7)
advisement
  information 527.1, 3
  news 532.1
  warning 668.1
  advice 695.1
adviser, advisor
  informant 527.5
  counsel 695.3
  (oracle 513.1)
  (teacher 540.1, 4)
  guide 694.6
advisory
  informative 527.13
  recommendatory 695.8
advocacy
  prompting 615.2
  advice 695.1
  patronage 707.2
  commendation 931.2
advocate n.
  upholder 711.4
  (friend 890.2)
  (sympathizer 914.2)
  defender 717.5
  deputy 759.1
  vindicator 937.4

attorney 968.1
advocate v. urge 615.7
  advise 695.4
  second 707.8
  commend 931.6
  plead for 937.6
advocation 619.1
advoke 741.7
advowson 995.3
adynamia 160.1
adynamic 160.10
adytum retreat 189.13
  room 191.16
  oracle 513.1
  sanctuary 666.3
adz, adze 253.6
aedile, edile 694.1
Aegir 192.8
aegis 717.2
aeolian, eolian 349.25
aeolian harp 417.2
Aeolus, Eolus 349.2
aeon, eon era 108.2
  indefinite time 109.2
  long time 110.3
aerage, aërage 338.6
aerate, aërate
  vaporize 336.5
  air 338.10
  blow up 349.24
  make effervesce 353.8
aeration, aëration
  vaporization 336.1
  (gaseity 334.1)
  effervescence 353.3
aerial, aërial
  high 206.13
  aeronautical 267a.37
  gaseous 334.7
  airy 338.11
aerialist, aërialist 269a.1
aerie, aërie 189.13
aeriferous, aëriferous
  gaseous 334.7
  aerial 338.11
aerification, aërification 336.1
aerify, aërify
  vaporize 336.5
  air 338.10
  (gasify 334.6)
aero, aëro n. 273a.1
aero, aëro v. 267a.30
aerobatics, aërobatics 267a.24
aeroboat, aëroboat 273a.3
aerobus, aërobus 273a.1
aerocurve, aërocurve 267a.3
aerodone, aërodone 273a.6
aerodonetic, aërodonetic 267a.37
aerodonetics, aërodonetics 267a.1
aerodrome, aërodrome 267a.28

aerodromics, aërodromics 267a.1
  (aerology 338.7)
aerodynamic, aërodynamic
  aeronautical 267a.37
  pneumatic 334.8
  aerologic 338.12
  anemological 349.28
aerodynamics, aërodynamics
  aeronautics 267a.2
  wind 349.16
  aerology 338.7
aerograph, aërograph 267a.29
aerographic, aërographic
  pneumatic 334.8
  aerologic 338.12
  anemological 349.28
aerography, aërography
  aeronautics 267a.2
  aerology 338.7
  wind 349.16
aerogun, aërogun 727.11
aerohydroplane, aërohydroplane 273a.3
aerolite, aërolite 318.3
aerological, aërological aerial 338.12
  anemological 349.28
aerology, aërology
  aeronautics 267a.2
  air 338.7
  wind 349.16
aeromancy, aëromancy 511.3
aeromarine, aëromarine 267a.37
aeromechanic, aëromechanic 269a.3
aeromechanical, aëromechanical
  aeronautical 267a.37
  pneumatic 334.8
  aerological 338.12
aeromechanics, aëromechanics
  aeronautics 267a.2
  aerology 338.7
aerometer, aërometer
  aviation 267a.29
  density 321.6
  weather gauge 338.8
  (gas 334.4)
aerometric, aërometric 338.12
aerometry, aërometry
  aeronautics 267a.2
  aerology 338.7
  wind 349.16
aeromotor, aëromotor 273a.11
  (engine 633.3)
aeronat, aëronat 273a.5
aeronaut, aëronaut 269a

aeronautical, aëronautical
  aviatorial 267a.37
  aerological 338.12
aeronautical engineer 269a.3
aeronautical engineering 267a.2
aeronautics, aëronautics 267a
  (aerology 338.7)
aeronautism, aëronautism 267a.1
aeronef, aëronef 273a.1
aeropathy, aëropathy 267a.1
aerophobia, aërophobia 267a.1
aerophotography, aërophotography 267a.2
aerophysical, aërophysical 267a.37
aerophysics, aërophysics
  aeronautics 267a.2
  aerology 338.7
aeroplane, aëroplane n. 273a.1
aeroplane, aëroplane v. 267a.30
aeroplaner, aëroplaner 269a.1
aeroplanist, aëroplanist 269a.1
aeropleustic, aëropleustic 267a.37
aeroscope, aëroscope
  aviation 267a.29
  weather gauge 338.8
aeroscopic, aëroscopic pneumatic 334.8
  aerologic 338.12
aeroscopy, aëroscopy
  aeronautics 267a.2
  aerology 338.7
aerosphere, aërosphere 338.1
aerostat, aërostat 273a.5
aerostatic, aërostatic
  aeronautical 267a.37
  pneumatic 334.8
  aerological 338.12
aerostatics, aërostatics
  aeronautics 267a.2
  aerology 338.7
aerostation, aërostation
  aeronautics 267a.2
  aerology 338.7
aerotechnical, aërotechnical
  aeronautical 267a.37
  aerological 338.12
aery, aëry
  chimerical 4.6
  gaseous 334.7
  airy 338.11

Aesculapius — Afrikander

Aesculapius
  convalescence 654.1
  medicine 662.19
Aesir 979.3
Aesop 846.3
aesthetic, esthetic *n.* 451.4
aesthetic, esthetic *adj.*
  sensuous 375.6
  artistic 845.16
  (tasteful 850.5)
aestheticize, estheticize 375.4
aesthetics, esthetics
  sensibility 375.1
  philosophy 451.4
  taste 850.1
aestival, aestivate etc.
  See estival etc.
aetheling See atheling
aetiological, aetiology
  See etiological etc.
afar 196.6
afeard, afeared 860.14
Afer 349.2
affability 894.1
affable sociable 892.12
  courteous 894.12
affair concern 151.2
  event 151.1
  topic 454.1
  business 625.1
  contest 720.1
  amour 897.3
affairs 151.2
affect be related 9.3
  influence 175.6
  (induce 615.8)
  tend 176.2
  qualify 469.3
  feign 544.6
  ~ the feelings 824.2
  assume 853.5
  (be ostentatious 882.6)
  affection 897.11
affectation
  ~ of knowledge 491.4
  (sophistry 477.1)
  mannerism 853
  (inelegance 579.1)
  (ostentation 882.1)
  (sanctimony 988.2)
affected style 579.3
  voice 583.5
  attempered 820.3
  impressed 821.7
  mannered 853.6
  (dissembling 544.8)
  (make-believe 545.13)
  grandiloquent 577.7
  (gaudy 851.8)
  (ostentatious 882.8)
  (sanctimonious 988.11)
  ~ with illness 655.23
be affected with 655.21
  easily affected 375.6

affecter
  mannerist 853.4
  (sophist 477.6)
  (pedant 492.4)
  (pretender 548.3)
  (bigot 606.3; 983a.6)
  (fop 854.1)
  (attitudinarian 882.5)
  (pietist 988.6)
affectibility
  physical ~ 375.1
  emotional ~ 822.1
affecting 830.11
affection *n.*
  ailment 655.1
  disposition 820
  feeling 821.1
  love 897.1
  (friendship 888.1)
have affection for 897.11
affection *v.* 897.11
affectional 821.4
affectionate
  amorous 897.14
  caressing 902.9
affettuoso 415.30
affiance *n.*
  belief 484.1
  betrothal 768.2
  hope 858.1
affiance *v.* 768.4
affidation 769.1
affidavit
  testimony 467.2
  deposition 535.2
  record 551.1
  promise 768.1
  legal declaration 969.6
affiliable 155.4
affiliate *v.* 155.3
affiliate *adj.* 155.4
affiliated related 9.6
  consanguine 11.7
affiliation
  consanguinity 11.1
  attribution 155.2
  lineage 167.2
  association 709.2
  sect 984.3
affinal 11.7
affinitive 9.6
affinity relation 9.1
  similarity 17.1
  agreement 23.1
  concord 714.1
  soul-mate 903.10
affirm confirm 467.9
  ratify 488.10
  assert 535.3
affirmance
  confirmation 467.3
  ratification 488.4
affirmant *n.* 488.5
affirmant *adj.* 535.6
affirmation
  testimony 467.2, 3
  ratification 488.4
  assertion 535
  (assent 488.1)

affirmative 535.6
  (assentive 488.11)
affirmatively 488.16; 535.7
affix *n.* adjunct 39.1
  syllable 561.3
affix *v.* add 37.3
  attach 43.6
afflation 349.1
afflatus wind 349.1
  genius 498.5
  divine ~ 985.1
afflict
  ~ physically 378.4
  ~ with disease 655.22
  (injure 659.8)
  ~ mentally 830.3
afflicted
  intoxicated 959.21
  hurt physically 378.6
  ~ with illness 655.23
  hurt mentally 828.13
affliction ailment 655.1
  bane 663.1
  adversity 735.1
  mental suffering 828.1
  source of pain 830.2
  (sorrow 837.4)
afflictive painful 378.7
  distressing 830.11
affluence 803.1
  (plenty 639.2)
  (prosperity 734.1)
affluent *n.* 348.1
affluent *adj.*
  approaching 286.3
  flowing 348.26
  abundant 639.7
  wealthy 803.8
afflux, affluxion 286.1
afford provide 637.4
  give 784.10
  yield 810.4
affranchise
  give franchise 748.10
  liberate 750.2
affranchisement
  freedom 748.1
  liberation 750.1
  privilege 922.2
affray 720.2
affrettando 415.32
africate *n.* 402.2
africate *v.* 331.3
affrication 331.1
affright *n.* 860.1
affright *v.* 860.10
affront *n.* offense 900.5
  indignity 929.2
affront *v.* defy 715.2
  aggrieve 830.5
  ~ danger 861.5
  give umbrage 900.10
  offend 929.3
affuse 337.5
affusion
  dispersion 73.1

  wetting 337.2
  baptism 998.5
affy 768.4
Afghan 560.4
afield 196.9
afire, aflame, aflicker 382.17
afloat existent 1.7
  unstable 149.6
  going on 151.5
  sailing 267.50
  aboard 267.53
  (at sea 341.6)
  rumored 532.8
  in preparation 673.13
get afloat 531.9
keep afloat 734.5
afluking 267.50
aflutter 149.6
afoot on foot 266.28
  in preparation 673.10, 13
  astir 682.23
go afoot 266.16
afore 116.5
afore-going
  preceding 62.4
  former 122.11
aforehand 116.6
afore-mentioned 62.4
  (prior 116.4)
  (foregoing 122.11)
aforenamed 62.4
aforesaid 62.4
  (repeated 104.6)
aforethought
  preceding 62.4
  premeditated 611.5
aforetime
  previously 116.5
  formerly 122.14
a fortiori
  still more 33.10
  reasoning 476.18
  evidentially 467.13
afoul 267.64
afraid 860.14
  (cowardly 862.4)
be afraid
  think 484.8
  suppose 514.6
  fear 860.8
  (hesitate 605.4)
  (shrink 623.9)
  (be cowardly 862.3)
afreet 980.2
  (fairy 979.9)
afresh secondly 90.6
  again 104.8
  newly 123.12
Afric *n.* 431.4
Afric *adj.* 431.9
African *n.* 431.4
African *adj.*
  racial 11.8
  negroid 431.9
African lethargy
  disease 655.6
  sleep 683.5
African school 451.9
Afrikander 57.3

Afro-American — agnostic

Afro-American 431.4
aft after 235.15
  astern 267.68
after 63.6
  time 117.3, 4
  place 235.14–17
  sequence 281.5
  pursuit 622.11
after all
  notwithstanding 30.8
  provided 469.8
  finally 476.20
after a while
  in future 121.9
  soon 132.15
  be after 620.3
  go after order 63.3
  time 117.2
  motion 281.3
afterage 124.9
afterbirth 65.2
  (birth 161.3)
afterbrain 450.2
afterclap
  afterpart 65.2
  effect 154.1
  disappointment 509.1
aftercome, aftercrop
  afterpart 65.2
  effect 154.1
afterdamp 334.2
afterglow
  decrement 39a
  afterpart 65.2
  light 420.1
aftergrass
  aftercrop 65.2
  grass 367.9
aftergrowth
  afterpart 65.2
  effect 154.1
afterguard 269.3
afterlife 121.2, 3
  (heaven 981.5)
afterlifetime 121.2
aftermath
  afterpart 65.2
  effect 154.1
  profit 775.2
aftermost 235.9
afternoon 126.2
afterpain 65.2
after part, afterpart
  sequel 65.2
  (tab 39.2)
  rear 235.1
afterpiece
  afterpart 65.2
  rear 235.1
  dramatic ~ 599.5
aftertaste
  afterpart 65.2
  taste 390.1
afterthought
  aftermath 65.2
  mature thought 451.2
  (reflection 505.4)
aftertime 121.2

afterwards 117.4
  (in future 121.9)
afterworld 121.3
aftmost 235.9
aga, agha 745.11
agacerie 617.1
again secondly 90.6
  repeated 104.6
  then 119.2
again and again
  repeatedly 104.8
  frequently 136.5
against
  opposite to 237.7
  opposed to 708.5
  (counteraction 179.6)
against the grain
  contrarily 14.7
  reversionally 145.7
  rough 256.19
  unwillingly 603.6
  difficult 704.12
  opposed to 708.5
  adverse 735.5
against the law 964.5
against the stream
  laborious 686.11
  difficult 704.12
  in opposition 708.5
go against
  counteract 179.3
  oppose 708.2
go against the grain
  roughen 256.11
  be difficult 704.5
  set at odds 713.8
  irritate 830.5, 7
agalloch 400.3
agama 986.1
agape *n.* 998.13
agape *adj.*
  open 260.15
  curious 455.5
  expectant 507.7
  astonished 870.6
Agapemone
  utopia 515.6
  abode of love 897.10
agate type 591.7
  gem 847.8
age *n.* era 108.2
  (date 114.4)
  indefinite time 109.2
  long time 110.3
  ancientness 124.1
  elderliness 128
come of age 131.4
for ages 110.11
from age to age 112.5
of age 131.5
ripe age
  old age 128.2
  adulthood 131.1
age *v.* make old 124.5
  grow old 128.8
  (deteriorate 659.6)
aged 124.6; 128.8, 9
  (senile 499.16)
agee 217.13
agency operation 170

  (instrumentality 631.1)
  (mediation 724.1)
  commission 755.1
agenda
  schedule 611.2
  tasks 625.2
agent cause 153.1
  actor's ~ 599.17
  medium 631.2
  (instrument 633.1)
  doer 690
  (servant 746.1)
  functionary 758.2
  deputy 759.1
  (steward 694.5)
  (broker 797.7)
  (lawyer 968.1)
  sales ~ 797.2
  (salesman 758.5)
agent provocateur 615.6
agglomerate
  cohere 46.8
  assemble 72.11
agglomeration
  coherence 46.1
  accumulation 72.6
agglutinate
  cement 46.7
  combine 48.3
agglutination 46.1
agglutinative languages 560.4
aggrandize
  increase 35.3
  enlarge 194.8
  ennoble 873.13
aggrandizement
  increase 35.1
  expansion 194.1
  glorification 873.6
aggravate
  increase 35.3
  exaggerate 549.2
  annoy 830.5
  exasperate 835.2
  provoke 900.10
aggravating
  annoying 830.12
  exasperating 835.5
aggravation
  increase 35.1
  annoyance 828.4
  source of ~ 830.2
  exasperation 835
  (exaggeration 549.1)
  resentment 900.1
aggregate *n.* all 50.2
  accumulation 72.6
  sum 84.3
in the aggregate 50.10
aggregate *v.*
  total 50.5
  assemble 72.11
  number 85.10
aggregation
  coherence 46.1
  combination 48.1
  accumulation 72.6

aggression 716.1
aggressive
  enterprising 682.18
  offensive 716.8
  combative 722.13
aggressor 716.4
aggrieve wrong 649.6
  distress 830.5
aggrieved
  pained 828.13
  sorrowful 837.11
aggroup 72.11
agha See **aga**
aghast
  terrified 860.14
  astonished 870.6
stand aghast
  be disappointed 509.3
  fear 860.8
  wonder 870.2
agile fast 274.13
  nimble 682.17
agility 682.2
Agincourt 722.5
agio 813.1
agiotage 794.2
agitate
  discompose 61.4
  shake 315.8
  discuss 461.17
  ~ a question 476.11
  excite 824.3
  trouble 830.5
agitated
  troublous 59.11
  shaking 315.13
  (turbulent 173.12)
  alarmed 669.4
  restless 682.21
  excited 824.9
  be agitated 315.9
agitatedly 315.14
agitation
  activity 171.2
  shaking 315
  excitation 824.1
  (turmoil 59.4)
  (restlessness 149.3)
  (excitement 825.3)
  (fear 860.3)
agitato 415.30
agitator
  instigator 615.6
  ringleader 694.1
  malcontent 710.3; 832.2
  (opponent 710.3)
  insurgent 742.3
  incendiary 913.1
aglet, aiglet 847.3
aglow
  burning 382.17
  shining 420.22
  illuminated 423.14
agnate 11.7
agnation 11.1
Agni fire 382.8
  deity 979.4
agnize 488.9; 762.2
agnomen 564.2
agnostic 989.4

agnosticism — airway

agnosticism
  skepticism 451.18
  irreligion 989.3
  (doubt 485.1)
Agnus Dei 990.2;
  998.7, 8
ago 122.8, 14
agog curious 455.5
  attentive 457.9
  vigilant 459.8
  expectant 507.7
  eager 865.17
  astonished 870.6
stand agog
  be disappointed
    509.3
  wonder 870.2
agoing 682.23
agone 122.8, 14
agonistic 159.11
agonistics 159.5
agonize
  suffer physically
    378.4
  maltreat 649.7
  suffer mentally
    828.9
  torture 830.6
agonizing
  378.7; 830.15
  (exciting 824.12)
agony death 360.1
  bodily pain 378.2
  excitement 825.2
  mental pain 828.3
in agony 830.19
agony column 531.4
agora 189.19
agoraphobia 860.4
agrarian rustic 183.3
  agricultural 371.9
agree accord 23.7, 8
  (be uniform 16.3)
  (conform 82.4)
  (concur 178.2)
  acquiesce 488.6, 7
  be concordant 714.2
  contract 769.5
agree to assent 488.6
  consent 762.2
agree to disagree
  489.4
agree with
  assent 488.6, 7
  be salubrious 656.4
not agree to 489.4
agreeable
  agreeing 23.9, 11
  willing 602.8
  concordant 714.4
  consenting 762.3
  pleasurable 829.7
  (melodious 413.27)
  satisfactory 831.7
  comely 845.10
agreeableness 829.1
agreed
  assentive 488.11, 12
  (concurrent 178.4)
  contracted 769.10
agreeing
  accordant 23.9

(uniform 16.5)
(conformable 82.8)
(concurrent 178.4)
harmonious 413.26
concordant 714.4
agreement accord 23
  (uniformity 16.1)
  (similarity 17.1)
  (conformity 82.1)
  (concurrence 178.1)
  ~ of sounds 413.1
  assent 488.1, 3
  co-operation 709.3
  concord 714.1
  consent 762.1
  compact 769.1
  (transaction 794.3)
agrémens, agréments
  413.10
agrestic rustic 183.3
  agricultural 371.9
agricultural 371.9
  (countrified 183.3)
  (terrestrial 342.13)
  (botanical 369.11)
agriculture 371
agriculturist 371.2
  (botanist 369.9)
  (workman 690.10)
  (rustic 876.5)
agrogeology, agrology 371.1
agronomic 371.9
agronomy 371.1
aground
  stuck 150.6
  shipwrecked 267.65
  in difficulty 704.11
  stranded 732.10
go aground 267.33
run aground 732.5
agua 337.1
ague shaking 313.3
  disease 655.6
aguish 383.8
aha! 838.12; 931.13
Ahasuerus 268.2
ahead before 234.9
  in advance 280.4;
    303.6
  forward 282.5
ahind 235.14
ahoy!
  navigation 267.69
  attention 457.10
  ship ahoy! 267.69
Ahriman 978.1
Ahura-Mazda 976.2
aid *n.* remedy 662.1
  assistance 707
  (instrumentality
    631.1)
  (means 632.1)
  (co-operation
    709.1)
  (benefit 784.4)
  (charity 906.2)
  assistant 711.1
  benefaction 784.4
  benefactor 912.1
aid *v.* 707.6
  (contribute 178.2)

(support 215.26)
(facilitate 705.4)
(serve 746.8)
(be benevolent
  906.5)
aide-de-camp, aid-de-camp assistant 711.1
  staff officer 745.11
aider assistant 711.1
  benefactor 912.1
aidful 707.12
aigrette, aigret 847.3
ail *n.* 655.1
ail *v.* 655.21; 828.9
aileron 273a.10
ailing 655.23
  (moribund 360.9)
ailment 655.1
aim *n.* direction 278.1
  meaning 516.1
  intention 620.2
  essay 675.1
take aim 278.4
aim *v.* ~ **high** 305.4
  mean 516.5
  intend 620.3
aim at direct 278.4
  intend 620.3
  (pursue 622.6)
  try to 675.3
  attack 716.5
aimless
  disorderly 59.8
  uncertain 475.9
  purposeless 621.21
air *n.*
  unsubstantiality 4.3
  boundlessness 180.4
  posture 184.2
  aeronautics 267a.19
  heavens 318.2
  lightness 320.2
  gas 334.2
  ether 338
  wind 349.1, 5
  tune 415.2
  (melody 413.4)
  appearance 448.4
  conduct 692.1
give the air 297.8
go on the air 532a.9
in the air aloft 206.19
  information 527.15
air *v.* begin 66.5
  aerate 338.10
  (gasify 334.6)
  (deodorize 399.4)
  cool 385.4
  publish 531.7
  refresh 689.2
air arm 726.9
air base 267a.28
air b'adder 334.5
air bubble 353.1
air-built 515.12
air bump 267a.19
air castle
  daydream 458.3
  fancy 515.4
air conditioner 338.6
air-conscious 267a.37
aircraft 273a

aircraft carrier
  273a.9; 726.11
aircraftsman 269a.2
air current 349.1
air-drawn 515.12
air duct 351.1
Airedale terrier 366.6
airfield 267a.28
airfoil 273a.10
air force 726.9
Air Force, U.S. 726.9
air gun firearm 727.10
  toy 840.16
air hole opening 260.1
  aeronautics 267a.19
  air passage 351.1
airing travel 266.4, 8
  ventilation 338.6
air line
  direct line 246.2
  aeronautics 267a.1,
    20
air liner 273a.1
air log 267a.29
air mail *n.* 592.4
by air mail 684.7
air-mail *v.* mail 270.9
  post 592.6
airman 269a.1
airmanship
  aeronautics 267a.1
  skill 698.1
air-minded 267a.37
airometer 338.8
air passage 351
airplane *n.* 273a.1
by airplane 270.12;
  684.7
airplane *v.* 267a.30
airplane carrier
  273a.9; 726.11
airplane makes 273a.4
airplane parts
  267a.29; 273a.10
airplanist 269a.1
air pocket 267a.19
airport 267a.28
Air Pump 318.6
air raid 716.1
airs affectation 853.1
  pretentions 882.2
  (pride 878.1)
  (vanity 880.2)
  (arrogance 885.1)
airscape view 448.2
  picture 556.10
air scoop 273a.10
airscrew
  propeller 273a.10
  wheel 312.4
air service 726.9
  (aeronautics 267a.1)
airship 273a.5
airsick 267a.37
airsickness
  aeronautics 267a.1
  indigestion 655.13
airspace 267a.19
air stream 349.1
airtight 261.6
airward 206.19
airway

694

air-wise — all abroad

air route 267a.20
  (itinerary 266.9)
  air passage 351.1
air-wise 267a.37
airwoman 269a.1
airworthy
  aeronautical 267a.37
  safe 664.10
airy chimerical 4.6
  light 320.7
  gaseous 334.7
  aery 338.11
  windy 349.25
  imaginary 515.12
  trifling 643.11
  cheerful 836.7
  ostentatious 882.8
aisle path 627.2
  church ~ 1000.3
ait 346.1
aitchbone, edgebone 235.5
ajar 260.15
ajutage See adjutage
Aka 560.4
akeldama See aceldama
akimbo
  oblique 217.9
  angular 244.5
akin 11.7
  (related 9.6)
  (connatural 17.13)
à la, à l', au
  ~ ~ mode, ~ ~
  king etc. 298.52
alabaster
  smooth 255.2
  white 430.3
à la carte 298.39
alack! 839.18
alacrity
  quickness 682.2
  (promptitude 132.3)
  (willingness 602.1)
  cheerfulness 836.2
Aladdin's lamp 993.4
alameda 627.2
alamode, à la mode 852.7
alarm *n.* noise 404.2
  call 550.16
  danger signal 669
  (noisemaker 404.4)
  (danger 665.1)
  (warning 668.1)
  fright 860.1
  air-raid ~ 669.1
  fright 860.1
alarm *v.* 669.3
  (frighten 860.10)
alarm clock 669.1
alarmed
  aroused 669.4
  frightened 860.14
alarmist 860.6
alarum See alarm
alarming
  warning 668.9
  (warning 669.5)
  frightening 860.18
alas 839.18

Alaska 383.4
alated 39.4
alb 999.1
alba 415.10
Albanian 560.4
Albany beef 298.18
albata white 430.3
  sham 545.6
albatross 366.22
albeit 30.8
alberca 343a.1
Alberich 193.5
albescence 430.1
albescent, albicant 430.8
albification 430.2
albificative 430.8
albify 430.6
albinism
  whiteness 430.1
  dim-sightedness 443.2
albinistic 430.8
Alborak 271.9
album
  memory book 505.6
  notebook 551.3
  book 593.2
albumen
  semiliquid 352.3
  protoplasm 357.3
albumin 357.3
albuminoid
  semiliquid 352.3
  protoplasma 357.3
Alcaic 597.13
alcaide, alcaid 745.9
alcalde official 745.9
  judge 967.1
alchemy 144.1
alcohol
  energizer 171.5
  medicine 662.5, 8
  intoxicant 959.4
alcoholic *n.* 959.11
alcoholic *adj.* 959.24
alcoholism 959.2
alcoholist 959.11
Alcoran 986.1
alcove 191.3, 22
  (recess 252.4)
Aldebaran 318.3
alder tree 367.6
  wood 635.3
alderman 745.9
Alderney 366.12
Aldine ~ book 593.1
  ~ binding 593.9
Aldus 593.1
ale 959.5
Alecto 173.6; 900.4
alee 236.8
alehouse 959.13
  (inn 189.8)
alembic
  conversion 144.4
  receptacle 191.11
  heater 386.1
alert *n.* 669.1
on the alert
  attentive 457.9
  vigilant 459.8

(ready 673.11)
  quick 682.17
alert *adj.*
  attentive 457.9
  vigilant 459.8
  sagacious 498.10
  quick 682.17
  be alert 682.15
  (be vigilant 459.4)
alertness 682.2
alesan 433.1
aleuromancy 511.3
Alexandrian school 451.9
Alexandrine 597.6
alexandrite 847.8
alexipharmic *n.* 662.12
alexipharmic *adj.* 662.25
alexiteric *n.* 662.12
alexiteric *adj.* 662.25
alfalfa 367.9
alforja 215.23
alfresco exterior 220.7
  outdoors 220.8;
  338.13
  airy 338.11
algae seaweed 367.3
  plants 369.4
algal 367.16
algebra 85.2
algebraist 85.6
algebraize 85.7
algid 383.8
algidity 383.1
algific 385.6
algologist 369.9
algology 369.1
Algonquin
  Indian 434.5
  language 560.4
algorism, algorithm 85.2
alias *n.* 565.3
alias *adv.* 18.6
alibi 937.2, 6
  (counterevidence 468.1)
  (loophole 671.4)
alien *n.* 57.3
  (outsider 220.3)
  (intruder 228.4)
  (incomer 294.4)
  (outcast 893.5)
alien *v.* 783.3
alien *adj.*
  irrelative 10.5
  foreign 57.4
alienable 783.5
alienage 57.1
alienate part 44.11
  transfer 783.3
  estrange 889.2
  set against 898.4
alienation
  insanity 503.1
  transfer 783.1
  enmity 889.1
  seclusion 893.2
  estrangement 898.1
alienism
  extraneousness 57.1

psychology 450.4
  (insanity 503.1)
alienist 450.5
alight *v.* land 267a.34
  dismount 292.8
  get down 306.5
alight *adj.*
  burning 382.17
  luminous 420.22
  illuminated 423.14
align, aline
  arrange 60.6
  level 213.6
alignment, alinement 278.3
alike 17.10
  (coincident 13.7)
  (uniform 16.5)
make alike
  uniform 16.4
  assimilate 17.8
alimentary
  eatable 298.49
  nutritious 662.26
alimentation 707.3
alimony 784.5, 6
aline, alinement See align etc.
aliquot partial 51.8
  numeral 84.7
aliquot part 84.2
alive *adj.* living 359.10
  attentive 457.9
  sagacious 498.10
  active 682.16
  vivacious 836.7
alive to
  responsive 375.6
  aware of 490.13
  (sagacious 498.10)
  perceptive 822.6
alive with 102.5
  be alive 359.6
become alive 359.7
become alive to 527.11
keep alive
  continue 143.3
  live 359.9
  preserve 670.3
alive *adv.* 274.14
alizarin, alizarine
  dye 428.4
  color 434.6
alkahest 335.4
alkahestic 335.9
alky 959.4
all *n.* 50.2
  (computation 37.2)
  (completeness 52.1)
  (everyone 78.5)
  (sum 84.3)
for all 50.12
not at all
  nowise 32.18
  none 87a.3
  never 107.3
  no 536.4
all *adj.* all gone 2.10
  every 78.13
all *adv.* 50.10
all abroad 495.12

Allah — ally

Allah 976.2
all along 110.11; 112.5
allargando 415.31
allay quiet 265.6
   moderate 174.5
   relieve 834.4
allayment
   modulation 174.2
   relief 834.1
all but 32.15; 197.12
all clear! 664.14
**all-comprehensive,
all-covering** 105.3
all-destroying 162.6
all-devouring
   all-destroying 162.6
   rapacious 789.15
   omnivorous 865.20;
     957.4
allegation
   testimony 467.2
   assertion 535.1
   statement 582.4
   pretext 619.1
   accusation 938.1
   ~ of facts 969.6
allege adduce 467.10
   assert 535.3
   say 582.6
   pretext 619.2
allegiance 939.4
allegorical 521.3
allegorize
   symbolize 521.2
   compare 464.2
allegory
   figure of speech
     521.1
   (comparison 464.1)
   story 594.2
allégresse 836.2
allegretto 415.6
allegro music 415.6, 32
   (fast 274.14)
   (tempo 413.30)
   cheerful 836.7
**alleluia, alleluiah,
alleluja**
   cheer 838.4, 12
   paean 931.4
   glorification 990.2,
     16
allemande
   music 415.7
   dance 840.7
all-embracing
   universal 78.11
   infinite 105.3
alleviate
   moderate 174.5
   relieve 834.4
alleviation
   decrease 36.1
   modulation 174.2
   relief 707.4; 834.1
alleviative 662.6
   (lenitive 834.3)
alley 627.2, 3
alley cat 59.5
alleyway 627.3
All-father 976.4
all-filling 105.3

all-fired, all-firedly
   31.24
all fours 840.12
all get out 52.4
all hail 292.13
Allhallowmas, Allhallows
   anniversary, 138.7
   holyday 998.13
Allhallowtide 138.7
all hands 78.5
alliance relation 9.1
   consanguinity 11.1
   junction 43.1
   combination 48.1
   concurrence 178.1
   association 709.2
   society 712.4
   form an alliance 48.4
   (form a party 712.7)
   in alliance 178.4
allied related 9.6
   consanguine 11.7
   connatural 17.13
   leagued 48.6
   concordant 714.4
alligation 43.1
alligator 366.18
alligator pear 298.31
all in 688.6
all in all
   on an average 29.5
   mainly 50.11
all-including 105.3
all-inclusive
   universal 78.11
   (inclusive 76.5)
   infinite 105.3
alliterate
   assonate 17.9
   rhyme 597.12
alliteration
   assonance 17.3
   repetition 104.1
   literary style 577.1
   rhyme 597.8
alliterative
   assonant 17.16
   literary style 577.6;
     597.13
all kinds of
   diversified 81.3
   multitude 102.2
all-knowing
   informed 490.15
   divine 976.12
all-knowingness 490.3
allness 52.1
allocate
   partition 44.10
   arrange 60.6
   appoint 609.11
   apportion 786.3
allocation
   arrangement 60.1
   apportionment 786.1
   location 184.5
   appointment 609.5
allocution 586
   (speech 582.2)
allod, allodial etc. See
   alod etc.

all one identical 13.6
   equivalent 27.9
   indifferent 866.4, 7
allopathic 662.25
allopathy 662.16
allot arrange 60.6
   grant 760.4
   appoint 609.11
   apportion 786.3
allot on, allot upon
   plan on 507.6
   rely on 484.7
   intend 620.3
allotment
   arrangement 60.1
   provisions 298.6
   appointment 609.5
   apportionment
     786.1, 2
   (part 51.1)
all out
   throughout 52.15
   at full speed 274.15
   erroneous 495.12
   completely 52.13
   universal 78.11
   everywhere 180.9
   unsuccessful 732.5
allow judge 480.6
   think 484.8
   acknowledge 488.9
   suppose 514.6
   confess 529.5
   permit 760.3
   consent 762.2
   give 784.8
   discount 813.2
allow for
   qualify 469.3
   excuse 918.3
   extenuate 937.8
allowable
   permissible 760.6
   concessional 784.14
   justifiable 937.10
allowance
   provisions 298.6
   qualification 469.1
   acknowledgment
     488.2
   confession 529.2
   permission 760.1
   contribution 784.5
   allotment 786.2
   discount 813.1
   extenuation 937.3
   stipend 973.2
make allowance
   qualify 469.3
   discount 813.2
   excuse 918.3
   extenuate 937.8
allowed given 784.14
   warranted 924.10
   not allowed 964.5
allowedly 469.7
allowing 8.8; 469.8
   (supposing 514.13)
alloy n. mixture 41.4
   (compound 48.2)
   solution 335.3

corruption 659.3
alloy v. mix 41.6
   combine 48.3
   corrupt 659.9
alloyage 41.1
alloy balance 319.5
all-possessed 503.12
all-powerful 976.12
all right
   accurate 494.11
   affirmation 535.8
all-round 698.11
All Saints' Day
   anniversary 138.7
   holyday 998.13
all-searching 461.24
all-seeing 976.12
all-sided 52.9
All Souls' Day
   anniversary 138.7
   holyday 998.13
allspice 393.1
all-star 599.28
all there
   attentive 457.9
   sane 502.5
all the same
   equivalent 27.9
   notwithstanding
     30.8
all the world 78.5
allude mean 516.7
   intimate 527.8
   (suggest 514.8)
all up extinct 2.10
   ended 67.9
   ~ ~ with 732.5, 12
allure lure 617.4
   enamor 897.13
allurement 617
   (attraction 157.3;
     288.1)
   (inducement 615.2)
   (seduction 961.4)
alluring 617.5
   (attractive 288.4;
     845.9)
   (delightful 829.8)
   (likable 897.17)
allusion 527.4
   (implication 516.1)
   (latency 526.2)
allusive
   approximative 9.7
   suggestive 514.11
   significative 516.8
   figurative 521.3
   implicative 526.7
alluvial
   horizontal 213.8
   terrestrial 342.9
alluvion, alluvium
   residue 40.2
   silt 270.2
   land 342.2
   overflow 348.3
   mud 352.4
all-wise 976.12
**all wool and a yard
wide** 494.12
ally n. 711.1
ally v. 48.4

Alma Mater — amaze

Alma Mater, alma mater 542.1
almanac
  chronology 114.5
  archive 551.2
almightily 31.15
almightiness 157.5
almighty
  omnipotent 157.8
  divine 976.12
  the Almighty 976.2
almighty dollar 800.1
almond 298.33
almoner
  almsgiver 784.7
  treasurer 801
  church officer 996.5
almonry 802.1
almost 32.15; 197.12
  (imperfectly 651.5)
alms donation 784.3
  charity 906.2
  give alms 990.13
almsgiver 784.7
  (philanthropist 911.1)
almsgiving *n.* 784.2; 906.2
almsgiving *adj.* 784.15; 906.7
almshouse
  poorhouse 189.11
  asylum 666.3
almsman giver 784.7
  donee 785.2
  almoner 996.5
almuce 999.1
alod, allod 748.5
alodial, allodial 748.12; 780.8
alodium, allodium 780.2
aloes bitter 395.3
  perfume 400.3
aloeswood 400.3
aloft on high 206.19
  ~ there! 267.69
  fly aloft, go aloft
  take off 267a.33
  soar 305.6
  lay aloft 267.10
alone *adj.*
  solitary 87.8
  (insular 44.12)
  unassisted 706.10
  secluded 893.10
  leave alone
  be conservative 141.5
  not interfere 748.11
  permit 760.3
  not alone 100.4
  stand alone 87.4
alone *adv.*
  simply 42.7
  singly 87.10
along
  at length 200.15
  forward 282.4
  along with
  with 37.9; 88.9
  and 37.10

through 631.5
right along 16.7
alongside
  parallel 216.5
  beside 236.9
  navigation 267.62
  heave alongside 267.26
aloof distantly 196.6
  aloft 206.19
  hold aloof
  be incredulous 487.3
  abstain 953.5
  keep aloof
  be absent 187.8
  keep distance 196.4
  abstain 953.5
  stand aloof
  do nothing 681.2
  discountenance 764.3
  be cautious 864.3
  seclude oneself 893.6
  abstain 953.5
alopecia 226.3
aloud 404.11
alow 207.11
alp 206.2
alpenstock 215.15
alpha 66.1
alpha and omega 50.2
alphabet *n.*
  rudiments 66.4
  letters 561.2
alphabet *v.* 561.6
alphabetarian 541.6
alphabetic 561.9
alphabetize
  classify 60.7
  letter 561.6
alpha ray 420.3
alpha test 461.3
alphitomancy 511.3
alpine 206.17
already
  previously 116.5
  until now 118.4
  (formerly 122.14)
alrighty 535.8
Alsatia 791.8
also additionally 37.8
  and 37.10
also-ran 732.4
altar
  hymenal ~ 903.3
  church ~ 1000.3
Altar 318.6
altar boy 400.6
altar carpet 223.2
alter *n.* 79.4
alter *v.* geld 38.7
  change 140.5, 6
  (convert 144.6)
alterabi¹ity 149.1
alterable 149.5
alterant
  modifier 140.4
  remedy 662.1
alteration
  change 140.1
  (modification 15.4)

music 415.5
ailment 655.1
alterative *n.* 140.4
  remedy 662.1
alterative *adj.* 149.5; 662.25
altercate 713.7
altercation
  quarrel 713.3
  contention 720.1
alter ego
  analogue 17.5
  self 79.4
  deputy 759.1
  friend 890.1
alternate *n.* 147.2
alternate *v.*
  be discontinuous 70.2
  recur 138.8
  vary 149.4
  oscillate 314.10
  (reciprocate 12.5)
  be irresolute 605.4
alternate *adj.*
  reciprocal 12.7
  periodic 138.10
  (successive 63.5)
  (discontinuous 70.4)
  oscillatory 314.12
alternately
  by turns 138.13
  to and fro 314.14
alternating 149.6
alternating personality 503.2
alternation
  permutation 84.4
  periodicity 138.2
  (discontinuity 70.1)
  (reversion 145.1)
  interchange 148.1
  oscillation 314.3
  (reciprocation 12.2)
  (changeableness 149.1)
  irresolution 605.1
alternative *n.*
  substitute 147.2
  choice 609.1
  plan 626.5
  have no alternative 601.10; 609a.2
alternative *adj.* **147.4**
alternator 147.2
althorn, alto horn 417.4
although, altho
  notwithstanding 30.8
  but 469.8
Alticamelus 206.7
altigraph 267a.29
altimeter
  altitude 206.8
  measure 244.3
  aviation 267a.29
altimetry
  altitude 206.8
  measurement 466.8
altitude height 206.1
  aeronautics 267a.21

altitudes 885.1
alto height 206.2
  high tone 410.2
  voice 413.14
  (vocalist 416.10)
  part 415.13
  singer 416.10
altogether *n.* 50.2
  the altogether 226.2
altogether *adv.* 50.10
  (fully 31.17)
  (completely 52.13)
alto-relievo 557.6
altruism 906.1
  (magnanimity 942.2)
altruist 911.1
altruistic 906.7
  (magnanimous 942.6)
alum 397.2
alumina 324.3
aluminous 324.6
aluminum 635.6; 800.15
alumnus 541.1, 5
alveary apiary 370.3
  workshop 691
alveolar 402.2
alveolate 252.10
alveolation 252.2
alveole 252.2
Alviss 193.5
always 112.5
  (invariably 16.7)
  (generally 78.15)
  (constantly 136.6)
  (habitually 613.13)
A.M., a.m. 125.1
amabile 415.30
amadou 388.6
amah guardian 664.3
  maidservant 746.2
amain violently 173.18
  hastily 684.7
amalgam 41.4
amalgamate mix 41.6
  combine 48.3, 4
amalgamation
  mixture 41.1
  combination 48.1
amanuensis 590.11
amaranthine 112.4
amarity
  bitterness 395.2
  gruffness 895.2
amass embody 50.4
  assemble 72.11
  store up 636.7
amassment
  accumulation 72.6
  acquisition 775.1
amateur
  dilettante 850.3
  votary 865.7
amateurish 699.14
amatory 897.14
amaurosis
  blindness 442.1
  disease 655.8
amaurotic 442.6
amaze *n.* 870.1

amaze — amphilogy

amaze *v.* 870.3
amazement
  astonishment 870.1
  (surprise 508.2)
  marvel 872.1
amazingly 31.21
Amazon
  warrioress 726.4
  heroine 861.3
ambages
  convolution 248.1
  circumlocution 573.3
  (quibble 477.3)
  circuit 629.1
ambagious
  convoluted 248.4
  circuitous 311.6
  circumlocutory 573.9
ambagiousness 248.1
ambagitory
  convoluted 248.4
  circuitous 311.6
ambassade, embassade 532.2
ambassador, embassador 759.2
ambeer, ambier 392a.7
amber 356a.1
ambergris 356a.1
ambidexter 607.4
ambidexterity
  dexterity 238.1
  proficiency 698.1
ambidextrous
  dexterous 238.3
  tergiversating 607.10
  skillful 698.11
ambient 227.4
ambiguity
  uncertainty 475.1
  quibble 477.3
  (circumlocution 573.3)
  equivocality 520.1, 2
  (unintelligibility 519.1)
  (imperspicuity 571.1)
  tautology 573.2
ambiguous
  uncertain 475.9
  obscure 519.7
  equivocal 520.5
ambit region 181.1
  (circuity 311.1)
  zone 230.2
  circuit 629.1
ambition
  intention 620.1
  aspiration 865.2
ambitious 865.18
amble *n.* 266.5
  (slowness 275.2)
amble *v.* 266.16
ambler 271.3
ambo 542.6; 1000.3
ambrose 400.2
ambrosia
  sweet drink 396.5
  (delicacy 298.9)
  perfume 400.2
ambrosial
  savory 394.7
  fragrant 400.10
ambrotype 591.6
ambry 1000.3
ambulance
  automobile 272.15
  hospital 662.17
ambulance chaser 968.1
ambulant 266.23
ambulate 266.16
ambulation 266.4
ambulatory *n.* 627.2
ambulatory *adj.* 266.23
ambuscade *n.* 530.1
ambuscade *v.* 530.5
ambush *n.* 530
  (concealment 528.1)
  (snare 545.4)
  (pitfall 667.1)
  in ambush 528.19
  lie in ambush
  hide 528.16
  ambush 530.5
ambush *v.* 530.5
  (ensnare 545.9)
ameba, amebic See **amoeba** etc.
âme damnée
  puppet 711.2
  serf 746.4
  henchman 886.2
  reprobate 949.1
ameer See **amir**
ameliorate 658.6, 8
amelioration 658.1
amen *v.* 488.10
amen *adv.* 488.15
amenability 926.1
amenable
  answerable 462.12
  unprejudiced 498.12
  accountable 926.11
amend
  improve 658.6, 8, 11
  reform 950.4
amendatory 30.6
amendment 658.1, 3
amends
  repayment 807.3
  reward 973.1
  atonement 952.1
  (compensation 30.2)
amenity 894.1, 3
Amenti 982.2
amentia
  mental deficiency 499.3
  insanity 503.1
amerce 974.3
amercement 974.2
American *n.* 188.9
American *adj.*
  racial 11.8
  native 188.11
American eagle 269a.1

American Indian languages 560.4
Americanism 563.5
Americanize 563.13
American plan 298.39
American Revolution 722.4
America the Beautiful 182.3
amethyst purple 437.1
  gem 847.8
amethystine 437.4
Amharic 560.4
amiability
  courtesy 894.1
  benevolence 906.1
amiable
  pleasurable 829.7
  courteous 894.12
  lovable 897.17
  benevolent 906.6
amianthine 385.8
amianthus 385.3
amicable 888.4
  (well-disposed 707.13)
amicably 888.5
amical 888.4
amice 999.1
amid among 41.11
  between 228.13
amidships 68.6
amidst among 41.11
  between 228.13
amir, ameer 745.5
amiss astray 304.5
  wrong 649.11
  do amiss 945.9
  go amiss 732.5
amity 888.1
  (concord 714.1)
  (peace 721.1)
ammeter
  electricity 158a.6
  aviation 267a.29
  automobile 272.16
ammonia
  energizer 171.5
  gas 334.2
  refrigerant 387.2
  pungency 392.2
ammonite 248.2
ammunition
  munition 727.13
  (detonator 406.6)
  liquor 959.4
amnemonic 506.8
amnesia 506.3
  (psychopathy 503.1)
amnesic 506.8
amnesty *n.*
  oblivion 506.1
  pardon 918.1
  acquittal 970.2
amnesty *v.* 970.3
amoeba, ameba
  microbe 193.4
  protoplasm 357.3
amoebaeum, amoebeum 597.2
amoebic, amebic
  infinitesimal 193.10

protoplasmic 357.9
amoebiform, amebiform 81.2
amoeboid, ameboid 193.10
amole 356.5
among amid 41.11
  between 228.13
amongst among 41.11
  between 228.13
amor 897.1
Amor 897.4
amorist 897.6
amorosa 897.7
amorosity 897.1
amoroso *n.* 897.6
amoroso *adv.* 415.30
amorous 897.14
amorousness 897.1
amorphia, amorphism 241.1
amorphous
  hermaphrodite 83.12
  formless 241.5
amortization 784.6
Amos 513.2
amotion 270.1
amount *n.*
  quantity 25.1, 2
  degree 26.1
  all 50.2
  sum 84.3
  ~ of money 800.10
  price 812.1
  gross amount all 50.2
  (computation 37.2)
  sum 84.3
  to the amount of 25.8
amount *v.*
  amount to equal 27.6
  total 50.5
  number 85.10
  cost 812.6
amour 897.3
amourette
  love affair 897.3
  god of love 897.4
amour-propre 880.1
amperage 158a.5
ampere, ampère 158a.5
  (measurement 466.3)
amperemeter 158a.6
Amphibia 366.18
amphibian *n.*
  seaplane 273a.3
  reptile 366.18
  animal 368.9
amphibian *adj.* 368.19
amphibious 41.10
amphibology 520.1
amphibolous 520.5
amphictyonic council 696.1
amphigoric 497.4
amphigory, amphigouri
  rigmarole 517.3; 584.2
  ridiculousness 855.1
amphilogy 520.1

amphitheater, amphitheatre
  field of view 441.6
  schoolroom 542.5
  theater 599.10
  arena 728.1
amphora 191.10
ample full 52.11
  spacious 180.6
  sizable 192.11
  broad 202.6
  plentiful 639.7
  (great 31.6)
  liberal 816.4
  satisfactory 831.7
ampliation 194.1
amplification
  expansion 194.1
  (exaggeration 549.1)
  rendition 522.2
  expatiation 573.4
amplify increase 35.3
  enlarge 194.8
  (exaggerate 549.2)
  expatiate 573.5
amplitude
  quantity 25.1
  degree 26.1
  greatness 31.1
  fullness 52.2
  size 192.1
  breadth 202.1
  plenty 639.2
amputate 38.6
amputation 38.2
amuck, amok n. 503.1
amuck, amok adj.
  maniac 503.13
  frenzied 824.10
amulet 993.2
amuse 840.20
  (please 829.4)
  (cheer 836.6)
amused 840.24
  (pleased 827.8)
amusement 840
  (pleasure 827.1; 829.1)
  place of amusement 840.14
  (theater 599.10)
  (casino 621.14)
amusing
  entertaining 840.22
  (pleasing 829.7)
  (witty 842.9)
  ridiculous 855.5
amylaceous 352.8
ana collection 72.7
  book 593.2
  narrative 594.2
  excerpts 596.2
Anabaptism 984.4
Anabaptist 984.14
anabranch 348.1
anachronism
  false time 115
  (untimeliness 135.1)
  error 495.1
anachronize 115.2

anachronous 115.3
  (untimely 135.6)
anaconda 366.19
Anacreontic n. 597.2
Anacreontic adj. 597.13
anacrusis 597.6
anaemia, anaemic See anemia etc.
anaesthesia, anaesthetic etc. See anesthesia etc.
anaglyph 557.6
anaglyphic 557.10
anaglyphy 557.1
anagnost 996.5
anagoge mystery 528.1
  mysticism 994.1
anagogic 528.17; 994.21
anagogics 994.1
anagram
  ambiguity 520.2
  cipher 561.5
  (enigma 533.2)
  wordplay 842.5
anagrammatic 533.6
anagrammatism
  equivocalness 520.1
  spelling 561.4
analecta 596.2
  (compilation 593.2)
analectic 596.5
analeptic
  restorative 660.18; 662.1
  remedial 662.25
analgesia
  insensibility 823.1
  pleasurelessness 828.2
  sadness 837.1
analogon 562.1
analogous 17.11
  (coincident 13.7)
  (comparable 464.6)
analogue
  correspondent 17.5
  (same 13.3)
  (opposite 14.2; 237.2)
  (equivalent 27.5)
  (inverse 218.3)
  equivalence 516.3
  word 562.1
analogy 17.1
analysis
  quantitative ~ 25.3
  dissection 44.4
  classification 60.2
  mathematics 85.2
  examination 461.3
  (experiment 463.1)
  reasoning 476.1
  declension 567.1
  synopsis 596.1
analyst
  examiner 461.13
  experimenter 463.6
analytical
  decomposing 49.5
  mathematical 85.12

  investigative 461.24
  experimental 463.12
  reasoning 476.13
  synoptical 596.5
analytical balance 319.5
analytic languages 560.4
analytic psychology 450.4
analyze, analyse
  dissect 44.9
  (decompose 49.3)
  examine 461.17
  parse 567.5
  describe 594.5
analyzer, analyser
  examiner 461.13
  experimenter 463.6
Anamnesis 998.7
anamorphoscope 555.2
anamorphose 555.4
anamorphosis
  distortion 243.1
  distorted vision 443.9
  misrepresentation 555.2
anamorphous 243.5
Ananias 548.5
anapaest, anapest 597.6
anapaestic, anapestic 597.13
anaphrodisia
  moderation 174.1
  indifference 866.1
anaphrodisiac n.
  moderator 174.3
  medicine 662.6
  lust-quencher 866.2
anaphrodisiac adj. 174.7
anarch
  anarchist 738.2
  insurgent 742.3
anarchic
  disorderly 59.8
  ungoverned 738.8
  (rebellious 742.7)
  (lawless 964.6)
anarchist
  anarch 738.2
  insurgent 742.3
  evildoer 913.1
anarchy disorder 59.1
  no authority 738.2
  (insurgence 742.2)
  (lawlessness 964.3)
anastatic 557.10
anastomose
  attach 43.6
  interlace 219.8
anastomosis
  junction 43.1
  interlacing 219.3
anastomotic 219.11
anastrophe
  inversion 218.2
  rhetoric 577.1
anathema 908.1
anathematize 908.4

  (defame 934.3)
anatomic 240.9
anatomist 368.2
anatomize dissect 44.9
  analyze 461.17
anatomy
  dissection 44.4
  thinness 203.5
  form 240.1
  texture 329.2
  (biology 357.5)
  zoology 368.1
  analysis 461.3
anatripsis, anatripsology 331.1
anatriptic 331.4
Anaximandrian 451.6
ancestor 166.1
ancestral
  patriarchal 124.7
  (former 122.10)
  parental 166.10
ancestry 166
  (origin 153.1)
  (filiation 155.2)
anchor n.
  fastening 45.2
  ship 273.14
  safeguard 666.2
  (obstacle 706.2)
  at anchor fast 150.5
  located 184.17
  quiescent 265.7
  navigation 267.63
  in shelter 664.10
anchor v. settle 184.14
  cast anchor 267.12
  (land 292.9)
  find refuge 666.5
  remain 683.8
anchorage
  retreat 189.13
  haven 666.4
anchored 150.5
anchoress 893.4
anchoritism, anchoretism 893.2
anchorite, anchoritess 893.4
  (religious 996.11)
anchoritic
  hermitic 893.9
  ascetic 955.3
anchoritism 955.1
ancien régime 875.1
ancient n.
  elderly 128.9
  ensign 550.13
ancient adj. 124.6
  (former 122.10)
ancient history 122.3
anciently 122.14
Ancient Mariner
  wanderer 268.2
  mariner 269.1
ancientness 124.1
ancillary 707.12
ancon 342.2
and n. 39.1
and conj. 37.10
  and all, and also 37.8, 10

andante — anneal

and *(continued)*
 and so forth 37.11
andante *n.* 415.8, 15
 (tempo 413.22)
andante *adv.* 415.31
andantino 415.8
andiron 386.3
Andra Kammeren 696.6
androgyne 83.5
androgynous 83.12
androlepsia 789.1
Andromeda 318.6
Andvari, Andwari 193.5
anear 286.2
aneath 207.11
anecdote 594.2
anecdotic 594.7
anecdotist 594.4
anele 998.14
anemia, anaemia
 weakness 160.3
 colorlessness 429.1
 ailment 655.5, 11
anemic, anaemic
 pale 429.6
 sickly 655.24
anemograph
 aviation 267a.29
 wind gauge 349.17
anemographic 349.28
anemography 349.16
anemological 349.28
anemology 349.16
anemometer
 aviation 267a.29
 ship 273.14
 wind gauge 349.17
 meter 466.4
 (recorder 553.3)
anemometric 349.28
anemometrograph 349.17
anemometry 349.16
anemoscope
 aviation 267a.29
 wind gauge 349.17
 ship 273.14
anent 9.10
aneroid 338.8
anesthesia, anaesthesia
 insensibility 376.1
 (numbness 381.1)
 languor 683.4
anesthetic, anaesthetic *n.*
 soporific 376.2
 (palliative 662.6)
 narcotic 381.3
anesthetic, anaesthetic *adj.* 376.5
anesthetist, anaesthetist 662.19
anesthetize, anaesthetize 662.24
anew secondly 90.6
 again 104.8
 newly 123.12
anfractuose 248.5
anfractuosity 248.1

anfractuous 248.4
angel
 messenger 534.1
 patron 599.17
 backer 711.4
 sweetheart 897.7
 endearment 902.4
 good person 948.1
 celestial being 977
 genius 979.12
 pastor 996.2, 5
angelic
 adorable 897.17
 righteous 944.3
 seraphic 977.4
 saintly 987.10
angelomachy 722.1
Angelus 550.16
anger *n.* 900.1
 (ill-humor 901.1)
 in anger 900.14
anger *v.*
 become angry 900.9
 make angry 900.10
angina 655.9
angina pectoris 655.12
angiography, angiology 329.2
angiospermous 369.11
ang e *n.* corner 244.2
 (nook 191.3)
 gliding ~ 267a.4
 aspect 448.4
 (viewpoint 441.4)
 at an angle 217.17
angle *v.* oblique 217.5
 (deviate 279.7)
 form an angle 244.4
 (bifurcate 91.5)
 grope 463.9
 fish 622.8
angle of yaw 267a.4
angler 622.5
angleworm 366.25
Anglican *n.*
 High Churchman 984.15
 ritualist 998.12
Anglican *adj.*
 ecclesiastical 995.9
 ritualistic 998.15
Anglicanism
 religion 984.5
 ritualism 998.11
Anglice 560.10
Anglicism 563.5
Anglicize, anglicize 563.13
angling 622.3
Anglophobia 860.4
Angora cat 366.4
 goat 366.9
angostura 395.3
angrily 900.14
angry 900.13
 (ill-humored 901.7)
 be angry 900.8
 become angry 900.9
 make angry 900.10
anguiform 248.6
anguilliform
 filamentary 205.7

eellike 248.6
anguilloid 248.6
anguine
 sinuous 248.6
 reptilian 366.27
anguineous 248.6
anguish 828.3
angular 244.5
 (bifurcate 91.7)
 (oblique 217.9)
 (rough 256.12)
 (notched 257.6)
angularity 244
 (obliquity 217.1)
angularness 244.1
angustifoliate, angustirostrate, angustisellate, angustiseptal 203.9
anhedonia
 pleasurelessness 828.2
 sadness 837.1
anhelation 688.2
anhelous 688.7
anhydrate dry 340.5
 preserve 670.4
anhydration
 drying 340.2
 preservation 670.2
anhydromyelia 340.2
anhydrous 340.7
anile 499.16
aniline, anilin 428.4
anility 499.5
 (effeminacy 160a.1)
anima life force 359.2
 spirit 994.11
anima bruta 994.11
animadversion 932.2
animadvert
 give attention 457.4
 censure 932.7
animal *n.* 366.2
 (mythical 83.7)
 (beast of burden 271.2)
animal *adj.* 366.26
 (zoological 368.11)
animalcular 193.10
animalcule 193.4
 (smallness 32.2)
 (animal 366.2)
animal husbandman 370.4
animal husbandry 370.1
animalian 366.26
animalism
 animality 364.1
 carnality 961.3
animalistic
 animal 366.26
 carnal 961.11
animality 364
animalization 364.2
animalize 364.2
animal kingdom 366.1
animal magnetism 994.6
animal spirits 836.1
anima mundi 359.3

animate *adj.* 359.10
 (organic 357.8)
animate *v.*
 strengthen 159.8
 stimulate 171.7
 impel 276.7
 vivify 359.8
 motivate 615.7
 refresh 689.2
 excite 824.2
 cheer 836.6
animated
 energetic 171.9
 living 359.10
 active 682.16
 vivacious 836.7
animation life 359.1
 vivification 359.4
 animalization 364.2
 activity 682.1
 excitation 824.1
 vivacity 836.2
animatism 984.10
animative
 animistic 317.6
 vivifying 359.11
animé 428.5
animism
 immaterialism 317.3
 religion 984.10
animist
 immaterialist 317.4
 religious 984.20
animistic
 immaterial 317.6
 religion 984.28
animosity
 enmity 889.1
 (hatred 898.1)
 resentment 900.1
animus
 propensity 602.2
 intention 620.1
 disposition 820.1
 desire 865.1
anisette 959.6
ankle *n.* angle 244.2
 legs 266.11
ankle *v.* 266.16
anklebone 366.21
ankle-deep deep 208.8
 shallow 209.4
anklet 847.7
ankus edge tool 253.6
 incentive 615.3
 spear 727.5
Anlage, anlage 153.3
anna 800.8
annalist
 chronographer 114.7
 chronicler 553.2
 (author 593.15)
 (narrator 594.4)
annals
 chronology 114.5
 record 551.1
 (book 593.1)
 history 594.2
Annamese 560.4
annatto, annotto 434.3, 6
anneal 673.6

annelidan — antichristian

annelidan 368.15
annex *n.* 39.1, 3
annex add 37.3
  (attach 43.6)
  appropriate 789.8
  steal 791.9
annexation
  adjunct 39.1
  junction 43.1
  (addition 37.1)
  appropriation 789.1
  theft 791.4
annexationist 43.4
annexion 43.1
annihilate
  destroy 162.4
  (nullify 2.6)
  extinguish 385.5
annihilation 162.2
  (nonexistence 2.3)
annihilative 162.6
anniversary 138.5
  (celebration 883.2)
annotation
  comment 522.4
  note 550.7
annotative 522.8
annotator
  scholiast 492.1
  commentator 524.2; 595.3
annotto See **annatto**
announce
  herald 116.3
  foretell 511.8
  proclaim 531.7
  (tell 582.6)
  declare 535.3
  (inform 527.7)
announcement
  prediction 511.1
  proclamation 531.1
  (information 527.1)
  declaration 535.1
announcer
  proclaimer 531.5
  radio ∼ 532a.6
  messenger 534.1
annoy vex 830.5
  (aggravate 835.1)
  provoke 900.10
annoyance evil 649.2
  vexation 828.4
  (aggravation 835.1)
  source of ∼ 830.2
  (provocation 900.5)
  resentment 900.1
annoying 830.12
  (aggravating 835.5)
annual *n.* plant 367.2
  yearbook 551.3
  journal 593.6
annual *adj.*
  yearly 138.11
  plant 367.17
annuity 784.5
annul
  counteract 179.4
  cancel 756.3
  (destroy 162.4)
annular 247.8
annularity 247.1

  (rotundity 249.1)
annulet 247.2
annulment 756.1
annulus 247.2
annunciate
  proclaim 531.7
  (tell 527.7)
  declare 535.3
  (inform 527.7)
annunciation
  proclamation 531.1
  declaration 535.1
Annunciation Day
  anniversary 138.7
  holyday 998.13
annunciator
  informant 527.5
  proclaimer 531.5
  announcer 534.1
annunciatory 531.11
  (informative 527.13)
anodyne *n.* 662.6
anodyne *adj.*
  moderative 174.7
  palliative 662.25
  relieving 834.7
anoint lubricate 332.4
  (coat 223.24)
  bribe 618.3
  chastise 972.6
  chrism 998.14
  (sanctify 987.8)
anointed 745.2
  the Anointed 976.5
anointment 332.1, 2
  (unctuousness 355.1)
anomalous
  unconformable 83.9
  (disorderly 59.8)
  formless 241.5
**anomalousness,
anomaly** 83.1
  (disorder 59.1)
anon in future 121.9
  soon 132.15
anon. 565.9
anonym, anonyme
  pseudonym 565.3
  anonymity 565.5
anonymity 565.5
anonymous 565.9
anoöpsia, anopia 443.1
anopsia
  blindness 442.1
  faulty vision 443.1
anorexia 866.1
another 15.9
  (repeated 104.6)
answer *n.*
  musical ∼ 415.14
  reply 462
  (gibe 930.3)
  (defense 937.2)
  refutal 479.1
  explanation 522.1
  (solution 481a.2)
  letter 592.2
answer *v.*
  be related 9.3

  reply 462.5, 8
  refute 479.2
  ∼ a letter 592.6
  ∼ a purpose 639.3
  avail 644.2
  pay 775.10
answer back 462.5
answer for
  represent 759.4
  promise 768.3, 8
  accept responsibility for 926.6
have to answer for
  be responsible for 926.5
  take the blame 932.10
answerable
  agreeing 23.9
  responsible 462.12
  amenable 926.5, 11
  blameworthy 932.14
answerable for 806.8
  be answerable for 768.3
answerer 462.4
answering 375.6; 462.11
ant insect 366.24
  worker 690.2
Antaeus, Antaios
  strong man 159.6
  giant 192.8
antagonism
  contrariety 14.1
  counteraction 179.1
  opposition 708.1
  belligerence 722.6
  enmity 889.1
antagonist 710.1
  (malcontent 832.2)
  (enemy 891.1)
antagonistic
  contrary 14.5
  disagreeing 24.6
  counteractive 179.5
  opposed 708.4
  belligerent 722.13
  unfriendly 889.3
antagonize
  oppose 708.2
  (counteract 179.3)
  alienate 889.2
antarctic 383.4
ante 621.3
antecede
  ∼ in order 62.2
  ∼ in time 116.3
antecedence
  precedence 62.1
  priority 116.1
antecedent *n.*
  precursor 64.1
  premise 116.2
antecedent *adj.*
  preceding 62.4
  prior 116.4
  (former 122.10)
antecedents 166.1
antechamber 191.17
antedate 115.2
antediluvian *n.* 130.1

antediluvian *adj.* 124.7
antefix 215.17
antelope speeder 274.6
  animal 366.10
antemeridian 125.3
antemundane 124.7
antenna 379.2
antepast
  serving 298.38
  foretaste 510.4
antepatriarchal 124.7
anteposition
  precedence 62.1
  contraposition 237.1
  precession 280.1
anterior
  preceding 62.4
  previous 116.4
  front 234.8
anteriority
  precedence 62.1
  priority 116.1
  front 234.1
anteroom 191.17
anteversion 311.2
anthelion 420.12
anthelmintic *n.* 662.11
anthelmintic *adj.* 662.25
anthem song 415.10, 11
  hymn 990.2
antheridium 357.4
anthesis 367.5
anthology 593.2; 597.4
anthozoan 368.13
anthracene 428.4
anthracite 388.2
anthrax 655.5, 18
anthropogeny, anthropography 372.4
anthropoid *n.* 366.16
anthropoid *adj.* 372.5
anthropologist 368.2
anthropology
  zoology 368.1
  mankind 372.4
anthropomancy 511.3
  (symbology 550.17)
**anthropomorphism,
anthropopathy** 984.4
anthropophagite 913.3
anthropos 372.1, 3
anthroposophy 372.4
anthropotomist 368.2
anthropotomy
  zoology 368.1
  mankind 372.4
anti contrary 14.5
  opposed 708.4
antiaircraft gun 727.11
antibody 662.12
antic *n.* caper 309.2
  prank 842.7
antic *v.* caper 309.5
  frolic 840.21
antichrist
  heretic 984.12
  irreligionist 989.4
Antichrist 989.4
antichristian *n.*
  heretic 984.12

antichristian — aplomb

antichristian (cont'd)
 irreligionist 989.4
antichristian adj.
 heterodox 984.22
 infidelic 989.7
Antichristian 989.7
anti-Christian 989.4
anti-Christianity
 984.1
 (infidelity 989.2)
anti-Christianize
 989.5
anticipant 507.7
anticipate
 antedate 115.2
 be beforehand 132.5
 (precede 116.3)
 expect 507.4
 (look forwards
 121.5)
 (hope 858.6)
 foresee 510.5
 (be prepared 673.9)
 (forearm 864.4)
anticipation
 prochronism 115.1
 prematurity 132.2
 intuition 477a.1
 expectation 507.1
 (hopefulness 858.2)
 foresight 510.1
 (preparation 673.1)
 in anticipation
 beforehand 116.6;
 132.12
 (in advance 280.4)
 in preparation
 673.13
anticipatory 132.8
 (foreseeing 510.6)
anticlimax
 bathos 497.1 ; 855.1
 figure of speech
 521.1
anticlinal 217.11
anticyclone 265.1
antidotal 662.25
antidote
 counteractant 179.2
 counteractive 662.12
Antietam 722.5
antifebrile n. 662.12
antifebrile adj. 662.25
antigropelos 225.28
antilogarithm 84.2
antiluetic 662.25
antimacassar 223.9
antimony 663.5
Antinomian 984.14
antinomy 964.1
Antinoüs 845.3
antiorgiastic 174.7
antiparallel 217.9
antipathy
 contrariety 14.1
 counteraction 179.1
 opposition 708.1
 dislike 867.2
 enmity 889.1
 hate 898.1
antiphon music 415.14
 hymnal ~ 990.2

antiphonal 462.11
antiphony 415.14
antiphrasis 563.1
antipodal
 contrary 14.5
 contrapositive 237.6
antipodal points 196.3
antipode 14.2
antipodean 196.5
antipodes
 distance 196.3
 contrapositives
 237.3
antipoints 237.3
antipole 14.2
antiquarian 122.5
antiquarianism 122.4
 (antiquities 124.2)
antiquarianize 122.7
antiquary
 antiquity 122.3
 antiquarian 122.5
 (annalist 553.2)
antiquate 124.5
antiquated
 superannuated 124.9
 (unfashionable
 852.10)
 elderly 128.9
antique n. 130.2
antique adj.
 old 124.6, 9
 type 591.8
antiquist 122.5
antiquities 124.2
 (antiquity 122.3)
antiquity
 ancient times 122.3
 oldness 124.1
anti-Scriptural
 984.22
antiseptic n. 662.8
 (cleanser 652.8)
antiseptic adj. 662.25
antiserum 662.12
antisocial 910.3
antisocialist 910.2
antispasmodic 662.12
antispast 597.6
antispastic 597.13
antisyphilitic 662.25
antithesis
 contrariety 14.1, 2
 (difference 15.1)
 (inverse 218.3)
 figure of speech
 521.1
antithesize 14.3
antithetic
 contrary 14.5
 contrapositive 237.6
 figurative 521.3
antitrades 349.9
antitype 22.1
antivenin, antivenine
 662.12
antler 253.2
antlia 250.4
Antlia 318.6
ant lion monster 83.7
 insect 366.24
antonomasia

figure of speech
 521.1
 nomenclature 564.1
antonomastic 521.3
antonym
 meaning 516.3
 word 562.1
 name 564.2
antonymous 516.11
antonymy 516.3
antre 252.3
antrum 252.2
Anubis 979.5
anus vitals 221.4
 buttock 235.5
anvil conversion 144.4
 supporter 215.2
 incus 418.5
 on the anvil
 intended 620.4
 in hand 625.10
 in preparation
 673.13
 (undertaken 676.3)
anvilsmith 690.6
anxiety
 care 459.1 ; 828.5
 expectation 507.3
 fearfulness 860.2
 desire 865.2
anxious
 apprehensive 860.14
 desirous 865.16
anxious seat 1000.3
any some 25.7
 part 51.1
 no choice 609a.1
 not any 87a.2
anyhow
 neglectfully 460.12
 anyway 627.9
anyway 627.9
anywhen 119.3
anywhichway 460.12
anywise 627.9
Anzac 726.6
A one, A 1
 supreme 33.8
 seaworthy 273.15
 best 648.9
 (paramount 642.14)
aorist n. 109.2
aorist adj. 109.5
aorta 350.4
apace promptly 132.14
 swiftly 274.14
 (hastily 684.7)
apache killer 361.8
 ruffian 913.2
Apache 913.3
apanage See **appanage**
aparejo 215.23
apart remote 10.7
 unconnected 44.12,
 14
 alone 87.8, 10
 distant 196.5
 away 196.11
apartment 191.16, 21
apartment house 189.3
apathetic

languid 683.14
 (inert 172.3)
 unfeeling 823.5
 (incurious 456.3)
 (indifferent 866.4)
 (irreligious 989.6)
apathy
 languor 683.4
 (inertness 172.1)
 (inaction 681.1)
 unfeeling 823.1
 (incuriosity 456.1)
 (indifference 866.1)
 (irreligion 989.1)
ape n. imitator 19.4
 monkey 366.16
ape v. 19.6
ape adj.
 imitation 19.12
 pseudo 545.13
aperçu 596.1
aperient n. 662.9
aperient adj.
 opening 260.21
 cathartic 662.25
apéritif 394.4
apertness, aperture
 260.1
apery 19.2
ape-ware copy 21.1
 sham 545.6
apex 210.1
aphelion 196.3
aphonia 581
 (silence 403.1)
aphonous 581.7
 (taciturn 585.4)
aphorism 496.1
aphoristic 496.5
aphoristically 496.6
aphorize 496.4
aphrodisia
 violent passion
 173.2
 sexual passion 961.3
aphrodisiac n.
 excitant 171.4
 love potion 865.10
aphrodisiac adj.
 171.12
Aphrodite
 beauty 845.3
 goddess 979.2
 love 897.4
aphroditous 171.12
aphthous fever 655.18
apiarist 370.4
apiary 370.3
apical 210.6
Apician 957.4
Apicius 957.2
apiculate 253.11
apiculture 370.1
apiculturist 370.4
apiece 79.12
apish imitative 19.12
 foolish 499.15
apishamore 223.10
aplomb stability 150.1
 verticality 212.1
 levelheadedness
 498.4

à plomb — apple-polishing

self-control 604.3
equanimity 826.3
à plomb 212.9
apnea, apnoea 655.5
Apocalypse 985.4
apocalyptic 985.7
Apocrypha 985.3
apocryphal
　puzzling 475.12
　erroneous 495.12
　heterodox 984.22
apodictal, apodeictal 474.8
apodictic, apodeictic
　certain 474.8
　demonstrative 478.3
apodixis 478.1
apodosis 67.1
apograph 21.2
apoise 267.50
Apollo, Apollon
　sun 318.4
　music 416.16
　wisdom 498.3
　poetry 597.9
　beauty 845.3
　god 979.2
Apollyon 978.1
apologetic n. 952.2
apologetic adj.
　excusing 937.9
　(pretexed 619.3)
　expiatory 952.6
apologize
　offer excuse 937.7
　express regret 952.5
　(recant 607.9)
apologizer 937.4
apologue
　figure of speech 521.1
　lesson 537.6
　story 594.2
apology
　makeshift 147.2
　atonement 952.2
　(admission 529.2)
　(vindication 937.2)
　(penitence 950.1)
　make apology 937.7
apophthegm, apoph-
　thegmatic etc. See apothegm etc.
apophyge 847.4
apophysis 250.2
apoplexy
　helplessness 158.2
　illness 655.3
aporia 475.1
aport 239.6
apostasy 607.2
　(dissent 489.1)
　(abandonment 624.1)
　(backsliding 661.1)
　(infidelity 940.2)
　(religion 984.2)
　(perversion 988.3)
apostate n. 607.5
　(reversionist 145.3)
　(unbeliever 485.4)
　(dissenter 489.3)

(insurgent 742.3)
(traitor 949.3)
(religion 984.12, 13; 988.5; 989.4)
apostate adj. 607.11
　(backsliding 661.4)
　(schismatic 984.23)
apostatize 607.8
　(abandon 624.3)
　(be faithless 940.7)
　(backslide 988.9)
aposteme 655.16
a posteriori 476.1, 18
apostle teacher 540.4
　disciple 541.2
　evangelist 985.6
apostleship 995.1
Apostolic n. 953.3
apostolic adj.
　evangelical 985.7
　papal 995.9
apostolic brief 592.2
Apostolic Church 983a.3
apostrophe
　figure of speech 521.1
　punctuation 550.8
　allocution 586.1
　soliloquy 589.1
apostrophic 589.4
apostrophize
　address 586.2
　soliloquize 589.3
apothecaries' measure 466.3
apothecary 662.21
apothegm, apophthegm 496.1
apothegmatic, apophthegmatic 496.5
apothegmatize, apophthegmatize 496.4
apotheosis
　glorification 873.6
　resurrection 981.8
　deification 991.2
apotheosize 991.6
apozem, apozema
　solution 335.3
　cauterant 384.11
apozemical 384.22
appall, appal
　horrify 830.7
　terrify 860.10
appalled
　shocked 828.13
　fear-struck 860.14
appalling vast 31.8
　shocking 830.13
　fearful 860.15
appanage, apanage
　inheritance 775.4
　bequest 784.6
apparatus
　instrument 633.1
　equipment 634.1
apparatus belli 727.1
apparel n. 225.1, 2
apparel v. 225.41
apparent

visible 446.4
　seeming 448.7
　plausible 472.6
　manifest 525.4
　(certain 474.8)
apparently
　presumably 472.7
　seemingly 448.8
　(visibly 446.6)
　(meaningly 516.12)
　(manifestly 525.7)
apparition
　illusion 443.9
　(appearance 448.3)
　specter 980a.1
apparitor 759.1
appassionato 415.30
appeal n.
　allocution 586.1
　~ to arms 722.3
　(duel 720.3)
　entreaty 765.2
　suit 969.6
　prayer 990.3
appeal v. cite 467.10
　address 586.2
　entreat 765.5
　claim 924.7
　litigate 969.10
appear attend 186.9
　become visible 446.2
　(become 1.5)
　(arrive 292.7)
　(be disclosed 529.6)
　seem 448.6
　(be manifest 525.3)
　~ unexpectedly 508.5
　~ in print 591.16
　~ at court 852.6
appearance
　apparition 443.9
　aspect 448.4
　(feature 240.2)
　(visibility 446.1)
　(fashion 852.1)
　probability 472.1
　false pretense 544.2
　personal ~ 599.8
　pretext 619.2
　specter 980a.1
　have the appearance of 448.6
　keep up appearances 852.6
appearanced 448.7
appeasable 723.7
appease
　moderate 174.5
　pacify 723.4
　(propitiate 990.13)
　relieve 834.4
appeasement 723.1
appellant
　claimant 924.4
　prosecutor 938.2
appellate v. 564.6
appellate adj. 966.7
appellate court 966.1
appellation
　designation 564.1, 2

title 877.1
appellative 564.2
append add 37.3
　(attach 43.6)
　place after 63.4
　be contiguous 199.3
appendage
　adjunct 39.1
　(addition 37.1)
　(accompaniment 88.1)
　tail 235.6
　hanger-on 886.2
appendicitis 655.5
appendix adjunct 39.1
　sequel 65.1
　end 67.1
　closure 261.1
apperception
　consciousness 450.1
　knowledge 490.1
　sagacity 498.2
apperceptive
　knowing 490.12
　sagacious 498.10
appercipient
　intellectual 450.8
　knowing 490.12
　sagacious 498.10
appertain
　be related 9.3
　enter into 56.2
　be included 76.2
　belong to 777.6
appetence 865.3
appetent 865.16
appetite 865.3
　(eating 298.1)
appetition 865.3
appetitive 865.16, 21
appetize 617.4; 865.14
appetizer food 298.38
　condiment 393.1
apéritif 394.4
appetizing
　savory 394.7
　tantalizing 617.5
　desirable 865.21
applaud 931.6
　(cheer 838.8)
applauder 935.1
applause 931.4
　(cheer 838.4)
apple pommel 215.23
　sphere 249.2
　fruit 298.31
　tree 369.8
apple green n. 435.2
apple-green adj. 435.6
apple grunt 298.12
applejack 959.6
apple of discord
　choice 609.6
　subject of dispute 713.5
apple of the eye 899.1
apple-pie order 58.4
in apple-pie order 58.7
apple-polisher 886.2
apple-polishing 886.1

applesauce — aptness

applesauce
 condiment 393.1
 sweet 396.3
 nonsense 497.5;
  517.2
apple tree 367.6
appliance means 632.1
 instrument 633.1
 equipment 634.1
 use 677.1
applicability
 relation 9.1
 aptness 23.2
 utility 644.1
applicable apt 23.10
 (relevant 9.8)
 usable 644.8
applicant 767.1
application
 close attention 457.2
 (thought 451.1)
 perseverance 604a.1
 use 677.1
 assiduity 682.5
 request 765.1
make application
  765.4
appliqué 847.3
apply
 ~ oneself 451.27;
  457.4
 ~ a remedy 662.24
 use 677.5
 make request 765.4
 appropriate 789.8
appoggiatura 413.10
appoint destine 601.9
 elect 609.11
 equip 634.2
 prescribe 741.5
 commission 755.4
 assign 786.3
 ordain 995.7
appointment
 election 609.5
 office 625.4
 order 741.1
 commission 755.2
 assignment 786.1
 engagement 892.3
 holy orders 995.6
appointments
 equipment 634.1
 belongings 780.1, 5
apportion
 partition 44.10
 arrange 60.6
 allot 786.3
 (distribute 73.3)
 (share 778.5)
apportionment
 arrangement 60.1
 allotment 786
 (division 44.1)
 (dispersion 73.1)
apposite related 9.6
 apt 23.10
apposition
 relation 9.1
 agreement 23.1
 nearness 197.1
 contiguity 199.1

appraisable 466.12
appraisal
 measurement 466.1
 (discrimination
  465.1)
 judgment 480.2
appraise
 measure 466.10
 judge 480.7
 value 812.4
appraisement 812.3
appreciable 466.12
appreciate
 increase 35.4
 enjoy 377.4
 relish 394.6
 realize 450.7
 valuate 466.10
 estimate 480.7
 know 490.9
 rate highly 642.8
 delight in 827.6
 display taste 850.4
 approve 931.5
appreciation
 increase 35.1
 knowledge 490.1
 discrimination 465.1
 valuation 466.1
 estimation 480.2
 approbation 931.1
apprehend
 sense 375.3
 believe 484.8
 know 490.9
 understand 518.4
 arrest 751.9
 seize 789.9
 fear 860.8
apprehensibility 518.1
apprehensib'e 518.5
apprehension
 idea 453.1
 knowledge 490.1
 understanding 498.1
 expectation 507.3
 arrest 751.3
 taking 789.1
 fearfulness 860.2
 (foreboding 511.6)
 (danger 665.1)
 (alarm 669.1)
apprehensive 860.14
apprehensiveness
  860.2
apprentice
 novice 541.6
 worker 690.2
 servant 746.1
apprenticeship 539.2
apprize, apprise 527.7
apprized 490.13
be apprized of 490.9
apprizer 527.5
approach n.
 nearing 286
 (advent 121.4)
 (nearness 197.1)
 arrival 292.1
 inlet 294.5
 path 627.2
approach

resemble 17.7
 ~ in time 121.6
 impend 152.2
 converge 290.2
 (near 197.6)
 move towards 286.2
 reach 292.7
 address 586.2
 bribe 618.3
approachable
 accessible 286.4
 easy 705.5
approaching 286.3
 (impending 152.3)
 (converging 290.3)
approbate 931.5
approbation 931
 (assent 488.1)
 (repute 873.1)
 (regard 928.1)
 (flattery 933.1)
approbatory 931.9
 (flattering 933.1)
appropinquate 286.2
appropinquation 286.1
appropinquity 197.1
appropriate v.
 possess 777.5
 allot 786.3
 take 789.8
 (acquire 775.6)
 (borrow 788.2)
 (steal 791.9)
 (assume 925.6)
appropriate adj.
 fit 23.11
 peculiar 79.8
 opportune 134.7
 language 578.4
 expedient 646.4
 (due 924.9)
appropriation
 possession 777.2
 allotment 786.1
 taking 789.1
 (acquisition 775.1)
 (theft 791.1)
 (assumption 925.3)
approval
 ratification 488.4
 approbation 931.1
 (assent 488.1)
 (consent 762.1)
on approval
 on trial 463.15
 optionally 609.17
approve ratify 488.10
 approbate 931.5
 (assent 488.6)
 (consent 762.2)
approved
 conventional 852.8
 uncensured 931.10
 (respected 928.9)
 orthodox 983a.7
approving 931.9
approximate v.
 resemble 17.7
 assimilate 17.8
 be near 197.5
 approach 286.2

approximate adj.
 286.3
approximately 32.17
approximation
 similarity 17.1
 mathematics 85.4
 nearness 197.1
 (relation 9.1)
 approach 286.1
approximative
 related 9.7
 (comparable 464.6)
 similar 17.4
 (accurate 494.11)
 approaching 286.3
appulse, appulsion
 contiguity 199.1
 clash 276.2
 approach 286.1
 convergence 290.1
appurtenance
 adjunct 39.1
 (accompaniment
  88.1)
 component 56.1
appurtenances
 equipment 634.1
 belongings 780.1, 5
appurtenant n. 39.1
appurtenant adj.
 relative 9.5
 apt 23.10
apricot n. 298.31
apricot adj. 434.10;
  436.6; 439.5
April fool 547.1
 (laughingstock
  857.1)
April showers 149.2
a priori 476.1, 18
apriorism 476.4
apron adjunct 39.1
 garment 225.20
 airdrome 267a.28
 clerical ~ 999.1
apron-string tenure
  777.1
apropos
 with regard 9.10
 appropriate 23.11
 pertinently 23.13
 by the way 134.11
apse 215.18; 1000.3
apt pertinent 23.10
 (relevant 9.8)
 ~ to 176.3
 (liable to 177.3)
 probable 472.5
 suitable 646.4
 skillful 698.11
 (teachable 539.7)
aptitude fitness 23.2
 tendency 176.1
 likelihood 177.1
 probability 472.1
 skill 698.2
 (genius 498.5)
 (learning 539.1)
 (propensity 602.2)
aptness
 pertinence 23.2
 skill 698.2

Apus 318.6
aqua 337.1
aquagreen 435.2
aquamarine
 color 435.23; 438.2
 gem 847.8
aqua pura 337.1
aquarium 370.3
 (collection 636.5)
Aquarius
 constellation 318.6
 water bearer 348.16
aquatic
 natatory 267.52
 watery 337.6
aquatics 267.1
aquatint 558.3
aqueduct 350.1
 (trench 259.2)
aqueous 337.6
Aquila 318.6
aquiline 245.8, 9
Ara 318.6
Arab
 vagabond 268.2;
  876.9
 horse 271.4
araba 272.4
arabesque
 music 413.10; 415.3
 ornamentation 847.3
Arabesque binding
 593.9
Arabic 560.4
arachis oil 356.3
arachnoid 368.18
arado 780.4
Aralu 982.2
Aramaic 560.4
Aranyaka 986.2
Araucan 560.4
Araucanian 434.5
Arawak 434.5
arbalest 727.9
arbiter 967.1
arbiter elegantiae,
 arbiter eleganti-
 arum 850.3
 (fashionable person
  852.5)
arbitrament 724.1
arbitrary
 irrelative 10.5
 unconformable 83.9
 dogmatic 474.15
 willful 606.7
 capricious 608.5
 authoritative 737.15
 autocratic 739.5
 unlimited 748.15
 dictatorial 885.8
 arbitrary 964.6
arbitrate
 adjudicate 480.6
 mediate 724.3
 compromise 774.2
arbitration
 conciliation 723.1
 mediation 724.1
arbitrator
 mediator 724.2
 (moderator 174.3)

judge 967.1
arbor, arbour
 retreat 189.13
 bower 191.22
 (garden 371.6)
 frame 215.8
arbor 312.5
arborary 367.15
Arbor Day 138.7
arboreal 367.15
arborescence 242.2
 (roughness 256.1)
arborescent
 ramous 242.6
 (rough 256.12)
 treelike 367.15
arboretum 371.6
arboricultural 371.9
arboriculture 371.1
arboriculturist 371.2
arboriform 242.6
arborization 242.2
arborvitae, arbor
 vitae 242.2
arbor vitae 450.2
arbour See arbor
arbutus 400.3
arc n. arch 215.18
 curve 245.2
arc v. 245.3
arcade
 arch 215.18; 245.2
 covered way 627.2
Arcadia 515.6
 (Heaven 981.1)
Arcadian rustic 183.3
 simple 703.4
 paradisiac 981.7
arcanal, arcane
 hidden 528.17, 21
 enigmatic 533.6
arcanum 533.2
arcature 215.18
arch n. 215.18; 245.2
 (convexity 250.6)
arch v. ~ over 223.27
 vault 245.3
 convex 250.8
arch adj. 702.6
archaeological, arche-
 ological 122.13
archaeologist, arche-
 ologist 122.5
archaeology, archeol-
 ogy 122.4
archaeus See archeus
archaic old 124.7, 9
 word 563.18
archaism
 antiquarianism
  122.4
 antiquity 124.2
 word 563.10
archangel 977.1, 2
archangelic 977.4
archbishop 996.5
archbishopric 995.3
archdeacon 996.5
archduchy 182.1
archduke 875.5
archebiosis 161.2
arched vaulted 245.5

convex 250.9
archenemy
 enemy 891.1
 Satan 978.1
archeological, arche-
 ologist etc. See
 archaeological etc.
archer shooter 284.8
 bowman 726.4
 sportsman 840.17
Archer 318.6
archery
 ballistics 284.9;
  727.2
 sport 840.11
archetypal 20.3
archetype
 prototype 22.1
 idea 453.1
archeus, archaeus
 359.3
archfiend 978.1
Archibald 727.11
archiepiscopacy 995.3
archiepiscopal 995.9
archigenesis 161.2
arching 245.1
archipelagic 346.4
archipelago 346.1
architect
 producer 164.1
 artist 559.1
 craftsman 690.5
architectonic 161.12
architectural
 structural 161.12
 formative 240.9
architecture
 arrangement 60.3
 construction 161.1
 form 240.1
 art 556.1
 ornamentation 847.1
architrave 210.4
archive 551.2
 (store 636.4)
archlute, archilute
 417.2
archon official 745.9
 judge 967.1
archtraitor 949.3
archway 215.18
arciform 245.5
arc lamp 423.3
arctic n. 383.4
arctic adj. 383.8
arctics 225.27
arcuate v. bow 245.3
 convex 250.8
arcuate adj. 245.5
arcuation 245.1
ardent violent 173.13
 hot 382.16
 eager 682.18; 865.17
 fervent 821.6
 friendship 888.1, 4
 amorous 897.14
 alcoholic 959.24
ardent spirits 959.4
ardor, ardour
 heat 382.1
 vehemence 574.3

eagerness 682.3
 fervor 821.2
 desire 865.2
 love 897.1
arduous steep 217.12
 laborious 686.10
 difficult 704.8
arduously 704.12
arduousness 704.1
are proportions 180.5
 measure 466.3
area region 181.1
 size 192.1
arear 283.8
arefact 340.5
arefaction 340.2
arena extent 180.1
 plot 181.3
 field of view 441.6
 scene of action 728
arenaceous, arenari-
 ous, arenose 330.8
arenosity 330.1
areola 247.2
Areopagus 966.1
Ares war 722.7
 god 979.2
aretaies ethics 926.4
 virtue 944.1
Aretinian syllables
 413.17
argal n. See argol
argal adv. 155.5
argali 366.8
argent, argenteous,
 argentine 430.8
argil softness 324.3
 soil 342.3
argillaceous 324.6
Argo 318.6
argol, argal 653.7
argon 334.2
Argonaut 463.6
argosy ship 273.1, 6
 navy 726.10
argot 563.4
argotic 563.16
argue show 467.7
 (talk 582.6)
 (converse 588.9)
 (quarrel 713.7)
 (contend 720.8)
 (litigate 969.10)
 reason 476.11
 mean 516.5
 indicate 550.18
 plead 937.6
 ~ at the bar 969.10
arguer 476.9
 (interlocutor 588.5)
argul See argol
argument
 argumentation
  476.2, 3
 (quarrel 713.3)
 (contention 720.1)
 (litigation 969.1)
 counterevidence
  468.1
 subject matter 516.4
 defense 937.2
 ~ at the bar 969.6

argumentation — arrogator

argumentation 476.2
 (interlocution
  588.4)
argumentative
 controversial 476.14
  (litigious 969.13)
 quarrelsome 901.9
Argus 441.9
Argus-eyed 459.8
argute 498.10
aria 415.2, 10
 (composition 54.2)
 (production 161.6)
Arianism 984.4
arid
 unproductive 169.4
 dry 340.7
 dull 843.5
aridity 340.1
Ariel speeder 274.7
 messenger 534.1
 fairy 979.9
Aries season 126a.1
 constellation 318.6
arietta, ariette 415.10
aright 648.14
ariose 413.27
arioso 415.3, 12, 30
arise originate 66.6
 (become 1.5)
 happen 151.3
 result 154.3
 ascend 305.4
 appear 446.2
arista point 253.2
 bristle 256.7
aristarchy 737.4
aristate 253.11
aristocracy
 government 737.4
 nobility 875.1, 2
 (society 852.4)
aristocrat 875.4
aristocratic 875.10
Aristotelian 476.5, 17
Aristotelianism 451.7
arithmetic
 mathematics 85.2
 accountancy 811.4
arithmetical 85.12
arithmetician 85.6
arithmograph, arithmometer 85.5
ark ship 273.1, 4
 refuge 666.3
arm n. member 51.4
 armature 158a.6
 supporter 215.2
 side 236.1
 lever 307.4
 ~ of the sea 343.1
 at arm's length
  196.11
 in arms
  infantile 127.7
  prepared 673.11
  armed 717.9
  warring 722.12
arm v. empower 157.7
 equip 634.2
 (provide 637.4)

(call to arms
 722.10)
 fortify 717.7
armada 726.10
armadillo 366.14
Armageddon
 battle 720.2
 war 722.1
armament
 equipment 634.1
 provision 673.1
 munitions 727.1
armature
 electricity 158a.6
 arms 727.1
armchair 215.22
armed 717.9
 (protected 664.11)
armed force 726.6
Armenian 560.4
armet 717.2
armful 25.2
armiger soldier 726.4
 nobleman 875.5
armigerous 722.13
arm in arm with 88.9
 friendly 888.4, 5
 sociably 892.13
armipotent 157.8
armistice 723.3
Armistice Day 138.7
armlet sleeve 225.31
 circle 247.2
 sea inlet 343.1
 ornament 847.7
arm of flesh 711.1
armor, armour 717.2
 (arms 727.1)
armored, armoured
 covered 223.28
 panoplied 717.9
 (protected 664.11)
armorial bearings
 550.12
armor-plated 223.28
armory, armoury
 auditorium 189.10
 store 636.4
 arms 727.1
 factory 691
arms insignia 550.12
 warfare 722.1
 weapons 727
 to arms! 722.15
 (attack 716.10)
 under arms 722.12
army multitude 102.2
 armed force 726.6
 (company 72.3)
arnatto See annatto
arnica 662.6
aroint!, aroynt!
 begone! 297.23
 curse! 908.7
aroma 400.1
aromatic n. 400.2
aromatic adj. 400.10
aromatize 400.9
around
 almost 32.15, 17
 near 197.8, 11, 12
 about 227.5

go around
 circuit 311.3
 be irresolute 605.4, 5
arouse stimulate 171.7
 inflame 173.8
 stimulate 615.7
 excite 824.2
aroynt See aroint
arpeggio chord 413.9
 music 415.15
arpent
 proportions 180.5
 length 200.6
arquebus, arquebusade See harquebus
 etc.
arraign accuse 938.4
 indict 969.10
arraignment
 accusation 938.1
 indictment 969.3
arrange accord 23.8
 ~ itself 58.5
 dispose 60.6
 (size 192.10)
 (prepare 673.6)
 include 76.3
 form 240.6
 music 415.26
 plan 626.9
 conciliate 723.4
 mediate 724.3
 settle 769.8
arrangement
 method 58.3
 disposition 60
 (order 58.1)
 (plan 626.1)
 (preparation 673.1)
 orchestration 413.3
 musical ~ 415.3, 21
 condition 469.2
 artistic ~ 556.5
 preparation 673.1
 adjustment 723.1
 settlement 769.3
 payment 807.1
make arrangements
 673.6
arranger 416.14
arrant absolute 31.12
 conspicuous 525.3
 notorious 531.10
 bad 649.8
 disreputable 874.8
 sinful 945.11
arras 847.6
arrastra, arrastre
 330.4
array n. method 58.3
 arrangement 60.3
 procession 69.3
 crowd 72.4
 multitude 102.2
 clothes 225.1
 armed force 726.6
 display 882.3
array v. arrange 60.6
 clothe 225.41
 equip 634.2
 adorn 847.11
arrayal

equipment 673.1
 display 882.3
arrear rear 235.1
 debt 806.2
 in arrear, in arrears
  incomplete 53.4
  behindhand 304.4
  in debt 806.9
  defaultant 808.9
arrears 806.2
arrector pili 383.2
arrest n.
 cessation 142.1
 hindrance 706.1
 restraint 751.3
 (arraignment
  969.4)
 put under arrest
  751.9
 under arrest 751.12
arrest v. stop 142.7
 ~ the thoughts
  451.33; 457.6
 restrain 751.9
arrière-pensée
 mental reservation
  477.4; 528.2
 ulterior motive
  615.1
arrish 65.2
arrival
 landing 267a.26
 reaching 292
 (cessation 142.1)
 (completion 729.1)
arrive happen 151.3
 reach 292.7
 (enter 294.6)
 (appear 446.2)
 (reach completion
  729.4)
arrive at
 come to 292.7
 ~ ~ the truth
  481a.4
arrogance 885.1
 (pride 878.1)
 (vanity 880.1)
 (ostentation 882.1)
 (disdain 930.1)
arrogant 885.8
 (proud 878.6)
 (vain 880.6)
 (contemptuous
  930.8)
arrogantly 885.11
 (contemptuously
  930.10)
arrogate
 usurp 737.13; 925.6
 (claim 924.7)
 appropriate 789.8
 assume 885.6
arrogation
 attribution 155.1
 ~ of authority 737.9
 dethronement 738.3
 usurpation 925.3
arrogator
 potentate 745.2
 taker 789.6
 usurper 925.4

arrosive 331.4
arrow speed 274.6
  missile 727.6
Arrow 318.6
arrowhead
  cuneiform 590.9
  weapon 727.6
arrowheaded, arrowy 253.13
arroyo stream 348.1
  water gap 350.1
arse 235.5
arsenal store 636.4
  factory 691
  armory 727.1
arsenic 663.5
arsenious oxide, arsenious acid 663.5
arson 384.5
arsonate 384.11
arsonist 384.6
art
  representation 554.1
  design 556.1
  work of art 556.8
  (decoration 847.1)
  vocation 625.5
  skill 698.2, 3
  artifice 702.3
Artemis moon 318.5
  chase 622.2
  goddess 979.2
arterialize 338.10
arteriosclerosis 655.5
artery vessel 350.4
  path 627.2
artful 702.6
  (false 544.7)
  (deceitful 545.12)
  (scheming 626.12)
Artful Dodger
  cunning person 702.4
  swindler 792.8
artfulness 702.1
  (falsehood 544.1)
art gallery 556.15
arthritis pain 378.1
  ailment 655.5
Arthropoda 368.8
  (fish 366.21)
arthrospore 193.4
artichoke 208.30
article section 51.2
  object 316.3
  tenet 484.3
  writing 590.3
  book section 593.7
  commentary 595.2
  stipulation 770.1
  merchandise 798.1
articled clerk 541.6
articles of agreement 770.1
articulate n. 368.8
articulate v.
  utter 580.8
  speak 582.6
articulate adj.
  arthropodal 368.18
  audible 402.10
  spoken 580.11

articulated 580.11
articulation joint 43.3
  word 562.1
  utterance 580.3
artifex 164.1
artifice 702.3
  (trick 545.3)
  (device 626.5)
artificer
  producer 164.1
  craftsman 690.5
artificial
  spurious 545.13
  speech 579.3
  affected 853.6
artillerist 726.4
artillery troops 726.8
  cannon 727.11
artilleryman 726.4
  (shooter 284.8)
artisan 690.5
artist
  painter etc. 559
  (producer 164.1)
  (workman 690.10)
  contriver 626.8
  craftsman 690.5
artiste musician 416.1
  artist 559.1
  actor 599.19
artistic
  graphic 556.19
  language 578.4
  beautiful 845.16
  (ornamental 847.12)
  (tasteful 850.5)
artistically 698.16
artistry art 556.6
  authorship 569.1
artist's proof 558.3
artless natural 674.9
  ingenuous 703.4
  (veracious 543.3)
  (inexperienced 699.14)
  (simple 849.3)
  (honest 939.7)
  (innocent 946.5)
artlessness 703
  (veracity 543.1)
  (simplicity 849.1)
  (honesty 939.1)
  (innocence 946.1)
art materials 556.16
art museum 556.15
arts 556
arts of design 554.1
  (ornament 847.1)
artware 556.8
arty 556.19; 845.16
arundinaceous 253.18
aruspex, aruspical etc. See haruspex etc.
Aryan 11.8
as 155.6
  as agreed 769.11
  as all creation 31.15
  as a matter of course generally 78.15
  consequently 154.7

(demonstrably 478.6)
  certainly 474.16
  necessarily 601.15
as a matter of fact
  actually 1.9
  truly 494.15
as a result 154.7
as a rule 78.15
  (conformably 82.12)
  (habitually 613.13)
as compared with 464.7
as for 9.10
as far as 106.8
as good as
  equivalent 27.9
  nearly 197.12
as good as one's word
  veracious 543.3
  observant 772.5
  reliable 939.6, 9
as if though 17.17
  supposedly 514.12
as it may be
  accordingly 8.7
  by chance 156.13
  possibly 470.7
as it were as if 17.17
  supposedly 514.12
  figuratively 521.4
as lief 602.11
as like as not 472.7
as long as
  while 106.9
  provided 469.8
as promised 769.11
as regards, as respects 9.10
as the case may be
  by chance 156.13
  possibly 470.7
as the crow flies 278.13
as they say
  proverbially 496.6
  rumored 532.10
  (by common report 527.15)
as things go
  accordingly 8.7
  eventually 151.8
  as usual 613.14
as though as if 17.17
  supposedly 514.12
as to 9.10
as usual
  permanently 141.8
  habitually 613.14
  (conformably 82.12)
as well 37.8
as well as 37.9, 10
  (with 88.9)
as you please 743.4; 886.6
as you were 613.14
Asa 979.3
asafetida, asafoetida
  bitter 395.3
  malodor 401.2
Asas 979.3

asbestic 385.8
asbestos
  fire extinguisher 385.3
  curtain 599.15
ascare 860.14
ascend be great 31.4
  be high 206.9
  incline 217.6
  aviate 267a.31
  mount 305.4
  (increase 35.4)
ascendance, ascendence 305.1
ascendancy, ascendency
  superiority 33.1
  (victory 731.3)
  dominion 737.2
  have the ascendancy
  be superior 33.6
  predominate 737.12
in ascendancy
  superior 33.7
  influential 175.10
  victorious 731.11
  ruling 737.15
ascendant
  superior 33.7
  influential 175.10
  ascending 305.7
  (elevated 307.8)
  victorious 731.11
  ruling 737.15
ascending
  acclivitous 217.10
  ascendant 305.7
ascension
  acclivity 217.2
  mounting 305.1
ascensional 305.7
Ascension Day 998.13
ascent
  motion upwards 305
  (elevation 307.1)
  (leap 309.1)
  acclivity 217.2
ascertain
  make certain 474.6
  decide 480.6
  discover 481a.3
ascertainment
  certification 474.2
  discovery 481a.1
ascetic n. recluse 893.4
  puritan 955.2
  (abstainer 953.3)
  (religious 996.11)
ascetic adj. 955.3
  (abstinent 953.6)
ascetical 942.5
asceticism
  self-denial 942.1
  austerity 955
  (abstinence 953.2)
ascribable
  attributable 155.4
  due 924.11
ascribe 155.3
ascription 155.1
ascititious
  extrinsic 6.2

aseptic — assignment

ascititious (continued)
  additional 37.7
  completing 52.12
aseptic 662.25
Asgard, Asgarth,
  Asgardhr 981.3
ash residue 40.2
  tree 367.6
  product of combustion 384.15
  wood 635.3
ashame disgrace 874.6
  humiliate 879.3
ashamed 879.5
ashcake 298.11
ash can 727.14
ashen pale 429.6
  whitish 430.9
  gray 432.4
ashes 362.1
ashore 342.14
  go ashore 292.9
Ash Wednesday
  anniversary 138.7
  holyday 998.13
ashy pale 429.6
  whitish 430.9
  gray 432.4
Asiatic 11.8
aside *n.*
  interjection 228.2
  secret 528.2
aside *adv.* apart 196.11
  beside 236.9
  sotto voce 405.11
  secretly 528.24
turn aside
  change 140.5
  deviate 279.7
  (turn 311.4)
  (disincline 616.3)
  disregard 458.5
  avert 706.5
asinine mulish 271.13
  absurd 497.4
  foolish 499.15
asininity 497.1
ask inquire 461.14
  request 765.4
  charge 794.5; 812.5
ask for one's hand
  inquire 461.14
  request 765.4
  propose 902.7
ask leave 760.5
askance, askant 236.8
  (obliquely 217.17)
look askance
  look 441.15
  squint 443.12
  disagree 489.4
  discountenance 764.3
  dislike 867.4
  disapprove 932.5
askew 217.13, 17
  (distorted 243.5)
aslant *adj.* 217.9
aslant, aslant-
  wise *adv.* 217.17
asleep dead 360.8
  inattentive 458.11

unwary 460.9
  sleeping 683.16
be asleep 683.9
fall asleep die 360.6
  go to sleep 683.9
aslope 217.9
Asmodeus 978.1
asomatous 317.6
asp 366.19
asparagus 298.30
Aspasia 962.2
aspect nature 5.3
  component 56.1
  posture 184.2
  look 441.2
  appearance 448.4
  (feature 240.2)
  (viewpoint 441.4)
aspergation
  sprinkling 337.2
  rite 998.5
asperge 337.5; 998.14
asperger 998.8
asperges 998.8
Asperges
  sprinkling 337.2
  rite 998.2
aspergillum
  sprinkler 337.3
  church 998.8
asperity
  roughness 256.1
  gruffness 895.2
  resentment 900.1
  irascibility 901.1
asperous 256.12
asperse
  disparage 934.3
  asperge 998.14
aspersion
  dispersion 73.1
  sprinkling 337.2
  (cleaning 652.2)
  malediction 908.1
  indignity 929.2
  disparagement 934.1
  rite 998.2, 5
asphalt, asphaltum *n.*
  smooth 255.2
  resin 356a.1
  pavement 627.4
asphalt *v.* 255.4
asphaltic 356a.3
asphyxiate 361.11
asphyxiating gas 334.2
asphyxiation
  suffocation 361.4
  ailment 655.5
aspic 298.19
aspirant
  candidate 767.1
  desirer 865.7
aspirate sibilate 409.3
  breathe 581.6
aspiration
  hopefulness 858.2
  ambition 865.2
aspire ascend 305.4
  intend 620.3
  desire 865.11
asport 270.8
asportation 270.2

asquint askance 236.8
  squint-eyed 443.14
look asquint
  look askance 441.15
  squint 443.12
ass rump 235.5
  donkey 271.10
  (animal 366.2)
  fool 501.1
  bullhead 606.3, 4
ass in lion's skin
  misfit 24.4
  impostor 548.3
  bungler 701
  bluff 887.2
  knave 949.1
assagai, assegai 727.5
assail attack 716.5
  pain 830.3
assailant 716.4
  (opponent 710.1)
  (combatant 726.1)
Assamese 560.4
assassin 361.8
assassinate 361.10
assassination 361.1
assault *n.* 716.1
assault *v.* 716.5
assaulter 716.4
assay *n.* analysis 461.3
  test 463.1
assay *v.* analyze 461.17
  test 463.8
assay balance 319.5
assayer 463.6
assegai See assagai
assemblage all 50.2
  gathering 72
  (quantity 31.3)
  (meeting 43.1)
  council 696.2
assemble 72.10, 11
  (accumulate 636.7)
  (attend church 990.1)
assemblée 696.2
assembler 696.8
assembly
  gathering 72.2
  (attendance 186.5)
  (social gathering 892.5)
  (divine service 990.7)
  auditorium 189.10
  council 696.2
  (conference 588.3)
  religious ~ 997.1
assemblyman 696.8
assembly room 189.10
  (meeting place 74.2)
  (theater 599.10)
assent *n.* 488
  (agreement 23.1)
  (concurrence 178.1)
  (affirmation 535.1)
  (willingness 602.1)
  (consent 762.1)
  (approval 931.1)
assent *v.* 488.6
  (agree 23.7)
  (concur 178.2)

(affirm 535.3)
(be willing 602.6)
(consent 762.2)
(approve 931.5)
assenter 488.5
assenting 488.11
  (concurrent 178.4)
  (willing 602.8)
  (consenting 762.3)
assertive 488.11
  (affirmative 535.6)
assert affirm 535.3
  ~ under oath 535.4
  insist 535.5
  say 582.6
  ~ a right 924.7
assertion
  affirmation 535.1
  statement 582.4
assertional, assertive, assertorial 535.6
asses' bridge 704.4
assess measure 466.10
  estimate 480.7
  charge 812.5
assessable
  measurable 466.12
  taxable 812.8
assessment
  measurement 466.1
  estimation 480.2
  tax 812.2
assessor 967.1
assets funds 800.2
  accounts 811.1
  property 780.7
  (wealth 803.1)
  (receipts 810.1)
asseverate 535.3
asseveration 535.1
asshead 501.1
assiduity 682.5
assiduous 682.19
  (studious 539.6)
assign attribute 155.3
  adduce 467.10
  pass judgment 480.9
  appoint 609.11
  commission 755.4
  transfer 783.3
  entrust 784.12
  allot 786.3
  impose a duty 926.7
assignable
  attributable 155.4
  transferable 270.11
assignat 800.6
assignation
  attribution 155.1
  assignment 783.1
  tryst 892.3
assignee
  consignee 758.1
  (transferee 270.5)
  recipient 785.2
assignee in fact 758.1
assignment
  attribution 155.1
  lesson 537.6
  appointment 609.5
  task 625.2

708

assimilate — asylum

commission 755.1
transfer 783.1
allotment 786.1
assimilate
uniform 16.4
similarize 17.8
agree 23.7, 8
convert 144.6
assimilation
adaptation 23.3
conversion 144.1
assist 707.6
assistance
remedy 662.1
aid 707.1
(benefit 784.4)
assistant n.
helpmate 711.1
servant 746.1
benefactor 912.1
assistant adj. 707.12
assister 912.1
assize
examination 461.3
measurement 466.1
trial 969.5
assizement 466.1
assizes 966.2
associate n.
assemble 72.10
accompanier 88.3
co-worker 690.4
confederate 711.1
staff 746.2
friend 890.3
associate v. relate 9.4
join 43.5
league 48.4
associate with
mix with 41.6
accompany 88.6
become a member 712.8
keep company with 892.9
associated related 9.6
accompanying 88.8
association
relation 9.1
accompaniment 88.2
intuition 477a.1
alliance 709.2
society 712.4
(company 72.3)
social relations 892.1
association of ideas 451.1
assoil, assoilzie 970.3
assonance
resemblance 17.3
agreement 23.1
rhyme 597.8
assonant
resembling 17.16
harmonious 413.26
rhyming 597.13
assonate
resemble 17.9
harmonize 413.24
assort 60.6
assortment

arrangement 60.1
miscellany 72.8
assuage
moderate 174.5
soften 324.4
qualify 469.3
relieve 834.4
assuagement
modulation 174.2
softening 324.2
relief 834.1
assuager
moderator 174.3
palliative 662.6
assuasive
moderative 174.7
softening 324.10
qualifying 469.6
palliative 662.25
relieving 834.7
assuetude 613.5
assume simulate 19.7
account for 155.3
wear 225.45
believe 484.8
suppose 514.6
feign 544.6
undertake 676.2
~ authority 737.13
appropriate 789.8
affect 853.5
arrogate 885.6
usurp 925.6
assumed name 565.3
assumer 514.5
assuming 885.8
assumption
conversion 144.1
accounting 155.1
premise 476.4
belief 484.2
expectation 507.2
supposition 514.1
~ of authority 737.9
receiving 785.1
hope 858.1
arrogance 885.1
usurpation 925.3
assumptive 514.9
assurance
stability 150.1
certainty 474.1, 2
(good chance 156.3)
belief 484.1
expectation 507.2
pledge 535.2
promise 768.1
guarantee 771.1
hope 858.1
(security 664.1)
impudence 885.2
assure
make certain 474.6
convince 484.10
vouch 535.4
promise 768.3
guarantee 771.6
give hope 858.8
I assure you
I'll warrant 535.8
I promise 768.8
assured

made sure 474.9
(demonstrated 478.4)
convinced 484.12
confident 858.9; 861.8
rest assured
be certain 474.5
believe 484.9, 17
I assure you 535.8
I promise 768.8
hope 858.6
assuredly
absolutely 31.16
certainly 474.16
yes 488.14
Assyrian 124.2
Assyriologist 122.5
Astarte
productiveness 168.1
moon 318.5
beauty 845.3
love 897.4
deity 979.6
asteism 856.1
asterisk 550.8
asterism
constellation 318.6
typography 550.8
astern after 235.15
aft 267.68
backward 283.8
go astern 267.25
asteroid 318.3
asteroidal 318.16
asthenia 160.1
asthenic n. 160.4
asthenic adj. 160.10
asthma 655.9
asthmatic 688.7
astigmatic 443.14
astigmatism 443.1
astir
in preparation 673.13
active 682.23
excited 824.9
astonish 870.3
(surprise 508.6)
astonished 870.6
(surprised 508.10)
astonishing vast 31.8
wonderful 870.8
(surprising 508.9)
astonishingly 31.21
astonishment
amazement 870.1
(surprise 508.2)
marvel 872.1
astound shock 824.3
frighten 860.10
astonish 870.3
(surprise 508.6)
astounding 860.15
astoundment 870.1
astraddle 215.31
Astraea 941.1
astragal
capital 215.17
ornament 847.4
astral n. 980a.1

astral adj. 318.16
astral body 994.12
(incorporeal being 317.2)
(double 980a.2)
astral spirits 980a.1
astray wide of 196.9
deviatively 279.9
amiss 304.5
uncertain 475.16
erroneous 495.12
go astray
deviate 279.5
err 495.7
fail 732.5
sin 945.9
lead **astray** 495.11
astriction
junction 43.1
contraction 195.1
astride 215.32
astringency
contraction 195.1
pungency 392.1
gruffness 895.2
astringent n. 195.3
astringent adj.
contractive 195.6
pungent 392.5
sour 397.6
penetrating 824.13
gruff 895.7
astringer 195.3
astrochemist 318.12
astrochemistry, astrognosy, astrography 318.10
astrologaster 318.13
astrologer 318.12, 13
(seer 513.2)
(diviner 994.16)
astrologian 318.13
astrological 318.16
(divinatory 994.23)
astrology stars 318.10
divination 511.4
(interpretation 522.5)
(symbology 550.17)
astromancer 318.13
astromancy 511.4
(stars 318.10)
astronomer 318.12
astronomical 318.16
astronomy, astrophotography, astrophotometry 318.10
astrophysicist 318.12
astrophysics 318.10
astute
discriminating 465.4
sagacious 498.10
cunning 702.6
asunder
unconnected 44.12, 14
distant 196.5
asylum
madhouse 503.8
hospital 662.17
refuge 666.3
(retreat 189.13)

asymptote — attention   710

asymptote 290.1
asymptotic 290.3
ataghan See yataghan
atar See attar
ataunt 267.67
atavism 145.1
atavistic 145.6
atelier 556.15
athanasia, athanasy 112.1
athanor 386.1
atheism 989.2
  (unbelief 485.1)
atheist 989.4
  (unbeliever 485.4)
atheistic 989.7
  (heterodox 984.22)
atheling, adeling 875.7
Athena wisdom 498.3
  goddess 979.2
athenaeum, atheneum 593.11
Athena Parthenos 948.2
athermancy 382.1
athirst 865.19
athlete 159.6
  (jumper 309.5)
athletic
  gymnastic 159.11
  exercising 686.10
athletics
  gymnastics 159.5
  exercise 686.2
  sports 840.10
at home, at-home *n.* 892.5
at home
  congenial 23.12
  here 186.20
  within 221.12
  comfortable 377.8
  versed 490.14
  accustomed 613.12
  skilled 698.14
  at ease 705.5; 748.20
  contented 831.6
  ~ ~ with 888.4
  be at home
    ~ ~ ~ in 705.3
    entertain 892.11
  feel at home
    feel free 748.8
    be pleased 827.5
    be content 831.3
  stay at home 265.5
athwart 219.12
  (transversely 217.18)
athwarthawse 267.53
athwartship, athwartships, athwartwise 219.12
Atlantean vast 31.8
  strong 159.10
  giantlike 192.15
  supporting 215.28
atlantes 847.4
Atlantides
  constellation 318.6
  divinities 979.8
Atlantis 515.6

atlas
  arrangement 60.3
  post 215.16
  archive 551.2
  (dictionary 593.4)
Atlas
  strong man 159.6
  support 215.25
atman, atma 994.10, 11
Atman 359.3
atmosphere
  surroundings 227.2
  aeronautics 267a.19
  air 338.1
  artistic ~ 556.5
atmospheric
  aerial 338.11
  blue 438.6
atmospherology 338.7
atoll 346.1
atom modicum 32.2
  (inextension 180a.1)
  diminutive 193.2
atomic 193.10
atomism 451.6
atomization 336.1
atomize 336.5
atomizer
  vaporizer 336.3
  sprinkler 337.3
  perfumer 400.5
atomy
  diminutive 193.2, 5
  thinness 203.5
atonal 414.4
at one agreeing 23.9
  concurrent 178.4
  unanimous 488.12
  in accord 714.4
atone
  harmonize 413.24
  expiate 952.4
  (compensate 30.4)
  (propitiate 990.13)
  recompense 973.3
atonement
  restitution 790.1
  repayment 807.3
  expiation 952
  (compensation 30.1, 2)
  (penitence 950.1)
  (penalty 974.1)
  (propitiation 990.5)
  recompense 973.1
  divine ~ 976.5, 9
atonic helpless 158.9
  silent 403.7
atony
  impotence 158.2
  weakness 160.1
atop 210.7
atrabilious 901.7
atrium
  vestibule 191.17
  ear 418.5
atrocious
  terrible 649.8
  disreputable 874.8
  cruel 907.9
  wicked 945.16
atrocity

  ill-treatment 649.4
  misuse 679.1
  offense 900.5
  malevolent act 907.4
  indignity 929.2
  crime 947.2
atrophy
  contraction 195.1
  ailment 655.11
  deterioration 659.2
atropine 662.7
Atropos 601.4
attach add 37.3
  join 43.6
  (suspend 214.6)
  dispossess 789.11
  enamor 897.13
  cite 969.10
attaché 746.1
attached 897.15
become attached to 897.12
attachment
  dispossession 789.2
  love 897.1
  fidelity 939.4
attack *n.* spasm 315.7
  vocal delivery 580.3
  ~ of illness 655.3
  assault 716
  (encounter 276.2)
  (fight 720.2)
  (campaign 722.4, 5)
  accusation 1003.1
attack *v.* assault 716.5
  (strike 276.8)
  (resist 719.3)
  (contend 720.8)
  (war 722.9)
  accuse 938.4
attacker 716.4
  (combatant 726.1)
attack plane 273a.2
attaghan See yataghan
attain reach 292.7
  accomplish 729.2
attainability 470.2
attainable
  approachable 286.4
  practicable 470.6
  not attainable 471.7
attainder taint 651.2
  condemnation 971.1
attainment
  arrival 292.1
  knowledge 490.2
  learning 539.1
  accomplishment 698.3; 729.1
  acquisition 775.1
attaint *n.* 379.1
attaint *v.*
  discolor 440a.2
  prove guilty 971.2
attaintment, attainture 971.1
attar, atar 400.2
attemper imbue 41.8
  moderate 174.5
attempered 820.3
attempt *n.* 675.1

  (experiment 463.1)
  (effort 686.1)
attempt *v.* 675.3
  (experiment 463.8)
  (undertake 676.2)
attend
  accompany 88.6
  ensue 117.2
  be present 186.9
  (be a spectator 444.3)
  listen 418.11
  be attentive 457.4
  ~ school 539.4
  doctor 662.24
  aid 707.10
  serve 746.8
  ~ divine service 990.14
attend to
  give attention 457.4
  care for 459.6
  ~ ~ business 625.8
  ~ ~ orders 743.2
  punish 972.5
attendance
  accompaniment 88.5
  (afterpart 65.2)
  (procession 69.3)
  (servants 746.6)
  presence 186.6
  (assembly 72.3)
  (theatergoers 599.24)
  (divine service 990.7)
attendant *n.*
  accompaniment 88.1, 3
  attender 186.7
  follower 281.2
  auxiliary 711.1
  servant 746.1
attendant *adj.*
  accompanying 88.8
  later 117.3
attender 186.7
  (spectator 444.1)
  (theatergoer 599.23)
attention *n.*
  hearing 418.2
  heed 457
  (thought 451.1)
  respect 928.1
pay attention
  attend 457.4
  (be careful 459.3)
  pay homage 928.5
pay attentions to
  pay respects 894.8
  court 902.7
pay no attention
  disregard 458.5
  neglect 460.4
  not observe 773.3
  snub 930.7
stand at attention
  attention 457.8
  await 507.5
attention *int.* 418.16; 457.10

attentive heedful 457.9
 (vigilant 459.8)
 respectful 928.8
attentiveness 457.1
attenuate v.
 decrease 36.4
 dilute 160.9
 thin 203.8
 rarefy 322.3
 pulverize 330.7
attenuate adj.
 thin 203.11
 finespun 205.7
attenuation
 decrease 36.1
 contraction 195.1
 thinness 203.4
 rarefaction 322.2
 deterioration 659.2
 (pulverization 330.2)
attest n.
 testimony 467.2
 certification 474.2
 attestation 535.1
attest v. testify 467.8
 adduce 467.10
 certify 474.6
 depose 535.4
 indicate 550.18
 promise 768.3
attestant 467.6
attestation
 testimony 467.2
 certification 474.2
 affirmation 535.1
 voucher 550.11
attestator, attester, attestor 467.6
attic n. loft 191.19
 (top 210.4)
 head 210.3
Attic adj. pure 42.5
 speech 578.4
 wit 842.1, 9
 refined 850.5
Atticism, atticism, Attic salt
 elegance 578.1
 wit 842.1
Attila 913.1
attire n. 225.1
attire v. 225.41
attitude
 circumstance 8.1
 posture 184.2
 frame of mind 820.1
attitudinarian 882.5
 (pretender 548.3)
 (affector 853.4)
 (fop 854.1)
 (hypocrite 988.6)
attitudinarianism 882.2
attitudinize 882.6
attorney
 functionary 758.2
 deputy 759.1
 lawyer 968.1
attract pull 288.3
 lure 617.4
 (tempt 865.14)

enamor 897.13
attract attention
 strike 457.6
 be ostentatious 882.6
attractant 288.2
attraction
 pulling power 157.3
 pull 288
 allurement 617.1
attractive
 drawing 288.4
 alluring 617.5
 (delightful 829.8)
 (likable 897.17)
 beautiful 845.9
 (tasteful 850.5)
attractiveness 617.1
attractivity 288.1
attractor, attrahent n. 288.2
 (lure 617.2)
attrahent adj. 288.4
attributable
 assignable 155.4
 (derivative 154.5)
 due 924.11
attribute n. 88.1
attribute v. 155.3
attribution 155
attrite 331.4
attrited 330.8
attrition 330.2
attritive 331.4
attritus 330.3
attune n. 413.1, 4
attune v.
 harmonize 413.24
 adapt 673.6
attune adj. 413.26
attunement 413.1
attuned 613.12
atween 228.13
aubade 415.3, 10, 17
auburn 433.5; 434.12
au courant 490.13
auction n. 796.2
 at auction, by auction 796.9
auction v. 796.6
auction bridge 840.12
auctioneer n.
 functionary 758.2
 salesman 797.5
auctioneer v. 796.6
audacious
 defiant 715.3
 daring 861.8
 insolent 885.9
audacity
 courage 861.1
 rashness 863.1
 insolence 885.2
audibility 418.1
 (sound 402.1)
audible
 hearable 402.10
 (auditory 418.13)
 heard 418.12
audience
 hearing 418.2
 (attender 186.7)

(spectators 444.2)
 (theatergoers 599.24)
 listeners 418.8
 conference 588.3
 council 696.2
give audience to 418.11
audient 418.7
audit n. 811.4
audit v. count 85.8
 examine 461.17
 take stock 811.8
audition
 musical ∼ 415.17
 hearing 418.1, 2
 examination 461.3
 trial 463.1
 conference 588.3
 performance 599.8
auditor hearer 418.7
 accountant 811.6
auditorium
 assembly 189.10
 theater 599.11
auditory n.
 audience 418.8
 auditorium 599.11
auditory adj. 418.13
 (acoustic 402.12)
auditory canal, auditory nerve, auditory tube 418.5
au fait aware 490.13
 capable 698.12
au fond 5.8
auf Wiedersehen 293.14
Augean stable 653.10
auger n. 262
auger v. 260.14
aught 51.1
augment n. 39.1
augment v.
 increase 35.3, 4
 (reinforce 37.4)
 enlarge 194.8
augmentation
 increase 35.1
 (addition 37.1)
 (expansion 194.1)
 adjunct 39.1
 music 415.5
augur n. 513.2
augur v.
 presage 511.7, 9
 ∼ well 858.8
augural 511.11
augury
 divination 511.2
 foreboding 511.6
 omen 512.1
august noble 642.10
 eminent 31.14; 873.18
 respected 928.9
Augustinian 996.11
Augustinianism 451.9
auk 310.3
auld 124.6
au naturel 298.52
aunt 11.3
aura emanation 349.1

sensation 380.1
 halo 420.13
 astral ∼ 980a.3; 994.12
 aural 418.13
aureate 436.6
aurelia 129.8
aureole circle 247.2
 halo 420.13
aureolin 436.4
au revoir 293.14
auricle 418.5
auricomous 436.6
auricular
 auditory 418.13
 confidential 528.21
auriculate 418.14
Auriga 318.6
auriphone 418.6
aurist
 otologist 418.10
 doctor 662.19
aurochs 366.13
aurora dawn 125.1
 nimbus 420.12, 13
 semidarkness 422.2
Aurora 125.1
aurora australis, aurora borealis 420.12
auscultate 418.11
auscultation 418.1
auscultator 418.6, 7
auspicate begin 66.5
 foreshow 511.9
auspice 512.1
 (prediction 511.1)
auspices
 protectorship 664.2
 supervision 693.2
 patronage 707.2
 (influence 175.1)
under the auspices of
 in charge of 693.7
 by authority of 737.17
auspicious
 opportune 134.7
 of good omen 512.4
 (predictive 511.11)
 (fortunate 734.8)
 propitious 858.11
Aussie 188.9
austere pungent 392.5
 severe 739.5
 gruff 895.7
 ascetic 955.3
austerity
 pungency 392.1
 severity 739.1
 gruffness 895.2
 asceticism 955.1
Austin friar 996.11
Austral 560.4
Australia 182.3
Australian n. 188.9
Australian adj. 188.11
Austroasiatic languages 560.4
austromancy 511.3
Austronesian languages 560.4

authentic — avoidless

authentic
  evidential 467.11
  authoritative 474.13
  genuine 494.12
  (real 1.8)
  (unimitated 20.3)
  (orthodox 82.10)
  (good 648.8)
  orthodox 983a.7
authenticate
  confirm 467.9
  demonstrate 478.2
authentication
  confirmation 467.3
  demonstration 478.1
  ratification 488.4
  (acceptance 771.3)
authenticity
  nonimitation 20.1
  genuineness 494.2
  (orthodoxy 983a.1)
author *n.* cause 153.1
  producer 164.1
  writer 593.15
  (recorder 553.1)
  (poet 597.10)
  (playwright 599.22)
  contriver 626.8
author *v.* 590.14
authoritative
  authentic 474.13;
    494.12
  (doctrinal 484.16)
  oracular 498.11
  directive 693.6
  ruling 737.15
  (influential 175.10)
  (commanding 741.8)
  (compulsory 744.3)
  (directing 693.6)
  orthodox 983a.7
authorities 745.8
authority
  testimony 467.4
  (warranty 771.1)
  wise man 500.1
  informant 527.5
  power 737
  (potency 157.1)
  (jurisdiction 965.1)
  commission 755.1
  warrant 760.2
authorization
  authority 737.1
  commission 755.1
  permission 760.1
authorize
  commission 755.4
  permit 760.4
  legitimatize 963.4
authorized 924.10
  (authoritative 737.15)
  (permissible 760.6)
authorship
  composition 54.2, 590.2
  (production 161.3)
  literary power 569.1
auto *n.* 272.15
auto *v.* 266.18

autobiographer 553.2
autobiographical 594.7
autobiography 594.2
autobolide, autobus, autocab etc. 272.15
autochthon 188.8
autochthonous 188.11
autocracy
  government 737.4
  despotism 739.2
autocrat 745.2
autocratic
  overruling 737.15, 16
  despotic 739.5
auto-da-fé 384.3
autodidactic 490.15
Autogiro, autogiro 273a.1
autograph
  inscription 551.1
  recorder 553.3
  name 564.2
  handwriting 590.3
  signature 550.11
autographic 551.9
autography
  signature 550.11
  name 564.2
  handwriting 590.1, 3
autohypnosis 994.6
autointoxication 655.13
autoist 268.10
autoluminescence 420.11
automat 298.42
automatic *n.* 727.10
automatic *adj.*
  self-moving 266.27
  instinctive 477a.4
  involuntary 601.14
automatism 994.5
automatist 994.14
automaton
  existence 1.1
  necessitarian 601.7
automobile *n.* 272.15
automobile *v.* 266.18
automobile *adj.* 266.27
automobilist 268.10
automotive 266.27
autonomous 748.17
autonomy
  government 737.4
  independence 748.3
autoplagiarism 791.1
autopsy *n.*
  post mortem 363.18
  sight 441.2
  examination 461.3
autopsy *v.* 461.17
autoptic
  distinct 446.5
  manifest 525.4
autorotation 267a.24
autosuggestion 994.6
autotruck 272.10, 15
autotype *n.*
  engraving 558.3
  type 591.6
autotype *v.* 591.14
autotypy

  engraving 558.1
  printing 591.1
autumn
  season 126a.4
  old age 128.2
autumnal 126a.6
autumnal equinox 126a.4
auxiliaries 726.6
auxiliary *n.* aid 707.5
  confederate 711
  (servant 746.1)
auxiliary *adj.*
  additional 37.7
  assistant 707.12
auxiliary language 560.5
avail *n.* use 644.1
  expedient 646.2
  benefit 648.2
  of no avail 645.8
avail *v.* suffice 639.3
  be useful 644.2
  benefit 648.6
  avail oneself of
    turn to account 134.6
    use 677.5
availability 644.1
available 644.8
avails profits 775.2
  receipts 810.1
avalanche 306.3
avania 812.2
avant-courier 64.1
avant-propos 64.2
avarice
  parsimony 819.1
  greed 865.4
avaricious 819.4
avast! cease! 142.8
  navigation 267.69
avatar
  transformation 140.2
  ~ **of Vishnu** 979.4
avaunt 297.23
ave! 883.7; 894.15
Ave Maria, Ave Mary 990.3
avenge 919.4
avengement 919.1
avenger 919.3
avenging 919.6
avenue hedge 371.6
  path 627.2, 3
  (inlet 294.5)
  (outlet 295.5)
aver
  acknowledge 488.9
  affirm 535.3
  say 582.6
average *n.* mean 29.1
  generality 78.4
  on an average 29.5
  (generally 78.15)
average *v.* 29.2
average *adj.*
  mean 29.3
  mediocre 736.3
averment
  testimony 467.2

  affirmation 535.1
Avernus 982.2
Averroism 451.10
aversation 603.1
averse contrary 14.5
  unwilling 603.5
  disliking 867.7
  (hating 898.5)
averseness 867.2
aversion
  unwillingness 603.1
  dislike 867.2
  (phobia 860.4)
  hatred 898.1, 2
  have an aversion for 867.4
avert 706.5
  (disincline 616.3)
  (remedy 662.24)
avert the eyes 441.17
  (not look 442.5)
Aves 366.22
Avesta 986.1
Avestan 560.4
aviary cote 189.7
  birdhouse 370.3
aviate 267a.30, 31
aviatic 267a.37
aviation 267a.1
  (air service 726.9)
aviator 269a.1
  (workman 690.10)
aviatorial 267a.37
aviatress, aviatrice, aviatrix 269a.1
avichi, avici 982.1
avicular 368.19
avid eager 682.18
  fervent 821.6
  desirous 865.17
avidity
  eagerness 682.3
  avarice 819.1
  greed 865.4
avigate 267a.30
avigation 267a.1
avigator 269a.1
avion 273a.1
avion-canon 273a.2
aviso tip 527.3
  news 532.1
  warning 668.1
  advice 695.1
avocado 308.31
avocation hobby 625.5
  diversion 840.1
avocational 625.11
avoid evade 623.6
  (recede 287.2)
  (be unwilling 603.4)
  (not observe 773.3)
  (dislike 867.4)
  (abstain 953.5)
  snub 930.7
avoidable 623.11
avoidance 623
  (truancy 187.5)
  (escape 671.1)
  (idleness 683.8)
  (seclusion 893.2)
  (abstinence 953.2)
avoidless 601.11

712

avolate flee 623.10
  escape 671.6
avolation
  avoidance 623.1
  escape 671.1
avouch *n.*
  affirmation 535.2
  promise 768.1
avouch *v.* testify 467.8
  affirm 535.4
  promise 768.3
avouchment
  affirmation 535.2
  promise 768.1
avow *n.* 535.2
avow *v.*
  acknowledge 488.9
  confess 529.5
  affirm 535.4
  promise 768.1, 3
avowal, avowance
  confession 529.2
  affirmation 535.2
  promise 768.1
avowed 525.4
avulsion
  sunderance 44.2
  extraction 301.2
await approach 121.6
  impend 152.2
  expect 507.5
  (wait 133.7)
awake *v.* 824.2
awake *adj.*
  attentive 457.9
  vigilant 459.8
  aware 490.13
  sagacious 498.10
  alert 682.17
  become awake to
    527.11
awaken
  stimulate 171.7
  be informed 527.11
  excite 824.2
award *n.*
  judgment 480.1
  trophy 733.1
  (reward 973.1)
award *v.*
  pass judgment 480.9
  give 784.8
  (reward 973.3)
aware 490.12, 13
  (sensible 375.6)
  (conscious 450.9)
  (sagacious 498.10)
  be aware of 450.7
awareness 490.1
away absent 187.10
  distantly 196.6
  hence 293.10
  begone 297.23
  escaped 671.7
  away back 122.14
awe *n.* respect 928.1
  fear 860.1
  wonder 870.1
awe *v.* daunt 860.11
  inspire fear 860.10
  astonish 870.3
    command respect
    928.7
aweather 236.8
awe-inspiring 860.15
awe-strike
  astonish 870.3
  command respect
    928.7
awe-struck
  fear-struck 860.14
  amazed 870.6
awful *adj.*
  terrible 649.8
  fearful 860.15
awful, awfully *adv.*
  remarkably 31.21,
    23
  badly 649.11
awhile 111.8
awkward
  pregnant 168.9
  grammar 579.3
  clumsy 699.12
  embarrassing 704.9
  unmanageable
    704.10
  annoying 830.12
  ungraceful 846.8
awkwardness
  pregnancy 168.2
  bungling 699.3
awkward squad
  bunglers 701
  raw recruits 726.5
awl 262
  (edge tool 253.6)
awless, aweless
  fearless 861.8
  unastonished 871.3
  brazen 885.10
  disrespectful 929.5
awl-shaped 253.11
A.W.O.L. 187.5, 10
  go A.W.O.L.
    play truant 187.8
    take French leave
    748.9
awn point 253.2
  bristle 256.7
awned 253.11
awning 223.2, 3
awny 253.11
awry
  crooked 217.13, 17
  (distorted 243.5)
  wrong 649.11
ax, axe cutter 253.6
  execution 975.4
  weapon 727.4
  give the ax 297.12
axial 222.4
axinomancy 511.3
axiom 496.2
  (premise 476.4)
axiomatic 496.5
axis 312.5
  (focus 74.1)
  (support 215.6)
  (center 222.2)
axle 312.5
  (support 215.6)
axle box 312.5
axlesmith 690.6
axle spindle, axletree
    312.5
axmaker, axemaker
    690.8
Axminster 219.5
ayah guardian 664.3
  lady's maid 746.2
aye, ay *n.*
  eternity 112.1
  vote 609.3
aye, ay *adv.*
  always 112.5
  yes 488.14
aye, aye! 267.69
Aymara 560.4
Azazel 978.2
azimuth
  horizon 213.4
  direction 278.2
azimuth circle 212.2
azoic inorganic 358.4
  lifeless 360.8
azote poison 663.5
  whip 975.1
Azrael death 360.2
  angel 977.1
Aztec 434.5
azure *n.* 438.2, 4
azure *v.* 438.5
azure *adj.* 438.6
azure stone 438.3
azurite blue 438.2
azygous 87.7

B

ba 994.11
B.A. 492.1
Baal
  productiveness
    168.1
  deity 979.6
  idol 991.4
baas
  superintendent
    694.1
  master 745.1
babble *n.* discord 414.2
  twaddle 517.3
  gossip 532.3
  chatter 584.2
  small talk 588.2
babble *v.* ripple 348.19
  murmur 405.5
  dote 503.9
  talk nonsense 517.6
  gossip 532.7
  be loquacious 584.4
babblement
  twaddle 517.5
  gossip 532.3
  chatter 584.2
  small talk 588.2
babbler dotard 501.3
  newsmonger 532.5
  chatterer 584.3
babbling 499.13
babe girl 129.5
  infant 129.6
  endearment 902.4
Babel turmoil 39.4
  discord 414.2
  gibberish 563.4
babirusa, babiroussa,
    babirussa 366.7
babish 499.16
Babism, Babiism
    984.11
Babist 984.21
baboo, babu
  scribe 590.11
  clerk 553.1
baboon monkey 366.16
  ugly 846.3
baby *n.* girl 129.5
  infant 129.6
  weakling 160.4, 5
  childish person
    501.4
  coward 862.2
  endearment 902.4
baby *v.* 161.9
baby *adj.*
  infantile 127.7
  little 193.8
baby blue 438.2
baby bunting 129.6
baby carriage 272.11
baby grand 417.6
babyhood
  infancy 127.3
  senility 499.5
babyish infantile 127.7
  senile 499.16
babyism 565.3
Babylonian 124.2
baccate 354.5
Bacchae 959.1
bacchanal, bacchana-
    lian
  drunken revelry
    959.3
  wassailer 959.11
bacchanalianism,
    bacchante 959.1
bacchic 959.21
Bacchus
  intoxication 959.1, 4
  god 979.2
bach *n.* 903.2
bach *v.* 904.4
bachelor
  academic degree
    877.3
  celibate 904.2
bachelor girl 904.3
bachelorhood 904.1
Bachelor of Arts 877.3
  (student 541.5)
bacillus 193.4
back *n.* rear 235.1, 3
  convexity 250.2
  ship 273.7
  back of beyond 196.3
  behind one's back
    behind 235.14
    surreptitiously
    528.24
  in back of 235.14
  on one's back
    impotent 158.8

back — bag

back (*continued*)
  horizontally 213.10
  sick 655.23
  unsuccessful 732.9
  turn one's back upon
  turn back 283.6
  repulse 289.2
  pay no attention 458.5
  ignore 460.5
  avoid 623.6, 10
  abandon 624.3
  oppose 708.2
  refuse 764.3
  be unsociable 893.7
  snub 930.7
back *v.* carry 270.8
  go back 283.5
  bet on 621.18
  aid 707.8
back an anchor 267.12
back and fill
  navigate 267.24
  alternate 314.10
  be uncertain 475.6
  be irresolute 605.4
back down
  go back 283.5
  recant 607.9
back out
  go back 283.5
  abandon 624.3
back the wrong horse
  err 495.7
  bungle 699.7
back up
  support 215.26
  go back 283.5
  motivate 615.7
  second 707.8
back water
  retard 275.7
  go astern 267.25
  back up 283.5
  recant 607.9
back *adj.* rustic 183.3
  rear 235.9
back *adv.*
  formerly 122.14
  rearward 235.16
  backward 283.8
back and forth
  interchangeably 148.5
  alternately 314.14
backache 378.1
back answer 930.3
  (retort 462.1)
backbite 934.3
backbiter 936.1
backbiting 934.1
backbone essence 5.2
  spine 235.4
  (foundation 215.3)
  (center 222.2)
  resolution 604.1
  courage 861.1
backcap 934.3
back country *n.* 183.1
back-country *adj.* 183.3

back door rear 235.1
  door 260.4
  escape 671.3
  covert way 530.4
backdown 725.2
backdrop 599.15
backer
  theater 599.17
  upholder 711.4
  (benefactor 912.1)
backfire 173.9
backflow 348.2
backfriend 891.1
backgammon 840.11
background
  distance 196.3
  surroundings 227.2
  rear 235.1
in the background
  behind 235.14
  secretly 528.24
  in disrepute 874.9
keep in the background
  conceal 528.10
  be modest 881.3
  (disrepute 874.4)
  (be humble 879.2)
  seclude oneself 893.6
backhand *n.* 276.3
backhand, backhanded *adj.*
  oblique 217.9
  indirect 311.6
  insulting 929.5
backhander 276.3
backhouse 653.9
backing 707.2
backlash 277.1
backlog
  firewood 388.3
  reserve fund 636.2
backpedal 275.7
backplate 717.2
backrope 273.10
back-scratcher
  sycophant 886.2
  flatterer 935.2
back-scratching 886.4
back seat
  inferiority 34.1
  seat 215.22
  rear 235.1
backset *n.* 735.3
backset *v.* 371.8
backsettler 188.6
backside 235.5
back side 235.1
backslapper
  sycophant 886.2
  flatterer 935.2
backslide *n.* 661.1
backslide *v.* 661.3
  (retrograde 283.5)
  (deteriorate 659.6)
  (be sinful 945.9)
  (fall from grace 988.9)
backslider 607.5
  (unbeliever 485.4)
  (recidivist 661.2)

(religion 984.12; 988.5; 989.4)
backsliding *n.* 661.1
  (regression 283.1)
  (apostasy 607.2)
  (deterioration 659.1)
  (heterodoxy 984.1)
  (perversion 988.3)
backsliding *adj.* 661.4
  (apostate 607.11)
  (heterodox 984.22)
backstage 599.28
back stairs stairs 305.2
  covert way 530.4
  backway 627.2
backstay 273.10
back street 627.3
backswept 235.9
backward *adj.*
  late 133.8
  uncultured 491.11
  reluctant 603.5
backward, backwards *adv.* late 133.11
  rearward 235.16; 283.8
backward and forward, backwards and forwards
  interchangeably 148.5
  alternately 314.14
backwardation 813.1
backwash 267a.16
backwater 283.2
in a backwater 893.10
backway
  covert way 530.4
  path 627.2
backwood, backwoods *adj.* 183.3
backwoods *n.* 183.1
  (inland 221.3)
backwoodsman
  backsettler 188.6
  woodsman 371.2
bacon 298.23
bacteria fungi 369.4
  blight 663.2
bactericidal 662.25
bactericide 662.8
bacteriologist 357.7
bacteriology 655.19
bacteriophobia 860.4
bacterium 193.4
bad *n.* evil 649.2
  (wrong 923.1)
  wickedness 945.1
bad *adj.* nasty 395.7
  evil 649.8
  (inferior 34.5)
  (inauspicious 512.5)
  (mean 643.12)
  (inexpedient 647.3)
  (imperfect 651.4)
  (insalubrious 657.3)
  (malevolent 907.6)
  (wrong 923.4)
  (reprehensible 932.14)

tainted 653.17
unwholesome 657.3
putrified 659.13
unsatisfactory 832.7
wicked 945.11
from bad to worse 735.10; 835.6
in a bad way
  sick 655.23
  impaired 659.12
  in danger 665.8
too bad
  regrettable 833.5
  disreputable 874.8
badaud 501.1
bad blood hate 898.1
  ill-humor 901.1
  malevolence 907.1
bad faith 940.2
  (dissembling 544.2)
  (nonobservance 773.2)
badge
  indication 550.2, 6, 12
  ~ of honor 733.1
  ~ of authority 747.1
badger *n.* 792.6
badger *v.*
  blackmail 791.13
  harass 830.5
bad habit 613.6
bad humor, bad humour 901.1
badinage
  witticism 842.4
  banter 856.1
bad influence 649.3
  (evil spirit 980.2)
bad luck 735.2
badly 649.11
badly off
  unfortunate 735.9
  poor 804.7
bad manners 895.1
badminton 840.11
badness 649
  (painfulness 830.1)
  (malevolence 907.1)
bad taste
  language 579.1
  vulgarity 851
bad-tempered 901.7
bad times 735.4
Baedeker
  itinerary 266.9
  guidebook 694.7
baff after 235.15
  astern 267.68
baffle *n.* 475.2
baffle *v.* perplex 475.8
  disappoint 509.2
  thwart 706.7
bafflement
  perplexity 475.2
  disappointment 509.1
baft after 235.15
  astern 267.68
bag *n.* hussy 129.5
  sack 101.4
  purse 802.2

bag — Baluchi

prostitute 962.2
in the bag 474.9
bag v. load 184.13
  bulge 250.7
  secure 775.6
  capture 789.9
  steal 791.9
bag and baggage 780.6
bagatelle music 415.3
  trifle 643.3
  game 840.11
baggage hussy 129.5
  luggage 270.4
  impediment 780.6
  strumpet 962.2
baggage car 272.19
baggage train 272.18
baggala 273.2
baggy 47.3
bagmaker 690.8
bagman 758.5; 797.2
bagnio 961.7
bagpipe n. whistle
  410.4
  instrument 417.4
bagpipe v. 416.18
bags multitude 102.2
  trousers 225.21
baguio 349.13
bah! nonsense 497.5
  pooh! 930.11
bahadur 877.2
bail n. ladle 191.14
  handle 215.7
  security 771.1, 2
  go bail
    be certain 474.5
    believe 484.7
    give security 771.5
bail ladle 270.10
  ~ out 267a.36
bailie 745.9
bailiff steward 694.5
  officer 745.9, 10
  retainer 746.1
  functionary 758.2
bailiwick
  territory 181.2
  city government
    737.4
  civil authorities
    745.9
  bureau 965.2
bairagi 996.8
Bairam 840.2
bairn 129.3
bait n. fulcrum 215.5
  lunch 298.35
  lure 617.2
  (snare 545.4)
  take the bait
    be credulous 486.3
    be deceived 547.3
bait v. ensnare 545.9
  lure 617.2
  fish 622.8
  torment 830.5
bake dry 340.5
  cook 384.18, 19
bakehouse 191.16;
  386.4
Bakelite 356a.1

baker 690.8
bakery
  cookroom 386.4
  market 799.4
bakeshop 799.4
bakestone 342.4
baksheesh, bakshish
  gratuity 784.3
  bribe 618.2
balance n.
  equality 27.1
  mean 29.1
  remains 40.1
  surplus 40.4
  stability 150.1
  symmetry 242.1
  weighing instrument 319.5
  (measure 466.4)
  comparison 464.1
  levelheadedness
    498.4
  sanity 502.1
  elegance 578.1
  money 800.10
  accounts 811.1
  equanimity 826.3
Balance n. 318.6
balance v. equal 27.6, 7
  compensate 30.5
  ~ the books 85.8
  symmetrize 242.3
  weigh 319.8
  compare 464.2
  discriminate 465.2
  measure 466.10
  waver 605.4
  decide between 609.7
  ~ accounts 807.7
    811.7
balanced
  symmetrical 242.4
  equitable 941.3
balance sheet 811.5
balcony 599.11
bald unclad 226.8
  hairless 226.10
  uninteresting 843.5
  unornamented 849.4
baldachin, baldaquin,
  baldakin
  canopy 223.3
  church 1000.3
Balder, Baldr
  beauty 845.3
  god 979.3
balderdash
  nonsense 497.5;
    517.2
  grandiloquence
    577.2
baldhead 226.3
bald-headed
  hairless 226.10
  unrigged 273.16
bald-headedness,
  baldness, baldpate
  226.1
bald-pated 226.10
bald-patedness 226.3
baldric zone 230.2
  circle 247.2

garment 225.34
Baldur See Balder
bale n. bundle 72.5
  load 190.1
  weight 319.1
  mental suffering
    828.1
bale v. 270.10
baleen 325.2
balefire 382.8
  (signal 423.5)
baleful painful 378.7
  harmful 649.10
balefully 31.23
Balinese 560.4
balista See ballista
balistraria 717.3
balk n. beam 215.12
  disappointment
    509.1
balk v. thwart 706.7
  disappoint 509.2
balked
  disappointed 509.4
  frustrated 732.9
balker 271.6
balky 606.6
ball n. sphere 249.2
  (rotation 312.4)
  projectile 284.5
  missile 727.14
  dance 840.6
  (party 892.5)
  game 840.11
  toy 840.16
  play ball 709.4
ball v. 249.5
ball up
  complicate 61.5
  confuse 458.9
  perplex 475.8
ballad n. 415.7, 10
ballad v.
  compose 415.26
  sing 416.20
ballade 597.2
ballader
  musician 416.14
  poet 597.10
ballad horn 417.4
ballast
  compensation 30.2
  counterweight 319.1
  stone 342.4
  levelheadedness
    498.4
  safeguard 666.2
  money 800.1
  equanimity 826.3
balled up
  confused 59.8, 12
  (misinterpreted
    523.3)
  bewildered 475.16
ballet
  musicale 415.17
  drama 599.3
  dance 840.7
ballet dancer, ballet
  girl 840.9
  (performer 599.19)
ballista, balista 727.9

ballistic 284.16
ballistics
  gunnery 284.9; 727.2
  knightly skill 722.2
ballonet, ballonette
  273a.12
balloon n.
  aerostat 273a.5
  elastic 325.2
balloon v. 267a.30
  balloon in 267a.34
balloonation 267a.1
ballooner 273.13
balloonery 267a.1
balloonist 269a.1
balloon sail 273.13
ballot n. list 86.1
  vote 609.3
ballot v. 609.10
ballot box 609.3
balloter 609.4
ballplayer 840.17
ballproof 664.11
ballroom 840.14
bally 31.24
ballyhack 162.1
ballyhoo n. noise 404.2
  publicity 531.3
  publicist 531.6
  sales talk 796.3
ballyhoo v.
  be noisy 404.6
  publicize 531.8
ballyhooer
  publicist 531.6
  solicitor 767.1; 797.4
ballywack, ballywrack
  162.1
balm n. lubricant 332.2
  perfume 400.2
  medicine 662.4, 6
balm v. 363.22
balm in Gilead
  solace 834.2
  hope 858.3
Balmoral 225.25
balmy n. 683.5
balmy adj.
  intoxicated 959.21
  fragrant 400.10
  imbecile 499.13
  insane 503.12
  sleep-inducing
    683.17
  relieving 834.7
balneal 337.6
balneary 652.4
balneation
  swimming 267.9
  bathing 652.2
  (watering 337.2)
balneatory 652.15
baloney 497.5; 517.2
balsam
  perfume 400.2, 3
  medicine 662.4
balsamic
  remedial 662.25
  relieving 834.7
Balthasar, Balthazar
  500.3
Baluchi 560.4

baluster — barbarism 716

baluster 215.16
balustrade
　support 215.16
　fence 232.2
bam *n.* sham 544.2
　hoax 545.3, 6
bam *int.* 406.13
bambino 129.6
bamboo 367.8
bamboozle *n.* 545.1
bamboozle *v.*
　perplex 475.8
　deceive 545.7
　(hoodwink 528.13)
　swindle 791.12
bamboozlement 545.1
bamboozler
　cheat 548.2
　swindler 792.8
ban *n.*
　prohibition 761.1
　curse 908.1
　under the ban 761.4
ban *v.* banish 297.11
　prohibit 761.2
banal 843.6
banality
　trite saying 496.3
　triteness 843.2
banana fruit 298.31
　plant 369.8
banana split 298.13
band *n.*
　fastening 45.2
　company 72.3
　line 200.4
　strip 205.5
　garment 231.1
　zone 230.2
　circle 247.2
　hair 256.3
　musicians 416.9
　instruments 417.1
　bandage 662.14
　party 712.1
band *v.* 43.5
band together
　league 48.4
　co-operate 709.4
bandage *n.*
　fastening 45.2
　supporter 215.2
　wrapper 223.11
　muffler 408a.3
　dressing 662.14
bandage *v.* tie 43.6
　repair 660.11
　dress wounds 662.24
bandbox 191.8
bandeau 225.25
banderole, banderol
　550.13
bandicoot 366.17
banding 847.3
bandit 792.3
band major 416.13
bandman 416.1
bandmaster 416.13
bandobust See **bundobust**
Band of Hope 953.4
bandog dog 366.6

guard 717.6
bandoleer 191.8
bandonion 417.4
bandore 417.2
bandy *v.*
　interchange 148.3
　brandish 315.8
　∼ about 531.7
　contend 720.8
bandy words
　argue 476.11
　converse 588.7
bandy, bandy-legged
　adj. 243.5
bane *n.* 663
　(evil 649.2)
　(adversity 735.1)
　(affliction 830.2)
bane *v.* 649.6
baneful 649.10
　(insalubrious 657.3)
banewort 663.6
bang *n.* hair 256.3
　blow 276.3
　clap 406.2
　(explosion 173.3)
　drug 662.7
bang *n.* See **bhang**
bang *v.* strike 276.8
　clap 406.7, 8
　(explode 173.9)
bang *adv.* 406.12
bang *int.* 406.13
banger
　large thing 192.6
　lie 546.2
　coin 800.4
banging vast 31.8
　huge 192.15
bangle 847.7
banish 297.11
　(exclude 55.3;
　　893.7)
　(dislocate 185.2)
　(transport 270.8)
　(punish 972.10)
banishment 297.3
　(exclusion 55.1;
　　893.7)
　(transportation
　　270.2)
　(emigration 295.2)
banister 215.16
banjo
　shovel 191.14; 386.3
　instrument 417.2
banjoist 416.3
banjorine, banjoukulele 417.2
bank *n.* shallow 209.2
　incline 217.2
　shore 342.2
　printing 591.5
　stakes 621.4
　hidden danger 667.1
　obstruction 706.2
　fortification 717.3
　treasury 802.1
　(storehouse 636.4)
　bank 840.12
bank *v.* aviate 267a.31
　store 636.7

bank on, bank upon
　rely on 484.7
　plan on 507.6
bankbook 811.5
banker
　moneylender 787.2
　financier 797.6
　treasurer 801
　game 840.12
bank examiner 811.6
bank holiday 840.5
banking 267a.24
bank note 800.6
bank roll 800.12
bankrupt *n.* 808.4
　(failure 732.4)
　(poor man 804.3)
bankrupt *v.* 804.6
　(break 808.7)
bankrupt *adj.* 808.10
　(poor 804.7)
go bankrupt 808.6
　(fail 732.5)
bankruptcy 808.2
　(want 640.3)
　(failure 732.1)
　(poverty 804.1)
banlieue, banlieu 227.2
banner *n.* caption 66.3
　advertisement 531.4
　flag 550.13
banner *adj.* 33.8
banneret 875.5
bannerman 531.6
bannerol 550.13
banquet *n.* 298.37
　(party 892.6)
banquet *v.* feast 298.44
　revel 840.21
banquette 717.3
banshee, banshie
　fairy 979.9
　spirit 980a.1
bant 203.8
bantam *n.* 193.2
Bantam *n.* 366.23
bantam *adj.* 193.8
bantam cock fop 854.1
　strutter 880.3
banter *n.* ridicule 856.1
　jesting 842.4
banter *v.* 856.4
　(joke 842.8)
　(taunt 930.6)
banterer 844
bantering 856.7
bantingize 203.8
bantling child 129.3
　bastard 167.5
Bantu languages 560.4
banty *n.*
　diminutive 193.2
　fowl 366.23
banty *adj.* 193.8
banyan 367.6
banyan day
　insufficiency 640.5
　fast day 956.2
baptism
　submergence 310.2
　wetting 337.2
　naming 564.1

rite 998.5
　(sanctification
　　987.2)
baptismal 998.15
Baptist 984.14
baptistery, baptistry
　998.5; 1000.3
baptize dilute 160.9
　submerge 310.5
　name 564.6
　administer rite
　　998.14
　(sanctify 987.8)
bar *n.* fastening 45.2
　line 200.4
　shallow 209.2
　shaft 215.13
　(pole 206.4)
　pry 307.4
　island 346.1
　bear 366.15
　music 413.12; 415.22
　obstacle 706.2
　insignia 747.4
　lock 752.3
　bullion 800.15
　barroom 959.13
　tribunal 966.1
　legal profession
　　968.2
at the bar
　practicing law 968.4
　in litigation 969.14
behind bars 751.12
bar *v.* exclude 55.3
　close 261.2
　obstruct 706.4
　prohibit 761.2
　exclude 893.7
bar out exclude 55.3
　lock out 719.4
bar *prep.*
　excepting 38.11
　excluding 55.7
baragouin
　twaddle 517.3
　jargon 563.4
barb *n.* point 253.2
　bristle 256.7
　horse 271.4
　speeder 274.6
　arrowhead 727.4
barb *v.* 253.9
barbaresque 851.7
barbarian *n.* alien 57.3
　vulgar speaker 579.2
　boor 876.7
　(vulgarian 851.4)
　savage 913.3
barbarian *adj.*
　alien 57.4
　language 563.15;
　　579.3
　vulgar 851.7
　(plebeian 876.11)
barbaric alien 57.4
　vulgar 851.7
barbarism word 563
　(ungrammaticism
　　568.1)
　inelegance 579.1
　vulgarity 851.1

barbarity — basal

barbarity
  vulgarity 851.1
  cruelty 907.3
barbarous
  savage 173.14
  language 563.15;
    579.3
  (inelegant 579.3)
  vulgar 851.7
  cruel 907.9
barbate 256.13, 14
barbecue *n.*
  meat 298.19
  festivity 840.2
barbecue *v.* 384.19
barbed
  clothed 225.46
  pointed 253.12
  bristly 256.14
barbed wire 253.2
barbel filament 205.1
  beard 256.5
barbellate
  barbed 253.12
  bristly 256.14
barbican tower 206.3
  fortification 717.3
barbigerous 256.13
barblet 253.2
barbule
  filament 205.1
  point 253.2
  beard 256.5
barbulate 256.14
barbwire 253.2
barcarole, barcarolle
  415.3, 10
bard singer 416.10
  poet 597.10
bard, barde 717.2
barded 225.46
bare *v.* divest 226.4
  open 260.12
  uncover 525.2
  disclose 529.3
bare *adj.* mere 32.11
  empty 187.11
  (wanting 640.11)
  unclad 226.8
  open 260.15
  manifest 525.4
  unornamented 849.4
bareback 226.8
  ride bareback 266.19
barebone 203.6
barefaced
  unconcealed 525.4
  brazen 885.10
barefoot 226.9
barefooted 804.7
bareheaded 928.8
barely
  scarcely 32.16
  nearly 197.12
bareness 226.2
bargain *n.*
  compact 769.1
  transaction 794.3
  cheapness 815.2
  at a bargain
    for sale 796.9
    at a discount 813.4

cheaply 815.11
blind bargain
  interchange 148.1
  uncertainty 475.5
  gamble 621.2
  (rashness 863.1)
  barter 794.3
  into the bargain 37.8
bargain *v.* 794.5
  (make terms 769.6)
  (sell 796.5)
  bargain for 507.6
bargain and sale
  783.1; 794.1
barge *n.* 273.4
barge *v.* 266.16
  barge in
    intrude 228.10
    enter 294.6
    blunder into 699.9
**bargee, bargeman,
  bargemaster, barger**
  269.2
barghest, barguest
  980.2
barite 635.6
baritone, barytone
  low tone 408.6
  voice 413.14
  (music 415.13)
  horn 417.4
barium sulphate 430.4
barium yellow 436.4
bark *n.* skin 223.12, 15
  shot 406.4
  (detonation 284.4)
  ~ of a dog 412.1
bark, barque *n.* 273.1, 2
bark *v.* explode 173.9
  (shoot 284.13)
  peel 226.5
  detonate 406.8
  bay 412.2
  threaten 909.2
  ~ at 932.8
**bark up the wrong
  tree** err 495.7
  bungle 699.7
barkbound
  bound 751.11
  prudish 853.7
barkeeper
  employee 746.1
  tapster 959.12
**barkentine, barquen-
  tine** 273.2
barker
  stageman 599.17
  pistol 727.10
  salesman 758.5
  solicitor 767.1; 797.4
bar!ey fodder 298.7
  plant 367.9
barleycorn 193.2
barm 320.3
barmaid
  maidservant 746.2
  bartender 959.12
barman
  employee 746.1
  bartender 959.12
barmaster 967.1

Barmecide feast 956.2
barmote 966.2
barmy leavening 320.8
  scatterbrained
    458.13
  foolish 499.15
barmybrained
  scatterbrained
    458.13
  foolish 499.15
barn 189.5
  (enclosure 232.1)
  (menagerie 370.3)
  (storehouse 636.4)
barnacle animal 368.8
  sycophant 886.2
barnacles 445.3
barney deception 545.3
  bungle 699.4
  quarrel 713.3
  contest 720.2
barnstorm
  aviate 267a.31
  troupe 599.26
barnstormer
  aeronaut 269a.1
  actor 599.19
barnstorming 267a.1
Barnumism 577.2
Barnumize 577.5
barnyard 232.1
barograph ship 273.14
  weather gauge 338.8
barographic 338.12
barometer
  aviation 267a.29
  ship 273.14
  weather gauge 338.8
barometric 338.12
barometrograph 338.8
**barometrography,
  barometry** 338.7
baron nobleman 875.5
  (title 877.2)
  husband 903.7
baronage 875.2
baronet 875.5
baronetcy 875.9
baronial 878.7
**Baron of the Ex-
  chequer** 967.1
baroque 83.10
baroscope 338.8
baroscopic 338.12
barouche 272.4
barque See **bark**
barquentine See **barkentine**
barrack *n.* camp 189.15
  roof 223.6
  fortification 717.4
barrack *v.* 930.6
barracker 936.1
barracks 189.4, 15
barracoon 717.4
barrage *n.*
  drumming 407.3
  salvo 716.2
barrage *v.* 716.6
barrage balloon
  273a.5
barranca 198.3

barratrous 940.10
barratry 940.2
barred netlike 219.11
  striate 440.10
barrel *n.*
  receptacle 191.11
  cylinder 249.3
  measure 466.3
barrel *v.* 274.4
barrel house 959.13
barrelmaker 690.8
barrel organ 417.5
barrel roll 267a.24
barren *n.* 169.2
barren *adj.*
  nugatory 158.11
  unproductive 169.4
  fruitless 645.8
barrenness 169.1
barrens 169.2
barricade *n.* 717.3
  (fence 232.2)
  (obstacle 706.2)
barricade *v.*
  obstruct 706.4
  fortify 717.7
barrier
  obstacle 706.2
  (closure 261.1)
  fortification 717.3
  (fence 232.2)
barring
  excepting 38.11
  excluding 55.7
barring out 719.2
barrister 968.1
barristerial 968.4
barroom 959.13
  (inn 189.8)
barrow hill 206.2
  handcart 272.11
  grave 363.13
bar shot 727.14
bar sinister
  fault 651.2
  stigma 874.2
  bastardy 964.1
bartender
  employee 746.1
  tapster 959.12
barter *n.* 794
  (reciprocation 12.2)
  (interchange 148.1)
  (business 625.1)
  (transfer 783.1)
  (sale 796.1)
barter *v.* 794.4
  (interchange 148.3)
  (sell 796.5)
bartizan 717.3
barton
  messuage 189.12
  yard 232.1
  farm 371.4
barway 260.4
baryta 430.4
baryta yellow 436.4
barytone See **baritone**
basal intrinsic 5.6
  original 153.9
  bottom 211.5
  (supporting 215.28)

basalt — battologize

basalt stone 342.4
  ceramics 384.14
bas bleu pedant 492.4
  affecter 853.4
bascule bridge 627.7
base *n.* number 84.2
  cause 153.1
  bottom 211
  (rudiment 153.3)
  (lowness 207.1)
  foundation 215.3
  voice 413.14
  singer 416.10
  at the base of 207.11
  base of operations
    plan 626.1
    point of attack 716.1
base *v.* 215.26
base *adj.* low 207.7
  infamous 649.8
  vulgar 851.6
  dastardly 862.5
  disreputable 874.8
  abject 886.4
  wicked 945.16
baseball 284.5
  game 840.11
baseboard 211.1
baseborn 876.11
based 211.5
  (supported 215.28)
  (evidential 467.11)
  be based on 215.27
baselard 727.3
baseless
  unsubstantial 4.5
  unauthentic 495.16
basement cellar 191.20
  (lowness 207.1)
  base 211.1
base-minded 945.14
baseness
  inferiority 34.1
  turpitude 945.2
bashaw tyrant 739.3
  ruler 745.7
  nobleman 875.4
bashful timid 862.4
  modest 881.5
bashfulness 881.1
bashi-bazouk 726.4
Bashkir 560.4
basic intrinsic 5.6
  original 153.9
  basal 211.5
basics facts 1.2
  essentials 642.4
basilica 1000.1
basilisk monster 83.7
  evil eye 441.8
basin receptacle 191.11
  bed 211.3
  cavity 252.2
  plain 344.1
  lavatory 652.5
  anchorage 666.4
basinet, bassinet 717.2
basis
  foundation 215.3, 4
  (base 211.1)
  premise 476.4
  reason 615.1

bask luxuriate 377.4, 5
  sun oneself 384.20
  prosper 734.5
  delight 827.5, 6
basket
  receptacle 191.9
  aerostat 273a.12
basketball, basket ball 840.11
basketful fill 52.3
  load 190.1
basketmaker 690.8
bas-relief 557.6
bass low tone 408.6
  voice 413.14
  voice part 415.13
  singer 416.10
Bassalia 208.3
Bassalian 208.12
basset *n.* 446.1
basset *v.* 446.2
basset horn 417.4
bassinet 191.9
bassinet See **basinet**
bassist 416.10
basso low tone 408.6
  voice 413.14
  singer 416.10
basso buffo, basso cantante 413.14
bassoonist 416.2
basso profundo
  low tone 408.6
  voice 413.14
bassus 415.13
  (voice 413.14)
bass viol, bass violin 417.3
Bast 979.5
bastard *n.*
  bantling 167.5
  counterfeit 545.6
bastard *adj.*
  spurious 545.13
  illegitimate 964.5
bastardy 964.1
baste strike 276.8
  cook 384.19
  beat 972.6
bastille, bastile 752.1
bastinado *n.* 972.3
bastinado *v.* 972.6
bastion 717.3
bat *n.*
  ~ of an eye 113.3
  battery 158a.6
  velocity 274.1, 6
  blow 276.3
  hammer 276.4
  animal 366.17
  madman 504.1
  jargon 563.4
  club 727.7
  spree 840.3
  toy 840.16
  drinking bout 959.3
  prostitute 962.2
bat *v.* ~ around 266.14
  strike 276.8
  ~ the eyes 443.11
  ~ out 460.6
Batan 560.4

batch *n.* quantity 25.2
  quantities 31.3
  (multitude 102.2)
  collection 72.5, 6
  lump 192.5
batch *v.* 72.11
bate decrease 36.3, 4
  deduct 38.4
  discount 813.2
bateau 273.4
bateau bridge 627.7
bated breath 581.3
bath 652.3, 4
  (pool 343a.1)
Bath chair 272.11
bathe *n.* 652.3
bathe *v.* swim 267.47
  wash 652.9
  (immerse 310.5)
bathhouse 652.4
bathing
  swimming 267.9
  cleansing 652.2
bathing suit 267.9
bathmism 359.2
bathometer 208.4
bathos
  absurdity 497.1
  ridiculousness 855.1
bathrobe 225.23
bathroom 652.4
  (hot bath 386.6)
baths 662.17
bathtub
  receptacle 191.11
  washbasin 652.5
bathyal 208.12
bathyal zone 208.3
bathybic
  deep-sea 208.12
  oceanic 341.5
bathycolpian, bathycolpic 208.13
bathygraphical 341.5
bathymetric
  deep-sea 208.12
  oceanic 341.5
bathymetry 341.3
bathypelagic, bathysmal 208.12
bathysophical 341.5
batik, battik art 556.9
  ornamentation 847.3
bating 55.7
batman 637.2
batoid 366.21
baton staff 215.15
  scepter 747.1
  bend sinister 874.2; 964.1
batophobia 860.4
Batrachia 366.18
batrachian *n.* 366.18
batrachian *adj.* 368.19
Batrachomyomachy, Batrachomyomachia 722.1
bats 503.12
batta 973.2
Battak, Batak 560.4
battalion 726.7
batten *n.* 215.12

batten *v.* 734.5
batten on, batten upon feed on 298.46
  sponge on 886.3
batter *n.* gluten 352.3
  (pulp 354.2)
  printing ~ 591.5
batter *v.* destroy 162.4
  strike 276.8
  discolor 440a.2
  maltreat 649.7
  damage 659.8
  inflict pain 830.6
  beat 972.6
battered 659.12
battering-ram
  hammer 276.4
  club 727.7
battery
  electricity 158a.6
  percussives 417.10
  attack 716.1
  military unit 726.7
  gun ~ 727.11
battle *n.* 720.2
  (war 722.5)
  half the battle
    important part 642.4
    success 731.1
battle *v.* fortify 717.7
  fight 720.8
  war 722.9
battle array
  in battle array
    prepared 673.11
    embattled 722.12, 14
battle array 722.1
battle-ax, battle-axe
  old woman 130.3
  weapon 727.4
  (knife 253.6)
battle cry call 550.16
  war cry 722.3
battled fortified 717.9
  in battle array 722.12
battledore 325.2
battledore and shuttlecock
  interchange 148.1
  game 840.11
battlefield 728.2
  (warfare 722.1)
  (slaughter 361.9)
battle flag 722.3
battleground
  discord 713.5
  battlefield 728.2
battle horn 722.3
battle line 728.2
battlement
  embrasure 257.4
  fortification 717.7
battleplane 273a.2
battler 726.1
battle royal 720.2
battleship 726.11
battle song 722.3
battological 573.8
battologize
  repeat 104.4
  tautologize 573.6

battology — beat

battology 573.2
  (repetition 104.1)
battue 622.2
batty imbecile 499.13
  insane 503.12
bauble trifle 643.3
  toy 840.16
  trinket 847.9
Baucis and Philemon
  elderly couple 130.4
  married couple
    903.9
bauxite 635.6
bavardage
  twaddle 517.3
  chatter 584.2
bavin 388.3
bawbee 643.3
bawd 962.4
bawdry 961.1
bawdy 961.9
bawdyhouse 961.7
bawl n. 839.1
bawl v.
  bellow 411.5; 412.2
  wail 839.9
  bawl out 932.8
bay n. horse 271.5
  sea inlet 343.1
  (recess 252.4)
  at bay
    in danger 665.8
    at an impasse 704.11
    up in arms 717.9
    on the defensive
      717.11
  keep at bay
    fend off 717.8
    resist 719.3
bay v. 412.2
bay adj. 433.5
bayadere, bayadeer
  840.9
bayard n. 271.5
Bayard n. horse 271.9
  paragon 650.3
bayard adj. 433.5
bayberry 400.3
bayberry oil 356.3
bayed 343.2
baygall 345.1
bay leaf 400.3
bay oil 356.3
bayonet n. 727.3
bayonet v. kill 361.12
  stab 716.5
bayonet leg 266.11
bayou 343.1
bay rum 400.3
bays trophy 733.1
  decoration 847.5
bay salt 336.3
bay window
  paunch 191.7
  curve 245.2
  window 260.5
bazaar, bazar 799.1
bazoo 260.2
B. C. 116.5
be 1.4
  (live 359.6)
  be it so 488.15

(consent 762.4)
be off depart 293.4
  begone! 297.23
  misinterpret 523.2
beach n. 342.2, 4
beach v. 267.33
beachcomber
  vagabond 268.2
  wave 348.10
beacon fire 382.8
  light 423.6
  observatory 441.5
  signal 423.5; 550.14
bead n. 847.4, 6
bead v. 847.11
beading 847.4
beadle 996.5
beadledom 737.7
beadlike 249.10
beadroll, beads
  prayers 990.3
  rosary 998.8
  tell one's beads
    990.11; 998.14
beadsman, bedesman
  pensioner 746.3
  religious 996.11
beadswoman, bedes-
  woman 746.3
beagle dog 366.6
  detective 528.9
  policeman 745.10
beak prow 234.3
  nose 250.4
  ornament 847.4
  judge 967.1
beaked 245.9
beaker 191.11
beaklike 245.9
be-all 50.2
beam n.
  breadth 202.1
  support 215.12
  side 236.1
  feather 256.8
  ship 273.7
  weighing instru-
    ment 319.5
  ~ of light 420.3
  ~ of hope 858.3
beam v. shine 420.17
  be beautiful 845.6
beaming 845.13
beam wind 349.10
beamy broad 202.6
  luminous 420.22
bean head 210.3
  vegetable 298.30
  brain 450.2
  trifle 643.3
  dollar 800.1, 8
beanery 298.42
beanfeast 840.2
beano 840.3
bean pole, beanstalk
  203.6
beany 503.12
bear n. animal 366.15
  proficient 700.1
  jobber 797.8
  beauty 845.3
  grouch 901.4

Bear n. Russian 188.9
  constellation 318.6
bear v. produce 161.9
  (be profitable
    775.10)
  (yield 810.4)
  support 215.26
  ~ on 215.27
  wear 225.45
  carry 270.8
  ~ heavily 319.8
  admit of 470.3
  ~ oneself 692.5
  lend support 707.7
  endure 826.6
bear down
  be violent 173.7
  force down 744.2
  domineer 885.5
bear down on, bear
  down upon
  sail for 267.26
  approach 286.2
  attack 716.5
  compel 744.2
bear in mind
  think 451.31
  take cognizance of
    457.4
  remember 505.11
bear in with 267.26
bear off
  oblique 217.5
  yaw 267.23, 24
  sail from 267.27, 28
  deviate 279.4
  turn aside 279.7
  abduct 791.11
bear sail 267.10
bear out
  corroborate 467.9
  demonstrate 478.2
bear up
  support 215.26
  approach 286.2
  persevere 604a.2
  resist 719.3
  solace 834.5
  keep up spirits 836.4
  brave 861.5
bear up for 267.26
bear upon
  be related 9.3
  influence 175.6
  urge 615.7
  compel 744.2
bear with
  be lenient 740.2
  permit 760.3
  endure 826.6
  forgive 918.3
bearable
  tolerable 648.11
  mediocre 736.3
  satisfactory 831.7
beard n. point 253.2
  hair 256.5, 7
  type 591.6
beard v. defy 715.2
  brave 861.5
bearded 256.13
beardless boyish 127.5

hairless 226.10
beardlessness 226.3
bearer carrier 271.1
  pallbearer 363.7
  messenger 534.1
  printing 591.5
  retainer 746.1
bear garden
  turmoil 59.4
  arena 728.1
bear grass 253.2
bearing n. relation 9.1
  posture 184.2
  fulcrum 215.5
  gait 266.5
  direction 278.1
  mien 448.4
  meaning 516.1
  conduct 692.1
  keep the bearing
    navigate 267.22
bearing adj. 23.10
bearings
  circumstances 8.4
  location 184.1
  get the bearings 278.7
  take bearings 267.39
bearish gruff 895.7
  irascible 901.7
bear leader 540.1
bear pit 370.3
bearskin 225.26
bear trap 545.4
beast violent 173.6
  animal 366.2
  savage 913.3
  carnal nature 961.3
beastly adj.
  execrable 649.8
  filthy 653.17
  odious 830.14
  carnal 961.11
beastly adv. 31.24
beast of burden
  carrier 271.2
  laborer 690.2
beat n. round 181.4
  itinerary 266.9
  pulsation 314.2
  (cadence 138.3)
  drumming 407.3
  rhythm 413.23
  news 532.1
  poetical ~ 597.6
  routine 613.4
  occupation 625.3
  path 627.2
  best 648.4
  ~ of drum 669.1;
    722.3
  sponger 886.2
beat v. excel 33.5
  (outstrip 303.4)
  repeat 104.4
  sail 267.19
  strike 276.8
  pulsate 314.9
  (recur 138.8)
  agitate 315.8
  pulverize 330.6
  drum 407.8
  nonplus 475.8

beat (continued)
~ against 708.2
~ off 717.8
defeat 731.9
batter 830.6
whip 972.6
beat about
~ ~ for 463.9
be uncertain 475.6
flounder 704.6
beat about the bush 477.8
(prevaricate 544.5)
(be circumlocutory 573.5)
(evade 623.6)
(circuit 629.2)
beat a retreat
go back 283.5
hasten off 293.5
flee 623.10
beat down
demolish 162.4
haggle 794.5
cheapen 815.7
domineer 885.5
beat it depart 293.5
begone! 297.23
flee 623.10
beat the air 645.6
beat the band 33.5
beat up agitate 315.8
churn 352.6
~ ~ against 708.3
batter 830.6
pummel 972.6
beat up for recruits 637.4
beat adj. inferior 34.5
nonplused 475.16
exhausted 688.6
defeated 732.12
penniless 804.7
beaten track
routine 613.4
path 627.2
beatific blissful 827.9
delightful 829.8
heavenly 981.7
beatification
bliss 827.2
sanctification 987.2
beatify delight 829.5
bless 987.8
beating defeat 732.3
whipping 972.3
(blow 276.3)
beatitude 827.2
beau fop 854.1
inamorato 897.6
beau ideal, beau idéal
paragon 650.2
(prototype 22.1)
a beauty 845.3
beau monde 852.4
beauteous 845.8
beautification 845.5
(decoration 847.1)
beautiful n. 845.1
beautiful adj. 845.8, 13
(shapely 242.5)
(pleasing 377.7)

(ornamental 847.12)
be beautiful 845.6
render beautiful 845.7
beautify
render beautiful 845.7
ornament 847.11
beauty 845
(symmetry 242.1)
beauty sleep 683.5
beaver pelt 223.12
hat 225.26
animal 366.17
armor 717.2
beaverette 223.12
becalm 265.6
becalmed 265.7
because 155.8
(causally 153.10)
(for this reason 462.13)
(by reason 476.21)
because of 155.5, 8
bechance 156.7
becharm lure 617.4
delight 829.5
enamor 897.13
conjure 992.4
bêche-de-mer, beche-le-mar 560.5
beck n. stream 348.1
sign 550.3
command 741.1
at beck and call
obedient 743.3
in subjection 749.6
at one's beck 707.12
beck v. 550.20
Becken bell 408.5
percussive 417.10
beckon signal 550.20
lure 617.4
becloud cloud 353.9
dim 422.6
(obfuscate 426.3)
confuse 458.9
conceal 528.10
become exist 1.5
originate 66.6
be converted into 144.8
beautify 845.7
behoove 926.5
become of 151.3
becoming
agreeing 23.9
expedient 646.4
(right 922.5)
due 924.9
comely 845.10
(ornamental 847.12)
becripple
disable 158.6
impair 659.8
bed n. layer 204.1
sea bottom 208.3
bottom 211.3
couch 215.24
plants 371.8
printing 591.5
marriage 903.1

go to bed
be quiescent 265.5
sleep 683.9
(repose 687.3)
bed v.
establish 184.11, 12
support 215.26
insert 300.5
~ down 370.7
bedarken
obscure 421.5
blacken 431.6
bedaub cover 223.24
paint 428.10
bedazzle glare 420.17
daze 443.13
confuse 458.9
bewilder 870.2
awe 928.7
bedbug 366.24
bedclothes, bedcover 223.9
bedding bed 215.24
(coverlet 223.9)
bedeck clothes 225.41
adorn 847.11
bedesman See **beadsman**
bedeswoman See **beadswoman**
bedevil
complicate 61.5
bewitch 992.4
(demonize 978.6)
bedevilment 992.1
bedew 337.5
bedfellow 890.3
bedgown 225.24
bedight v.
clothe 225.41
adorn 847.11
bedight adj.
clothed 225.46
adorned 847.14
bedim 422.6
bedizen clothe 225.41
adorn 847.11
bedizenment 225.1
bedlam turmoil 59.4
noise 404.2
discord 414.2
insanity 503.1
insane asylum 503.8
madman 504.1
bed'amite 504.1
bed of roses
comfort 377.2
prosperity 734.1
on a bed of roses
in comfort 377.9
prosperous 734.7
bedog 281.3
Bedouin 792.3
bedridden 655.23
bedrock n.
bottom 211.1
foundation 215.3
bedrock adj. 211.5
bedroom 191.16
bedspread 223.9
bedstead 215.24
bedtime 126.1

bedtime story 546.1
bedwarf 36.4
bee insect 366.24
busy ~ 682.10
worker 690.2
social gathering 892.5
bee in the bonnet
eccentricity 503.6
caprice 608.1
beech 367.6
beechwood 635.3
beef strength 159.1
meat 298.20
bovine 366.12
beef-brained 499.12
beefeater guard 717.6
yeoman 726.4, 7
beef extract 298.20
beefheaded 499.12
beefsteak 298.20
beef-witted 499.12
beefy 159.10
beehive
convexity 250.2
apiary 370.3
workshop 691
beekeeper 370.4
beekeeping 370.1
beeline
short way 197.2
direct line 246.2
(line 278.3)
in a beeline 278.13
make a beeline 278.6
Beelzebub 978.1, 2
beer 959.5
beer garden, beerhouse 959.13
beermaker 690.8
beery 959.21
beeswax n.
burnisher 255.3
cerate 356.6
beeswax v. 332.4
beet 298.30
beetle n. 366.24
beetle v. 214.5
(rise above 206.10)
beetle adj. 214.8
beetlehead 501.1
beetleheaded 499.12
beetroot, beet root 298.30
befall happen 151.3
chance 156.7
befit agree 23.7
(be expedient 646.3)
behoove 926.5
befitting
opportune 134.7
expedient 646.4
(ethical 926.12)
befog cloud 353.9
dim 422.6
conceal 528.10
befool
infatuate 503.11
deceive 545.10
before
in time 116.5; 122.14
in front 234.9

(in the presence of
    186.16)
  in advance 280.4
  in preference 609.18
beforehand 116.6
  (in advance 280.4)
  prematurely 132.12
  (unexpectedly
    508.11)
  (precipitately 684.7)
before-mentioned,
  before-said 62.4
beforetime 116.5
befoul 653.15
befoulment 653.2
befriend 707.6, 8
  (be friendly 888.2)
befriender 912.1
befringe edge 231.3
  side 236.4
befuddle confuse 458.9
  inebriate 959.18
befuddlement
  confusion 458.4
  drunkenness 959.1
beg n. 745.7
beg v. 765.4, 5, 6
  beg leave 765.4
  beg pardon 952.5
  beg the question
    477.8
  beg to differ 489.4
beget 161.10
  (vivify 359.8)
begetter
  producer 164.1
  parent 166.5
beggar n. 767.2
  (idler 683.7)
  (pauper 804.3)
  (vagabond 876.9)
beggar v. 83.8; 870.5
beggarly paltry 643.12
  poverty-stricken
    804.7
  vulgar 851.6
  disreputable 874.8
  servile 886.4
beggar-my-neighbor,
  beggar-my-neigh-
  bour 840.12
beggar's-lice, beggar-
  lice 253.2
beggar-ticks, beg-
  gar's-ticks 253.2
beggary
  mendicity 765.1
  poverty 804.2
begging the question
  477.4
begild 436.5
begin 66.5
  (become 1.5)
  (prepare 673.6)
  (undertake 676.2)
beginner 541.6
beginning n.
  commencement 66
  (prelude 64.2)
  (dawn 125.1)
  (birth 161.3)

(front 234.1)
(first attempt
  675.2)
cause 153.1
beginning and end
  50.2
beginning of the end
  162.1
from beginning to
  end 200.16
make a beginning
  66.5
beginning adj. 66.7
  (primitive 124.7)
begird 227.3
beglerbeg 745.7
begone! 287.5; 297.23
  (depart 293.11)
begrime
  discolor 440a.2
  dirty 653.15
begrudge
  be unwilling 603.4
  refuse 764.2
  be parsimonious
    819.3
  envy 921.2
begrudging 921.3
beguile deceive 545.7
  use artifice 702.5
  swindle 791.12
  reconcile 831.4
beguiler 548.1
béguin 865.1
begum empress 745.6
  princess 875.8
behalf 648.2
in behalf of
  in favor of 707.15
  instead of 755.6
  (as deputy 759.7)
on behalf of 707.15
behave 692.5
behave oneself
  conform to fashion
    852.6
  be courteous 894.7
behavior, behaviour
  692.1
behaviorism
  psychology 450.4
  conduct 692.1
behaviorist 692.7
behead 972.8
beheader 975.5
beheading 972.4
behemoth 192.8
behest 741.1
behind n. 235.1, 5
behind adv. prep.
  in back 235.14
  in the wake 281.5
  (after 622.11)
  behindhand 304.4
behindhand
  late 133.8, 11
  in arrears 304.4
  uncultured 491.11
  unfortunate 735.9
  defaultant 808.9
behold v. 441.10

(be a spectator
  444.3)
behold int. 457.10
beholden
  grateful 916.4
  obliged 926.10
beholder 444.1
behoof 648.2
behoove 926.5
beige 436.6
being existence 1.1
  (life 359.1)
  something 3.2
Bel 979.6
belabor, belabour
  strike 276.8
  chastise 972.6
belated late 133.8
  ignorant 491.10
belay attach 43.6
  cease 142.6
belay that!, belay
  there! cease! 142.8
  navigation 267.69
  silence 403.9
belaying pin 273.14
belch n.
  discharge 297.5
  (respiration 349.18)
  beer 959.5
belch v. 297.20
  (respire 349.23)
beldam, beldame
  crone 130.3
  grandmother 166.8
  fury 173.6
  shrew 901.4
  malevolent woman
    913.5
belduque knife 253.6
  weapon 727.3
beleaguer
  hem in 229.2
  besiege 716.5
bel-esprit 844
belfry tower 206.3
  head 210.3
belga 800.8
Belgian 271.4
Belgian hare 366.17
Belgium 182.3
Be'ial 978.1, 2
belie deny 536.2
  falsify 544.3
  oppose 708.2
belief 484
  (judgment 480.1)
  (credulity 486.1)
  (doctrine 983.2)
  (piety 987.1)
  (sect 984.3)
believable 484.15
  (plausible 472.6)
  (logical 476.16)
believability 484.5
  (reasonability
    476.7)
believe
  give credence 484.7
  (think 451.27)
  (presume 472.3)
  (be credulous 486.3)

(be pious 987.6)
  suppose 514.6
believe me!
  I assure you! 535.8
  I promise 768.8
not believe
  disbelieve 485.5
  astonished 870.2, 6
believer 987.4
believing 484.12
  (pious 987.10)
belike 472.7
belittle 36.4
  (disparage 934.3)
  (underestimate
    483.3)
bell n. capital 215.17
  peal 407.1
  tintinnabulum 408.5
  music instrument
    417.10
  signal 550.14
bell v. boom 406.9
  peal 407.6
  bellow 412.2
bell the cat 861.5
belladonna 663.6
bell, book and candle
  993.1
bellboy
  messenger 534.1
  attendant 746.1
bell cot, bell cote 189.7
belle woman 374.2
  a beauty 845.3
  fine lady 854.2
Belleau Wood 722.5
belles-lettres 560.8
bellhop
  messenger 534.1
  attendant 746.1
bellicism 722.6
bellicose 722.13
  (defiant 715.3)
bellicosity 722.6
bellied 250.9
belligerence 722.6
belligerent 722.13
  (contentious 720.12)
  (combatant 726.1)
belling 412.1
bell-like 245.10
bellman 534.1
bell mare 64.1
Bellona 722.7
bellow
  bawl 411.5; 412.2
  (be noisy 404.6)
  wail 839.9
bellows lungs 349.19
  blower 349.20
bellowsmaker 690.8
bell ringing 408.10
bellwether
  forerunner 64.1
  ram 366.8
  leader 694.1
belly n. 191.7
  (protuberance
    250.2)
belly v. 250.7
bellyache n. 378.1

bellyache — berry

bellyache v. 839.10
bellyacher 832.2
bellyband
 fastening 45.2
 garment 225.34
belly-bumper, belly-
 buster 272.13
bellyful fill 52.3
 (plenty 639.2)
 (redundance 641.1)
 satiety 869.1
belly-god 957.2
belly-whopper 272.13
belomancy 511.3
belong
 be related 9.3
 be included 76.2
 enter into 56.2
 be possessed by 777.6
 behoove 926.5
belonging 9.5
belongings 780.1, 5
beloved n. 897.7
beloved adj. 897.16
below less 34.7
 under 207.11
 ship 273.7
 in subjection 749.7
below there 864.9
belowstairs 207.11
belt n.
 fastening 45.2
 garment 225.34
 zone 230.2
 circle 247.2
 blow 276.3
 sea inlet 343.1
belt v.
 surround 227.3
 strike 276.8
 whip 972.6
beluga 366.21
belute 46.7
belvedere 441.5
bemire 653.15
bemist 422.6
bemoan 839.6
bemuse 959.18
bemused
 preoccupied 458.11
 intoxicated 959.21
ben n. 225.16
ben adv. 221.12
bench seat 215.22
 council 696.1
 official seat 747.5
 seat of justice 966.1
bencher judge 967.1
 lawyer 968.1
benchfellow 890.3
bench warmer 683.7
bend n. knot 45.6
 obliquity 217.1
 angle 244.2
 curvature 245.1
 protuberance 250.2
 deviation 279.1
 turn 311.2
bend v. tie 43.6
 conform 82.5
 tend 176.2

oblique 217.5
angle 244.4
curve 245.3
(deviate 279.4)
~ over 250.7
direct 278.4
deflect 279.6
crouch 308.7
turn 311.4
be pliant 324.5
submit 725.3
bend an ear 418.11
bend one's steps
 travel 266.12
 go to 266.22; 278.5
 pursue 622.6
bend the eye 441.11
bend the mind to
 think about 451.27
 give attention 457.4
 study 461.17
bendable 324.6
bender spree 840.3
 drinking bout 959.3
bends spasm 315.7
 cramps 378.1
 caisson disease 655.3
bend sinister
 stigma 874.2
 bastardy 964.1
bendsome 324.6
bendwise 217.15
beneath under 207.11
 in subjection 749.7
beneath one 940.9
benedicite 990.4
Benedicite 990.2
benedict 903.7
Benedict Arnold 949.3
benedictine 959.6
Benedictine 996.11
benediction
 thanksgiving 916.2
 blessing 931.2; 990.4
give benediction 990.12
benedictory 931.9
benefaction
 benefit 648.2
 gift 784.4
benefactor 912
 (giver 784.7; 816.2)
benefice 995.3
beneficence 906.2
 (goodness 648.1)
 (liberality 816.1)
beneficent 906.7
 (liberal 816.4)
beneficial good 648.12
 (useful 644.5)
 (helpful 707.12)
 salubrious 656.5
be beneficial 648.6
 (be useful 644.2)
beneficially 648.15
beneficiary
 recipient 785.2
 (heir 779.5)
 clergyman 996.5
benefit n. avail 644.1
 (use 677.1)

(help 707.1)
good 648.2
(gain 775.2)
estate 780.2
gift 784.4
(kindness 906.2)
benefit v. 648.6
 (be useful 644.2)
 (improve 658.8)
 (serve 707.10; 746.8)
 (be benevolent 906.5)
benefiter 912.1
benefit performance 599.8
benevolence tax 812.2
 kindness 906
 (aid 707.1)
 (charity 784.2)
 (friendship 888.1)
 (love 897.1)
 (mercy 914.1)
 (magnanimity 942.2)
benevolent 906.6
 (helpful 707.13)
 (friendly 888.4)
 (loving 897.14)
 (merciful 914.6)
 (magnanimous 942.6)
be benevolent 906.5
 (aid 707.6)
 (give 784.8)
 (be friendly 888.2)
benevolently 906.9
benevolist 911.1
Bengali 560.4
benight 442.3
benighted
 night-overtaken 126.7
 blind 442.6
 ignorant 491.10
benightedness 442.1
benign
 salubrious 656.5
 benevolent 906.6
benignant 906.6
benignity 906.1
benjamin 225.17
benjy 225.16
benny overcoat 225.17
 hat 225.26
bent n.
 tendency 176.1
 inclination 217.1, 2
 direction 278.1
 bent grass 367.9
 propensity 602.2
 aptitude 698.2
 affection 820.1
 penchant 865.1
bent adj.
 crooked 217.13
 distorted 243.5
 angular 244.5
 curved 245.4
 minded 820.4
bent on, bent upon
 desirous 865.11, 17
 resolved upon 604.8

(intending 620.4)
benthal 208.12
Benthamism 906.3
Benthamite 911.1
benthonic
 deep-sea 208.12
 oceanic 341.5
 animal 366.22
 algal 367.16
benthos
 sea bottom 208.3
 seaweed 367.3
ben trovato
 plausible 472.6
 imaginary 515.12
 trumped-up 546.6
 witty 842.9
benumb deaden 376.4
 numb 381.2
 freeze 385.4
 ~ emotionally 823.4
benumbed numb 381.3
 ~ emotionally 823.5
benumbedness 381.1
benzene 652.8
benzine, benzin
 oil 356.2
 solvent 652.8
benzoic acid 662.8
benzol, benzole 652.8
beplaster 933.2
bepraise 931.6
bepraisement 931.2
bequeath 784.13
bequeathable 270.11
bequest n. 270.3
 legacy 784.6
 (inheritance 775.4)
 (estate 780.3)
bequest v. 784.13
berate 932.8
berceuse song 415.9
 lullaby 834.1
bereave 789.11
bereaved
 deprived 776.6
 moneyless 804.7
bereavement
 death 360.1
 loss 776.1
 dispossession 789.2
bereft wanting 640.11
 deprived 776.6
 (dispossessed 789.16)
 moneyless 804.7
beretta See biretta
berg 383.5
bergamot 400.3
Bergsonism 451.13
beriberi 655.5
Berkeleian 317.4
Berkeleianism
 immaterialism 317.3
 philosophy 451.17
berlin 272.4, 15
berloque, breloque 407.3
berm, berme 627.2
Bernardine 996.11
berretta See biretta
berry fruit 298.31

money 800.1, 8
berserk, beserker
 173.6
berth abode 189.1
 bed 215.24
 office 625.4
Bertillon system
 550.17
beryl
 transparency 425.2
 green 435.3
 blue 438.2, 3
 gem 847.8
beryl blue *n.* 438.1
beryl-blue *adj.* 438.6
beryl green *n.* 435.2
beryl-green *adj.* 435.6
berylline green 435.6
 blue 438.6
beseech 765.5
 (ask pity 914.5)
 (pray 990.11)
beseechment
 entreaty 765.2
 prayer 990.3
beseem 926.5
beset hem in 229.2
 (surround 227.3)
 besiege 716.5
 entreat 765.5
 harass 830.5
 obsess 830.8
besetting
 prevalent 78.10
 habitual 613.11
 rife 639.7
beshrew 908.4, 7
beside excluding 55.7
 alongside 236.9
 (near 197.11)
 (parallelly 216.6)
 beside oneself
 rabid 503.13
 overwrought 824.10
 ~ with joy 827.10
besides
 additionally 37.8
 exclusive of 55.7
besiege hem in 229.2
 attack 716.5
 entreat 765.5
 obsess 830.8
besiegement 716.1
beslaver 933.2
beslime 653.15
beslubber 933.2
besmear cover 223.24
 paint 428.10
 discolor 440a.2
 befoul 653.15
besmirch
 discolor 440a.2
 befoul 653.15
besmoke, besmudge,
 besmut, besmutch
 653.15
besnow 430.6
besom 652.7
besot 959.18
besotted
 drunk 959.21
 obsessed 503.18

(prejudiced 481.10)
bespangle 847.11
bespangled
 luminous 420.22
 ornamented 847.13
bespatter splash 337.5
 discolor 440a.2
 dirty 653.15
 stigmatize 874.7
 insult 929.3
 flatter 933.2
 slander 934.3
bespeak
 pre-engage 132.5
 evince 467.7
 mean 516.5
 indicate 550.18
 commission 755.4
 ask for 765.4
bespeckle spot 440.4
 discolor 440a.2
 soil 653.15
bespectacled 445.10
bespice 392.4
besplatter, besplash
 653.15
bespot mottle 440.4
 discolor 440a.2
 soil 653.15
besprinkle imbue 41.8
 wet 337.5
 spot 440.a
best *n.*
 best clothes 225.13
 pick 648.4
 (choice 609.1)
 (perfection 650.1)
 do one's best 675.5
best *adj.* 648.9
 (supreme 33.8)
 (paramount 642.14)
 (perfect 650.5)
bestain 653.15
bestead 644.2
best girl 897.7
bestial savage 173.14
 brutal 907.9
 carnal 961.11
bestir oneself
 be active 682.12
 (work 686.6)
 hasten 684.3
best man
 companion 890.3
 wedding attendant
 903.4
bestow give 784.8
 ~ clerical benefice
 995.7
bestowal 784.1
bestower 784.7
bestraddle 215.27
bestrew 73.3
bestride
 be high 206.9
 sit on 215.27
bet *n.* 621.3
bet *v.* wager 621.18
 ~ on, ~ upon 474.5;
 484.7
betacism, betacismus
 583.1

betake oneself
 travel 266.12
 go to 266.22
 undertake 676.2
 use 677.5
beta ray 420.3
beta test 461.3
bête noire bane 663.1
 object of fear 860.7
 hate 898.2
 bugbear 980.4
bethel 1000.1
bethink 451.27
 bethink oneself
 think over 451.29
 remember 505.10
bethlehem 503.8
bethrall, bethral
 subjugate 749.5
 confine 751.8
betide 151.3
betimes 132.11, 15
bêtise 497.1
betoken evince 467.7
 foreshow 511.9
 mean 516.5
 indicate 550.18
betongue 932.8
betray appear 446.2
 inform on 527.10
 divulge 529.4
 deceive 545.7
 be faithless to 940.7
betrayal 940.4
 (information 527.1)
betrayer
 informer 527.6
 traitor 949.3
betroth 768.4
betrothal 768.2
betrothed *n.* 897.8
betrothed *adj.* 768.7
better *n.* 621.15
 all the better 831.9
 for better or for
 worse 78.15
 have the better of
 have advantage 33.6
 confute 479.2
better *v.* 658.8
 (benefit 648.6)
 (remedy 660.10)
better *adj.*
 superior 33.7
 (good 648.8)
 ~ for 658.7
 improved 658.14
 become better 658.6
 better and better
 831.9
 get better 689.3
 (return to health
 654.3)
better-advised 658.14
better half 903.5, 8
betterment 658.1
better off 658.14
betting 621.6
bettong, bettonga
 309.3
bettor 621.15
betty

hermaphrodite 83.5
mollycoddle 160a.3
old fogy 501.3
between 228.13
 between ourselves
 528.25
betweenbrain 450.2
between-decks 273.8
betwixt 228.13
 betwixt and between
 between 228.13
 mediocre 736.3
Beulah 981.1
bevel *n.*
 obliquity 217.1
 printing 591.5
bevel, beveled, bevelled *adj.* 217.9
bever 298.35
beverage drink 298.4
 (liquid 333.2)
 alcoholic drink
 959.4
bevue blunder 495.3
 bungle 699.4
bevy 72.4; 102.2
bewail 839.6
 (regret 833.2)
 (repent 950.3)
beware *v.* 864.3
 (warn 668.8)
beware *int.* 864.9
 (danger 665.10)
 (jiggers 668.11)
bewhiskered 256.13
bewilder confuse 458.9
 perplex 475.8
 astonish 870.3
bewildered
 confused 458.12
 perplexed 475.16
bewildering 475.12
bewilderment
 confusion 458.4
 perplexity 475.2
 (incomprehension
 491.3)
 astonishment 870.1
bewitch
 fascinate 617.4
 delight 829.5
 enamor 897.13
 spell 992.4
 (demonize 978.6)
bewitched 992.7
bewitcher 992.2
bewitchery
 allurement 617.1
 sorcery 992.1
 spell 993.1
bewitching
 delightful 829.8
 attractive 845.9
 witching 992.6
bewitchment 829.2
 sorcery 992.1
 spell 993.1
bewray 479.2
bey 745.7
beyond superior 33.9
 additionally 37.8
 farther 196.8

bezel, bezil 217.1
bezoar goat 366.9
bezonian 876.9
B-flat 366.24
Bhagavad-Gita 986.2
bhang, bang 662.7
  (poison 663.6)
bheesty, bheestie 348.16
bhikku 996.9
bhikshu 955.2; 996.8
bias n. influence 175.1
  tendency 176.1
  obliquity 217.1
  prejudice 481.3
  (bigotry 606.2)
  propensity 602.2
  disposition 820.1
  partiality 941a.1
bias v. influence 175.6
  (induce 615.8)
  oblique 217.5
  deviate 279.6
  prejudice 481.8
bias adj. 217.13
biased, biassed
  prejudiced 481.10
  partial 941a.3
bib n. apron 225.20
  napkin 652.7
bib v. drink 298.47
  tipple 959.15
bibacious 959.23
bibacity 959.1
bib and tucker 225.7
bibber n. 959.11
bibber v. 839.8
bibble-babble n.
  twaddle 517.3
  chatter 584.2
bibble-babble v. 517.6
bibi 374.2, 3
bible 273.14
Bible 985.2
Bible Christian 984.14
Biblical 985.7
biblioclasm
  destruction 162.1
  bibliology 593.18
biblioclast 165.1
bibliognost
  scholar 492.1
  bookman 593.14
bibliogony 593.18
bibliographer 593.14, 15
bibliographical 593.20
bibliography 593.3, 18
bibliokleptomania 593.18
bibliolater
  scholar 492.3
  idolater 991.5
biblio'atrous 991.7
bibliolatry
  bookishness 490.2
  hyperorthodoxy 983a.5
  worship 991.1
bibliological 593.20
bibliologist 593.14
bibliology

learning 490.2
  bibliography 593.18
bibliomancy
  divination 511.3
  bibliology 593.18
bibliomania 490.2
bibiomaniac 492.3
bibliopegic 593.20
bibliopegist 593.14
bibliopegy 593.9
bibliophagic 490.16
bibliophile 492.3
  (bookman 593.14)
bibliophilic 490.16
  (bibliological 593.20)
bibliophilism 490.2
bibliophilist 490.16
bibliophobia 593.18
bibliopolar 593.20
bibliopole 593.14
bibliopoly 593.18
bibliosoph
  scholar 492.1
  bookman 593.14
bibliothec
  library 593.11
  librarian 593.14
bibliothecary, bibliothetic 593.20
biblus, biblos 590.10
bibulosity 959.1
bibulous
  drinkable 298.51
  liquor-drinking 959.23
bice green 435.2, 4
  blue 438.2, 4
bicentenary, bicentennial hundred 98.8
  anniversary 138.5
bicephalous 90.3
bichloride 663.5
bicipital 90.3
bicker n. 713.3
bicker v. flutter 315.10
  quarrel 713.7
bickering 713.3
bico'or, bicolour 440.5
biconjugate 91.6
bicorn 245.6
bicuspid n. 253.3
bicuspid adj. 91.6
bicycle n. 272.14
bicycle v. 266.18
bid n. offer 763.1
  ~ at auction 796.2
bid v. command 741.4
  offer 763.2
  ~ at auction 796.6
bid fair
  have a chance 156.9
  tend 176.2
  be liable 177.2
  be possible 470.3
  be probable 472.2
  promise 511.10
  give hope 858.8
bid for intend 620.3
  offer 763.3
  (request 765.4)
  bargain 794.5

bid the banns 903.12
bidder 767.1
bidding
  command 741.1
  ~ at auction 796.2
  do one's bidding 743.2
biddy fowl 366.23
  female 374.8
  maidservant 746.2
bide wait 133.7
  be permanent 141.4
  wait 507.5
  endure 826.6
bide one's time
  wait 133.7; 507.5
  do nothing 681.2
bidental 90.3
bidet 271.3
biduous 89.4
biennial n. 138.5
biennial adj.
  periodic 138.11
  plant 367.17
bienséance
  conventionality 852.2
  politeness 894.1
bier 363.12
bifacial double 90.3
bilateral 236.7
bifarious 90.3
bifid 91.6
bifidity 91.1
bifold 90.3
biforked 91.7
biform 90.3
biformity 89.1
bifurcation 91.2
  (angularity 244.1)
  (divergence 291.1)
bifurcate v. 91.5
  (angle 244.4)
  (diverge 291.2)
bifurcate adj. 91.7
  (angular 244.5)
  (diverging 291.3)
big pregnant 168.9
  sizable 192.11
  (great 31.6)
  eminent 873.18
look big
  be defiant 715.2
  be proud 878.3
  be ostentatious 882.6
bigamist 903.5
bigamous 903.14
bigamy 903.2
big-bellied 194.11
  (stout 192.12)
big Bertha 727.11
big bug 642.5
big end main part 50.3
  greater share 786.2
big-eared 418.14
bigeminate 91.6
biggen increase 35.3
  enlarge 194.8
biggin 191.11
big gun 612.5
bighead 655.18
bighearted

generous 816.4
  charitable 906.7
  magnanimous 942.6
big house 752.1
bight circle 247.2
  sea inlet 343.1
big idea 453.1
big-league 642.10
bigness
  pregnancy 168.2
  size 192.1
  (greatness 31.1)
bigot 606.3
  (dogmatist 474.4)
  (affecter 853.4)
  (religious ~ 983a.6)
  (hypocrite 988.6)
bigoted 606.7
  (dogmatic 474.15)
  (unreasonable 477.10)
  (prejudiced 481.10)
  (unreasoning 499.17)
  (fanatical 503.18)
  (prudish 853.7)
  (hyperorthodox 983a.8)
  (pious 987.10)
  (overrighteous 988.12)
bigotry 606.2
  (conservatism 141.2)
  (dogmatism 474.3)
  (prejudice 481.3)
  (prudery 853.2)
  (hyperorthodoxy 983a.5)
  (sanctimony 988.2)
big shot 642.5
big-sounding
  loud 404.8
  grandiloquent 577.7
  affected 853.6
big stick 744.1
big talk 577.2
big-time 642.10
big top tent 223.5
  show 599.8
bigwig 642.5
bigwigged 642.10
Bihari, Behari 560.4
bijou, bijouterie 847.7
bijugate 89.5
bike 272.14
Bikol, Bicol 560.4
bilabiate 90.3
bilander 273.2
bilateral double 90.3
  two-sided 236.7
bilbo 727.3
bilboes 752.2
bile n. 901.1
bile v. boil 382.13
  cook 384.19
bilge n. bottom 211.1
  protuberance 250.2
bilge v. eliminate 42.4
  bulge 250.7
bilge pump 273.14
bilge water 653.6

biliary calculus — bite

biliary calculus 655.5
bilingual 560.9
bilious 901.7
bilk disappoint 509.2
  deceive 545.7
  swindle 791.12
bilker cheat 548.2
  swindler 792.8
bill *n.* nose 250.4
  promontory 250.5
  billhook 253.6
  advertisement 531.4
  ticket 550.11
  schedule 611.2
  (program 626.3)
  weapon 727.4
  security 771.1
  bank note 800.6
  ~ of accounts 811.3
bill *v.* list 86.3
  schedule 611.4
  enter accounts 811.7
bill and coo 902.7
billbug 366.24
billed 245.9
billet *n.* ticket 550.11
  epistle 592.2
  office 625.4
  ornament 847.4
billet *v.* lodge 184.12
  apportion 786.3
billet-doux
  epistle 592.2
  love letter 902.5
billhook 253.6
billiard ball 249.2
billiard room 840.14
billiards 840.11
billiard table 213.3
billingsgate
  slang 563.4
  profanity 908.2
billion *n.* 98.12
billion *adj.* 102.5
billionaire 803.2
billionth 98.29
bill of costs 86.1
bill of exchange
  security 771.1
  draft 800.7
bill of fare list 86.1
  menu 298.40
  schedule 611.2
bill of indictment
  accusation 938.1
  arraignment 969.3
bill of lading list 86.1
  statement 811.3
bill of mortality 360.3
bill of rights 969.6
bill of sale 771.1
billow *n.* 348.10
  (swell 194.2; 250.2)
billow *v.* roll 312.7
  surge 348.22
bil'owy 248.7
billposter 531.6
billy receptacle 191.11
  club 727.7
  chum 890.3
billycan 191.11
billycock hat 225.26

billy goat goat 366.9
  male animal 373.6
bimonthly 138.11
bin case 191.8
  cupboard 191.15
bina See vina
binary, binate 89.4
bind wrap 223.23
  edge 231.3
  compel 744.2
  tie 751.7
  (fasten 43.6)
  condition 770.2
  impose a duty 926.7
bind over 744.2
bind up join 43.5
  repair 660.11
binder 662.14
binder's board 635.4
bindery 691
binding *n.*
  bookbinding 593.9
  ornamentation 847.6
binding *adj.*
  compulsory 744.2
  (necessary 601.11)
  obligatory 926.9
bindle 72.5
bindle stiff 268.2
bine 367.4
Binet test 461.3
binge 959.3
binghi 188.8
bingo 406.2, 13
binocular 445.2
binomial 89.4
bioblast 357.4
biochemistry 359.5
biogen 357.4
biogenesis 161.2
biogenetic 357.10
biograph 445.6
biographer 553.2
  (author 593.15)
  (narrator 594.4)
biographical 594.7
biography 594.2
  (archive 551.2)
biological 357.11
biologist 357.7
biology 357.5; 359.5
bioluminescence
  420.11
bion 357.2
bionomics 368.1
biophore, biophor
  357.4
bioplasm 357.3
bioplasmic 357.9
biota 357.1
biotaxy
  taxonomy 60.2
  organic science
    357.5
biotic 357.8
biparous dual 89.4
  twin 90.3
bipartite
  separated 44.12
  bisected 91.6
bipartition 91.1
biped 366.1

biplane 273a.1
biplicity 89.1
biquadrate *n.* 95.1
biquadrate *v.*
  quadrate 95.3
  quadruplicate 96.2
biquadratic
  quaternary 95.4
  quadruplicate 96.3
birch *n.* tree 367.6
  wood 635.3
birch *v.* 972.6
birch oil 972.3, 6
bird oddity 83.4
  aeronaut 269a.1
  animal 366.22
  eye 441.9
birds of a feather
  analogue 17.5
  friends 890.4
bird of another
  feather 15.3
bird cage, bird-cage
  cote 189.7
  birdhouse 370.3
  dice box 621.8
birdcall 412.1
birdhouse cote 189.7
  aviary 370.3
bird ime *n.*
  cement 45.6
  snare 545.4
birdlime *v.* 545.9
birdman 269a.1
bird of freedom, bird
  of Jove, bird of
  Minerva, bird of
  night, bird of para-
  dise 366.22
Bird of Paradise 318.6
bird of passage 268.2
bird of prey
  bird 366.22
  taker 789.6
bird's-eye *n.* 392a.1
bird's-eye *adj.* 78.9
bird-witted 458.13
birdwoman 269a.1
birdy 413.10
bireme 273.3
biretta, berretta 999.1
birth cause 153.1
  childbirth 161.3
  (beginning 66.2)
  (pregnancy 168.2)
  ancestry 166.4
  nobility 875.1
birthday 138.5
birthday suit 223.12;
  226.2
birthmark 440a.1
birthplace 153.4
birthright
  birthday 138.5
  inheritance 775.4
  right 957.1
bis! again! 104.8
  bravo! 931.13
Bisayan See Visayan
biscuit
  pommel 215.23
  food 298.11, 12

dryness 340.4
  ceramics 384.14
bise 349.9, 11
bisect middle 68.4
  halve 91.4
  (divide 44.7)
bisected 91.6
bisection
  equidistance 68.3
  halving 91
  (division 44.1)
bisexual *n.* 83.5
bisexual *adj.* 83.12
bishop bustle 225.25
  drink 959.8
  clergyman 996.5
bishop coadjutor
  996.5
bishopric 995.3
bison 366.13
bisque soup 298.16
  ceramics 384.14
bissextile 138.7
bister, bistre 433.2
bistoury 253.6
bistro
  restaurant 298.42
  wine seller 959.13
bit modicum 32.2
  (pittance 640.5)
  piece 51.3
  short time 111.3
  short way 197.2
  taste 390.1
  minor role 599.7
  hindrance 706.2
  curb 752.2
  money 800.8
bit by bit
  gradually 26.5
  piecemeal 51.10
  severally 79.10
  slowly 275.11
do one's bit 360.6
not a bit 536.4
bitch *n.* slattern 59.5
  dog 366.6
  female animal 374.8
  strumpet 962.2
bitch *v.* 699.9
bite *n.* morsel 298.2
  lunch 298.35
  taste 390.1
  cheat 545.7
bite *v.* eat 298.44
  pain 378.4
  freeze 385.3
  be credulous 486.3
  be deceived 547.3
  swindle 791.12
  mental pain 830.3
bite in incise 259.3
  etch 558.5
bite off more than
  one can chew 676.2
bite the hand that
  feeds one 830.3
bite the dust die 360.6
  be defeated 732.5
bite the thumb at
  defy 715.2
  affront 929.3

biting — blast

bite (*continued*)
  bite the tongue
    be pungent 392.3
    not speak 585.3
biting acrid 171.10
  painful 378.7
  cold 383.8
  pungent 392.5
  vigorous 574.5
  penetrating 824.13
  distressing 830.15
  gruff 895.7
  censorious 932.11
bitter cold 383.8
  acrid 395.6
  (pungent 392.5)
  (sour 397.6)
  unpleasant 830.10
  gruff 895.7
  hating 898.5
  resentful 900.12
  ill-humored 901.7
  rancorous 907.6
bitter end *n.* 67.2
bitter-end *adj.* 141.7
bitter-ender
  conservative 141.3
  (irreconcilable 606.3)
  oppositionist 710.2
  malcontent 832.2
bitter-enderism 141.2
bitterly
  extremely 31.23
  coldly 383.13
bittern 366.22
bitterness
  acridness 395.2
  (pungency 392.1)
  (sourness 397.1)
  wretchedness 828.3
  regret 833.1
  enmity 889.1
  hate 898.1
  resentment 900.1
bitter pill 735.1; 830.2
bitters 395.3
bittersweet 396.8
bitumen 356a.1
bituminous *n.* 388.2
bituminous *adj.* 356a.3
bivalve 368.6
bivalvular double 90.3
  molluscan 368.16
bivouac *n.* 189.15
bivouac *v.* 184.15
biweekly 138.11
bizarre unusual 83.10
  absurd 497.4
bizarreness, bizarrerie 83.3
blab *n.* informer 527.6
  gossip 532.1
  chatter 584.2
  chatterer 584.3
blab *v.*
  inform on 527.10
  tattle 529.4
  be loquacious 584.4
blabber twaddle 517.3
  informer 527.6
  newsmonger 532.5

chatter 584.2
blabberer
  informer 527.6
  newsmonger 532.5
black *n.* horse 271.5
  color 431.1
  Negro 431.4
  mourning 839.4
black *v.* 431.6
black *adj.*
  nigrous 431.7
  (dark 421.7)
  evil 649.8
  wicked 945.16
blackamoor 431.4
black-and-blue
  black 413.7
  blue 438.6
  discolored 440a.3
black and white 556.3
  in black and white
    color 431.10
    written 590.15
  put in black and white 551.8
black art 992.1
blackball *n.* 893.3
blackball *v.*
  stigmatize 874.7
  exclude 893.7
  censure 932.7
blackberry 298.31
Black Bess 271.9
black bill 727.4
blackbird 366.22
blackboard 590.10
black-browed 961.8
black buck 366.10
blackcap 366.22
blackcoat 996.2
b'ackcock 366.22
blackdamp 334.2
Black Death 655.2
blacken darken 431.6
  (discolor 440a.2)
  stigmatize 874.7
  (vilify 934.3)
blackening 431.2
black eye
  discoloration 440a.1
  eye 443.5
  bruise 659.4
  give a black eye
    discolor 440a.2
    punish 972.6
blackface *n.*
  minstrel 416.10
  paint 431.5
blackface, black-faced *adj.* 431.9
blackfellow 431.4
b'ackfish 366.21
black flag 722.3
black gang 269.3
blackguard *n.* 949.1
blackguard *adj.*
  vulgar 851.7
  unprincipled 940.8
blackguardism
  vulgarity 851.1
  malediction 908.1
blackguardly 851.7

Black Hand 791.3
black hole 752.1
blackish 431.8
blackjack, black jack *n.* 727.7
blackjack *v.* club 361.10
  cudgel 972.6
black lead 332.2
blackleg scab 607.6
  disease 655.18
  swindler 792.8
black-letter 124.9
black list *n.* 893.3
black-list *v.*
  stigmatize 874.7
  exclude 893.7
  censure 932.7
black magic 992.1
blackmail *n.*
  extortion 791.3
  booty 793.1
  hush money 973.2
blackmail *v.* 791.13
Black Maria 272.7
Black Mass 992.1
blackness 431
  (darkness 421.1)
black-out 421.3
black pigment 431.5
black quarter 655.18
Black Saladin 271.9
black sheep 949.1
Black Shirt 712.6
blacksmith 690.6
black snake, blacksnake 975.1
black swan 650.3
blackwater 655.18
blacky *n.* 431.4
b'acky *adj.* 431.8
bladder bag 191.6
  bubble 353.1
blade stalk 215.14
  cutter 253.6
  foliage 367.4
  sharp fellow 682.10
  weapon 727.3
  fop 854.1
bladesmith 690.6
blague humbug 544.2
  deception 545.3
  lie 546.1
  boasting 884.1
blah, blah-blah
  nonsense 517.2, 3
  chatter 584.2
blain
  protuberance 250.2
  (blemish 848.1)
  sore 655.16
blamable 932.13
b!ame *n.*
  censure 932.2
  accusation 938.1
  shift the blame 938.4
  take the blame 932.10
blame *v.*
  confound 908.4
  reprehend 932.7
  accuse 938.4
  blame for, blame on,

blame upon 155.3
to blame
  reprehensible 932.13
  guilty 947.4
blame, blamed *adv.* 31.24
blameful 932.11
blameless 946.5
blameworthy 932.14
  (bad 649.8)
  (accusable 938.7)
  (unworthy 940.9)
  (unjustifiable 941a.4)
  (vicious 945.11)
  (guilty 947.4)
blanch decolor 429.5
  whiten 430.6
bland moderate 174.6
  hypocritical 544.8
  suave 894.13
  flattering 933.3
blandishment
  allurement 617.1
  endearment 902.3
blank *n.* 187.4
  (nonexistence 2.1)
blank *adj.*
  empty 187.11
  (nonexistent 2.7)
  (unsubstantial 4.5)
  closed 261.3
  incogitant 452.3
  expressionless 517.8
  unornamented 849.4
  look blank
    be disappointed 509.3
    be discontented 832.3
    wonder 870.2
blankbook 551.3
  (stationery 590.10)
blank cartridge
  nullity 4.2
  impotent 158.3
  false alarm 669.2
blanket
  cover 223.2, 9
  printing 591.5
blanketmaker 690.8
blank verse 597.1
blare *n.* noise 404.3
  brightness 420.1
blare *v.* be noisy 404.7
  bellow 412.2
blarney *n.* 933.1
blarney *v.* 933.2
blarneyer 935.2
blasé
  worldly wise 698.15
  life-weary 841.9
  (unastonished 871.3)
  indifferent 866.4
  sated 869.6
blaspheme 988.7
  (scoff 930.6)
blasphemer 988.4
blasphemous 988.10
blasphemy 988.1
blast *n.*

blast — bloat

explosion 173.3
gust 349.6
blare 404.3
bang 406.2
blast v. demolish 162.4
explode 173.9
blare 404.7
bang 406.8
blight 659.8; 663.2
blast int. 908.8
blast lamp 386.1
blastoderm 357.4
blastodermic 357.10
blastogenesis 161.2
blasty 349.25
blat 412.2
blatant noisy 404.9
bellowing 412.3
blate 412.2
blather, blether n.
twaddle 517.3
chatter 584.2
chatterer 584.3
blather, blether v.
584.4
blatherskite
nonsense 517.2
chatterer 584.3
boaster 884.3
blatter bleat 412.2
be loquacious 584.4
blaze n. notch 257.1
(mark 550.7)
fire 382.8
~ of light 420.4
landmark 550.10
in a blaze
burning 382.17
shining 420.22
blaze v. notch 257.5
(mark 550.19)
burn 382.13
~ up 384.17
flash 420.17
proclaim 531.7
blazer 225.16
blazing burning 382.17
shining 420.22
blazon proclaim 531.7
adorn 847.11
glorify 873.13
display 882.6
bleach n. 429.3
bleach v. fade 429.4, 5
whiten 430.6
bleachers
observatory 441.5
spectators 444.2
bleaching 429.2, 3
(whitening 430.2)
bleak
windswept 349.25
cold 383.8
blear v. 422.6
blear, bleared adj.
blurred 422.8
indistinct 447.5
blearedness 443.2
blear-eyed 443.15
bleary blurred 422.8
indistinct 447.5
bleat 412.2

bleb n. vessel 191.6
protuberance 250.2
bubble 353.1
sore 655.16
bleb v. 353.8
bleed
suffer physically
378.4
let blood 662.24
despoil 789.12
overcharge 814.3
suffer mentally 828.9
(be sad 837.6)
bleed white 688.5
bleeding
hemorrhage 299.6
bloodletting 662.15
bleeding heart
wretchedness 828.2
sorrow 837.3
pity 914.1
blemish n.
discoloration 440a.1
(mark 550.7)
(fault 651.2)
scar 659.4
disfiguration 848
(deformity 243.1)
(excrescence 250.2)
(defect 651.2)
(ugliness 846.1, 3)
vice 945.5
blemish deform 243.3
discolor 440a.2
(mark 550.19)
(disfigure 848.2)
soil 653.15
bruise 659.8
(uglify 846.5)
blemished
discolored 440a.3
disfigured 848.3
(deformed 243.5)
(defective 651.4)
blench shrink 277.3
flinch 623.9
be sensitive 822.4
blend n. 48.1
blend v. combine 48.3
(mix 41.6)
be converted 144.8
harmonize 413.24
be concordant 714.2
blending junction 43.1
combination 48.1
blend-word 563.9
Blenheim 722.5
blennorrhea, blennor-
rhoea 655.7
bless delight 829.5
praise 931.6
divine function
976.11
hallow 987.8
glorify 990.10
give benediction
990.12
bless my heart!
870.11
bless the Lord 990.16
bless us! 870.11
bless with 784.13

blessed 827.9
blessed event 161.3
blessedness 827.2
blessing
benefit 648.2
(prosperity 734.1)
grace 784.4
praise 931.2
benediction 990.4
give one's blessing
990.12
Blessing 998.7
blest 827.9
blest with 777.7
blether See blather
blight n. 663.2
(destroyer 165.1)
(decay 659.2)
(adversity 735.1)
(affliction 830.2)
blight v. 659.8
blighted 659.13
Blighty 182.3
blimp fat man 192.7
aerostat 273a.5
elastic 325.2
blind n. window 260.5
screen 424.3
ambush 530.1
deception 545.3
pretext 619.1
wager 621.3
artifice 702.3
blind v.
render blind 442.3
dazzle 443.13
conceal 528.10
hoodwink 545.7
blind adj.
dead drunk 959.22
sightless 442.6
(dim-sighted
443.15)
inattentive 458.10
obtuse 499.12
mechanical 601.14
insensible to 823.5
indifferent 866.4
be blind not see 442.4
not look 442.5
be ignorant 491.6
blind alley n.
closure 261.1
impasse 704.3
roadway 627.3
blind-alley adj. 442.6
blind baggage 528.6
b'inded blind 442.6
ignorant 491.10
blinders
eyeshade 424.4
goggles 445.3
blind faith 486.1
blind flight 267a.23
blind flying 267a.1
blindfold v. blind 442.3
hoodwink 545.7
blindfold, blindfolded
adj. blind 442.6
ignorant 491.10
be blindfolded 442.4
blind gut vitals 221.4

intestine 350.4
blind hookey 840.12
blind landing 267a.26
blindman's buff 840.11
blindness
sightlessness 442
(dim-sightedness
443.2)
ignorance 491.1
blind pig 959.13
blind-pigger 959.12
blind side
blindness 442.1
prejudice 481.3
credulity 486.1
bigotry 606.2
blind spot
prejudice 481.3
bigotry 606.2
blindstory 1000.3
blind tiger 959.13
blink n. glitter 420.5
reflection 420.10
blink v. shrink 277.3
glitter 420.18
wink 443.11
blench 623.9
blink at
not look 442.5
disregard 460.4
not observe 773.3
condone 918.3
blinkard 443.6
blinker 424.5
blinkers
eyelashes 256.6
eyeshade 424.4
eyes 441.7
blink-eyed 443.14
blinking 443.6
blinky glittery 420.23
blink-eyed 443.14
bliss 827.2
blissful 827.9
blister n.
vessel 191.6
protuberance 250.2
bubble 353.1
burn 384.8
sore 655.16
blemish 848.1
blister v. burn 384.18
(discolor 440a.2)
thrash 972.6
blister beetle
excitant 171.4
aphrodisiac 865.10
blithe 836.7
blitheness 836.1
blithesome 836.7
blitz n. 716.1
blitz v. 716.6
blitzkrieg
attack 716.1
warcraft 722.2
blizzard
windstorm 349.11, 12
snowstorm 383.6
bloak See bloke
bloat distend 194.8
blow up 349.24

bloated — blowy

bloated
  swollen 194.10
  (distorted 243.5)
  ~ with pride 878.6
blob *n.*
  protuberance 250.2
  bubble 353.1
  sore 655.16
blob *v.* bubble 353.8
  sound 405.7
blobber lip 848.1
block *n.* lump 192.5
  supporter 215.2
  solid 321.4
  hardness 323.3
  dolt 501.1
  engraving 558.3, 4
  writing tablet 590.10
  obstacle 706.2
  auction stand 796.2
  execution 975.4
  on the block 796.9
block *v.*
  hem in 229.2
  outline 230.3
  close 261.2
  hinder 706.4
  (delay 133.6)
  block in 466.10
  block out
    roughhew 161.8
    outline 230.3
    form 240.6
    plot 466.10
blockade *n.*
  closure 261.1
  obstruction 706.1, 2
  embargo 893.3
blockade *v.*
  hem in 229.2
  close 261.2
  obstruct 706.4
  barricade 717.7
  embargo 893.7
blockage
  closure 261.1
  hindrance 706.1
blockhead
  stupidity 499.2
  dolt 501.1
blockhouse hut 189.4
  fortification 717.4
blockish stupid 499.12
  clumsy 699.12
blockmaker 690.8
block print 558.3
block printing 558.2
bloke, bloak 373.2
blond, blonde 430.9
  (light-colored 429.7)
blood
  consanguinity 11.1
  kinsman 11.3
  gore 333.3
  life force 359.2
  bloodshed 361.1
  bloodstain 440a.2
  fop 854.1
  nobility 875.1
  let blood
    let out 297.13

    bleed 662.24
  stir the blood
    excite 824.2
    irritate 824.5
    anger 900.10
blood and iron 823.1
blood brother 11.3
bloodhound 366.6
bloodless pale 429.6
  anemic 655.24
  peaceful 721.4
  heartless 907.8
  innocent 946.5
bloodlessness 160.3; 655.5
bloodletting
  evacuation 297.5
  venesection 662.15
bloodline 166.4
blood poisoning
  infection 655.2
  poisoning 659.3
blood-red 434.9
blood relation 11.3
blood relationship 11.1
bloodshed
  killing 361.1
  warfare 722.1
bloodshedder 361.8
bloodshot 440a.3
blood sister 11.3
bloodstain 440a.2
  (redden 434.7)
bloodstained 361.15
  (discolored 440a.3)
bloodstone red 434.5
  gem 847.8
bloodsucker 789.6
bloodthirst
  cruelty 907.3
  unnatural desire 961.3
bloodthirsty
  murderous 361.15
  cruel 907.9
  bestial 961.11
blood vessel 350.4
blood-warm 382.15
bloodwite, bloodwit 974.1
bloody *v.* 440a.2
bloody *adj.*
  murderous 361.15
  red 434.9
  (fluid 333.7)
  execrable 649.8
  soiled 653.16
bloody *adv.* 31.24
bloody flux
  hemorrhage 299.6
  ailment 655.5
bloody-minded
  murderous 361.15
  cruel 907.9
bloody shirt 722.3
bloom *n.* flower 367.5
  heat flush 382.7
  reddening 434.4
  blueness 438.1
  health 654.1
  beauty 845.1
  in full bloom

    adult 131.5
    in health 654.4
    gorgeous 845.12
bloom *v.* vegetate 365.2
  be in health 654.2
  prosper 734.5
  be beautiful 845.6
bloomer 495.3
  pull a bloomer 495.9
bloomers 225.21, 25
blooming red 434.11
  healthy 654.4
  beautiful 845.12
blossom *n.*
  product 161.6
  flower 367.5
blossom *v.* bear 161.9
  vegetate 365.2
  prosper 734.5
blot *n.* error 495.2
  obliteration 552.1
  soil 653.3
  blemish 848.1
  stigma 874.2
  sin 945.5
blot *v.* darken 431.6
  discolor 440a.2
  obliterate 552.2
  soil 653.15
  stigmatize 874.7
  blot out excise 38.5
    destroy 162.4
    kill 361.10
blotch *n* soil 653.3
  blemish 848.1
  moral blemish 945.5
blotch *v.* darken 431.6
  discolor 440a.2
  soul 653.15
blotched 440.9
  (discolored 440a.3)
  (imperfect 651.4)
  (blemished 848.3)
blotchy dark 431.8
  spotted 440.9
  discolored 440a.3
blotter 652.7
blotto 959.22
blouse 225.8, 15, 18
blow *n.* knock 276.3
  (thrust 716.3)
  (whipping 972.3)
  windstorm 349.11
  flower 367.5
  surprise 508.2
  disappointment 509.1
  act 680.2
  calamity 735.3
  shock 830.2
  offense 900.5
blow *v.* depart 293.5
  puff 349.22, 23
  (emit 297.13)
  honk 404.7
  toot 410.8
  ~ a horn 416.18
  inform on 527.10
  publish 531.7
  flee 623.10
  be fatigued 688.4
  prosper 734.5

  boast 884.5
blow down 162.4
blow hot and cold
  vary 149.4
  quibble 477.8
  prevaricate 544.5
  be capricious 608.4
  (change 140.5)
  (be irresolute 605.4)
  (tergiversate 607.7)
blow in 818.3
blow off 73.3
blow one's brains out 361.10, 14
blow one's own horn
  be ostentatious 882.6
  boast 884.5
blow out
  explode 173.9
  extinguish 385.5
  detonate 406.8
blow over 122.6
blow the coals 824.2
blow the gaff
  inform on 527.10
  divulge 529.4
blow up
  demolish 162.4
  explode 173.9
  inflate 349.24
  (rarefy 322.3)
  ignite 384.17
  detonate 406.8
  excite 824.2
  reprove 932.8
blow upon
  disgrace 874.6
  defame 934.3
blower bellows 349.20
  (pump 333.6)
  (ventilator 338.6)
  boaster 884.3
blowgun 349.20
blowhard 884.3
blowhole
  opening 260.1
  air hole 351.1
  (outlet 295.5)
blowing 688.7
blown breathless 688.7
  proud 878.6
blowoff 67.1
blowout
  explosion 173.3
  feast 298.37
  detonation 406.2
  festival 840.2
blowpipe
  conversion 144.4
  blower 349.20
  (air passage 351.1)
  heater 386.1
blowth 367.5
blowtorch 386.1
blowtube 349.20
blowup
  explosion 173.3
  detonation 406.2
  reproof 932.3
blow valve 666.1
blowy 349.25

728

blowzed — bobble

blowzed 434.11
blowzy swollen 194.10
 red 434.11
 ugly 846.8
blub bubble 353.8
 sound 405.7
blubber n. 356.4
blubber v. bubble 353.8
 sound 405.7
 weep 839.8
bluchers 225.27
bludgeon 727.7
blue adj.
 unqualified 52.10
 cerulean 438.6
 bookish 490.16
 look blue
 be disappointed
  509.3
 feeling 824.8
 be discontented
  832.3
 be sad 837.6
blue v. 438.5
blue n. heavens 318.2
 color 438.2
 bluestocking 492.4;
  853.4
blueback 800.6
Bluebeard
 polygamist 903.5
 libertine 962.1
bluebell 438.3
blueberry 298.31
bluebird bird 366.22
 blue 438.3
blue blood
 nobility 875.1
 nobleman 875.4
blue-blooded
 intrinsic 5.6
 noble 875.10
bluebook 551.2
bluebreast 438.3
bluecoat 745.10
blue devils
 hallucination 503.5
 blues 837.1
bluefish 298.18
bluegrass 438.3
blueing See bluing
bluejacket 269.1
blue jay bird 366.22
 blue 438.3
bluejoint 367.9
blue light 669.1
Blue Monday, blue
 Monday 138.7
blue moon 110.3
 (indefinite time
  109.2)
blueness 438
blue peter 550.13
 hoist the blue peter
  267.16, 41
blue point 298.18
blue ribbon 733.1
blue ruin 162.1
blues uniform 225.8
 song 415.10
 sadness 837.1
bluestocking n.

pedant 492.4
 affecter 853.4
bluestocking adj.
 490.16
blue streak 274.6
bluff n.
 precipice 212.3
 false pretense 544.2
 deception 545.1
 impostor 548.3
 game 840.12
 boasting 884.1
 bluster 887.1
 blusterer 887.2
bluff v. deceive 545.7
 boast 884.5
 bluster 887.3
bluff adj. savage 173.14
 steep 217.12
 (vertical 212.8)
 blunt 254.3
 insolent 885.10
 gruff 895.7
bluffer impostor 548.3
 braggadocio 884.3
 blusterer 887.2
bluing, blueing 438.4
blunder n. error 495.3
 (absurdity 497.1)
 (folly 499.7)
 bungle 699.4
blunder v. err 495.9
 (be absurd 497.2)
 (fail 732.5)
 bungle 699.9
blunder away 699.9
blunder on, blunder
 upon
 chance upon 156.8
 bungle 699.7
blunderbuss
 bungler 701.1
 firearm 727.10
blunderer 701
blunderhead dolt 501.1
 bungler 701
blunderheaded
 stupid 499.12
 clumsy 699.12
blunt n. 800.1
blunt v. weaken 160.8
 moderate 174.5
 dull 254.3
 deaden 376.4
 dispirit 616.3
 impair 659.8
 ~ the sensibilities
  822.4
blunt adj. inert 172.3
 dull 254.3
 stupid 499.12
 abrupt 684.5
 frank 703.4
 gruff 895.7
bluntness 254
blunt-witted 499.12
blur n. soil 653.3
 blemish 868.1
 stigma 874.2
blur v. dim 422.6
 discolor 440a.2
 soil 653.15

blurb n. 531.3
blurb v. publicize 531.8
 praise 931.2
blurbist 531.6
blurred, blurry
 dim 422.8
 discolored 440a.3
 indistinct 447.5
blurt divulge 529.4
 speak 582.6
blush n.
 heat flush 382.7
 color 428.1
 reddening 434.4
 emotion 821.2
 modesty 881.1
blush v. redden 434.8
 turn color 824.8
 ~ from modesty
  881.4
blushing n. 881.1
blushing adj.
 red 434.11
 modest 881.5
bluster n. turmoil 59.4
 braggadocio 884.1
 swagger 887
bluster v. blow 349.22
 be defiant 715.2
 bully 860.12
 be boastful 884.5
 swagger 887.3
 (be ostentatious
  882.6)
 rage angrily 900.8
blusterer
 swaggerer 887.2
 (boaster 884.3)
 bully 913.2
blustering n. 887.1
blustering
 turbulent 173.12
 windy 349.25
 noisy 404.9
 blustery 887.4
blusterous, blustery
 turbulent 173.12
 windy 349.25
bo, boe 268.2
boa neckpiece 225.33
 serpent 366.19
boa constrictor 366.19
boar swine 366.7
 male animal 373.6
board n. lamina 204.2
 table 215.20
 flat 251.3
 food 298.5
 meal 298.34
 hardness 323.3
 plank 635.3
 council 696.1
 tribunal 966.1
 by the board 267.66
 on board here 186.20
 aboard 267.53
board v. copulate 43.8
 navigate 267.10
 attack 716.5
boarder lodger 188.4
 eater 298.41
boarding 716.1

boarding school 542.1
boards 599.1, 12
board walk 627.2
boarhound 366.6
boast n. 884.1
boast v. 884.5
 (exaggerate 549.2)
boaster 884.3
 (impostor 548.3)
 (egoist 880.3)
 (blusterer 887.2)
boastful 884.7
 (overestimated
  482.4)
 (magniloquent
  577.7)
 (proud 878.6)
 (vain 880.6)
boastfully 884.10
boasting 884
 (overestimation
  482.1)
 (exaggeration
  549.1)
 (magniloquence
  577.2)
 (vanity 880.1)
boat n.
 automobile 272.15
 vessel 273.1, 4
 aircraft 273a.1
 in the same boat 709.8
boat v.
 navigate 267.10
 transport 270.8
boatable 267.49
boater 269.2
boating 267.1
boatlike 245.11
boat line 273.10
boatman 269.2
boat race 274.4
boat-race 274.9
boat seaplane 273a.3
boatsetter 269.5
boat song 415.3
boatswain, bosun 269.4
boatwright 690.7
bob n.
 repetend 104.2
 fathomer 208.4
 plumb 212.5
 sled, skate 272.13
 shake 315.4
 gravity 319.2
 measure 466.4
 money 800.8
 obeisance 928.2
bob v. jerk 285.5
 caper 309.5
 oscillate 314.8
 shake 315.9
 make obeisance
  928.6
bob for grope 463.9
 fish 622.8
bobbery 404.2
bobbin 312.5
bobbish 654.4
bobble n. shake 315.4
 blunder 495.3
 bungle 699.4

bobble — bone

bobble v.
  oscillate 314.8
  shake 315.9
  bungle 699.9
bobby 745.10
bobcat 366.3
bobolink 366.22
bob skate, bobsled,
  bobsleigh 272.13
bobstay 273.10
bobtail 297.4
bobtailed 53.4
bocage 367.7
Boche, boche 188.9
  (German soldier
  726.4)
bodacious 885.9
bode 511.7, 9
bodice 225.18
bodiless 317.6
bodily *adj.*
  substantial 3.4
  material 136.8
  fleshly 364.4
bodily *adv.*
  substantially 3.5
  wholly 50.10
boding *n.* 511.6
boding *adj.* 511.11
bodkin 262
  (edge tool 253.6)
body *n.* being 3.2
  main part 50.3
  company 72.3
  crowd 72.4
  bodice 225.18
  enclosure 232.1
  fuselage 273a.10
  substance 316.2
  solid 321.4
  corpse 362.1
  person 372.3
  community 712.3
  religious order 984.3
  esoterics 994.12
  in a body
    wholly 50.10
    together 88.10
body *v.* 316.7
  body forth 554.7
body clothes 225.25
bodyguard escort 88.4
  protector 664.3
  guard 717.6
body corporate 712.5
body politic
  country 182.1
  (government 737.8)
  nation 372.2
boe See **bo**
Boehmenism 984.4
Boehmenist 984.14
Boeotian *n.* fool 501.1
  barbarian 876.7
Boeotian *adj.* 499.12
Boer War 722.4
bog *n.* 345.1
bog *v.* 345.2
bogey See **bogy**
boggart, boggard 980.4
boggle *n.* demur 485.2
  objection 489.2

  bungle 699.4
  fearfulness 860.2
boggle *v.*
  falter 475.6; 605.4
  demur 485.7
  object 489.4
  bungle 699.9
  (blunder 495.9)
  flounder 704.6
  disapprove 932.5
boggle-de-botch,
  boggle-dy-botch
  699.4
boggler 701
boggy 345.3
  (soft 324.6)
bogus *n.* 800.9
bogus *adj.* 545.13
bogy, bogey, bogie
  bugbear 980.4
  false alarm 669.2
Bohemian *n.* 83.4
Bohemian *adj.*
  unconformable 83.11
  uncouth 851.7
Bohemianism 83.2
bohunk alien 57.3
  Slav 188.9
  awkward fellow 701
boil *n.*
  protuberance 250.2
  sore 655.16
  (swelling 194.2)
boil *v.* bubble 353.8
  be hot 382.13
  cook 384.19
  ~ with passion
    825.7
  ~ with rage 900.8
boil down 201.4
boil over bubble 353.8
  rage 825.7
  become angry 900.8
boiled 959.21
boiler kettle 191.11
  caldron 386.1
boiler head 268.11
boilermaker 690.8
boiler room 404.4
boilersmith 690.6
boilerworks 691
boiling *n.*
  quantity 25.2
  bunch 72.5
  ebullition 384.7
boiling *adj.* 382.16
  boiling over
  fervent 821.6
  excited 824.10
boisterous
  turbulent 173.12
  (stormy 349.26)
  (blustering 887.4)
  hasty 684.5
  excited 824.11
  reckless 863.7
boisterousness 825.4
bold steep 217.12
  prominent 250.9
  seaworthy 273.15
  conspicuous 525.5
  vigorous 574.6

  defiant 715.3
  courageous 861.8
  brazen 885.10
boldface *n.* type 591.8
  insolent person 885.3
boldface, bold-faced
  adj. 591.18
boldness
  convexity 250.1
  courage 861.1
bole 50.3
bolero music 415.7
  dance 840.7
bollard pin 45.5
  ship 273.14
boll weevil 366.24
bollworm 366.25
bolo 727.3
Bologna sausage
  298.24
Bolshevik, bolshevik
  adj. 146.5; 742.7
Bolshevik, bo shevik
  n. radical 658.5
  insurgent 742.3
Bolsheviki 712.6
Bolshevism, bolshe-
  vism
  revolutionism 146.2;
    742.2
  reform 658.4
  socialism 737.6
Bolshevist, bolshevist
  n. insurgent 742.3
  radical 658.5
Bolshevist, bolshevist
  adj. 146.5; 742.7
Bolshie, bolshie 658.5;
  742.3
bolster *n.* 215.24
bolster *v.* 707.7
bo'ster up 215.26;
  707.7
bolt *n.*
  fastening 45.2
  (anchor 666.2)
  lightning 420.6
  weapon 727.5, 6, 14
  lock 752.3
bolt *v.* attach 43.6
  speed 274.9
  close 261.2
  eat 298.44
  secede 624.3
  refine 652.10
  ~ the door 666.6
  obstruct 706.4
  revolt 742.5
  prohibit 761.2
  eat greedily 957.3
bolt in 751.8
bolter sorter 60.4
  apostate 607.5
bolt from the blue
  lightning 420.6
  surprise 508.2
bolthead 191.11
boltmaker 690.8
boltrope 273.10
boltsmith 690.6
bolus bite 298.2
  pill 662.4

bomb *n.* firework 382.9
  boom 406.3
  missile 727.14
  (noisemaker 404.4)
bomb, bombard *v.*
  716.6
bombardier 726.4
bombardment 716.1, 2
bombardon 417.4
bombast twaddle 517.3
  grandiloquence
    577.2
  (exaggeration
    549.1)
  boasting 884.1
bombastic
  fantastic 497.4
  grandiloquent 577.7
  (diffuse 573.7)
  boastful 884.7
bomber
  aeronaut 269a.1
  battleplane 273a.2
  soldier 726.4
bombilate hum 405.6
  boom 406.9
  (rumble 407.6)
bombilation hum 405.2
  boom 406.3
  (rumble 407.1)
bombinate hum 405.6
  boom 406.9
bombination
  hum 405.2
  boom 406.3
bombing plane 273a.2
bomb ketch 726.11
bombproof 664.10, 11
bomb rack, bomb sight
  273a.10
bon 618.8
bona fide
  unfeigned 543.3
  in good faith 543.4
  genuine 494.12
  honorably 935.11
bona fides 939.4
  (veracity 543.1)
bonanza fund 636.2
  wealth 803.1
bona roba 962.2
bonbon 396.2
bond connection 45
  (link 9.2)
  (joint 43.3)
  shackle 752.2
  compact 769.1
  security 771.1
  (warrant 924.3)
  money 800.7
  allegiance 939.4
bondage 749.1
bonder 45.2
bonds 752.2
  (subjection 749.1)
  in bonds 740.6
bondslave, bondsman
  746.4
bondstone
  fastening 45.2
  stone 342.4
bone strength 159.4

bone-dry — bopeep

solid 321.4
 hardness 323.3
 dryness 340.4
 blunder 495.3
 translation 522.2
 counter 621.13
 dollar 800.1, 8
bone-dry 340.7
bonehead
 blunder 495.3
 stupidity 499.2
 dolt 501.1
 (ignoramus 493.1)
boneheaded 499.12
bone house 363.13
bon enfant
 sociable person 892.8
 well-wisher 911.1
bone of contention 713.5
 (question 461.10)
 (contention 720.1)
bone pot 363.11
boner 495.3
 pull a boner 495.9
bones corpse 362.1
 minstrel 416.10
 clappers 417.10
 end man 599.19
 dice 621.8
 refuse 645.4
bonesetter 662.19
boneshaker
 horse 271.3
 bicycle 272.14
boney See bony
bonfire fire 382.8
 celebration 883.1
bonhomie, bonhommie
 artlessness 703.1
 benevolence 906.1
bon mot 842.4
bonne guardian 664.3
 lady's maid 746.2
bonne bouche
 delicacy 298.9
 savings 636.2
bonnet hat 225.26
 automobile 272.16
 airplane 273a.10
bonny, bonnie
 hearty 836.11
 comely 845.10
bonnyclabber
 clot 321.5
 (sour articles 397.2)
 semiliquid 352.3
bon ton 852.1, 4
bonus surplus 641.1
 bribe 618.2
 gratuity 784.3
 reward 973.2
bon vivant
 epicure 850.3
 sociable person 892.8
 voluptuary 954a.1
bon voyage 293.14
bony, boney
 thin 203.11
 hard 323.5

bonze 996.9
bonzer 648.8
boob 501.1
 (dupe 547.1)
booby n. breast 250.3
 fool 501.1
booby v. 499.9
booby hatch
 cockpit 273a.10
 insane asylum 503.8
 prison 752.1
booby prize 733.1
boodle all 50.2
 bunch 72.5
 everyone 78.5
 bribe 618.2
 plunder 793.1
 money 800.1
boof 860.1
booger, boogerman 980.4
book n. section 51.2
 volume 593
 (production 161.6)
 (songbook 415.21)
 (edition 531.2)
 (narrative 594.2)
 (compendium 596.1)
 (playbook 599.16)
 (guide book 694.7)
 schedule 611.2
book v. list 86.3
 record 551.8
 schedule 611.4
 enter accounts 811.7
bookbinder 593.14
bookbinding 593.9, 10
bookboard 593.10
bookcase 593.13
 (cupboard 191.15)
book club 593.11
bookcraft 593.18
bookdealer 593.14
 (merchant 797.11)
booked 360.9
book end 593.13
bookery 593.11
book-fed 490.15
book-folder 593.14
bookful 490.15
bookholder 593.13
bookiness 490.2
booking 551.7
bookish 490.16
 (studious 539.6)
 (scholarly 541.9)
bookishness
 scholarship 490.2
 pedantry 491.4
bookkeeper
 recorder 553.1
 accountant 811.6
bookkeeping n. 811.4
bookkeeping adj. 811.10
book knowledge 490.2
book-learned 490.15, 16
 (bibliological 593.20)
bookless 491.9
booklore 490.2

(bibliology 593.18)
booklover 492.3
bookmaker n.
 bookman 593.14
 (workman 690.10)
 gambler 621.15
 craftsman 690.8
bookman scholar 492.1
 bookwright 593.14, 15
book-minded 490.16
bookmonger 492.3
Book of Mormon 986.1
bookplate 591.2
bookpress 593.13
book printer 591.12
bookrack, bookrest 593.13
bookroom 593.11
books 811.5
bookseller
 bookman 593.14
 salesman 797.2
bookselling 593.18
bookshelf 593.13
bookshop 593.12
bookstack 593.13
bookstall 593.12
book stamp 591.2
bookstand 593.12, 13
bookstore 593.12
book-taught, bookwise 490.15
bookworm 492.3
 (bookman 593.14)
bookwright
 bookman 593.14, 15
 wright 690.7
booky 490.16
booly, booley 268.2
boom n. shaft 215.13
 spar 273.12
 impulse 276.1
 roar 406.3
 (explosion 173.3)
 (rumble 407.1)
 (drum 407.3)
 obstruction 706.2
 fortification 717.3
boom v.
 navigate 267.10
 speed 274.9
 impel 276.7
 hum 405.6
 roar 406.9
 (be loud 404.5)
 (rumble 407.6)
 insect 412.2
boomerang
 recoil 277.1
 retaliation 718.1
 weapon 727.5
booming n. 406.3
booming adj. 404.8
boon benefit 648.2
 gift 784.3, 4
boon companion 892.8
boondoggle
 fastening 45.2
 cord 205.3
boonfellow 892.8

boor 876.5, 6
 (vulgarian 851.4)
boorish rustic 183.3
 (plebeian 876.12)
 uncouth 851.7
boost n. increase 35.1
 impulse 276.1
 aid 707.1
boost v. increase 35.3
 accelerate 267a.32
 impel 276.7
 lift 307.5
 publicize 531.8
 help 707.6
 extol 931.6
booster
 publicist 531.6
 commender 935.1
boot n. case 191.8
 footwear 225.27
 kick 276.3
 use 644.1
 advantage 648.2
 aid 707.1
 recruit 726.5
 gain 775.2
 bonus 784.3
 iron heel 975.3
 to boot 37.8
boot v. kick 276.8
 benefit 648.6
bootblack 746.1
booted 673.11
bootee 225.27
Boötes 318.6
booth hut 189.4
 compartment 191.2
 tent 223.5
 enclosure 232.1
 mart 799.1
bootikin 225.27
bootleg n. 959.9
bootleg v. 959.20
bootlegger 959.12
boot'egging 959.9
bootless useless 645.8
 unsuccessful 732.8
 nugatory 158.11
bootlick n. 886.2
bootlick v. 886.3
bootlicker 886.2
bootmaker
 shoemaker 225.40
 craftsman 690.8
boots footwear 225.27
 bootblack 746.1
booty gain 35.2
 spoils 793
 (gain 775.2)
booze n.
 drinking bout 959.3
 liquor 959.4
 drunkard 959.11
booze v. 959.15
booze fighter 959.11
boozer
 drunkard 959.11
 grogshop 959.13
boozy 959.21
bopeep, play at
 gaze 441.13
 hide 528.16

bordar — bound

bordar 188.3
Bordeaux 959.7
bordel
  prostitution 961.6
  brothel 961.7
border *n.*
  surroundings 227.2
  edge 231.1
  (side 236.1)
  (shore 342.2)
  hedge 371.6
  coulisse 599.15
  needlework 847.6
border *v.* be near 197.5
  be contiguous 199.3
  edge 231.3
  side 236.4
  touch 379.3
bordered 231.5
borderer 197.4
  (abutter 199.2)
bordering *n.* 231.2
bordering *adj.*
  near 197.8, 11
  marginal 231.4
borderland
  surroundings 227.2
  edge 231.1
bordure 231.1
bore *n.*
  diameter 202.3
  tube 260.6
  tide 348.9, 10
  annoyance 828.4
  tiresome person 841.4
bore *v.*
  perforate 260.14
  weary 841.5
  (sate 869.4)
boreal windy 349.25
  cold 383.8
Boreas 349.2
bored 841.9
  (incurious 456.3)
boredom 841.1
borer perforator 262
  insect 366.24
boric acid 662.8
boring 841.8
  (dull 843.5)
born 359.10
be born
  ~ so 5.5
  come to life 359.7
born on the wrong side of the blanket 161.9
born with a silver spoon in one's mouth 734.8
born days 110.4
borné 499.17
borough 189.16
borrel rustic 183.3
  unlearned 491.9
  uncouth 851.7
borrow imitate 19.6
  raise money 788.2
  (pawn 771.5)
  (appropriate 789.8)
  (charge 805.5)

  (go in debt 806.6)
  steal 791.9
borrowed 19.12
borrowed plumes
  disguise 545.5
  borrowing 788.1
borrower 806.4
borrowing 788
  (debt 806.1)
boscage, bosch, boschveld 367.7
bosh *n.*
  nonsense 517.2
  humbug 544.2
  untruth 546.1
  boasting 884.1
bosh *v.* 699.9
bosh *int.* 497.5
bosher 701
bosk, bosket, bosquet 367.7
bosky 367.15
bosom essence 5.2
  interior 221.2
  breast 250.3
  inmost mind 450.3
  (affections 820.2)
bosom friend
  friend 890.1
  liquor 959.4
boss *n.* relief 557.6
  printing 591.5
  superintendent 694.1
  political ~ 694.4
  master 745.1
  ornament 847.4
boss *v.* chase 250.8
  superintend 693.5
  rule 737.11
boss *adj.* 693.6
bossed 250.10
boss-eyed 443.14
bossism 693.1
bossy *n.* cow 366.12
  female animal 374.8
bossy *adj.*
  in relief 250.10
  directive 693.6
  dictatorial 737.15
boston 840.12
Boston bag 191.5
botanical 369.11
  (vegetable 367.14)
  (agricultural 371.9)
botanic garden 371.6
  (herbarium 369.2)
botanist 369.9
  (naturalist 357.7)
  (agriculturist 371.2)
botanize 369.10
botanomancy 511.3
botany 369
  (science 357.5;
  490.8)
botch *n.* 699.4
  (blunder 495.3)
  (failure 732.2)
botch *v.* repair 660.11
  bungle 699.9
  (blunder 495.9)
  (do carelessly 460.6)
botcher 701

botchery 699.3, 4
both *adj.* 89.6
both *pron.* 89.2
bother *n.* turmoil 59.4
  confusion 458.4
  perplexity 475.2
  bustle 682.6
  adversity 735.1
  trepidation 825.3
  annoyance 828.4
  trouble 830.2
bother *v.*
  confuse 458.9
  perplex 475.8
  embarrass 704.7
  annoy 830.5
botheration
  confusion 458.4
  perplexity 475.2
  adversity 735.1
  annoyance 828.4
  affliction 830.2
bothered 828.15
bothering 830.12
botherment
  perplexity 475.2
  adversity 735.1
  annoyance 828.4
  trouble 830.2
bothy 189.4
bottle *n.*
  receptacle 191.11
  alcoholic drink 959.4
bottle *v.* 670.4
bottle up
  conceal 528.10
  confine 751.8
bottle green 435.2
bottleholder 711.4
bottlemaker 690.8
bottlenose oil 356.4
bottle nose 959.2
bottling works 959.14
bottom *n.*
  ~ of the sea 208.3
  base 211.1, 3
  rump 235.5
  valley 252.5
  ship 273.1
  marsh 345.1
  resolution 604.1
  courage 861.1
at bottom 5.8
at the bottom of
  causal 153.9
  resulting from 154.5
from the bottom of one's heart
  truthfully 543.4
  heartily 821.9
  honestly 939.11
go to the bottom
  capsize 267.35
  sink 310.5
bottom *v.* 215.26
bottom *adj.*
  lowest 207.10
  basal 211.5
bottomless 208.9
bottomry 771.5
bottomry bond 771.1

bottoms dregs 40.2
  marsh 345.1
bottom sawyer 34.3
bottom water 208.3
bouche lining 224.1
  mouth 260.2, 3
  food 298.5
  pastry 298.12
bouderie 901.2
boudoir 191.16
bouge *n.* 250.2
bouge *v.* 250.7
bough member 51.4
  foliage 367.4
boughpot, bowpot 400.4
bought 245.2
bougie 423.7
bougie decimale 420.1
bouillon 298.16
boulder, bowlder
  sphere 249.2
  rock 342.4
boulevard
  roadway 627.3
  surroundings 227.2
bouleversement
  revolution 146.1
  destruction 162.1
boun 293.4
bounce *n.*
  outbreak 173.2
  dismissal 297.4
  joggle 315.4
  lie 546.2
  swagger 882.2
  brag 884.1
  bluster 887.1
bounce *v.* eject 297.8
  dismiss 297.12
  bang 406.7
  caper 309.5
  joggle 315.8
  be bombastic 577.5
  bluster 887.3
bounce upon
  meet 292.10
  surprise 508.6
bouncer ejector 297.6
  lie 546.2
  liar 548.5
  boaster 884.3
bouncing 192.12
bound *n.* edge 231.1
  limit 233.1
  leap 309.1
without bound 180.7
bound *v.*
  circumscribe 229.2
  edge 231.3
  limit 233.2
  speed 274.9
  ~ back 277.3
  leap 309.4
bound *adj.*
  shut in 229.4
  limited 233.3
  determined 604.7
  assured 474.9
  restrained 751.11
  promised 768.7
  obliged 926.10

boundary — bracket

bound for 620.4
be bound for 278.5
boundary n.
  outline 230.1
  edge 231.1
  fence 232.2
  limits 233.1
boundary adj. 233.3
bound bailiff 745.9
bounded 32.7
bounden 926.10
bounder
  vulgarian 851.4
  rascal 949.1
  libertine 962.1
boundless
  infinite 105.3
  eternal 112.4
  unlimited 180.7
boundlessness
  infinity 105.1
  illimitability 180.4
bounds outline 230.1
  edge 231.1
  (purlieus 197.3)
  (surroundings 227.2)
  limits 233.1
  have no bounds 112.2
  keep within bounds
  be moderate 174.4
  restrain 751.6
  prohibit 761.2
  out of bounds 641.5
  within bounds
  to a degree 32.13
  short of 304.5
  within reason 502.6
  moderately 174.8
bounteous, bountiful
  numerous 102.5
  plentiful 639.7
  liberal 816.4
  (charitable 906.7)
bounty aid 707.3
  gratuity 784.3
  liberality 816.1
  (charitableness 906.2)
  reward 973.2
bouquet
  fragrance 400.1
  nosegay 400.4
  ornament 847.5
  compliment 931.3
  give a bouquet 931.6
bourbon 959.6
Bourbon 141.3
bourdon staff 215.15
  drone bass 413.6, 14
  chorus 415.15
Bourdon tube 267a.29
bourgeois
  printing 591.7
  commoner 876.3
Bourgeois Gentilhomme 876.8
bourgeoisie
  mediocrity 736.1
  commonalty 876.1
bourgeon See burgeon
bourn, bourne

limit 233.1
destination 292.6
stream 348.1
bourrée music 415.7
  dance 840.7
bourse, Bourse 799.3
bouse n. 959.4
bouse v. 959.15
bouse, bowse v. 267.10
bouser 959.11
bousy 959.21
bout round 138.4
  act 680.2
  fight 720.2, 6
  spree 840.3
  drunken spree 959.3
boutade music 415.7
  caprice 608.1
  dance 840.7
  prank 842.7
boutonniere
  bouquet 400.4
  ornamentation 847.5
bovine n. 366.12
bovine adj.
  animal 366.26
  stupid 499.12
bow n. handle 215.7
  arching 245.1
  curve 245.2
  protuberance 250.2
  ship 273.7
  airplane 273a.10
  fiddlestick 417.13
  début 599.8
  sling 727.9
  ornament 847.3
  obeisance 928.2
  (greeting 894.4)
bow and arrow 727.9
bow v. convex 250.7
  violin 416.18
  submit 725.3
  kowtow 886.3
  make obeisance 928.6
  worship 990.9
bow and scrape
  be submissive 725.3
  truckle 886.3
  make obeisance 928.6
bowed
  arcuate 245.5
  convex 250.9
bowed-down
  stricken 837.13
  humbled 879.5
bowelless 914a.3
bowel movement 653.7
bowels depth 208.2
  vitals 221.4
  intestines 350.4
  mercy 914.1
bower retreat 189.13
  arbor 191.22
  (garden 371.6)
  anchor 666.2
  playing card 840.13
Bower of Bliss 981.2
bowie knife
  knife 253.6

weapon 727.3
bowing 245.1
bowknot 45.6
bowl n.
  receptacle 191.11
  cavity 252.2
  ceramics 384.14
  theater 599.10
  arena 728.1
  sport 840.11
bowl v. 312.7
bowl along
  walk 266.16
  speed 274.9
bowl down, bowl over floor 213.7
  fell 308.5
  startle 508.6
  astonish 870.3
bowler See boulder
bowlegs 266.11
bowlegged 243.5
  (bow-shaped 245.5)
bowler 225.26
bowline knot 45.6
  ship's rope 273.10
bowling 840.11
bowling alley 840.14
bowling green
  plane 213.3
  place of amusement 840.14
bowman
  shooter 284.8
  archer 726.4
bowpot See boughpot
bowse See bouse
bow-shaped 245.5
bowshot
  short way 197.2
  shot 284.4
bowsprit prow 234.3
  spar 273.12
bowstring n 975.4
bowstring v. 972.8
bow window 245.2
bowwow 366.6
bowwow theory 562.2
box n. house 189.3
  compartment 191.2
  case 191.8
  blow 276.3
  coffin 363.10
  printing 591.5
  theater 599.11
  ~ on the ear 900.5; 972.3
box v. strike 276.3
  fight 720.8
  ~ up 751.8
  cuff 972.6
box off 267.24
box the compass
  navigation 267.39
  direction 278.7
  turn round 283.6; 312.7
boxcar twelve 98.7
  railway car 272.19
  throw of dice 621.9
boxer 726.2
boxing 720.6

Boxing Day 138.7
boxmaker 690.8
box plait, box pleat 258.1
box wagon 272.19
boy lad 129.4
  (male 373.2)
  redcap 271.1
  retainer 746.1
boyar, boyard 875.5
boycott n.
  barring-out 719.2
  exclusion 893.3
  censure 932.2
boycott v. bar out 719.4
  censure 932.7
  stigmatize 874.7
boy friend 897.6
boyish 127.5
  (male 373.7)
boyishness 127.1
boylike 127.5
bra 225.25
brabble n.
  quarrel 713.3
  contest 720.2
brabble v. 713.7
brabblement 713.3
brabbler 901.4
brace n.
  fastening 45.2
  pair 89.2
  support 215.2, 11
  ship's rope 273.10
  music staff 415.22
  typography 550.8
  bandage 662.14
brace v. attach 43.6
  strengthen 159.8
  support 215.26
  navigate 267.10
  refresh 689.2
brace game 545.3
  (gambling 621.7)
bracelet circle 247.2
  ornament 847.7
bracer
  energizer 171.4
  supporter 215.2
  stimulant 662.5
  (pungency 392.2)
  alcoholic drink 959.10
braces
  fastening 45.2
  suspenders 214.3
brach, brachet
  dog 366.6
  female animal 374.8
brachiopod 368.17
brachygrapher 590.12
brachygraphic 590.16
brachygraphy 590.7
bracing n. 689.1
bracing adj.
  invigorating 656.5
  tonic 662.25
  refreshing 689.4
bracken, braken 367.8
bracket n.
  support 215.11, 17
  punctuation 550.8

bracket — break

bracket v. attach 43.6
  pair 89.3
brackish 392.6
bract, bractlet 367.4
brad pin 45.5
  coin 800.4
bradawl 262
Bradshaw 694.7
brae 206.2
brag n. game 840.12
  boast 884.1
  braggart 884.3
brag v. 884.5
braggadocio 884.1, 3
braggart n. 884.3
  (blusterer 887.2)
braggart adj. 884.7
braggartry, bragging
  n. 884.1
bragging adj. 884.7
Bragi, Brage
  poetry 597.9
  god 979.3
Brahma, Brahman
  world spirit 359.3
  divinity 976.2; 979.4
Brahman, Brahmin
  984.21; 996.8
Brahmana 986.2
Brahmanism, Brahmoism 984.11
Brahui 560.4
braid n. fastening 45.2
  cord 205.3
  network 219.4
  hair 256.3
braid v.
  interlace 219.8
  variegate 440.4
brail cord 205.3
  ship's rope 273.10
Braille, braille 442.2
brain n. vitals 221.5
  mind 450.1, 2
brain v. 361.10
brain box, brain case
  210.3
brain child
  work of art 556.8
  writing 590.3
  book 593.1
brain fever 503.3
brainless
  mindless 450a.2
  scatterbrained
    458.13
  unintelligent 499.11
brainpan 210.3
brains 450.1
  (intelligence 498.1)
brainsick
  confused 458.12
  insane 503.12
brain storm
  brilliant idea 453.1
  delirium 503.3
brainwork 451.1
brainy
  intellectual 450.8
  smart 498.10
brake v. 275.7
brakemaker 690.8

brakeman, brakie
  268.12
bramble adherer 46.3
  thorn 253.2
brambly 253.11
bran hull 223.14
  powder 330.3
brancard 272.12
branch n. member 51.4
  fork 91.2
  descendant 167.4
  angle 244.2
  stream 348.1
  animal kingdom
    366.1
  vegetable kingdom
    367.1
  foliage 367.4
  learning 537.7
  railway 627.5
branch v. 291.2
branch out
  bifurcate 91.5
  diverge 291.2
  expatiate 573.5
branched 242.6
branchia 349.19
branchial 368.18
branching n.
  bifurcation 91.2
  arborescence 242.2
  divergence 291.1
branching adj. 242.6
brand n. kind 75.2
  cauterant 384.11
  lighter 388.4
  torch 423.8
  mark 550.6, 7, 11
  weapon 727.3
  stigma 874.2
brand v. burn 384.18
  stigmatize 874.7
branding iron 384.11
brandish
  flourish 315.8
  (wave 314.11)
  flaunt 882.7
brand-new 123.9
brandy 959.6
brandy smash 959.8
brangle 713.7
brangler 710.2
branks 975.3
branle music 415.7
  dance 840.7
branny 330.8
brash n. rain 348.11
  rash 655.17
brash adj. brittle 328.4
  impudent 885.9
  gruff 895.7
brasier See brazier
brass n. mixture 41.4
  money 800.1
  impudence 885.2
brass adj. 439.5
brassard 550.12
brasses
  musicians 416.9
  instuments 417.4
brass buttons 225.8
brass-colored 439.5

brass farthing 643.3
brassière 225.25
brass knuckles 727.8
brass-smith 690.6
brass tacks facts 1.2
  essentials 642.4
  get down to brass
    tacks 79.6
brass wind 417.1, 4
brassworker 690.9
brassworks 691
brassy orange 439.5
  impudent 885.10
brat, bratling 129.1, 3
brattice, brattish
  lining 224.1
  partition 228.6
brattle n. 407.5
brattle v. 407.10
Bratwurst 298.24
bravado 884.1
brave n. soldier 726.4
  man of courage
    861.3
brave v. face 234.7
  endure 826.6
  dare 861.5
  (defy 715.2)
brave adj. hale 654.4
  courageous 861.8
bravery 861.1
bravo n. killer 361.8
  daring villain 863.3
  ruffian 913.2
bravo int. 931.13
  (hurrah! 838.12)
  (hail! 894.15)
bravura 415.10
brawl n. noise 404.2
  broil 713.4
  (contest 720.2)
brawl v. be noisy 404.6
  bawl 411.5
  quarrel 713.7
brawler
  oppositionist 710.2
  insurgent 742.3
brawn 159.1
brawny strong 159.10
  stout 192.12
bray n. 404.3
bray v. pulverize 330.6
  blare 404.7
  ululate 412.2
brayer 591.5
braystone 342.4
braze 384.19
brazen v. 885.7
brazen adj. 885.10
  (unaffected 823.6)
brazenface 885.3
brazenfaced
  impudent 885.10
  immodest 961.9
brazenness 885.2
brazier, brasier
  receptacle 191.1
  heater 386.1
Brazil nut 298.33
breach
  ~ of custom 83.2
  cleft 198.2

fault 651.2
  dissension 713.2
  violation 742.1
  infringement 925.3
  misfeasance 947.2
  violation of law
    964.2
breach of promise,
  breach of trust 940.2
breachy
  intervallic 198.5
  insubordinate 742.6
bread n. food 298.5, 11
  Eucharist 998.6
bread v. 298.43
bread and wine 998.6
breadbasket 191.7
breadfruit 298.31
breadmaker 690.8
breadstuff 298.11
breadth
  proportions 180.5
  width 202
break n.
  discontinuity 70.1
  (omission 53.2)
  interim 109a.1
  change 140.1
  pause 142.2
  chance 156.1
  electricity 158a.4
  interval 198.1, 2
  blunder 495.3
  dissension 713.2
  infraction 947.2
break, brake n. 272.4
brake n. handle 215.7
  automobile 272.16
  grove 367.7
  undergrowth 367.8
  hindrance 706.2
  (anchor 666.2)
  (restraint 752.2)
brake n. See break
break v. sunder 44.8, 9
  ~ a law 83.8; 964.4
  cease 142.6
  interrupt 142.7
  destroy 162.4
  ~ open 173.10
  turn ship 267.24
  ~ the fast 298.44
  cashier 297.12; 756.5
  be brittle 328.3
  tame 370.6
  publish 531.7
  (divulge 529.4)
  open 529.3
  be published 531.9
  train 537.10
  ~ a habit 614.2
  impair 659.6, 8
  cure 660.12
  disobey 742.4
  bankrupt 804.6;
    808.6
break a lance with
  joust 720.8
  attack 716.5
break away
  depart 293.4
  escape 671.6

breakable — bridegroom

break bread 298.44
break bulk
  trim ship 267.37
  unship 297.21
break camp 293.4
break cover 66.5
break down
  collapse 158.5
  demolish 162.4
  analyze 461.17
  deteriorate 659.6
  fail 732.5
break even 27.6
break forth
  appear 446.2
  be disclosed 529.6
break ground
  begin 66.5
  weigh anchor 267.15
  (embark 293.6)
break in
  open 260.11
  intrude 228.10
  enter 294.6
  tame 370.6
  train 537.10
  subdue 749.5
break into song
  416.21
break jail 671.6
break loose
  escape 671.6
  go free 750.4
break off cease 142.6
  disclaim 756.4
break one's back
  be clumsy 699.7
  fail 732.5
break one's heart
  837.6, 8
break one's word
  940.7
break on the wheel
  maltreat 649.7
  torture 830.6
  punish 972.8
break out
  originate 66.6
  break open 173.10
  ~ ~ ballast 267.37
  find vent 295.7
  sicken 655.21
  become excited
    824.6
break Priscian's
  head 568.2
break prison 750.4
break squares 713.7
break the ice
  begin 66.5
  prepare the way
    673.6
  make advances 888.3
break the neck of
  disable 158.6
  defeat 731.9
break the record
  excel 33.5
  triumph 731.6
break up
  disintegrate 44.9
  part 44.11

decompose 49.3
destroy 162.4
perish 162.5
be pulverized 330.7
disintegrate 659.7
damage 659.8
break water 267.43
break with part 44.11
  quarrel 713.7
breakable frail 160.11
  brittle 328.4
breakableness 328.1
breakaway 599.13
breakbone fever 655.6
breakdown
  revolution 146.1
  destruction 162.3
  bed 215.24
  physical ~ 655.1
  nervous ~ 655.14
  impairment 659.3
  dance 840.7
breaker cavity 252.2
  rider 268.8
  surf 348.10
  stockman 370.4
breakfast n. 208.34
breakfast v. 298.43, 44
breakneck steep 217.12
  hasty 684.5
  reckless 863.7
breakup
  dissection 44.4
  decomposition 49.1
  end 67.3
  revolution 146.1
  destruction 162.1, 3
  dissolution 659.2
breakwater
  buttress 215.10
  promontory 250.5
  anchorage 666.4
breast n. essence 5.2
  interior 221.2
  bosom 250.3
  ~ of fowl 298.25
  inmost mind 450.3
at the breast 127.7
breast v.
  confront 234.7
  oppose 708.3, 6
  resist 719.3
breast-high 206.13
breastplate 717.2
breastsummer 215.12
breastwork 717.3
breath instant 113.3
  breeze 349.5
  life force 359.2
  whisper 405.2; 581.3
  soul 994.11
hold one's breath
  be quiescent 265.5
  await 507.5
  not speak 585.3
  wonder 870.2
out of breath 688.7
under one's breath
  405.11
breathe ~ in 296.2
  ~ out 297.13
  respire 349.22

live 359.6
  (exist 1.4)
smell 398.7
evince 467.7
mean 516.5
tell privately 527.9
speak 528.12; 582.6
divulge 529.4
whisper 581.6
sigh 839.7
breathe freely
  be pleased 827.5
  be relieved 834.6
breathe one's last
  360.6
breathe revenge
  be angry 900.8
  be revengeful 919.5
not breathe
  be quiescent 265.5
  ~ ~ a word 528.11;
    585.3
breather nose 250.4
  exercise 686.2
breathing n.
  interim 109a.1
  respiration 349.18
  respite 687.2
breathing adj. 359.10
breathing spell
  interim 109a.1
  respite 687.2
  truce 723.3
breathless
  voiceless 581.7
  in haste 684.6
  fatigued 688.7
  ~ with emotion
    821.6
  eager 865.17
  astonished 870.6
breech n. 235.5
breech v. 225.41
breechcloth 225.22
breeches 225.21
breechloader 727.10
breed n. kind 75.2
  ancestry 166.4
  posterity 167.1
breed v.
  generate 161.10
  ~ stock 370.5
  rear 537.10
breeder 370.4
breeding
  procreation 161.2
  animal culture 370.1
  politeness 894.1
breeze n. turmoil 59.4
  wind 349.5
  broil 713.4
breeze v. speed 274.9
  blow 349.22
breezy windy 349.25
  (airy 338.11)
  lively 682.16
  cheerful 836.7
Breithablik, Breida-
  blik 981.3
breloque See berloque
brethren 997.1
Breton 560.4

breve note 413.6
  punctuation 550.8
brevet writ 741.3
  commission 755.1
  warrant 760.2
brevet rank 873.4
breviary prayer 990.3
  rituale 998.9
brevier 591.7
breviped, brevipen-
  nate 193.8
brevity
  transience 111.2
  shortness 201.1
  conciseness 572.1
brew n. 959.5
brew v. mix 41.6
  ~ a storm 349.22
  cook 384.19
brewer 959.12
brewery, brewhouse
  959.14
brewing n. 673.2
brewing adj.
  imminent 152.3
  afoot 673.10
brewmaster, brewster
  959.12
briar See brier
Briarean 159.10
Briareus
  strong man 159.6
  giant 192.8
briary See briery
bribe n. 618.2
  (compensation 30.3)
  (lure 617.2)
  (gift 784.3)
  (payment 809.2;
    973.2)
bribe v. 618.3
  (give 784.8)
  (purchase 795.3)
bribery 618
  (purchase 795.1)
bric-a-brac
  artware 556.8
  trinkets 847.9
brick n.
  hardness 323.3
  ceramics 384.14
  good thing 648.4
  man of honor 939.5
  good person 948.1
brick adj. 434.9
brickbat n.
  missile 727.14
  aspersion 929.2
brickbat v. 716.7
brickkiln 386.1
bricklayer 690.5
brickmaker 690.8
brick-red 434.9, 12
bricks 627.4
bricky 434.9
bridal n. 903.3
bridal adj. 903.14
bride 903.6
bridebed 903.1
bridechamber 897.10;
  903.3
bridegroom 903.6

bridesmaid — broad

bridesmaid
  companion 890.3
  wedding attendant 903.4
bridesman 903.4
bridewell 752.1
bridge *n.* bond 45.1
  dental ~ 253.3
  roadway 627.7
  game 840.12
bridge *v.* join 43.5
  reconcile 723.4
  compromise 774.2
bridgemaker 690.8
bridge passage 415.15
bridgework 253.3
bridle *n.*
  fastening 45.2
  restraint 752.2
bridle *v.*
  ~ a horse 370.7
  restrain 751.7
  simper 853.5
  ~ one's tongue 864.3
  act proudly 878.3
bridle up 900.9
bridle path 627.2
brief *n.* list 86.1
  compendium 596.1
  (miniature 193.3)
brief *adj.*
  inconsiderable 32.8
  momentary 111.7
  (instantaneous 113.4)
  short 201.5
  terse 572.3
  taciturn 585.4
to be brief 572.4
  (briefly 111.9)
brief case, brief bag 191.5
briefly
  in short time 111.9
  (instantaneously 113.6)
  soon 132.15
  in a word 572.4
  (in epitome 596.6)
briefness
  transience 111.2
  shortness 201.1
  terseness 572.1
brier, briar
  adherer 46.3
  thorn 253.2
  pipe 392a.6
briery, briary 253.11
brig ship 273.2, 7
  prison 752.1
brigade *n.* 726.7
brigade *v.* 60.8
brigade major, brigadier, brigadier general 745.11
brigand 792.3
brigandage 791.2
brigandine 717.2
brigantine 273.2
bright *adj.*
  luminous 420.22

bright-colored 428.14
  white 430.8
  alert 457.9
  intelligent 498.9, 10
  cheerful 836.7
  beautiful 845.12
  hopeful 858.11
  illustrious 873.17
be bright 420.17
bright-colored 428.14
brighten
  illuminate 420.20
  furbish 658.10
  cheer up 836.4, 14
bright-eyed 845.12
brightness 420.1
bright side 829.1
bright idea
  idea 453.1
  (wisdom 498.6)
  good plan 626.7
  witticism 842.4
brilliance
  brightness 420.1
  gorgeousness 845.2
  illustriousness 873.2
brilliant *n.* type 591.7
  gem 847.8
brilliant *adj.*
  music 416.24
  bright 420.22
  intelligent 498.10
  witty 842.9
  beautiful 845.13
  illustrious 873.17
be brilliant 498.8
brim 231.1
brimful 52.11
  (overfull 641.6)
brimmer 52.3
brimming 52.11
brimstone stone 342.4
  fumigator 388.7
brinded 440.10
brindisi 415.10
brindle *n.* 366.6
brindle *adj.* 440.10
brine *n.* ocean 341.1
  pungency 392.2
brine *v.* season 392.4
  preserve 670.4
bring induce 153.7
  carry 270.8
  sell for 812.6
bring about
  cause 153.6
  produce 161.8
  turn ship 267.24
  do 680.6
  accomplish 729.2
bring back 790.3
bring by the lee 267.24
bring down
  prostrate 213.7
  lower 308.5
  kill 361.10
bring forth
  bear 161.9
  show 525.2
bring forward

  appeal to 467.10
  propound 514.7
  show 525.2
  teach 537.9
  improve 658.8
  call to witness 969.10
bring home the bacon
  excel 33.5
  win 731.6
  acquire honor 873.12
bring home to
  attribute to 155.3
  prove 467.9
  convince 484.10
  accuse 938.4
  condemn 971.2
bring in induct 296.5
  ~ ~ a verdict 480.9
  yield 810.4
bring off prove 467.9
  deliver 672.2
bring on
  induce 153.7
  appeal to 467.10
  improve 658.8
bring out
  extract 301.6
  discover 481a.3
  show 525.2
  print 591.14
bring over
  convince 484.10
  induce 615.9
bring round
  turn ship 267.24
  convince 484.10
  render sane 502.4
  persuade 615.9
  (influence 175.6)
  cure 660.12
bring to convert 144.6
  turn ship 267.24
  be inactive 683.8
bring to bear
  relate 9.4
  bring into play 170.3
  influence 175.6
  render possible 470.4
  urge 615.7
  apply 677.5
  compel 744.2
bring to book
  evidence 467.9
  reprove 932.8
  punish 972.5
bring to light
  discover 481a.3
  manifest 525.2
  expose 529.3
bring to pass
  cause 153.6
  effectuate 729.2
bring to terms
  pacify 723.4
  mediate 724.3
bring up vomit 297.18
  breed 370.5
  ~ ~ an argument 476.11
  rear 537.10

bring up the rear 235.8
bring up with a round turn 142.6
brink 231.1
on the brink
  almost 32.15
  about to 121.11
  near 197.11
briny *n.* 341.1
briny *adj.* 392.6
briquette, briquet 388.1
brisk *v.* 689.2
brisk *adj.* brief 111.7
  active 171.9; 682.16
  vivacious 836.7
brisken 689.2
briskness 171.2; 682.1
bristle *n.* 256.7
  (point 253.2)
bristle *v.*
  be sharp 253.8
  abound 639.4
  (superabound 641.2)
bristle up
  project 250.7
  become angry 900.9
Bristol fashion 267.67
bristling *n.* 901.7
bristling *adj.*
  rough 256.14
  ~ with arms 717.9
  gruff 895.7
bristly 256.14
  (barbed 253.12)
britannia 430.3
britannia metal 545.6
britches 225.21
Briticism 563.5
British 188.11
Britisher 188.9
Briton 188.9
brittle 328.4
  (friable 330.9)
be brittle 328.3
brittleness 328
  (friability 330.1)
britska 272.4
broach *n.* 262
broach *v.* begin 66.5
  originate 153.6
  draw off 297.13
  propound 514.7
  publish 531.7
  allege 535.3
broach to 267.24, 34
broad *n.* girl 129.5
  pool 343a.1
  woman 374.2
  lamp 423.3
  loose woman 962.2
broad *adj.*
  extensive 31.7
  wide 202.6
  (large 192.11)
  unprejudiced 498.12
  positive 535.6
  risqué 961.9
as broad as long 27.9
grow broad, make broad 202.4

broad arrow 550.7, 11
broad awake
  attentive 457.9
  vigilant 459.8
  sagacious 498.10
  alert 682.17
broad-brimmed 202.6
broadcast n. 532a.4
broadcast v.
  disperse 73.3
  publish 531.7
  radiobroadcast 532a.9
broadcast adj. 73.4
broadcaster 532a.6
broadcasting
  publication 531.1
  radiocast 532a.4
broadcloth 219.5
broaden
  generalize 78.8
  expand 194.5, 8
  widen 202.4
broad-faced, broad-gauged, broad-headed, broad-leaved 202.6
broadloom 219.5
broadly 196.10
broad-minded 498.12
broadness 202.1
broad-ribbed 202.6
broadsheet 531.4
  (writing 590.3)
  (book 593.1)
broad-shouldered
  strong 159.10
  virile 159a.5
  broad 202.6
broadside side 236.1
  lamp 423.3
  handbill 531.4
  barrage 716.2
broadside on
  laterally 236.8
  afoul 267.64
broadsword 727.3
broad-tailed 202.6
broadwise 202.8
Brobdingnagian n.
  strong man 159.6
  giant 192.8
Brobdingnagian adj.
  strong 159.10
  giantlike 192.15
brocade cloth 219.5
  needlework 847.6
brocatel, brocatelle 847.6
brochure 593.1
Brocken specter 980a.1
brogan 225.27
brogue shoe 225.27
  dialect 563.5
  accent 580.4
  (inarticulation 583.1)
broidery 847.6
broil n. 713.4
  (turmoil 59.4)
  (war 722.5)

broil v. be hot 382.13
  cook 384.19
  quarrel 713.7
broiler fowl 298.25
  caldron 386.1
broiling 382.16
broke poor 804.7
  bankrupt 808.10
  go broke 808.6
broken
  discontinuous 70.4
  irregular 139.2
  rough 256.12
  tame 370.10
  impaired 659.12
  defeated 732.12
broken English 563.5
broken-down
  impaired 659.12
  crushed 837.13
brokenhearted
  wretched 828.16
  sad 837.13
broken meat 645.4
broken-winded
  sickly 655.24
  breathless 688.7
broker
  functionary 758.2
  deputy 759.1
  dealer 797.7
  (pawnbroker 787.2)
brokerage
  speculation 794.2
  fee 812.2
brokery 794.2
brolly
  umbrella 223.4
  parachute 273a.7
bromide, bromid
  conformist 82.3
  trite saying 496.3
  (joke 842.6)
bromidic 843.6
bromine, bromin 635.6
bronchial pneumonia 655.9
bronchial tube 351.3
bronchitis 655.9
bronco, broncho 271.3
broncobuster, bronchobuster
  rider 268.8
  stockman 370.4
bronchocele 655.5
bronchopneumonia 655.9
bronchus 351.3
Bronx cheer 930.2
  give the Bronx cheer 930.6
bronze n.
  sculpture 557.8
  precious metals 800.15
  impudence 885.2
bronze v. 433.3
bronze adj. 433.5
bronzesmith 690.6
brooch 847.7
brood n. kind 75.2
  multitude 102.2

progeny 167.1, 3
brood v. 370.8
brood over
  ponder 451.27
  remember 505.11
  mope 837.6
  nurse revenge 919.5
brooding 673.10
brook n. 348.1
brook v. 826.6
brooklet 348.1
broom n. plant 367.8
  brush 652.7
broom v. 652.12
broommaker 690.8
broomstick 203.6
broomtail 271.3
broose 274.4; 720.5
broth drink 298.4
  bouillon 298.16
brothel 961.7
  (sink 945.8)
brother kinsman 11.3
  analogue 17.5
  religious 996.11
brotherhood
  kinship 11.2
  (connaturalness 17.2)
  fraternal order 712.3
  fellowship 888.1
brother-in-law 11.3
Brother Jonathan 188.9
brotherliness 888.1
brotherly
  friendly 888.4
  benevolent 906.6
  (loving 897.14)
brougham 272.4, 15
brow summit 210.1
  edge 231.1
  face 234.4
browbeat
  intimidate 860.12
  (domineer 885.5)
  affront 929.3
brown n. 433.1
brown v. 433.3
brown adj. 433.4
Brown Bess 727.10
brown bill 727.4
brownie, browny 979.9
brownness 433
brownstone 342.4
brown study 458.3
  (dream 515.5)
browse 298.46
bruin 901.4
bruise n.
  discoloration 440a.1
  wound 659.4
bruise v.
  pulverize 330.6
  discolor 440a.2
  maltreat 649.7
  injure 659.8
  ~ the feelings 830.6
  beat 972.6
bruiser 726.2
bruit n.
  publicity 531.3

report 532.3
bruit v. 531.7
brumal wintery 126a.6
  cold 383.8
brummagem n. 545.6
brummagem adj.
  spurious 545.13
  gaudy 851.8
brunch 298.34
brunet, brunette 433.4
Brunswick blue 438.2, 4
Brunswick green 435.2, 4
brunt clash 276.2
  difficulty 704.4
  bear the brunt
  endure 826.6
  difficulty 704.6
  defend 717.8
brush n. waste 169.2
  backwoods 183.1
  tail 235.6
  point 253.2
  beard 256.5
  bristle 256.7
  plain 344.1
  wood 367.7, 8
  touch 379.1
  firewood 388.3
  painting 566.2
  paintbrush 556.16
  painter 559.2
  duster 652.7
  contest 720.2
  have a brush with 720.8
brush v. graze 199.3
  speed 274.9
  groom 370.7
  touch 379.3
  rustle 405.5
  sweep 652.12
brush away
  eject 297.8
  discard 678.3
  annul 756.3
brush up
  ~ ~ **the memory** 505.14
  furbish 658.10
brush wolf 366.5
brushwood
  undergrowth 367.8
  firewood 388.2
brusque savage 173.14
  impetuous 684.5
  gruff 895.7
brusquerie haste 684.1
  rudeness 851.1
  impetuosity 863.1
Brussels Biscuit 298.11
Brussels sprouts 298.30
brustle 405.5
brutal savage 173.14
  gruff 895.7
  cruel 907.9
brutality
  mindlessness 450a.1
  vulgarity 851.1

brutalize — bull

brutality (*continued*)
  cruelty 907.3
  (maltreatment 649.4)
brutalize
  render callous 823.4
  render rude 895.5
  vitiate 945.10
  (corrupt 659.9)
brute animal 366.2
  savage 913.3
brutification 851.1
brutified 851.7
brutify
  render callous 823.4
  render rude 895.5
brutish savage 173.14
  uncivilized 851.7
  cruel 907.9
  carnal 961.11
brutishness 851.1
brutum fulmen
  impotent 158.3
  failure 732.1
  compulsion 744.1
Brutus wig 256.4
  traitor 949.3
Bryanite 984.14
Bryophyta 369.5
bryozoan 368.17
bub brother 11.3
  boy 129.4
  liquor 959.5
Bubastis 979.5
bubble *n.*
  transient 111.4
  lightness 320.2
  air globule 353
  (unsubstantiality 4.3)
  delusion 495.5
  imagining 515.4
  deception 545.3
  dupe 547.1
  trifle 643.3, 5
  airy hopes 858.4
bubble *v.* ripple 348.19
  foam 353.8
  burble 405.7
  deceive 545.7
  swindle 791.12
bubble over 353.8
bubble and squeak 298.20
bubbling *n.* 353.3
bubbling, bubbly *adj.* 353.10
bubby boy 129.4
  breast 250.3
bubo
  protuberance 250.2
  sore 655.16
bubonic plague 655.2
bubonocele 250.2
buccaneer *n.* 792.5
buccaneer *v.* 791.10
buccaneering 791.2
Bucephalus 271.9
buck *n.* trestle 215.9
  caper 309.2
  male animal 373.6
  Negro 431.4
  Indian 434.5
  cleanser 652.8
  money 800.8
  fop 854.1
buck *v.* confront 234.7
  carry 270.8
  buckjump 309.5
  wash 652.9
buck and wing 840.8
buckaroo, buckayroo, buckeroo 268.8
buck basket 191.9
bucket *n.* pail 191.11
  ship 273.1
bucket *v.* ladle 270.10
  cheat 545.7
  swindle 791.12
bucketmaker 690.8
bucket shop 621.14
buck fever
  excitement 825.3
  trepidation 860.3
buckle *n.*
  fastening 45.2
  (supporter 215.2)
  distortion 243.1
  coil 248.2
buckle *v.* attach 43.6
  distort 243.3
buckle to
  be resolute 604.6
  undertake 676.2
  set to work 686.7
buckled 248.4
buckler 717.2
bucko 863.3
buck private 726.4
buckram
  bookbinding 593.10
  affectation 853.1
in buckram
  priggish 853.7
  dignified 878.7
bucksaw 257.3
bucktooth 253.3
buckwheat 367.9
bucolic *n.* poem 597.2
  poet 597.10
bucolic *adj.*
  poetry 597.13
  rustic 183.3
bud *n.* child 129.3
  rudiment 153.3
  brother 11.3
  flower 367.5
  in the bud 66.9
bud *v.* result 154.3
  grow 194.6
  ingraft 300.6
  grow 365.2
Buddha sage 500.1
  Divinity 976.2
  deity 979.4
buddhi 994.10
Buddhism 984.11
Buddhist 984.21
budding *n.* 194.3
budding *adj.* 127.5
buddy brother 11.3
  chum 890.3
budge *n.* 959.2
budge *v.* 264.2
budget bundle 72.5
  collection 72.7
  bag 191.4
  store 636.1
  funds 800.2
  financial ~ 811.3
budmash 949.1
bueno 648.8
buff *n.* bare skin 223.12
  nude 226.2
  in the buff 226.8
buff *v.* 255.4
buff *adj.* 436.6
buffalo *n.* 271.2; 366.13
buffalo *v.* 860.12
buffer obstacle 706.2
  guard 717.2
buffet *n.*
  cupboard 191.15
  blow 276.3
  restaurant 298.42
  disappointment 509.1
  affront 900.5
buffet *v.* confront 234.7
  strike 276.8
  joggle 315.8
  maltreat 649.7
  batter 659.8
  inflict pain 830.6
  beat 972.6
buffet the waves
  pitch 267.45
  have hard time 704.6
  oppose 708.3
  resist 719.3
buffo singer 416.10
  comedian 599.20
buffoon 599.20
  (fool 501.1)
  (laughingstock 857.1)
buffoonery
  acting 599.6
  wit 842.3
  (absurdity 497.1)
  (folly 499.6)
  (ridiculousness 855.1)
bug insect 366.24
  fanatic 504.2
  devotee 840.19
bugaboo
  false alarm 669.2
  bugbear 980.4
bugbear bane 663.1
  false alarm 669.2
  bugaboo 980.4
  (frightener 860.7)
bugger 699.9
buggy *n.* 272.4, 19
buggy *adj.* 503.12
bughouse *n.* 503.8
bughouse *adj.* 503.12
Bugi 560.4
bugle *n.* nose 250.4
  horn 417.4
  battle horn 722.3
  needlework 847.6
bugle *v.* toot 410.8
  blow a horn 416.18
bugler 416.2
buhrstone, burrstone 342.4
build *n.* 240.1
  (texture 329.1)
build *v.* 161.8
  (compose 54.4)
  (form 240.6)
build a chapel 267.24
builder
  producer 164.1
  craftsman 690.5
  organizer 626.8
building
  production 161.1, 7
  house 189.3
bulb sphere 249.2
  protuberance 250.2
  (swelling 194.2)
  lamp 423.11
bulbil, bulblet 250.2
bulbous 250.9
  (expanded 194.10)
  (rotund 249.6)
bulbul 416.11
Bulgarian 560.4
bulge *n.*
  advantage 33.2
  protuberance 250.2
  (swelling 194.2)
bulge *v.* 250.7
bulging 250.9
  (expanded 194.10)
bulk *n.* quantity 25.1
  main part 50.3
  size 192.1
  lump 192.5
bulk *v.* 31.4
bulkhead *n.*
  cover 223.6, 7
  partition 228.6
  safeguard 666.1
  obstacle 706.2
bulkhead *v.* 223.22
bulky sizable 192.11, 13
  (great 31.6)
  awkward 699.12
  unmanageable 704.10
  ungraceful 846.8
bull *n.* bullock 366.12
  male animal 373.6
  blunder 495.3
  (absurdity 497.1)
  (solecism 568.1)
  twaddle 517.3
  detective 528.9
  untruth 546.1
  epistle 592.2
  bullhead 606.4
  sore 655.16
  decree 741.2
  policeman 745.10
  jobber 797.8
bull in a china shop
  turmoil 59.4
  bungler 701
Bull *n.* 318.6
bull *v.*
  blunder 495.9
  talk nonsense 517.6
  lie 544.4
  bungle 699.9

bull *adj.* 192.11
bulla
  protuberance 250.2
  bubble 353.1
bulldog adherer 46.3
  dog 366.6
  resolution 604.4
  doggedness 606.4
  courage 861.4
bulldoze 860.12
bulldozer 913.2
bullet cone 249.4
  missile 727.14
  money 800.1
bullethead 606.3
bulletin list 86.1
  message 532.2
  record 551.1
  epistle 592.2
bulletin board list 86.1
  record 551.1
bulletmaker 690.8
bulletproof 664.11
bullfight 720.2
bullfighter 726.1
bullfrog 366.20
bullhead dolt 501.1
  obstinate person 606.3
  bungler 701
bullheaded 606.6
bullion metal 635.6
  money 800.15
bullion balance 319.5
bullnose 255.3
bullock bull 366.12
  male animal 373.6
bull ring 728.1
bull-roarer 404.4
Bull Run 722.5
bull's-eye center 222.2
  window 260.5
  ship 273.7
  shot 284.3
  lamp 423.2, 5
  target 620.2
Bull's Eye 318.3
bull terrier 366.6
bullwhack 975.1
bullwhacker 268.9
  (stockman 370.4)
bully *n.* ship 273.2
  canned beef 298.20
  bravo 863.3
  ruffian 913.2
  (blusterer 887.2)
bully *v.* 860.12
  (domineer 885.5)
  (bluster 887.3)
bully *adj.* good 648.8
  cheerful 836.7
bully *int.* 931.13
bully beef 298.20
bullyrag 830.5
bulrush 367.8
bulwark obstacle 706.2
  fortification 717.3
bulwarks 273.7
bum *n.* vagabond 268.2
  rump 235.5
  idler 683.7
  (neglector 460.3)

beggar 767.2
  spree 840.3; 959.3
  drunkard 959.11
bum *v.* hum 405.6
  idle 683.8
  beg 765.6
  tipple 959.15
bumbailiff 745.9
bumbershoot 223.4
bumblebee 366.24
Bumbledom 737.7
bummer
  vagabond 268.2
  idler 683.7
  beggar 767.2
bump *n.*
  protuberance 250.2
  clash 276.2
  joggle 315.4
  thud 408a.2
bump *v.* impel 276.7
  strike 276.8
  collide 276.9
  joggle 315.8
  bang 406.7
bump into 292.10
bump off 361.10
bumper fill 52.3
  large thing 192.6
bumping 192.15
bumpkin, bumkin
  spar 273.12
  rustic 876.5
bumptious 885.9
bumpy
  protuberant 250.9
  rough 256.12
bun head 210.3
  hair 256.3
  bread 298.11
bunce 800.1
bunch *n.* crowd 72.3-5
  (quantity 31.3)
  multitude 102.2
  protuberance 250.2
  clique 712.2
bunch *v.* league 48.4
  assemble 72.10, 11
  bulge 250.7
bunch-backed 243.5
bunco See bunko
buncombe, bunkum
  nonsense 517.2
  falsity 544.2
  deception 545.1
  grandiloquence 577.2
  boasting 884.1
  flattery 933.1
speak for Buncombe
  procrastinate 133.5
  boast 884.5
bund shore 342.2
  haven 666.4
Bund company 72.3
  confederacy 712.4
bunder 666.4
Bundesrat, Bundesrath 696.5
Bundesversammlung 696.4
bundle *n.* 72.5

bundle *v.* walk 266.16
  speed 274.9
bundle off start 284.14
  eject 297.8
bundle on 684.3
bundobust, bandobust 769.1
bung *n.* stopper 263.1
  bunghole 351.1
bung *v.* close 261.2
  throw 284.12
bungalow 189.3
bunghole 351.1
bungle *n.* 699.4
  (blunder 495.3)
  (foolish act 499.7)
  (failure 732.2)
bungle *v.* 699.9
  (blunder 495.9)
  (fail 732.5)
bungler 701
  (neglector 460.3)
  (ignoramus 493.1)
  (novice 541.6)
bungling *n.* 699.3
  (carelessness 460.2)
bungling *adj.* 699.12
bunk *n.* bed 215.24
  nonsense 517.2
  falsity 544.2
  deception 545.1
  untruth 546.1
  grandiloquence 577.2
  boasting 884.1
  flattery 933.1
bunk *v.* inhabit 186.10
  flee 623.10
bunker 191.8, 15
Bunker Hill 722.5
bunkhouse 189.4
bunkie 890.3
bunko, bunco *n.* 545.3
bunko, bunco *v.*
  cheat 545.7
  swindle 791.12
bunko steerer 548.2
bunkum See buncombe
bunny 366.17
bunt *n.* tail 235.6
  impulse 276.1
bunt *v.* 276.7
bunting 550.13
buntline 273.10
buoy *n.* ship 273.14
  lightness 320.2
  safeguard 666.1
buoy *v.* lighten 320.4
  give hope 858.7
buoyance 325.1
buoyancy
  navigation 267.1
  levity 320.1
  hopefulness 858.2
buoyant light 320.7
  (ascendant 305.7)
  elastic 325.5
  cheerful 836.7
  hopeful 858.9
make buoyant 320.4
bur, burr adherer 46.3

hull 223.14
  rough 256.2
bur See burr
burble ripple 348.19
  bubble 353.8; 405.7
burden, burthen *n.*
  load 190.1
  weight 319.1
  bane 663.1
  impediment 706.2
  hardship 735.1
  affliction 830.2
burden, bourdon *n.*
  ~ of a song 104.2
  tone 402.2
  drone bass 413.6, 14
  chorus 415.15
  ~ of a poem 597.7
burden *v.* add 37.3
  weight 319.8, 9
  task 686.8
  encumber 706.6
burdensome
  heavy 319.12
  laborious 686.10
  difficult 704.8
  impedimentary 706.8
  oppressive 830.16
bureau
  cupboard 191.15
  office 691
  civil department 745.9
  department 965.2
bureaucracy 737.7
bureaucrat 694.3
bureaucratic 737.15
burgee 550.13
burgeon, bourgeon *n.* 367.4, 5
burgeon, bourgeon *v.*
  bear 161.9
  grow 194.6; 365.2
burgess
  inhabitant 188.2
  freeman 748.6
burgh 189.16
burghal 189.22
burgher
  townsman 188.2
  freeman 748.6
burghmoot, burghmote 966.2
burglar 792.2
burglar alarm 669.1
  (signal 550.14)
burglarize 791.9
burglary 791.1, 4
burgle *n.* 791.1
burgle *v.* 791.9
burgomaster 745.9
burgrave 745.7
Burgundy purple 437.1
  wine 959.7
burial *n.*
  interment 363.1, 4
  (submergence 310.2)
  concealment 528.1
burial *adj.* 363.25
burial ground 363.14

burial place — busy 740

burial place 363.13
Buriat, Buryat 560.4
buried
  subterranean 208.10
  shut in 229.4
  interred 363.26
  concealed 528.17
  be buried 363.23
burin 558.4
burke 361.11
burker 361.8
burkite 361.8
burkundaz, burkundauze
  guardian 664.3
  bodyguard 717.6
burl 635.3
burlap cloth 219.5
  rough 256.2
burlesque *n.*
  caricature 21.3
  (misrepresentation 555.3)
  comedy 599.4
  ridicule 856.3
  (absurdity 497.1)
  (farce 855.2)
burlesque *v.*
  caricature 19.8
  ridicule 856.6
  (stultify 497.3)
burlesque *adj.*
  caricatural 19.13
  mock 856.7
  (farcical 855.5)
burlesquer 844
burletta 599.4
burly 192.12
Burmese 560.4
burn *n.* water 337.1
  stream 348.1
  hurt 378.1
  burned spot 384.8
  wound 659.2
burn *v.* be near 197.5
  dry 340.5
  cremate 363.21
  pain 378.4
  be hot 382.13
  torrefy 384.18
  (discolor 440a.2)
  be near 481a.7
  ~ with passion 825.7
  desire 865.11
  adore 897.11
  be angry 900.8
  execute 972.8
burn daylight 683.8
burn one's bridges 604.6
burn one's fingers 699.7
burn out 385.5
burn the candle at both ends
  waste 638.2
  redundance 641.3
  labor 686.6
  squander 818.3
  dissipate 954.3
burn the midnight oil
  study 539.4
  labor 686.6
burn up 830.5
burnable 384.22
burner 423.11
burning *n.*
  cremation 363.2
  cineration 384.3
burning *adj.*
  near 197.8
  hot 382.16, 17, 19
  (feverish 382.19)
  calefactive 384.22
  vehement 574.7
  fervent 821.6
  ~ with excitement 824.9, 10
  emotions 825.11
  desirous 865.17
  lustful 961.11
burning ghat
  crematory 363.17
  incinerator 384.12
burning glass 445.1
burning mountain 382.8
burnish *n.* 255.3
burnish *v.* polish 255.4
  rub 331.3
  beautify 847.11
burnished 420.22
burnisher 255.3
burnoose, burnous 225.15
burnsides 256.5
burnt heated 384.23
  dried 340.9
  red 434.11
burnt almond 433.1
burnt carmine, burnt crimson lake, burnt lake 434.2
burnt offering 990.6
burnt orange 439.1
burnt sienna, burnt umber 433.2
burr, buhr *n.* 342.4
burr, bur *n.*
  engraving 558.1
  printing 591.5
burr *n.* See **bur**
burr *v.* 410.6
burra, burra sahib 877.2
burro 271.10
burrow *n.* 252.3
burrow *v.* settle 184.14
  excavate 252.9
bursa 191.6
bursar 801
bursary 802.1
burst *n.* instant 113.5
  outbreak 173.2, 3
  ~ of speed 274.3
  detonation 406.2
  ~ of passion 825.5
  ~ of laughter 838.3
  ~ of anger 900.3
burst *v.* sunder 44.8
  explode 173.9
  be brittle 328.3
  detonate 406.8

impair 659.6, 8
  ~ into laughter 838.7, 10
  ~ into tears 839.8
  ~ into a passion 900.8, 9
  ~ with envy 921.2
burst forth
  originate 66.6
  grow 194.6
  appear 446.2
burst in
  open 260.11
  enter 294.6
burst into flame
  ignite 384.17
  become excited 824.6
burst out
  break open 173.10
  find vent 295.7
burst upon
  meet 292.10
  come unawares 508.5
ready to burst
  full 52.11
  crowded 72.13
  overfull 641.6
  excited 824.10
  excitable 825.11
  hot tempered 901.7
bury submerge 310.5
  inter 363.20
  conceal 528.10
bury oneself in 539.4
bury the hatchet 723.5
  (forgive 918.3)
burying 363.1, 4
bus vehicle 272.1, 6
  automobile 272.15
  ship 273.1
  aircraft 273a.1
busby 225.26
bush *n.* member 51.4
  waste 169.2
  provinces 183.1
  lining 224.1
  plain 344.1
  foliage 367.4
  woods 367.7
  plant 367.8
bush *v.* line 224.2
  timber 367.13
bushed
  bewildered 475.16
  fatigued 688.6
bushel
  quantities 31.3
  basket 191.9
  measure 466.2
busheler, busheller, bushelman 225.37
bushfighter 726.4
bushfighting 722.1
bushing 224.1
Bushman 431.4
bushranger 792.3
bushveld 367.7
bushwa 517.2
bushwhacker

edge tool 253.6
  soldier 726.4
bushy 256.13
business concern 151.1
  topic 454.1
  occupation 625
  pursuit 622.1)
  (undertaking 676.1)
  industry 682.5
  (duty 926.1)
  commerce 794.1
set up in business 184.14; 625.8
businesslike
  orderly 58.7
  occupational 625.11
  industrious 682.19
businessman 797.1
busk 279.4
buskin 599.3
buskined 599.28
buskins 225.27
buss *n.* ship 273.2
  kiss 894.4; 902.3
buss *v.* 902.8
bust *n.* breast 250.3
  figure 554.4
  (portrait sculpture 557.2)
  spree 840.3
  drinking bout 959.3
bust *v.* burst 44.8
  explode 173.9
  cashier 297.12
  be brittle 328.3
  impair 659.6, 8
  bust in intrude 228.10
  open 260.11
  enter 294.6
bustee 189.17
bustle *n.*
  activity 171.2
  undergarment 225.25
  agitation 315.1
  activity 682.6
  hurry 684.1
  excitement 825.3
  bluster 887.1
bustle *v.*
  be agitated 315.9
  stir about 682.12
  hurry about 684.3
bustling eventful 151.6
  active 682.21
busy *n.*
  inquisitive 455.2
  detective 528.9
  newsmonger 532.5
  meddler 682.11
busy *v.* occupy 625.6
  work 686.8
busy oneself
  engage in 625.7
  (be busy 682.13)
  (labor 686.6)
  meddle 682.14
busy *adj.* active 682.20
  (acting 680.7)
  (laboring 686.9)
  meddlesome 682.22
be busy

be otherwise occu-
    pied 135.3
be active 682.13
(busy oneself 625.7)
(work 686.6)
get busy 686.7
keep busy 686.8
busybody *n.*
    inquisitive 455.2
    newsmonger 532.5
    meddler 682.11
busybody *v.* 682.14
busybody *adj.* 682.22
but 30.8; 469.7, 8
no buts about it
    actually 1.9
    certainly 474.16
    truly 494.15
butcha 129.3
butcher *n.*
    slaughterer 361.8
    merchant 797.11
butcher *v.* 361.10
butchered 53.5
butcher shop 799.4
butchery 361.1, 7
butler 746.1
butt *n.* remains 40.1
    piece 51.3
    extremity 67.2
    receptacle 191.11
    impulse 276.1
    tobacco 392a.5
    aim 620.2
    laughingstock 857.1
butt *v.* 276.7
butt in
    intrude 228.10
    (enter 294.6)
    meddle 682.14
butte 206.2
butter *n.* softness 324.3
    pulp 354.2
    oil 356.4
    (semiliquid 352.3)
    suaviloquence 894.2
    flattery 933.1
butter *v.* 933.3
**butter-and-egg man,
    butter-and-egger**
    803.2
butterbox 188.9
buttercup
    yellow 436.3
    endearment 902.4
butterfingered 699.12
butterfingers
    bungling 699.3
    bungler 701
butterfly insect 366.24
    light filter 424.5
    variegation 440.2
    waverer 605.3
    beauty 845.4
buttermaker 690.8
buttermilk drink 298.4
    sour 397.2
butterscotch 396.2
butterwright 690.7
butterworker 690.9
buttery *n.*
    room 191.16, 20

storeroom 636.4
buttery *adj.*
    viscid 352.8
    unctuous 355.3
    suave 894.13
    flattering 933.3
buttinsky
    intruder 228.4
    (incomer 294.4)
    meddler 682.11
    (hinderer 706.3)
buttocks 235.5, 7
button *n.*
    fastening 45.2
    (suspender 214.3)
    diminutive 193.2
    chin 234.5
    protuberance 250.2
    trifle 643.3
    coin 800.4
button *v.* attach 43.6
    close 261.2
button up 751.8
buttonhold 586.2
buttonhole *n.* 400.4
buttonhole *v.*
    speak to 586.2
    be a bore 841.5
buttonholer 841.4
buttons 746.1
buttress *n.*
    support 215.2, 10
    fortification 717.3
buttress *v.*
    strengthen 159.8
    (reinforce 37.4)
    support 215.26
buttressing 215.10
butyraceous 355.3
buxom 836.11
buy *n.* 795.1
    good buy 815.2
buy *v.* 795.3
    buy and sell 794.4
    buy a pig in a poke
    chance 621.17
    be unclever 699.7
    be rash 863.5
    buy off 618.3
buyer user 677.4
    purchaser 795.2
    (merchant 797.1)
buying *n.* 795.1
buying *adj.* 795.5
buzz *n.* 532.3
buzz *v.* hum 405.6
    sibilate 409.3
    sound harshly 410.6
    insect 412.10
    question 461.15
buzz about
    rumor 531.7
    be published 531.9
buzzard 366.22
buzzer 669.1
buzz saw 257.3
B. V. D.'s 225.25
by beside 236.9
    through 278.16;
    631.5
by and by
    in future 121.9

soon 132.15
by and large
    mainly 50.11
    throughout 52.15
    generally 78.15
by the way
    incidentally 134.11
    (in connection 9.10)
    (incidentally 10.10)
    (between 228.13)
    (in passing 302.4)
    on the way 270.13
by-bid *n.* 796.2
by-bid *v.* 796.6
by-bidder 795.2
    (auction 796.2)
bye-bye! 293.14
by-end 620.2
bygone past 122.8
    forgotten 506.7
bylaw, byelaw 963.2
by-line 627.5
byname
    cognomen 564.2, 3
    nickname 565.3
by-pass
    devious way 279.3
    byroad 627.2
bypast 122.8
bypath
    devious way 279.3
    byway 627.2
byplay 550.3
byre 189.5
    (storehouse 636.4)
byroad
    devious way 279.3
    by-pass 627.2
byssin 219.5
byssus cloth 219.5
    nap 256.10
bystander
    neighbor 197.4
    spectator 444.1
    witness 467.6
by-talk 532.3
byway
    devious way 279.3
    bypath 627.2
byword maxim 496.1
    byname 564.3
    nickname 565.3
    laughingstock 857.1
    reproach 874.3
    (contempt 930.1)

C

cab taxicab 272.15
    translation 522.2
cabal *n.* plot 626.6
    clique 712.2
cabal *v.* 626.10
cabala, cabbala
    mystery 528.1
    esoteric science
    994.1
cabalic, cabbalic
    mysterious 528.17
    mystical 994.21
cabalism, cabbalism
    994.1

cabalist, cabbalist
    994.13
caballero 875.5
cabane 273a.10
cabaret inn 189.8
    restaurant 298.42
    night club 959.13
cabasset 717.2
cabbage *n.* 298.30
cabbage *v.*
    appropriate 789.8
    purloin 791.9
cabbagehead 501.1
cabbala, cabbalic etc.
    See cabala etc.
cabby, cabdriver 268.9
caber 215.12
cabin hut 189.4
    room 191.16
    cockpit 273a.10
cabin boy 269.3
cabinet
    cupboard 191.15
    room 191.16
    bower 191.22
    conservatory 371.6
    workshop 691
    council 696.1
cabinetmaker 690.5, 8
cable *n.*
    fastening 45.4
    cord 205.3
    cablegram 532a.3
    by cable 684.7
cable *v.* 532a.8
cablegram 532a.3
cable's length 200.6
cableway 627.6
cabman 268.9
caboodle all 50.2
    bunch 72.5
caboose galley 191.16
    railway car 272.19
    cookroom 386.4
cabriole 272.4
cabriolet
    carriage 272.4
    cart 272.5
    automobile 272.15
cacao butter 356.3
cachalot 192.8
cache *n.*
    hiding place 530.2
    store 636.4
cache *v.* conceal 528.10
    store 636.7
cachet 550.11
cachexia
    weakness 160.1
    ailment 655.5
cachinnation 838.3
cacique, cazique 745.3
cack 215.23
cackle *n.* chatter 584.2
    small talk 588.2
    laughter 838.3
cackle *v.* croak 412.2
    laugh 838.7
    exult 884.6
**cacodemon, cacodae-
    mon** 980.2
cacoëpistic 583.5

cacoëpy — calisthenics

cacoëpy
  bad diction 579.1
  mispronunciation 583.1
cacoëthes
  bad habit 613.6
  desire 865.1
cacoëthes scribendi 590.2
cacogenesis 83.6
cacographer 579.2; 590.11
cacographic 579.3
cacography
  poor diction 579.1
  (ungrammaticism 568.1)
  bad writing 590.6
cacology
  bad diction 579.1
  (ungrammaticism 568.1)
  speech defect 583.1
caconym 563.1
  (inelegance 579.1)
cacophonize 414.3
cacophonous 414.4
  (strident 410.9)
  (speech 583.5)
cacophony
  dissonance 414.1
  (stridor 410.1)
  inelegance 579.1
cad servant 746.1
  vulgarian 851.4
cadastral listed 86.4
  measuring 466.11
cadastration 466.8
cadastre, cadaster
  list 86.1
  measurement 466.8
cadaver 362.1
cadaverous
  corpselike 362.2
  pale 429.6
  unprepossessing 846.8
caddie, caddy
  case 191.8
  attendant 746.1
caddis fly 366.24
cadeau 784.3
cadence rhythm 138.3
  sinkage 306.1
  tone 402.2
  musical ~ 413.10, 21; 415.15
  poetical rhythm 597.6
cadent 413.29
cadenza 413.10; 415.15
cadet boy 129.4
  officer 745.11
cadet blue 438.2
cadge 765.6
cadger 767.2
cadi, kadi 967.1
cadmium 439.3
cadmium orange 439.1
cadmium yellow 436.1, 4
cadre 611.2

caduceus staff 215.15
  scepter 747.1
  wand 993.3
caducity
  transience 111.1
  impotence 158.1
  senility 499.5
  (degeneration 659.1)
caducous 111.6
caecal 261.3
caecum vitals 221.4
  closure 261.1
  intestine 350.4
Caelum 318.6
Caesar 745.3
Caesarism 737.4
caesura
  discontinuity 70.1
  stop 142.2, 5
  interval 198.1
  poetry 597.6
café 298.42
  (inn 189.8)
café au lait 433.1
café dansant 959.13
cafeteria 298.42
caffeine 171.5
caftan 225.15
cage *n.* case 191.8
  enclosure 232.1
  (menagerie 370.3)
  prison 752.1
cage *v.* 751.8
  (tame 370.6)
cageling 754.1
cagey 702.6
Cagliostro 548.3; 992.2
Cagot 893.5
cahot bump 250.2
  cavity 252.2
  joggle 315.4
cahoots
  association 709.2
  participation 778.1
  go cahoots
    league 48.4
    go shares 778.5
  in cahoots
    leagued 48.6
    co-operate 709.7
Cain 361.8
caïque 273.4
cairn, carn
  monument 363.15
  landmark 550.10
caisson case 191.8
  cavity 252.2
caisson disease
  spasm 315.7
  cramps 378.1
  illness 655.3
caitiff *n.* coward 862.2
  wretch 876.9
  savage 913.3
  knave 949.1
caitiff *adj.* 862.6
cajole deceive 545.10
  persuade 615.9
  flatter 933.2
cajoler 935.2

cajolery
  enticement 617.1
  flattery 933.1
  (dissimulation 544.2)
cake *n.* pastry 298.12
  (sweets 396.2)
  solid 321.4
  ~ of tobacco 392a.7
cake *v.* 321.7
cake-eater 902.6
cakewalk 840.7
calabash 191.12
calaboose 752.1
calambac, calambour 400.3
calamiform 253.18
calamine blue 438.2
calamitous 735.8; 830.17
calamity fatality 361.5
  misfortune 735.3
calando 415.31
calash
  headdress 225.26
  vehicle 272.4, 5
calathiform 252.10
calcareous 432.4
calcimine, kalsomine *n.* paint 428.5
  whitewash 430.5
calcimine, kalsomine *v.* paint 428.10
  whitewash 430.7
calcinate 384.18
calcination 384.3
calcinatory *n.* 384.12
calcinatory *adj.* 384.22
calcine 384.18
calcitrate 276.8
calcitration 276.3
calculable 85.11
calculate compute 37.5
  estimate 85.7
  judge 480.6
  think 484.8
  ~ in advance 511.7
  suppose 514.6
calculate on
  rely on 484.7
  plan on 507.6
  intend 620.3
calculated
  tending 176.3
  measured 466.13
  aforethought 611.5
calculating 498.11
calculating machine 85.5
calculation
  computation 37.2
  (total 50.2)
  numeration 85.1
  (accountancy 811.4)
  expectation 507.1
  circumspection 864.1
calculator
  counter 85.5
  mathematician 85.6
  accountant 811.6
calculus

numeration 85.1, 2
hardness 323.3
caldarium 386.6
  (lavatory 652.4)
caldron, cauldron
  conversion 144.4
  kettle 191.11
  boiler 386.1
calèche 272.5
Caledonian 188.9
calefaction 384
calefactive 384.22
  (warm 382.15)
calefactor 386.1
calefactory *n.* 386.1
calefactory *adj.* 384.22
calembour 842.5
calendar *n.*
  arrangement 60.3
  list 86.1
  chronology 114.5
  record 551.3
  schedule 611.2
calendar *v.* list 86.3
  chronicle 114.8
  record 551.8
  schedule 611.4
calendar watch 114.6
calender *n.* 255.3
calender *v.* 255.4
calends, kalends
  list 86.1
  chronology 114.5
calenture
  ~ of the brain 503.3
  sunstroke 503.4
  fever 655.4
calf youngling 129.7
  island 346.1
  bovine 366.12
  ice 383.5
  fool 501.1
  awkward boy 701
calf love 897.1
Caliban 846.3
caliber, calibre
  degree 26.1
  diameter 202.3
  (capacity 192.2)
  tube 260.6
  intelligence 498.1
calibrate
  graduate 26.2
  measure 466.10
calico cloth 219.5
  woman 374.5
calid 382.15
caliginous dark 421.7
  obscure 519.7
caligo 655.8
caliper, calliper 466.10
calipers, callipers 466.4
caliph, calif 745.5
caliphate, caliphship 737.3
calisthenic 686.10
calisthenics
  athletics 159.5
  physical education 537.5
  exercise 686.2

caliver — canard

beautification 845.5
caliver 727.10
calk, caulk
  repair 660.11
  nap 683.5
  defeat 731.10
calker, caulker
  end-all 67.4
  excellent thing 648.4
  alcoholic drink 959.10
calking iron 273.14
call *n.*
  human cry 411.1
  animal cry 412.1
  signal 550.16
  motive 615.1
  requirement 630.1
  ~ to arms 669.1; 722.3
  command 741.1
  social ~ 892.3
  at one's call 743.3
  (serving 746.9)
call *v.* cry 411.5; 412.2
  name 564.6
  accost 586.2
  meet a bet 621.18
  summons 969.10
  predestinate 976.10
  ~ to the ministry 995.7
be called 564.7
call a spade a spade
  speak plainly 576.2
  be artless 703.3
call attention to
  point out 457.7
  remind 505.15
call down 932.8
call for require 630.2
  cite 741.7
call forth
  resort to 677.5
  excite 824.2
call in 695.6
call in question
  doubt 485.6
  (disagree 489.4)
  (dispute 536.2)
call into existence 359.8
call into play 677.5
call it a day 142.6
call names
  curse 908.4
  insult 929.3
call on, call upon
  exhort 615.7
  command 741.4
  request 765.4
  visit 892.10
  claim 924.7
  impose a duty 926.7
call one's bluff 715.2
call out
  vociferate 411.7
  challenge 715.2
call over, call the roll 85.7
call to account

reprimand 932.8
  punish 972.5
call to arms 722.10
call to mind
  remember 505.10
  imagine 515.8
call to order
  command 741.4
  reprimand 932.8
  punish 972.5
call to the bar 968.3
call to witness
  appeal to 467.10
  arraign 969.10
call up
  remember 505.10
  imagine 515.8
  telephone 532a.7
  prompt 615.7
  call up 824.2
callant, callan 129.4
callboy 599.17
callidity 698.1
calligraph 590.5
calligrapher 590.11
calligraphy 590.1, 5
calling vocation 625.5
  (duty 926.1)
  holy orders 995.6
Calliope 597.9
calliope, calliophone
  noisemaker 404.4
  instrument 417.4
calliper, callipers See caliper etc.
callithump 59.4
callosity 323.1
callous *v.* 323.4
callous *adj.* hard 323.5
  ~ physically 376.5
  ~ emotionally 823.7
  (irreligious 989.6)
  heartless 907.8
  hardhearted 945.18
callousness 823.1
callow youthful 127.5
  immature 674.8
calm *n.*
  quiescence 265.1
  (inertness 172.1)
  no wind 349.15
calm *v.* moderate 174.5
  (compose 826.7)
  quiet 265.6
  dispirit 616.3
  ~ down 826.8
calm *adj.*
  equable 174.6
  smooth 213.8
  quiescent 265.7
  silent 403.6
  peaceful 721.4
  inexcitable 826.9
  (philosophical 451.38)
  (unastonished 871.4)
calmant, calmative *adj.*
  moderative 174.7
  palliative 662.25
  relieving 834.7

calmative *n.* 662.6
  (moderator 174.3)
calmly 826.12
calmness 826.2
calomel 662.9
caloric, caloricity 382.1
calorie, calory 382.10
calorific 382.16
calorimeter
  aviation 267a.29
  thermometer 389.1
calotte 999.1
calotype 556.18
calotypist 559.7
caloyer 996.11
calumet token 550.14
  peace offering, 723.2
calumniate 934.3
calumniation 934.1
calumniator 936.1
calumnious
  maledictory 908.6
  disparaging 934.4
calumny
  malediction 908.1
  detraction 934.1
calvary 1000.3
Calvary 363.14
calve 161.9
Calvinism
  predetermination 611.1
  religion 984.4
Calvinist 984.14
calyx 191.6
cam 272.16
camail 717.2
Cámara de Diputados 696.6
camaraderie 892.1
Cámara de Senadores 696.5
Cámara dos Deputados 696.6
camarilla
  council 696.2
  clique 712.2
camber
  convexity 250.1
  aeronautics 267a.3
cambist broker 797.7
  treasurer 801
Cambrian *n.* 188.9
Cambrian *adj.* 188.11
cambric 219.5
cambric tea 160.5
camel 271.2
  (animal 366.2)
camel-back 243.5
camel bird 474.6
cameleer 268.9
Camelidae, Cameloidea, camelopard 206.7
Camelopardalis 318.6
camelot 797.3
cameo sculpture 557.6
  (protuberance 250.2)
  (figure 554.4)
  beauty 845.4

cameo glass 557.6
camera 445.5
  (merchandise 798.3)
  (photography 556.4)
Camera dei Deputati 696.6
camera lucida 445.5
camera obscura 445.5
cameraman 559.7
camerated 191.23
Camilla 274.7
camisado, camisade 716.1
camisole 225.25
Camorra 791.3
camouflage *n.* 545.5
camouflage *v.* 528.10
camp *n.*
  encampment 189.15
  military ~ 728.2
camp *v.* encamp 184.15
  ~ on the trail of 281.3
camp meeting 990.7
campagna 344.1
campaign *n.*
  journey 266.8
  military ~ 722.4
campaign *v.*
  travel 266.12
  make war 722.9
campaigner 726.4
campaniform 245.10
campanile 206.3
campanular 245.10
camper 268.2
campestral 344.2
campfire 382.8
camphor 356a.1
cample *n.* 713.3
cample *v.* 713.7
campo square 189.19
  plain 344.1
campus green 367.11
  arena 728.1
camshaft 272.16
can *n.*
  receptacle 191.11
  piston 263.1
  dismissal 297.4
  water closet 653.9
  prison 752.1
can *v.* be able 157.6
  dismiss 297.12
  preserve 670.4
Canada 182.3
Canadian *n.* 188.9
Canadian *adj.* 188.11
canaille 876.1
canal narrow 203.3
  trench 259.2
  tube 260.6
  channel 350.1
  (seaway 267.8)
  (inlet 343.1)
  (passageway 627.2)
canalboat 273.4
canaliculate, canaliferous 259.4
canard aircraft 273a.1
  food 298.25
  report 532.3

canary — cap

canard (*continued*)
 falsehood 546.1
canary *n.*
 weakling 160.4
 bird 366.22
 songster 416.10, 11
 wine 959.7
canary *adj.* 436.6
canaster 392a.1
cancan 840.7
cancel *n.*
 musical notation 415.23
 obliteration 552.1
 cancellation 756.1
cancel *v.* excise 38.5
 destroy 162.4
 counteract 179.4
 obliterate 552.2
 annul 756.3
 ~ a debt 808.8
cancellate 219.11
cancellation
 interlacing 219.3
 obliteration 552.1
 annulment 756.1
cancelli 191.6
cancellous 219.11
cancer sore 655.16
 blight 663.2
 affliction 830.2
Cancer season 126a.1
 constellation 318.6
canch modicum 32.2
 piece 51.3
candelabrum 423.9
candent
 burning 382.17
 white 430.8
candid sincere 543.3
 frank 703.4
 (honest 939.7)
 fair 941.3
candidacy 763.1
candidate *n.*
 applicant 767.1
 aspirant 865.7
candidate *v.* 763.3
candied 396.8
candle 423.1, 7
candlebomb
 firework 382.9
 signal light 423.5
candle fly 423.13
candle-foot 157a.5
candlelight dusk 126.1
 light 420.7
 (candle 423.7)
 semidarkness 422.2
candlelighting 126.1
Candlemas
 anniversary 138.7
 holyday 998.13
candle power
 electricity 157a.5
 light 420.1
candlestand, candlestick 423.9
candlewick 388.4
candor, candour
 veracity 543.1
 sincerity 703.1

 (honesty 939.1)
candy *n.* 396.2
 (merchandise 798.3)
candy *v.*
 solidify 321.7
 sweeten 396.7
candymaker 690.8
cane *n.* staff 215.15
 club 727.7
 scourge 975.2
cane *v.* 972.6
canescence 430.1
canescent 430.8
Canes Venatici 318.6
cangle 713.7
Canicula 318.3
canicular 382.15
canicular days
 summer 126a.3
 hot weather 382.3
canicule 382.3
Canidae 366.5
canine *n.* 366.5, 6
canine *adj.* 366.26
canine appetite 865.4
canine madness 503.1
canister 191.8, 9, 11
canister shot 727.14
canker *n.* sore 655.16
 blight 663.2
 (corruption 659.2)
 (affliction 830.2)
canker *v.* 659.7, 9
cankered
 diseased 655.25
 putrified 659.13
 ill-humored 901.7
cankerworm 366.25
 (blight 663.2)
cannabis 662.7
canned 959.21
canned editorial 21.2
canned music
 duplicate 21.2
 music 415.3
cannel 388.2
cannery room 191.16
 storeroom 636.4
cannibal *n.*
 eater 298.41
 killer 361.8
 savage 913.3
cannibal *adj.*
 man-eating 298.48
 bloodthirsty 961.11
cannibalism 907.3; 961.3
cannibalistic 961.11
cannie See **canny**
cannikin 191.11
canning 670.2
cannon *n.* clash 276.2
 carom 276.3
 gun 727.11
cannon *v.* 276.8
cannonade *n.*
 boom 406.3
 drumming 407.3
 bombardment 716.1
cannonade *v.* 716.6
cannon ball
 sphere 249.2

 speed 274.6
cannon cracker 382.9
cannoneer, cannon fodder 726.4
cannular, cannulate, cannulated 260.16
cannon shot 727.14
cannot 158.4
canny, cannie
 sagacious 498.10
 cunning 702.6
 cautious 864.6
canoe 273.4
canon music 415.3
 measure 466.2
 tenet 484.3
 (doctrine 983.2)
 precept 697.1
 law 963.2
 clergyman 996.5
 rite 998.7, 9
cañon See **canyon**
canoness 996.12
canonical
 conformable 82.10
 authoritative 474.13
 (doctrinal 484.16)
 theological 983.4
 orthodox 983a.7
 scriptural 985.7
 ecclesiastical 995.9
canonicals 999
canonicate 995.3
canonics 983.1
canonist
 theologian 986.3
 orthodox 983a.4
canonization
 glorification 873.6
 beatification 987.2
 ordination 995.6
canonize
 beatify 987.8
 ordain 995.7
canonry 995.3
can opener 301.4
canopy 223.9, 3
 (sunshade 424.2)
canorous 413.27
cant *n.*
 obliquity 217.1
 file 255.3
 hypocrisy 544.2
 jargon 563.4
 (term 564.3)
 auction 796.2
 sanctimony 988.2
 pietist 988.6
cant *v.* incline 217.6
 turn ship 267.24
 impel 276.7
 throw 284.12
 dissemble 544.6
 jargon 563.13
 auction 796.6
 be sanctimonious 988.8
cant *adj.* 563.16
cantabile 415.3, 10
cantaloupe, cantaloup 298.32
cantankerous 901.7

744

cantata 415.10, 12
cantation 992.1
cantatrice 416.10
canteen
 receptacle 191.11
 restaurant 298.42
 store 799.4
canter *n.* run 274.3
 hypocrite 548.4
 pietist 988.6
canter *v.* 274.9
Canterbury 991.15
Canterbury tale 546.1
cantharis
 excitant 171.4
 aphrodisiac 865.10
canticle song 415.10
 hymn 990.2
cantico 840.6, 7
cantilever 215.11
cantillate 416.20
canting
 hypocritical 544.8
 (affected 853.6)
 sanctimonious 988.1
cantle modicum 32.2
 part 51.1
 saddle 215.23
cantlet part 51.1
 modicum 32.2
canto melody 415.2, 13
 verse 597.7
canton *n.* 181.2
canton *v.* 44.10
cantonment 189.1, 15
cantor 416.10, 13
cantorial side 239.2
cantrip, cantraip, cantrap *n.* 993.1
cantrip, cantraip, cantrap *adj.* 993.5
cantus figuratus, cantus firmus 415.4
cantus mensurabilis 415.5
cantus planus 415.4
canty 836.7
Canuck 188.9
canvas cloth 219.5
 tent 223.5
 sail 273.13
 picture 556.9
canvasback
 food 298.26
 bird 366.22
canvass *n.* 765.1
canvass *v.*
 investigate 461.17
 argue 476.11
 discuss 595.4
 solicit 765.4
canvasser 767.1; 797.4
canyon, cañon
 chasm 198.3
 water gap 350.1
canzon, canzonet 415.10
caoutchouc 325.2
cap *n.* summit 210.1
 capital 215.17
 lid 223.7
 (stopper 263.1)

headdress 225.26
firework 382.9
letter 561.1
foolscap 590.10
type 591.6
paper 635.4
by-bid 796.2
cap v. excel 33.5
  top 210.5
  cover 223.22
  ~ verses 597.12
  match 718.2
  complete 729.2
  by-bid 796.6
  salute 894.9
capability
  ability 157.2
  (capacity 5.4)
  skill 698.2
capable able 157.9
  effectual 644.7
  competent 698.11, 12
capacious
  spacious 180.6
  sizable 192.11
capacitate 52.7
capacitative 52.11
capacity
  character 5.4
  ability 157.2
  accommodation 192.2
  intellect 450.1
  function 625.3
  skill 698.2
cap and bells 599.4
cap-a-pie 52.15
caparison n.
  horsecloth 223.10
  wardrobe 225.2
  equipment 634.1
  armor 717.2
caparison v. 225.42
cape n. cloak 225.15
  promontory 250.5
cape v. 267.22
Cape cart 272.5
caper n. leap 309.2
  frolic 840.3
  prank 842.7
caper v.
  jump about 309.5
  frolic 840.21
capering, capersome 309.6
capful
  quantity 25.2
  modicum 32.2
capillament
  filament 205.1
  hair 256.3
capillary n. 205.1
capillary, capilliform adj. 205.7
capital n.
  town 189.16
  top 210.4
  crown 215.17
  letter 561.1
  type 591.6
  stock 636.2
  (means 632.1)

funds 800.2
(wealth 803.1)
make capital of
  pretext 619.2
  profit by 658.7; 775.7
capital adj.
  supreme 33.8
  top 210.6
  letter 561.9
  excellent 648.9
capitalist
  financier 797.6
  rich man 803.2
capitalize 775.7
capital punishment 972.4
capitation 812.2
capitol 717.4
capitular n. 996.5
capitular adj. 995.9
capitulary n.
  precepts 697.1
  ordinance 963.2
  ecclesiastic 996.5
capitulary adj. 995.9
capitulate 725.4
capitulation 725.2
capnomancy 511.3
cap of maintenance 747.2
capon n. 298.25
capon, caponize v. 38.7
caporal 694.1
capote 225.26
capper
  bunko steerer 548.2
  by-bidder 795.2
capping
  by-bidding 796.2
  salute 894.4
capriccetto 415.3
capriccio
  music 415.3
  caprice 608.1
capriccioso 415.30
caprice music 415.3
  whim 608.1, 2
capricious
  unconformable 83.9
  irregular 139.2
  uncertain 475.16
  whimsical 608.5
  (inconstant 149.6)
  (erratic 503.17)
  (irresolute 605.5)
  (tergiversating 607.10)
  be capricious 608.4
  (change 140.5)
  (be irresolute 605.4)
  (tergiversate 607.7)
capriciously 608.7
capriciousness 608.2
  (changeableness 149.1)
  (eccentricity 503.6)
  (irresolution 605.1)
  (tergiversation 607.1)
Capricorn 318.6
Capricornus 126a.1

capriole n. 309.2
capriole v. 309.5
capsheaf 210.1
capsicin, capsicum 393.1
capsizal, capsize n. 218.1
capsize v.
  turn over 218.5
  upset boat 267.35
capstan ship 273.14
  lifter 307.2
capstone 210.4
capsula 191.11
capsular
  vascular 191.23
  concave 252.10
capsule
  receptacle 191.6, 11
  wrapper 223.11
  hull 223.14
captain mariner 269.4
  chief 745.1, 11, 12
  (head 694.2)
captain general 745.11
captation 933.1
caption
  title 66.3; 564.2
  arrest 751.3
  capture 789.1
captious
  sophistical 477.9, 11
  capricious 608.5
  irascible 901.7
  faultfinding 932.11
captivate
  capture 751.9
  fascinate 617.4
  delight 829.5
  enamor 897.13
captivating
  delightful 829.8
  attractive 845.9
captivation
  allurement 617.1
  delightfulness 829.2
  spell 993.1
captive prisoner 754.1
  lover 897.6
  take captive
  subjugate 749.5
  capture 751.9
captivity 751.2
  in captivity 751.12
captor 789.6
capture n. arrest 751.3
  seizure 789.1, 5
capture v. arrest 751.9
  seize 789.9
capuche 999.1
Capuchin 996.11
caput 210.1
caput mortuum 40.2
car vehicle 272.15, 19
  gondola 273a.12
carabineer, carabinier 726.4
carack See carrack
caracole, caracol n. 309.2
caracole, caracol v.
  ride 266.19

caper 309.5
carafe 191.11
caramel 396.2
carapace shell 223.16
  shield 717.2
carat 319.4
caravan
  procession 69.3
  (travel 266.1)
  company 72.3
  vehicle 272.3, 19
caravansary, caravanserai 189.8
caravel, caravelle
  ship 273.1, 2
  battleship 726.11
carbarn 636.4
carbine 727.10
carbon residue 40.2
  burnt residue 384.15
  fuel 388.1
carbonaceous 388.10
Carbonaro 742.3
carbon copy
  duplicate 21.2
  (writing 590.3)
  record 551.1
carbon dioxide
  exudation 299.1
  gas 334.2
  refrigerant 387.2
  poison 663.5
carbonic acid 663.5
carbonization 384.3
carbonize 384.18
carbon lamp 423.3
carbon monoxide
  gas 334.2
  poison 663.5
carborundum 253.7
carboy 191.11
carbuncle
  protuberance 250.2
  red 434.5
  sore 655.16
  gem 847.8
carburetor 272.16
carcanet 847.7
carcass, carcase
  form 240.1
  corpse 362.1
  missile 727.14
carcinoma 655.16
carchariid 366.21
card n. oddity 83.4
  postcard 592.3
  schedule 611.2
  the card 494.4
card v.
  disentangle 60.9
  comb 652.11
cardboard
  bookbinding 593.10
  paper 635.4
cardcase 191.8
card game 840.12
cardialgia 655.13
cardigan jacket 225.16
cardinal n.
  cloak 225.15
  red 434.2, 5
  priest 996.5

cardinal — carry

cardinal *adj.* 33.8
cardinalate 995.3
cardinal bird 366.22
cardinal point 642.4
cardinal points 278.2
cardinal's hat 747.3; 999.1
cardinal virtues 944.1
card index 86.1
  (record 551.1)
  (store 636.4)
cardioid *n.* 245.2
cardioid *adj.* 245.12
carditis 655.12
cards divination 511.5
  game 840.12, 13
  in the cards 600.16
  on the cards
    imminent 152.3
    contingent 177.4
    possible 470.5
    probable 472.5
cardsharp cheat 548.2
  (proficient 700.1)
  gambler 621.15
  swindler 792.8
cardsharping
  deception 545.3
  gambling 621.6
care *n.*
  close attention 457.2
  heed 459
  (meticulousness 457.3)
  (accuracy 494.3)
  (forethought 510.2)
  (conscientiousness 939.2)
  task 625.2
  protectorship 664.2
  charge 693.1
  auspices 707.2
  hardship 735.1
  custody 751.4
  economy 817.1
  troubled thought 828.5
  trouble 830.2
  anxiety 860.2
  caution 864.1
  have a care 864.3, 9
  have care of 693.5
care *v.* 459.5
  care for
    look after 459.6
    value 642.8
    love 897.11
    desire 865.11
  not care
    be unwilling 603.4
    be apathetic 823.3
    be indifferent 866.3
    dislike 867.4
    disdain 930.5
careen incline 217.6
  ~ a boat 267.34
  repair 660.11
career
  course 264.3; 627.2
  race 274.4
  flow 348.2
  business 625.3

conduct 692.3
carefree 836.7
careful heedful 459.7
  (thoughtful 451.35)
  (attentive 457.9)
  (meticulous 494.11)
  (cautious 864.6)
  (conscientious 939.8)
  frugal 817.4
be careful
  take heed 459.3
  (be attentive 457.4)
  beware! 864.9
carefully 459.9
  (cautiously 864.8)
carefulness 459.1
  (caution 864.1)
careless untidy 59.9
  neglectful 460.8
  (clumsy 699.12)
  (reckless 863.6)
  diction 575.2
  insensible 823.5
  unconcerned 866.4
be careless 863.5
carelessly 460.12
  do carelessly 460.6
  (botch 699.9)
carelessness 460.1
  (incompetence 699.1)
  (recklessness 863.1)
  (indifference 866.1)
caress *n.* touch 379.1
  endearment 902.3
caress *v.* touch 379.3
  fondle 902.8
caressing *n.* 902.3
caressing, caressive *adj.* 902.9
caret deficiency 53.2
  typography 550.8
caretaker
  guardian 664.3
  functionary 758.2
careworn 828.16
cargo load 190.1
  freight 270.4
  baggage 780.6
caribou 366.11
caricatural
  imitative 19.13
  burlesque 856.7
caricature *n.*
  imitation 21.3
  (misrepresentation 555.3)
  exaggeration 549.1
  picture 556.9
  burlesque 856.3
caricature *v.*
  imitate 19.8
  burlesque 856.4
caricaturist
  artist 559.1
  humorist 844
caries ailment 655.16
  decay 659.2
carillon 417.10
cariole, carriole 272.4, 5, 13

cariosity 659.2
carious foul 653.17
  diseased 655.25
  putrefactive 659.13
cark *n.* 828.5
cark *v.* 828.10
carking 830.12
carl 876.5
carlish rustic 183.3
  uncouth 851.7
carload 190.1
carman 268.9
Carmelite 996.11
carminative *n.* 662.9
carminative *adj.* 662.25
carmine *n.* 434.2
carmine *v.* 434.7
carmine *adj.* 434.9
carminette 434.2
carnage 361.1
carnal fleshly 364.4
  sensual 961.11
  worldly 989.9
carnality 961.3
  (desire 865.6)
  (vice 945.1)
carnalize 364.3
carnal-minded
  sensual 961.11
  worldly 989.9
carnation
  fragrance 400.3
  red 434.2, 3, 5
carnelian red 434.2, 5
  gem 847.8
carnival show 599.8
  festival 840.2
carnivore 298.41
carnivorous 298.48
carnivorousness 298.1
carol *n.* 415.10
carol *v.* warble 412.2
  sing 416.20
  rejoice 838.5
caroler, caroller 416.10
Caroline 560.4
carom, carrom *n.* 276.3
carom, carrom *v.* 276.8
carotic 376.5
carousal revel 840.3
  (dissipation 954.2)
  drunken ~ 959.3
carouse *n.* revel 840.3
  drinking bout 959.3
carouse *v.* revel 840.21
  wassail 959.16
  (dissipate 954.3)
carousel See carrousel
carouser
  reveler 840.16
  wassailer 959.11
carp demur 485.7
  criticize 932.7
carpenter
  stage ~ 599.17
  craftsman 690.5
  (repairman 660.7)
carper 936.1
carpet floor 211.2

rug 223.8
  ground 342.1
on the carpet
  on foot 151.5
  in question 461.26
  planned 626.11
  intended 620.4
carpetbag 191.5
carpetbagger
  cheat 548.2
  rascal 702.4
  swindler 792.8
carpet knight fop 854.1
  sycophant 886.2
  sybarite 954a.1
carpetmaker 690.8
carping 932.11
carrack, carack 273.2
carrefour 219.2
carriable, carryable 320.7
carriage posture 184.2
  gait 266.5
  transportation 270.2
  vehicle 272.1, 4, 19
  mien 448.4
  conduct 692.1
carriage bow 727.9
carriage horse 271.3
carrier conveyer 271
  (driver 268.9)
  (vehicle 272.1)
  (ship 273.1)
  messenger 534.1, 2
  aircraft ~ 726.11
carrier pigeon
  carrier 271.1
  messenger 534.2
carriole See cariole
carrion corpse 362.1
  offal 653.6
carrom See carom
carronade 727.11
carrottop 256.3
carroty 434.12
carrousel, carousel
  whirligig 312.4
  merry-go-round 840.15
carry *n.* 270.2
carry *v.* escort 88.7
  tend 176.2
  support 215.26
  wear 225.45
  ~ sail 267.10
  transport 270.8
  induce 615.9
  ~ oneself 692.5
carry all before one 731.6
carry away
  charm 617.4
  abduct 791.11
  delight 829.5
  enamor 897.13
carry coals 879.2
carry coals to Newcastle waste 638.2
  redundance 641.3
  (labor in vain 645.6)
  (mismanage 699.7)

carry into effect 680.6
carry into execution
  complete 729.2, 3
  (do 680.6)
  observe 772.3
carry off 791.11
  (take away 789.10)
carry on
  continue 106.2; 143.3
  be violent 173.7
  persevere 604a.2
  practice 625.6
  do 680.6
  (pursue 622.6)
  be industrious 682.12
  conduct 692.4
  manage 693.4
  endure 826.6
  be angry 900.8
carry out do 680.6
  complete 729.2
  observe 772.3
carry over 811.7
carry the day 731.6
carry through
  do 680.6
  complete 729.2
  endure 826.6
carry weight
  have influence 175.7
  be important 642.7
carryable See carriable
carryall 272.4
carrying 270.2
carry-over 40.4
cart n. 272.5
cart v. 270.8
cartage 270.2
carte 86.1
carte blanche
  omnipotence 157.5
  permit 760.2
  liberality 816.3
give carte blanche 760.3
cartel trust 712.5
  challenge 715.1
  truce 723.3
  compact 769.1
cartel ship 723.3
carter 268.9
Cartesianism 451.11
cart horse 271.3
Carthusian 996.11
cartilage solid 321.4
  hardness 323.3
  gristle 327.2
cartilaginification 323.2
cartilaginous
  hard 323.5
  gristly 325.5
cartload 190.1
cartmaker 690.8
cartman 268.9
cartographer 466.9
cartographical 466.11
cartography

measurement 466.8
  map 626.2
carton case 191.8
  shot 284.4
  paper 635.4
cartoon
  caricature 21.3
  picture 556.9
cartoonist 559.1
cartouche, cartouch
  cartridge 727.13
  ornament 847.4
cartridge 727.13
cartulary list 86.1
  record 551.1
cart wheel
  inversion 218.1
  (whirl 312.2)
  money 800.8
cartwright 690.7
caruncle, caruncula 250.2
caruncular 250.9
carunculation 250.1, 2
carve cut 44.8
  produce 161.8
  form 240.6
  furrow 259.3
  sculpture 557.9
  (depict 554.7)
  engrave 558.5
  apportion 786.3
carvel See caravel
carver 559.4, 6
carving 557.1
caryatid post 215.16
  ornament 847.4
casa 189.3
Casanova 897.6
cascade 348.7
case n. state 7.1
  example 82.2
  oddity 83.4
  box 191.8
  frame 215.8
  pillowcase 223.9
  wrapper 223.11
  condition 469.2
  argument 476.3
  grammar 567.1
  printing ~ 591.5
  bookbinding 593.9
  addict 613.7
  business 625.1
  patient 655.20
  infatuation 897.1
  suit in law 969.1
case in point
  example 82.2
  (relevance 23.2)
  question 461.10
in any case still 469.8
  anyhow 627.9
in case
  provided 8.8; 469.8
  (supposing 514.13)
  in the event 151.8
make out a case 467.9
case v. wrap 223.23
  look at 441.11
  reconnoiter 461.22
caseation 321.3

caseharden
  strengthen 159.8
  inure 613.8
  make callous 823.4
casehardened
  insensible 376.5
  obstinate 606.6
  callous 823.7
  ~ in vice 945.18
casein adherer 46.3
  clot 321.5
  semiliquid 352.3
caseinogen 321.5
casemate camp 189.15
  fortification 717.3
casemated 717.9
casement frame 215.8
  window 260.5
caseous 321.8
casern, caserne 189.15
Casey Jones 268.11
cash money 800.1, 4, 13
  (payment 807.2)
  pay 807.8
in cash 803.8
cash down 807.11
cash on delivery 807.8, 11
cash account 811
cashbook
  record 551.3
  account book 811.5
cashbox 802.1
cashier n. 801
cashier v.
  dismiss 297.12
  depose 756.5
cashkeeper 801
cashmere cloth 219.5
  ~ shawl 225.15
Cashmere 366.9
Cashmere shawl 225.15
cash register
  calculator 85.5
  recorder 553.3
  money box 802.1
casing case 191.8
  wrapper 223.11
casino 621.14
cask 191.11
casket case 191.8
  coffin 363.10
Caslon 591.8
casque, casquetel 717.2
Cassandra
  prophet 513.2
  warning 668.3
Cassel yellow 436.4
cassideous 245.13
cassino 840.12
Cassiopeia, Cassiopeia's Chair 318.6
cassis 959.6
cassock priest 996.2
  clerical ~ 999.1
cast n. nature 5.3
  duplicate 21.2
  (sculpture 557.4)
  modicum 32.2
  computation 37.2

kind 75.2
  form 240.1
  tendency 176.1
  desquamation 223.13
  throw 284.3
  color 428.1
  glimpse 441.2
  aspect 448.4
  trait 550.6
  role 599.7
  dramatic ~ 599.18
  ~ of the dice 621.2
  aid 707.1
  disposition 820.1
cast v. scatter 73.3
  happen 151.3
  shed 226.6
  form 240.6
  turn ship 267.24
  throw 284.12
  vomit 297.18
  turn 311.4
  sculpture 557.9
  allot 786.3
  condemn 971.2
cast about
  turn ship 267.24
  grope 463.9
cast adrift eject 297.8
  release 750.2
cast a horoscope 511.7
cast a nativity 511.7
cast anchor
  settle 184.14
  anchor 267.12
  (land 292.9)
  be inactive 683.8
cast a shadow 422.6
  (shade 424.6)
cast aside
  postpone 133.4
  eject 297.8
  neglect 460.5
  put away 678.4
cast a slur
  stigmatize 874.7
  censure 932.7
  asperse 934.3
  accuse 938.4
cast a spell 992.4
  (spiritualism 994.19)
cast a traverse 267.39
cast away
  unmoor 267.15
  go aground 267.33
  waste 638.2
  squander 818.3
cast down 308.5
cast in one's lot with
  decide 609.8
  side with 709.5
cast in one's teeth
  taunt 930.6
  accuse 938.4
cast loose 267.15
cast lots 621.17
cast off undress 226.4
  unmoor 267.15
  discard 678.3

cast — catchword 748

cast (*continued*)
cast out 297.8
cast pearls before swine waste 638.2
  labor in vain 645.6
  be prodigal 818.3
cast sheep's eyes
  desire 865.11
  be modest 881.3
  eye amorously 902.7
cast skin 223.13
cast the gorge 297.18
cast the lead 208.7
cast up compute 37.5
  calculate 85.7
  happen 151.3
  vomit 297.18
cast up accounts 811.7
cast *adj.* 820.3
castaneous 433.5
castanets 417.10
castaway *n.*
  castoff 782.2
  outcast 893.5
castaway *adj.*
  stranded 732.10
  derelict 782.4
cast-by *n.* 782.2
cast-by *adj.* 782.4
caste kind 75.2
  class 712.1
  social class 873.4
castellan
  warden 664.3
  retainer 746.1
castellated 717.9
castellation 257.4
caster 191.11
castigate
  upbraid 932.8
  punish 972.5
castigation
  reproof 932.3
  punishment 972.1
castigator 936.2
castigatory 972.14
Castilian 560.4
casting
  duplicate 21.2
  computation 37.2
  numeration 85.1
casting weight
  inequality 28.1
  compensation 30.2
cast in the eye 443.1
cast iron *n.* 635.6
cast-iron *adj.* 604.7
castle house 189.3
  stronghold 717.4
castle-builder 515.7
castle-building *n.*
  preoccupation 458.3
  imagination 515.2
castle-building *adj.*
  preoccupied 458.11
  imaginative 515.14
castle-built 515.12
castle in Spain, castle in the air
  daydream 458.3
  fancy 515.4

castoff *n.*
  refuse 645.4
  derelict 782.2
castoff *adj.*
  abandoned 624.4
  derelict 782.4
castor cloth 219.5
  hat 225.26
Castor and Pollux
  corposant 420.11
  friends 890.5
castor oil oil 356.3
  cathartic 662.9
castor-oil plant 663.6
castrametation
  camp 189.15
  warcraft 722.2
castrate *n.*
  steer 366.12
  male animal 373.6
castrate *v.* 38.7
  (unman 158.7)
casual *n.* 156.1
casual *adj.*
  extrinsic 6.2
  disorderly 59.8
  occasional 134.9
  chance 156.12
  (accidental 621.20)
  uncertain 475.9
  nonobservant 773.5
casually 156.13
  (accidentally 621.22)
casualness 773.1
casualty
  happening 151.1
  fortuity 156.1
  fatality 361.5
  misfortune 735.3
casuist
  reasoner 476.9
  sophist 477.6
  deceiver 548.1
casuistic
  sophistical 477.9
  false 544.7
  ethical 927.12
casuistry
  sophistry 477.1
  falsehood 544.1
  ethics 926.4
casus belli
  ground of quarrel 713.5
  offense 900.5
cat pelt 223.12
  tractor 272.17
  catboat 273.2, 4
  animal 366.3, 4
  eye 441.9
  catalogue 593.3
  tipcat 840.11
  prostitute 962.2
  cat-o'-nine-tails 975.1
  black cat omen 512.2
  warning 668.3
catabasis 36.2
catabiased 217.13, 15
catachresis

figure of speech 521.1
  misinterpretation 523.1
catachrestic
  figurative 521.3
  misinterpreted 523.3
cataclasm 44.2
cataclysm
  debacle 162.3
  outbreak 173.2
  deluge 348.3
cataclysmic
  revolutionary 146.5
  destructive 162.6
catacomb 363.13
catacoustics 402.5
catafalque
  platform 215.21
  burial place 363.13
Catalan 560.4
catalepsy
  swoon 683.5
  hypnosis 994.6
cataleptic 265.7
catalexis 597.6
catalogue, catalog *n.*
  arrangement 60.3
  list 86.1
  record 551.3
  book 593.3
catalogue, catalog *v.*
  classify 60.7
  list 86.3
  record 551.8
catalysis
  decomposition 49.1
  dissolution 659.2
catalytic 49.5
catalyze 49.4
catamaran 273.4
catamenia 299.7
  (regularity 138.6)
catamenial 138.11
catamount, cata-mountain 366.3
cat-and-dog 901.9
cat-and-doggish 348.27
cataplasm 662.14
cataplexy swoon 683.5
  hypnosis 994.6
catapult *n.* 727.9
catapult *v.* 284.13
cataract
  waterfall 348.7
  blindness 442.1
  dim-sightedness 443.2
  ailment 655.8
catarrh
  salivation 299.5
  ailment 655.9
catarrhal pneumonia 655.9
catastrophe end 67.1
  final issue 154.1
  cataclysm 162.3
  disclosure 529.1
  finish 729.1
  misfortune 735.3

catastrophic
  revolutionary 146.5
  destructive 162.6
catawampous, catawampus 217.13, 15
catawamptious 217.13
catbird 366.22
catboat 273.2, 4
catcall *n.*
  noisemaker 404.4
  derision 930.2
catcall *v.* 930.6
catch *n.*
  fastening 45.2
  part music 415.12
  deception 545.3
  fault 651.2
  obstacle 706.2
  capture 789.5
catch *v.* hear 418.11
  discover 481a.3
  ~ unawares 508.5, 6
  understand 518.4
  seize 789.9
  (ensnare 545.9)
catch a crab 267.45
catch a disease 655.21
catch a likeness 554.7
catch at
  snatch at 789.13
  desire 865.11
catch a Tartar 699.7
catch at a straw 858.7
catch at straws
  overestimate 482.3
  be credulous 486.3
  be unskillful 699.7
  be rash 863.5
catch it 972.12
catch on 518.4
catch one's death 360.6
catch on fire 384.17
catch sight of 441.10
catch the eye
  appear 446.2
  meet with attention 457.6
catch up 789.9
catch-as-catch-can 720.7
catch basin 191.11
catch drain 191.11
catching
  transferable 270.11
  contagious 657.5
  taking 789.15
  attractive 845.9
catchpenny
  spurious 545.13
  paltry 643.12
  cheap 815.8
catchpole, catchpoll 745.9
catch question 461.16
catchup, ketchup 393.1
catchweed 253.2
catchword

catechesis — cazique

indication 550.11
locution 564.3
printing 591.2
catechesis 461.9
catechetic 461.24
catechism
  questioning 461.9
  creed 484.3
  (doctrine 983.2)
catechist 461.12
catechistic 461.24
catechize, catechise 461.15
catechumen
  convert 144.5
  novice 541.6
  convert 987.4
  layman 997.2
categorematic 75.6
categorical
  classificational 75.6
  certain 474.8, 15
  proposition 476.17
  demonstrative 478.3
  emphatic 535.6
categorization 60.2
category 75.1
catena fastening 45.4
  series 69.2
  network 219.4
catenarian, catenary 245.2
catenation 69.1
cater v.
  be diagonal 217.7
  victual 298.43
  provision 637.4
cater adv. 217.19
catercorner 217.3, 7, 15, 19
caterer 637.2
  (merchant 797.1)
caterpillar
  larva 129.8
  (worm 366.25)
  tractor 272.17
caterwaul n. 412.1
caterwaul v.
  stridulate 410.5
  mew 412.2
  court 902.7
cat-eyed 441.20
catgut 417.13
cathartic n. 662.9
  (cleanser 652.8)
cathartic adj.
  cleansing 652.15
  laxative 662.25
cathedral n. 1000.1
cathedral adj. 474.13
Catherine wheel 382.9
catheter 260.6
cathode luminescence 420.11
cathode ray 420.3
Catholic n. 984.16
catholic adj.
  universal 78.11
  authoritative 474.13
  unprejudiced 498.12
  orothodox 983a.7

Catholic adj.
  Catholical 984.25
  Christian 987.10
Catholic Church 983a.3
catholicism 78.1
Catholicism 984.6
  (Christianity 983a.2)
catholicity 78.1
Catholicization 144.2
catholicon 662.3
cat house 961.7
catling
  youngling 129.7
  kitten 366.4
cat nap 683.5
cat-o'-nine-tails 975.1
catoptrical 420.24
catoptrics 420.16
catoptromancy 511.3
cat's-eye 847.8
catskin 223.12
cat's paw knot 45.6
  dupe 547.1
  medium 631.2
  (instrument 633.1)
  puppet 711.2
cat's-tail 353.5
catstone stone 342.4
  landmark 550.10
cat-strip 273a.10
catsup See catchup
cattalo mongrel 41.5
  animals 366.13
cattle
  pack animals 271.2
  animal life 366.1, 12
catwalk 273a.12
Caucasian racial 11.8
  (nationality 188.9)
  whiteness 430.3
caucus assembly 72.2
  council 696.2
cauda 235.6
caudal final 67.8
  taillike 235.11
caudate
  pendanted 214.9
  caudal 235.11
caudation 235.6
caudex 215.14
caudiform 235.11
cauldron See caldron
caulicle 215.14
cauliflower 298.30
cauliflower ear 418.5
cauliflower-eared 418.14
caulis 215.14
caulk, caulker See calk etc.
Caurus, Corus 349.2
causable 161.11
causal 153.9
  (creational 161.11)
causality 153.5
causally 153.10
causate 153.6
causation 153.5
  (production 161.1)
causative n. 153.1

causative adj. 153.9
  (productive 161.11)
causativism, causativity 153.5
cause n. origin 153
  (motive 615.1)
  case at law 969.1
cause v. 153.6
  (arise 66.6)
  (produce 161.8)
causeless
  chance 156.12
  purposeless 621.21
causerie 588.2
causeuse 215.22
causeway, causey 627.3
causidical 969.13
caustic n. curve 245.2
  cauterant 384.11
caustic adj.
  acrid 171.10
  violent 173.11
  painful 378.7
  pungent 392.5
  intensely felt 821.5
  penetrating 824.13
  painful 830.15
  gruff 895.7
  malignant 907.6
causticity
  acrimony 171.3
  pungency 392.1
  gruffness 895.2
cauter, cauterant n. 384.11
cauterant adj. 384.22
cauterization 384.3
cauterize 384.18
cautery 384.3
caution n.
  good thing 648.4
  warning 668.1
  proficient 700.1
  security 771.1
  prudence 864
  (care 459.1)
  (forethought 510.2)
caution v. 668.6
cautionary 668.9
caution money 771.1
cautious 864.6
  (careful 459.7)
be cautious 864.3
  (be careful 359.3)
cautiously 864.8
  (carefully 459.9)
cavalcade 69.3
cavalier n. rider 268.8
  knight 875.5
  chivalrous person 894.6
  inamorato 897.6
  (escort 88.4)
cavalier adj.
  arrogant 885.8
  brusque 895.7
cavalier servente
  hanger-on 886.2
  lover 897.6
cavalry horses 271.3
  troops 726.8

cavalry horse
  horse 271.3
  war horse 726.12
cavalryman 726.4
cavatina 415.3
cave n. resort 74.2
  retreat 189.13
  cavern 252.3
  (cellar 191.20)
  (hole 260.1)
  stakes 621.4
  disaster 735.3
cave v.
cave in
  collapse 158.5
  be concave 252.8
  excavate 252.9
  open 260.11
  break down 659.6
  surrender 725.4
caveat warning 668.1
  decree 741.3
cave dweller 893.4
cave-in
  destruction 162.3
  disaster 735.3
cave man
  virile 159a.3
  recluse 893.4
cavendish 392a.1, 7
cave of Adullam
  desertion 624.1
  discontent 832.1
cave of Trophonius 859.1
cavern 252.3
cavernous 252.10
cavesson 752.2
cavetto 847.4
caviar 298.18
cavil n. 477.3, 4
cavil v. quibble 477.8
  demur 485.7
  object 489.4
  find fault 932.7
caviler, caviller
  quibbler 477.6
  faultfinder 936.1
caviling, cavilling
  quibbling 477.11
  critical 932.11
cavity
  compartment 191.2
  depth 208.2
  hollow 252.2
  (cleft 198.2)
  (furrow 259.1)
  (hole 260.1)
  (depression 308.1)
cavort n. 309.2
cavort v. caper 309.5
  frolic 840.21
cavy 366.17
caw
  sound harshly 410.6
  croak 412 2
cayenne 393 1
cayman 366 18
Cayuga 434.5
cayuse 271.3
cazique, cazic See oacique

cease — Ceratosaurus

cease *n.* 142.1
cease *v.* 142.6
  (end 67.5)
  (discontinue 70.3)
  (remain 265.5)
  (abandon 624.3)
  (disuse 678.2)
  (not do 681.2)
  (relax 687.4)
 cease! 142.8
  (forbear! 623.13)
  (enough! 639.9; 869.8)
  (don't! 761.6)
ceaseless
 continuous 69.6
 perpetual 112.4
ceaselessness 69.1
cecity 442.1
cedar tree 367.6
 perfume 400.3
 wood 635.3
cedar chest 191.8
cedarwood 400.3
cede surrender 725.4
 relinquish 782.3
 give 784.11
cedilla 550.8
ceil 224.2
ceiling roof 223.6
 line 224.2
 aeronautics 267a.19
celadon 435.2
celadonite 435.4
Celanese thread 205.2
 cloth 219.5
celebrant 990.8
celebrate
 commemorate 883.3
 (rejoice 838.5)
 (make merry 840.21)
 (do honor to 873.13)
 (laud 931.6)
 glorify 990.10
 observe ceremony 998.14
celebrated 873.16
celebrating *n.* 883.1
celebrating *adj.* 883.5
 (jubilant 838.9)
celebration
 commemoration 883
 (rejoicing 838.1)
 (festivity 840.2)
 (demonstration 882.3)
 (laudation 931.2)
 rite 998.2
 in celebration of 883.6
celebrity 873.1, 9
 (personage 642.5)
celerity 274.1
 (haste 684.1)
celery 298.30
celesta 417.10
celeste 417.12
celestial *n.* 977.1
Celestial *n.* 188.9
celestial *adj.*
 heavenly 318.16

divine 976.13
 angelic 977.4
 heavenly 981.7
Celestial *adj.* 188.11
celestial body 318.3
Celestial City
 utopia 515.6
 Zion 981.1
Celestial Empire 182.3
celestial equator 318.8
celestial hierarchy 977.2
celestial longitude, celestial meridian 318.8
celestial navigation 267a.1
celiac See coeliac
celibacy 904
 (continence 960.1)
 (monasticism 995.2)
celibate *n.* 904.2
 (monk 996.11)
celibate *adj.* 904.5
 (continent 960.2)
cell retreat 189.13
 compartment 191.2
 receptacle 191.6
 protoplasm 357.3
 sanctuary 666.3
 prison 752.1
cella 1000.1
cellar basement 191.20
 (cave 252.3)
 storeroom 636.4
cellaret 191.15
cellarway 260.4
cellist 416.3
cello 417.3
celloist 416.3
Cellophane 425.2
cellular
 vascular 191.23
 concave 252.10
 protoplasmic 357.9
cellule 191.2
cellulous 357.9
cembalo 417.6
cement *n.* glue 45.6
 (adhesive 46.3)
 (semiliquid 352.3)
 plaster 223.19
 hardness 323.3
 pavement 627.4
cement *v.*
 plaster 223.26
 solidify 321.7
cement, cemental *adj.* 323.5
cementation 46.1
cemetery 363.14
 (resting place 265.4)
cenobite 996.11
cenotaph 363.15
cense perfume 400.9
 thurify 998.14
censer, censor
 perfumer 400.5
 thurible 998.8

censer bearer
 perfumer 400.6
 thurifer 996.5
censor critic 480.5
 faultfinder 936.1
censorious 932.11
 (critical 480.13)
 (fastidious 868.4)
censorship 932.2
censurable 932.14
censure *n.* 932.2
 (criticism 480.3)
 (accusation 938.1)
censure *v.* 932.7
 (criticize 480.10)
 (complain 839.10)
 (maledict 908.4)
 (accuse 938.4)
censurer critic 480.5
 malcontent 832.2
 faultfind 936.1
census *n.* roll 86.2
 (statistics 85.3)
 record 551.2
census *v.*
 enumerate 85.7
 poll 86.3
cent trifle 643.3
 money 800.8
cental 98.8
centaur 83.7
Centaur, Centaurus 318.6
centavo 800.8
centenarian 130.1
centenary *n.* 98.8
centenary *adj.* 98.27
centennial *n.*
 hundred 98.8
 anniversary 138.5
centennial *adj.*
 centuple 98.27
 periodic 138.11
center, centre *n.* 222.2
 (middle 68.2)
 (focus 74.1)
 (backbone 235.4)
 (axis 312.5)
 in the center of 222.5
center, centre *v.*
 middle 68.4
 centralize 222.3
 (focus 74.3)
 converge 290.2
centerboard, centreboard 211.1
center of buoyancy 267a.5
center of gravity 222.2
center of pressure center 222.2
 aeronautics 267a.5
centesimal 99.3
centi- 98.27
centigram, centigramme
 hundred 98.8
 weight 319.4
centiliter, centilitre
 hundred 98.8
 measure 466.3
centime 800.8

centimeter, centimetre hundred 98.8
 length 200.6
 measure 466.3
centipede
 hundred 98.8
 insect 368.8
centistere 98.8
cento 597.2
central 222.4
 (middle 68.5)
centralism 222.1
centrality 222
 (convergence 290.1)
centralization
 combination 48.1
 centrality 222.1
centralize
 combine 48.3
 center 222.3
 converge 290.2
centrally 222.5
central point
 focus 74.1
 center 222.2
centre, centreboard
 See center etc.
centrical 222.4
 (convergent 290.3)
centricality 222.1
centrifugal 291.3
centrifugal blower 349.20
centripetal
 central 222.4
 converging 290.3
centroid 222.2
centroidal, centrolineal 222.4
centrosome 357.3
centrosymmetric 222.4
centrum, centry 222.2
centumvir, centumvirate 98.8
centuple *v.* 98.14
centuple *adj.* 98.27
centuplicate *v.* 98.14
centuplicate, centurial *adj.* 98.27
centurion
 hundred 98.8
 officer 745.11
century
 hundred 98.8
 time 108.1
 long time 110.3
ceorl 746.4
cephalalgia 378.1
cephalopodic 368.16
ceramic 557.10
ceramics 384.14
 (vase 191.10)
 (sculpture 557.7)
cerate *n.* wax 356.6
 palm 662.6
cerate *adj.* 355.3
Ceratopsia, Ceratopsidae 124.2
Ceratosaurus
 antiquity 124.2

behemoth 192.8
Cerberus
  monster 83.7
  watchdog 717.6
  god 982.4
cereal *n.* food 298.15
  crop 367.9
  plant 369.8
cereal *adj.* 298.49
cerebellum 450.2
cerebral
  phonetics 402.11
  intellectual 450.8
cerebrate 451.27
cerebration 451.1
cerebrum 450.2
cerecloth
  cover 223.2
  graveclothes 363.8
cerement
  plaster 223.19
  graveclothes 363.8
ceremonial *n.* 998.1
ceremonial *adj.* 998.15
  (ostentatious 882.10)
ceremonialism 998.11
ceremonialist 998.12
ceremonialize 998.14
ceremonious
  respectful 928.8
  ritual 998.15
ceremony 998.1
  (show 882.4)
  without ceremony 881.7
Ceres
  productiveness 168.1
  agriculture 371.3
  goddess 979.2
ceresin 356.6
cerise 434.2
cernuous 214.7
cerograph
  engraving 558.3
  writing 590.3
cerographer 559.6
cerographist 590.11
cerography
  painting 556.2
  engraving 558.1
  writing 590.1
ceromancy 511.3
ceroplastic 557.10
ceroplastics 557.1
certain special 79.7
  some 100.4
  sure 474.8
  (undoubting 484.12)
  (true 494.10)
  (manifest 525.4)
  (affirmative 535.6)
  for certain 474.16
  know for certain
    be certain 474.5
    doubt not 484.9
  make certain 474.6
certainly
  absolutely 31.16
  surely 474.16
  (actually 1.9)
  (truly 494.15)
  (affirmation 535.8)
  yes 488.14
certainty 474
  (actuality 1.2)
  (good chance 156.3)
  (assurance 507.2)
  for a certainty 31.16
certes
  certainly 474.16
  yes 488.14
certificate
  credential 467.4
  record 551.1
  security 771.1
  money 800.6, 7
certification
  assurance 474.2
  ratification 488.4
certify testify 467.8
  make certain 474.6
  ratify 488.10
  vouch 535.4
  promise 768.3
  guarantee 771.6
certiorari 969.6
certitude 474.1
cerulean *n.* 438.2
cerulean, cerulescent *adj.* 438.6
cespitose, caespitose 367.15
cess 812.2
cessation 142
  (end 67.1)
  (discontinuity 70.1)
  (quiescence 265.2, 3)
  (arrival 292.1)
  (abandonment 624.1)
  (disuse 678.1)
cession
  qualification 469.1
  surrender 725.2
  relinquishment 782.1
  concession 784.1
cesspool 653.8
cest 247.2
cestus fastening 45.2
  garment 225.34
  circle 247.2
cete 366.21
Cetus 318.6
Cgm. 319.4
chabouk, chabuk 975.1
chacma 366.16
chacona 415.7
chadar See **chuddar**
chafe rub 331.3
  pain 378.4
  heat 384.16
  irritate 824.5
  be impatient 825.6
  fret 828.10
  annoy 830.5
  be discontented 832.3
  be vexed 900.8
  excite anger 900.10
chafer 386.1
chaff *n.* remains 40.1
  hull 223.14
  lightness 320.2
  trumpery 643.5
  rubbish 645.4
  banter 856.1
  riffraff 876.2
chaff *v.* 856.4
chaffer 794.5
chafing dish 386.1
chagrin 828.4
chain *n.* fastening 45.4
  (shackle 752.2)
  series 69.2
  length 200.6
  range 206.2
  network 219.4
  pothook 386.3
  measure 466.4
  ornament 847.7
chain *v.* tie 43.6
  shackle 751.7
Chained Lady 318.6
chainmaker 690.8
chains 752.2
  in chains 751.11
chain shot 727.14
chain store 799.1
chair *n.* seat 215.22
  instructorship 540.6
  director 694.1
  official seat 747.5
  electrocution 972.4
  electric ~ 975.4
chair *v.*
  transport 270.8
  install 755.4
chair car 272.19
chairmaker 690.8
chairman 694.1
chaise 272.4, 5
chaise longue 215.22
chalcedony
  transparency 425.2
  gem 847.8
chalcograph 558.3
chalcographer 559.6
chalcography 558.1
Chaldean 318.13
chalet 189.3
chalice 191.11
chalk *n.* soil 342.3
  white 430.3
  drawing 556.3, 16
chalk *v.* mark 550.19
  draw 556.17
chalk out 626.9
chalkstone 342.4
chalkworker 690.9
chalky
  pulverulent 330.8, 9
  white 430.8
challenge *n.*
  barking 412.1
  questioning 461.9
  protest 489.2
  defiance 715.1
  accusation 938.1
challenge *v.*
  doubt 485.6
  (disagree 489.4)
  defy 715.2
  claim 924.7
  accuse 938.4
  ~ the jurors 969.10
Cham 560.4
chamber room 191.16
  council 696.1
chamber fellow 890.3
chamberlain 746.1
chambermaid 746.2
chamber music 415.3
Chamber of Deputies 696.6
chameleon
  changeableness 149.2
  reptile 366.18
  variegation 440.2
  waverer 605.3
Chameleon, Chamaeleon 318.6
chamfer *n.* 259.1
chamfer *v.* 259.3
chamfron 717.2
chamisal 367.7
chamois jumper 309.3
  animal 366.10
chamois, chammy
  pelt 223.12
  burnisher 255.3
Chamorro 560.4
champ *n.* bite 298.2
  champion 700.2; 726.1; 731.4
champ *v.* 298.45
  champ the bit
    be impatient 825.6
    be angry 900.7
champac, champak 400.3
champaca oil 400.3
champagne 959.7
champaign 344.1, 2
champain 874.2
champion *n.*
  best 648.4
  proficient 700.2
  upholder 711.4
  (sympathizer 914.2)
  defender 717.5
  combatant 726.1
  victor 731.4
  deputy 759.1
Champion *n.* 318.6
champion *v.* 937.6
champion *adj.* 33.8
championship 707.2
champlevé 847.13
chance *n.*
  quantity 25.2
  great quantity 31.3
  occasion 134.2
  absence of cause 156
  liability 177.1
  distance 196.1
  probability 472.1
  absence of aim 621
  by chance
    fortuitously 156.13

chance — charlatan

chance (*continued*)
(at random 59.12)
(accidentally 621.22)
possibly 470.7
good chance 156.3
(possibility 470.1)
(probability 472.1)
(certainty 474.1)
(assurance 507.2)
have a chance 470.3
have no chance 156.11
(be impossible 471.4)
take one's chance
gamble 621.17
attempt 675.3
chance *v.*
happen 156.7
risk 621.17
chance upon 156.8
chance, chanceful *adj.* 156.12
(accidental 621.20)
chancel 1000.3
chancellor 745.9
chance-medley 156.1
chancery 966.1, 2
chancre 655.16
chancy
chance 156.12
uncertain 475.14
risky 665.7
(hazardous 621.19)
chandelier 423.10
(pendant 214.2)
chandelle *n.* 267a.24
chandelle *v.* 267a.31
Chandi 979.4
chandler 797.1
change *n.*
alteration 140
(modification 15.4)
(novelty 123.1)
(conversion 144.1)
(dislocation 185.1)
(transference 270.1)
(tergiversation 607.1)
money 800.14
change *v.*
alter 140.5, 6
(differentiate 15.6)
(dissimilate 18.3)
(disturb 61.4)
(convert 144.6)
(vacillate 605.4)
(tergiversate 607.7)
interchange 148.3
move 264.6
transfer 270.6
barter 794.4
change color
get excited 824.8
blush 881.4
change hands
interchange 148.3
be transferred 783.4

change one's mind 607.7
change sides 607.7, 8
(abandon 624.3)
changeability 139.1
changeable
irregular 139.2
interchangeable 148.4
variable 149.5, 6
(fickle 608.6)
uncertain 475.16
be changeable 149.4
(be capricious 608.4)
changeableness 149
(transientness 111.1)
(alternation 314.3)
(irresolution 605.1)
(tergiversation 607.1)
(fickleness 608.3)
changeably 149.7
changeful
inconstant 149.6
(tergiversating 607.10)
uncertain 475.16
changefulness 149.1
changeless 141.6
changelessness 141.1
changeling
substitute 147.2
simpleton 501.1
elf child 980.6
change of life 128.3
changer 797.7
channel *n.* bed 211.3
isthmus 203.3
conduit 350.1
(trench 259.2)
(stream 348.1)
path 627.2
channel *v.* 259.3
chant *n.* song 415.10
religious ~ 990.2
chant *v.* 416.20
(glorify 990.10)
chantecler
cock 366.23
male animal 373.6
chanter
singer 416.10
bagpipe 417.4
chanticleer
cock 366.23
male animal 373.6
chantry 1000.1
chaos confusion 59.2
anarchy 738.2
chaotic
confused 59.8
anarchic 738.8
lawless 964.6
chap cleft 198.2
man 373.2
chaparajos 225.28
chaparral 367.7
chaparreras 225.28

chapatty, chupatty 298.12
chapbook 593.1
chapeau 225.26
chapel, chapellany 1000.1
chaperon *n.*
escort 88.4
guardian 664.3
chaperon *v.*
escort 88.7
(protect 664.6)
care for 459.6
chapfallen
dejected 837.9
humbled 879.5
chaplain 996.2, 5
chaplaincy 995.3
chaplet circle 247.2
flowers 400.4
trophy 733.1
ornament 847.5
chapman 797.1, 3
chaps 225.28
chapter *n.* section 51.2
subject 454.1
~ in a book 593.7
council 696.3
chapter *v.* 44.10
chapter and verse 494.16
chapter of accidents
circumstances 151.2
luck 156.1
chaqueta 225.16
char burn 384.18
do chars 746.8
charabanc 272.4
character *n.*
nature 5.3
(kind 75.2)
(particularity 79.2)
(tendency 176.1)
state 7.1
constitution 54.1
oddity 83.4
number 84.1
notation 415.23
eccentric 504.3
earmark 550.6
letter 561.1
(writing 590.9)
role 599.7
disposition 820.1
character *v.*
engrave 558.5
letter 561.6
characteristic *n.*
particularity 79.2
(nature 5.3)
earmark 550.6
trait 820.1
characteristic *adj.*
differentiative 15.8
peculiar 79.8
(intrinsic 5.7)
(characterized 820.3)
typical 550.21
characterization 599.7
characterize
personate 554.8

name 564.6
describe 594.5
charade riddle 533.2
drama 599.3
game 840.11
charbon 655.18
charcoal residue 40.2
carbon 384.15
fuel 388.2
black 431.3
drawing 556.3, 9, 16
charge *n.* task 625.2
custody 664.2
supervision 693.2
precept 697.1
attack 716.1
(encounter 276.2)
command 741.1
care 751.4
commission 755.1
price 812.1
accusation 938.1
curacy 995.3
in ~ in control 693.7
in custody 751.12
without charge 815.10
charge *v.* fill 52.7
enjoin 695.5
attack 716.5
command 741.4
commission 755.4
bargain 794.5
receive credit 805.5
assess 812.5
accuse 938.4
chargeability 947.1
chargeable
liable 806.8
assessable 812.8
blameworthy 932.14
(guilty 947.4)
charge account 811.1
chargé d'affaires 759.2
charged up 959.21
charger horse 271.3
war horse 726.12
chariot 272.1, 4
chariotee 272.4
charioteer 268.9
Charioteer 318.6
charitable
almsgiving 784.15
philanthropic 906.7
(liberal 816.4)
(merciful 914.6)
charitableness 906.2
(liberality 816.1)
charitably 906.9
charity
almsgiving 784.15
benevolence 906.1, 2
(aid 707.1)
(mercy 914.1)
charivari noise 404.2
discord 414.2
charlatan *n.*
impostor 548.3
(sciolist 493.2)
(affector 853.4)
(boaster 884.3)

charlatan — cheer

medicaster 662.19
**charlatan, charlatan-
 ish** *adj.* 491.13
charlatanism 853.1
charlatanry 544.2
 (pedantry 491.4)
Charles's Wain 318.6
Charley, Charlie
 beard 256.5
 night watchman
  717.6
Charley horse
 cramp 315.7; 378.1
 ailment 655.3
charlock 352.3
charlotte russe 298.12
charm *n.*
 allurement 617.1, 2
 beauty 845.1
 spell 993.1, 2
charm *v.* lure 617.4
 (attract 288.3)
 delight 829.5
 enamor 897.13
 conjure 992.4
charm-bound 992.7
charmed
 pleased 827.8
 enamored 897.14
 bewitched 992.7
charmer
 a beauty 845.3
 sorcerer 992.2
charming
 alluring 617.5
 (likable 897.17)
 delightful 829.8
 attractive 845.9
 (tasteful 850.5)
 bewitching 992.6
charm-struck 992.7
charnel house 363.13
Charon 982.4
chart *n.* 626.2
 (guidebook 694.7)
chart *v.*
 ~ a course 267.11
 map 626.9
charter *n.*
 commission 755.2
 grant 760.2
 compact 769.2
 law 963.2
charter *v.* grant 760.4
 legalize 963.4
chartered 924.10
chartreuse 959.6
chartulary list 86.1
 record 551.1
charwoman 746.2
chary
 economical 817.4
 parsimonious 819.4
 wary 864.6
Charybdis 346.8
chase *n.* grove 367.7
 printing ~ 591.5
 pursuit 622.7
 (search 461.2)
 steeplechase 720.5
chase *v.* escort 88.7
 boss 250.8

speed 274.9
repulse 289.2
~ out 297.8
engrave 558.5
pursue 622.7
 (follow 281.3)
chaser
 perforator 262
 music 415.3
 engraver 559.6
 act 599.5
 alcoholic drink
  959.10
chasing 558.1
chasm cleft 198.2, 3
 depth 208.2
 (cavity 252.2)
 (opening 260.1)
 water gap 350.1
chassé 840.8
chassepot 727.10
chasseur 726.4
chassis 272.16
chaste
 language 576.3
 elegant 578.4
 (tasteful 850.5)
 inornate 849.4
 pure 960.2
 (innocent 946.5)
chasten
 moderate 174.5
 simplify 849.2
 punish 972.5
chastened 826.10
chastise
 upbraid 932.8
 punish 972.5
chastisement
 reproof 932.3
 punishment 972.1
chastity
 unornamentation
  849.1
 purity 960.1
chasuble 999.1
chat *n.* gossip 532.3
 small talk 588.2
 (visit 892.3)
chat *v.* gossip 532.7
 converse 588.7
château 189.3
chatelaine 847.7
chatoyant 440.6
chatta 223.4
chattels 780.1, 4, 5
chatter *n.* clatter 407.5
 prattle 584.2
 (speech 582.1)
chatter *v.*
 clatter 407.10
 chirp 412.2
 gossip 532.7
 jabber 584.4
 (speak 582.6)
**chatterbag, chatter-
 basket, chatterbox**
 584.3
chatterer
 newsmonger 532.5
 chatterbox 584.3
 (speaker 582.5)

chattermag 584.3
chatty *n.* 191.11
chatty *adj.*
 loquacious 584.5
 conversational
  588.10
 sociable 892.12
chauffeur, chauffeuse
 268.10
 (carrier 271.1)
 (worker 690.10)
chaunt See **chant**
chaussure 225.27
chautauqua 537.8
chauvin *n.* 884.4
chauvin *adj.* 884.8
chauvinism
 overpatriotism
  549.1
 jingoism 884.2
 (militarism 722.6)
 (patriotism 906.4)
chauvinist 884.4
 (militarist 726.3)
chauvinistic
 overpatriotic 549.3
 jingoistic 884.8
 (patriotic 906.8)
 (militaristic 722.13)
chaw *n.* chew 298.2
 tobacco quid 392a.7
chaw *v.* chew 298.45
 ~ tobacco 392a.14
chawbacon 876.5
chay 272.5
cheap *n.* 799.1
cheap *adj.*
 paltry 643.12
 inexpensive 815.8
 be cheap 815.6
cheapen haggle 794.5
 reduce price 815.7
cheapening 815.3
cheap-Jack 797.3
cheaply 815.11
cheapness 815
cheat *n.* fraud 545.3
 (swindle 791.5)
 cheater 548.2
 swindler 792.8
cheat *v.* deceive 545.7
 swindle 791.12
cheater
 deceiver 548.2
 swindler 792.8
check *n.*
 cessation 142.1
 sound 402.2
 plaid 440.3
 examination 461.2
 experiment 463.5
 measure 466.2
 frustration 509.1
 identification 550.11
 counter 621.13
 hindrance 706.1, 2
 (anchor 666.2)
 misfortune 735.3
 restraint 751.1
 fetter 752.2
 cheque 800.7
hold in check

hinder 706.4
restrain 751.6
check *v.*
 ~ with 27.6
 ~ a calculation 85.8
 stop 142.7
 retard 275.7
 variegate 440.4
 examine 461.17
 counterevidence
  468.2
 hinder 706.4
 defeat 731.10; 732.3
 restrain 751.6
 (moderate 174.5)
check out 293.4
checked 81.3
checker, chequer
 440.4
**checkerboard,
 chequerboard** 440.3
checkered, chequered
 changeable 149.5
 mottled 440.8
**checkering, chequer-
 ing** 847.3
checkers, chequers
 checkerwork 440.3
 game 840.11
**checkerwork,
 chequerwork** 440.3
checkmate *n.*
 impediment 706.1
 (stoppage 142.1)
 utter defeat 732.3
 (hindrance 706.1)
checkmate *v.*
 thwart 706.7
 (stop 142.7)
 defeat 731.10
 (disable 158.6)
checkmated 732.12
checkrein
 hindrance 706.2
 restraint 752.2
checkstone 342.4
Chedreux 256.4
chee-chee 563.5
cheek support 215.11
 side 236.1
 screen 424.3
 impudence 885.2
 have the cheek 885.7
cheek See **chick**
cheek by cheek 236.9
cheek by jowl 88.9
cheeker 885.3
cheeky 885.9
cheep 412.2
cheer *n.* food 298.5
 happiness 827.2
 cheerfulness 836.1
 huzza 838.4
 (cry 411.1)
 (applause 931.4)
 hope 858.1
cheer *v.* refresh 689.2
 humor 707.11
 gladden 836.6
 (delight 829.5)
 (solace 834.5)
 (rejoice 838.5)

cheerer — chimes

cheer (continued)
  (amuse 840.20)
  huzza 838.8
  (cry 411.5)
  (exult 884.6)
  (applaud 931.6)
  encourage 858.8
  (embolden 861.7)
  bid godspeed 894.10
  applaud 931.6
cheer ship 267.41
cheer up 836.4, 14
cheerer 959.10
cheerful
  well-disposed 602.8
  gay 836.7
  (happy 827.9)
  (content 831.6)
  (optimistic 858.9)
be cheerful 836.4
make cheerful 836.6
cheerfully 836.13
cheerfulness 836
  (happiness 827.2)
  (content 831.1)
  (optimism 858.2)
cheering
  inspiriting 836.12
  (pleasing 829.7)
  encouraging 858.11
cheerless
  depressing 830.11
  sad 837.9
cheese food 298.29
  truth 494.4
  excellent thing 648.4
cheesecake 298.29
cheesecloth 219.5
cheeseparing n.
  remains 40.1
  parsimony 819.1
cheeseparing adj. 819.4
cheese it cease 142.8
  begone 297.23
  silence 403.9
  warning 668.11
cheesy 649.8
cheetah
  Felidae 366.3
  variegation 440.2
chef 746.1
chef de cuisine
  expert 700.1
  cook 746.1
chef d'œuvre 698.5
cheiromancy 511.3
chela disciple 541.2, 6
  pincers 781.3
chemical 316.2
chemical warfare 722.1
chemise 225.25
chemisette 225.33
chemist
  experimenter 463.6
  pharmacist 662.21
  (merchant 797.11)
chemistry 144.1
chemist's shop

pharmacy 662.18
  mart 799.4
chenille 219.5
cheque 800.7
chequer, chequer-
  board etc. See
  checker etc.
Cheremiss 560.4
cherish
  ~ an idea 451.31
  ~ a belief 484.8
  nourish 707.9
  foster feelings 824.2
  love 897.11
  caress 902.8
cheroot 392a.3
cherry n. fruit 298.31
  red 434.2, 5
cherry adj. 434.9
chersonese 250.5
cherub child 129.3
  endearment 902.4
  angel 977.1
cherubic 977.4
cherubim 977.1, 2
Cheshire cat 366.4
chess 840.11
chessboard 440.3
chest
  receptacle 191.8, 15
  breast 250.3
  money box 802.1
chest voice 408.6
chestnut horse 271.5
  nut 298.33
  color 433.5; 434.12
  trite saying 496.3
  stale news 532.1
  old joke 842.6
cheval-de-frise 253.2
chevalier 875.5
chevalier sans peur et
  sans reproche
  brave person 861.3
  good person 948.1
chevaux-de-frise 717.3
chevron zigzag 217.4
  insignia 747.4
chevronwise, chev-
  rony 217.16
chevrotain 366.11
chevy, chivy 622.2
chew n. chaw 298.2
  ~ of tobacco 392a.7, 10
chew v.
  masticate 298.45
  ~ tobacco 392a.14
chew the cud
  chew 298.45
  ponder 451.27
chew the rag
  argue 476.11
  converse 588.7
chewer 392a.11
chewing 298.1
chewink 366.22
Chianti 959.7
chiaroscuro 556.3
chiasma joint 43.3

crossing 219.1
chiasmal, chiasmic 219.9
chiasmus 218.2
chiaus 534.1
Chibcha 560.4
chic 847.14
  (fashionable 852.7)
chicane, chicanery
  sophistry 477.1
  deception 545.1, 3
  cunning 702.1
  sharp practice 940.5
chick
  youngling 129.3, 7
  chicken 366.23
  endearment 902.4
chick, cheek 424.3
chickabiddy
  child 129.3
  chicken 366.23
  endearment 902.4
chickadee 366.22
chickaree
  speeder 274.6
  animal 366.17
chicken
  youngling 129.1
  girl 129.5
  weakling 160.4, 5
  mollycoddle 160a.3
  food 298.25
  fowl 366.23
  coward 862.2
no chicken
  aged 128.8
  old woman 130.3
  adult 131.3
chicken coop
  enclosure 232.1
  animals 370.3
chickenhearted 862.4
chicken pox 655.6
chicken yard 232.1
chickling 129.7
chicky
  youngling 129.7
  chicken 366.23
chide 932.8
chider 936.2
chiding 932.3
chief n.
  Indian ~ 434.5
  principal 642.6
  ruler 745.1, 2
chief adj.
  supreme 33.8
  (paramount 642.14)
  first 66.8
  head 210.6
  foremost 234.8
  ruling 737.15
chiefdom 182.1
chiefery 737.3
chieftain 745.2
chieftaincy, chieftain-
  ry, chieftainship
  country 182.1
  authority 737.3
chiffon cloth 219.5
  transparency 425.2

chiffonier, chiffon-
  nier, chifforobe 191.15
chigetai, dzeggetai 271.10
chigger 366.24
chignon
  headdress 225.26
  hair 256.3
chigoe 366.24
chilblains 383.2
child urchin 129.3
  descendant 167.4
  childish person 501.4
  unsophisticate 703.2
  innocent 946.2
childbed, childbirth 161.3
childish puerile 127.5
  credulous 486.5
  senile 499.16
  ~ language 575.2
childishness
  childhood 127.1
  senility 499.5
childkind 129.2
childless 169.4
childlike puerile 127.5
  senile 499.16
  artless 703.4
  innocent 946.5
children
  childkind 129.2
  posterity 167.1
child's play
  trifle 643.3
  easy task 705.2
chili 393.1
chiliad
  thousand 98.10
  millennium 121.2
chiliadal 121.8
chiliagon, chilia-
  hedron, chiliaë-
  hedron, chiliarch 98.10
chill n. 383.2
chill v. cool 385.4, 7
  discourage 616.3
chill adj. 383.10
chilled 385.7
chilling 385.6
chilly 383.10
chime n. 413.1
chime v. agree 23.7
  ring 408.8
  harmonize 413.24
chime in with
  agree 23.7
  conform 82.4
  concur 488.7
  be concordant 714.2
chimer, chimere 999.1
chimera, chimaera
  monster 83.7
  imagining 515.4
chimerical 515.12
  (unreal 2.8)
  (imaginary 515.12)
  (spectral 980a.4)
chimes repetend 104.2

chimney — chorea

tintinnabula 417.10
 (bell 408.5)
chimney chasm 198.3
 tube 260.6
 smokeshaft 351.1
chimney corner
 home 189.2
 fireside 386.2
 (nook 191.3)
chimney sweep 652.6
chimpanzee 366.16
chin n. 234.5
Chin n. 560.4
chin v. 588.7
china 384.14
 (merchandise 798.3)
China 182.3
Chinaman 188.9
Chinaman's chance 156.4
China stone, china-ware 384.14
 (tableware 191.13)
chinch, chinche 366.24
chinchilla 223.12
chin-chin 588.7
chine ridge 206.2
 backbone 235.4
Chinese n.
 Chinaman 188.9
 yellowness 436.4
 language 560.4
Chinese adj. 188.11
chink n. cleft 198.2
 furrow 259.1
 money 800.1
Chink n. alien 57.3
 Chinaman 188.9
Chink adj. 188.11
chink v. 408.8
chinker 800.4
chinking 223.19
chinky 198.5
chin music 582.1
chinook 349.9
Chinook 560.5
chintz 219.5
chip n. modicum 32.2
 piece 51.3
 counter 621.13
 coin 800.1, 4, **7**
chip v. 44.8
 chip in
 contribute 707.6
 participate 709.6
 contribute 784.8
 pay one's share 807.6
chipmunk
 speeder 274.6
 animal 366.17
chipper
 healthy 654.4
 lively 682.16
 cheerful 836.7
chipping 32.2
chippy 962.2
chips
 ship's carpenter 269.3

carpenter 599.17; 690.5
chirk v.
 stridulate 410.5
 croak 412.2
chirk adj. 682.16
chirograph 590.3
chirographer 590.11
chirography 590.11
chiromancy 511.3
 (interpretation 522.5)
 (symbology 550.17)
chironomy 550.3
chiroplasty 662.16
chiropodist 662.19
chiropody 662.16
chiropractic 662.16, 19
chiropractor 662.19
chiropraxis 662.16
chirp, chirrup
 animal sounds 412.2
 sing 416.20
 rejoice 838.5
chirurgeon 662.19
chirurgery 662.16
chirurgical 662.25
chisel n.
 perforator 262
 sculptor's ~ 557.8
chisel v. produce 161.8
 form 240.6
 furrow 259.3
 sculpture 557.9
 engrave 558.5
 chisel in 228.10
chiseler, chiseller
 intruder 228.4
 sculptor 559
chiseling, chiselling 558.1
chit child 129.3
 dwarf 193.5
 epistle 592.2
chitchat gossip 532.3
 small talk 588.2
chitchatty 588.10
chiton 368.6
chitter 412.2
chitter-chatter 584.2
chitterlings 221.4
chitty 592.2
chivalrous
 military 722.13
 heroic 861.8
 courteous 894.12
 benevolent 906.6
 magnanimous 942.6
chivalry
 knightly skill 722.2
 tenure 777.1
 courage 861.1
 courtesy 894.1
 benevolence 906.1
 magnanimity 942.2
chivarros 225.28
chivvy, chivvy See chevy
chlamys 225.15
chloral 376.2
chloride of lime 652.8
chlorine gas 334.2

deodorant 399.2
decolorant 429.3
green 435.6
poison 663.5
chlorochrous 435.6
chloroform n. 376.2
 (palliative 662.6)
chloroform v. 376.4
chlorosis 655.11
chlorotic 655.24
chock, chock-full, choke-full 52.11
chocolate n.
 drink 298.4
 candy 396.2
chocolate adj. 433.4
Choctaw
 Indian 434.5
 unintelligibility 519.2
 jargon 563.4
choice n.
 selection 609
 (discretion 465.1)
 (decision 480.1)
 best 648.4
 at choice
 at will 600.5
 optionally 609.17
 by choice 609.18
 (voluntarily 600.5)
 have no choice
 be necessary 601.10
 have no alternative 609a.2
 take one's choice 609.7
 without choice
 necessarily 601.15
 choiceless 609a.3
 (neutral 628.3)
choice adj. 648.9
choiceful 609.15
choiceless 609a.3
 (necessary 601.11)
 (irresolute 605.5)
choicelessness 609a
 (necessity 601.1)
 (irresolution 605.1)
choicy
 choiceful 609.15
 finical 868.4
choir, quire
 chorus 416.12
 church section 1000.3
choirboy singer 416.10
 church singer 996.5
choir invisible 977.1
choirister See chorister
choirman 416.10
choirmaster 416.13
choke n.
 neckpiece 225.33
 automobile 272.16
choke v. close 261.2
 strangle 361.11
 extinguish 385.5
 overfill 641.4
 obstruct 706.4

choke off
 render mute 581.5
 hinder 706.4
chokeberry, choke-cherry 397.2
chokedamp 334.2
 (poison 663.5)
choke-full See chock-full
choker
 choking coil 157a.6
 neckpiece 225.33
chokidar 717.6
choking coil 158a.6
chokra 746.1
choky, chokey 752.1
choler anger 900.1
 irascibility 901.1
cholera 655.6, 18
choleric 901.7
chondric 323.5
chondrification 323.2
choose n. 609.1
choose v. 609.7
 (will 600.2)
 (decide 604.6)
choosing n. 609.1
choosing adj. 609.15
choosy, choosey
 choiceful 609.15
 finical 868.4
chop n. blow 276.3
 meat 298.27
 waves 348.10
 counter 550.11
chop v. cut 44.8
 change 140.5
chop and change 140.5
chopfallen 837.9
chophouse 298.42
choppiness 348.10
chopping 192.12
choppy rough 256.12
 flowing 348.26
chop suey, chop sooy 298.17
chor 792.1
choragic, choragus 694.1
choral, chorale n.
 music 415.10–12
 hymn 990.2
choral v. 416.20
choral adj.
 musical 415.28
 musicianly 416.24
choralcelo 417.5
choralist 416.10
choral service 415.17
choral symphony 416.12
 (musical performance 415.17)
chord n. 413.9
chord v.
 harmonize 413.24
 play chords 416.18
chore n. 625.2
chore v. 746.8
chorea
 twitching 315.6

chorine — chute

chorea (*continued*)
nervous disorder 655.14
chorine, chorist 416.10
chorister
musician 416.10, **13**
church ~ 996.5
chorographer 466.9
chorographic 466.11
chorography
topography 184.8
measurement 466.8
chorometry 466.8
chorus *n.*
repetend 104.2
outcry 411.2
song 415.12, 15
choir 416.12
unanimity 488.3
poetical ~ 597.7
in chorus
harmonious 413.26
unanimously 488.17
chorus *v.* 416.20
chorus girl
singer 416.10
actress 599.19
chose in possession 777.1
chosen 609.16
choucroute 397.2
chouse *n.* 545.3, 6, **7**
chouse *v.* 791.12
chow food 298.5
dog 366.6
chowchow *n.*
mixture 41.4
confusion 59.2
dog 366.6
chowder 298.16
chow mein 298.17
chrestomathy 72.7
chrism *n.* 998.4
chrism *v.* 998.14
chrismal, chrismale
cover 223.2
chrism cloth 998.4
chrismation, chrismatory, chrisom 998.4
chrisomloosing 998.5
Christ 976.5
christcross
cross 219.6
alphabet 561.2
christcross-row 561.2
christen name 564.6
baptize 998.14
Christendom
Church 983a.3
Christians 987.5
churchdom 995.1
christening
naming 564.1
baptism 998.5
Christian *n.*
good person 948.1
believer 987.4
(true believer 983a.4)
Christian *adj.*

orthodox 983a.7
religious 987.10
Christianity
religion 983a.2
Christendom 995.1
Christian Science
healing art 662.16
religion 984.9
Christian Scientist 984.14
Christmas *n.*
anniversary 138.7
holyday 998.13
Christmas *v.*
pass time 106.3
vacation 687.5
Christmastide 998.13
chroma 428.2
chromatic
tonal 413.28
colorific 428.12
chromatics 428.7
chromatin 357.3
chromatism 428.2
chromatogenous 428.12
chromatograph 428.8
chromatometer 428.8
(meter 466.4)
chromatophorous 428.12
chromatrope
chromoscope 428.8
optics 445.1
chrome *n.* 436.1, 4
chrome *v.* 436.5
chrome brick 384.14
chrome green 435.2, 4
chrome lemon 436.1
chrome orange 439.1
chrome yellow 436.1
chromic oxide 435.4
chromite 635.6
chromium green 435.2, 4
chromogen 428.3
chromolithograph 558.3
chromolithographer 559.6
chromolithography 558.1
chromometer, chromoscope 428.8
chromosome 357.3
chromosphere 318.4
chromotype 591.6
chromotypography 591.1
chromotypy, chromoxylography 591.1
chronic durable 110.9
continuing 143.4
chronicle *n.*
chronology 114.5
record 551.1
(writing 590.3)
(book 593.1)
narrative 594.2
chronicle *v.*
chronologize 114.8

record 551.8
chronicler
chronographer 114.7
annalist 553.2
chronogram 114.5
chronogrammatic 114.9
chronograph 114.6
chronographer
chronologist 114.7
recorder 553.2
(narrator 594.4)
chronographic 114.9
chronographical 594.7
chronography
chronometry 114.1
historiography 594.3
chronological 114.9
chronologist 114.7
chrono'ogize 114.8
chronology 114.1, 5
chronometer 114.6
chronometrical 114.9
chronometry 114
chronopher, chronoscope 114.6
chronoscopic 114.9
chronoscopy 114.1
chrysalis 129.8
chrysolite
transparency 425.2
green 435.3
gem 847.8
chrysolite green 435.2
chrysology 800.16
chrysoprase
green 435.3
gem 847.8
chrysoprase green 435.2
chthonian *n.*
diabolist 978.5
demonolater 991.5
chthonian *adj.*
hellish 982.5
demonolatrous 991.7
chubby 201.6
(stout 192.12)
(rotund 249.6)
chuck *n.* throw 284.3
ejection 297.1
dismissal 297.4
food 298.5, 20
chuck *v.*
eliminate 42.4
throw 284.12
eat 298.44
cluck 412.2
~ under the chin 902.8
chuck *adj.* 52.11
chuck-a-luck, chuck and toss 621.7
(game 840.11)
chucker thrower 284.7
ejector 297.6
chuck farthing 621.7
chuck-full See **chock-full**

chuckhole 252.2
chuckie 342.4
chuckle *n.* 838.3
chuckle *v.* **cluck** 412.2
laugh 838.7
exult 884.6
chucklehead
stupidity 499.2
dolt 501.1
bungler 701
chuckleheaded 499.12
chuck wagon 429.42
chuddar, chudder, chuddah 225.15
chuff 876.5
chum *n.* 890.3
chum *v.* 88.6
chummery 189.3
chummy
friendly 888.4
sociable 892.12
chump 501.1
(dupe 547.1)
chumpish 499.12
chumpy 201.6
chunk *n.* piece 51.3
lump 192.5
throw 284.3
chunk *v.* 284.12
chunky 201.6
chupatty See **chapatty**
chuprassy 534.1
church
denomination 542.4; 984.3
congregation 696.3
sect 712.1
Christendom 995.1
temple 1000.1
(assembly hall 189.10)
church 983a.3
church book 998.9
churchcraft 995.1
churchdom 995
churchly
ecclesiastical 995.9
churchlike 1000.6
churchman
clergyman 996.2
layman 997.2
believer 987.4
churchwarden 996.5
churchyard 363.14
churl serf 746.4
miser 819.2
peasant 876.5
churlish rustic 183.3
niggardly 819.4
uncouth 851.7
uncivil 895.7
irascible 901.7
churlishness 901.1
churn agitate 315.8
emulsify 352.6
chut 403.9
chute
parachute 273a.7; 666.1; 671.3
rapid 348.6
conduit 350.1
stampede 860.1

chuter, chutist 269a.2
chutney 393.1
Chuvash 560.4
chyle 333.2
chylification 333.1
chylifactive 333.7
chylify 335.5
cibarious 298.49
ciborium 998.8
cicada, cicala 366.24
cicatrice 659.4
cicatrix 551.5
cicatrization 660.5
cicatrize 660.16
 (close 261.2)
Cicero 582.5
cicerone 694.6
Ciceronian
 speech 578.4
 oratorical 582.12
cider 298.4
ci-devant 116.4
cigar 392a.3
cigarette, cigaret 392a.4
cigar store
 tobacconist 392a.12
 mart 799.4
cilia 256.3, 6
ciliate 256.13
ciliolum
 filament 205.1
 hair 256.3
cinch n. fastening 45.2
 saddle 215.23
 certainty 474.1
 dupe 547.1
 easy task 705.2
cinch v. tie 43.6
 ~ a saddle 370.7
 make certain 474.6
cinct 229.4
cincture n.
 circumscription 229.1
 zone 230.2
 enclosure 232.1
 circle 247.2
 ecclesiastical ~ 999.1
cincture v. 227.3
cinctured 227.4
cinders residue 40.2
 slag 384.15
 (coal 388.2)
Cinderella 746.2
cinema 599.9, 10
cinematograph, kinematograph
 camera 445.5
 magic lantern 445.6
 cinema 599.10
cinematographer 559.7
cinematography 556.4
cinemelodrama 599.9
cinerary 363.25
cineration 384.3
cinereal, cinerous 432.4
 (whitish 430.9)
cingle, cingulum 230.2

cinnabar 434.6
cinnamon n.
 condiment 393.1
 perfume 400.3
 brown 433.1
cinnamon adj. 433.4
cinque five 98.1
 throw of dice 621.9
cinquecento 554.9
cinquefoil 847.4
cipher n. nullity 4.2
 number 84.1
 zero 87a.1
 (nothing 2.2)
 cryptograph 528.5
 sign 550.2, 11
 letter 561.5
 cryptography 590.8
 nonentity 643.6
cipher v. compute 37.5
 calculate 85.7
 write ciphers 561.7
circa 32.17
Circe
 temptress 617.3
 sorceress 992.3
Circean, Circaean 992.5
Circinus 318.6
circle n. region 181.1
 ~ of houses 189.20
 round 247.2
 (zone 230.2)
 (turn 311.2)
 (circuit 629.1)
 measure 466.3
 clique 712.2
 social circle 892.7
 (society 712.4)
circle v.
 surround 227.3
 (curve 245.3)
 (round 247.7)
 circuit 311.3
 rotate 312.7
circlet circle 247.2
 chandelier 423.10
circuit n. round 138.4
 electricity 158a.4
 area 181.1
 beat 181.4
 zone 230.2
 journey 266.8, 9
 circuitous course 629
 (obliquity 217.1)
 (circle 247.2)
 (convolution 248.1)
 (deviation 279.3)
 (circuity 311.1)
 (turn 311.2)
circuit v. 311.3
 (circle 247.7)
circuit breaker 158a.6
circuit court 966.1
circuiteer 311.3
circuition 311.1
circuitman 158a.10
circuitous 311.6
 (oblique 217.9)
 (crooked 217.13)
 (convoluted 248.4)

 (deviative 279.8)
 (circumlocutory 573.9)
circuitously 311.7
 (deviatively 279.9)
circuity 311
 (convolution 248.1)
 (rotation 312.1)
circular n.
 handbill 531.4
 brochure 593.1
circular adj.
 round 247.8
 (curved 245.4)
 (rotund 249.6)
 encyclic 531.11
circularity 247
 (curvature 245.1)
 (rotundity 249.1)
circularize
 publicize 531.8
 correspond 592.6
circular letter 592.2
circular measure 466.3
circular note 805.2
circulate
 circuit 311.3
 rotate 312.7
 publish 531.7, 9
 ~ money 800.19, 20
circulating medium 800.1
circulation
 circuity 311.1
 rotation 312.1
 publication 531.1
 ~ of money 809.1
 in circulation 532.8
 (published 531.10)
circumambages 573.3
circumambient
 circumjacent 227.4
 circumscribed 229.4
 circuitous 311.6
circumambulate
 go round 227.3
 walk 266.16
 circuit 311.3
 (go round about 629.2)
circumambulation
 circumjacence 227.1
 circuity 311.1
 circuit 629.1
circumambulatory 311.6
circumanal, circumaxillary 227.4
circumbendibus 629.1
circumbuccal, circumbulbar, circumcallosal 227.4
circumcinct
 circumjacent 227.4
 circumscribed 229.4
circumcincture 227.1
circumcision 44.2
circumcorneal 227.4
circumduction
 circumjacence 227.1

obliteration 552.1
circumesophagal 227.4
circumference n.
 outline 230.1
 measure 466.3
circumference v. 227.3
circumferential
 circumjacent 227.4
 outlinear 230.4
circumflect v. 227.3
circumflect adj.
 circumjacent 227.4
 circuitous 311.6
circumfluence
 circumjacence 227.1
 circuity 311.1
circumfluent
 circumjacent 227.4
 circuitous 311.6
circumflex n. 550.8
circumflex v.
 go round 227.3
 circuit 311.3
circumflex adj.
 circumjacent 227.4
 circuitous 311.6
circumflexion 311.1
circumfluous 311.6
circumforaneous
 wandering 266.24
 circuitous 311.6
circumfuse 73.3
circumfusion
 dispersion 73.1
 rotation 312.1
circumgenital, circumintestinal 227.4
circumjacence 227
 (exteriority 220.1)
circumjacencies 227.2
circumjacent 227.4
circumlocute 573.5
circumlocution 573.3
 (quibble 477.3)
 (redundance 641.1)
circumlocutory 573.9
 (circuitous 311.6)
 (redundant 641.5)
circummigrate 311.3
circummigration 311.1
circumnavigable 311.6
circumnavigate
 navigate 267.10
 circuit 311.3
circumnavigation
 navigation 267.1
 circuity 311.1
circumnavigatory 311.6
circumnuclear 227.4
circumnutation 314.1
circumocular, circumorbital, circumpallial 227.4
circumpose 227.3
circumposition 227.1
circumrenal 227.4
circumrotatory 312.8
circumrotate 312.7

circumrotation — claptrap

circumrotation 312.1
circumscribe
  enclose 229.2
  (surround 227.3)
  (outline 230.3)
  restrict 761.2
circumscribed
  limited 32.7
  bound 229.4
  (outlined 230.4)
  (definite 233.3)
circumscript 229.4
circumscription
  surrounding 227.1
  enclosure 229
circumspect
  attentive 457.9
  prudent 498.11
  cautious 864.6
circumspection
  close attention 457.2
  caution 864.1
  (care 459.1)
circumstance
  phase 8
  condition 469.2
circumstances
  particulars 79.3
  affairs 151.2
  surroundings 227.2
  conditions 770.1
  assets 780.7
circumstantial
  conditional 8.5
  (extrinsic 6.2)
  (provisional 637.7)
  detailed 79.7
  evidential 467.11
circumstantial evidence
  evidence 467.1
  probability 472.1
circumstantiality
  meticulousness 457.3
  fastidiousness 868.1
circumstantiate
  confirm 467.9
  demonstrate 478.2
circumtonsillar, circumumbilical 227.4
circumvallation
  circumscription 229.1
  enclosure 232.1
  fortification 717.3
circumvascular 227.4
circumvent
  surround 227.3
  circuit 311.3
  deceive 545.8
  (be cunning 702.5)
  elude 623.8
  (defeat 731.9)
  thwart 706.7
circumvention
  circuity 311.1
  deception 545.1
  artifice 702.3
circumvolant 311.6
circumvolute 312.7

circumvolution
  convolution 248.1
  rotation 312.1
circumvolutory 312.8
circumvolve 312.7
circus circle 189.20
  show 599.8
  theater 599.10
  arena 728.1
cirrate 256.13
cirro-cumulus 353.5
cirrose
  filamentary 205.7
  hairy 256.13
  cloudy 353.11
cirro-stratus 353.5
cirrous hairy 256.13
  cloudy 353.11
cirrus filament 205.1
  coil 248.2
  cloud 353.5
cirsophthalmia 443.1
Cistercian 996.11
cistern 343a.1
cit 188.2
citadel 717.4
citation
  authority 467.4
  trophy 733.1
  warrant 741.3
  summons 969.2
cite exemplify 82.6
  adduce 467.10
  summon 741.7
  arraign 969.10
cithara 417.2
citharist 416.3
cither 417.2
citified 189.22
citizen
  inhabitant 188.1
  freeman 748.6
citizen of the world 911.1
citrange 41.5
citreous 436.6
citrine green 435.6
  yellow 436.6
  transparency 425.2
citron n. 436.3
citron adj. 436.6
citron yellow 436.1
cittern, cithern 417.2
city 189.16
city manager 745.9
city of the dead 363.14
cityscape view 448.2
  picture 556.10
city slicker 188.2
civet 400.2, 3
civic urban 189.22
  public 372.6
civic crown 733.1
civil public 372.6
  courteous 894.12
  secular 997.4
civilian 968.1
civility 894.1, 3
civilization
  culture 658.2
  civility 894.1
civilize cultivate 658.8

render civil 894.11
civilized 894.12
civism 906.4
civil law 963.2
civil war 722.1
civvies 225.9
clabber n. clot 321.5
  semiliquid 352.3
clabber v. 321.7
clachan 189.17
clack n.
  noisemaker 404.4
  clatter 407.5
  twaddle 517.3
  chatter 584.2
clack v. crack 406.7
  clatter 407.10
  cluck 412.2
  talk nonsense 517.6
  be loquacious 584.4
clacker 404.4
clacket 407.5
clad 225.46
claim n.
  allegation 619.1
  demand 741.2
  request 765.1
  estate 780.2
  right 922.2
  legal pleading 969.6
  have a claim upon 924.5
  have no claim upon 925.5
claim v. allege 619.2
  demand 741.6
  (request 765.4)
  ~ as due 924.7
  (assume 925.6)
  maintain 937.6
claimant
  respondent 462.4
  petitioner 767.1
  appellant 924.4
  accuser 938.2
clairaudience 994.7
clairaudient n. 994.15
clairaudient adj. 994.22
clairsentience 994.7
clairsentient 994.22
clairvoyance 994.7
  (intuition 477a.1)
  (foresight 510.1)
  (divination 511.2)
clairvoyant n. 994.15
clairvoyant adj. 994.22
  (intuitive 477a.4)
clam fish 298.18
  taciturn person 585.2
clamant noisy 404.9
  vociferous 411.8
clambake 840.2
  (party 892.6)
clamber 305.5
clamjamfry 645.4
clammy 352.8
clamor, clamour n.
  noise 404.2
  (discord 414.2)

clatter 407.5
vociferation 411.2
clamor, clamour v.
  silence 403.5
  vociferate 411.7
  ~ for 765.5
  complain 839.10
  ~ against 932.7
clamorous, clamourous noisy 404.9
  vociferous 411.8
  importunate 642.13
  turbulent 824.11
  wailing 839.13
  be clamorous 411.7
clamp n.
  fastening 45.2
  grip 781.2
clamp v. 43.6
clan race 11.4
  (party 712.1)
  kind 75.2
clandestine 528.21
clang n. tone 402.2
  noise 404.2
  birdcall 412.1
clang v. be noisy 404.6
  ring 408.8
clang color 402.2
  (resonance 408.1)
  (music 413.5)
clangor n. noise 404.2
  discord 414.2
clangor v.
  be noisy 404.6
  ring 408.8
clangorous 404.9
clang tint 402.2
clank ring 408.8
  sound harshly 410.6
clannish 75.6
clanship 709.2
clap n. bang 406.2, 4
  venereal disease 655.7
  applause 931.4
clap v. close 261.2
  bang 406.7, 8
  applaud 931.6
clap eyes on 441.10
clap hands 838.5
clap on 37.3
clap on the back
  approve 931.5
  urge 615.7
clap together 43.5
clap under hatches, clap up 751.8
clapboard n.
  coating 223.18
  board 635.3
clapboard v. 223.24
clapper
  noisemaker 404.4
  snapper 406.5
  claquer 599.23
clapperclaw 932.8
clappers 417.10
clapping 931.4
claptrap
  sophism 477.2
  twaddle 517.3

claque — cleave

untruth 546.1
pretext 619.1
claque 72.3
claqueur
 applauder 935.1
 theatergoer 599.23
clarence 272.4
clarendon 591.8
claret *n.* blood 333.3
 wine 959.7
claret *adj.* 434.9
clarification 652.2
clarify
 make intelligible
  518.3
 purify 652.9
clarinet 417.4
clarinetist, clarinet-
 tist 416.2
clarion horn 417.4
 battle horn 722.3
clarity
 transparency 425.1
 intelligibility 518.1
 elegance 578.1
clash *n.*
 collision 276.2
 discord 713.1
 contest 720.2
clash *v.*
 ~ with 15.5
 disagree 24.5
 counteract 179.3
 intrude 228.10
 collide 276.9
 bang 406.7
 sound harshly 410.6
 colors 428.11
 disaccord 713.6
 fight 720.8
 be unfriendly 889.2
clashing *n.*
 contrariety 14.1
 disagreement 24.1
 counteraction 179.1
 opposition 708.1
 discord 713.1
 hostility 889.1
clashing *adj.*
 contrary 14.5
 disagreeing 24.6
 counteractive 179.5
 colors 428.16
clashy 24.6
clasp *n.* fastening 45.2
 zone 230.2
 grip 781.1, 2
clasp *v.* attach 43.6
 cohere 46.5
 be near 197.5
 seize 789.9
 embrace 902.8
class *n.* kind 75
 (denomination
  542.4)
 animal kingdom
  366.1
 vegetable kingdom
  367.1
 study course 537.7
 students 541.8
 party 712.1

social ~ 873.4
ecclesiastical ~
 997.1
class *v.* 60.7
classfellow
 schoolmate 541.7
 companion 890.3
classical
 classificational 75.6
 old 124.7
 taste 850.5
 language 578.4
classicalism 560.3;
 578.1
classicism
 painting 556.6
 speech 560.3; 578.1
classicist
 scholar 492.1
 literary ~ 578.2
classics 560.8
classific 75.6
classification
 arrangement 60.2
 class 75.1
classificational, clas-
 sificatory 75.6
 (systematic 58.7)
classified 60.10
 (classificational
  75.6)
classify 60.7
classis 696.3
classman
 student 541.1
 companion 890.3
classmate
 schoolmate 541.7
 companion 890.3
classroom 542.5
classy
 beautiful 845.11
 smart 847.14
clatter *n.* 407.5
 (noise 404.2)
clatter *v.* rattle 407.10
 (be noisy 404.6)
 gossip 532.7
clattering, clattery
 noisy 404.9
 rattling 407.14
claudicate 266.16
claudication 266.5
clause section 51.2
 phrase 566.1
 passage 593.7
 condition 770.1
claustral 1000.6
claustrophobia 860.4
clavate 250.9
clavichord 417.6
clavichordist 416.4
clavicithern, clavi-
 cymbal, clavier
 417.6
claviharp 417.2
clavis key 260.10
 translation 522.2
claw *n.* adherer 46.3
 clutch 781.3
claw *v.* 789.9
claw hammer

dress clothes 225.14
hammer 276.4
claw-hammer coat
 225.14
clay plaster 223.19
 softness 324.3
 soil 342.1, 3
 mud 352.4
 corpse 362.1
 ceramics 384.14
clayey 324.6
claymore 727.3
clean *v.* 652.9
 clean out 297.14
 clean up 60.6
clean *adj.* 652.14
 (tidy 58.7)
 (uncorrupt 944.5)
 (innocent 946.5)
 (pure 960.2)
clean *adv.*
 utterly 52.14
 perfectly 650.6
clean bill of health
 654.1, 2
clean-cut 494.11
cleaner 652.6, 8
clean hands 946.1, 3, 5
cleaning 652.2
cleanliness 652.1
cleanly 652.14
cleanness 652
 (innocence 946.1)
 (purity 960.1)
cleanse 652.9
cleanser 652.8
clean-shaven 226.10
cleansing *n.* 652.2
cleansing *adj.*
 purifying 652.15
 antiseptic 662.25
clean slate void 187.4
 innocence 946.1
clean-speaking,
 clean-spoken 582.11
clean sweep 146.1
cleanup gain 35.2
 arrangement 60.5
clear *n.* 425.4
clear *v.*
 eliminate 42.4
 jump over 309.4
 purify 652.9
 disembarrass 705.4
 free 750.3
 ~ a profit 775.6
 settle accounts 807.7
 vindicate 937.5
 acquit 970.3
clear away
 dispel 73.3
 evacuate 297.14
clear for action
 trim ship 267.37
 prepare 673.8
 take precautions
  864.4
clear hawse 267.10
clear off 297.14
clear out
 depart 293.4
 evacuate 297.14

flee 623.10
clean 652.9
clear the decks
 eliminate 42.4
 arrange 60.6
 trim ship 267.37
 evacuate 297.14
 prepare 673.7
 take precautions
  864.4
clear the land 267.28
clear the skirts of
 937.5
clear the throat
 297.19
clear up arrange 60.6
 solve 481a.4
 make intelligible
  518.3
clear *adj.* pure 42.5
 empty 187.11
 audible 402.10
 clear-sounding
  413.27
 luminous 420.22
 distinct 446.5
 (apparent 448.7)
 intelligible 518.5
 (perspicuous 570.2)
 manifest 525.4
 (apparent 448.7)
 positive 535.6
 escaped 671.7
 free 748.12
 exempt 748.18
 unindebted 807.10
 innocent 946.5
keep clear of
 keep distance 196.4
 avoid 623.6
clearage 297.5
clearance
 altitude 267a.21
 evacuation 297.5
 payment 807.1
 vindication 937.1
 acquittal 970.1
clear coast
 safety 664.1
 facility 705.1
clear conscience
 946.1, 5
clear-cut limited 233.3
 accurate 494.11
 intelligible 518.5
clear-eyed 441.20
clearheaded 498.10
clearing space 180.3
 field 371.5
clearly 446.6
 (apparently 448.8)
clearness 518
 (perspicuity 570.1)
clear-sighted 441.20
clearstory See clere-
 story
clear-toned 413.27
clear-witted 498.10
cleat 45.5
cleavage 44.2
cleave *n.* 253.6
cleave *v.* cut 44.8

cleaver — closed

cleave (*continued*)
  (bisect 91.4)
  cohere 46.5
  open 260.11
cleaver 253.6
cleavers, clivers 253.2
cledge 342.3
clef 415.23
cleft *n.* chasm 198.2
  (separation 44.3)
  (cavity 252.2)
  (trench 259.2)
  (opening 260.1)
  notch 257.1
cleft *adj.* 91.6
clemency lenity 740.1
  compassion 914.1
clement mild 826.10
  merciful 914.6
  (lenient 740.4)
clench See clinch
Cleopatra 845.3
clepe 564.6
clepsydra 114.6
clerestory, clearstory
  story 191.18
  top 210.4
clergy 996
clergyman 996.2
  (theologian 983.3)
clergywoman 996.3, 12
cleric *n.* 996.2
cleric *adj.* 995.9
clerical *n.* 996.1, 2
clerical *adj.* 995.9
clerical error 495.3
clericalism 995.1
clericals 999.1
clerk scholar 492.1
  recorder 553.1
  scribe 590.11
  (workman 690.10)
  (servant 746.1)
  functionary 758.2
  agent 759.1
  salesman 797.2
  accountant 811.6
  clergyman 996.2, 5
clerk of works 694.5
clerkship 755.1
cleromancy 511.3
cleuch, cleugh 198.3
clever good 648.8
  skillful 698.11
  (sagacious 498.10)
  (cunning 702.6)
  witty 842.9
cleverness 698.1
  (cunning 702.1)
clew, clue *n.*
  sphere 249.2
  solution 522.1
  hint 527.4
  sign 550.2
clew, clue *v.* 461.16
cliché 496.3
click *n.* 45.2
click *v.* snap 406.7
  succeed 731.5
clicker 271.3
client
  dependent 746.3

customer 795.2
cliental 795.5
clientele
  attendance 88.5
  customers 795.2
clientship 749.2
cliff 212.3
  (height 206.2)
  (incline 217.2)
climacteric 128.3
climate latitude 181.5
  weather 338.4
climatology
  aeronautics 267a.2
  aerology 338.7
climatometer 267a.29
climax *n.* limit 52.4
  summit 210.1
  (supremacy 33.3)
  figure of speech
    521.1
climax *v.* 210.5
climb *n.* acclivity
    217.2
  ascent 305.1
climb *v.*
  aviate 267a.31
  ascend 305.5
  (improve 658.6)
climber 305.3
clime latitude 181.5
  weather 338.4
clinch *n.*
  fastening 45.2
  knot 45.6
  clamp 781.2
  word play 842.5
clinch *v.* attach 43.6
  make certain 474.6
  ~ an argument
    479.2
  complete 729.2
  settle 769.8
  clutch 781.4
  seize 789.9
clincher 479.1
cling 46.5
cling to
  be near 197.5
  persevere 604a.2
  ~ ~ a habit 613.10
  observe 772.3
  love 897.12
clinic patient 655.20
  hospital 662.17
clink *n.* 752.1
clink *v.* ring 408.8
  sound harshly 410.6
clinker residue 40.2
  cinder 384.15
  coin 800.1, 4
clinker-built 223.30
clinkstone 342.4
clinometer 244.3
clinquant 847.2
clint 342.4
Clio 594.3
clip *n.* fastening 45.2
  (grip 781.2)
  velocity 274.1
  blow 276.3

clip *v.* cut off 38.0
  (shorten 201.4)
  speed 274.9
  strike 276.8
clip the wings
  disable 158.6
  retard 275.7
  hinder 706.7
clipper horse 271.3
  ship 273.2
  seaplane 273a.3
  speeder 274.5
clipping
  modicum 32.2
  piece 51.3
  excerpt 596.2
clique *n.* kind 75.2
  conclave 696.2
  coterie 712.2
  (company 72.3)
clique *v.* 88.6
cliquish 712.9
cliquishness, cliquism
    481.4
clitter *n.* 407.5
clitter *v.* 407.10
clitterclatter 407.5
clivers See cleavers
cloaca conduit 350.1
  sewer 653.8, 9
cloak *n.* cover 223.2
  (disguise 545.5)
  garment 225.15
  pretext 619.1
  clerical ~ 999.1
cloak *v.* coat 223.24
  conceal 528.10
  (make a pretext
    619.2)
  protect 664.6
  guard 717.7
cloakmaker 690.8
cloam 342.3
clock *n.* 114.6
Clock *n.* 318.6
clock *v.* 114.8
clocksmith 690.6
clockwise 312.9
clockwork
  complexity 59.3
  mechanism 633.2
by clockwork
  regularly 16.7
  in order 58.8
clod lump 192.5
  clot 321.5
  soil 342.3
  dolt 501.1
  awkward fellow 701
  rustic 876.5
cloddish rustic 183.3
  uncouth 851.7
clodhopper
  shoe 225.27
  oaf 501.1
  awkward fellow 701
  rustic 876.5
clodhopping 183.3
clodpate 501.1
clodpated 499.12
clodpoll, clodpole
  dolt 501.1

awkward fellow 701
clog *n.*
  adherer 46.3
  shoe 225.27
  log 635.3
  hindrance 706.2
clog *v.* 706.4
clog dancer 840.9
clogmaker 690.8
cloison 228.6
cloissonné 384.14
cloisonné 847.13
cloister *n.*
  retreat 189.13
  courtyard 189.19
  covered way 627.2
  sanctuary 666.3
  monastery 1000.4
cloister *v.* 751.8
cloistered 1000.6
clonus, clonos, clonic
  spasm 655.3
close *n.* end 67
  (evening 126.1)
  (completion 729.1)
  plot 181.3
  square 189.19
  enclosure 232.1
come to a close 67.6
close *v.* end 67.5
  shut 261.2
  (stanch 348.24)
  (hinder 706.4)
  settle 769.8
close in 290.2
close with
  cohere 46.5
  converge 290.2
  concur 488.7
  attack 716.5
  fight with 720.8
  consent 762.2
  contract 769.8
close with the land
  navigate 267.26, 29
  approach 286.2
  make land 292.9
close *adj.*
  approximative 17.4
  copy 21.5
  fast 43.11
  crowded 72.13
  imminent 152.3
  (future 121.7)
  near 197.8
  (contiguous 199.4)
  narrow 203.9
  shut fast 261.6
  dense 321.8
  sultry 382.18
  phonetics 402.11
  concise 572.3
  taciturn 585.4
  stingy 819.4
  intimate 888.4
  unsociable 893.9
keep close
  keep secret 528.11
  retain 781.4
  seclude oneself
    893.6
closed 261.3

close call 671.2
closefisted, close-
 handed 819.4
close-haul 267.19, 24
close-hauled
 near 197.8
 sailing 267.50, 51, 54
close-mouthed 585.4
 (secretive 528.22)
closeness
 nearness 197.1
 secrecy 528.2
close quarters 197.2
close shave 671.2
closet cupboard 191.15
 (small place 184.4)
 hiding place 530.2
 storeroom 636.4
 be closeted with
  588.7
close-tongued 585.4
close to the wind
 near 197.8
 navigation 267.54,
  57
close-up 556.11
closing 261.1
closure joint 43.3
 cessation 142.3
 shutting 261
 (recess 252.4)
 (stopper 263.1)
 (obstruction 706.2)
 (contraction 795.1)
clot n. grume 321.5
 clod 342.3
 gluten 352.3
 obstruction 706.2
clot v. 321.7
clotbur 46.3
cloth textile 219.5
 (clothes 225.1)
 (material 635.5)
 tablecloth 223.2
 sail 273.13
 curtain 599.15
 profession 625.5
 napkin 652.7
 clergy 996.1
 canonicals 999.1
clothe 225.41
 (cover 223.22)
clothes 225.1
 (cloth 219.5)
 (canonicals 999.1)
clothesbasket 191.9
clotheshorse 215.9
clothesline 205.3
clothes pole 203.6
clothespress 191.15
clothier 225.36
clothing 225.1
 (cover 223.2)
 (wrap 384.13)
 (merchandise
  798.3)
clothmaker 690.8
Clotho 601.4
clothworker 690.9
cloth-yard shaft 727.6
cloture 142.3
cloud n. horde 72.4

multitude 102.2
haze 353.5
 (vapor 334.2)
 (moisture 339.1)
 (shade 424.1)
 (film 426.2)
 (screen 530.3)
adversity 735.4
gloomy outlook
 859.2
cloud on the horizon
 danger 665.1
 warning sign 668.3
 gloomy outlook
  859.2
gathering clouds
 omen 512.2
 danger 665.1
 warning sign 668.3
 adversity 735.4
in a cloud
 bewildered 475.16
 concealed 528.17
in the clouds
 aloft 206.19
 preoccupied 458.11
 imaginary 515.12
under a cloud
 unfortunate 735.9
 in disrepute 874.9
 secluded 893.10
 disapproved 932.9
 suspected 938.6
cloud v.
 overcloud 353.9
 dim 422.6
 (darken 421.5)
 opalesce 427.3
 conceal 528.10
cloud-built
 chimerical 4.6
 imaginary 515.12
cloudburst 348.11
cloud-capped 206.14
clouded
 obscure 519.7
 concealed 528.17
 dim 422.8
 mottled 440.7
 unfortunate 735.9
 gloomy 837.10
cloudiness 353.4
cloudland 515.6
cloudless light 420.22
 happy 827.9
cloudy
 overclouded 353.11
 (moist 339.7)
 (stormy 349.26)
 dim 422.8
 opaque 426.4
 obscure 519.7
clough 198.3
clout n. blow 276.3
 theft 791.4
clout v. 276.8
clove chasm 198.3
 condiment 393.1
 perfume 400.3
cloven bisected 91.6
 intervallic 198.5
cloven foot

malevolence 907.1
wickedness 945.1
cloven hoof
 earmark 550.6
 malevolence 907.1
 wickedness 945.1
 devilishness 978.3
clover trefoil 92.2
 grass 367.9
 well-being 377.2
 green 435.3
 prosperity 734.1
in clover
 in comfort 377.9
 prosperous 734.7
 happy 827.5
 pleasant 829.10
clown actor 599.20
 (humorist 844)
 awkward fellow
  701
 boor 876.5
 (vulgarian 851.4)
clownish rustic 183.3
 uncouth 851.7
cloy sate 869.4
 (overload 641.4)
 (weary 841.6)
cloyed 869.6
cloyedness 869.1
cloyer 869.2
cloying
 oversweet 396.8
 satiating 869.7
club n. resort 74.2
 clique 712.2
 (social group 892.7)
 cudgel 727.7
 (hammer 276.4)
 (rod 975.2)
 coercion 744.1
 playing card 840.13
club v. league 48.4
 ~ to death 361.10
club together
 co-operate 709.4
 keep company 892.9
clubbable, clubable
 club 712.9
 sociable 892.12
clubbability, clubabil-
 ity 892.1
clubbish 892.12
clubbism 892.1
clubfoot 211.4
 distortion 243.1
clubfooted 243.5
club law
 anarchy 738.2
 (lawlessness 964.3)
 coercion 744.1
clubman 852.5
club-shaped 250.9
club steak 298.20
clubwoman 852.5
cluck 412.2
clue See clew
clump bunch 72.5
 protuberance 250.2
 thud 408a.2
clumsiness 699.3
clumsy n 701

clumsy adj.
 awkward 699.12
 (thoughtless
  458.10)
 (careless 460.8)
 (stupid 499.12)
 (reckless 863.7)
 unmanageable
  704.10
 ungraceful 846.8
clunch 342.3
Cluniac 996.11
clunk 408a.2
cluricaune 979.9
cluster n. 72.5
cluster v. 72.10
clutch n.
 automobile 272.16
 grasp 781.1
 (seizure 789.1)
clutch v. grasp 781.4
 seize 789.9
clutches grasp 781.1, 3
 control 737.2
 in the clutches of
  749.6
clutter n. 407.5
clutter v. 407.10
Clydesdale 271.4
clypeiform 245.19
clyster, glyster 300.4
coacervation 72.6
coach n.
 vehicle 272.4, 15, 19
 teacher 540.1
coach v.
 transport 270.8
 tutor 537.9
 (prepare 673.6)
coach-and-four 272.8
coach house 191.16
coachmaker 690.8
coachman 268.8
 (workman 690.10)
coachsmith 690.6
coachwhip 550.13
coachwright 690.7
coachy 268.9
coact concur 178.2
 co-operate 709.4
coaction
 concurrence 178.1
 co-operation 709.1
 compulsion 744.1
coactive
 concurrent 178.4
 co-operative 709.7
 compulsory 744.3
 (restraining 751.13)
coadjument 709.1
 (concurrence 178.1)
coadjutant n. 711.1
coadjutant adj. 709.7
coadjute 709.4
coadjutement 709.1
coadjutor 711.1
coadjutorship, coad-
 juvancy 709.1
coadjuvant n. 711.1
coadjuvant adj. 709.7
 (concurrent 178.4)
coadunate v. 178.2

coadunate — coelenterate

coadunate *adj.*
  combined 48.5
  concurrent 178.4
coadunation
  combination 48.1
  concurrence 178.1
coagulate 321.7
  (conglomerate 46.8)
coagulation
  coherence 46.1
  thickening 321.3
coagulum clot 321.5
  gluten 352.3
coal *n.* residue 40.2
  spark 382.8
  ember 384.15
  fuel 388.2
  (mineral 635.6)
  black 431.3
coal *v.* 388.8
coal-black 431.7
coal car 272.19
coal dust 388.2
coaler 273.1
coalesce
  be identical 13.4
  combine 48.3
coalescence
  identity 13.1
  junction 43.1
  combination 48.1
coalescent
  coincident 13.7
  unific 87.9
coal gas 334.2
  (poison 663.5)
coalition
  junction 43.1
  combination 48.1
  association 709.2
  party 712.4
coalitional 709.7
coal oil 356.2
coalsack
  heavenly body 318.3
  nebula 420.12
coal shovel
  shovel 191.14
  fire iron 386.3
coaly
  carbonaceous 388.10
  black 431.7
coaptation 23.2
coarctate *v.* 195.4
coarctate *adj.* 203.9
coarctation
  narrowing 203.2
  hindrance 706.1
coarse rough 256.12
  coarse-grained 329.3
  harsh-sounding 410.9
  speech 579.3
  dirty 653.17
  unrefined 674.8
  vulgar 851.6
  (unprepossessing 846.8)
  obscene 961.9
coarse-grained

rough 256.12
  coarse 329.3
coarseness 851.1
coast *n.* edge 231.1
  shore 342.2
coast *v.* edge 231.3
  glide 266.20
  navigate 267.30
coastal
  bordering 231.4
  littoral 342.10
coaster 273.1
coast guard 717.6
coast guard cutter
  ship 273.1
  warship 726.11
coastland 342.2
coast line 213.4
coat *n.* layer 204.2
  cover 223.2, 12, 18
  garment 225.15, 16, 25
  fur 256.3
  ~ of paint 428.5
coat *v.*
  form layers 204.4
  cover 223.24
  clothe 225.41
  paint 428.10
coatee 225.16
coating layer 204.2
  cover 223.16, 18
  ~ of paint 428.5
coat of arms 550.12
coat of mail 717.2
coax persuade 615.9
  flatter 933.2
coaxer 615.6
cob 972.6
cobalt 438.4
cobalt green 435.2, 4
cobble *n.* stone 342.4
  pavement 627.4
cobble *v.* 660.11
cobbler 225.40
  (mender 660.7)
cobblestone
  stone 342.4
  pavement 627.4
cobbling 225.35
coble 273.4
cobra 366.19
cobweb filament 205.1
  lightness 320.2
  sophistry 477.1
  snare 545.4
  slight thing 643.5
Coca Cola 298.4
cocaine 662.7
cocher, cochero 268.9
cochineal 434.6
cochlea 418.5
cochlear 248.5
cock *n.* valve 263.2
  weather vane 338.9
  fowl 366.23
  male animal 373.6
cock *v.* 311.4
  cock the eye
    look askance 441.15
    squint 443.12
  cock up

be vertical 212.6
  project 250.7
cockade 550.12
cock-a-doodle *n.*
  cock 366.23
  male animal 373.6
cock-a-doodle *v.* 412.2
Cockaigne, Cockagne 515.6
cock-a-hoop
  elated 836.9
  exultant 884.9
cock-and-bull story 546.1
cockatrice
  monster 83.7
  (reptile 366.18)
  serpent 366.19
  evil eye 441.8
  deceiver 548.11
cockboat 273.4
cockcrow, cockcrowing 125.1
cocked hat 225.26
cocker wrinkle 258.3
  caress 902.8
cockerel fowl 366.23
  male animal 373.6
cocker spaniel 366.6
cocket 467.4
cockeye 443.4
cockeyed
  crooked 217.13
  drunk 959.21
  poor-sighted 443.14
cockle *n.*
  wrinkle 258.1
  boat 273.4
cockle *v.*
  contract 195.4
  wrinkle 258.3
cockleboat 273.4
cocklebur
  adherer 46.3
  rough 256.2
cockleshell
  shell 223.16
  boat 273.4
cockles of the heart
  essence 5.2
  inmost mind 450.3
cockloft 191.19
cockney *n.*
  townsman 188.2
  language 563.5
  plebeian 876.3
cockney *adj.* 876.11
cockneyese 563.5
cock of the walk
  best 648.4
  master 745.1
cockpit
  airplane 273a.10
  arena 728.1
Cockpit of Europe 182.3
cockroach 366.24
cockshut 126.1
cocksure 474.8
  (undoubting 484.12)
cockswain See coxswain

cocktail cloud 353.5
  alcoholic drink 959.8
cocky
  conceited 880.6
  pert 885.9
cocoa *n.* head 210.3
  drink 298.4
  brown 433.1
cocoa *adj.* 433.4
cocoa butter 356.3
coconscious 450.10
coconut 298.33
coconut brown 433.1
coconut oil, coconut butter 356.3
cocoon 129.8
cocotte 962.2
coction 384.7
Cocytean 982.5
Cocytus 982.5
cod hull 223.14
  fish 298.18
C.O.D., c.o.d. 807.11
coda 415.15
coddle caress 902.8
  ~ oneself 943.3
code *n.*
  cryptograph 528.5
  signal 550.15
  (telegraphy 532a.3)
  cipher 561.5
  cryptography 590.8
  precept 697.1
  ~ of morals 926.4
  ~ of laws 963.2
code *v.* codify 528.15
  cipher 561.7
codex
  manuscript 590.3
  book 593.1
codex rescriptus
  cryptograph 528.5
  manuscript 590.3
codfish 298.18
codfish aristocracy 876.8
codger oddity 83.4
  miser 819.2
codicil adjunct 39.1
  sequel 65.1
  testament 771.1
codification
  classification 60.2
  legislation 963.1
codify classify 60.7
  use code 528.15
  ~ laws 963.4
cod-liver oil 356.4
coeducation 537.4
coeducational 537.12
coefficiency
  accompaniment 88.1
  co-operation 709.1
coefficient
  number 84.2
  attendant 88.1
coelanaglyphic 557.6
Coelebs's wife 903.8
Coelentera 368.4
coelenterate 368.13

coeliac flux, coeliac
  passion 299.2
coemption 795.1
coemptional 795.5
coemptor 795.2
coequal *n.* 27.5
coequal *adj.*
  equal 27.8
  symmetrical 242.4
coequality 27.2
coerce 744.2
  (be severe 739.4)
coercion 744.1
  (despotism 739.2)
  (restraint 751.1)
coercive 744.3
  (severe 739.5)
coercive force 744.1
coetaneous 120.4
coeternal
  eternal 112.4
  synchronous 120.4
coeternity 112.1
  (long time 110.3)
coeval *n.* 120.2
coeval *adj.* 120.4
coevality
  equivalence 27.2
  synchronism 120.1
coexist coincide 1.4
  accompany 88.6
  synchronize 120.3
  be contiguous 199.3
coexistence
  synchronism 120.1
  (existence 1.1)
  accompaniment 88.1
  contiguity 199.1
coexistent 120.4
coextend 216.3
coextension
  equality 27.1
  parallelism 216.1
  symmetry 242.1
coextensive
  parallel 216.5
  symmetrical 242.4
coffee *n.*
  energizer 171.5
  drink 308.4
  brown 433.1
  stimulant 662.5
coffee *adj.* 433.4
coffeehouse 298.42
  (inn 189.8)
coffee mill 691
coffeepot 191.11
coffeeroom, coffee
  shop 298.42
coffer case 191.8
  (storehouse 636.4)
  treasury 802.1
cofferdam 55.2
coffin 363.10
coffinmaker 690.8
coffin nail 392a.4
cog *n.* tooth 253.3
  boat 273.4
  deception 545.3
cog *v.* quibble 477.8
  falsify 544.4
  deceive 545.7

cog a die cheat 545.7
  swindle 791.12
cogency potence 157.1
  cogent argument
    476.6
cogent 157. 8
coggle stone 342.4
  pavement 627.4
cogitable 470.5
cogitate 451.27
cogitation 451.1
cogitative 451.35
cognac 959.6
cognate related 9.6
  consanguine 11.7
  connatural 17.13
cognation relation 9.1
  (relevancy 23.2)
  consanguinity 11.1
cognition 490.1
cognitive
  intellectual 450.8
  cognizant 490.12
cognizability 518.1
cognizable
  knowable 490.18
  understandable
    518.5
cognizance 490.1
take cognizance of
  note 450.7
  bear in mind 457.4
cognizant 490.12, 13
  (conscious 450.9)
be cognizant of 490.9
cognomen *n.*
  name 564.2
  nickname 565.3
cognomen *v.* 564.6
cognominal 564.8
cognominate 564.6
cognomination
  564.1, 2
cognoscible 490.18
cogwheel 312.4
cohabit 186.10
cohabitation
  habitation 186.2
  marriage 903.1
coheir
  participator 778.3
  coparcener 779.5
coheirship
  inheritance 775.4
  participation 778.1
cohere 46.5
  (join 43.9)
  (solidify 321.7)
coherence
  agreement 23.1
  adherence 46
  (junction 43.1)
  (toughness 327.1)
  unity 87.1
  stability 150.1
coherent 46.9
  (dense 321.8)
  (viscid 352.8)
cohesion 46.1
  (density 321.1)
cohesive 46.9
  (dense 321.8)

(tough 327.5)
(viscid 352.8)
cohesiveness 46.2
  (toughness 327.1)
cohibit restrain 751.6
  prohibit 761.2
cohibition
  restraint 751.1
  prohibition 761.1
cohibitive 751.13
cohobate 336.5
cohobation 336.1
cohobator 336.3
cohort 726.7
coif, coiffure 225.26
coil *n.* length 200.3
  convolution 248.2
  (complexity 59.3)
  (curve 245.2)
  (circle 247.2)
  (turn 311.2)
  mortal ~ 362.1
  distiller 386.1
coil *v.* 248.3
  (curve 245.3)
coin *n.* 800.1, 4
coin, coign *n.* 244.2
  (nook 191.3)
coin *v.*
  produce 161.8
  invent 515.10
  trump up 544.3
  ~ words 563.14
  mint 800.20
coin money
  make profit 775.7
  become rich 803.6
coinage
  production 161.1, 6
  neologism 563.7
  money 800.1
coincide coexist 1.4
  be identical 13.4
  synchronize 120.3
  be contiguous 199.3
  concur 488.7
coincidence
  identity 13.1
  agreement 23.1
  synchronism 120.1
  contiguity 199.1
coincident
  identical 13.7
  (alike 17.10)
  joined 43.10
  concurrent 178.4
coincidental 13.7
coiner
  ~ of words 563.12
  minter 800.18
coinstantaneous 120.4
Cointreau 959.6
coistrel, coistril 862.2
coition 43.2
  (procreation 161.2)
coitus 43.2
cojuror 467.6
coke slag 384.15
  fuel 388.2
  (mineral 635.6)
colander, cullender
  sorter 60.4

porousness 260.7
colatorium 652.7
colature
  purification 652.2
  strainer 652.7
cold *n.*
  salivation 299.5
  frigidity 383
  disease 655.9
cold *adj.* dead 360.8
  frigid 383.8
  colorless 429.6
  gray 432.4
  blue 438.6
  dull 575.2
  unfeeling 823.5
  (irreligious 989.6)
  indifferent 866.4
  unfriendly 889.3
  discourteous 895.6
  heartless 907.8
  be cold 383.7
  render cold 385.4
cold blood 823.1
in cold blood
  intentionally 620.5
  dispassionately
    823.8
cold-blooded
  unfeeling 823.5
  inexcitable 826.9
  heartless 907.8
cold drink 396.5
  (cooling agent
    387.2)
cold feet 862.1
  get cold feet 862.3
cold frame 371.6
coldhearted
  dispassionate 823.5
  unfriendly 889.3
  heartless 907.8
coldly 383.13
coldness
  dispassion 822.1
  indifference 866.1
cold pack 387.1
cold-short 328.4
cold shoulder *n.* 930.4
  (disregard 460.1)
cold-shoulder *v.* 930.7
cold steel 727.3
cold storage 387.1
cold sweat
  trepidation 860.3
  repugnance 867.2
coleslaw 298.30
colic ache 378.1
  ailment 655.5
coliseum
  theater 599.10
  arena 728.1
Coliseum See Colos-
  seum
collaborate 709.4
collaboration 709.1
  (concurrence 178.1)
collaborative 709.7
  (concurrent 178.4)
collaborator 711.1
collapse *n.*
  prostration 158.2

collapse — column 764

collapse (*continued*)
  destruction 162.3
  contraction 195.1
  physical ~ 655.1
  impairment 659.3
  exhaustion 688.3
  failure 732.1, 3
  bankruptcy 808.2
collapse *v.*
  be impotent 158.5
  contract 195.4
  fall through 304.2
  break down 659.6
  fail 732.5
  go bankrupt 808.6
collar *n.*
  neckpiece 225.33
  circle 247.2
  foam 353.2
  shackle 752.2
collar *v.* 751.9; 789.9
collarband 247.2
collate compose 54.4
  liken 464.2
collateral *n.* 771.1
collateral *adj.*
  related 9.6
  consanguine 11.7
  synchronous 120.4
  parallel 216.5
  lateral 236.6
  evidential 467.11
collation meal 298.34
  comparison 464.1
collative 464.5
colleague
  accompanier 88.3
  co-worker 690.4
  confederate 711.1
  friend 890.1
colleagueship 709.2
collect *n.* 990.3
Collect *n.* 998.7
collect *v.*
  assemble 72.10, 11
  (accumulate 636.7)
  deduce 480.6
  understand 518.4
  acquire 775.6
collectanea
  assemblage 72.7
  book 593.2
  excerpts 596.2
collectarium 593.2
collected
  assembled 72.12
  composed 826.9
collection
  assemblage 72.1, 7
  (quantity 31.3)
  (store 636.1)
  book 593.2
  collectanea 596.2
  acquisition 775.1
  offertory 784.3; 990.6
collective 78.9
collectively
  wholly 50.10
  together 88.10
collectivism 737.6; 778.2

collectivist 778.4
collectivity 50.1
collector
  gatherer 72.9
  director 694.1
  official 745.7, 9
colleen 129.5
college
  insane asylum 503.8
  school 542.1
  prison 752.1
college ice 298.13
collegian
  student 541.3
  prisoner 754.1
collegiate *n.* 541.3
collegiate *adj.* 541.9; 542.9
collet 211.1
collibert 188.3
collide disagree 24.5
  intrude 228.10
  sail into 267.32
  clash 276.9
  encounter 720.8
  be unfriendly 889.2
collie 366.6
collier 273.1
colliery 252.2
colligate 72.11
colligation 72.1
collimate 216.4
collimation
  parallelism 216.1
  direction 278.1
collineate 216.4
collineation 216.1
colliquate
  liquefy 335.5
  melt 384.21
colliquation 335.1
colliquative 335.8
collision
  contrariety 14.1
  counteraction 179.1
  clash 276.2
  opposition 708.1
  contest 720.2
  accident 735.3
  hostility 889.1
in collision 267.64
collocate arrange 60.6
  assemble 72.11
collocation
  arrangement 60.1
  assemblage 72.1
  location 184.5
collocution 588.1
collocutor 588.5
collocutory 588.10
collogue 588.2
colloidality 352.1
collop 51.2
colloquial
  vernacular 563.16
  (linguistic 560.9)
  conversational 588.10
colloquialism 563.3
  (vernacular 560.2)
  (word 562.1)
colloquialist

colloquial speaker 563.11
  (linguist 560.7)
  conversationalist 588.5
colloquialize 563.13
colloquist 588.5
colloquize 588.7
colloquy 588.1
collotype 556.11
collude 709.4
collusion
  concurrence 178.1
  deception 545.1
  co-operation 709.1
collusive 545.12
colluvies 653.8
collyrium 662.6
cologne 400.3
colon stop 142.5
  intestine 350.4
  punctuation 550.8
colonel 745.11
colonial 188.5
colonist alien 57.3
  settler 188.5
  incomer 294.4
  (outgoer 295.4)
colonization 184.6
colonizer alien 57.3
  settler 188.5
colonnade series 69.2
  cloister 189.19
  covered way 627.2
colonnette 215.16
colony territory 181.2
  country 182.1
  settlement 188.10
colophon sequel 65.1
  printing 591.2
colophonate, colophony 356a.1
color, colour *n.*
  kind 75.2
  tone 402.2
  colorant 428.3
  redness 434.1
  aspect 448.4
  pretext 619.1
  extenuation 937.3
color, co'our *v.*
  tint 428.9
  (limn 556.17)
  redden 434.8
  disguise 544.3
  exaggerate 549.2
  pretext 619.2
  blush 881.4
  anger 900.7
  extenuate 937.8
colorable, colourable
  tingible 428.12
  plausible 472.6
  spurious 545.13
colorado 302a.15
colorant 428.3
coloration, colouration 428.2, 6
colorative, colourative 428.12
coloratura
  voice 413.14

singer 416.24
coloratura 415.10
color-blind, colour-blind 443.14
color blindness 443.1
colored, coloured 428.13
colored person 431.4
colorful, colourful
  bright 428.14
  variegated 440.5
colorific, colourific 428.12
colorifics, colourifics 428.7
colorimeter 428.8
coloring, colouring
  tone 402.2
  color 428.2, 3, 6
  qualification 469.1
  meaning 516.1
colorist, colourist 559.2
colorless, colourless
  hueless 429.6
  (weak 160.10)
  feeble 575.2
  become colorless 429.4
colorlessness, colourlessness 429
color photography 556.4
colors, colours 550.13
color sergeant 745.11
colory, coloury 440.5
colossal vast 31.8
  huge 192.15
  high 206.13
Colosseum, Coliseum 599.10
colossus
  strong man 159.6
  giant 192.8
  tower 206.3
colporteur, colporter
  vendor 797.3
  evangelist 996.4
colt
  youngling 129.4, 7
  horse 271.3
  fool 501.1
  awkward boy 701
colter, coulter 253.6
colt's-tail 353.5
colubrine 366.27
Columba 318.6
columbarium, columbary 189.7
Columbia 182.3
columbine 599.20
Columbus Day 138.7
columella 215.16
column
  procession 69.3
  tower 206.3
  post 215.16
  (cylinder 249.3)
  monument 363.15; 551.4
  printing 591.2
  book 593.7

military 726.7
columnar 215.29
  (cylindrical 249.8)
columnist 593.16
colure 318.8
colza oil 356.3
coulter See **colter**
coma
  insensibility 376.1
  swoon 683.5; 688.3
Coman 560.4
comate
  coworker 711.1
  companion 890.3
comatose
  insensible 376.5
  (numb 381.3)
  lethargic 683.15, 16
  apathetic 823.5
comb *n.* height 206.2
  tooth 253.2
  serration 257.2
  coal 388.2
  cleaner 652.7
comb *v.*
  disentangle 60.9
  curry 331.3
  clean 652.11
  whip 972.6
combat *n.*
  contest 720.2
  warfare 722.1
combat *v.* 720.8
  (war 722.9)
combatant 726
  (opponent 710.1)
  (assailant 716.4)
  (player 840.17)
combative
  aggressive 716.8
  belligerent 722.13
  (contentious 720.12)
combativeness 722.6
combat plane 273a.2
combe See **coomb**
comber 348.10
combination
  mixture 41.4
  (composition 54.1)
  union 48
  (minglement 41.1)
  (junction 43.1)
  (composition 54.1)
  permutation 84.4
  concurrence 178.1
  corset, undergarment 225.25
  association 709.2
  society 712.4
combinative
  conjunctive 43.13
  unific 87.9
combine *n.*
  junction 43.1
  society 712.4
combine *v.* join 43.5
  unite 48.3
  (mix 41.6)
  (unify 87.5)
  (form a party 712.7)
  enter into 56.2

concur 178.2
combined 48.5
  (unseparated 46.10)
comblike 253.11
combmaker 690.8
combure 384.18
comburent 384.22
combust 384.18
combustibility 384.10
combustible *n.* 388.1
combustible *adj.*
  384.22
combustion fire 382.8
  burning 384.3
come *v.* near 121.6
  (approach 286.2)
  happen 151.3
  chance 156.7
  arrive 292.7
come about
  happen 151.3
  improve 658.6
  reach completion
    729.4
come a cropper 306.6
come across
  meet 292.10
  discover 481a.3
  acquire 775.6
  give 784.9
  pay 807.6
come across with
  787.4
come again
  repeat 104.4
  recur 138.8
  farewell! 293.14
come and go
  recur 138.8
  alternate 314.10
come at arrive 292.7
  gain 775.6
come back
  revert 145.4
  regress 283.5
  answer 462.5
  retaliate 718.2
  bandy jokes 842.8
come between
  interject 228.7
  intermediate 631.3
come by
  acquire 775.6
  recover 775.9
  receive 785.3
come clean 529.5
**come down on, come
  down upon**
  be severe 739.4
  punish 972.5
come down with
  lend 787.4
  pay 807.6
come forth
  happen 151.3
  egress 295.6
  appear 446.2
  (become 1.5)
come forward
  appear 446.2
  volunteer 763.3

be ostentatious
  882.6
**come here!, come
  hither!** 286.6
come in
  give birth 161.9
  enter 294.6
  (arrive 292.7)
  be received 785.4
come in for
  inherit 775.8
  acquire 775.6
  receive 785.3
  (apportion 786.3)
come in with 582.6
come it speed 274.9
  divulge 529.4
  succeed 731.5
come it over
  have influence 175.8
  deceive 545.7
come near! 286.6
come of 154.3
come off
  be disjoined 44.6
  cease! 142.8
  happen 151.3
  nonsense! 497.5
  succeed 731.5, 6
come on ensue 63.3
  near 121.6
  happen 151.3
  impend 152.2
  come here! 286.6
  I dare you! 715.5
come out
  make a début 66.6;
    599.26
  result 154.3
  egress 295.6
  appear 446.2
  be disclosed 529.6
  be published 531.9
  be printed 591.16
**come out at the little
  end of the horn**
  776.2
come out with
  divulge 529.4
  utter 582.6
come over
  have influence 175.8
  deceive 545.7
  induce 615.10
  consent 762.2
come round
  recur 138.8
  be converted 144.8
  happen 151.3
  assent 488.9
  tergiversate 607.7
  improve 658.6
  recover 660.15
  be reconciled 723.5
  consent 762.2
  (be induced 615.10)
come short
  be inferior 34.4
  fall short 304.2
  disappoint 509.2
come through 807.6
come to equal 27.6

total 50.5
number 85.10
arrive 292.7
revive 359.7
recover 660.15
recuperate 689.3
side with 709.5
inherit 775.8
cost 812.6
come to a head 729.4
come to anchor
  settle 184.14
  anchor 267.12
  be inactive 683.8
come to blows 720.8
  (strike 276.8)
come together
  copulate 43.8
  take order 58.5
  assemble 72.10
  converge 290.2
  be reconciled 723.5
come to grief
  fail 732.5
  misfortune 735.6
  suffer 828.9
come to hand
  arrive 292.7
  appear 446.2
  be received 785.4
come to life 359.7
come to nothing
  cease to be 2.5
  be unproductive
    169.3
  fall through 304.2
  fail 732.5
come to oneself 689.3
come to pass
  fare 7.2
  happen 151.3
  reach completion
    729.4
come to terms
  concur 488.8
  (make a compact
    769.7)
  (compromise 774.2)
  (strike a bargain
    794.6)
  be reconciled 723.5
  surrender 725.4
come to the front
  excel 33.5
  front 234.7
  precede 280.2
  outstrip 303.4
  become famous
    873.12
come to the scratch
  720.8
come to time 82.5
come under 76.2
come up
  follow 281.3
  ascend 305.4
come upon
  meet 292.10
  appear 446.2
  discover 481a.3
  not expect 508.4
  surprise 508.6

come — commission

come (*continued*)
  (catch unprepared
    674.6)
  find 775.6
  claim 924.7
come up to scratch
  conform 82.5
  muster courage
    861.6
come what may
  certainly 474.16
  if necessary 601.15
  in any event 604.9
come with child
  168.6
not come up to 34.4
  (be unequal 28.2)
  (be smaller 195.5)
to come
  future 121.7
  imminent 152.3
come *int.*
  approach! 286.6
  cheer up! 836.14
come-at-able 286.4
comeback
  answer 462.1
  recovery 660.1
  gibe 930.3
comedian actor 599.20
  (humorist 844)
  dramatist 599.22
comedietta 599.4
comedown
  descent 306.1
  anticlimax 497.1
  disappointment
    509.1
  failure 732.1
  misfortune 735.3
comedy drama 599.4
  farce 855.2
  (humor 842.1)
comedy ballet 599.4
comeliness 845.1
  (symmetry 242.1)
comeling 294.4
comely speech 578.4
  good-looking 845.10
  (shapely 242.5)
come-off
  event 151.1
  escape 671.1, 4
come-on dupe 547.1
  lure 617.2
come-out 154.1
come-outer 607.5
  (sectarian 984.13)
comer 294.4
comestible 298.49
comestibles 298.5
comet
  heavenly body 318.3
  omen 512.2
cometary 111.7
comeuppance 924.2
  (punishment 972.1)
  (reward 973.1)
give one his comeuppance
  retaliate 718.2
  punish 972.6

comfit, comfiture
  396.3
comfort *n.*
  coverlet 223.9
  well-being 377.2
  (contentment
    831.1)
  relief 707.4
  solace 834.2
in comfort 377.9
take comfort
  be content 831.3
  be relieved 834.6
comfort *v.*
  content 831.4
  solace 834.5
comfortable *n.* 223.9
comfortable *adj.*
  easeful 377.8
  prosperous 734.7
  pleasant 829.7
  contented 831.6
comforter
  coverlet 223.9
  neckpiece 225.33
the Comforter 976.6
comforting
  gratifying 377.7;
    829.7
  consolatory 834.7
comfortless
  distressing 830.11
  disconsolate 837.12
comfort station 653.9
comfy 223.9
comic *n.* cartoon 556.9
  comedian 599.20
  humorist 844.1
comic *adj.* 855.5
  (humorous 842.9)
comical odd 83.10
  farcical 855.5
comicality 855.1
  (absurdity 497.1)
  (jocularity 842.2)
comic opera 599.3, 4
comic relief 599.7
coming *n.* 292.1
coming *adj.*
  eventual 151.7
  imminent 152.3
  (future 121.7)
  expected 507.8
  deserved 924.11
have it coming
  be due 924.5
  deserve punishment
    972.11
coming out début 66.1
  presentation 883.1
comitia 696.1
comity 894.1
comma stop 142.5
  punctuation 550.8
  (grammar 567.3)
command *n.*
  ~ of language 582.3
  (diction 569.1)
  authority 737.2
  (supervision 693.2)
  order 741
  (precept 697.1)

  ~ of temper 826.3
at one's command
  in charge 693.7
  by authority 737.17
  obedient 743.3, 4
  in possession 777.8
take command 737.13
under one's command 749.6, 7
command *v.*
  rise above 206.10
  ~ a view 441.10
  rule 737.11
  (superintend 693.5)
  order 741.4
  (authorize 737.10)
commandant 745.1, 11
commandeer
  compel 744.2
  appropriate 789.8
commander
  mariner 269.4
  chief 745.1, 11, 12
commander in chief
  745.11
commanding
  important 642.10
  mandatory 741.8
  (authoritative
    737.15)
commandment 741.1
comme il faut
  fashionable 852.7
  noble 875.10
commemorate 883.3
  (remember 505.10)
  (do honor to 873.13)
commemoration 883.1
  (memory 505.1)
  (memorial 551.4)
  (remembrance
    873.5)
in commemoration
  in memory 505.23
  in celebration 883.6
commemorative
  memorial 505.21
  celebrating 883.5
commence 66.5
commencement
  beginning 66.1
  cause 153.1
commend 931.6
  (flatter 933.2)
commendable 931.11
  (advisable 695.9)
commendably 931.12
  (well 648.14)
commendation 931.2
commendatory
  advisory 695.8
  approbatory 931.9
commender 935
commensurability
  23.2
commensurable 85.11
commensurate
  agreeing 23.9
  numerable 85.11
  adequate 639.6
  satisfactory 831.7
comment *n.*

  argument 476.2
  annotation 522.4
  statement 582.4
comment *v.* 582.6
comment upon
  discuss 476.11
  criticize 480.10
  explain 522.6
  dissertate 595.4
commentarial 595.5
commentary
  explanation 522.4
  treatise 595.2
commentate 595.4
commentation
  explanation 522.4
  treatise 595.2
commentator
  scholiast 492.1;
    524.2
  dissertator 595.3
commentatorial 522.8
commenter 595.3
commerce *n.*
  interlocution 588.1
  business 794.1
  (barter 625.1)
  game 840.12
commerce *v.* 588.7
commercial 794.10
commercialism 794.1
commercial paper
  800.7
commercial traveler
  758.5; 797.2
commination
  malediction 908.1
  threat 909.1
comminatory 909.3
commingle 41.6
comminute *v.* 330.6
  (disintegrate 44.9;
    49.3)
comminute *adj.* 330.8
comminution 330.2
commiserate
  pity 914.3
  condole 915.2
commiseration
  pity 914.1
  condolence 915.1
commissariat 637.1
  (provisions 298.6)
commissary
  supplier 637.2
  delegate 758.4
  deputy 759.1
commission *n.*
  condition 7.1
  task 625.2
  delegation 755
  (authority 737.1)
  percentage 786.2
  fee 812.2
out of commission
  659.12
commission *v.*
  send 270.9
  delegate 755.4
  (empower 157.7)
  (deputize 759.5)
  (grant 760.4)

commissionaire — comparative

commissionaire
  messenger 534.1
  official 745.9
  delegate 758.4
  deputy 759.1
commissioned 755.5
commissioner
  official 745.7, 9
  delegate 758.4
  deputy 759.1
commissure 43.3
commit n. 840.12
commit v. send 270.9
  ~ to memory 505.13
  (learn 539.3)
  ~ oneself to 609.8
  do 680.6
  delegate 755.4
  entrust 784.12
  ~ a crime 964.4
**commitment, commit-
  tal** 751.2
committed 768.7
committee
  council 696.1
  consignee 758.1
commix 41.6
commixture 41.1
commode 191.15
commodious 644.8
commodity 798.1
commodore 745.12
common n.
  park 189.21; 367.11;
    840.14
  plain 344.1
 in **common**
  relative 9.5
  on shares 778.9
common adj.
  correlative 12.6
  public 372.6
  well-known 490.17
  customary 613.11
  (prevalent 78.10)
  insignificant 643.10
  mediocre 736.3
  commonplace 843.6
  ordinary 849.3
  lowborn 876.11
**commonage, com-
  monalty** 876.1
  (people 372.2)
commoner
  student 541.4
  plebeian 876.3
common law
  tradition 124.3
  law 963.2
**common-law mar-
  riage** 903.2
commonly 613.13
  (invariably 16.7)
  (generally 78.15)
  (frequently 136.5)
commonness 136.1
**common or garden
  variety**
  mediocrity 736.1
  plain 849.1
commonplace n.
  topic 454.1

trite saying 496.3
  (triteness 843.2)
  memorandum 505.6
  record 551.1
commonplace v. 849.2
commonplace adj.
  well-known 490.17
  language 576.3
  usual 613.11
  insignificant 643.10
  mediocre 736.3
  trite 843.6
  ordinary 849.3
commonplace book
  memorandum book
    505.6
  notebook 551.3
commonplaceness
  843.2
common run
  rule 613.3
  commonalty 876.1
commons park 189.21
  provisions 298.6
  commonalty 876.1
common sense
  reasonableness
    476.7
  wisdom 498.3
common stock 778.1
**commonweal, com-
  mon weal**
  population 188.10
  nation 372.2
  public service 906.3
  (welfare 648.2)
commonwealth
  country 182.1
  population 188.10
  nation 372.2
  public welfare 906.3
commorant 188.1
commotion
  turmoil 59.4
  (brawl 713.4)
  agitation 315.1
  excitement 825.3
communal 372.6
communalism
  socialism 737.6
  collectivism 778.2
communalist 778.4
communalistic 778.8
communalization
  778.2
communalize 778.6
commune n. 181.2
commune v.
  with oneself 451.29
  converse 588.7
  ~ with God 990.11
communicable
  transferable 270.11
  contagious 657.5
  giveable 784.14
communicant
  informant 527.5
  worshiper 990.8
communicate
  tell 527.7
  speak 582.6
  correspond 592.6

give 784.8
  attend Communion
    998.14
  (attend service
    990.14)
communication
  junction 43.1
  information 527.1
  message 532.2
  written ~ 591.1, 2
  giving 784.1
communicative
  informative 527.13
  sociable 892.12
communicator
  informant 527.5
  correspondent 592.5
communion
  denomination 542.4
  interlocution 588.1
  party 712.1
  joint possession
    778.2
  religious order
    984.3
Communion 998.6, 7
Communion table
  1000.3
communiqué 532.2
communism
  socialism 737.6
  collectivism 778.2
  public welfare 906.3
communist
  collectivist 778.4
  humanitarian 911.1
communistic 778.8
  (co-operative 709.7)
communitarian 778.4
community
  population 188.10
  people 372.2
  group 712.3
  religious order
    984.3
community of interest
  888.1
community theater
  599.10
communization 778.2
communize 778.6
commutability 148.2
commutation
  compensation 30.1
  substitution 147.1
  interchange 148.1
  compromise 774.1
  barter 794.1
commutative 148.4
commute
  substitute 147.3
  interchange 148.3
  compromise 774.2
commuter 268.1
commutual 12.6
commutuality 12.1
compact n. 769
  (agreement 23.4;
    709.3)
  (promise 768.1)
  (transaction 794.3)

make a **compact**
    769.7
compact v.
  contract 195.4
  densify 321.7
compact adj.
  joined 43.10
  crowded 72.13
  unific 87.9
  short 201.5
  (compendious
    596.5)
  close 261.6
  dense 321.8
  (coherent 46.9, 10)
  concise 572.3
compaction
  whole 50.1
  composition 54.1
  unity 87.1
  contraction 195.1
compages whole 50.1
  unity 87.1
  structure 161.7
compagination 43.1
companion n.
  analogue 17.5
  accompanier 88.3
  ship 273.7
  companionway 305.2
  confederate 711.1
  knight 726.4
  friend 890.3
companion v. 88.6
companionable 892.12
companionize 88.6
companion ladder
  273.7
companionless 87.8
companionship
  accompaniment 88.2
  fellowship 892.1
companionway
  ship 273.7
  stairs 305.2
company
  assemblage 72.3
  (clique 712.2)
  accompaniment
    88.2
  theater 599.18
  guild 712.5
  (association 709.2)
  (firm 797.10)
  military 726.7
  social 892.2
in **company with** 88.9
comparability 464.1
  (similarity 17.1)
comparable 464.6
  (approximative 9.7)
  (similar 17.10)
 be **comparable** 464.4
  (resemble 17.7)
 not **comparable**
  irrelative 10.5
  dissimilar 18.5
comparative
  degree 26.3
  parallelistic 464.5
  (approximative 9.7)

comparatively — compliment 768

comparative (cont'd)
  (metaphorical 521.3)
comparatively
  to a degree 32.13
  as compared 464.7
  (relatively 9.9)
compare 464.2, 4
  (relate 9.4)
  (differentiate 15.6)
  compare notes
    exchange views 464.3
    advise with 695.6
  not compare with 18.2
comparison 464
  (relation 9.1)
  (difference 15.1; 18.1)
  (similarity 17.1)
  beyond comparison 33.8
compartment
  section 51.5
  region 181.1
  cell 191.2
compass n.
  degree 26.1
  extent 180.1
  area 181.1
  distance 196.1
  aviation 267a.29
  ship 273.14
  circuity 311.1
  music 413.15
  measure 466.4
  sphere of work 625.3
  circuit 629.1
  guide 694.6
  within compass
    moderately 174.8
    short of 304.5
    temperate 953.6
compass v.
  surround 227.3
  (circumscribe 229.2)
  limit 233.2
  circuit 311.3
  complete 729.2
compass course 267a.20
compassion n. 914.1
  (lenity 740.1)
compassion, compassionate v. 914.3
compassionate adj. 914.6
  (lenient 740.4)
compatibility
  agreement 23.1
  (possibility 470.1)
  concord 714.1
compatible
  agreeing 23.9
  (possible 470.5)
  concordant 714.4
compatriot 188.7
  (friend 890.8)
compeer equal 27.5

companion 890.3
compel 744.2
  (necessitate 601.8)
  (require 630.2)
  (be serene 739.4)
  (restrain 751.6)
compellation 564.1, 2
compelling 744.3
compend 596.1
compendious
  short 201.5
  inclusive 76.5
  abridged 596.5
  (concise 572.3)
compendium list 86.1
  abstract 596
  (contraction 195.1)
  (abbreviation 201.2)
  (conciseness 572.1)
  (book 593.1)
  (outline 626.2)
compensate
  recompense 30.4
  (equalize 27.7)
  (repay 807.9)
  counteract 179.4
  make restitution 790.3
  atone 952.4
  reward 973.3
compensating 30.6
compensation
  recompense 30
  (equalization 27.3)
  (counteraction 179.1)
  (compromise 774.1)
  (repayment 807.3)
  reparation 660.4
  (retaliation 718.1)
  consideration 784.3
  restitution 790.1
  atonement 952.1
  remuneration 973.1
  penalty 974.1
  in compensation 30.7
  (contrarily 14.7)
  make compensation
    compensate 30.4
    atone 952.4
compensatory
  compensating 30.6
  indemnificatory 790.5
  remunerative 973.5
compete 720.9
  (encounter 708.3)
competence
  ability 157.2
  sufficiency 639.1
  skill 698.1
competent able 157.9
  adequate 639.6
  effectual 644.7
  skillful 698.12
competition 720.1
  (opposition 708.1)
competitive 720.13
  (oppositional 708.4)
competitor
  opponent 710.4
  combatant 726.1

candidate 767.1
compilation
  composition 54.2
  collection 72.7
  book 593.2
  (excerpts 596.2)
  (anthology 597.4)
compile
  compose 54.4
  assemble 72.11
compiler 593.15
complacency
  obedience 743.1
  content 831.1
  courtesy 894.1
complacent
  courteous 894.12
  benevolent 906.6
complain 839.10
  (fret 828.10)
  (censure 932.7)
complain of 655.21
complainant 938.2
  (informer 527.6)
complainer 832.2
complaining 839.13
complaint
  ailment 655.1
  lamentation 839.1
  (discontent 832.1)
  accusation 938.1
complaisance 894.1
complaisant
  submissive 725.5
  lenient 740.4
  obedient 743.3
  courteous 894.12
  (benevolent 906.6)
complanate 251.5
complanation 251.1
complected 428.13
complection, complectioned See complexion etc.
complement
  analogue 17.5
  adjunct 39.1
  supplement 52.5
  number 84.2
complemental, complementary 12.6
complete v.
  accomplish 729.2
  (end 67.7)
  (effect 154.2)
  (produce 161.8)
  (perfect 650.4)
  (do 680.6)
  (succeed 731.5)
  settle 769.8
  (execute 771.7)
complete adj.
  absolute 31.12
  entire 52.9
  (whole 50.6)
  (perfect 650.5)
  completed 729.6
  render complete 52.7
completed 729.6
  (ended 67.9)
  (perfect 650.5)
completely 52.13

  (wholly 50.10)
  (perfectly 650.6)
completeness 52
  (whole 50.1)
  (unity 87.1)
completing
  completive 52.12
  finishing 729.5
  (ending 67.8)
completion
  accomplishment 729
  (end 67.1)
  (production 161.1)
  (arrival 292.1)
  settlement 769.3
completive 52.12; 729.5
complex n. 50.2
complex adj. 59.10
  (convoluted 248.4)
  (perplexing 475.12)
  (obscure 519.7)
  (enigmatic 533.6)
  (difficult 704.8)
complexion, complection state 7.1
  color 428.1, 9
  aspect 448.4
complexioned, complectioned 428.13
complexity 59.3
  (network 219.4)
  (convolution 248.1)
  (unintelligibility 519.1)
  (enigma 533.2)
  (imperspicuity 571.1)
  (dilemma 704.4)
compliance
  submission 725.1
  (conformity 82.1)
  obedience 743.1
  consent 762.1
  (willingness 602.1)
  observance 772.1
  civility 894.1
  in compliance with 743.4
compliant
  willing 602.8
  manageable 705.6
  submissive 725.5
  (conformable 82.8)
  (dutiful 926.8)
  obedient 743.3
  (servile 886.4)
  consenting 762.3
complicate 61.5
  (obscure 519.4)
complicated 59.10
  (difficult 704.8)
complication
  complexity 59.3
  predicament 704.2
complice 711.3
complicity 709.1
compliment n. 931.3
  (flattery 933.1)
  return the compliment

compliment — conceited

reciprocate 148.3
retaliate 718.2
compliment v.
  congratulate 896.2
  praise 931.6
  (flatter 933.2)
complimentary
  gratuitous 815.10
  approbatory 931.9
  (flattering 933.3)
compliments
  kind regards 894.3
  congratulations 896.1
complin, compline 990.7
complot n. 626.6
complot v. 626.10
comply conform 82.4
  submit 725.3
  obey 743.2
  consent 762.2
  (be willing 602.6)
  observe 772.3
compo
  composition 41.4
  plaster 223.19
component n. 56
  (member 51.4)
  be a component 56.2
component adj. 56.3
  (inclusive 76.5)
comport
  ~ with 23.7
  ~ oneself 692.5
comportment 692.1
compose
  constitute 54.4
  (be a component 56.2)
  arrange 60.6
  include 76.3
  conform 82.4
  produce 161.8
  moderate 174.5
  quiet 265.6
  ~ music 415.26
  (melodize 413.25)
  author 590.14
  ~ type 591.14
  ~ poetry 597.11
  ~ oneself 826.8
composed 826.9, 11
  be composed 826.5
composer
  ~ of music 416.14
  ~ of poetry 597.10
composing room 591.11
composing rule, composing stick 591.5
composite 41.9
composition
  mixture 41.4
  (compound 48.2)
  constitution 54
  (inclusion 76.1)
  production 161.1, 6
  plaster 223.19
  art 556.5, 8
  diction 569.1
  writing 590.2, **3**

typesetting 591.1
compromise 774.1
barter 794.1
atonement 952.1
compositor 591.12
compos mentis 502.5
compossibility 470.1
compossible 470.5
compost 653.7
composure
  quiescence 265.1
  calmness 826.2
  (restraint 751.1)
compotation
  drinking 298.**3**
  tippling 959.1
compote 298.12
compound n.
  mixture 41.4
  (composition 54.1)
  yard 232.1
compound v. join 43.5
  ~ for 147.3
  produce 161.8
  (prepare 673.6)
  compromise 774.2
comprador, compradore 637.2
comprehend
  include 76.3
  know 490.9
  understand 518.4
comprehensibility 518.1
comprehensible
  knowable 490.18
  intelligible 518.5
comprehension
  inclusion 76.1
  (composition 54.1)
  knowledge 490.1
  understanding 498.1
  past comprehension 519.6
comprehensive
  thorough 52.10
  inclusive 76.5
  universal 78.11
  sizable 192.11
compress n. 662.14
compress v.
  contract 195.4
  (shorten 201.4)
  (reduce 36.4)
  condense 321.7
compressed 572.3
compressibility
  contractibility 195.2
  rarity 322.1
compression
  contraction 195.1
  (shortening 201.2)
  (narrowing 203.2)
  (conciseness 572.1)
  (compendium 596.3)
  condensation 321.3
comprisal, comprizal 76.1
comprise, comprize
  compose 54.5
  include 76.3
  be comprised in 1.6

compromise n.
  arbitration 723.1
  mutual concession 774
  (mean 29.1)
  (compensation 30.1)
  (mid-course 628.1)
  (adjustment 769.3)
  atonement 952.1
compromise v.
  jeopardize 665.4
  compound 774.2
  (steer a middle course 628.2)
  (adjust 769.8)
compromised 768.7
  (obliged 926.10)
Compsognathus 124.2
comptometer 85.5
comptroller
  director 694.1
  master 745.1
compulsion 744
  (necessity 601.1)
  (unwillingness 603.3)
  (requirement 630.1)
  (despotism 739.2)
  (restraint 751.1)
compulsorily 744.4
  (of necessity 601.15)
compulsory 744.3
  (severe 739.5)
  (restraining 751.13)
  (necessary 601.11)
  (requisite 630.3)
  (authoritative 737.15)
compunction 950.1
  (regret 833.1)
compurgation
  testimony 467.2
  vindication 970.1
compurgator 467.6
computable
  numerable 85.11
  measurable 466.12
computation
  calculation 37.2
  numeration 85.1
  (estimation 466.1)
  (accountancy 811.4)
compute 37.5; 85.7
  (estimate 466.10)
  (keep accounts 811.7)
comrade 890.3
  (associate 711.1)
comradeship
  fellowship 709.2
  companionship 892.1
  (friendship 888.1)
Comus 992.2
con n. 754.1
con v. ponder 451.27
  memorize 505.13
  study 539.4
con v. See **conn**
con amore 602.11
conation

tendency 176.1
will 600.1
conative
  operative 170.4
  volitional 600.4
conatus 176.1
concamerate
  arch 245.3
  convex 250.7
concameration 215.18; 245.1, **2**
concatenation
  junction 43.1
  continuity 69.1
concave n. 252.8
concave v. 252.9
concave adj. 252.10
  (curved 245.4)
  be concave 252.8
concavity 252.2
conceal hide 528.10
  (cover 223.22)
  (blind 442.3)
  (render invisible 447.3)
  (latentize 526.5)
  (make a pretext 619.2)
  disguise 544.6
concealed blind 442.6
  hidden 528.17
  (invisible 447.4)
  (unknown 491.14)
  (latent 526.6)
  (secluded 893.10)
  be concealed 528.16
  (be invisible 447.2)
  (be latent 526.3)
concealment
  hiding 528
  (mask 225.11)
  (screen 424.3)
  (invisibility 447.1)
  (latency 526.1)
  (dissimulation 544.2)
  (disguise 545.5)
  (pretext 619.1)
  (cunning 702.1)
  (seclusion 893.2)
  hiding place 530.**2**
  (cover 223.2)
concede
  allow for 469.4
  acknowledge 488.9
  confess 529.5
  consent 762.2
  (be induced 615.10)
  give 784.11
conceded 488.14
conceit idea 453.1
  folly 499.6
  eccentricity 503.6
  fancy 515.1, 4
  caprice 608.1
  witticism 842.4, **5**
  foppery 853.3
  vanity 880.1
  (overestimation 482.1)
conceited
  opinionated 606.7

conceivability — concubitancy

conceited (*continued*)
  foppish 853.6
  vain 880.6
  (boastful 884.7)
conceivability
  possibility 470.1
  believability 484.5
  intelligibility 518.1
conceivable
  possible 470.5
  believable 484.15
  imaginable 515.15
  understandable 518.5
conceive
  originate 66.6
  be pregnant 168.6
  believe 484.8
  know 490.9
  suppose 514.6
  imagine 515.8
  understand 518.4
concent 413.1
concenter, concentre
  centralize 222.3
  converge 290.2
concentive 413.26
concento 413.9
concentralization
  centrality 222.1
  convergence 290.1
concentralize
  centralize 222.3
  converge 290.2
concentrate
  collect 72.10, 11
  contract 195.4
  centralize 222.3
  (focus 74.3)
  converge 290.2
  ponder 451.27
concentration
  accumulation 72.6
  contraction 195.1
  convergence 290.1
  (centrality 222.1)
  close attention 457.2
concentre See **concenter**
concentric
  parallel 216.5
  central 222.4
concentricity 216.1
concentual
  agreeing 23.9
  harmonious 413.26
  unanimous 488.12
concentus
  consensus 23.5
  attunement 413.1
concept 453.1
conception
  pregnancy 168.2
  mental faculty 450.1
  idea 453.1
  opinion 484.2
  creative thought 515.1
concern *n.*
  relation 9.1
  matter 151.1, 2
  care 459.1
  business 625.1
  importance 642.1
  company 712.5
  anxiety 828.5
  fearfulness 860.2
concern *v.*
  be related 9.3
  employ 625.6
concern oneself
  busy oneself 625.7
  meddle 682.14
not concern 10.3
concerning 9.10
concert *n.*
  agreement 23.1
  concurrence 178.1
  concord 413.1
  musicale 415.17
  (entertainment 840.2)
  band 417.1
  unanimity 488.3
  co-operation 709.1
in concert with
  co-operatively 709.8
  concordantly 714.5
concert *v.*
  harmonize 413.24
  orchestrate 415.26
  concertize 416.18
  plan 626.9
  co-operate 709.4
concert *adj.* 415.28
concertante 415.3
concert dance 840.7
concertgoer 416.15
concert grand 417.6
concert hall
  auditorium 189.10
  theater 599.10
concertina 417.4
concertinist 416.2
concertino 415.3
concertist 416.1
concertize 416.18
concertmaster, concertmeister 416.13
concert music, concerto, concertstück 415.3
concession
  qualification 469.1
  confession 529.2
  permission 760.1
  consent 762.1
  giving 784.1
  discount 813.1
concessional
  allowable 784.14
  discounting 813.3
conch shell 223.16
  music instrument 417.4
  ear 418.5
concha arch 215.18
  ear 418.5
conchate, conchiform 245.18
conchoid 245.2
conchoidal 245.18
conchology 223.21
concierge 717.6
conciliate
  win over 615.9
  pacify 723.4
  (mediate 724.3)
  satisfy 831.4
  be courteous 894.7
conciliation
  pacification 723.1
  (mediation 724.1)
  atonement 952.1
conciliatory
  pacificatory 723.6
  (concordant 714.4)
  courteous 894.12
  forgiving 918.5
  atoning 952.6
concinnate 578.4
concinnity
  agreement 23.1
  elegant style 578.1
  beauty 845.1
concise terse 572.3
  (short 201.5)
  (compendious 596.5)
  taciturn 585.4
be concise 572.2
concisely 572.4
  (briefly 111.9)
conciseness
  laconism 572
  (contraction 195.1)
  (shortness 201.1)
  (compendium 596.3)
  pauciloquy 585.1
concision 201.2
conclave 696.2, 3
  (conference 588.3)
conclude end 67.5
  think likely 472.3
  judge 480.6
  suppose 514.6
  decide 604.6
  settle 769.8
concluding 729.5
conclusion sequel 65.1
  end 67.1
  final issue 154.1
  judgment 480.1
  (conviction 484.2)
  completion 729.1
  settlement 769.3
in conclusion 476.20
conclusive final 67.8
  ended 67.9
  answering 462.11
  evidential 467.11
  decisive 474.10
  (demonstrative 478.3)
  (manifest 525.4)
  completive 729.5
  mandatory 741.8
conclusively 67.11
conclusiveness 478.1
conclusory 67.8
concoct produce 161.8
  imagine 515.10
  trump up 544.3
  devise 626.9
concoction
  composition 54.2
  production 161.1, 6
  (preparation 673.1)
  lie 546.1
concomitance
  accompaniment 88.1
  synchronism 120.1
  concurrence 178.1
concomitant *n.* 88.1
concomitant *adj.*
  accompanying 88.8
  synchronous 120.4
  concurrent 178.4
concord
  agreement 23.1
  chord 413.9
  (music 415.1)
  unanimity 488.3
  harmony 714
  (peace 721.1)
  (friendship 888.1)
in concord 413.26
concordance
  agreement 23.1
  (concurrence 178.1)
  music 413.1
  unanimity 488.3
  book 593.3
  concord 714.1
concordant
  agreeing 23.9
  (concurrent 178.4)
  music 413.26
  unanimous 488.12
  harmonious 714.4
  (pacific 721.4)
  (pacificatory 723.6)
  (friendly 888.4)
be concordant 714.2
concordantly 714.5
  (unanimously 488.17)
  (in concert 709.8)
concordat 769.2
Concord buggy 272.4
concordia discors 414.1
concourse
  junction 43.1
  assemblage 72.1
  convergence 290.1
  council 696.2
concremation 384.3
concrete *n.*
  plaster 223.19
  solid 321.4
  (conglomerate 46.4)
  hardness 323.3
  pavement 627.4
concrete *v.* 321.7
concrete *adj.* 323.5
concreteness 3.1
concretion
  coherence 46.1
  solid 321.3, 4
concubinage 903.2; 961.6
concubine 962.3
  (wife 903.8)
concubitancy 903.1

concubitous — configuration

concubitous 903.15
concupiscence
 desire 865.2, 6
 sexual lust 961.3
concupiscent 961.11
concur
 accompany 88.6
 synchronize 120.3
 coact 178.2
 (agree 23.7)
 converge 290.2
 (focus 74.3)
 assent 488.7
 (consent 762.2)
 co-operate 709.4
concurrence
 junction 43.1
 synchronism 120.1
 coaction 178
 (agreement 23.1, 5)
 (assent 488.1)
 convergence 290.1
 unanimity 488.3
 co-operation 709.1
 observance 772.1
concurrent
 joined 43.10
 synchronous 120.4
 coactive 178.4
 (agreeing 23.9)
 (co-operative 709.7)
 parallel 216.5
 converging 290.3
 unanimous 488.12
concurrently 178.5
concussion
 shock 173.4
 clash 276.2
cond See conn
condemn
 censure 932.7
 blame 938.4
 convict 971.2
 (judge 480.9)
condemnation
 censure 932.2
 blame 938.1
 conviction 971
condemnatory
 censorious 932.11
 accusatory 938.5
 damnatory 971.4
condemned 971.5
condensation
 contraction 195.1
 shortening 201.2
 densification 321.3
 (precipitation 40.2)
 compendium 596.1
condense
 shorten 201.4
 (be concise 572.2)
 (abridge 596.4)
 densify 321.7
condensed 572.3
condescend 878.3
condescendence 878.1
condescending 878.6
condescension 878.1
condescensive 878.6
condign 924.11

condiment 393
 (food 298.5)
condisciple 541.7
condition n. state 7.1
 (predicament 8.3)
 (order 58.1)
 qualification 469.2
 hypothesis 514.1
 stipulation 770
 rank 873.4
on condition
 provided 8.8; 469.8
 (conditionally 469.7; 769.4)
condition v.
 limit 233.2
 stipulate 770.2
conditional n. 514.1
conditional adj.
 modal 7.3
 circumstantial 8.5
 (provisional 637.7)
 qualifying 469.6
 dependent 475.15
 hypothetical 476.17
 stipulatory 770.3
conditionally
 provisionally 7.4;
  770.4
 allowedly 469.7
 (if possible 470.8)
conditioned 32.7
conditions 770
condole 915.2
 (sympathize 914.3)
condolence 915
send one's condolences 915.2
condonation 918.1
condone 918.3
conduce
 contribute 153.8
 tend 176.2
 (serve 644.2; 707.10)
 concur 178.2
conducement
 tendency 176.1
 aid 707.1
conducive
 tending 176.3
 (useful 644.5; 677.8)
 (aiding 707.12)
 instrumental 631.4
conduciveness 176.1
conduct n. usage 677.2
 behavior 692
 (action 680.1)
 direction 693.1, 2
conduct v.
 escort 88.7
 (precede 280.2)
 carry 270.8
 direct 278.4
 ~ music 416.22
 carry on 692.4
 (officiate 625.9)
 ~ oneself 692.5
 direct 693.4
conduction
 motion 264.1
 transportation 270.2

conductional, conductive 270.11
conductor escort 88.4
 electricity 158a.8
 railroad 268.12
 carrier 271.1
 music 416.13
 director 694.1, 6
conduit 350
 (tunnel 252.3)
 (trench 259.2)
 (inlet 294.5)
 (outlet 295.5)
 (passage 302.1)
 (passageway 627.2)
conduplicate v. 89.3
conduplicate adj. 89.4
condyle 250.2
cone 249.4
conelike 249.9
cone pulley 307.2
cone-shaped 249.9
 (concave 252.10)
Conestoga wagon,
Conestoga wain
 272.3
confab, confabulate v.
 588.7
confabulation 588.1, 3
confabulator 588.5
confabulatory 588.10
confection
 composition 54.1
 clothes 225.4
 sweet 396.2
 medicine 662.4
confectioner 797.11
confectionery
 sweets 396.2
 mart 799.4
confederacy
 co-operation 709.1
 association 709.2
 society 712.4
confederate n. 711.1, 3
Confederate n. 712.6
confederate v. 48.4
 (co-operate 709.4)
confederate, confederated adj. 48.6
confederation
 association 709.2
 society 712.4
confer parley 588.8
 bestow 784.8
 (deliver 783.3)
 ~ an honor 873.13
 confer with 695.6
conference
 hearing 418.2
 parley 588.3
 (consultation 695.2)
 council 696.2, 3
conferential 588.10
conferment
 bestowment 784.1
 holy orders 995.6
conferrer 784.7
conferva, confervoid
 n. 367.3
confervoid adj. 367.16

confess
 acknowledge 488.9
 admit a mistake
  495.10
 unbosom 529.5
 (tell the truth 543.2)
 (repent 950.3)
 shrive 998.14
confession belief 484.4
 acknowledgment
  488.2
 shrift 529.2
 (penitence 950.1)
 make confession
  998.14
confessional n.
 confession 529.2
 rite 998.2
 confession stall
  1000.3
confessional adj.
 529.8
confessionary n.
 confessional 529.2
 rite 998.2
confessionary adj.
 529.8
confessions 594.2
confessor 996.2
confessory 529.8
confidant 890.1
 (associate 711.1)
confide trust 484.7
 entrust 784.12
 hope 858.6
confidence
 certainty 474.1
 belief 484.1
 expectation 507.2
 private matter 533.1
 hope 858.1
 (security 664.1)
 courage 861.1
 have confidence in
  484.7
 in confidence 528.25
confidence game 545.3
 (swindle 791.5)
confidence man
 cheat 548.2
 swindler 792.8
confident n. 890.1
confident adj.
 assured 474.9
 convinced 484.12
 emphatic 535.6
 hopeful 858.9
 fearless 861.8
 feel confident 858.6
confidential
 reliable 484.15
 secret 528.21
confidentially 528.25
confidential communication 533.1
confiding
 trustful 484.13
 (credulous 486.5)
 artless 703.4
configuration
 outline 230.1

confine — Congressional medal

configuration (cont'd)
  form 240.1
  constellation 318.6
confine n. edge 231.1
  enclosure 232.1, 2
confine v.
  circumscribe 229.2
  limit 233.2
  restrain 751.8
  (intern 221.8)
confined special 79.7
  narrow 203.9
  bigoted 606.7
  sick 655.23
  imprisoned 751.12
confinement
  birth 161.3
  circumscription 229.1
  restraint 751.2
in confinement 751.12
confines region 181.1
  edge 231.1
  (purlieus 197.3)
  bounds 233.1
confirm
  stabilize 150.4
  corroborate 467.9
  (affirm 535.3)
  make certain 474.6
  demonstrate 478.2
  ratify 488.10
  (settle 769.9)
  impose 998.14
confirmation
  corroboration 467.3
  (affirmation 535.1)
  certification 474.2
  demonstration 478.1
  ratification 488.4
  (contract 769.4)
  sacrament 998.3
confirmatory 467.11
confirmed
  established 150.5
  inveterate 613.12
confiscate take 789.11
  sequestrate 974.3
confiscation
  dispossession 789.2
  sequestration 974.2
confiture 396.3
conflagrant 384.22
conflagrate 384.17
conflagration
  fire 382.8
  burning 384.3
conflagrative 162.6
conflagrator 384.6
conflation 54.2
conflict n.
  contrariety 14.1
  counteraction 179.1
  opposition 708.1
  (disagreement 24.1)
  discord 713.1
  contention 720.1, 2
  (attack 716.1)
  (battle 722.5)
  hostility 889.1
in conflict with 708.5
conflict v. differ 15.5

disagree 24.5
counteract 179.3
intrude 228.10
~ with evidence 468.2
disaccord 713.6
be unfriendly 889.2
conflicting
  contrary 14.5
  counteractive 179.5
  opposing 708.4
  adverse 735.8
confluence
  junction 43.1
  convergence 290.1
  flow 348.2
confluent 290.3
conflux
  assemblage 72.1
  convergence 290.1
confluxible, confocal 290.3
conform
  agree 23.7
  adapt 82.4, 5
  (be uniform 16.3)
  (agree 23.7)
  (be wont 613.10)
  (be fashionable 852.6)
  concur 488.7
conformable
  agreeing 23.9
  (concurrent 178.4)
  adaptable 82.8, 9
  (uniform 16.5)
  (regular 80.3)
  (customary 613.11)
  (compliant 725.5)
  (conventional 852.8)
  (orthodox 983a.7)
  ~ to law 963.5
conformably 82.12
conformance
  agreement 23.1
  conformity 82.1
conformation
  agreement 23.1
  conformity 82.1
  production 161.1
  formation 240.1, 3
conformist 82.3
conformity
  agreement 23.1
  (concurrence 178.1)
  adaptation 82
  (uniformity 16.1)
  (custom 613.2)
  (compliance 725.1)
  (convention 852.2)
  (orthodoxy 983a.1)
  symmetry 242.1
  truth 494.1
  accuracy 494.3
in conformity with 82.12
confound v.
  complicate 61.5
  destroy 162.4
  confuse 458.9

be indiscriminate 465a.2
perplex 475.8
confute 479.2
frustrate 706.7
defeat 731.10
astonish 870.3
curse 908.4
confound int. 908.7
confounded 649.8
confoundedly 31.24
confraternity
  association 709.2
  fraternal order 712.3
  fellowship 888.1
confrere
  confederate 711.1
  friend 890.3
confront front 234.7
  oppose 237.5; 708.3
  compare 464.2
  resist 719.3
confrontment 464.1
Confucianism 984.11
Confucianist 984.21
Confucius 500.1; 986.3
confuse
  complicate 61.5
  (obscure 519.4)
  daze 443.13
  distract 458.9
  be indiscriminate 465a.2
  perplex 475.8
  (render unintelligible 519.4)
confused
  disorderly 59.6
  (misinterpreted 523.3)
  (imperspicuous 571.2)
  indistinct 447.5
  distracted 458.12
  uncertain 475.11
confusion
  disorder 59.2
  (mixture 41.4)
  (formlessness 241.2)
  (imperspicuity 571.1)
  distraction 458.4
  perplexity 475.2
in confusion
  disorderly 59.13
  excitably 825.12
confutable 479.4
confutation 479
  (answer 462.1)
  (negation 536.1)
  (pleadings 969.6)
confutative 479.3
  (countervailing 468.3)
  (negatory 536.3)
confute 479.2
  (answer 462.5)
  (countervail 468.2)
  (dispute 536.2)
con game 545.3

congé departure 293.1
  dismissal 297.4
  ornament 847.4
congeal 321.7
  thicken 321.7
  freeze 385.4
congelation
  coherence 46.1
  refrigeration 385.1
congener n. 17.5
congener, congeneric adj. 9.6
congenerous
  related 9.6
  (included 76.4)
  connatural 17.13
congenial
  agreeing 23.9
  concordant 714.4
congeniality
  agreement 23.1
  concord 714.1
congenital 5.6
congeries, congestion 72.6
congestive fever 655.4
conglaciate 385.4
cong'obation 72.6
conglomerate n.
  accumulation 72.6
  solid 321.4
conglomerate v.
  cohere 46.8
  assemble 72.10
  (solidify 321.7)
conglomeration
  coherence 46.1
  accumulation 72.6
  solid 321.4
conglutinate 46.7
conglutination 46.1
Congoleum 223.8
Congo tobacco 663.6
  (tobacco 392a.1)
congratulate 896.2
  congratulate oneself
  rejoice 838.5
  be proud 878.4
  boast 884.5
congratulation 896
congratulatory 896.3
congregate 72.10
congregation
  assemblage 72.1
  (worshipers 990.8)
  audience 418.8
  council 696.2, 3
  laity 997.1
congregational 997.4
Congregationalist 984.14
Congreso Nacional 696.4
congress
  assembly 72.2
  convergence 290.1
  conference 588.3
  council 696.2, 4
congressional 696.9
Congressional medal 733.2

Congressional Record 551.2
congressman 696.8
  (statesman 694.4)
  (official 745.9)
Congreve 388.5
congruence 23.1
congruent 23.9
congruity
  agreement 23.1
  (conformity 82.1)
  symmetry 242.1
congruous
  agreeing 23.9
  colors 428.18
conical 249.9
conifer 369.8
coniferous 369.11
coniform 249.9
conjecturable 514.10
conjectural 514.9
conjecturality 514.3
conjecture n. 514.1
conjecture v. 514.6
conjecturer 514.5
conjoin join 43.5
  be contiguous 199.3
conjoint joined 43.10
  combined 48.5
conjointly 43.14
  (together 88.10)
conjugal 903.14
conjugate v. 567.5
conjugate adj.
  combined 48.5
  coupled 89.5
  etymological 562.9
conjugation
  junction 43.1
  pair 89.2
  contiguity 199.1
  grammar 567.1
  association 709.2
conjunct 43.10
conjunction
  junction 43.1
  concurrence 178.1
  contiguity 199.1
  part of speech 567.2
  association 709.2
in conjunction
  ~ ~ with 37.9
  jointly 43.14
  with 88.9, 10
conjunctive
  connective 43.13
  combined 48.5
  unific 87.9
conjunctivitis 655.8
conjuncture
  occasion 8.2
  junction 43.1
  crisis 134.4
  association 709.2
conjuration
  adjuration 765.2
  incantation 992.1
  (delusion 545.2)
  charm 993.1
conjure deceive 545.7
  entreat 765.5
  exorcise 992.4

conjure up
  remember 505.10
  imagine 515.8, 9
conjuror 992.2
  (legerdemainist 548.6)
conk head 210.3
  nose 250.4
con man cheat 548.2
  swindler 792.8
conn, cond 267.11
connate intrinsic 5.6
  related 9.6
  consanguine 11.7
  original 153.9
connatural related 9.6
  uniform 16.5
  corresponding 17.13
  (akin 11.7)
connaturalness 17.2
  (consanguinity 11.1)
  (identity 13.1)
connature
  uniformity 16.1
  similarity 17.2
connect be related 9.3
  relate 9.4
  (compare 464.2)
  join 43.5
  be contiguous 199.3
connected 9.6
become connected
  with 712.8
connecting 87.9
connecting rod 272.16
connection, connexion
  relation 9.1
  kinsman 11.3
  junction 43.1, 3
  (fastening 45.2)
  bond 45.1
  coherence 46.1
  kind 75.2
  contiguity 199.1
  mediator 724.2
  deputy 759.1
in connection with 9.10
  (by the way 134.11)
connectional, connexional 87.9
connective n. 45.1
connective adj.
  conjunctive 43.13
  unific 87.9
  comparative 464.5
conning tower 273.7
conniption 900.2
connivance
  deception 545.1
  toleration 760.1
connivant
  deceptive 545.12
  scheming 702.6
connive
  disregard 460.4
  tolerate 760.3
  not observe 773.3
  condone 918.3
connivent 286.3
conniving

deceptive 545.12
  scheming 702.6
  knavish 940.8
connoisseur
  critic 480.5
  scholar 492.1
  expert 700.1
  epicure 850.3
connotate 550.18
connotation
  meaning 516.1
  indication 550.1
connotative 550.21
connote denote 467.7
  mean 516.5
  (imply 526.4)
  indicate 550.18
connubial 903.14
conoid n. 249.4
conoid adj. 249.9
conquer 731.9
conquerable 158.9
conquered 732.12
conqueror 731.4
conquest victory 731.3
  subjugation 749.1
conquistador 731.4
cons 476.3
consanguine n. 11.3
consanguine adj. 11.7
consanguineous 11.7
  (related 9.6)
  (connatural 17.13)
consanguinity 11
  (relation 9.1)
  (connaturalness 17.2)
  (ancestry 166.1)
conscience
  knowledge 490.1
  sense of duty 926.3
  (conscientiousness 939.2)
conscience-smitten,
  conscience-stricken 950.5
conscientious
  copy 21.5
  scrupulous 939.8
  (careful 459.7)
  (precise 494.11)
  (particular 868.4)
  (ethical 926.12)
  (just 941.3)
conscientiousness 939.2
  (care 459.1)
  (particularity 868.1)
  (conscience 926.3)
conscientious objector 721.7
conscionable 939.8
conscious 490.12, 13
  (sensible 375.6)
be conscious of 450.7
consciousness
  intellect 450.1
  knowledge 490.1
  (sensation 375.2)
conscript n. 726.5
conscript v. 744.2

conscription 744.1
consecrate
  devote 677.5
  dedicate 873.13
  sanctify 987.8
  ordain 995.7
consecrated 987.11
consecration
  glorification 873.6
  sanctification 987.2
  ordination 995.6
Consecration 998.7
consecution
  sequence 63.1
  continuity 69.1
consecutive
  continuous 69.6
  (successive 63.5)
  later 117.3
consecutively
  continuously 69.7
  gradually 275.11
consecutiveness
  sequence 63.1
  continuity 69.1
consension 23.5; 488.3
consensual
  agreeing 23.9
  unanimous 488.12
consensus 488.3
consent n.
  unanimity 488.3
  (concurrence 178.1)
  acquiescence 762
  (assent 488.1)
  (willingness 602.1)
  (permission 760.1)
  (promise 768.1)
  (approval 931.1)
with one consent 488.12, 17
consent v.
  concur 488.7
  not refuse 762.2
  (assent 488.6)
  (be willing 602.6)
  (be induced 615.10)
  (permit 760.3)
  (promise 768.3)
  (approve 931.5)
consentaneity 23.5; 488.3
consentaneous
  agreeing 23.9
  concurrent 178.4
consentaneousness 23.5
consentant 762.3
consenter 488.5
consentience 488.3
consentient
  agreeing 23.9
  unanimous 488.12
  consenting 762.3
consenting 762.3
  (assenting 488.11)
  (willing 602.8)
  (permissive 760.6)
consentive
  agreeing 23.9
  consenting 762.3

consequence — constitute

consequence
  greatness 31.2
  effect 154.1
  (sequel 65.1)
  (eventuality 151.1)
  influence 175.1
  importance 642.1
  authority 737.2
  eminence 873.3
  take the consequences 972.12
consequent n. 154.1
consequent adj.
  succeeding 63.5
  resultant 154.6
consequential
  resultant 154.6
  deducible 478.5
  important 642.10
  (distinguishable 873.16)
  arrogant 885.8
consequently 154.7
  (accordingly 8.7)
  (hence 155.5)
  (demonstrably 478.6)
conservate 670.3
conservation
  permanence 141.1
  preservation 670.1
  (storing 636.6)
conservatism 141.2
  (bigotry 606.2)
  (preservation 670.1)
conservatist, conservative n. 141.3
  (irreconcilable 606.3)
Conservative n. 712.6
conservative adj.
  unchanging 141.7
  preservative 670.5
  be conservative 141.5
conservatoire 542.1
conservatory n.
  greenhouse 371.6
  (bower 191.22)
  (hothouse 386.5)
  school 542.1
  store 636.4
conservatory adj. 670.5
conserve n.
  preserve 396.3
  medicine 662.4
conserve v. 670.3
consider
  think over 451.29
  (give attention 457.4)
  take heed of 459.5
  study 461.17
  judge 480.6
  think 484.8
  suppose 514.6
  stop to consider
    be uncertain 475.6
    be irresolute 605.4
considerable n. 31.3
considerable adj.
  great 31.6
  numerous 102.5
  sizable 192.11
  important 642.10
considerable, considerably adv. 31.15
considerate
  careful 459.7
  (thoughtful 451.35)
  judicious 498.11
  benevolent 906.6
consideration
  equivalent 147.2
  thought 451.1
  (examination 461.3)
  (dissertation 595.1)
  idea 453.1
  attention 457.1
  qualification 469.1
  estimation 480.2
  motive 615.1
  importance 642.1
  gift 784.3
  payment 807.2
  benevolence 906.1
  respect 928.1
  recompense 973.1
  be under consideration 457.6
  in consideration of
    in compensation 30.7; 973.6
    since 155.8
    provided 469.8
  take into consideration
    include 76.3
    bear in mind 457.4
    discriminate 465.2
  under consideration
    in question 461.26
    planned 626.11
    (in preparation 673.13)
considered 611.6
  all things considered
    considering 451.39
    if possible 470.8
    probably 472.7
    on the whole 480.14
considering 155.8
consign send 270.9
  appoint 609.11
  ~ to prison 751.9
  commission 755.4
  ~ property 783.3
  entrust 784.12
consignation 783.1
consignee 758
  (transferee 270.5)
consignificant 516.11
consignment
  appointment 609.5
  commission 755.1
  ~ of property 783.1
  giving 784.1
  apportionment 786.1
consilience 178.1
consilient 178.4
consimilarity 17.1
consist be 1.6
  be composed of 54.3
consistence
  uniformity 16.1
  symmetry 242.1
consistency
  uniformity 16.1
  agreement 23.1
  unity 87.1
  symmetry 242.1
  density 321.1
consistent
  uniform 16.5
  agreeing 23.9
  (conformable 82.8)
  be consistent 23.7
consistently 82.12
consistory 696.3
consociate n.
  confederate 711.1
  friend 890.3
consociate v.
  league 48.4
  keep company 892.9
consociation 892.1
consolation
  solace 834.2
  condolence 915.1
  religious ~ 976.6
consolatory 834.7
console n.
  support 215.11, 17
  table 215.20
console v. solace 834.5
  condole 915.1
consolidate join 43.5
  combine 48.3
  condense 321.7
  (agglomerate 46.8)
consolidation
  junction 43.1
  coherence 46.1
  condensation 321.3
  association 709.2
consommé 298.16
consonance
  uniformity 16.1
  agreement 23.1
  attunement 413.1
consonant n. 402.2
  (letter 561.1)
consonant adj.
  agreeing 23.9
  harmonious 413.26
  colors 428.18
consonate 413.24
consort n.
  accompanier 88.3
  confederate 711.1
  friend 890.3
  spouse 903.5
consort v. agree 23.7
  accompany 88.6
  keep company 892.9
consortship 892.1
conspectus 596.1
  (outline 230.1; 626.2)
conspicuous
  distinct 446.5
  manifest 525.5
  (gaudy 851.8)
  eminent 642.10
  famous 873.16
conspicuousness
  visibility 446.1
  manifestness 525.1
conspiracy plot 626.6
  complicity 709.1
conspiracy of silence 460.1
conspirator 626.8
conspire concur 178.2
  plot 626.10
  (maneuver 702.5)
  co-operate 709.4
conspirer 626.8
constable 745.9, 10
  (detective 528.9)
constablewick, constabulary
  jurisdiction 737.4
  sheriffwick 745.10
  bureau 965.2
constancy
  regularity 16.2
  durability 110.1
  permanence 141.1
  stability 150.1
  (resolution 604.1)
  accuracy 494.3
  perseverance 604a.1
  (frequency 136.1)
  observance 772.2
  faithfulness 939.4
constant
  uniform 16.5
  (regular 80.3; 138.9)
  continuous 69.6
  (monotonous 104.7)
  durable 110.9
  perpetual 112.4
  continual 136.4
  unchanged 141.6
  (unchangeable 150.7)
  accurate 494.11
  persistent 604a.3
  observant 772.5
  faithful 939.10
  be constant 143.2
constantly
  invariably 16.7
  continually 136.6
  (perpetually 112.5)
  (habitually 613.13)
constellation
  stars 318.6
  elite 873.9
consternation 860.1
constipate 321.7
constipated 321.8
constipation
  closure 261.1
  costiveness 321.1
  ailment 655.13
constituency
  electorate 609.4
  clique 712.2
constituent n.
  component 56.1
  voter 609.4
constituent adj. 56.3
constitute
  compose 54.4
  (be a component 56.2)
  create 161.8

constituted — contest

enact 963.4
constituted 963.5
  be constituted by 1.6
constitution nature 5.3
  composition 54.1
  production 161.1
  form 240.1
  (texture 329.1)
  law 963.2
constitutional *n.* 266.4
  (exercise 686.2)
constitutional *adj.*
  authorized 924.10
  legal 963.5
constitutionality 963.1
constitutionalize 963.4
constitutive 153.9
constrain hinder 706.4
  compel 744.2
  restrain 751.6
constrained
  restrained 751.10
  modest 881.5
constraint
  contraction 195.1
  hindrance 706.1
  compulsion 744.1
  restraint 751.1
  (dissuasion 616.1)
  (subjection 749.1)
  modesty 881.1
constrict 195.4
  (reduce 36.4)
constriction
  contraction 195.1
  narrowing 203.2
  hindrance 706.1
  restraint 751.1
constrictive 751.13
constrictor
  contractor 195.3
  serpent 366.19
constringe 195.4
constringency 195.1
constringent *n.* 195.3
constringent *adj.* 195.6
construable 522.8
construct 161.8
  (compose 54.4)
  (form 240.6)
construction
  composition 54.1
  production 161.1, 7
  (formation 240.3)
  form 240.1
  rendition 522.2
  under construction 673.13
constructional 161.11
constructive
  productive 161.11
  (formative 240.7)
  evidence 467.11
  implicative 526.7
constructor 164.1
construe *n.* 522.2
construe *v.* 522.6
construed 526.7
consubstantiate 48.3
consubstantiation 998.6

consuetude 613.2
consuetudinary 613.11
consul 759.2
consular 759.6
consulship 737.3
consult confer 588.8
  advise with 695.6
consultant 662.19
consultation 588.3
  (advice 695.2)
consultative 695.8
consume
  decrease 36.3
  decompose 49.3
  eat 298.44
  burn 384.18
  waste 638.2
  decay 659.7
  use up 677.6
  squander 818.3
consumer eater 298.41
  user 677.4
consuming 378.7; 830.15
consummate *v.*
  top 210.5
  complete 729.2
  (perfect 650.4)
consummate *adj.*
  absolute 31.12
  unqualified 52.10
  complete 729.6
  (perfect 650.5)
consummation
  limit 52.4
  end 67.1
  final issue 154.1
  completion 729.1
consumpt 638.1
consumption
  decrease 36.1
  destruction 162.1
  contraction 195.1
  eating 298.1
  disease 655.10, 11
  decay 659.2
  use 677.1
  loss 776.1
consumptive 655.25
contact *n.*
  contiguity 199.1
  touch 379.1
  in contact 199.4
contact *v.*
  be contiguous 199.3
  touch 379.3
contact *int.* 267a.38
contactual
  contiguous 199.4
  touchable 379.5
contagion
  transference 270.1
  infection 655.2
  (insalubrity 657.1)
contagious
  transferable 270.11
  infectious 657.5
contagious disease 654.1
contain 76.3
  be contained in 1.6
container 191.1

contaminate
  imbue 41.8
  soil 653.15
  disease 655.22
  corrupt 659.9
contaminated
  diseased 655.25
  corrupt 945.15
contamination
  hybridism 563.8
  defilement 653.2
  infection 655.2
  corruption 659.3
contango 813.1
contemn 930.5
contemper 48.3
contemplate
  scrutinize 441.12
  ponder 451.27
  (give attention 457.4)
  study 461.17
  expect 507.4
  foresee 510.5
  intend 620.3
contemplation
  scrutiny 441.2
  thought 451.1
  expectation 507.1
  intention 620.1
  in contemplation
  in question 461.26
  (under consideration 454.3)
  for the purpose of 620.6
contemplative 451.35
  (studious 539.6)
contemporaneity 120.1
contemporaneous 120.4
contemporary *n.* 120.1
contemporary *adj.* 120.4
contemporize
  coexist 1.4
  synchronize 120.3
contempt 930
  (disrespect 929.1)
  beneath contempt 643.12
  in contempt of 24.10
contemptible
  paltry 643.12
  bad 649.8
  odious 830.14
  disreputable 874.8
contemptuous
  defiant 715.3
  arrogant 885.8
  disdainful 930.8
  (derisive 856.7)
  (disrespectful 929.5)
  be contemptuous of 930.5
contemptuously 930.10
  (arrogantly 885.11)
contemptuousness 930.1
contend argue 476.11

maintain 535.3
  ~ against 708.2
  contest 720.8
  (quarrel 713.7)
  (attack 716.5)
  (war 722.9)
contend for
  fight for 720.10
  defend 937.6
contend with 720.8
  (encounter 708.3)
contender
  opponent 710.4
  combatant 726.1
contending 720.11
content *n.*
  capacity 192.2
  contentment 831
  (serenity 826.2)
  (cheerfulness 836.1)
content *v.* 831.4
content *adj.*
  assentive 488.11
  (willing 602.8)
  consentant 762.3
  tolerant 826.9
  satisfied 831.6
  (pleased 827.8)
  (cheerful 836.7)
  be content 831.3
  (endure 826.6)
  not content 603.5
contented 831.6
  (cheerful 836.7)
contentedly 831.8
contention
  argumentation 476.2
  quarrel 713.3
  strife 720
  (opposition 708.1)
  (warfare 722.1)
contentious
  combative 722.13
  quarrelsome 901.9
  (discordant 24.6)
contentiousness
  discord 713.1
  warlikeness 722.6
  (contention 720.1)
  (irascibility 901.1)
contentment 831.1
  (comfort 377.2)
contents
  component part 56.1
  filling 190
  (interior 221.2)
  book 593.7
  synopsis 596.1
conterminal 233.3
conterminous
  ending 67.8
  synchronous 120.4
  contiguous 199.4
contest *n.* 720.1, 2
  (argument 476.2)
  (quarrel 713.3, 4)
  (attack 716.1)
  (battle 722.5)
  (sports 840.10)
contest *v.* argue 476.11
  contend 720.8

contestable — contrate wheel

contestable
  uncertain 475.9
  illogical 477.10
contestant
  opponent 710.4
    (gamester 840.17)
  combatant 726.1
contestation 720.1
context
  accompaniment 88.1
  printing 591.2
contexture 329.1
contiguity
  nearness 197.1
  contact 199
contiguous near 197.8
  touching 199.4;
    379.4
  be contiguous 199.3
contiguousness 199.1
continence
  chastity 960.1
  (celibacy 904.1)
  (temperance 953.1)
continent *n.* 342.1
continent *adj.* 960.2
  (celebate 904.5)
  (temperate 953.6)
continental *n.* 643.3
continental *adj.* 342.9
continentals 225.8
contingence
  liability 177.1
  contiguity 199.1
  expectation 507.1
contingency
  extrinsicality 6.1
  crisis 134.4
  happening 151.1
    (occasion 8.2)
  fortuity 156.1
  (possibility 470.1)
  liability 177.1
  uncertainty 475.5
  expectation 507.1
contingent *n.*
  expectation 507.1
  aid 707.5
  share 786.2
  quota 807.2
contingent *adj.*
  extrinsic 6.2
  circumstantial 8.5
  eventual 151.7
  resultant 154.6
  chance 156.12
  liable 177.4
  contiguous 199.4
  qualifying 469.6
  possible 470.5
  uncertain 475.15
    (occasional 134.9)
  conditional 770.3
continual
  perpetual 112.4
  constant 136.4
  (continuing 143.4)
continually
  invariably 16.7
  constantly 136.6
continuance
  durability 110.1

posteriority 117.1
  ~ in action 143
  (continuation 63.2)
  (repetition 104.1)
  (frequency 136.1)
  (permanence 141.1)
  (perseverance
    604a.1)
continuant sequel 65.1
  sound 402.2
continuation
  adjunct 39.1
  sequence 63.2
  sequel 65.1
  continuance 143.1
  (continuity 69.1)
continue endure 106.2
  (elapse 109.3)
  (endure 110.5)
  (tarry 133.7)
  ~ in action 143.2
  (do frequently
    136.2)
  (abide 141.4)
  (persevere 604a.2)
  reverberate 408.7
continued 69.6
continuing
  ~ in time 106.4
  (durable 110.9)
  uninterrupted 143.4
  (continuous 69.6)
  (perpetual 112.4)
  (constant 136.4)
continuity
  uniformity 16.1
  consecutiveness 69
  (gradation 58.2)
  continuance 143.1
continuous 69.6
  (successive 63.5)
  (monotonous 104.7)
  (continuing 143.4)
continuously 69.7
  (lengthwise 200.15)
contort distort 243.3
  convolve 248.3
contorted 243.5
contortion 243.1
contortional 243.6
contortionist 599.21
contortive 243.6
contour *n.*
  outline 230.1
  form 240.1
  lineaments 448.5
contour *v.* 230.3
contra
  contrarily 14.7
  contrapositive 237.6
  counterevidence
    468.5
contraband
  prohibited 761.4
  illicit 964.5
contrabandist 792.1
contrabass 417.3
contrabassist 416.3
contraclockwise 283.8
contract *n.*
  compact 769.1
  (promise 768.1)

pledge 771.1
  card game 840.12
contract *v.*
  compress 195.4
  (decrease 36.3, 4)
  (shorten 201.4)
  (narrow 203.7)
  promise 768.4
  covenant 769.5
  (promise 768.3)
contract matrimony
  903.13
contract bridge 840.12
contracted 195.6
  (narrow 203.9)
contractibility 195.2
contractile 195.6
contractility 195.2
contraction
  compression 195
  (decrease 36.1)
  (shortening 201.2)
  (narrowing 203.2)
  (closure 261.1)
  (conciseness 572.1)
  (compendium
    596.3)
  shorthand 590.7
contractive
  decreasing 36.5
  constringent 195.6
contractor
  constrictor 195.3
  builder 690.5
contractual 769.10
contradict
  be contrary 14.3
  counteract 179.3
  deny 536.2
  (countervail 468.2)
  (dissent 489.4)
  oppose 708.2
contradiction
  contrariety 14.1
  counteraction 179.1
  answer 462.1
  denial 536.1
  (disproof 468.1)
  (protest 489.2)
  opposition 708.1
contradictory
  contrary 14.5
  evidence 468.3
  denying 536.3
  (confutative 479.3)
  opposing 708.4
contradistinction 14.1
contraindicate 616.2
contraindication
  dissuasion 616.1
  warning 668.1
contralto
  low tone 408.6
  voice 413.14
contraoctave 413.19
contrapose 237.4
contraposita 237.3
contraposition 237
  (contrariety 14.1)
  (inversion 218.1)
contrapositive *n.* 237.3

contrapositive *adj.*
  237.6
  (contrary 14.5)
contrapposto 237.1
contraption 123.2
contrapuntal 415.28
contrapuntist 416.14
contraremonstrance
  462.1
contrariety
  opposition 14
  (difference 15.1)
  (counteraction
    179.1)
  (inversion 218.1)
  (contraposition
    237.1)
  opposition 708.1
contrarily
  conversely 14.7;
    468.5
  (differently 15.10)
  (otherwise 18.6)
  (notwithstanding
    30.8)
  (counteractively
    179.6)
  (inversely 218.8)
contrariness 708.1
contrariwise
  contrarily 14.7
  crosswise 219.12
  conversely 468.5
  opposed to 708.5
contrary *n.* 14.2
  (inverse 218.3)
  (opposite 237.2)
  **on the contrary, to
    the contrary**
  contrarily 14.7
  counterevidence
    468.5
contrary *adj.*
  opposite 14.5
  (different 15.7)
  (counteractive
    179.5)
  (inverted 218.6)
  (contrapositive
    237.6)
  (oppositional
    708.4)
  ~ to evidence 468.3
  denying 536.3
  obstinate 606.6
  capricious 608.5
  adverse 735.8
  be contrary 14.3;
    708.2
  go contrary to 14.3
contrast *n.*
  contrariety 14.1
  comparison 464.1
contrast *v.*
  oppose 237.5
  compare 464.2
  contrast with 14.3
  (differ 15.5)
  (be unlike 18.2)
contrasted 14.5
contrastive 464.5
contrate wheel 312.4

contravallation
  fence 232.2
  fortification 717.3
contravene
  be contrary 14.3
  counteract 179.3
  counterevidence 468.2
  deny 536.2
  thwart 706.7
  oppose 708.2
contravention
  denial 536.1
  opposition 708.1
  violation of law 964.2
contrecoup 277.1
contrectation 379.1
contretemps 735.3
  (untimeliness 135.2)
contribute
  conduce to 153.8
  tend 176.2
  (serve 644.2)
  concur 178.2
  provide 637.4
  benefit 648.6
  aid 707.6
  give 784.8
contribution 784.5
contributor
  correspondent 592.5
  donor 784.7
contributory
  helpful 707.12
  tributary 784.14
contrite 950.5
contrition 950.1
contriturate 330.6
contrivance
  object 316.3
  scheme 626.5
  (artifice 702.3)
  (expedient 646.2)
  instrument 633.1
contrive induce 153.7
  produce 161.8
  invent 515.10
  plan 626.9
  succeed in 731.5
contriver 626.8
contriving
  scheming 702.6
  conniving 940.8
control n.
  airplane 273a.10
  dominion 737.2
  (influence 175.2)
  (potency 157.1)
  (jurisdiction 965.1)
  restraint 751.1
  spirit 980a.1; 994.6
get control of 175.9
have control of 737.12
in control 693.7
under control
  obedient 743.3
  in subjection 749.6
  under restraint 751.10
control v.

  aviate 267a.31
  superintend 693.5
  rule 737.11, 12
  (influence 175.8)
  restrain 751.6
control oneself 953.5
controller
  master 745.1
  director 694.1
controlment 693.2
controls 273a.10
control stick 273a.10
controversial
  argumentative 476.14
  quarrelsome 901.9
controversialist 476.9
  (disputant 726.1)
controversion
  argumentation 476.2
  denial 536.1
controversy 476.2
  (interlocution 588.4)
  (quarrel 713.3)
  (contention 720.1)
in controversy with 708.4
controvert 536.2
controvertible
  uncertain 475.9
  (debatable 476.15)
  (untenable 485.11)
  (unauthentic 495.16)
  illogical 477.10
contumacious
  obstinate 606.6
  insubordinate 742.6
contumacy
  obstinacy 606.1
  disobedience 742.1
contumelious
  arrogant 885.8
  maledictory 908.6
  insulting 929.5
  contemptuous 930.8
  derogatory 934.4
contumely
  insolence 885.2
  discourtesy 895.2
  malediction 908.1
  indignity 929.2
  contempt 930.1
  reproach 932.3
  detraction 934.1
contund, contuse 330.6
contusion 330.2
conundrum 533.2
  (equivocal 520.2)
convalesce 654.3
convalescence
  health 654.1
  recuperation 660.5
convalescent 660.17
be convalescent 654.3
convection 270.2
convenance 852.2
convene 72.11
convenience
  instrument 633.1
  leisure 685.1

at one's convenience 684.2, 4
conveniences 632.1
convenient
  opportune 134.7
  comfortable 377.8
  expedient 646.4
conveniently 646.6
convent 1000.4
conventicle
  assembly 72.2
  council 696.3
  chapel 1000.1
convention
  assembly 72.2
  council 696.2, 3
  (conference 588.3)
  precept 697.1
  truce 723.3
  compact 769.1
conventionality 852.2
  (custom 613.2)
conventional n. 852.1
conventional adj.
  contractual 769.10
  fashionable 852.8
  (conformable 82.9)
  (habitual 613.11)
  orthodox 983a.7
conventionalism 852.2
conventionalist 82.3
conventionality 852.2
  (conformity 82.1)
conventionalize 82.5
  (be fashionable 852.6)
conventual n. 996.11
conventual adj.
  monasterial 995.9
  claustral 1000.6
converge 290.2
  (focus 74.3)
  (near 197.6)
  (centralize 222.3)
  (approach 286.2)
convergence 290
  (meeting 72.1)
  (focus 74.1)
  (nearness 197.1)
  (centrality 222.1)
convergent
  approaching 286.3
  concurrent 290.3
  (centrical 222.4)
converging 290.3
  (approaching 286.3)
conversable
  interlocutory 588.10
  sociable 892.12
conversant
  versed 490.14
  used to 613.12
  skilled in 698.14
be conversant with 490.9
conversation 588.1
  (argumentation 476.2)
  (speech 582.1)
conversational
  interlocutory 588.10

  (spoken 582.10)
  sociable 892.12
conversationalist 588.5
  (talker 582.5)
conversazione 892.5
converse n.
  the contrary 14.2
  conversation 588.1
converse v. 588.7
  (argue 476.11)
  (speech 582.6)
converse adj. 14.5
  (opposite 237.6)
conversely
  contrarily 14.7
  counterevidence 468.5
converser 588.5
conversible 144.9
conversion
  gradual change 144
  (change 140.1)
  proselytism 537.3
  religious ~ 987.3
convert n.
  proselyte 144.5
  religious 987.4
convert v.
  change 140.6; 144.6
  convince 484.10
  restore 660.8
  reform 950.4
  religion 987.9
converted 987.7, 12
be converted 144.8
  (change 140.5)
convertible
  equivalent 27.9
  transformable 144.9
  interchangeable 148.4
convex v. 250.7, 8
convex adj.
  bowed 245.5
  excurved 250.9
  (expanded 194.10)
  (curved 245.4)
  (rotund 249.6)
convexed 245.5
convexity 250
convexo-concave 245.6
convey transport 270.8
  mean 516.5
  utter 582.6
  commission 755.4
  assign 783.3
  plagiarize 789.8
  steal 791.9
  ~ away 791.11
conveyable 270.11
conveyance
  transportation 270.2
  vehicle 272.1
  ~ of property 783.1
conveyancer 968.5
conveyer, conveyor 271.1
convict n.
  prisoner 754.1
  criminal 949.2

convict — copulate

convict *v.*
  convince 484.10
  find guilty 971.2
conviction
  certainty 474.1
  confutation 479.1
  belief 484.2
  (judgment 480.1)
  expectation 507.2
  persuasion 537.3
  hope 858.1
  condemnation 971.1
convince
  confute 479.2
  assure 484.10
  (teach 537.3)
  (persuade 615.9)
convinced
  assured 474.9
  believing 484.12
convincement
  certainty 474.1
  belief 484.2
convincing
  conclusive 474.10
  demonstrative 478.3
  be convincing 484.10
convivial 892.12
conviviality
  festivity 840.2
  good-fellowship 892.2
convocate 72.11
convocation
  assembly 72.2
  council 696.2, 3
  (ecclesiastic 995.5)
convoke 72.11
convolute 312.2
convoluted 248.4
  (complex 59.10)
  (circuitous 311.6)
convolutely 248.7
convolution
  winding 248
  (complexity 59.3)
  (curvature 245.1)
  (circuity 311.1)
  (circuit 629.1)
  whirl 312.2
convolve 248.3
  (interlace 219.8)
  (curve 245.3)
  (turn 311.4)
convoy *n.* escort 88.4
  safe-conduct 664.3
  guard 717.6
  naval ~ 726.11
convoy *v.* escort 88.7
  (protect 664.6)
  navigate 267.42
  carry 270.8
convulse *n.* 315.7
convulse *v.*
  discompose 61.4
  agitate 315.8
  pain 378.4
  torture 830.6
convulsed 828.13
convulsion
  turmoil 59.4
  outbreak 173.2

  spasm 315.6, **7**
  (pain 378.1)
  seizure 655.3
  revolution 742.2
  frenzy 825.4, 5
  fit of anger 900.2
  in convulsions 315.14
convulsive
  turbulent 173.12
  agitated 315.13
coo 412.2
cook *n.* 746.1
cook *v.* destroy 162.4
  heat 384.19
  (prepare 673.6)
  falsify 544.3
cook one's goose
  ruin 162.4
  defeat 731.9
cooker 386.1
cookery
  cookroom 191.16; 386.4
  apparatus 386.1
  preparation 673.2
cookhouse
  lunch room 298.42
  cookroom 191.16; 386.4
cookie See cooky
cooking 673.2
cookroom room 191.16
  kitchen 386.4
  (workshop 691)
cookshack, cookshop 298.42
cookstove 386.1
cooky, cookie 298.12
cool *v.*
  moderate 174.5
  (compose 826.7)
  make cold 385.4
  discourage 616.3
  refresh 689.2
cool down, cool off
  become sane 502.3
  compose oneself 826.8
cool one's heels
  wait 133.7
  do nothing 681.2
  idle 683.8
cool *adj.* equable 174.6
  chilly 383.10
  gray 432.4
  blue 438.6
  levelheaded 498.11
  inexcitable 826.9
  (cautious 864.7)
  (unastonished 871.4)
  unexcited 826.11
  indifferent 866.4
  unfriendly 889.3
  discourteous 895.6
  grow cool 826.8
coolant 387.2
cooled 385.7
cooler
  refrigerator 387
  (ventilator 338.6)
  (fan 349.21)

  prison 752.1
coolheaded
  levelheaded 498.11
  inexcitable 826.9
coolhouse
  conservatory 371.6
  refrigerator 387.1
coolie, cooly 271.1
cooling *n.* 385.1
cooling *adj.* 385.6
cooling system 338.6
coolness cold 383.1
  dispassion 822.1
  composure 826.2
  (caution 864.2)
  estrangement 898.1
coom, coomb 388.2
coomb, combe 252.5
coon raccoon 366.17
  Negro 431.4
  cunning person 702.4
coon's age 110.3
coop *n.*
  enclosure 232.1
  (cote 189.7)
  (menagerie 370.3)
  coup-cart 272.5
  coupé 272.15
  lamp 423.3
  prison 752.1
coop *v.* 751.8
co-operate, coöperate 709.4
  (league 48.4)
  (concur 178.2)
  (be concordant 714.2)
co-operation, coöperation 709
  (concurrence 178.1)
  (unanimity 488.3)
  (concord 714.1)
  (participation 778.1)
  in co-operation 709.7, 8
co-operative, coöperative, 709.7
  (leagued 48.6)
  (concurrent 178.4)
  (helpful 707.12)
  (in league 712.10)
  (communistic 778.8)
co-operatively, coöperatively 709.8
  (concordantly 714.5)
co-operator, coöperator 711.1
co-opt, coöpt 609.7, 11
co-optation, coöptation 609.1
co-optive, coöptive 609.14
co-ordinate, coördinate *v.* 60.8
co-ordinate, coördinate *adj.* equal 27.8
  concurrent 178.4
  symmetrical 242.4

778

co-ordinates, coördinates 466.7
co-ordination, coördination
  equalization 27.3
  symmetry 242.1
coot 504.1
cootie 366.24
cop *n.* 745.10
cop *v.* 791.9
copaiba 356.3
copal, copaline, copalite 428.5
coparcenary
  coheirship 775.4
  participation 778.1
coparcener
  participator 778.3
  coheir 779.5
copartner
  accompanier 88.3
  ally 711.1
  participator 778.3
  companion 890.3
copartnership
  accompaniment 88.2
  association 709.2
  company 712.5
  participation 778.1
cope *n.* 999.1
cope *v.* 720.9
copeck See kopeck
Copenhagen 271.9
copestone
  completion 729.1
  stone 342.4
copier 19.4
coping layer 204.1
  top 210.4
coping stone top 210.4
  completion 729.1
copious
  numerous 102.5
  productive 168.7
  verbose 573.7
  plentiful 639.7
  liberal 816.4
copiousness 639.2
copper *n.* red 434.2
  metal 635.6
  policeman 745.10
  money 800.8, 15
copper *v.* 621.18
copperhead 366.19
copperplate 558.2, **3**
copper red 434.2
coppersmith 690.6
copperworks 691
coppery 433.5
coppet 367.8
coppice *n.* 367.7, **8**
coppice *v.* 367.13
coprolite 653.7
copse *n.* 367.7, **8**
copse *v.* 367.13
copsewood 367.7, **8**
copsy 367.15
Coptic 560.4
copula coition 43.2
  fastening 45.2
copulate *v.* attach 43.6

have sexual congress 43.8
(procreate 161.10)
(fructify 168.4)
copulate *adj.* 43.10
copulation
junction 43.1
coition 43.2
(procreation 161.1)
copulative 43.13
copy *n.* imitation 21
(same 13.3)
(counterpart 17.5)
(reproduction 163.1)
(counterfeit 545.6)
(representation 554.3)
(picture 556.9)
prototype 22.2
music score 415.21
news 532.1
record 551.1
manuscript 590.3
typescript 591.2
book 593.1
pattern 626.2
read copy 591.17
copy *v.* imitate 19.5
emulate 19.10
represent 554.7
transcribe 590.13
copybook book 593.1
textbook 593.5
copycat *n.* 19.4
copycat *v.* 19.6
copyhold *n.* 780.2
copyhold *adj.* 780.8
copyholder 591.12
copying 19.1
copyist imitator 19.4
artist 559.1
writer 590.11
copyman 593.16
copy paper 590.10
copyreader 591.13
copyright 760.2
copy writer 531.6
coquelicot 434.2
coquet *n.* 607.4
coquet, coquette *v.*
be irresolute 605.4
be capricious 608.4
be affected 853.5
flirt 902.7
flatter 933.2
coquetry
capriciousness 608.2
foppery 853.3
flirtation 902.1
flattery 933.1
coquette 902.6
coquettish
fickle 608.6
flirtatious 902.10
Cora See Kore
coracle 273.4
coral *n.* animal 368.4
gem 847.8
coral *adj.* 434.10
coralliform 368.13
coralline 434.10

coral snake 366.19
corbeau 435.2
corbeil 191.9
corbel 215.11, 12, 17
cord 205.3
(ligament 45.4)
(supporter 215.2)
cordage capacity 192.2
ropework 205.4
(rigging 273.9)
cordate 245.12
cordial *n.*
pungency 392.2
sweet drink 396.5
medicine 662.4
alcoholic drink 959.4, 6
cordial *adj.*
pleasing 377.7; 829.7
well-disposed 602.8
ardent 821.6
friendly 888.4
courteous 894.12
benevolent 906.6
cordiality
willingness 602.7
ardor 821.2
friendliness 888.1
cordiform 245.12
cording 205.4
cordite 727.13
cordon fence 232.2
(zone 230.2)
circle 247.2
sanitary ~ 666.1; 670.2
decoration 733.1
cordon bleu 733.1
cordonnet 247.2
corduroy *n.*
cloth 219.5
rough 256.2
corduroy *adj.* 259.4
corduroys 225.21
corduroy road 256.2
cordwainer 225.40
core essence 5.2
center 222.2
(middle 68.2)
corelation 12.1
coremaker 690.8
coriaceous 327.5
corium 223.12
cork *n.* lid 223.7
stopper 263.1
lightness 320.2
cork *v.* close 261.2
confine 751.8
corker
effective retort 479.1
excellent thing 648.4
paragon 650.3
cork jacket 666.1
corkmaker 690.8
corkscrew *n.*
coil 248.2
opener 260.10
perforator 262
extractor 301.4

corkscrew *v.* 248.3
corkscrew *adj.* 248.5
corkscrewy 248.5
corky shrunk 195.6
light 320.7
dry 340.7
lively 682.16
Corliss engine 633.3
cormorant 957.2
corn *n.*
protuberance 250.2
fodder 298.7
plant 367.9
sore 655.16
money 800.1
corn *v.* solidify 321.7
preserve 670.4
corn bread 298.11
corncob 392a.6
cornea 441.7
corned 959.21
corned beef 298.20
corneous 323.5
corner *n.* nook 191.3
angle 244.2
hiding place 530.2
impasse 704.3
monopoly 777.2
in a corner
secretly 528.24
at an impasse 704.11
corner *v.* angle 244.4
place in difficulty 704.7
checkmate 731.10
monopolize 777.5
cornered
angular 244.5
at an impasse 704.11
cornerstone
foundation 215.3
stone 342.4
salient point 642.4
cornet horn 417.4
officer 745.11
cornettist 416.2
corn-fed 192.12
corn god 371.3
cornhusk 223.14
cornhusking 892.5
cornice top 210.4
ornament 847.4
corniculate, cornific 253.19
cornification 323.2
cornified
hornlike 253.19
hard 323.5
corniform, corniferous 253.19
corno 417.4
corn oil 356.3
cornopean 417.4
corn shuck 223.14
corn shucking 892.5
corn sirup 396.4
cornucopia 639.2
cornute convex 250.9
hornlike 253.19
cornwallis 840.6
corny 843.6
corollary adjunct 39.1

deduction 480.1
corona top 210.4
capital 215.17
circle 247.2
nimbus 420.13
chandelier 423.10
Corona Australis 318.6
coronach 839.3
(music 415.8)
coronation 755.2
(celebration 883.1)
coroner 662.19
coronet circle 247.2
royal insignia 747.1
jewel 847.7
corporal *n.*
officer 745.11
communion cloth 1000.3
corporal *adj.*
material 316.8
fleshly 364.4
corporality 316.1
corporate
joined 43.10
leagued 48.6
corporation
paunch 191.7
(corpulence 192.4)
company 712.5
(firm 797.10)
corporational, corporative 48.6
corporeal
material 316.8
(substantial 3.4)
fleshly 364.4
corporealist 316.6
corporeality 316.1
corporealization 316.4
corporealize 316.7
corporeity 316.1
(substantiality 3.1)
corporify 316.7
corporosity 192.4, 7
corposant 420.11
corps company 72.3
corpse 362.1
army ~ 726.7
corps de réserve 636.2
corps diplomatique 759.2
corpse *n.*
thin person 203.6
dead body 362
tobacco 392a.5
corpse *v.* 361.10
corpselike 362.2
corpulence 192.4
(thickness 202.2)
(rotundity 249.1)
corpulent 192.12
(big-bellied 194.11)
corpus 316.2
Corpus Christi 998.13
corpuscle 32.2
corpuscular 193.10
corpus delicti 947.3
corpus juris 697.1
Corpus Juris Civilis 963.2

corradiation — cottager

corradiation
  focus 74.1
  convergence 290.1
corral *n.* 232.1
  (menagerie 370.3)
corral *v.*
  circumscribe 229.2
  ~ animals 370.7
correal 43.10
correct *v.*
  undeceive 545a.2
  improve 658.8, 11
  remedy 660.10
  right 922.3
  reprove 932.8
  punish 972.5
stand corrected
  932.10
correct *adj.*
  orderly 58.7
  accurate 494.11
  speech 578.4
  conventional 852.8
  right 922.5
  virtuous 944.3
  orthodox 983a.7
correctable 658.16
correction
  revision 658.3
  reparation 660.4
  reproof 932.3
  punishment 972.1
make corrections
  658.11
corrective *n.* 662.1
  (cure 660.5)
corrective *adj.* 662.25
  (improving 658.15)
corregidor 745.9
correlate *n.* 17.5
correlate *v.* 12.4
correlation 12
  (relation 9.1)
correlative *n.* 17.5
correlative *adj.*
  correspondent 12.6
  connatural 17.13
  (relative 9.5)
  interchangeable
    148.4
be correlative 12.4
correlativity 12.1
correspond
  be related 9.3
  (answer to 462.8)
  correlate 12.4
  agree 23.7
  equal 27.6
  conform 82.4
  write to 592.6
  be concordant 714.2
correspondence
  correlation 12.1
  similarity 17.1
  agreement 23.1
  (conformity 82.1)
  symmetry 242.1
  letter writing 592
  concord 714.1
correspondence
  school 542.1
correspondent *n.*

analogue 17.5
letter writer 592.5
journalist 593.16
(reporter 758.1)
accused 938.3
correspondent *adj.*
  correlative 12.6
  connatural 17.13
  agreeing 23.9
  adequate 639.6
corresponding
  correlative 12.6
  connatural 17.13
  equivalent 27.9
corresponsive 178.4
corridor
  vestibule 191.17
  path 627.2
corrigendum 495.2
corrigible 658.16
corrival 710.4
corrivalry 720.1
corroborant
  invigorating 656.5
  tonic 662.25
corroborate
  confirm 467.9
  (ratify 488.10)
  demonstrate 478.2
corroboration
  confirmation 467.3
  (ratification 488.4)
  demonstration 478.1
in corroboration
  467.13
corroborative 467.11
corrode burn 384.18
  disintegrate 659.6
  ~ the mind 830.7
corroding
  painful 378.7
  mentally ~ 830.15
corrosion 659.2
  (pulverization
    330.2)
corrosive *n.* 384.11
corrosive *adj.* 649.10
corrosive sublimate
  663.5
corrugate *v.*
  contract 195.4
  roughen 256.11
  wrinkle 258.3
  furrow 259.3
corrugate *adj.*
  rough 256.12
  folded 258.4
  furrowed 259.4
corrugated
  rough 256.12
  folded 258.4
  furrowed 259.4
corrugation
  contraction 195.1
  roughness 256.1, 2
  wrinkle 258.1
corrupt *v.*
  adulterate 41.8
  bribe 618.3
  taint 653.14, 15
  spoil 659.7, 9
  (demoralize 945.10)

corrupt *adj.*
  foul 653.17
  diseased 655.25
  decayed 659.13
  dishonest 940.8
  wicked 945.15
corrupted 945.15
corrupting 649.10
corruption
  adulteration 41.2
  barbarism 563.1
  defilement 653.2
  infection 655.2
  pus 655.16
  deterioration 659.2
  wordplay 842.5
  dishonesty 940.5
  vice 945.2, 6
corsage bodice 225.18
  ornamentation
    847.5
corsair ship 273.2
  pirate 792.5
corse 362.1
corselet, corslet, cor-
  set 225.25
corseting 219.5
cortege, cortège
  adjunct 39.2
  attendance 88.5
  (afterpart 65.2)
  (procession 69.3)
Cortes, Cortes Geraes
  696.4
cortex cover 223.2
  peel 223.15
cortical 223.32
Corus See **Caurus**
coruscate
  glitter 420.18
  ~ intellectually
    498.8
coruscation 420.4
corvette, corvet
  ship 273.2
  warship 726.11
Corvus 318.6
corybantiasm 503.1
Corybantic
  dithyrambic 503.13
  orgiastic 954.5
coryphaeus
  teacher 540.1
  director 694.1
coscinomancy 511.3
cosey, cosie See **cozy**
cosiness 377.2
Cos lettuce 298.30
cosmetics paint 428.5
  merchandise 798.3
  beauty 845.5
  (ornamentation
    847.3)
cosmic, kosmic 318.15
cosmism 318.9
cosmogonal 318.15
cosmogonist 318.11
cosmogony 318.9
cosmographer 318.11
cosmographic 318.15
cosmographist 318.11
cosmography 318.9

cosmologist 318.11
cosmology
  existence 1.3
  science 451.22
cosmopolitan
  urban 189.22
  public 372.6
  social 892.12
  public-spirited 906.8
cosmopolitanism
  906.3
cosmopolite 911.1
cosmorama 448.2
cosmos, kosmos
  arrangement 60.3
  world 318.1
cosmotheism 984.10
Cossack 726.4
Cossack post 234.2
cosset *n.* 899.1
cosset *v.* 902.8
cost *n.* 812.1
at cost 815.11
cost *v.* 812.6
costate 259.4
costermonger 797.3
costive 321.8
costiveness 321.1
costless 815.10
costliness 814.1
costly 814.5
costume *n.*
  clothes 225.1, 10
  suit 225.7
  (canonicals 999.1)
  theatrical ~ 599.13
costume *v.* 225.41, 42
costumer
  clothier 225.36
  stageman 599.17
costumery 225.1
costumier
  clothier 225.36
  stageman 599.17
cosy See **cozy**
cot abode 189.4, 7
  bed 215.24
cote abode 189.4, 7
  messuage 189.12
  (enclosure 232.1)
  menagerie 370.3)
  farm 371.4
cotenancy 778.1
cotenant 778.3
coterie kind 75.2
  clique 712.2
  (social group
    892.7)
coterminous 120.4
cothurned 599.28
cothurnus 599.3
cotidal 341.5
cotillion, cotillon
  840.7
cotise, cotice 231.3
cotquean
  mollycoddle 160a.3
  old fogy 501.3
cotta 999.1
cottage 189.3, 4
cottager, cotter, cot-
  tar, cottier 188.3

cotton *n.*
 thread 205.2
 cloth 219.5
 dressing 662.14
cotton *v.* agree 23.7
 be concordant 714.2
 be friendly 888.2
 become enamored 897.12
cotton belt 183.1
cotton mill 691
cottonseed oil 356.3
cottontail 366.17
cotyledon 367.4
couch *n.* layer 204.1
 seat 215.22
 bed 215.24
couch *v.* recline 213.5
 (sit 308.6)
 depress 308.4
 lurk 526.3
 lie hid 528.16
 phrase 566.3
 repose 687.3
couchancy 213.2
couchant, couché 213.9
couchmaker 690.8
cough *n.* 655.9
cough *v.* 349.23
 cough up
 confess 529.5
 pay 807.6
cough sirup 662.6
coulee bed 211.3
 water gap 350.1
couleur de rose
 auspicious 512.4
 optimism 858.11
coulisse 599.12, 15
couloir 198.3
coulomb 158a.5
coulometer 158a.6
council *n.*
 conference 588.3
 assemblage 696.2
 (tribunal 966.1)
council *adj.* 696.9
council fire 588.3; 696.2
councilor, councillor
 counselor 696.7
 official 745.9
counsel *n.*
 advice 695.1
 adviser 695.3
 lawyer 968.1
 take counsel
 consider 451.21
 take advice 695.7
counsel *v.*
 confer 588.8
 advise 695.4
counselor, counsellor
 adviser 695.3
 councilor 696.7
 lawyer 968.1
count *n.*
 computation 37.2
 sum 84.3
 numeration 85.3
 nobleman 875.5

count *v.*
 enumerate 85.7
 have influence 175.7
 estimate 480.7
 be important 642.7
count noses
 census 86.3
 enumerate 85.7
 census 86.3
count on, count upon
 rely on 484.7
 (presume 472.3)
 plan on 507.6
count out
 eliminate 42.4
 exclude 55.3
count up
 compute 37.5
 calculate 85.7
 not count 643.7
countable 85.11
countenance *n.*
 face 234.4
 appearance 448.5
 patronage 707.2
 keep in countenance
 urge 615.7
 lend one's favor 707.8
 give hope 858.8
 encourage 861.7
 approve 931.5
countenance *v.*
 lend one's favor 707.8
 approve 931.5
 not countenance
 not agree to 489.4
 refuse 764.3
 disapprove 932.5
counter *n.*
 number 84.1
 calculator 85.5
 table 215.20
 stern 235.7
 ship 273.7
 type 591.6
 gambling 621.13
 retaliation 718.1
 shopboard 799.1
 token 800.7
 over the counter 796.9
counter *adj.*
 contrary 14.5
 contrapositive 237.6
 countervailing 468.3
counter *adv.* 708.5
counteract
 be contrary 14.3
 compensate 30.5
 run counter 179.3
 (recoil 277.3)
 (withstand 719.3)
 (restrain 751.6)
 thwart 706.7
 oppose 708.2
counteractant *n.*
 counteragent 179.2
 antidote 662.12
counteractant *adj.* 179.5

counteraction
 opposition 179.1; 708.1
 (contrariety 14.1)
 (compensation 30.1)
 (retroaction 277.1)
 (restraint 751.1)
 hindrance 706.1
counteractive *n.*
 counteragent 179.2
 antidote 662.12
counteractive *adj.* 179.5
 (contrary 14.5)
 (oppositional 708.4)
counteractively 179.6
 (contrarily 14.7)
counterbalance *n.*
 compensation 30.2
 counteractant 179.2
 counterweight 319.1
counterbalance *v.*
 compensate 30.5
 counteract 179.4
 counterweigh 319.8
counterblast
 counteractant 179.2
 answer 462.1
 retaliation 718.1
counterchange *n.*
 interchange 148.1
 recrimination 938.1
counterchange *v.* 148.3
 (reciprocate 12.5)
countercharge *n.* 462.1
countercharge *v.* 938.4
countercharm 993.1
countercheck *n.* 706.2
countercheck *v.* 706.4
counterclaim *n.* 30.2
counterclaim *v.* 462.6
counterclockwise
 backward 283.8
 rotatively 312.9
countercurrent 348.8
counterevidence 468 (defense 937.2)
counterfeit *n.* 545.6
 (copy 21.1)
counterfeit *v.*
 disguise 528.10
 falsify 544.3, 6
 (simulate 19.7)
 (be deceptive 545.11)
 coin 800.20
 affect 853.5
counterfeit *adj.* 545.13
 (imitation 19.12)
 (disguised 528.20)
 (false 544.7)
counterfeiter
 imitator 19.4
 coiner 800.18
 (swindler 792.8)
counterfeiting 544.1
 (simulation 19.3)

counterflow, counterflux 348.8
counterfoil 550.11
counterirritant 662.12
counterjumper 797.2
countermand *n.* 756.1
countermand *v.* 756.3
countermarch *n.* 283.3
countermarch *v.* 283.5
countermark 550.11
countermine *n.*
 cavity 252.2
 intrigue 626.6
 fortification 717.3
countermine *v.*
 counterplot 626.10
 entrench 664.6
 thwart 706.7
countermotion 264.1
countermovement 283.3
counterorder *n.* 756.1
counterorder *v.* 756.3
counterpane 223.9
counterpart
 analogue 17.5
 (same 13.3)
 (opposite 14.2; 237.2)
 (inverse 218.3)
 duplicate 21.2
 (duplication 90.1)
counterplot *n.*
 plot 626.6
 opposition 708.1
counterplot *v.* 626.10
counterpoint *n.*
 the contrary 14.2
 concord 413.2
 music 415.4
counterpoint *v.* 415.26
counterpoise *n.*
 compensation 30.2
 counteractant 179.2
 counterweight 319.1
counterpoise *v.*
 compensate 30.5
 counteract 179.4
 counterweigh 319.8
counterpoison 662.12
counterpole 14.2
 (opposite 237.2)
counterproject 718.1
counterprotest 468.1
counterrevolution
 revolution 146.1
 revolt 742.2
counter scale 319.5
counterscarp
 trench 259.2
 fortification 717.3
countersign *n.* 550.11
countersign *v.*
 endorse 488.10
 (confirm 467.9)
 sign 550.19
countersignature, counterstamp 550.11
counterstatement 462.1, 2
counterstroke 718.1
countertendency 719.1

countervail — cover

countervail
  be unequal 28.2
  compensate 30.5
  counteract 179.3
  ~ evidence 468.2
  (confute 479.2)
countervailing *n.* 30.2
countervailing *adj.*
  compensating 30.6
  evidence 468.3
  (confutative 479.3)
counterweight
  compensation 30.2
  counterbalance 319.1
counterwork
  be contrary 14.3
  counteract 179.3
  thwart 706.7
  oppose 708.2
countess 875.6
counting 85.1
countinghouse 799.1
countless 105.3
countrified, countryfied 183.3
  (agricultural 371.9)
  (uncouth 851.7)
country *n.*
  region 181.1
  land 182
  (territory 181.2)
  (government 737.8)
  provinces 183
  (inland 221.3)
  (plain 344.1)
  jury 967.2
country *adj.* 183.3
country cousin 11.3
countryman 876.5
countryseat 189.3
countryside 183.1
counts 79.3
on all counts
  wholly 50.10
  throughout 52.15
county 181.2
county seat 189.16
coup instant 113.3
  coup-cart 272.5
  coupé 272.15
  masterstroke 626.7
  feat 680.2
  thrust 716.3
  lucky stroke 731.2
coup-cart 272.5
coup de grâce
  end-all 67.4
  (deathblow 361.6)
  finishing stroke 729.1
  pity 914.3
coup de main
  feat 680.2
  attack 716.1
coup de maître
  master stroke 698.5
  great success 724.7
coup de soleil 384.9
coup d'essai 675.2
coup d'état
  stroke 626.7
  feat 680.2
  revolution 742.2
coup de théâtre 599.6
coup d'œil 441.2
coupé 272.15
couple *n.*
  analogue 17.5
  fastening 45.2
  pair 89.2
couple *v.* attach 43.6
  league 48.4
  ~ with 88.6
  pair 89.3
  marry 903.12
coupled 89.5
coupled with
  with 37.9; 88.9
  accompanying 88.8
coupler 45.2
couplet pair 89.2
  verse 597.7
coupling junction 43.1
  fastening 45.2
coupon 800.7
courage 861
  (resolution 604.1)
  muster courage 861.6
courageous 861.8
  (warlike 722.13)
  (fearless 858.10)
  be courageous 861.5
courante, courant
  music 415.7
  dance 840.7
courier
  messenger 534.1
  (traveller 268.5)
  guide 694.6
course *n.* method 58.3
  continuity 69.1
  ~ of time 109
  round 138.4
  ~ of events 151.2
  tendency 176.1
  layer 204.1
  motion 264.3
  travel 266.1, 8
  itinerary 266.9
  voyage 267.6
  race 274.4
  direction 278.1
  serving 298.38
  flow 348.2
  channel 350.1
  ~ of study 537.7
  career 625.3
  692.3
  measure 626.7
  path 627.2
  (itinerary 266.9)
  (airway 267a.20)
  (line 278.3)
  arena 728.1
of course
  consequently 154.7
  (demonstrably 478.6)
  certainly 474.16
  yes 488.14
  (willingly 602.11)
  of necessity 601.15
  no wonder! 871.5
run its course
  end 67.6
  elapse 109.3
  reach completion 729.4
take a course
  pursue 622.6
  conduct oneself 692.5
take its course
  continue 143.2
  happen 151.3
course *v.* flow 348.17
  move 264.6
  travel 266.12
  sail 267.22
  hunt 622.7
courser horse 271.3
  speeder 274.6
  huntsman 622.4
coursing 622.2
court *n.*
  attendance 88.5
  house 189.3
  square 189.19
  vestibule 191.17
  yard 232.1
  (plot 181.3)
  council 696.1
  play ground 840.14
  society 852.4
  social circle 892.7
  tribunal 966.1–4, 6
in court 969.14
court *v.* allure 617.4
  solicit 765.4; 865.13
  curry favor 886.3
  woo 902.7
court-baron 966.2
court card
  trump 626.7
  playing card 840.13
courteous 894.12
  (genteel 852.9)
  (respectful 928.8)
  be courteous 894.7
courteously 894.14
courter 897.6
courtesan, courtezan 962.2
courtesy 894
  (respect 928.1)
courthouse
  town 189.16
  court 966.6
courtier
  hanger-on 886.2
  flatterer 935.2
courtierly 933.3
courting 902.2
courtlet 966.2
courtly 894.12
court-martial 966.5
court of admiralty, Court of Appeal 966.2
Court of Arches, Arches Court 966.4
court of assize, court of attachments, court of chancery 966.2
court of claims 966.1, 3
court of conscience, court of equity 966.1
court of errors 966.3
court of honor 939.1; 966.1
court of probate 966.2
court plaster 662.14
courtroom 966.6
courtship 902.2
courtyard
  square 189.19
  yard 232.1
cousin 11.3
cousinhood 11.2
couturière 225.38
couvert 298.39
cove nook 191.3
  (recess 252.4)
  chasm 198.3
  arch 215.18
  cave 252.3
  sea inlet 343.1
  man 373.2
covenant *n.*
  compact 769.1
  (promise 768.1)
  pledge 771.1
covenant *v.* 769.5
  (promise 768.3)
covenantor 488.5
Coventry 893.3
cover *n.*
  covering 223.2, 7, 9
  (mask 225.11)
  (concealment 530.3)
  (disguise 545.5)
  (safeguard 666.1)
  meal 298.39
  hiding place 530.2
  bookbinding 593.9
  pretext 619.1
  refuge 666.3
from cover to cover 200.16
under cover
  covered 223.28
  in hiding 528.19
  secretly 528.24
  deceptively 545.15
  safe 664.10
cover *v.*
  compensate 30.4
  include 76.3
  superimpose 223.22
  (clothe 225.41)
  close 261.2
  incubate 370.8
  paint 428.10
  conceal 528.10
  (make a pretext 619.2)
  report 531.7
  meet a bet 621.18
  protect 664.6
  guard 717.7
cover ground 274.9
cover up
  substitute 147.3
  conceal 528.10

coverage 223.2
coverchief 225.26
covered 223.28
covered waggon
 272.19
covered wagon 272.3
covering *n.* 223
 (layer 204.2)
 (bedding 215.24)
 (exterior 220.2)
 (investment 225.1)
 (wrap 384.13)
 (sunshade 424.2)
covering *adj.* 223.29
coverlet, coverlid
 223.9
 (bedding 215.24)
 (wrap 384.13)
covert *n.*
 retreat 189.13
 cover 223.2
 den 252.3
 feather 256.8
 grove 367.7
 hiding place 530.2
 (shelter 424.1)
 refuge 666.3
covert *adj.*
 covered 223.28
 secret 528.21
 (invisible 447.4)
coverture cover 223.2
 hiding place 530.2
 refuge 666.3
 marriage 903.1
covert way 530.4
covet desire 865.11
 envy 921.2
coveting 865.2
covetous
 avaricious 819.4
 greedy 865.20
 envious 921.3
covetousness 865.4
covey company 72.3
 crowd 72.4
 multitude 102.2
covin 545.1
covinous 545.12
cow *n.* bovine 366.12
 female animal 374.8
cow *v.* 860.12
co-walker 980a.2
coward *n.* 862.2
 (shirker 623.4)
 be a coward 862.3
coward *adj.* 862.4
cowardice 862
 (irresolution 605.2)
 (fear 860.1)
cowardly 862.4
 (weak-willed 605.6)
 (afraid 860.14)
 be cowardly 862.3
 (shrink 623.9)
cowbird 366.22
cowboy rider 268.8
 stockman 370.4
 (workman 690.10)
cow byre 189.5
cower

crouch 207.5; 308.7
 quail 860.8
 be cowardly 862.3
 grovel 886.3
cowering
 cowardly 862.5
 obsequious 886.4
cowgirl rider 268.8
 stockman 370.4
cowherd 370.4
cowhide *n.* 975.1
cowhide *v.* 972.6
cowkeeper 370.4
cowl airplane 273a.10
 monk 996.11
 clerical ~ 999.1
cowled
 covered 223.28
 vestmented 999.3
cowling 273a.10
cowlstaff 215.15
cow pox 655.6
cowpuncher
 cowboy 268.8
 stockman 370.4
cowrie, cowry 800.3
cowshed 189.5
co-work 709.4
co-worker 690.4
co-working
 concurrence 178.1
 co-operation 709.1
cox 269.5
coxcomb 854.1
coxcombry
 foppery 853.3
 vanity 880.1
coxcomical
 foppish 853.6
 vain 880.6
coxswain, cockswain
 n. 269.5
coxswain *v.* 267.11
coy timid 862.4
 demure 881.5
 coquettish 902.10
coyote 366.5
coze *n.* 588.2
coze *v.* 588.7
cozen deceive 545.7
 swindle 791.12
cozenage 545.1
cozener cheat 548.2
 swindler 792.8
cozy, cozey, cozie
 comfortable 377.8
 chatty 588.10
 sociable 892.12
C.P.A. 811.6
crab *n.* fish 298.18
 animal 368.8
 malcontent 832.2
Crab *n.* 318.6
crab *v.* aviate 267a.31
 complain 839.10
crab apple 397.2
crabbed
 complex 59.10
 (obscure 519.7)
 sour 397.6
 difficult 704.8
 gruff 895.7

ill-humored 901.7
crabbedness 901.1
crabbing 267a.24
crabby 901.7
crablike 283.7
crabs 89.2
crabsidle 236.5
 (deviate 279.7)
crack *n.* instant 113.3
 ~ of dawn 125.1
 short way 197.2
 cleft 198.2
 (opening 260.1)
 furrow 259.1
 blow 276.3
 snap 406.1, 2
 (shot 284.4)
 attempt 675.1
 proficient 700.1
crack *v.* sunder 44.8
 furrow 259.3
 open 260.11
 strike 276.8
 be brittle 328.3
 snap 406.7, 8
 (explode 173.9)
 solve 481a.14
 impair 659.6
 ~ a joke 842.8
 boast 884.5
 ~ a bottle 892.11;
  959.15
crack down on 716.5
crack on
 ~ ~ sail 267.16;
  274.9
 accelerate 274.10
crack up
 collide 276.9
 crash 267a.35
crack *adj.* best 648.9
 skillful 698.11
crackajack *n.*
 superior 33.4
 excellent thing
  648.4
 proficient 700.1
crackajack *adj.*
 good 648.8
 skillful 698.11
crackbrain 504.1
crackbrained 503.12
cracked
 harsh-sounding
  410.9
 insane 503.12
cracker bread 298.11
 dryness 340.4
 firecracker 382.9
 noisemaker 404.4
 snapper 406.5
cracker bonbon
 firework 382.9
 noisemaker 404.4
crackle *n.*
 ceramics 384.14
 snap 406.1
crackle *v.* 406.7
crackling 406.1
crack-loo, crackaloo
 621.7
crack of doom

end 67.1
 doomsday 121.2
 destruction 162.2
 destiny 601.3
crackpot oddity 83.4
 madman 504.1, 3
cracksman 792.2
crack-up
 destruction 162.3
 collision 276.2
 crash 267a.27
 accident 735.3
cradle *n.*
 beginning 66.1
 infancy 127.3
 origin 153.4
 bassinet 191.9
 bed 215.24
 network 219.4
 cavity 252.2
 (furrow 259.1)
 in the cradle 127.7
cradle *v.* lodge 184.12
 support 215.26
 nurse 707.9
cradlemaker 690.8
cradlesong song 415.9
 soothing 834.1
craft ship 273.1
 trade 625.5
 skill 698.1
 cunning 702.1
 (deception 545.1)
craftiness 702.1
 (skill 698.1)
craftsman 690.5
craftsmanship 680.3
craftworker 690.5
crafty 702.6
 (deceitful 545.12)
crag height 206.2
 (spire 253.4)
 precipice 212.3
 rock 342.4
cragged, craggy
 256.12
craichy 160.12
cram *n.* fill 52.3
 crowd 72.4
 study 539.1
 lie 546.2
cram *v.*
 assemble 72.11
 expand 194.8
 densify 321.7
 tutor 537.9
 study 539.4
 gorge 957.3
cram down one's
 throat
 convince 484.10
 force upon 744.2
crambo rhyme 597.8
 game 840.11
crambo clink, crambo
 jingle 597.3
cram-full, crammed
 full 52.11
 overfull 641.6
crammer tutor 540.1
 lie 546.2
 liar 548.5

cramp — credulous

cramp *n.* spasm 315.7
　pain 378.1
　ailment 655.3
cramp *v.* disable 158.6
　contract 195.4
　impair 659.8
　hinder 706.4
cramped little 193.8
　style 579.3
cranberry fruit 298.31
　sour 397.2
　red 434.5
cranch See **craunch**
crane *n.* basket 191.9
　angle 244.2
　lifter 307.2
　bird 366.22
　pothook 386.3
Crane *n.* 318.6
crane *v.* 441.13
craniology, cranio-
　scopy 450.4
cranium 210.3
crank oddity 83.4
　handle 215.7
　automobile 272.16
　eccentricity 503.6
　eccentric 504.1, 3
　caprice 608.1
　malcontent 832.2
　witticism 842.4
　punishment 975.3
cranky
　unsteady 160.12
　sickly 655.24
cranny nook 191.3
　(small place 184.4)
　cleft 198.2
　furrow 259.1
crap *n.* dice 621.9
　rubbish 645.4
crap *v.* 972.8
crape *n.* cloth 219.5
　mourning 839.4
crape *v.* 248.3
crapehanger
　marplot 706.3
　spoilsport 837.5
　(pessimist 859.4)
crap game 621.8
craps deuce 89.2
　dice 621.8, 9
crap shooter 621.15
crap shooting 621.8
crapulence
　overindulgence
　　954.1
　gluttony 957.1
　drunkenness 959.1
crapulent
　drunken 959.21
　gluttonous 957.4
　intemperate 954.4
crapulous
　intemperate 954.4
　gluttonous 957.4
　drunken 959.21
crash *n.*
　destruction 162.3
　cloth 219.5
　clash 276.2
　crack-up 267a.27

bang 406.2, 4
failure 732.1
accident 735.3
bankruptcy 808.2
crash *v.* destroy 162.4
　intrude 228.10
　collide 276.9
　crack up 267a.35
　be brittle 328.3
　bang 406.7, 8
　fail 732.5
　go bankrupt 808.6
crash *int.* 406.13
crash dive 267.5
crasher 228.4
crash landing 267a.26
crasis nature 5.3
　combination 48.1
　constitution 54.1
crass
　absolute 31.12
　dense 321.8
　viscid 352.8
　ignorant 491.8
　stupid 499.12
　vulgar 851.6
　crude 851.7
crassamentum
　clot 321.5
　gluten 352.3
crassitude
　density 321.1
　viscidity 352.1
crate
　receptacle 191.8, 9
　automobile 272.15
　aircraft 273a.1
　coffin 363.10
crater depth 208.2
　cavity 252.2
　embouchure 260.3
Crater 318.6
craunch, cranch *n.*
　298.2
craunch, cranch *v.*
　disintegrate 44.9
　chew 298.45
　pulverize 330.6
　grind 331.3
　sound harshly 410.6
cravat necktie 225.33
　bandage 662.14
crave request 765.4
　~ after 865.11
craven *n.* 862.2
craven *adj.* 862.5
craving *n.* 865.2
craving *adj.* 865.19
craw 191.7
crawdad 366.21
crawfish *n.*
　sea food 298.18
　animal 366.21
　apostate 607.5
crawfish *v.*
　back up 283.5
　recant 607.9
crawl *n.* 275.2
crawl *v.*
　be protracted 110.7
　go slow 275.6
　back up 283.5

recant 607.9
grovel 886.3
crawling
　groveling 886.4
　slow 275.9
　~ with 52.11
crawly 380.6
crayfish
　sea food 298.18
　animal 366.21
crayon 556.16
craze *n.* 503.7
　(whim 608.1)
　(phobia 860.4)
　(passion 865.5)
craze *v.* dement 503.11
　crack 659.6, 8
crazed 503.12
craziness 503.1
crazy frail 160.11
　absurd 497.4
　insane 503.12
　(idiotic 499.13)
crazy about 897.15
crazy quilt 70.1
creak 410.5, 412.2
cream *n.* drink 298.4
　semiliquid 352.3
　foam 353.2
　oil 356.4
　salience 642.4
　best 648.4
　good person 948.1
cream *adj.*
　whitish 430.9
　yellow 436.6
cream puff
　mollycoddle 160a.3
　food 298.12
creamy whitish 430.9
　yellow 436.6
crease *n.* 258.1
crease *v.* 258.3
create produce 161.8
　(cause 153.6)
　invent 515.10
　divine function
　　976.7
created being 366.2
creation
　production 161.1, 6
　(art 556.8)
　world 318.1
all creation
　limit 52.4
　boundlessness 180.4
in all creation 318.17
creational 161.11
creative
　productive 161.11
　(causal 153.9)
　(formative 240.7)
　imaginative 515.11
creative imagination
　imagination 515.1
　poetic inspiration
　　597.9
creativeness 20.1
creator cause 153.1
　producer 164.1
　poet 597.10
Creator 976.2

creature being 3.2
　product 161.6
　food 298.5
　animal 366.2
　person 372.3
　puppet 711.2
　liquor 959.4
creature comfort
　food 298.5
　comfort 377.2
creature of habit
　613.7
credence belief 484.1
　prothesis 1000.3
give credence to
　484.7
give no credence to
　485.6
credenda 484.3
credential
　evidence 467.4
　(warranty 771.1)
　voucher 550.11
　record 551.1
credibility 484.5
　(possibility 470.1)
　(probability 472.1)
　(reasonability
　　476.7)
credible 484.15
　(possible 470.5)
　(plausible 472.6)
　(logical 476.16)
credit *n.*
　credence 484.1
　merit 648.1
　pecuniary ~ 805
　(security 771.1)
　(loan 787.1)
　(note 800.7)
　entry 811.2
　reputation 873.1
　virtue 944.1
do credit to 931.7
give credit to
　believe 484.7
　credit 805.4
　(lend 787.4)
　approve 931.5
give no credit to
　485.6
on credit 805.7
to one's credit 780.9
credit *v.* believe 484.7
　extend credit 805.4
　~ to account 811.7
creditable
　reputable 873.15
　praiseworthy 931.11
　honorable 939.7
　virtuous 944.3
credited 805.6
credit instrument
　805.2
credit man, creditor
　805.3
　(lender 787.2)
credo 484.3
Credo 998.7
credulity 486
　(belief 484.1)
credulous 486.5

784

(trustful 484.13)
(deceivable 545.14)
be credulous 486.3
  (believe 484.7)
creed 484.3
  (doctrine 983.2)
creed-bound 606.7
  (hyperorthodox
  983a.8)
creek cleft 198.2
  sea inlet 343.1
  stream 348.1
Creek 434.5
creep *n.* 275.2
creep *v.* walk 266.16
  go slow 275.6
  ~ in 294.6
  tingle 380.4
  grovel 886.3
creep out 529.6
creep with
  be numerous 102.4
  abound 639.4
creeper plant 367.8
  hack writer 593.15
creepers shoes 225.27
  clothes 225.32
creeping 275.9
creeps sensation 380.1
  coldness 383.2
  trepidation 860.3
creepy tingly 380.6
  fearful 860.15
creese, kris 727.3
cremate
  ~ a corpse 363.21
  burn 384.18
cremation
  ~ of corpses 363.2
  burning 384.3
cremator 384.12
crematory
  deadhouse 363.17
  incinerator 384.12
crème de cacao
  959.6
crème de la crème
  best 648.4
  good person 948.1
crème de menthe
  green 435.3
  liqueur 959.6
Cremona 417.3
cremor 335.3
crena 257.1
crenate 257.6
crenation, crenature
  257.2
crenel, crenelle 257.1
crenelate, crenellate *v.*
  257.5
crenelate, crenellate
  adj. 257.6
**crenelation, crenella-
  tion** 257.2
crenula 257.2
crenulate *v.* 257.5
crenulate *adj.* 257.6
crenulation 257.2
creole 57.3
crepe, crêpe 219.5
crêpé 248.4

crepe de Chine 219.5
crepitant 406.10
crepitate 406.7
crepitation 406.1
crepuscle 126.1
  (morning 125.1)
crepuscular 126.5
  (morning 125.3)
  (dim 422.8)
crepuscule
  morning 125.1
  evening 126.1
  (semidarkness
  422.2)
crescendo
  increasing 35.6, 7
  music 415.30
crescent *n.*
  ~ of houses 189.20
  semicircle 245.2
  moon 318.5
crescent *adj.*
  increasing 35.6
  crescent-shaped
  245.6
crescentiform 245.6
crescent-shaped
  245.6, 7
  (horn-shaped
  253.19)
crescive 35.6
cress 298.30
crest *n.*
  pinnacle 206.2
  summit 210.1
  (supremacy 33.3)
  feathers 256.8
  insignia 550.12
  pride 878.1
crest *v.* 210.5
crested 256.13
crestfallen
  dejected 837.9
  humbled 879.5
cretaceous 430.8
crevasse chasm 198.3
  depth 208.2
crevice 198.2
  (opening 260.1)
crew company 72.3
  population 188.10
  party 712.1
  staff 746.7
crib *n.* case 191.8
  bassinet 191.9
  frame 215.8
  bed 215.24
  translation 522.2
  gambling den 621.4
  brothel 961.7
crib *v.* 791.9
cribbage 840.12
cribbed 751.12
cribber 271.6
cribble, cribellum
  260.7
criblé 558.1
cribriform 260.17
crick *n.* creek 348.1
  pain 378.1
crick *v.* 410.5
cricket seat 215.22

insect 366.24
  game 840.11
cricketer 840.17
crier 534.1
crime
  criminality 945.6
  misdemeanor 947.2
  violation of law
  964.2
Crimean War 722.4
criminal *n.* 949.2
criminal *adj.*
  dishonest 940.8
  guilty 947.4
  illegal 964.5
criminal conversation
  961.6
criminality
  wrongdoing 945.6
  guilt 947.1
  (vice 945.1)
  lawlessness 964.1
criminate 938.4
crimination 938.1
criminatory 938.5
crimp *n.* cheat 548.2
  abductor 792.7
crimp *v.*
  convolve 248.3
  notch 257.5
  kidnap 791.11
crimp *adj.* 330.9
crimper cheat 548.2
  abductor 792.7
crimson *n.* 434.2
crimson *v.*
  redden 434.7
  turn color 824.8
  blush 881.4
crine 256.3
cringe
  ~ to 725.3
  grovel 886.3
cringing 886.4
crinite 256.13
crinkle *n.* 258.1
crinkle *v.*
  convolve 248.3
  roughen 256.11
  wrinkle 258.3
crinkled angular 244.5
  rough 256.12
crinkly 256.12
crinoid 368.5
crinoidal, crinoidean
  368.14
crino!ine cloth 219.5
  dress 225.19
crinose 256.13
cripple *n.* 655.20
  (impotent 158.3)
cripple *v.*
  disable 158.6
  (weaken 160.8)
  (render useless
  645.7)
  impair 659.8
  (afflict 655.22)
crippled
  impotent 158.8
  lame 655.24
  (impaired 659.12)

crisis
  critical situation
  134.4
  (predicament 8.3;
  704.2)
  (turning point
  145.2)
  (eventuality 151.1)
  climax 210.1
crisp *v.*
  roughen 256.11
  coil 248.3
crisp *adj.*
  brittle 328.4
  pulverable 330.9
  terse 572.3
Crispin 225.40
crisscross *n.*
  cross 219.6
  alphabet 561.2
  game 840.11
crisscross *v.* 219.7
criterion
  prototype 22.1
  (rule 80.1)
  test 463.1
  measure 466.2
crithomancy 511.3
critic censor 480.5
  (commentator
  524.2)
  (judge 967.1)
  expositor 595.3
  connoisseur 850.3
  faultfinder 936.1
critical
  circumstantial 8.5
  crucial 134.8
  discriminating
  465.4
  commentarial 595.5
  urgent 642.13
  precarious 665.7
  ticklish 704.7
  discontented 832.5
  censorious 932.11
  (judicial 480.13)
  (disparaging 934.4)
critical point 134.4
  (turning point
  145.2)
criticism
  philosophy 451.15
  examination 461.3
  discrimination 465.1
  judgment 480.3
  (comment 522.4)
  commentary 595.2
  censure 932.2
  (detraction 934.1)
criticize, criticise
  discriminate 465.2
  judge 480.10
  comment upon
  595.4
  exercise taste 850.4
  censure 932.7
  (complain 839.10)
  (detract 934.3)
criticizer, criticiser
  595.3

critique — crow

critique n.
  examination 461.3
  discrimination 465.1
  criticism 480.3
  commentary 595.2
  (comment 522.4)
critique v.
  criticize 480.10
  comment upon 595.4
critter being 3.2
  creature 366.2
croak 360.6
  kill 361.10
  sound harshly 410.6
  forebode 511.9
  speech defect 583.2
  complain 839.10
croaker killer 361.8
  frog 366.20
  doctor 662.19
  malcontent 832.2
Croat 726.4
crocein, croceine 428.4
crochet note 413.6, 12
  needlework 847.6
crock n. pot 191.11
  horse 271.6
  ceramics 384.14
crock v. 959.18
crockery 384.14
  (tableware 191.13)
crocodile 366.18
crocodile tears
  hypocrisy 544.2
  affectation 853.1
crocodilian 366.18
crocus 436.3
Croesus 803.2
croft close 181.3
  enclosure 232.1
  field 371.5
cromlech 363.15
cromorna 417.12
crone
  old woman 130.3
  mollycoddle 160a.3
  dotard 501.3
cronk 412.2
Cronus See Kronos
crony chum 890.3
  boon companion 892.8
crook n. staff 215.15; 747.3
  angle 244.2
  curve 245.2
  pot hook 386.3
  thief 792.1
  criminal 949.2
  pastoral staff 999.1
crook v. oblique 217.5
  distort 243.3
  angle 244.4
  curve 245.3
  deviate 279.6
  crook the elbow 950.15
crookbacked 243.5
crookbilled 245.9
crooked oblique 217.13

(distorted 243.5)
(deviative 279.8)
(circuitous 311.6; 629.3)
angular 244.5
dishonest 940.8
crooked-backed 243.5
crookedness 217.1
  (distortion 243.1)
crooked stick 901.4
crooken oblique 217.5
  distort 243.3
crooknosed 245.9
croon n. 415.10
croon v. 416.20
crooner 416.10
crop n. stomach 191.7
  handle 215.7
  breast 250.3
  hair 256.3
  vegetable life 367.1
  store 636.3
  (agriculture 371.7)
  produce 775.2
crop v. cut off 38.6
  graze 298.46
  harvest 371.8
  gather 775.6
  pluck 789.9
crop-ear 418.5
crop-eared 418.14
crop forth 529.6
crop out
  appear 446.2
  be disclosed 529.6
crop up
  originate 66.6
  happen 151.3
  be disclosed 529.6
cropper 306.2
croquet 840.11
croquette 298.19
crore 98.11
crosier, crozier
  staff 215.15
  insignia 747.3
  pastoral staff 999.1
cross n. mongrel 41.5
  staff 215.15
  cruciform 219.6
  tombstone 363.15
  signature 488.4
  bane 663.1
  impediment 706.2
  hardship 735.1
  trouble 830.2
  crucifixion 975.4
  crucifix 998.8
Cross n. 318.6
cross v. mix 41.6
  counteract 179.3
  intersect 219.7
  navigate 267.10
  pass 302.2
  thwart 509.2
  oppose 708.2
  refuse 764.4
  cross swords 720.8
  (war 722.9)
cross up
  inform on 527.10
  betray 940.7

cross adj.
  crossed 219.9, 10
  opposed 708.4
  ill-humored 901.7
  (angry 900.13)
cross adv. 219.12
cross prep. 708.5
cross and pile, cross or pile 621.7
crossarm 158a.9
crossbar n.
  cable pole 158a.9
  cross 219.6
crossbar v. 219.7
crossbeam 215.12
crossbill 366.22
crossbow 727.9
crossbred 41.10
crossbreed n. 41.5
crossbreed v. 41.6
crossbreeding 563.8
cross-country race 720.5
crosscurrent
  counteractant 179.2
  opposition 708.1
crosscut 246.2
crosscut saw 257.3
crossed mongrel 41.10
  cross 219.9, 10
  frustrated 732.9
cross-examination 461.9
  (examination 461.3)
  (trial 969.5)
cross-examine 461.15
  (try 969.11)
cross-examiner 461.12
cross-eye 443.1
cross-eyed 443.14
cross-fertilization 161.2
cross-fertilize 168.4
cross fire
  interchange 148.1
  counteractant 179.2
  opposition 708.1
  gunfire 716.2
cross-grained adj.
  rough 256.12
  obstinate 606.6
  irascible 901.7
cross-grained adv. 219.12
crosshatch 259.3
crossing n. 219
crossing adj. 219.9
cross-interrogate 461.15
cross-interrogation 461.9
cross-interrogator 461.12
crossjack 273.13
crossjack yard 273.12
crosslike 219.10
crossness 901.1
Cross of Merit 733.2
crosspatch 901.4
crosspoint 219.2
cross-pollinate 168.4

cross-pollination 161.2
cross-purpose
  mistake 495.2
  variance 713.2
  at cross-purposes
    contrary 14.5
    in disagreement 24.10
    in disorder 59.13
    mistaken 495.13
    in a dilemma 704.11
    in opposition 708.4
    at loggerheads 713.10
    inimical 889.3
  be at cross-purposes
    be contrary 14.3
    disagree 24.5
    mistake 495.8
    misinterpret 523.2
cross-question 461.15
cross-questioner 461.12
cross-questioning 461.9
crossroad 219.2
  (roadway 627.3)
crossroads 189.17
  at the cross-roads 525.7
crossruff 314.3
cross-shaped 219.10
cross-staff 215.15
crosstie 215.12
crosstree 273.12
crosswalk, crossway n. 219.2
crossway, crossways, crosswise adv. 219.12
  (laterally 236.8)
crotch fork 91.2
  angle 244.2
crotched
  bifurcate 91.7
  angular 244.5
crotchet
  eccentricity 503.6
  punctuation 550.8
  caprice 608.1
  (quirk 481.3)
crotchety
  eccentric 503.17
  capricious 608.5
croton oil 356.3
crouch squat 207.5
  stoop 308.7
  be submissive 725.3
  quail 860.8
  fawn 886.3
crouched 207.7
crouching
  submissive 725.3
  obsequious 886.4
crouch ware 384.14
croup rump 235.5
  disease 655.9, 18
croupier 694.5
crow n. crowbar 307.4
  bird 366.22
  black 431.3

Negro 431.4
laughter 838.3
eyesore 846.3
Crow *n.* 318.6
crow *v.* croak 412.2
 speech defect 583.2
 laugh 838.7
 exult 884.6
crowbait horse 271.6
 corpse 362.1
crowbar 307.4
crowd *n.*
 company 72.3, 4
 (multitude 102.2)
 ~ of sail 273.13
 music instrument
  417.2, 3
 clique 712.2
 masses 876.1
crowd *v.*
 assemble 72.10
 be numerous 102.4
 densify 321.7
crowd sail
 speed 274.9
 set sail 267.16
crowded packed 72.13
 (full 52.11)
 (overfull 641.6)
 populous 102.5
crowdy, crowdie
 298.15
crowfoot 550.8
crown *n.* summit 210.1
 capital 215.17
 circle 247.2
 chandelier 423.10
 trophy 733.1
 sovereignty 737.2
 royal ~ 747.2
 insignia 747.4
 money 800.5, 8
 ornament 847.5, 7
crown *v.* top 210.5
 complete 729.2
 (perfect 650.4)
 ~ with success
  731.5
 enthrone 755.4
 glorify 873.13
Crown Derby 384.14
crowned head 745.2
crowning
 supreme 33.8
 completing 729.5
 (ending 67.8)
crown of thorns 830.2
crown post 215.16
crown wheel 312.4
crow's-feet 258.1
crow's-nest
 height 210.1
 ship 273.7
 observatory 441.5
crowstone 342.4
crozier See **crosier**
crucial
 circumstantial 8.5
 critical 134.8
 crosslike 219.10
 demonstrative 478.3
 urgent 642.13

cruciate 219.10
cruciation
 bodily pain 378.2
 mental pain 828.6
crucible
 conversion 144.4
 receptacle 191.11
 heater 386.1
 experiment 463.5
crucified 828.13
crucifix cross 219.6
 holy cross 998.8
crucifixion
 bodily pain 378.2
 mental pain 828.6
 execution 972.4
cruciform *n.* 219.6
cruciform *adj.* 219.10
crucify cross 219.7
 pain 378.4
 maltreat 649.7
 torture 830.6
 execute 972.8
crude
 gaudy-colored
  428.15
 speech 579.3
 unfinished 674.8
 (incomplete 53.4)
 uncouth 851.7
crudity 674.2
cruel
 painful 378.7; 830.15
 gruff 895.7
 brutal 907.9
 (savage 173.14)
 (murderous 361.15)
 (severe 739.5)
 (pitiless 914a.3)
cruelly 31.23
cruelty 907.3
 (maltreatment
  649.4)
 (torture 828.6)
cruet
 receptacle 191.11
 church vessel 998.8
cruise *n.* 267.6
cruise *v.* 267.10, 42
cruiser traveler 268.1
 aircraft 273a.1
 warship 726.11
cruising 267.1
cruller 298.12
crumb *n.*
 modicum 32.2
 piece 51.3
 diminutive 193.2
 powder 330.3
 lice 366.24
crumb *v.* 330.6
crumble *n.* 330.3
crumble *v.*
 decrease 36.3
 decompose 49.3
 weaken 160.7
 perish 162.5
 powder 330.6, 7
 (break 328.3)
 decay 659.7
crumbling *n.* 49.1
crumbling *adj.*

antiquated 124.9
deteriorating 659.11
crumbly 330.9
 (brittle 328.4)
crump *n.* 408a.2
crump *v.* oblique 217.5
 bang 406.7
 sound harshly 410.6
crump *adj.*
 crooked 217.13
 distorted 243.5
crumpet 210.3
crumple *n.* 258.1
crumple *v.*
 contract 195.4
 roughen 256.11
 wrinkle 258.3
crumple up
 destroy 162.4
 contract 195.4
crunch *n.* 298.2
crunch *v.*
 disintegrate 44.9
 chew 298.45
 pulverize 330.6
 grind 331.3
 sound harshly 410.6
crunk 412.2
cruor 333.3
crupper 235.5
crusade, Crusades
 722.4
cruse 191.11
crush *n.* fill 52.3
 crowd 72.4
 pulp 354.2
 infatuation 897.1
crush *v.*
 disintegrate 44.9
 destroy 162.4
 contract 195.4
 be brittle 328.3
 pulverize 330.6
 pulp 354.4
 sound harshly 410.6
 confute 479.2
 break 659.8
 conquer 731.9
 subdue 749.5
 humiliate 879.3
crushable *n.* 225.26
crushable *adj.* 328.4
crushed
 defeated 732.12
 wretched 828.16
 ~ by grief 837.13
crusher 479.1
crushing
 vigorous 574.6
 painful 830.13
crust *n.*
 incrustation 223.16
 impudence 885.2
crust *v.* 223.25
crustacean *n.* 368.8
 (fish 366.21)
crustacean *adj.* 368.18
crusty
 audacious 885.9
 gruff 895.7
 irascible 901.7
crutch fork 91.2

support 215.2, 15
 angle 244.2
Crutched Friar 996.11
crux cross 219.6
 difficulty 704.2
Crux 318.6
cry *n.* human ~ 411
 (exclamation 580.5)
 animal ~ 412.1
 (call 550.16)
 publicity 531.3
 rumor 532.3
 cheer 838.4
 sob 839.1, 2
cry *v.* call 411.5
 (be noisy 404.6)
 (exclaim 580.9)
 ululate 412.2
 ~ abroad 531.7
 plead 765.5
 cheer 838.8
 sob 839.8, 9
 complain 839.10
 cry down
  censure 932.7
  disparage 934.3
 cry for 865.11
 cry havoc 722.10
 cry out
  vociferate 411.7
  proclaim 531.7
 cry out against
  advise against 616.2
  deprecate 766.2
  censure 932.7
 cry quits 725.4
 cry to 765.5
 cry up 931.6
 cry wolf
  falsify 544.3
  false alarm 669.3
  frighten 860.10
  ready to cry 839.14
crying *n.*
 vociferation 411.1
 weeping 839.2
crying *adj.*
 vociferous 411.8
 ululant 412.3
 urgent 642.13
cryolite glass 384.14
crypt
 compartment 191.2
 burial place 363.13
 hiding place 530.2
 money vault 802.1
 church ~ 1000.3
cryptic vague 475.11
 hidden 528.17
 (latent 526.6)
 enigmatic 533.6
cryptogram
 concealment 528.5
 cipher 561.5
cryptogrammic 528.22
cryptograph
 concealment 528.5
 (unintelligibility
  519.2)
 cipher 561.5
cryptographic
 secret 528.23

cryptography — cupel

cryptographic (cont'd)
  steganographic
    590.17
cryptography
  concealment 528.5
  cipher 561.5
  steganography
    590.8
cryptology 528.5
crystal
  hardness 323.3
  water 337.1
  stone 342.4
  snowflake 383.6
  transparency 425.2
  divination 511.5
crystal-clear 425.4
crystal-gazer 513.2
crystal gazing 511.3
crystalline *n.* 425.4
crystalline *adj.* 321.8
crystallinity 425.1
crystallization
  solidification 321.3
  (refrigeration
    385.1)
  hardening 323.2
crystallize 321.7
  (harden 323.4)
crystallized, crystalloid 323.5
crystallomancy 511.3
  (symbology 550.17)
crystallose 396.4
crystal vision 994.7
ctenidia 349.19
cub *n.*
  youngling 129.4, 7
  unrefined person
    851.4
cub *v.* 161.9
Cuba 182.3
cubby
  small place 184.4
  compartment 191.2
  room 191.16
  hiding place 530.2
cubbyhole
  small place 184.4
  (inextension
    180a.1)
  compartment 191.2
  room 191.16
  hiding place 530.2
cubbyhouse 184.4
cube *n.*
  third power 92.3
  angle 244.2
cube *v.* 93.2
cubeb 393.1
cubed 244.5
cubes 621.8
cubic 244.5
cubicle 191.16
cubic measure 466.3
cubiform 244.5
cubism 556.6
  (modernism 123.3)
cubist *n.* 559.1
  (modernist 123.4)
cubist *adj.* 556.19
cubit 200.6

cubitiere 717.2
cucking stool 975.3
cuckold 903.7
cuckoldry 961.6
cuckoo *n.*
  imitator 19.4
  aeronaut 269a.1
  battleplane 273a.2
  bird 366.22
  songbird 416.11
cuckoo *v.* 412.2
cuckoo *adj.* 503.12
cuculla 999.1
cucumber
  vegetable 298.30
  green 435.2
cud 298.2
cuddle 902.8
cuddlesome, cuddly
  902.9
cuddy 271.10
cudgel *n.* 727.7
  (hammer 276.4)
  (rod 975.2)
take up the cudgels
  aid 707.8
  attack 716.5
  fight 720.8
  wage war 722.9
cudgel *v.* 972.6
cudgel one's brains
  505.14
cudgeling 972.3
cue nature 5.3
  tail 235.6
  hair 256.3
  hint 527.4
  sign 550.2
  role 599.7
  waiting line 599.23
  function 625.3
  humor 820.1
give the cue
  remind 505.10
  hint 527.8
  (signal 550.20)
cuff *n.*
  wristband 225.31
  blow 276.3
  (whipping 972.3)
  handcuff 752.2
cuff *v.* strike 276.8
  chastise 972.6
cui bono 620.5; 645.10
cuirass 717.2
cuirassier 726.4
cuisine meal 298.39
  preparation 673.2
cul-de-lampe
  support 215.11
  engraving 558.1
  ornament 847.3
cul-de-sac
  closure 261.1
  (recess 252.4)
  roadway 627.3
  impasse 704.3
culinary 298.49
culinary art 673.2
cull *n.* 547.1
cull *v.* 609.7

cullender See colander
cullet 211.1
cullion 949.1
cully 547.1
culm stalk 215.14
  coal 388.2
culmen 210.1
culminal 210.6
culminate top 210.5
  complete 729.3, 4
culminating 210.6
culmination
  final issue 154.1
  summit 210.1
  completion 729.1
culpa 460.1
culpability 947.1
culpable 932.14
  (unworthy 940.9)
  (vicious 945.11)
  (guilty 947.4)
culpose 460.8
culprit convict 754.1
  felon 949.2
cult belief 484.3
  religious ~ 984.3, 4
cultism 984.2
cultist 984.13, 14
cultivate till 371.8
  (grow 367.12)
  sensitize 375.4
  train 537.10
  improve 658.8
  ~ the soil 673.6
  foster 707.9
  become friendly
    888.3
  civilize 894.11
cultivated
  taste 850.1, 5
  polite 894.12
cultivation
  agriculture 371.1
  learning 490.2
  training 537.2
  culture 658.2; 894.1
  preparation 673.3
  refinement 850.1
cultivator
  agriculturist 371.2
  countryman 876.5
cultural
  educational 537.12
  (schoolish 542.9)
  improving 658.16
culture
  animal ~ 370
  agriculture 371.1
  learning 490.2
  cultivation 658.2
  refinement 850.1
  civilization 894.1
culverin 727.11
culvert 350.1
cumber *n.* 319.1
cumber *v.*
  weight 319.9
  encumber 706.6
cumbersome
  hulky 192.13
  heavy 319.12

awkward 699.12
impedimentary
  706.8
oppressive 830.16
cumbrance 319.1
cumbrous
  hulky 192.13
  heavy 319.12
  awkward 699.12
  impedimentary
    706.8
  oppressive 830.16
cum laude 873.8, 20
cummerbund
  garment 225.34
  circle 247.2
cumshaw
  gratuity 784.3
  reward 973.2
cumulation
  assemblage 72.6
  acquisition 775.1
cumulative
  assembling 72.14
  evidence 467.11
cumulo-stratus 353.5
cumulous 353.11
cumulus 353.5
cunctation 133.2
cunctatious 133.9
cuneate 244.5
cuneiform, cuniform *n.* 590.1, 9
cuneiform,
  cuniform *adj.*
  angular 244.5
  writing 590.15
cuneus 244.2
cunning *n.* 702
  (sagacity 498.2)
  (stealth 528.3)
  (falsehood 544.1)
  (deceit 545.1)
  (skill 698.1)
  (rascality 940.1, 4)
cunning *adj.*
  well-laid 611.6
  crafty 702.6
  (knowing 490.12)
  (sagacious 498.10)
  (deceitful 545.12)
  (false 544.7)
  (evasive 623.12)
  (scheming 626.12)
  (skillful 698.11)
be cunning 702.5
  (deceive 545.7)
cunningly 702.7
cup *n.*
  receptacle 191.11
  cavity 252.2
  fate 601.3
  trophy 733.1
  alcoholic drink
    959.4
Cup *n.* 318.6
cup *v.* 662.24
cupbearer 746.1
cupboard closet 191.15
  (storehouse 636.4)
  coffer 802.1
cupel *n.* 384.12

788

cupel v. 384.18
cupellation
 vaporization 336.1
 burning 384.3
cupful quantity 25.2
 fill 52.3
 load 190.1
Cupid love 897.4
 god 979.2
cupidity avarice 819.1
 greed 865.4
cupidon 897.4
Cupid's bow, Cupid's-
 dart 897.5
cupmaker 690.8
cupola tower 206.3
 arch 215.18
 roof 223.6
cupped 252.10
cupping 662.15
cur dog 366.6
 coward 862.2
 scoundrel 949.1
curability 660.6
curable 658.16
 (remediable 662.27)
curaçao, curaçoa
 959.6
curacy 995.3
curate 996.2, 5
curative 662.25
 (restorative
  660.18)
 (relieving 834.7)
curator
 librarian 593.14
 caretaker 664.3
 steward 694.5
 functionary 758.2
curb n.
 frame 215.8
 edge 231.1
 hindrance 706.2
 restraint 751.1
 fetter 752.2
 (dissuasion 616.1)
 stock exchange
  799.3
curb v. retard 275.7
 hinder 706.4
 restrain 751.6
 (moderate 174.5)
curb bit 706.2
curb market 799.3
curbstone, kerbstone
 limit 233.1
 stone 342.4
 pavement 627.4
curcuma paper 463.5
curd n. clot 321.5
 semiliquid 352.3
curd, curdle v. 321.7
cure n.
 restoration 660.5
 remedy 662.1
 curacy 995.3
cure v. remedy 660.12
 (better 658.8)
 (relieve 834.4)
 preserve 670.4
 (prepare 673.6)
 punish 972.5

curé 996.2
cure-all 662.3
cureless 859.7
curfew 126.1
curia 966.1, 4
curial 966.7
curing 660.5
 (remedy 662.1)
curio 556.8
curiosity oddity 83.4
 inquisitiveness 455
 (questioning 461.9)
 (meddlesomeness
  682.8)
 phenomenon 872.1
curious unusual 83.10
 inquisitive 455.5
 (inquiring 461.24)
 (meddlesome
  682.22)
 exact 494.11
 artistic 845.16
 anxious 865.16
be curious 455.3
curiously 31.21
curl n. coil 248.2
 (curve 245.2)
 hair 256.3
curl v. coil 248.3
 (curve 245.3)
 fold 258.3
 sneer 930.6
curl cloud 353.5
curler 386.1
curlicue, curlycue n.
 248.2
 (curve 245.2)
curlicue, curlycue v.
 248.3
curling 840.11
curling iron 386.1
curl paper 256.3
curly 248.4
curmudgeon 819.2
currant 298.31
currency
 publicity 531.3
 money 800.1
current n.
 electricity 158a.1
 flow 348.2
current adj.
 existent 1.7
 prevalent 78.10
 present 118.2
 going on 151.5
 well-known 490.17
 rumored 532.8
 (published 531.10)
 familiar 613.11
 conventional 852.8
curricle 272.4, 5
curricular 272.22
curriculum 537.7
currish
 churlish 895.7
 irascible 901.7
curry n. 298.17
curry v.
 rub down 331.3
 cook 384.19
 season 392.4

curry favor 886.3
 (flatter 933.2)
currycomb 370.7
curse n. trifle 643.3
 bane 663.1
 (adversity 735.1)
 affliction 830.2
 malediction 908.1, 3
curse v.
 maledict 908.4
 swear 908.5
cursed
 execrable 649.8
 cantankerous 901.7
 damned 908.6
 wicked 945.16
cursedly 31.24
cursitor 968.1
cursive n. 590.9
cursive adj. 591.8
cursory
 inconsiderable 32.8
 transient 111.6
 superficial 209.4
 offhand 458.9
 perfunctory 460.8
 hasty 684.5
curst 901.7
curt short 201.5
 terse 572.3
 taciturn 585.4
 gruff 895.7
curtail 201.4
 (reduce 36.4)
 (deduct 38.4)
curtailment
 decrease 36.1
 contraction 195.1
 shortening 201.2
 (deduction 38.1)
curtain n.
 encore 104.2
 screen 424.3
 stage ~ 599.15
 fortification 717.3
behind the curtain
 invisible 447.4
 aware of 490.13
 in private 528.24
curtain v. 528.10
curtain call
 encore 104.2
 drama 599.5
curtain lecture 932.3
curtain raiser
 beginning 66.1
 music 415.3
 act 599.5
curtains end 67.1
 destruction 162.2
 death 360.1
curtain tune 415.3
curtate short 201.5
 terse 572.3
curtilage 232.1
curtness 585.1
curtsy, curtsey n.
 928.2
 (greeting 894.4)
curtsy, curtsey v.
 928.6
curule 696.9

curvation 245.1
curvature 245
 (obliquity 217.1)
 (circularity 247.1)
 (convolution 248.1)
curve n. girl 129.5
 curvature 245.1, 2
 woman 374.2
curve v. bend 245.3
 (oblique 217.5)
 (round 247.6)
 (wind 248.3)
 (deviate 279.4)
 turn 311.4
curved 245.4
 (oblique 217.9)
 (round 247.8)
 (rotund 249.6)
 (concave 252.10)
 (deviative 279.8)
curvet n. caper 309.2
 turn 311.2
curvet v. caper 309.5
 frolic 840.21
curving n. 245.1
curving adj. 245.4
curvy 245.4
cush, cusha
 cow 366.12
 female animal 374.8
cushat 366.22
cushion
 bedding 215.24
 softness 324.3
cusp angle 244.2
 point 253.2
 ornament 847.4
cusped 253.11
cuspidate v. 253.9
cuspidate adj. 253.11
cuspidation 847.3
cuspidor 191.1
cuss n. 908.3
cuss v. 908.5
cussed 901.7
cussedness 606.1
cuss word 908.3
custodian
 guardian 664.3
 jailer 753.1
custody
 protectorship 664.2
 imprisonment 751.4
 retention 781.1
in custody 751.12
take into custody
 751.9
custom
 tradition 124.3
 usage 613.2
 (conformity 82.1)
 (wont 677.1)
 (convention 852.2)
 business ~ 794.1
 (sale 796.4)
 clientele 795.2
 tax 812.2
customary
 traditional 124.8
 habitual 613.11
 (prevalent 78.10)
 (regular 80.3)

customer — cynosure

customary (*continued*)
  (conformable 82.9)
  (prescriptive 697.2)
  conventional 852.8
  orthodox 983a.7
customer person 372.3
  client 795.2
customs union 712.4
custos music 415.23
  guardian 664.3
  jailer 753.1
cut *n.* degree 26.1
  decrease 36.1
  piece 51.3
  rank 71.1
  absentation 187.5
  cleft 198.2, 3
  (disjunction 44.3)
  lamina 204.2
  form 240.1
  notch 257.1
  furrow 259.1, 2
  blow 276.3
  hurt 378.1
  woodcut 558.3
  manner 627.1
  wound 659.4
  thrust 716.3
  share 786.2
  discount 813.1
  mental pain 830.2
  rank 873.4
  gibe 930.3, 4
  (disregard 460.1)
cut of one's jib
  feature 240.2
  appearance 448.5
cut *v.* geld 38.7
  imbue 41.8
  sunder 44.8
  dilute 160.9
  destroy 162.4
  form layers 204.4
  form 240.6
  notch 257.5
  furrow 259.3
  open 260.11
  hasten off 293.5
  ~ to pieces 361.12
  reap 371.8
  pain physically 378.4
  freeze 385.3
  colors 428.11
  pretermit 460.7
  sculpture 557.9
  engrave 558.5
  discount 813.2
  cheapen 815.7
  irritate 824.5
  pain mentally 830.3
  snub 930.7
  (disregard 460.5)
  (exclude 893.7)
cut a crab 267.46
cut across 302.2
cut a dash
  be distinguished 873.10
  splurge 882.6
cut a dido 309.5
cut a figure
  appear 448.6
  be distinguished 852.6; 873.10
  (be important 642.7)
  splurge 882.6
cut along 274.9
cut and come again 104.4
cut and run
  hasten off 293.5
  flee 623.10
cut blocks with a razor quibble 477.8
  misuse 679.2
  be unskillful 699.7
cut capers
  caper 309.5
  frolic 840.21
cut down
  demolish 162.4
  fell 213.7; 308.5
  kill 361.12
cut in 228.10
cut loose 173.7
cut no ice
  be small 32.4
  be unimportant 643.7
cut off deduct 38.6
  disjoin 44.7
  cease 142.6
  shorten 201.4
  hasten off 293.5
  kill 361.10
  hinder 706.4
  disinherit 789.11
  isolate 893.7
cut one's coat according to one's cloth
  exercise skill 698.9
  economize 817.3
  take precautions 864.4
cut one's eye 441.15
cut one's eyeteeth 131.4
cut one's stick 293.5
cut one's throat 699.7
cut out excel 33.5
  excise 38.5
  exclude 55.3
  substitute 147.3
  destroy 162.4
  plan 626.9
cut short stop 142.7
  destroy 162.4
  shorten 201.4
  be concise 572.2
  render mute 581.5
cut stick depart 293.5
  flee 623.10
cut the knot 705.4
cut the mustard
  be able 157.6
  succeed 731.5
cut up
  disintegrate 44.9
  destroy 162.4
  be violent 173.7
  distress 830.3

dissatisfy 832.4
grieve 837.8
disconsolate 837.13
misbehave 851.5
criticize 932.7
cut *adj.* 959.21
cut off 776.6
cut out for 698.12
cut up 828.16
cut and dried
  predetermined 611.5
  ready-prepared 673.12
  conventional 852.8
cutaneous 223.32
cutaway coat 225.14
cutcherry, cutchery
  office 745.9
  treasury 802.1
  bureau 965.2
cute sagacious 498.10
  clever 698.11
  witty 842.9
cuticle, cuticula 223.12
cuticular 223.32
cutie 129.5
cutis 223.12
cutlass 727.3
cutlery
  edge tools 253.6
  merchandise 798.3
cutlet 298.27
cutpurse 792.6
cutter tooth 253.3
  knife 253.6
  sled 272.13
  ship 273.2
  warship 726.11
cutthroat *n.*
  killer 361.8
  ruffian 913.2
cutthroat *adj.* 720.13
cutting *n.* piece 51.3
  excerpt 596.2
cutting *adj.*
  acrid 171.10
  violent 173.11
  sharp 253.11
  cold 383.8
  intensely felt 821.5
  penetrating 824.13
  painful 830.15
  gruff 895.7
  censorious 932.11
cuttlefish 368.6
cutty stool 950.1
cutwater 273.7
cutworm 366.25
cwt. 319.4
cyan 438.2
cyanic 438.6
cyanide, cyanid 663.5
cyanin 438.4
cyanine blue 438.2
cyanogen 438.4
Cyanophyceae 369.4
cyathus, kyathos 191.14
Cybele
  maternity 166.3
  world 318.1

goddess 979.2
cycad 369.6, 8
cycadaceous 369.11
cycle *n.* series 69.2
  era 108.2
  round 138.4
  circle 247.2
  vehicle 272.14
  circuit 629.1
cycle *v.* 266.18
cyclian, cyclic 138.10
cycloid 247.4
cycloidal 247.8
cyclone 349.13
  (storm 173.5)
cyclone cellar 666.3
cyclonic 345.26
Cyclopean vast 31.8
  strong 159.10
  giantlike 192.15
cyclopedia, cyclopaedia
  knowledge 490.7
  book 593.3
Cyclops monster 83.7
  strong man 159.6
  giant 192.8
cyclostome 368.19
cygnet 366.22
cylinder
  rotundity 249.3
  automobile 272.16
  record 551.6
cylinder head 272.16
cylindrical 249.8
  (columnar 215.29)
cylindricality 249.1
cylindroid *n.* 249.3
cylindroid *adj.* 249.8
cyma 847.4
cymatium, cymation 215.17
cymbaler, cymbaleer 416.8
cymbals 417.10
cymbiform 245.11
cymophane 440.2
cymophanous 440.7
cynanche 655.9
cynic spoilsport 837.5
  pessimist 859.4
  recluse 893.4
  misanthrope 910.2
  disparager 936.1
  ascetic 955.2
cynical
  pessimistic 837.15
  ironical 856.7
  misanthropic 910.3
  contemptuous 930.8
  disapprobatory 932.11
cynicism
  pessimism 837.1; 859.1
  discourtesy 895.2
  misanthropy 910.1
  contempt 930.2
  asceticism 955.2
Cynicism 451.7
cynosure sign 550.10
  guide 694.6

celebrity 873.9
Cynosure 318.3
Cynthia 318.5
Cynthian 318.16
cypress 839.4
  (funeral 363.4)
cypress, cyprus 427.2
Cyprian n. 962.2
Cyprian adj. 961.10
Cyprus earth 433.2
Cyrenaicism 451.7
cyst vessel 191.6
  wrapper 223.11
cystic 191.23
cystis 223.11
cystocarp 357.4
cytologist 368.2
cytology
  organic science 357.5
  zoology 368.1
cytoplasm 357.3
cytoplasmic 357.9
czar, tsar 745.3
czarevitch, tsarevitch 745.3
czarevna, tsarevna 875.8
czarina, tsarina 745.6
czarism, tsarism 737.4
Czech 188.9
Czechoslovak, Czecho-Slovak 560.4

D

d. 800.8
D.A. 968.1
dab n. modicum 32.2
  blow 276.3
  attempt 675.1
  proficient 700.1
dab v. strike 276.8
  paint 428.10
dabber 591.5
dabb e splash 337.5
  befoul 653.15
  dally 683.8
dabbler
  sciolist 493.2
  artist 559.1
dablet 32.2
dabster 700.1
da capo 415.23
dace 89.2
dachshund 366.6
dacker, daiker 149.4
dacoit 792.3
dactyl 597.6
dactylic 597.13
dactyliomancy 511.3
dactylogram, dactylograph 550.7
dactylography
  dumb show 550.3
  symbology 550.17
dactylology
  deafness 419.5
  dumb show 550.3
dactylonomy 85.1

dad 166.6
Dadaism 556.6
Dadaist 556.19
daddle deceive 545.7
  swindle 791.12
daddy 166.6
daddy longlegs 206.6
dado n. 211.1
dado v. 231.3
daduchus, dadouchos 996.10
daedal complex 59.10
  diversified 81.3
  variegated 440.5
Daedalian 698.11
Daedalus
  aeronaut 269a.1
  daredevil 863.2
daemon
  tutelary deity 979.12
  demon 980.2
daemon, daemoniac
  etc. See demon etc.
daeva See deva
daffy 503.12
Dafla 560.4
daft 503.12
dagger obelisk 550.8
  weapon 727.3
daggle
  hang down 214.4
  befoul 653.15
dago alien 57.3
  Italian 188.9
dagoba, dagaba 1000.2
Dagon 991.4
daguerreotype n. 556.11
daguerreotype v. 556.18
daguerreotypist 559.7
dahabeah 273.4
dah'ia 438.2, 3
daiker See dacker
Dail Eireann, Dail 696.6
dai'y n. 593.6
daily adj. 138.11
daily adv. 136.6
daily bread 298.5
daimio, daimyo 875.4
daimon 979.12
dainty n. 298.9
  (treat 829.3)
dainty adj. slight 32.10
  frail 160.11
  savory 394.7
  pleasing 829.7
  pretty 845.8
  refined 850.5
  fastidious 868.4
dairy room 191.16
  storehouse 636.4
  mart 799.4
dais table 215.20
  platform 215.21
  (horizontal 213.3)
  seat 215.22
  rostrum 542.6
daisy 648.4
daisy-clipping 267a.25
dak, dawk 534.1

dak bungalow 189.8
dakhma See dokhma
Dakota 434.5
dale 252.5
dalliance 902.3
dallier 683.7
dally delay 133.5, 7
  go slow 275.5
  be irresolute 605.4
  trifle 643.9
  idle 683.8
  play with 840.21
  make love 902.7
dalmatic 999.1
Daltonism 443.1
dam n. mother 166.7
  pool 343a.1
  obstruction 706.2
dam v. 261.2
  (stanch 348.24)
  (hinder 706.4)
damage n.
  bill of account 86.1
  impairment 659.3
  loss 776.1
  statement 811.3
  charge 812.1
damage v. 659.8
  (harm 649.6)
damages
  reparation 973.2
  fine 974.2
damaging 649.10
damascene 440.4
damask cloth 219.5
  red 434.2
dame girl 129.5
  old woman 130.3
  woman 374.2, 3
  instructress 540.2
  lady 875.6
damn v. curse 908.4, 5
  censure 932.7
  condemn 971.2
damn int. 908.7
damnability
  badness 649.1
  turpitude 945.2
damnable
  execrable 649.8
  wicked 945.16
damnably 31.24
damnation 971.1
damnatory
  execrable 649.8
  maledictory 908.6
  censorious 932.11
  defamatory 934.4
  accusatory 938.5
  condemnatory 971.4
damned
  execrable 649.8
  cursed 908.6
damnification 649.1
damnify 649.6
damning 467.11
damnum 659.3
Damocles 935.2
Damon and Pythias 890.5
damosel, damozel See damsel

damp n. gas 334.2
  moisture 339.1
  ~ of the spirits 837.4
damp v.
  moderate 174.5
  wet 337.5
  extinguish 385.5
  muffle 408a.4
  discourage 616.3
  hinder 706.7
  ~ the spirits 837.8
  dull 843.4
damp adj. 339.7
dampen
  moderate 174.5
  wet 337.5
  moisten 339.5
  muffle 408a.4
  ~ the spirits 837.8
dampened 405.9
damper bread 298.11
  fire iron 386.3
  discouragement 616.1
  marplot 706.3
  spoilsport 837.5
damper pedal 408a.3 417.11
dampness 339.1
dampproof 340.11
damsel, damozel 129.5
damson 437.1
Dan 373.3
  from Dan to Beersheba 180.9
Danaë 803.2
dance n. flutter 315.5
  ball, steps 840.6–8
  (caper 309.2)
  (party 892.5)
dance v.
  flutter 315.10
  (oscillate 314.8)
  glitter 420.18
  trip 840.21
  (caper 309.5)
dance attendance
  wait 133.7
  serve 746.8
  court favor 886.3
  (pay one's respects 894.8)
dance on nothing 972.13
dance hall 840.14
dance music 415.7
dance of death 840.7
dancer 840.9
  (performer 599.19)
dance time 413.22
dancing 840.6
dander anger 900.1
  temper 901.1
dandi See dandy
Dandie Dinmont, Dandie 366.6
dandified
  foppish 853.6
  vain 880.6
dandify 847.11
dandiprat 193.5

dandle — day 792

dandle 902.8
dandruff 653.6
dandy *n.* ship 273.2
  excellent thing 648.4
  fop 854.1
dandy, dandi *n.* 272.12
dandy *adj.* 648.8
dandy fever 655.6
dandy horse 272.14
dandyism 853.3
danger peril 665
  (warning 668.1)
  (alarm 669.1)
  source of ~ 667
be in danger 665.6
in danger
  liable 177.3
  sick 655.23
  endangered 665.8
dangerous 665.7
  (fearful 860.15)
danger signal 669.1
dangle *n.* 214.1
dangle *v.* depend 214.4
  oscillate 314.8
  flaunt 882.7
dangler
  follower 281.2
  hanger-on 886.2
Daniel 513.2
Danish 560.4
Danish balance 319.5
dank 339.7
danse macabre 840.7
danseuse 840.9
  (performer 599.19)
dap 622.8
dapper little 193.8
  trim 845.11
  smart 847.14
dapperling 193.5
dapple *v.* gray 432.3
  mottle 440.4
dapple *adj.* 440.7
  dappled gray 432.4
  mottled 440.7
dapple-gray 432.4
Darby and Joan
  elderly couple 130.4
  married couple 903.9
dare *n.* 715.1
dare *v.* face 234.7
  defy 715.2
  brave 861.5
dare say
  think likely 472.3
  believe 484.8
  suppose 514.6
I dare say, I daresay
  there is a probability 472.3
  I believe 484.17
daredevil 863.2
daring *n.*
  defiance 715.1
  courage 861.1
daring *adj.*
  defiant 715.3
  courageous 861.8
  reckless 863.7

showy 882.8
  (conspicuous 525.5)
dark *n.* darkness 421.1
  ignorance 491.1
  secrecy 528.2
dark *v.* darken 421.5
  blacken 431.6
dark *adj.*
  lightless 421.7
  (nocturnal 126.6)
  (dim 422.8)
  (opaque 426.4)
  dark-colored 431.7
  (dull 428.19)
  blind 442.6
  indistinct 447.5
  ignorant 491.10
  obscure 519.7
  hidden 528.17
  sad 837.10
  dishonest 940.8
be dark 421.4
grow dark 421.5
in the dark
  at night 421.10
  ignorant 491.10
  concealed 528.17
  secretly 528.24
Dark Ages 108.2
dark-colored 431.7
Dark Continent 491.2
darken cloud 353.9
  obscure 421.5
  (dim 422.6, 7)
  (shade 424.6)
  (obfuscate 426.3)
  overshadow 422.6
  blacken 431.6
  blind 442.3
  look black 824.8
darkening *n.*
  dusk 126.1
  blackening 431.2
darkening *adj.* 421.9
darkey See **darky**
dark horse 491.2
darkish dim 422.8
  blackish 431.8
  indistinct 447.5
dark lantern 423.2
darkle 421.5
  (grow dim 422.7)
darkling, darkly 421.10
  (dimly 422.10)
darkmans 126.3
dark nebula 420.12
darkness
  lightlessness 421
  (night 126.3)
  (dimness 422.1)
  blackness 431.1
  ignorance 491.1
  unintelligibility 519.1
  (imperspicuity 571.1)
  latency 526.1
darksome dark 421.7
  dim 422.8
  blackish 431.8
darky, darkey

night 126.3
  lantern 423.2
  Negro 431.4
darling *n.* child 129.3
  sweetheart 897.7
  favorite 899.1
  endearment 902.4
darling *adj.* 897.16
darn *v.* 660.11
darn *int.* 908.8
darned 31.24
darning cotton 205.2
dart *n.* speed 274.6
  spear 727.5, 6
dart *v.* speed 274.9
  throw 284.12
  ~ to and fro 684.3
darveesh, darvish, darwaysh, darwesh See **dervish**
darwan See **durwaun**
Darwinism 161.5
  (philosophy 451.21)
darzee 225.37
dash *n.* modicum 32.2
  tincture 41.3
  bond 45.1
  energy 171.1
  spurt 274.3
  taste 390.1
  mark 550.7, 8
  code 550.15
  ~ of the pen 590.1
  verve 682.1
  haste 684.1
  race 720.5
  courage 861.1
  splurge 882.1
make a dash
  spurt 274.11
  be resolute 604.6
  attack 716.5
dash, dashee *n.* 784.3
dash *v.* imbue 41.8
  spurt 274.11
  strike 276.8
  throw 284.12
  ~ down 308.5
  mark 550.19
  attack 716.5
  dishearten 837.8
dash off
  compose 54.4
  hasten off 293.5
  sketch 556.17
  write 601.21
dash on speed 274.9
  hasten 684.3
dash one's hope
  disappoint 509.2
  (fail 732.5)
  despair 859.6
dash *int.* 908.8
dashed
  frustrated 732.9
  dejected 837.13
  abashed 879.5
dashedly 31.24
dashing smart 847.14
  ostentatious 882.8
dastard *n.* 862.2
dastard *adj.* 862.5

dastardly 862.5
dastardy 862.1
dastur, dustoor
  custom 613.2
  fee 973.2
dasturi, dustoori 973.2
data evidence 467.1
  logic 476.4
  hypothesis 514.1
date *n.* 114.4
date *v.* 114.8
dateless
  timeless 107.2
  eternal 112.4
  prehistoric 124.7
datum logic 476.4
  hypothesis 514.1
daub *n.* scribble 517.7
  bad likeness 555.2
  soil 653.3
  blemish 848.1
daub *v.*
  cover 223.24, 26
  lubricate 332.4
  paint 428.10
  scribble 517.7
  soil 653.15
dauber 559.1
daubing 223.19
daubster 559.1
daughter, daughter-in-law 167.4
daughterly 167.6
daughter of joy 962.9
daunt 860.11
dauntless 861.8
  (fearless 858.10)
davenport
  cupboard 191.15
  seat 215.22
David and Jonathan 890.5
Davidist 984.14
Davy Jones 341.2; 979.10
Davy Jones's locker
  sea bottom 208.3
  ocean 341.1
daw 501.1
dawdle *n.*
  slow goer 275.4
  idler 683.7
dawdle *v.*
  delay 133.5, 7
  go slow 275.5
  idle 683.8
  (be irresolute 605.4)
dawdler
  slow goer 275.4
  idler 683.7
dawdling 683.2
dawk See **dak**
dawn *n.*
  forerunner 64.1
  daybreak 125.1
  (beginning 66.1)
dawn *v.* 116.3
dawnlight 125.1
day period 108.1
  daylight 420.8
day after day

repeatedly 104.8
long 110.11
constantly 136.6
day and night 136.6
day by day
repeatedly 104.8
regularly 138.12
day in, day out
long 110.11
constantly 136.6
days of the week
138.7
from day to day
138.12
Dayak See Dyak
day bed 215.22, 24
day b'indness 443.2
daybook record 551.3
(journal 593.6)
account book 811.5
daybreak 125.1
daydream *n.*
muse 458.3
imagination 515.5
daydream *v.*
muse 458.6
imagine 515.9
daydreamer 515.7
daydreaming *n.*
preoccupation
458.3
imagination 515.2
daydreaming *adj.*
515.14
daydreamy 458.11
daylight dawn 125.1
light 420.8
(sun 318.4)
daylights 441.7
daymare
hallucination 503.5
dream 515.5
Day of Judgment
end 67.1
doomsday 121.2
day of reckoning
919.1
day-peep 125.1
dayshine 420.8
day sight 443.2
dayspring 125.1
daystar 318.3, 4
daytide, daytime 420.8
daze *n.* 458.4
in a daze 458.12
daze *v.* glare 420.17
dazzle 443.13
confuse 458.9
perplex 475.8
bewilder 870.3
awe 928.7
dazed numb 381.3
confused 458.12
dazy 458.12
dazzle *n.* 458.4
dazzle *v.* glare 420.17
daze 443.13
(blind 442.3)
confuse 458.9
bewilder 870.3
awe 928.7
dazzlement 420.1

dazzler
excellent thing
648.4
a beauty 845.3
dazzling 845.13
deacon *n.* 996.5
deacon *v.* falsify 544.3
intone 990.10
deaconry 995.3
dead *n.*
midnight 126.4
corpse 362.1
silence 403.1
dead one
slow goer 275.4
neglector 460.3
idler 683.7
dead *adj.*
unqualified 52.10
antiquated 124.9
inert 172.3
lifeless 360.8
(extinct 2.10)
insensible 376.5
numb 381.1
nonresonant 408a.6
dull-colored 428.19
colorless 429.6
blind 442.6
language 563.10, 18
languid 683.14
asleep 683.16
exhausted 688.6
dead to
insensible 823.5
indifferent 866.4
dead-alive 688.6
dead beat *n.*
idler 683.7
sponger 886.2
dead-beat *adj.*
impotent 158.8
exhausted 688.6
**dead-color, dead-
colour** *n.* 428.5
**dead-color, dead-
colour** *v.* 428.10
dead-drunk 959.22
deaden
disable 158.6
moderate 174.5
dull 376.4
(numb 381.2)
muffle 408a.4
~ emotionally 823.4
relieve 834.4
dead end *n.*
closure 261.1
roadway 627.3
dead-end *adj.* 442.6
deadened
insensible 376.5
numb 381.2
deader 362.1
deadfall snare 545.4
pitfall 667.2
dead hand 748.5
deadhead 599.23;
815.5
dead heat 27.4
dead letter
impotent 158.3

unmeaningness
517.1
dereliction 927.1
dead lift
exertion 686.1
difficulty 704.1
deadlock *n.*
standstill 265.3
obstruction 706.1
(stop 142.1)
impasse 704.3
stalemate 732.3
deadlock *v.*
obstruct 706.4
(stop 142.7)
stalemate 731.10
deadly 361.16
(destructive 162.6)
(harmful 649.10)
insalubrious 657.3
dead'y sin 947.2
deadman 158a.9
dead march
slow motion 275.2
funeral 363.4
music 415.8
dead marine 191.11
deadness 823.1
dead pledge 771.1
dead reckoning
numeration 85.1
measurement 466.1
dead set
standstill 265.3
impasse 704.3
attack 716.1
dead stand 265.3
dead weight
difficulty 704.1
impediment 706.2
deadwood 33.2
deaf *v.* 419.7
deaf *adj.*
unhearing 419.8
inattentive 458.10
be deaf 419.6
deaf to
unwilling 603.6
incompliant 764.5
insensible to 823.5
indifferent 866.4
deaf and dumb
deaf 419.8
voiceless 581.7
**deaf-and-dumb
alphabet**
dactylology 419.5
dumb show 550.3
deaf-dumb
deaf 419.8
voiceless 581.7
deaf-dumbness
deafness 419.1
aphonia 581.1
deaf ears
deafness 419.1
impenitence 951.1
deafen be loud 404.5
make deaf 419.7
render mute 581.5
deafened 419.8
deafening 404.8

deaf-mute *n.*
surdomute 419.3
mute 581.2
deaf-mute *adj.*
deaf 419.8
voiceless 581.7
deaf-muteness 419.1
deaf-mutism
deafness 419.1
aphonia 581.1
deafness 419
deal *n.*
quantity 25.2; 31.3
compact 769.1
apportionment
786.1
transaction 794.3
deal *v.*
apportion 786.3
traffic 794.4
deal in 794.7
(sell 796.5)
deal out
arrange 60.6
disperse 73.3
give 784.8
deal with
discuss 595.4
conduct 692.4
trade with 794.8
punish 972.5
dealbate 430.6
dealbation 430.2
dealer 797.1
dealings acts 680.2
commerce 794.1
have dealings with
trade with 794.8
be friendly 888.2
dean senior 130.5
master 745.1
church dignitary
996.5
deanery
ecclesiastical ~
995.3
parsonage 1000.5
deanship 128.4
dear *n.*
sweetheart 897.7
endearment 902.4
dear *adj.* costly 814.5
loved 897.16
be dear 814.2
hold dear 897.11
dear *adv.* 814.7
dearborn 272.4
dear-bought 814.6
dearly 814.7
dearness 814
dearth 640.2
deary, dearie 902.4
death 360
(end 67.1)
(cessation 142.1)
(extinction 162.2)
at death's door 360.9
till death long 110.11
always 112.5
**death agony, death
bed** 360.1
death bell 363.5

deathblow — decided

deathblow
  end-all 67.4
  defeat 732.3
death camass 663.6
deathday 360.1
death feud 919.1
death fire 382.8
deathful 361.16
deatnify 361.10
deathless
  eternal 112.4
  fame 873.19
death light light 423.7
  warning 668.3
death ike
  deathly 360.10
  corpselike 362.2
  unprepossessing 846.8
deathly
  deathlike 360.10
  mortal 361.16
death rate 360.1
death rattle 360.1
death sentence 971.1, 2
death's-head 837.4
death song 839.3
death-stricken 360.8
death stroke
  end-all 67.4
  death 360.1
death-struck 360.8
deathtrap 545.4
death warrant 971.1
deathwatch 360.1
debacle, débâcle
  revolution 146.1
  destruction 162.3
  downfall 306.3
  deluge 348.3
debar preclude 706.4
  prohibit 761.2
  exclude 893.7
debark 292.9
debarkation 292.2
  (disembarkment 292.1)
debarment 55.1
debase depress 308.4
  (lower 207.6)
  corrupt 659.9
  (demoralize 945.10)
  degrade 874.7
  depreciate 934.3
debased low 207.7
  degenerate 945.15
debasement
  lowness 207.1
  depression 308.1
  deterioration 659.1
  disgrace 874.1
  turpitude 945.2
debatable
  uncertain 475.9
  (argumental 476.15)
  illogical 477.10
debate *n.* 476.2
  (interlocution 588.4)
debate *v.* argue 476.11
  (converse 588.9)
  be undecided 605.4

debater 476.9
debauch *n.* orgy 954.2
  (spree 840.3)
  drinking bout 959.3
debauch *v.*
  corrupt 659.9
  dissipate 954.3
  wassail 959.16
  violate 961.8
debauched
  depraved 945.15
  dissipated 954.5
  unchaste 961.10
debauchee, debaucher 962.1
debauchery
  dissipation 954.2
  (merrymaking 840.4)
  unchastity 961.2
debauchment 961.2, 4
debenture
  voucher 771.1
  (credit 805.2)
  money order 800.7
debilitate
  weaken 160.8
  sicken 655.22
debilitated 160.10
debilitation 160.1
debility
  weakness 160.1
  ailment 655.1
debit *n* debt 806.1
  entry 811.2
debit *v.* 811.7
debonair, debonaire 836.7
debouch *n.*
  departure 293.1
  outlet 295.5
debouch *v.*
  issue forth 293.4
  discharge 295.7
  let out 297.13
débouché 293.1
debouchment
  embouchure 260.3
  departure 293.1
debris, débris
  remains 40.1
  silt 270.3
  attritus 330.3
  rubbish 645.4
  (oddments 51.6)
debt 806
  (borrowing 788.1)
  be in debt 806.5
  go in debt 806.6
  in debt 806.7
  (poor 804.7)
  (defaultant 808.9)
debtee 805.3
debtor 806.4
  (defaulter 808.3)
debunk 545a.2
debunkment 545a.1
debus 292.8
debut beginning 66.1
  (first attempt 675.2)
  theatrical ~ 599.8
  presentation 883.1

  coming-out party 892.5
make one's debut
  begin 66.6
  stage 599.26
debutant actor 599.19
  unsophisticate 703.2
debutante 541.6
deca-, dec- 98.20
decade ten 98.6
  time 108.1
decadence
  deterioration 659.1
  turpitude 945.2
decadent 659.11
decagon ten 98.6
  angle 244.2
decagonal 98.20
decagram, decagramme ten 98.6
  weight 319.2
decahedral 98.20
decahedron 98.6
décalage 267a.3
decalescence 382.1
decalescent 382.16
decaliter, decalitre ten 98.6
  measure 466.3
decalogue decalog 926.4
Decalogue, Decalog 98.6
decameter, decametre ten 98.6
  measure 466.3
decamp
  depart 293.4, 5
  flee 623.10
decampment
  departure 293.1
  flight 623.2
decanal side 238.2
decant 270.6
decanter 191.11
decapitate 972.8
decapitation 972.4
decapitator 975.5
decapod, decare 98.6
decarnate
  disembodied 317.6
  spectral 980a.4
decastere 98.6
decasyl'abic 98.20
decasyllable 98.6
decay *n.* 659.2
  (destruction 162.1)
  (malodor 401.2)
  (putrescence 653.4)
  (disease 655.1)
  (blight 663.2)
decay *v.*
  decompose 659.7
  suffer misfortune 735.6
decayed foul 653.17
  putrified 659.13
decease 360.1
deceased *n.* 362.1
deceased *adj.* 360.8
deceit 545.1, 3
  (falsification 544.1)

  cunning 702.1
deceitful 545.12
  (false 544.7)
  (dishonest 940.8)
deceivability 486.1
deceivable 545.12, 14
  (gullible 486.5)
deceive 545.7
  (mislead 495.11)
  (hoodwink 528.13)
  (misinform 538.2)
  (dissemble 544.6)
  (dupe 547.2)
  (misrepresent 555.4)
  (be cunning 702.5)
  (swindle 791.12)
be deceived err 495.7
  be duped 547.3
deceiver 548
  (traitor 949.3)
deceiving *n.* 545.1
deceiving *adj.* 545.12
decelerate 275.7
deceleration 275.3
decemvirate 98.6
decency 960.1
decennary ten 98.6
  decade 108.1
decennial *n.* 138.5
decennial *adj.* 138.11
decennium ten 98.6
  decade 108.1
decent
  clothed 225.46
  tolerable 648.11
  comely 845.10
  decorous 960.2
deception
  ~ of vision 443.9
  trick 545.3
  (falsehood 544.1; 546.1)
  (misrepresentation 555.1)
  (artifice 702.3)
  (swindle 791.5)
  (improbity 940.1)
  (dishonesty 940.5)
deceptive
  sophistical 477.9
  deceitful 545.12
  (delusive 495.15)
  (false 544.7)
  (cunning 702.6)
  (dishonest 940.8)
be deceptive 545.7
  (dissemble 544.6)
deceptively 545.15
decession 293.1
dechristianize 989.5
deci- 98.20
decide
  contribute 153.8
  determine 474.6; 480.6
  (will 600.2)
  (choose 609.7, 8)
  resolve 604.6
decided
  absolute 31.12
  ended 67.9

decidedly — decretal

certain 474.8, 9
emphatic 535.6
determined 604.7, 8
decidedly
  absolutely 31.16
  certainly 474.16
deciduary 111.6
deciduous
  transient 111.6
  descending 306.7
  herbal 367.14
  withered 659.12
**decigram, deci-
gramme** ten 98.6
  weight 319.4
deciliter, decilitre
466.3
decillion 98.13
decimal *n.* 84.2
decimal *adj.*
  numeral 84.7
  tenth 98.20; 99.3
decimalization 99.1
decimalize 99.2
decimate deduct 38.4
  disintegrate 44.9
  tenth 99.2
  weaken 160.8
  slaughter 361.10
  ravage 659.8
decimation 99.1
decimeter, decimetre
466.3
decipher solve 481a.4
  (manifest 525.2)
  decode 561.7
decipherability 518.1
decipherable 518.5
decision
  determination
    480.1; 620.1
  (choice 609.1)
  (verdict 969.8)
  resolution 604.1
decisive
  critical 134.8
  evidential 467.11
  certain 474.8
  conclusive 474.10
  (judicial 480.11)
  mandatory 741.8
decisively 474.16
deck *n.* floor 211.2
  roof 223.6
  ship 273.8
  airplane 273a.10
  ~ of cards 840.13
  below deck 207.11
  on deck
    aboard 267.53
    available 644.8
deck *v.*
  trim sail 267.16
  equip 634.2
  adorn 847.11
  deck out 225.41
decked 273.16
deck hand 269.3
deckie 269.3
deckle-edged 674.8
declaim
  make a speech 582.7

(address 586.2)
~ against 932.7
declamation
  rhetoric 577.1
  speech 582.2, **3**
declamatory
  bombastic 577.7
  oratorical 582.12
declaration
  testimony 467.**2**
  report 527.1
  proclamation 531.1
  affirmation 535.1
  statement 582.4
  decree 741.3
  legal pleading 969.6
declaration of faith
484.4
  (theology 983.2)
declaration of rights
969.6
declaration of war
  dissension 713.2
  wager of battle
    722.3
**declarative, declara-
tory**
  promulgatory
    531.11
  affirmative 535.6
declare proclaim 531.7
  affirm 535.3
  (signify 516.5)
  indicate 550.18
  say 582.6
déclassé 893.5
declension
  decrease 36.1
  descent 306.1
  grammar 567.1
  rejection 610.1
  deterioration 659.1
  refusal 764.1
  religious ~ 988.3
declinate 217.11
declination
  obliquity 217.1
  deviation 279.1
  divergence 291.1
  descent 306.1
  ~ and right ascen-
    sion 466.7
  rejection 610.1
  deterioration 659.1
  refusal 764.1
declinatory
  rejective 610.3
  refusing 764.5
declinature 764.1
decline *n.*
  subsidence 36.2
  ~ of day 126.1
  ~ of life 128.**2**
  declivity 217.2
  slump 304.1
  sinkage 306.1
  deterioration 659.1
  (disease 655.1)
  ~ in price 815.3
  on the decline
    sickly 655.24
    deteriorating 659.11

decline *v.*
  decrease 36.3
  weaken 160.7
  incline 217.6
  recede 287.2
  lose ground 304.**2**
  sink 306.4
  inflect 567.5
  deteriorate 659.6
  (age 124.5; 128.7)
  languish 683.10
  suffer misfortune
    735.6
  refuse 764.**2**
  (reject 610.2)
  ~ in price 815.7
declined
  declivitous 217.11
  rejected 610.3
declining aged 128.8
  declivitous 217.11
  deteriorating 659.11
declivate, declivitous
217.11
  (descending 306.7)
declivity 217.2
  (descent 306.1)
declivous 217.11
decoction
  solution 335.3
  boiling 384.7
  cauterant 384.11
decode solve 481a.4
  (manifest 525.2)
  decipher 561.7
decollate 972.8
decollation 972.4
décolleté low 207.8
  in negligee 225.47
decolor, decolour
429.5
  (discolor 440a.2)
decolorant 429.3
decolorate 429.6
decoloration 429.2
  (whitening 430.**2**)
decompose
  segment 44.9
  disintegrate 49.**3**
  decay 659.7
decomposed
  disintegrated 49.5
  decayed 659.13
  become decomposed
    49.3
decomposing 49.**5**
decomposition
  disintegration 49
  (waste 638.1)
  decay 659.2
decompound 49.3
deconsecrate 756.5
deconsecration 756.2
decorate speech 577.4
  ornament 847.11
  (paint 428.10)
  (art 556.17)
  (beautify 845.7)
decoration
  trophy 733.1
  ornament 847.1
  (art 556.1)

  (beautifying 845.5)
Decoration Day 138.7
decorative 847.11
decorous seemly 646.4
  conventional 852.8
  deferential 928.8
  decent 960.2
decorticate 226.5
decortication 226.1
decorum
  conventionality
    852.2
  propriety 922.1
  ethics 926.4
  decency 960.1
decoy *n.* 617.2
  (attractor 288.2)
  (snare 545.4)
decoy *v.* 617.4
  (attract 288.3)
  (ensnare 545.9)
decoy duck
  bunko steerer 548.2
  lure 617.2
decrassify 652.9
decrease *n.*
  in degree 36
  (subtraction 38.1)
  (diminution 174.2)
  (shortening 201.2)
  (waste 638.1)
  (deterioration
    659.1)
  (loss 776.1)
  in size 195.1
decrease *v.* 36.3, 4
  (mitigate 174.5)
  (contract 195.4)
  (descend 306.4)
decreasing 36.5
decreasingly 36.6
decree *n.*
  judgment 480.1
  command 741.3
  (proclamation
    531.1)
  (law 963.2)
decree *v.*
  pass judgment 480.9
  command 741.4
  (legalize 963.4)
decreement, decreet
741.3
decrement
  decrease 36.1; 39a
  (deduction 38.1)
  contraction 195.1
  waste 638.1
  loss 776.1
decrepit aged 128.8
  impotent 158.8
  weak 160.13
  senile 499.16
  worn out 659.12
  (infirm 655.24)
decrepitate 406.7
decrepitation 406.1
decrescence 36.1
decrescendo 36.5, 6
decrescent 36.5
decretal *n.* 741.3
decretal *adj.* 741.8

decrete — defiant

decrete 741.3
decretive, decretory 741.8
decry censure 932.7
  disparage 934.3
Decuma 601.4
decumbency 213.2
decumbent 213.9
decuple 98.20
decurrence 306.1
decurrent
  descending 306.7
  flowing 348.26
decursive 306.7
decurtate short 201.5
  terse 572.3
decussate v. 219.7
decussate adj. 219.9
decussation joint 43.3
  crossing 219.1
decorous 647.3
dedicate devote 677.5
  consecrate 873.13
dedication
  book ~ 593.7
  glorification 873.6
deditician 748.6
deduce deduct 38.4
  think likely 472.3
  infer 480.6
  (reason 476.10)
  suppose 514.6
  etymologize 562.7
deducible
  deductive 38.8
  inferable 478.5
  (evidential 467.11)
deduct subtract 38.4
  (reduce 36.4)
  (shorten 201.4)
  (take away 789.10)
  discount 813.2
deduction
  subtraction 38
  (shortening 201.2)
  decrement 39a
  qualification 469.1
  reasoning 476.1
  inference 480.1
  (interpretation 522.1)
  discount 813.1
  in deduction 38.10
deductive
  subtractive 38.8
  reasoning 476.17
  deducible 478.5
deed
  transference 270.3
  act 680.2
  security 771.1
  exploit 861.2
deed poll 771.1
deem judge 480.6
  think 484.8
  suppose 514.6
deemster 967.1
deep n. depth 208.2, 3
  ocean 341.1
deep adj. great 31.6
  profound 208.8
  (low 207.7)

(descending 306.7)
  loud 404.8
  resonant 408.9
  deep-dyed 428.13
  learned 490.15
  wise 498.11
  obscure 519.7
  language 574.9
  cunning 702.6
  deep-felt 821.8
deep-bosomed 208.13
deep-colored 428.13
deep-dye 428.9
deep-dyed
  deep-colored 428.13
  wicked 945.18
deep-echoing 408.9
deepen increase 35.3
  render deep 208.6
  (hollow out 252.9)
deep-felt 821.8
  (penetrating 824.13)
deep-laid 702.6
deepmouthed
  resonant 408.9
  barking 412.3
deepness 208.1
deep-pitched 408.9
deep-read 490.15
deep-rooted
  stable 150.5
  sound 159.12
  deep 208.8
  interior 221.9
  inveterate 613.12
deep sea n. 208.3
deep-sea adj. 208.12
deep-sea lead
  fathomer 208.4
  measure 466.4
deep-seated
  stable 150.5
  deep 208.8
deep-set 408.9
deep water
  in deep water 704.11
deer 366.11
deerdog, deerhound 366.6
deer tiger 366.3
deev See daeva
deface deform 243.5
  discolor 440a.2
  obliterate 552.2
  damage 659.8
  (blemish 848.2)
defaced 848.3
  (deformed 243.5)
defacement
  distortion 243.1
  blemish 848.1
de facto 1.9
defalcate 808.5
defalcation
  deficiency 53.2
  contraction 195.1
  shortcoming 304.1
  nonpayment 808.1
defalcator 808.3
defamation 934.1
  (scandal 532.4)

(malediction 908.1)
defamatory 934.4
  (damnatory 908.6)
  (disapprobatory 932.11)
defame degrade 874.7
  detract 934.3
  (anathematize 908.4)
defamer 936.1
default n.
  shortcoming 304.1
  neglect 460.1
  nonobservance 773.1
  debt 806.2
  nonpayment 808.1
in default
  incomplete 53.4
  imperfect 651.4
in default of
  empty 187.11
  for want of 640.13
default v. 808.5
defaultant n. 808.3
defaultant adj. 808.9
  (indebted 806.7)
defaulter
  swindler 792.8
  defalcator 808.3
  (debtor 806.4)
  delinquent 949.1
defeasance 756.1
defeasible 479.4
defeat n. 732.3
  (hindrance 706.1)
  (victory 731.3)
  (subjection 749.1)
defeat v. confute 479.2
  conquer 731.9
  (thwart 706.7)
  (subjugate 749.5)
defeater 731.4
defecate
  let out 297.13
  purify 652.9
defecation
  evacuation 297.5
  excrement 299.2
  purification 652.2
  (elimination 42.2)
defect decrement 39a
  deficiency 53.2
  fault 651.2
  ailment 655.1
  (blemish 848.1)
  vice 945.5
defection 624.1
  (apostasy 607.2)
  (revolt 742.2)
defective
  incomplete 53.4
  erroneous 495.12
  imperfect 651.4
  vicious 945.11
defedation, defoedation 659.3
defend guard 717.7, 8
  (care for 459.6)
  (protect 664.6)
  (preserve 670.3)
  justify 937.6

(answer 462.6)
  (law 969.10)
defendant
  respondent 462.4
  accused 938.3
  (vindicator 937.4)
  (litigant 969.9)
defender
  respondent 462.4
  champion 717.5
  (protector 664.3)
  (benefactor 912.1)
  vindicator 937.4
  (defendant 938.3)
Defender of the Faith 717.5
defense, defence
  guard 717
  (protection 664.2)
  (preservation 670.2)
  (resistance 719.1)
  vindication 937.2
  (answer 462.2)
  (law 969.6)
in defense 717.11
defenseless, defenceless helpless 158.9
  (unstrengthened 160.15)
  unprotected 665.9
defensible
  tenable 717.10
  vindicable 937.10
defensive 717.9
  (protective 664.12)
on the defensive 717.8, 11
defensively 717.11
defer 133.4
defer to
  acknowledge 488.9
  submit 725.3
  respect 928.4
deference
  submission 725.1
  obedience 743.1
  respect 928.1
in deference to 928.10
deferential
  submissive 725.5
  obedient 743.3
  respectful 928.8
  (dutiful 926.8)
deferment 133.2
  (neglect 460.1)
deferred payment 806.2
defiance
  challenge 715
  (threat 909.1)
  courage 861.1
bid defiance to 715.2
in defiance of
  in disagreement 24.10
  in opposition 708.6
  (notwithstanding 30.8)
defiantly 715.4
defiant 715.3
  (bellicose 722.13)

defiantly — delicacy

(rebellious 742.7)
(threatening 909.3)
defiantly 715.4
deficiency
 inferiority 34.1
 incompleteness 53.1, 2
 (shortcoming 304.1)
 (insufficiency 640.1)
 imperfection 651.1
 vice 945.5
deficient
 incomplete 53.4
 (insufficient 640.8)
 short of 304.3
 imperfect 651.4
 (inferior 34.5)
 be deficient 304.2
deficit
 deficiency 53.2
 debt 806.2
defile *n.* 198.5
 (narrow 203.3)
 (passage 302.1)
defile *v.* march 266.21
 discolor 440a.2
 dirty 653.15
 corrupt 659.9
 stigmatize 874.7
 debauch 961.8
defiled 653.17
defilement
 pollution 653.2
 corruption 659.3
 defloration 961.4
defiler 962.1
define stabilize 150.4
 circumscribe 229.2
 outline 230.3
 limit 233.2
 interpret 522.6
 characterize 564.6
defined
 limited 233.3
 obvious 525.4
definer 524.1
definite special 79.7
 limited 233.3
 audible 402.10
 distinct 446.5; 518.5
 certain 474.8
 accurate 494.11
 manifest 525.4
 resolute 604.7
 right 922.6
definitely 474.16
definition
 intelligibility 518.1
 interpretation 522.1
 (meaning 516.1)
 (dictionary 593.4)
 (description 594.1)
 characterization 564.1
definitional 522.8
definitive final 67.8
 definitional 522.8
 emphatic 535.6
deflagrable 384.22
deflagrate
 explode 173.9

burn 384.18
deflagration 384.3
deflect oblique 217.5
 curve 245.3
 deviate 279.6
 (side 236.4)
 avert 706.5
deflection, deflexion, deflexure
 obliquity 217.1
 deviation 279.1
defloration 961.4
deflower
 corrupt 659.9
 ravish 961.8
defluent 348.26
defluxion 348.2
defoedation See **defedation**
deform 243.3
 (uglify 846.5)
 (blemish 848.2)
deformation 243.1
deformed 243.5
 (imperfect 651.4)
 (disfigured 848.3)
deformity 243.1
 (ugliness 846.1)
 (blemish 848.1)
defraud 791.12
 (deceive 545.7)
defrauder 792.8
defray 807.6
defrayer 807.5
defrayment 807.1
deft 698.11
defunct *n.* 362.1
defunct *adj.* 360.8
 (extinct 2.10)
defy *n.* 715.1
defy *v.* face 234.7
 challenge 715.2
 (threaten 909.2)
 be courageous 665.5; 861.5
dégagé free 748.20
 inexcitable 826.9
degeneracy
 deterioration 659.1
 turpitude 945.2
degenerate *n.* 949.1
degenerate *v.* 659.6
degenerate *adj.*
 deteriorating 659.11
 depraved 945.15
degeneration 659.1
deglutition 298.1
degradation
 deterioration 659.1
 disgrace 874.1
 turpitude 945.2
degrade corrupt 659.9
 (demoralize 945.10)
 defame 874.7
 humiliate 879.3
 depreciate 934.3
degrade oneself 874.5
degraded 945.15
degrading 874.8
degree grade 26
 musical ~ 413.11

music staff 415.22
 measure 466.3
 rank 873.4
by degrees
 gradually 26.5
 piecemeal 51.10
 slowly 275.11
degreewise 26.5
degust taste 390.3
 relish 394.6
degustation 390.2
dehisce 260.13
dehiscence 260.9
dehiscent
 intervallic 198.5
 gaping 260.15
dehort dissuade 616.2
 deprecate 766.2
dehortation
 dissuasion 616.1
 (advice 695.1)
 admonition 668.1
 deprecation 766.1
dehortative *n.*
 deterrent 616.1
 deprecation 766.1
dehortative *adj.*
 dissuasive 616.4
 advisory 695.8
 deprecative 766.3
dehortatory 766.3
dehydrant 340.3
dehydrate dry 340.5
 preserve 670.4
dehydration
 drying 340.2
 preservation 670.2
dehydrator 340.3
deification
 glorification 873.6
 apotheosis 981.6; 991.2
deify glorify 873.13
 apotheosize 991.6
deign consent 762.2
 be proud 878.3
deil 978.1
deism 984.4; 989.3
deist 989.4
deistic
 heterodox 984.22
 nullifidian 989.8
deity 979.1–6
Deity 976.2
deject 837.8
dejecta 299.2
dejected 837.9
dejection
 evacuation 297.5
 excretion 299.1
 sadness 837.1
dejecture 299.1
deka-, dek- 98.20
delaminate 204.4
delamination 204.3
delation 938.1
delator informer 527.6
 accuser 938.2
delay *n.* 133.2
 (protraction 110.2)
 (retardation 275.3)
 (neglect 460.1)

without delay
 instantly 113.6
 promptly 132.14
 (hastily 684.7)
delay *v.*
 be late 133.4, 6, 7
 (protract 110.6)
 (pretermit 460.7)
 retard 275.7
 hinder 706.4
delayage 133.2
delayed 133.8
de´aying 133.9
dele excise 38.5
 destroy 162.4
 obliterate 552.2
delectability
 savoriness 394.1
 pleasurableness 829.1
delectable
 savory 394.7
 pleasurable 829.7
delectate 827.5
delectation 827.2
delectus 593.2
delegate *n.* 758.4; 759.1
delegate *v.* send 270.9
 commission 755.4
 (deputize 759.5)
delegation 755.1
delete excise 38.5
 destroy 162.4
deleterious
 harmful 649.10
 unwholesome 657.3
deletion 552.1
delft, delf, delftware 384.14
deliberate *v.*
 ponder 451.27
 advise with 695.6
deliberate *adj.*
 slow 275.8
 measured 466.13
 leisurely 685.4
deliberated 466.13
deliberately
 tardily 133.13
 intentionally 620.5
 (premeditatedly 611.7)
deliberation
 thought 451.1
 (attention 457.2)
 circumspection 864.1
deliberative 451.35
delicacy nicety 15.2
 frailty 160.1
 food 298.9
 (savory 394.3)
 (treat 829.3)
 discrimination 465.1
 exactness 494.3
 delicate health 655.1
 crux 704.4
 beauty 845.1
 taste 850.1

delicate — demolishment

delicacy (*continued*)
  fastidiousness 868.1
  (scrupulousness 603.2)
  point of honor 939.2
  decorum 960.1
delicate slight 32.10
  frail 160.11
  thin 203.10
  soft 324.6
  fragile 328.4
  fine 329.3
  savory 394.7
  soft-colored 428.17
  discriminating 465.4
  exact 494.11
  ticklish 704.8
  pleasing 829.7
  beautiful 845.8
  taste 850.5
  fastidious 868.4
  decorous 960.2
delicatessen 799.4
delicious savory 394.7
  pleasant 829.7
delict 947.2
delight *n.* 827.2
  to one's delight 829.10
delight *v.* joy 827.5
  please 829.5
  (cheer 836.6)
  (amuse 840.20)
  rejoice 838.5
  exult 884.6
  delight in
  relish 394.6
  enjoy 827.6
delighted
  well-disposed 602.8
  pleased 827.8
delightful 829.8
  (alluring 617.5)
delightfully 829.10
delightfulness 829.2
Delilah 962.2
delimit
  circumscribe 229.2
  limit 233.2
delimitate 229.2
delineate
  outline 230.3
  depict 554.7
  outline 626.9
delineation
  outline 230.1; 626.2
  marking 550.7
  depiction 554.1
  (description 594.1)
delineator 554.6
delineatory
  outlinear 230.4
  representative 554.9
  (descriptive 594.7)
delinquency
  shortcoming 304.1
  nonpayment 808.1
  moral ~ 945.3
  (violation of law 964.2)
  misdeed 947.2

delinquent *n.*
  defaulter 808.3
  reprobate 949.1, 2
delinquent *adj.* 808.9
deliquesce
  decrease 36.4
  liquefy 335.5
deliquescence 335.1
deliquescent
  decreasing 36.5
  liquescent 335.8
  flowing 348.26
deliquium
  helplessness 158.2
  fatigue 688.3
delirament 503.7
deliriant, delirifacient 663.4
delirious
  insane 503.14
  (ill 655.23)
  impassioned 821.6
  overwrought 824.10
  unquiet 825.9
delirium
  insanity 503.3
  (ailment 655.4, 5)
  fury 825.4
delirium tremens 959.2
delisk 367.3
delitescence 526.1
  (invisibility 447.1)
delitescent 526.6
  (invisible 447.4)
deliver
  transfer to 270.7
  utter 580.8; 582.6
  ~ a speech 582.7
  ~ in childbirth 662.24
  rescue 672.2
  (redeem 660.9)
  (liberate 750.2)
  relieve 707.6
  convey 783.3
  give 784.9
  deliver oneself 750.4
  deliver the goods
  do thoroughly 729.3
  succeed 731.5
deliverable 672.3
deliverance
  transference 270.1
  rescue 672
  (escape 671.1)
  (liberation 750.1)
  relief 707.4
  conveyance 783.1
  giving 784.1
  relief 834.1
deliverer 912.2
delivery birth 161.3
  transference 270.1
  enunciation 580.3
  declamation 582.3
  conveyance 783.1
  giving 784.1
dell 252.5
delocalization 270.1
delocalize 270.6
Delphian oracle

Delphic oracle
  oracle 513.1
  equivocalness 520.1
  hidden meaning 526.1
delta four 95.2
  promontory 250.5
delubrum 1000.2
delude 545.7
deluder 548.1
deludher 545.7
deluding *n.* 545.2
deluding *adj.* 495.15
deluge *n.*
  flood 348.2, 3, 11
  superabundance 641.1
deluge *v.*
  overrun 303.3
  submerge 310.5
  wet 337.5
  flood 348.18
  overfill 641.4
delusion illusion 443.9
  deception 545.2
  (sorcery 992.1)
  sophism 477.2
  error 495.5
  (hallucination 503.5)
  (imagining 515.4)
  (heresy 984.1)
delusive
  illusive 495.15
  deceptive 545.12
delve excavate 252.9
  cultivate 371.8
  seek 461.16
  ~ into 461.17
demagogue, demagog *n.* speaker 582.5
  ringleader 694.1
  insurgent 742.3
  malcontent 832.2
demagogue, demagog *v.* 582.7
demagogy 737.4
demand *n.*
  requirement 630.1
  requisition 741.2
  estate 780.2
  market 796.1
  price 812.1
  right 922.2
  in demand
  requisite 630.3
  salable 796.7
  desired 865.21
demand *v.* ask 461.14
  require 741.5
  (request 765 4)
  charge 812 5
  ~ a right 924 7
  (assume 925.6)
demantoid 435.3
demarcate
  partition 44.10
  circumscribe 229.2
  outline 230.3
  limit 233.2
dematerialize
  immaterialize 317.5

  spiritualize 994.20
demean
  conduct oneself 692.5
  submit 725.3
  disgrace oneself 874.5
  humble oneself 879.2
demeanor, demeanour mien 448.4
  (fashion 852.1)
  conduct 692.1
démêlé 713.3
demency 503.1
dement *n.* 504.1
dement *v.* 503.11
  (derange 61.2)
dement *adj.* 503.12
dementation 503.1
demented 503.12
  (deranged 61.6)
dementia, dementia paralytica, dementia praecox 503.1
demerit 945.1
Demeter
  productiveness 168.1
  agriculture 371.3
  goddess 979.2
demi- 91.6
demibastion 717.3
demigod hero 861.3
  good person 948.1
  godling 979.1
demijohn 191.11
demi-jour 422.2
demilune moon 318.5
  fortification 717.3
demimondaine, demimonde
  plebeian 876.3
  prostitute 962.2
demirep 962.2
demise *n.* death 360.1
  conveyance 783.1
demise *v.* 787.6
demised 360.8
demisemiquaver 413.6
demission 757.1
demit abdicate 738.6
  resign 757.2
demitint *n.* 428.1
demitint *v.* 259.3
demitone 402.2
Demiurge 976.2
demiurgic 161.11
demivolt, demivolte 309.1
demobilize
  disband 44.11
  release 750.2
democracy
  government 737.4
  (country 182.1)
  commonalty 876.1
democrat 876.3
Democrat 712.6
demoiselle 129.5
demolish 162.4
demolishment 162.1

demolition — denunciatory

demolition 162.1
demolitionary 162.6
demon, daemon
  violent 173.6
  evildoer 913.4
  tutelary spirit 979.12
  devil 980.2
  (bane 663.1)
  (Satan 978.1)
demonetize 800.19
demoniac, daemoniac *n.* 504.1
demoniac, daemoniac *adj.*
  furious 824.10
  malevolent 907.9
  wicked 945.17
  fiendish 980.9
  (satanic 978.7)
  (hellish 982.5)
demonianism, daemonianism
  diabolism 978.4
  sorcery 992.1
demoniast 978.5
demonifuge, daemonifuge 993.1
demonism, daemonism
  diabolism 978.4
  demon worship 991.1
demonist, daemonist 978.5
demonize, daemonize
  diabolize 978.6
  bedevil 992.4
demonolater, daemonolater
  diabolist 978.5
  demon worshiper 991.5
demonolatrous, daemonolatrous 991.7
demonolatry, daemonolatry
  diabolism 978.4
  demon worship 991.1
demonologist, daemonologist 978.5
demonology, daemonology
  diabolism 978.4
  demon worship 991.1
  sorcery 992.1
demonomancy, daemonomancy
  diabolism 978.4
  sorcery 992.1
demonophobia, daemonophobia 860.4
demonry, daemonry
  diabolism 978.4
  sorcery 992.1
demonstrable 478.3
demonstrate
  evidence 467.7
  prove 478.2
  (prove true 494.8)

manifest 525.2
  (explain 522.6)
  indicate 550.18
demonstrated 478.4
  (assured 474.9)
demonstration
  proof 478
  manifestation 525.1
  indication 550.1
  show 882.3
demonstrational 525.4
demonstrative
  demonstrating 478.3
  (evidential 467.11)
  (conclusive 474.10)
  manifestative 525.4
  indicative 550.21
  passionate 825.10
  caressing 902.9
demonstrator 524.1
demoralization
  deterioration 659.1
  turpitude 945.2
demoralize
  vitiate 945.10
  (corrupt 659.9)
demoralized
  unmanned 158.10
  corrupt 945.15
demos 876.1
Demosthenean, Demosthenian 582.12
Demosthenes 582.5
demotic 590.15
demulce 324.4
demulcent *n.* 662.6
demulcent *adj.*
  moderative 174.7
  softening 324.10
  palliative 662.25
  relieving 834.7
demulsion 324.2
demur *n.* delay 133.2
  misgiving 485.2
  objection 489.2
  scruple 603.2; 939.2
  indecision 605.1
  timidity 860.2
demur *v.*
  be uncertain 475.6
  hang in doubt 485.7
  object 489.4
  scruple 603.4
  show indecision 605.4
demure *v.* 932.5
demure *adj.*
  composed 826.9
  serious 837.16
  prudish 853.7
  modest 881.5
demureness
  equanimity 826.3
  gravity 837.2
demurity 826.3
demurrage 133.2
demurral delay 133.2
  indecision 605.1
  timidity 860.2
demurrer 937.2; 969.6
demurring 603.5

demy student 541.4
  stationery 590.10
den resort 74.2
  retreat 189.13
  room 191.16
  cave 252.3
  prison 752.1
  ~ of thieves 791.8
  sink of iniquity 945.8
denary 98.20
denaturalize 659.9
denaturalized 83.10
dendriform 242.6
dendritic, dendroid
  arborescent 242.6
  arborary 367.15
  botanic 369.11
dendrologist 369.9
dendrology 369.1
dengue 655.6
deniable 475.9
denial negation 536.1
  (disproof 468.1)
  (confutation 479.1)
  (protest 489.2)
  (retraction 607.3)
  (rejection 610.1)
  refusal 764.1
  prohibition 761.1
  demurrer 937.2
  temperance 953.1
take no denial
  be obstinate 606.5
  (persist 604a.2)
  compel 744.2
denigrate 431.6
denigration 431.2
denim 219.5
denization 184.7
denizen *n.*
  inhabitant 188.1
  citizen 748.6
denizen *v.* 184.16
denizenation 184.7
denizenize 184.16
denominate 564.6
denomination
  kind 75.2
  school 542.4
  appellation 564.1, 2
  sect 712.1
  religious ~ 984.3
denominational
  classificational 75.6
  partisan 712.9
  sectarian 984.23
denominationalism 984.2
denominationalist 984.13
denominative 75.6
denominator 84.2
denotation
  meaning 516.1
  indication 550.1
denotative 550.21
denote specify 79.5
  show 467.7
  mean 516.5
  indicate 550.18
denouement end 67.1

final issue 154.1
  solution 481a.2
  disclosure 529.1
  finish 729.1
denounce
  censure 932.7
  (maledict 908.4)
  accuse 938.4
denouncement
  censure 932.2
  accusation 938.1
dense crowded 72.13
  compact 321.8
  (coherent 46.9)
  (thick 202.7)
  luxuriant 365.4
  ignorant 491.8
  stupid 499.12
densen 321.7
density
  compactness 321
  (thickness 202.2)
  stupidity 499.2
dent *n.*
  indentation 252.2
  (depression 308.1)
  notch 257.1
  tooth 253.3
  mark 550.7
dent *v.* indent 252.9
  notch 257.5
  (depress 308.4)
dental tooth 253.3
  sound 402.2
dentate 257.6
dented 252.10
dentelated, dentellated 257.6
denticle tooth 253.3
  (projection 250.2)
  serration 257.2
denticulation
  tooth 253.3
  serration 257.2
denticule, dentification 257.2
dentiform 253.20
dentifrice 662.8
dentil capital 215.17
  tooth 253.3
  serration 257.2
dentilation, dentile 257.2
dentilingual 402.11
dentist 662.19
dentistry 662.16
dentoid 253.20
denudation 226.2
denude 226.4
denuded
  wanting 640.11
  deprived 776.6
denunciate
  censure 932.7
  accuse 938.4
denunciation
  malediction 908.1
  threat 909.1
  censure 932.2
  accusation 938.1
denunciatory
  censorious 932.11

deny — deprive

denunciatory (cont'd)
  accusatory 938.5
deny negate 536.2
  (oppose 468.2)
  (confute 479.2)
  (doubt 485.6)
  (dissent 489.4)
  (reject 610.2)
  recant 607.9
  prohibit 761.2
  refuse 764.2
deny oneself
  refuse 764.4
  seclude oneself 893.6
  be abstinent 953.5
  propitiate 990.13
denying 536.3
deobstruent n. 662.9
deobstruent adj. 662.25
deodand 974.2
deodar tree 367.6
  wood 635.3
deodorant n.
  deodorizer 399.2
  purifier 652.8
deodorant adj. 399.2
deodorization
  fumigation 399.2
  disinfection 652.2
deodorize
  fumigate 399.4
  (ventilate 338.10)
  disinfect 652.13
deodorizer 652.8
deontology 926.4
deordination 59.1
deorganization 61.1
deorganize 61.2
deoxidization 140.2
depart differ 15.5
  (start 66.5)
  (absent oneself 187.8)
  (emerge 295.6)
  (disappear 449.2)
  leave 293.4, 5
  die 360.6
depart from
  deviate 279.4
  abandon 624.3
departed n. 362.1
departed adj.
  extinct 2.10
  gone 293.9
  dead 360.8
departer 295.3, 4
departing 293.8
department class 75.1
  (compartment 51.5)
  region 181.1
  function 625.3
  bureau 745.9; 965.2
departmental
  classificational 75.6
  bureaucratic 737.15
department store 799.1
departure
  difference 15.1
  leaving 293

(absence 187.1)
  (embarkment 267.2)
  (recession 287.1)
  (egress 295.1)
  (emigration 295.2)
  (disappearance 449.1)
  (flight 623.2)
  death 360.1
depend hang 214.4
  be dependent 475.7
depend on
  result from 154.3
  evidence 467.7
  trust in 484.7
  be dependent 749.3
to be depended on
  infallible 474.14
  believable 484.15
  trustworthy 940.9
dependability 939.3
dependable
  veracious 543.3
  infallible 474.14
  believable 484.15
  authentic 494.12
  safe 664.10
  trustworthy 939.9
dependence
  relation 9.1
  coherence 46.1
  pendency 214.1
  belief 484.1
  subjection 749.1
dependency
  relation 9.1
  subjection 749.1
  possession 777.1
dependent, dependant n. 746.3
dependent adj.
  contingent 177.3, 4; 475.15
  (occasional 134.9)
  (provisional 637.7)
  resulting 154.5
  pendent 214.7
  subject 749.6
  (slavish 886.4)
  be dependent 475.7
depending 475.15
deperdite 776.6
deperdition 776.1
dephlegmation 340.2
dephlegmatory 340.7
depict delineate 554.7
  (paint 428.10)
  (limn 556.17)
depicter, depictor
  delineator 554.6
  artist 559.1
depiction 554.1
  (description 594.1)
depictive 554.9
  (descriptive 594.7)
depicture n. 554.1
depicture v. 554.7
depilation 226.3
depilous 226.10
deplete
  evacuate 297.14
  (empty 187.9)

use up 638.2; 677.6
depletion
  emptiness 187.3
  waste 638.1
  exhaustion 640.4
  loss 776.1
deplorability 830.1
deplorable
  terrible 649.8
  disastrous 735.8
  grievous 830.11
  disreputable 874.8
deplore regret 833.2
  lament 839.6
deploy 194.5, 8
deployment 194.1
depone 535.4
deponent 467.6
depopulate
  evict 297.10
  dispeople 893.8
depopulation
  eviction 297.2
  dispeoplement 893.2
deport 297.11
  (transport 270.8)
deportation 297.3
  (transportation 270.2)
deportment 692.1
deposal
  ejection 297.1
  dethronement 738.3
  deposition 756.2
  (dismissal 297.4)
depose testify 467.8
  affirm 535.4
  (tell the truth 543.2)
  (promise 768.3)
  dethrone 738.5
  divest of office 756.5
  (dismiss 297.12)
deposit n. dregs 40.2
  silt 270.3
  security 771.1
  (payment 807.2; 809.2)
on deposit 771.9
deposit v. place 184.10
  precipitate 321.7
  store 636.7
depositary 801
deposition
  location 184.5
  dislocation 185.1
  ejection 297.1
  testimony 467.2
  affirmation 535.1
  record 551.1
  dethronement 738.3
  deposal 756.2
  legal pleading 969.6
depository 636.4
  (room 191.16)
  (treasury 802.1)
deposit slip 805.2
depot stop-off 266.10
  storehouse 636.4
depotentiate 158.6
depot ship 726.11

depravation 659.1
deprave 659.9
depraved 945.15
depravedness, depravity 945.2
  (deterioration 659.1)
deprecate
  remonstrate 766.2
  (dissuade 616.2)
  discommend 932.6
deprecation 766
  (discussion 616.1)
  (advice 695.1)
deprecatory
  remonstratory 766.3
  modest 881.6
depreciate
  discount 813.2
  cheapen 815.7
  disparage 934.3
  (underestimate 483.3)
  (discommend 932.6)
depreciation
  decrease 36.1
  discount 813.1
  cheapening 815.3
  detraction 934.1
  (underestimation 483.1)
  (disapprobation 932.1)
depreciative 813.3
depreciator 936.1
depredate 791.10
depredation 791.2
depredator 792.1
depress dent 252.9
  lower 308.4
  sadden 837.8
  damp 842.4
depressed
  dented 252.10
  (low 207.7)
  downcast 308.9
depressing 830.11
depression
  cavity 252.2
  (lowness 207.1)
  (depth 208.1)
  notch 257.1
  lowering 308
  (descent 306.1)
  sadness 837.1, 4
depressive 830.11
deprivation
  want 640.3
  ~ of power 738.3
  deposal 756.2
  dispossession 789.2
  (loss 776.1)
  (disentitlement 925.2)
deprivative 789.15
deprive
  ~ of power 158.6
  ~ of authority 738.5
  ~ of office 756.5
  (dismiss 297.12)
  take from 789.11

800

deprived empty 187.11
bereft 776.6
(forfeited 925.10)
be deprived 776.6
de profundis
lamentation 839.17
penitently 950.6
depth pit 208.2, 4
(lowness 207.1)
pitch 413.13
wisdom 498.3
beyond one's depth
too deep 208.14
impossible 471.7
unintelligible 519.6
in the depths 837.9
depth bomb 727.14
depthless
inconsiderable 32.8
shallow 209.4
depurate 652.9
depurative
antiseptic 662.25
egressive 295.9
purifying 652.15
deputation 755.1
deputative 759.6
depute send 270.9
commission 755.4
deputize 759.5
deputize 755.4
(depute 759.5)
deputy n. 759
(substitute 147.2)
(intermediary 228.5)
(messenger 534.1)
(mediator 724.2)
(servant 746.1)
(broker 797.7)
(agent 690.1)
(steward 694.5)
(lawyer 968.1)
be deputy 759.4
deputy adj. 759.6
deputy sheriff 745.10
deracinate
destroy 162.4
root out 297.17
derail 142.7
derange
disarrange 61.2
(mix 41.6)
(disorder 59.7)
(dislocate 185.2)
(unform 241.4)
dement 503.11
sicken 655.22
deranged
disordered 61.6
(disorderly 59.8)
insane 503.12
derangement 61
(disorder 59.1)
(inversion 218.1)
deray 59.2
derby hat 225.26
mute 417.11
Derby 274.4; 720.5
Derby day
anniversary 138.7
racing 720.5

derelict n. ship 273.1
land 342.2
danger 667.1
castoff 782.2; 893.5
derelict adj.
abandoned 624.4
castoff 782.4
outcast 893.10
dereliction
relinquishment 782.1
~ of duty 927
(neglect 460.1)
(evasion 623.1)
moral ~ 945.3
nonfeasance 947.2
deride ridicule 856.1
(disparage 934.3)
jeer 930.6
derision
ridicule 856.1
(detraction 934.1)
laughingstock 857.1
object of scorn 874.3
scoffing 930.2
derisive 856.7
(insulting 929.5)
(contemptuous 930.8)
(disparaging 934.4)
derivable
attributable 155.4
deducible 478.5
derivation cause 153.1
derivative 154.1
attribution 155.1
ancestry 166.4
etymology 562.4
derivational
resulting from 154.5
attributable 155.4
derivative n.
derivation 154.1
word 562.1
derivative adj.
resulting from 154.5
attributable 155.4
etymological 562.9
derive result 154.3
attribute 155.3
deduce 480.6
etymologize 562.7
get 775.6
receive 785.3
derived 154.5
derm, derma 223.12
dermatogen 223.15
dermatological 223.32
dermatologist 662.19
dermatology 223.20
dermatophytic, dermatoplastic 223.32
dermatoplasty 223.20
dermic 223.32
dermis 223.12
dern! 908.8
dernier cri
novelty 123.2
fashion 852.1
derogate
disgrace 874.5, 6

detract 934.3
derogation
disgrace 874.1
detraction 934.1
derogator 936.1
derogatory
disreputable 874.8
detractory 934.4
derrick 307.2
derring-do 861.1
dervish, darveesh
ascetic 955.2
religious 984.18; 996.7
descant n.
prelude 64.2
music 415.2-4, 12, 13, 15
(polyphony 413.2)
(voice 413.14)
dissertation 595.1
descant v. sing 416.20
expatiate 573.5
discuss 595.4
descanter 595.3
descend incline 217.6
land 267a.34
go down 306.4
(decrease 36.3)
(plunge 310.4)
gravitate 319.7
descendant 167.1
(youngling 129.1)
descendent 306.7
descending
declivitous 217.11
descendent 306.7
descension 306.1
descent ancestry 166.4
(origin 153.1)
posterity 167.1
declivity 217.2
motion downwards 306
(depression 308.1)
(plunge 310.1)
inheritance 775.4
describe
~ a circle 311.3
(circle 247.7)
tell 527.7
characterize 564.6
relate 594.5
(depict 554.7)
(phrase 566.3)
(write 590.14)
description kind 75.2
account 594
(explanation 522.1)
(representation 554.1)
descriptive 594.7
(interpretative 522.8)
(depictive 554.9)
descry see 441.10
discover 481a.3
desecrate misuse 679.2
dishonor 929.3
commit sacrilege 988.7
desecration

misuse 679.1
sacrilege 988.1
desert n. 169.2
(dryness 340.4)
(plain 344.1)
(open space 180.3)
merit 648.1
due 924.2
(punishment 972.1)
(reward 973.1)
virtue 944.1
give one his deserts
retaliate 718.2
punish 972.5
desert v. 624.3
(apostatize 607.8)
(flee 623.10)
desert adj. 187.11
deserted
unoccupied 187.11
forsaken 893.10
deserter 607.5
(runagate 623.5)
(abandoner 624.2)
desertful 931.11
desertion
abandonment 624.1
(apostasy 607.2)
loneliness 893.2
desert rat 188.6
deserve
be entitled to 924.5
be praiseworthy 931.7
deserved 924.11
deserving
entitled to 924.11
worthy 931.10
deshabille 225.23
desiccate 340.5
desiccated 340.9
desiccation 340.2
desiccative n. 340.3
desiccative adj. 340.10
desiccator 340.3
desiderant n. 865.7
desiderant adj. 865.16
desiderate
require 630.2
desire 865.11
desideration
requirement 630.1
desire 865.1, 8
desiderative 865.16
desideratum
requirement 630.1
desire 865.8
desiderium 865.1
design n.
meaning 516.1
representation 554.1
(ornament 847.1)
art 556.1
intention 620.1
plan 626.1, 2
(copy 22.2)
by design 620.5
design v. limn 556.17
intend 620.3
plan 626.9
designate
specify 79.5

designation — determinate

designate *(continued)*
  call attention to 457.7
  (indicate 550.18)
  name 564.6
  (phrase 566.3)
  appoint 609.11
designation kind 75.2
  indication 550.1
  appellation 564.1, 2
  appointment 609.5
designer artist 559.1
  planner 626.8
designing *n.*
  representation 554.1
  art 556.1
  (composition 54.2)
designing *adj.*
  scheming 702.6
  dishonest 940.8
designless 621.21
desinence 142.1
desirability 646.1
desirable
  expedient 646.4
  (advisable 695.9)
  to be desired 865.21
  (palatable 394.7)
  (pleasurable 829.7)
  (satisfactory 831.7)
desire *n.* will 600.1
  wish 865
  (requirement 630.1)
  (hope 858.1)
  (love 897.1)
  (lust 961.3)
  have no desire 866.3
  (be insensible 823.3)
desire *v.* 865.11
  (prefer 609.9)
  (want 630.2)
  (love 897.11)
desired 865.21
desirer 865.7
desiring, desirous 865.16
  (lustful 961.11)
desirously 865.22
desist cease 142.6, 8
  abandon 624.3
desistance 142.1
desk cupboard 191.15
  table 215.20
  clergy 996.1
désœuvré 683.12
desolate *v.*
  destroy 162.4
  damage 659.8
  depopulate 893.8
desolate *adj.*
  unoccupied 187.11
  disconsolate 837.12
  forsaken 893.10
desolating 830.17
desolation
  destruction 162.1
  damage 659.3
  wretchedness 828.3
  loneliness 893.2
despair *n.* 859.1

(wretchedness 828.3)
(sadness 837.1)
in despair 859.7
(wretched 828.16)
(disconsolate 837.12)
despair *v.* 859.5
(be sad 837.6)
despairing 859.7
despatch See **dispatch**
despecificate 15.6
despect 930.1
desperado thief 792.3
  bravo 863.3
  ruffian 913.2
  criminal 949.2
desperate *adj.*
  absolute 31.12
  hopeless 859.7
  rash 863.7
desperate, desperately *adv.* 31.22
desperation
  excitement 825.2
  recklessness 863.1
  hopelessness 859.1
in desperation 173.18
despicable bad 649.8
  odious 830.14
  disreputable 874.8
despisal 930.1
despise 930.5
not to be despised 642.10
despite *n.* 907.1
despite *prep.* 30.8
despiteful 907.6
despoil damage 659.8
  strip 789.12
  plunder 791.10
despoiler 789.6
Despoina world 318.1
  goddess 979.2; 982.4
despond
  lose heart 837.6
  despair 859.5
despondency 837.1
  (hopelessness 859.1)
despondent 837.9
despot tyrant 739.3
  potentate 745.2
despotic 739.5
  (authoritative 737.15)
despotism 739.2
  (lawlessness 964.3)
despumate 652.9
despumation 652.2
desquamate
  form layers 204.4
  scale 226.7
desquamation
  lamination 204.3
  cast skin 223.13
  divestment 226.1
desquamative 226.11
dess, dass 204.1
dessert 298.12, 28
destinate 601.9
destination end 67.1

goal 292.6
(resting place 265.4)
(port 666.4)
destiny 601.3
intention 620.2
destine mean 516.5
  ordain 601.9
  (predetermine 611.3)
  intend 620.3
destined 601.13
  (imminent 152.3)
  (predetermined 611.5)
destinism 601.6
destinist 601.7
destiny 601.3
  (imminence 152.1)
  (predetermination 611.1)
  (fortune 621.1)
destitute
  wanting 640.11
  moneyless 804.7
destitution want 640.3
  poverty 804.1
desto 415.32
destrier, destrer 726.12
destroy ruin 162.4
  (nullify 2.6)
  (injure 649.6)
  (impair 659.8)
  (discard 678.3)
  (abrogate 756.3)
destroyed 162.7
  (extinct 2.10)
  (lost 776.5)
be destroyed 162.5
destroyer 165
  warship 726.11
  evildoer 913.1
destruction 162
  (waste 638.1)
  (impairment 659.3)
  (abolition 756.1)
  (loss 776.1)
destructive 162.6
  (fatal 361.16)
  (harmful 649.10)
desuetude 678.1
  (nonprevalence 614.1)
  (abandonment 624.1)
desultory
  disorderly 59.8
  diversified 81.3
  irregular 139.2
  (discontinuous 70.4)
  inconstant 149.6
  deviative 279.8
  agitated 315.13
  digressive 573.7
desynonymize 15.6
detach disjoin 44.7
  (loosen 47.2)
  appoint 609.11
detached remote 10.7
  disconnected 44.12

incoherent 47.3
abstracted 458.11
detachment
  disjunction 44.1
  part 51.1
  abstraction 458.3
  party 712.1
  military unit 726.7
detail *n.* part 51.1
  particular 79.3
  trivia 643.4
in detail
  piecemeal 51.10
  severally 79.12
detail *v.*
  specialize 79.6
  enumerate 85.7
  appoint 609.11
  assign 786.3
detailed 79.7
  (circumstantial 8.5)
detain delay 133.6
  hinder 706.4
  hold 781.4
detect 481a.3
detectaphone 418.6
detection 481a.1
detective 528.9
  (investigator 461.13)
  (constable 745.10)
detective story 594.2
detent 45.2
detention
  hindrance 706.1
  confinement 751.2
  retention 781.1
détenu 754.1
deter
  disincline 616.3
  daunt 860.11
deterge 652.9
detergent *n.*
  cleanser 652.8
  antiseptic 662.25
detergent *adj.* 652.15
deteriorate
  degenerate 659.6
  (age 124.5; 128.7)
  (perish 162.5)
  (run to waste 638.3)
  (relapse 661.3)
  (backslide 988.9)
  impair 659.8
  suffer misfortune 735.6
deteriorated 659.12
deteriorating 659.11
deterioration 659
  (destruction 162.1)
  (waste 638.1)
  (disease 655.1)
  (relapse 661.1)
  (perversion 988.3)
determent
  dissuasion 616.1
  hindrance 706.1
determinable
  directable 278.9
  measurable 466.12
determinant 153.1
determinate

special 79.7
limited 233.3
certain 474.8
intended 620.4
determination
end 67.1
decision 480.1
(will 600.1)
(choice 609.1)
revelation 481a.1
resolution 604.1
purpose 620.1
determinative
final 67.8
evidential 467.11
(demonstrative 478.3)
(judicial 480.11)
conclusive 474.10
determine end 67.5
specify 79.5
contribute 153.8
influence 175.6
circumscribe 229.2
outline 230.3
limit 233.2
direct 278.4
make certain 474.6
decide 480.6
(make a decision 609.8)
discover 481a.3, 4
(explain 462.7)
resolve 604.6
(will 600.2)
induce 615.9
purpose 620.3
determined
assured 474.9
resolved 604.7, 8
(willful 606.6)
determinism 601.6
determinist 601.7
deterministic 601.12
deterrent 706.8
detersion 652.2
detersive 662.25
detest 898.3
(dislike 867.4)
detestable 649.8
detestation
dislike 867.2
hatred 898.1
dethrone
discrown 738.5
depose 756.5
dethronement
discrownment 738.3
deposal 756.2
detonate
explode 173.9
bang 406.8
(be noisy 404.6)
detonating 173.17
detonation
explosion 173.3
(shot 284.4)
report 406.2
detonator 388.4
(noisemaker 404.4)
(noise 406.6)
(explosive 727.13)

detorsion 243.1
detour, détour n. 629.1
(deviation 279.3)
detour v. 311.3
detract deduct 38.4
disparage 934.3
(underestimate 483.3)
(discommend 932.6)
detracting 934.4
detraction 934
(underestimation 483.1)
(ridicule 856.1)
(malediction 908.1)
(disapprobation 932.1)
(accusation 938.1)
detractor 936
(pessimist 859.4)
detrain 292.8
detriment 659.3
detrimental 649.10
detrital 330.8
detrition 330.2
detritus remains 40.1
(oddments 51.6)
silt 270.3
attritus 330.3
detrude
force out 297.13
depress 308.4
detruncate 38.6
detruncation 38.2
detrusion
ejection 297.1
depression 308.1
detrusive 308.9
deuce two 89.2
throw of dice 621.9
devil 978.1
go to the deuce 162.5
deuce-ace three 92.2
throw of dice 621.9
deuced 830.19
deucedly very 31.24
painfully 830.19
deuterogamist 903.5
deuterogamy 903.2
deva, daeva
god 976.2; 979.1
demon 980.2
devachan 981.4
devaloka 981.4
devastate
destroy 162.4
damage 659.8
desolate 893.8
devastating 845.13
devastation
destruction 162.1
(waste 638.1)
damage 659.3
desolation 893.2
develop, develope
cause 153.6
grow 194.6
enlarge 194.8
evolve 313.2
train 537.10
improve 658.6, 8
elaborate 673.6

development, develoopement
result 154.1
evolution 161.5
growth 194.3
training 537.2
improvement 658.1
Devi 979.4
deviability 149.1
deviant 279.8
deviate differ 15.5
change 140.5
(tergiversate 607.7)
oblique 217.5
turn 279.4, 6
(sidle 236.5)
(curve 245.3)
(navigation 267.24)
(diverge 291.2)
(turn 311.4)
not deviate
be straight 246.3
go directly 278.6
deviation
difference 15.1
nonuniformity 16a.1
unconformity 83.1
irregularity 139.1
change 140.1
obliquity 217.1
turn 279
(divergence 291.1)
deviative
different 15.7
unconformable 83.9
irregular 139.2
indirect 279.8
(oblique 217.9)
(curved 245.4)
(circuitous 311.6; 629.3)
device object 316.3
deception 545.3
sign 550.2
cipher 561.5
plan 626.1
contrivance 626.5
(way 627.1)
(expedient 646.2)
instrument 633.1
artifice 702.3
devices means 632.1
tactics 692.2
devil n.
windstorm 349.12
archenemy 891.1
evildoer 913.4
rogue 949.1
Satan 978.1
fallen angel 978.2
demon 980.2
little ~ 980.3
between the Devil and the deep blue sea 704.11
go to the devil
perish 162.5
become wicked 945.9
the devil take the hindmost! 623.13
the devil and all

all 50.2
everyone 78.5
devil v. cook 384.19
season 392.4
devil-dodger 996.2
devil dog
marine 269.1; 726.10
aeronaut 269a.1
devilfish 366.21
devil-god deity 979.1
idol 991.4
deviling 980.3
devilish
damnable 649.8
malevolent 907.9
wicked 945.17
satanic 978.7
(hellish 982.5)
demoniac 980.9
devilishly 31.24
devilishness 978.3
devilkin 980.3
devil lore 978.4
devil-may-care
reckless 863.7
indifferent 866.4
devilry
diabolism 978.4
sorcery 992.1
devil's bones 621.8
devilship 978.3
devil's tattoo 407.3
devil worship 991.1
devil worshiper 991.5
devious 279.8
(circuitous 311.6)
devisable 270.11
devise n. 784.6
devise v.
produce 161.8
invent 515.10
plan 626.9
bequeath 784.13
devised 626.11
devisee
transferee 270.5
recipient 785.2
deviser 164.1
devitalize
unman 158.7
weaken 160.8
sicken 655.22
devoid empty 187.11
wanting 640.11
devoirs
compliments 894.3
respects 928.3
devolution
deterioration 659.1
transference 783.2
devolve 783.4
devolve on 926.5
Devonshire cream 352.3
devote destine 601.9
employ 625.6
use 677.5
consecrate 873.13
devote oneself to
give attention 457.4
study 461.17
be resolute 604.6

devote (*continued*)
  busy oneself with 625.7
  undertake 676.2
devoted
  doomed 512.5
  destined 601.13
  given to 613.12
  obedient 743.3
  friendship 888.4
  loving 897.14
  pious 987.10
devotee fanatic 504.2
  sportsman 840.19
  votary 865.7
  religious ~ 987.4
devotion
  close attention 457.2
  resolution 604.1
  (eagerness 682.3)
  friendship 888.1
  love 897.1
  constancy 939.4
  piety 987.1
  (reverence 928.1)
  worship 990.1
devotional 990.15
devotionalist 987.4
devotionist 990.8
devotions 990.7
devour destroy 162.4
  eat 298.44
  be credulous 486.3
  use up 677.6
  eat greedily 957.3
devourer 298.41
devourment 298.1
devout fervent 821.6
  pious 987.10
  worshipful 990.15
devoutless 989.6
devoutly 821.9
dew 339.2
Dewali
  anniversary 138.7
  festival 840.2
dewan, diwan 745.4, 5, 9
dew-beater 211.4
dewdrop 339.2
dewy 339.9
dexter *n.* 238.2
dexter, dexterical *adj.* 238.3
dexterity
  dextrality 238.1
  skill 698.1
  (facility 705.1)
dexterous, dextrous
  dextral 238.3
  skillful 698.11
dextrad 238.5
dextral 238.3
dextrality 238
dextrally 238.5
dextrocardial, dextrocerebral, dextrocular 238.3
dextrocularity, dextroduction 238.1
dextrogyrate 238.3
dextrogyration 238.1

dextromanual, dextropedal 238.3
dextrorotation 238.1
dextrorse 238.3
dextrose 396.4
dextrosinistral
  dextral 238.3
  sinistral 239.5
dextroversion 238.1
dey 745.7
dg. 319.4
dhobi, dhoby, dhobee, dhobey, dhobie 652.6
dhoti, dhooti 225.22
dhow 273.2
dhu 431.7
diable 978.1
diablerie, diablery
  diabolism 978.4
  sorcery 992.1
diabolical
  damnable 649.8
  malevolent 907.9
  wicked 945.17
  devilish 978.7
  demoniacal 980.9
diabolism
  devil lore 978.4
  sorcery 992.1
diabolist 978.5
  (sorcerer 992.2)
diabolize
  demonize 978.4
  bedevil 992.4
diabolology 978.4
diacaustic 245.2
diaconicon, 1000.3
diacritical
  differentiative 15.8
  discriminating 465.4
  distinctive 550.21
diadem
  royal insignia 747.1
  jewel 847.7
diaeresis, dieresis
  dissection 44.4
  decomposition 49.1
  typography 550.8
  poetical ~ 597.6
diagnose
  identify 13.5
  distinguish 465.2
diagnosis
  discrimination 465.1
  interpretation 522.1
  disease 655.19
diagnostic *n.*
  particularity 79.2
  test 463.1
  earmark 550.6
diagnostic *adj.*
  differentiative 15.8
  distinctive 79.8
  discriminating 465.4
  interpretative 522.8
  indicative 550.21
diagnostication 465.1
diagnostics
  interpretation 522.5
  pathology 655.19

diagonal *n.* 217.3
diagonal *adj.* 217.15
  be diagonal 217.7
diagonality 217.1
diagonally, diagonalwise 217.19
diagram *n.* 626.2
diagram *v.* 230.3; 626.9
dial *n.* timepiece 114.6
  measure 466.4
dial *v.* 466.10
dialect *n.*
  brogue 563.5
  (language 560.1)
  diction 591.1
dialect, dialectal *adj.* 563.16
  (linguistic 560.9)
dialectalize 563.13
dialectic *n.* 476.9
dialectic *adj.* 476.14
dialectician
  reasoner 476.9
  philologist 560.7
  colloquialist 563.11
dia'ecticism, dialectics 476.1
dialectologist 560.7; 563.11
dialogist 588.5
dialogize 588.7
dialogue, dialog *n.*
  interlocution 588.1
  drama 599.3
  script 599.16
dialogue, dialog *v.* 588.7
diameter 202.3
diametrical 237.6
diamond angle 244.2
  transparency 425.2
  type 591.7
  treasure 648.4
  playing card 840.13
  gem 847.7
  good person 948.1
diamond in the rough
  unformed 241.3
  undevelopment 674.3
  unsophisticate 703.2
  vulgarian 851.4
  good person 948.1
diamond cut diamond 718.1
Diana
  moon god 318.5
  chase 622.2
  spinster 904.3
  good woman 948.2
  goddess 979.2
diapason
  music 413.1, 15
  organ stop 417.12
  tuning fork 417.13
diaper
  garment 225.22, 32
  ornamentation 847.3
diaphane *n.* 425.2
diaphane *adj.* 425.4
diaphaneity 425.1

diaphanous 425.4
diaphonic 414.4
diaphony 414.1
diaphoresis
  perspiration 299.4
  uncertainty 475.1
diaphragm
  middle 68.2
  partition 228.6
diarchy 737.4
diarrhea, diarrhoea
  excrement 299.2
  ailment 655.5
diary
  chronology 114.5
  record 551.3
  (journal 593.6)
diaskeuast 593.16
diastase 320.3
diastatic 320.8
diaster 161.1
diastole 194.2
diatessaron 413.11
diathermancy 382.1
diathermanous, diathermic 382.21
diathesis nature 5.3
  temperament 820.1
diaton 193.4
diatomaceous, diatomic 193.10
diatomite 635.6
diatonic 413.28
diatonic scale 413.16
diatribe lecture 582.2
  malediction 908.1
  tirade 932.3
dib *n.* money 800.1
  token 800.7
dib *v.* 622.8
dibble *n.* 262
dibble *v.*
  cultivate 371.8
  fish 622.8
dibbler 622.5
dice angle 244.2
  divination 511.3, 5
  gambling 621.8
  (game 840.11)
diced 244.5
dicer hat 225.26
  gambler 621.15
dichotomize 91.4
dichotomous 91.6
dichotomy 91.1
dichroic 443.14
dichroism 440.1
dichromic 440.5
dick detective 528.9
  declaration 582.4
  policeman 745.10
dickens 978.1
dicker *n.* ten 98.6
  interchange 148.1
  compact 769.1
  barter 794.3
dicker *v.* 794.5
dickey, dicky
  ass 271.10
  bird 366.22
dickeybird, dickybird 366.22

dicotyledonous 369.11
Dictaphone
　sound device 418.6
　recorder 553.3
dictate n. axiom 496.2
　urge 615.2
　precept 697.1
　decree 741.3
　law 963.2
dictate v. enjoin 695.5
　command 741.4
　domineer 885.5
dictation
　command 737.2
　decree 741.3
　law 963.2
dictator
　director 694.1, 4
　ruler 745.1, 2
dictatorial
　dogmatic 474.15
　opinionated 606.7
　directing 693.6
　advisory 695.8
　authoritative 737.15
　despotic 739.5
　arrogant 885.8
dictatorship
　authority 737.3
　despotism 739.2
dicature 737.2, 3
diction 569
　(language 560.1)
　(verbiage 562.3)
　(grammar 567.1)
　(utterance 580.3)
dictionary 593.4
　(list 86.1)
　(definition 522.1)
Dictograph 418.6
dictum maxim 496.1, 2
　affirmation 535.1
　remark 582.4
　precept 697.1
　command 741.1
　law 963.2
didactic
　instructive 537.12
　advisory 695.8
　preceptive 697.2
didactics 537.1
didder n. shake 315.4
　coldness 383.2
　trepidation 825.3
didder v. shake 315.9
　be cold 383.7
diddle n. 959.4
diddle v. deceive 545.7
　swindle 791.12
diddler cheat 548.2
　swindler 792.8
dido 309.2
die n. mold 22.3
　angle 244.2
　perforator 262
　chance 621.2
　dice 621.8
die v. expire 360.6
　(cease 2.5)
　(end 67.6)
　(deteriorate 659.6)
　extinguish 385.5

disappear 449.2
die away
　cease 2.5; 142.6
　decrease 36.3
　disappear 449.2
die dunghill 360.6
die for 865.11
die game
　die fighting 360.6
　persevere 604a.2
　be impenitent 951.2
die hard
　be obstinate 606.5
　resist 719.3
die in one's shoes
　continue 143.3
　persevere 604a.2
　be executed 972.13
die out
　cease to be 2.5
　extinguish 385.5
　disappear 449.2
diecious See dioecious
die-hard, diehard n.
　conservative 141.3
　oppositionist 710.2
　malcontent 832.2
die-hard adj. 141.7
diemaker 690.8
diencephalon 450.2
dieresis See diaeresis
Diesel engine, Diesel 633.3
diet food 298.8
　remedy 662.15
　legislature 696.4
dietary food 298.8
　remedy 662.15
dietetic of food 298.49
　dietary 662.26
dietetics 662.15
Dieu, dieu 976.2
differ be contrary 14.3
　vary 15.5
　(be unlike 18.2)
　dissent 489.4
　disaccord 713.6
difference n.
　variance 15
　(contrariety 14.1)
　(dissimilarity 18.1)
　(inequality 28.1)
　(comparison 464.1)
　disparity 24.2
　sum 84.3
　~ of opinion 489.1
　dissension 713.2
　settle differences
　reconcile 723.4
　be reconciled 723.5
　compromise 774.2
difference v. 15.6
difference engine 85.5
different 15.7
　(unrelated 10.5)
　(contrary 14.5)
　(ununiform 16a.2)
　(dissimilar 18.4)
　(diversified 81.3)
　be different 15.5
differentia nicety 15.2

particularity 79.2
differential n.
　nicety 15.2
　number 84.2
　automobile 272.16
differential adj.
　differentiative 15.8
　numeral 84.7
differential psychology 450.4
differentiate
　difference 15.6
　(change 140.6)
　(compare 464.2)
　(discriminate 465.2)
　specify 79.5
differentiation
　mathematics 85.4
　discrimination 465.1
　(difference 15.1)
differently 15.10
　(contrarily 14.7)
　(otherwise 18.6)
differing 15.7
　(disagreeing 24.6)
　(unequal 28.3)
difficile 704.8
difficult not easy 704.8
　(complicated 59.10)
　(laborious 686.10)
　unmanageable 704.10
　fastidious 868.4
　be difficult 704.5
difficulty
　arduousness 704
　(adversity 735.1)
　obstacle 706.2
　poverty 804.1
in difficulties 806.5, 7
in difficulty 704.11
with difficulty 704.12
　(laboriously 686.11)
diffidence doubt 485.2
　fearfulness 860.2
　modesty 881.1
diffident fearful 860.14
　modest 881.5
diffluent 348.26
diffuse v.
　disperse 73.3
　pervade 186.12
　publish 531.7
　be diffused 186.12
diffuse adj.
　verbose 573.7
　(grandiloquent 577.7)
　(loquacious 584.5)
　(redundant 641.5)
　copious 639.7
　be diffuse 573.5
　(be loquacious 584.4)
diffusely 573.10
diffuse nebula 420.12
diffuseness 573
　(verbiage 562.3)
　(grandiloquence 577.2)
　(loquacity 584.1)

(redundance 641.1)
diffusion
　imbuement 41.2
　dispersion 73.1
　(permeation 186.5)
　~ of light 420.10
　publication 531.1
diffusive
　dispersive 73.5
　lavish 639.7
dig n. resort 74.2
　blow 276.3
　bookworm 492.3
　gibe 930.3
dig v. excavate 252.9
　(deepen 208.6)
　speed 274.9
　cultivate 371.8
　labor 686.6
dig for 461.16
dig in 664.6
dig out
　hasten off 293.5
　extract 301.5
　discover 481a.3
dig up extract 301.5
　discover 481a.3
　acquire 775.6
dig up the tomahawk 722.9
digamist 903.5
digamous 903.14
digamy 903.2
digenesis 161.2
digenetic 161.11
digest n. list 86.1
　dissertation 595.1
　compendium 596.1
　pandect 963.2
digest v. classify 60.7
　heat 384.16
　ponder 451.27
　revise 658.11
　submit to 725.3
　brook 826.6
digestible 662.26
digestion 60.2
digestive 662.26
digger
　Australian 188.9
　excavator 252.7
diggings resort 74.2
　location 184.1
　abode 189.1
dight n. 32.2
dight v. adorn 847.11
　clothe 225.41
dight adj. 225.46
digit number 84.1
　finger 379.2; 781.3
digitate 253.11
digitated 44.12
digladiation 720.1
diglot 560.9
dignification 873.6
dignified
　ennobled 873.18
　proud 878.7
dignify 873.13
dignity greatness 31.2
　importance 642.1
　nobility 873.3

digraph — dip

dignity (*continued*)
  pride 878.1
digraph 561.1
digress deviate 279.5
  ~ from subject 573.5
digression
  obliquity 217.1
  deviation 279.1
  excursus 573.3
  circuit 629.1
digressive 573.7
digs resort 74.2
  location 184.1
  abode 189.1
dihedral 236.7
dijudicate 480.6
dijudication 480.1
dike, dyke fence 232.2
  trench 259.2
  pool 343a.1
  channel 350.1
  fortification 717.3
dilaceration 44.2
dilapidate 659.8
dilapidated 659.12
dilapidation 659.2
  (destruction 162.1)
dilatant 194.10
dilatation
  distention 194.1
  convexity 250.1
dilatation of the heart 655.12
dilate distend 194.5, 8
  bulge 250.7
  blow up 349.24
  expatiate 573.5
dilation
  distention 194.1
  (increase 35.1)
  (thickness 202.2)
  convexity 250.1
  expatiation 573.4
dilatoriness
  delay 133.2
  indolence 683.3
dilatory 133.9
  (slow 275.8)
  (neglectful 460.8)
  (indolent 683.13)
be dilatory 133.5
dilemma
  perplexity 475.2
  logic 476.4
  alternate choice 609.1
  predicament 704.4
  (question 461.10)
  (enigma 533.2)
in a dilemma
  uncertain 475.16
  in a predicament 704.11
dilettante *n.*
  sciolist 493.2
  artist 559.1
  connoisseur 850.1
  votary 865.7
dilettante *adj.* 491.12
dilettantism

slight knowledge 491.3
  virtuosity 850.2
diligence
  vehicle 272.6
  close attention 457.2
  industry 682.5
diligent 682.19
  (studious 539.6)
dill, dillseed 393.1
dillydallier
  waverer 605.3
  idler 683.7
dillydally *v.*
  delay 133.5, 7
  go slow 275.5
  be irresolute 605.4
  idle 683.8
dillydally, dillydallying *adj.*
  dilatory 133.9
  slow 275.8
dilogy 573.2
diluent *n.* 335.4
diluent *adj.*
  solvent 335.9
  watery 337.6
dilute imbue 41.8
  weaken 160.9
  (thin 203.8)
  (water 337.5)
diluted 160.10
  (watery 337.6)
dilution 337.2
diluvian 124.7
diluvium
  residue 40.2
  silt 270.3
dim *v.* obscure 422.6
  (darken 421.5)
  (shade 424.6)
  (obfuscate 426.3)
  decolor 429.5
  tarnish 440a.2
  ~ the eyes 443.13
dim *adj.* faint 405.9
  semidark 422.8
  (dark 421.7)
  pale 429.6
  indistinct 447.5
  obscure 519.7
grow dim 422.7
dime 800.8
dime novel 594.2
dimensions
  proportions 180.5
  size 192.1
dim-eyed 443.15
dimidiate *v.* 91.4
dimidiate *adj.* 91.6
dimidiation 91.1
diminish
  decrease 36.3, 4
  (deduct 38.4)
  qualify 469.3
diminished 38.11
diminishment 36.1
  (contraction 195.1)
diminuendo 415.15, 30
diminution
  decrease 36.1

(contraction 195.1)
  (waste 638.1)
  modulation 174.2
  depression 308.1
  music 415.5
diminutive *n.* 193.2
diminutive *adj.* 193.8
diminutiveness 193.1
  (quantity 32.1)
dimity 219.5
dimly 422.10
  (darkly 421.10)
dimmish, dimish, dimmy 422.8
dimness
  faintness 405.1
  semidarkness 422
  (darkness 421.1)
  (paleness 429.1)
dim-out 421.3
dimple cavity 252.2
  notch 257.1
dimpsy *n.* 126.1
dimpsy *adj.* 422.8
dim-sighted
  poor-sighted 443.15
  (blind 442.6)
  obtuse 499.12
be dim-sighted 443.10
dim-sightedness 443.2
  (blindness 442.1)
din *n.* 404.2
din *v.* repeat 104.4
  be loud 404.5
din in the ear
  repeat 104.4
  (be loquacious 584.4)
  drum 407.8
dinamode 171.6
dinar 800.8
dine 298.43, 44
dine with Duke Humphrey 956.3
diner
  dining car 272.19
  eater 298.41
diner-out 298.41
ding 408.8
ding-a-ling *n.* 407.1
ding-a-ling *v.* 408.8
dingdong *n.* 407.1
  (repetition 104.1)
  (drumming 407.11)
dingdong *v.* 408.8
dingdong *adj.*
  uniform 16.5
  repetitional 104.7
  tedious 841.8
dingdong *adv.* 604.9
dinge *n.* 431.4
dinge *v.* 440a.2
dinghy, dingy, dingey
  railway car 272.19
  boat 273.2, 4
dingle *n.* valley 252.5
  door 260.4
dingle *v.* 408.8
dingo 366.5
dingy *n.* 431.4
dingy *adj.*

blurred 422.8
  dark 431.8
  gray 432.4
  discolored 440a.3
dining car 272.19
dining hall, dining room 191.16
dinky
  inconsiderable 32.6
  diminutive 193.8
dinner *n.* meal 298.34
  party 892.6
dinner *v.* 298.43, 44
dinner clothes 225.14
dinner coat 225.14, 16
dinosaur
  antiquity 124.2
  (animal 366.2)
  behemoth 192.8
dinosaurian *n.* 192.8
dinosaurian, dinotherian *adj.* 192.15
Dinotherium
  antiquity 124.2
  behemoth 192.8
dint *n.* potence 157.1
  dent 252.2
  notch 257.1
  blow 276.3
  mark 550.7
by dint of
  potently 157.10
  through 631.5
  (by means of 632.4)
dint *v.* dent 252.9
  notch 257.5
diocesan 996.5
diocese territory 181.2
  ecclesiastical 995.3
dioecious, diecious 357.10
Diogenes
  recluse 893.4
  misanthrope 910.2
Diomedes and Sthenalus 890.5
Dionaea 545.4
Dionysus, Dionysos
  agriculture 371.3
  drama 599.1
  intoxication 959.1
  god 979.2
dioptrics 420.16
diorama view 448.2
  picture 556.10
dip *n.*
  declivity 217.2
  cavity 252.2
  (depression 308.1)
  direction 278.1
  plunge 310.1
  candle 423.7
  pickpocket 792.6
  curtsy 928.2
dip *v.*
  signal ship 267.41
  aviate 267a.31
  ladle 270.10
  direct 278.4
  plunge 310.4, 5
  (insert 300.7)
  (descend 306.4)

~ snuff 392a.14
signal 550.20
curtsy 928.6
tipple 959.15
baptize 998.14
dip into
  glance at 441.14;
    461.19
  study 539.4
**diphenylchloroarsine,
  diphenylchlorar-
  sine** 334.2
diphtheria 655.6
diphthong 402.2
diphyletic dual 89.4
  lineal 167.7
diplegia 655.15
diplex 158a.12
diploma
  credential 467.4
  voucher 550.11
  record 551.1
  commission 755.1
diplomacy tact 698.4
  cunning 702.2
  mediation 724.1
diplomat, diplomate
  strategist 702.4
  diplomatist 759.2
diplomatic n. 700.4
diplomatic adj.
  cunning 702.6
  mediatory 724.4
diplomatic agent
  759.2
  (mediator 724.2)
diplomatical 702.4
diplomatics
  cunning 702.2
  mediation 724.1
diplomatism 724.1
diplomatist
  strategist 702.4
  diplomat 759.2
dipper 191.14
Dipper 318.6
dipsas 83.7
  (serpent 366.19)
dipsey, dipsie, dipsy n.
  plumb 208.4
  measure 466.4
**dipsey, dipsie,
  dipsy** adj. 208.12
dipsomania
  insanity 503.1
  alcoholism 959.2
dipsomaniac 504.1
diptych list 86.1
  record 551.1
Diras violent 173.6
  Furies 900.4
  mythical beings
    980.5
dire terrible 649.8
  disastrous 735.8
  painful 830.13
  fearful 860.15
direct n. 415.23
direct v. pilot 267.11
  point 278.4
  ~ music 416.22
  mean 516.5

teach 537.9
manage 693.4
(conduct 692.4)
(rule 737.11)
command 741.4
direct adj.
  lineal 167.7
  straight 246.5
  straightforward
    278.8
  frank 703.4
direct adv. 278.13
directable 278.9
directing n. 693.1
directing adj. 693.6
  (conducting 692.6)
  (ruling 737.15)
  (jurisdictional
    965.4)
direction course 278
  (right 238.2)
  (left 239.2)
  teaching 537.1
  guidepost 550.10
  management 693
  (conduct 692.1)
  (advice 695.1)
  (command 737.2)
  (jurisdiction 965.1)
  precept 697.1
  order 741.1
in the direction of
  278.12
directional 278.10
directionally 278.11
directive
  directional 278.9, 10
  directing 693.6
directly soon 132.15
  straightforward
    278.13
  (straightly 246.6)
directness 246.1
Directoire 554.9
director
  teacher 540.4
  manager 694
  (chief 642.6)
  (master 745.1)
directorate 542.8
directorship
  managership 693.3
  authority 737.3
directory book 593.3
  guide 694.6, 7
  council 696.3
direful 860.15
diremption 44.2
direption 791.2
dirge 839.3
  (music 415.8)
dirgelike 839.15
  (funereal 363.25)
dirigible n. 273a.5
dirigible adj. 278.9
dirk 727.3
dirt n. rain 348.11
  windiness 349.14
  scandal 532.4
  filth 653.5
  (stain 848.1)
  obscenity 961.1

heap dirt upon 874.7
dirt v. 653.15
dirt-cheap 815.6, 8
dirtied 653.16
dirty v. 653.15
  (corrupt 659.9)
dirty adj.
  stormy 349.26
  cloudy 353.11
  blurred 422.8
  opaque 426.4
  unclean 653.16
  (muddy 352.9)
  disreputable 874.8
  obscene 961.9
Dis 979.2; 982.4
disability
  impotence 158.1
  ailment 655.1
disable 158.6
  (render useless
    645.7)
  (impair 659.8)
disabled 158.8
disablement 158.1
disabusal 545a.1
disabuse 545a.2
  (disclose 529.3)
disaccord n.
  difference 15.1
  disagreement 24.1
  discord 713.1
disaccord v.
  differ 15.5
  disagree 24.5; 713.6
disaccordance 24.1
disaccordant 15.7
disadvantage
  inexpedience 647.1
  obstacle 706.2
disadvantageous
  inexpedient 647.3
  detrimental 649.10
disaffect 616.3
disaffected 889.3
disaffection
  dissent 489.1
  dislike 867.1
  hate 898.1
disaffirm 536.2
disaffirmation 536.1
disagree differ 15.5
  disaccord 24.5
    713.6
  dissent 489.4
  (doubt 485.6)
  be insalubrious
    657.2
disagreeable
  unsavory 395.5
  unpleasant 830.10
  (dislikable 867.9)
disagreeableness
  830.1
disagreeing 24.6
  (differing 15.7)
  (dissimilar 18.4)
  (unconformable
    83.9)
  (dissenting 489.5)
  (quarrelsome 901.9)
disagreement

disaccord 24
  (irrelation 10.1)
  (difference 15.1)
  (unconformity
    83.1)
  nonconformity 83.2
  dissent 489.1
  variance 713.2
  (opposition 708.1)
in disagreement with
  24.10
  (notwithstanding
    30.8)
disallow deny 536.2
  prohibit 761.2
  refuse 764.2
  disapprove 932.5
disallowance 761.1
disannul 756.3
disappear
  cease to be 2.5
  vanish 449.2
  (depart 293.4)
cause to disappear
  552.2
disappearance 449
  (departure 293.1)
  (egress 295.1)
disappeared 449.5
disappearing n. 449.1
disappearing adj.
  449.4
disappoint
  defeat expectation
    509.2
  (disillusion 545a.2)
  dissatisfy 832.4
disappointed 509.4
  (regretful 833.3)
  (discontented
    832.5)
be disappointed 509.3
disappointing 832.6
  (disappointment
    509.5)
disappointment 509
  (disillusionment
    545a.1)
  (failure 732.1)
  (discontent 832.1)
  (regret 833.1)
  (hopelessness
    859.1)
disapprobation
  discountenance
    764.1
  disapproval 932
  (dissent 489.1)
  (disrepute 874.1)
  (malediction 908.1)
  (derision 930.2)
  (detraction 934.1)
disapprobatory 932.11
  (disparaging 934.4)
disapproval 932.1
  (dissent 489.1)
  (dislike 867.1)
disapprove
  discountenance
    764.3
  object to 932.5
  (dissent 489.4)

disapproved — disconnected 808

disapprove (*cont'd*)
  (dislike 867.4)
  (condemn 971.2)
disapproved 932.12
disapprover 936.1
disapproving 932.11
disarm
  disable 158.6
  render useless 645.7
  reconcile 831.4
  propitiate 914.4
disarrange 61.2
  (dislocate 185.2)
disarrangement 61.1
disarray 59.2
disassociation
  irrelation 10.1
  disjunction 44.1
disaster fatality 361.5
  misfortune 735.3
disastrous
  harmful 649.10
  calamitous 735.8; 830.17
disavow deny 536.2
  recant 607.9
disavowal denial 536.1
  recantation 607.3
disband part 44.11
  disperse 73.3
  demobilize 750.2
disbar depose 756.5
  (dismiss 297.12)
  degrade 874.7
  disbench 968.4
disbark 292.9
disbelief
  unbelief 485.1
  (incredulity 487.1)
  infidelity 989.2
disbelieve 485.5
  (be irreligious 989.5)
disbeliever
  irreligionist 989.4
  (unbeliever 485.4)
disbelieving 989.7
disbench depose 756.5
  degrade 874.7
  disbar 968.4
disbowel 297.16
disbranch 44.9
disburden
  unpack 297.21
  lighten 320.4
  ~ one's mind 529.5
  ease 705.4
  (relieve 834.4)
disburse 809.3
disbursement 809.1
disc See **disk**
discal 220.7
discalceate, discalced 226.9
discanonization 756.2
discanonize 756.5
discard eliminate 42.4
  disuse 678.3
  (excise 38.5)
  (destroy 162.4)

(eject 297.8)
(reject 610.2)
(abandon 624.3)
(relinquish 782.3)
discarded 495.17
discarnate
  disembodied 317.6
  spectral 980a.4
discept differ 15.5
  argue 476.11
disceptation 476.2
disceptator 476.9
discern see 441.10
  (be discerning 498.7)
  discover 481a.3
  judge 480.6
  know 490.9
  understand 518.4
discernibility 446.1
discernible
  visible 446.4
  knowable 490.18
  manifest 525.4
discerning 498.10
  be discerning 498.7
discernment
  vision 441.1
  discrimination 465.1
  intuition 477a.1
  sagacity 498.2
discerptible 44.13
discerption 44.2
discharge *n.*
  explosion 173.3
  (impulse 276.1)
  shot 284.4
  dismissal 297.4
  (egress 295.1)
  excretion 299.1
  detonation 406.2
  gunfire 716.2
  completion 729.1
  release 750.1
  (acquittal 970.1)
  receipt 771.4
  observance 772.1
  payment 807.1
  ~ of duty 926.2
discharge *v.*
  explode 173.9
  shoot 284.13
  exude 295.7
  dismiss 297.12
  let out 297.13
  ~ the duties of 625.9
  ~ a function 644.3
  do 680.6
  transact 692.4
  complete 729.2
  exempt 748.10
  release 750.2
  (acquit 970.3)
  ~ an obligation 772.3, 4; 926.2
  pay 807.7
disciple convert 144.5
  pupil 541.2
  (follower 281.2)
  school 542.4

religious 985.6
believer 987.4
disciplinarian
  teacher 540.1
  tyrant 739.3
disciplinary 537.12
discipline *n.*
  method 58.3
  science 490.7
  training 537.2
  restraint 751.1
  punishment 972.1
discipline *v.* 537.10
disclaim deny 536.2
  recant 607.9
  (resign 757.2)
  reject 610.2
  abrogate 756.4
  refuse 764.2
disclamation
  denial 536.1
  recantation 607.3
  (resignation 757.1)
  refusal 764.1
disclamatory
  resigning 757.3
  declinatory 764.5
disclose open 260.12
  reveal 529.3
  (discover 481a.3)
  (manifest 525.2)
  (inform 527.7, 10)
  (undeceive 545a.2)
  indicate 550.18
disclosed
  manifest 525.4
  revealed 529.7
  become disclosed 313.2
  be disclosed 529.6
  (appear 446.2)
  (be informed 527.11)
disclosive 529.8
  (informative 527.13)
disclosure
  appearance 448.1
  (manifestation 525.1)
  (information 527.1)
  (publication 531.1)
  (undeception 545a.1)
  discovery 481a.1
  revelation 529
discobolus, discobolos 284.7
discoid broad 202.6
  laminated 204.5
  exterior 220.7
  circular 247.8
  flat 251.5
discolor, discolour *n.* 440a.1
discolor, discolour *v.*
  decolor 429.5
  stain 440a.2
  (mark 550.19)
discoloration, discolouration
  decoloration 429.2

stain 440a
(mark 550.7)
bruise 659.4
discolored, discoloured 440a.3
  (spotted 440.9)
  (imperfect 651.4)
discolorment, discolourment
  decoloration 429.2
  stain 440a.1
discomfit 731.9
discomfited 732.12
discomfiture 732.3
discomfort pain 378.1
  pain 828.1
discomforted 828.14
discommend 932.6
  (detract 934.3)
discommendable 932.13
discommendation 932.1
  (detraction 934.1)
discommode
  hinder 706.4
  distress 830.3
discommodious 647.3
discommodity 647.1
discompose
  derange 61.4
  (change 140.6)
  agitate 315.8
  confuse 458.9
  excite 824.3
  distress 830.3
  anger 900.10
discomposed
  deranged 61.6
  displeased 828.14
discomposure
  derangement 61.1
  confusion 458.4
  pain 828.1
disconcert
  discompose 61.4
  confuse 458.9
  perplex 475.8
  disappoint 509.2
  daunt 860.11
  embarrass 704.7
  frustrate 706.7
  dissatisfy 832.4
  blight one's hopes 859.6
disconcerted 732.9
disconcerting
  embarrassing 704.9
  unsatisfactory 832.6
disconcertion
  confusion 458.4
  perplexity 475.2
disconformity 83.2
discongruity
  difference 15.1
  disagreement 24.1
disconnect 44.7
  (part 51.7)
  (discontinue 70.3)
disconnected
  irrelative 10.5
  disjoined 44.12

disconnectedness — disdainful

discontinuous 70.4
irregular 139.2
diction 575.2
disconnectedness, disconnected, disconnexion
  disjunction 44.1
  (irrelation 10.1)
  discontinuity 70.1
disconsolate 837.12
  (in despair 859.7)
discontent 832
  (dissent 489.1)
  (disappointment 509.1)
  (displeasure 828.2)
  (regret 833.1)
  (sadness 837.1)
  (complaint 839.1)
discontented 832.5
  (dissentient 489.5)
  (disappointed 509.4)
  (displeased 828.14)
  (regretful 833.3)
  (sad 837.9)
  be discontented 832.3
  (complain 839.10)
discontinuance 142.1
  (end 67.1)
  (discontinuity 70.1)
  (abandonment 624.1)
  (disuse 678.1)
discontinuation
  discontinuity 70.1
  cessation 142.1
discontinue
  interrupt 70.3
  (disjoin 44.7)
  cease 142.6
  (end 67.5)
  (disuse 678.2)
discontinued 70.4
discontinuity 70
  (disjunction 44.1)
  (periodicity 138.2)
discontinuous 70.4
  (disjoined 44.12)
  (periodic 138.10)
  (fitful 139.2)
  be discontinuous 70.2
discontinuously 70.5
  (irregularly 139.3)
discord n.
  disagreement 24.1
  dissonance 414
  (noise 404.2)
  (stridor 410.1)
  disaccord 713.1
  (dissent 489.1)
  (opposition 708.1)
  (enmity 889.1)
discord v. 414.3
discordance
  difference 15.1
  disagreement 24.1
  discord 713.1
  (dissent 489.1)
discordant
  different 15.7
  disagreeing 24.6

(irrelative 10.5)
dissonant 414.4
(strident 410.9)
(speech 583.5)
colors 428.16
at variance 713.9
(dissentient 489.5)
(quarrelsome 901.9)
be discordant 414.4
(be harsh 410.6)
discordantly 24.9
discount n.
  decrement 39a
  ~ in price 813
  at a discount
  marked down 813.4
  in disrepute 874.9
  in disfavor 932.12
discount v.
  deduct 38.4
  ~ a price 813.2
discountenance n.
  refusal 764.1
  disapprobation 932.1
discountenance v.
  disconcert 706.7
  oppose 708.2
  refuse 764.3
  disapprove 932.5
discounting 813.3
discourage
  disincline 616.3
  deject 837.8
  daunt 860.11
discouraged 837.9
discouragement 616.1
discourse n.
  reasoning 476.1
  lesson 537.6
  speech 582.1, 2
  interlocution 588.1
  dissertation 595.1
discourse v.
  drift 267.23
  expound 537.11
  declaim 582.7
  converse 588.7
  dissertate 595.4
discourser
  conversationalist 588.5
  dissertator 595.3
discoursive
  conversational 588.10
  dissertative 595.5
discourteous 895.6
  (insolent 885.9)
  (disrespectful 929.5)
  be discourteous 895.4
  (disrespect 929.3)
discourteously 895.8
discourtesy 895
  (vulgarity 851.1)
  (insolence 885.2)
  (disrespect 929.1)
discous 202.6
discover see 441.10
  find 481a.3

(manifest 525.2)
(learn 539.3)
disclose 529.3
indicate 550.18
discover itself
  appear 446.2
  be disclosed 529.6
discoverable
  knowable 490.18
  intelligible 518.5
discovery
  detection 481a.1
  (solution 462.3)
  disclosure 529.1
discredit n.
  doubt 485.2
  disrepute 874.1
discredit v.
  doubt 485.6
  defame 874.7
  disparage 934.3
discreditable
  disreputable 874.8
  unworthy 940.9
discredited 495.17
discreet
  discriminating 465.4
  wise 498.11
  cautious 864.6
discrepancy
  difference 15.1
  disparity 24.2
  (impossibility 471.1)
discrepant
  different 15.7
  disagreeing 24.6
discrepate 15.5
discrete
  unconnected 44.12
  discontinuous 70.4
discretion
  discrimination 465.1
  (judgment 480.1)
  (wisdom 498.3)
  (will 600.1)
  (choice 609.1)
  (taste 850.1)
  caution 864.1
  at one's discretion 600.5
discretional
  discriminative 465.4
  (selective 609.15)
  optional 600.4
discretionary
  discriminating 465.4
  volitional 600.4
  (self-determined 748.17)
  arbitrary 964.6
discretive
  unconnected 44.12
  discontinuous 70.4
discriminate 465.2, 3
  (differentiate 15.6)
  (be discerning 498.7)
  (select 609.7)
  not discriminate 465a.2

discriminating
  perceptive 465.4
  wise 498.11
  not discriminating 465a.3
discrimination
  distinction 465
  (difference 15.1)
  (meticulousness 457.3)
  (estimation 466.1)
  (judgment 480.1)
  (exactness 494.3)
  (wisdom 498.3)
  (will 600.1)
  (choice 609.1)
  (taste 850.1)
  (fastidiousness 868.1)
  grammatical ~ 578.1
discriminative 498.11
  (differentiative 15.8)
  (selective 609.15)
  (tasteful 850.5)
  (fastidious 868.4)
discrown
  dethrone 738.5
  depose 756.5
disculpate
  vindicate 937.5
  acquit 970.3
disculpation
  vindication 937.1
  acquittal 970.1
disculpatory 937.9
discursive
  wandering 266.24
  deviative 279.8
  argumentative 476.14
  digressive 573.7
  dissertative 595.5
discus
  projectile 284.5
  sport 840.11
discuss eat 298.44
  taste 390.3
  ponder 451.27
  investigate 461.17
  argue 476.11
  (examine 461.17)
  talk over 588.8
  dissertate 595.4
  advise with 695.6
discussion
  eating 298.1
  tasting 390.2
  dispute 461.9
  argumentation 476.2
  (dissertation 595.1)
  conference 588.3
disdain n. 930.1
  (indifference 866.1)
  (arrogance 885.1)
disdain v. 930.5
disdainful
  arrogant 885.8
  contemptuous 930.8

disease — disintegrate

disdainful (*cont'd*)
(disrespectful 929.5)
disease *n.* 655
(deterioration 659.1)
(bane 663.1)
disease *v.* 655.22
diseased 655.25
disembark 292.9
(anchor 267.12)
disembarkation, disembarkment 292.2
disembarrass 705.4
disembodied
discarnate 317.6
spectral 980a.4
disembody
disperse 73.3
disincarnate 317.5
spiritualize 994.20
disembogue
exude 295.7
let out 297.13
disemboguement 297.5
disembowel 297.16
disembowelment
suicide 361.3
execution 972.4
disembroil 60.9
disemplane 292.8
disenable 158.6
disenchant
undeceive 545a.2
discourage 616.3
disenchanting 545a.3
disenchantment 545a.1
disencumber 705.4
disencumbrance 705.1
disendow 756.5
disendowment 756.2
disengage disjoin 44.7
disembarrass 705.4
free 750.3
disengaged idle 683.12
free 748.12
disengagement
disjunction 44.1
liberation 750.1
disentangle
unravel 60.9
(simplify 42.3)
(separate 44.7)
solve 481a.4
disembarrass 705.4
free 750.3
disentanglement 705.1
disenthrall, disenthral 750.2
disenthrallment, disenthralment 750.1
disenthrone
discrown 738.5
depose 756.5
disenthronement
discrownment 738.3
deposal 756.2
disentitle 925.7
(dispossess 789.11)
disentitled 925.10
disentomb 363.24

disentombment 363.19
disequalize 15.6
disestablish 756.5
disestablishment 756.2
disesteem
disrepute 874.1
disrespect 929.1
disapprobation 932.1
disestimation 929.1
disfavor, disfavour *n.*
dislike 867.1
disrepute 874.1
hate 898.1
disrespect 929.1
in disfavor 932.12
disfavor, disfavour *v.*
oppose 708.2
dislike 867.4
disfellowship *n.* 297.3
(exclusion 893.3)
disfellowship *v.* 297.11
disfiguration 898.1
disfigure deform 243.3
damage 659.8
(uglify 846.5)
(blemish 848.2)
disfigured 848.3
(deformed 243.5)
disfigurement
distortion 243.1
blemish 848.1
(ugliness 846.1)
disfranchise 925.7
disfranchised 925.10
disfranchisement 925.2
disgorge let out 297.13
vomit 297.18
make restitution 790.3
repay 807.9
disgorgement 297.5
disgrace *n.*
dishonor 874.1
humiliation 879.1
abomination 923.1
disgrace *v.*
dishonor 874.6
humiliate 879.3
disgraced 874.9
disgraceful
disreputable 874.8
evil 945.16
disgruntle 832.4
(disappoint 509.2)
disgruntled 832.5
(disappointed 509.4)
disguise *n.* 545.5
(cover 223.2)
(mask 225.11)
(concealment 528.1; 530.3
(dissemblance 544.2)
(pretext 619.1)
in disguise 528.20
disguise *v.*
conceal 528.10
(make a pretext 619.2)

falsify 544.3, 6
inebriate 959.18
disguised
intoxicated 959.21
in disguise 528.20
(spurious 545.13)
disguiser 528.7
disgust *n.*
dejection 837.1
ennui 841.2
repugnance 867.2
(displeasure 828.2)
disgust *v.* repel 830.7
(be unsavory 395.4)
(weary 841.6)
(displease 867.6)
(be hateful 898.4)
disgusted
displeased 828.14
(abhorrent 898.5)
sick of 841.9
disgusting nasty 395.7
foul 653.17
odious 830.14
dish *n.* plate 191.12
food 298.38
merchandise 798.3
dish *v.*
destroy 162.4
concave 252.9
dishabille, deshabille 225.23
(nudity 226.2)
in dishabille 225.47
disharmonious 24.6
disharmony
disagreement 24.1
disorder 59.1
dishearten
discourage 616.3
daunt 860.11
dissatisfy 832.4
deject 837.8
(unman 158.7)
disheartened 837.9
(unmanned 158.10)
disheartening
distressing 830.11
unsatisfactory 832.6
dished concave 252.10
frustrated 732.9
disherison 789.1
dishevel 61.2
disheveled, dishevelled loose 47.3
scattered 73.4
dishevelment 59.1
dishmaker 690.8
dishonest 940.8
(false 544.7)
(deceitful 545.12)
(thieving 791.14)
(wicked 945.11, 13)
be dishonest 940.6
(falsify 544.3)
(misrepresent 555.4)
dishonestly 940.13
dishonesty
fraud 545.3
improbity 940.1
(falsehood 544.1)

810

(deception 545.1)
(theft 791.1)
(injustice 941a.1)
dishonor, dishonour *n.*
disrepute 874.1
disrespect 929.1
improbity 940.1
dishonor, dishonour *v.* not pay 808.5
disgrace 874.6
be disrespectful 929.3
(disparage 934.3)
dishonor oneself 874.5
dishonorable, dishonourable
disreputable 874.8
unprincipled 940.8
dishonorable discharge 297.4
dishpan 652.5
dishwasher
cleaner 652.6
scullion 746.1
dishwater 653.6
dishwiper 652.6
disillude 545a.2
disillusion *n.* 545a.1
disillusion *v.* 545a.2
(disappoint 509.2)
disillusioning 545a.3
disillusionment 545a.1
(disappointment 509.1)
(disclosure 529.1)
disillusive 545a.3
disincarnate
disembody 317.5
spiritualize 994.20
disinclination 603.1
(dissuasion 616.1)
(dislike 867.1)
disincline
dissuade 616.3
(avert 706.5)
(restrain 751.6)
cause dislike 867.6
disinclined
unwilling 603.5
averse to 867.7
disinfect 652.13
disinfectant *n.*
fumigator 388.7
purifier 652.8
antiseptic 662.8
disinfectant *adj.* 662.25
disinfection
sanitation 652.2
cure 660.5
disingenuous
false 544.7
dishonest 940.8
disinherit 789.11
disinheritance 789.2
disinherited 776.6
disinhume 363.24
disintegrate
break up 44.9
decompose 49.3
pulverize 330.6, 7

decay 659.7
disintegrated
  decomposed 49.5
  pulverulent 330.8
disintegration
  decomposition 49.1
  decay 659.2
disinter
  exhume 363.24
  discover 481a.3
disinterest 942.1
disinterested
  unprejudiced 498.12
  impartial 941.3
  unselfish 942.5
disinterment 363.19
disinthrall, disinthral
  See **disenthrall**
disintricate 42.3
disinvigorate 158.6
disinvolve 42.3
  (disentangle 60.9)
disjecta membra
  disjunction 44.1
  confusion 59.2
  flotsam 73.2
disjoin 44.7
  (loosen 47.2)
  (part 51.7)
  (segregate 55.4)
  (discontinue 70.3)
disjoined 44.12
  (discontinuous 70.4)
  be disjoined 44.6
disjoint v. disjoin 44.7
  displace 61.3
  dislocate 185.2
disjoint adj. 44.12
disjointed
  disorderly 59.8
  impotent 158.8
  diction 575.2
disjointure 44.1
disjunct
  disjoined 44.12
  discontinuous 70.4
disjunction 44
  (incoherence 47.1)
  (decomposition 49.1)
  (dispersion 73.1)
disjunctive
  disjoined 44.12
  discontinuous 70.4
disk, disc lamina 204.2
  exterior 220.2
  front 234.1
  circle 247.2
  record 417.9; 551.6
dislikable
  unpleasant 830.10
  unlikable 867.9
  (unsavory 395.5)
dislike n. 867
  (displeasure 828.2)
  (phobia 860.4)
  (enmity 889.1)
  (hate 898.1)
  (resentment 900.1)
  (disesteem 932.1)
  cause dislike 867.6

(excite hatred 898.4)
dislike v. 867.4
  (hate 898.3)
  (resent 900.6)
  (disesteem 932.5)
disliked 867.8
  (unloved 898.6)
disliking 867.7
  (unfriendly 889.3)
  (hating 898.5)
  (resenting 900.12)
dislocate disjoin 44.7
  displace 61.3
  remove 185.2; 270.6
dislocated
  disorderly 59.8
  removed 185.3
dislocation
  disjunction 44.1
  displacement 61.1
  removal 185
  (change 140.1)
  (transference 270.1)
dislocatory 185.3
dislodge
  dislocate 185.2
  evict 297.9
dislodgment, dislodgement
  dislocation 185.1
  removal 270.1
  eviction 297.2
disloyal 940.10
disloyalty 940.2
dismal gloomy 421.8
  dull-colored 428.19
  dreadful 649.8
  depressing 830.11
  gloomy 837.10
  (sullen 901.8)
dismals blues 837.1
  sullens 901.2
dismantle
  demolish 162.4
  undress 226.4
  render useless 645.7
  (unprepare 674.5)
  (disuse 678.2)
  damage 659.8
dismast
  demolish 162.4
  render useless 645.7
  injure 659.8
dismay n. 860.1
dismay v.
  perplex 475.8
  daunt 860.11
dismayed 860.14
dismaying 860.15
dismember
  dissect 44.9
  disperse 73.3
  execute 972.8
dismemberment
  dissection 44.4
  punishment 972.2
dismiss
  discharge 297.12
  (depose 756.6)
  release 750.2

relinquish 782.3
dismissal
  discharge 297.4
  (deposal 756.2)
  release 750.1
Dismissal 998.7
dismount alight 292.8
  get down 306.5
  render useless 645.7
disniche 185.2
disobedience 742
  (anarchy 738.2)
  (nonobservance 773.1, 2)
  (dereliction 927.1)
  (violation 964.2)
disobedient
  insubordinate 742.6
  (defiant 715.3)
  (nonobservant 773.5)
  (lawless 964.6)
  impious 988.10
disobey 742.4
  (disregard 773.3)
disobeying 742.6
disobliging 907.7
disomatous 90.3
disorder n.
  confusion 59
  (derangement 61.1)
  (formlessness 241.1)
  ailment 655.1
  anarchy 738.2
  in disorder
  disorderly 59.8
  in confusion 59.13
disorder v.
  put out of order 59.7
  derange 61.2
  (dislocate 185.2)
  sicken 655.22
disordered
  disorderly 59.8
  deranged 61.6
disorderliness 59.1
disorderly
  without order 59.8
  (deranged 61.6)
  (misplaced 185.5)
  (neglectful 460.8)
  (indiscriminate 465a.3)
  (purposeless 621.21)
  anarchic 738.8
  malefactory 945.13
  lawless 964.6
  be disorderly 59.6
disorganization
  derangement 61.1
  destruction 162.1
  dissolution 659.2
  anarchy 738.2
disorganize
  derange 61.2
  destroy 162.4
  damage 659.8
disorganized
  disorderly 59.8

anarchic 738.8
  lawless 964.6
disorientation 279.1
disown deny 536.2
  recant 607.9
  reject 610.2
  disclaim 756.4
  disinherit 789.11
disowned 782.4
disownment 536.1
dispatch, despatch n. 532.2
dispatch, despatch v.
  send out 297.13
  eat 298.44
  kill 361.10
disparage 934.3
  (ridicule 856.4)
  (disrespect 929.3)
  (scoff 930.6)
  (discommend 932.6)
disparagement
  malediction 908.1
  detraction 934.1
  (ridicule 856.1)
  (disrespect 929.1)
  (scoffing 930.2)
  (disapprobation 932.1)
disparager 936.1
disparaging 934.4
  (derisive 856.7)
  (disrespectful 929.5)
  (disapprobatory 932.11)
disparate
  dissimilar 18.4
  unequal 28.3
  unconnected 44.12
disparity
  dissimilarity 18.1
  disagreement 24.2
  (impossibility 471.1)
  inequality 28.1
  (difference 15.1)
  dissension 713.2
dispart disjoin 44.7
  interval 198.4
  open 260.11
dispassion
  unfeeling 823.1
  inexcitability 826.1
dispassionate
  unprejudiced 498.12
  unfeeling 823.5
  inexcitable 826.9
  indifferent 866.4
  impartial 941.3
  disinterested 942.5
dispatch, despatch n.
  velocity 274.1
  ejection 297.1
  message 532.2
  epistle 592.2
  performance 680.1
  expedition 682.2
  haste 684.1
  completion 729.1
dispatch, despatch v.
  send 270.9

dispatch bearer — disrelish

dispatch (*continued*)
  send out 297.13
  eat 298.44
  kill 361.10
  ~ a letter 592.6
  do 680.6
  transact 692.4
  accomplish 729.2
dispatch bearer 534.1
dispatch boat 273.4
dispel disperse 73.3
  (dislocate 185.2)
  destroy 162.4
  repulse 289.2
dispensable 645.8
dispensary 662.18
dispensation
  destiny 601.3
  decree 741.3
  exemption 760.1
  relinquishment 782.1
  giving 784.1
  apportionment 786.1
  give dispensation 748.10
dispensatory 662.4, 18
dispense disperse 73.3
  give out 784.8
  apportion 786.3
  vend 796.5
  dispense with
  not use 678.5
  exempt 748.10
dispenser 662.21
dispeople evict 297.10
  depopulate 893.8
dispeoplement 893.2
dispermous 89.4
dispermy 89.2
disperse part 44.11
  scatter 73.3
  (dislocate 185.2)
  (diverge 291.2)
  apportion 782.3
dispersed 73.4
  (diverging 291.3)
dispersion
  scattering 73
  (disjunction 44.1)
  (permeation 186.5)
  (divergence 291.1)
  ~ of light 420.10
  apportionment 786.1
dispersive 73.5
dispirit
  discourage 616.3
  deject 837.8
dispirited 837.9
displace
  dislocate 61.3
  remove 185.2; 270.6
  (eject 297.8)
  dismiss 297.12
  depose 756.5
displacement
  dislocation 61.1
  removal 185.1; 270.1
  (ejection 297.1)
  draft 208.5

deposal 756.2
displacency
  dislike 867.1
  disapprobation 932.1
display *n.*
  appearance 448.1
  spectacle 448.2
  manifestation 525.1
  ostentation 882.1
  make a display 882.6
display *v.* evince 467.7
  manifest 525.2
  indicate 550.18
  flaunt 882.7
displease
  give displeasure 830.3
  dissatisfy 832.4
  cause dislike 867.6
displeased 828.14
  (discontented 832.5)
  (disliking 867.7)
  (abhorrent 898.5)
  (resentful 900.12)
displeasing
  unsavory 395.5
  unpleasant 830.10
  (ugly 846.9)
  unsatisfactory 832.6
displeasure 828.2
  (painfulness 830.1)
  (discontent 832.1)
  (dislike 867.1)
  (resentment 900.1)
displume 789.12
disport 840.21
disposal
  arrangement 60.1
  use 677.1
  sale 796.1
  at one's disposal
  offered 763.4
  in possession 777.8
  place at one's disposal 763.2
dispose arrange 60.6
  influence 175.6
  tend 176.2
  induce 615.9
  dispose of
  confute 479.2
  use 677.5
  complete 729.2
  relinquish 782.3
  give 784.8
  sell 796.5
disposed
  arranged 60.10
  tending 176.3
  minded 620.4
  (willed 600.3)
  dispositioned 820.4
disposition nature 5.3
  (tendency 176.1)
  state 7.1
  method 58.3
  arrangement 60.1
  location 184.5
  use 677.1
  bent of mind 820.1

(propensity 602.2)
dispositioned 820.4
dispossess
  evict 297.9
  take from 789.11
  (disentitle 925.7)
dispossessed 789.16
  (bereft 776.6)
dispossession 789.2
  (loss 776.1)
  (disentitlement 925.2)
dispossessor 789.6
disposure 60.1
dispraise *n.* 932.1
dispraise *v.* 932.6
dispread, disspread *v.* 73.3
dispread, disspread *adj.* 73.4
  (diverging 291.3)
disprize
  underestimate 483.3
  scorn 930.5
disproof
  counterevidence 468.1
  (negation 536.1)
  confutation 479.1
disproportion 24.2
disproportionate 24.6
disproportionateness 24.2
disprovable 479.4
disproval
  counterevidence 468.1
  confutation 479.1
disprove 479.2
  (countervail 468.2)
disputable
  uncertain 475.9
  (untenable 485.11)
  illogical 477.10
  (incredible 485.11)
disputant
  arguer 476.9
  oppositionist 710.2
  combatant 726.1
disputation 476.2
disputatious
  argumentative 476.14
  (litigious 969.13)
  quarrelsome 901.9
dispute *n.*
  questioning 461.9
  argument 476.2
  (litigation 969.1)
  protest 489.2
  quarrel 713.3
  in dispute 461.26
dispute *v.* argue 476.11
  (converse 588.9)
  (litigate 969.10)
  doubt 485.6
  deny 536.2
  (confute 479.2)
  quarrel 713.7
disputed 461.25
disqualification
  impotence 158.1

812

unfitness 674.1
  incompetence 699.1
  disentitlement 925.2
disqualified
  impotent 158.8
  unfitted 674.7
  incompetent 699.15
  disentitled 925.10
disqualify
  disable 158.6
  (render useless 645.7)
  disentitle 925.7
disquiet *n.*
  restlessness 149.3
  agitation 315.1
  excitement 825.3
  uneasiness 828.2
disquiet *v.*
  agitate 315.8
  excite 824.2
  vex 830.5
  frighten 860.10
disquieted
  displeased 828.14
  frightened 860.14
disquieting 860.15
disquietude
  restlessness 149.3
  agitation 315.1
  excitement 825.3
  trepidation 860.3
disquiparancy 10.1
disquiparent
  irrelevant 10.6
  unequal 28.3
disquisition
  lesson 537.6
  dissertation 595.1
  (discussion 476.2)
disquisitive 595.5
disregard *n.*
  inattention 458.1
  neglect 460.1
  (slight 930.4)
  nonobservance 773.1
disregard *v.*
  pay no attention 458.5
  neglect 460.4
  (not do 681.2)
  (be insensible to 823.3)
  not observe 773.3
  (disobey 742.4)
  endure 826.6
  excuse 918.3
  snub 930.7
disregardance 460.1
disregarded
  neglected 460.10
  unrespected 929.6
disregarder 460.3
disregardful
  inattentive 458.10
  neglectful 460.8
  (nonobservant 773.5)
  indifferent 823.5
disre'ated 10.5
disrelish *n.* 867.1

disrelish v. 867.4
(hate 898.3)
disremember 506.4
disreputability 874.1
(improbity 940.1)
disreputable 874.8
(ignoble 876.11)
(dishonorable 940.8)
(unworthy 940.9)
disreputably 874.11
disrepute 874
(disapprobation 932.1)
be in disrepute 874.4
in disrepute 874.9
disrespect 929
(insolence 885.2)
(discourtesy 895.1)
(contempt 930.1)
(disparagement 934.1)
disrespectful 929.5
(discourteous 895.6)
(disdainful 930.8)
(disparaging 934.4)
be disrespectful 929.3
(disparage 934.3)
disrobe 226.4
disrupt 162.4
disruption
sunderance 44.2
destruction 162.1
dissension 713.2
dissatisfaction
pain 828.1
discontent 832.1
dissatisfactory 832.6
dissatisfied 832.5
dissatisfy 832.4
(disappoint 509.2)
dissect
analyze 44.9; 461.3
(decompose 49.3)
dissection 44.4; 461.3
(decomposition 49.1)
disseize, disseise 789.11
disseizin, disseisin 789.2
disseizor, disseisor 789.6
disselboom 215.13
dissemblance
dissimilarity 18.1
dissimulation 544.2
(flattery 933.1)
(sanctimony 988.2)
dissemble
disguise 528.10
dissimulate 544.6
(deceive 545.7, 11)
(pretext 619.2)
(be sanctimonious 988.8)
dissembler
deceiver 548.1
hypocrite 988.6
dissembling n. 544.2
(pedantry 491.4)

(sanctimony 988.2)
dissembling adj. 544.8
(affected 853.6)
disseminate
disperse 73.3
publish 531.7
~ learning 537.9
disseminated 73.4
be disseminated 186.12
dissemination
dispersion 73.1
publication 531.1
disseminator 531.5
dissension 713.2
(dissent 489.1)
(contention 720.1)
(enmity 889.1)
sow dissension
set at odds 713.8
excite hatred 898.4
dissent n.
nonconformity 83.2
disagreement 489
(unbelief 485.1)
(negation 536.1)
(unwillingness 603.1)
(recantation 607.3)
(refusal 764.1)
(discontent 832.1)
(disapproval 932.1)
(sectarianism 984.2)
dissension 713.2
dissent v. 489.4
(disagree 24.5)
(deny 536.2)
(be unwilling 603.4)
(recant 607.9)
(refuse 764.2)
(disapprove 932.5)
dissenter 489.3
(separatist 44.5)
(nonconformist 83.4)
(apostate 607.5)
(insurgent 742.3)
(sectarian 984.13)
dissentience 489.1
dissentient n. 489.3
dissentient adj. 489.5
(disagreeing 24.6)
(contradictory 536.3)
(discordant 713.9)
(discontented 832.5)
dissenting 489.5
(unwilling 603.5)
(unconsenting 764.5)
(sectarian 984.23)
dissentingly 489.7
dissepiment 228.6
dissert, dissertate 595.4
dissertation 595
(discussion 476.2)
(speech 582.2)
(book 593.1)
(prose 598.1)
dissertative 595.5

dissertator 595.3
(commentator 524.2)
(author 593.15)
disserve 649.6
disservice
ill-service 649.4
malevolent act 907.4
disserviceable 649.10
dissever 44.8
(discontinue 70.3)
disseverance 44.2
dissidence
disagreement 24.1
dissent 489.1
discord 713.1
dissident
disagreeing 24.6
(discordant 713.9)
dissentient 489.5
dissiliency 173.2
dissimilar 18.4
(different 15.7)
(ununiform 16a.2)
(disagreeing 24.6)
(diversified 81.3)
(novel 123.10)
dissimilarity 18
(difference 15.1)
(nonuniformity 16a.1)
(novelty 123.1)
dissimilation 18.1
dissimilitude
difference 15.1
dissimilarity 18.1
disparity 24.2
dissimulate 544.6
dissimulation 544.2
(concealment 528.1)
(deception 545.1)
(pretext 619.1)
dissimulator
deceiver 548.1
hypocrite 988.6
dissipate
destroy 162.4
waste 638.2
use up 677.6
squander 818.3
(lose 776.3)
overindulge 954.3
(carouse 959.16)
dissipated lost 776.5
prodigal 818.4
licentious 954.5
debauched 961.10
dissipater, dissipator 954a.1
dissipation
dispersion 73.1
pleasure 377.1
waste 638.1
loss 776.1
prodigality 818.1
licentiousness 954.2
(spree 840.3, 4)
(drunkenness 959.1)
debauchery 961.2
dissipative
dispersive 73.5

prodigal 818.4
dissociability 893.1
dissociable, dissocial 893.9
dissociality 893.1
dissocialize 893.6
dissociate 44.7
dissociation
irrelation 10.1
disjunction 44.1
~ of personality 503.2
dissogeny 161.2
dissolubility 335.2
dissoluble
divisible 44.13
liquefactive 335.8
dissolute
vicious 945.15
dissipated 954.5
debauched 961.10
dissolution
decomposition 49.1
destruction 162.1
death 360.1
(end 67.1)
disappearance 449.1
decay 659.2
abrogation 756.1
dissolutional 335.8
dissolvability 335.2
dissolvable
divisable 44.13
liquefactive 335.8
dissolve n. 449.1
dissolve v.
cease to be 2.5
decompose 49.3
destroy 162.4
soften 324.4
liquefy 335.5
disappear 449.2
annul 756.3
~ in tears 839.8
dissolvent n. 335.4
dissolvent adj. 335.9
dissolving view 449.1
dissonance
difference 15.1
disagreement 24.1
music 414.1
discord 713.1
dissonant
different 15.7
discordant 414.4
disspread See dispread
dissuade 616.2
(remonstrate 766.2)
dissuasion 616.1
(advice 695.1)
(restraint 751.1)
(remonstrance 766.1)
dissuasive 616.4
dissuitable inapt 24.7
inexpedient 647.3
dissyllabic 561.9
dissyllable 561.3
distad 196.6
distaff 374.5
distain discolor 440a.2

distal — dithyrambic 814

distain (*continued*)
  soil 653.15
distal 196.5
distance *n.*
  ~ of time 110.1
  remoteness 196
  (length 200.1)
  (measurement 466.1)
  at a distance 196.6
  keep one's distance
    be distant 196.4
    avoid 623.6
    be modest 881.3
    respect 928.4
    snub 930.7
distance *v.* excel 33.5
  (gain the ascendancy 731.8)
  outstrip 303.4
distant 196.5
  (long 200.12)
  be distant 196.4
  (be long 200.8)
distantly far 196.6
  widely 196.10
distaste 867.1
distasteful
  unsavory 395.5
  unpleasant 830.10
distemper *n.*
  color 428.3
  disease 655.18
distemper *v.* 428.10
distemperature 655.1
distend increase 35.3
  expand 194.5, 8
  blow up 349.24
distended 260.15
distensive 194.10
distention 193.1
distich couplet 89.2
  verse 597.7
distichous 91.6
distill, distil
  trickle 295.7
  extract 301.7
  vaporize 336.5
  trickle 348.19
distillage 348.4
distillation
  egress 295.1
  extraction 301.3
  trickle 348.4
  vaporization 336.1
distiller crucible 386.1
  liquor ~ 959.12, 14
distillery 959.14
distinct different 15.7
  unconnected 44.12
  audible 402.10
  visible 446.5
  (apparent 448.7)
  clear 518.5
  obvious 525.4
distinction
  difference 15.1
  greatness 31.2
  discrimination 465.1
  elegance 578.1
  importance 642.1
  repute 873.1, 3

  scholastic honor 873.8
  nobility 875.1
distinction without a difference
  equivalence 27.2
  no choice 609a.1
make a distinction 465.3
distinctive
  differentiative 15.8
  unconnected 44.12
  peculiar 79.8
  savory 394.7
  discriminative 465.4
  typical 550.21
distinctly 446.6
  (apparently 448.8)
distinctness
  visibility 446.1
  ~ of articulation 580.3
distingué
  distinguished 873.16
  noble 875.10
distinguish see 441.10
  discriminate 465.2, 3
  (differentiate 15.6)
  judge 480.6
  recognize 481a.6
  characterize 564.6
  confer distinction 873.13
distinguishability 518.1
distinguishable
  knowable 490.18
  intelligible 518.5
distinguished
  different 15.7
  superior 33.7
  special 79.7
  notable 642.10
  famous 873.16
  noble 875.10
be distinguished 873.10
Distinguished Conduct Medal, Distinguished Flying Cross, Distinguished Service Cross etc. 733.2
distinguishing
  discriminating 465.4
  (differentiative 15.8)
  typical 550.21
distinguishment 465.1
distort deform 243.3
  (crook 217.5)
  (uglify 846.5)
  (blemish 848.2)
  sophisticate 477.7
  misinterpret 523.2
  misteach 538.2
  falsify 544.3
  misrepresent 555.4
distorted
  deformed 243.5
  (crooked 217.13)

  (imperfect 651.4)
  (disfigured 848.3)
  erroneous 495.12
distortion
  deformity 243
  (crookedness 217.1)
  (ugliness 846.1)
  anamorphosis 443.9
  sophistry 477.1
  misinterpretation 523.1
  misteaching 538.1
  falsification 544.1
  misstatement 546.1
  misrepresentation 555.1, 2
distortive 243.6
distract 458.8, 9
distracted
  inattentive 458.11
  bewildered 475.16
  (delirious 503.14)
  overwrought 824.10
distraction
  inattention 458.3, 4
  delirium 503.3
  excitement 825.2
distrain seize 789.9
  attach 969.10
distraint
  distress 789.2
  fine 974.2
distraught
  absent-minded 458.11
  bewildered 475.16
  (delirious 503.14)
distress *n.*
  bodily pain 378.1
  distraint 789.2
  poverty 804.1
  displeasure 828.1
  (adversity 735.1)
  fine 974.2
distress *v.* 830.3
distressed
  impoverished 804.7
  suffering 828.13
distressing 830.11
distressingly 31.23
distribute arrange 60.6
  disperse 73.3
  ~ type 591.15
  apportion 786.3
distribution
  arrangement 60.1
  dispersion 73.1
  apportionment 786.1
distributor 272.16
district *n.* 181.1
district *v.* 44.10
district attorney 968.1
distrust *n.* doubt 485.2
  (suspiciousness 487.2)
  (fearfulness 860.2)
  jealousy 920.1
distrust *v.* doubt 485.6
  (be incredulous 487.3)

  (fear 860.8)
  be jealous 920.2
distrustful 485.10
disturb
  discompose 61.4
  (change 140.6)
  agitate 315.8
  confuse 458.9
  perplex 475.8
  embarrass 704.7
  excite 824.3, 4
  annoy 830.5
disturbance
  turmoil 59.4
  (brawl 713.4)
  discomposure 61.1
  agitation 315.1
  confusion 458.4
disturbed
  turbulent 173.12
  (agitated 315.13)
  alarmed 669.4
  displeased 828.14, 15
disunion
  disagreement 24.1
  disjunction 44.1
  disorder 59.1
disunite disjoin 44.7
  sow dissension 713.8
disunited 713.10
disunity
  disagreement 24.1
  disjunction 44.1
  disorder 59.1
disuse, disusage *n.* 678.1
  (discontinuance 142.1)
  (nonprevalence 614.1)
  (abandonment 624.1)
  (relinquishment 782.1)
disuse *v.* 678.2
  (discontinue 142.6)
  (reject 610.2)
  (abandon 624.3)
  (render useless 645.7)
  (relinquish 782.3)
disused
  antiquated 124.9
  out of use 678.6
disutilize 678.2
disvaluation 932.1
disvalue 932.6
ditch *n.* trench 259.2
  channel 350.1
  fortification 717.3
Ditch *n.* 343.1
ditch *v.* 623.6
ditheism 984.10
dither *n.*
  coldness 383.2
  trepidation 825.3
dither *v.* 383.7
dithery 383.8
dithyramb 597.2
dithyrambic *n.* 597.10

dithyrambic — dizzy

dithyrambic *adj.*
  rabid 503.13
  verse 597.13
ditto *n.* duplicate 21.2
  equal 27.5
  repetend 104.2
ditto *v.*
  be identical 13.4
  imitate 19.5
  equal 27.6
  duplicate 90.2
  repeat 104.4
  concur 488.7
ditto *adv.*
  identically 13.8
  again 104.8
ditty 415.10
ditty bag, ditty box 191.5
diurnal
  transient 111.6
  daily 138.11
diuturnal 110.9
diuturnity 110.1
diva 599.19
divagate 279.5
divagation 279.1
divan seat 215.2
  throne 747.5
  tribunal 966.1
  council 696.1
divaricate *v.*
  differ 15.5
  bifurcate 91.5
  open 260.11
  deviate 279.4
  diverge 291.2
divaricate *adj.*
  bifurcate 91.7
  diverging 291.3
divarication
  nonuniformity 16a.1
  bifurcation 91.2
  deviation 279.1
  divergence 291.1
dive *n.*
  low resort 189.9
  navigation 267.5
  aerobatics 267a.24
  plunge 310.1
  (swimming 267.9)
  grogshop 959.13
  brothel 961.7
dive *v.*
  submarine 267.43
  swim 267.47
  aviate 267a.31
  plunge 310.4
  examine 461.17
dive bomber 273a.2
divellicate 44.9
diver 310.3
diverge differ 15.5
  bifurcate 91.5
  oblique 217.5
  deviate 279.4
  divaricate 291.2
  (separate 44.7)
  (spread 73.3)
divergence
  difference 15.1
  nonuniformity 16a.1

dissimilarity 18.1
disparity 24.2
unconformity 83.1
bifurcation 91.2
obliquity 217.1
deviation 279.1
divarication 291
(division 44.1)
(spread 73.1)
divergent
  different 15.7
  dissimilar 18.4
  disagreeing 24.6
  unconformable 83.9
  bifurcate 91.7
  diverging 291.3
diverging
  divergent 291.3
  (dispread 73.4)
  bifurcate 91.7
divers different 15.7
  diversified 81.3
  numerous 102.5
diverse 15.7
diversified 81.3
  (different 15.7)
  (ununiform 16a.2)
  (dissimilar 18.4)
diversiform 81.2
diversify
  change 140.5, 6
  colors 440.4
diversion
  change 140.1
  deviation 279.1
  apostasy 607.2
  amusement 840.1
diversity
  difference 15.1
  dissimilarity 18.1
  (nonuniformity 16a.1)
  multiformity 81.1
  ~ of opinion 489.1
divert deviate 279.6
  ~ attention 458.8
  deceive 545.7
  deter 616.3
  amuse 840.20
diverting 840.22
divertisement 840.1
divertissement
  music 415.3
  drama 599.5
Dives 803.2
divest unclothe 226.4
  ~ of office 756.5
  dispossess 789.11
divested unclad 226.8
  deprived 776.6
divestiture 226.11
divestiture 226.1
divestment
  unclothing 226
  dispossession 789.2
divesture *n.* 226.1
divesture *v.* 226.4
divide *n.* 206.2
divide *v.*
  graduate 26.2
  disjoin 44.7
  partition 44.10, 11

(part 51.7)
(segregate 55.4)
(bisect 91.4)
(diverge 291.2)
classify 60.7
calculate 85.7
discriminate 465.2
measure 466.10
select 609.7
vote 609.10
share 778.5
(halve 91.4)
(distribute 786.3)
divided 44.12
  (partial 51.8)
dividend part 51.1
  number 84.2
  share 786.2
dividers 466.4
dividuous 44.13
divinable 511.12
divination
  prediction 511.2–5
  (intuition 477a.1)
  (interpretation 522.5)
  (sorcery 992.1)
  (spiritualism 994.4, 9)
  omen 512.1
  supposition 514.1
divinatory 511.11
  (intuitive 477a.4)
  (psychic 994.23)
divine *n.*
  theologian 983.3
  clergyman 996.2
divine *v.*
  predict 511.7, 9
  (religion 994.17)
  foresee 510.5
  suppose 514.6
divine *adj.*
  beautiful 845.13
  godly 976.13
  (heavenly 981.7)
  theological 983.4
  religious 983a.7
divine healing
  healing art 662.16
  religion 984.9
diviner 513.2
  (sorcerer 992.2)
  (psychic 994.16)
divine right 737.1
Divine Science Church 984.9
divine service 990.7
  (meeting 72.2)
diving 267.9
diving bell, diving boat, diving helmet etc. 310.3
divining 511.2
divining rod, divining stick
  divination 511.5
  wand 993.3
divinity god 979.1–6
  theology 983.1
Divinity 976.1, 2
divisible 44.13

(partial 51.8)
division
  disjunction 44.1
  (bisection 91.1)
  (divergence 291.1)
  part 51.1
  classification 60.2
  class 75.1
  mathematics 85.4
  region 181.1
  botany 367.1
  music 413.10; 415.15
  school class 541.8
  ~ of a book 593.7
  election 609.3
  party 712.1
  dissension 713.2
  military ~ 726.7, 10
  apportionment 786.1
  religious faction 984.3
divisional, divisionary, divisive 75.6
divisor 84.2
divorce *n.*
  disjunction 44.1
  matrimonial ~ 905
divorce *v.* disjoin 44.7
  unmarry 905.4
divorcé, divorcee, divorcée 905.1
divorcement
  disjunction 44.1
  divorce 905.1
divulgation 529.1
  (publication 531.1)
divulgatory 529.8
divulge
  communicate 527.7
  disclose 529.4
  (manifest 525.2)
  (inform on 527.10)
  (say 582.6)
  publish 531.7
  become public 531.9
divulgence 529.1
  (manifestation 525.1)
divulsion 44.2
divvy *n.*
  dividend 51.1
  share 786.2
divvy *v.*
  partition 44.10
  share 778.5
  apportion 786.3
diwan See **dewan**
dixi 535.8
Dixie, Dixie Land 515.6
dizen clothe 225.41
  adorn 847.11
dizenment 225.1
dizzard 501.1
dizziness
  faulty sight 443.7
  delirium 503.3
dizzy *n.* 501.2
dizzy *v.* 458.9
dizzy *adj.*
  confused 458.12
  stupid 499.12, 15

do — dog's age

dizzy *(continued)*
  delirious 503.14
  intoxicated 959.21
do *n.* act 680.2
  command 741.1
do *v.* fare 7.2
  agree 23.7
  produce 161.8
  visit 186.9
  solve 481a.4
  deceive 545.7
  suffice 639.3
  avail 644.2
  perform 680.6
  (pursue 622.6)
  complete 729.2
  swindle 791.12
  be satisfactory
    831.5, 9
  be doing 625.7
do again 104.4
do as others do
  conform 82.5
  be fashionable 852.6
do away with
  destroy 162.4
  (abrogate 756.3)
  eject 297.17
do for destroy 162.4
  kill 361.10
  defeat 731.9
  serve 746.8
  punish 972.5
do into 522.6
do like 19.5
do over 223.24
do to death 361.10
do up arrange 60.6
  repair 660.11
  fatigue 688.5
do up brown 729.3
do without 678.5
have to do with
  be related 9.3
  be employed in
    680.6
  (busy oneself with
    625.7)
  conduct 692.4
  participate in 709.6
not do 681.2
  (procrastinate
    133.5)
  (cease 142.6)
  (be quiescent 265.5)
  (neglect 460.4)
  (abstain 623.7)
do *int.* 765.9
do-all factotum 690.3
  servant 746.1
doable 470.6
doat, doating See dote
  etc.
dobbin 271.3
dobson 366.24
doc 662.19
doch-an-dorrach,
doch-an-dorroch,
doch-an-dorris
  959.10
docile tame 370.10
  willing 602.9

(teachable 539.7)
(manageable 705.6)
submissive 725.5
docility
  intelligence 498.1
  willingness 602.3
  (susceptibility
    615.5)
docimastic 463.12
docimasy
  analysis 461.3
  test 463.1
docity 498.1
dock *n.* tail 235.6
  airdrome 267a.28
  stage 599.12
  storehouse 636.4
  anchorage 666.4
  dockyard 691
  witness box 966.6
dock *v.* 38.6
docker 269.7
docket *n.* list 86.1
  superscription
    550.11
  record 551.1
  schedule 611.2
  security 771.1
  on the docket 461.26
docket *v.* list 86.3
  ticket 550.19
  record 551.8
  schedule 611.4
  enter accounts 811.7
dock gate 350.2
dock hand, dock-
walloper 269.7
dockyard 691
doctor *n.* breeze 349.5
  learned man 492.1
  loaded die 621.8
  mender 660.7
  physician 662.19
  (professional
    690.10)
  academic degree
    877.3
doctor *v.*
  adulterate 41.8
  falsify 544.3
  corrupt 659.9
  repair 660.11
  apply a remedy
    662.24
  ~ accounts 811.9
doctored 545.13
Doctor Honoris
Causa 873.8
Doctor of Divinity
  996.2
Doctor of Philosophy
  877.3
doctrinaire *n.*
  dogmatist 474.4
  pedant 492.4
  theorist 514.5
doctrinaire *adj.* 474.15
doctrinal
  authoritative 474.13
  creedal 484.16
  educational 537.12
  theological 983.4

doctrinalism 983.1
doctrinarian *n.*
  pedant 492.4
  theorist 514.5
doctrinarian *adj.* 983.4
doctrinary
  dogmatic 474.15
  doctrinal 983.4
doctrine belief 484.3
  (maxim 496.2)
  (theology 983.2)
  knowledge 490.7
doctrine of inference,
doctrine of terms,
doctrine of the
judgment 451.4
document
  credential 467.4
  writing 590.3
  (record 551.1)
documentary 467.11
dodad See doodad
dodder 160.6
doddering aged 128.8
  impotent 158.8
  unsteady 160.12
  senile 499.16
dodecahedron 244.2
dodge *n.* quibble 477.3
  deception 545.3
  evasion 623.1
  expedient 646.2
  artifice 702.3
dodge *v.* change 140.5
  move 264.6
  recoil 277.3
  (turn aside 279.7)
  quibble 477.8
  shy at 603.4
  avoid 623.6, 9
  snub 930.7
dodger handbill 531.4
  shirker 623.4
  cunning person
    702.4
dodgery cunning 702.1
  sharp practice
    940.5
dodo 130.2
Dodona 513.1
doe speeder 274.6
  deer 366.11
  female animal 374.8
doegling oil 356.4
doer 690.1
  (actor 680.4)
doff undress 226.4
  greet 894.9
dog *n.* foot 211.4
  horse 271.6
  canine 366.6
  male animal 373.6
  airs 882.2
  scoundrel 949.1
  gone to the dogs
    945.15
  go to the dogs
    perish 162.5
    suffer misfortune
      735.6
    become poor 804.5
    go bankrupt 808.6

    become wicked
      945.9
dog *v.* follow 281.3
  chase 622.7
dogcart 272.5
dog days
  summer 126a.3
  hot weather 382.3
doge 745.3
dog-ear *n.* 258.1
dog-ear *v.* 258.3
dog-eared 418.14
dogfight 720.2
dogfish 366.21
dog flea 366.24
dogged
  persistent 604a.3
  obstinate 606.6
doggedness
  resolution 604.1
  obstinacy 606.1
dogger 273.2
doggerel, doggrel *n.*
  bad poetry 597.3
  nonsense verse
    855.1
doggerel, doggrel *adj.*
  rhetoric 579.3
  vulgar 851.6
  ridiculous 855.5
doggish churlish 895.7
  irascible 901.7
doggone! 908.8
doghole 189.6
doghouse
  small place 184.4
  kennel 189.6
  contrabass 417.3
  in the doghouse
    932.12
dogie 366.12
dog in the manger
  marplot 706.3
  spoilsport 837.5
  self-seeker 943.2
dog Latin 563.4
dogma 484.3
  (doctrine 983.2)
dogmatic
  certain 474.15
  (prejudiced 481.10)
  (fanatic 503.18)
  (bigoted 606.7)
  (hyperorthodox
    983a.8)
  assertive 535.6
dogmatics 983.1
dogmatism 474.3
  (bigotry 606.2)
  (hyperorthodoxy
    983a.5)
dogmatist 474.4
  (zealot 504.2)
  (opinionist 606.3)
  (bigot 983a.6)
dogmatize
  be certain 474.7
  be prejudiced 481.7
  assert positively
    535.5
dogs 225.27
dog's age 110.3

816

dog's chance 156.4
dog's-ear n. 258.1
dog's-ear v. 258.3
dog ship 273a.1
dog-sick 867.7
dogs of war 727.11
Dog Star 318.3
dog tent 223.5
dog-tired 688.6
dogtooth, dog tooth 253.3
dogtrot n. 275.2
 (gait 266.5)
 (run 274.3)
dogtrot v. 275.5
dog-weary 688.6
doily, doyley 652.7
doing n. event 151.1
 action 680.1
doing adj. 151.5
doings affairs 151.2
 acts 680.2
doit dolt 501.1
 trifle 643.3
 (money 800.8)
 bungler 701
doited 499.16
dokhma, dakhma 363.13
dolcan 417.12
dolce 415.30
doldrums blues 837.1
 sullens 901.2
 in the doldrums 837.9
dole n. modicum 32.2
 part 51.1
 pittance 640.5
 alms 784.3
 allotment 786.2
 sorrow 837.3
 payment 973.2
dole v. 786.3
dole out
 dispense 784.8
 be parsimonious 819.3
doleful 837.9
dolefuls blues 837.1
 sullens 901.2
do-little 683.7
doll dowel 45.5
 girl 129.5
 miniature 193.3
 figure 554.4
 toy 840.16
dollar, dollar bill 800.8
dollar mark 550.2
dollhouse
 small place 184.4
 toy 840.16
dollish, doll-like 127.7
dollmaker 690.8
dolly 272.10
dolmen 363.15
dolomite 342.4
dolor, dolour 828.1
do'orific dolorous 830.9
dolorously 31.23
dolphin 366.21
dolphin striker 273.12

dolt 501.1
doltish 499.12
dom 877.4
 (Mister 373.3)
domain class 75.1
 region 181.1
 country 182.1
 property 780.4
Domdaniel
 gambling hell 621.14
 den 945.8
dome n. tower 206.3
 head 210.3
 arch 215.18
 roof 223.6
 arc lamp 423.3
dome v. 223.22
Domesday book 551.3
domestic n. 746.1
 (worker 690.10)
domestic adj.
 domiciliary 188.12
 native-grown 367.17
 tame 370.10
 stay-at-home 893.9
domestic animal 366.1
domesticate
 settle 184.14
 naturalize 184.16
 tame 370.6
 habituate 613.8
domesticated
 domestic 188.12
 (naturalized 184.19)
 tame 370.10
domestication
 naturalization 184.7
 taming 370.2
 habituation 613.5
domesticity 893.1
domicile 189.1
domiciled
 inhabited 186.14
 domesticated 188.12
domiciliary n. 188.3
domiciliary adj. 188.12
domiciliary visit 461.8
domiciliated 188.12
domina 374.2, 3
dominance 737.2
dominant n. 413.6, 7
dominant adj.
 supreme 33.8
 influential 175.10
 ruling 737.15
dominate 737.12
 (influence 175.8)
domination
 dominion 737.2
 despotism 739.2
 celestial hierarchy 977.2
domineer
 tyrannize 739.4
 overbear 885.5
 (bully 860.12)
domineering n.
 tyranny 739.2
 overbearance 885.1
domineering adj.
 tyrannical 739.5
 overbearing 885.8

be domineering 885.5
Dominican 996.11
dominie 540.1
dominion region 181.1
 country 182.1
 authority 737.2
 (supremacy 33.3)
 (supervision 693.2)
 (victory 731.3)
 (jurisdiction 965.1)
 celestial hierarchy 977.2
Dominion Day 138.7
domino mask 225.11
 masquerader 528.7
dominoes 840.11
domus 189.1
don n. man 373.2
 learned man 492.1
 teacher 540.1
 nobleman 875.4
Don n. 373.3
don v. 225.43
dona 875.6
doña 374.2, 3
donate 784.8
donation 784.1, 3
donation party 784.1; 892.5
donative n. 784.3
donative adj. 784.14
donator 784.7
done impotent 158.8
 cooked 298.50
 exhausted 688.6
 completed 729.6
be done for 162.5
being done 852.7
done brown 158.8
done for extinct 2.10
 (destroyed 162.7)
 ended 67.9
 impotent 158.8
 dead 360.8
 dying 360.9
 worn out 659.12
 finished 729.6
 defeated 732.12
done up
 impotent 158.8
 impaired 659.12
 exhausted 688.6
 defeated 732.12
done with ended 67.9
 disused 678.6
donee transferee 270.5
 recipient 785.2
donga 252.5
donjon
 stronghold 717.4
 prison 752.1
Don Juan 962.1
donkey ass 271.10
 fool 501.1
 bullhead 606.3, 4
 bungler 701
donkey's years 110.3
donna 374.2, 3
Donnybrook Fair 59.4
donor 784.7
do-nothing n. 683.7
do-nothing adj.

inactive 681.3
indolent 683.13
do-nothingism, do-nothingness
 inaction 681.1
 indolence 683.3
Don Quixote
 romanticist 515.7
 knight-errant 861.3
donship 875.9
don't! 761.6
 (cease! 142.8)
 (God forbid! 766.5)
doodad, dodad 316.3
doodle, doudle 416.18
doodlesack 410.4; 417.4
dooly, doolie, doolee, doley, dooli 272.12
doom n. end 67.1
 destruction 162.2
 destiny 601.2
 (death 360.1)
 predetermination 611.1, 3
 condemnation 971.1
doom v. destine 601.9
 assess 812.5
 condemn 971.2
 (judge 480.9)
doomage
 assessment 812.2
 fine 974.2
doomed
 inauspicious 512.5
 destined 601.13
doomsday end 67.1
 hereafter 121.2
till doomsday 112.5
door 260.4
 (inlet 294.5)
 (outlet 295.5)
at one's door 197.11
behind closed doors 528.24
doorjamb 215.16
doorkeeper 717.6
doormaker 690.8
doormat
 weakling 160.4
 rug 652.7
doorpost
 post 215.16
 portal 260.4
doorsill 215.3
doorstone 342.4
doorway 260.4
 (path 627.2)
dope n. fuel 388.1
 information 527.1
 addict 613.7
 drug 662.7
dope v. imbue 41.8
 lubricate 332.4
 anaesthetize 376.4
 medicate 662.24
dope out solve 481a.4
 predict 511.7
dope fiend 613.7
dopester 513.2
dopey stupid 499.12
 languid 683.14

Dorado — dovetail

Dorado 318.6
do-re-mi *n.* 413.16
do-re-mi *v.* 416.20
dormancy
  inertness 172.1
  (inaction 681.1)
  latency 526.1
dormant inert 172.3
  (quiescent 265.7)
  (inactive 681.3; 683.12)
  latent 526.6
  sleeping 683.16
dormant partner 711.1
dormer 260.5
dormitory 191.16
dormouse 683.7
dorp 189.17
dorsad 235.17
dorsal rear 225.10
  posterial 235.10
dorsum back 235.3
  ridge 250.2
dose *n.* quantity 25.2
  part 51.1
  venereal disease 655.7
  ~ of medicine 662.4
  portion 786.2
dose *v.* 662.24
dosology 662.16
doss bedroom 191.16
  bed 215.24
  sleep 683.5
dosser, dorser 191.9
dossil wrapper 223.11
  stopper 263.1, 2
  dressing 662.14
dot *n.* modicum 32.2
  inextension 180a.1
  (small place 184.4)
  diminutive 193.2
  music mark 415.23
  mark 550.7, 8
  code 550.15
  dowry 784.6
on the dot
  on the instant 113.6
  punctually 132.13
dot *v.* mark 550.19
  endow 784.13
  dot the i's 494.6
dotage senility 499.5
  nonsensical talk 517.3
dotard *n.* 501.3
dotard *adj.* 499.15, 16
dotardism 499.5
dotardy 499.15, 16
dotate 784.8, 13
dotation 784.1, 6
dote, doat
  ~ insanely 503.9
  talk nonsense 517.6
  (act foolishly 499.10)
dote on 897.11
doting, doating *n.* 517.3
doting, doating *adj.*
  aged 128.8
  senile 499.16

crazy 503.14
dotty unsteady 160.12
  insane 503.12
douanier 745.9
Douay Bible 985.2
double *n.*
  analogue 17.5
  duplicate 21.2
  substitute 147.2
  fold 258.1
  etheric ~ 980a.2
on the double 274.14
double *v.* imitate 19.5
  increase 35.3
  middle 68.4
  duplicate 90.2
  substitute 147.3
  fold 258.1
  turn round 283.6
  turn 311.4
  circumvent 623.6
  quickmarch 684.8
double back 283.6
double the fist
  defy 715.2
  threaten 909.2
double up 158.6
double *adj.*
  duplicate 90.3
  (dual 89.4)
  equivocal 520.5
  dissembling 544.8
  treacherous 940.12
double-aspect theory 994.3
double-cross
  inform on 527.10
  betray 940.7
doubled
  duplicate 90.3
  folded 258.4
double-dealer
  deceiver 548.1
  (traitor 949.3)
  tergiversator 607.4
double-dealing *n.*
  duplicity 544.2
  treachery 940.4
double-dealing *adj.*
  dissembling 544.8
  treacherous 940.12
double-decker 273a.1
double-distilled 171.10
double Dutch
  unintelligibility 519.2
  jargon 563.4
double-dyed 428.13
double-edged
  acrid 171.10
  sharp 253.11
double-entendre
  ambiguity 520.2
  witticism 842.5
  risqué story 851.3
double entente 520.2
double-faced
  double 90.3
  dissembling 544.8
  treacherous 940.12
doubleganger 980a.2

doublehanded
  dissembling 544.8
  treacherous 940.12
double-headed 90.3
doublehearted, double-minded
  dissembling 544.8
  irresolute 605.5
  treacherous 940.12
doubleness 544.2
double personality 503.2
double-quick 274.14
double-reef 267.38; 864.4
double-ripper, double-runner 272.13
double-shot 171.7
double sight 443.1
doublet pair 89.2
  coat 225.16
double-tongued
  dissembling 544.8
  (equivocal 520.5)
  treacherous 940.12
doubling
  duplication 90.1
  lining 224.1
  fold 258.1
  ~ of the masts 273.12
doublure 224.1
doubly 90.4
doubt *n.*
  uncertainty 475.1
  unbelief 485.2
  (suspiciousness 487.2)
  (fearfulness 860.2)
  jealousy 920.1
  religious ~ 989.3
beyond doubt 474.12
  (truly 494.15)
have no doubt
  be certain 474.5
  believe 484.9
have one's doubts 485.6
in doubt
  uncertain 475.9
  doubtful 485.10
no doubt
  undoubtedly 474.16
  to be sure 488.14
doubt *v.*
  be uncertain 475.6
  disbelieve 485.6
  (be incredulous 487.3)
  (dispute 536.2)
  (fear 860.8)
  (be irreligious 989.5)
  be jealous 920.2
not to doubt 474.5
doubtable
  uncertain 475.9
  unbelievable 485.11
doubter 989.4
doubtful
  uncertain 475.9

(disputed 461.25)
(improbable 473.3)
(equivocal 520.5)
(irresolute 605.5)
unbelieving 485.10
(incredulous 487.4)
unbelievable 485.11
unsafe 665.7
nullifidian 989.8
be doubtful 485.6
doubtfully 475.17
doubtfulness
  uncertainty 475.1
  unbelief 485.2, 3
  (improbability 473.1)
doubtless *adj.*
  indubious 474.12
  believing 484.12
doubtless *adv.* 488.14
douceur
  bribe 618.2
  gratuity 784.3
douche *n.* 337.3
douche *v.* 337.5
doudle See doodle
dough softness 324.3
  gluten 352.3
  pulp 354.2
  money 800.1
doughboy
  dumpling 298.11
  soldier 726.4
doughface 605.3
dough-faced 324.6
  (weak-willed 605.6)
  (servile 886.4)
doughhead 501.1
dough-headed 499.12
doughnut 298.12
doughty strong 159.10
  courageous 861.8
doughy soft 324.6
  viscid 352.8
  pulpy 354.5
Douma See Duma
dour 739.5
douse, dowse *n.* 276.3
douse, dowse *v.*
  destroy 162.4
  reduce sail 267.38
  strike 276.8
  submerge 310.5
  extinguish 385.5
dout 385.5
dove bird 366.22
  unsophisticate 703.2
  innocent 946.2
Dove 976.6
dove-colored, dove-coloured 432.4
dovecot, dovecote 189.7
dove-gray 432.4
dovelike 946.5
dovetail *n.* 43.3
dovetail *v.* agree 23.7
  attach 43.6
  interlace 219.8
  (interject 228.8)

dovetailed — draper

(insert 300.5)
dovetailed 244.5
dowager matron 374.2
  widow 905.3
dowdy *n.* slattern 59.5
  pastry 298.12
dowdy *adj.* 59.9
dowel 45.5
dower *n.* 784.6
  (estate 780.3)
dower *v.* 784.13
dowerless 804.7
down *n.* hill 206.2
  smooth 255.2
  plumage 256.9
  nap 256.10
  lightness 320.2
  softness 324.3
  plain 344.1
down *v.* eat 298.44
  fell 308.5
  confute 479.2
  be credulous 486.3
  be deceived 547.3
down *adj.*
  descending 306.7
  dejected 837.9
down *adv.* 207.11;
  306.8
down helm 267.70
down to the ground
  52.15
down-and-out *n.*
  804.3
down-and-out *adj.*
  poor 804.7
  in disrepute 874.9
down-and-outer
  804.3
downbear 308.4
downbeat 413.23
downcast *n.* 308.2
  (descent 306.1)
downcast *adj.*
  descending 306.7
  downthrown 308.9
  dejected 837.9
  look downcast 837.6
downcome 306.1
down-Easter 188.9
downfall
  destruction 162.1
  descent 306.1
  rainstorm 348.11
  defeat 732.3
downfallen 837.13
downflow
  stream 348.2
  rain 348.11
downgate 217.2
downgrade *n.* 217.2
  (descent 306.1)
  on the downgrade
  659.11
downgrade *adv.* 306.8
downhaul 273.10
downhearted 837.9
downhill *n.* 217.2
downhill *adj.* 217.11
downhill *adv.* 306.8
  go downhill
  weaken 160.7

incline 217.6
  deteriorate 659.6
  suffer misfortune
  735.6
downland 207.3
downline 306.8
downpour
  stream 348.2
  rainstorm 348.11
downright *adj.*
  absolute 31.12
  unqualified 52.10
  frank 703.4
downright *adv.* 31.16
downstairs
  below 207.11
  down 306.8
downstream, down-
  street 306.8
downthrow 308.2
downthrown 308.9
  (prostrate 213.9)
downtown 306.8
downtrodden
  subjugated 749.6
  in disrepute 874.9
downward 306.8
downwards 207.11
down-wash 267a.16
downwith 306.8
down-wind 267a.34
downy *n.* 215.24
downy *adj.*
  nappy 256.15
  soft 324.7
dowry 784.6
  (inheritance 775.4)
dowse See **douse**
dowser 992.2
doxologize 990.10
doxology
  sacred music 415.11
  paean 990.2
doxy 962.3
doyen 130.5
doyley See **doily**
doze *n.* 683.5
doze *v.* 683.9
dozen 98.7
dozy 683.15
dr. 319.4
drab *n.* modicum 32.2
  slattern 59.5
  strumpet 962.2
drab *adj.*
  dull-colored 428.19
  colorless 429.6
  gray 432.4
drabble 653.15
drabbletail 59.5
drabbletailed 59.9
drachm 319.4
drachma 800.8
Draco statesman 694.4
  tyrant 739.3
Draconian 739.5
draff dregs 40.2
  offal 653.6
draft, draught *n.*
  decrement 39a
  list 86.1
  depth 208.5

pull 285.2
  drink 298.4
  air flow 349.1
  music score 415.21
  drawing 556.9
  writing 590.3
  abstract 596.1
  plan 626.2
  dose 662.4
  recruits 726.5
  conscription 744.1
  check 800.7
  (credit instrument
  805.2)
  dram of liquor
  959.10
draft, draught *v.*
  compose 54.4
  outline 230.3; 626.9
  draw up 590.14
  appoint 609.11
  impanel 611.4
  conscript 744.2
draft off dispel 73.3
  remove 185.2
  transfer 270.6
draft chair 215.22
draftee 726.5
draft horse 271.3
draftsman, draughts-
  man 559.1
  (delineator 554.6)
drag *n.* adherer 46.3
  pulling power 157.3
  influence 175.1
  smoother 255.3
  aeronautics 267a.13
  carriage 272.4
  sled 272.13
  slowness 275.3
  attraction 288.1
  smoke 392a.10
  hindrance 706.2
  (restraint 752.2)
drag *v.* escort 88.7
  be protracted 110.7
  (elapse 109.3)
  smooth 255.4
  go slow 275.5
  pull 285.4
  attract 288.3
  smoke 392a.14
  drawl 583.2
drag in foist in 10.4
  interject 228.8
drag on
  be protracted 110.7
  continue 143.2
drag out 481a.3
drag up 307.6
draggle
  hang down 214.4
  pull 285.4
draggletail 59.5
draggletailed 59.9
dragoman
  driver 268.9
  interpreter 524.1
  guide 694.6
dragon monster 83.7
  violent 173.6
  reptile 366.18

ill-humored person
  901.4
dragonfly 366.24
dragonnade, dragoon-
  ade attack 716.1
  punishment 972.2
dragoon *n.*
  attacker 716.4
  soldier 726.4
dragoon *v.*
  coerce 744.2
  intimidate 860.12
drag sail, drag sheet
  706.2
drain *n.*
  leakage 295.1
  conduit 350.1
  sewer 653.8
drain *v.* leak out 295.7
  evacuate 297.14
  dry 340.5
  use up 638.2; 677.6
  filter 652.10
  ~ of resources
  789.12
  squander 818.3
drain the cup
  drink 298.47
  tipple 959.15
drainage
  leakage 295.1
  evacuation 297.5
  drying 340.2
  sanitation 652.2
drained 187.11
draisine, draisene
  272.14
drake monster 83.7
  bird 366.22
  male animal 373.6
drakestone 342.4
dram
  drink 298.4; 959.10
  weight 319.4
  measure 466.3
  stimulus 615.3
drama 599
  (personation
  554.2)
dramalogue 599.3
dramatic singer 416.24
  verse 597.13
  theatrical 599.28
  spectacular 882.9
dramatics 599.2
dramatis personae
  599.18
  (coworkers 690.4)
dramatist 599.22
  (author 593.15)
dramatize 599.25
  (write 590.14)
dramatizer 599.19, 22
dramaturgic
  dramatic 599.28
  spectacular 882.9
dramaturgist 599.22
dramaturgy 599.2
dramshop 959.13
drap d'or 847.6
drape 225.41
draper 225.36

drapery — drift 820

drapery clothes 225.1
  ornamentation 847.6
drastic acrid 171.10
  gruff 895.7
drat! 908.8
drather 609.2
draught See **draft**
draughts 840.11
draughtsman See
  draftsman
Dravidian languages
  560.4
draw *n.* tie 27.4
  pulling power 157.3
  attendance 186.6
  pull 285.2
  attraction 288.1
  allurement 617.1
  chance 621.2, 10
draw *v.*
  compose 54.4
  influence 175.6
  pull 285.4
  attract 288.3
  smoke 392a.14
  limn 556.17
  (represent 554.7)
  derive 775.6
draw a bead on 716.6
draw back
  recoil 277.3
  (recede 283.5)
  shrink 623.9
draw in
  contract 195.4
  (narrow 203.7)
  take in 296.2
draw in one's horn
  humble oneself
    879.2
  surrender 725.4
  recant 607.9
draw lots 621.17
draw near
  ~ ~ in time 121.6
  impend 152.2
  approach 286.2
draw off
  let out 297.13
  drain 340.5
  avert 706.5
draw on
  ~ ~ in time 121.6
  happen 151.3
  impend 152.2
  influence 175.6
  lure 617.4
  seduce 897.13
draw oneself up
  307.7
draw out
  protract time 110.6
  lengthen 200.9
  extract 301.5, 6
  discover 481a.3
  show 525.2
  expatiate 573.5
draw the curtain
  conceal 528.10
  disclose 529.3
draw the line
  discriminate 465.2

  choose 609.7
draw the longbow
  exaggerate 549.2
  (lie 544.4)
  boast 884.5
draw up
  compose 54.4
  take order 58.5
  pick up 307.6
  draft 590.14
  describe 594.5
  plan 626.9
drawback
  decrement 39a
  objection 489.2
  disadvantage 647.1
  fault 651.2
  obstacle 706.2
  discount 813.1
drawbridge
  bridge 627.7
  escape 671.3
drawer
  cupboard 191.15
  artist 559.1
drawers 225.21, 25
drawing *n.*
  traction 285.1
  attraction 288.1
  art 556.3, 9
  (representation
    554.1)
  plan 626.2
drawing *adj.*
  tractional 285.6
  attracting 288.4
drawing card 617.2
drawing room
  room 191.16
  society 852.4
  social circle 892.7
drawing-room car
  272.19
drawknife 253.6
drawl *n.*
  slowness 275.1
  speech defect 583.1
drawl *v.*
  lengthen 200.9
  go slow 275.5
  ~ one's words 583.2
drawly 583.5
drawn 27.9
drawshave 253.6
dray cart 272.5
  sled 272.13
dray horse 271.3
drayman 268.9
dread *n.* 860.1
dread *v.* 860.8
dreadful *n.* 594.2
dreadful *adj.* vast 31.8
  deplorable 649.8
  shocking 830.13
  fearful 860.15
dreadful *adv.*
  extremely 31.23
  badly 649.11
dreadfully 31.23
dreadnought, dread-
  naught
  overcoat 225.17

  man-of-war 726.11
dream *n.* muse 458.3
  imagination 515.5
  (unsubstantiality
    4.3)
  (delusion 495.5)
  a beauty 845.3
dream *v.* muse 458.6
  (think 451.27)
  suppose 514.6
  imagine 515.9
  invent 515.10
  intend 620.3
dream-born, dream-
  built 515.14
dreamer 515.7
dreamery 515.4
dreaming *n.*
  preoccupation 458.3
  imagination 515.2
dreaming *adj.*
  preoccupied 458.11
  imagining 515.14
dreamland
  imagination 515.6
  sleep 683.5
dreamy
  chimerical 4.6
  preoccupied 458.11
  (thoughtful 451.37)
  imaginative 515.14
  sleepy 683.15
dreamy-eyed,
  dreamy-minded
  515.14
drear dismal 837.10
  tedious 841.8
  dull 843.5
drearihead, dreari-
  hood 841.3
drearisome
  tedious 841.8
  dull 843.5
dreary gloomy 421.8
  dull-colored 428.19
  gray 432.4
  disheartening
    830.11
  dismal 837.10
  tedious 841.8
  dull 843.5
dredge *n.*
  excavator 252.7
  dredger 307.2
dredge *v.*
  assemble 72.11
  dig out 301.1
  pick up 307.6
dredger
  excavator 252.7
  dredge 307.2
dreggy 653.16
dregs remains 40.2
  (condensation
    321.3)
  (rubbish 645.4)
  (offal 653.6)
  ~ of society 876.2
  ~ of vice 949.5
drench *n.* drink 298.4
  alcoholic drink
    959.10

drench *v.* soak 337.5
  overfill 641.4
drenched
  drunk 959.21
  overfull 641.6
drencher 348.11
drenching 337.6
Dresden blue 438.2
dress *n.* 225.1, 7, 19
dress *v.* uniform 16.4
  accord 23.8
  equalize 27.7
  clothe 225.41, 43
  lubricate 332.4
  falsify 544.3
  personate 554.8
  equip 634.2
  repair 660.11
  ~ wounds 662.24
  decorate 847.11
  whip 972.6
be dressed in 225.45
dress down 972.6
dress the ground
  cultivate 371.8
  prepare 673.6
dress circle 599.11
dress coat 225.14
dresser table 215.20
  doctor 662.19
dressing clothes 225.1
  bandage 662.14
  reproof 932.3
  whipping 972.3
dressing gown 225.23
dressing jacket
  225.16, 23
dressmaker 225.38
dressmaking 225.35
dress shirt 225.18
dress suit 225.14
Dreyse rifle 727.10
dribble *n.*
  trickle 348.4
  twaddle 517.3
dribble *v.*
  leak out 295.7
  trickle 348.19
  purl 405.5
driblet, dribblet 32.2
  by driblets 51.10
dried 340.9
dried up
  shrunk 195.6
  wasted 638.4
drier
  dehydrator 340.3
  paint 428.5
drift *n.*
  accumulation 72.6
  tendency 176.1
  (intention 620.1)
  distance 196.1
  course 264.3
  aeronautics 267a.14
  silt 270.3
  direction 278.1
  deviation 279.1
  flow 348.2
  meaning 516.1
drift *v.* course 264.6
  sail 267.23

driftage — druggist

aviate 267a.30
deviate 279.5
idle 683.8
~ with the stream 705.3
drift along 282.2
drift away 287.2
driftage course 264.3
  flow 348.2
drifter wanderer 268.2
  neglector 460.3
  fisherman 622.5
driftless 621.21
drift sail 706.2
driftway 267.7
driftwood 635.3
drill *n.* cloth 219.5
  perforator 262
  monkey 366.16
  training 537.2
  exercise 686.2
drill *v.*
  perforate 260.14
  train 537.10
driller 252.7
drink *n.*
  nonalcoholic 298.4
  ocean 341.1
  alcoholic 959.4, 10
drink *v.* quaff 298.47
  (swallow 296.3)
  ~ tobacco 392a.14
  tipple 959.15
drink in 298.47
drink off 959.15
drink to pledge 883.4
  toast 959.17
drinkable *n.* 298.4
drinkable *adj.* 298.51
drinker 959.11
drinking *n.*
  potation 298.3
  tippling 959.1
drinking *adj.* 959.23
drinking bout 959.3
  (spree 840.3)
drinking song 415.10
drinking water 337.1
drip *n.* top 210.4
  trickle 348.4
  bore 841.4
drip *v.* leak out 295.7
  be moist 339.6
  trickle 348.19
dripping *n.* 356.4
dripping *adj.* 339.8
dripple trickle 348.19
  purl 405.5
dripproof 340.11
drippy 348.27
dripstone 342.4
drisk drizzle 348.11
  mist 353.5
drive *n.* crowd 72.4
  energy 171.1
  travel 266.7, 8
  enterprise 682.1, 4
  haste 684.1
drive *v.* postpone 133.4
  excavate 252.9
  travel 266.18
  drift 267.23

aviate 267a.31
  propel 284.10
  ~ stock 370.7
  fish 622.8
  hasten 684.2
  work 686.8
  conduct 693.4
  besiege 716.5
  compel 744.2
  barter 794.5
drive at mean 516.5
  aim 620.3
drive away
  dispel 73.3
  repulse 289.2
drive back 289.2
drive home 729.3
drive in
  intrude 228.10
  insert 300.5
drive on
  advance 282.2
  keep going 682.12
drive out 297.8
drive stakes 184.15
drivel *n.*
  twaddle 517.3
  verbosity 573.1
drivel *v.*
  salivate 297.19
  ~ insanely 503.9
  talk nonsense 517.6
  (dote 499.10)
  be verbose 573.5
driveler, driveller
  dotard 501.3
  chatterer 584.3
driveling 499.13
driver traveler 268.9
  automobilist 268.10
  propeller 284.6
driveway 627.3
drizzle *n.* 348.11
drizzle *v.* 348.25
drizzling 348.27
drizzly 348.27
droit 922.2
  (due 924.1)
droll witty 842.9
  comical 855.5
drollery wit 842.1
  comicality 855.1
drome 267a.28
dromedary
  giraffe 206.7
  camel 271.2
drone *n.*
  slow goer 275.4
  bee 366.24
  tone 413.6, 14
  bagpipe 417.4
  idler 683.7
drone *v.* 405.6
droning 407.13
dronish, drony 683.14
drool *n.*
  twaddle 517.3
  verbosity 573.1
drool *v.*
  salivate 297.19
  ~ insanely 503.9
  talk nonsense 517.6

be verbose 573.5
droop *n.*
  pendency 214.1
  gait 266.5
  descent 306.1
  bore 841.4
droop *v.* depend 214.4
  descend 306.4
  sicken 655.21
  deteriorate 659.6
  languish 683.10
  tire 688.4
  despond 837.6
droop-eared 418.14
drooping weak 160.12
  sickly 655.24
  fatigued 688.6
drop *n.* modicum 32.2
  advantage 33.2
  pause 142.2
  pendant 214.2
  platform 215.21
  declivity 217.2
  sphere 249.2
  descent 306.1
  fall 310.1
  trickle 348.4
  dram of liquor 959.10
  gallows 975.4
at the drop of the hat
  first 66.9
  willingly 602.11
drop by drop
  gradually 26.5
  piecemeal 51.10
drop in the bucket
  modicum 32.2
  pittance 640.5
  trifle 643.3
drop in the eye 959.10
drop *v.* cease 142.6
  collapse 158.5
  weaken 160.7
  give birth 161.9
  prostrate 213.7
  leak out 295.7
  descend 306.4
  depress 308.4
  fell 308.5
  fall 310.4
  gravitate 319.7
  trickle 348.19
  kill 361.10
  abandon 624.3
  disuse 678.2
  faint 688.4
  lose 776.2
  relinquish 782.3
drop dead 360.6
drop from the clouds 508.5
drop in
  intrude 228.10
  insert 300.5
  visit 892.10
drop off
  decrease 36.3
  die 360.6
  fall asleep 683.9
drop the curtain 67.7
drop the subject

disregard 458.5
  ignore 460.5
drop curtain 599.15
drop-dry
  seaworthy 273.15
  watertight 664.10
drop game 545.3
drophead 66.3
droplet 32.2
droppings 653.7
drop serene 442.1
dropsical
  swollen 194.10
  (overfull 641.6)
  hydropic 655.25
dropsicalness 194.1
dropsy swelling 194.1
  ailment 655.5
droshki, drosky 272.4
dross dregs 40.2
  (rubbish 645.4)
  (offal 653.6)
  slag 384.15
drought, drouth
  dryness 340.1
  want 640.3
  thirst 865.3
droughty, drouthy
  dry 340.7
  thirsty 865.19
drouk 337.5
drove crowd 72.4
  multitude 102.2
drover 370.4
drown submerge 310.5
  die 360.7
  kill 361.11
  muffle 408a.4
  mute 581.5
  founder 732.5
drown the shamrock 959.15
drowning
  death 360.1
  (killing 361.1)
  execution 972.4
drowse *n.* 683.5
drowse *v.* 683.9
drowsiness 683.4
  (fatigue 688.1)
  (weariness 841.1)
drowsy 683.15
  (fatigued 688.6)
drub defeat 731.9
  beat 972.6
drubbing 732.3
drudge *n.*
  seaman 269.3
  toiler 690.2
drudge *v.* 686.6
drudgery 686.3
  (industry 682.5)
drug *n.* 662.4, 7
  (merchandise 798.3)
drug *v.* imbue 41.8
  anesthetize 376.4
  medicate 662.24
druggery 662.18
drugget cloth 219.5
  rug 652.7
druggist 662.21
  (merchant 797.11)

drugstore — dulcify   **822**

drugstore
  restaurant 298.42
  (pharmacy 662.18)
  mart 799.4
druid prophet 513.2
  priest 996.10
druid stone 342.4
drum *n.* resort 74.2
  repetend 104.2
  dive 189.9
  cylinder 249.3
  thrum 407.3
  drummer 416.4, 7
  percussive 417.10
  festivity 840.2
  party 892.5, 6
drum *v.* repeat 104.4
  thrum 407.8
  (pulsate 314.9)
  beat time 416.19
  drum out 297.8, 11
drum corps
  drummers 416.7
  corps 726.7
drumfire
  drumming 407.3
  (boom 406.3)
  barrage 716.2
drumhead
  music 417.13
  court 966.1, 5
drum major
  conductor 416.13
  officer 745.11
  festivity 840.2
  party 892.5
drummer
  tympanist 416.7
  salesman 758.5; 797.2
drumming *n.* 407.3
  (repetition 104.1)
  (pulsation 314.2)
drumming *adj.* 407.11
  (repeated 104.6)
drumstick
  thigh 266.11
  fowl 298.25
  music 417.13
drunk *n.* spree 959.3
  drunkard 959.11
drunk *adj.* 959.21, 22
  be drunk 959.19
  get drunk 959.15
  make drunk 959.18
drunkard 959.11
  (addict 613.7)
drunken *v.* 959.15
drunken *adj.* 959.21, 23
  (intemperate 954.4)
drunkenness 959
  (intemperance 954.1)
druther 609.2
dry *n.* 953.4
dry *v.* empty 187.11
  dehydrate 340.5
  cure 670.4
  (prepare 673.6)
  exhaust 789.12
  dry up shrink 195.4
  run to waste 638.3

wither 659.6
dry *adj.* not wet 340.7
  unsavory 395.5
  harsh-sounding 410.9
  style 575.2; 579.3
  (speech 576.3)
  dull 843.5
  (boring 841.8)
  thirsty 865.19
  cynical 932.11
  be dry 340.7
  run dry 638.3
dryad wood 367.7
  nymph 979.8
dryasdust *n.*
  antiquary 122.5
  bore 841.4
dry-as-dust *adj.*
  wearying 841.8
  dull 843.5
dry cell 158a.6
dry-clean 652.9
dry cleaner 652.6
dry cleaning 652.2
dry goods
  textile 219.5
  merchandise 798.3
dry ice ice 383.5
  refrigerant 387.2
drying *n.*
  siccation 340.2
  preservation 670.2
drying *adj.* 340.10
dry measure 466.3
dryness 340
dry nurse *n.*
  tutor 540.1
  guardian 664.3
  assistant 711.1
dry-nurse *v.*
  train 537.10
  nourish 707.9
dry point 558.1, 4
dry rot 659.2
  (blight 663.2)
duad 89.2
duadic, dual 89.4
  (double 90.5)
dualism duality 89.1
  philosophy 451.20
  ditheism 984.10
duality 89
dual personality 503.2
duarchy 737.4
dub *n.* analogue 17.5
  duplicate 21.2
  substitute 147.2
dub *v.* imitate 19.5
  double 90.5
  substitute 147.3
  name 564.2
dubash
  functionary 758.2
  deputy 759.1
dubiety, dubiosity
  uncertainty 475.1
  doubt 485.2
dubious
  uncertain 475.9
  doubtful 485.10
  unsafe 665.7

nullifidian 989.8
dubiousness 475.1
dubitable
  uncertain 475.9
  unbelievable 485.11
dubitate
  be uncertain 475.6
  doubt 485.6
dubitation
  uncertainty 475.1
  doubt 485.2
dubitative
  uncertain 475.9
  doubtful 485.10
  nullifidian 989.8
ducat 800.5
duchess 875.6
duchy 182.1
duck *n.* oddity 83.4
  zero 87a.1
  lowness 207.4
  seaplane 273a.3
  food 298.25
  bird 366.22
  person 372.3; 373.2
  endearment 902.4
duck *v.* move 264.6
  dodge 277.3
  plunge 310.4, 5
  shy at 603.4
  avoid 623.9
duck and run, duck out 623.10
duck egg 87a.1
duck fit 900.2
duck green 435.2
ducking 310.2
ducking stool 975.3
duckling
  youngling 129.3, 7
  poultry 298.25
  endearment 902.4
duct tube 260.6
  conduit 350.1
ductibility 324.1; 325.1
ductible 324.6
ductile flexible 324.6
  (manageable 705.6)
  (obedient 743.3)
  elastic 325.5
ductility
  flexibility 324.1
  (obedience 743.1)
  elasticity 325.1
dud nullity 4.2
  impotent 158.3
  garment 225.1–3, 5
  shortcoming 304.1
  false alarm 669.2
  failure 732.1, 4
dude tourist 268.1
  fop 854.1
Dudelsack 417.4
dudgeon
  weapon 727.3
  pique 900.2
duds
  clothes 225.1, 2, 5
  belongings 780.1, 5
due *n.* debt 806.1
  privilege 922.2

entitlement 924.1
due *adj.* fit 646.4
  unpaid 806.9
  becoming 924.9
  (right 922.5)
  (just 941.3)
be due to
  result from 154.3
  be entitled to 924.5
due to
  resulting from 154.5
  entitled to 924.11
  obliged to 926.10
in due time
  in time 109.6
  in future 121.9
  early 132.11
  soon 132.15
  opportunely 134.10
due bill 800.7
duel *n.* 720.3
duel *v.* 720.8
duelist, duellist 726.1
duello 720.3
dueness 924
  (expedience 646.1)
  (right 922.1)
  (justice 941.1)
duenna escort 88.4
  instructress 540.2
  custodian 664.3
dues debt 806.1
  assessment 812.2
  (rent 810.2)
  deserts 924.2
duet, duettino 415.12
duettist 416.1
duffel bag 191.5
duffer oddity 83.4
  ignoramus 493.1
  dolt 501.1
  sham 545.6
  trifle 643.3
  bungler 701
  thief 792.1
  counterfeiter 800.18
duffy See **duppy**
dug 250.3
dugout hut 189.4
  cave 252.3
  trench 259.2
  boat 273.4
  refuge 666.3
  fortification 717.3
duit 643.3
  (money 800.8)
duke 875.5
  (potentate 745.2)
dukedom
  country 182.1
  nobility 875.9
dulcet sweet 396.8
  melodious 413.27
  (soft 405.9)
  pleasing 829.7
dulcetness 413.4
dulciana 417.12
dulcifluous
  sweet 396.8
  melodious 413.27
dulcification 324.2
dulcify moderate 174.5

soften 324.4
sweeten 396.7
dulcimer 417.2
Dulcin 396.4
Dulcinea 897.7
dulcitude 396.1
duledge 45.5
dulia 990.1
dull *v.* moderate 174.5
  blunt 254.2
  deaden 376.4
  muffle 408a.4
  decolor 429.5
  ~ the sensibilities 823.4
  relieve 834.4
  sadden 837.8
dull *adj.* weak 160.10
  inert 172.3
  blunt 254.3
  insensible 376.5
  faint 405.9
  nonresonant 408a.6
  ~ of hearing 419.8
  dim 422.8
  dull-colored 428.19
  (dark 421.8)
  colorless 429.6
  gray 432.4
  stupid 499.12
  style 575.2
  languid 683.14
  unemotional 823.5
  dismal 837.10
  prosaic 843.5
  (prose 598.4)
  (boring 841.8)
be dull 843.3
dullard *n.* 501.1
dullard *adj.* 499.12
dullardism 499.2
dullbrained 499.12
dull-colored 428.19
dull-eared 419.8
dullhead 501.1
dull-headed 499.12
dullish 254.3
dullness, dulness
  weakness 160.1
  bluntness 254.1
  ~ of hearing 419.1
  languor 683.4
  apathy 823.1
  prosaism 843
  (weariness 841.1)
dull-pated 499.12
dull-sighted 443.15
dullsome 843.5
dull-witted 499.12
dully 501.1
dulse 367.3
duly 924.12
  (rightly 922.7)
Duma, Douma 696.4
dumb ignorant 491.8
  stupid 499.12
  voiceless 581.7
  (taciturn 585.4)
not so dumb 498.9
dumbbell 501.1
dumb crambo 840.11
dumbhead 501.1

dumbness 581.1
dumb show
  gesticulation 550.3
  pantomime 599.3
dumb-waiter 307.3
dumfound, dumbfound
  disappoint 509.2
  strike dumb 581.5
  amaze 870.3
dumdum bullet 727.14
dummy *n.*
  substitute 147.2
  impotent 158.3
  dolt 501.1
  mute 581.2
  printing 591.2
  nonentity 643.6
  sleeping partner 683.7
  cards 840.13
dummy *v.* 585.3
dump *n.* abode 189.1, 4
  dive 189.9
  tune 415.2
  wasteyard 645.4
  sty 653.10
  dirge 839.3
dump *v.* unload 297.21
  sell 796.5
dumpcart 272.2, 5
dump truck 272.10, 15
dump wagon 272.2
dumpish sad 837.9
  sullen 901.8
dump'ing
  fat man 192.7
  food 298.11, 12
dumps
  melancholy 837.1
  sullens 902.2
dumpy 201.6
  (little 193.8)
dun *n.* horse 271.5
  dunner 805.3
dun *v.* 765.5
dun *adj.* dim 422.8
  gray 432.4
dunce
  ignoramus 493.1
  dolt 501.1
dunderhead 501.1
dune 206.2
dung 653.7
  (excrement 299.2)
  (malodor 401.2)
dungeon 752.1
dunghill *n.* 653.8
dunghill *adj.*
  dastardly 862.5
  ignoble 876.11
dunghill fowl 366.23
dungy 653.17
Dunker 984.14
dunner 805.3
dun-white 430.9
duo 415.12
duodecillion 98.13
duodecimal 98.22; 99.3
duodecimo *n.*
  miniature 193.3

book size 593.8
duodecimo *adj.* 193.8
duodenal twelfth 98.22
  visceral 221.11
duodenary 98.22
duodenum vitals 221.4
  intestine 350.4
duologue
  interlocution 588.1
  drama 599.3
duomo 1000.1
dupability 486.1
dupable 486.5
dupe *n.*
  duplicate 21.2
  gull 547
  (ignoramus 493.1)
  (fool 501.1)
  (laughingstock 857.1)
be the dupe of 547.3
dupe *v.*
  imitate 19.5
  duplicate 90.2
  repeat 104.4
  fool 545.10
duplex *n.* 189.3
duplex *adj.*
  double 90.3
  (dual 89.4)
  electric 158a.12
  equivocal 520.5
duplexity duality 89.1
  equivocalness 520.1
duplicate *n.* copy 21.2
  (reproduction 163.1)
  tally 550.11
  record 551.1
  credit 805.2
duplicate *v.*
  imitate 19.5
  (reproduce 163.2)
  double 90.2
  repeat 104.4
duplicate *adj.* 90.3
duplication
  imitation 19.1
  duplicate 21.2
  doubling 90
  repetition 104.1
duplicature 258.1
duplicity duality 89.1
  falsehood 544.2
  (deception 545.1)
  treachery 940.4
duppy, duffy 980a.1
durability
  lastingness 110
  (perpetuity 112.1)
  (slowness 275.1)
  permanence 141.1
durable lasting 110.9
  (continuing 106.4)
  (perpetual 112.4)
  (unchangeable 150.7)
  permanent 141.6
durableness 141.1
durance 751.2
duration time 106.1

(course 109.1)
  permanence 141.1
durbar
  auditorium 189.10
  council 696.2
  tribunal 966.1
duress
  compulsion 744.1
  imprisonment 751.2
Durga 979.4
during 106.7, 9
durity 323.1
durn 260.4
durwaun, darwan, durvan 717.6
dusk *n.* twilight 126.1
  semidarkness 422.2
dusk *v.* 422.7
dusk *adj.*
  evening 126.5
  dark 421.8
  dim 422.8
  dark-colored 431.8
dusken 422.7
duskingtide 126.1
dusky evening 126.5
  gloomy 421.8
  dim 422.8
  dark-colored 431.8
dust *n.* turmoil 59.4
  lightness 320.2
  powder 330.3
  (sandstorm 349.12)
  dryness 340.4
  corpse 362.1
  trifle 643.3
  rubbish 645.4
  dirt 653.5
  money 800.1
in the dust
  humbled 879.5
  worshiping 990.15
dust *v.*
  hasten off 293.5
  flee 623.10
dust one's jacket 972.6
dust bowl 183.1
dustcloth, duster 652.7
dustman sweep 652.6
  sleep 683.5
dustoor, dustoori See **dastur** etc.
dust storm 349.12
dusty powdery 330.8
  dirty 653.16
Dutch *n.*
  unintelligibility 519.2
  language 560.4
  jargon 563.4
Dutch *adj.* 188.11
Dutch auction 796.2
Dutch concert
  discord 414.2
  concert 415.17
Dutch courage
  cowardice 862.1
  intoxication 959.1, 4
Dutcher, Dutchman 188.9

Dutch treat — east

Dutch treat 892.5
dutiable 812.8
dutiful duteous 926.8
 (submissive 725.5)
 (obedient 743.3)
 reverent 928.8
dutifully 926.13
duty task 625.2
 tax 812.2
 compliments 894.3
 obligation 926
 (liability 177.1)
 reverence 928.1, 3
 divine service 990.7
 rite 998.1
do duty
 officiate 625.9
 accept responsibility 926.6
 perform a rite 998.14
do one's duty
 discharge one's responsibility 926.6
 (be honorable 939.6)
 be virtuous 944.2
on duty 682.20
put a duty on 812.5
duty-bound 926.10
duumvirate 737.4
dwarf *n.* midget 193.5
 elf 979.9
dwarf *v.* 36.4
dwarf, dwarfed, dwarfish *adj.* 193.9
dwell
 be permanent 141.4
 inhabit 186.10
 (stay 265.5)
dwell on, dwell upon
 repeat 104.4
 (tautologize 573.6)
 remember 505.11
 be boresome 841.5
 nurse revenge 919.5
dweller
 inhabitant 188.1
 horse 271.6
dwelling, dwelling place 189.1
dwindle
 decrease 36.3
 sicken 655.21
dwt. 319.4
dyad pair 89.2
 microbe 193.4
Dyak, Dayak 560.4
Dyaus
 paternity 166.2
 deity 979.4
dye *n.* 428.1, 3, 4
dye *v.* 428.9
dyestuff color 428.3
 dye 428.4
dying *n.* 360.1
dying *adj.*
 moribund 360.9
 eager 865.17
dying day 360.1
dyke See **dike**
dynamic potent 157.8
 electric 158a.12
 energetic 171.9

impulsive 276.10
dynamics force 159.3
 mechanics 276.5
 (kinetics 264.4)
dynamistic 276.10
dynamite 727.13
dynamiter 863.3
dynamize 171.7
dynamo 158a.7
 (engine 633.3)
dynamoelectric 158a.12
dynamometer
 aviation 267a.29
 mechanics 276.6
dynastic 737.16
dynasty 737.2
dyophone 418.6
dysentery
 excrement 299.2
 ailment 655.5
dysmerogenesis 161.2
dysmeromorph 357.3
dysmorphophobia 860.4
dyspepsia 655.13
dyspeptic 655.25
dysphonia 581.1
dysphoria 149.3
dyspnea, dyspnoea
 respiration 349.18
 fatigue 688.2
dyspneal, dyspnoeal 688.7
dzeggetai, dziggetai See **chigetai**

E

each every 78.13
 apiece 79.12
each and every 78.5
each other 12.3
eager expectant 507.7
 avid 682.18
 ardent 821.6
 (willing 602.8)
 desirous 865.17
eagerness
 avidity 682.3
 (willingness 602.1)
 (resolution 604.1)
 ardor 821.2
 desire 865.2
eagle aeronaut 269a.1
 speeder 274.6
 bird 366.22
 eye 441.9
 insignia 550.12;
 747.4
 gold piece 800.5
Eagle 318.6
eagle boat 726.11
eagle eye 441.7
 (discernment 498.2)
eaglelike 245.9
eagle-winged 274.13
eaglewood 400.3
eagre, hygre 348.10
ean 161.9
ear hearing 418.1, 5

light shield 424.5
 attention 457.1
all ears
 listening 418.15
 attentive 457.9
be all ears
 listen 418.11
 pay attention 457.4
by the ears 713.10
have the ear of
 convince 484.10
 be a friend of 888.2
earache 378.1
 (ailment 655.5)
ear-deafening 404.8
eardrop 214.2
eardrum 418.5
eared 418.14
earful 418.1
earing 273.10
earl 875.5
earldom country 182.1
 nobility 875.9
earless 419.8
earlier prior 116.4, 5
 lower 207.9
earliness 132
Earl of Coventry 840.12
early *n.* 132.4
early *adj.* 132.7
 (timely 134.7)
be early 132.5
early *adv.* 132.11
 (opportunely 134.10)
early bird 132.4
earmark *n.*
 particularity 79.2
 indication 550.6
earmark *v.* 550.19
ear muff 225.26
 (wrap 384.13)
earn 775.6
earnest *n.* 771.1
 (payment 807.2; 809.2)
in earnest
 sincere 543.4
 resolutely 604.9
 enterprising 682.18
 honest 939.11
earnest *adj.*
 resolute 604.7
 important 642.12
 enterprising 682.18
 ardent 821.6
 serious 837.16
earnestly 604.9
earnestness
 intentness 682.3
 heartiness 821.2
earnings 775.2
 (receipts 810.1)
 (remuneration 973.2)
earphone
 sound device 418.6
 phone 532a.5
ear-piercing
 loud 404.8
 shrill 410.10

earreach
 short way 197.2
 earshot 418.4
earring pendant 214.2
 ornament 847.7
earshot
 short way 197.2
 hearing 418.4
out of earshot
 405.11; 419.9
earsplitting 404.8
earth ground 211.2
 plane 213.3
 world 318.1, 3
 land 342.1
 corpse 362.1
on earth 180.9
earthborn 876.11
earthenware 384.14
earth flax 385.3
earthling person 372.3
 irreligionist 988.4;
  989.4
earthly worldly 318.14
 terrestrial 342.9
 unspiritual 989.9
earthly-minded 989.9
earthquake 173.2
 (shake 315.4)
earthwork 717.3
earthworm 366.25
earthy worldly 318.14
 terrestrial 342.9
 unspiritual 989.9
ear trumpet 418.6
earwig 366.24
earwitness 467.6
ease *n.* comfort 377.2
 style 578.1
 leisure 685.1
 repose 687.1
 facility 705.1
 relief 707.4
 prosperity 734.1
 content 831.1
at ease
 in comfort 377.9
 all's well! 664.14
 at rest 687.8
 easygoing 705.5
 prosperous 734.7
 free 748.20
 content 831.6
ease *v.* decrease 36.4
 facilitate 705.4
 take from 789.11
 relieve 834.4
 ease off 279.7
ease the helm 267.11,
  24, 70
ease up 275.7
easeful 377.8
easel table 215.20
 art 556.16
easement
 relief 707.4; 834.1
 estate 780.2
ease-off 275.3
easily 705.8
easiness 705.1
easing 834.7
east *n.* 278.2

east v. 278.5
east adj. 278.10
eastabout 278.11
easter n. 349.11
Easter n.
  anniversary 138.7
  holyday 998.13
easter v. 278.5
easterly n. 349.11
easterly adj. 278.10
easterly adv. 278.11
eastern 278.10
Easterner 57.3
easternly 278.10
easting 196.1
eastward 278.11
easy adj. slow 275.8
  comfortable 377.8
  credulous 486.5
  graceful 578.4
  leisurely 685.4
  not difficult 705.5
  lenient 740.4
  inexcitable 826.9
  be easy 705.3
easy adv.
  silently 403.8
  carefully 459.9
  easily 705.8
  cautiously 864.8
  not easy 704.8
  render easy 705.4
easy come, easy go 818.5
easy-flowing 705.5
easygoing docile 602.9
  irresolute 605.5
  easy-running 705.5
  lenient 740.4
  inexcitable 826.9
  content 831.6
  indifferent 866.4
easy-osey, easy-osie, easy-running 705.5
Easy Street 705.1
eat devour 298.44
  (swallow 296.3)
  (gormandize 957.3)
  submit to 725.3
  brook 826.6
eat away 659.7
eat crow, eat humble pie recant 607.9
  be submissive 725.3
  be humiliated 879.2
eat one's head off 957.3
eat one's words 607.9
  (apologize 952.5)
eat the wind out of, eat to windward of 267.20
eat up 486.3
eatable 298.49
eatables 298.5
eater 298.41
eating n. 298
eating adj. 298.48
eating house 298.42
eats 298.5
eau 337.1
Eau de Cologne 400.3

eau de Javelle 429.3
eau de vie 959.6
eavesdrop n. 348.4
eavesdrop v. 418.11
eavesdropper
  listener 418.7
  inquisitive 455.2
  informer 527.6
ébauche 556.9
ebb n.
  subsidence 36.2
  (waste 638.1)
  reflux 283.2
  tide 348.9
  deterioration 659.1
  at a low ebb
  inconsiderable 32.8
  less 34.7
  low 207.11
  depressed 308.9
  wasted 638.4
  insufficient 640.8
  sick 655.23
  impaired 659.12
ebb v. decrease 36.3
  go back 283.5
  recede 287.2
  deteriorate 659.6
ebb and flow n.
  alternation 314.3
  tide 348.9
ebb and flow v.
  alternate 314.10
  billow 348.22
ebbing 36.2
ebb tide
  subsidence 36.2
  lowness 207.2
  reflux 283.2
  tide 348.9
  insufficiency 640.1
ebenezer 1000.1
Ebionite 984.14
Eblis 978.1
E-boat 726.11
ebon 431.3
ebony n. tree 367.6
  black 431.3, 4
  wood 635.3
ebony adj. 431.7
éboulement 162.1
ebriety 959.1
ebullate, ebulliate
  bubble 353.8
  boil 382.13; 384.19
ebullience
  bubbling 353.3
  boiling 384.7
ebullient
  boiling 382.16
  excited 824.10
ebulliometer, ebullioscope 384.7
ebullition
  bubbling 353.3
  (activity 171.2)
  (agitation 315.2)
  boiling 384.7
  excitement 825.3
eburine 430.3
écarté 840.12
ecbatic 155.4

eccentric n.
  oddity 83.4
  (original 20.2)
  queer person 504.3
eccentric adj.
  unconformable 83.9
  irregular 139.2
  exterior 220.7
  idiocratic 503.17
  (inconstant 149.6)
  (capricious 608.5)
eccentricity
  exteriority 220.1
  idiosyncrasy 503.6
  (oddity 83.3)
  (capriciousness 608.2)
ecchymoma, ecchymosis 299.1
ecclesiarch 996.5
ecclesiastic n. 996.2
ecclesiastic adj.
  canonical 985.7
  churchly 995.9
  (claustral 1000.6)
ecclesiolater 991.5
ecclesiolatry 991.1
ecclesiology 995.1
eccrinology 299.8
eccrisis 299.1
ecdemic 220.7
ecderon 223.12
ecdysis 226.1
echelon n.
  deviation 279.2
  attack 716.1
echelon v.
  methodize 60.8
  deviate 279.7
echinate 253.11
Echinodermata 368.7
echinodermatous, echinoid 368.14
echinulate 253.11
echinus 215.17
echo n. imitator 19.4
  duplicate 21.2
  repetend 104.2
  reverberation 408.2
  (rebound 277.1)
  answer 462.1
echo v. imitate 19.5
  repeat 104.4
  reverberate 408.7
  acknowledge 462.5
  concur 488.7
echoer 19.4
echoless 403.6
eclampsia spasm 315.7
  illness 655.3
éclat 873.1
eclectic
  choosing 609.15
  remedy 662.25
eclecticism
  philosophy 451.9
  choice 609.1
  medicine 662.16
  religious ~ 984.2
eclipse n.
  obscuration 421.3
  disappearance 449.1

in eclipse
  invisible 447.4
  concealed 528.17
eclipse v. excel 33.5
  obscure 421.5
  blind 442.3
  disappear 449.2
  hide 528.10, 16
  eclipsed 447.4
ecliptic 318.8
eclogue 597.2
ecologist, oecologist 368.2
ecology, oecology
  organic science 357.5
  zoology 368.1
economical 817.4
  (parsimonious 819.4)
  be economical 817.3
  (save 636.8)
economics 693.3
economist 817.1
economize 817.3
economy method 58.3
  husbandry 693.3
  thrift 817
  (saving 670.1)
  (parsimony 819.1)
ecphonesis
  outcry 411.2
  exclamation 580.5
ecru brown 433.4
  yellow 436.6
ecstasis swoon 683.5
  trance 994.6
ecstasy delight 827.2
  (fervor 821.2)
  trance 994.6
ecstatic n. 994.14
ecstatic adj.
  fanciful 515.13
  overjoyed 827.10
  delightful 829.8
ectoderm 223.12
ectogenous 161.11
ectoplasm
  protoplasm 357.3
  luminescence 420.11
  emanation 980a.3
  (spiritualism 994.5)
ectoplasy 980a.3; 994.5
ectropion 218.1
ectype 21.1
ecumenical, oecumenical universal 78.11
  unprejudiced 498.12
ecumenical council 696.3
ecumenicity, oecumenicity 78.1
eczema 655.17
edacious 957.4
edacity 957.1
Edda 986.1
eddish 65.2
eddy n. whirl 312.2
  whirlpool 348.8
eddy v. rotate 312.7

edema — egoistic

eddy (*continued*)
 surge 348.21
edema, oedema
 swelling 194.1
 ailment 655.5
edematous, oedematous swollen 194.10
 spongy 324.9
 dropsical 655.25
Eden 515.6
 (heaven 981.1)
Edenic 981.7
edentate 254.3
edge *n.* advantage 33.2
 acrimony 171.3
 summit 210.1
 border 231
 (extremity 67.2)
 (purlieus 197.3)
 (surroundings 227.2)
 (limit 233.1)
 (side 236.1)
 (threshold 260.4)
 (shore 342.2)
 pungency 392.1
 have the edge on 33.6
 on edge 507.7
edge *v.* border 231.3
 lateralize 236.4, 5
 sharpen 253.9
 edge in 228.8, 10
 edge off 279.7
edgebone See **aitchbone**
edged
 bordered 231.5
 (fringed 256.17)
 sharp 253.11
edgestone limit 233.1
 stone 342.4
edge tool 253.6
 (arms 727.3)
edgeways, edgewise 236.8
edging
 bordering 231.2
 ornament 847.6
edgy 244.5
edible 298.49
edibles 298.5
edict 741.3
 (proclamation 531.1)
 (law 963.2)
edification
 production 161.1
 teaching 537.1
 learning 539.1
 spiritual ~ 987.2
edifice structure 161.7
 house 189.3
edificial 161.12
edify build 161.8
 educate 537.9
 religion 987.8
edifying
 educational 537.12
 beneficial 648.12
edile See **aedile**
edit write 590.14
 abridge 596.4

revise 658.11
edition 531.2
 (book 593.1)
editor
 journalist 593.16
 commentator 595.3
editorial 595.2
editorialize 590.14
educate 537.9
educated 490.15
 (taught 537.13)
 (skilled 698.13)
 be educated 539.3
educatee 541.1
education 537.1
 (learning 490.2; 539.1)
 (preparation 673.1)
educational 537.12
 (informative 527.13)
 (pedagogic 540.7)
 (scholarly 541.9)
 (schoolish 542.9)
educator 540.1
educatress 540.2
educe 481a.3
educt 40.3
eduction
 decrement 39a
 result 40.3
edulcorate
 sweeten 396.7
 purify 652.9
edulcoration
 sweetening 396.6
 purification 652.2
Eduskunta 696.5
eel 248.2
eellike 248.6
eelspear
 edge tool 253.6
 spear 727.5
eerie, eery 980a.4
efface 552.2
effacement 552.1
effect *n.* result 154
 (sequel 65.1)
 (eventuality 151.1)
 (product 161.6)
 musical ~ 415.20
 appearance 448.4
 meaning 516.1
 be the effect of 154.3
 go into effect 729.4
 in effect 5.8
 (truly 494.15)
 put into effect
 do 680.6
 effectuate 729.2
 to that effect 522.9
effect *v.* induce 153.7
 do 680.6
 complete 729.2
effective
 substantial 3.4
 able 157.9
 influential 175.10
 effectual 644.7
 practical 646.5
effectively
 energetically 171.13

with effect 175.11
effects
 belongings 780.1
 (equipment 634.1)
 merchandise 798.1
effectual able 157.9
 operative 170.4
 influential 175.10
 effective 644.7
 (adequate 639.6)
effectually
 mainly 50.11
 by and large 52.15
effectuate 729.2
 (effect 154.2)
effectuation
 production 161.1
 performance 680.1
 completion 729.1
effeminacy 160a
effeminate *n.* 160a.3
effeminate *v.* 160.4
effeminate *adj.*
 hermaphrodite 83.12
 unmanly 160a.5
 (weak 160.10)
 (female 374.11)
 (cowardly 862.4)
effemination 160a.2
effeminize geld 38.7
 feminize 160a.4
 (unman 158.7)
effendi 877.2
effervesce
 leaven 320.6
 bubble 353.8
effervescence
 bubbling 353.3
 (activity 171.2)
 (agitation 315.2)
 excitement 825.3
effervescent
 agitated 315.13
 airy 338.11
 bubbling 353.10
effervescive 353.10
effete aged 128.8
 nugatory 158.11
 weak 160.12
 useless 645.8
 worn out 659.12
efficacious able 157.9
 operative 170.4
 influential 175.10
 effectual 644.7
efficacy ability 157.2
 utility 644.1
 competence 698.1
efficiency
 ability 157.2
 utility 644.1
 proficiency 698.1
efficient able 157.9
 operative 170.4
 businesslike 625.11
 effectual 644.7
 competent 698.12
effigy copy 21.1
 figure 554.4
efflation 349.1
efflorescence

flowing 161.4
 incrustation 223.16
 pulverulence 330.1
 powder 330.3
efflorescent 330.8
effluence 295.1
 (flow 348.2)
effluent *n.* 348.1
effluent *adj.* 295.9
effluviate 398.5
effluvious 398.8
effluvium fume 334.2
 odor 398.1
 miasma 663.5
 spiritual ~ 980a.3
efflux 295.1
efform 240.6
efformation
 production 161.1
 formation 240.1, 3
effort attempt 675.1
 action 680.2
 exertion 686.1
 make an effort 675.3
effrontery 885.2
effulge 420.17
effulgence 420.1
effulgent 420.22
effuse 295.7
effusion egress 295.1
 evacuation 297.5
 excretion 299.1
 loquacity 584.1
 (diffuseness 573.1)
effusive
 egressive 295.9
 loquacious 584.5
eft 366.18
eftsoon
 subsequently 117.4
 soon 132.15
e.g. 82.14
egad 535.8
egest 297.13
egesta 299.2
egestion 297.5
egestive 297.22
egg *n.* rudiment 153.3
 food 298.28
 ovum 357.4
egg *v.*
 egg on urge 615.7
 hasten 684.2
egg and dart 847.4
egg glass 114.6
eggplant 298.30
egg-shaped 247.9
 (spheric 249.7)
eggshell shell 223.16
 fragility 328.2
eggshell porcelain 384.14
egg white 352.3
ego self 79.4
 (mind 450.3)
 psyche 994.11
egohood 79.4
egoism 880.1
egoist 880.3
 (boaster 884.3)
 (self-seeker 943.2)
egoistic 880.6

826

egotism — electromechanics

egotism 880.1
  (selfishness 943.1)
egotistical
  opinionated 606.7
  vain 880.6
  (selfish 943.4)
egregious
  unconformable 83.9
  absurd 497.4
  exaggerated 549.3
  important 642.10
  eminent 873.18
egregiously
  remarkably 31.21
  eminently 33.10
egress *n.* 295.1, 5
  (departure 293.1)
  (ejection 297.1)
  (extraction 301.1)
  (passage 302.1)
  (escape 671.1)
egress *v.* 295.6
  (escape 671.6)
egression 295.1
egret bird 366.22
  ornamentation 847.3
egurgitate 297.18
Egypt 182.3
Egyptian 560.4
Egyptologist 122.5
eiderdown
  coverlet 223.9
  softness 324.3
eidolon idea 453.1
  phantom 980a.1
  idol 991.4
eidouranion 318.10
eight 98.4
Eighteenth Amendment 761.1
eighth 98.18
eight-oar 273.4
eighty 98.7
Eileithyia 161.3
Einstein theory 451.11
eisegesis 523.1
eisegetical 523.3
eisteddfod
  assembly 72.2
  musical performance 415.17
either 609.17
ejaculate eject 297.8
  (project 284.11)
  cry out 411.7
  exclaim 580.9
ejaculation
  ejection 297.1
  (projection 284.2)
  evacuation 297.5
  outcry 411.2
  exclamation 580.5
ejaculative, ejaculatory 284.16
eject eliminate 42.4
  expel 297.8
  (displace 185.2)
  (project 284.11)
  (exude 295.7)
  (extract 301.5)
  (discard 678.3)
  (dispossess 789.11)

ejecta, ejectamenta 299.2
ejection
  elimination 42.2
  expulsion 297
  (exclusion 55.1)
  (displacement 185.1)
  (projection 284.2)
  (egress 295.1)
  (extraction 301.1)
  excretion 299.1
ejective 297.22
  (egressive 295.9)
  (excretory 299.10)
ejector 297.6
eke *v.* 35.3
eke out fill 52.7
  protract 110.6
eke *adv.* 37.8
ekka 272.4
elaborate *v.*
  perfect 658.8
  prepare the way 673.6
  complete 729.2
elaborate *adj.*
  high-wrought 673.11
  laborious 686.10
elaboration
  preparation 673.1
  completion 729.1
  ornamentation 847.1
élan 276.2
eland 366.10
élan vital 359.2
elapse 109.3
  (continue 106.2)
  (pass 122.6)
elapsed 122.8
elapsing 109.4
elastic *n.* 325.2
elastic *adj.*
  flexible 324.6
  springy 325.5
  be elastic 325.3
  (recoil 277.3)
elasticity
  strength 159.1
  flexibility 324.1
  springiness 325
  (recoil 277.1)
elasticize 325.4
elate *v.* cheer 836.6
  make proud 878.5
elate, elated *adj.*
  overjoyed 827.10
  cheerful 836.9
  jubilant 838.9
  hopeful 858.9
  proud of 878.6
  exultant 884.9
elation 880.1
elbow *n.* joint 43.3
  angle 244.2
  protuberance 250.2
  fold 258.1
  at one's elbow handy 673.11
  near 197.11

elbow *v.* angle 244.4
  impel 276.7
elbow one's way
  advance 282.2
  forge ahead 682.12
elbowchair 215.22
elbow grease
  rubbing 331.1
  labor 686.3
elbowroom
  room 180.2
  free scope 748.2
elbow shaker 621.15
elbow shaking 621.8
eld antiquity 122.2
  oldness 124.1
elderliness 128.1
elder *n.*
  old person 130.1, 5
  (veteran 700.3)
  church ~ 996.5
elder *adj.* older 124.10
  senior 128.9
elderliness 128.1
elderly 128.8
elderman 996.5
eldership 128.4
eldest oldest 124.10
  senior 128.9
El Dorado, Eldorado 803.1
Eleaticism 451.6
elect *n.* best 648.4
  Christians 987.5
elect *v.*
  choose 609.7, 11
  predestinate 976.10
  call to ministry 995.7
elect *adj.*
  destined 601.13
  select 609.16
  best 648.9
election
  mathematical permutation 84.4
  choice 609.1, 3
  holy orders 995.6
electioneering 609.3
elective 609.14, 15
  (voluntary 602.10)
elector 609.4
electoral 609.14
electorate
  constituency 609.4
  jurisdiction 737.3
electragist 158a.10
electric *n.* 272.15
electric *adj.*
  electrical 158a.12
  fast 274.13
  exciting 824.12
  excitable 825.9
electrical engineer 158a.10
electrical transcription 532a.4
electric blue 438.2
electric cable 158a.8
electric chair 975.4
electric clock, electric column 158a.6

electric current 158a.1
electric eye 158a.6
electric field 158a.1
electric heater 158a.6
electrician
  electrotechnician 158a.10
  (workman 690.10)
  stage ~ 599.17
electricity
  electrics 158a
  (fuel 388.1)
  (illuminant 420.15)
  (telephony 532a.1)
  speed 274.6
  heat 382.1
electricize 158a.11
electric light 420.7; 423.3
  (electricity 185a.1)
electric lighting 420.14
electric locomotive 158a.7
electric meter, electric railway 158a.6
electrics 158a.3
electric spark 158a.1
electric switch 158a.6
electric units 158a.5
electrification
  electricity 158a.1
  excitation 824.1
electrifier 158a.10
electrify
  electricize 158a.11
  startle 508.6
  excite 824.3
  astonish 870.3
electrifying 158a.12
electrocute 972.8
electrocution 972.4
electrocutioner 975.5
electrodynamic 158a.12
electrodynamometer 158a.6
electrokinetic 158a.12
electrolier 423.10
electroluminescence 420.11
electrolysis
  decomposition 49.2
  remedy 662.15
electrolyte 158a.6
electrolytic 662.25
electrolyzation
  decomposition 49.2
  remedy 662.15
electrolyze
  decompose 49.4
  electrify 158a.11
  ~ surgically 662.24
electromagnet
  electricity 158a.6
  attractor 288.2
electromagnetic 158a.12
electromagnetism 158a.1
electromechanics 158a.3

electrometer — emancipate 828

electrometer 158a.6
electrometric 158a.12
electrometry 158a.3
electromobile
　electricity 158a.7
　automobile 272.15
electromotion 158a.1
electromotive 158a.12
electromotivity 158a.1
electromotor 158a.7
electron
　modicum 32.2
　electricity 158a.5
　diminutive 193.2
electronegative
　158a.12
electropathy 158a.3
electrophone
　electricity 158a.6
　sound device 418.6
electrophorus 158a.6
electrophysiology
　158a.3
electroplate 223.24
electropositive, electroreceptive 158a.12
electroscope 158a.6
electroscopic, electrostatic 158a.12
electrotechnician
　158a.10
electrotechnics, electrotherapy, electrothermics 158a.3
electrotype n.
　engraving 558.3
　type 591.6
electrotype v. 558.5
electuary 662.4
eleemosynary 784.15;
　906.7
elegance
　linguistic ~ 578.1
　　(taste 850.1)
　beauty 845.1
　ornateness 847.1
　civility 894.1
elegant savory 394.7
　speech 578.4
　　(tasteful 850.5)
　beautiful 845.8
　ornate 847.13
elegiac n. 597.6
elegiac adj.
　poetry 597.1, 13
　dirgelike 839.15
　　(funereal 363.25)
elegiacs 597.1
elegiast 597.10
elegy funeral 363.4
　poem 597.2
　lamentation 839.3
element
　component 56.1
　cause 153.1
　substance 316.2
　mineral 635.6
　in one's element
　　at home 23.12
　　at ease 705.5; 748.20
　　content 831.6
elemental n. 979.7

elemental adj.
　unmixed 42.6
　beginning 66.7
elementary
　intrinsic 5.6
　unmixed 42.6
　beginning 66.7
　original 153.9
　basal 211.5
elementary school
　542.1
elements
　rudiments 66.4
　Eucharist 998.6
elemi 428.5
elench 477.2
elenchize 477.7
elephant
　behemoth 192.8
　pack animal 271.2
　　(animal 366.2)
elephantiasis 055.5
elephantine
　huge 192.15
　dull 843.5
Eleutherian 748.12
eleutherism 748.1
elevate erect 212.7
　raise 307.5
　　(heighten 206.12)
　　(improve 658.6)
　ennoble 873.13
elevated n. 627.5
elevated adj.
　high 206.13
　intoxicated 959.21
　uplifted 307.8
　　(ascendant 305.7)
　language 574.8
　exalted 873.18
　proud 878.6
　magnanimous 942.6
elevatedly 307.10
elevating 307.9
elevation
　height 206.1, 2
　raising 307
　　(ascent 305.1)
　　(improvement
　　658.1)
　~ of expression
　　574.4
　ground plan 626.2
　honor 873.3, 6
　~ of spirit 942.2
　the Elevation 998.7
elevator
　airplane 273a.10
　lift 307.3
elevatory 307.9
eleven 98.7
eleventh 98.21
eleventh hour 126.1
elf child 129.3
　dwarf 193.5
　fairy 979.9
elf child 980.6
elfenfolk 979.9
elfin dwarf 193.9
elfish 979.15
elflock 256.3
elicit induce 153.7

extract 301.6
　discover 481a.3
　　(manifest 525.2)
elide 55.3
eligible 646.4
eliminant n. 40.3
eliminant adj. 297.22
eliminate
　simplify 42.4
　　(sift 652.10)
　exclude 55.3
　eject 297.17
　extract 301.5
　discard 678.3
elimination
　simplification 42.2
　exclusion 55.1
　destruction 162.2
　evacuation 297.5
　extraction 301.1
eliminative
　egressive 295.9
　ejective 297.22
　　(excretory 299.10)
elision
　sunderance 44.2
　shortening 201.2
elite the great 873.9
　best 648.4
　nobility 875.2
　　(society 852.4)
elixir essence 5.2
　remedy 662.3, 4
elixir of life 662.3
elk 366.11
ell 200.6
ellipse 247.3
ellipsis
　shortening 201.2
　punctuation 550.8
　grammar 572.1
ellipsoid 247.3
　　(sphere 249.2)
elliptic 572.3
elliptical
　oblong 200.14
　short 201.5
　oval 247.9
elm 367.6
elocute 582.7
elocution 582.1, 2, 3
　　(diction 569.1)
elocutionary 582.12
elocutionist 582.5
elongate 200.9
elongated 200.12, 14
elongation
　distance 196.1
　lengthening 200.5
elope 623.10
elopement flight 623.2
　escape 671.1
eloper fugitive 623.5
　defaulter 808.3
eloquence 582.3
　　(loftiness 574.4)
　　(fluency 584.1)
eloquent
　meaningful 516.8
　lofty 574.8
　oratorical 582.12
　　(fluent 584.5)

be eloquent 582.8
else other 15.9
　additionally 37.8
elsehow, elseways
　18.6
elsewhere
　preoccupied 458.11
　absent 187.15
elsewhither 187.15
elsewise 18.6
elucidate
　exemplify 82.6
　make intelligible
　　518.3
　　(explain 522.6)
　illustrate 554.7
elucidation
　exemplification 82.2
　explanation 522.1
elucidative 522.8
elude quibble 477.8
　evade 623.6
　　(escape 671.6)
　　(defeat 731.9)
　　(not observe 773.3)
eludible 623.11
elusion 623.1
　　(escape 671.1)
elusive
　deceptive 545.12
　evasive 623.12
elusory
　deceptive 545.12
　untrue 546.6
　evasive 623.12
elute 652.9
elution 652.2
elutriate 652.9
elutriation 652.2
Elysian
　delightful 829.8
　paradisiac 981.7
Elysium 981.2
elytrin, elytron
　223.17
Elzevir n.
　miniature 193.3
　book 593.1
Elzevir adj. 591.8
emaciated thin 203.11
　meager 640.9
emaciation
　contraction 195.1
　thinness 203.4
　ailment 655.11
émail 438.2
emanant 295.9
emanate ensue 117.2
　result 154.3
　egress 295.6
emanation
　egress 295.1
　excretion 299.1
　exsufflation 349.1
　effervescence 353.3
　odor 398.1
　light 420.1
　spiritual ~ 980a.3
emanative 295.9
emancipate
　deliver 672.2
　disembarrass 705.4

emancipation — emissary

liberate 750.2
emancipation
  deliverance 672.1
  liberation 750.1
  (freedom 748.1)
emancipator 912.2
emasculate v. geld 38
  unman 158.7
emasculate adj. 158.10
emasculation 158.2
embalm
  ~ a corpse 363.22
  preserve 670.4
embalmer 363.6
embalmment 363.3
embankment
  shore 342.2
  roadway 627.3
  breakwater 666.4
  obstruction 706.2
  fortification 717.3
embargo n.
  deadlock 265.3
  prohibition 761.1
  blockade 893.3
embargo v. 893.7
embark begin 66.5
  ship 270.9
  depart 293.6
  (weigh anchor 267.15)
  undertake 676.2
  invest 787.5
embarkation
  ship 273.1
  departure 293.1
  (embarkment 267.2)
embarkment
  beginning 66.1
  departure 293.1
embarrass
  perplex 475.8
  bother 704.7
  hinder 706.4
embarras de richesses
  superabundance 641.1
  wealth 803.1
embarrassed 804.7
embarrassing 704.9
  (perplexing 475.12)
embarrassment
  perplexity 475.2
  predicament 704.2
  hindrance 706.1
  trouble 735.1
embassade See **ambassade**
embassador See **ambassador**
embassage 532.2
embassy
  message 532.2
  commission 755.1
  envoys 759.2
embattle 717.7
embattled
  fortified 717.9
  in battle array 722.12
embay 229.3
embed, imbed

establish 184.11
  support 215.26
  insert 300.5
  (internalize 221.8)
embedded
  located 184.17
  shut in 229.4
embedment 300.3
embellish
  speech 577.4
  ornament 847.11
embe'lishing 847.12
embellishment
  music 413.10
  ornament 847.1
ember 40.2
embers 384.15
  (coal 388.2)
embezzle 791.9
embezzlement 791.1
embezzler 792.8
embitter
  aggravate 835.2
  envenom 900.10
emblazon color 428.9
  adorn 847.11
  display 882.6
emblem 550.2, 12; 747.1
emblematic
  exemplary 82.11
  typical 550.21
  representative 554.9
embodied 316.8
embodiment
  combination 48.1
  whole 50.1
  composition 54.1
  corporealization 316.4
embody join 43.5
  combine 48.3
  form a whole 50.4
  include 76.3
  corporify 316.7
  represent 554.7
embo'den 861.7
  (hearten 858.8)
embolism
  interjection 228.2
  closure 261.1
  obstruction 706.2
embolus closure 261.1
  obstruction 706.2
embonpoint 192.4
embosom 229.3
embosomed
  located 184.17
  interjacent 228.11
  shut in 229.4
emboss boss 250.8
  engrave 558.5
  (ornament 847.11)
embossed 250.10
embosser 559.6
embossment 557.6
embouchement, embouchure 260.3
embow bow 245.3
  convex 250.8
embowed 245.5
embowel 297.16

embrace n.
  welcome 892.4
  accolade 894.4
  hug 902.3
embrace v.
  include 76.3
  surround 227.3
  adopt 609.7
  consent 762.2
  hold 781.4
  seize 789.9
  receive a friend 888.3
  welcome 892.11
  hug 902.8
  (greet 894.9)
embracement 609.1
embrangle, imbrangle 61.5
embranglement 713.4
embrasure
  battlement 257.4
  window 260.5
embrocation 662.6
embroider
  variegate 440.4
  falsify 544.3
  exaggerate 549.2
  speech 577.4
  ornament 847.11
embroidery
  adjunct 39.2
  exaggeration 549.1
  literary ~ 577.1
  redundance 641.1
  ornamentation 847.1, 6
embroil
  discompose 61.4
  set at odds 713.8
embroiled 713.10
embroilment
  turmoil 59.4
  brawl 713.4
  contest 720.2
embrown 433.3
embryo
  rudiment 153.3
  (undevelopment 674.3)
  germ 357.4
in embryo first 66.9
  original 153.9
  in preparation 673.13
  immature 674.8
embryologist 357.7
embryology
  life science 359.5
  zoology 368.1
embryonic
  beginning 66.7
  original 153.9
  infinitesimal 193.10
  germinal 357.10
  immature 674.8
embryotic 674.8
embus 293.6
emeer See **emir**
emend 658.8, 11
emendation 658.1, 3
emendatory 662.25

  (improving 658.15)
emerald n.
  green 435.2, 3
  gem 847.8
emerald adj. 435.6
emerald green n. 435.2, 4
emerald-green adj. 435.6
emeraude 435.2
emerge egress 295.6
  (depart 293.4)
  appear 446.2
emergence
  egress 295.1
  (escape 671.1)
  appearance 448.1
emergency
  crisis 134.4
  (predicament 8.3)
  (eventuality 151.1)
  emergence 295.1
emergency landing 267a.26
emergent 295.9
emeritus 928.9
emersion 295.1
emery n.
  sharpener 253.7
  mineral 635.6
emery v. 255.4
emery board, emery paper 255.3
emesis 297.5
emetic n. 297.5; 662.10
emetic adj. 662.25
émeute 742.2
emigrant alien 57.3
  migrant 268.3
  outgoer 295.4
emigrate
  migrate 266.15
  go out 295.8
emigration
  migration 266.3
  exodus 295.2
émigré alien 57.3
  migrant 268.3
  outgoer 295.4
emigree 268.3
eminence
  greatness 31.2
  height 206.1, 2
  elevation 307.1
  importance 642.1
  distinction 873.3
Eminence 996.5
eminent great 31.14
  superior 33.7
  high 206.13
  (elevated 307.8)
  important 642.10
  distinguished 873.18
eminent domain 744.1
eminently 33.10
emir, emeer
  potentate 745.5
  prince 875.7
  title 877.2
emissary
  secret agent 528.8

emission — enclosure 830

emissary (*continued*)
  delegate 758.4
  deputy 759.2
  (messenger 534.1)
emission 297.1
emissive 297.22
emit exude 295.7
  let out 297.13
  publish 531.7
  utter 580.8; 582.6
emitted, emitting
  297.22
Emmanuel 976.5
emmet 366.24
emollient *n.*
  lubricant 332.2
  balm 662.6
emollient *adj.*
  softening 324.10
  lubricant 332.5
  palliative 662.25
  relieving 834.7
emolument 973.2
  (gain 775.2)
emote 599.26
emotion 821.1
  (affection 820.1)
emotionable 822.6
emotional
  feeling 821.4
  sensitive 822.6
emotional instability,
  emotionalism 503.2
emotionalize 599.26
emotive 821.4
empale, empalement
  See **impale** etc.
empanel See **impanel**
empeirema, empirema 476.3
empennage tail 235.6
  airplane 273a.10
emperor 745.2
empery 182.1; 737.2
emphasis tone 402.2
  music 413.23
  stress 535.1
  accentuation 580.4
  give emphasis to
    642.9
emphasize
  insist upon 535.5
  accentuate 580.8
  stress 642.9
emphatic loud 404.8
  insistent 535.6
  significant 642.11
emphatically 31.21
empire country 182.1
  dominion 737.2
Empire Day 138.7
empirema See **empeirema**
empiric 548.3
empirical
  experimental 463.12
  (tentative 675.6)
  half-learned 491.13
empiricism
  philosophy 451.11
  experiment 463.2
  affectation 491.4

ethics 926.4
emplacement
  location 184.5
  platform 215.21
emplane 293.6
employ *n.*
  occupation 625.1, 4
  use 677.1
  service 749.2
employ *v.* busy 625.6
  use 677.5
  commission 755.4
  in one's employ
    746.9
  employ oneself
    busy oneself 625.7
    work 680.6
employed used 677.7
  busy 682.20
be employed in 625.7
employee, employé,
  employe
  hireling 690.2
  retainer 746.1
  functionary 758.2
employer user 677.4
  master 745.1
employment
  business 625.1
  use 677.1, 3
  operation 680.1
  work 686.3
  service 749.2
empoison infect 655.21
  poison 659.10
emporium 799.1
empower enable 157.7
  (strengthen 159.8)
  commission 755.4
  grant 760.4
empress 745.6
  (noblewoman 875.6)
  (princess 875.8)
  (title 877.2)
empressement
  eagerness 682.3
  fervor 821.2
  desire 865.2
emprise, emprize
  enterprise 676.1
  exploit 861.2
emptiness 187.3
  (depletion 640.4)
emption 795.1
emptional 795.5
emptor 795.2
empty *n.* 191.11
empty *v.*
  evacuate 297.14
  (dislocate 185.2)
  ~ one's glass 298.47
  dry 340.5
empty *adj.*
  nugatory 158.11
  void 187.11
  (unsubstantial 4.5)
  (wanting 640.11)
  incogitant 452.3
  ignorant 491.8
  empty-headed
    499.14

empty-handed 640.12
empty-headed
  mindless 450a.2
  incogitant 452.3
  scatterbrained
    458.13
  ignorant 491.8
  unintelligent 499.14
empty-headedness
  unintellectuality
    450a.1
  incogitance 452.1
  unintelligence
    499.4
empty-minded 499.14
empty-noddled,
  empty-pated,
  empty-skulled
  scatterbrained
    458.13
  unintelligent 499.14
empurple 437.3
empyreal 318.16
empyrean *n.* 318.2
empyrean *adj.*
  celestial 318.16
  delightful 829.8
empyreuma 401.1
empyreumatic 401.4
emu apple 397.2
emulate
  imitate 19.10
  vie with 648.7
  compete with 720.9
emulation 720.1
emulator 710.4
emulous 720.13
emulsification 352.2
emulsify 352.6
emulsion 352.3
emulsive 352.7
emulsoid 352.3
emunctory *n.* 295.5
emunctory *adj.* 295.9
enable empower 157.7
  grant 760.4
enablement 157.2
enact
  personate 554.8
  act out 599.26
  do 680.6
  transact 692.4
  execute 729.2
  decree 741.4
  legislate 963.4
enactment 963.2
  (decree 741.3)
enallage 521.1
enamel *n.*
  ceramics 384.14
  paint 428.5
  (coating 223.18)
enamel *v.* coat 223.24
  paint 428.10
enameler, enameller
  559.2
enamelware 384.14
enamor, enamour
  897.13
enamored, enamoured
  897.14, 15

become enamored
  897.12
enanthema 655.16
en bloc 50.10
encage, incage 751.8
encamp 184.15
encampment
  camp 189.15
  military ~ 728.2
encarnadine See **incarnadine**
encase, encasement
  See **incase** etc.
encaustic
  engraving 558.3
  writing 590.3
encaustic painting
  556.2
enceinte *n.* close 181.3
  enclosure 232.1
enceinte *adj.* 168.9
encephalitis lethargica disease 655.6
  sleep 683.5
encephalon 450.2
enchain 751.7
enchant delight 829.5
  cast a spell 992.4
enchanted
  overjoyed 827.10
  bewitched 992.7
enchanter 992.2
enchanting
  fascinating 617.4
  delightful 829.8
  attractive 845.9
  bewitching 992.6
enchantment
  allurement 617.1
  delight 827.2; 829.2
  love 897.1
  bewitchery 992.1
  spell 993.1
enchantress
  temptress 617.3
  a beauty 845.3
enchase attach 43.6
  incase 223.23
  infold 229.3
  incise 259.3
  engrave 558.5
enchasement 223.1
enchiridion 593.1
enchymatous 194.10
encincture *n.*
  surrounding 227.1
  circumscription
    229.1
  enclosure 232.1
encincture *v.* 227.3
encircle include 76.3
  surround 227.3
  (circle 247.7)
  circuit 311.3
enclasp, inclasp 229.3
enclave 181.3
enclose, inclose
  include 76.3
  surround 227.3
  circumscribe 229.2
  (internalize 221.8)
enclosure, inclosure

enclothe — energy

close 181.3
circumscription 229.1
close 232.1
  (square 189.19)
  (receptacle 191.1)
  (wrapper 223.11)
  (zone 230.2)
  (closure 261.1)
  (menagerie 370.3)
  (prison 752.1)
enclothe 225.41
encomiast 935.1
encomiastic 931.9
encomium
  approbation 931.2
  flattery 933.1
encompass
  include 76.3
  surround 227.3
  circuit 311.3
  lay siege to 716.5
encompassment
  surrounding 227.1
  besiegement 716.1
encore n. 104.2
encore v. 931.6
encore adv.
  again 104.8
  bravo! 931.13
encounter n.
  clash 276.2
  meeting 292.4
  contest 720.2
  (attack 716.1)
encounter v.
  experience 151.4
  intrude 228.10
  collide 276.9
  meet 292.10
  confront 708.3
  contend with 720.8
encourage
  incite 615.7
  help 707.11
  comfort 834.5
  give hope 858.8
  embolden 861.7
encouraging 858.11
encouragement
  motivation 615.2
  patronage 707.2
  comfort 834.2
  give encouragement 615.7
Encratism 953.2
Encratite 953.3
encraty 953.2
encrimson 434.7
encroach
  intrude 228.10
  overstep 303.5
  infringe 925.6
  impose upon 941a.2
encroachment
  intervention 228.3
  overstepping 303.1
  infringement 925.3
encrust 223.25
encuirassed 223.28
encumber, incumber
  add 37.3

weight 319.9
  burden 706.6
encumbered, incumbered
  hindered 706.9
  in debt 806.7
encumbrance, incumbrance
  weight 319.1
  impediment 706.2
encyclic 531.11
encyclical
  handbill 531.4
  letter 592.2
encyclopedia, encyclopaedia
  knowledge 490.7
  book 593.3
  (storehouse 636.4)
encyclopedic, encyclopaedic 78.9
encyst 229.2
end n.
  termination 67
  (afterpart 65.2)
  (cessation 142.1)
  (eventuality 151.1)
  (extinction 162.2)
  (edge 231.1)
  (death 360.1)
  (completion 729.1)
  final issue 154.1
  limit 233.1
  intention 620.2
  share 786.2
at the end of one's rope dying 360.9
  nonplused 475.16
  destitute 640.11
  at an impasse 704.11
  impoverished 804.7
come to an end 67.6
  (die 360.6)
end to end 199.4
from end to end
  everywhere 180.9
  lengthwise 200.16
no end of
  greatly 31.15
  multitude 102.2, 5, 6
  infinite 105.3
  long 200.12
on end 212.9
to the end
  throughout 52.15; 67.12
  (to completion 729.8)
  in order 620.6
without end
  infinite 105.3
  eternal 112.4
  always 112.5
  (infinitely 105.4)
  unlimited 180.7
  long 200.12
end v. 67.5, 6, 7
  (cease 142.1)
  (reach completion 729.4)
end in smoke
  fall through 304.2

fail 732.5
  (collapse 158.5)
end-all 50.2; 67.4
endamage 659.8
endanger 665.4
  (threaten 909.2)
endangered 665.8
endangerment 665.1
endbrain 450.2
endear 897.11, 13
endearment 902.3, 4
endeavor, endeavour n. 675.1
  (pursuit 622.1)
  (effort 686.1)
endeavor, endeavour v. 675.3
  (pursue 622.6)
endebted, endebtment
  See indebted etc.
ended 67.9
  (completed 729.6)
endemic n. 655.1
endemic adj.
  peculiar 79.8
  native 188.11
  epidemic 657.5
endenizen 184.16
ender 67.4
enderon 223.12
en déshabillé 225.47
endew See endue
ending n. 67.1
ending adj. 67.8
  (completing 729.5)
endive 298.30
endless
  continuous 69.6
  infinite 105.3
  (numerous 102.5)
  eternal 112.4
  (durable 110.9)
  unlimited 180.7
endlessly 112.5
endlong 200.15
end man
  minstrel 416.10
  blackface actor 599.19
endocrinology 221.6
endogenous
  herbal 367.14
  botanic 369.11
endome 223.22
end on 267.64
endoplasm 357.3
endorse, indorse
  confirm 467.9
  ratify 488.10
  (guarantee 771.6)
  second 707.8
  approve 931.5
endorsee, indorsee 270.5
endorsement, indorsement
  ratification 488.4
  (acceptance 771.3)
  signature 550.11
  inscription 551.1
endorser, indorser 488.5

endosmosic 302.3
endosmosis 302.1
endosmotic 302.3
endothelium 223.12
endow empower 157.7
  dower 784.13
endowed
  talented 698.13
  possessing 777.7
endowment
  character 5.4
  talent 698.2
  (ability 157.2)
  bestowal 784.1, 6
endue, endew
  empower 157.7
  clothe 225.41
  surround 227.3
endurable 110.9
endurance
  durability 110.1
  permanence 141.1
  perseverance 604a.1
  sufferance 826.4
endure last 106.2
  (be durable 110.5)
  be eternal 112.2
  be permanent 141.4
  (exist 1.4)
  continue 143.2
  persevere 604a.2
  bear 826.6
  (be content 831.3)
  forgive 918.3
not to be endured 830.18
enduring
  permanent 141.6
  remembered 505.18
  persevering 604a.3
  forbearant 826.10
endways, endwise
  lengthwise 200.15
  vertically 212.9
enema clyster 300.4
  syringe 337.3
enemy time 106.1
  foe 891
  (opponent 710.1)
energetic
  vigorous 171.9
  (potent 157.8)
  active 682.16
  industrious 682.19
  make energetic 171.7
energetically 171.13
energic, energico 171.9
energid 171.6
energist 171.4
energize
  electrify 158a.11
  give energy 171.7
  (strengthen 159.8)
  vivify 359.8
energizer 171.4
energizing 171.11
energumen
  madman 504.1, 2
  devotee 840.19
energy vigor 171
  (potence 157.1)

enervate — enough 832

energy (*continued*)
 (strength 159.1)
 (exertion 686.1)
 activity 682.1
enervate 158.7
 (weaken 160.8)
enervated
 unmanned 158.10
 language 575.2
enervation
 weakening 160.2
 feeble style 575.1
enface 590.13
en famille 892.13
enfeeble weaken 160.8
 sicken 655.22
enfeebled 688.6
enfeeblement 160.2
enfeoff 783.3
enfeoffment 783.1
enfilade rake 200.11
 perforate 260.14
 pass through 302.2
enflame See **inflame**
enfold, enfoldment
 See **infold** etc.
enforce urge 615.7
 enjoin 695.5
 compel 744.2
 require 924.7
enforcement 744.1
enframement 231.1
enfranchise
 give franchise
  748.10
 liberate 750.2
 grant 760.4
enfranchised 924.10
enfranchisement
 freedom 748.1
 liberation 750.1
 privilege 922.2
engage
 pre-engage 132.5
 induce 615.9
 occupy 625.6
 fight 720.8
 commission 755.4
 promise 768.3
 (undertake 676.2)
 (contract 769.5)
engage in
 busy oneself with
  625.7
 undertake 676.2
 (pursue 622.6)
engaged
 intent on 457.9
 busy 682.20
 betrothed 768.7
become engaged
 768.4
be engaged
 be otherwise occu-
  pied 135.3
 be doing 625.7
engagement
 office 625.4
 undertaking 676.1
 contest 720.2
 promise 768.2
 (contract 769.1)

transaction 794.3
 social ~ 892.3
engagement book
 memorandum book
  505.6
 notebook 551.3
engagement ring 902.5
engaging
 alluring 617.5
 delightful 829.8
 attractive 845.9
engarrison 717.7
engender 161.10
engild 436.5
engine
 automobile 272.16
 machine 633.2
 types of ~ 633.3
engine driver 268.11
engineer
 engineman 268.11
 craftsman 690.5
 military ~ 726.4
engineering 633.2
engineman 268.11
 (workman 690.10)
enginery 633.2
engird 227.3
England 182.3
English *n.* 560.4
English *adj.*
 British 188.11
 language 560.9
Eng'ish horn 417.4
Englishman 188.9
English-speaking
 582.11
engobe 428.5
engorge
 swallow 296.3
 overeat 957.3
engorgement
 reception 296.1
 overfullness 641.1
 satiety 869.1
engraft, ingraft
 attach 43.6
 infix 300.6
 (add 37.3)
 ~ plants 371.8
 inculcate 537.9
engrafted, ingrafted
 613.12
engrail 256.11
engrain 847.11
en grand seigneur
 878.8
engrave incise 259.3
 enchase 558.5
 (mark 550.19)
 (depict 554.7)
 (print 591.14)
 (ornament 847.11)
engraved 558.6
engraver 559.6
 (workman 690.10)
engraving 558.3
 (marking 550.7)
 (representation
  554.1)
engross absorb 451.30

~ **the thoughts**
 457.6
 write 590.13
 possess 777.5
engrossed
 thoughtful 451.36
 ~ in 457.9
 preoccupied 458.11
engrossment
 preoccupation 458.3
 writing 590.3
 possession 777.2
engu'f, ingulf
 destroy 162.4
 swallow 296.3
 submerge 310.5
 overfill 641.4
engulfment 310.2
enhance increase 35.3
 exaggerate 549.2
 improve 658.8
enhancement
 increase 35.1
 expansion 194.1
 improvement 658.1
enharmonic *n.* 413.9
enharmonic *adj.*
 413.28; 415.28
enharmonic diesis
 413.11
enigma 533.2
 (complexity 59.3)
 (question 461.10)
 (ignorance 491.2)
 (unintelligibility
  519.2)
 (concealment 528.6)
 (dilemma 704.4)
enigmatic 533.6
 (complex 59.10)
 (perplexing 475.12)
 (unintelligible
  519.6)
enisle 346.3
enjoin advise 695.5
 command 741.4
 impose a duty 926.7
enjoy
 ~ physically 377.4
 relish 394.6
 possess 777.4
 ~ mentally 827.6
enjoy oneself 827.5
enjoyer 677.4
enjoyment 827.1
enkindle
 stimulate 171.7
 inflame 173.8
 ignite 384.17
 excite 824.2
enlarge increase 35.3
 (reinforce 37.4)
 expand 194.5, 8
 (be increased 35.4)
 (stretch 325.3)
 (exaggerate 549.2)
 ~ the mind 537.9
 expatiate 573.5
 liberate 750.2
enlarged 35.5
enlargement
 increase 35.1

expansion 194.1
 (exaggeration
  549.1)
 expatiation 573.4
 liberation 750.1
enleagued 48.6
enlighten
 illuminate 420.20
 inform 527.7
 (explain 522.6)
 (teach 537.9)
enlightened 490.15
 (wise 498.11)
en'ightener 527.5
enlightenment
 lighting 420.14
 learning 490.2
 information 527.1
 instruction 537.1
enlist appoint 609.11
 engage 615.9
 use 677.5
 side with 709.5
 (second 707.8)
 become a member
  712.8
 (join 43.5)
 (~ in the army
  722.11)
 commission 755.4
enliven
 stimulate 171.7
 cheer 836.6
 amuse 840.20
enlivenment
 invigoration 159.2
 refreshment 689.1
en masse wholly 50.10
 co-operatively
  709.8
enmesh ensnare 545.9
 ~ in difficulty 704.6
enmist 422.6
enmity 889
 (discord 713.1)
 (dislike 867.1)
 (hatred 898.1)
 (malevolence 907.1)
ennea-, enne- 98.19
ennead 98.5
enneahedral 98.19
enneastyle *n.* 98.5
enneastyle *adj.* 98.19
ennoble 873.13
ennui 841.1
enormity
 greatness 31.1
 hugeness 192.3
 crime 947.2
enormous vast 31.8
 huge 192.15
enormously 31.20
enough *n.* 639.1
 have **enough** 639.3;
  869.5
 (feel disgust 867.5)
enough *adj.* 639.6
enough and to spare
 plenty 639.2, 7
 redundance 641.1, 5
 liberality 816.1
good enough

enough — entrancing

tolerable 648.11
bravo! 931.13
more than enough
  redundance 641.1, 7
  satiety 869.1
not enough 640.8
enough *int.*
  cease! 142.8
  (that's sufficient!
    639.9)
  don't! 761.6
  satiety 869.8
en passant
  in passing 111.8;
    302.4
  by the way 134.11
  on the way 270.13
enquire, enquirer etc.
  See inquire etc.
enrage vex 830.5
  aggravate 835.2
  anger 900.11
en rapport related 9.6
  agreeing 23.9
  in accord 714.4
enrapture
  lure 617.4
  delight 829.5
  enamor 897.13
enraptured
  overjoyed 827.10
  in love 897.14
enravish 829.5
enravished 827.10
enravishing
  alluring 617.5
  delightful 829.8
  attractive 845.9
enravishment
  intoxication 824.1
  delightfulness 829.2
enrich speech 577.4
  improve 658.8
  richen 803.7
  ornament 847.11
enrichment 658.1
enrobe 225.41
enroll, enrol list 86.3
  record 551.8
  become a member
    712.8
  (enlist in the army
    722.11)
  commission 755.4
enrollment, enrolment
  551.7
en route 270.13; 282.5
ens 1.1
ensample
  prototype 22.1
  example 82.2
  warning 668.1
ensanguine 440a.2
ensanguined 361.15
ensate 253.15
ensconce
  conceal 528.10
  protect 664.6
ensconced 184.17
ensemble all 50.2
  ~ of musicians
    416.9, 12

choir 416.12
ensepulcher, ensepulchre 363.20
enshrine infold 229.3
  inter 363.20
  glorify 873.13
  consecrate 987.8
  deify 991.6
enshrinement
  glorification 873.6
  consecration 987.8
  deification 991.2
ensiform 253.15
ensign
  emblem 550.2, 12, 13
  standard-bearer
    726.4
  officer 745.11, 12
  ~ of authority
    747.1
ensilage 298.7
enslave 749.5
enslaved 749.6
enslavement 749.1
ensnare, insnare 545.9
  (ambush 530.5)
  (lure 617.4)
  (seize 789.9)
ensphere 227.3
enstamp
  engrave 558.5
  print 591.14
ensue succeed 63.3
  be subsequent 117.2
  eventuate 151.3
  result 154.3
ensuing
  succeeding 63.5
  later 117.3
ensure 474.6
entablature 210.4
entail cause 153.6
  tie up 781.4
entailed 780.8
entangle
  complicate 61.5
  interlace 219.8
  ensnare 545.9
  ~ in difficulty 704.7
  set at odds 713.8
entangled 59.10
  (difficult 704.8)
entanglement
  complexity 59.3
  (network 219.4)
  (dilemma 704.4, 5)
  fortification 717.3
  love affair 897.3
entasia spasm 315.7
  illness 655.3
entelechy 161.5
entente cordiale
  agreement 23.4
  concord 714.1
  compact 769.1
  cordiality 888.1
enter begin 66.5
  list 86.3
  converge 290.2
  go in 294.6
  (intrude 228.10)
  (arrive 292.7)

record 551.8
  ~ the stage 599.26
  become a member
    712.8
  ~ accounts 811.7
enter into
  be a component 56.2
  (participate 778.5)
  be included 76.2
enter on, enter upon
  begin 66.5
  undertake 676.2
  set to work 686.7
enter the lists 720.8
enteric fever 655.6
entering 294.8
**enteritis, enterography, enteropathy,
enterotomy** 221.6
enterprise *n.*
  undertaking 676.1
  (pursuit 622.1)
  (business 625.1)
  initiative 682.4
  exploit 861.2
enterprise *v.* 676.2
enterpriser 694.1
enterprising
  active 682.18
  (energetic 171.9)
  courageous 861.9
entertain
  ~ an idea 451.31
  bear in mind 457.4
  ~ a feeling 821.3
  amuse 840.20
  ~ guests 892.11
entertaining 840.22
entertainment
  repast 298.34
  theatrical ~ 599.8
  amusement 840.1
  party 892.5
entêté 606.6
enthrall, enthral
  enslave 749.5
  confine 751.8
enthrallment, enthralment
  subjection 749.1
  confinement 751.2
enthrone install 755.4
  exalt 873.13
enthronement
  coronation 755.2
  exaltation 873.6
enthusiasm
  craze 503.7
  vehemence 574.3
  eagerness 682.3
  fervor 821.2
  hopefulness 858.2
enthusiast
  fanatic 504.2
  (live wire 682.10)
  idealist 515.7
  devotee 840.19
  votary 865.7
enthusiastic
  fanatical 503.18
  rhapsodic 515.13
  ardent 821.6

(willing 602.8)
  hopeful 858.9
  eager 865.9
enthymematic 476.17
enthymeme 476.5
entice 617.4
enticement 617.1
entincture 41.8
entire *n.* all 50.2
  stallion 271.3
  male animal 373.6
entire *adj.* whole 50.6
  complete 52.9
entirely wholly 50.10
  (fully 31.17)
  completely 52.13
entirety whole 50.1
  completeness 52.1
entitle name 564.6
  warrant 760.4
  (give a right 924.8)
entitled 924.5, 11
entitlement 924.1
entity existence 1.1
  integer 87.3
entomb, intomb
  inter 363.20
  confine 751.8
entombment, intombment
  interment 363.1
  confinement 751.2
entomologist 368.2
entomology 368.1
entomotomist 368.2
entomotomy 368.1
entourage 227.2
entozoan, entozoon
  193.4
entrails vitals 221.4
  intestines 350.4
entrain 293.6
entrammel
  impede 706.4
  fetter 751.7
entrance *n.*
  vestibule 191.17
  portal 260.4
  ship 273.7
  ingress 294.1, 5
  (insertion 300.1)
  reception 296.1
entrance *v.*
  delight 829.5
  cast a spell 992.4
  place in a trance
    994.19
entranced
  dreaming 515.14
  overjoyed 827.10
entrancement
  intoxication 824.1
  delightfulness 829.2
  bewitchment 992.1
  spell 993.1
entranceway
  vestibule 191.7
  (path 627.2)
  portal 260.4
  inlet 294.5
entrancing
  alluring 617.5

entrant — equal

entrancing (*cont'd*)
  delightful 829.8
  attractive 845.9
  bewitching 992.6
entrant *n.*
  incomer 294.4
  novice 541.6
  contestant 710.4
entrant *adj.* 294.8
entrap 545.9
entreat 765.5
  (offer 763.2)
  (ask pity 914.5)
entreaty
  beseechment 765.2
  prayer 990.3
entrée, entrée
  ingress 294.1
  reception 296.1
  food 298.38
entrench, intrench
  ~ on 303.5
  safeguard 664.6
  fortify 717.7
entrenchment, intrenchment
  trench 259.2
  overstepping 303.1
  channel 350.1
  fortification 717.3
entrepôt
  storehouse 636.4
  mart 799.1
entrepreneur
  impresario 599.17
  director 694.1
entrust, intrust
  commission 755.4
  (grant 760.4)
  commit 784.12
  invest 787.5
  credit 805.4
entry vestibule 191.17
  portal 260.4
  race horse 271.8
  ingress 294.1, 5
  reception 296.1
  record 551.1, 7
  item 811.2
  make an entry
  record 551.8
  accounting 811.7
entryway portal 260.4
  inlet 294.5
  (conduit 350.1)
entwine, intwine 219.8
  (convolve 248.3)
enucleate 522.6
enucleation 522.1
enumerate
  compute 37.5
  include 76.3
  number 85.7
enumeration 85.1
enunciate
  proclaim 531.7
  declare 535.3
  pronounce 580.8
  speak 582.6
enunciation
  proclamation 531.1
  declaration 535.1

utterance 580.3
  (diction 569.1)
  delivery 582.3
enunciative
  promulgatory 531.11
  vocal 580.11
enunciator
  proclaimer 531.5
  announcer 534.1
enunciatory 531.11
enure See **inure**
envelop *v.* wrap 223.23
  clothe 225.41
  infold 229.3
envelope, envelop *n.*
  wrapper 223.11
  (enclosure 232.1)
  aerostat 273a.12
envenom infect 655.22
  poison 659.10
  aggravate 835.2
  excite hatred 898.4
  anger 900.10
envenomed
  poisonous 657.3
  malevolent 907.6
envious 921.3
  (jealous 920.3)
environ 227.3
environal 184.18
environment 227.1, 2
environmental 184.18
environs 227.2
  (nearness 197.3)
envisage 220.6
envoy delegate 758.4
  ambassador 759.2
  (messenger 534.1)
envy *n.* 921
  (jealousy 920.1)
envy *v.* 921.2
  (be jealous 919.2)
enwrap, inwrap
  cover 223.23
  clothe 225.41
  infold 229.3
  engross 451.30
enzyme, enzym 320.3
enzymic 320.8
eolian See **aeolian**
eolith 124.2
Eolus See **Aeolus**
eon See **aeon**
Eos 125.1
epacme 62.1
epact era 108.2
  excess 641.1
epagoge 476.1
epagogic 476.17
eparch 745.9
epaulet, epaulette
  insignia 747.4
  decoration 847.3
epenthetic 228.12
ephemeral *n.* 111.4
ephemeral *adj.* 111.6
ephemerality 111.1
ephemerid
  ephemeral 111.4
  insect 366.24
ephemeris
  calendar 114.5

record 551.3
  journal 593.6
ephemeron 111.4
ephialtes 828.7
ephor 967.1
epic *n.*
  narrative 594.2
  poem 597.2
epic *adj.* 594.7; 597.13
epicarp 223.15
epicedial 839.15
epicedium 839.3
epicene *n.* 83.5
epicene *adj.*
  multiform 81.2
  hermaphrodite 83.12
épicier 851.4
epicranium 210.3
epicure
  connoisseur 850.3
  sensualist 954a.1
  gourmand 957.1
epicurean *n.*
  connoisseur 850.3
  sensualist 954a.1
  gourmand 957.2
epicurean *adj.* 954.4
epicureanism
  sensualism 954.1
  gluttony 957.1
Epicureanism 451.8
epicurism eating 298.1
  virtuosity 850.2
  (fastidiousness 868.1)
epicycle 247.4
epicyclic train 633.2
epicycloid 247.4
epidemic *n.* 655.2
epidemic *adj.*
  prevalent 78.10; 639.7
  contagious 657.5
epidermic 223.32
epidermis 223.12
epigenesis 161.2
epigram 496.1
  (witticism 842.4)
epigrammatic 572.3
epigrammatist 844
epigrammatize 496.4
epigraph 550.5
epilepsy
  twitching 315.6
  illness 655.3, 14
epilogue, epilog
  sequel 65.1
  (end 67.1)
  drama 599.5
Epimenides 500.3
Epiphany 998.13
epiphenomenon 994.3
episcopal 995.9
Episcopalian *n.* 984.14
episcopalian *adj.* 995.9
episcopalianism 995.1
episcopacy 995.1, 2
episcopal ring 999.1
episcopate 995.3
episode adjunct 39.1
  discontinuity 70.1

event 151.1
  digression 573.3
episodic
  incidental 10.8
  parenthetical 228.11
  digressive 573.7
epistemology 451.4
epistle 592.2
  (telegram 532a.3)
Epistle part of the Mass 998.7
  Scripture 985.4
Epistle side 238.2
epistolarian *n.* 592.5
epistolarian *adj.* 592.7
epistolize 592.6
epistyle 210.4
epitaph 363.16; 550.5
epitasis spasm 315.7
  illness 655.3
epithalamic 903.14
epithalamium 903.3
epithelium 223.12
epithem, epithema, epitheme 662.14
epithet name 564.2
  oath 908.3
epitome 596.1
  (abbreviation 201.2)
  (conciseness 572.1)
  in epitome
  in a word 572.4
  in short 596.6
epitomist 201.3
epitomization 201.2
epitomize
  shorten 201.4
  abridge 596.4
epitomizer 201.3
epizootic *n.* 655.18
epizootic *adj.* 657.5
epoch 108.2
epochal 138.10
epode 597.2
eponym 564.2
eponymy 562.4
epopee 597.1, 2
epopoean 597.13
epopoeia 597.1, 2
epopoeist 597.10
epoptae 996.10
epos 597.2
Epsom salts 662.9
epulation 298.1
epurate 652.9
epuration 652.2
equable uniform 16.5
  moderate 174.6
equal *n.* match 27.5
  (synonym 516.3)
  substitute 147.2
equal *v.* 27.6
equal on a par 27.8
  (compensative 30.6)
  (synonymous 516.11)
  parallel 216.5
  symmetrical 242.4
  adequate 639.6
  equitable 941.3
  equal to able 157.9

prepared for 673.11
competent 698.12
satisfactory 831.7
not equal to 699.15
render equal 27.7
  (harmonize 23.8)
equaling, equalling 27.3
equality 27
  (identity 13.1)
equalization 27.3
  (compensation 30.1)
equalize adjust 27.7
  (compensate 30.4)
  level 213.6
  smooth 255.4
equalized 27.9
equally 27.10
equanimity 826.3
equate 27.7
equation
  equalization 27.3
  mathematics 85.4
equator middle 68.2
  map line 550.9
equatorial 68.5
equerry
  stockman 370.4
  retainer 746.1
equestrian n. 268.8
equestrian adj. 271.12
equestrienne 268.8
equibalanced 27.9
equidistance n.
  middle 68.3
  (interjacence 228.1)
  parallelism 216.1
equidistance v. 216.4
equidistant 216.5
equilibration 27.3
equilibrium
  equivalence 27.2
  stability 150.1
equine n. 271.3
equine adj.
  equestrian 270.12
  animal 366.26
equinoctial circle, equinox 318.8
equip clothe 225.42
  furnish 634.2
  (provide 637.4)
  (prepare 673.6)
equipage vehicle 272.8
  accouterments 634.1
  (effects 780.5)
equiparant
  related 9.6
  equal 27.8
equipment
  accouterments 634
  preparation 673.1
equipoise, equipollence 27.2
equipollent n. 27.5
equipollent adj. 27.9
equiponderance 27.2
equiponderant 27.2
equiponderate 319.8
equipped 634.3
  (provided 637.6)

(prepared 673.11)
equisetaceous 369.11
equitable 941.3
  (unprejudiced 498.12)
equitant 223.30
equitation 266.7
equity justice 941.1
  law 963.2
equivalence
  equality 27.2
  (sameness 13.2)
  (similarity 17.1)
  ~ of meaning 516.3
equivalent n.
  analogue 17.5
  equal 27.5
  (synonym 516.3)
  compensation 30.2
  substitute 147.2
equivalent v. 27.7
equivalent adj.
  correlative 12.6
  tantamount 27.9
  (coincident 13.7)
  (analogous 17.11)
  (compensative 30.6)
  (synonymous 516.11)
equivocacy 475.1
equivocal
  uncertain 475.9
  ambiguous 520.5
  (obscure 519.7)
  be equivocal 520.4
equivocality
  uncertainty 475.1
  ambiguity 520.1, 2
equivocalness 520.1
equivocate
  quibble 477.8
  (be circumlocutory 573.5)
  (evade 623.6)
  employ ambiguity 520.3
  prevaricate 544.5
equivocation
  quibbling 477.4
  (equivocalness 520.1)
  (circumlocution 573.3)
  (tergiversation 607.1)
  (evasion 623.1)
  prevarication 544.1
equivocator
  quibbler 477.6
  (waverer 605.3)
  (tergiversator 607.4)
  dissembler 548.1, 5
equivoque, equivoke
  equivocation 477.4
  ambiguity 520.1, 2
  wordplay 842.5
  double-entendre 851.3
era 108.2
  (date 114.4)
eradicate

exclude 55.3
  destroy 162.4
  eject 297.17
  extract 301.5
eradication
  exclusion 55.1
  destruction 162.2
  extraction 301.1
erase excise 38.5
  destroy 162.4
  rub out 331.3
  kill 361.10
  obliterate 552.2
Erastian 984.14
Erastianism 984.4
erasure rubbing 331.1
  obliteration 552.1
Erato 416.16
ere 116.5
ere long 132.15
ere now
  previously 116.5
  formerly 122.14
Erebus 982.4
erect v. build 161.8
  upend 212.7
  raise 307.5
erect adj.
  vertical 212.8
  uplifted 307.8
  stand erect 212.6
erectile 307.9
erection
  production 161.1, 7
  house 189.3
  elevation 212.4
  raising 307.1
erective 307.9
erectly 307.10
erectness 212.1
erector 307.2
eremite 893.4
eremitic 893.9
eremitism 893.2
erenow
  previously 116.5
  formerly 122.14
Eretrian school 451.7
erewhile, erewhiles
  previously 116.5
  formerly 122.14
erg
  electricity 158a.5
  energy 171.6
ergal 171.1
ergo 155.5
ergophobia 683.3
ergotism 476.2
ergotize reason 476.11
  demur 485.7
  object 489.4
Erinyes
  Furies 900.4
  mythical beings 980.5
Erinys 173.6
eriometer 445.1
eristic 476.9
eristical 476.14
Eristic school 451.7
ermelin, ermilin 223.12

ermine pelt 223.12
  animal 366.17
  malodor 401.2
  robe of state 747.2
erne, ern 366.22
erode decrease 36.3
  decompose 49.3
  disintegrate 659.7
Eros love 897.1, 4
  god 979.2
erosion 49.1; 659.2
  (pulverization 330.2)
erotic amorous 897.14
  concupiscent 961.11
err be wrong 495.7
  (misjudge 481.5)
  (misinterpret 523.2)
  sin 945.9
errability 475.4
errable 475.14
errancy 475.4
errand message 532.2
  task 625.2
  commission 755.1
errant
  deviative 279.8
  erroneous 495.12
errata 593.7
erratic n. 504.3
erratic adj.
  irregular 139.2
  deviative 279.8
  eccentric 503.17
  (inconstant 149.6)
  (capricious 608.5)
erraticism 503.6
  (capriciousness 608.2)
erratum 495.2
errhine n. 349.18
errhine adj. 349.30
erroneous 495.12
  (illogical 477.10)
  (false 544.7)
  (untrue 546.6)
  (imperfect 651.4)
  (abortive 732.8)
  (heterodox 984.22)
be erroneous 495.6
error fallacy 495
  (sophistry 477.1, 2)
  (misjudgment 481.1)
  (misinterpretation 523.1)
  (falsehood 544.1; 546.1)
  (misrepresentation 555.1)
  (fault 651.2)
  (wrong 923.1)
  (heterodoxy 984.1)
  mistake 495.2
  sinfulness 945.1
  sin 947.2
be in error 495.7
in error 495.13
ersatz 147.2
erst 122.10, 14

erstwhile — estrangement

erstwhile, erstwhiles 122.14
erubescence 434.1, 4
erubescent 434.13
eruct, eructate 297.20
eructation 297.5
erudite 490.15
  (wise 498.11)
erudition 490.2
erumpent 295.9
eruption
  outbreak 173.2
  (debacle 162.3)
  egress 295.1
  evacuation 297.5
  detonation 406.2
  outburst of passion 825.5
eruptive 295.9
eruptivity 297.5
erysipelas, erythema 655.17
erythroblast 357.3
escadrille 726.10
escalade *n.*
  ascent 305.1
  attack 716.1
escalade *v.*
  climb 305.5
  attack 716.5
escalator 307.3
  (stairs 305.2)
escalier 305.2
escalop, escallop *n.*
  curl 248.2
  serration 257.2
escalop, escallop *v.*
  curl 248.3
  notch 257.5
escaloped, escalloped 257.6
escapable 623.11
escapade caprice 608.1
  frolic 840.3
escape *n.* 671
  (egress 295.1)
  (flight 623.2)
  (refuge 666.3)
  (deliverance 672.1)
  (liberation 750.1)
escape *v.*
  get away 671.6
  (find vent 295.7)
  (elude 623.6, 10)
  (be safe 664.4)
  (go free 750.4)
  forget 506.4
escaped 671.7
  (free 748.12)
escapee 671.5
escapement 671.1
escaper, escapist 671.5
escarp trench 259.2
  fortification 717.3
escarpment
  stratum 204.1
  precipice 212.3
eschar lamina 204.2
  incrustation 223.16
escharotic *n.* 384.11
escharotic *adj.*

acrid 171.10
pungent 392.5
escheat *n.*
  reversion 145.1
  forfeiture 974.2
escheat *v.* 145.4
escheatment 974.2
eschew
  have no use for 867.4
  abstain 953.5
eschewal 953.2
escopette, escopet 727.10
escort *n.*
  accompanier 88.4
  (lover 897.6)
  guardian 664.3
  guard 717.6
escort *v.* 88.7
  (precede 280.2)
  (protect 664.6)
escritoire 191.15
escudo 800.8
esculent 298.49
escutcheon
  insignia 550.12
  hatchment 551.4
esker, eskar 206.2
Eskimo 560.4
esophagus, oesophagus 350.4
esoteric *n.* 994.13
esoteric *adj.*
  special 79.7
  occult 528.17; 994.21
  obscure 519.7
esotericism, esoterics 994.1
esotropia 443.1
espalier 232.2
especial 79.7
especially
  principally 33.10
  in particular 79.11
Esperantido, Esperanto 560.5
espial sight 441.2
  reconnoitering 461.8
  discovery 481a.1
espièglerie 842.7
espier 528.8
espionage espial 441.2
  reconnoitering 461.8
  (vigilance 459.2)
esplanade plane 213.3
  path 627.2
espousal
  adoption 609.1
  spouse 903.5
espousals 903.2
espouse adopt 609.7
  ~ a cause 707.8
  (side with 709.5)
  marry 903.13
  defend 937.6
espousement 903.3
esprit sagacity 498.2
  wit 842.1
esprit de corps

sociality 892.1
  co-operation 709.2
esprit fort 989.4
espy see 441.10
  discover 481a.3
esquire armiger 726.4
  nobleman 875.5
  lover 897.6
Esquire 877.2
essay *n.* trial 463.1
  writing 590.3
  dissertation 595.1
  (prose 598.1)
  attempt 675
  (effort 686.1)
essay *v.* try 463.8
  attempt 675.3
  (undertake 676.2)
essayer 463.6
essayist
  experimenter 463.6
  dissertator 595.3
  (author 593.15)
esse 1.1
essence *n.*
  quintessence 5.2
  (interior 221.2)
  (truth 494.1)
  (salient point 642.4)
  odor 398.1
essence *v.* 400.9
essenced 400.10
essential *n.*
  essence 5.2
  requirement 630.1
essential *adj.* real 1.8
  intrinsic 5.6
  (component 56.3)
  absolute 31.12
  basal 211.5
  necessary 630.3
  important 642.14
essentiality 630.1
essentially
  intrinsically 5.8
  (substantially 3.5)
  absolutely 31.16
essentials facts 1.2
  fundamentals 642.4
establish
  stabilize 150.4
  originate 153.6
  create 161.8
  place 184.11, 14
  (remain 265.5)
  confirm 467.9
  demonstrate 478.2
  enact 963.4
establish oneself 184.14
  (become stable 150.3)
established
  stable 150.5
  (permanent 141.6)
  well-founded 474.9
  inveterate 613.12
  conventional 852.8
establishment
  stability 150.1
  production 161.1
  placement 184.6

demonstration 478.1
  company 712.5
  mart 799.1
estafette, estafet 534.1
estaminet 298.42
estate state 7.1
  class 75.1
  messuage 189.12
  property 780.1, 2
  (inheritance 775.4)
esteem *n.*
  reputability 873.1
  respect 928.1
  approbation 931.1
esteem *v.* judge 480.6
  consider 484.8
  honor 873.13
  hold dear 897.11
  respect 928.4
  appreciate 931.5
esthetic, estheticize
etc. See **aesthetic** etc.
Esthonian See **Estonian**
estimable
  measurable 466.12
  (good 648.8)
  reputable 873.15
  in high esteem 928.9
  praiseworthy 931.11
  (virtuous 944.4)
  honorable 939.7
estimate *n.*
  measurement 466.1
  judgment 480.2
estimate *v.*
  calculate 85.7
  measure 466.10
  judge 480.7
  consider 484.8
estimation
  numeration 85.1
  measurement 466.1
  (discrimination 465.1)
  judgment 480.2
  valuation 812.3
  respect 928.1
  approbation 931.1
estival, aestival 382.15
estivate, aestivate 683.9
estivation, aestivation 683.5
estoile 98.1
Estonian, Esthonian 560.4
estop 706.4
estoppel 706.1
Estotiland 515.6
estrade 215.21
estrange part 44.11
  alienate 889.2, 898.4
estranged
  alienated 889.3
  isolated 893.10
estrangement
  enmity 889.1
  seclusion 893.2
  alienation 898.1

estrapade 972.2
estreat 974.3
estuous, aestuous 384.22
esurient n. 865.7
esurient adj. 865.19
étalage 882.1
État Major 745.8
etc., et cetera, et caetera 37.11
etch n. 558.1
etch v. incise 259.3
 engrave 558.5
etcher 559.6
etching n. 558.1, 3
etching ball, etching ground, etching varnish 558.4
Eternal n. 976.2
eternal adj. 112.4
 (infinite 105.3)
 (timeless 107.2)
be eternal 112.2
eternal feminine 374.5
eternalize 112.3
eterne 112.4
eternity
 long time 110.3
 everlastingness 112.1
 (infinity 105.1)
 (timelessness 107.1)
 heaven 981.1
eternize 112.3
ether
 boundlessness 180.4
 sky 318.2
 lightness 320.2
 gas 334.2
 (rarity 322.1)
 air 338.1
 anesthetic 376.2
 refrigerant 387.2
ethereal
 chimerical 4.6
 light 320.7
 (rare 322.4)
 gaseous 334.7
 aerial 338.11
etherealism 334.1
ethereality
 rarity 322.1
 gaseity 334.1
etherealization 336.1
etherealize
 vaporize 336.5
 spiritualize 994.20
etherification 336.1
etheriform 338.11
etherify 336.5
ethical moral 926.12
 (expedient 646.4)
 (right 922.5)
 honorable 939.7
ethical culture 984.4
ethical nihilism 989.3
ethicism 984.4
ethics 926.4
 (right 922.1)
Ethiop, Ethiope 431.4
Ethiopian n.
 Negro 431.4

language 560.4
Ethiopian adj.
 racial 11.8
 negroid 431.9
ethnic 984.28
ethnography, ethnology 372.4
ethological 926.12
ethology
 zoology 368.1
 ethics 926.4
ethonomics 926.4
ethylene 376.2
etiolate decolor 429.5
 whiten 430.6
etiolated 429.6
etiolation
 colorlessness 429.1, 2
 whitening 430.2
etiological, aetiological 490.19
etiology, aetiology
 attribution 155.1
 life science 359.5
 science 490.7
 pathology 655.19
etiquette 852.2
étourderie
 inattention 458.1
 bungle 699.4
 (blunder 495.3)
étude 415.3
etymological 562.9
 (philological 560.9)
etymologist 560.7
 (lexicologist 562.5)
etymologize 562.7
etymology 562.4
 (philology 560.6)
etymon root 153.3
 word 562.1
eucalyptus tree 367.6
 wood 635.3
Eucharist 998.6
eucharistial 998.8
eucharistic 998.15
euchology 998.9
euchre n. 840.12
euchre v. 731.9
euchred 732.12
eucrasy 41.1
eudaemonism, eudemonism
 philosophy 451.7
 benevolence 906.1
eudaemonist, eudemonist 911.1
eudiometer 338.8
eudiometrical 338.12
eudiometry 338.7
eugenics 658.2
eulogist 935.1
eulogistic 931.9
eulogize 931.6
 (overestimate 482.3)
eulogy trophy 733.1
 approbation 931.2
 (overestimation 482.1)
Eumenides

violents 173.6
 Furies 900.4
 avenger 919.3
 mythical beings 980.5
eumerogenesis 161.2
eunuch 158.3
eunuchize 38.7
eupepsia 654.1
euphemism
 figure of speech 521.1
 diction 577.1; 578.1
 affectation 853.1
 flattery 933.1
euphemist
 rhetorician 577.3
 man of taste 850.3
 affecter 853.4
euphemistic
 figurative 521.3
 rhetorical 577.6
 grammar 578.4
 affected 853.6
euphemize
 speech 577.4
 affect 853.5
euphemy 933.1
euphonious
 melodious 413.27
 speech 578.4
euphonium 417.4
euphonon 417.2
euphony music 413.1
 speech 578.1
euphoria 654.1
Euphrosyne 836.1
euphuism
 figure of speech 521.1
 affected speech 577.1; 578.1; 579.1
 affectation 853.1
euphuist
 rhetorician 577.3; 579.2
 affecter 853.4
euphuistic
 figurative 521.3
 rhetorical 577.6
 grammar 578.4
 affected 853.6
euphuize 853.5
eupnea, eupnoea 349.18
Eurasian 41.5
eureka 481a.9
euripus 343.1
Euroclydon 349.9
European 11.8
European plan 298.39
Eurus 349.2
eurythmics, eurhythmics
 symmetry 242.1
 physical education 537.5
 exercise 686.2
eurythmy, eurhythmy 242.1
Eusebian 984.14
Eustachian tube 418.5

Euterpe 416.16
euthanasia 360.1
euthenics 658.2
eutrophy 707.3
evacuate leave 293.4
 void 297.14
 (empty 187.9)
 abandon 624.3
evacuation
 elimination 42.2
 departure 293.1
 voidance 297.5
 excrement 299.1
 abandonment 624.1
evacuator 893.5
évacué migrant 268.3
 outcast 893.5
evadable, evadible 623.11
evade quibble 477.8
 avoid 623.6
 (not observe 773.3)
 (not pay 808.5)
evaluate 812.4
evanescence
 transience 111.1
 disappearance 449.1
evanescent
 transient 111.6
 infinitesimal 193.10
 (inappreciable 32.9)
 disappearing 449.4
evangel
 glad tidings 532.1
 messenger 534.1
evangelical 983a.7; 985.7
evangelist
 apostle 985.6
 revivalist 996.4
Evangelist 985.4
evaporability 336.2
evaporate v.
 cease to be 2.5
 be transient 111.5
 vaporize 336.5
 dehydrate 340.5
 disappear 449.2
 preserve 670.4
evaporate, evaporated adj. 340.9
evaporation
 vaporization 336.1
 dehydration 340.2
 effervescence 353.3
 preservation 670.2
evaporative
 volatile 336.7
 drying 340.10
evaporator
 vaporizer 336.3
 dehydrator 340.3
evaporize 340.5
evasible 623.11
evasion
 quibbling 477.4
 secrecy 528.2
 avoidance 623.1
 (pretext 619.1)
 (nonobservance 773.1)
 (nonpayment 808.1)

evasive — evolved

evasion (*continued*)
  (dereliction 927.1)
  artifice 702.3
evasive
  quibbling 477.11
  secretive 528.22
  elusive 623.12
  (sly 702.6)
  (nonobservant 773.5)
eve 126.1
  on the eve of
  previously 116.5
  about to 121.11
evection 61.1
even *n.* 126.1
even *v.* equal 27.6
  level 213.6
  smooth 255.4
  (flatten 251.4)
  ~ the score 718.2; 807.7
even *adj.*
  uniform 16.5
  (measured 466.13)
  equal 27.8
  moderate 174.6
  horizontal 213.8
  parallel 216.5
  symmetrical 242.4
  straight 246.5
  flat 251.5
  smooth 255.5
  accurate 494.11
  neutral 628.3
  get even with
  retaliate 718.2
  (repay 807.9)
  (revenge 919.4)
  (punish 972.5)
  pay 807.7
even *adv.* 33.10; 469.8
even break tie 27.4
  even chance 156.2
  even odds 621.5
evenhanded 941.3
evening *n.* 126.1, 2
  (close 67.3)
  (daylight 420.8)
  (semidarkness 422.2)
evening *adj.* 126.5
  (dim 422.8)
evening dress, evening gown 225.14
evening song 415.3
evenness
  regularity 16.2
  equality 27.1
  symmetry 242.1
evensong
  eventide 126.1
  vespers 990.7
even Stephen 27.4, 8
event
  occurrence 151.1
  (occasion 8.2)
  contest 720.2
  at all events
  notwithstanding 30.8
  provided 469.8

of course 474.16
resolutely 604.9
in any event
  provided 469.8
  resolutely 604.9
  anyhow 627.9
in the event of
  in case 151.8
  provided 469.8
  expectantly 507.9
eventful
  stirring 151.6; 682.23
  momentous 642.10
eventide 126.1
eventual final 67.8
  future 121.7
  ultimate 151.7
  resultant 154.6
eventuality
  futurity 121.4
  contingency 151
  (effect 154.1)
eventually
  ultimately 121.9; 151.8
  at last 133.12
eventuate 151.3
eventuation
  eventuality 151.1
  effect 154.1
ever 112.5
ever and anon
  always 112.5
  constantly 136.6
ever so 102.6
ever-changing 149.5
everduring 112.4
evergreen
  continuous 69.6
  durable 110.9
  eternal 112.4
  evernew 123.8
  herbal 367.14
everlasting 112.4
  (durable 110.9)
everlastingness 112.1
everliving 112.4
evermore 112.5
ever-new 123.8
ever-recurring 104.6
eversible 149.5
eversion 218.1
  (change 140.1)
  (evolution 313.1)
evert 218.4
every *adv.* 78.13; 138.10
every bit 52.15
everybody 78.5
everyday
  constant 136.4
  customary 613.11
  commonplace 843.6
  ordinary 849.3
every man Jack 78.5
every now and then, every once in a while
  irregularly 59.12
  repeatedly 104.8

everyone, every one 78.5
  (all 50.2)
every other 138.10
everything 50.2
everyway 278.15
everywhence, everywhere all over 180.9
  everywhither 278.15
every which way
  ununiformly 16a.3
  in disorder 59.13
  everywhither 278.15
  (deviatively 279.9)
everywhither
  everywhere 180.9
  everyway 278.15
evict *n.* 893.5
evict *v.* 297.9
  (dispossess 789.11)
eviction 297.2
  (dispossession 789.2)
evictor 297.6
evidence *n.*
  testimony 467
  (trace 551.5)
  demonstration 478.1
  manifestation 525.1
  indication 550.1
  give evidence 467.8
  (lawsuit 969.10)
  in evidence 446.4
evidence *v.*
  appear 448.6
  evince 467.7, 10
  (demonstrate 478.2)
  (manifest 525.2)
  disclose 529.3
  indicate 550.18
evident visible 446.4
  distinct 446.5
  manifest 525.4
  (certain 474.8)
  (demonstrated 478.4)
  (intelligible 518.5)
  make evident 529.3
evidential 467.11
  (demonstrative 478.3)
  (indicative 550.21)
evidentially 467.13
evidently 525.7
  (meaningly 516.12)
evil *n.* bad 649.2
  (bane 663.1)
  (adversity 735.1, 3)
  (wrong 923.1)
  wickedness 945.1
  misdeed 947.2
  do evil 649.6
  the Evil One 978.1
evil *adj.* bad 649.8
  (adverse 735.8)
  wicked 945.11
evil *adv.* 649.11
evil-affected 945.11
evil-disposed
  malevolent 907.6
  wicked 945.11

evildoer 913
  (bane 663.1)
  (wrongdoer 949.2)
evildoing *n.* vice 945.6
  (malevolence 907.1)
  misdeed 947.2
evildoing *adj.* 945.13
  (malevolent 907.6)
  (dishonest 940.8)
evil eye eye 441.8
  malevolence 907.1
  wickedness 945.1
  spell 993.1
evil-eyed 945.11
evil-favored
  unprepossessing 846.8
  vicious 945.11
evilhearted 945.14
evil-hued 945.11
evil-looking
  ugly 846.8
  vicious 945.11
evil-minded 945.14
evil-qualitied
  evil 649.8
  wicked 945.11
evil-savored 945.11
evilspeaking
  profanity 908.2
  detraction 934.1
evil-starred
  inauspicious 512.5
  unfortunate 735.9
evince evidence 467.7
  (demonstrate 478.2)
  (manifest 525.2)
  disclose 529.3
  indicate 550.18
evincement 525.1
evirate geld 38.7
  unman 158.7
eviscerate 297.16
  (extract 301.5)
eviscerated 4.5
evoke induce 153.7
  prompt 615.7
  entreat 765.5
  excite 824.2
evolute 313.2
evolution
  mathematics 85.4
  development 161.2
  motion 264.1
  turn 311.2
  unfoldment 313
  (circuity 311.1)
  elaboration 673.1
  action 680.1
evolutional, evolutionary 313.3
evolutionism
  evolution 161.5
  (philosophy 451.21)
  ethics 926.4
evolutionist, evolutive 313.3
evolve produce 161.8
  extract 301.5
  unfold 313.2
  discover 481a.3
evolved 154.5

838

evolvement — exchange

evolvement
　extraction 301.1
　evolution 313.1
evulgate
　divulge 529.4
　publish 531.7
evulgation
　disclosure 529.1
　publication 531.1
evulsion 301.1
ewe sheep 366.8
　female animal 374.8
ewer 191.11
exacerbate
　inflame 173.8
　aggravate 835.2
exacerbation
　increase 35.1
　violence 173.1
　aggravation 835.1
exacerbescent 835.5
exact *v.* extract 301.6
　require 741.5
　force from 744.2
　dictate 885.5
　~ dues 924.7
　assume 925.6
　~ duty 926.7
exact *adj.* copy 21.5
　limited 233.3
　accurate 494.11
　(careful 459.7)
　(literal 516.9)
　(perspicuous 570.2)
　(faithful 772.5)
to be exact 494.16
exacting
　ticklish 704.8
　strict 739.5
　discontented 832.5
　greedy 865.20
　fastidious 868.4
exaction
　demand 741.2
　tax 812.2
　imposition 925.3
exactitude
　meticulousness 457.3
　accuracy 494.3
　fastidiousness 868.1
exactly
　certainly 474.16
　to be sure 488.14
　accurately 494.16
　(literally 19.14)
exactment 812.2
exactness
　meticulousness 457.3
　accuracy 494.3
　(discrimination 465.1)
　(perspicuity 570.1)
exaggerate
　increase 35.3
　magnify 549.2
　(enlarge 194.8)
　(overestimate 482.3)
　(lie 544.4)

(misrepresent 555.4)
(be bombastic 577.5)
(overdo 641.3)
(boast 884.5)
(flatter 933.2)
exaggerated 549.3
　(overestimated 482.4)
　(grandiloquent 577.7)
　(redundant 641.5)
　(ostentatious 882.8)
exaggeration
　increase 35.1
　magnification 549
　(enlargement 194.1)
　(overestimation 482.1)
　(falsification 544.1)
　(untruth 546.2)
　(misrepresentation 555.1)
　(grandiloquence 577.2)
　(redundance 641.1)
　(aggravation 835.1)
　(ostentation 882.1)
　(boasting 884.1)
　(flattery 933.1)
exalt increase 35.3
　elevate 307.5
　honor 873.13
　extol 931.6
　sanctify 987.8
　glorify 990.10
exaltation
　height 206.1
　elevation 307.1
　honor 873.3, 6
　magnanimity 942.2
　sanctification 987.2
　religious ~ 990.2
exalted high 206.13
　eminent 873.18
　noble 875.10
　magnanimous 942.6
exam, examen 461.3
examinant 461.13
examination
　scrutiny 441.2
　inquiry 461.3, 4, 9
　(hearing 418.2)
　(attention 457.2)
　(trial 463.1; 969.5)
examine
　scrutinize 441.12
　inquire 461.15, 17, 18
　(give attention 457.4)
　(reason 476.10)
　(criticize 480.10)
　(try 969.11)
　~ judicially 480.8
　~ the books 811.8
examiner 461.13
example *n.*
　prototype 22.1
　(guide 540.4)
exemplification 82.2

(relevance 23.2)
　warning 668.1
for example
　for instance 82.14
　by the way 134.11
good example
　paragon 650.2
　good person 948.1
make an example of 972.5
set an example 22.4
example *v.*
　prototype 22.4
　exemplify 82.6
exanimate
　lifeless 360.8
　languid 683.14
exanthema 655.17
exarch regent 745.7
　bishop 996.5
exasperate
　inflame 173.8
　irritate 824.5
　annoy 830.5
　aggravate 835.2
　anger 900.10
exasperating 830.12
exasperation
　violence 173.1
　aggravation 835.1
　resentment 900.1
exasperative 835.5
ex cathedra
　authoritative 474.13
　affirmatively 535.7
　with authority 737.17
　arrogantly 885.11
excavate dig 252.9
　(deepen 208.6)
　dig out 301.5
excavation 252.2
excavator 252.7
　(workman 690.10)
exceed excel 33.5
　(outstrip 303.4)
　rise above 206.10
exceeding
　superior 33.7
　remaining 40.6
exceedingly 31.15
excel
　be superior 33.5
　(be better 648.5)
　be skillful 698.7
excellence
　goodness 648.1
　(superiority 33.1)
　virtue 944.1
Excellency 877.2
excellent good 648.8
　virtuous 944.3
excellently 648.14
excelsior *n.* 591.7
excelsior *adj.* 305.7
except *v.*
　take exceptions 469.5
　reject 610.2
except *prep.*
　excepting 38.11

excluding 55.7
except *conj.* 8.8
excepted 748.18
excepting 55.7
　(notwithstanding 30.8)
exception
　exclusion 55.1
　oddity 83.4
　conditon 469.2
　objection 489.2; 932.1
　exemption 748.1; 777a.1
　prodigy 872.1
　demurrer 937.2
take exception
　qualify 469.5
　demur 485.7
　object 489.4
　resent 900.6
　disapprove 932.5
without exception 16.7
exceptionable
　qualifying 469.6
　intolerable 649.9
　objectionable 932.13
exceptional
　exclusive 55.6
　unusual 83.10
　(disagreeing 24.6)
　(superexcellent 648.10)
　qualifying 469.6
　remarkable 642.10
exceptionality 83.3
exceptious 901.9
excerpt *n.*
　record 551.1
　extract 596.1, 2
　selection 609.1
excerpt *v.* 609.7
excerption 609.1
excess *n.*
　exaggeration 549.1
　superfluity 641.1
　(surplus 40.4)
　overindulgence 954.1
in excess
　excessive 641.5
　intemperate 954.4
excess *adj.* 641.5
excessive
　immense 31.9
　exaggerated 549.3
　superfluous 641.5
　(undue 925.8)
　(unjust 941a.3)
　price 814.6
　intemperate 954.4
excessively 31.20
exchange *n.*
　interchange 148.1
　(transfer 783.1)
　retaliation 718.1
　barter 794.1
　(reciprocation 12 2)
　stock ~ 799.3
　(gambling establishment 621.14)

exchange — exercise 840

exchange (*continued*)
  barroom 959.13
give in exchange
  718.2
in exchange 148.5
exchange *v.*
  interchange 148.3
    (reciprocate 12.5)
  (substitute 147.3)
  (transfer 783.3)
  barter 794.4
exchangeable
  interchangeable
    148.4
  commercial 794.10
exchequer funds 800.2
  treasury 802.1
exchequer bill 800.7
excise *n.* 812.2
excise *v.* 38.5
  (discard 678.3)
exciseman 745.9
excision 38.2
excitability 825
  (irritability 901.1)
excitable 825.8
  (irritable 901.7)
excitably 825.12
excitant *n.* 171.4
excitant *adj.* 171.11
excitation 824
  (agitation 315.1)
excitative, excitatory
  171.11
excite
  stimulate 171.7
  inflame 173.8
  agitate 315.8
  sensitize 375.4
  impassion 824.2
    (incite 615.7)
excited
  alarmed 669.4
  wrought up 824.9
    (agitated 315.13)
  become excited 824.6
    (anger 900.9)
  be excited 824.7
excitedly 824.14
excitement 824.1;
  825.2
    (agitation 315.1)
    (incitement 615.2)
exciting
  energizing 171.11
  tantalizing 617.6
  thrilling 824.12
    (piquant 392.5)
exclaim *n.*
  outcry 411.2
  exclamation 580.5
exclaim *v.*
  cry out 411.7
  ejaculate 580.9
    (say 582.6)
  ~ **against** 932.7
exclamation
  outcry 411.2
  ejaculation 580.6
    (figure of speech
      521.1)

exclamation point
  550.8
exclude
  eliminate 42.4
  leave out 55.3
  eject 297.8
  banish 297.11
  reject 610.2
  prohibit 761.2
  ostracize 893.7
excluded 55.5
  (extraneous 57.4)
excluding 38.11 ; 55.6
exclusion
  elimination 42.2
  noninclusion 55
  banishment 297.3
  rejection 610.1
  ostracism 893.3
exclusive
  unmixed 42.6
  excluding 55.6
    (extraneous 57.4)
  special 79.7
  prohibitive 761.3
exclusive of
  excepting 38.11
  excluding 55.7
exclusively 87.10
excogitate
  think 451.27
  devise 515.10
excogitation
  thought 451.1
  creative thought
    515.1
excogitative 451.35
excommunicate 297.11
excommunication
  banishment 297.3
  anathema 908.1
ex-convict 754.1
excoriate 226.5
excoriation 226.1
excrement 299.1, 2
    (exudation 295.1)
    (evacuation 297.5)
    (offal 653.6)
    (dung 653.7)
excrementitious
  653.17
excrescence
  protrusion 250.1, 2
  morbid growth
    655.16
excrescential 250.9
excreta 299.1, 2
    (dung 653.7)
excrete 297.13
    (exude 295.7)
excretes 299.2
excretion
  evacuation 297.5
  excrement 299
excretionary, excretory 299.10
    (exudative 295.9)
    (ejective 297.22)
excruciate pain 378.4
  torture 830.6
excruciating 378.7 ;
  830.15

exculpate
  vindicate 937.5
  acquit 970.3
    (forgive 918.3)
exculpation
  vindication 937.1
  acquittal 970.1
    (forgiveness 918.1)
exculpatory 937.9
excursion
  obliquity 217.1
  journey 266.8
  circuity 311.1
  sight-seeing 441.3
  circuit 629.1
excursionist
  traveler 268.1
  sight-seer 444.1
excursive 279.8
excursus
  dissertation 595.1
  digression 573.3
excurvate 250.7
excurvation 250.1
excurvature
  curvature 245.1
  convexity 250.1
excurved curved 245.4
  convex 250.9
excusable 937.10
    (justifiable 941.4)
excuse *n.*
  exemption 777a.1
  pardon 918.1
  justification 937.2
    (counterevidence
      468.1)
    (pretext 619.1)
    (apology 952.2)
  acquittal 970.1
excuse *v.*
  exempt 748.10;
    777a.2
  forgive 918.3
  vindicate 937.5
  justify 937.6
    (apologize 952.5)
  acquit 970.3
excused
  exempt 748.18
  forgiven 918.6
excusing 937.9
    (pretexed 619.3)
execrable
  deplorable 649.8
  odious 830.14
  disreputable 874.8
execrate hate 898.3
  curse 908.4, 5
    (berate 932.8)
execration
  abomination 876.2
  hate 898.1
  malediction 908.1
execute music 416.18
  do 680.6
  conduct 692.4
  complete 729.2
  ~ **an agreement**
    769.8
  observe 772.3
  put to death 972.8

executed 972.13
execution
  production 161.1
  music 415.20; 416.17
  performance 680.1
    (conduct 692.1)
  completion 729.1
  settlement 769.3
  attachment 789.2
  capital punishment
    972.4
executioner 975.5
    (killer 361.8)
executive *n.*
  director 694.1
  officer 694.3; 745.9
executive *adj.* 693.6
    (ruling 737.15)
    (jurisdictional
      965.4)
executor, executrix
  producer 164.1
  agent 690.1
exegesis 522.1, 5
exegete 524.1
exegetic 522.8
exegetics 522.5
exemplar
  prototype 22.1
  example 82.2
  good example 948.1
exemplary
  exemplifying 82.11
  virtuous 944.3
exemplification
  example 82.2
  illustration 522.4
exemplificative 522.8
exemplify
  example 82.6
  symbolize 521.2
  illustrate 522.6
exemplifying 82.11
exempt *v.* free 748.10
    (acquit 970.3)
  release 777a.2
exempt *adj.*
  free 748.18
  unpossessed of
    777a.3
exempt from
  unmixed 42.6
  not having 187.13
exempted 748.18
exemption
  condition 469.2
  release 672.1
  permission 760.1
  freedom 748.1
  nonpossession,
    777a.1
  impunity 970.2
exenterate 297.16
exequatur 755.1
exequial 363.25
exequies 363.4
exercise *n.*
  agency 170.1
  training 537.2
  lesson 537.6
  task 625.2
  hygiene 656.2

exercise — expect

use 677.1
action 680.1
exertion 686.2
  (walk 266.4)
divine service 990.7
exercise v.
  train 537.10
  employ 625.6; 677.5
  do 680.6
exercising 686.10
exercitation
  training 537.2
  use 677.1
  action 680.1
  exercise 686.2
exert
  ~ energy 171.7
  use 677.5
exert oneself 686.5
  (try hard 675.4)
exertion
  attempt 675.1
  effort 686
  (energy 171.1, 2)
  (difficulty 704.1)
exertive 170.4
exfiltration 295.1
  (trickle 348.4)
exfoliate
  form layers 204.4
  scale 226.7
exfoliation
  lamination 204.3
  divestment 226.1
exfoliatory 226.11
exgorgitate emit 295.7
  spout 348.20
exhalation
  evaporation 336.1
  humidification 339.1
  expiration 349.18
  effervescence 353.3
  odor 398.1
exhale let out 297.13
  emit vapor 336.5
  expire 349.23
  ~ an odor 398.5
exhaust
  weaken 160.8
  evacuate 297.14
  emit vapor 336.5
  dry 340.5
  use up 638.2; 677.6
  fatigue 688.5
  drain 789.12
  squander 818.3
exhausted
  extinct 2.10
  impotent 158.8
  worn out 659.12
  tired out 688.6
exhaustion
  impotence 158.2
  emptiness 187.3
  exhalation 336.1
  waste 638.1
  depletion 640.4
  fatigue 688.3
  loss 776.1
exhaustive
  thorough 52.10

complete 729.6
exhaustless
  infinite 105.3
  plentiful 639.7
exhaust pipe 272.16
exhibit n.
  display 448.2; 882.3
  (show 525.1)
  evidence 467.4
  theatrical ~ 599.8
exhibit v.
  appear 448.6
  evidence 467.7
  manifest 525.2
  indicate 550.18
  flaunt 882.7
exhibition
  exposition 448.1, 2
  manifestation 525.1
  theatrical ~ 599.8
  parade 882.3
exhibitioner 541.4
exhibitive 550.21
exhilarate
  strengthen 159.8
  refresh 689.2
  cheer 836.6
exhilarating 836.12
exhilaration
  invigoration 159.2
  refreshment 689.1
  cheerfulness 836.6
exhort urge 615.7
  advise 695.4
exhort against 616.2
exhortation
  lecture 582.2
  (religion 998.2)
  persuasion 615.4
  (advice 695.1)
exhumation 363.19
exhume
  antiquarianism 122.7
  disinter 363.24
exigency crisis 134.4
  (predicament 8.3)
  necessity 630.1
  (desire 865.1)
  want 640.3
  urgency 642.2
exigent urgent 642.13
  (requisite 630.3)
  strict 739.5
  discontented 832.5
exiguity
  fewness 103.1
  littleness 193.1
  (narrowness 203.1)
exiguous sparse 103.3
  little 193.8
exile n.
  banishment 297.3
  exclusion 893.3
  outcast 893.5
exile v. 297.11
  (exclude 893.7)
  (punishment 972.10)
exilement 893.3
exility 203.1
exist 1.4

(be present 186.8)
(live 359.6)
not exist 2.4
existence being 1
  (substantiality 3.1)
  (essence 5.2)
  (presence 186.1)
  something 3.2
  come into existence
  become 1.5
  originate 66.6
  happen 151.3
  come to life 359.7
  in existence 1.7
existent 1.7
  (substantial 3.4)
  (present 186.13)
existing
  existent 1.7
  (living 359.10)
  present 118.2
existless 2.7
existlessness 2.1
exit n. 295.1, 5
  (departure 293.1)
  (disappearance 449.1)
  (path 627.2)
exit v. egress 295.6
  leave stage 599.26
exode 599.4, 5
exodus egress 295.1
  drama 599.5
ex officio
  authentic 494.12
  authoritative 737.15
  by right 922.7
exogenous 367.14
exomorphic 220.7
exonerate
  disembarrass 705.4
  vindicate 937.5
  acquit 970.3
  (exempt 748.10)
  (forgive 918.3)
exonerated
  disembarrassed 705.7
  acquitted 970.4
exoneration
  vindication 937.1
  acquittal 970.1
  (exemption 748.1)
  (forgiveness 918.1)
exorability 914.1
exorable 914.6
exorbitance
  exaggeration 549.1
  excess 641.1
  (undueness 925.1)
  (injustice 941a.1)
  overcharge 814.1
exorbitant
  immense 31.9
  overdone 549.3
  excessive 641.5
  high-priced 814.6
exorbitantly 31.20
exorbitation 279.1
exorcise, exorcize 992.4
exorcism

conjuration 992.1
spell 993.1
exorcist 992.2
exordium 64.2
exosmic 302.3
exosmosis 302.1
exosmotic 302.3
exostosis
  protuberance 250.2
  sore 655.16
exoteric
  comprehensible 518.5
  obvious 525.4
exotic n. 367.2
exotic adj.
  irrelative 10.5
  extraneous 57.4
  unusual 83.10
  plant 367.17
expand increase 35.3
  enlarge 194.5, 8
  (be increased 35.4)
  (broaden 202.4)
  (be elastic 325.3)
  (exaggerate 549.2)
  evolve 313.2
  blow up 349.24
  expatiate 573.5
expanded
  larger 194.10
  (hulky 192.13)
  open 260.15
expanding 573.4
expanse extent 180.1
  size 192.1
  (expansion 194.1)
  breadth 202.1
  plain 344.1
expansile 194.9
expansion
  extent 180.1
  size 192.1
  enlargement 194
  (increase 35.1)
  (thickness 202.2)
  (exaggeration 549.1)
expansional 194.9
expansive
  spacious 180.6
  expansional 194.9
  broad 202.6
ex parte 481.10
expatiate
  wander 266.14
  descant 573.5
  (be loquacious 584.4)
expatiation 573.4
expatriate n. 893.5
expatriate v. 297.11
expatriation 297.3
  (emigration 295.2)
expect believe 484.8
  anticipate 507.4
  (look forward 121.5)
  (presume 472.3)
  (foresee 510.5)
  (hope 858.6)

expectancy — expository

expect (*continued*)
  (be unastonished 871.2)
  suppose 514.6
  intend 620.3
not expect 508.4
expectancy 780.2
expectant 507.7
  (hopeful 858.9)
expectantly 507.9
expectation 507
  (imminence 152.1)
  (foresight 510.1)
  (hopefulness 858.2)
  (unastonishment 871.1)
in expectation 507.7
expected 507.8
  (future 121.7)
  (imminent 152.3)
  (unastonished 871.3)
expectorate 297.19
expedience 646
  (timeliness 134.1)
  (utility 644.1)
  (right 922.1)
  (dueness 924.1)
expedient *n.*
  contrivance 626.5
  medium 631.2
  shift 646.2
  (device 626.5)
  (means 632.1)
  tactics 692.2
expedient *adj.*
  opportune 134.7
  fitting 646.4
  (fit 23.11)
  (politic 498.11)
  (good 648.8)
  (advisable 695.9)
  (right 922.5)
  (due 924.9)
  (ethical 926.12)
  (just 941.3)
be expedient 646.3
  (befit 23.7)
  (be timely 134.5)
expediently 646.6
  (opportunely 134.10)
expedite
  hasten 684.2
  aid 707.6
expedition
  journey 266.8
  ejection 297.1
  dispatch 682.2
  (velocity 274.1)
  (punctuality 132.3)
  haste 684.1
  military ~ 722.4
expeditious
  fast 274.13
  quick 682.17
  (prompt 132.9)
  hasty 684.5
expel eliminate 42.4
  eject 297.8
  (project 284.11)
expellee 893.5

expeller 297.6
expend
  discharge 297.13
  use up 638.2; 677.6
  ~ itself 683.10
  spend 809.3
  (pay 807.6)
expended 807.10
expenditure
  waste 638.1
  loss 776.1
  disbursement 809
  (purchase 795.1)
  (pay 807.2)
  accounts payable 811.1
expense 812.1
expenseless 815.10
expenses 809.1
expensive 814.5
expensiveness 814.1
experience *n.*
  event 151.1
  knowledge 490.2
  skill 698.4
  sensation 821.1
experience *v.*
  undergo 151.4
  ~ an emotion 821.3
experienced 698.15
  (wise 498.11)
experiment *n.* 463
  (trial 675.1)
experiment *v.* 463.8
  (seek 461.16)
  (test 461.17)
  (try 675.3)
experimental
  probative 463.12
  undecided 475.10
experimental engineer 463.6
experimentalism 463.1
experimentally 463.14
experimentation 463.1
experimentee, experimenter 463.6
expert *n.* 700.1
expert *adj.* 698.11
expertness 698.1
expiable 937.10
expiate atone 952.4
  divine function 976.9
expiation 952.1
  (propitiation 990.5)
expiatory 952.6
expiration end 67.1
  exsufflation 349.1
expire end 67.6
  elapse 109.3
  let out 297.13
  exhale 349.23
  die 360.6
expired 122.8
expiry 67.1
explain
  exemplify 82.6
  interpret 522.6
  (solve 481a.4)
  (elucidate 518.3)
  (show 525.2)

  (tell 527.7)
explain away 523.2
explainer 524.1
  (informant 527.5)
explanation
  exemplification 82.2
  interpretation 522.1
  (attribution 155.1)
  (answer 462.3)
  (solution 481a.2)
  (meaning 516.1)
  (instruction 537.1)
  (description 594.1)
  (reason 615.1)
in explanation 522.9
explanatory 522.8
  (descriptive 594.7)
expletive *n.*
  adjunct 39.1
  pleonasm 573.2
  exclamation 580.5
  redundance 641.1
  oath 908.3
expletive *adj.* 641.5
explicability 518.1
explicable
  attributable 155.4
  understandable 518.5
explication 522.1
explicative 522.8
explicator 524.1
explicit
  demonstrative 478.5
  clear 518.5; 525.4
  (meaning 516.8)
  (affirmative 535.6)
  (perspicuous 570.2)
explode
  detonate 173.9; 406.8
  (shoot 284.13)
  confute 479.2
  fail 732.5
  become excited 824.6
  (rage 825.7)
  become angry 900.9
exploded past 122.8
  discredited 495.17
  disapproved 932.12
exploder 406.5
exploit *n.* deed 680.2
  heroic act 861.2
exploit *v.* 677.5
exploitation 461.8
exploration 461.3
exploratory 461.24
explore *n.* 461.3
explore *v.* 461.17
  (grope 463.9)
explorer 268.1
explosible 173.17
explosion
  detonation 173.3
  (impulse 276.1)
  (shot 284.4)
  (gunfire 716.2)
  report 406.2
  failure 732.1

  outburst of passion 825.5
  outburst of anger 900.3
explosive *n.*
  sound 406.2
  ammunition 727.13
  (noisemaker 404.4)
  (detonator 406.6)
explosive *adj.*
  detonating 173.9
  fulminant 406.10
exponent number 84.2
  interpreter 524.1)
  (informant 527.5)
  deputy 759.1
exponential
  numeral 84.7
  indicative 550.21
export, exportation 295.3
  (extraction 301.1)
expose divest 226.4
  open 260.12
  confute 479.2
  display 525.2
  (visibilize 446.3)
  disclose 529.3
  (discover 481a.3)
  ~ to danger 665.4, 5
  ~ to infamy 874.7; 934.3
expose oneself
  be liable 177.2
  appear 446.2
exposé
  confutation 479.1
  disclosure 529.1
  description 594.1
exposed
  liable to 177.3
  open 260.15
  airy 338.11
  windswept 349.25
  visible 446.4
  ~ to danger 665.6, 8
  unprotected 665.9
exposit explain 522.6
  teach 537.11
exposition
  exhibition 448.1, 2; 882.3
  confutation 479.1
  explanation 522.1
  display 525.1
  disclosure 529.1
  description 594.1
  dissertation 595.1
  bazaar 799.1
expositive
  interpretative 522.8
  revealing 529.8
expositor
  interpreter 524.1
  (teacher 540.1)
  speaker 582.5
  dissertator 595.3
expository
  interpretative 522.8
  (informative 527.13)
  (descriptive 594.7)

revealing 529.8
dissertative 595.5
ex post facto 117.4
expostulate
  advise 695.4
  deprecate 766.2
  (dissuade 616.2)
  reprove 932.8
expostulation
  deprecation 766.1
  (discussion 616.1)
  (advice 695.1)
  protest 489.2
  reproof 932.3
expostulative
  dissuasive 616.4
  advisory 695.8
  deprecative 765.3
expostulatory 766.3
exposure
  ~ to air 338.6
  visibility 446.1
  appearance 448.1
  confutation 479.1
  discovery 481a.1
  disclosure 529.1
  photograph 556.11
  ~ to danger 665.2
expound explain 522.6
  teach 537.11
expounder
  interpreter 524.1
  speaker 582.5
expounding
  explanation 522.1
  dissertation 595.1
express *n.*
  expressman 271.1
  message 532.2
  messenger 534.1
  mail 592.4
  by express 270.12
express *v.* ship 270.9
  extract 301.7
  betoken 467.7
  mean 516.5
  make known 527.7
  phrase 566.3
  (word 562.6)
  (speak 582.6)
  voice 580.8
  hasten 684.2
express *adj.*
  special 79.7
  explicit 525.4
  (meaning 516.8)
  (affirmative 535.6)
  intended 620.4
expression
  extraction 301.3
  tone 402.2
  music 415.20; 416.17
  mien 448.4
  meaning 516.1
  manifestation 525.1
  word 562.1
  locution 564.3
  phrase 566.1
  (figure of speech 521.1)
  phraseology 569.1
  utterance 580.3

enunciation 582.3
statement 582.4
give expression to
  express 566.3
  voice 580.8
  speak 582.6
expressionism 556.6
expressionist 556.19
expressionless 517.8
expressive
  significative 516.8
  (graphic 518.6)
  sensitive 822.6
expressman 271.1
express train
  train 272.18
  speed 274.6
exprobrate 932.8
exprobration
  reproach 932.3
  accusation 938.1
expropriate 782.3
expropriation 782.1
expugnable 665.9
expuition 299.5
expulsion
  elimination 42.2
  ejection 297.1, 3
  (exclusion 55.1)
  exsufflation 349.1
expunge excise 38.5
  destroy 162.4
  obliterate 552.2
expurgate *v.* 652.9
expurgate *adj.* 652.14
expurgation 652.2
expurgative 652.15
expurge 652.9
exquisite *n.* 854.1
exquisite *adj.*
  savory 394.7
  superexcellent 648.10
  delightful 829.8
  beautiful 845.8
exquisitely 31.15
exsiccate 340.5
exsiccated 340.9
exsiccation 340.2
exsiccative *n.* 340.3
exsiccative *adj.* 340.10
exsiccator 340.3
exspuition 299.5
exsufflation
  expiration 349.1
  exorcism 992.1
extant 1.7
extemporaneous
  brief 113.4
  occasional 134.9
  improvised 612.4
extemporaneously 612.5
extemporary 134.9
extempore *n.*
  music 415.16
  impromptu 612.1
  unpreparation 674.1
extempore *adj.* 113.5
extempore *adv.*
  promptly 132.14
  by the way 134.11

offhand 612.5
extemporization
  improvisation 612.1
  unpreparation 674.1
extemporize 612.3
  (be unprepared 674.4)
extemporizer 612.2
extend increase 35.3
  continue 106.2; 143.3
  ~ time 110.6
  expand 194.5, 8
  (stretch 325.3)
  be distant 196.4
  be long 200.8
  lengthen 200.9
  expatiate 573.5
extended
  protracted 110.10
  spacious 180.6
  lengthened 200.12
  broad 202.6
  open 260.15
extensibility
  flexibility 324.1
  elasticity 325.1
extensible
  flexible 324.6
  elastic 325.5
extensile
  flexible 324.6
  elastic 325.5
extension
  increase 35.1
  (expansion 194.1)
  adjunct 39.1
  addition 39.3
  continuation 63.2
  continuance 143.1
  space 180.1
  lengthening 200.5
extensive
  far-reaching 31.7
  (comprehensive 76.5)
  (prevalent 78.10)
  (abundant 639.7)
  spacious 180.6
  far-reaching 200.12
  broad 202.6
extensively 180.8
  (widely 196.10)
extent quantity 25.1
  (measurement 466.1)
  degree 26.1
  size 192.1
  distance 196.1
  (length 200.1)
to a great extent 31.15
extenuate
  decrease 36.4
  weaken 160.8
  thin 203.8
  sicken 655.22
  vindicate 937.8
extenuated 203.11
extenuating
  qualifying 469.6
  vindicative 937.9

extenuating circumstance
  qualification 469.1
  vindication 937.3
  (loophole 671.4)
extenuation
  decrease 36.1
  thinness 203.4
  vindication 937.3
  (loophole 671.4)
extenuative *n.* 937.3
extenuative *adj.* 937.9
exterior *n.*
  external 220.2
  (cover 223.2)
  appearance 448.5
  picture 556.10
exterior *adj.*
  extraneous 57.4
  external 220.6
  (extrinsic 6.2)
exteriority 220
  (extrinsicality 6.1)
  (extraneousness 57.1)
  (circumjacence 227.1)
exteriorization 220.1
exteriorize
  externalize 220.5
  materialize 316.7
exterminate
  destroy 162.4
  eject 297.17
  extract 301.5
extermination
  destruction 162.2
  extraction 301.1
exterminator 165.1
extern *n.* 57.3
  (outsider 220.3)
extern *adj.* 220.7
external *n.* 220.2
external *adj.*
  extraneous 57.4
  exterior 220.7
  objective 316.10
externality, externalization 220.1
externalize
  exteriorize 220.6
  materialize 316.7
externally, exterrestrial, exterritorial 220.7
extinct
  nonexistent 2.10
  (destroyed 162.7)
  (dead 360.8)
  past 122.8
  antiquated 124.9
become extinct
  cease to be 2.5
  (perish 162.5)
  become obsolete 124.5
extincteur 385.3
extinction
  destruction 162.2
  (nonexistence 2.3)
  (end 67.1)
  (death 360.1)

extinguish — eyeservant

extinction (cont'd)
  obscuration 421.3
  obliteration 552.1
extinguish
  destroy 162.4
  ~ fire 385.5
  (~ light 421.6)
extinguisher 385.3
extinguishment
  destruction 162.2
  obscuration 421.3
extirpate excise 38.5
  (discard 678.3)
  destroy 162.4
  eject 297.17
  extract 301.5
extirpation
  destruction 162.2
  extraction 301.1
extirpatory 162.6
extispex 513.2
extispicious 511.11
extispicy 511.3
extol, extoll
  eulogize 931.6
  glorify 990.10
extoller 935.1
extort extract 301.6
  force from 744.2
  wrest from 789.11
  rob 791.13
  overcharge 814.3
extortion
  rapacity 789.4;
    819.1
  theft 791.3
  overcharge 814.1
extortionate
  tyrannical 739.5
  exorbitant 814.6
  avaricious 819.4
  grasping 865.20
extortionist 789.6
extra n. 599.19
extra adj. 37.7
extra adv.
  additionally 37.8
  overplus 641.7
extract n. record 551.1
  excerpt 596.1, 2
  selection 609.1
extract v.
  ~ roots 85.7
  withdraw 301.5, 6
  (eject 297.8)
  elicit 301.6
  select 609.7
  ~ teeth 662.24
extraction
  ancestry 166.4
  (race 11.4)
  withdrawal 301
  (egress 295.1)
  (ejection 297.1)
  selection 609.1
extractor 301.4
extradite
  banish 297.11
  (transport 270.8)
  (punishment 972.10)
extradition n. 297.3

(transportation 270.2)
extradition v. 297.11
extrados 220.2
extraembryonic, extraenteric, extragalactic 220.7
extrajudicial 964.5
extralateral 220.7
extrality 220.1
extramarginal
  external 220.6
  subconscious 450.10
extramatrical, extramedullary, extramolecular etc. 220.7
extramundane
  exterior 220.7
  immaterial 317.6
  supernatural 976.14
extramural 220.7
extraneity 220.1
extraneous
  irrelative 10.5
  additional 37.7
  alien 57.4
  (extrinsic 6.2)
  (excluded 55.5)
  exterior 220.7
extraneousness 57
  (extrinsicality 6.1)
  (exteriority 220.1)
extraordinarily 31.21
extraordinary
  unusual 83.10
  (remarkable 31.13)
  (superexcellent 648.10)
  memorable 642.10
  wonderful 870.7
extraplacental, extrapolar, extraprovincial etc. 220.7
extraterrene, extraterrestrial
  exterior 220.7
  cosmic 318.15
extraterritorial 220.7
extraterritoriality 220.1
extratribal, extratubal, extratympanic etc. 220.7
extravagance
  expensiveness 814.1
  prodigality 818.1
  excess 641.1
  exaggeration 549.1
  (absurdity 497.1)
extravagant
  immense 31.9
  (fanatic 503.18)
  violent 173.11
  fantastic 497.4
  fanciful 515.13
  exaggerated 549.3
  verbose 573.7
  abundant 639.7
  excessive 641.5
  high-priced 814.6
  prodigal 818.4
  vulgar 851.6

boastful 884.7
extravagantly 31.15
extravaganza
  caricature 21.3
  fancy 515.4
  drama 599.3
extravagate 549.2
extravasate n. 299.1
extravasate v.
  exude 295.7
  let out 297.13
extravasation
  evacuation 297.5
  excretion 299.1
extraventricular 220.7
extreme n.
  limit 52.4; 233.1
  extremity 67.2
in the extreme 31.19
extreme adj.
  absolute 31.12
  final 67.8
  violent 173.11
  overwrought 549.3
extremely 31.19
  (utterly 52.14)
extreme unction 998.3, 4
extremism 549.1
extremist 710.2
extremity limit 52.4
  end 67.2
  (edge 231.1)
  crisis 134.4
  foot 211.4
  exaggeration 549.1
  impasse 704.3
  wretchedness 828.3
extricable 672.3
extricate extract 301.5
  deliver 672.2
  disembarrass 705.4
  free 750.3
extrication
  extraction 301.1
  deliverance 672.1
extrinsic 6.2
  (circumstantial 8.5)
  (extraneous 57.4)
  (exterior 220.7)
extrinsicality 6
  (extraneousness 57.1)
  (exteriority 220.1)
extrude eject 297.8
  expel 297.13
extrusion 297.1
extrusive 297.22
exuberance
  verbosity 573.1
  plenty 639.2
  (redundance 641.1)
exuberant
  verbose 573.7
  plentiful 639.7
exuberate 639.4
exudate n. 299.1
exudate v. 295.7
exudation
  egress 295.1
  (ejection 297.1)
  excretion 299.1

humidification 339.1
exudative 295.9
  (ejective 297.22)
  (excretory 299.10)
exude 295.7
  (let out 297.13)
  (excrete 299.9)
  (trickle 348.19)
exult rejoice 838.5
  boast 884.6
exultant
  jubilant 838.9
  hopeful 858.9
  boastful 884.9
exultantly 884.10
exultation
  rejoicing 838.1
  boasting 884.1
exulting
  overjoyed 827.10
  elated 836.9
  boasting 884.9
exundate 348.18
exundation 348.3
exuviae
  cast skin 223.13
  excrements 299.2
  (offal 653.6)
exuvial 226.11
exuviate 226.6
exuviation 226.1
eye n. circle 247.2
  opening 260.1
  sight 441.1, 2, 7
  intention 620.1
all eyes
  attentive 457.9
  vigilant 459.8
an eye for an eye
  interchange 148.1
  retaliation 718.1
  revenge 919.1
have an eye to
  bear in mind 457.4
  intend 620.3
  desire 865.11
have eyes for 897.11
keep an eye on 459.6
under one's eyes 446.6
with an eye to 620.6
eye v. 441.12, 13
eyeball 441.7
eyebrow pencil 845.5
eyeful look 441.2
  a beauty 845.3
eyeglass, eyeglasses 445.3
eyelash hair 256.6
  eye 441.7
eyeless 442.6
eyelet circle 247.2
  opening 260.1
eyelid 441.7
eye opener
  surprise 508.2
  alcoholic drink 959.10
eyepiece 445.3
eyereach 441.6
eyeservant
  shirker 623.4

844

idler 683.7
eyeservice 927.1
eyeshade, eyeshield 424.4
eyeshot 441.2, 6
eyesight 41.1
eyes of wall 443.4
eyesore 846.3
  (blemish 848.1)
eyetooth 253.3
eyewash
  medicine 662.6
  flattery 933.1
eyewater
  eyewash 662.6
  liquor 959.4
eyewitness
  spectator 444.1
  witness 467.6
eyre 966.2
eyot 346.1
eyrie, eyry 189.13
Ezekiel 513.2

F

Fabian policy
  delay 133.2
  conservatism 141.2
  inaction 681.1
  caution 864.1
fable n.
  figure of speech 521.1
  falsehood 546.1
  story 594.2
fable v. 521.2
fableist 594.4
fabric structure 161.7
  textile 219.5
  (material 635.5)
  (merchandise 798.3)
  form 240.1
  texture 329.1
fabricate
  produce 161.8
  imagine 515.10
  trump up 544.3
fabricated 546.6
fabrication
  production 161.1
  falsification 544.1
  lie 546.1
fabricative 161.11
fabricator 548.5
fabulist liar 548.5
  storyteller 594.4
fabulous vast 31.8
  fictitious 515.12
  (unreal 2.8)
  (mythical 979.14)
  exaggerated 549.3
  legendary 594.7
façade 234.1, 4
face n.
  exterior 220.2
  front 234.1
  visage 234.4
  countenance 448.5
  impudence 885.2
face to face

before 234.9
opposite to 237.7
to one's face 525.7
in the face of
  in the presence of 186.16
  in defiance of 708.6
make faces
  deform 243.3
  look ugly 846.4
  show dislike 867.4
  be disrespectful 929.3
on the face of it
  apparently 448.8
  presumably 472.7
  manifestly 525.7
face v. coat 223.24
  line 224.2
  front 234.7
  oppose 237.5; 708.3
  paint 428.10
  resist 719.3
face about 283.6
face the music
  brave 861.5
  suffer punishment 972.12
face ague pain 378.1
  nervous disorder 655.14
face card 840.13
facecloth 652.7
face guard 717.2
face powder 330.3
facer 959.10
facet exterior 220.2
  front 234.1
facetiae 842.4
facetious 842.9
facetiousness 842.2
facia 234.1
facial 331.1
facile flexible 324.6
  (docile 602.9)
  easy 705.5
facilitate 705.4
  (aid 707.6)
facilities 705.1
facility
  flexibility 324.1
  skill 608.1
  ease 705
  (freedom 748.1)
facing n.
  coating 223.18
  lining 224.1
facing adj. 237.6
facsimile n.
  duplicate 21.2
  (same 13.3)
  representation 554.3
facsimile v. 19.5
fact reality 1.2
  (certainty 474.1)
  (truth 494.1)
  event 151.1
  evidence 467.1
in fact actually 1.9
  in truth 494.14
  (certainly 474.16)
  indeed 535.8

faction party 712.1
  discord 713.1
  sect 984.3
factionist 984.13
factious
  disagreeing 24.6
  quarrelsome 901.9
factitious
  spurious 545.13
  fictitious 546.6
factor
  component 56.1
  number 84.2
  cause 153.1
  agent 690.1
  steward 694.5
  functionary 758.2
factory 691
factotum
  do-all 690.3
  servant 746.1
factual real 1.8
  true 494.10
factuality 1.2
factum record 551.1
  memorial 594.2
facula 420.4
faculative 760.6
facultate 760.4
faculty
  intellect 450.1
  professorate 540.5
  vocation 625.5
  aptitude 698.2
  (ability 157.2)
faculty psychology 450.4
facund 582.12
facy 885.9
fad 608.1
  (craze 503.7)
fadaise 496.3
faddiness 608.2
faddish
  infatuated 503.12
  whimsical 608.5
faddishness 608.2
faddism craze 503.7
  whimsicality 608.2
faddist 504.2
faddle trifle 643.9
  dawdle 683.8
fade v.
  cease to be 2.5
  be transient 111.5
  weaken 160.7
  grow dim 422.7
  pale 429.4, 5
  (discolor 440a.2)
  disappear 449.2
  meet a bet 621.18
  deteriorate 659.6
  (age 124.5; 128.7)
fade adj. 391.2
fadeaway 449.1
faded 659.12
fadeless 873.19
fade-out 449.1
fadge 23.8
fading n. 429.2
fading adj. 128.8
fadmonger 504.2

eyeservice — failure

fadmongering
  infatuated 503.12
  whimsical 608.5
fadmongery
  craze 503.7
  whimsicality 608.2
faecal, faeces See fecal etc.
faërie, faëry n. 979.9
faery, faerie adj. 979.15
faex populi 876.2
Fafnir 192.8
fag n.
  hermaphrodite 83.5
  cigarette 392a.4
  drudgery 686.3
  fatigue 688.1
  drudge 690.2
fag v. work 686.6, 8
  tire 688.4, 5
  serve 746.8
fag end remains 40.1
  extremity 67.2
fagged 688.6
fagger 690.2
faggery, fagging 686.3
fagot, faggot
  bundle 72.5
  hermaphrodite 83.5
  firewood 388.3
fagotto 417.12
fagot vote 609.3
faïence 384.14
fail n.
  without fail 474.16
fail v. weaken 160.7
  sicken 655.21
  be unsuccessful 732.5
  (collapse 158.5)
  (perish 162.5)
  (fall short 304.2)
  (blunder 495.9)
  (be useless 645.5)
  (labor in vain 645.6)
  (mismanage 699.7)
  (bungle 699.9)
  (lose 776.2)
  not observe 773.3
  go bankrupt 808.6
  not keep faith 940.7
not fail 939.6
failed 732.11
failing n. 945.4
failing adj.
  incomplete 53.4
  unsuccessful 732.7
failing prep. 640.13
faille 219.5
failure
  unsuccessful person 732.4
  (misfit 24.4)
  (impotence 158.1)
  (shortcoming 304.1)
  (blunder 495.3)
  (disappointment 509.1)
  (labor in vain 645.3)

fain — fall 846

failure (*·ontinued*)
 (adversity 735.1, 3)
 (bankruptcy 808.2)
 (bankrupt 808.4)
 nonobservance
  773.1
 dereliction 927.1
 vice 945.3, 4
 nonfeasance 947.2
 be a failure 732.5
fain *adj.* willing 602.8
 desirous 865.16
fain *adv.*
 willingly 602.11
 desirably 865.22
faineance
 inertness 172.1
 indolence 683.3
fainéant *n.* 683.7
fainéant *adj.*
 inert 172.3
 indolent 683.13
faint *n.* 688.3
faint *v.* collapse 158.5
 swoon 688.4
faint *adj.* weak 160.13
 faint-sounding
  405.9
 (quiet 403.6)
 dim 422.8
 pale 429.6
 indistinct 447.5
 sickly 655.24
 fatigued 688.6
 be faint 405.4
faint *adv.* 405.11
faintheart 862.1
fainthearted 862.4
fainting 688.3
faintish 655.24
faintly slightly 32.12
 sound 405.11
 (voicelessly 581.9)
faintness
 weakness 160.1
 ~ of sound 405
 (nonresonance
  408a.1)
 fatigue 688.3
fair *n.* woman 374.2
 womankind 374.5
 bazaar 799.1
 festival 840.2
fair *adj.*
 inconsiderable 32.8
 rainless 340.8
 light-colored 429.7
 blond 430.9
 probable 472.5
 tolerable 648.11
 mediocre 736.3
 comely 845.10
 just 941.3
 (unprejudiced
  498.12)
 (right 922.5)
 (conscientious
  939.8)
 be fair 941.2
 for fair
  absolutely 31.16
  for certain 474.16

fair *adv.* 52.14
fair and square 941.3
fairing 784.3
fairish
 inconsiderable 32.8
 mediocre 736.3
fairly
 essentially 5.8
 justly 941.5
fairness, fair play
  941.1
 (honesty 939.1)
fair sex 374.5
fair-spoken
 suave 894.13
 flattering 933.3
fairway seaway 267.8
 runway 267a.28
fair-weather sailor
  269.1
fairy *n.*
 hermaphrodite 83.5
 sprite 979.9
fairy *adj.*
 imaginary 515.12
 fairylike 979.15
fairyfolk 979.9
fairy godmother
 giver 784.7
 good genius 979.12
fairyism 979.13
fairyland utopia 515.6
 fairies 979.9
fairylike 515.12
fairy ring 993.5
fairy tale
 falsehood 546.1
 story 594.2
fait accompli 729.1
faith belief 484.1
 (sect 984.3)
 (piety 987.1)
 expectation 507.2
 hope 858.1
 fidelity 939.4
 **give faith to, have
  faith** 484.7
 (be pious 987.6)
 keep faith with
  observe 772.4
  be honorable 939.6
 not keep faith with
  not observe 773.3
  be faithless 940.7
 take on faith 486.3
 the faith, the Faith
  983a.1
**faith curer,
  faith-curist**
 doctor 662.19
 religious 984.19
faithful copy 21.5
 (lifelike 17.15)
 accurate 494.11
 obedient 743.3
 observant 772.5
 constant 939.10
 orthodox 983a.7
 pious 987.10
 be faithful to 772.3
 the faithful
  believers 484.6

 Christians 987.5
faithfully 772.6
 (literally 19.14)
faithfulness 939.4
faith healer 662.19
faith healing 662.16
faithless
 unbelieving 485.9
 false 544.7
 unfaithful 940.10
 (untrue 546.6)
 infidelic 989.7
 be faithless 940.7
 (apostatize 607.8)
faithlessness 940.2;
  989.2
faithworthy 940.9
fake *v.* sham 544.6
 falsify 554.3
 affect 853.5
fake *n.* sham 544.2
 deception 545.3, 6
 lie 546.1
 impostor 548.3
 artifice 702.3
fake *adj.* 545.13
fakement copy 21.1
 dissimulation 544.2
 (simulation 19.3)
 deception 545.3, 6
 artifice 702.3
faker impostor 548.3
 peddler 797.3
fakir, fakeer
 beggar 767.2
 ascetic 955.2
 Moslem 996.7
falcade 309.2
falcate 245.20
falcation 244.2
falchion angle 244.2
 weapon 727.3
falciform 245.20
falcon bird 366.22
 thief 792.1
falconer 727.11
falculate 245.20
fall *n.* autumn 126a.4
 destruction 162.1
 declivity 217.2
 veil 225.12
 descent 306.1, 2
 drop 310.1
 waterfall 348.7
 rainfall 348.11
 death 360.1
 relapse 661.1
 defeat 732.3
fall *v.* happen 151.3
 perish 162.5
 incline 217.6
 descend 306.4, 6
 drop 310.4
 rain 348.25
 relapse 661.3
 faint 688.4
 fail 732.5, 6
 ~ in price 815.7
 sin 945.9
fall aboard 267.32
fall astern 235.8
fall away 36.3

fall back
 regress 283.5
 relapse 661.3
**fall back on, fall
  back upon** 637.4;
  677.5
fall dead die 360.6
 fail 732.5
fall down
 drift 267.23
 fall through 304.2
 descend 306.4, 6
 fail 732.5
 make obeisance
  928.6
fall flat
 fall through 304.2
 fail 732.5
 be dull 843.3
fall for
 be credulous 486.5
 be deceived 547.3
 become enamored
  897.12
fall foul of
 collide 276.9
 encounter 708.3
 quarrel 713.7
 contend with 720.8
fall from grace 661.3
 (be sinful 945.9)
 (religion 988.9)
fall in
 form a series 69.4
 happen 151.3
fall into 144.8
fall into line 69.4
fall into the hands of
  785.4
fall in with
 agree 23.7
 conform 82.4
 converge 290.2
 discover 481a.3
 concur 488.7
 accord 714.2
 consent 762.2
fall off decrease 36.3
 be disjoined 44.6
 deteriorate 659.6
fall on one's feet
  734.6
fall out happen 151.3
 oppose 708.2
 quarrel 713.7
 cease friendship
  889.2
fall short
 not reach 304.2
 disappoint 509.2
 (be incomplete 53.3)
 (be smaller 195.5)
 (be insufficient
  640.6)
 (be imperfect 651.3)
 (not complete
  730.2)
 (fail 732.5)
fall through
 fall short 304.2
 fail 732.5
fall to begin 66.5

eat 298.44
undertake 676.2
set to work 686.7
fall together 195.4
fall to the ground
 perish 162.5
 fall through 304.2
 fail 732.5
fall under
 be included 76.2
 be subjugated 749.3
fall upon
 discover 481a.3
 not expect 508.4
 attack 716.5
 let **fall** drop 308.4
 make known 527.7
 divulge 529.4
 utter 582.6
fallacious
 illogical 477.10
 erroneous 495.12
 (heterodox 984.22)
 untrue 546.6
fallacy 495.1
 (sophistry 477.1, 2)
 (heterodoxy 984.1)
fallen 961.10
fallen angel
 reprobate 949.1
 devil 978.2
fall guy 147.2
fallibility 475.4
fallible
 uncertain 475.14
 (untenable 485.11)
 illogical 477.10
falling 217.11
falling sickness
 twitching 315.6
 illness 655.3
falling star 318.3
falling weather 348.11
fallow
 unproductive 169.4
 yellow 436.6
 uncultivated 674.10
 (inactive 683.12)
 lie fallow
  be unprepared 674.4
  lie idle 683.8
false
 erroneous 495.12
 (illogical 477.10)
 untruthful 544.7
 (deceitful 545.12)
 (cunning 702.6)
 (dishonest 940.8)
 (sanctimonious 988.11)
 spurious 545.13
 untrue 546.6
 apostate 607.11
 suave 894.13
 faithless 940.10
false alarm
 alarm 669.2
 failure 732.4
false bottom 545.4
false face 225.11
false front
 false pretense 544.2

disguise 545.5
affectation 853.1
falsehearted 940.10
falsehood
 untruthfulness 544
 (error 495.1)
 (deception 545.1)
 (exaggeration 549.1)
 (improbity 940.1)
 lie 546.1
falseness 544.1
false pretenses 619.1
falsetto n.
 high tone 410.2
 voice 413.14
 speech defect 583.1
falsetto adj. 415.28
falsification
 untruthfulness 544.1
 (deception 545.1)
 (misrepresentation 555.1)
 lie 546.1
falsified 544.7
falsifier 548.5
falsify pervert 544.3, 4
 (sophisticate 477.7)
 (mislead 495.11)
 (deceive 545.7)
 (exaggerate 549.2)
 (misrepresent 555.4)
 (be dishonest 940.6)
 ~ accounts 811.9
falsity error 495.1
 falsehood 544.1
 faithlessness 940.2
falter go slow 275.5
 be uncertain 475.6
 demur 485.7
 stammer 583.3
 be irresolute 605.4
 (be afraid 860.8)
 despair 859.5
falx 244.2
fame 873.1
 (importance 642.1)
famed 873.16
familiar n. 979.12
familiar adj.
 well-known 490.17
 customary 613.11
 commonplace 843.6
 presumptuous 885.9
 friendship 888.4
 intimate 892.12
 affable 894.12
 familiar with
  versed in 490.14
  used to 613.12
  skilled in 698.14
familiarity
 knowledge 490.1
 acquaintance 888.1
 intimacy 892.1
familiarization 613.5
familiarize 613.8
 (train 537.10)
familiar spirit 979.12
Familist 984.14

familistère 712.3
family n. race 11.4
 (extraction 166.4)
 (party 712.1)
 household 11.5
 kind 75.2
 posterity 167.1
 population 188.10
 animal kingdom 366.1
 vegetable kingdom 367.1
family adj. racial 11.8
 classificational 75.6
 ancestral 166.10
family circle 892.7, 13
family tree 166.4
famine 640.3
famine-stricken 640.9
famish 819.3
famished
 meager 640.9
 hungry 865.19
famous 873.16
famously 31.21
fan n. blower 349.20
 (ventilator 338.6)
 (cooler 387.1)
 search 461.2
 fanatic 504.2
 motion-picture ~ 599.23
 sport 840.19
 votary 865.7
fan v.
 strike out 276.8; 732.5
 ventilate 338.10
 (blow 349.22)
 cool 385.4
 search 461.16
 refresh 869.2
 whip 972.6
fan the flame
 inflame 173.8
 ignite 384.17
 nourish 707.9
 rouse feeling 824.2
 (aggravate 835.2)
fanatic 504.2
 (dogmatist 474.4)
 (opinionist 606.3)
 (religion 983a.6)
 (hypocrite 988.6)
fanatical
 obsessed 503.18
 (dogmatic 474.15)
 (prejudiced 481.10)
 (opinionated 606.7)
 (hyperorthodox 983a.8)
 (pious 987.10)
 (overrighteous 988.12)
 extravagant 515.13
 overzealous 821.6
fanaticism 503.7
 (dogmatism 474.3)
 (bigotry 606.2)
 (fervor 821.2)
fanciable 515.15
fancical 515.12

fanciful
 fantastic 83.10
 imaginary 515.12
 whimsical 608.5
fancy n.
 daydream 458.3
 imagination 515.1, 4
 caprice 608.1
 (notion 453.1)
 pugilists 726.2
 humor 842.1
 desire 865.1
 love 897.1
 have a fancy for 897.11
 take a fancy to
  like 827.6
  desire 865.11
  become enamored 897.12
 take one's fancy
  please 829.4
  titillate 865.14
fancy v. judge 480.6
 believe 484.8
 (think 451.27)
 suppose 514.6
 imagine 515.8
 desire 865.11
 (prefer 609.9)
 love 897.11
fancy adj.
 fanciful 515.12
 excessive 641.5
 ornate 847.13
 showy 882.8
fancy-born, fancy-bred, fancy-built 515.12
fancy diving 310.1
fancy-formed, fancy-framed 515.12
fancy-free 748.12
fancy man 962.1
fancymonger 515.7
fancy stocks 800.9
fancywork 847.6
fancy-woven, fancy-wrought 515.12
fandangle 882.8
fandango music 415.7
 dance 840.7
fane 1000.1
fanfare blare 404.3
 celebration 883.1
fanfaron n.
 celebration 883.1
 boaster 884.3
 swaggerer 887.2
fanfaron adj. 884.7
fanfaronade
 ostentation 882.1
 celebration 883.1
 boasting 884.1
fanfaronading n. 884.1
fanfaronading adj. 884.7
fang tooth 253.3
 poison 663.3
 clutch 737.2
fanlight 260.5
fanlike 202.6

fan mail 592.4
fanmaker 690.8
fanon
 canonicals 999.
 sacrament cloth 1000.3
fan scale 319.5
fan-shaped
 expanded 194.10
 broad 202.6
fantad See fantod
fantail hat 225.26
 tail 235.6
fan-tan 621.7
fantasia music 415.3
 fancy 515.4
fantasied 515.12
fantasque n. 515.4
fantasque adj. 515.12
fantast 515.7
fantastic
 unusual 83.10
 absurd 497.4
 imaginary 515.12
 whimsical 608.5
fantasticality 608.2
fantasticate 515.8
fantasy, phantasy
 fancy 515.1, 4
 (unsubstantiality 4.3)
 (illusion 495.5)
 desire 865.1
fantoccini 599.8
fantocine 554.4
fantod, fantad 503.5
faqueer, faquir See fakir
far 196.5, 6
 by far 31.15
 far and away 31.15
 far and near 196.10
 far and wide
  greatly 31.15
  widely 196.10
  (extensively 180.8)
 far from it
  dissimilar 18.5
  amiss 304.5
  not at all 536.4
 thus far
  to a degree 32.13
  so far 233.3, 4
 too far 641.7
farad 158a.5
faraway distant 196.5
 preoccupied 458.11
farce untruth 546.1
 comedy 599.4
 trifle 643.3
 ridiculousness 855.2
 (burlesque 856.3)
farcical drama 599.28
 ridiculous 855.5
 (absurd 497.4)
farcicality 855.1
farcist actor 599.20
 dramatist 599.22
far cry 196.2
fardel 72.5
fare n. food 298.5
 price 812.1

fare v. do 7.2
 eat 298.44
fare well
 succeed 731.5
 prosper 734.5
far-embracing 31.7
farewell n.
 leave-taking 293.2
 aftertaste 390.1
 loss 776.7
farewell v. 293.4, 7
farewell int. 293.14
far-extending 31.7
far-famed
 extensive 31.7
 renowned 873.16
farfetched 10.7
far-flung
 extensive 31.7
 spacious 180.6
far-flying, fargoing 31.7
far-gone insane 503.12
 impaired 659.12
 in love 897.14
 drunk 959.21
far-heard
 extensive 31.7
 far-famed 873.16
farina 330.3
farinaceous 330.8
farm n.
 farmhouse 189.3
 poorhouse 189.11
 grange 371.4
 source of supply 636.2
 asylum 666.3
farm v. 371.8
farmer 371.2
 (workman 690.10)
 (rustic 876.5)
farmhouse 189.3
farming 371.1
farmstead 371.4
 (messuage 189.12)
farmyard 232.1
faro 840.12
far-off 196.5
farrago 59.2
far-ranging 31.7
far-reaching 31.7; 200.12
farrier 370.4
farriery 370.1
farrow
 multitude 102.2
 young 167.3
farse 998.9
farseeing
 clear-sighted 441.20
 foreseeing 510.6
farseeingness 510.1
farsighted
 clear-sighted 441.20
 presbyopic 443.14
 foreseeing 510.6
 (sagacious 498.10)
farsightedness
 presbyopia 443.1
 sagacity 498.2
 foresight 510.1

far-spread, far-spreading, far-stretched 31.7
farther 196.8
farthest 67.8
farthing fourth 97.2
 trifle 643.3
 money 800.8
farthingale 225.19
fasces 747.1
Fasci 712.6
fascia strip 205.5
 garment 225.34
 circle 247.2
 ornament 847.4
fasciate 247.8
fascicle section 51.2
 cluster 72.5
fascicled 72.12
fascicule 51.2
fascinate lure 617.4
 thrill 824.2
 delight 829.5
 astonish 870.3
 enamor 897.13
fascinated 897.14
fascinating
 delightful 829.8
 attractive 845.9
 bewitching 992.6
fascination
 obsession 503.7
 allurement 617.1
 intoxication 824.1
 delightfulness 829.2
 astonishment 870.1
 spell 993.1
fascinator 845.3
fascine 72.5
Fascism 737.4
Fascisti 712.6
fash 830.5
fashion n. state 7.1
 form 240.1
 (appearance 448.4)
 manner 627.1
 style 852
 in fashion 852.7
 out of fashion 124.9
fashion v.
 produce 161.8
 form 240.6
 create 976.7
fashionable 852.7
 (smart 847.14)
 be fashionable 852.6
 (conform 82.5)
fashionably 852.11
fashioned 161.13
fast n.
 fastening 45.2
 anniversary 138.7
 cord 205.2
 ship's rope 273.10
 fasting 956.2
 holytide 998.13
fast v. 956.3
fast adj. secure 43.11
 fixed 150.5, 6
 close 261.6
 speedy 274.13
 (sudden 113.5)

(hasty 684.5)
 music 415.33
 friendship 888.1, 4
 licentious 961.10
 make fast attach 43.6
 (stabilize 150.4)
 bind 751.7
fast adv.
 securely 43.15
 swiftly 274.14
 go fast 274.9
 hold fast
  navigation 267.69
  be resolute 604.6
  persevere 604a.2
  restrain 751.6
 stand fast
  be permanent 141.4
  continue! 143.5
  be quiescent 265.5
  resist 719.3
fast and loose 608.5
fast day 640.5; 956.2
fast-dyed 428.13
fasten attach 43.6
 (stabilize 150.4)
 close 261.2
 ~ a quarrel 713.8
 restrain 751.7
 seize 789.9
fasten oneself upon
 attend 746.8
 fawn 886.3
fastener, fastening 45.2
 (suspender 214.3)
 (supporter 215.2)
 (anchor 666.2)
 (shackle 752.2)
 (grip 781.2)
fasthold refuge 666.3
 stronghold 717.4
fastidious 868.4
 (discriminative 465.4)
 (precise 494.11)
 (choosy 609.15)
 (oversensitive 822.6)
 (tasteful 850.5)
 (prudish 853.7)
 (conscientious 939.8)
 be fastidious 868.3
 (discriminate 465.2)
fastidiousness 868
 (discrimination 465.1)
 (preciseness 494.3)
 (scrupulousness 603.2)
 (taste 850.1)
 (prudery 853.2)
 (conscientiousness 939.2)
fastigium 210.4
fasting n. 956
fasting adj. 956.4
fastness 717.4
fat n. 356.1, 4
fat in the fire 59.4
fat of the land

fleshpots 298.10
plenty 639.2
prosperity 734.1
fat *adj.*
 corpulent 192.12
 unctuous 355.3
 moneyed 803.8
 grow fat 734.5
fatal 361.16
 (destructive 162.6)
fatalism 601.6
fatalist 601.7
fatalistic 601.12
fatality
 casualty 361.5
 destiny 601.3
fata morgana
 luminescence 420.11
 (illusion 495.5)
 (imagining 515.4)
 apparition 443.9
fate 601.3
 (imminence 152.1)
 (fortune 156.1)
 (predetermination 611.1)
fated, fateful 601.13
Fates 601.4
fathead 501.1
fatheaded 499.12
father *n.* senior 130.5
 parent 166.6
 priest 996.2
 the Fathers 983.3; 985.6
father *v.*
 father upon 155.3
fatherhood 166.2
Fatherhood 976.1
father-in-law
 kinsman 11.3
 father 166.6
fatherland 182.2
 (home 189.2)
fatherless 158.9
fatherly
 paternal 166.10
 benevolent 906.6
Father of Lies 978.1
fathership 166.2
Father Time
 time 106.1
 elder 130.1
fathom *n.* 200.6
fathom *v.*
 sound 208.7; 461.17
 measure 466.10
 solve 481a.4
 (explain 462.7)
 know 490.9
 understand 518.4
fathomable 466.12
fathomer, fathometer 208.4
 (sea 273.14)
fathomless 208.9
fatidic 511.11
fatigue *n.* labor 686.3
 tiredness 688.1
 (lassitude 683.4)
 (weariness 841.1)
fatigue *v.* 688.5

(tax 686.8)
(weary 841.5)
fatigued 688.6
fatiguesome, fatiguing 688.8
 (laborious 686.10)
 (wearying 841.8)
fatiloquent 511.11
fatling 298.19
fatness 192.4
fatten enlarge 194.7, 8
 (oil 355.2)
 feed on 298.46
 improve 658.8
 prosper 734.5
 sponge on 886.3
fatty *n.* 192.7
fatty *adj.* 355.3
fatty degeneration 655.12
fatuitous
 nugatory 158.11
 (unsubstantial 4.5)
 absurd 497.4
 foolish 499.15
 useless 645.8
fatuity
 unsubstantiality 4.4
 incogitance 452.1
 absurdity 497.1
 folly 499.6
fatuous
 nugatory 158.11
 absurd 497.4
 foolish 499.15
 useless 645.8
fat-witted 499.12
faubourg 227.2
fauces 350.4
faucet 263.2
faugh 867.11
fault cleft 198.2
 mistake 495.2
 defect 651.2
 (weakness 160.1)
 (blemish 848.1)
 vice 945.5
 sin 947.2
 at fault
 misinformed 491.10
 erroneous 495.12, 13
 imperfect 651.4
 unsuccessful 732.7
 in fault 947.4
faultfinder
 malcontent 832.2
 censor 936.1
 (pessimist 859.4)
faultfinding *n.* 932.2
faultfinding *adj.* 932.11
faultful 495.12
faultiness 651.1
fault'ess perfect 650.5
 innocent 946.5
 (pure 960.2)
faultlessness 650.1
fault-slip 495.3
faulty illogical 477.10
 erroneous 495.12
 imperfect 651.4
 blameworthy 932.14

vicious 945.11
guilty 947.4
faun wood 367.7
 deity 979.11
fauna
 organic matter 357.1
 animal life 366.1
Faunus 367.7
faussebraie, fausse-braye 717.3
fauteuil 215.22
fautor 711.4
faux air 443.9
faux-bourdon 413.2
faux pas 495.3
 (bungle 699.4)
 (failure 732.2)
favaginous, faveolate 252.10
favi!ous 432.4
favonian 349.25
Favonius 349.2
favor, favour *n.*
 influence 175.1
 face 234.4
 appearance 448.4, 5
 epistle 592.2
 benefit 648.2
 patronage 707.2
 token 733.1
 indulgence 740.1
 permission 760.1
 gift 784.4
 be in favor of 931.5
 be in favor with 931.8
 in favor
 in good odor 873.15
 approved 931.10
 in favor of
 on behalf of 707.15
 approving 931.9
 in one's favor 648.15
favor, favour *v.*
 resemble 17.7
 prefer 609.9
 befriend 707.8
 permit 760.3
 ~ with 784.10
 be unfair 941a.2
favorable, favourable
 opportune 134.7
 auspicious 512.4
 willing 602.8
 beneficial 648.12
 helpful 707.13
 propitious 858.11
favored, favoured 748.18
favorer, favourer
 upholder 711.4
 (friend 890.2)
 well-wisher 889.2; 911.1
favorite, favourite *n.*
 race horse 271.8
 darling 899
 (loved one 897.7)
favorite, favourite, *adj.* 897.16

favoritism, favouritism 888.1; 941a.1
favose 252.10
fawn *v.*
 give birth 161.9
 truckle 886.3
 (flatter 933.2)
fawn *adj.* 433.4
fawner 886.2
 (flatterer 935.2)
fawnery, fawning *n.* 886.1
 (flattery 933.1)
fawning *adj.* 886.4
 (flattering 933.3)
fay whiteness 430.2
 fairy 979.9
faze, phase
 confuse 458.9
 daunt 860.11
 disconcert 706.7
 distress 830.3
F.B.I. 528.9
fealty 939.4
fear *n.* 860
 (trepidation 315.1)
 (uncertainty 475.1)
 (irresolution 605.2)
 (alarm 669.1)
 (cowardice 862.1)
 in fear 860.14, 16
fear *v.* 860.8
 (distrust 485.6)
fearful vast 31.8
 shocking 830.13
 afraid 860.14
 (alarmed 669.3, 4)
 frightful 860.15
 (ominous 512.5)
 (dangerous 665.7)
 cowardly 862.4
 wonderful 870.7
fearfulness 860.2
 (distrust 485.2)
 (foreboding 511.6)
 (irresolution 605.1)
fear-inspiring 860.15
fearless
 confident 858.10
 courageous 861.8
fearlessness 861.1
fearnought, fearnaught 225.17
fearsome 860.15
fear-struck 860.14
feasibility 470.2
feasible 470.6
feast *n.*
 anniversary 138.7
 banquet 298.37
 (festivity 840.2)
 holyday 998.13
feast *v.*
 banquet 298.44, 46
 luxuriate 377.4
 revel 840.21
feasting 298.1
feat deed 680.2
 success 731.2
 exploit 861.2
feather *n.* kind 75.2
 plume 256.8, 9

feather — feme

feather *(continued)*
  lightness 320.2
  wave 348.10
  irresolution 605.3
  trifle 643.3
  ornament 847.3
a feather in one's cap
  victory 731.3
  trophy 733.1
  (honor 873.7)
in fine feather
  sound 159.12
  in health 654.4
feather *v.* row 267.46
  aviate 267a.31
feather the oar
  row 267.46
  exercise skill 698.9
feather one's nest
  store up 636.8
  provide against 673.7
  prosper 734.5
  make money 803.6
  take precautions 864.4
  look after one's own interest 943.3
feather bed 324.3
featherbrain 501.2
featherbrained 458.13
featheredge
  edge 231.1
  sharp edge 253.5
featheredged 253.11
feathering 256.9
feathers bed 215.24
  clothes 225.1
feathery
  plumose 256.16
  light 320.7
  downy 324.7
  fickle 608.6
featly 682.25
feature *n.*
  component 56.1
  particularity 79.2
  form 240.2
  earmark 550.6
  salient point 642.4
feature *v.*
  resemble 17.7
  star 599.25
  emphasize 642.9
features face 234.4
  lineaments 448.5
feaze See **feeze**
febricity 655.4
  (flush 382.7)
febrifugal 662.25
febrifuge 662.12
febrile
  feverish 382.19
  impassioned 821.6
  excited 824.9
febrility 655.4
fecal, faecal
  excretionary 299.10
  foul 653.17
feces, faeces
  dregs 40.2
  excrement 299.2

  dung 653.7
Fechner's law 994.3
feck 25.1
feculence
  excrement 299.2
  dung 653.7
  (dregs 40.2)
feculent
  excretory 299.10
  foul 653.17
fecund 168.7
fecundate 168.4
  (procreate 161.10)
fecundation 161.2
fecundative 168.8
fecundity 168.1
federal 48.6
federalism 737.4
Federalist 712.5
federalize, federate *v.* 48.4
federate *adj.* 48.6
federation
  association 709.2
  society 712.4
federative 48.6
fed-up, fed up 869.6
fee *n.* estate 780.2
  (inheritance 775.4)
  gratuity 784.3
  pay 807.2
  assessment 812.2
  compensation 973.2
fee *v.* 973.3
feeble weak 160.10
  (infirm 655.24)
  (impaired 659.12)
  faint 405.9
  illogical 477.10
  weak-minded 499.13
  language 575.2
feeble-eyed 443.15
feeble-minded
  imbecile 499.13
  weak-willed 605.6
feeble-mindedness 499.3
feebleness
  weakness 160.1
  ~ of expression 575
feebly 32.12
feed *n.* 298.5, 7, 34, 37
feed *v.* dine 298.43, 44
  (provide 637.4)
  tend stock 370.7
  stoke 388.8
  (fire 384.17)
feed on eat 298.46
  sponge on 886.3
feeder aircraft 273a.1
  stream 348.1
  role 599.7
  foil 599.19
  provider 637.2
feeding 298.1
fee-faw-fum
  bogy 980.4
  object of fear 860.7
feel *n.* 379.1
feel *v.*
  sense 375.3; 477.3
  touch 379.3

  sound out 461.15
  grope 463.9
  (examine 461.17)
  suppose 514.6
  emotion 821.3
  (experience 151.4)
feel for
  sympathize 906.5
  pity 914.3
  condole 915.2
feel in one's bones 510.5
feel like 602.6
feel one's way 463.9
  (try 675.3)
feel out 461.15
feel the pulse
  sound out 461.15
  grope 463.9
not feel like 603.4
feeler bristle 256.7
  tactile organ 379.2
  leading question 461.10
  test 463.4
feeling *n.*
  sensation 375.1, 2
  touch 379.1
  emotion 821
  (affection 820.1)
  (sensibility 822.1)
  love 897.1
feeling *adj.* 821.4
feeze *n.* 860.3
feeze, feaze *v.*
  disentangle 60.9
  confuse 458.9
  daunt 860.11
  distress 830.3
feign sham 544.6
  (simulate 19.7)
  affect 853.5
feigned 545.13
feint deception 545.3
  pretext 619.1
  artifice 702.3
feldspar 635.6
felicitate 896.2
felicitation 896.1
felicitous apt 23.10
  opportune 134.7
  well-expressed 578.4
  delightful 829.8
felicity style 578.1
  skill 698.2
  happiness 827.2
Felidae 366.3
feliform 366.26
Felinae 366.3
feline *n.* 366.3, 4
feline *adj.*
  animal 366.26
  furtive 528.21
  sly 702.6
fell *n.* hill 206.2
  pelt 223.12
  fur 256.3
  plain 344.1
fell *v.* demolish 162.4
  prostrate 213.7
  (flatten 251.4)

  overthrow 308.5
  kill 361.10
fell *adj.* dire 860.15
  cruel 907.9
fellah 876.5
felloe See **felly**
fellow *n.*
  analogue 17.5
  (equivalent 27.5)
  accompanier 88.3
  person 372.3
  man 373.2
  schoolman 492.1
  companion 890.3
  inamorato 897.6
fellow *v.*
  fellow with 27.6
fellow *adj.* 88.8
fellow citizen 188.7
fellow creature
  person 372.3
  fellow man 890.9
fellow feeling
  friendship 888.1
  love 897.1
  benevolence 906.1
  pity 914.1
fellowless 28.4
fellow man 890.9
fellow pupil 890.3
fellowship
  accompaniment 88.2
  partnership 709.2
  fraternal order 712.3
  (social group 892.7)
  scholarship 873.8
  friendship 888.1
  companionship 892.1
  religious ~ 984.3
fellow student 541.7
fellow sufferer 890.3
fellow townsman 188.7
fellow worker
  co-worker 690.4
  confederate 711.1
  companion 890.3
felly, felloe 247.2
felo-de-se 361.3
felon 949.2
felonious
  unprincipled 940.8
  wicked 945.16
felony crime 947.2
  violation of law 964.2
Felsöház 696.5
felt *n.* 219.5
felt *v.* 219.8
feltmaker *n.* 690.8
felucca 273.2
female *n.* 374
  (girl 129.5)
female *adj.* 374.11
  (effeminate 160a.5)
femality 374.5
feme, feme covert 903.8

850

feme sole — fibrovascular

feme sole 904.3
feminality
  effeminacy 160a.1
  womankind 374.5
feminine *n.* 374.1
feminine *adj.*
  effeminate 160a.5
  female 374.11
femininity
  effeminacy 160a.1
  womankind 374.5
feminism 374.9
feminist 374.10
feminity 374.5
feminization 160a.2
feminize 160a.4
femme 374.2
femme de chambre 746.2
fen pool 343a.1
  marsh 345.1
fence *n.*
  enclosure 232.2
  (obstacle 706.2)
  mid-course 628.1
  fortification 717.3
  receiver 792.9
  on the fence
  uncertain 475.16
  neutral 628.3
fence *v.*
  (protect 664.6)
  quibble 477.8
  defend 717.7
  fight 720.8
  fence in
  circumscribe 229.2
  condition 770.2
fenceless
  helpless 158.9
  defenseless 665.9
fencer 726.1
fencible 726.6
fend avert 706.5
  defend 717.7, 8
fender
  automobile 272.16
  fireguard 386.2
  guard 717.2
fenestra 260.1
fenestration 260.5
Fenian 742.3
fenny 345.3
Fenrir 192.8
feod See feud
feoffee trustee 779.4
  legatee 785.2
feoffor, feoffer 784.7
ferae naturae 366.1
feral savage 173.14
  funereal 363.25
  ferocious 907.9
feria 840.2, 5
ferial 687.7
ferine savage 173.14
  ferocious 907.9
ferity 907.3
ferment *n.*
  leaven 320.3
  effervescence 353.3
  (activity 171.2)
  (agitation 315.2)

bustle 682.6
excitement 825.3
anger 900.2
in a ferment 59.13
ferment *v.*
  leaven 320.6
  effervesce 353.8
  (be agitated 315.12)
  sour 397.4
fermentation 353.3
fermentative, fermenting 320.8
fern 367.8; 369.6
fernint, ferninst See fornent
fernlike 242.6
fern seed 993.5
ferocious 173.14; 907.9
ferociousness
  violence 173.1
  fury 825.4
ferocity 907.3
ferret *n.* 366.17
ferret *v.*
  ferret out pry 455.4
  hunt out 461.16
  discover 481a.3
ferret-eyed 441.20
ferriage, ferryage 270.2
Ferris wheel 840.15
ferrotype 556.11
ferruginous 433.5
ferruminate 46.7
ferry *n.* boat 273.4
  pass 627.7
ferry *v.* 270.8
ferryage See ferriage
ferryman 269.2
fertile
  productive 168.7
  imaginative 515.11
fertility 168.1
fertilization
  procreation 161.2
  productiveness 168.1
fertilize
  fructify 168.4
  cultivate 371.8
fertilizer 653.7
fertilizing 168.8
ferule
  punishment 972.1
  scourge 975.2
fervency heat 382.1
  eagerness 682.3
  passion 821.1
fervent, fervid
  hot 382.16
  passionate 821.6
  (willing 602.8)
  (devout 990.15)
  excited 824.9
  eager 865.17
fervor heat 382.1
  eagerness 682.3
  passion 821.1
  (fanaticism 503.7)
  (excitement 825.2)
  (happiness 827.2)
  love 897.1

Fescennine 961.9
fescenninity 961.1
fescue 367.9
fess, 'fess 529.5
festa 298.37
festal holiday 687.7
  festive 840.22
  convivial 892.12
fester *n.* 655.16
fester *v.* 659.7
festival
  anniversary 138.7
  festivity 840.2
  (celebration 883.1)
  (entertainment 892.5)
festive festal 840.22
  convivial 892.12
festivity 840.2
  (celebration 883.1)
  (conviviality 892.2)
  (dissipation 954.2)
festoon curve 245.2
  decoration 847.5
festooned 847.13
fetch *n.* likeness 17.6
  deception 545.3
  wraith 980a.2
fetch *v.* carry 270.8
  reach 292.7
  cost 812.6
fetch about 267.24
fetch and carry
  carry 270.8
  truckle 886.3
fetch up reach 292.7
  rear 537.10
fetcher 845.3
fetching 845.9
fete, fête
  festival 840.2
  (celebration 883.1)
  gala 882.3
fête champêtre 892.5
fete day
  anniversary 138.5
  gala day 840.5
  (red-letter day 883.2)
feticide, foeticide 361.2
fetid, foetid 401.4
  (nasty 395.7)
  (foul 653.17)
fetish, fetich
  idol 991.4
  talisman 993.2
fetisheer, fetisher 992.2
fetishism, fetichism
  idolatry 991.1
  sorcery 992.1
fetishist, fetichist 991.5
fetishistic, fetichistic 991.7
fetishization, fetichization 991.2
fetishize, fetichize 991.6
fetor, foetor 401.1
  (odor 398.1)

(corruption 653.2)
(putrescence 653.4)
(decay 659.2)
fetter *n.* 752.2
  (obstacle 706.2)
fetter *v.* 751.7
  (fasten 43.6)
fettle *n.*
  condition 7.1
  fine ~ 654.1
  in fine fettle 654.4
fettle *v.* arrange 60.6
  deck 634.2
fetus, foetus 153.3
feud quarrel 713.3
  fight 720.2
  at feud 713.10
feud, feod 780.2
feudal
  government 737.16
  subject 749.6
  estate 780.8
feudalism, feudality
  government 737.4
  serfdom 749.1
feu de joie 883.1
feuille-morte 433.1
fever delirium 503.3
  illness 655.4
  (flush 382.7)
  excitement 825.2
  (fervor 821.2)
fever heat 825.2
feverish hot 382.19
  (sick 655.23)
  hasty 684.5
  impassioned 821.6
  excited 824.9
  restless 825.9
  reckless 863.7
few 103.3
  (inconsiderable 32.8)
  (infrequent 137.2)
  a few a number 100.1
  small number 103.2
  (modicum 32.2)
few and far between 103.3
  not a few 102.5
fewer 103.4
fewness 103
  (infrequency 137.1)
fez 225.26
F.F.V.s 875.2
fiacre 272.4
fiancé 897.8
fiasco 732.1
fiat 741.3
fib *n.* 546.1
fib *v.* 544.4
fibber 548.5
fibbery 544.1
fiber, fibre
  filament 205.1
  texture 329.1
fibril, fibrilla 205.1
fibrous
  filamentary 205.7
  tough 325.5
fibrovascular, fibry 205.7

fibster — filch 852

fibster 548.5
ficelle 545.3
Fichteanism 451.11
fickle
  uncertain 475.16
  capricious 608.6
  (inconstant 149.6)
  (irresolute 605.5)
  (tergiversating 607.10)
  faithless 940.10
fickleness 608.3
  (changeableness 149.1)
  (irresolution 605.1)
  (tergiversation 607.1)
fico 643.3
fictile 324.6
  (formative 240.7)
fiction
  imagining 515.4
  falsehood 546.1
  story 594.2
fictitious
  imaginary 515.12
  spurious 545.13
  false 546.6
fictive spurious 545.13
  fictitious 546.6
fid 392a.7
fiddle *n.*
  violinist 416.3
  violin 417.3
fiddle *v.* violin 416.18
  trifle 643.9
fiddledeedee
  nonsense 497.5; 517.2
  bah! 930.11
fiddle-faddle *n.*
  nonsense 517.2
  (absurdity 497.1)
  trifle 643.3
fiddle-faddle *v.*
  procrastinate 133.5
  talk nonsense 517.6
  trifle 643.9
  dillydally 683.8
fiddle-faddle *adj.*
  nonsensical 517.9
  trivial 643.11
fiddle-faddle *int.* 497.5
fiddler 416.3
fiddlery 416.17
fiddlestick bow 417.13
  trifle 643.3
fiddlesticks
  nonsense! 497.5
  bah! 930.11
fiddlestring 417.13
fidelity accuracy 494.3
  veracity 543.1
  constancy 939.4
  (adherence 772.2)
fidfad *n.* 643.3
fidfad *adj.* 643.11
fidget *n.* 684.1
fidget *v.*
  twitch 315.11
  bustle 684.2
  be excited 824.7

  (be impatient 825.6)
fidgetiness
  twitching 315.6
  restlessness 682.6
  trepidation 825.3
fidgets
  restlessness 149.3; 682.6
  twitching 315.6
  nervous disorder 655.14
  trepidation 825.3
fidgety
  restless 149.6; 682.21
  agitated 315.13
  irresolute 605.5
  nervous 825.9; 860.14
fiducial firm 150.5
  confidential 484.15
fie shame 874.12
  censure 932.16
fief 780.2
field extent 180.1
  region 181.1
  plot 181.3
  the country 183.1
  airdrome 267a.28
  grassland 367.11
  farm 371.5
  sphere of work 625.3
  contestants 710.4
  arena 728.1
  athletic ~ 840.14
field artillery 726.8
field day racing 720.5
  festivity 840.2
  display 882.3
fielder 268.12
field glass 445.2
field gun 727.11
field marshal 745.11
field of blood
  aceldama 361.9
  battlefield 728.2
field of vision 441.6
fieldpiece 727.11
fieldwork 717.3
fie'dworker 690.9
fiend violent 173.6
  addict 613.7
  monster 913.4
  Satan 978.1
  demon 980.2
fiendish cruel 907.9
  wicked 945.17
  demoniac 980.9
fierce violent 173.11
  savage 173.14
  warlike 722.13
  frenzied 824.10
  passionate 825.10
  furious 900.13
  cruel 907.9
fierceness
  violence 173.1
  fury 825.4
fieri facias 963.2
fiery violent 173.13
  hot 382.16, 17

  red 434.9
  fervent 821.6
  excited 824.10
  passionate 825.10
  angry 900.13
  hot-tempered 901.7
fiery cross fire 382.8
  alarm 669.1
  rallying signal 722.3
fiesta 840.2
fife *n.* whistle 410.4
  instrument 417.4
fife *v.* 416.17, 18
fifer 416.2
fifteen 98.7
fifth 99.1
fifty 98.7
fifty-fifty
  equivalent 27.9
  mixed 41.9
  half-and-half 91.3, 6
  neutral 628.3
  go fifty-fifty
    compromise 774.2
    go shares 778.5
fig *n.* condition 7.1
  clothes 225.1
  fruit 298.31
  trifle 643.3
fig *v.*
  fig out clothe 225.41
    adorn 847.11
fig. 626.2
fight *n.* 720.2, 6
  (quarrel 713.3)
  (war 722.5)
fight *v.* resist 719.3
  contend 720.8
  (quarrel 713.7)
  (attack 716.5)
  (war 722.9)
  fight it out 720.8
  fight one's way
    be industrious 682.12
    work 686.6
    war 722.9
  fight shy of
    be reluctant 603.4
    avoid 623.6
    be fearful 860.8
  fight the tiger 621.18
fighter
  battleplane 273a.2
  combatant 726.1
fighting *n.* 722.1
fighting *adj.* 722.13
fighting chance 156.4
fighting cock
  combatant 726.1
  courage 861.4
fig leaf 225.3
figment 515.4
figmental 515.12
figural 84.7
figurant actor 599.19
  dancer 840.9
figurate 84.7
figuration 240.1, 3
figurative
  exemplary 82.11

  numeral 84.7
  symbolic 521.3
  (ornate 577.6)
  representative 554.9
figure *n.* number 84.1
  form 240.1
  (aspect 448.4)
  sign 550.2
  representation 554.4
  (art 556.8)
  (sculpture 557.4)
  outline 626.2
  consequence 642.1
  personage 642.5
  price 812.1
  eyesore 846.3
  celebrity 873.1, 9
  ostentation 882.1
figure *v.* compute 37.5
  calculate 85.7
  form 240.6
  appear 448.6
  imagine 515.8
  symbolize 521.2
  represent 554.7
  be distinguished 873.10
  be ostentatious 882.6
  figure in 37.5
  figure on 620.3
  figure out
    compute 37.5
    calculate 85.7
    solve 481a.4
  figure up
    compute 37.5
    calculate 85.7
figure caster 318.13
figured 577.6
figure dancer 840.9
figurehead
  insignia 550.12
  figure 554.4
figure-of-eight knot 45.6
figure of fun 857.1
figure of speech 521
  (phrase 566.1)
  (ornament 577.1)
figurer 559.4
figure work 847.3
figurine 554.4
figuriste 559.4
Fiji 560.4
filaceous 256.13
filament *n.* thread 205
  (ligament 45.4)
  hair 256.3
  lamp 423.11
filament *v.* 205.6
filamentary
  threadlike 205.7
  hairy 256.13
filament lamp 423.13
filamentous
  hairy 256.13
  filamented 205.7
  (thin 203.10)
filamentule 256.3
filch *n.* theft 791.4
  stolen goods 793.1

filch v. 791.9
filcher 792.1
file n.
 classification 60.3
 series 69.2
 list 86.1
 (store 636.4)
 case 191.8
 smoother 255.3
 (sharpener 253.7)
 grinder 330.4
 cunning person 702.4
 military unit 726.7
 pickpocket 792.6
in file 69.7
on file
 arranged 60.10
 on record 551.10
file v. classify 60.7
 give continuity 69.5
 list 86.3
 sharpen 253.9
 smooth 255.4
 pass through 302.2
 grind 330.6
 abrade 331.3
 store away 636.7
file off cut off 38.6
 march 266.21
 diverge 291.2
filed 60.10
file firing 716.2
filet de sole 298.18
filial 167.6
filiate 155.3
filiation
 consanguinity 11.1
 (relation 9.1)
 attribution 155.2
 lineage 167.2
filibeg 225.19
filibuster n.
 filibusterer 706.3
 oppositionist 710.2
 freebooter 792.3
filibuster v.
 procrastinate 133.5
 hinder 706.4
 plunder 791.10
filibusterer 706.3
filibustering 791.2
filicoid
 arborescent 242.6
 botanic 369.11
filiform
 threadlike 205.7
 hairy 256.13
filigree network 219.4
 ornamentation 847.3
filing 330.2
filings remains 40.1
 raspings 330.3
Filipino 188.9
fill n.
 full measure 52.3
 (plenty 639.2)
 (redundance 641.1)
 satiety 869.1
have one's fill
 have enough 639.2

be satiated 869.5
fill v.
 make complete 52.7
 (load 184.13)
 (line 224.2)
 (overload 641.4)
 (sate 869.4)
 pervade 186.12
 plug 261.2
 ~ an office 625.9
 provide 637.4
 teeth 662.24
 possess 777.4
fill in fill 52.7
 substitute 147.3
 shallow 209.3
fill one's shoes
 substitute 147.3
 represent 759.4
fill out expand 194.5
 rotund 249.5
 pad 573.5
fill the bill
 suffice 639.3
 avail 644.2
 complete 729.3
fi'l time 106.3
fill up
 compensate 30.4
 restore 660.8
filler 271.3
fillet fastening 45.2
 strip 205.5
 circle 247.2
 bandage 662.14
 ornament 847.3 4
fill-in 147.2
filling 190.1
 (lining 224.1)
fillip n. blow 276.3
 incentive 615.3
fillip v. throw 284.12
 excite 824.2
filly girl 129.5
 horse 271.3
 female animal 374.8
film layer 204.2
 coating 223.18
 semitransparency 427.2
 photography 556.11
 motion picture 599.9
filmlike 204.5
filmy laminated 204.5
 fine 329.3
 dim 422.8
filmy-eyed 443.15
filoplume 256.8
filter n.
 porousness 260.7
 refiner 652.7
filter v.
 ~ into 294.6
 percolate 295.7
 refine 652.10
filth dirt 653.5
 (malodor 401.2)
 obscenity 961.1
filthify 653.15
filthiness 653.2
filthy foul 653.17
 obscene 961.9

filthy lucre gain 775.2
 money 800.1
 wealth 803.1
filtrate percolate 295.7
 refine 652.10
filtration 295.1
fimbria fringe 231.2
 hair 256.3
fimbriated
 fringed 256.17
 (edged 231.5)
fimbriation 231.2
fimbricate 256.17
fimicolous 653.17
fin five 98.1
 swimming 267.9
 airplane 273a.10
 light shield 424.5
final n. 461.3
final adj. ending 67.8
 (hindermost 235.9)
 (completing 729.5)
 eventual 151.7
 evidential 467.11
 decisive 474.10
 mandatory 741.8
final cause cause 153.1
 objective 620.2
finale end 67.1
 final issue 154.1
 drama 599.5
 finish 729.1
finality 67.1
finally
 conclusively 67.11
 at last 133.12
 permanently 141.8
 eventually 151.8
 in conclusion 476.20
finance 800.1
finances 800.2
financial 800.21
financier 797.6
 (moneylender 787.2)
finback 366.21
finch 366.22
find n.
 discovery 481a.1
 treasure 648.4
 acquisition 775.2
find v.
 give birth 161.9
 decide 480.6
 pass judgment 480.9
 discover 481a.3
 provide 637.4
 acquire 775.6
find fault with 932.7
find favor 931.8
find in one's heart 865.11
find one's account in
 profit by 644.2
 use 677.5
 succeed 731.5
find oneself 186.9
find out
 make certain 474.6
 discover 481a.3, 4
find up 481a.3
fin de siècle 659.11

finding decision 480.1
 (verdict 969.8)
 discovery 481a.1
 explanation 522.1
 acquisition 775.2
finding store 799.1
fine n. 974.2
 (charge 812.2)
in fine 67.11; 476.20
fine v. 974.2
 (charge 812.5)
fine adj. little 193.8
 thin 203.10
 rare 322.4
 fine-grained 329.3
 powdery 330.8
 rainless 340.8
 discriminating 465.4
 exact 494.11
 good 648.8
 in health 654.4
 beautiful 845.13
 ornate 847.13
 refined 850.5
 fastidious 868.4
fine arts 556.1
fine-draw 660.11
fine-grained 329.3
finery clothes 225.13
 (gaudiness 851.2)
 frippery 847.2
fines herbes 393.1
fine-spoken
 suave 894.13
 flattering 933.3
finespun thin 203.10
 attenuate 205
 hairsplitting 477.11
finesse n.
 discrimination 465.1
 skill 698.1
 subtlety 702.1
 good taste 850.1
finesse v. 702.5
fine-still n. 336.3
finestill v. 336.5
fine-toned 413.27
finger n. feeler 379.2
 pointer 694.6
 hold 781.3
at one's finger's end 197.11
have a finger in
 intrude 228.10
 meddle 682.14
have a finger in the pie
 contribute 153.8
 have to do with 680.6
 meddle 682.14
 participate 709.6
have at one's fingers' ends
 know well 490.10
 memorize 505.13
finger v. 379.3
finger bowl 652.5
fingerling 193.5
fingernail 781.3

finger post — fish

finger post sign 550.10
  guide 694.6
fingerprint mark 550.7
  track 551.4
fingersmith 792.6
fingerstall
  wrapper 223.11
  dressing 662.14
fingerstone 342.4
fingle-fangle 643.3
finial 847.4
finical trifling 643.11
  fastidious 868.4
  (discriminative 465.4)
  (choosy 609.15)
  (prudish 853.7)
finicality 457.3
finicalness, finickiness 868.1
finicking, finikin
  trifling 643.11
  fastidious 868.4
finis 67.1
finish *n.*
  symmetry 242.1
  grammatical ~ 578.1
  skill 698.3
  completion 729.1
  (end 67.1)
finish *v.* end 67.5
  destroy 162.4
  kill 361.10
  confute 479.2
  complete 729.2
finish off
  destroy 162.4
  kill 361.10
  complete 729.2
finished absolute 31.12
  ended 67.9
  symmetrical 242.4
  dead 360.8
  skilled 698.13
  completed 729.6
finisher end-all 67.4
  effective retort 479.1
  finishing touch 729.1
finishing 729.5
finite 32.7
Finland 182.3
finnan haddie, finnan haddock 298.18
Finno-Ugric languages 560.4
fiord, fjord 343.1
fioritura 413.10
fipple flute 417.4
fir tree 367.6
  green 435.2
  wood 635.3
fire *n.* energy 171.1
  flame 382.8
  (light 420.1)
  vehemence 574.3
  eagerness 682.3
  gunfire 716.2
  fervor 821.2
  excitement 825.2

between two fires 665.8
be under fire 722.9
go through fire and water
  persevere 604a.2
  defy danger 665.5
  try one's best 675.5
  be courageous 861.5
  be rash 863.5
in the fire 673.13
  (in hand 625.10, 13)
on fire 382.17
open fire begin 66.5
  attack 716.6, 10
under fire 665.8
fire *v.* stimulate 171.7
  explode 173.9
  shoot 284.13; 716.6
  dismiss 297.12
  ignite 384.17
  detonate 406.8
  impassion 824.2
  ~ a salute 883.3
fire away begin 66.5
  set to work 686.7
fire up
  become excited 824.6
  become angry 900.9
  tipple 959.15
fire alarm 669.1
  (signal 550.14)
firearm 727.10
fireball fuel 388.1
  missile 727.14
fire barrel 388.1
fireboard 386.2
fireboat 726.11
firebolt 420.6
firebox 386.1
firebrand lighter 388.4
  instigator 615.6
  incendiary 913.1
firebrat 366.24
firebrick 384.14
fire brigade 385.3
firebug 384.6
fire clay 384.14
firecracker 382.9
  (noisemaker 404.4)
  (detonator 406.6)
fire cross 669.1
firedamp 334.2
firedog 386.3
firedrake, firedragon 420.11
fire-eater
  violent 173.6
  rash person 863.2
  chauvinist 884.4
  ill-humored person 901.4
  evildoer 913.1
fire-eating *n.* 863.1
fire-eating *adj.* 863.7
fire engine 385.3
fire escape
  stairs 305.2
  escape 671.3
fire extinguisher 385.3
fire fighter 385.1

fire fly 423.13
  (insect 366.24)
  (luminescence 420.11)
fireguard 386.2
fire hook, fire iron 386.3
fire light light 420.7
  semidarkness 422.2
firelock 727.10
fireman
  railroader 268.12
  fire fighter 385.3
fire net 671.3
fire-new 123.9
fireplace 386.2
fireproof 385.8
firer 384.6
fire-red 434.9
fire-resisting 664.11
fire screen 386.2
fireside home 189.2
  fireplace 386.2
fire tongs 386.3
firetrap 545.4
firewater 959.4
firewood 388.3
fireworks
  pyrotechnics 382.9
  shot 406.2
  gunfire 716.2
fireworm worm 366.25
  glowworm 423.13
fire worship
  fire 382.11
  idolatry 991.1
fire worshiper
  pyrolator 382.11
  idolater 991.5
fir green 435.2
firing fuel 388.1
  detonation 406.2
  gunfire 716.2
firkin 191.11
firm *n.* 712.5
  (merchants 797.10)
firm *adj.* fast 43.11
  crowded 72.13
  durable 110.9
  stable 150.5
  strong 159.12
  close 261.6
  solid 321.8
  rigid 323.5
  well-founded 474.9
  resolute 604.7
  obstinate 606.6, 7
  unprecarious 664.10
  strict 739.5
  friendship 888.1, 4
  loyal 939.10
  orthodox 983a.7
make firm 150.4
remain firm 265.5
stand firm
  be stable 150.3
  be quiescent 265.5
  be resolute 604.6
  resist 719.3
firm *adv.* 43.15
firmament
  boundlessness 180.4

854

heavens 318.2
firman decree 741.3
  license 760.2
firmly 43.15
firmness
  stability 150.1
  (resolution 604.1)
  strength 159.1
first *n.* beginning 66.1
  scholastic honor 873.8
first *adj.*
  beginning 66.8
  foremost 234.8
  preceding 280.3
at first sight
  at sight 441.23
  apparently 448.8
  manifestly 525.7
from first to last 52.15
first *adv.* at first 66.9
  (formerly 122.14)
  in advance 280.4
  in preference 609.18
first aid 662.15
first and last 87.7
first blush 66.1
at the first blush
  at first sight 441.23
  apparently 448.8
  manifestly 525.7
first-born 128.9; 130.5
First Cause 976.2
First Chamber 696.5
first-chop, first-class 648.9
first come, first served 609a.1
First day 687.2
first edition 593.1
First Families of Virginia 875.2
firsthand
  unimitated 20.3
  evidential 467.11
first line van 234.2
  ~ ~ of defense 726.6, 10
firstling 130.5
firstly 66.9
first-nighter 599.23
first-rate *n.* 726.11
first-rate *adj.* 648.9
  (paramount 642.14)
first-rater 648.4
first water
of the first water
  supreme 33.8
  best 648.9
  eminent 873.18
firth chasm 198.3
  sea inlet 343.1
fisc 802.1
fiscal 800.21
fiscalize 800.19
fish *n.* food 298.18
  animal 366.21
  dupe 547.1
  counter 621.13
fish to fry 625.2

855 fish — flair

fish v. 622.8
 fish for seek 461.16
  grope 463.9
  court 865.13
 fish for compliments
  880.4
 fish in troubled wa-
  ters 704.6
 fish out
  hunt out 461.16
  discover 481a.3
 fish up 307.6
 fish culture 370.1
 fish day 956.2
 fisher, fisherman 622.5
  (sportsman 840.17)
 fishery
  aquarium 370.3
  fishing 622.3
 Fishes 318.6
 fish fry 840.2
 fish glue 45.6
 fishify 544.4
 fishing 622.3
 fishing boat 273.1
 fishmonger
  vendor 797.3
  merchant 797.11
  (provider 637.2)
 fish out of water
  misfit 24.4
  bungler 701
 fishpond ocean 341.1
  pond 343a.1
  aquarium 370.3
 fish story
  falsehood 546.1
  (exaggeration
   549.1)
  boast 884.1
fishtail 267a.31
fishtailing 267a.24
fishwife 797.3, 11
fishworm 366.25
fishy piscatory 366.26
 improbable 473.3
 (untrue 546.6)
 dishonest 940.8
fissile 328.4
fissility 328.1
fission 44.2
fissural 198.5
fissure 198.2
 (disjunction 44.3)
fist
 handwriting 590.1, 4
 attempt 675.1
 grasp 781.3
 shake the fist
  defy 715.2
  threaten 909.2
fisticuffs 720.6
fistula 260.6
fistular, fistulose
 260.16
fit n. spasm 315.6, 7
 delirium 503.3
 caprice 608.1
 ~ of illness 655.3
 excitement 825.4
 ~ of laughter 838.3
 ~ of crying 839.2

 ~ of anger 900.2
 by fits and starts
  irregularly 59.12
  discontinuously
   70.5
  (fitfully 139.3)
  agitatedly 315.14
  capriciously 608.7
 in fits 315.14
fit v. accord 23.7, 8
 equalize 27.7
 conform 82.4
 clothe 225.42
 equip 634.2
 prepare 673.6
 beautify 845.7
 fit out clothe 225.42
  equip 634.2
  (provide 637.4)
fit adj. adapted 23.11
 opportune 134.7
 expedient 646.4
  (right 922.5)
  (due 924.9)
  (just 941.3)
 in health 654.4
 refreshed 689.5
 fit for 698.12
fitchew animal 366.3
 malodor 401.2
fitful
 irregular 139.2
 (discontinuous
  70.4)
 inconstant 149.6
 uncertain 475.16
 rabid 503.13
 capricious 608.5
fitfully 139.3
fitfulness 139.1
fitness aptitude 23.2
 (timeliness 134.1)
 expedience 646.1
 (right 922.1)
 (dueness 924.1)
 preparedness 673.4
fitted 698.12
fitting opportune 134.7
 expedient 646.4
fittings 634.1
 (wardrobe 225.2)
fittyfied 503.13
five 98.1
fivefold v. 98.14
fivefold adj. 98.15
five hundred 840.12
fiver fivesome 98.1
fix n.
 predicament 8.3;
  704.2
 standstill 265.3
 perplexity 475.2
 in a fix
  bewildered 475.16
  in difficulty 704.11
fix v. quantify 25.5
 ~ a burden 37.3
 attach 43.5, 6
 arrange 60.6
 methodize 60.8
 stabilize 150.4
 destroy 162.4

establish 184.10, 11
limit 233.2
form 240.6
solidify 321.7
kill 361.10
~ a limit 465.2
make certain 474.6
true 494.7
determine 604.6
bribe 618.3
repair 660.11
prepare 673.6, 7
retaliate 718.2
defeat 731.9
settle 769.8
take revenge 919.4
right 922.3
prescribe 963.4
punish 972.5
fix up arrange 60.6
 repair 660.11
 conciliate 723.4
fix upon
 discover 481a.3
 choose 609.7
fixation fixity 150.1
 location 184.5
fixed fast 43.11
 special 79.7
 durable 110.9
 immovable 150.5, 6
 (permanent 141.6)
 limited 233.3
 quiescent 265.7
 (inert 172.3)
 assured 474.9
 resolute 604.7
 inveterate 613.12
 conventional 852.8
fixed idea idea 453.1
 prejudice 481.2
 monomania 503.7
fixed star 318.3
fixer 660.7
fixings 56.1
fixity 150.1
 (permanence 141.1)
 (inertness 172.1)
 (quiescence 265.1)
 (inaction 681.1)
fixture fixity 150.1
 equipment 634.1
 appointment 741.1
 property 780.4
fizgig 382.9
fizz, fiz n. foam 353.2
 alcoholic drink
  959.8
fizz, fiz v. bubble 353.8
 sibilate 409.3
fizzle n.
 shortcoming 304.1
 failure 732.1
fizzle v. bubble 353.8
 extinguish 385.5
 sibilate 409.3
fizzle out
 weaken 160.7
 fall through 304.2
 extinguish 385.5
 fail 732.5
fizzy 353.10

fjord See fiord
flabbergast 870.3
flabbergastation 870.1
flabby soft 324.6
 pulpy 354.5
flabelliform
 expanded 194.10
 broad 202.6
flabellum 349.21
flaccid weak 160.10
 soft 324.6
flaccidity
 flexibility 324.1
 feeble style 575.1
flag n. caption 66.3
 lamina 204.2
 floor 211.2
 flat 251.3
 flagstone 342.4
 foliage 367.4
 ensign 550.13
 pavement 627.4
flag v.
 weaken 160.7
 go slow 275.5
 sicken 655.21
 languish 683.10
 tire 688.4, 5
flagellate v. 972.6
flagellate adj. 368.12
flagellation
 penance 952.3
 asceticism 955.1
 whipping 972.3
flagelliform 205.7
flageolet 417.4, 12
flagging n. floor 211.2
 pavement 627.4
flagging adj.
 sickly 655.24
 weary 841.9
flagitious
 scandalous 649.8
 wicked 945.16
flagman
 signaler 668.4
 train guard 717.6
flag of truce 723.3
flagon 191.11
flagpole 206.4
flagrancy
 manifestness 525.1
 publicity 531.3
 turpitude 945.2
flagrant
 absolute 31.12
 unconformable 83.9
 absurd 497.4
 conspicuous 525.5
 notorious 531.10
 terrible 649.8
 wicked 945.16
flagship 726.11
flagstaff 206.4
flagstone lamina 204.2
 flat 251.3
 stone 342.4
 pavement 627.4
flail hammer 276.4
 whip 972.6
flair
 discrimination 465.3

flake — fleck

flair (*continued*)
  sagacity 498.2
  taste 850.1
flake *n.* lamina 204.2
  powder 330.3
  snowflake 383.6
flake *v.*
  form layers 204.4
  scale 226.7
flaky laminated 204.5
  divestitive 226.11
  rough 256.12
  pulverulent 330.8
flam *n.*
  falsehood 544.2
  deception 545.3
  lie 546.1
flam *v.* deceive 545.7
  swindle 791.12
flam *adj.* 545.12
flambeau lighter 388.4
  torch 423.8
flamboyant
  rhetorical 577.6
  ostentatious 882.8
flame *n.* fire 382.8
  (luminary 423.1)
  light 420.4
  excitement 825.2
  love 897.1, 6
flame *v.* escort 88.7
  burn 382.13
  in flames 382.17
  flame up 824.6
flamen 996.10
flameproof 385.8
flame projector, flame thrower 727.11
flaming violent 173.13
  burning 382.17
  red 434.9
  orange 439.5
  fervent 821.6
  excited 824.10
  gaudy 851.8
  flamboyant 882.8
  boastful 884.7
flamingo 366.22
Flammenwerfer 727.11
flanch 231.1
flange edge 231.1
  protuberance 250.2
flank *n.* 236.1
flank *v.* side 236.4
  protect 664.6
flanked 236.7
flanking 236.6
flannel 219.5
flap *n.* adjunct 39.2
  lamina 204.2
  pendant 214.2
  tail 235.6
  airplane 273a.10
  blow 276.3
  flutter 315.5
  clap 406.7
flap *v.* hang 214.4
  slap 276.8
  shake 315.8, 10
flapcake 298.12
flapdoodle 517.2

flap-eared 418.14
flapjack 298.12
flapper girl 129.5
  tail 235.6
  reminder 505.5
flapperhood 127.1
flapperish 127.5
flare *n.*
  explosion 173.3
  firework 382.9
  signal light 423.5
flare *v.* explode 173.9
  flash 420.17
flare up
  become excited 824.6
  (rage 825.7)
  become angry 900.9
flare-up
  firework 382.9
  signal light 423.5
  outburst of anger 900.3
flaring
  gaudy-colored 428.15
  gaudy 851.8
  showy 882.8
flash *n.* instant 113.3
  explosion 173.3
  finery 225.13
  flame 382.8
  ~ of light 420.4
  ~ of lightning 420.6
  flashlight 423.3
  glimpse 441.2
  cant 563.16
  impulse 612.1
  ~ of wit 842.4
flash *v.* explode 173.9
  flare 420.17
  be witty 842.8
flash back
  answer 462.5
  bandy jokes 842.8
flash up 824.6
flash *adj.*
  spurious 545.13
  cant 563.16
flasher 423.3
flashing 847.13
flash in the pan
  nullity 4.2
  impotent 158.3
  shortcoming 304.1
  labor in vain 645.3
  false alarm 669.2
  failure 732.1, 4
flashlight flash 420.4
  lamp 423.3, 5
flashy
  gaudy-colored 428.15
  rhetorical 577.6
  gaudy 851.8
  affected 853.6
  showy 882.8
flask, flasket 191.11
flat *n.* suite 191.21
  shallow 209.2
  horizontal 213.3
  surface 251.2

  smooth 255.2
  tire 272.16
  flatcar 272.19
  plain 344.1
  note 413.6
  fool 501.1
  (dupe 547.1)
  stage 599.15
  gambling 621.14
  hidden danger 667.1
flat *v.* 428.10
flat out
  fall through 304.2
  fail 732.5
flat *adj.* inert 172.3
  horizontal 213.8
  (low 207.7)
  plane 251.5
  smooth 255.5
  insipid 391.2
  phonetics 402.11
  nonresonant 408a.6
  off-key 414.4
  dull-colored 428.19
  positive 535.6
  moneyless 804.7
  obtuse 823.5
  dismal 837.10
  uninteresting 843.5
  render flat 251.4
flat *adv.* 251.6
  (horizontally 213.10)
flatboat 273.4
flatcar 272.19
flatfoot
  detective 528.9
  policeman 745.10
flat-footed 703.4
flatiron
  smoother 255.3
  heater 386.1
flatness planeness 251
  dullness 843.1
flat spin 267a.24
flatten level 213.6
  make flat 251.4
  smooth 255.4
  flatten out 267a.34
flattener 67.4
flatter deceive 545.10
  please 829.4
  adulate 933.2
  (overestimate 482.2)
  (exaggerate 549.2)
  (truckle to 886.3)
  (praise 931.6)
flatter oneself
  presume 472.3
  hope 858.7
flattercap, flatterer 935.2
  (sycophant 886.2)
flattering 933.3
  (sycophantic 886.4)
  (approbatory 931.9)
flatteringly 933.4
flattery 933
  (overestimation 482.1)

  (dissimulation 544.2)
  (exaggeration 549.1)
  (sycophancy 886.1)
  (commendation 931.2, 3)
flat tire tire 272.16
  bore 841.4
flatulence 334.1
flatulent
  gaseous 334.7
  airy 338.11
  windy 349.31
  style 575.2
  grandiloquent 577.7
  (diffuse 573.7)
flatus 349.1
flatwise 251.6
flatworm 366.25
flaunt 882.7
flaunting
  gaudy-colored 428.15
  grandiloquent 577.7
  gaudy 851.8
  ostentatious 882.8
  (conspicuous 525.5)
flautist 416.2
flauto 417.12
flavor, flavour *n.* 390.1
flavor, flavour *v.*
  imbue 41.8
  taste 390.3
  season 392.4
flavorful, flavourful 394.7
flavoring, flavouring 393.1
flavorless, flavourless 391.2
flavorous, flavourous
  gustable 390.4
  savory 394.7
flavorsome, flavoursome 394.7
flavory, flavoury 394.7
flaw *n.* cleft 198.2
  gust 349.6
  sophism 477.2
  error 495.2
  fault 651.2
  (blemish 848.1)
  moral defect 945.5
flaw *v.* 349.22
flawy 349.25
flax *n.* 205.2
flax *v.* 972.6
flaxen, flaxen-haired 436.6
flay 226.5
flea jumper 309.3
  insect 366.24
flea in the ear
  tip 527.3
  advice 695.1
fleabite 643.3
flea-bitten 440.9
flèche 253.4
fleck 440.4

flecked, fleckered
  440.9
flection, flexion
  curvature 245.1, 2
  fold 258.1
  deviation 279.1
fledgling, fledgeling
  129.1, 7
flee hasten off 293.5
  take flight 623.10
  (desert 624.3)
  (escape 671.6)
fleece n. pelt 223.12
  hair 256.3, 10
  softness 324.3
fleece v. strip 789.12
  rob 791.10, 12
  impoverish 804.6
  overcharge 814.3
fleeced 804.7
fleecy 324.7
fleer n. ridicule 856.1
  gibe 930.3
fleer v. 930.6
fleet n. flotilla 273.6
  flight 623.2
  navy 726.10
Fleet n. 752.1
fleet v.
  cease to be 2.5
  be transient 111.5
  disappear 449.2
fleet adj. brief 111.7
  shallow 209.4
  fast 274.13
  nimble 682.17
fleeting 111.6
Fleet Street 593.17
Flemish 560.4
Flemish horse 273.10
flesh meat 298.19
  animality 364.1
  man 372.1
  carnality 961.3
  in the flesh
    in person 186.17
    living 359.10
  flesh and blood
    being 3.2
    corpulence 192.4
    materiality 316.1
    animality 364.1
flesh color n. 434.3
flesh-color adj. 434.10
flesh-devouring 961.11
flesh-eater 298.41
flesh-eating 298.48
fleshly
  material 136.8
  physical 364.4
  (human 372.5)
  carnal 961.11
fleshpots eating 298.10
  prosperity 734.1
  gain 775.2
  wealth 803.1
fleshy stout 192.12
  pulpy 354.5
fleuron 847.3
flex 245.1
flexibility 324.1; 325.1

flexible, flexile 324.6;
  325.5
flexion See flection
flexuose 248.4
flexuosity zigzag 217.4
  convolution 248.1
flexuous zigzag 217.16
  convoluted 248.4
  (flowing 348.26)
  flexible 324.6
flexure
  curvature 245.1
  fold 258.1
flibbertigibbet 980.2
flick jerk 285.5
  flutter 315.10
flicker n.
  flutter 315.5
  bird 366.22
  glimpse 441.2
flicker v. vary 149.4
  flutter 315.10
  glitter 420.18
  (fade 422.7)
flickering
  irregular 139.2
  burning 382.17
flickery, flicky 420.23
flier, flyer
  aeronaut 269a.1
  speeder 274.5
  handbill 531.4
  gamble 621.2
flies 599.12
flight n. horde 72.4
  multitude 102.2
  hull 223.14
  course 264.3
  aeronautics 267a.1
  volitation 267a.23
  velocity 274.1
  ~ of steps 305.2
  music 413.10
  ~ of fancy 515.1
  (exaggeration
    549.1)
  avoidance 623.2
  (retreat 287.1)
  (departure 293.1)
  (escape 671.1)
  air squadron 726.9
  ~ of arrows 727.6
  put to flight
    repel 717.5
    vanquish 731.9
  take flight
    hasten off 293.5
    flee 623.10
flight v. 284.13
flight path 267a.3
flighty
  scatterbrained
    458.13
  delirious 503.14
  fanciful 515.13
flimflam n.
  humbug 544.2
  fraud 545.1, 3
  caprice 608.1
flimflam v.
  deceive 545.7
  swindle 791.12

flimflam adj. 545.12
flimflammer
  cheat 548.2
  swindler 792.8
flimflammery 545.1
flimsiness 160.1
flimsy n. 590.3, 10
flimsy adj. frail 160.11
  thin 203.10
  rare 322.4
  soft 324.6
  illogical 477.10
  trivial 643.11
flinch recoil 277.3
  shrink 623.9
  (be afraid 860.8)
  (be cowardly 862.3)
flinder 51.3
fling n. throw 284.3
  attempt 675.1
  spree 840.3
  dance 840.7
  gibe 930.3
  (retort 462.1)
  have a fling
    have a chance 156.9
    scoff 930.6
  have one's fling
    be active 682.12
    be law 738.4
    be free 748.8
    revel 840.21
    dissipate 954.3
  take a fling at 716.5
fling v. 284.12
fling away
  waste 638.2
  discard 678.3
  squander 818.3
fling down 308.5
flinger 284.7
flint hardness 323.3
  stone 342.4
  lighter 388.4
flinthearted 907.8
flintworker 690.9
flip n. 959.8
flip v. 285.5
flip adj. glib 584.5
  impertinent 885.9
flippancy 885.2
flippant 885.9
flipper
  swimming 267.9
  airplane 273a.10
  scene 599.15
flirt n.
  tergiversator 607.4
  coquette 902.6
flirt v. throw 284.12
  jerk 285.5
  coquet 608.4; 853.5;
    902.7
flirtation
  capriciousness
    608.2
  coquetry 902.1
flirtatious 608.6;
  902.10
flit elapse 109.3
  be transient 111.5
  vary 149.4

course 264.6
travel 266.12
fly 267a.30
speed 274.9
hasten off 293.5
flitch 236.1
flitter n.
  modicum 32.2
  piece 51.3
  fritter 298.12
  flutter 315.5
flitter v. vary 149.4
  flutter 315.10
flivver
  automobile 272.15
  shortcoming 304.1
  trifle 643.3
  failure 732.1
float n. raft 273.5
  airplane 273a.10
  lightness 320.2
  ice 383.5
float v. stabilize 150.4
  navigate 267.44, 46
  transport 270.8
  soar 305.6
  be light 320.5
  (rise 305.4)
  blow 349.22
floater
  wanderer 268.2
  voter 609.4
  politics 702.4
floating n. 267.9
floating adj.
  sailing 267.50
  rumored 532.8
floating battery 726.11
floating debt 806.1
floatstone 342.4
floaty 320.7
floccillation
  twitching 315.6
  nervous disorder
    655.14
floccose nappy 256.15
  downy 324.7
floccule 330.3
flocculence 324.1
flocculent
  nappy 256.15
  downy 324.7
  pulverulent 330.8
flocculose 324.7
flock n. crowd 72.4
  multitude 102.2
  laity 997.1
flock v.
  assemble 72.10
  ~ together 88.6
  ~ to 709.5
flocky 324.7
flog hasten 684.2
  whip 972.6
flood n.
  quantities 31.3
  progression 282.1
  water 337.1
  deluge 348.2, 3, 11
  floodlight 423.3
  superabundance
    641.1

flood — fluorite

flood (*continued*)
  prosperity 734.1
flood *v.* wet 337.5
  stream 348.17
  overfill 641.4
floodgate limit 233.1
  sluice 350.2
flood-hatch 350.2
flood lamp,
  floodlight *n.* 423.3
floodlight *v.* 420.20
floodlighting 420.14
floodmark 466.5
floodproof 340.11
flood tide
  increase 35.1
  height 206.5
  advance 282.1
  tide 348.9
floor *n.* story 191.18
  stratum 204.1
  sea bottom 208.3
  bottom 211.2, 3
  plane 213.3
  platform 215.21
  flat 251.3
  deck 273.8
  on the floor 461.26
floor *v.*
  prostrate 213.7
  fell 308.5
  nonplus 475.8
  confute 479.2
  defeat 731.9
floored
  nonplused 475.16
  at an impasse 704.11
  defeated 732.12
floorer
  effective retort 479.1
  puzzle 533.2
flooring 211.2
flop *n.* bed 215.24
  fall 306.2
  flutter 315.5
  failure 732.1, 4
  take a flop 306.6
flop *v.*
  drop down 306.4
  flap 315.10
  fail 732.5
flophouse 189.4, 8
flora
  organic matter 357.1
  vegetable life 367.1
  botany 369.1
Flora 367.1
floral 367.14
florescence
  flowering 161.4
  bloom 367.5
floressence 400.2
floret 367.5
floriculture 371.1
floriculturist 371.2
florid music 416.24
  gaudy-colored 428.15
  red 434.11
  rhetorical 577.6

(figurative 521.3)
  healthy 654.4
  gaudy 851.8
  ostentatious 882.8
Florida Water 400.3
floridity 577.1
florification 367.5
florin 800.8
florist
  agriculturist 371.2
  merchant 797.11
floscule 367.5
flotilla fleet 273.6
  navy 726.10
flotsam
  scattering 73.2
  derelict 782.2
flounce *n.* fringe 231.2
  fold 258.1
  gait 266.5
flounce *v.* fold 258.3
  walk 266.16
  jerk 285.5
  caper 309.5; 840.21
flounder vary 149.4
  pitch 267.45
  wallow 311.5
  stagger 315.9
  falter 475.6; 605.4
  be clumsy 699.9
  be in difficulty 704.6
flour 330.3
flourish *n.*
  music 413.10
  blare 404.3
  rhetoricalness 577.1
  ornamentation 847.3
  ostentation 882.1
  celebration 883.1
  (demonstration 882.3)
flourish *v.*
  brandish 315.8
  grow rank 365.2
  declaim 582.7
  be in health 654.2
  prosper 734.5
  be famous 873.10
  boast 884.5
flourishing
  luxuriant 365.4
  prosperous 734.7
floury 330.8
flout *n.* insult 929.2
  gibe 930.3
flout *v.* 930.6
flow *n.* course 264.3
  fluid 347
  air 348.1
  water 348.2
  (inflow 294.1)
  (outflow 295.1)
flow *v.* elapse 109.3
  hang down 214.4
  course 264.6
  stream 348.17
  blow 349.22
  purl 405.5
  abound 639.4
  flow from 154.3
  flow in 294.6
  flow out 295.7

flow over
  overrun 303.3
  overflow 348.18
  superabound 641.2
flower *n.*
  essence 5.2
  product 161.6
  blossom 367.5
  rhetoricalness 577.1
  excerpt 596.2
  best 648.4
  merchandise 798.3
  beauty 845.1, 4
  ornament 847.5
  good person 948.1
flower *v.* bear 161.9
  vegetate 365.2
  prosper 734.5
flowerage
  vegetation 365.1
  bloom 367.5
flower bed 371.6
floweret 367.5
flowering
  blossoming 161.4
  bloom 367.5
flowerlike 845.8
flowerpot vase 191.10
  firework 382.9
flowery
  rhetorical 577.6
  (figurative 521.3)
  ornate 847.13
  gaudy 851.8
  ostentatious 882.8
flowing *n.* 348.2
flowing *adj.*
  hanging 214.7
  streaming 348.26
  style 578.4
flu 655.9
fluctuate recur 138.8
  vary 149.4
  (be capricious 608.4)
  oscillate 314.8
  be irresolute 605.4
  (be capricious 608.4)
fluctuating 149.6
fluctuation
  changeableness 149.1
  oscillation 314.1
  uncertainty 475.1
  irresolution 605.1
fluctuosity 314.1
flue nap 256.10
  tube 260.6
  lightness 320.2
  smokeshaft 351.1
  dirt 683.5
flue cleaner 652.6
fluency 584.1
  (eloquence 582.3)
fluent *n.* 84.2
fluent *adj.*
  flowing 348.26
  (fluid 333.7)
  style 578.4
  voluble 584.5
  (eloquent 582.12)

fluently 584.6
fluey nappy 256.15
  downy 324.7
fluff girl 129.5
  plumage 256.9
  nap 256.10
  lightness 320.2
fluffy nappy 256.15
  downy 324.7
Flügelhorn 417.4
flugelman See fugleman
fluid *n.*
  electricity 158a.1
  liquid 333.2
  (beverage 298.4)
  (water 337.1)
  (semiliquid 352.3)
fluid *adj.* 333.7
  (liquefied 335.7)
fluidification 335.1
fluidify 335.5
fluidity 333
fluidization 335.1
fluke fortuity 156.1
  angle 244.2
  chance 621.2
  lucky stroke 731.2; 734.2
flukiness 156.6
fluking 267.50
fluky 156.12
flume tube 260.6
  conduit 350.1
flummadiddle, flumadiddle, flummydiddle 517.2
flummery
  nonsense 517.2
  flattery 933.1
flummox, flummux, flummix
  confuse 458.9
  perplex 475.8
  confound 706.7
  defeat 731.10
  fail 732.5
flummoxed 732.9
flump *n.* 408a.2
flump *v.* 306.4
flunk *n.* 732.1
flunk *v.* shirk 623.8
  fail 732.5
  be cowardly 862.3
flunked 732.11
flunker shirker 623.4
  failure 732.4
  coward 862.2
flunky, flunkey
  stagehand 599.17
  menial 690.2
  failure 732.4
  retainer 746.1
  (attendant 88.3)
  sycophant 886.2
flunkyism, flunkeyism 886.1
fluorescence
  luminescence 420.11
  transparency 425.1
fluorite, fluor spar 635.6

flurry — foist

flurry *n.*
  agitation 315.1
  gust 349.6
  snowstorm 383.6
  confusion 458.4
  bustle 682.6
  hurry 684.1
  excitement 825.3
  bluster 887.1
flurry *v.* agitate 315.8
  confuse 458.9
  excite 824.3
flush *n.* gush 348.5
  heat glow 382.7
  (fever 655.4)
  color 428.1; 434.4
  emotion 821.2
  rejoicing 838.1
  ~ at cards 840.13
  blush 881.1
flush *v.* glow 382.13
  redden 434.8
  cleanse 652.9
  turn color 824.8
  blush 881.4
  anger 900.7
flush *adj.* full 52.11
  horizontal 213.8
  flat 251.5
  intoxicated 959.21
  abundant 639.7
  healthy 654.4
  affluent 803.8
flushed
  intoxicated 959.21
  red 434.11
  impassioned 821.6
  excited 824.9
  cheerful 836.9
  jubilant 838.9
  hopeful 858.9
  ~ with pride 878.6
  exultant 884.9
  ~ with anger 900.13
fluster *n.*
  agitation 315.1
  confusion 458.4
  bustle 682.6
  excitement 825.3
  bluster 887.1
fluster *v.*
  confuse 458.9
  excite 824.3
flusterate, flustrate 458.9
flusteration, flustration 458.4
flustered 959.21
flustery 458.12
flute *n.*
  hermaphrodite 83.5
  instrument 417.4
  organ stop 417.12
flute *v.* fold 258.3
  furrow 259.3
fluting 259.1
flutist 416.2
flutter *n.* spurt 274.3
  shake 315.5
  (pulsation 314.2)
  tremolo 407.2
  gamble 621.2

  bustle 682.6
  hurry 684.1
  excitement 825.3
  in a flutter 315.14
flutter *v.* vary 149.4
  shake 315.8, 10
  (pulsate 314.9)
  tremolo 407.7
  glitter 420.18
  bustle 682.12
  hurry about 684.3
  agitate 824.3
  be excited 824.7
fluttery 420.23
fluvial, fluviatile 348.26
fluviograph 348.13
fluviology, fluvioterrestrial 348.14
flux converson 144.1
  changeableness 149.1
  course 264.3
  excretion 299.1
  ~ and reflux 314.3; 348.9
  fusion 335.1, 3
  flow 348.2
  melt 384.21
  ailment 655.5
fluxation 149.1
fluxion 84.2; 85.2
fluxional 84.7
fly *n.* adjunct 39.2
  midge 193.2
  carriage 272.4
  insect 366.24
fly in the ointment
  evil 649.2
  source of distress 830.2
on the fly 264.10
fly *v.* cease to be 2.5
  elapse 109.3
  be transient 111.5
  aviate 267a.30, 31
  speed 274.9
  hasten off 293.5
  fade 429.4
  disappear 449.2
  flee 623.10
fly about 531.9
fly after 281.3
fly a kite 788.2
  (charge 805.5)
fly at 716.5
fly away 293.5
fly back 277.3
fly in the face of
  be contrary 14.3
  oppose 708.2
  resist 719.3
  revolt 742.5
fly into a passion
  excitement 824.6
  become angry 900.9
fly off deviate 279.7
  diverge 291.2
  excitement 824.6
fly off at a tangent
  deviate 279.7
  diverge 291.2

  excitement 824.6
  become angry 900.9
fly off the handle
  die 360.6
  excitement 824.6
  become angry 900.9
fly out
  break open 173.10
  become angry 900.9
fly to 664.8
flyabout 273a.1
flyblown foul 653.17
  putrefied 659.13
flyboat 273.4
fly-by-night 273.13
flycatcher 366.22
flyer See flier
fly-fish 622.8
flying *n.*
  aeronautics 267a.1
  velocity 274.1
flying *adj.* 111.6
flying boat 273a.3
flying circus 269a.1
flying colors
  trophy 733.1
  celebration 883.1
  (demonstration 882.3)
flying column 726.7
flying corps 726.9
Flying Dutchman
  wanderer 268.2
  mariner 269.1
  fancy 515.4
flying fish
  jumper 309.3
  fish 366.21
Flying Fish 318.6
flying jib, flying kites 273.13
flying machine 273a.1
flyman 599.17
flyspeck
  modicum 32.2
  inextension 180a.1
  diminutive 193.2
flytrap 545.4
flywheel
  automobile 272.16
  wheel 312.4
foal *n.*
  youngling 129.7
  horse 271.3
foal *v.* 161.9
foam *n.* froth 353.2
  insignificancy 643.5
foam *v.* froth 353.8
  fume 825.7
  ~ with rage 900.8
foaming rabid 503.13
  raging 824.10
  angry 900.13
foamy light 320.7, 8
  frothy 353.10
fob, fub *n.* 191.4
fob, fub *v.* 545.7
focal central 222.4
  converging 290.3
focalization 290.1
  (focus 74.1)
  (centrality 222.1)

focalize 74.3
focal point 74.1
focus *n.* 74
  (center 222.2)
  (convergence 290.1)
  (axis 312.5)
focus *v.* 74.3
  (converge 290.2)
fodder *n.* 298.7
fodder *v.* 370.7
foe 891.1
foehn 349.9
foeman 891.1
foeticide, foetid etc.
  See feticide etc.
fog *n.*
  aeronautics 267a.19
  cloud 353.5
  grass 367.9
  confusion 458.4
  vagueness 475.3
fog *v.* cloud 353.9
  dim 422.6
  perplex 475.8
in a fog
  bewildered 475.16
  concealed 528.17
fog bell signal 550.14
  alarm 669.1
fogey, fogeyish etc.
  See fogy etc.
foggage 367.9
fogged
  confused 458.12
  bewildered 475.16
foggy cloudy 353.11
  dim 422.8
  opaque 426.4
  confused 458.12
  bewildered 475.16
  stupid 499.12
  obscure 519.7
foghorn signal 550.14
  alarm 669.1
  (warning 668.3)
fogram, fogrum
  fogey 130.2
  conservative 141.3
  liquor 959.4
fogy, fogey
  conservative 141.3
  dotard 501.3
fogyish, fogeyish 141.7
fogyism, fogeyism 141.2
foible 945.4
foil *n.*
  the contrary 14.2
  lamina 204.2
  frustration 509.1
  actor 599.19
  weapon 727.3
  ornament 847.4
foil *v.* frustrate 509.2
  thwart 706.7
foiled 732.9
foin *n.* 276.3; 716.3
foin *v.* 276.8
foist *n.* 273.3
foist *v.*
  foist in drag in 10.4

fold — foppery 860

foist (*continued*)
  interject 228.8
  intrude 228.10
foist off 545.7
fold *n.* bond 45.1
  lamina 204.2
  enclosure 232.1
  double 258
  (angle 244.2)
  laity 997.1
fold *v.* 258.3
  fold one's arms
  do nothing 681.2
  idle 683.8
foldable, folded 258.4
folder handbill 531.4
  brochure 593.1
folding doubling 258.2
  bookbinding 593.9
foliaceous 204.5
foliage 367.4
foliate 85.9
foliated 204.5
foliation
  lamination 204.3
  foliage 367.4
  ornamentation 847.3
folio case 191.8
  page number 590.2
  book 593.1, 7
foliole 367.4
folk
  population 188.10
  people 372.2
Folketing, Folkething 696.6
folklore
  tradition 124.3
  mythology 979.13
folks 11.3
folk song 415.10
Folkvang, Folkvangr 981.3
follicle
  compartment 191.2
  hull 223.14
  cavity 252.2
follicular 260.16
follicule 252.2
follow resemble 17.7
  emulate 19.10
  come after 63.3; 281.3
  (accompany 88.6)
  be subsequent 117.2
  seek 461.16
  understand 518.4
  pursue 622.6
  (be behind 235.8)
  follow a course
  sail 267.22
  go directly 278.6
  follow from
  result from 154.3
  be proved by 478.2
  follow out 604a.2
  follow suit 19.10
  follow up
  continue 143.3
  seek 461.16
  pursue 622.6

follower
  successor 281.2
  (afterpart 65.2)
  (accompanier 88.3)
  (pursuer 622.4)
  (puppet 711.2)
  disciple 541.2
  school 542.4
  retainer 746.1
  devotee 840.19
  hanger-on 886.2
  suitor 897.6
following *n.* order 63.1
  attendance 88.5
  (follower 281.2)
  posterity 117.1
  motion 281.1
following *adj.*
  succeeding 63.5
  later 117.3
  deducible 478.5
folly 499.6, 7
  (nonsense 517.2)
  (unskillfulness 699.1)
  (rashness 863.1)
foment inflame 173.8
  agitate 315.8
  heat 384.16
  nourish 707.9
  excite 824.2
  soothe 834.4
fomentation
  agitation 315.1
  lotion 662.6
fond *n.* 215.3
fond *adj.* 897.11, 14, 15
fondant 396.2
fondle 902.8
fondling pet 899.1
  endearment 902.3
fondness desire 865.1
  love 897.1
font source 153.2
  fountain 348.5
  type 591.6
  baptistery 998.5; 1000.3
fontanel, fontanelle 260.1
food 298.5
  (sustenance 707.3)
  (merchandise 798.3)
foodstuff 298.5
fool *n.* simpleton 501
  (wiseacre 500.2)
  (madman 504.1)
  (dupe 547.1)
  (bungler 699.5)
  comedian 599.20
  make a fool of
  deceive 545.10
  make ridiculous 856.5
  (stultify 497.3)
  make a fool of one-self
  act the fool 499.9
  be ridiculous 855.3
fool *v.*
  act the fool 499.9

  deceive 545.10
  (mislead 495.11)
  (dupe 547.2)
  (ridicule 856.5)
fool around
  behave foolishly 499.9
  trifle 643.9
fool away
  waste 638.2
  squander 818.3
fool *adj.* 499.15
fool duck 366.22
foolery
  absurdity 497.1
  folly 499.6
  buffoonery 842.3
foolhardihood 863.1
foo hardy 863.7
fooling 842.3
foolish absurd 497.4
  (trivial 643.11)
  silly 499.15
  (irrational 477.10)
  (senseless 517.8)
  (inexpedient 647.3)
  look foolish
  be disreputable 874.4
  feel small 879.2
foolishness
  absurdity 497.1
  (ridiculousness 855.1)
  folly 499.6
  (irrationality 477.5)
  nonsense 517.2
foolscap
  stationery 590.10
  paper 635.4
fool's mate 732.3
fool's paradise
  unsubstantiality 4.4
  prejudgment 481.2
  delusion 495.5
  airy hopes 858.4
foot *n.* length 200.6
  base 211.1, 4
  (foundation 215.3)
  metrical ~ 597.6
  infantry 726.8
  at the feet of
  near 197.11
  in subjection 749.6
  under 749.7
  worshiping 990.15
  at the foot of 207.11
  foot by foot 51.10
  go on foot 266.16
  on foot existent 1.7
  continuing 106.4
  going on 151.5
  operative 170.4
  afoot 266.28
  in question 461.26
  in preparation 673.13
  astir 682.23
foot *v.* 266.16
  foot the bill 807.6

foot up 37.5
footage 200.1
foot-and-mouth disease 655.18
football 840.11
footballer 840.17
footboy 746.1
footbridge 627.7
foot-candle
  electricity 157a.5
  light 420.1
footfall gait 266.5
  beat 407.3
footgear 225.27
Foot Guards 726.7
foothold 215.4
  (leverage 175.3)
footing
  circumstance 8.1
  degree 26.1
  computation 37.2
  rank 71.1
  numeration 85.1
  position 184.1
  foothold 215.4
  fee 807.2
  rank 873.4
  on a footing with 27.8
footlicker 886.2
footlicking 886.4
footlights
  illumination 420.7
  stage 599.1, 14
foot-loose
  wandering 266.24
  free 748.12
footman
  infantryman 726.4
  retainer 746.1
footmark 550.4
  (trace 551.5)
footpad 792.4
footpath 627.2
footprint 550.4, 7
foot race 274.4; 720.5
foot racer 274.5
footrest 215.4
footrope 273.10
footslog 266.16
footslogger, foot soldier 726.4
footsore 688.6
footstep 550.4
footstone stone 342.4
  tombstone 363.15
footstool 215.22
foot warmer 386.1
footwear
  clothes 225.27
  merchandise 798.3
foot-weary 688.6
footwork 266.4
foozle *n.* 699.4
fooz'e *v.* 699.9
fop 854
  (affecter 853.4)
  (attitudinarian 882.5)
foppery
  dandyism 853.3
  vanity 880.1

foppish
  dandified 853.6
  vain 880.6
for *prep.* 620.6
for all me 79.11
for all that 30.8;
    469.8
for as much as, for-
  asmuch as 155.8
for ever See **forever**
for ever and a day
    110.11
for the most part
  absolutely 31.16
  generally 78.15
  (habitually 613.13)
for the reason that
    155.8
for *conj.* 155.8
  (by reason 476.21)
for because 155.8
forage *n.* 298.7
  (grass 367.9)
forage *v.*
  victual 298.43
  search 461.16
  provision 637.4
  pillage 791.10
foramen 260.1
foraminifer 193.4
foraminiferous 368.12
foraminous 260.18
foraminule 260.1
foraminulous 260.18
foray attack 716.1
  (fight 720.2)
  (battle 722.5)
  pillage 791.2
forbear
  pretermit 460.7
  not use 678.5
  not do 681.2
  endure 826.6
  take pity 914.3
  abstain 953.5
  (avoid 623.6)
forbearance
  disuse 678.1
  lenity 740.1
  sufferance 826.4
  (submission 725.1)
  mercy 914.1
  indulgence 918.1
  temperance 953.1
forbearant
  unprejudiced 498.12
  lenient 740.4
  permissive 760.6
  meek 826.10
  (submissive 725.5)
  merciful 914.6
  forgiving 918.5
forbid 761.2
forbiddance 761.1
forbidden fruit
  knowledge 490.6
  temptation 617.1
  prohibition 761.1
forbidding
  prohibitive 761.3
  odious 830.14
  ugly 846.6

force *n.* quantity 25.1
  company 72.3
  crowd 72.4
  potence 157.1
  strength 159.1
  agency 170.1
  energy 171.1
  violence 173.1
  brutality 450a.1
  meaning 516.1
  grammatical ∼
    574.1
  military 726.6
  compulsion 744.1
  (despotism 739.2)
by force
  with strength 159.14
  violently 173.18
  compulsorily 744.4
  (of necessity
    601.15)
in force 170.4
force, foss *n.* 348.7
force *v.*
  ∼ plants 371.8
  urge 615.7
  compel 744.2
  rape 961.8
force down 739.4;
    744.2
force from
  compel 744.2
  take 789.11
force one's way
  advance 282.2
  pass 302.2
force open 173.10
force upon 744.2
force bed 371.6
forced remote 10.7
  labored 579.3
  involuntary 603.5
  be forced 601.10
forced labor 603.3
forceful potent 157.8
  energetic 171.9
  language 574.5
force of friction 157.4
force of inertia 157.1
forceless 158.8
  (uninfluential
    175a.2)
forcemeat 298.19
forceps
  extractor 301.4
  pincers 781.2
forcible potent 157.8
  strong 159.10
  energetic 171.9
  language 574.5
  compulsory 744.3
forcibly
  energetically 171.13
  violently 173.18
  compulsorily 744.4
ford *n.* 627.7
ford *v.* 302.2
fore *n.* 234.1
fore *adj.*
  preceding 62.4
  prior 116.4
  former 122.10

front 234.8
fore and aft
  throughout 52.15
  lengthwise 200.16
  nautical 267.68
fore-and-after
  hat 225.26
  ship 273.2
fore-and-aft rig 225.8
forearm
  prepare for 673.7
  take precautions
    864.4
  (anticipate 510.5)
forebears 166.1
forebode 511.7, 9
  (forewarn 668.7)
  (threaten 909.2)
foreboding *n.* 511.6
  (forewarning 668.2)
  (apprehension
    860.2)
  (threatening 909.1)
  (clairvoyance
    994.7)
foreboding *adj.* 511.11
  (ominous 512.3)
  (forewarning
    668.10)
forebrace 273.10
forebrain 450.2
forecast *n.*
  foresight 510.1
  prediction 511.1
forecast *v.*
  foresee 510.5
  predict 511.7
  plan ahead 626.9
forecast *adj.* 511.13
forecaster 513.2
foreclose 706.4
foredawn, foreday
    125.1
foredestiny 611.1
foredoom *n.*
  destiny 601.3
  (imminence 152.1)
  predetermination
    611.1, 3
foredoom *v.* 601.9
foredoomed 601.13
forefather 166.1
forefend See **forfend**
forefinger 379.2
forefoot, fore foot
    211.4
forefront 234.1
foreganger 273.10
foregather, fore-
  gathering See **for-**
  gather etc.
foreg'ance, fore-
  gleam, foreglimpse
    510.1
forego
  ∼ in order 62.2
  ∼ in time 116.3
  ∼ in motion 280.2
forego See **forgo**
foregoing
  preceding 62.4
  former 122.11

  (prior 116.4)
foregone past 122.8
  predetermined 611.5
foregone conclusion
    611.1
  (forethought 510.2)
foreground 234.1
in the foreground
  before 234.9
  conspicuous 525.5
fore-gut vitals 221.4
  intestine 350.4
forehand 611.5
forehead 234.4
foreign
  irrelative 10.5
  alien 57.4
foreigner 57.3
foreignism 563.1
forejudge 481.6
  (foresee 510.5)
forejudgment, fore-
  judgement 481.2
foreknow 510.5
foreknowledge 510.3
  (prediction 511.1)
foreknown 511.13
foreland 250.5
forelooper, foreloper,
  forelouper 64.1
foreman 694.1
  (master 745.1)
foremast 273.12
forementioned 62.4
foremost first 66.8
  headmost 234.8
  preceding 280.3
forenamed 62.4
forenoon 125.1
forensic 968.4
foreordain
  predetermine 611.3
  predestinate 976.10
foreordination 611.1
fore part, forepart
    234.1
forepole 206.4
forerank 234.2
forerigging 273.9
foreroyal 273.13
forerun
  ∼ in order 62.2
  ∼ in time 116.3
  (presage 511.9)
  anticipate 132.5
  ∼ in motion 280.2
forerunner
  precursor 64.1
  (van 234.2)
  (messenger 534.1)
  (preparer 673.5)
  ship's rope 273.10
foresee 132.5; 510.5
  (look forwards
    121.5)
  (forejudge 481.6)
  (expect 507.4)
  (predict 511.7)
  (forewarn 668.7)
  (be prepared 673.9)
foreseeing 510.6
  (predictive 511.11)

foreseeingly — forsaken

foreseeingly 510.7
foreseen 507.8; 511.13
foreshadow 511.9
foresheet 273.7, 10
foreshore 342.2
foreshorten 201.4
foreshow 511.9
foreshown 511.13
foreside 234.1
foresight 510
  (wisdom 498.3)
  (expectation 507.1)
  (prediction 511.1)
  (preparation 673.1)
  (clairvoyance 994.7)
  with foresight 510.7
foresighted 510.6
forest
  backwoods 183.1
  woods 367.7
forestall
  be early 132.5
  (be prior 116.3)
  (anticipate 121.5; 510.5)
  possess 777.5
forestallment 777.2
forestay 273.10
forester 371.2
forestry woods 367.7
  silviculture 371.1
foretack 273.10
foretackle 273.11
foretaste *n.* 510.4
foretaste *v.*
  anticipate 132.5
  foresee 510.5
foretell 511.7
foretelling 511.1
forethought 510.2
  (care 459.1)
  (forejudgment 481.2)
  (preparation 673.1)
  (caution 864.1)
foretime 122.2
foretoken *n.* 512.1
  (precursor 64.1)
foretoken *v.* 511.9, 10
foretold 511.13
foretop 273.7
forever *n.* 112.1
forever, for ever, forevermore *adv.* 112.5
forewarn 668.7
  (foresee 510.5)
  (forebode 511.9)
  (threaten 909.2)
forewarning *n.* 668.2
  (foreboding 511.6)
  (threat 909.1)
forewarning *adj.* 668.10
  (foreboding 511.11)
  (threatening 909.3)
forewisdom 510.3
foreword 64.2
foreyard 273.12
forfeit *n.* 974.2
forfeit *v.* 776.2
forfeit *adj.* lost 776.5

forfeiture loss 776.1
  (disentitlement 925.2)
  fine 974.2
forfend, forefend
  avert 706.5
  defend 717.7
  prohibit 761.2
forgather, foregather 72.10
forgathering, foregathering 72.1
forge *n.* furnace 386.1
  workshop 691
forge *v.* produce 161.8
  falsify 544.3
  (simulate 19.7)
  coin 800.20
forge ahead
  advance 282.2
  be industrious 682.12
forged
  spurious 545.13
  (illegal 964.5)
  trumped-up 546.6
forger imitator 19.4
  smith 690.6
  coiner 800.18
forgery
  falsehood 544.1
  (simulation 19.3)
  sham 545.6
  lie 546.1
  counterfeit 800.9
forget *n.* 506.1
forget *v.*
  neglect 460.4, 5
  not remember 506.4
  (escape notice 458.7)
  (forgive 918.3)
forget it!
  never mind! 460.13
  you are welcome 784.17
forget oneself
  be inattentive 458.5
  neglect 460.4
  become angry 900.9
  misdemean oneself 945.9
forgetful
  neglectful 460.8
  oblivious 506.8
  (heedless 458.10)
  be forgetful 506.5
forgetfulness 506.1
forgive 918.3
  (forget 506.6)
  (be reconciled 723.5)
  (acquit 970.3)
forgiven 918.6
forgiveness 918
  (acquittal 970.1)
forgiving 723.7; 918.5
forgo, forego 624.3; 782.3
forgotten past 122.8

unremembered 506.7
unthanked 917.4
fork *n.*
  bifurcation 91.2
  angle 244.2
  stream 348.1
fork *v.* 91.5
  (angle 244.4)
fork out give 784.8
  pay out 807.6; 809.3
forked 91.7
  (angular 244.5)
  (diverging 291.3)
forking 91.2
  (divergence 291.1)
forlana See **furlana**
forlorn
  disconsolate 837.12
  hopeless 859.7
  forsaken 893.10
forlorn hope
  disappointment 509.1
  hopelessness 859.3
form *n.* condition 7.1
  arrangement 60.3
  kind 75.2
  seat 215.22
  shape 240
  (texture 329.1)
  (aspect 448.4)
  school 541.8
  printing 591.5
  method 627.1
  formula 697.1
  law 963.2
  rite 998.1
form *v.* compose 54.4
  (be a component 56.2)
  take order 58.5
  produce 161.8
  (prepare 673.6)
  shape 240.6
  (convert 144.6)
  (fashion 852.1)
  train 537.10
  create 976.7
formable 324.6
  (formative 240.7)
formal
  conditional 7.3
  formative 240.7, 9
  definitive 535.6
  style 579.3
  strict 739.5
  taste 850.5
  priggish 853.7
  dignified 878.7
  ceremonial 998.15
formalism
  strictness 739.1
  lip worship 988.2
  ceremonialism 998.11
formalist
  conformist 82.3
  affecter 853.4
  pietist 988.6
  ritualist 998.12
formality

conventionality 852.2
affectation 853.1
law 963.2
rite 998.1
formalize 963.4
format 240.1
formation
  composition 54.1
  production 161.1
  conformation 240.1
formative
  productive 161.11
  formational 240.7
  flexible 324.6
formature 240.3
formed 820.3
  be formed of 54.3
former preceding 62.4
  past 122.10
  (prior 116.4)
  (older 124.10)
formerly 122.14
  (first 66.9)
  (previously 116.5)
  (until now 118.4)
  (then 119.2)
  (lately 123.13)
  (once 137.5)
formication 380.1
formicative 380.6
formidable
  terrible 860.15
  difficult 704.6
forming 56.3
formless 241.5
formlessness 241
  (disorder 59.1)
Formosan 560.4
formula rule 80.1
  number 84.1
  axiom 496.2
  precept 697.1
  law 963.2
  magic ~ 993.1
  rite 998.1
formular 998.15
formulary *n.*
  axiom 496.2
  precept 697.1
  law 963.2
  ritual 998.1, 9
formulary *adj.* 998.15
formulate
  produce 161.8
  author 590.14
  ~ laws 963.4
formulist 998.12
Fornax 318.6
fornent, fornenst
  near 197.11
  beside 236.9
fornication 961.2
fornicator 962.1
fornicatress 962.2
fornix 215.18
forsake 624.3
  (apostatize 607.8)
  (backslide 988.9)
forsaken
  unoccupied 187.11
  abandoned 624.4

forlorn 893.10
lovelorn 898.6
Forseti, Forsete 979.3
forsooth yes 488.14
  truly 494.15
  (affirmation 535.8)
Första Kammaren
  696.5
forswear deny 536.2
  falsify 544.4
  recant 607.9
  reject 764.2
forswearing 607.3
forsworn 544.7
fort 717.4
fortalice 717.3
forte 698.2
forth 282.5
forthcoming
  imminent 152.3
  preparing 673.10
forthright *adj.* 703.4
forthright, forth-
  rights *adv.* 132.14
fortnwith 132.14, 15
fortification 717.3, 4
  (fence 232.2)
fortified 717.9
fortify imbue 41.8
  strengthen 159.8
  (reinforce 37.4)
  corroborate 467.9
  refresh 689.2
  defend 717.7
fortissimo 415.15, 30
fortitude
  sufferance 826.4
  courage 861.1
  cardinal virtue
    944.1
fortnightly 138.11
fortress 717.4
fortuitous
  extrinsic 6.2
  chance 156.12
  (accidental 621.20)
fortuitously 156.13
  (accidentally
    621.22)
fortuity 156.1, 6
Fortuna 156.1
fortunate *n.* 734.4
fortunate *adj.*
  opportune 134.7
  auspicious 512.4
  lucky 734.8
  (successful 731.11)
  be fortunate 734.6
Fortunate Islands
  981.2
Fortunatus 865.9; 993.4
fortune luck 156.1
  (chance 621.1)
  event 594.2
  fate 601.3
  wealth 803.1
  make a fortune 803.6
  make one's fortune
    734.5
  tell fortunes 511.7
fortune hunter 943.2
fortuneless

luckless 735.9
poor 804.2
Fortune's wheel
  chance 156.1
  wheel 312.4
  fate 601.3
  wheel of chance
    621.11
fortunetell 511.7
fortuneteller, fortune-
  telling 513.2
forty 98.7
forty-five 727.10
forty-niner 463.6
forum square 189.19
  school 542.6
  tribunal 966.1
forward *v.*
  contribute 153.8
  transfer to 270.7
  impel 276.7
  motivate 615.7
  improve 658.8
  hasten 684.2
  conduct 692.4
  aid 707.6
forward *adj.*
  premature 132.8
  front 234.8
  versed in 490.14
  expected 507.8
  ready 602.8
  eager 682.18
  meddlesome 682.22
  vain 880.6
  impudent 885.9
forward *adv.*
  frontward 234.10
  onward 282.5
  (hither 278.12)
forward-looking
  282.3; 658.15
forwhy 155.6
foss See force
fosse, foss
  trench 259.2
  fortification 717.3
fossil *n.* remains 40.1
  fogey 130.2
  antiquities 124.2
  (corpse 362.1)
  hardness 323.3
  bore 841.4
fossil *adj.* 124.7
fossilation, fossilifi-
  cation 323.2
fossilify 323.4
fossilization 323.2
  (paleontology
    357.6)
fossilize 323.4
fossilized
  antique 124.7
  aged 128.8
  hard 323.5
fossil man 124.2
fossilogy 122.4
foster feed 298.43
  ~ an idea 451.31
  care for 459.6
  ~ a belief 484.8
  train 537.10

protect 664.6
nourish 707.9
~ feelings 824.2
fosterage 707.2
foster child 167.4
foster father 166.6
foster mother 166.7
fou 959.21
fougasse 252.2
foul *v.*
  ~ the anchor 267.12
  collide 276.9
  dirty 653.15
foul *adj.*
  stormy 349.26
  nasty 395.7
  bad 649.8
  filthy 653.17
  (fetid 401.4)
  odious 830.14
  disreputable 874.8
  vicious 945.16
  obscene 961.9
foulmouthed
  maledictory 908.6
  obscene 961.9
  (vulgar 851.6)
foul play killing 361.1
  molestation 649.4
  malevolence 907.4
  treachery 940.4
  (deception 545.1)
foul-spoken
  maledictory 908.6
  obscene 961.9
foumart, foulmart
  animal 366.3
  malodor 401.2
found originate 153.6
  create 161.8
  establish 184.11
  support 215.26
foundation
  substantiality 3.1
  stability 150.2
  establishment 184.6
  support 215.3
  (precursor 64.1)
  (rudiment 153.3)
  (base 211.1)
  (backbone 235.4)
  (preparation 673.1)
  premise 476.4
foundation stone 215.3
founder *n.*
  producer 164.1
  planner 626.8
founder *v.*
  capsize 267.35
  sink 310.5
  fail 732.5
foundered 732.10
foundling find 775.2
  derelict 782.2
  waif 876.9
  outcaste 893.5
foundry, foundery
  691
fount source 153.2
  fountain 348.5
  type 501.6

source of supply
  636.2
fountain source 153.2
  water 348.5
  source of supply
    636.2
fountainhead
  source 153.2
  (fountain 348.5)
  height 210.1
four 95.2, 4
  on all fours
    identically 13.8
    agreeing 23.9
    horizontally 213.10
    unanimous 488.12
    humbly 879.7
four-decker 273a.1
four flush *n.* 544.2
four-flush *v.*
  dissemble 544.6
  deceive 545.7
  bluff 884.5
fourflusher
  impostor 548.3
  bluff 887.2
four-flushing 544.2
fourfold *v.* 96.2
fourfold *adj.*
  quarternary 95.4
  quadruplicate 96.3
four hundred, the
  society 852.4
  élite 875.2
Fourierism 906.3
four-in-hand 272.4, 9
four million, the 876.1
four-oar 273.4
fourpence 800.8
four-poster 215.24
fourragère 733.1
fourscore 98.7
four-sided 236.7
foursome 95.2
foursquare *n.* 95.1
foursquare *adj.*
  square 95.4
  rectangular 244.5
fourteenth 98.23
fourth *n.* quarter 97.2
  fraction 101.1
fourth *adj.* 96.3
fourth arm 726.9
fourth-dimensional
  105.3
fourth estate 593.17
fourthly 96.5
Fourth of July 138.7
fourth-rate
  imperfect 651.4
  paltry 643.12
  mediocre 736.3
four-wheeler 272.4
fowl food 298.25
  animal 366.1, 22, 23
fowling piece 727.10
fox pelt 223.12
  animal 366.5
  cunning person
    702.4
fox and geese 840.11
foxglove 663.6

foxhound — freethinking

foxhound 366.6
fox hunting 622.2
fox paw 495.3
foxtail 367.9
fox terrier 366.6
fox trot music 415.7
  dance 840.7
foxy 433.5
fracas turmoil 59.4
  noise 404.2
  broil 713.4
fraction part 51.1
  (modicum 32.2)
  turmoil 59.4
  number 84.2; 101.1
  broil 713.4
Fraction 998.7
fractional partial 51.8
  (divided 44.12)
  (incomplete 53.4)
  numeral 84.7
  numerical 101.2
fractious 901.7
fracture n. 198.2
  (separation 44.3)
fracture v. 328.3
fraenum See frenum
fragile frail 160.11
  (unsubstantial 4.5)
  (dainty 32.10)
  brittle 328.4
fragility frailty 160.1
  brittleness 328.1
fragment part 51.1
  (modicum 32.2)
  (fraction 101.1)
  (particle 193.2)
  excerpts 596.2
fragmentary
  partial 51.8
  fractional 101.2
fragrance 400
  (odor 398.1)
fragrant 400.10
  (pleasing 377.7)
  (odorous 398.8)
  be fragrant 400.8
frail n. girl 129.5
  hammer 276.4
  woman 374.2
frail v. 972.6
frail adj. weak 160.11
  (unsubstantial 4.5)
  (dainty 32.10)
  fragile 328.4
  weak-willed 605.6
  morally ~ 945.12
  unchaste 961.10
frailty weakness 160.1
  fragility 328.1
  moral ~ 945.4
frame n. nature 5.3
  edge 231.1
  support 215.8
  form 240.1
  substance 316.2
  printing 591.5
  false charge 938.1
  false conviction 971.1
frame v. produce 161.8
  imagine 515.10

plan 626.9
  trump up a charge 938.4
  convict falsely 971.2
frame up
  trump up a charge 938.4
  convict falsely 971.2
framed 820.3
frame of mind 820.1
  (propensity 602.2)
frame-up
  trumped-up charge 938.1
  false conviction 971.1
framework
  support 215.8
  outline 230.1
  form 240.1
franc 800.8
France 182.3
franchise
  freedom 748.1
  privilege 922.2
Franciscan 996.11
Francophobia 860.4
Franco-Prussian War 722.4
franc-tireur 726.4
frangibility 328.1
frangible frail 160.11
  brittle 328.4
frank sincere 543.3
  candid 703.4
  (honest 939.7)
frankalmoign, frankalmoine, frankalmoigne 748.5
frankfurter, frankforter 298.24
frankhearted
  veracious 543.3
  artless 703.4
frankincense 400.3
frankly 703.5
frantic
  turbulent 173.12
  rabid 503.13
  overwrought 824.10
frappé 298.13
fratch 713.7
fraternal
  consanguine 11.7
  concordant 714.4
  friendly 888.4
  benevolent 906.6
fraternal order 712.3
fraternity kinship 11.2
  association 709.2
  fraternal order 712.3
  fellowship 888.1
fraternization
  association 709.2
  sociality 892.1
fraternize league 48.4
  co-operate 709.4
  be concordant 714.2
  be friendly 888.2
  (be benevolent 906.5)

associate 892.9
fratricide 361.2, 8
Frau 374.2, 3
fraud
  deception 545.1, 3, 6
  (falsification 544.1)
  (swindle 791.5)
  (dishonesty 940.5)
  impostor 548.3
  defrauder 792.8
fraudulence 545.1
  (dishonesty 940.5)
fraudulent
  spurious 545.13
  (dishonest 940.8)
  (illegal 964.5)
fallacious 546.6
fraught full 52.11
  ~ with 777.7
Fräulein 374.4
fray n. 720.2
  (brawl 713.4)
fray v. rub 331.3
  quarrel 713.7
frayed 659.12
frazil 383.5
frazzle 688.5
freak
  monstrosity 83.6
  (prodigy 872.1)
  eccentricity 503.6
  eccentric 504.3
  caprice 608.1, 2
freakery 608.2
freakish unusual 83.10
  capricious 608.5
freckle
  discoloration 440a.1
  mark 550.7
freckled 440.9
fredaine 840.3
free v. deliver 672.2
  disembarrass 705.4
  relieve 707.6
  exempt 748.10
free adj.
  unconnected 44.12
  unconditional 52.10
  at liberty 748.12
  (volitional 600.4)
  (voluntary 602.10)
  (escaped 671.7)
  (unburdened 705.7)
  (liberated 750.5)
  gratuitous 815.10
  liberal 816.4
  licentious 961.10
be free 748.8
free from
  unmixed 42.6
  empty 187.11
  go free 750.4
  (escape 671.6)
free-acting 748.12
free and easy
  cheerful 836.7
  sociable 892.12
freebooter
  soldier 726.4
  independent 748.7
  brigand 792.3

freeborn, free-bred 748.12
free-burning 384.22
freed 750.5
  (exempt 748.18)
freedman 748.6
freedom leisure 685.1
  liberty 748
  (free will 600.1)
  (laxity 738.1)
  (liberation 750.1)
freedom of speech 748.1
free-for-all 720.2
free-going 748.12
freehearted
  liberal 816.4
  charitable 906.7
  magnanimous 942.6
freehold n.
  free land 748.5
  (realty 780.4)
  estate 780.2
freehold adj.
  free 748.12
  estate 780.8
free lance
  author 593.15
  freebooter 726.4
  independent 748.7
  free liver 954a.1
  free living n. 954.2
  free-living adj. 954.5
  free love 961.6
  free-lovism 897.1
freely willingly 602.11
  without restraint 748.21
  (at will 600.5)
  (permissibly 760.7)
freeman 748.6
Freemason 994.13
Freemasonic 994.21
Freemasonry
  secrecy 528.2
  fellowship 709.2
  esoterics 994.1
free-moving 748.12
free play
  facility 705.1
  freedom 748.2
freer 912.2
free-speaking
  speaking 582.11
  free 748.12
free speech 748.1
free-spirited 748.12
free-spoken
  speaking 582.11
  frank 703.4
freestone 342.4
freethinker
  independent 748.7
  latitudinarian 984.14; 989.4
freethinking n.
  unbelief 485.1
  latitudinarianism 989.3
freethinking adj.
  unprejudiced 498.14
  free 748.12

latitudinarian 989.8
free thought
  unbelief 485.1
  latitudinarianism 989.3
free-tongued
  frank 703.4
  free 748.12
free trade
  independence 748.3
  commerce 794.1
free trader, freetrader 748.7
free verse 597.1
free will 600.1
free-working 748.12
freezable 385.6
freeze
  be quiescent 265.5
  anesthetize 376.4
  be cold 383.7
  refrigerate 385.4
  preserve 670.4
freezer 387.1
freezing n.
  anaesthetic 376.2
  refrigeration 385.1
freezing adj.
  cold 383.8
  refrigerative 385.6
freezing mixture 387.2
freight n. load 190.1
  freightage 270.2, 4
  weight 319.1
  by freight 270.12
freight v. fill 52.7
  load 184.13
  ship 270.9
  weight 319.9
freightage
  transportation 270.2
  fee 812.2
freight car 272.19
freighter carrier 271.1
  train 272.18
  ship 273.1
freight train 272.18
freight yard 636.4
French n. 560.4
French adj.
  native 188.11
  language 560.9
French bulldog 366.6
French disease 655.7
French gray n. 432.1
French-gray adj. 432.4
French harp, French horn 417.4
French leave 187.5
take French leave
  play truant 187.8
  (shirk 623.8)
  flee 623.10
  take liberty 748.9
Frenchman 188.9
French nude 433.1
French Revolution 722.4
Frenchy 188.9
frenetic 503.13
frenum, fraenum 45.1

frenzied, phrensied
  turbulent 173.12
  (agitated 315.13)
  rabid 503.13
  overwrought 824.10
frenzy, phrensy
  violence 173.1
  delirium 503.3
  seizure 655.3
  fury 825.4
  (spasm 315.7)
frequence
  frequency 136.1
  attendance 186.6
frequency 136.1
  (repetition 104.1)
  (continuance 143.1)
frequent v.
  attend 186.9
  resort to 186.11
  trade with 794.8
frequent adj.
  oftentime 136.3
  (repeated 104.6)
  (periodic 138.10)
  persevering 604a.3
  habitual 613.11
frequentative 136.3
frequenter
  attender 186.7
  habitué 613.7
  guest 890.7
frequently 136.5
  (repeatedly 104.8)
  (periodically 138.12)
  (habitually 613.13)
fresco n. paint 428.5
  painting 556.9
fresco v. 428.10
fresh n. stream 348.1
  freshman 541.4
fresh adj.
  additional 37.7
  new 123.8
  intoxicated 959.21
  cold 383.8
  sound 654.4
  refreshed 689.5
  impertinent 885.9
get fresh 885.7
freshen
  breeze up 349.22
  cool 385.4
  refresh 689.2
freshen the way 267.16
freshet 348.1, 3
freshman 541.4
fret n. network 219.4
  irritation 828.4
  source of pain 830.2
  ornament 847.4
fret v. rub 331.3
  pain 378.4
  be impatient 825.6
  chafe 828.10
  vex 830.5
  be discontented 832.3
  move 837.6
  complain 839.10

  embroider 847.11
  be vexed 900.8, 10
  grumble 901.6
fretful 901.8
fretted 219.9
fretwork
  network 219.4
  ornamentation 847.3
Freudianism 450.4
Frey, Freyr
  productiveness 168.1
  god 979.3
Freya, Freyja, Freyia
  beauty 845.3
  love 897.4
  goddess 979.3
friability 330.1
  (brittleness 328.1)
friable 330.9
friandise 850.2
friar 996.11
friarhood 995.2
Friar Rush 980.2
friar's lantern 420.11
friary 1000.4
fribb'e n.
  triviality 643.2, 3
  trinket 847.9
  fop 854.1
fribble v.
  slight 460.6
  trifle 643.9
  dawdle 683.8
fribble adj. 643.11
fribblery 643.2
fribbling 643.11
fricandeau, fricando 298.19
fricandel, fricandelle 298.19
fricassee n. 298.17
fricassee v. 384.19
frication 331.1
fricative n. 402.2
fricative adj. 331.4
friction n.
  counteraction 179.1
  rubbing 331
  discord 713.1
friction v. 331.3
frictional 331.4
frictionize 331.3
fried 959.21
friend 890
  (sympathizer 914.2)
be friends 888.2
become friends 888.3
friend at court
  influence 175.5
  upholder 711.4
  deputy 759.1
friends with 888.4
make friends 888.3
friendless
  helpless 158.9
  unfriended 893.10
friendliness 888.1
friendly adj. 888.4
  (well-disposed 707.13)

  (concordant 714.4)
  (sociable 892.12)
  (benevolent 906.6)
be friendly 888.2
  (be sociable 892.9)
  (love 897.11)
  (be benevolent 906.5)
become friendly 888.3
friendly adv. 888.5
friendship 888
  (concord 714.1)
  (peace 721.1)
  (comradeship 892.1)
  (love 897.1)
  (benevolence 906.1)
frier See **fryer**
frieze top 210.4
  cloth 219.5
  ornament 847.4
frigate ship 273.2
  warship 726.11
Frigg, Frigga
  heavens 318.2
  marriage 903.1
  goddess 979.3
fright n. game 840.12
  eyesore 846.3
  fear 860.1
fright, frighten v. 860.10
  (alarm 669.3)
frightened 860.14
frightening n. 860.5
frightening adj. 860.15
frightful vast 31.8
  dreadful 830.13, 14
  ugly 846.6
  fearful 860.15
  (alarming 669.5)
frightfully 31.23
frigid cold 383.8
  style 575.2
  unfeeling 823.5
  indifferent 866.4
Frigidaire, frigidarium 387.1
frigidity cold 383.1
  ~ of expression 575.1
  dispassion 822.1
frigiferous, frigoric, frigorific 385.6
frigorify 385.4
frijol, frijole, frejol 298.30
frill adjunct 39.2
  fringe 231.2
  literature 577.1
  redundance 641.1
  ornament 847.2, 6
frillery adjunct 39.2
  redundance 641.1
  frippery 847.2, 6
  (ostentation 882.1)
frilling 847.2, 6
frilly 882.8
fringe n. edge 231.1, 2
  hair 256.3
  embroidery 549.1

fringe — fudge

fringe (*continued*)
  needlework 847.6
fringe *v.* edge 231.3
  side 236.4
fringed 256.17
  (edged 231.5)
frippery finery 225.13
  trifles 643.5
  frillery 847.2
  (tawdriness 851.2)
  (ostentation 882.1)
Frisian 560.4
frisk *n.* caper 309.2
  search 461.2
  frolic 840.3
frisk *v.* prance 266.19
  caper 309.5
  search 461.16
  rollic 838.5
  frolic 840.21
frisker 840.17
frisket 591.5
frisky capersome 309.6
  lively 682.16
  playful 836.10
frith chasm 198.3
  sea inlet 343.1
  copse 367.7, 8
fritter *n.*
  modicum 32.2
  flitter 298.12
fritter *v.*
 fritter away
  decrease 36.4
  waste 638.2
  squander 818.3
Fritz German 188.9
  German soldier 726.4
frivol
  act the fool 499.9
  trifle 643.9
frivolity folly 499.6
  triviality 643.2
frivolous
  quibbling 477.11
  fickle 608.6
  trivial 643.11
  (foolish 499.15)
friz, frizz *n.* 256.3, 4
friz, frizz *v.* curl 248.3
  fold 258.3
  fry 384.19
frizzle *n.* 256.3
frizzle *v.* curl 248.3
  (curve 245.3)
  fold 258.3
  fry 384.19
frizzly, frizzy 248.4
frock *n.*
  garment 225.3, 7, 15
  clerical ~ 999.1
frock *v.* 995.7
frock coat 225.14, 16
frog
  Frenchman 188.9
  jumper 309.3
  animal 366.20
  ornament 847.3
Froggy 188.9
frogskin 800.6

frolic *n.*
  amusement 840.3
  (caper 309.2)
  prank 842.7
frolic *v.* 840.21
  (caper 309.5)
frolicker 840.17
frolicsome 836.10
frond, frondescence 367.4
frondeur
  insurgent 742.3
  malcontent 832.2
  faultfinder 936.1
front *n.* forepart 234
  (beginning 66.1)
  (precession 280.1)
  wig 256.4
  false pretense 544.2
  disguise 545.5
  auditorium 599.11
  resistance 719.1
  mediator 724.2
  battlefield 728.2
  deputy 759.1
  affectation 853.1
  display 882.1
  effrontery 885.2
get in front of 280.2
in front before 234.9
in advance 280.4
front *v.*
  confront 224.7
  oppose 237.5
front for
  substitute 147.3
  represent 759.4
front *adj.* first 66.8
  fore 234.8
frontad 234.10
frontage 234.1
frontal *n.* front 234.1
  altar front 1000.3
frontal *adj.* 234.8
frontier 231.1
  (limit 233.1)
frontispiece
  prelude 64.2
  front 234.1
front rank 234.2
frore, froren
  cold 383.8
  frozen 385.7
frost *n.* ice 383.5
  lens 424.5
  failure 732.1
frost *v.* opalesce 427.3
  whiten 430.6
frost-beaded 383.9
frostbite 383.2
frostbitten 383.8
frost-bound, frost-chequered 383.9
frosted hoary 383.9
  opalescent 427.4
  white 430.8
frost-fettered 383.9
frost-hoar 383.5
frosting 847.3
frost-nipped 383.8
frost-rent, frost-riven 383.9

frost smoke 353.5
frostwork 847.3
frosty hoary 383.9
  opalescent 427.4
  white 430.8
frosty-faced, frosty-whiskered 383.9
froth *n.* dregs 40.2
  foam 353.2
  insignificancy 643.5
froth *v.* foam 353.8
~ **at the mouth** 503.9
~ **up** 900.9
frothy light 320.7, 8
  foamy 353.10
  style 575.2
  rhetorical 577.6
  fickle 608.6
  trivial 643.11
  showy 882.8
frounce 258.3
frouzy See **frowzy**
frow 374.2
froward 606.6
  (ill-humored 901.7)
frown *n.*
  sullen look 901.3
  reproving look 932.4
frown *v.* 901.6
  (resentment 900.7)
frown at 895.4
frown down 932.5
frown upon
  discourage 837.8
  disapprove 932.5
frowning 837.10
frowst, froust 401.1
frowsty, frousty, frowy foul 653.17
  decayed 659.13
frowzy, frouzy
  untidy 59.9
  foul 653.17
  decayed 659.13
frozen cold 383.8
  refrigerated 385.7
  (icy 383.9)
frozen music art 556.1
  architecture 847.1
frozen pudding 298.13
fructiferous 168.7
fructification
  procreation 161.2
  flowering 161.4
  productiveness 168.1
  (copulation 43.2)
fructify bear 161.9
  fertilize 168.4
  (copulate 43.8)
  improve 658.6
  prosper 734.5
fructose 396.4
frugal
  economical 817.4
  temperate 953.6
frugality
  economy 817.1
  temperance 953.1
fruit *n.* result 154.1

866

  product 161.6
  food 298.31
  profit 775.2
fruit *v.* 161.9
fruitarian *n.* 953.3
fruitarian *adj.* 953.6
fruitarianism 953.2
fruitful 168.7
  (producible 161.11)
  (profitable 644.6)
be fruitful 35.4
fruitfulness 168.1
fruition
  flowering 161.4
  pleasure 827.1
fruitless
  unproductive 169.4
  useless 645.8
  unsuccessful 732.8
fruit wood 635.3
frumenty 298.15
frump *n.* slattern 59.5
  crone 130.3
  shrew 901.4
frump *v.* 901.6
frumpish 59.9
frumps 901.2
frustrate *v.*
  neutralize 179.4
  disappoint 509.2
  thwart 706.7
frustrated 732.9
  (unaccomplished 730.3)
frustrater 706.3
frustration
  disappointment 509.1
  failure 732.1
frustum 51.1
fry *n.*
  multitude 102.2
  youngling 129.1
  festivity 840.2
fry *v.* 384.19
fryer, frier
  youngling 129.7
  food 298.25
  fowl 366.23
frying pan 191.11
  cooker 386.1
fub See **fob**
fuchsin, fuchsine 434.6
fucoid *n.* 367.3
fucoid *adj.* 367.16
fucus 367.3
fud rump 235.5
  tail 235.6
fuddle *n.*
  confusion 458.4
  intoxication 959.1, 3, 4
fuddle *v.*
  confuse 458.9
  inebriate 959.15, 18
fuddled 959.21
fuddler 959.11
fudge candy 396.4
  nonsense 497.5; 517.2
  (trumpery 643.5)

bungle 699.4
fudgy 699.12
fuel *n.* 388
　(electricity 158a.1)
　(gas 334.2)
　(oil 356.1)
　(illuminant 420.15)
fuel *v.* 388.8
　(fire 384.17)
fugacious 111.6
fugacity 111.1
fugitive *n.*
　runaway 623.5
　(escaper 671.5)
　outlaw 949.2
fugitive *adj.*
　transient 111.6
　runaway 623.12
fugleman, flugelman
　prototype 22.1
　leader 694.1
fugler 22.1
fugue *n.* music 415.3
　insanity 503.1
fugue *v.* 415.26
fulcrum 215.5
　(lever 307.4)
fulcrumage 175.3
　(fulcrum 215.5)
fulfill, fulfil 729.2
fulfillment, fulfilment
　completion 729.1
　observance 772.1
　~ of duty 926.2
fulgent, fulgid 420.22
fulgor, fulgour 420.1
fulgorous, fulgourous, fulgurant 420.22
fulgurate
　explode 173.9
　flash 420.17
fulguration
　explosion 173.3
　flash 420.4, 6
fulgurite tube 260.6
　explosive 727.13
fuliginosity
　dimness 422.1
　opacity 426.1
fuliginous
　blurred 422.8
　opaque 426.4
full *n.* fullness 52.2, 3
　satiety 869.1
　to the full
　utterly 52.14
　sufficiently 639.8
full *v.* 652.9
full *adj.* great 31.6
　complete 52.11
　(packed 72.13)
　(plenty 639.7)
　(overfull 641.6)
　(satiated 869.6)
　detailed 79.7
　stout 192.12
　(rotund 249.6)
　drunk 959.21
　loud 404.8
　resonant 408.9
　full-colored 428.13

　unlimited 748.15
full age 131.1
full-armed 717.9
full blast 157.1
　at full blast 274.15
　go at full blast 274.9
full bloom
　adulthood 131.1
　bloom 367.5
　good health 654.1
full-blown adult 131.5
　full-sized 192.14
full-charged 52.11
full cry
　in full cry
　loudly 404.11
　in pursuit 622.10
full dress 225.14
　in full dress 847.14
fullface 591.8
full-faced 591.18
full feather 225.13
　in full feather
　prepared 673.11
　prosperous 734.7
　affluent 803.8
full-fed 954.4
full-flavored 392.5
full-formed 192.14
full-fraught 52.11
full-grown adult 131.5
　full-sized 192.14
full house fill 52.3
　cards 840.13
full measure 52.3
　(plenty 639.2)
fullmouthed 411.8;
　412.3
fullness, fulness
　greatness 31.1
　completeness 52.2
　fullness of the heart 821.1
　(happiness 827.2)
　in the fullness of time in time 109.6
　in future 121.9
　(eventually 151.8)
　opportunely 134.10
full sail
　in full sail 274.15
full-size 192.9
full-sized 192.14
full tilt directly 278.13
　actively 682.25
　hastily 684.7
　recklessly 863.8
full-toned 413.27
fully completely 52.13
　amply 639.8
fulmar 366.22
fulminant *n.* 420.6
fulminant *adj.* 406.10
fulminate
　explode 173.9
　detonate 406.8
　(be noisy 404.6)
　maledict 908.4
　threaten 909.2
　~ against 932.8
fulmination
　explosion 173.3

　(shot 284.4)
　detonation 406.2
　lightning 420.6
fulness See **fullness**
fulsome nasty 395.7
　(malodorous 401.4)
　bad 649.8
　foul 653.17
　odious 830.14
　disreputable 874.8
　flattering 933.3
　lewd 961.9
fulvous 436.6
fumble *n.* 699.4
fumble *v.* derange 61.2
　feel 379.3
　grope 463.9
　bungle 699.9
fumbler 701
fume *n.*
　effluvium 334.2
　foam 353.2
　odor 398.1
　excitement 825.3
　fit of anger 900.2
fume *v.*
　be violent 173.7
　vaporize 336.5
　smolder 382.13
　rave 503.9
　rage 825.7
　fret 828.10
　be angry 900.8
fumigant
　deodorant 399.2
　disinfectant 652.8;
　662.8
fumigate fume 336.5
　deodorize 399.4
　perfume 400.9
　disinfect 652.13
fumigation
　vaporization 336.1
　deodorization 399.2
　disinfection 652.2
fumigator
　incense 388.7
　perfumer 400.5
　purifier 652.8
　disinfectant 662.8
fuming
　smoldering 382.17
　excited 824.10
　angry 900.13
fumistery 392a.13
fun 840.1
　in fun 842.10
　make fun of
　joke about 842.8
　ridicule 856.4
　deride 930.6
funambulist
　acrobat 599.21
　proficient 700.1
function *n.*
　agency 170.1
　business 625.3
　(utility 644.1)
　(career 692.3)
　(duty 926.1)
　usage 677.2

　rite 998.1
function *v.* 680.5
functional
　official 625.11
　formal 998.15
functional psychology 450.4
functionary *n.*
　officer 694.3
　official 745.9
　consignee 758.2
functionary *adj.* 998.15
fund *n.* 636.2
　(means 632.1)
　(plenty 639.2)
　(savings 817.2)
fund *v.* store 636.7
　supply 637.4
　invest 787.5
fundament 235.5
fundamental *n.*
　fact 1.2
　essence 5.2
　tone 402.2
　essential 642.4
fundamental *adj.*
　intrinsic 5.6
　original 153.9
　basal 211.5
　(supporting 215.28)
　important 642.14
fundamentally 31.16
fundamental tone 402.2
funds 800.2
　(supplies 636.2)
　(wealth 803.1)
　in funds 803.8
funèbre, funebrial 363.25
funeral *n.*
　procession 69.3
　burial 363.4
　(dirge 839.3)
　painful loss 776.1
funeral *adj.* 363.25
funeral home 363.17
funeralize 363.20
funeral march
　slow motion 275.2
　dirge 839.3
funeral parlor 363.17
funeral pile
　cremation 363.2
　death fire 382.8
funerary 363.25
funereal burial 363.25
　(sad 837.9)
　(dirgelike 839.15)
　gloomy 421.8
　dismal 837.10
fungate 365.2
fungi 369.4
fungible 148.4
fungiform
　convex 250.9
　herbal 367.14
　botanic 369.11
fungoid 367.14
fungologist 369.9
fungology 369.1

fungosity — Gabriel 868

fungosity 250.1, 2
fungous 367.14
fungus
 protuberance 250.2
 vegetation 367.2
 malodor 401.2
 blight 663.2
funicle 45.4
 (cord 205.3)
funicular 205.7
funk n. fear 860.1
 cowardice 862.1
 coward 862.2
funk v. smoke 382.13
 use tobacco 392a.14
 stink 401.3
 shirk 623.8
 be afraid 860.8
 scare 860.10
 be cowardly 862.3
funked 392a.15
funker shirker 623.4
 coward 862.2
funking 862.4
funk hole cellar 191.20
 hiding place 530.2
 refuge 666.3
funky cigar 392a.15
 cowardly 862.4
funnel tube 260.6
 (conduit 350.1)
 smokeshaft 351.1
funnel-shaped
 concave 252.10
 cone-shaped 249.9
funnies 556.9
funny n. 273.4
funny adj. odd 83.10
 humorous 842.9
 ridiculous 855.5
funnyman 599.20
 (humorist 844)
fur pelt 223.12
 hair 256.3
 scum 653.6
 merchandise 798.3
furacious 791.14
furacity 791.6
furbelow 231.2
furbish polish 255.4
 improve 658.10
 adorn 847.11
furcate v. 91.5
furcate adj. 91.7
 (angular 244.5)
 (diverging 291.3)
furcation 91.2
 (divergence 291.1)
furcula fork 91.2
 angle 244.2
furcular 91.7
furculum fork 91.2
 angle 244.2
 wishbone 993.4
furfur 653.6
furfuraceous 330.8
Furies violents 173.6
 anger 900.4
 (evildoers 913.5)
 mythical beings 980.4
furious

violent 173.11, 12
rabid 503.13
hasty 684.5
frenzied 824.10
passionate 825.10
reckless 863.7
infuriated 900.13
furiously 31.22
furiousness
 violence 173.1
 fury 825.4
furl 312.7
furlana, forlana, forlane music 415.7
 dance 840.7
furlong 200.6
furlough 760.2
furnace stove 386.1
 (incinerator 384.12)
 foundry 691
Furnace 318.6
furnish bear 161.9
 equip 634.2
 provide 637.4
 (store 636.7)
 give 784.10
furnished 634.3
furnishing 673.1
furnishment
 equipment 634.1
 provision 673.1
furniture
 equipment 634.1
 merchandise 798.3
furor violence 173.1
 insanity 503.1, 3
 eagerness 682.3
 fervor 821.2
 passion 825.4
 violent anger 900.3
furrow n. 259
 (cavity 252.2)
 (fold 258.1)
furrow v. 259.3
furrowed 259.4
 (rough 256.12)
Fürst 875.7
further n. 282.1
further v. 707.6
further adj. 37.7
further adv.
 additionally 37.8
 beyond 196.8
furtherance
 progression 282.1
 improvement 658.1
 aid 707.1
in furtherance of 707.15
furthermore 37.8
furthersome 707.12
furtive
 surreptitious 528.21
 thievish 791.14
furtiveness 528.3
furunc'e
 protuberance 250.2
 sore 655.16
furuncular 250.9
fury violence 173.1
 violent 173.6
 delirium 503.3

passion 825.4
anger 900.3
ill-humored person 901.4
evildoer 913.1
malevolent woman 913.5
demon 980.5
furze 367.8
fuscous 433.4
fuse, fuze n.
 lighter 388.4
 wick 423.12
fuse, fuze v.
 attach 43.6
 combine 48.3
 (mix 41.6)
 melt 384.21
 (liquefy 335.5)
fusee, fuzee 388.5
fuselage 273a.10
fusel oil 356.3
fusiform 253.17
fusil 727.10
fusilier, fusi'eer
 attacker 716.4
 soldier 726.4
fusillade n.
 slaughter 361.1
 barrage 716.2
fusillade v. 716.6
fusion mixture 41.1
 combination 48.1
 liquefaction 335.1
 melting 384.2
 association 709.2
fuss n. turmoil 59.4
 agitation 315.1
 bustle 682.6
 hurry 684.1
 excitement 825.3
 ostentation 882.1
 bluster 887.1
make a fuss
 give importance to 642.8
 bustle 682.12
 complain 839.10
 reprehend 932.7
fuss v. confuse 458.9
 trifle 643.9
 bustle 680.12; 684.3
 fret 825.6
 complain 839.10
fuss-budget 832.2
fuss-budgety 832.5
fussy bustling 682.21
 fidgety 825.9
fust 401.1
fustee, fustie 41.5
fustian n. cloth 219.5
 twaddle 517.3
 bombast 577.2
fustian adj. 577.7
fustigate 972.6
fustigation 972.3
fusty antiquated 124.9
 foul 653.17
 decayed 659.13
futhorc, futharc, futhork, futhark alphabet 561.2

writing 590.9
futile nugatory 158.11
 useless 645.8
 hopeless 859.7
futility
 absurdity 497.1
 folly 499.6
 uselessness 645.2
 hopelessness 859.1
futtock 273.7
future n. time 121.2
 fiancé 897.8
in future 121.9
 (subsequently 117.4)
 (sometime 119.4)
 (soon 132.15)
 (eventually 151.8)
future adj.
 hereafter 121.7
 (subsequent 117.3)
 (imminent 152.3)
 expected 507.8
futures 621.6
futurism 556.6
 (modernism 123.3)
futurist n. artist 559.1
 (modernist 123.4)
futurist adj. 556.19
futuristic 123.11
futurity 121.2
 (posteriority 117.1)
 (anticipation 507.1; 510.1)
futurize 123.7
fuze, fuzee See fuse etc.
fuzzy 447.5
fylfot 993.2

G

gab n. mouth 260.2
 speech 582.1
 gabble 584.2
have the gift of gab 582.8
gab v. 582.6
gabardine cloth 219.5
 cloak 225.15
 apron 225.20
gabble n.
 twaddle 517.3
 chatter 584.2
gabble v. gobble 412.2
 talk nonsense 517.6
 be inarticulate 583.2
 be loquacious 584.4
gabby n. 501.1
gabby adj. 584.5
gabelle 812.2
gaberlunzie 876.9
gable 236.1
gable end
 extremity 67.2
 top 210.4
 side 236.1
Gabriel
 messenger 534.1
 angel 977.1

gad — game

gad *n.*
  wandering 266.2
  wanderer 268.2
gad *v.* 266.14
Gadaba 560.4
gadabout 268.2
gadding 266.2
gadfly 366.24
gadget 316.3
  (contrivance 626.5)
Gaea, Gaia
  world 318.1
  agriculture 371.3
  goddess 979.2
Gaekwar, Gaekwad 745.4
Gaelic 560.4
gaff edge tool 253.6
  spar 273.12
  noise 404.2
  outcry 411.2
  speech 582.1
  spear 727.5
gaffer elder 130.1
  grandfather 166.8
  stagehand 599.17
  superintendent 694.1
  rustic 876.5
gag *n.* muffler 408a.3
  acting device 599.6
  restraint 752.2
  witticism 842.4
gag *v.*
  render mute 581.5
    (silence 403.5)
  ~ in acting 599.26
  restrain 751.7
gage challenge 715.1
  security 771.1
gage, gageable etc.
  See gauge etc.
gaggle 412.2
gaging See gauging
gagtooth 253.3
gaiety, gayety 836.1
Gaikwar See Gaekwar
gaillard See galliard
gain *n.* increase 35.2
  benefit 648.2
  acquisition 775.2
    (success 731.1)
    (booty 793.1)
    (receipts 810.1)
    (remuneration 973.2)
gain *v.* fatten 194.7
  reach 292.7
  acquire 775.6
  receive 785.3
gain a point 731.5
gain ground
  accelerate 274.10
  progress 282.2
gain the day 731.6
gain time
  temporize 110.6
  be early 132.5
  procrastinate 133.5
gain upon
  approach 286.2

  become habitual 613.9
gainer 310.1
gainful
  profitable 644.6
  remunerative 775.12
gaining 775.1
gainless 645.8
gainsay *n.* 536.1
gainsay *v.* deny 536.2
  oppose 708.2
gairish See garish
gait pace 266.5
  journey 266.8
  velocity 274.1
  way 627.1
gaiter 225.28
gala festival 840.2
  display 882.3
galactic circle 318.7
gala day 840.5
Galahad, Sir 861.3
galanty show, galanty show
  show 599.8
  amusement 840.15
galavant See gallivant
galaxy crowd 72.4
  multitude 102.2
  constellation 318.7
  elite 873.9
galbe outline 230.1
  form 240.1
Galcha 560.4
gale 349.5, 11
galeate, galeiform 245.13
Galen 662.19
galilee 191.17
galiongee, galionji 269.1
galiot, galleot 273.2
gall *n.* bitter 395.3
  (pungency 392.2)
  bane 663.1
  vexation 830.2
  impudence 885.2
  anger 900.1
  rancor 901.1
  malevolence 907.1
gall *v.* rub 331.3
  pain 378.4
  vex 830.5
gallant *n.* 897.6
gallant *adj.*
  courageous 861.8
  courteous 894.12
gallantry
  courage 861.1
  courtesy 894.1
  love 897.1
  courtship 902.2
gallanty show See galanty show
galleass 273.2, 3
galled 828.15
galleon 273.2
galleot, See galiot
gallery
  vestibule 191.17
  trench 259.2

  audience 418.8
  observatory 441.5
  spectators 444.2
  balcony 599.11
  covered way 627.2
  collection 636.5
galley
  cookroom 191.16; 386.4
  ship 273.3; 273.7
  printing 591.5
  punishment 972.2 975.3
galley proof 591.3
galley-west 173.18; 217.13
galleyworm 368.8
galliard, gaillard
  music 415.7
  dance 840.7
  humorist 844
Gallic 188.11
Gallicism, gallicism 563.5
Gallicize, gallicize 563.13
Gallic Wars 722.4
galligaskins 225.28
gallimaufry 41.4
gallinaceous 366.26
galling
  annoying 830.12
  malevolent 907.6
galliot See galiot
gallipot 191.11
gallivant, galavant
  wander 266.14
  make love 902.7
gallon 466.3
galloon 847.6
gallop *n.* 274.3
gallop *v.*
  be transient 111.5
  run 274.9
  (ride 266.19)
ga'lopade, galopade 840.7
galloper 271.3
Gallophobia 860.4
Galloway 271.4
gallows *n.*
  suspenders 214.3
  gibbet 975.4
gallows *adj.*
  good 648.8
  impudent 885.9
gallows *adv.* 31.15
gallows bird 949.2
gallstone 655.5
galluses 214.3
gally 885.9
galoot oaf 501.1
  awkward fellow 701
galop 840.7
galopade See gallopade
galore *n.*
  quantities 31.3
  plenty 639.2
galore *adv.*
  in abundance 102.6
  plentifully 639.8

galosh, galoshe 225.27
galvanic
  electric 158a.12
  exciting 824.12
  excitable 825.9
galvanic pile 158a.6
galvanism
  electricity 158a.1
  excitation 824.1
galvanist 158a.10
galvanization 158a.1
galvanize
  electrify 158a.11
  excite 824.3
galvanometer
  electricity 158a.6
  aviation 267a.29
galvanometric 158a.12
galvanoscope 158a.6
galvanoscopic 158a.12
galvanothermometer 389.1
Galways 256.5
gama grass 367.9
Gamaliel 492.4
gamashes 225.28
gamb, gambe 266.11
gambado *n.*
  legging 225.28
  caper 309.2
  dance 840.8
gambado *v.* 309.5
gamble *n.* 621.2
  (speculation 463.3)
  (uncertainty 475.1)
  (rashness 863.1)
gamble *v.*
  be certain 474.5
  believe 484.7
  chance 621.17
  (be rash 863.5)
gambler 621.15
  (player 840.17)
  (rash person 863.4)
gambling 621.6
  (rashness 863.1)
gamboge 436.4
gambol *n.* caper 309.2
  frolic 840.3
gambol *v.* caper 309.5
  frolic 840.6
game *n.* teeth 253.3
  food 298.26
  animal life 366.1
  resolution 604.1
  objective 620.2
  ~ of chance 621.7
  pursuit 622.1
  scheme 626.1
  policy 692.2
  contest 720.2
  artifice 702.3
  sport 840.1, 11, 12
  laughingstock 857.1
  courage 861.1
make game of
  ridicule 856.4
  (fool 545.10)
  deride 930.6
game *v.*
  gamble 621.17
  play 840.21

game — gate

game *adj.*
  willing 602.8
  resolute 604.7
  courageous 861.8
gamecock
  resolution 604.4
  combatant 726.1
  courage 861.4
gamekeeper
  stockman 370.4
  caretaker 664.3
gamesome 836.10
gamester
  gambler 621.15
  player 840.17
  (contestant 710.1)
gametangium, gamete 357.4
gametic 161.11
gametophore, gametophyte 357.4
gamic
  productional 161.11
  germinal 357.10
gamin 876.9
gaming 621.6
gaming house 621.14
gammadion 993.2
gamma ray 420.3
gammer
  old woman 130.3
  grandmother 166.8
  matron 374.2
gammon *n.*
  twaddle 517.3
  falsehood 544.2
  deception 545.1
gammon *v.* feign 544.6
  deceive 545.7
gammoner 792.8
gammy 166.9
gamp
  umbrella 223.4
  midwife 662.19
gamut 413.16
gamy 392.5
gander bird 366.22
  male animal 373.6
ganef, ganof 792.6
Ganesa, Ganesha 979.4
gang *n.* company 72.3
  (clique 712.2)
  party 712.4
  staff 746.7
gang *v.* league 48.4
  assemble 72.10
  associate 88.6
  go 264.6
  ~ along 293.4
gangboard 627.7
ganger 694.1
gangling, gangly 203.11
gangplank
  ship 273.7
  bridge 627.7
gangrene *n.*
  mortification 360.1
  ailment 655.16
gangrene *v.* 659.7
gangrened

diseased 655.25
  decayed 659.13
gang tooth 253.3
gangway *n.* ship 273.7
  way 627.7
gangway *int.* 260.22
ganja 662.7
gantlet 972.3
gantlet See gauntlet
gaol, gaolbird etc. See jail etc.
gap *n.*
  interval 198.1, 2, 3
  opening 260.1
  water gap 350.1
gap *v.* gape 260.13
  yawn 683.9
gape *n.* 260.1
gape *v.* yawn 260.13; 683.9
  gaze 441.13
  be curious 455.3
  yearn 865.11
  wonder 870.2
gaping *n.* 260.9
gaping *adj.*
  intervallic 198.5
  expectant 507.7
garage room 191.16
  automobile 272.16
garb *n.* 225.1
garb *v.* 225.41
garbage 653.6
  (malodor 401.2)
  (rubbish 645.4)
garble
  segregate 55.4
  distort 243.4
  misinterpret 523.2
  falsify 544.3; 811.9
  misrepresent 555.4
garbled 53.5
garçon 746.1
garden *n.* park 189.21
  plantation 371.5
  (bower 191.22)
  (herbarium 369.2)
  source of supply 636.2
  beautiful 845.4
garden *v.* 371.8
garden *adj.* 849.3
gardener 371.2
gardening 371.1
garden party 892.5
gare 266.10
Gargantua 192.8
Gargantuan 192.15
gargle 337.5
gargoyle, gurgoyle 350.1
garish, gairish
  bright 420.22
  gaudy-colored 428.15
  gaudy 851.8
  (conspicuous 525.5)
  (ostentatious 882.5)
garland
  circle 247.2
  flowers 400.4

anthology 593.2
  597.4
  trophy 733.1
  (insignia 550.12)
  decoration 847.5
garlic
  condiment 393.1
  malodor 401.2
garment 225.1, 3
garmenture 225.1
garmentworker 690.9
garner *n.* 636.4
garner *v.* 636.7
garnet red 434.5
  mineral 635.6
  gem 847.8
garnish *n.* 847.1
garnish *v.* 847.11
garnishee 758.1
garnishment 847.1
Garo 560.4
garran, garron 271.3
garret attic 191.19
  head 210.3
garrison *n.*
  population 188.10
  stronghold 717.4
  guard 717.6
  troops 726.7
garrison *v.*
  guard 664.6
  engarrison 717.7
garrisoned 188.13
garron See garran
garrote, garrotte *n.*
  strangulation 361.4
  execution 972.4
garrote, garrotte *v.*
  disable 158.6
  strangle 361.11
  execute 972.8
garroter, garrotter
  strangler 361.8
  ruffian 913.2
  executioner 975.5
garrulity 584.1
garrulous 584.5
garter fastening 45.2
  suspender 214.3
  decoration 733.1
garter-blue 438.6
garth close 181.3
  enclosure 232.1
gas *n.*
  automobile 272.16
  vapor 334.2
  (fluid 333.2)
  (fuel 388.1)
  (illuminant 420.15)
  gasoline 356.2
  anesthetic 376.2
  light 420.7
  twaddle 517.3
  chatter 584.2
  boasting 884.1
gas *v.*
  talk nonsense 517.6
  be loquacious 584.4
gasbag
  chatterer 584.3
  boaster 884.3
Gascon 884.3

gasconade *n.* 884.1
gasconade *v.* 884.5
gasconading 884.7
gaseity 334
  (fluidity 333.1)
gaselier 423.10
gaseous
  chimerical 4.6
  vaporous 334.7
  (volatile 336.7)
gas fitter 690.5
gash *n.* cleft 198.2
  notch 257.1
  furrow 259.1
  twaddle 517.3
  wound 659.4
gash *v.* cut 44.8
  notch 257.5
  furrow 259.3
gasification 336.1
gasiform 334.7
gasify
  make gaseous 334.6
  (liquefy 335.5)
  vaporize 336.5
gas jet 382.8
gasket 273.10
gaskins 225.29
gas lamp 423.2
gaslight light 420.7
  lamp 423.2
gaslighting 420.14
gaslit 423.14
gasoline, gasolene
  automobile 272.16
  oil 356.2
  (fuel 388.1)
  (illuminant 420.15)
gasometer 334.4
gasp breathe 349.23
  be hot 382.13
  ail 655.21
  be fatigued 688.4
  yearn 865.11
Gaspar 500.1
gasper 392a.4
gasping 655.24
gassy gaseous 334.7
  (flatulent 349.31)
  grandiloquent 577.7
  loquacious 584.5
  pompous 882.8
  boastful 884.7
gastric 191.23
gastriloquist 580.6
gastriloquous 580.13
Gastrolobium 663.6
gastrology 298.1
gastromancy 511.3
gastronome 957.2
gastronomy
  eating 298.1
  gluttony 957.1
gastropodous 368.16
gastroscope 445.1
gastroscopic 445.9
gastroscopy 445.7
gasworks 691
gat 727.10
gate floodgate 350.2
  portal 260.4

870

gatekeeper — generous

(obstacle 706.2)
valve 263.2
automobile 272.16
dismissal 297.4
ingate 294.5
gatekeeper 717.6
gate man 599.17
gatepost 215.16
gateway 260.4
(path 627.2)
gatewright 690.7
gather *n.* 258.1
gather *v.*
assemble 72.10, 11
grow 194.6
fold 258.3
brew 349.22
harvest 371.8
presume 472.3
deduce 480.6
suppose 514.6
interpret 522.6
acquire 775.6
gather up 307.6
gather way 267.16, 21
gatherer 72.9
gathering
assemblage 72.1, **2**
abscess 655.16
council 696.2
social gathering 892.5
(assembly 72.2)
(festivity 840.2)
Gatling gun 727.11, 12
gator 366.18
gauche 699.12
gaucherie
bungle 699.4
vulgarity 851.1
gaud 847.9
gaudery finery 225.13
frippery 847.2
tawdriness 851.2
(ostentation 882.1)
gaudiness 851.2
(finery 225.13)
gaudy
overcolorful 428.15
tawdry 851.8
(conspicuous 525.5)
(ornate 847.13)
(ostentatious 882.8)
gauge, gage *n.*
measure 466.2, 4
(sign 550.2)
printing 591.5
gauge, gage *v.*
size 192.10
measure 466.10
estimate 480.7
gaugeable, gageable 466.12
gauger, gager 745.9
gauging, gaging 466.1
gaumy, gawmy 352.8
gaunt, gant 203.11
(distorted 243.5)
gauntlet glove 225.30
challenge 715.1
armor 717.2
fling down the

gauntlet
quarrel 713.7
challenge 715.2
gaunty 203.11
gaup, gawp 441.13
gaur 366.13
Gauri 979.4
Gautama 986.3
gauze veiling 225.12
light filter 424.5
semitransparency 427.2
dressing 662.14
gavel
emblem of authority 747.1
rent 810.2
dues 812.2
gavelkind
tenure 777.1
coheirship 778.1
gavelock 307.4
gavial 366.18
gavotte, gavot
music 415.7
dance 840.7
gaw 441.13
gawk *n.* oaf 501.1
awkward fellow 701
gawk *v.* 441.13
gawkhammer *n.* 701
gawkhammer *adj.* 699.12
gawky *n.* oaf 501.1
awkward fellow 701
gawky *adj.*
thin 203.11
awkward 699.12
ungraceful 846.8
gawmy See gaumy
gawp See gaup
gay
intoxicated 959.21
gay-colored 428.14
cheerful 836.7
smart 847.14
showy 882.8
wanton 961.10
gayety See gaiety
gay-colored 428.14
gaze *n.* 441.2
gaze *v.* 441.11, 13
gazebo 441.5
gazel, ghazel 597.2
gazelle
speeder 274.6
animal 366.10
gazer 444.1
gazette 593.6
gazetted 808.6, **10**
gazetteer 551.2
gazingstock
laughingstock 857.1
curiosity 872.1
Ge 979.2
geanticlinal 245.4
geanticline 245.2
gear *n.*
fastening 45.2
cordage 205.4
vestment 225.1
automobile 272.16

rigging 273.9
wheel 312.4
equipment 634.1
in gear 673.11
out of gear
disorderly 59.8
impotent 158.8
dislocated 185.3
unprepared 674.7
gear *v.* 634.2
gearbox, gear shifter 272.16
gearing, gear wheel, gearwheel 312.4
gecko 366.18
gee agree 23.7
concur 488.7
be concordant 714.2
Geechee 431.4
gee-gee 271.8
geezer 83.4
Gegenschein 420.12
Gehenna 982.1
geisha 840.9
Geist genius 498.5
ghost 980a.1
psyche 994.11
gelatin, gelatine
gluten 352.3
jelly 396.3
gelatinate 321.7
gelatination 321.3
gelatinity 352.1
gelatinization 321.3
gelatinize 321.7
gelatinous, gelatose 352.8
geld 38.7
(unman 158.7)
gelding horse 271.3
male animal 373.6
gelée 396.3
gelid cold 383.8
frozen 385.7
gelidity 383.1
gelignite 727.13
gelt 800.1
gem treasure 648.4
precious stone 847.8
good person 948.1
Gemara 985.5
Gemaric 985.8
geminate *v.* 90.2
geminate *adj.* 90.3
gemination
duplication 90.1
procreation 161.2
Gemini 89.2; 318.6
gemma 153.3
gemmation 194.3
gemmule 153.3
gemot, gemote 72.2
gemshorn 417.12
gendarme
soldier 726.4
constable 745.10
gender 75.2, 3
genealogy 166.4
general *n.* all 50.2
alarm 669.1
factotum 690.3
officer 745.11

servant 746.1, **2**
masses 876.1
general *adj.*
generic 78.9
(well-known 490.17)
(common 613.11)
public 372.6
be general 78.7
in general 78.15
General Assembly 696.4
general council 696.3
generalissimo 745.11
generality mean 29.1
universality 78.1
generalization
generality 78.1
reasoning 476.1
generalize
universalize 78.8
reason 476.10
generally 78.15
(invariably 16.7)
(on an average 29.5)
(always 112.5)
(habitually 613.13)
general practitioner 662.19
generalship
managership 693.3
warcraft 722.2
general store 799.1
generant 161.11
generate
electrify 158a.11
beget 161.10
(copulate 43.8)
(cause 153.6)
(reproduce 163.2)
(fecundate 168.4)
generation race 11.4
era 108.2
lifetime 110.4
procreation 161.2
(coition 43.2)
(reproduction 163.1)
(productiveness 168.1)
ancestry 166.4
man 372.1
generative
productive 161.11
procreative 168.8
generator cause 153.1
electricity 158a.7
(engine 633.3)
producer 164.1
automobile 272.16
generic 78.9
generosity 816.1
(charitableness 906.2)
(magnanimity 942.2)
generous
profuse 102.5
liberal 816.4
(charitable 784.15; **906.7**)

genesis — get 872

generous (continued)
  (magnanimous 942.6)
genesis cause 153.1
  generation 161.2, 3
  (beginning 66.2)
  lexicology 562.4
genet, genette 223.12
genet See jennet
genethlialogy 511.4
genetic intrinsic 5.6
  productive 161.11
genetic psychology 450.4
genetics
  organic science 357.5
  zoology 368.1
Geneva band, Geneva gown 999.1
genial
  productive 161.11
  pleasing 377.7; 829.7
  warm 382.15
  well-disposed 602.8
geniality
  willingness 602.1
  cheerfulness 836.1
geniculate 244.5
genie 980.2
genista 367.8
genital 161.11
genitor 166.5
genius intellect 450.1
  mental power 498.5
  talent 698.2
  proficient 700.1
  familiar spirit 979.12
genius loci 979.12
genre kind 75.2, 3
  art 556.6, 19
gens race 11.4
  kind 75.2
gent man 373.2
  vulgarian 851.4
genteel noble 875.10
  polite 894.12
  (fashionable 852.9)
gentile n. 984.20
  (unbeliever 989.4)
gentile adj. racial 11.8
  pagan 984.28
gentilism 984.10
gentility race 11.4
  nobility 875.1
  politeness 894.1
  (fashion 852.3)
gentle v. soften 324.4
  tame 370.6; 749.5
gentle adj.
  moderate 174.6
  slow 275.8
  tame 370.10
  fa'nt 405.9
  lenient 740.4
  meek 826.10
  polite 894.12
gentlefo'k, gentlefolks 875.3
gentleman man 373.2

nobleman 875.4
man of honor 939.5
gentlemanly
  male 373.7
  noble 875.10
  (genteel 852.9)
  courteous 894.12
gentleman's agreement, gentlemen's agreement
  agreement 23.4
  compact 769.1
gentleness 740.1
gentlewoman 374.2
gentlewomanly 374.11
Gentoo 984.21
gentry 875.3
genuflect 928.6
  (worship 990.9; 998.14)
genuflection, genuflexion 928.2
  (worship 990.1; 998.2)
genuine 494.12
  (unimitated 20.3)
  (good 648.8)
genuineness 494.2
genus kind 75.2
  animal kingdom 366.1
  vegetable kingdom 367.1
geodesic
  worldly 318.14
  geographic 342.13
  measuring 466.11
geodesist, geodecist
  cosmologist 318.11
  land 342.6
  measurer 466.9
  (mathematician 85.6)
geodesy
  cosmology 318.9
  land 342.5
  measurement 466.8
  (mathematics 85.2)
geodete
  cosmologist 318.11
  measurer 466.9
geodetic
  worldly 318.14
  geographic 342.13
  measuring 466.11
geodynamics 318.9
geognost 342.6
geognostic 342.13
geognosy land 342.5
  mineralogy 358.2
geographer
  cosmologist 318.11
  land 342.6
geographic 342.13
geographics 342.5
geography
  topography 184.8
  land 342.5
geoid 249.2
geological 342.13
geologist 342.6

geology 358.2
  (science of land 342.5)
geomancer 513.2
geomancy 511.3
geomant 513.2
geometer 85.6
  (measurer 466.9)
geometric 85.12
geometrician 85.6
geometry 85.2
  (measurement 466.8)
geomorphology 240.4
geophilous 342.9
Geophone, geophone 418.6
geophysics, geopolitics 342.5
geoponic 371.9
  (terrestrial 342.13)
geoponics 371.1
  (science 342.5)
georama 448.2
georgic n.
  agriculture 371.1
  poem 597.2
georgic adj.
  agricultural 371.9
  verse 597.13
geoscopy 358.2
geosynclinal 245.4
geosyncline 245.2
gephyrean 368.15
germ rudiment 153.3
  (undevelopment 674.3)
  microbe 193.4
  embryo 357.4
germal 357.10
German n.
  native 188.9
  language 560.4
  square dance 840.7
German adj.
  Germanic 188.11
  linguistic 560.9
germane, german n. 11.3
germane, german adj.
  related 9.6
  consanguine 11.7
  apt 23.10
Germanic 188.11
Germanophobia 860.4
German silver 545.6
Germany 182.3
germicidal 662.25
germicide 662.8
germinal
  original 153.9
  embryonic 357.10
germinate
  result from 154.3
  grow 194.6; 365.2
germination
  procreation 161.2
  growth 194.3
gerocomy 128.5
gerontal 128.8
gerontology 128.5
gerrymander n. 702.2

gerrymander v. 702.5
gerrymandering 702.2
Gerth 192.8
gest, geste
  romance 515.4
  deed 680.2
Gestalt psychology 450.4
gestant 168.9
gestate 168.6
gestation 673.1
gesticulate 550.20
gesticulation, gesture n. 550.3
  (acting 599.6)
gesture v. 550.20
  (motion 264.5)
get
  be converted into 144.8
  induce 153.7
  generate 161.10
  speed 274.9
  arrive 292.7
  hasten off 293.5
  hear 418.11
  nonplus 475.8
  understand 518.4
  learn 539.3
  acquire 775.6
  receive 785.3
  vex 830.5
  punish 972.5
get about
  be published 531.9
  recover 660.15
get ahead
  increase 35.4
  precede 280.2
  progress 282.2
  improve 658.6
get ahead of
  excel 33.5
  outstrip 303.4
get along
  depart 293.4
  begone! 297.23
  be mediocre 736.2
get along with 714.2
get around
  be published 531.9
  evade 623.6
get at solve 481a.4
  acquire 775.6
get away
  recede 287.2
  depart 293.4
  begone! 297.23
  escape 671.6
get back retreat 283.5
  recover 775.9
get back at 718.2
  (punish 972.5)
get behind lag 281.4
  second 707.8
get by 736.2
get chummy with 888.3
get clear escape 671.6
  become free 750.4
get down eat 298.44

descend 306.5
crouch 308.7
get in gather 72.11
acquire 775.6
get it 972.12
get left 732.5
get off depart 293.4
escape 671.6
get on don 225.43
prosper 734.5
**get on the band
 wagon** concur 488.7
be fashionable 852.6
comply obsequious-
 ly 886.3
get out eject 297.17
extract 301.5
publish 531.7
print 591.14
escape 671.6
get over
recover 660.15
surmount 731.7
be reconciled to
 830.3
get religion 987.7
get round 660.15
get the better of
recover 660.15
trick 702.5
triumph over 731.8
get there 731.5
get to begin 66.5
be distant 196.4
arrive 292.7
get together
assemble 72.11
come to terms 488.8
acquire 775.6
get through do 680.6
complete 729.2
spend 809.3
terminate 67.7
get up produce 161.8
ascend 305.4
stand up 307.7
study 539.4
trump up 544.3
recover 660.15
prepare 673.6
rouse feeling 824.2
get-at-able 286.4
getaway
make a getaway
 671.6
getting 35.2
get-together
assembly 72.2
party 892.5
Gettysburg 722.5
getup
composition 54.1
form 240.1
enterprise 682.4
get-up-and-get 682.4
gewgaw trifle 643.3
toy 840.16
trinket 847.9
geyser fountain 348.5
hot springs 382.5
gharry, gharri 272.4
gharry-wallah 268.9

ghastly pale 429.6
terrible 649.8
ugly 846.8
frightful 860.15
ghat, ghaut 203.3
ghazel See gazel
Gheber, Ghebre 984.21
ghee, ghi 356.4
gherkin 397.2
ghetto 189.16
ghost n.
substitute 147.2
ghost writer 593.15
specter 980a.1
psyche 994.11
give up ∼ 360.6
lay ghosts 992.4
raise ghosts
conjure 992.4
hold a séance 994.18
ghost v.
substitute 147.3
ghostwrite 590.14
ghost dance 992.1
ghostified
haunted 980a.5
bewitched 992.7
ghostlike 846.8
ghostly 980a.4
 (spiritual 994.22)
ghost story 546.1
ghost word 562.1
ghostwrite
substitute 147.3
author 590.14
ghostwriter
substitute 147.2
author 593.15
ghoul
vampire 913.4;
 992.3
fiend 980.2
ghoulish 980.9
ghurry period 108.1
timepiece 114.6
ghyll See gill
G.I. 726.4
giant n.
strong man 159.6
colossus 192.8
(tall person 206.6)
giant adj. 192.15
Giant Hunter 318.6
giantlike 192.15
giaour pagan 984.20
infidel 989.4
gib cat 366.4
tomcat 373.6
gibber n.
twaddle 517.3
jargon 563.4
chatter 584.2
gibber v.
talk nonsense 517.6
be inarticulate
 583.2
be loquacious 584.4
gibberish
twaddle 517.3
(unintelligibility
 519.2)
jargon 563.4

gibbet n. 975.4
gibbet v.
stigmatize 874.7
expose to infamy
 934.3
execute 972.8
gibblegabble n.
twaddle 517.3
chatter 584.2
gibblegabble v.
talk nonsense 517.6
be loquacious 584.4
gibbose rotund 249.6
convex 250.9
gibbosity 250.1
gibe, jibe n. 930.3
 (retort 462.1)
 (indignity 929.2)
 (personality 934.2)
gibe, jibe v. 930.6
gibe v. See jibe
giddiness
flightiness 458.2
 (folly 499.6)
delirium 503.3
illness 655.13
giddy
confused 458.12, 13
 (empty-headed
 499.1)
 (reckless 863.6)
delirious 503.14
fickle 608.6
tipsy 959.21
giddybrain 501.2
giddy-brained 458.13
giddyhead 501.2
**giddy-headed, giddy-
 pated, giddy-witted**
 458.13
gif 469.8
gift talent 698.2
donation 784.3
(compensation 30.3)
(thing transferred
 270.3)
(bribe 618.2)
(gratuity 815.4)
(charity 906.2)
(reward 973.2)
(oblation 990.6)
gifted 698.13
giftlike 815.10
gift of the gab 582.3
 (fluency 584.1)
gig n. cart 272.5
boat 273.4
gig v. 622.8
gigantic vast 31.8
huge 192.15
gigantomachy 722.1
giggle n. 838.3
gigg'e v. 838.7
gig lamps 445.3
gigolo 962.1
gigster 271.3
Gila monster 366.18
Gilbertese 560.4
gild n. See guild
gild v. coat 223.24
paint 428.10
yellow 436.5

gild the pill
deceive 545.7
tempt 617.4
make pleasant
 829.6
flatter 933.2
gilded
intoxicated 959.21
yellow 436.6
gilding yellow 436.3
ornament 847.2
gill, ghyll
valley 252.5
stream 348.1
gill man 373.2
lungs 349.19
measure 466.3
gillie, gilly
townsman 188.2
servant 746.1
gilt n. yellow 436.3
money 800.1, 5, 15
ornament 847.2
gilt adj. yellow 436.6
ornamented 847.13
gilt-edge, gilt-edged
 648.9
gimbal fulcrum 215.5
axis 312.5
gimbaljawed 584.5
gimcrack n.
trifle 643.3
toy 840.16
trinket 847.9
gimcrack adj.
frail 160.11
fragile 328.4
paltry 643.12
gimcrackery 643.5
gimcrackiness 160.1
gimcracky frail 160.11
paltry 643.12
gimlet 262
gimlet eye 441.7;
 443.4
gimlet-eyed 441.20
gimmal fulcrum 215.5
axis 312.5
gimp orderly 58.7
spruce 845.11
gimp See jimp
gimper 269a.1
gin n. snare 545.4
engine 633.2
distilled liquors
 959.6
gin v. 66.5
gin conj. 469.8
gin fizz 959.8
ginger energy 171.1
horse 271.5
pungency 392.1
condiment 395.1
verve 462.1
ginger ale 396.5
gingerbread n.
money 800.1
frippery 847.2
**gingerbread,
 gingerbready** adj.
 160.11
gingerly adj. 864.6

gingerly — glare

gingerly *adv.*
  moderately 174.8
  cautiously 864.8
  (carefully 459.9)
gingham cloth 219.5
  umbrella 223.4
gingle See **jingle**
ginny 959.21
gin rickey, gin sling 959.8
gip bitch 366.6
  female animal 374.8
gipon 225.15
gipsy See **gypsy**
giraffe 206.7
Giraffe 318.6
girandole
  firework 382.9
  candleholder 423.9
girasol, girasole 847.3
gird tie 43.6
  strengthen 159.8
  surround 227.3
  scoff 930.6
gird up one's loins
  strengthen 159.8
  prepare oneself 673.8
girder fastening 45.2
  beam 215.12
  aerostat 273a.12
girdle *n.*
  fastening 45.2
  garment 225.25, 34
  zone 230.2
  (enclosure 232.1)
  circle 247.2
girdle *v.* 227.3
girl maiden 129.5
  (female 374.2)
  mare 271.3
  female animal 374.8
  maidservant 746.2
  inamorata 897.7
girleen 129.5
girl friend 897.7
girlish 127.5
  (female 374.11)
girlishness 127.1
girllike 127.5
girly 129.5
giro 273a.1
girt *n.* saddle 215.23
  garment 225.34
  zone 230.2
girt *adj.* 227.4
girth *n.*
  fastening 45.2
  saddle 215.23
  garment 225.34
  zone 230.2
girth *v.* 43.6
gisarme 727.4
gist essence 5.2
  (substance 516.4)
  (salient point 642.4)
  center 222.2
  point 454.1
gîte abode 189.1
  resting place 265.4
gittern 417.2

give be pliant 324.5
  (be elastic 325.3)
  provide 637.4
  present 784.8
  (deliver 270.7;
  783.3)
  (bribe 618.3)
  (offer 763.2)
  (pay 807.6)
  (be benevolent 906.5)
  (reward 973.3)
  discount 813.2
give a leg lift 307.5
  help 707.6
give and take
  compensate 30.5
  interchange 148.3
  retaliate 718.2
  compromise 774.2
  barter 794.4
  deal justly 941.2
give a shoulder 707.6
give away
  divulge 529.4
  discard 678.3
  relinquish 782.3
  present 784.8
give back 790.3
give birth to
  cause 153.6
  bear 161.9
  (vivify 359.8)
give ear listen 418.11
  pay attention 457.4
give forth
  sound 402.7
  publish 531.7
give ground
  promise 511.10
  surrender 725.4
give in
  surrender 725.4
  consent 762.2
give it to
  reprove 932.8
  punish 972.5
give off 297.13
give oneself airs
  be proud 878.3
  be ostentatious 882.6
  (affect 853.5)
  (be vain 880.4)
  (bluster 887.3)
give one's hand 903.13
give out
  weaken 160.7
  let out 297.13
  publish 531.7
  dispense 784.8
give over cease 142.6
  abandon 624.3
  despair 859.5
give place to
  substitute 147.3
  avoid 623.6
give points to
  equalize 27.7
  tip 527.9
give rise to

cause 153.6
  generate 161.10
give thanks 990.11
give the lie to
  doubt 485.6
  deny 536.2
give the reins to
  facilitate 705.4
  be lax 738.4
  allow freedom 748.10
  (permit 760.3)
give the sack 297.12
give the slip
  elude 623.6
  escape 671.6
give tongue
  vociferate 411.7
  bark 412.2
  proclaim 531.7
  voice 580.8
  utter 582.6
give up
  not understand 519.5
  abandon 624.3
  (cease 142.6)
  (resign 757.2)
  disuse 678.2
  surrender 725.4
  abdicate 738.6
  relinquish 782.3
  part with 784.11
give voice
  voice 580.8
  utter 582.6
give way
  weaken 160.7
  row 267.45, 69
  be brittle 328.3
  submit 725.3, 4
  lose heart 837.6
  ~ to tears 839.8
  despair 859.5
  be modest 881.3
give-and-take *n.*
  interchange 148.1
  retaliation 718.1
  equity 941.1
give-and-take *adj.* 148.4
given
  circumstantial 8.5
  assumed 514.9
  bestowed 784.14
  (gratuitous 815.10)
  given to 613.12
given up dying 360.9
  hopeless 859.7
giver 784.7
giving 784
  (liberality 816.1)
  (charitableness 906.2)
gizzard stomach 191.7
  vitals 221.4
glabrate, glabrescent 255.5
glabrous
  hairless 226.10
  smooth 255.5
glacé 255.5

glaciable 385.6
glacial 383.9
glacial epoch 383.5
glaciarium 840.14
glaciate 385.4
glaciation
  hardening 323.2
  ice 383.5
  refrigeration 385.1
glacier, glacieret 383.5
glacification 385.1
glacis declivity 217.2
  fortification 717.3
glad pleased 827.8
  (cheerful 836.7)
  pleasing 829.7
gladden 836.6
  (delight 829.5)
  (rejoice 838.5)
  (amuse 840.20)
glade valley 252.5
  light beam 420.3
gladiate 253.15
gladiator 726.1
gladiatorial 722.13
gladiatorism 720.2
gladly 602.11
gladness 827.2
  (cheerfulness 836.1)
gladsome glad 827.8
  pleasing 829.7
Gladstone 191.5
glair 352.3
glaive 727.3
glamorous, glamourous 992.6
glamour, glamor *n.*
  magic 992.1
  spell 993.1
glamour *v.* 992.4
glance *n.* touch 379.1
  flash 420.4
  glimpse 441.2
  signal 550.3
  at a glance 441.23
glance *v.* polish 255.4
  turn aside 279.7
  touch 379.3
  shine 420.17
  look 441.14
  signal 550.20
glance at
  look at 441.14
  examine curiously 461.19
  hint at 527.8
glance off
  turn aside 279.7
  diverge 291.1
glance over 539.4
glance round 441.1
gland vitals 221.5
  aerostat 273a.12
  duct 350.1
glanders 655.18
glandule 221.5
glare *n.*
  brightness 420.1
  glower 441.2
glare *v.* shine 420.17
  glower 441.13

glare-eyed — glottological

daze 443.13
stand out 446.2
glare-eyed 443.14
glaring absolute 31.12
  bright 420.22
  gaudy-colored 428.15
  distinct 446.5
  conspicuous 525.5
  gaudy 851.8
  ostentatious 882.8
glaringly 31.21
glass tumbler 191.11
  fragility 328.2
  ceramics 384.14
  thermometer 389.1
  transparency 425.2
  telescope 445.2
  mirror 445.4
glasses 445.3
glasshouse
  fragility 328.2
  conservatory 371.6
Glassite 984.14
glasslike 425.4
glassmaker 690.8
glassware
  ceramics 384.14
  (tableware 191.13)
  merchandise 798.3
glasswork 384.14
glassworker 690.9
glassworks 691
glassy smooth 255.5
  glossy 420.22
  dim 422.8
  transparent 425.4
  colorless 429.6
glauconite 435.4
glaucous 435.6
glaucous green 435.2
glaver 933.2
glaze *n.*
  smoothness 255.1
  sleet 383.5
  paint 428.5
glaze *v.* polish 255.4
  paint 428.10
gleam *n.*
  modicum 32.2
  light 420.1, 3, 4
gleam *v.* shine 420.17
  be distinguished 873.10
gleaming 420.22
glean deduce 480.6
  select 609.7
  acquire 775.6
gleaning
  accumulation 72.6
  crop 636.3
glebe soil 342.3
  ecclesiastical ~ 995.3
  pastorate 1000.5
glee part music 415.12
  happiness 827.2
  cheerfulness 836.1
gleeful 836.8
gleemaiden, gleeman 416.10
glen 252.5

glib 584.5
glide *n.*
  aerobatics 267a.24
  sound 402.2
glide *v.* elapse 109.3
  be converted into 144.8
  course 264.6
  slide 266.20
  aviate 267a.31
glider 273a.6
gliding boat 273.4
gliding machine 273a.6
glim modicum 32.2
  fire 382.8
  light 420.1
  luminary 423.1
  glimpse 441.2
  eyes 441.7
glime *n.* 441.2
glime *v.*
  look askance 441.15
  squint 443.12
glimmer *n.*
  glitter 420.5
  (semidarkness 422.2)
  hint 527.4
  ~ of hope 858.3
glimmer *v.* 420.18
  (fade 422.7)
glimmering 527.4
  (slight knowledge 491.3)
glimmery 420.23
glimpse *n.* 441.2
glimpse *v.* 441.10
glims eyes 441.7
  spectacles 445.3
glint *n.* light 420.1, 4
  glimpse 441.2
glint *v.* shine 420.17
  glimpse 441.10, 14
glisk 420.18
glissade *n.* 306.3
glissade *v.*
  glide 266.20
  slide 306.4
glissando slide 306.3
  music 415.20
glisten *n.* 420.5
glisten *v.* 420.18
glister *n.* 420.5
glister *v.* 420.18
glitter *n.*
  sparkle 420.5
  show 882.1
glitter *v.*
  sparkle 420.18
  be distinguished 873.10
  be ostentatious 882.6
glittering
  ornate 847.13
  gaudy 851.8
  showy 882.8
glittery 420.23
gloam *n.* 126.1
gloam *v.* 422.7
gloaming 126.1

gloat
  luxuriate in 377.4
  gaze 441.13
  delight in 827.6
  exult 884.6
globate 249.7
globe sphere 249.2
  world 318.1
  light ~ 423.11
globelike 249.7
globe-trotter
  traveler 268.1
  sight-seer 444.1
globe-trotting
  travel 266.1
  sight-seeing 441.3
globoid *n.* 249.2
globoid *adj.* 249.7
globosity 249.1
globous, globular 249.7
globule modicum 32.2
  sphere 249.2
  bubble 353.1
glochideous 256.14
glochidiate 253.12
glockenspiel 417.10
glomeration 72.6
gloom *n.*
  darkness 421.2
  (semidarkness 422.2)
  shadow 422.3
  sadness 837.1
  sullenness 901.3
  gloomy person 901.4
gloom *v.* darken 421.5
  grow dim 422.7
glooming dusk 126.1
  sullenness 901.2, 3
gloomth
  darkness 421.2
  shadow 422.3
gloomy dark 421.8
  (shadowy 422.9)
  dull-colored 428.19
  dismal 837.10
  (funereal 363.25)
Gloria
  doxology 990.2
  part of Mass 998.7
glorification
  honor 873.6
  praise 931.2
  sanctification 987.2
  worship 990.2
glorify honor 873.13
  boast 884.5
  praise 931.6
  bless 976.11
  sanctify 987.8
  worship 990.10
gloriole 420.13
glorious
  intoxicated 959.21
  beautiful 845.13
  illustrious 873.17
glory *n.* halo 420.13
  gorgeousness 845.2
  renown 873.1, 2
  praise 931.2
  divinity 976.2

  spiritual aura 980a.3
  heaven 981.1
  glorification 990.2
gone to glory 360.8
go to glory
  perish 162.5
  die 360.6
  deteriorate 659.6
glory *v.* rejoice 838.5
  take pride in 878.4
  exult 884.6
glory be!
  hurrah! 838.12
  hail! 883.7
Glory be to God! 916.5
glory hole
  small place 184.4
  compartment 191.2
  store 636.4
  rubbish heap 645.4
gloss *n.*
  glossary 86.1
  smoothness 255.1
  sheen 420.1
  interpretation 522.2
  falsehood 546.1
  dictionary 593.4
  pretext 619.1
  elegance 845.1
  veneer 882.1
  extenuation 937.3
gloss *v.* coat 223.24
  polish 255.4
  paint 428.10
  whitewash 430.7
gloss over
  whitewash 430.7
  neglect 460.4
  sophisticate 477.7
  falsify 544.3
  pretext 619.2
  extenuate 937.8
glossarist 524.2
glossary index 86.1
  explanation 522.5
  dictionary 593.4
glossic 561.4
glossographer
  commentator 524.2
  philologist 560.7
glossography 562.4
glossological
  linguistic 560.9
  lexical 562.8
  terminological 564.9
glossologist 560.7
  (lexicologist 562.5)
glossology
  linguistics 560.6
  lexicology 562.4
  nomenclature 564.1
glossotype 561.4
glossy smooth 255.5
  shining 420.22
  specious 545.13
  pretty 845.11
glottis 580.2
glottogonic 562.9
glottogony 562.4
glottological 560.9

glottologist — go

glottologist 560.7
glottology 560.6
glout *n.* 901.3
glout *v.* 901.6
glove clothes 225.30
 challenge 715.1
glovemaker 690.8
glover 225.36
glow *n.*
 heat flush 382.7
 shine 420.1
 color 428.1
 redness 434.1, 4
 vehemence 574.3
 ardor 821.2
 beauty 845.1
 spiritual aura
  980a.3
glow *v.* burn 382.13
 shine 420.17
 redden 434.8
 ~ with excitement
  824.8
 be distinguished
  873.10
glower *n.* 441.2
glower *v.*
 glare 441.13
 look sullen 901.6
glowering
 frowning 837.10
 surly 901.8
glowfly 423.13
glowing
 intoxicated 959.21
 burning 382.17
 shining 420.22
 red 434.9, 11
 orange 439.5
 vehement 574.7
 fervent 821.6
 excited 824.9
 beauty 845.13
glow lamp 423.3
glowworm
 worm 366.25
 firework 423.13
gloze *n.* 933.1
gloze *v.* shine 420.17
 whitewash 430.7
 pretext 619.2
 flatter 933.2
 extenuate 937.8
glucose 396.4
glue *n.* 45.6
 (adhesive 46.3)
 (semiliquid 352.3)
glue *v.* 46.7
 (attach 43.6)
gluemaker 690.8
gluey 352.8
glum sad 837.9
 (discontented
  832.5)
 sullen 901.8
 look glum 832.3
glume 223.14
glut *n.*
 overfullness 641.1
 satiety 869.1
glut *v.* overfill 641.4
 sate 869.4

gorge 957.3
gluteal 235.10
gluten cement 45.6
 paste 352.3
glutenous, glutinous
  352.8
 (tough 327.5)
glutinize 352.6
glutinosity
 tenacity 46.2
 viscidity 352.1
glutose 352.8
glutted 869.6
glutter 420.5
glutton 957.2
 (eater 298.41)
gluttonize 957.3
gluttonous 957.4
 (intemperate 954.4)
 be gluttonous 957.3
gluttony 957.1
 (eating 298.1)
 (greed 865.4)
 (intemperance
  954.1)
glycerin, glycerine *n.*
 oil 356.1
 (lubricant 332.2)
 balm 662.6
glycerin, glycerine *v.*
  332.4
glycerogel oil 356.1
 balm 662.6
**glycerogelatin, gly-
 cerogelatine** 356.1
glycerol 662.6
glycoprotein 352.3
glyph 557.6
glyphic 557.10
glyphograph 558.3
glyphography 558.1
glyptic
 carving 557.10
 engraving 558.6
glyptician, 559.6
glyptics 558.1
glyptograph 558.3
glyptographer 559.6
glyptography 558.1
glyptotheca
 gallery 556.15; 636.5
 sculpture 557.1
glyster See **clyster**
G-man 528.9
gnarl *n.*
 complexity 59.3
 protuberance 250.2
gnarl *v.* distort 243.3
 show resentment
  900.7
 threaten 909.2
gnarled complex 59.10
 protuberant 250.9
 rough 256.12
 dense 321.8
gnarly 256.12
gnash *n.* 298.2
gnash *v.* grind 331.3
 ~ one's teeth
  839.11; 900.7
gnat ephemerid 111.4
 midge 193.2

 insect 366.24
gnaw chew 298.45
 abrade 331.3
 pain 378.4
 wear away 659.7
 rankle 830.7
gnawer 366.17
gnome maxim 496.1
 mythical being
  979.7, 9
gnomic 496.5
gnomon 114.6
gnostic
 knowing 490.12
 wise 498.11
Gnostic 984.21
Gnosticism
 philosophy 451.9
 (ism 984.4)
 religion 984.11
gnu, gnu goat 366.9, 10
go *n.* circumstance 8.1
 predicament 8.3;
  704.2
 agreement 23.4
 part 51.1
 period 108.1
 event 151.1
 energy 171.1
 examination 461.3
 attempt 675.1
 act 680.2
 enterprise 682.1, 4
 contest 720.2
 success 731.2
 bargain 769.1
 game 840.11
 fashion 852.1
 all the go 852.7
 make a go of 731.5
 on the go 264.10
go *v.* cease to be 2.5
 move 264.6
 advance 282.2
 recede 287.2
 depart 293.4
 pass 302.2
 fade 429.4
 disappear 449.2
go a-begging 765.6
go about
 wander 266.14
 turn ship 267.24
 circuit 311.3
 be published 531.9
 undertake 676.2
go ahead begin 66.5
 improve 658.6
 keep going 682.12
go ahead of
 order 62.2
 motion 280.2
go all out speed 274.9
 do thoroughly 729.3
go along 293.4;
  297.23
go along with
 concur 178.3
 co-operate 709.5
go away part 44.11
 recede 287.2, 5
 depart 293.4; 297.23

 disappear 449.2
go back return 104.5
 regress 283.5; 287.2
go back on
 abandon 624.3
 not keep faith
  773.4; 940.7
go back over 461.20
go bad 659.7
go before order 62.2
 time 116.3
 front 234.7
 precede 280.2
go below 267.43
go beyond 303.2
go by conform 82.5
 elapse 109.3
 be past 122.6
go down
 capsize 267.35
 descend 306.4
 sink 310.5
 find credence 484.11
 deteriorate 659.6
 suffer misfortune
  735.6
 be borne 826.6
 be tolerated 831.5
go Dutch 807.6
go for
 be credulous 486.3
 be deceived 547.3
 attack 716.5
 become enamored
  897.12
go forth depart 293.4
 be published 531.9
go in 294.6
go in for
 resolve upon 604.6
 adopt 609.7
 pursue 622.6
 undertake 676.2
go into 595.4
go it speed 274.9
 act 680.5
 bestir oneself 682.12
go it blind 621.17
go off happen 151.3
 explode 173.9
 (shoot 284.13)
 turn aside 279.7
 diverge 291.2
 depart 293.4
 die 360.6
 detonate 406.8
 deteriorate 659.6
 get excited 824.6
 marry 903.13
go on last 106.2
 continue 143.2, 3
go out cease 142.6
 egress 295.6
 extinguish 385.5
 undertake 676.2
go over repeat 104.4
 traverse 302.2
 examine 461.15, 17
 apostatize 607.8
 succeed 731.5
go round
 be inverted 218.5

876

surround 227.3
circuit 311.3
(circumambulate 629.2)
be induced 615.10
go the whole hog
be thorough 52.8
persevere 604a.2
do thoroughly 729.3
go through
experience 151.4
penetrate 302.2
complete 729.2
spend 809.3
feel 821.3
move deeply 824.4
go to be distant 196.4
travel 266.22
go towards 278.5
go under 162.5
go up ascend 305.4
die 360.6
fail 732.5
go bankrupt 808.6
go west 360.6
go with agree 23.7
accompany 88.6
concur 178.3; 488.7
be contiguous 199.3
go without saying
be certain 474.17
be manifest 525.3, 8
go wrong 732.5
go-about 268.2
goad n. 615.3
goad v. impel 276.7
~ a horse 370.7
urge 615.7
hasten 684.2
goads 621.8
goal end 67.1
destination 292.6
(resting place 265.4)
intention 620.2
go-ahead n. 682.4, 10
go-ahead adj.
progressive 282.3; 658.15
enterprising 682.18
go-as-you-please n. 274.4; 720.5
go-as-you-please adj. 748.12
goat substitute 147.2
horse 271.6, 8
jumper 309.3
game 840.12
libertine 962.1
Goat 318.6
goatee 256.5
goat god 979.11
goatherd 370.4
goatish 961.11
goat's-hair 353.5
goatstone 342.4
gob quantity 25.2
quantities 31.3
piece 51.3
accumulation 72.6
lump 192.5
mouth 260.2

mariner 269.1
bite 298.2
solid 321.4
gobang, goban 840.11
gobbet modicum 32.2
bite 298.2
gobble eat 298.44
gabble 412.2
eat greedily 957.3
gobble up, gobble down 486.3
gobbler turkey 366.23
male animal 373.6
gobe-mouche 547.1
go-between
intermediary 228.5
mediator 724.2
negotiator 758.3
(interpreter 524.1)
(interlocutor 588.5)
(medium 631.2)
(deputy 759.1)
goblet 191.11
goblin 980.4
(frightener 860.7)
gobo 424.5
go-by neglect 460.1
avoidance 623.1
snub 930.4
gocart 272.11
god good person 948.1
deity 979.1–6
God world spirit 359.3
Deity 976
for God's sake! 765.9
God forbid!
by no means! 489.9
(no! 536.4)
deprecation 766.6
(don't! 761.6)
censure 932.16
God help you! 914.7
God knows! 491.17
so help me God!
upon oath 535.8
I promise! 768.8
under God 976.15
godchild 771.2
goddess
sweetheart 897.7
good woman 948.2
deity 979.1–6
go-devil
tractor 272.17
handcar 272.21
godfather 771.2
Godforsaken, godforsaken
unoccupied 187.11
remote 196.5
Godhead, godhood 976.1
godless 989.6
godlike
righteous 944.3
divine 976.13
godling 979.1
godly divine 976.13
pious 987.10
godmother 771.2
god of love 897.2
godown 636.4

God's acre 363.14
God's board 1000.3
God's country 182.2
godsend
benefit 648.2
(prosperity 734.1)
gain 775.2
godship 976.1
Godspeed, God-speed, God speed
leave-taking 293.2, 4
good luck 858.12
wish Godspeed
be benevolent 906.5
express approbation 931.5
goer traveler 268.1
horse 271.3
speeder 274.5
outgoer 295.4
Gog and Magog 192.8
go-getter 682.10
go-getterism 682.4
goggle n. 441.7
goggle v. turn 311.4
gaze 441.13
squint 443.12
goggled 445.10
goggle-eyed 443.14
goggles
eveshade 424.4
spectacles 445.3
going n. 293.1
going adj. 360.9
get going begin 66.5
set to work 686.7
going about
general 78.7
rumored 532.8
going on
happening 151.5
in preparation 673.13
goings on affairs 151.2
conduct 692.1
goiter, goitre 655.5
Golconda 803.1
gold n. yellow 436.3
metal 635.6
money 800.5
Gold, Goldi n. 560.4
gold adj. 436.6
gold brick 545.6
gold digger 902.6
golden v. 436.5
golden adj. 436.6
golden age
prosperity 734.3
pleasure 827.3
golden apple 617.1
go'den buck 298.29
golden calf 991.4
golden-haired 436.6
golden mean
mean 29.1
(mediocrity 736.1)
(mid-course 628.1)
moderation 174.1
keep the golden mean
be moderate 174.4
steer a middle

course 628.2
(be mediocre 736.2)
golden pheasant 436.1
goldenrod 436.3
golden rule
axiom 496.2
precept 697.1
golden yellow 436.1, 6
goldfinch 366.22
Goldfish 318.6
goldflower 436.3
gold piece
yellow 436.3
coin 800.5
goldsmith 690.6
gold star 733.1
goldstone 342.4
goldworker 690.9
golf 840.11
golf ball 284.5
golf links 840.14
Golgotha, golgotha 363.14
Goliath
strong man 159.6
giant 192.8
gomashta, gomastah
functionary 758.2
deputy 759.1
gombo See **gumbo**
gombroon 384.14
gonad 221.5
Gondi 560.4
gondola flatcar 272.19
boat 273.4
aerostat 273a.12
gondolier 269.2
gone extinct 2.10
past 122.8
absent 187.10
departed 293.9
dead 360.8
disappeared 449.5
forgotten 506.7
hopeless 859.7
be gone depart 293.4
disappear 449.2
gone on 897.15
gone out 124.9
gone west 360.8
gone-by past 122.8
antiquated 124.9
goneness 688.3
goner failure 732.4
forlorn hope 859.3
gonfalon 550.13
gong n. bell 408.5
music instrument 417.10
signal 550.14
gong v. 408.8
Gongorism 579.1
Gongorist 579.2
gongoristic 579.3
gonidium 193.4
goniometer, goniometry 244.3
gonoph, gonof See **ganef**
gonorrhea, gonorrhoea 655.7
goo 352.3

goober — Gothic

goober, goober pea 298.33
good *n.* 648.2
  (prosperity 734.1)
  (right 922.1)
 to the good
  sufficiently 639.8
  to one's credit 780.9
good *adj.* full 52.11
  savory 394.7
  authentic 494.12
  excellent 648.8
  (expedient 646.4)
  (pleasing 829.7)
  (praiseworthy 931.11)
  salubrious 656.5
  skilled 698.14
  solvent 800.22
  benevolent 906.6
  right 922.5
  just 941.3
  virtuous 944.3
 as good as gold 648.10
 be good
  farewell! 293.14
  be excellent 648.5
 be good for 656.4
 do good benefit 648.6
  (be useful 644.2)
  be benevolent 906.5
 for good long 110.11
  always 112.5
  permanently 141.8
 for good and all
  throughout 52.15
  permanently 141.8
 good for useful 644.5
  salubrious 656.5
 good for you! 931.13
good *int.*
  very well! 831.9
  bravo! 931.13
good afternoon 292.13; 894.4
good behavior
  deportment 692.1
  courtesy 894.1
  virtue 944.1
Good Book 985.2
good breeding 894.1
good-by, good-bye 293.2, 14
 bid good-by 293.7
 good-by to . . . 776.7
good cheer 298.10
good day
  welcome 292.13
  (farewell 293.14)
  greeting 894.4
good faith 939.4
 in good faith 543.4
good feeling 906.1
good fellow
  boon companion 892.8
  philanthropist 911.1
good-fellowship 892.2
good folk, the 979.9

good form 852.2
good-for-nothing, good-for-naught *n.*
  idler 683.7
  wretch 949.1
good-for-nothing, good-for-naught *adj.* 645.8
  (nugatory 158.11)
Good Friday
  anniversary 138.7
  holyday 998.13
good humor
  cheerfulness 836.1
  courtesy 894.1
good-humored, good-humoured
  courteous 894.12
  benevolent 906.6
good lack! 870.11
good-looking 845.10
good luck
  farewell! 293.14
  prosperity 734.2
  (fortune 156.1)
  God speed! 858.12
  hail! 894.15
goodly great 31.6
  sizable 192.11
  comely 845.10
goodman man 373.2
  husband 903.7
good morning
  welcome! 292.13
  (farewell! 293.14)
  greeting 894.4
good morrow
  welcome! 292.13
  greeting 894.4
good nature
  cheerfulness 836.1
  benevolence 906.1
good-natured 906.6
goodness
  excellence 648
  (benevolence 906.1)
  virtue 944.1
 for goodness' sake 765.9
 goodness gracious! 870.11
good night
  farewell! 293.14
  greeting 894.4
good office
  mediation 724.1
  kindness 906.2
goods textile 219.5
  freight 270.4
  information 527.1
  skill 698.2
  belongings 780.1
  (equipment 634.1)
  merchandise 798.1
good Samaritan
  philanthropist 911.1
  benefactor 912.1
  unselfish 942.3
Good Shepherd 976.5
goods train 272.18
goods waggon 272.19
good temper

  cheerfulness 836.1
  courtesy 894.1
Good Templar 953.4
good turn
  benefit 648.2
  aid 707.1
  favor 784.4
  (kindness 906.2)
 do a good turn
  do good to 648.6
  help 707.6
  be benevolent 906.5
goodwife
  good woman 374.2
  wife 903.8
good will, goodwill
  willingness 602.1
  benevolence 906.1
  (peace 721.1)
  (friendship 888.1)
goody
  mollycoddle 160a.3
  delicacy 298.9
  good woman 374.2
goof 504.1
go-off beginning 66.1
  event 151.1
  departure 293.1
goofy 503.12
goose *n.* food 298.25
  bird 366.22
  hisser 409.2
  fool 501.1
  game 840.11
goose *v.* 380.5
gooseberry
  chaperon 88.4; 664.3
  fruit 298.31
  falsehood 546.1
  exaggeration 549.1
gooseberry-eyed 443.14
gooseboy 370.4
goose chase
  inutility 645.2
  failure 732.1
goose egg 87a.1
  (nothing 2.2)
goose flesh 383.2
goose grass 253.2
gooseherd 370.4
goose step *n.*
  gait 266.5
  routine 613.4
goose-step *v.* 266.16
goosy, goosey 380.7; 499.15
gopher 366.17
gopura 206.3
Gordian knot
  knot 45.6
  complexity 59.3
  dilemma 704.4
gore *n.* joint 43.3
  airplane 273a.10
  blood 333.3
  bloodshed 361.1
gore *v.* 260.14
gorge *n.*
  stomach 191.7
  chasm 198.3
  (valley 252.5)

  water gap 350.1
  gullet 350.4
gorge *v.* overfill 641.4
  sate 869.4
  overeat 957.3
gorged overfull 641.6
  satiated 869.6
gorgeous
  colorful 428.14
  beautiful 845.13
  ornate 847.13
gorgeousness 845.2
gorger 957.2
gorgerin 215.17
Gorgon monster 83.7
  object of fear 860.7
  sorceress 992.3
Gorgonian 860.15
gorilla killer 361.8
  monkey 366.16
  thief 792.3
  ruffian 913.2
gormandize 957.3
gormandizer 957.2
gormandizing 957.4
gorse 367.8
gory
  murderous 361.15
  (discolored 440a.3)
  red 434.9
  soiled 653.16
gosling novice 541.6
  unsophisticate 703.2
gospel doctrine 484.3
  truth 494.1
  glad tidings 532.1
Gospel
  scriptures 985.2, 4
  communion rite 998.7
Gospel side 239.2
gospel truth 484.3
gossamer *n.*
  filament 205.1
  cloth 219.5
  lightness 320.2
  transparency 425.2
gossamer *adj.*
  fine 329.3
  gossamery 425.4
gossamery
  chimerical 4.6
  frail 160.11
  light 320.7
  fine 329.3
  transparent 425.4
gossip *n.* rumor 532.3
  (chat 588.2)
  newsmonger 532.5
  (inquisitive 455.2)
  (talker 582.5)
  (chatterer 584.3)
  (meddler 682.11)
gossip *v.* 532.7
  (talk 582.6)
gossipry 532.3
Goth 876.7
Gothamite
  wiseacre 500.2
  fool 501.1
Gothic 591.7
Gothic, gothic 851.7

Gothicism
  barbarism 579.1
  vulgarity 851.1
gouache color 428.3
  painting 556.9
gouge *n.*
  perforator 262
  cheat 545.7
gouge *v.*
  excavate 252.9
  ream 260.14
  blind 442.3
  swindle 791.12
goulash 298.17
gourmand
  connoisseur 850.3
  sensualist 954a.1
  glutton 957.2
gourmet
  connoisseur 850.1
  sensualist 954a.1
  glutton 957.2
gout pain 378.1
  ailment 655.5
goût 394.2
gouty 378.6; 655.25
govern manage 693.4
  rule 737.11
governed 737.14
governess
  instructress 540.2
  custodian 664.3
governing 737.15
government
  management 693.1
  (command 737.2)
  (jurisdiction 965.1)
  system of ~ 737.4
  authorities 745.8
governmental
  directing 693.6
  authoritative 737.15
governor father 166.6
  guardian 664.3
  director 694.1
  ruler 745.1, 9
governorship 693.3
gowk oaf 501.1
  awkward fellow 701
gown *n.*
  garment 225.3, 19
  clerical ~ 999.1
gown *v.* 225.41
G.P. 662.19
gr. 319.4
grab *n.* theft 791.4
  booty 793.1
grab *v.* seize 789.9
  be avaricious 819.3
grab-all 191.5
grab bag 621.10
grabble 379.3
grace *n.* music 413.10
  elegance 578.1
  indulgence 760.1
  favor 784.4
  beauty 845.1
  good taste 850.1
  kindness 906.1
  mercy 914.1
  thanksgiving 916.2
  forgiveness 918.1

  conscience 926.3
  divine ~ 976.6
  sanctification 987.2
  prayer 990.3
  by the grace of God 922.7
  say grace 990.11
Grace *n.* 877.2
  the Graces 845.3
grace *v.*
  beautify 845.7
  honor 873.13
graceful elegant 578.4
  beautiful 845.8
  courteous 894.12
graceless
  inelegant 579.3
  awkward 699.12
  homely 846.8
  uncouth 851.7
  virtueless 945.11
  impenitent 951.4
  irreligious 989.6
grace note 413.6, 10
gracile 203.10
gracious
  well-disposed 602.8
  courteous 894.12
  benevolent 906.6
graciously 602.11
gradatim
  gradually 26.5
  in order 58.8
  continuously 69.7
  slowly 275.11
gradation *n.*
  degree 26.1
  graduation 58.2
  continuity 69.1
  rank 71.1
gradation *v.* 26.2
gradational 26.4
grade *n.* degree 26.1
  rank 71.1; 873.4
  incline 217.2
  school 541.8; 542.1
  at grade 219.12
  make the grade
  be able 157.6
  succeed 731.5
grade *v.*
  partition 44.10
  classify 60.7
  size 192.10
grade school 542.1
gradient 217.2
gradin, gradine 215.19
gradual
  gradational 26.4
  continuous 69.6
  slow 275.8
gradually
  by degrees **26.5**
  by gradations 69.7
  slowly 275.11
graduate *n.*
  student 541.5
  proficient 700.1
graduate *v.*
  gradation 26.2
  partition 44.10
  classify 60.7

  give continuity 69.5
  size 192.10
  measure 466.10
  take a degree 873.12
graduation
  adaptation 23.3
  degree 26.1
  gradation 58.2
  arrangement 60.1
  measure 466.4
gradus 593.4
Graeae Graiae 992.3
graff 259.2
graffito 847.3
graft *n.*
  bribery 618.1
  machiavellianism 702.2
  plunder 793.1
  dishonesty 940.5
graft *v.* attach 43.6
  ingraft 300.6
  ~ plants 371.8
  inculcate 537.9
grafter 702.4
graham bread 298.11
grail 342.4
grain *n.* nature 5.3
  modicum 32.2
  kind 75.2
  tendency 176.1
  diminutive 193.2
  rough 256.2
  fodder 298.7
  weight 319.4
  texture 329.1
  powder 330.3
  disposition 820.1
  in the grain 5.6
  with a grain of salt
  conditionally 469.7
  unbelievingly 485.12
grain *v.* dye 428.9
  ornament 847.11
grain-eating 298.48
grain elevator 636.4
grain-fed 192.12
grain oil 356.3
grallatorial 267.52
gram, gramme 319.4
grama 367.9
gramarye, gramary 992.1
gramercy 916.5
graminivore 298.41
graminivorous 298.48
grammar *n.*
  rudiments 66.4
  language 567
  diction 569.1
  textbook 593.5
grammar *v.* 567.5
  (linguistics 560.6)
grammarian 560.7
grammarless 491.9
grammar school 542.1
grammatical 567.6
grammaticize 567.5
gramme See **gram**
gramophone 417.9
gramp, grampa 166.8
grampus

  fat man 192.7
  whale 366.21
granam See **grannam**
granary 636.4
grand *n.*
  thousand 98.10
  piano 417.6
grand *adj.* great 31.6
  sizable 192.11
  language 574.8
  important 642.10
  excellent 648.8
  beautiful 845.13
  eminent 873.18
  (august 31.14)
  dignified 878.7
  ostentatious 882.8
grandam, grandame
  old woman 130.3
  grandmother 166.9
grandam, granddam 166.9
grandchild 167.1, 4
granddad, grandad 166.8
granddaughter 167.4
grand duke 875.5
grande dame
  fine lady 854.2
  proud person 878.2
grandee 875.4
  (personage 642.5)
grandeur
  greatness 31.2
  ~ of expression 574.4
  importance 642.1
  distinction 873.3
grandfather 166.8
  (elder 130.1)
grandiloquence 577.2
  (exaggeration 549.1)
  (diffuseness 573.1)
  (redundance 641.1)
  (affectation 853.1)
grandiloquent 577.7
  (exaggerated 549.3)
  (diffuse 573.7)
  (redundant 641.5)
  (affected 853.6)
  (ostentatious 882.8)
grandiloquently 577.8
grandiose 577.7
grandiosity 577.2
grandisonant 577.7
grand juror 967.3
grandma, grandmamma, grandmammy 166.8
Grand Mogul 745.3
grandmother
  mollycoddle 160a.3
  ancestor 166.9
  (old woman 130.3)
  dotard 501.3
grandpa, grandpapa 166.8
Grand Gachem 745.1
Grand Seignior, Grand Signor 745.5

grandsire, grandsir 166.8
grandson 167.4
grandstand n.
　observatory 441.5
　spectators 444.2
grandstand v. 882.6
grandstander, grandstand player 882.5
grand strategy 722.2
grand style 569.1
grand tactics 722.2
Grand Turk 745.5
grand vizier 745.9
grange
　farmhouse 189.3
　farm 371.4
granger 371.2
Grani 271.9
granite
　hardness 323.3
　stone 342.4
granivore 298.41
granivorous 298.48
grannam, granam 166.9
granny
　old woman 130.3
　grandmother 166.9
　newsmonger 532.5
　obstetrician 662.19
　nurse 662.20
　nursemaid 664.3
grant n.
　qualification 469.1
　permit 760.2
　gift 784.3
　privilege 922.2
grant v.
　allow for 469.4
　acknowledge 488.9
　confess 529.5
　permit 760.4
　(commission 755.4)
　consent 762.2
　give 784.8
　(deliver 783.3)
granted 488.14
grantee
　transferee 270.5
　recipient 785.2
Granth, Grunth 986.1
granting 8.8; 469.8
grantor 784.7
granular 330.8
granularity 330.1
granulate v.
　solidify 321.7
　(harden 323.4)
　crumble 330.6, 7
granulate adj. 330.8
granulation 330.1, 2
granule modicum 32.2
　grain 330.3
granulet 330.3
granulitization 330.2
granulitize, granulize 330.6
grape fruit 298.31
grapeshot 727.14
grapefruit 298.31
grapeshot 727.14

grapes of wrath 900.1
grapevine
　covert way 530.4
　rumor 532.3
　dance 840.8
grapevine telegraph
　covert way 530.4
　rumor 532.3
graphic
　intelligible 518.6
　(expressive 516.8)
　pictorial 556.19
　vigorous 574.5
　descriptive 594.7
　(depictive 554.9)
graphically 556.19
graphic arts 556
graphite
　lubricant 332.2
　mineral 635.6
graphologist 590.11
graphology 590.1
　(symbology 550.17)
graphomania 590.2
graphomaniac 590.11
graphometer 244.3
graphophone 417.9
graphotype 558.3
grapnel
　fastening 45.2
　(grip 781.2)
　anchor 666.2
grapple attach 43.6
　seize 789.9
grapple with
　resist 719.3
　contend with 720.8
grapple iron, grappler 45.2
grappling iron
　fastening 45.2
　anchor 666.2
grasp n. handle 215.7
　understanding 498.1
　control 737.2
　hold 781.1
grasp v. cohere 46.5
　understand 518.4
　grip 781.4
　seize 789.9
　be avaricious 819.3
　~ at 865.11
grasping n. 865.4
grasping adj.
　rapacious 789.15
　greedy 865.20
grass n. spring 126a.2
　verdure 367.9, 11
　(fodder 298.7)
　green 435.3
grass v. floor 213.7
　fell 308.5
grass-eater 298.41
grass-eating 298.48
grass green n. 435.2
grass-green adj. 435.6
grasshopper
　lowness 207.4
　jumper 309.3
　insect 366.24
grassland 367.11
　(plain 344.1)

(field 371.5)
grassplot, grassplat
grassland 367.11
greenyard 371.6
grass widow, grass widower 905.3
grasswidowhood 905.2
grassy 367.14
grate n. sorter 60.4
　network 219.4
　fire iron 386.3
grate v. grind 330.6
　abrade 331.3
　pain 378.4
　sound harshly 410.6, 7
　(rasp 331.3)
　(discord 414.3)
　~ upon the feelings 830.5, 7
grated 219.11
grateful
　gratifying 377.7; 829.7
　thankful 916.4
be grateful 916.3
gratefulness 916.1
grater rough 256.2
grinder 330.4
gratification
　relish 394.2
　pleasure 827.1
　source of ~ 829.3
gratified 827.8
gratify feed 298.43
　indulge 740.3
　permit 760.3
　satisfy 829.4
　(render content 831.4)
　make proud 878.5
gratifying
　physically ~ 377.7
　mentally ~ 829.7
grating n. sorter 60.4
　network 219.4
　fire iron 386.3
grating adj.
　harsh-sounding 410.9
　distressing 830.15
gratis 815.10
　(unpaid 806.9)
gratitude 916
gratuitous
　assumed 514.9
　voluntary 602.10
　gratis 815.10
　(free 748.14, 19)
gratuitousness 815.4
gratuity gift 784.3
　(reward 973.2)
gratuitousness 815.4
gratulate 896.2
gratulation 896.1
gratulatory 896.3
gravamen
　salient point 642.4
　accusation 938.1
grave n. cavity 252.2
　trench 259.2
　burial place 363.13

(resting place 265.4)
abode of dead 982.1
grave v.
　excavate 252.9
　incise 259.3
　inter 363.20
　engrave 558.5
grave adj. great 31.6
　painful 378.7
　dull-colored 428.19
　important 642.12
　deplorable 649.8
　composed 826.9
　distressing 830.15
　solemn 837.16
　heinous 945.16
graveclothes 363.8
gravel n.
　granule 330.3
　sand 342.4
gravel v. floor 213.7
　fell 308.5
　nonplus 475.8
　confute 479.2
　defeat 731.9
graveled, gravelled
　nonplused 475.16
　at an impasse 704.11
　(helpless 158.9)
　defeated 732.12
graven image 991.4
　(figure 554.4)
graveolence 401.1
graveolent 401.4
graver tool 558.4
　artist 559.4, 6
gravestone 363.15
graveyard 363.14
gravid 168.9
gravidity, gravidness 168.2
gravitate tend 176.2
　descend 306.4
　be attracted 319.7
gravitation
　pulling power 157.3
　tendency 176.1
　weight 319.1
gravitational, gravitative 319.11
gravity
　pulling power 157.3
　(attraction 288.1)
　tendency 176.1
　weight 319
　~ of expression 574.1
　importance 642.2
　staidness 826.3
　solemnity 837.2
gravy
　semiliquid 352.3
　easy task 705.2
gray, grey n.
　horse 271.5
　color 432.1
gray, grey v. 432.3
gray, grey adj.
　aged 128.8
　gray-colored 432.4
　(dull 428.19)

(light-colored 429.7)
(whitish 430.9)
grayback, greyback 366.24
graybeard, greybeard 130.1
gray-colored, grey-colored 432.4
gray-headed, grey-headed 128.8
gray matter 450.1, 2
grayness, greyness 432
gray sour 429.3
gray-white, grey-white 430.9
graze n. 379.1
graze v.
 touch 199.3; 379.3
 strike 276.8
 pasture 298.43
 browse 298.46
 rub 331.3
grazier 370.4
grease n. oil 356.1
 (lubricant 332.2)
 bribe 618.2
 money 800.1
 flattery 933.1
grease v. 332.4
 grease the palm
 bribe 618.3
 pay 807.6
 grease the wheels
 grease 332.4
 facilitate 705.4
greased lightning 274.6
grease paint 599.13
greaser alien 57.3
 Mexican 188.9
greasy 355.3
great n. 873.9
great adj.
 considerable 31.6
 pregnant 168.9
 violent 173.11
 big 192.11
 important 642.10
 excellent 648.8
 eminent 873.18
 magnanimous 942.6
 be great 31.4
great-circle track 246.2
greatcoat 225.17
greaten increase 35.3
 enlarge 194.8
greater
 superior 33.7
 higher 206.15
 become greater 35.4
greatest 33.8
great go 461.3
great-grandchildren 167.1
great-grandfather 166.8
great-grandmother 166.9
great gun

masterstroke 626.7
 personage 642.5
Greatheart, Mr. 942.3
greathearted
 liberal 816.4
 magnanimous 942.6
great hundred 98.8
greatly 31.15
Great Mogul 745.3
greatness
 quantity 31.1
 (superiority 33.1)
 (boundlessness 105.1)
 (size 192.1)
 (importance 642.1)
 pregnancy 168.2
 renown 873.3
Great Spirit, the 976.2
great unwashed 876.1
greaves
 leggings 225.28
 armor 717.2
grebe 310.3
Grecian 188.9
greed
 covetousness 865.4
 gluttony 957.1
greedy
 avaricious 819.4
 desirous 865.20
 gluttonous 957.4
 greedygut, greedy-guts 957.2
Greek n. native 188.9
 unintelligibility 519.2
 language 560.4
 jargon 563.4
 swindler 792.8
 be Greek to 519.3
Greek adj. 519.6
Greek calends
 at the Greek calends 107.3
green n.
 verdure 367.9, 10, 11
 greenyard 371.6
 color 435.2
 ~ in the eye 491.1
green v. 435.5
green adj. new 123.8
 youthful 127.5
 sour 397.6
 verdant 435.6
 credulous 486.5
 ignorant 491.8
 (unaccustomed 614.3)
 remembered 505.18
 vigorous 654.4
 immature 674.8
 inexperienced 699.14
 ~ with jealousy 920.3
greenback 800.6
green bag 968.1
green book 551.2
green cheese 318.5
Green Cloth, Green-cloth 966.2

greener
 ignoramus 493.1
 novice 541.6
 dupe 547.1
 unsophisticate 703.2
greenery 367.9
green-eyed 920.3
green goods 545.6
greengrocer 797.11
greengrocery 799.4
greenhood 435.1
greenhorn
 ignoramus 493.1
 (fool 501.1)
 novice 541.6
 (bungler 701)
 dupe 547.1
 unsophisticate 703.2
greenhornism 491.1
greenhouse 371.6
 (bower 191.22)
Greenland 383.4
green light 423.5; 550.14
greenness color 435
 ignorance 491.1
green ocher 435.4
greenroom 599.12
greens
 vegetables 298.30
 grass 367.9
greensickness 655.11
greenstone 342.4
greensward 367.10
greeny
 ignoramus 493.1
 novice 541.6
 dupe 547.1
 unsophisticate 703.2
greenyard
 grassland 367.11
 grassplot 371.6
greet accost 586.2
 weep 839.8
 hail 894.9
 (welcome 892.11)
greeting
 hail 894.4
 (welcome 892.4)
 (obeisance 928.2)
gregale 349.9
gregarine n. 193.4
gregarine adj. 368.12
gregarious 892.12~
Gregorian 256.4
Gregorian chant 415.4
grenade 727.14
grenadier 726.4
Grendel 192.8
grewsome See gruesome
grey, grey matter etc. See gray etc.
greyhound
 speeder 274.6
 dog 366.6
grid n. network 219.4
 fire iron 386.3
 stage 599.12
grid v. 384.19
griddle n. 386.1, 3

griddle v. 384.19
griddlecake 298.12
gridelin 437.1
gridiron
 network 219.4
 fire iron 386.3
 stage 599.12
grief
 misfortune 735.3
 sorrow 837.3
 (wretchedness 828.3)
 in grief 837.11
grievance evil 649.2
 source of ~ 830.2
 wrong 923.1
grieve sorrow 837.6, 8
 (suffer 828.9, 11)
 (pain 830.3, 4)
 mourn 839.6
grieved
 pained 828.13
 sorrowful 837.11
griever 363.7
grievous
 deplorable 649.8
 distressing 830.11
 sad 837.9
grievously 31.23
griffado, griffe 41.5
griffin
 mongrel 41.5
 newcomer 57.3
griffin, griffon 83.7
griffonage 590.6
grig 622.8
grill n. network 219.4
 restaurant 298.42
grill v. be hot 382.13
 cook 384.19
 cross-examine 461.15
grille 219.4
grilling 461.9
grillroom 298.42
grillwork 219.4
grim resolute 604.7
 dreadful 830.13
 solemn 837.16
 unprepossessing 846.8
 gruff 895.7
 sullen 901.8
grimace n.
 distortion 243.1
 affectation 853.1
grimace v.
 deform 243.3
 make faces 846.4
 show dislike 867.4
grimacer actor 599.20
 affecter 853.4
grimalkin 366.4
grime n. 653.5
grime v. 440a.2
grim-faced
 unprepossessing 846.8
 pitiless 914a.3
Grimm's law 402.5
grim-visaged
 solemn 837.16

grimy — groveling

grim-visaged (cont'd)
  unprepossessing 846.8
  pitiless 914a.3
grimy blurred 422.8
  discolored 440a.3
  dirty 653.16
grin *n.* 838.2
grin *v.* 838.6
  grin at
    ridicule 856.4
    scoff 930.6
grind *n.*
  bookworm 492.3
  study 539.1
  routine 613.4
  labor 686.3
grind *v.*
  ~ off 38.6
  sharpen 253.9
  smooth 255.4
  abrade 331.3
  pain 378.4
  sound harshly 410.6
  ~ the organ 416.18
  tutor 537.9
  study 539.4
  aggrieve 649.6
  toil 686.6
  tyrannize 739.4
  ~ one's teeth 900.7
grinder
  rotary gap 158a.6
  tooth 253.3
  pulverizer 330.4
  tutor 540.1
grindery 799.4
grinding
  tyrannical 739.5
  painful 830.15
  malevolent 907.6
grindstone
  sharpener 253.7
  grinder 330.4
grip *n.* handbag 191.5
  trench 259.2
  spasm 315.7
  tessera 550.11
  sceneshifter 599.17
  control 737.2
  grasp 781.1, 2
  (fastener 45.2)
  (seizure 789.1)
  handshake 894.4
grip *v.* grasp 781.4
  seize 789.9
gripe *n.* pain 378.1
  ailment 655.5
  control 737.2
  grip 781.1
gripe *v.* pain 378.4
  grip 781.4
  seize 789.9
  stint 819.3
  vex 830.5
  complain 839.10
grippe, grip 655.3, 9
gripper 591.5
gripping 819.4
gripsack 191.5
grisaille
  grayness 432.1

painting 556.2
grisard 130.1
grisette
  proletarian 876.3
  strumpet 962.2
grisly 846.8
grist quantity 25.2
  supply 637.1
  bring grist to the mill 775.7
gristle solid 321.4
  cartilage 327.2
gristly 325.5
gristmill 330.4
grit *n.*
  strength 159.1
  rough 256.2
  texture 329.1
  powder 330.3
  stone 342.4
  resolution 604.1
  (perseverance 604a.1)
  courage 861.1
grit *v.* 604.6
gritty hard 323.5
  granular 330.8
  resolute 604.7
  courageous 861.8
grizzle *n.* hair 256.3, 4
  horse 271.5
grizzle *v.* whiten 430.6
  gray 432.3
grizzled white 430.8
  gray 432.4
grizzly *n.* 901.4
grizzly *adj.*
  white 430.8
  gray 432.4
grizzly bear
  bear 366.15
  grouch 901.4
groan *n.* 839.1
groan *v.* blow 349.22
  sound harshly 410.6
  moan 839.9
groat 800.8
grocer 797.11
  (provider 637.2)
grocery food 298.6
  (provisions 637.1)
  (merchandise 798.3)
  store 799.4
grog *n.* 959.4
grog *v.* 959.15
grog blossom 959.2
groggery 959.13
groggy
  intoxicated 959.21
  stupid 499.12
grogshop 959.13
groin 244.2
groom *n.*
  stockman 370.4
  stableman 746.1
  bridegroom 903.6
groom *v.*
  tend stock 370.7
  upbraid 932.8
  whip 972.6
grooming 932.3

groomsman
  stableman 746.1
  friend 890.3
  wedding attendant 903.4
groove *n.* cavity 252.2
  furrow 259.1
  printing 591.6
  routine 613.4
  path 627.2
groove *v.* 259.3
grooving plane 255.3
grope feel 379.3
  experiment 463.9
  (examine 461.17)
  grope in the dark
    be blind 442.4
    be ignorant 491.6
    be in difficulty 704.6
gross *n.*
  main part 50.3
  number 98.8
gross *adj.*
  absolute 31.12
  whole 50.6
  unconformable 83.9
  absurd 497.4
  speech 579.3
  flagrant 649.8
  vulgar 851.6
  (unprepossessing 846.8)
  disreputable 874.8
  vicious 945.16
  impure 961.9
gross-headed 499.12
grossièreté 851.1
grossly 31.20
grossness 961.1
gross profit 775.2
grotesque
  unusual 83.10
  (absurd 497.4)
  (ridiculous 855.5)
  deformed 243.5
  speech 579.3
  ugly 846.6
grotto 191.22
grouch *n.*
  malcontent 832.2
  ill-humor 901.2
  grouchy person 901.4
grouch *v.*
  complain 839.10
  grumble 901.6
grouchy
  discontented 832.5
  ill-humored 901.7
ground *n.* region 181.1
  position 184.1
  base 211.2
  plane 213.3
  foundation 215.3
  land 342.1
  (realty 780.4)
  paint 428.5
  evidence 467.1
  premise 476.4
  motive 615.1
  (cause 153.1)

keep one's ground
  be permanent 141.4
  be stable 150.3
  be resolute 604.6
ground *v.*
  stabilize 150.4
  floor 213.7
  support 215.26
  go aground 267.33
  fell 308.5
  train 537.10
ground on 155.3
ground bait 617.2
ground crew 269a.3
grounded stuck 150.6
  in difficulty 704.11
  stranded 732.10
grounded on
  based on 211.5
  evidential 467.11
ground hog 366.17
ground-hog day 138.7
groundless
  unsubstantial 4.5
  illogical 477.10
  unauthentic 495.16
ground log 466.4
groundman 158a.10
groundnut oil 356.3
ground plan 626.2
grounds dregs 40.2
  realty 780.4
ground school 269a.3
ground swell 348.10
groundwork
  substantiality 3.1
  foundation 215.3
  (precursor 64.1)
  (rudiment 153.3)
  (base 211.1)
  (preparation 673.1)
  substance 316.2
group *n.*
  company 72.3
  bunch 72.5
  party 712.2, 3
  squadron 726.9
  sect 984.3
group *v.*
  arrange 60.6, 7
  assemble 72.11
  size 192.10
grouping
  arrangement 60.1
  class 75.1
grouse *n.* food 298.26
  bird 366.22
grouse *v.* 839.10
grouser 832.2
grout *n.* 223.19
grout *v.* 901.6
grouty 901.7
grove cluster 72.5
  valley 252.5
  copse 367.7
grovel crouch 207.5
  creep 275.6
  fawn 886.3
groveler, groveller 886.2
groveling, grovelling 886.4

grow — guinea hen

grow increase 35.4
 be converted into 144.8
 produce 161.8
 expand 194.6
 become high 206.11
 vegetate 365.2
 raise 367.12
 cultivate 371.8
 grow from 154.3
 grow into 144.8
 grow over 303.3
 grow together 46.5
 grow up 194.6; 305.4
 grow upon one 613.9
grower 371.2
 (producer 164.1)
growing 35.6
growl blow 349.22
 sound harshly 410.6
 snarl 412.2
 complain 839.10
 be rude 895.4
 show resentment 900.7
 (be irascible 901.5)
 threaten 909.2
growler bucket 191.11
 carriage 272.4
 malcontent 832.2
growling 901.7
grownup n. 131.3
grown-up adj. 131.5
growth
 conversion 144.1
 evolution 161.5
 expansion 194.3
 excrescence 250.2
 vegetable life 367.1
grub n. larva 129.8
 diminutive 193.2
 food 298.5
grub v. eat 298.44
 drudge 686.6
 grub up eat 298.44
 extract 301.5
 discover 481a.3
grubbery 298.5
grubby 59.9
grubstreet writer 593.15
grudge n. 900.1
 bear a grudge 907.5
grudge v.
 be unwilling 603.4
 refuse 764.2
 be parsimonious 819.3
 envy 921.2
grudgeful 919.6
grudging n. 921.1
grudging adj.
 unwilling 603.5
 parsimonious 819.4
 envious 921.3
grudgingly 603.6
grue 594.2
gruel weakness 160.5
 cereal 298.15
 semiliquid 352.3
grueler, grueller 533.2

gruesome, grewsome 846.8
gruff
 harsh-sounding 410.9
 discourteous 895.7
 (ill-humored 901.7)
 (malevolent 907.6)
gruffness 895.2
 (ill-humor 901.1)
grum
 harsh-sounding 410.9
 sullen 901.8
grumble n. 839.1
grumble v.
 sound harshly 410.6
 complain 839.10
 grouch 901.6
grumbler 832.2
 (pessimist 837.5)
 (lamenter 839.5)
grumbling 901.7
grume clot 321.5
 blood 333.3
 gluten 352.3
 (pulp 354.2)
grumose 321.8
grumous 352.8
 (pulpy 354.5)
grumpy 901.8
Grundy, Mrs. 851.2
Grundyism 852.2
grunt n. 158a.10
grunt v.
 animal sound 412.2
 complain 839.10
grunter 158a.10
Grunth See **Granth**
gruntle 412.2
Grus 318.6
G string 225.22
guano 653.7
guarantee n.
 pledge 535.2
 promise 768.1
 security 771.1, 2
guarantee v.
 vouch 535.4
 promise 768.3
 warrant 771.6
 (indorse 488.10)
guarantor 771.2
guaranty 771.1
 (warrant 924.3)
guard n.
 railroader 268.12
 printing 591.5
 defense 717.1, 2
 defender 717.6
 (watcher 444.1)
 (protector 664.3)
 (policeman 745.10)
 (jailer 753.1)
 military unit 726.7
 off one's guard
 unwary 460.9
 inexpectant 508.7
 (inattentive 458.11)
 (unprepared 674.7)
 on guard, on one's guard

vigilant 459.8
 cautious 864.6
guard v. protect 664.6
 (preserve 670.3)
 defend 717.7
guard against
 provide against 673.7
 take precautions 864.4
guarded
 vigilant 459.8
 conditional 770.3
 cautious 864.6
guardful 459.8
guardhouse 752.1
guardian n.
 protector 664.3
 (guard 717.6)
 tutelary genius 979.12
guardian adj. 664.12
guardian angel
 guardian 664.3
 familiar spirit 979.12
 (benefactor 912.1)
guardianship 664.2
guardless 665.9
guardrail 666.1
guardroom 752.1
guard ship 726.11
guardsman 726.4
Guarnerius, Guarnieri, guarneri 417.3
gubernatorial
 supervisory 693.6
 authoritative 737.15
guddle 622.8
gudgeon n. axis 312.5
 dupe 547.1
gudgeon v.
 deceive 545.7
 swindle 791.12
guerdon n. 973.1
guerdon v. 973.3
Guernsey 366.12
guerrilla, guerilla
 warfare 722.1
 soldier 726.4
guess n. 514.1
 rough guess 514.2
guess v.
 believe 484.8
 suppose 514.6
guesser 514.5
guess-rope, guesswarp 273.10
guesswork 514.1
guessworker 514.5
guest incomer 294.4
 visitor 890.7
guest rope 273.10
guff twaddle 517.3
 chatter 584.2
guffaw n. 838.3
guffaw v. 838.7
guggle ripple 348.19
 bubble 353.8
 purl 405.5
 cackle 412.2

gugu 188.9
guib, guiba 366.10
Guicowar See **Gaekwar**
guidable 278.9
guidance
 teaching 537.1
 protectorship 664.2
 direction 693.1
 auspices 707.2
guide n.
 prototype 22.1
 teacher 540.4
 guidepost 550.10
 printing 591.5
 director 694.6
 (interpreter 524.1)
 (informant 527.5)
 (adviser 695.3)
 tutelary genius 979.12
 spirit control 980a.1; 994.14
guide v. escort 88.7
 (precede 280.2)
 pilot 267.11
 herd 370.7
 teach 537.9
 direct 693.4
 be guided by 82.4
guideboard
 sign 550.10
 guide 694.6
guidebook 694.7
 (itinerary 266.9)
 (outline 626.2)
guideless 158.9
guidepost sign 550.10
 guide 694.6
guider 694.6
guidon 550.13
guild, gild 712.5
guildhall 799.2
guile deceit 545.1
 (falsehood 544.1)
 cunning 702.1
guileful 545.12
guileless
 veracious 543.3
 artless 703.4
 (honest 939.7)
guillemet 550.8
guilloche 847.3
guillotine n.
 printing 591.5
 execution 972.4
 ax 975.4
guillotine v. 972.8
guilt 947
guiltless 946.5
guiltlessness 946.1
guilty 947.4
 (culpable 932.14)
 find guilty 971.2
guimpe 225.33
guinea alien 57.3
 yellow 436.3
 money 800.5, 8
guinea fowl
 food 298.25
 fowl 366.23
guinea hen 374.8

guinea pig
  animal 366.17
  experimentee 463.7
guipure 847.6
guise cover 223.2
  clothes 225.1
  appearance 448.4
  disguise 545.5
  pretext 619.1
  way 627.1
  conduct 692.1
guiser
  masquerader 528.7
  actor 599.20
guitar 417.2
guitarist 416.3
Gujarati 560.4
gulch chasm 198.3
  (cavity 252.2)
  water gap 350.1
gulden 800.8
gules 434.2
gulf interval 198.1, 3
  depth 208.2
  sea inlet 343
  eddy 348.8
gulfweed 367.3
gulfy rotating 312.8
  vortical 348.26
  gulflike 343.2
gull *n.* bird 366.22
  deception 545.2, 3
  dupe 547.1
  deceiver 548.2, 3
  swindler 792.8
gull *v.* dupe 545.10
  swindle 791.12
Gullah 431.4
gullery 545.2
gullet water gap 350.1
  (tube 260.6)
  esophagus 350.4
gullibility 486.1
gullible 486.5
  (deceivable 545.14)
gully chasm 198.3
  (cavity 252.2)
  water gap 350.1
gullyhole 350.1
gulosity 957.1
gulp *n.* 298.4
gulp *v.* swallow 296.3
  eat 298.44
  eat greedily 957.3
gulp down
  swallow 296.3
  be credulous 486.3
gulph See gu'f
gum *n.* cement 45.6
  shoe 225.27
  gluten 352.3
  resin 356a.1
  tree 367.6
gum *v.* cement 46.7
  deceive 545.7
  ~ up 699.9
gum arabic 662.6
gumbo, gombo *n.*
  soup 298.16
  soil 342.3
  semiliquid 352.3, 4
gumbo *adj.* 352.9

gumboil
  protuberance 250.2
  sore 655.16
gum elastic 325.2
gummose 352.8
gummosis 352.1
gummous 356a.3
gummy viscid 352.8
  (tough 327.5)
  resinous 356a.3
gumption
  sagacity 498.2
  enterprise 682.4
gumshoe *n.*
  shoe 225.27
  detective 528.9
  policeman 745.10
gumshoe *v.* 528.16
gumshoe man 745.10
gum spirit 356.3
gumwood 635.3
gun *n.*
  accelerator 272.16
  airplane 273a.10
  shooter 284.8
  lifter 307.2
  killer 361.8
  firearm 727.10, 11
  thief 792.1
  gunman 913.2
cut the gun 142.7
gun *v.*
  accelerate 267a.32
  shoot 284.13
  seek 461.16
guna 402.2
gunate 561.8
gunboat 726.11
guncotton 727.13
gunfire shot 406.2
  attack 716.2
  (explosion 173.3)
  (shot 284.4)
gunflint 727.10
gunge, gunj 799.1
gunlock 727.10
gunmaker 690.8
gunman shooter 284.8
  killer 361.8
  ruffian 913.2
gun mount 273a.10
gunner shooter 284.8
  soldier 726.4, 8
gunnery
  ballistics 284.9;
  727.2
  knightly skill 722.2
gunpowder 727.13
gunshot
  short way 197.2
  shot 284.4; 406.2
gunsmith 690.6
gup 532.3
gurge *n.* whirl 312.2
  eddy 348.8
gurge *v.* rotate 312.7
  eddy 348.21
gurgle ripple 348.19
  bubble 353.8
  purl 405.5
  (resonate 408.7)
gurglet 348.8

gurgoyle See gargoyle
gurnard 366.21
gurry 645.4
guru scholar 492.1
  teacher 540.1
  holy man 996.8
gush *n.* flow 348.2, 5
  (egress 295.1)
  loquacity 584.1
  fervor 821.2
gush *v.*
  ~ out 295.7
  flow 348.17, 20
  be loquacious 584.4
gushing 821.6
gushy 584.5
gusset joint 43.3
  support 215.11
  airplane 273a.10
gust wind 349.6
  relish 394.2
  outburst of passion 825.5
  aesthetic taste 850.1
gustable
  eatable 298.49
  tastable 390.4
gustation 390.2
gustatory 390.4
gustful
  flavorous 390.4
  savory 394.7
gusto pleasure 377.1
  relish 394.2
  (taste 390.1)
  fervor 821.2
  aesthetic taste 850.1
gusty windy 349.25
  flavorous 390.4
  savory 394.7
gut *n.* tube 260.6
  sea inlet 343.1
gut *v.* demolish 162.4
  disembowel 297.16
  strip 789.12
  plunder 791.10
guts strength 159.1
  vitals 221.4
  intestines 350.4
  pungency 392.1
  resolution 604.1
  courage 861.2
guttae 215.17
gutta serena
  blindness 442.1
  ailment 655.8
gutter conduit 350.1
  printing 591.5
gutt'e 957.3
guttler 957.2
guttling 957.1
guttural *n.* 402.2
guttural *adj.*
  phonetics 402.11
  speech 583.5
guy *n.* fastening 45.2
  cord 205.3
  supporter 215.2
  ship's rope 273.10
  person 372.3
  man 373.2

anchor 666.2
  tether 752.2
guy *v.* depart 293.5
  flee 623.10
  ridicule 856.4
guzzle *n.* drink 298.4
  spree 959.3
  alcoholic drink 959.4, 10
  drunkard 959.11
guzzle *v.* drink 298.47
  gluttonize 957.3
  tipple 959.15
guzzler 959.11
guzzling 957.1
gybe See jibe
Gymir 192.8
gymkhana
  contest 720.5
  festival 840.2
gymnasial 542.9
gymnasium
  auditorium 189.10
  school 542.1
  arena 728.1
  sports 840.14
gymnast 159.6
gymnastic
  athletic 159.11
  gymnasial 542.9
  exercising 686.10
gymnastics
  athletics 159.5
  physical education 537.5
  exercise 686.2
  sports 840.10
gymnosophist 953.3
  984.21
gymnosophy
  abstinence 953.2
  religion 984.11
gymnospermous 369.11
gynaeceum, gynaecium 374.7
gynandroid 83.5
gynandrous 83.12
gynarchy 737.5
gynecic, gynaecic 374.11
gynecologist, gynaecologist 662.19
gynecology, gynaecology 662.16
gyneolatry 897.1
gyniatrics 662.16
gynocracy 737.5
gyp, *n.* bitch 366.6
  female animal 374.8
  fraud 545.3
  (swindle 791.5)
  servant 746.1
gyp *v.* 791.12
gypper 792.8
gypsum 635.6
gypsy, gipsy 268.2
Gypsy, Gipsy 560.4
gyral 312.8
gyrate 312.7
gyration 312.1

gyrational — half measure

gyrational, gyratory
 312.8
gyre n. 312.2
gyre v. 312.7
gyro, gyrocar, gyro-
 compass 312.4
gyromancy 511.3
gyrometer, gyroplane
 312.4
gyroscope
 airplane 273a.10
 rotator 312.4
gyroscopic 312.8
gyrostat 312.4
gyrostatic 312.8
gyrostatics 312.6
gyrowheel 312.4
gyve 752.2

H

Habakkuk 513.2
habanera music 415.7
 dance 840.7
habeas corpus
 law 963.2
 summons 969.2
haberdasher
 hatter 225.39
 (workman 690.10)
 merchant 797.1
haberdashery
 headdress 225.26
 tailoring 225.35
 merchandise 798.3
habergeon 717.2
habi'liment 225.1
habilitate 225.41
habilitation 698.2
habit n. nature 5.3
 clothes 225.1, 3, 7
 custom 613
 (regularity 16.2)
 (rule 80.1)
 convention 852.2
become a habit 613.9
in the habit of 613.12
not in the habit of
 614.3
habit v. 225.42
habitancy
 occupancy 186.2
 population 188.10
habitant 188.1, 5
habitat resort 74.2
 location 184.1
habitate 186.10
habitation
 occupation 186
 abode 189.1
habitual n. 613.7
habitual adj.
 orderly 58.7
 customary 613.11
 (prevalent 78.10)
 (regular 80.3)
 (conformable 82.9)
 (repeated 104.6)
 (frequent 136.3)
 (conventional
  852.8)

become habitual
 613.9
habitually 613.13
 (invariably 16.7)
 (generally 78.15)
 (always 112.5)
 (frequently 136.5)
habituate tame 370.6
 inure 613.8
 (train 537.10)
 (naturalize 184.16)
habituated 613.12
 (adapted 82.7)
habituation 613.5
 (naturalization
  184.7)
habitude 613.1
habitué
 attender 186.7
 frequenter 613.7
 guest 890.7
hachure 550.9
hacienda
 messuage 189.12
 farm 371.4
 property 780.4
hack n. horse 271.3
 carriage 272.4
 author 593.15
 drudge 690.2
hack v. cut 44.8
 kill 361.12
hackamore 752.2
hackbut, hagbut
 727.10
hackee 274.6
hackery 272.5
hackle n. 256.9
hackle v. cut 44.8
 comb 652.11
hackman 268.9
hackney n. horse 271.3
 vehicle 272.4, 6
hackney, hack-
 neyed adj. 843.6
hacky 268.9
haddock 298.18
Hadean 982.5
Hades god 979.2;
 982.4
 hell 982.1, 2
hadj, haj 266.8
hadji, haji
 wanderer 268.2
 priest 996.7
Haeckelism 161.5
haematobic, haemato-
 bious See hemato-
 bic etc.
haemorrhage, haem-
 orrhoid, See hemor-
 rhage etc.
haemorrhoea, haem-
 orrhea See hemor-
 rhea
haft, heft 215.7
hag crone 130.3
 ugly 846.3
 malevolent
  woman 913.5
 witch 992.3
hagbut See hackbut

Haggai 513.2
haggard thin 203.11
 pale 429.6
 rabid 503.13
 weary-looking
  688.6
 wild-eyed 824.10
 unprepossessing
  846.8
haggis 298.19
haggle cut 44.8
 chaffer 794.5
Hagiographa 985.3
hagiography 983.1
hagiolatry 983a.5
hagiology 983.1
hagride 992.4
hagridden 992.7
ha-ha fence 232.2
 trench 259.2
 conduit 350.1
 fortification 717.3
haik 225.15
hail n. ice 383.5
 greeting 894.4
hail v. accost 586.2
 greet 894.9
 approve 931.5
hail int.
 welcome! 292.13
 attention! 457.10
 hurrah! 838.12
 celebration 883.7
 greetings! 894.15
 (bravo! 931.13)
hail fellow well met,
 hail-fellow-well-
 met 892.12
Hail Mary 990.3
hailstone, hailstorm
 383.5
hair modicum 32.2
 weakness 160.5
 inextension 180a.1
 diminutive 193.2
 short way 197.2
 narrowness 203.1
 fur 256.3
 (filament 205.1)
 trifle 643.3
to a hair 494.16
hairbreadth, hairs-
 breadth
 short way 197.2
 narrowness 203.1
hairbreadth escape
 671.2
haircloth 219.5
haircut, hair-do 256.3
hairif, harif 253.2
hairless 226.10
hairlessness 226.3
hairpin 45.5
hairsplitting n.
 discrimination 465.1
 quibbling 477.4
 overscrupulous-
 ness 868.1
 hypercriticism
  932.2
hairsplitting adj.
 quibbling 477.11

overscrupulous
 868.4
hypercritical 932.11
hairy 256.13
 (filamentous 205.7)
hairy-chested 159a.5
haj, hajj See hadj
haji, hajji See hadji
hakim
 potentate 745.5
 judge 967.1
halberd, halbert 727.4
halberdier 726.4
halcyon
 equable 174.6
 auspicious 512.4
 (fortunate 734.8)
 peaceful 721.4
 pleasant 829.9
halcyon days
 prosperity 734.3
 pleasure 827.3
hale strong 159.10
 healthy 654.4
ha'f n.
 bisection 91.3
 fraction 101.1
half, half after adv.
 114.10
half-and-half n. 91.3
half-and-half adj.
 equivalent 27.9
 mixed 41.9
 incomplete 53.4
 halved 91.6
 neutral 628.3
half an eye 441.2
half-baked
 incomplete 53.4
 half-learned 491.12
 half-witted 499.13
 immature 674.8
 inexperienced
  699.14
 uncompleted 730.3
ha'f-blind 443.15
half blood 41.5
half-blooded, half-
 bred 41.10
half-breed n. 41.5
half-breed adj. 41.10
half-caste n. 41.5
half-caste adj. 41.10
half cock
 at half cock 674.12
half-cocked
 immature 674.8
 uncompleted 730.3
half crown, half dol-
 lar 800.8
half-famished 865.19
halfhearted
 irresolute 605.5
 apathetic 823.5
 indifferent 866.4
halfheartedness 605.1
half-learned 491.12
half-light 422.2
half-mast 669.3
half measure
 irresolution 605.1
 mid-course 628.1

half-moon — handfasting

half measure (cont'd)
  by half measures 53.6
half-moon
  crescent 245.2
  moon 318.5
  fortification 717.3
half past 114.10
halfpenny trifle 643.3
  money 800.8
half-pint 193.8
half-seas over 959.21
half speed
  at half speed 174.8
half-starved
  meager 640.9
  hungry 865.19
half tone, half-tone 558.1
half-truth 546.3
  (secrecy 528.2)
halfway adj. 32.7
halfway adv. 68.6
  go halfway 628.2
half-wit 501.1
half-witted 499.13
halieutics 622.3
halitosis 401.1
hall house 189.3
  auditorium 189.10
  vestibule 191.17
  mart 799.2
hallelujah, halleluiah n. cheer 838.4
  paean 931.4
  glorification 990.2
  (celebration 883.1)
hallelujah, halleluiah int.
  hurrah! 838.12
  (hail! 883.7)
  praise God! 990.16
halliard See halyard
hallmark, hall mark 550.11
hallo, halloa See hollo
halloo v. shout 411.5
  accost 586.2
halloo int.
  attention 457.10
  (salutation 586.3)
  hunting 622.12
  wonder 870.11
hallow
  celebrate 883.3
  bless 976.11
  sanctify 987.8
Hallowday, Halloween, Hallowmas 138.7
hallowed
  sacred 976.13
  sanctified 987.11
hallucination
  optical illusion 443.9
  mental disorder 503.5
  (delusion 495.5)
  (imagining 515.4)
hallucinational 495.15
hallucinosis 503.5
hallway 191.17

halma 840.11
halo circle 247.2
  nimbus 420.13
  glory 873.2
halomancy 511.3
halse 350.4
halt n. cessation 142.1
  cripple 655.20
  respite 687.2
  impasse 704.3
at the halt
  quiescent 265.8
  inactive 681.4
halt v. stop 142.6, 7
  be weak 160.6
  go slow 275.5
  stammer 583.3
  sicken 655.21
halt adj. 655.24
halter fastening 45.2
  restraint 752.2
  hangman's noose 975.4
halting speech 579.3
  crippled 655.24
halve bisect 91.4
  share 778.5
halved 91.6
halver 91.3
halvers
  equalization 27.3
  half 91.3
  go halvers 778.5
halves 27.3
  by halves 53.6
  do by halves
    do carelessly 460.6
    not complete 730.2
    (mismanage 699.7)
  go halves 778.5
  (halve 91.4)
halving 91.1
halyard, halliard 273.10
ham messuage 189.12
  village 189.17
  thigh 266.11
  meat 298.23
  hamfatter 599.19
  telegrapher 532a.6
hamadryad
  wood 367.7
  nymph 979.8
hamal, hammal, hamaul 746.1
hamate 245.8
Hambletonian 271.4
Hamburg steak, hamburg steak 298.20
hamfatter 599.19
hamiform 245.8
Hamitic languages 560.4
hamlet 189.17
hammer n.
  repetend 104.2
  knocker 276.4
  malleus 418.5
  bring to the hammer, bring under the hammer 796.5
hammer v.

repeat 104.4
  stammer 583.3
  plod 686.6
hammer at
  do frequently 136.2
  think hard 451.28
  labor 686.6
hammer out
  roughhew 161.8
  form 240.6
  think hard 451.28
  do carelessly 460.6
  work out 729.2
hammer and tongs
  resolutely 604.9
  lustily 686.11
hammerhead 366.21
hammering 686.3
hammersmith 690.6
hammock 215.24
hammy 599.28
hamper n.
  receptacle 191.1, 9
  hindrance 706.2
hamper v.
  weight 319.9
  hinder 706.4, 6
hampering 706.1
hamstring
  disable 158.6
  cripple 659.8
hamulate 245.8
hanaper 802.1
hand n. length 200.6
  paw 211.4
  side 236.1
  seaman 269.3
  person 372.3
  pointer 550.10; 694.6
  signature 550.11
  handwriting 590.1, 4
  tool 631.2
  worker 690.2
  aid 707.1
  puppet 711.2
  clutches 781.3
  cards 840.13
a good hand at 698.14
at hand
  imminent 152.3
  present 186.13
  near 197.8
  available 644.8
from hand to hand 270.12
go hand in hand
  accompany 88.6
  synchronize 120.3
  concur 178.3
  co-operate 709.5
  be concordant 714.2
hand in glove
  with 88.9
  concurrent 178.4
  co-operative 709.7, 8
have a hand in
  contribute to 153.8
  be employed in 680.6
  meddle in 682.14
  participate in 709.6

have in hand
  be doing 625.7
  (undertake 676.2)
  (do 680.6)
  possess 777.4
have no hand in 681.2
have on one's hands 625.7
helping hand
  aid 707.1
  assistant 711.1
  benefactor 912.1
in hand
  in preparation 673.13
  (being done 625.13)
  possessed 777.8
in the hands of
  by authority of 737.17
  in subjection 749.6
  in charge of 693.7
on hand
  in store 636.9
  available 644.8
  possessed 777.8
on the other hand
  notwithstanding 30.8
  (contrarily 14.7)
  (otherwise 18.6)
  laterally 236.8
  evidence 468.5
out of hand 132.14
hand v.
  transfer 270.7; 783.3
  (pass 302.2)
  give 784.9
hand down
  transfer 783.3
  immortalize 873.13
hand it to 34.4
hand out
  pay out 807.6
  display 882.7
hand over
  transfer to 270.7; 783.3
  give 784.9
  pay 807.6
hand and glove 888.4
handbag bag 191.5
  purse 802.2
handbarrow 272.11, 12
handbill 531.4
handbook book 593.1
  guidebook 694.7
handbreadth 200.6
handcar 272.21
handcart 272.5, 11
handclap, hand clapping 931.4
handclasp 894.4
handcuff n. 752.2
handcuff v.
  disable 158.6
  impair 659.8
  shackle 751.7
handfast n. 768.2
handfast v. 768.4
handfasting 768.2

handful quantity 25.2
  modicum 32.2
  a few 103.2
hand grenade 727.14
handicap n.
  race 274.4; 720.5
  hindrance 706.2
handicap v.
  equalize 27.7
  encumber 706.6
handicraft trade 625.5
  handiwork 680.3
handicraftsman 690.5
hand-in-hand adj.
  joined 43.10
  friendly 888.4
hand in hand adv.
  jointly 43.14
  with 88.9
  concurrent 178.4
  co-operatively 709.8
  (concordantly 714.5)
  friendly 888.5
  sociably 892.9, 13
handiwork
  product 161.6
  handicraft 680.3
  manual labor 686.3
handkerchief 652.7
handle n. hold 215.7
  name 564.2
  pretext 619.1
  handle to one's name 877.1
handle v. pilot 267.11
  touch 379.3
  discuss 595.4
  use 677.5
  conduct 692.4
  manage 693.4
handle bar
  handle 215.7
  moustache 256.5
handling 379.1
handmade 161.13
handmaid
  ~ of theology 451.4
  minister 631.2
  servant 746.2
  (auxiliary 711.1)
hand-me-down n. 225.4
hand-me-down adj.
  secondhand 124.6
  impaired 659.12
hand of glory 511.5
hand organ 417.5, 7
handout 784.3
hand over hand, hand over fist
  swiftly 274.14
  hastily 684.7
hand over head
  neglectfully 460.12
  hastily 684.7
  recklessly 863.8
handpost sign 550.10
  guide 694.6
handrail 666.1
hand running 69.7
handsaw 257.3

hands down 705.8
handsel, hansel n.
  security 771.1
  gift 784.3
handsel, hansel v.
  begin 66.5
  give security 771.5
handshake n. 894.4
handshake v. 886.3
handshaker 886.2
handshaking 886.1
hands off
  forbear! 623.13
  resist 719.6
  don't! 761.6
handsome
  liberal 816.4
  beautiful 845.8
  magnanimous 942.6
handspike 307.4
handstaff handle 215.7
  weapon 727.7
hand to hand, hand-to-hand 199.4
handwriting
  signature 550.11
  writing 590.1, 3, 4
handwriting on the wall destiny 601.3
  warning sign 668.3
handy
  close-at-hand 197.8
  available 644.8
  ready 673.11
  skillful 698.11
handy man 700.1
hang n.
  pendency 214.1
  knack 698.2
hang v.
  procrastinate 133.5
  depend 214.4
  suspend 214.6
  be dependent 475.7
  execute 972.8
hang about
  wait 133.7
  frequent 186.11
  be near 197.5
hang around
  wait 133.7
  frequent 186.11
  be dependent 475.7
hang around with 88.6
hang back
  procrastinate 133.5
  (move slowly 275.5)
  be uncertain 475.6
  demur 485.7
  be reluctant 603.4
  be irresolute 605.4
  shrink 623.9
hang by a thread 665.6
hang fire
  be late 133.3
  procrastinate 133.5
  cease 142.6
  be unproductive 169.3
  be inert 172.2

  be uncertain 475.6
  be reluctant 603.4
  be irresolute 605.4
  do nothing 681.2
  languish 683.10
  not complete 730.2
hang in the balance
  be late 133.3
  be dependent 475.7
hang on
  accompany 88.6
  be dependent 475.7
  persevere 604.7
hang on the sleeve of
  serve 746.8
  fawn 886.3
hang out
  reside 186.10
  frequent 186.11
hang out one's shingle 625.8
hang over
  impend 152.2
  overhang 214.5
hang together
  agree 23.7
  join 43.5
  be joined 43.9
  cohere 46.5
  co-operate 709.4
hang up 133.4
hang upon 154.3; 749.3
hangar 267a.28
hanged 972.13
hanger caption 66.3
  pendent 214.2, 3
  grove 367.7
  weapon 727.3
hanger-on
  follower 281.2
  (accompanier 88.3)
  sycophant 886.2
  (dependent 746.3)
hanging n.
  pendency 214.1, 2
  stage 599.15
  tapestry 847.6
  execution 972.4
hanging adj.
  pendent 214.7
  declivitous 217.11
hangman 975.5
hangnail 214.2
hangout resort 74.2
  habitat 189.13
hang-over 959.1
hank fastening 45.2
  piece 51.3
  lump 192.5
hanker 865.11
hankering 865.2
hanky-panky
  deception 545.2
  cunning 702.1
hansel See **handsel**
hansom, hansom cab 272.5, 6
Hanswurst
  actor 599.20
  buffoon 844.1
hant 980a.1

Hanuman 979.4
hap n. event 151.1
  fortuity 156.1
hap v. happen 151.3
  chance 156.7
haphazard n. 156.1
  at **haphazard** 59.12
  (by chance 156.13)
haphazard adj. 59.8
  (chance 156.12)
  (indiscriminate 465a.3)
  (purposeless 621.21)
hapless 735.9
haplology 195.1
haply 470.7
happen occur 151.3
  chance 156.7
happen what may
  without fail 474.16
  if necessary 601.15
  in any event 604.9
  recklessly 863.8
happening n.
  event 151.1
  fortuity 156.1
happening adj. 151.5
happenstance
  event 151.1
  fortuity 156.1
happily 827.13
happiness 827.2
  (cheerfulness 836.1)
happy apt 23.10
  opportune 134.7
  intoxicated 959.21
  auspicious 512.4
  well-expressed 578.4
  joyful 827.9
  (cheerful 836.7)
happy dispatch 361.3
happy-go-lucky 674.11
happy hunting grounds 981.1
happy land 981.1
Happy Valley 515.6
hara-kiri suicide 361.3
  execution 972.4
haram See **harem**
harangue n.
  lesson 537.6
  verbosity 573.1
  lecture 582.2
harangue v.
  expound 537.11
  perorate 573.5
  declaim 582.7
harass fatigue 688.5
  torment 830.5
  obsess 830.8
  intimidate 860.12
harassing 830.12
harbinger 64.1
  (omen 512.1)
  (informant 527.5)
  (messenger 534.1)
harbor, harbour n.
  sea inlet 343.1
  haven 666.4

harbor — harness

harbor (*continued*)
  in harbor 664.10
  make the harbor 666.5
harbor, harbour *v.*
  lodge 184.12
  ~ an idea 451.31
  protect 664.6
  ~ revenge 919.4
harborless, harbourless unplaced 185.4
  unprotected 665.9
hard *n.* 686.3
hard *adj.*
  strong 159.10
  rigid 323.5
  (inelastic 326.3)
  (tough 327.5)
  (severe 739.5)
  insensible 376.5
  painful 378.7
  unripe 397.6
  phonetics 402.11
  ~ of hearing 419.8
  difficult 704.8
  callous 823.7
  acute 830.15
  heartless 907.8
  hardened in vice 945.18
  impenitent 951.3
  alcoholic 959.24
  become hard 323.4
  be hard upon 716.5
  go hard with
    be difficult 704.5
    fail 732.5
    suffer 735.5; 828.9
  hard upon
    near 197.11
    censorious 932.11
  render hard 323.4
hard *adv.*
  hard alee, hard aweather etc. 267.70
  hard by 197.11
  hard and fast 267.65
  hard-bitten 606.6
  hard-boiled
    sophisticated 698.14
    severe 739.5
    tough 945.18
  hard cash 800.4
  hard-earned
    laborious 686.10
    difficult 704.8
harden
  strengthen 159.8
  indurate 323.4
  (solidify 321.7)
  (mineralize 358.3)
  inure 613.8
  render callous 823.4
hardened
  insensible 376.5
  callous 823.7
  ~ in vice 945.18
  impenitent 951.3
  impious 988.10
hardening
  induration 323.2
  inurement 613.5
  ~ of the arteries 655.5
hard-favored, hard-favoured, hard-featured 846.8
hardfisted 819.4
hard-fought
  laborious 686.10
  difficult 704.8
hardheaded
  sagacious 498.10
  strict 739.5
hardhearted
  callous 823.7
  heartless 907.8
  (pitiless 914a.3)
  vicious 945.18
hardihood
  courage 861.1
  effrontery 885.2
hard labor 972.2
hardly
  scarcely 32.16
  infrequently 137.3
  nearly 197.12
  with difficulty 704.12
hardmouthed 606.6
hardness
  rigidity 323
  (inelasticity 326.1)
  (toughness 327.1)
  (severity 739.1)
  ~ of hearing 419.1
  difficulty 704.1
  callousness 823.1
  hardness of heart
    callousness 823.1
    malevolence 907.1
    pitilessness 914a.1
    wickedness 945.1
    impenitence 951.1
hardpan 211.1
hard pressed
  in haste 684.6
  in difficulty 704.11
  (hindered 706.9)
hard pushed 684.6
hard run
  in haste 684.6
  in difficulty 704.11
hard-set
  obstinate 606.6
  in difficulty 704.11
Hard-shell *n.* 141.3
hard-shell *adj.*
  conformable 82.10
  conservative 141.7
  uncompromising 739.5
hardship 735.1
  (difficulty 704.1)
hardtack 298.11
hard times 735.3
hard up
  in difficulty 704.11
  poor 804.7
hard-visaged 846.8
hardware
  hardness 323.3
  merchandise 798.3
hardwood
  hardness 323.3
  wood 635.3
hard-working 682.19
  (laboring 686.9)
hardy strong 159.10
  plant 367.17
  hale 654.4
  courageous 861.8
hare speeder 274.6
  food 298.26
  rabbit 366.17
Hare 318.6
harebrain 501.2
harebrained
  scatterbrained 458.3
  reckless 863.7
harefoot 211.4
harelip 848.1
harem, haram
  seraglio 374.7
  (polygamy 903.2)
  abode of love 897.10
harif, hariffe See **hairif**
hariolate 511.7
hariolation 511.2
hark *v.* listen 418.11
  pay attention 457.4
  hark back
    go back 283.5
    revert 457.5
hark *int.* 418.16; 457.10
harken, harkener See **hearken** etc.
harl 205.2
harlequin
  changeableness 149.2
  variegation 440.2
  actor 599.20
Harlequin 274.7
harlequinade
  comedy 599.4
  buffoonery 842.3
harlequin snake 366.19
harlot 962.2
harlotry 961.6
harm *n.* evil 649.2
  (malevolence 907.1)
  damage 659.3
  do no harm 648.6
harm *v.* hurt 649.6
  damage 659.8
harmattan wind 349.9
  heat 382.4
harmful 649.10
  (destructive 162.6)
  (insalubrious 657.3)
  (deteriorating 659.11)
  (baneful 663.7)
  (malevolent 907.6)
harmless
  innocuous 648.13
  (impotent 158.8)
  (salubrious 656.6)
  (innocent 946.5)
  perfect 650.5

preserved 670.6
harmonic 413.26; 415.28
harmonica 417.1, 4
harmonic close 415.15
harmonichord 417.2, 6
harmonicon 417.4
harmonics 415.24
  (concord 413.1)
harmonic tone 413.8
harmonious
  agreeing 23.9
  (conformable 82.8)
  orderly 58.7
  music 413.26
  (beautiful 845.8)
  colors 428.18
  concordant 714.4
  (friendly 888.4)
  be harmonious 413.24
harmoniphon 417.4
harmonist 416.1, 14
harmonium 417.5
harmonization
  orchestration 413.3
  musical piece 415.3
harmonize
  accord 23.7, 8
  (conform 82.4)
  (concur 178.2)
  (pacify 723.4)
  (mediate 724.3)
  order 58.6
  methodize 60.8
  symmetrize 242.3
  ~ tones 413.24
  orchestrate 415.26
  be concordant 714.2
harmonizer 416.14
harmony
  agreement 23.1
  order 58.1
  symmetry 242.1
  concord 413.1; 714.1
  (music 415.1)
  harmonics 415.24
  elegance 578.1
  (peace 721.1)
  (friendship 888.1)
  in harmony with 23.9
    (uniform 16.5)
  be in harmony with 714.2
    (be at peace 721.3)
  harmony of the spheres stars 318.3
    concord 413.1
harness *n.*
  fastening 45.2
  safety belt 158a.6
  wardrobe 225.2
  uniform 225.8
  parachute 273a.7
  equipment 634.1
  restraint 752.2
  in harness
    prepared 673.11
    (equipped 634.3)
    in action 680.7
    busy 682.20
    in subjection 749.6
harness *v.* attach 43.6

888

clothe 225.41
~ a horse 370.7
equip 634.2
prepare 673.6
arm 717.7
harness cask 191.11
harnessed 717.9
harness race 720.5
harp *n.* 417.2, 4
harp *v.*
 harp upon
  repeat 104.4
  (maintain 143.3)
  (tautologize 573.6)
  be boresome 841.5
Harpagon 819.2
harper 416.3
harping *n.* 104.1
harping *adj.*
 repetitional 104.7
 tedious 841.8
harpist 416.3
harpoon
 edge tool 253.6
 spear 727.5
harpoon log 466.4
harpsichord 417.6
harpsichordist 416.4
harpy taker 789.6
 thief 792.1
 miser 819.2
 vampire 913.4
 sorceress 992.3
Harpy 980.2
harquebus, arquebus, harquebuse, harquebuss 727.10
harquebusade, arquebusade 662.6
harridan
 ugly person 846.3
 strumpet 962.2
harrier 366.6
harrow *n.* spike 253.2
 smoother 255.3
harrow *v.*
 smooth 255.4
 cultivate 371.8
 pain 378.4
 torture 830.6
 terrify 860.10
harrowed
 haggard 824.10
 tortured 828.13
harrowing 830.13
harry attack 716.5
 harass 830.5
harrycane See **hurricane**
harsh acrid 171.10
 painful 378.7; 830.15
 pungent 392.5
 harsh-sounding 410.9
 (discordant 414.4)
 style 579.3
 severe 739.5
 (pitiless 914a.3)
 penetrating 824.13
 gruff 895.7
 (malevolent 907.6)
be harsh 410.6

harshly 739.6
harshness
 acrimony 171.3
 raucousness 410.1
 (discord 414.1)
 (speech 583.1)
 severity 739.1
hart deer 366.11
 male animal 373.6
hartal 719.2
hartebeest 366.10
hartshorn 392.2
harum-scarum *n.* 863.2
harum-scarum *adj.*
 turbulent 173.12
 reckless 863.7
harum-scarum *adv.* 59.13
haruspex, aruspex 513.2
haruspical, aruspical 511.11
haruspicate, aruspicate 511.7
haruspice, aruspice 513.2
haruspicy, aruspicy 511.2, 3
harvest *n.* crop 636.3
 (agriculture 371.7)
 benefit 648.2
 gain 775.2
harvest *v.* reap 371.8
 gather 775.6
has-been 124.9
hash *n.* mixture 41.4
 confusion 59.2
 meat 298.19
 bungle 699.4
 botcher 701
hash *v.*
 disintegrate 44.9
 botch 699.9
hash up mix 41.6
 repeat 104.4
hashed 53.5
hashish 662.7
 (tobacco 392a.1)
hasp *n.* 45.2
 (anchor 666.2)
hasp *v.* 43.6
hassock 215.22
hastate 253.14
haste *n.* velocity 274.1
 hurry 684
 (promptness 132.3)
 (activity 682.2)
 be in haste 684.4
 in haste
  in a hurry 684.6
  hastily 684.7
haste *v.* speed 274.9
 hasten 684.2
hasteful 684.5
hasteless 685.4
hasten speed 274.9
 ~ off 293.5
 hurry 684.2, 3
 (accelerate 274.10)
 aid 707.6
hastily 684.7

 (suddenly 113.7)
 (promptly 132.14)
 (swiftly 274.14)
hastiness 132.2
Hastings 722.5
hastish 684.5
hasty *v.* 684.2
hasty *adj.*
 hurried 684.5
 (brief 111.7)
 (sudden 113.5)
 (fast 274.13)
 impulsive 825.9, 11
 hot-tempered 901.7
hasty pudding 298.15
hat headdress 225.26
 (sunshade 424.2)
 mute 417.11
hatbox 191.8
hatch *n.* door 260.4
 ship 273.7
 cockpit 273a.10
 under hatches
  dead 360.8
  imprisoned 751.12
  poor 804.7
hatch *v.*
 generate 161.10
 enchase 259.3
 incubate 370.8
 ~ up 515.10
 trump up 544.3
 design 556.17
 concoct 626.9
 plot 626.10
hatchel 652.11
hatchet 253.6
 (arms 727.4)
hatchet face 203.5
hatchet-faced 203.11
hatchet man
 killer 361.8
 ruffian 913.2
hatching birth 161.3
 incubation 673.1
hatchment
 insignia 550.12
 achievement 551.4
hatchway door 260.4
 ship 273.7
hate *n.*
 bombardment 716.1
 detestation 898
 (discord 713.1)
 (dislike 867.1)
 (enmity 889.1)
 (resentment 900.1)
 (malice 907.1)
hate *v.* 898.2
 (dislike 867.4)
 (bear malice 907.5)
hated 898.6
 (disliked 867.8)
hateful horrible 649.8
 odious 830.14
 reprehensible 898.4, 7
 invidious 907.6
 be hateful 898.4
 (repel 830.7)
hathi 271.2
hating 898.5

 (disliking 867.7)
 (unfriendly 889.3)
hat-in-hand 886.5
hatmaker 690.8
hatrack 271.7
hatred dislike 867.2
 detestation 898.1
 (phobia 860.4)
 (revengefulness 919.2)
hatter 225.39
hatti-humayun, hatti-humaiun, hatti-sherif 741.3
hattock 72.5
hauberk 717.2
haugh 367.11
haughtiness 885.1
 (pride 878.1)
haughty 885.8
 (proud 878.6)
 (contemptuous 930.8)
haul *n.* freight 270.4
 pull 285.2
 catch 789.5
 theft 791.4
 booty 793.1
haul *v.* navigate 267.10
 turn ship 267.24
 transport 270.8
 pull 285.4
 haul down
  navigate 267.10
  ~ one's flag 725.4
 haul off, haul to 267.24
haulage
 transportation 270.2
 drawing 285.1
hauling 285.1
haulm 215.14
haulyard See **halyard**
haunch rump 235.5
 flank 236.1
haunt *n.* resort 74.2
 ghost 980a.1
haunt *v.*
 attend 186.9, 11
 obsess 830.8
 (fear 860.13)
 (regret 833.2)
 (harass 860.13)
haunted
 spectered 980a.5
 bewitched 992.7
Hausa 560.5
hautboy 417.4
hauteur 885.1
haut goût 392.1
haut monde 875.2
Havana 392a.1
have *n.* fraud 545.3
 rich man 803.2
have *v.* confute 479.2
 know 490.9
 possess 777.4
 have done with
  cease 142.6
  abandon 624.3
  disuse 678.2
  relinquish 782.3

haven — hearing

have (*continued*)
  have it excel 33.5
    solve 481a.4
    believe 484.8
  have it in one 698.7
  have on 225.45
  have up 969.10
  not have 777a.3
haven 666.3
  (destination 292.6)
  (stronghold 717.4)
have-not 804.3
haversack 191.5
havildar 745.11
havior, haviour 692.1
havoc
  destruction 162.1
  damage 659.3
  play havoc 659.8
haw 583.3
Hawaiian 560.4
hawk *n.* bird 366.22
  eye 441.9
  thief 792.1
hawk *v.*
  salivate 297.19
  vend 796.5
  hawk about 531.7
  hawk at 716.5
hawker 797.3
hawking 622.2
hawkshaw 528.9
hawse bag 273.14
hawsehole 273.7
hawse hook 273.14
hawsepiece 273.7
hawsepipe 273.14
hawser
  fastening 45.2
  ship's rope 273.10
hawser clamp 273.14
hawse timber 273.7
hawsing iron 273.14
hay bed 215.24
  fence 232.2
  fodder 298.7
  (grass 367.9)
  hit the hay 683.9
haycock 72.5
hay fever
  salivation 299.5
  ailment 655.9
hayloft 636.4
haymaker 276.3
haymow, hayrick
  stack 72.5
  store 636.2
hayrif See hairif
hayseed 876.5
hayward 717.6
hazard *n.*
  fortuity 156.1
  chance 621.2, 3, 7
  danger 665.1
  at all hazards 604.9
hazard *v.*
  chance 621.17
  endanger 665.4
hazarder 621.15
hazardous 665.7
haze *n.* mist 353.5
  (moisture 339.1)
  vagueness 475.3
  confusion 458.4
  in a haze
    bewildered 475.16
    concealed 528.17
haze *v.* wander 266.14
  mist 353.9
  idle 683.8
  banter 856.4
hazel 433.4
hazel oil 972.3, 6
hazy cloudy 353.11
  dim 422.8
  opalescent 427.4
  indistinct 447.5
  bewildered 475.16
  confused 458.12
  obscure 519.7
he 373.1
head *n.* caption 66.3
  class 75.1
  top 210.1, 3
  capital 215.17
  headdress 225.26
  front 234.1
  promontory 250.5
  plane 255.3
  ship 273.7
  foam 353.2
  person 372.3
  headache 387.1
  intellect 450.1, 2
  subject 454.1
  portrait 556.9
  title 564.2
  synopsis 596.1
  water closet 653.9
  chief 694.2
  master 745.1
  above one's head
    aloft 206.19
    unintelligible 519.6
  at the head of
    paramount 642.14
    in charge 693.7
    ruling 737.15
    eminent 873.18
  bring to a head 729.2
  from head to foot 200.16
  head and head 267.64
  head and shoulders
    throughout 52.15
    hastily 684.7
  head on 267.64
  over one's head
    too deep 208.14
    overmuch 641.7
head *v.*
  come before 62.2
  begin 66.5
  tend 176.2
  top 210.5
  go before 280.2
  (front 234.7)
  gravitate 319.7
  direct 693.4
  rule 737.11
  head away 267.27
  head into
    sail into 267.32
    attack 716.5
head *adj.* first 66.8
  top 210.6
headache 378.1
  (ailment 655.5)
head and front 642.4
headboard 210.4
headclothes, head-dress 225.26
  (wig 256.4)
head earing 273.10
header 306.2; 310.1
  take a header
    fall 306.6
    plunge 310.4
head gate valve 263.2
  (outlet 295.5)
  floodgate 350.2
headgear 225.26
head-hunter 361.8
heading caption 66.3
  (prelude 64.2)
  front 234.1
  precession 280.1
  superscription 550.11
  title 564.2
headkerchief 225.26
headland 250.5
  (height 206.2)
headlight 423.4
headline *n.* 66.3
headline *v.* 599.25
headliner 599.19
headlong *adj.*
  steep 217.12
  hasty 684.5
  (sudden 113.5)
  reckless 863.7
headlong *adv.*
  violently 173.18
  swiftly 274.14
  hastily 684.7
  precipitately 863.8
headman 745.1
headmold, headmould 210.4
headmost
  foremost 234.8, 9
  preceding 280.3, 4
head over heels
  inversely 218.8
  rotatively 312.9
  hastily 684.7
  recklessly 863.8
headphone
  sound device 418.6
  phone 532a.5
headpiece
  head 210.1, 3, 4
  headdress 225.26
  brain 450.2
  engraving 558.1
  armor 717.2
  ornament 847.3
headquarters
  resort 74.2
  abode 189.1
headship 737.3
  (supremacy 33.3)
headsman 975.5
headspring 153.2
headstall 752.2
headstone
  foundation 215.3
  support 215.18
  tombstone 363.15
headstrong 606.6
headward 234.10
headway room 180.2
  navigation 267.7
  progression 282.1
  improvement 658.1
  make headway
    navigation 267.21
    progress 282.2
    improve 658.6
headwear 798.3
head wind
  counteractant 179.2
  aeronautics 267a.19
  wind 349.10
  hindrance 706.2
  opposition 708.1
headwork 451.1
heady frothy 353.10
  odorous 398.8
  fragrant 400.10
  obstinate 606.6
heal cure 660.12
  be cured 660.16
heal-all 662.3
healing *n.* 660.5
  (remedy 662.1)
healing *adj.* 662.25
health 654
  in health 654.4
healthful
  in health 654.4
  salubrious 656.5
  (beneficial 648.12)
healthfulness 656.1
healthless 655.24
healthy
  in health 654.4
  (sound 159.12)
  salubrious 656.5
heap *n.*
  quantities 31.3
  accumulation 72.4, 6
  (store 636.1)
  automobile 272.15
  aircraft 273a.1
heap *v.*
  assemble 72.11
  accumulate 636.7
hear listen 418.11
  sit in judgment 480.8
  (try 969.11)
  overhear 527.11
  hear out, hear say, hear tell of 418.11
hearable 402.10
heard 418.12
hearer 418.7
hear, hear! 931.13
hearing *n.*
  music 415.17
  interview 418.2
  earshot 418.4
  examination 461.3
  trial 463.1
  conference 588.3
  performance 599.8

hearing — heavyweight

council 696.2
reproof 932.3
trial 969.5
give a hearing
listen 418.11
test 463.6
hearing adj. 418.13
hearken, harken v.
listen 418.11
pay attention 457.4
hearken, harken int. 418.16
hearkener, harkener 418.7
hearsay n.
evidence 467.1
rumor 532.3
hearsay adj. 467.11
hearse n.
automobile 272.15
burial 363.9, 10, 12
hearse v. 363.20
heart essence 5.2
vitals 221.4
center 222.2
(interior 221.2)
inmost mind 450.3
(affections 820.2)
disposition 820.1
emotions 821.1, 2
game 840.12, 13
courage 861.1
love 897.1
soul 994.11
at heart 821.9
by heart 505.22
(literally 19.14)
from a full heart 829.10
go to one's heart 824.4
have at heart 865.11
know by heart
know well 490.10
memorize 505.13
learn by heart 505.13
(learn 539.3)
to one's heart's content
willingly 602.11
without stint 639.8
successfully 731.12
with pleasure 829.10
contentedly 831.8
heartache
wretchedness 828.3
sorrow 837.3
heart and soul
throughout 52.15
willingly 602.6, 11
resolutely 604.9
lustily 686.11
heartily 821.9
heartblood, heart's blood essence 5.2
life force 359.2
heartbreaker 256.3
heartbreaking 830.13
heartbroken
wretched 828.16
sad 837.13
heartburn

indigestion 655.13
enmity 889.1
jealousy 920.1
heartburning
discontent 832.1
regret 833.1
enmity 889.1
heart-corroding 830.13
heart disease 655.12
hearten 858.8
(embolden 861.7)
heart failure
death 360.1
ailment 655.12
heartfelt
deep-felt 821.8
(devout 990.15)
delightful 829.8
heartgrief
discontent 832.1
sorrow 837.3
hearth home 189.2
fireplace 386.2
family circle 892.7
hearthstone
home 189.2
fireside 386.2
heartily
willingly 602.11
heart and soul 821.9
heartiness 821.2
heartless
unfeeling 823.4
hardhearted 907.8
(severe 739.5)
(pitiless 914a.3)
relentless 919.6
wicked 945.11
heartlike 245.12
heart of hearts
inmost mind 450.3
soul 994.11
heart of oak
strength 159.4
hardness 323.3
courage 861.1
heartquake 860.3
heart-rending 830.13
heart-robbing
alluring 617.5
delightful 829.8
heart's blood See **heartblood**
heartscalded
pained 828.16
sad 837.13
heartsick
disconsolate 837.12
disliking 867.7
satiated 869.6
heartsickening 830.13
heartsome 858.9
heart-stirring 824.12
heart-stricken
pained 828.16
sad 837.13
heart-swe'ling, heart-thrilling 824.12
heart-wounding 830.13

hearty
intoxicated 959.21
hale 654.4
ardent 821.6
cheerful 836.11
friendly 888.4
heat n. hotness 382
race 720.5
fervor 821.2
excitement 825.2
hot temper 900.1
sexual desire 961.3
in heat 961.11
heat v. warm 384.16
impassion 824.2
heated 384.23
(hot 382.16)
heater 386
heath waste 169.2
plain 344.1
vegetation 367.8
heathen n. 984.20
(unbeliever 485.4)
heathen adj.
uncivilized 851.7
heathenish 984.28
heathen Chinee 188.9
heathenish 851.7
heathenism 984.10
heather 367.8
heating n. 384.1
heating adj. 384.22
heatstroke 503.4
heat wave 382.1, 3
heaume 717.2
heave n. throw 284.3
wave 348.10
heave v.
navigate 267.10
throw 284.12
vomit 297.18
lift 307.5
billow 348.22
~ with emotion 824.7
~ a sigh 839.7
heave down 267.34
heave in sight 446.2
heave out 267.16
heave round 267.24
heave the hook 267.12
heave the gorge 297.18
heave the lead
sound 208.7
measure 466.10
heave the log
navigate 267.10
measure 466.10
heave to
turn ship 267.24
be inactive 683.8
heave ho! 267.69
heaven
boundlessness 180.4
sky 318.2
(air 338.1)
utopia 515.6
bliss 827.2
paradise 981
(afterlife 121.3)

for heaven's sake 765.9
good heavens! 870.11
Heaven be praised
hurrah! 838.12
gratitude 916.5
hallelujah! 990.16
Heaven forbid! 766.5
heaven-born
majestic 873.18
righteous 944.3
heaven-kissing 206.14
heavenly
celestial 318.16; 981.7
delightful 829.8
beautiful 845.13
divine 976.13
angelic 977.4
heavenly body 318.3
Heavenly City
utopia 515.6
Zion 981.1
heavenly host 977.1
heavenly-minded
righteous 944.3
pious 987.10
heavenward 305.8
heaven-wide 78.11
heave offering 990.6
heaves 655.18
heaviness
pregnancy 168.2
weight 319.1
sadness 837.1
heaving 825.3
Heaviside layer 338.2
heavy n.
heavyweight 192.7
role 599.7
tragedian 599.19
heavy adj. great 31.6
pregnant 168.9
inert 172.3
steep 217.12
weighty 319.12
stupid 499.12
profound 519.7
diction 574.9
dramatic 599.28
~ on hand 641.5
consequential 642.12
burdensome 649.11
lethargic 683.14, 15
laborious 686.10
difficult 704.8
cumbrous 830.16
dull 843.5
be heavy 319.8
heavy-armed 717.9
heavy-handed 699.12
heavy-hearted 837.9
heavy-laden
encumbered 706.9
careworn 828.16
heavy water 337.1
heavyweight n.
superior 33.4
big man 192.7
personage 642.5

heavyweight — hell-diver 892

heavyweight adj.
  642.10
hebdomadal 138.11
Hebe 845.3
hebetate v. 823.4
hebetate adj. 499.12
hebetation 823.1
hebetic 127.6
hebetude
  stupidity 499.2
  languor 683.4
  insensibility 823.1
hebetudinous
  stupid 499.12
  languid 683.14
Hebraic 984.26
Hebraism 984.7
Hebraist
  philologist 560.7
  Judaist 984.17
Hebrew n. Jew 188.9
  unintelligibility
    519.2
  language 560.4
  jargon 563.4
  Judaist 984.17
Hebrew adj.
  racial 11.8
  Jewish 188.11
  Judaical 984.26
Hebrewism 984.7
Hecate, Hekate 318.5
hecatomb
  hundred 98.8
  sacrifice 990.6
heck hatch 260.4
  ship 273.7
heckelphone 417.4
heckle comb 652.11
  harass 830.5
hectare 466.3
hectic n.
  heat flush 382.7
  reddening 434.4
  emotion 821.2
hectic adj.
  feverish 382.19
  red 434.11
hectic fever
  heat flush 382.7
  fever 655.4
hectic flush
  heat flush 382.7
  reddening 434.4
  fever 655.4
  emotion 821.2
hecto-, hect- 98.27
hectogram, hecto-
  gramme 319.4
hectoliter, hectolitre
  466.3
hectometer, hecto-
  metre 466.3
hector n. 863.3
Hector n. 861.3
hector v. 860.12
hedge n. edge 231.1
  fence 232.2
  border 371.2
hedge v.
  compensate 30.5
  surround 227.3

hedge in
  circumscribe 229.2
  hinder 706.4
  condition 770.2
hedgehog spine 253.2
  animal 366.17
hedgehop 267a.31
hedgehopping 267a.24
hedgerow 232.2
hedgesmith 690.6
hedonic
  pleasure 377.7;
    827.11
  philosophical 451.38
hedonics 836.1
hedonism
  physical pleasure
    377.1
  philosophy 451.7, 11
  spiritual pleasure
    827.1
  cheer 836.1
hedonist
  philosophical 451.38
  sensualist 954a.1
heed n. attention 457.1
  care 459.1
  custody 664.2
  caution 864.1
give heed 457.4
take heed
  be careful 459.3, 5
  be cautious 864.3
heed v. listen 418.11
  note 450.7
  be attentive 457.4
  care 459.5
  not heed 458.5
heedful
  attentive 457.9
  careful 459.7
heedfulness 457.1
heedless
  inattentive 458.10
  (forgetful 506.8)
  (reckless 863.7)
  careless 460.8
  shiftless 674.11
heedlessness 458.1
  (recklessness 863.1)
heel n. foot 211.4
  supporter 215.2
  rear 235.1, 7
  ship 273.7
on the heels of 197.11
heel v.
  turn ship 267.24
  careen 267.34
  deviate 279.4
  follow 281.3
  turn 311.4
  equip 634.2
heel over 267.35
heel-and-toe 840.8
heeled 959.21
hee'er follower 281.2
  hanger-on 886.2
heel of Achilles 665.2
heelpiece n. 235.1
heelpiece v. 660.11
heels over head
  inversely 218.5

rotatively 312.9
hastily 684.7
recklessly 863.8
heeltap 40.2
Hefner candle 420.1
heft n. main part 50.3
  weight 319.1
  strain 686.1
heft n. See **haft**
heft v. 319.8
hefty potent 157.8
  strong 159.10
  heavy 319.12
  laborious 686.10
  difficult 704.8
Hegelianism 451.11
hegemonic
  supreme 33.8
  directive 693.6
  ruling 737.15
hegemony 737.3
he-goat goat 366.9
  male animal 373.6
heifer girl 129.5
  calf 366.12
  female animal 374.8
heigh-ho! 839.18
height n.
  degree 26.1
  advantage 33.2
  altitude 206.1, 2
  (promontory 250.5)
  (spire 253.4)
  summit 210.1
  (perfection 650.1)
  pitch 413.13
at its height
  great 31.6
  beyond 33.9
height v. 206.12; 307.5
heighten increase 35.3
  make high 206.12
  elevate 307.5
  exaggerate 549.2
  aggravate 835.2
heightening
  expansion 194.1
  aggravation 835.1
Heimdall, Heimdallr
  979.3
Heinie, Heine
  German 188.9
  soldier 726.4
heinous evil 649.8
  disreputable 874.8
  wicked 945.16
heir descendant
  167.1, 4
  inheritor 779.5
  (inheritance 775.4)
  (beneficiary 785.2)
heir apparent, heiress
  167.4
heirloom 775.4
heir presumptive
  167.4
heirship, heirship
  movables 775.4
Hekate See **Hecate**
Hel
  goddess 979.3; 982.4
  Hades 982.2

Helen of Troy 845.3
heliacal 318.16
helical, helicoid 248.5
Helicon 597.9
helicopter 273a.1
heliochrome, helio-
  chromotype 556.11
heliochromy 556.4
helioengraving
  558.2, 3
Heliogabalus 954a.1
heliogram
  telegram 532a.3
  signal 550.14
heliograph
  telegraph 532a.5
  signal 550.14
  photograph 556.11
  engraving 558.3
heliographic 420.24
heliography 420.16
heliogravure 558.1
heliolater 382.11;
  991.5
heliolatrous 991.7
heliolatry 382.11;
  991.1
heliology, heliometer,
  heliometry 420.16
Helios 318.4
helioscope 445.1
heliotherapy
  photics 420.16
  healing art 662.16
heliotrope
  fragrance 400.3
  purple 437.1
  gem 847.8
heliotype
  photograph 556.11
  engraving 558.3
heliotypy 558.1
helium 334.2
helix 248.2
hell depth 208.2
  gambling den 621.14
  prison 752.1
  mental suffering
    828.6
  eyesore 846.3
  den 945.8
  infernal regions 982
go to hell
  perish 162.5
  become sinful 945.9
he'l broke loose
  turmoil 59.4
  noise 404.2
  discord 414.2
hellbender spree 840.3
  drinking bout 959.3
hell-bent
  swiftly 274.14
  recklessly 863.8
  go hell-bent 274.9
hellborn
  wicked 945.17
  satanic 978.7
hellcat vio'ent 173.6
  daredevil 863.2
  evildoer 913.1, 5
hell-diver 269a.1

hellebore 663.6
hellebore red 434.2
Hellenist 560.7
hell-fire 982.1
hell-fired 31.24
hellgrammite, hellgamite, hellgramite 366.24
hellhag 913.5
hellhound
  violent 173.6
  fiend 913.4
  reprobate 949.1
hellion violent 173.6
  evildoer 913.1
hellish
  damnable 649.8
  malignant 907.9
  wicked 945.17
  infernal 982.5
  (satanic 978.7)
  (demoniac 980.9)
hellishly 31.24
hello attention 457.10
  greeting 894.4
  say hello 894.9
helm n. handle 215.7
  ship 273.7
  direction 693.1
  armor 717.2
  authority 747.6
  at the helm 693.7
  helm alee 267.70
  take the helm 693.4
helm v. 267.11
helmage 267.1
helmet 717.2
  (headdress 225.26)
helminthic n. 662.11
helminthic adj. 662.25
helminthologist 368.2
helminthology 368.1
helmsman
  steersman 269.5
  guide 694.6
helot 746.4
help n. remedy 662.1
  employee 690.2
  aid 707.1
  assistant 711.1
  retainer 746.1
  staff 746.7
  benefaction 784.4
  benefactor 912.1
help v. benefit 648.6
  (improve 658.8)
  aid 707.6
  (contribute 178.2)
  (utility 644.1)
  (render a service 644.3)
  (facilitate 705.4)
  (serve 746.8)
  (blessing 784.4)
help oneself to 789.8
helper assistant 711.1
  benefactor 912.1
helpful 707.12
  (useful 644.5; 677.8)
  (beneficial 648.12)
  (co-operative 709.7)

(serving 746.9)
(benevolent 906.6)
helping n. 298.38
helping adj. 707.12
helpless
  impotent 158.9
  (unstrengthened 160.15)
  (unprotected 665.9)
  (infirm 655.24)
  dead drunk 959.22
helplessness 158.2
helpmate, helpmeet
  assistant 711.1
  spouse 903.8
  benefactor 912.1
helter-skelter adj. 59.8
helter-skelter adv.
  in disorder 59.13
  neglectfully 460.12
  carelessly 863.8
  hastily 684.7
helve 215.7
hem n. 231.1, 2
hem v. edge 231.3
  fold 258.3
hem in
  circumscribe 229.2
  (surround 227.3)
  confine 751.8
hem int. 870.11
he-man 159a.3
hematobious, haematobious
  intrinsic 5.6
  productional 161.11
hemeralopia 443.2
hemeralopic 443.15
hemi- 91.6
hemicrania 378.1
hemicycle 247.5
hemiplegia
  insensibility 376.1
  paralysis 655.15
hemisect 91.4
hemisphere half 91.3
  region 181.1
hemispheric 250.9
hemlock suicide 361.3
  tree 367.6
  bitter 395.3
  wood 635.3
  execution 972.4
hemorrhage, haemorrhage
  bleeding 299.6
  ailment 655.5
hemorrhea, hemorrhoea 299.6
hemorrhoid, haemorrhoid 655.16
hemp cord 205.3
  drug 662.7
hen food 298.25
  fowl 366.23
  female 374.2, 8
  source of supply 636.2
henbane 663.6
hence therefore 155.5
  (accordingly 8.7)

(consequently 154.7)
(logically 476.19)
away 293.10
henceforth, henceforwards 121.10
henchman
  servant 746.1
  (inferior 34.3)
  hanger-on 886.2
henhearted 862.4
henhussy
  mollycoddle 160a.3
  old fogy 501.3
henna n. 439.1, 2
henna adj. 433.5
henotheism 984.10
henotheist 984.20
henpecked
  obedient 743.3
  in subjection 749.6
henry 158a.5
hep 490.12
hepatic 369.11
hepatize 641.4
Hephaestus, Hephaistos fire 382.8
  smith 690.6
  god 979.2
hepta-, hept- 98.17
heptad seven 98.3
  microbe 193.4
heptagon seven 98.3
  angle 244.2
heptagonal, heptahedral 98.17
heptahedron 98.3
heptamerous 98.17
heptameter 98.3
heptangular 98.17
heptarchy 98.3
heptastich seven 98.3
  stanza 597.7
Heptateuch 98.3
her 374.1
Hera, Here
  marriage 903.1
  goddess 979.2
Heracliteanism 451.6
Heraclitus 839.5
herald n. 64.1
  (informant 527.5)
  (messenger 534.1)
herald v.
  be prior 116.3
  (presage 511.9)
  precede 280.2
  foretell 511.8
  proclaim 531.7
heraldry 550.12
herb n. 367.1, 2
herb v. 371.8
herbaceous 367.14
herbage
  vegetation 365.1
  vegetable life 367.1
herbal 367.14
  (botanical 369.11)
herbalist 369.9
herbalize
  botanize 369.10
  harvest 371.8

herbarium 369.2
  (garden 371.6)
herbarize 371.8
Herbartianism 451.11
herbivore 298.41
herbivority 298.1
herbivorous 298.48
herborist 369.9
herborization 369.1
herborize
  botanize 369.10
  cultivate 371.8
Herculean vast 31.8
  strong 159.10
  giantlike 192.15
  laborious 686.10
  difficult 704.8
Hercules
  strong man 159.6
  giant 192.8
  support 215.25
  hero 861.3
herd n. crowd 72.4
  multitude 102.2
herd v. assemble 72.10
  ~ together 88.6
  aviate 267a.31
  cattle 370.7
herd boy, herder, herdsman 370.4
  (workman 690.10)
  (servant 746.1)
Herdsman 318.6
here
  in this place 186.20
  hither 292.12
  from here 293.10
  from here out 180.9
  here and there
    scatteringly 73.6
    sparsely 103.5
  where 186.22
  not here 187.15
Here See Hera
hereabout, herabouts
  here 186.20
  nearly 197.12
hereadays 118.3
hereafter n.
  the future 121.2
  postexistence 121.3
  (heaven 981.5)
hereafter adj. 121.7
hereafter, hereafterward adv. 121.9
hereby 631.5
hereditament
  inheritance 775.4
  property 780.4
hereditary
  intrinsic 5.6
  lineal 167.7
  estate 780.8
heredity 167.2
herein 221.12
hereon 117.4
heresy 984.1
  (misbelief 485.1)
  (delusion 495.5)
  (infidelity 989.2)
heresyphobia 860.4

heretic 984.12
  (separatist 44.5)
  (nonconformist 83.4)
  (unbeliever 485.4; 989.4)
  (dissenter 489.3)
  (apostate 607.5)
heretical
  disbelieving 485.9
  heterodox 984.22
  (erroneous 495.12)
  (infidelic 989.7)
heretofore n. 122.2
heretofore adv.
  previously 116.5
  formerly 122.14
hereupon 117.4
herewith with 88.9
  by means of 632.4
herif See hairif
heritable n. 775.4
heritable adj. 783.5
heritage lineage 167.2
  inheritance 775.4
heritance 775.4
heritor 779.5
hermaphrodite n. 83.5
hermaphrodite adj. 83.12
hermaphrodite brig 273.2
hermaphroditic 83.12
hermeneut 524.1
hermeneutic 522.8
hermeneutics 522.5
Hermes
  messenger 534.1
  spokesman 582.5
  god 979.2
hermit 893.4
  (ascetic 955.2)
  (religious 996.11)
hermitage
  retreat 189.13
  sanctuary 666.3
  seclusion 893.2
hermitary, hermitic 893.9
hermitism 893.2
hermitize 893.6
hermitry 893.2
hernia 655.5
hero actor 599.19
  brave person 861.3
  great man 873.9
  good example 948.1
  demigod 979.1
heroic verse 597.13
  courageous 861.8
  magnanimous 942.6
heroics 884.1
heroic verse 597.1
Heroin 662.7
heroine actress 599.19
  brave person 861.3
  celebrity 873.9
  demigoddess 979.1
heroism bravery 861.4
  magnanimity 942.2
heron 366.22
hero worship

homage 931.2
idolatry 991.1
herpes 655.17
herpetologist 368.2
herpetology 368.1
herpetotomist 368.2
herpetotomy 368.1
Herr 373.3
herring virgin 129.5
  fish 298.18
herringbone 219.5
herring pond 341.1
herself 79.4
hesitancy
  uncertainty 475.1
  irresolution 605.1
  scruple 939.2
hesitant 605.5
hesitate
  procrastinate 133.5
  be uncertain 475.6
  demur 485.7
  stammer 583.3
  be reluctant 603.4
  be irresolute 605.4
  (be afraid 860.8)
hesitating 605.1
hesitation pause 142.2
  uncertainty 475.1
  (doubt 485.2)
  stammering 583.1
  scrupulousness 603.2; 939.2
  irresolution 605.1
  (fearfulness 860.2)
Hesper, Hesperus 318.3
Hessian
  soldier 726.4
  niggard 819.2
hessians 225.27
hest 741.1
Hestia home 189.2
  goddess 979.2
heteroclite
  unconformable 83.9
  hermaphrodite 83.12
  irregular 139.2
heterodox
  heretic 485.9
  heretical 984.22
  (materialistic 316.9)
  (erroneous 495.12)
  (infidelic 989.7)
heterodoxy 984.1
  (misbelief 485.1)
  (fallacy 495.1)
heterogamous 357.10
heterogamy
  dissimilarity 18.1
  generation 161.2
heterogeneity
  difference 15.1
  nonuniformity 16a.1
  multiformity 81.1
  (irrelation 10.1)
heterogeneous
  different 15.7
  mixed 41.9
  multiform 81.2
  (unrelated 10.5)

heterogenesis 161.2
heterogenetic 161.11
heteromorphism 16a.1
heteronomy 737.4
heteronym
  equivalence 516.3
  word 562.1
heteropathic 662.25
heteropathy 662.16
heterotopia
  transformation 140.2
  dislocation 185.1
heterotopic 185.3
heterotropia 443.3
hetman 745.11
hew cut 44.8
  form 240.6
hew down 213.7; 308.5
hex n. 992.2, 3
hex v. 992.4
hexa-, hex- 98.16
Hexabiblos, hexabromide 98.2
hexachord six 98.2
  music 413.18
  instrument 417.2
hexacosihedroid 98.2
hexad six 98.2
  microbe 193.4
hexaglot 560.9
hexagon six 98.2
  angle 244.2
hexagonal 98.16
hexagram 98.2
hexahedral 98.16
hexahedron six 98.2
  angle 244.2
hexamerous 98.16
hexameter six 98.2
  versification 597.6
hexangular 98.16
hexapod, hexapody, hexarchy 98.2
hexastich six 98.2
  stanza 597.7
Hexateuch six 98.2
  Scriptures 985.3
hexatomic 98.16
hexavalent 98.2
hey! 457.10
  (halloo! 586.3)
heyday n.
  jubilation 838.1
  festivity 840.2
heyday int. 870.11
hg. 319.4
hi! 457.10
hiate interval 198.4
  gape 260.13
hiation, hiatus
  interval 198.1
  opening 260.1
hibernal 383.8
hibernate 683.9
hibernation 683.5
Hibernian n. 188.9
Hibernian adj. 188.11
Hibernicism
  blunder 495.3
  language 563.5

hiccius-doccius 959.21
hiccup, hiccough n. 349.18
hiccup, hiccough v. 349.23
hic jacet 363.16, 27
hick n. 876.5
hick adj. 183.3
hidalgo 875.4
hidden blind 442.6
  concealed 528.17
  (invisible 447.4)
  (obscure 519.7)
  (latent 526.6)
hide n. skin 223.12
  race horse 271.8
hide v. conceal 528.16
  lie hid 528.16
  (~ oneself 893.6)
  disguise 544.6
  whip 972.6
hide one's face
  be humble 879.2
  be modest 881.3
hide and hair 52.15
hide-and-seek 840.11
hideaway resort 74.2
  hiding place 530.2
  (retreat 189.13)
hidebound
  bigoted 606.7
  bound 751.11
  illiberal 819.4
  prudish 853.7
hideous odious 830.14
  ugly 846.6
hide-out resort 74.2
  hiding place 530.2
hiding
  concealment 528.1
  ambush 530
  go in hiding 528.16
  in hiding 528.19
hiding place 530.2
  (retreat 189.13)
  (shelter 424.1)
  (refuge 666.3)
  (escape 671.3)
hidlings, hidlins 530.2
hie go 264.6
  ~ to 266.22
  speed 274.9
hiemal, hyemal 383.8
hierarch 996.5
hierarchic 995.9
hierarchy 995.1
hieratic 590.15
hieroglyph 590.9
hieroglyphic 590.15
  (literal 561.9)
hierography 983.1
hierolatry 991.1
hierology 983.1
hieromancy 511.3
hieromonach 996.11
Hieronymite 893.4
hierophant 996.2, 10
hieroscopy 511.3
higgle 794.5
higgledy-piggledy 59.13

higgler — hip

higgler 797.3
high n. 542.1
high adj. great 31.6
  elevated 206.13
  (large 192.11)
  (long 200.12, 13)
  intoxicated 959.21
  haut goût 298.50
  strong-flavored 392.5
  rank 395.7
  fetid 401.4
  shrill 410.10
  foul 653.17
  expensive 814.5
  eminent 873.18
  noble 875.10
  proud 878.6
  magnanimous 942.6
  become high 206.11
  be high 206.9
  from on high 981.7
  on high 206.19
  (elevatedly 307.10)
high and dry
  stuck 150.6
  safe 664.10
  in difficulty 704.11
  stranded 732.10
high and low 180.9
high and mighty
  eminent 873.18
  proud 878.6
  arrogant 885.8
highball, high ball 959.8
highbinder
  killer 361.8
  thief 792.3
  ruffian 913.2
highborn 875.10
high-brow n. 492.4
high-brow v. 930.7
high-brow adj. 490.16
High-Church 998.15
High-churchism 984.5; 998.11
High-churchman
  Anglican 984.15
  ritualist 998.12
high-colored, high-coloured 428.14
high day 840.5
High Dutch
  unintelligibility 519.2
  jargon 563.4
higher 33.7; 206.15
higher education 490.2
Higher Thought 984.9
higher-up 33.4
highest supreme 33.8
  top 210.6
highfalutin, high-faluting, highfaluten n. bombast 577.2
  boasting 884.1
highfalutin, highfaluting, highfaluten adj.
  exaggerated 549.3

bombastic 577.7
proud 878.6
ostentatious 882.8
boastful 884.7
arrogant 885.8
high-fed 954.4
high-flavored 392.5
highflier, highflyer
  fanatic 504.2
  imaginer 515.7
  proud person 878.2
high-flown
  fantastic 497.4
  fanciful 515.13
  exaggerated 549.3
  grandiloquent 577.7
  proud 878.6
  vain 880.6
  ostentatious 882.8
  boastful 884.7
  arrogant 885.8
highflying
  exaggerated 549.3
  grandiloquent 577.7
  ostentatious 882.8
high-geared 157.8
high hand 739.2
highhanded
  strict 739.5
  arrogant 885.8
high-hat v. 930.7
high-hat adj. 885.8
high-headed
  proud 878.6
  arrogant 885.8
high horse 885.1
  get on one's high horse 878.3
  (be arrogant 885.4)
highjacker, hijacker 792.4
high jinks 840.2
highland n.
  hinterland 183.1
  heights 206.2
highland adj. 206.17
Highland fling 840.7
high life society 852.4
  nobility 875.2
high liver 954a.1
high living 954.2
high-low 225.27
high-mettled
  excitable 825.8
  courageous 861.8
  proud 878.6
high-minded
  proud 878.6
  honorable 939.7
  magnanimous 942.6
high-muck-a-muck 642.5
Highness 877.2
high-pitched
  high 206.13
  shrill 410.10
high-pressure
  high-powered 157.8
  forcible 744.3
high-priced 814.5
high priest 996.5, 6
high-principled 939.7

high-reaching
  high 206.13
  aspiring 865.18
highroad 627.3
high roller 818.2
high school 542.1
high sea 341.1
high-seasoned 392.5
high-set 206.13
high-souled 878.6
high-sounding
  loud 404.8
  shrill 410.10
  grandiloquent 577.7
  (ostentatious 882.8)
  affected 853.6
high-spirited 861.8
high spirits 836.1
high-stepper 271.3
high-strung 825.8
high-swelling 878.6
hight n. See height
hight v. 564.7
high-tasted 392.5
high tide fullness 52.3
  height 206.5
  tide 348.9
  prosperity 734.1
high time
  leeway 133.2
  timeliness 134.3
hightoby 792.4
high-toned
  shrill 410.10
  proud 878.6
  ostentatious 882.8
high water
  fullness 52.3
  height 206.5
  tide 348.9
high-water mark
  limit 233.1
  water mark 466.5
highway 627.3
highwayman 792.4
highways and byways 627.3
hijacker See highjacker
high-wrought
  superexcellent 648.10
  elaborate 673.11
  excited 824.10
high yellow 41.5
hike n. increase 35.1
  walk 266.4
hike v. 266.16
hike up 35.3
hiker 268.6
hilarious 836.8
hilarity 836.3
hill 206.2
  (incline 217.2)
  (promontory 250.5)
  (elevation 307.1)
hillbilly 188.6
hillock 206.2
hil'side 217.2
hilly 206.17
hilt 215.7
him 373.1

himself 79.4
hind n. deer 366.11
  female animal 374.8
  peasant 876.5
hind adj. 235.9
hindbrain 450.2
hinder v. 706.4
  (delay 133.6)
  (stop 142.7)
  (counteract 179.3)
  (close 261.2)
  (oppose 708.2)
  (resist 719.3)
  (checkmate 731.10)
  (restrain 751.6)
  (prohibit 761.2)
hinder adj. 235.9
hinderer 706.2, 3
  (meddler 682.11)
hindering 706.8
  (restrictive 751.13)
hindermost 235.9
  (ending 67.8)
hind-gut vitals 221.4
  intestine 350.4
hindhand 235.9
hindhead 235.1
hind leg 266.11
hindmost 235.9
hindquarter 235.5
hindrance 706
  (anchor 666.2)
  (opposition 708.1)
  (checkmate 732.3)
  (restraint 751.1)
  (prohibition 761.1)
Hindu, Hindoo 994.13
Hinduism, Hindooism religion 984.11
  (Hinduism 451.5)
  occultism 994.1
Hindustani, Hindostani, Hindoostani 560.4, 5
Hindu triad 976.3
hinge n. joint 43.3
  fold 258.1
  swivel 312.5
hinge v. 475.7
hinge on, hinge upon 154.3
hingle 312.5
hinny 271.11
hint n. taste 390.1
  supposition 514.2
  intimation 527.4
  (slight knowledge 491.3)
  (reminder 505.5)
  indication 550.1
hint v. 527.8
  (remind 505.15)
  (suggest 514.8)
  (imply 526.4)
hinted 526.7
  (insinuated 527.14)
hinterland
  the country 183.1
  inland 221.3
  rear 235.1
hip rump 235.5
  flank 236.1

hip — hokeypokey

hip (*continued*)
  on the hip 749.6
hip See **hyp**
hip boot 225.27
hipped
  hypochondriac 503.16
  in love 897.15
hipping, hippen 225.22
hippish 503.16
hippo 192.8
hippocampus
  monster 83.7
  animal 366.21
Hippocrates 662.19
hippodrome
  theater 599.10
  arena 728.1
hippogriff, hippogryph 83.7
hippophagism 298.1
hippopotamic 192.13
hippopotamus 192.8
hiram 72.3
hircarra, hircarrah 534.1
hircocervus 83.7
hirdie-girdie 218.8
hire *n.* price 812.1
  wages 973.2
  for hire, on hire 763.4
hire *v.* bribe 618.3
  commission 755.4
  lease to 787.6
  lease from 788.3
  (purchase 795.3)
hired man 690.2; 746.1
hirsuite, hispid 256.13
hispidity 256.1
hispidulous 256.14
hiss *n.*
  sibilation 409.1
  derision 930.2
hiss *v.* sibilate 409.3
  serpent sound 412.2
  scoff 930.6
hissing *n.*
  sibilation 409.1
  object of scorn 874.3
  derision 930.2
hissing *adj.* 409.4
hist! silence! 403.9
  attention! 457.10
histogenesis 161.2
histologist 368.2
histology
  texture 329.2
  (science of form 240.4)
  zoology 368.1
historian 553.2
  (author 593.15)
  (narrator 594.4)
historical 594.7
historiographer 553.2
historiographical 594.7
historiography 594.3
historize 594.5
  (write 590.14)
history 594.2

(archive 551.2)
(writing 590.3)
(book 593.1)
histrio 599.19
histrionic 599.28
histrionics 599.2
hit *n.* blow 276.3
  success 731.2
  (luck 156.1)
  criticism 932.2
make a hit
  succeed 731.5
  enamor 897.13
hit *v.*
  chance upon 156.8
  impress 171.8
  travel 266.12
  strike 276.8
  (whip 972.6)
  shoot 284.13
  reach 292.7
  meet 292.10
  touch 379.3
hit back 718.2
hit for 286.2
hit it
  electrify 158a.11
  solve 481a.4
  succeed 731.5
hit it off
  be concordant 714.2
  be friendly 888.2
hit off imitate 19.6
  caricature 19.8
  agree 23.7
  represent 554.7
hit the nail on the head solve 481a.4
  exercise skill 698.9
  succeed 731.5
hit upon
  chance upon 156.8
  discover 481a.3
hit-and-run 268.10
hitch *n.* joint 43.3
  knot 45.6
  pause 142.2
  gait 266.5
  difficulty 704.4
  obstacle 706.2
hitch *v.* agree 23.7
  tie 43.6
  walk 266.16
  jerk 285.5
  (shake 315.8)
  ~ a horse 370.7
  marry 903.12
hitch horses
  agree 23.7
  league 48.4
  concur 178.2
  be concordant 714.2
hitch up add 37.3
  ~ ~ horses 370.7
hitchhike *n.* 266.4
hitchhike *v.* 266.16
hitchhiker 268.6
hither
  here 186.20; 292.12
  to here 278.12
hitherto
  previously 116.5

formerly 122.14
hit-off 21.1
hive *n.* horde 72.4
  multitude 102.2
  apiary 370.3
  workshop 691
hive *v.* settle 184.14
  swarm 370.9
hives 655.17
Hler 192.8
H.M.S. 726.11
Ho *n.* 560.4
ho *int.* 457.10
hoar *n.* 383.5
hoar *adj.* aged 128.8
  white 430.8
hoard *n.* 636.1
  (quantity 31.3)
  (accumulation 72.6)
hoard *v.* 636.7
hoarfrost 383.5
hoarfrosted 383.9
hoariness 430.1
hoarse 410.9
  (speech 583.5)
hoarstone 551.4
hoary old 124.6
  aged 128.8
  frosty 383.9
  white 430.8
hoax *n.* canard 532.3
  deception 545.3
  falsehood 546.1
  false alarm 669.2
hoax *v.* 545.7
hoaxee 547.1
hoaxer 548.1
hoaxproof 487.4
hob shelf 215.19
  fireplace 386.2
hob-and-nob 883.4
hobble *n.* gait 266.5
  perplexity 475.2
  predicament 704.2
  fetters 752.2
hobble *v.* walk 266.16
  go slow 275.5
  flounder 699.9
  fetter 751.7
hobbledehoy 129.4
hobby
  velocipede 272.14
  avocation 625.5
  diversion 840.1
ride a hobby
  repeat 104.4
  be boresome 841.5
hobbyhorse 840.1
hobbyhorsical 625.11
hobgoblin elf 979.9
  bogy 980.4
hobnail 876.5
hobnailed 183.3
hobnob 883.4
hobo, hoboe *n.* 268.2
  (neglector 460.3)
  (idler 683.7)
hobo, hoboe *v.* 266.14
hoboism
  wandering 266.2
  indolence 683.3

Hobson's choice 609a.1
  (necessity 601.1)
  (compulsion 744.1)
Hoch! 838.12
hock *n.* legs 266.11
  wine 959.7
  in hock 771.9
hock *v.* disable 158.6
  cripple 659.8
  pawn 771.5
hockey 840.11
hock shop 787.3
hocus *n.*
  deception 545.3
  drugged liquor 959.4
hocus *v.*
  adulterate 41.8
  falsify 544.3
  deceive 545.7
hocus-pocus *n.*
  nonsense 517.2
  deception 545.2, 3
  (sorcery 992.1)
  cunning 702.1
  magic formula 993.1
hocus-pocus *v.* 545.7
hod receptacle 191.1
  supporter 215.2
hodge 876.5
hodgepodge
  mixture 41.4
  (accumulation 72.8)
  confusion 59.2
hoe 371.8
hoecake 298.11
hog *n.* slattern 59.5
  swine 366.7
  monopolist 943.2
  glutton 957.2
hog *v.* 777.5
hogan 189.4
hogback 206.2
hogger 268.11
hoggish
  greedy 865.20
  gluttonous 957.4
hog's-back 206.2
hogshead 466.3
hog-tie tie 43.6
  disable 158.6
  impair 659.8
  fetter 751.7
hogwash
  nonsense 517.2
  garbage 653.6
Hohlee See **Holi**
hoick 267a.31
hoiden See **hoyden**
hoi polloi 876.1
hoist
  ~ sail 267.16
  ~ a banner 267.41; 550.20
  lift 307.5
hoity-toity!
  defiance 715.5
  wonder 870.11
hokeypokey
  deception 545.2

896

hokum — homemade

cunning 702.1
hokum nonsense 517.2
  deception 545.1
  acting 599.6
hold n.
  leverage 175.3
  compartment 191.2
  room 191.20
  bottom 211.1
  footing 215.4
  handle 215.7
  ship 273.7
  stronghold 717.4
  control 737.2
  possession 777.1
  grip 781.1
  treasury 802.1
get hold of 775.6
hold v. cohere 46.5
  include 76.3
  be permanent 141.4
  cease 142.6
  continue 143.2
  occur 151.3
  support 215.26
  believe 484.8
  ~ an office 625.9
  do nothing 681.2
  defend 717.7
  restrain 751.6
  possess 777.4
  retain 781.4
hold a brief for
  second 707.8
  represent 759.4
hold a close wind
  267.19
hold back
  reserve 636.8
  hinder 706.4
  restrain 751.6
  (disincline 616.3)
  retain 781.4
  stint 819.3
  abstain 953.5
hold forth
  expound 537.11
  declaim 582.7
hold good
  be permanent 141.4
  be reasonable
    476.12
  demonstrate 478.2
  be true 494.5
hold in hand 737.12
hold off
  procrastinate 133.5
  repulse 289.2
hold on wait 133.7
  be permanent 141.4
  cease! 142.8
  continue 143.2
  persevere 604a.2
hold one's ground
  be permanent 141.4
  (maintain 670.3)
  be stable 150.3
  be resolute 604.6
  (be obstinate
    606.5)
  resist 719.3
  war 722.9

retain 781.4
hold one's hand
  cease 142.6
  abandon 624.3
hold one's own
  repel 717.8
  resist 719.3
  dominate 737.12
  retain 781.4
hold one's peace,
  hold one's tongue
  585.3
  (keep secret 528.11)
hold out
  continue 106.2;
    143.2
  maintain 535.3
  persevere 604a.2
  be obstinate 606.5
  resist 719.3
  offer 763.2
hold the bag 932.10
hold together
  agree 23.7
  join 43.5
  be joined 43.9
  cohere 46.5
  be true 494.5
  co-operate 709.4
hold up agree 23.7
  delay 133.6
  support 215.26
  be true 494.5
  persevere 604a.2
  hinder 706.4
  lend support 707.7
  rob 791.9
  overcharge 814.3
  display 882.7
  approve 931.5
hold water agree 23.7
  be reasonable 476.12
  demonstrate 478.2
  be true 494.5
hold with 488.6
not hold water 495.6
holdall 191.5
holdback 706.2
ho'der 779.1
holdfast
  fastening 45.2
  clamp 781.2
holding
  messuage 189.12
  possession 777.1
  property 780.1, 2
hold-off 133.2
holdup delay 133.2
  robbery 791.1
holdup man 792.4
hole degree 26.1
  rank 71.1
  resort 74.2
  location 184.1
  small place 184.4
  house 189.3
  dive 189.9
  retreat 189.13
  receptacle 191.2, 3
  hold 191.20
  depth 208.2
  bottom 211.1

cavity 252.2
  cave 252.3
  opening 260.1
  (cleft 198.2)
  hiding place 530.2
  fault 651.2
  sty 653.10
  predicament 704.2, 3
  rank 873.4
  moral defect 945.5
hole-and-corner
  528.21
Holi, Hoolee
  anniversary 138.7
  festival 840.2
holiday n.
  neglect 460.2
  vacation 687.2
  red-letter day 840.5
  (anniversary 138.5)
  (celebration 883.2)
holiday v. 687.5
holiday adj. 687.7
holiness divinity 976.2
  piety 987.1
Holiness 877.4
Holland gin, Hol-
  lands 959.6
hollo v. 411.5
hollo int. 457.10
hollow n.
  compartment 191.2
  depth 208.2
  cavity 252.2
hollow v. 252.9
  (depress 308.4)
hollow adj.
  incomplete 53.4
  empty 187.11
  concave 252.10
  (open 260.15)
  resonant 408.9
  sophistical 477.9
hollow adv. 52.14
hollowed 252.10
hollowhearted 545.12
hollowness
  concavity 252.1
  false pretense 544.2
holm marsh 345.1
  island 346.1
holoblastic 357.10
holocaust 990.6
holograph 590.3
holothurian 368.14
holotony spasm 315.7
  illness 655.3
Holstein 366.12
holt 367.7
holus-bo'us
  hastily 684.7
  precipitately 863.8
holy
  righteous 944.3;
    987.10
  (pure 960.2)
  sacred 976.13
  scriptural 985.7
  hallowed 987.11
Holy City 981.1
holyday, holy day
  998.13

Holy Father 996.5
Holy Ghost 976.6
Holy Grail 998.8
Holy Joe 996.2
holy-minded 944.3;
  987.10
holy of holies
  room 191.16
  sanctuary 1000.3
holy orders 995.6
holy place 1000.2
Holy Spirit 976.6
holystone 273.14
holy terror
  violent 173.6
  evildoer 913.1
Holy Thursday
  holytide 998.13
holy water 998.2, 8
Holy Week 998.13
Holy Willie 988.6
Holy Writ 985.2
homage
  reverence 928.1, 2
  praise 931.2
  allegiance 939.4
  worship 990.1
pay homage to 928.5
  (pay respects
    894.8)
  (worship 990.9)
homaloid plane 213.3
  flat 251.2
homaloidal 213.8;
  251.5
hombre 373.2
home resort 74.2
  abode 189.2
  (resting place
    265.4)
  (parsonage 1000.5)
  poorhouse 189.11
  destination 292.6
  insane asylum
    503.8
  hospital 662.17
  asylum 666.3
  down home 186.21
  drive home to 484.10
  from home 187.10
  reach home 666.5
homebred 851.6
home-brew 959.9
home-coming 292.3
homecroft
  messuage 189.12
  farm 371.4
homefelt 821.8
home-grown 367.17
homeless
  unplaced 185.4
  forsaken 893.10
homelike 849.3
homeliness 846.1
homely
  comfortable 377.8
  language 576.3
  ugly 846.6
  simple 849.3
  rude 851.6
  common 876.11
homemade 161.19

homeopathic — hooter

homeopathic, homoeopathic
  inconsiderable 32.8
  remedial 662.25
homeopathic dose 32.2
homeopathy, homoeopathy 662.16
home reserves 726.6
Homeric epic 594.7
  verse 597.13
Homeric laughter 838.3
home rule
  government 737.4
  independence 748.3
homesick 833.3
homesickness 833.1
homespun *n.*
  cloth 219.5
  rough 262.2
homespun *adj.*
  simple 42.5
  homemade 161.13
  rough 256.12
  coarse 329.3
  language 576.3
  plain 849.3
  rude 851.6
  common 876.11
homestead
  abode 189.2, 12
  farm 371.4
homesteader 188.5
homester 188.7
homestretch 67.3
home-towner 188.7
homeward bound 292.12
homicidal 361.15
homicide 361.1
homiletic 537.12
homily 595.1
homing pigeon
  carrier 271.1
  messenger 534.2
hominine 372.5
hominy 298.15
homish 849.3
homo
  homosexual 83.5
  man 372.1; 373.2
  human being 372.3
homocentric 222.4
homoeopathic, homoeopathy See homeopathic etc.
homogeneity
  relation 9.1
  uniformity 16.1
  similarity 17.1
  simpleness 42.1
homogeneous
  uniform 16.5
  simple 42.5
homogenesis 161.2
homoiousia 17.1
homoiousian 17.11
Homoiousianism 984.2
homologize 23.7, 8
homologous

uniform 16.5
equivalent 27.9
homology relation 9.1
  uniformity 16.1
homonym, homonyme
  equivalence 516.3
  ambiguity 520.2
  word 562.1
homonymous 520.5
homonymy 520.1
homoousia 13.1
homoousian 13.6
Homoousianism 984.4
homophonic 402.12
homophonous 413.26
homophony
  acoustics 402.5
  unisonance 412.1
homosexual *n.*
  hermaphrodite 83.5
  libertine 962.1
homosexual *adj.* 83.12
homosexuality 961.3
Homo sapiens 372.1
homozygosity 42.1
homunculus 193.5
hone 253.7
honest
  veracious 543.3
  honorable 939.7
  (artless 703.4)
  chaste 960.2
honest Injun 535.8
honestly 935.11
honesty veracity 543.1
  probity 939.1
  (artlessness 703.1)
  (justice 941.1)
  chastity 960.1
honey *n.* sweets 396.2
  excellent thing 648.4
  endearment 902.4
  (sweetheart 897.7)
honey *v.* sweeten 396.7
  flatter 933.2
honeybee 366.24
honey bunch 902.4
honeycomb *n.*
  cavity 252.2
  porousness 260.7
honeycomb *v.* 260.14
honeycombed 260.17
  (hollow 252.10)
honeycomb stomach 191.7
honeyfogle, honeyfugle 933.2
honeymoon
  pleasure 827.3
  marriage 903.3
honeymouthed
  suave 894.13
  flattering 933.3
honeysweet 396.8
honey-tongued
  suave 894.13
  flattering 933.3
honk *n.* 404.3
honk *v.* toot 404.7
  quack 412.2
honor, honour *n.*

trophy 733.1
demesne 780.4
repute 873.1, 7, 8
honorific 877.1, 2
respect 928.1
praise 931.2
probity 939.1
do honor to 873.13
  (celebrate 883.3)
in honor of 883.6
render honor to
  honor 873.13
  pay homage to 928.5
upon my honor
  I'll warrant 535.8
  I promise 768.8
honor, honour *v.*
  prefer 609.9
  ~ a bill 807.6
  render honor to 873.13
  respect 928.4
  esteem 931.5
  worship 990.9
honorable, honourable
  reputable 873.15
  venerable 928.9
  upright 939.7
  (observant 772.5)
  (ethical 926.12)
be honorable 939.6
Honorable, Honourable 877.5
honorableness, honourableness 939.1
honorably, honourably 935.11
honorarium
  gratuity 784.3
  reward 973.2
honorary 815.10
honor bright
  upon my word 535.8
  (truly 494.15)
  (truthfully 543.4)
  (honestly 939.12)
  I promise 768.8
honored, honoured
  distinguished 873.16
  respected 928.9
honorific 873.15
honor man 541.4
honors
  examination 461.3
  scholastic honor 873.8
do the honors
  entertain 892.11
  pay homage to 928.5
honor society 873.8
hooch 959.4, 9
hood headdress 225.26
  automobile 272.16
  airplane 273a.10
  thief 792.3
  clerical ~ 999.1
hooded 223.28
hoodlum thief 792.3
  ruffian 913.2
hoodmold 210.4
hoodoo *n.*

898

bad influence 649.3
voodoo 992.1
jinx 993.2
hoodoo *v.*
  bring bad luck 735.7
  bewitch 992.4
hoodoo *adj.* 992.5
hoodooed 735.9
hoodwink
  blindfold 442.3
  (conceal 528.13)
  deceive 545.7
hoodwinked 491.10
hooey *n.* 517.2
hooey *int.* 497.5
hoof *n.* 211.4
hoof *v.* 266.16
hoofbeat 407.2
hoofer 268.6
hook *n.*
  fastening 45.2
  (suspender 214.3)
  angle 244.2
  curve 245.2
  anchor 273.14; 666.2
  snare 545.4
  finger 781.3
by hook or by crook 627.10
hook *v.* attach 43.6
  angle 244.4
  curve 245.3
  ensnare 545.9
  catch 789.9
  steal 791.9
hook in ensnare 545.9
  induce 615.9
hook up tie 43.6
  league 48.4
hookah, hooka 392a.6
hook and eye 45.2
hook and ladder 671.3
hooked 245.8
hooker 273.1, 2
hooklike, hook-nosed 245.8
hookup junction 43.1
  association 709.2
hooky 187.5
  (avoidance 623.1)
  (dereliction 927.1)
play hooky 187.8
Hoolee See Holi
hooligan 913.2
hoop *n.* 247.2
hoop *v.* 411.5
hoople 247.2
hoop skirt 225.19
hoosegow, hoosgow, hoosegaw 752.1
hoosier *n.* 876.5
hoosier *adj.* 183.3
hoosierdom 183.1
hoot *n.* modicum 32.2
  trifle 643.3
  derision 930.2
hoot *v.* call 411.5
  ululate 412.2
  scoff 930.6
hooter
  modicum 32.2
  alarm 669.1

hoot owl 366.22
hop n. gait 266.5
　journey 266.8
　flight 267a.23
　departure 293.1
　leap 309.1
　opium 662.7
　dance 840.6
　on the hop
　moving 264.10
　active 682.20
hop v. walk 266.16
　speed 274.9
　depart 293.4
　leap 309.4
hop off
　take off 267a.33
　depart 293.4
hop the twig 360.6
hop to it 686.7
hop up
　intensify 157.7
　key up 171.7
hope n. 858
　(expectation 507.2)
　(desire 865.1)
　beyond hope
　successfully 731.12
　prosperously 734.9
　hopeless 859.7
　irreformable 945.19
　give up hope 859.5
　in hopes 858.9
　past ~ hopeless **859.7**
　irreformable 945.19
hope v. 858.6
　(expect 507.4)
hope against hope 858.7
hope for 865.11
　(expect 507.4)
hope for the best 858.7
hope chest 191.8
hopeful n. 129.1
hopeful adj.
　probable 472.5
　sanguine 858.9
　(expectant 507.7)
　(cheerful 836.7)
　be hopeful 858.7
hopefulness 858.2
　(cheerfulness 836.1)
hopeless
　despairing 859.7
　(impossible 471.6)
　(unpromising 512.5)
　(pessimistic 837.15)
　irreformable 945.19
hopelessness 859
　(impossibility 471.1)
　(disappointment 509.1)
Hopi 434.5
hopoff
　aeronautics 267a.25
　departure 293.1
hop-o'-my-thumb 193.5
hopped up 959.21
hopper

receptacle 191.1
jumper 309.3
hopple 751.7
hopples 752.2
hops 959.5
hop-sacking 219.5
hopscotch 840.11
hop skip and jump
　caper 309.2
　agitatedly 315.14
　hastily 684.7
　game 840.11
horde crowd 72.4
　masses 876.1
horehound 400.3
horizon
　sky line 213.4
　(distance 196.3)
　(outline 230.1)
　aeronautics 267a.22
　vista 441.6
　on the horizon 507.8
horizontal n. 213.3
　(flat 251.2)
horizontal adj. 213.8
　(low 207.7)
　(flat 251.5)
be horizontal 213.5
render horizontal 213.6
horizontality 213
　(lowness 207.1)
horizontalize 213.6
horizontally 213.10
　(flat 251.6)
horn n. cup 191.11
　pommel 215.23
　sphere 249.2
　point 253.2
　airplane 273a.10
　noisemaker 404.4
　music instrument 417.4
　alarm 669.1
horns of a dilemma
　perplexity 475.2
　logic 476.4
　dilemma 704.4
horn v.
horn in
　intrude 228.10
　meddle 682.14
hornbook 593.5
horned
　crescent-shaped 245.6
　hornlike 253.19
horned lizard, horned toad 366.18
horner 416.2
hornet
　battleplane 273a.2
　insect 366.24
hornet's nest
　danger 667.1
　predicament 704.2
　trouble 830.2
hornify 323.4
hornist 416.2
hornlike
　crescent-shaped 245.6

corniform 253.19
horn of plenty 639.2
hornpipe music 415.7
　horn 417.4
　dance 840.7
hornwork 717.3
horny
　crescent-shaped 245.6
　hornlike 253.19
　hard 323.5
horography 114.1
horologe 114.6
horological 114.9
horologist 114.7
horologium 114.9
Horologium 318.6
horology 114.1
horometrical 114.9
horometry 114.1
horoscope, horoscopy 511.4
horrib'e adj. vast 31.8
　terrible 649.8
　odious 830.14
　ugly 846.6
　fearful 860.15
horrible, horribly adv. 31.23
horrid terrible 649.8
　odious 830.14
　ugly 846.6
　vulgar 851.6
　fearful 860.15
horrified
　shocked 828.13
　terrified 860.14
horrify appal 830.7
　(be hateful 898.4)
　terrify 860.10
horrifying
　odious 830.14
　ugly 846.6
horripilate 383.7
horripilation 383.2
horror
　hypochondria 837.1
　fear 860.1
　abhorrence 867.2
　the horrors 959.2
horror-stricken
　828.13 ; 860.14
hors de combat
　impotent 158.8
　(infirm 655.24)
　exhausted 688.6
　checkmated 731.10
　defeated 732.12
put hors de combat 158.6
hors d'œuvre 394.4
horse n.
　suspender 214.3
　trestle 215.9
　steed 271.3
　(animal 366.2)
　man 373.2
　translation 522.2
　cavalry 726.8
a horse of another color 15.3
a horse on one 735.2

hold one's horses 133.7
horse v. 270.8
horse and foot 726.8
horse and horse 27.8
horse artillery 726.8
horseback 206.2
horsebacker 268.8
horse box, horsecar 272.20
horsecloth 223.10
horse coper
　cheat 548.2
　crafty rascal 702.4
　swindler 792.8
horse doctor 662.19
horse fiddle 404.4
horseflesh 271.3
horsefly 366.24
Horse Guards 726.7
horselaugh n. 838.3
horselaugh v. 838.7
horse litter 272.12
horseman 268.8
horsemanship
　riding 266.7
　animal culture 370.1
　skill 698.1
horse marine 269.1
horseplay 842.3
horsepower 157.1
horse racing
　game of chance 621.7
　racing 720.5
　sport 840.11
horse-radish 393.1
horse sense 498.3
horseshoe
　crescent 245.2
　dress circle 599.11
horseshoer 370.4
horsetail 369.6
horsewhip 972.6
horsewoman 268.8
horsy, horsey 271.12
hortation 615.4
　(advice 695.1)
hortative 695.8
hortatory
　homiletic 537.12
　persuasive 615.11
horticultural 371.9
　(botanical 369.11)
horticulture 371.1
horticulturist 371.2
　(botanist 369.9)
Horus 979.5
hosanna n. cheer 838.4
　paean 931.4
　glorification 990.2
hosanna int.
　hurrah 838.12
　praise God 990.16
hose stockings 225.29
　tube 260.6
　(conduit 350.1)
　washer 652.7
Hosea 513.2
hosier 225.36
hosiery
　stockings 225.29

hospice — huddle

hosiery (*continued*)
  merchandise 798.3
hospice inn 189.8
  hospital 662.17
hospitable
  liberal 816.3, 4
  sociable 892.12
hospital inn 189.8
  infirmary 662.17
  (resort 189.14)
  (asylum 503.8)
Hospitaler 996.11
hospitality
  liberality 816.1
  reception 892.4
hospital ship 726.11
hospodar 745.3
host crowd 72.4
  multitude 102.2
  armed force 726.6
  proprietor 779.2
  friend 890.6
  ~ of hell 978.2;
    980.1
  Eucharist 998.6, 8
hostage 771.2
hostel, hostelry 189.8
hostess
  proprietress 779.2
  host 890.6
hostile contrary 14.5
  disagreeing 24.6
  opposed 708.4
  unfriendly 889.3
  be hostile to 708.2
hostility *n.*
  opposition 708.1
  belligerence 722.1, 6
  enmity 889.1
  (hatred 898.1)
hostler, ostler
  stockman 370.4
  retainer 746.1
hot *n.* 382.1
hot *v.* 384.16
hot *adj.* violent 173.13
  near 197.8; 481a.8
  torrid 382.16
  (sweaty 299.11)
  (calefactive 384.22)
  (heated 384.23)
  peppery 392.5
  syncopated 415.29
  red 434.9
  orange 439.5
  fervent 821.6
  excited 824.9
  angry 900.13
  hot-tempered 901.7
  in heat 961.11
  be hot
  be near 197.5
  burn 382.13
hot air heat 382.4
  (air 338.1)
  (chinook wind
    349.9)
  twaddle 517.3
  untruth 546.1
  chatter 584.2
  boasting 884.1
hotbed *n.* origin 153.4

productiveness
  168.3
  garden 371.6
hot-blooded
  intrinsic 5.6
  hot 382.16
  rash 863.7
hotbox 312.5
hot-brained 863.7
hot cake 298.12
hotchpot, hotchpotch
  mixture 41.4
  confusion 59.2
hot dog 298.24
hotel house 189.3
  inn 189.8
hôtel Dieu 662.17
hôtelier, hotelkeeper
  779.2
hotfoot 684.7
hothead 901.4
hotheaded
  violent 173.13
  excitable 825.10
  impetuous 863.7
  hot-tempered 901.7
hothouse 371.6
  (heater 386.5)
hot iron 384.11
hotness 382.1
hot-press 255.4
hot-short 328.4
hot-shot 274.5
hot spring
  hot water 382.5
  health resort 662.17
hotspur
  violent 173.6
  rash person 863.2
  ill-humored person
    901.4
hot-tempered 901.7
Hottentot
  Negro 431.4
  barbarian 876.7
hot water heat 382.5
  (water 337.1)
  predicament 704.2
  trouble 830.2
  in hot water 704.11
hot wave 382.3
hot wind 382.4
hough disable 158.6
  cripple 659.8
hound *n.* dog 366.6
  (pursuer 622.4)
  scoundrel 949.1
hound *v.* follow 281.3
  chase 622.7
hound on urge 615.7
  hasten 684.2
hound-dog 366.6
houppe'ande 225.15
hour period 108.1
  the time 114.2
  from hour to hour
    138.12
  hour after hour
  long 110.11
  constantly 136.6
hourglass 114.6
houri 845.3

hourly *adj.* 138.11
  (frequent 136.3)
hourly *adv.* 136.6
house *n.* race 11.4
  (extraction 166.4)
  assembly 72.2
  dwelling 189.3
  astrology 318.8;
    511.4
  audience 418.8
  (spectators 444.1)
  theater 599.10, 11
  legislature 696.6
  company 712.5
  (firm 797.10)
  before the house
    461.26
house *v.* lodge 184.12
  protect 664.6
houseboat 273.4
housebreaker 792.2
housebreaking 791.1
house dog 717.6
housefly 366.24
household *n.*
  family 11.5
  population 188.10
  home 189.2
household *adj.*
  well-known 490.17
  common 613.11
  commonplace 843.6
  ordinary 849.3
householder 188.3
  (proprietor 779.2)
household troops
  726.7
household words 576.1
housekeeper
  householder 188.3
  manager 694.5
housekeeping 693.3
  set up housekeeping
    184.14
housel *n.* 998.6
housel *v.* 998.14
houseless 185.4
housemaid 746.2
house of cards
  weakness 160.5
  fragility 328.2
House of Commons
  696.6
**house of correction,
  house of detention**
  752.1
house of God 1000.1
**House of Lords,
  House of Peers**
  senate 696.5
  nobility 875.2
House of Representatives 696.6
house-raising 892.5
housetop *n.* top 210.4
  roof 223.5
housewares 798.3
housewarming 892.5
housewife 191.4
housewifery 693.3
housewright 690.7
housing abode 189.1

horsecloth 223.10
  cloak 225.15
  airdrome 267a.28
housings 717.2
Houyhnhnm 271.4
hovel 189.4
hover impend 152.2
  be high 206.9
  rove 266.14
  aviate 267a.30
  soar 305.6
  be light 320.5
  be irresolute 605.4
how why 155.6
  inquiry 461.27
  in what way 627.8
  (by means of 632.4)
  and how! 535.8
howbeit 30.8
how come 461.27
**how-do-you-do, how-
  do-ye, how-d'ye-do,
  how-de-do** 8.3;
  704.2
however
  gradually 26.5
  notwithstanding
    30.8
  but 469.7, 8
  anyhow 627.9
howitzer 727.11
howl *n.* ululation 412.1
  wail 839.1
howl *v.* blow 349.22
  yowl 411.5; 412.1
  wail 839.9
howler
  funny mistake 405.3
  blunder 495.3
  (absurdity 497.1)
  lie 546.2
howling *n.* 412.1
howling *adj.* vast 31.8
  ululant 412.3
howsoever 26.5
hoy 273.4
hoyden, hoiden
  tomboy 129.5
  virile 159a.3
  rude person 851.4
hub circle 247.2
  axis 312.5
  fireplace 386.2
hubble circle 247.2
  axis 312.5
hubbly 250.9
hubbub turmoil 59.4
  agitation 315.1
  noise 404.2
  (outcry 411.2)
  bustle 682.6
hubby 250.9
huckleberry 298.31
huckster 797.3
huddle *n.*
  confusion 59.2
  conference 588.3
  go into a huddle
  assemble 72.10
  confer 588.8
huddle *v.*
  derange 61.2

900

assemble 72.10
be near 197.5
don 225.43
Hudibrastic
verse 597.13
burlesque 856.7
hue *n.* 428.1
hue and cry
outcry 411.2
search 461.2
chase 622.2
alarm 669.1
hue *v.* give cry 411.7
color 428.9
hued 428.13
hueless 429.6
huff *n.* quarrel 713.3
dudgeon 900.2
huff *v.* distend 194.8
puff 349.22, 24
quarrel 713.7
intimidate 860.12
anger 900.10
offend 929.3
huffy 901.7
hug *n.*
welcome 892.4
embrace 894.4;
902.3
hug *v.* cohere 46.5
be near 197.5
~ a belief 606.5
hold 781.4
seize 789.9
receive a friend 888.3
welcome 892.11
embrace 902.8
hug oneself
be pleased 827.5
be content 831.3
rejoice 838.5
be proud of 878.4
boast 884.5
hug the shore, hug the land
be near 197.5
navigate 267.30
approach 286.2
huge 192.15
(vast 31.8)
hugeness 192.3
huggermugger *n.* 528.2
in huggermugger 528.24
huggermugger *v.* 528.11
huggermugger *adj.*
confused 59.8
secret 528.21
huggermugger *adv.*
in disorder 59.13
secretly 528.24
huggermuggery 528.2
Huguenot 984.14
hula 840.7
hulk main part 50.3
ship 273.1
hulky large 192.13
awkward 699.12
ungraceful 846.8

hull *n.*
main part 50.3
saddle 215.23
husk 223.14
hull *v.* peel 226.5
shoot 284.13
hullabaloo, hullaballoo 404.2
(outcry 411.2)
raise a hullabaloo 404.6
hum *n.*
faint sound 405.2
(bombilation 406.3)
(rumble 407.1)
falsehood 546.1
hum *v.* drone 405.6
(bombilate 406.9)
insect sound 412.2
sing 416.20
deceive 545.7
human *n.* 372.3
human *adj.* 372.5
(fleshly 364.4)
humane
cultural 537.12
charitable 906.7
compassionate 914.6
humanism
philosophy 451.11
education 537.4
humanistic
human 372.5
cultural 537.12
humanitarian *n.* 911.1
humanitarian *adj.* 906.7
humanitarianism
mankind 372.4
benevolence 906.1
humanities
studies 537.4
belles-lettres 560.8
humanity man 372.1
lenity 740.1
humanitarianism 906.1
compassion 914.1
humanize 894.11
humankind 372.1
humble *v.* 879.3
humble oneself
submit 725.3
be humble 879.2
be penitent 950.3
worship 990.9
humble *adj.*
inferior 34.5
plebeian 876.11
(unimportant 643.10)
lowly 879.4
(submissive 725.5)
(meek 826.10)
(ignoble 876.11)
(modest 881.5)
(servile 886.4)
be humble 879.2
humbled 879.5
humblehearted,

humble-minded 879.4
humbleness 879.1
humbly 879.7
humbug *n.*
nonsense 517.2
falsehood 544.2
deception 545.1
deceiver 548.1, **3**
swindler 792.8
humbug *v.* 545.7
humbugger
deceiver 548.1
swindler 792.8
humdinger
excellent thing 648.4
man of action 682.10
humdrum *n.* 841.3
humdrum *adj.*
uniform 16.5
repetitional 104.7
tedious 841.8
Humean 989.8
humectate 337.5
humectation
watering 337.2
moisture 339.1
humid 339.7
humidification 339.1
humidify 339.5
humidity 339.1
humidor
humidity 339.4
tobacco jar 392a.2
humify 339.5
humiliate
humble 879.3
(disgrace 874.6)
disrespect 929.3
humiliated 879.2
humiliating
disreputable 874.8
humbling 879.6
humiliation
disgrace 874.1
mortification 879.1
humility 879
(submission 725.1)
(modesty 881.1)
(servility 886.1)
(piety 987.1)
Humism 989.3
Humist 989.4
hummer
speeder 274.5
man of action 682.10
humming 407.13
hummingbird 366.22
hummock 206.2
humor, humour *n.*
nature 5.3
tendency 176.1
fluid 333.2, 3
caprice 608.1
mood 820.1
(propensity 602.2)
wit 842.1
in the humor
willing 602.8
disposed 820.4
out of humor

discontented 832.5
sad 837.9
ill-humored 901.7
(displeased 828.14)
humor, humour *v.*
oblige 707.11
indulge 740.3
permit 760.3
please 829.4
flatter 933.2
humoresque 415.3
humorist, humourist 844
humorous, humourous witty 842.9
(amusing 840.22)
funny 855.5
humorsome, humoursome
capricious 608.5
ill-humored 901.7
humoul See **hamal**
hump *n.* 250.2
hump *v.* carry 270.8
speed 274.9
humpback 366.21
humpbacked 243.5
humph! 870.11
humpty-dumpty 192.7
humus 342.3
Hun destroyer 165.1
Hungarian, German 188.9
German soldier 726.4
hunch piece 51.3
protuberance 250.2
hunchbacked 243.5
hundi 800.7
hundred
number 98.8; 102.5
territory 181.2
hundredfold 98.27
hundredth 98.27; 99.3
hundred weight 319.4
Hundred Years' War 722.4
Hungarian *n.* 188.9
Hungarian *adj.* 188.11
Hungarian goulash 298.17
hunger *n.* 865.3
hunger *v.* 865.11, 12
hungry 865.19
be hungry 865.12
hunk
quantities 31.3
piece 51.3
lump 192.5
Hunker 141.3
Hunkerism 141.2
hunkers 235.5
hunks 819.2
hunky *n.* alien 57.3
Hungarian 188.9
hunky *adj.* 27.8
hunt *n.* search 461.2
chase 622.2
hunt *v.* seek 461.16
chase 622.7
hunt down 481a.3

hunter — hygiastics 902

hunt in couples
 resemble 17.7
 co-operate 709.4
hunt out
 search for 461.16
 discover 481a.3
hunter horse 271.3
 huntsman 622.4
 (shooter 284.8)
hunting 622.2
 (slaughter 361.7)
Hunting Dogs 318.6
huntsman rider 268.8
 pursuer 622.4
 (killer 361.8)
 (sportsman 840.17)
hunt the slipper 840.11
hurdle *n.* sled 272.13
 jump 309.1
hurdle *v.* 309.4
hurdler 309.3
hurdle race 274.4;
 720.5
hurdling 840.11
hurdy-gurdist 416.6
hurdy-gurdy 417.7
hurl *n.* 284.3
hurl *v.* throw 284.12
 attack 716.7
hurler 284.7
hurly-burly
 agitation 315.1
 excitement 825.3
hurrah, hurra *n.* 838.4
 (cry 411.2)
hurrah, hurra *v.* 838.8
 (cry 411.5)
hurrah, hurra *int.*
 838.12
 (hail! 883.7)
 (bravo! 931.13)
hurricane
 windstorm 349.11
 festivity 840.2
 party 892.5
hurried hasty 684.5
 excitable 825.9
hurriedly 684.7
hurry *n.*
 velocity 274.1
 haste 684.1
 excitement 825.3
hurry *v.*
 speed 274.9
 ~ away 293.5
 urge 615.7
 hasten 684.2, 3
hurry up
 accelerate 274.10
 hasten 684.2, 3, 8
**hurry-scurry, hurry-
 skurry** *n.* 825.3
**hurry-scurry, hurry-
 skurry** *adv.*
 hastily 684.7
 carelessly 863.8
hurst 367.7
hurt *n.* pain 378.1
 harm 649.2
 damage 659.3
 affliction 830.2

hurt *v.* collide 276.9
 pain 378.4
 suffer physically
 378.5
 harm 649.6
 (be malevolent
 907.5)
 damage 659.8
 suffer mentally
 828.9
 ~ the feelings
 830.3; 900.10
hurt *adj.*
 ~ physically 378.6
 (ailing 655.23)
 damaged 659.12
 ~ mentally 828.13
 offended 900.12
hurtful 649.10
 (painful 830.9)
hurtfulness 649.1
hurting *n.* 659.3
hurting *adj.*
 physically painful
 378.6, 7
 mentally painful
 828.13; 830.9
hurtle impel 276.7
 collide 276.9
hurtless 648.13
husband *n.*
 manager 694.1
 married man 903.7
husband *v.*
 save 636.8; 673.7
 take precaution
 864.4
husbandless 904.5
husbandman 371.2
husbandry
 agriculture 371.1
 management 693.3
 economy 817.1
hush *n.* 403.1
hush *v.*
 moderate 174.5
 quiet 265.6
 silence 403.4, 5
 (mute 581.5)
 muffle 408a.4
 ~ up 528.11
hush *adj.*
 quiescent 265.7
 silent 403.6
hush *int.* 403.9
 (speech 585.6)
hushcloth 408a.3
hushed *adj.*
 quiescent 265.7
 silent 403.6
hush money
 bribe 618.2
 payment 973.2
husk *n.* 223.14
husk *v.* 226.5
husking bee 892.5
husky *n.*
 sledge dog 271.2
 dog 366.6
husky *adj.*
 strong 159.10

dry 340.7
harsh-sounding
 410.9
 (speech 583.5)
hussar 726.4
hussy bag 191.4
 insolent person
 885.3
 strumpet 962.2
hustings
 rostrum 542.6
 arena 728.1
 court 966.1
hustle *n.*
 activity 171.2
 bustle 682.6
 haste 684.1
hustle *v.*
 derange 61.2
 escort 88.7
 impel 276.7
 joggle 315.8
 bustle 682.12
 (work 686.6)
 hurry 684.2, 3
hustler speeder 274.5
 man of action
 682.10
 (worker 690.2)
hustling 682.21
huswife See house-
 wife
hut, hutch 189.4
huzoor 877.2
 (Mister 373.3)
huzza *n.* 838.4
huzza *v.* 838.8
 (cry 411.5)
huzza *int.* 838.12
hyacinth
 fragrance 400.3
 blue 438.2, 3
 gem 847.8
hyacinthine 437.4
Hyades, Hyads 979.8
hyaena See hyena
hyalescence 425.1
hyalescent 425.4
hyaline heavens 318.2
 ocean 341.1
 transparency 425.2
hyalinocrystalline
 425.1
hyalite 425.2
hybrid *n.*
 mongrel 41.5
 word 563.8
hybrid *adj.* 41.10
hybridism 563.8
hybridize 41.6
Hydra monster 83.7
 productiveness
 168.3
 constellation 318.6
hydragogue 348.26
Hydra-headed 163.3
hydraulic ram 333.6
hydraulics 348.14
hydrochloric acid
 429.3
hydrocyanide 663.5

hydrocycle 272.14
hydrodynamic 333.8
hydrodynamics
 hydrology 333.4
 water 348.14
hydrodynamometer
 348.13
hydrogen 334.2
hydrographer 341.4
hydrographic 341.5
hydrography 341.3
hydroid 368.13
hydrokinetics
 hydrology 333.4
 water 348.14
hydrol 337.1
hydrology 333.4
hydrolysis 49.2
hydrolyze 49.4
hydromancy 511.3
hydromechanics
 348.14
hydromel 396.5
hydrometer 333.5
hydrometric 333.8
hydrometry 333.4
hydropathic 662.25
hydropathist 662.19
hydropathy 662.16
hydrophobia 503.1
hydrophone
 fluidometer 333.5
 sound device 418.6
hydropic
 swollen 194.10
 dropsical 655.25
hydroplane *n.*
 boat 273.4
 seaplane 273a.3
hydroplane *v.* 267a.30
hydroplaning 267a.1
hydropot 953.3
hydroscope 114.6
hydrostat 333.5
hydrostatic 333.8
hydrostatics
 aeronautics 267a.2
 hydrology 333.4
 water 348.14
hydrotherapy 662.16
hydrotic, hydrous
 337.1
hydrozoal 368.13
Hydrus 318.6
hyemal See hiemal
hyena, hyaena
 animal 366.3
 savage 913.3
 scoundrel 949.1
hyetograph 348.12
**hyetography, hyetol-
 ogy** 348.15
**hyetometer, hyetome-
 trograph** 348.12
**Hygeia, Hygea,
 Hygia, Hygiaea**
 654.1
hygiastics, hygiene
 656.2
 (therapeutics
 662.16)

hygienic 656.5
hygienist 656.3
hygre See eagre
hygric 339.10
hygrodeik 339.4
hygrograph
 aviation 267a.29
 ship 273.14
 humidity 339.4
hygrology 339.3
hygrometer
 aviation 267a.29
 humidity 339.4
hygrometric 339.10
hygrometry 339.3
hygrophanous 339.10
hygroscope 339.4
hygroscopic 339.10
hygroscopy 339.3
hygrostat 339.4
hygrothermal 339.10
hyle 316.2
hylic 316.8
hylicist 316.6
hylism, hylology, hy-
 lotheism 316.5
hylotheist 316.6
hylotheistic 316.9
hylozoism 317.3
hylozoist 317.4
hymen, hymeneal n.
 903.3
hymeneal adj. 903.14
Hymen 192.8
hymn n.
 sacred music 415.11
 glorification 990.2
hymn v. 990.10
hymnal, hymnbook
 music 415.21
 church 998.10
hymner 416.10
hymnist 416.14
hymnody
 composition 54.2
 sacred music 415.11
hymnographer 416.14
hymnography 415.24
hymnologist 416.14
hymnology
 composition 54.2
 music 415.11, 24
hyoscyamus 662.7
hyp, hip n. 503.2
hyp, hip v. 837.8
hypallage 218.2
hyperbatic 218.6
hyperbaton 218.2
hyperbola 245.2
hyperbole 549.1
 (figure of speech
 521.1)
hyperbolic 549.3
hyperbolize 549.2
hyperborean
 distant 196.5
 cold 383.8
hypercritical
 discontented 832.5
 fastidious 868.4
 censorious 932.11

hypercriticism
 prejudice 481.3
 discontent 832.1
 fastidiousness
 868.1
hyperdulia 990.1
Hyperion sun 318.4
 beauty 845.3
hypernormal 976.14
hyperorthodox 983a.8
 (dogmatic 474.15)
 (fanatical 503.18)
 (bigoted 606.7)
hyperorthodoxy
 983a.5
 (dogmatism 474.3)
 (fanaticism 503.7)
 (bigotry 606.2)
hyperphysical
 immaterial 317.6
 supernatural
 976.14
 (spiritual 994.22)
hyperphysics 994.1
hypertrophic 194.10
hypertrophy
 overexpansion 194.4
 ~ of the heart
 655.12
hyphen bond 45.1
 punctuation 550.8
hypnoidal state 994.6
hypnology
 hypnotic sleep 683.5
 mesmerism 994.6
hypnosis
 insensibility 376.1
 hypnotic sleep 683.5
 trance 994.6
hypnotic n.
 anesthetic 376.2
 sleep inducer 683.6
hypnotic adj.
 soporific 662.25
 sleep-inducing
 683.17
hypnotism n.
 fascination 617.1
 hypnotic sleep
 683.5
 mesmerism 994.6
hypnotist 994.13
hypnotize
 anesthetize 376.4
 charm 617.4
 mesmerize 994.19
hypocaust 386.1
hypochondria
 psychosis 503.2
 dejection 837.1
hypochondriac n.
 837.5
 (eccentric 504.1)
hypochondriac adj.
 psychoneurotic
 503.16
 sad 837.14
hypocrisy 544.2
 (sanctimony 988.2)
hypocrite n.
 canter 548.4

 (affecter 853.4)
 (attitudinarian
 882.5)
 religious ~ 988.6
hypocrite, hypocriti-
 cal adj. 544.8
 (affected 853.6)
 (sanctimonious
 988.11)
hypocrize 544.6
hypodermic 223.32
hypostasis
 substantiality 3.1
 substance 316.2
hypostatic 3.4
hypothec 771.1
hypothecate 771.5
hypothecation 771.1
hypothesis
 accounting for 155.1
 premise 476.4
 (philosopheme
 451.24)
 theory 514.1
hypothesist 514.5
hypothesize
 account for 155.3
 theorize 514.6
hypothetical
 uncertain 475.12
 proposition 476.17
 theoretical 514.9
 (imaginary 515.12)
hyppish
 hypochondriac
 503.16
 dejected 837.14
hyps 503.2; 837.1
hypsographic
 altimetric 206.18
 measuring 466.11
hypsography
 altitude 206.8
 measurement 466.8
hypsometer
 altitude 206.8
 aviation 267a.29
hypsometric
 hypsographic 206.18
 measuring 466.11
hypsometry
 altitude 206.8
 measurement 466.8
hypsophobia 860.4
hysteria
 psychosis 503.2
 nervous disorder
 655.14
hysterical
 psychoneurotic
 503.15
 uncontrolled 608.5
 overwrought 824.10
 frightened 860.14
hysterics
 psychosis 503.2
 nervous disorder
 655.14
 frenzy 825.4
hysteron proteron
 218.2

I

I 79.4
 the I 994.11
iamb, iambic n. 597.6
iambic adj. 597.13
iambus 597.6
Ibanag 560.4
ibex 366.9
ibid., ibidem 13.8
Icarus
 aeronaut 269a.1
 daredevil 863.2
ice smooth 255.2
 frozen dessert
 298.13
 frozen water 383.5
 (refrigeration
 385.1)
 freeze 385.4
 refrigerant 387.2
 on ice 474.9
ice age 383.5
ice bag 387.1
ice bear 366.15
iceberg 383.5
iceblink 420.10
iceboat 273.4
icebound
 bound 229.4; 751.11
 frozen out 383.9
icebox 387.1
ice-built 383.9
ice canoe 273.4
icecap 383.5
ice chest 387.1
ice-cold 383.9
ice cream 298.13
ice-cream cone
 cone 249.4
 food 298.13
ice-cream soda
 298.4, 13
iced tea 298.4
icehouse 387.1
Iceland 383.4
Icelandic 560.4
icelike 383.9
ice machine 387.1
ice pack ice 383.5
 cooler 387.1
icequake, ice storm
 383.5
ice yacht 273.4
icicle 383.5
Ichabod 874.3
ichnite 550.4
ichnography art 556.1
 plan 626.2
ichnolite 550.4
ichor 333.2, 3
ichorous 333.7
ichthyocol 352.3
ichthyologist 368.2
ichthyology 368.1
ichthyomancy 511.3
ichthyotomist 368.2
ichthyotomy 368.1
icon copy 21.1
 figure 554.4
 sacred image 998.8

iconic 554.9
iconoclasm 984.1
iconoclast
　destroyer 165.1;
　　913.1
　heretic 984.12
iconoclastic 984.22
iconoduly 991.1
iconography 554.1
iconolatry 991.1
icosahedron 244.2
icterine 436.6
　(discolored 440a.3)
icterus
　yellowness 436.2
　ailment 655.5
ictus spasm 315.7
　music 413.23
　accent 580.4
　meter 597.6
　seizure 655.3
icy 383.9
　(frozen 385.6)
idea
　modicum 32.2
　notion 453.1
　(thought 451.1)
　(conviction 484.2)
　supposition 514.2
　give an idea of 537.9
　have no idea 491.6
ideaed, idea'd, idea-
　genous 453.2
ideal n. 52.4
ideal adj. 515.12
　(unreal 2.8)
idealism
　immaterialism 317.3
　(spiritualism 994.4)
　philosophy 415.14
　fancy 515.2
　art 556.6
idealist
　immaterialist 317.4
　visionary 515.7
idealistic
　imaginary 515.12
　romantic 594.7
ideality, idealization
　515.2, 4
idealize imagine 515.8
　spiritualize 994.20
ideate 453.1
ideational 453.2
idee 453.1
idée fixe idea 453.1
　prejudice 481.2
　monomania 503.7
identical 13.6
　(equivalent 27.9)
　be identical 13.4
identically 13.8
identification
　identity 13.1
　comparison 464.1
identify 481a.6
identity 13
　(similarity 17.1)
　(equivalence 27.2)
　(individuality 79.2)
ideogram, ideograph

character 561.1
　writing 590.9
ideology 450.4
ideophone
　sound symbol
　　402.4
　word 562.1
ideophonetics 402.5
ideophonous 402.12
Ides of March 601.3
id est 522.9
idiocrasy
　particularity 79.2
　tendency 176.1
　eccentricity 503.6
　temperament 820.1
idiocratic
　intrinsic 5.6
　peculiar 79.8
　tending to 176.3
　eccentric 503.17
idiocy 499.3
　(insanity 503.1)
idiologism 569.1
idiom
　language 560.1;
　　563.5
　phrase 566.1
　diction 569.1
idioplasm 357.3
idioplasmic 357.9
idiosyncrasy
　particularity 79.2
　eccentricity 503.6
　(oddity 83.3)
　temperament 820.1
idiosyncratic
　intrinsic 5.6
　peculiar 79.8
　tending to 176.3
　eccentric 503.17
idiot 501.1
　(impotent 158.3)
　(madman 504.1)
idiotic 499.13
　(crazy 503.12)
idioticon
　language 563.5
　dictionary 593.4
idiotism
　mental deficiency
　　499.3
　phrase 566.1
idle v. 683.8
　(do nothing 681.2)
idle adj.
　trivial 643.11
　useless 645.8
　inactive 683.12
　(inert 172.3)
idlehood 683.2
idleman 683.7
idleness 683.2
　(rest 142.2)
　(inertness 172.1)
　(inaction 681.1)
　(leisure 685.1)
　(dereliction 927.1)
idler 683.7
　(dawdler 275.4)

(neglector 460.3)
(beggar 767.2)
idleset n. 683.2
idleset adj. 683.12
idleship 683.7
idlesse, idling n. 683.2
idling adj. 683.12
Ido 560.5
idol n. desire 865.8
　sweetheart 897.7
　favorite 899.1
　fetish 991.4
　(figure 554.4)
idol v. 991.6
idolater 991.5
　(pagan 984.20)
idolatrize 991.6
idolatrous 991.7
　(pagan 984.28)
　(worshiping 990.15)
idolatry
　adoration 897.1
　idol worship 991
　(paganism 984.10)
idolism, idolization
　897.1
idolize adore 897.11
　idolatrize 991.6
　(revere 928.4)
　(worship 990.9)
idolizer 991.5
　(worshiper 990.8)
idoloclast 165.1
idolodulia, idoloman-
　cy, idolomania 991.1
idolothyte 990.6
idolothytic 991.7
idolum 980a.1
idoneous 23.11
idyl, idyll 597.2
idylist, idyllist 597.10
idyllic 597.13
if 8.8; 469.8
　(supposing 514.13)
i' faith 535.8
igloo, iglu 189.4
igneous 382.17
ignis fatuus 420.11
　(unsubstantiality
　　4.3)
　(illusion 443.9)
　(specter 980a.1)
ignite 384.17
　(light 420.21)
ignited 382.17
igniter 388.4
ignition
　automobile 272.16
　fire 382.8
　kindling 384.4
ignoble vulgar 851.6
　disreputable 874.8
　lowborn 876.11
　(unimportant
　　643.10)
　(renownless 874.10)
　(humble 870.4)
ignominious 874.8
ignominy 874.1
ignoramus 493
　(fool 501.1)
　(novice 541.6)

(dupe 547.1)
(bungler 701)
ignorance 491
　(unintelligence
　　499.1)
　(unskillfulness
　　699.1)
　plead ignorance
　　937.6
ignorant n. 493.1
ignorant adj. 491.8
　(unintelligent
　　499.11)
　(unaccustomed
　　614.3)
　(immature 674.8)
　(inexperienced
　　699.14)
　be ignorant 491.6
　(not understand
　　519.5)
　(be inexperienced
　　699.6)
ignorantism 491.1
ignorantly 491.16
ignore neglect 460.5
　(not observe 773.3)
　be incredulous
　　487.3
　be ignorant 491.6
　not observe 773.3
　excuse 918.3
　snub 930.7
ignored 460.10
ignorer 460.3
Igorot, Igorote 560.4
iguana 366.18
ileum 350.4
Ilithyia See Eileithyia
　161.3
ilium 221.4
ilk 13.6
ill n. 649.2
　bear ill 825.6
ill adj. bad 649.8
　sick 655.23
　feel ill 655.21
ill adv. 649.11
　ill at ease 828.14
ill off
　unfortunate 735.9
　ill-provided 640.12
　impoverished 804.7
ill-adapted 24.7
ill-advised
　indiscriminate
　　465a.3
　illogical 477.10
　foolish 499.15
　inexpedient 647.3
　ill-managed 699.17
ill-affected 901.7
ill'apse n. 294.1
illapse v. 144.8
illaqueate 545.9
ill-assorted 24.8
illation 480.1
illative 478.5
illaudable 932.13
ill-balanced 28.3
ill-behaved 895.6

ill blood — imbricate

ill blood hate 898.1
  ill-humor 901.1
  malevolence 907.1
ill-boding 512.5
ill-bred 895.6
ill breeding 895.1
  (vulgarity 851.1)
ill-conditioned
  evil 649.8
  difficult 704.8
  discourteous 895.6
  malevolent 907.6
  vicious 945.11
ill-contrived
  inexpedient 647.3
  evil 649.8
  ill-managed 699.17
  malevolent 907.6
ill-defined 447.5
ill-digested 674.8
ill-disposed evil 649.8
  ill-humored 901.7
  (vindictive 919.6)
  malevolent 907.6
  vicious 945.11
ill-disposedness 907.1
illegal 964.5
  (fraudulent 545.13)
  (prohibited 761.4)
illegality 964
  (prohibition 761.1)
illegally 964.7
illegibility 519.1
illegible 519.6
render illegible
  552.2
illegitimacy 964.1
illegitimate n. 167.5
illegitimate adj.
  spurious 545.13
  illegal 964.5
ill-fated 512.5
ill-favored, ill-
  favoured 846.8
ill-furnished 640.12
ill-humor, ill-
  humour 901
  (gruffness 895.2)
  (resentment 900.1)
  (malevolence 907.1)
  (misanthropy 910.1)
ill-humored, ill-
  humoured 901.7
  (gruff 895.7)
  (angry 900.13)
  (malevolent 907.6)
  (misanthropic
  910.3)
illiberal
  bigoted 606.7
  parsimonious 819.4
  (selfish 943.4)
illiberality
  bigotry 606.2
  parsimony 819.1
  (selfishness 943.1)
  incivility 895.1
illicit 964.5
illicitness 964.1
illimitability
  infinity 105.1
  boundlessness 180.4

illimitable
  infinite 105.3
  eternal 112.4
  unlimited 180.7
  unrestricted 748.15
illimited 105.3
illiteracy 491.1
illiterate n. 493.1
illiterate adj. 491.9
illiterature 491.1
ill-judged
  indiscriminate
  465a.3
  illogical 477.10
  foolish 499.15
  unskillful 699.17
ill-judging 481.9
ill-looking 846.8
ill-made 243.5
i'l-managed 699.17
ill-mannered 895.6
  (vulgar 851.6)
ill-matched 28.3
ill nature
  ill-humor 901.1
  malignity 907.1
ill-natured 907.6
illness 655.1
illogical 477.10
  (irrelevant 10.6)
  (improbable 473.3)
  (questionable
  485.11)
  (unauthentic
  495.16)
illogicality 477.5
ill-omened 512.5
  (dangerous 665.7)
ill-proportioned 243.5
ill-qualified 699.15
ill-requited 917.4
ill-seasoned 135.6
ill-smelling 401.4
ill-sorted 24.8
ill-spent 645.8
ill-starred
  inauspicious 512.5
  unfortunate 735.9
ill-tasted 395.5
ill-tempered 901.7
ill-timed inapt 24.7
  untimely 135.6
ill-treat 649.7
  (be severe 739.4)
ill-treatment
  maltreatment 649.4
  malevolence 907.3
illume 420 20
illuminant n.
  light 420.15
  (electricity 158a.1)
  (oil 356.1)
  (fuel 388.1)
  luminary 423.1
illuminant adj. 420.22
illuminate v.
  ignite 384.17
  light 420.20
  color 428.9
  explain 518.3
  kindle emotion
  824.2

adorn 847.11
inebriate 959.18
illuminate adj. 420.22
illuminated
  intoxicated 959.21
  light 420.22
  lit 423.14
illuminati 492.1
illuminating gas 334.2
illumination
  radiation 420.1, 14
  (luminary 423.1)
  engraving 558.1
  adornment 847.1
  celebration 883.1
illumine light 420.20
  kindle emotion
  824.2
ill-usage
  ill-treatment 649.4
  misuse 679.1
  abuse 907.3
ill-use n.
  ill-treatment 649.4
  misuse 679.1
ill-use v.
  maltreat 649.7
  misuse 679.2
illusion
  fallacy of vision
  443.9
  (unsubstantiality
  4.3)
  delusion 495.5
  (hallucinosis 503.5)
  (imagining 515.4)
illusive
  sophistical 477.9
  delusive 495.15
  deceptive 545.12
illusory
  chimerical 4.6
  sophistical 477.9
  delusive 495.15
  (imaginary 515.12)
  deceptive 545.12
  false 546.6
illustrate
  exemplify 82.6;
  522.6
  depict 554.7
  adorn 847.11
illustration
  example 82.2
  exemplification
  522.4
  representation 554.1
  engraving 558.1
  adornment 847.1
illustrative
  exemplary 82.11
  exemplificative
  522.8
  (graphic 518.6)
  representative 554.9
illustrious 873.17
illustriousness 873.2
ill will enmity 889.1
  malevolence 907.1
  envy 921.1
ill wind
  windstorm 349.11

bad influence 649.3
hindrance 706.2
adversity 735.2
Ilokano 560.4
image n. likeness 17.6
  copy 21.1
  (representation
  554.3)
  (picture 556.9)
  appearance 448.4
  idea 453.1
  figure of speech
  521.1
  figure 554.4
image v. 515.8
imagerial 515.12
imagery
  imagination 515.1
  fancy 515.4
  figure of speech
  521.1
  representation 554.1
imaginable
  possible 470.5
  fanciable 515.15
  (presumable 514.10)
imaginal 515.12, 15
imaginary n. 515.4
imaginary adj.
  numeral 84.7
  fanciful 515.12
  (unreal 2.8)
  (chimerical 4.6)
  (illusory 495.15)
  (suppositional
  514.9)
  (mythical 979.14)
imagination 515
imaginative 515.11
imagine judge 480.6
  believe 484.8
  suppose 514.6
  fancy 515.8
imagined 515.12
imaginer 515.7
imagining n. 515.1, 4
  (illusion 443.9)
  (hallucination
  503.5)
imagining adj. 515.11
imam, imaum 996.7
Imam, Imaum 745.5
imbecile n. 501.1
  (madman 504.1)
imbecile adj.
  helpless 158.9
  absurd 497.4
  idiotic 499.13
  (insane 503.12)
imbecility
  impotence 158.1
  helplessness 158.2
  absurdity 497.1
  mental deficiency
  499.3
imbed See embed
imbibe 296.2
imbibition 296.1
imbibitory 296.6
imbrangle See em-
  brangle
imbricate v. 223.27

imbricate — imparity

imbricate *adj.* 223.30
imbrication
　covering 223.1
　ornamentation 847.3
imbroglio
　confusion 59.2
　predicament 704.2
　broil 713.4
imbue infuse 41.8
　(pervade 186.12)
　(interpenetrate 228.9)
　infix 300.5
　saturate 337.5
　tinge 428.9
　inculcate 537.9
imbued
　combined 48.5
　addicted to 613.12
　~ with emotion 821.7
imbuement
　impregnation 41.2
　infixion 300.1
imburse 803.7
imitable 19.12
imitate copy 19.5
　(duplicate 90.2)
　(personate 554.8)
　(act 599.26)
　appropriate 789.8
imitated 19.11
imitatee 22.1
imitation *n.*
　copying 19.1
　(sham 545.6)
　(representation 554.1)
　copy 21.1
imitation *adj.* 19.12
　(sham 545.13)
imitative 19.12
　(representative 554.9)
imitator copyist 19.4
　disciple 542.4
immaculacy 652
　(innocence 946.1)
　(purity 960.1)
immaculate
　perfect 650.5
　clean 652.14
　(pure 960.2)
immaculateness 652.1
immalleability 323.1
immalleable 323.5
immanence 5.1
immanent 5.6
Immanuel 976.5
immaterial
　incorporeal 317.6
　(unsubstantial 4.5)
　(supernatural 976.4)
　(spectral 980a.4)
　(spiritual 994.22)
　unimportant 643.10
immaterialism
　idealism 317.3
　(spiritualism 994.4)
　philosophy 415.17

immaterialist 317.4
　(psychist 994.13, 14)
immateriality
　incorporeality 317
　(unsubstantiality 4.1)
　incorporeal being 317.2
　unimportance 643.1
　specter 980a.1
immaterialize
　unsubstantialize 317.5
　spiritualize 994.20
immature
　incomplete 53.4
　new 123.8
　youthful 127.5
　premature 132.8
　unprepared 674.8
　(ignorant 491.9)
　(imperfect 651.4)
immaturity
　youth 127.1
　(newness 123.1)
　prematurity 132.2
　nonpreparation 674.2
　(incompleteness 53.1)
　(imperfection 651.1)
immeasurability 105.1
immeasurable
　infinite 105.3
　unlimited 180.7
immeasurably 31.19
immediate
　continuous 69.6
　instantaneous 113.4
　punctual 132.9
　imminent 152.3
immediately
　instantly 113.6
　promptly 132.14
　(hastily 684.7)
immediateness 113.1
immedicable 859.7
Immelmann turn 267a.24
immelodious 414.4
immemorial 124.8
immense vast 31.8
　infinite 105.3
　spacious 180.6
　huge 192.15
immensity
　greatness 31.1
　infinity 105.1
　hugeness 192.3
immerge 310.5
immergence 310.2
immerse
　submerge 310.5
　(insert 300.7)
　baptize 998.14
immersed 229.4
immersion
　submergence 310.2
　(submarine 267.5)
　(insertion 300.2)
　(bathing 652.2)

　baptism 998.5
immethodical
　disorderly 59.8
　irregular 139.2
　inconstant 149.6
immigrant alien 57.3
　migrant 268.3
　incomer 294.4
immigrate 266.15
immigration
　migration 266.3
　entrance 294.2
imminence 152
　(expectation 507.1)
　(destiny 601.3)
imminent 152.3
　(future 121.7)
　(immediate 132.9)
　(approaching 286.3)
　(expected 507.8)
　(destined 601.13)
　(threatening 909.3)
　be imminent 152.2
　(await 507.5)
　(threaten 909.2)
immingle 41.6
immiscibility 47.1
immiscible 47.3
immission 296.1
immit 296.2, 5
immitigability 919.2
immitigable
　irremediable 859.7
　unforgiving 919.6
immix 41.6
immixture 41.1
immobile 265.7
immobility 150.1
　(inertness 172.1)
　(quiescence 265.1)
　(inaction 681.1)
　(inactivity 683.1)
immobilize 43.6
immoderate
　exaggerated 549.3
　excessive 641.5
　intemperate 954.4
immoderately 31.20
immoderation
　exaggeration 549.1
　overindulgence 954.1
immodest 961.9
immodesty 961.1
immolate 990.13
immolation 990.6
immoral 945.11
immorality 945.1
immortal
　everlasting 112.4
　fame 873.19
immortality
　everlastingness 112.1
　fame 873.5
immortalization 873.6
immortalize
　perpetuate 112.3
　make famous 873.13
　preserve 976.8
immotile, immotive 265.7

immovability 150.1
　(obstinacy 606.1)
immovable
　durable 110.9
　fixed 150.5, 6
　(inert 172.3)
　(quiescent 265.7)
　obstinate 606.6, 7
　(resistant 719.5)
immundity 653.1
immune free 748.18
　exempt 777a.3
immunity
　hygiene 656.2
　exemption 672.1; 777a.1
　freedom 748.1
　privilege 922.2
　impunity 970.2
immunize 748.10; 777a.2
immunology 655.19
immure 751.8
immutability
　stability 150.1
　(permanence 141.1)
　inflexibility 323.1
　divine attribute 976.2
immutable
　unchangeable 150.7
　inflexible 323.5
imp
　youngling 129.1, 3
　bad fairy 980.3
impack 300.5
impact clash 276.2
　contact 379.1
impair weaken 160.8
　deteriorate 659.6
　damage 659.8
　(disable 158.6)
　(destroy 162.4)
　(harm 649.6)
　(afflict 655.22)
impaired 659.12
　(unsound 160.13)
　(imperfect 651.4)
　(infirm 655.24)
　(blemished 848.3)
impairment 659.3
　(destruction 162.1)
　(disease 655.1)
impale, empale
　perforate 260.14
　crucify 972.8
impalement, empalement
　perforation 260.8
　execution 972.4
impalpable
　infinitesimal 193.10
　immaterial 317.6
　powdery 330.8
impanation 998.6
impanel, empanel
　list 86.3
　schedule 611.4
　~ a jury 969.10
imparadise 829.5
imparadised 827.10
imparity 28.1

impart — implicated

impart
  communicate 527.7
  (tell 582.6)
  give 784.8
impartial
  unprejudiced 498.12
  (unbiased 748.16)
  neutral 628.3
  just 941.3
  disinterested 942.5
impartiality 941.1
impartibility 321.2
impartible 321.10
impassable
  unpierceable 261.5
  blind 442.6
  impracticable 471.7
impasse 704.3
  (obstacle 706.2)
  at an impasse 704.11
impassibility
  unfeeling 823.1
  sufferance 826.4
impassible
  unfeeling 823.5
  indifferent 866.4
impassion 824.2
impassionable 822.6
impassioned
  vehement 574.7
  fervent 821.6
  amorous 897.14
impassive
  unfeeling 823.5
  (incurious 456.3)
  indifferent 866.4
impassivity
  unfeeling 823.1
  sufferance 826.4
impatience 825.1, 2
impatient 825.8
  (in haste 684.6)
  eager 865.17
  be impatient 825.6
impeach accuse 938.4
  arraign 969.10
impeachable 932.14
  (accusable 938.7)
impeachment
  deposition 738.3
  accusation 938.1
  arraignment 969.3
impeccability
  perfection 650.1
  innocence 946.1
impeccable 650.5
impeccancy 650.1
impecuniosity 804.1
impecunious 804.7
impede 706.4
  (counteract 179.3)
impedient 706.8
impediment 706.1, 2
impedimenta
  equipment 634.1
  impediments 706.2
  luggage 780.6
impedimentary, impeditive 706.8
impel drive 276.7
  motivate 615.7
  (move 264.7)

  (propel 284.10)
impellent 276.10
  (propulsive 284.15)
impend
  be imminent 152.2
  (approach 121.6; 286.2)
  overhang 214.5
impendence 152.1
impending
  imminent 152.3
  (immediate 132.9)
  (approaching 286.3)
  (expected 507.8)
  (threatening 909.3)
  overhanging 214.8
impenetrability 321.1
impenetrable
  solid 321.8
  hard 323.5
  unintelligible 519.6
impenitence 951
impenitent 951.3
  be impenitent 951.2
imperative n.
  decree 741.3
  duty 926.1
imperative adj.
  necessary 630.3
  authoritative 737.15
  imperious 739.5
  mandatory 741.8
  compulsory 744.3
  obligatory 926.9
imperator 745.2
imperatorial
  authoritative 737.15
  autocratic 739.5
imperceptibility
  invisibility 447.1
  latency 526.1
imperceptible
  infinitesimal 193.10
  slow 275.8
  invisible 447.4
  unknowable 491.15
imperceptive, impercipient 376.5
imperfect
  defective 651.4
  (inferior 34.5)
  (partial 51.8)
  (incomplete 53.4)
  (distorted 243.5)
  (erroneous 495.12)
  (wanting 640.11)
  (tolerable 648.11)
  (bad 649.8)
  (impaired 659.12)
  (immature 674.8)
  (mediocre 736.3)
  (blemished 848.3)
  vicious 945.11
  be imperfect 651.3
  (fall short 304.2)
imperfection
  inferiority 34.1
  faultiness 651
  (incompleteness 53.1)

  (distortion 243.1)
  (shortcoming 304.1)
  (inadequacy 640.1)
  (want 640.3)
  (immaturity 674.2)
  (mediocrity 736.1)
  (ugliness 846.1)
  vice 945.5
imperfectly
  slightly 32.12
  to a limited extent 651.5
imperforate 261.4
imperforation 261.1
imperial case 191.8
  beard 256.5
  sovereign 737.16
imperialism 737.4
imperialistic 737.16
imperiality 737.2
imperil 665.9
imperilment 665.1
imperious
  authoritative 737.15
  tyrannical 739.5
  arrogant 885.8
imperishable
  eternal 112.4
  unchangeable 150.7
  fame 873.19
impermanence 111.1
impermanent 111.6
impermeability
  closure 261.1
  density 321.1
impermeable
  unpierceable 261.5
  solid 321.8
impersonal
  general 78.14
  objective 316.10
  impartial 941.3
  disinterested 942.5
impersonate 554.8
impersonation 554.2
imperspicuity
  unintelligibility 519.1
  ~ of expression 571
imperspicuous
  obscure 519.7
  style 571.2
  (complex 59.10)
impersuasibility 606.1
impersuasible 606.7
impertinence
  irrelation 10.1
  insolence 885.2
impertinent
  irrelevant 10.6
  insolent 885.9
imperturbability 826.1
  (unastonishment 871.1)
imperturbable
  inexcitable 826.9
  (philosophical 451.38)
  (unastonishable 871.4)
  content 831.6
imperturbation

  quiescence 265.1
  inexcitability 826.2
  (insensibility 823.1)
impervious
  unpierceable 261.5
  insensible 376.5
  ~ to light 426.4
  impracticable 471.7
  callous 823.7
  hardened 945.18
imperviousness 261.1
impetiginous 653.17
impetigo 655.17
impetrate 765.5
impetration
  entreaty 765.2
  prayer 990.3
impetuosity
  violence 173.1
  haste 684.1
  excitability 825.1
  recklessness 863.1
impetuous hasty 684.5
  (sudden 113.5)
  impulsive 825.11
  reckless 863.7
impetus 276.1
  give an impetus 276.7
impiety 988
  (mockery 930.2)
  (wickedness 945.1)
  (irreligion 989.1)
impignorate v. 771.5
impignorate adj. 771.9
impinge 379.3
impious 988.10
  (sinful 945.11)
  (irreligious 989.6)
  be impious 988.7
implacability 919.2
  (hatred 898.1)
implacable 919.6
implant
  establish 184.11
  interject 228.8
  introduce 296.5
  infix 300.5
  plant 371.8
  inculcate 537.9
implantation 300.1
implanted
  intrinsic 5.6
  located 184.17
implausibility 485.3
implausible
  impossible 471.6
  improbable 473.3
  unbelievable 485.11
implead 969.10
implement 633.1
  (equipment 634.1)
implete 52.7
impletion 52.3
implex 41.9
impliability 323.1
impliable 323.5
implicate mean 516.5
  imply 527.8
  accuse 938.4
implicated
  related 9.6
  implied 526.7

implication — improbity

implicated (*continued*)
  be implicated in 56.2
implication
  complexity 59.3
  meaning 516.1
  intimation 527.4
  (latency 526.2)
  indication 550.1
  by implication 526.7
implicative
  inferential 526.7
  indicative 550.21
implicit, implied 526.7
  (hinted 527.14)
imploration
  entreaty 765.2
  prayer 990.3
imploratory 765.7
implore 765.5
imply show 467.7
  be probable 472.2
  mean 516.5
  be latent 526.4
  intimate 527.8
  indicate 550.18
impolicy 699.2
impolite 895.6
impolitic 647.3
imponderabilia, imponderability 320.1
imponderable
  chimerical 4.6
  thin 203.10
  light 320.7
  (immaterial 317.6)
imponderables 320.1
imponderous 320.7
import *n.* ingress 294.3
  meaning 516.1
  importance 642.1
import *v.*
  bring in 296.5
  insert 300.5
  mean 516.5
  be important 642.7
importance 642
  (greatness 31.2)
  (superiority 33.1)
  (precedence 62.1)
  (eminence 873.3)
  give importance to 642.8
  of importance 642.10
  of no importance 643.10, 13
important 642.10
  (great 31.6)
  (eventful 151.6)
  (influential 175.10)
  (memorable 505.19)
  (distinguished 873.16)
  be important 642.7
importation
  ingress 294.3
  (reception 296.1)
  insertion 300.1
imporosity 321.1
imporous 321.8
importunate
  urgent 642.13
  (solicitous 765.8)

compulsory 744.3
harassing 830.12
importune *v.* 765.5
importune *adj.* 830.12
importunity
  entreaty 765.2
  prayer 990.3
impose intrude 228.10
  ~ type 591.14
  task 686.8
  inflict 739.4
  prescribe 741.5
  levy 812.5
  exact dues 924.7
  assume 925.6
  ~ a duty 926.7
  command respect 928.7
  confirm 998.14
impose on, impose upon deceive 545.7
  be unfair 941a.2
imposer 228.4
imposing stout 192.12
  grandiloquent 577.7
  important 642.10
  exciting 824.12
  stately 873.18
  dignified 878.7
  ostentatious 882.8
imposition
  intervention 228.3
  lesson 537.6
  deception 545.1
  demand 741.2
  undue ~ 925.3
  ~ of hands 998.3
impossibility 471
  (no chance 156.5)
  (hopelessness 859.1)
impossible
  numeral 84.7
  not possible 471.6
  (hopeless 859.7)
  refused 764.6
  be impossible 471.4
  (have no chance 156.11)
impost *n.* 812.2
impost *v.* 812.5
impostor 548.3
  (sciolist 493.2)
  (masquerader 528.7)
  (boaster 884.3)
  (usurper 925.4)
imposture 545.1
  (simulation 19.3)
impotence 158
  (weakness 160.1)
  (unproductiveness 169.1)
  (uninfluentiality 175a.1)
  (insufficiency 640.1)
  (inutility 645.1)
  (failure 732.1)
impotent *n.* 158.3
  (weakling 160.4)
impotent *adj.* 158.8
  (weak 160.10)

(unproductive 169.4)
(useless 645.8)
(harmless 648.13)
(infirm 655.24)
(ineffectual 732.8)
be impotent 158.4
impound *v.* 751.8
impoverish
  weaken 160.8
  exhaust 638.2
  use up 677.6
  despoil 789.12
  render poor 804.6
impoverished 804.7
impracticability 471.2
impracticable
  infeasible 471.7
  obstinate 606.6
imprecate
  entreat 765.5
  curse 908.4
imprecation
  entreaty 765.2
  malediction 908.1
  prayer 990.3
imprecatory
  supplicatory 765.7
  maledictory 908.6
impregnable
  hard 323.5
  invulnerable 664.11
impregnant 168.9
impregnate
  imbue 41.8
  combine 48.3
  fructify 168.4
  (procreate 161.10)
  infix 300.5
  saturate 337.5
  inculcate 537.9
impregnated 48.5
impregnation
  imbuement 41.2
  (interjection 228.2)
  (ingress 294.1)
  combination 48.1
  procreation 161.2
  infixion 300.1
impresario
  entrepreneur 599.17
  director 694.1
imprescriptible 922.6
impress *n.*
  impression 154.1
  indentation 252.2
  mark 550.6, 7
  imprint 558.3
  print 591.2
impress *v.* strike 171.8
  cause sensation 375.5
  engrave 558.5
  print 591.14
  conscript 744.2
  crimp 791.11
  excite feeling 824.2
impressed
  believing 484.12
  affected 821.7
  be impressed with 821.3

impressibility
  physical ~ 375.1
  susceptibility 615.5
  emotional ~ 822.1
impressible 324.6
impression
  effect 154.1
  form 240.1
  indentation 252.2
  sensation 375.2
  appearance 448.4
  idea 453.1
  (conviction 484.2)
  supposition 514.2
  edition 531.2
  mark 550.6, 7
  engraving 558.3
  print 591.1
  emotion 821.1
  make an impression 171.8; 451.33
  under the impression 484.12
impressionable
  flexible 324.6
  physically ~ 375.6
  emotionally ~ 822.6
impressionism 556.6
impressionist *n.* 559.1
impressionist *adj.* 556.19
impressive
  sensitive 375.6
  believable 484.15
  vigorous 574.5
  dramatic 599.28
  important 642.10
  exciting 824.12
  (deep-felt 821.8)
  dignified 878.7
impressment 744.1
imprimatur 760.2
imprint *n.* caption 66.3
  indentation 252.2
  edition 531.2
  mark 550.7
  engraving 558.3
  print 591.2
  printer's ~ 593.7
imprint *v.*
  engrave 558.5
  print 591.14
imprison 751.8
  (intern 221.8)
imprisoned 751.12
  be imprisoned 754.2
imprisonment 751.2
improbability 473
  (small chance 156.4)
  (doubt 485.3)
improbable 473.3
  (doubtful 475.9)
  (illogical 477.10)
  (incredible 485.11)
  be improbable 473.2
improbity 940
  (falsehood 544.1, 2)
  (deception 545.1)
  (theft 791.1)
  (wrong 923.1)

impromptu — inanity

(injustice 941a.1)
(vice 945.1)
impromptu *n.*
  music 415.16
  extempore 612.1
  unpreparation 674.1
impromptu *adv.* 612.5
improper inapt 24.7
  foolish 499.15
  ungrammatical 568.3
  inelegant 579.3
  unfit 647.3
  untasteful 851.6
  wrong 923.4
  (undue 925.8)
  unworthy 940.9
  indecent 961.9
impropriate
  possess 777.5
  appropriate 789.8
impropriation
  possession 777.2
  taking 789.1
improprietor 779.2
impropriety
  unfitness 24.3
  barbarism 563.1
  solecism 568.1
  inelegance 579.1
  inexpedience 647.1
  bad taste 851.1
  wrong 923.1
  misdemeanor 945.6
  indecency 961.1
improvable 658.16
  (restorative 660.19)
  (remediable 662.27)
improve
  ~ the occasion 134.6; 658.7
  become better 658.6
  (increase 35.3)
  (rise 305.4)
  (elevate 307.5)
  (teach 537.9)
  (benefit 648.6)
  (return to health 654.3)
  (remedy 660.10)
  (recover 660.15)
  (mitigate 834.4)
  better 658.6, 8
  prosper 734.5
improved 658.14
be improved 658.7
improvement 658
  (increase 35.1)
  (progress 282.1)
  (rise 305.1)
  (elevation 307.1)
  (restoration 660.1)
  make an improvement 658.8, 11
improvidence 674.1
  (neglect 460.1)
improvident
  shiftless 674.11
  (negligent 460.8)
  unthrifty 818.4
  rash 863.6
improving 658.15

(restorative 660.18)
(remedial 662.25)
improvisation
  music 415.16
  extemporization 612.1
  unpreparation 674.1
improvisator
  musician 416.10
  speaker 582.5
  poet 597.10
improvise
  invent 515.10
  extemporize 612.3
improvised 612.4
improviser, improvisor 612.2
imprudence
  stupidity 499.7
  rashness 863.1
  (carelessness 460.1)
  (folly 499.6)
imprudent
  indiscriminate 465a.3
  inexpedient 647.3
  rash 863.6
  (careless 460.8)
impudence 885.2
  (discourtesy 895.1)
impudent 885.9
  (discourteous 895.6)
impudicity 961.1
impugn deny 536.2
  censure 932.7
impugnation, impugnment 708.1
impuissance 158.1
impulse
  impelling 276
  (thrust 716.3)
  (propulsion 284.1)
  blind ~ 477a.1; 601.2
  sudden thought 612
  motive 615.2
  give an impulse to
  propel 284.14
  motivate 615.7
  help 707.6
impulsion
  impulse 276.1
  motivation 615.2
impulsive
  impellent 276.10
  (propulsive 284.15)
  instinctive 477a.4
  unpremeditated 612.4
  (involuntary 601.14)
  (unprepared 674.7)
  hasty 684.5
  impetuous 825.11
  reckless 863.7
  be impulsive 612.3
impulsively 612.5
impunctual 133.8
impunity
  escape 671.1
  exemption 970.2

(restorative 660.18)
with impunity 664.13
impure speech 579.3
  unclean 653.16
  unchaste 961.9
  (wicked 945.11)
  be impure 961.8
impurity
  ~ of speech 579.1
  uncleanness 653.1
  unchastity 961
  (vice 945.1)
imputable
  attributable 155.4
  blameworthy 932.14
  (accusable 938.7)
imputation
  attribution 155.1
  stigma 874.2
  blame 932.2
  accusation 938.1
imputative 938.5
impute attribute 155.3
  accuse 938.4
in 221.12; 294.8
  be in for it 972.11
  in for it 768.7
  in so far as, in that 155.8
inability
  impotence 158.1
  incompetence 699.1
inabstinence 954.1
inaccessibility 471.2
inaccessible
  distant 196.5
  impracticable 471.7
inaccordance 24.1
inaccordant 24.6
inaccuracy 495.4
  (neglect 460.1)
  (imperspicuity 571.1)
inaccurate
  incorrect 495.14
  (imperspicuous 571.2)
  ungrammatical 568.3
inaction
  inertness 172.1
  voluntary ~ 681; 683.1
  (permanence 141.1)
  (rest 142.2)
inactivate 683.11
  (mitigate 174.5)
inactive inert 172.3
  latent 526.6
  do-nothing 681.3
  idle 683.12
  (quiescent 265.7)
  (leisured 685.3)
  (reposing 687.6)
  be inactive 683.8
  (be quiescent 265.5)
  (shirk 623.8)
  (do nothing 681.2)
inactivity
  inertness 172.1
  latency 526.1
  idleness 683
  (quiescence 265.1)

(repose 687.1)
inadept 699.11
inadequacy
  inequality 28.1
  inferiority 34.1
  impotence 158.1
  insufficiency 640.1
  (shortcoming 304.1)
  (inutility 645.1)
  (imperfection 651.1)
  incompetence 699.1
inadequate
  unequal 28.3
  incomplete 53.4
  short of 304.3
  insufficient 640.8
  (ineffectual 158.11)
  (useless 645.8)
  (imperfect 651.4)
  incompetent 699.15
  unsatisfactory 832.6
inadequately 640.13
inadequation
  inequality 28.1
  inferiority 34.1
inadmissible
  inapt 24.7
  exclusive 55.6
  inexpedient 647.3
  intolerable 649.9
inadvertence
  inattention 458.1
  neglect 460.1
  mistake 495.2
inadvertent
  inattentive 458.10
  neglectful 460.8
  shiftless 674.11
inadvertently 458.14
inadvisability 647.1
inadvisable 647.3
  (bad 649.8)
inaffable 895.6
inalienable
  incommunicable 781.7
  indefeasible 922.6
inamorata 897.7
inamorato 897.6
in-and-out
  changeable 149.7
  windingly 248.8
  alternately 314.14
inane nugatory 158.11
  (unsubstantial 4.5)
  unthinking 452.3
  absurd 497.4
  (senseless 517.8)
  foolish 499.15
  trivial 643.11
  vain 645.8
inanimate
  inorganic 358.4
  lifeless 360.8
inanimation 683.1
inanition
  helplessness 158.2
  want 640.3
inanity
  unsubstantiality 4.4

inappealable — inclasp 910

inanity *(continued)*
  incogitance 452.1
  absurdity 497.1
  (nonsense 517.2)
  folly 499.6
  triviality 643.2
  worthlessness 645.2
inappealable 474.10
inappetence
  insensibility 823.1
  indifference 866.1
inappetent 866.4
inapplicability
  irrelation 10.1
  unfitness 24.3
inapplicable, inapposite 10.6
  (inapt 24.7)
inappreciable
  infinitesimal 193.10
  unimportant 643.10
inapprehensible
  stupid 499.12
  unintelligible 519.6
inappropriate
  inapt 24.7
  inexpedient 647.3
  (wrong 923.4)
  (undue 925.8)
inapt unfit 24.7
  (inapposite 10.6)
  impotent 158.8
  absurd 497.1
  inexpedient 647.3
  unskillful 699.11
inaptitude
  unfitness 24.3; 647.1
  impotence 158.1
  uselessness 645.1
  unskillfulness 699.1
inarch 300.6
inarticulate
  dumb 581.7
  indistinct 583.5
  be inarticulate 583.2
inarticulated 583.5
inarticulation 583.1
inartificial
  natural 674.9
  artless 703.4
  simple 849.3
inartificiality 703.1
inartistic 846.6
inasmuch 26.5
  inasmuch as 155.8
inattention 458
  (neglect 460.1)
  (clumsiness 699.1)
  (nonobservance 773.1)
  (recklessness 863.1)
  (indifference 866.1)
inattentive 458.10
  (deaf 419.8)
  (incurious 456.3)
  (neglectful 460.8)
  (forgetful 506.8)
  (inexpectant 508.7)
  (clumsy 699.12)
  (insensible 823.5)
  (reckless 863.6)
  (indifferent 866.4)

be inattentive 458.5
  (not think 452.2)
  (be negligent 460.4)
inattentively 458.14
inaudibility 403.1;
  419.2
inaudible
  soundless 403.6
  indistinct 405.9
  unhearable 419.9
inaugural
  preceding 62.4
  beginning 66.7
inaugurate begin 66.5
  install 755.4
inauguration
  beginning 66.1
  installation 755.2
  (celebration 883.1)
inauspicious
  inopportune 135.6
  ill-omened 512.5
  (predictive 511.11)
  (unfortunate 735.9)
inbeing 5.1
inborn 5.6
  (dispositional 820.5)
inbound 294.8
inbred 5.6
Inca Indian 434.5
  chief 745.3
incage See **encage**
incalculability 105.1
incalculable 105.3
incalculably
  extremely 31.19
  infinitely 105.4
  (numerously 102.6)
incalescence 382.1
in camera 528.24
incandent 382.17
incandesce
  burn 382.13
  heat 384.16
incandescence
  heat 382.1
  light 420.1
incandescent 382.17
incandescent light
  light 420.7
  lamp 423.3
incantation
  conjuration 992.1
  magic formula 993.1
incantator 992.2
incantatory 992.5
incapability
  impotence 158.1
  incompetence 699.1
incapable *n.* 158.3
incapable *adj.*
  impotent 158.8
  incompetent 699.15
incapacious 203.9
incapacitate
  disable 158.6
  weaken 160.8
  sicken 655.22
incapacity
  impotence 158.1
  ignorance 491.3

unintelligence 499.1
incompetence 699.1
incarcerate 751.8
incarceration 751.2
incarmined 434.9
incarn 316.7
incarnadine *n.* 434.3
incarnadine, encarnadine *v.* 434.7
incarnadine *adj.*
  434.10
incarnate *v.* 316.7
  (animalize 364.3)
incarnate *adj.*
  intrinsic 5.6
  embodied 316.8
  vicious 945.16
incarnation 316.4
  the Incarnation 976.5
incase, encase
  wrap 223.23
  infold 229.3
incasement, encasement case 191.8
  covering 223.1
incautious 863.6
incautiousness 863.1
incendiarism
  destruction 162.1
  arson 384.5
incendiary *n.*
  arsonist 384.6
  instigator 615.6
  firebrand 913.1
incendiary *adj.*
  destructive 162.6
  malevolent 907.6
incensation 400.7
incense *n.*
  fumigator 388.7
  fragrance 400.1, 3
  suaviloquence 894.1
  flattery 933.1
  oblation 990.6
  thurification 998.1
incense *v.*
  perfume 400.9
  excite hatred 898.4
  anger 900.10
  thurify 998.14
incense burner 400.5
incense wood 400.3
incensory
  perfumer 400.5
  thurible 998.8
incentive 615.3
incept 66.5
inception
  beginning 66.1
  cause 153.1
inceptive
  procreative 168.8
  ingressive 294.8
inceptor 541.5
incertitude 475.1
incessant
  continuous 69.6
  repetitional 104.6
  perpetual 112.4
  constant 136.4
incessantly 136.6
  (perpetually 112.5)

incest 961.3
incestuous 961.11
inch *n.*
  modicum 32.2
  short way 197.2
  length 200.6
by inches
  piecemeal 51.10
  slowly 275.11
inch by inch
  gradually 26.5
  piecemeal 51.10
  slowly 275.11
inch *v.*
  ~ **along** 275.5
  measure 466.10
inchoate *v.* 66.5
inchoate *adj.*
  beginning 66.7
  preparing 673.10
inchoation 66.1
inchoative 66.7
incident *n.* 151.1
incident *adj.* 177.3
incidental
  extrinsic 6.2
  circumstantial 8.5
  independent 10.8
  occasional 134.9
  going on 151.5
  chance 156.12
  contingent 177.4
  dependent 475.15
incidentally 134.11
incidental music 415.3
incinerate
  cremate 363.21
  burn 384.18
incineration
  cremation 363.2
  burning 384.3
incinerator 384.12
  (furnace 386.1)
incipience 66.1
incipient 66.7
incircumspect 460.9
incise sunder 44.8
  furrow 259.3
  open 260.11
  engrave 558.5
incision cleft 198.2
  furrow 259.1
  wound 659.4
incisive forceful 171.9
  violent 173.11
  vigorous 574.5
  intensely felt 821.5
incisor 253.3
Incitatus 271.9
incite induce 153.7
  inflame 173.8
  instigate 615.7
  (excite 824.2)
incitement 615.2
  (influence 175.1)
  (impulse 612.1)
incivic 910.3
incivility
  inelegance 851.1
  discourtesy 895.1
incivism 910.1
inclasp See **enclasp**

inclemency — incontestable

inclemency
  violence 173.1
  cold 383.1
  cruelty 907.3
  unmercifulness 914a.1
  (severity 739.1)
inclement cold 383.8
  unmerciful 914a.3
  (severe 739.5)
inclination
  tendency 176.1
  (bias 481.3)
  (intention 620.1)
  obliquity 217.1
  direction 278.1
  descent 306.1
  propensity 602.2
  disposition 820.1
  desire 865.1
  obeisance 928.2
  partiality 941a.1
incline *n.* 217.1, 2
  (precipice 212.3)
  (ascent 305.1)
  (descent 306.1)
incline *v.*
  influence 175.6
  (induce 615.8)
  tend 176.2
  slope 217.6
  direct 278.4
  gravitate 319.7
incline one's ear 457.4
incline to
  be willing 602.6
  prefer 609.9
inclined tending 176.3
  oblique 217.9
  sideling 236.6
  willing 602.8
  (minded 600.3)
  (desirous 865.16)
  disposed 620.4; 820.4
inclined plane 217.2
inclinometer 267a.29
inclose, inclosure See enclose etc.
include 76.3
included 76.4
be included 76.2
including
  inclusive of 37.9
  (with 88.9)
  comprehending 76.4
inclusion 76
inclusive 76.5
  (component 56.3)
  inclusive of 37.9
inclusory 76.5
incog
  unknown 491.14
  incognito 528.20
incogitable 452.4
incogitancy 452
  (unintellectuality 450a.1)
incogitant 452.3
  (mindless 450a.2)

(unintelligent 499.11)
(empty-headed 499.14)
incognitive 491.8
incognito *n.*
  masquerader 528.7
  disguise 545.5
incognito *adj.*
  unknown 491.14
  disguised 528.20
incognito *adv.* 528.24
incognizability 519.1
incognizable
  unknowable 491.15
  inunderstandable 519.6
incognizance 491.1
incognizant 491.8
incognoscible 491.15
incoherence
  nonadhesion 47
  (disjunction 44.1)
  delirium 503.3
incoherent 503.14
incombustibility 385.2
incombustible 385.8
income ingress 294.1
  receipts 810.1
  (gain 775.2)
  (assets 780.7)
  (funds 800.2)
  (remuneration 973.2)
incomer 294.4
  (alien 57.3)
  (intruder 228.4)
incoming *n.*
  ingress 294.1
  receipts 810.1
incoming *adj.* 294.8
incommensurability 10.1
incommensurate
  irrelative 10.5
  unsatisfactory 832.6
incommode
  hinder 706.4
  distress 830.3
incommodious 647.3
incommodity 647.1
incommunicable
  inexpressible 517.11
  inalienable 781.7
incommutable 150.7
incomparable 33.8
incompassion
  uncharitableness 907.2
  pitilessness 914a.1
incompassionate
  unbenevolent 907.7
  pitiless 914a.3
incompatibility 15.1
incompatible
  different 15.7
  disagreeing 24.6
  (impossible 471.6)
incompetence
  impotence 158.1
  (insufficiency 640.1)
  (inutility 645.1)

unskillfulness 699.1
incompetent *n.* 158.3
incompetent *adj.*
  impotent 158.8
  (insufficient 640.8)
  unskillful 699.15
  (useless 645.8)
incomplete 53.4
  (partial 51.8)
  (short 304.3)
  (insufficient 640.8)
  (imperfect 651.4)
  (immature 674.8)
  (uncompleted 730.3)
be incomplete 53.3
incompletely 53.6
  (partly 51.9)
  (unfinished 730.4)
incompleteness 53
  (shortcoming 304.1)
  (insufficiency 640.1)
  (imperfection 651.1)
  (immaturity 674.2)
  (noncompletion 730.1)
incomplex 42.6
incompliance 764.1
incompliant 764.5
incomposite 458.10
incomprehensibility
  infinity 105.1
  unintelligibility 519.1
incomprehensible
  infinite 105.3
  unknowable 491.15
  unintelligible 519.6
incomprehension 491.1
incompressibility 321.1
incompressible 321.8
inconceivability
  unbelievability 485.3
  unintelligibility 519.1
inconceivable
  unusual 83.10
  incogitable 452.4
  impossible 471.6
  improbable 473.3
  unbelievable 485.11
  ununderstandable 519.6
  wonderful 870.7
inconcinnity
  unfitness 24.3
  ugliness 846.1
inconclusive 477.10
incondite 851.7
inconformable 15.7
inconformity 15.1
incongruence 24.1
incongruent 24.6
incongruity
  difference 15.1
  disagreement 24.1
incongruous
  different 15.7

disagreeing 24.6
  colors 428.16
  illogical 477.10
  absurd 497.4
  foolish 499.15
  ungrammatical 568.3
inconnection, inconnexion
  irrelation 10.1
  disjunction 44.1
inconsequence
  irrelation 10.1
  unimportance 643.1
inconsequent
  irrelevant 10.6
  illogical 477.10
inconsequential
  illogical 477.10
  unimportant 643.10
inconsequentiality 643.1
inconsiderable
  small 32.8
  (few 103.3)
  (diminutive 193.8)
  fractional 101.2
  unimportant 643.10
inconsiderate
  unthinking 452.3
  inattentive 458.10
  neglectful 460.8
  unbenevolent 907.7
inconsideration 458.1
inconsistency
  difference 15.1
  unfitness 24.3
  unconformity 83.1
  sophism 477.2
  absurdity 497.1
  folly 499.6
inconsistent
  contrary 14.5
  disagreeing 24.6
  indiscriminate 465a.3
  illogical 477.10
  absurd 497.4
  foolish 499.15
inconsolable 837.12
  (in despair 859.7)
inconspicuous 447.4
inconstancy
  irregularity 139.1
  changeableness 149.1
  fickleness 608.3
  irresolution 605.1
  infidelity 940.2
inconstant
  irregular 139.2
  changeable 149.6
  (transient 111.6)
  (erratic 503.17)
  (irresolute 605.5)
  (fickle 608.6)
  uncertain 475.16
  nonobservant 773.5
  faithless 940.10
inconstantly 149.7
incontestability 474.1
incontestable 474.10

incontestably — indelicacy

incontestably 474.16
incontinence 961.2
  (intemperance 954.1)
incontinent 961.10
  (unrestrained 748.13)
  (intemperate 954.4)
  (dissipated 954.5)
incontinently 132.14
incontrollable
  obstinate 606.6
  unmanageable 704.10
incontrovertibility 474.1
incontrovertible
  sound 150.5
  conclusive 474.10
incontrovertibly 474.16
inconvenience 647.1
inconvenient
  inopportune 135.6
  unsuitable 647.3
  embarrassing 704.9
inconvertible 143.4
inconvincibility 487.1
inconvincible 487.4
incorporal 317.6
incorporality 317.1
incorporate v.
  join 43.5
  combine 48.3
  (form a party 712.7)
  include 76.3
  materialize 316.7
incorporate adj. 317.6
incorporated 48.6
incorporation
  combination 48.1
  inclusion 76.1
  association 709.2
incorporeal n.
  immateriality 317.2
  (unsubstantiality 4.3)
  (spirit 994.11)
  specter 980a.1
incorporeal adj. 317.6
  (unsubstantial 4.5)
  (spectral 980a.4)
incorporeity
  immateriality 317.1, 2
  (unsubstantiality 4.1)
  specter 980a.1
incorporeous 317.6
incorrect
  inaccurate 495.14
  (illogical 477.10)
  ungrammatical 568.3
  inelegant 579.3
  wrong 923.4
incorrigibility 606.1
incorrigible
  obstinate 606.6
  hopeless 859.7

irreformable 945.19
incorruptibility
  health 654.1
  trustworthiness 939.3
incorruptible 940.9
incorruption
  health 654.1
  innocence 946.1
incrassate
  expand 194.5
  thicken 321.7
incrassation 321.3
increase n.
  in degree 35
  (addition 37.1)
  (ascent 305.1)
  (improvement 658.1)
  ~ in number 102.3
  ~ in size 194.1
  ~ in temperature 384.1
  on the increase 35.6
increase v.
  ~ in degree 35.3, 4
  (reinforce 37.4)
  (ascend 305.4)
  (improve 658.6)
  ~ in size 194.6, 7
  enlarge 194.8
  exaggerate 549.2
increased 35.5
  (added 37.7)
  be increased 35.4
increasing 35.6
increasingly 35.7
incredibility 485.3
  (improbability 473.1)
incredible vast 31.8
  unusual 83.10
  unbelievable 485.11
  (improbable 473.3)
  wonderful 870.7
incredibly 31.21
incredulity 487
  (unbelief 485.1)
  (skepticism 989.3)
incredulous
  hard of belief 487.4
  (unbelieving 485.9)
  nullifidian 989.8
  be incredulous 487.3
incremate 363.21
incremation 363.2
increment
  increase 35.1
  (addition 37.1)
  adjunct 39.1
  expansion 194.1
increpation 932.3
increscent 318.5
incretionary 35.6
incriminate 938.4
incrimination 938.1
incriminatory 938.5
incrust cover 223.25
  line 224.2
incrustation
  coating 223.16

lining 224.1
incubate 370.8
incubation cause 153.1
  birth 161.3
  maturation 673.1
incubator origin 153.4
  animals 370.3
incubus weight 319.1
  hallucination 503.5
  dream 515.5
  nightmare 828.7
  object of fear 860.7
  evil spirit 980.2
inculcate 537.9
inculcation 537.1
inculpable 946.6
  (vindicable 937.10)
inculpate 938.4
inculpation 938.1
inculpatory 938.5
incultivation, inculture 674.2
incumbency
  weight 319.1
  office 625.4
  church 995.3
incumbent n.
  inhabitant 188.1
  rector 996.5
incumbent adj.
  overhanging 214.8
  overlying 223.30
  heavy 319.12
  incumbent on, incumbent upon 926.5, 9
incumber, incumbered etc. See encumber etc.
incunabula
  beginning 66.1
  infancy 127.3
  cause 153.1
  book 593.1
incur 177.2
incurable 859.7
incuriosity 456
  (impassiveness 823.1)
  (unconcern 866.1)
incurious 456.3
  (inattentive 458.10)
  (impassive 823.5)
  (unconcerned 866.4)
  be incurious 456.2
incursion n.
  encroachment 228.3
  overstepping 303.1
  attack 716.1
incursive 716.8
incurvation 252.1
incurvature
  curvature 245.1
  concavity 252.1
incurve 245.3
incurved
  curved 245.4
  concave 252.10
incus 418.5
indaba 588.3
indagate 461.17
indagation 461.3

indagative 461.24
indagator 461.13
indebted, endebted
  in debt 806.7
  grateful 916.4
  obliged 926.10
indebtment, endebtment 806.1
indecency nudity 226.2
  immodesty 961.1
indecent unclad 226.8
  immodest 961.9
indeciduous 150.7
indecipherable 519.6
indecision
  uncertainty 475.1
  (doubt 485.2)
  irresolution 605.1
indecisive
  vague 475.11
  irresolute 605.5
  (inconstant 149.6)
indeclinable 150.5
indecorous
  speech 579.3
  unseemly 647.3
  vulgar 851.6
  indecent 961.9
indecorum
  bad taste 851.1
  misdemeanor 945.6
indeed
  absolutely 31.16
  certainly 474.16
  yes 488.14
  truly 494.15
  (actually 1.9)
  I assure you 535.8
  really! 870.11
indefatigability
  perseverance 604a.1
  industry 682.5
indefatigable
  persevering 604a.3
  industrious 682.19
indefeasible
  unchangeable 150.7
  inevitable 601.11
  inalienable 922.6
indefectibility 650.1
indefectible, indefective 650.5
indefensible
  defenseless 158.9
  unjustifiable 941a.4
indeficient 650.5
indefinite
  general 78.14
  infinite 105.3
  aoristic 109.5
  indistinct 447.5
  vague 475.11
  obscure 519.7
indefinitely 31.19
indefiniteness 475.3
indeliberate 612.4
indelible
  unchangeable 150.7
  unforgettable 505.20
  deep-felt 821.8
indelicacy
  bad taste 851.1

912

immodesty 961.2
indelicate
  vulgar 851.6
  indecorous 961.9
indemnification
  compensation 30.1;
    973.1
  relief 707.4
  restitution 790.1
  atonement 952.1
indemnificatory
  compensating 30.6
  restitutive 790.5
indemnify
  compensate 30.4;
    973.3
  make restitution
    790.3
indemnity
  compensation 30.1;
    973.1
  amnesty 918.1
  atonement 952.1
  impunity 970.2
indent *n.* notch 257.1
  mark 550.7
indent *v.* list 86.3
  dent 252.9
  notch 257.5
  contract 769.5
  invoice 811.7
indentation
  concavity 252.1, 2
  notch 257.1
indented 252.10
indention 257.1
indenture
  compact 769.1
  pledge 771.1
independence
  irrelation 10.1
  freedom 748.1, 3
  wealth 803.1
Independence Day
  138.7
independent *n.* 748.7
Independent *n.* 984.14
independent *adj.*
  irrelative 10.5
  free 748.12, 17
indescribable
  immense 31.10
  wonderful 870.8
indescribables 225.21
indestructible 150.7
indeterminable 475.11
indeterminate
  general 78.14
  infinite 105.3
  chance 156.12
  vague 475.11
  (equivocal 520.5)
  obscure 519.7
indetermination
  fortuitousness 156.6
  uncertainty 475.1
  irresolution 605.1
indevotion 989.1
indevotional, indevout 989.6
index *n.*
  classification 60.3

  number 84.2
  list 86.1
  face 234.4
  indication 550.2
  typography 550.8
  dictionary 593.4
  of a book 593.7
index *v.* classify 60.7
  list 86.3
  indicate 550.18
Index Expurgatorius,
  Index Librorum
  Prohibitorum 761.1
indexterity 699.1
India 182.3
Indian *n.*
  constellation 318.6
  red 434.5
  stoic 823.2
  savage 913.3
Indian *adj.* 11.8
Indian gift 784.3
Indian giver
  dissembler 548.1
  schemer 702.4
  giver 784.7
Indian red 434.2
Indian summer 126a.4
Indian yellow 436.4
India-rubber, india-
  rubber 325.2
indicant *n.* 550.2
indicant *adj.* 550.21
indicate specify 79.5
  call attention to
    457.7
  denote 467.7
  (manifest 525.2)
  be probable 472.2
  mean 516.5
  intimate 527.8
  signify 550.18
  (evidence 467.7)
  (portend 511.9)
indicated 550.22
  (predicted 511.13)
indication
  manifestation 525.1
  intimation 527.4
  signification 550
  (evidence 467.1)
indicative
  significative 516.8;
    550.21
  (evidential 467.11)
  (predictive 511.11)
  suggestive 526.7
  be indicative 550.18
indicator
  airplane 267a.29
  witness 467.6
  sign 550.2
indicia 550.2
indicolite 438.3
indict accuse 938.4
  arraign 969.10
indiction era 108.2
  declaration 531.1
  decree 741.3
indictment
  accusation 938.1
  arraignment 969.3

indifference
  insensibility 823.1
  unconcern 866
  (incuriosity 456.1)
  (inattention 458.1)
  (apathy 823.1)
  (disdain 930.1)
  (irreligion 989.1)
indifferent
  inconsiderable 32.8
  insipid 391.2
  mediocre 736.3
  (unimportant
    643.10)
  (imperfect 651.4)
  insensible 823.5
  (regardless 460.8)
  (indolent 683.13)
  unconcerned 866.4
  (incurious 456.3)
  (inattentive 458.10)
  (neutral 628.3)
  (apathetic 823.5)
  (irreligious 989.6)
  be indifferent 866.3
indifferently 866.6
indigena 188.8
indigenal 188.11
indigence 804.1
  (want 640.3)
indigenous
  intrinsic 5.6
  native 188.11
  native-grown 367.17
indigent 804.7
indigested 674.8
indigestible 657.4
indigestion 655.13
indigitation 85.4
indignant 900.12
indignation 900.1
indignity 929.2
  (provocation 900.5)
  (malediction 908.1)
  (gibe 930.3)
  (snub 930.4)
  (personality 934.2)
indigo 438.4
indiligence 683.3
indirect
  resultant 154.6
  deviative 279.8
  (oblique 217.9)
  circuitous 311.6
  implied 526.7
indiscernible
  invisible 446.4
  unknowable 491.15
indiscerptibility
  completeness 52.1
  indivisibility 321.2
indiscerptible
  joined 43.12
  indivisible 321.10
indiscreet
  indiscriminate
    465a.3
  inexpedient 647.3
  rash 863.6
  improper 940.9
indiscrete 48.5
indiscretion

  foolish act 499.7
  (blunder 495.3)
  rashness 863.1
  (folly 499.6)
  misdeed 947.2
indiscretionary
  465a.3
indiscriminate
  extensive 31.7
  mixed 41.9
  disorderly 59.8
  diversified 81.3
  undiscriminating
    465a.3
  (purposeless
    621.21)
  be indiscriminate
    465a.2
indiscriminating
  465a.3
indiscrimination 465a
indispensability 630.1
indispensable 630.3
indispose 616.3
indisposed
  unwilling 603.5
  ill 655.23
indisposition
  unwillingness 603.1
  illness 655.1
indisputability 474.1
indisputable 474.10
indisputably 474.16
indissolubility 321.2
indissoluble
  joined 43.12
  unchangeable 150.7
  indivisible 321.10
indissolvability 321.2
indissolvable
  unchangeable 150.7
  indivisible 321.10
indistinct
  faint-sounding
    405.9
  dim 422.8
  indistinguishable
    447.5
  (hidden 528.17)
  undiscriminating
    465a.3
  vague 475.11
  obscure 519.7
  (inarticulate 583.5)
indistinction 465a.1
indistinctness 422.1
indistinguishable
  coincident 13.7
  indistinct 447.5
  without distinction
    465a.3
  vague 475.11
  unknowable 491.15
  unintelligible 519.6
indisturbance
  quiescence 265.1
  composure 826.1
indite compose 54.4
  write 590.14
inditement
  composition 54.2
  authorship 590.2

individible — inexactness

individible 321.10
  (whole 50.8)
individual *n.*
  integer 87.3
  organism 357.2
  person 372.3
individual *adj.*
  whole 50.6
  classificational 75.6
  special 79.7
  one 87.6
  subjective 317.7
  human 372.5
individuality 79.2
  (identity 13.1)
  (unusualness 83.3)
  (unity 87.1)
individualize 79.6
individually 87.10
indivisibility
  tenacity 46.2
  completeness 52.1
  inseparability 321.2
indivisible 321.10
Indo-Chinese languages 560.4
indocile 606.6
indocility
  impotence 158.1
  obstinacy 606.1
  (unwillingness 603.1)
indoctrinate 537.9
indoctrination 537.1
Indo-European languages 560.4
indolence 683.3
  (inattention 458.1)
  (neglect 460.1)
  (dereliction 927.1)
indolent *n.* 683.7
indolent *adj.* 683.13
  (dilatory 133.9)
  (slow 275.8)
  (negligent 460.8)
  (indifferent 823.5)
indomitable
  resolute 604.7
  (resistant 719.5)
  persevering 604a.3
indoor 221.9
indoors, indoor 221.12
indorse, indorsee etc.
  See endorse etc.
Indra rain 348.11
  thunder 406.4
  deity 979.4
indraft, indraught 294.1
in dubio 475.9
indubious
  certain 474.12
  believing 484.12
indubitable
  undeniable 474.10
  (believable 484.15)
  (manifest 525.4)
indubitably 474.16
induce cause 153.7
  (produce 161.8)
  persuade 615.9
  (influence 175.6)

be induced 615.10
  (consent 762.2)
inducement 615.2
  (cause 153.1)
  (allurement 617.1)
inducive 615.11
induct bring in 296.5
  instate 755.4
  church 995.7
induction
  reasoning 476.1
  drama 599.5
  church 995.6
inductional 615.11
inductive
  reasoning 476.17
  persuasive 615.11
  (provocative 617.5)
indue See endue
indulge
  ~ one's fancy 609.7
  humor 740.3
  permit 760.3
  favor 784.10
  delight in 827.6
  please 829.4
  ~ oneself 943.3
  ~ one's appetites 954.3; 957.3
indulgence
  lenity 740.1
  permission 760.1
  forgiveness 918.1
  intemperance 954.1
indulgent
  unprejudiced 498.12
  lenient 740.4
  permissive 760.6
  benevolent 906.6
  intemperate 954.4
indurate *v.* 323.4
indurate *adj.* 323.5
induration
  hardness 323.1, 2
  physical ~ 376.1
  emotional ~ 823.1
  impenitence 951.1
Indus 318.6
industrious 682.19
  (energetic 171.9)
  (studious 539.6)
  (persevering 604a.3)
  (laboring 686.9)
industry
  vocation 625.5
  assiduity 682.5
  (perseverance 604a.1)
  work 686.3
indweller 188.1
indwelling *n.* 5.1
indwelling *adj.* 5.6
inearth 363.20
inebriant *n.* 959.4
inebriant *adj.* 959.24
inebriate *v.* 959.18
inebriate, inebriated *adj.* 959.21
inebriating, inebriative 959.24
inebriety 959.1

inebrious 959.21
inedible
  unsavory 395.5
  (dislikable 867.9)
  unpleasant 830.10
ineducation 491.1
ineffable
  immense 31.10
  inexpressible 517.11
  wonderful 870.8
ineffective
  impotent 158.8, 11
  (useless 645.8)
  uninfluential 175a.2
  abortive 732.8
  (insufficient 640.8)
ineffectiveness 175a.1
ineffectual
  nugatory 158.11
  unproductive 169.4
  uninfluential 175a.2
  insignificant 643.10
  abortive 732.8
ineffectuality
  impotence 158.1
  noninfluence 175a.1
  unimportance 643.1
inefficacious
  impotent 158.8
  uninfluential 175a.2
  useless 645.8
  abortive 732.8
inefficacy
  impotence 158.1
  noninfluence 175a.1
  uselessness 645.1
  failure 732.1
inefficiency
  impotence 158.1
  (inutility 645.1)
  unskillfulness 699.1
inefficient
  impotent 158.8
  (insufficient 640.8)
  (ineffectual 732.8)
  unproficient 699.11
  become inefficient 699.10
inelastic 326.3
  (inflexible 323.5)
inelasticity 326
  (inflexibility 323.1)
inelegance
  ~ of diction 579
  (barbarism 563.1)
  ugliness 846.1
  bad taste 851.1
  indecency 961.1
inelegant
  speech 579.3
  (barbarous 563.15)
  (ungrammatical 568.3)
  ungraceful 699.12
  unprepossessing 846.1
  unrefined 851.6
  indecent 961.9
ineligible 647.3
ineluctability 474.1
ineluctable 601.11
inept impotent 158.8

  (useless 645.8)
  absurd 497.4
  inexpedient 647.3
ineptitude
  impotence 158.1
  absurdity 497.1
  folly 499.6
  uselessness 645.1
inequal disparate 28.3
  rough 256.12
inequality 24.2; 28
  (difference 15.1)
  (superiority 33.1)
  (inferiority 34.1)
inequation 28.1
inequitable 941a.3
inequity 941a.1
ineradicable 150.7
inerrability 946.1
inerrable, inerrant 474.14
inert passive 172.3
  (stable 150.5)
  (quiescent 265.7)
  (inactive 681.3; 683.12)
  latent 526.6
  languid 683.14
  be inert 172.2
  (not do 681.2)
inert gas 334.2
inertia inertness 172.1
  quiescence 265.1
  latency 526.1
  indolence 683.3
inertness 172
  (permanence 141.1)
  (noninfluence 175a.1)
  (quiescence 265.1)
  (inaction 681.1; 683.1)
inerudite 491.9
inerudition 491.1
inescapable 601.11
inesculent
  unsavory 395.5
  unpleasant 830.10
inessential 10.6
inestimable
  superexcellent 648.10
  priceless 814.5
inevasible 601.11
inevitability
  certainty 474.1
  necessity 601.1
inevitable 601.11
  (unavoidable 474.11)
  (requisite 630.3)
inevitably 154.7
inexact
  inaccurate 495.14
  (imperspicuous 571.2)
  grammar 575.2
inexactitude 495.4
inexactness 495.4
  (neglect 460.1)
  (imperspicuity 571.1)

914

inexcitability 826
  (restraint 751.1)
  (insensibility 823.1)
  (unastonishment 871.1)
inexcitable 826.9
  (philosophical 451.38)
inexcitably 826.12
inexcusable 941a.4
inexecution 730.1
inexertion 683.3
inexhaustibility 105.1
inexhaustible
  infinite 105.3
  plentiful 639.7
inexistence 2.1
  (unsubstantiality 4.1)
inexistent 2.7
inexorability 914a.1
inexorable
  inevitable 601.11
  resolute 604.7
  (obstinate 606.6)
  strict 739.5
  pitiless 914a.3
  unforgiving 919.6
inexpectant 508.7
  (unwary 460.9)
  (unprepared 674.7)
inexpectation 508
  (miscalculation 481.1)
  (nonpreparation 674.1)
inexpected 508.8
inexpedience 647
  (untimeliness 135.1)
  (inutility 645.1)
  (wrong 923.1)
  (undueness 925.1)
  mismanagement 699.2
inexpedient 647.3
  (untimely 135.6)
  (foolish 499.15)
  (useless 645.8)
  (bad 649.8)
  (wrong 923.4)
  (undue 925.8)
  (unworthy 940.9)
  (unjust 941a.3)
inexpensive 815.8
inexpensiveness 815.1
inexperience 699.1
  (ignorance 491.1)
  (unaccustomedness 614.1)
inexperienced 699.14
  (ignorant 491.8)
  (artless 703.4)
inexpert 699.11
inexpertness 699.1
inexpiable 941a.4
inexplicability 519.1
  (enigma 533.3)
inexplicable 519.6
  (enigmatic 533.6)
inexpressible
  immense 31.10

unutterable 517.11
wonderful 870.8
inexpressibles 225.21
inexpressive 517.8
inexpugnable 664.11
inextensible, inextensile 323.5
inextension
  nonexpansion 180a
  (smallness 32.1)
  littleness 193.1
  immateriality 317.1
inextensive 180a.2
in extenso
  throughout 52.15
  diffusely 573.10
inextinguishable
  unchangeable 150.7
  passionate 825.11
in extremis 704.11
inextricable
  complex 59.10
  impracticable 471.7
infallibility 474.1
infallibilism 474.3
infallibilist 474.4
infallible 474.14
infamous
  terrible 649.8
  disreputable 874.8
  nefarious 945.16
infamy 874.1
infancy beginnng 66.1
  babyhood 127.3
infant n. baby 129.6
  (offspring 167.4)
  childish person 501.4
infant adj. 127.7
infanta 875.8
infanticide
  killer, killing 361.2
  sacrifice 990.6
infantile babyish 127.7
  senile 499.16
infantile paralysis 655.15
infantry
  children 129.2
  troops 726.8
infantryman 726.4
infarct
  closure 261.1
  obstruction 706.1
infarcted 261.4
infarction
  closure 261.1
  obstruction 706.1
infare 892.5
infatuate n.
  fanatic 504.2
  lover 897.6
infatuate v.
  obsess 503.11
  enamor 897.13
infatuate adj. 897.14
infatuated
  credulous 486.5
  fanatical 503.18
  (prejudiced 481.10)
  (opinionated 606.7)
  enamored 897.11, 14

infatuation
  prejudice 481.3
  credulity 486.1
  folly 499.6
  craze 503.7
  love 897.1
infeasibility 471.2
infeasible 471.7
infect imbue 41.8
  disease 655.22
  corrupt 659.9
  excite 824.2
infection
  transference 270.1
  contagion 655.2
  (insalubrity 657.1)
  (poison 663.4)
  excitation 824.1
infectious
  transferable 270.11
  contagious 657.5
infectious disease 655.1, 6
infecund 169.4
infelicitous inapt 24.7
  inexpedient 647.3
  wretched 828.16
infelicity
  inexpedience 647.1
  unskillfulness 699.1
  wretchedness 828.3
infer
  think likely 472.3
  deduce 480.6
  (reason 476.10)
  suppose 514.6
  mean 516.5
  interpret 522.6
  intimate 527.8
inferable See inferrible
inference
  deduction 476.1; 480.1
  (interpretation 522.1)
  supposition 514.1
  intimation 527.4
  indication 550.1
by inference
  evidentially 467.13
  implicative 526.7
inferential
  logical 476.16
  deducible 478.5
  construable 522.8
  implicative 526.7
  indicative 550.21
inferentialism 476.1
inferior n. 34.3
  (nonentity 643.6)
  (servant 746.1)
inferior adj.
  subordinate 34.5
  (unimportant 643.10)
  (bad 649.8)
  (second-rate 651.4)
  lower 207.9
be inferior 34.4
  (be smaller 195.5)
inferiority 34

  (shortcoming 304.1)
inferiority complex 34.2
infernal
  damnable 649.8
  malevolent 907.9
  wicked 945.17
  hellish 982.5
  (satanic 978.7)
infernally 31.24
infernal machine 727.14
inferno 982.1
inferred 526.7
inferrible, inferable
  logical 476.16
  deducible 478.5
infertile 169.4
infertility 169.1
infest overrun 303.3
  torment 830.5
infestation bane 663.1
  molestation 830.2
infibulation 43.1
infidel n. pagan 984.20
  irreligionist 989.4
  (unbeliever 485.4)
infidel adj.
  skeptical 485.10
  pagan 984.28
  infidelic 989.7
infidelic
  skeptical 485.10
  disbelieving 989.7
  (heterodox 984.22)
  (pagan 984.28)
infidelity
  faithlessness 940.2
  (apostasy 607.2)
  irreligion 989.2
  (paganism 984.10)
infiltrate imbue 41.8
  (interpenetrate 228.9)
  enter 294.6
  instill 296.5
  seep 337.5
infiltration
  imbuement 41.2
  (interjection 228.2)
  ingress 294.1
  passage 302.1
  seepage 337.2
infiltrative 337.6
infinite
  illimitable 105.3
  (vast 31.8)
  (numerous 102.5)
  eternal 112.4
  unlimited 180.7
  divine 976.12
be infinite 105.2
the Infinite 976.2
Infinite Being 976.2
infinitely
  extremely 31.19
  illimitably 105.3
  (perpetually 112.5)
infinitesimal 193.10
  (inappreciable 32.9)
infinitude 105.1

infinity — ingénue

infinity
  illimitability 105
  eternity 112.1
  boundlessness 180.4
  divine attribute 976.2
infirm weak 160.13
  irresolute 605.5
  (cowardly) 862.4)
  sickly 655.23
  (impotent 158.8)
  (impaired 659.12)
  unsafe 665.7
  morally ~ 945.12
infirmary 662.17
infirmity
  ~ of age 128.2
  weakness 160.1
  irresolution 605.1
  disease 655.1
  moral ~ 945.4
infix insert 300.5
  (add 37.3)
  inculcate 537.9
infixed 5.6
infixion 300.1
inflame, enflame
  stir up 173.8
  ignite 384.17
  excite 824.2
  ~ with love 897.13
  anger 900.10
inflamed
  violent 173.13
  hot 382.17, 19
  red 434.11
inflammability 384.10
inflammable 384.22
inflammation
  ignition 384.4
  sore 655.16
inflammatory 384.22
inflate increase 35.3
  distend 194.8
  blow up 349.24
  (rarefy 322.3)
  render vain 880.5
inflated
  blown up 349.27
  preposterous 497.4
  grandiloquent 577.7
  pompous 882.8
  boastful 884.7
inflation
  distention 194.1
  (increase 35.1)
  sufflation 349.1
  (rarefaction 322.2)
  grandiloquence 577.2
  pomposity 882.1
inflect curve 245.3
  conjugate 567.5
inflection, inflexion
  change 140.1
  angle 244.2
  curvature 245.1
  tone 402.2
  grammar 567.1
inflectional 567.6
inflectional languages 560.4

inflexibility
  rigidity 323.1
  (stability 150.1)
  (straightness 246.1)
  (inelasticity 326.1)
  (resolution 604.1)
  (obstinacy 606.1)
  (severity 739.1)
  pitilessness 914a.1
inflexible rigid 323.5
  (unchangeable 150.7)
  (straight 246.5)
  (inelastic 326.3)
  (resolute 604.7)
  (obstinate 606.6)
  (unmanageable 704.10)
  (severe 739.5)
  unforgiving 919.6
inflict impose 741.5
  ~ pain 830.1
  ~ punishment 972.5
infliction bane 663.1
  adversity 735.1
  mental suffering 828.1
  source of pain 830.2
  punishment 972.1
inflictive 972.14
inflorescence 161.4; 367.5
inflow n.
  inpour 294.1
  insufflation 349.1
inflow v. 294.6
influence n. sway 175
  (advantage 33.2)
  (agency 170.1)
  (motivation 615.2)
  (instrumentality 631.1)
influencer 175.5
  authority 737.2
have influence 175.7, 8
  (dominate 737.12)
influence v.
  change 140.6
  contribute 153.8
  influential person 175.5
  sway 175.6
  (induce 615.8)
  prejudice 481.8
influenced 941a.3
influencer 175.5
influential 175.10
  (potent 157.8)
  (persuasive 615.11)
  (authoritative 737.15)
be influential 175.7
influentiality 175.1
influenza 655.9
influx, influxion 294.1
infold, enfold
  envelop 229.3
  fold 258.3
infoldment, enfoldment 258.2
inform v. form 240.6

  apprize 527.7
  (point out 457.7)
  (explain 522.6)
  (disclose 529.3)
  (teach 537.9)
  (tell 582.6)
inform against, inform on 527.10
  (divulge 529.4)
  (accuse 938.4)
  (betray 940.7)
  (testify 969.10)
inform adj.
  formless 241.5
  deformed 243.5
informal
  unconformable 83.9, 11
  colloquial 563.16
  natural 849.3
informality
  nonconformity 83.2
  nonobservance 773.1
informant 527.5
  (herald 64.1)
  (interpreter 524.1)
  (messenger 534.1)
  (guide 694.6)
  (accuser 938.2)
information
  formation 240.3
  knowledge 490.2
  communication 527.1
  (intelligence 498.1)
  (disclosure 529.1)
  (instruction 537.1)
  (warning 668.1)
  news 532.1
  prosecution 969.6
informative
  formative 240.7
  communicative 527.13
  (interpretative 522.8)
  (disclosive 529.8)
  (instructive 537.12)
informed
  aware 490.13
  enlightened 490.15
  (wise 498.11)
  (educated 537.13)
  become informed 527.11
  (be disclosed 529.6)
  (learn 539.3)
informer 527.6
  (accuser 938.2)
  (traitor 949.3)
informity 241.1
infraction
  overstepping 303.1
  violation 742.1
  (nonobservance 773.2)
  infringement 925.3
  wrongdoing 945.6
  misdeed 947.2
  lawbreaking 964.2
infrangibility 321.2

infrangible 321.10
infrequency 137
  (fewness 103.1)
infrequent 137.2
  (few 103.3)
  (spasmodic 139.2)
infrequently 137.3
  (sparsely 103.5)
infrigidate 385.4
infrigidation 385.1
infrigidative 385.6
infringe
  overstep 303.5
  ~ a law 83.8
  violate 742.4
  (disregard 773.3)
  encroach 925.6
infringement
  nonconformity 83.2
  overstepping 303.1
  violation 742.1
  (nonobservance 773.2)
  encroachment 925.3
  misfeasance 947.2
  violation of law 964.2
infructuose 169.4
infumate dry 340.5
  smoke-cure 670.4
infumation 340.2
infundibular
  cone-shaped 249.9
  concave 252.10
infundibulate 249.9
infuriate v.
  inflame 173.8
  irritate 824.5
  enrage 900.11
infuriate adj.
  turbulent 173.12
  angry 900.13
infuriated 900.13
infuscate 431.6
infuscation 431.2
infuse imbue 41.8
  (interpenetrate 228.9)
  infix 300.5
  inculcate 537.9
infusibility 321.2
infusible 321.10
infusion
  mixture 41.2, 3
  infixion 300.1
  baptism 998.5
Infusoria 368.3
infusorial 368.12
infusorian, infusorium 193.4; 368.12
ingate inlet 294.5
  conduit 350.3
ingathering 72.1
ingeminate 90.3
ingemination 90.1
ingenerate 5.6
ingenious
  imaginative 515.11
  skillful 698.11
ingenit, ingenite 5.6
ingénue actor 599.19
  unsophisticate 703.2

916

ingenuity 698.1
ingenuous 703.4
  (veracious 543.3)
  (honest 939.7)
ingenuousness 703.1
  (veracity 543.1)
ingest imbibe 296.2
  eat 298.44
ingesta 298.5
ingestion
  imbibition 296.1
  eating 298.1
ingestive 296.6
ingle fire 382.8
  fireplace 386.2
inglenook, ingle nook, ingleside
  home 189.2
  fireside 386.2
inglorious 874.8, 10
ingloriousness 874.1
ingluvies 191.7
ingoing n. 294.1
ingoing adj. 294.8
ingot metal 635.6
  bullion 800.15
ingraft, ingrafted See engraft etc.
ingrain n. 329.1
ingrain v. 428.9
ingrain adj.
  textural 329.3
  fast-dyed 428.13
ingrained
  intrinsic 5.6
  combined 48.5
  textural 329.3
  inveterate 613.12
ingrate 917.3
ingratiate 886.3
ingratiating 894.13
ingratiation 886.1
ingratitude 917
ingravidate 319.9
ingravidation 168.2
ingredient 56.1
ingress 294.5
  (reception 296.1)
  (insertion 300.1)
  (passage 302.1)
ingression 294.1
ingressive 294.8
ingulf See engulf
ingurgitate 296.3
ingurgitation 296.1
inhabit 186.10
  (settle 184.14)
inhabitance
  habitation 186.2
  abode 189.1
inhabitant 188.1, 10
  (people 372.2)
inhabited 186.14
inhalation
  reception 296.1
  inspiration 349.18
inhale take in 296.2
  inspire 349.23
  ~ tobacco 392a.14
  smell 398.7
inhalement 296.1
inharmonious

different 15.7
discordant 414.4
colors 428.16
inharmony 15.1
inhere 56.2
inherence 5.1
inherent
  intrinsic 5.6
  (component 56.3)
  (subjective 317.7)
  (dispositional 820.5)
  instinctive 477a.4
inherit 775.8
inheritable 783.5
inheritance
  lineage 167.2
  heritage 775.4
  (estate 780.3)
  (bequest 784.6)
  (receipt 810.1)
inherited
  intrinsic 5.6
  lineal 167.7
inheritor 779.5
inhesion 5.1
inhibit hinder 706.4
  restrain 751.6
  prohibit 761.2
inhibition
  hindrance 706.1
  restraint 751.1
  prohibition 761.1
inhibitive
  hindering 706.8
  restrictive 751.13
  prohibitive 761.3
inhospitable 893.9
inhospitality 893.1
inhuman
  cruel 907.9
  diabolical 980.9
inhumane 907.9
inhumanity 907.3
inhumation 363.1
inhume 363.20
inimical contrary 14.5
  opposed 708.4
  bellicose 722.13
  unfriendly 889.3
inimitable
  unequaled 28.4
  supreme 33.8
  (nonimitation 20.4)
  (perfect 650.5)
iniquitous
  unjust 941a.3
  wicked 945.11
iniquity
  injustice 941a.1
  wickedness 945.1
inirritability 826.1
inirritable 826.9
initial n.
  beginning 66.1
  letter 561.1
initial v. 561.6
initial adj. 66.7
initiary 296.7
initiate n. 541.6
initiate v. begin 66.5
  preinstruct 537.9

initiated 698.13
initiation
  reception 296.1
  preinstruction 537.1
initiative n.
  beginning 66.1
  enterprise 682.4
take the initiative 66.5
initiative adj. 66.7
initiatory
  beginning 66.7
  introductory 296.7
inject interject 228.3
  insert 300.5
  (introduce 296.5)
  ~ a fluid 337.5
injection
  counteractant 179.2
  insertion 300.1
injudicial 964.5
injudicious
  indiscriminate 465a.3
  foolish 499.15
  (ill-managed 699.17)
  inexpedient 647.3
  rash 863.6
injunction
  precept 697.1
  (advice 695.1)
  command 741.1
  prohibition 761.1
injure harm 649.6
  damage 659.8
  (afflict 655.22)
  (blemish 848.2)
injured
  impaired 659.12
  (infirm 655.24)
  (blemished 848.3)
  pained 828.13
  offended 900.12
injurious 649.10
  (deteriorating 659.11)
injury harm 649.2
  damage 659.3
  (blemish 848.1)
  grievance 830.2
injustice 941a
  (wrong 923.1)
  (undueness 925.1)
ink black 431.2, 5
  writing fluid 590.10
inkhorn 590.10
inkle fastening 45.2
  cord 205.3
inkling
  supposition 514.2
  hint 527.4
  (slight knowledge 491.3)
inkpot 590.10
inkslinger 590.11
  (author 593.15)
inkslinging 590.1
inkstand, inkwell 590.10
inky, inky-black 431.7

inlaid 847.13
inland n.
  interior 221.3
  land 342.1
inland adj.
  interior 221.10
  midland 342.9
in-law 11.3
inlay n. lining 224.1
  insert 300.3
inlay v. line 224.2
  infix 300.5
  ~ colors 440.4
inlayer, inlaying 224.1
inlet chasm 198.3
  entrance 294.5
  (portal 260.4)
  (conduit 350.1)
  sea 343
  (recess 252.4)
in loco fit 23.11
  in place 184.20
  expedient 646.4
inlook n. 461.5
inlook v. 461.17
inlooker looker 444.1
  examiner 461.13
inlooking 461.5
inly 221.12
inmate 188.1
in medias res
  mediumly 29.4
  midway 68.6
  between 228.13
in memoriam
  in memory 363.27;
    505.23
  in commemoration 883.6
inmost 221.9
inn 189.8
  (restaurant 298.42)
  (barroom 959.13)
innate intrinsic 5.6
  instinctive 477a.4
innavigable 471.7
inner n.
  interior 221.2
  vitals 221.4
  shot 284.4
inner adj. 221.9
inner man
  stomach 191.7
  vitals 221.4
  inmost mind 450.3
  (ego 79.4)
  (affections 820.2)
  psyche 994.11
innermost n. 221.2
innermost adj. 221.9
inner tube 272.16
innholder
  (householder 188.3)
innings land 342.2
  marsh 345.1
  profits 775.2
innkeeper 779.2
innocence 946
  (immaculacy 652.1)
  (artlessness 703.1)
  (purity 960.1)

innocent — insertion

innocent *n.* child 129.3
  childish person 501.4
  unsophisticate 703.2
  ~ person 946.2
innocent *adj.*
  harmless 648.13
  guiltless 946.5
  (undefiled 652.14)
  (artless 703.4)
  (uncorrupt 944.5)
  (pure 960.2)
innocuous 648.13
innominables 225.21
innominate 565.9
innominate bone 235.5
innovate 140.7
innovation 140.3
  (novelty 123.1)
  (neology 563.7)
innovator 563.12
innoxious 648.13
  (salubrious 656.6)
innuendo
  insinuation 527.4
  censure 932.2
innumerable 105.3
  (numerous 102.5)
innumerably 105.4
  (numerously 102.6)
innutritious 657.4
inobservance
  inattention 458.1
  nonfulfillment 773.1
inobservant
  inattentive 458.10
  unwary 460.9
  unfaithful 773.5
inobtainable 471.7
inoculable 657.5
inoculate insert 300.5
  inculcate 537.9
inoculated 48.5
inoculation
  insertion 300.1
  inculcation 537.1
inodorous 399.5
  be inodorous 399.3
inodorousness 398
inoffensive
  harmless 648.13
  unobjectionable 937.10
inominous 512.5
inoperative 158.11
  (useless 645.8)
inopportune 135.6
  (inexpedient 647.3)
inopportunity 135.1
  (inexpedience 647.1)
inordinacy
  exaggeration 549.1
  excess 641.1
  (undueness 925.1)
  (injustice 941a.1)
  overindulgence 954.1
inordinate
  immense 31.9
  (fanatic 503.18)

exaggerated 549.3
excessive 641.5
(undue 925.8)
(unjust 941a.3)
intemperate 954.4
inordinately 31.20
inorganic, inorganized 358.4
inorganization 358.1
inornate 849.4
inosculate attach 43.6
  combine 48.3
  interlace 219.8
inosculation
  junction 43.1
  combination 48.1
  interlacing 219.3
  convolution 248.1
inpatient 655.20
in petto
  in the thoughts 454.4
  secretly 528.24
  intended 620.4
inpour *n.* 294.1
inpour *v.* 294.6
in propria persona 186.17
inquest
  inquiry 461.1, 3
  jury 967.2
  trial 969.5
inquietude
  restlessness 149.3
  agitation 315.1
  excitement 825.3
  uneasiness 828.2
  discontent 832.1
  trepidation 860.3
inquire, enquire 461.14, 15
inquirent 461.24
inquirer, enquirer
  inquisitive 455.2
  questioner 461.12
  (interlocutor 588.5)
  learner 541.1
inquiring, enquiring *n.* 461.1
inquiring, enquiring *adj.* 461.24
  (curious 455.5)
  (pursuing 622.10)
inquiry, enquiry
  search 461.1, 10
  (curiosity 455.1)
  (dissertation 595.1)
  trial 969.5
  make inquiry 461.14
inquisite, inquisit 461.14
inquisition *n.*
  inquiry 461.1, 3
  persecution 907.3
  tribunal 966.1
  trial 969.5
inquisition *v.* 461.14
inquisitional 461.24
inquisitionist 461.12
inquisitive *n.* 455.2
  (inquirer 461.12)
  (gossip 532.5)

inquisitive *adj.* 455.5
  (inquiring 461.24)
inquisitiveness 455.1
  (questioning 461.9)
inquisitor
  inquirer 461.12
  tyrant 739.3
inquisitorial
  inquiring 461.24
  (curious 455.5)
  (litigious 969.13)
  tyrannical 739.5
in re 9.10
inroad *n.*
  encroachment 228.3
  (ingress 294.1)
  overstepping 303.1
  damage 659.3
  attack 716.1
  make an inroad 716.5
inroad *v.* 716.5
inrun 294.1
inrush *n.* inflow 294.1
  insufflation 349.1
inrush *v.* 294.6
insalubrious 657.3
  (harmful 649.10)
  (baneful 663.7)
  be insalubrious 657.2
insalubrity 657
ins and outs 156.1
insane 503.12
  be insane 503.9
  drive insane 503.11
  go insane 503.10
  insane asylum 503.8
  (hospital 662.17)
insanify 503.11
insanity 503
  (derangement 61.1)
  (idiocy 499.3)
insatiable, insatiate
  greedy 865.20
  appetite 957.4
inscience 491.1
inscient 491.8
inscribe list 86.3
  record 551.8
  engrave 558.5
  letter 561.6
  write 590.13
inscribed 590.15
inscriber 559.6
inscript record 551.1
  writing 590.3
inscription
  epitaph 363.16
  record 551.1
  writing 590.3
inscroll record 551.8
  write 590.13
inscrutability 519.1
inscrutable 519.6
  (enigmatic 533.6)
insculpture
  sculpture 557.9
  engrave 558.5
insect midge 193.2
  bug 366.24
insecticide 361.2
insectile 368.18
insecure

918

uncertain 475.14
unsafe 665.7
insecurity
  uncertainty 475.1
  precariousness 665.1
insensate
  insensible 376.5
  absurd 497.4
  unintelligent 499.11
  foolish 499.15
  insane 503.12
insensibility
  physical ~ 376
  (numbness 381.1)
  moral ~ 823
  (incuriosity 456.1)
  (inexcitability 826.1)
  (indifference 866.1)
insensible
  physically ~ 376.5
  (numb 381.3)
  morally ~ 823.5
  (inattentive 458.10)
  (inexcitable 826.9)
  (indifferent 866.4)
  ungrateful 917.3
  be insensible
  ~ ~ physically 376.3
  ~ ~ emotionally 823.3
  (not heed 458.5)
  render insensible
  stun 376.4
  dull 823.4
insensibly 823.8
insensitive
  physically ~ 376.5
  emotionally ~ 823.5
insensitiveness 823.1
insentience
  physical ~ 376.1
  emotional ~ 823.1
inseparability
  tenacity 46.2
  indivisibility 321.2
inseparable
  joined 43.12
  indivisible 321.10
  (coherent 46.9, 10)
  (whole 50.8)
inseparableness 46.2
insert *n.* 300.3
insert *v.*
  introduce 300.5
  (foist in 10.4)
  (add 37.3)
  (internalize 221.8)
  (interject 228.8)
  (perforate 260.14)
  (enter 294.6)
  (bring in 296.5)
  (immerse 310.5)
  record 551.8
insertion
  insert 300.1, 3
  (addition 37.1)
  (adjunct 39.1)
  (placement 184.5)
  (ingress 294.1)

inset — institutive

(reception 296.1)
(immersion 310.2)
recording 551.7
needlework 847.6
inset *n.* 300.3
inset *v.* 300.5
inseverable 43.12
inside *n.*
  contents 190.1
  interior 221.2
  (side 236.1)
  vitals 221.4
inside *adj.* 221.9
inside *adv.* 221.12, 13
  inside and out 52.15
inside out 218.6
inside track
  advantage 33.2
  best chance 156.3
  influence 175.1
insidious
  deceptive 545.12
  sly 702.6
  dishonest 940.8
insight
  discrimination 465.1
  intuition 477a.1
  (knowledge 490.1)
  clairvoyance 994.7
insignia ensign 550.12
  (trophy 733.1)
  ~ of authority 747
insignificance
  unmeaningness 517.1
  unimportance 643
  (smallness 32.1)
insignificant *n.* 643.3, 6
insignificant *adj.*
  inconsiderable 32.8
  meaningless 517.8
  unimportant 643.10
insincere
  hypocritical 544.8
  (flattering 933.3)
  affected 853.6
  suave 894.13
insincerity 544.2
  (flattery 933.1)
insinuate
  intrude 228.10
  insert 300.5
  (interject 228.8)
  intimate 527.8
  (imply 526.4)
  ingratiate 886.3
insinuate oneself 294.6
insinuated 526.7
  (hinted 527.14)
insinuation
  intervention 228.3
  (ingress 294.1)
  insertion 300.1
  intimation 527.4
  (latency 526.2)
  reprehension 932.2
insinuative 526.7
insipid
  wishy-washy 160.14
  tasteless 391.2
  (**unsavory** 395.5)

(indifferent 866.5)
style 575.2
mediocre 736.3
prosy 843.5
insipidity 391
insist 476.11
insist on, insist upon
  repeat 104.4
  emphasize 535.5
  be determined 604.6
  contend for 720.10
  compel 744.2
  stipulate 770.2
  demand 924.7
insistence
  motivation 615.2
  urgency 642.2
insistent
  emphatic 535.6
  urgent 642.13
  (importunate 765.8)
in situ 184.20
insnare See ensnare
insobriety 959.1
insociable, insocial 893.9
insolate sun-dry 340.5
  sun 384.20
insolation
  drying 340.2
  heating 382.1
  sunstroke 384.9
insolence 885.2
  (discourtesy 895.1)
  (disrespect 929.1)
  (disdain 930.1)
  (snub 930.4)
insolent defiant 715.3
  arrogant 885.9
  (discourteous 895.6)
  insulting 929.5
  be insolent 885.7
  (disrespect 929.3)
  (snub 930.7)
insolently 885.11
  (contemptuously 930.10)
insolubility 321.2
insoluble
  indivisible 321.10
  unintelligible 519.6
insolvency 808.2
  (insufficiency 640.1)
  (arrears 806.2)
insolvent *n.* 808.4
insolvent *adj.* 808.10
  (indebted 806.7)
  become insolvent 808.6
insomnia 682.9
insomnious, insomnolent 682.24
insouciance
  apathy 823.1
  indifference 866.1
  (incuriosity 456.1)
  (inattention 458.1)
insouciant
  apathetic 823.5
  (regardless 460.8)

indifferent 866.4
inspect
  scrutinize 441.12
  examine 461.17
  (give attention 457.4)
inspection
  scrutiny 441.2
  examination 461.3
inspector looker 444.1
  examiner 461.13
  supervisor 694.1
inspiration
  inhalation 296.1; 349.18
  insufflation 349.1
  brilliant idea 453.1
  (wisdom 498.6)
  intuition 477a.1
  genius 498.5
  creative thought 515.1
  impulse 612.1
  motivation 615.2
  feeling 821.1
  excitation 824.1
  divine ~ 985.1
  religion 987.2
inspirational 477a.4
inspirator 349.20
inspire
  inhale 296.2; 349.23
  stimulate 615.7
  uplift 658.8
  rouse feeling 824.2
  cheer 836.6
  ~ spiritually 987.8
inspired 985.7
inspirit inspire 615.7
  rouse feeling 824.2
  cheer 836.6
  encourage 858.8
inspiriting
  cheering 836.12
  encouraging 858.11
inspissate 321.7
  (thicken 202.5)
  (viscidize 352.6)
inspissation 321.3
  (viscidization 352.2)
instability
  inconstancy 149.1
  irresolution 605.1
  precariousness 665.1
install inaugurate 66.5
  originate 153.6
  create 161.8
  establish 184.11
  instate 755.2
  ~ clergy 995.7
installation
  inauguration 66.1; 755.2
  establishment 184.6
  holy orders 995.6
installment, instalment part 51.1
  payment 807.2
  by installments 51.10
instance *n.*

example 82.2
instigation 615.2
request 765.3
for instance 82.14
instance *v.*
  exemplify 82.6
  adduce 467.10
instant *n.* 113.3
in an instant 113.6
instant *adj.*
  instantaneous 113.4
  present 118.2
  imminent 152.3
  urgent 642.13
  quick 682.17
instant *adv.* 113.6
instantaneity 113
  (transience 111.1)
instantaneous 113.4
  (brief 111.7)
  (punctual 132.9)
instantaneously 113.6
  (briefly 111.9)
instanter, instantly
  instantly 113.6
  promptly 132.14
instate 755.4
instauration 660.5
instead
  as a substitute 147.5
  in behalf of 755.6
instigate 615.7
  (impel 276.7)
instigation 615.2
  (impulse 276.1)
instigator 615.6
instill, instil
  imbue 41.8
  introduce 296.5
  infix 300.5
  inculcate 537.9
instillation 300.1
instinct *n.*
  intuition 477a.1
  (intellect 450.1)
  involuntariness 601.2
instinct *adj.* 777.7
instinctive
  intrinsic 5.6
  intuitive 477a.4
  involuntary 601.14
  (impulsive 612.4)
instinctively 477a.5
institute *n.*
  school 542.1
  society 712.4
institute *v.*
  inaugurate 66.5
  originate 153.6
  create 161.8
institution
  custom 613.2
  society 712.4
  law 963.2
  ordination 995.6
  ~ of sacrament 998.1
institutional 542.9
institutive
  original 153.9

instruct — intempestivity

institutive (*continued*)
　intrusive 228.12
instruct teach 537.9
　(inform 527.7)
　advise 695.5
　direct 741.4
instructed 490.15
instruction
　teaching 537.1
　(information 527.1)
　precept 697.1
　(advice 695.1)
　order 741.1
instructive
　educational 537.12
　(informative 527.13)
　preceptive 697.2;
　741.8
instructor 540.1
　(pedant 492.4)
instrument *n.*
　melody part 415.13
　musical ~ 417
　medium 631.2
　(means 632.1)
　(agent 690.1)
　implement 633
　puppet 711.2
　deputy 759.1
　security 771.1
　negotiable ~ 800.7
　(credit ~ 805.2)
　instrument *v.* 415.26
instrumental
　musical 415.28
　serviceable 631.4
　(operative 170.4)
　(conducive to 176.3)
　(mechanical 633.5)
　(useful 644.5;
　677.8)
　be instrumental
　631.3
　(influence 175.6)
　(be useful 644.2)
instrumentalist 416.1
instrumentality 631
　(agency 170.1)
　(influence 175.1)
　(means 632.1)
　(utility 644.1)
　(aid 707.1)
　(mediation 724.1)
instrumentate 415.26
instrumentation
　composition 54.2
　orchestration 413.3
instrument board
　aviation 267a.29
　airplane 273a.10
insubmission 742.1
insubordinate 742.6
insubordination 742.1
　(anarchy 738.2)
insubstantial
　unsubstantial 4.5
　immaterial 317.6
　(supernatural 976.14)
　(spectral 980a.4)
　(spiritual 994.22)

uncertain 475.14
illogical 477.10
unauthentic 495.16
deceptive 545.13
insubstantiality
　unsubstantiality 4.1
　immateriality 317.1
insubstantiate 316.7
insubstantiation 316.4
insufferable 830.18
　(dislikable 867.9)
　(hateful 898.7)
insufficiency
　impotence 158.1
　inadequacy 640
　(incompleteness 53.1, 2)
　(shortcoming 304.1)
　(inutility 645.1)
　(imperfection 651.1)
　(insolvency 808.2)
insufficient
　inadequate 640.8
　(deficient 53.4)
　(incompetent 158.8)
　(useless 645.8)
　(imperfect 651.4)
　(ineffective 732.8)
　unsatisfactory 832.6
　be insufficient 640.6
　(fall short 304.2)
insufficiently 640.13
　(slightly 32.12)
insufflation 349.1
insular *n.* 346.2
insular *adj.*
　irrelative 10.5
　separate 44.12
　(alone 87.8)
　regional 181.6
　bigoted 606.7
insularity 44.1
insulate *v.* 44.7
insulate *adj.* 345.3
insulated 346.4
insulation 44.1
insulse stupid 499.12
　dull 843.5
insulsity 499.2
insult *n.* 929.2
　(insolence 885.2)
　(malediction 908.1)
　(gibe 930.3)
　(personality 934.2)
insult *v.*
　give umbrage 900.10
　affront 929.3
　(be insolent 885.7)
　(disparage 934.3)
insulting
　insolent 885.9
　disrespectful 929.5
　(disparaging 934.4)
insuperability 471.2
insuperable 471.7
insupportable 830.18
insuppressible
　unmitigable 173.16
　obstinate 606.6
insurance
　promise 768.1

guarantee 771.1
insure
　make certain 474.6
　guarantee 771.6
insurer 758.2
insurgence 742.2
　(anarchy 738.2)
insurgent *n.* 742.3
　(separatist 44.5)
　(dissenter 489.3)
　(apostate 607.5)
　(antagonist 710.3)
insurgent *adj.* 742.7
　(revolutionary 146.5)
insurmountable 471.7
insurrect 742.5
　(revolutionize 146.4)
insurrection 742.2
insurrectionary 742.7
　(revolutionary 146.5)
insusceptibility
　physical ~ 376.1
　emotional ~ 823.1
insusceptible 823.5
intact whole 50.7
　complete 52.9
　unchanged 141.6
　perfect 650.5
　preserved 670.6
　keep intact 670.3
intaglation 558.3
intaglio die 22.3
　modeling 557.6
　engraving 558.3, 4
intaglio printing 558.2
intaglio rilievo 557.6
intangible
　infinitesimal 193.10
　immaterial 317.6
integer whole 50.1
　number 84.1
　item 87.3
integral *n.* whole 50.1
　number 84.2
integral *adj.*
　whole 50.6
　component 56.3
　numeral 84.7
integrality
　completeness 52.1
　unity 87.1
integrant *n.* 56.1
integrant *adj.* 56.3
integrate *v.* 50.4
integrate *adj.* 50.6
integration whole 50.1
　mathematics 85.4
integrity whole 50.1
　completeness 52.1
　probity 939.1
　(virtue 944.1)
integument 223.2, 12
　(layer 204.2)
intellect 450
intellection 451.1
intellectual *n.* 492.1
intellectual *adj.* 450.8
　(scholarly 490.16)
　(intelligent 498.9)

(studious 539.6)
intellectuality 450.1
intellectualize
　think 451.27
　(rationalize 450.6)
　reason 476.10
intelligence
　intellect 450.1
　understanding 498
　(knowledge 490.1)
　(experience 698.4)
　information 527.1
　news 532.1
intelligence quotient 498.1
intelligencer
　informant 527.5
　messenger 534.1
intelligence test 461.3
intelligency 450.1
intelligent
　knowing 490.12
　understanding 498.9
　(intellectual 450.8)
　(sane 502.5)
　be intelligent 498.7
　(understand 518.4)
　(know what's what 698.8)
intelligential 527.13
intelligentsia 492.1
intelligibility 518
　(manifestness 525.1)
　(perspicuity 570.1)
intelligible 518.5
　(expressive 516.8)
　(manifest 525.4)
　(perspicuous 570.2)
　be intelligible 518.2
　render intelligible 518.3
　(explain 522.6)
intelligibly 518.7
intelligize think 451.27
　reason 476.10
intemperance
　exaggeration 459.1
　inabstinence 954
　(excess 641.1)
　(prodigality 818.1)
　(gluttony 957.1)
　(drunkenness 959.1)
　(incontinence 961.2)
intemperate
　overdone 549.3
　inabstinent 954.4
　(excessive 641.5)
　(unrestrained 748.13)
　(prodigal 818.4)
　(gluttonous 957.4)
　(drinking 959.23)
　(incontinent 961.10)
　be intemperate 954.3
　(be prodigal 818.3)
　(tipple 959.15)
intempestive 135.6
intempestivity 135.1
　(anachronism 115.1)

intend — interlinking

intend mean 516.5
  purpose 620.3
  (premeditate 611.3)
  (pursue 622.6)
  (plan 626.9)
  (undertake 676.2)
intendant 694.1
intended n. 897.8
intended adj.
  purposed 620.4
  (willed 600.3)
  (predetermined 611.5)
  betrothed 768.7
intense great 31.6
  forceful 171.9
  violent 173.11
  acute 375.7
  colorful 428.14
intensely 31.15
intensification 35.1
intensify increase **35.3**
  give more power 157.7
  stimulate 171.7
intensifying 35.6
intensity
  greatness 31.1
  energy 171.1
  violence 173.1
  loudness 404.1
intensive 35.6
intent n.
  meaning 516.1
  intention 620.1
to all intents and purposes
  equally 27.10
  mainly 50.11
  throughout 52.15
  intentionally 620.5
intent adj.
  attentive 457.9
  (industrious 682.19)
  resolved 604.8
  avid 865.17
intention
  meaning 516.1
  purpose 620
  (tendency 176.1)
  (will 600.1)
  (resolution 604.1)
  (predetermination 611.1)
  (motive 615.1)
  (plan 626.1)
  (undertaking 676.1)
  goal 620.2
intentional 620.4
intentionally 620.5
  (voluntarily 600.5)
  (premeditatedly 611.7)
intentness
  close attention 457.2
  earnestness 682.3
inter 363.20
interact 12.5
interaction
  agency 170.1
  interworking 680.1

interactionism 994.3
interagency 724.1
interagent
  medium 631.2
  agent 690.1
  mediator 724.2
interbreed 41.6
interbreeding 41.1
intercalary 228.11
intercalate 228.8
intercalation 228.2
intercede
  mediate 724.3
  divine function 976.9
interceder 724.2
intercept
  hinder 706.4
  seize 789.9
interception 706.1
interceptor 273a.10
intercession
  mediation 724.1
  prayer 990.3
  divine ~ 996.5
intercessor 724.2
intercessory 724.4
interchange n.
  mutual change 148
  (reciprocation 12.2)
  (transposition 270.1)
  (retaliation 718.1)
  (transfer 783.1)
  (barter 794.1)
  interlocution 588.1
  ~ of views 588.3
interchange v. 148.3
  (reciprocate 12.5)
  (substitute 147.3)
  (transplace 185.2)
  (retaliate 718.2)
  (transfer 783.3)
  (barter 794.4)
interchangeability 148.2
interchangeable
  exchangeable 148.4
  (reciprocal 12.7)
  commercial 794.10
interchangeably 148.5
intercollegiate 148.4
intercolumnar 228.11
intercommunicate 892.9
intercommunication 527.1
intercommunion 892.1
interconnect
  correlate 12.4
  interlace 219.8
interconnected 12.6
interconnection
  correlation 12.1
  junction 43.1
  bond 45.1
  unity 87.1
  interlacing 219.3
intercostal 228.11
intercourse
  junction 43.1
  business ~ 704.1

social ~ 892.1
intercross 219.7
intercrossing 219.2
intercurrence
  interjacence 228.1
  passage 302.1
intercurrent
  interchangeable 148.4
  interjacent 228.11
  passing 302.3
interdenominational 148.4
interdepend 12.4
interdependence 12.1
interdependent 12.6
interdict n. 761.1
interdict v. 761.2
interdiction 761.1
interdigitate 219.8
  (interject 228.8)
interdigitation
  junction 43.1
  interlacing 219.3
interest n.
  relation 9.1
  influence 175.1
  curiosity 455.1
  importance 642.1
  good 648.2
  patronage 707.2
  party 712.1
  estate 780.2
  premium 806.3
  right 922.2
in one's interest 648.15
take an interest in
  be curious 455.3
  love 897.11
  be benevolent 906.5
take no interest
  be apathetic 822.3
  (be incurious 456.2)
  be indifferent 866.3
interest v.
  be related 9.3
  excite 824.2
  please 829.4
  amuse 840.20
interested
  partial 941a.3
  selfish 943.4
interesting 617.5
interfacial 228.11
interfere
  counteract 179.3
  intrude 228.10
  (disagree 24.5)
  meddle 682.14
  hinder 706.4
  mediate 724.3
  not interfere 748.11
interference
  counteraction 179.1
  meddling 682.8
  hindrance 706.1
  mediation 724.1
interferent 228.12
interferer 228.4
interferometer 193.7
interfuse combine 48.3

  disperse 73.3
  interpenetrate 228.9
  (infuse 41.8)
interfusion
  mixture 41.1
  dispersion 73.1
intergrown 228.11
interim n. 109a
  (interruption 70.1)
  (spare time 685.1)
  in the interim 109a.3
interim adv. 109a.3
interior n.
  inside 221.2, 3
  (middle 68.2)
  (insides 190.1)
  (center 222.2)
  inland 342.1
  picture 556.10
interior adj. 221.9
interiority 221
  (intrinsicality 5.1)
  (interjacence 228.1)
interjacence 228
  (equidistance 68.3)
  (interiority 221.1)
interjacent 228.11
  (middle 68.5)
  (interior 221.9)
be interjacent 228.7
interject 228.8
  (introduce 10.4; 296.5)
  (add 37.3)
  (insert 300.5)
interjection
  interpolation 228.2
  (addition 37.1)
  (impregnation 41.2)
  (ingress 294.1)
  (reception 296.1)
  (insertion 300.1)
  part of speech 567.2
interjoin, interknit,
interlace 219.8
  (mix 41.6)
  (join 43.7)
  (combine 48.3)
  (convolve 248.3)
interlacement, interlacery
  mixture 41.1
  interweavement 219.3
interlacing 847.3
interlard 228.8
  (mix 41.6)
interlarding 41.1
interleaf, interleave
  interlace 219.8
  interject 228.8
interleague 48.4
interline 224.2
interlineal 228.11
interlinear, interlineary 522.7
interlineation 228.2
interlining 224.1
interlink 219.8
  (join 43.7)
  (combine 48.3)
interlinking 43.1

interlocation — interspersion

interlocation 228.1
interlock 219.8
interlocking 43.1
interlocular 228.11
interlocution 588
  (argumentation 476.2)
  (speech 582.1)
interlocutor
  inquirer 461.12
  interpreter 524.1
  conversationalist 588.5
  (talker 582.5)
  mediator 724.2
  deputy 759.1
interlocutory
  conversational 588.10
  mediatory 724.4
interlocutress, interlocutrice, interlocutrix 524.1
interlope 228.10
interloper 228.4
interlude n.
  pause 142.2
  interim 109a.1
  music 415.15
  drama 599.5
interlude v. 109a.2
intermarriage
  mixture 41.1
  marriage 903.1
intermarry mix 41.6
  interwed 903.13
intermaxillary 228.11
intermeddle 682.14
intermeddler 682.11
  (intruder 228.4)
intermeddling 682.8
  (intervention 228.3)
intermediacy 631.1
intermedial
  instrumental 631.4
  mediatory 724.2
intermediary n.
  intermedium 228.5
  medium 631.2
  mediator 724.2
intermediary adj.
  mean 29.3
  interjacent 228.11
  instrumental 631.4
  mediatory 724.4
intermediate n. 724.2
intermediate v.
  subserve 631.3
  mediate 724.3
intermediate adj.
  mean 29.3
  (neutral 628.3)
  interjacent 228.11
  (middle 68.5)
  instrumental 631.4
intermediation
  instrumentality 631.1
  mediation 724.1
  (intervention 228.3)
intermediator 724.2
intermediatory 724.4

intermedium
  mean 29.1
  bond 45.1
  intermediary 228.5
  medium 631.2
  mediator 724.2
interment 363
intermessage 532.2
intermessenger 534.1
intermezzo 415.15
intermigration 266.3
interminability
  infinity 105.1
  boundlessness 180.4
interminable
  infinite 105.3
  eternal 112.4
  long 200.12
interminate 105.3
intermingle 41.6
  (combine 48.3)
intermission
  discontinuity 70.1
  interim 109a.1
  pause 142.2
  respite 687.2
intermit
  be discontinuous 70.2
  interlude 109a.2
  recur 138.8
  interrupt 142.7
intermittence
  interim 109a.1
  periodicity 138.2
  (discontinuity 70.1)
  irregularity 139.1
  pause 142.2
intermittent n. 655.4
intermittent adj.
  periodic 138.10
  (discontinuous 70.4)
  irregular 139.2
intermittently 70.5
intermix 41.6
  (combine 48.3)
intermixture 41.1
intermolecular, intermundane 228.11
intermutation 148.1
intern, interne n.
  inhabitant 188.1
  interior 221.2
  doctor 662.19
  occupant 779.1
intern v.
  internalize 221.8
  imprison 751.8
intern, internal adj. 221.9
  (intrinsic 5.6)
  (subjective 317.5)
internal-combustion engine 633.3
internality, internalization 221.1
internalize 221.8
internally 221.12
internals 221.4
internasal 228.11
international

interchangeable 148.4
  public 372.6
  cosmopolitan 892.12
international auxiliary language, international language 560.5
interneciary 361.16
internecine
  destructive 162.6
  deadly 361.16
internecion 361.1
internecive
  destructive 162.6
  deadly 361.16
interneural 228.11
internist 662.19
internment 751.2
internodal 228.11
internuncio
  mediator 724.2
  diplomatist 759.2
  (messenger 534.1)
interoceanic, interosseal 228.11
interpellate 461.15
interpellation
  questioning 461.9
  allocution 586.1
interpenetrate
  interfuse 228.9
  (infuse 41.8)
  (pervade 186.12)
  enter 294.6
  pass through 302.2
interpenetration
  ingress 294.1
  passage 302.1
interplanetary 228.11
interpleader 724.2
interpolar 228.11
interpolate 228.8
interpolation
  mathematics 85.4
  interjection 228.2
  (impregnation 41.2)
  music 415.16
interpose
  intervene 228.7, 8, 9
  (add 37.3)
  (interrupt 70.3)
  (meddle 682.14)
  mediate 724.3
interposed 228.11
interposition
  interjacence 228.1, 3
  (intermeddling 682.8)
  mediation 724.1
interpret 522.6
  (solve 481a.4)
  (elucidate 518.3)
  (understand 518.4)
  (show 525.2)
  (tell 527.7)
interpretation 522
  (answer 462.3)
  (solution 481a.2)
  (meaning 516.1)
  (description 594.1)
interpretative 522.8

(informative 527.13)
(descriptive 594.7)
interpreter 524
  (oracle 513.1)
  (prophet 513.2)
  (informant 527.5)
  (teacher 540.1)
  (interlocutor 588.5)
  (guide 694.6)
  (go-between 724.2)
  (spokesman 759.1)
interradial 228.11
interregnum
  interim 109a.1
  pause 142.2
  (inaction 681.1)
  interval 198.1
  no authority 738.1
interreign 109a.1
interrelate 12.4
interrelated 12.6
interrelation
  correlation 12.1
  junction 43.1
interrenal 228.11
interrogate 461.15
interrogation 461.9
  (figure of speech 521.1)
interrogation point
  question 461.11
  punctuation 550.8
interrogative 461.24
interrogator 461.12
interrogatory 461.9
interrupt
  discontinue 70.3
  stop 142.7
  (end 67.7)
  intrude 228.10
  hinder 706.4
interrupted 70.4
interrupter 228.4
interruption
  discontinuity 70.1
  interim 109a.1
  pause 142.2
  interval 198.1
  intervention 228.3
  hindrance 706.1
interruptive 228.12
interscapular 228.11
interscholastic 148.4
intersect 219.7
intersection joint 43.3
  interval 198.1
  crossing 219.1, 2
  (roadway 627.3)
interseptal 228.11
intersidereal 318.16
intersow 73.3
interspace n.
  interval 198.1
  interior 221.2
interspace v. 198.4
interspaced 198.5
intersperse
  disperse 73.3
  interpenetrate 228.9
interspersion
  dispersion 73.1

922

intersprinkle — intrusion

interjection 228.2
intersprinkle 73.3
interstate 148.4
interstellar
  interjacent 228.11
  intersidereal 318.16
interstice 198.1
interstitial 228.11
intertanglement 41.1
intertexture
  mixture 41.1
  juncture 43.1
  interlacing 219.3
  texture 329.1
intertie 219.8
intertribal 148.4
intertwine 219.8
  (mix 41.6)
intertwist *n.* 219.4
intertwist *v.* 219.8
interurban 148.4
interval *n.* degree 26.1
  discontinuity 70.1
  period 108.1
  interim 109a.1
  pause 142.2
  interspace 198
  (separation 44.1)
  (omission 53.2)
  music 413.11
at intervals
  irregularly 59.12
  discontinuously 70.5
interval *v.*
  interlude 109a.2
  interspace 198.4
intervaled, intervalled, intervallic 198.5
intervalvular, intervascular 228.11
intervene
  interlude 109a.2
  interpose 228.7, 10
  (interrupt 70.3; 142.7)
  mediate 724.3
intervener 724.2
intervenience 228.1
intervenient, intervening 228.11, 12
intervention
  interposition 228.3
  (ingress 294.1)
  (insertion 300.1)
  (intermeddling 682.8)
  passage 302.1
  mediation 724.1
interventional 724.4
interventricular, intervertebral 228.11
interview
  hearing 418.2
  conference 588.3
interviewer 593.16
interweave 219.8
  (mix 41.6)
  (interject 228.8)
interweavement 219.3
interwed 903.13

interwork 12.5
interworking
  agency 170.1
  interaction 680.1
intestate 552.4
intestinal 221.11
intestine vitals 221.4
  bowels 350.4
  (tube 260.6)
inthrall, inthral
  enslave 749.5
  confine 751.8
intimacy
  friendship 888.1
  familiarity 892.1
intimate *n.*
  waist 225.18
  undergarment 225.25
  friend 890.1
intimate *v.* mean 516.5
  hint 527.8
  (indicate 550.18)
intimate *adj.*
  joined 43.10
  special 79.7
  near 197.8
  interior 221.9
  friendly 888.4
  familiar 892.12
intimated 526.7
intimation
  supposition 514.2
  monition 527.1, 4
intimidate 860.12
  (domineer 885.5)
  (threaten 909.2)
intimidation 860.5
  (threat 909.1)
intinction 998.6
intitule 564.6
intolerable
  unacceptable 649.9
  insufferable 830.18
intolerance
  prejudice 481.3
  bigotry 606.2
  (hyperorthodoxy 983a.5)
  impatience 825.1
intolerant
  dissentient 489.5
  bigoted 606.7
  (prejudiced 481.10)
  impatient 825.8
intomb, intombment. See **entomb** etc.
intonate 416.20
intonated 402.11
intonation tone 402.2
  (voice 580.1)
  orchestration 413.3
  music 413.23; 415.20
intone 416.20
  (glorify 990.10)
intorsion 248.1
intort interlace 219.8
  convolve 248.3
in toto 50.10
intoxation 655.2
intoxicant
  poison 663.4

inebriant 959.4
intoxicate thrill 824.2
  inebriate 959.18
intoxicated 959.21
intoxication
  poisoning 655.2
  excitation 824.1
  excitement 825.2
  drunkenness 959.1
intoxicating 959.24
intracellular 221.9
intractability
  inflexibility 323.1
  obstinacy 606.1
intractable
  inflexible 323.5
  obstinate 606.6
  unmanageable 704.10
  insubordinate 742.6
intrados 221.2
intralobular, intramarginal, intramolecular etc. 221.9
intransient 110.9
intransigency 604.1
intransigent *n.* 606.3
intransigent *adj.*
  resolute 604.7
  bigoted 606.7
intransitive 110.9
in transitu
  passing 111.8
  on the way 270.13
intransmutable
  durable 110.9
  unchangeable 150.7
intransparent 426.4
intra-uterine 221.9
intravasation 228.3
intravascular, intravenous, intraventricular 221.9
intrench, intrenchment See **entrench** etc.
intrepid 861.8
intrepidity 861.1
intricacy 59.3
  (puzzle 533.2)
  (dilemma 704.4)
intricate 59.10
  (difficult 704.8)
intrigant
  deceiver 548.1
  planner 626.8
  schemer 702.4
  libertine 962.1
intrigue *n.*
  influence 175.4
  plot 626.6
  cunning 702.1
  love affair 897.3
intrigue *v.* plot 626.10
  use artifice 702.5
  seduce 961.8
intrigued 827.8
intriguer
  deceiver 548.1
  schemer 702.4
intriguing

  scheming 702.6
  attractive 845.9
  conniving 940.8
intrinsic 5.6
  (characteristic 79.8)
  (internal 221.9)
  (subjective 317.7)
be intrinsic 5.5
intrinsicality 5
  (interiority 221.1)
intrinsically 5.8
  (truly 494.15)
introceptive 296.6
introduce precede 62.3
  begin 66.5
  innovate 140.7
  usher in 280.2
  bring in 296.5
  insert 300.5
  (interject 228.8)
introducer 164.1
introducible 296.7
introduction
  prelude 64.2
  innovation 140.3
  interjection 228.2
  reception 296.1
  insertion 300.1
  music 415.15
  drama 599.5
  presentation 894.3
introductory
  beginning 66.7
  introductive 296.7
  (preliminary 62.4)
introit 294.5
Introit psalm 990.2
  part of Mass 998.7
introitus 294.5
intromission
  intervention 228.3
  reception 296.1
intromissive 296.6
intromit 296.2
intromittent 296.6
introspect 461.17
introspection
  look 441.2
  inlooking 461.5
introsusception, introversion 218.1
introvert 218.4
intrudance 228.3
intrude
  intervene 228.10
  (foist in 10.4)
  (be untimely 135.3)
  (interrupt 142.7)
  (enter 294.6)
  (insert 300.5)
  overstep 303.5
  meddle 682.14
intruder 228.4
  (alien 57.3)
  (incomer 294.4)
  (meddler 682.11)
intrusion
  intervention 228.3
  (untimeliness 135.1)
  (ingress 294.1)
  overstepping 303.1

intrusive — invoke

intrusion (*continued*)
  meddling 682.8
intrusive
  disagreeing 24.6
  intervenient 228.12
  meddlesome 682.22
  hindering 706.8
intrusiveness 682.8
intrust See **entrust**
intuit 477a.3
intuition 477a
  (intellect 450.1)
  (knowledge 490.1)
  (divination 511.2)
  (clairvoyance 994.7)
intuitional 477a.4
intuitionism 926.4
intuitive 477a.4
intuitive knowledge 477a
  (knowledge 490.1)
intuitively 477a.4
intuitivism 477a.1, 2
intumescence
  swelling 194.1
  convexity 250.1, 2
  ailment 655.16
intussuscept 14.4; 218.4
intussusception 218.1
intwine See **entwine**
inundate
  overrun 303.3
  submerge 310.5
  wet 337.5
  overflow 348.18
  overfill 641.4
inundation
  submergence 310.2
  overflow 348.3
inunderstandable 519.6
inurbane 183.3
inure, enure
  habituate 613.8
  (train 537.10)
  (prepare 673.6)
  render callous 823.4
inured
  insensible 376.5
  habituated 613.12
  callous 823.7
  hardened in vice 945.18
inurement 613.5
  (preparation 673.1)
inurn 363.20
inusitate
  unusual 83.10
  unused 678.7
inusitation
  unaccustomedness 614.1
  disuse 678.1
inutile 645.8
inutility 645
  (impotence 158.1)
  (waste 638.1)
  (inadequacy 640.1)
  (inexpedience 647.1)

(unskillfulness 699.1)
invade intrude 228.10
  overstep 303.5
  attack 716.5
invader 716.4
invaginate 14.4; 218.4
invagination 218.1
invalescence 655.1
invalid *n*. 655.20
invalid *adj*.
  nugatory 158.11
  illogical 477.10
  abrogated 756.6
invalidate
  disable 158.6
  weaken 160.8
  disprove 479.2
  sicken 655.22
  abrogate 756.3
  disentitle 925.7
invalidation
  weakening 160.2
  disproof 479.1
invalidism 655.1
invalidity
  impotence 158.1
  ailment 655.1
invaluable
  useful 644.6
  superexcellent 648.10
  priceless 814.5
invariability
  regularity 16.2
  tedium 841.3
invariable
  uniform 16.5
  unchangeable 150.7
invariably 16.7
  (generally 78.15)
  (always 112.5)
  (constantly 136.6)
  (habitually 613.13)
invasion
  encroachment 228.3
  (ingress 294.1)
  attack 716.1
  (campaign 722.4)
invasive
  intrusive 228.12
  incursive 716.8
invective
  malediction 908.1
  railing 932.3
  disparagement 934.1
inveigh 932.7
inveigle 617.4
  (ensnare 545.9)
invent cause 153.6
  imagine 515.10
  trump up 544.3
invented 546.2
invention
  composition 54.2
  causation 153.5
  production 161.1, 6
  falsification 544.1
  lie 546.1
  contrivance 626.5
inventive 515.11

inventor 164.1
inventorial 86.4
inventory *n*. 86.1
inventory *v*.
  count 85.8
  list 86.3
  take stock 811.8
inverse *n*.
  the contrary 14.2
  (counterpart 17.5)
  reverse 218.3
inverse *v*. 218.4
inverse *adj*.
  contrary 14.5
  contrapositive 237.6
inversely 218.8
  (contrarily 14.7)
inversion
  reversal 218
  (contrariety 14.1)
  (derangement 61.1)
  (change 140.1)
  (reversion 145.1)
  (contraposition 237.1)
  anastrophe 577.1
invert 14.4; 218.4
  (change 140.6)
  (revert 145.4)
invertebracy 158.2
Invertebrata 368.10
invertebrate *n*.
  weakling 160.4
  animal 368.10
invertebrate *adj*.
  nugatory 158.11
  frail 945.12
inverted 218.6
  (reverse 14.5)
be inverted 218.5
invest empower 157.7
  clothe 225.41
  surround 227.3
  besiege 716.5
  install 755.4
  entrust 784.12
  ~ money 787.5; 817.3
  (expend 809.3)
  ~ in 795.3
  ordain 995.7
investigate
  examine 461.17
  (criticize 480.10)
  ~ judicially 480.8
investigation 461.3
  (trial 463.1)
  (dissertation 595.1)
investigative 461.24
investigator
  examiner 461.13
  detective 528.9
investiture
  investment 225.1
  installation 755.2
  holy orders 995.6
investment
  cover 223.2
  clothing 225
  (canonicals 999.1)
  besiegement 716.1
  endowment 784.1

  lending 787.1
make investments 673.7
investor
  contributor 784.7
  financier 797.6
inveterate
  traditional 124.8
  established 150.5
  confirmed 613.12
invidious
  annoying 830.12
  malignant 907.6
  envious 921.3
invigilation 459.2
invigorate
  strengthen 159.8
  energize 171.7
  cheer 836.6
invigorating
  bracing 656.5
  tonic 662.25
invigoration
  strengthening 159.2
  refreshment 689.1
inviolability 939.3
inviolable
  secret 528.21
  right 922.6
  trustworthy 940.9
inviolate
  unchanged 141.6
  secret 528.21
invisibility 447
  (latency 526.1)
  (concealment 528.1)
invisible
  infinitesimal 193.10
  imperceptible 447.4
  (latent 526.6)
  (hidden 528.17, 18)
be invisible 447.5
render invisible 528.10
invisible ink 528.5
invitation offer 763.1
  request 765.1
invitatory 765.7
invite allure 617.4
  offer 763.2
  request 765.4
  call to the ministry 995.7
inviting 617.5
  (delightful 829.8)
invocate 765.5
invocation
  allocution 586.1
  request 765.1
  benediction 931.2
  prayer 990.3, 4
  incantation 993.1
  rite 998.2
invocative, invocatory 765.7
invoice *n*. list 86.1
  statement 811.3
invoice *v*. list 86.3
  enter accounts 811.7
invoke address 586.2
  entreat 765.5
  pray 990.11

924

involucrum — irresistible

involucrum 223.11
involuntariness 601.2
involuntary
 instinctive 477a.4
 unwitting 601.14
 (impulsive 612.4)
 (unintentional 621.20)
 unwilling 603.5
involution
 complexity 59.3
 (imperspicuity 571.1)
 mathematics 85.4
 convolution 248.1
involve
 complicate 61.5
 include 76.3
 cause 153.6
 infold 229.3
 show 467.7
 mean 516.5
 (imply 526.4)
 indicate 550.18
 ~ in difficulties 704.6
involved
 complex 59.10
 (perplexing 475.12)
 (enigmatic 533.6)
 (imperspicuous 571.2)
 implied 526.7
 in debt 806.7
 (poor 804.7)
involvement 59.3
 (dilemma 704.4)
invulnerable 664.11
 (defensible 717.10)
inward interior 21.9
 (intrinsic 5.6)
 ingoing 294.8
inwardness 221.1
inwards 221.4
inweave 219.8
inwrap See **enwrap**
inwrought 5.6
iodine 662.8
ion 193.2
Ionian philosophy 451.6
Ionic
 philosophical 451.38
 type 591.8
 verse 597.13
iota modicum 32.2
 trifle 643.3
I O U pledge 771.1
 commercial paper 800.7
ipse dixit
 it is certain 474.17
 affirmation 535.1
ipso facto 1.9
I.Q. 498.1
iracund 901.7
iracundity 901.1
irascent 900.13
irascibility 901.1
 (excitability 825.1)
 (gruffness 895.2)
 (resentment 900.1)

irascible 901.7
 (sensitive 822.6)
 (excitable 825.8)
 (gruff 895.7)
 (angry 900.13)
 be irascible 901.5
irate 900.13
ire 900.1
ireful 900.13
Ireland 182.3
iridal 440.6
iridesce 440.4
iridescence
 opalescence 427.1
 variegation 440.1
iridescent 427.4; 440.6
iridization 440.1
iridize 440.4
iridosmine 323.3
iris n. 440.2
Iris n. 534.1
iris v. 440.4
irisation 440.1
irised 440.6
Irish n.
 language 560.4
 temper 900.1
Irish adj. 188.11
Irish bull 495.3
Irisher 188.9
Irishism blunder 495.3
 language 563.5
Irishman 188.9
Irishman's hurricane 265.1; 349.15
Irish stew 298.17
irk n. 841.3
irk v. be fatigued 688.4
 annoy 830.5
 bore 841.5
irk adj. 841.9
irked 828.15
irksome difficult 704.8
 annoying 830.12
 boresome 841.8
iron n. strength 159.4
 smoother 255.3
 hardness 323.3
 heater 386.1
 metal 635.6
 firearm 727.10
 have many irons in the fire 682.13
 in irons 751.11
 irons in the fire 625.2
iron v. 255.4
iron adj. 604.7
iron age 735.4
iron-bound coast
 shore 342.2
 danger 667.1
ironclad n. 726.11
ironclad adj.
 covered 223.28
 armored 717.9
Iron Cross 733.2
iron-gray, iron-grey 432.4
ironhanded 739.5
ironhearted 861.8
ironical
 figurative 521.3

 derisive 856.7
 discourteous 895.7
 contemptuous 930.8
 disapprobatory 932.11
Iron Maiden of Nuremberg 975.3
ironmaker 690.8
irons 752.2
ironsmith 690.6
ironstone stone 342.4
 ore 635.6
ironstone china 384.14
ironworker 690.9
ironworks 691
irony
 figure of speech 521.1
 ridicule 856.1
 discourtesy 895.2
 sarcasm 930.2
Iroquois 434.5
irradiance 420.1
irradiate v. 420.20
irradiate, irradiated adj. 420.22
irradiation 420.1, 14
irrational
 numeral 84.7
 illogical 477.10
 (absurd 497.4)
 (foolish 499.15)
 unintelligent 499.11
irrationality 477.5
 (absurdity 497.1)
 (foolishness 499.6)
irreclaimable
 hopeless 859.7
 irreformable 945.19
irreconcilable n.
 obstinate person 606.3
 (conservative 141.3)
 oppositionist 710.2
 malcontent 832.2
irreconcilable adj.
 different 15.7
 disagreeing 24.6
 unwilling 603.5
 bigoted 606.7
 at enmity 889.3
irreconciliation 889.1
irrecoverable
 past 122.8
 hopeless 859.7
irredeemable 859.7
irreducible
 uncongenial 24.8
 complex 59.10
 unchangeable 150.7
irreformable
 hopeless 859.7
 lost 945.19
irrefragability 474.1
 (proof 478.1)
irrefragable 474.10
irrefragably 474.16
irrefutability 474.1
irrefutable 474.10
irrefutably 474.16
irregular n. 726.4
irregular adj.

 ununiform 16a.2
 unequal 28.3
 disorderly 59.8
 diversified 81.3
 unconformable 83.9
 fitful 139.2
 (discontinuous 70.4)
 (transient 111.6)
 inconstant 149.6
 (erratic 503.17)
 distorted 243.5
 rough 256.12
irregularity
 nonuniformity 16a.1
 disorder 59.1
 unconformity 83.1
 ~ of recurrence 139
 roughness 256.1
irregularly
 disorderly 59.12
 (by chance 156.13)
 fitfully 139.3
 (discontinuously 70.5)
irrelation 10
 (unfitness 24.3)
 (disconnection 44.1)
 (multifariousness 81.1)
 (unconformity 83.1)
irrelative 10.5
irrelevance
 irrelation 10.1
 (unfitness 24.3)
 unimportance 643.1
irrelevant
 inapplicable 10.6
 (inapt 24.7)
 (illogical 477.10)
 unimportant 643.10
irrelevantly 10.9
irreligion 989
 (indifference 866.1)
 (impiety 988.1)
irreligionist 989.4
 (materialist 316.6)
 (misbeliever 984.12)
 (worldling 988.4)
irreligious 989.6
 (indifferent 866.4)
 (impious 988.10)
 be irreligious 989.5
 (disbelieve 485.5)
irremediable 859.7
irremissible 941a.4
irremovable 150.5
irreparable 859.7
irrepentance 951.1
irreprehensible 946.6
irrepressible
 unmitigable 173.16
 obstinate 606.6
 free 748.13
 impulsive 825.11
irreproachable, irreprovable 946.6
irresilient 326.3
irresistible
 demonstrative 478.3
 necessary 601.11

irresoluble — jabber

irresoluble 150.7
irresolute 605.5
  (inconstant 149.6)
  (undecided 475.10)
  (uncertain 475.16)
  (tergiversating 607.10)
  (fickle 608.6)
  (choiceless 609a.3)
be irresolute 605.4
  (change 140.5)
  (tergiversate 607.7)
  (be capricious 608.4)
  (be afraid 860.8)
irresolutely 605.7
irresolution 605
  (changeableness 149.1)
  (uncertainty 475.1)
  (tergiversation 607.1)
  (fickleness 608.3)
  (choicelessness 609a.1)
  (fearfulness 860.2)
  (cowardice 862.1)
irresolvable 87.9
irresolved 605.5
irrespective 10.5
irrespectively 10.9
irresponsibility 964.3
irresponsible
  fickle 608.6
  exempt 748.18
  lawless 964.6
irretrievable
  unchangeable 150.7
  hopeless 859.7
  (lost 776.5)
irrevealable 528.21
irreverence
  disrespect 929.1
  impiety 988.1
irreverent
  disrespectful 929.5
  impious 988.10
irreversible
  unchangeable 150.7
  resolute 604.7
  hopeless 859.7
irrevocable
  unchangeable 150.7
  necessary 601.11
  resolute 604.7
  mandatory 741.8
  hopeless 859.7
irrigate dilute 160.9
  water 337.5
irrigation 337.2
  (cleaning 652.2)
irriguous 339.8
irrision
  derision 856.1
  contempt 930.2
irritability 901.1
  (excitability 825.1)
irritable 901.7
  (excitable 825.8)
irritate inflame 173.8
  excite 824.5
  (aggravate 835.2)

  annoy 830.5
  incense 900.10
irritated 828.15
irritating 830.12
  (exciting 824.12)
irritation
  violence 173.1
  annoyance 828.4
  pique 900.1
  (excitation 824.1)
  (aggravation 835.1)
irritative 835.5
irruption
  intervention 228.3
  (ingress 294.1)
  invasion 716.1
irruptive
  intrusive 228.12
  invasive 716.8
Irvingite 984.14
Isaiah 513.2
Iscariot 949.3
Iscariotic 940.12
Iscariotism 940.4
ischialgia pain 378.1
  nervous disorder 655.14
Ishmael 893.5
isinglass 352.3
Isis productiveness 168.1
  deity 979.5
Islam 984.8
Islamic 984.27
Islamite 984.18
island *n.*
  separation 44.1
  isle 346
island *v.* 346.3
island *adj.* 346.4
islander 346.2
Islands of the Blessed 981.2
islandy 345.4
isle *n.* 346.1
isle *v.* 346.3
islesman 346.2
islet 346.1
ism, -ism belief 484.3
  denomination 542.4
  cult 984.3
isobar
  thermodynamics 338.5
  map line 550.9
isobaric 338.12
isobathic 27.9
isocheimal 383.12
isochronal
  equivalent 27.9
  periodic 138.10
  (chronological 114.9)
isochrone 120.4
isochronism 120.1
isochronize 120.3
isochronon 114.6
isochronous
  synchronous 120.4
  periodic 138.10
isogamous 357.10
isogamy

  similarity 17.2
  generation 161.2
isogenesis 161.2
isogloss 563.5
isolate separate 44.7
  segregate 55.4
  insulate 346.3
  seclude 893.7
isolated
  irrelative 10.5
  separate 44.12
  (alone 87.8)
  insular 346.4
  secluded 893.10
isolating languages 560.4
isolation
  separation 44.1
  (aloneness 87.1)
  segregation 55.2
  seclusion 893.2
isolationist 748.7
isometric 338.12
isometric line 338.5
isomorph 240.5
isomorphic 240.10
isomorphism 240.5
isonomy 27.2
isoperimetric 27.9
isopiestic 338.12
isoplere 338.5
isopolity 27.2
isotherm 550.9
isothermal 382.24
isothermal region 338.2
isotonic 413.26
isotropy 27.2
Israelite *n.* Jew 188.9
  Judaist 984.17
Israelite *adj.* 984.26
Israelitism 984.7
issuance egress 295.1
  appearance 448.1
  publication 531.1
issue *n.* focus 74.1
  result 154.1
  posterity 167.1
  egress 295.1
  question 461.10
  (topic 454.1)
  publication 531.1, **2**
  (book 593.1)
  ailment 655.5
at issue on foot 151.5
  dissentient 489.7
  denied 536.3
  in opposition 708.4
  contending 720.11
issue *v.* disperse 73.3
  eventuate 151.3
  result 154.3
  depart 293.4
  egress 295.1
  (escape 671.6)
  flow 348.17
  blow 349.22
  appear 446.2
  publish 531.7
  be published 531.9
  print 591.14
  ~ money 800.19

issueless 169.4
ist 984.13
isthmus bond 45.1
  narrow 203.3
  promontory 250.5
it, It 880.3
Italian *n.* native 188.9
  language 560.4
Italian *adj.* 188.11
italic 591.8
itch *n.*
  sensation 380.3
  rash 655.17
  desire 865.1
itch *v.* sensation 380.4
  ~ after 865.11
itching *n.* 865.1
  (excitability 825.1)
itching *adj.* 865.16
itching palm 865.1
itchy 380.6
item *n.* adjunct 39.1
  part 51.1
  particulars 79.3
  integer 87.3
  note 551.1
  account entry 811.2
item *adv.* 37.8
itemize
  specialize 79.6
  tell in detail 594.6
iterate 104.4
  (tautologize 573.6)
iteration 104.1
iterative 104.6
Ithunn, Ithun 979.3
itineracy 266.1
itinerant *n.* 268.2
itinerant *adj.* 266.23
itinerarian 268.2
itinerary *n.*
  route 266.9
  (seaway 267.8)
  (airway 267a.20)
  (path 627.2)
  wanderer 268.2
  directory 694.7
itinerary *adj.* 266.23
itinerate 266.12
itineration 266.1
itself 79.4
Ivan Ivanovitch 188.9
ivories
  piano keys 417.13
  dice 621.8
ivory *n.* tooth 253.3
  smooth 255.2
  white 430.3
ivory *adj.* 430.9
ivory black 431.5
ivory-white 430.9
izzard 67.1

J

jab *n.* blow 276.3
  attempt 675.1
  thrust 716.3
  gibe 930.3
jab *v.* 276.8
jabber *n.*

jabber — jazz

twaddle 517.3
jargon 563.4
chatter 584.2
jabber *v.*
 talk nonsense 517.6
 be inarticulate 583.2
 be loquacious 584.4
jacal 189.4
jacent 213.9
jacinth 847.8
jack *n.* ass 271.10
 spar 273.12
 lifter 307.2
 rotator 312.4
 tobacco 392a.2
 flag 550.13
 money 800.1
 playing card 840.13
Jack *n.*
 mariner 269.1
 man 373.2
jack *v.*
 jack up increase 35.3
 reprove 932.8
jack-a-dandy
 humorist 844
 fop 854.1
Jack afloat 269.1
jackal animal 366.5
 puppet 711.2
 sycophant 886.2
jackanapes 854.1
jackaroo, jackeroo 57.3
jackass ass 271.10
 hawse bag 273.14
jack-at-a-pinch
 friend in need 890.1
 help 912.1
jack boot, jackboot 225.27
jackdaw 366.22
jacker 622.5
jacket *n.*
 wrapper 223.11
 skin 223.12
 coat 225.16
 bookbinding 593.9
jacket *v.* clothe 225.41
 whip 972.6
Jack Frost 383.5
Jack-in-office 694.3
Jack-in-the-green 844
jack-in-the-pulpit 876.8
Jack Ketch 975.5
jackknife
 edge tools 253.6
 plunge 310.1
jackleg 792.8
Jack-of-all-trades 700.1
jack-o'-lantern, jack-o'-lanthorn
 luminescence 420.11
 lantern 423.2
jack pot stakes 621.4
 card playing 840.12
jackpudding 599.20
jack rabbit
 lowness 207.4
 hare 366.17

jacks 840.11
jackscrew 307.2
jackstay 273a.10
jackstone 342.4
jackstones 840.11
jackstraw
 nonentity 643.6
 puppet 711.2
jack-tar, jacky 269.1
Jacob 305.2
Jacobin 742.3
Jacobinic 742.7
Jacob's ladder
 ship's rope 273.10
 stairs 305.2
Jacquard, jacquard 219.5
Jacquerie 742.2
jactancy 884.1
jactation
 shaking 315.3
 boasting 884.1
jactitate 315.9
jaculate 284.11
jaculation 284.2
jaculator 284.7
jaculatory 284.16
jade *n.* horse 271.6
 wreck 659.5
 gem 847.8
 bad woman 949.4
 strumpet 962.2
jade *v.* tire 688.4, 5
 bore 841.5
 sate 869.4
jaded 869.6
jadu, jadoo 649.3
jag, jagg *n.*
 quantity 25.2
 part 51.1
 load 52.3; 190.1
 tooth 253.3
 notch 257.1
 freight 270.4
 spree 959.3
jag *v.* notch 257.5
 carry 270.8
Jagatai 560.4
Jagannath, Jagan-natha, Juggernaut 979.6
jäger, jager 726.4
jagged rough 256.12
 notched 257.6
 (angular 244.5)
jaggy 257.6
jaguar animal 366.3
 variegation 440.2
jail, gaol *n.* 752.1
jail, gaol *v.* 751.8
jailbird, gaolbird
 prisoner 754.1
 criminal 949.2
jailer, gaoler 753.1
 (protector 664.3)
 (guard 717.6)
Jain, Jaina 984.21
Jainism 984.11
jake 876.1
jakes dung 653.7
 water closet 653.9
Jakun 560.4

jalousie 424.3
jam *n.* gluten 352.3
 preserve 396.3
Jam *n.* 745.4
jam, jamb *n.* 704.2
 in a jam 704.11
jam, jamb *v.*
 attach 43.6
 ~ **in** 228.8
Jamaica rum 959.6
jamb, jambe
 post 215.16
 leg 266.11
 armor 717.2
jamboree 840.2
James 268.10
jampan 272.12
Jane 374.2
jangle *n.* discord 414.2
 quarrel 713.3
jangle *v.*
 sound harshly 410.7
 quarrel 713.7
jangly 410.9
Janizary, Janissary 726.4
Jansenism 984.4
janty See **jaunty**
Janus deceiver 548.1
 tergiversator 607.4
Janus-faced
 dissembling 544.8
 treacherous 940.12
Jap alien 57.3
 Japanese 188.9
japan *n.* paint 428.5
 blackening 431.5
Japan *n.* 182.3
japan *v.* 428.10
Japanese
 nationality 188.9
 yellowness 436.4
 language 560.4
jaquima 752.2
jar *n.*
 receptacle 191.11
 joggle 315.4
 (concussion 173.4)
 start 508.3
 discord 713.1
jar *v.*
 ~ **with** 15.5
 disagree 24.5
 joggle 315.8
 sound harshly 410.1
 (be discordant 414.3)
 startle 508.6
 disaccord 713.6
 shock 824.3
 annoy 830.5
Jardin des Plantes 371.6
jardiniere 191.10
jargon *n.*
 twaddle 517.3
 lingo 563.4
 (unintelligibility 519.2)
 (language 560.1)
 (term 564.3)
 gem 847.8

jargon *v.* 563.13
jargoner 563.11
jargonish 563.16
jargonist 563.11
jarring *n.*
 disagreement 24.1
 discord 713.1
jarring *adj.*
 disagreeing 24.6
 harsh-sounding 410.9
 (discordant 414.4)
jarvey 268.9
jasey 256.4
jasmine, jasmin 400.3
jasper man 373.2
 green 435.3
 red 434.5
 gem 847.8
jasper ware 384.14
jaundice *n.*
 yellowness 436.2
 (discoloration 440a.1)
 ailment 655.5
jaundice *v.*
 yellow 436.5
 prejudice 481.8
jaundiced
 yellow 436.6
 (discolored 440.3)
 ill-humored 901.7
 jealous 920.3
 partial 941a.3
jaunt *n.* 266.4, 8
jaunt *v.* 266.14
jaunting car 272.5
jaunty, janty
 cheerful 836.7
 pretty 845.11
 smart 847.14
 showy 882.8
Javanese 560.4
javelin 727.5
jaw *n.* 584.2
jaw *v.*
 be loquacious 584.4
 reprove 932.8
jaw-box 584.3
jawbreaker 577.2
jawbreaking 577.7
jawfall 837.1
jawfallen 837.9
jawing 932.3
jaws pair 89.2
 mouth 260.2
 embouchure 260.3
jawsmith 582.5
jawy 584.5
jay dupe 547.1
 chatterer 584.3
jay bird 366.22
jaywalker 268.6
jazz *n.* 415.6, 7
 (dance 840.7)
jazz *v.* copulate 43.8
 syncopate 416.18
jazz up
 intensify 157.7
 key up 171.7
 syncopate 416.18
jazz, jazzed *adj.* 415.29

jazzer — jittery

jazzer 416.1
jazz stick 417.13
jazzy
  syncopated 415.29
  gaudy 851.8
  showy 882.8
jealous 920.3
  (envious 921.3)
be jealous 920.2
  (envy 921.2)
jealousy doubt 485.2
  envious suspicion 920
  (envy 921.1)
Jean Baptiste 188.9
Jean Crapaud
  France 182.3
  Frenchman 188.9
jeans 225.21
jeer *n.* 930.3
jeer *v.* 930.6
jehad See jihad
Jehovah 976.2
Jehu 268.9
jejune
  incomplete 53.4
  unproductive 169.4
  empty 187.11
  insipid 391.2
  feeble style 575.2
  lacking 640.11
  uninteresting 843.5
jejunity
  insipidity 391.1
  ~ of style 575.1
  dullness 843.1
jejunum vitals 221.4
  intestine 350.4
jell 321.7
jellification 321.3
jellify 321.7
  (pulpify 354.4)
jelly *n.* gluten 352.3
  preserve 396.3
  light filter 424.5
jelly *v.* 321.7
jellyfish
  weakling 160.4
  fish 368.4
jemadar 745.11
jemmy 307.4
je ne sais quoi
  particularity 79.2
  object 316.3
  what's-its-name 565.4
jennet, genet
  horse 271.4
  ass 271.10
jeopard hazard 621.17
  endanger 665.4
jeopardize 665.4
jeopardy *n.*
  hazard 621.2
  danger 665.1
jeopardy *v.* 665.4
jerboa 309.3
jereed, jerrid 727.5
jeremiad, jeremiade
  lamentation 839.1
  malediction 908.1
  tirade 932.3

Jeremiah
  prophet 513.2
  lamenter 839.5
jerk *n.* yank 285.3
  (shake 315.4)
  twitching 315.6
  fool 501.1
by jerks 70.5
jerk *v.* throw 284.12
  yank 285.5
  (shake 315.8)
  twitch 315.11; 824.7
jerkin 225.16
jerks twitching 315.6
  nervous disorder 655.14
jerkwater town 189.17
jerky 315.13
jerrid See jereed
Jerry *n.* German 188.9
  German soldier 726.4
jerry *adj.*
  jerry-built 160.11
  cognizant 490.12
  spurious 545.13
jerry-build 545.7
jerry-building
  house 189.3
  deception 545.6
jerry-built
  unsubstantial 160.11
  spurious 545.13
jerry shop 959.13
Jerry sneak 862.2
jersey 219.5
Jersey 366.12
Jerusalem pony 271.10
Jesse, Jessie, Jessy 972.1
Jesse James 792.10
jest *n.* trifle 643.3
  witticism 842.4
  ridicule 856.1
  laughingstock 857.1
in jest in fun 842.10
  in ridicule 856.8
jest *v.* joke 842.8
  banter 856.4
jestbook 842.4
jester comedian 599.20
  humorist 844
jestingstock 857.1
Jesuit deceiver 548.1
  evangelist 996.4
  monk 996.11
jesuitic
  sophistical 477.9
  false 544.7
jesuitism, Jesuitry 477.1; 544.1
Jesus 976.5
jet *n.* essence 5.2
  center 222.2
  spout 348.5
  (egress 295.1)
  lamp 423.11
  black 431.3
  type 591.6
jet *v.* jerk 285.5
  flow out 295.7
  spout 348.20

jet-black 431.7
jetsam 782.2
jettison *n.* 782.2
jettison *v.* 678.3
jetty *n.*
  promontory 250.5
  anchorage 666.4
jetty *adj.* 431.7
jeu de mots 842.5
jeu d'esprit 842.4
Jew Hebrew 188.9
  Judaist 984.17
jewel axis 312.5
  treasure 648.4
  ornament 847.7
  favorite 899.1
  endearment 902.4
  good person 948.1
jeweler, jeweller 797.11
jewelry, jewellery 847.7
  (merchandise 798.3)
Jewish racial 11.8
  Hebrew 188.11
  Judaical 984.26
Jewism 984.7
jew's-harp, jews'-harp 417.1
Jezebel
  malevolent woman 913.5
  jade 949.4
  strumpet 962.2
jib *n.* face 234.4
  sail 273.13
jib *v.* 277.3
jib, jibb *v.*
  change 140.5
  turn ship 267.24
jibbah, jibba, jibbeh 225.15
jibber
  talk nonsense 517.6
  be loquacious 584.4
jibber the kibber
  signal ship 267.41
  signal 550.20
jib boom, jibboom
  prow 234.3
  spar 273.12
jibe See gibe
jibe, gibe 23.7
  (concur 178.2)
not jibe 24.5
jibe, gybe
  change 140.5
  turn ship 267.24
  (deviate 279.4)
jibstay 273.10
jiff, jiffy 113.3
in a jiffy 113.6
jig *n.* joggle 315.4
  music 415.7
  Negro 431.4
  dance 840.7
jig *v.* jerk 285.5
  joggle 315.8
jigger *n.*
  supporter 215.2
  cart 272.5

bicycle 272.14
streetcar 272.20
object 316.3
flea 366.24
man 373.2
jiggerman 668.4
jiggers!
  warning 668.11
  beware! 864.9
jigget, jiggit
  jerk 285.5
  joggle 315.8
jiggle *n.* 315.4
jiggle *v.* jerk 285.5
  joggle 315.8
jihad, jehad 722.4
jilt *n.* 548.1
jilt *v.* deceive 545.7
  be faithless 940.7
jilter 548.1
Jim Crow 431.4
Jim Crow car 272.20
jim-dandy 648.4
jimjams 959.2
jimmy meat 298.22
  pry 307.4
jimp, gimp
  orderly 58.7
  spruce 845.11
Jimson weed 663.6
jingal, gingall 727.11
gingall See jingal
jingle, gingle *n.*
  confusion 458.4
  poem 597.2
  rhyme 597.8
jingle, gingle *v.*
  ring 408.8
  confuse 458.9
jingled 959.21
jingler 800.4
jingo *n.* 884.4
by jingo! 535.8
jingo *adj.* 884.8
jingoism
  overpatriotism 549.1
  chauvinism 884.2
  (prejudice 481.4)
jingoist *n.* 884.4
jingoist *adj.* 884.8
jingoistic 549.3
jinni, jinnee 980.2
jinrikisha, jinricksha 272.5, 11
jinx *n.*
  bad influence 649.3
  hoodoo 993.2
jinx *v.* 735.7
jinxed 735.9
jipper 384.19
jitneur, jitneuse 268.10
jitney
  diminutive 193.2
  omnibus 272.15
  money 800.8
jitterbug
  music lover 416.15
  dancer 840.9
jitters *n.* 825.3; 860.3
jittery 860.14

jiujitsu, jiujutsu See
  jujitsu
jiva potence 157.1
  life force 359.2
  soul 994.11
jivatma 994.11
Joan of Arc 861.3
job event 151.1
  aircraft 273a.1
  task 625.2, 4
  deed 680.2
  theft 791.4
  dishonest act 940.5
on the job
  attentive 457.9
  vigilant 459.8
  alert 682.17
jobation 932.3
jobber cheat 548.2
  crafty rascal 702.4
  dealer 797.8
jobbernowl 501.1
jobbernowlism 499.2
jobbery
  machiavellianism
    702.2
  sharp practice 940.5
jobbing 794.2
job printer 591.12
Job's comforter
  sad person 837.5
  pessimist 859.4
jock 268.8
Jock 188.9
jockey n.
  saddle 215.23
  rider 268.8
  cheat 548.2
  cunning person
    702.4
  swindler 792.8
jockey v. cheat 545.7
  swindle 791.12
jockeyism 545.1
Jocks 726.4
jocose merry 836.8
  witty 842.9
jocosity 842.2
jocular merry 836.8
  witty 842.9
jocularity 842.2
  (merriment 836.3)
jocund merry 836.8
  jolly 840.22
jocundity
  pleasurableness
    829.1
  merriment 836.3
Joel 513.2
Joe Miller
  old joke 842.6
  (repetition 104.3)
  humorist 844
jog n.
  slow motion 275.2
  (gait 266.5)
  impulse 276.1
  joggle 315.4
jog v. walk 266.16
  impel 276.7
  jerk 285.5
  joggle 315.8

jog on continue 143.2
  walk 266.16
  go slow 275.5
  advance 282.2
  be mediocre 736.2
jogger 505.5
joggle n. 315.4
joggle v. jerk 285.5
  jolt 315.8
jog trot n.
  slow motion 275.4
  routine 613.4
jog-trot v. 275.5
jog-trot adj.
  uniform 16.5
  repetitional 104.7
  habitual 613.11
  tedious 841.8
John 373.2
John Bull
  England 182.3
  Englishman 188.9
John Doe 643.6
John Hancock 488.4
Johnny, Johnnie
  man 373.2
  soldier 726.4
johnnycake 298.11
Johnny Crapaud 188.9
Johnny on the spot
  punctual 132.9
  attentive 457.9
Johnsonian 577.7
join unite 43.5
  (mix 41.6)
  (combine 48.3)
  (unify 87.5)
  be joined 43.9
  (cohere 46.5)
  league 48.4
  assemble 72.10
  be near 197.5, 7
  be contiguous 199.3
  meet 292.10
  touch 379.3
  side with 709.5
  become a member
    712.8
  (enlist 722.11)
  bear company 892.9
join forces 48.4
  (co-operate 709.4)
join hands 709.5
join in 709.6
join issue
  argue 476.11
  deny 536.2
  quarrel 713.7
  fight 720.8
joinder 43.1
joined 43.10
be joined 43.9
joiner
  junction 43.4
  abutter 199.2
  sociable person
    892.8
joining
  junction 43.1, 3
  (addition 37.1)
  meeting 292.4
joint n.

juncture 43.3
  (fastening 45.2)
  member 51.4
  abode 189.1
  dive 189.9
  fold 258.1
  meat 298.19
  gambling 621.14
  sink of iniquity
    945.8
  brothel 961.7
out of joint
  inapt 24.7
  disorderly 59.8
  impotent 158.8
  dislocated 185.3
  amiss 649.11
joint adj.
  joined 43.10
  combined 48.5
  accompanying 88.8
  concurrent 178.4
jointer 255.3
jointly 43.14
  (with 37.9)
  (together 88.10)
joint operation
  co-operation 709.1
  warfare 722.1
joint stock
  co-operation 709.2
  participation 778.1
joint tenancy 778.1
joint tenant 778.3
jointure
  coheirship 775.4
  joint tenancy 778.1
joist 215.12
joke n. trifle 643.3
  witticism 842.4
  ridicule 856.1
  laughingstock 857.1
no joke reality 1.2
  gravity 642.2
old joke 842.6
  (repetition 104.3)
  (trite saying 496.3)
  (triteness 843.2)
joke v. jest 842.8
  banter 856.4
joker man 373.2
  playing card 840.13
  humorist 844
jokul, jökul 383.5
jole See jowl
jollification 840.2
jollity 836.3; 840.2
  (conviviality 892.2)
jolly n.
  marine 269.1; 726.10
  boat 273.4
jolly v.
  banter 856.4
  flatter 933.2
jolly adj.
  intoxicated 959.21
  merry 836.8
  jovial 840.22
  convivial 892.12
jolly adv. 31.15
jolly jumper 273.13
jolt n. impulse 276.1

joggle 315.4
  (concussion 173.4)
  start 508.3
jolt v. walk 266.16
  impel 276.7
  joggle 315.8
  startle 508.6
  shock 824.3
jolterhead, jolthead
  501.1
jolterheaded, jolt-
  headed 499.12
Jonah n.
  mariner 269.1
  prophet 513.2
  bad influence 649.3
Jonah v. 735.7
Jonahed 735.9
jongleur singer 416.10
  poet 597.10
jonquil 436.3
jonquil yellow 436.1
Jophiel 977.1
jordan, jorden 191.11
jornada 266.8
jorum 191.11
joseph 225.16
Joseph prophet 513.2
  interpreter 524.1
Joseph's coat 440.2
Joseph Smith 513.2
Joseph Surface 548.4
Joshua 513.2
joskin 876.5
joss luck 156.1
  idol 991.4
joss house 1000.1
jostle, justle n.
  impulse 276.1
  joggle 315.4
jostle, justle v.
  disagree 24.5
  counteract 179.3
  impel 276.7
  joggle 315.8
  disaccord 713.6
  joust 720.8
joss stick
  incense 400.2
  fumigator 388.7
jot n. modicum 32.2
  inextension 180a.1
  diminutive 193.2
  mark 550.7
  trifle 643.3
jot v.
jot down 551.8
jotting record 551.1
  writing 590.3
Jotunn, Jotun, Jötunn
  192.8
joule 158a.5
jounce n. 315.4
jounce v. 315.8
journal
  chronology 114.5
  record 551.3
  (list 86.1)
  book 593.6
  narrative 594.2
  account book 811.5
journal box 312.5

journalism — Jupiter 930

journalism
  recording 551.7
  authorship 590.2
  writing 593.17
journalist 593.16
  (publisher 531.5)
  (recorder 553.1)
journey *n.* 266.8
  (voyage 267.6)
  (passage 302.1)
journey *v.*
  travel 266.12
  ~ by water 267.10
journeyer 268.1
journeying 266.1
journeyman
  timepiece 114.6
  craftsman 690.5
joust, just *n.* 720.2
joust, just *v.* 720.8
jouster, juster 726.1
jouvence blue 438.2
Jove paternity 166.2
  god 979.2
jovial merry 836.8
  jolly 840.22
  convivial 892.12
joviality
  merriment 836.3
  amusement 840.1
  jollity 840.2
Jovinianist 984.14
jowl, jole 236.1
joy *n.* 827.2
  (cheerfulness 836.1)
joy *v.* enjoy 827.5, 6
  rejoice 838.5
  exult 884.6
joyance 827.2
joyful happy 827.9
  merry 836.8
joyless
  depressing 830.1
  sad 837.9
joyous 836.8
joy ride *n.* 266.7
joy-ride *v.* 266.18
joy-rider 268.10
joy stick 273a.10
J. P. 967.1
Juang 560.4
juba 415.7
jubbah, jibbah 225.15
jibba, jibbeh See **jub-bah**
jube 1000.3
jubilant
  overjoyed 827.10
  gay 836.9
  rejoicing 838.9
  (celebrating 883.5)
  exultant 884.9
jubilate rejoice 838.5
  celebrate 883.3
  exult 884.6
jubilation 838.1
  (celebration 883.1)
jubilee
  anniversary 138.5
  celebration 883.1
  (rejoicing 838.1)
  (festivity 840.2)

Judaical 984.26
Judaism 984.7
Judaist
  sectary 984.14
  Hebraist 984.17
Judas deceiver 548.1
  traitor 949.3
Judas kiss
  duplicity 544.2
  treachery 940.4
judge *n.*
  connoisseur 850.3
  magistrate 967
  (critic 480.5)
  (mediator 724.2)
judge *v.* decide 480.6
  (administer justice 965.3)
  (try 969.11)
  believe 484.8
  suppose 514.6
  exercise taste 850.4
judgmatic
  judicial 480.11
  wise 498.11
  juridical 965.4
judgment, judgement
  mental faculty 450.1
  decision 480
  (conviction 484.2)
  (interpretation 522.1)
  (judicature 965.1)
  (verdict 969.8)
  wisdom 498.3
  (discrimination 465.1)
  punishment 972.1
  divine ~ 976.5
pass judgment, pronounce judgment 480.9
  (condemn 971.2)
sit in judgment 480.8
  (administer justice 965.3)
  (try 969.11)
judgment seat 966.1
judicate 480.6
judication 480.1
judicative 965.4
  (tribunal 966.7)
judicator 967.1
judicatory *n.*
  supervision 693.2
  dominion 737.2
  jurisdiction 965.1
  tribunal 966.1
judicatory *adj.*
  judicial 480.11
  juridical 965.4
judicature
  judgment 480.1
  supervision 693.2
  jurisdiction 737.2; 965.1
  tribunal 966.1
judicial
  judicatory 480.11
  wise 498.11
  juridical 965.4

judiciary *n.* 966.1
judiciary *adj.*
  judicial 480.11
  judicatory 965.4
judicious 498.11
  (judicial 480.12)
judiciousness 498.3
jug *n.*
  receptacle 191.11
  ceramics 384.14
  prison 752.1
jug *v.* 751.8
Juggernaut
  avatar 979.6
  idol 991.4
Juggernaut See **Jagannath**
juggle *n.*
  deception 545.3
  artifice 702.3
juggle *v.* 545.7
juggler
  deceiver 548.2, 6
  (proficient 700.1)
  acrobat 599.21
  cunning person 702.4
jugglery
  deception 545.2
  cunning 702.1
jugulate 361.12
jugulum 45.1
juice
  electricity 158a.1
  fluid 333.2
juiceless 340.7
juicer
  electrician 158a.10
  stagehand 599.17
juicy fluid 333.7
  moist 339.7
jujitsu, jujutsu 720.7
jujube 396.3
julep 396.5
jumble *n.* 59.2
  (mixture 41.4)
jumble *v.*
  derange 61.2
  be indiscriminate 465a.2
jumbo *n.*
  large thing 192.6
  behemoth 192.8
Jumbo *n.* 271.2
jumbo *adj.* 192.15
jump *n.*
  advantage 33.2
  gait 266.5
  journey 266.8
  flight 267a.23
  leap 309.1
have the jump on 33.6
on the jump
  moving 264.10
  active 682.20
jump *v.*
  play truant 187.8
  walk 266.16
  leap 309.4
  pretermit 460.7
  startle 508.6

evade 623.6
escape 671.6
jump about
  caper 309.5
  toss 315.9
jump at
  rush upon 622.9
  be precipitate 684.4
  catch at 789.13
  desire 865.11
jump down one's throat 900.8
jump on 972.5
jump over 303.2
jump up 307.7
jumper
  electricity 158a.8
  coat 225.16
  sled 272.13
  leaper 309.3
  (athlete 840.17)
jumpers 225.32
jumping 686.2
jumping bean, jumping jack 309.3
jumping-off place
  village 189.17
  distant point 196.3
jump-off 66.1
junction union 43
  (addition 37.1)
  (mixture 41.1)
  (coherence 46.1)
  (combination 48.1)
  contiguity 199.1
  railway 627.5
juncture
  circumstance 8.2
  joint 43.3
  (fastening 45.2)
  crisis 134.4
jungle
  complexity 59.3
  resort 74.2
  woods 367.7
jungly 365.4
junior *n.* 541.4
junior *adj.* 34.5
juniority
  inferiority 34.2
  youth 127.1
juniper tree 367.6
  wood 635.3
junk ship 273.2
  rubbish 645.4
junket *n.*
  journey 266.8
  meal 208.34, 37
  picnic 840.2
junket *v.* 840.21
junk heap 645.4
Juno 979.2
Juno Curitis, Juno Quiritis 722.7
Juno Lucinia 161.3
Juno Pronuba 903.1
junta 696.1
junto 712.2
jupe 225.16, 18, 19
jupes 225.25
Jupiter
  paternity 166.2

planet 318.3
god 979.2
Jupiter Fulgur, Jupiter Fulminator 420.6
Jupiter Pluvius 348.11
Jupiter Tonans 406.4
jupon 225.19
jurat 967.1
juridical
  judicial 480.11
  legal 963.5
  jurisdictive 965.4
jurisconsult 968.1
jurisdiction
  supervision 693.2
  authority 737.2
  legal authority 965
jurisdictional
  administrative 693.6
  juridical 965.4
jurisprudence 963.3
jurisprudent n. 968.1
jurisprudent adj.
  legal 963.5
  barristerial 968.4
jurisprudentialist, jurist 968.1
juristic 480.11
juror 967.3
jury 967.2
jury chancellor, juryman 967.3
jussive n. 567.1
jussive adj. 741.8
just n., v. See joust
just adj.
  reasonable 476.16
  accurate 494.11
  fair 941.3
  (unprejudiced 498.12)
  (expedient 646.4)
  (right 922.5)
  (due 924.9)
  (conscientious 939.8)
  (legal 963.5)
  righteous 944.4; 988.10
just adv. 494.16
juste-milieu
  mean 29.1
  moderation 174.1
juster See jouster
justice fairness 941
  (right 922.1)
  (dueness 924.1)
  (honesty 939.1)
  (legality 963.1)
  cardinal virtue 944.1
  judge 967.1
  do justice to
  eat heartily 298.44
  do one's duty 926.6
  extenuate 937.8
  be fair 941.2
in justice
  rightfully 922.7
  justly 941.5
  retributive justice

nemesis 941.1
punishment 972.1
seat of justice 966.1
see justice done 941.2
justice of the peace 967.1
justiciar, justiciary 967.1
justifiable
  logical 476.16
  vindicable 937.10
  (right 922.5)
justification
  printing 591.2
  vindication 937.1, 2
  (apology 952.2)
  religion 987.2
justificatory 937.9
justifier 937.4
justify
  ~ type 591.14
  vindicate 937.5, 6
  (apologize 952.5)
  sanctify 976.11
justifying 937.9
justle See jostle
justly 941.5
justness 941.1
just now
  instantly 113.6
  recently 123.13
jut overhang 214.5
  project 250.7
jute 205.3
Jutland 722.5
jutting 214.8
jutty
  promontory 250.5
  anchorage 666.4
juvenescence 127.1
juvenile n.
  youngling 129.1
  actor 599.19
juvenile adj. 127.5
juvenilify 127.4
juvenility 127.1
juxtapose
  place near 197.7
  compare 464.2
juxtaposit
  place near 197.7
  compare 464.2
juxtaposition
  nearness 197.1
  contiguity 199.1
in juxtaposition
  near 197.11
  beside 236.9
juxtapositional
  near 197.8
  contiguous 199.4

K

kaama 366.10
Kabyle 560.4
kachahri See cutcherry
Kachin 560.4
kadi, kadee See cadi

Kaffir, Kafir 984.20
Kafiri 560.4
Kaiser 745.3
kaiserism 737.4
kajawah 272.12
kaleidophon, kaleidophone 445.1
kaleidoscope
  changeableness 149.2
  chromoscope 428.8
  scope 445.1
kaleidoscopic
  changeable 149.5
  variegated 440.5
kalends See calends
Kali 979.4
Kalki 979.6
Kalmuck, Kalmuk 560.4
Kalpa eon 108.2
  indefinite time 109.2
kalsomine See calcimine
Kama 897.1, 4
kamarupa 994.12
Kamasin, Kamassin 560.4
kame 206.2
kamseen, kamsin See khamsin
Kanarese 560.4
kangaroo 309.3
  (animal 366.2)
Kantianism 451.11
kaolin, kaoline
  soil 342.3
  ceramics 384.14
Kapelle 416.8, 11
Kapellmeister 416.13
Karaism 984.7
Karaite 984.17
Kara-Kalpak, Karen 560.4
karma 941.1
karroo, karoo 169.2
karyokinesis 264.4
karyokinetic 264.9
karyoplasm 357.3
karyoplasmic 357.9
karyosome 357.3
Kashmiri, Kasubian, Kashubian 560.4
katar, kuttar 727.3
Kavi, Kawi 560.4
kayak 273.4
kayo n. 67.4
kayo v. 67.7
Kazan Tatar 560.4
keck 297.18
keddah 232.1
  (closure 261.1)
kedge n. 666.2
kedge v. 267.10
keel n. bottom 211.1
  ship 273.7
  airplane 273a.10
keel v. incline 217.6
  careen 267.34
keel over
  be inverted 218.5
  capsize 267.35

keelboat 273.2
keelhaul, keelhale
  torture 830.6
  punish 972.5
keelson, kelson
  bottom 211.1
  ship 273.7
keen n. 839.3
keen v. 839.6
keen adj.
  forceful 171.9, 10
  violent 173.11
  sharp 253.11
  sensible 375.7
  cold 383.8
  pungent 392.5
  odorous 398.8
  discriminating 465.4
  sagacious 498.10
  good 648.8
  eager 682.18; 865.17
  emotion 821.5, 6
  penetrating 824.13
  witty 842.9
  gruff 895.7
  ~ about 897.15
keen-edged 253.11
keener mourner 363.7
  crafty rascal 702.4
keenness
  sharpness 253.1
  sagacity 498.2
  sharp appetite 865.3
keen-sighted 441.20
keen-witted
  sagacious 498.10
  witty 842.9
keep n.
  nourishment 298.5
  custody 664.2; 751.4
  aid 707.1
  stronghold 717.4
  prison 752.1
  retention 781.1
for keeps 112.5
keep v.
  be permanent 141.4
  continue 143.2
  stabilize 150.4
  inhabit 186.10
  reserve 636.8
  preserve 670.3
  sustain 707.7
  restrain 751.6
  observe 772.3
  retain 781.4
  celebrate 883.3; 998.14
  immortalize 976.8
keep at 604a.2
keep at it
  do frequently 136.2
  continue 143.3, 5
  persevere 604a.2
  be industrious 682.12
keep away
  be absent 187.8
  keep distance 196.4
  avoid 623.6
keep back delay 133.6

keeper — kidnaping

keep (*continued*)
  keep secret 528.11
    (latentize 526.5)
  reserve 636.8
  not use 678.5
  hinder 706.4
  restrain 751.6
  retain 781.4
keep body and soul together
  keep alive 358.9
  be in health 654.2
keep company
  accompany 88.6
  consort 892.9
  (be friends 888.2)
keep dark 528.11
keep from
  keep secret 528.11
  hinder 706.4
  restrain 751.6
  abstain 953.5
keep going
  carry on 143.3
  move 264.6
  persevere 604a.2
  be industrious 682.12
  keep moving! 682.26
keep house 184.14
keep off
  keep distance 196.4
  forbear! 623.13
  avert 706.5
  fend off 717.8
  hands off! 719.6
  don't 761.6
keep off and on
  vary 149.4
  be irresolute 605.4
  be capricious 608.4
keep on
  do frequently 136.2
  continue 143.2
  persevere 604a.2
  be industrious 682.12
keep one's counsel 528.11
keep one's hand in 613.10
keep tab 459.6
keep the field 722.9
keep the peace
  be moderate 174.4
  be concordant 714.2
  (be reconciled 723.5)
  be at peace 721.3
keep together 709.4
keep to oneself
  keep secret 528.11
  not speak 585.3
keep under
  dominate 737.12
  restrain 751.6
keep up
  continue 143.3
  support 215.26
  keep pace 274.12
  persevere 604a.2
  preserve 670.3

stimulate 824.2
keeper stockman 370.4
  guardian 664.3
  jailer 753.1
keeping
  agreement 23.1
  conformity 82.1
  symmetry 242.1
  coloring 428.2
  protectorship 664.2
  preservation 670.1
  retention 781.1
in keeping with 82.12
out of keeping
  inapt 24.7
  unconformable 83.9
  inexpedient 647.3
keeping room 191.16
keepsake 505.5
kef 683.4
keg 191.11
kelly 225.26
kelp 367.3
kelpie, kelpy
  horse 271.9
  water sprite 979.10
kelson See **keelson**
kelt 41.5
kelter See **kilter**
ken *n.* sight 441.1, 6
  knowledge 490.1
ken *v.* see 441.10, 11
  know 490.9
  understand 518.4
kennel crowd 72.4
  doghouse 189.6
  (enclosure 232.1)
  (menagerie 370.3)
  conduit 350.1
keno 840.12
kenosis 942.1
Kentucky bluegrass 367.9
kepi 225.26
Képviselőház 696.6
kerbstone See **curbstone**
kerchief
  garment 225.26, 33
  napkin 652.7
kern, kerne *n.* 876.5
kern *v.* 321.7
kerned 591.18
kernel essence 5.2
  center 222.2
  (middle 68.2)
  nut 298.33
kerosene 356.2
ketch 273.2
ketchup See **catchup**
kettle
  receptacle 191.11
  boiler 386.1
  kettledrum 417.10
kettledrum *n.*
  drum 417.10
  festivity 840.2
  party 892.5
kettledrum *v.* 416.19
kettledrummer 416.7
kettlemaker 690.8
kettle of fish

predicament 8.3
confusion 59.2
kevel pin 45.5
  ship 273.14
key *n.* opener 260.10
  (stopper 263.1)
  (medium 631.2)
  island 346.1
  tone 402.2
  note 413.7, 13
  color tone 428.2
  clew 550.2
  interpretation 522.1
  motive 615.1
  main thing 642.4
  anchorage 666.4
  emblem of authority 747.3
key *n.* See **quay**
key *v.*
key up
  stimulate 171.7
  intensify 157.7
keyhole 260.1
keynote
  prototype 22.1
  note 413.7
  salient point 642.4
keystone
  support 215.18
  motive 615.1
  salient point 642.4
  completion 729.1
kg. 319.4
khaki *n.* 225.8
khaki *adj.* 433.4
khamsin, khamseen
  wind 349.9, 12
  heat 382.4
khan inn 189.8
  prince 745.5; 875.7
  honorifics 877.2
khansamah, khansaman caterer 637.2
  steward 746.1
khanum 875.6
Kharia, Khasi 560.4
khedive 745.7
khidmatgar, khidmutgar, khitmatgar, khitmutgar 746.1
Khmer 560.4
khoja 540.1
Khond, Khowar 560.4
kiack 1000.1
kiang, kyang
  ass 271.10
  animal 366.2
kibitka 272.4
kibosh *n.* end-all 67.4
  destruction 162.2
  nonsense 517.2
kibosh *v.* finish 67.7
  disable 158.6
  destroy 162.4
  silence 403.5
kick *n.* energy 171.1, 3
  foot 211.4
  blow 276.3
  recoil 277.1
  pungency 392.1
  protest 489.2

verve 682.1
purse 802.2
thrill 827.1
kick *v.* strike 276.8
  recoil 277.3
  eject 297.8
  dismiss 297.12
  protest 489.4
  object 708.2; 932.5
  complain 839.10
kick against
  oppose 708.2
  resist 719.3
kick against the pricks
  labor in vain 645.6
  be unclever 699.7
  resist 719.3
  be rash 863.5
kick back 277.3
kick downstairs 297.12
kick in
  contribute 784.8
  pay 807.6
kick off 360.6
kick one's heels
  wait 133.7
  do nothing 681.2
  idle 683.8
kick over the traces
  revolt 742.5
  violate the law 964.6
kick the beam
  be unequal 28.2
  be small 32.4
  be inferior 34.4
  fall short 304.2
  measure 466.10
  be insufficient 640.6
  be imperfect 651.3
kick the bucket 360.6
kick up a dust
  be violent 173.7
  be noisy 404.6
  bestir oneself 682.12
  quarrel 713.7
  bluster 887.3
  vent anger 900.8
kick up one's heels 360.6
kicker foot 211.4
  malcontent 832.2
kickoff 66.1
kicks trousers 225.21
  shoes 225.27
kickshaw, kickshaws
  delicacy 298.9
  meat 298.19
  trifle 643.3
  toy 840.16
  trinket 847.9
kickup 273.1
kid youngling 129.3, 7
  goat 366.9
kiddish 127.5
kiddy 366.9
kidnap 791.11
kidnaper, kidnapper 792.7
kidnaping, kidnapping 791.1

932

kidney kind 75.2
  vitals 221.4
kids 225.30
kike alien 57.3
  Jew 188.9
kilderkin 191.11
Kilkenny cats 713.1
kill stop 142.7
  slay 361.10
  (execute 972.8)
  extinguish 421.6
  be killed 361.13
  kill by inches
    pain 378.4
    torture 830.6
  kill oneself 361.14
  kill the fatted calf
    celebrate 883.3
    give reception 892.11
  kill time idle 683.8
    play 840.21
  kill two birds with one stone 682.12
killer slayer 361.8
  (destroyer 165.1)
  (executioner 975.5)
  dolphin 366.21
killick 666.2
killing n. slaying 361
  (execution 972.4)
  success 731.2
killing adj.
  murderous 361.15
  captivating 617.4
  delightful 829.8
  beautiful 845.13
  ridiculous 855.5
killing time 126.4
kill-joy marplot 706.3
  sad person 837.5
kiln n. 386.1
kiln v. 340.5
Kilo kilocycle 158a.5
  kilogram 319.4
kilo- 98.28
kilocycle
  thousand 98.10
  electricity 158a.5
kilogram, kilogramme
  thousand 98.10
  weight 319.4
kiloliter, kilolitre
  thousand 98.10
  measure 466.3
kilometer, kilometre
  thousand 98.10
  length 200.6
  measure 466.3
kilowatt 158a.5
kilt 225.19
kilter, kelter 7.1
  in kilter 58.7
  out of kilter
    disorderly 59.8
    unprepared 674.7
kimono 225.23
kin 11.3
kinaesthetic See kinesthetic
kind n. 75.2

(nature 5.3)
give in kind 718.2
pay in kind 807.9
kind adj. 906.6
kindergarten
  education 537.4
  school 542.1
kindergartner, kindergartener 540.1
kindhearted 906.6
kindle induce 153.7
  give birth 161.9
  stimulate 171.7
  inflame 173.8
  ignite 384.17
  (light 420.21)
  excite 824.2
  become angry 900.9
kindling n.
  ignition 384.4
  firewood 388.3
kindling adj. 384.22
kindly 906.6
kindness grace 784.4
  benevolence 906.1, 2
  (benefit 784.4)
kind of as if 17.17
  somewhat 32.14
kindred
  consanguinity 11.1
  kinsmen 11.3
  consanguine 11.7
  (related 9.6)
kine 366.12
kinematic
  kinetic 264.9
  impulsive 276.10
kinematics
  kinetics 264.4
  aeronautics 267a.2
  mechanics 276.5
kinematograph See cinematograph
kinesiatric 264.9
kinesiatrics, kinesis 264.4
kinesodic kinesthetic, kinaesthetic 264.9
kinetic motion 264.9
  impulsive 276.10
kinetic energy 171.1
kinetics motion 264.4
  aeronautics 267a.2
  mechanics 276.5
kinetogenic 264.9
kinetophone 418.6
kinetoscope 445.6
kinetoscopic 264.9
king sovereign 745.2
  (prince 875.7)
  (title 877.2)
  playing card 840.13
kingbird 366.22
kingcraft 693.3
kingdom 182.1
  (territory 181.2)
kingdom come
  utopia 515.6
  heaven 981.1
kingfisher 366.22
kinghood

dominion 737.2, 3
nobility 875.9
King James Bible 985.2
kinglike, kingly 737.16
  (noble 875.10)
kingmaker
  influence 175.5
  politician 694.4
king of beasts 366.3
King of Heaven 976.5
King of Kings 972.2, 5
kingpin 745.1
king post 215.16
King's Bench 752.1
King's Birthday 138.7
king's English 560.3
king's evil 655.10
kingship
  country 182.1
  dominion 737.2, 3
  nobility 875.9
kink n. coil 248.2
  (complexity 59.3)
  pain 378.1
  eccentricity 503.6
  caprice 608.1
  expedient 646.2
kink v. 248.3
kinky curly 248.4
  eccentric 503.17
  capricious 608.5
kinship 11.1
  (relation 9.1)
kinsman 11.3
kiosk house 189.3
  bower 191.22
kip bedroom 191.16
  bed 215.24
kipper n. 298.18
kipper v. 670.4
Kiranti, Kirghiz 560.4
kirk 1000.1
kirsch, kirschwasser 959.6
kirtle 225.15, 19
kismet, kismat 601.3
kismetic 601.13
kiss n. touch 379.1
  candy 396.2
  greeting 894.4
  endearment 902.3
kiss v. touch 379.3
  greet 894.9
  make love 902.8
  kiss the rod 725.3
kissable 902.9
kisser face 234.4
  mouth 260.2
kiss-me-quick 256.3
kiss of peace 998.2
kist 363.10
Kiswahili 560.5
kit bunch 72.5
  kind 75.2
  youngling 129.7
  receptacle 191.5, 8, 9, 11
  kitten 366.4
kitchen stomach 191.7

room 191.16
  cookroom 386.4
kitchener 386.1
kitchenmaid 746.2
kitchenman 746.1
kitchenware 798.3
kite sail 273.13
  aircraft 273a.1, 8
  check 800.9
kite balloon, kite sausage 273a.5
kith 11.3
kithless alone 87.8
  friendless 893.10
kitling
  youngling 129.7
  kitten 366.4
kitten n.
  weakness 160.5
  youngling 129.3, 7
  cat 366.4
kitten v. 161.9
kittenish 127.7
kittereen 272.6
kittle v. 380.5
kittle, kittlish adj. 380.7
kitty kitten 366.4
  gambling pot 621.4
kit violin 417.3
kiver 223.2
kiwi 269a.1
Klang, Klangfarbe 402.2
klavier 417.6
klaxon n.
  noisemaker 404.4
  alarm 669.1
klaxon v. 404.7
kleptomania
  insanity 503.1
  thievishness 791.6
kleptomaniac n. 504.1
kleptomaniac adj. 503.12
klieg eyes 443.4
klieg light, kleig light 423.3
knack 698.2
knap 206.2
knapsack 191.5
knave
  playing card 840.13
  rascal 949.1
knavery
  cunning 702.1
  (deceit 545.1)
  improbity 940.1
knavish 940.8
  (wicked 945.11)
knead mix 41.6
  form 240.6
  soften 324.4
  rub 331.3
  handle 379.3
kneading 379.1
knee joint 43.3
  angle 244.2
fall on one's knees
  be submissive 725.3
  entreat 765.5
  truckle 886.3

knee breeches — krans 934

knee (*continued*)
  beg for mercy 914.5
  thank 916.3
  make obeisance 928.6
  ask forgiveness 952.5
knee breeches 225.21
knee-deep
  deep 208.8
  shallow 209.4
knee-high 206.13
kneel submit 725.3
  beg 765.5
  truckle 886.3
  beg for mercy 914.5
  make obeisance 928.6
  (worship 990.9)
kneeling 928.2
  (worship 990.1)
knell 363.5
  (dirge 839.3)
knez, kniaz 875.7
knickerbockers,
  knickers 225.21
knickknack
  trifle 643.3
  toy 840.16
  trinket 847.9
knife *n.* cutter 253.6
  (perforator 262)
  (arms 727.3)
  woodcarver's ~ 557.8
  operation 662.15
knife *v.* 361.12
knife-edge 253.5
knife-edged 253.11
knife plait, knife pleat 258.1
knifesmith 690.6
knight
  combatant 726.4
  nobleman 875.5
  cavalier 894.6
  humanitarian 911.1
knightage 875.2
knight-errant
  defender 717.5
  hero 861.3
  cavalier 894.6
  humanitarian 911.1
knight-errantry
  knightly skill 722.2
  quixotism 863.1
  benevolence 906.1
  magnanimity 942.2
knighthood
  knightly skill 722.2
  nobility 875.9
knight of the road
  vagabond 268.2
  highwayman 792.4
knight service, knight's service 777.1
knit contract 195.4
  interlace 219.8
knit the brow
  express discontent 832.3

look sullen 901.6
knob head 210.3
  suspender 214.3
  sphere 249.2
  protuberance 250.2
knobbed 250.9
knobby upland 206.17
  protuberant 250.9
knobstick 607.6
knock *n.* blow 276.3
  criticism 932.2
knock *v.* strike 276.8
  bang 406.7
  criticize 932.7
knock about 266.14
knock down
  demolish 162.4
  floor 213.7
  fell 308.5
  auction off 796.6
  deject 837.8
knock in the head
  finish 67.7
  kill 361.10
knock off
  terminate 67.7
  cease 142.6
  die 360.6
  do carelessly 460.6
  write 590.14
  complete 729.2
knock out finish 67.7
  roughhew 161.8
  destroy 162.4
  form 240.2
  do carelessly 460.6
  write 590.14
knock together 161.8
knock under 725.3
  (repent 950.3)
knock up 688.5
knocker handle 215.7
  disparager 936.1
knock-kneed 243.5
  (angular 244.5)
knockout end-all 67.4
  destruction 162.2
  excellent thing 648.4
  victory 731.3
  beauty 845.3
knockout drops
  drug 662.7
  drugged liquor 959.4
knoll hill 206.2
  summit 210.1
knot *n.* bond 45.3
  (connection 43.3)
  (network 219.4)
  complexity 59.3
  length 200.6
  distortion 243.1
  sphere 249.2
  protuberance 250.2
  hair 256.3
  solid 321.4
  dilemma 704.4
  hindrance 706.2
  clique 712.5
  ornament 847.3
knot *v.* attach 43.6

interlace 219.8
  distort 243.3
knotted complex 59.10
  rough 256.12
  dense 321.8
  difficult 704.8
knotty
  protuberant 250.9
  rough 256.12
  dense 321.8
  difficult 704.8
knout 975.1
know *n.*
  knowledge 490.1
  information 527.1
know *v.*
  recognize 481a.6
  have knowledge of 490.9
  (be informed of 527.11)
  be a friend of 888.2
have one to know 527.7
know a hawk from a handsaw, know a thing or two 698.8
know one's onions
  know well 490.10
  be skillful 698.8
know one's own mind 604.5
know one's way about 698.8
know on which side one's bread is buttered
  be selfish 943.3
  be experienced 698.8
know the ropes
  know well 490.10
  be skillful 698.8
know the time of day 698.8
know what's what
  discriminate between 465.3
  be skillful 698.8
  (know well 490.10)
  (be intelligent 498.7)
not know 491.6
knowability 518.1
knowable
  cognizable 490.18
  understandable 518.5
knowing
  cognizant 490.12
  (sagacious 498.10)
  intelligent 498.9, 11
  cunning 702.6
knowingly 620.5
know-it-all *n.* 880.3
know-it-all *adj.* 880.6
knowledge
  cognition 490
  (intelligence 498.1)
  (education 537.1)
  (skill 698.1)
  information 527.1

to one's knowledge 490.20
knowledgeable 490.12
known
  ascertained 490.17
  ~ by 550.22
  ~ as 564.8
  become known 529.6
make known
  inform 527.7
  (indicate 550.18)
  (tell 582.6)
  divulge 529.4
  publish 531.7
knuckle *n.*
  angle 244.2
  meat 298.19
knuckle *v.* 725.3
knuckle to
  set to work 686.7
  submit 725.3
knuckle-duster 727.8
knur, knurr 250.2
knur and spell 840.11
knurl *n.* 250.2
knurl *v.* 256.11
knurled, knurly 256.12
knyaz See knez
kobold 979.9
K.O. *n.* end-all 67.4
  destruction 162.2
  victory 731.3
K.O. *v.* finish 67.7
  destroy 162.4
Kodagu 560.4
kodak *n.* 445.5
kodak *v.* 556.18
kodaker 559.7
kodakry 556.4
Koh-i-noor, Koh-i-nur, Kohinoor 650.3
Kohistani, Koibal 560.4
Koine 560.5
kolinsky 223.12
Kongoese 560.4
koniology 330.5
koodoo See kudu
kop 206.2
kopeck, kopek 800.8
kopje 206.2
Koran 986.1
Kore, Cora
  world 318.1
  agriculture 371.3
  goddess 979.2
Korwa 560.4
kos 200.6
kosmic, kosmos See cosmic etc.
kowtow, kotow *n.* 928.2
kowtow, kotow *v.*
  be submissive 725.3
  truckle 886.3
  make obeisance 928.6
kraal 189.17
krait 366.19
kraken 83.7
krans, krantz 212.3

kraut 298.30
kriegspiel, Kriegsspiel 722.2
kris See creese
Krishna 979.6
krone 800.8
Kronos, Cronus
  time 106.1
  god 979.2
kudos 873.1
kudu, koodoo 366.10
Kuki 560.4
kukri 727.3
Kultur learning 490.2
  culture 658.2
Kumyk 560.4
Kunstlied 415.10
Kunzite 434.5
kurbash 975.1
Kurdish, Kurukh 560.4
kutcherry See cutcherry
kuttar, kuttaur See katar
kyack 215.23
kyang See kiang
kyathos See cyathus
kyphosis 243.1
kyphotic 243.5
Kyrie eleison 990.3; 998.7

L

L addition 39.3
  railway 627.5
laager, lager
  camp 189.15
  fortification 717.3
lab 691
labarum 550.13
labefaction 659.3
labefy 659.8
label n. 550.11, 19
label v. 564.6
labellum 231.1
labial n. 402.2
labial adj. 231.4
labiodental, labiovelar 402.2
labis 191.14
labium 231.1
labor, labour n.
  birth 161.3
  work 686.3
  (task 625.2)
  (industry 682.5)
labor, labour v.
  ~ for 620.3
  work 686.6
  (be busy 625.6)
labor under
  experience 821.3
  suffer 828.9
laboratory 691
Labor Day 138.7
labored, laboured
  diction 579.3
  elaborate 673.11

laborer, labourer 690.2
laboring, labouring 686.9
laboring oar 686.5
laborious
  arduous 686.10
  (fatiguing 688.8)
  difficult 704.8
laboriously 686.11
  (with difficulty 704.12)
laboriousness 682.5
labor of love
  voluntary labor 602.2
  favor 784.4
  gratuity 815.4
  amusement 840.1
  kindness 906.2
  magnanimity 942.2
labrum 231.1
labyrinth
  complexity 59.3
  (convolution 248.1)
  (enigma 533.2)
  ear 418.5
labyrinthian, labyrinthic, labyrinthine 59.10
  (convoluted 248.4)
  (perplexing 475.12)
lac 428.5
lac, lakh 98.10
lace n. fastening 45.2
  tissue 219.4, 5
  transparency 425.2
  needlework 847.6
lace v. imbue 41.8
  sew 43.6
  whip 972.6
laced mutton 962.2
lacerable 328.4
lacerate
  disintegrate 44.9
  pain 378.4
  wound 659.8
  torture 830.6
  ~ the heart 837.8
lacerated 828.13
laceration
  sunderance 44.2
  hurt 378.1
  wound 659.4
Lacerta 318.6
lacery tissue 219.4
  transparency 425.2
laches neglect 460.1
  nonobservance 773.1
Lachesis 601.4
lachryma 839.2
lachrymal, lacrimal 839.14
lachrymals, lacrimals
  blues 837.1
  tears 839.2
lachrymation 839.2
lachrymator 334.2
lachrymatory n. 839.2
lachrymatory, lachrymose adj. 839.14

lacing fastening 45.2
  lacery 219.4
laciniate, laciniform, laciniose 256.17
lack n.
  deficiency 53.2
  want 640.3
  (shortcoming 304.1)
  (need 630.1)
  poverty 804.1
lack v. fall short 304.2
  want 640.6
  (be incomplete 53.3)
  (need 630.2)
  be poor 804.4
lackadaisical
  indolent 683.13
  indifferent 866.4
lackadaisy!
  alas! 839.18
  wonder 870.11
lack-brain 501.1
lacker See lacquer
lackey 746.1
  (attendant 88.3)
  (worker 690.10)
lacking
  absent 187.10
  short of 304.3
  wanting 640.11
  deprived 776.6
  be found lacking
  fall short 304.2
  be insufficient 640.6
lackluster, lacklustre
  dim 422.8
  colorless 429.6
lackwit 501.1
lackwitted 499.11
Laconian, laconic n. 585.2
laconic adj.
  concise 572.3
  (short 201.5)
  taciturn 585.4
laconically 585.5
laconism
  conciseness 572.1
  taciturnity 585.1
laconize 572.2
lacquer, lacker n. 428.5
  (resin 356a.1)
lacquer, lacker v. 428.10
  (coat 223.24)
  (resin 356a.2)
lacrosse 840.11
lactarene, lactarine 352.3
lactation 352.2
lacteal 352.7
lactescence
  semiliquidity 352.1
  whiteness 430.1
lactescent 430.8
lactiferous 352.7
lactoprotein 352.3
lactose 396.4
lactovegetarian n. 298.41

lactovegetarian adj. 298.48
lacuna interval 198.1
  cavity 252.2
lacuscular 343a.3
lacustrian n. 343a.2
lacustrian, lacustrine adj. 343a.3
lad boy 129.4
  man 373.2
ladder stairs 305.2
  escape 671.3
laddie 129.4
lade fill 52.7
  load 184.13
  ladle 270.10
  weight 319.9
laden full 52.11
  pregnant 168.9
  possessing 777.7
ladies' man 854.1
lading load 52.3; 190.1
  stowage 184.5
  freight 270.4
  weight 319.1
  cargo 780.6
ladino mongrel 41.5
  horse 271.6
ladle n. 191.14
ladle v. 270.10
lady bitch 366.6
  woman 374.2
  noblewoman 875.6
  wife 903.8
Lady 877.2
Lady Day
  anniversary 138.7
  holyday 998.13
ladyfinger
  mollycoddle 160a.3
  firework 382.9
lady in waiting 746.2
ladylike
  effeminate 160a.5
  female 374.11
  noble 875.10
  courteous 894.12
ladylove 897.7
Lady Nicotine 392a.1
Lady of the Lake 992.3
lady's maid 746.2
Ladyship 877.2
lag n.
  slowness 275.3
  prisoner 754.1
lag v. go slow 275.5
  loiter 281.4
  extradite 207.11
  dawdle 683.8
  arrest 751.9
laggard n.
  slow goer 275.4
  idler 683.7
laggard adj.
  reluctant 603.5
  indolent 683.13
lagger 754.1
lagniappe, lagnappe 784.3
lagoon, lagune
  sea inlet 343.1
  pool 343a.1

la grippe — language 936

la grippe 655.9
Lagting, Lagthing 696.5
Lahnda 560.4
laic 997.2
laical 997.4
laicize 997.3
laid up 655.23
lair resort 74.2
  retreat 189.13
  den 252.3
laird
  proprietor 779.2
  nobleman 875.4
Lais 962.2
laisser-aller, laisser aller, laissez aller, laissez faire, laisser faire n.
  conservatism 141.2
  neglect 460.1
  inaction 681.1
  noninterference 748.4
laisser aller, laisser faire v.
  be conservative 141.5
  do nothing 681.2
  be lax 738.4
  not interfere 748.11
  be composed 826.5
laissez-faire adj. 681.3
laissez-faireism
  conservatism 141.2
  noninterference 748.4
laity 997
lake pool 343a
  stream 348.1
  dye 428.4
  red 434.2
lake dweller 343a.2
lakelet 343a.1
laker 343a.2
lakh See lac
lakish 343a.3
Lakshmi 979.4
laky 434.9
lam hasten off 293.5
  flee 623.10
lama potentate 745.3
  priest 996.9
Lamaism 984.11
Lamaist 984.21
Lamarckism 161.5
lamb n.
  youngling 129.3, 7
  meat 298.22
  sheep 366.8
  unsophisticate 703.2
  endearment 902.4
  innocent 946.2
lamb v. 161.9
lambaste strike 276.8
  beat 972.6
lambency 379.1
lambent
  touching 379.4
  luminous 420.22
lambent flame

glimmer 420.5
  genius 498.5
Lambeth 1000.5
lambkin
  youngling 129.3, 7
  sheep 366.8
lamblike meek 826.10
  innocent 946.5
Lamb of God 976.5
lambskin 223.12
lamb's wool 959.8
lame n. 655.20
lame v. disable 158.6
  cripple 659.8
lame adj.
  incomplete 53.4
  crippled 655.24
  (impaired 659.12)
  unsuccessful 732.8
lame duck 808.4
lamella 204.2
lamellar, lamellated 204.5
lamellation 204.3
lamellibranch 368.16
lament n. 839.1
  (music 415.8)
lament v. 839.6
  (grieve 828.11; 837.6)
  (regret 833.2)
  (condole 915.2)
  (repent 950.3)
lamentabile 415.30
lamentable
  deplorable 649.8
  (regrettable 833.4)
  grievous 830.11
  sad 837.9
lamentably 31.23
lamentation 839
  (regret 833.1)
  (condolence 915.1)
  (penitence 950.1)
lamenter 363.7
  (grumbler 832.2)
lamenting n. 839.1
lamenting adj. 839.13
  (regretting 833.3)
lamentingly 839.17
lamia vampire 913.4
  demon 980.2
  witch 992.3
lamina layer 204.2
  (piece 51.3)
  incrustation 223.16
  foliage 367.4
laminate v. 204.4
laminate adj.
  laminated 204.5
  rough 256.12
laminated 204.5
  (covered 223.28)
lamination 204.3
luminous 204.5
Lammas 998.13
lamp n. 423.1, 2
  (light 420.1)
lamp v. 441.10
lampadedromy 274.4; 720.5
lampblack 431.5

lampfly 423.13
lampful 423.14
lamping 420.22
lampion 423.2
lamplight 420.7
lamplighted, lamplit 423.14
lampmaker 690.8
Lampong 560.4
lampoon n. 934.2
  (sarcasm 856.2)
lampoon v. 934.3
lampooner 936.1
lamprey 368.9
lamps 441.7
lamp shade 424.5
  (cover 223.2)
lampstand 423.9
lampwick
  lighter 388.4
  wick 423.12
Lamut 560.4
lanate nappy 256.15
  (smooth 255.5)
  downy 324.7
Lancasterian 541.9
lance n.
  perforator 262
  spear 727.5
lance v.
  open 260.11, 14
  throw 284.12
lance corporal 745.11
lancelike 253.14
Lancelot 861.3
lanceolate 253.14
lancer 726.4
lancers 840.7
lancet arch 215.18
  knife 253.6
  perforator 262
lanciform 253.14
lancinate
  pain physically 378.4
  pain mentally 830.3
lancination
  bodily pain 378.2
  mental pain 828.6
land n. region 181.1
  country 182.1
  ground 342
  realty 780.4
  by land, on land 342.17
land v.
  aeronautics 267a.34
  (alight 306.5)
  arrive 292.2
  (anchor 267.12)
  induce 615.9
landau 272.4
landaulet, landaulette 272.15
landed
  praedial 371.9
  propertied 780.8
landed interest 779.3
Landessprache 560.2
landgrave 875.5
landholder 779.2
landing

platform 215.21
  aeronautics 267a.26
  airdrome 267a.28
  arrival 292.2
  (disembarkment 267.3)
  perron 305.2
  anchorage 666.4
landing field 267a.28
landing gear 273a.10
landing stage 292.6
landlady 779.2
landlocked 229.4
landlord 779.2
  (host 890.6)
landlouper, landloper 268.2
landlouping, landloping 266.24
landlubber
  mariner 269.1
  landsman 342.7
landman 342.7
landmark
  boundary 233.1
  mark 550.10
land of behest, Land of Beulah 515.6
land of bondage 182.3
land-office business 734.1
land of Nod 683.5
Land of Promise 515.6
Land of Regrets 182.3
Land of the Leal 981.1
Land of the Midnight Sun, Land of the Rose, Land of the Shamrock etc. 182.3
landowner 779.2
land pirate 792.1, 8
landplane 273a.1
land rat 792.1
landreeve 694.5
landscape view 448.2
  picture 556.10
landscape gardening 845.5
landscapist 559.2
land shark 792.8
landslide, landslip 306.2
landsman
  landlubber 269.1
  landman 342.7
Landsting, Landsthing 696.5
Landsturm 726.5
landward 183.3
Landwehr 726.5
lane 627.2, 3
langrage, langrel 727.14
landspiel 417.2
langsyne 122.2
language
  speech 560; 582.1
  (dialect 563.5)
  colloquialism 563.3
  diction 569.1

langue d'oc — latently

profanity 908.2
**langue d'oc, langue
d'oïl** 560.4
langue du pays 560.2
languid weak 160.12
style 575.2
sickly 655.24
indolent 683.14
(slow 275.8)
(weary 841.9)
apathetic 823.5
languish
decrease 36.3
weaken 160.7
sicken 655.21
become languid
 683.10
despond 837.6
affect 853.5
yearn for 865.11
languishing 853.6
languor
weakness 160.1
inertness 172.1
lassitude 683.4
(slowness 275.1)
(fatigue 688.1)
(weariness 841.1)
laniard See lanyard
laniate destroy 162.4
damage 659.8
lank *n.* 203.6
lank, lanky *adj.* 203.11
(long-legged
 200.13)
(tall 206.13)
lant 299.3
lantern, lanthern
window 260.5
light 423.1, 2
lantern fly 423.13
lantern-jawed 203.11
lantern jaws 203.5
lantern light 420.7
lanuginose
nappy 256.15
downy 324.7
lanyard, laniard
273.10
Laodicean *n.* 605.3
Laodicean *adj.*
irresolute 605.5
apathetic 823.5
indifferent 866.4
Laodiceanism
irresolution 605.1
indifference 866.1
Lao-tzu, Lao-tse
986.3
lap *n.* adjunct 39.2
abode 189.1
lamina 204.2
supporter 215.2
drink 298.4; 959.4
circuit 620.1
lap *v.* drink 298.47
~ over 303.2
plash 348.19
touch 379.3
murmur 405.5
tipple 959.15
lap dog 366.6

lapel adjunct 39.2
fold 258.1
lapicide 559.6
lapidarian 558.6
lapidary *n.* 559.6
lapidary *adj.*
hard 323.5
engraved 558.6
lapidate
stone 284.12; 716.7
kill 361.10
pelt 972.7
lapidation 361.1
lapidator 361.8
lapideous hard 323.5
engraved 558.6
lapidification 323.2
lapidify 323.4
lapidity 323.2
lapidose 323.5
lapis lazuli blue 438.3
gem 847.8
Lapp 560.4
lappet 39.2
lap robe 223.9
lapse *n.*
subsidence 36.2
~ of time 109.1
pause 142.2
conversion 144.1
sinkage 306.1
~ of memory 506.3
relapse 661.1
loss 776.1
moral 947.2
lapse *v.* elapse 109.3
(pass 122.6)
be converted into
 144.8
sink 306.4
deteriorate 659.6
relapse 661.3
become lost 776.4
err 945.9
lapsed 122.8
lapstone 342.4
lapstreak 223.30
**lapsus calami, lapsus
linguae** 495.3
Laputa 515.6
lapwing 366.22
lar 979.12
larboard *n.* 239.2
larboard *adj.* 239.5
larboard *adv.* 239.6
larcenist 792.1
larcenous 791.14
larceny 791.1
larch 367.6
lard *n.* 356.4
lard *v.* 332.4
lardaceous 355.3
larder room 191.16
storeroom 636.4
lard oil 356.4
lardy 355.3
lares 189.2
lares and penates
979.2
large great 31.6
sizable 192.11
~ as life 192.14

(long 200.12)
(broad 202.6)
(high 206.13)
exaggerated 549.3
at large
diffusely 573.10
free 748.12
(escaped 671.7)
(liberated 750.5)
become larger 194.5
(increase 35.4)
go at large 748.8
largehearted
liberal 816.4
charitable 906.7
magnanimous
 942.6
largely 31.15
largeness
quantity 31.1
size 192.1
large order
hearty meal 298.36
lie 546.2
difficult task 704.1
largess, largesse
gratuity 784.3
reward 973.2
largo, larghetto
415.8, 31
lariat 45.2
lark *n.* ascent 305.3
bird 366.22
songbird 416.11
frolic 840.3
lark *v.* 266.19
larmier 210.4
larrikin 913.2
larrup strike 276.8
whip 972.6
larruping 394.7
larum noise 404.2
alarm 669.1
larva chrysalis 129.8
(worm 366.25)
diminutive 193.2
specter 980a.1
laryngismus
spasm 315.7
illness 655.3
laryngitis 655.9
larynx windpipe 351.3
vocal organs 580.2
lascivious 961.11
lasciviousness 961.3
lash *n.* eyelash 256.6
incentive 615.3
whip 975.1
lash *v.* tie 43.6
inflame 173.8
anchor 267.12
~ a horse 370.7
urge 615.7
hasten 684.2
bind 751.7
reprove 932.8
whip 972.6
lashings 31.3
lass 129.5
lassitude
weakness 160.1

languor 683.4
(fatigue 688.1)
(weariness 841.1)
lasso, lazo
fastening 45.2
noose 247.2
last *n.* die 22.3
end 67.1
graver 558.4
last *v.* continue 106.2
(endure 110.5)
be permanent 141.4
last *adj.* final 67.8
(hindermost 235.9)
eventual 151.7
foregoing 122.11
at last finally 67.11
at length 133.12
eureka 480a.9
at long last
at last 133.12
finally! 481a.9
lasting 110.9
(continuing 106.4)
lastingness
durability 110.1
permanence 141.1
lastly 476.20
last straw
final cause 153.1
provocation 900.5
Last Supper 998.6
last word
a novelty 123.2
fashion 852.1
lasty durable 110.9
permanent 141.6
latch *n.* 45.2
latch *v.* 43.6
latchet 45.2
latchkey 260.10
late *adj.*
former 122.10
new 123.8
tardy 133.8
(slow 275.8)
late-lamented 360.8
be late 133.3
late *adv.* 133.11
of late 123.13
too late 135.6
late-lamented 360.8
lately 123.13
(formerly 122.14)
latency 526
(invisibility 447.1)
(unintelligibility
 519.1)
lateness 133
latent inert 172.3
delitescent 526.6
(invisible 447.4)
(obscure 519.7)
(concealed 528.17)
be latent 526.3
(escape notice
 447.2)
latentiate 526.5
(conceal 528.10)
latently 526.9
(secretly 528.24)

later — lay

later 117.3, 4
  (succeeding 63.5)
  (future 121.7)
laterad 236.8
lateral side 236.6
  phonetics 402.11
laterality 236.1
lateralize 236.5
laterally 236.8
  (obliquely 217.17)
  (crosswise 219.12)
  (deviatively 279.9)
latest 118.2
latex 333.2
lath thinness 203.5
  strip 205.5
  board 635.3
lathe conversion 144.4
  territory 181.2
lathee, lathi 215.15
lather n. foam 353.2
  soap 356.5
lather v. 972.6
lath-legged, lathy
  long-legged 200.13
  thin 203.11
laticostate, latidentate
  202.6
latigo 215.23
Latin 560.4
latitancy latency 526.1
  concealment 528.1
latitant latent 526.6
  lying hid 528.19
latitat 969.2
latitude extent 180.1
  region 181.5
  breadth 202.1
  map line 550.9
  scope 748.2
latitude and longitude
  location 184.1
  co-ordinates 466.7
latitudinarian n.
  984.14; 989.4
latitudinarian adj.
  unprejudiced 498.12
  freethinking 989.8
latitudinarianism
  religion 984.4
  freethinking 989.3
latrant 412.3
latration 412.1
latria 990.1
latrine 653.9
latrocinium 791.2
latter 122.11
Latter-day Saint
  984.14
latterly 123.13
lattice frame 215.8
  network 219.4
  window 260.5
latticed 219.11
latticework
  frame 215.8
  network 219.4
laud n.
  laudation 931.2
  paean 990.2
laud v. praise 931.6
  (celebrate 883.3)

glorify 990.10
laudable 931.11
laudanum 662.7
laudation praise 931.2
  (celebration 883.1)
  glorification 990.2
laudatory 931.9
lauder 935.1
Laudism 984.5
Laudist 984.15
lauds 990.7
laugh n. 838.3
laugh v. 838.7
  (be cheerful 836.5)
laugh at
  ridicule 856.4
  jeer 930.6
laugh in one's sleeve
  laugh 838.7
  ridicule 856.4
  affront 929.3
  scoff 930.6
laugh off 460.5
laugh to scorn 715.2;
  930.6
  (ridicule 856.4)
laughable 855.5
  (amusing 840.22)
laughing n. 838.3
laughing adj. 838.10
laughing gas gas 334.2
  anesthetic 376.2
laughing jackass
  366.22
laughingly 838.11
laughingstock 857
  (dupe 547.1)
  (buffoon 844.1)
laughter 838.3
  (merriment 836.3)
  (amusement 840.1)
laughter-loving 836.8
launch n. 273.4
launch v.
  begin 66.5; 284.14
  throw 284.12
launch forth
  start 284.14
  undertake 676.2
launch into
  undertake 676.2
  set to work 686.7
launch out
  expatiate 573.5
  attack 716.5
launder 652.9
laundress 652.6
  (worker 690.10)
laundry 652.4
  (workshop 691)
laundryman 652.6
laureate 597.10
laurel trophy 733.1
  decoration 847.5
Lautverschiebung
  402.5
lava residue 40.2
  semiliquid 352.3
  slag 384.15
lavabo
  washing 652.2
  washbasin 652.5

Lavabo 998.7
lavadero 652.5
lavage enema 300.4
  cleansing 652.2
lavaliere, lavalier,
  lavalière 214.2
lavandera, lavandero
  652.6
lavation 652.2
lavational 652.15
lavatory n.
  washing 652.2
  washroom 652.4
  (room 191.16)
  (hot bath 386.6)
  (toilet 653.9)
lavatory adj. 652.15
lave 652.9
lavement 300.4
lavender n. 400.3
lavender adj. 437.4
lavender blue 438.2
lavish n. 31.3
lavish v.
  give freely 784.10
  squander 818.3
  (overdo 641.3)
  (be intemperate
  954.3)
lavish adj.
  profuse 102.5
  bountiful 639.7
  (redundant 641.5)
  liberal 816.4
  prodigal 818.4
lavishment 639.2
law n. rule 80.1
  axiom 496.2
  precept 697.1
  indulgence 760.1
  statute 963.2
  jurisprudence 963.3
  (decree 741.3)
  at law 969.14
  by law 963.6
  practice law 968.3
  within the law 963.5
law v. 969.10
law-abiding
  obedient 743.3
  upright 939.7
law agent 968.1
lawbreaking 964.2
lawful permitted 760.6
  legal 963.5
lawfulness 963.1
lawgiver 694.4
lawless
  unconformable 83.9
  anarchic 738.8
  disobedient 742.6
  (nonobservant
  773.5)
  unprincipled 940.8
  licentious 964.6
lawlessness
  anarchy 738.2
  illegality 964.3
lawlike 963.5; 939.7
lawn cloth 219.5
  grassland 367.11
  greenyard 371.6

938

lawn sleeves 999.1
law of the Medes and
  Persians
  permanence 141.1
  stability 150.2
lawsuit 969
  (dispute 476.2)
  (accusation 938.1)
lawyer n. 968
  (mediator 724.2)
  (deputy 759.1)
lawyer v.
  practice law 968.3
  prosecute 969.10
lax v. 324.4
lax adj.
  incoherent 47.3
  flexible 324.6
  neglectful 460.8
  diction 575.2
  shiftless 674.11
  indolent 683.13
  slack 738.7
  (lenient 740.4)
  (unconstrained
  748.13)
  nonobservant 773.5
  loose-moraled
  945.12
  be lax 738.4
laxate 324.4
laxation 324.1, 2
laxative n. 662.9
laxative adj. 662.25
laxity
  incoherence 47.1
  flexibility 324.1
  neglect 460.1
  slackness 738
  (lenity 740.1)
  (freedom 748.1)
  nonobservance
  773.1
  dereliction 927.1
  improbity 940.1
  ~ of morals 945.3
laxness 773.1
lay n.
  arrangement 60.3
  song 415.2, 10
  poem 597.2
lay n. See lea
lay v. moderate 174.5
  level 213.6
  relieve 834.4
lay about one
  act vigorously
  682.12
  labor 686.6
  besiege 716.5
  chastise 972.6
lay a course for
  267.22, 26
lay aside
  segregate 55.4
  postpone 133.4
  remove 185.2
  disregard 458.5
  neglect 460.5
  reserve 636.8
  put away 678.4
  (reject 610.2)

(relinquish 782.3)
lay at 716.5
lay away sail 267.27
  store 636.7
  (put 184.10)
lay bare divest 226.4
  disclose 529.3
lay by
  postpone 133.4
  lie to 267.14
  reserve 636.8
  prepare 673.7
  put away 678.4
  lie idle 683.8
  take precautions 864.4
lay by the heels
  destroy 162.4
  defeat 731.9
  capture 751.9
  catch 789.9
lay claim to
  claim 741.6
  demand 924.7
lay down
  place 184.10
  level 213.6
  careen 267.19, 34
  ~ ~ one's life 360.6
  insist upon 535.5
  pay down 807.6
lay down one's arms
  make peace 723.5
  surrender 725.4
lay down the law
  dogmatize 474.7
  insist upon 535.5
  rule 737.12
  command 741.4
  domineer 885.5
lay eyes on 441.10
lay for
  sail for 267.22, 26
  approach 286.2
lay hands on
  acquire 775.6
  seize 789.9
  discover 841a.3
  confirm 998.14
lay hold of 789.9
lay in sail for 267.26
  eat 298.44
  store 636.7
  (provide 637.4)
  prepare for 673.7
lay into attack 716.5
  fight 720.8
lay it on
  be bombastic 577.5
  overload 641.4
  flatter 933.2
lay it on thick
  cover 223.24
  overload 641.4
  flatter 933.2
lay off cease! 142.8
  hush 403.4
  silence! 403.9
  idle 683.8
lay on strike 276.8
  beat 972.6
lay one's account for

believe 484.7
  plan on 507.6
lay oneself out 673.8
lay out destroy 162.4
  level 213.6
  kill 361.10
  ~ ~ a corpse 363.22
  plan 626.9
  expend 809.3
  upbraid 932.8
lay over
  be late 133.3
  postpone 133.4
  cover 223.22
lay to
  attribute to 155.3
  lie to 267.14
  lie idle 683.8
lay up lie to 267.14
  store up 636.7
  be ill 655.21
  put away 678.4
lay waste
  destroy 162.4
  damage 659.8
lay *adj.* 997.4
lay brother 996.11
layer lamina 204
  (piece 51.3)
  (cover 223.2)
  atmosphere 338.2
layette 225.32
lay figure
  prototype 22.1
  figure 554.4
  nonentity 643.6
layman 997.1, 2
layout wardrobe 225.2
  plan 626.2
layover 266.12
lazaretto, lazar house 662.17
laze *n.* 683.3
laze *v.* 683.8
laziness 683.3
lazo See **lasso**
lazulite 438.3
lazy *v.* 683.8
lazy *adj.* 683.13
lazybones, lazybone, lazyboots etc. 683.7
lazzarone 683.7
lb. 319.4
lea, lay 367.11
leach lixiviate 295.7
  solubilize 335.6
  purify 652.9
leaching 295.1
leachy 335.8
lead *n.*
  superiority 33.1
  precedence 62.1
  electricity 158a.8
  fathomer 208.4
  plumb 212.5
  roofing 223.6
  horse 271.3
  precession 280.1
  gravity 319.2
  measure 466.4
  leading role 599.7
  protagonist 599.19

mineral 635.6
in the lead
  before 234.9
  in advance 280.4
take the lead
  excel 33.5
  come before 62.2; 280.2
  begin 66.5
  direct 693.4
  dominate 737.12
lead *v.* excel 33.5
  come before 62.2
  have influence 175.8
  tend 176.2
  go before 280.2
  (outstrip 303.4)
  gravitate 319.7
  music 416.22
  direct 693.4
  rule 737.11
lead by the nose
  have influence 175.8
  dominate 737.12
lead captive
  subjugate 749.5
  capture 751.9
lead off 66.5
lead on lure 617.2
  direct 693.4
lead one a dance 623.6
lead the way
  begin 66.5
  direct 693.4
lead to the altar 903.13
leadable 278.9
leaded 172.3
leaden
  dim 422.8
  dull-colored 428.19
  colorless 429.6
  gray 432.4
  languid 683.14
leader *n.*
  fastening 45.4
  forerunner 64.1
  horse 271.3
  music director 416.13
  typography 550.8
leading article 595.2
  director 694.1, 6
  (master 745.1)
  counsel 968.1
leadership
  managership 693.3
  authority 737.3
  (supremacy 33.3)
leader writer
  journalist 593.16
  commentator 595.3
leading *n.* 280.1
leading *adj.*
  supreme 33.8
  first 66.8
  preceding 280.3
leading article 595.2
leading lady, leading man 599.19

leading question 461.10
leading strings 752.2
hold in leading strings
  subjugate 549.5
  restrain 751.6
in leading strings
  infantile 127.7
  pupil 541.9
  obedient 743.3
  in subjection 749.6
leaf lamina 204.2
  foliage 367.4
  tobacco 392a.1
  handbill 531.4
  page 593.7
  paper 635.4
leafage 367.4
leaf green 435.2
leafless 226.8
leaflet foliage 367.4
  handbill 531.4
  brochure 593.1
leafstalk 367.4
leafy 256.12
league *n.* length 200.6
  association 709.2
  society 712.4
in league
  combined 48.6
  (co-operative 709.7)
  co-operating 709.4
league *v.* join 43.5
  combine 48.4
  (co-operate 709.4)
  (form a party 712.7)
leagued 48.6
  (co-operative 709.7)
leak *n.* crack 198.2
  egress 295.1
leak *v.* run out 295.7
  (waste 638.3)
  be watery 337.4
  divulge 529.4
leak out
  find vent 295.7
  be disclosed 529.6
leakage 295.1
  (waste 638.1)
  (escape 671.1)
  (loss 776.1)
leakproof 340.11
leaky 295.9
leam 420.3
lean *v.* tend 176.2
  gravitate 319.7
lean on, lean upon
  rest on 215.27
  rely on 484.7
  be dependent 749.3
  hope 858.6
lean towards
  be willing 602.6
  prefer 609.9
lean *adj.* thin 203.11
  (little 193.8)
  (tall 206.13)
  (distorted 243.5)
  meager 640.9

lean-faced 203.11
leaning n.
  tendency 176.1
  obliquity 217.1
  propensity 602.2
  disposition 820.1
  penchant 865.1
  partiality 941a.1
  have a leaning to 888.2
leaning adj. 176.3
lean-minded 499.11
lean-to 189.4
lean-witted 499.11
leap n. 309
  a leap in the dark
    uncertainty 475.5
    gamble 621.2
    (speculation 463.3)
    (rashness 863.1)
  by leaps and bounds 274.14
leap v.
  ~ over 303.2
  jump 309.4, 5
  (ascend 305.4)
  leap to the eye
    be evident 474.17
    be manifest 525.3, 8
leaper 309.3
leapfrog 840.11
leaping 309.6
leap year 138.7
learn teach 537.9
  acquire knowledge 539.3
  (discover 481a.3)
  (memorize 505.13)
  (be informed 527.11)
learned 490.15
  (intellectual 450.8)
  (wise 498.11)
  (scholarly 541.9)
learner 541
learning
  knowledge 490.2
  (education 537.1)
  acquisition of ~ 539
lease n.
  transference 270.3
  estate 780.2
lease v.
  ~ to 787.6
  ~ from 788.3
lease and release 783.1; 794.1
leased 771.10
leasehold n. 780.2
leasehold adj. 780.8
leash n. 92.2
  hold in leash
    hinder 706.4
    subjugate 749.5
    restrain 751.6
leash v. tie 43.6
  bind 751.7
least 34.6
  at least 32.13
  not in the least 536.4
leather n.

saddle 215.23
pelt 223.12
toughness 327.2
bookbinding 593.10
purse 802.2
leather v. 972.6
leatherette 223.12
leathermaker 690.8
leatherneck 269.1; 726.10
leathery 327.5
leave n.
  departure 293.1
  permission 760.1
  by leave 760.7
leave v. part 44.11
  depart 293.4, 5
  abandon 624.3
  permit 760.3
  bequeath 784.13
  be left 40.5
  leave in the cold
    neglect 460.4
    snub 930.7
  leave in the lurch
    outstrip 303.4
    circumvent 545.8
    abandon 624.3
  leave no stone unturned
    search 461.16
    persevere 604a.2
    (do thoroughly 729.3)
    try one's best 675.5
    go all lengths 682.12
  leave off
    cease 142.6, 8
    abandon 624.3
    disuse 678.2
    don't! 761.6
  leave out
    exclude 55.3
    neglect 460.4
    not observe 773.3
leaven n.
  component 56.1
  cause 153.1
  ferment 320.3
  poison 663.4
leaven v.
  ferment 320.6
  qualify 469.3
  corrupt 653.15; 659.9
leavening n. 320.3
leavening adj. 320.8
leaver 295.4
leaving n. 293.1
leaving adj. 293.8
leavings remains 40.1
  rubbish 645.4
leave-taking 293.1, 2
lecher 962.1
lecherous 961.11
lechery 961.3
lecithoprotein 352.3
lectern desk 542.6
  pulpit 1000.3
lection 522.2
lectionary 998.9

lector teacher 540.3
  clerical reader 996.5
lecture n. lesson 537.6
  speech 582.2
  (allocution 586.1)
  (dissertation 595.1)
  reproof 932.3
lecture v.
  expound 537.11
  declaim 582.7
  (address 586.2)
  reprove 932.8
lecturer teacher 540.3
  speaker 582.5
  clergyman 996.5
lectureship 540.6
led captain 886.2
ledge height 206.2
  shelf 215.19
  edge 231.1
ledger record 551.3
  (list 86.1)
  account book 811.5
lee 236.2
  in the lee of 234.9
leech adherer 46.3
  bloodletting 662.15
  doctor 662.19
  sycophant 886.2
leechcraft 662.16
leechlike 886.4
leek condiment 393.1
  malodor 401.2
leek green n. 435.2
leek-green adj. 435.6
leer n. look 441.2, 8
  dumb show 550.3
  ridicule 856.1
leer v.
  look leeringly 441.16
  signal 550.20
leery, leary wily 702.6
  wary 864.6
lees 40.2
lee shore 667.1
leewan 747.5
leeward n. 236.2
leeward adj. 236.8; 267.58
  (direction 278.14)
leeway reprieve 133.2
  room 180.2
  navigation 267.7
  aeronautics 267a.14
  shortcoming 304.1
  free scope 748.2
  give leeway 748.10
  make leeway 267.21, 23
left n. 239.2
left adj.
  remaining 40.6
  sinistral 239.5
  departed 293.9
left-handed sinistromanual 239.5
  clumsy 699.12
  insulting 929.5
left-handed marriage 903.2

left-handedness 239.1
left-hander 239.4
leftness 239.1
leftover 40.1, 4
  (oddments 51.6)
leftward 239.6
leg n. member 51.4
  electricity 158a.4
  post 215.16
  side 236.1
  journey 266.8
  limbs 266.11
  meat 298.25
  swindler 792.8
  obeisance 928.2
leg v.
  leg it walk 266.16
  depart 293.5
  flee 623.10
legacy
  transference 270.3
  bequest 784.6
  (inheritance 775.4)
  (estate 780.3)
legal permitted 760.6
  legitimate 963.5
  (just 941.3)
legal holiday 840.5
legality 963
  (justice 941.1)
legalization 963.1
legalize 963.4
  (decree 741.4)
legalized 963.5
legally 963.6
legal right 965.1
legal tender 800.1
legatary 785.2
legate 759.2
legatee
  transferee 270.5
  heir 779.5
  recipient 785.2
legation 755.1
legato 415.15, 30
leg bail 623.2
  give leg bail 623.10
legend 594.2
  (archive 551.2)
legendary
  fabulous 515.12
  (mythical 979.14)
  traditional 594.7
legerdemain 545.2, 3
legerdemainist 548.6
  (sorcerer 992.2)
leggiero 415.30
legging 225.28
leggy 200.13
leghorn 225.26
legibility 518.1
legible 518.5
legion crowd 72.4
  multitude 102.2
  military unit 726.7
legionary, légionnaire 726.4
legislate 963.4
legislation
  government 693.1
  law 963.1
legislative 963.5

Legislative Assembly — let

Legislative Assembly
  696.6
legislative council
  696.5
legislator
  statesman 694.4
  congressman 696.8
legislature
  assembly 72.2
  government 693.1
  parliament 696.4
  legislation 963.1
legist 968.1
legitimacy 963.1
legitimate n. 599.3
legitimate v. 963.3
legitimate adj.
  logical 476.16
  authentic 494.12
  drama 599.28
  permitted 760.6
  justifiable 937.10
  legal 963.5
legitimate drama
  599.3
legitimatize 963.4
leg of lamb 298.22
Legree, Simon 599.19
legume vessel 191.6
  hull 223.14
  vegetable 367.2
  food 298.30
legumen 223.14
legumin 321.5
leguminous 367.4
Leibnitzianism 451.11
leiocephalous, lio-
  cephalous 255.5
leiodermatous, lio-
  dermatous 255.5
leisure 685
  (interim 109a.1)
  (idleness 683.2)
  (vacation 687.2)
at one's leisure
  tardily 133.13
  leisurely 684.2, 4
leisured idle 683.12
  leisurely 685.3
leisureliness 275.1
leisurely adj.
  slow 275.8
  unhurried 685.4
  be leisurely 275.5
leisurely adv.
  tardily 133.13
  slowly 275.10
leitmotiv, leitmotif
  music 415.19
  topic 454.1
leman 897.6
lemma hull 223.14
  premise 476.4
lemon n. fruit 298.31
  sour 397.2
  yellow 436.3
lemon adj. 436.6
lemonade drink 298.4
  sweet beverage
    396.5
  (cooling agent
    387.2)

lemon chrome, lemon
  yellow n. 436.1, 4
lemon-yellow adj.
  436.6
lemur 366.16
lemures 980a.1
lend 787.4
  (give credit 805.4)
lend an ear 418.11, 16
lend a hand
  render a service
    644.3
  aid 707.6
lend oneself to
  assent 488.6
  second 707.8
  participate 709.6
lender 787.2
  (creditor 805.3)
lending 787
length distance 196.1
  longness 220
  (measurement
    466.1)
  portion 200.3
at length
  at last 133.12
  lengthwise 200.15
  diffusely 573.10
go the whole length
  be thorough 52.8
  persevere 604a.2
  try one's best 675.5
  do thoroughly 729.3
length and breadth
  all 50.2
  boundlessness 180.4
  world 318.1
lengthen increase 35.3
  time 110.6
  elongate 200.9
lengthened
  protracted 110.10
  elongated 200.12
lengthening 35.6
lengthwise
  at length 200.15
  flatwise 251.6
lengthy long 200.12
  high 206.13
  (long-legged
    200.13)
  verbose 573.7
leniency 740.1
  (compassion 914.1)
lenient
  softening 324.10
  unprejudiced 498.12
  mild 740.4
  (moderate 174.6)
  (lax 738.7)
  (compassionate
    914.6)
  permissive 760.6
be lenient 740.2
lenify moderate 174.5
  qualify 469.3
lenitive n.
  lubricant 332.2
  palliative 662.6
  (relief 834.3)
lenitive adj.

moderative 174.7
  softening 324.10
  lubricant 332.5
  qualifying 469.6
  palliative 662.25
  relieving 834.7
lenitude, lenity 740.1
  (laxity 738.1)
  (compassion 914.1)
lens eye 441.7
  optics 445.1, 3
lent 787.7
Lent fast day 640.5
  fast 956.2
  holytide 998.13
lenten period 138.11
  fasting 956.4
lenticular, lentiform
  lens-shaped 245.15
  convex 250.9
lentiginous
  pulverulent 330.8
  dirty 653.17
lentigo 440a.1
lentitude
  slowness 275.1
  languor 683.4
lentitudinous 683.14
lento 415.31
lentoid 245.15
lentor slowness 275.1
  viscidity 352.1
  languor 683.4
Leo
  constellation 318.6
  lion 366.3
Leonine 597.13
Leonine verse 597.1
leopard pelt 223.12
  animal 366.3
  variegation 440.2
leper 893.5
Lepidodendraceae
  369.7
lepidodendroid 369.11
lepidote 330.8
Lepisma 366.24
leprechaun 979.9
leprosy 655.6
leprous 655.25
Lepus 318.6
lerret 273.4
Lesbian n.
  hermaphrodite 83.5
  Sapphist 962.2
Lesbian adj. 83.12
Lesbianism 961.3
lese majesty, lèse-
  majesté 742.2; 940.4
less adj.
  inferior 34.5
  fewer 103.4
  grow less 36.3
less adv. 34.7
no less 639.1
less prep. minus 38.11
  without 187.16
lessee lodger 188.4
  tenant 779.1
  recipient 785.2
lessen 36.3, 4
  (mitigate 174.5)

lessening
  decrease 36.1
  contraction 195.1
lesser 34.5
lesson
  instruction 537.6
  warning 668.1
give a lesson to 972.5
read a lesson
  teach 537.11
  reprove 932.7
lessor 787.2
  (creditor 805.3)
let n. 706.2
let v. hinder 706.4
  permit 760.3
  lease 787.6
let a-be 460.7
let alone with 37.9
  excluding 55.7
  be conservative
    141.5
  be quiescent 265.5
  pretermit 460.7
  not use 678.5
  do nothing 681.2
  not complete 730.2
  not interfere 748.11
  abstain 953.5
let be
  be conservative
    141.5
  pretermit 460.7
  let alone 681.2
let bygones be by-
  gones 918.3
  (forget 506.6)
let down
  depress 308.4
  humiliate 879.3
let drive 716.5
let fly
  propel 284.12, 13
  attack 716.5
let go
  neglect 460.4
  do nothing 681.2
  allow freedom
    748.10
  liberate 750.2, 6
  relinquish 782.3
  restore 790.3
let have 784.8
let in interject 228.8
  admit 296.2
  tip 527.9
  divulge 529.4
  deceive 545.7, 10
let it go
  ignore 460.5, 13
  forgive 918.3
let loose 750.2
let off explode 173.9
  shoot 284.13
  dismiss 297.12
  exempt 748.10
  acquit 970.3
let on 529.4
let oneself in for
  704.6
let out dispel 73.3
  lengthen 200.9

let — libertine

let out *(continued)*
  dismiss 297.12
  give vent to 297.13
  (exude 295.7)
  divulge 529.4
  utter 582.6
  ~ ~ at 716.5
  liberate 750.2
let slip
  be too late 135.5
  neglect 460.4
  divulge 529.4
  do nothing 681.2
  not complete 730.2
  lose 776.2
  relinquish 782.3
let the cat out of the bag 529.4
let up decrease 36.3
  intermit 109a.2
  cease! 142.8
  retard 275.7
let well enough alone
  be conservative 141.5
  be content 831.3
  be cautious 864.3
  abstain 953.5
  to let 763.4
let *adj.* leased 771.10
  loaned 787.7
let-alone principle
  conservatism 141.2
  noninterference 748.4
letdown
  disappointment 509.1
  failure 732.1
  humiliation 879.1
lethal 361.16
lethargic
  languid 683.14, 15
  apathetic 823.5
lethargus 683.5
lethargy
  languor 683.4
  apathy 823.1
Lethe oblivion 506.1
  river of hell 982.3
Lethean
  forgetful 506.8
  Stygian 982.5
lethiferous 361.16
letter *n.*
  literality 516.2
  mark 550.11
  alphabet 561.2
  type 591.6
  epistle 592.2, 4
  (message 532.2)
  to the letter 19.14
  (exactly 494.16)
  (faithfully 772.6)
letter *v.* initial 561.6
  correspond 592.6
letter card 592.3
letter carrier 534.2
  (carrier 271.1)
letter drop 592.4
lettered
  learned 490.15

literal 561.9
lettergram 532a.3
  (epistle 592.2)
letter of credit 805.2
letter of marque 791.7
letterpress news 532.1
  print 591.2
  press 591.10
letters learning 490.2
  literature 560.8
  narrative 594.2
letter writer 592.5
Lettish 560.4
lettuce
  vegetable 298.30
  paper money 800.6
letup decrease 36.1
  discontinuity 70.1
  respite 109a.1; 687.2
  pause 142.2
  retardation 275.3
leucocyan 438.4
leucocythemia, leucocythaemia 655.11
leucoderma 430.1
leucorrhea, leucorrhoea 299.1
leukemia, leukaemia 655.11
levant, levanter *n.* 349.9
Levant *n.* 278.2
levant *v.* 623.10
levee porch 191.17
  trench 259.2
levee, levée
  assembly 72.2
  party 892.5
level *n.*
  equality 27.1, 4
  floor 191.18
  layer 204.1
  horizontal 213.3
  (flat 251.2)
  smooth 255.2
  plain 344.1
  measure 466.4
on a level equal 27.8
  horizontally 213.10
  (flat 251.6)
  honest 939.7, 11
level *v.* uniform 16.4
  equalize 27.7
  demolish 162.4
  horizontalize 213.6
  (flatten 251.4)
  smooth 255.4
  fell 308.5
level at direct 278.4
  aim 620.3
  shoot at 716.6
level off 267a.34
level *adj.* uniform 16.5
  equal 27.8
  horizontal 213.8
  flat 251.5
  smooth 255.5
  just 941.3
level *adv.* 213.10
levelheaded
  wise 498.11
  inexcitable 826.9

levelheadedness
  mental poise 498.4
  equanimity 826.3
lever 307.4
  (leverage 175.3)
  (fulcrum 215.5)
leverage 175.3
  (advantage 33.2)
  (fulcrum 215.5)
  (lever 307.4)
leviable 812.8
leviathan 192.8
levigate mix 41.6
  smooth 255.4
  pulverize 330.6
levigation
  mixture 41.1
  smoothness 255.1
  pulverization 330.2
levin 420.6
levirate 903.2
levitate 320.4
levitative 320.7
Levite 996.6
Levitical 995.6
levity
  lightness 320.1
  ~ of mind 499.6
  fickleness 608.3
  triviality 643.2
  merriment 836.3
  rashness 863.1
levy *n.*
  mobilization 72.1
  recruits 726.5
  tax 812.2
levy *v.* seize 789.9
  assess 812.5
lewd 961.9, 10, 11
lewdness 961.3
lex 963.2
lexical 562.8
lexicographer 560.7
  (author 593.15)
  (professional 690.10)
lexicographical 562.8
lexicography 562.4
lexicological 562.8
  (philological 560.9)
lexicologist 560.7
lexicology 562.4
  (philology 560.6)
lexicon 593.4
lexigraphical 562.8
lexigraphy
  lexicology 562.4
  writing 590.1
lexiphanic 577.7
lexiphanicism 577.2
ley See lea
lex non scripta, lex scripta
  precept 697.1
  law 963.2
lex talionis 718.1
leze majesty See lese majesty
liabilities 811.1
liability
  likelihood 177
  (tendency 176.1)

  probability 472.1
  exposure 665.2
  debt 806.1
  duty 926.1
liable tending to 176.3
  subject to 177.3
  (unprotected 665.9)
  answerable 462.12
  probable 472.5
  chargeable 806.8
  amenable 926.11
  be liable 177.2
  (tend 176.2)
  not liable 748.18
liaison 897.3
  (seduction 961.5)
liar 548.5
  be a liar 544.4
libation drink 298.4
  alcoholic drink 959.10
  oblation 990.6
libel *n.*
  defamation 934.2
  (accusation 938.1)
  lawsuit 969.6
libel *v.* 934.3
libelant, libellant 938.2
libelee, libellee 938.3
libeler, libeller 936.1
libelous, libellous 934.4
Liberal *n.* 712.6
liberal *adj.*
  extensive 31.7
  unprejudiced 498.12
  plentiful 639.7
  free 748.12
  generous 816.4
  (charitable 784.15; 906.7)
  (magnanimous 942.6)
  be liberal 816.3
  (be charitable 906.5)
liberal education
  learning 490.2
  education 537.4
liberalism 748.1
liberalistic 748.12
liberality 816
  (giving 784.2)
  (charitableness 906.2)
  (magnanimity 942.2)
liberally 816.5
liberate deliver 672.2
  set at liberty 750.2
  (acquit 970.3)
liberated 750.5
  (free 748.12)
liberation
  release 750
  (escape 671.1)
  (freedom 748.1)
  (acquittal 970.1)
  deliverance 672.1
liberator 912.2
libertine *n.* 962

942

libertine *adj.*
  freethinking 498.12
  uncontrolled 748.13
libertinism 961.2
liberty
  opportunity 134.2
  freedom 748.1
  permission 760.1
at liberty 748.12
set at liberty 750.2
take a liberty
  make free with 748.9
  arrogate 885.6
  be disrespectful 929.3
liberty hall 748.2
libidinous 961.11
Libra season 126a.1
  constellation 318.6
librarian
  bookman 593.14
  curator 694.5
library retreat 189.13
  room 191.16
  newspaper 591.11
  bookroom 593.11
librate 314.8
libration 314.1, 3
libratory 314.12
librettist poet 597.10
  dramatist 599.22
libretto
  music score 415.21
  (book 593.1)
  poetry 597.2
  playbook 599.16
license, licence *n.*
  laxity 738.2
  freedom 748.1
  permission 760.1, 2
  (privilege 922.2)
  academic degree 877.3
license, licence *v.*
  760.4
  (commission 755.4)
licensed, licenced
  lax 738.7
  exempt 748.18
  warranted 924.10
licentiate 877.3
licentious
  dissipated 954.5
  wanton 961.10
  lawless 964.6
licentiousness
  anarchy 738.2
  dissipation 954.2
  wantonness 961.2
lich 362.1
lichen fungi 369.4
  rash 655.17
lich gate, lych gate
  portal 260.4
  graveyard 363.14
lich-house 363.17
licit permitted 760.6
  legal 963.5
licitly 760.7
lick *n.*
  modicum 32.2
  velocity 274.1

  blow 276.3
  touch 379.1
  music 415.16
  attempt 675.1
  stroke of work 686.3
lick *v.* eat 298.44
  touch 379.3
  nonplus 475.8
  defeat 731.9
  whip 972.6
lick into shape
  form 240.6
  train 537.10
lick the dust
  submit 725.3
  be defeated 732.6
  be humiliated 879.2
  toady 886.3
lick and a promise, a 460.2
licked 732.12
lickerish, liquorish
  desirous 865.19
  lustful 961.11
lickety-brindle,
  lickety-cut, lickety-split 274.14
licking touch 379.1
  defeat 732.3
lickpenny 819.2
lickspit, lickspittle *n.* 886.2
lickspittle *v.* 886.3
licorice, liquorice 396.2
lictor 745.9
lid cover 223.7
  (stopper 263.1)
  hat 225.26
lie *n.* 546.1
  (falsification 544.1)
  (exaggeration 549.1)
lie *v.*
  be located 184.9
  be present 186.8
  recline 213.5
  ~ at anchor 267.13
  falsify 544.4
  (misinform 538.2)
  (deceive 545.7)
  (exaggerate 549.2)
  (misrepresent 555.4)
lie along 267.34
lie along the shore 267.30
lie around
  surround 227.3
  (be exterior 220.4)
  idle 683.8
lie athwart 267.13
lie by lie to 267.14
  lie idle 683.8
lie down
  recline 213.5
  shirk 623.8
  idle 683.8
  repose 687.3
lie in
  consist in 1.6

  be located 184.9
  sail for 267.26
lie in wait
  await 507.5
  ambush 530.5
  do nothing 681.2
lie low be low 207.5
  hide 528.16
lie off lie to 267.14
  idle 683.8
lie on 215.27
lie over
  impend 152.2
  overlie 223.27
lie to
  navigation 267.14
  lie idle 683.8
lie up lie to 267.14
  sail 267.22
  lie idle 683.8
lie under
  be liable 177.2
  underlie 207.5
lie-abed 683.7
lied 415.10
Liederkranz 416.12
lief 602.8
would as lief
  be willing 602.6
  prefer 609.9
liege potentate 745.2
  subject 746.5
  (inferior 34.3)
liege man, liegeman 746.5
lien 771.1
  (credit 805.2)
lientery
  excrement 299.2
  dung 653.7
lieu 184.3
in lieu of 147.5; 755.6
lieutenant
  officer 745.11, 12
  deputy 759.1
lieutenant colonel 745.11
lieutenant commander 745.12
lieutenant general 745.11
lieutenant governor 745.9
life lifetime 110.4
  affairs 151.2
  vitality 359
  (existence 1.1)
  (spirit 994.11)
  animal ~ 364.1; 366.1
  biography 594.2
  business career 625.3
  animation 682.1
  (energy 171.1)
  career 692.3
  vivacity 836.2
for life 110.11
lifeblood essence 5.2
  life force 359.2
lifeboat boat 273.4
  safeguard 666.1

  escape 671.3
life buoy ship 273.14
  safeguard 666.1
  (escape 671.3)
life force 359.2
life-giving
  procreative 168.8
  vivifying 359.11
life guard 664.3
lifeguard 717.6
lifeless inert 172.3
  dead 360.8
  dull-colored 428.19
  colorless 429.6
  languid 683.14
lifelike alike 17.15
  (faithful 21.5)
  description 594.7
life line
  ship's rope 273.10
  escape 671.3
lifelong 110.9
life net 671.3
life preserver
  safeguard 666.1
  blackjack 727.7
life raft 671.3
lifesaver
  protector 664.3
  lifeguard 717.6
life-size 192.9
life-sized 192.14
life-weary 841.9
life-while 110.4
lift *n.* ride 266.7
  aeronautics 267a.12
  ship's rope 273.10
  elevation 307.1
  (improvement 658.1)
  elevator 307.3
  heavens 318.2
  atmosphere 338.1
  stage 599.12
  aid 707.1
  theft 791.4
  stolen goods 793.1
lift *v.* elevate 307.5
  improve 658.8
  plagiarize 789.8
  steal 791.9
lift a finger
  attempt 675.3
  act 680.5
lift the hand against
  attack 716.5
  (resist 719.3)
  fight 720.8
lift up one's head 878.3
lift up the eyes 441.11
lift up the voice 411.7
not lift a finger
  do nothing 681.2
  idle 683.8
lifter erector 307.2
  thief 792.1
lifting 791.1
ligament 45.4
  (cord 205.3)

ligation — limited 944

ligation junction 43.1
  bond 45.1
ligature 591.6
light *n.* state 7.1
  skylight 260.5
  speed 274.6
  lighter 388.4, 5
  luminary 423.1
  illumination 420
  eyesight 441.1
  aspect 448.4
  (viewpoint 441.4)
  explanation 522.1
  enlightenment 527.1
  come to light 529.6
  give light 420.17
  shed light upon
    illuminate 420.20
    make intelligible
      518.3
light *v.* land 267a.34
  alight 292.8
  get down 306.5
  ignite 384.17
  illuminate 420.20, 21
  (electricity
    158a.11)
  light into
    set to work 686.7
    attack 716.5
    fight 720.8
    punish 972.5
  light out 293.5
  light up
    illuminate 420.20
    kindle emotion
      824.2
    cheer up 836.4, 14
  light upon
    chance upon 156.8
    meet 292.10
    discover 481a.3
    acquire 775.6
light *adj.*
  inconsiderable 32.8
  weightless 320.7
  (rare 322.4)
  airy 338.11
  luminous 420.22
  light-colored 429.7
  whitish 430.9
  fickle 608.6
  trivial 643.11
  easy 705.5
  lighthearted 836.7
  loose-moraled
    945.12
  wanton 961.10
  be light 320.5
light-blue 438.6
light-colored 429.7
  (whitish 430.9)
  (gray 432.4)
lighted 423.14
lighten *n.* 420.6
lighten *v.*
  levitate 320.4
  illuminate 420.20
  facilitate 705.4
  (ease 834.2)
lighter boat 273.4
  igniter 388.4

lighterman 269.2
lightface 591.8
light-faced 591.18
light filter 424.5
light-fingered 791.14
light-footed
  fast 274.13
  nimble 682.17
lightheaded 503.14
lightheadedness 503.3
lighthearted 836.7
lighthouse
  beacon 423.5
  observatory 441.5
  landmark 550.10
lighthouseman 668.4
lighting ignition 384.4
  illumination 420.14
light-legged 274.13
lightless 421.7
light-minded 608.6
lightness 320.1
  (rarity 322.1)
lightning speed 274.6
  thunderbolt 420.6
  omen 512.2
lightning rod 666.1
light of the World
  976.5
lights lungs 349.19
  eyes 441.7
  stage 599.14
lightsome fickle 608.6
  lighthearted 836.7
lightweight
  weakling 160.4
  a nobody 643.6
lignaloes 400.3
ligneous 367.15
lignite 388.2
ligulate
  filamentary 205.7
  tongue-shaped
    245.21
ligule 205.5
likable, likeable
  pleasurable 829.7
  lovable 897.17
  (attractive 617.5)
like *n.* fancy 865.1
  love 897.1
  and the like 37.11
  the like
    similar 17.4
    kind 75.2
like *v.* relish 394.6
  liken 464.2
  seem likely 472.2
  delight in 827.6
  love 897.11
  (desire 865.11)
  (approve 931.5)
  like better 609.9
like *adj.*
  similar 17.10, 12
  (relevant 9.8)
  (comparable 464.6)
  (representative
    554.9)
  likely 472.5
likelihood
  liability 177.1

possibility 470.1
probability 472.1
(good chance 156.3)
likely *adj.*
  tending to 176.3
  (liable to 177.3)
  possible 470.5
  probable 472.5
  comely 845.10
  not likely 473.4
  think likely 472.3
  (expect 507.4)
likely *adv.* 472.7
like-minded
  agreeing 23.9
  unanimous 488.12
  (concurrent 178.4)
  concordant 714.4
like-mindedness
  consensus 23.5
  unanimity 488.3
  concord 714.1
liken 464.2
likeness
  similarity 17.1, 6
  (equivalence 27.2)
  copy 21.1
  (representation
    554.1, 3
  (picture 556.9)
likening 464.1
likewise 37.8
likin 812.2
liking fancy 865.1
  (propensity 602.2)
  (preference 609.2)
  love 897.1
  take a liking to
    897.12
lilac *n.* 400.3
lilac *adj.* 437.4
Lilliputian, Lili-
  putian *n.* 193.5
Lilliputian, Lili-
  putian *adj.* 193.9
lilt *n.* rhythm 138.3
  oscillation 314.5
  music 413.21; 415.6
lilt *v.* sing 416.20
  rejoice 838.5
lily
  mollycoddle 160a.3
  plant 369.8
  perfume 400.3
  white 430.3
lily-livered 862.4
lily of the valley 400.3
lily-white 430.8
limation
  pulverization 330.2
  rubbing 331.1
limb member 51.4
  leg 266.11
  lever 307.4
  foliage 367.4
  rascal 949.1
limber 324.6
limbic, limbiferous
  231.4
limbo
  imprisonment 751.2
  prison 752.1

abode of the dead
  982.1
in limbo
  imprisoned 751.12
  suffering 828.13
Limbu 560.4
limbus 752.1
lime *n.* cement 45.6
  fruit 298.31
  tree 367.6
  sourness 397.2
  deodorant 399.2
  decolorant 429.3
  snare 545.4
  mineral 635.6
lime *v.* 545.9
limeade 298.4; 396.5
lime-juicer
  Englishman 188.9
  mariner 269.1
limekiln 386.1
limelight light 420.7
  spotlight 423.3
  publicity 531.3
  drama 599.14
  in the limelight
    publicly 531.12
    acting 599.29
Limerick 597.2
limestone 342.4
limewater 337.1
limey
  Englishman 188.9
  mariner 269.1
limit *n.*
  consummation 52.4
  end 67.1
  capacity 192.2
  edge 231.1
  bounds 233.1
  go the limit
    be thorough 52.8
    persevere 604a.2
    do thoroughly 729.3
  to the limit
    completely 52.13
    utterly 52.14
    to perfection 650.6
limit *v.*
  circumscribe 229.2
  bound 233.2
  qualify 469.3
  prohibit 761.2
limitable, limital 233.3
limitarian 984.14
limitary
  boundary 233.3
  restrictive 751.13
limitation
  circumscription
    229.1
  qualification 469.1
  restraint 751.1
  estate 780.2; 783.1
limitative
  circumstantial 8.5
  qualifying 469.6
  restraining 751.13
limited
  ~ in quantity 32.7
  special 79.7
  moderate 174.6

limitless — liquor

~ in size 193.8
narrow 203.9
bound 233.3
 (circumscribed
 229.4)
shallow 499.17
limitless *adj.*
 infinite 105.3
 eternal 112.4
 unlimited 180.7;
  748.15
limn depict 554.7
 (paint 428.10)
 design 556.17
limner
 delineator 554.6
 artist 559.1
limnery 556.1
limniad 979.10
limoniad 367.11; 979.8
limousine 272.15
limp *n.* 266.5
limp *v.* be weak 160.6
 walk 266.16
 go slow 275.5
limp *adj.* 324.6
limpid
 transparent 425.4
 perspicuous 518.5
limpidity
 transparency 425.1
 intelligibility 518.1
limy 432.4
linaloa, linaloe 400.3
Lincoln's Birthday
 138.5, 7
linctus 662.4
linden tree 367.6
 wood 635.3
line *n.*
 agreement 23.1
 degree 26.1
 fastening 45.4
 series 69.2
 procession 69.3
 conformity 82.1
 length 200.4, 6
 cord 205.3
 direction 278.3
 ~ of music 415.21
 measure 466.4
 mark 550.7
 engraving 558.1
 ~ of writing 590.3
 epistle 592.2
 ~ of poetry 597.7
 vocation 625.5
 path 627.2
 career 692.3
 troops 726.6
 between the lines
  526.9
 get into line 82.5
 in a line
  continuously 69.7
  (lengthwise 200.15)
  straight 246.5
 in line with 278.13
 out of line 83.9
line *v.*
 interline 224.2
 edge 231.3

line up arrange 60.6
 list 86.3
 schedule 611.4
 ~ ~ with 709.5
lineage
 ancestry 166.4
 (race 11.4)
 posterity 167.2
lineal racial 11.8
 ancestral 166.10
 progenial 167.7
lineament
 particularity 79.2
 earmark 550.6
lineaments
 outline 230.1
 face 234.4
 features 448.5
 (feature 240.2)
linear
 continuous 69.6
 straight 246.5
linear measure 200.6
 (measure 466.3)
lineation 550.7
line letter 442.2
lineman 158a.10
linen thread 205.2
 cloth 219.5
 sheet 223.9
 clothes 225.1
 merchandise 798.3
linene, linenette
 219.5
line of action 692.1
line of battle
 procession 69.3
 battlefield 728.2
line-of-battle ship
 726.11
line of circumvalla-
 tion 233.1
line of defense 726.6
line of march 278.3
liner 273.1
lines fastening 45.4
 outline 230.1
 lineaments 448.5
 art 556.6
 role 599.7, 16
 fortification 717.3
 reins 752.2
line-up, lineup
 list 86.1
 schedule 611.2
linger *v.*
 be protracted 110.7
 (continue 106.2)
 delay 133.5, 7
 go slow 275.5
 lag 281.4
 dawdle 683.8
lingerer
 slow goer 275.4
 idler 683.7
lingerie
 undergarments
  225.25
 merchandise 798.3
lingering
 protracted 110.10
 slow 275.8

lingo, lingua
 language 560.1
 jargon 563.4
linguadental 402.11
lingua franca 560.5
 (language 563.6)
lingual 560.9
linguiform 245.21
linguipotence 560.6
linguist, linguister,
 lingster
 interpreter 524.1
 scholar 560.7
linguistic 560.9
 (verbal 562.8)
linguistics 560.6
 (lexicology 562.4)
 (grammar 567.1)
lingulate 245.21
liniment 662.6
lining interlining 224
 (contents 190.1)
 ornamentation 847.3
link *n.* bond 45.1
 fastening 45.2
 (connection 9.2)
 (joint 43.3)
 member 51.4
 rank 71.1
 intermediary 228.5
 torch 423.8
 measure 466.3
link *v.* join 43.5
 attach 43.6
 (relate 9.4)
 (combine 48.3)
 interlace 219.8
linn pond 343a.1
 waterfall 348.7
linnet 366.22
linoleum cloth 219.5
 rug 223.8
linotype *n.* 591.6
linotype *v.* 591.14
linotypist 591.12
linseed oil 356.3
linsey-woolsey *n.*
 cloth 219.5
 rough 256.2
linsey-woolsey *adj.*
 mixed 41.9
 rough 256.12
 coarse 329.3
linstock 388.5
lint wrapper 223.11
 dressing 662.14
lintel top 210.4
 beam 215.12
linter 189.4
lint-white 430.8
liocephalous, lio-
 dermatous etc. See
 leiocephalus etc.
lion animal 366.3
 courage 861.4
 prodigy 872.1
 celebrity 873.9
Lion 318.6
lioness 374.8
lionhearted 861.8
lionization 873.6
lionize

show curiosity 455.3
honor 873.13
lion's share
 main part 50.3
 majority 100.2
 too much 641.1
 share 786.2
 undue 925.3
lip edge 231.1
 protuberance 250.2
 speech 582.1
 impertinence 885.2
lip homage
 flattery 933.1
 (dissimulation
  544.2)
 (pretext 619.1)
 sanctimony 988.2
lipothymy 688.3
lippitude 443.2
lip reading 419.5
lip server 988.6
lip service
 flattery 933.1
 sanctimony 988.2
lipstick *n.* color 434.6
 beautifying 845.5
lipstick *v.* 434.7
lip wisdom 499.6
lip worship 988.2
lip worshiper 988.6
liquation 382.1
liquefacient 335.4
liquefaction
 fluidity 333.1
 liquidization 335
 (melting 384.2)
liquefactive, liquefia-
 ble 335.8
liquefied 335.7
 (fluid 333.7)
liquefier 335.4
liquefy, liquesce 335.5
 (melt 384.21)
liquescence 335.1
liquescent 335.8
liqueur
 sweet drink 396.5
 alcoholic 959.4
 distilled 959.6
liquid *n.* drink 298.4
 fluid 333.2
liquid *adj.* fluid 333.7
 (liquefied 335.7)
 (watery 337.6)
 phonetics 402.11
liquidable 335.8
liquid air 387.2
liquidate 807.7
liquidation 807.1
liquidator 801
 (payer 807.5)
liquidity 333.1
liquidize 335.5
liquid measure 466.3
liquor *n.* drink 298.4
 fluid 333.2
 intoxicating ~
  959.4–10
 (merchandise 798.3)
liquor *v.*
 lubricate 332.4

liquorice — load

liquor (*continued*)
  tope 959.15
liquorice See licorice
liquorish 959.23
liquorish See lickerish
liquorist 959.12
lira 800.8
lisle 219.5
lisp *n.* 583.1
lisp *v.*
  sibilate 409.3
  speak 583.2
lisping 583.5
lissome, lissom 324.6
list *n.* catalogue 86
  (record 551.1)
  (dictionary 593.4)
  strip 205.5
  obliquity 217.1
  hem 231.2
list *v.* classify 60.7
  give continuity 69.5
  catalogue 86.3
  incline 217.6
  careen 267.34
  listen 418.11
  pay attention 457.4
  record 551.8
  think fit 600.2
  choose 609.9
  desire 865.11
  love 897.11
listed
  catalogued 86.4
  striate 440.10
listel 847.4
listen *v.*
  hearken 418.11
  pay attention 457.4
  listen in 418.11
listen *int.* hark! 418.16
  attend! 457.10
listener 418.5, 7
listener-in
  eavesdropper 418.7
  radio 532a.6
listless languid 683.14
  indifferent 866.4
  (inattentive 458.10)
lists 728.1
lit intoxicated **959.21**
  illuminated 423.14
litany prayer 990.3
  rite 998.2, 9
liter, litre 466.3
literal imitated 19.11
  (faithful 772.5)
  meaning 516.9
  (exact 494.11)
  lettered 561.9
  verbal 562.8
  written 590.15
  scriptural 983a.7
literalism, literality 516.2
literally 19.14
  (exactly 494.16)
  (verbally 562.11)
  (faithfully 772.6)
literati 492.1
literatim 19.14

literature
  learning 490.2
  advertisement 531.4
  belles-lettres 560.8
lithe, lithesome 324.6
lithification 323.2
lithify 323.4
  (mineralize 358.3)
lithium 635.6
lithograph *n.* 558.3
lithograph *v.* 558.5
lithographer 559.6
lithographic 558.6
lithography, lithogravure 558.1
lithoid 323.5
  (inorganic 358.4)
lithomancy 511.3
lithophone 418.6
lithotint 558.3
lithotype 591.6
Lithuanian 560.5
litigable 969.13
litigant *n.*
  disputant 726.1
  accused 938.3
  suitor 969.9
litigant *adj.*
  contentious 901.9
  litigious 969.13
litigate
  quarrel 713.7
  prosecute 969.10
  (dispute 476.11)
litigation
  argumentation 476.2
  dispute 713.3
  contention 720.1
  lawsuit 969.1
  in litigation 969.14
litigator 969.9
litigious
  contentious 901.9
  litigant 969.13
  (disputatious 476.14)
litmus paper 463.5
litotes 521.1
litre See liter
litter *n.* confusion 59.2
  multitude 102.2
  young 167.3
  stretcher 215.24
  vehicle 272.12
  bier 363.12
  rubbish 645.4
litter *v.* derange 61.2
  bed down 370.7
littérateur, litterateur
  scholar 492.1
  author 593.15
little *n.*
little by little
  gradually 26.5
  piecemeal 51.10
  slowly 275.11
little one 129.3
little *adj.*
  inconsiderable 32.6
  diminutive 193.8
  (short 201.5)
  (narrow 203.9)

  bigoted 606.7
  insignificant 643.10
  disreputable 874.8
make little of
  underestimate 483.3
  deem unimportant 643.8
  be easy 705.3
  disdain 930.5
too little 640.8
little *adv.* 193.11
Little Fox 318.6
little go 461.3
Little Joe four 95.2
  throw of dice 621.9
Little Lord Fauntleroy 160a.3
little Mary 191.7
littleness
  quantity 32.1
  inferiority 34.1
  diminutiveness 193
  (shortness 201.1)
  (narrowness 203.1)
little people 979.9
little theater 599.10
littoral *n.* 342.2
littoral *adj.*
  bordering 231.4
  coastal 342.10
liturgical 998.15
liturgics 998.11
liturgy 998.1, 7, 9
lituus staff 215.15
  horn 417.4
livable, liveable 359.12
live *v.*
  be permanent 141.4
  inhabit 186.10
  be alive 359.6
  (exist 1.4)
  be famous 873.10
live and let live
  laissez faire 681.2
  not interfere 748.11
live by one's wits
  be deceptive 545.7
  exercise skill 698.9
  be cunning 702.5
  swindle 791.12
  be dishonest 940.6
live fast 954.3
live from hand to mouth
  be unprepared 674.4
  be poor 804.4
live high 954.3
live in a glass house
  visible 446.2
  defy danger 665.5
  be rash 863.5
live in clover 734.5
live *adj.*
  burning 382.17
  attentive 457.9
  lively 682.16
livelihood 625.1
liveliness
  activity 682.1
  vivacity 836.2
livelong 110.9
lively

  energetic 171.9
  capersome 309.6
  vivid 375.7
  style 574.6
  active 682.16
  feeling 821.5
  vivacious 836.7
step lively
  speed 274.9
  bestir oneself 682.12
  make haste! 684.8
liver 221.5
liver-colored 433.5
liverwort 369.5
liverwurst 298.24
livery wardrobe 225.2
  uniform 225.8
liveryman 748.6
livestock 366.1
live wire
  electricity 157a.4, 8
  man of action 682.10
livid
  black-and-blue 431.7
  gray 432.4
  purple 437.4
  blue 438.6
  discolored 440a.3
livid-brown 433.5
lividity
  blackness 431.1
  purpleness 437.2
living *n.* life 359.1
  business 625.1
  benefice 995.3
living *adj.* 359.10
  (existing 1.7)
living force
  potence 157.1
  life force 359.2
living pledge 771.1
living room 191.16
Livonian 560.4
lixiviate
  percolate 295.7
  solubilize 335.6
  purify 652.9
lixiviation
  percolation 295.1
  solubilization 335.1
  purification 652.2
lixiviator 652.8
lixivium
  solution 335.3
  solvent 652.8
lizard 366.18
Lizard 318.6
llama 271.2
llano 344.1
lo! attend! 457.10
  wonder 870.11
load *n.*
  quantities 31.3
  fill 52.3
  lading 190.1
  aeronautics 267a.8
  freight 270.4
  weight 319.1
  impediment 706.2
  hardship 735.1
  trouble 830.2

946

load — loneliness

load v. fill 52.7
  (overload 641.4)
  place in 184.13
  (store 636.7)
  weight 319.9
  encumber 706.6
loaded 959.21
loader 269.7
load-line mark 466.5
loadstar See **lodestar**
loadstone, lodestone 288.2
  (lure 617.1)
loaf n. lump 192.5
  loafing 683.2
  Eucharist 998.6
loaf v. 683.8
loafer vagabond 268.2
  idler 184.1
  (neglector 460.3)
loafing n. 683.2
loafing adj. 683.12
loam 342.1, 3
loamy 324.6
loan n. 787.1
  (security 771.1)
  (credit 805.1)
loan v. 784.7
loath, loth
  unwilling 603.5
  disliking 867.7
loathe 898.3
  (dislike 867.4)
loathful 830.14
loathing
  abhorrence 867.2
  hate 898.1
loathly 603.6
loathsome nasty 395.7
  foul 653.17
  odious 830.14
  (dislikable 867.9)
lobby n. 191.17
  (portal 260.4)
  (entrance 294.5)
lobby v. 175.6
lobbyism 175.4
lobbyist 615.6
lobe member 51.4
  pendant 214.2
  ear 418.5
lobelia 434.5
loblolly 352.3, 5
loblolly pine 400.3
lobo 366.5
lobscouser 269.1
lobster food 298.18
  animal 368.8
  red 434.5
  awkward fellow 701
lobular pneumonia 655.9
lobulate 44.8
lobule member 51.4
  ear 418.5
locable 184.18
local n. 184.1
local adj. 181.6
local color 428.1
locale 184.1
localism 563.5

locality 184.1
localization 184.5
localize 184.10
locate 184.10, 14
located 184.17
location
  placement 184.5
  (region 181.1)
  farm 371.4
locational 184.18
  (regional 181.6)
loch sea inlet 343.1
  lake 343a.1
Lochaber ax 727.4
lock n.
  fastening 45.2
  hair 256.3
  stopper 263.1
  standstill 265.3
  floodgate 350.2
  fetter 752.3
  fence 792.9
lock v. attach 43.6
  interlace 219.8
  close 261.2
  conceal 528.10
  ~ the door 666.6
  obstruct 706.4
lock horns
  quarrel 713.7
  fight 720.8
lock out 719.4
lock up close 261.2
  confine 751.8
locker
  cupboard 191.15
  safe 802.1
locket
  ornament 847.7
  love token 902.5
lockjaw 655.5
lockmaker 690.8
lockout
  exclusion 55.1
  strike 719.2
locksmith 690.6
lock, stock, and barrel 50.2
lockup 752.1
loco v. 503.11
loco adj. 503.12
locomobile n. 272.15
locomobile adj. 266.27
locomote 264.6
locomotion
  motion 264.2
  (navigation 267.1)
  (progression 282.1)
  travel 266.1
locomotive n.
  leg 266.11
  train 272.19
  engine 633.3
locomotive adj.
  self-moving 266.27
  engine 633.5
locomotor 633.5
locomotor ataxia 655.14
locoweed 663.6
locular 191.23
loculus 191.6

locum tenens
  substitute 147.2
  inhabitant 188.1
  deputy 759.1
locus location 184.1
  topic 454.1
  water closet 653.9
locus standi
  footing 215.4
  rank 873.4
locust insect 366.24
  (blight 663.2)
  prodigal 818.2
locution word 562.1
  expression 564.3
  phrase 566.1
  phraseology 569.1
  utterance 580.3
  speech 582.1
lode attractor 288.2
  fund 636.2
lodestar, loadstar
  attractor 288.2
  cynosure 550.10
lodestone See **loadstone**
lodge n. 189.3
lodge v. quarter 184.12
  inhabit 186.10
  ~ a complaint 938.4
lodger 188.4; 779.1
lodging 189.1
lodginghouse 189.8
lodgment, lodgement
  location 184.5
  abode 189.1
loess residue 40.2
  silt 270.3
loft attic 191.19
  head 210.3
  balcony 599.11
loftiness height 206.1
  ~ of expression 574.4
  (oratory 582.3)
lofty high 206.13
  (elevated 307.8)
  airy 338.11
  language 574.8
  grandiloquent 577.7
  exalted 873.18
  proud 878.6
  ostentatious 882.8
  arrogant 885.8
  magnanimous 942.6
lofty-minded 878.6
log
  velocimeter 274.8
  firewood 388.3
  measure 466.4
  record 551.3
  recorder 553.3
  wood 635.3
  account book 811.5
loganberry 298.31
logarithm 84.2
logarithmic 84.7
logbook record 551.3
  account book 811.5
log cabin 189.4
logger 371.2
loggerhead 501.1

at loggerheads
  at variance 713.10
  contending 720.11
  at enmity 889.2, 3
  go to loggerheads 720.8
loggia 191.17
logic 451.4
  (reasoning 476.1)
logical 476.16
  (possible 470.5)
  (plausible 472.6)
  (credible 484.15)
logicality 476.7
logicalization 476.1
logicalize 476.10
logically 476.18
  (hence 155.5)
logician 476.9
logistic 451.4
log line
  velocimeter 274.8
  measure 466.4
logogram 561.5
logogrammatic 533.6
logographer 590.12
logographic 590.16
logography 590.7
logogriph 561.5
logogriphic 533.6
logomach 476.9
logomachic 476.14
logomachize 476.11
logomachy
  argument 476.2
  warfare 722.1
logometer 466.4
  (calculator 85.5)
logometric 84.7
Logos
  world spirit 359.3
  Deity 976.5
logotype 591.6
logrolling 709.1
logy 172.3
loin rump 235.5
  side 236.1
  meat 298.19
loincloth 225.22
loiter wait 133.7
  go slow 275.5
  lag 281.4
  dawdle 683.8
loiterer 275.4
Loki, Loke
  giant 192.8
  god 979.3; 982.4
  evil 980.2
loll recline 213.5
  lounge 683.8
  repose 687.3
loller 683.7
lollipop 396.2
lollop 683.8
lolloping 192.15
lolly ice 383.5
  lollipop 396.2
loma 206.2
Lombard Street 799.3
lone 87.6
loneliness 893.2

lonely — loophole

lonely, lonesome
  alone 87.8
  solitary 893.10
long *v.* 865.11
long *adj.*
  lengthy 200.12
  (large 192.11)
  (distant 196.5)
  (tall 206.13)
  verbose 573.7
  be long 200.8
  for ever so long 110.11
long *adv.* 110.11
  no longer 122.14
  long ago 122.2, 14
longanimity
  sufferance 826.4
  indulgence 918.1
longanimous
  long-suffering 826.10
  forgiving 918.5
long-arm balance 319.5
longbow 727.9
long-continued, long-continuing 110.10
long dozen 98.7
long-drawn-out
  protracted 110.10
  verbose 573.7
longear 271.10
long-eared 418.14
longéron 273a.10
longeval 110.9
longevity 128.1
  (durability 110.1)
longevous 110.9
long face
  solemnity 837.2
  sullenness 901.3
long-faced 837.16
long green 800.6
longhand 590.4
  in longhand 590.15
longhead 500.1
long head
  wisdom 498.3
  foresight 510.1
longheaded 498.10
  (farsighted 510.6)
longheadedness
  wisdom 498.3
  foresight 510.1
long home 363.13
longhorn native 188.8
  bovine 366.12
  veteran 700.3
long hundredweight 319.4
longiloquence 573.1
longiloquent 573.7
longing *n.* 865.2
  have a longing 865.11
longing *adj.* 865.16
longinquity 196.1
longish 200.12
longitude
  region 181.5
  distance 196.1

length 200.1
map line 550.9
longitudinal 273a.12
longitudinally 200.15
long-lasting 110.9
long-legged 200.13
  (lean 203.11)
  (tall 206.13)
long-limbed 200.13
long-lived 110.9
long-lost 776.5
longness 200.1
long-pending 110.10
long pig 362.1
longshanks
  tall person 206.6
  legs 266.1
longshoreman 269.7
long-sighted
  presbyopic 443.14
  foreseeing 510.6
long-sightedness
  presbyopia 443.1
  sagacity 498.2
  foresight 510.1
longsome 200.12
long-standing 110.9
long-suffering *n.*
  longanimity 826.4
  compassion 914.1
  indulgence 918.1
long-suffering *adj.*
  lenient 740.4
  forbearant 826.10
  compassionate 914.6
  forgiving 918.5
long ton 319.4
long-winded
  protracted 110.10
  verbose 573.7
  (loquacious 584.5)
loo 840.12
looby fool 501.1
  awkward fellow 701
  boor 876.5
look *n.* modicum 32.2
  sight 441.2
  appearance 448.4
look *v.* tend 176.2
  gaze 441.11, 13
  appear 448.6
  (be manifest 525.3)
  give attention 457.4
look about
  look at 441.11
  be vigilant 459.4
  be cautious 864.3
look after
  give attention 457.4
  care for 459.6
  superintend 693.5
look a gift horse in the mouth
  be fastidious 868.3
  be ungrateful 917.2
look ahead 510.5
look at
  gaze upon 441.11, 12
  give attention 457.4
  examine 461.17, 18
look away 441.17

(not look 442.5)
look back
  retrospect 122.7
  remember 505.10
look before one leaps
  prepare for 673.7
  take precautions 864.4
look black
  disagree 489.4
  discountenance 764.3
  feeling 824.8
  be discontented 832.3
  discourage 837.8
  be discourteous 895.4
  be sullen 901.6
  disapprove 932.5
look daggers
  be angry 900.7
  threaten 909.2
look down one's nose
  look askance 441.15
  be proud 878.3
  snub 930.7
look down upon 930.5
look for seek 461.16
  expect 507.4
look forth 446.2
look forward
  expect 507.4
  (futurity 121.5)
  foresee 510.5
look in 892.10
look into
  give attention 457.4
  examine 461.17
look like
  resemble 17.7
  appear 448.6
look on attend 186.9
  (be a spectator 444.3)
  see 441.10, 11
look one in the face
  be artless 703.3
  be proud 878.3
look out
  be attentive 457.4, 10
  be careful 459.4
  care for 459.6
  seek 461.16
  expect 507.4
  beware! 864.3, 9
look over
  scrutinize 441.12
  give attention 457.4
  examine 461.17
look through 461.17
look to
  give attention 457.4
  care for 459.6
  call upon 926.7
look up increase 35.4
  hunt up 461.16
  improve 658.6
  prosper 734.5
  rise in price 814.2
  hope 858.8

visit 892.10
look up to
  honor 873.13
  respect 928.4
  admire 931.5
not look 442.5
  (look away 441.17)
looker
  spectator 444.1, 2
  beauty 845.3
look-in 441.2
looking 441.18
looking glass 445.4
  (glass 384.14)
lookout watch 441.2
  observatory 441.5
  outlook 441.6
  view 448.2
  vigil 459.2
  intention 620.1
  concern 625.1
  sentinel 668.2
  (watcher 444.1)
  guard 717.6
be on the lookout 459.4
on the lookout
  attentive 457.9
  vigilant 459.8
  in search 461.24
  expectant 507.7
  cautious 864.3
looks
  appearance 448.4
  good ~ 845.1
look-through 441.2
loom *n.* handle 215.7
  airplane 273a.10
  ~ of the land 342.2
loom *v.* be great 31.4
  impend 152.2
  grow dim 422.7
  appear 446.2
loom large 525.3
looming *n.* 443.9
looming *adj.* 152.3
loon diver 310.3
  oaf 501.1
  madman 504.1
  awkward fellow 701
  boor 876.5
  rascal 949.1
loony, luny *n.*
  fool 501.1
  madman 504.1
loony, luny *adj.*
  imbecile 499.13
  insane 503.12
loop *n.*
  fastening 45.2
  electricity 158a.4
  curve 245.2
  circle 247.2
  acrobatics 267a.24
  circuit 629.1
loop *v.* surround 227.3
  aviate 267a.31
loop in 158a.11
loop the loop 267a.31
loophole opening 260.1
  observatory 441.5

948

alternative 626.5
escape 671.4
 (outlet 295.5)
 (pretext 619.1)
 (refuge 666.3)
 (extenuation 937.3)
fortification 717.3
looping the loop 267a.24
loose *n.* 748.1
loose *v.* disjoin 44.7
 ~ the anchor 267.15
 liberate 750.3
loose *adj.*
 unconnected 44.12
 incoherent 47.3
 hanging 214.7
 deviative 279.8
 neglectful 460.8
 illogical 477.10
 diction 575.2
 shiftless 674.11
 lax 738.7
 free 748.12
 (escaped 671.7)
 (liberated 750.5)
 nonobservant 773.5
 loose-moraled 945.12
 wanton 961.10
loosen slacken 47.2
 (disjoin 44.7)
 free 750.3
looseness
 incoherence 47.1
 laxity 738.1
 dereliction 927.1
 ~ of morals 945.3
loose tongue 584.1
loot *n.* 793.1
loot *v.* 791.10
looting 791.14
lop 38.6
lope *n.* 274.3
lope *v.* 274.9
lop-eared 418.14
loper 228.4
lopped 53.5
lopper *n.* 321.5
lopper *v.* 321.7
lopsided
 unequal 28.3
 topheavy 218.7
loquacious 584.5
 (diffuse 573.7)
 be loquacious 584.4
 (be diffuse 573.5)
loquaciously 584.6
loquacity 584
 (verbiage 562.3)
 (diffuseness 573.1)
lorcha 273.2
lord *n.* master 745.1
 proprietor 779.2
 nobility 875.2, 4
Lord *n.* title 877.2
 God 976.2
lord *v.*
lord it over
 dominate 737.12

be domineering 885.5
 (bully 860.12)
Lord Chancellor 967.1
lording 875.4
Lord Justice 967.1
lord lieutenant 745.9
lordling 875.4
lordly noble 873.18
 proud 878.7
 arrogant 885.8
Lord Mayor 745.9
Lord of Misrule 701
lord of the ascendant 745.1
Lord's day
 vacation 687.2
 holyday 998.13
lordship
 authority 737.3
 proprietorship 777.3
 nobility 875.9
Lordship title 877.2
 judge 967.1
Lord's Prayer 990.3
Lord's Supper 998.6
Lord's table 1000.3
 (eucharist 998.6)
lore 490.2
Lorelei, Lurlei
 siren 617.3
 mythical being 980.2
Lorettine 996.11
lorgnette, lorgnon 445.3
lorica 717.2
loricate 223.24
loricated 223.28
lorication 223.1
lorn 893.10
lorry 272.10, 15
lose forget 506.4
 not understand 519.5
 be defeated 732.6
 incur loss 776.2
 lose caste 874.5
lose ground
 retard 275.7
 decline 304.2
lose heart
 despond 837.6
 despair 859.5
lose oneself 475.6
lose one's head
 be uncertain 475.6
 act the fool 499.9
 go mad 503.10
lose one's heart 897.12
lose out 732.6
lose sight of
 be blind 442.4
 disappear 449.2
 neglect 460.4
 forget 506.4
 not complete 730.2
losel *n.* prodigal 818.2
 vagabond 876.9
 good-for-nothing 949.1

losel *adj.* 818.4
loss decrease 36.1
 decrement 39a
 death 360.1
 damage 659.3
 privation 776
 (destruction 162.1)
 (waste 638.1)
 (dispossession 789.2)
 (disentitlement 925.2)
at a loss
 bewildered 475.16
 (irresolute 605.5)
 (in difficulty 704.11)
 desirous 865.16
lost extinct 2.10
 bewildered 475.16
 forgotten 506.7
 not won 732.11
 gone out of one's possession 776.5
 (destroyed 162.7)
 (irretrievable 859.7)
 (forfeited 925.10)
 distracted 824.10
 disconsolate 837.12
 ~ in iniquity 945.15
 sinful 945.19
 impenitent 951.4
lost sheep 949.1
lot *n.* state 7.1
 quantity 25.2
 quantities 31.3
 bunch 72.5
 kind 75.2
 multitude 102.2
 fortune 156.1
 field 371.5
 fate 601.3
 chance 621.1, 2
 gambling 621.6
 share 786.2
 price 812.1
by lot 786.5
fall to one's lot
 chance 156.7
 be received 785.4
 be the duty of 926.5
lota, lotah 191.11
loth See loath
Lothario lover 897.6
 libertine 962.1
lotion cleanser 652.8
 balm 662.6
Lot's wife 455.2
lottery
 gambling 621.10
 game 840.12
lotto 621.10; 840.12
lotus-eater, lotos-eater 683.7
loud
 loud-sounding 404.8
 (thundering 406.11)
 (shrill 410.10)
 (vociferous 411.8)
 gaudy-colored 428.15
 gaudy 851.8

 (conspicuous 525.5)
 (ostentatious 882.8)
 be loud 404.5
loudly 404.11
loudmouthed 411.8
loudness 404
loud-speaker 418.6
loud-spoken 582.11
lough 343a.1
louis d'or 800.5
lounge *n.*
 vestibule 191.17
 seat 215.22
lounge *v.* 683.8
lounger 683.7
lour, louring See lower etc.
lousiness 653.2
lousy bad 649.8
 unclean 653.18
lout oaf 501.1
 awkward fellow 701
 bumpkin 876.5
loutish rustic 183.3
 hulky 192.13
 uncouth 851.7
louver, louverwork
 ventilator 338.6
 air passage 351.1
Louvre 636.5
lovable 897.17
love *n.* desire 865.1
 compliments 894.3
 affection 897
 (concord 714.1)
 (friendship 888.1)
 (benevolence 906.1)
 sweetheart 897.7
 endearment 902.4
 fall in love 897.12
 for love 815.10
 in love 897.11, 14, 15
Love *n.*
 world spirit 359.3
 God 976.2
love *v.* 897.11
 (desire 865.11)
 (be friendly 888.2)
love affair 897.3
love apple 308.30
lovebird 897.9
loved 897.16
loved one 897.7
 (favorite 899.1)
 (endearment 902.4)
love feast 897.1; 998.13
love knot 733.1
loveless 898.6
love letter
 epistle 592.2
 endearment 902.5
loveliness 845.1
lovelock 256.3
lovelorn in love 897.14
 forsaken 898.6
lovely
 delightful 829.8
 beautiful 845.8
 (pleasing 377.7)
 lovable 897.17

love-maker — lumberjack

love-maker 897.6
love-making 902
love potion
  excitant 171.4
  aphrodisiac 865.10
lover 897.6
  (escort 88.4)
  (flirt 902.6)
lovering, loverly 897.14
love seat 215.22
lovesick, lovesome 897.14
love song 415.10
loving 897.14
  (benevolent 906.6)
loving cup
  trophy 733.1
  pledge 894.3
loving-kindness 906.1
low *v.* 412.2
low *adj.*
  inconsiderable 32.8
  unelevated 207.7
  (short 201.5)
  (deep 208.8)
  faint 405.9
  speech 579.3
  cheap 815.8
  vulgar 851.6
  disreputable 874.8
  (ignoble 876.11)
  humble 879.4
  wicked 945.16
  obscene 961.9
be low 207.5
bring low
  depress 308.4
  degrade 874.7
  humble 879.3
  depreciate 934.3
laid low weak 160.12
  sick 655.23
  impaired 659.12
run low 36.3
lowborn, lowbred 876.11
  (humble 879.4)
low-brow
  unlearned 491.9
  ignoramus 493.1
low comedy 855.2
low-cut 207.8
low-down 527.2
lower *v.*
  decrease 36.4
  make low 207.6
  deepen 208.6
  depend 214.4
  excavate 252.9
  ~ sail 267.38
  depress 308.4
  cheapen 815.7
  sadden 837.8
  humble 879.3
lower oneself 874.5
lower, lour *v.*
  impend 152.2
  darken 421.5
  grow dim 422.7
  look downcast 837.6
  look sullen 901.6

threaten 909.2
  (portend 511.9)
lower *adj.*
  inferior 34.5
  nether 207.9
lower case letter 561.1
  type 591.6
lower house 696.6
lowering *n.* 308.1
  (descent 306.1)
lowering, louring *adj.*
  imminent 152.3
  gloomy 421.8
  ominous 512.5
  (threatening 909.3)
  dismal 837.10
lowermost
  lowest 207.10
  bottom 211.5
lower world 982.1
lowest least 34.6
  nethermost 207.10
  bottom 211.5
Low German 560.4
lowland
  provinces 183.1
  lowness 207.3
lowliness 879.1
lowly 879.4
  (ignoble 876.11)
low-lying 207.7
low-minded
  vulgar 851.6
  wicked 945.14
lown oaf 501.1
  awkward fellow 701
  rascal 949.1
low-necked 207.8
lowness
  lack of height 207
  (shortness 201.1)
  (depth 208.1)
  (base 211.1)
  (horizontality 213.1)
  faintness 405.1
  depression 837.1
low-priced 815.8
low relief 557.6
low-spirited 837.9
low tide lowness 207.2
  tide 348.9
low-toned 431.8
low water
  lowness 207.2
  tide 348.9
  insufficiency 640.1
  poverty 804.1
low-water mark
  at low-water mark
  inconsiderable 32.8
  insufficient 640.8
loxodromic, loxotic 217.9
loy 191.14
loyal obedient 743.3
  observant 772.5
  faithful 939.10
loyalty 939.4
Loyolite 996.11
lozenge angle 244.2

incense 400.2
l. tn. 319.4
lubber mariner 269.1
  oaf 501.1
  idler 683.7
  awkward fellow 701
  (ignoramus 493.1)
Lubberland 515.6
lubberly hulky 192.13
  clumsy 699.12
  uncouth 851.7
lubric 961.11
lubricant *n.*
  lubricator 332.2
  oil 356.1
lubricant *adj.* 332.5
  (unctuous 355.3)
lubricate oil 332.4
  (smooth 255.4)
  facilitate 705.4
lubricated 959.21
lubrication 332
  (unctuousness 355.1)
lubricator 332.2
lubricity
  lubrication 332.1
  (smoothness 255.1)
  unctuousness 355.1
  lasciviousness 961.3
lubricous
  lubricant 332.5
  (smooth 255.5)
  lascivious 961.11
lubritorium -y 332.3
lucence shine 420.1
  transparency 425.1
lucent *n.* 425.4
lucent *adj.* 420.22
lucerne, lucern 367.9
lucid luminous 420.22
  transparent 425.4
  sane 502.5
  perspicuous 518.5
lucid interval 502.1
lucidity shine 420.1
  transparency 425.1
  sanity 502.1
  intelligibility 518.1
  (perspicuity 570.1)
lucifer 388.5
Lucifer star 318.3
  Satan 978.1
lucimeter 445.1
luck fortune 156.1
  (chance 621.1)
  prosperity 734.2
  (success 731.1)
in luck 734.8
out of luck 735.9
luckily 734.9
luckless 735.9
lucky opportune 134.7
  auspicious 512.4
  fortunate 734.8
lucrative 775.12
lucre gain 775.1, 2
  money 800.1
Lucretia 948.2
lucubration
  thought 451.1
  writing 590.2

luculent 420.22
ludicrous 855.5
  (absurd 497.4)
  (amusing 840.22)
ludicrousness 855.1
  (absurdity 497.1)
luetic 655.25
luff *n.* side 236.3
  lifter 307.2
luff *v.* 267.19
luff round 267.24
lug *n.* adjunct 39.2
  load 52.3; 190.1
  handle 215.7
  face 234.4
  freight 270.4
  spar 273.12
  pull 285.2
  tobacco 392a.1
  car 418.5
lug *v.* carry 270.8
  pull 285.4
lug in foist in 10.4
  interject 228.8
luggage baggage 270.4
  impedimenta 780.6
luggage van 272.19
lugger 273.2
lugs finery 225.13
  airs 882.2
  (vanity 880.2)
lugsail 273.12
lugubrious 837.10
luke nothing 2.2
  zero 87a.1
lukewarm tepid 382.15
  (cool 383.10)
  irresolute 605.5
  dispassionate 823.5
  indifferent 866.4
lukewarmness
  irresolution 605.1
  dispassion 822.1
  indifference 866.1
lull *n.* pause 142.2
  (quiescence 265.2)
  silence 403.1
  respite 687.2
lull *v.* moderate 174.5
  quiet 265.6
lullaby song 415.9
  (sleep-inducer 683.6)
  soothing 834.1
lumbago pain 378.1
  ailment 655.5
lumbar 235.10
lumber *n.*
  confusion 59.2
  rubbish 645.4
  wood 635.3
  (tree 367.6)
  stores 636.1
  impedimenta 706.2
lumber *v.* walk 266.16
  go slow 275.5
  be awkward 699.2
  encumber 706.6
lumberer 787.2
lumbering 846.8
lumberjack, lumberman 371.2

lumber room — macaroni

lumber room 636.4
  (room 191.16)
lumbriciform, lumbricine 248.6
lumen 420.1
luminant *n.*
  light 420.15
  luminary 423.1
luminant *adj.* 420.22
luminary *n.* light 423
  (electricity 158a.1)
  (brightness 420.1)
  sage 500.1
luminary *adj.* 423.14
  (luminous 420.22)
luminate, lumine 420.20
luminesce 420.19
luminescence
  light 420.11
  spiritualistic glow 980a.3
luminosity 420.1, 2
luminous light 420.22
  (luminary 423.14)
  intelligible 518.5
luminous energy 420.1
lummox oaf 501.1
  awkward fellow 701
lump *n.*
  quantities 31.3
  main part 50.3
  piece 51.3
  accumulation 72.6
  mass 192.5, 7
  protuberance 250.2
  weight 319.1
  solid 321.4
  awkward fellow 701
lump *v.* join 43.5
  combine 48.3
  assemble 72.11
lumper 690.2
lumping 846.8
lumpish hulky 192.13
  heavy 319.12
  dense 321.8
  ignorant 491.8
  stupid 499.12
  languid 683.14
  clumsy 699.12
  ungraceful 846.8
  uncouth 851.7
lumpkin 876.5
lumpy 319.12
Luna 318.5
lunacy 503.1
lunar
  moon-shaped 245.7
  lunular 318.16
lunar caustic 384.11
lunatic *n.* 504.1
lunatic *adj.* 503.12
lunation 108.1
lunch *n.* morsel 298.2
  meal 298.34, 35;
  892.6
lunch *v.* feed 298.43
  eat 298.44
lunch counter 298.42
luncheon *n.*

morsel 298.2
meal 298.34, 35
party 892.6
luncheon *v.* 298.44
luncher 298.41
lunchroom 298.42
lunette 717.3
lung vitals 221.4
  respiration 349.19
  (voice 580.2)
  noisemaker 404.4
lunge *n.* 276.3; 716.3
lunge *v.* walk 266.16
  strike 276.8
lungmotor 349.20
luniform 245.7
lunkhead dolt 501.1
  bungler 701
lunula 245.2
lunular
  moon-shaped 245.7
  lunar 318.16
lunule 245.2
luny See loony
lupine 789.15
Lupus 318.6
lurch *n.*
  obliquity 217.1
  oscillation 314.5
  sway 315.4
lurch *v.* incline 217.6
  pitch 267.45
  topple 306.6
  oscillate 314.8
  flounder 315.9
  deceive 545.7
  steal 791.9
  swindle 791.12
lurcher 366.6
lure *n.*
  music instrument 417.4
  allurement 617.2
  (attractor 288.2)
  (snare 545.4)
  (bribe 618.2)
lure *v.* 617.4
  (attract 288.3)
  (ensnare 545.9)
  (tempt 865.14)
lurid gloomy 421.8
  pale 429.6
  reddish-brown 433.5
  obscene 961.9
lurk *n.* 530.1
lurk *v.*
  be latent 526.3
  (escape notice 447.2)
  lie hid 528.16
  ambush 530.5
lurking 526.6
Lurlei See Lorelei
luscious savory 394.7
  sweet 396.8
  (pleasurable 829.7)
  (desirable 865.21)
lush *n.* liquor 959.4
  drunkard 959.11
lush *v.* 959.15
lush *adj.* drunk 259.21
  luxuriant 365.4

grow lush 365.2
lusher 959.11
lushy 259.21
lusory 840.22
lust *n.* desire 865.4
  sexual ~ 961.3
lust *v.* 865.11
luster, lustre *n.*
  time 108.1
  shine 420.1
  luminary 423.1
  chandelier 423.10
  radiant beauty 845.2
  illustriousness 873.2
luster, lustre *v.* 255.4
lusterware, lustreware 384.14
lustful 961.11
  (desirous 865.16)
lustihood
  strength 159.1
  corpulence 192.4
lustily loudly 404.11
  laboriously 686.11
lustiness 159.1
lustless
  unmanned 158.10
  weak 160.10
lustration
  cleansing 652.2
  penance 952.3
lustre See luster
lustrous
  luminous 420.22
  illustrious 873.17
lustrum 108.1
lusty strong 159.10
  (virile 159a.5)
  stout 192.12
lutanist 416.2
lute *n.* cement 45.6
  instrument 417.2
lute *v.* 46.7
luteolous, luteous 436.6
luter 416.3
lutescent 436.6
Lutheran 984.14
lutist 416.2
lutose marshy 345.3
  muddy 352.9
lux 420.1
luxate 185.2
luxation 44.1
luxuriance 168.1
luxuriant fertile 168.7
  growing rank 365.4
  abundant 639.7
luxuriate
  grow rank 365.2
  revel in 377.4
  delight in 827.6
  indulge freely 954.3
luxurious
  comfortable 377.8
  pleasant 829.7
  intemperate 954.4
luxuriousness 954.1
luxury
  delicacy 298.9

  comfort 377.2
  extravagance 641.1
  indulgence 954.1
lycanthrope 980.7
lycanthropic 503.12
lycanthropy 503.1
lyceum
  education 537.8
  school 542.1
lych gate See lich gate
lycopodiaceous 369.11
lyddite 727.13
Lydian 415.8
lye 652.8
lying *n.* 544.1
lying *adj.*
  recumbent 213.9
  untruthful 544.7
lymph fluid 333.2
  water 337.1
  transparency 425.2
lymphatic *n.* 350.4
  (gland 221.5)
lymphatic *adj.*
  fluid 333.7
  watery 337.6
  languid 683.14
lynch 972.8
lyncher 975.5
lynching 972.4
lynch law
  anarchy 738.2
  coercion 744.1
lynx animal 366.3
  eye 441.9
lynx-eyed
  sharp-sighted 441.20
  vigilant 459.8
Lyra 318.6
lyre 417.2
Lyre 318.6
lyrebird 366.22
lyric *n.* 597.2
lyric *adj.* singer 416.24
  poetry 597.13
lyrical
  melodious 413.27
  musical 415.28
  poetical 597.13
lyrichord 417.6
lyrico-dramatic, lyrico-epic 597.13
lyrist 416.14
  musician 416.3
  poet 597.10
lyssophobia 860.4

M

ma 166.7
ma'am 374.3
Mab 979.9
macabre, macaber 846.7
macadam
  smooth 255.2
  pavement 627.4
macadamize 255.4
macaroni 854.1

macaronic — magneto

macaronic n.
  word 563.8
  bad poetry 597.3
  burlesque 856.3
macaronic adj. 856.7
macaronicism 563.8
macaroon 298.12
Macassar oil 356.3
mace condiment 393.1
  club 727.7
  scepter 747.1
mace-bearer 745.9
macerate soak 337.5
  pulp 354.4
macerater, macerator 354.3
maceration
  soaking 337.2
  pulpification 354.1
  penance 952.3
  asceticism 955.1
machete 727.3
Machiavel, Machiavelli deceiver 548.1
  schemer 626.8;
  702.4
Machiavellian n.
  626.8; 702.4
Machiavellian, Machiavelian adj.
  false 544.8
  crafty 702.6
  dishonest 940.8
Machiavellianism
  falsity 544.2
  political cunning 702.2
Machiavellist n. 702.4
Machiavellist adj. 702.6
machicolated 717.9
machicolation
  embrasure 257.4
  fortification 717.3
machinate plot 626.10
  maneuver 702.5
machination plot 626.6
  artifice 702.3
machinator
  schemer 626.8
  strategist 702.4
machine
  vehicle 272.14, 15
  aircraft 273a.1
  mechanism 633.2
  confederacy 712.4
machine gun 727.11
machine gunner 726.4
machinelike 633.5
machinery 633.2
machinist stage 599.17
  craftsman 690.5
macilence 203.4
macilent 203.11
mackerel fish 298.18
  variegation 440.2
  procurer 962.4
mackerel sky
  cloud 353.5
  variegation 440.2
mackinaw 219.5
Mackinaw 225.16

mackintosh
  cloth 219.5
  raincoat 225.17
mackle n. 591.2
mackle v. 591.14
macrobiotic 110.9
macrocosm, macrocosmos 318.1
macrogamete 357.4
macrograph 590.3
macrography 590.1
macrology 573.2
macron 550.8
macrospore 357.4
mactation 990.6
macula
  discoloration 440a.1
  blemish 848.1
maculate v.
  spot 440.4
  discolor 440a.2
  soil 653.15
maculate adj.
  discolored 440a.3
  (blemished 848.3)
  spotted 440.9
maculation
  variegation 440.1
  discoloration 440a.1
  defilement 653.2
  blemish 848.1
macule n.
  discoloration 440a.1
  mackle 591.2
  blemish 848.1
macule v. 591.14
maculose
  spotted 440.9
  discolored 440a.3
mad
  turbulent 173.12
  insane 503.12
  furious 824.10
  angry 900.13
  drive one mad 900.11
  go mad 503.10
  mad about 897.15
madam, madame
  mistress 374.2, 3
  (title 877.2)
  procuress 962.4
mad apple 298.30
madbrain n. 863.2
madbrain adj. 863.7
madbrained
  insane 503.12
  rash 863.6
madcap n.
  violent 173.6
  madman 504.1
  buffoon 844
  rash person 863.2
madcap adj.
  hotheaded 825.10
  reckless 863.7
madden inflame 173.8
  dement 503.11
  irritate 824.5
  enrage 900.11
maddened 503.12
madder n. dye 428.4

color 434.2, 6
madder v. 434.7
madder bloom 428.4
madder blue 438.2
madder extract 428.4
madder orange 439.1
madder violet 437.1
madder yellow 436.1
madding crowd 682.7
made 161.13
  be made of 54.3
madefaction 337.2
madefy 337.5
Madeira 959.7
mademoiselle 374.4
madhouse 503.8
madid 339.7
madman 504
  (fool 501.1)
madness
  insanity 503.1
  frenzy 825.4
Madonna
  good woman 948.2
  Virgin Mary 977.3
madrigal
  music 415.12
  poem 597.2
madrigalist 416.14
madstone 993.2
Madurese 560.4
Maecenas 711.4
maelstrom 348.8
maenad 959.1
maestro
  musician 416.1, 12
  teacher 540.1
maffick 883.3
mag n.
  magneto 158a.7;
  272.16
  chatter 584.2
  chatterer 584.3
mag, meg n. 800.8
mag v. 584.4
magazine
  journal 593.6
  (edition 531.2)
  storeroom 636.4
magazine gun 727.10
magazinist 593.15
Magdalen, Magdalene 950.2
mage 992.2
magenta 434.2; 437.4
maggot larva 129.8
  diminutive 193.2
  eccentricity 503.6
  fancy 515.4
  caprice 608.1
maggoty
  eccentric 503.17
  fanciful 515.12
  capricious 608.5
  filthy 653.17
  decayed 659.13
Magi 500.3
magian n. 992.2
Magian n. 500.1
magian adj. 992.5
Magian adj. 984.21
Magianism

religion 984.11
  sorcery 992.1
magic n. 992.1
  (delusion 545.2)
magic v. 992.4
magic adj. 992.5
magic carpet 993.4
magic circle 992.1
magician 992.2
  (legerdemainist 548.6)
magic lantern
  lantern 423.2
  projector 445.6
  (motion pictures 599.9)
magilp See megilp
magiric, magirology 673.2
Magism 992.1
magisterial
  dogmatic 474.15
  arrogant 885.8
magistracy
  authority 737.3
  jurisdiction 965.1
magistrate
  officer 694.3
  executive 745.9
  judge 967.1
magistrateship, magistrature 737.3
magma mixture 41.4
  stratum 204.1
Magna Charta, Magna Carta 769.2
magna cum laude 873.20
magnanimity 942.2
  (generosity 816.1)
  (benevolence 906.1)
  (charitableness 906.2)
magnanimous 942.6
  (generous 816.4)
  (charitable 906.7)
magnate
  personage 642.5
  nobleman 875.3
magnesite, magnesium 635.6
magnet n. 288.2
  (lure 617.1)
magnet v. 288.3
magnetic 158a.12
magnetic force 157.3
magnetic friction 157.4
magnetism 157.3
  (electricity 158a.1)
  (attraction 288.1)
  (allurement 617.1)
magnetite 288.2
magnetize
  electrify 158a.11
  influence 175.6
  attract 288.3
  mesmerize 376.4
  entrance 994.19
magneto
  electricity 158a.7
  automobile 272.16

magnetoelectric — make

magnetoelectric
 158a.12
magnetoelectricity
 158a.1
magnetology 158a.3
magnetometer 158a.6
magnetomotive
 158a.12
magneton 193.2
magnetophone 418.6
magnetoscope 158a.6
magnetotelegraph
 532a.5
Magnificat 990.2
magnification
 increase 35.1
 exaggeration 549.1
 (enlargement 194.1)
 glorification 990.2
magnificence
 gorgeousness 845.2
 pomp 882.1
magnificent
 beautiful 845.13
 imposing 882.8
magnifico 875.4
 (personage 642.5)
magnifier 445.1
magnify increase 35.3
 exaggerate 549.2
 (enlarge 194.8)
 (overestimate
 482.3)
 eulogize 931.6
 glorify 990.10
magnifying glass
 445.1
magniloquence 577.2
 (boasting 884.1)
magniloquent 577.7
 (boastful 884.7)
magnitude
 quantity 25.1
 greatness 31.1
 size 192.1
magnitudinous 31.8
magnolia tree 367.6
 wood 635.3
magpie bird 366.22
 chatterer 584.3
magsman 792.8
magus 992.2
Magus 500.1; 984.21
Magyar 560.4
maharaja, maharajah
 745.4
maharani, maharanee
 empress 745.6
 princess 875.8
mahat 359.3
mahatma sage 500.1
 proficient 700.1
 occultist 994.13
Mahican 434.5
mah!stick See maulstick
mahogany n.
 table 215.20
 tree 367.6
 wood 635.3
mahogany adj. 433.5
mahout 268.9

Mahratti See Marathi
maid n. girl 129.5
 minister 631.2
 maidservant 746.2
 (nursemaid 664.3)
 (worker 690.10)
 spinster 904.3
maid v. 746.8
maidan 367.11
maiden n. girl 129.5
 spinster 904.3
 guillotine 975.4
maiden adj. 66.8
maidenhead, maidenhood 904.1
maiden speech 66.1
maidhood 904.1
maid of all work
 factotum 690.3
 servant 746.1, 2
maid of honor
 companion 890.3
 bridesmaid 903.4
maidservant 746.2
mail n.
 plumage 256.9
 mailman 534.2
 post 592.4
 (freight 270.4)
 armor 717.2
 by mail 270.12
mail v. 270.9; 592.6
mail adj. 592.7
mailable 270.11
mailbag, mailbox
 592.4
mail carrier 534.2
mailclad 717.9
mail coach
 vehicle 272.6
 mail carrier 534.2
mailed 717.9
mailer, mailman 534.2
 (correspondence
 592.4)
 (workman 690.10)
mail-order house
 799.1
mailplane
 aircraft 273a.1
 mail carrier 534.2
maim disable 158.6
 damage 659.8
main n. pipe 260.6
 ocean 341.1
 mainland 342.1
 conduit 350.1
in the main
 essentially 5.8
 absolutely 31.16
 principally 33.10
 mainly 50.11
main adj.
 supreme 33.8
 (paramount 642.14)
 first 66.8
main chance
 best chance 156.3
 salient point 642.4
 good 648.2
mainland 342.1

mainly
 principally 33.10
 on the whole 50.11
 in the main 642.15
mainmast 273.12
mainpernor, mainprise, mainprize
 771.2
mains
 messuage 189.12
 farm 371.4
mainsail 273.13
mainsheet 273.10
mainspring
 source 153.2
 motive 615.1
mainstay n.
 supporter 215.2
 (anchor 666.2)
 ship's rope 273.10
mainstay v. 215.26
maintain
 be permanent 141.4
 continue 143.3
 operate 170.2
 support 215.26
 argue 476.11
 assert 535.3
 preserve 670.3
 conduct 692.4
 lend support 707.7
 possess 777.4
 retain 781.4
 justify 937.6
maintainer 215.2
maintenance
 permanence 141.1
 continuance 143.1
 agency 170.1
 support 215.1
 preservation 670.1
 aid 707.1
 sustenance 707.3
maintop 273.7
maire 745.9
maize 367.9
majestic
 sovereign 737.16
 noble 873.18
 imposing 882.8
 dignified 878.7
majesty
 importance 642.1
 sovereignty 737.2
 king 745.2
 nobility 873.3
 deity 976.2
majolica 384.14
Majolica earth 434.2
major n. 745.11
major adj. 33.7
major-domo
 steward 694.5
 retainer 746.1
major general 745.11
majority
 plurality 100.2
 (superiority 33.1)
 adulthood 131.1
major key 413.7
majuscule letter 561.1
 type 591.6

Makassar 560.4
make n.
 composition 54.1
 kind 75.2
 form 240.1
make v.
 compose 54.4
 convert 144.6
 cause 153.6
 produce 161.8
 reach 292.7
 recognize 481a.6
 understand 518.4
 perform 680.6
 accomplish 729.2
 compel 744.2
 ~ a compact 769.8
 (execute 771.7)
 divine creation
 976.7
make a clean breast
 529.5
 (tell the truth
 543.2)
make a dead set
 oppose 708.2
 attack 716.5
make after 622.6
make a leg 928.6
make a long arm
 exert oneself 686.5
 reach 789.13
make amends
 atone 952.4
 (compensate 30.4)
 reward 973.3
make a motion
 propound 514.7
 propose 763.2
make a mountain
 out of a molehill
 549.2
make a mouth
 show distaste 867.4
 express disapproval
 932.5
make a point of
 insist upon 604.6
 contend for 720.10
 compel 744.2
 stipulate 770.2
 demand 924.7
 be honorable 939.6
make a shift
 substitute 147.3
 use 677.5
make a stand
 oppose 708.2
 resist 719.3
make at 267.26
make away with
 destroy 162.4
 (discard 678.3)
 kill 361.10
 abduct 791.11
make believe
 feign 544.6
 (act 599.26)
 affect 853.5
make bold
 dare 861.5
 presume 885.6

make-believe — male

make (*continued*)
  be disrespectful 929.3
make both ends meet
  have money 803.5
  economize 817.3
make bricks without straw 471.5
  (labor in vain 645.6)
  (not know what one is about 699.7)
make common cause with 709.5
make for
  sail for 226.26
  go towards 278.5
  approach 286.2
make free with
  appropriate 789.8
  take a liberty 748.9
  be disrespectful 929.3
make good
  compensate 30.4
  fill 52.7
  stabilize 150.4
  confirm 467.9
  demonstrate 478.2
  supply a defect 637.4
  remedy 660.10
  complete 729.2
  succeed 731.5
  prosper 734.5
  keep faith 772.4; 939.6
  acquit oneself 926.6
  atone 952.4
make haste
  speed 274.9
  hurry 684.3, 8
make hay while the sun shines
  turn to account 134.6
  (take advantage 698.10)
  be industrious 682.12
make head against
  oppose 708.3
  surmount 731.7
make heavy weather 267.31
make her number 267.41
make land
  navigate 267.29
  approach 286.2
make light of
  ignore 460.5
  underestimate 483.3
  deem unimportant 643.8
  be easy 705.3
  endure 826.6
  disdain 930.5
make love 902.7
make much of
  exaggerate 549.2
  give importance to 642.8

be friendly 888.2
show love for 897.11
praise 931.6
make no bones 602.6
make nothing of
  underestimate 483.3
  not understand 519.5
  deem unimportant 643.8
  be easy 705.3
  fail 732.5
  be unastonished 871.2
make off 293.4, 5
make off with 791.9, 11
make one's mark
  succeed 731.5
  prosper 734.5
make one's mouth water
  anticipate 507.4
  tantalize 617.4; 865.14
  (eat 298.44)
make one's peace with 831.3
make one's way
  advance 282.2
  pass 302.2
  forge ahead 682.12
  succeed 731.5
  prosper 734.5
make out see 441.10
  demonstrate 478.2
  discover 481a.3, 4, 6
  know 490.9
  understand 518.4
make over
  transfer 270.7; 783.7
  reconstruct 660.14
  give 784.9
make peace 723.4, 5
make sail 267.16
make sternway 267.21, 25
make sure
  stabilize 150.4
  examine 461.17
  make certain 474.6
  assure oneself 484.10
  persuade oneself 615.10
  take precautions 864.4
make terms 769.6
make the best of
  overestimate 482.3
  use 677.5
  submit 725.3
  compromise 774.2
  endure 826.6
make the most of
  overestimate 482.3
  exaggerate 549.2
  profit by 658.7
  use 677.5
  (take advantage of 698.10)
  compromise 774.2

make the worst of 482.5
make time
  temporize 110.6
  procrastinate 133.5
  speed 274.9
make up
  compensate 30.4
  fill 52.7
  compose 54.4
  ~ ~ leeway 282.2
  paint 428.10
  imagine 515.10
  set type 591.14
  supply a defect 637.4
  be reconciled 723.5
  ~ ~ accounts 811.7
  beautify 845.7
  (ornament 847.11)
make up one's mind
  decide 480.6
  be convinced 484.10
  resolve 604.6
  decide upon 609.8
  persuade oneself 615.10
make up to
  approach 286.2
  address 586.2
  make friends with 888.3
make use of
  use 677.5
  appropriate 789.8
make water 297.15
make way
  open up! 260.22
  navigation 267.21
  pass 302.2
make way for
  substitute 147.3
  open 260.11
  turn aside 279.7
  avoid 623.6
  facilitate 705.4
  be courteous 894.7
make wing 267a.30
make-believe *n.*
  dissimulation 544.2
  (acting 599.6)
  sham 545.6
make-believe *adj.*
  imitation 19.12
  spurious 545.13
  (affected 853.6)
  dramatic 599.28
make-peace 724.2
maker producer 164.1
  poet 597.10
  craftsman 690.8
Maker 976.2
makeshift *n.*
  substitute 147.2
  pretext 619.1
  expedient 646.2
makeshift *adj.* 147.4
make-up
  composition 54.1
  wardrobe 225.2
  form 240.1
  paint 428.5

book 593.7
stage requisites 599.13
beautifying 845.5
(ornamentation 847.3)
makeweight
  inequality 28.1
  compensation 30.2
  complement 52.5
makings 56.1
Malachi 513.2
malachite 435.3
malachite green 435.4
malacologist 368.2
malacology
  shell 223.21
  zoology 368.1
maladjusted 699.15
maladminister 699.3
maladministration 699.2
maladroit 699.12
malady 655.1
Malaga 959.7
Malagasy 560.4
malaise
  physical ~ 378.1
  mental ~ 828.1
malapert *n.* 885.3
  (discourteous person 895.3)
malapert *adj.* 885.9
malapertness 885.2
malappropriate 24.7
malaprop
  blunder 495.3
  misnomer 565.2
  ridiculousness 855.1
Malaprop, Mrs. 701
malapropian 565.8
  (ungrammatical 568.3)
  (inelegant 579.3)
malapropism
  blunder 495.3
  misnomer 565.2
  (missaying 563.1)
  (ungrammaticism 568.1)
  ridiculousness 855.1
malapropish, malapropos 565.8
malaria disease 655.6
  miasma 663.5
Malay *n.* 560.4
Malay *adj.* 11.8
Malayalam 560.4
malconformation 243.1
malcontent *n.*
  oppositionist 710.3
  insurgent 742.3
  grumbler 832.2
  (pessimist 837.5)
malcontent *adj.* 832.5
mal de mer 655.13
mal du pays 833.1
male *n.* 373.6
  (boy 129.4)

954

male — manhood

male adj. 373.7
  (virile 159a.5)
maledict v. 908.4
maledict adj. 908.6
malediction 908
  (insult 929.2)
  (disapprobation 932.1)
  (detraction 934.1, 2)
maledictory 908.6
  (defamatory 934.4)
malefaction
  malevolent act 907.4
  misdeed 947.2
malefactor
  evildoer 913.1
  wrongdoer 949.2
malefactory 945.13
malefic
  harmful 649.10
  malevolent 907.6
maleficence 907.1, 4
maleficent 907.6
malevolence 907
  (badness 649.1)
  (maltreatment 649.4)
  (enmity 889.1)
  (ill-humour 901.1)
  (incompassion 914a.1)
  (revengefulness 919.2)
  (evildoing 945.6)
malevolent n. 913.1
malevolent adj. 907.6
  (violent 173.11)
  (bad 649.8)
  (harmful 649.10)
  (hateful 898.7)
  (ill-humored 901.7)
  (revengeful 919.6)
  (evildoing 945.13)
  be malevolent 907.5
  (maltreat 649.7)
malevolently 907.10
malfeasance
  mismanagement 699.2
  evil conduct 945.6
  misdeed 947.2
  (violation of law 964.2)
malfeasant 945.13
malfeasor
  evildoer 913.1
  wrongdoer 949.2
malformation 243.1
malformed 243.5
malice 907.1
  (hate 898.1)
  bear malice
  be malevolent 907.5
  (hate 898.2, 3)
  harbor revenge 919.5
  with malice
  intentionally 620.5
  malevolently 907.10
malicious 907.6

  (hateful 898.7)
malign v.
  stigmatize 874.7
  slander 934.3
malign adj. 907.6
malignance
  hurtfulness 649.1
  malevolence 907.1
malignant
  harmful 649.10
  irascible 901.7
  malevolent 907.6
  (bad 649.8)
malignity 907.1
  (evildoing 945.6)
malik 877.2
malinger
  dissemble 544.6
  (ail 655.21)
  (be inactive 683.8)
  shirk 623.8
malingerer
  pretender 540.3
  shirker 623.4
  (idler 683.7)
malingery 623.1
  (idleness 683.2)
malison 908.1
malkin, mawkin 59.5
mall 627.2
mall See maul
mallard food 298.26
  bird 366.22
malleability 324.1
malleable 324.6
mallet
  hammer 276.4
  sculptor's ~ 557.8
malleus 418.5
mallow 437.1
malnutrition 655.5
malodor, malodour 401.1
malodorous, malodourous 401.4
  (odorous 398.8)
  be malodorous 401.3
malpractice 945.6
malt, malted milk 298.4
Maltese cat 366.4
  language 560.4
malt liquor 959.5
Malto 560.4
maltose 396.4
maltreat 649.7
  (misuse 679.2)
  (be malevolent 907.5)
  (punish 972.5)
maltreatment 649.4
  (misusage 679.1)
  (malevolence 907.1)
malversation
  rapacity 819.2
  evil conduct 945.6
Mameluke, Mamaluke 726.4
mamma, mama 166.7
mamma 250.3
mammal 368.9
  (animal life 366.1)

mammalian
  convex 250.9
  animalian 366.26
  vertebrate 368.19
mammalogist 368.2
mammalogy 368.1
mammiferous, mammiform 250.9
mammilla 250.3
mammillary 250.9
mammillation 250.3
mammon 800.1
Mammon 978.2
mammoth n.
  antiquity 124.2
  behemoth 192.8
mammoth adj. 192.15
mammy mother 166.7
  negress 431.4
  nursemaid 664.3
man n.
  human kind 372.1
  person 372.3
  male 373.2, 4
  (adult 131.3)
  worker 690.2
  retainer 746.1
  brave person 861.3
  inamorato 897.6
  husband 903.7
  like a man 604.9
  to a man 488.17
man v.
  furnish men 634.2
  garrison 717.7
man about town 854.1
manacle n. 752.2
manacle v. 751.7
manage n. 266.7
manage v. pilot 267.11
  direct 693.4
  succeed in 731.5
  (conduct 692.4)
  (rule 737.11)
manageable 705.6
  (docile 602.9)
management
  direction 693.1
  (conduct 692.1)
  skill 698.4
manager 599.17 694.1
managership 693.3
mañana 121.2, 9
manas 994.10
man-at-arms 726.4
manavel, manarvel 791.9
manbird 269a.1
Manchu 560.4
manciple 637.2
Mandaean 984.21
Mandaeism 984.11
mandamus 741.3
mandarin
  orange 439.2
  official 745.7
mandate decree 741.3
  commission 755.1
mandatory
  preceptive 697.2
  commanding 741.8

mandible 260.2
Mandingo 431.4
mando-bass, mandocello, mandola etc. 417.2
mandolin 417.2
mandolinist 416.3
mandrel, mandril 312.5
mandrill 366.16
manducate 298.45
manduction 298.1
mane 256.3
man-eater eater 298.41
  killer 361.8
  fish 366.21
  cannibal 913.3
manège, manege
  riding 266.7
  animal culture 370.1
manes 994.11
maness 374.2
maneuver, manoeuvre n. action 680.2
  artifice 702.3
maneuver, manoeuvre v.
  navigate 267.42
  plot 626.10
  be cunning 702.5
maneuverer, manoeuvrer 702.4
maneuvering, manoeuvring
  cunning 702.1
  warcraft 722.2
maneuvers, manoeuvres
  navigation 267.4
  aerobatics 267a.24
  warcraft 722.2
man Friday
  assistant 711.1
  retainer 746.1
manful 159a.5
manfully 604.9
manganese 635.6
Mangar 560.4
mange itch 380.3
  disease 655.18
manger
  compartment 191.2
  enclosure 232.1
mangle n. 255.3
mangle v.
  disintegrate 44.9
  smooth 255.4
  damage 659.8
mangled 53.5
mango, mangosteen 298.31
mangy itchy 380.6
  diseased 655.25
man-hater 910.2
manhead 131.1
manhole 260.1
manhood
  adulthood 131.1
  virility 159a.1
  mankind 373.4
  courage 861.1

man hunter — marble

man hunter 528.9
mania insanity 503.1
　craze 503.7
　(passion 865.5)
maniac *n.* 504.1
maniac *adj.* 503.12, 13
manic-depressive
　503.15
Manichaeism,
　Manicheism 451.9
manichord 417.6
manicure 652.9; 662.24
manifest *n.* list 86.1
　train 272.18
　statement 811.3
manifest *v.* list 86.3
　~ itself 446.2
　evince 467.7
　(demonstrate 478.2)
　show 525.2
　(visibilize 446.3)
　(appear 448.6)
　(explain 522.6)
　(disclose 529.3)
　indicate 550.18
manifest *adj.*
　visible 446.4
　evident 525.4
　(apparent 448.7)
　(certain 474.8)
　(meaning 516.8)
　(intelligible 518.5)
　(disclosed 529.7)
　(perspicuous 570.2)
be manifest 525.3
　(appear 448.6)
become manifest
　446.2
make manifest 529.3
manifestable 525.6
manifestation
　appearance 448.1
　showing 525
　(visibility 446.1)
　(disclosure 529.1)
　indication 550.1
manifestative 525.4
manifestly 525.7
　(apparently 448.8)
manifesto
　proclamation 531.1
　decree 741.3
manifold *n.* 272.16
manifold *v.* 590.13
manifold *adj.*
　multiform 81.2
　numerous 102.5
manikin, mannikin
　dwarf 193.5
　figure 554.2
man in the moon
　moon 318.5
　fancy 515.4
maniple 726.7
manipulate
　aviate 267a.31
　handle 379.3
　use 677.5
　maneuver 702.5
manipulation 680.1
manipulator 677.4
mankind

humankind 372
male sex 373.4
manlihood
　adulthood 131.1
　virility 159a.1
manlike virile 159a.5
　anthropoid 372.5
　male 373.7
manliness
　virility 159a.1
　courage 861.1
manly virile 159a.5
　(adult 131.5)
　male 373.7
　courageous 861.8
　honorable 939.7
manna 396.2
mannequin, manikin
　554.4
manner kind 75.2
　method 627.1
　(fashion 852.1)
　conduct 692.1
all manner of 81.3
in a manner
　as if 17.17
　to a degree 32.13
　supposedly 514.12
　figuratively 521.4
manner of speaking
　diction 569.1
　utterance 580.3
mannered style 579.3
　affected 853.6
mannerism
　particularity 79.2
　affectation 853.1
　(inelegance 579.1)
mannerist 853.4
mannerly 894.12
manners
　behavior 692.1
　good ~ 894.1
　bad ~ 895.1
mannify 159a.4
mannikin See manikin; mannequin
mannish 159a.5
　(male 373.7)
Manobo 560.4
manoeuvre, manoeuvres etc. See maneuver etc.
man of all work
　factotum 690.3
　menial 746.1
man of letters 492.1
man of mark
　personage 642.5
　celebrity 873.9
man of means 803.2
man of pleasure
　954.1
man of science 492.5
Man of Sorrows 976.5
man of straw
　sham 545.6
　nonentity 643.6
　puppet 711.2
　bankrupt 808.4
man of the world
　sophisticate 700.3

fashionable 852.5
man-of-war 726.11
manor
　messuage 189.12
　property 780.4
manor house 189.3
manorial 780.8
manse 1000.5
mansion 189.3
manslaughter 361.1
manslayer 361.8
manstopping bullet
　727.14
mansuetude 894.1
manta cloth 219.5
　cloak 225.15
mantel 215.19
mantelet 225.15
mantelet, mantlet
　717.3
mantelletta, mantellone cloak 225.15
　canonicals 999.1
mantelpiece, mantelshelf 215.19
mantevil 225.15
manticore, manticora
　83.7
mantilla 225.15
mantle *n.* cover 223.2
　(shade 424.1)
　cloak 225.15
　plumage 256.9
　lamp 423.11
　emblem of authority 747.1
　clerical ~ 999.1
mantle *v.* spread 194.5
　coat 223.24
　clothe 225.41
　redden 434.8
　bubble 353.8
　flush 824.8
　blush 881.4
　anger 900.7
mantlet See mantelet
mantologist 513.2
mantology 511.2
mantrap 545.4
mantua cloth 219.5
　cloak 225.15
mantuamaker 225.38
manual book 593.1, 5
　guidebook 694.7
　rituale 998.9
manufactory 691
manufactural 161.11
manufacture *n.*
　production 161.1
　(preparation 673.1)
　handiwork 680.3
manufacture *v.* 161.8
manufacturer 164.1
　(workman 690.8)
manufacturing 161.11
manumission 750.1
manumit 750.2
manumitter 912.2
manure *n.* 653.7
manure *v.* 371.8
manus 781.3
manuscript *n.* 590.1, 3

manuscript *adj.*
　590.15
man without a country 893.5
Manx 560.4
many numerous 102.5
　(great 31.6)
　frequent 136.3
　masses 876.1
not many 103.3
too many
　superfluity 641.1
　superfluous 641.5
many-colored, manycoloured 440.5
　(colorful 428.14)
many-headed monster 876.1
many-hued 440.5
manyplies 191.7
many-sided
　multiform 81.2
　changeable 149.5
　multilateral 236.7
many-tongued 532.8
Maori 560.4
map *n.* face 234.4
　plan 626.2
　(topography 184.8)
　(guidebook 694.7)
map *v.* 626.9
　(prepare 673.6)
maple tree 367.6
　wood 635.3
maple sirup 396.4
mar deform 243.3
　discolor 440a.2
　damage 659.8
　botch 699.9
　thwart 706.7
marabou 41.5
Marabout 893.4
Marah 395.3
marantic
　contractive 195.6
　thin 203.11
maraschino 959.6
marasmic
　contractive 195.6
　thin 203.11
marasmoid, marasmous 203.11
marasmus
　contraction 195.1
　ailment 655.11
　deterioration 659.2
Marathi, Mahratti
　560.4
marathon 274.4
maraud 791.10
marauder
　soldier 726.4
　pillager 792.1
marbelize 440.4
marble *n.*
　sphere 249.2
　smooth 255.2
　hardness 323.3
　stone 342.4
　variegation 440.2
　sculpture 557.8
　writing tablet 590.10

marble — martyrdom

marble *v.* 440.4
marbled 440.7
marblehearted 907.8
marc See mark
marcescence 659.2
marcescent 659.12
march *n.* beat 181.4
  limit 233.1
  walk 266.4, 5
  music 415.8
  path 627.2
  on the march 264.10
march *v.*
  ~ with 199.3
  walk 266.16
  parade 882.6
march off 293.4
marchioness 875.6
marchpane, marzipan 298.9
march of time 109.1
marconigram 532a.3
Mardi gras 840.2
mare horse 271.3
  female animal 374.8
Marengo 271.9
mare's-nest 546.1
mare's-tail 353.5
margarine 356.4
margin *n.* room 180.2
  edge 231.1
  surplus 641.1
  free scope 748.2
margin *v.* edge 231.3
  side 236.4
marginal *n.* 522.4
marginal *adj.* 231.4
marginate edge 231.3
  side 236.4
margrave 875.5
margravine 875.6
mariage de convenance 903.2
marigold 439.1, 2
marigraph 348.13
marijuana, marihuana 662.7
marimba 417.10
marinate 670.4
marine *n.* bottle 191.11
  mariner 269.1
  ships 273.6
  blue 438.2
  combatant 726.10
marine *adj.*
  nautical 267.48
  oceanic 341.5
marine chronometer 114.6
Marine Corps 726.10
marine green 435.2
mariner 269
  (workman 690.10)
Mariology, Maryoltry 984.6
Mariology, Maryology 984.6
marionette
  figure 554.4
  puppet 840.15, 16
marish *n.* 345.1
marish *adj.* 345.3

marital 903.14
maritime
  nautical 267.48
  oceanic 341.5
marjoram 393.1
mark *n.* degree 26.1
  rank 71.1
  particularity 79.2
  limit 233.1
  notation 415.23
  endorsement 488.4
  dupe 547.1
  indication 550.1, 2, 4, 6, 7
  (trace 551.5)
  (blemish 440a.1)
  (punctuation 567.3)
  goal 620.2
  importance 642.1
  repute 873.1
below the mark
  inconsiderable 32.8
  less 34.7
  under 207.11
  imperfect 651.4
beside the mark 304.5
beyond the mark
  ahead 303.6
  overmuch 641.7
hit the mark
  impress 171.8
  succeed 731.5
of mark 31.13
over the mark 33.9
up to the mark
  equal 27.8
  sufficient 639.6
  good 648.11
  competent 698.12
  right 922.5
mark, marc *n.* 800.8
mark *v.* note 450.7
  give attention 457.4
  call attention to 457.7
  indicate 550.19
  (blemish 440a.2)
  (record 551.8)
  (engrave 558.5)
  (write 590.13)
  letter 561.6
  emphasize 642.9
mark down
  record 551.8
  discount 813.2
  cheapen 815.7
mark off
  circumscribe 229.2
  outline 230.3
  record 551.8
mark out
  mark 550.19
  appoint 609.11
  plan 626.9
  prescribe 741.5
mark time
  time 114.8
  wait 133.7; 507.5
  be quiescent 265.5
  do nothing 681.2
marked

remarkable 31.13
  superior 33.7
  peculiar 79.8
  emphatic 535.6
  indicated 550.22
  important 642.10
  distinguished 873.16
marked down
  at a bargain 796.9
  price reduced 813.4; 815.9
marker 363.15
market *n.*
  purchasers 677.4
  sale 796.1
  mart 799.1
go to market 675.3
in the market
  in search of 461.24
  offered 763.4
on the market 796.9
market *v.* shop 795.4
  sell 796.5
marketability 796.4
marketable 796.7
  (commercial 794.10)
marketer 795.2
marketing 798.2
market overt 799.1
market place
  square 189.19
  mart 799.1
in the market place 525.7
markhor, markhoor 366.9
marking mark 550.7
  engraving 558.1
marksman
  shooter 284.8
  expert 700.1
marksmanship 698.1
markswoman 284.8
marl soil 342.1, 3
  mineral 635.6
marlinespike, marlinspike, marlingspike 307.4
marm 374.3
marmalade 396.3
marmoreal 430.8
marmoset, marmozet 366.16
marmot pelt 223.12
  animal 366.17
  idler 683.7
Marne 722.5
maroon *n.* red 434.2
  fugitive 623.5
maroon *v.* flee 623.10
  abandon 782.3
  isolate 893.7
marplot botcher 701
  hinderer 706.3
  mischiefmaker 913.1
marquee 223.3
Marquesan 560.4
marquetry, marqueterie 440.3
marquis 875.5
marquisate 875.9

marquise 223.3
marquisette 219.5
marriage
  mixture 41.1
  matrimony 903
  (union 43.1)
give in marriage 903.12
marriageability 903.1
marriageable
  mature 131.5
  nubile 903.15
marriage broker 903.11
marriage of convenience 903.2
married 903.14, 16
marrow essence 5.2
  center 222.2
marrowless
  unmanned 158.10
  weak 160.10
marry *v.* 903.12, 13
marry *adv.* 535.8
marry come up!
  I defy you 715.5
  censure 932.16
Mars planet 318.3
  war-god 722.7
  god 979.2
Mars brown 433.1
marsh 345
  (waste 169.2)
  (mud 352.5)
marshal *n.* 745.10, 11
marshal *v.* 60.6
Marshall 560.4
Marshalsea 752.1
marsh gas 334.2
marshy 345.3
  (soaked 339.8)
  (muddy 352.9)
  (soft 324.6)
marsupial 191.23
Mars violet 437.1
mart 799
martello tower 206.3
  stronghold 717.4
marten 223.12
martial 722.13
martiality 722.6
martial law
  militarism 737.4
  anarchy 738.2
  coercion 744.1
martin 366.22
martinet 739.3
martingale, martingal
  ship's rope 273.10
  checkrein 752.2
Martinmas 998.13
martyr *n.*
  sufferer 828.8
  ascetic 955.2
martyr *v.* pain 378.4
  torture 830.6
martyrdom
  killing 361.1
  bodily pain 378.2
  mental pain 828.6
  self-sacrifice 942.1
  asceticism 955.1

martyrize — materiate

martyrdom (*cont'd*)
 punishment 972.2
martyrize pain 378.4
 torture 830.6
 (punish 972.9)
marvel *n.*
 wonder 870.1
 prodigy 872.1
marvel *v.* 870.2
marvelous, marvellous unusual 83.10
 wonderful 870.7
 (stupendous 31.8)
marvelously, marvellously 31.21
Marxism 737.6
Maryolatry, Maryology See Mariolatry etc.
marzipan See marchpane
mascara 845.5
mascot, mascotte
 luck 621.16
 good-luck charm 993.2
masculine *n.*
 man 159a.3
 male 373.1
masculine *adj.*
 virile 159a.5
 male 373.7
masculinity 159a.1
masculinize 159a.4
mash *n.* mixture 41.4
 confusion 59.2
 pulp 354.2
 infatuation 897.1
have a mash on 897.1
mash *v.* soften 324.4
 pulverize 330.6
 pulp 354.4
 (viscidize 352.6)
masher pulper 354.3
 fop 854.1
masjid 1000.1
mask *n.* visor 225.11
 (cover 223.2)
 (concealment 528.1)
 (screen 530.3)
 (disguise 545.5)
 masquerader 528.7
 masque 599.3
 actor 599.19
 pretext 619.1
mask *v.* conceal 528.10
 disguise 544.6
masker
 masquerader 528.7
 actor 599.19
masnad See musnud
masochism 961.3
mason 690.5
Mason 994.13
Masonic 994.21
Masonry 994.1
Masora, Masorah 985.5
masque mask 225.11
 drama 599.3

masquerade
 costume 225.10
 disguise 545.5
 (mask 225.11)
masquerader 528.7
 (impostor 548.3)
mass *n.*
 quantity 25.1
 quantities 31.3
 main part 50.3
 accumulation 72.6
 (store 636.1)
 size 192.1
 lump 192.5
 weight 319.1
 solid 321.4
 commonalty 876.1
Mass, Mess *n.* 998.7
 (divine service 990.7)
mass *v.* 72.11
massacre *n.* 361.1
massacre *v.* 361.10
massage *n.*
 rubbing 331.1
 handling 379.1
massage *v.*
 knead 324.4
 rub 331.3
 handle 379.3
 treat 662.24
massager, massageuse, massagist 331.2
Mass book 998.9
masser, masseur, masseuse 331.2
 (worker 690.10)
massicot 436.4
massive sizable 192.11
 heavy 319.12
 dense 321.8
massy 192.11
mast cable pole 158a.9
 spar 273.12
 nuts 298.33
before the mast 267.53
mastaba, mastabah 363.13
master *n.* boy 129.4
 sage 500.1
 teacher 540.1
 proficient 700.1
 victor 731.4
 ruler 745
 (superior 33.4)
 (chief 642.6)
 (director 694.1)
 (head 694.2)
 skipper 745.12
 proprietor 779.2
 title 877.2, 3
be master of
 know well 490.10
 be skillful 698.7
 rule 737.11
master of
 skilled in 698.14
 in possession of 777.7
Master *n.* 373.3

master *v.*
 understand 518.4
 learn 539.3
 conquer 731.9
 dominate 737.12
 subjugate 749.5
 ~ one's feelings 826.8
 ~ one's passions 944.2
masterful, masterly 698.11
master mariner 269.4
mastermind
 mental genius 492.2
 sage 500.1
 proficient 700.1
Master of Arts 877.3
 (student 541.5)
master of ceremonies
 stageman 599.17
 amusement 840.18
Master of the Rolls 967.1
masterpiece
 work of art 556.8
 masterwork 698.5
 (excellence 648.4)
 (perfection 650.3)
master sergeant 745.11
mastership skill 698.1
 dominion 737.2
master stroke
 plan 626.7
 masterpiece 698.5
 great success 731.2
masterwork
 work of art 556.8
 masterpiece 698.5
mastery skill 698.1
 dominion 737.3
 (influence 175.2)
 (victory 731.3)
masthead
 torture 830.6
 punish 972.5
mastic *n.* cement 45.6
 semiliquid 352.3
 resin 356a.1
mastic *adj.* 356a.3
masticate chew 298.45
 pulp 354.4
mastication 298.1
mastiff 366.6
mastigophoran, mastigopod 193.4
mastodon 124.2
mastologist 368.2
mastology 368.1
mat *n.* bedding 215.24
 network 219.4
 hair 256.3
 doormat 652.7
go to the mat 720.8
mat *v.* 219.8
matador 361.8
match *n.*
 analogue 17.5
 equal 27.5
 lucifer 388.5
 (luminary 423.1)

contest 720.2
 boxing ~ 720.6
 marriage 903.1
match *v.*
 resemble 17.7
 imitate 19.5
 equal 27.6
 pair 89.3
 size 192.10
 parallelize 216.4
 liken 464.2
 give in kind 717.2
matchless
 unequaled 28.4
 supreme 33.8
 (best 648.9)
 virtuous 944.3
matchlock 727.10
matchmaker
 craftsman 690.8
 marriage broker 903.11
mate *n.* analogue 17.5
 (equal 27.5)
 accompanier 88.3
 mariner 269.4
 drink 298.4
 confederate 711.1
 officer 745.12
 chum 890.3
 spouse 903.5
mate *v.* 89.3
mater, materfamilias 166.7
material *n.*
 textile 219.5
 (merchandise 798.3)
 matter 316.2
 substance 635
material *adj.*
 corporeal 316.8
 (substantial 3.4)
 important 642.10
materialism 316.5
 (irreligion 989.3)
materialist 316.6
 (irreligionist 989.4)
materialistic 316.9
 (heterodox 984.22)
 (irreligious 989.8)
materiality
 corporeity 316
 (substantiality 3.1)
 material 316.2
 importance 642.1
materialization
 corporealization 316.4
 (specter 980a.1)
 (spiritualism 994.5)
 appearance 448.1
 manifestation 525.1
materialize
 corporealize 316.7
 (spiritualism 994.18)
 appear 446.2
 manifest itself 525.2
materia medica 662.16
materiate *adj.* 316.8
materiate *v.* 316.7

958

matériel 634.1
maternal
 ancestral 166.10
 benevolent 906.6
maternity 166.3
mathematic 85.2
mathematical
 arithmetical 85.12
 (accounting 811.10)
 exact 494.11
mathematician 85.6
 (measurer 466.9)
mathematics, mathesis 85.2
 (measurement 466.8)
matin, matinal 125.3
matinee 892.5
matins morning 125.1
 prayers 990.7
matmaker 690.8
matrass, mattrass 191.11
matriarch 166.7
matriarchate, matriarchy 737.5
matricide 361.2
matriculate 86.3
matrimonial 903.14
matrimony
 mixture 41.1
 marriage 903.1
 (sacrament 998.3)
matrix die 22.3
 perforator 262
 type 591.6
matron woman 374.2
 housekeeper 694.5
 wife 903.8
matronage 374.5
matronal 374.11
matronhood 374.5
matronize v.
 care for 459.6
 supervise 693.5
matronly 374.11
matronship 374.5
matter n.
 concern 151.1, 2
 excrement 299.2
 material 316.2
 (something 3.2)
 subject 454.1
 subject matter 516.4
 manuscript 590.3
 business 625.1
 trouble 704.2; 735.1
 in the matter of 9.10
matter v. 642.7
 not matter 643.7, 13
matter in hand
 topic 454.1
 task 625.2
 (undertaking 676.1)
matter of course 613.3
matter of fact n. 843.1
matter-of-fact adj.
 language 576.3
 artless 703.4
 commonplace 843.6
 (prosaic 598.4)
 ordinary 849.3

matting 219.4
mattock 253.6
mattrass See matrass
mattress 215.24
maturate
 prepare 673.6
 complete 729.2, 4
maturation
 evolution 161.5
 elaboration 673.1
maturative 662.12
mature v.
 become adult 131.4
 ripen into 144.8
 perfect 650.4
 improve 658.6
 prepare 673.6
 complete 729.2, 4
mature adj.
 adult 131.5
 prepared 673.11
 completed 729.6
maturescence 131.1
maturescent 131.5
maturity
 adulthood 131.1
 (oldness 124.1)
 ripeness 673.4
 reach maturity 729.4
matutinal 125.3
matzoth 298.11
maudlin drunk 959.21
 foolish 499.15
 indolent 683.13
 sentimental 822.7
mauger, maugre 30.8
maul, mall n. 276.4
maul, mall v.
 maltreat 649.7
 batter 659.8
maulstick, mahlstick 215.15
maund, maun 191.9
maunder
 digress 573.5
 mumble 583.2
 be loquacious 584.4
maundering 573.7
Maundy Thursday
 anniversary 138.7
 holyday 998.13
mausoleum 363.13
mauve 437.4
maverick
 newcomer 57.3
 calf 366.12
mavis, mavie
 bird 366.22
 songbird 416.11
maw 191.7
mawkin See malkin
maxilla 260.2
maxim topic 454.1
 tenet 484.3
 aphorism 496
 (phrase 566.1)
 (witticism 842.4)
 precept 697.1
 (rule 80.1)
maximal
 supreme 33.8
 top 210.6

Maximalist 712.6
maximate, maximize 549.2
maximum n.
 limit 52.4
 summit 210.1
 (supremacy 33.3)
maximum adj.
 supreme 33.8
 top 210.6
Maya Indian 434.5
 language 560.4
May apple, mayapple 663.6
maybe 470.7
May Day 138.7
Mayfair 852.4
May fly
 ephemerid 111.4
 insect 366.24
mayhap, mayhappen, mayhaps 470.7
Maying
 go a-Maying 840.21
mayor 745.9
mayoralty 965.1
maypole 206.4
 (shaft 215.13)
mazard 234.4
Mazda 976.2
maze 59.3
 (convolution 248.1)
 in a maze 475.16
mazed
 confused 458.12
 bewildered 475.16
 (delirious 503.14)
mazement 870.1
mazuma 800.1
mazurka, mazourka
 music 415.7
 dance 840.7
mazy 59.10
 (convoluted 248.4)
M.C.
 stageman 599.17
 member of congress 696.8
me 79.4
mead grassland 367.11
 sweet drink 396.5
meadow 367.11
 (plain 344.1)
 (field 371.5)
meadow brook 435.2
meager v. 203.8
meager, meagre adj.
 incomplete 53.4
 thin 203.11
 feeble 575.2
 insufficient 640.9
 (inconsiderable 32.8)
 paltry 643.12
meal fodder 298.7
 repast 298.34
 powder 330.3
mealy 330.8
mealymouthed
 hypocritical 544.8
 suave 894.13
 flattering 933.3

mealymouthedness 933.1
mean n. 29
 (middle 68.1)
 (mid-course 628.1)
 (mediocrity 736.1)
 (compromise 774.1)
in the mean
 mediumly 29.4
 midway 68.6
mean v.
 signify 516.5
 (imply 526.4)
 intend 630.3
mean business 604.5
mean adj.
 average 29.3
 middle 68.5
 interjacent 228.11
 paltry 643.12
 (bad 649.8)
 miserly 819.4
 disreputable 874.8
 (ignoble 876.11)
 abject 886.4
 selfish 943.4
meander n.
 complexity 59.3
 convolution 248.1
meander v. wind 248.3
 (turn 311.4)
 (flow 348.17)
 wander 266.14
 deviate 279.5
 (circuit 629.2)
meandering n. 248.1
meandering, meandrous adj.
 complex 59.10
 convoluted 248.4
meaning n. 516
 (explanation 522.1)
meaning, meaningful adj. 516.8
 (graphic 518.6)
meaningless 517.8
 (absurd 497.4)
 (foolish 499.15)
meaningly 516.12
meanness
 inferiority 34.1
 selfishness 943.1
means
 ~ of support 625.1
 method 627.1
 medium 631.2
 resources 632
 (instrumentality 631.1)
 (instrument 633.1)
 (provision 637.1)
 (expedient 646.2)
 (aid 707.1)
 (sustenance 707.3)
 assets 780.7
 funds 800.2
 (wealth 803.1)
by all means
 assent 488.15
 (willingly 602.11)
 (permission 760.7)
 anyhow 627.9

meant — meet

means (*continued*)
 by means of
  with 632.4
  (by the agency
   170.5)
  (through 631.5)
  (by the aid of
   707.14)
 by no means
  nowise 32.18
  God forbid! 489.9
  no 536.4
  refusal 764.7
meant 526.7
 not meant 621.20
meantime, meanwhile *n.* 109a.1
 in the meantime
  109a.3
meantime, meanwhile *adv.* 109a.3
measles 655.6
measly 643.12
measurable 466.12
measuration 466.1
measure *n.*
 quantity 25.1, 2
 degree 26.1
 rhythm 138.3
 moderation 174.1
 size 192.1
 stratum 204.1
 music 413.12, 21;
  415.2, 15
 gauge 466.1, 2, 4
 (calculator 85.5)
 (sign 550.2)
 poetry 597.6, 7
 procedure 626.7
 action 680.2
 portion 786.2
 beyond measure
  extremely 31.19
  overmuch 641.7
measure *v.*
 graduate 26.2
 gauge 466.10
 (quantify 25.5)
 measure swords
  720.8
measured
 rhythmic 413.29
 metrical 466.13
 (regular 16.5; 80.3)
 temperate 953.6
measured music 415.5
measure for measure
 compensation 30.1
 interchange 148.1
 retaliation 718.1
 justice 941.1
measureless 105.3
measurement
 quantity 25.1
 ~ of time 114.1
 size 192.1
 ~ of length 200.6
 mensuration 466
 (numeration 85.1)
 (distance 196.1)
 (length 200.1)
measurer 466.4, 9

measures 632.1
measure signature
 415.23
measuring *n.* 466.1
measuring *adj.* 466.11
measuring machine
 466.4
meat *n.*
 food 298.5, 19
 nut 298.33
meat *v.* 298.43
meatus 418.5
mechanic 690.5
 (repairman 660.7)
mechanical
 involuntary 601.14
 machinelike 633.5
 (instrumental
  631.4)
mechanics 276.5
 (kinetics 264.4)
mechanism 633.2
Mechlin lace 847.6
Médaille Militaire
 733.2
medal medallion 557.6
 trophy 733.2
 (insignia 550.12;
  747.4)
 (monument 551.4)
Medal for Valor 733.2
medalist, medallist
 700.2
medallion
 sculpture 557.6
 medal 733.2
Medal of Honor 733.2
meddle 682.14
 (intrude 228.10)
 (pry 455.4)
meddler 682.11
 (intruder 228.4)
 (gossip 532.5)
 (hinderer 706.3)
meddlesome 682.22
 (prying 455.5)
meddlesomeness 682.8
 (inquisitiveness
  455.1)
meddling *n.* 682.8
meddling *adj.* 682.22
meden agan 174.1
medial mean 29.3
 middle 68.5
 interjacent 228.11
mediant 413.7
mediastinum 228.6
mediate *v.*
 subserve 631.3
 intercede 724.3
 (accord 714.3)
 (conciliate 723.4)
 divine function
  976.9
mediate *adj.*
 middle 68.5
 interjacent 228.11
mediation
 instrumentality
  631.1
 intercession 724
 (agency 170.1)

 (intervention 228.3)
 (conciliation 723.1;
  918.2)
 divine ~ 976.5
mediator 724.2
 (moderator 174.3)
 (intermediary
  228.5)
 (interlocutor 588.5)
 (medium 631.2)
 (deputy 759.1)
 (lawyer 968.1)
mediatorial 631.4
mediatory 724.4
 (pacificatory 723.6)
medic, medick, medical *n.* 662.19
medical *adj.* 662.25
**medical examiner,
 medical man** 662.19
medicament 662.4
medicaster
 impostor 548.3
 surgeon 662.19
medicate imbue 41.8
 remedy 662.24
medicinal *n.* 662.4
medicinal *adj.* 662.25
medicine remedy 662.4
 healing art 662.16
 (disease 655.19)
 medicine man 662.19
 alcoholic drink
  959.4
medicine man
 doctor 662.19
 sorcerer 992.2
mediciner, medico
 662.19
mediety 91.3
medieval, mediaeval
 124.7
medieval history 122.3
medievalism, mediaevalism
 antiquarianism
  122.4
 Dark Ages 491.5
medievalist, mediaevalist 122.5
mediocre *n.* 643.6;
 736.1
mediocre *adj.* 736.3
 (medium 29.3)
 (moderate 174.6)
 (unimportant
  643.10)
 (tolerable 648.11)
 (imperfect 651.4)
 be mediocre 736.2
mediocrity
 insignificancy 643.6
 mediocreness 736
 (mean 29.1)
 (moderation 174.1)
 (mid-course 628.1)
 (imperfection 651.1)
meditate ponder
 451.27
 purpose 620.3
meditation
 thought 451.1

 preoccupation 458.3
meditative 451.35
mediterranean
 midland 68.5
 inland 221.10; 342.9
 interjacent 228.11
medium *n.* mean 29.1
 (middle 68.1)
 moderation 174.1
 surroundings 227.2
 intermediary 228.5
 color 428.3
 instrumentality
  631.2
 (key 260.10)
 (means 632.1)
 agent 690.1
 mediator 724.2
 spiritualistic ~
  994.14
medium *adj.*
 mean 29.3
 middle 68.5
 interjacent 228.11
 mediocre 736.3
mediumism 994.4
mediumistic 994.22
mediumize 994.18
medley *n.*
 mixture 41.4
 confusion 59.2
 miscellany 72.8
 music 415.3
medley *adj.* 41.9
**medulla, medulla
 oblongata** 450.2
medullary 324.9
medusa 368.4
Medusa 992.3
medusiform 368.13
meed allotment 786.1
 ~ of praise 931.2
 reward 973.1
meek
 forbearant 826.10
 (submissive 725.5)
 humble 879.4
 (modest 881.5)
meeken 879.3
meekhearted 879.4
meekly 879.7
meekness 879.1
 (modesty 881.1)
meerschaum 392a.6
meet *n.* 72.2
meet *v.* agree 23.7
 join 43.5
 assemble 72.10, 11
 conform 82.4
 be contiguous 199.3
 front 234.7
 collide 276.9
 converge 290.2
 arrive together
  292.10
 touch 379.3
 concur 488.7
 ~ a bet 621.18
 ~ requirements
  639.3
 confront 708.3
 observe 772.3

960

confront danger
 861.5
meet halfway
 be willing 602.6
 be reconciled 723.5
 mediate 724.3
 compromise 774.2
 be benevolent 906.5
meet the eye
 appear 446.2
 meet with attention
  457.6
meet with
 experience 151.4
 discover 481a.3
meet *adj.*
 opportune 134.7
 expedient 646.4
 (fit 23.11)
 (ethical 926.12)
 (just 941.3)
meeting junction 43.1
 assembly 72.2
 (divine service
  990.7)
 contiguity 199.1
 clash 276.2
 convergence 290.1
 encounter 292.4
 council 696.2
meetinghouse 1000.1
 (assembly hall
  189.10)
meg *See* mag
megacoulomb, mega-
 cycle, megafarad
 etc. 158a.5
megalith 363.15
megalomania 482.1
megalosaur, megalo-
 saurian 192.8
Megalosaurus
 antiquity 124.2
 behemoth 192.8
megaphone
 noisemaker 404.4
 sound device 418.6
Megarianism 451.7
megascope 445.6
megatherian 192.15
Megatheriidae 124.2
Megatherium 192.8
 antiquity 124.2
 behemoth 124.2
megavolt, megawatt
 158a.5
megilp, megilph,
 meguilp resin 356a.1
 paint 428.5
megohm 158a.5
megohmmeter 158a.6
megrim 378.1
megrims
 twitching 315.6
 psychosis 503.2
 disease 655.18
 blues 837.1
mehtar 652.6
Meistersinger
 singer 416.10
 poet 597.10
Meithei 560.4

melancholia 503.2
melancholy *n.* 837.1
melancholy *adj.*
 gloomy 421.8
 depressing 830.11
 sad 837.9
 (sullen 901.8)
Melanesian 431.4
mélange 41.4
Melchior 500.3
melee turmoil 59.4
 contest 720.2
Melibean, Meliboean
 597.13
melic
 melodious 413.27
 musical 415.28
melinite 727.13
meliorate 658.6, 8
melioration 658.1
melliferous 396.8
mellifluence 413.4
mellifluent sweet 396.8
 melodious 413.27
mellifluous
 resonant 408.9
 speech 578.4
mellisonant
 melodious 413.27
 speech 578.4
mellophone 417.4
mellow *v.*
 ripen 144.8; 673.6
 soften 324.4
 improve 658.8
mellow *adj.* aged 128.8
 mature 131.5
 intoxicated 959.21
 soft 324.4
 tobacco 392a.15
 resonant 408.9
 mellisonant 413.27
 soft-colored 428.17
 prepared 673.11
mellowness 673.4
mellow-toned 413.27
melodeon 417.5
melodia 417.12
melodica 417.5
melodics 415.24
 (melody 413.4)
melodion 417.2
melodious 413.27
 (pleasing 377.7)
 (musical 415.28)
melodist 416.10, 14
melodize
 compose 415.26
 play 416.18
 (harmonize 413.25)
melodizer 416.14
melodrama
 drama 599.3
 sensationalism 824.1
melodramatic 824.12
melodramatics 599.2
melodramatist 599.22
melodramatize 599.25
melody
 tunefulness 413.4
 (tone 402.2)
 (music 415.1)

(beauty 845.4)
 song 415.2
melon 298.32
Melpomene 599.1
melt combine 48.3
 be transient 111.5
 be converted into
  144.8
 liquefy 335.5
 (soften 324.4)
 fuse 384.21
 disappear 449.2
 ~ into tears 839.8
 relent 914.3
 excite pity 914.4
melt away
 cease to be 2.5
 decrease 36.3
 (waste 638.3)
 disappear 449.2
meltable 335.8
melted
 liquefied 335.7
 molten 384.24
 penitent 950.5
melting *n.*
 liquefaction 335.1
 fusion 384.2
melting *adj.* 335.8
melting pot
 conversion 144.4
 United States 182.3
mem 505.10
member *n.* part 51.4
 (component 56.1)
 person 372.3
become a member
 712.8
member *v.* 505.10
membrane layer 204.2
 skin 223.12
membranous 204.5
memento
 memory 505.1, 5
 monument 551.4
memento mori 837.4
memoir
 memorandum
  505.5, 8
 record 551.1
 dissertation 595.1
memoirs 594.2
memorabilia
 affairs 151.2
 memories 505.8;
  594.2
 record 551.1
 notabilia 642.3
memorable
 rememberable
  505.19
 notable 642.10
memorandize 551.8
 (remind 505.16)
memorandum *n.*
 list 86.1
 reminder 505.6
 record 551.1
 term 770.1
memorandum *v.* 551.8
memoria 363.15; 551.4
memorial *n.*

monument 363.15
 tombstone 363.15
 memoir 505.5, 8;
  594.2
 (memento 505.7)
 record 551.1, 4
memorial *adj.* 505.21;
 883.5
Memorial Day 138.7
memorialist 553.2
memorialization 883.1
memorialize 883.3
 (remember 505.10)
memoried 505.17
memorize 505.13
 (learn 539.3)
memory
 recollection 505
 (store 636.4)
 posthumous fame
  873.5
 commemoration
  883.1
from memory 505.22
in memory
 hic jacet 363.27
 in remembrance
  505.23
 in commemoration
  883.6
memory book
 memorandum 505.6
 notebook 551.3
memoryless 506.8
mem-sahib
 mistress 374.2, 3
 title 877.2
menace *n.*
 villain 599.19
 threat 909.1
menace *v.*
 impend 152.2
 threaten 909.2
menacing
 imminent 152.3
 threatening 909.3
ménage, menage
 home 189.2
 husbandry 693.3
menagerie 370.3
 (enclosure 232.1)
 (collection 636.5)
mend *n.* 658.1
mend *v.*
 improve 658.6, 8
 repair 660.1
 reconcile 723.4
mend one's fences
 723.5
mendacious 544.7
mendacity lying 544.1
 lie 546.1
mender 660.7
mendicancy 765.1
mendicant *n.*
 beggar 767.2
 monk 996.11
mendicant *adj.* 765.7
mendicate 765.6
mendicity
 beggary 765.1
 poverty 804.2

mending — messengers

mending 660.4
menfolk, menfolks 373.4
menhaden oil 356.4
menhir 550.10
menial worker 690.2
  servant 746.1
meniscus
  crescent 245.2
  lens 445.1
menopause 128.3
Mensa 318.6
mensal 1000.3
menses 299.7
  (regularity 138.6)
Menshevik, menshevik 712.6
menstrual 138.11
menstruum 335.4
mensurable 466.12
mensurable music 415.5
mensural 466.11, 12
mensurate 466.10
mensuration 466.1
mensurational, mensurative 466.11
mental 450.8
mental age 498.1
mental deficiency 499.3
  (insanity 503.1)
mental healer
  doctor 662.19
  religious 984.19
mental healing 984.9
mental image 515.4
mentality 450.1
mentalize 451.27
mental philosophy 450.4
  (philosophy 451.4)
mental ratio 498.1
mental reservation
  equivocation 477.4
  secrecy 528.2
  (half truth 546.3)
  ulterior motive 615.1
mentals 450.1
Mental Science 984.9
Mental Scientist 984.19
mentation 451.1
menticulture
  learning 490.2
  culture 658.2
mention *n.*
  information 527.1
  statement 582.4
mention *v.*
  specify 79.5
  make known 527.7
  say 582.1
  not to mention 37.9
mentor sage 500.1
  adviser 695.3
  (teacher 540.4)
mentum 234.5
menu list 86.1
  food 298.40
  schedule 611.2

Mephistophelean, Mephistophelian 945.17
Mephistopheles 978.1
mephitic
  stenchy 401.4
  poisonous 657.3
mephitis fume 334.2
  stench 401.1
  miasma 663.5
mercantile 794.10
mercantilism 794.1
mercantile marine
  marine 273.6
  navy 726.10
mercenary *n.*
  soldier 726.4
  employee 746.1
mercenary *adj.* 819.4
mercer 225.36
merchandise 798
  (supplies 636.1)
merchandising 798.2
merchant 797
  (tobacconist 392a.12)
  (bookdealer 593.14)
  (workman 690.10)
  (buyer 795.2)
  (barkeeper 959.12)
merchantable 796.7
merchantman 273.1
merchant marine
  marine 273.6
  navy 726.10
merchantry
  commerce 794.1
  tradespeople 797.9
merchant ship 273.1
merciful 914.6
  (benevolent 906.6)
merciless 914a.3
mercilessness 914a.1
mercurial
  inconstant 149.6
  moving 264.8
  fast 274.13
  fickle 608.6
  restless 825.9
Mercurochrome 662.8
mercury speed 274.6
  thermometer 389.1
  metal 635.6
Mercury
  speeder 274.7
  planet 318.3
  messenger 534.1
  commerce 794.1
  god 979.2
mercury lamp 423.3
mercy lenity 740.1
  compassion 914.1
  (benevolence 906.1)
  at the mercy of
  contingent 177.4
  in the power of 749.5, 6
  cry you mercy
  God forbid! 766.5
  have pity! 914.7
  forgive me! 918.7
  for mercy's sake

please! 765.9
  have pity! 914.7
  have no mercy 914a.2
mercy seat 966.1
mere *n.* ocean 341.1
  sea inlet 343.1
  lake 343a.1
mere *adj.* 32.11
merels 840.11
merely 32.13
meretricious
  false 545.13
  gaudy 851.8
  whorish 961.10
meretrix 962.2
merge combine 48.3
  be converted into 144.8
  submerge 310.5
merge in
  enter into 56.2
  be included 76.2
merge into
  change 140.5
  be converted into 144.8
merged 228.11
  be merged in 56.2
merger 712.5
Merida 433.1
meridian *n.* noon 125.2
  latitude 181.5
  summit 210.1
  map line 550.9
meridian *adj.*
  noon 125.4
  summital 210.6
meringue 298.12
merit *n.*
  excellence 648.1
  desert 924.2
  virtue 944.1
merit *v.* 923.5
merited, meriting 924.11
meritorious
  praiseworthy 931.11
  virtuous 944.3
Merlin 992.2
merlon 717.3
mermaid, merman
  monster 83.7
  spirit of the sea 341.2
  water spirit 979.10
merogenesis 161.2
merriment
  mirth 836.3
  (rejoicing 838.1)
  (jocularity 842.2)
  amusement 840.2
merry
  intoxicated 959.21
  mirthful 836.8
  make merry
  play 840.21
  (rejoice 838.5)
  (celebrate 883.3)
  joke 842.8
  ridicule 856.5
merry-andrew 599.20
merry-go-round

whirligig 312.4
carrousel 840.15
merrymaking 840.2
  (rejoicing 838.1)
  (conviviality 892.2)
merrythought 993.4
mesa 344.1
mésalliance
  disagreement 24.1
  fault 651.2
  ill-assorted marriage 903.1
mescal 663.6
meseems 484.17
mesencephalon 450.2
mesh network 219.4
  snare 545.4
mesial, mesian
  middle 68.5
  interjacent 228.11
mesilla 344.1
mesmeric 683.17
mesmerism
  fascination 617.1
  hypnotic sleep 683.5
  hypnotism 994.6
mesmerist 994.13
mesmerize
  anesthetize 376.4
  charm 617.4
  hypnotize 994.19
mesne 217.6
mesne lord 779.2
mesoblast 357.4
mesoblastic 357.10
mesogaster 221.4
mesquite grass 367.9
mess *n.*
  quantities 31.3
  mixture 41.4
  confusion 59.2
  meal 298.34
  bungle 699.4
  predicament 704.2
  share 786.2
  in a mess 704.11
  make a mess of
  derange 61.2
  botch 699.9
mess *v.* 298.43, 44
mess up
  derange 61.2
  botch 699.9
Mess See Mass 998.7
message
  dispatch 532.2
  (information 527.1)
  (telegram 532a.2)
  epistle 592.2
Messalina 962.2
messenger
  ship's rope 273.10
  courier 534
  (forerunner 64.1)
  (traveller 268.5)
  (informant 527.5)
  (delegate 758.4)
  (deputy 759.1)
messengers
  clouds 353.5
  omen 512.2
  warning sign 668.3

Messiah 976.5
mess jacket 225.14
messmate 890.3
messuage house 189.3
 (farm 371.4)
 property 780.4
messy 59.9
mestee 41.5
metabatic 264.8
metabolic 240.8
metabolism 140.2
metabolize 140.6
metacenter, meta-
 centre 222.2
metachronism
 anachronism 115.1
 error 495.1
metage 466.1
metagenesis
 transformation
  140.2
 generation 161.2
metagenetic 149.5
metageometry 85.2
metagrammatism
  561.4
metakinesis 264.4
metakinetic 264.9
metal soil 342.3
 mineral 635.6
metalepsis 521.1
metallography, metal-
 lurgy 358.2
metalwork 847.3
metalworker 690.9
metamorphose 140.6
metamorphosis 140.2
metamorphotic 81.2
metaphor 521.1
 (comparison 464.1)
 (equivalence 516.3)
metaphorical 521.3
 (comparative 464.5)
metaphorically 521.4
metaphorize 521.2
metaphrase 522.2
 (paraphrase 21.4)
metaphrast 524.1
metaphrastic
 literal 516.9
 interpretative 522.8
metaphysic 451.4
metaphysical 994.21
metaphysician, meta-
 physicist 994.13
metaphysics
 existence 1.3
 philosophy 451.4
 esoteric science
  994.1
metaplasm 357.3
metaplasmic 357.9
metaprotein 352.3
metapsychical 994.21
metapsychics 994.1
metapsychist 994.13
metasomatism, meta-
 somatosis 140.2
metastasis
 transformation
  140.2
 dislocation 185.1

inversion 218.2
transference 270.1
metastatic 270.11
metathesis
 transformation
  140.2
 dislocation 185.1
 inversion 218.2
 transference 270.1
 figure of speech
  521.1
metathetic
 dislocated 185.3
 transferable 270.11
métayer system 777.1
mete measure 466.10
 ~ out 784.8
 apportion 786.3
metempiric 519.7
metempsychosis 140.2
metencephalon 450.2
meteor
 heavenly body 318.3
 cloud 353.5
meteoric brief 111.7
 turbulent 173.12
 brilliant 420.22
meteorite 318.3
meteorograph 267a.29
meteoroid, meteoro-
 lite 318.3
meteorological
 aerologic 338.12
 nephological 353.12
meteorologist 513.3
meteorology
 aeronautics 267a.2
 aerology 338.7
 nephology 353.6
meter, metre n.
 length 200.6
 musical rhythm
  413.21
 measure 466.3, 4
 versification 597.6
meter, metre v. 466.10
methane 334.2
metheglin 396.5
methinks 484.17
method system 58.3
 (rule 80.1)
 music 415.20
 way 627.1
 (plan 626.1)
 (means 632.1)
 (conduct 692.1)
 (fashion 852.1)
methodical
 orderly 58.7
 (uniform 16.5)
 (constant 80.3)
 (businesslike
  625.11)
 regular 138.9
methodically 58.8
Methodism 984.4
Methodist 984.14
methodize order 58.6
 arrange 60.8
methodologist 82.3
Methuselah 130.1
methylene 428 4

metic alien 57.3
 settler 188.5
 incomer 294.4
meticulous
 exact 494.11
 (careful 459.7)
 observant 772.5
 fastidious 868.4
meticulousness
 minute attention
  457.3
 (care 459.1)
 (discrimination
  465.1)
 (exactness 494.3)
 fastidiousness 868.1
métier, metier 625.5
métis 41.5
metonym
 equivalence 516.3
 word 562.1
metonymy 521.1
 (substitution 147.1)
metope 215.17
metoposcopist 234.6
metoposcopy
 physiognomy 234.6
 interpretation 522.5
metrical
 rhythmic 413.29
 mensural 466.11, 13
 poetic 597.13
metric system 466.3
metric ton 319.4
metrology 466.8
metronome
 timepiece 114.6
 music 417.13
metronomic 114.9
metronomic mark
  415.23
metropolis
 town 189.16
 center 222.2
metropolitan n. 996.5
metropolitan adj.
 urban 189.22
 central 222.4
mettle
 resolution 604.1
 disposition 820.1
 courage 861.1
mettlesome
 resolute 604.7
 excitable 825.8
 courageous 861.8
meum et tuum 780.1
mew n. retreat 189.13
 den 252.3
 refuge 666.3
mew v. shed 226.6
 miaow 412.2
 ~ up 751.8
 (wail 839.9)
mewl 412.2
Mexican n. 188.9
Mexican adj. 188.11
Mexico 182.3
mezzanine
 floor 191.18
 balcony 599.11
Mezzofanti 492.2

mezzo-relievo, mezzo-
 rilievo 557.6
mezzo-soprano
  413.14
mezzo termine 68.1
mezzotint n. 558.3
mezzotint v. 259.3
mgrm. 319.4
mian mister 373.3
 master 745.5
 title 877.2
miaow, miaou 412.2
miasm fume 334.2
 mephitis 401.1
 infection 655.2
 mephitic air 663.5
miasma
 mephitis 401.1
 infection 655.2
 mephitic air 663.5
mica
 opalescence 427.2
 mineral 635.6
micaceous 204.5
Micah 513.2
Micawber
 neglector 460.3
 idler 683.7
Micawberish 133.9
Micawberism 133.2
Michael 977.1
Michaelmas 998.13
mick alien 57.3
 Irishman 188.9
mickle 31.6
microbe 193.4
 (animal 366.2)
microbic 193.10
micrococcus 193.4
microcosm 193.3
microcosmography,
 microcosmology
  193.6
microgamete 357.4
micrograph 590.3
micrography
 micrology 193.6
 writing 590.1
micrology 193.6
micrometer
 littleness 193.7
 aviation 267a.29
micrometry 267a.2
micromorph 193.5
micron 193.2
microorganic 193.10
microorganism 193.4
microphone
 sound device 418.6
 radio 532a.5
microphotography,
 microphysics 193.6
microphyte 193.4
microscope
 littleness 193.7
 scope 445.1
Microscope 318.6
microscopic
 infinitesimal 193.10
 scopic 445.9
microscopist 445.8
Microscopium 318.6

microscopy — millionaire 964

microscopy
  micrology 193.6
  optics 445.7
microspore, micro-
zoon, microzyme
etc. 193.4
micturate 297.15
micturition 299.3
mid *n.* 68.1
mid *adj.* 68.5
'mid *prep.* among 41.11
  between 228.13
Midas 803.2
midbrain 450.2
mid-course 628
  (middle 68.1)
  (mediocrity 736.1)
  (compromise 774.1)
midday *n.* 125.2
midday *adj.* 125.4
midden 653.8
middle *n.* 68
  (mean 29.1)
  (interior 221.2)
  (center 222.2)
  (interjacence 228.1)
  (mid-course 628.1)
in the middle
  midway 68.6
  (mediumly 29.4)
  during 106.7
  centrally 222.5
middle *v.*
  put in middle 68.4
  centralize 222.3
middle *adj.*
  medial 68.5
  (mean 29.3)
  (central 222.4)
  interjacent 228.11
middle age 131.2
Middle Age 491.5
middle-class 736.3
middle classes 736.1
middle ground
  mean 29.1
  (compromise 774.1)
  mid-course 628.1
middleman
  mediator 724.2
  (deputy 759.1)
  negotiator 758.3
middlemost
  middle 68.5
  central 222.4
middle of the road
628.1
  (mean 29.1)
middle term
  mean 29.1
  middle 68.1
middling *adj.*
  inconsiderable 32.8
  mediocre 736.3
  (tolerable 648.11)
middling *adv.* 32.14
middy 225.18
midge
  diminutive 193.2, 5
  insect 366.24
midget 193.5
mid-gut 221.4

midland *n.*
  inland 221.3
  land 342.1
midland *adj.*
  inland 221.10; 342.9
  interjacent 228.11
midmost *n.* 68.1
midmost *adj.*
  middle 68.5
  central 222.4
midnight 126.4
  (darkness 421.1)
midnight blue 438.2
midnight oil 420.7
midrib 228.6
midriff middle 68.2
  partition 228.6
midship 68.5
midships 68.6
midst *n.* 68.1
in the midst
  among 41.11
  midway 68.6
  between 228.13
midst *prep.*
  among 41.11
  between 228.13
midsummer
  season 126a.3
  hot weather 382.3
Midsummer Day 138.7
midway *adj.* 68.5
midway *adv.* 68.6
  (mediumly 29.4)
  (between 228.13)
  (mid-course 628.4)
midwife
  minister 631.2
  obstetrician 662.19
midwifery birth 161.3
  obstetrics 662.16
midyear 461.3
mien aspect 448.4
  conduct 692.1
miff quarrel 713.3
  dudgeon 900.2
might greatness 31.1
  potence 157.1
  strength 159.1
  violence 173.1
with might and main
  violently 173.18
  laboriously 686.11
  (actively 682.25)
mightily 31.15
mightless 158.8
mighty *adj.* great 31.6
  potent 157.8
  strong 159.10
  huge 192.15
  authoritative 737.15
  eminent 873.18
  proud 878.6
mighty *adv.* 31.15
mignonette 435.2, 3
migraine 378.1
migrant
  traveler 268.3
  outgoer 295.4
migrate 266.15
migration 266.3
migrational 266.24

migrator 268.3
migratory 266.24
mikado 745.3
mike
  microscope 193.7
  microphone 418.6;
    532a.5
milady woman 374.2
  title 877.2
milch cow 636.2
mild moderate 174.6
  warm 382.15
  insipid 391.2
  lenient 740.4
  meek 826.10
  gentle 894.12
milden 324.4
mildew *n.* 659.2
  (blight 663.2)
mildew *v.* 659.7
mildewed
  antiquated 124.9
  foul 653.17
  decayed 659.13
mildness 740.1
mile 200.6
mileage
  length 200.1
  payment 973.2
milepost, milestone
550.10
miliaria 655.17
milieu 227.2
militancy 722.6
militant *n.* 726.3, 4
militant *adj.* 722.13
militarism
  martiality 722.6
  (chauvinism 884.2)
  stratocracy 737.4
militarist 726.3
  (chauvinist 884.4)
militaristic 722.13
  (chauvinistic 884.8)
military *n.* 726.6
military *adj.* 722.13
Military Cross, mili-
tary medal 733.2
military school 542.3
militaster 726.4
militate
  militate against
    counteract 179.3
    oppose 708.2
militia 726.6
  (guard 717.6)
milk *n.* drink 298.4
  fluid 333.2
  white 430.3
milk *v.* 370.7
milk and water *n.*
160.5
milk-and-water *adj.*
  wishy-washy 160.14
  insipid 391.2
  mediocre 736.3
milkiness *n.*
  opalescence 427.1
  whiteness 430.1
milk-livered 862.4
milkmaid 746.2
milk shake 298.4

milk sickness 655.18
milksop
  weakling 160.4
  mollycoddle 160a.3
  (coward 862.2)
milk-white 430.8
milky
  semiliquid 352.7
  opalescent 427.4
  white 430.8
Milky Way 318.7
mill *n.*
  aeromotor 273a.11
  pulverizer 330.4
  machine 633.2
  trifle 643.3
  workshop 691
  boxing match 720.6
  money 800.8
mill *v.* notch 257.5
  fight 720.8
  thrash 972.6
millboard 635.4
millenary *n.*
  thousand 98.10
  millennium 121.2
millenary *adj.* 98.28
millennial
  thousandth 98.28
  hereafter 121.8
millennium
  thousand 98.10
  century 108.1
  hereafter 121.2
  utopia 515.6
  prosperity 734.3
millepede, milleped
  thousand 98.10
  insect 368.8
miller 726.2
millesimal 99.3
millet seed 193.2
milli- 98.28
milliad 98.10
milliard 98.12
millier 319.4
milligram, milli-
gramme
  thousand 98.10
  weight 319.4
milliliter, millilitre
  thousand 98.10
  measure 466.3
millimeter, millimetre
  thousand 98.10
  measure 466.3
milliner 225.39
millinery
  headdress 225.26
  haberdashery 225.35
  merchandise 798.3
  needlework 847.6
million
  number 98.11; 102.5
  wealth 800.11
  the masses 876.1
  (people 372.2)
for the million
  intelligible 518.5
  easy 705.5
long million 98.12
millionaire 803.2

millionth — minstrel show

millionth 98.29
millipede, milliped
  See millepede
millpond 341.1
millpool 343a.1
millrace, mill run 348.2
millstone
  gravity 319.2
  grinder 330.4
  impediment 706.2
millwright 690.7
milord 877.2
miloti blue 438.2
milori green 435.2
milreis 800.8
milt rudiment 153.3
  sperm 357.4
mime *n.*
  imitator 19.4
  masquerader 528.7
  actor 599.20
mime *v.* 19.6
mimeograph 19.5
mimer, mimic *n.*
  imitator 19.4
  masquerader 528.7
  actor 599.20
mimic *v.* 19.6
  (personate 554.8)
  (act 599.26)
mimic *adj.* 19.12
mimicker 19.4
mimicry 19.2
Mimir 192.8
mimmation 567.1
mimographer 599.22
mina, minah 366.22
minacious 909.3
minacity 909.1
minaret 206.3
minatory 909.3
mince *n.* 298.19
mince *v.*
  disintegrate 44.9
  walk 266.16
  go slow 275.5
  ~ the truth 544.5
  clip words 583.2
  be affected 853.5
  be fastidious 868.3
  show off 882.6
  extenuate 937.8
mincemeat 298.19
mincing trifling 643.11
  prudish 853.7
mind *n.*
  intellect 450.1
  (intelligence 498.1)
  attention 457.1
  opinion 484.2
  will 600.1
  will power 604.2
  obstinacy 606.1
  intention 620.1
  desire 865.1
  psyche 994.10, 11
  give the mind to
  give attention 457.4
  study 461.17
  have a mind to
  be willing 602.6

intend 620.3
desire 865.11
have in mind
  think 451.30, 31
  remember 505.11
  mean 516.5
  intend 620.3
have on one's mind 451.30
keep in mind 505.11
to one's mind
  agreeable 829.7
  to one's taste 850.6
  fancied 897.16
Mind *n.*
  world spirit 359.3
  God 976.2
mind *v.*
  be attentive 457.4
  be careful 459.3, 5
  care for 459.6
  remember 505.10
  remind 505.15
  be willing 602.6
  intend 620.3
  be cautious 864.3
  object to 867.4
mind one's business
  be incurious 456.2
  be attentive 457.4
  be careful 459.3
  not interfere 748.11
mind one's eye
  be careful 459.4
  beware 864.3, 9
mind one's P's and
  Q's be careful 459.3
  be cautious 864.3
  behave 894.7
  be virtuous 944.2
mind out
  be attentive 457.4, 10
  be careful 459.4
  beware 864.3, 9
never mind
  no matter! 460.13; 643.14
  who cares? 866.7
not mind
  be apathetic 823.3
  be indifferent 866.3
of one mind
  agreeing 23.9
  concurrent 178.4
  unanimous 488.12
  concordant 714.4
on the mind 454.4
mind cure 662.16
minded tending 176.3
  disposed 620.4; 820.4
  (willed 600.3)
mindful
  attentive 457.9
  careful 459.7
  recollective 505.17
mindfulness 457.1
mindless
  reasonless 450a.2
  (incogitant 452.3)
  inattentive 458.10
  careless 460.8

unintelligent 499.11
forgetful 506.8
insensible 823.5
indifferent 866.4
mindlessness 450a.1
mind's eye 505.1
mind-stuff theory 451.19
mine *n.* cavity 252.2
  snare 545.4
  intrigue 626.6
  fund 636.2
  (plenty 639.2)
  hidden danger 667.1
  fortification 717.3
mine *v.* demolish 162.4
  excavate 252.9
  (perforate 260.14)
  damage 659.8
  entrench 664.6
  sap 716.5
mine layer 726.11
Minenwerfer 727.11
miner excavator 252.7
  (workman 690.10)
  military 726.4
mineral *n.* 635.6
  (inorganic matter 358.1)
mineral *adj.* 358.4
mineralize 358.3
  (harden 323.4)
mineral kingdom 358.1
mineralogize 358.3
mineralogy 358.2
mineral oil 662.9
mineral pigment 428.4
mineral water
  water 337.1
  cathartic 662.9
Minerva
  wisdom 498.3
  goddess 979.2
mine ship, mine sweeper 726.11
mine thrower 727.11
mingle mix 41.6
  (join 43.5)
  keep company 892.9
minglement 41.1
miniature *n.*
  diminutive 193.3
  (compendium 596.1)
  picture 556.9
in miniature 193.11
miniature *adj.*
  inconsiderable 32.6
  diminutive 193.8
miniaturist 559.2
minify 36.4
minikin
  inconsiderable 32.6
  little 193.8
minim modicum 32.2
  diminutive 193.2
  note 413.6, 12
  measure 466.3
Minimalist 712.6
minimifidian *n.* 989.4
minimifidian *adj.*
  unbelieving 485.9
  irreligious 989.7

minimifidianism
  unbelief 485.1
  infidelity 989.2
minimize
  decrease 36.4
  underestimate 483.3
minimum
  modicum 32.2
  inferiority 34.1
minion type 591.7
  darling 899.1
minish 36.4
minister *n.*
  instrument 631.2
  (agent 690.1)
  officer 694.3
  deputy 759.1, 2
  clergyman 996.2
minister *v.*
  subserve 631.3
  perform a rite 998.14
minister to
  doctor 662.24
  aid 707.6
  serve 746.8
  (care for 459.6)
ministerial
  instrumental 631.4
  ecclesiastical 995.9
  (pastoral 996.15)
ministering 746.9
ministrant 707.12
ministration
  supervision 693.2
  aid 707.1
  rite 998.1
ministress 996.3
ministry
  supervision 693.2
  aid 707.1
  church 995.1
  clergy 996.1
  rite 998.1
minium 434.6
miniver, mink 223.12
Minnesänger, minnesinger
  singer 416.10
  poet 597.10
minnie 727.11
minnow 193.2
minor *n.* 129.1
minor *adj.* 34.5
Minorite 996.11
minority
  inferiority 34.2
  a few 103.2
  youth 127.1
minor key 413.7
Minos
  statesman 694.4
  judge 967.1
  god 982.4
Minotaur 83.7
minster 1000.1
minstrel *n.*
  musician 416.1, 10
  poet 597.10
minstrel *v.* 416.20
minstrel show
  musicale 415.17

minstrelsy — misemployment

minstrel show (cont'd)
  show 599.8
minstrelsy music 415.3
  musicians 416.1
  poetry 597.1
mint n. die 22.3; 558.4
  quantities 31.3
  pungency 392.2
  condiment 393.1
  candy 396.2
  perfume 400.3
  manufactory 691
mint v. form 240.6
  coin 800.20
mintage 800.1
minter 800.18
mint julep 959.8
minuend 38.3
minuet music 415.7
  dance 840.7
minuetic 415.28
minus n. 38.3
minus adj.
  nonexistent 2.7
  absent 187.10
  short of 304.3
  lacking 640.11
  deprived of 776.6
minus prep. less 38.11
  without 187.10
minuscular 561.9
minuscule letter 561.1
  type 591.6
minute n. period 108.1
  instant 113.3
  time 114.2
  measure 466.3
  note 551.1
  compendium 596.1
  account entry 811.2
minute v. 811.7
minute adj.
  inconsiderable 32.6
  detailed 79.7
  (circumstantial 8.5)
  little 193.8
  insignificant 643.10
minuteman 726.6
minuteness 457.3
minutes 551.2
minutiae
  particulars 79.3
  (smallness 32.3)
  diminutives 193.2
  trivia 643.4
minx brat 129.1
  insolent person 885.3
  strumpet 962.2
mir population 188.10
  sir 373.3
  potentate 745.5
  title 877.2
miracle 872.1
miracle play 599.3
miraculous 870.7
mirage 443.9
mire n. 345.1
  (mud 352.5)
  (dirt 653.5)
mire v. sink 310.5
  bog 345.2

mirk, mirky etc. See murk etc.
mirror n.
  prototype 22.1
  (paragon 650.2)
  plumage 256.9
  looking glass 445.4
  (glass 384.14)
mirror v. 19.5
mirth 836.3
mirth-loving, mirthful 836.8
miry, mirey 345.3
  (muddy 352.9)
mirza sir 373.3
  prince 745.4, 5; 875.7
  title 877.2
  (mister 373.3)
misadministration 699.2
misadventure 735.3
misadvised 699.17
misalliance
  misrelation 10.2
  disagreement 24.1
misanthrope 910.2
misanthropic 910.3
  (ill-humored 901.7)
  (selfish 943.4)
misanthropy 910
  (ill-humor 901.1)
  (selfishness 943.1)
misapplication
  misinterpretation 523.1
  misuse 679.1
  (perversion 243.2)
  mismanagement 699.2
misapply
  sophisticate 477.7
  misinterpret 523.2
  misuse 679.2
  (pervert 243.4)
  mismanage 699.8
misapprehend 523.2
misapprehension
  mistake 495.2
  misinterpretation 523.1
misappropriate 679.2
misappropriation 679.1
misarrange 61.2
misarrangement 61.1
misbecome 923.3
misbecoming 647.3
misbegotten
  deformed 243.5
  bastard 964.5
misbehave
  be vulgar 851.5
  misdemean oneself 945.9
misbehaving 945.13
misbehavior, misbehaviour
  vulgarity 851.1
  unmannerliness 895.1
  wrongdoing 945.6
misbelief

unbelief 485.1
  heterodoxy 984.1
  (delusion 495.5)
misbelieve
  disbelieve 485.5
  err 495.7
misbeliever 984.12
  (unbeliever 989.4)
misbelieving 984.22
miscalculate 481.5
  (err 495.7)
miscalculation 481.1
  (inexpectation 508.1)
  (disappointment 509.1)
miscall 565.6
miscarriage 732.1
miscarried 732.8
miscarry
  give birth 161.9
  fall short 304.2
  fail 732.5
miscarrying 732.8
miscegenate mix 41.6
  intermarry 903.13
miscegenation 903.1
miscegenator 903.5
miscegenetic 903.14
miscellanea
  collection 72.8
  record 551.1
miscellaneous 41.9
miscellany
  mixture 41.4
  collection 72.8
  record 551.1
  book 593.2; 597.4
  excerpts 596.2
mischance 735.3
mischief 649.2
  (bane 663.1)
full of mischief 649.10
mischief-maker 913.1
mischief-making
  mischievous 649.10
mis-cite
  misinterpret 523.2
  falsify 544.3
  misrepresent 555.4
miscomputation 481.1
  (error 495.1)
miscompute 481.5
misconceive 523.2
misconception
  error 495.2, 5
  (misjudgment 481.1)
  misinterpretation 523.1
misconduct n.
  mismanagement 699.2
  misbehavior 851.1
  unmannerliness 895.1
  wrongdoing 945.6
misconduct v. 699.8
misconduct oneself 945.9
misconjecture n. 481.1

misconjecture v. 481.5
misconstruction
  distortion 243.2
  misinterpretation 523.1
  (misjudgment 481.1)
  (error 495.1)
  falsification 544.1
misconstrue
  distort 243.4
  misjudge 481.5
  misinterpret 523.2
  (err 495.7)
misconstruing 243.2
miscorrect 538.2
miscreance 485.1
miscreant n.
  knave 949.1
  heretic 984.12
  irreligionist 989.4
miscreant adj.
  heretic 485.9
  heterodox 984.22
  infidelic 989.7
miscreation 83.6
miscreated 964.5
miscue n. 495.3
miscue v. 495.9
misdate n. 115.1
misdate v. 115.2
misdated 115.3
misdeed 947.2
  (violation of law 964.2)
misdeem
  misjudge 481.5
  misinterpret 523.2
misdemeanant 949.2
misdemeanor, misdemeanour
  evil conduct 945.6
  crime 947.2
  violation of law 964.2
misdescribe 538.2
misdevotion 988.2
misdirect distort 243.4
  mislead 495.11
  misteach 538.2
  misuse 679.2
  mismanage 699.8
misdirection
  distortion 243.2
  misteaching 538.1
  misuse 679.1
  mismanagement 699.2
misdo 945.9
misdoing vice 945.6
  misdeed 947.2
misdoubt n.
  doubt 485.2
  jealousy 920.1
misdoubt v. 920.2
miseducate 538.2
miseducation 536.1; 538.1
miseducative 538.4
mise en scène 599.2
misemploy 679.2
misemployment 679.1

miser 819.2
miserable
    paltry 643.12
    wretched 828.16
miserably
    extremely 31.23
    slightly 32.12
Miserere 990.2
miserly 819.4
misery pain 378.1
    wretchedness 828.3
    (adversity 735.1)
    (sorrow 837.3)
misesteem, misestimate 481.5
misestimation 481.1
misexplain 523.2
misexplanation, misexplication 523.1
misfeasance
    mismanagement 699.2
    wrongdoing 945.6
    misdeed 947.2
misfeasor 949.2
misfire n. 732.1
misfire v. 732.5
misfit 24.4
    (impotent 158.3)
    (failure 732.4)
misfortune 735.3
    (evil 649.2)
    (predicament 704.2)
    (failure 732.1)
misgiving doubt 485.2
    scruple 603.2; 939.2
    apprehension 860.2
    (foreboding 511.6)
misgovernment 699.2
misguidance
    misteaching 538.1
    mismanagement 699.2
misguide
    mislead 495.11
    misteach 538.2
    mismanage 699.8
misguided 699.17
mishap 735.3
mishmash 59.2
Mishmi 560.4
Mishnah, Mishna 985.5
Mishnaic 985.8
misidentify 495.8
misinform 538.2
    (mislead 495.11)
    (lie 544.4)
    (deceive 545.7)
misinformation 538.1
misinformed
    ignorant 491.10
    mistaught 538.3
misinstruct 538.2
misinstruction 538.1
misinstructive 538.4
misintelligence 538.1
misinterpret
    distort 243.4
    sophisticate 477.7
    misexplain 523.2
    (misjudge 481.5)

(err 495.7)
(mislead 495.11)
(misrepresent 555.4)
misinterpreted 523.3
misinterpretation
    distortion 243.2
    misexplanation 523
    (misjudgment 481.1)
    (error 495.1)
    (misrepresentation 555.1)
misjoinder 24.3
misjoined 24.8
misjudge 481.5
    (reason ill 477.7)
    (overestimate 482.3)
    (underestimate 483.3)
    (err 495.7)
    (misinterpret 523.2)
misjudging 481.9
misjudgment, misjudgement 481
    (sophistry 477.1)
    (error 495.1)
    (inexpectation 508.1)
    (disappointment 509.1)
    (misinterpretation 523.1)
mislay displace 61.3
    lose 776.2
mislead 495.11
    (sophisticate 477.7)
    (misinform 538.2)
    (falsify 544.3)
    (deceive 545.7)
    (misrepresent 555.4)
    (be dishonest 940.6)
misleading
    sophistical 477.9
    misteaching 538.1
    deceptive 545.12
    dishonest 940.8
mislike 867.4
mismanage 699.8
    (labor in vain 645.6)
mismanagement 699.2
mismatch n. 24.3
mismatch v. differ 15.5
    disagree 24.5
mismatched 24.8
mismatchment 24.3
mismate 24.5
mismated 24.8
misname 565.6
misnamed 565.7
misnaming 565.1
misnomer n. 565
misnomer v. 565.6
misogamist
    celibate 904.2
    misanthrope 910.2
misogamy 904.1
misogynist
    celibate 904.2
    misanthrope 910.2
misogyny 904.1

misplace 61.3
misplaced
    uncongenial 24.8
    (irrelevant 10.6)
    unconformable 83.9
    dislocated 185.5
    (disorderly 59.8)
misplacement
    displacement 61.1
    dislocation 185.1
misprint 495.2
misprision
    secrecy 528.2
    misdemeanor 945.6
misprision of treason
    revolt 742.2
    treachery 940.4
    misdemeanor 945.6
misprize, misprise
    underestimate 483.3
    scorn 930.5
mispronounce 583.4
mispronunciation
    blunder 495.3
    bad diction 579.1
    speech defect 583.1
misproportion 243.1
misproportioned 243.5
misquote
    misinterpret 523.2
    falsify 544.3
    misrepresent 555.4
misreading 523.1
misreckon 481.5
    (err 495.7)
misreckoning 481.1
misreference, misrelation 10.2
misremember 506.5
misremembrance 506.1
misrender
    distort 243.4
    misinterpret 523.2
misreport n.
    mistake 495.2
    misrepresentation 555.1
misreport v.
    falsify 544.3
    misrepresent 555.4
misrepresent
    distort 243.4
    pervert 555.4
    (sophisticate 477.7)
    (mislead 495.11)
    (misinterpret 523.2)
    (misteaching 538.2)
    (falsify 544.3)
    (deceive 545.7)
    (exaggerate 549.2)
    (be dishonest 940.6)
misrepresentation
    distortion 243.2
    misstatement 546.1
    perversion 555
    (error 495.1)
    (misinterpretation 523.1)
    (misteaching 538.1)
    (falsification 544.1)
    (deception 545.1)

(exaggeration 549.1)
misrepresented 555.6
misrule n.
    mismanagement 699.2
    anarchy 738.2
misrule v. 699.8
miss n. girl 129.5
    mistake 495.2
    failure 732.1
Miss n. 374.4
miss v. miscarry 304.2
    pretermit 460.7
    not understand 519.5
    need 640.6
    bungle 699.9
    fail 732.5
    lose 776.2
miss fire 732.5
miss stays
    about-ship 267.24
    miscarry 304.2
    fail 732.5
Missa 998.7
missal 998.9
missal stand 1000.3
missay 583.4
missaying
    barbarism 563.1
    wordplay 842.5
missel bird 366.22
misshape n. 243.1
misshape v. 243.3
misshapen 243.5
    (ugly 846.7)
missile 727.6, 14
    (shot 284.4)
    (projectile 284.5)
missing
    nonexistent 2.7
    absent 187.10
    disappeared 449.5
missing link
    deficiency 53.2
    oddity 83.4
mission task 625.2
    commission 755.1
missionary
    teacher 540.4
    evangelist 996.4
missis 374.3
missive 592.2
Missouri
    from Missouri 485.10
misspell 523.2
misspelling 523.1
misspend 818.3
misstate falsify 544.3
    (mislead 495.11)
    misrepresent 555.4
misstatement
    mistake 495.2
    falsification 544.1
    lie 546.1
    misrepresentation 555.1
misstep 495.3
missy 129.5
mist n. rain 348.11
    haze 353.5

mist — moderation

mist (*continued*)
 (moisture 339.1)
 (shade 424.1)
mist *v.* haze 353.9
 dim 422.6
mistake *n.* 495.2
 (misjudgment 481.1)
 (misinterpretation 523.1)
 (fault 651.2)
 make a mistake 495.8
mistake *v.* 495.8
 (misinterpret 523.2)
mistaken 495.13
 be mistaken 495.7
mistaught 538.3
misteach 538.2
 (mislead 495.11)
 (misrepresent 555.4)
misteaching *n.* 538
 (misrepresentation 555.1)
misteaching *adj.* 538.4
Mister 373.3
 (title 877.2)
misterm 565.6
misthink 481.5
mistime misdate 115.2
 ill-time 135.4
mistimed 135.6
mistral 349.9, 11
mistranslate 523.2
mistranslation 523.1
mistress woman 374.2
 schoolmistress 540.2
 master 745.1
 proprietress 779.2
 inamorata 897.7
 kept woman 962.3
 (paramour 903.8)
Mistress 374.3
 (title 877.2)
mistrust *n.*
 doubt 485.2
 (fearfulness 860.2)
 jealousy 920.1
mistrust *v.*
 doubt 485.6
 (fear 860.8)
 be jealous 920.2
mistrustful 485.10
misty cloudy 353.11
 (moist 339.7)
 dim 422.8
 opaque 426.4
 opalescent 427.4
 indistinct 447.5
 obscure 519.7
misunderstand 523.2
 (misjudge 481.5)
 (not understand 519.5)
misunderstanding
 mistake 495.2
 misinterpretation 523.1
 variance 713.2
misunderstood 523.3
misusage

ill-treatment 649.4
misuse 679.1
misuse *n.* 679
 ~ of words 523.1
 misemployment 679
 (perversion 343.2)
 (waste 638.1)
misuse *v.*
 maltreat 649.7
 misemploy 679.2
 (pervert 243.4)
misventure 735.3
mite modicum 32.2
 (pittance 640.5)
 child 129.3
 diminutive 193.2, 5
 insect 366.24
 trifle 643.3
 coin 800.8
miter, mitre *n.*
 joint 43.3
 headdress 747.3
 clerical hat 999.1
miter, mitre *v.* 43.6
mithridate 662.12
mitigate
 modulate 174.2
 (reduce 36.4)
 (inactivate 683.11)
 qualify 469.3
 relieve 834.4
 (improve 658.13)
mitigation
 decrease 36.1
 modulation 174.2
 qualification 469.1
 relief 707.4; 834.1
 extenuation 937.3
mitigative 469.6
mitigator 174.3
Mitis green 435.2
mitosis 161.5
mitt, mitten 225.30
 (wrap 384.13)
mittimus
 dismissal 297.4
 writ 741.3
 judge 967
mix *n.* mixture 41.4
 confusion 59.2
 muddle 704.2
mix *v.* mingle 41.6
 (join 43.5)
 (combine 48.3)
 (interlace 219.8)
 (variegate 440.4)
 keep company 892.9
 mix up
 derange 61.2, 5
 (mix 41.6)
 side with 709.5
mixed composite 41.9
 (variegated 440.5)
 phonetics 402.11
mixen 653.8
mixer 892.8
mixture 41
 (junction 43.1)
 (combination 48.1, 2)
 (composition 54.1)
 (jumble 59.2)

(miscellany 72.8)
 (multiformity 81.1)
 (solution 335.3)
 (variegation 440.1)
mix-up mixture 41.4
 confusion 59.2
 contest 720.2
mizzenmast
 stern 235.7
 mast 273.12
mizzle *n.* 348.11
mizzle *v.* depart 293.5
 drizzle 348.25
 flee 623.10
mnemonic *n.* 505.5
mnemonic *adj.* 505.17
mnemonics, Mnemosyne 505.9
moan *n.* 839.1
moan *v.* blow 349.22
 sough 405.5
 lament 839.9
moat trench 259.2
 channel 350.1
 fortification 717.3
mob *n.* crowd 72.3, 4, 8
 (multitude 102.2)
 clique 712.2
 masses 876.1
mob *v.* 930.6
mobcap 225.26
mobile
 changeable 149.5
 expressive 822.6
mobility
 changeableness 149.1
 expressibility 822.1
 commonalty 876.1
mobilization
 assemblage 72.1
 motion 264.1
 military ~ 722.3
mobilize
 make movable 264.7
 ~ troops 722.10
mobocracy 738.2
moccasin 225.27
mock *n.* sham 545.6
 gibe 930.3
mock *v.* imitate 19.6
 laugh at 838.7
 ridicule 856.4
 scoff 930.6
mock *adj.*
 imitation 19.12
 pseudo 545.13
 derisive 856.7
mocker 19.4
mockery
 unsubstantiality 4.3
 imitation 19.2
 sophism 477.2
 false pretense 544.2
 sham 545.6
 ridicule 856.1
 derision 930.2
 (impiety 988.1)
mock-heroic *n.* 597.1
mock-heroic *adj.*
 verse 597.13
 farcical 855.5

burlesque 856.7
mocking 104.7
mockingbird
 imitator 19.4
 bird 366.22
 songbird 416.11
mock moon, mock sun 420.12
modal extrinsic 6.2
 conditional 7.3
 circumstantial 8.5
modality
 extrinsicality 6.1
 state 7.1
mode state 7.1
 music 413.20
 syllogism 476.5
 fashion 852.1
model *n.*
 duplicate 21.2
 prototype 22.1
 (outline 626.2)
 measurement 466.2
 figure 554.4
 precept 697.1
 good example 948.1
model *v.*
 ~ after 19.10
 form 240.6
 sculpture 557.9
 (depict 554.7)
modeler, modeller 559.4
modeling, modelling 557.1
 (composition 54.2)
modelmaker 690.8
moderate *v.*
 temper 174.5
 (reduce 36.4)
 (weaken 160.8)
 (inactivate 683.11)
 (pacify 723.4)
 (restrain 751.6)
 (compose 826.7)
 retard 275.7
 qualify 469.3
 mediate 724.3
moderate *adj.*
 inconsiderable 32.8
 tempered 174.6
 (mediocre 736.3)
 (restrained 751.10)
 slow 275.8
 lenient 740.4
 cheap 815.8
 temperate 953.6
 be moderate 174.4
moderately
 somewhat 32.14
 (tolerably 736.4)
 in moderation 174.8
moderation
 moderateness 174
 (mean 29.1)
 (reduction 36.1)
 (lenity 740.1)
 (restraint 751.1)
 contentment 831.1
 temperance 953.1
 in moderation 174.8
 (midway 628.4)

968

moderations — monger

moderations 461.3
moderato 174.6
moderator
 temperer 174.3
 (palliative 662.6)
 lamp ~ 423.11
 mediator 724.2
 judge 967.1
modern *n.* 123.4
modern *adj.* 123.11
modernism
 newness 123.3
 (vogue 852.1)
 art 556.6
modernist *n.*
 neoterist 123.4
 artist 559.1
modernist *adj.* 556.19
modernistic 123.11
modernity, modern-
 ization 123.3
modernize 123.7
modernizer 123.4
modest
 inconsiderable 32.8
 diffident 881.5
 (humble 879.4)
 decent 960.2
 be modest 881.3
modestly 881.7
modesty
 diffidence 881
 (underestimation
 483.1)
 (humility 879.1)
 decency 960.1
modicum
 minimum 32.2
 pittance 786.2
modifiability 149.1
modifiable
 convertible 144.9
 changeable 149.5
modification
 change 140.1
 (variation 15.4)
 tone 402.2
 qualification 469.1
modificatory 469.6
modifier 140.4
modify quantify 25.5
 change 140.6
 (differentiate 15.6)
 qualify 469.3
modillion 215.11, 17
modish 852.7
modiste 225.38
modulate *v.*
 change 140.5, 6
 moderate 174.5
 qualify 469.3
modulate *adj.* 174.6
modulation
 change 140.1
 moderation 174.2
 (pacification 723.1)
 tone 402.2
 orchestration 413.3
modulative 174.7
modulator 174.3
module prototype 22.1
 integer 87.3

diameter 202.3
modulus 84.2
modus operandi
 method 627.1
 usage 677.2
 conduct 692.1
mofussil 181.2
mog 264.6
mogul 642.5
Mogul 745.3
mohair 219.5
Mohammed 513.2;
 986.3
Mohammedan *n.*
 984.18
Mohammedan *adj.*
 984.27
Mohammedanism
 984.8
Mohawk Indian 434.5
 savage 913.3
Mohock 913.2
mohur 800.5
moider confuse 458.9
 perplex 475.8
 embarrass 704.7
moidore 800.5
moiety part 51.1
 half 91.3
moil *n.* 686.3
moil *v.* 686.6
moiler 690.2
Moira 601.4
moist *v.* wet 337.5
 moisten 339.5
moist *adj.* 339.7
 (sweaty 299.11)
 (watery 337.6)
 (rainy 348.27)
 (cloudy 353.11)
 be moist 339.6
moisten wet 337.5
 humidify 339.5
moisture 339
moistureproof 340.11
moke network 219.4
 ass 271.10
 Negro 431.4
molar 253.3
molasses
 adherer 46.3
 semiliquid 352.3
 sweetening 396.4
mold, mould *n.*
 die 22.3
 kind 75.2
 form 240.1
 soil 342.1, 2
 fungi 369.4
 decay 659.2
mold, mould *v.*
 form 240.6
 (convert 144.6)
 model 557.9
 decay 659.7
 create 976.7
moldable, mouldable
 324.6
molder, moulder *n.*
 559.4
molder, moulder *v.*
 659.7

molding, moulding
 847.4
moldy, mouldy
 antiquated 124.9
 foul 653.17
 decayed 659.13
mole tower 206.3
 pelt 223.12
 protuberance 250.2
 promontory 250.5
 (blemish 848.1)
 discoloration 440a.1
 morbid growth
 655.16
 anchorage 666.4
 embankment 706.2
 fortification 717.3
molecular 193.10
molecule
 modicum 32.2
 diminutive 193.2
mole-eyed 443.15
molehill
 diminutive 193.2
 lowness 207.4
 trifle 643.3
moleskin 223.12
molest 830.5
 (hurt 649.6)
molestation
 ill-treatment 649.4
 affliction 830.2
moll 374.2
molla, mollah See
 mullah
mollescence 324.2
mollescent 324.10
mollification
 modulation 174.2
 (pacification 723.1)
 softening 324.2
 relief 834.1
mollifier 174.3
mollify
 modulate 174.5
 (pacify 723.4)
 soften 324.4
 relieve 834.4
mollifying, mollitious
 324.10
mollusca 368.9
molluscan molluscoid
 368.16
Molluscoida, mollusk
 368.6
molly
 hermaphrodite 83.5
 mollycoddle 160a.3
mollycoddle 160a.3
 (weakling 160.4)
 (coward 862.2)
Moloch 991.4
molt, moult 226.6
molten 384.24
 (hot 382.16)
molybdenum 635.6
molybdomancy 511.3
moment period 108.1
 instant 113.2
 cause 153.1
 influence 175.1
 momentum 276.1

importance 642.1
 authority 737.2
 for the moment 111.8
momentary 113.4
 (brief 111.7)
momentous 642.10
 (eventful 151.6)
momentum 276.1
Mon 560.4
monachal
 monkish 995.9
 monastic 1000.6
monachism 995.2
monad *n.* unit 87.2
 diminutive 193.2
 microbe 193.4
 psychon 994.2
monad *adj.* 87.8
monadic 87.8
monarch 745.2
monarchic 737.16
monarchy 737.4
monas 87.2
monastery 1000.4
monastic *n.* 996.11
monastic *adj.*
 monkish 995.9
 claustral 1000.6
monasticism 995.2
 (celibacy 904.1)
Monday 106.3
monde 852.4
monecious See mo-
 noecious
moner, moneron 193.4
monetary 800.21
monetize 800.19
money 800
 (assets 780.7)
 come into money
 803.6
 for money 775.13
 make money
 profit 775.7
 acquire wealth 803.6
 money down 807.11
moneybag 802.2
moneybags
 riches 803.1
 rich man 803.2
money broker 787.2
moneyed 803.8
moneyer
 financier 797.6
 coiner 800.18
moneygrub, money-
 grubber 819.2
moneygrubbing *n.*
 775.1
moneygrubbing *adj.*
 819.4
moneylender 787.2
 (financier 797.6)
moneyless 804.7
money-making 775.1
moneymonger 787.2
money order
 epistle 592.2
 commercial paper
 800.7
money's worth 812.3
monger 797.1, 3

Mongolian — moonlight

Mongolian n. 560.4
Mongolian adj. 11.8
  (native 188.11)
mongoose 366.17
mongrel n. hybrid 41.5
  dog 366.6
  scoundrel 949.1
mongrel adj.
  hybrid 41.10
  language 579.3
  vulgar 851.6
'mongst among 41.11
  between 228.13
moniker, monicker,
  monica name 564.2
  nickname 565.3
moniliform 249.10
monism 451.19
monition
  intimation 527.1
  dehortation 616.1
  warning 668.1
monitor student 541.1
  director 694.1
  warning sign 668.3
  adviser 695.3
  (teacher 540.4)
  warship 726.11
monitorial 541.9; 695.8
monitory
  predictive 511.11
  advisory 527.13;
    695.8
  dissuasive 616.4
  warning 668.9
monitory letter 592.2
monk monkey 366.16
  ferret 366.17
  religious 996.11
  (celibate 904.2)
monkey imitator 19.4
  brat 129.1
  supporter 215.2
  hammer 276.4
  animal 366.16
  mortgage 771.1
  eyesore 846.3
  laughingstock 857.1
  temper 900.1
monkey jacket 225.16
monkey rail 273.7
monkey-rigged 273.16
monkeyshine 842.3, 7
monkhood 995.2
monkish 995.9
monk's cloth
  cloth 219.5
  rough 256.2
monkshood 663.6
monniker See moniker
Monoceros 318.6
monochord
  concord 413.1
  instrument 417.6, 13
monochordist 416.4
monochrome
  colorlessness 429.1
  picture 556.19
monocle 445.3
monocled 445.10
monoclinous 83.12

monocoque 273a.1
monocotyledonous
  369.11
monocracy 737.4
monocular
  poor-sighted 443.14
  monocled 445.10
monocularity 443.1
monocycle 272.14
monodic
  acoustic 402.12
  unisonance 413.26
monodrama 599.3
monodramatic 599.28
monodramatist 599.22
monody
  unisonance 412.1
  song 415.3
  poem 597.2
  dirge 839.3
monoecious, monoe-
  cious 357.10
monogamist 903.5
monogamous 903.14
monogamy 903.2
monogenesis 161.2
monogram 550.11;
  561.5
monogrammatic 533.6
monograph
  writing 590.3
  description 594.1
  dissertation 595.1
monographist
  writer 590.11
  dissertator 595.3
monography 590.1
monogynist 903.5
monogynous 903.14
monogyny 903.2
monolith
  tombstone 363.15
  (rock 342.4)
  monument 551.4
monologic 589.4
monologist
  speaker 582.5
  soliloquist 589.2
monologize, mono-
  loguize 589.3
  (act 599.26)
monologue, mono-
  log n. speech 582.2
  soliloquy 589.1
  drama 599.3
monologue, mono-
  log v. 589.3
monology 589.1
monomachy 720.3
monomania 503.1, 7
  (bigotry 606.2)
  (passion 865.5)
monomaniac n. 504.1
monomaniac adj.
  503.2
monophonous
  acoustic 402.12
  unisonance 413.26
monophthong 402.2
monoplane 273a.1
monoplanist 269a.1
monopolist

restrictionist 751.5
self-seeker 943.2
monopolize 777.5
monopoly trust 712.5
  possession 777.2
monospermous 87.9
monostich 572.1
monosyllabic 561.9
monosyllable
  syllable 561.3
  word 562.1
monotheism
  theism 983.1
  ism 984.4
monotheist
  theist 983.1
  cultist 984.14
monotheistic 983a.7
monotone 104.1
monotonous
  uniform 16.5
  repetitional 104.7
  (continuous 69.6)
  unchanged 141.6
  style 575.2
  tedious 841.8
  (dull 843.5)
monotony
  regularity 16.2
  equality 27.1
  tedium 841.3
  (dullness 843.1)
monotype 591.6
Monroe Doctrine
  748.4
monsieur 373.3
Monsignor 877.4
Mons Mensae 318.6
monsoon rain 348.11
  wind 349.9
monster n.
  monstrosity 83.6
  behemoth 192.8
  ugly thing 846.3
  evildoer 913.4
monster adj. 192.15
monstrance case 191.8
  church 998.8
monstrosity
  monster 83.6
  (prodigy 872.1)
  hugeness 192.3
  deformity 243.1
monstrous
  immense 31.9
  unusual 83.10
  huge 192.15
  deformed 243.5
  absurd 497.4
  ugly 846.6
  vulgar 851.6
  wonderful 870.7
  nefarious 945.16
monstrously 31.20
monte 840.12
Montes 560.4
montgolfier 273a.5
month 108.1
  (date 114.4)
month after month
  long 110.11
  constantly 136.6

month in, month out
  long 110.11
  constantly 136.6
monthlies 299.7
monthly n. 593.6
monthly adj. 138.11
monthly epact 108.2
monticle, monticule
  206.2
montiform 206.17
Montpellier green
  435.2
monument tower 206.3
  tombstone 363.15
  record 551.4
  (memorial 505.7)
monumental
  huge 192.15
  high 206.13
  statuesque 557.10
monumentalize 112.3
monumentary 557.10
moo 412.2
mooch, mouch n. 547.2
mooch, mouch v.
  play truant 187.8
  ~ over 264.6
  wander 266.14
  ~ off 623.10
  idle 683.8
  beg 765.6
  steal 791.9
moocha 225.22
moocher, moucher
  idler 683.7
  beggar 767.2
mood nature 5.3
  state 7.1
  tendency 176.1
  humor 820.1
in the mood
  willing 602.8
  disposed 820.4
not in the mood 603.5
moodiness 901.2
moody glum 837.9
  sullen 901.8
moon n. month 108.1
  changeableness
    149.2
  heavenly body 318.5
  (moonlight 420.9)
moon v. 458.6
moonbeam 420.3, 9
moon-blind, moon
  blindness, moon-
  blink 443.2
mooncalf
  monstrosity 83.6
  fool 501.1
moon dog 420.12
moon-eyed 443.14
moonfaced 192.12
moonglade, moonglow
  420.9
moonless 421.7
moonlight n.
  light 420.9
  (moon 318.5)
  (semidarkness
    422.2)
  pink 434.3

moonlight — moss

illicit liquor 959.9
moonlight *v.* 959.20
moonlighter 959.12
moonlighting 959.9
moonlike 245.7
moonlit 423.14
moonraker 273.13
moonraking 458.3
moonsail 273.13
moonshade
  shadow 422.3
  light shield 424.5
moonshine
  nullity 4.2
  month 108.1
  moonlight 420.9
  sophism 477.2
  nonsense 517.2
  (absurdity 497.1)
  (trumpery 643.5)
  false pretense 544.2
  untruth 546.1
  pretext 619.1
  illicit liquor 959.9
moonshiner 959.12
moonshining 959.9
moonstone stone 342.4
  transparency 425.2
  gem 847.8
moon-struck 503.12
moony, mooney 458.11
moor *n.* hill 206.2
  plain 344.1
  (waste 169.2)
  (open space 180.3)
  marsh 345.1
moor *v.* tie 43.6
  locate 184.14
  anchor 267.12
  tether 751.7
moored fast 150.5
  located 184.17
mooring drag 666.2
mooring mast 267a.28
moorings
  fastening 45.2
  anchor 666.2
  haven 666.4
mooring swivel 273.14
moory 345.3
moose 366.11
moot *v.* 476.11
moot *adj.* 475.9
mooted
  doubtful 475.9
  assumed 514.9
mooter 476.9
mop *n.* hair 256.3
  cleaner 652.7
mop *v.* 652.9
mope *n.* idler 683.7
  sad person 837.5
mope *v.* walk 266.16
  be sad 837.6
  sulk 901.6
mope-eyed 443.14
moper 683.7
mopes blues 837.1
  sulks 901.2
mopish glum 837.9
  sulky 901.8
moppet child 129.1

endearment 902.4
mopsy, mopsey
  endearment 902.4
  strumpet 962.2
mopus dreamer 515.7
  money 800.1
mora 597.6
moraine residue 40.2
  silt 270.3
moral *n.* likeness 17.6
  conclusion 480.1
  maxim 496.1
moral *adj.*
  ethical 926.12
  upright 939.7
  virtuous 944.3
morale 926.4
moralism 451.11
moralistic 926.12
morality drama 599.3
  ethics 926.4
  virtue 944.1
moralize
  discuss 476.11
  sermonize 537.11
morals 926.4
  (right 922.1)
morass 345.1
moration, moratorium 133.2
moratory 133.8
morbid 655.25
morbidity 655.1
morbific 657.3
morceau
  modicum 32.2
  music 415.3
  writing 590.3
mordacious
  pungent 392.5
  gruff 895.7
  malignant 907.6
mordacity
  pungency 392.1
  gruffness 895.2
  malignity 907.1
mordant *n.* 428.4
mordant *adj.*
  acrid 171.10
  pungent 392.5
  vigorous 574.5
  gruff 895.7
mordent 413.10
Mordvinian 560.4
more *adj.* 37.7
more *adv.* beyond 33.9
  additionally 37.8
  all the more 33.10
  more or less 25.7
no more
  extinct 2.10
  (destroyed 162.7)
  past 122.8
  dead 360.8
morendo 415.30
moreover 37.8
Moresque 847.3
Morgan 271.4
morganatic marriage 903.2
morganite 434.5
morgue

deadhouse 363.17
  filing room 591.11
moribund 360.9
  (ailing 655.23)
morion 717.2
Morisco 847.3
Mormon
  polygamist 903.5
  sectary 984.14
Mormonism 984.4
morn 125.1
morning 125.3
  (beginning 66.1)
  (earliness 132.1)
  (semidarkness 422.2)
in the morning 125.5
morning dress 225.23
mornings 125.5
morning song 415.3
morningtide, morntime 125.1
Moro 560.4
morocco 593.10
morology 499.6
moron
  ignoramus 493.1
  simpleton 501.1
moronic 499.13
moronity 499.3
morose 901.8
morosis 499.3
  (insanity 503.1)
morosity 901.2
Morpheau 683.15
morpheme 562.1
Morpheus 683.5
morphine 662.7
morphological 240.9
morphologist 368.2
morphology
  form 240.4
  organic science 357.5
  zoology 368.1
morphon 357.2
morphotic 240.7
morris dance 840.7
morrow 121.2
Morse code 550.15
  (telegraphy 532a.3)
morsel modicum 32.2
  (piece 51.3)
  food 298.2, 9
mortal *n.* 372.3
mortal *adj.*
  transient 111.6
  fatal 361.16
  human 372.5
  fatiguing 688.8
  tedious 841.8
mortal *adv.* 31.15
mortality
  transience 111.1
  death rate 360.1
  man 372.1
mortally 31.15
mortal sin 947.2
mortar *n.*
  conversion 144.4
  plaster 223.19
  (cement 45.6)

  weapon 727.9, 11
mortar *v.* 223.26
mortarboard 550.11
mortgage *n.* 771.1
  (loan 787.1)
  (credit 805.2)
mortgage *v.* 771.5
mortgagee
  trustee 779.4
  lender 787.2
  (creditor 805.3)
mortgagor, mortgager
  possessor 779.1
  debtor 806.4
mortician 363.6
mortification
  death 360.1
  gangrene 655.16
  vexation 828.4
  source of ~ 830.2
  discontent 832.1
  humiliation 879.1
  penance 952.3
  asceticism 955.1
mortified
  diseased 655.25
  putrefied 659.13
  chagrined 828.13
mortify putrefy 659.7
  vex 830.5
  dissatisfy 832.4
  humiliate 879.3
mortifying
  annoying 830.12
  unsatisfactory 832.6
mortise, mortice *n.* 43.3
mortise, mortice *v.*
  attach 43.6
  interlace 219.8
  ~ type 591.14
mortmain 748.5
  in mortmain 781.7
mortuary *n.* 363.17
mortuary *adj.*
  of death 360.8, 10
  funereal 363.25
mortuous
  deathlike 360.10
  fatal 361.16
mosaic *n.*
  ceramics 384.14
  checkerwork 440.3
  (mixture 41.4)
  art 556.9
mosaic *adj.*
  multiform 81.2
  checkered 440.8
mosaic gold 545.6
Mosaic Law 985.3
Moselle 959.7
mosey, mosy
  go slow 275.5
  depart 293.4
Moslem *n.* 984.18
Moslem *adj.* 984.27
Moslemism 984.8
mosque, mosk 1000.1
mosquito 366.24
mosquito boat 726.11
mosquito fleet 726.10
moss nap 256.10

mossback — move

moss (*continued*)
  elastic 325.2
  marsh 345.1
  vegetation 367.2
  plant 369.5
  green 435.2, 3
  money 800.1
mossback 141.3
moss-backed 128.8
moss green 435.2
moss-grown
  antiquated 124.9
  herbal 367.14
  moldy 659.13
mosstrooper
  soldier 726.4
  brigand 792.3
mossy 367.14
most
  extremely 31.19
  almost 32.15
  at most 32.13
  the most 33.10
mosy See mosey
mot maxim 496.1
  witticism 842.4
Motazilite 984.18
mote modicum 32.2
  diminutive 193.2
  lightness 320.2
  trifle 643.3
  mote in the eye
    prejudice 481.2
    bigotry 606.2
motet
  sacred music 415.11
  hymn 990.2
moth insect 366.24
  blight 663.2
  (destroyer 165.1)
  (decay 659.2)
moth-eaten
  antiquated 124.9
  aged 128.8
  deteriorated 659.13
  trite 843.6
mother 166.7
Mother Carey's
  chicken bird 366.22
  omen 512.2
  warning sign 668.3
motherhood 166.3
mother-in-law
  kinsman 11.3
  mother 166.7
motherland 182.2
motherly
  maternal 166.10
  benevolent 906.6
Mother of God 977.3
mother-of-pearl
  opalescence 427.2
  variegation 440.2
mothership 166.3
mother superior
  mistress 745.1
  nun 996.12
mother wit 498.1
motif music 415.19
  topic 454.1
  needlework 847.6

motile 264.8
motility 264.1
motion *n.*
  movement 264
  (travel 266.1)
  (progression 282.1)
  (activity 682.1)
  topic 454.1
  signal 550.3
  resolution 626.1
  offer 763.1
  proposal 765.3
  go through the motions 19.7
  in motion 264.8
  set in motion
    move 264.7
    start 284.14
    use 677.5
motion *v.* 550.20
motionless 265.7
  (inert 172.3)
  (inactive 681.3; 683.12)
motion picture 599.9
  (photograph 556.11)
motion-picture projector 445.6
motivate 615.7
  (influence 175.6)
  (move 264.7)
  (impel 276.7)
  (propel 284.10)
motivation 615.2
  (cause 153.1)
  (impulse 276.1)
motive *n.* music 415.19
  theme 454.1
  consideration 615
  (cause 153.1)
  (explanation 522.1)
  (intention 620.1)
  ostensible ~ 619.1
motive *v.* 615.7
motive *adj.* 264.8
motley *n.*
  variegation 440.1
  comedy 599.4
motley *adj.*
  multiform 81.2
  variegated 440.7
motophone 418.6
motor *n.*
  automobile 272.15, 16
  machine 633.2
motor *adj.* 264.8
motorboat 273.4
motorbus, motorcar 272.6, 15
motorcycle *n.* 272.14
motorcycle *v.* 266.18
motoring, motorism 266.7
motorist 268.10
motorium 264.1
motorman 268.11
motte, mott 367.7
mottle 440.4
mottled 440.7
motto maxim 496.1
  (phrase 566.1)

device 550.5
mouch See mooch
mouchard
  informer 527.6
  detective 528.9
mouflon, moufflon 366.8
mouillé 402.11
mould, mouldable etc.
  See mold etc.
moult See molt
mound hill 206.2
  (incline 217.2)
  (promontory 250.5)
  grave 363.13
  embankment 706.2
  fortification 717.3
mount *n.* height 206.2
  horse 271.3
mount *v.* be great 31.4
  be high 206.9
  aviate 267a.31
  ascent 305.4
  (increase 35.4)
  lift 307.5
  ~ up to 812.6
  display 882.6
mountain
  height 206.2
  (elevation 307.1)
  gravity 319.2
mountained 206.17
mountaineer
  backsettler 188.6
  traveler 268.1
mountain gun 727.11
mountain lion 366.3
mountainous 206.17
mountebank
  impostor 548.3
  actor 599.20
mounted infantry 726.8
mounting 305.1
mourn 839.6
  (grieve 828.11; 837.6)
mourner 363.7
mourners' bench 950.1; 1000.3
mournful
  grievous 830.11
  sorrowful 837.11
  plaintive 839.13
  (funereal 363.25)
mourning *n.*
  clothes 225.6
  lamentation 839.1, 4
  (funeral 363.4)
in mourning
  in black 431.10
  lamenting 839.13
mourning *adj.* 839.13
mouse *n.*
  diminutive 193.2
  animal 366.17
  discoloration 440a.1
  black eye 443.5
mouse *v.* 461.16
mouse over
  ponder 451.27
  study 461.18

mouse-eared 418.14
mousehole 260.1
mousehound 366.17
mouser 366.4
mousetrap 545.4
mousquetaire glove 225.30
mousseline, mousseline de soie 219.5
mousseux 353.10
moustache See mustache
mouth *n.* opening 260.1
  embouchure 260.3
  (inlet 294.5)
  (outlet 295.5)
  eater 298.41
  sea inlet 343.1
mouth *v.* talk 582.6, 7
  mumble 583.2
mouthful
  quantity 25.2
  modicum 32.2
  fill 52.3
  bite 298.2
mouth organ 417.4
mouthpiece
  embouchure 260.2, 3
  music instrument 417.13
  informant 527.5
  spokesman 582.5
  deputy 759.1
  lawyer 968.1
mouthwash 662.8
mouth-watering *n.* 865.3
mouth-watering *adj.*
  appetizing 394.7; 865.21
  tantalizing 617.4
mouthy 577.7
movability, moveability 149.1
movable, moveable *n.*
  inheritance 775.4
  property 780.5
movable, moveable *adj.*
  changeable 149.5
  transferable 270.11
movableness, moveableness 264.1
move *n.* motion 264.1
  attempt 675.1
  act 680.2
on the move
  moving 264.10
  departing 293.10
  active 682.20
move *v.* influence 175.6
  remove 185.2
  set in motion 264.6
  (travel 266.12)
  (progress 282.2)
  (propel 284.10)
  transfer 270.6
  impel 276.7
  blow 349.22
  propound 514.7
  motivate 615.7, 9
  (influence 175.6)

972

act 680.5
advise 695.4
propose 763.2
excite 824.2
move aside 279.7
move away
 recede 287.2
 depart 293.4
move forward 282.2
move heaven and
 earth
 persevere 604a.2
 try hard 675.4, 5
 go all lengths 682.12
move off recede 287.2
 depart 293.4
move out 295.6
move to nod 894.9
 make obeisance
 928.6
moved 821.7
moveless 265.7
movement
 motion 264.1
 (travel 266.1)
 removal 270.1
 music 415.15
 gesture 550.3
 action 680.1
 bustle 682.6
movements 633.2
mover creator 164.1
 wanderer 268.2
movie 599.9
movie-goer 599.23
movieland 599.1, 9
moving n.
 dislocation 185.1
 motion 264.1
 removal 270.1
moving adj. 264.8
 (traveling 266.23)
 (progressive 282.3)
moving picture 599.9
moving staircase 307.3
mow n. stack 72.5
 haymow 636.4
mow v. cut off 38.6
 smooth 255.4
 reap 371.8
mow down
 demolish 162.4
 fell 213.7
 cut down 308.5
moxa 384.11
mozzetta, mozetta
 999.1
M.P. 696.8
Mr. 373.3
Mrs. 374.3
Mru 560.4
much v.
 make much of 897.11
 caress 902.8
much adv. 31.15
much of a muchness
 approximative 9.7;
 17.14
 superfluity 641.1
too much
 superfluity 641.1
 excessive 641.5

overmuch 641.7
much ado about nothing
 overestimation 482.1
 (exaggeration
 549.1)
 disappointment
 509.1
 triviality 643.2, 9
 boasting 884.1
much cry and little
 wool
 overestimation 482.1
 disappointment
 509.1
 triviality 643.2
 boasting 884.1
muchness 31.1
mucid viscid 352.8
 slimy 653.17
mucidness 352.1
mucilage cement 45.6
 gluten 352.3
muck mud 352.4
 filth 653.5, 7
 money 800.1
mucker 306.2
 come a mucker 306.6
muckrake 934.3
muckraker 936.1
 (scandalmonger
 532.5)
mucksy 352.9
muckworm 819.2
mucky 352.9
 (dirty 653.16)
mucor 659.2
mucosity 352.1
mucous
 lubricant 332.5
 viscid 352.8
mucronate 253.11
mucronation 253.1
muculent
 lubricant 332.5
 viscid 352.8
mucus lubricant 332.2
 fluid 333.2
 semiliquid 352.3
mud 352.4
 (dirt 653.5)
muddle n.
 confusion 59.2;
 458.4
 perplexity 475.2
 predicament 704.2
in a muddle
 bewildered 475.16
 in difficulty 704.11
muddle v.
 derange 61.2
 complicate 61.5
 confuse 458.9
 be indiscriminate
 465a.2
 perplex 475.8
muddle away
 waste 638.2
 squander 818.3
muddled
 bewildered 475.16
 intoxicated 959.21

muddleheaded
 confused 458.12
 stupid 499.12
muddlement
 confusion 458.4
 perplexity 475.2
muddy mucky 352.9
 (soft 324.6)
 (soaked 339.8)
 (marshy 345.3)
 (pulpy 354.5)
 (dirty 653.16)
 blurred 422.8
 opaque 426.4
 obscure 519.7
muddybrained 499.12
mudhole 352.5
mud lark
 race horse 271.8
 sweep 652.6
 vagabond 876.9
mudstone 342.4
muezzin 996.7
muff n.
 mollycoddle 160a.3
 clothes 225.30
 (wrap 384.13)
 beard 256.5
 bungle 699.4
 bungler 701
muff v. 699.9
muffin 298.11
muffle
 ~ up 225.41
 silence 403.5
 mute 408a.4; 581.5
 keep secret 528.11
 mumble 583.2
muffled faint 405.9
 nonresonant 408a.6
muffler veil 225.12
 neckpiece 225.33
 (wrap 384.13)
 mute 408a.3
mufti clothes 225.9
 judge 967.1
 priest 996.7
mug cup 191.11
 face 234.4
 mouth 260.2
 man 373.2
 ceramics 384.14
mugger, muggar,
 muggur 366.18
muggy moist 339.7
 sultry 382.18
mughouse 959.13
mugient 412.3
mugwump
 apostate 607.5
 personage 642.5
Muharram 840.2
Mukden 722.5
mulatto 41.5
 (negro 431.4)
mulberry 437.4
mulct n. 974.2
mulct v.
 swindle 791.12
 fine 974.3
mule mongrel 41.5
 (animal 366.2)

obstinate person
 606.3
 stubbornness 606.4
muleteer 268.9
muley head 366.12
muliebrity 160a.1
muliebrous 160a.5
mulish asinine 271.13
 obstinate 606.6
mull n. height 206.2
 promontory 250.5
 failure 732.1
mull v. heat 384.16
 sweeten 396.7
 ~ over 451.27
mullah, mulla
 scholar 492.1
 teacher 540.1
 priest 996.7
mullet 98.1
mulligan mixture 41.4
 stew 298.17
mulligatawny 298.16
mullion 215.16
multangular 244.5
multicolor 440.1
multicolored 440.5
multifarious
 multiform 81.2
 (irrelative 10.5)
 (ununiform 16a.2)
 numerous 102.5
multifariousness 81.1
 (irrelation 10.1)
multiferous 102.5
multifid 51.8
multifold
 multiform 81.2
 numerous 102.5
multiform 81.2
 (dissimilar 18.4)
multiformity 81
 (nonuniformity
 16a.1)
 (mixture 41.1)
multilateral
 many-sided 236.7
 multiangular 244.5
multilocular 191.23
multiloquence 584.1
 (eloquence 582.3)
multiloquent 584.5
 (eloquent 582.12)
mu'tiparity 168.1
multiparous 168.8
multipartite 44.12
multiphase 81.2
multiplane 273a.1
multiple n.
 number 84.2
 multiplier 102.3
multiple adj. 102.5
multiple personality
 503.2
multiplex
 multiform 81.2
 electric 158a.12
multiplicand
 number 84.2
 multiple 102.3
multiplication
 mathematics 85.4

multiplication table — must

multiplication (cont'd)
　multiplicity 102.3
　procreation 161.2
　productiveness 168.1
multiplication table 102.3
multiplicator 84.2
multiplicity 102.1
multiplied 102.5
multiplier
　number 84.2
　multiple 102.3
multiply increase 35.4
　calculate 85.7
　pluralize 100.3
　become numerous 102.4
　give birth 161.9
　generate 161.10
　be productive 168.5
multiplying 35.6
multipotent 157.8
multisegmental 44.12
multisonous 404.9
multitude crowd 72.4
　large number 102.2
　(plurality 100.1)
　the masses 876.1
multitudinous 102.5
multitudinousness 102.1
multure 330.2
mum *adj.*
　voiceless 581.7
　taciturn 585.4
mum *int.* 585.6
mumble chew 298.45
　mutter 583.2
mumble-the-peg 840.11
Mumbo Jumbo
　god 979.2
　bogy 980.4
　fetish 993.2
mummer
　masquerader 528.7
　actor 599.19, 20
mummery
　disguise 545.5
　sanctimony 988.2
mummification
　drying 340.2
　corpse 362.1
　embalmment 363.3
　(paleontology 357.6)
　preservation 670.2
mummify dry 340.5
　embalm 363.22
　preserve 670.4
mummy dryness 340.4
　corpse 362.1
　brown 433.1, 2
mummy-brown 433.4
mump deceive 545.7
　mumble 583.2
　beg 765.3
mumper 767.2
mumpish sad 837.9
　grumpy 901.8
mumps blues 837.1
　sulks 901.2

mumpsimus 495.1
munch *n.* 298.2
munch *v.* 298.45
Munchausenism 549.1
muncheel 272.12
mundane
　worldly 318.14
　unspiritual 989.9
mundatory 652.8
mundivagant 266.24
municipal 189.22
municipality
　town 189.16
　city government 737.4
　civil authorities 745.9
　bureau 965.2
municipium 189.16
munificence 816.1
munificent 816.4
muniment 717.3
muniments 771.1
munition 634.2
munitions
　equipment 634.1
　armament 727.1, 13
munshi, moonshee
　scholar 492.1
　teacher 540.1
Muong 560.4
murder *n.* 361.1
murder *v.* 361.10
　murder the King's English
　be ungrammatical 568.2
　stammer 583.3
　swear 908.5
murderer 361.8
murderous 361.15
　(cruel 907.9)
muricate, muriculate 253.11
murk, mirk *n.* 421.2
murk, mirk *v.*
　darken 421.5
　blacken 431.6
　discolor 440a.2
murk, mirk *adj.*
　gloomy 421.8
　opaque 426.4
　dark-colored 431.8
murky, mirky
　gloomy 421.8
　opaque 426.4
　dark-colored 431.8
　discolored 440a.3
　dismal 837.10
Murmi 560.4
murmur *n.*
　faint sound 405.2
　(trill 407.2)
　muted voice 581.3
　complaint 839.1
murmur *v.*
　ripple 348.19
　blow 349.22
　sound faintly 405.2
　(resonate 408.7)
　speak softly 581.6
　complain 839.10

murmured 405.9
murmurer 832.2
murmuring 405.10
murrain 655.18
Murray 694.7
murrey cloth 219.5
　red 434.2
murshid 996.7
muscatel 959.7
muscle *n.* 159.1
muscle *v.* 159.9
　muscle in 228.10
muscoid 369.11
muscular 159.10
muse *n.*
　preoccupation 458.3
　dream 515.5
　poet 597.10
Muse *n.* music 416.16
　belles-lettres 560.8
　poetry 597.9
　(god 979.1)
muse *v.* ponder 451.27
　abstract oneself 458.6
museful 451.35
musette 417.4
museum studio 556.15
　store 636.5
mush *n.*
　umbrella 223.4
　face 234.4
　mouth 260.2
　march 266.4
　cereal 298.15
　pulp 354.2
mush *v.* 266.16
mushroom *n.*
　umbrella 223.4
　vegetable 298.30
　plant 369.4
　upstart 876.8
mushroom *adj.* 876.11
mushy 160.14
music *n.* 413.4; 415
　(composition 54.2; 590.3)
　(harmony 413.1)
　(polyphony 413.2)
music *v.*
　set to music 415.26
　play music 416.18
musical *n.* 415.17
musical *adj.*
　melodious 413.27
　musiclike 415.28
　musicianly 416.24
　be musical 416.22
musical comedy
　musicale 415.17
　drama 599.4
musicale 415.17
musical glasses 417.1
musicality 413.4
musicalize
　set to music 415.26
　play music 416.18
music box 417.8
music case 417.13
music demy 415.21
music director 416.13
music drama 415.17

music-flowing 413.27
music hall 599.10
musician 416
musicianship 416.17
music lyre 417.13
music-mad 415.28
musicmonger 416.15
musico 416.1
musicoartistic, musicodramatic 415.28
musicofanatic 416.15
music of the spheres
　order 58.1
　stars 318.3
　concord 413.1
musicographer 416.1
musicography 415.24
musicological 415.28
musicologist 416.1
musicology 415.24
musicomania 415.25
musicomechanical 415.28
musicophilosophical 415.28
musicophobia 415.25
musicopoetic 415.28
music rack 417.13
music roll 415.21; 417.13
music supervisor 416.13
music-tongued 413.27
music wire 417.13
musing 458.3
musk 400.2, 3
musk bag 191.6
musket 727.10
musketeer
　shooter 284.8
　soldier 726.4
musketoon, musketry 727.10
muskmelon 298.32
Muskogee 560.4
musk ox 366.13
muskrat 223.12
muslin cloth 219.5
　sheet 223.9
　sail 273.13
　semitransparency 427.2
musnud, masnad
　seat 215.22
　council 696.1
　throne 747.5
muss *n.* mixture 41.4
　confusion 59.2
muss *v.*
　muss up 61.2
　(disorder 59.7)
mussal lighter 388.4
　torch 423.8
mussuk, mussuck 191.11
Mussulman 984.18
mussy untidy 59.9
　soiled 653.16
must *n.* 659.2
must, musth *n.* 961.3
must, musth *adj.* 961.11

mustache, moustache
256.5
mustang 271.3
mustard
 productiveness
  168.3
 condiment 393.1
mustard gas 334.2
mustard seed 193.2
mustee 41.5
musteline 433.4
muster *n.*
 mobilization 72.1
 schedule 611.2
 council 696.2
muster *v.*
 assemble 72.10, 11
 enumerate 85.7
musth See must
musty foul 653.17
 decayed 659.13
mut See mutt
mutability
 irregularity 139.1
 changeableness
  149.1
mutable
 irregular 139.2
 changeable 149.5
mutate 140.5, 6
mutation 140.1, 2
mutatis mutandis
 148.5
mute *n.* mourner 363.7
 sound 402.2
 muffler 408a.3
 sourdine 417.11
 dummy 581.2
 actor 599.19
mute *v.* 408a.4; 581.5
mute *adj.*
 unsounded 403.7
 nonresonant 408a.6
 voiceless 581.7
 (silent 403.6)
 taciturn 585.4
 be mute 581.4
muted faint 405.9
 nonresonant 408a.7
muteness
 aphonia 581.1
 (silence 403.1)
 taciturnity 585.1
mutescence
 silence 403.1
 nonresonance 408a.1
 aphonia 581.1
mutilate cut off 38.6
 disintegrate 44.9
 destroy 162.4
 deform 243.3
 damage 659.8
mutilated 53.5
mutilation
 excision 38.2
 distortion 243.1
 impairment 659.4
mutineer *n.* 742.3
mutineer *v.* 742.5
mutineering 742.2
mutinous 742.7
mutinousness 742.1

mutiny *n.* 742.2
 (revolution 146.1)
mutiny *v.* 742.5
mutism 581.1
mutt, mutt dog 366.6
 fool 501.1
mutter *n.* 839.1
mutter *v.*
 sound faintly 405.5
 speak softly 581.6
 mumble 583.2
 complain 839.10
 threaten 909.2
mutton meat 298.22
 sheep 366.8
mutton chops 256.5
muttonhead 501.1
muttonheaded 499.12
mutual
 correlative 12.6
 interchangeable
  148.4
mutuality 12.1
mutually 88.10
mutule 215.17
mux *n.* mixture 41.4
 confusion 59.2
mux *v.* 61.2
muzzle *n.* nose 250.4
 mouth 260.2
 embouchure 260.3
 muffler 408a.3
 restraint 752.2
muzzle *v.* disable 158.6
 restrain 751.7
 render mute 581.5
 (silence 403.5)
muzzle-loader 727.10
muzzler 349.10
muzzy
 intoxicated 959.21
 confused 458.12
mycetoid, mycological
 369.11
mycologist 369.9
mycology 369.1
myelencephalon 450.2
myna, mynah 366.22
Mynheer 373.3
myology 329.2
myomancy 511.3
myoneurosis 655.14
myopia 443.1
myopic 443.14
myriad *n.* 98.10
myriad *adj.* 102.5
myriagram, myria-
 gramme 319.4
myriameter 466.3
Myrmidon 726.4
myrrh bitter 395.3
 fragrance 400.3
myrtle tree 367.6
 green 435.2, 3
 wood 635.3
 love 897.5
myrtle green 435.2
myself 79.4
mystae 996.10
mysterious
 indistinct 447.5
 vague 475.11

 obscure 519.7
 hidden 528.17, 21
 enigmatic 533.6
 occult 994.21
mystery
 concealment 528.1
 enigma 533.2
 drama 599.3
 vocation 625.5
 cabala 994.1
 rite 998.1, 3
mystic *n.* 994.13
mystic *adj.*
 obscure 519.7
 hidden 528.17
 enigmatic 533.6
 occult 994.21
mysticism 994.1
 (philosophy 451.23)
 (concealment 528.4)
mysticize 526.5
mystification
 sophistry 477.1
 concealment 528.1
 (unintelligibility
  519.1)
 (dissimulation
  544.2)
mystify perplex 475.8
 (conceal 528.14)
 (puzzle 533.4)
 sophisticate 477.7
mytacism 583.1
myth imagining 515.4
 falsehood 546.1
mythical
 imaginary 515.12
 legendary 594.7
 mythological 979.14
mythicism 984.10
mythification 515.1
mythmaker, mythog-
 rapher 515.7
mythological
 imaginary 515.12
 mythical 979.14
mythology
 mythical lore 979.13
 religion 984.10
mythomania 544.1
mythomaniac 548.5

N

nab deceive 545.7
 arrest 751.9
 catch 789.9
 swindle 791.12
nabob
 personage 642.5
 viceroy 745.7
 rich man 803.2
nacelle 273a.10
nacre
 opalescence 427.2
 variegation 440.2
nacreous, nacrous
 opalescent 427.4
 iridescent 440.6
nadir nothing 2.2
 base 211.1

nadiral 211.5
naevoid, naevus See
 nevoid etc.
nag *n.* 271.3
nag *v.* 713.7
Naga 560.4
nagging *n.* 932.3
nagging *adj.* 901.7
naggy 271.3
Nahum 513.2
naiad 979.10
naïf See naïve
naik, naig, naigue,
 naique, 745.11
nail *n.* pin 45.5
 (suspender 214.3)
 length 200.6
 point 253.2
 hardness 323.3
 fingernail 781.3
 coin 800.4
 on the nail now 118.3
 punctually 132.13
 money down 807.11
nail *v.* attach 43.6
 see 441.10
 recognize 481a.6
 nail one's colors to
  the mast 604.6
nailery 691
naïve, naïf *n.* 703.2
naïve, naive, naïf *adj.*
 credulous 486.5
 artless 703.4
 (inexperienced
  699.14)
naïveté, naïvete 703.1
naked unclad 226.8
 pure 494.13
 manifest 525.4
 plain 849.4
naked eye 441.7
namby-pamby *n.* 160.4
namby-pamby *adj.*
 wishy-washy 160.14
 mediocre 736.3
 sentimental 853.6
namda, numda
 223.8, 10
name *n.*
 appellation 564.2
 (word 562.1)
 distinction 642.1
 celebrity 873.1, 9
 bear the name of
  564.7
 in the name of
 on behalf of 707.15
 by authority of
  737.17
name *v.* adduce 467.10
 call 564.6
 appoint 755.4
named 62.4
nameless
 immense 31.10
 anonymous 565.9
 renownless 874.10
namely 79.13; 522.9
namer 564.5
namesake 564.2
naming 564.1

nammad — nay

nammad 223.8
Nanna 979.3
nanny goat goat 366.9
  female animal 374.8
nanoid 193.9
naos 1000.1, 2
nap *n.* pile 256.10
  texture 329.1
  doze 683.5
  game 840.12
nap *v.* 683.9
Napaea, Napea 979.8
nape 235.1
naphtha, naphthalene 356.2
naphthol, naphtol 428.4
napiform 245.22
napkin 652.7
napoleon
  gold piece 800.5
  game 840.12
Napoleonic Wars 722.4
napoo, napooh *v.* 162.4
napoo, napooh *adj.* 2.10
napping
  preoccupied 458.11
  inexpectant 508.7
nappy pily 256.15
  (textural 329.3)
  intoxicated 959.21
  sleepy 683.15
Naraka 982.1
Narcissus 845.3
narcosis 376.1
  (numbness 381.1)
narcotic *n.* 662.7
  (alleviative 174.3)
  (anesthetic 376.2)
narcotic *adj.*
  anesthetic 381.3
  insalubrious 657.3
  palliative 662.25
  relieving 834.7
narcotization 376.1
narcotize 376.4
narghile, nargile, nargileh 392a.6
nark *n.* 527.6
nark *v.* 527.10
Narragansett 271.4
narrate 594.5
narration 594.1
narrative *n.* 594.2
  (writing 590.3)
  (book 593.1)
narrative *adj.* 594.7
narrator 594.4
  (annalist 553.2)
  (author 593.15)
  (prose writer 598.2)
narrow *n.* strait 203.3
  (gorge 198.3)
  gulf 343.1
narrow *v.*
  contract 195.4
  taper 203.7
  qualify 469.3
narrow *adj.*
  slender 203.9

(contracted 195.6)
(little 193.8)
phonetics 402.11
shallow 499.17
bigoted 606.7
prudish 853.7
narrowing 203.2
  (contraction 195.1)
narrow-minded 606.7
  (prejudiced 481.10)
  (unreasoning 499.17)
  (hyperorthodox 983a.8)
narrow-mindedness
  prejudice 481.3
  bigotry 606.2
narrowness 203
narrow-souled, narrow-spirited 606.7
narthex 191.17
narwhal, narwal, narwhale 366.21
nary 187.7
nasal *n.*
  of the nose 349.30
  sound 402.2
nasal *adj.* 583.5
nasalize 583.2
nasal twang 583.1
nascent 66.7
Nastrond, Naströnd 982.2
nasty *v.* 653.15
nasty *adj.*
  unpalatable 395.7
  (malodorous 401.4)
  filthy 653.17
  odious 830.14
  obscene 961.9
natal beginning 66.7
  native 188.11
natation
  swimming 267.9
  bathing 652.2
natational 267.52
natatorium, natatory *n.* 652.4
natatory *adj.* 267.52
nation race 11.4
  country 182.1
  population 188.10
  people 372.2
national racial 11.8
  public 372.6
national anthem
  song 415.10
  martial music 722.3
national council 696.3
National Guard 726.6
nationalism 737.6
nationality race 11.4
  nationalities 188.9
  nation 372.2
  patriotism 906.4
national school 542.2
National Socialist party 712.6
native *n.* 188.8
native *adj.*
  intrinsic 5.6

indigenous 188.11
native-grown 367.17
natural 703.4
simple 849.3
nativity birth 161.3
  horoscope 511.4
natty 845.11
natural *n.* note 413.6
  idiot 501.1
  throw of dice 621.9
natural *adj.*
  intrinsic 5.6
  instinctive 477a.4
  pure 494.13
  ~ diction 576.3; 578.4
  impulsive 612.4
  untouched 674.9
  artless 703.4
  simple 849.3
natural child 167.5
natural history 357.5
naturalism 556.6
naturalist 357.7
  (zoologist 368.2)
  (botanist 369.9)
naturalization
  domestication 184.7
  (conversion 144.1)
  acclimatization 613.5
naturalize
  domesticate 184.16
  acclimatize 613.8
naturalized
  domestic 188.12
  (domesticated 184.19)
  native 367.17
  habituated 613.12
  (adapted 82.7)
naturally 154.7
natural philosophy 316.5
  (philosophy 451.4)
natural science
  matter 316.5
  organic science 357.5
nature essence 5.3
  (kind 75.2)
  (particularity 79.2)
  constitution 54.1
  world 318.1
  animal ~ 364.1; 961.3
  inartificiality 703.1
  disposition 820.1
state of nature
  the nude 226.2
  natural state 674.3
Nature
  world spirit 359.3
  God 976.2
naught, nought
  nothing 2.2
  zero 87a.1
  insignificancy 643.3, 6
bring to naught
  destroy 162.4
  fail 732.5

naughtiness 945.6
naughty 945.11, 13
naughty pack, naughty-pack 962.2
naumachia 720.4
nausea illness 655.13
  repugnance 867.2
nauseant *n.*
  unsavoriness 395.3
  emetic 662.10
  sickener 867.3
  cloyer 869.2
nauseant *adj.*
  nasty 395.7
  foul 653.17
nauseate 830.7
  (be unsavory 395.4)
  (disgust 841.6)
  (displease 867.6)
nauseated sick 655.23
  displeased 828.14
  (disliking 867.7)
  be nauseated 867.5
nauseating nasty 395.7
  foul 653.17
  odious 830.14
nauseous foul 653.17
  odious 830.14
nautch 840.6
nautch girl 840.9
nautical 267.47
  (oceanic 341.5)
nautical mile 200.6
nautiloid 368.16
nautilus 368.6
naval 267.48
naval auxiliary 726.11
naval brigade, naval militia 726.10
naval officer 745.12
naval reserve 726.10
navarch mariner 269.4
  officer 745.12
nave center 222.2
  circle 247.2
  axis 312.5
  church 1000.3
navel *n.* 222.2
navel *adj.* 222.4
navicular, naviform 245.11
navigable 267.49
  (seaworthy 273.15)
navigate sail 267.10
  aviate 267a.30
navigation 267
  (navy 726.10)
navigator 269.1
navvy 690.2
navy tobacco 392a.7
  blue 438.2
  naval forces 726.10
  (navigation 267.1)
  (mariner 269.1)
  (marine 273.6)
navy blue *n.* 438.2
navy-blue *adj.* 438.6
Navy Cross 733.2
nawab
  potentate 745.4, 5
  honorifics 877.2
nay *n.* 609.3

nay *adv.* 536.4
Nazarene Christ 976.5
 Christian 987.4
naze 250.5
Nazi 712.6
Nazism 737.4
neap *n.* lowness 207.2
 shaft 215.13
neap *adj.* 207.7
near *v.*
 ~ in time 121.6
 approach 286.2
 (converge 290.2)
near *adj.*
 approximative 17.14
 imitation 19.12
 imminent 152.3
 (future 121.7)
 close 197.8, 9
 (contiguous 199.4)
 nearer 197.9
 pseudo 545.13
 stingy 819.4
 intimate 888.4
near *adv.* almost 32.15
 close to 197.11, 12
 (around 227.5)
 (beside 236.9)
 be near 197.5
 bring near 17.8
 go near, come near
  286.2
 near the mark
  almost 32.15
  close 197.8
 near the wind
  close 197.8
  navigation 267.57
nearabout, near-
 abouts 197.11
near-at-hand
 imminent 152.3
 (immediate 132.9)
 near 197.8
nearaway, nearaways
 197.12
near-beer 959.5
near-by *adj.* 197.8
near by, near-by *adv.*
 197.11, 12
nearest 197.10
nearing *n.* 286.1
 (nearness 197.1)
nearing *adj.* 286.3
nearly almost 32.15
 about 32.17
 near 197.12
nearmost 197.10
nearness 197
 (contiguity 199.1)
 (approach 286.1)
near-sight 443.1
nearsighted
 myopic 443.14
 obtuse 499.12
 bigoted 606.7
nearsightedness 443.1
neat *v.* 60.6
neat *adj.* pure 42.5
 orderly 58.7
 (clean 652.14)
 symmetrical 242.5

terse 572.3
 style 576.3
 well-expressed
  578.4
 appearance 845.11
neaten 60.6
neat-handed 698.11
neatherd 370.4
neat's-foot oil 356.4
neb nose 250.4
 point 253.2
nebula stars 318.3
 nimbus 420.12
nebular 318.16
nebule 353.5
nebulosity 353.4
nebulous
 celestial 318.16
 cloudy 353.11
 dim 422.8
 obscure 519.7
nebulousness 422.5
necessarily
 consequently 154.7
 of necessity 601.15
 (unwillingly 603.6)
necessary *n.*
 requirement 630.1
 privy 653.9
necessary *adj.*
 inescapable 601.11
 (inevitable 474.11)
 (choiceless 609a.3)
 (compulsory 744.3)
 requisite 630.3
 be necessary 601.10
 if necessary 601.15
 render necessary
 necessitate 601.8
 require 630.2
necessitarian *n.* 601.7
necessitarian *adj.*
 601.12
necessitarianism 601.6
necessitate
 make necessary
  601.8
 require 630.2
 compel 744.2
necessitous
 requisite 630.3
 poverty-stricken
  804.7
necessity
 inevitability 601
 (choicelessness
  609a.1)
 (compulsion 744.1)
 requirement 630.1
 indigence 804.1
 of necessity
 consequently 154.7
 necessarily 601.15
 (compulsorily
  744.4)
 neck *n.* bond 45.1
 narrow 203.3
 promontory 250.5
 type 591.6
 run neck and neck
  274.12
 neck *v.*

make love 902.7
 hang 972.8
neck and heels 52.15
neckband
 neckpiece 225.33
 circle 247.2
necker 897.6
neckerchief 225.33
necklace circle 247.2
 ornament 847.7
neck or nothing 604.9
neckpiece, necktie
 225.33
neckwear
 clothes 225.33
 merchandise 798.3
necrology 594.2
necromancer 992.2
necromancy 992.1
 (divination 511.2)
necromantic 992.5
necropolis 363.14
necropsy 363.18
necroscopic 363.25
necroscopy 363.18
necrosis
 ailment 655.16
 decay 659.2
nectar 396.5
 (drink 298.4)
 (delicacy 298.9)
nectareous 396.8
 (savory 394.7)
neddy 271.10
need *n.*
 deficiency 53.2
 requirement 630.1
 (necessity 601.1)
 (desire 865.1)
 want 640.3
 poverty 804.1
 if need be 601.15
need *v.* require 630.2
 want 640.6
needfire 382.8
needful *n.* 800.1
needful *adj.*
 necessary 601.11
 requisite 630.3
needle point 253.2
 perforator 262
 foliage 367.4
 graver 558.4
 pointer 694.6
needle in a haystack
 475.5
needle gun 727.10
needlelike 253.11
needlemaker 690.8
needle point
 cloth 219.5
 needlework 847.6
needless 641.5
needlewoman 225.38
needlework 847.6
needs must 601.15
needy 804.7
ne'er-do-well 949.1
nefarious
 horrible 649.8
 disreputable 874.8
 iniquitous 945.16

negate deny 536.2
 refuse 764.2
negation
 nonexistence 2.1
 denial 536
 (disproof 468.1)
 (confutation 479.1)
 (dissent 489.2)
 (retraction 607.3)
 (rejection 610.1)
 refusal 764.1
negative *n.* die 22.3
 print 556.11
 impress 558.4
negative *v.*
 disprove 479.2
 deny 536.2
 refuse 764.2
 disapprove 932.5
negative *adj.*
 nonexistent 2.7
 contrary 14.5
 numeral 84.7
 electronegative
  157a.12
 denying 536.3
 (dissentient 489.5)
negatively 536.4
negativeness 2.1
negatory
 countervailing 468.3
 negative 536.3
 (confutative 479.3)
 declinatory 764.5
neglect *n.*
 negligence 460
 (inattention 458.1)
 (inexactness 495.4)
 (nonpreparation
  674.1)
 (inaction 681.1;
  683.1)
 (noncompletion
  730.1)
 (nonobservance
  773.1)
 (recklessness 863.1)
 (dereliction 927.1)
 (slight 930.4)
 delinquency 945.3
neglect *v.*
 be negligent 460.4
 (be inattentive
  458.5)
 (not do 681.2)
 (not complete
  730.2)
 (not observe 773.3)
 not use 678.5
 snub 930.7
neglectful 460.8
 (dilatory 133.9)
 (inadequate 304.3)
 (inattentive 458.10)
 (forgetful 506.8)
 (lax 738.7)
neglectfully 460.12
neglective 460.8
neglector 460.3
 (shirker 623.4)
 (idler 683.7)
 (bungler 701)

negligee — neutrality

negligee 225.23
 in negligee 225.47
negligence 460.1
 (inattention 458.1)
 (laxity 738.1)
negligent n. 460.3
negligent adj. 460.8
 (inattentive 458.10)
 (shiftless 674.11)
 (indolent 683.13)
 (nonobservant 773.5)
 (reckless 863.6)
 be negligent 460.4
negligently 460.12
negotiability 470.2
negotiable
 transferable 270.11; 783.5
 practicable 470.6
 mediatory 724.4
negotiant 724.2
negotiate
 jump over 309.4
 ~ a peace 723.4
 mediate 724.3
 succeed in 731.5
 make terms 769.6
 transfer 783.3
 bargain 794.5
negotiation
 mediation 724.1
 compact 769.1
 barter 794.3
negotiator
 mediator 724.2
 go-between 758.3
 deputy 759.1
negress, negrillo 431.4
Negrillo 193.5
negrine 431.9
Negritic, Nigritic 193.9
Negrito 193.5
negro n. black 431.4
 slave 746.4
Negro n. 431.4
 (nationalities 188.9)
negro adj. 431.7
Negro adj. 11.8; 431.7
 (native 188.11)
negrohead 392a.7
Negroid n. 431.4
Negroid adj.
 racial 11.8
 black 431.7
negroize 431.6
negro minstrel 416.10
negus 959.8
neif See nieve
neigh nicker 412.2
 exult 884.2
neighbor, neighbour n.
 bystander 197.4
 (abutter 199.2)
 acquaintance 890.1
neighbor, neighbour v.
 be near 197.5, 7
 be contiguous 199.3
 touch 379.3
neighbor, neigh-
bour adj. 197.8
neighborer, neighbourer 197.4
neighborhood, neighbourhood
 region 181.1
 nearness 197.1
 surroundings 227.2
 in the neighborhood 197.8
neighboring, neighbouring near 197.8
 circumjacent 227.4
neighborly, neighbourly
 friendly 888.4
 sociable 892.12
 courteous 894.12
neigher 271.3
neither 610.4
 neither here nor there remote 10.7
 nowhere 187.14
nemesis 941.1
Nemesis avenger 919.3
 punishment 972.1
neocriticism 451.11
Neo-Darwinism 161.5
Neo-Hegelianism 451.14, 16
neoimpressionism 556.6
neoimpressionist n. 559.1
neoimpressionist adj. 556.19
Neo-Lamarckism 161.5
neolith 124.2
neological 563.17
neologism 563.7
 (word 562.1)
neologist
 modernist 123.4
 word-coiner 563.12
 (linguist 560.7)
neologize
 innovate 140.7
 coin words 563.14
neology 563.7
 (newness 123.1)
 (innovation 140.3)
neon 334.2
neon lamp 423.3
neophobia 860.4
neophyte
 convert 144.5
 novice 541.6
 believer 987.4
Neoplatonism, Neo-Platonism 451.7
 (ism 984.4)
Neo-Scholasticism 451.10
neoteric n. 123.4
neoteric adj. new 123.8
 modern 123.11
 neologic 563.17
neoterism 563.7
neoterist
 modernist 123.4
 word-coiner 563.12
neoterize 563.14
nepenthe 662.7
nephalism 953.2
 (sobriety 958.1)
nephalist 953.3
nephelognosy 353.6
nephelometer 353.7
nephelometric 353.12
nephesh 994.11
nephew 11.3
nephograph 353.7
nephological 353.12
nephology 353.6
nephoscope
 aviation 267a.29
 clouds 353.7
Nephthys 979.5
ne plus ultra
 supremacy 33.3, 8
 limit 52.4; 233.1
 distance 196.3
 summit 210.1
 perfection 650.1
nepotism
 consanguinity 11.1
 favoritism 941a.1
 selfishness 943.1
nepotist 943.2
Neptune planet 318.3
 spirit of the sea 341.2
 god 979.2
 deity 979.10
Nereid
 spirit of the sea 341.2
 nymph 979.10
nerve n.
 strength 159.1
 courage 861.1
 impudence 885.2
 get on one's nerves
 sound harshly 410.7
 irritate 830.5
nerve v. 861.7
 nerve oneself 861.6
nerveless
 unmanned 158.10
 weak 160.10
 feeble style 575.2
 inexcitable 826.9
nervous
 vigorous 574.5
 excitable 825.9
 fearful 860.14
nervousness 825.3; 860.3
nervy 885.9
nescience 491.1
nescient 491.8
nese 250.4
ness 250.5
nest n.
 multitude 102.2
 origin 153.4
 retreat 189.13
 airdrome 267a.28
nest v. settle 184.14
 inhabit 186.10
nest egg 636.2
 (savings 817.2)
nester 188.5
nestle inhabit 186.10
 protect 664.6
 snuggle 902.8
nestling 129.7
Nestor elder 130.1
 sage 500.1
 adviser 695.3
net n. bag 191.4
 tissue 219.4, 5
 aerostat 273a.12
 snare 545.4
Net n. 318.6
net v. interlace 219.8
 gain 775.6
nether 207.9
nethermost
 lowest 207.10
 bottom 211.5
nether world 982.1
netlike 219.11
net profit gain 775.2
 receipts 810.1
netting tissue 219.4, 5
 veiling 225.12
nettle n. 253.2
 (bane 663.1)
nettle v. vex 830.5
 anger 900.10
nettled 828.15
nettle rash 655.17
network 219.4
 (complexity 59.3)
neural 235.10
neuralgia 378.1
neurasthenia
 helplessness 158.2
 psychosis 503.2
 nervous disorder 655.14
neurasthenic 503.15
neuritis pain 378.1
 nervous disorder 655.14
neurologist 662.19
neurology 329.2
neuroparalysis 655.15
neurosis
 psychosis 503.2
 nervous disorder 655.14
neurotic
 psychoneurotic 503.15
 drugs 662.25
neuroticism 655.14
neuter neutral 628.3
 indifferent 866.4
neutral impartial 628.3
 (intermediate 29.3)
 (without choice 609a.3)
 pacifistic 721.4
 indifferent 866.4
 be neutral, remain neutral 628.2
 (have no choice 609a.2)
neutrality
 mid-course 628.1
 (mean 29.1)
 (choicelessness 609a.1)

neutralization — nihilist

pacifism 721.1
indifference 866.1
neutralization 30.1
  (counteraction 179.1)
neutralize
  compensate 30.4
  counteract 179.4
neutralizer 179.2
névé 383.5
never 107.3
  never a one
    nothing 2.2
    nobody 187.7
never-dying, never-ending, never-fading 112.4
nevermore 107.3
never-tiring
  persevering 604a.3
  industrious 682.19
nevertheless
  notwithstanding 30.8
  however 469.7, 8
  anyhow 627.9
nevoid, naevoid 440.5
nevus, naevus
  variegation 440.2
  discoloration 440a.1
new additional 37.7
  recent 123.8
  (unaccustomed 614.3)
  (unused 678.7)
  inexperienced 699.14
Newari 560.4
new birth
  revival 660.2
  regeneration 987.3
newborn new 123.8
  infantile 127.7
newcomer alien 57.3
  (incomer 294.4)
  novice 541.6
newfangle 123.2
newfangled 123.10
  (unique 83.10)
  (changed 140.8)
newfanglement 123.1, 2
new-fashion, new-fashioned
  modern 123.11
  fashionable 852.7
Newfoundland 366.6
Newgate 752.1
New Jerusalem
  utopia 515.6
  Celestial City 981.1
newly 123.12
newlywed 903.6, 9
new-made 123.9
new-model 660.14
newness
  recentness 123
  (immaturity 127.1)
  (innovation 140.3)
  (neology 563.7)
  unaccustomedness 614.1

news tidings 532
  (information 527.1)
  newspaper 593.6
newsbill 532.2
newsboy 534.1
news editor, newsman 593.16
newsmonger 532.5
  (inquisitive 455.2)
  (informant 527.5)
  (chatterer 584.3)
newsmongery 532.3
  (inquisitiveness 455.1)
newspaper 593.6
newspaperman 593.16
newsprint news 532.1
  print 591.2
news vendor, newsy n. 534.1
newsy adj. 532.9
newt 366.18
New Testament 985.4
New Thought 984.9
New Thoughtist 984.19
New Year's Day 138.7
next adj. 63.5
next adv. 117.4
next door to 197.11
next friend 759.1
next of kin 11.3
nexus 45.1
niagara 348.2, 7
Niasese 560.4
nib extremity 67.2
  summit 210.1
  shaft 215.13
  nose 250.4
  point 253.2
nibble n. 298.2
nibble v. eat 298.44, 45
  be credulous 486.3
  be deceived 547.3
  criticize 932.7
nibs personage 642.5
  judge 967.1
nice savory 394.7
  discriminating 465.4
  exact 494.11
  good 648.8
  ticklish 704.8
  pleasant 829.7
  refined 850.5
  fastidious 868.4
  scrupulous 939.8
  virtuous 944.3
nicety subtlety 15.2
  meticulousness 457.3
  discrimination 465.1
  exactness 494.3
  taste 850.1
  fastidiousness 868.1
  point of honor 939.1
niche nook 191.3
  (small place 184.4)
  (corner 244.2)
  ~ in the hall of fame 873.5
nick n.
  ~ of time 134.4

notch 257.1
  (mark 550.7)
  type 591.6
  throw of dice 621.9
  in the nick of time 134.10
  (expediently 646.6)
nick v. notch 257.5
  (mark 550.19)
  cheat 545.7
  succeed 731.5
  rob 791.9, 12
nicked 257.6
nickel 800.8, 15
nicker 412.2
nickname n. 565.3
  (name 564.2)
nickname v. 565.6
  (name 564.6)
Nicobarese 560.4
nicotia 392a.1, 9
nicotian
  tobacco 392a.1
  tobacco user 392a.11
nicotine, nicotin
  tobacco 392a.9
  poison 663.5
nicotinic 392a.15
nicotinism 392a.10
nictate 443.11
nictation 443.6
nidorosity 401.1
nidorous 401.4
nidorulent 398.8
nidus origin 153.4
  retreat 189.13
niece 11.3
niello 847.3
nieve, neif 781.3
Niflheim, Nifelheim, Niflheimr 982.2
nifty 845.8
niggard 819.2
niggardly
  paltry 643.12
  parsimonious 819.4
nigger n. alien 57.3
  capstan 273.14
  light shield 424.5
  Negro 431.4
  slave 746.4
nigger in the woodpile latent 526.1
  hidden thing 528.6
nigger v. 384.18
nigger adj. 431.9
niggerhead 392a.7
niggerish 431.9
niggerling 431.4
niggertoe 298.33
niggle copulate 43.8
  scoff 930.6
niggling 643.11
nigh v. 286.2
nigh adj. 197.8
nigh adv. almost 32.15
  near 197.11, 12
night n. 126.3
  (darkness 421.1)
  at night
    nightly 126.8
    in the dark 421.10

night adj. 126.6
night and day 136.6
night-black dark 421.7
  black 431.7
night blindness 443.2
nightcap
  headdress 225.26
  alcoholic drink 959.10
night-clad, night-cloaked 421.7
  (nocturnal 126.6)
night clothes 225.24
night club 959.13
night-dark dark 421.7
  black 431.7
night-enshrouded 421.7
nightfall 126.1
night-fallen 126.6
night-filled, night-hid 421.7
nightgown 225.24
nighthawk 272.15
nightingale
  bird 366.22
  songbird 416.11
night letter 532a.3
  (epistle 592.2)
nightly adj. 126.6
nightly adv. 126.8
night-mantled 421.7
nightmare
  hallucination 503.5
  dream 515.5
  mental suffering 828.7
  object of fear 860.7
nights 126.8
night song 990.7
nightshade 663.6
nightshirt 225.24
nighttime n. 126.3
nighttime adj. 126.6
night-veiled 421.7
nightwalker 268.7
nightwalking n. 266.6
night walking, night-wandering adj. 266.25
night watchman 717.6
nightwear 798.3
nigrescence 431.1
nigrescent 431.8
nigrification 431.2
nigrify 431.6
nigrine 431.7
nigrities, nigritude 431.1
nigrosine, nigrosin 431.5
nigrous 431.7, 9
nihil 2.2
nihilism
  nonexistence 2.1
  anarchy 738.2
  (lawlessness 964.3)
  irreligion 989.3
nihilist
  destroyer 165.1
  evildoer 913.1
  irreligionist 989.4

nihilistic — nonadmission

nihilistic 738.8
nihility
  nonexistence 2.1
  nullity 4.2
  insignificancy
    643.3, 6
nil nothing 2.2
  zero 87a.1
Nile green 435.2
nilgai, nilgau, nilghai,
  nilghau 366.10
nill *n.* 603.1
nill *v.*
  be unwilling 603.4
  refuse 764.2
Nilometer 348.13
nimble fast 274.13
  agile 682.17
nimble-fingered 698.11
nimble-footed
  fast 274.13
  sprightly 682.17
nimble-witted
  sagacious 498.10
  witty 842.9
nimbleness 682.2
nimbus cloud 353.5
  light 420.12, 13
nimiety 641.1
Nimrod 622.4
  (shooter 284.8)
nincompoop 501.1
nine 98.5
  the Nine 416.16
ninefold 98.19
ninepin 840.11
ninety 98.7
ninny, ninnyhammer
  501.1
ninnyism 499.6
ninth 98.19
Niobe 839.5, 14
nip *n.* bite 298.2
  drink 298.4
  pain 378.1
  pungency 392.1
  dram 959.10
nip *v.* cut off 38.6
  cut 44.8
  destroy 162.4
  cut short 201.4
  pain 378.4
  freeze 385.3
  be pungent 392.3
  seize 789.9
  steal 791.9
  tipple 959.15
nip in the bud
  destroy 162.4
  kill 361.10
  avert 706.5
niphablepsia
  blindness 442.1
  dim-sightedness
    443.2
nipper 959.10
nippers adherer 46.3
  pince-nez 445.3
  pincers 781.2, 3
nipping 383.8
nipple 250.3
nippy 383.8

nirvana
  nonexistence 2.1
  heaven 981.1
nisi prius 969.2
nisse, nis 979.9
nisus 176.1
nit 366.24
nitch *n.* 257.1
nitch *v.* 257.5
nitency 420.1
niter, nitre
  energizer 171.5
  pungency 392.2
nitidous 420.22
nitric acid 384.11
nitrogen gas 334.2
  poison 663.5
nitroglycerin, nitro-
  glycerine 727.13
nitrous oxide
  gas 334.2
  anesthetic 376.2
nitwit 501.1
Niue 560.4
niveous 430.8
nix nothing 2.2
  zero 87a.1
  nobody 187.7
  water nymph 979.10
nixie 979.10
nixie, nixy 87a.1
Nizam 745.4, 5
Njorth, Njord 979.3
no *v.* 536.2
no *adj.* 87a.2
no *adv.* 536.4
  (dissent 489.8)
say no dissent 489.4
  deny 536.2
  refuse 764.2
  disapprove 932.5
No. 84.1
no-account 645.8
Noachian 124.6
Noah's ark
  mixture 41.4
  miscellany 72.8
Noah's Dove 318.6
Noatun 981.3
nob head 210.3
  personage 642.5
  nobleman 875.4
Nobel prize 733.1
nobi'itate 873.13
nobility
  greatness 31.2
  importance 642.1
  eminence 873.3
  élite 875.1, 2
  (gentility 852.3)
  (society 852.4)
noble *n.* 875.4
  (personage 642.5)
noble *v.* 642.10
noble *adj.* great 31.6
  reputable 873.15
  illustrious 873.18
  highborn 875.10
  (genteel 852.9)
  title 877.5
  dignified 878.7
  honorable 939.7

  virtuous 944.3
noble gas 334.2
nobleman 875.4
nob.e-minded
  magnanimous 942.6
  virtuous 944.3
noblesse 875.1, 2
noblewoman 875.6
nobody nothing 2.2
  no one 187.7
  nonentity 643.6
  (nullity 4.2)
  (commoner 876.4)
nocent 649.10
nociassociation 688.3
nock 257.1
noctambulant 266.25
noctambulation 266.6
noctambule, noctam-
  bulist 268.7
noctilucence 420.11
noctivagant 126.6
noctivagous 266.25
noctograph 442.2
nocturnal night 126.6
  dark 421.7
nocturne 415.3
nod *n.*
  ~ of assent 488.1
  sign 550.3
  command 741.1
  greeting 894.4
  obeisance 928.2
  ~ of approval 931.7
nod *v.* signal 550.20
  get sleepy 683.9
  greet 894.9
  make obeisance
    928.6
nod to its fall
  perish 162.5
  fall 306.6
  collapse 659.6
nodding 214.7
noddle head 210.3
  brain 450.2
noddy 501.1
node joint 43.3
  protuberance 250.2
  dilemma 704.4
nodose
  protuberant 250.9
  rough 256.12
nodosity
  convexity 250.1, 2
  roughness 256.1
nodular
  protuberant 250.9
  rough 256.12
nodulate 250.8
nodulated 256.12
nodulation
  convexity 250.1, 2
  roughness 256.1
nodule 250.2
nodulose 250.9
nodulus 250.2
nodus 704.4
Nogai 560.4
noggin cup 191.11
  head 210.3
  brain 450.2

no-good 645.8
noise *n.* sound 402.1
  racket 404.2
  (clatter 407.5)
  (discord 414.2)
noise *v.* sound 402.7
  make noise 404.6
  ~ abroad 531.7
noiseless 403.6
noisemaker 404.4
  (fireworks 382.9)
noisome nasty 395.7
  (fetid 401.4)
  bad 649.8
  harmful 649.10
  foul 653.17
  unwholesome 657.3
  odious 830.14
noisiness 404.1
noisy rackety 404.9
  blustering 887.4
  be noisy 404.6
  (clatter 407.10)
nolition, nolleity 603.1
nol-pros
  abandon 624.3
  annul 756.3
noma 655.16
nomad *n.* 268.2
nomad, nomadic *adj.*
  266.24
nomadism 266.2
nomancy 511.3
no man's land 728.2
nom de guerre, nom
  de plume 565.3
nomen 564.2
nomenclator 564.5
nomenclature *n.* 564
nomenclature *v.* 564.6
nominal
  unsubstantial 4.5
  titular 564.8
  (verbal 562.8)
  price 815.8
nominalism 451.10
nominally 79.13
nominate name 564.6
  appoint 755.4
  call to the ministry
    995.7
nomination
  ~ of a race horse
    271.8
  appellation 564.1, 2
  appointment 755.2
  holy orders 995.6
nominative 454.2
nominee 758.1
nomistic 963.5
nomography, nomol-
  ogy 963.3
nomothetic 963.5
Nona 601.4
nona-, non- 98.19
nonacceptance 764.1
nonaccomplishment,
  nonachievement
    730.1
nonadhesion 47.1
nonadhesive 47.3
nonadmission 55.1

nonage — noose

nonage nine 98.5
 youth 127.1
nonagenarian 130.1
nonagon 98.5
nonagreement 489.1
 (negation 536.1)
nonanticipative 508.6
nonapparent 447.4
nonappearance
 absentation 187.5
 invisibility 447.1
nonary *n.* 98.5
nonary *adj.* 98.19
nonassent 489.1
 (disapproval 932.1)
nonattendance 187.5
nonattendant 187.10
nonbeing 2.1
nonce 118.2
 for the nonce 118.3
 nonce word 563.7
nonchalance
 dispassion 823.1
 (disregard 460.1)
 inexcitability 826.2
 indifference 866.1
nonchalant
 dispassionate 823.5
 inexcitable 826.9
 indifferent 866.4
non-Christian *n.*
 984.20
 (unbeliever 989.4)
non-Christian *adj.*
 984.28
nonclerical 997.4
noncohesion 47.1
noncohesive 47.3
noncombatant 721.2
noncommissioned officer 745.11
noncommittal 864.2
noncompletion 730
 (incompleteness 53.1)
 (shortcoming 304.1)
 (neglect 460.1)
 (imperfection 651.1)
noncomp'iance
 nonconformity 83.2
 disobedience 742.1
 refusal 764.1
 (dissent 489.1)
 (disapproval 932.1)
 nonobservance 773.1
noncompos 504.1
non compos mentis 503.12
nonconcurrence 489.1
nonconducive 175a.2
nonconductibility 175a.1
nonconductive 175a.2
nonconformable 83.9
nonconformance 83.2
nonconformist
 original 83.4
 (sectarian 984.13)
 dissenter 489.3

nonconformity 83.2
 (dissent 489.1)
 (sectarianism 984.2)
nonconsenting 764.5
noncontent
 dissenter 489.3
 malcontent 710.3
 insurgent 742.3
 grumbler 832.2
non-co-operation 927.1
nondescript *n.* 83.4
nondescript *adj.* 83.10
none, None *n.* 990.7
none *adv.* 87a.2
 (nonexistent 2.11)
none *pron.* 2.2
 (zero 87a.1)
nonecclesiastical 997.4
nonego 6.1
nonentity
 nonexistence 2.1
 nullity 4.2
 nobody 643.6
non esse 2.1
nonessential
 extrinsic 6.2
 irrelevant 10.6
 unimportant 643.10
nonesuch, nonsuch
 oddity 83.4
 best 648.4
 prodigy 872.1
nonexistence 2
 (absence 187.2)
nonexistent 2.7
 (absent 187.10)
nonexpansion 180a.1
nonexpansive 180a.2
nonexpectation 508.1
nonextension
 nonexpansion 180a.1
 immateriality 317.1
nonexteriority, non-externality 317.1
nonfeasance 945.6;
 947.2
nonfeasor 949.2
nonfulfillment, non-fulfillment
 disappointment 509.1
 noncompletion 730.1
 failure 732.1
 nonobservance 773.1
 derelection 927.1
nonidentical 18.4
nonillion 98.13; 102.5
noninclusion 55.1
noninfluence 175a
noninterference
 laissez faire 681.2
 nonintervention 748.4
nonintervention 748.4
nonius 466.4
non-Jew 984.20
non-Jewish 984.28
nonjurant
 dissentient 489.5
 heterodox 984.22

nonjuring 984.22
nonjuror
 dissenter 489.3
 religious dissenter 984.13
nonlegal 964.5
nonministerial 997.4
non-Mohammedan *n.* 984.20
non-Mohammedan *adj.* 984.28
nonobservance
 nonconformity 83.2
 inattention 458.1
 nonfulfillment 773
 (neglect 460.1)
 (evasion 623.1)
 (disobedience 742.1)
 (faithlessness 940.2)
 derelection 927.1
nonoccupation 187.3
nonobservant
 unconformable 83.9, 11
 (unaccustomed 614.3)
 inattentive 458.10
 unwary 460.9
 unfaithful 773.5
 (negligent 460.8)
 (evasive 623.12)
 (disobedient 742.6)
nonpareil
 unequaled 28.4
 type 591.7
 best 648.4
nonpartisan 748.7
nonpastoral 997.4
nonpayment 808
 (evasion 623.1)
 (arrears 806.2)
nonperformance
 noncompletion 730.1
 nonobservance 773.1
 derelection 927.1
nonplus *n.*
 perplexity 475.2
 impasse 704.3
nonp'us *v*
 perplex 475.8
 (be difficult 704.5)
 thwart 706.7
 checkmate 731.10
nonplusation, nonplussation 704.3
nonplused, nonplussed
 perplexed 475.16
 at an impasse 704.11
nonpreparation 674
 (neglect 460.1)
 (inexpectation 508.1)
nonpresence 187.1
nonprevalence
 unaccustomedness 614.1
 disuse 678.1
nonprevalent 678.7
nonreligious 997.4
nonresidence 187.3
nonresident 187.10

nonresistance
 do-nothingism 681.2
 submission 725.1
 obedience 743.1
 forbearance 826.4
nonresisting
 submissive 725.5
 obedient 743.3
nonresonant 408a.6
nonsense
 absurdity 497.1
 (folly 499.6)
 senselessness 517.2
 (trumpery 643.5)
 talk nonsense 517.6
 (be absurd 497.2)
 (prattle 584.4)
nonsensical
 absurd 497.4
 (illogical 477.10)
 (ridiculous 855.5)
 foolish 499.15
 unmeaning 517.8
nonsensicality 497.1
nonsensification 517.2
nonsensify 517.5
nonsonant *n.* 402.2
nonsonant *adj.* 403.7
nonsubjective 316.10
nonsubsistence 2.1
nonsuccess 732.1
nonsuch See nonesuch
nonsuit *n.* 732.3
nonsuit *v.*
 defeat 731.10
 ∼ at law 971.2
nonsuited 732.12
nontransparency 426.1
nontransparent 426.4
nonunderstanding 499.12
 (incogitant 452.3)
nonuniform 16a.2
nonuniformity 16a
 (diversity 18.1)
 (multiformity 81.1)
 (unconformity 83.1)
 (roughness 256.1)
nonuplet 98.5
nonvocal *n.* 402.2
nonvocal *adj.* 581.7
noodle head 210.3
 brain 450.2
 fool 501.1
nook 191.3
 (small place 184.4)
 (angle 244.2)
 (recess 252.4)
noological 450.8
noology 450.4
noon *n.* 125.2
noon *adj.* 125.4
noonday 125.2
no one, no-one
 nothing 2.2
 nobody 187.7
nooning, noontide, noontime 125.2
nooscopic 450.8
noose *n.*
 fastening 45.2
 circle 247.2

noose — notwithstanding

noose (*continued*)
　snare 545.4
　hanging 972.4
　hangman's ~ 975.4
noose *v.* 972.8
norimon 272.12
norm, norma
　measure 466.2
　precept 697.1
Norma 318.6
normal *n.* mean 29.1
　vertical 212.2
　school 542.1
normal *adj.*
　intrinsic 5.6
　mean 29.3
　orderly 58.7
　sane 502.5
　customary 613.11
normality
　normalcy 80.2
　sanity 502.1
　mediocrity 736.1
normalize 58.6
Norn giant 192.8
　Fates 601.4
north *n.* 278.2
north *adj.* 278.10
north and south 237.3
northeast 278.10
northeaster, norther 349.11
northerly, northern 278.10
Northerner 57.3
northern lights 420.12
northing 196.1
North Pole 383.4
North Star star 318.3
　cynosure 550.10
　guiding star 694.6
northward 278.10, 11
northwest 278.10
northwester 349.11
Northwest Passage 311.1
norward 278.11
Norway 182.3
Norwegian 560.4
nor'wester 349.11
nose *n.* prow 234.3
　olfactory organ 250.4
　(smell 398.4)
　tube 260.6
　airplane 273a.10
　detective 528.9
under one's nose
　near 197.11
　before 234.9
　in sight 446.6
　openly 525.7
　defiantly 715.4
nose *v.* smell 398.7
　pry 455.4
　nasalize 583.2
nose down 267a.31
nose in 228.10
nose into 267.32
nose out pry 455.4
　hunt out 461.16
　smell out 481a.7

nose over, nose up 267a.31, 34
nose bag 191.4
nose dive *n.*
　aerobatics 267a.24
　dive 310.1
nose-dive *v.*
　aviate 267a.31
　dive 310.4
nosee-um 366.24
nosegay
　fragrance 400.1
　bouquet 400.4
　ornament 847.5
nosehole nose 250.4
nostril 351.2
olfactories 398.4
noser 349.10
nose ring 847.7
nosey See **nosy**
nosology 655.19
　(therapeutics 662.16)
nostalgia 833.1
nostalgic 833.3
nostology 128.5
nostril nose 250.4
　air hole 351.2
　olfactories 398.4
nostrum plan 626.5
　remedy 662.2
nosy, nosey *n.* 455.2
nosy, nosey *adj.*
　odorous 398.8
　fetid 401.4
　inquisitive 455.5
not 536.4
not a little 31.15
not bad 648.11
not guilty 946.5
not half 535.8
not proven 479.5
notabilia 642.3
notability
　greatness 31.2
　importance 642.1
　personage 642.5
　distinction 873.1, 3
　celebrity 873.9
　nobilty 875.2
　(nobleman 875.4)
notable *n.*
　personage 642.5
　celebrity 873.9
　nobility 875.2
　(nobleman 875.4)
notable *adj.*
　remarkable 31.13
　conspicuous 525.5
　important 642.10
　distinguished 873.16
notab'y 31.21
notary recorder 553.1
　legist 968.1
notation
　mathematics 85.4
　music 415.23
　(note 413.6)
　record 551.1
　account entry 811.2
notch *n.* degree 26.1
　rank 71.1 ; 873.4

chasm 198.3
　nick 257
　(angle 244.2)
　(cavity 252.2)
　(mark 550.7)
notch *v.* 257.5
　(mark 550.19)
notched 257.6
　(angular 244.5)
　(rough 256.12)
note *n.* tone 402.2
　woodnote 412.1
　musical ~ 413.6, 11, 13
　(notation 415.23)
　song 415.2
　color tone 428.2
　attention 457.1
　indication 550.2, 7
　record 551.1
　printing 591.2
　epistle 592.2
　(message 532.2)
　compendium 596.1
　importance 642.1
　security 771.1
　money 800.6, 7
　account entry 811.2
　repute 873.1
make a note of 551.8
　(memorandize 505.16)
of note 873.16
take no note of
　disregard 458.5
　neglect 460.4
　not observe 773.3
　snub 930.7
note *v.*
　take cognizance 450.7
　give attention 457.4
　mark 550.19
　record 551.8
　enter accounts 811.7
notebook
　memorandum book 505.6
　record 551.3
　(stationery 590.10)
　(book 593.1)
noted
　well-known 490.17
　distinguished 873.16
note of hand 800.7
noteworthy
　remarkable 31.13
　special 79.7
　unusual 83.10
　important 642.10
　wonderful 870.7
　distinguished 873.16
nothing
　nonexistence 2.2
　(thing of naught 4.2)
　(zero 87a.1)
　insignificancy 643.3, 6
nothing doing
　quiescent 265.7
　refusal 764.7

do nothing
　forbear 681.2
　idle 683.8
for nothing 815.10
nothing else but
　actually 1.9
　certainly 474.16
　truly 494.15
nothingness
　nonexistence 2.1
　(unsubstantiality 4.1)
　insignificance 643.1
notice *n.*
　attention 457.1
　criticism 480.3
　information 527.1
　(warning 668.1)
　proclamation 531.1
　advertisement 531.4
　commentary 595.2
　decree 741.3
bring to notice 457.7
give notice
　inform 527.7
　warn 668.6
notice *v.* see 441.10
　take cognizance 450.7
　give attention 457.4
　heed 459.5
　recognize 481a.6
noticeable
　remarkable 31.13
　visible 446.4
　manifest 525.4
　conspicuous 525.5
notification
　information 527.1
　proclamation 531.1
　warning 668.1
　decree 741.3
notifier 527.5
notify 527.7
notion idea 453.1
　supposition 514.2
　caprice 608.1
　merchandise 798.3
have no notion of
　dissent 489.4
　disapprove 932.5
notional 515.12
notionalist, notionist 514.5
notoriety
　publicity 531.3
　fame 873.1
notorious
　well-known 490.17
　public 531.10
　famous 873.16
　disreputable 874.8
Notre Dame 977.3
Notus 349.2
notwithstanding
　nevertheless 30.8
　(in disagreement 24.10)
　(excepting 55.7)
　(counteractively 179.6)

nougat — nursery tale

(in defiance of 708.6)
conditionally 469.7
nougat 396.2
nought See **naught**
noun 564.4
  (part of speech 567.2)
nourish feed 298.43
  nurture 707.9
nourishment
  food 298.5
  hygiene 656.2
  sustenance 707.3
nous
  world spirit 359.3
  mind 450.1
nouveau riche 876.8
  (rich man 803.3)
novaculite 253.7
Nova Scotian 188.9
novate 1'0.7
novation
  innovation 140.3
  choice 609.1
Nova Zembla 383.4
novel *n.* 594.2
  (writing 590.3)
  (book 593.1)
novel *adj.* 123.10
  (dissimilar 18.4)
  (unimitated 20.3)
  (unique 83.10)
novelist author 593.15
  storyteller 594.4
novelize
  innovate 140.7
  narrate 594.5
  (write 590.14)
novelty 123.1, 2
  (dissimilarity 18.1)
  (nonimitation 20.1)
  (innovation 140.3)
novena nine 98.5
  time 108.1
novenary 98.19
Novial 560.5
novice tyro 541.6
  (ignoramus 493.1)
  religious ~ 996.12
novitiate, noviciate
  apprenticeship 539.2
  novice 541.6
novocain 662.7
  (anesthetic 376.2)
now 118.1
  now or never 134.10
nowadays 118.3
now and then
  sometimes 119.4
  occasionally 137.4
nowanights 118.3
noway, noways
  nowise 32.18
  no 536.4
nowhence, nowhere 187.14
nowhereness 186.2
nowhither 187.14
nowise
  in no degree 32.18
  no 536.4

noxious nasty 395.7
  harmful 649.10
  foul 653.17
  unwholesome 657.3
  odious 830.14
noyade 972.4
nozzle nose 250.4
  embouchure 260.3
  tube 260.6
  sprinkler 337.3
nth 52.4
nuance 15.2
nub essence 5.2
  point 454.1
nubbin
  diminutive 193.2
  pommel 215.23
nubilate 353.9; 422.6
nubilated 422.8
nubilation
  cloudiness 353.4
  dimness 422.5
  opacity 426.1
nubile mature 131.5
  marriageable 903.15
nubility 903.1
nubilous cloudy 353.11
  dim 422.8
  opaque 426.4
nuclear central 222.4
  protoplasmic 357.9
nucleolar 357.9
nucleolus center 222.2
  protoplasm 357.3
nucleoprotein 352.3
nucleus essence 5.2
  rudiment 153.3
  center 222.2
nude *n.* 226.2
nude *adj.* unclad 226.8
  unadorned 849.4
nudge *n.* 550.3
nudge *v.* 550.20
nudity bareness 226.2
  (skin 223.12)
  unadornment 849.1
nugacious
  nugatory 158.11
  trifling 643.11
  useless 645.8
nugacity
  absurdity 497.1
  folly 499.6
  unimportance 643.1
  futility 645.2
nugae 643.4
nugatory
  ineffectual 158.11
  (unsubstantial 4.5)
  trifling 643.11
  useless 645.8
nuggar 273.4
nugget lump 192.5
  gold 800.15
nuisance evil 649.2
  vexation 830.2
  (bane 663.1)
  bore 841.4
null
  nonexistent 2.7
  empty 187.11
  render null 2.6

nullah chasm 198.3
  valley 252.5
null and void
  unproductive 169.4
  empty 187.11
  abrogated 756.6
  illegal 964.5
  declare null and void 756.3
nullibicity, nullibility 187.2
nullification
  compensation 30.1
  annulment 756.1
nullifidian *n.* 989.4
nu lifidian *adj.*
  unbelieving 485.9
  irreligious 989.8
nullify
  nonexistence 2.6
  compensate 30.4
  counteract 179.4
  annul 756.3
  (destroy 162.4)
  not pay 808.5
nullity
  nonexistence 2.1
  nonentity 4.2
  insignificancy 643.3, 6
numb *v.* deaden 376.4
  benumb 381.2
  freeze 385.4
  ~ emotionally 823.4
numb *adj.*
  insensible 376.5
  unfeeling 381.3
  apathetic 823.5
number *n.*
  section 51.2
  kind 75.2
  numeral 84
  (quantity 25.1)
  a ~ of 100.1; 102.2
  cadence 402.2
  rhythm 413.21
  edition 531.2
  (book 593.1)
  act 599.5
number *v.*
  compute 37.5
  ~ among 76.3
  enumerate 85.7
numberable 85.11
numbering 85.1
numberless 105.3
numbers
  quantity 25.1
  multitude 102.2
  meter 597.6
number one 79.4
numbing 383.8
numbness
  unfeeling 381
  (insensibility 376.1)
  apathy 823.1
numda See **namda**
numen 979.12
numerable 85.11
numeral *n.* 84.1
numeral, numerary *adj.* 84.7

numerate
  compute 37.5
  number 85.7
  (estimate 466.10)
numeration 85
  (estimation 466.1)
  (accountancy 811.4)
numerative
  numeral 84.7
  numerable 85.11
numerator 84.2
numerical 84.7
numerosity 102.1
numerous 102.5
  be numerous 102.4
numerously 102.6
numerousness 102
  (greatness 31.1)
  (plurality 100.1)
  (profusion 639.2)
numismatic 800.21
numismatics 800.16
nummary, nummiform 800.21
numskull
  stupidity 499.2
  dolt 501.1
  (ignoramus 493.1)
numskulled 499.12
numskullery 499.2
nun
  clergywoman 996.3
  religieuse 996.12
  (spinster 904.3)
Nunc Dimittis 990.2
nunciate 531.5
nunciative 531.11
nuncio, nuntio
  messenger 534.1
  diplomatist 759.2
nuncupative
  evidential 467.11
  informative 527.13
  oral 582.10
nunnation 567.1
nunnery 1000.4
nuptial 903.14
nuptials 903.3
nurse *n.* sister 662.20
  (professional 690.10)
  custodian 664.3
nurse *v.*
  ~ an idea 451.31
  ~ a sick person 662.24
  watch over 664.6
  preserve 670.3
  nourish 707.9
nurseling See **nursling**
nursemaid 664.3
nursery
  infancy 127.3
  origin 153.4
  room 191.16
  garden 371.6
  school 542.1
nurserymaid 664.3
nurseryman 371.2
nursery rhyme 597.2
nursery tale

nursery tale (cont'd)
  falsehood 546.1
  story 594.2
nursling, nurseling 129.6
nurture n.
  nourishment 298.5
  sustenance 707.3
nurture v. feed 298.43
  ~ an idea 451.31
  ~ a belief 484.8
  train 537.10
  nourish 707.9
nut oddity 83.4
  head 210.3
  food 298.33
  madman 504.1, 2, 3
  devotee 840.19
  nut to crack
    puzzle 533.2
    dilemma 704.1
Nut 979.5
nutate 314.8
nutation 314.1
nut-brown 433.4
nutlet 298.33
nutmeg 393.1
nut oil 356.3
nutriment 298.5
nutrition 707.3
nutritious, nutritive
  edible 298.49
  healthful 656.5
  alimentary 662.26
nutshell
  modicum 32.2
  cover 223.16
  (hull 223.14)
  in a nutshe'l 193.11
nutty spicy 392.5
  imbecile 499.13
  insane 503.12
nux vomica 663.6
nuzzle deceive 545.7
  fondle 902.8
Nyaya 451.5
nyctalopic 443.15
nylon thread 205.2
  cloth 219.5
nymph larva 129.8
  divinity 979.8
nymphical 979.15
nymphid 367.7
nymphomania 961.3
nystagmic 443.14
nystagmus 443.1

O

O! 870.11
oaf dolt 501.1
  awkward fellow 701
  changeling 980.6
oafdom 499.2
oafish stupid 499.12
  clumsy 699.12
oak strength 159.4
  hardness 323.3
  tree 367.6; 369.8
  wood 635.3
oakum 205.3

oar oarsman 269.2
  paddle 273.14
  lie upon one's oars
    shirk 623.8
    do nothing 681.2
    lie idle 683.8
    relax 687.4
oarlock fulcrum 215.5
  pivot 312.5
oarsman 269.2
oasis 44.1
oath
  affirmation 535.2
  pledge 768.1
  curse 908.3
  under oath 768.6
oath helper 467.6
oatmeal 298.15
oats fodder 298.7
  plant 367.9
Obadiah 513.2
obbligato n. 88.1
obbligato adj. 88.8
obconical 245.17
obduracy
  obstinacy 606.1
  insensibility 823.1
  hardness of heart 907.1
  wickedness 945.1
  impenitence 951.1
obdurate
  obstinate 606.6
  strict 739.5
  hardened in vice 945.18
  impenitent 951.3
obeah, obi
  sorcery 992.1
  charm 993.2
obeah doctor 992.2
obedience
  compliance 743
  (submission 725.1)
  (subjection 749.1)
  (observance 772.1)
  (servility 886.1)
  obeisance 928.2
obedient 743.3
  (submissive 725.5)
  (serving 746.9)
  (subject 749.6)
  (observant 772.5)
  (servile 886.4)
  (dutiful 926.8)
  be obedient 743.2
  (serve 746.8)
obediently 743.4
obeisance 928.2
  (greeting 894.4)
  (worship 990.1; 998.2)
make obeisance 928.6
  (worship 990.9; 998.14)
  (idolatrize 991.6)
obeisant
  submissive 725.5
  obsequious 886.6
  deferential 928.8
obelisk tower 206.3
  tombstone 363.15

typography 550.8
monument 551.3
Oberon 979.9
obese 192.12
  (big-bellied 194.11)
  (chubby 201.6)
obesity 192.4
obey conform 82.5
  be obedient 743.2
  (submit 725.3)
  (be subject 749.3)
  (observe 772.3)
obfuscate
  obscure 421.5
  dim 422.6
  opaque 426.3
obfuscated
  intoxicated 959.21
  opaque 426.4
obfuscation
  obscuration 421.3
  opacity 426.1
  drunkenness 959.1
obfuscous 426.4
obi, obia, obiah See obeah
obit 360.3
obiter 134.11
obiter dictum 134.11
  (between 228.13)
obituary
  necrology 360.3
  biography 594.2
object n. article 316.3
  (something 3.2)
  (contrivance 626.5)
  experimentee 463.7
  meaning 516.1
  intention 620.2
  eyesore 846.3
  be an object 642.7
object v.
  take exception 469.5
  demur 485.7
  protest 489.4
  oppose 708.2
  dislike 867.4
  disapprove 932.5
objectify 220.6
objection protest 489.2
  obstacle 706.2
  disapprobation 932.1
  demurrer 937.2
  have no ~ 762.2
raise objections
  take exception 469.5
  demur 485.7
  protest 489.4
objectionable
  inexpedient 647.3
  intolerable 649.9
  uncommendable 932.13
  unjustifiable 941a.4
objective extrinsic 6.2
  material 316.10
  goal 620.2
objectiveness 6.1
objectivity 3.1
object lesson 82.2

objet d'art 556.8
objurgate 932.8
objurgation 932.3
objurgatory 932.11
oblation 990.6
  (gift 784.3)
  (atonement 952.1)
oblectate 827.5
oblectation 827.2
obligation
  necessity 601.1
  (requirement 630.1)
  compulsion 744.1
  promise 768.1
  condition 770.1
  debt 806.1
  duty 926.1
  (liability 177.1)
fulfill an obligation
  772.3, 4; 926.6
under obligation
  grateful 916.4
  obliged 926.10
obligatory
  mandatory 741.8
  compulsory 744.3
  incumbent on 926.9
  (required 630.3)
oblige
  accommodate 707.11
  compel 744.2
  (necessitate 601.8)
  (require 630.2)
  impose a duty 926.7
obliged grateful 916.4
  under obligation 926.10
  (required 630.3)
  (promised 768.7)
  be obliged 601.10
  much obliged! 916.5
obligement 744.1
obliging
  courteous 894.12
  benevolent 906.6
  (helpful 707.13)
obliquate 217.5
obliquation 279.1
oblique v. 217.5
  (curve 245.3)
  (deviate 279.7)
oblique adj. 217.9
  (cross 219.9)
  (angular 244.5)
  (curved 245.4)
  (deviative 279.8)
obliquely 217.17
  (crosswise 219.12)
  (laterally 236.8)
  (deviatively 279.9)
ob'ique motion 279.2
obliquity
  divergence 217
  (angularity 244.1)
  (curvature 245.1)
  (deviation 279.2)
  (circuit 629.1)
  immorality 945.1
obliterate
  destroy 162.4
  (nullify 2.6)
  efface 552.2

obliterated — obtuse

obliterated 552.3
obliteration
  extinction 162.2
  (nonexistence 2.3)
  effacement 552
  (oblivion 506.1)
oblivion
  nonexistence 2.1
  forgetfulness 506
  forgiveness 918.1
  fall into oblivion
    506.4
oblivious 506.8
obliviousness 506.1
oblong, oblongated
  200.14
oblongitude 200.2
oblongitudinal 200.14
obloquy
  disrepute 874.1
  malediction 908.1
  censure 932.2
  detraction 934.1
obmutescence
  aphonia 581.1
  taciturnity 585.1
obmutescent
  voiceless 581.7
  taciturn 585.4
obnoxious
  ~ to 177.5
  nasty 395.7
  horrible 649.8
  foul 653.17
  odious 830.14
  (hateful 898.7)
  disreputable 874.8
obnubilated 422.8
obnubilation
  cloudiness 353.4
  dimness 422.5
  opacity 426.1
oboe 417.4
oboist 416.2
obovate, obovoid 247.9
obreption 775.5
obreptitious 528.21
obscene 961.9
  (vulgar 851.6)
obscenity 961.1
  (vulgarity 851.1)
  (vice 945.1)
obscurantism 491.1
obscuration
  ~ of light 421.3
  vagueness 475.3
  unintelligibility
    519.1
  latency 526.1
obscure n. 421.1
obscure v.
  darken 421.5
  (render unintelligible 519.4)
  dim 422.6
  blind 442.3
  conceal 528.10
  (confuse 61.5)
obscure adj.
  dark 421.7
  dim 422.8
  blind 442.6

indistinct 447.5
vague 475.11
illogical 477.10
unintelligible 519.7
  (complex 59.10)
  (equivocal 520.5)
  (latent 526.6)
  (imperspicuous
    571.2)
  hidden 528.17
renownless 874.10
  (ignoble 876.11)
obscurity
  nullity 4.2
  darkness 421.1
  dimness 422.1
  vagueness 475.3
  unintelligibility
    519.1
  (imperspicuity
    571.1)
  latency 526.1
  insignificancy
    643.3, 6
  (commoner 876.4)
obsecrate 765.5
obsecration
  entreaty 765.2
  prayer 990.3
obsecrationary, obsecratory 765.7
obsequial 363.25
obsequies 363.4
obsequious 886.4
  (submissive 725.5)
  (compliant 743.3)
  (ingratiating
    894.13)
  (obeisant 928.8)
obsequiousness 886.1
  (obedience 743.1)
  (obeisance 928.2)
observable
  visible 446.4
  manifest 525.4
observance
  conformity 82.1
  espial 441.2
  attention 457.1
  custom 613.2
  (convention 852.2)
  conduct 692.1
  fulfillment 772
  (obedience 743.1)
  celebration 883.1
  ~ of duty 926.2
  orthodoxy 983a.1
  rite 998.1
Observant n. 996.11
observant adj.
  attentive 457.9
  vigilant 459.8
  faithful 772.5
  (obedient 743.3)
  (honorable 939.7)
observation
  conformity 82.1
  espial 441.2
  idea 453.1
  attention 457.1
  statement 582.4
  (assertion 535.1)

observance 772.1
orthodoxy 983a.1
observation balloon
  273a.5
observatory 318.10
observe conform 82.5
  see 441.10
  note 450.7
  give attention 457.4
  remark 582.6
  comply with 772.3
  (obey 743.2)
  celebrate 998.14
not observe 773.3
  (neglect 460.4)
  (evade 623.6)
observer
  aeronaut 269a.1
  spectator 444.1
obsess craze 503.11
  haunt 830.8
  (harass 860.13)
  demonize 978.6
obsessed
  fanatical 503.18
  (opinionated 606.7)
  bewitched 992.7
obsession
  prejudice 481.2, **3**
  mania 503.7
  bewitchment 993.1
obsidional 716.8
obsolesce
  antiquate 124.5
  be obsolescent 678.2
obsolescence
  archaism 563.10
  disuse 678.1
obsolescent
  word 563.18
  disused 678.6
obsolete v. 678.2
obsolete adj.
  antiquated 124.9
  (past 122.8)
  exploded 495.17
  word 563.18
  disused 678.6
  become obsolete 124.5
obsoletism
  word 563.10
  disuse 678.1
obstac'e 706.2
  (wall 232.2)
  (closure 261.1)
  (stopper 263.1)
  (difficulty 704.1)
  (impasse 704.3)
  (restraint 752.2)
obstacle race 840.11
obstetrician
  minister 631.2
  doctor 662.19
obstetrics birth 161.3
  healing art 662.16
obstinacy
  stubbornness 606
  (immovability
    150.1)
  (unwillingness
    603.1)
  (resolution 604.1)

(perseverance
  604a.1)
disobedience 742.1
obstinate 606.6
  (firm 150.5)
  (tough 327.5)
  (resolute 604.7)
  (unmanageable
    704.10)
  (resistant 719.5)
  be obstinate 606.5
  (be resolute 604.5)
  (persist 604a.2)
obstinately 606.8
obstipation 261.1
obstreperous
  noisy 404.9
  obstinate 606.6
obstruct 706.4
  (stanch 348.24)
obstruction 706.1, **2**
  (closure 261.1)
obstructionist
  counteractant 179.2
  hinderer 706.3
  oppositionist 710.2
obstructive n.
  counteractant 179.2
  hinderer 706.2, **3**
  oppositionist 710.2
obstructive adj. 706.8
obstruent 706.8
obtain exist 1.4
  induce 153.7
  acquire 775.6
  receive 785.3
obtainable 470.6
obtainment 775.1
obtenebrate 421.5
obtenebration 421.3
obtest 765.5
obtestation
  entreaty 765.2
  prayer 990.3
obtrude intrude 228.10
  meddle 682.14
obtruder 228.4
obtruncate 38.6
obtruncation
  excision 38.2
  shortening 201.2
obtrusion
  intrusion 228.3
  meddling 682.8
  hindrance 706.1
obtrusive
  intrusive 228.12
  meddlesome 682.22
  hindering 706.8
  gaudy 851.8
  forward 885.9
obtund
  moderate 174.5
  blunt 254.2
  deaden 376.4
  dull the feelings
    823.4
obtundent 823.5
obtundity
  bluntness 254.1
  insensibility 823.1
obtuse blunt 254.3

obtuse *(continued)*
　insensible 376.5
　stupid 499.12
　apathetic 823.5
obtuseness 499.2
obumbrate 421.5
obumbration 421.3
obverse
　the contrary 14.2
　front 234.1
obviate
　anticipate 132.5
　avert 706.5
obvious distinct 446.5
　manifest 525.4
　(intelligible 518.5)
ocarina 417.4
occasion *n.*
　circumstance 8.2
　time 134.2
　(chance 621.1)
　event 151.1
　cause 153.1
　reason 615.1
have occasion for
　630.2
occasion *v.* 153.6
occasional *adj.*
　incidental 134.9
　infrequent 137.2
　dependent 475.15
occasionally 137.4
　(sporadically 70.5)
occident 278.2
occidental 278.10
Occidental 560.5
occiput 235.1
occlude 261.2
occlusion 261.1
occlusive 402.2
occult *v.* 528.10, 16
occult *adj.*
　obscure 519.7
　hidden 528.17
　(latent 526.6)
　esoteric 994.21
　(supernatural
　　976.14)
occultate
　disappear 449.2
　hide 528.10, 16
occultation
　disappearance 449.1
　concealment 528.1
occulting screen
　screen 424.3
　shield 717.2
occultism 994.1
　(concealment 528.4)
occultist *n.* 994.13
occultist *adj.* 994.21
occupancy
　habitation 186.2
　possession 777.1
occupant
　inhabitant 188.1
　possessor 779.1
occupation
　habitation 186.2
　business 625.1, 5
　(undertaking 676.1)
　(work 686.3)
　possession 777.1
occupational 625.11
occupied
　inhabited 188.13
　thoughtful 451.36
　intent 457.9
　busy 682.20
be occupied with
　625.7
occupier 188.1
occupy inhabit 186.10
　engross 451.30
　busy 625.6
　~ a post 737.11
　possess 777.4
occupy oneself with
　be attentive 457.4
　engage in 625.7
　(undertake 676.2)
occupy the chair
　superintend 693.5
　rule 737.11
　preside 965.3
occur happen 151.3
　suggest itself 451.32
occurrence
　circumstance 8.1
　event 151.1
　appearance 448.1
ocean quantities 31.3
　sea 341
　(seaway 267.8)
ocean-going 267.48
oceanic 341.5
　(nautical 267.48)
Oceanid
　spirit of the sea
　　341.2
　nymph 979.10
ocean liner 273.1
oceanographer 341.4
oceanographic 341.5
oceanography 341.3
Oceanus
　spirit of the sea
　　341.2
　god 979.10
oceanward 341.8
ocelot 440.2
ocher, ochre 433.2;
　439.3
ocherous, ochreous
　yellow 436.6
　orange 439.5
ochlocracy 738.2
o'clock 114.10
octa-, oct- 98.18
octad eight 98.4
　microbe 193.4
octagon eight 98.4
　angle 244.2
octagonal, octahedral
　98.18
octahedron eight 98.4
　angle 244.2
octameter 98.4
octan, octangular
　98.18
Octans, Octant 318.6
octant 267a.29
octastich 597.7
Octateuch eight 98.4
　Scriptures 985.3
octave *n.* eight 98.4
　time 108.1
　music 413.19
　stanza 597.7
octave *v.* 416.18
octavo 593.8
octennial 138.5
octet, octette
　eight 98.4
　part music 415.12
octillion 98.13
octo-, oct- 98.18
octodecimo 593.8
octofid 99.3
octogenarian 130.1
octonary *n.* 98.4
octonary *adj.* 98.18
octoon 41.5
octopus
　animal 366.21; 368.6
　ugly thing 846.3
octoroon 41.5
octosyllable 98.4
octroi, octroy 812.2
octuple 98.18
ocular *n.* eye 441.7
　eyeglass 445.3
ocular *adj.* 441.18
oculate 445.10
oculist
　observer 444.1
　optician 445.8
　doctor 662.19
oculus 441.7
od 994.7
O.D. 269.1
odalisque, odalisk
　746.4
odd dissimilar 18.4
　unequal 28.3
　remaining 40.6
　unusual 83.10
　(absurd 497.4)
　(ridiculous 855.5)
　unique 87.7
　eccentric 503.17
oddity
　unusualness 83.3, 4
　eccentricity 503.6
oddly 31.21
oddments
　remains 40.1
　parts 51.6
odds difference 15.1
　inequality 28.1
　advantage 33.2
　gambling 621.5
　variance 713.2
at odds
　disagreeing 24.6
　dissentient 489.7
　opposed 708.4
　at loggerheads
　　713.10
long odds
　small chance 156.4
　(improbability
　　473.1)
　gambling 621.5
odds and ends
　remains 40.1

mixture 41.4
　parts 51.6
　rubbish 645.4
ode 597.2
Odelsting, Odelsthing
　696.6
odeum 599.10
Odin, Othin
　paternity 166.2
　wisdom 498.3
　war 722.7
　god 979.3
odious nasty 395.7
　horrible 649.8
　foul 653.17
　execrable 830.14
　(ugly 846.9)
　(dislikable 867.9)
　(hateful 898.7)
　disreputable 874.8
odium
　disrepute 874.1
　hate 898.1
odontalgia 378.1
odontoid convex 250.7
　toothlike 253.20
odophone 418.6
odor, odour 398
　(fragrance 400.1)
have an odor 398.5
odoriferous 398.8
　(fragrant 400.10)
odorize 400.9
　(scent 398.6)
odorous, odourous
　smelling 398.8
　(fragrant 400.10)
　fetid 401.4
odyl, odyle 994.6
oecologist, oeco'ogy
　See ecologist etc.
oecumenic, oecumenicity See ecumenic
　etc.
oedema, oedematous
　See edema etc.
Oedipean 462.11
Oedipus prophet 513.2
　interpreter 524.1
oenomancy 511.3
oenophilist 959.11
oesophagus See
　esophagus
oestrous 961.11
oestrous cycle,
　oestrum, oestrus
　961.3
œuvre 161.6
off *v.* 226.4
off *adj.* odd 83.10
　tainted 401.4;
　　653.17; 659.13
　erroneous 495.12
　crazy 503.12, 14
off *adv.* 196.6
　all off 67.9
offal rubbish 645.4
　filthy refuse 653.6
　(dregs 40.2)
　(excrements 299.2)
off and on
　by turns 138.13

offbeat — old-timer

changeably 149.7
alternately 314.14
 (irresolutely 605.7)
offbeat 413.23
off-color, off-colour
 428.16
offcut 591.2
offend repel 830.7
 give umbrage 900.10
 affront 929.3
 sin 945.9
 ~ against the law
  964.4
offender 949.2
offended
 displeased 828.14
 resentful 900.12
offense, offence
 attack 716.1
 provocation 830.2
 resentment 900.1, 5
 indignity 929.2
 misdeed 947.2
 violation of law
  964.2
 give offense 900.10
  (annoy 830.5)
 take offense 900.6
offensive n. 722.2
 on the offensive 716.9
offensive adj.
 nasty 395.7
 foul 653.17
 aggressive 716.8
 combative 722.13
 odious 830.14
 indecent 961.9
offer n.
 proffer 763
 proposal 765.3
 make an offer 902.7
offer v. allege 535.3
 proffer 763.2
 (volunteer 602.7)
 (give 784.8)
 ~ **for sale** 796.5
 bid 796.6
offer oneself 763.3
offering n. gift 784.3
 (offer 763.1)
 oblation 990.6
offering adj. 763.4
offertory
 music 415.11, 14
 offering 784.3; 990.6
 hymn 990.2
Offertory 998.7
offhand adj.
 cursory 458.10
 perfunctory 460.8
offhand adv.
 promptly 132.14
 by the way 134.11
 extemporaneously
  612.5
 do offhand 161.8
office agency 170.1
 room 191.16
 cockpit 273a.10
 tip 527.3
 appointment 609.5
 business 625.4

workshop 691
 bureau 745.9; 965.2
 commission 755.1
 divine service 990.7
hold office
 manage 693.5
 have authority
  737.11
office-bearer 694.3
office boy 746.1
officer
 officeholder 694.3
 military ~
  745.11, 12
  (soldier 726.4)
 civil ~ 746.9
officer of the day
 745.11
official n. officer 694.3
 attaché 746.1
official adj.
 authentic 494.12
 directive 693.6
 functional 625.11
 authoritative 737.15
 public ~ 745.9
officialism 737.7
officiant officer 694.3
 official 745.9
officiate
 perform duties 625.9
  (conduct 692.4)
 minister 631.3
 do service 746.8
 perform a rite 998.14
officious 682.22
officiousness 682.8
offing 213.4
 (distance 196.3)
 (outline 230.1)
offprint duplicate 21.2
 print 591.2
offscourings, offscum
 dregs 40.2
 offal 653.6
  (rubbish 645.4)
 ~ **of society** 876.2
offset n.
 compensation 30.2
 descendant 167.4
 counteractant 179.2
 imprint 591.2
offset v.
 compensate 30.5
 counteract 179.4
 print 591.14
offshoot adjunct 39.1
 member 51.4
 result 154.1
 descendant 167.4
 foliage 367.4
off side 238.2
offspring result 154.1
 product 161.6
 progeny 167.1
 descendant 167.4
  (youngling 129.1)
offtake 39a
oft 136.5
often adj. 136.3
often adv.
 repeatedly 104.8

frequently 136.5
 habitually 613.13
 not often 137.3
oftenness 136.1
oftentime adj. 136.3
**oftentime, oftentimes,
 oftly** adv. 136.5
oftness 136.1
ofttime adj. 136.3
**ofttime, ofttimes, oft-
 whiles** adv. 136.5
ogam, ogham
 alphabet 561.2
 language 563.5
 writing 590.1
ogdoad 98.4
ogee arch 215.18
 ornament 847.4
ogive 215.18
ogle n. eye 441.7
 amorous glance
  902.1
ogle v. eye 441.12, 13
 stare rudely 895.4
 flirt 902.7
ogre, ogress
 monster 83.7
 object of fear 860.7
 evildoer 913.4, 5
 demon 980.2
ogum See ogam
ohm, ohmage 158a.5
ohmic 158a.12
ohmmeter 158a.6
oil n. fat 356
  (lubricant 332.2)
  (fuel 388.1)
  (illuminant 420.15)
 painting 556.9
 balm 662.6
 flattery 933.1
oil v. lubricate 332.4
 bribe 618.3
 flatter 933.2
oilcloth 219.5
oiled 959.21
oil gauge 272.16
oiling 332.1
oil of myrcia 400.3
oil paint 428.5
oilpaper, oil silk 425.2
oilskins 225.17
oilstone 253.7
oily unctuous 355.3
  (smooth 255.5)
  (lubricant 332.5)
 bland 894.13
 flattering 933.3
ointment
 lubricant 332.2
 balm 662.6
 money 800.1
 unction 998.4
Oireachtas 696.4
Ojibway, Ojibwa 434.5
**O.K., OK., okay,
 okeh** n. 488.4
**O.K., OK., okay,
 okeh** v.
 endorse 488.10
 approve 931.5
O.K., OK., okay,

okeh adv. 535.8
okapi 206.7
old ancient 124.6
  (past 122.8)
  (former 122.10)
  (senile 499.16)
 elderly 128.9
 be old
  be ancient 124.4
  be elderly 128.6
 grow old 124.5; 128.7
 of old 122.14
 old age 128.2
  (oldness 124.1)
  (senility 499.5)
Old Clootie 978.1
old country 182.2
olden v.
 make old 124.5
 grow old 128.8
olden adj. 124.6
older, oldest
 elder 124.10
  (former 122.10)
 senior 128.9
Old Faithful 382.5
**oldfangled, old-
 fashioned** 124.9
  (unfashionable
   852.10)
Old Gentleman, the
 978.1
Old Glory 550.13
old gold n. 439.1
old-gold adj. 439.5
**Old Gooseberry, Old
 Harry** 978.1
old maid game 840.12
 spinster 904.3
old-maidish 904.5
old man elder 130.1
  (grandfather 166.8)
 father 166.6
 mariner 269.4
 husband 903.7
Old Nick 978.1
oldness
 ancientness 124
  (age 128.2)
  (maturity 131.1)
 elderliness 128.1
Old Poker 978.1
Old Probabilities
 513.3
old salt mariner 269.1
 veteran 700.3
old school 141.3
Old Scratch 978.1
old soldier
 tobacco 392a.5
 shirker 623.4
 veteran 700.3
old song
 trite saying 496.3
 trifle 643.3
old story
 trite saying 496.3
 stale news 532.1
 love 897.1
Old Testament 985.3
old-timer
 native 188.8

old-timy — oont

old-timer (*continued*)
  veteran 700.3
old-timy 124.9
old woman
  oldster 130.3
  (grandmother 166.9)
  mollycoddle 160a.3
  mother 166.7
  dotard 501.3
  wife 903.8
old-womanish 499.16
  (effeminate 160a.5)
old-womanishness 499.5
  (effeminacy 160a.1)
old-world 124.9
oleaginous, oleic 355.3
olein 356.1
olent 400.10
oleo
  oleomargarine 356.4
  curtain 599.15
oleomargarine, oleomargarin, oleo oil 356.4
oleoresin 356a.1
  (oil 356.3)
olericultural 371.9
olericulture 371.1
oleum 356.1
olfaction 398.2, 3
olfactories 398.4
  (nose 250.4)
olfactory 398.9
olibanum 400.3
olid 401.4
oligarch 745.2
oligarchic 737.16
oligarchy 737.4
olio 41.4
olivaceous 435.6
olive *n.* tree 367.6
  green 435.2
  wood 635.3
olive *adj.* brown 433.4
  green 435.6
olive branch
  descendant 167.4
  peace offering 723.2, 4
olive-drab 225.8
olive green *n.* 435.2
olive-green *adj.* 435.6
olive oil 356.3
olivine 435.3
olla-podrida
  mixture 41.4
  (miscellany 72.8)
  confusion 59.2
ology 490.7
Olympian 981.7
Olympus 981.2
omasum 191.7
omber, ombre 840.12
ombrometer 348.12
omega 67.1
omelet, omelette 298.28
omen *n.* foretoken 512
  (precursor 64.1)
  (prediction 511.1)

(sign 550.1)
(warning 668.3)
(threat 909.1)
good ~ 858.1
of good omen
  auspicious 512.4
  propitious 858.11
omen *v.* 511.7, 9
  (forewarn 668.7)
ominous
  predictive 511.11
  (indicative 550.21)
  (dangerous 665.7)
  (forewarning 668.10)
  portentous 512.3, 5
  (unfortunate 735.9)
  (threatening 909.3)
omission
  deficiency 53.2
  (interval 198.1)
  exclusion 55.1
  neglect 460.1
  mistake 495.2
  failure 732.1
  nonobservance 773.1
  delinquency 945.3
  sin of ~ 947.2
omit exclude 55.3
  pretermit 460.7
  not observe 773.3
omitted
  nonexistent 2.7
  absent 187.10
omnibus
  vehicle 272.6
  automobile 272.15
omnifarious 81.2
omnific 168.8
omniform 81.2
omniformity 81.1
omnigenous 81.2
omnipotence
  almightiness 157.5
  divine attribute 976.2
Omnipotence 976.2
omnipotent
  almighty 157.8
  divine 976.12
the Omnipotent 976.5
omnipresence
  ubiquity 186.4
  divine attribute 976.2
omnipresent 976.12
omniscience
  knowledge 490.3
  divine attribute 976.2
omniscient
  informed 490.15
  divine 976.12
the Omniscient 976.5
omnium-gatherum
  mixture 41.4
  confusion 59.2
  miscellany 72.8
omnivore 298.41
omnivorous
  eating 298.48
  greedy 865.20

gluttonous 957.4
omnivorousness 298.1
omophagist 298.41
omophagous 298.48
omoplatoscopy 511.3
ompnalos 222.2
onager ass 271.10
  animal 366.2
once formerly 122.14
  (then 119.2)
one time 137.5
at once
  instantly 113.6, 7
  promptly 132.14
  (hastily 684.7)
once and again 137.4
once for all
  finally 67.11
  once 137.5
  definitely 604.9
  chosen 609.17
once in a while 137.4
once more 104.8
  (twice 90.5)
once-over 441.2
  give the once-over
  scrutinize 441.12
  glance at 461.19
once upon a time 122.14
on-dit 532.3
one *n.* unit 87.2
  person 372.3
be at one
  concur 488.7
  be concordant 714.2
one *adj.* identical 13.6
  whole 50.6
  single 87.6
  unique 87.7
  married 903.16
one by one
  separately 44.14
  severally 79.12
  individually 87.10
one and all 50.2
  everyone 78.5, 13
  unanimously 488.17
one another 12.3
one day 122.14
one-eyed 443.14
one half 101.1
one-horse little 193.8
  paltry 643.12
  mediocre 736.3
Oneida 434.5
oneirocritic 524.1
oneirocriticism, oneirology 522.5
oneiromancy 511.3
oneness identity 13.1
  singleness 87.1
one or two 100.1
oner 648.4
onerous heavy 310.12
  laborious 686.10
  difficult 704.8
  impedimentary 706.8
  oppressive 830.16
oneself 79.4
  for oneself 943.5

one-sided
  unilateral 236.7
  distorted 243.5
  prejudiced 481.10
  unjust 941a.3
one-sidedness 481.3
one-step music 415.7
  dance 840.7
one third 101.1
on-go 282.1
ongoing *n.*
  course 264.3
  progression 282.1
ongoing *adj.*
  progressive 282.3
  improving 658.16
onion
  vegetable 298.30
  condiment 393.1
  malodor 401.2
onionpeel, onionskin 425.2
onlooker 444.1
only to a degree 32.13
  simply 42.7
  unique 87.7
  if only! 865.23
  only-begotten 87.7
onomancy 511.3
onomasticon 593.4
onomatopoeia, onomatopoësis, onomatopoesy 521.1; 562.2
Onondaga 434.5
onrush course 264.3
  flow 348.2
onset beginning 66.1
  attack 716.1
onslaught 716.1
ontogenesis 161.5
ontogenetic 161.11
  (evolutional 313.3)
ontogeny
  evolution 161.5
  organic science 357.5
ontoogism 451.15
ontology
  existence 1.3
  cosmology 451.22
onus
  impediment 706.2
  duty 926.1
onward
  frontward 234.10
  forward 282.5
onychomancy, onycomancy 511.3
onyx 847.8
oöcyte 357.4
oodles 31.3
oecium 357.4
oof, ooftish 800.1
oofy 803.8
oögamous 357.10
oögamy
  dissimilarity 18.1
  germ 357.4
oögenesis 161.2
oögonium 357.4
oont 271.2

oöphyte — opposite

oöphyte 357.4
oöphytic 357.10
oösperm, oösphere,
 oöspore 357.4
oösporous 357.10
ooze n. leakage 295.1
 mud 352.4
ooze v. leak out 295.7
 (trickle 348.19)
 be watery 337.4
 ~ out 529.6
oozing 295.1
oozy infiltrative 337.6
 marshy 345.3
 muddy 352.9
opacity 426
opacous 426.4
opal 440.2
opalesce 427.3
opalescence 427.1
opalescent
 semitransparent
  427.4
 iridescent 440.6
opaline n. 427.2
opaline adj. 427.4
opalize 427.3
opaque n. 424.4
opaque v. 426.3
opaque adj. 426.4
 (dark 421.7)
opaqueness 426.1
ope 260.11
open n. 338.3
open v. begin 66.5
 grow 194.6
 unclose 260.12
 (separate 198.4)
 evolve 313.2
 disclose 529.3
 ~ an account 794.8
open one's eyes
 be informed 527.11
 wonder 870.2
open one's mouth
 speak 582.6
 wonder 870.2
open up begin 66.5
 disclose 529.3, 5
open adj.
 unclosed 260.15
 (hollow 252.10)
 phonetics 402.11
 visible 446.4
 uncertain 475.9
 unprejudiced 498.12
 manifest 525.4
 (disclosed 529.7)
 (public 531.10)
 sincere 543.3
 unprotected 665.9
 frank 703.4
 honest 939.7
in the open
 outdoors 220.9;
  338.13
 openly 525.7
lay open divest 226.4
 open 260.11
 show 525.2
 disclose 529.3
open to

liable to 177.3
 (unprotected 665.9)
 easy 705.5
openable 260.20
open account 811.1
open-and-shut
 assured 474.9
 obvious 525.4
 predetermined 611.5
open air 338.3
open court
in open court
 openly 525.7
 publicly 531.12
open-eared
 eared 418.14
 attentive 457.9
opener
 beginning 66.1
 device 260.10
 (medium 631.2)
open-eyed
 curious 455.5
 attentive 457.9
 vigilant 459.8
 expectant 507.7
openhanded 816.4
openhearted
 veracious 543.3
 artless 703.4
 generous 816.4
 honest 939.7
open house 816.3
keep an open house
 892.11
opening n.
 beginning 66.1
 occasion 134.2
 space 180.3
 hole 260
 (cleft 198.2)
 (inlet 294.5)
 (outlet 295.5)
 (passage 302.1)
 (loophole 671.4)
 appearance 448.1
opening adj. 260.21
openly 525.7
open market 799.1
open-minded 498.12
openmouthed
 vociferous 411.8
 curious 455.5
 attentive 457.9
 expectant 507.7
 greedy 865.20
 astonished 870.6
open order 716.1
Open sesame! 260.22
open-sesame
 passkey 260.10
 password 550.11
 magic formula 993.1
open spaces 180.3
opera production 161.6
 music 415.3, 10, 12,
  17, 21
 poetry 597.2
 drama 599.3
 playbook 599.16
opéra ballet 415.17
opera glass 445.2

operagoer 416.15
opera hat 225.26
opera house 599.10
operate
 produce 153.7; 161.8
 act 170.2; 680.5
 pilot 267.11
 remedy 662.24
operate upon
 motivate 615.7
 work on feelings
  824.2
operatic
 operative 170.4
 musical 415.28
operating 170.4
operation agency 170.1
 action 680.1
 warfare 722.1
in operation 170.4
 (acting 680.7)
put in operation 677.5
operative
 operating 170.4
 (instrumental 631.4)
 (acting 680.7)
 agent 690.1
be operative 170.2
operator
 speculator 621.15
 surgeon 662.19
 user 677.4
 agent 690.1
opercled, operculate
 261.3
operculum lid 223.7
 closure 261.1
operetta
 musicale 415.17
 drama 599.3
operose
 laborious 686.10
 difficult 704.8
ophicleide 417.4
ophidian n. 366.19
ophidian, ophio-
 logic adj. 366.27
ophiologist 368.2
ophiology 368.1
ophiomancy 511.3
ophiomorphous 366.27
ophite 440.2
Ophiuchus 318.6
ophiuran 368.14
ophthalmia 443.1
ophthalmic 441.18
ophthalmologist
 662.19
opiate 662.7
 (alleviative 174.3)
 (anesthetic 376.2)
 (sleep-inducer
  683.6)
opine judge 480.6
 think 484.8
 suppose 514.6
opinion n. 484.2
 (idea 453.1)
 (judgment 480.1)
be of the opinion
 484.8
in my opinion 484.17

opinion v. 480.6
opinionated
 dogmatic 474.15
 bigoted 606.7
 (zealotic 503.18)
opinionatedness 606.2
opinioned 474.15
opinionist 606.3
 (dogmatist 474.4)
 (zealot 504.2)
opisthograph 590.3
opisthography 590.1
opium 662.7
 (poison 663.6)
opium eater 683.7
opium poppy 663.6
oppidan n. 188.2
oppidan adj. 189.22
oppidum 189.17
opponent 710
 (assailant 716.4)
 (combatant 726.1)
 (malcontent 832.2)
 (gamester 840.17)
 (enemy 891.1)
opportune 134.7
 (expedient 646.4)
opportunely 134.10
 (expediently 646.6)
opportuneness 134.1
opportunism 646.1
opportunist 605.3
opportunity
 occasion 134.2, 3
 (chance 156.1;
  621.1)
 expedience 646.1
have an opportunity
 156.9
seize the opportunity
 134.6; 682.12
oppose
 be contrary 14.3
 ~ change 141.5
 confront 234.7
 contrapose 237.4, 5
 compare 464.2
 ~ evidence 468.2
 (confute 479.2)
 deny 536.2
 be hostile to 708.2
 (be unwilling 603.4)
 (counteract 179.3)
 (thwart 706.7)
 (resist 719.3)
 (contend 720.8)
 (restrain 751.6)
opposed contrary 14.5
 ~ to change 141.7
 hostile 708.4
 (unwilling 603.5)
 adverse 735.8
be opposed to
 be contrary 14.3
 oppose 708.2
opposer 710.2
 (malcontent 832.2)
opposing contrary 14.5
 adverse 735.8
opposite n.
 the contrary 14.2
 (counterpart 17.5)

opposite — order

opposite (*continued*)
  contraposition 237.2
    (inverse 218.3)
  opponent 710.1
  opposites 237.3
opposite *adj.*
  contrary 14.5
  contrapositive 237.6
    (inverted 218.6)
  adverse 735.8
 be opposite 237.5
 opposite to 237.7
oppositely 468.5
opposition
  contrariety 14.1
  ~ to change 141.2
  counteraction
    179.1, 2
  contraposition 237.1
  comparison 464.1
  counterevidence
    468.1
  hostility 708
    (disagreement 24.1)
    (hindrance 706.1)
    (discord 713.1)
    (resistance 719.1)
    (contention 720.1)
    (restraint 751.1)
  opponents 710.1
  disapprobation 932.1
 in opposition
  in disagreement
    24.10
  opposite 237.7
  opposed 708.4, 5
    (counteractively
    179.6)
  adverse 735.8
oppositional
  contrary 14.5
  opposing 708.4
    (counteractive
    179.5)
    (resistant 719.5)
    (contentious 720.11)
oppositionary 179.5
oppositionist
  counteractant 179.2
  opponent 710.1
    (hinderer 706.3)
**oppositious, opposi-
tive** 179.5
opposure
  counteraction 179.1
  opposition 708.1
oppress weigh 319.8
  aggrieve 649.6
  tyrannize 739.4
  subjugate 749.5
oppression
  ill-treatment 649.4
  despotism 739.2
  subjugation 749.1
  affliction 830.2
  depression 837.4
oppressive
  heavy 319.12
  sultry 382.18
  tyrannical 739.5
  burdensome 830.16
oppressor tyrant 739.3

evildoer 913.1
opprobrious 874.8
opprobrium
  infamy 874.1
  malediction 908.1
oppugn
  counteract 179.3
  oppose 708.2
oppugnacy
  resistance 719.1
  enmity 889.1
oppugnance
  counteraction 179.1
  opposition 708.1
  resistance 719.1
oppugnant *n.*
  counteractant 179.2
  opponent 710.1
oppugnant *adj.*
  counteractive 179.5
  opposing 708.4
  resistant 719.5
  inimical 889.3
oppugnation
  opposition 708.1
  resistance 719.1
  enmity 889.1
oppugner 179.2
opsimathy 537.1
opt 609.7
optable 865.21
optant 609.15
optate 609.7
optation 609.1
optative *n.* 865.8
optative *adj.* 865.16
optical 420.24
optician 445.8
  (workman 690.10)
optic nerve 441.7
optics eyes 441.7
  photics 420.16
  optometry 445.7
  (vision 441.1)
optimates 875.2
optime
  learned man 492.1
  student 541.4
optimism
  overestimation 482.1
  hopefulness 858.2
    (cheerfulness 836.1)
optimist 858.5
  (commender 935.1)
optimistic 858.9
  (cheerful 836.7)
option 609.1
  (will 600.1)
at the option of
  609.17
optional
  volitional 600.4
  elective 609.14
  (voluntary 602.10)
  permissive 760.6
optionally 609.17
  (voluntarily 600.5)
optometer 445.1
optometrist
  optician 445.8
  doctor 662.19
optometry 445.7

optophone 418.6
opulence plenty 639.2
  wealth 803.1
opulent 803.8
opus product 161.6
  music 415.3
    (composition 54.2)
  writing 590.3
  book 593.1
opuscule, opuscle
  593.1
or *n.* 436.1
or *conj.* 609.17
oracle
  wise saying 496.2
  sage 500.1
  prophet 513
    (interpreter 524.1)
    (adviser 695.3)
oracular
  answering 462.11
  dogmatic 474.15
  vague 475.11
  profound 498.11
  predictive 511.11
oral *n.* 461.3
oral *adj.*
  evidence 467.11
  spoken 582.10
    (verbal 562.8)
    (vocal 580.11)
oraler 621.15
orally 582.13
oral method 419.5
orange *n.* sphere 249.2
  fruit 298.31
  color 439
orange *adj.* 439.5
orangeade 298.4
**orangeberry, orange-
bird** 439.2
orange madder 439.1
Orangemen's Day
  138.7
orangery 371.6
orange shellac 439.3
orange vermilion 439.1
**orangutan, orangou-
tang, orangoutan,
oranutan** 366.16
Oraon 560.4
orate 582.7
oration *n.* 582.2
oration *v.* 582.7
orator 582.5
oratorical 582.12
oratorio
  part music 415.12
  musicale 415.17
oratory
  elocution 582.3
    (loftiness 574.4)
    (fluency 584.1)
  chapel 1000.1
orb region 181.1
  zone 230.2
  circle 247.2
  sphere 249.2
  heavenly body 318.3
  eye 441.7
  sphere of work 625.3
  royal insignia 747.1

orbic, orbicular 249.7
  (round 247.8)
**orbicularity, orbicula-
tion** 249.1
orbit region 181.1
  zone 230.2
  circle 247.2
  heavens 318.8
  path 627.2
  circuit 629.1
orby 249.7
orchard grove 367.7
  arboretum 371.6
  source of supply
    636.2
orchestra
  musicians 416.9
  instruments 417.1
  audience 418.8
orchestral
  symphonious 413.26
  musical 415.28
  of orchestras 416.24
orchestra pit 599.12
orchestrate 60.8
  harmonize 413.24
  instrumentate
    415.26
orchestrater 416.14
orchestration
  instrumentation
    413.3
  musical piece 415.3
    (arrangement 60.3)
orchestrion 417.8
orchid plant 369.8
  beauty 845.4
orchotomy 158.2
ordain
  pass judgment 480.9
  destine 601.9
  command 741.4
    (will 600.2)
  commission 755.4
  grant 760.4
  enact 963.4
  predestinate 976.10
  ~ to the ministry
    995.7
ordained
  destined 601.13
  warranted 924.10
  ~ to the ministry
    996.7
ordeal test 463.1
  ~ of battle 722.1
  trial 735.1
  mental suffering
    828.1
  sorcery 992.1
order *n.* condition 7.1
  regularity 58
  (arrangement 60.1)
  (rule 80.1)
  class 75.1
  kind 75.2
  animal kingdom
    366.1
  vegetable kingdom
    367.1
  denomination 542.4
  sect 712.1

990

~ of battle 722.1
command 741.1
(precept 697.1)
money ~ 800.7
social ~ 873.4
religious ~ 984.3
at one's orders
 obedient 743.3, 4
 in subjection 749.7
by order 741.9
give an order 741.4
in order 58.7, 8
 (arranged 60.10)
in order to 620.6
out of order
 disorderly 59.8
 unconformable 83.9
 unprepared 674.7
put in order 60.6
 (touch up 658.10)
 (prepare 673.6)
to order 741.9
under one's orders
 749.6
order v.
 regulate 58.6
 arrange 60.6
 pass judgment
  480.9
 direct 693.4
 command 741.4
 (authorize 737.10)
 (legalize 963.4)
orderless 59.8
 (shapeless 241.5)
orderliness 58.4
 (arrangement 60.3)
 (care 459.1)
orderly n. 746.1
orderly adj. 58.7
 (uniform 16.5)
 (arranged 60.10)
 (regular 80.3)
 (symmetrical 242.4)
 (careful 459.7)
 (businesslike
  625.11)
be orderly, become
 orderly 58.5
orderly officer 745.11
order of the day
 circumstances 151.2
 schedule 611.2
 decree 741.3
 fashion 852.2
Order of the Purple
 Heart 733.2
ordinal 998.9
ordinance order 741.1
 law 963.2
 rite 998.1
ordinary mean 29.3
 table d'hôte 298.39
 customary 613.11
 insignificant 643.10
 mediocre 736.3
 homely 846.6
 plain 849.3
ordinate and abscissa
 466.7
ordination
 arrangement 60.1

decree 741.3
appointment 755.2
holy order 995.6
ordnance 727.11
ordonnance 963.2
ordure 653.7
 (excrement 299.2)
ore 635.6
oread 979.8
orectic 865.16
Oregon Jargon 560.5
organ n.
 music instrument
  417.5
 implement 633.1
organ v. 416.18
organdy, organdie
 219.5
organ-grinder 416.6
organic
 formative 240.9
 organized 357.8
organic chemistry
 357.5
organism
 arrangement 60.3
 living being 357.1, 2
organist 416.5
organity 357.1, 2
organization
 arrangement 60.1
 (plan 626.1)
 production 161.1
 organic matter 357.1
 religious ~ 984.3
organize v. order 58.6
 methodize 60.8
 create 161.8
organized
 intoxicated 959.21
 organic 357.8
organizer
 planner 626.8
 director 694.1
organography, orga-
 nology 240.4
 (science of texture
  329.2)
organotherapy 662.16
organ point
 low tone 408.6
 key 413.7
orgasm outbreak 173.2
 spasm 315.7
orgasmic, orgastic
 173.12
orgiastic 954.5
orgy debauch 954.2
 (spree 840.3)
 drinking bout 959.3
oriel 260.5
orient n. 278.2
orient v. 278.7
orient adj.
 oriental 278.10
 luminous 420.22
orientate 278.7
orientation
 direction 278.1
 habituation 613.5
orifice 260.1
 (inlet 294.5)

oriflamme, oriflamb
 550.13
Origenism 984.4
origin cause 153.1
 (beginning 66.2)
 (descent 166.4)
 etymology 562.4
original n.
 prototype 22.1
 (nonimitation 20.2)
 nonconformist 83.4
 native 188.8
 manuscript 590.3
original adj.
 intrinsic 5.6
 primary 66.7
 peculiar 79.8
 unconformable 83.11
 (dissimilar 18.4)
 (unimitated 20.3)
 causal 153.9
 (creational 161.11)
 native 188.11
 basal 211.5
 imaginative 515.11
originality
 nonimitation 20.1
 (dissimilarity 18.1)
 nonconformity 83.2
 creative thought
  515.1
 will 600.1
originate begin 66.6
 cause 153.6
 result 154.3
 invent 515.10
 author 590.14
origination
 composition 54.2
 causation 153.5
 production 161.1, 6
 authorship 590.2
originative 161.11
 (causal 153.9)
originator 164.1
 (author 593.15)
oriole bird 366.22
 songbird 416.11
Orion, Orion's Belt
 318.6
orismological 564.9
orismology
 terminology 562.4
 nomenclature 564.1
orison 990.3
Oriya 560.4
Ormazd 976.2
ormolu 545.6
ornament n.
 music 413.10; 415.20
 ornate speech 577
 (figure of speech
  521.1)
 trophy 733.1
 decoration 847
ornament v.
 speech 577.4
 decorate 847.11
 (paint 428.10)
 (art 556.17)
 (engrave 558.5)
 (beautify 845.7)

ornamental 847.12
 (artistic 845.16)
ornamentalism 556.6
ornamentalist 559.1
ornamentation
 ornate speech 577.1
 decoration 847.1, 3
ornamented, ornate
 rhetorical 577.6
 adorned 847.13
 (gaudy 851.8)
 (ostentatious 882.8)
ornately 577.8
ornateness
 rhetoricalness 577.1
 ornamentation 847.1
ornation, ornature
 847.1
orniscopy 511.3
Ornithischia 124.2
ornithologist 368.2
ornithology 368.1
ornithomancy 511.3
ornithopod, Ornitho-
 poda 124.2
ornithotomist 368.2
ornithotomy 368.1
orotund 577.7
orotundity
 rotundity 249.1
 grandiloquence
  577.2
 pomposity 882.1
Orpheus 416.16
orpiment 436.4
orrery 318.10
orthodiagonal n.
 212.2
orthodiagonal adj.
 244.5
orthodox n. 484.6
orthodox adj.
 conformable 82.10
 (authentic 494.12)
 authoritative 474.13
 (doctrinal 484.16)
 conventional 852.8
 religion 983a.7
orthodoxy 983a
 (conformity 82.1)
 (belief 484.1)
 (authenticity 494.2)
orthoëpist 560.7
orthoëpy
 lexicology 562.4
 pronunciation 580.3
orthogenesis 161.2
orthogonal 244.5
 (vertical 212.8)
orthogonality 212.1
orthographic projec-
 tion 556.1
orthographize 561.8
orthography 561.4
orthological 494.11
orthology 494.3
orthometric 244.5
orthometry
 measurement 466.8
 versification 597.5
orthopedics, ortho-
 paedics 662.16

orthopedist — outlay 992

orthopedist, orthopae-
  dist 662.19
orthopraxy 662.16
orthopter 273a.1
orts remains 40.1
  rubbish 645.4
oryx 366.10
oscillate
  fluctuate 149.4
  electrify 158a.11
  vibrate 314.8
  (recur 138.8)
  be irresolute 605.4
oscillation
  vibration 314
  (changeableness
    149.1)
  irresolution 605.1
oscillator 314.6
oscillatory
  vibratory 314.12
  irresolute 605.5
oscillograph, oscil-
  lometer, oscillo-
  scope 314.7
oscitancy
  gaping 260.9
  drowsiness 683.4
oscitant gaping 260.15
  sleepy 683.15
oscitate 683.9
oscitation 683.4
osculate
  be contiguous 199.3
  contact 379.3
osculation joint 43.3
  contiguity 199.1
  contact 379.1
  kiss 894.4; 902.3
osculatory
  contiguous 199.4
  pax 998.8
Osiris deity 979.5
  god 982.4
Osmanli 560.4
osmosis 302.1
osmotic 302.3
osseous 323.5
Ossetic 560.4
ossification 323.2
ossified 323.5
ossify 323.4
ossuary
  funeral urn 363.11
  burial place 363.13
ostensibility 472.1
ostensible
  apparent 448.7
  plausible 472.6
  manifest 525.4
  (pretexed 619.3)
ostensibly 619.4
ostent
  appearance 448.4
  ostentation 882.1
ostentation 882
  (finery 225.13)
  (exaggeration
    549.1)
  (frippery 847.2)
  (gaudiness 851.2)
  (affectation 853.1)

(pride 878.1)
(vanity 880.1)
(arrogance 885.1)
ostentatious
  gaudy-colored
    428.15
  grandiloquent 577.7
  pretentious 882.8
  (conspicuous 525.5)
  (exaggerated 549.3)
  (ornate 847.13)
  (gaudy 851.8)
  (affected 853.6)
  (proud 878.6)
  (vain 880.6)
  be ostentatious 882.6
  (affect 853.5)
  (bluster 887.3)
ostentatiously 882.11
ostentatiousness 882.1
osteography, osteol-
  ogy 240.4
osteopath 662.19
osteopathy 662.16
osteophone 418.6
ostiary
  embouchure 260.3
  doorkeeper 717.6
ostium 260.6
ostler See hostler
ostracism 297.3
  (exclusion 893.3)
ostracize 297.11
  (exclude 55.3;
    893.7)
ostrich 274.6
Ostyak, Ostiak 560.4
otalgia 378.1
other different 15.9
  additional 37.7
  no other same 13.3
  unit 87.2
othergates, other-
  guess, otherhow 18.6
otherness 15.1
othersome 15.9
otherways, otherwise
  18.6
  (contrarily 14.7)
  (differently 15.10)
  (notwithstanding
    30.8)
Othin See Odin
otic 418.13
otiose
  unproductive 169.4
  languid 683.14
otiosity
  unproductiveness
    169.1
  indolence 683.3
otography 418.9
otologist aurist 418.10
  doctor 662.19
otology, otopathy,
  otoplasty 418.9
otorhinolaryngol-
  ogist 418.10
otorrhea 418.9
otoscope 418.6
otoscopy 418.9
ottar See attar

ottava 413.19
otter brown 433.1
otterhound 366.6
otto See attar
ottoman 215.22
oubliette 752.1
ough! 874.12
ouija 994.5
ounce 319.4
ouphe 980.3
Our Lady 977.2
ourselves 372.2
ousel See ouzel
ousia 994.11
oust eject 297.8, 9
  (dispossess 789.11)
  depose 756.5
ouster eviction 297.2
  ejector 297.6
ousting 297.1
out v. 162.4; 385.5
out adj.
  dissimilar 18.4
  odd 83.10
  dead drunk 950.22
  erroneous 495.12
  be out 523.2
  be out of it 156.11
  from out to out 200.16
  just out 123.9
  out at elbows, out at
    heels poor 804.7
  in disrepute 874.9
out adv. 220.8
out of
  wanting 640.11
  escaped 671.7
out prep. 38.11
out-and-out
  absolute 31.12
  unqualified 52.10
outbalance excel 33.5
  outweigh 319.10
outbid 794.5
outbound 295.9
outbrave 885.7
outbrazen face 234.7
  outface 885.7
outbreak
  beginning 66.1
  eruption 173.2
  egress 295.1
  revolt 742.2
  ~ of passion 825.5
outburst
  eruption 173.2
  (debacle 162.3)
  egress 295.1
  ~ of passion 825.5
  ~ of laughter 838.3
  ~ of anger 900.3
outcast n. outlet 295.5
  pariah 893.5
  (alien 57.3)
  (vagabond 876.9)
outcast adj. 893.10
outcaste 893.5
outcome result 154.1
  egress 295.1
  outlet 295.5
  produce 775.2
outcoming 295.1

outcrop n. 446.1
outcrop v. 446.2
outcropping 446.1
outcry n.
  vociferation 411.2
  (noise 404.2)
  auction 796.2
  wail 839.1
outcry v. 796.6
outdo excel 33.5
  outstrip 303.4
  defeat 731.9
outdone 732.12
outdoor 220.7
outdoors n. 338.3
outdoors adv.
  outside 220.8
  in the open 338.13
outer, outermost 220.7
outface 885.7
outfit n. company 72.3
  messuage 189.12
  wardrobe 225.2
  equipment 634.1
  clique 712.2
  military unit 726.7
outfit v. clothe 225.42
  equip 634.2
outfitter 225.36
outflank 731.9
outflanked 732.12
outflow 295.1
outgate 295.5
outgeneral 731.9
outgo n. egress 295.1
  outlet 295.5
outgo v. 303.4
outgoer 295.4
outgoing n.
  egress 295.1
  expenditure 809.1
outgoing adj. 295.9
outgrow 194.6; 365.2
outgrowth result 154.1
  (sequel 65.1)
  product 161.6
  excrescence 250.2
out-Herod excel 33.5
  exaggerate 549.2
outhouse 653.9
outing 266.8
outjump 303.4
outland 57.4
outlander 57.3
outlandish
  irrelative 10.5
  alien 57.4
  unusual 83.10
  eccentric 503.17
  language 563.15;
    579.3
  uncouth 851.7
outlast 110.8
outlaw n. horse 271.6
  outcast 893.5
  criminal 949.2
outlaw v. 207.11
  (exclude 893.7)
out'aw, outlawed adj.
  964.5
outlawry 964.1
outlay 809.1

outleap — overconfident

outleap 303.4
outlet chasm 198.3
  exit 295.5
  (portal 260.4)
  (valve 263.2)
  (conduit 350.1)
  (path 627.2)
  (loophole 671.4)
outlie 196.4
outline *n.*
  contour 230
  (enclosure 232.1)
  lineaments 448.5
  drawing 556.9
  writing 590.3
  synopsis 596.1
  plan 626.2
  (copy 22.2)
  (arrangement 60.3)
  (compendium 596.1)
  (schedule 611.2)
  (undevelopment 674.3)
outline *v.*
  contour 230.3
  (circumscribe 229.2)
  plan 626.9
outlinear, outlined
  230.4
  (circumscribed 229.4)
outlines 66.4
outlive outlast 110.8
  be permanent 141.4
outlook *n.* 448.2
out'ook *v.* 885.7
outlying
  remaining 40.6
  exterior 220.7
outmaneuver, out-
  manoeuvre
  circumvent 545.8
  defeat 731.9
outmarch 303.4
outnumber 102.4
out-of-date
  anachronous 115.3
  antiquated 124.9
  (untimely 135.6)
  (unfashionable 852.10)
out of doors
  outside 220.9
  outdoors 338.3, 13
out-of-the-way
  remote 10.7; 196.5
  isolated 893.10
out-of-work 683.12
outpatient 655.20
outplay, outpoint 33.5
outpoise 319.10
outpost distance 196.3
  surroundings 227.2
  edge 231.1
  van 234.2
outpour 205.1
output 775.2
outrage *n.*
  ill-treatment 649.4
  injury 659.3
  misuse 679.1

resentment 900.5
  malevolent act 907.4
  indignity 929.2
  crime 947.2
outrage *v.*
  maltreat 649.7
  give umbrage 900.10
  affront 929.3
outrageous
  immense 31.9
  exaggerated 549.3
  disreputable 874.8
outrank excel 33.5
  precede 62.2
outré odd 83.10
  absurd 497.4
  exaggerated 549.3
outreach extend 196.4
  circumvent 545.8
outreckon 482.3
outride 303.4
outrigger shaft 215.13
  ship 273.2
outright 52.10
outrival excel 33.5
  outstrip 303.4
outrun 303.4
outrun the constable
  be in debt 806.5, 6
  squander 818.3
outscouring 653.6
outset
  beginning 66.1
  departure 293.1
outside *n.*
  exterior 220.2
  (side 236.1)
  limit 233.1
  appearance 448.5
outside *adj.*
  extraneous 57.4
  exterior 220.7
outside *adv.* 220.8
outsider 57.3
  (outcast 893.5)
outskirt distance 196.3
  edge 231.1
outskirts 227.2
outspan 292.8
outspeak 582.6
outspoken
  spoken 582.10
  frank 703.4
  (veracious 543.3)
  be outspoken 932.7
outspread *v.* 202.4
outspread *adj.* 202.6
outstanding
  remaining 40.6
  exterior 220.7
  prominent 642.10
  due 806.9
  notable 873.16
outstart 66.1
outstep 303.4
outstretch
  extend 196.4
  be long 200.8
  broaden 202.4
outstretched
  lengthened 200.12
  broad 202.6

outstrip excel 33.5
  speed 274.9
  outrun 303.4
  (lead 280.2)
outtalk 584.4
out-Tory 33.5
outvie rival 648.7
  compete with 720.9
outward 220.7
  (extrinsic 6.2)
outward-bound
  departing 293.10
  egressive 295.9
outwardly, outwards
  220.8
outwear 110.8
outweigh excel 33.5
  outbalance 319.10
outwit
  circumvent 545.8
  defeat 731.9
outwitted 732.12
outwork 717.3
outworn
  antiquated 124.9
  exploded 495.17
ouzel, ousel 366.22
oval *n.* 247.3
  (sphere 249.2)
oval *adj.* 247.9
  (spheric 249.7)
ovarian 357.10
ovary 357.4
ovate 247.9
ovation
  procession 69.3
  celebration 883.1
oven 386.1
over *v.* 67.5
over *adj.*
  superior 33.7
  remaining 40.6
  ended 67.9
  past 122.8
  higher 206.15
  be all over end 67.6
  perish 162.5
over *adv.*
  beyond 33.9
  aloft 206.19
  too 641.7
over again, over and over 104.8
  (twice 90.5)
over and above
  beyond 33.9
  additionally 37.8
  (extra 641.7)
  remaining 40.6
over *prep.* 106.7
over all 200.16
overabound 641.2
overact act 599.26
  overdo 641.3
  be affected 853.5
overacted 853.6
overage 40.4; 641.1
overalls 225.21
overanxiety 865.2
overarch 223.27
overawe daunt 860.11
  dominate 737.12

command respect 928.7
overbalance excel 33.5
  counteract 179.4
  overweigh 319.10
  overdo 641.3
overbalanced
  unequal 28.3
  topheavy 218.7
overbear excel 33.5
  overdo 641.3
  predominate 737.12
  domineer 885.5
overbearance 885.1
overbearing
  tyrannical 739.5
  domineering 885.8
overblown 641.5
overboard 267.66
  go overboard 267.36
  man overboard!
  navigation 267.69
  to the rescue! 672.4
overbridge 627.7
overbrim 641.2
overbuild 641.3
overburden *n.* 641.1
overburden *v.*
  overload 641.4
  (weight 319.9)
  aggrieve 649.6
  overtask 686.8
  overload 706.6
overburn, overbuy,
  overcarry 641.3
overcast *v.* cloud 353.9
  overshadow 422.6
overcast *adj.*
  cloudy 353.11
  overshadowed 422.9
overcautious 864.6
overcertify 641.3
overcharge *n.* 814.1
overcharge *v.*
  exaggerate 549.2
  ornament 577.4
  overdo 641.3
  charge too much 814.3
overcharged 641.6
overcloud cloud 353.9
  dim 422.6
overclouded 353.11
overcoat 225.17
overcome *v.*
  persuade 615.9
  surmount 731.7
  defeat 731.9
overcome *adj.*
  defeated 732.12
  ~ with grief 837.13
  drunk 959.21, 22
  be overcome 661.3
overcoming 824.12
overcommend
  exaggerate 549.2
  overdo 641.3
  boast 884.5
overconfidence 863.1
overconfident
  credulous 486.5
  incautious 863.6

overconscientious — override

overconscientious
  fastidious 868.4
  overscrupulous
    939.8
overcorrect 641.3
overcount
  overestimate 482.3
  overdo 641.3
overcritical
  fastidious 868.4
  censorious 932.11
overcriticalness
  fastidiousness 868.1
  hypercriticism 932.2
overcrop 641.3
overcrossing 219.2
overcut, overdare,
  overdevelop 641.3
overdevelopment 194.4
overdistention 194.4
overdo
  carry too far 641.3
  (overestimate 482.3)
  (exaggerate 549.2)
  (squander 818.3)
  overwork 686.6
  overact 853.5
  overindulge 954.3
overdone
  immense 31.9
  overcooked 298.50
  exaggerated 549.3
  (ostentatious 882.8)
  excessive 641.5
  affected 853.6
overdose *n.*
  superfluity 641.1
  cloyer 869.2
overdose *v.*
  overfeed 641.4
  sate 869.4
overdraw
  exaggerate 549.2
  misrepresent 555.4
  overdo 641.3
  ~ one's account
    818.3
overdress *n.* 225.15
overdress *v.* 641.3
overdrive *n.* 272.16
overdrive *v.* 686.8
overdue
  anachronous 115.3
  late 133.8
overdye 641.3
overeager 865.17
overeat 957.3
overestimate *n.* 482.1
overestimate *v.* 482.3
  (misjudge 481.5)
  (exaggerate 549.2)
  (overdo 641.3)
  (flatter 933.2)
overestimated 482.4
  (exaggerated 549.3)
overestimation 482
  (misjudgment
    481.1)
  (exaggeration
    549.1)
  (redundance 641.1)
  (vanity 880.1)

  (boasting 884.1)
  (flattery 933.1)
overexpand 641.3
overexpansion 194.4
  (redundance 641.1)
overexpose 641.3
overfed
  satiated 869.6
  gluttonous 957.4
overfeed overfill 641.4
  sate 869.4
overflow *n.*
  inundation 348.3
  plenty 639.2
  superabundance
    641.1
overflow *v.*
  overrun 303.3
  inundate 348.18
  superabound 641.2
overflowing 641.6
overfly 641.3
overfull 641.6
  (packed 72.13)
  (swollen 194.10)
  (satiated 869.6)
overfullness 641.1
  (overexpansion
    194.4)
overgo overrun 303.2
  overdo 641.3
overgorge sate 869.4
  overeat 957.3
overgreat
  exaggerated 549.3
  excessive 641.5
overgrow spread 194.5
  overrun 303.3; 365.2
  superabound 641.2
overgrown
  immense 31.9
  hulky 192.13
  expanded 194.10
  excessive 641.5
overgrowth 194.4
overhang *n.* 214.1
overhang *v.* 214.5
  (rise above 206.10)
  (overlie 223.27)
  (project 250.7)
overhanging
  imminent 152.3
  impending 214.8
  (above 206.16)
  (overlying 223.30)
overhasty 825.11
overhaul count 85.8
  scrutinize 441.12
  examine 461.17
  repair 660.11
  take stock 811.8
  upbraid 932.8
overhead 206.19
overhear hear 418.11
  be informed 527.11
overheat 384.16
overindulge
  be intemperate 954.3
  (be prodigal 818.3)
  be gluttonous 957.3
overindulgence 954.1
overindulgent 954.4

overjoyed 827.10
overjump
  overpass 303.2
  outstrip 303.4
  overdo 641.3
overking 745.2
overlabor, overlabour
  overdo 641.3
  overwork 686.6
overlade 641.4
overladen 641.6
overlap overlie 223.27
  overrun 303.2
overlapping 223.30
  (overhanging 214.8)
overlarge 641.3
overlay *n.* cover 223.2
  printing 590.5
  odds 621.5
overlay *v.* cover 223.22
  (form layers 204.4)
  exaggerate 549.2
  overdo 641.3
  overburden 706.6
overlayer 223.2
overleap
  overpass 303.2
  outstrip 303.4
overliberal 818.4
overlie 223.27
  (overtop 206.10)
  (overhang 214.5)
overlift 641.3
overline 66.3
overload *n.* 641.1
overload *v.*
  overfill 641.4
  (fill 52.7)
  (load 190.2)
  (sate 869.4)
  ornament 577.4
  overburden 706.6
overlook
  rise above 206.10
  pay no attention
    458.5
  neglect 460.4
  examine 461.17
  superintend 693.5
  not observe 773.3
  excuse 918.3
  snub 930.7
  bewitch 992.4
overlooked 460.10
overlooker 694.1
overlord master 745.1
  potentate 745.2
overly
  inordinately 31.20
  overmuch 641.7
overlying 223.30
  (above 206.16)
  (overhanging 214.8)
overman
  director 694.1
  master 745.1
overmaster 731.9
overmastered 824.10
overmastering 824.12
overmatch excel 33.5
  (be unequal 28.2)
  defeat 731.9

overmeasure *n.* 641.1
overmeasure *v.*
  overestimate 482.3
  overdo 641.3
overmodest 853.7
  (modest 881.5)
overmost 210.6
overmuch
  exaggerated 549.3
  redundant 641.5
  overly 641.7
overnice 868.4
overnicety 868.1
overofficious 682.22
overparticular 868.4
overpass *n.*
  overrunning 303.1
  path 627.2
  bridge 627.7
overpass *v.* excel 33.5
  overreach 303.2
overpatriotic
  exaggerated 549.3
  jingoistic 884.8
overpay 641.3
overpicture 549.2
overplay 641.3
overplus *n.*
  surplus 40.4
  superfluity 641.1
overplus *adj.* 641.5
overplus *adv.*
  additionally 37.8
  extra 641.7
overpower 731.9
overpowering 824.12
overpraise *n.*
  overestimation 482.1
  (flattery 933.1)
  exaggeration 549.1
  redundance 641.1
  boasting 884.1
overpraise *v.*
  overestimate 482.3
  (extol 931.6)
  (flatter 933.2)
  exaggerate 549.2
  overdo 641.3
  boast 884.5
overprize 482.3
overproduce 641.3
overproud 880.6
overrate 482.3
overreach
  overpass 303.2
  cheat 545.8
  (be cunning 702.5)
  overdo 641.3
  defeat 731.9
overreckon
  overestimate 482.3
  overdo 641.3
overrefined 477.11
overrefinement 477.4
overreligious
  ascetic 955.3
  hyperorthodox
    983a.8
override excel 33.5
  overrun 303.2
  outstrip 303.4
  overdo 641.3

994

overrighteous — pacha

thwart 706.7
conquer 731.9
dominate 737.12
tyrannize 739.4
revoke 756.3
overrighteous 988.11
(fanatical 503.18)
overrule rule 737.12
revoke 756.3
overruling
supreme 33.8
authoritative 737.15
overrun *n.*
overrunning 303.1
surplus 641.1
overrun *v.*
pervade 186.12
spread 194.5
overpass 303.2, 3, 4
overgrow 305.2
type 591.14
superabound 641.2
overrun *adj.* 194.10
overrunning
overpassing 303
redundance 641.1
overscrupulous
fastidious 868.4
overconscientious 939.8
overscrupulousness 868.1
oversea *adj.* alien 57.4
absent 187.10
oversea, overseas *adv.*
abroad 57.5
transmarine 341.7
oversee 693.5
overseer 694.1
oversensitive
~ physically 375.6
~ emotionally 822.6
(fastidious 868.4)
overset *n.* surplus 40.4
overthrow 308.2
excess 641.1
overset *v.* invert 218.4
capsize 267.35
overthrow 308.5
overdo 641.3
defeat 731.9
overshade 422.6
overshadow
cloud 353.9
overshade 422.6
overshadowment 421.3
overshine 420.20
overshoe 225.27
overshoot
land 267a.34
overrun 303.2
exaggerate 549.2
overdo 641.3
oversight
inattention 458.1
neglect 460.1
mistake 495.2
supervision 693.2
failure 732.1
nonobservance 773.1
overskirt 225.19
oversleep 683.9

oversmoke cloud 353.9
overshadow 422.6
oversoul 359.3
oversow 641.3
overspeak
exaggerate 549.2
overdo 641.3
overspend 641.3
overstate
exaggerate 549.2
misrepresent 555.4
overstatement 549.1
overstep *n.* 303.1
overstep *v.* 303.2, 5
overstock 641.4
overstrain
overestimate 482.3
overdo 641.3
overtask 686.8
overstretch 641.3
overstride 303.2
overstudy 641.3
oversubtle
hairsplitting 477.11
fastidious 868.4
oversubtlety 868.1
oversupply *n.* 641.1
oversupply *v.* 641.4
overswarm 641.2
oversweet 396.8
overt 525.4
overt act 680.2
overtake
come up with 292.7
overrun 303.2
inebriate 959.18
be overtaken 661.3
overtask, overtax 686.8
(misuse 679.2)
overtell 549.2
overthrow *n.*
revolution 146.1;
742.2
destruction 162.1
inversion 218.1
overturn 308.2
defeat 732.3
overthrow *v.*
destroy 162.4
invert 218.4
overturn 308.5
confute 479.2
conquer 731.9
revolutionize 742.5
overthrown
upset 308.9
vanquished 732.12
overthwart *v.* 706.7
overthwart *adj.*
crosswise 219.12
opposed 708.4
overtired 688.6
overtone 402.2; 413.8
overtop excel 33.5
rise above 206.10
(top 210.5)
(overlie 223.27)
climb over 305.5
overtrustful 486.5
overture prelude 64.2
music 415.15

peace offering 723.2
offer 763.1
proposal 765.3
make an overture 763.2
overturn *n.*
revolution 146.1;
742.2
destruction 162.1
inversion 218.1
overthrow 308.2
vanquishment 732.3
overturn *v.*
destroy 162.4
invert 218.4, 5
capsize 267.35
overthrow 308.5
confute 479.2
conquer 731.9
revolutionize 742.5
overvaluation 482.1
overvalue 482.3
overweening
excessive 641.5
overconfident 863.6
vain 880.6
arrogant 885.8
overweigh excel 33.5
outweigh 319.10
overestimate 482.3
overdo 641.3
overload 641.4
overweight
overbalance 319.10
overload 641.4
(weight 319.9)
overwhelm
destroy 162.4
confute 479.2
superabound 641.2
overfill 641.4
overburden 706.6
defeat 731.9
astound 870.3
overwhelming
evidential 467.11
exciting 824.12
astonishing 870.7
overwise 880.6
overwork 686.6, 8
overwrought
immense 31.9
exaggerated 549.3
(ostentatious 882.8)
excessive 641.5
overexcited 824.10
affected 853.6
overzealous 503.18;
821.6
(hyperorthodox 983a.8)
(pious 987.10)
ovicell 357.4
ovicular, oviferous 357.10
oviform 247.9
oviparous 357.10
ovoid *n.* 247.3
ovoid *adj.* 247.9
ovolo 847.4
ovule 247.3
ovum oval 247.3

egg 357.4
owe 806.5
owelty 27.2
owing in debt 806.9
due 924.11
owing to
resulting from 154.5
since 155.8
owl bird 366.22
fool 501.1
owllight 126.1
own *v.*
acknowledge 488.9
confess 529.5
possess 777.4
own *adj.* 777.8
on one's own 600.5
owner 779.2
ownership 777.3
(property 780.1)
ox pack animal 271.2
bovine 366.12
male animal 373.6
Oxford Group movement 984.5
Oxford shoe, Oxford tie 225.27
oxgoad edge tool 253.6
spear 727.5
oxidation 384.3
oxide, oxid 384.15
oxidize burn 384.18
rust 659.7
oxreim fastening 45.2
cord 205.3
oxygen 334.2
oxygenize 338.10
oxygon 244.2
oyez, oyes 418.16;
457.10
oyster 298.18
oyster plant 298.30
oz. 319.4
ozocerite 356.6
ozone gas 334.2
air 338.1
ozonometer 267a.29

P

pa 166.6
pa, pah 717.4
pabulation 298.5
pabulatory 298.48
pabulum
nourishment 298.5
material 316.2
pace *n.* gait 266.5
(slowness 275.2)
velocity 274.1
keep pace equal 27.6
synchronize 120.3
concur 178.3
keep up with 274.12
pace *v.* walk 266.16
row 267.46
measure 466.10
pace *adv.* 760.7
pacer 271.3
pacha, pachadom etc.
See **pasha** etc.

pachydermatous — palatable

pachydermatous
  insensible 376.5
  callous 823.7
  hardened 945.18
pacifiable 723.7
pacific equable 174.6
  peaceable 721.4
  (concordant 714.4)
  pacificatory 723.6
  meek 826.10
pacifics 723.2
pacification
  modulation 174.2
  conciliation 723
  (concord 714.1)
  (mediation 724.1)
  treaty 723.3
pacificator 724.2
pacificatory 723.6
  (concordant 714.4)
  (mediatory 724.4)
pacifism 721.1
pacifist 721.2
pacifistic 721.4
pacify moderate 174.5
  quiet 265.6
  conciliate 723.4
  (harmonize 23.8)
  (accord 714.3)
  (mediate 724.3)
  (propitiate 990.13)
  relieve 834.4
pack *n.*
  quantities 31.3
  crowd 72.4
  bundle 72.5
  parachute 273a.7
  impediment 706.2
  ~ of cards 840.13
  strumpet 962.2
pack *v.* fill 52.7
  arrange 60.6
  assemble 72.11
  expand 194.8
  carry 270.8
  hasten off 293.5
  weight 319.9
  store 636.7
  (load 184.13)
pack away 636.7
pack in 300.5
pack off
  hasten off 293.5
  repulse 289.2
pack on sail
  set sail 267.16
  speed 274.9
package 72.5
pack animal 271.2
packed 72.13
  (full 52.11)
  (overfull 641.6)
packet bundle 72.5
  ship 273.1
packet boat 534.2
pack horse 271.2, 3
packing stowage 184.5
  contents 190.1
  stopper 263.1
packsaddle 215.23
packthread 205.2
packtong See paktong

pact, paction 769.1
Pactolus 803.1
pad *n.* paw 211.4
  horse 271.3
  frog 366.20
  foliage 367.4
  thud 408a.2
  footprint 550.4
  notebook 551.3
pad *v.* fill 52.7
  expand 194.8
  walk 266.16
  weight 319.9
  ~ a speech 573.5
pad the hoof 266.16
padded 573.7
padding contents 190.1
  stopper 263.1
  softness 324.3
  pleonasm 573.2
  redundance 641.1
paddle *n.* gait 266.5
  oar 273.14
paddle *v.* walk 266.16
  row 267.46
  splash 337.5
paddle one's own canoe
  have one's will 600.2
  conduct oneself 692.5
  be independent 748.8
paddle boat 273.1
paddock yard 232.1
  frog 366.20
Paddy, Paddywhack, Paddywack 188.9
padishah 745.3
padlock fastening 45.2
  stopper 263.1
  lock 752.3
padnag 271.3
padre 996.2
padrone 745.1
paean, pean
  sacred music 415.11
  plaudit 931.4
  worship 990.2
  (rejoicing 838.1)
  (celebration 883.1)
  (thanksgiving 916.2)
paederast See pederast
paediatrics See pediatrics
paedotribe, pedotribe 540.1
pagan *n.* 984.20
  (unbeliever 485.4; 989.4)
  (idolater 991.5)
pagan *adj.* 984.28
  (infidelic 989.7)
  (idolatrous 991.7)
paganism 984.10
  (infidelity 989.2)
  (idolatry 991.1)
page *n.*
  printed ~ 591.2
  book 593.7
  paper 635.4

attendant 746.1
page *v.* 85.9
pageant
  spectacle 448.2
  drama 599.3
  role 599.7
  elaborate display 882.3
pageantry
  spectacle 448.2
  elaborate display 882.3
paginate 85.9
pagoda tower 206.3
  temple 1000.1
pah *n.* See pa
pah *int.* 867.11
Pahari 560.4
paid 807.10
pail 191.11
paillasse, palliasse 215.24
pain *n.* bread 298.11
  physical ~ 378
  (ailment 655.1, 5)
  mental ~ 828, 830
  affliction 830.2
  penalty 974.1
pain *v.*
  ~ physically 378.4
  (afflict 655.22)
  ~ mentally 830.1
  (hurt 649.6)
  (be malevolent 907.5)
pained
  ~ physically 378.6
  ~ mentally 828.13
painful
  ~ physically 378.7
  careful 459.7
  laborious 686.10
  difficult 704.8
  ~ mentally 830.9
  (harmful 649.10)
painfully 31.23
painless 827.9
pains
  close attention 457.2
  care 459.1
  exertion 686.1
  penalty 974.1
  take pains
  try one's best 675.5
  exert oneself 686.5
painstaking *n.* 682.5
painstaking *adj.*
  careful 459.7
  diligent 682.19
  laborious 686.10
paint *n.* color 428.5
  (coating 223.18)
  deception 545.6
paint *v.* 428.10
  (coat 223.24)
  (depict 554.7)
  (limn 556.17)
paint the lily 641.3
paint the town red
  revel 840.21
  (celebrate 883.3)
  carouse 959.16

paintable 845.16
paintbrush 556.16
painted 556.19
painter
  ship's rope 273.10
  artist 559.2, 3
  (workman 690.10)
Painter's Easel 318.6
painting
  coloring 428.5, 6
  art 556.2, 9
  (composition 54.2)
  (representation 554.1)
painty 556.19
pair *n.* analogue 17.5
  couple 89.2
  horses 272.9
  cards 840.12, 13
  lovers 897.9
  wedded ~ 903.9
pair *v.* league 48.4
  couple 89.3
  pair off average 29.2
  league 48.4
  marry 903.13
paired 89.5
pair-oar 273.4
pajama, pyjama 225.23
pakka See pucka
paktong, packtong 545.6
pal *n.* 890.3
pal *v.* 88.6
palace house 189.3
  room 191.16
palace car 272.19
paladin
  champion 717.5
  combatant 726.1
  hero 861.3
palaeocrystic, palaeography etc. See paleocrystic etc.
palaeotype, paleotype 561.4
palaeotypography, paleotypography 591.1
palaestra, palestra
  athletics 159.5
  school 542.1
  arena 728.1
palaestrian, palestrian *n.* 159.6
palaestrian, palestrian *adj.*
  athletic 159.11
  gymnasial 542.9
palaestric, palestric 686.10
palaestrics, palestrics 686.2
palaetiology, paletiology 155.1
palais 189.3
palanquin, palankeen 272.12
palatable 394.7
  (pleasing 377.7; 829.7)
  (flavorful 390.4)

(desirable 865.21)
palatableness 394.1
palatal 402.2
palate 390.1
palatial palace 189.23
　ostentatious 882.8
palatinate 182.1
palatine 745.7
Palau, Palaung 560.4
palaver *n.*
　twaddle 517.3
　speech 582.1
　chatter 584.2
　conversation 588.1
　conference 588.3
　council 696.2
palaver *v.*
　talk nonsense 517.6
　be loquacious 584.4
　converse 588.7
　confer 588.8
palazzo 189.3
pale *n.* region 181.1
　post 215.16
　outline 230.1
　edge 231.1
　limit 233.1
　fence 232.2
　~ of the church 995.1
pale *v.*
　grow dim 422.7
　fade 429.4, 5
　turn color 824.8
　take fright 860.8
pale *adj.* dim 422.8
　pallid 429.6
　yellow 436.6
　indistinct 447.5
　sickly 655.24
　excited 824.9
　turn pale
　　lose color 429.4
　　be afraid 860.8
palea 223.14
paleface 430.2
pale-faced 429.6
Pale Horse 360.2
paleness 429.1
　(dimness 422.1)
paleocrystic, palaeocrystic 124.7
paleography, palaeography
　antiquarianism 122.4
　linguistics 560.6
　(interpretation 522.5)
paleolith, palaeolith 124.2
paleological, palaeological 122.13
paleologist, palaeologist 122.5
paleontologist, palaeontologist 368.2
paleontology, palaeontology
　antiquarianism 122.4
　zoology 368.1

paleotype, paleotypography See **paleotype** etc.
Paleozoic, Palaeozoic 124.7
paleozoology, palaeozoology 122.4
palestra, palestrian See **palaestra** etc.
paletiology See **palaetiology**
paletot 225.15, 17
palette, palette knife 556.16
pale-yellow 436.6
palfrey 271.3
Pali 560.4
palimpsest
　cryptograph 528.5
　writing 590.3
palindrome
　inversion 218.2
　wordplay 842.5
palindromic 218.6
paling 232.2
palingenesis
　reproduction 163.1
　regeneration 660.2
palinode poem 597.2
　retraction 607.3
palinodist 597.10
palisade
　precipice 212.3
　post 215.16
　fence 232.2
　fortification 717.3
pall *n.*
　graveclothes 363.8
　coffin 363.10
　repugnance 867.2
　pallium 999.1
pall *v.* 869.4
　(weary 841.6)
palladium 666.1
pallbearer 363.7
pallet bed 215.24
　art 556.16
palliate
　moderate 174.5
　relieve 834.4
　(improve 658.13)
　(remedy 662.24)
　extenuate 937.6
palliation relief 834.1
　extenuation 937.3
palliative *n.*
　alleviative 662.6
　(moderator 174.3)
　(anesthetic 376.2)
　(lenitive 834.3)
　extenuative 937.3
palliative *adj.*
　qualifying 469.6
　alleviative 662.25
　relieving 834.7
　extenuative 937.9
pallid 429.6
pallidity 429.1
pallium 999.1
pall-mall, pallone 840.11
pallor 429.1

palm *n.* length 200.6
　tree 367.6
　plant 369.8
　wood 635.3
　trophy 733.1
　hand 781.3
　bear the palm
　　excel 33.5
　　win 731.6
　　acquire honor 873.12
palm *v.* handle 379.3
　bribe 618.3
　steal 791.9
palmate 257.6
palmer wanderer 268.2
　religious 996.11
palmiped 219.11
pa'mist 513.2
palmistry 511.3
　(interpretation 522.5)
　(symbology 550.17)
palmitin 356.1
palm oil oil 356.3
　bribe 618.2
palmy
　auspicious 512.4
　pleasant 829.9
　cheerful 836.7
palp 379.2
palpability 379.1
palpable
　material 316.8
　touchable 379.5
　distinct 446.5
　manifest 525.4
palpate 379.3
palpation 379.1
palpitant
　pulsatory 314.12
　drumming 407.11
palpitate pulsate 314.9
　flutter 315.10
　drum 407.8
　~ with emotion 824.7
palpitation
　pulsation 314.2
　flutter 315.5
　pain 378.1
　drumming 407.3
　~ of the heart 655.12
　trepidation 825.3; 860.3
pa'pus 379.2
palsgrave 875.5
palsied helpless 158.9
　paralytic 376.5; 655.25
　irresolute 605.5
palsy *n.*
　helplessness 158.2
　insensibility 376.1
　paralysis 655.15
palsy *v.* 376.4
palsy *adj.* 892.12
palter quibble 477.8
　prevaricate 544.5
　shift 605.4
　not keep faith 773.4
paltriness 643.1

paltry
　unimportant 643.12
　(inconsiderable 32.8)
　(bad 649.8)
　(mediocre 736.3)
　(contemptible 930.9)
　disreputable 874.8
paludal 345.3
Pampango, Pampanga 560.4
pampas 344.1
　(grassland 367.11)
pamper 943.3
pampered 954.4
pamphlet 593.1
pamphleteer 595.3
pan *n.* receptacle 191.11
　face 234.4
pan *n.* wood 367.7
　deity 979.11
pan *v.* 384.19
panacea 662.3
　(cure 660.5)
panache feathers 256.8
　ornament 847.3
panama 225.26
Panama 182.3
Pan-American, Pan-Anglican 78.12
panax 662.3
pancake *n.*
　landing 267a.26
　griddlecake 298.12
pancake *v.* 267a.34
pancratiast
　athlete 159.6
　victor 731.4
pancreas 221.5
pandal 191.22
Pandean pipes
　whistle 410.4
　instrument 417.4
pandect
　knowledge 490.7
　dissertation 595.1
　compendium 506.1
　code of laws 963.2
pandemia 655.2
pandemic 657.5
pandemonium
　turmoil 59.4
　noise 410.2
　discord 414.2
Pandemonium 982.1
pander, pandar *n.* 962.4
pander, pandar *v.*
　minister 631.3
　aid 707.6
　serve 746.8
　fawn 886.3
pandiculation
　swelling 194.1
　gaping 260.9
　drowsiness 683.4
pandit See **pundit**
pandora 417.2
Pandora's box 649.2; 858.3
pandowdy 298.12

pane — parallelogram

pane lamina 204.2
  window pane 260.5
  glass 384.14
paned 440.7
panegyric 931.2
panegyrical 931.9
panegyrist 935.1
panegyrize 931.6
panel list 86.1, 2
  lamina 204.2
  saddle 215.23
  partition 228.6
  schedule 611.2
  litigants 938.3
  jury 967.2
  parties litigant 969.9
panel house 961.7
paneling, panelling, panelwork 847.3
pang pain 378.1
  mental pain 828.1
  pangs of conscience 950.1
Pangasinan 560.4
pangen, pangene 357.4
pangenesis 161.2
Pangloss 492.4
panhandle 765.6
panhandler 767.2
panic 860.1
  panic-struck 860.14
panisc, panisk
  wood 367.7
  deity 979.11
Panjabi 560.4
panjandrum 642.5
pannier basket 191.9
  dress 225.19
  bustle 225.25
panoplied 717.9
panoply n.
  safeguard 717.2
  arms 727.1
panoply v. 664.6
panopticon 752.1
panorama view 448.2
  picture 556.10
panoramic 78.9
panpharmacon 662.3
Panpipes whistle 410.4
  instrument 417.4
panpsychism 317.3
panpsychist 317.4
pansophical 490.19
pansophy 490.3
pansy
  hermaphrodite 83.5
  purple 437.1
pant pulsate 314.9
  breathe 349.23
  be hot 382.13
  be fatigued 688.4
  ~ with excitement 824.7
  ~ for 865.11
pantalets, pantalettes 225.21
pantaloon 599.20
pantaloons 225.21
pantelegraph 532a.5
pantheism

philosophy 451.19
  religion 984.10
pantheist 984.20
pantheistic 984.28
pantheon gods 979.1
  temple 1000.1
panther animal 366.3
  variegation 440.2
  courage 861.4
pantile roofing 223.6
  bread 298.11
  gutter tile 359.1
panting n.
  labored breathing 688.2
  trepidation 825.3
panting adj. 688.7
pantisocracy 737.4
pantological 490.19
pantologist 492.2
pantology 490.3
pantometer 244.3
pantomime
  dumb show 550.3
  acting 599.3
pantomimist 599.19
pantophagic 957.4
pantophagist
  eater 298.41
  glutton 957.2
pantophagous 298.48
pantophagy
  eating 298.1
  gluttony 957.1
pantry room 191.16
  storeroom 636.4
pants
  pantaloons 225.21
  airplane 273a.10
panurgy 698.1
pap father 166.6
  nipple 250.3
  gluten 352.3
  pulp 354.2
papa father 166.6
  Pope 996.5
papacy 995.4
papal 995.9
papal brief 592.2
paper n. thinness 203.5
  white 430.3
  writing 590.3
  (record 551.1)
  newspaper 593.6
  treatise 595.1
  foolscap 635.4
  security 771.1
paper v. coat 223.24
  ~ the house 599.25
paper credit 805.2
papermaker 690.8
paper money 800.6
papery 160.11
Paphian n. 962.2
Paphian adj. 961.10
papier-mâché 635.4
papilionaceous 242.6
papilla 250.3
papillary, papillose 250.9
papillote 256.3
papish

Roman Catholic 984.25
  papal 995.9
papism 984.6
papist, Papist n. 984.16
papist, Papist adj.
  papish 984.25
  papal 995.9
papistry 984.6
papoose 129.6
pappose, pappous 256.13
pappus 256.7
pappy 166.6
paprika, paprica 393.1
Papuan 431.4
papule
  protuberance 250.2
  sore 655.16
papulose 250.9
papyrus 590.10
  (paper 635.4)
par 27.2
  above par
    beyond 33.9
    good 648.8
  below par
    inconsiderable 32.8
    under 207.11
    imperfect 651.4
    at a discount 813.4
  on a par equal 27.8
    equivalent 27.9
  under par
    inconsiderable 32.8
    less 34.7
  up to par 648.11
parable
  figure of speech 521.1
  lesson 537.6
  story 594.2
parabola 245.2
parabolic 521.3
paracentesis 297.5
parachronism
  anachronism 115.1
  error 495.1
parachute
  aircraft 273a.7
  safeguard 666.1
  escape 671.3
parachutist 269a.2
Paraclete 976.6
parade n.
  procession 69.3
  path 627.2
  ostentation 882.1, 3
parade v. march 266.21
  show off 882.6
paradigm
  prototype 22.1
  grammar 567.1
paradisaic
  delightful 829.8
  heavenly 981.7
paradise
  park 189.21; 367.7
  gallery 441.5
  utopia 515.6
  balcony 599.11

bliss 827.2
  place of **amusement** 840.14
  heaven 981.1
paradox
  absurdity 497.1
  dilemma 704.4
paradoxal 475.12
paradoxical
  inconsistent 497.4
  unintelligible 519.6
paraesthesia See **paresthesia**
paraffin, paraffine 356.2
paragon
  perfection 650.2
  (prototype 22.1)
  ~ of beauty 845.3
  good person 948.1
paragram
  ambiguity 520.2
  wordplay 842.5
paragraph
  section 51.2
  typography 550.8
  phrase 566.1
  passage 593.7
paragrapher, paragraphist 593.16
parakeet 366.22
paraleipsis, paralipsis, paralepsis 460.1
parallel n.
  analogue 17.5
  equal 27.5
  parallelism 216.2
  typography 550.8
parallel v.
  resemble 17.7
  imitate 19.5
  equal 27.6
  relate 9.4
  coextend 216.3
  compare with 464.2, 4
parallel adj.
  analogous 17.11
  coextensive 216.5
  symmetrical 242.4
parallelepiped, parallelepipedon
  parallel 216.2
  angle 244.2
parallelepipedal 216.5
paralleler 216.2
parallelinerved 216.5
parallelism
  similarity 17.1
  agreement 23.1
  equivalence 27.2
  coextension 216
  symmetry 242.1
  comparison 464.1
parallelistic 464.5
parallelization
  coextension 216.1
  comparison 464.1
parallelize relate 9.4
  compare 464.2
parallelodrome 216.5
parallelogram

parallelogrammatic — parsley

parallel 216.2
  angle 244.2
parallelogrammatic, parallelogrammic 216.5
parallelograph, parallelometer 216.2
parallelotropism 216.1
paralogical 477.10
paralogism
  syllogism 476.5
  sophistry 477.1, 2
paralogist 477.6
paralogistic 477.10
paralogize 477.7
paralogy 477.1
paralysis
  helplessness 158.2
  insensibility 376.1
  palsy 655.15
paralytic
  helpless 158.9
  palsied 376.5; 655.25
paralyze disable 158.6
  deaden 376.4
  (numb 381.2)
  startle 508.6
  ~ emotionally 823.4
  dumfound 870.3
paramecium 193.4
parameter 153.1
paramount *n.*
  chief 642.6
  master 745.1
  potentate 745.2
paramount *adj.*
  supreme 33.8
  highest 210.6
  most important 642.14
  (best 648.9)
  ruling 737.15
paramountcy 33.3
  (importance 642.1)
paramour lover 897.6
  mistress 962.3
  (wife 903.8)
paranoia
  insanity 503.1
  craze 503.7
paranoiac 504.1
paranomia 503.1
parapet fence 232.2
  fortification 717.3
paraph 550.11
paraphernalia
  equipment 634.1
  belongings 780.1, 5
paraphrase *n.* 522.2
  (copy 21.4)
paraphrase *v.* 522.7
  (caricature 19.9)
paraphrast 524.1
paraphrastic 522.8
paraplegia 655.15
paraselene 420.12
  (moon 318.5)
parasite 886.2
  (adherent 46.3)
  (dependent 746.3)
parasitic
  grasping 789.15

sycophantic 886.4
parasitism 886.1
parasitology 655.19
parasol 223.4
paratrooper 269a.2
paratroops 726.9
parboil 384.19
Parca 601.4
parcel *n.* part 51.1
  bundle 72.5
  ~ of land 371.5
parcel *v.*
  partition 44.10
  ~ out 60.6
  apportion 786.3
parcel post 592.4
parch dry 340.5
  be hot 382.13
  burn 384.18
parched dried 340.9
  thirsty 865.19
parching 382.16
parchment
  stationery 590.10
  (paper 635.4)
  bookbinding 593.10
  security 771.1
pard accompanier 88.3
  ally 700.1
  companion 890.3
pardie, parde, pardi, pardy 494.15
pardner 711.1
pardon *n.*
  forgiveness 918.1
  acquittal 970.1
  I beg your pardon!
  dissent 489.9
  forgive me 918.7
pardon *v.* forgive 918.3
  acquit 970.3
pardon me!
  dissent 489.9
  forgive me! 918.7
pardonable 937.10
pare cut off 38.6
  (reduce 36.4)
  form layers 204.4
  peel 226.5
  cheapen 815.7
paregoric *n.* 662.6
paregoric *adj.*
  palliative 662.25
  relieving 834.7
parenchyma 316.2
parenchymatous 316.8
parent 166.5
parentage 166.1
parental 166.10
parenthesis
  discontinuity 70.1
  punctuation 550.8
parenthetic
  incidental 10.8
  interjacent 228.11
parenthetically
  incidentally 10.10
  by the way 134.11
  (between 288.13)
paresis ailment 655.5
  paralysis 655.15
paresthesia, paraes-

thesia
  sensation 380.1
  nervous disorder 655.14
par excellence 33.10
parget coat 223.24
  paint 428.10
parhelic circle, parhelion 420.12
  (sun 318.4)
pariah
  despised person 876.9
  outcast 893.5
pariah dog 366.6
paries lining 224.1
  side 236.1
parietal 236.6
pari mutuel 621.7, 12
paring modicum 32.2
  remains 40.1
  piece 51.3
  shavings 330.3
Paris green 435.4
parish territory 181.2
  laity 997.11
  go on the parish 804.5
parishioner 997.2
parish lantern 318.5
Paris white 430.4
Paris yellow 436.4
parity
  similarity 17.1
  equality 27.1
park *n.*
  pleasance 189.21
  (garden 371.6)
  valley 252.5
  verdure 367.7, 11
  place of amusement 840.14
  ~ of artillery 727.11
park *v.* 184.10, 14
parker 223.9
Parkinson's disease 655.15
parkway 627.3
parlance
  language 560.1
  diction 569.1
  common ~ 576.1
parlando *n.* 415.20
parlando *adv.* 415.30
parley *n.*
  conference 588.3
  (consultation 695.2)
  mediation 724.1
  (peace offering 723.2)
parley *v.* talk 582.6
  address 586.2
  converse 588.7
  confer 588.8
parliament 696.4
parliamentary
  congressional 696.9
  deputy 759.1
parliamentary agent 724.2
parliamentary train 272.18
parlor, parlour 191.16

parlor car 272.19
parlormaid 746.2
parlous *adj.* 665.7
parlous *adv.* 31.15
Parnassian 597.10
Parnassus 597.9
parochial
  regional 181.6
  bigoted 606.7
parochialism 481.4
parodic 19.13
parodist 844
parody *n.*
  caricature 21.3
  burlesque 856.3
  (absurdity 497.1)
  (wordplay 842.5)
parody *v.*
  caricature 19.8
  burlesque 856.6
parol, parole *adj.* 582.10
parole *n.* speech 582.1
  promise 768.1
  (guarantee 771.1)
  on parole 751.12
parolist 754.1
paronomasia
  assonance 17.3
  ambiguity 550.2
  wordplay 842.5
paronymous 9.6; 562.9
parotid 221.5
paroxysm spasm 315.7
  delirium 503.3
  seizure 655.3
  frenzy 825.4
  fit of anger 900.2
parquet floor 211.2
  checkerwork 440.3
  auditorium 599.11
parquetry
  checkerwork 440.3
  ornamentation 847.3
parricide 361.2
parrot imitator 19.4
  bird 366.22
  chatterer 584.3
parrotism, parrotry 19.2
parry quibble 477.8
  confute 479.2
  (answer 462.5)
  avoid 623.6
  fend off 717.8
parse analyze 461.17
  grammaticize 567.5
Parsi, Parsee *n.* 382.11; 991.5
Parsi, Parsee *adj.* 984.21
Parsiism, Parseeism 382.11; 991.1
parsimonious 819.4
  (economical 817.4)
  (selfish 943.4)
  be parsimonious 819.3
parsimony 819
  (economy 817.1)
  (selfishness 943.1)
parsley 393.1

parsnip — pass

parsnip 298.30
parson 996.2
parsonage 1000.5
  (home 189.2)
parsoness 996.3
part *n.* portion 51;
  786.2
  (component 56.1)
  (fraction 101.1)
  music 415.15, 21
  ~ of a book 593.7
  role 599.7
  function 625.3
form a part 56.2
for my part 79.11
in part
  to a degree 32.13
  partly 51.9
on the part of
  apropos 9.10
  on behalf of 707.15
part and parcel 56.1
part by part 51.10
play a part
  dissemble 544.6
  act 599.26
  do 680.6
  participate 709.6
  be affected 853.5
play one's part
  officiate 625.9
  conduct oneself
    692.1
take the part of
  second 707.8
  side with 709.5
part *v.* disjoin 44.7
  (segregate 55.4)
  (diverge 291.2)
  separate 44.11
  interval 198.4
  open 260.11
  depart 293.4
part company 713.7
part with
  discard 678.3
  relinquish 782.3
  give up 784.11
partake 778.5
partaker 778.3
partaking 778.1
parterre plane 213.3
  auditorium 599.11
parthenogenesis 161.2
Parthenope 980.2
partial unequal 28.3
  fractional 51.8
  (divided 44.12)
  (incomplete 53.4)
  (imperfect 651.4)
  special 79.7
  fractional 101.2
  prejudiced 481.10
  unfair 941a.3
partial to
  desirous of 865.16
  enamored of 897.15
partial eclipse 422.2
partiality
  inequality 28.1
  prejudice 481.3
  preference 609.2

liking 865.1
favoritism 888.1
injustice 941a.1
partially
  to a degree 32.13
  partly 51.9
partibility 44.1
partible 44.13
particeps criminis
  711.3
participant 778.3
participate do 680.6
  co-operate 709.6
  share 778.5
  (enter into 56.2)
  (halve 91.4)
  (apportion 786.3)
participation
  co-operation 709.1
  sharing 778
participative 778.7
participator 778.3
particle modicum 32.2
  (piece 51.8)
  (powder 330.3)
  diminutive 193.2
not a particle 2.2
**parti-color, parti-
  colour** 440.1
**parti-colored, parti-
  coloured** 440.5
  (colorful 428.14)
particular *n.* part 51.1
  event 151.1
give particulars 79.6
in particular 79.11
particular *adj.*
  classificational 75.6
  special 79.7
  exact 494.11
  eccentric 503.17
  noteworthy 642.10
  fastidious 868.4
  (conscientious
    939.8)
not particular 831.6
particularity
  speciality 79.2
  (nature 5.3)
  meticulousness
    457.3
  fastidiousness 868.1
  (conscientiousness
    939.2)
particularization
  reasoning 476.1
  indication 550.1
particularize
  differentiate 15.6
  specialize 79.6
  reason 476.10
  tell in detail 594.6
particularly
  remarkably 31.21
  principally 33.10
  singly 87.10
particulars
  speciality 79.3
  account 594.1
parting 44.1
parting cup 959.10
Partington, Mrs. 701

partisan, partizan
  follower 281.2
  upholder 711.4
  party 712.1
  halberd 727.4
partisan, partizan *adj.*
  712.9
partisanism 984.2
partisanship
  co-operation 709.2
  partiality 941a.1
partition *n.*
  interjacence 228.6
  apportionment 786.1
partition *v.*
  divide 44.10
  apportion 786.3
Partlet fowl 366.23
  female animal 374.8
partly
  to a degree 32.13
  in part 51.9
  (incompletely 53.6)
part music 415.12
partner *n.*
  accompanier 88.3
  ally 711.1
  participator 778.3
  companion 890.3
  spouse 903.5
partner *v.* 48.4
partnership
  accompaniment 88.2
  association 709.2
  company 712.5
  (concurrence 178.1)
  participation 778.1
go in partnership
  league 48.4
  co-operate 709.5
part of speech 567.2
partridge food 298.26
  color 433.2
parts intellect 450.1
  intelligence 498.1
  talents 698.2
part song 415.12
parturiency 168.2
parturient 168.9
parturition 161.3
part-way 32.7
party *n.* person 372.3
  co-worker 690.4
  association 712
  (company 72.3)
  (denomination
    542.4)
  (association 709.2)
  political ~ 712.6
  social gathering
    892.5
  (festivity 840.2)
  sect 984.3
be a party to
  have to do with
    680.6
  participate 709.6
form a party 712.7
  (league 48.4)
give a party 892.11
party *adj.* 79.8
party-color, party-

colour etc. See
  parti-color etc.
party line 228.6
par value 812.3
Parvati 979.4
parvenu *n.* 876.8
  (newness 123.5)
  (nouveau riche
    803.3)
parvenu *adj.* 876.11
parvenuism 851.1
parvitude 193.1
pas degree 26.1
  rank 71.1; 873.4
  dance 840.8
paschal 138.11; 998.15
pasear *n.* 266.4
pasear *v.* 266.13, 16
pasha, pacha
  personage 642.5
  ruler 745.7
  nobleman 875.4
pashalik, pashalic
  authority 737.3
  nobility 875.9
pashaship, pachaship
  authority 737.3
  nobility 875.9
pasigraphic 590.16
pasigraphy
  language 560.5
  shorthand 590.7
pasilaly 560.5
pasquil, pasquinade
  934.2
pasquinader 936.1
pass *n.*
  predicament 8.3
  crisis 134.4
  (eventuality 151.1)
  chasm 198.3
  (passage 302.1)
  narrow 203.3
  passkey 260.10
  thrust 276.3; 716.3
  password 550.11
  path 627.2
  way 627.7
  safe-conduct 664.2
  predicament 704.2
  permit 760.2
  free ticket 815.4
make a pass at 716.3
pass *v.* excel 33.5
  elapse 109.3
  be past 122.6
  happen 151.3
  move 264.6
  transfer to 270.7
  ~ along 282.2
  go through 302.2
  overrun 303.2
  ~ and repass 314.10
  disappear 449.2
  stand the test 463.11
  give up 519.5
  not bet 621.18
  refuse 764.2
  make over to 783.3
  give 784.9
  graduate 873.12
  ~ a law 963.4

1000

passable — patent

let pass neglect 460.4
  do nothing about 681.2
  not observe 773.3
  excuse 918.3
not pass
  be inferior 34.4
  be imperfect 651.3
pass away
  cease to be 2.5
  end 67.6
  be transient 111.5
  be past 122.6
  cease 142.6
  die 360.6
pass by elapse 109.3
  be past 122.6
  overrun 303.2
  escape notice 458.7
  slight 460.4
  not observe 773.3
  snub 930.7
pass current
  conform 82.5
  find credence 484.11
  be published 531.9
  be fashionable 852.6
pass in one's checks 360.6
pass in review 505.10
pass muster
  conform 82.5
  stand the test 463.11
  suffice 639.3
  be good 648.5
  be praiseworthy 931.7
pass off egress 295.6
  dissemble 544.6
  affect 853.5
pass on
  advance 282.2
  die 360.6
pass out
  cease to be 2.5
  egress 295.6
  disappear 449.2
  overdrink 959.19
pass over
  exclude 55.3
  transfer to 270.7
  traverse 302.2
  die 360.6
  disregard 458.5
  slight 460.4, 6
  pretermit 460.7
  glance at 461.19
  side with 709.5
  exempt 748.10
  not observe 773.3
  transfer 783.3
  give 784.9
  excuse 918.3
pass the buck 938.4
pass the hat 765.6
pass through
  experience 151.4
  penetrate 302.2
  feel 821.3
pass up neglect 460.4
  pretermit 460.7
  avoid 623.6

not observe 773.3
  snub 930.7
passable
  inconsiderable 32.8
  tolerable 648.11
  (presentable **845.15**)
  mediocre 736.3
  satisfactory 831.7
passably 32.14
passacaglia, passacaglio 415.7
passage section 51.2
  transition 144.3
  vestibule 191.17
  chasm 198.3
  portal 260.4
  course 264.3
  travel 266.1, 3, 8
  voyage 267.6
  transference 270.1
  motion through 302
  (opening 260.1)
  channel 350.1
  music 413.10; 415.13, 15
  ~ in a book 593.7
  extract 596.1
  path 627.2
  (inlet 294.5)
  (outlet 295.5)
  transaction 680.2
  ~ at arms 720.2
passageway
  vestibule 191.17
  portal 260.4
  channel 350.1
  path 627.2
passbook 811.5
passé
  antiquated 124.9
  exploded 495.17
  worn 659.12
passed 122.8
passenger car 272.19
passe-partout
  passkey 260.10
  safe-conduct 664.2
passer-by
  wanderer 268.2
  spectator 444.1
pas seul 840.7
passim 186.22
passing great 31.6
  elapsing 109.4
  transient 111.6
  penetrating 302.3
  hasty 684.5
in passing
  transiently 111.8
  by the way 134.11
  on the way 270.13
  en passant 302.4
passing bell 363.5
passion mania 503.7
  (desire 865.5)
  vehemence 574.3
  eagerness 682.3
  emotion 821.1, 2
  fury 825.4
  mental suffering 828.1, 6
  love 897.1

anger 900.3
  lust 961.3
in a passion 900.13
passionate
  vehement 574.7
  fervent 821.6
  excitable 825.10
  amorous 897.13
  hot-tempered 901.7
passionless 823.5
Passion music 415.11, 12
Passion Week 998.13
passive inert 172.3
  (inactive 681.3)
  submissive 725.5
  obedient 743.3
  meek 826.10
passiveness
  inertness 172.1
  inaction 681.1
  obedience 743.1
  sufferance 826.4
passivism 681.1
passivity
  inertness 172.1
  latency 526.1
  inaction 681.1
  (inactivity 683.1)
  submission 725.1
  obedience 743.1
  sufferance 826.4
passkey 260.10
passman 541.4
passometer 553.3
Passover 998.13
passport
  passkey 260.10
  safe-conduct 664.2
  warrant 741.3
  pass 760.2
password
  passkey 260.10
  answer 462.1
  sign 550.11
  battle cry 722.3
past n. 122.2, 3
  (priority 116.1)
in the past 122.14
past adj.
  bygone 122.8, 9
  (prior 116.4)
  antiquated 124.9
paste n.
  mixture 41.4
  cement 45.6
  gluten 352.3
  pulp 354.2
  sham 545.6
  frippery 847.2
  gaudery 851.2
paste v. **cement** 46.7
  strike 276.8
pasteboard pulp 354.2
  paper 635.4
pasteboardy 160.11
pastel art 556.16
  description 594.1
pastelist, pastellist 559.1
pasticcio copy 21.1
  mixture 41.4

pastille, pastil, pastile n. 400.2
pastille, pastil v. 400.9
pastime 840.1
pastiness 354.1
past master 700.1
pastor 996.2
pastoral n. 415.3, 10
pastoral adj.
  rustic 183.3
  poem 597.13
  ecclesiastical 995.9
  (ministerial 996.15)
pastorate
  ministry 995.3
  parsonage 1000.5
pastose 556.19
past perfect 122.9
pastry 298.12
pasture n.
  enclosure 232.1
  pasturage 298.7
  grassland 367.11
pasture v. 298.43
pasty n. 298.12
pasty adj. **soft** 324.6
  viscid 352.8
  pulpy 354.5
pat n. **paw** 211.4
  blow 276.3
  sound 408a.2
  caress 902.3
pat v. **strike** 276.8
  beat time 416.19
  caress 902.8
pat juba 416.19
pat oneself on the back 884.5
pat on the back
  urge 615.7
  comfort 834.5
  encourage 858.8
  approve 931.5
  flatter 933.2
pat adj. **apt** 23.10
  fixed 150.5
  known 490.17
  resolute 604.7
patch n.
  modicum 32.2
  plot 181.3
  airplane 273a.10
  field 371.5
  ~ of light 420.3
  blemish 848.1
patch v. 140.6
patch up
  repair 660.11
  reconcile 723.4
  mediate 724.3
  compromise 774.2
patchwork
  mixture 41.4
  disconnection 70.1
  check 440.3
pate head 210.3
  brain 450.2
patella 191.10
patent n. 760.2
patent v. 760.4
patent adj. **open** 260.15
  distinct 446.5

patent medicine — pay

patent (continued)
  manifest 525.4
  permissive 760.6
patent medicine 662.2
pater father 166.6
  ecclesiastic title 877.4
patera
  receptacle 191.11, 12
  ornament 847.4
  sacramental cup 998.8
paterero See pedrero
paterfamilias
  patriarch 166.6
  master 745.1
paterissa 215.15; 999.1
paternal
  ancestral 166.10
  benevolent 906.6
paternity 166.2
  (filiation 155.2)
paternoster, Pater Noster prayer 990.3
  part of Mass 998.7
path track 550.4
  way 627.2
  (short cut 246.2)
  (doorway 260.4)
  (itinerary 266.9)
  (line 278.3)
  (entranceway 294.5)
  (passage 302.1)
  (mid-course 628.1)
  (detour 629.1)
  (career 692.3)
pathetic 830.11
pathfinder 673.5
pathless 261.4
pathogeny 655.19
pathognomonic 550.21
pathognomy 550.1
pathological illusion 503.5
pathological lying
  insanity 503.1
  falsehood 544.1
pathology 655.19
  (therapeutics 662.16)
pathomania 503.1
pathoneurosis, pathopsychosis 503.2
pathos 821.1
pathway 627.2
patience
  perseverance 604a.1
  sufferance 826.4
  (content 831.1)
  game 840.12
patient n. 655.20
patient adj.
  persevering 604a.3
  long-suffering 826.10
  (content 831.6)
patois 563.4, 5
  (language 560.1)
patriarch elder 130.1
  ancestor 166.1
  paterfamilias 166.6
  head 694.2

master 745.1
  church dignitary 996.5
patriarchal old 124.7
  aged 128.8
  ancestral 166.10
patriarchate, patriarchship, patriarchy 737.3, 4
patrician n. 875.4
patrician adj. 875.10
patrimony 775.4
patriot 911.1
patriotic 906.8
  (chauvinistic 884.8)
patriotism 906.4
  (chauvinism 884.2)
patristicism 451.9
patrol n. 717.6
patrol v. travel 266.12
  keep watch 664.7
patrolman guard 717.6
  constable 745.10
patrol wagon 272.7
patron attender 186.7
  captain 269.4
  theater 599.17
  guardian 664.3
  upholder 711.4
  (giver 816.2)
  (benefactor 912.1)
  master 745.1
  deputy 759.1
  customer 795.2
patronage
  protectorship 664.2
  auspices 693.2
  fosterage 707.2
  (influence 175.1)
  clientage 795.2
patronize
  supervise 693.5
  aid 707.8
  trade with 794.8
  arrogate 885.6
patronizer 795.2
patronizing 885.8
patronymic 564.2
patten bottom 211.1
  shoe 225.27
patter n.
  drumming 407.3
  twaddle 517.3
  language 560.1
  jargon 583.4
  acting device 599.6
patter v. strike 276.8
  drum 407.8
  talk nonsense 517.6
  talk 582.6
  be loquacious 584.4
  act 599.26
patterer 582.5
pattern n.
  prototype 22.1
  (example 82.2)
  (paragon 650.2)
  form 240.1
  measurement 466.2
  plan 626.2
  good example 948.1
pattern v. 240.6

patternmaker 690.8
patty, patty-cake, patty shell 298.12
patulous
  expanded 194.10
  open 260.15
pauciloquent 585.4
pauciloquy 585.1
paucity fewness 103.1
  scarcity 640.2
Paul Jones 792.5
Paul Pry n.
  inquisitive 455.2
  (gossip 532.5)
  meddler 682.11
  (intruder 228.4)
Paul-Pry v. 455.4
Paul Revere 534.1
paunch 191.7
paunched 194.11
paunchiness 192.4
paunchy 194.17
  (stout 192.12)
pauper 804.3
  (beggar 767.2)
pauperism 804.1
pauperize 804.6
pause n.
  discontinuity 70.1
  interim 109a.1
  delay 133.2
  stop 142.2
  (quiescence 265.2)
  (inaction 681.1)
  (idleness 683.2)
  music 413.12
  notation 415.23
  respite 687.2
pause v.
  discontinue 70.3
  stop 142.6
  (remain 265.5)
  (not do 681.2)
  (relax 687.4)
  be uncertain 475.6
  demur 485.7
  be irresolute 605.4
pave n. floor 211.2
  coating 223.18
  pavement 627.4
pave v. coat 223.24
  smooth 255.4
pave the way
  prepare 673.6
  facilitate 705.4
pavement floor 211.2
  coating 223.18
  roadway 627.4
paver 673.5
pavestone stone 342.4
  pavement 627.4
pavilion house 189.3
  cover 223.2, 3, 5
paving floor 211.2
  coating 223.18
  pavement 627.4
pavior, paviour 673.5
Pavo 318.6
pavonian, pavonine
  blue 438.6
  iridescent 440.6
paw n. foot 211.4

hand 781.3
paw v. 379.3
pawky
  sagacious 498.10
  cunning 702.6
pawl 45.2
pawn n.
  ~ of necessity 600.7
  pledge 771.1
  pawnbroker 787.2, 3
  in pawn 771.9
pawn v. 771.5
  (borrow 788.2)
pawnbroker 787.2
pawnbrokery 786.3
pawnshop 787.3
pax n. peace 721.1
  kiss of peace 998.2, 7
  osculatory 998.8
pax int. 403.9
Pax Britannica, Pax Ecclesiae, Pax Romana 721.1
Pax Dei, pax Dei 721.1
pax vobiscum!
  farewell! 293.14
  peace be with you! 721.5
  best wishes! 894.15
pay n. payment 807.2
  (compensation 30.3)
  (disbursement 809.2)
  punishment 972.1
  remuneration 973.2
  in one's pay 746.9
pay v.
  retaliate 718.2
  be profitable 775.10
  make payment 807.6
  (give 784.8)
  (purchase 795.3)
  (expend 809.3)
  yield 810.4
  punish 972.5
  reward 973.3
  (compensate 30.4)
not pay 808.5
  (evade 623.6)
  (swindle 791.12)
pay back
  reciprocate 148.3
  retaliate 718.2
pay court to
  curry favor 886.3
  woo 902.7
pay dearly for one's whistle
  be unskillful 699.7
  pay exorbitantly 814.4
pay home 718.2
pay off
  turn ship 267.24
  settle accounts 807.7
pay one in his own coin retaliate 718.2
  repay 807.9
pay one's way
  defray 807.6
  economize 817.3

payer — pedometer

pay out
  make payment
    807.6, 7
  expend 809.3
  punish 972.5
pay size, pay the
  devil 814.4
pay the piper
  pay for 807.6
  be punished 972.12
pay through the nose
  814.4
pay up 807.7
payer 807.5
paying
  profitable 775.12
  remunerative 973.5
paying guest 188.4
paymaster 801
  (payer 807.5)
payment
  defrayment 807
  (compensation 30.3)
  (security 771.1)
  (disbursement
    809.2)
  punishment 972.1
  remuneration 973.2
  (bribe 618.2)
  make payment 807.6
  (reward 973.3)
paynim n. 984.20
paynim adj. 984.28
pay-off end 67.1
  final issue 154.1
  payment 807.2
pea sphere 249.2
  vegetable 298.30
  plant 369.8
peace
  quiescence 265.1
  comfort 377.2
  silence 403.1
  peacefulness 721
  (concord 714.1)
  (friendship 888.1)
  truce 723.3
  at peace 721.3, 4
  (concordant 714.4)
peace of mind
  calmness 826.2
  content 831.1
peaceable
  equable 174.6
  pacific 721.4
  meek 826.10
peaceful equable 174.6
  quiescent 265.7
  comfortable 377.8
  restful 687.6
  pacific 721.4
  inexcitable 826.9
  meek 826.10
peacefulness
  comfort 377.2
  peace 721.1
peacemaker 724.2
  (judge 967.1)
peaceman, peace man
  721.2
peace offering
  pacification 723.2

offering 784.3
oblation 990.6
  (atonement 952.1)
peace officer 745.10
peace pipe
  token 550.14
  peace offering 723.2
peach n. fruit 298.31
  good thing 648.4
  a beauty 845.3
peach v.
  inform on 527.10
  blab 529.4
peach adj. 434.10;
  436.6
peacher 527.6
peachery 371.6
peacoat 225.16
peacock n. fowl 366.23
  male animal 373.6
  variegation 440.2
  strutter 880.3
Peacock n. 318.6
peacock v.
  act proudly 878.3
  strut 882.6
peacock blue n. 438.2
peacock-blue adj.
  438.6
peacockery
  vanity 880.1
  ostentation 882.2
peacockish vain 880.6
  ostentatious 882.8
Peacock throne 747.5
peafowl 366.23
peag, peage 800.3
pea green n. 435.2
pea-green adj. 435.6
peahen fowl 366.23
  female animal 374.8
peak n. pinnacle 206.2
  summit 210.1
  (spire 253.4)
  promontory 250.5
peak v. top 210.5
  sicken 655.21
peaked 203.11
peal n. boom 406.3, 4
  ~ of laughter 838.3
  ~ of applause 931.4
peal v. boom 406.9
  roll 407.1, 6
  ring 408.8
  toot 410.8
pean See paean
peanut
  diminutive 193.2
  nut 298.33
  trifle 643.3
peanut oil 356.3
pear 298.31
pearl tooth 253.3
  type 591.7
  treasure 648.4
  gem 847.8
  good person 948.1
pearl adj.
  whitish 430.9
  gray 432.4
pearl-gray 432.4
pearlike 245.17

pearliness 427.1
pearl white 430.4
pearly
  opalescent 427.4
  soft-colored 428.17
  whitish 430.9
  gray 432.4
  iridescent 440.6
peasant 876.5
  (farmer 371.2)
  (serf 746.4)
peasantry 876.1
peasecod 223.14
peashooter 273a.2
pea soup n. 353.5
pea-soup adj. 353.11
peat 388.1
peat bog 345.1
peba 366.14
pebble
  diminutive 193.2
  sphere 249.2
  stone 342.4
peccability
  badness 649.1
  sinfulness 945.1
  guilt 947.1
peccable 945.11
peccadillo 947.2
peccancy
  badness 649.1
  immorality 945.1
  sin 947.2
peccant
  erroneous 495.12
  (imperfect 651.4)
  bad 649.8
  foul 653.17
  diseased 655.25
  decayed 659.13
  disreputable 874.8
  sinning 945.15
  guilty 947.4
peccary swine 366.7
  malodor 401.2
peck n.
  quantities 31.3
  multitude 102.2
  food 298.5
  measure 466.3
peck v. eat 298.44
  criticize 932.7
pecker 250.4
peckerwood 366.22
pecket 342.4
peckish 865.19
peckle 342.4
Pecksniff 548.4
pecky 348.26
pectinate 253.11
pectoral cross 999.1
peculate 791.9
peculation 791.1
peculator 792.8
peculiar
  differentiative 15.8
  classificational 75.6
  special 79.8
  (intrinsic 5.7)
  (characterized
    820.3)
  unusual 83.10

eccentric 503.17
peculiarity
  particularity 79.2
  unusualness 83.3
  eccentricity 503.6
  earmark 550.6
  diction 569.1
  trait 820.1
peculiarly
  remarkably 31.21
  principally 33.10
pecuniary 800.21
pecunious 803.8
pedagogic 540.7
  (educational 537.12)
  (scholastic 542.9)
pedagogue, pedagog
  pedant 492.4
  teacher 540.1
pedagogy 537.1
pedal 211.4
pedal point
  low tone 408.6
  key 413.7
pedant
  conformist 82.3
  scholar 492.4
  (teacher 540.1)
  (affecter 853.4)
pedantic
  sciolistic 491.12
  grandiloquent 577.7
  priggish 853.7
pedantry
  minute attention
    457.3
  prejudice 481.3
  bookishness 491.4
  (quackery 544.2)
  bigotry 606.2
  affectation 853.1
peddle dawdle 683.8
  vend 796.5
peddler, pedlar 797.3
peddler's French
  563.4
peddling
  trifling 643.11
  miserly 819.4
pederast, paederast
  962.1
pederero See pedrero
pedestal 215.3
pedestrian n. 268.6
pedestrian adj. 266.23
pedestrianism 266.4
pedestrianize 266.16
pediatrics, paediatrics
  662.16
pedicel 215.14
pedicellate 215.30
pedicle stalk 215.14
  flower 367.5
pedicular 653.18
pediculosis 653.12
pediculous 653.18
pedicure clean 652.9
  chiropody 662.24
pedigree 166.4
pediment top 210.4
  base 215.3
pedometer 553.3

pedotribe — penny-a-liner 1004

pedotribe See paedotribe
pedrero, pederero 727.11
peduncle stalk 215.14
　flower 367.5
pedunculate 215.30
peek n. 441.2
peek v. 441.13
peel n. layer 204.2
　cover 223.15
　stronghold 717.4
peel v. cut off 38.6
　~ off 44.6
　form layers 204.4
　pare 226.4
peeler 745.10
peeling 223.15
peel tower 717.4
peep n.
　~ of day 125.1
　glimpse 441.2
peep v. chirp 412.2
　peer 441.13
　pry 455.4
peep out
　look about 441.11
　appear 446.2
　reconnoiter 461.22
　be disclosed 529.6
peeper eye 441.7
　informer 527.6
peephole
　opening 260.1
　observatory 441.5
Peeping Tom
　inquisitive 455.2
　informer 527.6
peep show show 599.8
　amusement 840.15
peer n. equal 27.5
　nobleman 875.4
peer v. gaze 441.13
　appear 446.2
　pry 455.4
　seek 461.16, 17
peerage 875.2
peerless
　unequaled 28.4
　supreme 33.8
　(best 648.9)
　(eminent 873.18)
　virtuous 944.3
peevish 901.7
peewee
　diminutive 193.2
　bird 366.22
peg n. degree 26.1
　pin 45.5
　(suspender 214.3)
　(supporter 215.2)
　rank 71.1
　tooth 253.3
　stopper 263.1
　leg 266.11
　blow 276.3
　throw 284.3
　drink 298.4
　alcoholic drink 959.10
peg v. walk 266.16
　speed 274.9

strike 276.8
throw 284.12
see 441.10
recognize 481a.6
plod 686.6
peg away
　persevere 604a.2
　be industrious 682.12
　plod 686.6
peg out
　cease to be 2.5
　weaken 160.7
　die 360.6
　tire 688.4
　fail 732.5
　tether 751.7
Pegasus horse 271.9
　constellation 318.6
pegology 348.14
pegomancy 511.3
peg tops 225.21
peignoir 225.23
peine forte et dure 972.1
pelagic 341.5
pelagic zone 208.3
pelerine 225.15
pelf gain 775.2
　money 800.1
pelisse 225.15
pellet 249.2
pellicle layer 204.2
　skin 223.12
　coating 223.18
pell-mell, pellmell
　hastily 684.7
　excitably 825.12
pellucid
　luminous 420.22
　transparent 425.4
　perspicuous 518.5
pellucidity 425.1
pelmatozoan 368.14
Peloponnesian War 722.4
peloria 242.1
pelt n. skin 223.12
　fur 256.3
　race horse 271.8
　blow 276.3
pelt v. strike 276.8
　throw 284.12
　shoot 284.13
　stone 716.7; 972.7
peltate 245.19
peltry 223.12
peludo 366.14
pemphigus 655.17
pen n.
　messuage 189.12
　enclosure 232.1
　(cote 189.7)
　grassland 367.11
　farm 371.4
　writing ~ 590.10
　writer 590.11
　prison 752.1
pen v. write 590.13
　confine 751.8
pen in
　circumscribe 229.2

(enclose 232.3)
confine 751.8
penal 972.14
penalization
　punishment 972.1
　penalty 974.1
penalize
　inflict penalty 974.3
　(sentence 971.2)
　(punish 972.5)
　inflict penance 998.14
penal servitude 972.2
penalty
　punishment 972.1
　penal retribution 974
　(penance 952.3)
penance
　atonement 952.3
　(penitence 950.1)
　(propitiation 990.5)
　(sacrament 998.3)
　penalty 974.1
do penance 952.4
　(repent 950.3)
　(propitiate 990.13)
penates home 189.2
　familiar spirit 979.12
penchant
　tendency 176.1
　liking 865.1
　(propensity 602.2)
　(love 897.1)
pencil n.
　~ of light 420.3
　drawing 556.3, 9, 16
　writing ~ 590.10
in pencil 556.19
pencil v. draw 556.17
　write 590.13
pencraft 590.1, 2
pend depend 214.4
　be dependent 475.7
pendant, pendent n.
　adjunct 39.1
　analogue 17.5
　hanging 214.2
　(supporter 215.2)
pendeloque 214.2
pendency
　interim 109a.1
　hanging 214
　(support 215.1)
pendent, pendant adj. 214.7
　be pendent 214.4
pendente lite
　uncertainly 475.17
　meanwhile 109a.3
pendicle 214.2
pending adj. 214.7; 475.15
pending prep. 106.7
pendragon 745.3
pendulant 214.7
pendulate
　oscillate 314.8
　be irresolute 605.4
pendulation
　oscillation 314.1

irresolution 605.1
penduline n. 214.2
penduline adj. 214.7
pendulosity 214.1
pendulous
　hanging 214.7, 8
　oscillatory 314.12
pendulum
　pendant 214.2
　oscillator 314.6
penetrability 518.1
penetrable
　pervious 260.20
　understandable 518.5
penetral, penetralia 221.2
penetrate
　pervade 186.12
　perforate 260.14
　enter 294.6
　pass through 302.2
　make an impression 451.33
　see through 481a.5
　understand 518.4
　~ the feelings 824.4
penetrating
　odorous 398.8
　sagacious 498.10
　~ emotionally 824.13
　(deep-felt 821.8)
penetration
　imbuement 41.2
　pervasion 186.5
　perforation 260.8
　ingress 294.1
　passage 302.1
　discrimination 465.1
　sagacity 498.2
penfold See pinfold
penguin
　aeronaut 269a.1
　aircraft 273a.1
　diver 310.3
peninsula 250.5
penitence 950
　(regret 833.1)
　(lamentation 839.1)
　(penance 952.3)
penitent n. 950.2
penitent adj. 950.5
　(regretful 833.3)
　be penitent 950.3
penitentiary n.
　prison 752.1
　confessor 996.2, 5
penitentiary adj. 950.5
penknife 253.6
penmaker 690.8
penman 590.11
　(author 593.15)
penmanship 590.1
pen name 565.3
pennant 550.13
penner 590.11
penniless 804.7
　(bankrupt 808.10)
pennon 550.13
penny 800.8
penny-a-liner 593.15

penny ante 840.12
penny dreadful 594.2
pennyweight 319.4
penny wisdom 818.1
penny-wise 819.4
  penny-wise and
    pound-foolish
  foolish 499.15
  capricious 608.5
  prodigal 818.4
pennyworth
  value 812.3
  bargain 815.2
penology 972.1
penscript 590.1, 3
penseroso 837.9
pensile 214.7
pensility 214.1
pension 784.5
pensionary n.
  hireling 746.1
  pensioner 746.3
  recipient 785.2
pensionary adj. 785.5
pensioner
  student 541.4
  dependent 746.3
  recipient 785.2
pensive
  thoughtful 451.35
  sad 837.9
pensively 451.39
pensiveness 451.1
penstock 349.1, 2
pent up shut in 229.4
  imprisoned 751.12
penta-, pent- 98.15
pentachord 413.18
pentacle 98.1
pentad n. five 98.1
  microbe 193.4
pentad adj. 98.15
pentagon five 98.1
  angle 244.2
pentagonal 244.5
pentagram 98.1
pentahedral 244.5
pentahedron 244.2
pentalpha 98.1
pentameter five 98.1
  versification 597.6
pentapody, pentarchy
  98.1
pentastich five 98.1
  stanza 597.7
Pentateuch five 98.1
  Scriptures 985.3
pentathlon 98.1
pentavalent 98.15
pentaconter 273.3
Pentecost 998.13
Penthesilea 861.3
penthouse 189.3
pentrough 350.1
penultimate 67.10
penumbra 422.3
penurious 819.4
penury poverty 804.1
  parsimony 819.1
penwoman
  writer 590.11
  author 593.15

peon messenger 534.1
  soldier 726.1
peonage 603.3
people n.
  kinsmen 11.3
  race 11.4
  population 188.10
  persons 372.2
  subjects 746.5
  masses 876.1
  laity 997.1
people v.
  multiply 102.4
  inhabit 186.10
pep n. energy 171.1
  vigorous style 574.2
  liveliness 682.1
pep v.
pep up 171.7
pepper n. energy 171.1
  seasoning 393.1
  verve 682.1
pepper v. season 392.4
  bombard 716.6
pepper-and-salt n.
  219.5
pepper-and-salt adj.
  440.7
peppercorn n. 643.3
peppercorn adj. 815.8
peppercorn rent 815.1
peppermint
  pungency 392.2
  condiment 393.1
  candy 396.2
peppery
  pungent 392.5
  hot-tempered 901.7
peppy energetic 171.9
  language 574.6
  lively 682.16
pepsin, pepsine 320.3
pepsinate 320.6
peptic leavening 320.8
  digestive 665.26
per 631.5
peradventure 470.7
peragrate 266.12
perambulate 266.16
perambulation 266.4
perambulator 272.11
perambulatory 266.23
percale cloth 219.5
  sheet 223.9
perceivability 446.1
perceivable
  visible 446.4
  manifest 525.4
perceive sense 375.3
  hear 418.11
  see 441.10
  note 450.7
  judge 480.6
  recognize 481a.6
  know 490.9
  understand 518.4
per cent, percent 84.6
percentage ratio 84.6
  portion 786.2
  discount 813.1
perceptibility 446.1
perceptible

visible 446.4
knowable 490.18
manifest 525.4
perception
  hearing 418.1
  vision 441.1
  consciousness 450.1
  idea 453.1
  knowledge 490.1
  sagacity 498.2
perceptive
  sensible 375.6; 822.6
  discriminating 465.4
  cognitive 490.12
  sagacious 498.10
perceptivity
  physical ∼ 375.1
  intuition 477a.1
  emotional ∼ 822.1
perch n. abode 189.1
  shaft 215.13
  post 215.16
  landing 267a.26
perch v. settle 184.14
  inhabit 186.10
  be high 206.9
  get down 306.5
  sit 308.6
perchance 470.7
  (by chance 156.13)
Percheron 271.4
percipience
  consciousness 450.1
  sagacity 498.2
percipient
  intellectual 450.8
  knowing 490.12
  sagacious 498.10
percolate
  filter 295.7; 652.10
  solubilize 335.6
  infiltrate 337.5
  trickle 348.19
percolation
  filtration 295.1
  trickle 348.4
percolative 295.9
percolator 191.11
percontation 461.1
percontatorial 461.24
per contra
  contrarily 14.7
  counterevidence
    468.5
percursory 460.8
  offhand 458.10
  perfunctory 460.8
percuss 406.8
percussion clash 276.2
  detonation 406.2
percussion fire 716.2
percussion instrument
  417.10
perdie See pardie
perdition
  destruction 162.1
  defeat 732.3
  loss 776.1
  go to perdition
  perish 162.5
  deteriorate 659.6
perdu, perdue 528.17

perdurability 112.1
perdurable
  durable 110.9
  everlasting 112.4
perdurant 112.4
perdure 106.2
peregrinate 266.12, 14
peregrination
  266.1, 2, 8
peregrinator 268.2, 6
peremptory
  emphatic 535.6
  resolute 604.7
  authoritative 737.15
  arbitrary 739.5
  compulsory 744.3
  obligatory 926.9
perennate 106.2
perennial
  continuous 69.6
  durable 110.9
  (unchangeable
    150.7)
  eternal 112.4
  plant 367.17
perenniality 112.1
perennialize 112.3
perfect v.
  bring to perfection
    650.4
  improve 658.8
  elaborate 673.6
  complete 729.2
perfect adj.
  absolute 31.12
  unqualified 52.10
  complete 729.6
  faultless 650.5
  (supreme 33.8)
  (superexcellent
    648.10)
not perfect 651.4
perfected 729.6
  (perfect 650.4)
perfection
  faultlessness 650
  (superiority 33.1)
  (summit 210.1)
  (superexcellence
    648.3)
  philosopher's stone
    650.3
  improvement 658.1
  elaboration 673.1
  completion 729.1
to perfection 650.6
perfectionism 926.4
perfectly 650.6
  (completely 52.13)
perfidious 940.12
  (false 544.7)
  (deceptive 545.12)
perfidy 940.4
  (dissembling 544.2)
perflate 338.10
perflation 338.6
  (wind 349.1)
perforate v. 260.14
  (insert 300.5)
  (penetrate 302.2)
perforate adj. 260.15
perforation 260.1, 8

perforator — perplexity

perforator 262
 (knife 253.6)
perforce
 by force of 744.4
 (unwillingly 603.6)
 necessarily 601.15
perform produce 161.8
 operate 170.2
 ~ music 416.18
 act 599.26
 ~ a function 644.3
 do 680.6
 complete 729.2
 ~ a duty 926.6
 ~ a rite 998.14
performable 470.6
performance
 production 161.1
 product 161.6
 music 415.17, 20
 musicianship 416.17
 theatrical ~ 599.6, 8
 action 680.1, 2
 completion 729.1
 observance 772.1
 ~ of duty 926.2
performer
 musician 416.1
 doer 690.1
 affecter 853.4
performing 680.7
perfumatory 400.10
perfume n. 400.1, 2
 (odor 398.1)
perfume v.
 fumigate 336.5
 scent 400.9
 (odorize 398.6)
perfumed 400.10
perfumer 400.5, 6
 (merchant 797.11)
perfumery 400.2
perfumizer 400.5
perfumy 400.10
perfunctorize 460.6
perfunctory
 incomplete 53.4
 neglectful 460.8
 (inadequate 304.3)
pergola 191.22
perhaps n. 470.1
perhaps, perhazard adv. 470.7
 (supposedly 514.12)
peri beauty 845.3
 fairy 979.9
Periander 500.3
periapt 993.2
pericarp vessel 191.6
 hull 223.14
pericranium 210.3
periderm, peridium 223.15
peridot green 435.3
 gem 847.8
perihelion 197.4
peril n. 665.1
peril v. 665.4
perilous 665.7
 (fearful 860.15)
perimeter
 outline 230.1

edge 231.1
perimetric 230.4
period degree 26.1
 end 67.1
 time 106.1
 ~ of time 108
 (date 114.4)
 stop 142.5
 limit 233.1
 menses 299.7
 music 415.15
 punctuation 550.8
periodic 138.10
 (successive 63.5)
 (discontinuous 70.4)
 (frequent 136.3)
periodical 593.6
periodically 138.12
 (in order 58.8)
 (frequently 136.5)
periodicity 138.2
 (discontinuity 70.1)
 (repetition 104.1)
 (reversion 145.1)
peripatetic n. 268.2, 6
peripatetic adj. 266.23
peripateticate 266.16
peripheral 230.4
periphery
 surroundings 227.2
 outline 230.1
 edge 231.1
periphrase, -sis 573.3
periphrastic 573.9
periplus 267.1
periscope 445.1
perish
 be destroyed 162.5
 (cease 2.5)
 (deteriorate 659.6)
 (fail 732.5)
 die 360.6
perishability 111.1
perishable 111.6
perished 162.7
 (extinct 2.10)
peristalsis 221.6
peristaltic 248.6
peristyle series 69.2
 cloister 189.19
perivisceral 220.7
periwig 256.4
periwinkle 298.18
perjure 544.4
perjurer 548.5
perjury 544.1
perk v. jerk 285.5
 act proudly 878.3
 perk up lift up 307.5
 recuperate 689.3
 cheer up 836.4, 14
 exalt oneself 878.3
perk adj. 878.6
perks 973.2
perky 878.6
perlustrate 441.12
perlustration 441.2
permanence
 uniformity 16.1
 durability 110.1
 changelessness 141
 (continuance 143.1)

(stability 150.1)
(inertness 172.1)
(quiescence 265.1)
(preservation 670.1)
(inaction 681.1;
 683.1)
permanent n. 256.3
permanent adj.
 durable 110.9
 (continuing 106.4)
 (perpetual 112.4)
 unchanged 141.6
 (stable 150.5)
 (unchangeable 150.7)
 (unmoved 265.7)
 inveterate 613.12
be permanent 141.4
make permanent 141.6
 (stabilize 150.4)
Permanent Court of International Justice 966.1
permanently
 for a long time 110.11
 (perpetually 112.5)
 without change 141.8
permanent wave 256.3
permeable 260.20
permeate
 pervade 186.12
 interpenetrate 228.9
 pass through 302.2
permeation
 imbuement 41.2
 (interjection 228.2)
 pervasion 186.5
 passage 302.1
Permian 560.4
permissible 760.6
 (warranted 924.10)
permissibly 760.7
 (willingly 602.11)
 (freely 748.21)
permission 760
 (authority 737.1)
 (freedom 748.1)
 (consent 762.1)
 (privilege 922.2)
permissioned, permissive 760.6
 (consenting 762.3)
permit n. 760.2
permit v. 760.3
 (empower 157.7)
 (allow freedom 748.10)
 (consent 762.2)
permitted 760.6
 (legal 963.5)
not permitted 761.4
permutability
 interchangeableness 148.2
 changeableness 149.1
permutable 149.5
permutation
 change 140.1

interchange 148.1
permute 148.3
pernavigate 267.10
pernicious 649.10
perorate
 speak at length 573.5
 declaim 582.7
peroration sequel 65.1
 prolixity 573.1
 speech 582.2
peroxide n.
 decolorant 429.3
 antiseptic 662.8
peroxide v. 429.5
perpend n. 228.6
perpend v. 451.27
perpendicular n. 212.2
perpendicular adj. 212.8
 (straight 246.5)
perpendicular adv. 212.9
perpendicularity 212.1
 (straightness 246.1)
perpetrate 680.6
perpetration 680.1
perpetrator 690.1
perpetual 112.4
 (infinite 105.3)
 (durable 110.9)
 (constant 136.4)
 (continuing 143.4)
perpetually 112.5
 (invariably 16.7)
 (infinitely 105.4)
 (constantly 136.6)
perpetuate
 eternalize 112.3
 continue 143.3
 (stabilize 150.4)
 immortalize 976.8
perpetuation
 perpetuity 112.1
 continuance 143.1
perpetuity
 continuity 69.1
 eternity 112
 (durability 110.1)
perplex
 complicate 61.5
 (obscure 519.4)
 confuse 458.9
 bewilder 475.8
 fill with doubt 485.8
 (mystify 533.4)
 (be difficult 704.5)
perplexed
 confused 59.8
 complex 59.10
 (obscure 519.7)
 bewildered 475.16
perplexing 475.12
 (enigmatic 533.6)
 (embarrassing 704.9)
perplexity
 complexity 59.3
 (unintelligibility 519.1)
 confusion 458.4
 bewilderment 475.2

perquisite — perverted

(incomprehension 491.3)
(dilemma 704.4)
perquisite gain 775.2
  boodle 793.1
  pay 973.2
perquisition 461.4
perquisitor 461.12
perron platform 215.21
  stairs 305.2
per saltum
  discontinuously 70.5
  suddenly 113.7
  agitatedly 315.14
perscrutate 461.18
perscrutation 461.4
perscrutator 461.13
per se
  essentially 5.8
  alone 87.10
persecute harm 649.6
  torment 830.5
persecution
  ill-treatment 649.4
  abuse 907.3
Persephassa, Persephone world 318.1
  agriculture 371.3
  goddess 979.2; 982.4
Perseus
  constellation 318.6
  hero 861.3
perseverance 604a
  (continuance 143.1)
  (resolution 604.1)
  (obstinacy 606.1)
  (sedulity 682.5)
perseverant 604a.3
persevere
  continue 143.2
  persist 604a.2
  (keep on 136.2)
  (be resolute 604.5)
  (be obstinate 606.5)
  (plod 686.6)
  (do thoroughly 729.3)
persevering 604a.3
  (stable 150.5)
  (resolute 604.7)
  (sedulous 682.19)
perseveringly 604a.4
  (resolutely 604.9)
Persian cat 366.4
  language 560.4
Persian earth 434.2
persiflage
  witticism 842.4
  banter 856.1
persist endure 106.2
  be permanent 141.4
  (maintain 670.3)
  continue 143.2
  persevere 604a.2
  (keep on 136.2)
  (be resolute 604.5)
  (be obstinate 606.5)
persistence
  uniformity 16.1
  durability 110.1
  permanence 141.1

perseverance 604a.1
  (frequency 136.1)
  (continuance 143.1)
persistent
  durable 110.9
  unchanged 141.6
  continuing 143.4
  persevering 604a.3
person being 3.2
  human 372.2, 3
in person 186.17
personable 845.10
personage
  person 372.3
  man of mark 642.5
  (nobleman 875.4)
persona grata
  friend 890.1
  favorite 899.1
personal physical 3.4
  special 79.7
  subjective 317.7
  human 372.5
  property 780.8
personality self 79.4
  personal property 780.5
  discourtesy 895.1
  personal remark 934.2
  (sarcasm 856.2)
  (malediction 908.1)
  (indignity 929.2)
  (gibe 930.3)
personal property 780.5
personate 554.8
  (simulate 19.7)
  (act 599.26)
personation 554.2
  (simulation 19.3)
  (acting 599.6)
personification
  figure of speech 521.1
  personation 554.2
personify
  embody 316.7
  symbolize 521.2
  personate 554.8
personnel
  components 56.1
  staff 746.7
perspective
  distance 196.1
  vista 441.6
  scene 448.2
  art 556.5
perspicacious
  discriminating 465.4
  sagacious 498.10
perspicacity
  vision 441.1
  discrimination 465.1
  sagacity 498.2
perspicuity
  sagacity 498.2
  intelligibility 518.1
  (manifestness 525.1)
  ~ of expression 570
perspicuous

sagacious 498.10
  intelligible 518.5
  manifest 525.4
perspiration 299.4
  (exudation 295.1)
  (offal 653.6)
perspire 295.7
  (be moist 339.6)
perspiry 299.11
perstringe
  do carelessly 460.6
  glance at 461.19
persuadability 602.3
  (susceptibility 615.5)
persuadable 498.12
persuade
  convince 484.10
  induce 615.9
  (cause 153.7)
  (influence 175.6)
persuade oneself 615.10
persuasibility 602.3
persuasible
  unprejudiced 498.12
  docile 602.9
persuasion kind 75.2, 3
  belief 484.2
  proselytism 537.3
  denomination 542.4
  inducement 615.4
  (influence 175.1)
  (advice 695.1)
  sect 984.3
persuasive n. 615.4
persuasive adj.
  believable 484.15
  inducive 615.11
  (influential 175.10)
persuasiveness 615.4
pert vain 880.6
  impertinent 885.9
pertain
  be related 9.3
  be included 76.2
  belong 777.6
  behoove 926.5
pertinacious
  persistent 604a.3
  obstinate 606.6
pertinacity
  perseverance 604a.1
  obstinacy 606.1
pertinence 23.2
pertinent
  ~ to 9.5
  apt 23.10
  (relevant 9.8)
  pointed 550.22
not pertinent 10.6
pertinently 23.13
  (relatively 9.9)
perturb
  discompose 61.4
  agitate 315.8
  confuse 458.9
  excite 824.3
perturbance 860.3
perturbate
  agitate 315.8
  excite 824.3

perturbation
  turmoil 59.4
  discomposure 61.1
  restlessness 149.3
  activity 171.2
  agitation 315.1
  confusion 458.4
  excitation 824.1
  excitement 825.3
  trepidation 860.3
perturbed 828.14
pertussis 655.9
peruke 256.4
perusal
  examination 461.3
  study 539.1
peruse examine 461.17
  study 539.4
pervade
  permeate 186.12
  (imbue 41.8)
  interpenetrate 228.9
  pass through 302.2
pervading 821.8
pervasion
  imbuement 41.2
  permeation 186.5
  passage 302.1
perverse
  obstinate 606.6
  (ill-humored 901.7)
  unmanageable 704.10
  scurrile 895.6
perversion
  distortion 243.2
  sophistry 477.1
  misinterpretation 523.1
  misteaching 538.1
  falsification 544.1
  misstatement 546.1
  misrepresentation 555.1
  apostasy 607.2
  corruption 659.3
  misuse 679.1
  impiety 988.3
perversity
  obstinacy 606.1
  gruffness 895.2
  ill-humor 901.1
pervert n.
  hermaphrodite 83.5
  apostate 607.5
  (reversioner 145.3)
  (backslider 661.2; 988.5)
  degenerate 949.1
  heretic 984.12
pervert v. distort 243.4
  sophisticate 477.7
  misinterpret 523.2
  misteach 538.2
  falsify 544.3
  (mislead 495.11)
  misrepresent 555.4
  corrupt 659.9
  misuse 679.2
perverted
  hermaphrodite 83.12
  erroneous 495.12, 15

pervicacious — philosophism

perverted (*continued*)
  wicked 945.15
  impious 988.10
pervicacious 606.6
pervigilium 682.9
pervious
  penetrable 260.20
  egressive 295.9
  transparent 425.4
pes 211.4
peseta, peso 800.8
pessimism
  underestimation 483.1
  gloominess 837.1
  hopelessness 859.1
pessimist
  sad person 837.5
  (malcontent 832.2)
  cynic 859.4
  (detractor 936.1)
pessimistic 837.15
  (hopeless 859.7)
pessimize
  underestimate 483.3
  be sad 837.8
pest pestilence 655.2
  bane 663.1
  nuisance 830.2
  bore 841.4
pester 830.5
pesthole
  contagion 655.2
  unhealthfulness 657.1
pesthouse 662.17
pestiferous 657.5
pestilence
  epidemic 655.2
  (evil 649.2)
  bane 663.1
  scourge 830.2
pestilent 657.5
pestle 330.4
pet *n.* favorite 899.1
  dudgeon 900.2
  endearment 902.4
pet *v.* make love 902.7
  caress 902.8
  flatter 933.2
pet *adj.* 807.16
petal 367.4
petard 727.14
peter *n.* 191.5
peter *v.*
  peter out
    cease to be 2.5
    weaken 160.7
    fail 732.5
peterero See **pedrero**
Peter Funk 795.2
peterman
  fisherman 622.5
  safecracker 792.2
petiole stalk 215.14
  foliage 367.4
petite 193.8
petite noblesse 875.3
petition *n.*
  request 765.1
  prayer 990.3
petition *v.* 765.4

(pray 990.11)
petitionary 765.7
petitioner 767
petit larceny 791.1
petit mal 655.3
petkin 902.4
petrel 366.22
petrescence, petrifaction 323.2
petrifactive, petrific, petrified 323.5
petrify harden 323.4
  (solidify 321.7)
  (mineralize 358.3)
  freeze 385.4
  startle 508.7
  stun 824.3
  terrify 860.10
  dumfound 870.3
petrol
  automobile 272.16
  gasoline 356.2
petrolatum oil 356.2
  balm 662.6
petroleum 356.2
  (fuel 388.1)
  (illuminant 420.15)
petrology 358.2
petronel 727.10
petter 897.6
petticoat *n.*
  garment 225.16, 19, 25
  woman 374.2
petticoat *adj.* 160a.5
pettifog argue 476.11
  quibble 477.8
pettifogger 968.1
pettifoggery
  deception 545.1
  cunning 702.1
  dishonesty 940.5
pettifogging
  quibbling 477.11
  dishonest 940.8
pettish 901.7
petty little 193.8
  trivial 643.11
  (inconsiderable 32.8)
  (mediocre 736.3)
  disreputable 874.8
petty cash 800.14
petty larceny 791.1
petty officer 745.11
petulance
  insolence 885.2
  ill-humor 901.1
petulant 901.7
pew
  compartment 191.2
  seat 215.22
  church ~ 1000.3
pewter mixture 41.4
  white 430.3
pfennig 800.8
Phaëthon 318.4
phaeton 272.4, 15
phalansterianism 906.3
phalanx party 712.1
  military unit 726.7

phantasize 515.8
phantasm
  apparition 443.9
  delusion 495.5
  figment 515.4
  specter 980a.1
phantasmagoria
  illusion 443.9
  view 448.2
  fancy 515.4
phantasmagoric 515.12
phantasmagorist 515.7
phantasmal, phantasmic 515.12
phantast 515.7
phantasy See **fantasy**
phantom *n.*
  apparition 443.9
  (unsubstantiality 4.3)
  (appearance 448.3)
  (imagining 515.4)
  specter 980a.1
phantom *adj.*
  imaginary 515.12
  spectral 980a.4
phantomnation 562.1
pharisaical
  hypocritical 544.8
  sanctimonious 988.11
pharisaism
  hypocrisy 544.2
  sanctimony 988.2
  (dissemblance 544.2)
Pharisaism 984.7
pharisee
  hypocrite 548.4
  lip worshiper 988.6
Pharisee 984.17
pharmaceutics 662.16
pharmaceutist, pharmacist 662.21
  (professional 690.10)
pharmacology 662.16
pharmacon 662.4
pharmacophobia 860.9
pharmacopoeia 662.4
  pharmacist 662.21
pharmacy
  healing art 662.16
  drugstore 662.18
pharos
  observatory 441.5
  landmark 550.10
phase *n.*
  circumstance 8.1
  transition 144.3
  aspect 448.4
phase *v.* See **faze**
phasis
  circumstance 8.1
  aspect 448.4
phasm
  apparition 443.9
  specter 980a.1
pheasant 298.25, 26
phenix See **phoenix**
phenomenon
  event 151.1

view 448.2
  prodigy 872.1
phial 191.11
Phi Beta Kappa 873.8
philabeg 225.19
Philadelphia lawyer 702.4
philander *n.*
  flirtation 902.1
  philanderer 902.6
philander *v.* 902.7
philanderer 902.6
philanthropic 906.7
  (almsgiving 784.15)
philanthropist 911
  (giver 784.7)
philanthropy 906.1, 2
  (giving 784.2)
philharmonic *n.* 416.15
philharmonic *adj.* 415.28
Philippi 722.5
philippic
  malediction 908.1
  tirade 932.3
Philippine mahogany 635.3
Philistine *n.*
  conformist 82.3
  barbarian 876.7
  enemy 891.1
Philistine *adj.*
  unlearned 491.9
  commonplace 849.3
Philistinism 491.4
philological 560.9
  (verbal 562.8)
philologist 560.7
  (grammarian 567.4)
philologize 562.7
philology 560.6
  (lexicology 562.4)
  (grammar 567.1)
philomel 416.11
philosoph, philosophe
  philosopher 476.9
  sophist 477.6
philosophaster 477.6
philosophastry 477.1
philosopheme 476.3
  (philosophy 451.24)
philosopher 476.9
  (sage 500.1)
philosophers' stone, philosopher's stone
  perfection 650.3
  panacea 662.3
  wealth 803.1
philosophical
  of philosophy 451.38
  wise 498.11
  unruffled 826.9
philosophicalness 826.3
Philosophical Pleiad 500.3
philosophicohistorical, philosophicojuristic, philosophicolegal etc. 451.38
philosophism 477.1, 2

1008

philosophist — physiognomist

philosophist, philoso-
  phister sophist 477.6
  philosopher 492.6
philosophistic *adj.*
  477.9
philosophize *v.*
  think 451.34
  reason 476.10
philosophy
  thought 451.4
  (Darwinism 161.5)
  (sophistry 477.1)
  (knowledge 490.8)
  (esoteric sciences 994)
  equanimity 826.3
philter, philtre
  excitant 171.4
  aphrodisiac 865.10
  love charm 993.2
phlebotomize 297.13
phlebotomy
  evacuation 297.5
  bloodletting 662.15
Phlegethon 982.3
phlegm
  semiliquid 352.3
  languor 683.4
  apathy 823.1
phlegmatic
  languid 683.14
  apathetic 823.5
phlogistic, phlogotic
  382.17
pho!, phoh! 497.5
phobe 504.1
phobia 860.4
  (craze 503.7)
  (dislike 867.1)
  (hatred 898.1)
phobic 504.1
phobophobia 860.4
Phoebe five 98.1
  moon god 318.5
  throw of dice 621.9
Phoebus, Phoebus
  Apollo sun 318.4
  god 979.2
phoenix, phenix
  monster 83.7
  paragon 650.3
phonate 402.7
phonation
  sounding 402.3
  utterance 580.3
phone *n.*
  sound device 418.6
  telephone 532a.5
  syllable 561.3
phone *v.* 532a.7
phoneme 402.2
phonetic
  sounded 402.11
  acoustic 402.12
  speech 561.10
  vocal 580.11
  spoken 582.10
phoneticize 402.8
phonetic law 402.5
phonetics
  acoustics 402.5
  (linguistics 560.6)

spelling 561.4
phonetism 402.5
phonetist 402.6
phonic
  sounded 402.11
  acoustic 402.12
  auditory 418.13
  vocal 580.11
  spoken 582.10
phonics 402.5
phonocamptic 402.12
phonogram 402.4
  (letter 561.1)
phonograph
  sound symbol 402.4
  music instrument
    417.9
  (recorder 553.3)
phonographer
  acoustician 402.6
  stenographer 590.12
phonographic 590.16
phonograph record
  phonograph 417.9
  record 551.6
phonography
  acoustics 402.5
  spelling 561.4
  shorthand 590.7
phonolite 342.4
phonologist 560.7
phonology
  acoustics 402.5
  lexicology 562.4
phony, phoney *n.* 545.6
phony, phoney *adj.*
  545.13
phoo!
  nonsense! 497.5
  bah! 930.11
phosphate drink 298.4
  mineral 635.6
phosphoprotein 352.3
Phosphor 318.3
phosphoresce 420.19
phosphorescence
  420.11
Phosphorus 318.3
photic 420.24
photics 420.16
photo *n.* 556.11
photo *v.* 556.18
photodrama 599.9
photoelectric cell
  158a.6
photoengraver 559.6
photoengraving
  558.1, 3
photogenic 420.24
photograph *n.* 556.11
  (representation
    554.3)
photograph *v.* 556.18
photographer 559.7
  (workman 690.10)
photographic
  photics 420.24
  pictorial 556.19
photographic telescope 445.5
photography
  photics 420.16

art 556.4
  (camera 445.5)
photogravure
  photography 556.4
  engraving 558.1
photointaglio 558.3
photokinesis 264.4
photokinetic 264.9
photolithograph 558.3
photolithographer
  559.6
photolithography
  photics 420.16
  engraving 558.1
photological 420.24
photology 420.16
photoluminescence
  420.11
photometeor 420.12
photometer
  aviation 267a.29
  optics 445.1
  (photics 420.16)
  (meter 466.4)
photometric 420.24
photometry
  aeronautics 267a.2
  photics 420.16
photomicrography
  micrology 193.6
  photics 420.16
photomicroscope 445.5
photomicroscopy
  193.6
photophobia 860.4
photophone 418.6
photophony 402.5
photoplay 599.9
  (play 599.3)
photoplayer 599.19
photoplaywright
  599.22
photosphere 318.4
phototelegraphy, phototherapy 420.16
phototypy 591.1
phrase *n.* section 51.2
  musical ∼ 415.15
  maxim 496.1
  expression 566
  (figure of speech
    521.1)
  phraseology 569.1
phrase *v.* 566.3
  (word 562.6)
  (voice 580.8)
  (speak 582.6)
phrasemonger
  phrasemaker 566.2
  rhetorician 577.3
phrasemongery 577.2
phraseogram, phraseograph 566.1
phraseological 564.9;
  565.7
phraseology
  nomenclature 564.1
  (phrase 566.1)
  diction 569.1
  (language 560.1)
  (verbiage 562.3)
phrasing

orchestration 413.3
  diction 569.1
phrasy 566.4
phrenesia, phrenesis
  503.3
phrenetic *n.* 504.1
phrenetic *adj.* 503.14
phrenitis 503.3
phrenologist 234.6
phrenology
  physiognomy 234.6
  mind 450.4
  (symbology 550.17)
phrensied, phrensy
  See frenzied etc.
phrontistery 542.1
Phrygian 560.4
Phryne 962.2
phthiriasis 653.12
phthisical 655.25
phthisis 655.10
phthongal *n.* 402.2
phthongal *adj.* 402.11
phut
  gone phut 2.10
phylacteric
  aphoristic 496.5
  talismanic 992.5
phylactery
  maxim 496.1
  talisman 993.2
phyletic racial 11.8
  ancestral 166.10
phylogenetic
  racial 11.8
  ancestral 166.10
phylogeny
  evolution 161.5
  organic science
    357.5
phylum kind 75.2
  animal kingdom
    366.1
  vegetable kingdom
    367.1
physic *n.* 662.4, 9
physic *v.* 662.24
physical
  substantial 3.4
  material 316.8
  fleshly 364.4
physical culture 845.5
physical education
  537.5
physical science 316.5
physician 662.19
physicism 316.5
physicist 316.6
physicker 662.19
physicomorphism
  984.4
physics
  decomposition 49.2
  physical science
    316.5
  knowledge 490.8
  (study 537.7)
physiogenesis, physiogeny 161.5
physiognomic 79.2;
  550.6
physiognomist 234.6

physiognomy — Pietà

physiognomy
  face 234.4, 6
  countenance 448.5
  physiognomics 522.5
physiological 357.11
physiological psychology 450.4
physiologist 368.2
physiology
  science of life 359.5
  (biology 357.5)
  zoology 368.1
physique 364.1
phytivorous 298.48
phytobiological, phytochemical 369.11
phytobiology, phytochemistry 369.1
phytogenesis 161.2
phytogenous 369.11
phytography 369.1
phytological 369.11
phytologist 369.9
phytology 369.1
phytomer, phyton 369.3
phytophagan 298.41
phytophagous 298.48
phytophagy 298.1
phytotomist 369.9
phytotomy 369.1
phytozoan, Phytozoaria, phytozoon 193.4
pi See pie
piacular 952.6
piaffer n. 266.5
piaffer v. 266.16
pianette 417.6
pianissimo n. 415.8, 15
pianissimo adv.
  softly 405.11
  music 415.30
pianist 416.4
pianistic 415.28
piano n.
  soft music 415.8, 15
  pianoforte 417.6
piano adv.
  softly 405.11
  music 415.30
pianoforte, Pianola 417.6
pianologue 415.3
piano player 417.4
piano-player roll 551.6
piano-violin 417.6
piazza square 189.19
  porch 191.17
pibroch music 415.8
  battle horn 722.3
pica 591.7
picacho 206.2
picaresque 554.9
picaroon 792.3
picayune 643.3
picayunish
  inconsiderable 32.8
  petty 643.11
picayunishness 32.1
piccolo whistle 410.4

instrument 417.4
piccoloist 416.2
pice 643.3
pick n. ax 253.6
  plectrum 417.13
  best 648.4
  (choice 609.1)
pick v. eat 298.44
  harvest 371.8
  strum 416.18
  choose 609.7
  cleanse 652.10
  procure 775.6
  pluck 789.9
pick a bone with 713.7
pick and choose
  discriminate 465.2
  choose 609.7
pick one's steps
  be careful 459.3
  be cautious 864.3
pick out
  eliminate 42.4
  segregate 55.4
  extract 301.5
  select 609.7
pick to pieces
  disintegrate 44.9
  destroy 162.4
  criticize 932.7
pick up
  take up 307.6
  improve 658.6
  arrest 751.9
  acquire 775.6
pickaninny child 129.3
  Negro 431.4
  brown 433.1
pickax, pickaxe 253.6
Pickelhering 599.20
picket n. post 215.16
  guard 717.6
  military ∼ 726.7
  tether 752.2
picket v. tie 43.6
  circumscribe 229.2
  go on strike 719.4
  tether 751.7
  punish 972.5
picket fence
  fence 232.2
  teeth 253.3
pickings profits 775.2
  booty 793.1
pickle n.
  predicament 8.3; 704.2
  sour 397.2
  (condiment 393.1)
  spotlight 423.3
pickle v. season 392.4
  preserve 670.4
  inebriate 959.18
pickle-herring 599.20
pick-me-up
  energizer 171.4
  stimulant 662.5
  alcoholic drink 959.10
pickpocket n. 792.6
pickpocket v. 791.9

pickpocketry 791.1
pickpurse 792.6
picksmith 690.6
pickthank
  meddler 682.11
  sycophant 886.2
  flatterer 935.2
pickup ride 266.7
  acceleration 274.2
  convalescence 654.1
  bargain 815.2
  loose woman 962.2
picky
  choiceful 609.15
  finical 868.4
picnic meal 298.34
  easy task 705.2
  festivity 840.2
  (party 892.6)
pico 210.1
pictorial
  graphic 556.19
  artistic 845.16
picture n. likeness 17.6
  view 448.2
  picturization 554.1
  work of art 556.9
  (copy 21.1)
  (representation 554.3)
  a beauty 845.3
out of the picture 34.5
picture v.
  imagine 515.8
  depict 554.7
  (describe 594.5)
picture card 840.13
picture hat 225.26
picture house 599.10
picturer
  delineator 554.6
  artist 559.1
picturesque
  pictorial 556.19
  artistic 845.16
picturization
  depiction 554.1
  (description 594.1)
  picture 556.9
picturize 554.7
piddle 683.8
piddling 643.11
pidgin English,
  pigeon English 560.5
pie n. pastry 298.12
  (sweets 396.2)
  easy task 705.2
pie, pi n. 591.6
pie, pi v.
  derange 61.2
  ∼ type 591.15
piebald n. 271.5
piebald adj. 440.7
piece n. part 51.3
  short way 197.2
  length 200.3
  lunch 298.35
  work of art 556.8
  stageplay 599.3
  role 599.7
  firearm 727.10
  portion 786.2

coin 800.4
  strumpet 962.2
fall to pieces
  ∼ together 43.5
  be disjoined 44.6
  decompose 49.3
  perish 162.5
  be brittle 328.3
  be pulverized 330.7
  disintegrate 659.7
in pieces 330.8
of a ∼ uniform 16.5
  analogous 17.11
  agreeing 23.9
  simple 42.5
  unanimous 488.12
piece by piece 51.10
to pieces
  completely 31.22
  violently 173.18
piece v. change 140.6
  snack 298.44
pièce de résistance 298.9
piecemeal 51.10
piece of one's mind 932.2
pieceworker 690.9
piecrust 223.16
pied n. 211.4
pied adj.
  mottled 440.7
  type 591.18
pie-dog See pye-dog
pie-eyed 959.21
pier support 215.10, 16
  anchorage 666.4
pierce
  perforate 260.14
  (insert 300.5)
  (penetrate 302.2)
  kill 361.12
  ∼ physically 378.4
  freeze 385.3
  be loud 404.5
  be strident 410.7
  wound 659.8
  ∼ emotionally 824.4; 830.3
  grieve 837.8
pierceless 261.4
piercer 262
piercing n. 260.8
piercing adj.
  violent 173.11
  painful 378.7
  cold 383.8
  pungent 392.5
  odorous 308.8
  shrill 410.10
  (loud 404.8)
  sagacious 498.10
  intensely felt 821.5
  emotionally ∼ 824.13
  (deep-felt 821.8)
  gruff 895.7
pier glass 445.4
Pierian 597.13
Pierides music 416.16
  poetry 597.9
Pietà 998.8

1010

pietism — pinfold

pietism 988.2
pietist
  pious person 987.4
  hypocrite 988.6
    (affecter 853.4)
pietistic pious 987.10
  sanctimonious 988.11
piety 987
  (faith 484.1)
  (reverence 928.1)
  (virtue 944.1)
piffle 517.2
pig *n.* slattern 59.5
  swine 366.7
  ingot 635.6
  glutton 957.2
  a pig in a poke
  blind bargain 148.1; 794.3
  uncertainty 475.5
  gamble 621.2
pig *v.* 72.10
pigeon *n.* food 298.26
  bird 366.22
  dupe 547.1
pigeon *v.* 791.12
pigeon English See pidgin English
pigeonhearted 862.4
pigeonhole *n.*
  arrangement 60.3
  small place 184.4
  compartment 191.2
    (recess 252.4)
  opening 260.1
pigeonhole *v.*
  postpone 133.4
  put aside 678.4
pigeon house 189.7
pigeon post
  carrier 271.1
  mail 534.2
pigeonwing 840.8
piggery 232.1
piggin 191.11
piggish greedy 865.20
  gluttonous 957.4
piggy, piggie 366.7
pighead 606.3
pigheaded
  stupid 499.12
  obstinate 606.6
pig iron 635.6
pig Latin 563.4
pigman 370.4
pigment *n.* 428.3
pigment *v.* 428.9
pigmentation 428.6
pigmy See pygmy
pignorate 771.9
pignoration, pignus 771.1
pigpen
  enclosure 232.1
  filthy place 653.10
pigs' feet 298.23
pigskin 593.10
pigsticker knife 253.6
  sled 272.13
  bayonet 727.3
pigsty hovel 189.4

enclosure 232.1
  filthy place 653.10
pigtail pendant 214.2
  tail 235.6
  hair 256.3
  tobacco 392a.7
pigwidgeon, pigwidgin, Pigwiggen 193.5
pike *n.* pinnacle 206.2
  fish 298.18
  idler 683.7
  spear 727.5
pike *v.* depart 293.4
  bet 621.18
  shirk 623.8
pikeman 726.4
piker
  gambler 621.15
  shirker 623.4
  idler 683.7
pikestaff pole 206.4
  staff 215.15
pilaster tower 206.3
  post 215.16
  ornament 847.4
pilau, pilaw 298.19
pile *n.*
  quantities 31.3
  accumulation 72.6
  structure 161.7
  pole 206.4
  point 253.2
  bristle 256.7
  nap 256.10
  texture 329.1
  ~ of money 800.11
pile *v.* load 52.7
  weight 319.9
  accumulate 636.7
pile it on
  be bombastic 577.5
  overdo 641.4
pile up total 50.5
  assemble 72.11
  go aground 267.33
  exaggerate 549.2
  overdo 641.4
pile driver 276.4
pile dweller 343a.2
pileous 256.13
piles 655.16
pilfer *n.* 791.1, 4
pilfer *v.* 791.9
pilferer 792.1
pilgarlic 876.9
pilgrim *n.*
  wanderer 268.2
  palmer 996.11
pilgrim *v.* 266.12
pilgrimage *n.* 266.8
pilgrimage *v.* 266.12
pill sphere 249.2
  cigarette 392a.4
  medicine 662.4
  bore 841.4
pillage *n.*
  plunder 791.2
  booty 793.1
pillage *v.* 791.10
pillager 792.1
pillar stability 150.2
  tower 206.3

post 215.16
gravestone 363.15
monument 551.4
writing tablet 590.10
~ of the state 642.5; 873.9
refuge 666.3
~ of the church 873.9; 987.4
from pillar to post
transferably 270.12
circuitously 311.7
alternately 314.14
  (irresolutely 605.7)
pillarist, pillar saint
  recluse 893.4
  religious 996.11
Pillars of Hercules
  limit 233.1
  landmark 550.10
pillion 215.23
pillory 975.3
pillow *n.*
  bedding 215.24
  softness 324.3
  (resting place 265.4)
pillow *v.* 215.26
pillowcase, pillow slip 223.9
pilon 784.3
pilose 256.13
pilosity 256.1
pilot *n.* mariner 269.5
  aeronaut 269a.1
  guide 694.6
  clergyman 996.2
pilot *v.*
  ~ a ship 267.11
  aviate 267a.31
  direct 693.4
pilotage
  navigation 267.1
  aeronautics 267a.1
  direction 693.1
pilot balloon 463.4
pilot boat 273.4
pilot burner 382.8
pilot engine 463.4
pilot light fire 382.5
  light 423.5
pilotship
  navigation 267.1
  aeronautics 267a.1
pilous 256.13
pilpul 476.2
pilpulist 476.9
pilpulistic 476.14
Piltdown man 124.2
pily 256.15
pimento 393.1
pimp 962.4
pimpernel 393.1
pimple rising 250.2
  sore 655.16
  (swelling 194.2)
pin *n.* fastener 45.5
  (suspender 214.3)
  (supporter 215.2)
  point 253.2
  perforator 262
  stopper 263.1
  leg 266.11

axis 312.5
trifle 643.3
pin *v.* 43.6
pin down
  bind 744.2
  restrain 751.7
pinafore 225.20
pinakotheke, pinacotheca 556.15; 636.5
pin and web 655.8
pince-nez 445.3
pincers, pinchers
  adherer 46.3
  nippers 781.2, 3
pinch *n.* crisis 134.4
  (predicament 704.2)
  small place 184.4
  pain 378.1
  necessity 630.1
  exigency 642.2
  trifle 643.3
  difficulty 704.4
  hardship 735.1
  arrest 751.3
  theft 791.4
  at a pinch 704.12
pinch *v.*
  contract 195.4
  sail 267.19
  pain 378.4
  arrest 751.9
  steal 791.9
  stint 819.3
pinchback 225.8
pinchbeck *n.* 847.2
pinchbeck *adj.* 545.13
pinched thin 203.11
  in difficulty 704.11
  impoverished 804.7
pinchers See pincers
pinchfist, pinchgut 819.2
pinchgut money
  pittance 640.5
  parsimony 819.1
pinch-hit 147.3
pinch hitter 147.2
pinching *n.* 819.1
pinching *adj.*
  cold 383.8
  niggardly 819.4
pinchpenny 819.2
Pindaric 597.13
pine *n.* saddle 215.23
  point 253.2
  tree 367.6
  wood 635.3
pine *v.* sicken 655.21
  languish 683.10
  grieve 837.6
  (suffer 828.11)
  desire 865.11
pineapple fruit 298.31
  tree 369.8
pine cone 249.4
pine needle point 253.2
  foliage 367.4
pine oil 356.3
pinery, pinetum 371.6
pinfold, penfold
  enclosure 232.1
  prison 752.1

Ping-pong — pitiless 1012

Ping-pong
 photograph 556.11
 game 840.11
pinguefaction 355.1
pinguefy fatten 194.7
 (oil) 355.2)
 lubricate 332.4
pinguescence 355.1
pinguid 355.3
pinguitude 192.4
pinhole 260.1
pinion *n.* feather 256.8
 fetter 752.2
pinion *v.* tie 43.6
 shackle 751.7
pink *n.* 434.3
 in the pink 654.4
 the pink of 845.1
pink *v.* notch 257.5
 perforate 260.14
 strike 276.8
pink *adj.* 434.10
pinkeye, pink eye 655.8
pinkify 434.7
pink spiders
 hallucination 503.5
 delirium tremens 959.2
pinky 434.10
pin money
 allowance 784.5
 petty cash 800.14
pinnace 273.2, 4
pinnacle peak 206.2
 summit 210.1
 spire 253.4
pin point 193.2
pinprick
 inextension 180a.1
 diminutive 193.2
 superficiality 209.1
 trifle 643.3
pins and needles 381.1
pint 466.3
pinto *n.* 271.5
pinto *adj.* 440.7
pin wheel, pinwheel 382.9
pioneer
 precursor 64.1
 teacher 540.4
pious 987.10
 (believing 484.12)
 (virtuous 944.4)
 (worshipful 990.15)
 be pious 987.6
 (believe 484.7)
pip 648.4
pipal tree 367.6
 wood 635.3
pipe *n.* tube 260.6
 (conduit 350.1)
 (air passage 351.1)
 ~ of tobacco 392a.2
 whistle 410.4
 horn 417.4
 pipe dream 458.3; 515.5
 easy task 705.2
pipe *v.* blow 349.22
 toot 410.8
 cry 411.5

warble 412.2
blow a horn 416.18
sing 416.20
see 441.10, 11
weep 839.8
pipe down
 hush 403.4, 9
 silence! 585.6
pipe off imitate 19.6
 depart 293.4
 die 360.6
 see 441.10
 call attention to 457.7
pipe up 416.21
piped 260.16
pipe dream
 preoccupation 458.3
 imagining 515.4, 5
pipe-dreaming
 preoccupied 458.11
 imaginative 515.14
pipeful 392a.2
pipelayer 702.4
pipelaying
 intrigue 626.6
 machiavellianism 702.2
pipelike 260.16
pip emma 126.2
pipe of peace
 token 550.14
 peace offering 723.2
pipe organ 417.5
piper 416.2
pipes boatswain 269.4
 bagpipes 417.4
pipette, pipet 260.6
pipkin 191.11
pippin 648.4
piquancy
 pungency 392.1
 diction 574.2
 excitation 824.1
piquant pungent 392.5
 (exciting 824.12)
 savory 394.7
 aphoristic 496.5
 style 574.6
 emotion 821.5
pique *n.* 900.1, 2
pique *v.* aviate 267a.31
 dive 310.4
 irritate 824.5
 annoy 830.5
 anger 900.10
 pique oneself 878.4
piqué 219.5
piqued 828.15
piracy 791.2
piragua ship 273.2
 boat 273.4
pirate *n.* mariner 269.1
 thief 792.1, 5
pirate *v.*
 plagiarize 789.8
 steal 791.9, 10
piratery, piratry 791.2
piratical 791.14
pirogue 273.4
pirouette *n.*
 inversion 218.1

whirl 312.2
pirouette *v.* 312.7
pis aller
 substitute 147.2
 expedient 646.2
piscation, piscatology 622.3
piscator 622.5
piscatorial, piscatory
 fishy 366.26
 vertebrate 368.19
Pisces
 constellation 318.6
 marine creatures 366.21
 fishes 368.9
pisciculture 370.1
piscina conduit 350.1
 washbasin 652.5
 church basin 1000.3
piscinal, piscine 366.26
Piscis Volans 318.6
pish! nonsense! 497.5
 bah! 930.11
pismire, pissant 366.24
pistareen 643.3
pistol *n.* 727.10
pistol *v.* 284.13
piston stopper 263.1
 automobile 272.16
pit *n.* depth 208.2
 cavity 252.2
 (hole 260.1)
 grave 363.13
 audience 418.8
 pitfall 545.4; 667.2
 parquet 599.11
 stock exchange 799.3
 hell 982.1
pit *v.* 252.9
pit against
 compare 464.2
 oppose 708.2
 set at odds 713.8
pitapat *n.*
 pulsation 314.2
 flutter 315.5
 patter 407.3
 trepidation 825.3
pitapat *adj.* 314.12
pitapatation
 pulsation 314.2
 flutter 315.5
 patter 407.3
 heart disease 655.12
 trepidation 825.3; 860.3
pitch *n.* degree 26.1
 rank 71.1
 ~ camp 184.15
 height 206.1
 inclination 217.1, 2
 ~ and toss 267.45
 aeronautics 267a.11
 throw 284.3
 resin 356a.1
 tone 402.2
 musical ~ 413.13
 black 431.3
 performance 599.8
pitch *v.* erect 212.7

incline 217.6
throw 284.12
topple 306.6
plunge 310.4
oscillate 314.8
~ about 315.9
flounder 605.4
be excited 824.7
pitch in begin 66.5
 eat 298.44
 set to work 686.7
pitch into
 attack 716.5
 fight 720.8
pitch upon
 meet 292.10
 discover 481a.3
 get 775.6
 choose 609.7
pitch and toss 621.7
pitch-black, pitch-dark dark 421.7
 black 431.7
pitcher
 receptacle 191.11
 thrower 284.7
pitchfork *n.* 417.13
pitchfork *v.* 284.12
pitchhole 252.2
pitch pipe 417.13
pitchy resinous 356a.3
 dark 421.7
 black 431.7
piteous 830.11
piteously 31.23
pitfall *n.* snare 545.4
 (ambush 530.1)
 trapfall 667.2
 (pit 208.2)
pitfall *v.* 545.9
pith essence 5.2
 (substance 516.4)
 strength 159.1
 center 222.2
 (interior 221.2)
 point 454.1
 resolution 604.1
 courage 861.1
pith helmet, pith hat 225.26
pithless
 unmanned 158.10
 weak 160.10
pithy spongy 324.9
 pulpy 354.5
 aphoristic 496.5
 meaningful 516.8
 terse 572.3
 language 574.6
pitiability 830.1
pitiable
 deplorable 649.8
 grievous 830.11
pitiful paltry 643.12
 (contemptible 930.9)
 deplorable 649.8
 disreputable 874.8
 compassionate 914.6
pitiless 914a.3
 (severe 739.5)
 (heartless 907.8)

pitilessness — plaque

(cruel 907.9)
(relentless 919.6)
be pitiless 914a.2
pitilessness 914a
  (severity 739.1)
  (relentlessness 919.2)
Pitot tube, Pitot's tube 267a.29
pittance modicum 32.2
  insufficiency 640.5
  (quantity 25.2)
  allowance 784.5
  allotment 786.2
pitter-patter n.
  flutter 315.5
  patter 407.3
  trepidation 825.3
pitter-patter v.
  flutter 315.10
  drum 407.8
pittite 418.8
pituitary 221.5
pituite 352.3
pituitous 352.8
pitwright 690.7
pity n.
  tender feeling 821.1
  compassion 914
  (benevolence 906.1)
for pity's sake! 914.7
take pity on 914.3
what a pity!
  regret 833.5
  alas! 839.18
pity v. 914.3
pitying 914.6
pivot n. joint 43.3
  axis 312.5
pivot v.
  turn round 283.6
  turn 311.4
pivotal 222.4
pix See pyx
pixilated 503.12
pixilation 503.1
pixy, pixie fairy 979.9
  imp 980.3
pizzicato 415.20
placable
  pacifiable 723.7
  forgiving 918.5
placard n. 531.4
placard v. 531.8
placate 723.4
placation 723.2
  (propitiation 990.5)
placative, placatory 723.6
place n.
  circumstance 8.1
  rank 71.1
  (gradation 58.2)
  occasion 134.2
  position 184.1, 3
  abode 189.1
  dive 189.9
  square 189.19
  restaurant 298.42
  office 625.4
  roadway 627.3
  rank 873.4

in one's place 755.6
in place orderly 58.7
  in position 184.20
in place of
  instead of 147.5
  in behalf of 755.6
out of place
  inapt 24.7
  disorderly 59.8
  unconformable 83.9
  misplaced 185.5
  inexpedient 647.3
take the place of 147.3
place v. arrange 60.6
  locate 184.10
  remember 505.10
  invest 787.5
  sell 796.5
placeman 758.2
placement 184.5
placenta 65.2
placet 741.3
placid quiescent 265.7
  inexcitable 826.9
placidity 265.1; 826.2
placket, placket hole 260.1
plafond 223.6
plagiarism
  falsehood 544.1
  (simulation 19.3)
  theft 791.1
  (borrowing 788.1)
plagiarist
  imitator 19.4
  thief 792.1
plagiarize falsify 544.3
  appropriate 789.8
  steal 791.9
plagihedral 217.9
plague n.
  epidemic 655.2
  bane 663.1
plague v.
  scourge 830.2
  torment 830.5
plagued 828.15
plaguesome 830.12
plague spot
  contagion 655.2
  unhealthfulness 657.1
plaguily 31.24
plaguy adj. 704.9
plaguy adv. 31.24
plaice 298.18
plaid n. cloth 219.5
  cloak 225.15
  check 440.3
plaid adj. 440.8
plaidoyer 476.3
plain n. 344
  (open space 180.3)
  (country 183.1)
  (horizontal 213.3)
  (flat 251.2)
plain adj. mere 32.11
  unmixed 42.5
  horizontal 213.8
  (champaign 344.2)
  flat 251.5

audible 402.10
dull-colored 428.19
distinct 446.5; 518.5
obvious 525.4
language 576.3
artless 703.4
economical 817.4
homely 846.6
simple 849.3
make plain 525.2
plain adv. 52.14
plain clothes 225.9
plain-clothes man 528.9
  (constable 745.10)
plain dealing
  veracity 543.1
  justice 941.1
plain English
  intelligibility 518.1
  common parlance 576.1
plainly 576.4
plainness
  language 576
  simplicity 849.1
plain sailing 705.1
plain song 415.4
plain speaking n.
  intelligibility 518.1
  (manifestness 525.1)
  (perspicuity 570.1)
  veracity 543.1
  sincerity 703.1
plain-spoken
  speaking 582.11
  frank 703.4
plaint 839.1
  (cry 411.3)
plaintful 839.13
  (sorrowful 837.11)
plaintiff 938.2
  (claimant 924.4)
plaintive 839.13
  (funereal 363.25)
plait n. lamina 204.2
  network 219.4
  hair 256.3
  pleat 258.1
plait v. interlace 219.8
  pleat 258.3
plan n. intention 620.1
  scheme 626
  (arrangement 60.3)
  (schedule 611.2)
  (way 627.1)
  (undertaking 676.1)
  (policy 692.2)
  (guidebook 694.7)
plan v. 626.9
  (predetermine 611.3)
  (prepare 673.6)
plan on
  expect 507.6
  (prepare for 673.7)
  intend 620.3
planchette 994.5
planchment 223.6
plane n.
  horizontal 213.3

(flat 251.2)
smooth 255.2
smoother 255.3
aeroplane 273a.1
plane v. smooth 255.4
  (flatten 251.4)
  aviate 267a.30
  soar 305.6
  be light 320.5
plane adj.
  horizontal 213.8
  flat 251.5
  smooth 255.5
planeness 251.1
planer 255.3
plane sailing 705.1
planet
  heavenly body 318.3
  astral influence 601.3
planetarium 318.10
planetary 318.16
planetary nebula 420.12
planetesimal 318.16
planetoid 318.3
planetoidal 318.16
planet-stricken, planet-struck 512.5
planimetry 466.8
planish 255.4
plank lamina 204.2
  flat 251.3
  platform 626.4
  bridge 627.7
  board 635.3
plankton 367.3
planktonic
  animal 366.26
  algal 367.16
planned 626.11
  (in preparation 673.13)
planner 626.8
planning 626.12
plant n. herb 367.1, 2
  deception 545.3
  apparatus 634.1
  workshop 691
  property 780.4
plant v.
  establish 184.11
  infix 300.5
  inter 363.20
  sow 371.8
  (grow 367.12)
  conceal 528.10
plantain 298.31
plantation
  settlement 188.10
  vegetable life 367.1
  farm 371.4, 6
plant-eating 298.48
planter settler 188.5
  horse 271.6
  obstacle 706.2
  landowner 779.2
planting 300.1
plantlet 367.2
plant life 367.1
plant louse 366.24
plaque 557.6

plash — pleasing 1014

plash n. puddle 343a.1
  trickle 348.4
  rain 348.11
plash v. splash 348.19
  murmur 405.5
plashy sodden 339.8
  marshy 345.3
  muddy 352.9
plasma
  protoplasm 357.3
  gem 847.8
plasmatic
  formative 240.8
  protoplasmic 357.9
plasmation 240.3
plasmic
  formative 240.8
  protoplasmic 357.9
plasome 357.4
plaster n.
  wrapper 223.11
  coating 223.19
  (cement 45.6)
  poultice 662.14
plaster v. coat 223.26
  ~ up 660.11
  dress wounds 662.24
  inebriate 959.18
plasterwork 223.19
plastic n. 557.8
plastic adj.
  changeable 149.5
  formative 240.7, 8
  flexible 324.6
plasticine 557.8
plasticity
  changeableness 149.1
  flexibility 324.1
plat n. tract 181.3
  network 219.4
  pleat 258.1
  plain 344.1
  field 371.5
plat v. interlace 219.8
  pleat 258.3
plate n. dish 191.12
  (merchandise 798.3)
  lamina 204.2
  flat 251.3
  meat 298.19
  food 298.38
  engraving 558.2, 3, 4
plate v.
  form layers 204.4
  coat 223.24
plateau hill 206.2
  plain 344.1
  (horizontal 213.3)
plated 545.13
plate fulcrum scale 319.5
plate glass 384.14
plate horse 271.8
platen 591.5
plater 271.8
platform n.
  foundation 215.3
  estrade 215.21
  (floor 211.2)
  (horizontal 213.3)
  (stage 599.12)

rostrum 542.6
politics 626.4
(policy 692.2)
arena 728.1
platform v. 582.7
platinum 430.3
platinum blond 430.9
platinumsmith 690.6
platitude 496.3
  (triteness 843.2)
platitudinize 843.3
platitudinous 843.6
Plato
  philosopher 476.9
  learned man 492.2
  sage 500.1
Platonic
  immaterial 317.6
  philosophical 451.38
  inexcitable 826.9
Platonic love 960.1
Platonism
  immaterialism 317.3
  philosophy 451.7, 17
  platonic love 960.1
Platonist
  immaterialist 317.4
  philosopher 476.9
platoon company 72.3
  military unit 726.7
Plattdeutsch 560.4
platter plate 191.12
  lamina 204.2
  flat 251.3
platyhelminth 368.5
  (worms 366.25)
plaudit 931.4
plausibility
  ostensibility 472.1
  (reasonability 476.7)
  believability 484.5
plausible
  ostensible 472.6
  (possible 470.5)
  (logical 476.16)
  sophistical 477.9
  believable 484.15
  dissembling 544.8
  flattering 933.3
play n. agency 170.1
  influence 175.1
  ~ of colors 440.1
  drama 599.1, 3
  gambling 621.3, 6
  operation 680.1
  exercise 686.2
  free scope 748.2
  amusement 840.1
  at play 840.25
  come into play 170.3
  have play
    operate 170.2
    have influence 175.7
  in play
    operative 170.4
    in action 680.7
    in jest 842.10
play v. vary 149.4
  operate 170.2
  ~ music 416.18
  (melodize 413.25)

act 599.26
  (represent 554.8)
  gamble 621.17
  operate 677.5
  do 680.5, 6
  frolic 840.21
play a trick 545.10
play fair 941.2
play false
  dissemble 544.6
  deceive 545.7
play first fiddle
  excel 33.5
  (be important 642.7)
  dominate 737.12
play gooseberry
  chaperon 88.7
  care for 459.6
play off
  palm off 545.7
  practice 677.5
play out 160.7
play safe 864.4
play second fiddle
  be inferior 34.4
  obey 743.2
  be subordinate 749.3
  be in disrepute 874.4
play the game 941.2
play the ponies 621.17
play to the gallery 882.6
play truant 187.8
  (shirk 623.8)
play upon 545.7, 10
play with 460.6
play with fire
  defy danger 665.5
  be unskillful 699.7
  be rash 863.5
playa shore 342.2
  plain 344.1
play-act
  dissemble 544.6
  act 599.26
  be affected 853.5
play-acting
  dissimulation 544.2
  acting 599.2, 6
playbook 599.16
  (book 593.1)
playboy 840.17
playcraftsman 599.22
play day 840.5
played out ended 67.9
  tired out 688.6
player musician 416.1
  gambler 621.15
  combatant 726.1
  frolicker 840.17
  (contestant 710.1)
player piano 417.6
playfellow 890.3
playful 836.10; 840.23
playfully 840.25
playground
  arena 728.1
  place of amusement 840.14
playhouse
  small place 184.4

theater 599.10
  (arena 728.1)
playing field 728.1
playland 599.1
playmate 890.3
playreader 599.17
playroom 191.16
plaything 840.16
play upon words 842.5
playwoman 599.19
playwork 599.6
playwright 599.22
  (author 593.15)
  (professional 690.10)
plaza 189.19
plea argument 476.3
  defense 937.2
  (answer 462.2)
  (counterevidence 468.1)
  (pretext 619.1)
  (law 969.6)
make a plea 937.6
plead adduce 467.10
  pretext 619.2
  entreat 765.5
  justify 937.6
  (answer 462.6)
  practice law 968.3
  argue at the bar 969.10
plead guilty 950.3
pleader 968.1
pleading defense 937.2
  litigation 969.6
pleasance park 189.21
  place of amusement 840.14
pleasant rainless 340.8
  pleasing 829.7
  (melodious 413.27)
  witty 842.9
pleasantness 829.1
pleasantry
  amusement 840.1
  wit 842.1
pleasant-sounding 413.27
please choose 609.9
  give pleasure 829.4
  (satisfy 831.4)
  (amuse 840.20)
  (gratify 865.15)
if you please
  obedience 743.4
  entreaty 765.9
please oneself
  be free 748.8
  be selfish 943.3
pleased 827.8
  (satisfied 831.6)
  (amused 840.24)
be pleased 827.5
pleasing
  ~ physically 377.7
  (palatable 394.7)
  (sweet 396.8)
  (fragrant 400.10)
  ~ in color 428.18
  ~ mentally 829.7
  (good 648.8)

pleasurable — plumb bob

(cheering 836.12)
(amusing 840.22)
comely 845.10
pleasurable 829.7
  (melodious 413.27)
  (amusing 840.22)
  (desirable 865.21)
pleasurableness 829
  (beauty 845.1)
pleasurably 829.10
pleasure *n.*
  physical ~ 377
  will 600.1
  (willingness 602.1)
  mental ~ 827, 829
  (amusement 840.1)
  source of ~ 829.3
  at one's pleasure
    737.17
  at pleasure 600.5
    (optionally 609.17)
  with pleasure
    willingly 602.11
    happily 827.13
pleasure *v.*
  enjoy 377.4
  delight 827.6
pleasure-giving *n.*
  829.1
pleasure-giving *adj.*
  829.7
pleasurer 840.17
pleat *n.* 258.1
pleat *v.*
  interlace 219.8
  fold 258.3
pleb student 541.4
  plebeian 876.3
plebeian *n.* 876.3
plebeian *adj.*
  ordinary 849.3
  proletarian 876.11
  (rustic 183.3)
  (uncouth 851.7)
plebiscite 609.3
  (decree 741.3)
plectron, plectrum
  417.13
pledge *n.* vow 535.2
  promise 768.1
  security 771.1
  token 894.3
  hold in pledge 771.8
  redeem one's pledge
    keep faith 772.4;
      939.6
    do one's duty 926.6
  take the pledge 953.5
    (sobriety 958.2)
pledge *v.*
  promise 768.3
  give security 771.5
  drink to 883.4
pledged
  promised 768.7
  pawned 771.9
pledget
  wrapper 223.11
  stopper 263.1
  bandage 662.14
Pleiades cluster 72.5
  constellation 318.6

divinities 979.8
plein-airist 559.2
plenary great 31.6
  full 52.11
  unlimited 748.15
plenary council 696.3
plenilune 318.5
plenipo 157.7
plenipotent *n.* 759.2
plenipotent *adj.*
  potent 157.8
plenipotentiary
  759.6
plenipotentiary *n.*
  759.2
plenipotentiary *adj.*
  potent 157.8
  deputy 759.6
plenitude
  fullness 52.2
  plenty 639.2
plenteous, plentiful
  numerous 102.5
  ample 639.7
  be plentiful 639.4
plentifully 639.8
plenty *n.*
  quantities 31.3
  multitude 102.2
  amplitude 639.2
  (fullness 52.2)
  (fill 52.3)
  (numerousness
    102.1)
  (store 636.1)
  (fund 636.2)
  (redundance 641.1)
  (wealth 803.1)
  (satiety 869.1)
plenty *adj.*
  numerous 102.5
  ample 639.7
  (great 31.6)
  (full 52.11)
  (redundant 641.5)
plenty *adv.*
  greatly 31.15
  in abundance 102.6
  plentifully 639.8
plenum
  boundlessness 180.4
  materiality 316.1
  world 318.1
  council 696.2
pleny 52.11
pleonasm
  tautology 573.2
  (repetition 104.1)
  redundance 641.1
pleonastic 573.8
  (redundant 641.5)
plerophory 484.2
plethora
  redundance 641.1
  satiety 869.1
plethoric
  swollen 194.10
  overfull 641.6
pleuron 236.1
plexal, plexiform
  219.11
plexure, plexus 219.4

pliability 324.1
  (docility 602.3)
pliable 324.6
  (weak-willed 605.6)
pliancy 324.1
  (weak will 605.2)
  (facility 705.1)
pliant 324.6
  (docile 602.9)
  (manageable 705.6)
  (submissive 725.5)
  (obedient 743.3)
  (servile 886.4)
  be pliant 324.5
plica 258.1
plicate *v.* 258.3
plicate, plicatile *adj.*
  258.4
plication 258.1, 2
plicatulate 258.4
plicature 258.1, 2
pliciferous, pliciform
  258.4
pliers extractor 301.4
  pincers 781.2
plight *n.*
  predicament 8.3;
    704.2
  (state 7.1)
  (misfortune 735.3)
  promise 768.1
  security 771.1
plight *v.* 768.3, 4
Plimsoll mark, Plimsoll line 466.5
plinth 211.1; 215.3
plod walk 266.16
  go slow 275.5
  persevere 604a.2
  toil 686.6
plodder 690.2
plodding *n.*
  perseverance 604a.1
  drudgery 686.3
plodding *adj.* 682.19
  (persevering
    604a.3)
plop *v.*
  ~ **down** 184.10;
    306.6
  plunge 310.4
  bubble 353.8
  sound 405.7
plop *adv.* 113.7
plot *n.* tract 181.3
  plain 344.1
  field 371.5
  plan 626.2, 6
  (artifice 702.3)
plot *v.*
  measure 466.10
  conspire 626.10
plow, plough
  furrow 259.3
  navigate 267.10
  aviate 267a.31
  cultivate 371.8
  prepare 673.6
  fail 732.5
plowboy, ploughboy
  agriculturist 371.2
  rustic 876.5

plowing, ploughing
  673.3
plow horse 271.3
plowman, ploughman
  agriculturist 371.2
  rustic 876.5
plowshare, ploughshare 253.6
plowwright, ploughwright 690.7
pluck *n.*
  resolution 604.1
  courage 861.1
pluck *v.* jerk 285.5
  harvest 371.8
  strum 416.18
  cheat 545.7
  fail 732.5
  pick 789.9
  fleece 789.12
  swindle 791.12
pluck a crow with
  quarrel 713.7
  reprove 932.8
pluck up
  destroy 162.4
  extract 301.5
  ~ ~ **courage** 861.6
plucked 732.11
plucky resolute 604.7
  courageous 861.8
plug *n.* remains 40.1
  electricity 158a.6
  stopper 263.1
  horse 271.6
  blow 276.3
  ~ **of tobacco** 392a.7
  publicity 531.3
  wreck 659.5
plug *v.* continue 143.3
  close 261.2
  go slow 275.5
  strike 276.8
  shoot 284.13
  publicize 531.8
  persevere 604a.2
  plod 686.6
plug in 158a.11
plugger 531.6
plug hat 225.26
plug-ugly 913.2
plum 437.1
plumage 256.9
plumate 256.16
plumb *n.* vertical 212.2
  plummet 212.5
  gravity 319.2
  measure 466.4
plumb *v.* sound 208.7
  plum 212.7
  close 261.2
  measure 466.10
plumb, plum *adj.*
  unqualified 52.10
  vertical 212.8
plumb, plum *adv.*
  utterly 52.14
  à plomb 212.9
plumbago 332.2
plumb bob
  fathomer 208.4
  plumb 212.5

plumber — point

plumb bob (*continued*)
  measure 466.4
plumber 690.5
  (repairman 660.7)
plumbless 208.9
plumb line *n.*
  fathomer 208.4
  plumb 212.5
  measure 466.4
plumb-line *v.*
  sound 208.7
  plumb 212.7
plum-colored 437.4
plumcot 41.5
plume feather 256.8
  pen 590.10
  ornament 847.3
plumigerous 256.16
plummet
  fathomer 208.4
  plumb 212.5
  gravity 319.2
  measure 466.4
plumose 256.16
plump *n.* 408a.2
plump *v.*
  ~ down 184.10;
   306.6
  ~ upon 292.10
  plunge 310.4
  vote 609.10
plump *adj.* full 52.11
  stout 192.12
  (rotund 249.6)
plump *adv.* 113.7
plumper 609.3
plumpness 192.4
plumule sprout 167.4
  feather 256.8
plunder *n.* gain 35.2
  pillage 791.2
  booty 793.1
plunder *v.* 791.10
plunderbund 712.4
plunderer taker 789.6
  pillager 792.1
plundering 791.14
plunge *n.* dive 310
  (submergence
   267.5)
  speculation 621.2
  bathing place 652.4
  predicament 704.2
plunge *v.* pitch 267.45
  swim 267.47
  dive 310.4
  (insert 300.7)
  (descend 306.4)
  gravitate 319.7
  bet 621.18
  hasten 684.4
plunge into
  study 539.4
  undertake 676.2
  set to work 686.7
plunger diver 310.3
  pump 333.6
  gambler 621.15
plunk *n.* blow 276.3
  thud 408a.2
  coin 800.1
plunk *v.*

~ down 184.10
  strike 276.8
  plunge 310.4
  croak 412.2
  strum 416.18
plunk *adv.* 113.7
pluperfect 122.9
plural 100.4
pluralism 451.20
plurality number 100
  majority 100.2
  (numerousness
   102.1)
pluralize 100.3
plurative 100.4
plurify 100.3
plus *n.* 37.2
plus *v.* 37.3
plus *adj.* 37.7
plus *conj.* 37.8, 10
plus fours 225.21
plush 256.10
Pluto planet 318.3
  god 979.2; 982.4
  (satan 978.1)
plutocracy, plutocrat
  803.2
plutonic 382.23
Plutonic 982.5
Plutus 803.2
pluviograph 348.12
pluviography 348.15
pluviometer
  aviation 267a.29
  rain gauge 348.12
pluviometry 348.15
pluvioscope 348.12
pluvious 348.27
ply *n.* lamina 204.2
  pleat 258.1
ply *v.* pleat 258.3
  sail 267.19
  employ 677.5
  exert 686.5
  entreat 765.5
  ~ a trade 625.8;
   794.7
ply the oar
  row 267.46
  exert oneself 686.5
P.M., p.m. 126.2
pneuma
  life force 359.2
  spirit 994.11
pneumatic
  gaseous 334.8
  aerial 338.11
pneumatics
  aeronautics 267a.2
  gas 334.3
  (air 338.7)
  wind 349.16
pneumatize 338.10
pneumatogram 532.2
pneumatograph
  662.22
pneumatologic 338.12
pneumatology 334.3
pneumatometer
  gas 334.4
  remedy 662.22
pneumatoscope 334.4

pneumatotherapy
  662.16
pneumonia 655.9
pneumonic 655.25
poach 791.9
poacher 792.1
poachy 345.3
pock
  protuberance 250.2
  pustule 655.16
  scar 659.4
  blemish 848.1
pocket *n.*
  floor plug 157a.6
  bag 191.4
  vessel 191.6
  funds 800.2
  treasury 802.2
pocket *v.* load 184.13
  receive 785.3
  take 789.9
  put up with 826.6
pocket the affront
  be submissive 725.3
  endure 826.6
  forgive 918.3
pocket *adj.* 193.8
pocketbook
  memorandum book
   505.6
  notebook 551.3
  book 593.1
  purse 802.2
pocket chronometer
  114.6
pocketknife 253.6
pocket money 800.14
pocket pistol 191.11
pocket-size 193.8
pococurante *n.* 822.2
pococurante *adj.*
  unfeeling 823.5
  indifferent 866.4
pod *n.* bag 191.4
  vessel 191.6
  paunch 191.7
  hull 223.14
pod *v.* 226.5
podagra pain 378.1
  ailment 655.5
podagric
  378.6; 655.25
podesta 967.1
podex 235.5
podite 266.11
podura 366.24
poeci'onym
  equivalence 516.3
  word 562.1
poecilonymic 516.11
poem 597.2
poesy *n.* 597.1, 2, 4, 9
poesy *v.* 597.12
poet 597.10
  (author 593.15)
poetaster poet 597.10
  affecter 853.4
poethood 597.11
poetic 574.8; 597.13
poeticize 597.12
poetic justice 941.1
poetic license 597.5

poetico-philosophical
  597.13
poetics 597.1, 5
poetization 597.5
poet laureate 597.10
poet-laureateship
  597.11
poetry 597
pogrom 361.1
poignancy
  acrimony 171.3
  pungency 392.1
  diction 574.2
poignant acrid 171.17
  sharp 253.11
  painful 378.7
  pungent 392.5
  style 574.6
  emotion 821.5
poilu 726.4
point *n.*
  circumstance 8.1
  degree 26.1
  modicum 32.2
  extremity 67.2
  rank 71.1
  integer 87.3
  period of time 108.1
  stop 142.5
  acrimony 171.3
  inextension 180a.1
  (small place 184.4)
  location 184.1
  diminutive 193.2
  height 206.2
  summit 210.1
  cloth 219.5
  chin 234.5
  promontory 250.5
  sharp end 253.2
  (bristle 256.7)
  ~ of the compass
   278.2
  topic 454.1
  question 461.10
  tip 527.3
  mark 550.2, 7, 8
  stonecutter's ~
   557.8
  spirit 574.2
  intention 620.2
  ~ of a joke 842.4
  needlework 847.6
at the point of the
  sword
  violently 173.18
  at war 722.14
  severely 739.6
  by force 744.4
beside the point 10.6
come to the point
  specialize 79.6
  argue 476.11
  be concise 572.2
  speak plainly 576.2
in point 23.10
in point of 9.10
in point of fact 494.15
on the point of
  about to 121.11
  near 197.11
to the point apt 23.10

1016

terse 572.3
  in plain words 576.4
  material 642.10
point v. tend 176.2
  sharpen 253.9
  direct 278.4
  gravitate 319.7
point at
  call attention to
    457.7
  aim 620.3
  be unpolite 895.4
  show disrespect
    929.3
  scoff 930.6
point out
  specify 79.5
  call attention to
    457.7
  (inform 527.7)
  indicate 550.18
point to
  attribute to 155.3
  direct 278.4
  be probable 472.2
  (portend 511.9)
  mean 516.5
  indicate 550.18
point-blank
  directly 278.13
  in plain words 576.4
point d'appui 215.5
pointed
  remarkable 31.13
  sharp-cornered
    244.5
  sharp 253.11
  emphatic 535.6
  indicated 550.22
  terse 572.3
  language 574.6
pointedly
  remarkably 31.21
  intentionally 620.5
pointer dog 366.6
  tip 527.3
  sign 550.2, 10
  guide 694.6
pointillism 556.6
pointless blunt 254.3
  dull 843.5
point of departure
  293.3
point of honor 939.1
point of view 441.4
point-to-point race
  720.5
poise n. equality 27.1
  gait 266.5
  mental ~ 498.4
  (experience 698.4)
  equanimity 826.3
poise v.
  equalize 27.7
  weigh 319.8
  measure 466.10
poised 826.9
poison n. 663.4, 5, 6
  (infection 655.2)
  (insalubrity 657.1)
poison v. kill 361.10
  infect 655.22

corrupt 659.10
poisoned 655.25
poisoner 361.8
poison gas 334.2
  (poison 663.5)
  (war 727.15)
poisoning
  infection 655.2
  corruption 659.3
  execution 972.4
poison ivy 663.6
poisonous 657.3
  (baneful 663.7)
poisonousness 657.1
poison sumac 663.6
poke n. fastening 45.2
  bag 191.16
  slow goer 275.4
  blow 276.3
  yoke 752.2
  purse 802.2
poke v. attach 43.6
  ~ out 250.7
  go slow 275.5
  impel 276.7
  strike 276.8
  ~ up the fire 384.17
  dawdle 683.8
  attack 716.5
poke fun at
  ridicule 856.4
  scoff 930.6
poker
  fire iron 386.3
  game 840.12
  goblin 980.4
pokerish 323.5
pokeweed 663.6
poking, poky, pokey
  slow 275.8
  petty 643.11
polacre 273.2
polar 210.6
polar bear 366.15
polar co-ordinates
  466.7
polar front 383.4
polaric 210.6
Polaris star 318.3
  cynosure 550.10
  guiding star 694.6
polariscope 445.1
polarity
  duality 89.1
  counteraction 179.1
  contraposition 237.1
polar lights 420.12
polar star 318.3
pole length 200.6
  stick 206.4
  extremity 210.1
  spar 215.12, 13
  tail 235.6
  mast 273.12
  oar 273.14
  axis 312.5
from pole to pole
  180.9
  (widely 196.10)
poleax, poleaxe 727.4
polecat animal 366.3
  malodor 401.2

polemic n.
  argument 476.2
  arguer 476.9
polemic adj.
  argumentative
    476.14
  quarrelsome 901.9
polemicist, polemist
  476.9
polemics 476.2
polemize 476.11
polemoscope 445.1
polestar
  attractor 288.2
  star 318.3
  cynosure 550.10
  guiding star 694.6
police n. 745.10
police v. 60.6
police commissioner
  745.10
police dog 366.6
policedom, police in-
  spector, policeman,
  etc. 745.10
police station 752.1
policewoman 745.10
policy conduct 692.2
  (program 611.2)
  (plan 626.1)
  (platform 626.4)
  (way 627.1)
  artifice 702.3
poliomyelitis 655.15
polish n.
  smoothness 255.1
  grammatical ~
    578.1
  culture 658.2
  elegance 845.1
  refinement 850.1
  politeness 894.1
  (gentility 852.3)
Polish n. 560.4
polish v.
  burnish 255.5
  rub 331.3
  furbish 658.10
  beautify 847.11
  render polite 894.11
polish off kill 361.10
  complete 729.2
polished smooth 255.5
  shining 420.22
  speech 578.4
  polite 894.12
polite 894.12
polite society 852.4
politeness 894.1
politic wise 498.11
  expedient 646.4
  crafty 702.6
  cautious 864.6
political economy
  693.3
politician, politico
  statesman 694.4
  Machiavellian 702.4
politics 702.2
polity country 182.1
  policy 692.2
polka music 415.7

dance 840.7
poll n. census 86.2
  (count 85.3)
  head 210.3
  vote 609.3
  schedule 611.2
poll v. enumerate 85.7
  census 86.3
  vote 609.10
  schedule 611.4
pollage 812.2
pollard n. 367.6
pollard v. cut off 38.6
  cut short 201.4
pollard adj. 193.9
pollen, pollinate 168.4
pollinization, pollen-
  ization 161.2
polliwog 129.7; 366.20
polls 609.3
poll tax 812.2
pollute befoul 653.15
  corrupt 659.9
  inebriate 959.18
pollution
  defilement 653.2
  infection 655.2
  corruption 659.3
  turpitude 945.2
polly 19.4
pollywog See polliwog
polo 840.7
poltergeist
  spirit 980a.1
  spirit control
    994.5, 14
poltroon n. 862.2
poltroon adj. 862.5
poltroonery 862.1
polyandrist 903.5
polyandrium, poly-
  andrion 363.14
polyandrous 903.14
polyandry 903.2
polychord 417.2
polychrest 662.3
polychromatic 428.12
polychrome n. 440.1
polychrome adj.
  variegated 440.5
  picture 556.19
polychrome v. 440.4
polychromism 440.5
polyclinic 662.17
polydipsia 865.3
polygamist 903.5
polygamous 903.14
polygamy 903.2
polygastric 191.23
polyglot linguist 492.7
  linguistic 560.9
  dictionary 593.4
polygon court 189.19
  angle 244.2
polygonal 244.5
polygraphic 590.16
polygraphy 590.7
polygynist 903.5
polygynous 903.14
polygyny 903.2
polyhedral 236.7
polylogy 584.1

polyloquent — portal

polyloquent 584.5
polymeter 267a.29
Polymnia 416.16
polymorphism 81.1
polymorphous 81.2
polyonym
  equivalence 516.3
  word 562.1
polyonymic 516.11
polyp animal 368.4
  sore 655.16
polyparous, polypean 368.13
Polyphemus
  strong man 159.6
  giant 192.8
polyphonic 415.28
polyphony
  acoustics 402.5
  harmony 413.2
  (counterpoint 415.4)
polypus
  protuberance 250.2
  sore 655.16
polyscope 445.1
polysyllabic 561.9
polysyllable 561.3
polytechnic 542.1
polytheist 984.20
polytheism 984.10
polytheistic 984.28
pomade n. oil 356.1
  perfume 400.2
pomade v. 332.4
pomander 400.2
pomato 41.5
pomatum oil 356.1
  perfume 400.2
Pomeranian 366.6
pommel horn 215.23
  sphere 249.2
pomological 369.11
pomologist 369.9
pomology 369.1
Pomona
  vegetation 367.1
  botany 369.1
pomp 882.1
pompadour 256.3
Pompeii 434.3
pom-pom 727.11
pomposity
  grandiloquence 577.2
  (affectation 853.1)
  ostentation 882.1
  arrogance 885.1
pompous
  grandiloquent 577.7
  (affected 853.6)
  ostentatious 882.8
  arrogant 885.8
poncho 225.15
pond ocean 341.1
  pool 343a.1
  (store 636.4)
ponder 451.27
ponderable
  material 316.8
  heavy 319.12
ponderance 319.1
ponderate 319.8

ponderation
  weight 319.1, 3
  thought 451.1
  estimation 480.2
ponderosity 319.1
ponderous
  hulky 192.13
  heavy 319.12
  language 574.9
  style 579.3
  consequential 642.12
  unmanageable 704.10
  dull 843.5
pondy 343a.3
poniard 727.3
pons 450.2
pons asinorum 704.4
pontiff 996.5
pontifical n. 998.9; 999.1
pontifical adj. 995.9
pontificate 995.4
Pontius Pilate 967.1
pontoon, ponton
  float 273.5
  bridge 627.7
pony, poney n.
  diminutive 193.2
  horse 271.3, 8
  translation 522.2
  money 800.1
pony v.
  pony up 807.6
pony adj. 193.8
poodle 366.6
pooh, pooh-pooh, poohpooh n. 930.2
pooh, pooh-pooh, poohpooh v. 930.6
pooh, pooh-pooh, poohpooh int.
  nonsense! 497.5
  bah! 930.11
pooh-pooh theory, poohpooh theory 562.2
pool n. pond 343a
  stakes 621.4
  bathing place 652.4
  co-operation 709.2
  trust 712.5
  game 840.11
pool v. 709.4
pool room
  gambling house 621.14
  sports 840.14
poonghie, poonghee, poongee 996.9
poop stern 235.7
  ship 273.7
poor n. 804.3
poor adj.
  incomplete 53.4
  weak 160.13
  thin 203.11
  illogical 477.10
  style 575.2
  meager 640.9
  paltry 643.12
  (bad 649.8)

  sickly 655.24
  impoverished 804.7
  (unfortunate 735.9)
  (in debt 806.7)
  (bankrupt 808.10)
  wretched 828.16
be poor 804.4
become poor 804.5
poorhouse
  almshouse 189.11
  asylum 666.3
poor in spirit 879.4
poorish 160.13
poorling 804.3
poorly 655.23, 24
poorness 34.1
poor-sighted 443.14
poor-spirited 862.4
pop n. father 166.6
  sweet beverages 396.5
  bang 406.2
pop v. bubble 353.8
  bang 406.8
  shoot 716.5
pop in intrude 228.10
  enter 294.6
  insert 300.5
pop off 360.6
pop up appear 446.2
  be unexpected 508.5
pop adv. 113.7
  (unexpectedly 508.11)
pope 996.5
popedom 995.4
Pope Joan 840.12
popery 984.6
popgun
  noisemaker 404.4
  toy 840.16
popinjay 854.1
popish
  Roman Catholic 984.25
  papal 995.9
poplar 367.6
poplin 219.5
poppycock 517.2
poppycockish
  absurd 497.4
  nonsensical 517.9
populace 876.1
popular n. 415.17
popular adj.
  well-known 490.17
  familiar 613.11
  in demand 796.7; 865.21
  conventional 852.8
  celebrated 873.16
  well-beloved 897.16
  estimable 928.9
  in favor 931.10
  lay 997.4
popularity
  celebrity 873.1
  (approbation 931.1)
  popular regard 897.1
popularize
  make intelligible 518.3

  make easy 705.4
  make pleasant 829.6
popular psychology 450.4
popular song 415.10
populate
  multiply 102.4
  inhabit 186.10
population 188.10
  (people 372.2)
populous
  crowded 72.13
  thronged 102.5
  peopled 186.15
porbeagle 366.21
porcelain 384.14
porch 191.17
  (portal 260.4)
porcupine spine 253.2
  animal 366.17
pore n. opening 260.1
  outlet 295.5
  duct 350.4
pore v.
pore over
  scrutinize 441.12
  study 461.18; 539.4
poriferan 368.13
porism question 461.10
  deduction 480.1
pork 298.23
pork barrel 793.1
pork chop 298.23, 27
porker 366.7
pornographic 961.9
pornography 961.1
porosity 260.7
porous
  sievelike 260.17
  (hollow 252.10)
  egressive 295.9
  leachy 335.8
porousness 260.7
porphyry 342.4
porpoise n.
  largeness 192.7, 8
  dolphin 366.21
porpoise v. 267a.31
porpoise oil 356.4
porraceous 435.6
porridge cereal 298.15
  semiliquid 352.3
porringer 191.12
port posture 184.2
  left 239.2
  porthole 260.5
  gait 266.5
  airplane 273a.10
  outlet 295.5
  mien 448.4
  haven 666.4
  wine 959.7
in port 664.10
make port 666.5
put into port 267.26
port v. 267.24, 70
port adj. 239.5, 6
portable little 193.8
  transferable 270.11
  light 320.7
portage 270.2, 4
portal

1018

portamento — posteriority

vestibule 191.17
  opening 260.4
  (edge 231.1)
  (inlet 294.5)
  (path 627.2)
portamento 270.1
portance 266.5
portative little 193.8
  transferable 270.11
portcullis
  obstacle 706.2
  fortification 717.3
porte-cochere 260.4
porte-monnaie 802.2
portend 511.7, 9
  (forerun 116.3)
  (indicate 550.18)
  (forewarn 668.7)
  (threaten 909.2)
portendance, portent, portention
  foreboding 511.6
  forewarning 668.2
portentous
  predictive 511.11
  (fearful 860.15)
  ominous 512.3
  (threatening 909.3)
porter carrier 271.1
  (workman 690.10)
  doorkeeper 717.6
porterage 270.2
porterhouse steak 298.20
portfire 388.4
portfolio case 191.8
  book 593.13
  managership 693.3
  office 745.9
  authority 747.1
  bureau 965.2
porthole opening 260.1
  window 260.5
  ship 273.7
portico series 69.2
  vestibule 191.17
portiere 424.3
portion n.
  quantity 25.2
  part 51.1
  (fraction 101.1)
  destiny 601.3
  share 786.2
  (participation 778.1)
portion v.
  partition 44.10
  apportion 786.3
portional partial 51.8
  fractional 100a.2
portly 192.12
portmanteau 191.5
  (merchandise 798.3)
portmanteau word 563.9
  (word 562.1)
  (conciseness 572.1)
portmantologism 563.9
portrait likeness 17.6
  portraiture 556.1, 9
  (copy 21.1)

(representation 544.3)
portraitist 559.2
portraiture
  representation 554.1
  portrait 556.1, 9
portray 554.7
  (limn 556.17)
  (describe 594.5)
portrayal 554.1
portrayer
  delineator 554.6
  artist 559.1
portreeve 745.9
portside left 239.2
  airplane 273a.10
portsider 239.4
port tack 239.2
Portuguese n.
  native 188.9
  language 560.4
Portuguese adj. 188.11
posada 189.8
pose n. posture 184.2
  ostentation 882.2
pose v. perplex 475.8
  (be difficult 704.5)
  ~ as 554.8
  be ostentatious 882.6
  (affect 853.5)
Poseidon
  spirit of the sea 341.2
  god 979.2, 10
poser inquirer 461.12
  puzzle 533.2
  (question 461.10)
  (dilemma 704.4)
  attitudinarian 882.5
posit 514.7
position
  circumstance 8.1
  rank 71.1
  location 184.1
  proposition 476.4
  belief 484.3
  hypothesis 514.1
  affirmation 535.1
  statement 582.4
  appointment 609.5
  office 625.4
  ~ in society 873.4
in position 184.20
positional 184.18
positive n. 556.11
positive adj. real 1.8
  absolute 31.12
  numeral 84.7
  electropositive 157a.12
  certain 474.8
  dogmatic 474.15
  (prejudiced 481.10)
  (bigoted 606.7)
  (hyperorthodox 983a.8)
  convinced 484.12
  accurate 494.11
  emphatic 535.6
  authoritative 737.15
  peremptory 739.5
  right 922.6

positively
  absolutely 31.16
  certainly 474.16
  to be sure 488.14
positiveness
  dogmatism 474.3
  affirmation 535.1
positivism
  physicism 316.5
  philosophy 451.13
  dogmatism 474.3
  (bigotry 606.2)
  (hyperorthodoxy 983a.5)
positivist 474.4
  (opinionist 606.3)
  (bigot 983a.6)
positivistic
  dogmatic 474.15
  bigoted 606.7
posnet 191.11
posologist 662.21
posology 662.16
posse company 72.3
  party 712.1
  armed force 726.7
possess know 490.9
  craze 503.11
  have 777.4
  (retain 781.4)
  demonize 978.6
possess oneself of 789.8
possessed
  insane 503.12
  possessing 777.7, 8
  bewitched 992.7
  like all possessed
    greatly 31.15
    swiftly 274.14
possession hold 777
  (retention 781.1)
  property 780.1
  bewitchment 993.1
come into possession 775.6
  (change hands 783.4)
take possession
  acquire 775.6
  appropriate 789.8
possessor 779
possessorship 777.3
possibile 470.1
possibilitate 470.4
possibility
  liability 177.1
  conceivability 470
  (chance 156.3)
  (reasonability 476.7)
  (credibility 484.5)
  latency 526.1
possible
  numeral 84.7
  liable 177.4
  conceivable 470.5
  (plausible 472.6)
  (logical 476.16)
  (credible 484.15)
  potential 526.6
be possible 470.3

(have a chance 156.9)
if possible 470.8
  (conditionally 469.7)
make possible 763.2
not possible 471.6
render possible 470.4
possibles 800.1
possibly 470.7
  (supposedly 514.12)
possum
  play possum 458.5
  feign 544.6
post n. stake 45.5
  position 184.1
  stratum 204.1
  pole 206.4
  upright 215.16
  (verticality 212.1)
  messenger 534.1, 2
  landmark 550.10
  mail 592.4
  appointment 609.5
  office 625.4
at one's post 926.6, 13
post v. list 86.3
  place 184.10
  mail 270.9; 592.6
  speed 274.9
  ~ bills 531.8
  record 551.8
  bet 621.18
  pay down 807.6
  ~ accounts 811.7
  stigmatize 874.7
post adj. 592.7
postage 592.4
postal 592.7
postal card 592.3
postal clerk, post boat 534.2
postbox 592.4
postboy rider 268.8
  messenger 534.1
  mailman 534.2
  postilion 694.6
post car 534.2
post card, postcard 592.3
postcart 534.2
post chaise 272.4
post coach 534.2
Postcommunion 998.6, 7
postdate 115.2
postdiluvian 117.3
posted 490.15
poster n.
  advertisement 531.4
  postrider 534.1
  post horse 534.2
poster v. 531.8
posteriad 235.17
posterior n. 235.1
posterior adj.
  later 117.3
  rear 235.9
posteriority
  subsequence 117
  (sequence 63.1; 281.1)

posteriormost — powder

posteriority (*cont'd*)
  (futurity 121.1)
  rear 235.1
  rump 235.5
posteriormost 235.9
posteriors 235.5
posterity 167
  (futurity 121.1)
postern *n.* rear 235.1
  portal 260.4
postern *adj.* 235.9
Post Exchange 799.4
postexist 1.4
postexistence 121.3
postface 65.1
postfix *n.*
  afterpart 65.2
  rear 235.1
postfix *v.* 37.3
postgeniture 167.2
posthaste 274.14; 684.7
post horn 417.4
post horse horse 271.3
  mail carrier 534.2
posthumous
  later 117.3
  post-mortem 360.11
postilion, postillion
  rider 268.8
  guide 694.6
postliminary 117.3
  (later 133.10)
postlude 65.1
postman 534.2
postmark 592.4
postmaster 534.2
post meridiem 126.2
postmistress 534.2
post-mortem *n.*
  autopsy 363.18
  examination 461.3
post-mortem *v.* 461.17
post-mortem, post-
  mortuary *adj.* 360.11
postmundane 360.11
post office 592.4
post-office car 534.2
post-office order
  epistle 592.2
  money 800.7
postpone 133.4
  (pretermit 460.7)
postponement 133.2
postprandial 117.3
postrider 534.1
postscript adjunct 39.1
  sequel 65.1
  epistle 592.2
posttonic
  sounded 402.11
  pretonic 580.11
postulant
  petitioner 767.1
  religion 996.12
postulate *n.*
  premise 64.2; 476.4
  (axiom 496.2)
  hypothesis 514.1
postulate *v.* 514.7
postulation
  hypothesis 514.1
  request 765.1

postulational 514.9
postulatory 765.7
postulatum 514.1
posture
  circumstance 8.1
  position 184.2
posturer 882.5
posy bouquet 400.4
  motto 550.5
  anthology 593.2; 597.4
  ornament 847.5
  love token 902.5
  compliment 931.3
pot *n.*
  quantities 31.3
  transformer 158a.6
  paunch 191.7
  vase 191.10
  receptacle 191.11
  race horse 271.8
  ceramics 384.14
  boiler 386.1
  stakes 621.4
  loving cup 733.1
  ~ of money 800.11
  go to pot perish 162.5
  deteriorate 659.6
  fail 732.5
  suffer misfortune 735.6
  go bankrupt 808.6
  become wicked 945.9
pot *v.* shoot 284.13
  preserve 670.4
potable *n.* drink 298.4
  alcoholic drink 959.4
potable *adj.* 298.51
potassium 635.6
potation
  drinking 298.3
  drink 298.4
  tippling 959.1, 3
  alcoholic drink 959.4, 10
potato 298.30
potbellied 194.11
potbelly paunch 191.7
  fat man 192.7
potboiler writing 590.3
  book 593.1
  hack writer 593.15
pot companion 892.8
potence power 157
  (strength 159.1)
  (energy 171.1)
  influence 175.1
potency
  potence 157.1
  influence 175.1
  potentiality 470.1
potent powerful 157.8
  (strong 159.10)
  (productive 168.7)
  (energetic 171.9)
  influential 175.10
  authoritative 737.15
potentate ruler 745.2
  (head 694.2)
  (prince 875.7)
  raja 745.4

  sultan 745.5
potential unreal 2.8
  potent 157.8
  electric 158a.12
  possible 470.5
  latent 526.6
potential energy 171.1
potentiality
  potence 157.1
  possibility 470.1
  latency 526.1
potentialize 171.7
potentiate 159.8
potentiometer 267a.29
pother *n.* turmoil 59.4
  trepidation 825.3
  annoyance 828.4
  bother 830.2
pother *v.*
  embarrass 704.7
  annoy 830.5
pothole 252.2
pothook
  fire iron 386.3
  scribbling 517.4; 590.6
pothouse 959.13
pothunter 767.1
potion drink 298.4
  medicine 662.4
  alcoholic drink 959.10
potluck chance 156.1
  gamble 621.2
  social meal 892.6
potpourri mixture 41.4
  perfume 400.2
  music 415.3
potshot *n.* shot 284.13
  reckless bet 621.3
potshot *v.* 284.13
pottage 298.16
potted 959.21
potter, putter
  dawdle 683.8
  (trifle 643.9)
  squander 818.3
potter's field
  aceldama 361.9
  graveyard 363.14
potter's wheel 144.4
pottery 384.14
  (vase 191.10)
potty 191.11
pot-valiance 959.1
pot-valiant 959.21
pot-valor 959.1
pot-valorous 959.21
pot-walloper
  dishwasher 652.6
  scullion 746.1
pouch bag 191.4
  purse 802.2
pouched rat 366.17
poulard 298.25
poultice *n.*
  semiliquid 352.3
  bandage 662.14
poultice *v.*
  dress wounds 662.24
  foment 834.4
poultry 298.25

pounce *n.* leap 309.1
  plunge 310.1
  claw 781.3
pounce *v.* leap 309.4
  plunge 310.4
pounce upon
  surprise 508.6
  attack 716.5
  seize 789.13
pound *n.* kennel 189.6
  enclosure 232.1
  (menagerie 370.3)
  weight 319.4
  (measurement 466.3)
  dog ~ 323.1
  drumming 407.3
  prison 752.1
  money 800.4, 8
pound *v.*
  ~ together 41.6
  repeat 104.4
  pulverize 330.6
  drum 407.8
  beat time 416.19
  ~ out 460.6
poundage
  capacity 192.2
  weight 319.1
  impost 812.2
  discount 813.1
pound-folly 818.1
pound-foolish 818.4
pour *n.* 348.11
pour *v.* flow 348.17
  rain 348.25
  abound 639.4
pour forth
  let out 297.13
  utter 582.6
  be loquacious 584.4
pour in
  converge 290.2
  inflow 294.6
pour oil on troubled
  water pacify 723.4
  make pleasant 829.6
pour on wet 337.5
  give freely 784.10
pour out emit 295.7
  let out 297.13
  (flow 348.23)
pourboire 784.3
Pour le mérite 733.2
pourparler
  conference 588.3
  council 696.2
pourpoint 225.15
pousse-café 959.10
pou sto 215.4
pout bulge 250.7
  sulk 901.6
poverty
  feeble style 575.1
  indigence 804
  (want 640.3)
  (bankruptcy 808.2)
poverty-stricken 804.7
powder *n.* power 157.1
  dust 330.3
  (littleness 193.2)
  flight 623.2

1020

powder — precede

gunpowder 727.13
beautifying 845.5
powder *v.* speed 274.9
  pulverize 330.6, 7
  beautify 845.7
powderiness 330.1
powdering 847.3
powder mill 691
powder puff 160a.3
powdery 330.8
power quantities 31.3
  (multitude 102.3)
  number 84.2
  potence 157.1
  (strength 159.1)
  influence 175.1
  country 182.1
  loudness 404.1
  vigorousness 574.1
  authority 737.1
  privilege 922.2
  celestial hierarchy 977.2
in one's power 693.7
in the power of 749.6
power behind the throne
  influence 175.5
  politician 694.4
powerful *adj.*
  potent 157.8
  (strong 159.10)
  loud 404.8
  language 574.5
  authoritative 737.15
powerful, powerfully *adv.* 31.15
powerless 158.8
  (week 160.10)
  (uninfluential 175a.2)
  render powerless 158.6
  (weaken 160.8)
  (render useless 645.7)
powerlessness 158.1
  (uninfluentiality 175a.1)
power of attorney 755.1, 4
power plant
  aeromotor 273a.11
  machine 633.2
powwow *n.*
  conference 588.3
  council 696.2
powwow *v.* 588.8
pox
  venereal disease 655.7
  rash 655.17
poyou 366.14
praam, praham 273.2, 4
practicability 470.2
practicable
  feasible 470.6
  utilitarian 644.5
  practical 646.5
practical
  substantial 3.4
  operative 170.4
  businesslike 625.11
  utilitarian 644.5
  expedient 646.5
Practical Christianity 984.9
practical joke 842.7
  (trick 545.3)
practically 5.8
practice *n.*
  mathematics 85.4
  training 537.2
  custom 613.2, 3
  (convention 852.2)
  vocation 625.5
  preparation 673.1
  usage 677.2
  exercise 686.2
  conduct 692.1
in practice
  prepared 673.11
  in use 677.7
out of practice 699.16
practice, practise *v.*
  train 537.10
  employ 625.6
  prepare 673.8
  use 677.5
  do 680.6
practice upon
  experiment 463.8
  deceive 545.7
practiced, practised 698.13
  (prepared 673.11)
practitioner
  doctor 662.19
  doer 690.1
prad 271.3
praecognitum 467.1
praedial, predial
  agricultural 371.9
  landed 780.8
praefect See **prefect**
praefoliation, prefoliation 367.4
praelect, praelection etc. See **prelect** etc.
praemunire, premunire 974.2
praenomen, prenomen 564.2
praetor, pretor 967.1
pragmatic
  dogmatic 474.15
  opinionated 606.7
  utilitarian 644.5
  practical 646.5
pragmatical
  priggish 853.7
  conceited 880.6
pragmatic sanction 769.2
pragmatism
  philosophy 451.16
  expedience 646.1
praham, prahm See **praam**
prahu See **proa**
prairie 344.1
  (waste 169.2)
  (open space 180.3)
  (horizontal 213.3)
  (flat 251.2)
  (grassland 367.11)
prairie dog 366.17
prairie schooner 272.3
praise *n.*
  thanksgiving 916.2
  commendation 931.2
  (flattery 933.1)
  worship 990.2
beyond praise
  perfect 650.5
  praiseworthy 931.11
sing praises
  praise 931.6
  (honor 873.13)
  worship 990.10
praise *v.* 931.6
  (flatter 933.2)
praise meeting 990.7
praiser 935.1
praiseworthy 931.11
  (good 648.8)
  (virtuous 944.4)
be praiseworthy 931.7
Prakrit 560.4
pralltriller 413.10
pram 272.11
pram, prame See **praam**
prana life force 359.2
  theosophy 994.10
  spirit 994.11
prance *n.* gait 266.5
  caper 309.2
prance *v.* walk 266.16
  frisk 266.19
  caper 309.5
prancer 271.3
prank *n.* caper 309.2
  caprice 608.1
  joke 842.7
  (trick 545.3)
  (frolic 840.3)
prank *v.* caper 309.5
  adorn 847.11
pranked, prankt 847.14
prankish
  playful 840.23
  waggish 842.9
pranky 840.23
prate *n.* twaddle 517.3
  chatter 584.2
prate *v.*
  talk nonsense 517.6
  gossip 532.7
  be loquacious 584.4
prattle *n.*
  twaddle 517.3
  speech 582.1
  chatter 584.2
  chat 588.2
prattle *v.*
  talk nonsense 517.6
  gossip 532.7
  be loquacious 584.4
pravity 945.2
prawn 298.18
praxis grammar 567.1
  practice 680.1; 692.1
pray request 765.4
  worship 990.11
pray! 765.9
prayer request 765.1
  ~ of thanks 916.2
  worship 990.3
say one's prayers 990.11
prayer book
  holystone 273.14
  sacred articles 998.9
prayer meeting 990.7
prayer wheel 990.3; 998.8
preach *n.* 582.2
preach *v.*
  expound 537.11
  declaim 582.7
  (address 586.2)
  (religion 996.14)
preacher teacher 540.3
  lecturer 582.5
  clergyman 996.2
preacheress 996.3
preachification, preaching 582.2
preachment
  lesson 537.6
  lecture 582.2
preadamite *n.* 130.1
preadamite *adj.* 124.7
preamb'e *n.* 64.2
preamble *v.* 62.3
preapprehension
  prejudice 481.2
  foreknowledge 510.3
  foreboding 511.6
prearrange 611.3
prearrangement
  predetermination 611.1
  preparation 673.1
prebend 995.3
prebendary 996.5
precarious
  transient 111.6
  uncertain 475.14
  unsafe 665.7
precariousness
  uncertainty 475.1
  danger 665.1
precatory 765.7
precaution *n.*
  forewarning 668.2
  (caution 864.1)
  preparation 673.1
  (care 459.1)
  (protection 664.2)
take precautions
  prepare for 673.7
  play safe 864.4
  (be careful 459.3)
  (safeguard 664.9)
precaution *v.* 668.7
precautious
  preparatory 673.10
  cautious 864.6
precede
  ~ in worth 35.2
  ~ in order 62.2
  ~ in time 116.3
  ~ in motion 280.2
  (guide 88.7)
  (front 234.7)

precedence — predominant

precede (*continued*)
  (outstrip 303.4)
precedence
  superiority 33.1
  anteposition 62
  (precession 280.1)
  (preference 609.2)
  (importance 642.1)
  priority 116.1
  rank 873.4
take precedence
  excel 33.5
  precede 62.2
precedent *n.*
  prototype 22.1
  precursor 64.1
  judgment 480.1
precedent *adj.*
  ~ in order 62.4
  ~ in time 116.4
  ~ in motion 280.3
preceding
  ~ in order 62.4
  (introductory 296.7)
  (preparatory 673.10)
  ~ in time 116.4
  foregoing 122.11
  ~ in motion 280.3
precentor
  choirmaster 416.13
  teacher 540.1
  leader 694.1
  choir chaplain 996.5
precept tenet 484.3
  axiom 496.2
  rule 697
  (principle 80.1)
  (advice 695.1)
  (law 963.2)
  command 741.1
  permit 760.2
preceptive
  prescriptive 697.2
  (according to rule 82.9)
  mandatory 741.8
preceptor 540.1
preceptoral, preceptorial 540.7
preceptress 540.2
precession
  precedence 62.1
  priority 116.1
  going before 280
  (front 234.1)
precessional 280.3
precinct region 181.1
  territory 181.2
  nearness 197.1
precincts 227.2
precious *n.* 902.4
precious *adj.*
  great 31.6
  unqualified 52.10
  superexcellent 648.10
  expensive 814.5
  loved 897.16
precious, preciously *adv.* 31.15
precious metal 800.15

precious stone 847.8
precipice 212.3
  (height 206.2)
  (incline 217.2)
precipitance
  suddenness 113.2
  haste 684.1
  recklessness 863.1
precipitate *n.* 40.2
  (condensation 321.3)
precipitate *v.* fell 308.5
  gravitate 319.7
  condense 321.7
  rain 348.25
  hasten 684.2
precipitate *adj.*
  premature 132.8
  hasty 684.5
  impetuous 863.7
  (sudden 113.5)
be precipitate 684.4
precipitately
  hastily 684.7
  (suddenly 113.7)
  (beforehand 132.12)
  recklessly 863.8
precipitation
  dregs 40.2
  prematurity 132.2
  silt 270.3
  downthrow 308.2
  condensation 321.3
  rainfall 348.11
  haste 684.1
  recklessness 863.1
precipitous 217.12
  (vertical 212.8)
précis 596.1
precise special 79.7
  limited 233.3
  accurate 494.11
  (scrupulous 939.8)
  distinct 518.5
  strict 739.5
  taste 850.5
  prudish 853.7
  meticulous 868.4
precisely
  punctually 132.13
  certainly 474.16
  to be sure 488.14
  accurately 494.16
  (literally 19.14)
preciseness
  meticulousness 457.3
  fastidiousness 868.1
precisian *n.*
  conformist 82.3
  stickler 739.3
  purist 850.3
  affecter 853.4
precisian *adj.* 739.5
precisianism
  strictness 739.1
  affectation 853.1
  hyperorthodoxy 983a.5
precision
  meticulousness 457.3

  accuracy 494.3
  (discrimination 465.1)
  intelligibility 518.1
  fastidiousness 868.1
precision balance 319.5
preclude hinder 706.4
  prohibit 761.2
preclusion
  exclusion 55.1
  hindrance 706.1
preclusive
  exclusive 55.6
  hindering 706.8
precocious
  premature 132.8
  (immature 674.8)
  pert 885.9
precocity 132.2
  (immaturity 674.2)
precognition 510.3
precognize 510.5
precompose 54.4
preconceive 481.6
preconception 481.2
preconcert *n.* 611.1
preconcert *v.* 611.3
  (plan 626.9)
preconcertion 673.1
precurrent 511.11
precurse be prior 116.3
  herald 511.8
precursive 511.11
precursor 64.1
  (premise 116.2)
  (vanguard 234.2)
  (omen 512.1)
  (messenger 534.1)
  (preparer 673.5)
be the precursor
  be prior 116.3
  herald 511.8
precursory 62.4
  (prelusive 64.3)
  (prior 116.4)
predacean 298.41
predaceous, predacious eating 298.48
  thievish 791.14
predacity
  rapacity 789.4
  thievishness 791.6
predatory
  rapacious 789.15
  thievish 791.14
predecessor 64.1
predella shelf 215.19
  altar 1000.3
predestinarianism 611.1
predestinate 976.10
predestination 611.1
  (destiny 601.3)
predestine
  predetermine 611.3
  (destine 601.9)
  preordain 976.10
predestined 611.5
  (destined 601.13)
predetermination 611
  (destiny 601.3)

  (intention 620.1)
predetermine 611.3
  (destine 601.9)
  (plan 626.9)
predetermined
  assured 474.9
  preordained 611.5
  (destined 601.13)
  (intended 620.4)
predial See praedial
predicament
  circumstance 8.3
  (state 7.1)
  class 75.1
  plight 704.2
  (crisis 134.4)
  (misfortune 735.3)
in a predicament 704.11
predicate *n.* 535.1
predicate *v.*
  predict 511.7
  propound 514.7
  affirm 535.3
predicate *adj.* 511.13
predication
  prediction 511.1
  affirmation 535.1
predicative, predicatory 535.6
predict 511.7
  (foresee 510.5)
  (religion 994.17)
predictable 511.12
prediction 511
  (foreknowledge 510.3)
  (omen 512.1)
  (indication 550.1)
  (clairvoyance 994.7)
make a prediction 511.7
predictional 535.6
predictive 511.11
  (prescient 510.6)
  (indicative 550.21)
  (forewarning 668.10)
  (psychic 994.23)
predictor 513.2
predilection
  tendency 176.1
  prejudice 481.2
  preference 609.2
  (liking 865.1)
  predisposition 820.1
predisposed
  tending 176.3
  willing 602.8
  minded 820.4
predisposition
  tendency 176.1
  prejudice 481.2
  preference 609.2
  preparation 673.1
  affection 820.1
predominance
  superiority 33.1
  (potence 157.1)
  dominion 737.2
predominant
  supreme 33.8

predominate — prepare

influential 175.10
  (potent 157.8)
  ruling 737.15
  (directing 693.6)
predominate excel 33.5
  rule 737.12
predomination
  superiority 33.1
  dominion 737.2
pre-eminence
  superiority 33.1
  (eminence 31.2;
    873.3)
  importance 642.1
pre-eminent
  supreme 33.8
  (eminent 873.18)
  highest 210.6
  almighty 976.12
pre-eminently 33.10
  (supremely 31.18)
pre-emption 795.1
pre-engage 132.5
pre-engagement 768.2
pre-establish 611.3
pre-exist exist 1.4
  be prior 116.3
pre-existence 116.1
pre-existent 116.4
preface n. 64.2
Preface n. 998.7
preface v. 62.3
prefatory 62.4
prefect, praefect
  student 541.1
  official 745.9
prefecture 737.3
prefer choose 609.9
  (desire 865.11)
  (like 897.11)
  ~ charges 938.4
  ~ a claim 969.10
preferable
  preferential 609.15
  improved 658.14
preferably 609.18
preference
  choice 609.2
  (precedence 62.1)
  (liking 865.1)
  favorite 899.1
  by preference 609.18
preferential 609.15
preferment
  improvement 658.1
  favorite 899.1
  ecclesiastical ~
    995.6
prefiguration 512.1
prefigurative 82.11
prefigure 511.9
  (indicate 550.18)
prefigurement
  prediction 511.1
  (sign 550.1)
  omen 512.1
  (precursor 64.1)
prefix n. adjunct 39.1
  prelude 64.2
  syllable 561.3
prefix v. 62.3
prefixture 64.2

preglacial 124.7
pregnable
  helpless 158.9
  vulnerable 665.9
pregnancy
  fertility 168.1
  parturience 168.2
  (birth 161.3)
pregnant fertile 168.7
  enceinte 168.9
  meaningful 516.8
  verb 572.3
  significant 642.11
  be pregnant 168.6
prehend 789.9
prehensile
  retentive 781.5
  seizing 789.15
prehensility 781.1
prehension
  retention 781.1
  seizure 789.1
prehistoric 124.7
preinstruct 537.9
preinstruction 537.1
prejudge 481.6
**prejudgment, pre-
  judgement** 481.2
  (forethought 510.2)
prejudicate 481.6
prejudication 481.2
prejudice n.
  prepossession
    481.2, 3
  (bigotry 606.2)
  preference 609.2
  harm 649.2
  partiality 941a.1
prejudice v. bias 481.8
  impair 659.9
prejudiced
  biased 481.10
  (dogmatic 474.15)
  (unreasonable
    477.10)
  (unreasoning
    499.17)
  (fanatical 503.18)
  (bigoted 606.7)
  (hyperorthodox
    983a.8)
  partial 941a.3
  be prejudiced 481.7
prejudicial 649.10
prejudicious 481.10
prelacy 995.1, 2
prelate 996.5
prelatic 995.9
prelation 609.2
prelect, praelect
  expound 537.11
  lecture 582.7
prelection, praelection
  lesson 537.6
  lecture 582.2
prelector, praelector
  teacher 540.3
  lecturer 582.5
prelibation 510.4
preliminary n. 64.2
preliminary adj. 62.4
  (introductory 296.7)

(preparatory
  673.10)
prelude n. preface 64.2
  (beginning 66.1)
  music 415.15
prelude v. 62.3
**preludial, preludious,
preluxive, prelusory**
  62.4
premature 132.8
  (untimely 135.6)
  (unexpected 508.8)
  (immature 674.8)
prematurely 132.12
  (unexpectedly
    508.11)
prematurity 132.2
  (untimeliness 135.1)
  (immaturity 674.2)
premeditate 611.3
  (intend 620.3)
premeditated
  measured 466.13
  aforethought 611.5
premeditation 611.1
premier n. 745.9
premier adj. 66.7
première danseuse
  proficient 700.1
  dancer 840.9
premiership
  managership 693.3
  authority 737.3
premise, premiss n.
  postulate 64.2
  region 181.1
  proposition 476.4
  (philosopheme
    451.24)
  (axiom 496.2)
premise v.
  precede 62.3
  herald 511.8
premises region 181.1
  evidence 467.1
premiums
  surplus 641.1
  gratuity 784.3
  interest 806.3
  reward 973.2
  at a premium 814.7
premolar 253.3
premonish 668.7
premonishment
  foreboding 511.6
  forewarning 668.2
premonition
  foreknowledge 510.3
  foreboding 511.6
  forewarning 668.2
  (clairvoyance 994.7)
premonitor omen 512.1
  warning sign 668.3
premonitory
  predictive 511.11
  forewarning 668.10
Premonstratensian
  996.11
premunire See prae-
  munire
prenomen See praeno-
  men

prenotation 511.6
prenotice
  prenotion 481.2
  foreboding 511.6
  forewarning 668.2
prenotification 668.2
prenotify 668.7
prenotion
  prejudice 481.2
  foreknowledge
    510.3
  foreboding 511.6
  forewarning 668.2
prentice, 'prentice n.
  apprentice 541.6
  worker 690.2
  servant 746.1
prentice, 'prentice adj.
  541.9
preoccupancy 777.1
preoccupation 458.3
preoccupied
  thoughtful 451.36
  distracted 458.11
  (engrossed 457.9)
preoption 609.2
preordain
  predetermine 611.3
  predestinate 976.10
preordination 611.1
preparation
  orchestration 413.3
  training 537.2
  authorship 590.2
  making ready 673
  (arrangement 60.1)
  (production 161.1)
  (foundation 215.3)
  (forethought 510.2)
  (equipment 634.1)
  (provision 637.1)
  in preparation 673.13
  (planned 626.11)
  (undertaken 676.3)
  make preparations
    673.6
preparationist 673.5
preparative n. 673.1
preparative adj. 673.10
preparator 673.5
preparatory n. 673.1
preparatory adj.
  preceding 62.4
  preparing 673.10
  (preliminary 62.4)
  (provisional 637.7)
preparatory school
  542.1
prepare cook 384.19
  author 590.14
  ready 673.6
  (arrange 60.6)
  (begin 66.5)
  (produce 161.8)
  (train 537.10)
  (plan 626.9)
  (equip 634.2)
  (provide 637.4)
prepare for 673.7
  (plan on 507.6)
prepare oneself 673.8

prepared — pressman

prepared
 ready 673.11
 (equipped 634.3)
 (provided 637.6)
 skilled 698.13
 be prepared 673.9
 (be provided 637.5)
preparedness 673.4
preparer 673.5
 (forerunner 64.1)
 (trainer 540.1)
prepense 611.5
 (intended 620.4)
prepollence
 superiority 33.1
 dominion 737.2
prepollent
 influential 175.10
 ruling 737.15
preponderance
 superiority 33.1
 majority 100.2
 dominion 737.2
preponderant
 influential 175.10
 ruling 737.15
preponderate
 excel 33.5
 predominate 737.12
preponderation
 superiority 33.1
 majority 100.2
preposition 567.2
prepossess 481.8
prepossessed
 prejudiced 481.10
 obsessed 503.18
 partial 941a.3
prepossessing
 alluring 617.5
 delightful 829.8
prepossession
 prejudice 481.2, 3
 preference 609.2
 preoccupancy 777.1
 partiality 941a.1
preposterous
 immense 31.9
 absurd 497.4
 fanciful 515.13
 exaggerated 549.3
 unwarranted 925.9
preposterously 31.20
prepotency
 superiority 33.1
 (potence 157.1)
 dominion 737.2
prepotent
 influential 175.10
 (potent 157.8)
 ruling 737.15
prepublication 511.1
Pre-Raphaelite *n.*
 122.5
Pre-Raphaelite *adj.*
 124.7
Pre-Raphaelitism
 122.4
prerequisite *n.*
 condition 469.2;
 770.1

prerequirement
 630.1
prerequisite *adj.* 630.3
prerogative
 authority 737.1
 privilege 748.1;
 922.2
presa 415.23
presage *n.*
 foreknowledge 510.3
 prediction 511.1
 foreboding 511.6
 omen 512.1
presage *v.* 511.7, 9
 (forerun 116.3)
presageful 511.11
presagement 511.1
presager 512.1
presbyopia 443.1
presbyopic 443.14
presbyter 996.2
Presbyterian 984.14
presbytery
 council 696.3
 (church 995.5)
 presbyterate 995.3
 clergy 996.1
 church section
 1000.3
 parsonage 1000.5
prescience 510.3
prescient 510.6
 (predictive 511.11)
prescribe direct 693.4
 advise 695.4
 order 741.5
 (require 630.2)
 entitle 760.4
 impose a duty 926.7
 ordain 963.4
prescript *n.*
 axiom 496.2
 precept 697.1
 command 741.1
 law 963.2
prescript *adj.* 697.2;
 741.8
prescription
 axiom 496.2
 custom 613.2
 nostrum 662.2
 precept 697.1
 command 741.1
 possession 777.2
 privilege 922.2
 law 963.2
prescriptive
 customary 613.11
 preceptive 697.2
 mandatory 741.8
 conventional 852.8
presence
 presentness 186
 (existence 1.1)
 apparition 443.9
 mien 448.4
 conduct 692.1
 breeding 894.1
 specter 980a.1
 in the presence of
 before 186.16
 near 197.11

presence chamber
 191.16
presence of mind
 levelheadedness
 498.4
 equanimity 826.3
present *n.*
 present time 118.1
 gift 784.3
 (thing transferred
 270.3)
 at present 118.3
present *adj.* 186.13
 (existent 1.7)
 (situate 184.17)
 be present 186.8, 9
 (exist 1.4)
 not present 187.10
present *v.* exhibit 525.2
 appear 448.6
 adduce 467.10
 tell 527.7
 allege 535.3
 expound 537.11
 indicate 550.18
 phrase 566.3
 utter 582.6
 dramatize 599.25
 provide 637.4
 offer 763.2
 give 784.8
present arms
 salute 894.9
 pay homage to 928.5
present itself
 happen 151.3
 appear 446.2
 suggest itself 451.32
present oneself
 attend 186.9
 volunteer 763.3
 pay respects 894.8
presentable
 tolerable 648.11
 (pretty 845.15)
 ~ **in society** 852.7
presentation
 appearance 448.1
 exhibition 525.1
 plan 626.1
 offer 763.1
 giving 784.1
 ~ **at court** 883.1
 introduction 894.3
 ecclesiastical ~
 995.6
presenter 784.7
presentient 511.11
presentiment
 intuition 477.1
 foreknowledge 510.3
 foreboding 511.6
presentimental 511.11
presently 132.15
presentment
 information 527.1
 giving 784.1
 arraignment 969.3
preserval 670.1
preservation
 permanence 141.1
 conservation 670

 (storing 636.6)
 (protection 664.2)
 (defense 717.1)
preservative *n.* 670.2
preservative *adj.*
 141.7; 670.5
 (protective 664.12)
preserve *n.* 396.3
preserve *v.*
 keep 670.3, 4
 (sustain 143.3)
 (reserve 636.8)
 (protect 664.6)
 (prepare 673.6)
 (safeguard 717.7)
 immortalize 976.8
preserved 670.6
 (safe 664.10)
preserver 670.2
preshow 511.9
preside
 superintend 693.5
 rule 737.11
 entertain 892.11
 administer justice
 965.3
presidency 737.3
president 745.9
presidentship 737.3
presignify 511.9
press *n.* crowd 72.4
 cupboard 191.15
 smoother 255.3
 journalism 593.17
 (printing 591.1)
 urge 615.2
 ~ **of business** 682.7
 compulsion 744.1
 go to press 591.16
press *v.* smooth 255.4
 weigh 319.8
 urge 615.7
 hasten 684.2
 compel 744.2
 entreat 765.5
 (offer 763.2)
 crimp 791.11
 ~ **one's suit** 902.7
press down
 depress 308.4
 force down 744.2
press forward
 advance 282.2
 hasten 684.3
press in
 intrude 228.10
 enter 294.6
 insert 300.5
press on elapse 109.3
 advance 282.2
 keep going 682.12
 hasten 684.3
press out 301.7
press agent *n.* 531.6
press-agent *v.* 531.8
presser 255.3
pressing urgent 642.13
 (requisite 630.3)
 hasty 684.5
 tyrannical 739.5
pressman
 printer 591.12

journalist 593.16
press revise 591.3
pressroom 591.11
pressure
  influence 175.1
  aeronautics 267a.9
  gravity 319.1
  urgency 642.2
  adversity 735.1
  authority 737.2
  compulsion 744.1
presswork 591.1
prestidigitation 545.2
prestidigitator 548.6
prestige
  superiority 33.1
  influence 175.1
  importance 642.1
  dominion 737.2
  renown 873.3
prestissimo 415.32
presto *n.* 415.6
presto *adv.*
  instantly 113.6
  fast 415.32
presumable
  probable 472.5
  conjecturable 514.10
  (imaginable 515.15)
presumably 472.7
presume
  think likely 472.3
  (expect 507.4)
  judge 480.6
  preconceive 481.6
  believe 484.8
  suppose 514.6
  take a liberty 748.9
  hope 858.6
  arrogate 885.6
presumption
  evidence 467.1
  probability 472.1
  preconception 481.2
  belief 484.2
  expectation 507.2
  supposition 514.1
  hope 858.1
  overconfidence 863.1
  arrogance 885.1
presumptive
  evidential 467.11
  probable 472.5
  supposititious 514.9
  arrogant 885.8
presumptive evidence
  evidence 467.1
  probability 472.1
presumptuous
  arrogant 885.8
  impertinent 885.9
presuppose
  preconceive 481.6
  presurmise 514.6
presupposition
  premise 64.2; 476.4
  preconception 481.2
  presumption 514.1
presurmise *n.* 510.2
presurmise *v.* 514.6
pretend feign 544.6

(act 599.26)
(pretext 619.2)
allege 535.3
affect 853.5
(be ostentatious 882.6)
pretended 545.13
(pretexed 619.3)
pretender
  impostor 548.3
  (actor 599.19)
  (attitudinarian 882.5)
  (usurper 925.4)
  affecter 853.4
  braggart 884.3
pretense, pretence
  dissimulation 544.2
  (simulation 19.3)
  (acting 599.6)
  pretext 619.1
  affectation 853.1
  ostentation 882.1
  boasting 884.1
pretension
  dissimulation 544.2
  grandiloquence 577.2
  pretext 619.1
  affectation 853.1
  ostentation 882.1, 2
  boasting 884.1
  privilege 922.2
pretentious vain 880.6
  (overestimated 482.4)
  ostentatious 882.8
  (proud 878.6)
  affected 853.6
  boastful 884.7
pretentiousness 882.1
preterhuman 976.14
preterience 111.1
preterient 111.6
preterit, preterite 122.9
preterition 122
  (priority 116.1)
pretermit 460.7
  (postpone 133.4)
preternatural
  unusual 83.10
  supernatural 976.14
pretext *n.* 619
  (concealment 528.1)
  (disguise 545.5)
  (untruth 546.1)
  (evasion 623.1)
  (loophole 671.4)
  (excuse 937.2)
pretext *v.* 619.2
pretonic
  sounded 402.11
  posttonic 580.11
pretor See **praetor**
pretty *adj.* 845.8
pretty *adv.*
  greatly 31.15
  somewhat 32.14
  (imperfectly 651.4)
pretypify 511.9
prevail exist 1.4

excel 33.5
be general 78.7
~ upon 615.9
triumph 731.6
predominate 737.12
prevailing
  prevalent 78.10
  going on 151.5
  plentiful 639.7
  conventional 852.8
prevalence
  superiority 33.1
  generality 78.2
  frequency 136.1
  common practice 613.2
prevalent
  existent 1.7
  general 78.10
  (extensive 31.7)
  (common 613.11)
  going on 151.5
  influential 175.10
  plentiful 639.7
  predominant 737.15
  conventional 852.8
prevaricate
  quibble 477.8
  falsify 544.4, 5
  (equivocate 520.3)
prevarication
  equivocation 477.4
  falsification 544.1
  lie 546.1
prevaricator 548.5
prévenance 894.1
prevene precede 62.2
  be prior 116.3
prevenience 132.2
  (immaturity 674.2)
prevenient
  preceding 62.4
  premature 132.8
  (immature 674.8)
prevent 706.5
  (remedy 662.24)
preventable 623.11
preventative *n.* 179.2
preventative *adj.* 706.8
prevention
  prejudice 481.2
  hindrance 706.1
preventive
  counteractant 179.2
  prophylactic 662.8
  (hindrance 706.2)
preventive *adj.*
  exclusive 55.6
  remedial 662.25
  hindering 706.8
preview *n.* 461.7
preview *v.* 461.21
previous prior 116.4
  (preceding 62.4)
  (former 122.10)
  (earlier 132.10)
  premature 132.8
previously 116.5
  (then 119.2)
  (formerly 122.14)
previousness 116.1

prevision *n.* 510.1
prewar *v.* 668.7
prey quarry 620.2
  defeated 732.4
  booty 793.1
  sufferer 828.8
fall a prey to
  be defeated 732.6
  become subjected 749.3
price *n.*
  consideration 147.2
  odds 621.5
  worth 648.1
  interest 806.3
  cost 812
  reward 973.1
  penalty 974.1
beyond price
  useful 644.6
  superexcellent 648.10
  expensive 814.5
price *v.* 812.4
priced 812.7
priceless
  superexcellent 648.10
  dear 814.5
prick *n.* point 253.2
  incentive 615.3
prick *v.*
  perforate 260.14
  ~ a horse 370.7
  pain physically 378.4
  tingle 380.4
  urge 615.7
  hasten 684.2
  pain mentally 830.3
prick up the ears
  listen 418.11
  be curious 455.3
  pay attention 457.4
prick-eared 418.14
prickle *n.*
  adherer 46.3
  point 253.2
  sensation 380.1
prickle *v.* 380.4
prickly 253.11
  (bristly 256.14)
prickly heat 655.17
prick song 415.4
pricky 253.11
pride 878
  (vanity 880.1)
  (ostentation 882.1)
  (arrogance 885.1)
prie-dieu 215.22
priest 996.2, 6
priestcraft 995.1
priestess 996.3
priesthood
  sacerdotalism 995.1, 3
  clergy 996.1
priestly, priest-ridden 995.9
  (ministerial 996.15)
prig *n.* thief 792.1
  prude 853.4

prig — prize

prig *(continued)*
  fop 854.1
  vain person 880.3
prig *v.* 791.9
prigger 792.1
priggery 880.1
priggish
  thievish 791.14
  prudish 853.7
  vain 880.6
priggishness 853.2
prim 853.7
prima buffa 599.19
primacy
  supremacy 33.3
  (importance 642.1)
  dominion 737.2
  church 995.3
prima donna
  singer 416.10
  actress 599.19
  principal 642.6
  proficient 700.1
prima facie
  at sight 441.23
  presumably 472.7
primal 66.7
primary *n.*
  school 542.1
  election 609.3
primary *adj.*
  intrinsic 5.6
  supreme 33.8
  beginning 66.7
  original 153.9
  basal 211.5
  paramount 642.14
primate 996.5
primatial council 696.3
prime *n.*
  beginning 66.1
  dawn 125.1
  ∼ of life 127.1
  cause 153.1
  best 648.4
  canonical office 990.7
in one's prime 131.6
past one's prime 128.8
prime *v.* paint 428.10
  tutor 537.9
  prepare 673.6
prime *adj.*
  supreme 33.8
  beginning 66.7
  numeral 84.7
  primitive 124.7
  early 132.7
  paramount 642.14
  best 648.9
  prepare 673.6
primed drunk 959.21
  prepared 673.11
  skilled 608.13
prime minister 745.9
prime mover
  cause 153.1
  creator 164.1
  motive 615.1
primer
  automobile 272.16
  paint 428.5

type 591.7
textbook 593.5
primeval
  primitive 124.7
  (beginning 66.7)
  original 153.9
primigenial
  beginning 66.7
  lineal 167.7
priming 428.5
primitive *n.*
  native 188.8
  word 562.1
primitive *adj.*
  beginning 66.7
  primeval 124.7
  original 153.9
  native 188.11
  basal 211.5
primogenial
  beginning 66.7
  primitive 124.7
  lineal 167.7
primogenitary
  senior 128.9
  lineal 167.7
primogeniture
  seniority 128.4
  lineage 167.2
  inheritance 775.4
primogenous 128.9
primordial
  unimitated 20.3
  primitive 124.7
  original 153.9
primordium
  cause 153.1
  microbe 193.4
  motive 615.1
primp 847.11
  (dress 225.44)
primrose pink 434.3, 5
  yellow 436.3
prince 875.7
  (potentate 745.2)
  (title 877.2)
Prince Albert coat 225.14
princely
  sovereign 737.16
  munificent 816.4
  illustrious 873.18
  noble 875.10
  magnanimous 942.6
Prince of Darkness 978.1
Prince of Peace 976.5
princess 875.8
  (empress 745.6)
  (title 877.2)
principal *n.*
  organ stop 417.12
  chief 642.6
  master 745.1
  fund 799.2
principal *adj.*
  supreme 33.8
  (paramount 642.14)
  first 66.8
principality
  country 182.1
  (region 181.2)

archangel 977.1, 2
principally 33.10
principia
  rudiments 66.4
  axiom 496.2
  precept 697.1
principle
  essence 5.2
  rule 80.1
  cause 153.1
  substance 316.2
  life ∼ 359.2; 994.11
  tenet 484.3
  axiom 496.2
  (premise 476.4)
  motive 615.1
  precept 697.1
  moral ∼ 926.4
  probity 939.1
Principle
  world spirit 359.3
  God 976.2
prink adorn 847.11
  be affected 853.5
  show off 882.6
print *n.*
  indentation 252.2
  edition 531.2
  news 532.1
  mark 550.4, 7
  photograph 556.11
  engraving 558.3
  letterpress 591.2
  type 591.6
in print 591.18
out of print 552.4
print *v.* engrave 558.5
  (mark 550.19)
  stamp 591.14
printed 591.18
printed matter 591.2
  (copy 21.1)
printer, printer's devil 591.12
  (workman 690.10)
printing
  engraving 558.2
  typography 591
  (composition 54.2)
  (edition 531.2)
printing press 591.10
printless 552.4
printworks 691
prior *n.* 996.11
prior *adj.*
  preceding 62.4
  previous 116.4, 5
  (former 122.10)
  (earlier 132.10)
be prior 116.3
prioress 996.12
priority
  superiority 33.1
  ∼ in time 116
  (precedence 62.1)
  (preterition 122.1)
  (precession 280.1)
  front 234.1
priory 1000.4
prism angle 244.2
  spectroscope 428.8
  optics 445.1

prismatic
  angular 244.5
  chromatic 428.12
  iridescent 440.6
prismoid 244.2
prison 752
  (enclosure 232.1)
  (stronghold 717.4)
in prison 751.12
prisoner captive 754
  accused 938.3
take prisoner
  arrest 751.9
  capture 789.9
prissy 160a.3
pristine 124.7
  (former 122.10)
prithee! 765.9
prittle-prattle *n.*
  chatter 584.2
  chat 588.2
prittle-prattle *v.* 588.7
privacy secrecy 528.2
  secret 533.1
  seclusion 893.2
Privatdocent 540.1
private *n.*
  residence 189.1
  soldier 726.4
private *adj.*
  special 79.7
  confidential 528.21
  secluded 893.10
in private 528.24
privateer *n.*
  warship 726.11
  pirate 792.5
privateer *v.* 791.10
privateering 791.2
privately 881.7
privation loss 776.1
  deprivation 789.2
  poverty 804.1
privative 789.15
privilege *n.*
  freedom 748.1
  immunity 777a.1
  right 922.2
  (permission 760.1)
  (due 924.1)
privilege *v.*
  grant 760.4
  exempt 777a.2
privileged
  exempt 748.18
  warranted 924.10
privity bond 45.1
  knowledge 490.1
privy *n.* 653.9
in privy 528.24
privy *adj.*
  ∼ to 490.13
  private 528.21
  secluded 893.10
privy council 696.1
privy seal, privy signet 747.2
prize *n.*
  leverage 175.3
  pry 307.4
  good 648.2, 4
  trophy 733.1

1026

prize — production

(reward 973.1)
(gain 775.2)
booty 793.1
prize *v.* break 173.10
appraise 466.10
estimate 480.7
rate highly 642.8
hold dear 897.11
esteem 931.5
prize fight 720.6
prize fighter 726.2
prize fighting 720.6
prizeman 700.2
prizer 767.1
prize ring 728.1
proa, prahu 273.2
pro and con
argument 476.3, 18
reasons 615.1
probabilism 473.1
probability 177.1; 472
(good chance 156.3)
(reasonability 476.7)
(credibility 484.5)
(assurance 507.2)
in all probability 472.7
probabilize 472.4
probable likely 472.5
(logical 476.16)
(credible 484.15)
propitious 858.11
be probable 472.2
(have a chance 156.9)
make probable 472.4
probable cause 473.1
probably 472.7
probate 771.1
probate court 966.1, **2**
probation
examination 461.3
experiment 463.1
demonstration 478.1
probationary
experimental 463.12
demonstrative 478.3
student 541.9
probationer
student 541.6
nurse 662.20
probative
experimental 463.12
demonstrative 478.3
probatory 541.9
probe *n.*
perforator 262
examination 461.3
probationist 662.20
probe *v.*
examine 461.15, 17, 18
(grope 463.9)
measure 466.10
probity 939
(truth 494.1)
(veracity 543.1)
(right 922.1)
(justice 941.1)
(virtue 944.1)
problem

question 461.**10**
enigma 533.2
(topic 454.1)
(dilemma 704.4)
problematic
unbelievable 485.11
enigmatic 533.6
(perplexing 475.12)
proboscis 250.4
procacious 885.9
procacity
insolence 885.**2**
irascibility 901.1
procedure
measure 626.7
usage 677.2
conduct 692.1
(way 627.1)
(action 680.1)
proceed elapse 109.3
result from 154.3
advance 282.2
act 680.5
conduct 692.4
proceeding event 151.1
act 680.2
conduct 692.1
proceedings
affairs 151.2
record 551.2
lawsuit 969.1
proceeds profits 775.**2**
receipts 810.1
procerity 206.1
process
protuberance 250.**2**
procedure 692.1
in process 673.13
procession
gradation 58.**2**
continuity 69.3
(attendance 88.5)
parade 882.2
processional 998.**2**
procès-verbal
testimony 467.**2**
record 551.1
legal pleadings 969.6
prochronism
anachronism 115.1
error 495.1
proclaim *n.*
proclamation 531.1
decree 741.3
proclaim *v.*
herald 116.3
foretell 511.8
announce 531.7
(manifest 525.2)
(say 582.6)
~ the banns 903.12
proclaimer
publisher 531.5
announcer 534.1
proclamation
prediction 511.1
announcement 531.1
decree 741.3
proclamatory 531.11
(informative 527.13)
proclive 217.**11**

proclivity
tendency 176.1
propensity 602.**2**
disposition 820.1
partiality 865.1
proclivous 217.11
proconsul 759.2
proconsular 759.6
proconsulship 737.3
procrastinate
delay 133.4, 5
(pass time 106.3)
(move slowly 275.5)
(not do 681.2)
waste time 683.8
procrastinating 133.9
(neglectful 460.8)
procrastination
delay 133.2
(neglect 460.1)
indolence 683.3
procrastinator 460.3
procreant 168.8
procreate 161.10
(copulate 43.8)
(reproduce 163.2)
(fecundate 168.4)
procreation 161.2
(coition 43.2)
(reproduction 163.1)
(productiveness 168.1)
procreative 168.8
(productive 161.11)
(reproductive 163.3)
procreator 166.5
Procrustean 739.5
Procrustean bed 975.3
proctor steward 694.5
functionary 758.2
deputy 750.1
lawyer 968.1
proctorship 693.3
procumbent 213.9
procuration
agency 170.1
mandate 755.1
acquisition 775.1
procurator
steward 694.5
lawyer 968.1
procure effect 153.7
induce 615.9
acquire 775.6
purchase 795.3
procurement
agency 170.1
acquisition 775.1
procurer 962.4
prod impel 276.7
urge 615.7
hasten 684.2
prodigal *n.* 818.2
(neglector 460.3)
prodigal *adj.*
profuse 102.5
abundant 639.7
(wasteful 638.5)
(redundant 641.5)
(liberal 816.4)
(intemperate 954.4)
extravagant 818.4

wayward 945.11
be prodigal 818.3
(overdo 641.3)
(be intemperate 954.3)
prodigality
plenty 639.2
(redundance 641.1)
extravagance 818
(waste 638.1)
(intemperance 954.1)
prodigal son
prodigal 818.2
penitent 950.2
prodigiosity 83.6
prodigious vast 31.8
unusual 83.10
huge 192.15
wonderful 870.7
prodigy
monstrosity 83.6
genius 492.2
(proficient 700.1)
nonesuch 648.4
wonder 872
prodromal 62.4
prodromus 64.1
produce *n.*
increase 35.2
product 161.6
profits 775.2
merchandise 798.1
produce *v.* cause 153.6
create 161.8
(compose 54.4)
(form 240.6)
(vivify 359.8)
(prepare 673.6)
bear 161.9
(be profitable 775.10)
(yield 810.4)
be productive 168.5
lengthen 200.9
exhibit 525.2
author 590.14
dramatize 599.25
do 680.6
accomplish 729.2
producer cause 153.1
creator 164
(author 593.15)
(craftsman 690.5)
(workman 690.8)
theater 599.17
producible
productional 161.11
manifestable 525.6
product sum 84.3
production 161.6
(effect 154.1)
(handiwork 680.3)
crop 636.3
gain 775.2
productible 161.11
production
composition 54.2
creation 161
(causation 153.5)
(formation 240.3)
(preparation 673.1)

productive — prolificate 1028

production (cont'd)
  product 161.6
  (art 556.8)
  lengthening 200.5
  exhibition 525.1
  writing 590.2, 3
  book 593.1
  theater 599.8
  achievement 729.1
productive
  creative 161.11
  (causal 153.9)
  fertile 168.7
  (potent 157.8)
  (profitable 644.6)
  imaginative 515.11
  gainful 775.12
  be productive 168.5
productiveness, productivity 168
  (utility 644.1)
proem 64.2
  (beginning 66.1)
proemial
  preceding 62.4
  beginning 66.7
proemium 64.2
profanation
  misuse 679.1
  sacrilege 988.1
profane adj.
  impious 988.10
  unspiritual 989.9
profane v.
  misuse 679.2
  commit sacrilege 988.7
profanity
  swearing 908.2
  impiety 988.1
profess assert 535.3
  pretend 544.6
  allege 619.2
  affect 853.5
profession
  ~ of faith 484.4
  assertion 535.1
  allegation 619.1
  vocation 625.5
  promise 768.1
professional 625.11
professionally 625.14
professor
  affirmant 488.5
  learned man 492.1
  teacher 540.1
professorate 540.5
professorial 540.7
professorship 540.6
proffer n. 763.1
proffer v. 763.2
  (volunteer 602.7)
proficiency
  knowledge 490.2
  skill 157.1
  (ability 157.2)
proficient n. 700
proficient adj. 698.11
  (able 157.9)
proficient in 698.14
  (versed in 490.14)
profile n. outline 230.1

side 236.1
form 240.1
lineaments 448.5
portrait 556.9
profile v. 230.3
profit n. increase 35.2
  avail 648.2
  gain 775.2
  (success 731.1)
  (remuneration 973.2)
profit v. avail 644.2
  benefit 648.6
  make money by 775.7
profit by
  turn to account 134.6
  be better for 658.7
  use 677.5
  (take advantage of 698.10)
profitability 644.1
profitable useful 644.6
  (productive 168.7)
  (beneficial 648.12)
  expedient 646.4
  gainful 775.12
  be profitable 775.10
  (produce 161.9)
profitably 775.13
profitless 645.8
profit-sharing 778.8
profligacy 945.2
profligate n. 962.1
profligate adj.
  vicious 945.15
  dissolute 961.10
profluence 348.2
profluent
  progressive 282.3
  flowing 348.26
pro formâ 82.13
profound
  absolute 31.12
  deep 208.8
  deep-felt 821.8
  learned 490.15
  wise 498.11
  obscure 519.7
  language 574.9
  cunning 702.6
profundity depth 208.1
  wisdom 498.3
profuse
  numerous 102.5
  verbose 573.7
  abundant 639.7
  (redundant 641.5)
  liberal 816.4
  prodigal 818.4
profuseness 573.1
profusion
  quantities 31.5
  plenty 639.2
  (numerousness 102.1)
  (redundance 641.1)
  prodigality 818.1
  in profusion 102.5
profusive 639.7
prog vagabond 268.2

food 298.5
progenerate 161.10
progeneration 161.2
progenerative 168.8
progenitive 163.3
progenitor 166.1, 5
progeniture 167.1
progeny
  ancestry 166.4
  posterity 167.1
progeny 167.1
progger 268.2
prognose 511.7
prognosis
  prediction 511.1
  (foreknowledge 510.3)
  diagnosis 522.1
  disease 655.19
prognostic n.
  prediction 511.1
  omen 512.1
  disease 655.19
prognostic adj.
  predictive 511.11
  interpretative 522.8
prognosticate 511.7, 9
prognostication
  prediction 511.1
  omen 512.1
  symptomatology 655.19
program, programme
  list 86.1
  notice 531.4
  schedule 611.2
  (outline 230.1)
  (plan 626.3)
  (policy 692.2)
program v. 611.4
program music 415.3
progress n.
  conversion 144.1
  velocity 274.1
  advance 282.1
  (locomotion 264.2)
  (success 731.1)
  improvement 658.1
  in progress
  progressively 282.4
  in preparation 673.13
  make progress
  progress 282.2
  (be active 682.12)
  (succeed 731.5)
  improve 658.6
progress v.
  advance 282.2
  (move 264.6)
  improve 658.6
progression
  gradation 58.2
  continuity 69.1
  mathematics 84.6
  advancement 282
  improvement 658.1
progressive n. 658.5
Progressive n. 712.6
progressive adj.
  continuous 69.6
  advancing 282.3

(time 109.4)
(moving 264.8)
forward-looking 658.15
progressively 282.4
progressiveness 282.1
progressivism 658.3
prohibit 761.2
  (deny 536.2)
  (hinder 706.4)
  (restrain 751.6)
prohibited 761.4
  (illegal 964.5)
prohibition
  exclusion 55.1
  forbiddance 761
  (denial 536.1)
  (hindrance 706.1)
  (restraint 751.1)
  (illegality 964.1)
  temperance 953.2
prohibitionary 761.3
prohibitionist 953.4
prohibitive
  exclusive 55.6
  forbidding 761.3
project n.
  intention 620.1
  plan 626.1
  (undertaking 676.1)
project v.
  overhang 214.5
  protrude 250.7
  traject 284.11
  plan 626.9
projectile n.
  trajectile 284.5
  missile 727.14
projectile adj. 284.16
projecting
  overhanging 214.8
  protuberant 250.9
projection
  convexity 250.1, 2
  tooth 253.3
  trajection 284.2
  plan 626.1
  ground plan 626.2
projector
  magic lantern 445.6
  planner 626.8
  enterpriser 694.1
prolation 415.5
prolegomenon 64.2
prolepsis
  premise 64.2
  anachronism 115.1
proletarian n. 876.3
proletarian adj. 876.11
proletariat 876.1
proliferate
  generate 161.10
  be productive 168.5
proliferation
  generation 161.2
  productiveness 168.1
proliferous, prolific 168.7
  be prolific 35.4
prolificacy 168.1
prolificate 35.4

prolification — proper

prolification, prolificity 168.1
prolify 161.9
prolix verbose 573.7
 plentiful 639.7
 boresome 841.8
prolixity
 verbosity 573.1
 profusion 639.2
prolocutor
 lecturer 540.3
 spokesman 582.5
 deputy 759.1
prologize 62.3
prologue prelude 64.2
 drama 599.5
prolong time 110.6
 (delay 133.4)
 continue 143.3
 lengthen 200.9
prolongation
 continuation 63.2
 posteriority 117.1
 delay 133.2
 continuance 143.1
 lengthening 200.5
prolonged
 protracted 110.10
 elongated 200.12, 14
prolusion 64.2
promenade n.
 travel 266.4, 8
 path 627.2
 dance 840.6
 parade 882.3
promenade v.
 travel 266.13, 16
 parade 882.6
promenade concert 415.17
Promethean 359.11
prominence
 greatness 31.2
 height 206.1
 convexity 250.1
 manifestness 525.1
 importance 642.1
 fame 873.3
prominent high 206.13
 protuberant 250.9
 distinct 446.5
 conspicuous 525.5
 important 642.10
 eminent 873.18
prominently
 remarkably 31.21
 eminently 33.10
promiscuity 465a.1
promiscuous
 mixed 41.9
 disorderly 59.8
 (indiscriminate 465a.3)
 (purposeless 621.21)
promise n. pledge 768
 (undertaking 676.1)
 (consent 762.1)
 (contract 769.1)
 (guarantee 771.1)
 hope 858.1
 keep one's promise
 keep faith 772.4

 be honorable 939.6
 of promise 858.11
promise v.
 be probable 472.2
 expect 507.4
 foretoken 511.10
 pledge 768.3
 (depose 535.4)
 (undertake 676.2)
 (consent 762.2)
 (contract 769.5)
 (guarantee 771.6)
 give hope 858.8
 threaten 909.2
promising
 probable 472.5
 auspicious 512.4
 promissory 768.6
 propitious 858.11
promissory 768.6
promissory note
 pledge 771.1
 commercial paper 800.7
promontory
 height 206.2
 point 250.5
promorphologist 368.2
promorphology
 form 240.4
 zoology 368.1
promote
 subserve 631.3
 advance 658.8
 aid 707.6
 (facilitate 705.4)
promoter 626.8
promotion
 improvement 658.1
 aid 707.1
prompt n. 505.5
prompt v.
 remind 505.15
 hint 527.8
 instigate 615.7
 (influence 175.6)
 (impel 276.7)
 advise 695.4
prompt adj.
 punctual 132.9
 ready 602.8
 businesslike 625.11
 quick 682.17
promptbook
 memorandum book 505.6
 notebook 551.3
 playbook 599.16
prompter
 reminder 505.5
 stageman 599.17
 instigator 615.6
 adviser 695.3
prompting
 reminder 505.5
 motivation 615.2
promptitude
 punctuality 132.3
 quickness 682.2
promptly 132.14
 (briefly 111.9)
 (hastily 684.7)

promptness
 punctuality 132.3
 (haste 684.1)
 willingness 602.1
promulgate 531.7
promulgation 531.1
promulgator 531.5
pronation 218.1
prone v.
 prostrate 213.7
 fell 308.5
prone adj.
 ~ to 176.3
 prostrate 213.9
 willing 602.8
 disposed 820.4
proneness
 tendency 176.1
 recumbency 213.2
 propensity 602.2
 affection 820.1
proneur 935.1
prong fork 91.2
 angle 244.2
 point 253.2
 stream 348.1
pronghorn 366.10
pronoun 564.4
 (parts of speech 567.2)
pronounce
 declare 535.3
 enunciate 580.8
 say 582.6
pronounced
 absolute 31.12
 distinct 446.5
 conspicuous 525.5
pronouncement
 proclamation 531.1
 declaration 535.1
 statement 582.4
 decree 741.3
pronto 132.14
pronunciamiento, pronunciamiento
 proclamation 531.1
 decree 741.3
pronunciation
 affirmation 535.1
 phonology 562.4
 enunciation 580.3
pronunciative 535.6
proof n. test 463.1
 demonstration 478.1
 (evidence 467.1)
 (undeniability 474.1)
 indication 550.1
 engraving 558.3
 draft 626.2
proof adj.
 sound 159.12
 impregnable 323.5
 insensible 376.5
proof against
 invulnerable 664.11
 resolute 604.7
 (resistant 719.5)
 (defensible 717.10)
 steeled 823.7
proofer 591.12

proofread 591.17
proofreader 591.13
 (workman 690.10)
proofroom 591.11
proof sheet 590.3
prop n.
 supporter 215.2
 (fastening 45.2)
 leg 266.11
 propeller 273a.10;
 284.6
 wheel 312.4
prop v. support 215.26
 lend support 707.7
propaedeutic 537.12
propaedeutics 537.4
propaganda, propagandism 537.3
propagandist
 teacher 540.4
 evangelist 996.4
propagate
 procreate 161.10
 (reproduce 163.2)
 publish 531.7
 ~ learning 537.9
propagation
 procreation 161.2
 (reproduction 163.1)
 (productiveness 168.1)
 publication 531.1
propagative
 procreative 168.8
 educational 537.12
propagator 531.5
propagatory 531.11
propel 284.10
 (move 264.7)
 (transfer 270.6)
 (impel 276.7)
propellant, propellent n. 284.6
propellent adj. 284.15
propeller leg 266.11
 airplane 273a.10
 driver 284.6
 wheel 312.4
propeller race 267a.16
propelling n. 284.1
propelling adj. 284.15
prope'ment 284.1
propend 602.6
propeuse tending 176.3
 willing 602.8
 disposed 820.4
propension 820.1
propensity
 willingness 602.2
 (aptitude 698.2)
 disposition 820.1
 liking 865.1
proper adj.
 peculiar 79.8
 opportune 134.7
 speech 578.4
 (tasteful 850.5)
 fit 646.4
 comely 845.10
 conventional 852.8
 right 922.5

proper — prostrate 1030

proper (*continued*)
  (due 924.9)
  just 941.3
  orthodox 983a.7
think proper
  be willing 602.6
  choose 609.9
proper, properly *adv.* 31.15
propertied 780.8
properties 599.13
property nature 5.3
  particularity 79.2
  earmark 550.6
  belongings 780
  (equipment 634.1)
  (possession 777.1)
  (wealth 803.1)
prophecy 511.1
  (religion 994.17)
prophesy 511.7
prophet
  predictor 512.2
  (astrologer 318.13)
  (interpreter 524.1)
  (biblical 985.6)
  (sorcerer 992.2)
  (psychic 994.16)
  preacher 996.5
the Prophets 985.3
prophetic 511.11
  (scriptural 985.7)
prophylactic *n.*
  counteractant 179.2
  medicine 662.8
prophylactic *adj.*
  sanitary 656.5
  remedial 662.25
  protective 664.12
  conservative 670.5
  hindering 706.8
prophylaxis 670.2
propinquant 197.8
propinquity 197.1
propitiate pacify 723.4
  mediate 724.3
  content 831.4
  pity 914.4
  atone 952.4
  divine function 976.9
  offer sacrifice 990.13
propitiation
  pacification 723.1
  (worship 990.5)
  atonement 952.1
  divine function 976.5
propitiative 724.4
propitiator 724.2
  (judge 967.1)
propitiatory
  pacificatory 723.6
  mediatory 724.4
  atoning 952.6
propitious
  opportune 134.7
  auspicious 512.4; 858.11
  (fortunate 734.8)
  helpful 707.13
proplasm 22.1

proponent 937.4
proportion
  mathematical ~ 84.6; 85.4
  dimension 180.5
  size 192.1
  symmetry 242.1
  comparison 464.1
  (relation 9.1)
  elegance 578.1
  share 786.2
out of proportion
  inapt 24.7
  inordinately 31.20
proportionable, proportional 464.6
proportionality 242.1
proportionate *adj.*
  approximative 9.7
  agreeing 23.9
  comparable 464.6
  adequate 639.6
proportionate *v.* 242.3
proportioned 242.4
proposal
  hypothesis 514.1
  intention 620.1
  plan 626.1
  offer 763.1
  proposition 765.3
propose
  ~ a discussion 476.11
  propound 514.7
  allege 535.3
  intend 620.3
  offer 763.2
  ~ marriage 902.7
propositio 476.3
proposition
  topic 454.1
  question 461.10
  argument 476.3, 4
  axiom 496.2
  hypothesis 514.1
  plan 626.1
  offer 763.1
  proposal 765.3
propound
  propose 514.7
  allege 535.3
proprietary 779.2
proprieties 852.2
proprietor 779.2
  (householder 188.3)
  (master 745.1)
  (host 890.6)
proprietorship 777.3
propriety fitness 23.2
  language 578.1
  expedience 646.1
  conventionality 852.2
  right 922.1
  ethics 926.4
proprio motu 600.5
propugnaculum 717.4
propulsion 284
  (impulse 276.1)
propulsive 284.15
  (impulsive 276.10)
propulsor 284.6

prore 234.3
pro re nata
  respectively 79.12
  conditionally 770.4
prorogate 133.4
prorogation 133.2
proruption 295.1
prosaic style 575.2
  language 576.3
  unpoetic 598.4
  workaday 625.11; 686.9
  wearisome 841.8
  dull 843.5
  (stupid 499.12)
  ordinary 849.3
prosaicism
  trite saying 496.3
  dullness 843.1
prosaism prose 598.1
  dullness 843.1
proscenium
  front 234.1
  stage 599.12
proscenium box 599.11
proscribe
  banish 297.11
  prohibit 761.2
  condemn 971.2
proscription
  banishment 297.3
  prohibition 761.1
  ban 908.1
  condemnation 971.1
proscriptive 761.3
prose *n.*
  trite saying 496.3
  writing 598
  prosaism 843.1
prose *v.*
  write prose 598.3
  be prosaic 843.3
prosecute
  continue 143.3; 604a.2
  pursue 622.6
  (practice 625.6)
  carry on 680.6
  conduct 692.4
  sue 969.10
  (impeach 938.4)
prosecuting attorney 968.1
prosecution
  pursuit 622.1
  lawsuit 969.1
prosecutor
  accuser 938.2
  prosecuting attorney 968.1
proselyte
  convert 144.5
  disciple 541.2
  believer 987.4
proselytism 537.3
proselytization 144.2
prosencephalon 450.2
proser 841.8
Proserpina, Proserpine world 318.1
  agriculture 371.3
  goddess 979.2; 982.4

prosing style 575.2
  boring 841.8
  dull 843.5
prosody 597.5
prosopopoeia 521.1
prospect vista 441.6
  view 448.2
  probability 472.1
  expectation 507.1
  (futurity 121.1)
  (imminence 152.1)
  foresight 510.1
  picture 556.10
  intention 620.1
  hope 858.1
in prospect
  expected 507.8
  (future 121.7)
  (imminent 152.3)
  intended 620.4
prospection
  expectation 507.1
  foresight 510.1
prospective 507.8
  (future 121.7)
  (foreseeing 510.6)
prospectively 121.9
prospector, prospecter 463.6
prospectus list 86.1
  synopsis 596.1
  schedule 611.2
  (outline 230.1)
  (program 626.3)
prosper 734.5
prosperity
  success 731.1
  weal 734.1
  (fortune 156.1)
  (good 648.2)
  (success 731.1)
  (wealth 803.1)
prosperous 512.4
  (successful 731.11)
  (wealthy 803.8)
be prosperous 734.5
prosperously 734.9
prospicience 510.1
prostate 221.5
prostitute *n.* 962.2
prostitute *v.*
  corrupt 659.9
  misuse 679.2
  debauch 961.8
prostitute *adj.* 961.10
prostitution
  perversion 659.2
  misuse 679.1
  harlotry 961.6
prostrate *v.*
  destroy 162.4
  disable 158.6
  supinate 213.7
  fell 308.5
  exhaust 688.5
  grieve 837.8
prostrate oneself
  submit 725.3
  be servile 886.3
  make obeisance 928.6

prostrate — provincialism

(idolatrize 991.6)
prostrate *adj.*
  impotent 158.8
  supine 213.9
  (low 207.7)
  (downthrown 308.9)
  sick 655.23
  exhausted 688.6
  submissive 725.5
  servile 886.4
  obeisant 928.8
  worshiping 990.15
  fall prostrate 306.6
  lie prostrate 213.5
prostration
  impotence 158.2
  destruction 162.1
  collapse 195.1
  recumbency 213.2
  (lowness 207.1)
  downthrow 308.2
  physical ~ 655.1
  nervous ~ 655.14
  exhaustion 688.3
  wretchedness 828.3
  sorrow 837.3
  servility 886.1
  obeisance 928.2
  (worship 990.1)
prosy style 575.2
  wearisome 841.8
  dull 843.5
  ordinary 849.3
prosyllogism 476.5
protagonist
  actor 599.19
  proficient 700.1
pro tanto 32.13
protasis prelude 64.2
  axiom 496.2
protean *n.*
  semiliquid 352.3
  actor 599.19
protean *adj.*
  multiform 81.2
  changeable 149.5
  actor 599.28
protect 664.6
  (chaperon 88.7)
  (care for 459.6)
  (preserve 670.3)
  (defend 717.7)
protected 664.12
  (armed 722.12)
protecting 664.12
protection
  safekeeping 664.2
  (preservation 670.1)
  (defense 717.1)
  auspices 693.2
  patronage 707.2
  (influence 175.1)
  custody 751.4
protectionist 751.5
protective *n.* 662.8
protective *adj.*
  remedial 662.25
  protecting 664.12
  (preservative 670.5)
  (defensive 717.9)
protector
  guardian 664.3

(safeguard 666.1)
  (defender 717.5)
  (guard 717.6)
  (jailer 753.1)
  (benefactor 912.1)
  regent 745.7
protectorate
  country 182.1
  authority 737.3
protectorship
  country 182.1
  guardianship 664.2
  authority 737.3
protégé
  dependent 746.3
  guest 890.7
proteide, proteid
  semiliquid 352.3
  protoplasma 357.3
proteiform
  multiform 81.2
  changeable 149.5
protein semiliquid 352.3
  protoplasm 357.3
proteinaceous 357.9
pro tempore 111.8
proteolysis 49.2
protervity 901.1
protest *n.*
  dissent 489.2
  (negation 536.1)
  affirmation 535.1
  refusal 764.1
  deprecation 766.1
  ~ of indebtedness 808.1
  under protest
  dissentingly 489.7
  unwillingly 603.6
  (compulsorily 744.4)
protest *v.* demur 485.7
  dissent 489.4
  (deny 536.2)
  affirm 535.3
  oppose 708.2
  refuse 764.2
  deprecate 766.2
  ~ a debt 808.5
  object 932.5, 7
protestant *n.* 489.3
  (sectarian 984.13)
Protestant *n.* 984.14
protestant *adj.*
  dissentient 489.5
  (sectarian 984.23)
  refusing 764.5
protestantism 489.2
Protestantism 984.4
protestation
  protest 489.2
  affirmation 535.1
protester 489.3
Proteus 149.2
prothesis 1000.3
prothonotary, proton-
  otary 553.1
protocol
  schedule 611.2
  plan 626.2
  treaty 769.2

protogenal, protogen-
  ic 153.9
proton
  electricity 158a.5
  microbe 193.4
protoplasm
  prototype 22.1
  plasm 357.3
protoplasmic
  formative 240.8
  plasmic 357.9
prototypal 20.3
prototype *n.* 22
  (paragon 650.2)
prototype *v.* 22.4
Protozoa 368.3
protozoal 368.12
protozoan *n.*
  protozoon 193.4
  protoplasm 357.3
protozoan *adj.*
  protoplasmic 357.9
  of protozoa 368.12
protozoic 368.12
protozoologist 368.2
protozoology
  zoology 368.1
  pathology 655.19
protozoon 193.4
protract time 110.6
  (delay 133.4)
  continue 143.3
  lengthen 200.9
  expatiate 573.5
protracted
  prolonged 110.10
  (slow 275.8)
  lengthened 200.12
  verbose 573.7
protraction
  delay 133.2
  lengthening 200.5
protrude 250.7
protrusion 250.1
protuberance 250.1, 2
protuberant 250.9
protuberate 250.7, 8
proud pleased 827.8
  dignified 873.18
  self-esteeming 878.6
  (vain 880.6)
  (pretentious 882.8)
  (boastful 884.7)
  (arrogant 885.8)
  be proud 878.3, 4
  (be vain 880.4)
  do proud
  make proud 878.5
  extol 931.6
  flatter 933.2
  make proud 878.5
proud flesh
  protuberance 250.2
  morbid growth 655.16
proudhearted 878.6
proudling 878.2
proudly 878.8
  (arrogantly 885.11)
prove
  ~ an estimation 85.8

eventuate 151.3
  test 463.8
  show 467.9
  demonstrate 478.2
  ~ true 494.7, 8
  indicate 550.18
  engrave 558.5
  take a proof 591.14
  experience 821.3
proved, proven
  tried 463.13
  demonstrated 478.4
  (assured 474.9)
Provençal 560.4
provender *n.*
  298.5, 6, 7
  (provisions 637.1)
provender *v.*
  victual 298.43
  provision 637.4
proverb 496.1
proverbial
  well-known 490.17
  aphoristic 496.5
proverbially 496.6
proverbs 840.11
provide
  supply 637.4
  (provision 298.43)
  (equip 634.2)
  (store 636.7)
  (prepare 673.6)
  prepare for 673.7
  give 784.10
  be provided 637.5
  (reserve 636.8)
provided *adj.* 637.6
  (equipped 634.3)
  (prepared 673.11)
provided *conj.* 8.8;
  469.8
  (conditionally 7.4)
  (supposing 514.13)
providence
  provision 637.1
  preparation 673.1
  (forethought 510.2)
  aid 707.1
  God 976.4
Providence 976.2
provident 673.10
  (foresighted 510.6)
providential
  opportune 134.7
  fortunate 734.8
provider 637.2
providing *n.* 637.1
providing *conj.* 469.8
province class 75.1
  region 181.1, 2
  the country 183.1
  sphere of work 625.3
  career 692.3
provincial
  regional 181.6
  rustic 183.3
  (uncouth 851.7;
  876.12)
  bigoted 606.7
provincialism
  partisanship 481.4
  language 563.5

provision — psychophysics

provision n.
  food 298.5
  condition 469.2
  supply 637
    (means 632.1)
    (equipment 634.1)
  preparation 673.1
  aid 707.1
  stipulation 770.1
  make provision for
    provide for 637.4; 784.10
    prepare for 673.7
provision v.
  victual 298.43
  purvey 637.4
  (equip 634.2)
provisional
  circumstantial 8.5
  transient 111.6
  substitutional 147.4
  experimental 463.12
  qualifying 469.6
  dependent 475.15
  provisory 637.7
  preparatory 673.10
  conditional 770.3
provisionally 7.4; 770.4
provisionary 475.15
provisions food 298.6
  equipment 634.1
  (sustenance 707.3)
  stores 636.1
proviso 469.2
  (conditions 770.1)
  with this proviso 469.8
provisory
  transient 111.6
  qualifying 469.6
  dependent 475.15
  provisional 637.7
  conditional 770.3
provocation
  motivation 615.2
    (cause 153.1)
  excitation 824.1
  vexation 830.2
  resentment 900.5
    (indignity 929.2)
provocative n. 615.3
provocative adj.
  tantalizing 617.5
    (inductive 615.11)
  exciting 824.12
  attractive 845.9
  desirable 865.21
provoke induce 153.7
  incite 615.7
  excite 824.2
  irritate 824.5
  vex 830.5
  aggravate 835.2
  anger 900.10
provoked 828.15
  (resentful 900.12)
provoking 830.12
provost 745.9
prow 234.3
  (ship 273.7)
prowess 861.1

prowl wander 266.14
  sneak 528.16
prowl after
  seek 461.16
  pursue 622.6
prowler 792.1
proximal 197.8
proximate v. 286.2
proximate adj.
  succeeding 63.5
  near 197.8
proximation 286.1
proximity 197.1
  (contiguity 199.1)
proximo 121.9
proxy substitute 147.2
  commission 755.1
  deputy 759.1
  by proxy 147.5; 755.6
prude prig 853.4
  fop 854.1
  vain person 880.3
prudence
  caution 864.1
    (care 459.1)
  (wisdom 498.3)
  (forethought 510.2)
  cardinal virtue 944.1
prudent wise 498.11
  cautious 864.6
  (careful 459.7)
prudery 853.2
  (bigotry 606.2)
  (fastidiousness 868.1)
  (modesty 881.1)
prudish 853.7
  (bigoted 606.7)
  (fastidious 868.4)
  (modest 881.5)
  (hyperorthodox 983a.8)
  (sanctimonious 988.11)
prune n. fruit 298.31
  trifle 643.3
prune v. cut off 38.6
  ~ plants 371.8
prunes and prisms 853.1
pruriency
  desire 865.1
  lasciviousness 961.3
prurient
  itching 380.6
  lustful 961.11
prurigo, pruritus 380.3
prussic acid 663.5
pry n.
  leverage 175.3
  lever 307.4
  inquisitive 455.2
  meddler 682.11
pry v.
  ~ open 173.10
  peer 441.13
  be curious 455.4
  (meddle 682.14)
  seek 461.16, 17
  reconnoiter 461.22
pry out
  hunt out 461.16

  discover 481a.3
prying 455.5
  (meddlesome 682.22)
psalm n.
  sacred music 415.11
  glorification 990.2
Psalm n. 998.10
psalm v. 990.10
psalmbook 998.10
psalmody 415.11
psalm singer 416.10
psalter 998.10
psalterium 191.7
psaltery 417.2
Psaltery 998.10
psammous 330.8
psephomancy 511.3
pseudo imitation 19.12
  spurious 545.13
  (approximative 17.14)
pseudologia phantastica 544.1
pseudologist, pseudologue 548.5
pseudology
  falsehood 544.1
  barbarism 563.1
pseudonym, pseudonyme, pseudonymity 565.3
pseudonymous 565.7
pseudoscope 445.1
pseudosyllogism
  syllogism 476.5
  sophism 477.2
pshaw!, psha!
  nonsense! 497.5
  pooh! 930.11
psora itch 380.3
  rash 655.17
psoriasis 655.17
psoric 380.6
psorophthalmia 443.1
psychasthenia 503.2
psychasthenic 503.15
psyche mirror 445.4
  intellect 450.1
  spirit 994.11
  (self 79.4)
  (life force 359.2)
  (mind 450.3)
psychiasis cure 662.16
  religion 984.9
psychiatrist
  psychologist 450.5
  (insanity 503.1)
  doctor 662.19
psychiatry
  psychology 450.4
  (insanity 503.1)
  ward 662.17
psychic
  intellectual 450.8
  spiritualist 994.14, 22
psychical 994.22
  (immaterial 317.6)
  (supernatural 976.14)
  (spectral 980a.4)

  psychical research, psychicism 994.2
psychicist 994.13
psychic monism, psychics 994.2
psychism
  immaterialism 317.3
  psychical research 994.2
psychist
  immaterialist 317.4
  psychicist 994.13
psychoanalysis 450.4
psychoanalyst 450.5
psycho-asthenics, psychobiochemistry, psychobiology etc. 450.4
psychognosis 994.2
psychognostic 994.22
psychographer 450.5
psychographist 994.14
psychography
  psychology 450.4
  spirit writing 994.5
psychokinesia 503.1
psycholepsy 503.2
psychological 450.8
psychological logic 451.4
psychological moment 134.4
psychological warfare 722.1
psychologist 450.4
psychologize 994.19
psychology 450.4
  (philosophy 451.4)
psychomancy
  divination 511.3
  necromancy 992.1
  spiritism 994.4
psychomantic 994.22
psychometer
  psychologist 450.5
  psychic 994.15
psychometric 994.22
psychometry
  psychology 450.4
  psychical research 994.2, 7
psychon 994.2
psychonomics 450.4
psychopath
  psychologist 450.5
  madman 504.1
psychopathic 503.15
psychopathic hospital
  asylum 503.8
  hospital 662.17
psychopathologist 450.5
psychopathology 662.16
psychopathy
  psychology 450.4
  psychosis 503.2
psychophysicist
  psychologist 450.5
  psychist 994.13
psychophysics
  psychology 450.4

psychical research
 994.3
psychophysiologist
 994.13
psychoplasm 994.2
**psychopompos, psy-
 chopomp** 88.4
psychorrhagy 994.5
psychosensory 994.22
psychosis 503.2
 (ailment 655.14)
psychosome 994.3
psychotechnology
 450.4
psychotherapeutics
 662.16
psychotherapist 450.5
psychotherapy
 psychology 450.4
 healing art 662.16
psychotic 503.12
psychrometer 339.4
psychrometry 339.3
Pteridophyta 369.6
ptisan 662.4
ptyalism 299.5
ptyalize 207.19
pub inn 189.8
 grogshop 959.13
puberty 127.2
pubes 256.3
pubescence
 adolescence 127.2
 hair 256.1, 2
pubescent
 adolescent 127.6
 hairy 256.13
public *n.*
 population 188.10
 inn 189.8
 people 372.2
 grogshop 959.13
public *adj.*
 of people 372.6
 made public 531.10
 become public 531.9
 in public 531.12
 make public 531.7
 (divulge 529.4)
publican 959.12
publication
 promulgation 531
 (production 161.6)
 (manifestation
 525.1)
 (information 527.1)
 (disclosure 529.1)
 printing 591.1
 book 503.1
 for publication 531.12
public enemy 891.2
public house inn 189.8
 grogshop 959.13
publicist
 advertiser 531.6
 journalist 593.16
 writer 595.3
 legist 968.1
publicity 531.3
 (information 527.1)
publicize 531.8
publicly 531.12

public opinion
 belief 484.3
 unanimity 488.3
public servant 911.1
public spirit 906.4
publish
 promulgate 531.7
 (manifest 525.2)
 (tell 527.7)
 (divulge 529.4)
 (say 582.6)
 (write 593.19)
 print 591.14
 ~ **the bans** 903.12
published 531.10
 (reported 532.8)
 be published 531.9
publisher
 promulgator 531.5
 (journalist 593.16)
 bookman 593.14
publishing
 publication 531.1
 printing 591.1
puce brown 433.4
 purple 437.4
pucelage, pucellage
 spinsterhood 904.1
 virginity 960.1
puck 980.3
Puck speeder 274.7
 fairy 979.9
pucka, pucker
 dense 321.8
 valid 494.14
pucker *n.*
 wrinkle 258.1
 confusion 458.4
 perplexity 475.2
 dudgeon 900.2
 in a pucker
 confused 458.12
 bewildered 475.16
 excited 824.9
 angry 900.13
pucker *v.*
 contract 195.4
 wrinkle 258.3
 ~ **the mouth** 397.5
puckery 258.4
pud 211.4
pudder 59.4
pudding food 298.12
 softness 324.3
 semiliquid 352.3
puddle pool 343a.1
 mudhole 352.5
puddler 690.5
pudge 192.7
pudgy stout 192.12
 stubby 201.6
pudicity 960.1
pueblo 189.17
puerile childlike 127.5
 senile 499.16
 (effeminate 160a.5)
 language 575.2
puerility 499.5
puerperal 168.9
puff *n.* food 298.12
 ~ **of air** 349.4
 smoke 392a.10

publicity 531.3
 boast 884.1
puff *v.* distend 194.8
 blow 349.22, 23, 24
 smoke 392a.14
 be fatigued 688.4
 boast 884.5
 (exaggerate 549.2)
 eulogize 931.6
 flatter 933.2
puff up distend 194.8
 blow up 349.24
 render vain 880.5
puffball 369.4
puffed 878.6
 (vain 880.6)
 (arrogant 885.8)
puffer 935.1
puffery 884.1
 (exaggeration
 549.1)
puffing swelling 194.1
 panting 688.7
puffy 194.10
 (hulky 192.13)
pug dog 366.6
 footprint 550.4
 pugilist 726.2
pugged 201.6
puggree, puggry
 225.26
pugh!
 nonsense! 497.5
 bah! 930.11
pugilism 720.6
 (sports 840.10)
pugilist 726.2
 (player 840.17)
pugnacious 722.13
 (quarrelsome 901.9)
pugnacity 722.6
 (irascibility 901.1)
pug-nosed
 snubbed 201.6
 deformed 243.5
puisne 127.8
puissance
 potence 157.1
 strength 159.1
puissant potent 157.8
 strong 159.10
 authoritative 737.15
puke 297.18
pukka See pucka
pulchritude 845.1
pu'chritudinous 845.8
Pulcinella 599.20
pule chirp 412.2
 weep 839.8
Pulitzer prize 733.1
pull *n.*
 pulling power 157.3
 influence 175.1
 handle 215.7
 draw 285.2
 attraction 288.1
 drink 298.4
 proof 591.3
 allurement 617.1
 effort 686.1
 alcoholic drink
 959.10

pull *v.* row 267.46
 draw 285.4
 (transfer 270.6)
 attract 288.3
 smoke 392a.14
 engrave 558.5
 take a proof 591.14
 do 680.6
 strain 686.5
pull an oar
 render a service
 644.3
 work 680.6
 co-operate 709.6
pull back
 be reluctant 603.4
 shrink 623.9
pull down
 demolish 162.4
 fell 308.5
pull foot
 depart 293.5
 flee 623.10
 pull in 751.6
pull off 680.6
pull oneself together
 834.6
pull one's leg 933.2
pull out
 aviate 267a.31
 extract 301.5
 secede 624.3
pull over 33.2
pull the strings
 influence 175.6
 control 693.5
pull through 660.15
pull together 700.4
 (concur 178.2)
 (be concordant
 714.2)
pull to pieces
 disintegrate 44.9
 destroy 162.4
 criticize 932.7
pull up cease 142.6
 aviate 267a.31
 extract 301.5
 reprove 932.8
 arraign 969.10
pull up stakes 293.4
pullet
 youngling 129.3, 7
 food 298.25
pulley 307.2
pulling *n.* 288.1
pulling *adj.* 285.6
Pullman car 272.19
pull-out 267a.24
pullulate
 be productive 168.5
 grow 194.6; 365.2
pullulation
 productiveness
 168.1
 growth 194.3
pull-up 267a.24
pulmonary 349.29
pulmonic 655.25
pulmotor
 respirator 349.20
 remedy 662.22

pulp — purchase

pulp *n.* 354.2
  (semiliquid 352.3)
pulp *v.* 354.4
  (jellify 352.6)
pulpalgia 354.1
pulpboard pulp 354.2
  paper 635.4
pulpectomy, pulpefaction 354.1
pulper, pulpifier 354.3
pulpify 354.4
pulpiness 354
  (semiliquidity 352.1)
pulpit platform 215.21
  rostrum 542.6
  clergy 996.1
  church 1000.3
pulpiteer, pulpiter 996.2
pulpitis, pulpotomy 354.1
pulpy 354.5
  (soft 324.6)
  (semiliquid 352.7)
pulsate 314.9
  (recur 138.8)
  (flutter 315.10)
  (drum 407.8)
pulsating
  periodic 138.10
  rhythmic 413.29
pulsation throb 314.2
  (rhythm 138.3)
  (flutter 315.5)
  (repeated sound 407.1)
  (drumming 407.3)
  trepidation 825.3
pulsative
  periodic 138.10
  rhythmic 413.29
pulsatory
  periodic 138.10
  palpitant 314.12
pulse *n.* throb 314.2
  vegetable 367.2
  rhythm 413.23
pulse *v.* 314.9
pulsion 276.1
pulsive
  impulsive 276.10
  propulsive 284.15
pulverable 330.9
  (brittle 328.4)
pulverization 330.2
pulverize 330.6
  (disintegrate 44.9; 49.3)
pulverizer 330.4
pulverous 330.8
pulverulence 330
  (brittleness 328.1)
pulverulent 330.8, 9
puma 366.3
pumice *n.*
  burnisher 255.3
  stone 342.4
pumice *v.* 255.4
pummel strike 276.8
  beat 972.6
pump *n.* shoe 225.27

instrument 333.6
pump *v.* distend 194.8
  question 461.15
pump up
  distend 194.8
  blow up 349.24
pumpernickel 298.11
pumpkin, punkin 298.30
pumpkin head 501.1
pumpkin-headed 499.12
pump room 662.17
pun *n.*
  assonance 17.3
  witticism 842.5
  (equivoque 520.2)
pun *v.* assonate 17.9
  joke 842.8
punch *n.* die 22.3
  energy 171.1
  perforator 262
  horse 271.4
  blow 276.3
  hammer 276.4
  drink 298.4
  pungency 392.1
  sweet drink 396.5
  graver 558.4
  vigor 574.2
  actor 599.20
  verve 682.1
  alcoholic drink 959.8
Punch *n.* 844
punch *v.*
  perforate 260.14
  strike 276.8
punch in, punch out 114.8
Punch-and-Judy show 599.8
punch bowl
  receptacle 191.11
  alcoholic drink 959.8
puncheon
  receptacle 191.11
  perforator 262
  board 635.3
puncher
  perforator 262
  cowboy 268.8
  hammer 276.4
punchinello 599.20
punch pliers 262.1
punchy 201.6
punctate, punctated 440.9
punctilio
  point of etiquette 852.2
  punctiliousness 868.1
  point of honor 939.2
punctiliosity 939.2
punctilious
  exact 494.11
  strict 739.5
  observant 772.5
  fastidious 868.4
  scrupulous 939.8

punctiliousness
  conventionality 852.2
  fastidiousness 868.1
punctual prompt 132.9
  (instantaneous 113.4)
  (timely 134.7)
  regular 138.9
  exact 494.11
  observant 772.5
  punctilious 868.4; 939.8
be punctual 132.6
punctuality
  promptness 132.3
  (regularity 138.1)
  (expedition 682.2)
  (haste 684.1)
  punctiliousness 868.1
  scrupulosity 939.2
punctually 132.13
punctuate *v.*
  ~ sentences 567.5
  emphasize 642.9
punctuate *adj.* 567.6
punctuation
  mark 550.8
  grammar 566.3
puncture *n.*
  perforation 260.1
  wound 659.4
puncture *v.* 260.14
puncturer 262
pundit, pandit
  scholar 492.1
  teacher 540.1
  lawyer 968.1
  priest 996.8
pundita 540.2
pung 272.13
pungency
  piquancy 392
  (acrimony 171.3)
  (sourness 397.1)
  odorousness 398.1
  ~ of diction 574.2
pungent painful 378.7
  piquant 392.5
  (acrid 171.10)
  (flavorful 390.4)
  (tart 397.6)
  (exciting 824.12)
  odorous 398.8
  style 574.6
  intensely felt 821.5
  wit 842.9
be pungent 392.3
render pungent 392.4
Punic Wars 722.4
punish 972.5
  (requite 718.2)
  (take revenge 919.4)
  (penalize 974.3)
punishment 972
  (revenge 919.1)
  (reward 973.1)
  (penalty 974.1)
punition 972.1
punitive
  revengeful 919.6

punishing 972.14
punk *n.* child 129.3
  bread 298.11
  tinder 388.6
punk *adj.* 649.8
punkah, punka 349.21
punkie 366.24
punkin See pumpkin
punner, punster 844
punt *n.* 273.4
punt *v.* row 267.46
  bet 621.18
punter 621.15
puny small 32.6, 10
  dwarfed 193.9
  meager 640.9
  trivial 643.11
pup *n.*
  youngling 129.4, 7
  stream 348.1
  dog 366.6
pup *v.* 161.9
pupa 129.8
pupil eyes 441.7
  student 541.1
pupilage 539.2
pupilize, pupillize 537.9
pupillary 541.9
puppet
  miniature 193.3
  dupe 547.1
  figure 554.4
  nonentity 643.6
  cat's-paw 711.2
  (servant 746.1)
  (sycophant 886.2)
  doll 840.16
puppet show
  show 599.8
  amusement 840.15
puppy
  youngling 129.4, 7
  dog 366.6
  fop 854.1
puppyism 853.3
puppy love 897.1
pup tent 223.5
pur See purr
purana 986.2
purblind
  dim-sighted 443.15
  obtuse 499.12
  bigoted 606.7
purblindness
  dim-sightedness 443.2
  prejudice 481.3
  bigotry 606.2
purchase *n.*
  leverage 175.3
  footing 215.4
  tackle 273.11
  buying 795
  (bribery 618.1)
  (acquisition 775.1)
  (expenditure 809.1)
purchase *v.*
  bribe 618.3
  buy 795.3
  (hire 788.3)
  (pay for 807.6)

1034

purchase money — put

(spend 809.3)
purchase money 147.2
purchaser user 677.4
  buyer 795.2
purdah veil 225.12
  harem 374.7
  screen 424.3
pure simple 42.5
  unmixed 42.5
  music 415.28
  genuine 494.12, 13
  guileless 543.3
  speech 576.3; 578.4
  clean 652.14
  artless 703.4
  inornate 849.4
  chaste 960.2
  (immaculate 652.14)
  (uncorrupt 944.4)
  (innocent 946.5)
  holy 987.10
pure-blooded 875.10
purebred 5.6
purée 352.3
purely
  absolutely 31.16
  to a degree 32.13
  simply 42.7
purfle 231.3
purgation
  purification 652.2
  penance 952.3
purgative n. 662.9
purgative adj.
  cleansing 652.15
  cathartic 662.25
purgatory
  affliction 735.1
  mental suffering 828.6
  penance 952.3
  abode of dead 982.1
purge
  evacuate 297.14
  purify 652.9
  (eliminate 42.3)
  shrive 952.4
purification
  cleansing 652.2
  (elimination 42.2)
  (improvement 658.1)
  sanctification 987.2
purificative 652.15
purifier 652.8
purify cleanse 652.9
  (eliminate 42.3)
  (better 658.8)
  sanctify 987.8
purism 853.1
purist
  linguistic ~ 578.2
  man of taste 850.3
  affecter 853.4
puritan prude 853.4
  (bigot 983a.6)
  (pietist 988.6)
  ascetic 955.2
Puritan 984.14
puritanical
  prudish 853.7

(hyperorthodox 983a.8)
  (sanctimonious 988.11)
  ascetic 955.3
puritanism
  asceticism 955.1
  hyperorthodoxy 983a.5
purity
  no mixture 42.1
  elegance 578.1
  immaculateness 652.1
  unornamentation 849.1
  chastity 960
  (immaculacy 652.1)
  (virtue 944.1)
  (innocence 946.1)
purl n. 959.8
purl v. edge 231.3
  ripple 348.19
  murmur 405.5
purlieu 227.2
  (nearness 197.3)
  (bounds 231.1)
purloin 791.9
purloiner 792.1
purpie 437.4
purple n. color 437.1
  robe of state 747.2
purple v. 437.3
purple adj. 437.4
purple and fine linen 377.2
purple passage, purple patch 577.1
  (ornamentation 847.1)
purplescent 437.4
purport n. 516.1
purport v. 516.5
purpose n.
  meaning 516.1
  intention 620.1
  (will 600.1)
on purpose 620.5
serve the purpose 639.5
purpose v. mean 516.5
  resolve 604.6
  intend 620.3
purposeless 621.21
  (haphazard 59.8)
  (indiscriminate 465a.3)
purposely 620.5
  (voluntarily 600.5)
purpure 437.1
purr, pur hum 405.6
  animal sound 412.2
purree 436.4
pur sang 875.10
purse n. funds 800.2
  wallet 802.2
  (bag 191.4, 5)
  wealth 803.1
purse v. 195.4
purse bearer 801
purser seaman 269.3
  provider 637.2

treasurer 801
purse race 720.5
purse strings 802.2
pursuance
  continuance 143.1
  pursuit 622.1
in pursuance of 622.11
pursuant n. 622.4
pursuant adj. 622.10
  pursuant to 620.6
pursue follow 281.3
  seek 461.16
  run after 622.6
  (be behind 235.8)
  (intend 620.3)
  (practice 625.6)
  (engage in 676.2)
  exercise 680.6
pursuer
  pursuant 622.4
  (follower 281.2)
  suitor 897.6
pursuit chase 622
  (sequence 63.1; 281.1)
  (search 461.2)
  (undertaking 676.1)
  business 625.1
in pursuit 622.10, 11
pursuit plane 273a.2
pursy 194.10
purulent 653.17
purusha 994.11
purvey victual 298.43
  provision 637.4
purveyance 637.1
purveyor 637.2
  (merchant 797.1)
purview 620.1
purwannah 760.2
pus excrement 299.2
  (offal 653.6)
  fluid 333.2
  semiliquid 352.3
  sore 655.16
Puseyism 984.5
Puseyite 984.15
push n. gang 72.3
  crowd 72.4
  crisis 134.4
  impulse 276.1
  (propulsion 284.1)
  enterprise 682.4
  clique 712.2
  attack 716.1
push v. impel 276.7
  (propel 284.10)
  try hard 675.4
  hasten 684.2
push aside
  postpone 133.4
  neglect 460.5
  put away 678.4
  spurn 930.7
push back 289.2
push down
  aviate 267a.31
  depress 308.4
push forward
  advance 282.2
  aid 707.6

push off 293.4
push on
  advance 282.2
  keep going 682.12, 26
  hasten 684.3
pushball 840.11
push bicycle 272.14
push car, pushcart 272.11, 21
pusher 273a.1
pushing
  enterprising 682.18
  meddlesome 682.22
  hasty 684.5
push-over
  weakling 160.4
  dupe 547.1
pusillanimity 862.1
pusillanimous
  cowardly 862.4
  dastardly 862.5
puss face 234.4
  cat 366.4
pussy girl 129.5
  cat 366.4
pussyfoot walk 266.16
  move warily 864.3
pustule
  protuberance 250.2
  sore 655.16
put n. fool 501.1
  game 840.12
  rustic 876.5
put v. place 184.10
  impel 276.7
  throw 284.12
  hasten off 293.5
  phrase 566.3
  invest 787.5
put about
  turn ship 267.24
  (turn back 283.6)
  (turn 311.4)
  bruit about 531.7
put a flea in one's ear 527.9
put a good face on
  deceive 545.7
  pretext 619.2
  endure 826.6
  be cheerful 836.4
  be hopeful 858.7
  act proudly 878.3
  set off 882.6
  extenuate 937.8
put an end to
  terminate 67.7
  stop 142.7
  destroy 162.4
  (abrogate 756.3)
  kill 361.10
  hinder 706.5
put aside
  postpone 133.4
  remove 185.2
  disregard 458.5
  neglect 460.5
  put away 678.4
put away eat 298.44
  set aside 678.4
  divorce 905.4

putation — quackery 1036

put back
  turn back 283.6
  impair 659.8
  restore 660.8
put by 636.8
put down
  attribute 155.3
  destroy 162.4
  place 184.10
  record 551.8
  conquer 731.9
  subjugate 749.5
  pay down 807.6
  degrade 874.7
  depreciate 934.3
put forth
  grow 194.6; 365.2
  propound 514.7
  tell 527.7
  publish 531.7
  allege 535.3
  utter 582.6
  aid 707.6
  offer 763.2
  display 882.7
put in intrude 228.10
  sail for 267.26
  land 292.9
  enter 294.6
  insert 300.5
put in mind
  resemble 17.7
  remind 505.15
put in one's oar
  intrude 228.10
  meddle 682.14
put in possession
  527.7
put in practice
  use 677.5
  do 680.5, 6
  perform 729.2
put into one's head
  527.7
put off postpone 133.4
  undress 226.4
  navigate 267.16, 27
  (embark 293.6)
  avoid 623.6
put on don 225.43
  feign 544.6
  deceive 545.7
  stage 599.25
  affect 853.5
  be ostentatious 882.6
put on airs
  act proudly 878.3
  be ostentatious 882.6
put one in his place
  930.7
put one's cards on the table
  confess 529.5
  be honorable 939.6
put one's hand to the plow, put one's shoulder to the wheel
  undertake 676.2
  set to work 686.7
put on one's thinking cap 451.27

put on side
  be proud 878.3
  be ostentatious 882.6
put on the grill 461.15
put out destroy 162.4
  put externally 220.5
  extinguish 385.5
  confuse 458.9
  perplex 475.8
  disappoint 509.2
  embarrass 704.7
  displease 830.3
  dissatisfy 832.4
  blight hopes 859.6
  humiliate 879.3
put out of one's head
  disregard 458.5
  forget 506.6
put out of the way
  361.10
put the cart before the horse
  invert 218.4
  be foolish 499.9
  be unskillful 699.7
put to bed
  lodge 184.12
  print 591.14
put to death
  kill 361.10
  execute 972.8
put together join 43.5
  (mix 41.6)
  combine 48.3
  assemble 72.11
  make 161.8
put to it 475.8
put to rights
  arrange 60.6
  right 922.3
put to sea 267.15
  (embark 293.6)
put to shame
  disgrace 874.6
  humiliate 879.3
put to silence
  silence 403
  (muzzle 581.5)
  confute 479.2
put to sleep 376.4
put to the question
  461.15
put to use 677.5
put up build 161.8
  store up 636.7
put up to teach 537.9
  instigate 615.7
put up with
  substitute 147.3
  brook 826.6
  (be content 831.3)
putation 514.1
putative
  attributable 155.4
  believed 484.14
  supposititious 514.9
put-off delay 133.2
  pretext 619.1
put-on
  make-believe 544.2
  affectation 853.1
put-out

nonplused 475.16
  disappointed 509.4
putrefacient 657.3
putrefaction
  filthiness 653.4
  decay 659.2
putrefactive
  foul 653.17
  septic 657.3
  corrupt 659.13
putrefy, putresce
  659.7
  (become putrid 653.14)
putrescence
  filthiness 653.4
  decay 659.2
putrid bad 649.8
  foul 653.17
  (nasty 395.7)
  (fetid 401.4)
  decayed 659.13
putridity
  filthiness 653.4
  (fetor 401.1)
  decay 659.2
puttee, putty, puttie 225.28
putter See potter
putting green 367.11
putty cement 45.6
  softness 324.3
put-up 611.5
puzzle *n*.
  perplexity 475.2
  enigma 533.2
  (unintelligibility 519.2)
puzzle *v*. 475.6, 8
  (mystify 533.4)
puzzle out 481a.4
puzzleheaded 499.12
puzzlement 475.2
puzzlepated 499.12
puzzling
  perplexing 475.12
  enigmatic 533.6
  (unintelligible 519.6)
pye-dog 366.6
pyemia, pyaemia 655.2
pygmy, pigmy *n*. 193.5
Pygmy, Pigmy *n*. 431.4
pygmy, pigmy *adj*. 193.9
pyjama See **pajama**
pylon tower 206.3
  airdrome 267a.28
pyorrhea, pyorrhoea 655.5
pyramid
  accumulation 72.8
  tower 206.3
  angle 244.2
  cone 249.2
  monument 363.15
  bets 621.3
pyramidal
  angular 244.5
  conical 249.9
pyramidion 244.2
pyramids 840.11

pyre cremation 363.2
  death fire 382.8
pyrethrum yellow 436.1
pyretic 382.19
pyrexia 655.4
  (flush 382.7)
pyriform 245.17
pyrite 635.6
pyrogenic, pyrognostic 382.20
pyrognostics 382.12
pyrolater 382.11; 991.5
pyrolatry 382.11; 991.1
pyrological 382.20
pyrology 382.12
pyromancy 511.3
pyromania 384.5
pyromaniac 384.6
pyrometer
  aviation 267a.29
  heat 389.1
pyrophobia 860.4
pyrosis 655.13
pyrotechnical 382.20
pyrotechnics
  fireworks 382.9
  pyrology 382.12
pyroxylin, pyroxyline 727.13
Pyrrhonic
  philosophical 451.38
  skeptical 485.10
  nullifidian 989.8
Pyrrhonism
  philosophy 451.6, 18
  questioning 461.9
  skepticism 485.2
  irreligion 989.3
Pyrrhonist 989.4
Pyrrhonize 451.34
Pythagorean 953.3
Pythagoreanism 451.6
Pythagoric 451.38
Pythagorism 953.2
Pythagorize 451.34
Pythia, Pythian 513.2
python
  serpent 366.19
  prophet 513.2
Python 83.7
pythonic 511.11
pythonism 511.2
pyx, pix case 191.8
  reagent 463.5
  ciborium 998.8

Q

Q.E.D. 478.7
quack *n*.
  impostor 548.3
  (sciolist 493.2)
  medicaster 662.19
quack *v*. 412.2
quack *adj*. 491.13
quackery
  false pretense 544.7
  (sophistry 477.1)
  (pedantry 491.4)
  affectation 853.1

quackish — queen

quackish 491.13
quacksalver
　impostor 548.3
　medicaster 662.19
quad square 189.19
　yard 232.1
　horse 271.3
　quadraplane 273a.1
　quadrat 591.9
Quadragesima 956.2
quadragesimal 956.4
quadrangle
　square 95.1
　plaza 189.19
　yard 232.1
　rectangle 244.2
quadrangular
　square 95.4
　rectangular 244.5
quadrant n.
　rectangle 244.2
　measure 244.3;
　　466.3, 4
　semicircle 247.5
　airplane 273a.10
quadrant adj. 244.5
quadrat 591.9
quadrate n. 244.2
quadrate v. agree 23.7
　square 95.3
quadrate adj. 244.5
quadratic 95.4
quadrature 244.2
quadrennial 138.5
quadric 95.4
quadricycle 272.14
quadrifid
　quaternary 95.4
　quadrisected 97.4
quadrifoliate 97.4
quadriform 95.4
quadrifurcate 97.4
quadrigeminal
　quadruplicate 96.3
　quadrisected 97.4
quadrilateral n.
　square 95.1
　rectangle 244.2
quadrilateral adj.
　square 95.4
　four-sided 236.7
　rectangular 244.5
quadrille
　square dance 840.7
　game 840.12
quadrillion 98.13;
　102.5
quadrilogy, quadri-
　nomial n. 95.1
quadrinomial adj. 95.4
quadripartite 97.4
quadripartition 97.1
quadripinnate, quad-
　riplanar 97.4
quadrisection 97
quadriserial 97.4
quadrivalent 95.4
quadrivial 97.4
quadroon 41.5
quadrumanal 97.4
quadruped 366.1
quadruplane 273a.1

quadruple v. 96.2
quadruple adj. 96.3
quadruple adv. 96.4
quadruplet 95.2
quadruplex v. 96.2
quadruplex adj. 96.3
quadruplicate v. 96.2
quadruplicate adj. 96.3
quadruplication 96
quaere 461.10
quaestor, questor 801
quaff drink 298.47
　tipple 959.15
quaggy 345.3
quagmire mire 345.1
　predicament 704.2
quail n. 298.26
quail v. shrink 623.9
　be afraid 860.8
　be cowardly 862.3
quaint odd 83.10
　trim 845.11
quake n.
　earthquake 173.2
　shake 315.4
quake v. shake 315.9
　be cold 383.7
　~ with excitement
　　824.7
Quaker 984.14
Quaker-drab,
　Quaker-gray 432.4
Quaker gun 158.3
Quakerish 853.7
quaking 825.3
qualification
　change 140.1
　modification 469
　training 537.2
　talent 698.2
　(ability 157.2)
　condition 770.1
　discount 813.1
　extenuation 937.3
qualificatory
　modificatory 469.6
　conditional 770.3
qualified 698.12
　(able 157.9)
qualify
　quantify 25.5
　change 140.6
　limit 233.2
　modify 469.3
　train 537.10
　prepare 673.6
quality nature 5.3
　particularity 79.2
　earmark 550.6
　disposition 820.1
　nobility 875.1
qualm n. doubt 485.2
　scruple 603.2 ; 939.2
　nausea 655.13
　apprehension 860.2
　repugnance 867.2
　have qualms 860.8
qualm v. 485.7
qualmish
　doubtful 485.10
　sick 655.23
qualmishness

suspiciousness 487.2
　nausea 655.13
qualm-sick, qualmy
　655.23
quandary 475.2
　(dilemma 704.4)
quantify 25.5
　(measure 466.10)
quantitative 25.6
quantity amount 25.2
　(number 84.1)
　(size 192.1)
　(measurement
　　466.1)
　greatness 31.3
　(accumulation 72.6)
　(store 636.1)
　(plenty 639.2)
quantum
　quantity 25.1
　portion 786.2
quarantine
　stop-off 266.10
　safeguard 666.1
　confinement 751.2
quarantine flag 668.3
quarrel n.
　dispute 713.3
　(argument 476.2)
　(contest 720.2)
　(enmity 889.1)
　(litigation 969.1)
　arrow 727.6
quarrel v. 713.7
　(argue 476.11)
　(contend 720.8)
quarreling, quarrel-
　ling 720.1
quarrelsome 901.9
　(discordant 713.9)
　(litigious 969.13)
quarrelsomeness 901.1
　(contentiousness
　　722.6)
quarry game 620.2
　fund 636.2
quarrystone 342.4
quart fourth 97.2
　measure 466.3
quarter n. fourth 97.2
　semester 108.1
　region 181.1
　side 236.7
　direction 278.3
　~ and tierce 716.3
　lenity 740.1
　money 800.8
　mercy 914.1
at close quarters
　197.11
come to close quar-
　ters approach 286.2
　fight 720.8
give quarter
　be lenient 740.2
　relent 914.3
give no quarter
　kill 361.10
　be pitiless 914a.2
　(be severe 739.4)
　revenge 919.4
quarter v.

quadrisect 97.3
　lodge 184.12
quarter-cut, quar-
　tered 97.4
quarter evil 655.18
quartering 97.1
quarterly 593.6
quartermaster
　provider 637.2
　officer 745.11, 12
quartern 97.2
quarters 189.1, 12, 15
quarterstaff 727.7
quartet, quartette
　four 95.2
　part music 415.12
　(choir 416.12)
quartic, quartile 95.4
quarto 593.8
quartz hardness 323.3
　stone 342.4
　transparency 425.2
quash destroy 162.4
　conquer 731.9
　subdue 749.5
　annul 756.3
quashee, quashie 431.4
quasi
　approximative 17.14
　as if 17.17
　imitation 19.12
　supposedly 514.12
　spurious 545.13
　so-called 565.7
quassation 315.3
quassative 315.13
quassia 395.3
quaternary n. 95.2
quaternary adj. 95.4
quaternion 95.2
quaternity 95.1
quatrain 597.7
quatre 95.2
quatrefoil
　quaternity 95.1
　ornament 847.4
quattrocento 554.9
quaver n. shake 315.4
　tremolo 407.2
　note 413.6
　trepidation 825.3
quaver v. vary 149.4
　tremolo 407.7
　(resonate 408.7)
　warble 416.20
　voice 583.2
　~ with excitement
　　824.7
　shake 315.9
　(be afraid 860.9)
quavering 825.3
quay, key 666.4
quean jade 949.4
　strumpet 962.2
queasiness 867.2
queasy sick 655.23
　displeased 828.14
　(disliking 867.7)
　fastidious 868.4
Quechuan 560.4
queen
　hermaphrodite 83.5

queen bee — quill

queen *(continued)*
  empress 745.6
  playing card 840.13
  good woman 948.2
queen bee 366.24
queencraft 693.3
queenly 737.16
  (noble 875.10)
Queen of Heaven
  977.3
queen of night 318.5
Queen's Bench 752.1
queen's English 560.3
queer *n.* 83.5
queer *adj.* odd 83.10
  hermaphrodite 83.12
  eccentric 503.17
  spurious 545.13
  counterfeit 800.9
queer fish oddity 83.4
  eccentric 504.3
queerly 31.21
queerness 503.6
Queer Street 804.1
quell destroy 162.4
  moderate 174.5
  quiet 265.6
  conquer 731.9
  subdue 749.5
quench destroy 162.4
  extinguish 385.5
  (darken 421.6)
  dispirit 616.3
  satisfy 829.4
quenchless 865.20
querier
  inquisitive 455.2
  inquirer 461.12
querimonious 839.13
querist
  inquisitive 455.2
  inquirer 461.12
quern, quernstone
  330.4
querulosity 901.1
querulous *n.* 901.7
querulous *adj.*
  complaining 839.13
  fastidious 868.4
query *n.* 461.10
query *v.* 461.14, 15
quest *n.* 461.2
  (pursuit 622.1)
  in quest of 461.24
  (in pursuit 622.10)
quest *v.* 461.16
question *n.*
  inquiry 461.10
  (topic 454.1)
  (subject of dispute
  713.5)
  enigma 533.2
  beyond question
  474.16
  in question
    on foot 151.5
    at issue 461.26
    (under considera-
    tion 454.3)
  unsafe 665.7
  out of the question
    impracticable 471.7

(hopeless 859.7)
  dissent 489.5
  rejected 610.3
  refused 764.6
  undue 925.9
without question
  474.12
question *v.*
  inquire 461.14, 15
  be uncertain 475.6
  doubt 485.6
questionable
  uncertain 475.9
  (doubtful 461.25)
  illogical 477.10
  unbelievable 485.11
  dishonest 940.8
questionary 461.10
questioner
  inquisitive 455.2
  inquirer 461.12
  (interlocutor 588.5)
  learner 541.1
question extraordi-
  naire 461.9
questioning *n.* 461.9
  (curiosity 455.1)
questioning *adj.* 461.24
questionist
  inquirer 461.12
  student 541.1, 4
questionless *adj.*
  indubious 474.12
  believing 484.12
questionless *adv.*
  474.16
question mark *n.*
  question 461.11
  punctuation 550.8
question-mark *v.*
  461.15
questionnaire 461.10
question stop 461.11
questman 996.5
questor See quaestor
queue afterpart 65.2
  series 69.2
  pendant 214.2
  tail 235.6
  hair 256.3
  waiting line 599.23
quibble *n.* cavil 477.3
  (circumlocution
  573.3)
  (evasion 623.1)
  ambiguity 520.2
  wordplay 842.5
quibble *v.* cavil 477.8
  (prevaricate 544.5)
  (be circumlocutory
  573.5)
  (evade 623.6)
  object 489.4
  find fault 932.7
quibbler
  caviler 477.6
  dissembler 548.1
quibbling *n.* 477.4
quibbling *adj.* 477.11
quiblet 477.3
quick *n.* 822.3
  to the quick

physically 375.8
  mentally 822.8
quick *adj.* brief 111.7
  instantaneous 113.4
  brisk 171.9
  fast 274.13
  living 359.10
  sagacious 498.10
  ready 682.17
  (prompt 132.9)
  skillful 698.11
  intensely felt 821.5
  impulsive 825.11
  hot-tempered 901.7
quick *adv.* 274.14
quicken
  strengthen 159.8
  operate 170.2
  stimulate 171.7
  inflame 173.8
  accelerate 274.10
  vivify 359.7, 8
  hasten 684.2
  refresh 689.2
  aid 707.6
  rouse feeling 824.2
quick-lunch 298.42
quickly
  promptly 132.14
  swiftly 274.14
  (hastily 684.7)
quickmarch 684.8
quickness
  activity 171.2
  velocity 274.1
  alertness 682.2
  (promptitude 132.3)
  (skill 698.1)
quicksand mire 345.1
  hidden danger 667.1
quicksandy 345.3
quicksilver *n.*
  changeableness
  149.2
  energy 171.5
  speed 274.6
quicksilver *adj.* 264.8
quick-witted
  sagacious 498.10
  witty 842.9
quid *n.* essence 5.2
  cud 298.2
  tobacco 392a.7
  money 800.8
quid *v.* 392a.14
quidam 372.3
quiddit 477.3
quiddity essence 5.2
  quibble 477.3, 4
  witticism 842.4
quidnunc
  inquisitive 455.2
  (inquirer 461.12)
  newsmonger 532.5
quid pro quo
  reciprocation 12.2
  compensation 30.2
  substitute 147.2
  interchange 148.1
  (barter 794.1)
  co-operation 709.1
  retaliation 718.1

witty reply 842.4
  reward 973.1
quiesce 403.4
quiescence
  stillness 265
  (permanence 141.1)
  (cessation 142.1)
  (stability 150.1)
  (inertness 172.1)
  (inaction 681.1;
  683.1)
  (repose 687.1)
  (peace 721.1)
  silence 403.1
  latency 526.1
quiescent still 265.7
  (immovable 150.5)
  (inert 172.3)
  (inactive 681.3;
  683.12)
  (reposing 687.6)
  silent 403.7
  latent 526.6
be quiescent 265.5
  (stop 142.6)
  (not do 681.2)
  (be inactive 683.8)
  (repose 687.3)
quiet *n.*
  quiescence 265.1
  (repose 687.1)
  silence 403.1
  peace of mind 826.2
quiet *v.*
  moderate 174.5
  still 265.6
  silence 403.4, 5
  muffle 408a.4
  dispirit 616.3
quiet *adj.*
  equable 174.6
  quiescent 265.7
  silent 403.6
  (faint 405.9)
  inexcitable 826.9
keep quiet
  be quiescent 265.5
  be silent 403.3
  silence 403.9
quietism
  mental calmness
  826.2
  content 831.1
  ism 984.4
quietist
  contented person
  831.2
  sectary 984.14
quietly silently 403.8
  modestly 881.7
quietsome 403.6
quietude
  quiescence 265.1
  silence 403.1
  mental calmness
  826.2
quietus end-all 67.4
  (deathblow 361.6)
  death 360.1
  defeat 732.3
  acquittance 970.1
quill *n.* point 253.2

1038

quill — racket

feather 256.8
pen 590.10
quill v. 258.3
quill driver 590.11
quill driving 590.1
quillet 477.3
quill pig 366.17
quilt n. 223.9
quilt v. 440.4
quin-, quino- 98.15
quinary 98.15
quince 436.3
quincuncial 98.15
quincunx 98.1
quindecennial, quindecim, quindecima, quindene 98.7
quinine, quinin
 nine 98.5
 throw of dice 621.9
quino- See quinquinquefid 99.3
quinquennial 138.5
quinquennium 108.1
quinquepartite 99.3
quinquesect 99.2
quinquesection 99.1
quinsy 655.9
quint five 98.1
 throw of dice 621.9
quintain target 620.2
 game 840.11
quintal 319.4
quinteroon See quintroon
quintessence
 essence 5.2
 superexcellence 648.3
 perfection 650.1
quintet, quintette
 five 98.1
 part music 415.12
quintillion 98.13
quintroon, quinteroon 41.5
quintuple v. 98.14
quintuple adj. 98.15
quintuplet 98.1
quintuplicate v. 98.14
quintuplicate adj. 98.15
quinze 840.12
quip
 eccentricity 503.6
 caprice 608.1
 witticism 842.4
 gibe 930.3
quire choir 416.12
 stationery 590.10
 paper 635.4
 church section 1000.3
quire See choir
quirk quibble 477.3
 prejudice 481.3
 eccentricity 503.6
 caprice 608.1
 witticism 842.4
quirt 975.1
quisby 83.10
quit v. part 44.11

cease 142.6
 leave 293.4
 abandon 624.3
 pay 807.7
 requite 973.3
quit adj.
 quit of 776.6
quitclaim
 transference 270.3
 release 750.1
quite greatly 31.15
 utterly 52.14
 not quite 32.15
quits n.
 equivalence 27.2
 quittance 952.1
quits adj. 27.9
 get quits with 807.7
quittance
 cessation 142.1
 departure 293.1
 abandonment 624.1
 acquittance 771.4
 payment 807.1
 atonement 952.1
 acquittal 970.1
 recompense 973.1
quitter 623.4
quiver n. case 191.8
 agitation 315.4, 5
 tremolo 407.2
 trepidation 825.3
quiver v. vary 149.4
 flutter 315.10
 (oscillate 314.8)
 be cold 383.7
 tremolo 407.7
 ~ with emotion 822.4
 ~ with excitement 824.7
 ~ with rage 900.8
qui vive
 on the qui vive
 attentive 457.9
 vigilant 459.8
 alert 682.17
 excited 824.9
Quixote 515.7
quixotic
 visionary 515.12
 rash 863.7
quixotism
 idealization 515.2
 rashness 863.1
quixotize 515.8
quiz n.
 inquisitive 455.2
 examination 461.3, 9
 inquirer 461.12
 joke 842.4, 7
 ridicule 856.1
 laughingstock 857.1
quiz v. 461.15
quizzer 461.12
quizzical curious 455.5
 ridiculous 855.5
 derisive 856.7
quizzify 461.15
quizzing glass 445.3
quizzish, quizzy 455.5
quoad hoc 9.10

quod 752.1
quod erat demonstrandum 478.7
quodlibet
 question 461.10
 quibble 477.3
 point of joke 842.4
quoil See coil
quoin angle 244.2
 printing 591.5
quoit 284.5
quoits 840.11
quondam 122.10
quorum 696.2
quota quantity 25.2
 number 84.2
 share 786.2
 contingent 807.2
quotation
 imitation 19.1
 example 82.2
 authority 467.4
 price 812.1
quotation mark 550.8
 (punctuation 567.3)
quote n. 550.8
quote v.
 exemplify 82.6
 adduce 467.10
quotient 84.2
quotiety
 quantity 25.2
 frequency 136.1
quotum quantity 25.2
 number 84.2

R

Ra, Re sun god 318.4
 deity 979.5
raband See roband
rabat, rabato 225.33
rabbet 43.6
rabbi 996.6
rabbinism 984.7
rabbinist 984.17
rabbit
 productiveness 168.3
 pelt 223.12
 food 298.26
 hare 366.17
 coward 862.2
rabbit-foot, rabbit's-foot 993.2
rabbitskin 223.12
rabble crowd 72.4
 masses 876.1
Rabelaisian 856.7
rabid maniac 503.13
 impassioned 821.6
 overwrought 824.10
 eager 865.17
 infuriated 900.13
rabies 503.1
raccoon, racoon 366.17
race n. tribe 11.4
 (extraction 166.4)
 (nationality 188.9)
 kind 75.2
 course 264.3
 velocity 274.3, 4

stream 348.1, 2
 channel 350.1
 human ~ 372.1
 pungency 392.1
 chase 622.2
 business career 625.3
 career 692.3
 contest 720.5
 sport 840.11
 run a race
 speed 274.9
 work 680.6
 conduct oneself 692.5
 compete 720.9
race v. speed 274.9
 compete 720.9
racecourse arena 728.1
 play ground 840.14
race horse 274.6
racer
 automobilist 268.10
 race horse 271.8
 automobile 272.15
 speeder 274.5
rachial, rachidial 235.12
rachis 235.4
rachitic 655.25
rachitis, rhachitis 655.5
racial tribal 11.8
 (native 188.11)
 classificational 75.6
 ancestral 166.10
racing 686.2
rack n. case 191.8
 frame 215.8
 slow motion 275.2
 clouds 353.5
 bodily pain 378.2
 mental pain 828.6
 punishment 972.2
 torturer 975.3
on the rack
 physical pain 378.6
 expectant 507.7
 mental pain 828.13
rack v. pain 378.4
 maltreat 649.7
 refine 652.10
 torture 830.6
 punish 972.5
rack the brains
 think hard 451.28
 try to recall 505.14
rackabones
 thin person 203.6
 horse 271.7
 wreck 659.5
racker 271.3
racket n. turmoil 59.4
 agitation 315.1
 noise 404.2
 (discord 414.2)
 clatter 407.5
 business 625.1
 game 840.11
racket, racquet n.
 elastic 325.2
 toy 840.16

racket — rake 1040

racket v. 404.6
rackety 404.9
racking 378.7; 830.15
rack rent, rackrent 810.2
raconteur 594.4
racoon See **raccoon**
racquet See **racket**
racy pungent 392.5
  (acrid 171.10)
  style 574.6
  lively 821.5
raddle 219.8
radial 291.3
radiance light 420.1
  gorgeousness 845.2
  illustriousness 873.2
radiant n. 312.5
radiant adj.
  diverging 291.3
  luminous 420.22
  beautiful 845.13
  illustrious 873.17
radiant energy 420.1
radiate v.
  disperse 73.3
  diverge 291.2
  shine 420.17
radiate, radiated adj. 242.4
radiation
  symmetry 242.1
  divergence 291.1
  illumination 420.1, 14
  spiritual ~ 980a.3
radiator
  automobile 272.16
  heater 386.1
radical n. root 153.3
  reformer 658.5
  (nonconformist 83.4)
Radical n. 712.6
radical adj.
  intrinsic 5.6
  thorough 52.10
  numeral 84.7
  revolutionary 146.5; 742.7
  original 153.9
  basal 211.5
  important 642.14
radicalism 658.3
radically 31.16
radicated
  herbal 367.14
  inveterate 613.12
radication, radicle 153.3
radiculose 367.14
radio n.
  aviation 267a.29
  radiogram 532a.3
  wireless 532a.5
  (electricity 158a.6)
radio v. 532a.8
radioactive, radio-active
  energetic 171.9
  calefactive 384.22
radioactivity 171.2

radiobroadcast 532a.9
radiobroadcaster, radiobserver 532a.6
radiogram
  skiagram 422.4
  telegram 532a.3
  picture 556.12
radiograph 532a.8
radiography 556.4
radiolarian n. 193.4
radiolarian adj. 368.12
radiological 420.24
radiology 420.16
radiometer
  photics 420.16
  optics 445.1
radiophone
  sound device 418.6
  radio 532a.5
radiophonic 532a.10
radiophony
  acoustics 402.5
  telephony 532a.1
  (electricity 158a.1)
radio receiver 532a.5
radioscopy 420.16
radiotelegram 532a.3
radiotelegraph n. 532a.5
radiotelegraph v. 532a.8
radiotelegraphic 532a.10
radiotelegraphy 532a.1
radiotelephone 532a.5
radiotelephonic 532a.10
radiotelephony 532a.1
radiotherapy
  photics 420.16
  healing art 662.16
radio transmitter 532a.5
radiotrician
  electrician 158a.10
  radio 532a.6
radish
  vegetable 298.30
  condiment 393.1
radium cloth 219.5
  cauterant 384.11
radius length 200.4
  diameter 202.3
  circle 247.2
radius rod 272.16
radix number 84.2
  root 153.3
R.A.F. 726.9
raff rubbish 645.4
  riffraff 876.2
raffle n. 621.10
raffle v. 621.17
raft n. quantities 31.3
  float 273.5
raft v. 270.8
rafter 215.12
rag n. modicum 32.2
  cloth 219.5
  garment 225.3
  sail 273.13
  ragtime 413.22; 415.6

  curtain 599.15
rag v.
  ~ out, ~ up 225.43
  syncopate 416.18
  banter 856.4
  chide 932.8
ragabash, ragabrash 876.1, 9
ragamuffin 876.9
rag doll 840.16
rage n. violence 173.1
  delirium 503.3
  passion 825.4
  fashion 852.1
  anger 900.3
all the rage 852.7
in a rage 900.13
rage v.
  be violent 173.7
  blow 349.22
  rave 503.9; 825.7
  (become excited 824.6)
  bluster 887.3
  storm angrily 900.8
ragged rough 256.12
  worn 659.12
ragging 932.3
raging
  turbulent 173.12
  (stormy 349.26)
  rabid 503.13
  frenzied 824.10
  angry 900.13
ragout 298.17
ragpicker 876.9
rags remains 40.1
  clothes 225.1
  tatters 225.5
  rubbish 645.4
  paper money 800.6
in rags 804.7
ragtag 876.1
ragtime tempo 413.22
  music 415.6, 7
  (dance 840.7)
ragtimer 416.1
raid n. attack 716.1
  (campaign 722.4)
  pillage 791.2
raid v. 716.5
rail n. thinness 203.5
  fence 232.2
  railroader 268.12
  railway 627.5
by rail 270.12
rail v.
  rail at 932.8
  (maledict 908.4)
rail in
  circumscribe 229.2
  confine 751.8
railing 232.2
raillery 856.1
  (scoffing 930.2)
railroad n. 627.2
railroad v. ride 266.18
  speed 274.9
  hasten 684.2
railroader 268.12
  (workman 690.10)
railway 627.5

  (train 272.18)
raiment 225.1, 3
rain n. 348.11
rain v. shower 348.25
  be abundant 639.4
rainbow
  variegation 440.2
  omen 512.2
raincoat 225.17
rainfall 348.11
rain gauge 348.12
rainless 340.8
rain or shine
  without fail 474.16
  come what may 601.15
  resolutely 604.9
  perseveringly 604a.4
rainproof 340.11
rainspout rain 348.11
  whirlwind 349.13
rainstorm 348.11
rain water water 337.1
  rain 348.11
rainy 348.27
  (moist 339.7)
  (stormy 349.26)
rainy day 735.4
for a rainy day 510.7
raise n. 35.1
raise v. increase 35.3
  produce 161.8
  erect 212.7
  boss 250.8
  elevate 307.5
  (heighten 206.12)
  leaven 320.6
  grow 367.12
  breed 370.5
  cultivate 371.8
  rouse feeling 824.2
  exalt 873.13
raise a dust
  be violent 173.7
  bestir oneself 682.12
  quarrel 713.7
raise a hue and cry
  proclaim 531.7
  censure 932.7
raise Cain, raise the roof
  be violent 173.7
  be noisy 404.6
  rage 825.7
  vent anger 900.8
raise money 788.2
raise the dead 267.15
raise the wind 788.2
raise up erect 212.7
  rouse feeling 824.2
raised 250.10
raiser 371.2
  (producer 164.1)
raisin fruit 298.31
  purple 437.1
raising 307.1
raison d'être 620.2
raja, rajah 745.4
Rajasthani 560.4
Rajput 726.3
rake n. thinness 203.5
  pull 285.2

cleaner 652.7
reprobate 949.1
libertine 962.1
rake v. enfilade 200.11
　pull 285.4
　~ out 301.5
　cultivate 371.8
　search 461.16
　clean 652.11
　debauch 954.3
　rake over the coals 932.8
rake up
　assemble 72.11
　acquire 775.6
　rouse feeling 824.2
rakehell n.
　reprobate 949.1
　libertine 962.1
rakehell, rakehell-ish adj. 961.10
rake-off gain 35.2
　commission 786.2
raker 215.2
rakery 961.2
raking 932.3
rakish 961.10
　(dissipated 954.5)
rallentando 415.15, 31
rally n. 722.3
rally v. arrange 60.6
　improve 658.6
　recover 660.15
　recuperate 689.3
　call to arms 722.10
　banter 856.4
　encourage 861.7
　rally round
　take order 58.5
　side with 709.5
rallying cry call 550.16
　battle cry 722.1
rallying point 74.2
ram n. stopper 263.1
　hammer 276.4
　sheep 366.8
　male animal 373.6
　warship 726.11
　club 727.7
Ram n. 318.6
ram v.
　ram down 321.7
　ram in 300.5
Rama 979.4
Ramadan, Ramazan
　anniversary 138.7
　fast 956.2
ramage 367.4
ramble n. 266.4, 8
ramble v.
　wander 266.14
　deviate 279.5
　~ in delirium 503.9
　digress 573.5
　be loquacious 584.4
rambler 268.2
rambling
　irregular 139.2
　inconstant 149.6
　deviative 279.8
　preoccupied 458.11
　delirious 503.14

digressive 573.7
rambunctious 173.12
ramificate 291.2
ramification
　member 51.4
　bifurcation 91.2
　descendant 167.4
　arborescence 242.2
　divergence 291.1
ramiform 242.6
ramify bifurcate 91.5
　(angle 244.4)
　diverge 291.2
Ramillie, Ramilie 256.4
rammer stopper 263.1
　hammer 276.4
ramose 242.6
ramp n. incline 217.2
　fraud 545.3
　(swindle 791.5)
ramp v. climb 305.5
　caper 309.5
　steal 791.9
　swindle 791.12
　frolic 840.21
rampage 173.7
rampageous, rampagious 173.12
rampant
　prevalent 78.10
　turbulent 173.12
　vertical 212.8
　elevated 307.8
　abounding 639.7
　overwrought 824.11
　(vehement 825.10)
　licentious 961.10
rampart fence 232.2
　obstacle 706.2
　fortification 717.3
ramrod stopper 263.1
　hammer 276.4
ramroddy 323.5
ramshackle 659.12
Ran 192.8
rana 745.4
ranch, ranche,
rancheria n. 371.4
　(messuage 189.12)
ranch v. 371.8
rancho house 189.4
　village 189.17
　farm 371.4
rancid foul 653.17
　(nasty 395.7)
　(malodorous 401.4)
　putrefied 659.13
rancor, rancour
　enmity 889.1
　resentment 900.1
　(revengefulness 919.2)
　ill-humor 901.1
　malignity 907.1
rancorous
　resentful 900.12
　(revengeful 919.6)
　malevolent 907.6
randan turmoil 59.4
　boat 273.4
　spree 840.3

drinking bout 959.3
randem 272.9
random n. 156.1
　at random
　irregularly 59.12
　(by chance 156.13)
　uncertainly 475.17
random adj.
　disorderly 59.8
　(chance 156.12)
　uncertain 475.9
randy spree 840.3
　drinking bout 959.3
ranee See **rani**
range n. degree 26.1
　series 69.2
　rank 71.1
　class 75.1
　extent 180.1
　region 181.1
　size 192.1
　distance 196.1
　mountains 206.2
　direction 278.3
　cookstove 386.1
　music 413.15
　earshot 418.4
　~ of vision 441.6
　scope 748.2
　close range 197.2
　long range 196.2
　out of range
　unhearable 419.9
　beyond 196.8
　within range
　contingent 177.4
　near 197.11
range v. arrange 60.6
　be included 76.2
　size 192.10
　be distant 196.4
　wander 266.14
　~ the coast 267.30
　range itself 58.5
ranger caretaker 664.3
　overseer 694.1
　brigand 792.3
rani, ranee
　empress 745.6
　princess 875.8
rank n. degree 26.1
　series 69.2
　station 71.1
　(gradation 58.2)
　military unit 726.7
　social class 873.4
　nobility 875.1
　of rank 875.10
rank v. have place 1.4
　arrange 60.6
　classify 60.7
　precede 62.2
　occupy a place 71.2
　estimate 480.7
rank adj.
　absolute 31.12
　luxuriant 365.4
　nasty 395.7
　fetid 401.4
　foul 653.17
　bad 649.8
　disreputable 874.8

flagrant 945.16
grow rank 365.2
rank and file
　procession 69.3
　army 726.6
　commonalty 876.1
rankle
　be remembered 505.12
　fester 659.7
　be painful 830.7
　nurse revenge 919.5
rankling n. 900.1
rankling adj. 919.7
ransack n. 461.2
ransack v.
　search 461.16
　pillage 791.10
ransom n. 672.1
ransom v.
　redeem 660.9
　deliver 672.2
　recover 790.4
　expiate 952.4
rant n. twaddle 517.3
　verbosity 573.1
　bombast 577.2
　(exaggeration 549.1)
　boasting 884.1
rant v. rave 503.9
　talk nonsense 517.6
　perorate 573.1
　(be loquacious 584.4)
　declaim 582.7
　act 599.26
　rage 825.7
　bluster 887.3
　rage angrily 900.8
rantan, ran-tan
　turmoil 59.4
　drumming 407.3
　spree 840.3
　drinking bout 959.3
ranter talker 584.3
　blusterer 887.2
　lip worshiper 988.6
ranting n. 825.4
ranting adj.
　rabid 503.13
　frenzied 824.10
rantipole n. 863.2
rantipole adj. 863.7
rap n. blow 276.3
　trifle 643.3
　(money 800.8)
　gibe 930.3
　criticism 932.2
　rapscallion 949.1
　sentence 971.1
rap v. strike 276.8
　bang 406.7
　swear 535.4
　criticize 932.7
rap out affirm 535.5
　exclaim 580.9
　speak 582.6
　~ ~ an oath 908.5
rapacious
　predacious 789.15
　(thieving 791.14)

rapacity — rattlebrained

rapacious (*continued*)
 avaricious 819.4
 greedy 865.20
 gluttonous 957.4
rapacity
 predacity 789.4
 thievishness 791.6
 avarice 819.1
 greed 865.4
 gluttony 957.1
rape *n.* robbery 791.2
 debauchment 961.4
rape *v.* 789.9; 961.8
rape oil 356.3
rapee See **rappee**
raper 962.1
Raphael 977.1
raphe 43.3
rapid *n.* 348.6
rapid *adj.*
 instantaneous 113.4
 steep 217.12
 fast 274.13
rapidity
 velocity 274.1
 quickness 682.2
rapids 348.6
 (danger 667.1)
rapier 727.3
rapine 791.2
rapparee 792.3
rappee, rapee 392a.8
rappel 722.3
rapper lie 546.2
 oath 908.3
rappist 994.14
rapport relation 9.1
 agreement 23.1
 concord 714.1
 sympathy 888.1
 in rapport related 9.6
 *agreeing 23.9
 in accord 714.4
rapprochement
 pacification 723.1
 sympathy 888.1
rapscallion 949.1
rapt thoughtful 451.36
 intent 457.9
 preoccupied 458.11
 overjoyed 827.10
raptor 789.6
raptorial 789.15
 (thieving 791.14)
rapture
 delight 827.2
 love 897.1
 trance 994.6
rapturous
 overjoyed 827.10
 delightful 829.8
 in love 897.14
rara avis rarity 83.4
 personage 642.5
 nonesuch 648.4
 prodigy 872.1
 celebrity 873.9
rare *n.* 51.1
rare *adj.* unusual 83.10
 (unimitated 20.3)
 (superexcellent 648.10)

sparse 103.3
infrequent 137.2
thin 203.10
underdone 298.50
tenuous 322.4
 (light 320.7)
exceptional 642.10
not rare 136.3
raree show show 599.8
 amusement 840.15
rarefaction
 expansion 194.1
 attenuation 322.2
rarefactive 322.5
rarefied thin 203.10
 attenuated 322.4
rarefy dilute 160.9
 expand 194.8
 thin 203.8
 attenuate 322.3
rare gas 334.2
rarely 137.3
rarity fewness 103.1
 infrequency 137.1
 oddity 83.3, 4
 tenuity 322
 (lightness 320.1)
 prodigy 872.1
rascal 949.1
 (deceiver 548.1)
rascality 940.1
 (cunning 702.1)
rascally 940.8
 (cunning 702.6)
rase See **raze**
rash *n.* 655.17
rash *adj.*
 impulsive 612.4
 incautious 863.6
 (dangerous 665.7)
 be rash 863.5
 (gamble 621.17)
rasher piece 51.3
 lamina 204.2
rashness 863
 (carelessness 460.1)
 (folly 499.6)
 (gamble 621.2)
 (danger 665.3)
rasorial 366.26
rasp *n.* 330.4
rasp *v.* grind 330.6
 abrade 331.3
 pain 378.4
 sound harshly 410.6
 comb 652.11
raspberry fruit 298.31
 catcall 930.2
 give the raspberry 930.6
rasper 704.1
raspings remains 40.1
 filings 330.3
rasure 552.1
rat *n.* headdress 225.26
 hair 256.3
 animal 366.17
 deserter 607.5, 6
 scoundrel 949.1
 traitor 949.3
rat *v.*
 inform on 527.10

desert 624.3
ratan See **rattan**
rataplan *n.* 407.3
rataplan *v.* 407.8
ratchet tooth 253.3
 printing 591.5
rate *n.* degree 26.1
 velocity 274.1
 interest 806.3
 worth 812.3
 at a great rate 274.14
 at any rate
 notwithstanding 30.8
 of course 474.16
 resolutely 604.9
 anyhow 627.9
rate *v.* quantify 25.5
 measure 466.10
 estimate 480.7
 value 642.8; 812.4
 reprove 932.8
rated 812.7
rath *n.* 717.4
rathe, rath *adj.* 132.8
rathe, rath *adv.* 132.11
rather *n.* 609.2
rather *v.* 609.9
rather *adv.*
 somewhat 32.14
 (imperfectly 651.5)
 ~ than 147.5
 yet 469.7
 preferably 609.18
 had rather 609.9
ratherish 32.14
ratification
 confirmation 467.3
 endorsement 488.4
 (confirmation 769.4)
 (acceptance 771.3)
ratify confirm 467.9
 indorse 488.10
 (record 551.8)
 (confirm 769.9)
 (guarantee 771.6)
rating 932.3
ratio degree 26.1
 mathematical ~ 84.6
 comparison 464.1
 (relation 9.1)
 ration 786.2
ratiocinate 476.10
ratiocination 476.1
ratiocinative 476.13
ratiocinator 476.9
ration provisions 298.6
 (equipment 634.1)
 allotment 786.2
rational *n.*
 attribution 155.1
 reason 615.1
rational *adj.*
 numeral 84.7
 intellectual 450.8
 reasoning 476.13
 logical 476.16
 intelligent 498.9
 wise 498.11
 (philosophical 451.38)

sane 502.5
rationale
 attribution 155.1
 reason 615.1
 (explanation 462.3; 522.1)
rationalism
 philosophy 451.11
 reasoning 476.1
 irreligion 989.3
rationalist 476.9
rationalistic 989.8
rationality
 mentality 450.1
 reasoning 476.1
 reasonableness 476.7
 wisdom 498.3
 sanity 502.1
rationalization 476.1
rationalize
 think 451.27
 (intellectualize 450.6)
 reason 476.10
rational psychology 450.4
rationate 476.10
ratline, ratlin, ratling *n.*
 supporter 215.2
 ship's rope 273.10
ratline *v.* 267.10
rat poison 663.5
rats! 497.5
ratsbane 663.5
rat's-tail, rattail
 tail 235.6
 hair 256.3
rattan 407.3
rattan, ratan 975.2
rat-tat, rat-tat-tat, rattattoo, rat-tattle 407.3
ratten 158.6
rattle *n.*
 noisemaker 404.4
 clatter 407.5
 (noise 404.2)
 clapper 417.10
 confusion 458.4
 twaddle 517.3
 chatterer 584.3
 predicament 704.2
 trouble 735.1
 prison 752.1
rattle *v.* clatter 407.10
 (be noisy 404.6)
 confuse 458.9
 (discompose 61.4)
 talk nonsense 517.6
 be loquacious 584.4
rattlebones
 thin person 203.6
 clappers 417.10
rattlebox 404.4
rattlebrain 501.2
rattlebrained
 scatterbrained 458.1
 empty-headed 499.14

1042

rattled 458.12
rattlehead 501.2
rattleheaded
　scatterbrained
　　458.13
　empty-headed
　　499.14
rattler
　train 272.18, 19
　rattlesnake 366.19
rattletrap 584.3
rattletraps 780.1, 5
rattlety-bang, rat-
　tling *n.* 407.5
rattling, rattly *adj.*
　407.14
rattrap 545.4
raucity 410.1
　(speech 583.1)
raucous 410.9
　(discordant 414.4)
raucousness 410.1
ravage *n.*
　destruction 162.1
　ill-treatment 649.4
　damage 659.3
ravage *v.* destroy 162.4
　damage 659.8
rave
　~ insanely 503.9
　bluster 887.3
　rage 825.7; 900.8
　~ against 932.8
ravel
　disentangle 60.9
　complicate 61.5
　interlace 219.8
　(disorder 59.7)
　solve 481a.4
raveled, ravelled 59.10
ravelin 717.3
raveling, ravelling
　59.3
raven *n.* bird 366.22
　black 431.3
raven, ravin, ravine *v.*
　desire 865.11
　eat greedily 957.3
raven, raven-
black *adj.* 431.7
ravening
　turbulent 173.12
　rapacious 789.15
　desirous 865.19, 20
ravenous
　rapacious 789.15
　greedy 865.20
　gluttonous 957.4
ravenousness 865.4
raver 887.2
ravine *n.* chasm 198.3
　(narrow 203.3)
　(valley 252.5)
　(trench 259.2)
　water gap 350.1
ravin, ravine *v.* See
　raven
raving *n.*
　delirium 503.3
　fury 825.4
raving *adj.*
　rabid 503.13, 14

frenzied 824.10
beautiful 845.13
raving mad
　rabid 503.13
　infuriated 900.13
ravish seize 789.9
　delight 829.5
　debauch 961.8
ravished 827.10
ravisher taker 789.6
　debaucher 962.1
ravishing
　delightful 829.8
　beautiful 845.13
ravishment rape 791.2
　intoxication 824.1
　delight 827.2
　delightfulness 829.2
raw *n.*
　bare skin 223.12
　the nude 226.2
　sore point 822.3
　in the raw 226.8
raw *adj.* new 123.8
　youthful 127.5
　unclad 226.8
　windswept 349.25
　painful 378.7
　cold 383.8
　gaudy-colored
　　428.15
　ignorant 491.8
　immature 674.8
　inexperienced
　　699.14
　crude 851.7
rawboned 203.11
rawhide 975.1
raw material 635.1
rawness 674.2
raw sienna, raw um-
　ber 433.2
ray fish 366.21
　~ of light 420.3
　~ of hope 858.3
rayless 442.6
rayon thread 205.2
　cloth 219.5
ray therapy 420.16
raze, rase
　demolish 162.4
　level 213.6
　fell 308.5
　erase 331.3
　obliterate 552.2
razor 253.6
razorback 366.7
razoredge 253.5
razz 930.2
razzia
　destruction 162.1
　attack 716.1
　pillage 791.2
razzle-dazzle *n.*
　turmoil 59.4
　discomposure 61.1
　noisemaker 404.4
　confusion 458.4
razzle-dazzle *v.* 458.9
Re See Ra
reach *n.* degree 26.1
　extent 180.1

distance 196.1
shaft 215.13
sea inlet 343.1
plain 344.1
earshot 418.4
authority 737.2
scope 748.2
beyond reach
　beyond 196.8
　impossible 471.7
in the reach of 221.13
out of reach
　beyond 196.8
　unhearable 419.9
　impracticable 471.7
within reach
　present 186.13
　near 197.11
　practicable 470.6
　easy 705.5
reach *v.* equal 27.6
　~ to 196.4
　transfer to 270.7
　arrive at 292.7
　(reach completion
　　729.4)
　bribe 618.3
　~ to take 789.13
reach out
　extend 196.4
　be long 200.8
reaching 292.1
reach-me-down 659.12
react 277.3
　(counteract 179.3)
reaction recoil 277.1
　(counteraction
　　179.1)
　(retaliation 718.1)
　resistance 719.1
reactionary *n.*
　conservative 141.3
　recalcitrant 277.2
　apostate 607.5
　malcontent 832.2
　(opposer 710.3)
reactionary *adj.*
　conservative 141.7
　reversionary 145.6
　counteractive 179.5
　recoiling 277.4
　(regressive 283.7)
　apostate 607.11
reactionaryism
　conservatism 141.2
　apostasy 607.2
reactionist *n.*
　conservative 141.3
　reactionary 277.2
　malcontent 832.2
reactionist *adj.* 141.7
reactive 277.4
read *v.*
　interpret 522.6
　study 539.4
　indicate 550.18
read between the
　lines 522.6
read oneself in 995.8
read *adj.* 490.14
readable 578.4
reader

reading glass
　445.1, 3
advertisement 531.4
teacher 540.3
lecturer 582.5
proofreader 591.13
journalist 593.16
anagnost 996.5
readership 540.6
readily 705.8
readiness
　punctuality 132.3
　tendency 176.1
　willingness 602.1
　preparedness 673.4
　quickness 682.2
　(skill 698.1)
in readiness 673.11
reading
　scholarship 490.2
　version 522.2
　study 539.1
　~ in 995.6
reading desk 1000.3
reading glass 445.1, 3
reading notice 531.4
readjust accord 23.8
　equalize 27.7
　reset 494.7
　restore 660.8
readjustment
　equalization 27.3
　restoration 660.1
readmit 296.2
ready *n.*
　preparation 673.1
　cash 800.13
ready *v.* 673.6
ready *adj.*
　alert 457.9
　expectant 507.7
　willing 602.8
　available 644.8
　prepared 673.11
　(equipped 634.3)
　quick 682.17
　skillful 698.11
　be ready 673.9
　make ready 673.6
　(provide 637.4)
　not ready 674.7
readying 673.1
ready-cooked, ready-
　cut, ready-formed
　etc. 673.12
ready-mades 225.4
ready money 800.13
reaffirm 535.5
reagent
　experiment 463.5
　agent 690.1
real *adj.* actual 1.8
　(substantial 3.4)
　(tangible 316.8)
　numeral 84.7
　true 494.10, 12
　literal 516.9
　property 780.8
real *adv.* 31.15
real estate 780.4
　(land 342.1)
realgar 434.6

realism — receipt

realism
  philosophy 451.10
  truth 494.1
  art 556.6
realistic real 494.10
  description 594.7
reality 1.2
  (substantiality 3.1)
  (truth 494.1)
  (real thing 494.4)
  in reality
    actually 1.9
    in truth 494.15
realization 729.1
realize note 450.7
  recognize 481a.6
  believe 484.8
  know 490.9
  understand 518.4
  accomplish 729.2
  ~ a profit 775.7
  sell for 796.5
really actually 1.9
  to be sure 488.14
  truly 494.15
really-truly 494.15
  (actually 1.9)
realm region 181.1
  country 182.1
  population 188.10
  nation 372.2
  sphere of work 625.3
real McCoy 494.4
  (reality 1.2)
real presence 998.6
realty 780.4
  (land 342.1)
ream *n.*
  stationery 590.10
  paper 635.4
ream *v.* 260.14
reamer 262
reanimate
  revive 660.13
  (recreate 163.2)
  refresh 689.2
  (vivify 359.8)
reanimation 660.2
  (reproduction 163.1)
reap harvest 371.8
  gain 775.6
reap the benefit of
  profit by 644.2; 658.7
  utilize 677.5
  succeed 731.5
  be rewarded 973.4
reaper 371.2
Reaper 360.2
reappear repeat 104.5
  recur 138.8
  appear 446.2
  return 660.15
reappearance 104.1
rear *n.* 235
  (afterpart 65.2)
  in the rear 235.14
rear *v.* produce 161.8
  be high 206.9
  erect 212.7
  pitch 267.45
  elevate 307.5
  breed 370.5

train 537.10
rear *adj.* 235.9
  (ending 67.8)
rear admiral 745.12
rear guard 235.2
rearmost 235.9
rearward *n.* 235.1, 2
rearward *adj.* 235.9
rearward *adv.*
  hindward 235.16
  backward 283.8
reason *n.*
  intellect 450.1
  wisdom 498.3
  motive 615.1
  (cause 153.1)
  (attribution 155.1)
  (explanation 462.3;
    522.1)
  (reasoning 476.8)
  bring to reason
    convince 484.10
    render sane 502.4
    persuade 615.9
  by reason of 155.5, 8
  in reason
    in moderation 174.8
    sanely 502.6
    rightfully 922.7
    in justice 941.5
reason *v.* think 451.27
  (intellectualize
    450.6)
  rationalize
    476.10, 11
  (examine 461.17)
  ~ with 588.8
reasonability 476.7
  (possibility 470.1)
  (probability 472.1)
  (credibility 484.5)
reasonable
  moderate 174.6
  logical 476.16
  (plausible 472.6)
  (credible 484.15)
  intelligent 498.9
  wise 498.11
  sane 502.5
  inexpensive 815.8
  vindicable 937.10
  (justifiable 941.4)
  be reasonable
    logical 476.12
    be intelligent 498.7
reasonableness
  wisdom 498.3
  cheapness 815.1
reasoner 476.9
  (interlocutor 588.5)
reasoning *n.* 476
  (dissertation 595.1)
reasoning *adj.*
  intellectual 450.8
  rational 476.13
reasonless
  mindless 450a.2
  unintelligent 499.11
  insane 503.12
reassemble 72.10
reassert 535.5
reassurance

certification 474.2
  hope 858.1
reassure assure 474.6
  give hope 858.8
reassuring 858.11
reasty, reasy
  foul 653.17
  rancid 659.13
reave 789.9
rebate *n.*
  decrement 39a
  discount 813.1
rebate *v.*
  moderate 174.5
  discount 813.2
rebatement
  decrease 36.1
  decrement 39a
  discount 813.1
rebec, rebeck 417.3
rebel *n.* 742.3
  (dissenter 489.3)
  (apostate 607.5)
  (opposer 710.3)
rebel *v.* 742.5
  (revolutionize
    146.4)
  (strike 719.4)
rebeller
  insurgent 742.3
  malcontent 832.2
rebellion 742.2
  (revolution 146.1)
  (strike 719.2)
  in open rebellion
    715.4
rebellious 742.7
  (revolutionary
    146.5)
  (defiant 715.3)
  (resistant 719.5)
  (anarchic 738.8)
rebirth revival 660.2
  regeneration 987.3
reboant 412.3
reborn 987.12
rebound *n.* recoil 277.1
  (elasticity 325.1)
  reverberation 408.2
rebound *v.* recoil 277.3
  reverberate 408.7
rebuff *n.* recoil 277.1
  resistance 719.1
  defeat 732.3
  refusal 764.1
  discourtesy 895.2
  snub 930.4
rebuff *v.* refuse 764.4
  snub 930.7
rebuild *n.* 272.16
rebuild *v.* 660.14
rebuke *n.* 932.3
rebuke *v.* 932.8
rebuker 936.2
rebus 533.2
rebut answer 462.5, 6
  refute 479.2
  (countervail 468.2)
  (dispute 536.2)
rebuttal
  answer 462.1, 2
  (defense 937.2)

refutal 479.1
  (negation 536.1)
in rebuttal 468.5
rebutter 462.2
  (law 969.6)
recalcitrance 719.1
recalcitrant *n.* 277.2
recalcitrant *adj.*
  recoiling 277.4
  obstinate 606.6
  resistant 719.5
  unruly 742.6
recalcitrate
  recoil 277.3
  resist 719.3
recalcitration
  recoil 277.1
  resistance 719.1
recalesce 382.13
recalescence 382.1
recalescent 382.16
recall *n.*
  memory 505.1
  ~ of ambassadors
    713.2
  beyond recall 859.7
recall *v.*
  recognize 481a.6
  remember 505.10
  recant 607.9
  ~ to life 660.13
  revoke 756.3
recant 607.9
  (dissent 489.4)
  (deny 536.2)
  (abandon 624.3)
  (disclaim 756.4)
  (repent 950.3)
  (apologize 952.5)
recantation 607.3
  (dissent 489.1)
  (negation 536.1)
  (rejection 610.1)
  (abandonment
    624.1)
  (abrogation 756.1)
  (resignation 757.1)
  (repentance 950.1)
recapitulate
  recount 85.7
  repeat 104.4
  recount 594.5
recapitulation
  recount 85.3
  repetend 104.2
  retelling 594.1
  summary 596.1
recede regress 283.5
  (recoil 277.3)
  move back 287.2
  (diverge 291.2)
  (shrink 623.9)
recedence
  recession 287.1
  surrender 725.2
receding
  regressive 283.7
  recessive 287.3
receipt *n.* answer 462.1
  axiom 496.2
  contrivance 626.5
  nostrum 662.2

receipt — recoil

precept 697.1
security 771.4
reception 785.1
voucher 807.4
~ of money 810
 (gain 775.2)
 gift 784.3, 5, 6
receipt v. 462.5
receipts profits 775.2
 income 810.1
 (assets 780.7)
 (remuneration 973.2)
 accounts 811.1
receive include 76.3
 admit 296.2
 believe 484.7
 assent 488.6
 get 785.3
 (acquire 775.6)
 (take 789.7)
 welcome 892.11
received
 authoritative 474.13
 known 490.17
 come to hand 785.4
 conventional 852.8
 orthodox 983a.7
be received 484.11
receiver
 receptacle 191.1
 telephone ~ 418.6; 532a.5
 believer 484.6
 recorder 553.3
 recipient 785.2
 ~ of stolen goods 792.9
 treasurer 801
 believer 987.1
receiving n. 785
 (acquisition 775.1)
receiving adj. 785.5
receiving set 532a.5
recency 123.1
recension 85.1
recent 123.8
 (foregoing 122.11)
recently 123.13
recentness 123.1
receptacle 191
 (enclosure 232.1)
reception
 inclusion 76.1
 admission 296
 (ingress 294.1)
 (insertion 300.1)
 conference 588.3
 receiving 785.1
 (taking 789.1)
 hospitality 892.4
 (arrival 292.5)
 party 892.5
 welcome 894.3
reception hall 191.17
receptive
 admissive 296.6
 flexible 324.6
 recipient 785.5
 hospitable 892.12
receptual 296.6
recess interim 109a.1

pause 142.2
nook 191.3
(angle 244.2)
interior 221.2
cavity 252.4
(closure 261.1)
hiding place 530.2
refuge 666.3
respite 687.2
seclusion 893.2
recession
 motion from 287
 (recoil 277.1)
 (regression 283.1)
 (departure 293.1)
 (avoidance 623.1)
 divergence 291.1
 surrender 725.2
recessive 283.7
Rechabite 953.3
Rechabitism 953.2
réchauffé n.
 stale news 532.1
 old joke 842.6
réchauffé adj.
 repeated 104.6
 reheated 384.23
recheck n. 461.6
recheck v. 461.20
recherché
 unusual 83.10
 fashionable 852.7
recidivation
 progression 283.1
 degeneration 659.1
 relapse 661.1
recidive 661.3
recidivism
 progression 283.1
 degeneration 659.1
 relapse 661.1
 (apostasy 607.2)
recidivist 607.5
 (backslider 661.2)
recidivistic 661.4
 (apostate 607.11)
recidivous
 regressive 283.7
 relapsing 661.4
 sinful 945.19
recipe axiom 496.2
 nostrum 662.2
 precept 697.1
recipience 785.1
 (acquisition 775.1)
recipient n.
 receptacle 191.1
 receiver 785.2
recipient adj.
 receptive 296.6
 receiving 785.5
reciprocal n. 84.2
reciprocal adj.
 correlative 12.7
 (interchangeable 148.4)
 numeral 84.7
 alternate 314.12
 retaliatory 718.4
reciprocality 12.2
reciprocally 148.5
 (vice versa 14.7)

reciprocate v.
 interchange 148.3
 alternate 314.10
 concur 488.7
 be concordant 714.2
 retaliate 718.2
reciprocate adj.
 reciprocal 12.7
 interchangeable 148.4
 alternate 314.12
reciprocation
 correlation 12.2
 (exchange 794.1)
 interchange 148.1
 alternation 314.3
 retaliation 718.1
reciprocative
 reciprocal 12.7
 interchangeable 148.4
 alternate 314.12
be reciprocative 12.5
reciprocator 12.3
reciprocity 12.2
recision 38.2
recital repetend 104.2
 musicale 415.17
 lesson 537.6
 speech 582.2
 narration 594.1
recitalist 416.1
recitation lesson 537.6
 speech 582.2
recitationalism 582.3
recitative 415.10
recite enumerate 85.7
 speak 582.6, 7
 ~ the rosary 990.11; 998.14
reciter 582.5
reck n. 459.1
reck v. 459.5
reckless
 turbulent 173.12
 rash 863.7
 (heedless 458.10)
 (careless 460.8)
 (clumsy 699.12)
 (daring 715.3)
recklessly 863.8
 (carelessly 460.12)
recklessness 863.1
 (carelessness 460.1)
reckon compute 37.5
 ~ among 76.3
 calculate 85.7
 (estimate 466.10)
 judge 480.6
 think 484.8
 suppose 514.6
reckon on
 rely on 484.7
 plan on 507.6
 intend 620.3
reckon up total 50.5
 calculate 85.7
reckon without one's host
 misjudge 481.5
 err 495.7
 be foolish 499.9

unclever 699.7
be rash 863.5
reckoner 811.6
reckoning
 computation 37.2
 sum 84.3
 numeration 85.1
 (estimation 466.1)
 expectation 507.1
 payment 807.1
 accounts 811.1
 reward 973.1
reclaim
 redeem 660.9; 952.4
 (reform 658.12)
 claim 741.6
 recover 790.4
 revindicate 924.7
 regenerate 950.4
reclamation
 made land 342.2
 restoration 660.1
 demand 741.2
 atonement 952.1
réclame 531.3
reclinate 248.4
reclination 213.2
recline lie 213.5
 (sit 308.6)
 ~ on 215.27
 repose 687.3
recluse 893.4
 (ascetic 955.2)
reclusion 893.2
recognition
 acknowledgment 488.2; 894.3
 knowledge 490.1
 memory 505.1
 thanks 916.2
recognitor 967.3
recognizability 518.1
recognizable
 distinct 446.5
 intelligible 518.5
 indicated 550.22
recognizance
 knowledge 490.1
 indemnity 771.1
recognize see 441.10
 take cognizance 457.4
 realize 481a.6
 (identify 13.5)
 acknowledge 488.9
 know 490.9
 remember 505.10
 admit 760.3
 show gratitude 916.3
recognized
 known 490.17
 conventional 852.8
 be recognized 175.9
recoil n. reaction 277
 (reversion 145.1)
 (counteraction 179.1)
 (reflux 283.2)
 (recession 287.1)
 (elasticity 325.1)
 (retaliation 718.1)
 reluctance 603.2

recoil — recurrent

recoil (*continued*)
  scruple 939.2
recoil v. react 277.3
  (revert 145.4)
  (counteract 179.3)
  (turn aside 279.7)
  (recede 283.5)
  (be elastic 325.3)
  shy at 603.4
  shrink 623.9
Recollect, Recollet *n.* 996.11
recollect *v.* 505.10
recollectable 505.19
recollected
  remembered 505.18
  composed 826.9
recollection 505.1, 4
  (reconsideration 451.2)
recollective 505.17
recomember 505.10
recommend
  advocate 615.7
  advise 695.4
  commend 931.6
recommendation
  advice 695.1
  commendation 931.2
recommendatory 695.8
recompensation
  compensation 30.1
  atonement 952.1
recompense *n.*
  compensation 30.1
  atonement 952.1
  reward 973.1
recompense *v.*
  compensate 30.4
  atone 952.4
  reward 973.3
recompensive 30.6
recompose 54.4
reconcilable
  agreeing 23.9
  concordant 714.4
reconcile accord 23.8
  conform 82.4
  conciliate 723.4
  (be concordant 714.3)
  content 831.4
be reconciled to 831.3
become reconciled 723.5
  (forgive 918.3)
reconcile oneself to 826.6
reconcilement
  conformity 82.1
  conciliation 723.1
reconciler 724.2
reconciliation
  adaptation 23.3
  conformity 82.1
  conciliation 723.1
  (concord 714.1)
reconciliatory 723.6
recondite
  obscure 519.7
  hidden 528.17

recondition 660.13
reconnaissance, reconnoissance
  scrutiny 441.2
  reconnoitering 461.8
reconnoiter, reconnoitre
  look about 441.11
  examine 461.22
reconnoiterer, reconnoitrer
  investigator 461.13
  spy 528.8
reconnoitering, reconnoitring 461.8
reconsider
  think over 451.29
  re-examine 461.20
  revise 658.11
reconsideration
  mature thought 451.2
  recollection 505.4
  revision 658.3
reconstitute 660.8
reconstitution 660.1
reconstruct
  reproduce 163.2
  remodel 660.14
reconstruction
  reproduction 163.1
  remaking 660.3
reconstructive 163.3
reconversion
  reversion 145.1
  revival 660.2
reconvert 660.8
recook 384.19
record *n.* list 86.1
  chronology 114.5
  register 551
  (indication 550.1)
  (writing 590.3)
  (book 593.1)
  (muniments 771.1)
off the record 528.25
on record 551.10
record *v.* list 86.3
  register 551.8
  (write 590.13)
recordation 551.7
record book 551.3; 811.5
  (list 86.1)
  (stationery 590.10)
  (book 593.1)
  (journal 593.6)
recorded music 415.3
recorder
  phonograph 417.9
  registrar 553
  (writer 590.11)
  (author 593.15)
  accountant 811.6
  judge 967.1
recording *n.* 551.1
recording *adj.* 551.9
recount *n.* 85.3
recount *v.*
  recapitulate 85.7
  repeat 104.4
  relate 594.5

recountal 104.2
recounter 199.1
recoup
  indemnify 790.3
  redeem 952.4
recourse refuge 666.3
  use 677.1
have recourse to 677.5
recover redeem 660.9
  rally 660.15
  (improve 658.6)
  (recuperate 689.3)
  get back 775.9
  (retake 789.14)
  take back 790.4
recoverability 660.6
recoverable 658.16
recovery
  restoration 660.1
  (improvement 658.1)
  ~ of strength 689.1
  retrieval 775.3
  (resumption 789.3)
  restitution 790.2
recreancy 607.2
recreant *n.*
  apostate 607.5
  coward 862.2
  knave 949.1
recreant *adj.*
  apostate 607.11
  dastardly 862.5
  dishonest 940.8
  wicked 945.11
recreate
  reproduce 163.2
  reconstruct 660.14
  amuse 840.20
recreation
  reproduction 163.1
  reconstruction 660.3
recreational 840.22
recreative
  reproductive 163.3
  amusing 840.22
recrement 40.2
recriminate
  reproach 932.7
  countercharge 938.4
  (retaliate 718.2)
recrimination 938.1
  (retaliation 718.1)
recriminatory
  retaliatory 718.4
  accusatory 938.5
recrudency, recrudescence 661.1
recrudescent 661.4
recruit *n.*
  newcomer 57.3
  novice 541.6
  aid 707.5
  conscript 726.5
recruit *v.*
  reinforce 37.4; 707.6
  restrengthen 159.8
  replenish 637.4
  ~ strength 654.3
  restore 660.8
  recuperate 689.3

~ troops 722.10
recruital 660.5
recruiting 722.3
rectal 221.11
rectangle
  vertical 212.2
  quadrangle 244.2
rectangular
  oblong 200.14
  quadrangular 244.5
rectangularity 212.1
rectification
  revision 658.3
  reparation 660.4
rectify
  graduate 26.2
  straighten 246.4
  improve 658.8
  remedy 660.10
  right 922.3
rectilinear 246.5
rectilinearity 246.1
rectitude 939.1; 944.1
recto right 238.2
  book 593.7
rector director 694.1
  master 745.1
  clergyman 996.5
rectoress, rectress, rectrix 745.1
rectory
  rectorship 995.3
  parsonage 1000.5
rectum vitals 221.4
  intestine 350.4
rectus in curia 946.6
recubant 217.9
reculade 283.1
recumbency 213.2
recumbent
  oblique 217.9
  horizontal 213.9
  (downthrown 308.9)
recuperate 689.3
recuperation
  restoration 660.1
  convalescence 660.5
  refreshment 689.1
  restitution 790.1
recuperative 660.18
  (refreshing 689.4)
  (restitutive 790.5)
recur repeat 104.5
  (do frequently 136.2)
  reoccur 138.8
recur to
  revert to 457.5
  be remembered 505.12
  use 677.5
recure *n.* 660.5
recure *v.* 660.12
recurrence
  repetition 104.1
  (renewal 660.2)
  periodicity 138.2
recurrent
  repetitional 104.6
  frequent 136.3
  periodic 138.10
  (discontinuous 70.4)

recurvature 245.1
recurve 245.3
recusancy
  nonconformity 83.2
  dissent 489.1
  (sectarianism 984.2)
  (perversion 988.3)
  disclamation 536.1
  refusal 764.1
  impenitence 951.1
recusant *n.* 489.3
  (nonconformist 83.4)
  (sectarian 984.13)
recusant *adj.*
  dissentient 489.5
  (sectarian 984.23)
  denying 536.3
  refusing 764.5
  impenitent 951.3
recusation 764.1
recusative 764.5
red *n.* color 434.2, 6
  radical 658.5
  in the red 776.5
Red *n.*
  Russian 188.9
  revolutionist 742.3
red *v.* 434.7
red *adj.*
  revolutionary 146.5
  rubicund 434.9, 11
  radical 742.7
  turn red 824.8
redact compose 54.4
  devise 658.11
redan 717.3
redargue 479.2
redargution 479.1
red blindness 443.1
red book 551.2
redbreast 434.5
redcap 271.1
red cent trifle 643.3
  money 800.8
redcoat 726.4
red-crested 434.12
Red Cross 662.17
redden color 434.7, 8
  blush 881.4
  anger 900.7
redding 434.6
reddish-brown,
  reddish-yellow 433.5
reddition
  rendition 522.2
  restitution 790.1
redeem
  substitute 147.3
  reclaim 660.9
  deliver 672.2
  recover 775.9
  make restitution 790.4
  pay 807.6
  reform 950.4
  (compensate 30.4)
  atone 952.4; 976.9
  give salvation 987.9
redeemable 672.3
redeemer 912.2
Redeemer 976.5

redemption
  restoration 660.1
  deliverance 672.1
  recovery 775.3
  restitution 790.2
  performance 926.2
  atonement 952.1
  divine function 976.5
  salvation 987.3
  (repentance 950.1)
redemptioner 295.4
redemptive 790.5
red-eyed 443.14
red-faced 434.11
red flag flag 550.13
  warning sign 668.3
  danger signal 669.1
red-handed
  killing 361.15
  in the act 680.8; 947.5
redheaded 434.11
red heat 382.2
red herring 617.2
red-hot violent 173.13
  hot 382.16
  fervent 821.6
  excited 824.9
red-ink 434.7
redintegration 660.1
redivivus 660.17
red lead 434.6
red-letter day
  importance 642.3
  holiday 840.5
  (celebration 883.2)
red light
  signal light 423.5
  signal 550.14
  warning sign 668.3
  danger signal 669.1
red-light district 961.7
redness
  heat flush 382.7
  color 434
redolence 398.1
  (fragrance 400.1)
redolent odorous 398.8
  fragrant 400.10
redouble increase 35.3
  reduplicate 90.2
redoubt 717.3
redoubtable 860.15
redound
  contribute 153.8
  tend 176.2
redpoll 366.12
red rag tongue 379.2
  provocation 900.5
Red Republican 742.3
redress *n.*
  reparation 660.4; 973.1
  relief 707.4
  repayment 807.3
  atonement 952.1
redress *v.*
  remedy 660.10
  right 922.3
  atone 952.4

red ribbon 733.1
red-short 328.4
redskin Indian 434.5
  savage 913.3
redstart 434.5
red tape delay 133.2
  routine 613.4
red-tapism
  routine 613.4
  officialism 737.7
red-tapist 694.3
redtop 367.9
reduce decrease 36.4
  (deduct 38.4)
  (contract 195.4)
  (shorten 201.4)
  (take away 789.10)
  weaken 160.8
  dilute 160.9
  thin 203.8
  ~ sail 267.38
  ~ the speed 275.7
  depress 308.4
  ~ to ashes 384.18; 363.21
  analyze 461.17
  qualify 469.3
  sicken 655.22
  conquer 731.9
  impoverish 804.6
  discount 813.2
  cheapen 815.7
  humiliate 879.3
reduced
  impaired 659.12
  conquered 732.12
  poor 804.7
  ~ in price 815.9
reduct 38.4
reductio ad absurdum
  counterevidence 468.1
  reasoning 476.6
  confutation 479.1
reduction
  decrease 36.1
  (subtraction 38.1)
  (diminution 174.2)
  (shortening 201.2)
  mathematics 85.4
  conversion 144.1
  contraction 195.1
  depression 308.1
  discount 813.1
reductive 36.5
redundance 641
  (surplus 40.4)
  (fill 52.3)
  (overexpansion 194.4)
  (overrunning 303.1)
  (overestimation 482.1)
  (exaggeration 549.1)
  (tautology 573.2)
  (grandiloquence 577.2)
  (plenty 639.2)
  (satiety 869.1)
  (undueness 925.1)

  (intemperance 954.1)
redundant *n.*
  surplus 40.4
  redundance 641.1
redundant *adj.* 641.5
  (exaggerated 549.3)
  (tautological 573.8)
  (grandiloquent 577.7)
  (prodigal 639.7)
  (useless 645.8)
  (undue 925.8)
  (intemperate 954.4)
reduplicate
  redouble 90.2
  repeat 104.4
reduplication
  imitation 19.1
  (reproduction 163.1)
  duplication 90.1
  repetition 104.1
reduplicative 104.6
red wine 959.7
redwood tree 367.6
  wood 635.3
re-echo *n.*
  repetition 104.2
  reverberation 408.2
  answer 462.1
re-echo *v.*
  imitate 19.5
  repeat 104.4
  resonate 408.7
  (rebound 277.3)
  (roll 407.6)
  answer 462.5
re-echoing 104.6
reechy foul 653.17
  rancid 659.13
reed weakness 160.5
  tube 260.6
  mouthpiece 417.13
  pen 590.10
  spear 727.5
  ornament 847.4
reedbird 366.22
reeding 847.3
reed instrument 417.4
reedlike, reedy 253.18
reef *n.* shallow 209.2
  promontory 250.5
  island 346.1
  hidden danger 667.1
reef *v.*
  reduce sail 267.38
  retard 275.7
reefer
  refrigerator car 272.19
  refrigerator 387.1
reek *n.* 334.2
reek *v.* vaporize 336.5
  be watery 337.4
  be moist 339.6
  be hot 382.13
  smell strong 398.5
  stink 401.3
  (be unclean 653.14)
reeking
  vaporous 336.7
  soaked 339.8

reeky — regal

reeking (*continued*)
  hot 382.17
  odorous 398.8
  fetid 401.4
reeky odorous 398.8
  fetid 401.4
  foul 653.17
reel *n.* whirl 312.2
  spool 312.5
  boom 406.3
  roll 407.1
  music 415.7
  dance 840.7
reel *v.* pitch 267.45
  rotate 312.7
  oscillate 314.8
  flounder 315.9
  eddy 348.21
  be drunk 959.19
re-embody join 43.5
  combine 48.3
re-encounter 292.4
re-enforce, re-enforcement See reinforce etc.
re-enliven 689.2
re-enter 245.3
re-entrance, re-entry 292.3
re-establish
  reproduce 163.2
  restore 660.8
re-establishment
  reproduction 163.1
  restoration 660.1
reeve official 745.9
  functionary 758.2
re-examination
  reconsideration 451.2
  reinquiry 461.6
  revision 658.3
re-examine
  reconsider 451.29
  reinquire 461.20
refashion
  reproduce 163.2
  reconstruct 660.14
refect 689.2
refection
  nourishment 298.5
  refreshment 298.34; 689.1
refectory 191.16
refer
  refer to
    be related 9.3
    include 76.3
    attribute to 155.3
    cite 467.10
    advise with 695.6
referable
  relative to 9.5
  attributable 155.4
referee *n.*
  mediator 724.2
  judge 967.1
referee *v.* 724.3
reference
  relation 9.1
  attribution 155.1
  authority 467.4

indication 550.2
with reference to 9.10
reference book 593.3
reference mark 550.2
referendary 967.1
referendum 609.3
referential
  suggestive 514.11
  figurative 521.3
refine rarefy 322.3
  sensitize 375.4
  split hairs 477.8
  cleanse 652.10
  improve 658.8
  elaborate 673.6
refined speech 578.4
  elegant 845.8
  taste 850.1, 5
  fastidious 868.4
  polite 894.12
refinement nicety 15.2
  rarefaction 322.2
  discrimination 465.1
  exactness 494.3
  ~ of speech 578.1
  cultivation 658.2
  elegance 845.1
  taste 850.1
  fastidiousness 868.1
  courtesy 894.1
  (gentility 852.3)
  probity 939.2
refiner, refinery 652.7
refit 660.8
reflect imitate 19.5
  reverberate 408.7
  ponder 451.27
  ~ upon 932.7
reflectance 420.10
reflecting 498.11
reflection, reflexion
  duplicate 21.2
  repetend 104.2
  recoil 277.1
  (reflux 283.2)
  reverberation 408.2
  light 420.10
  thought 451.1, 2
  (attention 457.2)
  idea 453.1
  recollection 505.4
  censure 932.2
reflective 451.35
reflector 445.4
reflex *n.*
  duplicate 21.2
  recoil 277.1
  (elasticity 325.1)
reflex *adj.* 283.7
refluence reflux 283.2
  ebb 348.9
refluent
  recoiling 277.4
  regressive 283.7
reflux
  subsidence 36.2
  recoil 277.1
  regression 283.2
  ebb 348.9
refocillation
  invigoration 159.2
  refreshment 689.1

reform *n.* 658.4
  (regeneration 660.2)
reform *v.*
  convert 144.7
  reproduce 163.2
  reconstruct 660.14
  (improve 658.12)
  repent 950.4
  (recant 607.9)
  (be converted 987.7)
  regenerate 987.9
reformation
  conversion 144.2
  reproduction 163.1
  reform 658.3
  reconstruction 660.3
  regeneration 987.3
reformational 658.16
reformative 163.3
reformatory *n.*
  school 542.1
  reform school 658.3
  prison 752.1
reformatory *adj.* 658.16
reformer 658.5
reform school
  school 542.1
  reformatory 658.3
  prison 752.1
refound 144.7
refraction
  deviation 279.1
  ~ of light 420.10
  distorted vision 443.9
refractometer 420.16
refractory
  obstinate 606.6
  unmanageable 704.10
  insubordinate 742.6
refrain *n.*
  repetend 104.2
  chorus 415.15
  poetry 597.7
refrain *v.*
  cease 142.6
  ~ from doing 681.2
  be temperate 953.5
  (avoid 623.7)
refreeze 385.4
refreezing 385.1
refresh cool 385.4
  freshen 689.2
  (strengthen 159.8)
  (improve 658.9)
  (revive 660.13)
  (relieve 834.4)
  regale 829.4
refreshed 689.5
refresher 959.10
refreshing
  pleasing 377.7
  bracing 689.4
  (restorative 660.18)
  pleasant 829.7
refreshment
  invigoration 159.2
  food 298.34
  bracing 689.1

(revival 660.2)
(relief 834.1)
  treat 829.3
refrigerant *n.* 387.2
refrigerant *adj.* 385.6
refrigerate
  anesthetize 376.4
  freeze 385.4
  preserve 670.4
refrigerating machine 387.1
refrigeration
  anesthetic 376.2
  freezing 385
  (ice 383.5)
  preservation 670.2
refrigerative *n.* 387.2
refrigerative *adj.* 385.6
refrigerator 387.1
  (merchandise 798.3)
refrigerator car 272.19
reft 44.12
refuge 666.3
  (retreat 189.13)
  (hiding place 530.2)
  (escape 671.3)
  (stronghold 717.4)
take refuge 666.5
refugee 623.5
  (escaper 671.5)
refulgence 420.1
refulgent 420.22
refund 807.9
refusal
  nonconsent 764
  (dissent 489.1)
  (negation 536.1)
  (unwillingness 603.1)
  (rejection 610.1)
  (disapproval 932.1)
  pre-emption 795.1
refuse *n.* 645.4
  (dregs 40.2)
  (oddments 51.6)
  (trumpery 643.5)
  (offal 653.6)
refuse *v.* 764.2
  (dissent 489.4)
  (deny 536.2)
  (be unwilling 603.4)
  (be obstinate 606.5)
  (reject 610.2)
  (disapprove 932.5)
refusing 764.5
  (dissenting 489.5)
  (unwilling 603.5)
refutable
  uncertain 475.9
  confutable 479.4
refutal, refutation 479.1
  (negation 536.1)
refutative 479.3
  (countervailing 468.3)
refute 479.2
  (dispute 536.2)
regain
  ~ strength 689.3
  recover 775.9
regal 737.16

regale — re infecta

regale n.
 delicacy 298.9
 feast 298.37
 refreshment 689.1
 treat 829.3
 amusement 840.1
regale v. feed 298.43
 feast 298.44
 refresh 689.2
 give pleasure 829.4
 entertain 840.20
regalia
 sovereignty 737.2
 royal insignia 747.1
regard n. look 441.2
 attention 457.1
 care 459.1
 repute 873.1
 love 897.1
 respect 928.1
 approbation 931.1
 without regard to
 irrelevantly 10.9
 notwithstanding 30.8
 with regard to 9.10
regard v.
 be related 9.3
 look at 441.11
 note 450.7
 judge 480.6
 believe 484.8
 study 539.4
 hold dear 897.11
 respect 928.4
regardful
 attentive 457.9
 careful 459.7
regardless
 inattentive 458.10
 neglectful 460.8
 insensible 823.5
 unconcerned 866.4
regardless of
 notwithstanding 30.8
 (in disagreement 24.10)
 conditionally 469.7
 defiant 715.3
regards
 compliments 894.3
 respects 928.3
 send one's regards 894.8
regatta
 race 274.4; 720.5
 festival 840.2
regelate 385.4
regelation 385.1
regency 755.3
regenerate v.
 convert 144.7
 (revolutionize 146.4)
 reproduce 163.2
 revive 660.13
 reform 950.4
 redeem 987.9
regenerate adj. 987.12
regeneration
 conversion 144.2

reproduction 163.1
revival 660.2
(reform 658.4)
divine function 976.6
religious ~ 987.3
regenerative 163.3
regenesis, re-genesis 163.1
regent ruler 745.7
 deputy 759.3
regicide 361.2
regime, régime
 circumstance 8.1
 regimen 662.15
 management 693.1
 rule 737.2
regimen diet 298.8
 remedy 662.15
 government 693.1
 rule 737.2
regiment 726.7
 (company 72.3)
regimentals 225.8
Reginn, Regin 193.5
region 181
 (compartment 51.5)
 (location 184.1)
 (land 342.1)
regional 181.6
 (locational 184.18)
regionalism 563.5
register n. list 86.1
 chronology 114.5
 heater 386.1
 music 413.15
 organ stop 417.12
 record 551.1
 (arrangement 60.3)
 (writing 590.3)
 recorder 553.1
 schedule 611.2
 account book 811.5
register v.
 simulate 19.7
 list 86.3
 indicate 550.18
 record 551.18
 represent 554.7
 act 599.26
 schedule 611.4
 affect 853.5
registrar
 recorder 553.1
 accountant 811.6
registration 551.7
registry list 86.1
 chronology 114.5
 record 551.1
 recording 551.7
 account book 811.5
reglet 591.5
regnal 737.15
regnant
 influential 175.10
 ruling 737.15
regorge 790.3
regrade 283.5
regrate possess 777.5
 purchase 795.3
 retail 796.5
regrater 797.1

regress n. 283.1
 (recession 287.1)
regress v. revert 145.4
 retrogress 283.5
 (recede 287.2)
 (relapse 661.3)
regression 283
 (reversion 145.1)
 (recession 287.1)
 (relapse 661.1)
 (perversion 988.3)
regressive
 reversionary 145.6
 retrogressive 283.7
 (reactionary 277.4)
 (recessive 287.3)
 (relapsing 661.4)
regret n. 833
 (disappointment 509.1)
 (discontent 832.1)
 (lamentation 839.1)
 (remorse 950.1)
regret v. 833.2
 (bewail 839.6)
 (repent 950.3)
regretful 833.3
 (disappointed 509.4)
 (discontented 832.5)
 (remorseful 950.5)
regrettable bad 649.8
 lamentable 833.4
regular n. 726.6
regular adj.
 uniform 16.5
 (conformable 82.9)
 (measured 466.13)
 (monotonous 841.8)
 unqualified 52.10
 orderly 58.7
 constant 136.4
 methodical 138.9
 (frequent 136.3)
 symmetrical 242.4
 smooth 255.5
 habitual 613.11
regular adv. 16.7; 138.12
regularity
 uniformity 16.2
 (sameness 13.2)
 (rule 80.1)
 (routine 613.4)
 (monotony 841.3)
 order 58.1
 periodicity 138
 symmetry 242.1
regularize
 symmetrize 242.3
 codify 963.4
regularly
 invariably 16.7
 periodically 138.12
regulate accord 23.8
 order 58.6
 methodize 60.8
 qualify 469.3
 render true 494.7
 govern 693.4
 right 922.3
 legislate 963.4
 be regulated by 82.4

regulation
 method 58.3
 government 693.1
 precept 697.1
 (rule 80.1)
 law 963.2
regulative 693.6
regulator 540.4
regulus 635.6
regurgitate
 go back 283.5
 flow back 348.17
 restore 790.3
regurgitation
 reflux 283.2
 backflow 348.2
rehabilitate 660.8
rehabilitation 660.1
 (restitution 790.1)
rehash n. 104.2
rehash v. repeat 104.4
 paraphrase 522.7
rehearsal
 repetend 104.2
 music 415.18
 narration 594.1
 preparation 673.1
rehearse
 enumerate 85.7
 repeat 104.4
 recount 594.5
 ~ a speech 589.3
 ~ a play 599.26
 prepare 673.8
reheat 384.19
reichsmark 800.8
Reichsrat, Reichsrath 696.5
Reichstag 696.6
reidentification 505.1
reidentify
 recognize 481a.6
 remember 505.10
reign n. influence 175.1
 dominion 737.2
reign v. 737.11
reign of terror
 anarchy 738.2
 despotism 739.2
 fear 860.5
reimburse
 indemnify 790.3
 repay 807.9
reimbursement
 repayment 807.3
 indemnity 973.2
rein n. 752.2
 (bond 45.2)
reincarnate 316.7
reincarnation 316.4
reincarnationism 994.1
reincarnationist 994.13
reindeer
 pack animal 271.2
 animal 366.11
rein v.
 rein in retard 275.7
 restrain 751.6
re infecta
 quiescent 265.8
 amiss 304.5

reinforce, re-en-
 force n. 215.2
reinforce, re-en-
 force v.
 increase 35.3
 add to 37.4
 strengthen 159.8
 replenish 637.4
 restore 660.8
 assist 707.6
reinforcement, re-en-
 forcement
 increase 35.1
 addition 37.1
 adjunct 39.1
 supporter 215.2
 replenishment 637.1
 aid 707.5
reinless 748.13
 (lax 738.7)
reins fastening 45.4
 direction 693.1
 restraint 752.2
reinstate 660.8; 790.3
reinstatement
 restoration 660.1
 restitution 790.1
reinvest 790.3
reinvestment
 restoration 660.1
 restitution 790.1
reinvigorate
 youthify 127.4
 restrengthen 159.8
 refresh 689.2
 (revive 660.13)
reinvigoration
 invigoration 159.2
 refreshment 689.1
reis 800.8
Reis Effendi 694.4
reissue n. 591.2
reissue v.
 reprint 591.14
 remonetize 800.19
reiterate v. 104.4
reiterate, reiterat-
 ed adj. 104.6
reiteration 104.1
 (duplication 90.1)
reiterative 104.6
Rejang 560.4
reject eliminate 42.4
 exclude 55.3
 eject 297.8
 be incredulous 487.3
 (disbelieve 485.5)
 repudiate 610.2
 (deny 536.2)
 discard 678.3
 refuse 764.2
 despise 930.5
 disapprove 932.5
rejected
 exploded 495.17
 not chosen 610.3
 jilted 898.6
rejection
 elimination 42.2
 exclusion 55.1
 ejection 297.1
 objection 489.2

repudiation 610
 (denial 536.1)
 (recantation 607.3)
 refusal 764.1
 disapprobation 932.1
rejective
 declinatory 610.3
 refusing 764.5
rejectment 55.1
rejoice 838.5
 delight 829.5
 cheer 836.6
 exult 838.5
 (be cheerful 836.5)
 (celebrate 883.3)
 (exult 884.6)
rejoice in 827.6
rejoicing n. 838
 (merriment 836.3)
 (merrymaking
 840.2)
 (celebration 883.1)
rejoicing adj. 838.9
rejoin
 reassemble 72.10
 meet 292.10
 answer 462.5
rejoinder 462.1, 2
rejuvenate
 youthify 127.4
 revive 660.13
rejuvenation 660.2
rejuvenesce 127.4
rekindle relight 384.17
 revive 660.13
 ~ feelings 824.2
relapse n. 661
 (reversion 145.1)
 (apostasy 607.2)
 (deterioration
 659.1)
relapse v. 661.3
 (retrovert 145.4)
 (retrograde 283.5)
 (deteriorate 659.6)
relapsing 661.4
 (retrograde 283.7)
relate
 be related 9.3, 4
 (connect 43.5)
 (compare 464.2)
 enumerate 85.7
 say 582.6
 narrate 594.5
related connected 9.6
 consanguine 11.7
 be related 9.3
 (answer to 462.8)
relation
 relationship 9
 (relevancy 23.2)
 (comparison 464.1)
 consanguinity 11.1
 (ancestry 166.1)
 (posterity 167.1)
 kinsman 11.3
 narration 594.1
relational 9.5
relationship 9.1
relative n. 11.3
relative adj.
 relational 9.5

 (correlative 12.6)
 (under considera-
 tion 454.3)
 comparative 26.3
relatively
 in relation 9.9
 (pertinently 23.13)
 (comparatively
 464.7)
 to a degree 32.13
relativism 451.11
relativity 450.12
relator 594.4
relax loosen 47.2
 retard 275.7
 soften 324.4, 5
 do nothing 681.2
 languish 683.10
 rest 687.4
 (cease 142.6)
 relent 914.3
relaxation
 incoherence 47.1
 weakness 160.1
 modulation 174.2
 softening 324.2
 repose 687.1
 laxity 738.1
 diversion 840.1
 dereliction 927.1
relaxed
 incoherent 47.3
 flexible 324.6
relay 636.2
relay race 274.4; 720.5
release n. death 360.1
 deliverance 672.1
 liberation 750.1
 (acquittal 970.1)
 permission 760.1
 receipt 771.4
 exemption 777a.1
 relinquishment
 781.1
 restitution 790.2
 receipt in full 807.4
release v. deliver 672.2
 exempt 748.10;
 777a.2
 free 750.2
 (acquit 970.3)
 relinquish 782.3
 let go 790.3
released dead 360.8
 exempted 748.18
relegate exclude 55.3
 send 270.9
 eject 297.8
 banish 297.11
 discard 678.3
 entrust 784.12
relegation
 exclusion 55.1
 banishment 297.3
relent
 be moderate 174.4
 be pliant 324.5
 submit 725.3
 take pity 914.3
relentless
 resolute 604.7
 persevering 604a.3

severe 739.5
unforgiving 919.6
 (heartless 907.8)
 (ruthless 914a.3)
 impenitent 951.3
relentlessness 919.2
 (ruthlessness
 914a.1)
relessee 785.2
relevance 23.2
 (relation 9.1)
relevant 23.10
 (like 17.10)
reliability
 certainty 474.1
 solvency 800.17
 trustworthiness
 939.3
reliable sound 150.5
 infallible 474.14
 believable 484.15
 authentic 494.12
 veracious 543.3
 safe 664.10
 solvent 800.22
 trustworthy 940.9
reliance belief 484.1
 expectation 507.2
 hope 858.1
relic
 antiquity 124.2
 memento 505.5
 vestige 551.5
relics remains 40.1
 mortal remains
 362.1
 sacred ~ 998.8
relict 905.3
relief outline 230.1
 sculpture 557.6, 7
 (composition 54.2)
 (protuberance
 250.2)
 (figure 554.4)
 remedy 662.1
 help 707.4
 easement 834
 (restoration 660.1)
 (refreshment 689.1)
 in high relief
 distinct 446.5
 conspicuous 525.5
 sculptured 557.11
 in low relief 557.11
 in relief raised 250.10
 sculptured 557.11
relieve cure 660.12
 help 707.6
 ease 834.4
 (remedy 662.24)
 (refresh 689.2)
relieved 834.6
relieving 834.7
 (restorative 660.18)
 (remedial 662.25)
relievo 557.6
relight rekindle 384.17
reillumine 420.21
religieuse 996.12
religion
 theology 983.1
 sect 984.3

religionist — Renaissance

(belief 484.3)
piety 987.1
religionist
  believer 987.4
  pietist 988.6
religious *n.*
  believer 987.4
  religieux 996.11
religious *adj.*
  exact 494.11
  conscientious 939.8
  godly 976.13
  theological 983.4
  pious 987.10
religiousness 987.1
relinquish
  abandon 624.3
  (recant 607.9)
  abdicate 738.6
  ~ property 782.3
  (disuse 678.3)
  ~ hope 859.5
relinquished
  abandoned 624.4
  surrendered 782.4
relinquishment
  abandonment 624.1
  (recantation 607.3)
  (resignation 757.1)
  surrender 725.2
  ~ of property 782
  (disuse 678.1)
reliquary case 191.8
  monument 551.4
  shrine 998.8; 1000.2
reliquiae
  antiquities 124.2
  mortal remains 361.1
relish *n.*
  pleasure 377.1
  condiment 393.1
  savor 394.2
  (taste 390.1)
  desire 865.1
have no relish for 866.3
with relish 836.13
relish *v.*
  enjoy 377.4; 827.6
  savor 394.6
  (taste 390.3)
relucent 420.22
reluct resist 719.3
  fight 720.8
reluctance
  unwillingness 603.1
  (dislike 867.1)
  resistance 719.1
reluctant 603.5
reluctate resist 719.3
  fight 720.8
reluctation 719.1
relume 384.17; 420.21
rely *v.*
rely on
  trust in 484.7, 17
  hope 858.6
remain be left 40.5
  continue 106.2
  be permanent 141.4

(persist 143.2)
be present 186.8
be quiescent 265.5
(stop 142.6)
(settle 184.14)
remainder
  remains 40.1
  (redundance 641.1)
  posteriority 117.1
  estate 780.2
remainderman 779.5
remains
  remainder 40.1
  (oddments 51.6)
  corpse 362.1
  vestige 551.5
remake
  reproduce 163.2
  reconstruct 660.14
remaking
  reproduction 163.1
  reconstruction 660.3
remand 741.4
remanent
  additional 37.7
  remaining 40.6
remanet 40.1
remark *n.* 582.4
  (assertion 535.1)
  (utterance 580.3)
remark *v.*
  give attention 457.4
  say 582.6
  feel 821.3
remarkable
  notable 31.13
  unusual 83.10
  important 642.10
  (distinguished 873.16)
  wonderful 870.7
remarkably
  notably 31.21
  eminently 33.10
remarry 903.13
remediable 658.16
  (restorative 660.19)
  (curable 662.27)
remedial 662.25
  (salubrious 656.5)
  (improving 658.15)
  (restorative 660.18)
  (relieving 834.7)
remediless 859.7
remedy *n.*
  counteractant 179.2
  cure 662
  (restoration 660.5)
  relief 707.4
  money 800.1
beyond remedy 859.7
remedy *v.*
  repair 660.10, 11, 12
  (better 658.8)
  (cure 662.23)
  (relieve 834.4)
  right 922.3
remember
  recollect 505.10
  remind 505.15
rememberable
  memorable 505.19

notable 642.10
remembered 505.18
be remembered 505.12
remembrance *n.*
  memory 505.1, 5
  monument 551.4
  posthumous fame 873.5
  commemoration 883.1
have no remembrance 506.4
in remembrance
  in memory of 505.23
  in celebration 883.5, 6
remembrance *v.* 505.15
remembrancer 505.5
remembrances 894.3
remiform 245.16
remiges 256.8
remigrate
  go back 283.5
  go out 295.8
remigration
  progression 283.1
  return 292.3
  exodus 295.2
remind 505.15
  (hint 527.8)
remindal, reminder 505.5
  (hint 527.4)
remindful 505.17
reminisce 505.10
reminiscence 505.4
reminiscent 505.17
remise, remiss *v.* 748.10
remiss *adj.*
  neglectful 460.8
  (lax 738.7)
  reluctant 603.5
  shiftless 674.11
  indolent 683.13
  nonobservant 773.5
  sinful 945.11
remissible 937.10
remission pause 142.2
  modulation 174.2
  laxity 738.1
  forgiveness 918.1
  absolution 970.1
remissive 918.5
remissness 683.3
remit decrease 36.4
  interrupt 142.7
  be moderate 174.4
  exempt 748.10
  restore 790.3
  forgive 918.3
  acquit 970.3
remittance 807.2
remittent *n.* 655.4
remittent *adj.* 138.10
remitter 790.2
remnant 40.1
remodel
  regenerate 144.7
  (revolutionize 146.4)
  reconstruct 660.14

(reform 658.12)
remodelment 660.3
remonetize 800.19
remonstrance
  protest 489.2
  deprecation 766.1
  (dissuasion 616.1)
  (advice 695.1)
  reproof 932.3
remonstrant 766.3
remonstrate
  advise 695.4
  deprecate 766.2
  (dissuade 616.2)
  reprove 932.8
remonstrative 765.3
remonstratory 766.3
remora adherer 46.3
  hindrance 706.2
remorse 950.1
  (regret 833.1)
remorseful 950.5
  (regretful 833.3)
remorseless
  revengeful 919.6
  impenitent 951.3
remote unrelated 10.7
  distant 196.5
remoteness 196.1
remotion 270.1
remount 271.3
removable 270.11
removal
  deduction 38.1
  exclusion 55.1
  dislocation 185.1
  (ejection 297.1)
  transference 270.1
  departure 293.1
  evacuation 297.5
  extraction 301.1
remove *n.* degree 26.1
  rank 71.1
  food 308.28
  class 541.8
remove *v.* deduct 38.4
  disjoin 44.7
  exclude 55.3
  destroy 162.4
  displace 185.2
  interval 198.4
  transfer 270.6
  eject 297.8
  depart 293.4
  extract 301.5
  discard 678.3
  ~ from office 756.5
removed 196.5
removement 270.1
remuda 72.4
remunerate
  profit 644.2
  recompense 973.2
remuneration 973.1
  (gain 775.2)
remunerative
  profitable 644.5
  gainful 775.12
  compensative 973.5
renaissance, renascence 660.2
Renaissance 554.9

renascent — replace

renascent
  reproductive 163.3
  renewed 660.17
rencontre, rencounter n.
  contiguity 199.1
  meeting 292.4
  contest 720.2
rencounter v. 292.10
rend sever 44.8
  be brittle 328.3
rend the air
  be loud 404.5
  vociferate 411.7
  (wail 839.6)
rend the ears
  be loud 404.5
  be strident 410.7
rend the heart 837.8
render convert 144.6
  ~ music 416.18
  interpret 522.6
  perform 680.6
  give 784.8
render up 790.3
rendering 522.2
  (paraphrase 21.4)
rendezvous n. 72.1; 74.2
rendezvous v. 72.10
rendition
  interpretation 522.2
  restitution 790.1
renegade n.
  apostate 607.5
  (insurgent 742.3)
  (traitor 949.3)
  fugitive 623.5
renegade adj. 607.11
renege, renig n. 756.1
renege, renig v.
  abandon 624.3
  abrogate 756.3
renew
  remember 505.10
  revive 660.13
  (reproduce 90.2)
  (repeat 104.4)
  (renovate 123.6)
  (refresh 689.2)
renewal 660.2
  (reproduction 90.1)
  (repetition 104.1)
  (newness 123.1)
renewed 660.17
  (new 123.8)
renewer 660.7
reniform 245.14
renitence
  counteraction 179.1
  rigidity 323.1
  elasticity 325.1
  unwillingness 603.1
  resistance 719.1
renitent
  counteractive 179.5
  rigid 323.5
  elastic 325.5
  unwilling 603.5
  resistant 719.5
rennet bag 191.7
renounce abjure 536.2

recant 607.9
  (disclaim 756.4)
  (resign 757.2)
  reject 610.2
  abdicate 738.6
  relinquish 782.3
  abstain 953.5
renouncement
  recantation 607.3
  refusal 764.1
  temperance 953.1
renovate 660.13
renovation 660.2
  (newness 123.1)
renovator, renovater 660.7
renovize 660.13
renown 873.1
renowned 873.16
renownless 874.10
  (ignoble 876.11)
rent n.
  tenement 189.3
  cleft 198.2
  receipts 810.2
  (dues 812.2)
rent v. open 260.11
  ~ to 787.6
  ~ from 788.3
  (purchase 795.3)
rentage, rental 810.2
renter lodger 188.4
  tenant 779.1
rent-free 815.10
rent-roll 810.2
renunciant 757.3
renunciation
  recantation 607.3
  (resignation 757.1)
  surrender 725.2
  refusal 764.1
  relinquishment 781.1; 782.1
  temperance 953.1
renunciative
  recanting 607.12
  resigning 757.3
renunciatory 757.3
reoccupy
  recover 775.9
  retake 789.14
reorganization 660.1
reorganize
  regenerate 144.7
  re-establish 660.8
  (reform 658.12)
rep 949.1
repair n. 660.4
  (improvement 658.1)
  (refreshment 689.1)
out of repair 659.12
repair v. go to 266.22
  mend 660.11
  (better 658.8)
  (remedy 662.23)
  atone for 952.4
repairer, repairman 660.7
  (workman 690.10)
repair ship 726.11
reparability 660.6

reparation
  restoration 660.4
  restitution 790.1
  repayment 807.3
  atonement 952.1
  (penalty 974.1)
  reward 973.1
reparative
  compensating 30.6
  restorative 660.18
  rewarding 973.5
repartee n.
  answer 462.1
  persiflage 842.4
repartee v.
  acknowledge 462.5
  bandy jokes 842.8
repartition 786.1
repass 302.2
repast 298.34
repay retaliate 718.2
  make repayment 807.9
  (compensate 30.4)
  reward 973.3
repayment
  reimbursement 807.3
  reward 973.2
repeal n. 756.1
repeal v. 756.3
repeat n. 104.2
repeat v. imitate 19.5
  iterate 104.4
  (duplicate 90.2)
  (frequency 136.2)
  (maintain 143.3)
  (reproduce 163.2)
  (tautologize 573.6)
  (be loquacious 584.4)
  (renew 660.13)
  reaffirm 535.5
repeatal 104.1
repeated 104.6
  (frequent 136.3)
  (dingdong 407.11)
  (habitual 613.11)
  be repeated 408.7
repeatedly 104.8
  (twice 90.5)
  (frequently 136.5)
repeater
  timepiece 114.6
  voter 609.4
  politics 702.4
  firearm 727.10
repel repulse 289.2
  reject 610.2
  deter 616.3
  avert 706.5
  resist 719.3
  refuse 764.4
  revolt 830.7
  (be unsavory 395.4)
  (disgust 841.6)
  (displease 867.6)
  (be hateful 898.4)
  exclude 893.7
repellency 289.1
repellent
  repulsive 289.3; 653.17

resistant 719.5
  odious 830.14
  (ugly 846.9)
repent v. 950.3
  (confess 529.5)
  (recant 607.9)
  (regret 833.2)
  (bewail 839.6)
  (be converted 987.7)
  do penance 952.4
repent adj. 275.9
repentance 950.1
  (confession 529.2)
  (recantation 607.3)
  (lamentation 839.1)
  (redemption 987.3)
  (religion 998.3)
repentant n. 950.2
repentant adj. 950.5
repercuss v.
  recoil 277.3
  repulse 289.2
  detonate 406.8
  reverberate 408.7
repercussion
  repetend 104.2
  recoil 277.1
  detonation 406.2
  reverberation 408.2
  music 415.20
repercussive
  recoiling 277.4
  repulsive 289.3
  reverberative 408.9
repertory
  repertoire 599.7
  story 636.4
repertory theater 599.7
repetend
  number 84.2
  repetition 104.1
repetition
  imitation 19.1
  repetend 104.2
  (duplication 90.1)
  (frequency 136.1)
  (recurrence 138.2)
  (continuance 143.1)
  (reproduction 163.1)
  (sound 407.1)
  (twice-told tale 496.3)
  (tautology 573.2)
  (renewal 660.2)
  (retold story 842.6)
repetitional, repetitious 104.6
  (tautological 573.8)
  (tedious 841.8)
rephrase 522.7
repine
  be discontented 832.3
  regret 833.2
  grieve 837.6
replace
  substitute 147.3
  restore 660.8
  (return 790.3)

1052

replacement
  substitution 147.1
  restoration 660.1
replenish fill 52.7
  reinforce 637.4
replenishment 637.1
replete *v.* fill 52.7
  replenish 637.4
replete *adj.* full 52.11
  (overfull 641.6)
  ample 639.7
repletion
  overfullness 641.1
  (plenty 639.2)
  satiety 869.1
replevin *n.* bail 771.1
  recovery 775.3
  restitution 790.2
replevin *v.*
  recover 775.9
  take back 790.4
replevy *n.* 790.2
replevy *v.*
  recover 775.9
  seize 789.9
  take back 790.4
replica 21.2
replicate 462.5
replication 462.1, 2
replier 462.4
reply *n.*
  answer 462.1, 2
  (defense 937.2)
  letter 592.2
reply *v.*
  reverberate 408.7
  answer 462.5, 6
  ~ by mail 592.6
report *n.*
  detonation 406.2
  note 413.6
  (explosion 173.3)
  (shot 284.4)
  music 415.14
  judgment 480.1, 3
  information 527.1
  publication 531.1, 3
  rumor 532.3
  record 551.2
  description 594.1
  commentary 595.2
  renown 873.1
  by common report
    527.15
    (rumor 532.10)
report *v.*
  pass judgment 480.9
  tell 527.7
  (record 551.8)
  make known 531.7
  (~ news 532.6)
  narrate 594.5
reportage
  publication 531.1
  rumor 532.3
reporter
  informant 527.5
  journalist 593.16
  (publisher 531.5)
repose *n.*
  quiescence 265.1
  rest 687

(inaction 681.1;
  683.1)
(sleep 683.5)
repose *v.* recline 213.5
  rest on 215.27
  be quiescent 265.5
  (not do 681.2)
  rest 687.3
  (lie idle 683.8)
  (sleep 683.9)
**repose on one's
  laurels**
  pause 142.6;
  rest 265.5
  do nothing 681.2
  relax 687.4
reposed 687.6
reposeful
  quiescent 265.7
  restful 687.6
reposing
  quiescent 265.7
  dead 360.8
  reposeful 687.6
  (inactive 683.12, 16)
reposit 636.7
  (put 184.10)
reposition 184.5
repository 636.4
repossess 775.9
repossession 775.3
repoussé *n.* 847.3
repoussé *adj.* 250.10
reprehend 932.7, 8
reprehensibility 947.1
reprehensible
  hateful 898.7
  blameworthy 932.14
  (bad 649.8)
  (wrong 923.4)
  (unworthy 940.9)
  (unjustifiable
    941a.4)
  (vicious 945.11)
reprehension 932.2, 3
represent
  denote 467.7
  mean 516.5
  tell 527.7
  typify 550.18
  delineate 554.7
  (simulate 19.7)
  (paint 428.10)
  (symbolize 521.2)
  (limn 556.17)
  (describe 594.5)
  (act 599.26)
  be deputy 759.4
  (substitute for
    147.3)
  (be commissioned
    755.5)
representation
  copy 21.2
  exhibition 448.2
  information 527.1
  delineation 554
  (imitation 19.1)
  (simulation 19.3)
  (art 556.8)
  (picture 556.9)
  (description 594.1)

(acting 599.6)
representative *n.*
  example 82.2
  congressman 696.8
  deputy 759.1
  (agent 690.1)
representative *adj.*
  peculiar 79.8
  exemplary 82.11
  typical 550.21
  illustrative 554.9
  (imitative 19.12)
  (descriptive 594.7)
  deputy 759.6
repress blunt 254.2
  muffle 408a.4
  restrain 751.6
  (counteract 179.3)
  (compose 826.7)
  ~ one's feelings
    826.8
repression
  secrecy 528.2
  subjugation 749.1
  restraint 751.1
  (counteraction
    179.1)
repressionary, repressive 751.13
reprieval 672.1
reprieve *n.* delay 133.2
  release 672.1
  pardon 970.1
reprieve *v.*
  liberate 750.2, 6
  pardon 970.3
reprimand *n.* 932.3
reprimand *v.* 932.8
reprimander 936.2
reprint *n.*
  duplicate 21.2
  (reproduction 163.1)
  print 591.2
reprint *v.*
  engrave 558.5
  print 591.14
reprisal
  retaliation 718.1
  resumption 789.3
  revenge 919.1
  in reprisal 718.5
reprise 39a
reprises 789.3
reproach *n.*
  stigma 874.2
  reproof 932.3
  accusation 938.1
reproach *v.*
  censure 932.7
  accuse 938.4
reproachful 932.11
reproachfully 932.15
reprobacy
  improbity 940.1
  wickedness 945.1
reprobate *n.* 949.1
reprobate *v.* 932.7
reprobate *adj.*
  lost 776.5
  unprincipled 940.8
  wicked 945.11
  unregenerate 988.10

reprobation 932.2
reproduce
  imitate 19.5
  repeat 104.4
  beget 161.10
  recreate 163.2
  (procreate 161.10)
reproducer 417.9
reproduction
  imitation 19.1
  duplicate 21.2
  duplication 90.1
  repetition 104.1
  recreation 163
  (generation 161.2)
  (revival 660.2)
reproductive
  recreative 163.3
  procreative 168.8
reproof 932.3
  (accusation 938.1)
reprovable 932.14
reproval 932.3
reprove 932.8
reprover 936.2
reptant, reptatorial
  275.9
reptile animal 366.18
  toady 886.2
  scoundrel 949.1
Reptilia 366.18
reptilian
  snakish 366.27
  groveling 886.4
republic
  country 182.1
  nation 372.2
  government 737.4
republican 876.3
Republican 712.6
republicanism 737.4
republic of letters
  560.8
repudiate
  exclude 55.3
  not admit 489.4
  recant 607.9
  (disclaim 756.4)
  reject 610.2
  (deny 536.2)
  ~ a debt 808.5
repudiation
  exclusion 55.1
  recantation 607.3
  (abrogation 756.1)
  rejection 610.1
  (denial 536.1)
  ~ of a debt 808.1
repudiative
  recanting 607.12
  resigning 757.3
repugnance
  contrariety 14.1
  disparity 24.2
  counteraction 179.1
  opposition 708.1
  resistance 719.1
  abhorrence 867.2
  (displeasure 828.2)
  (hatred 898.1)
  enmity 889.1

repugnant — resolute

repugnant
  contrary 14.5
  disagreeing 24.6
  counteractive 179.5
  denying 536.3
  opposed 708.4
  resistant 719.5
  odious 830.14
  (dislikable 867.9)
  inimical 889.3
repugnate 708.2
repulse *n.*
  recoil 277.1
  repulsion 289.1
  resistance 719.1
  defeat 732.3
  refusal 764.1
repulse *v.*
  repel 289.2; 717.8
  reject 610.2
  resist 719.3
  refuse 764.4
repulsion
  repelling 289
  resistance 719.1
repulsive
  repellent 289.3
  nasty 395.7
  (malodorous 401.4)
  foul 653.17
  resistant 719.5
  odious 830.14
  (ugly 846.9)
  (dislikable 867.9)
repurchase *n.* 795.1
repurchase *v.* 795.3
reputability 873.1
  (probity 939.1)
  (virtue 944.1)
reputable
  estimable 873.15
  (great 31.14)
  (noble 875.10)
  honorable 939.7
reputation 873.1
repute good ~ 873.1
  (importance 642.1)
  (approbation 931.1)
  bad ~ 874.1
request *n.* 765
  (demand 741.2)
  (orison 990.3)
in request 630.3
request *v.* 765.4
  (claim 741.6)
  (pray 990.11)
requiem 839.3
require need 630.2
  (necessitate 601.8)
  want 640.6
  demand 741.5
  compel 744.2
  charge 812.5
  ~ dues 924.7
  ~ duty 926.7
required
  requisite 630.3
  (obligatory 926.9)
  ordered 741.9
  compulsory 744.3
requirement need 630
  (necessity 601.1)

  (want 640.3)
  (compulsion 744.1)
  (desire 865.1)
  demand 741.2
requisite *n.*
  condition 469.2;
    770.1
  requirement 630.1
requisite *adj.* 630.3
  (necessary 601.11)
  (urgent 642.13)
  (compulsory 744.3)
requisition
  demand 741.2
  (requirement 630.1)
  request 765.1
requital
  retaliation 718.1
  (punishment 972.1)
  reward 973.1
in requital 718.5
requite
  reciprocate 148.3
  retaliate 718.2
  show gratitude 916.3
  repay 973.3
rerebrace 717.2
reredos 1000.3
rescind disjoin 44.7
  revoke 756.3
  (recant 607.9)
rescission
  sunderance 44.2
  revokement 756.1
rescript copy 21.1
  answer 462.1
  rewriting 590.3
  epistle 592.2
  decree 741.3
  (law 963.2)
rescription
  answer 462.1
  epistle 592.2
rescuable 672.3
rescue *n.*
  deliverance 672.1
  relief 707.4
to the rescue! 672.4;
    707.16
rescue *v.*
  deliver 672.2
  (redeem 660.9)
  help 707.6
rescuer 912.2
Rescuer 318.6
research 461.2, 3
resection 44.1
reseda 435.3
resemblance
  similarity 17.1
  copy 21.1
  bear resemblance
    17.7
resemble 17.7
  (be comparable
    464.4)
resent 900.6
  (dislike 867.4)
resentful 900.12
  (displeased 828.14)
  (ill-humored 901.7)
  (revengeful 919.6)

  be resentful 900.6
resenting 900.12
  (disliking 867.7)
resentment 900
  (displeasure 828.2)
  (dislike 867.1)
  (hate 898.1)
  (ill-humor 901.1)
  (revengefulness
    919.2)
reservation
  condition 469.2
  taciturnity 584.1
  with a reservation
    469.7; 770.4
reserve *n.*
  secrecy 528.2
  taciturnity 585.1
  fund 636.2
  modesty 881.1
have in reserve 637.5
  (reserve 636.8)
in reserve
  imminent 152.3
  in store 636.9
  preparatory 673.10
reserve *v.*
  postpone 133.4
  keep secret 528.11
  appoint 609.11
  save 636.8
  preserve 670.3
  not use 678.5
reserved
  secretive 528.22
  taciturn 585.4
  modest 881.5
reserve militia 726.6
reserves fund 636.2
  (funds 800.2)
  (savings 817.2)
  military ~ 726.6
reservoir *n.*
  fountain 153.2
  pool 343a.1
  store 636.4
  fund 636.2
reservoir *v.* 636.7
reset sharpen 253.9
  transplant 371.8
  readjust 494.7
reside 186.10
  (settle 184.14)
residence
  habitation 186.2
  abode 189.1
resident *n.*
  inhabitant 188.1
  intern 662.19
  minister 759.2
  clerical ~ 996.5
resident *adj.* 186.14
residential 186.14
residentiary
  inhabitant 188.1
  clerical ~ 996.5
resider 188.1
residual, residuary
  40.6
residue, residuum
  40.1, 2
resign submit 725.3

  abdicate 738.6
  ~ one's office 757.2
  (renounce 607.9)
  (abandon 624.3)
  relinquish 782.3
resign oneself
  submit 725.3
  obey 743.2
  endure 826.6
resignation
  submission 725.1
  (sufferance 826.4)
  (contentment 831.1)
  (humility 879.1)
  obedience 743.1
  demission 757
  (recantation 607.3)
  (relinquishment
    624.1; 782.1)
resigned
  submissive 725.5
  obedient 743.2, 3
  meek 826.10
  (content 831.6)
  (humble 879.4)
resignful, resigning
  757.3
resignment 757.1
resile 277.3
resilience reflux 283.2
  elasticity 325.1
resilient
  regressive 283.7
  elastic 325.5
resin *n.* **adherer** 46.3
  gum 356a
resin *v.* 356a.2
resinate, resinoid
  356a.1
resinous 356a.3
resipiscence 950.1
resist withstand 719.3
  (counteract 179.3)
  (thwart 706.7)
  (oppose 708.2)
  (attack 716.5)
  refuse 764.4
resistance
  aeronautics 267a.13
  toughness 327.1
  withstanding 719
  (opposition 708.1)
  (defense 717.1)
resistant tough 327.5
  resisting 719.5
  (unyielding 323.5)
  (obstinate 606.6)
  (oppositional 708.4)
resisting 719.5
  (rebellious 742.7)
resistless 601.11
resistor 158a.6
resolute
  determined 604.7
  (persevering
    604a.3)
  (obstinate 606.6)
  (earnest 682.18)
  (resistant 719.5)
  courageous 861.8
  constant 939.10
  be resolute 604.5

1054

resolutely — restlessness

(persevere 604a.2)
(be obstinate 606.5)
resolutely 604.9
  (perseveringly 604a.4)
resoluteness
  resolution 604.1
  courage 861.1
resolution
  dissection 44.4
  decomposition 49.1
  conversion 144.1
  (change 140.1)
  orchestration 413.3
  topic 454.1
  analysis 461.3
  solution 481a.2
  explanation 522.1
  determination 604
  (firmness 150.1)
  (strength 159.1)
  (will 600.1)
  (perseverance 604a.1)
  (obstinacy 606.1)
  (eagerness 682.3)
  (courage 861.1)
  purpose 620.1
  plan 626.1
  dissolution 659.2
resolutive *n.* 335.4
resolutive *adj.* 335.9
resolve *n.*
  resolution 604.1
  purpose 620.1
resolve *v.* change 140.6
  liquefy 335.5
  analyze 461.17
  judge 480.6
  solve 481a.4
  mean 516.5
  determine 604.6
  (will 600.2)
  (decide 609.8)
  resolve into 144.6, 8
resolved 604.7, 8
  (intending 620.4)
resolvent *n.* 335.4
resolvent *adj.*
  decomposing 49.5
  dispersive 73.5
  solvent 335.9
resonance 408
resonance box 417.13
resonant *n.* 408.3
resonant *adj.* 408.9
  (rolling 407.11)
resonate 408.7
  (roll 407.6)
resorb 296.4
resorbence 296.1
resorbent 296.6
resort *n.*
  meeting place 74.2
  habitat 189.13
  (hideaway 530.2)
  expedient 646.2
  (means 632.1)
  refuge 666.3
  use 677.1
  last resort
    necessity 601.5

(expedient 646.2)
refuge 666.3
resort *v.*
  frequent 186.11
  go to 266.22
  use 677.5
re-sort *v.* 72.10
resound *n.* 408.2
resound *v.*
  be loud 404.5
  reverberate 408.7
  (sound 402.7)
re-sound 402.7
resounding 408.9
resource
  reserve source 636.2
  expedient 646.2
  refuge 666.3
  last resource 601.5
    (means 632.1)
resourceful 698.11
resources means 632.1
  (provision 637.1)
  stock 636.2
  assets 780.7
  pecuniary 800.2
respect *n.* aspect 448.4
  attention 457.1
  repute 873.1
  deference 928
  (courtesy 894.1)
  (piety 987.1)
  command respect 928.7
  in no respect 536.4
  in respect to, with respect to 9.10
respect *v.*
  acknowledge 488.9
  observe 772.3
  regard 928.4
respectability
  mediocrity 736.1
  probity 939.1
  (reputability 873.1)
respectable
  reputable 873.15
  honorable 939.7
respected 928.9
  (approved 931.10)
respectful 928.8
  (courteous 894.12)
  (dutiful 926.8)
respective special 79.7
  apportioned 786.4
respectively
  severally 79.12
  each to each 786.5
respectless
  inattentive 458.10
  neglectful 460.8
respects
  compliments 894.3
  regards 928.3
  in all respects
    mainly 50.11
    throughout 52.15
  pay one's respects
    show courtesy 894.8
    (visit 802.10)
    pay homage to 928.5
respiration 349.18

respirator 349.20
respire 349.23
respirometer 662.22
respite *n.*
  interim 109a.1
  delay 133.2
  pause 142.2
  (idleness 683.2)
  recess 687.2
  reprieve 970.1
respite *v.* delay 133.2
  reprieve 970.3
resplendence
  brightness 420.1
  illustriousness 873.2
resplendent
  bright 420.22
  beautiful 845.13
  illustrious 873.17
respond *n.* 462.1
respond *v.* agree 23.7
  answer 462.5, 8
  be concordant 714.2
  feel 821.3
respondence 462.1
respondent *n.*
  answerer 462.4
  accused 938.3
respondent *adj.* 462.11
response
  music 415.14, 15
  answer 462.1
  concord 714.1
  feeling 821.1
  sympathy 888.1
  ecclesiastical ~ 990.2
responsibility
  solvency 800.17
  duty 926.1
  fix the responsibility
    attribute 155.3
    blame 938.4
  take the responsibility
    exercise volition 600.2
    bear the blame 932.10
responsible
  answerable 462.12
  solvent 800.22
  amenable 926.11
responsions 461.3
responsive
  flexible 324.6
  elastic 325.5
  sensible 375.6
  answering 462.11
  unprejudiced 498.12
responsory
  music 415.11, 14
  anthem 990.2
ressaidar, ressaldar 745.11
rest *n.* remains 40.1
  interim 109a.1
  pause 142.2
  (inaction 681.1)
  (idleness 683.2)
  foundation 215.3
  fulcrum 215.5

quiescence 265.1
(inertness 172.1)
silence 403.1
music 413.12
repose 687.1
at rest
  quiescent 265.7, 8
  dead 360.8
  beneath the sod 363.28
  all's well! 664.14
  at ease 687.8
  content 831.6
  put at rest 265.6
rest *v.*
  be permanent 141.4
  pause 142.6
  be quiescent 265.5
  be at anchor 267.13
  weigh 319.8
  be dependent 475.7
  do nothing 681.2
  repose 687.3
  be content 831.3
  rest on
    be supported 215.27
    rely on 484.7
  rest on one's oars
    pause 142.6
    shirk 623.8
    do nothing 681.2
    lie idle 683.8
    relax 687.4
restate 522.7
restatement 104.2
restaurant 298.42
  (inn 189.8)
restaurateur 779.2
restful quiescent 265.7
  comfortable 377.8
  subdued 405.9
  reposeful 687.6
restfulness 377.2
resthouse, rest house 189.8
resting 265.7
resting place
  fulcrum 215.5
  stand 265.4
  destination 292.6
  grave 363.13
restitute 790.3
restitution
  restoration 660.1
  return 790
restitutionist 984.14
restitutive 790.3
restive averse 603.5
  obstinate 606.6
  insubordinate 742.6
  incompliant 764.5
  nervous 860.14
restless unquiet 149.6
  (moving 264.8)
  turbulent 173.12
  agitated 315.13
  active 682.21
  excitable 825.9
  tremulous 860.14
restlessness
  disquiet 149.3
  agitation 315.1

restorable — retreat 1056

restlessness (cont'd)
  activity 682.6, 9
  excitement 825.3
  trepidation 860.3
restorable 658.16
  (recoverable 660.19)
restorableness 660.6
restoral 790.1
restoration
  reinstatement 660
  (reversion 145.1)
  (reproduction 163.1)
  (improvement 658.1)
  (refreshment 689.1)
  restitution 790.1
restorative n. 662.1
  (cure 660.5)
restorative adj.
  revivatory 660.18
  (salubrious 656.5)
  (improving 658.15)
  (remedial 662.25)
  (refreshing 689.4)
  (relieving 834.7)
  restitutive 790.5
restore
  render sane 502.4
  reinstate 660.8
  (recreate 163.2)
  (vivify 359.8)
  (better 658.8)
  (reform 658.12)
  (deliver 672.2)
  (refresh 689.2)
  (relieve 834.4)
  (right 922.3)
  return 790.3
restrain limit 233.2
  circumscribe 229.2
  qualify 469.3
  curb 751.6
  (moderate 174.5)
  (counteract 179.3)
  (disincline 616.3)
  (hinder 706.4)
  (oppose 708.2)
  (compel 744.2)
  (prohibit 761.2)
  (compose 826.7)
  simplify 849.2
restrainable 743.3
restrained
  speech 578.4
  under restraint 751.10
  (moderate 174.6)
  inornate 849.4
  temperate 953.6
restraining 751.13
  (compulsory 744.3)
restraint
  circumscription 229.1
  elegance 578.1
  hindrance 706.1
  curb 751
  (moderation 174.1)
  (counteraction 179.1)
  (discussion 616.1)
  (opposition 708.1)

(compulsion 744.1)
(prohibition 761.1)
equanimity 826.3
simplicity 849.1
temperance 953.1
under restraint
  circumscribed 229.4
  restrained 751.10
restrict
  circumscribe 229.2
  limit 233.2
  qualify 469.3
  hinder 706.4
  restrain 751.6
  prohibit 761.2
restricted
  special 79.7
  narrow 203.9
restriction
  junction 43.1
  circumscription 229.1
  qualification 469.1
  hindrance 706.1
  restraint 751.1
  prohibition 761.1
restrictionist 751.5
restrictive
  qualifying 469.6
  restraining 751.13
  (hindering 706.8)
  prohibitive 761.3
restringe 751.6
rest room 653.9
resty 606.6
result n.
  remainder 40.3
  consequence 154.1
  (eventuality 151.1)
  product 161.6
  conclusion 480.1
result v. ensue 117.2
  eventuate 151.1
  be the effect 154.3
resultant n. result 40.3
  effect 154.1
resultant adj. 154.6
resulting 154.5
resume repeat 104.4, 5
  recover 660.15;
    775.9
  retake 789.14
résumé
  review 594.1
  summary 596.1
resumption
  revival 660.2
  reoccupation 789.3
  (recovery 775.3)
resupinate, resupine 213.9
resupination 213.2
resurge 660.15
resurgence
  reproduction 163.1
  revival 660.2
resurgent 163.3
resurrect 660.15
resurrection
  revival 660.2
  afterlife 981.6
resuscitate 660.13

(refresh 658.9)
resuscitation 660.2
retable 215.19
retail n. 796.1
retail v. disperse 73.3
  sell 796.5
retail adj. 794.10
retailer 797.1
retailing 798.2
retain stabilize 150.4
  remember 505.11
  reserve 636.8
  keep 781.4
  (possess 777.4)
retainer escort 88.4
  (retinue 746.6)
  guardian 664.3
  bodyguard 717.6
  servant 746.1
retaining 781.5
retainment 781.1
retake recover 775.9
  resume 789.14
retaliate 718.2
  (reciprocate 12.5)
  (interchange 148.3)
  (repay 807.9)
  (revenge 919.4)
retaliation 718
  (reciprocation 12.2)
  (compensation 30.1)
  (interchange 148.1)
  (reaction 277.1)
  (punishment 972.1)
in retaliation 718.5
retaliatory 718.4
  (revengeful 919.6)
retard n. 275.3
retard v. delay 133.6
  slow down 275.7
  hinder 706.4
retardation
  delay 133.2
  slowdown 275.3
  hindrance 706.1
retardment 706.1
retch 297.18
retell repeat 104.4
  recapitulate 594.5
  (tell 527.7)
retention
  memory 505.2
  keeping 781
  (tenacity 46.2)
  (possession 777.1)
  (seizure 789.1)
retentive
  recollective 505.17
  retaining 781.5
retentivity
  memory 505.2
  retention 781.1
reticella 219.5
reticence
  secrecy 528.2
  taciturnity 584.1
reticent
  secretive 528.22
  taciturn 585.4
reticle 219.4
reticular 219.11
reticulation 219.3

reticule, reticulum
  handbag 191.5
  network 219.4
Reticulum 318.6
retiform 219.11
retimber 367.13
retina 441.7
retinue adjunct 39.2
  attendance 88.5
  (afterpart 65.2)
  (procession 69.3)
  (servants 746.6)
retiral 757.1
retire
  be concave 252.8
  go back 283.5
  recede 287.2
  (shrink 623.9)
  depart 293.4
  disappear 449.2
  hide 528.16
  resign 757.2
  be modest 881.3
  seclude oneself 893.6
retired 893.10
retirement
  progression 283.1
  recession 287.1
  resignation 757.1
  seclusion 893.2
retiring
  concave 252.10
  color 438.6
retort n.
  conversion 144.4
  interchange 148.1
  receptacle 191.11
  vaporizer 336.3
  heater 386.1
  answer 462.1
  (gibe 930.3)
  refutal 479.1
  retaliation 718.1
  witty ～ 842.4
  recrimination 938.1
retort v. answer 462.5
  retaliate 718.2
  bandy jokes 842.8
  ～ an accusation 938.4
retort courteous 718.1
retortion 311.2
retouch 660.11
retrace 461.20
retrace one's steps
  go back 283.5
  recant 607.9
retract recant 607.9
  (deny 536.2)
  revoke 756.3
retraction
  repulsion 289.1
  recantation 607.3
  (negation 536.1)
  (abrogation 756.1)
  (resignation 757.1)
retread 272.16
retreat n.
  resort 74.2; 189.13
  (resting place 265.4)
  (hideaway 530.2)

retreat — reverse

progression 283.1
recession 287.1
  (avoidance 623.1)
  departure 293.1
  refuge 666.3
  (hiding place 530.2)
  seclusion 893.2
sound a retreat 283.5
retreat v. incline 217.6
  be concave 252.8
  go back 283.5
  (revert 145.4)
  recede 287.2
  depart 293.4
retreating 252.10
retrench excise 38.5
  cut off 38.6
  shorten 201.4
  economize 817.3
retrenchment
  deduction 38.1
  shortening 201.2
  economy 817.1
retribution
  retaliation 718.1
  repayment 807.3
  punishment 972.1
  (penalty 974.1)
  reward 973.1
retributive
  retaliatory 718.4;
    972.5
  rewarding 973.5
retrievable 658.16
retrieval
  restoration 660.1
  recovery 775.3
retrieve redeem 660.9
  (deliver 672.2)
  recover 775.9; 790.4
retriever 366.6
retroaction
  recoil 277.1
  (counteraction
    179.1)
  regression 283.1
retroactive
  retrospective 122.12
  counteractive 179.5
  recoiling 277.4
retrocede
  regress 283.5
  recede 287.2
retrocedence 287.1
retrocedent 287.3
retrocession
  regression 283.1
  (reversion 145.1)
  (recession 287.1)
  deterioration 659.1
retroflection, retro-
  flexion 218.1
retrogradation
  regression 283.1
  (recession 287.1)
  (relapse 661.1)
  deterioration 659.1
retrograde v.
  invert 14.4
  regress 283.5
  (recede 287.2)
  (relapse 661.3)

(backslide 988.9)
  deteriorate 659.6
retrograde adj.
  regressive 283.7
  (relapsing 661.4)
  (heterodox 984.22)
  degenerate 659.11
retrogress
  regress 283.5
  (recede 287.2)
  deteriorate 659.6
retrogression
  regression 283.1
  (reversion 145.1)
  (relapse 661.1)
  deterioration 659.1
retrogressive
  reversionary 145.6
  regressive 283.7
  (recessive 287.3)
  deteriorating 659.11
retrospect n. 505.4
retrospect v. 122.7
retrospect adj. 122.12
retrospection 505.4
  (preterition 122.1)
  (reconsideration
    451.2)
retrospective 122.12
retroussé
  snubbed 201.6
  upturned 307.8
retroversion
  reversion 145.1
  inversion 218.1
  turn 311.2
retrovert revert 145.4
  (relapse 661.3)
  (backslide 988.9)
  invert 218.4
retrude 289.2
retrusion 289.1
return n.
  repetition 104.1
  periodicity 138.2
  reversion 145.1
  recoil 277.1
  reflux 283.2
  arrival 292.3
  answer 426.1
  recovery 660.1
  retaliation 718.1
  appointment 755.2
  restitution 790.1
  repayment 807.3
  reward 973.2
in return 30.7
return v. repeat 104.5
  recur 138.8
  revert 145.4
  reciprocate 148.3
  regress 283.5
  (recoil 277.3)
  reverberate 408.7
  answer 462.5
  summarize 551.8
  recover 660.15
  relapse 661.3
  retaliate 718.2
  appoint 755.2
  give back 790.3
  yield 810.4

reward 973.3
return to repeat 104.4
revert to 457.5
returnable 148.4
returns census 86.2
  record 551.2
  profits 775.2
  receipts 810.1
reune 43.5; 72.10
reunion union 43.1
  reconciliation 723.1
  party 892.5
  (assembly 72.2)
reunite unite 43.5
  reconcile 723.4
revamp change 140.6
  repair 660.11
reveal open 260.12
  ~ itself 446.2
  disclose 529.3, 4
  (discover 481a.3)
  (manifest 525.2)
  indicate 550.18
revealed visible 446.4
  manifest 525.4
  disclosed 529.7
  divinely ~ 985.7
  become revealed
    446.2
revealing 529.8
revealment 529.1
reveille 550.16
revel n. 840.2, 3
revel v.
  luxuriate 377.4
  delight in 827.6
  rejoice 838.5
  frolic 840.21
  (be intemperate
    954.3)
  wassail 959.16
  (dissipate 954.3)
revelation
  appearance 448.1
  discovery 481a.1
  disclosure 529.1
  (manifestation
    525.1)
Revelation 985.4
revelational
  revealing 529.8
  apocalyptic 985.7
revelatory 529.8
  (informative 527.13)
reveler, reveller
  frolicker 840.17
  wassailer 959.11
revelment, revelry
  rejoicing 838.1
  festivity 840.2
  (dissipation 954.2)
revenant 980a.1
revendicate
  reclaim 741.6; 924.7
  recover 775.9
revendication
  reclamation 741.2
  recovery 775.3
revenge n. 919
  (retaliation 718.1)
  (resentment 900.1)
  (punishment 972.1)

in revenge 718.5
take revenge 919.4
  (retaliate 718.2)
  (punish 972.5)
revenge v. 919.4
revengeful 919.6
  (retaliatory 718.4)
  (resentful 900.12)
  (pitiless 914a.3)
be revengeful 919.5
revengefulness 919.2
  (hatred 898.1)
  (malevolence 907.1)
  (ruthlessness
    914a.1)
revenue 810.1
  (funds 800.2)
revenue cutter 273.1
reverb, reverberate
  408.7
  (roll 407.6)
reverberating 408.9
reverberation
  repetend 104.2
  resound 408.2
  (rebound 277.1)
  (rumble 407.1)
  answer 462.1
reverberatory 386.1
revere
  hold dear 897.11
  respect 928.4
  worship 990.9
revered 928.9
reverence
  veneration 928.1, 2
  (piety 987.1)
  worship 990.1
  priest 996.2, 5
Reverence n. 877.2
reverence v.
  venerate 928.4
  worship 990.9
reverend 996.2
reverent
  reverential 928.8
  (dutiful 926.8)
  pious 987.10
  worshipful 990.15
reverential
  venerative 928.8
  pious 987.10
  worshipful 990.15
reverie, revery
  muse 458.3
  (thought 451.3)
  dream 515.5
in a reverie 458.11
  (thoughtful 451.37)
reversal
  reversion 145.1
  inversion 218.1
  regression 283.1
  tergiversation 607.1
reverse n.
  the contrary 14.2
  reversion 145.1
  inversion 218.1, 3
  rear 235.1
  regression 283.1
  ~ of the shield 468.1
  tergiversation 607.1

reverse — rhetoric 1058

reverse (*continued*)
  misfortune 735.3
  game 840.12
reverse *v.*
  invert 14.4; 218.4
  (change 140.6)
  revert 145.4
  revoke 756.3
reverse *adj.*
  contrary 14.5
  (inverted 218.6)
  contrapositive 237.6
reversed
  reverted 145.5
  inverted 218.6
reverseless 150.7
reversement, reverse turn 267a.24
reversi, reversis 840.12
reversion
  posteriority 117.1
  return 145
  (periodicity 138.2)
  (recoil 277.1)
  (regression 283.4)
  (relapse 661.1)
  (perversion 988.3)
  inversion 218.1
  progression 283.1
  reconversion 660.2
  inheritance 775.4
  estate 780.2
  succession 783.2
  restitution 790.1
reversional
  regressive 145.6
  transferable 783.5
reversionally 145.7
reversionary *n.* 779.5
reversionary *adj.*
  regressive 145.6
  restitutive 790.5
reversioner
  reversionist 145.3
  heir 779.5
reversionist
  reversioner 145.3
  apostate 607.5
reversis See **reversi**
reverso 593.7
revert
  return 104.5; 145.4
  (invert 218.4)
  (recoil 277.3)
  regress 283.5
  hark back 457.5
revertal 145.1
reverted 145.5
revertible 790.5
revery See **reverie**
revest 790.3
review *n.*
  reconsideration 451.2
  examination 461.3, 6
  criticism 480.3
  (comment 522.4)
  recollection 505.4
  retelling 594.1
  commentary 595.2
  summary 596.1
  drama 599.3

revision 658.3
parade 882.3
pass under review
  scrutinize 441.12
  examine 461.17
  (criticize 480.10)
review *v.*
  scrutinize 441.12
  reconsider 451.29
  examine 461.17, 20
  criticize 480.10
  remember 505.10
  retell 594.5
  comment upon 595.4
  revise 658.11
reviewer critic 480.5
  (commentator 524.2)
  essayist 595.3
  (author 593.15)
revile
  anathematize 908.4
  scoff 930.6
  (be impious 988.7)
  abuse 932.8
revilement 932.3
reviler 936.2
revindicate 924.7
revise *n.* copy 21.1
  rewriting 590.3
  proof 626.2
  revision 658.3
revise *v.* rewrite 590.13
  emend 658.11
reviser 593.16
revision copy 21.1
  re-examination 461.6
  rewriting 590.3
  emendation 658.3
revisit 186.11
revival
  restoration 660.2
  (repetition 104.1)
  (reproduction 163.1)
  (vivification 359.4)
  (improvement 658.1)
  (reform 658.4)
  (refreshment 689.1)
  religious ~ 990.7
revivalist 996.4
revivatory 660.18
  (refreshing 689.4)
revive
  come to life 359.7
  remember 505.10
  resuscitate 660.13
  (repeat 104.4)
  (reproduce 163.2)
  (vivify 359.8)
  recover 660.15
  refresh 689.2, 3
  (strengthen 159.8)
  rouse feelings 824.2
reviver
  renovator 660.7
  tonic 662.5
  intoxicant 959.10
revivification
  invigoration 159.2
  revival 660.2

(vivification 359.4)
refreshment 689.1
revivify revive 660.13
  refresh 689.2
reviviscence 660.2
reviviscent 660.18
revocation
  recantation 607.3
  repeal 756.1
revocatory
  denying 536.3
  recanting 607.12
revoke recant 607.9
  repeal 756.3
  (deny 536.2)
revokement
  recantation 607.3
  repeal 756.1
revolt *n.*
  insurgence 742.2
  (revolution 146.1)
  (secession 624.1)
  (strike 719.2)
  (anarchy 738.2)
revolt *v.*
  disagree 489.4
  rebel 742.5
  (revolutionize 146.4)
  (secede 624.3)
  (strike 719.4)
  repel 830.7
  ~ against 898.3
  disapprove 932.5
  scandalize 932.9
revolter 742.3
revolting nasty 395.7
  foul 653.17
  odious 830.14
revolute 146.1
revolution *n.*
  radical change 146
  (change 140.1)
  aeronautics 267a.18
  rotation 312.1
  warfare 722.1
  revolt 742.2
revolution *v.* 146.4
revolutionary *n.* 742.3
revolutionary *adj.*
  revolutional 146.5
  rebellious 742.5
  (anarchic 738.8)
revolutionism
  bolshevism 146.2
  revolt 742.2
revolutionist 742.3
  (opposer 710.3)
revolutionize
  change radically 146.4
  (change 140.6)
  (reorganize 144.7)
  revolt 742.5
revolve recur 138.8
  rotate 312.1
  ponder 451.27
revolver 727.10
revolving door 312.4
revulsion
  reversion 145.1

revolution 146.1
inversion 218.1
recoil 277.1
revulsionary 145.6
revulsive
  revolutionary 146.5
  recoiling 277.4
  tergiversating 607.11
reward *n.* prize 733.1
  deserts 924.2
  recompense 973
  (compensation 30.3)
  (gain 775.2)
  (gift 784.3)
  (punishment 972.1)
  in reward 973.6
reward *v.* 973.3
  (compensate 30.4)
  (award 784.8)
  (repay 807.9)
rewarding 973.5
rewed 903.13
reword repeat 104.4
  paraphrase 522.7
rewording 522.2
rewrite *n.* copy 21.1
  rewriting 590.3
rewrite *v.* 590.13
rewrite man, rewriter 593.16
reynard animal 366.5
  cunning person 702.4
rez-de-chaussée 191.18
rhabdomancy 511.3
rhachitis See **rachitis**
Rhadamanthus, Rhadamanthys
  justice 941.1
  judge 967.1
  god 982.4
Rhaeto-Romanic 560.4
rhamphoid 245.9
rhapsodical
  extravagant 497.4
  fanciful 515.13
  poetry 597.13
rhapsodist
  singer 416.10
  fanatic 504.2
  imaginer 515.7
  poet 597.10
rhapsodize
  employ absurdity 497.2
  idealize 515.8
rhapsody
  disconnection 70.1
  music 415.3
  fancy 515.4
  poem 597.2
Rhea maternity 166.3
  world 318.1
  goddess 979.2
rheometer, rheostat 158a.6
rhetor
  rhetorician 577.3
  speaker 582.5
rhetoric diction 569.1

ornateness 577.1
oratory 582.3
rhetorical ornate 577.6
 eloquent 582.12
rhetorician
 phrasemonger 577.3
 speaker 582.5
rheum saliva 299.5
 fluid 333.2
 disease 655.9
rheumatism pain 378.1
 ailment 655.5
rheumy 333.7
Rhine wine 959.7
rhino 800.1
rhipidate
 expanded 194.10
 broad 202.6
rhizanthous 367.14
rhizopod 193.4
rhizopodous 368.12
rhomb 244.2
rhombencephalon
 450.2
rhombic 244.5
rhombohedron, rhomboid, rhombus 244.2
rhubarb 298.30
rhumb 278.2
rhyme, rime *n.*
 assonance 17.3
 music 413.21
 poetry 597.1, 2, 6, 8
rhyme, rime *v.*
 assonate 17.9
 make rhymes 597.12
rhymeless, rimeless 598.4
rhyming, riming *n.* 597.5
rhyming, riming *adj.*
 assonant 17.16
 poetry 597.13
rhymester, rimester 597.10
rhyming dictionary
 dictionary 593.4
 poetry 597.8
rhythm
 recurrence 138.3
 (repetition 104.1)
 (pulsation 314.2)
 oscillation 314.5
 music 413.21
 elegance 578.1
 poetry 597.6
rhythmic, rhythmics *n.* 415.24
 (rhythm 413.21)
rhythmic *adj.*
 periodic 138.10
 musical 413.29
 metrical 466.13
 poetic 597.13
rhythmical accent 597.6
rhythmize
 musicalize 415.26
 play music 416.18
rialto 799.1
riant 836.7

riata 45.2
rib supporter 215.2
 protuberance 250.2
 wife 903.8
ribald *n.* 851.4
ribald *adj.*
 vulgar 851.6
 obscene 961.9
ribaldry
 vulgarity 851.1
 profanity 908.2
 obscenity 961.1
riband 733.1
ribband 205.5
ribbed 259.4
ribbon strip 205.5
 decoration 733.1
 reins 752.2
ribby 203.11
riboast 972.6
rice grain 330.3
 sprig 367.4
 plant 367.9
ricebird food 298.26
 bird 366.22
ricelike 249.11
rich fertile 168.7
 tobacco 392a.15
 flavorsome 394.7
 oversweet 396.8
 resonant 408.9
 rich-colored 428.14
 rhetorical 577.6
 abundant 639.7
 wealthy 803.8
 beautiful 845.13
 ornate 847.13
 ridiculous 855.5
 be rich 803.4
 grow rich 734.5
Richard Roe 643.6
richen 803.7
riches 803.1
 (funds 800.2)
richling 803.2
richly 31.15
ricinus oil 356.3
rick stack 72.5
 hayrick 636.4
ricketish 160.12
rickets 655.5
rickety
 unsteady 160.12
 ugly 846.8
rickrack 257.2
ricksha, rickshaw 272.5
ricochet *n.* 277.1
ricochet *v.* 277.3
ricochet fire 716.2
rid *v.* release 672.2
 ~ oneself of 678.3
rid *adj.* 776.6
 get rid of
 eliminate 42.4
 eject 307.17
 kill 361.10
 deliver 672.2
 discard 678.3
 free oneself 750.4
riddance

elimination 42.2
escape 671.1
deliverance 672.1
loss 776.1
 good ~ 776.7
relinquishment 782.1
riddle *n.* sorter 60.4
 network 219.4
 porousness 260.7
 enigma 533.2
 (unintelligibility 519.2)
 (ambiguity 520.2)
 (wordplay 842.5)
 refiner 652.7
riddle *v.* sort 60.6
 perforate 265.16
 shoot 284.13; 361.10
 refine 652.10
riddling 533.6
ride *n.* 266.7, 8
ride *v.* continue 143.2
 be high 206.9
 travel 266.18
 (navigate 267.10)
 (aviate 267a.30)
 at anchor 267.13
 float 267.44
 carry 270.8
 let it ride
 maintain 143.3
 neglect 460.4
 do nothing 681.2
ride and tie
 by turns 138.13
 ride 266.7
 alternate 314.10, 14
ride at anchor
 anchor 267.13
 be inactive 683.8
ride easy 267.13
ride hard 274.9
ride herd
 care for 459.6
 watch over 664.6
ride out
 navigate 267.31
 ~ the storm 664.4
ride over 303.2
ride roughshod
 be violent 173.7
 tyrannize 739.4
 be domineering 885.5
 violate the law 964.4
ride shanks' mare 266.16
ride the beam 267a.31
rider adjunct 39.1
 horseman 268.8
 horse 271.3
ridge bond 45.1
 hill 206.2
 (promontory 250.5)
 spine 235.4
 protuberance 250.2
 gold 800.15
ridgebone 235.4
ridgepole 215.12
ridicule *n.*

derision 856
 (detraction 934.1)
 derision 930.2
ridicule *v.* 856.4; 930.6
 (fool 545.10)
 (disparage 934.3)
ridiculous 855.5
 (absurd 497.4)
 (trivial 643.11)
 be ridiculous 855.3
 (be absurd 497.2)
ridiculousness 855
 (absurdity 497.1)
 (buffoonery 842.3)
riding territory 181.2
 travel 266.7
 exercise 686.2
rife prevalent 78.10
 profuse 102.5
 rumored 532.8
 plentiful 639.7
rifeness 78.2
riff rapid 348.6
 music 415.16
riffle shake 315.4
 stream 348.6, 10
riffraff rubbish 645.4
 commonalty 876.2
rifle *n.* spotlight 423.3
 firearm 727.10
rifle *v.* shoot 284.13
 search 461.16
 pillage 791.10
rifleman shooter 284.8
 soldier 726.4
rifler 792.1
rifles 726.8
rift cleft 198.2
 dissension 713.2
rig *n.* wardrobe 225.2
 suit 225.7
 vehicle 272.8
 rigging 273.9
 equipment 634.1
 frolic 840.3
 prank 842.7
rig *v.* clothe 225.42
 equip 634.2
 ~ the market 794.9
rigadoon music 415.7
 dance 840.7
rigamarole See **rigmarole**
rigged 273.16
rigger lineman 158a.10
 aircraftsman 269a.3
rigging
 wardrobe 225.2
 ship 273.9
 (cordage 205.4)
 equipment 634.1
Riggs' disease 655.5
right *n.* side 238.2
 truth 494.1
 authority 737.1
 privilege 748.1; 922.2
 (permission 760.1)
 (due 924.1)
 estate 780.2
 propriety 922

right — rising

right (*continued*)
  (expedience 646.1)
  (good 648.2)
  (ethics 926.4)
  (probity 939.1)
  (justice 941.1)
by rights 922.7
have a right 924.5
have no right 925.5
right *v.* 922.3
  (remedy 660.10)
right itself 660.16
right *adj.*
  substantial 3.4
  dextral 238.3
  straight 246.5
  true 494.10, 11
  sane 502.5
  seemly 646.4
  conventional 852.8
  morally ~ 922.5
  (expedient 646.4)
  (due 924.9)
  (ethical 926.12)
  (justifiable 937.10)
  upright 939.7
  fair 941.3
  virtuous 944.3
  orthodox 983a. 7
as is right
  rightfully 922.7
  (duly 924.12)
  fairly 941.5
at right angles 212.9
put right 660.10
right *adv.*
  greatly 31.15
  accurately 494.16
  affirmation 535.8
right away
  instantly 113.6
  promptly 132.14
rightabout, right-about-face *n.* 607.1
send to the right-about
  repulse 289.2; 764.4
  eject 297.8
rightabout-face *v.* 283.6
right-and-left
  extensively 180.8
  laterally 236.8
  around 227.5
right angle *n.* 212.2
right-angle, right-angular *adj.* 244.5
  (vertical 212.8)
right ascension 466.7
righteous
  virtuous 944.3
  godly 987.10
righteousness 944.1
right field 238.2
rightful proper 922.5
  fair 941.3
  lawful 963.5
rightfully 922.7
right hand *n.*
  right 238.2
  assistant 711.1

right-hand, right-handed *adj.* 238.3
right-handedness 238.1
right line 246.2
rightly 922.7
  (duly 924.12)
right-minded
  sane 502.5
  honorable 939.7
  virtuous 944.3
righto 535.8
right smart of 31.15
rightward 238.5
right whale 366.21
right wing 141.3
rigid hard 323.5
  accurate 494.11
  severe 739.5
rigidity
  hardness 323.1
  accuracy 494.3
  severity 739.1
rigidness 323.1
  (straightness 246.1)
rigmarole, rigamarole
  twaddle 517.3
  chatter 584.2
rigor, rigour
  violence 173.1
  rigidity 323.1
  coldness 383.1, **2**
  accuracy 494.3
  severity 739.1
rigorous violent 173.11
  rigid 323.5
  cold 383.8
  accurate 494.11
  severe 739.5
  unforgiving 919.6
rig-out 225.2
Rigsdag, Riksdag 696.4
rile foul 653.15
  vex 830.5
  anger 900.10
riled 828.15
rill, rillet 348.1
rim *n.* edge 231.1
  automobile 272.16
rim *v.* 231.3
rime *n.* cleft 198.2
  frost 333.5
rime *n.* See **rhyme**
rime *v.* See **ream; rhyme**
rime-frosted 383.9
rimeless See **rhymeless**
rimer 262
rimery, rimester See **rhymery** etc. 597.5
rimiform 259.4
rimose, rimous 198.5
rimple *n.* 258.1
rimple *v.* 258.3
rimulose 198.5
rimy 597.13
rind skin 223.12
  peel 223.15
rinderpest 655.18

rindle 348.1
ring *n.*
  fastening 45.2
  (suspender 214.3)
  circle 247.2
  tintinnabulation 408.4
  clique 712.2
  society 712.4
  arena 728.1
  insignia 747.3
  ornament 847.7
  love token 902.5
ring *v.* surround 227.3
  tintinnabulate 408.8
ring down
  terminate 67.7
  ~ ~ the curtain 599.26
ring in begin 66.5
  time 114.7
  substitute 147.3
ring off 585.6
ring out 114.8
ring the bell 731.5
ring the changes
  repeat 104.4
  change 140.6
  vary 149.4
ring up 599.26
ringdove bird 366.22
  songbird 416.11
ringent 260.15
ringer likeness 17.6
  substitute 147.2
  cheat 548.2
  swindler 792.8
ring-in 147.2
ringing *n.* 408.4
ringing *adj.* 408.10
ringleader 694.1
ringlet circle 247.2
  hair 256.3
ringlike 247.8
ringside 441.5
ringtail 366.22
ringworm 655.17
rink 840.14
rinse 652.9
riot *n.* turmoil 59.4
  broil 713.4
  mutiny 742.2
riot *v.*
  be violent 173.7
  luxuriate in 377.4
  mutiny 742.5
  delight in 827.6
rioter 742.3
riotous
  turbulent 173.12
  (troublous 59.11)
  mutinous 742.7
rip *n.* horse 271.6
  reprobate 949.1
  libertine 962.1
rip *v.* 260.11
rip up 824.2
R.I.P. 363.29
riparian 342.10
rip cord 273a.7
ripe *v.* 650.4

ripe *adj.* aged 128.8
  mature 131.5
  cheese 298.50
  tobacco 392a.15
  prepared 673.11
  complete 729.2, 4, 6
ripen
  be converted into 144.8
  perfect 650.4
  improve 658.6
  mature 673.6
  complete 729.2, 4
ripeness 673.4
ripicolous 342.10
riposte, ripost *n.* 426.1
riposte, ripost *v.* 462.**5**
rip panel 273a.12
ripple *n.* rough 256.2
  agitation 315.4
  stream 348.6, 10
ripple *v.* flow 348.19
  murmur 405.5
riprap *n.* 215.3
riprap *v.* 215.26
ripsaw 257.3
Ripuarian 342.10
risaldar See **ressaldar** 745.11
rise *n.* increase 35.1
  cause 153.1
  evolution 161.5
  height 206.2
  acclivity 217.2
  ascent 305.1
  (improvement 658.1)
  answer 462.1
rise *v.* originate 66.2
  result from 154.3
  be high 206.9
  incline 217.6
  ascend 305.4
  (increase 35.4)
  (improve 658.6)
  be light 320.5
  appear 446.2
  ~ from the grave 660.15
  ~ in the world 734.5
  ~ in price 814.2
rise above
  be great 31.4
  surmount 206.10;
  731.7
  (overhang 214.5)
rise to the occasion 612.3
rise up
  become high 206.11
  ascend 305.4
  stand up 307.7
  revolt 742.5
risibility 838.3
risible
  prone to laugh 838.10
  ridiculous 855.5
risibles 838.3
rising *n.* swelling 194.2
  acclivity 217.2

1060

protuberance 250.2
ascent 305.1
sore 655.16
revolt 742.2
rising *adj.* 217.10
risk *n.* gamble 621.2
danger 665.1
at one's own risk
926.13
risk *v.* chance 621.17
endanger 665.4, 5
invest 787.5
risky dangerous 665.7
(hazardous 621.19)
ticklish 704.8
risqué 961.9
risqué story 851.3
ritardando 415.15, 31
rite 998
last rites
funeral 363.4
extreme unction
998.4
ritornel, ritornelle
prelude 64.2;
repetend 104.2
music 415.15
Ritter 875.5
ritual *n.* 998.1, 9
(ceremony 882.4)
ritual *adj.* 998.15
ritualism
religion 984.5
ceremonialism
998.11
ritualist
Anglican 984.15
ceremonialist 998.12
ritualistic 998.15
(ceremonial 882.10)
rituality 998.1, 11
ritzy 882.8
rival *n.*
opponent 710.4
combatant 726.1
rival *v.* excel 33.5
emulate 648.7
compete with 720.9
rival *adj.* 720.13
rivalry
competition 720.1
envy 921.1
in rivalry 720.13
rive sunder 44.8
be brittle 328.3
rivel *n.* 258.1
rivel *v.*
wrinkle 258.3
dry 340.5
river 348.1, 2
riverain, riverine 342.9
river gunboat 726.11
river horse 192.8
rivet *n.* 45.5
rivet *v.* attach 43.6
~ the attention
457.6
rivulation
interlacing 219.3
convolution 248.1
rivulet 348.1

rivulose 248.4
riziform 249.11
Ro 560.5
roach hair 256.3
insect 366.24
road sea inlet 343.1
haven 666.4
path 627.2
(itinerary 266.9)
roadway 627.3
(crossroad 219.2)
go on the road 266.12
on the road
absent 187.10
on the way 270.13;
286.5
roadbook 694.7
road cart 272.5
road hog
automobilist 268.10
monopolist 943.2
road horse 271.3
road map 694.7
roadstead
sea inlet 343.1
haven 666.4
roadster horse 271.3
automobile 272.15
roadway 627.3
(seaway 267.8)
(airway 267a.20)
roam 266.14
roamer 268.2
roan *n.* horse 271.5
bookbinding 593.10
roan *adj.* 433.5
Roan Barbary 271.9
roanoke 800.3
roar *n.* noise 404.2
boom 406.3
roll 407.1
~ of laughter 838.3
roar *v.*
be violent 173.7
blow 349.22
boom 406.9
roll 407.6
laugh 838.7
wail 839.9
roarer
strong man 159.6
violent 173.6
horse 271.6
blusterer 887.2
evildoer 913.1
roaring 31.8
roast *n.* 296.9
roast *v.* be hot 382.13
cook 384.19
cross-examine
461.15
ridicule 856.4
upbraid 932.8
roaster fowl 298.25
hot day 382.3
roasting *n.*
cross-examination
461.9
reproof 932.3
roasting *adj.* 382.16
rob *n.* 352.3

rob *v.* 791.9
rob Peter to pay Paul
compensate 30.4
steal 791.9
be unjust 941a.2
roband, robbin 273.10
robber taker 789.6
thief 792.1
robbery 791.1
robe *n.* coverlet 223.9
garment 225.3
cloak 225.15
insignia 747.2
robe *v.* 225.41
robe-de-chambre
225.23
robes clothes 225.1
canonicals 999.1
robin 366.22
Robin Goodfellow
979.9
Robin Hood
outlaw 792.10
philanthropist 911.1
robin's egg blue 438.2
roborant *n.* 662.5
roborant *adj.*
invigorating 656.5
tonic 662.25
robust strong 159.10
healthy 654.4
robustness 159.1
roc, rock *n.* 83.7
rochet 999.1
rock *n.*
stability 150.2
oscillation 314.5
shake 315.4
solid 321.4
hardness 323.3
stone 342.4
refuge 666.3
hidden danger 667.1
missile 727.14
coin 800.1, 4
on the rocks
aground 267.65
in danger 665.8
in difficulty 704.11
stranded 732.10
bankrupt 808.10
rock *v.* pitch 267.45
stone 284.12; 716.7
oscillate 314.8
shake 315.8, 9
kill 361.10
pelt 972.7
rockaway 272.4
rock bottom *n.*
bottom 211.1
bedrock 215.3
rock-bottom *adj.*
lowest 207.10
bottom 211.5
rocker seat 215.22
network 219.4
rocket speed 274.6
ascent 305.3
skyrocket 382.9
signal light 423.5
(signal 550.14)

projectile 727.14
rocking chair 215.22
rocking stone 314.6
rocklike 323.5
rock oil 356.2
rock pile 972.2
rockweed 367.3
rocky unsteady 160.12
rough 256.12
hard 323.5
rococo 83.10
rod length 200.6
stick 215.13, 15
(cylinder 249.3)
killer 361.8
measure 466.4
firearm 727.10
scepter 747.1
gunman 913.2
scourge 975.2
(club 727.7)
wand 993.3
rodent, Rodentia
366.17
rodlike 323.5
rodman killer 361.8
gunman 913.2
Rodomont, Rodomonte 884.3
rodomontade *n.*
twaddle 517.3
peroration 572.1
verbosity 573.1
bombast 577.2
boasting 884.1
rodomontade *v.*
talk nonsense 517.6
perorate 572.5
be diffuse 573.5
roe rudiment 153.3
fish eggs 298.18
eggs 357.4
deer 366.11
female animal 374.8
roebuck 366.11
Roentgen ray, Röntgen ray 420.3
rogation
request 765.1
prayer 990.3
rogatory 765.7
rogue horse 271.6
rascal 949.1
(deceiver 548.1)
roguery 940.1
rogue's march 297.2
roguish playful 840.23
waggish 842.9
roil foul 653.15
vex 830.5
anger 900.10
roister brag 882.5
bluster 887.3
roisterer 887.2
rokelay See **roguelaure**
Roland 650.3
a Roland for an Oliver
interchange 148.1
(barter 794.1)

role — rosy-cheeked

Roland (*continued*)
  retaliation 718.1
role, rôle
  drama 599.7
  (part 51.1)
  function 625.3
  career 692.3
roll *n.* roster 86.2
  (count 85.3)
  length 200.3
  coil 248.2
  cylinder 249.3
  gait 266.5
  aerobatics 267a.24
  rotation 312.1
  wave 348.10
  boom 406.3
  rumble 407.1
  throw of dice 621.9
  bank ~ 800.12
roll *v.* smooth 255.4
  move 264.6
  walk 266.16
  pitch 267.45
  aviate 267a.31
  goggle 311.4
  rotate 312.7
  oscillate 314.8
  flounder 315.9
  billow 348.22
  rumble 407.6
  (resonate 408.7)
  trill 412.2
  roll about 311.5
  roll on elapse 109.3
  move 264.6
  advance 282.2
roll call 86.2
roller fastening 45.2
  cylinder 249.3
  smoother 255.3
  rotator 312.4
  pulverizer 330.4
  wave 348.10
  (oscillation 314.1)
  bandage 662.14
roller coaster 840.15
rollick revel 838.5
  bluster 887.3
rollicking 836.10
rolling *n.*
  aerobatics 267a.24
  rotation 312.1
  rumble 407.1
rolling *adj.* wavy 248.7
  rumbling 407.11
rolling mill 691
rolling pin
  cylinder 249.3
  smoother 255.3
rolling stock 272.18
rolling stone
  changeableness 149.2
  rotator 312.4
romaine 298.30
roman 591.8
Roman balance 319.5
Roman candle
  firework 382.9
  signal light 423.5

Roman Catholic 984.16, 25
Roman Catholicism 984.6
romance *n.* fancy 515.4
  falsehood 546.1
  story 594.2
romance *v.*
  employ absurdity 497.2
  romanticize 515.8
  (lie 544.4)
  storify 594.5
romancer
  imaginer 515.7
  fabricator 548.5
  storyteller 594.4
Romani See **Romany**
Romanism 984.6
Romanist 984.16
Roman-nosed 245.9
romantic *n.* 515.7
romantic *adj.*
  imaginary 515.12
  story 594.7
  sentimental 822.7
romanticism
  idealization 515.2
  painting 556.6
romanticist *n.* 515.7
romanticist *adj.* 515.12
romanticize 515.8
Romany, Rommany
  vagabond 268.2
  language 560.4; 563.5
Romeo 897.6
Romeo and Juliet 807.9
romp *n.* hoyden 129.5
  frolic 840.3
romp *v.*
  be violent 173.7
  caper 309.5
  frolic 840.21
rompers 225.25, 32
rompish
  capersome 309.6
  playful 840.23
rondeau music 415.3
  poem 597.2
rondel, rondelle 247.2
rondel, rondelet 597.2
rondino, rondo, rondoletto 415.3
rondure 247.2
Ronga 560.4
ronyon, ronion 949.1
rood cross 219.6
  crucifix 998.8
rood screen 1000.3
roof *n.* home 189.2
  cover 223.6
  (top 210.4)
  (sunshade 424.2)
roof *v.* 223.22
roofing 223.6
rooflike 223.33
rook *n.* bird 366.22
  swindler 792.8
rook *v.* 791.12

rookery retreat 189.13
  slum 653.10
rookie, rooky
  newcomer 57.3
  recruit 541.6; 726.5
room *n.*
  occasion 134.2
  space 180.1
  place 184.3
  chamber 191.16
  capacity 192.2
  class 541.8
  scope 748.2
  make room
    open 260.11
    show respect 928.4
room *v.* lodge 184.12
  inhabit 186.10
roomage space 180.1
  capacity 192.2
roomer 188.4
rooming house 189.8
roommate 890.3
roomstead space 180.1
  room 191.16
  capacity 192.2
roomy spacious 180.6
  broad 202.6
  airy 338.11
  comfortable 377.8
roorback, roorbach 934.2
roost *n.* abode 189.1
  bed 215.24
roost *v.* settle 184.14
  inhabit 186.10
  sit 308.6
rooster cock 366.23
  male animal 373.6
root *n.* number 84.2
  origin 153.3
  (base 211.1)
  word 562.1
  motive 615.1
root *v.*
  root for 931.6
  root up eject 297.17
    extract 301.5
    discover 481a.3
  root and branch 52.15
root beer drink 298.4
  sweet beverages 396.5
rooted
  traditional 124.8
  stable 150.5
  located 184.17
  bigoted 606.7
  inveterate 613.12
rooter 840.19
rope cord 205.3
  (ligament 45.4)
  (shackle 752.2)
  (supporter 215.2)
  cigar 392a.3
  free scope 748.2
  hanging 972.4
  hangman's noose 975.4
  give rope
    be lax 738.4

    allow freedom 748.10
  rope of sand
    incoherence 47.1
    weakness 160.5
ropeband See **roband**
ropedancer
  acrobat 599.21
  proficient 700.1
ropedancing 698.1
ropemaker 690.8
ropes influence 175.4
  rigging 273.9, 10
rope's end 975.1
ropewalker 700.1
ropeway 627.6
ropework, roping
  cordage 205.4
  rigging 273.9
ropy stringy 205.7
  tough 325.5
  viscid 352.8
roquelaure 225.15
roral, roric 339.9
rorqual 366.21
rory-tory, rory-cum-tory 882.8
rosary prayer 990.3
  beadroll 998.8
roscid 339.9
Roscius 599.19
rose *n.* sprinkler 337.3
  fragrance 400.3
  pink 434.3, 5
  beauty 845.4
  under the rose 528.24
rose *adj.* 434.10
roseate pink 434.10
  optimistic 858.11
rose cold 655.9
rose-colored
  pink 434.10
  optimistic 858.11
rosehead 337.3
rose oil 400.3
Rosetta stone 590.3
rosette 847.3
rose water 400.3
rosewood 635.3
Rosicrucian 994.13
Rosicrucianism 994.1
rosin *n.* 356a.1
rosin *v.* rub 331.3
  resin 356a.2
Rosinante 271.6, 7, 9
rosiny 356a.3
roster roll 86.2
  schedule 611.2
rostrate, rostriform, rostroid 245.9
rostrum
  platform 215.21
  prow 234.3
  pulpit 542.6
rostulate 245.9
rosy pink 434.10, 11
  auspicious 512.4
  blooming 845.12
  optimistic 858.11
rosy-cheeked 845.12

rot n.
  nonsense 517.2
  decay 659.2
  (malodor 401.2)
  (putrescence 653.4)
rot v. 659.7
rota roll 86.2
  round 138.4
Rota 966.4
rotary n. 273a.11
rotary adj. 312.8
rotary blower 349.20
rotary converter,
  rotary gap 158a.6
rotate 312.7
rotating 312.8
rotation round 138.4
  revolution 312
  (circuity 311.1)
  in rotation 138.13
rotational, rotative 312.8
rotatively 312.9
rote
  by rote 505.22
rotifer 193.4
rotograph
  photograph 556.11
  engraving 558.3
rotogravure
  photography 556.4
  photograph 556.11
  engraving 558.2, 3
rotor, rotor ship 273.1
rotten bad 649.8
  foul 653.17
  decayed 659.13
  wicked 945.15
rottenness 659.2
rottenstone 342.4
rotter 949.1
rotund v. 249.5
  (curve 245.3)
  (round 247.6)
rotund adj.
  stout 192.12
  round 249.6
  (corpulent 192.12)
  (chubby 201.6)
  (curved 245.4)
  (circular 247.8)
rotunda 189.3
rotundate 249.6
rotundity, rotundness 249.1
  (corpulence 192.4)
  (curvature 245.1)
  (circularity 247.1)
roturier 876.3
rouble See ruble
roué 949.1
rouge n. red 434.2, 6
  beautifying 845.5
rouge v. redden 434.7
  beautify 845.7
rouge et noir 840.12
  (game of chance 621.7)
rough n. picture 556.9
  writing 590.3
  outline 626.2

vulgarian 851.4
ruffian 913.2
  (boor 876.7)
in the rough
  roughly 256.18
  unfinished 674.8
rough v.
  ~ in 230.3
  roughen 256.11
rough adj.
  violent 173.11
  unsmooth 256.12
  (ununiform 16a.2)
  (notched 257.6)
  (furrowed 259.4)
  (textural 329.3)
  pungent 392.5
  harsh-sounding 410.9
  unfinished 674.8
  penetrating 824.13
  ungraceful 846.8
  uncouth 851.7
  (unformed 241.6)
  gruff 895.7
rough-and-tumble 59.4
roughcast n. 223.19
roughcast v.
  plaster 223.26
  form 240.6
  rough out 256.11
roughcast adj.
  rough 256.12
  unfinished 674.8
rough diamond
  unformed 241.3
  undevelopment 674.3
  unsophisticate 703.2
  vulgarian 851.4
  good person 948.1
rough-edged 674.8
roughen 256.11
roughhew
  do off-hand 161.8
  form 240.6
  rough out 256.11
roughhewn
  rough 256.12
  (unformed 241.6)
  unfinished 674.8
roughhouse
  be violent 173.7
  misbehave 851.5
roughly nearly 197.12
  unsmoothly 256.18
roughneck 851.4
  (boor 876.7)
roughness 256
  (nonuniformity 16a.1)
  (texture 329.1)
roughrider 268.8
roughscuff 876.1
roulade n. 413.10; 415.15
roulade v. 416.20
rouleau
  accumulation 72.6
  cylinder 249.3

money 800.4
roulette 621.7
roulette wheel 621.11
Roumanian See Rumanian
rounce handle 215.7
  printing 591.5
rouncy 271.3
round n. degree 26.1
  series 69.2
  rank 71.1
  revolution 138.4
  beat 181.4
  footing 215.4
  circle 247.2
  cylinder 249.3
  itinerary 266.9
  part music 415.12
  routine 613.4
  business 625.3
  circuit 629.1
  fight 720.6
  cards 840.12
go the rounds
  wander 266.14
  be published 531.9
make the round of 311.3
round v.
  ~ in 72.10
  make round 247.6
  (circle 227.3)
  (curve 245.3)
  rotund 249.5
  bulge 250.7
  ~ a point 267.24
  turn 311.4
  rotate 312.7
  ~ up animals 370.7
  ~ a period 578.3
  ~ out 729.2
round adj.
  circumjacent 227.4
  circular 247.8
  rotund 249.6
  positive 535.6
in round numbers 29.5
round adv. 227.5
roundabout n.
  circle 247.2
  merry-go-round 840.15
roundabout adj.
  circumjacent 227.4
  circuitous 311.6
  (convoluted 248.4)
  (deviative 279.8)
  (circumlocutory 573.5)
in a roundabout way 311.7
round about adv.
  around 227.5
  deviatively 279.9
  circuitously 311.7
  rotatively 312.9
round and round
  by turns 138.13
  windingly 248.8
  rotatively 312.9

alternately 314.14
rounded
  circular 247.8
  rotund 249.6
  phonetics 402.11
roundel circle 247.2
  poem 597.2
rounder 949.1
rounders 840.11
round-faced 192.12
roundhead alien 57.3
  Swede 188.9
roundhouse ship 273.7
  blow 276.3
  carbarn 636.4
  water closet 653.9
  workshop 691
  prison 752.1
roundlet 247.2
roundness
  circularity 247.1
  rotundity 249.1
  constable 745.10
round peg in a round hole 23.6
round robin
  epistle 592.2
  solicitation 765.1
round-shouldered 243.5
roundtop 215.21
round trip 266.8
roundup 72.4
roup n. 796.2
roup v. 796.6
rouper 797.5
roupingwife 797.1
rouse
  stimulate 171.7; 615.7
  inflame 173.8
  agitate 315.8
  excite 824.2
rouser 508.2
rousing vast 31.8
  energizing 171.11
roustabout
  longshoreman 269.7
  worker 690.2
rout n. crowd 72.4
  attendance 88.5
  agitation 315.1
  defeat 732.3
  festivity 840.2
  masses 876.1
  party 892.5
rout v.
  ~ type 591.14
  defeat 731.9
rout out eject 297.8
  (dislocate 185.2)
  clean 652.9
route
  routine 58.3; 613.4
  itinerary 266.9
  path 627.2
routine system 58.3
  custom 613.4
  (regularity 16.2)
  (rule 80.1)
  (round 138.4)

rove — Ruksh

routine (*continued*)
　business 625.3
rove wander 266.14
　deviate 279.5
rover wanderer 268.2
　brigand 792.3
roving *n.* 266.2
roving *adj.*
　inconstant 149.6
　deviative 279.8
　digressive 573.7
roving commission 475.5
row *n.* turmoil 59.4
　series 69.2
　roadway 627.3
　quarrel 713.4
a hard row to hoe 704.1
row *v.*
　paddle 267.45, 46, 69
　quarrel 713.7
row dry 267.46
row in the same boat 88.6
rowboat 273.4
rowdy *n.* 913.2
rowdy *adj.* 851.7
rowdydow
　turmoil 59.4
　noise 404.2
rowdyish 851.7
rowdyism 851.1
rowel point 253.2
　incentive 615.3
rowen 65.2
rower 269.2
rowlock fulcrum 215.5
　pivot 312.5
royal sail 273.13
　sovereign 737.16
Royal Highness 877.2
royalist 737.16
royal road 705.1
royalty
　sovereignty 737.2
　sovereign 745.2
　nobility 875.2
ruach 994.11
rub *n.* crisis 134.4
　friction 331.1
　touch 379.1
　difficulty 704.4
　hardship 735.1
　trouble 830.2
rub *v.* graze 199.3
　smooth 255.4
　frictionize 331.3
　touch 379.3
　massage 662.24
　~ one's hands 838.5
　~ one's eyes 870.2
rub down grind 330.6
　groom 370.7
　chastise 972.6
rub off 38.6
rub on go slow 275.5
　advance 282.2
rub out excise 38.5
　rub 331.3
　obliterate 552.2

rub the wrong way 256.11; 713.8
rub up 658.10
rub-a-dub 407.3
rubber *n.*
　overshoe 225.27
　elastic 325.2
　massager 331.2
　game 840.12
rubber *v.* gaze 441.13
　sight-see 444.3
　be curious 455.3
rubber check 800.9
rubberneck *n.*
　excursionist 268.1
　sight-seer 444.1
　inquisitive 455.2
rubberneck *v.*
　gaze 441.13
　sight-see 444.3
　be curious 455.3
rubberneck *adj.* 455.5
rubbernecker
　excursionist 268.1
　sight-seer 444.1
　inquisitive 455.2
rubbing 331.1
rubbish
　nonsense 517.2
　trumpery 643.5
　refuse 645.4
　　(dregs 40.2)
　　(oddments 51.6)
　　(waste 638.1)
　　(offal 653.6)
　riffraff 876.2
rubbishy 517.9
rubble 645.4
rubble car 272.19
rube oaf 501.1
　awkward fellow 701
　rustic 876.5
rubefaction 434.4
rubelle 434.2
rubeola 655.6
rubescence 434.1, 4
rubescent 434.13
rubiate *n.* 434.6
rubiate *adj.* 434.9
Rubicon 233.1
　cross the Rubicon
　　begin 66.5
　　overstep 303.5
　　decide upon 609.8
rubicund 434.9, 11
rubicundity
　heat flush 382.7
　redness 434.1
rubificative 434.13
rubify 434.7
rubiginous 433.5
rubine, rubin 434.6
ruble, rouble 800.8
rubric law 963.2
　rituale 998.9
rubricate *v.* 434.7
rubricate *adj.* 434.9
rubrication 434.4
rubricity 434.1
rubrific 434.13
rubstone 253.7

ruby red 434.2, 5
　type 591.7
　gem 847.8
ruck *n.*
　generality 78.4
　wrinkle 258.1
　furrow 259.1
　masses 876.1
ruck *v.* 258.3
ruckle *n.* 407.5
ruckle *v.* 407.10
rucksack 191.5
ruckus turmoil 59.4
　noise 404.2
　broil 713.4
ructation 297.5
ruction turmoil 59.4
　noise 404.2
　broil 713.4
rud, rudd *n.* 434.1, 6
rud, rudd *v.* 434.7
rudder handle 215.7
　stern 235.7
　ship 273.7
　airplane 273a.10
　guidance 693.1
　authority 747.6
rudder bar 273a.10
rudderless 158.8
rudderpost stern 235.7
　ship 273.7
ruddiness 434.1
ruddle *n.* 434.6
ruddle *v.* 434.7
ruddy *adj.*
　red 434.9, 11
　beautiful 845.12
ruddy *v.* 434.7
ruddy-complexioned 434.11
ruddy duck 366.22
rude savage 173.14
　harsh-sounding 410.9
　unlearned 491.9
　speech 579.3
　unfinished 674.8
　vulgar 851.6, 7
　　(unformed 241.6)
　discourteous 895.6
　　(disrespectful 929.5)
rudeness 895.1
rudiment
　beginning 66.4
　origin 153.3
　　(base 211.1)
　　(foundation 215.3)
　　(undevelopment 674.3)
　microbe 193.4
rudimental
　beginning 66.7
　infinitesimal 193.10
　immature 674.8
rudimentary
　beginning 66.7
　infinitesimal 193.10
　abecedarian 541.9
　immature 674.8
rue *n.* 395.3

rue *v.* 833.2
　(repent 950.3)
rueful
　grievous 830.11
　sad 837.16
ruff
　neckpiece 225.33
　drumming 407.3
ruffian 913.2
ruffianism
　vulgarity 851.1
　brutality 907.3
ruffle *n.* wrinkle 258.1
　drumming 407.3
　expedient 646.2
　trepidation 825.3
ruffle *v.* derange 61.2
　(disorder 59.7)
　roughen 256.11
　wrinkle 258.3
　agitate 315.8
　drum 407.8
　beat time 416.19
　discompose 824.3
　vex 830.5
　anger 900.10
ruffled
　convoluted 248.4
　rough 256.12
　annoyed 828.15
rufous
　reddish-brown 433.5
　red 434.9
rug bedding 215.24
　cover 223.8, 9
　mat 652.7
Rugby 840.11
rugged strong 159.10
　rough 256.12
　difficult 704.8
　ungraceful 846.8
ruggedness 256.1
rugmaker 690.8
rugose, rugous, rugulose 256.12
rugosity 256.1
ruin *n.* remains 40.1
　destruction 162.1
　defeat 732.3
　go to ruin
　perish 162.5
　　(fail 732.5)
　go bankrupt 808.6
ruin *v.* destroy 162.4
　　(injure 649.6)
　bankrupt 804.6
　deflower 961.8
ruination 162.1
ruined
　unsuccessful 732.12
　bankrupt 808.6, 10
　irremediable 859.7
ruiner 165.1
ruinous
　destructive 162.6
　　(harmful 649.10)
　disastrous 735.8
　desolating 830.17
rukh See roc
Ruksh 271.9

1064

rule *n.* prototype 22.1
  mean 29.1
  principle 80
  (order 58.1)
  measure 466.2, 4
  (calculator 85.5)
  tenet 484.3
  axiom 496.2
  custom 613.3
  precept 697.1
  command 737.2
  law 963.2
  by rule 82.12
Rule *n.* 318.6
rule *v.*
  measure 466.10
  pass judgment 480.9
  sway 737.11
  (superintend 693.5)
  (command 741.4)
  rule out 552.1
rule of thumb
  experiment 463.2
  intuition 477a.1
  mismanagement 699.2
by rule of thumb 463.14
ruler measure 466.4
  master 745.1, 2
ruling *n.* 963.2
ruling *adj.*
  supreme 33.8
  authoritative 737.15
  (directing 693.6)
rum *n.*
  card game 840.12
  liquor 959.4
  distilled liquors 959.6
rum *adj.* odd 83.10
  good 648.8
rumal 225.26
Rumanian, Roumanian 560.4
rumble *n.* seat 215.22
  back seat 235.1
  boom 406.3
  roll 407.1
rumble *v.*
  ripple 348.19; 405.5
  boom 406.9
  roll 407.6
rumble seat
  seat 215.22
  back seat 235.1
  automobile 272.16
rumbling 407.11
rumbumptious, rumbustical, rumbustious 173.12
rumen 191.7
ruminate chew 298.45
  ponder 451.27
rumination
  chewing 298.1
  thought 451.1
rummage *n.*
  confusion 59.2
  search 461.2
  rubbish 645.4

rummage *v.* 461.16
rummer 191.11
rummy oddity 83.4
  card game 840.12
  drunkard 959.11
  liquor dealer 959.12
rumor, rumour 532.3
rumored, rumoured 532.8
rump remains 40.1
  buttocks 235.5
  meat 298.20
rumple *n.* 258.1
rumple *v.* derange 61.2
  (disorder 59.7)
  roughen 256.11
  wrinkle 258.3
rumpus turmoil 59.4
  (violence 173.1)
  noise 404.2
  broil 713.4
rumrunner 959.12
rumrunning 959.9
rumshop 959.13
run *n.* mean 29.1
  generality 78.2, 4
  succession 104.1
  continuance 143.1
  length 200.3
  course 264.3
  journey 266.8
  ship 273.7
  speed 274.3
  (gait 266.5)
  direction 278.1
  sequence 281.1
  stream 348.1, 2
  music 413.10
  custom 613.2, 4
  path 627.2
  attack 716.1
  contest 720.2
  race 720.5
  freedom 748.1
have a run
  travel 266.13
  be fashionable 852.6
  be famous 873.10
in the long run
  on an average 29.5
  (generally 78.15)
  mainly 50.11
  eventually 121.9
on the run
  moving 264.10
  active 682.20
run *v.* continue 106.2
  elapse 109.3
  happen 151.3
  course 264.6
  pilot 267.11
  float 267.44
  speed 274.9
  (make haste 684.3)
  liquefy 335.5
  flow 348.17
  melt 384.21
  manage 693.4
  smuggle 791.9
  run a blockade 267.10

run afoul, run foul 267.32; 708.3
run about 266.14
run after
  pursue 622.6
  lionize 873.10, 13
run against
  impel 276.7
  oppose 708.2
run amuck
  be violent 173.7
  go mad 503.10
  rage 825.7
run a rig 840.21
run away 293.5
run counter to
  be contrary 14.3
  counteract 179.3
  counterevidence 468.2
  oppose 708.2
run down
  sail into 267.32
  pursue 622.9
  impaired 659.12
  disused 678.6
  attack 716.5
  disparage 934.3
run hard
  aggrieve 649.6
  in difficulty 704.11
  suffer adversity 735.5
run in foist in 10.4
  interject 228.8
  sail into 267.32
  arrest 751.9
run in the blood 5.5
run into
  be converted into 144.8
  sail into 267.32
run in with the land
  sail toward 267.26
  approach 286.2
  make land 292.9
run mad 825.7
  (become excited 824.6)
run mad after 865.11
run off
  hasten off 293.5
  flee 623.10
  abduct 791.11
  cheapen 815.7
run on endure 106.2
  continue 143.2
run out end 67.6
  elapse 109.3
  past 122.8
  antiquated 124.9
  exude 295.7
run out a warp 267.12
run over
  enumerate 85.7
  overrun 303.3
  look over 441.12, 14
  think over 451.27
  glance at 461.19
  study 539.2
  recount 594.5

superabound 641.2
run riot
  be violent 173.7
  exaggerate 549.2
  superabound 641.2
  be active 682.12
  mutiny 742.5
  rage 825.7
  be intemperate 954.3
run the chance
  be liable 177.2
  risk 665.5
run the gantlet
  navigate 267.10
  risk 665.5
  brave 861.5
run through
  be uniform 16.3
  pervade 186.12
  exude 295.7
  kill 361.12
  spend 809.3
  squander 818.3
run to seed
  aged 128.8
  wasted 638.3, 4
  deteriorate 659.6
  become inefficient 699.10
run up increase 35.4
  improve 658.6
  ~ ~ a bill 806.6
  (charge 805.5)
run wild
  be violent 173.7
  rage 825.7
runabout
  wanderer 268.2
  carriage 272.4
  automobile 272.15
runagate
  apostate 607.5
  fugitive 623.5
run-around
  neglect 460.1
  avoidance 623.1
runaway *n.*
  apostate 607.5
  fugitive 623.5
runaway *adj.* 623.12
rundle circle 247.2
  cylinder 249.3
  wheel 312.4
  stream 348.1
rundlet 191.11
rune letter 561.1
  character 590.9
  magic 992.1
runer bard 416.10
  poet 597.10
runes poetry 597.1
  magic signs 993.1
runesmith 597.10
rung degree 26.1
  rank 71.1
  footing 215.4
  cylinder 249.3
runic 590.15; 597.13
runic alphabet, Runic alphabet 561.2

run-in — saddle

run-in quarrel 713.3
   contest 720.2
runlet, runnel 348.1
runner member 51.4
   horse 271.3
   airplane 273a.10
   tackle 273.11
   lifter 307.2
   conduit 350.3
   foliage 367.4
   messenger 534.1
   (traveller 268.5)
   solicitor 767.1;
     797.2, 4
   procurer 962.4
runner and tackle
   273.11
running
   continuously 69.7
   exercise 686.2
running account 811.1
running board 272.16
running head 66.3
runnion See ronyon
runoff 295.1
runout 623.2
runt
   diminutive 193.2, 5
   horse 271.6
   insignificancy 643.6
runty 193.9
runway 267a.28
rupee 800.8
rupia 655.17
rupture *n.* cleft 198.2
   ailment 655.5
   dissension 713.2
rupture *v.* 328.5
rural 183.3
   (agricultural 371.9)
rural district 183.1
ruralism 893.2
ruralize 183.2
rurigenous 183.3
ruse, ruse de guerre
   702.3
rush *n.* outbreak 173.2
   course 264.3
   dash 274.3
   flow 348.2, 5
   plant 367.8
   trifle 643.3
   haste 684.1
rush *v.*
   be violent 173.7
   flow 348.17
   ~ to a conclusion
     481.6; 486.3
   hasten 684.2, 3
rushlight light 420.7
   semidarkness 422.2
   candle 423.7
rusk 298.11
russet 433.5
Russia 182.3
Russian *n.* native 188.9
   language 560.4
Russian *adj.* 188.11
Russian bank 840.12
Russian bath 382.6

Russo-Japanese War
   722.4
rust *n.* fungi 369.4
   red 434.5
   decay 659.2
   blight 663.2
rust *v.* redden 434.7
   corrode 659.7
rust-cankered, rust-
   eaten 659.13
rustic *n.* 876.5
   (farmer 371.2)
rustic *adj.* 183.3
   (agricultural 371.9)
   (uncouth 851.7)
   (plebeian 876.12)
rusticate seclude 893.6
   banish 297.11
   countrify 183.2
rustication
   banishment 297.3
   seclusion 893.2
rusticity
   vulgarity 851.1
   incivility 895.1
rustle *n.* 405.2
rustle *v.* swish 405.5
   hustle 682.12
rustler
   man of action 682.10
   thief 792.1
rustly 405.10
rustproof 159.12
rust-red 433.5
rust-worn 659.13
rusty
   antiquated 124.9
   aged 128.8
   reddish-brown 433.5
   rust-eaten 659.13
   idle 683.12
   out of practice
     699.16
   sullen 901.8
   become rusty 699.10
rut furrow 259.1
   routine 613.4
   (rule 80.1)
   path 627.2
   sexual desire 961.3
   in a rut 16.7
   get in a rut 613.10
ruth 914.1
ruthful 914.6
ruthless 914a.3
   (severe 739.5)
   (cruel 907.9)
   (relentless 919.6)
ruthlessness 914a.1
   (relentlessness
     919.2)
rutilant, rutilous
   420.22
ruttish, rutty 961.11
rye plant 367.9
   distilled liquors
     959.6
ryot serf 746.4
   peasant 876.5

S

s. 800.8
Sabaean, Sabean *adj.*
   984.21
Sabaean, Sabean *n.*
   991.5
Sabaeanism, Sabean-
   ism
   religion 984.11
   star worship 991.1
Sabaism, Sabeism
   382.11; 991.1
Sabaist 382.11; 991.5
Sabaoth 726.6
sabbat 992.1
Sabbatarian *n.*
   ascetic 955.2
   formalist 998.12
Sabbatarian *adj.*
   955.3
Sabbatarianism
   asceticism 955.1
   hyperorthodoxy
     983a.5
   formalism 998.11
Sabbath
   vacation 687.2
   holyday 998.13
Sabbathbreaker 988.4
Sabbath school 542.1
sabbatic 687.7
sabbatism 983a.5
sabe See savvy
Sabeism See Sabaism
Sabellianism 984.4
saber, sabre *n.* 727.3
saber, sabre *v.*
   kill 361.12
   stab 716.5
saber-toothed tiger
   124.2
sabine See savin
Sabir 560.5
sable *n.* pelt 223.12
   color 431.1
sable *adj.* 431.7
sabotage
   destruction 162.1
   revolt 742.2
sabre See saber
sabreur 726.1
sabuline, sabulose
   330.8
sabulosity 330.1
sac bag 191.4, 6
   wrapper 223.11
sacatra 41.5
saccharin,
   saccharine *n.* 396.4
saccharine *adj.* 396.8
saccharinity 396.1
saccharization 396.6
saccharize 396.7
saccharose 396.4
saccular 191.23
saccule, sacculus 191.6
sac de nuit
   handbag 191.5
   nightclothes 225.24

sacellum 1000.1
sacerdotal 995.9
sacerdotalism 995.1, 3
sachem
   personage 642.5
   master 745.1
   chief 745.3
sachet 400.5
sack *n.* bag 191.4
   dismissal 297.4
   pillage 791.2
sack *v.* dismiss 297.12
   secure 775.6
   take 789.9
   pillage 791.10
sackage 791.2
sackbut 417.4
sackcloth and ashes
   mourning 839.4
   penance 952.3
sack coat 225.16
sacking cloth 219.5
   rough 256.2
sackmaker 690.8
sacrament 998.1, 3, 6
sacramental *n.* 998.1, 8
sacramental *adj.*
   998.15
sacramentalism 998.11
sacramentalist 998.12
sacrarium 1000.2, 3
sacred holy 976.13
   scriptural 985.6
   hallowed 987.11
sacred music 415.11
   (glorification 990.2)
sacrifice *n.*
   destruction 162.1
   oblation 990.6
   (atonement 952.1)
   (idolatry 991.3)
   make a sacrifice 942.4
sacrifice *v.* 784.11
sacrificial 952.6
sacrilege 988.1
sacrilegious 988.10
sacring bell 550.16
sacrist, sacristan 996.5
sacristy 1000.3
sacrosanct
   inviolable 922.6
   sacred 976.13
   hallowed 987.11
sad great 31.6
   sodden 384.23
   sad-colored 428.19
   gray 432.4
   deplorable 649.8
   grievous 830.11
   unhappy 837.9
   (funereal 363.25)
   (wretched 828.16)
   (discontented 832.5)
   (sullen 901.8)
   be sad 837.6
   (despair 859.5)
   (be sullen 901.6)
sad-colored 428.19
sadden 837.8
saddle *n.* seat 215.23
   meat 298.19

1066

seat of power 747.5
in the saddle
 prepared 673.11
 in charge 693.7
saddle v. weight 319.9
 ~ a horse 370.7
saddle on add 37.3
 attach 43.6
 attribute to 155.3
saddle with add 37.3
 lodge 184.12
 encumber 706.6
 impose a duty 926.7
 accuse of 938.4
saddlebag bag 191.4
 saddle 215.23
saddle blanket, saddlecloth 223.10
saddle horse, saddler 271.3
saddle skirt 215.23
Sadducee 984.17
sadiron
 smoother 255.3
 heater 386.1
sadism 961.3
sadly extremely 31.23
 indeed 535.8
 unhappily 837.17
sadness 837
 (wretchedness 828.3)
 (discontent 832.1)
 (weariness 841.1)
 (sullenness 901.2)
safe n.
 cupboard 191.15
 money box 802.1
 (hiding place 530.2)
safe adj.
 unscathed 654.5
 secure 664.10
 uninjured 670.6
 cautious 864.6
 be safe 664.4
 (escape 671.6)
 on the safe side
  safe 664.10
  cautious 864.6
 render safe 664.6
safeblower, safebreaker, safecracker 792.2
safeblowing, safebreaking, safecracking 791.1
safe-conduct
 escort 88.4
 passkey 260.10
 protection 664.2, 3
 guard 717.6
 passport 760.2
safe-deposit vault 802.1
 (storehouse 636.4)
safeguard n.
 protection 664.2
 safety device 666
 (shield 223.2)
 (protector 664.3)
 guard 717.2

safe-conduct 760.2
safeguard v.
 protect 664.6
 defend 717.7
safehold refuge 666.3
 stronghold 717.4
safekeeping
 protection 664.2
 preservation 670.1
safely 664.13
safemaker 690.8
safety razor 253.6
 bicycle 272.14
 security 664
 in safety 664.10
 seek safety 664.8
 (take refuge 666.5)
safety belt 158a.6
safety pin, safety razor, safety valve 666.1
safety zone 666.3
saffron n. 436.3
saffron adj. 436.6
sag n. obliquity 217.1
 droop 306.1
 price decline 815.3
sag v. incline 217.6
 curve 245.3
 drift 267.23
 droop 306.4
 depreciate 815.7
saga 594.2
sagacious 498.10, 11
 (sage 500.4)
 (farsighted 510.6)
 (clever 698.11)
 (cunning 702.6)
sagacity 498.2, 3
 (farsightedness 510.1)
 (experience 698.4)
 (cunning 702.1)
sagaman 594.4
sagamore 745.3
sage n.
 condiment 393.1
 wise man 500
 (scholar 492.2)
 (adviser 695.3)
sage adj. 498.11
sageness 498.3
Sagitta, Sagittarius 318.6
sagittal 253.13
Sagittary 83.7
sagum 225.15
Sahara 169.2
sahib, saheb
 gentleman 373.2
 (master 745.1)
 title 877.2
Sahibah 374.2, 3
saic 273.2
said n. See sayid
said adj.
 preceding 62.4
 spoken 582.9
 it is said 532.10
sail n. voyage 267.6
 ship 273.1

ship's canvas 273.13
put on sail
 set sail 267.16
 speed 274.9
take in sail
 be moderate 174.4
 reduce sail 267.38
 retard 275.7
under sail
 moving 264.10
 afloat 267.54
 forward 282.5
sail v. 267.10
sail against the wind 267.18
sail before the wind 734.5
sail close to the wind, sail fine 267.19
sail free 267.17
sail into
 run afoul of 267.32
 attack 716.5
 fight 720.8
sail near the wind
 sail 267.19
 exercise skill 698.9
 be dishonest 940.6
sail with the wind 267.17
sail under false colors
 dissemble 544.6
 assume 925.6
sailboat, sailer 273.2, 4
sailing n. 267.1
sailing adj. 267.49
sailing master 269.4
sail loft 273.7
sailmaker 690.8
sailor voyager 268.1
 mariner 269.1
sailplane 273a.6
saint n.
 good person 948.1
 angel 977.1
 apostle 985.6
 Christian 987.4
saint v. sanctify 987.8
 canonize 995.7
St. Anthony's fire 655.17
St. Bernard 366.6
St. Elmo's fire 420.11
saintly
 righteous 944.3
 pious 987.10
St. Patrick's Day, St. Swithin's Day 138.7
saint's day 138.5
saintship 987.1
Saint-Simonianism 906.3
St. Vitus's dance
 twitching 315.6
 illness 655.14
Saiva Siddhanta, Shaiva Siddhanta 451.5
Sakai 560.4

sake
 for the sake of
 since 155.8
 for the purpose of 620.6
 on behalf of 707.15
salaam, salam n.
 greeting 894.4
 obeisance 928.2
salaam, salam v. 928.6
salability, saleability 796.4
salable, saleable 796.7
 (commercial 794.10)
salacious 961.11
salacity 961.3
salad 41.4
salade See sallet
salamander
 monster 83.7
 reptile 366.18
 heater 386.1
 fire iron 386.3
 elemental spirit 979.7
salamandrine 384.22
salame, salami 298.24
Salamis 722.5
sal ammoniac, salammoniac
 energizer 171.5
 pungency 392.2
salary 973.2
sale 796
 (barter 794.1)
 for sale offered 763.4
 to sell 796.9
saleability, saleable See salability etc.
salesman 758.5; 797.2
sales manager 797.2
salesmanship 796.1
sales resistance, sales talk 796.3
salience
 convexity 250.1
 manifestness 525.1
 importance 642.1
salient n. 250.2
salient adj.
 prominent 250.9
 conspicuous 525.5
 important 642.10
salient point 642.4
 (essence 5.2)
salina 343a.1
saline 392.6
saliva 299.5
salivant 297.22
salivary 332.5
salivate 297.19
 (excrete 299.9)
salivation 299.5
 (evacuation 297.5)
sallet, salade 717.2
sallow pale 429.6
 yellow 436.6
sally n. handle 215.7
 outlet 295.5
 attack 716.1

sally — sanitation

sally (*continued*)
  (battle 722.5)
  witticism 842.4
sally *v.* 293.4
sally port
  covert way 530.4
  escape 671.3
  fortification 717.3
salmagundi
  mixture 41.4
  stew 298.17
salmi 298.17
salmon fish 298.18
  color 434.3, 10
salmon brick 384.14
saloon 959.13
  (inn 189.8)
salsify 298.30
salt *n.* mariner 269.1
  seasoning 393.1
  mineral 635.6
  salience 642.4
  cathartic 662.9
  veteran 700.3
  money 800.1
  wit 842.1
  below the salt 876.13
salt *v.* season 392.4
  cure 670.4
  falsify accounts 811.9
  salt away, salt down 636.1
salt *adj.* 392.6
saltant 315.13
saltarello music 415.7
  dance 840.7
saltate 309.4
saltation 309.1
saltatorial 315.13
saltatory *n.* 309.3
saltatory *adj.* 309.6
saltimbank, saltimbanque 548.3
salt marsh 344.1
salt of the earth
  best 648.4
  commonalty 876.1
  philanthropist 911.1
  good person 948.1
salt pan, saltpan 344.1
saltpeter, saltpetre
  energizer 171.5
  pungency 392.2
salt water 341.1
saltworker 690.9
saltworks 691
salty 392.6
salubrious 656.5
  (beneficial 648.12)
  (restorative 660.18)
  (remedial 662.25)
  be salubrious 656.4
salubrity 656
salutary
  beneficial 648.12
  (helpful 707.12)
  salubrious 656.5
  (remedial 662.25)
salutation
  allocution 586.1

greeting 894.4
homage 928.2
salutatory
  speech 582.2
  allocution 586.1
salute *n.*
  celebration 883.1
  greeting 894.4
  homage 928.2
salute *v.*
  signal ship 267.41
  signal 550.20
  accost 586.2
  greet 894.9
  pay homage to 928.5
salvage
  reclamation 660.1
  redemption 775.3
  fee 812.2
  discount 813.1
  compensation 973.2
salvation
  reclamation 660.1
  preservation 670.1
  deliverance 672.1
  divine function 976.5
  redemption 987.3
salve *n.*
  lubricant 332.2
  balm 662.6
  money 800.1
  flattery 933.1
salve *v.* lubricate 332.4
  relieve 834.4
salver 191.12
salvo shot 284.4; 406.2
  barrage 716.2
  saving clause 770.1
  salute 883.1
  excuse 937.2
sal-volatile 392.2
samadhi 994.6
sambar, sambur 366.11
sambo mongrel 41.5
  Negro 431.4
Sambo 431.4
same 13.3, 6; 27.9
  (analogue 17.5)
  (copy 21.1)
at the same time
  notwithstanding 30.8
  meanwhile 109a.3
sameliness
  regularity 16.2
  (sameness 13.2)
  tedium 841.3
samely 16.5
sameness identity 13.2
  (similarity 17.1)
  (equivalence 27.2)
  regularity 16.2
  tedium 841.3
samesome 16.5
samiel wind 349.9, 12
  hot wind 382.4
samisen 417.2
Samkhya See **Sankhya**
Sammael 978.1

sammy 352.8
Sammy
  American 188.9
  soldier 726.4
Samoan 560.4
Samotherium 206.7
samovar 191.11
samp 298.15
sampan 273.4
sample *n.* example 82.2
  taster 390.1
sample *v.*
  exemplify 82.6
  taste 390.3
Sampson
  Dominie ~ 492.2
Samson, Sampson 159.6
Samuel 513.2
samurai 875.3
sanable 658.16
sanative
  restorative 660.18
  curative 662.25
  (salubrious 656.5)
sanatorium 662.17
  (resort 189.14)
sanatory
  restorative 660.18
  curative 662.25
sanctification
  divine function 976.6
  purification 987.2
sanctified
  hallowed 987.11
  sanctimonious 988.11
sanctify sanction 760.4
  bless 976.11
  purify 987.8
  (bless 990.12)
sanctimonious 988.11
  (dissembling 544.8)
  (affected 853.6)
  be sanctimonious 988.8
sanctimony 988.2
  (dissemblance 544.2)
  (bigotry 606.2)
  (affectation 853.1)
  (piety 987.1)
sanction *n.*
  permission 760.1, 2
  approval 931.1
sanction *v.*
  ratify 488.10
  permit 760.4
  approve 931.5
  legalize 963.4
sanctioned 924.10
sanctity 987.1
sanctuary refuge 666.3
  (retreat 189.13)
  (stronghold 717.4)
  temple 1000.1, 3
sanctum sanctorum
  retreat 189.13
  room 191.16
  sanctuary 666.3

Holy of Holies 1000.3
Sanctus
  doxology 990.2
  Mass 998.7
Sanctus bell 550.16
sand *n.* granule 330.3
  stone 342.4
  resolution 604.1
  hidden danger 667.1
  ~ in the eyes 683.4
  courage 861.1
sand *v.* 255.4
sandal shoe 225.27
  sandalwood 400.3
sandbag *n.* 727.7
sandbag *v.* 972.6
sandbagger 792.3
sandbank, sand bar
  shallow 209.2
  hidden danger 667.1
sand-blind 442.6
sand dune 206.2
sand flea 366.24
sandglass 114.6
sand hog 252.7
sandman 683.5
sandpaper *n.* 255.3
sandpaper *v.* 255.4
sandpiper 366.22
sandstone 342.4
sandstorm 349.12
  (dust 330.3)
sandwich 228.8
sandwich boy, sandwich man 531.6
sandy granular 330.8
  redheaded 434.12
  yellow 436.6
Sandy 188.9
sane logical 476.16
  sound-minded 502.5
  (intelligent 498.9)
  become sane 502.3
  render sane 502.4
sanely 502.6
sane-minded 502.5
saneness 502.1
sangar 717.3
sang-froid, sangfroid
  levelheadedness 498.4
  dispassion 822.1
  composure 826.2
Sangraal, Sangreal 998.8
sanguinary 361.15
sanguine
  murderous 361.15
  red 434.9, 11
  hopeful 858.9
sanguisuge 662.15
Sanhedrin, Sanhedrim 696.1
sanies 333.2
sanious 333.7
sanitarian 656.3
sanitarium 662.17
  (asylum 503.8)
sanitary 656.5
sanitation

sanity — sault

cleansing 652.2
hygiene 656.2
sanity
  soundness of mind 502
  health 654.1
Sankhya, Samkhya 451.5
sannyasi, sannyasin
  beggar 767.2
  ascetic 955.2
  religious 996.8
sans 187.16
sans-culotte
  revolutionist 742.3
  ragamuffin 876.9
sans-culottic 146.5; 742.1
sans-culottism 146.2; 742.2
Sanskrit
  antiquity 124.2
  language 560.4
Sanskritist 560.7
sans pareil 33.8
sans peur et sans reproche
  perfect 650.5
  noble 873.18
  beyond praise 931.11
  honorable 939.7
  innocent 946.5
sans souci
  in comfort 377.9
  insensible 823.5
  content 831.6
  indifferent 866.4
Santali 560.4
santon recluse 893.4
  priest 996.7
sap *n.* essence 5.2
  trench 259.2
  fluid 333.2
  fool 501.1
sap *v.* weaken 160.8
  excavate 252.9
  injure 659.8
  mine 716.5
sap green 435.4
saphead 501.1
sapheaded 499.12
sapid
  flavorous 390.4
  palatable 394.7
sapidity 390.1
sapience 498.3
sapient *n.* 500.1
sapient *adj.* 498.11
sapless weak 160.10
  dry 340.7
sapling
  youngling 129.1
  tree 367.6
saponaceous 355.3
saponacity 355.1
saporous
  flavorous 390.4
  palatable 394.7
sapper excavator 252.7
  military ~ 726.4
Sapphic 597.13

sapphire blue 438.2, 3
  gem 847.8
Sapphism 961.3
Sapphist 962.2
sappy youthful 127.5
  fluid 333.7
  foolish 499.15
saprogenic foul 653.17
  putrefactive 659.13
saraband music 415.7
  dance 840.7
Sarasvati, Saraswati 979.4
Saratoga trunk 191.8
sarcasm ridicule 856.1
  discourtesy 895.2
  derision 930.2
  (detraction 934.1)
sarcastic
  derisive 856.7
  discourteous 895.7
  contemptuous 930.8
  disapprobatory 932.11
  (disparaging 934.4)
sarcology 662.16
sarcoma
  protuberance 250.2
  ailment 655.16
sarcophagus 363.10
sard 847.8
Sardanapalus 954a.1
sardar See sirdar
sardine 298.18
sardonic
  contemptuous 930.8
  disapprobatory 932.11
sardonic grin
  smile 838.2
  ridicule 856.1
sardonyx red 434.5
  gem 847.8
sargasso, sargassum 367.3
sark 225.18, 25
sarmentum
  member 51.4
  foliage 367.4
sarsen stone 342.4
sartor 225.37
sartorial 225.48
sash frame 215.8
  garment 225.34
  circle 247.2
  screen 424.3
sashay move 264.6
  walk 266.16
  depart 293.4
sash curtain 424.3
Sassak 560.4
sastra See shastra
Satan 978
  (evil 649.2)
  (demon 980.2)
satanic
  malevolent 907.9
  wicked 945.17
  devilish 978.7
  (demoniac 980.9)
  (hellish 982.5)

Satanism
  diabolism 978.4
  sorcery 992.1
satchel 191.5
sate 869.4
  (fill 52.7)
satellite
  follower 281.2
  (accompanier 88.3)
  (puppet 711.2)
  hanger-on 886.2
satiate *v.*
  satisfy 829.4
  sate 869.4
  (overload 641.4)
  overeat 957.3
satiate, satiated 869.6
  (full 52.11)
  (overfull 641.6)
satiation 869.1
satiety 869
  (plenty 639.2)
  (redundance 641.1)
  (weariness 841.2)
satin cloth 219.5
  smooth 255.2
  softness 324.3
satiny 324.8
satire
  figure of speech 521.1
  poetry 597.1, 2
  burlesque 856.3
  derision 930.2
satirical
  figurative 521.3
  ironical 930.8
  disapprobatory 932.11
satirist poet 597.10
  lampooner 936.1
satirize
  burlesque 856.6
  lampoon 934.3
satisfaction
  gratification 377.1
  adequacy 639.1
  reparation 660.4
  duel 720.3
  observance 772.1
  payment 807.1
  content 831.1
  (pleasure 827.1)
  satiety 869.1
  performance 926.2
  atonement 952.1
  compensation 973.1
give satisfaction
  duel 720.8
  atone 952.4
satisfactional 952.6
satisfactory
  pleasing 377.7
  believable 484.15
  adequate 639.6
  tolerable 648.11
  satisfying 831.7
  (agreeable 829.7)
  (desirable 865.21)
be satisfactory 463.11
satisfied

convinced 484.12
content 831.6
  (pleased 827.8)
satiated 869.6
satisfy feed 298.43
  stand the test 463.11
  ~ oneself 474.6
  convince 484.10
  suffice 639.3
  consent 762.2
  observe 772.3
  pay 807.7
  gratify 829.4
  content 831.4
  sate 869.4
  ~ an obligation 926.6
  compensate 973.3
satisfying
  believable 484.15
  satisfactory 831.7
satrap 745.7
Satsuma ware 384.14
saturate imbue 41.8
  fill 52.7
  (overload 641.4)
  (sate 869.4)
  soak 337.5
saturated full 52.11
  (overfull 641.6)
  (satiated 869.6)
  soaked 339.8
saturation fill 52.3
  soaking 337.2
  satiety 869.1
Saturn time 106.1
  planet 318.3
  sun 318.4
  god 979.2
saturnalia
  turmoil 59.4
  festival 840.2
  debauch 954.2
saturnalian 954.5
Saturnian 829.9
saturnine 837.10
satyr wood 367.7
  ugliness 846.3
  libertine 962.1
  deity 979.11
satyric 961.11
satyrism 961.3
sauce *n.* mixture 41.4
  pulp 354.2
  condiment 393.1
  impertinence 885.2
sauce *v.* 885.7
sauce-alone 393.1
saucebox 885.3
  (discourteous person 895.3)
saucepan 191.11
saucer plate 191.12
  eye 443.4
saucer eye 441.7; 443.4
saucer-eyed 443.14
sauciness 885.2
saucy 885.9
sauerkraut food 298.30
sour article 397.2
sault 348.7

saunter — scape

saunter n.
 walk 266.4, 5
 slow motion 275.2
saunter v.
 wander 266.14
 walk 266.16
 go slow 275.5
saurian 366.18
Saurischia, sauropod, Sauropoda 124.2
sausage balloon 273a.5
 meat 298.24
savage n.
 barbarian 876.7
 brute 913.3
savage adj.
 ferocious 173.14
 warlike 722.13
 uncivilized 851.7
 furious 900.13
 cruel 907.9
savagery
 vulgarity 851.1
 cruelty 907.3
savanna, savannah 344.1
savant 492.1
 (sage 500.1)
 (proficient 700.1)
Savara 560.4
save v. reserve 636.8
 preserve 670.3
 rescue 672.2
 economize 817.3
 atone 976.9
 redeem 987.9
save up 636.8
 (be economical 817.3)
save prep. 38.11; 55.7
save-all n.
 economist 817.1
 miser 819.2
save-all adj. 819.4
saved 672.4
savin, savine 367.6
saving n.
 preservation 670.1
 economy 817.1, 2
saving 817.4
saving prep. 55.7
saving clause 770.1
 (condition 469.2)
savings 636.2
savior, saviour 912.2
Saviour 976.5
Savitar sun 318.4
 deity 979.4
savoir-faire
 experience 698.4
 manners 894.1
savoir-vivre 894.1
savor, savour n.
 taste 389.1
 relish 394.2
 odor 398.1
savor, savour v.
 taste 390.3
 flavor 392.4
savor of
 resemble 17.7

taste of 394.6
savoriness, savouriness 394
savorless, savourless 391.2
savory, savoury n. 298.9
 (palatable 394.3)
savory, savoury adj.
 palatable 394.7
 (pleasing 377.7)
 (flavorful 390.4)
 fragrant 400.10
 be savory 394.5
savvy, savvey n.
 knowledge 490.1
 understanding 498.1
savvy, savvey v.
 know 490.9
 understand 518.4
saw n. ten 98.6
 tool 257.3
 (cutter 253.6)
 maxim 496.1
saw v. cut 44.8
 sound harshly 410.6
 violin 416.18
 ~ the air 550.20
saw off 361.10
sawbones 662.19
sawbuck ten 98.6
 trestle 215.9
sawder n. 933.1
sawder v. 933.2
sawdust remains 40.1
 powder 330.3
sawfish 366.21
sawfly 366.24
sawhorse 215.9
sawlike 257.6
sawmaker 690.8
sawmill 691
Sawney, Sawnie, Sawny
 Scotchman 188.9
 oaf 501.1
 awkward fellow 701
saw tooth
 tooth 253.3
 serration 257.2
saw-toothed 257.6
sawyer 706.2
sax, saxcornet, saxhorn 417.4
Saxon 576.3; 578.4
saxophone 417.4
saxophonist 416.2
saxtuba 417.4
say n. round 138.4
 cloth 219.5
 assertion 535.1
 speech 582.2, 4
 conversation 588.1
 have one's say 535.3
say v. answer 462.5
 suppose 514.6
 assert 535.3
 utter 582.6
 (argue 476.11)
 (tell 527.7)
 (divulge 529.4)

(announce 531.7)
(express 566.3)
(voice 580.8)
(declaim 582.7)
(chatter 584.4)
(soliloquize 589.3)
say over 104.4
sayid, sayyid 745.5
saying maxim 496.1
 (phrase 566.1)
 affirmation 535.1
 statement 582.4
say-so 741.1
sc. See scilicet
scab n.
 incrustation 223.16
 itch 380.3
 blackleg 607.6
 sore 655.16
 wound 659.4
 blemish 848.1
scabbard 191.8
scabby
 laminated 204.5
 rough 256.12
 disreputable 874.8
scabies itch 380.3
 ailment 655.17, 18
scabious 380.6
scabrous 256.12
scad quantities 31.3
 multitude 102.2
scaddle 293.5
scads 31.3
scaffold
 foundation 215.3
 frame 215.8
 execution 975.4
scagliola
 plaster 223.19
 sham 545.6
scalawag, scallawag
 horse 271.6
 rascal 949.1
scald n. 384.8
scald, skald n. 597.10
scald v. 382.13
scaldic, skaldic 597.13
scalding 382.16
scale n. degree 26.1
 piece 51.3
 series 69.2
 rank 71.1
 lamina 204.2
 incrustation 223.16
 powder 330.3
 music 413.15, 16
 measure 466, 4
 draw to scale 466.10
scale v.
 form layers 204.4
 flake 226.7
 climb 305.5
 weigh 319.7
 escalade 716.5
scale beam 319.5
scalene 243.5
scales balance 319.5
 ~ of Justice 941.1
 hold the scales
 measure 466.10

judge 480.8
scaliness 204.3
scallawag See scalawag
scallion 298.30
scallop n. curl 248.2
 serration 257.2
scallop v. curl 248.3
 notch 257.5
scalloped 257.6
scalp 226.5
scalpel 253.6
scaly laminated 204.5
 (covered 223.28)
 divestitive 226.11
 rough 256.12
scamp n. 949.1
scamp v. 460.6
 (not complete 730.2)
scamper n. dash 274.3
 haste 684.1
scamper v. speed 274.9
 hasten off 293.5
 hasten 684.3
scampish 940.8
 (evildoing 945.13)
scan look at 441.11, 12
 examine 461.17
 glance at 461.19
 know 490.9
 study 539.4
 poetry 597.12
scandal gossip 532.4
 (defamation 934.1)
 disgrace 874.1, 2
 abomination 923.1
scandalize 932.9
be scandalized 932.5
scandalmonger 532.5
 (slanderer 936.1)
scandalmongery 532.4
scandalous
 terrible 649.8
 disreputable 874.8
 wicked 945.16
scandent 305.7
Scandinavian n. 188.9
Scandinavian adj. 188.11
scanning, scansion 597.5
scansorial 305.7
scant
 inconsiderable 32.8
 sparse 103.3
 narrow 203.9
 scarce 640.10
scantiness
 incompleteness 53.1
 scarcity 640.2
scantling
 modicum 32.2
 beam 215.12
scanty
 inconsiderable 32.8
 incomplete 53.4
 sparse 103.3
 narrow 203.9
 scarce 640.10
scape n.
 scenic view 448.2

1070

scape — schoolmaid

picture 556.10
escape 671.1
scape *v.* 671.6
scapegoat
  substitute 147.2
  sacrifice 990.6
scapegrace
  bravo 863.3
  rascal 949.1
scaphoid 245.11
Scapin liar 548.5
  knave 949.1
scapular
  feather 256.8
  monk's ~ 999.1
scapulimancy 511.3
scar *n.* precipice 212.3
  shore 342.2
  mark 550.7; 551.5
  wound 659.4
  blemish 848.1
scar *v.* 659.8
scarab 993.2
Scaramouch
  actor 599.20
  buffoon 844
scarce incomplete 53.4
  sparse 103.3; 640.10
  (infrequent 137.2)
  (inconsiderable 32.8)
make oneself scarce
  be absent 187.8
  depart 293.4
  flee 623.10
scarcely barely 32.16
  infrequently 137.3
  nearly 197.12
scarcity fewness 103.1
  dearth 640.2
scare *n.* 860.1
scare *v.*
  ~ up 775.6
  frighten 860.10
scarecrow
  ugly thing 846.3
  object of fear 860.7
scared 860.14
scarehead 66.3
scaremonger 860.6
scaremongering 860.5
scare-sinner 860.7
scarf veil 225.12
  neckpiece 225.33
  ecclesiastical ~ 999.1
scarfskin 223.12
scarify notch 257.5
  torture 830.6
scarlatina 655.6
scarlet *n.* 434.2
scarlet *v.* 434.7
scarlet *adj.* red 434.9
  whorish 961.10
scarlet fever 655.6
scarlet runner 298.30
Scarlet Woman 983.a.3
scarp stratum 204.1
  precipice 212.3
  trench 259.2
  fortification 717.3

scarpines
  punishment 972.2
  iron heel 975.3
scathe, scath *n.*
  harm 649.2
  damage 659.3
scathe, scath *v.*
  harm 649.6
  damage 659.8
  distress 830.3
scatheful, scathful 649.10
scatheless, scathless
  perfect 650.5
  preserved 670.6
scatter *n.* 74.2
scatter *v.* derange 61.2
  disperse 73.3
  (diverge 291.2)
  dive 189.9
scatter to the winds
  disperse 73.3
  destroy 162.4
  confute 479.2
  waste 638.2
  throw away 678.3
  squander 818.3
scatterbrain 501.2
scatterbrained 458.13
  (empty-headed 499.14)
scattered 73.4
scattergood 818.2
scattering *n.* 73.1
scattering *adj.* 73.5
scatteringly 73.6
scatterling 268.2
scavenger 652.6
scene
  surroundings 227.2
  view 448.2
  picture 556.10
  theater 599.5, 15
  ~ of action 728.1
  passion 825.5
  anger 900.3
behind the scenes
  causally 153.10
  invisible 447.4
  aware of 490.13
  in private 528.24
  drama 599.29
scene painter 559.2, 17
scene plot 599.16
scenery
  costume 225.10
  view 448.2
  stage 599.15
sceneshifter 599.17
scenewright
  painter 559.2
  drama 599.17
scenic dramatic 599.28
  spectacular 882.9
scenist painter 559.2
  drama 599.17
scenograph
  picture 556.10
  artist 559.1
scenographic 556.19
scenography 556.1

scent *n.* smell 398.1, 3
  (fragrance 400.1)
  perfume 400.2
  intimation 527.4
  spoor 550.4
get scent of 527.11
scent *v.*
  smell 398.5, 6, 7
  perfume 400.9
  detect 481a.7
scent bag 400.5
scented 400.10
scenter 400.5
scentless 399.5
scepter, sceptre 747.1
sceptic, scepticism etc.
  See skeptic etc.
schatchen 903.11
schedule *n.* list 86.1
  prospectus 611.2
  (outline 230.1)
  (plan 626.2)
  (program 626.3)
  (policy 692.2)
schedule *v.* list 86.3
  book 611.4
Schellingism, Schellingianism 451.12
schema, schematism 60.3
scheme *n.*
  arrangement 60.3
  purpose 516.1
  plan 626.2
  (way 627.1)
scheme *v.* 626.10
  (maneuver 702.5)
schemeful 702.6
schemer planner 626.8
  intrigant 702.4
scheming
  planning 626.12
  designing 702.6
  dishonest 940.8
schemist 702.4
scherzo 415.6
schism
  religious faction 984.3
  dissension 713.2
  (dissent 489.1)
schismatic *n.*
  apostate 607.5
  sectarian 984.13
schismatic *adj.* 984.23
  (dissentient 489.5)
schismatism 984.2
schismatist
  apostate 607.5
  sectarian 984.13
schizomycete 193.4
schizophrenia 503.2
schnapps liquor 959.5
  distilled liquors 959.6
schnorrer 767.2
scholar
  learned man 492
  (sage 500.1)
  (bookman 593.14)
  student 541.1, 4

scholarly
  bookish 490.16
  (intellectual 450.8)
  (studious 539.6)
  pupillary 541.9
  (educational 537.12)
  (pedagogic 540.7)
  (schoolish 542.9)
scholarship
  learning 490.2
  (literature 560.8)
  scholastic honor 873.8
scholastic *n.*
  scholar 492.1
  student 541.1
  theologian 983.3
scholastic *adj.*
  bookish 490.16
  (studious 539.6)
  educational 537.12
  (pedagogic 540.7)
  scholarly 541.9
  academic 542.9
Scholasticism 451.10
scholiast scholar 492.1
  commentator 524.2; 595.3
scholiastic 522.8
scholium axiom 496.2
  annotation 522.4
school *n.* horde 72.4
  ~ of belief 484.3
  study course 537.7
  class 541.8
  denomination 542.4
  art 556.6, 7
  sect 712.1
  religious order 984.3
school *v.* teach 537.9
  study 539.4
school board 542.8
schoolbook 593.5
schoolboy boy 129.4
  student 541.1
school companion 541.7
schoolcraft
  learning 490.2
  teaching 537.1
school desk 542.6
schooldame 540.2
schoolery
  learning 490.2
  teaching 537.1
schoolfellow
  schoolmate 541.7
  companion 890.3
schoolgirl girl 129.5
  student 541.1
schoolhouse 542.1
schooling 537.1
schoolish 542.9
  (educational 537.12)
  (pedagogic 540.7)
  (scholarly 541.9)
schoolkeeper 540.1
schoolma'am, schoolmarm 540.2
schoolmaid girl 12?
  student 541.?

schoolman — scranch

schoolman
  scholar 492.1
  student 541.1
  theologian 983.3
schoolmaster 540.1
schoolmastery *n.* 540.6
schoolmastery,
  schoolmasterish,
  schoolmasterly *adj.*
  540.7
schoolmate 541.7
schoolmiss girl 129.5
  student 541.1
schoolmistress 540.2
schoolroom
  room 191.16
  classroom 542.5
schoolteacher 540.1
schoolteacherish,
  schoolteachery 540.7
school of thought
  philosophy 451.4
  denomination 542.4
schooner cup 191.11
  ship 273.2
Schopenhauerism
  451.12
schottische, schottish
  840.7
schweizerkäse 298.29
sciagram, sciagraph
  etc. See skiagram
sciatica pain 378.1
  nervous disorder
  655.14
science
  knowledge 490.7
  skill 698.3
scientific
  knowledge 490.19
  exact 494.11
scientist 492.5
  (professional
  690.10)
scilicet, scil., sc. 522.9
scimitar, scimiter
  727.3
scintilla
  modicum 32.2
  fire 382.8
  light 420.5
scintillate
  glitter 420.18
  ~ intellectually
  498.8
  be witty 842.8
scintillating 420.23
scintillation fire 382.8
  light 420.5
  flash of wit 842.4
sciolism 491.3
sciolist 493.2
  (charlatan 548.3)
sciolistic 491.12
sciomancy 511.3
scion member 51.4
  descendant 167.4
  (youngling 129.1)
scissile 44.13
scission 44.2
  ~ors 253.6

scissors-smith 690.6
scissure 198.2
scobs remains 40.1
  filings 330.3
scoff *n.* food 298.5
  meal 298.34
  gibe 930.3
scoff *v.* eat 298.44
  jeer 930.6
  (ridicule 856.4)
  (disapprove 932.5)
  (disparage 934.3)
  (be impious 988.7)
scoffer 988.4
scoffing 930.2
  (raillery 856.1)
  (impiety 988.1)
scold *n.* shrew 901.4
  chider 936.2
scold *v.* 932.8
scolding 932.3
scolecid, scolecoid
  248.6
scollop *n.* curl 248.2
  serration 257.2
scollop *v.* curl 248.3
  notch 257.5
sconce *n.* head 210.3
  top 210.4
  candleholder 423.9
  brain 450.2
  fortification 717.3
  fine 974.2
sconce *v.* 974.3
scone 298.11
scoop *n.* ladle 191.14
  perforator 262
  news 532.1
scoop *v.*
  excavate 252.9
  ladle 270.10
scoot *n.* 272.13
scoot *v.* speed 274.9
  hasten off 293.5
scooter vehicle 272.14
  ship 273.2
scope degree 26.1
  occasion 134.2
  extent 180.1
  size 192.1
  optics 445.1
  meaning 516.1
  sphere of work 625.3
  freedom 748.2
  have free scope 748.8
scopic optical 441.18
  visual 445.9
scorch *n.* run 274.3
  burn 384.8
scorch *v.* speed 274.9
  dry 340.5
  be hot 382.13
  burn 384.18
  (discolor 440a.2)
scorcher
  automobilist 268.10
  speeder 274.5
scorching
  violent 173.13
  hot 382.16
score *n.* sum 84.3

list 86.1
twenty 98.7
notch 257.1
furrow 259.1
music 415.21
  (arrangement 60.3)
  (composition 590.3)
  (book 593.1)
mark 550.7
playbook 599.16
credit 805.1
debt 806.1
account 811.1, 3
charge 812.1
settle the score
retaliate 718.2
punish 972.5
score *v.*
compose 54.4
arrange 60.8
calculate 85.7
list 86.3
notch 257.5
furrow 259.3
music 415.26
mark 550.19
 ~ a success 731.5
upbraid 932.8
scoreboard, score
  sheet 551.1
scorer 416.14
scores 102.2
scoria dregs 40.2
  slag 384.15
scoriaceous 384.22
scorification 384.3
scorifier 191.11
scorify 384.18
scorn *n.* 930.1
scorn *v.* 930.5
scornful 930.8
Scorpio 318.6
scorpion 366.24; 368.3
Scorpion 318.6
scot price 812.1
  payment 973.2
Scot 188.9
scotch *n.* 257.1
scotch *v.* notch 257.5
  injure 659.8
  thwart 706.7
Scotch *adj.* 188.11
scotched 732.9
Scotchman 188.9
Scotch reel 840.7
scot-free
  escaped 671.7
  free 748.12
  gratuitous 815.10
go scot free
  escape 671.6
  be free 750.4
scotia 847.4
Scotism 451.10
Scotland 182.3
scotograph 556.12
scotomy 443.1
Scotsman 188.9
Scotticism 563.5
Scottish 188.11
scoundrel 949.1

scour *n.* 274.3
scour *v.* smooth 255.4
  travel 266.12
  speed 274.9
  rub 331.3
  search 461.16
  clean 652.9
scourge *n.* bane 663.1
  affliction 735.1
  infliction 830.2
  evildoer 913.1
  instrument of pun-
    ishment 975
scourge *v.* 972.6
scourings dregs 40.2
  offal 653.6
scout *n.*
  forerunner 64.1
  (van 234.2)
  aeronaut 269a.1
  person 372.3
  man 373.2
  feeler 463.4
  spy 528.8
  patrol boat 726.11
  servant 746.1
scout *v.*
  reconnoiter 461.22
  spurn 610.2; 930.5
  scoff 930.6
scout out
  hunt out 461.16, 22
  discover 481a.3
scow 273.4
scowl *n.*
  sullen look 901.3
  reproving look 932.4
scowl *v.* 901.6
scowling 901.8
scrabble *n.* 517.4
scrabble *v.*
  ~ up 305.5
  scribble 517.7
  write 590.13
scrag *n.*
  thin person 203.6
  horse 271.7
scrag *v.* 972.8
scraggy dwarfed 193.9
  thin 203.11
  rough 256.12
scram *v.* 623.10
scram *int.* 297.23
scramble *n.*
  turmoil 59.4
  pursuit 622.1
  hurry 684.1
  predicament 704.2
  broil 713.4
  contest 720.2
scramble *v.* mix 41.6
  ~ up 305.5
  hustle 682.12
  hurry about 684.3
  contend 720.8
  ~ for 789.13
scrambling 684.5
scranch
  pulverize 330.6
  grind 331.3
  sound harshly 410.6

1072

scrannel 643.12
scrap *n.* modicum 32.2
　remains 40.1
　piece 51.4
　child 129.3
　diminutive 193.2
　taste 390.1
　quarrel 713.3
　contest 720.2
scrap *v.* quarrel 713.7
　fight 720.8
scrapbook
　memory book 505.6
　notebook 551.3
scrape *n.* scraper 652.7
　predicament 704.2
　obeisance 928.2
　in a scrape 704.11
scrape *v.* graze 199.3
　grind 330.6
　abrade 331.3
　sound harshly 410.6
　violin 416.18
　engrave 558.5
　comb 652.11
　make obeisance
　　928.6
scrape acquaintance
　888.3
scrape off 38.6
scrape together
　assemble 72.11
　acquire 775.6
scraper hat 225.26
　cleaner 652.7
scrapper 726.1
scrapple 298.19
scrapworks 691
scratch *n.* nothing 2.2
　(zero 87a.1)
　diminutive 193.2
　furrow 259.1
　mark 550.7
　bad likeness 555.2
　wound 659.4
scratch *v.* furrow 259.3
　abrade 331.3
　sound harshly 410.6
　scribble 517.7
　~ out 552.2
　draw 556.17
　write 590.13
　maltreat 649.7
　wound 659.8
scratch *adj.* 156.12
scratch hit 156.1
scrawl *n.* 517.4
scrawl *v.*
　be unmeaning 517.7
　scribble 590.13
scrawny 203.11
screak
　stridulate 410.5
　scream 411.5; 412.2
scream *n.*
　funny mistake 495.3
　wail 839.1
　latest scream
　　novelty 123.2
　　fashion 852.1
scream *v.* blow 349.22

stridulate 410.5
cry 411.5; 412.2
　(wail 839.9)
screamer *n.*
　caption 66.3
　funny mistake 495.3
screaming
　gaudy-colored
　　428.15
　gaudy 851.8
　ridiculous 855.5
screech
　stridulate 410.5
　scream 411.5; 412.2
screech owl 366.22
screed *n.*
　modicum 32.2
　list 86.1
　lecture 582.2
　writing 590.3
screed *v.* 584.4
screen *n.* sorter 60.4
　network 219.4
　cover 223.2
　(mask 225.11)
　(concealment 530.3)
　(disguise 545.5)
　(safeguard 666.1)
　porousness 260.7
　shade 424.3
　(concealment 528.1;
　　530.3)
　cinema 599.9
　stage 599.15
　refiner 652.7
　guard 717.2
screen *v.* sort 60.6
　shade 424.6
　conceal 528.10
　(cover 223.22)
　(blind 442.3)
　refine 652.10
　protect 664.6
　guard 717.7
screened
　covered 223.28
　indistinct 447.5
screw *n.* pin 45.5
　distortion 243.1
　coil 248.2
　key 260.10
　horse 271.6
　propeller 284.6
　rotator 312.4
　jailer 753.1
　miser 819.2
　a screw loose
　　fault 651.2
　obstacle 706.2
　discord 713.1
screw *v.* attach 43.6
　distort 243.3
　convolve 248.3
　force 744.2
　extort 791.13
　scrimp 819.3
screw up attach 43.6
　strengthen 159.8
　wind up 673.6
screwball oddity 83.4
　madman 504.1, 3

screwy crooked 217.13
　spiral 248.5
　absurd 497.4
　crazy 503.12, 17
scribble *n.*
　scrawl 517.4
　scribbling 590.6
scribble *v.*
　scrawl 517.7
　write 590.13
scribblemania 590.2
scribblement 590.6
scribbler writer 590.11
　hack writer 593.15
scribble-scrabble *n.*
　517.4
scribble-scrabble *v.*
　scribble 517.7
　write 590.13
scribbly 590.15
scribe *n.* writer 590.11
　(recorder 553.1)
　author 593.15
　priest 996.6
scribe *v.* 590.13
scrimmage 720.2
scrimp *n.* 819.2
scrimp *v.* 819.3
scrimp *adj.*
　inconsiderable 32.8
　sparse 103.3
　scarce 640.10
scrimp *adv.* 103.5
scrimption
　modicum 32.2
　a few 103.2
　pittance 640.5
scrimpy
　inconsiderable 32.8
　sparse 103.3
　scarce 640.10
scrip bag 191.4
　writing 590.1, 3
　money 800.7
　purse 802.2
script
　writing 590.1, 3, 9
　type 591.8
　playbook 599.16
scription record 551.1
　writing 590.1
scriptural
　written 590.15
　orthodox 983a.7
　Biblical 985.7
scripture truth 494.1
　writing 590.1, 3, 9
Scripture 985.2
scrive *n.* 590.1, 3
scrive *v.* 590.13
scrivello 253.3
scrivener scribe 590.11
　notary 968.1
scrivening 590.1
scrod 298.18
scrofula 655.10
scroll *n.* list 86.1
　writing 590.3; 590.10
　ornamentation 847.3
scroll *v.* 590.13
scrollhead 847.4

scrub *n.* plant 367.8
　insignificancy 643.6
scrub rub 331.3
　wash 652.9
scrubber 652.7
scrubby dwarfed 193.9
　stubby 201.6
　paltry 643.12
　vulgar 851.6
　disreputable 874.8
scruff 235.1
scrumptious 394.7
scrunch *n.* 298.2
scrunch *v.* chew 298.45
　pulverize 330.6
　grind 331.3
　sound harshly 410.6
scruple *n.*
　modicum 32.2
　weight 319.4
　misgiving 485.2
　objection 489.2
　unwillingness 603.2
　(fastidiousness
　　868.1)
　apprehension 860.2
　conscience 939.2
scruple *v.*
　hang in doubt 485.7
　object 489.4
　be reluctant 603.4
　disapprove 932.5
scrupulosity 487.2
scrupulous
　doubtful 485.10
　observant 772.5
　fastidious 868.4
　(unwilling 603.5)
　conscientious 939.8
　(careful 459.7)
　(precise 494.11)
　(veracious 543.3)
scrupulousness
　reluctance 603.2
　fastidiousness 868.1
　(preciseness 494.3)
　conscientiousness
　　939.2
scrutinize
　look at 441.12
　examine 461.17
　(give attention
　　457.4)
scrutinizer
　spectator 444.1
　examiner 461.13
scrutiny look 441.2
　examination 461.3
　(attention 457.2)
scud *n.* dash 274.3
　rain 348.11
　gust 349.6
　foam 353.2
　clouds 353.5
scud *v.* float 267.44
　speed 274.9
scuff 659.4
scuffle contest 720.2
　(brawl 713.4)
　contend 720.8
scuffler 726.1

scull — seaworthy

scull n. 273.14
scull v. 267.46
scullery room 191.16
   cookroom 386.4
scullery maid 746.2
scullion
   dishwasher 652.6
   servant 746.1
sculpt v. 557.9
sculpt, sculptile adj.
   557.11
sculptograph 556.11
sculptography 556.4
sculptor 559.4, 5
   (workman 690.10)
Sculptor 318.6
sculptural 557.10
sculpturation 557.3
sculpture n.
   production 161.1
   formation 240.3
   figure 554.4
   art 557
   (composition 54.2)
   (representation
   554.1)
sculpture v. form 240.6
   insculpture 557.9
sculptured glass 557.6
sculpturer 559.4
sculpturesque 557.10
scum n. dregs 40.2
   foam 353.2
   offal 653.6
   riffraff 876.2
   (the wicked 949.5)
scum v. 353.8
scupper 350.1
scurf powder 330.3
   offal 653.6
   (dregs 40.2)
scurfy
   laminated 204.5
   rough 256.12
   pulverulent 330.8
   dirty 653.17
scurrile, scurril
   rude 895.6
   maledictory 908.6
   insulting 929.5
   derogatory 934.3
scurrility
   malediction 908.1
   indignity 929.2
   gibe 930.3
   aspersion 934.1
   vulgarity 961.1
scurrilous rude 895.6
   maledictory 908.6
   insulting 929.5
   (derisive 856.7)
   derogatory 934.4
   vulgar 961.9
scurry, skurry n.
   dash 274.3
   hurry 684.1
scurry, skurry v.
   speed 274.9
   hurry 684.3
scurvy paltry 643.12
   abominable 649.8

vulgar 851.6
wicked 945.11
scut 235.6
scutate 245.19
scutcheon
   insignia 550.12
   hatchment 551.4
scuttle n.
   receptacle 191.1
   cup 191.11
   gait 266.5
   dash 274.3
   haste 684.1
scuttle v. destroy 162.4
   walk 266.16
   capsize 267.35
   speed 274.9
   submerge 310.5
   hasten 684.3
scuttle butt 273.7
scutum 717.2
Scutum 318.6
Scylla and Charybdis
   609.6
   between Scylla and
   Charybdis
   in danger 665.8
   in a dilemma 704.11
scyphiform, scyphose
   252.10
scythe angle 244.2
   cutter 253.6
scythesmith 690.6
'sdeath! 870.11; 932.16
sea
   great quantity 31.3
   (multitude 102.2)
   ocean 341.1
   (seaway 267.8)
   wave 348.10
   blue 438.3
   at sea afloat 267.54
   ocean 341.6
   bewildered 475.16
   (ignorant 491.10)
   erroneous 495.12
   by sea 341.8
   put to sea 267.16
sea bank, seabeach
   342.2
sea blue 438.2
seaboard, seacoast
   342.2
sea cow 192.8
sea devil 341.2
sea dog 269.1
sea duck 310.3
seafarer 269.1
seafaring n. 267.1
seafaring, seago-
   ing adj. 267.48
   (oceanic 341.5)
sea gull diver 310.3
   bird 366.22
sea horse monster 83.7
   animal 366.21
sea-kindly
   seaworthy 273.15
   safe 664.10
sea king 792.5
seal n. die 22.3

pelt 223.12
oil 356.2
animal 366.21
endorsement 488.4
~ of secrecy 528.2
mark 550.7, 11
(authority 467.4)
die 558.4
bookbinding 593.10
insignia 747.2
seal v. close 261.2
   endorse 488.10
   conceal 528.10
   mark 550.19
   determine 604.6
   complete 729.2
   marry 903.12
sea lane 267.8
seal-brown 433.4
sealed
   unknown 491.14
   contracted 769.10
sealed book
   ignorance 491.2
   unintelligibility
   519.2
   concealment 528.5
   secret 533.1
sea legs 267.1
sea lentil, sea lettuce
   367.7
sea line 213.4
sea lion 366.21
seal oil 356.4
sealskin 223.12
seam 43.3
sea-maid 979.10
seaman, sea man
   spirit of the sea
   341.2
   merman 979.10
seamanship
   navigation 267.1
   skill 698.1
seamark 550.10
seamless 50.7
Sea Monster 318.6
seamstress 225.38
Seanad Eirann 696.5
séance assembly 72.2
   council 696.2
   spiritualism 994.4
seapiece 556.10
sea pig 366.21
seaplane 273a.3
seaplane carrier
   273a.9; 726.11
seaport 666.4
sear v. shrink 195.4
   dry 340.5
   burn 384.18, 19
   wither 659.6
sear, sere adj.
   shrunk 195.6
   dried 340.9
   callous 823.4
sea rat 269.1
search n. hunt 461.2, 3
   (pursuit 622.1)
   inquirer 461.12
   in search of 461.24

search v.
   nose out 455.4
   seek 461.16, 17
   (grope 463.9)
searcher 461.12
searching severe 739.5
   painful 830.15
searchlight 423.3
seared
   hardened in vice
   945.18
   impenitent 951.3
searing 830.15
seascape view 448.2
   picture 556.10
sea serpent 83.7
Sea Serpent 318.6
seashore 342.2
seasick
   be seasick 297.18
seasickness 655.13
seaside n. 342.2
seaside adj. 342.10
sea slug 298.18
season n.
   time 106.1; 126a
   (period 108.1)
   spice 392.4
   in season 126a.6
   out of season
   inapt 24.7
   anachronous 115.3
season v. imbue 41.8
   habituate 613.8
   cure 670.4
   prepare 673.6
seasonable fit 23.11
   timely 134.7
   (expedient 646.4)
seasonal season 126a.6
   periodic 138.10
seasonality 126a.1
seasoned spiced 392.5
   habituated 613.12
   experienced 698.15
seasoning
   mixture 41.2, 3
   condiment 393.1
   habituation 613.5
seat n. position 184.1
   abode 189.1
   chair 215.22
   rump 235.5
   pew 1000.3
seat v. place 184.10
   ~ oneself 308.6
sea urchin 368.5
sea wall 215.10
seawan, seawant See
   sewan
seaward 341.8
seaway room 180.2
   waterway 267.8
   (itinerary 266.9)
   (sea 341.1)
   (channel 350.1)
seaweed 367.3
seaworthy
   seakindly 273.15
   (navigable 267.49)
   safe 664.10

sebaceous 355.3
sebkha, sebka 344.1
sec 113.3
secant cutting 44.12
  cross 219.9
secede 624.3
  (dissent 489.4)
  (apostatize 607.8)
  (revolt 742.5)
seceder 607.5
  (dissenter 489.3)
secern 297.13
secernment
  evacuation 297.5
  excretion 299.1
secesh, secesher 607.5
secession 624.1
  (dissent 489.1)
  (apostasy 607.2)
  (revolt 742.2)
secessionist 607.5
  (insurgent 742.3)
seclude
  ~ oneself 893.6
  (be concealed 528.16)
  exclude 893.7
secluded 893.10
  (concealed 528.17)
seclusion
  retreat 189.13
  retirement 893.2, 3
  (aloneness 87.1)
  (concealment 528.1)
  (avoidance 623.1)
second n. period 108.1
  instant 113.3
  alto 415.13
  measure 466.3
second v. 707.8
  (side with 709.5)
second adj. 90.3
secondariness 34.1
  (sequence 63.1)
secondary n.
  inferior 34.3
  substitute 147.2
  deputy 759.1
secondary adj.
  inferior 34.5
  duplicate 90.3
  resultant 154.6
  mediocre 736.3
seconder 711.4
second-best 736.3
second childhood 499.5
second fiddle 34.1, 3
  (nonentity 643.6)
secondhand
  imitation 19.12
  old 124.6
  impaired 659.12
  (used 677.7)
  at second hand 467.13
secondly 90.6
second nature 613.1
second-rate
  paltry 643.12
  imperfect 651.4
  (inferior 34.5)
  mediocre 736.3

second self 17.5
second sight
  intuition 477a.1
  clairvoyance 994.7
second-sighted 994.22
second thoughts 658.3
  on second thoughts 658.17
secrecy
  concealment 528.2
  (half truth 546.3)
  (taciturnity 585.1)
  secret 533.1
secret n. 533
  (latency 526.1)
  (secrecy 528.2)
  (concealment 528.6)
  in secret 528.24
  in the secret 490.13
  make no secret of 525.2
secret adj. 528.21
  (latent 526.6)
  (enigmatic 533.5)
  keep secret 528.11
  (not speak 585.3)
secreta
  excrements 299.2
  part of Mass 998.7
secret agent 528.8
secrétaire
  cupboard 191.15
  table 215.20
secretariat office 745.9
  bureau 965.2
secretary
  cupboard 191.15
  table 215.20
  scribe 590.11
  (recorder 553.1)
  (workman 690.10)
  (servant 746.1)
  functionary 758.2
  agent 759.1
Secretary of State 694.4
secrete let out 297.13
  conceal 528.10
secret ink 528.5
secretion
  evacuation 297.5
  excretion 299.1
  concealment 528.1
secretionary, secretitious 299.10
secretive
  excretory 299.10
  reticent 528.22
  (taciturn 585.4)
secretiveness 528.2
  (secret 533.1)
secretly 528.24
  (latently 526.9)
secretory 299.10
sect kind 75.2, 3
  school 542.4
  class 712.1
  religious ~ 984.3, 4
  (belief 484.3)
  (creed 983.2)
sectarial

classificational 75.6
partisan 712.9
sectarian n.
  dissenter 489.3
  religious ~ 984.13, 23
  (nonconformist 83.4)
  (dissentient 489.5)
  (apostate 607.5)
sectarian adj.
  classificational 75.6
  partisan 712.9
sectarianism, sectarism 984.2
  (nonconformity 83.2)
  (dissent 489.1)
sectary n.
  follower 281.2
  dissenter 489.3
  partisan 711.4
  religious ~ 984.13, 14
sectary adj.
  classificational 75.6
  partisan 712.9
  denominational 984.23
sectator 281.2
section n.
  disjunction 44.1
  part 51.1, 2
  class 75.1
  region 181.1
  music 415.15
  typography 550.8
  printed ~ 591.2
  ~ of a book 593.7
  military unit 726.7
section v. 44.7
sectional partial 51.8
  classificational 75.6
  regional 181.6
sectionize 44.7
sector part 51.1
  semicircle 247.5
secular n. 997.2
secular adj.
  centuple 98.27
  periodic 138.11
  temporal 989.9
  lay 997.4
secularism 984.2
secularist 989.4
secularization 756.2
secularize
  discannonize 756.5
  laicize 997.3
secundines 65.2
secure v. attach 43.6
  close 261.2
  pre-engage 132.5
  preserve 670.3
  defend 717.7
  restrain 751.7
  acquire 775.6
  hold fast 781.4
  receive 785.3
secure adj. fast 43.11
  well-founded 474.9

safe 664.10
pledged 771.9
securely firmly 43.6
safely 664.13
security safety 664.1
  guaranty 771
  (loan 787.1)
  (credit 805.2)
  (payment 807.2; 809.2)
  hope 858.1
  give security 771.5
  in security 664.10
sedan 272.12, 15
Sedan 722.5
sedan limousine 272.15
sedate calm 826.9
  serious 837.16
sedative n. 662.6
  (alleviative 174.3)
  (sleep-inducer 683.6)
sedative adj.
  moderative 174.7
  (sleep-inducing 683.17)
  palliative 662.25
  relieving 834.7
sedentary 265.7
sedge 367.8
sedilia 1000.3
sediment dregs 40.2
  (condensation 321.1)
  silt 270.3
sedimental 40.6
sedition revolt 742.2
  treason 940.4
seditionist
  malcontent 832.2
  incendiary 913.1
seditious 742.7
seduce lure 617.4
  enamor 897.13
  debauch 961.8
seducer tempter 617.3
  libertine 962.1
seduction
  allurement 617.1
  debauchment 961.4
seductive 617.5
  (attractive 288.4)
seductress 617.3
sedulity 682.5
  (perseverance 604a.1)
sedulous
  industrious 682.19
  (studious 539.6)
  (persevering 604a.3)
  desirous 865.16
see n. look 441.2
  diocese 995.3, 4
see v. behold 441.10
  (be a spectator 444.3)
  (discover 481a.3)
  (be discerning 498.7)
  note 450.7

seeable — self-depreciation 1076

see *(continued)*
  give attention 457.4
  make certain 474.6
  recognize 481a.6
  deem 484.8
  know 490.9
  understand 518.4
  meet a bet 621.18
  have seen better days 735.6
  not see
    be blind 442.4
    not understand 519.5
  see after 461.16
  see daylight
    see through 481a.5
    understand 518.4
  see fit will 600.2
    be willing 602.6
    choose 609.9
  see it through
    continue 143.3
    persevere 604a.2
  see life 840.21
  see one's way
    foresee 510.5
    be skillful 698.8
    be easy 705.3
  see service 722.11
  see the light
    become 1.5
    originate 66.6
    come to life 359.7
    appear 446.2
    understand 518.4
    be published 531.9
  see to
    give attention 457.4
    care for 459.6
    superintend 693.5
  see through
    detect 481a.5
    understand 518.4
seeable visible 446.4
  manifest 525.4
seed *n.* modicum 32.2
  rudiment 153.3
  posterity 167.1
  young 167.3
  diminutive 193.2
  sperm 357.4
  gone to seed 124.9
seed *v.* 371.8
seedling plant 367.2
  tree 367.6
seedtime 126a.2
seedy unwell 655.23
  shabby 659.12
  fatigued 688.6
  needy 804.7
seeing *n.* 441.1
seeing *adj.* 441.18
seeing *conj.* 155.8
  (accordingly 8.7)
seeing glass 445.4
seek search 461.16
  (follow 281.3)
  bid for 763.3
  solicit 765.4
seeker 461.12
seem

  ~ likely 472.2
  appear 448.6
  (be manifest 525.3)
seeming *n.*
  optical illusion 443.9
  appearance 448.4
seeming *adj.* 448.7
seemingly
  apparently 448.8
  presumably 472.7
  supposedly 514.12
seemly *adj.*
  opportune 134.7
  language 578.4
  (tasteful 850.5)
  fit 646.4
  comely 845.10
seemly *adv.* 514.12
seep leak out 295.7
  (trickle 348.19)
  infiltrate 337.5
seepage leakage 295.1
  (trickle 348.4)
  infiltration 337.2
seepy 337.6
seer spectator 444.1
  fanatic 504.2
  prophet 513.2
  (astrologer 318.13)
  (psychic 994.16)
  visionary 515.7
seersucker 219.5
seesaw *n.*
  alternation 314.3
  oscillator 314.6
  game 840.15
seesaw *v.*
  alternate 314.10
  be irresolute 605.4
seethe soak 337.5
  be hot 382.13
  stew 384.19
  fume 825.7
  be angry 900.8
seething hot 382.16
  ~ with excitement 824.10
segar See **cigar**
segment *n.* 51.1
segment *v.* 44.9
segno 415.23
segregate
  separate 44.7
  exclude 55.4
  classify 60.7
  discriminate 465.2
  select 609.7
segregated
  remote 10.7
  incoherent 47.3
segregation
  disjunction 44.1
  exclusion 55.2
seigneur 745.1
seignior mister 373.3
  master 745.1
  gentleman 875.4
seigniorial 780.8
seigniory, seignory
  authority 737.3
  proprietorship 777.3

  nobility 875.9
seilenos See **silenus**
seisin See **seizin**
seismic 314.13
seismicity 314.4
seismograph
  mechanics 276.6
  oscillation 314.7
  recorder 553.3
seismographic 314.13
seismography 314.4
seismological 314.13
seismology 314.4
seismometer
  mechanics 276.6
  recorder 553.3
seismometry 314.4
seismoscope 314.7
seize
  commandeer 744.2
  arrest 751.9
  lay hold of 789.9
  (ensnare 545.9)
  (abduct 791.11)
  (assume 925.6)
seized of 777.7
seizin, seisin 777.1
  (property 780.1)
seizure spasm 315.7
  ictus 655.3
  arrest 751.3
  capture 789.1, 5
  (retention 781.1)
  booty 793.1
  assumption 925.3
seldom, seldomly 137.3
seldomness 137.1
seldseen 137.2
select *n.* 648.4
select *v.* specify 79.5
  choose 609.7
  (discriminate 465.3)
select *adj.*
  selected 609.16
  best 648.9
selection 609.1
  make a selection 609.7
selective 609.15
  (discriminating 465.4)
selectman 745.9
Selene, Selena 318.5
self 79.4; 994.11
  (identity 13.1)
self-abasement
  humility 879.1
  unselfishness 942.1
self-abasing 942.5
self-abnegation 942.1
self-absorbed 943.4
self-absorption 943.1
self-accusation 950.1
self-accusing 950.5
self-acting 266.27
self-activity 600.1
self-admiration 880.1
self-advancement 943.1
self-applauding 880.6
self-applause, self-

  approbation 880.1
self-assuming, self-aware, se.f-besot etc. 943.4
self bow 727.9
self-centered, self-centred 943.4
self-command
  levelheadedness 498.4
  self-control 604.3
  equanimity 826.3
self-communing 451.1
self-complacency
  content 831.1
  vanity 880.1
self-complacent 880.6
self-conceit 880.1
self-condemnation
  penitence 950.1
  self-conviction 971.1
self-condemned 971.5
self-condemning 950.5
self-confidence
  courage 861.1
  self-esteem 878.1
  vanity 880.1
self-confident
  self-esteeming 878.6
  vain 880.6
self-conquest 604.3
self-consideration 943.1
self-considerative 943.4
self-consistent 23.9
  be self-consistent 23.7
self-content *n.* 880.1
self-content *adj.* 880.6
self-contradiction 497.1
self-contradictory
  impossible 471.6
  illogical 477.10
  inconsistent 497.4
self-control
  will power 604.3
  (temperance 953.1)
  equanimity 826.3
self-controlled 826.9
self-convicted
  penitent 950.5
  self-condemned 971.5
self-conviction
  conviction 484.2
  penitence 950.1
self-deception
  credulity 486.1
  delusion 495.5
self-defense, self-defence 717.1
  in self-defense 717.11
self-delusion 486.1
self-denial
  self-control 604.3
  unselfishness 942.1
  temperance 953.1
self-denying 942.5
self-depreciation 483.1

self-destruction — send

self-destruction 361.3
self-determination
  voluntarism 600.1
  independence
    748.1, 3
self-determined 748.17
self-devoted 942.5
self-devotion 942.1
self-directing 748.17
self-ease 377.1
self-educated 490.15
self-education 539.1
self-endeared 880.6
self-esteem
  pride 878.1
  vanity 880.1
self-evident 525.4
  be self-evident 525.3
self-examination 461.5
self-existent 1.8
self-flattering 880.6
self-forgetful 942.5
self-forgetfulness
  942.1
self-glorification 880.1
  (boasting 884.1)
self-governed, self-
  governing 748.17
self-government
  self-control 604.3
  independence 748.3
  autonomy 737.4
self-gratulation 880.1
selfhood 79.4
self-humiliation 950.1
self-immolation 942.1;
  990.6
self-importance
  pride 878.1
  vanity 880.1
self-important 880.6
self-indulgence
  selfishness 943.1
  intemperance 954.1
self-indulgent
  selfish 943.4
  intemperate 954.4
self-instruction 539.1
self-interest
  vanity 880.1
  selfishness 943.1
self-interested
  vain 880.6
  selfish 943.4
selfish 943.4
  (parsimonious
    819.4)
  (egotistical 880.6)
  (misanthropic
    910.3)
  be selfish 943.3
selfishly 943.5
selfishness 943
  (parsimony 819.1)
  (vanity 880.1)
  (misanthropy 910.1)
self-jealous 943.4
self-jealousy 943.1
self-laudation, self-
  love 880.1
self-loving 880.6

self-luminous 423.14
self-made
  homemade 161.13
  self-taught 490.15
self-mastery 604.3
self-moving 266.27
self-murder 361.3
self-neglectful 942.5
self-occupation 943.1
self-occupied 943.4
self-opinionated
  dogmatic 474.15
  bigoted 606.7
  vain 880.6
self-persuasion 484.2
self-pleaser 943.2
self-pleasing 943.1, 4
self-possessed
  resolute 604.7
  composed 826.9
self-possession
  levelheadedness
    498.4
  self-control 604.3
  equanimity 826.3
self-praise 880.1
self-praising 880.6
self-preservation 717.1
self-propelling 266.27
self-protection 717.1
self-puffery 884.1
self-recording 551.9
self-reliance
  self-control 604.3
  courage 861.1
self-reliant
  resolute 604.7
  independent 748.17
  confident 861.8
self-renouncement
  942.1
self-renouncing 942.5
self-reproach 950.1
self-reproachful 950.5
self-respect
  pride 878.1
  vanity 880.1
self-respecting
  proud 878.6
  vain 880.6
self-restrained 826.9
self-restraint
  self-control 604.3
  equanimity 826.3
  (restraint 751.1)
  temperance 953.1
self-righteous
  hypocritical 544.8
  sanctimonious
    988.11
self-sacrifice 942.1
self-sacrificing 942.5
selfsame 13.3
selfsameness 13.2
self-satisfaction 880.1
self-satisfied 880.6
self-seeker 943.2
  (egoist 880.3)
self-seeking n. 943.1
self-seeking adj. 943.4
self-solicitude 943.1

self-starter 272.16
self-subjection, self-
  subordination 942.1
self-sufficiency
  vanity 880.1
  unsociality 893.1
  selfishness 943.1
self-sufficient
  vain 880.6
  selfish 943.4
self-taught 490.15
self-tormenter, self-
  tormentor 837.5
self-unconscious 942.5
self-will 606.1
self-willed 606.6
self-worship 880.1
  (selfishness 943.1)
self-worshiping 880.6
sell n. fraud 545.3
  falsehood 546.1
sell v. deceive 545.7
  persuade 615.9
  vend 796.5
  (barter 794.4)
sell for 812.6
sell one's life dearly
  719.3; 722.9
sell oneself 940.6
sell out
  inform on 527.10
  sell 796.5
  betray 940.7
seller 797.2
  (salesman 758.5)
selliform 250.9
sellout 796.1
Selung 560.4
selvage, selvedge 231.2
Semang 560.4
semanteme 562.1
semantic 560.9
semantics 560.6
semantic tone 402.2
semaphore 550.14
semasiological 560.9
semasiology 560.6
sematic
  indicative 550.21
  symptomatic 668.9
semblance
  similarity 17.1
  copy 21.1
  appearance 448.4
  false pretense 544.2
  (simulation 19.3)
  pretext 619.1
semeiology, semiology
  interpretation 522.5
  indication 550.1
  pathology 655.19
semeiological, semio-
  logical 522.8
semeiotic, semiotic
  550.21
semeiotics, semiotics
  interpretation 522.5
  indication 550.1
semen rudiment 153.3
  sperm 357.4
semester 108.1

semi- 91.6
semibarbarian 913.3
semibreve 413.6, 12
semicircle
  crescent 245.2
  hemicycle 247.5
semicircular 245.6
semicolon stop 142.5
  punctuation 550.8
semidark 422.8
semidarkness 422.2
  (gloom 421.2)
semidiaphaneity 427.1
semidiaphanous 427.4
semifluid n. 352.3
semifluid adj. 352.7
semifluidity 352.1
semiliquid n. 352.3
  (pulp 354.2)
semiliquid adj. 352.7
  (pulpy 354.5)
semiliquidity 352
  (pulpiness 354.1)
semilunar
  crescentlike 245.6, 7
  celestial 318.16
seminal 153.9
seminar 541.8
seminary class 541.8
  school 542.1
semination 673.3
Seminole 434.5
semioccasionally 137.4
semiology, semiotic
  etc. See semeiology
semiopaque, semi-
  pellucid 427.4
semipellucidity 427.1
semiquaver 413.6
semisphere 91.3
Semitic languages
  560.4
semitonal 413.28
semitone tone 402.2
  music 413.11
semitransparency 427
semitransparent 427.4
semivowel 402.2
sempervirent
  durable 110.9
  eternal 112.4
  evernew 123.8
sempiternal 112.4
sempiternity 112.1
  (long time 110.3)
sempstress See seam-
  stress
sen 800.8
Senado 696.5
senary 98.16
Sénat 696.5
senate assembly 72.2
  council 696.4, 5
Senato 696.5
senator 696.8
senatorial 696.9
senatorship 693.3
senatus 696.5
send dispatch 270.9
  start 284.14

send-off — sequacity 1078

send (continued)
  radiobroadcast
    532a.9
send about one's
  business
  repulse 289.2
  eject 297.8
send away
  repulse 289.2
  eject 297.8
send back 408.7
send for 741.7
send forth
  start 284.14
  let out 297.13
  publish 531.7
send off start 284.14
  repulse 289.2
send out
  commission 755.4
  let out 297.13
send packing
  repulse 289.2
  eject 297.8
send to Coventry
  banish 297.11
  exclude 893.7
send-off
  beginning 66.1
  leave-taking 293.2
Seneca 434.5
Seneca oil 356.2
senectitude 128.2
senectuous 128.8
Senegambian 431.4
senesce 128.7
senescence 128.2
senescent 128.9
seneschal
  steward 694.5
  official 745.9
  retainer 746.1
seneschalship, seneschalsy, seneschalty
  country 182.1
  authority 737.3
senhor mister 373.3
  gentleman 875.4
senhora 374.3
senhorita 374.4
senile n. 501.3
senile adj.
  impotent 158.8
  foolish 499.16
  (old 124.6)
  (aged 128.8)
senile dementia 499.5
senility
  impotence 158.2
  foolishness 499.5
  (oldness 124.1)
  (age 128.2)
  (degeneration 659.1)
senior n. elder 130.5
  student 541.4
  master 745.1
senior adj. 128.10
seniority 128.4
sennit fastening 45.2
  cord 205.3

señor mister 373.3
  gentleman 875.4
señora 374.3
señorita 374.4
sensate 375.3
sensation
  physical sense 375.2
  emotion 821.1
  wonder 870.1
  phenomenon 872.1
sensational
  language 574.5
  exciting 824.12
sensationalism
  philosophy 451.11
  excitement 824.1
sense n.
  sensation 375.2
  ~ of touch 379; 380
  ~ of taste 390.1
  ~ of smell 398.3
  ~ of hearing 418.1
  ~ of sight 441.1
  reasonableness 476.7
  intelligence 498.1, 3
  meaning 516.1
  (explanation 522.1)
  ~ of obligation 916.1
  ~ of duty 926.3
  in a sense 514.12
sense v. feel 375.3
  ~ intuitively 477a.3
  understand 518.4
senseless
  insensible 376.5
  incogitant 452.3
  absurd 497.4
  unintelligent 499.11
  foolish 499.15
  insane 503.12
  meaningless 517.8
senselessness 517.1
sense of shame 879.1
senses intellect 450.1
  intelligence 498.1
  sanity 502.1
  come to one's senses 502.2
sensibility
  physical ~ 375
  discrimination 465.1
  knowledge 490.1
  emotional ~ 822
  (feeling 821.1)
sensible
  material 316.8
  sensitive 375.6
  logical 476.16
  cognizant 490.12
  intelligent 498.9
  wise 498.11
  emotionable 822.6
  be sensible
  be sensitive 375.3
  emotion 822.4
  render sensible 375.4
sensism 451.15
sensitive flexible 324.6
  physically ~ 375.6

emotionally ~ 822.6
  (irascible 901.7)
sensitiveness
  physical 375.1
  emotional 822.1
sensitive plant 822.1
sensitivity 465.1
sensitize 375.4
sensorium, sensory n. 450.2
sensory adj. 821.4
sensual
  voluptuous 377.7; 954.4
  carnal 961.11
sensualist 954a
  (bad person 949.1)
sensuality
  pleasure 377.1
  indulgence 954.1
  carnality 961.2
sensualization 364.2
sensualize
  animalize 364.3
  indulge oneself 954.3
sensuosity 377.1
sensuous
  sensitive 375.6
  voluptuous 377.7; 954.4
  feeling 821.4
sentence n.
  music 415.15
  judgment 480.1
  (verdict 969.8)
  maxim 496.1
  phrase 566.1
  statement 582.4
  condemnation 971.1
sentence v.
  pass judgment 480.9
  (administer justice 965.3)
  condemn 971.2
sententious
  aphoristic 496.5
  laconic 572.3
  language 574.6
  bombastic 577.7
  taciturn 585.4
sentience 821.1
sentient sensible 375.6
  feeling 821.4
  emotionable 822.6
sentiment idea 453.1
  feeling 821.1
  sensibility 822.1
sentimental
  tenderhearted 822.7
  affected 853.6
sentimentality 822.1
sentinel, sentry
  warner 668.4
  guard 717.6
sepal 367.4
separability 44.1
separable 44.13
separate v.
  disjoin 44.7, 9, 11
  (disentangle 60.9)

(diverge 291.2)
  segregate 55.4
  bifurcate 91.5
  interval 198.4
  open 260.11
  analyze 461.17
  discriminate 465.2
  select 609.7
  refine 652.10
separate adj.
  different 15.7
  unconnected 44.12
separately 44.14
separate maintenance 905.1
separation
  disjunction 44.1
  (interval 198.1)
  (divergence 291.1)
  segregation 55.2
  bifurcation 91.2
  divorce 905.1
separatist 607.5
  (dissenter 489.3)
  (insurgent 742.3)
  (sectarian 984.13)
separative 49.5
sepawn, sepon See supawn
sepia n. 433.2
sepia adj. 433.5
sepian 41.5
sepoy 726.4
sept kind 75.2
  ancestry 166.4
sept- 98.17
septal 228.11
septate 99.3
septenary n. 98.3
septenary adj. 98.17
septennate 98.3
septennial 138.5
septet, septette
  seven 98.3
  part music 415.12
septic morbid 655.25
  putrefactive 657.3
septicemia, septicaemia 655.2
septillion 98.13
septuagenary, septuagesimal 98.26
Septuagint 985.3
septulum, septum 228.6
septuor 98.3
septuple 98.17
sepulcher, sepulchre 363.13
  (shrine 1000.2)
sepulchral
  burial 363.25
  resonant 408.9
sepulture n. 363.1
sepulture v. 363.20
sequacious
  succeeding 63.5
  flexible 324.6
sequacity 324.1

sequel — session

sequel, sequelant 65.1
  (sequence 63.1;
    281.1)
  (end 67.1)
  (posteriority 117.1)
  (consequence 154.1)
  (tail 235.6)
sequence order 63
  (sequel 65.1)
  (continuity 69.1)
  (pursuit 622.1)
  posteriority 117.1
  motion 281
sequential
  succeeding 63.5
  continuous 69.6
  subsequent 117.3
  resultant 154.6
  deducible 478.5
sequester 789.11; 974.3
sequestered 893.10
sequestrate 974.3
sequestration
  dispossession 789.2
  confiscation 974.2
seraglio, serai
  harem 374.7
  abode of love 897.10
seraph saint 948.1
  angel 977.1
seraphic
  delightful 829.8
  lovely 897.17
  righteous 944.3
  angelic 977.4
  saintly 987.10
seraphim 977.2
seraphine 417.5
seraskier 745.11
Serbo-Croatian 560.4
serdab 191.20
sere See sear
serena 415.10
serenade *n.*
  charivari 404.2;
    414.2
  music 415.3, 10,
    12, 17
  courtship 902.2
serenade *v.* sing 416.20
  bid godspeed 894.10
  woo 902.7
serenader 416.10
serenata 415.3, 12
serene
  luminous 420.22
  transparent 425.4
  inexcitable 826.9
serenity
  quiescence 265.1
  mental ~ 826.2
  (content 831.1)
serf 746.4
  (peasant 876.5)
serfage, serfdom 749.1
serge 219.5
sergeant, serjeant
  745.11
sergeant-at-law,
  serjeant-at-law
  968.1

serial *n.* section 51.2
  journal 593.6, 7
serial *adj.*
  continuous 69.6
  periodic 138.10
serially 69.7
seriate 60.8
seriatim
  continuously 69.7
  gradually 275.11
sericeous smooth 255.5
  velvety 324.8
series succession 69.2
  (gradation 58.2)
  (continuation 63.2)
  number 84.1
  round 138.4
  form a series 69.4
  in series 58.8
serif 591.6
seriocomic 855.5
serious great 31.6
  resolute 604.7
  important 642.12
  solemn 837.16
seriously
  absolutely 31.16
  indeed 535.8
  resolutely 604.9
seriousness 642.2
  in all seriousness
    535.8; 703.5
sermon *n.* lesson 537.6
  lecture 582.2
  (dissertation 595.1)
  (religion 990.7;
    998.2)
sermon *v.*
  expound 537.11
  preach 582.7
sermoner 996.2
sermonet, sermonette
  582.2
sermonist 582.5
sermonize
  expound 537.11
  preach 582.7
  (religion 996.14)
seroon 72.5
serosity 333.1
serous 333.7
Serpens, Serpent *n.*
  318.6
serpent *n.* coil 248.2
  snake 366.19
  firework 382.9
  hisser 409.2
  horn 417.4
  organ stop 417.12
  deceiver 548.1
  evildoer 913.1
  scoundrel 949.1
  the serpent, the Old
    Serpent 978.1
serpent *v.* 248.3
Serpent Bearer 318.6
serpentiform, serpen-
  tile snakelike 248.6
  reptilian 366.27
serpentine *v.* 248.3

serpentine *adj.*
  sinuous 248.6
  reptilian 366.27
serpentine green 435.2
serpentinoid, serpen-
  tinous 248.6
serpentoid
  sinuous 248.6
  reptilian 366.27
serrate *v.* 257.5
serrate, serratic, ser-
  ratile *adj.* 257.6
  (angular 244.5)
serration, serrature
  257.2
serried crowded 72.13
  dense 321.8
serum
  counteractant 179.2
  fluid 333.2
  medicine 662.12
servage 749.1
servant *n.*
  minister 631.2
  retainer 746
  (inferior 34.3)
  (attendant 88.3)
  (agent 690.1)
  (worker 690.10)
  (auxiliary 711.1)
  (puppet 711.2)
  (functionary 758.2)
  (deputy 759.1)
  (sycophant 886.2)
servant *v.* 746.8
servant girl 746.2
servant of God 996.2, 5
servantry 746.7
serve
  ~ an apprentice-
    ship 539.4
  officiate 625.9
  be instrumental
    631.3
  suffice 639.3
  avail 644.2
  (answer 462.9)
  be beneficial 648.6
  work 680.6
  help 707.10
  war 722.11
  obey 743.2
  attend 746.8
  (be in servitude
    749.4)
  (be obedient 743.2)
serve one out
  retaliate 718.2
  punish 972.5
serve one right
  be fair 941.2
  punish 972.5
  get one's deserts
    973.4
serve one's turn 644.2
serve time 754.2
service *n.*
  cordage 205.4
  rigging 273.9
  food 298.38, 39
  office 625.4

benefit 648.2
utility 644.1
use 677.1
aid 707.1
military ~ 722.1
act of grace 784.4
rite 998.1
at your service 743.4
do service help 707.10
  toady 886.3
pay respects 894.8
  worship 990.9
in the service of
  707.15
render a service
  be useful 644.3
  (aid 707.6)
  be benevolent 906.5
service *v.* 660.11
serviceability 644.1
serviceable
  instrumental 631.4
  useful 644.5
  (beneficial 648.12)
  (helpful 707.12)
  (serving 746.9)
service call 722.3
service company 726.7
serviceman 726.4
service medal 733.2
serviette 652.7
servile copy 21.5
  (lifelike 17.15)
  obsequious 886.4
  (submissive 725.5)
  (compliant 743.3)
  (dependent 749.6)
  (humble 879.4)
  (flattering 933.3)
be servile 886.3
servility 886
  (obedience 743.1)
  (humility 879.1)
  (flattery 933.1)
serving *n.*
  cordage 205.4
  rigging 273.9
  ~ of food 298.38
serving *adj.*
  serviceable 644.5
  attending 746.9
  (helping 707.12)
  (obedient 743.3)
  (in subjection 749.6)
servitor student 541.4
  servant 746.1
servitorial 749.6
servitorship 749.2
servitrix 746.2
servitude
  subjection 749.1
  service 749.2
sesame grass 367.9
sesqui– 87.6
sesquipedalian 577.7
sesquipedalianism
  577.2
sessile 47.10; 321.10
sessility 321.2
session assembly 72.2
  council 696.2, 3

sessions — settle

sessions court 966.2
 jury 967.2
sestet six 98.2
 part music 415.12
 stanza 597.7
sestina 597.2
set n. coherence 46.1
 series 69.2
 kind 75.2
 bunch 72.5
 tendency 176.1
 posture 184.2
 ~ of rooms 191.21
 form 240.1
 course 264.3
 direction 278.1
 music 415.3
 radio 532a.5
 stage-set 599.15
 clique 712.2
Set, Seth n. deity 979.5
 god of evil 980.2
set v. attach 43.6
 stabilize 150.4
 place 184.10
 form 240.6
 sharpen 253.9
 settle 306.4
 solidify 321.7
 plant 371.8
 true 494.7
 ~ type 591.14
 prepare 673.6
 prescribe 741.5;
  963.4
 lease 787.6
set about begin 66.5
 (pursue 622.6)
 undertake 676.2
 set to work 686.7
set abroach
 begin 66.5
 disperse 73.3
set afloat 153.6
set against
 compare 464.2
 oppose 708.2
 set at odds 713.8
 excite hatred 898.4
set agoing begin 66.5
 impel 276.7
 aid 707.6
set apart
 segregate 44.7; 55.4
 interval 198.4
 discriminate 465.2
 select 609.7
 appoint 609.11
 reserve 636.8
set aside
 segregate 55.4
 postpone 133.4
 remove 185.2
 disregard 458.5
 neglect 460.5
 (renounce 536.2)
 reserve 636.8
 put away 678.4
 annul 756.3
 refuse 764.3
 not observe 773.3

set at defiance
 defy 715.2
 (rebel 742.5)
 violate the law 964.4
set at ease
 content 831.4
 comfort 834.5
set at large 750.2
set at naught
 underestimate 483.3
 (show insensibility
  823.3)
 reject 610.2
 deem unimportant
  643.8
 oppose 708.2
 defy 715.2
 disobey 742.4
 disdain 930.5
set before
 inform 527.7
 prefer 609.9
 put to choice 609.12
set by postpone 133.4
 reserve 636.8
 put aside 678.4
set by the ears
 set at odds 713.8
 excite hatred 898.4
 anger 900.10
set down
 attribute to 155.3
 place 184.10
 record 551.8
 humiliate 879.3
 dishonor 929.3
 reprove 932.8
set eyes on 441.10
set fire to 384.17
set forth depart 293.4
 evidence 467.7
 propound 514.7
 show 525.2
 tell 527.7
 allege 535.3
 expound 537.11
 indicate 550.18
 depict 554.7
 utter 582.6
 describe 594.5
set forward
 depart 293.4
 undertake 676.2
 aid 707.6
set free
 undeceive 545a.2
 deliver 672.2
 liberate 750.2
 (loose 44.7)
set in begin 66.5
 begin raining 348.25
 begin storming
  349.22
set no store by
 underestimate 483.3
 deem unimportant
  643.8
 be contemptuous of
  930.5
set off
 compensate 30.5

depart 293.4
beautify 845.7
display 882.6
set on urge 615.7
 hasten 684.2
set one back 812.6
set one's back up
  878.3
set one's cap
 desire 865.11
 love 897.12; 902.7
set one's face against
 avoid 623.6
 oppose 708.2
 resist 719.3
 refuse 764.3
 spurn 930.7
 disapprove 932.5
set one's house in
  order
 prepare 673.7
 atone 952.4
set out arrange 60.6
 depart 293.4
 (start 66.5)
 adorn 847.11
set over 755.4
set right teach 537.9
 undeceive 545a.2
 remedy 660.10
 right 922.3
 vindicate 937.5
set sail 267.16
set store by
 give credence 484.7
 rate highly 642.8
 esteem 931.5
set the fashion 852.6
set the teeth on edge
 be sour 397.5
 sound harshly 410.7
 (rasp 331.3)
 offend 830.7
set to begin 66.5
 undertake 676.2
 quarrel 713.7
 fight 720.8
set to rights 922.3
set to work use 677.5
 get busy 686.7
 prescribe 741.5
set up begin 66.5
 cause 153.6
 strengthen 159.8
 build 161.8
 erect 212.7
 rear 307.5
 print 591.14
 (compose 54.4)
 restore 660.10
 refresh 689.2
 aid 707.6
 right 922.3
set upon 716.5
set adj. fast 43.11
 sharpened 253.11
 determined 604.7, 8
 bigoted 606.7
 habitual 613.11
 ready 673.11
 trite 843.6

~ against 898.5;
  900.12
get set 673.8
set on 865.17
seta 256.7
setaceous
 pointed 253.11
 bristly 256.14
setal 256.14
setback
 hindrance 706.1
 misfortune 735.3
setdown
 humiliation 879.1
 reproof 932.3
get a setdown 879.2
set gun snare 545.4
 hidden danger 667.1
setiferous, setiform,
 setigerous 256.14
setoff
 compensation 30.2
 departure 293.1
 imprint 591.2
 discount 813.1
setose 256.14
setout beginning 66.1
 departure 293.1
 display 882.3
settee 215.22
setter 366.6
setting
 surroundings 227.2
 background 235.1
 densification 321.3
setting hen 366.23
settle n. shelf 215.19
 seat 215.22
settle v.
 methodize 60.8
 conform 82.4
 stabilize 150.4
 establish 184.14
 (inhabit 186.10)
 (remain 265.5)
 quiet 265.6
 sink 306.4
 gravitate 319.7
 kill 361.10
 make certain 474.6
 prove 478.2
 confute 479.2
 decide 480.6
 determine 604.6
 reconcile 723.4
 defeat 731.9
 arrange 769.8
 (compromise 774.2)
 pay 807.7
 take revenge 919.4
 punish 972.5
settle accounts
 retaliate 718.2
 pay 807.7
 punish 972.5
settle down
 be moderate 174.4
 locate 184.14
 (become stable
  150.3)
 land 267a.34

1080

settle one's hash
 ruin 162.4
 defeat 731.9
 punish 972.5
settle the land 267.28
settle upon
 choose 609.7
 endow 784.13
settled ended 67.9
 stable 150.5
 assured 474.9
 resolute 604.7
 bigoted 606.7
 defeated 732.12
settlement dregs 40.2
 territory 181.2
 country 182.1
 colonization 184.6
 colony 188.10
 reconciliation 723.1
 arrangement 769.3
 (compromise 774.1)
 deed 771.1
 ~ of an estate 780.2
 payment 807.1
settler alien 57.3
 end-all 67.4
 habitant 188.5
 incomer 294.4
 effective retort 479.1
settlings 40.2
settlor 784.7
set-to quarrel 713.3
 argument 476.2
 contest 720.2, 6
setula, setule 256.7
setup n.
 composition 54.1
 form 240.1
 predetermination 611.1
set up adj. 803.8
seven, sevener 98.3
seven-league boots 993.4
seven seas 341.1
seventh 98.17
seventh heaven
 bliss 827.2
 glory 981.1
seventieth 98.26
seventy 98.7
sever
 differentiate 15.6
 sunder 44.8
 discriminate 465.2
severable 44.13
several special 79.7
 numerous 102.5
severalize
 differentiate 15.6
 discriminate 465.2
severally
 separately 44.14
 respectively 79.12
 individually 87.10
severance 44.2
severe acrid 171.10
 violent 173.11
 painful 378.7 : 830.15
 cold 383.8

pungent 392.5
 accurate 494.11
 style 576.3
 strict 739.5
 (hard 323.5)
 (authoritative 737.15)
 (coercive 744.3)
 (cruel 907.9)
 (pitiless 914a.3)
 (imperative 926.9)
 penetrating 824.13
 inornate 849.4
 censorious 932.11
 be severe 739.4
 (ill-treat 649.7)
severely
 extremely 31.22
 harshly 739.6
severity
 acrimony 171.3
 violence 173.1
 cold 383.1
 pungency 392.1
 ~ of language 575.1
 strictness 739
 (hardness 323.1)
 (pitilessness 914a.1)
 simplicity 849.1
 gruffness 895.2
 cruelty 907.3
Sèvres ware 384.14
sew 43.6
sewage 653.7
sewan, seawan 800.3
sewer conduit 350.1
 filth 653.8
sewerage
 sanitation 652.2
 filth 653.7
sex kind 75.2, 3
 womankind 374.5
sex- 98.16
sexagenarian 130.1
sexagenary n. 98.7
sexagenary adj.
 sixtieth 98.25
 number 99.3
sexagesimal
 number 98.3
 sixtieth 98.25
sexennial 98.16
sexlike, sexly 75.7
sexpartite sixth 98.16
 divided 99.3
sext 990.7
Sextans, Sextant 318.6
sextant
 measure 244.3
 semicircle 247.5
sextennial 138.5
sextet, sextette
 six 98.1
 part music 415.12
 stanza 597.7
sextillion 98.13
sextipartite 99.3
sextipartition 90.1
sextodecimo 593.8
sexton 996.5
sextuple v. 98.14

sextuple adj. 98.16
sextuplet 98.2
sexual 75.7
sexual intercourse 43.2
sh! 403.9
shabbiness 34.1
shabby paltry 643.12
 worn 659.12
 miserly 819.4
 disreputable 874.8
shabby-genteel 851.6
shack hut 189.4
 brakeman 268.12
shackle n. 752.2
 (fastening 45.2)
 (obstacle 706.2)
shackle v. 751.7
 (fasten 43.6)
 (hinder 706.4)
shackled 751.11
shad 298.18
shad-bellied coat, shadbelly 225.16
shade n.
 ~ of difference 15.2
 degree 26.1
 modicum 32.2
 gradation 58.2
 veil 225.12
 shadow 422.3
 screen 424
 (cover 223.2)
 (cloud 353.5)
 color 428.1
 specter 980a.1
 soul 994.11
in the shade
 inferior 34.5
 shadowy 422.10
 concealed 528.17
 in disrepute 874.9
the shades
 death 360.1
 Hades 982.1
shade v.
 ~ off 26.2
 cloud 353.9
 shadow 422.6
 (obscure 421.5)
 screen 424.6
 paint 428.10
 darken 431.6
 conceal 528.10
shaded 422.9
shad fly 111.4
shading 556.5
shadow n.
 unsubstantiality 4.3
 duplicate 21.2
 degree 26.1
 modicum 32.2
 remains 40.1
 thinness 203.5
 thin person 203.6
 follower 281.2
 (accompanier 88.3)
 semidarkness 422.3
 (gloom 421.2)
 (shade 424.1)
 imagining 515.4

picture 556.5
 hanger-on 886.2
 specter 980a.1
 soul 994.11
shadow v. follow 281.3
 (pursue 622.6)
 cloud 353.9
 shade 422.6
 paint 428.10
 darken 431.6
shadow forth
 foreshadow 511.9
 represent 554.7
shadowed dim 422.8
 vague 475.11
 obscure 519.7
shadow figure 556.9
shadowgram, shadowgraph
 skiagram 422.4
 picture 556.13
shadowgraphy 422.4
shadowing 421.3
shadow of death 360.1
shadowy adj.
 chimerical 4.6
 shady 422.9
 (gloomy 421.8)
 indistinct 447.5
 obscure 519.7
shadowy adv. 422.10
shady 422.9
 (dark 421.7)
 shady side 128.2
shaft tower 206.3
 pole 206.4
 depth 208.2
 support 215.7, 13
 (mast 273.12)
 cavity 252.2
 monument 363.15
 air passage 351.1
 spear 727.5, 6
shaft grave tomb 363.13
shag n. hair 256.3
 nap 256.10
 texture 329.1
 tobacco 392a.1
 search 461.2
 chase 622.2
shag v. 622.7
shagged, shaggy 256.13
shagreen 223.12
shah 745.3
shahzada, shahzadah 875.7
shaitan, sheitan
 violent 173.6
 windstorm 349.12
 fiend 913.4
Shaitan 978.1
Shaiva Siddhanta See Saiva Siddhanta
shake n. instant 113.3
 earthquake 173.2
 agitation 315.4, 5
 (concussion 173.4)
 (jerk 285.3)
 (fear 860.3)

shake — shatterbrained 1082

shake (continued)
  tremolo 407.2
  shingle 635.3
shake v. vary 149.4
  be weak 160.6
  weaken 160.8
  agitate 315.8
  (jerk 285.5)
  quiver 315.9, 10
  (oscillate 314.8)
  (be afraid 860.9)
  be cold 383.7
  ~ belief 485.8
  voice 583.2
  tremolo 407.7
  dissuade 616.3
  disorder 655.22
  impair 659.8
  ~ emotionally 824.3
  be excited 824.7
shake down 791.13
shake hands
  be reconciled 723.5
  (forgive 918.3)
  ~ with laughter 838.7
  make friends 888.3
  greet 894.9
shake off 297.17
shake the head
  dissent 489.4
  deny 536.2
  refuse 764.2
  disapprove 932.5
shake up 315.8
shakedown bed 215.24
  theft 791.3, 4
shaken 659.12
Shaker 984.14
shaking n.
  agitation 315.3
  (fear 860.3)
  ~ of hands 723.1
  trepidation 825.3
shaking adj.
  agitated 315.13
  laughing 838.10
shako 225.26
shaky unsteady 160.12
  agitated 315.13
  cold 383.8
  voice 583.5
  unsafe 665.7
  fearful 860.14
  morally ~ 945.12
shale
  incrustation 223.16
  soil 342.3
shale oil 356.2
shallop ship 273.2
  boat 273.4
shallot
  vegetable 298.30
  condiment 393.1
shallow n. shoal 209.2
  hidden danger 667.1
shallow v. 209.3
shallow adj.
  inconsiderable 32.8
  depthless 209.4
  half-learned 491.12

shallow-minded 499.17
  trivial 643.11
shallowbrained, shallow-headed, shallow-minded etc. 499.17
shallowness
  depthlessness 209
  half-learning 491.3
shallowpate 501.1
sham n.
  dissimulation 544.2
  (simulation 19.3)
  (pretext 619.1)
  counterfeit 545.6
sham v. feign 544.6
  (simulate 19.7)
  (be deceptive 545.11)
  affect 853.5
sham Abram
  dissemble 544.6
  shirk 623.8
sham adj. 545.13
  (imitation 19.12)
  (false 544.7)
sham Abram, sham Abraham
  sailor 269.6
  pretender 548.3
  shirker 623.4
shaman n. 992.2
shaman adj. 992.5
shamaness 992.3
shamanism 992.1
Shamash
  sun god 318.4
  gods 979.6
shamble n. 266.5
shamble v. walk 266.16
  go slow 275.5
shambles 361.9
shame n.
  disgrace 874.1
  abomination 923.1
  modesty 960.1
  feel shame 879.2
  for shame! 874.12; 932.16
shame v.
  disgrace 874.6
  humiliate 879.3
shamed 879.2, 5
shamefaced 881.5
shameful
  deplorable 649.8
  disreputable 874.8
  evil 945.16
shamefully 874.11
shameless
  brazen 885.10
  wicked 945.11
  immodest 961.9
Shamianah 223.3
shammy, shamoy See chamois
shampoo 652.9
shamrock alien 57.3
  trefoil 92.2
  green 435.2, 3

Shan 560.4
shandrydan, shandradan 272.5
shanghai 791.11
shanghaier 792.7
shank handle 215.7
  post 215.16
  leg 266.11
  meat 298.19
  type 591.6
shanks' mare 266.11
Shantung 219.5
shanty hut 189.4
  discoloration 440a.1
  black eye 443.5
shape n.
  condition 7.1
  form 240.1
  (aspect 448.4)
  apparition 443.7
  illusion 443.9
  phantom 980a.1
in shape 58.7
out of shape 243.5
put in shape
  arrange 60.6
  repair 660.11
shape v. conform 82.4
  form 240.6
  ~ a course 267.11; 626.9
shape one's course
  go towards 278.5
  pursue 622.6
  conduct oneself 692.5
shapeless 241.5
  (orderless 59.8)
shapelessness 241.1
shapeliness 242.1
shapely
  symmetrical 242.5
  comely 845.10
share n. 786.2
  (part 51.1)
  (participation 778.1)
share v.
  participate 778.5
  (enter into 56.2)
  (~ in 709.6)
  apportion 786.3
share and share alike 778.5, 9
shareholder, sharer 778.3
shark fish 366.21; 368.9
  adept 700.1
  swindler 792.8
sharp n. note 413.6
  cheat 548.2
  gambler 621.15
  adept 700.1
  swindler 792.8
sharp v. 545.7
sharp adj.
  acrid 171.10
  violent 173.11
  steep 217.12
  sharp-cornered 244.5

  keen 253.11
  (rough 256.12)
  (bristly 256.14)
  sensible 375.7
  painful 378.7
  pungent 392.5
  odorous 398.8
  phonetics 402.11
  shrill 410.10
  off-key 414.4
  alert 457.9
  sagacious 498.10
  (clever 698.11)
  quick 682.17
  cunning 702.6
  intensely felt 821.5
  penetrating 824.13
  painful 830.15
  gruff 895.7
  censorious 932.11
be sharp 253.8
look sharp
  be careful 459.4
  be attentive 457.4, 10
  be alert 682.15
  make haste! 684.8
  beware 864.3, 9
sharp-cornered 244.5
sharp-eared 418.14
sharp-edged 253.11
sharpen
  stimulate 171.7
  inflame 173.8
  make sharp 253.9
  sensitize 375.4
  excite 824.2
sharper
  sharpener 253.7
  cheat 548.2
  gambler 621.15
  swindler 792.8
sharpness
  violence 173.1
  keenness 253
  pungency 392.1
  sagacity 498.2
sharp practice
  deception 545.1, 3
  cunning 702.1
  dishonesty 940.5
sharp-set 865.19
sharpshooter
  shooter 284.8
  gambler 621.15
  soldier 726.4
sharp-sighted 441.20
sharp-witted 498.10
shastra, sastra 986.2
shatter
  disintegrate 44.9
  destroy 162.4
  be brittle 328.3
  dement 503.11
  damage 659.8
  ~ one's hopes 859.6
shatterbrain 501.2
shatterbrained
  scatterbrained 458.13
  insane 503.12

shattery— shingle

shattery frail 160.11
  fragile 328.4
shave n. 546.1
shave v. cut off 38.6
  form layers 204.4
  smooth 255.4
  swindle 791.12
  cheapen 815.7
shaven 226.10
shaver 129.3
shaving modicum 32.2
  piece 51.3
  thinness 203.5
  lamina 204.2
  strip 205.5
shavings
  remains 40.1
  parings 330.3
shaw 367.7
shawl 225.15
shay 272.5
she 374.1, 11
sheaf 72.5
shear cut off 38.6
  ~ sheep 370.7
  fleece 789.12
shears 253.6
sheath n. case 191.8
  wrapper 223.11
sheathe
  moderate 174.5
  wrap 223.23
  line 224.2
  clothe 225.41
  close 261.2
sheathe the sword 723.5
sheathing
  wrapper 223.11
  coating 223.18
  lining 224.1
shebang house 189.3
  messuage 189.12
shebeen 959.13
shed n. hut 189.4
  airdrome 267a.28
shed v. dispel 73.3
  slough 226.6
shed blood 361.10
shee, sidhe 979.9
sheen n. 420.1
sheen, sheeny adj. 420.22
sheep animal 366.8
  laity 997.1
sheepfold 232.1
sheepherder 370.4
sheepish 881.5
sheep laurel 663.6
sheep rot 655.18
sheep's eyes
  longing 865.1
  flirtation 902.1
sheepshank 45.6
sheer n.
  obliquity 217.1
  deviation 279.1
sheer v. oblique 217.5
  turn ship 267.24
  deviate 279.4
sheer off recede 287.2

avoid 623.9
sheer adj. mere 32.11
  pure 42.5
  unqualified 52.10
  vertical 212.8
  steep 217.12
  transparent 425.4
sheer pole 273.12
sheers cloth 219.5
  transparency 425.2
sheet lamina 204.2
  coverlet 223.9
  (merchandise 798.3)
  ship's rope 273.10
  white 430.3
  advertisement 531.4
  book 593.1
  newspaper 593.6
  paper 635.4
sheeting 223.9
sheet music 415.21
sheetwork 591.1
she-goat goat 366.9
  female animal 374.8
sheik, sheikh
  potentate 745.3
  prince 875.7
  priest 996.7
sheitan See shaitan
shekel 800.1
shelf cupboard 191.15
  height 206.2
  ledge 215.19
  hidden danger 667.1
shelfworn 659.12
shell n.
  cover 223.14, 16
  boat 273.4
  coffin 363.10
  ear 418.5
  shield 717.2
  projectile 727.14
shell v. peel 226.5
  bombard 716.6
shell out give 784.8
  pay 807.6
  disburse 809.3
shellac, shellack,
  shell-lac n. 428.5
shellac v. 428.10
shellback
  mariner 269.1
  veteran 700.3
shellfish 366.21
shell game 545.3
shell jacket 225.14
shellproof 664.11
shellshock
  psychosis 503.2
  neurosis 655.14
shellworker 690.9
shelter n. cover 223.2
  (shade 424.1)
  (concealment 530.3)
  refuge 666.3
in shelter 664.10
take shelter 664.8
shelter v. lodge 184.12
  protect 664.6
  guard 717.7
shelty, sheltie 271.3

shelve postpone 133.4
  (pretermit 460.7)
  incline 217.6
  put aside 678.4
shelved
  neglected 460.10
  unsalable 796.8
shenanigan 842.3, 7
shend 659.8
Sheol 982.1
shepherd
  herdsman 370.4
  leader 694.6
  pastor 996.2
sherbet 298.13
sherif, shereef
  ruler 745.7
  prince 875.7
sheriff 745.10
sheriffry, sheriffwick
  constabulary 745.10
  bureau 965.2
Sherlock Holmes 529.9
sherry 959.7
Shetland pony 271.3
shew See show
she-wolf fury 173.6
  shrew 901.4
  malevolent woman 913.5
Shiah See Shiite
shibboleth 550.11
shield n. cover 223.2
  (shade 424.1)
  (safeguard 666.1)
  insignia 550.12
  guard 717.2
shield v.
  protect 664.6
  guard 717.7
shieldlike 245.19
shift n. change 140.1
  conversion 144.1
  substitute 147.2
  dislocation 185.1
  waist 225.18
  undergarment 225.25
  transference 270.1
  shuffle 315.4
  quibble 477.3
  deception 545.3
  pretext 619.1
  subterfuge 623.1
  expedient 646.2
  (device 626.5)
  (means 632.1)
  artifice 702.3
shift v. change 140.5
  (tergiversate 607.7)
  be converted into 144.8
  vary 149.4
  move 264.6
  turn ship 267.24
  transfer 270.6
  deviate 279.4, 6
  shuffle 315.9
  quibble 477.8
  be irresolute 605.4

shift for oneself
  conduct oneself 692.5
  be independent 748.8
  be alone 893.10
shift off
  postpone 133.4
  avoid 623.6
shifting use 783.2
shiftless
  improvident 674.11
  (negligent 460.8)
  indolent 683.13
shifty transient 111.6
  wily 702.6
  (evasive 623.12)
  treacherous 940.12
Shiite, Shiah 984.18
shikar n. 622.2
shikar v. 622.7
shikari, shikaree 622.4
Shilha, Shilluh 560.4
shillelagh, shillalah,
  shillelah, shillala,
  shillely 727.7
shilling 800.4, 8
shilly-shally n. 605.1, 3
shilly-shally v. 605.4
shilly-shally adj. 605.5
shilly-shally adv. 605.7
shilly-shallyer, shil-
  lishallier 605.3
shimmer n. 420.5
shimmer v. 420.18
shimmery 420.23
shimmy, shimmey
  chemise 225.25
  dance 840.7
shin n. 266.11
shin v. 305.5
Shina 560.4
shindig 840.6
shindy turmoil 59.4
  broil 713.4
shine n. turmoil 59.4
  smoothness 255.1
  light 420.1, 8
  Negro 431.4
  display 882.1
  fancy 897.1
  moonshine liquor 959.9
shine v. polish 255.4
  rub 331.3
  give light 420.17
  ~ intellectually 498.8
  furbish 658.10
  be skillful 698.7
  be beautiful 845.6
  be distinguished 873.10
shine upon
  illuminate 420.20
  second 707.8
shiner black eye 443.5
  coin 800.4
shingle n.
  roofing 223.6
  coating 223.18
  granule 330.3

shingle — shortcoming

shingle (*continued*)
  stone 342.4
  board 635.3
shingle *v.* coat 223.24
  whip 972.6
shingled 223.30
shingles 655.17
shingling 223.6
shining
  luminous 420.22
  white 430.8
  gorgeous 845.13
  illustrious 873.17
shinny, shinney 840.11
shinplaster 800.1, 6
shintiyan, shintyan 225.21
Shinto, Shintoism 984.11
Shintoist 984.21
shiny 420.22
ship *n.* vessel 273
  (man-of-war 726.11)
  airplane 273a.1, 5
ship *v.* load 184.13
  transport 270.8, 9
shipload 190.1
shipman 269.1
shipmate 890.3
shipment
  transportation 270.2
  freight 270.4
  export 295.3
ship of the desert 271.2
ship of the line, ship of war, ship-of-war 726.11
shipplane 273a.1
shippon, shippen 189.5
shipshape
  orderly 58.7
  navigation 267.67
  (rigged 273.16)
shipworm 366.25
shipwreck *n.*
  destruction 162.3
  accident 735.3
shipwreck *v.*
  destroy 162.4
  go aground 267.33
shipwrecked 732.10
shipwright 690.7
shipyard 691
shire 181.2
Shire 271.4
shirk *n.* 623.4
  (absentee 187.6)
shirk *v.* avoid 623.8
  (play truant 187.8)
  (be unwilling 603.4)
  (be inactive 683.8)
  ~ off 623.10
  disobey 742.4
  ~ out of 808.5
shirker 623.4
  (neglector 460.3)
  (idler 683.7)
  (coward 862.2)
shirking 623.1
  (truancy 187.5)

(idleness 683.2)
shirr 258.3
shirt, shirtwaist 225.18
Shiva See **Siva**
shivaree noise 404.2
  discord 414.2
shive modicum 32.2
  lamina 204.2
shiver *n.* modicum 32.2
  piece 51.3
  strip 205.5
  shake 315.4
  (fear 860.3)
  trepidation 825.3
shiver *v.*
  disintegrate 44.9
  destroy 162.4
  shake 315.9
  (be afraid 860.9)
  be brittle 328.3
  be cold 383.7
  break 659.8
  ~ with excitement 824.7
make one shiver 385.4
shivering *n.* 383.2
shivering *adj.* 383.8
shivers shaking 315.3
  coldness 383.2
  trepidation 860.3
shivery fragile 328.4
  pulverulent 330.9
  cold 383.8
shizoku 875.4
shoal *n.* horde 72.4
  multitude 102.2
  shallow 209.2
  hidden danger 667.1
shoal *v.* 209.3
shoal water 209.2
shoaly 209.5
shoat 366.7
shock *n.* stack 72.5
  concussion 173.4
  hair 256.3
  clash 276.2
  agitation 315.4
  start 508.3
  ailment 655.14, 15
  discord 713.1
  blow 735.3
  excitement 825.2
  source of pain 830.2
shock *v.*
  electrify 158a.11
  startle 508.6; 824.3
  repel 830.7
  astonish 870.3
  scandalize 932.9
shock absorber 272.16
shocked 828.13
shocking terrible 649.8
  painful 830.13
  (vulgar 851.6)
  fearful 860.15
  disreputable 874.8
shockingly 31.23
shock tactics 722.2
shod 225.46
shoddy *n.* 645.4
shoddy *adj.* 545.13

shoe supporter 215.2
  footwear 225.27
  merchandise 798.3
shoemaker
  cobbler 225.40
  craftsman 690.8
shoemaking 225.35
shog concussion 173.3
  clash 276.2
  shock 315.4
shogi 840.11
shogun 745.3
shoo! 297.23
shoot *n.*
  descendant 167.4
  shot 284.4
  rapid 348.6
  conduit 350.1
  foliage 367.4
  pang 378.1
shoot *v.* explode 173.9
  grow 194.6
  ~ballast 267.37
  float 267.44
  row 267.46
  speed 274.9
  advance 282.2
  fire 284.13
  (discharge 173.9)
  kill 361.10
  photograph 556.18
  bestir oneself 682.12
  fire upon 716.6
  execute 972.4
shoot craps 621.17
shoot down 361.10
shoot off one's mouth 584.4
shoot straight
  be honorable 939.6
  be fair 941.2
shoot the sun 267.39
shoot up increase 35.4
  grow 194.6; 365.2
  project 250.7
  ascend 305.4
  improve 658.6
shooter
  gunner, archer 284.8
  (hunter 622.4)
  firearm 727.10
shooting hunting 622.2
  (slaughter 361.7)
  sport 840.11
  execution 972.4
shooting gallery 840.14
shooting iron 727.10
shooting star
  heavenly body 318.3
  omen 512.2
shop *n.* workshop 691
  (business 625.1)
  store 799.1
keep a shop
  transact business 625.8
  trade 794.7
shop *v.* 795.4
shopboard 799.1
shopkeeper 797.1

shoplifter 792.1
shoplifting 791.1
shopman 797.1
shopmate 890.3
shopper 795.2
shopworn
  impaired 659.12
  depreciated 815.9
shore *n.*
  supporter 215.2
  coast 342.2
  (edge 231.1)
on shore 342.14
shore *v.*
shore up 215.26
shoreless 180.7
short *n.*
  deficiency 53.2
  breve 550.8
  shortage 640.2
in short 572.9
  (shortly 201.7)
  (in epitome 596.6)
short *adj.*
  inconsiderable 32.8
  incomplete 53.4
  momentary 111.7
  not long 201.5
  (little 193.8)
  (low 207.7)
  (compendious 596.5)
  inadequate 304.3
  brittle 328.4
  crumbly 330.9
  terse 572.3
  brusque 895.7
at short notice
  briefly 111.9
  promptly 132.14
make short work of
  destroy 162.4
  bestir oneself 682.12
  hasten 684.3
  complete 729.2
  win easily 731.5
  punish 972.5
render short 201.4
short of less 34.7
  minus 38.11
  unreached 304.3
  wanting 640.11
  imperfect 651.4
short *adv.* 201.8
shortage
  deficiency 53.2
  shortcoming 304.1
  scarcity 640.2
short and sweet 572.3
short-arm balance 319.5
shortbread 298.12
short-breathed 688.7
shortcake 308.12
shortcoming
  inequality 28.1
  motion short of 304
  (inferiority 34.1)
  (incompleteness 53.1)
  (insufficiency 640.1)

1084

(imperfection 651.1)
(fault 651.2)
(noncompletion 730.1)
(failure 732.1)
short-commons
  pittance 640.5
  meager diet 956.2
short cut
  short way 197.2
  crosscut 246.2
shorten 201.4
  (reduce 36.4)
  (deduct 38.4)
  (contract 195.4)
  (be concise 572.2)
  (abridge 596.4)
shorten sail
  reduce sail 267.38
  retard 275.7
shortening
  abbreviation 201.2
  (decrease 36.1)
  (contraction 195.1)
  (conciseness 572.1)
  fat 356.4
shortfall 304.1
shorthand *n.* 590.7
shorthand *adj.* 590.16
shorthand *v.* 590.13
shorthanded 640.12
shorthorn
  newcomer 57.3
  bovine 366.12
short-lived 111.6
shortly briefly 111.9; 201.7
  soon 132.15
shortness
  transience 111.2
  briefness 201
  (littleness 193.1)
  (lowness 207.1)
  ~ of breath 688.2
for shortness' sake 572.4
shorts 225.21, 25
shortsighted
  myopic 443.14
  obtuse 499.12
  bigoted 606.7
shortsightedness
  myopia 443.1
  prejudice 481.3
  bigotry 606.2
short step 197.2
short-winded 688.7
short-witted 499.11
shot
  counteractant 179.2
  speed 274.6
  discharge 284.4
  (explosion 173.3)
  (gunfire 716.2)
  shooter 284.8
  report 406.2
  rough guess 514.2
  signal 550.14
  photograph 556.11
  gamble 621.3, 9

attempt 675.1
dead ~ 700.1
missile 727.14
price 812.1
alcoholic drink 959.10
payment 973.2
a shot in the locker
  last resort 600.5
  necessity 601.5
  reserve fund 636.2
have a shot at 156.9
take a shot at 716.5
shote 366.7
shotgun 727.10
shot-putter 284.7
shoulder *n.*
  support 215.2, 10, 11, 19
  ridge 250.2
  type 591.6
give the cold shoulder 289.2
on the shoulders of
  aloft 206.19
  elevatedly 307.10
  through 631.5
shoulder to shoulder
  concurrently 178.5
  side by side 236.9
  co-operatively 709.8
shoulder *v.*
  support 215.26
  carry 270.8
  impel 276.7
  ~ arms 673.8
  lend support 707.7
  ~ a musket 722.9
shout *n.* cry 411.1
  ~ of laughter 838.3
  cheer 838.4
  ~ of applause 931.4
shout *v.* cry 411.5
  ~ out 411.7
  (be noisy 404.6)
  laugh 838.7
  cheer 838.8
shove *n.* gang 72.3
  crowd 72.4
  impulse 276.1
shove *v.* 276.7
shove off
  navigate 267.16, 27
  depart 293.4
  die 360.6
shove on move 264.6
  depart 293.4
shovel *n.* 252.7
shovel *v.* 270.10
shovel hat 999.1
shovelhead 366.21
show *n.*
  occasion 134.2
  (chance 156.1)
  illusion 443.9
  spectacle 448.2
  appearance 448.4
  possibility 470.1
  manifestation 525.1
  false pretense 544.2
  performance 599.8

pretext 619.1
affectation 853.1
ostentation 882.1, 3
make a show
  simulate 19.7
  dissemble 544.6
  affect 853.5
  be ostentatious 882.6
show *v.* appear 448.6
  evince 467.7, 9
  demonstrate 478.2
  manifest 525.2
  (visibilize 446.3)
  (direct attention 457.7)
  (explain 522.6)
  disclose 529.3
  teach 537.9
  indicate 550.18
show fight defy 715.2
  defend 717.8
show forth 525.2
show off 882.7
  (be proud 878.3)
  (boast 884.5)
show one his place 930.7
show one's cards 529.5
show one's colors
  signal ship 267.41
  be truthful 543.2
  manifest oneself 525.2
  signal 550.20
show one's face
  attend 186.9
  manifest oneself 525.2
show one's teeth
  show fight 715.2
  show resentment 900.7
show the door
  be discourteous 895.4
  prohibit 761.2
  eject 297.8
show the heels 623.10
show up happen 151.3
  attend 186.9
  appear 446.2
  confute 479.2
  display 525.2
  expose 529.3
  make ridiculous 856.5
showdown
  manifestation 525.1
  disclosure 529.1
shower *n.* horde 72.4
  sprinkler 337.3
  rain 348.11
  bath 652.3, 4
  donation party 784.1
shower *v.* 348.25
shower down
  be abundant 639.4
  give 784.10
  be liberal 816.3
showery 348.27

showing-off 882.2
show-off display 525.1
  attitudinarian 882.5
show of hands 609.3
showup
  appearance 448.1
  display 525.1
  disclosure 529.1
showy
  gaudy-colored 428.15
  grandiloquent 577.7
  gaudy 851.8
  (ornate 847.13)
  ostentatious 882.8
  (conspicuous 525.5)
shrapnel 727.14
  (shot 284.4)
shred *n.* modicum 32.2
  piece 51.3
  strip 205.5
shred *v.* 205.6
shrew 901.4
  (scold 936.2)
shrewd
  sagacious 498.10
  (knowing 490.12)
  (clever 698.11)
  cunning 702.6
shrewdness 498.2
shrewish 901.7
shriek *n.* stridor 410.2
  ~ of laughter 838.3
shriek *v.*
  stridulate 410.5
  cry 411.5
  laugh 838.7
shrievalty
  government 737.4
  constabulary 745.10
  bureau 965.2
shrift confession 529.2
  penance 952.3
shrill *v.*
  stridulate 410.5
  cry 411.5
shrill *adj.* 410.10
  (loud 404.8)
shrimp *n.*
  diminutive 193.2, 5
  fish 298.18
shrimp *v.* 622.8
shrine case 191.8
  burial place 363.13, 15
  monument 551.4
  reliquary 998.8
  holy place 1000.2
shrink contract 195.4
  (decrease 36.3)
  recoil 277.3
  demur 603.4
  flinch 623.9
  (recede 287.2)
  (be cowardly 862.3)
  (dislike 867.4; 898.3)
  be sensitive 822.4
shrinkage
  decrease 36.1
  (waste 638)

shrinking — sideling

shrinkage (continued)
  decrement 39a
shrinking n.
  contraction 195.1
  reluctance 603.2
  scruple 939.2
shrinking adj.
  reluctant 603.5
  modest 881.5
  timid 862.4
  (evasive 623.12)
shrive atone 952.4
  give absolution 998.14
shrivel shrink 195.4
  dry 340.5
  wither 659.6
shriveled, shrivelled
  shrunk 195.6
  thin 203.11
shroud n.
  supporter 215.2
  cover 223.2
  ship's rope 273.10
  graveclothes 363.8
shroud v. clothe 225.41
  conceal 528.10
  (cover 223.22)
  protect 664.6
  guard 717.7
shrouded
  obscure 519.7
  enigmatic 533.6
shrub 367.8
shrubbery 371.6
shrug n. 550.3
shrug v. 550.20
shrug the shoulders
  dissent 489.4
  submit 725.3
  endure 826.6
  express discontent 832.3
  dislike 867.4
  show contempt 930.5
  express disapproval 932.5
shrunk, shrunken 195.6
  (dwarfed 193.9)
shruti See sruti
shuck 223.14
shucks 643.5
shudder 383.7
make one shudder 830.7
shudder at
  dislike 867.4
  hate 898.3
shuffle n.
  interchange 148.1
  gait 266.5
  shift 315.4
  quibble 477.3
  evasion 623.1
  dance 840.8
shuffle v. derange 61.2
  (mix 41.6)
  interchange 148.3
  vary 149.2
  walk 266.16

go slow 275.5
  shift 315.9
  quibble 477.8
  (prevaricate 544.5)
  be irresolute 605.4
  (change 140.5)
  (tergiversate 607.7)
shuffle off 623.6
shuffle the cards
  change 140.6
  gamble 621.17
  prepare 673.7
shuffler quibbler 477.6
  dissembler 548.1
  waverer 605.3
  (tergiversator 607.4)
shun avoid 623.6
  (dislike 867.4)
  snub 930.7
shunt postpone 133.4
  transfer 270.6
  shift 279.6
  put aside 678.4
shush 403.1, 4, 5, 9
shut n.
  elimination 42.2
  ~ of day 126.1
shut v. 261.2
shut down
  terminate 67.7
  cease 142.6
  stop 142.7
  silence 403.5
shut in
  circumscribe 229.2
  confine 751.8
shut one's eyes to
  disregard 458.5
  ignore 460.5
  (conceal 528.10)
  be incredulous 487.3
  tolerate 760.3
  not observe 773.3
  forgive 918.3
shut one's mouth 585.3
shut out exclude 55.3
  defeat 731.9
  prohibit 761.2
shut up close 261.2
  confute 479.2
  not speak 585.3
  confine 751.8
shut up shop
  terminate 67.7
  cease 142.6
  abandon 624.3
  vacation 687.5
shut adj.
  ~ out 55.5; 732.12
  ~ in 229.4
  closed 261.3
shut-eye 683.5
shutter 424.3
shuttle n. 314.6
shuttle v. 314.10
shuttlecock n. 605.3
shuttlecock v. 314.10
shuttlewise 314.12
shuttle-witted 458.13

shy n. throw 284.3
  attempt 675.1
shy v. recoil 277.3
  (turn aside 279.7)
  (recede 283.5)
  throw 284.12
  quibble 477.8
  demur 485.7; 603.4
  shrink 623.9
  (be cowardly 862.3)
  take fright 860.8
shy adj.
  incomplete 53.4
  timid 862.4
  (evasive 623.12)
  (afraid 860.14)
  modest 881.5
shy of
  reluctant 603.5
  wanting 640.11
  wary 864.6
  disliking 867.7
Shylock 787.2
shyster rascal 949.1
  lawyer 968.1
Siam 182.3
Siamese 560.4
sib 11.7
Siberia 383.4
Siberian 383.8
sibilant 409.4
sibilate 409.3
sibyl 513.2
sibylline 511.11
Sibylline Oracles 513.1
sic 19.14
siccaneous, siccant 340.7, 10
siccate 340.5
siccation 340.2
siccative n. 340.3
siccative adj. 340.10
siccity 340.1
sick n. illness 655.1
  sick persons 655.20
sick adj. 655.23
  make one sick 830.7
sick of
  displeased 828.14
  weary 841.9
  disliking 867.7
  satiated 869.6
sick bay ship 273.7
  hospital 662.17
sickbed 662.17
sicken be sick 655.21
  make sick 655.22
  repel 830.7
  (be unsavory 395.4)
  (displease 867.6)
  feel disgust 867.5
sickened 828.14
sickener
  unsavoriness 395.3
  overdose 641.1
  source of distress 830.2
  nauseant 867.3
  cloyer 869.2
sickening nasty 395.7

foul 653.17
  odious 830.14
sickish 655.23
sickle angle 244.2
  cutter 253.6
sicklelike 245.20
sickling 655.20
sickly v. 655.22
sickly adj. pale 429.6
  infirm 655.24
sickness illness 655.1
  repugnance 867.2
sickroom 662.17
side n.
  extraction 166.4
  hillside 217.2
  edge 231.1
  flank 236
  (superficies 220.2)
  (right 238.2)
  (left 239.2)
  aspect 448.4
  actor's lines 599.16
  party 712.1
  airs 882.2
side by side with 88.9
  beside 236.9
  (near 197.11)
  co-operatively 709.8
from side to side 314.14
on all sides 227.5
on the side
  additionally 37.8
  beside 236.9
over the side 267.66
side v.
  ~ up 60.6
  postpone 133.4
  flank 236.4
  sidle 236.5
  put aside 678.4
side with 709.5
  (second 707.8)
  (join 712.8)
side adj. 236.6
side arms 727.3
sideboard 191.15
sideburns 256.5
sidecar 272.5
sided 236.7
side door portal 260.4
  covert way 530.4
by a side door
  circuitously 311.7
  surreptitiously 528.21, 24
side glance 902.1
side issue 39.1
side-kick, sidekicker
  confederate 711.1
  pal 929.2
side light light 420.1
  lamp 423.4
  information 527.1
side line 625.5
sideling, sidelong adj. 236.6
sideling, sidelings, sidelins, side-long adv. 236.8, 9

1086

(deviatively 279.9)
side meat 298.23
side partner
  associate 711.1
  companion 890.3
sideral, sidereal 318.16
siderite 288.2
side road 279.3
sideromancy 511.3
sidesaddle 215.23
side show 599.8
sideslip n. 267a.24
sideslip v. sidle 236.5
  aviate 267a.31
sidesman 996.5
side step 623.1
sideswipe n. 276.3
sideswipe v. 276.8
sidetrack
  turn aside 279.7
  (side 236.4)
  avert 706.5
sidewalk 627.2
sideways 236.8
side-wheeler
  horse 271.3
  ship 273.1
sidewinder horse 271.3
  blow 276.3
sidewise adj.
  obliquely 217.17
  sidelong 236.6
sidewise adv. 236.8
  (obliquely 217.17)
  (crosswise 219.12)
sidhe See **shee**
siding 635.3
sidle incline 217.6
  lateralize 236.5
  (deviate 279.7)
Sidney 650.3
siege 716.1
  lay siege to 716.5
  raise a siege 723.5
siege artillery 727.11
siegecraft 722.2
siege train 727.11
Siena 434.6
sienna brown 433.1
  color 433.2
siesta 683.5
sieve n. sorter 60.4
  network 219.4
  porousness 260.7
  refiner 652.7
sieve v. sort 60.6
  refine 652.10
sievelike 260.17
sieve pit 260.1
Sif 979.3
sift segregate 55.4
  sort 60.6
  analyze 461.17
  discriminate 465.2
  select 609.7
  refine 652.10
  (eliminate 42.4)
sifter sorter 60.4
  network 219.4
  porousness 260.7
sifting 461.3

sigh n.
  suspiration 349.18
  faint sound 405.2
  ~ of relief 834.1, 6
  lamentation 839.1
sigh v. blow 349.22
  suspire 349.23
  sough 405.5
  lament 839.7
  ~ for 865.11
sight n.
  quantities 31.3
  vision 441.1, 2, 4, 6
  spectacle 448.2
  appearance 448.4
  ~ for sore eyes
    829.3; 845.3
  eyesore 846.3
  phenomenon 872.1
  at sight
    promptly 132.14
    as seen 441.23
  come in sight 446.2
    (be disclosed 529.6)
  in sight
    visible 446.4
    openly 525.7
  in sight of near 197.11
    visibly 446.6
  keep in sight
    look at 441.11
    bear in mind 457.4
    care for 459.6
  keep out of sight
    ignore 460.5
    conceal 528.10
  out of sight
    inordinately 31.20
    utterly 52.14
    absent 187.10
    beyond 196.8
    invisible 447.4
  within sight
    present 186.13
    hopeful 858.11
sight v.
  ~ land 267.29
  see 441.10
sighthole 441.5
sightless blind 442.6
  invisible 447.4
sightlessness 442.1
sightly 845.10
sightproof 447.4
sight reading 415.18
sights eyes 441.7
  spectacles 445.3
sight-see travel 266.12
  be spectator 444.3
sight-seeing 441.3
sight-seer
  excursionist 268.1
  spectator 444.1
  (inquisitive 455.2)
sight-shot 441.6
sigil
  endorsement 488.4
  seal 550.11
sigmoid
  crescent-shaped
    245.6

convoluted 248.4
sign n. notation 415.23
  indication 550.1, 2,
    10, 14
  (evidence 467.1)
  (omen 512.1)
  (warning 668.3)
  trace 551.5
  letter 561.1
  prodigy 872.1
  sign of the times
    omen 512.1
    indication 550.1
    warning sign 668.3
sign v. endorse 488.10
  (record 551.8)
  (write 590.13)
  mark 550.19, 20
  letter 561.6
signal n. 550.2, 14
  (warning 668.3)
  alarm ~ 669.1
signal v.
  navigation 267.41
  sign 550.20
  (tip 527.9)
  (warn 668.6)
signal adj. great 31.6
  important 642.10
  (eventful 151.6)
signaler, signaller
  668.4
signalize signal 550.20
  confer distinction
    873.13
  celebrate 883.3
signally 31.21
signature
  notation 415.23
  endorsement 488.4
  identification 550.11
  (authority 467.4)
  inscription 551.1
  name 564.2
  handwriting 590.3
  printing 591.2
signboard 550.10
signed 769.10
signet
  endorsement 488.4
  seal 550.11
  insignia 747.2
significance
  meaning 516.1
  importance 642.1
  consequence 873.3
significant n. 516.4
significant adj.
  evidential 467.11
  meaningful 516.8
  indicative 550.21
  important 642.11
signification
  meaning 516.1
  indication 550.1
significative 550.21
signify mean 516.5
  intimate 527.8
  indicate 550.17
  (portend 511.9)
  be important 642.7

sign language 550.3
sign manual
  ratification 488.4
  inscription 551.1
  name 564.2
  handwriting 590.3
sign of the cross
  benediction 990.4
  ritual 998.2
  **make the sign of the
    cross** 990.12; 998.14
signor, signior
  mister 373.3
  (title 877.2)
  gentleman 875.4
signora 374.3
  (nobility 875.6)
signorina 374.4
signorino 373.3
signpost sign 550.10
  guide 694.6
Sigyn 979.3
sike 348.1
Sikh 984.21
**sikhara, sikhra, sikra,
  sikar, sikara** 206.3
Sikhism 984.11
silence n.
  soundlessness 403
  (quiescence 265.1)
  (aphonia 581.1)
  taciturnity 585.1
  (latency 526.1)
  (secrecy 528.2)
  in silence
    silently 403.8
    secretly 528.24
  keep silence
    be silent 403.3
    not speak 585.3
    (be mute 581.4)
silence v. **disable** 158.6
  kill 361.10
  hush 403.4, 5
  (mute 581.5)
  confute 479.2
  defeat 731.10
silence cloth, silencer
  408a.3
silent
  soundless 403.6, 7
  (quiet 265.7)
  (faint 405.9)
  (inaudible 419.9)
  (aphonous 581.7)
  taciturn 585.4
  become silent 403.4
  be silent
    be toneless 403.3
    silence! 403.9
    be taciturn 585.3
  render silent 403.5
silently 403.8
silent partner 711.1
silenus, seilenos
  wood 367.7
  deity 979.11
silhouette n.
  outline 230.1
  form 240.1
  skiagram 422.4

silhouette — singsong

silhouette (*continued*)
 lineaments 448.5
 picture 556.9
silhouette *v.* 230.3
silica 635.6
silica brick 384.14
silique 191.6
siliquose 191.23
silk thread 205.2
 cloth 219.5
 smooth 255.2
 softness 324.3
 light filter 424.5
 transparency 425.2
 king's counsel 968.1
silken smooth 255.5
 velvety 324.8
silk gown 968.1
silkworm 366.25
silky smooth 255.5
 velvety 324.8
sill base 215.3
 seat 215.22
 fool 501.1
silliness 499.6
silly *n.* 501.1
silly *adj.*
 credulous 486.5
 absurd 497.4
 foolish 499.15
silo 636.4
silt *n.* residue 40.2
 drift 270.3
 mud 352.4
silt *v.* 209.3
silvan, sylvan
 rustic 183.3
 arborary 367.15
silver *n.*
 silverware 191.13
 white 430.3; 432.1
 metal 635.6
 money 800.15
silver *v.* whiten 430.6
 gray 432.3
silver *adj.* white 430.8
 gray 432.4
silverfish, silver fish 366.24
silver-gray 432.4
silver lining 858.3
silver nitrate 384.11
silver screen 599.9
silversmith 690.6
Silver Star Medal 733.2
silverware 191.13
 (merchandise 798.3)
silvery
 silver-toned 413.27
 white 430.8
 gray 432.4
silvicultural 371.9
silviculture 371.1
silviculturist 371.2
simar 999.1
simian 499.15
similar *n.* 17.4
similar *adj.* alike 17.10
 (uniform 16.5)
 (faithful 21.5)

(equivalent 27.9)
 (comparable 464.6)
be similar 17.7
render similar 17.8
similarity 17.1
 (identity 13.1)
 (sameness 13.2)
 (uniformity 16.1)
 (agreement 23.1)
 (equivalence 27.2)
 (comparison 464.1)
similarly 37.8
simile *n.*
 comparison 464.1
 figure of speech 521.1
 (equivalence 516.3)
simile *v.*
 similize 464.2
 symbolize 521.2
similitude *n.*
 similarity 17.1
 copy 21.1
 comparison 464.1
 simile 521.1
similitude, similize *v.*
 liken 464.2
 symbolize 521.2
simmer bubble 353.8
 be hot 382.13
 stew 384.19
 ~ with passion 825.7
 be angry 900.8
simmering hot 382.16
 ~ with excitement 825.11
simoleon 800.1
simon-pure 494.13
simoom, simoon
 wind 349.9
 hot wind 382.4
simous 243.5
simp 501.1
simper 838.2, 5, 6
simpering 853.6
simple *n.* 662.4
simple *adj.* mere 32.11
 unmixed 42.5
 credulous 486.5
 ignorant 491.8
 simple-minded 499.13
 language 576.3; 578.4
 artless 703.4
 easy 705.5
 plain 849.3
 (tasteful 850.5)
render simple
 disinvolve 42.3
 strip of ornament 849.2
simplehearted
 veracious 543.3
 artless 703.4
simple-minded
 imbecile 499.13
 artless 703.4
 (simple 849.3)
simp'eness 42.1

Simple Simon, simpleton 501.1
 (dupe 547.1)
simpletonianism 499.6
simple-witted 499.13
simplicity
 no mixture 42.1
 ignorance 491.1
 mental deficiency 499.3
 language 576.1; 578.1
 artlessness 703.1
 plainness 849
simplify
 disinvolve 42.3
 (disentangle 60.9)
 clarify 518.3
 strip of ornament 849.2
simply
 to a degree 32.13
 purely 42.7
 solely 87.10
simulate imitate 19.7
 dissemble 544.6
 affect 853.5
simulated 545.13
simulation 19.3
simultaneous 120.4
simultaneousness 120.1
sin *n.* eyesore 846.3
 vice 945.1
 (violation of law 964.2)
 (impiety 988.1)
 misdeed 947.2
sin *v.* err 495.7
 commit sin 945.9
 (be impious 988.7)
Sinaean, Sinaeic *n.* 188.9
Sinaean, Sinaeic *adj.* 188.11
sinapism
 counteractive 662.12
 poultice 662.14
since *adv.* 117.4; 155.8
 (accordingly 8.7)
 (for this reason 462.13)
 (by reason 476.21)
 long since 122.14, 15
sincere
 veracious 543.3
 frank 703.4
 ardent 821.6
sincerely 703.5
sincerity
 veracity 543.1
 candor 703.1
 (honesty 939.1)
Sindhi 560.4
sinecure 705.2
sine qua non
 necessity 630.1
 salient point 642.4
 condition 770.1
sinew ligament 45.4
 strength 159.1

sinewless
 unmanned 158.10
 weak 160.10
sinewy 159.10
sinful 945.11
 (impious 988.10)
 (ungodly 989.6)
 be sinful 945.9
sinfully 945.20
sinfulness 945.1
 (guilt 947.1)
sing *n.* 415.17
sing *v.* blow 349.22
 warble 412.2
 vocalize 416.20
 (melodize 415.27)
 confess 529.5
 compose poetry 597.12
 rejoice 838.5
 (be cheerful 836.5)
sing out 411.7
sing small 879.2
sing the same song
 be boresome 841.5
 repeat 104.4
singe *n.* 384.8
singe *v.* be hot 382.13
 burn 384.18
singer 416.10
Singhalese, Sinhalese 560.4
singing 415.17
single *n.* 235.6
single *v.*
 single out 609.7
single *adj.* simple 42.5
 one 87.6
 unmarried 904.5
single blessedness 904.1
single combat 720.3
single-decker 273a.1
single-foot *n.* 266.5
single-foot *v.* 266.16
single-footer 271.3
singlehanded
 alone 87.8
 easily 705.8
 unassisted 706.10
singlehearted
 artless 703.4
 constant 939.10
single path 635.3
single-minded 703.4
singleness
 oneness 87.1
 ~ of heart 703.1; 939.4
 ~ of purpose 604a.1
 celibacy 904.1
single-seater 273a.1
singly simply 42.7
 individually 87.10
Sing Sing 752.1
singsong *n.* 415.17
singsong *adj.*
 uniform 16.5
 repetitional 104.7
 (dingdong 407.11)
 tedious 841.8

Singspiel — skeleton

Singspiel 415.17
singular special 79.7
  unusual 83.10
  one 87.6
  unique 87.7
singularity
  particularity 79.2
  unusualness 83.3
singularly 31.21
Sinhalese See **Singhalese**
Sinic 188.9
sinister
  sinistral 239.5
  ominous 512.5
  bad 649.8
  adverse 735.8
  dishonest 940.8
sinistra 239.3
sinistrad 239.6
sinistral *n.* 239.4
sinistral *adj.* left 239.5
  inauspicious 512.5
sinistrality 239
sinistrally 239.6
sinistration 239.1
sinistrodextral
  dextral 238.3
  sinistral 239.5
sinistrogyrate 239.5
sinistrogyration 239.1
sinistromanual, sinistrorsal, sinistrorse etc. 239.5
sink *n.*
  agreement 23.1
  cavity 252.2
  sinkage 306.1
  washbasin 652.5
  ~ of corruption 653.8; 945.8
sink *v.* cease to be 2.5
  be transient 111.5
  destroy 162.4
  deepen 208.6
  prostrate 213.7
  excavate 252.9
  capsize 267.35
  recede 287.2
  decline 306.4
  depress 308.4
  submerge 310.5
  gravitate 319.7
  disappear 449.2
  ignore 460.5
  conceal 528.10
  deteriorate 659.6
  relapse 661.3
  languish 683.10
  tire 688.4
  fail 732.5
  suffer misfortune 735.6
  invest 787.5
  despond 837.6
  sadden 837.8
sink or swim
  without fail 474.16
  (perseveringly 604a.4)
  resolutely 604.9

sinkage draft 208.5
  decline 306.1
sinker
  doughnut 298.12
  gravity 319.2
sinkhole 252.2
sinking fund
  fund 636.2
  investment 787.1
sinless 946.5
  (pure 960.2)
sinner *n.* 949.2
  (worldling 988.4)
  (irreligionist 989.4)
sinner *v.* 945.9
Sinn Feiner 742.3
Sinologist 560.7
sinter residue 40.2
  silt 270.3
sinuate 248.4
sinuation 248.1
sinuose 248.4
  (complex 59.10)
sinuosity 248.1
  (curvature 245.1)
sinuous 248.4
  (circuitous 311.6)
sinus vessel 191.6
  cavity 252.2
Sioux 434.5
sip *n.* modicum 32.2
  drink 298.4
  taste 390.1
  swig 959.10
sip *v.* drink 298.47
  taste 390.3
  tipple 959.15
siphon, syphon 260.6
sir Mister 373.3
  title 877.2
sircar, sirkar 745.8
sirdar, sardar
  chief 745.4, 11
  honorifics 877.2
sire father 166.6
  man 373.2
  sir 373.3
  title 877.2
siren
  spirit of the sea 341.2
  noisemaker 404.4
  (whistle 410.4)
  signal 550.14
  temptress 617.3
  alarm 669.1
  malevolent woman 913.5
  mermaid 979.10
  mythical being 980.2
  sorceress 992.3
siriasis
  sunstroke 384.9
  mental disorder 503.4
Sirius 318.3
sirkar See **sircar**
sirloin 298.20
sirocco wind 349.9
  hot wind 382.4
sirrah sir 373.3

  title 877.2
Sir Roger de Coverley 840.7
sirup, syrup
  adherer 46.3
  semiliquid 352.3
  sweetening 396.4
sise, size 98.2
siskin 366.22
sissification 160a.2
sissify 160a.4
sissy *n.* sister 11.3
  mollycoddle 160a.3
  (coward 862.2)
sissy, sissyish *adj.* 160a.5
sister kinsman 11.3
  analogue 17.5
  nurse 662.20
  nun 996.12
sisterhood
  kinship 11.2
  fraternal order 712.3
  sisterliness 888.1
sister-in-law 11.3
sisterly
  friendly 888.4
  benevolent 906.6
Sisyphean labor
  difficult task 704.1
  noncompletion 730.1
Sisyphus 471.3
sit
  ~ on 215.27
  seat oneself 308.6
  incubate 370.8
sit down 184.14; 308.6
  (recline 213.5)
sit in 709.6
sit on the fence 628.2
  (be irresolute 605.4)
  (tergiversate 607.7)
sit up wait 133.7
  be attentive 457.4
  work nights 686.6
sit-down strike 719.2
site 184.1
sith 155.8
sitiophobia 860.4
sitting
  incubation 673.1
  council 696.2
  séance 994.4
sitting room 191.16
situal 184.18
situate *v.* 184.10
situate *adj.* 184.17
  (present 186.13)
situation
  circumstance 8.1
  affairs 151.2
  location 184.1, 5
  condition 469.2
  office 625.4
sit-upons 225.21
situs 184.1
Siva, Shiva 979.4
Sivatherium 206.7
six, sixer 98.2
sixfold 98.16

six-footer 206.6
six gun 727.10
six of one and half a dozen of the other
  equivalence 27.2
  no choice 609a.1
sixpence 800.8
six-shooter 727.10
sixteenmo 593.8
sixth 98.15, 16; 99.1
sixth sense
  instinct 477a.1
  clairvoyance 994.7
sixtieth 98.25
sixty 98.7
sizable, sizeable 192.11
  (great 31.6)
  (spacious 180.6)
sizar, sizer
  student 541.4
  pensioner 746.3
size *n.*
  character 5.4
  cement 45.6
  dimensions 192
  (quantity 25.1)
  (greatness 31.1)
  (expansion 194.1)
  (measurement 466.1)
  semiliquid 352.3
size *n.* See **sise**
size *v.* arrange 60.6
  gauge 192.10
  measure 466.10
  judge 480.7
size up
  scrutinize 441.12
  examine 461.17
  measure 466.10
  judge 480.7
size stick 466.4
sizing 352.3
sizz 409.3
sizzle speed 274.9
  sibilate 409.3
  (snap 406.7)
  be angry 900.8
sizzling 382.16
sjambok 975.1
skald, skaldic See **scald** etc.
skate *n.* horse 271.6
  sled 272.13
  fish 366.21
  wreck 659.5
  spree 959.3
skate *v.* 266.20
skating 840.11
skean 727.3
skedaddle speed 274.9
  flee 623.10
skedaddler
  fugitive 623.5
  defaulter 808.3
skeel 191.11
skeesicks, skeezix 949.1
skeletal 203.11
skeleton remains 40.1
  main part 50.3

skeleton at the feast — slack

skeleton (*continued*)
  thinness 203.5
  thin person 203.6
  frame 215.8
  outline 230.1
  corpse 362.1
  synopsis 596.1
  outline 626.2
skeleton at the feast 837.4
skeleton in the closet
  secret 533.1
  evil 649.2
  bane 663.1
  mortification 830.2
skelter off 293.5
skeptic, sceptic 989.4
  (misbeliever 984.12)
skeptical
  doubtful 485.10
  (incredulous 487.4)
  irreligiously 989.6
  (heterodox 984.22)
  be skeptical 485.6
skepticism, scepticism
  philosophy 451.18
  questioning 461.9
  doubt 485.2
  (incredulity 487.1)
  religious ~ 989.3
skepticize, scepticize 485.6
  (be incredulous 487.3)
sketch *n.*
  drawing 556.9
  description 594.1
  abstract 596.1
  plan 626.2
  (compendium 596.1)
  (schedule 611.2)
sketch *v.* outline 230.3
  form 240.6
  draw 556.17
  act in a ~ 599.26
  outline 626.9
sketcher 559.1
sketchy
  incomplete 53.4
  feeble style 575.2
  uncompleted 730.3
skew *n.* 217.1
skew *v.* oblique 217.5
  sidle 236.5
  deviate 279.6
skew *adj.* 217.13
skewback 215.18
skewbald *n.* 271.5
skewbald *adj.* 440.7
skewer 45.5
ski *n.* shoes 225.27
  sled 272.13
ski *v.* 266.20
skiagram, sciagram
  shadowgram 422.4
  picture 556.13
skiagraph, sciagraph
  skiagram 422.4
  picture 556.13
skiagrapher, sciagrapher 559.7

skiagraphy, sciagraphy shadow 422.4
  photography 556.4
skibby 188.9
skid *n.* supporter 215.2
  sled 272.13
  airplane 273a.10
  hindrance 706.2
skid *v.* sideslip 236.5
  aviate 267a.31
skiff 273.4
skill 698
  (ability 157.2)
  (knowledge 490.1)
  (genius 498.5)
  (readiness 682.2)
  (cunning 702.1)
  (facility 705.1)
skilled 698.13, 14
  (versed in 490.14)
  (prepared 673.11)
skillet pan 191.11
  cooker 386.1
skillful, skilful 698.11
  (able 157.9)
  (cunning 702.6)
  be skillful 698.7
skillfully, skilfully 698.16
skim graze 199.3
  glide 266.20
  float 267.44
  speed 274.9
  glance at 441.14; 461.19
  slight 460.6
  clean 652.9
skimble-scamble, skimble-skamble *n.* 517.3
skimble-scamble, skimble-skamble *adj.* 517.9
skimmer 225.26
skimmington
  procession 69.3
  ride 266.7
skimp *v.* slight 460.6
  scrimp 819.3
skimp, skimping, skimpy *adj.*
  inconsiderable 32.8
  incomplete 53.4
  sparse 103.3
  scarce 640.10
  parsimonious 819.4
skin *n.* layer 204.2
  cuticle 223.12
  peel 223.15
  (exterior 220.2)
  swindler 792.8
  purse 802.2
  skinflint 819.2
by the skin of one's teeth 671.6
skin *v.* excel 33.5
  peel 226.5
  ~ over 660.16
  defeat 731.9
  fleece 789.12
  overcharge 814.3

skin and bones 203.5
skin-deep
  inconsiderable 32.8
  shallow 209.4
skinflint 819.2
skin friction 267a.3
skinful fill 52.3
  satiety 869.1
skin game 545.3
skinned 732.12
skinny thin 203.11
  cutaneous 223.32
skiogram, skiograph 556.13
skip play truant 187.8
  walk 266.16
  hasten off 293.5
  caper 309.5
  pretermit 460.7
  evade 623.6
  flee 623.10
  escape 671.6
  gambol 840.21
skip bail 623.6
skip over
  overrun 303.2
  glance at 441.14; 461.19
  slight 460.6
skipjack jumper 309.3
  upstart 876.8
skipper hut 189.4
  mariner 269.4
  jumper 309.3
  master 745.12
skipper's daughters 348.10
skippet case 191.8
  basket 191.9
skirmish *n.* 720.2
skirmish *v.* 720.8
skirmisher 726.4
skirt *n.* adjunct 39.2
  pendant 214.2
  dress 225.19
  edge 231.1
  woman 374.2
skirt *v.* surround 227.3
  edge 231.3
  side 236.4
skirting 231.2
skit 934.2
skittish
  capersome 309.6
  capricious 608.5
  excitable 825.8
  fearful 860.14
  timid 862.4
  shy 881.5
skittles 840.11
skive cut off 38.6
  form layers 204.4
skiver 593.10
skulk sneak 528.16
  be cowardly 862.3
skulking
  furtive 528.21
  cowardly 862.5
skull 194.6
skullcap 225.26
skunk pelt 223.12

animal 366.3
  malodor 401.2
skunk cabbage 401.2
skurry See scurry
sky *n.*
  boundlessness 180.4
  heavens 318.2
  (air 338.1)
  blue 436.2, 3
  beneath the sky
  on earth 318.17
  outdoors 338.13
  to the sky 52.14
sky *v.* 267.46
sky-aspiring 865.18
sky blue *n.* 438.2
sky-blue *adj.* 438.6
sky-clad 226.8
sky-gazer 273.13
sky-high 206.14
skylark 305.3
skylarker 840.17
skylarking 840.2
skylight 260.5
sky line 213.4
sky parlor 191.19
sky pilot 996.2
skyrocket ascent 305.3
  firework 382.9
  signal light 423.5
skysail 273.13
skyscape view 448.2
  picture 556.10
skyscraper
  building 189.3
  tower 206.3
  height 210.1
skysail 273.13
skyscraping 206.14
skyward aloft 206.19
  up 305.8
skywrite 531.8
skywriter 531.6
skywriting
  aeronautics 267a.1
  publicity 531.4
slab *n.* lamina 204.2
  tabletop 215.20
  flat 251.3
  puddle 343a.1
  mud 352.4, 5
  gravestone 363.15
  monument 551.4
  board 635.3
  filth 653.5
slab *adj.* 352.8, 9
slabber 297.19
slabby 352.8, 9
slabstone 342.4
slack, sleck *n.* 388.2
slack *v.*
  extinguish 385.5
  shirk 623.8
  disobey 742.4
slack *adj.*
  incoherent 47.3
  weak 160.12
  inert 172.3
  slow 275.8
  neglectful 460.8
  reluctant 603.5

1090

slacken — slide

insufficient 640.8
shiftless 674.11
indolent 683.13
lax 738.7
nonobservant 773.5
loose-moraled 945.12
slacken loosen 47.2
  retard 133.6; 275.7
  moderate 174.5
  relax 687.4
  hinder 706.4
  relieve 834.4
slacker 623.4
  (neglector 460.3)
slackness laxity 738.1
  nonobservance 773.1
  dereliction 927.1
slacks 225.21
slag dregs 40.2
  (rubbish 645.4)
  (offal 653.6)
  scoria 384.15
slake moderate 174.5
  satisfy 829.4
  relieve 834.4
  ~ one's thirst 959.15
slam n. blow 276.3
  gibe 930.3
  criticism 932.2
slam v. close 261.2
  strike 276.8
  bang 406.7
  criticize 932.7
slam the door in one's face
  avoid 623.6
  oppose 708.2
  repulse 764.4
  snub 930.7
slam-bang v. 406.7
slam-bang adv.
  bang 406.12
  recklessly 863.8
slammock, slummock 59.5
slammocky, slummocky 59.9
slander n. 934.1
  (scandal 532.4)
  (accusation 938.1)
slander v. 934.3
  (vilify 908.4)
slanderer 936.1
  (scandalmonger 532.5)
slanderous 934.4
slang n. 563.4
  (inelegance 579.1)
slang v. 563.13
slang adj. 563.16
slangster 563.11
slangy 563.16
  (inelegant 579.3)
slant n.
  glimpse 441.2
  aspect 448.4
slant v. 217.6
slant adj. 217.9
slantwise 217.17
slap n. blow 276.3

(whipping 972.3)
attempt 675.1
insult 929.2
slap v.
  ~ on 37.3
  ~ down 184.10
  strike 276.8
  clap 406.7
  chastise 972.6
slap adv. 113.7
slap-bang bang 406.12
  hastily 684.7
  precipitately 863.8
  (carelessly 460.12)
slapdash n. 460.2, 3
slapdash v.
  paint 428.10
  do carelessly 460.6
slapdash adj. 428.13
slapdash adv.
  hastily 684.7
  (suddenly 113.7)
  carelessly 863.8
slap in the face
  affront 900.5
  insult 929.2
  punishment 972.3
slapper 192.6
slapping vast 31.8
  huge 192.15
slapstick
  comedy 599.4, 6
  farce 855.2
slash cut 44.8
  cheapen 815.7
slashing 574.6
slat thinness 203.5
  airplane 273a.10
  strip 205.5
  gravestone 363.15
slate n. ballot 86.1
  roofing 223.6
  stone 342.4
  writing tablet 590.10
  schedule 611.2
  platform 626.4
slate v. list 86.3
  schedule 611.4
slater 271.8
slather 31.3
slating 223.6
slattern 59.5
  (vulgarian 851.4)
slatternly untidy 59.9
  (unclean 653.16)
  (uncouth 851.7)
  awkward 699.12
slaughter n. 361.1, 7
slaughter v. 361.10
slaughterer 361.8
slaughterhouse 361.9
slaughterous 361.15
Slav 188.9
slave n. minister 631.2
  drudge 690.2
  serf 746.4
  slave to 749.6
slave v. labor 686.6
  enslave 749.5
slaver n. ship 273.1
  twaddle 517.3

slaver v.
  salivate 297.19
  ~ insanely 503.9
  talk nonsense 517.6
  flatter 933.2
slaverer 935.2
slavery
  forced labor 603.3
  toil 686.3
  subjection 749.1
slave trade 795.1
slavey 746.1, 2
slavish 886.4
  (dependent 749.6)
slavishness 886.1
Slavonic 188.11
slaw 298.30
slay 361.10
slayer 361.8
slaying 361.1
sleave 59.3
sleazy 160.11
sleck See **slack**
sled n. 272.13
sled v. slide 266.20
  transport 270.8
sledding 840.11
sledge n. 272.13
sledge v. 270.8
sledge dog 271.2
sleek v. 255.4
sleek adj. smooth 255.5
  unctuous 355.3
  pretty 845.11
sleeker 255.3
sleep n. 683.5
  (quiescence 265.1)
  (insensibility 376.1)
  (repose 687.1)
  go to sleep 683.8, 9
  (repose 687.3)
sleep v. be inert 172.2
  idle 683.8
  slumber 683.9
sleep upon
  postpone 133.4
  think over 451.29
sleep with one eye open 459.4
sleeper n. beam 215.12
  railway car 272.19
  wager 621.3
  slumberer 683.7
sleep-bringing, sleep-causing, sleep-inducing 683.17
  (sedative 174.7)
sleepiness 683.4
sleeping inert 172.3
  dead 360.8
  inattentive 458.11
  unwary 460.9
  asleep 683.16
  (quiescent 265.7)
  (reposing 687.6)
sleeping bag 191.4
sleeping car 272.19
sleeping draught 683.6
sleeping partner
  idler 683.7
  partner 711.1

sleeping sickness
  disease 655.6
  sleep 683.5
sleepless vigilant 459.8
  industrious 682.19
  wakeful 682.24
sleeplessness 682.9
sleep of the just 683.5
sleep-producing, sleep-provoking, sleep-soothing etc. 683.17
sleep-swollen 683.15
sleepwalk n. 266.6
sleepwalk v. 266.17
sleepwalker 268.7
sleepwalking n. 266.6
sleepwalking adj. 266.25
sleepy 683.15
  (weary 841.9)
  get sleepy 683.9
  (be fatigued 688.4)
sleepyhead 683.7
sleet 383.5
sleeve 225.31
  up one's sleeve 528.24
sleeveless
  nugatory 158.11
  fickle 608.6
  useless 645.8
sleigh 272.13
sleight skill 698.2
  artifice 702.3
sleight of hand 545.2
Sleipnir, Sleipner 271.9
slender
  inconsiderable 32.8
  narrow 203.9, 10
  meager 640.9
  trivial 643.11
slenderize 203.8
sleuth, sleuthhound 528.0
slew, slue n. 31.3
slew v. See **slue**
slice n. piece 51.3
  lamina 204.2
slice v. cut 44.8
  form layers 204.4
slick n. 191.14
slick v. polish 255.4
  lubricate 332.4
  paint 428.10
slick adj.
  smooth 255.5
  unctuous 355.3
  alert 457.9
  clever 698.11
  sly 702.6
slicker raincoat 225.17
smoother 255.3
  crafty rascal 702.4
slidder n. 306.3
slidder v. 306.4
sliddery
  smooth 255.5
  unctuous 355.3
slide n. smooth 255.2
  descent 306.3

slide — slubberer 1092

slide *v.* elapse 109.3
  course 264.6
  glide 266.20
  descend 306.4
slide back 661.3
slide rule 466.4
slide valve 263.2
slight *n.* neglect 460.1
  nonobservance 773.1
  snub 930.4
slight *v.*
  neglect 460.4, 5, 6
  (not complete 730.2)
  not observe 773.3
  be disrespectful 929.3
  snub 930.7
slight *adj.*
  inconsiderable 32.8
  incomplete 53.4
  frail 160.11
  (unsubstantial 4.5)
  little 193.8
  thin 203.10
  superficial 209.4
  rare 322.4
  feeble 575.2
  meager 640.9
  trivial 643.11
slighted 460.10
slightly
  in small degree 32.12
  little 193.11
slight-made 203.10
slily 702.7
slim *n.* 203.6
slim *v.* 203.8
slim *adj.* sparse 103.3
  narrow 203.8, 9
  meager 640.9
  sly 702.6
slime mud 352.4
  filth 653.5
slimsy frail 160.11
  thin 203.10
slimy 653.17
sling *n.* throw 284.3
  bandage 662.14
  slingshot 727.9
  alcoholic drink 959.8
sling *v.*
  miscarry 161.9
  ~ the lead 208.7
  suspend 214.6
  throw 284.12
slingshot 727.9
slink *n.* 862.2
slink *v.* miscarry 161.9
  sneak 528.16
  be cowardly 862.3
  slink away flee 623.10
  be in disrepute 874.4
slinky 203.11
slip *n.* modicum 32.2
  youngling 129.1
  diminutive 193.2
  thinness 203.5
  strip 205.5
  pillowslip 223.9

undergarment 225.25
  aeronautics 267a.3
  slide 306.3
  blunder 495.3
  proof 591.3
  evasion 623.1
  dockyard 691
  bungle 699.4
  failure 732.1
  misdeed 947.2
make a slip 732.5
slip of the pen, slip of the tongue 495.3
  (misstatement 583.1)
slip *v.* elapse 109.3
  slide 306.4
  blunder 495.9
  bungle 699.4
  become inefficient 699.10
  fail 732.5
  give 784.8
  err 945.9
slip away
  play truant 187.8
  flee 623.10
  escape 671.6
slip back 661.3
slip in 294.6
slip on 225.43
slip one's breath 360.6
slip over slight 460.6
  glance at 461.19
slip the cable 623.10
slip the collar
  escape 671.6
  go free 750.4
slip through the hands escape 671.6
  lose 776.2
slip up blunder 495.9
  bungle 699.9, 10
  fail 732.5
slipknot, slip knot 45.6
slippage 306.3
slipper 225.27
slippery
  transient 111.6
  smooth 255.5
  (lubricous 332.5)
  unctuous 355.3
  uncertain 475.14
  tergiversating 607.10
  precarious 665.7
  cunning 702.6
  treacherous 940.12
slippy alert 457.9
  precarious 665.7
slipshod untidy 59.9
  diction 575.2
slipslap, slipslop *n.*
  blunder 495.3
  twaddle 517.3
  malapropism 565.2
slipslap, slipslop *adj.*
  solecistic 568.3
  diction 575.2
slipstream 267a.16

slip-up blunder 495.3
  failure 732.1
slish 44.8
slit *n.* cleft 198.2
  furrow 259.1
slit *v.* sever 44.8
  furrow 259.3
  open 260.11
slithery smooth 255.5
  unctuous 355.3
sliver modicum 32.2
  strip 205.5
slob ice 383.5
  awkward fellow 701
slobber salivate 297.19
  wet 337.5
sloe 431.3
sloe-black, sloe-colored 431.7
sloe gin 959.6
slogan 722.3
slojd, sloid See **sloyd**
sloop 273.2
sloop of war 726.11
slop *n.* mud 352.4, 5
  filth 653.5
slop *v.* spill 297.13
  splash 337.5
  overflow 348.18
slope *n.* 217.1, 2
slope *v.* incline 217.6
  depart 293.5
  flee 623.10
sloping
  oblique 217.9-11
  (ascending 305.7)
  (descending 306.7)
  sideling 236.6
sloppy untidy 59.9
  sodden 339.8
  marshy 345.3
  muddy 352.9
  (dirty 653.16)
  diction 575.2
slops 225.4
slosh *n.* mud 352.4
  ice 383.5
  filth 653.5
slosh *v.*
  overflow 348.18
  plash 348.19
  murmur 405.5
sloshy 352.9
slot 260.1
sloth 683.3
sloth bear 366.15
slothful 683.13
slouch *n.* gait 266.5
  awkward fellow 701
slouch *v.* crouch 207.5
  walk 266.16
  go slow 275.5
  dawdle 683.8
slouching 846.8
slouchy 59.9
slough *n.*
  cast skin 223.13
  peel 223.15
  marsh 345.1
  offal 653.6
  mortification 655.16

predicament 704.2
slough *v.* 226.6
Slough of Despond
  misery 828.3
  sadness 837.1
  despair 859.1
sloughy 226.11
sloven slattern 59.5
  (uncleanness 653.13)
  (bungler 701)
  wagon 272.2
Slovenian 560.4
slovenly untidy 59.9
  (neglectful 460.8)
  (unclean 653.16)
  (uncouth 851.7)
  diction 575.2
  awkward 699.12
slovenry 59.1
  (neglect 460.1)
  (uncleanness 653.1)
slow *v.*
  slow down
  retard 133.6; 275.7
  moderate 174.5
slow *adj.* late 133.8
  equable 174.6
  leisurely 275.8
  (protracted 110.10)
  (languid 683.14)
  (leisurely 685.4)
  stupid 499.12
  reluctant 603.5
  dull 843.5
  be slow 730.2
slow *adv.* 275.10
  go slow 275.5
slow-burning 384.22
slow coach 275.4
  (idler 683.7)
slow-crawling, slow-creeping 275.8
slowdown 275.3
slow-foot *n.* 275.4
slow-foot, slow-footed, slowgoing *adj.* 275.8
slowly tardily 133.13
  leisurely 275.10
  music 415.32
slow motion 275.2
slow-moving 275.8
slowness 275
  (durability 110.1)
  (unwillingness 603.1)
  (languor 683.4)
slow-paced 275.8
slowpoke 275.4
slow time 275.2
slow-up 275.3
sloyd, slojd 537.5
slubber *n.* 653.5
slubber *v.*
  discolor 440a.2
  soil 653.15
  botch 699.9
slubberer slattern 59.5
  bungler 701

sludge — smitch

sludge mud 352.4
 ice 383.5
 filth 653.5
sludgy 352.9
slue *n.* See slew
slue, slew *v.* 217.5
slug *n.* part 51.1
 slow goer 275.4
 mollusk 368.6
 idler 683.7
 missile 727.14
 gold piece 800.5
 token 800.7
 nugget 800.15
slug *v.* 275.5
slugabed, sluggard
 slow goer 275.4
 idler 683.7
sluggardize 683.11
sluggish inert 172.3
 stupid 499.12
 languid 683.14
 apathetic 823.5
sluggishness
 weakness 160.1
 slowness 275.1
 languor 683.4
sluice limit 233.1
 flow 348.2
 floodgate 350.2
 (outlet 295.5)
sluice gate 350.2
slum 653.10
slumber *n.* 683.5
slumber *v.*
 be inert 172.2
 (not do 681.2)
 (be inactive 683.8)
 sleep 683.9
slumberer 683.7
slumbering 172.3
slumberland 683.5
slumberous 683.15
slummock, slummocky
 See slammock etc.
slump *n.*
 subsidence 36.2
 pastry 298.12
 decline 304.1
 drop 306.1
 price decline 815.3
slump *v.*
 lose ground 304.2
 drop 306.4
 depreciate 815.7
slung shot 727.14
slur *n.* music 415.20
 notation 415.23
 printing 591.5
 stigma 874.2
 aspersion 934.1
 reproach 938.1
slur *v.* discolor 440a.2
 slight 460.6
 glance at 461.19
 pretext 619.2
 stigmatize 874.7
 asperse 934.3
 extenuate 937.8
 reproach 938.4
slurry 440a.2

slush mud 352.4
 ice 383.5
 loquacity 584.1
 filth 653.5
slushy muddy 352.9
 effusive 584.5
slut slattern 59.5
 (vulgarian 851.4)
 bitch 366.6
 woman 374.2
 female animal 374.8
 jade 949.4
 strumpet 962.2
sluttish 59.9
sly sagacious 498.10
 furtive 528.21
 cunning 702.6
 (evasive 623.12)
slyboots 702.4
slyness 702.1
 (stealth 528.3)
smack *n.*
 modicum 32.2
 tincture 41.3
 ship 273.2
 blow 276.3
 taste 390.1
 (savor 394.2)
 pungency 392.1
 kiss 894.4; 902.3
smack *v.* strike 276.8
 taste 390.3
 bang 406.7
 kiss 902.8
smack of
 resemble 17.7
 savor of 394.6
smack the lips
 rejoice 838.5
 relish 377.4; 394.6; 827.6
smack *adv.* 113.7
smacker 800.8
small! *adj.*
 inconsiderable 32.6
 (inferior 34.5)
 diminutive 193.8
 bigoted 606.7
 insignificant 643.10
 be small 32.4
 feel small 879.2
small *adv.* 193.11
small arm 727.10
small beer
 insignificancy 643.5, 6
 liquor 959.5
smallclothes 225.21, 25, 32
smaller inferior 34.5
 fewer 103.4
 contracted 195.6
be smaller 195.5
 (be inferior 34.4)
smallest
 most inferior 33.6
 least 34.6
small fry *n.*
 diminutive 193.2, 5
 insignificance 643.5, 6

small-fry *adj.* 643.12
small hours 125.1
smallness quantity 32
 (inextension 180a.1)
 (size 193.1)
 (powder 330.3)
 (insignificance 643.1)
 inferiority 34.1
smallpox 655.6
smalls trousers 225.21
 clothes 225.25, 32
 examination 461.3
small talk 588.2
smally 32.12
smalt 438.4
smaragdine 435.6
smart *n.* 378.1
smart *v.*
 ~ with pain 378.5
 ~ under 821.3
smart *adj.* alert 457.9
 shrewd 498.10
 (clever 698.11)
 quick 682.17
 intensely felt 821.5
 witty 842.9
 trim 845.11
 chic 847.14
 (clothed 225.46)
 (fashionable 852.7)
 impudent 885.9
get smart 885.7
smart aleck 885.3
smart-alecky 885.9
smarten 847.11
smart money 973.2
smartness 682.2
smart set 852.4
smarty *n.* 885.3
smarty *adj.* 885.9
smash *n.*
 destruction 162.3
 collision 276.2
 pulp 354.2
 success 731.2
 failure 732.1, 3
 accident 735.3
 alcoholic drink 959.8
go to smash 162.5
to smash 173.18
smash *v.*
 disintegrate 44.9
 destroy 162.4
 collide 276.6
 soften 324.4
 pulverize 330.6
 pulp 354.4
 break 659.8
smasher pulper 354.3
 fence 792.9
 counterfeiter 800.18
smashup
 collision 276.2
 accident 735.3
smatter 32.2
smatterer 493.2
smattering 491.3
smear *n.*
 quantities 31.3

glissando 415.20
soil 653.3
blemish 848.1
smear *v.* cover 223.24
 lubricate 332.4
 paint 428.10
 discolor 440a.2
 soil 653.15
smeared 422.8
smell *n.* modicum 32.2
 odor 398.1
smell *v.* scent 398.5, 7
 be fragrant 400.8
 stink 401.3
 detect 481a.7
smell a rat
 detect 481a.7
 suspect 485.6
smell of the lamp 577.5
smell out
 hunt out 461.16
 find 481a.7
smell to heaven
 stink 401.3
 (be unclean 653.14)
 be shameful 874.12
smeller 250.4
smell-feast 886.2
smelling *n.* 398.2
smelling *adj.*
 odorous 398.8
 fetid 401.4
smelling bottle 400.5
smelling salts
 energizer 171.5
 pungency 392.2
 aromatic 400.2
 tonic 662.5
smelly odorous 398.8
 fetid 401.4
smelt burn 384.18
 temper 673.6
smidgen, smidge 32.2
smile *n.*
 rejoicing 838.2
 ~ of contempt 930.2
 swig of liquor 959.10
smile *v.*
 be cheerful 836.4
 rejoice 838.6
 ~ at 856.4
smile upon
 second 707.8
 greet 894.9
smiling *n.* 838.2
smiling *adj.* 836.7
smirch *n.* black 431.3
 soil 653.3
 blemish 848.1
 stigma 874.2
 moral blemish 945.5
smirch *v.* darken 431.6
 discolor 440a.2
 soil 653.15
smirk *n.*
 sardonic grin 838.2
 ridicule 856.1
smirk *v.* 838.6; 853.5
smitch 32.2

smite — snarl

smite strike 276.8
 impress 824.2
 chastise 972.5, 6
smith 690.6
smither modicum 32.2
 piece 51.3
 smith 690.6
smithereen
 modicum 32.2
 piece 51.3
 to smithereens 173.18
smithier, smithy 690.6
smitten 897.14, 15
smock *n.* cloak 225.15
 apron 225.20
smock *v.* 258.3
smockface 160a.1
smock-faced 160a.5
smog 353.5
smoke *n.*
 transient 111.4
 smut 330.3
 tobacco 392a.2, 10
 black 431.3
 unimportance 643.5
 dirt 653.5
smoke *v.*
 vaporize 336.5
 dry 340.5
 cloud 353.9
 smolder 382.13
 ~ tobacco 392a.14
 darken 431.6
 discolor 440a.2
 soil 653.15
 cure 670.4
 banter 856.4
 be angry 900.8
smoke bomb 727.14
smoke-dry dry 340.5
 cure 670.4
smokejack 312.4
smoker
 smoking car 272.19
 tobacco user 392a.11
 smoking room
  392a.13
 party 892.5
smoke room, smokery
 392a.13
smoke screen
 screen 424.3
 shield 717.2
smokestack tube 260.6
 chimney 351.1
smokestone 342.4
smoke talk 586.1
smoking *n.*
 vaporization 336.1
 tobacco 392a.10
smoking *adj.* 382.17
smoking car 272.19
smoking jacket
 225.16, 23
smoking room 392a.13
smoky vaporous 336.7
 blurred 422.8
 opaque 426.4
 discolored 440a.3
 unclean 653.16

smolder, smoulder
 be inert 172.2
 (not do 681.2)
 (be inactive 683.8)
 burn 382.13
 be latent 526.3
 be angry 900.8
smoldering, smoul-
 dering inert 172.3
 burning 382.17
smooth *n.* 255.3
smooth *v.* uniform 16.4
 moderate 174.5
 level 213.6
 smoothen 255.4
 (flatten 251.4)
 (lubricate 332.4)
 prepare the way
  673.6
 facilitate 705.4
smooth *adj.*
 equable 174.6
 horizontal 213.8
 hairless 226.10
 not rough 255.5
 (flat 251.5)
 (lubricous 332.5)
 unctuous 355.3
 specious 545.13
 suave 894.13
 flattering 933.3
smoothbore 727.11
smoothen 255.4
smoother 255.5
smooth-faced
 hairless 226.10
 dissembling 544.8
smoothly 705.8
smoothness 255
 (flatness 251.1)
 (lubrication 332.1)
smooth sailing 705.1
smooth-shaven 226.10
smooth-spoken,
 smooth-tongued
 hypocritical 544.8
 suave 894.13
 flattering 933.3
smot soil 653.3
 blemish 848.1
 moral blemish 945.5
smother
 moderate 174.5
 suffocate 361.11
 extinguish 385.5
 silence 403.5
 muffle 408a.4
 keep secret 528.11
 mute 581.5
 restrain 751.6
smotheration 361.4
smothered 641.6
smoulder, smoulder-
 ing See smolder etc.
smriti 986.2
smudge *n.* fire 382.8
 black 431.3
 soil 653.3, 5
 blemish 848.1
 stigma 874.2
 moral blemish 945.5

smudge *v.*
 darken 431.6
 discolor 440a.2
 soil 653.15
smudgy dark 431.8
 discolored 440a.3
smug 853.7
smuggle 791.9
smuggle in
 foist in 10.4
 interject 228.8
smuggler 792.1
smut *n.* residue 40.2
 powder 330.3
 fungi 369.4
 black 431.3
 dirt 653.5
 blight 663.2
 obscenity 961.1
smut *v.* darken 431.6
 discolor 440a.2
smutch *n.* black 431.3
 soil 653.3
 blemish 848.1
 stigma 874.2
 moral blemish 945.5
smutch *v.* darken 431.6
 discolor 440a.2
 soil 653.15
smutty dark 431.8
 discolored 440a.3
 dirty 653.16
 obscene 961.9
snack *n.* modicum 32.2
 piece 51.3
 lunch 298.35
 share 786.2
 go snacks 778.5
snack *v.* 298.44
snaffle *n.*
 hindrance 706.2
 bit 752.2
snaffle *v.* 791.9
snag *n.* horn 253.2
 tooth 253.3
 fault 651.2
 hidden danger 667.1
 obstacle 706.2
snag *v.* 789.9
snagged, snaggled
 253.11
snaggletooth 253.3
snail slow goer 275.4
 mollusk 368.6
snaillike 275.8
snail's pace 275.2
 at a snail's pace
  275.10
snake *n.* coil 248.2
 serpent 366.19
 firework 382.9
 hisser 409.2
 deceiver 548.1
 evildoer 913.1
 scoundrel 949.1
snake *v.* 285.4
snake in the grass
 latent 526.1
 hidden thing 528.6
 deceiver 548.1
 evil 649.2

bane 663.1
 hidden danger 667.1
 secret enemy 891.1
 evildoer 913.1
 scoundrel 949.1, 3
snakestone 248.2
snaky sinuous 248.4
 reptilian 366.27
snap *n.* spell 109a.1
 energy 171.1
 bite 298.2
 cold weather 383.3
 taste 390.1
 pungency 392.1
 sound 406
 snapshot 556.11
 verve 682.1
 easy task 705.2
 bargain 815.2
 have a snap at 932.2
snap *v.* sunder 44.8
 close 261.2
 be brittle 328.3
 bubble 353.8
 crack 406.7
 photograph 556.18
 be rude 895.4
 show resentment
  900.7
snap at
 catch at 789.13
 assail 830.3
snap off one's head
 900.8
snap one's fingers at
 defy 715.2
 disdain 930.5
snap up 789.9
snap *adj.* 612.4
snapdragon 840.11
snapper
 noisemaker 404.4
 cracker 406.5
snapping 406.10
snappish 901.7
snappy energetic 171.9
 fast 274.13
 cold 383.8
 pungent 392.5
 newsy 532.9
 lively 682.16
snap shooter 559.7
snapshot *n.* 556.11
snapshot *v.* 556.18
snapshotter 559.7
snare *n.* string 417.13
 sophism 477.2
 trap 545.4
 (ambush 530.1)
 (lure 617.2)
 (pitfall 667.2)
 (artifice 702.3)
snare *v.* trap 545.9
 catch 789.9
 steal 791.9
snare drum 417.10
snarl *n.* 713.3
snarl *v.* blow 349.22
 sound harshly 410.6
 growl 412.2
 be rude 895.4

show resentment
  900.7
  (be irascible 901.5)
  threaten 909.2
snarled complex 59.10
  difficult 704.6
snarleyyow, snarle-
  yow 366.6
snatch n.
  modicum 32.2
  piece 51.3
  by snatches
    piecemeal 51.10
    irregularly 59.12
    discontinuously 70.5
snatch v. jerk 285.5
  catch 789.9
  steal 791.9
snatch at
  pursue 622.9
  strip 789.12, 13
snatch a verdict
  deceive 545.7
  use artifice 702.5
snath, snathe, snead
  215.7
sneak n. coward 862.2
  knave 949.1
sneak v. steal 528.16
  be cowardly 862.3
sneak out of
  avoid 623.8, 10
  escape 671.6
sneakers 225.27
sneaking
  cowardly 862.5
  dishonest 940.8
sneak thief 792.1
sneer n. 930.3
  (disapprobation
   932.1)
  with a sneer
    insolently 885.11
    contemptuously
     930.10
sneer v.
  crowd sail 267.16
  scoff 930.6
  (disparage 934.3)
sneeze n. 349.18
sneeze v. exhale 349.23
  sibilate 409.3
sneeze at ignore 460.5
  disdain 930.5
sneeze gas 334.2
snick 32.2
snicker n.
  laughter 838.3
  ridicule 856.1
  scornful laugh 930.2
snicker v. laugh 838.7
  ridicule 856.1
  scoff 930.6
snide n. horse 271.6
  sham 545.6
  counterfeit 800.9
snide adj. 545.13
sniff inhale 349.23
  smell 398.7
  sibilate 409.3
  detect 481a.7

sniff out
  hunt out 461.16
  find 481a.7
sniffle inhale 349.23
  sibilate 409.3
sniffy 885.8
snifter 959.10
snifting valve 666.1
snigger n.
  laughter 838.3
  ridicule 856.1
  scornful laugh 930.2
snigger v. laugh 838.7
  ridicule 856.4
  scoff 930.6
sniggle n. 545.4
sniggle v. 545.9
snip n. modicum 32.2
  piece 51.3
  diminutive 193.2
  tailor 225.37
  seaman 269.3
  share 786.2
  go snips 778.5
snip v. 44.8
snipe n. food 298.26
  cigarette 392a.5
snipe v. shoot 284.13
  fire upon 716.6
sniper 726.4
snippet modicum 32.2
  diminutive 193.2
snip-snap 713.3
snipsnapsnorum
  840.12
snitch n. modicum 32.2
  nose 250.4
  informer 527.6
snitch v. 791.9
snitcher 527.6
snivel 839.8
sniveling 886.4
snivy, snivey 606.6
snob shoemaker 225.40
  scab 607.6
  rude person 851.4
  insolent person
   885.3
  sycophant 886.2
snobbery 885.1
snobbish 885.8
snood
  headdress 225.26
  ornament 847.3
snoop, snooper n.
  inquisitive 455.2
  meddler 682.11
snoop v. 455.4
snoopy 455.5
snoot 250.4
snooty 885.8
snooze, snoozle n.
  683.5
snooze, snoozle v.
  683.9
snoozy 683.15
snore sibilate 409.3
  sound harshly 410.6
  sleep 683.9
snork, snort 409.3;
  412.2

snorter 159.6
snotty 885.8
snout nose 250.4
  airplane 273a.10
  tobacco 392a.1
snow ship 273.2
  ice 383.6
  white 430.3
  drug 662.7
snowball
  accumulation 72.6
  snow 383.6
snowbank 383.6
snowberg 383.5
snow blanket, snow
  blast 383.6
snow-blind
  blind 442.6
  dim-sighted 443.15
snow blindness
  blindness 442.1
  dim-sightedness
   443.2
  (blindness 442.1)
snowblink 420.10
snowbound 383.9
snowdrift
  accumulation 72.6
  snow 383.6
snowdust, snowfall,
  snowflake 383.6
snowshoe shoe 225.27
  sled 272.13
snowslide, snowslip
  slide 306.3
  snow 383.6
snow-white, snowy
  430.8
snub n. 930.4
  (disregard 460.1)
  (discourtesy 895.1)
  (indignity 929.2)
snub v. cut off 38.6
  cut short 201.4
  repulse 289.2
  impede 706.4
  rebuff 930.7
  (disregard 460.5)
  (exclude 893.7)
  (be discourteous
   895.4)
snub, snubbed adj.
  201.6
snubbing post 215.16
snub-nosed
  snubbed 201.6
  deformed 243.5
snuff n. tobacco 392a.8
  odor 398.1
  up to snuff
    aware of 490.13
    competent 698.12
    cunning 702.6
snuff v. draw in 296.2
  inhale 349.23
  smell 398.7
  sibilate 409.3
snuff out
  destroy 162.4
  extinguish 385.5

snarled — soapy

snuff bottle, snuffbox
  392a.8
snuff color 433.1
snuffcolored 433.4
snuff dipper, snuffer
  392a.11
snuffle inhale 349.23
  sibilate 409.3
  nasalize 583.2
  cant 988.8
snuffman 392a.12
snuffy
  of snuff 392a.15
  dirty 653.16
snug adj. close 261.6
  seaworthy 273.15
  comfortable 377.8
  secure 664.10
  prepared 673.11
  content 831.6
  unsociable 893.9
snug v.
  snug down 267.38
snuggle 902.8
snugness 377.2
so thus 8.6; 627.8
  analogous 17.12
  provided 469.8
  even so
   notwithstanding
    30.8
  yes! 488.14
  just so yes! 488.14
  exactly 494.16
  so as 469.8
  so be it! 488.15
  so far 233.4
  so far so good! 931.13
  so that 469.8
  so to speak as if 17.17
  figuratively 521.4
soak n. blow 276.3
  spree 959.3
  drunkard 959.11
soak v. strike 276.8
  drench 337.5
  ~ up 340.5
  overcharge 814.3
  tipple 959.15
soaker rain 348.11
  drunkard 959.11
so-and-so 565.4
soap n. oil 356.5
  (cleaner 652.8)
  bribe 618.2
  flattery 933.1
soap v. wash 652.9
  flatter 933.2
soap the ways 332.4
soapbox, soap box n.
  215.21
soapbox v. 582.7
soapboxer 582.5
soap bubble 353.1
soapmaker 690.8
soapstone 342.4
soapy bubbling 353.10
  unctuous 355.3
  suave 894.13
  flattering 933.3

soar — solely 1096

soar be great 31.4
  be high 206.9
  aviate 267a.30
  fly aloft 305.6
  be light 320.5
soaring 206.13
sob *n.* 839.1
sob *v.* blow 349.22
  sough 405.5
  weep 839.8
  (cry 411.6)
sober *v.*
  moderate 174.5
  render sane 502.4
sober down
  be moderate 174.4
  become sane 502.3
  humble oneself 879.2
sober *adj.*
  substantial 3.4
  equable 174.6
  dull-colored 428.19
  gray 432.4
  thoughtful 451.35
  wise 498.11
  sane 502.5
  language 576.3
  composed 826.9
  solemn 837.16
  temperate 953.6
  unintoxicated 958.3
sobriety
  levelheadedness 498.4
  sanity 502.1
  staidness 826.3
  temperance 953.1
  unintoxicatedness 958
  (abstinence 953.2)
sobriquet 565.3
soc 965.1
socage 777.1
so-called
  spurious 545.13
  nominal 564.8
  quasi 565.7
soccer 840.11
sociability 892.1
sociable *n.*
  carriage 272.4
  party 892.5
sociable *adj.* 892.12
  (friendly 888.4)
be sociable 892.9
social 892.12
social democracy 737.6
social evil 961.6
sccialism
  government 737.6
  collectivism 778.2
  public welfare 906.3
socialist
  collectivist 778.4
  humanitarian 911.1
Socialist 712.6
socialistic 778.8
sociality 892
social-minded 892.12
social science 906.3
  (man 372.4)

social service 602.4
social worker 602.5
societal 372.6
society company 88.2
  people 372.2
  community 712.4
  (association 709.2)
  fashionable ~ 852.4
  social circle 892.7
  religious order 984.3
  parish 997.1
Socinianism 984.4
sociology 906.3
  (man 372.4)
sock *n.* hose 225.29
  blow 276.3
  wind gauge 338.9
  comedy 599.4
sock *v.* 276.8
sockdolager
  end-all 67.4
  effective retort 479.1
socket case 191.8
  cavity 252.2
socle, zocle 215.3
Socrates
  philosopher 476.9
  learned man 492.2
  sage 500.1
Socratic 451.38
Socratic method 461.8
Socratism 451.7
Socratist 476.9; 492.6
Socratize 451.34
sod *n.* soil 342.3
  turf 367.10
sod *v.* 371.8
soda drink 298.4
  sweet beverages 396.5
sodality
  association 709.2
  fraternal order 712.3
  fellowship 888.1
sodden *v.* 337.5
sodden *adj.*
  drunk 259.21
  soaked 339.8
  boiled 384.23
sodium carbonate 652.8
sodomist, sodomite
  hermaphrodite 83.5
  libertine 962.1
sodomy 961.3
sofa 215.22
soft *n.*
  mollycoddle 160a.3
  fool 501.1
soft *adj.* weak 160.10
  effeminate 160a.5
  (cowardly 862.4)
  moderate 174.6
  not hard 324.6
  (formative 240.7)
  (muddy 352.9)
  (pulpy 354.5)
  (weak-willed 605.6)
  soppy 339.8
  marshy 345.3
  phonetics 402.11

faint 405.9
  (quiet 403.6)
  melodious 413.27
  soft-colored 428.17
  credulous 486.5
  foolish 499.15
  out of practice 699.16
  easy 705.5
  lenient 740.4
  tender 822.7
  meek 826.10
  amorous 897.14
  compassionate 914.6
  morally infirm 945.12
render soft 324.4
soft drink 298.4
soften moderate 174.5
  make soft 324.4
  muffle 408a.4
  qualify 469.3
  relieve 834.4
  excite pity 914.4
  extenuate 937.8
softened faint 405.9
  soft-colored 428.17
  penitent 950.5
softening *n.*
  mollification 324.2
  relief 834.1
  extenuation 937.3
softening *adj.* 324.10
softening of the brain 655.5
soft goods 798.3
softhead 501.1
softhearted
  tenderhearted 822.7
  benevolent 906.6
  compassionate 914.6
softheartedness 914.1
softness pliability 324
  tenderness 821.1; 822.2
soft pedal *n.*
  muffler 408a.3
  sourdine 417.11
soft-pedal *v.*
  hush 403.4, 5
  muffle 408a.4
soft sawder *n.*
  suaviloquence 894.2
  flattery 933.1
soft-sawder *v.* 933.2
soft-sawderer 935.2
soft snap 705.2
soft soap *n.* soap 356.5
  suaviloquence 894.2
  flattery 933.1
soft-soap *v.* 933.2
soft-soaper 935.2
soft-sounding 405.9; 413.27
soft-spoken
  speaking 582.11
  suave 894.13
soft-toned 413.27
softwood 635.3
softy, softie fool 501.1
  weakling 160.4

mollycoddle 160a.3
soggy 339.8
soho!
  attention! 457.10
  (salutation 586.3)
  halloo! 622.12
soi-disant 565.7
soil *n.* region 181.1
  the country 183.1
  land 342.1, 3
  defilement 653.3
  (stain 848.1)
  moral blemish 945.5
soil *v.* discolor 440a.2
  dirty 653.15
  (blemish 848.2)
soilage
  defilement 653.3
  vice 945.5
soiled 653.16
  (blemished 848.3)
soiree, soirée 892.5
sojourn *n.* 189.1
sojourn *v.* 186.10
sojourner 188.1
soke territory 181.2
  jurisdiction 965.1
Sol 318.4
solace *n.* 834.2
solace *v.* 834.5
  (cheer 836.6)
solano 382.4
solar 318.16
solar system 318.3
solatium 973.1, 2
sold
  sold on 827.8
solder *n.* 45.6
solder *v.* 46.7
soldering 46.1
soldier *n.* sailor 269.6
  shirker 623.4
  idler 683.7
  warrior 726.4
  (shooter 284.8)
soldier *v.* shirk 623.8
  idle 683.8
soldierly 722.13
  (courageous 861.8)
soldier's wind
  calm 265.1
  beam wind 349.10
soldiery 726.6
soldo 800.8
sole *n.* foot 211.1, 4
  supporter 215.2
  fish 298.18
sole *adj.* 87.6, 7
solecism
  sophism 477.2
  blunder 495.3
  ungrammaticism 568.1
  (barbarism 563.1)
  (inelegance 579.1)
solecistic 568.3
  (inelegant 579.3)
solecize 568.2
solely simply 42.7
  alone 87.10

solemn
  declaration 535.6
  important 642.12
  serious 837.16
  commemorative 883.5
  religious 987.10
  reverential 990.15
  ritual 998.15
solemnity
  importance 642.2
  gravity 837.2
  pomp 882.1
  rite 998.1
solemnization 883.1
solemnize
  celebrate 883.3
  ritualize 998.14
sol-fa *n.* scale 413.16
  solmization 415.18
sol-fa *v.* 416.20
sol-faist 416.10
solfeggio 415.18
solferino 434.2
solicit request 765.4
  court 865.13
solicitant 865.7
solicitation 765.1
  (persuasion 615.4)
solicitor
  functionary 758.2
  deputy 759.1
  petitioner 767.1
  salesman 797.2, 4
  attorney 968.1
solicitous
  careful 459.7
  requesting 765.7
  desirous 865.16
solicitude care 459.1
  anxiety 828.5; 860.2
  caution 864.1
  desire 865.2
solid *n.* 321.4
  (conglomerate 46.4)
solid *adj.*
  substantial 3.4
  complete 52.9
  crowded 72.13
  stable 150.5
  dense 321.8
  (thick 202.7)
  well-founded 474.9
  unanimous 488.12
  learned 490.15
  valid 494.14
  wise 498.11
  resolute 604.7
  solvent 800.22
solidarity
  completeness 52.1
  unity 87.1
solidate 321.7
solidification
  coherence 46.1
  densification 321.3
  (refrigeration 385.1)
solidify combine 48.3
  densify 321.7
  (conglomerate 46.8)

  (thicken 202.5)
  (harden 323.4)
solidity
  completeness 52.1
  stability 150.1
  strength 159.1
  density 321.1
  (thickness 202.2)
  wisdom 498.3
  solvency 800.17
solidungulate 366.26
soliloquist 589.2
soliloquize 589.3
  (speak 582.6)
soliloquizing 589.4
soliloquy 589
soliped 366.26
solitaire game 840.12
  recluse 893.4
solitary one 87.6
  alone 87.8
  in solitude 893.10
solitude 893.2
  (aloneness 87.1)
solitudinarian 893.4
solitudinous 893.10
solleret 717.2
solmizate 416.20
solmization 415.18
  (sol-fa 413.17)
solo 415.12
solo flight 267a.23
soloist 416.1
Solomon
  learned man 492.2
  sage 500.1
  judge 967.1
Solon 500.3
solubility 335.2
  (fluidity 333.1)
soluble 335.8
solubilization 335.1
solubilize 335.5
solus one 87.6
  alone 87.8
solution *n.* cement 45.6
  discontinuity 70.1
  fusion 335.3
  orchestration 413.3
  discovery 481a.2
  explanation 522.1
  (answer 462.3)
solution *v.* 43.6; 46.7
solve liquefy 335.5
  unriddle 481a.4
  (explain 522.6)
  (manifest 525.2)
solvency 800.17
solvent *n.* 652.8
solvent *adj.*
  decomposing 49.5
  dissolvent 335.9
  diluent 337.6
  able to pay 800.22
  (unindebted 807.10)
Soma 979.4
somatic 136.8
somatism 316.5
somatist 316.6
somatological 316.9
somatologist 316.6
somatology 316.5

somber, sombre *n.* 421.2
somber, sombre *v.*
  darken 421.5
  blacken 431.6
somber, sombre *adj.*
  gloomy 421.8; 837.10
  dim 422.8
  dull-colored 428.19
  dark-colored 431.8
  gray 432.4
sombrero 225.26
some quantity 25.7
  somewhat 32.14
  more than one 100.4
somebody person 372.3
  personage 642.5
  celebrity 873.9
  be somebody
  be important 642.7
  be distinguished 873.10
someday 119.4
somegate, somehow
  in some way 155.7
  by some means 627.10
someone 372.3
someplace 186.23
somersault, summersault 218.1
  (whirl 312.2)
somerset, summerset 218.1
something thing 3.2
  ~ else 15.3
  object 316.3
  personage 642.5
sometime *adj.* 122.10
sometime, sometimes *adv.* 119.4
  (in future 121.9)
  (once 137.5)
somewhat 32.14
  (partly 51.9)
somewhere
  there 186.21
  someplace 186.23
  ~ else 187.15; 458.11
somnambulant 266.25
somnambulate 266.17
somnambulation 266.6
somnambulator, somnambule, somnambulist 268.7
somnial, somniative 683.15
somnifacient 683.6
somniferous, somnific
  sleepy 683.15
  sleep-inducing 683.17
somnify 683.11
somnivolent 683.7
somnolence 683.4
somnolent
  sleepy 683.15
  sleep-inducing 683.17
somnolism 683.5
Somnus 683.5
son 167.1, 4

sonance 402.1
sonant *n.*
  sound 402.1, 2
  letter 561.1
sonant *adj.* 402.9
sonata, sonatina 415.3
sonation 402.3
sondation 402.3
Sonderbund 769.2
song clamor 404.2
  tune 415.2, 10
  (melody 413.4)
  poetry 597.1, 2
  trifle 643.3
  for a song 815.11
song and dance 599.5
songbird 416.10, 11
songbook 415.21
  (book 593.1)
songful
  melodious 413.27
  musical 415.28
song hit 415.10
song-play 415.17
songster bird 366.2
  songbook 415.21
  singer 416.10, 11
soniferous 402.9
sonification 402.3
son-in-law 167.4
sonly 167.6
sonnet 597.2
sonneteer 597.10
sonny boy 129.4
  descendant 167.4
Son of God 976.5
son of the soil 876.5
sonorescence 402.1
sonorescent 402.9
sonority
  loudness 404.1
  resonance 408.1, 3
  (sound 402.1)
sonorous loud 404.8
  resonant 408.9
  (sounding 402.9)
  high-sounding 577.7
sonship 167.2
soon 132.15
  (briefly 111.9)
  (in future 121.9)
  too soon
  beforehand 132.12
  untimely 135.6
sooner *n.* 188.5
sooner *adv.* 609.18
  sooner or later
  sometime 119.4
  eventually 121.9
soot *n.* residue 40.2
  powder 330.3
  black 431.3, 5
  dirt 653.5
soot *v.* darken 431.6
  discolor 440a.2
sooth *n.* truth 494.1
  veracity 543.1
  by my sooth
  I'll warrant 535.8
  I promise 768.8
  in sooth, sooth to say
  truly 494.15

sooth — sound

sooth (*continued*)
  truthfully 543.4
sooth *adj.* 494.10
sooth *adv.* 494.15
soothe moderate 174.5
  (render insensible 376.4)
  quiet 265.6
  relieve 834.4
  flatter 933.2
soothfast *adj.* 543.3
soothfast *adv.*
  truly 494.15
  truthfully 543.4
soothing
  subdued 405.9
  melodious 413.27
  relieving 834.7
soothsay *n.*
  axiom 496.2
  divination 511.2
  omen 512.1
soothsay *v.* 511.7
soothsayer 513.2
  (sorcerer 992.2)
soothsaying 511.2
sooty blurred 422.8
  dark 431.8
  discolored 440a.3
  unclean 653.16
sop *n.* modicum 32.2
  mollycoddle 160a.3
  fool 501.1
  bribe 618.2
sop *v.* 337.5
soph 541.4
Sophi See **Sophy**
sophism 477.1, 2
  (absurdity 497.1)
sophist
  false reasoner 477.6
  (reasoner 476)
  (philosopher 492.6)
  (affecter 853.4)
  deceiver 548.1
sophister student 541.4
  deceiver 548.1
sophistical 477.9
  (absurd 497.4)
sophisticate *n.* 700.3
sophisticate *v.*
  adulterate 41.8
  reason ill 477.7
  (mislead 495.11)
  (misrepresent 555.4)
  falsify 544.3
  corrupt 659.9
sophisticated
  adulterated 545.13
  worldly-wise 698.15
sophistication
  adulteration 41.2
  corruption 659.3
  experience 698.4
sophistic syllogism
  syllogism 476.5
  sophism 477.2
sophistry
  false reasoning 477.1
  (philosophy 451.4)

(misjudgment 481.1)
(affectation 491.4)
(fallacy 495.1)
(misteaching 538.1)
(quackery 544.2)
sophism 477.2
deception 545.1
sophomore 541.4
sophomoric 541.9
Sophy, Sophi 745.3
sopite 376.4
sopor
  insensibility 376.1
  swoon 683.5; 688.3
soporific *n.*
  anesthetic 376.2
  sleep inducer 683.6
soporific *adj.*
  palliative 662.25
  sleep-inducing 683.17
soppy 339.8
soprano
  high tone 410.2
  voice 413.14
  voice part 415.13
Sorbian 560.4
sorcer 992.4
sorcerer 992.2
  (prophet 513.2)
  (legerdemainist 548.6)
  (diabolist 978.5)
sorceress 992.3
sorcerous 992.5
sorcery 992
  (divination 511.2)
  (spell 993.1)
sordellina 417.4
sordes dregs 40.2
  riffraff 876.2
sordid
  niggardly 819.4
  covetous 865.20
sordine See **sourdine**
sordo softly 405.11
  nonresonant 408a.6
  music 415.30
sore *n.* hurt 378.1
  inflammation 655.16
  (swelling 194.2)
  (wound 659.4)
sore *adj.* painful 378.7
  distressing 830.15
  discontented 832.5
  angry 900.13
sorely 31.23
soreness
  discontent 832.1
  resentment 900.1
sorghum, sorgo, sorgho 396.4
sorites 476.5
soritical 476.17
sororal
  consanguine 11.7
  friendly 888.4
  benevolent 906.6
sorority kinship 11.2
  fraternal order 712.3
  sisterliness 888.1

sororize
  be friendly 888.2
  associate 892.9
sorrel *n.* horse 271.5
  reddish-brown 433.5
sorrow *n.* grief 837.3
  (affliction 830.2)
  remorse 950.1
sorrow *v.*
  grieve 837.6, 8
  (suffer 828.11)
  mourn 839.6
sorrowful, sorrowing, sorrow-struck, sorrow-torn 837.11
  (funereal 363.25)
  (wretched 828.16)
  (lamenting 839.13)
sorry paltry 643.12
  wretched 828.16
  regretful 833.2, 3
  vulgar 851.2
  remorseful 950.5
  be sorry for 833.2
  (repent 950.3)
  not sorry 827.8
sort *n.* degree 26.1
  kind 75.2
  (nature 5.3)
  all sorts
    mixture 41.4
    diversified 81.3
    multitude 102.2
  of a sort
    dissimilar 18.4
    mediocre 736.3
  of sorts
    diversified 81.3
    mediocre 736.3
  out of sorts
    disorderly 59.8
    unwell 655.23
    sad 837.9
    ill-humored 901.7
  sort of as if 17.17
    somewhat 32.14
sort *v.*
  ~ out 55.4
  arrange 60.6
  size 192.10
  ~ with 892.9
sortable fit 23.11
  opportune 134.7
  suitable 646.4
sortal 75.6
sorter 60.4
sortie 716.1
sortilege
  divination 511.3
  sorcery 992.1
sorting 60.1
sortition 621.6
sorty
  classificational 75.6
  diversified 81.3
SOS 669.1
soso, so-so *adj.*
  inconsiderable 32.8
  somewhat 32.14
  mediocre 736.3
  (unimportant 643.10)

(tolerable 648.11)
(imperfect 651.4)
sossle, sozzle 653.5
sot *n.* fool 501.1
  drunkard 959.11
sot *v.* fool 545.10
  tipple 959.15
soteriology 976.5
sotnia 726.7
sottage 499.6
sottise 499.7
sottish stupid 499.12
  bibulous 959.23
sotto voce
  in a whisper 405.11
  (voicelessly 581.9)
  secretly 528.24
sou 800.8
soubrette actor 599.19
  lady's maid 746.2
soubriquet See **sobriquet**
soufflé 298.28
sough *n.* conduit 350.1
  sink 653.8
sough *v.* blow 349.22
  murmur 405.5
soul essence 5.2
  person 372.3
  genius 498.5
  emotions 821.1
  theosophy 994.10
  psyche 994.11
  (life force 359.2)
  (mind 450.3)
  (affections 820.2)
  not a soul
    nothing 2.2
    nobody 187.7
Soul
  world spirit 359.3
  God 976.2
soulless
  languid 683.14
  unfeeling 823.5
soul mate 903.10
soul-sick 837.12
soul-stirring, soul-subduing 824.12
  (deep-felt 821.8)
sound *n.*
  bladder 191.6; 334.5
  fathomer 208.4
  sea inlet 343.1
  tone 402.2
  ~ of a trumpet 404.3; 669.1
  animal ~ 412.1
  melody 413.4
  earshot 418.4
  articulate ~ 562.1; 580.3
sound *v.* fathom 208.7
  produce sound 402.7
  toot 404.7
  reverberate 408.7
  ring 408.8
  whistle 410.8
  ~ a horn 416.18
  examine 461.15, 17
  measure 466.10
  ~ a trumpet 531.7

1098

sound — spark

utter 580.8
~ a fanfare 883.3
sound an alarm
  signal 550.20
  alarm 669.3
  (warn 668.6)
  scare 860.10
sound a tatto
  toot 404.7
  drum 407.8
  beat time 416.19
sound off 403.4, 9
sound out 461.15
sound *adj.*
  substantial 3.4
  great 31.6
  fast 43.11
  conformable 82.10
  stable 150.5
  strong 159.12
  infallible 474.14
  logical 476.16
  true 494.12, 14
  wise 498.11
  perfect 650.5
  healthy 654.4
  safe 664.10
  preserved 670.6
  solvent 800.22
  orthodox 983a.7
soundable 310.6
soundboard 417.13
sounded 402.11
  (vocal 580.12)
sounding *n.*
  depth 208.4
  sonation 402.3
sounding *adj.* 402.9
soundings 208.4
  in soundings 267.54
  take soundings 208.7
sounding lead, sounding machine 208.4
sound law 402.5
soundless
  abysmal 208.9
  silent 403.6
soundlessness 403.1
soundness
  stability 150.1
  ~ of mind 502.1
  ~ of body 654.1
  solvency 800.17
  ~ of doctrine 983a.1
sound shifting 402.5
soup power 157.1
  aeronautics 267a.19
  food 298.16
  semiliquid 352.3
  fog 353.5
in the soup 704.11
soup-and-fish 225.14
soupçon
  modicum 32.2
  tincture 41.3
  taste 390.1
souper 114.6
soupy 353.11
sour *v.* acidify 397.4
  aggravate 835.2
sour *adj.* tart 397.6
  (pungent 392.5)

(bitter 395.6)
off-key 414.4
gruff 895.7
ill-humored 901.7
sourbelly 837.5
sourbread
  bread 298.11
  sour 397.2
source 153.1
  (fountain 348.5)
sour cream 397.2
sourdine, sordine *n.*
  mute 408a.3
  music 417.11
sourdine, sordine *adj.*
  408a.6
sourdook drink 298.4
  sour 397.2
sourdough 188.8
soured sour 397.6
  ill-humored 901.7
souren 397.4
sour grapes sour 397.2
  unattainability 471.2
  lame excuse 619.1
cry sour grapes
  dissemble 544.6
  pretext 619.2
souring vinegar 397.2
  acidification 397.3
sourness 397
  (pungency 392.1)
  (bitterness 395.2)
sour-sweet 396.8
souse *n.* spree 959.3
  drunkard 959.11
souse *v.* plunge 310.4
  submerge 310.5
  wet 337.5
  tipple 959.15, 18
soutane 999.1
souter, soutar 225.40
south *n.* 278.2
south, southeast *adj.*
  278.10
southeaster, souther
  349.11
southerly, southern
  278.10
Southern Cross 318.6
Southerner 57.3
southern lights 420.12
southing 196.1
southpaw 239.3
South Pole 383.4
southward 278.10, 11
southwester 349.11
souvenir
  memento 505.5
  trophy 551.4
sovereign *n.*
  suzerain 737.16
  potentate 745.2
  gold piece 800.5
sovereign *adj.*
  supreme 33.8
  independent 748.17
sovereignty
  dominion 737.2
  (supremacy 33.3)
  deity 976.2
soviet 696.4

sovietism 737.6
sow *n.* swine 366.7
  female animal 374.8
  ingot 635.6
sow *v.* disperse 73.3
  plant 371.8
sow broadcast
  disperse 73.3
  waste 638.2
  squander 818.3
sow one's wild oats
  carouse 840.21
  sin 945.9
  debauch 954.3
sow the seeds of
  cause 153.6
  teach 537.9
sow the wind and reap the whirlwind
  be unskillful 699.7
  fail 732.5
  suffer the consequences 972.12
  be rewarded 973.4
sowar 726.4
sow-belly 298.23
sower 371.2
sowing 673.3
Soyot 560.4
sozzle See **sossle**
spa 662.17
  (resort 189.14)
space *n.* degree 26.1
  time 106.1
  period 108.1
  occasion 134.2
  extension 180
  interval 198.1
  music 415.22
  type 591.9
space *v.* arrange 60.6
  interval 198.4
spaced 198.5
spacious
  extensive 180.6
  (sizable 192.11)
  broad 202.6
spade *n.*
  shovel 191.14; 252.7
  playing card 840.13
spade *v.* ladle 270.10
  cultivate 371.8
spahi, spahee 726.4
span *n.* pair 89.2
  period 108.1
  short time 111.3
  proportions 180.5
  distance 196.1
  (length 200.1)
  short way 197.2
  (shortness 201.1)
  breadth 202.1
  arch 215.18
  of horses 272.9
  ship's rope 273.10
  bridge 627.7
span *v.* resemble 17.7
  join 43.5
  pair 89.3
  measure 466.10
spangle *n.* 847.2
spangle *v.* 847.11

spangled
  luminous 420.22
  ornamented 847.13
Spaniard 188.9
spaniel dog 366.6
  sycophant 886.2
Spanish 560.4
Spanish-American War 722.4
Spanish Armada 722.5
Spanish fly
  excitant 171.4
  aphrodisiac 865.10
Spanish green 435.2
Spanish-walnut oil
  356.3
spank *n.* 276.3
spank *v.* speed 274.9
  whip 972.6
spanker
  large thing 192.6
  sail 273.13
spanker boom 273.12
spanking vast 31.8
  huge 192.15
spar *n.*
  suspender 214.3
  support 215.12, 13
  ship 273.12
  boxing match 720.6
spar *v.* argue 476.11
  quarrel 713.7
  fight 720.8
spar down 267.10
spar-decker 273.1
spare *v.* preserve 670.3
  not use 678.5
  refrain from 681.2
  be lenient 740.2
  exempt 748.10
  relinquish 782.3
  give up 784.11
  abstain 953.5
to spare
  remaining 40.6
  in reserve 636.9
  superfluous 641.5
spare *adj.*
  additional 37.7
  remaining 40.6
  thin 203.11
  in reserve 636.9
  meager 640.9
  superfluous 641.5
  economical 817.4
spared 748.18
be spared 359.9
sparerib 203.6
spare room 180.2
spare time 685.1
  (interim 109a.1)
  (vacation 687.2)
sparge *n.* 337.3
sparge *v.* 337.5
sparing meager 640.9
  economical 817.4
  parsimonious 819.4
  temperate 953.6
sparingly 817.5
spark *n.* modicum 32.2
  electricity 158a.1
  ~ of life 359.2

spark — speculation

spark (*continued*)
  fire 382.8
  light 420.5
  wit 844
  fop 854.1
  lover 897.6
spark *v.* bubble 353.8
  glitter 420.18
  court 902.7
sparker igniter 388.4
  suitor 897.6
sparkle *n.* 420.5
sparkle *v.* bubble 353.8
  glitter 420.18
  be witty 824.8
sparkler 382.9
sparkling
  effervescent 353.10
  glittery 420.23
  style 574.4
  excited 824.9
  cheerful 836.7
  witty 842.9
  beauty 845.13
spark plug 272.16
sparks
  electrician 158a.10
  telegrapher 532a.6
sparrer 726.2
sparrow 366.22
sparse
  inconsiderable 32.8
  scattered 73.4
  scanty 103.3
  scarce 640.10
sparsely
  scatteringly 73.6
  meagerly 103.5
  (infrequently 137.3)
sparseness 103.1
  (infrequency 137.1)
sparsim
  scatteringly 73.6
  sparsely 103.5
Spartacus 742.3
Spartan *n.*
  taciturn person 585.2
  stoic 823.2
Spartan *adj.* 739.5
spasm
  convulsion 315.7
  (violence 173.1)
  (pain 378.1)
  seizure 655.3
  fury 825.4
spasmodic
  irregular 139.2
  (discontinuous 70.4)
  (transient 111.6)
  (infrequent 137.2)
  inconstant 149.6
spasmodically 70.5
spastic 139.2
spat *n.* rudiment 153.3
  young 167.3
  quarrel 713.3
spat *v.*
  give birth 161.9
  quarrel 713.7
spathic 204.5

spatter sprinkle 73.3
  splash 337.5
  discolor 440a.2
  dirty 653.15
spatula ladle 191.14
  painter's ~ 556.16
  modeler's ~ 557.8
spavined 655.24
spawn *n.*
  rudiment 153.3
  young 167.3
spawn *v.* 161.9
spay 38.7
speak
  signal ship 267.41
  signal 550.20
  talk 582.6
  (argue 476.11)
  (tell 527.7)
  (divulge 529.4)
  (announce 531.7)
  (gossip 532.7)
  (assert 535.3)
  (express 566.3)
  (voice 580.8)
  (exclaim 580.9)
  (declaim 582.7)
  (chatter 584.4)
  (converse 588.7)
  (soliloquize 589.3)
speak by the card
  be careful 459.3
  be truthful 543.2
  phrase 566.3
speak daggers 932.8
speak for 937.6
speak for itself
  show 467.7
  be intelligible 518.2
  be manifest 525.3, 8
  indicate 550.18
speak one fair 894.7
speak one's mind
  speak out 582.6
  be artless 703.3
  (be truthful 543.2)
speak out
  manifest oneself 525.2
  be artless 703.3
speak up
  break silence 582.6
  defend 937.6
speak volumes
  show 467.7
  be intelligible 518.2
  indicate 550.18
speak with 588.7
speak-easy 959.13
speaker
  sound device 418.6
  talker 582.5
  (gossip 532.5)
  (chatterer 584.3)
  (conversationalist 588.5)
  (soliloquist 589.2)
  director 694.1
  deputy 759.1
speaking *n.* 582.3
speaking *adj.*
  alike 17.15

  talking 582.11
speaking of
  apropos 9.10
  incidentally 134.11
speaking trumpet 418.6
spear *n.* stalk 215.14
  weapon 727.5
  (knife 253.6)
  (perforator 262)
spear *v.* 260.14
spearlike 253.14
spearman 726.4
special
  classificational 75.6
  specific 79.7
  (circumstantial 8.5)
  noteworthy 642.10
special delivery 592.4
by special delivery 270.12
specialist 662.19
speciality 79
specialize
  differentiate 15.6
  particularize 79.6
specially 79.11
special pleading 477.1
  (pretext 619.1)
  (defense 937.2)
specialty
  contract 769.1
  pledge 771.1
specie 800.4
species kind 75.2
  animal kingdom 366.1
  vegetable kingdom 367.1
specific *n.* 662.1
specific *adj.*
  classificational 75.6
  special 79.7
  limited 233.3
specification
  condition 469.2
  mention 527.1
  indication 550.1
  stipulation 770.1
specifications 594.1
  (outline 626.2)
specific gravity 321.1
specificness 79.1
specify designate 79.5
  limit 233.2
  call attention 457.7
  (inform 527.7)
  (indicate 550.18)
  name 564.6
  tell in detail 594.6
specimen
  example 82.2
  taster 390.1
speciosity 477.1
specious
  plausible 472.6
  sophistical 477.9
  spurious 545.13
  suave 894.13
  flattering 933.3
speck *n.* modicum 32.2
  inextension 180a.1

  diminutive 193.2
  mark 550.7
  soil 653.3
  blemish 848.1
speck *v.* spot 440.4
  discolor 440a.2
  soil 653.15
specked 440.9
  (imperfect 651.4)
speckle *n.* mark 550.7
  soil 653.3
  blemish 848.1
speckle *v.* spot 440.4
  discolor 440a.2
  soil 653.15
speckled, speckledy 440.9
  (blemished 848.3)
spectacle sight 448.2
  (display 525.1)
  drama 599.3
  phenomenon 872.1
  show 882.3
spectacled 445.10
spectaclemaker 690.8
spectacles 445.3
spectacular
  dramatic 599.28
  ostentatious 882.9
spectator 444
  (attender 186.7)
  (theatergoer 599.23)
be a spectator 444.3
  (attend 186.9)
  (look 441.11)
specter, spectre
  eyesore 846.3
  ghost 980a
  (optical illusion 443.9)
specter-haunted, spectre-haunted 980a.5
spectral 980a.4
  (chimerical 4.6)
  (immaterial 317.6)
  (supernatural 976.14)
  (spiritual 994.22)
spectrograph, spectroheliogram 556.14
spectroscope
  chromoscope 428.8
  scope 445.1
spectrum
  variegation 440.2
  apparition 443.9
speculate
  ponder 451.27
  gamble 621.17
  (experiment 463.10)
  venture 675.3
  business 794.9
speculation
  vision 441.1
  scrutiny 441.2
  thought 451.1
  supposition 514.1
  chance 621.2, 6
  (experiment 463.3)
  business 794.2
  game 840.12

1100

speculative
  thoughtful 451.35
  experimental 463.12
  undecided 475.9,
    10, 14
  (hazardous 621.19)
  supposititious 514.9
speculator
  theorist 514.5
  gambler 621.15
  (experimenter
    463.6)
speculum
  plumage 256.9
  mirror 445.4
sped 729.6
speech language 560.1
  diction 569.1
  talk 582
  (utterance 580.3)
  (chatter 584.2)
  (allocution 586.1)
  (dissertation 595.1)
  conversation 588.1
  make a speech 582.7
speechcraft
  linguistics 560.6
  oratory 582.3
speech defect 583.1
speechification 582.2
speechifier 582.5
speechify 582.7
speechless 581.7
  (silent 585.4)
speechlore 560.6
speechmaker 582.5
**speech melody, speech
  sound, speech tune**
  402.2
speed *n.*
  character 5.4
  aeronautics 267a.17
  velocity 274.1
  (haste 684.1)
  success 731.1
speed *v.* go fast 274.9
  (make haste 684.3)
  hasten 684.2
  aid 707.6
  succeed 731.5
  prosper 734.5
speed up 274.10
  (hasten 684.2)
speedboat 273.4
speed maniac, speeder
  automobilist 268.10
  goer 274.5
speedily 132.14
speedometer
  automobile 272.16
  velocimeter 274.8
  recorder 553.3
speed-up 274.2
speedway 627.3
speed writing 590.7
speedy 274.13
  (sudden 113.5)
  (hasty 684.5)
spell *n.* time 106.1
  period 108.1
  interim 109a.1
  distance 196.1

short way 197.1
~ of work 686.3
respite 687.2
witchery 993
  (sorcery 992.1)
  (trance 994.6)
spell *v.* study 539.4
  orthographize 561.8
  charm 992.4
spellbind orate 582.7
  cast a spell 992.4
spellbinder 582.5
spellbinding 992.6
spellbound
  astonished 870.6
  bewitched 992.7
**spelldown, spelling,
  spelling bee** etc.
  561.4
spell-struck 992.7
spence room 191.16
  storeroom 636.4
spencer 225.16
Spencerianism 161.5
spend
  ~ time 106.3;
    625.6, 7
  discharge 297.13
  use up 638.2; 677.6
  expend 809.3
  (purchase 795.3)
  be liberal 816.3
  squander 818.3
spend-all, spender
  818.2
spending 809.1
spending money 800.14
spendthrift 818.2
spent impotent 158.8
  weak 160.10
  worn out 659.8
  tired out 688.6
  expended 807.10
sperm rudiment 153.3
  oil 356.2
  germ 357.4
spermatic
  procreative 168.8
  germinal 357.10
spermatize 168.4
spermatocyte 357.4
**spermatogenetic,
  spermatoid, spermatophoral** 357.10
spermatophore 357.4
Spermatophyta 369.8
spermatozoal 357.10
spermatozoid, spermatogonium 357.4
sperm oil 356.4
spew vomit 297.18
  spit 297.19
sphacelate *v.* 659.7
sphacelate *adj.*
  diseased 655.25
  decayed 659.13
sphacelation 655.16
sphere *n.* degree 26.1
  class 75.1
  extent 180.1
  region 181.1
  ball 249.2

(oval 247.3)
(rotation 312.4)
world 318.1
heavenly body 318.3
atmosphere 338.1
~ of business 625.3
arena 728.1
rank 873.4
sphere *v.* orb 249.2
  rotund 249.5
spherical 249.6
  (circular 247.8)
sphericity 249.1
spherify 249.5
spheroid *n.* 249.2
spheroid *adj.* 249.7
spheroidicity 249.1
spheroidize 249.5
spherule, spherulite
  249.2
sphery 318.16
sphinx 83.7
sphinx oracle 513.2
  equivocalness 520.1
  the Sphinx
  wisdom 498.3
  enigma 533.2
  deity 979.5
sphygmometer 662.22
spiccato note 413.6
  music 415.15, 20
spice *n.* modicum 32.2
  tincture 41.3
  taste 390.1
  condiment 393.1
  odor 398.1
spice *v.* 392.4
spiced
  flavorsome 390.4
  seasoned 392.5
  (flavorful 390.4)
spick 57.3
spick-and-span 123.9
spiculate *v.* 253.9
spiculate *adj.* 253.11
spicule, spiculum 253.2
spicy pungent 392.5
  (exciting 824.12)
  fragrant 400.10
spider pan 191.11
  insect 368.8
  skillet 386.1
spiel *n.* speech 582.2
  sales talk 796.3
spiel *v.* 582.6, 7
spieler cheat 548.2
  stageman 599.17
  solicitor 767.1; 797.4
  swindler 792.8
spigot stopper 263.1
  valve 263.2
spike *n.* pin 45.5
  point 253.2
  stopper 263.1
spike *v.* disable 158.6
  (checkmate 731.10)
  perforate 260.14
spike one's guns
  disable 158.6
  hinder 706.7
spiked 253.11
  (bristly 256.14)

spiketail 225.14
spike team three 92.2
  team 272.9
spiky 253.11
spile pole 206.4
  stopper 263.1
spilehole 351.1
spileworm 366.25
spiling 206.4
spill *n.* strip 205.5
  stopper 263.1
  fall 306.2
  upset 308.2
  ~ blood 361.10;
    722.9
  lighter 388.4
spill *v.* pour out 297.13
  upset 308.5
  overflow 348.18
  divulge 529.4
  waste 638.2
  squander 818.3
spill the beans 529.4
spin *n.* ride 266.7
  aerobatics 267a.24
  whirl 312.2
spin *v.* ride 266.18
  aviate 267a.31
  rotate 312.7
  eddy 348.21
  fabricate 544.3
  ~ a long yarn 549.2;
    573.5
  fish 622.8
spin out
  protract time 110.6
  lengthen 200.9
  expatiate 573.5
spina 235.4
spinach 298.30
spinal 215.31; 235.12
spinal column 235.4
spindle handle 215.7
  axis 312.5
**spindle-legged,
  spindle-shanked**
  long-legged 200.13
  thin 203.11
spindlelegs, spindleshanks
  thin person 203.6
  legs 266.11
spindling, spindly
  203.11
spindrift 353.2
spine ridge 206.2
  backbone 235.4
  point 253.2
spinel, spinelle 847.8
spineless 945.12
spinet 417.6
spinner
  airplane 273a.10
  liar 548.5
  narrator 594.4
spinney 367.7
spinosity
  sharpness 253.1
  gruffness 895.2
spinous pointed 253.11
  gruff 895.7
spinozism 451.11

spinster — spokesman

spinster 904.3
spinsterhood 904.1
spinsterish, spinsterly 904.5
spinulescent, spinuliferous, spinulose 253.11
spiny pointed 253.11
  difficult 704.8
spiracle opening 260.1
  air hole 351.1
spiral *n.* coil 248.2
  (turn 311.2)
  aerobatics 267a.24
  ornamentation 847.3
spiral *v.* 267a.31
spiral *adj.* 248.4
spiral balance 319.5
spiral nebula 420.12
spiral stairs 305.2
spirant 402.2
spire *n.* tower 206.3
  summit 210.1
  stalk 215.14
  point 253.4
spire *v.* be high 206.9
  ascend 305.6
spiriferous 248.5
spirit *n.* essence 5.2
  nature 5.3
  genius 498.5
  meaning 516.1
  vigorous style 574.2
  animation 682.1
  (energy 171.1)
  mood 820.1
  ardor 821.2
  courage 861.1
  specter 980a.1
  (incorporeity 317.2)
  psyche 994.11
  (life force 359.2)
  (mind 450.3)
spirit *v.* 615.7
spirit away 791.11
spirit up
  stimulate 615.7
  rouse feeling 824.2
spirited style 574.6
  active 682.16
  cheerful 836.7
  courageous 861.8
spiritful cheerful 836.7
  courageous 861.8
spiritism 994.4
spiritist 994.14
spiritistic 994.22
spiritize
  immaterialize 317.5
  spiritualize 994.20
spiritless
  dispassionate 823.5
  sad 837.9
  weary 841.9
  cowardly 862.4
spirit rapper 994.14
spirit rapping 994.5
spirits
  cheerfulness 836.1
  distilled liquors 959.4, 6
  in good spirits 836.7

  in low spirits 837.9
spiritual *n.* 415.11
spiritual *adj.*
  intellectual 450.8
  spectral 980a.4
  (immaterial 317.6)
  (supernatural 976.14)
  heavenly-minded 987.10
  psychical 994.22
spiritual director 996.2
spiritualism 994.4
  (immaterialism 317.3)
  (divination 511.2)
spiritualist 994.14
  (immaterialist 317.4)
spiritualistic 994.22
spirituality
  immateriality 317.1
  piety 987.1
spiritualize
  immaterialize 317.5
  spiritize 994.20
spiritual-minded 987.10
spiritual-mindedness 987.1
spirituosity 317.1
spirituous 959.24
spiritus 5.2
spirit writing 994.5
spirograph 662.22
spiroid 248.5
spirometer 662.22
spirt, spirtle See spurt etc.
spissitude
  density 321.1
  viscidity 352.1
spit *n.* likeness 17.6
  point 253.2
  saliva 299.5
  rotator 312.4
  turnspit 386.3
spit *v.* empale 260.14
  expectorate 297.19
  rain 348.25
spit upon 930.5
spit curl 256.3
spite malignity 907.1
  envy 921.1
in spite of 30.8
  (in disagreement 24.10)
  (counteractively 179.6)
  (in defiance of 708.6)
spiteful 907.6
  (hateful 898.7)
spitfire violent 173.6
  ill-humored person 901.4
spitting 299.5
spitting image 17.6
spittle 299.5
spittoon 191.1
spitz 366.6

splanchnic
  visceral 221.11
  textural 329.3
splanchnological 329.3
splanchnology
  enterology 221.6
  texture 329.2
splash *n.* swash 348.5
  splurge 882.1
make a splash 873.10
splash *v.* spill 297.13
  splatter 337.5
  swash 348.19
  murmur 405.5
  dirty 653.15
  splurge 882.6
splashy marshy 345.3
  muddy 352.9
  showy 882.8
splatter splash 337.5
  dirty 653.15
splay window 260.5
  ornament 847.4
splayfoot *n.* 211.4
splayfoot *adj.* 243.5
spleen anger 900.1
  irascibility 901.1
spleeny *adj.*
  angry 900.13
  irascible 901.7
splendid bright 420.22
  beautiful 845.13
  ornate 847.13
  illustrious 873.17
  showy 882.8
splendor, splendour
  brightness 420.1
  importance 642.1
  gorgeousness 845.2
  illustriousness 873.2
  pomp 882.1
splendorous, splendrous
  bright 420.22
  beautiful 845.13
  illustrious 873.17
splenetic angry 900.13
  irascible 901.7
splenic fever 655.18
splice *n.* 43.3
splice *v.* tie 43.6
  interlace 219.8
  repair 660.11
  marry 903.12
splice the main brace 959.15
splint *n.*
  supporter 215.2
  bandage 662.14
splint *v.* 662.24
splinter *n.*
  modicum 32.2
  piece 51.3
  thinness 203.5
  strip 205.5
splinter *v.*
  disintegrate 44.9
  be brittle 328.3
splinternew 123.9
splintery 328.4
split *n.* cleft 198.2
  dissension 713.2

split *v.* part 44.8, 10, 11
  (bisect 91.4)
  open 260.11
  be brittle 328.3
  inform on 527.10
  blab 529.4
  quarrel 713.7
  apportion 786.3
  ~ with laughter 838.7
split hairs
  discriminate 465.2
  quibble 477.8
  be hypercritical 868.3
split one's sides 838.7
split the difference
  average 29.2
  compromise 774.2
  go shares 778.5
split the ears
  be loud 404.5
  be strident 410.7
  deafen 419.7
split up
  partition 44.10, 11
  apportion 786.3
  divorce 905.4
split *adj.* 44.12
split personality 503.2
splitsaw 257.3
splurge *n.* 882.1
splurge *v.* 882.6
splutter *n.*
  activity 171.2
  flutter 315.5
  bustle 682.6
  hurry 684.1
  bluster 887.1
splutter *v.*
  salivate 297.19
  flutter 315.10
  sputter 583.2
  hurry about 684.3
  bluster 887.3
spode 384.14
spoil *n.* 793.1
spoil *v.* impair 659.7, 8
  botch 699.9
  thwart 706.7
  indulge 704.5
  plunder 791.10
  satiate 869.4
spoiler
  airplane 273a.10
  plunderer 792.1
spoilsport
  marplot 706.3
  sad person 837.5
spoke radius 200.4
  hindrance 706.2
spoken 582.10
  (verbal 562.8)
  (enunciatory 580.11)
  (conversational 588.10)
spokesman
  informant 527.5
  speaker 582.5
  (interlocutor 588.5)
  deputy 759.1

(interpreter 524.1)
(mediator 724.2)
(lawyer 968.1)
spokeswoman 759.1
spoliate 791.10
spoliation 791.2
spoliative 791.14
spondaic 597.13
spondee 597.6
spondulics, spondulix 800.1
sponge *n.* stopper 263.1
  animal 368.4
  blotter 652.7
  dressing 662.14
  sponger 815.5
  sycophant 886.2
  drunkard 959.11
sponge *v.* dry 340.5
  ~ out 552.2
  wash 652.9
  squeeze from 789.11
  extort 791.13
  ~ a debt 808.8
  be a dependent 886.3
sponger 886.2
  (beggar 767.2)
sponging 886.4
sponging house 752.1
spongiose, spongious 368.13
spongy porous 260.17
  rare 322.4
  soft 324.9
  marshy 345.3
  pulpy 354.5
sponsion 771.2
sponsor witness 467.6
  guarantor 771.2
  become sponsor for 768.3
  be sponsor for 926.5
sponsorial 771.11
sponsorship 771.2
spontaneity 600.1
spontaneous
  instinctive 477a.4
  involuntary 601.14
  voluntary 602.10
  (impulsive 612.4)
  (free 748.1)
spontoon 727.5
spoof *n.* 545.1, 3
spoof *v.* 545.10
spoofery 545.1
spook 980a.1
spooky 980a.4
spool 312.5
spoon *n.* ladle 191.14
  lover 897.6
spoon *v.* fish 622.8
  make love 902.7
spoondrift 353.2
spooner 807.6
spoonerism
  blunder 495.3
  ridiculousness 855.1
spoon food 298.8
spoonful
  quantity 25.2
  modicum 32.2
spooning 902.1

spoon meat, spoon victual 298.8
spoony, spooney *n.*
  fool 501.1
  lover 897.6
spoony, spooney *adj.*
  foolish 499.15
  amorous 897.14
spoor 550.4
sporaceous 330.8
sporadic
  scattered 73.4
  irregular 139.2
  epidemic 657.5
sporadically 70.5
  (occasionally 137.4)
sporadic disease 655.1
spore 330.3
sporocarp, sporocyst, sporocyte 357.4
sporogenous
  productional 161.11
  germinal 357.10
sporophorous 161.11
sporophyte 357.4
sporous 330.8
sport *n.* gambler 621.15
  hunting 622.2
  exercise 686.2
  amusement 840.1, 10, 11
  (swimming 267.9)
  (contest 720.2)
  sportsman 840.17
  in sport
    playfully 840.25
    in jest 842.10
sport *v.* wear 225.45
  gamble 621.17
  hunt 622.7
  play 840.21
  flaunt 882.7
  sport one's oak 893.6
sporting 622.2
sportive 836.10; 840.23
sport of kings
  game of chance 621.7
  horseracing 720.5
  game 840.11
sportsman
  gambler 621.15
  huntsman 622.4
  gamester 840.17
sportswear 798.3
sportula 784.3
sporty gaudy 851.8
  showy 882.8
sporule 330.3
sposh mud 352.4
  filth 653.5
sposhy marshy 345.3
  muddy 352.9
spot *n.*
  inextension 180a.1
  location 184.1
  short way 197.2
  spotlight 423.3; 599.14
  discoloration 440a.1
  mark 550.7
  soil 653.3

blemish 848.1
stigma 874.2
moral blemish 945.5
in spots
  irregularly 59.12
  scatteringly 73.6
  sparsely 103.5
on the spot
  on the instant 113.6
  now 118.3
  promptly 132.14
  here 186.20
  dying 360.9
spot *v.* mottle 440.4
  discolor 440a.2
  (mark 550.19)
  see 441.10
  discover 481a.3, 6
  reidentify 505.10
  soil 653.15
spotless perfect 650.5
  clean 652.14
  (pure 960.2)
spotlight light 420.7
  lamp 423.3
  publicity 531.3
  limelight 599.14
  in the spotlight
    publicly 531.12
    acting 599.29
spot news 532.1
spotted 440.9
  (discolored 440a.3)
  (imperfect 651.4)
  (blemished 848.3)
spotter
  aeronaut 269a.1
  informer 527.6
  spy 528.8, 9
spotting 847.3
spotty 440.9
spousage 903.1
spousal 903.14
spousals 903.3
spouse
  accompanier 88.3
  married person 903.5
spousehood 903.1
spouseless 904.5
spout *n.*
  stream 348.5, 7, 11
  conduit 350.1
  (outlet 295.5)
  pawnshop 787.3
spout *v.* flow out 295.7
  let out 297.13
  jet 348.20
  declaim 582.7
  be loquacious 584.4
  act 599.26
  pawn 771.5
spouty 345.3
sprain weaken 160.2
  injure 659.8
sprawl
  outstretch 200.8
  recline 213.5
  fall 306.6
  repose 687.3
spray *n.* member 51.4
  shot 284.4; 406.2

atomizer 336.3
sprinkler 337.3
jet 348.5
foam 353.2
foliage 367.4
flowers 400.4
perfumer 400.5
barrage 716.2
ornamentation 847.5
spray *v.* atomize 336.5
  sprinkle 337.5
spread *n.* caption 66.3
  dispersion 73.1
  (increase 35.1)
  extent 180.1
  size 192.1
  expansion 194.1
  distance 196.1
  breadth 202.1
  coverlet 223.9
  meal 298.34, 37
  publicity 531.4
spread *v.* disperse 73.3
  (increase 35.3)
  (diverge 291.2)
  generalize 78.8
  expand 194.5, 8
  broaden 202.4
  open 260.11
  ~ sail 267.16
  publish 531.7
  be published 531.9
spread *adj.* 194.10
spread eagle *n.* 884.2, 4
spread-eagle *v.*
  fall 306.6
  overthrow 308.5
  exaggerate 549.2
  boast 884.5
spread-eagle *adj.*
  overpatriotic 549.3
  jingoistic 884.8
spread-eagleism
  overpatriotism 549.1
  jingoism 884.2
spreadhead 66.3
spree *n.* frolic 840.3
  (dissipation 954.2)
  drinking bout 959.3
spree *v.* revel 840.21
  wassail 959.16
sprig member 51.4
  youngling 129.1
  foliage 367.4
sprightly
  nimble 682.17
  cheerful 836.7
  witty 842.9
spring *n.*
  season 126a.2
  source 153.2
  strength 159.1
  ship's rope 273.10
  recoil 277.1
  leap 309.1
  elasticity 325.1
  fountain 348.5
  motive 615.1
  source of supply 636.2
spring *v.*
  ~ from 154.5

spring balance — squash

spring (*continued*)
  give birth 161.9
  speed 274.9
  ~ off 293.5
  leap 309.4
  ~ forth 446.2
spring a leak
  be defective 651.3
  break 659.6
spring a mine
  demolish 162.4
  surprise 508.6
  attack 716.6
spring a surprise
  508.6
spring back 277.3
  (be elastic 325.3)
spring up
  originate 66.6
  happen 151.3
  grow 194.6
  ascend 305.4
  appear 446.2
spring upon
  surprise 508.6
  seize 789.13
spring balance 319.5
springbok, springbuck
  366.10
spring chicken 366.23
springe *n.* 545.4
springe *v.* 545.9
spring fever 683.7
spring gun snare 545.4
  hidden danger 667.1
springhead 153.2
springiness 325.1
springs 662.17
spring scale 319.5
springtail 366.24
springtide
  season 126a.2
  youth 127.1
spring tide
  increase 35.1
  fullness 52.3
  height 206.5
  tide 348.9
springtime 126a.2
springtrap 545.4
spring water 337.1
springy 325.5
sprinkle *n.* 348.11
sprinkle *v.* add to 37.3
  imbue 41.8
  scatter 73.3
  wet 337.5
  rain 348.25
  spot 440.4
  asperge 998.14
sprinkler 337.3
sprinkling
  modicum 32.2
  mixture 41.2, 3
  baptism 998.5
sprint *n.* 274.3
sprint *v.* 274.9
sprit descendant 167.4
  shaft 215.13
  spar 273.12
sprite fairy 979.9
  imp 980.3

spirit 980a.1
sprocket 253.3
sprout *n.*
  descendant 167.4
  foliage 367.4
  upstart 876.8
sprout *v.*
  ~ from 154.3
  bear 161.9
  grow 194.6; 365.2
sprouting 194.3
spruce *n.* tree 367.6
  wood 635.3
spruce *v.* 60.6
spruce up clean 652.9
  adorn 847.11
  (dress 225.44)
spruce *adj.*
  orderly 58.7
  trim 845.11
  smart 847.14
  (fashionable 852.7)
sprue dregs 40.2
  type 591.6
sprung
  intoxicated 959.21
  impaired 659.12
spry active 682.17
  spirited 836.7
spud 191.14
spuddy 201.6
spume *n.* 353.2
spume *v.* 353.8
spunk, sponk
  tinder 388.6
  resolution 604.1
  enterprise 682.4
  courage 861.1
  anger 900.1
sponk See **spunk**
spun-out
  protracted 110.10
  verbose 573.7
spur *n.* member 51.4
  electricity 158a.6
  promontory 250.5
  point 253.2
  incentive 615.3
spur *v.*
  ~ a horse 370.7
  urge 615.7
  hasten 684.2
  (accelerate 274.10)
spur gearing 312.4
spurious 545.13
  (approximative 17.14)
  (imitation 19.12)
  (unauthentic 495.16)
  (disguised 528.20)
  (false 544.7)
  (untrue 546.6)
  (pretexed 619.3)
  (affected 853.6)
spuriously 545.15
spurn *n.* 930.4
spurn *v.* reject 610.2
  scorn 930.5, 7
spurt, spirt *n.*
  short time 111.3
  dash 274.3

jet 348.5
impulse 612.1
exertion 686.3
spurt, spirt *v.*
  dash ahead 274.11
  pour out 297.13
  jet 348.20
spurtle, spirtle *n.*
  spurt 274.3
  flow 348.4, 5
spurtle, spirtle *v.*
  348.19, 20
sputter *n.* flutter 315.5
  fuss 682.6
  hurry 684.1
  bluster 887.1
sputter *v.*
  salivate 297.19
  flutter 315.10
  sibilate 409.3
  splutter 583.2
  bluster 887.3
sputum 299.5
spy *n.* informer 527.6
  secret agent 528.8
  (watcher 444.1)
  (investigator 461.13)
spy *v.* 441.10
spy out
  look about 441.11
  reconnoiter 461.22
  discover 481a.3
spyglass 445.2
squab *n.*
  weakling 160.4
  fat man 192.7
  seat 215.22
  food 298.26
  bird 366.22
squab *adj.* 201.6
squabble *n.* 713.3
squabble *v.* 713.7
squabby 201.6
squad company 72.3
  party 712.1
  military unit 726.7
squadron 726.7, 9, 10
squalid untidy 59.9
  unclean 653.16
  ugly 846.8
squall *n.* turmoil 59.4
  wind 349.6
  broil 713.4
squall *v.* blow 349.22
  cry 411.5; 412.2
  wail 839.9
squall cloud 353.5
squally 349.25
squalor disorder 59.1
  uncleanness 653.1
  (ugliness 846.1)
squamose 204.5
squamosity 204.3
squander 818.3
  (waste 638.2)
  (overdo 641.3)
  (lose 776.3)
  (be intemperate 954.3)
squanderer 818.2
squandering 818.1

1104

(dissipation 776.1)
squantum 840.2
square *n.*
  quadrilateral 95.1
  block 189.18
  plaza 189.19
  (plot 181.3)
  vertical 212.2
  instrument 212.5
  yard 232.1
  rectangle 244.2
  hearty meal 298.36
  measure 466.4
square *v.* accord 23.8
  equalize 27.7
  compensate 30.5
  quadrate 95.3
  plumb 212.7
  true 494.7
  bribe 618.3
square the circle
  471.5
square up
  compensate 30.5
  sketch 556.17
  fight 720.8
  square with 23.7
square *adj.* equal 27.8
  quadrilateral 95.4
  rectangular 244.5
  accurate 494.11
  fair 941.3
square *adv.*
  vertically 212.9
  accurately 494.16
square chain 466.3
square dance 840.7
square deal 941.1
  give a square deal
  941.2
square-dealing 941.3
squarehead alien 57.3
  Scandinavian 188.9
  dolt 501.1
square inch 180.5
square link 466.3
square meal 298.36
**square measure,
  square meter,
  square pole** etc.
  466.3
square rig 225.8
square-rigger 273.2
square rod 466.3
square shooter 939.5
square shooting 941.1
square yard
  proportions 180.5
  measure 466.3
squash *n.* blow 276.3
  vegetable 298.30
  mud 352.4
  pulp 354.2
  game 840.11
squash *v.* destroy 162.4
  floor 213.7
  flatten 251.4
  soften 324.4
  pulp 354.4
  silence 403.5
  sibilate 409.3
  confute 479.2

squashy soft 324.6
  sodden 339.8
  marshy 345.3
  viscid 352.8, 9
  pulpy 354.5
squat v. settle 184.14
  crouch 207.5
  sit 308.6
squat adj. stubby 201.6
  (little 193.8)
  low 207.7
squatter 188.5
squattish, squatty
  201.6
squaw woman 374.2
  wife 903.8
squawk squall 412.2
  confess 529.5
squawkie 599.9
squawky 410.9
squeak
  stridulate 410.5
  cry 411.5; 412.2
  confess 529.5
squeaker 527.6
squeaky 410.9
squeal
  stridulate 410.5
  cry 411.5; 412.2
  inform on 527.10
  (betray 940.7)
squealer 527.6
  (traitor 949.3)
squeamish sick 655.23
  fastidious 868.4
  (unwilling 603.5)
squeamishness 868.1
squeeze n.
  duplicate 21.2
  crowd 72.4
  crisis 134.4
  representation 554.3
  narrow escape 671.2
  difficulty 704.4
  embrace 894.4
squeeze v. imitate 19.5
  contract 195.4
  ~ out 301.7
  densify 321.7
  force from 744.2
  wring from 789.11
  extort 791.13
squeezers 840.12
squeezing
  extraction 301.3
  extortion 791.3
squelch destroy 162.4
  floor 213.7
  flatten 251.4
  silence 403.5
  confute 479.2
  discomfit 731.9
squelcher 479.1
squelchy soft 324.6
  marshy 345.3
  muddy 352.9
squib firework 382.9
  fuse 388.4
  wick 423.12
  lampoon 934.2
  (ridicule 856.2)
squid 368.6

squidgy 201.6
squiffer 417.4
squiffy 959.21
squinch, squint n.
  443.3
squinch, squint v.
  look askance 441.15
  squint 443.12
squint-eyed, squinty
  443.14
squire n.
  attendant 746.1
  nobleman 875.4
  lover 897.6
  (escort 88.4)
squire v. escort 88.7
  court 902.7
squirearchy, squir-
  archy 875.3
squireen 875.4
squirm wiggle 315.9
  be excited 824.7
squirrel
  speeder 274.6
  animal 366.17
squirt n. child 129.3
  jet 348.5
squirt v. 297.13
squish 396.3
squishy soft 324.6
  muddy 352.9
S. R. O. 186.6
sruti, shruti 986.2
stab n. wound 659.4
  attempt 675.1
  thrust 716.3
stab v.
  perforate 260.14
  kill 361.12
  pain physically
    378.4
  wound 659.8
  attack 716.5
  pain mentally 830.3
stability n.
  uniformity 16.1
  firmness 150
  (permanence 141.1)
  (inertness 172.1)
  (quiescence 265.1)
  (resolution 604.1)
  (obstinacy 606.1)
  (inaction 681.1)
  (inactivity 683.1)
  aeronautics 267a.7
stabilization 150.1
stabilize 150.3, 4
  (sustain 143.3)
stabilized 150.5
stabilizer 273a.10
stable n. barn 189.5
  (storehouse 636.4)
  filthy place 653.10
stable adj.
  substantial 3.4
  durable 110.9
  firm 150.5
  (uniform 16.5)
  (permanent 141.6)
  (inert 172.3)
  (quiescent 265.7)
  (resolute 604.7)

(persevering 604a.3)
  sound 159.12
  well-founded 474.9
  unprecarious 664.10
  be stable 150.3
stableboy 370.4
stable equilibrium
  150.1
stableman
  stockman 370.4
  retainer 746.1
staccato n. note 413.6
  music 415.15, 20
staccato adv. 415.30
staccato mark 415.23
stack n. quantities 31.3
  bunch 72.5
  bookstack 593.13
stack v. 636.7
  stack the cards 611.3
  stack up 27.6
stadholder, stadt-
  holder 745.9
stadium theater 599.10
  arena 728.1
staff pole 206.4
  support 215.2, 15
  music 415.22
  landmark 550.10
  council 696.1
  weapon 727.7
  officials 745.8
  personnel 746.7
  scepter 747.1, 3
  pastoral ~ 999.1
staff officer 745.11
staff of life 298.5, 11
stag n. deer 366.11
  male animal 373.6
  party 892.5
stag v.
  stag the market 794.9
stage n. degree 26.1
  time 106.1
  period 108.1
  transition 144.3
  layer 204.1
  frame 215.8
  platform 215.21
  vehicle 272.6
  scene 448.2
  rostrum 542.6
  theater 599.1, 12
  arena 728.1
stage v. 599.25
stage box 599.11
stagecoach 272.6
stage coachman 268.9
stagecraft 599.2
  (acting 599.6)
stage direction 697.1
stage director 599.17
stagedom 599.1
stage fright
  nervousness 825.3
  fear 860.3
stagehand 599.17
  (workman 690.10)
stage'and 599.1
stageman, stage man-
  ager 599.17
stage play 599.3

stage player, stager
  599.19
stagery 599.2
stage-set, stage set-
  ting 448.2; 599.15
stage-struck 599.28
stage whisper 581.3
stageworthy 599.28
stagey See stagy
stagger n. gait 266.5
  aeronautics 267a.3
  attempt 675.1
stagger v. vary 149.4
  zigzag 217.8
  walk 266.16
  go slow 275.5
  flounder 315.9
  falter 475.6; 605.4
  startle 508.6
  dissuade 616.3
  agitate 824.3
  astonish 870.3
  be drunk 959.19
staggered 217.16
staggerer
  surprise 508.2
  puzzle 533.2
staggering 485.11
staggers
  twitching 315.6
  disease 655.18
staghound 366.6
stagnancy 172.1
stagnant inert 172.3
  (quiescent 265.7)
  (inactive 681.3;
    683.12)
  foul 653.17
stagnate be inert 172.2
  be quiescent 265.5
  (not do 681.2)
  (be inactive 683.8)
stagnation
  inertness 172.1
  (quiescence 265.1)
  inaction 681.1
  (inactivity 683.1)
stagy, stagey
  theatrical 599.28;
    882.9
  affected 853.6
staid wise 498.11
  composed 826.9
  serious 837.16
staidness 826.3
stain n. color 428.1, 3, 9
  discoloration 440a.1
  (mark 550.7)
  soil 653.3
  blemish 848.1
  stigma 874.2
  moral blemish 945.5
stain v.
  discolor 440a.2
  (blemish 848.2)
  soil 653.15
  (corrupt 659.9)
  stigmatize 874.7
stained glass 556.9
stainless
  perfect 650.5
  clean 652.14

stair — standpoint

stainless (*continued*)
  (innocent 946.5)
stair degree 26.1
  rank 71.1
  footing 215.4
  stairway 305.2
staircase, stairway
  305.2
stake *n.* pin 45.5
  post 215.16
  burning 384.3
  wager 621.3, 4
  security 771.1
  estate 780.2
  payment 807.2
  execution 975.4
at stake
  intended 620.4
  pledged 771.9
stake *v.* 621.17, 18
  stake out tie 43.6
  tether 751.7
stake horse, staker
  271.8
stake race 720.5
stalactite, stalagmite
  224.1
stale *n.* 299.3
stale *v.* 297.15
stale *adj.*
  antiquated 124.9
  insipid 391.2
  tainted 653.17
  (nasty 395.7)
  impaired 659.13
  trite 843.5, 6
stalemate *n.* 732.3
stalemate *v.* 731.10
stalk *n.* handle 215.7
  stem 215.14
  gait 266.5
  foliage 367.4
stalk *v.*
  ~ about 78.7
  walk 266.16
  hunt 622.7
  strut 878.3
stalker 622.4
stalking 528.3
stalking-horse
  horse 271.3
  ambush 530.1
  pretext 619.1
stall *n.* delay 133.2
  hut 189.4
  compartment 191.2
  tent 223.5
  enclosure 232.1
  aerobatics 267a.24
  theater 599.11
  mart 799.1
  diocese 995.3
  church 1000.3
stall *v.*
  procrastinate 133.5
  cease 142.6
  stop 142.7
  aviate 267a.31
stallion
  studhorse 271.3
  male animal 373.6

stalwart strong 159.10
  stout 192.12
stamin 219.5
stamina strength 159.1
  resolution 604.1
  (perseverance
  604a.1)
  courage 861.1
stammel cloth 219.5
  red 434.2
  color 434.6
stammer 583.3
stammering *n.* 583.1
stammering *adj.* 583.5
stamp *n.*
  die 22.3; 558.4
  kind 75.2
  form 240.1
  ratification 488.4
  mark 550.6, 7, 11
  type 591.6
stamp *v.* form 240.6
  walk 266.16
  engrave 558.5
  letter 561.6
  print 591.14
  complete 729.2
  ~ the foot 900.8
stamp out
  destroy 162.4
  extinguish 385.5
stampede 860.1
stamping ground
  haunt 74.2
  habitat 189.13
stance 215.4
stanch, staunch *v.*
  close 261.2
  stop a flow 348.24
  repair 660.11
stanch, staunch *adj.*
  sound 159.12
  close 261.6
  resolute 604.7
  hale 654.4
  loyal 939.10
stanchion post 215.16
  ship 273.7
**stanchless, staunch-
  less** 825.11
stand *n.* degree 26.1
  rank 71.1
  cessation 142.1
  position 184.1
  base 215.3
  footing 215.4
  table 215.20
  standstill 265.3
  vegetable life 367.1
  performance 599.8
  impasse 704.3
  resistance 719.1
at a stand
  permanently 141.8
  inactive 681.4
  at an impasse 704.11
take one's stand
  argue 476.11
  insist upon 535.5
  be resolute 604.6
  plead 619.2
  resist 719.3

demand 924.7
stand *v.* exist 1.4
  continue 106.2
  be present 186.8
  be quiescent 265.5
  resist 719.3
  endure 826.6
  brave 861.5
stand a chance
  have a chance 156.9
  be liable 177.2
  be possible 470.3
stand by
  be near 197.5
  navigation 267.69
  second 707.8
  defend 717.8
stand fair to
  have a chance 156.9
  tend to 176.2
  be liable to 177.2
  be probable 472.2
  promise 511.10
stand fire 861.5
stand for
  sail for 267.26
  typify 550.18
  represent 759.4
  candidacy 763.3
stand in good stead
  644.2
**stand in one's own
  light** 699.7
stand off
  procrastinate 133.5
  keep distance 196.4
  sail from 267.27
  recede 287.2
stand off and on
  267.24, 27
stand on 215.27
stand on one's ground
  defend 717.8
  resist 719.3
**stand on one's own
  legs**
  have one's will 600.2
  be independent 748.8
stand out
  project 250.7
  loom 446.2
  be obstinate 606.5
stand over
  be late 133.3
  postpone 133.4
stand pat
  be permanent 141.4
  be stable 150.3
  be resolute 604.6
  (be obstinate 606.5)
  not bet 621.18
stand the racket
  972.12
stand to one's guns
  861.5
stand to reason
  be certain 474.5
  be reasonable 476.12
  (demonstrate 478.2)
  be manifest 525.3
  be right 922.4
stand up

be vertical 212.6
rise up 307.7
stand the test 463.11
be true 494.5
stand up for
  approve 931.5
  defend 937.6
standard *n.*
  prototype 22.1
  (rule 80.1)
  (paragon 650.2)
  degree 26.1
  base 215.3
  post 215.16
  measurement 466.2
  ensign 550.13
  precept 697.1
  moral principle
  926.4
  good example 948.1
standard *adj.*
  mean 29.3
  authoritative 474.13
  type 591.8
  orthodox 983a.7
standard-bearer
  soldier 726.4
  officer 745.11
standardize 58.6
standard time 114.3
stand-by 599.19
standee 599.23
Ständerat, Ständerath
  696.5
stand-in
  substitute 147.2
  influence 175.1
standing
  circumstance 8.1
  degree 26.1
  rank 71.1; 873.4
  durability 110.1
  permanence 141.1
  position 184.1
  footing 215.4
standing army 726.6
standing order
  rule 80.1; 613.3
  law 963.2
standing room 186.6
stand of arms 727.1
standoff tie 27.4
  delay 133.2
**standpat, standpat-
  ter** *n.* 141.3
  (irreconcilable
  606.3)
standpat *adj.*
  conservative 141.7
  unchangeable 150.7
  resolute 604.7
**standpattism, stand-
  patism**
  conservatism 141.2
  (bigotry 606.2)
  inaction 681.1
standpipe 260.6
standpoint
  position 184.1
  viewpoint 441.4
  (aspect 448.4)

standstill — stay

standstill *n.*
  stand 265.3
  (cessation 142.1)
  impasse 704.3
at a standstill
  permanently 141.8
  quiescent 265.8
  inactive 681.4
  at an impasse 704.11
standstill *adj.* 141.7
stand-up 212.8
stanza music 415.15
  poetry 597.7
  act 599.5
stapes 418.5
staple *n.* pin 45.5
  main part 50.3
  raw material 635.1
  store 636.2, 4
  emporium 799.1
staple *adj.* stable 150.5
  marketable 796.7
star *n.*
  heavenly body 318.3
  (luminary 423.1)
  asterisk 550.8
  actor 599.19
  astral influence 601.3
  principal 642.6
  proficient 700.1
  badge of honor 733.1
  insignia 747.4
  ornament 847.3
under the stars
  on earth 318.17
  outdoors 338.13
star *v.*
  headline 599.25, 26
  be distinguished 873.12
starboard *n.*
  right 238.2
  airplane 273a.10
starboard *v.* 267.24, 70
starboard *adj.* 238.3
starboard tack 238.2
starbright 420.22
starch 352.3
Star Chamber 966.2
starched hard 323.5
  priggish 853.7
  dignified 878.7
starchy hard 323.5
  viscid 352.8
stare *n.* 441.2
stare *v.* gaze 441.13
  be curious 455.3
  marvel 870.2
stare one in the face
  await 121.6
  impend 152.2
  be manifest 525.3
starfish fish 366.21
  animal 368.5
stargazer
  moonsail 273.13
  astronomer 318.12, 13
stargazing 318.10
staring distinct 446.5
  conspicuous 525.5

stark *adj.*
  absolute 31.12
  mere 32.11
  rigid 323.5
stark *adv.* 52.14
stark-blind 442.6
stark-mad 503.12
stark-naked 226.8
stark-staring
  absolute 31.12
  distinct 446.5
  conspicuous 525.5
starless 421.7
starlight light 420.1
  semidarkness 422.2
starlike
  stellular 253.21
  shining 420.22
starling 366.22
starlit luminous 420.22
  illuminated 423.14
Star of the Sea 977.3
starry starlike 253.21
  celestial 318.16
  luminous 420.22
Stars and Stripes 550.13
star-spangled 318.16
Star-Spangled Banner 550.13
star-studded 318.16
  (luminous 420.22)
start *n.* beginning 66.1
  departure 293.1
  ~ of surprise 508.3
get a head start
  be beforehand 132.5
  precede 280.2
start *v.* begin 66.5
  happen 151.3
  set going 284.14
  (impel 276.7)
  depart 293.4
  jump 309.4
  ~ in surprise 508.4
  startle 508.6
  propound 514.7
  crack 659.6
  set to work 686.7
  take fright 860.8
start up project 250.7
  ascend 305.4
  jump 309.4
  appear 446.2
starter 271.8
starting post 293.3
startle
  stagger belief 485.8
  surprise 508.6
  agitate 824.3
  frighten 860.10
  astonish 870.3
startled alarmed 669.4
  frightened 860.14
startling
  surprising 508.9
  frighening 860.15
startlish 825.8
starvation want 640.3
  fasting 956.1
starve
  freeze 383.7 ; 385.4

be poor 804.4
be parsimonious 819.3
  fast 956.3
starved thin 203.11
  frozen 383.8
  meager 640.9
  hungry 865.19
  (fasting 956.4)
starveling *n.* 804.3
starveling *adj.*
  thin 203.11
  meager 640.9
stash conceal 528.10
  store 636.7
state *n.* condition 7
  (predicament 8.3)
  (order 58.1)
  station 71.1
  ~ of affairs 151.2
  territory 181.2
  country 182.1
  (government 737.8)
  population 188.10
  nation 372.2
  pomp 882.1
lie in state 363.22
the States 182.3
state *v.* affirm 535.3
  expound 537.11
  say 582.6
state *adj.* 372.6
statecraft 693.3
stated 150.5
Statehouse, State house 966.6
stately grand 873.18
  dignified 878.7
  ostentatious 882.8
statement topic 454.1
  testimony 467.2
  proposition 476.3
  report 527.1
  assertion 535.1
  remark 582.4
  description 594.1
  account 811.3
  legal pleadings 969.6
statemonger 694.4
state paper 551.2
stateroom
  room 191.16
  ship 273.7
States-General 696.4
statesman 694.4
  (congressman 696.8)
  (official 745.9)
statesmanship 693.3
state-wide 78.11
static electric 158a.12
  inert 172.3
  of weight 319.12
statics force 159.3
  gravity 319.6
station *n.* degree 26.1
  rank 71.1 ; 873.4
  position 184.1
  stop-off 266.10
  airdrome 267a.28
  office 625.4
  police ~ 752.1

station *v.* 184.10
stationary 265.7
  (permanent 141.6)
  (stable 150.5)
stationery
  writing 590.10
  merchandise 798.3
station house 752.1
statist 694.4
statistical 85.12
  (accounting 811.10)
statistician 85.6
statistics 85.3
statuary *n.*
  figure 554.4
  sculpture 557.1
  sculptor 559.4
statuary *adj.* 557.10
statue 554.4
  (monument 551.4)
  (art 556.8)
  (sculpture 557.4)
  (beauty 845.4)
statuelike 265.7
statuesque 557.10
stature 206.1
status
  circumstance 8.1
  degree 26.1
  rank 71.1 ; 873.4
  class 75.1
  position 184.1
status quo 141.1
statute 963.2
statute mile 200.6
statutory 963.5
staunch, staunchless
  See stanch etc.
stave *n.* pole 206.4
  support 215.2, 15
  music staff 415.22
  stanza 597.7
  stick 635.3
stave *v.*
stave in
  excavate 252.9
  open 260.11
stave off 706.5
staving 31.8
stay *v.* cohere 46.5
  delay 133.2
  stop 142.1, 2
  cord 205.3
  supporter 215.2
  ship's rope 273.10
  airplane 273a.10
  perseverance 604a.1
  respite 687.2
  hindrance 706.2
stay *v.* cohere 46.5
  continue 106.2 ; 143.3
  postpone 133.4
  wait 133.7
  be permanent 141.4
  stop 142.6, 7
  be stable 150.3
  inhabit 186.10
  (remain 265.5)
  support 215.26
  quiet 265.6
  await 507.5
  persevere 604a.2

stay-at-home — stereotype 1108

stay (*continued*)
  remedy 660.12
  hinder 706.4
stay it out
  continue 143.3
  persevere 604a.2
stay one's hand
  cease 142.6
  (relax 687.4)
  abandon 624.3
stay-at-home
  quiescent 265.7
  unsociable 893.9
stays 225.25
staysail 273.13
stead location 184.1
  place 184.3
  avail 644.1
in one's stead 755.6
in the stead of 147.5
steadfast, stedfast
  durable 110.9
  constant 136.4;
    939.10
  stable 150.5
  resolute 604.7
  persistent 604a.3
  (attentive 457.9)
be steadfast 143.2
steadiness
  uniformity 16.1
  regularity 138.1
  perseverance 604a.1
steady uniform 16.5
  (regular 80.3; 138.9)
  constant 136.4
  stable 150.5
  persistent 604a.3
  unprecarious 664.10
  inexcitable 826.9
  steadfast 939.10
steady-handed,
  steady-nerved 826.9
steal *n.* theft 791.4
  stolen goods 793.1
  bargain 815.2
steal *v.*
  ~ along 275.5
  sneak 528.16
  thieve 791.9
  (appropriate 789.8)
steal a march upon
  be beforehand 132.5
  precede 280.2
  outstrip 303.4
  circumvent 545.8
  (be cunning 702.5)
  seize an opportunity
    682.12
steal off 623.10
steal one's thunder
  706.7
steal upon 508.5
stealage theft 791.1
  stolen goods 793.1
stealer 792.1
stealing 791.1
stealings 793.1
stealth
  furtiveness 528.3
  (cunning 702.1)
  stealing 791.1

by stealth 528.24
stealthy furtive 528.21
  (cunning 702.6)
  cautious 864.6
stealy 791.14
steam *n.* power 157.1
  vapor 334.2
  water 337.1
  cloud 353.5
  hot water 382.5
by steam 684.7
under steam 267.54
steam *v.*
  navigate 267.10, 42
  vaporize 336.5
  be hot 382.13
  heat 384.19
steamboat *n.* 273.1
steamboat *v.* 267.10
steamer *n.*
  automobile 272.15
  ship 273.1
  by steamer 270.12
steamer *v.* 267.10
steam heat 382.1
steaming 336.1
steamship 273.1
steamy 336.7
stearin, stearine 356.1
steatite 342.4
stedfast See **steadfast**
steed 271.3
steel *n.*
  strength 159.4
  knife 253.6
  sharpener 253.7
  hardness 323.3
  lighter 388.4
  measure 466.4
  metal 635.6
  weapon 727.3
steel *v.*
  strengthen 159.8
  ~ the heart 823.4;
    951.2
steel oneself 604.6
steel blue 438.2
steel-gray 432.4
steel helmet 717.2
steelmaker 690.8
steelworks 691
steelyard 319.5
steep *n.* 212.3
  (height 206.2)
steep *v.* 337.5
steep *adj.* high 206.13
  precipitous 217.12
  (vertical 212.8)
  (descending 306.7)
  profound 519.7
  excessive 641.5
  difficult 704.8
steeple tower 206.3
  spire 253.4
steeplechase
  race 274.4; 720.5
  jumping 309.1
  hunting 622.2
steepy 217.12
steer *n.* cattle 366.12
  male animal 373.6
  tip 527.3

steer *v.* pilot 267.11, 26
  direct 693.4
steer a middle course
  628.2
  (be mediocre 736.2)
  (compromise 774.2)
steer clear of
  turn aside 279.7
  avoid 623.6
  snub 930.7
steer for
  go towards 278.5
  approach 286.2
steer one's course
  go towards 278.5
  pursue 622.6
  conduct 692.5
steerage
  navigation 267.1
  direction 278.1;
    693.1
steerageway 267.7
steering gear 273.7
steering wheel 272.16
steersman 694.6
steganogram 528.5
steganography 528.5;
  590.8
Stegosauria 124.2
stein 191.11
steinbok 366.10
stellar 318.16
stellate, stelliform,
  stellular 253.21
stelography 590.1
stem *n.* origin 153.3
  family tree 166.4
  stalk 215.14
  prow 234.3
  tube 260.6
  leg 266.11
  foliage 367.4
  type 591.6
from stem to stern
  200.16
stem *v.* 708.3
stem the tide
  stop 142.7
  resist 719.3
  surmount 731.7
stem-winder
  timepiece 114.6
  ship 273.1
stench *n.* 401.1
stench *v.* close 261.2
  stop a flow 348.24
stenchy 401.4
stencil 556.17
stenciling, stencilling
  847.3
stenographer 590.12
  (recorder 553.1)
  (workman 690.10)
stenographic 590.16
stenography 590.7
stenotype 591.6
stenotypist 590.12
stenotypy 590.7
stent See **stint**
stentor 404.4
stentorian 404.8
  (vociferous 411.8)

step *n.* degree 26.1
  rank 71.1
  short way 197.2
  footing 215.4
  gait 266.5
  velocity 274.1
  music 413.11
  footprint 550.4
  measure 626.7
  action 680.2
in step 23.9
keep in step
  conform 82.5
  synchronize 120.3
  be fashionable 852.6
out of step 83.9
step by step
  gradually 26.5
  in order 58.8
  continuously 69.7
  slowly 275.11
step *v.* walk 266.16
  speed 274.9
  measure 466.10
step aside 279.7
step down
  decrease 36.4
  electrify 158a.11
step up increase 35.3
  intensify 157.7
  electrify 158a.11
  key up 171.7
stepchild 167.4
step dance 840.7
step dancer 840.9
stepdaughter 167.4
stepfather 166.6
step-in 225.25
stepladder 305.2
stepmother 166.7
steppe 344.1
steppe murrain 655.18
stepper horse 271.3
  speeder 274.5
steppingstone
  bond 45.1
  bridge 627.7
  medium 631.2
  safeguard 666.1
steps stairs 305.2
  means 632.1
take steps plan 626.9
  prepare 673.7
  act 680.5
  take action 692.4
  take precautions
    864.4
stepson 167.4
stepstone bridge 627.7
  medium 631.2
stercoraceous 653.17
stercoration 653.7
stere 466.3
stereognosis 379.1
stereognostic 379.4
stereometry 466.8
stereopticon 445.6
stereoscope 445.1
stereotype *n.*
  engraving 558.3
  type 591.6
stereotype *v.* fix 150.4

stereotyped — stillness

engrave 558.5
print 591.14
stereotyped fixed 150.5
  trite 843.6
stereotypic 591.18
stereotypist 591.12
stereotypy 591.1
sterile nugatory 158.11
  unproductive 169.4
  useless 645.8
  abortive 732.8
sterility 169.1
sterilize, sterilise 38.7
sterling n. 800.1
sterling adj.
  genuine 494.12
  silver 800.21
  virtuous 944.3
stern n. 235.1, 5, 7
  (ship 273.7)
stern adj.
  accurate 494.11
  resolute 604.7
  severe 739.5
  gruff 895.7
sternpost stern 235.7
  ship 273.7
stern sheets 273.7
sternutation
  sneeze 349.18
  sibilation 409.1
sternutative, sternutator n. 349.18
sternutative adj.
  sturnutatory 349.30
  sibilant 409.4
sternway 267.7
stern-wheeler 273.1
stertorious, stertorous 410.9
  (speech 583.5)
stet 150.4, 8
stethometer 662.22
stethoscope
  sound device 418.6
  remedy 662.22
stevedore n.
  longshoreman 269.7
  carrier 271.1
  worker 690.2
stevedore v. 184.13
stew n. mixture 41.4
  food 298.17
  confusion 458.4
  bustle 682.6
  predicament 704.2
  trepidation 825.3
  fit of anger 900.2
  drunkard 959.11
  brothel 961.7
  prostitute 962.2
stew v. be hot 382.13
  seethe 384.19
  think 451.28
  rage 825.7
  fret 828.10
  fume angrily 900.8
  inebriate 959.18
steward seaman 269.3
  caterer 637.2
  agent 690.1
  manager 694.5

retainer 746.1
functionary 758.2
deputy 759.1
treasurer 801
stewardess
  aircraftsman 269a.3
  seaman 269.3
stewardship 693.3
stewpan 386.1
Stheno 992.3
sthula sharira, sthula sarira 994.10
stichomancy 511.3
stick n. all 50.2
  sum 84.3
  cable pole 158a.9
  pole 206.4
  rod 215.13, 15
  mast 273.12
  propeller 273a.10
  wheel 312.4
  dryness 340.4
  fool 501.1
  wood 635.3
  awkward fellow 701
  club 727.7
  bore 841.4
  scourge 975.2
  for the stick 50.12
stick v. cohere 46.5
  (join 43.9)
  continue 106.2; 143.3
  cease 142.6
  perforate 260.14
  be quiescent 265.5
  nonplus 475.8
  compose type 591.14
  persevere 604a.2
  (plod 686.6)
  checkmate 731.10
stick around 133.7
stick at demur 485.7
  be reluctant 603.4
stick by 707.8
stick fast
  be stable 150.3
  be quiescent 265.5
  be resolute 604.6
  at an impasse 704.6
stick in one's gizzard
  disgust 830.7
  give umbrage 900.10
stick in the mud
  be in difficulty 704.6
  fail 732.5
stick it out
  continue 143.3
  persevere 604a.2
  resist 719.3
stick out
  protrude 250.7
  persevere 604a.2
stick to one's guns 604.6; 604a.2
stick up
  vertical 212.6, 7
  project 250.7
  raise 307.5
  rob 791.9
stick up for
  second 707.8
  approve 931.5

defend 937.6
sticker adherer 46.3
  thorn 253.2
  puzzle 533.2
stickiness
  tenacity 46.2
  viscidity 352.1
sticking 46.1
stick-in-the-mud n.
  conservative 141.3
  slow goer 275.4
  idler 683.7
stick-in-the-mud adj. 141.7
stickit 732.7
stickle
  be reluctant 603.4
  be obstinate 606.5
  ~ for 720.10
  haggle 794.5
stickler bigot 606.3
  disciplinarian 739.3
sticks 183.1
stick-to-itive
  coherent 46.9
  persistent 604a.3
  retentive 781.5
stick-to-itiveness
  tenacity 46.2
  perseverance 604a.1
stickum 45.6
sticky sweaty 299.11
  moist 339.7
  viscid 352.8
  (coherent 46.9)
stiff n. vagabond 268.2
  horse 271.6
  slow goer 275.4
  corpse 362.1
  neglector 460.3
  idler 683.7
  bore 841.4
stiff adj. steep 217.12
  dead drunk 959.22
  rigid 323.5
  dead 360.8
  style 579.3
  bigoted 606.7
  excessive 641.5
  severe 739.5
  ungraceful 846.8
  priggish 853.7
  dignified 878.7
stiff-backed 606.7
stiffen
  electrify 158a.11
  harden 323.4
stiff neck, stiffneck
  pain 378.1
  bigotry 606.2
  ailment 655.5
stiff-necked
  bigoted 606.7
  prudish 853.7
  dignified 878.7
stiffness
  stability 150.1
  affectation 853.1
stifle suffocate 361.11
  extinguish 385.5
  silence 403.5
  muffle 408a.4

keep secret 528.11
mute 581.5
stifled 405.9
stifling 382.18
stigma
  discoloration 440a.1
  mark 550.7
  blemish 848.1
  infamy 874.2
  moral blemish 945.5
stigmatic 440a.3
  (imperfect 651.4)
  (blemished 848.3)
stigmatism
  discoloration 440a.1
  mark 550.7
  blemish 848.1
  stigma 874.2
stigmatize, stigmatise
  spot 440.4
  discolor 440a.2
  (blemish 848.2)
  give a bad name 874.7
  (vilify 908.4; 934.3)
stile post 215.16
  stairs 305.2
  obstacle 706.2
stiletto
  perforator 262
  weapon 727.3
still n. vaporizer 336.3
  crucible 386.1
  silence 403.1
  picture 556.9, 11
  distillery 959.14
still v. moderate 174.5
  quiet 265.6
  silence 403.5
still adj. equable 174.6
  quiescent 265.7
  silent 403.6
  (aphonous 581.7)
keep still
  be silent 403.3
  silence 403.9
  not speak 585.3
stand still
  be permanent 141.4
  (not do 681.2)
  be quiescent 265.5
still adv.
  notwithstanding 30.8
  until now 118.4
still alarm 669.1
stillatitious 348.26
stillborn dead 360.8
  abortive 732.8
  fall stillborn 732.5
stiller 959.12
still hunt n.
  search 461.2
  stealth 528.3
  chase 622.2
still-hunt v.
  seek 461.16
  chase 622.7
stillicide 348.4
still life 556.9
stillness
  quiescence 265.1

stillroom — stooge 1110

stillness (*continued*)
  (repose 687.1)
  silence 403.1
stillroom room 191.16
  storeroom 636.4
stillstand 265.3
stilly quiescent 265.7
  silent 403.6
stilt 215.2
  on stilts aloft 206.19
  elevatedly 307.10
  exaggerated 549.3
  grandiloquent 577.7
  arrogant 885.8
stilted elevated 307.8
  exaggerated 549.3
  pedantic 577.7
  priggish 853.7
  dignified 878.7
  arrogant 885.8
stimulant
  energizer 171.4
  tonic 662.5
stimulate
  strengthen 159.8
  animate 171.7
  inflame 173.8
  sensitize 375.4
  incite 615.7
  refresh 689.2
  excite 824.2
stimulating
  suggestive 514.11
  exciting 824.12
stimulation
  invigoration 159.2
  provocation 615.2
  refreshment 689.1
  excitation 824.1
stimulative 514.11
stimulator, stimulater 171.4
stimulus
  energizer 171.4
  incentive 615.3
sting *n.*
  aviation 267a.29
  prickle 380.1
  poison 663.3
  mental pain 830.2
sting *v.* pain 378.4
  tingle 380.4
  be pungent 392.3
  irritate 824.5
  provoke 830.5
  excite anger 900.10
stinger 663.3
stinginess 819.1
stinging
  pungent 392.5
  exciting 824.13
  annoying 830.12
  gruff 895.7
stingo 959.5
stingy 819.4
stink *n.* 401.1
stink *v.* 401.3
stinkball, stink bomb, stinkbush 401.2
stink cat animal 366.3
  malodor 401.2
stinker cigar 392.3

malodor 401.2
stinking 401.4
stinko 959.21
stinkpot, stinkstone, stinkweed etc. 401.2
stint, stent *n.*
  degree 26.1
  task 625.2
  scarcity 640.2
  parsimony 819.1
stint *v.* limit 233.2
  scrimp 819.3
stinted 640.9
stinting
  parsimonious 819.4
  temperate 953.6
stintless 639.7
stipe 215.14
stipend 973.2
stipendiary
  recipient 785.2
  receiving 785.5
stipple *n.* 558.1
stipple *v.* paint 428.10
  dapple 440.4
  engrave 558.5
stipulate
  contend for 720.10
  negotiate 769.6
  condition 770.2
stipulation
  condition 469.2; 770.1
  promise 768.1
  contract 769.1
stipulatory 770.3
stipule 367.4
stir *n.* turmoil 59.4
  activity 171.2
  motion 264.1
  agitation 315.1
  ~ of air 349.5, 15
  bustle 682.6
  prison 752.1
  excitement 825.1
  make a stir give importance to 642.8
  bustle 682.12
stir *v.* stimulate 171.7
  move 264.6
  agitate 315.8
  sensitize 375.4
  rustle 405.5
  ~ a question 476.11
  be active 682.12
  excite 824.2, 3
  not stir
  be quiescent 265.5
  do nothing 681.2
  stir up mix 41.6
  energize 171.7
  inflame 173.8
  agitate 315.8
  excite 824.2
stirps origin 153.3
  ancestry 166.4
stirring eventful 151.6
  energetic 171.9
  momentous 642.10
  astir 682.23
stirrup
  supporter 215.2

saddle 215.23
  ship's rope 273.10
  stapes 418.5
stirrup cup 959.10
stitch *n.* joint 43.3
  piece 51.3
  (particle 193.2)
  tailor 225.37
  pain 378.1
stitch *v.* 43.6
stitching 593.9
stitch in time 132.2
stiver 800.8
stoa 191.17
stoat animal 366.17
  malodor 401.2
stob stake 45.5
  post 215.16
stoccado, stoccata 716.3
stock *n.* quantity 25.2
  origin 153.3
  ancestry 166.4
  (race 11.4)
  necktie 225.33
  soup 298.16
  credence 484.1
  fool 501.1
  drama 599.7
  raw material 635.1
  fund 636.2
  assets 780.7
  merchandise 798.1
  funds 800.2
  in stock in store 636.9
  in possession 777.8
stock *v.* store 636.7
  supply 637.4
stock *adj.*
  habitual 613.11
  trite 843.6
stock *adv.* 52.14
stockade 717.3
stockbreeding 370.1
stockbroker 797.7
stockbroking 794.2
stock car 272.19
stock company
  troupe 599.18
  firm 712.5
stock exchange 799.3
stockholder 370.4
stock horse 271.3
stocking 225.29
stock in trade
  supply 636.1
  (means 632.1)
  (merchandise 798.1)
  assets 780.7
stockjobber 797.8
stockjobbing 794.2
stockkeeper, stockman 370.4
  (driver 268.9)
  (workman 690.10)
stock room 636.4
stocks shackle 752.2
  commercial paper 800.7
  pillory 975.3
stock-still 265.7
stocky 201.6

stockyard 232.1
stodgy stubby 201.6
  viscid 352.8
stogie, stogy 392a.3
stogy 225.27
stoic *n.* 823.3
stoic *adj.*
  enduring 826.10
  disinterested 942.5
Stoic *adj.* 451.38
stoicism
  insensibility 823.1
  sufferance 826.4
  disinterest 942.1
Stoicism
  philosophy 451.8
  ethics 926.4
  abstemiousness 953.2
stoke 388.8
  (fire 384.17)
stokehold 273.7
stoker
  railroader 268.12
  mariner 269.3
stole 999.1
stolid 499.12
stolidity 499.2
stomach *n.* belly 191.7
  (vitals 221.4)
  taste 390.1
  hunger 865.3
  have no stomach for 867.4
stomach *v.*
  submit to 725.3
  brook 826.6
stomach-ache 378.1
  (ailment 655.5)
stomacher 225.25
stomachic
  vascular 191.23
  visceral 221.11
stone *n.* weight 319.4
  solid 321.4
  hardness 323.3
  rock 342.4
  (mineral 635.7)
  gravestone 363.15
  sculpture 557.8
  lithography 558.4
  writing tablet 590.10
  pavement 627.4
  gallstone 655.5
  missile 727.14
stone *v.* throw 284.12
  kill 361.10
  lapidate 716.7
  pelt 972.7
stone-blind 442.6
stone-broke 804.7
stone-colored 432.4
stone-dead 360.8
stone-deaf 419.8
stonelike 323.5
stoneshot 284.4
stone's throw 197.2
stoneware 384.14
stony hard 323.5
  penniless 804.7
stonyhearted 907.8
stooge 599.19

stook 72.5
stool *n.* seat 215.22
  dung 653.7
  between two stools
    704.11
stool *v.*
  disembowel 297.16
  inform on 527.10
stool of repentance
  950.1
stool pigeon
  informer 527.6
  bunko steerer 548.2
  decoy 617.2
stoop *n.*
  receptacle 191.11
  porch 191.17
stoop *v.* crouch 308.7
  (get down 306.5)
  submit 725.3
  degrade oneself
    874.5
  truckle 886.3
stoop to conquer
  be cunning 702.5
  be proud 878.3
stop *n.* delay 133.2
  cessation 142.1, 5
  (standstill 265.3)
  stopper 263.1
  stop-off 266.10
  organ ~ 417.12
  impasse 704.3
  hindrance 706.2
stop *v.* halt 142.6, 7
  (end 67.5, 7)
  (discontinue 70.3)
  (remain 265.5)
  (quiet 265.6)
  (abandon 624.3)
  (not do 681.2)
  (checkmate 731.10)
  close 261.2
  silence 403.5
  render mute 581.5
  hinder 706.4
  (delay 133.6)
stop in one's tracks
  361.10
stop one's mouth
  581.5
  (silence 403.5)
stop short 304.2
  (not complete 730.2)
stopcock 263.2
stopgap
  substitute 147.2
  stopper 263.1
  expedient 646.2
stop light lamp 423.4
  signal 550.14
stopover sojourn 189.1
  stop-off 266.10
stoppage end 67.1
  cessation 142.1
  hindrance 706.1
stopper end-all 67.4
  lid 223.7
  plug 263
  (closure 261.1)
  (obstacle 706.2)

stopping
  cessation 142.1
  stopper 263.1
stopping place
  stopover 189.1
  stop-off 266.10
stopple 263.1
stop watch 114.6
storage 636.4, 6
store *n.* credence 484.1
  fund 636
  (quantity 31.3)
  (accumulation 72.6)
  (sustenance 707.3)
  (merchandise 798.1)
  market 799.1
be in store for 152.2
  (await 507.5)
have in store for
  destine 601.9
  be provided 637.5
in store
  imminent 152.3
  in stock 636.9
  ~ **for** 673.10
  in possession 777.8
store *v.*
  stow away 636.7
  (load 184.13)
  (put 184.10)
  supply 637.4
store clothes 225.4
storehouse 636.4
  (barn 189.5)
  (treasury 802.1)
storekeeper 797.1
storeroom 636.4
  (room 191.16)
storeship ship 273.1
  naval auxiliary
    726.11
storge 897.2
storied 594.7
storier liar 548.5
  narrator 594.4
storify 594.5
stork birth 161.3
  bird 366.22
storm *n.* horde 72.4
  tempest 173.5
  (rainstorm 348.11)
  (snowstorm 383.6)
  (agitation 315.1)
  wind 349.11-14
  (dust storm 330.3)
  thunderstorm 406.4
  attack 716.1
  passion 825.5
  anger 900.3
by storm 173.18
storm *v.*
  be violent 173.7
  blow 349.22
  attack 716.5
  rage 825.7; 900.8
  bluster 887.3
storm cellar 666.3
storm cloud 353.5
storm door 260.4
storm in a teacup
  overestimation 482.1
  triviality 643.2

**stormproof, storm-
tight** 340.11
stormy
  turbulent 173.12
  tempestuous
    349.25, 26
stormy petrel
  bird 366.22
  omen 512.2
  warning sign 668.3
Storting, Storthing
  696.4
story *n.* sum 84.3
  news article 532.1
  falsehood 546.1
  narrative 594.2
  joke 842.4
story, storey *n.*
  floor 191.18
  layer 204.1
story *v.* 544.4
storyteller liar 548.5
  narrator 594.4
storytelling 594.1
stot steer 366.12
  male animal 373.6
stoup, stoop
  receptacle 191.11
  church 1000.3
stour 59.4
stout strong 159.10
  sound 159.12
  corpulent 192.12
  (big-bellied 194.11)
  (chubby 201.6)
  (rotund 249.6)
  courageous 861.8
stouthearted 861.8
stoutness 159.1
stove
  electricity 157a.6
  heater 386.1
  (merchandise 798.3)
stove coal 388.2
stovehouse
  conservatory 371.6
  heater 386.1
  fire iron 386.3
stove lifter 386.3
stovepipe 260.6
stovepipe hat 225.26
stovewood 388.3
stow cease 142.6
  store 636.7
  (load 184.13)
stowage location 184.5
  capacity 192.2
stowaway 528.6
strabismal 443.14
strabismus
  faulty vision 443.1
  squint 443.3
Strad, Stradivarius
  417.3
straddle *n.* 266.5
straddle *v.* walk 266.16
  bet 621.18
  remain neutral 628.2
  (be irresolute 605.4)
  (tergiversate 607.7)

**straddle, straddle-
back, straddle-
legged** *adv.* 215.31
strafe *n.* 716.1
strafe *v.*
  bombard 716.6
  upbraid 932.8
straggle
  wander 266.14
  stray 279.5
straggler 268.2
straggling
  unconnected 44.12
  disorderly 59.8
straight *n.* 840.13
straight *adj.*
  fixed 150.5
  rectilinear 246.5
  (vertical 212.8)
  (direct 278.8)
  accurate 494.11, 12
  veracious 543.3
  honest 939.7
be straight 246.3
put straight
  straighten 246.4
  undeceive 545a.2
  remedy 660.10
  right 922.3
set straight
  remedy 660.10
  pacify 723.4
  reform 950.4
straight *adv.*
  promptly 132.14
  straightly 246.6
  directly 278.13
  accurately 494.16
go straight
  be straight 246.3
  go directly 278.6
straightaway 278.8
straightedge 466.4
straighten
  rectify 246.4
  mediate 724.3
  settle 769.8
straightforward *adj.*
  direct 278.8
  sincere 543.3
  artless 703.4
straightforward *adv.*
  278.13
straight-lined 246.5
straightness 246
  (verticality 212.1)
straight-up 212.8
  (steep 217.12)
**straight-up-and-
down** vertical 212.8
  accurate 494.11
  honest 939.7
straightway
  promptly 132.14
  directly 278.13
strain *n.* kind 75.2
  ancestry 166.4
  (race 11.4)
  agency 170.1
  outbreak 173.2
  pull 285.2
  tone 402.2

strain — stretch 1112

strain (*continued*)
 tune 415.2
 (melody 413.4)
 music 415.15
 exaggeration 549.1
 style of speech 569.1
 poetry 597.7
 exertion 686.1
strain *v.* weaken 160.8
 operate 170.2
 filter 295.7
 overstep 303.5
 overestimate 482.3
 exaggerate 549.2
 misrepresent 555.4
 overdo 641.3
 clean 652.10
 sprain 659.8
 strive 686.5
 task 686.8
strain a point
 overstep 303.5
 exaggerate 549.2
 not observe 773.4
 be undue 925.6
strained 686.10
strainer
 porousness 260.7
 refiner 652.7
strait *n.* crisis 134.4
 chasm 198.3
 narrow 203.3
 gulf 343.1
 predicament 704.2
 (misfortune 735.3)
strait *adj.*
 narrow 203.9
 straitlaced 606.7
straitened
 in difficulty 704.11
 impoverished 804.7
strait jacket 752.2
strait-laced
 bigoted 606.7
 prudish 853.7
 (hyperorthodox 983a.8)
 (sanctimonious 988.11)
straits 804.1
strait-waistcoat 752.2
strake 273.7
stramash 713.4
stramonium 662.7
strand *n.* cord 205.3
 shore 342.2
strand *v.* 267.33
stranded stuck 150.6
 in difficulty 704.11
 aground 732.10
strange irrelative 10.5
 extraneous 57.4
 odd 83.10
 (unknown 491.14)
 eccentric 503.17
 wonderful 870.7
 strange to say 870.9
strangely 31.21
strangeness 83.3
stranger 57.3
 a stranger to
 ignorant 491.8

inexperienced 699.14
strangle disable 158.6
 contract 195.4
 suffocate 361.11
 execute 972.8
stranglement 195.1
strangler killer 361.8
 ruffian 913.2
strangling 972.4
strangulate 195.4
strangulation
 contraction 195.1
 suffocation 361.4
 execution 972.4
strap *n.*
 fastening 45.4
 cord 205.3
 sharpener 253.7
 credit 805.1
 lash 975.1
strap *v.* tie 43.6
 dress wounds 662.24
 bind 751.7
 whip 972.6
straphanger 268.1
strap oil 972.4, 6
strappado 972.2
strapped 804.7
strapper 192.6
strapping
 strong 159.10
 stout 192.12
strapwork 847.3
strata See stratum
stratagem 702.3
 (trick 545.3)
 (device 626.5)
strategics 692.2
strategist
 schemer 626.8; 702.4
 politician 694.4
 tactician 700.4
strategy 692.2; 722.2
strath 252.5
strathspey music 415.7
 dance 840.7
stratification 204.3
stratified, stratiform 204.5
stratify 204.4
stratocracy 737.4
stratosphere
 height 206.1
 aeronautics 267a.19
 atmosphere 338.2
stratum 204.1
 (horizontal 213.3)
stratus 353.5
straw *n.* remains 40.1
 tube 260.6
 fodder 298.7
 lightness 320.2
 trifle 643.3
 in the straw 168.9
straw *adj.* 436.6
straw bail 545.1
straw basher 225.26
strawberry 298.31
straw bid
 deception 545.1
 auction 796.2

straw bidder 548.2
strawboard 635.4
straw bond 545.1
straw boss 694.1
straw hat 225.26
straw-ride 266.7
straw vote 609.3
stray *n.*
 vagabond 268.2; 876.9
 outcast 893.5
stray *v.* wander 266.14
 deviate 279.5
 err 495.7
stray *adj.*
 scattered 73.4
 unconformable 83.9
 deviative 279.8
straying
 unconformable 83.9
 erroneous 495.12
streak *n.* nature 5.3
 line 200.4
 thinness 203.5
 furrow 259.1
 speed 274.6
 ~ of light 420.3
 mark 550.7
 frame of mind 820.1
 streak of luck
 success 731.1
 good fortune 734.2
streak *v.* furrow 259.3
 striate 440.4
streaked
 netlike 219.11
 striate 440.10
stream *n.*
 electricity 158a.1
 outbreak 173.2
 course 264.3
 water 348
 (fluid 347.1)
 (channel 350.1)
 flow 348.2
 air 349.1
 light 420.3
 go with the stream
 conform 82.5
 advance 282.2
 be fashionable 852.6
 comply obsequiously 886.3
stream *v.*
 assemble 72.10
 course 264.6
 flow 348.17
 blow 349.22
 abound 639.4
streamer caption 66.3
 flag 550.13
streaming
 incoherent 47.3
 scattered 73.4
 flowing 348.26
streamlet 348.1
streamliner 272.18
streamy 348.26
street
 stock exchange 621.14
 roadway 627.3

the street 799.3
street Arab
 vagabond 268.2; 876.9
 (outcast 893.5)
streetcar 272.20
streetwalker 962.2
streetwalking *n.* 961.6
streetwalking *adj.* 961.10
strength
 quantity 25.1
 greatness 31.1
 vigor 159
 (potence 157.1)
 (energy 171.1)
 (resolution 604.1)
 toughness 327.1
 pungency 392.1
 language 574.1
 ~ of mind 604.2
 health 654.1
strengthen
 increase 35.3
 invigorate 159.8
 (reinforce 37.4)
 (empower 157.7)
 (energize 171.7)
 (refresh 689.2)
 feed 298.43
strengthener 215.2
strengthening 159.2
strengthless 160.10
strengthlessness 160.1
strengthy 159.10
strenuous
 energetic 171.9
 industrious 682.19
 laborious 686.10
 difficult 704.8
Strephon 897.6, 9
stress *n.*
 aeronautics 267a.9
 tone 402.2
 music 413.23
 emphasis 535.1
 accent 580.4
 necessity 630.1
 urgency 642.2
 strain 686.1
 difficulty 704.4
 hardship 735.1
 by stress of
 necessarily 601.15
 compulsorily 744.4
stress *v.*
 emphasize 535.5; 642.9
 accent 580.8
stretch *n.* period 108.1
 extent 180.1
 distance 196.1
 lengthening 200.5
 walk 266.4
 elasticity 325.1
 plain 344.1
 exaggeration 549.1
 strain 686.1
 spell of work 686.3
 at a stretch
 continuously 69.7
 during 106.7

stretch *v.*
  distend 194.5, 8
  lengthen 200.9
  overstep 303.5
  be elastic 325.3
  blow up 349.24
  overestimate 482.3
  exaggerate 549.2
  misrepresent 555.4
  overdo 641.3
  hang 972.8
stretch a point
  be unconformable 83.8
  overstep 303.5
  exaggerate 549.2
  connive at 760.3
  not keep faith 773.4
  be undue 925.6
stretch out
  extend 196.4
  be long 200.8
stretch the legs 266.16
stretchable 325.5
stretched 194.10
stretcher
  litter 215.24; 272.12
  lie 546.2
  (exaggeration 549.1)
stretchy elastic 325.5
  sleepy 683.15
strew 73.3
strewn 73.4
stria furrow 259.1
  variegation 440.1
striate *v.* 440.4
striate *adj.* 440.10
striated 259.4
striation 440.1
stricken
  wretched 828.16
  ~ by grief 837.13
strict copy 21.5
  (lifelike 17.15)
  accurate 494.11
  (literal 516.9)
  severe 739.5
  (orthodox 82.10)
  meticulous 868.4
  conscientious 939.8
striction
  hindrance 706.1
  restraint 751.1
strictness
  severity 739.1
  orthodoxy 983a.1
stricture
  narrowing 203.2
  obstruction 706.1
  restraint 751.1
  censure 932.2
stride *n.* distance 196.1
  gait 266.5
  velocity 274.1
  make strides
    speed 274.9
    (progress 282.2)
    improve 658.6
stride *v.* 266.16
stridence 410.1

strident 410.9
  (discordant 414.4)
  (speech 583.5)
stridor 410
  (discord 414.1)
  (speech 583.1)
stridulate 410.5
stridulation
  stridor 410.1
  animal sound 412.1
  insect sound 412.2
strife quarrel 713.3
  contention 720.1
  at strife 713.10
striga 256.7
strigate, strigose
  bristly 256.14
  striate 440.10
strike *n.* type 591.6
  labor ~ 719.2
  (revolt 742.2)
strike *v.* operate 170.2
  impress 171.8; 824.2
  hit 276.8
  (attack 716.5)
  (whip 972.6)
  shoot 284.13
  reach 292.7
  go on strike 719.4
  (revolt 742.5)
strike a balance
  equalize 27.7
  average 29.2
  be moderate 174.4
  measure 466.10
  compromise 774.2
  settle accounts 807.7
strike a bargain 794.6
  (agree 488.8)
  (make a compact 769.7)
strike all of a heap
  startle 508.6
  agitate 824.3
  frighten 860.10
  astonish 870.3
strike camp 293.4
strike dumb
  dumfound 581.5; 870.3
  shock 824.3
  frighten 860.10
strike hands 888.3
strike home
  impress 171.8
  attack 716.5
strike in with
  concur 488.7
  side with 709.5
strike it rich 803.6
strike off
  exclude 55.3
  print 591.14
  discount 813.2
strike off the rolls
  dismiss 297.12
  depose 756.5
strike oil 731.5
strike out excise 38.5
  exclude 55.3
  destroy 162.4
  fan 276.8

  hasten off 293.5
  obliterate 552.2
  plan 626.9
  fail 732.5
strike root 175.9
strike the iron while it is hot 134.6
strike up
  begin to play 416.21
  make friends 888.3
striking
  conspicuous 525.5
  dramatic 599.28
  important 642.10
  wonderful 870.7
strikingly 31.21
string *n.* series 69.2
  procession 69.3
  company 72.3
  cord 205.3
  (ligament 45.4)
  music 417.13
  party 712.1
string *v.* tie 43.6; 751.7
  give continuity 69.5
  tune 413.24
  flatter 933.2
string together
  arrange 60.6
  give continuity 69.5
  string up 972.8
string alphabet 442.2
stringency 739.1
stringent acrid 171.10
  severe 739.5
  (authoritative 737.15)
  (imperative 926.9)
  gruff 895.7
stringer 268.12
string instrument 417.2
stringpiece 215.12
strings influence 175.4
  musicians 416.3, 9
  instruments 417.1, 2
  condition 770.1
stringy
  filamentary 205.7
  tough 325.5
  viscid 352.8
striolate 440.10
strip *n.* line 200.4
  shred 205.5
strip *v.* divest 226.4
  peel 226.5
  fleece 789.12
  plunder 791.10
stripe *n.* nature 5.3
  kind 75.2
  line 200.4
  blow 276.3
  mark 550.7
  insignia 747.4
  character 820.1
stripe *v.* 440.4
stripes 225.8
stripling 129.1
stripped unclad 226.8
  moneyless 804.7
strive attempt 675.3
  exert oneself 686.5

  contend 720.8
stroke *n.* blow 276.3
  spasm 315.7
  ~ of death 360.1
  mark 550.7
  ~ of the pen 590.1
  illness 655.3
  act 680.2
  affliction 830.2
stroke of luck 731.2
  (fortune 621.1)
  at a stroke 113.7
stroke *v.* 379.3
stroke the wrong way 256.11
stroll *n.* walk 266.4
  slow motion 275.2
stroll *v.* wander 266.14
  walk 266.16
  go slow 275.5
strong great 31.6
  vigorous 159.10
  (potent 157.8)
  (virile 159a.5)
  energetic 171.9
  tough 327.5
  strong-flavored 392.5
  (flavorful 390.4)
  rank 395.7
  odorous 398.8
  fetid 401.4
  phonetics 402.11
  language 574.5
  foul 653.17
  hale 654.4
  emotions 821.5
  alcoholic 959.24
  be strong 159.7
  by a strong arm 744.4
  render strong 159.8
strong in
  versed in 490.14
  skilled in 698.14
strong arm *n.*
  strength 159.1
  coercion 744.1
strong-arm *v.*
  use force 159.9
  coerce 744.2
strong-arm *adj.* 744.3
strongbox 802.1
  (hiding place 530.2)
strong drink 959.4
strongheaded 498.9
stronghold
  fastness 717.4
  (prison 752.1)
  treasury 802.1
strong language 908.2
strongly 159.14
strong man 159.6
strong-minded
  intelligent 498.9
  resolute 604.7
strongness 159.1
strong point 476.6
strong room 802.1
strong-scented, strong-smelling 398.8

strong-willed — stupor 1114

strong-willed
  resolute 604.7
  obstinate 606.6
strop *n.* fastening 45.4
  cord 205.3
  sharpener 253.7
strop *v.* 253.9
strophe 597.7
structural
  architectural 161.12
  formative 240.9
  (formal 7.3)
  (textural 329.3)
structural botany 240.4
structural psychology 450.4
structure junction 43.1
  construction 161.7
  house 189.3
  form 240.1
  (texture 329.1)
struggle *n.*
  pursuit 622.1
  attempt 675.1
  exertion 686.1
  contention 720.1, 2
struggle *v.*
  strive 686.5, 6
  (try hard 675.4)
  be in difficulty 704.6
  ~ against 719.2
  contend 720.8
struggler 726.1
strum 416.18
struma 655.5
strummer 416.3
strumpet
  ugly person 846.3
  harlot 962.2
strut *n.*
  supporter 215.2
  beam 215.12
  gait 266.5
  airplane 273a.10
  ostentation 882.2
strut *v.* walk 266.16
  act proudly 878.3
  be pompous 882.6
  swagger 887.3
strut one's stuff
  act 599.26
  exercise skill 698.9
  show off 882.6
strutter 880.3
strychnine, strychnin 663.5
stub extremity 67.2
  tail 235.6
  tobacco 392a.5
  counterfoil 550.11
stubbed 201.6
stubble remains 40.1
  refuse 645.4
stubborn rigid 323.5
  obstinate 606.6
  (tough 327.5)
  (unmanageable 704.10)
  (resistant 719.5)
  strict 739.5
stubbornness 606.1

stubby 201.6
  (stout 192.12)
  (thick 202.7)
  (distorted 243.5)
  (rotund 249.6)
stucco *n.* 223.19
  (cement 45.6)
stucco *v.* 223.26
stuck fast 150.6
  nonplused 475.16
  at an impasse 704.11
  stranded 732.10
stuck on 897.15
stuck-up proud 878.6
  arrogant 885.8
stud suspender 214.3
  beam 215.12
  protuberance 250.2
  stallion 271.3
  male animal 373.6
studded
  thronged 102.5
  pointed 253.11
  luminous 420.22
  spotted 440.9
studding 215.12
studding sail 273.13
student 541.1
  (scholar 492.1)
studhorse
  stallion 271.3
  male animal 373.6
studied
  measured 466.13
  premeditated 611.5
studio room 191.16
  artist's ~ 556.15
  (workshop 691)
studious
  thoughtful 451.35
  scholarly 539.6
  (intellectual 450.8)
  (bookish 490.16)
  (industrious 682.19)
studiously 620.5
study *n.* copy 21.1
  retreat 189.13
  room 191.16
  thought 451.1
  (examination 461.3)
  (dissertation 595.1)
  close attention 457.2
  preoccupation 458.3
  learning 539.1
  work of art 556.8, 9
  actor 599.19
study *v.*
  scrutinize 441.12
  ponder 451.27
  examine 461.17, 18
  learn 539.4
  intend 620.3
stuff *n.*
  ~ and nonsense 4.2
  matter 316.2
  absurdity 497.1
  nonsense 517.2
  materials 635.2
  trumpery 643.5
  rubbish 645.4
  skill 698.2

stuff-gownsman 968.1
stuff *v.* fill 52.7
  (line 224.2)
  expand 194.8
  plug 261.2
  weight 319.9
  deceive 545.10
  overeat 957.3
stuffed 641.6
stuff gown, stuff-gownsman 968.1
stuffing contents 190.1
  (lining 224.1)
  vitals 221.4
  stopper 263.1
stuffy dense 321.8
  sultry 382.18
  obstinate 606.6
  angry 900.13
  sullen 901.8
stuggy 201.6
stultification 497.1
stultified 732.9
stultify
  counteract 179.3
  render absurd 497.3
  make ridiculous 856.5
stultify oneself
  act the fool 499.9
  be ridiculous 855.3
stultiloquence 497.1
stultiloquent 497.4
stumble *n.* trip 306.2
  blunder 495.3
  bungle 699.4
stumble *v.* trip 306.6
  flounder 315.9
  falter 475.6; 605.4
  blunder 495.9
  stammer 583.3
  bungle 699.9
  fail 732.5
stumble on
  chance upon 156.8
  discover 481a.3
stumbling block, stumbling stone 706.2
  (difficulty 704.1)
stump *n.* remains 40.1
  piece 51.3
  staff 215.15
  platform 215.21
  leg 266.11
  shader 556.16
  challenge 715.1
stump *v.* travel 266.12
  walk 266.16
  go slow 275.5
  depart 293.5
  nonplus 475.8
  declaim 582.7
  challenge 715.2
  checkmate 731.10
stump up 807.6
stumped 475.16
stumper 533.2
stumpy 201.6
  (distorted 243.5)
stun stupefy 376.4

  ~ with noise 404.5
  deafen 419.7
  startle 508.6
  ~ emotionally 823.4
  shock 824.3
  terrify 860.10
  dumfound 870.3
Stundism
  religion 984.4
  sectary 984.14
stunned
  deafened 419.8
  terrified 860.14
stunner a beauty 845.3
  prodigy 872.1
stunning
  beautiful 845.13
  terrifying 860.15
stunt *n.* theater 599.6
  feat 680.2
stunt *v.* shorten 201.4
  aviate 267a.31
stunted dwarfed 193.9
  meager 640.9
stunter, stunt man 269a.1
stupa
  monument 363.15
  shrine 1000.2
stupe *n.* 662.14
stupe *v.* 834.4
stupefaction
  languor 683.4
  unfeeling 823.1
  astoundment 870.1
stupefied
  unfeeling 826.5
  terrified 860.14
stupefy stun 376.4
  (numb 381.2)
  startle 508.6
  ~ emotionally 823.4
  terrify 860.10
  dumfound 870.3
stupendous vast 31.8
  unusual 83.10
  huge 192.15
  wonderful 870.7
stupendously 31.21
stupid *n.* 501.1
stupid *adj.*
  credulous 486.5
  ignorant 491.8
  absurd 497.4
  unintelligent 499.12
  (clumsy 699.12)
  (dull 843.5)
stupidhead 501.1
stupid-headed 499.12
stupidity
  absurdity 497.1
  unintelligence 499.2, 7
  (unskillfulness 699.1)
  (dullness 843.1)
stupor
  anesthesia 376.1
  languor 683.4
  swoon 688.3
  apathy 823.1
  astoundment 870.1

stuprate — subordinate

stuprate 961.8
stupration 961.4
sturdy substantial 3.4
  strong 159.10
    (virile 159a.5)
sturgeon 298.18
stutter *n.* 583.1
stutter *v.* 583.3
sty hovel 189.4
  enclosure 232.1
    (menagerie 370.3)
  filthy place 653.10
Stygian dark 421.8
  diabolic 945.17
  infernal 982.5
style *n.* state 7.1
  kind 75.2
  chronology 114.5
  form 240.1
  music 415.20, 30
  art 556.6
  graver 558.4
  designation 564.2
  diction 569.1
  pen 590.10
  manner 627.1
  fashion 852.1
style *v.* 564.6
  (phrase 566.3)
stylet 262
stylish 852.7
stylist 578.2
stylite recluse 893.4
  religious 996.11
stylograph 590.10
stylography 590.1
styptic 397.6
Styx 982.3
Styxian 982.5
suan pan 85.5
suasible 602.9
suasion 615.4
suasive 615.11
suave, suave-mannered, suave-spoken 894.13
  (unctuous 355.3)
suaviloquence
  suavity 894.2
  flattery 933.1
suaviloquent
  suave 894.13
  flattering 933.3
suavity 894.2
  (unctuousness 355.1)
sub *n.* inferior 34.3
  substitute 147.2
  submarine 726.11
sub *adj.* 34.5
subacidity 397.1
subahdar, subadar 745.11
subalpine 206.17
subaltern *n.*
  inferior 34.3
  officer 745.11
subaltern *adj.* 34.5
subaqueous 208.11
subastral 318.14
subaudition 527.4
subbase 215.3

subbasement 191.20
subchaser 726.11
subcommittee 696.1
subconscious *n.* 450.3
subconscious *adj.*
  extramarginal 220.6
  subliminal 450.10
subcontraoctave 413.19
subcontrariety 237.1
subcontrary
  contrary 14.5
  contrapositive 237.6
subcutaneous 223.32
subdean 996.5
subdichotomy 91.1
subdititious 147.4
subdivision
  disjunction 44.1
  part 51.1
  class 75.1
  bisection 91.1
  military unit 726.7
subdivisional, subdivisive 75.6
subdominant 413.7
subdual 732.3
  (victory 731.3)
  (subjection 749.1)
subduct 38.4
subduction 38.1
subdue moderate 174.5
  muffle 408a.4
  conquer 731.9
  subjugate 749.5
  relieve 834.4
subdued faint 405.9
  soft-colored 428.17
  conquered 732.12
  meek 826.10
subduer 731.4
subeditor 593.16
suberose 320.7
subfamily, subgenus, subgroup 75.2
subhastation 796.2
subitaneous 113.5
subito instantly 113.6
  suddenly 113.7
subjacency
  inferiority 34.1
  lowness 207.1
subjacent 207.9
subject *n.* topic 454.1
  (problem 461.10)
  experimentee 463.7
  matter 516.4
  liege 746.5
subject *v.* 749.5
subject *adj.* 749.6
  (submissive 725.5)
  (obedient 743.3)
  (slavish 886.4)
be subject 749.3
  (submit 725.3)
not subject 748.18
subject to
  liable to 177.3
  provided 469.8
  dependent 475.15
subjected 749.6
be subjected to 177.2

subjection
  inferiority 34.2
  subjugation 749
    (submission 725.1)
    (subdual 732.3)
    (obedience 743.1)
    (constraint 751.1)
in subjection 749.6
  (serving 746.9)
subjective
  intrinsic 5.6
  immaterial 317.7
  (internal 221.9)
  intellectual 450.8
  topical 454.2
subjectivity 5.1
subject matter 516.4
subjoin 63.4
subjoinder 462.1
sub judice 461.26
subjugate 749.5
  (defeat 731.9)
  (arrest 751.9)
subjugation 749.1
  (subdual 732.3)
subjugator 731.4
subjunction 43.1
subjunctive 37.7
subkingdom
  animal kingdom 366.1
  vegetable kingdom 367.1
sublapsarian 984.14
sublation 38.1
sublease
  ~ to 787.6
  ~ from 788.3
sublet 787.6
sublevate 307.5
sublevation 307.1
sublieutenant 745.11
sublimate *n.*
  dregs 40.2
  silt 270.3
sublimate *v.*
  elevate 307.5
  vaporize 336.5
sublimate *adj.* 320.7
sublimation
  elevation 307.1
  vaporization 336.1
sublime *v.* 336.5
sublime *adj.*
  high 206.13
  language 574.8
  beautiful 845.13
  exalted 873.18
  (great 31.14)
  magnanimous 942.6
Sublime Porte 745.8
subliminal *n.* 450.3
subliminal *adj.* 220.6; 450.10
subliminal self 79.4
sublimity height 206.1
  ~ of expression 574.4
  importance 642.1
  gorgeousness 845.2
  high dignity 873.3
  magnanimity 942.2

sublineation 550.7
sublunar 318.14
submarine *n.* 726.11
  (ship 273.1)
submarine *v.* 716.6
submarine *adj.* 208.11
submarine chaser 726.11
submediant 413.7
submerge
  destroy 162.4
  navigate 267.43
  plunge 310.5
submergence
  draft 208.5
  navigation 267.5
  plunging 310.2
  (insertion 300.2)
submerse 310.5
submersible
  submergible 310.6
  submarine 726.11
submersion draft 208.5
  submergence 310.2
submission
  yielding 725
  (conformity 82.1)
  (obedience 743.1)
  (subjection 749.1)
  (sufferance 826.4)
  (humility 879.1)
  offer 763.1
  proposal 765.3
submissive
  manageable 705.6
  yielding 725.5
  (conformable 82.8)
  (pliant 324.6)
  (obedient 743.3)
  (subject 749.6)
  (meek 826.10)
  (humble 879.4)
  (servile 886.4)
  (dutiful 926.8)
be submissive
  be yielding 725.3
  be obedient 743.2
submissiveness
  submission 725.1
  obedience 743.1
submit propound 514.7
  yield 725.3
  (obey 743.2)
  (be subject 749.3)
  (be humble 879.2)
  (repent 950.3)
  offer 763.2
submit to
  acknowledge 488.9
  endure 826.6
submittal 725.1
submultiple *n.* 84.2
submultiple *adj.* 84.7
suborder 75.2
subordinacy
  inferiority 34.1
  (sequence 63.1)
  subjection 749.1
subordinate *n.* 34.3
subordinate *adj.*
  inferior 34.5
  subject 749.6

subordination — succession 1116

subordination
  inferiority 34.1
  method 58.3
  subjection 749.1
suborn 618.3
subornation 618.1
subpoena *n.*
  warrant 741.3
  summons 969.2
subpoena *v.* 741.7
subrent
  ~ to 787.6
  ~ from 788.3
subreption
  falsehood 544.1
  acquisition 775.5
subreptitious 544.7
subrogate 147.3
subrogation 147.1
sub rosa 528.24
subscribe
  endorse 488.6, 10
  second 707.6, 8
  give 784.8
subscriber
  endorser 488.5
  contributor 784.7
subscript adjunct 39.1
  sequel 65.1
subscription
  endorsement 488.4
  contribution 784.5
subsequence 117.1
subsequent
  succeeding 63.5
  posterior 117.3
  (future 121.7)
  (later 133.10)
subsequently 117.4
  (in future 121.9)
subserve
  contribute 153.8
  be instrumental 631.3
  (be useful 644.2)
  (serve 707.10; 746.8)
subservience
  inferiority 34.2
  instrumentality 631.1
  (utility 644.1)
  servility 886.1
subservient
  instrumental 631.4
  (conducive to 176.3)
  (useful 644.5; 677.8)
  assistant 707.12
  submissive 725.5
  servile 886.4
subside decrease 36.3
  sink 306.4
  gravitate 319.7
  deteriorate 659.6
subsidence
  decrease 36.2
  sinkage 306.1
subsidiary *n.* 34.3
subsidiary *adj.*
  extrinsic 6.2
  assistant 707.12
  (conducive 176.3)
subsidize 618.3

subsidy aid 707.3
  contribution 784.5
  pay 807.2
sub silentio 403.8
subsist exist 1.4
  (live 359.6)
  remain 40.5
  continue 106.2
  be permanent 141.4
subsistence
  existence 1.1
  nourishment 298.5
  sustenance 707.3
subsistent 1.7
subsoil interior 221.2
  soil 342.3
subspecies
  subgenus 75.2
  animal kingdom 366.1
  vegetable kingdom 367.1
substance essence 5.2
  (interior 221.2)
  (salient point 642.4)
  quantity 25.1
  matter 316.2
  (something 3.2)
  meaning 516.4
  materials 635.1
  funds 800.2
in substance 572.4
substandard 563.2, 15
substantial
  substantive 3.4
  (real 1.8)
  sizable 192.11
  material 316.8
  solid 321.8
  true 494.13
  important 642.10
  solvent 800.22
substantialism 316.5
substantialist 316.6
substantiality
  substantivity 3.1
  (existence 1.1)
  materiality 316.1
substantialize 316.7
substantially
  substantively 3.5
  essentially 5.8
  mainly 50.11
substantiate
  materialize 316.7
  confirm 467.9
  demonstrate 478.2
  (prove true 494.8)
substantiation 478.1
substantify 316.7
substantive 3.4
substantivity 3.1
substitute *n.*
  substitution 147.2
  (deputy 759.1)
  understudy 599.19
substitute *v.*
  replace 147.3
  (represent 759.4)
  (transfer 783.3)
  interchange 148.3
substitution

compensation 30.1
  replacement 147
  (transfer 783.1)
substitutive 148.4
substratum
  substantiality 3.1
  stratum 204.1
  foundation 215.3
  interior 221.2
  substance 316.2
substruction, substructure 215.3
subsultus
  twitching 315.6
  nervous disorder 655.14
subsume 76.3
subtend 237.5
subterfuge
  quibbling 477.4
  secrecy 528.2
  hiding place 530.2
  pretext 619.1
  evasion 623.1
  expedient 646.2
  refuge 666.3
  artifice 702.2
subterrane 252.3
subterranean 208.10
subtile delicate 32.10
  thin 203.10
  light 320.7
  rare 322.4
  fine 329.3
  cunning 702.6
subtilization 322.2
subtilize rarefy 322.3
  split hairs 477.8
subtilty rarity 322.1
  sagacity 498.2
  deception 545.1
  cunning 702.1
subtitle 593.7
subtle delicate 32.10
  thin 203.10
  light 320.7
  rare 322.4
  fine 329.3
  discriminating 465.4
  sagacious 498.10
  cunning 702.6
  refined 850.5
  nice 868.4
subtlety nicety 15.2
  rarity 322.1
  discrimination 465.1
  hairsplitting 477.8
  exactness 494.3
  sagacity 498.2
  deception 545.1
  cunning 702.1
  taste 850.1
  nicety 868.1
  point of honor 939.2
subtract deduct 38.4
  (reduce 36.4)
  calculate 85.7
subtraction
  deduction 38.1, 3
  (decrease 36.1)
  mathematics 85.4
subtractive 38.8

subtrahend
  subtraction 38.3
  number 84.2
subulate 253.11
suburb 189.16
suburban urban 189.22
  circumjacent 227.4
suburbs 227.2
subvene 292.7
subvention
  support 215.1
  foundation 215.3
  arrival 292.1
  aid 707.1, 3
  subsidy 784.5
subversal
  inversion 218.1
  overthrow 308.2
subversion
  revolution 146.1
  destruction 162.1
  inversion 218.1
  overthrow 308.2
subversionary, subversive 162.6
subvert destroy 162.4
  (countervail 468.2)
  invert 218.4
  overthrow 308.5
subvocal 580.11
subway
  underground 252.3
  train 272.18
  railway 627.5
succedaneum 147.2
succeed follow 63.3
  be subsequent 117.2
  substitute 147.3
  be successful 731.5
  (make progress 282.2)
  (accomplish 729.2)
  (prosper 734.5)
  (make profit 775.7)
  inherit 775.8
  devolve 783.4
not succeed 732.5
succeeding
  following 63.5
  later 117.3
  successful 731.11
succentor 996.5
success
  fortunate outcome 731
  (luck 156.1)
  (progress 282.1)
  (accomplishment 729.1)
  (prosperity 734.1)
  (profit 775.2)
successful 731.11
  (prosperous 734.8)
  be successful 731.5
successfully 731.12
succession
  gradation 58.2
  order 63.1
  continuity 69.1, 2
  repetition 104.1
  time 117.1
  lineage 167.2

notion 281.1
transfer 783.2
in succession 69.7
successive
 following 63.5
 continuous 69.6
 later 117.3
successor 281.2
succinct short 201.5
 terse 572.3
succinctorium 999.1
succor, succour n.
 707.1, 5
succor, succour v.
 707.6
succorer, succourer
 912.1
succory, succotash
 298.30
succubus, succub, suc-
 cube 980.2
succulence 352.1
succulent
 eatable 298.49
 fluid 333.7
 semiliquid 352.7
 pulpy 354.5
succumb faint 688.4
 submit 725.3
 be defeated 732.6
succussion 315.3
succussive 315.13
such 17.4, 12
such and such, such a
 one 565.4
suchlike 17.4, 12
suchness 5.2
suck n. drink 298.4
 swig of liquor 959.10
suck v. draw in 296.2
 draw off 297.13
 drink 298.47
suck the blood of
 789.12
sucker dupe 547.1
 parasite 886.2
suckle 707.9
suckling 129.6
sucrose 396.4
suction 296.1
Sudanese 431.4
sudarium
 perspiration 299.4
 hot bath 386.6
 napkin 652.7
 veronica 993.2
sudatory n.
 perspiration 299.4
 hot bath 386.6
 (bath 652.4)
sudatory adj. 299.11
sudden n. 113.2
 of a sudden
 suddenly 113.7
 short 201.8
sudden adj.
 abrupt 113.5
 (brief 111.7)
 (fast 274.13)
 (unexpected 508.8)
 (hasty 684.5)
 impulsive 825.11

suddenly
 abruptly 113.7
 (unexpectedly
 508.11)
 (hastily 684.7)
 short 201.8
suddenness 113.2
sudor, sudoresis 299.4
sudoric 299.11
suds foam 353.2
 soap 356.5
 beer 959.5
sudsy 353.10
sue request 765.4
 woo 902.7
 prosecute 969.10
suet 356.4
suffect 147.3
suffer
 experience 151.4;
 821.3
 ~ physically 378.4
 ail 655.21
 have trouble 735.5, 6
 permit 760.3
 endure 826.6
 ~ mentally 828.9
 (be sad 837.6)
sufferance
 physical pain 378.1
 permission 760.1
 endurance 826.4
 (submission 725.1)
 mental pain 828.1
sufferer
 sick person 655.20
 victim 828.8
suffering n.
 physical ~ 378.1
 mental ~ 828.1
 penalty 974.1
suffering adj.
 ~ physically 378.6
 (ailing 655.23)
 ~ mentally 828.13
suffice
 be sufficient 639.3
 avail 644.2
 not suffice 640.6
sufficiency
 ability 157.2
 adequacy 639
 (fill 52.3)
 competence 698.1
sufficient
 economical 817.4
 satisfactory 831.7
 enough 639.6
 (effectual 644.7)
 be sufficient 639.3
 render sufficient
 639.5
sufficiently 639.8
 (fully 31.17)
suffix n. adjunct 39.1
 afterpart 65.2
 rear 235.1
 syllable 561.3
suffix v. 63.4
sufflate distend 194.8
 blow up 349.24
sufflation

distention 194.1
inflation 349.1
suffocate
 asphyxiate 361.11
 overfill 641.4
suffocating
 sultry 382.18
 fetid 401.4
suffocation 361.4
Suffolk 271.4
suffragan 996.5
suffrage 609.3
suffragette
 feminist 374.10
 voter 609.4
suffragettism
 feminism 374.9
 election 609.3
suffragism 609.3
suffuse 41.8
suffusion
 imbuement 41.2
 emotion 821.2
 blush 881.1
Sufi 984.18
Sufism, Sufiism 984.8
sugar n.
 sweetening 396.4
 money 800.1
 endearment 902.4
sugar v. sweeten 396.7
 bribe 618.3
Sugarbowl of the
 World 182.3
sugar-coat 396.7
sugar-coating, sugari-
 ness 396.1
sugarplum 396.2
sugarsweet, sugary
 396.8
sugar-water 396.5
suggest mean 516.5
 intimate 527.8
 (remind 505.15)
 (propose 514.8)
 advise 695.4
suggest itself 451.32
suggester 615.6
suggestion taste 390.1
 supposition 514.2
 hint 527.4
 (reminder 505.5)
 (implication 516.1)
 indication 550.1
 plan 626.1
 advice 695.1
 proposal 765.3
suggestive
 remindful 505.17
 allusive 514.11
 significative 516.8
 implicative 526.7
 indicative 550.21
 descriptive 594.7
suggestum 215.21
suicide
 self-murder 361.3
 self-murderer 361.4
 commit suicide 361.14
suit n. series 69.2
 kind 75.2
 attendance 88.5

frock 225.7
request 765.1
love ~ 902.2
lawsuit 969.1
prayer 990.3
bring suit 969.10
do suit and service
 743.2
suit v. agree 23.7
 (be expedient 646.3)
 accord 23.8
 conform 82.4
 beautify 845.7
suit the occasion
 134.5
 (be expedient 646.3)
suitability 646.1
 (right 922.1)
 (dueness 924.1)
suitable fit 23.11; 646.4
 (right 922.5)
 opportune 134.7
 adequate 639.6
suitcase, suit case
 191.5
suite series 69.2
 attendance 88.5
 (afterpart 65.2)
 apartment 191.21
 music 415.3
suiting 23.9
suitor petitioner 767.1
 lover 897.6
 accuser 938.2
 litigant 969.9
sulcate 259.4
sulcus 259.1
sulfur See sulphur
sulk 901.6
sulks 901.2
 in the sulks 901.8
sulky n. 272.4
sulky adj.
 obstinate 606.6
 sullen 901.8
 (sad 837.9)
sullen obstinate 606.6
 sad 837.9
 sulky 901.8
 be sullen 901.6
sullenness, sullens
 901.2
 (sadness 837.1)
sully discolor 440a.2
 dirty 653.15
 stigmatize 874.7
sulphidic, sulphitic
 83.11
sulphite 83.4
 (original 20.2)
sulphur, sulfur
 fumigator 388.7
 mineral 635.6
sulphur-bottom 366.21
sulphur-colored 436.6
sulphuric acid
 cauterant 384.11
 decolorant 429.3
sulphur yellow 436.1
Sultan 745.5
sultana 745.6

sultry — superimposition

sultry hot 382.18
  obscene 961.9
sum *n.* quantity **25.1, 2**
  all 50.2
  (computation 37.2)
  number 84.3
  (count 85.3)
  ~ of money
    800.10, 11
sum and substance
  meaning 516.4
  compendium 596.1
  important part 642.4
sum *v.* 85.7
sum up compute 37.5
  calculate 85.7
  (keep accounts
    811.7)
  recount 594.5
sumless 105.3
summa cum laude
  873.20
summarily 132.14
summarize 551.8
summary *n.*
  ~ of facts 594.1
  synopsis 596.1
  (outline 230.1;
    626.2)
summary *adj.*
  brief 111.7
  punctual 132.9
  short 201.5
  terse 572.3
summation sum 84.3
  numeration 85.1
  computation 37.2
  (total 50.2)
summer season 126a.3
  beam 215.12
  hot weather 382.3
summer complaint
  655.6
summer day 382.3
summer heat 382.2
summerhouse
  house 189.3
  conservatory 371.6
summersault, summerset See **somersault** etc.
summertide, summertime 126a.3
summery
  seasonal 126a.6
  warm 382.15
summing up 104.2
summit 210
  (supremacy 33.3)
  (height 206.2)
  (perfection 650.1)
summital 210.6
  (perfect 650.5)
summon
  cite 741.7; 969.10
  ~ spirits 994.18
summon up
  remember 505.10
  imagine 515.8
  rouse feeling 824.2
summons *n.* call 550.16
  warrant 741.3

subpoena 969.2
summons *v.* 969.10
sump puddle 343a.1
  marsh 345.1
  sink 653.8
sumpter 271.2, 3, 11
sumption 476.4
sumptuary
  monetary 800.21
  liberal 816.4
sumptuous 882.8
sun *n.*
  heavenly body 318.3
  (heat 382.3)
  (daylight 420.8)
  (luminary 423.1)
  sunstroke 384.9
  sun arc 423.3
under the sun
  existent 1.7
  everywhere 180.9
  on earth 318.14, 17
  outdoors 338.13
sun *v.* sun-dry 340.5
  heat 384.20
sun arc 423.3
sunbeam 420.3, 8
sunbonnet 225.26
sunburn *n.* 384.8
sunburn *v.* 433.3
sunburned, sunburnt
  burnt 384.23
  red 433.5; 434.11
sunburst 420.8
sundae 298.13
Sundanese 560.4
Sunday *n.*
  vacation 687.2
  holyday 998.13
Sunday *v.*
  pass time 106.3
  vacation 687.5
Sunday best 225.13
Sunday school 542.1
sunder 44.8
sunderance 44.2
sundial 114.6
sundog 420.12
sundown
  nightfall 126.1
  hat 225.26
sundowner 268.2
sundry 102.5
sun-dry 340.5
sunfisher
  broncho 271.3
  buckjumper 309.3
sunflower 369.8
sunglass 445.1
sunglasses
  eyeshade 424.4
  spectacles 445.3
sun-go-down 126.1
sun hat, sun helmet
  225.26
  (sunshade 424.2)
sunk deep 208.8
  depressed 252.10
  nonplused 475.10
  sad 837.13
sunken deep 208.8
  depressed 252.10

sunk fence 717.3
sun lamp 423.3
sunless 421.7
sunlight 420.8
  (sun 318.4)
sunlit 423.14
Sunna, Sunnah 124.3
Sunnite 984.18
sunny warm 382.15
  luminous 420.22
  palmy 829.9
  cheerful 836.7
sunnyasee, sunnyasi
  See **sannyasi**
sunny side 734.8; 829.1
sunrise dawn 125.1
  east 278.2
at sunrise 125.5
sunscald 384.8
sunset nightfall 126.1
  (daylight 420.8)
  west 278.2
  death 360.1
sunsetty 126.5
sunshade
  umbrella 223.4
  shield 424.2
  (cover 223.2)
  (headdress 225.26)
sunshine
  daylight 420.8
  prosperity 734.3
  happiness 827.2
  cheerfulness 836.1
sunshiny warm 382.15
  luminous 420.22
sun spark 420.3, 8
sun spot 423.3
sunstone 847.8
sunstroke heat 384.9
  mental disorder
    503.4
  (ailment 655.5)
sun tan 433.1
sunup 125.1
sun worship, sun worshiper 382.11
sup *n.* modicum 32.2
  drink 298.4
  taste 390.1
  alcoholic drink
    959.10
sup *v.* eat 298.44
  drink 298.47
  taste 390.3
  tipple 959.15
supawn, sepawn, sepon 298.15
super *n.*
  supernumerary
    599.19
  supervisor 694.1
super *adj.* 648.10
superability 470.2
superable 470.6
superabound 641.2
  (be plentiful 639.4)
superabundance 641.1
superabundant
  profuse 102.5
  redundant 641.5
superabundantly 31.20

superadd 37.3
superaddition 37.1
superaltar 215.19
superannuated
  antiquated 124.9
  aged 128.8
  impotent 158.8
superannuation
  old age 128.2
  impotence 158.2
superb
  superexcellent
    648.10
  beautiful 845.13
superbness 648.3
supercargo 694.1
supercilious 885.8
  (contemptuous
    930.8)
superconscious 450.10
supercurious 455.5
supereminence
  importance 642.1
superexcellence
  648.3
spereminent 33.8
supererogation 641.1
superexcellence 648.3
  (perfection 650.1)
superexcellent 648.10
  (exceptional 83.10)
  (perfect 650.5)
superfetate *v.* 168.6
superfetate *adj* 168.9
superfetation
  addition 37.1
  pregnancy 168.2
superficial
  inconsiderable 32.8
  shallow 209.4;
    499.17
  exterior 220.7
  prejudiced 481.10
  half-learned 491.12
  trivial 643.11
  hasty 684.5
superficiality
  shallowness 209.1
  half-learning 491.3
superficies 220.2
superfine 648.10
superfluent 320.7
superfluity
  redundance 641.1
  (surplus 40.4)
  (tautology 573.2)
  (satiety 869.1)
  frippery 847.2
superfluous 641.5
  (surplus 40.6)
  (tautological 573.8)
  (useless 645.8)
superheat 384.16
superhuman *n.* 33.4
superhuman *adj.*
  976.14
superimpose add 37.3
  change 140.6
  cover 223.22
superimposed 223.30
superimposition 223.1

1118

superincumbency — surdomute

superincumbency
 319.1
superincumbent
 overhanging 214.8
 overlying 223.30
 heavy 319.12
superinduce
 change 140.6
 induce 153.7
superintend 693.5
 (rule 737.11)
superintendence
 supervision 693.2
 authority 737.3
superintendent 694.1
superior *n.*
 superior being 33.4
 director 694.2
 master 745.1
superior *adj.*
 greater 33.7
 (good 648.8)
 higher 206.15
 top 210.6
 be superior 33.5
 (be better 648.5)
superioress 996.12
superiority 33
 (eminence 31.2)
 (precedence 62.1)
 (majority 100.2)
 (importance 642.1)
 (excellence 648.3)
 (perfection 650.1)
 have superiority
 have advantage 33.6
 predominate 737.12
superlative 33.8
superlatively 33.10
 (supremely 31.18)
superman 33.4
supernal high 206.13
 celestial 981.7
supernatant
 overlying 223.30
 light 320.7
 (ascendant 305.7)
supernatural
 unusual 83.10
 divine 976.14
 (immaterial 317.6)
 (angelic 977.4)
 (spiritual 980a.4;
 994.22)
 metaphysical 994.21
supernaturalism 994.1
supernaturalist 994.13
supernormal
 unusual 83.10
 supernatural 976.14
supernumerary *n.*
 adjunct 39.1
 actor 599.19
supernumerary *adj.*
 additional 37.7
 remaining 40.6
 spare 636.9
 superfluous 641.5
superphysical
 immaterial 317.6
 supernatural 976.14
superplus 40.4; 641.1

superpose add 37.3
 cover 223.22
superposition
 addition 37.1
 covering 223.1
supersaturate 641.4
supersaturation 641.1
superscription 550.11
 (signature 550.3)
supersedable 147.4
supersede
 substitute 147.3
 disuse 678.2
superseder 147.2
**supersensible, super-
 sensual** 976.14
 (immaterial 317.6)
supersession 147.1
superstition
 credulity 486.1
 religious ~ 984.1
superstitious 486.5
superstratum 220.2
superstructure 161.7
supertonic 413.7
supervene
 be added 37.6
 be subsequent 117.2
 happen 151.3
supervenient
 extrinsic 6.2
 additional 37.7
supervention
 posteriority 117.1
 happening 151.1
supervise 693.5
 (preside 965.3)
supervision 693.2
supervisor 694.1
supervisory 693.6
supinate
 prostrate 213.7
 fell 308.5
supination 213.2
supine prostrate 213.9
 languid 683.14
 apathetic 823.5
supineness
 languor 683.4
 (inattention 458.1)
 (neglect 460.1)
 apathy 823.1
supper *n.* 298.34
supper *v.* feed 298.43
 eat 298.44
supplant 147.3
 (succeed 63.3)
supplantation 147.1
supplanter 147.2
supple 324.6
supplement
 adjunct 39.1
 complement 52.5
 sequel 65.1
**supplemental, supple-
 mentary**
 additional 37.7
 (surplus 641.5)
 completing 52.12
**suppliant, suppli-
 cant** *n.* 767.1

**suppliant, suppli-
 cant** *adj.* 765.7
supplicate
 entreat 765.5
 (ask pity 914.5)
 pray 990.11
supplication
 entreaty 765.2
 prayer 990.3
supplicatory 765.7
supplier 637.2
supplies
 provisions 298.6
 equipment 634.1
 (provision 637.1)
 (sustenance 707.3)
 stores 636.1
 (merchandise 798.1)
 (funds 800.2)
supply *n.* fund 636.2
 provision 637.1
supply *v.* provide 637.4
 (provision 298.43)
 (equip 634.2)
 (store 636.7)
 give 784.10
support *n.*
 suspender 214.3
 upholding 215
 (fastening 45.2)
 (leverage 175.3)
 (suspension 214.1)
 (anchor 666.2)
 corroboration 467.3
 preservation 670.1
 aid 707.1, 3
support *v.*
 operate 170.2
 hold up 215.26
 (sustain 143.3)
 keep alive 359.9
 corroborate 467.3
 demonstrate 478.2
 protect 664.6
 preserve 670.3
 aid 707.7
 endure 826.6
 defend 937.6
supportance 707.1
supported 215.28
 be supported 215.27
supporter
 suspender 214.3
 upholder 215.2;
 711.4
 insignia 550.12
supporting 215.28
 (basal 211.5)
supportive 467.11
supposable 514.10
supposal premise 476.4
 supposition 514.1
suppose
 think likely 472.3
 judge 480.6
 believe 484.8
 presume 514.6
 (think 451.27)
supposer 514.5
supposed 514.9
supposedly
 possibly 470.7

 theoretically 514.12
 (perhaps 470.7)
supposing *n.* 514.1
supposing *conj.*
 provided 8.8
 assuming 514.13
 (provided 469.8)
supposition 514
suppositional 514.9
 (imaginary 515.12)
supposititious
 presumptive 514.9
 (unreal 2.8)
 fictitious 546.6
 (unattested 468.4)
supposititiousness
 514.3
suppress destroy 162.4
 silence 403.5
 keep secret 528.11
 mute 581.5
 overpower 731.9
 subdue 749.5
 restrain 751.6
suppressed 732.12
suppression
 destruction 162.1
 secrecy 528.2
**suppurant, suppura-
 tive** 662.13
supralapsarian 984.14
supraliminal 450.10
suprarenal 221.5
supremacy
 superiority 33.3
 (summit 210.1)
 (importance 642.1)
 dominion 737.2
supreme highest 210.6
 greatest 33.8
 (vast 31.8)
 (paramount 642.14)
 (best 648.9)
 (perfect 650.5)
 ruling 737.15
 almighty 976.12
Supreme Being 976.2
Supreme Court
 966.2, 3
supremely 33.10
supremeness 33.3
surcease *n.* 142.1
surcease *v.* 142.6
surcharge *n.* 641.1
surcharge *v.*
 overload 641.4
 falsify accounts
 811.9
surcingle 45.2
surcoat 225.17
surd *n.* 402.2
surd *adj.* numeral 84.7
 silent 403.7
 (mute 581.8)
 deaf 419.8
surdimutism
 deafness 419.1
 aphonia 581.1
surdity 419.1
surdomute
 deaf-mute 419.3
 mute 581.2

sure — sustentation

sure certain 474.8
  (believing 484.12)
  authentic 494.12
  safe 664.10
  trustworthy 940.9
feel sure
  be certain 474.5
  believe 484.9
to be sure
  certainly 474.16
  yes 488.14
sure-enough
  certain 474.8
  true 494.10
sure-footed
  careful 459.7
  dextrous 698.11
surely
  certainly 474.16
  yes 488.14
surety certainty 474.1
  security 664.1; 771.1, 2
surf waves 348.10
  foam 353.2
surface *n.*
  exterior 220.2
  texture 329.1
below the surface 526.9
surface *v.* 267.43
surface *adj.* 220.7
surfeit *n.*
  superfluity 641.1
  satiety 869.1
surfeit *v.* overfill 641.4
  sate 869.4
surfeited 869.6
surfeiter 869.2
surge *n.* rotation 312.1
  flow 348.2
  eddy 348.8
  wave 348.10
  (swell 194.2; 250.2)
  ~ of sound 404.1
surge *v.*
  assemble 72.10
  flow back 283.5
  flow out 295.7
  roll 312.7
  flow 348.17, 20, 21, 22
  grow louder 404.5
surgeon 662.19
surgery 662.16
surgical 662.25
surliness 895.2
surly uncivil 895.7
  sullen 901.8
surmise *n.* 514.1
surmise *v.* judge 480.6
  believe 484.8
  suppose 514.6
surmiser 514.5
surmount
  rise above 206.10
  top 210.5
  climb over 305.5
  overcome 731.7
surmountable
  helpless 158.9
  practicable 470.6
surname 564.2

surpass 33.5
  (outstrip 303.4)
  (gain the ascendancy 731.8)
surpassing 33.7
surpassingly 33.10
surplice 999.1
surplus *n.*
  remainder 40.4
  excess 641.1
surplus *adj.*
  additional 37.7
  remaining 40.6
  superfluous 641.5
surprisable 508.9
surprisal 716.1
surprise *n.*
  inexpectation 508.2
  astonishment 870.1
by surprise 508.11
  (unpreparedly 674.12)
surprise *v.*
  be unexpected 508.6
  (catch unprepared 674.6)
  astonish 870.3
surprised
  inexpectant 508.10
  astonished 870.6
be surprised 870.2
surprise party
  surprise 508.2
  party 892.5
surprising
  unexpected 508.9
  astonishing 870.7
surprisingly 31.21
surrealism 556.6
surrealist *n.* 559.1
surrealist *adj.* 556.19
surrebound 408.7
surrebut 462.6
  (law 969.10)
surrebuttal, surrebutter 462.2
surrejoin 462.6
  (law 969.10)
surrejoinder 462.2
  (law 969.6)
surrender *n.*
  abandonment 624.1
  submission 725.2
  relinquishment 782.1
surrender *v.*
  relinquish 624.3; 782.3
  submit 725.4
  (be defeated 732.5)
  abdicate 738.6
surreptitious
  secret 528.21
  deceptive 545.13
surreptitiously 528.24
surrogate *n.*
  substitute 147.2
  deputy 759.1
surrogate *v.* 147.3
surrogation 147.1
surround
  encompass 227.3

  (circumscribe 229.2)
  eat 298.44
surrounded 229.4
surrounding 227.4
surroundings 227.2
  (nearness 197.3)
  (outline 230.1)
  (edge 231.1)
surtout 225.17
surveillance
  vigilance 459.2
  supervision 693.2
survey *n.*
  scrutiny 441.2
  examination 461.3
  measurement 466.1
survey *v.*
  look at 441.11
  measure 466.10
surveying 466.8
surveyor
  measurer 466.9
  supervisor 694.1
surveyor's area measure 466.3
survival surplus 40.4
  durability 110.1
survive remain 40.5
  outlast 110.8
  be permanent 141.4
  recover 660.15
surviving 40.6
Surya sun 318.4
  deity 979.4
susceptibility
  liability 177.1
  physical ~ 375.1
  impressibility 615.5
  (persuadability 602.3)
  exposure 665.2
  emotional ~ 822.1
susceptible
  flexible 324.6
  physically ~ 375.6
  emotionally ~ 822.6
susception 785.1
susceptive
  liable to 177.3
  physically ~ 375.6
  emotionally ~ 822.6
susceptivity
  liability 177.1
  physical ~ 375.1
  exposure 665.2
  emotional ~ 822.1
suscitate 153.7
suspect *v.* believe 484.8
  doubt 485.6
  suppose 514.6
  be jealous 920.2
suspect *adj.* 485.11
suspected 938.6
suspectful 485.10
suspend
  postpone 133.4
  interrupt 142.7
  hang 214.6
suspended inert 172.3
  pendent 214.7
  latent 526.7

suspended animation 683.1
suspender 214.3
  (fastening 45.2)
  (supporter 215.2)
suspenders 45.2
suspensation 214.1
suspense pause 142.2
  inertness 172.1
  uncertainty 475.1
  expectation 507.3
  irresolution 605.1
in suspense
  inert 172.3
  uncertain 475.15
  expectant 507.7
  latent 526.6
suspension
  postponement 133.2
  pause 142.2
  pendency 214.1
  (support 215.1)
  orchestration 413.3
suspension of arms 723.3
suspicion *n.*
  modicum 32.2
  doubt 485.2
  suspiciousness 487.2
  supposition 514.2
  hint 527.4
  apprehension 860.2
  jealousy 920.1
above suspicion 946.6
under suspicion
  on trial 463.15
  suspected 938.6
suspicion *v.*
  suspect 485.6
  suppose 514.6
suspicious
  doubtful 485.10, 11
  (incredulous 487.4)
  wary 864.6
suspiciousness 487.2
  (doubt 485.2)
suspiration 349.18; 839.1
suspire 349.23
sustain
  continue 106.2; 143.3
  (stabilize 150.4)
  (preserve 670.3)
  strengthen 159.8
  operate 170.2
  support 215.26; 707.7
  feed 298.43
  corroborate 467.9
  demonstrate 478.2
  act 599.26
  maintain 670.3
  endure 826.6
  justify 937.6
sustained 143.4
sustainer 215.2
sustenance
  support 215.1
  nourishment 298.5
  aid 707.3
sustentacular 215.28
sustentation
  permanence 141.1

sustentational — sweetness

nourishment 298.5
preservation 670.1
sustenance 707.3
sustentational, sustentative 215.28
susurrate 405.5
susurration 405.2
susurringly 405.11
susurrous 405.10
sutler 797.3
sutlerage, sutlery
  restaurant 298.42
  store 799.4
suttee suicide 361.3
  self-sacrifice 942.1
  sacrifice 990.6
sutteeism
  suicide 361.3
  sacrifice 990.6
suture 43.3
suzerain *n.*
  sovereign 737.16
  potentate 745.2
suzerain *adj.* 33.8
suzerainty 737.2
svarabhakti 402.2
swab *n.* oaf 501.1
  mop 652.7
  awkward fellow 701
swab *v.* dry 340.5
  wash 652.9
swacked 959.21
swad quantity 25.2
  quantities 31.3
  crowd 72.4
  lump 192.5
swaddle tie 43.6
  clothe 225.41
  bind 751.7
swaddling clothes 225.32
  in ~ 127.7
swag *n.*
  obliquity 217.1
  droop 306.1
  oscillation 314.5
  booty 793.1
swag *v.* hang 214.4
  incline 217.6
  curve 245.3
  droop 306.4
  oscillate 314.8
swagbellied 194.11
swagbelly 191.7
swage 174.5
swagger *n.* gait 266.5
  ostentation 882.2
  braggadocio 884.1
  bluster 887.1
swagger *v.* walk 266.16
  act proudly 878.3
  strut 882.6
  be boastful 884.5
  bluster 887.3
swaggerer
  strutter 880.3
  blusterer 887.2
swagman, swagsman
  vagabond 268.2
  fence 792.9
Swahili 560.4, 5
swain peasant 876.5

inamorato 897.6
swainish 183.3
swallow *n.*
  speeder 274.6
  bird 366.22
swallow *v.*
  take in 296.3
  eat 298.44
  be credulous 486.3
  (believe 484.7)
  be deceived 547.3
  submit to 725.3
  put up with 826.6
  be swallowed 484.11
swallow up
  destroy 162.4
  consume 638.2
  use up 677.6
  take all 789.12
swallowtail, swallow-tailed coat 225.14
swamp *n.* 345.1
swamp *v.* 162.4
swamped 732.10
swampy 345.3
  (soaked 339.8)
swan 366.22
swan dive 310.1
swank *n.* 882.2
swank *adj.* 882.8
swanker 878.2
swan song
  music 415.3, 17
  performance 599.8
swap *n.*
  interchange 148.1
  barter 794.3
swap, swop *v.*
  interchange 148.3
  bang 406.7
  barter 794.4
swap horses 148.3
swapping 148.1
sward 367.10
swarm *n.* horde 72.4
  multitude 102.2
swarm *v.*
  assemble 72.10
  be numerous 102.4
  climb 305.5
  hive 370.9
  abound 639.4
  (superabound 641.2)
swarming
  crowded 72.13
  profuse 102.5
swart gloomy 421.8
  dark-colored 431.7
swarth, swarthiness, swartness 431.1
swash *n.* 348.5
swash *v.*
  splash 337.5; 348.19
  murmur 405.5
swashbuckle 887.3
swashbuckler 887.2
swashbucklery 887.1
swashy 339.8
swastika, suastica, svastika 993.2
swat *n.* 276.3
swat *v.* 276.8

swatch 51.3
swath, swathe 72.5
swathe tie 43.6
  clothe 225.41
  bind 751.7
sway *n.* influence 175.1
  obliquity 217.1
  oscillation 314.5
  shake 315.4
  rule 737.2
  (potence 157.1)
sway *v.* change 140.6
  vary 149.4
  influence 175.6
  incline 217.6
  pitch 267.45
  oscillate 314.8
  shake 315.8, 9
  bias 481.8
  induce 615.8
  rule 737.11
swear *n.* oath 535.2
  curse 908.3
swear *v.* testify 467.8
  depose 535.4
  (be truthful 543.2)
  (promise 768.3)
  curse 908.5
swear at
  disagree 24.5
  of colors 428.11
  curse 908.5
swear by 484.7
  (depose 535.4)
swear falsely 544.4
swear in 768.5
swear off 953.5
swearing
  adjuration 535.2
  profanity 908.2
swearword 908.3
sweat *n.*
  perspiration 299.4
  labor 686.3
  trepidation 860.3
  by the sweat of one's brow 686.11
sweat *v.* perspire 295.7
  (excrete 299.9)
  (be hot 382.13)
  think hard 451.28
  cross-examine 461.15
  work 686.6, 8
sweat bath 382.6
sweater, sweat shirt 225.16
sweatshop 691
sweaty 299.11
  (exudative 295.9)
  (moist 339.7)
  (hot 382.16)
Swede 188.9
Swedenborg 986.3
Swedenborgian 984.14
Swedenborgianism 984.4
Swedish *n.* 560.4
Swedish *adj.* 188.11
sweep *n.* course 109.1
  extent 180.1
  curvature 245.1

oar 273.14
deviation 279.1
sweepstake 621.7;
  720.5; 840.11
dishwasher 652.6
vagabond 876.9
sweep *v.* curve 245.3
  course 264.6
  glide 266.20
  speed 274.9
  touch 379.3
  rustle 405.5
  strum 416.18
  clean 652.12
  plunder 791.10
sweep away
  destroy 162.4
  eject 297.8
  discard 678.3
  annul 756.3
sweep out
  evacuate 297.14
  clean 652.9
sweepback 267a.3
sweeper sweep 652.6
  ship 726.11
  vagabond 876.9
sweeping
  extensive 31.7
  (comprehensive 76.5)
  (prevalent 78.10)
  thorough 52.10
sweepings
  residue 40.2
  rubbish 645.4
sweepstake, sweepstakes
  race 274.4; 720.5
  game of chance 621.7
  horse race 840.11
sweet *n.* 902.4
sweet *adj.*
  saccharine 396.8
  (pleasing 377.7)
  (savory 394.7)
  fragrant 400.10
  melodious 413.27
  soft-colored 428.17
  pleasant 829.7
  lovable 897.17
sweet on 897.15
sweetbread 298.21
sweeten
  saccharize 396.7
  make pleasant 829.6
sweetening
  sweetener 396.4
  saccharization 396.6
sweet-flowing 413.27
sweet grass 400.3
sweetheart, sweetie *n.*
  lover 897.6, 7
  endearment 902.4
sweetheart *v.* 902.7
sweetmeat 396.2
  (delicacy 298.9)
  (dessert 298.12)
  (savory 394.3)
  (treat 829.3)
sweetness 396

sweet oil — symbolize 1122

sweet oil 356.3
sweet pea 400.3
sweet potato
  vegetable 298.30
  ocarina 417.4
sweet-scented, sweet-
  smelling 400.10
sweet-sounding 413.27
swell *n.*
  swelling 194.2;
    250.1, 2
  wave 348.10
  ~ of sound 404.1
  notation 415.23
  fop 854.1
  nobleman 875.4
swell *v.* bulge 250.7
  billow 348.22
  blow up 349.24
  grow louder 404.5
  ~ with emotion
    824.7
  act proudly 878.3
  splurge 882.6
  ~ with rage 900.8
  extol 931.6
swell *adj.* good 648.8
  fashionable 852.7
swelled head 880.1
swelled-headed 878.6
  (vain 880.6)
swelling *n.*
  expansion 194.1, 2
  convexity 250.1, 2
  sound 404.1
  sore 655.16
swelling *adj.*
  protuberant 250.9
  grandiloquent 577.7
  excited 824.9
  heart 824.12
  pompous 882.8
swell mob, swellmobs-
  man 792.6
swelter *n.*
  perspiration 299.4
  heat 382.2
swelter *v.* 382.13
sweltering 382.16
swerve *n.*
  obliquity 217.1
  deviation 279.1
swerve *v.*
  change 140.5
  oblique 217.5
  deviate 279.4
  ~ off 287.2
  demur 603.4
  shrink 623.9
swift *n.* 366.22
swift *adj.* 274.13
  (sudden 113.5)
  (hasty 684.5)
swifter 273.10
swiftly 274.14
  (hastily 684.7)
swiftness 274.1
swig *n.* drink 298.4
  alcoholic drink
    959.10
swig *v.* drink 298.47
  swill 959.15

swill *n.* drink 298.4
  garbage 653.6
  alcoholic drink
    959.10
swill *v.* drink 298.47
  tipple 959.15
swillbowl, swiller,
  swilltub 959.11
swim bathe 267.46
  be light 320.5
  luxuriate in 377.4
swim against the
  stream 704.6
swim with the stream
  conform 82.5
  concur 488.7
  idle 683.8
  take it easy 705.3
  be fashionable 852.6
swimming *n.*
  bathing 267.9
  faulty sight 443.7
  delirium 503.3
go in swimming
  267.46
swimming *adj.* 458.12
swimmingly
  easily 705.8
  successfully 731.12
  prosperously 734.9
swimming pool 652.4
  (pool 343a.1)
swindle *n.* 545.3; 791.5
swindle *v.* 791.12
  (deceive 545.7)
  (not pay 808.5)
swindler 792.8
  (cheat 548.2)
swine slattern 59.5
  pig 366.7
swineherd 370.4
swing *n.* rhythm 138.3
  agency 170.1
  influence 175.1
  extent 180.1
  bed 215.24
  gait 266.5
  thrust 276.3; 716.3
  oscillation 314.5
  musical rhythm
    413.21
  music 415.6
  operation 680.1
  scope 748.2
  amusement 840.15
swing *v.* vary 149.4
  depend 214.4
  walk 266.16
  pitch 267.45
  turn 311.4
  oscillate 314.8
  shake 315.8
  be irresolute 605.4
  tergiversate 607.7
  be hanged 972.13
swing in with 709.5
swing round
  turn ship 267.24
  turn round 283.6
swinge singe 384.18
  chastise 972.6

swingeing, swinging
  31.8
swingy 415.29
swinish greedy 865.20
  gluttonous 957.4
  carnal 961.11
swink *n.* 686.3
swink *v.* 686.6
swipe *n.* 373.2
swipe *v.* 791.9
swipes 959.5
swirl *n.* whirl 312.2
  eddy 348.8
swirl *v.* rotate 312.7
  eddy 348.21
swirly 312.8
swish rustle 405.5
  sibilate 409.3
Swiss *n.* 188.9
Swiss *adj.* 188.11
Swiss guards 726.7
switch *n.* member 51.4
  interchange 148.1
  hair 256.3
  twig 367.4
  trade 794.3
  whip 975.2
switch *v.*
  interchange 148.3
  shift 279.6
  trade 794.4
  whip 972.6
switch off
  electricity 158a.11
  extinguish 421.6
switch on
  electrify 158a.11
  light 420.21
switchback 627.5
swivel *n.* whirl 312.2
  axis 312.5
  gun 727.11
swivel *v.*
  turn round 283.6
  turn 311.4
  rotate 312.7
swiveleye 443.4
swiveleyed 443.14
swizzle *n.* 959.8
swizzle *v.* 959.15
swollen
  expanded 194.10
  (hulky 192.13)
  (convex 250.9)
  (overfull 641.6)
  proud 878.6
  boastful 884.7
swollenness 250.1
swoon *n.* coma 683.5
  faint 688.3
swoon *v.* collapse 158.5
  faint 688.4
swoop *n.* 310.1
at one fell swoop
  suddenly 113.7
  violently 173.18
  seizure 789.17
swoop *v.* 310.4
swoop down upon
  789.13
swop See swap
sword *n.*

warfare 722.1
weapon 727.3
  (knife 253.6)
  coercion 744.1
at swords' points
  722.14
sword *v.* 361.12
swordfish 298.18
Swordfish 318.6
sword-in-hand
  prepared 673.11
  under arms 722.12
swordlike 253.15
sword of Damocles
  667.1
swordsman 726.1
sword stick 727.3
Sybarite 954a.1
Sybaritic 954.4
sycophancy 886.1
  (flattery 933.1)
sycophant 886.2
  (adherent 46.3)
  (follower 281.2)
  (dependent 746.3)
  (flatterer 935.2)
sycophantic 886.4
  (flattering 933.3)
syllabic 561.9
syllabification 567.1
syllabify 566.5
syllable phone 561.3
  word 562.1
syllabus list 86.1
  compendium 596.1
  (book 593.1)
syllepsis 567.1
syllogism
  reasoning 476.1
  logic 476.5
syllogist 476.9
syllogistic 476.1, 17
syllogize
  philosophize 451.34
  reason 476.10
sylph 979.7, 9
sylphidine 979.15
sylvan See silvan
sylvestrian 367.15
symbol number 84.1
  notation 415.23
  emblem 550.2, 12
  letter 561.1
symbolic
  exemplary 82.11
  figurative 521.3
  typical 550.21
  representative 554.9
symbolically 550.23
symbolic logic 451.4
symbolism
  cryptography 528.5
  indication 550.1
  art 556.6
  esoterics 994.1
  religion 998.1
symbolist 556.19
symbolization 550.1
symbolize mean 516.5
  figure 521.2
  (represent 554.7)
  latentize 526.5

symbology — tablet

typify 550.18
symbology 550.17
symmetrical
  equal 27.8
  form 242.4
  (orderly 58.7)
  (comely 845.10)
make symmetrical 242.3
symmetrize 242.3
symmetry
  equality 27.1
  order 58.1
  form 242
  (beauty 845.1)
  elegance 578.1
sympathetic
  friendly 888.4
  loving 897.14
  benevolent 906.6
  pitying 914.6
sympathetic ink 528.5
sympathetic magic 992.1
sympathize
  be concordant 714.2
  be friendly 888.2
  have fellow feeling 906.5
  commiserate 914.3
  condole 915.2
sympathizer
  upholder 711.4
  (pitier 914.2)
  friend 890.1
  philanthropist 911.1
sympathizing 906.6
sympathy
  understanding 488.3
  tender feeling 821.1
  friendship 888.1
  love 897.1
  (concord 714.1)
  fellow-feeling 906.1
  pity 914.1
  condolence 915.1
symphonic 415.28
symphonion 417.5
symphonious 413.26
symphonist 416.1, 14
symphonize
  harmonize 413.24
  play music 416.18
symphony
  music 413.1; 415.3, 15
  concord 714.1
symphony orchestra 416.9
symphysis 43.1
symposium
  collection 72.7
  drinking 298.3
  book 593.2
  festivity 840.2
  compotation 959.1
symptom 550.1
symptomatic
  indicative 550.21
  warning 668.9
symptomatological 522.8

symptomatology
  interpretation 522.5
  indication 550.1
  pathology 655.19
synaeresis, syneresis
  combination 48.1
  composition 54.1
synagogue 1000.1
synchronization
  agreement 23.1
  synchronism 120.1
  music 413.1
synchronize agree 23.7
  ~ in time 120.3
  harmonize 413.24
synchronized 23.9
synchronous
  simultaneous 120.4
  harmonious 413.26
be synchronous 120.3
synchysis 218.2
synclinal 217.11
syncopate
  contract 195.4
  rhythmize 416.18
syncopated 415.29
syncopation
  contraction 195.1
  tempo 413.22
  music 415.6
syncopator 416.1
syncope elision 44.2
  helplessness 158.2
  contraction 195.1
  shortening 201.2
  grammar 572.1
  swoon 688.3
syncretic 61.6
syncretism
  unfitness 24.3
  religion 984.2
syncretize 48.3
syndic official 745.9
  judge 967.1
syndicate n.
  directorate 542.8
  council 696.1
  trust 712.5
syndicate v. 48.4
synecdoche 521.1
syneresis See synaeresis
synergetic
  concurrent 178.4
  co-operative 709.7
synergism 709.1
synergistic
  concurrent 178.4
  co-operative 709.7
synergize 178.2
synergy
  concurrence 178.1
  co-operation 709.1
syngenetic 5.6
synizesis
  combination 48.1
  composition 54.1
synod 696.2, 3
  (ecclesiastic 995.5)
synodical 696.9
synonym, synonyme
  equivalence 516.3

(analogue 17.5)
(equivalent 27.5)
  word 562.1
  name 564.2
synonymic 13.7; 516.11
synonymicon 593.4
  (synonym 516.3)
synonymity 13.1
synonymize 516.6
synonymous
  coincident 13.7
  meaning 516.11
  (equivalent 27.9)
synonymy
  identity 13.1
  equivalence 516.3
synopsis list 86.1
  grammar 567.1
  compendium 596.1
synopsize 596.4
synoptic short 201.5
  grammar 567.6
  compendious 596.5
synovia 332.2
synovial 332.5
syntactical 567.6
syntagma 60.3
syntax 567.1
syntaxis 60.1
syntectic 655.25
synthesis
  combination 48.1
  composition 54.1
  reasoning 476.1
synthetic 476.17
syphilis 655.7
syphilitic 655.25
syphilophobia 860.4
syphon See siphon
Syriac 560.4
syringe n. 337.3
syringe v. 337.5
syrinx whistle 410.4
  instrument 417.4
  larynx 580.2
syrtis 667.1
syrup See sirup
Syryenian 560.4
system method 58.3
  (arrangement 60.1)
  (rule 80.1)
  method 627.1
  (plan 626.1)
systematic
  orderly 58.7
  (uniform 16.5)
  (arranged 60.10)
  (classificational 75.6)
  (businesslike 625.11)
  regular 138.9
systematically 58.8
systematization 60.2
systematize order 58.6
  methodize 60.8
systole
  contraction 195.1
  ~ and diastole 314.3
syzygy 199.1

T

T 219.6
to a T 494.16
tab adjunct 39.2
  (afterpart 65.2)
  airplane 273a.10
  tabloid 599.3
  drop 599.15
tabacin 392a.1
tabacosis 392a.10
tabacum 392a.1
tabard 225.15
tabaret 219.5
tabasco 393.1
tabby n. cat 366.4
  newsmonger 532.5
tabby adj. 440.10
tabefaction 195.1
tabefy decrease 36.3
  decompose 49.3
  shrink 195.4
tabernacle abode 189.1
  church 1000.1
tabes 195.1
tabescent
  contractive 195.6
  withered 659.12
tabes dorsalis 655.14
tabetic, tabid
  contractive 195.6
  thin 203.11
  diseased 655.25
  wasted 659.12
table n.
  arrangement 60.3
  ~ of contents 86.1; 593.7
  lamina 204.2
  hill 206.2
  plane 213.3
  stand 215.20
  flat 251.3
  food 298.5
  meal 298.34
  plain 344.1
  writing tablet 590.10
  on the table
    in question 461.26
    openly 525.7
    planned 626.11
    ready 673.11
table v. postpone 133.4
  abandon 624.3
  put aside 678.4
tableau list 86.1
  view 448.2
  picture 556.9
  drama 599.5
tablecloth 223.2
table d'hôte 298.39
tableland hill 206.2
  plain 344.1
Table Mountain 318.6
tablespoon 191.14
tablet list 86.1
  lamina 204.2
  flat 251.3
  gravestone 363.15
  record 551.3
  monument 551.4

table talk — take

tablet *(continued)*
  stationery 590.10
table talk 532.3
table turning 994.5
tableware 191.13
  (merchandise 798.3)
tablier 225.20
tablinum 191.17
tabloid *n.* 599.3
tabloid *adj.* 204.5
taboo, tabu *n.* 761.1
taboo, tabu *v.* 761.2
taboo, tabu *adj.* 761.4
tabor, tabour 417.10
taborer, tabourer 416.7
taboret, tabouret
  seat 215.22
  percussive 417.10
tabular arranged 60.10
  laminated 204.5
tabula rasa void 187.1
  obliteration 552.1
tabulate classify 60.7
  give continuity 69.5
  list 86.3
tabulation 551.7
tace 403.9
tachometer 267a.29
tachygrapher 590.12
tachygraphic 590.16
tachygraphy 590.7
tacit implied 526.7
  wordless 581.7
taciturn 585.4
  (secretive 528.22)
taciturnist 585.2
taciturnity 585
  (secrecy 528.2)
taciturnly 585.5
tack *n.* pin 45.5
  cordage 205.4
  point 253.2
  ship's rope 273.10
  direction 278.1
  deviation 279.2
  path 627.2
tack *v.*
  ~ on 37.3
  ~ together 43.5
  attach 43.6
  change 140.5
  wear ship 267.24
  (deviate 279.4)
tackle *n.*
  fastening 45.2
  cordage 205.4
  ship 273.9, 11
  litter 307.2
  equipment 634.1
tackle *v.*
  undertake 676.2
  set to work 686.7
tackling rigging 273.9
  equipment 634.1
tacky, tackey *n.* 659.5
tacky *adj.* viscid 352.8
  shabby 659.12
tact contact 379.1
  discrimination 465.1
  skill 698.4
  (wisdom 498.3)
  good taste 850.1

tactful
  discriminating 465.4
  graceful 894.12
tactician
  strategist 700.7
  proficient 702.4
tactics
  navigation 267.4
  conduct 692.2
  military ~ 722.2
tactile 379.5
tactility 379.1
taction
  contiguity 199.1
  contact 379.1
tactless 465a.3
tactual 379.5
tad 129.3
tadpole 129.7; 366.20
taenia, tenia
  strip 205.5
  capital 215.17
taffeta, taffety 219.5
taffrail log 466.2
taffy candy 396.2
  flattery 933.1
Taffy 188.9
tag *n.* modicum 32.2
  adjunct 39.2
  fastening 45.2
  sequel 65.1
  extremity 67.2
  horn 253.2
  sheep 366.8
tag *v.* add 37.3
  follow 281.3
  label 550.19
  name 564.6
Tagalog, Tagal 560.4
tag end 67.2
tagtail
  follower 281.2
  hanger-on 886.2
Tahitian 560.4
tail *n.* extremity 67.2
  pendant 214.2
  rear 235.1, 5, 6
  (afterpart 65.2)
  hair 256.3
  airplane 273a.10
  follower 281.2
  eye 441.7
  waiting line 599.23
tail *v.* 281.3
  (pursue 622.6)
tail off 36.3
tailage See tallage
tail coat 225.14
tailed pendanted 214.9
  caudal 235.11
tail end extremity 67.2
  rear 235.1, 7
tailless 38.9
tailleur 225.37
taillight 423.4
taillike 235.11
tailor 225.37
  (workman 690.10)
tailoring 225.35
tailor-made 161.13
tailpiece pendant 214.2
tail 235.1, 6

music 415.15
  engraving 558.1
  ornament 847.3
tail plane 273a.10
tailrace 350.1
tail spin 267a.24
tail wind 267a.19
taint *n.*
  discoloration 440a.1
  defect 651.2
  soil 653.3
  infection 655.2
  stigma 874.2
  moral blemish 945.5
taint *v.* discolor 440a.2
  soil 653.15
  disease 655.22
  corrupt 659.9
  stigmatize 874.7
tainted fetid 401.4
  imperfect 651.4
  unclean 653.17
  diseased 655.25
  corrupt 659.13;
    945.15
take *n.* gain 35.2
  profits 775.2
  catch 789.5
  theft 791.4
  booty 793.1
  receipts 810.1
take *v.* carry 270.8
  eat 298.44
  consider 484.8
  suppose 514.6
  understand 518.4
  submit to 725.3
  appropriate 789.7, 8
  (acquire 775.6)
  (receive 785.3)
  (assume 925.6)
  steal 791.9
  put up with 826.6
  delight 829.5
take aback 508.6
take a back seat
  be inferior 34.4
  be modest 881.3
take about 459.6
take account of 811.8
take a dare 861.5
take advantage of
  677.5
  (make the most of
    698.10)
take after
  resemble 17.7
  emulate 19.10
take amiss 900.6
  (dislike 867.4)
take away
  decrease 36.4
  deduct 38.4
  remove 185.2
  seize 789.10
  abduct 791.11
take back
  recant 607.9
  (apologize 952.5)
  recover 790.4
take breath 689.3
  (relax 687.4)

take by storm
  attack 716.5
  triumph 731.6
  seize 789.9
take care
  be careful 459.3
  be cautious! 864.3, 9
take care of
  kill 361.10
  care for 459.5, 6
  (protect 664.6)
  (preserve 670.3)
  (help 707.10)
  (defend 717.7)
  (minister to 746.8)
  punish 972.15
take charge of
  protect 664.6
  arrest 751.9
take down eat 298.44
  lower 308.4, 5
  degrade 874.1, 7
  humiliate 879.3
  reprove 932.8
  depreciate 934.3
take effect
  happen 151.3
  operate 170.2
take fire ignite 384.17
  become excited
    824.6
  become angry 900.9
take for granted
  presume 472.3
  believe 484.7
  be credulous 486.3
  suppose 514.6
take from
  decrease 36.4
  deduct 38.4
  dispossess 789.11
take heart
  be comforted 831.3
  cheer up 836.4, 14
  be hopeful 858.7
  take courage 861.6
take hold cohere 46.5
  gain influence 175.9
  seize 789.9
take horse 266.19
take in include 76.3
  attend 186.9
  (be a spectator
    444.3)
  shorten 201.4
  receive 296.2; 785.3
  eat 298.44
  hear 448.11
  see 441.10
  understand 518.4
  deceive 545.7, 10
take in hand
  train stock 370.5
  discipline 537.10
  undertake 676.2
  (work 686.6)
take into account
  include 76.3
  bear in mind 457.2
  discriminate 465.2
  allow for 469.4
take into one's head

1124

take-in — tallow

intend 620.3
desire 865.11
take issue with 708.2
take it
  not weaken 159.6
  consider 484.8
  suppose 514.6
take it easy idle 683.8
  rest 686.3
  go easily 705.3
  be composed 826.5
  be cautious 864.3, 9
take it or leave it
  609a.2
take it out of
  weaken 160.8
  punish 972.5
  chastise 972.6
take leave part 44.11
  depart 293.7
  abandon 624.3
  take liberty 748.9
take measures
  plan 626.9
  prepare 673.7
  take action 692.4
  take precautions
    864.4
take no account of
  disregard 458.5
  neglect 460.4
  not observe 773.3
  disdain 930.5
take no notice of
  disregard 458.5
  neglect 460.4
  not observe 773.3
  snub 930.7
take no part in
  do nothing 681.2
  abstain 953.5
take off imitate 19.6
  begin 66.5
  obliterate 162.4
  remove 185.2
  undress 226.4
  airplane 267a.33
  depart 293.4, 5
  abduct 791.11
  discount 813.2
take on
  undertake 676.2
  fight 720.8
  fret 828.10
  be discontented
    832.3
  grieve 837.6
  complain 839.10
  be angry 900.8
**take one's breath
  away**
  astonish 870.3
  awe 928.7
take one's medicine
  972.12
take one's time
  go slow 275.5
  (be leisurely 685.2)
  dawdle 683.8
take one's leisure
  685.2
take out

hasten off 293.5
extract 301.5
take part in
  do 680.6
  participate 709.6
take place 151.3
take root
  gain influence 175.9
  settle 184.14
  become habitual
    613.9
take shipping 293.6
take silk 968.3
take stock count 85.8
  scrutinize 441.12
  examine 461.17
  give credence 484.7
  take account of
    811.8
take the air
  travel 266.13
  fly 267a.30
take the back track
  283.5
**take the bull by the
  horns**
  be resolute 604.6
  undertake 676.2
  set to work 686.7
  be courageous 861.5
  be rash 863.5
take the cake
  excel 33.5
  win 731.6
  acquire honor 873.12
take the field 722.9
take the rap
  substitute 147.3
  take the blame
    932.10
  be punished 972.12
take the reins
  direct 693.4
  assume authority
    737.13
take the road 266.12
**take the wind out of
  one's sails**
  disable 158.6
  thwart 706.7
**take time by the fore-
  lock**
  be early 132.5
  turn to account 134.6
take to
  ~ ~ a habit 613.10
  pursue 622.6
  use 677.5
  like 827.6
  fancy 865.11
  become enamored
    897.12
take to heart
  be sensitive 822.4
  suffer 828.9
  be discontented
    832.3
  be dejected 837.6
  resent 900.6
take to task
  reprove 932.8
  accuse 938.4

punish 972.5
take up pick up 307.6
  discuss 595.4
  adopt 609.7
  undertake 676.2
  (pursue 622.6)
  second 707.8
  arrest 751.9
  borrow 788.2
  buy up 795.3
  reprove 932.8
take upon oneself
  will 600.2
  undertake 676.2
  (resolve 604.6)
  (intend 620.3)
take up the gauntlet
  720.8
take up with
  associate with 88.6
  confer 588.8
  use 677.5
  advise with 695.6
  brook 826.6
  be content 831.3
  make friends with
    888.3
take-in 35.2
take-off copy 21.1, 3
  decrement 39a.1
  beginning 66.1
  aeronautics 267a.25
  departure 293.1, 3
taker 789.6
takin 366.9
taking n.
  appropriation 789
  (acquisition 775.1)
  (theft 791.1)
  pain 828.1
  dudgeon 900.2
taking adj.
  alluring 617.5
  contagious 657.5
  catching 789.15
  (thieving 791.14)
  delightful 829.8
talapoin 996.9
tale sum 84.3
  handle 215.7
  narrative 594.2
talebearer
  informer 527.6
  newsmonger 532.5
  aptitude 698.2
talent 698.2
  (genius 498.5)
talented 698.13
talesman 967.3
talion 718.1
talionic 718.4
taliped 243.5
talipes 243.1
talisman 993.2
  (luck 156.1)
talismanic 992.5
talk n. rumor 532.3
  lesson 537.6
  language 560.1
  (dialect 563.5)
  diction 569.1
  speech 582.1, 2

(chatter 584.2)
allocution 586.1
conversation 588.1
talk v. confess 529.5
  gossip 532.7
  speak 582.6
  (argue 476.11)
  (tell 527.7)
  (divulge 529.4)
  (assert 535.3)
  (express 566.3)
  (voice 580.8)
  (exclaim 580.9)
  (declaim 582.7)
  (chatter 584.4)
  (converse 588.7)
  (soliloquize 589.3)
talk big
  be bombastic 577.5
  (exaggerate 549.2)
  be ostentatious
    882.6
  boast 884.5
  bluster 887.3
  threaten 909.2
talk over
  discuss 588.8
  persuade 615.9
  advise with 695.6
talk shop 851.5
talk to
  address 586.2
  reprove 932.9
talkative 584.5
talkativeness 584.1
talked-about 873.16
**talkee-talkee, talky-
  talky**
  ungrammaticism
    568.1
  speech defect 583.1
  chatter 584.2
talker speaker 582.5
  (gossip 532.5)
  (chatterer 584.3)
  (conversationalist
    588.5)
  (soliloquist 589.2)
talkfest 588.1
talkie 599.9
talking 582.1
talking-to 932.3
talky 584.5
talky-talk 584.2
tall great 31.6
  absolute 31.12
  sizable 192.11
  high 206.13
  (long 200.12)
  (long-legged 200.13)
  (lanky 203.11)
  exaggerated 549.3
  grandiloquent 577.7
  ostentatious 882.8
  boastful 884.7
tallage, tailage 812.2
tall order
  big undertaking
    676.1
  difficult task 704.1
tallow fat 356.4
  candle 423.7

tallow-faced — taskmaster

tallow-faced 429.6
tall story
  falsehood 546.1
  boast 884.1
tally *n.* sum 84.3
  (count 85.3)
  list 86.1
  mark 550.11
  credit 805.1
  account 811.1
tally *v.* agree 23.7
  conform 82.4
  list 86.3
tallyho *n.* 272.4
tallyho *int.* 622.12
tallyman 797.1
talma 225.15
Talmud 985.5
Talmudic 985.8
Talmudism 984.7
Talmudist 984.17
talon adherer 46.3
  clutch 737.2; 781.3
talus 217.2
tam 225.26
Tamashek 560.4
tambo drummer 416.7
  blackface actor 599.19
tamboura, tambura 417.2
tambouret 417.10
tambourgi 416.7
tambourine
  drummer 416.7
  percussion instrument 417.10
  blackface actor 599.19
tame *v.* moderate 174.5
  domesticate 370.6
  break in 537.10
  subdue 749.5
tame *adj.* inert 172.3
  moderate 174.6
  domesticated 370.10
  feeble 575.2
  apathetic 823.5
  meek 826.10
tame cat 160a.3
tameless 173.14
Tamil 560.4
taming 370.2
tam-o'-shanter 225.26
tamp *n.* 276.4
tamp *v.* 276.8
tamper change 140.6
  bribe 618.3
  corrupt 659.9
  meddle 682.14
tampion, tompion 263.1
tampon stopper 263.1
  dressing 662.14
tam-tam 417.10
tan *v.* brown 433.3
  whip 972.6
tan *adj.* 433.4
tana See thana
Tanagra 433.1
tandem *n.* team 272.9
  bicycle 272.14

tandem *adv.* 200.15
tandle 382.8
tan-faced 433.4
tang tine 253.2
  fang 253.3; 663.3
  taste 390.1
  (savor 394.2)
  pungency 392.1
tangelo 41.5
tangency
  contiguity 199.1
  contact 379.1
tangent *n.* 199.2
tangent *adj.*
  contiguous 199.4
  touching 379.4
tangerine 439.1, 2
tangibility 3.1
tangible material 316.8
  (real 1.8)
  (substantial 3.4)
  touchable 379.5
  valid 494.14
  sufficient 639.6
Tangier 439.3
tangle *n.* 59.3
tangle *v.*
  complicate 61.5
  interlace 219.8
  contend with 720.8
tangled
  complex 59.10
  difficult 704.6
tangle-legs 959.4
tangly 59.10
tank *n.*
  receptacle 191.11
  tractor 272.17
  pond 343a.1
  (store 636.4)
  drunkard 959.11
tank *v.*
  tank up 959.15
tankage 192.2
tankard 191.11
tank car 272.19
tanked 959.21
tanker 726.11
tank town 189.17
tanna See thana
Tannenberg 722.5
tannic acid, tannin 663.5
tan-skinned 433.4
tantalization 617.1
tantalize
  tempt 617.4; 865.14
  harass 830.5
  seduce 897.13
tantalizing
  alluring 617.5
  (exciting 824.12)
  desirable 865.21
tantalum 635.4
tantamount 27.9
tantara, tantarara 404.3
tanti 642.11
tantivy 274.14
tantra 986.2
tantrum 900.2
Taoism 984.11

Taoist 984.21
Tao Tê Ching 986.1
tap *n.* kind 75.2
  root 153.3
  stopper 263.1
  faucet 263.2
  (outlet 295.5)
  blow 276.3
  hammer 276.4
  taproom 959.13
on tap 644.8
tap *v.* open 260.11
  strike 276.8
  draw off 297.13
  bang 406.7
tap dance 840.7
tap dancer 840.9
tape strip 205.5
  bandaging 662.14
  liquor 959.4
tapeline 205.5
tape measure 466.4
taper *n.* lighter 388.4
  light 423.1, 7
  wick 423.12
taper *v.* 203.7
tapered, tapering
  narrow 203.9
  pointed 253.11
tapestry cloth 219.5
  art 556.9
  needlework 847.6
tapis
on the tapis
  on foot 151.5
  in question 461.26
  intended 620.4
  planned 626.11
tapper 276.4
tapping 297.5
taproom 959.13
taproot 153.3
tapster, tapstress
  employee 746.1
  bartender 959.12
tar *n.* mariner 269.1
  resin 356a.1
  pavement 627.4
tar *v.* 223.24
tar and feather
  torture 830.6
  affront 929.3
  punish 972.5
taradiddle See tarradiddle
tarantella music 415.7
  dance 840.7
tarantism, tarentism
  twitching 315.6
  nervous disorder 655.14
tarboosh 225.26
tardily 133.13
tardiness 133.1
tardy 133.8
  (slow 275.8)
tare decrement 39a
  weed 645.4
  discount 813.1
target butt 620.2
  armor 717.2
Targum *n.* 522.2

Targum, Targumize *v.* 522.7
Targumic 522.8
tariff 812.2
tarn 343a.1
Tarnhelm 993.4
tarnish *n.*
  blemish 848.1
  stigma 874.2
tarnish *v.*
  decolor 429.5
  discolor 440a.2
  soil 653.15
  stigmatize 874.7
tarp tarpaulin 223.3
  raincoat 225.17
tarpan horse 271.4
  fish 298.18
tarpaulin cloth 219.5
  canopy 223.3
  raincoat 225.17
  mariner 269.1
tarradiddle *n.* lie 546.1
  liar 548.5
tarradiddle *v.* 544.4
tarriance 133.2
tarry *v.* wait 133.7
  (protract 110.6)
  (continue 106.2)
  be permanent 141.4
  be quiescent 265.5
  await 507.5
tarry *adj.* 356a.3
tart *n.* hussy 129.5
  pastry 298.11
  loose woman 961.2
tart *adj.* sour 397.6
  (pungent 392.5)
  gruff 895.7
tartan ship 273.2
  check 440.2
tartar sour 397.2
  scum 653.5
  ill-humored person 901.4
Tartarean
  cruel 907.9
  infernal 982.5
tartar emetic 663.5
tartarize 397.4
Tartarus 982.2
tartness
  sourness 397.1
  gruffness 895.2
tartufe, tartuffe
  hypocrite 548.4
  pietist 988.6
tartufery, tartuffery 988.2
tartufian, tartuffian
  hypocritical 544.8
  sanctimonious 988.11
Tarzan 159.6
task *n.* lesson 537.6
  job 625.2
  (labor 686.3)
  difficulty 704.1
  commission 755.1
task *v.* tax 686.8
  exact 741.5
taskmaster 694.1

1126

tassel — teeth

tassel pendant 214.2
  needlework 847.6
tastable, tasteable 390.4
taste *n.* modicum 32.2
  flavor 390
  (savor 394.2)
  discrimination 465.1
  elegance 578.1
  refinement 850
  (fastidiousness 868.1)
  have no taste for
  be indifferent 866.3
  dislike 867.4
  in bad taste
  language 579.3
  inelegant 851.6
  in good taste 850.5
  to one's taste
  savory 394.7
  agreeable 829.7
  after one's fancy 850.6
  liked 897.16
taste *v.* savor 390.3
  be savory 394.5
  ~ of 394.6
  experience 821.3
tasteful savory 394.7
  speech 578.4
  in good taste 850.5
  (discriminating 465.4)
  (esthetic 845.16)
  (simple 849.3)
  (fastidious 868.4)
tastefully 850.7
tasteless insipid 391.2
  speech 579.3
  dull 843.5
  inelegant 851.6
tastelessness
  insipidity 391.1
  inelegance 579.1
taster 390.1
tasting 390.2
tasty savory 394.7
  in good taste 850.5
tatoo See **tattoo**
tatou, tatouay 366.14
tats 621.8
tatter modicum 32.2
  piece 51.3
  rag 225.5
tatterdemalion 876.9
Tattersall's 799.4
tatting 847.6
tattle *n.* gossip 532.3
  small talk 588.2
tattle *v.*
  inform on 527.10
  blab 529.4
  gossip 532.7
tattler, tattletale
  informer 527.6
  newsmonger 532.5
tattoo, tatoo *n.*
  pony 271.3
  fanfare 404.3
  drumming 407.3
tattoo, tatoo *v.*

toot 404.7
  drum 407.8
  beat time 416.19
  spot 440.4
tau 219.6
taught 490.15
  (educated 537.13)
taunt *n.* 930.3
taunt *v.* jeer 930.6
  (ridicule 856.4)
  reproach 938.4
tauromachy 720.2
Taurus 318.6
taut 43.11
tautological 573.8
  (repetitional 104.6)
tautologize
  repeat 104.4
  battologize 573.6
tautology 573.2
  (repetition 104.1)
  (grandiloquence 577.2)
  (redundance 641.1)
tautophonic 473.8
tautophony 573.2
tavern inn 189.8
  (restaurant 298.42)
  grogshop 959.13
Tavghi 560.4
tawdriness 851.2
  (frippery 847.2)
tawdry
  spurious 545.13
  gaudy 851.8
tawny *n.* 433.1
tawny, tawney *adj.*
  tan 433.4
  yellow 436.6
tax *n.* 812.2
tax *v.* weight 319.9
  employ 677.5
  task 686.8
  (fatigue 688.5)
  exact 741.5
  entreat 765.5
  assess 812.5
  accuse 938.4
taxable 812.8
taxation 812.2
taxi *n.*
  taxicab 272.6, 15
  taxiplane 273a.1
taxi, taxy *v.*
  ride 266.18
  aviate 267a.31
taxicab *n.* 272.6, 15
taxicab *v.* 266.18
taxidermist 368.2
taxidermy 368.1
taxiing, taxying 267a.25
taxing 938.1
taxiplane 273a.1
taxis 60.1
taxonomic 75.6
taxonomist 368.2
taxonomy
  classification 60.2
  zoology 368.1
t.b. 655.10
T D 392a.6

tea energizer 171.5
  drink 298.4
  stimulant 662.5
  social meal 892.6
teach 537.9
  (inform 527.7)
  (prepare 673.6)
teach fishes to swim 641.3
teachable 539.7
  (docile 602.9)
teacher
  instructor 540
  (interpreter 524.1)
  (preparer 673.5)
  (professional 690.10)
  (advisor 695.3)
teacherage 189.2
teacheress 540.2
teacherly, teachery 540.7
teaching *n.*
  doctrine 484.3
  instruction 537
  (information 527.1)
  (preparation 673.1)
teaching *adj.* 537.12
tea gown 225.23
Teague 188.9
tea hound 902.6
teak 367.6
teakwood 635.3
teal food 298.26
  bird 366.22
team *n.* series 69.2
  company 72.3
  horses 272.9
  party 712.1
team *v.* 48.4
teammate 711.1
teamster 268.9
  (carrier 271.1)
tea party 892.4, 6
teapot 191.11
teapoy 215.20
tear *n.* teardrop 839.2
  spree 840.3
  drinking bout 959.3
  in tears 839.14
  (wretched 828.16)
  shed tears 839.8
tear *v.* sever 44.8
  ~ **down** 162.4
  be violent 173.7
  open 260.11
  speed 274.9
  be brittle 328.3
  ~ **away from** 789.11
  rage 825.7
tear one's hair 839.11
tear out
  hasten off 293.5
  extract 301.5
tear to pieces
  disintegrate 44.9
  destroy 162.4
  damage 659.8
tear bottle, teardrop 830.2
tearful 839.14
  (sorrowful 837.11)

tearfully 839.17
tear gas 334.2
tease 830.5
teaser example 82.2
  advertisement 531.4
  difficult task 704.1
teaser curtain 599.15
teasing 830.12
teaspoon 191.14
teat 250.3
tea urn 191.11
tec 528.9
technicality
  term 564.3
  formulary 697.1
techniphone 418.6
technique art 556.5
  skill 698.3
technological 564.9
technology
  nomenclature 564.1
  skill 698.3
techy 901.7
tectiform 223.33
tectology 240.4
ted 73.3
Te Deum 990.2
  (sacred music 415.11)
  (rejoicing 838.1)
  (thanksgiving 916.2)
tedge 350.3
tedious 841.8
  (uniform 16.5)
  (repetitional 104.7)
tedium 841.3
  (sameness 13.2)
  (regularity 16.2)
tee-hee See **te-hee**
teem
  be numerous 102.4
  give birth 161.9
  be productive 168.5, 6
  abound 639.4
teemful 168.7
teeming crowded 72.13
  profuse 102.5
  productive 168.7
  pregnant 168.9
  abundant 639.7
teemless 169.4
teen-age 127.5
teens 127.1
teeny, teeny-weeny 193.8
teepee See **tepee**
teeter *n.* 314.3, 6
teeter *v.*
  be weak 160.6
  alternate 314.10
teeter-totter *n.*
  alternation 314.3, 6
  game 840.15
teeter-totter *v.*
  alternate 314.10
  be irresolute 605.4
teeth tooth 253.3
  serration 257.2
  between the teeth 405.11

teetotal — tendency

teeth (*continued*)
in the teeth of
 in spite of 704.12
 in defiance of 708.6;
  715.4
teetotal whole 50.6
 abstinent 953.6
teetotaler, teetotaller
  953.3
teetotalism 953.2
 (sobriety 958.1)
teetotum spinner 312.4
 toy 840.16
teg 366.8
tegmental 223.31
tegument 223.2
tegumentary 223.31
te-hee, teehee 856.4
teinoscope 445.2
telamon post 215.16
 ornament 847.4
telegram *n.* 532a.3
 (message 532.2)
 (epistle 592.2)
telegram *v.* 532a.8
telegraph *n.*
 speed 274.6
 telegram 532a.3, 5
 (electricity 158a.6)
 signal 550.14
by telegraph 684.7
telegraph *v.* 532a.8
telegrapheme 532a.3
telegrapher 532a.6
telegraphic fast 274.13
 wireless 532a.10
telegraphic alphabet
  550.15
telegraphone
 telephonograph
  532a.5
 recorder 553.3
telegraphy
 telephony 532a.1
 (electricity 158a.1)
 (code 550.15)
 signal 550.14
telekinesis
 kinetics 264.4
 spiritualism 994.5
telekinetic
 kinetic 264.9
 psychic 994.22
telemotor 273.7
telencephalon 450.2
teleological 620.4
teleology 620.1
telepathic 994.22
telepathist 994.15
telepheme 532a.2
telephone *n.* 532a.5
telephone *v.* 532a.7
telephone call 532a.2
telephoner 532a.6
telephone wire 158a.8
telephonic 532a.10
telephonograph
 telegraphone 532a.5
 recorder 553.3
telephony
 acoustics 402.5
 communication 532a

(electricity 158a.1)
telescope *n.* 445.2
Telescope, Tele-
  scopium *n.* 318.6
telescope *v.* 572.2
telescope word 563.9
telesm 993.2
telethermometer 389.1
Teleut 560.4
televise 532a.9
television 532a.1
televisional 532a.10
televisor 532a.6
televisual
 visual 441.19
 of television 532a.10
telfer, telferage See
 telpher etc.
tell *n.* 588.1
tell *v.* enumerate 85.7
 have influence 175.7
 show 467.7
 inform 527.7, 10
 (explain 522.6)
 divulge 529.4
 publish 531.7
 say 582.6
 narrate 594.5
 be important 642.7
tell it not in Gath!
  932.16
tell it to the marines!
  497.5
tell off 85.7
tell tale 529.4
tell the world 535.8
teller informant 527.5
 storyteller 594.4
 treasurer 801
telling *n.*
 numeration 85.1
 information 527.1
 (disclosure 529.1)
 ~ of beads 998.2
telling *adj.*
 influential 175.10
 graphic 518.6
 significant 642.11
 exciting 824.12
telltale hint 527.4
 informer 527.6
 (traitor 949.3)
 newsmonger 532.5
 indication 550.1
telluric worldly 318.14
 terrestrial 342.9
Tellus, Tellus Mater
 world 318.1
 goddess 979.2
telpher, telfer 627.6
telpherage, telferage
  270.4
telpherway 627.6
Telugu 560.4
temblor 173.2
temerarious, temeri-
  tous 863.6
temerity 863.1
temerous 863.6
temper *n.* nature 5.3
 state 7.1
 hardness 323.1

frame of mind 820.1
 anger 900.1
have a temper 901.5
lose one's temper
  900.9
 (become excited
  824.6)
 (rage 825.7)
temper *v.*
 moderate 174.5
 harden 323.4
 qualify 469.3
 prepare 673.6
tempera 428.3
temperament
 nature 5.3
 constitution 54.1
 frame of mind 820.1
temperance
 moderation 174.1
 cardinal virtue 944.1
 abstemiousness 953
 (self-control 604.3)
 (continence 960.1)
temperate
 moderate 174.6
 abstemious 953.6
 (sober 958.3)
be temperate 953.5
make temperate 174.5
temperature 382.1
tempered
 moderate 174.6
 music 415.28
 affected 820.3
temperer 174.3
tempest storm 173.5
 windstorm 349.11
 excitement 825.5
 festivity 840.2
 party 892.5
tempest in a teapot
 overestimation 482.1
 (exaggeration
  549.1)
 triviality 643.2
tempestive 134.7
tempestivity 134.1
tempest-tossed 824.10
tempestuous
 turbulent 173.12
 stormy 349.26
 excited 824.11
tempestuousness 825.4
Templar 996.11
temple side 236.1
 church 1000
 (assembly hall
  189.10)
tempo 413.22
set the tempo 58.6
temporal
 temporary 111.6
 chronological 114.9
 worldly 318.14
 earthly 989.9
temporarily 111.8
temporary
 transient 111.6
 (provisional 637.7)
 substitutional 147.4
temporization 702.1

temporize
 protract 110.6
 procrastinate 133.5
 use artifice 702.5
temporizer 943.2
temporizing
 cunning 702.6
 improbity 940.8
tempt
 ~ **the appetite** 394.5
 lure 617.4
 attempt 675.3
 excite desire 865.14
 seduce 897.13
temptation 617.1
tempter 617.3
the Tempter 978.1
tempting
 appetizing 394.7
 alluring 617.5
 (attractive 288.4)
 (inductive 615.11)
temptress 617.3
temulence 959.1
temulent 959.21
ten 98.6
tenable
 believable 484.15
 defensible 717.10
tenacious
 adhesive 46.9
 (tough 327.5)
 viscid 352.8
 persistent 604a.3
 (resolute 604.7)
 obstinate 606.6
 retentive 781.5
tenacity
 adhesiveness 46.2
 (toughness 327.1)
 (retention 781.1)
 perseverance 604a.1
 (resolution 604.1)
 obstinacy 606.1
 stinginess 819.1
tenaille, tenail 717.3
tenancy 777.1
tenancy in common
  778.1
tenant *n.*
 inhabitant 188.1
 possessor 779.1
tenant *v.* 186.10
Ten Commandments
  926.4
tend incline 176.2
 (be liable 177.2)
 (serve 644.2; 707.10)
 ~ **towards** 278.4
 gravitate 319.7
 ~ **stock** 370.7
 attend 457.4
 subserve 631.3
 work for 746.8
tendance, tendence
  749.2
tendency
 inclination 176
 (nature 5.3)
 (characteristic 79.2)
 (liability 177.1)
 (direction 278.1)

tender — terroristic

(bias 481.3)
(intention 620.1)
propensity 602.2
disposition 820.1
tender n. ship 273.1
  naval auxiliary
   726.11
  offer 763.1
tender v. soften 324.4
  ~ to 707.6
  offer 763.2
tender adj.
  dainty 32.10
  youthful 127.5
  soft 324.6
  oversensitive 375.6
  soft-colored 428.17
  tenderhearted 822.7
  affectionate 897.14
  benevolent 906.6
  compassionate 914.6
tender-conscienced
  939.8
tenderfoot
  newcomer 57.3
  novice 541.6
  (ignoramus 493.1)
  unsophisticate 703.2
  recruit 726.5
tenderhearted
  softhearted 822.7
  benevolent 906.6
  compassionate 914.6
tenderling
  mollycoddle 160a.3
  weakling 160.4
tenderness
  affection 821.1
  tender susceptibility
   822.2
  compassion 914.1
tending 176.3
  (liable to 177.3)
  (disposed 820.4)
tendon 45.4
tendril member 51.4
  filament 205.1
  coil 248.2
  foliage 367.4
tenebrity 421.1
tenebrous 421.7
tenement
  house 189.3, 12
  suite 191.21
  property 780.4
tenet 484.3
tenfold 98.20
ten-gallon hat 225.26
tenia See taenia
tenné tan 433.1
  yellow 436.6
tenner, tener 98.6
tennis 840.11
Tenno 745.3
tenor state 7.1
  tendency 176.1
  direction 278.1
  tone 402.2
  high tone 410.2
  voice 413.14
  (vocalist 416.10)
  voice part 415.13

singer 416.10
  meaning 516.1
tenoroon 417.4
tenor violin 417.3
tenpins 840.11
ten-pounder 727.11
tense rigid 323.5
  phonetics 402.11
tensibility 325.1
tensible, tensile 325.5
tensility 325.1
tension strength 159.1
  stretch 200.5
ten-strike 731.2
tent cover 223.2, 5
  (camp 189.15)
  (sunshade 424.2)
  stopper 263.1
  dressing 662.14
tentacle 781.3
tentage 223.5
tentative
  substitutional 147.4
  experimental 463.12
  (provisional 637.7)
  undecided 475.10
tenterhook 214.3
  on tenterhooks 507.7
tenth n. 812.2
tenth adj. 98.20; 99.3
tentmaker 690.8
tent pegging 840.11
tenuity smallness 32.1
  thinness 203.4
  rarity 322.1
tenuous
  chimerical 4.6
  thin 203.10
  rare 322.4
tenure time 106.1
  possession 777.1
  (property 780.1)
tenure in free alms
  748.5
tepee, teepee hut 189.4
  tent 223.5
tepefaction 384.1
tepefy 384.16
tephramancy 511.3
tepid 382.15
  (cool 383.10)
tepidarium 386.6
teraphim 511.5
teratism
  unconformity 83.1
  monstrosity 83.6
teratogenic 83.10
teratology
  monstrosity 83.6
  distortion 243.1
tercentenary
  hundred 98.8
  anniversary 138.5
tercentennial 98.8
tercet, terzet
  three 92.2
  note 413.6
  stanza 597.7
terebration 260.1, 260.8
tergal 235.10
tergiversant n. 607.4

tergiversant adj.
  607.10
tergiversate
  change one's mind
   607.7
  (change 140.5)
  (be irresolute 605.4)
  (be capricious
   608.4)
tergiversating 607.10
  (changeful 149.6)
  (irresolute 605.5)
  (fickle 608.6)
tergiversation 607
  (change 140.1)
  (changeableness
   149.1)
  (equivocation 477.4)
  (irresolution 605.1)
  (fickleness 608.3)
  (abandonment
   624.1)
tergiversator 607.4
  (equivocator 477.6)
  (waverer 605.3)
tergum 235.3
term n. end 67.1
  station 71
  time 106.1
  period 108.1
  limit 233.1
  word 562.1
  name 564.3
  estate 780.2
term v. 564.6
termagant fury 173.6
  shrew 901.4
  malevolent woman
   913.5
terminable 233.3
terminal n. end 67.1
  limit 233.1
  stop-off 266.10
  destination 292.6
  ornament 847.4
terminal adj. final 67.8
  limitary 233.3
  arriving 292.11
terminate 67.5–7
termination end 67.1
  (eventuality 151.1)
  (completion 729.1)
  limit 233.1
terminological 564.9
terminology
  lexicology 562.4
  nomenclature 564.1
terminus end 67.1
  limit 233.1
  stop-off 266.10
  destination 292.6
termite insect 366.24
  worker 690.2
termless infinite 105.3
  unlimited 180.7
terms
  circumstance 8.1
  reconciliation 723.1
  conditions 770.1
tern 93.3
ternal triplicate 93.3
  tripartite 94.2

ternary n. 92.2
ternary adj. 93.3
terpsichore
  dancing 840.6
  dancer 840.9
Terpsichore 416.16
terpsichorean 840.9
terra 318.1
terrace plane 213.3
  roadway 627.3
terra cotta n.
  ceramics 384.14
  modeling clay 557.8
terra-cotta adj. 433.5
terra firma
  ground 211.2
  foundation 215.3
  land 342.1
  on terra firma
   on land 342.14
   safe 664.10
terrain region 181.1
  land 342.1
terra incognita 491.2
  (enigma 533.2)
terraqueous
  worldly 318.14
  terrestrial 342.9
terra rosa 434.2
terra sienna, terra
  umbra 433.2
terra verde 435.2, 4
terrene n. world 318.1
  land 342.1
terrene adj.
  worldly 318.14
  terrestrial 342.9
terrestrial
  worldly 318.14
  earthly 342.9
  mundane 989.9
terret 45.2
terre-verte 435.2, 4
terrible vast 31.8
  very bad 649.8
  fearful 860.15
terribly 31.23
terrier list 86.1
  dog 366.6
  account 811.1
terrific vast 31.8
  shocking 830.13
  frightful 860.15
terrifically 31.22
terrified 860.14
terrify 860.10
terrifying 860.15
terrine 191.11
territorial 181.6
territory 181.1
  (country 182.1)
terror fear 860.1
  (alarm 669.1)
  evildoer 913.1
terrorful 860.15
terrorism
  anarchy 738.2
  fear 860.5
terrorist
  alarmist 860.6
  evildoer 913.1
terroristic 738.8

terrorize — theopathy

terrorize 860.12
terror-striking 860.15
terror-struck 860.14
terry cloth 219.5
terse
 aphoristic 496.5
 concise 572.3
 (short 201.5)
tertian 138.11
tertiary 93.3
tertium quid
 mixture 41.4
 hermaphrodite 83.5
terzet See tercet
terzetto three 92.2
 part music 415.12
tessellate 440.4
tessellated
 checkered 440.8
 ornamented 847.13
tessellation 440.3
tessera
 checkerwork 440.3
 sign 550.2, 11
test *n.*
 examination 461.3
 measure 466.2
 experiment 463.1
 stand the test
 pass muster 463.11
 be true 494.5
test *v.* examine 461.17
 experiment 463.8
testa 223.14
testaceography 223.21
testaceous 223.32
testament
 testimony 467.2
 covenant 771.1
 will 784.6
testamur 467.4
testate testify 467.8
 depose 535.4
 promise 768.3
testator 784.7
testatory 467.11
tested 463.13
testee 463.7
tester canopy 223.3
 experimenter 463.6
testicle 357.4
testification 467.2
testificatory 467.11
testifier 467.6
testify *v.*
 give evidence 467.8
 (inform 527.10)
 (law 969.10)
 acknowledge 488.9
 depose 535.4
 indicate 550.18
 promise 768.3
testimonial *n.*
 testimony 467.2
 token 550.2
 monument 551.4
 (memorial 505.7)
testimonial *adj.* 467.11
testimony
 evidence 467.2
 (affirmation 535.1)
 (lawsuit 969.6)

token 550.2
testis 357.4
teston 800.8
testy 901.7
tetanus spasm 315.7
 illness 655.3
 ailment 655.5
tête-à-tête *n.*
 seat 215.22
 conversation 588.2
tête-à-tête *adj.*
 dual 89.4
 conversational
 588.10
 sociable 892.12
tête à tête *adv.* 236.9
tether *n.* 752.2
tether *v.* tie 43.6
 bind 751.7
tethered 150.5
tetrachord 413.18
tetract, tetractinal 95.4
tetrad *n.* four 95.2
 microbe 193.4
tetrad *adj.* 95.4
tetragon 95.1
tetragram 95.1
tetrahedral
 quadrilateral 236.7
 angular 244.5
 pointed 253.11
tetrahedroid, tetrahedron
 quaternity 95.1
 angle 244.2
tetralogy, tetraphony 95.1
tetraploid 96.3
tetrapody 95.1
tetrarch 745.7
tetraseme 597.6
tetrastich 597.7
tetravalent 95.4
tetter 655.17
tewel 386.1
text prototype 22.2
 topic 454.1
 subject matter 516.4
 letterpress 591.2
 book 593.5, 7
 playbook 599.16
textbook 593.5
textile *n.* 219.5
 (texture 329.1)
textile *adj.*
 netlike 219.11
 textural 329.3
textual literal 983a.7
 Scriptural 985.7
textualist 983a.4
textural
 formative 240.9
 of texture 329.3
texture mixture 41.4
 textile 219.5
 form 240.1
 fabric 329
 (roughness 256.1)
Thais 962.2
thakur, thackoor
 potentate 745.4
 idol 991.4

thalassa!, thalatta!
 481a.9
Thales 500.3
Thalia 599.1
thallogen 369.4
thalloid 369.11
Thallophyta 369.4
thana, thanah 752.1
thanatophobia 860.4
thane, thegn 875.5
thank 916.3
 thank you! 916.5
thankful 916.4
thankfulness 916.1
thankless
 unacceptable 830.10
 ungrateful 917.3
thank offering
 thanksgiving 916.2
 oblation 990.6
thanks 916.2
 return thanks
 thank 916.3
 say grace 990.11
 thanks to 155.8
thanksgiving
 gratitude 916.2
 worship 990.3
Thanksgiving Day
 138.7
thank-you-ma'am
 bump 260.2
 cavity 252.2
 rut 259.1
 shake 315.4
that 79.10
 at that 37.8
 that being so 8.7
 that is to say
 namely 79.13
 in explanation 522.9
thatch roofing 223.6
 hair 256.3
thaumatrope 445.1
thaumaturge 992.2
thaumaturgic 992.5
thaumaturgy 992.1
thaw *n.*
 liquefaction 335.1
 melting 384.2
thaw *v.*
 liquefy 335.5
 (soften 324.4)
 melt 384.21
 calm the mind 826.8
 relent 914.3
thearchy
 government 737.4
 Deity 976.4
theater, theatre
 audience 418.8
 vista 441.6
 schoolroom 542.5
 drama 599.1
 playhouse 599.10
 (assembly hall 189.10)
 arena 728.1
theatergoer, theatre-goer 599.23
 (attender 186.7)
 (spectator 441.1)

1130

theater of war 728.2
theatricable 599.28
theatrical *n.* 599.19
theatrical *adj.*
 dramatic 599.28
 affected 853.6
 showy 882.9
theatricality 599.8
theatricalize 599.25
theatricals 225.10
theatrician 599.17
theatrics 599.2
theatromania 599.1
theatron 599.10, 12
theatrophobia 599.1
theca vessel 191.6
 hull 223.14
theft 791
 (appropriation 789.1)
thegn See thane
theism
 monotheism 983.1
 ism 984.4
 piety 987.1
theist
 monotheist 983.3
 believer 987.4
theistic
 monotheistic 983a.7
 heterodox 984.22
thematic 454.2
theme music 415.19
 topic 454.1
 writing 590.3
 dissertation 595.1
theme song 415.10
Themis 941.1
themselves 79.4
then when 106.6
 at that time 119.2
 (previously 116.5)
 (formerly 122.14)
 (once 137.5)
 hence 155.5
 just then 113.6
thence
 henceforth 121.10
 hence 155.5; 293.10
thenceforth 121.10
theocracy
 government 737.4
 divine government 976.4
 prelacy 995.1
theocratic 995.9
theodicy 987.1
theodolite 244.3; 466.4
theogony
 generation 161.2
 theology 979.1
theologian, theological *n.* 983.3
 (clergyman 996.2)
theologian, theological *adj.* 983.4
theologue, theolog 983.3
theology 983
theomancy 511.3
theopantism 984.10
theopathy 987.1

theophany
  apparition 980a.1
  divine revelation 985.1
theopneustic 985.7
theopneusty 985.1
theorbist 416.3
theorbo 417.2
theorem topic 454.1
  premise 476.4
  axiom 496.2
  hypothesis 514.1
theoretical 514.9
  (imaginary 515.12)
theoretically 514.12
theoretics 514.4
theorist 514.5
theorize
  account for 155.3
  hypothesize 514.6
theory
  accounting for 155.1
  belief 484.3
  hypothesis 514.1
  (idea 453.1)
theory of evolution 161.5
theory of knowledge 451.4
theosophical 994.21
theosophist 994.13
theosophy 994.1
theotherapy
  healing art 662.16
  religion 989.9
therapeutic 662.25
therapeutics, therapy 662.16
  (disease 655.19)
there 186.21
thereabouts, thereabout about 32.17
  there 186.21
  nearly 197.12
thereafter
  subsequently 117.4
  (in future 121.9)
  henceforth 121.10
thereby 9.10; 631.5
therefore hence 155.5
  (accordingly 8.7)
  (consequently 154.7)
  (logically 476.19)
  (because 615.13)
  this being so 480.14
therein apropos 9.10
  internally 221.12
thereon, thereover, thereto etc. 9.10
theretofore 116.5
thereupon 117.4
therewith with 88.9
  by means of 632.4
theriaca 662.12
theriacal 662.25
therm, therme 382.10
thermae
  hot springs 382.5
  hot bath 386.6
  (baths 652.4)
  health resort 662.17
thermal 382.16

thermal unit 382.10
thermantidote 349.21
thermic fever 503.4
thermodynamics
  atmosphere 338.5
  pyrology 382.12
thermoelectrometer 389.1
thermogenesis 382.1
thermograph
  aviation 267a.29
  ship 273.14
thermoluminescence 420.11
thermolysis 49.2
thermolyze 49.4
thermometer 389
  (meter 466.4)
thermometrograph, thermophile 389.1
Thermopylae 722.5
thermostat
  aviation 267a.29
  thermometer 389
theroid 961.11
theropod, Theropoda 124.2
Thersites 936.1
thesaurus 593.4
  (storehouse 636.4)
Theseus 861.3
thesis topic 454.1
  premise 476.4
  hypothesis 514.1
  writing 590.3
  dissertation 595.1
Thesmophoros 371.3
Thespian n. 599.19
Thespian adj. 599.28
Thespis 599.1
Thetis
  spirit of the sea 341.2
  sea nymph 979.10
theurgist 992.2
theurgy 992.1
thew 45.4
thews 159.1
thick n. 68.1
  in the thick of
    among 41.11
    between 228.13
  the thick of things 682.7
thick v. thicken 202.5
  densify 321.7
thick adj.
  numerous 102.5
  broad 202.7
  (large 192.11)
  dense 321.8
  viscid 352.8
  opaque 426.4
  stupid 499.12
  guttural 583.5
  friendly 888.4
thick and thin
  through thick and thin
    throughout 52.15
    to the end 67.12
    violently 173.18

  perseveringly 604a.4
  (laboriously 686.11)
thick-ankled, thick-bodied 202.7
thickbrained 499.12
thick-coming
  numerous 102.5
  repetitional 104.6
  frequent 136.3
thicken increase 35.3
  broaden 202.5
  densify 321.7
  (viscidize 352.6)
thickening 321.3
  (viscidization 352.2)
thicket cluster 72.5
  grove 367.7
thick-girthed
  big-bellied 194.11
  thick 202.7
thickhead 501.1
thickheaded 499.12
thickness 202.2
  (expansion 194.1)
  (density 321.1)
thick-pated 499.12
thickset stubby 201.6
  (stout 192.12)
  (thick 202.7)
  dense 321.8
thick-skinned
  insensible 376.5
  callous 823.7
  hardened 945.18
thickskull, thickwit 501.1
thick-witted 499.12
thief 792
thieve 791.9
thievery 791.1
thieves' Latin 563.4
thieving, thievish 791.14
  (taking 789.15)
  (dishonest 940.8)
thievishness 791.6
thigh flank 236.1
  ham 266.11
thill tower 206.3
  shaft 215.13
thiller, thill horse 271.3
thimbleful 32.2
thimblerig n. 545.3
thimblerig v.
  deceive 545.7
  swindle 791.12
thimblerigger 792.8
thimblerigging 545.3
thin v. dilute 160.9
  slim 203.8
  rarefy 322.3
thin out excise 38.5
  ~ ~ plants 371.8
thin adj. sparse 103.2
  slim 203.10
  (little 193.8)
  (long-legged 200.13)
  rare 322.4
  insipid 391.2
  transparent 425.4
  meager 640.9

  become thin 203.8
  (contract 195.4)
thing something 3.2
  object 316.3
the thing
  the very thing 23.6
  the right thing 922.1
thingumbob, thingumabob 316.3
  (what's-its-name 565.4)
things wardrobe 225.2
  belongings 780.1, 5
think n. 484.2
think v.
  cogitate 451.27
  (intellectualize 450.6)
  (reason 476.10)
  take thought of 459.5
  judge 480.6
  believe 484.8
  suppose 514.6
not think
  incogitance 452.2
  (be inattentive 458.5)
  neglect 460.4
not to be thought of
  inconceivable 452.4
  impossible 471.6
  (hopeless 859.7)
  rejected 610.3
  prohibited 761.4
  refused 764.6
  unwarranted 925.9
  objectionable 932.13
think back 505.10
think best 609.7
think better of
  recant 607.9
  reconsider 658.11
  repent 950.3
think fit will 600.2
  be willing 602.6
  choose 609.9
think highly of
  respect 928.4
  approve 931.5
think ill of 932.5
think no more of
  disregard 458.5
  (forget 506.6)
  ignore 460.5
  forgive 918.3
think nothing of
  underestimate 483.3
  deem unimportant 643.8
  be easy 705.3
  disdain 930.5
think of 620.3
think out 515.10
think out loud 589.3
think over 451.27, 29
  (study 461.17)
think up 515.10
thinkable 470.5
thinker 500.1
thinking n.
  thought 451.1

thinking — through

thinking (*continued*)
  opinion 484.2
thinking *adj.* 451.35
thinner 428.5
thinness 203.4
  (littleness 193.1)
thin-skinned
  physically ~ 375.6
  emotionally ~ 822.6
  (irascible 901.7)
  fastidious 868.4
third *n.* triality 92.3
  trisection 94.1
  fraction 101.1
third *adj.* 93.3
third degree *n.* 461.9
third-degree *v.*
  cross-examine 461.15
thirdly 93.5
third-rate
  paltry 643.12
  imperfect 651.4
  mediocre 736.3
thirds
  coheirship 775.4
  bequest 784.6
thirst *n.* 865.3
  (drinking 298.3)
thirst *v.* be dry 340.6
  desire 865.11
thirsty dry 340.7
  desirous 865.19
thirteen 98.7
thirteenth 98.23
thirty 67.1
Thirty Years' War 722.4
this 79.9
this-a-way 8.6
thistle 253.2
thistledown
  lightness 320.2
  irresolution 605.3
thistly 253.11
thither there 186.21
  hither 278.12
thole *n.* pin 45.5
  fulcrum 215.5
thole *v.* 826.6
Thomism 451.10
thong fastening 45.2
  cord 205.3
  lash 975.1
Thor, Thorr 979.3
thorax 250.3
thorn adherer 46.3
  bramble 253.2
  (bane 663.1)
  evil 649.2
  annoyance 830.2
thorny brambly 253.11
  difficult 704.8
  gruff 895.7
thorough
  absolute 31.12
  complete 52.10
  businesslike 625.11
thoroughbred *n.*
  horse 271.3
  nobleman 875.4

thoroughbred *adj.*
  intrinsic 5.6
  thoroughly skilled 698.13
  noble 875.10
thoroughfare 627.3
thoroughgoing
  absolute 31.12
  thorough 52.10
thoroughly 52.13
  do thoroughly 729.3
  (persevere 604a.2)
thoroughpaced 31.12
thorp, thorpe 189.17
Thoth wisdom 498.3
  deity 979.5
though 30.8; 469.8
thought modicum 32.2
  cogitation 451
  idea 453.1
  attention 457.1
  opinion 484.2
  give thought to
    think about 451.27
    give attention 457.4
  lost in thought
    thoughtful 451.36
    preoccupied 458.11
thoughtful
  pensive 451.35
  (studious 539.6)
  careful 459.7
  prudent 498.11
thoughtfully 451.39
thoughtfulness 451.1
thoughtless
  incogitant 452.3
  (mindless 450a.2)
  inattentive 458.19
  (clumsy 699.12)
  scatterbrained 458.13
  (empty-headed 499.14)
  careless 460.8
  (reckless 863.6)
  shiftless 674.11
  be thoughtless 863.5
thoughtlessness
  incogitance 452.1
  inattention 458.1
  (folly 499.6)
  (clumsiness 699.1)
  (recklessness 863.1)
thought-provoking 454.2
thought reader 994.15
thought reading, thought transference 994.8
thousand 98.10; 102.5
thousand and one 102.2, 5
thousandth 98.28
thrall *n.* slave 746.4
  subjection 749.1
  confinement 751.2
  hold in thrall 751.8
thrall *adj.* 749.6
thralldom, thraldom 749.1
thrash pulverize 330.6

~ **out** 461.17
  defeat 731.9
  whip 972.6
Thraso 884.3
thrasonical 884.7
thraw, thrawart, thrawn 217.13
thread *n.* series 69.2
  weakness 160.5
  filament 205.2
thread *v.* arrange 60.6
  give continuity 69.5
  pass through 302.2
threadbare
  worn 659.12
  trite 843.6
threadlike, thready 205.7
  (thin 203.10)
threat 909
  (warning 668.1)
  (defiance 715.1)
  (intimidation 860.5)
  (malediction 908.1)
threaten impend 152.2
  (approach 121.6)
  menace 909.2
  (portend 511.9)
  (endanger 665.4)
  (forewarn 668.7)
  (defy 715.2)
  (intimidate 860.12)
  (maledict 908.4)
threatening
  imminent 152.3
  ominous 512.5
  menacing 909.3
  (foreboding 511.6)
  (dangerous 665.7)
  (forewarning 668.10)
  (defiant 715.3)
three 92.2, 4
three-cornered 94.2
three-decker 189.3
threefold *v.* 93.2
threefold *adj.* 93.3
threefold *adv.* 93.4
three-footed, three-forked 94.2
three-in-hand 272.9
Three in One 976.3
three-master 273.2
Three Musketeers 890.5
three-parted 94.2
threepence, three-penny bit 800.8
three-ply 93.3
three-point landing 267a.26
three-pronged 94.2
three R's 537.7
threescore 98.7
three sheets in the wind 959.21
three-sided
  tripartite 94.2
  trilateral 236.7
threnetic 839.15
threnody 839.3

thresh pulverize 330.6
  whip 972.6
threshold
  vestibule 191.17
  (edge 231.1)
  portal 260.4
  at the threshold of 197.11
thrice 93.4
thrift 817.1
thriftless
  improvident 674.11
  prodigal 818.4
thrifty 817.4
thrill *n.* tingle 380.1
  excitement 825.2
  (feeling 821.1)
  pleasure 827.1
thrill *v.* tingle 380.4
  excite 824.2
  be excited 824.7
  (feel 821.3)
thriller 594.2
thrilling
  exciting 824.12
  delightful 829.8
  shocking 830.13
thrillingly 824.14
thrive 734.5
thriving 734.7
throat 350.4
throaty 583.5
throb *n.*
  pulsation 314.2
  (flutter 315.5)
  pain 378.1
  drumming 407.3
  rhythm 413.23
  trepidation 825.3
throb *v.* pulsate 314.9
  (flutter 315.10)
  drum 407.8
  (resonate 408.7)
  ~ **with emotion** 824.7
throe birth ~ 161.3
  spasm 315.7
  (pain 378.1)
  seizure 655.3
throne *n.*
  sovereignty 737.2
  royal seat 747.5
throne *v.*
  enthrone 755.4
  exalt 873.13
thrones 977.2
throng *n.* 72.4
throng *v.* 72.10
throttle *n.* 273a.10
throttle *v.*
  disable 158.6
  close 261.2
  retard 275.7
  strangle 361.11
  muffle 408a.4
  render mute 581.5
  seize 789.9
through during 106.7
  byway of 278.16; 631.5
  (by the agency of 170.5)

(by means of 632.4)
(by aid of 707.14)
through and through
 52.15
throughout *adv.* 52.15
 (wholly 50.10)
throughout *prep.* 106.7
throw *n.* fling 284.3
 (impulse 276.1)
 ~ of the dice 621.2, 9
 exertion 686.1
throw *v.*
 give birth 161.9
 fling 284.12
 nonplus 475.8
throw about 267.24
throw away
 waste 638.2
 discard 678.3
 (eject 297.8)
 squander 818.3
**throw a wet blanket
  on** moderate 174.5
 discourage 616.3
 hinder 706.7
throw a wrench
 render useless 645.7
 thwart 706.7
throw cold water on
 moderate 174.5
 discourage 616.3
 hinder 706.7
 dull 842.4
throw down
 destroy 162.4
 fell 308.5
throw down the glove
 716.2
**throw dust in one's
  eyes** blind 442.3
 hoodwink 545.7
 pretext 619.2
**throw good money
  after bad** 818.3
throw in 228.8
throw in the towel
 725.4
throw into the shade
 excel 33.5
 outstrip 303.4
 conceal 528.10
 humiliate 879.3
**throw oneself at the
  feet of** submit 725.3
 entreat 765.5
 truckle 886.5
 beg for mercy 914.5
throw open
 open 260.11
 receive 296.2
throw out eject 297.8
 propound 514.7
 discard 678.3
throw out of gear
 disjoin 44.7
 displace 61.3
 dislocate 185.2
throw over
 exclude 55.3
 destroy 162.4
 eject 297.8
 abandon 624.3

discard 678.3
 annul 756.3
 relinquish 782.3
throw the bull 544.4
throw together
 mix 41.6
 do carelessly 460.6
throw up
 vomit 297.18
 abandon 624.3
 relinquish 782.3
throwback 145.1
thrower 284.7
thrown
 nonplused 475.16
 ~ away 638.4
 (useless 645.8)
 ~ out 704.11
thrum *n.* 407.3
thrum *v.* hum 405.6
 drum 407.8
 purr 412.2
 strum 416.18
 beat time 416.19
thrummer 416.3
thrush bird 366.22
 songbird 416.11
 disease 655.9
thrust *n.*
 aeronautics 267a.10
 impulse 276.1, 3
 attack 716.3
 gibe 930.3
thrust *v.* 276.7
thrust in
 intrude 228.10
 enter 294.6
 insert 300.5
thrust upon 784.10
**Thruthvang, Thruth-
  vangr, Thrymheim**
 981.3
thud *n.* 408a.2
thud *v.* 408a.5
thug killer 361.8
 thief 792.3
 ruffian 913.2
thuggee 361.1
thumb *n.* 379.2
 all thumbs 699.12
 under one's thumb
  749.6
thumb *v.* touch 379.3
 ~ over 539.4
 thumb one's nose at
  715.2
thumbprint mark 550.7
 evidence 551.4
thumbs down 361.17
thumbscrew 975.3
thump *n.* blow 276.3
 thud 408a.2
thump *v.* strike 276.8
 drum 407.8; 416.19
 thud 408a.5
 beat 972.6
thumper 192.6
thumping vast 31.8
 huge 192.15
thunder *n.* boom 406.4
 (explosion 173.3)
 rain 348.11

omen 512.2
thunder *v.* boom 406.9
 (be loud 404.5)
 ~ forth 531.7
 bluster 887.3
 threaten 909.2
thunder against
 maledict 908.4
 berate 932.8
thunder and lightning
 219.5
thunderblast 406.4
thunderbolt
 velocity 274.6
 lightning 420.6
 (thunder 406.4)
 surprise 508.2
thunderburst 406.4
 (storm 173.5)
thunderclap
 thunder 406.4
 surprise 508.2
thundercloud
 cloud 353.5
 (thunder 406.4)
 omen 512.2
 warning sign 668.3
thundercrack 406.4
thunder-gust
 rain 348.11
 windstorm 349.11
thunderhead
 cloud 353.5
 omen 512.2
 warning sign 668.3
thunderheaded 353.11
thundering vast 31.8
 huge 192.15
 explosive 406.11
 (loud 404.8)
 booming 407.10
thunderlight 420.6
thunderpeal 406.4
**thunderplump, thun-
  dershower** 348.11
thundersquall
 rain 348.11
 (thunder 406.4)
 windstorm 349.11
thunderstroke
 thunder 406.4
 lightning 420.6
thunderstruck 870.6
thunder tube 260.6
thurible
 perfumer 400.5
 ecclesiastical ~
  998.8
thurifer
 perfumer 400.6
 acolyte 996.5
thurification
 perfuming 400.7
 rite 998.2
thurify perfume 400.9
 cense 998.14
thus so 8.6
 literally 19.14
 hence 155.5
 in this way 627.8
thusly 155.5
thwack *n.* 276.3

thwack *v.* 276.8
thwart *v.* 509.2; 706.7
 (oppose 708.2)
 (resist 719.3)
 (checkmate 731.10)
thwart *adv.* 219.12
thwarted
 disappointed 509.4
 frustrated 732.9
thwartly, thwartwise
 219.12
thyme 393.1
thyroid 221.5
thyrsus 215.15
tiara
 emblem of authority
  747.2, 3
 jewel 847.7
 church 999.1
Tibetan 560.4
tic douloureux 655.14
tick *n.* instant 113.3
 animal 368.8
 ticktock 407.4
 mark 550.7
 credit 805.1
tick *v.* snap 406.7
 ticktock 407.9
 (pulsate 314.9)
 mark 550.19
 extend credit 805.4
tick off
 call attention to
  457.7
 record 551.8
ticker timepiece 114.6
 heart 221.4
 beard 256.5
 recorder 553.3
ticket *n.*
 the very thing 23.6
 ballot 86.1; 609.3
 truth 494.4
 token 550.11
 platform 626.4
ticket *v.* 550.19
ticket of leave 760.2
ticking 219.5
tickle *n.* 380.2
tickle *v.* titillate 380.5
 delight 829.4, 5
 amuse 840.20
tickle the palm
 bribe 618.3
 pay 807.6
tickled 827.10
tickler 959.10
tickling 380.2
ticklish
 titillative 380.7
 uncertain 475.14
 precarious 665.7
 difficult 704.8
ticktack
 noisemaker 404.4
 tick 407.8
ticktick, ticktoc 407.4
 (pulsation 314.2)
tidal 348.26
**tidal current, tidal
  wave** 348.9, 10
 (danger 697.1)

tidbit — timeworn 1134

tidbit delicacy 298.9
  good thing 648.4
tiddlywinks 840.11
tide *n.* time 106.1
  ocean 341.1
  flow 348.2
  tidal current 348.9
  prosperity 734.1
  go with the tide
    705.3
tide *v.*
  tide over
    pass time 106.3
    be safe 664.4
    surmount 731.7
tide gate tide 348.9
  floodgate 350.2
tidemark 466.5
tiderace, tideway 348.9
tidiness 58.4
tidings 532.1
  give tidings of 531.7
tidy *n.* 223.9
tidy *v.* 60.6
tidy *adj.* orderly 58.7
  (careful 459.7)
  (clean 652.14)
  sizable 192.11
  tolerable 648.11
  trim 845.11
tie *n.* equality 27.4
  bond 45
  (connection 9.2)
  beam 215.12
  necktie 225.33
  notation 415.23
  security 771.1
  allegiance 939.4
tie *v.* equal 27.6
  attach 43.6
  restrain 751.7
  tie down bind 744.2
    restrain 751.7
  tie one's hands
    disable 158.6
    hinder 706.7
    restrain 751.7
  tie the knot 903.12
  tie up tie 43.6
    wrap 223.23
    bind 751.7
    condition 770.2
    hold 781.4
  tie up with
    league 48.4
    associate 88.6
tie beam 45.2
tied equivalent 27.9
  ~ down 926.10
tie-in relation 9.1
  junction 43.1
  association 709.2
tier series 69.2
  layer 204.1
  apron 225.20
tierce third 92.3
  canonical hour 990.7
Tiergarten 370.3
tie-up junction 43.1
  association 709.2
  strike 719.2
tiff *n.* quarrel 713.3

dudgeon 900.2
tiff *v.* 713.7
tiffin 298.34
tig See tyg
tigella, tigelle 367.4
tigellate 367.14
tiger violent 173.6
  pelt 223.12
  animal 366.3
  stockman 370.4
  faro bank 621.4
  groom 746.1
  cheer 838.4
  (cry 411.1)
  courage 861.4
  savage 913.3
tight fast 43.11
  narrow 203.9
  drunk 959.21
  close 261.6
  stingy 819.4
  trim 845.11
  hold tight 781.4
tighten attach 43.6
  contract 195.4
tightfisted 819.4
tights 225.10
tight squeeze
  small place 184.4
  narrow escape 671.2
  predicament 704.2
tightwad 819.2
Tigré 560.4
tigress fury 173.6
  female animal 374.8
  shrew 901.4
  malevolent woman
    913.5
Tigriña, Tigrina,
  Tigrinya 560.4
tike See tyke
tilaka 550.11
tilbury 272.5
tilde 550.8
tile roofing 223.6
  ceramics 384.14
  pavement 627.4
tilemaker 690.8
tiler, tyler 717.6
tile red 434.2
tilestone stone 342.4
  pavement 627.4
tilewright 690.7
tiling 223.6
till *n.* soil 342.3
  cashbox 802.1
till *v.* 371.8
till *prep.* 106.8
tillage 371.1
tiller handle 215.7
  ship 273.7
  lifter 307.2
  agriculturist 371.2
  cashbox 802.1
  ~ of the soil 876.5
tilmus twitching 315.6
  nervous disorder
    655.14
tilpah 223.10
tilt *n.*
  inclination 217.1, 2
  descent 306.1

contest 720.2
  run a tilt attack 716.5
  joust 720.8
tilt *v.* incline 217.6
  ~ over 218.5
  throw 284.12
  attack 716.5
  joust 720.8
tilt at windmills
  imagine 515.8
  labor in vain 645.6
tilted 217.9
tilth 371.1
tilting 840.11
tiltyard 728.1
timber *n.* beam 215.12
  ship 273.1
  spars 273.12
  trees 367.6, 7
  wood 635.3
timber *v.* 367.13
timberland 367.7
timber topper 309.3
timber topping 309.1
timberwright 690.7
timbre, timber 402.2
  (resonance 408.1)
  (music 413.5)
timbrel *n.* 417.10
timbrel *v.* 416.18
time *n.* duration 106
  occasion 134.2
  tempo 413.22
  leisure 685.1
  abreast of the times
    modern 123.11
    fashionable 852.7
  another time 119.1
  at any time 119.3
  at times
    sometimes 119.4
    occasionally 137.4
  behind time
    overdue 115.3
    late 133.11
  behind the times
    antiquated 124.9
    uncultured 491.11
  be on time 132.6
  for a time
    meanwhile 109a.3
    temporarily 111.8
  for the time being
    meanwhile 109a.3
    now 118.3
  from time to time
    137.4
  in good time
    eventually 121.9
    opportunely 134.10
  in no time
    briefly 111.9
    instantly 113.6
    promptly 132.14
  in time
    in due time 109.8
    in future 121.9
    early 132.11
    opportunely 134.10
    in tempo 413.29
  keep time time 114.8
    be punctual 132.6

comply obsequious-
  ly 886.3
lose no time
  be industrious
    682.12
  hasten 684.3
lose time 683.8
many times
  repeatedly 104.8
  frequent 136.3, 5
on time 132.13
take time
  pass time 106.3
  wait 133.7
  do nothing 681.2
take time out
  interlude 109a.2
  vacation 687.5
the time being 118.1
time *v.* regulate 58.6
  measure 114.8
time and again 104.8
time ball 114.6
time clock 553.3
time-honored, time-
  honoured old 124.6
  famous 873.19
  venerable 928.9
time immemorial 122.3
timekeeper 114.6
timeless dateless 107.2
  (eternal 112.4)
  untimely 135.6
timelessness 107
  (eternity 112.1)
timeliness 134
  (fitness 23.2)
  (expedience 646.1)
timely *adj.* 134.7
  (early 132.7)
  (expedient 646.4)
  be timely 134.5
  (be expedient
    646.3)
timely *adv.* 134.10
timenoguy 273.10
time of day 114.2
timeous 134.7
time out 109a.1 ; 687.2
time out of mind
  122.14
timepiece 114.6
timepleaser
  tergiversator 607.4
  self-seeker 943.2
timer 114.6
timeserver
  tergiversator 607.4
  sycophant 886.2
  self-seeker 943.2
timeserving *n.* 886.1
timeserving *adj.*
  tergiversating
    607.10
  cunning 702.6
  obsequious 886.4
  improbity 940.8
time signature 415.23
timeworn
  antiquated 124.9
  aged 128.8
  worn 659.12

timid cowardly 862.4
 (weak-willed 605.2)
 (afraid 860.14)
 shy 881.5
timidity
 fearfulness 860.2
 (uncertainty 475.1)
 (irresolution 605.2)
 (cowardice 862.1)
 shyness 881.1
timocracy 803.2
Timon 910.2
Timon of Athens
 rich man 803.2
 recluse 893.4
timor 860.2
timorous timid 862.4
 shy 881.5
timothy 367.9
timpan See tympan
timpanist 416.7
timpano, tympano 417.10
tin n. can 191.11
 metal 635.6
 money 800.1
tin v. 670.4
tinct n. 428.1
tinct v. 428.9
tinct adj. 428.13
tinction color 428.3
 coloring 428.6
tinctorial 428.12
tincture n.
 modicum 32.2
 tinge 41.3
 color 428.1, 2, 3
tincture v. imbue 41.8
 color 428.9
tinder 388.6
tinderbox heater 386.1
 tinder 388.6
tine 253.2
ting 408.8
tinge n.
 modicum 32.2
 tincture 41.3
 taste 390.1
 color 428.1
tinge v. imbue 41.8
 color 428.9
 discolor 440a.2
tingle n. pain 378.1
 sensation 380.1
tingle v.
 ~ with pain 378.5
 thrill 380.1
 ring 408.8
 ~ with excitement 824.7
tingling 825.2
tingly 380.6
tin hat 717.2
tinhorn n. 643.6
tinhorn adj. 643.12
tink 408.8
tinker n. 690.5
 (mender 660.7)
tinker v. 660.11
tinker's damn 643.3
tinkle n. 408.4
tinkle v. 408.8

tinny 803.8
Tino 560.4
tin-pan alley 416.1
tin-pot, tin-potty 643.12
tinsel n. sham 545.6
 frippery 847.2
 gaudery 851.2
tinsel adj. 545.13
tinsmith 690.6
tint n. 428.1
tint v. 428.9
tintamarre, tintamar 404.2
tinted 428.13
tintinnabulant 408.10
tintinnabulate 408.8
tintinnabulation 408.4
 (roll 407.1)
tintinabulum bell 408.5
 chimes 417.10
tintype 556.11
tiny 193.8
tip n. extremity 67.2
 summit 210.1
 information 527.3
 (reminder 505.5)
 (warning 668.1, 2)
 bribe 618.2
 advice 695.1
 gratuity 784.3
 at the tip of one's tongue 582.6
tip v. top 210.5
 cover 223.22
 inform 527.9
 signal 550.20
 (warn 668.6)
 bribe 618.3
 present 784.8
 ~ the hat 894.9
tipcat 840.11
tip-off 527.3
tipper 527.5
tippet pendant 214.2
 neckpiece 225.33
 canonicals 999.1
tipple n. 959.4
tipple v. tope 959.15
 (be intemperate 954.3)
 inebriate 959.18
tippler 959.11
tipsification 959.1
tipsifier 959.4
tipsify 959.15
tipstaff 745.9
tipster predictor 513.2
 informant 527.5
tipsy 959.21
tiptoe n. 266.5
 on tiptoe up 206.19
 expectant 507.7
 stand on tiptoe 206.9
tiptoe v. 266.16
tiptoe adv. 206.19
tiptop n. 210.1
tiptop adj.
 supreme 33.8
 top 210.6
 best 648.9
Tipura 560.4

tirade lecture 582.2
 malediction 908.1
 berating 932.3
tire n. clothes 225:1
 noose 247.2
 fatigue 688.1
tire, tyre n. 272.16
tire v. clothe 225.41
 be fatigued 688.4
 fatigue 688.5
 bore 841.5
tired fatigued 688.6
 bored 841.7, 9
tired-armed, tired-eyed, tired-faced 688.6
tiredness
 fatigue 688.1
 ennui 841.1
Tiresias 513.2
tiresmith 690.6
tiresome
 fatiguesome 688.8
 annoying 830.12
 boresome 841.8
tiro See tyro
tisane 662.4
Tisiphone 900.4
tissue main part 50.3
 accumulation 72.6
 network 219.4, 5
 texture 329.1
 transparency 425.2
tissue paper 425.2
tit diminutive 193.2
 nipple 250.3
 pony 271.3
Titan
 strong man 159.6
 giant 192.8
 sun god 318.4
Titania 979.9
titanic vast 31.8
 huge 192.15
 strong 195.10
titanium 635.6
Titanomachy 722.1
titbit 298.9
 (savory 394.3)
tit for tat
 interchange 148.1
 retaliation 718.1
give tit for tat
 retaliate 718.2
 repay 807.9
tithable 812.8
tithe n. 812.2
tithe adj. 99.3
tithing 181.2
tithingman 745.9
titian 433.5; 434.12
titillate tickle 380.5
 tempt 617.4; 865.14
 delight 829.5
 amuse 840.20
titillation
 pleasure 377.1
 tickling 380.2
titillative
 pleasing 377.7
 ticklish 380.7

titivate, tittivate 847.11
title n. caption 66.3
 superscription 550.11
 name 564.2
 ~ of a book 593.7
 estate 780.2
 honorific 877
 right 922.2
 have a title to 924.5
 have no title to 925.5
 titles of nobility 875.5–8
title v. 564.6
titled 875.10
title deed 771.1
title page 66.3
titmouse
 diminutive 193.2
 bird 366.22
titrate 461.17
titration 461.3
titter n. 838.3
titter v. 838.7
tittle n. modicum 32.2
 inextension 180a.1
 diminutive 193.2
tittle v. 532.7
tittle-tattle n.
 gossip 532.3
 small talk 588.2
tittle-tattle v.
 gossip 532.7
 converse 588.7
tittle-tattler
 newsmonger 532.5
titty 250.3
titubant 583.5
titubate topple 306.6
 stammer 583.3
titubation 583.1
titular 564.8
 (verbal 562.8)
titule 564.6
tivoli 840.11
tmesis 218.2
tn. 319.4
TNT, T.N.T. 727.13
to until 106.8
toward 278.17
for 620.6
toad jumper 309.3
 animal 366.20
 ugly thing 846.3
 toady 886.2
toadeat 886.3
toadeater 886.2
toadeating n. 886.1
toadeating adj. 886.4
toadstabber
 knife 253.6
 bayonet 727.3
toadstool 369.4
toady n. 886.2
 (flatterer 935.2)
toady v. 886.3
to-and-fro n. 314.3
to-and-fro adj. 314.12
to and fro adv.
 interchangeably 148.5

toast — toot

to and fro (*continued*)
   (changeably 149.7)
   alternately 314.14
 go to and fro
   alternate 319.10
toast *n.* 854.2
toast *v.* be hot 382.13
   heat 384.19
   pledge 883.4
   drink to 959.17
toaster 386.1
toasting 382.16
toastmaster 840.18
toasty 382.15
tobacco 392a
   (merchandise 798.3)
 use tobacco 392a.14
tobacco camphor
   392a.9
tobaccoism 392a.10
tobaccoite 392a.11
tobaccolike 392a.15
tobaccoman 392a.12
tobacconist 392a.12
   (merchant 797.11)
tobacco pipe 392a.6
to-be 121.7
toboggan *n.* 272.13
 go on the toboggan
   160.7
toboggan *v.* 266.20
tobogganing 840.11
toby cup 191.11
   cigar 392a.3
toccata, toccatina
   415.3
**tocogony, tocology,
   tokology** birth 161.3
   obstetrics 662.16
tocsin 669.1
 ring the tocsin 669.3
Toda 560.4
today, to-day *n.* 118.1
today, to-day *adv.*
   118.3
toddle *n.* 266.5
toddle *v.* walk 266.16
   depart 293.4
   go slow 275.5
toddler 129.6
toddy 959.8
to-do predicament 8.3;
   704.2
   turmoil 59.4
   excitement 825.3
toe *n.* 211.4
toe *v.*
 toe the mark 82.5
toffee, toffy 396.2
toft messuage 189.12
   farm 371.4
   property 780.4
tog 225.1, 3, 16
toga 747.1
together with 88.10
   (jointly 43.14)
   co-operatively 709.8
 together with
   with 37.9, 10
   among 41.11
   with 88.9
toggery 225.1

toggle, toggel pin 45.5
   ship 273.14
toil *n.* 686.3
toil *v.* 686.6
toile 219.5
toiler 690.2
toilet clothes 225.1
   lavatory 652.4
   water closet 653.9
toiletry 798.3
toilette 225.1
toilet water 400.2
toils 545.4
toilsome
   laborious 686.10
   difficult 704.8
toilworn 688.6
Tokay 959.7
token memento 505.5
   sign 550.2
   (omen 512.1)
   (warning 668.3)
   trophy 551.4; 733.1
   currency 800.7
   ~ of regard 894.3
 in token of 550.23
tokology See **tocology**
tolbooth, tollbooth
   prison 752.1
   market 799.2
Toledo 727.3
tolerable
   inconsiderable 32.8
   moderately good
   648.11
   (imperfect 651.4)
   tolerably well 654.4
   mediocre 736.3
tolerably 32.14
   (imperfectly 651.5)
   (moderately 736.4)
tolerance lenity 740.1
   sufferance 826.4
tolerant
   unprejudiced 498.12
   lenient 740.4
   permissive 760.6
   forbearant 826.10
tolerate be lax 738.4
   be lenient 740.2
   permit 760.3
   endure 826.6
 be tolerated 831.5
toleration lenity 740.1
   (laxity 738.1)
   permission 760.1
   sufferance 826.4
   benevolence 906.1
toll *n.* ringing 408.4
   (roll 407.1)
   tax 812.2
toll *v.* 408.8
   (roll 407.6)
tollhouse 799.2
tolling 363.5
tom tomcat 366.4
   male animal 373.6
tomahawk
   hatchet 253.6; 722.3
   weapon 727.4
tomato 298.30
tomb *n.* 363.13

 the Tombs 752.1
tomb *v.* 363.20
tombola 621.10
tomboy hoyden 129.5
   virile 159a.3
   rude person 851.4
tombstone 363.15
tomcat cat 366.4
   male animal 373.6
Tom, Dick, and Harry
   nonentities 643.6
   commonalty 876.1
tome 593.1
tomentose 256.15
tomfool, Tom Fool *n.*
   501.1
tomfool *v.* 499.9
tomfoolery 842.3
   (absurdity 497.1)
   (folly 499.6)
tomjon See **tonjon**
tommy
   Englishman
   provisions 298.6
   bread 298.11
   soldier 726.4
Tommy Atkins 726.4
tommyrot nullity 4.2
   nonsense 517.2
**tommy noddy, tom-
   noddy** 501.1
Tom o' Bedlam 504.1
**tomorrow, to-mor-
   row** *n.* 121.2
**tomorrow, to-mor-
   row** *adv.* 121.9
Tom Pepper 548.5
tompion See **tampion**
Tom Thumb 193.5
tomtit 193.2
tom-tom drum 417.10
   call to arms 722.3
ton weight 319.4
   fashion 852.1
tonal 413.28
tonalist 416.15
tonality 402.2
   (music 413.5)
tonant 404.8, 9
tone *n.* nature 5.3
   state 7.1
   strength 159.1
   tendency 176.1
   sound 402.2
   (resonance 408.1)
   (music 413.5)
   (note 413.6)
   (voice 580.1)
   tune 413.4
   degree 413.11
   air 415.2
   color 428.1, **2**
   painting 556.5
   manner 627.1
   mood 820.1
tone *v.* intone 416.20
   color 428.9
 tone down
   moderate 174.5
   harmonize 413.24
   decolor 429.5
 tone up 413.24

tone color 402.2
toneless silent 403.6, 7
   nonresonant 408a.6
tone painting 413.3
tone poem 415.3
tone poet 416.14
tong 712.6
tonga 272.5
Tongan 560.4
tongs 781.2
tongue shaft 215.13
   promontory 250.5
   feeler 379.2
   taste 390.1
   tone 402.2
   language 560.1
   (dialect 563.5)
   utterance 580.3
tonguefence 476.2
tonguefencer 476.9
tongue-lash 932.8
tongue-lashing 932.3
tongueless 581.7
tonguelike 245.21
tongue-tied 581.7
   (silent 585.4)
tonic *n.* sound 402.2
   hygiene 656.2
   medicine 662.5
   (pungency 392.2)
   intoxicant 959.4
tonic *adj.*
   sounded 402.11
   tonal 413.28
   invigorating 656.5
   remedial 662.25
tonicity 159.1
tonic key 413.7
tonic section 415.13
tonic spasm 655.3
tonitruone 417.10
tonjon, tomjon 272.12
tonnage, tunnage
   capacity 192.2
   weight 319.1
   impost 812.2
tonneau 272.16
tonsillitis 655.9
tonsure symbol 550.11
   church 999.1
tonsured 226.10
tontine 784.5
too inordinately 31.20
   additionally 37.8
   overly 641.7
tool *n.* medium 631.2
   instrument 633.1
   equipment 634.1
   puppet 711.2
   (sycophant 886.2)
   deputy 759.1
tool *v.* engrave 558.5
   (ornament 847.11)
   manage 693.4
tooling
   bookbinding 593.9
   ornamentation 847.3
toolsmith 690.6
toot *n.* blare 404.3
   spree 840.3; 959.3
toot *v.* blare 404.7
   whistle 410.8

1136

~ a horn 416.18
toot one's own horn 884.5
tooter musician 416.2
  horn 417.4
tooth *n.* pin 45.5
  dental 253.3
  (projection 250.2)
  rough 256.2
  texture 329.1
  taste 390.1
tooth *v.* 257.5
toothache 378.1
  (ailment 655.5)
tooth and nail
  violently 173.18
  resolutely 604.9
  lustily 686.11
toothdrawer 662.19
toothed 257.6
toothful 959.10
toothing plane 255.3
toothless 254.3
toothlike 253.20
tooth paste 662.8
toothsome 394.7
tootle *n.* 404.3
tootle *v.* blare 404.7
  whistle 410.8
  ~ a horn 416.18
tootsy 211.4
top *n.* summit 210.1, **2**
  head 210.3
  tent 223.5
  roof 223.6
  lid 223.7
  automobile 272.16
  spinner 312.4
  toy 840.16
at the top of one's voice 404.11
at the top of the tree
  atop 210.7
  paramount 642.14
  eminent 873.18
from top to bottom 200.16
on top
  additionally 37.8
  atop 210.7
over the top 716.10
top *v.* excel 33.5
  rise above 206.10
  crown 210.5
  cover 223.22
top *adj.* supreme 33.8
  uppermost 210.6
  (perfect 650.5)
toparchy 182.1
topaz yellow 436.**3**
  gem 847.8
top boots 225.27
tope *n.* tower 206.3
  monument 363.15
  grove 367.7
  shrine 1000.2
tope *v.* 959.15
topee, topi 225.26
topek See **tupek**
toper 959.11
topgallant *n.* 210.1
topgallant *adj.* 210.6

topgallant mast
  height 210.1
  spar 273.12
top hat 225.26
top-heavy
  unequal 28.3
  lopsided 218.7
  drunk 959.21
Tophet, Topheth 982.1
top-hole supreme 33.8
  first-class 648.9
topi See **topee**
topiary 847.13
topic 454
  (problem 461.10)
topical 181.6
top kick 745.11
topknot hair 256.**3**
  feathers 256.8
toploftiness 885.1
toplofty proud 878.6
  arrogant 885.8
topmast 273.12
top milk 356.4
topmost supreme 33.8
  top 210.6
top-notch
  supreme 33.8
  best 648.9
topnotcher best 648.4
  expert 700.1
topographer 466.9
topographical
  regional 181.6
  (locational 184.18)
  measuring 466.11
topography
  geography 184.8
  measurement 466.8
toponymy, toponomy 564.1
topophone 418.**6**
topper 225.26
topple
  be unequal 28.**2**
  perish 162.5
  fall 306.6
  collapse 659.6
topsail 273.13
top sawyer chief 642.6
  (superior 33.4)
  expert 700.1
  master 745.1
top sergeant 745.11
topside *n.* top 210.**2**
  ship 273.7
topside *adv.* atop 210.**7**
  on deck 267.53
topsman 975.5
topsy-turvification 218.1
topsy-turvify 218.4
topsy-turvy *n.* 59.2
  (disorderly 59.8)
  turn topsy-turvy 218.4
  (disorder 59.7)
  (derange 61.2)
topsy-turvy *adv.* 218.8
topsy-turvydom 218.1
tor 206.2
torch *n.* lighter 388.4

light 423.1, **7**
torch *v.* 622.8
torchlight dusk 126.1
  light 420.7
  torch 423.8
torch race 720.5
torch singer 416.10
torch song 415.10
torch staff 423.9
toreador, torero 726.1
to-rights 494.16
torment *n.*
  bodily pain 378.2
  bane 663.1
  mental pain 828.6
  punishment 972.2
torment *v.* pain 378.4
  harass 830.5, 6
tormented 828.15
tormenting
  painful 378.7
  annoying 830.12
tormentor wing 599.15
tormina pain 378.1
  ailment 655.5
torminous 378.6
tornado 349.11, **13**
torose 250.9
torpedinous 683.14
torpedo *n.*
  automobile 272.15
  killer 361.8
  firework 382.9
  missile 727.14
  gunman 913.2
torpedo *v.* 716.6
torpedo boat, torpedo-boat destroyer 726.11
torpedoist 726.4
torpescence
  languor 683.4
  apathy 823.1
torpescent 683.14
torpid inert 172.3
  languid 683.14
  apathetic 823.5
torpidity languor 683.4
  apathy 823.1
torpids 274.4; 720.5
torpor inertness 172.1
  languor 683.4
  apathy 823.1
torporific
  insensible 376.**5**
  (numb 381.3)
  languid 683.14
torque
  aeronautics 267a.9
  ornament 847.7
torrefaction 384.1
torrefy, torrify
  dry 340.5
  burn 384.18
torrent outbreak 173.2
  speed 274.6
  flood 348.2
torrid 382.16
torridity 382.1
torsion
  convolution 248.1
  aeronautics 267a.**9**

torso 50.3
tort wrong 923.1
  breach 925.3
  misdeed 947.**2**
torticollis pain 378.1
  ailment 655.5
tortile 248.4
tortility 248.1
tortious 923.4
tortoise
  support 215.25
  slow goer 275.4
tortoiselike 275.8
tortoise shell *n.* 440.**2**
tortoise-shell *adj.* 440.6
tortoise-shell cat 366.4
tortuosity 248.1
tortuous
  convoluted 248.4
  (complex 59.10)
  (circuitous 311.6)
  dishonest 940.8
torture *n.*
  bodily pain 378.2
  ill-treatment 649.4
  mental suffering 828.6
  (cruelty 907.3)
  punishment 972.2
torture *v.* distort 243.3
  pain physically 378.4
  maltreat 649.7
  pain mentally 830.6
  (punish 972.6)
tortured 828.13
torturous 378.7
torus 847.4
Tory
  conservative 141.**3**
  party 712.6
Toryism 141.2
tosh 517.2
toss *n.*
  even chance 156.2
  gamble 621.2
toss *v.* be excited 824.7
toss and turn
  be uncertain 475.6
  be irresolute 605.4
  be excited 824.7
toss off drink 298.47
  do carelessly 460.6
  drink liquor 959.15
toss the head
  ignore 460.5
  show contempt 930.5
  act proudly 878.3
toss up 621.17
tossel See **tassel**
tosspot 959.11
tossup
  even chance 156.**2**
  gamble 621.2
tot *n.* computation 37.**2**
  all 50.2
  child 129.**3**
tot *v.* 50.5
total *n.*
  computation 37.**2**
  all 50.2
  (sum 84.**3**)

total — tract 1138

total v. compute 37.5
  amount to 50.5
  calculate 85.7
  number 85.10
total adj. whole 50.6
  comprehensive 52.10
total abstinence 953.2
totaling, totalling
  computation 37.2
  numeration 85.1
totality whole 50.1
  completeness 52.1
totalizator, totalisator
  record 551.1
  pari-mutuel 621.12
totalizer list 86.1
  pari-mutuel 621.12
totally 50.10
  (fully 31.17)
  (completely 52.13)
total war 722.1
tote n. all 50.2
  totalizator 86.1;
    551.1
  handle 215.7
  freight 270.4
tote v. total 50.5
  escort 88.7
  carry 270.8
tote fair 941.2
totem 550.11
totem pole 206.4
totient 84.2
totitive 84.7
toto caelo 50.10
totter n. 266.5
totter v. vary 149.4
  be weak 160.6
  walk 266.16
  go slow 275.5
  flounder 315.9
  collapse 659.6
tottering
  unsteady 160.12
  deteriorating 659.11
tottery
  unsteady 160.12
  unsafe 665.7
tottle n.
  computation 37.2
  all 50.2
tottle v. compute 37.5
  total 50.5
tottlish 160.12
Toucan 318.6
touch n. modicum 32.2
  tincture 41.3
  contiguity 199.1
  sensation 379
  taste 390.1
  music 415.20
  musicianship 416.17
  signal 550.3
  act 680.2
  request 765.1
  in touch with 9.6
touch v. be related 9.3
  equal 27.6
  be contiguous 199.3
  feel 379.1
  ~ the guitar 416.18
  slight 460.6

glance at 461.19
  grope 463.9
  (examine 461.17)
  discuss 595.4
  beg from 765.6
  ~ emotionally 824.4
  excite pity 914.4
not touch 678.5
touch the hat 894.9
touch the wind 267.19
touch up 658.10
touchable 379.5
touched insane 503.12
  tainted 653.17;
    659.13
  impressed 821.7
  pitying 914.6
  remorseful 950.5
touchhole 351.1
touching n. 199.1
touching adj.
  contiguous 199.4
  tangent 379.4
  distressing 830.11
touching prep. 9.10
touchstone 463.5
touchwood 388.6
touchy 901.7
tough n. 913.2
tough adj.
  violent 173.11
  rigid 323.5
  resistant 327.5
  (hard 323.5)
  viscid 352.8
  (coherent 46.9)
  obscure 519.7
  obstinate 606.6
  laborious 686.10
  difficult 704.8
  hardened in vice
    945.18
be tough 327.3
toughen 327.4
toughness
  tenacity 46.2
  resistance 327
  (hardness 323.1)
  (viscidity 352.1)
toupee 256.4
tour n. journey 266.8
  circuit 629.1
tour v. 266.12
tour de force 698.5
tourer 268.1
touring car 272.15
tourism 266.2
tourist n. 268.1
tourist v. 266.12
touristic 266.23
touristry 266.2
  (traveler 268.1)
tourmaline, turmaline
  847.8
tournament
  contest 720.2
  sports event 840.10
tourney n. 720.2
tourney v. 720.8
tourniquet
  stopper 263.1
  bandage 662.14

tournure bustle 225.25
  outline 230.1
  form 240.1
  gait 266.5
  lineaments 448.5
touse n. turmoil 59.4
  broil 713.4
touse, tousle v. 61.2
tousled 59.9
tout n. lookout 459.2
  predictor 513.2
  tipster 527.5
  scout 528.8
  solicitor 767.1; 797.4
  commender 935.1
tout v.
  look about 441.11
  reconnoiter 461.22
  watch 664.7
  solicit 765.4
keep tout
  be vigilant 459.4
  keep watch 664.7
tout ensemble all 50.2
  the nude 226.2
touter predictor 513.2
  tipster 527.5
  salesman 758.5
  solicitor 767.1; 797.4
  commender 935.1
tout le monds 78.5
tow n.
  take in tow pull 285.4
  aid 707.6
tow v. 285.4
towage drawing 285.1
  fee 812.2
toward, towardly 705.6
towel n. 652.2
  (merchandise 798.3)
towel v. 972.6
tower n. stability 150.2
  structure 161.7
  house 189.3
  height 206.2, 3
  (spire 253.4)
  observatory 441.5
  refuge 666.3
  stronghold 717.4
Tower n. 752.1
tower v. be great 31.4
  be high 206.9, 10
  ascend 305.6
towering vast 31.8
  huge 192.15
  high 206.13
tower of silence 363.13
towheaded 430.9
  (light-colored
    429.7)
towing path 627.2
towline 205.3
town region 181.2
  metropolis 189.16
  society 852.4
  social circle 892.7
townee, towner 188.2
town hall market 799.2
  courthouse 966.6
townhouse
  poorhouse 189.11
  asylum 666.3

courthouse 966.6
town house 189.3
township
  territory 181.2
  town 189.16
  measure 466.3
townsman 188.2
town talk 532.3
  (chitchat 588.2)
towny 188.2
towpath 627.2
tow-row 713.3
toxemia, toxaemia
  655.2
toxic n. 663.4
toxic adj. 657.3
toxicant n.
  poison 663.4
  intoxicant 959.4
toxicant adj. 657.3
toxicology 663.4
toxicophobia 860.4
toxophilite 840.17
toy n. 840.16
  (merchandise 798.3)
toy v. play 840.21
  make love 902.7
toy dog 366.6
trace n. taste 390.1
  mark 550.4
  vestige 551.5
  (evidence 467.1)
  (indication 550.1)
  picture 556.9
trace v. outline 230.3
  hunt 461.16
  (follow 281.3)
  mark 550.19
  delineate 554.7
  etymologize 562.7
  transcribe 590.13
trace out
  discover 481a.3
  spell out 561.8
trace to 155.3
traceable 155.4
tracery network 219.4
  curve 245.2
  ornamentation 847.3
trachea 351.3
tracheate 368.18
tracheocele 655.5
tracheophone 418.6
trachoma 655.8
tracing duplicate 21.2
  drawing 556.9
  writing 590.3
track n. spoor 550.4
  (trace 551.5)
  routine 613.4
  path 627.2
  (line 278.3)
  on the track 622.10
track v. walk 266.16
  hunt 461.16
  (follow 281.3)
  (pursue 622.6)
trackless 261.4
tract
  ~ of time 109.1
  plot 181.3
  (land 342.1)

field 371.5
brochure 593.1
dissertation 595.1
tractability 324.1
 (docility 602.3)
 (susceptibility 615.5)
tractable flexible 324.6
 (docile 602.9)
 submissive 725.5
Tractarian 984.15
Tractarianism 984.5
tractate 595.1
tractile
 tractional 285.6
 flexible 324.6
tractility 324.1
traction 285
 (transportation 270.2)
traction engine 272.17
tractive 285.6
tractor 272.15, 17
trade *n.*
 interchange 148.1
 ~ wind 349.9
 vocation 625.5
 barter 794.1, 3
 (business 625.1)
trade *v.*
 interchange 148.3
 barter 794.4, 8
 (sell 796.5)
trade-mark, trademark
 mark 550.11
 name 564.2
trade name 564.2
trader, tradesman 797.1
tradespeople 797.9
trade-union, trades-union 712.4
trading *n.*
 interchange 148.1
 barter 794.1
trading *adj.* 794.10
tradition 124.3
traditional
 immemorial 124.8
 legendary 594.7
 conventional 852.8
traditionalism 451.13
traditional logic 451.2
traditive
 traditional 124.8; 594.7
 conventional 852.8
traduce 934.3
traducent 934.4
traducer 936.1
Trafalgar 722.5
traffic *n.* 794.1
traffic *v.* 794.4
trafficker 797.1
traffic light 550.14
tragedian actor 599.19
 dramatist 599.22
tragedy drama 599.3
 misfortune 735.3
tragical
 dramatic 599.28

desolating 830.17
tragicomedy 599.3, 4
tragicomic
 drama 599.28
 comic 855.5
trail *n.* afterpart 65.2
 attendance 88.5
 odor 398.1
 spoor 550.4
 path 627.2
 hit the trail
 travel 266.12
 depart 293.4
 on the trail
 near discovery 480a.8
 pursuing 622.10
trail *v.*
 hang down 214.4
 go slow 275.5
 follow 281.3
 pull 285.4
 hunt 461.16
 (pursue 622.6)
trail blazer 673.5
trailer 272.16
train *n.* afterpart 65.2
 (tail 235.6)
 series 69.2
 procession 69.3
 attendance 88.5
 pendant 214.2
 vehicle 272.18
 ~ of thought 451.1;
  476.1
 military ~ 726.7
 in the train of 281.5
 serving 746.9
 lay a train plot 626.10
 prepare 673.6
train *v.* pull 285.4
 ~ stock 370.5
 teach 537.10
 (habituate 613.8)
 (prepare 673.6)
trainband 726.6
trainbearer
 follower 281.2
 attendant 746.1
trained 698.13
trainer rider 268.8
 aircraft 273a.1
 stockman 370.4
 teacher 540.1
 (preparer 673.5)
training 537.2
 (preparation 673.1)
traipse, trapes *n.* 59.5
traipse, trapes *v.*
 go slow 275.5
 travel 266.14, 16
trait particularity 79.2
 contact 379.1
 lineament 448.5
 earmark 550.6
 habit 613.1
traitor 949.3
 (informer 527.6)
 (deceiver 548.1)
 (turncoat 607.5)
traitorous 940.12
traject 284.11

trajectile *n.*
 projectile 284.5
 missile 727.14
trajectile *adj.* 284.16
trajection 284.2
trajectory 627.2
tra-la-la! 838.12
tralatition 521.1
tralatitious 521.3
tram *n.*
 streetcar 272.20
 railway 627.5
tram *v.* 266.18
tramcar 272.20
tramline 627.5
trammel *n.* 752.2
trammel *v.*
 impede 706.4
 fetter 751.7
tramontane *n.*
 alien 57.3
 wind 349.9
tramontane *adj.*
 alien 57.4
 distant 196.5
 outlandish 851.7
tramp *n.* walk 266.4
 traveler 268.2, 6
 (neglector 460.3)
 (idler 683.7)
 (beggar 767a)
 (vagabond 876.9)
tramp *v.*
 wander 266.14
 walk 266.16
tramper 268.6
trample
 trample in the dust
 destroy 162.4
 overthrow 308.5
 conquer 731.9
 subdue 749.5
 trample upon
 aggrieve 649.6
 tyrannize 739.4
 violate 742.4
 domineer 885.5
 scorn 930.5
tramroad, tramway 627.5
trance *n.* muse 458.3
 dream 515.5
 swoon 683.5
 ecstasy 994.6
 (spell 993.1)
 in a trance 515.14
trance *v.* 992.4
tranquil equable 174.6
 quiescent 265.7
 peaceful 721.4
 inexcitable 826.9
tranquilization, tranquillization 174.2
tranquilize, tranquillize moderate 174.5
 (pacify 723.4)
 (compose 826.7)
 (content 831.4)
 quiet 265.6
tranquillity, tranquility quiescence 265.1
 (peace 721.1)

~ **of mind** 826.2
transact
 ~ business 625.8;
  794.8
 perform 680.6
 conduct 692.4
transaction
 event 151.1
 action 680.1, 2
 (conduct 692.1)
 business ~ 794.3
 (compact 769.1)
transalpine 196.5
transanimation 140.2
transatlantic 196.5
transcalency 382.1
transcalent 384.22
transcend
 be great 31.4
 excel 33.5
 (be better 648.5)
transcendence
 superiority 33.1
 (overrunning 303.1)
 (perfection 650.1)
transcendent
 unequaled 28.4
 supreme 33.8
transcendental
 obscure 519.7
 metaphysical 994.21
transcendentalism
 philosophy 451.17
 unintelligibility 519.1
 esoteric science 994.1
transcendentalist 994.13
transcribe
 imitate 19.5
 translate 522.6
 write 590.13
transcriber 590.11
transcript
 duplicate 21.2
 music score 415.21
transcription
 imitation 19.1
 duplicate 21.2
 (writing 590.3)
transept 1000.3
transeunt 111.6
transfer *n.*
 duplicate 21.2
 translocation 270.1
 vehicle 272.15
 ~ of property 783
 (substitution 147.1)
 (exchange 148.1)
 (barter 794.1)
transfer *v.*
 translocate 270.6, 7
 (dislocate 185.2)
 (pass 302.2)
 transport 270.8
 ~ property 783.3
 (substitute 147.3)
 (exchange 148.3)
transferable, transferrable
 removable 270.11

transferee — traps

transferable (*cont'd*)
  negotiable 783.5
transferee 270.5
transference
  translocation 270
  (interchange 148.1)
  (displacement
    185.1)
  (moving 264.2)
  ~ of property 783.1
transferrer 271.1
transfiguration
  transformation
    140.2
  rite 998.2
transfigure 140.6
transfix 260.14
transfixed 150.6
transforation 260.1
transform 140.6
transformable 144.9
transformation 140.2
  (conversion 144.1)
transformation scene
  599.15
transformer
  alterant 140.4
  electricity 158a.6
transformism 140.2
transfuse imbue 41.8
  transfer 270.6
  ~ blood 662.24
transfusion
  imbuement 41.2
  transference 270.1
transgress
  overstep 303.5
  violate 742.4
  sin 945.9
  violate the law 964.4
transgression
  overstepping 303.1
  violation 742.1
  wrongdoing 945.1
  misdeed 947.2
  lawbreaking 964.2
transgressive 742.6
  (nonobservant
    773.5)
  (lawless 964.6)
transgressor 949.2
transhape, tranship
  etc. See **transshape**
  etc.
transience 111.1, 4
  (instantaniety
    113.1)
  (changeableness
    149.1)
  (swiftness 274.1)
transient *n.*
  ephemeral 111.4
  lodger 188.4
  traveler 268.1
transient *adj.* 111.6
  (inconstant 149.6)
transiently 111.8
transilience
  revolution 146.1
  passage 302.1
transilient
  revolutionary 146.5

passing 302.3
transillumination
  425.1
transit transition 144.3
  measure 244.3; 466.4
  transference 270.1
in transit 270.13
transit instrument
  267a.29
transition 270.1
  (passage 302.1)
transitional
  convertible 144.9
  changeable 149.5
  moving 264.8
transition sound 402.2
transitive, transitory
  111.6
translate
  transfer 270.6
  render 522.6
  (manifest 525.2)
  cipher 561.7
  ~ words 562.7
  transfer bishop
    995.7
translation
  transference 270.1
  rendition 522.2
  (paraphrase 21.4)
  lexicology 562.4
  ~ to heaven 981.6
  bishopric transfer
    995.6
translative
  figurative 521.3
  interpretative 522.8
translator 524.1
translatory 522.8
transliterate 561.7
translocate
  dislocate 185.2
  transfer 270.6
translocation
  transformation
    140.2
  dislocation 185.1
  transference 270.1
translucence 425.1
translucent
  transparent 425.4
  perspicuous 518.5
transmarine
  distant 196.5
  oversea 341.7
transmigrate 266.15
transmigration
  transformation
    140.2
  transition 144.3
  migration 266.3
transmissible 270.11
transmission
  translocation 270.1
  automobile 272.16
  ~ of property 783.1
transmissive 783.5
transmit transfer 270.6
  (pass 302.2)
  radiobroadcast
    532a.9
  hand over 783.3

transmittal
  translocation 270.1
  assignment 783.1
transmitting set,
transmitting station
  532a.5
transmogrification
  140.2
transmogrifier 140.4
transmogrify 140.6
transmutable
  convertible 144.9
  interchangeable
    148.4
transmutation 140.2
  (conversion 144.1)
transmute 140.6
transom beam 215.12
  air passage 351.1
transparency 425
transparent
  luminous 420.22
  translucent 425.4
  perspicuous 518.5
be transparent 425.3
transpicuity
  transparency 425.1
  intelligibility 518.1
transpicuous
  transparent 425.4
  perspicuous 518.5
transpierce 260.14
transpire happen 151.3
  be disclosed 529.6
transplant
  dislocate 185.2
  transfer 270.6
  reset 371.8
transplantation
  dislocation 185.1
  transference 270.1
transpontine 196.5
transport *n.* ship 273.1
  aircraft 273a.1
  troopship 726.11
  excitement 825.2
  delight 827.2
  ~ of love 897.1
transport *v.*
  convey 270.8
  banish 297.11
  (punish 972.10)
  delight 829.5
transportable 270.11
transportation
  transition 144.3
  conveyance 270.2
  (traction 285.1)
  banishment 297.3
transported 827.10
transporter 271.1
transposal
  interchange 148.1
  inversion 218.1
  transference 270.1
transpose
  invert 14.4; 218.4
  interchange 148.3
  (transplace 185.2)
  transfer 270.6
  ~ music 415.26;
    416.18

transposition
  transformation
    140.2
  interchange 148.1
  dislocation 185.1
  inversion 218.1
  transference 270.1
transshape, transhape
  140.6
transship, tranship
  185.1
transshipment, tran-
shipment
  dislocation 185.1
  transportation 270.2
transubstantiate 140.6
transubstantiation
  transformation
    140.2
  sacrament 998.6
transudate 299.1
transudation
  egress 295.1
  excretion 299.1
  passage 302.1
transudative 295.9
transude 295.7
transume 270.6
transumption 270.1
transumptive 270.11
transvection 270.2
transverse *v.* 140.6
transverse *adj.*
  oblique 217.14
  aerostat 273a.12
transversely
  obliquely 217.18
  crosswise 219.12
transversion 219.1
trap *n.* mouth 260.2
  trap door 260.4
  cart 272.5
  stone 342.4
  snare 545.4
  (lure 617.2)
  (pitfall 667.2)
  (artifice 702.3)
  trap door 599.12
fall into a trap
  be deceived 547.3
  be clumsy 699.7
trap *v.* close 261.2
  ensnare 545.9
trapan See **trepan**
trap door door 260.4
  trap 545.4
  stage 599.12
  pitfall 667.2
trapes See **traipse**
trapezohedron 244.2
trapfall snare 545.4
  pitfall 667.2
trapper 622.4
trappings adjunct 39.2
  wardrobe 225.2
  equipment 634.1
  belongings 780.1, 5
  frippery 847.2
Trappist 996.11
traprock 342.4
traps adjunct 39.2
  wardrobe 225.2

1140

equipment 634.1
belongings 780.1, 5
trapse See traipse
trash n. nonsense 517.2
　trumpery 643.5
　rubbish 645.4
　riffraff 876.2
trash v. 678.3
trashy twaddly 517.9
　paltry 643.12
traulism 583.1
trauma neurosis 655.14
　wound 659.4
traumatic 662.25
travail birth 161.3
　labor 686.3
trave 215.12
travel n. 266
　(locomotion 264.2)
　(progress 282.1)
travel v. 266.12
　(move 264.6)
traveler, traveller
　journeyer 268
　(workman 690.10)
　salesman 758.5;
　797.2
traveling, travelling
　travel 266.1
　itinerant 266.23
　(moving 264.8)
traveling bag 191.5
traveling man, traveling salesman 758.5
　(traveler 268.1)
travelogue, travelog 582.2
travel-worn 266.26
traversal 536.1
traverse n. 215.12
traverse v.
　counteract 179.3
　travel 266.12
　navigate 267.10
　pass 302.2
　deny 536.2
　thwart 706.7
traverse a yard 267.10
travesty n.
　caricature 21.3
　(misrepresentation 555.3)
　comedy 599.4
　burlesque 856.3
　(absurdity 497.1)
travesty v.
　caricature 19.8
　burlesque 856.6
travis, traviss 215.12
trawl pull 285.4
　fish 622.8
trawler ship 273.1
　fisherman 622.5
tray 191.12
treacherous 940.12
　(false 544.7)
　(deceitful 545.12)
　(cunning 702.6)
treachery 940.4
　(deception 545.1)
　(cunning 702.1)
treacle

semiliquid 352.3
sweetening 396.4
tread n. velocity 274.1
　beat 407.3
tread v. 266.16
tread down
　tyrannize 739.4
　domineer 885.5
tread on the heels of
　be near 197.5
　follow 281.3
　approach 286.2
tread the stage 599.26
tread underfoot
　destroy 162.4
　conquer 731.9
　tyrannize 739.4
　subdue 749.5
　degrade 874.7
　domineer 885.5
　scorn 930.5
treadmill rotator 312.4
　punishment 975.3
treason revolt 742.2
　treachery 940.4
treasonist 949.3
treasonous 940.12
treasure n. store 636.1
　good thing 648.4
　funds 800.2
treasure v.
　~ the memory of 505.11, 12
　store up 636.7
　(acquire 775.6)
　rate highly 642.8
　hold dear 897.11
treasure house
　storehouse 636.4
　treasury 802.1
treasurer 801
　(functionary 758.2)
treasure-trove 648.2
treasury
　~ of words 593.4
　storehouse 636.4
　bank 802
treasury bill 800.7
treat n. delight 829.3
　(pleasure 377.3)
　amusement 840.1
treat v. discuss 595.4
　~ a disease 662.24
　deal with 692.4
　negotiate 769.6
　~ oneself to 827.6
　give pleasure 829.4
　entertain 840.20
treatise writing 590.3
　dissertation 595.1
　(book 593.1)
treatment art 556.5
　medical ~ 662.15
　usage 677.2
treaty 769.2
treble n.
　high tone 410.2
　voice 413.14
　voice part 415.13
　speech defect 583.1
treble v. 93.2
treble adj. 93.3

trebly 93.4
trebuchet, trebucket
　weapon 727.9
　cucking stool 975.3
trecento 554.9
treck, trecker See trek etc.
tree n. ancestry 166.4
　mast 273.12
　plant 367.6
　(wood 635.3)
　impasse 704.3
　gallows 975.4
tree v. nonplus 475.8
　corner 704.7
　checkmate 731.10
treed nonplused 475.16
　cornered 704.11
treelike
　arborescent 242.6
　arborary 367.15
treenail, trenail 45.5
tree of knowledge 490.6
tree of life 450.2
trefoil three 92.2
　ornament 847.4
trek, treck n. 266.3, 8
trek, treck v.
　travel 266.12, 15
　pull 285.4
trekker, trecker 268.1, 3
trellis network 219.4
　fence 232.2
tremble n. shake 315.4
　tremolo 407.2
　trepidation 825.3
tremble v. vary 149.4
　be weak 160.6
　shake 315.9
　be cold 383.7
　tremolo 407.7
　~ with excitement 824.7
　be afraid 860.9
tremellose 352.8
tremendous
　appalling 830.13
　frightful 860.15
tremendously 31.15
tremolando, tremulando 407.2, 12
tremolant 407.12
tremolo n. 407.2
tremolo v. trill 407.7
　warble 416.20
tremoloso 407.12
tremor
　earthquake 173.2
　shake 315.4
　~ of excitement 825.3
tremulant 407.12
tremulous
　agitated 315.13
　tremulant 407.12
　voice 583.5
　irresolute 605.5
　fearful 860.14
trenail See treenail
trench n. furrow 259.2

(cleft 198.2)
(cavity 252.2)
channel 350.1
fortification 717.3
trench v.
trench on
　be near 197.5
　overstep 303.5
　violate 742.4
　infringe 925.6
trenchant
　forceful 171.9
　emphatic 535.6
　terse 572.3
　vigorous 574.5
　telling 642.11
　intensely felt 821.5
　brusque 895.7
　criticism 932.11
trencher 191.12
trench gun 727.11
trench warfare 722.1
trend n. tendency 176.1
　direction 278.1
trend v. tend 176.2
　direct 278.4
　deviate 279.4
trepan n. 262
trepan, trapan n.
　deception 545.3, 4
　deceiver 548.1
trepan v. 260.14
trepan, trapan v.
　ensnare 545.9
　swindle 791.12
trepang 298.18
trephine n. 262
trephine v. 260.14
trepidate 315.9
trepidation, trepidity
　agitation 315.1
　excitement 825.3
　fear 860.3
trespass n.
　overstepping 303.1
　violation 742.1
　sin 947.2
　lawbreaking 964.2
trespass v.
　intrude 228.10
　(enter 294.6)
　overstep 303.5
　violate 742.4
　sin 945.9
　violate the law 964.4
trespassage 303.1
trespasser 228.4
tress 256.3
trestle, trestle legs, trestlework etc. 215.9
tret 813.1
trews 225.21
trey three 92.2
　throw of dice 621.9
triad three 92.2
　microbe 193.4
　chord 413.9
triadelphous 94.2
triadic 92.4
trial n.
　examination 461.3

trial — tripedal

trial (*continued*)
 (hearing 418.2)
 experiment 463.1
 attempt 675.1
 difficulty 704.2
 trouble 735.1
 suffering 828.1
 affliction 830.2
 lawsuit 969.5
 punishment 972.1
 on trial
 experiment 463.15
 in litigation 969.14
trial *adj.* 92.4
trial and error *n.* 463.1
trial-and-error *adj.* 463.12
trialism, triality 92
 (triplication 93.1)
trialogue
 interlocution 588.1
 drama 599.3
triangle three 92.2
 angle 244.2
 music instrument 417.10
 pillory 975.3
Triangle, Triangulum 318.6
triangular
 tripartite 94.2
 angular 244.5
triarch trinal 92.4
 tripartite 94.2
triarchy 737.4
tribal racial 11.8
 classification 75.6
tribe race 11.4
 company 72.3
 crowd 72.4
 kind 75.2
triboluminescence, tribophosphorescence 420.11
tribulation
 suffering 828.1
 affliction 830.2
tribunal *n.* 966
 (council 696.1)
tribunal *adj.* 966.7
 (judicative 965.4)
tribune rostrum 542.6
 judge 967.1
tributary *n.* 348.1
tributary *adj.* 784.14
tribute
 contribution 784.5
 payment 807.2; 973.2
 commendation 931.2
 pay tribute
 pay homage 928.5
 commend 931.6
tricapsular 94.2
trice *n.* 113.3
 in a trice 113.6
trice *v.*
 trice up 43.6
tricennial 138.5
Triceratops 124.2
trichinopoly 392a.3
trichogenous, trichoid 256.13

trichosis 226.1
trichotomic, trichotomous 94.2
trichotomy 94.1
trichroism 440.1
trichromic 440.5
trick *n.*
 particularity 79.2
 optical illusion 443.9
 delusion 495.5
 foolish act 499.7
 deception 545.3
 (contrivance 626.5)
 (dishonesty 940.5)
 trait 550.6
 habit 613.1
 knack 698.2
 artifice 702.3
 prank 842.7
trick *v.* deceive 545.7
 intrigue 702.5
 play pranks 842.8
 trick up
 clothe 225.41
 adorn 847.11
trick *adj.*
 imitation 19.12
 pseudo 545.13
tricker 548.1, 6
trickery
 deception 545.1
 cunning 702.1
 buffoonery 842.3
 frippery 847.2
 sharp practice 940.5
trickle *n.* 348.4
trickle *v.*
 leak out 295.7
 dribble 348.19
 purl 405.5
trick of eyesight 443.9
trickster
 deceiver 548.1, 6
 crafty rascal 702.4
 swindler 792.8
tricksy crafty 702.6
 playful 836.10
 pretty 845.11
 smart 847.14
 dishonest 940.8
tricky
 deceptive 545.12, 13
 crafty 702.6
 dishonest 940.8
tricolor, tricolour *n.*
 variegation 440.2
 flag 550.13
tricolor *adj.* 440.5
tricorn, tricornered, tricuspid 94.2
tricycle 272.14
trident *n.* 92.2
trident *adj.* 94.2
tried tested 463.13
 friendship 888.4
 trustworthy 940.9
triennial *n.* 138.5
triennial *adj.*
 periodic 138.11
 plant 367.17
trifid 94.2
trifle *n.* 643.3, 4

 (smallness 32.2)
 (trinket 847.9)
trifle *v.* slight 460.6
 quibble 477.8
 act the fool 499.9
 fribble 643.9
 potter 683.8
 make love 902.7
trifle with slight 460.6
 fool 545.10
 be disrespectful 929.3
trifler
 neglector 460.3
 sciolist 493.2
trifling
 meaningless 517.8
 trivial 643.11
 (absurd 497.4)
trifloral, trifoliate 94.2
triforium 1000.3
triform 94.2
trifurcate 94.2
trig *n.* 85.2; 244.3
trig *adj.* orderly 58.7
 trim 845.11
trigamist 903.5
trigamy 903.2
trigeminal neuralgia 378.1
trigger 215.7
triglyph 215.17
trigon three 92.2
 triangle 244.2
trigonal
 tripartite 94.2
 triangular 244.5
trigonometry
 mathematics 85.2
 measurement 244.3
trigraph 561.1
trilateral
 tripartite 94.2
 three-sided 236.7
 triangular 244.5
triliteral 94.2
trill *n.* trickle 348.4
 tremolo 407.2
 (ornament 413.10)
 (musical effect 415.20)
trill *v.* trickle 295.7
 ripple 348.19
 purl 405.5
 tremolo 407.7
 warble 412.2; 416.20
trillando 407.12
trillet, trilletto 407.2
trillion 98.13
trillo 407.2
 (ornament 413.10)
trilogic 93.3
trilogy triality 92.1
 drama 599.16
trim *n.* condition 7.1
 clothes 225.1
 in trim orderly 58.7
 shipshape 267.67
 put in trim
 arrange 60.6
 prepare 673.6
trim *v.* equalize 27.7

arrange 60.6
form 240.6
be irresolute 605.4
neutral 628.2
defeat 731.9
cheapen 815.7
decorate 847.11
berate 932.8
whip 972.6
trim sail 267.16, 37
trim up 60.6
trim *adj.*
 orderly 58.7
 symmetrical 242.5
 navigation 267.51
 shipshape 267.67
 spruce 845.11
trimerous 94.2
trimmed
 navigation 267.51
 rigged 273.16
 defeated 732.12
trimmer 605.3
 (tergiversator 607.4)
trimming *n.*
 edging 231.2
 ornament 847.6
 reproof 932.3
 dishonesty 940.5
trimming *adj.* 607.10
Trimurti 976.3
trinal, trine three 92.4
 triplicate 93.3
Trinitarian 984.14
Trinitarianism 984.4
trinitrotoluene 727.13
trinity, Trinity 92.1
Trinity Sunday 998.13
trinket trifle 643.3
 toy 840.16
 gewgaw 847.9
trinomial *n.* 92.2
trinomial *adj.* 94.2
trio three 92.2
 part music 415.12
triolet 597.2
trionym 92.2
trip *n.* journey 266.8
 stumble 306.2
 blunder 495.3
 bungle 699.4
 misdeed 947.2
trip *v.* travel 266.12
 walk 266.16
 speed 274.9
 stumble 306.6
 caper 309.5
 blunder 495.9
 ensnare 545.9
 bungle 699.9
 fail 732.5
 skip 840.21
 err 945.9
tripalmitin 356.1
tripartite 94.2
tripartition 94.1
tripe vitals 221.4
triplane 273a.1
 rubbish 645.4
tripedal, tripetalous 94.2

triphthong 402.2
Tripitaka 986.1
triplane 273a.1
triple v. increase 35.3
 triplicate 93.2
triple adj. 93.3
triple crown 747.3;
 999.1
triplet three 92.2
 note 413.6
 stanza 597.7
triplex 93.3
triplicate n. 93.1
triplicate v. 93.2
triplication 93
 (triality 92.1)
triplicity triality 92.1
 triplication 93.1
triplopia 92.2
triply 93.4
tripod three 92.2
 table 215.20
 seat 215.22
 fire iron 386.3
 oracle 513.1
tripodic 94.2
tripos 461.3
tripot 621.14
tripper 268.1
tripping 578.4
tripsis 330.2
Triptolemus, Tripto-
 lemos 371.3
triquetrel 94.2
triquetrous 236.7
trireme three 92.2
 galley 273.3
Trisagion 990.2
trisected 94.2
trisection 94
triseme three 92.2
 versification 597.6
triskelion, triskele
 92.2
trismus 655.5
triste 837.10
tristful 837.9
tristich 597.7
trisul 92.2
trite 843.6
 (well-known 490.17)
triteness 843.2
 (platitude 496.3)
 (old joke 842.6)
tritheism 984.4, 10
Triton
 spirit of the sea
 341.2
 deity 979.10
triturate 330.6
trituration 330.2
triumph n.
 procession 69.3
 victory 731.3
 exultation 838.1
 celebration 883.1
triumph v.
 be victorious 731.6, 8
 exult 838.5; 884.6
triumphal arch
 trophy 733.1
 celebration 883.1

triumphant
 victorious 731.11
 exultant 884.9
triumpher 731.4
triumvirate three 92.2
 government 737.4
triune 92.4
Triune 976.3
triunity 92.1
trivet table 215.20
 seat 215.22
 fire iron 386.3
trivia 643.4
 (smallness 32.3)
trivial
 superficial 209.4
 meaningless 517.8
 trifling 643.11
 (inconsiderable
 32.8)
 (nugatory 158.11)
 (foolish 499.15)
 (mediocre 736.3)
 (ridiculous 855.5)
 trite 843.6
triviality
 trite saying 496.3
 unimportance
 643.2, 3
 triteness 843.2
troat 412.2
trocar, trochar 262
trochaic 597.13
troche 400.2
trochee 597.6
trochilic 312.8
trochilics 312.6
troglodyte 893.4
troglodytic 893.9
troll n.
 part music 415.12
 mythical being 980.2
troll v. pull 285.4
 turn 311.4
 roll 312.7
 sing 416.20
 fish 622.8
troller 622.5
trolley, trolly n.
 272.20, 21
trolley, trolly v. 266.18
trolley car 158a.7
trollop slattern 59.5
 (vulgarian 851.4)
 strumpet 962.2
trombone horn 417.4
 organ stop 417.12
trombonist 416.2
troop company 72.3
 party 712.1
 military unit 726.7
trooper 726.4, 12
troops 726.6
troopship 726.11
trope 521.1
trophoplasm 357.3
trophoplasmic 357.9
trophy memento 551.4
 prize 733
 (sign 550.2)
 (insignia 550.12)
 (monument 551.4)

(honor 873.7)
(reward 973.1)
tropical exotic 367.17
 hot 382.16
 figurative 521.3
tropopause, tropo-
 sphere
 aeronautics 267a.19
 atmosphere 338.2
trot n.
 old woman 130.3
 run 274.3
 translation 522.2
trot v. 274.9
trot out show 525.2
 show off 882.7
troth belief 484.1
 truth 494.1
 veracity 543.1
 promise 768.1
 engagement 768.2
 fidelity 939.4
by my troth
 upon my word!
 535.8
 (truthfully 543.4)
 I promise! 768.8
trothless
 untruthful 544.7
 untrue 546.6
 untrustworthy
 940.11
trothplight n. 768.2
trothplight v. 768.4
trothplight adj. 768.7
trotter foot 211.4
 leg 266.11
 horse 271.3
 meat 298.23
troubadour
 singer 416.10
 poet 597.10
trouble n. turmoil 59.4
 exertion 686.1
 predicament 704.2
 adversity 735.1
 annoyance 828.4
 affliction 830.2
 in trouble 704.11
 (unfortunate 735.9)
 take trouble 686.5
trouble v.
 discompose 61.4
 agitate 315.8
 ask for 765.4
 annoy 830.5
 trouble oneself 686.5
troubled
 displeased 828.14
 annoyed 828.15
trouble man
 electrician 157a.10
 repairman 660.7
trouble shooter
 electrician 158a.10
 repairman 660.7
trouble shooting 660.4
troublesome
 inexpedient 647.3
 laborious 686.10
 difficult 704.8
 annoying 830.12

troublous
 tumultuous 59.11
 turbulent 173.12
 agitated 315.13
trou-de-loup 545.4
trough trench 259.2
 (cavity 252.2)
 aeronautics 267a.19
 conduit 350.1
 washbasin 652.5
trounce reprove 932.8
 thrash 972.6
troupe n. company 72.3
 theatrical ~ 599.18
troupe v. 599.26
trouper 599.19
trouse, trouserettes,
 trousers 225.21
trousseau 225.2
trout 298.18
trouveur, trovatore
 597.10
trover 775.2, 3
 (finding 481a.1)
trow judge 480.6
 believe 484.8
 (think 451.27)
 know 490.9
 suppose 514.6
trowel 191.14
truancy 187.5
 (avoidance 623.1)
 (dereliction 927.1)
truant n.
 absentee 187.6
 shirker 623.4
 delinquent 949.1
truant adj. 187.10
truantism 187.5
truce delay 133.2
 armistice 723.3
 (pause 142.2)
 (peace 721.1)
a truce to 142.8
truce of God 723.3
trucidation 361.1
truck n.
 vehicle 272.10, 15, 19
 nonsense 517.2
 trumpery 643.5
 rubbish 645.4
 barter 794.1
have no truck with
 ignore 460.5
 exclude 893.7
 snub 930.7
truck v.
 transport 270.8
 barter 794.4
truckage 270.2
truck car 272.19
truck driver 268.10
truckle
 be submissive 725.3
 fawn 886.3
 (flatter 933.2)
truckle bed 215.24
truckler 886.2
truckling 886.4
truckman driver 268.9
 automobilist 268.10
truck system 794.1

truculence — tugboat 1144

truculence 907.3
truculent 907.9
trudge walk 266.16
  go slow 275.5
true v. 494.7
true adj.
  ~ to life 17.15
  straight 246.5
  unerroneous 494.10
  (real 1.8)
  (certain 474.8)
  (right 922.5)
  (orthodox 983a.7)
  veracious 543.3
  observant 772.5
  reliable 939.9
  faithful 939.10
be true 494.5, 10
not true oblique 217.9
  erroneous 495.12
  untrue 546.6
true bill
  accusation 938.1
  indictment 969.3
true blue n. 939.4
true-blue n. 939.5
true-blue adj.
  true 494.13
  veracious 543.3
  faithful 939.10
  orthodox 983a.7
truehearted
  veracious 543.3
  upright 939.7, 10
truelove 897.1, 7
truelove knot 902.5
trueman, truepenny 939.5
true-speaking
  veracious 543.3
  speaking 582.11
truffle 298.30
truism 496.2
trull 962.2
truly
  absolutely 31.16
  to be sure 488.14
  verily 494.15
  (actually 1.9)
  (intrinsically 5.8)
  (certainly 474.16)
  (affirmation 535.8)
  (truthfully 543.4)
trump n.
  master stroke 626.7; 698.4
  good thing 648.4
  paragon 650.3
  cards 840.13
  man of honor 939.5
  good person 948.1
trump v.
  ~ up 544.3
  defeat 731.10
trump card
  masterstroke 626.7; 698.5; 731.2
  (salient point 642.4)
trumped-up
  spurious 545.13
  untrue 546.6
trumpery n.

nonsense 517.2
trifles 643.5
trumpery adj.
  nonsensical 517.9
  paltry 643.12
trumpet n.
  whistle 410.4
  horn 417.4
  battle horn 722.3
trumpet v.
  ~ forth 531.7
  boast 884.5
trumpet call 550.16
trumpeter
  musician 416.2
  messenger 534.1
  boaster 884.3
trumpet-tongued, trumpet-voiced
  loud 404.8
  shrill 410.10
truncate cut off 38.6
  (shorten 201.4)
  deform 243.3
truncated 53.5
truncation
  excision 38.2
  shortening 201.2
  distortion 243.1
truncator 201.3
truncheon club 727.7
  (rod 975.2)
  scepter 747.1
trundle 312.7
  (start 284.14)
trundle bed 215.24
trunk main part 50.3
  origin 155.3
  family tree 166.4
  case 191.8
  stalk 215.14
  nose 250.4
trunks 267.9
trunnion 312.5
truss n. bundle 72.5
  beam 215.12
  airplane 273a.10
truss v. tie 43.6
  assemble 72.11
trust n. belief 484.1
  expectation 507.2
  syndicate 712.5
  commission 755.1
  estate 780.2
  credit 805.1
  hope 858.1
on trust 805.7
take on trust
  believe 484.7
  be credulous 486.3
trust v. believe 484.7, 8
  hope 858.6
trustee
  consignee 758.1
  possessor 779.4
  treasurer 801
truster 484.6; 987.4
trustful
  confiding 484.13
  (credulous 486.5)
  artless 703.4
  trustworthy 940.9

trustless 940.11
trustworthiness 939.3
trustworthy
  infallible 474.14
  believable 484.15
  authentic 494.12
  veracious 543.3
  safe 664.10
  reliable 939.9
trusty veracious 543.3
  trustworthy 940.9
truth verity 494
  (fact 1.2)
  (essence 5.2)
  (certainty 474.1)
  (right 922.1)
  (probity 939.1)
  (orthodoxy 983a.1)
  axiom 496.2
  veracity 543.1
  fidelity 939.4
in truth truly 494.15
  (certainly 474.16)
  (affirmation 535.8)
  truthfully 543.4
speak the truth
  confess 529.5
  be truthful 543.2
  (be honorable 939.6)
Truth
  world spirit 359.3
  God 976.2
  Christ 976.5
truth-declaring, truthful 543.3
be truthful 543.2
truthfully 543.4
  (truly 494.15)
truthfulness 543.1
truth-loving, truth-speaking 543.3
try n. 675.1
try v. examine 461.15
  test 463.8
  judge 480.8
  (administer justice 965.3)
  (prosecute 969.11)
  attempt 675.3, 4
  (struggle 686.5, 6)
try conclusions
  reason 476.10
  contend with 720.8
try it on 463.8
try one
  be difficult for 704.5
  have trouble 735.5
try out 463.8
tryer-out 463.6
trying 704.9
tryout hearing 418.2
  trial 463.1
try square 212.5
tryst, trysting place
  rendezvous 74.2
  assignation 892.3
tryworks 691
tsar, tsarevitch etc.
  See czar etc.
T square 212.5
Tuamotuan 560.4
tub n.

receptacle 191.11
automobile 272.15
ship 273.1
bath 652.3
washtub 652.5
tub v. 652.9
tuba horn 417.4
  organ stop 417.12
tubate 260.16
tubby stout 192.12
  stubby 201.6
tube subway 252.3
  pipe 260.6
  (conduit 350.1)
  (air passage 351.1)
  tire 272.16
  train 272.18
  lamp 423.11
  railway 627.5
tubercle
  protuberance 250.2
  ailment 655.16
tubercular 655.25
tuberculosis 655.10
tuberculous
  tuberous 250.9
  consumptive 655.25
tuberose 400.3
tuberosity
  convexity 250.1
  protuberance 250.2
  swelling 655.16
tubman 968.1
tubular, tubulate 260.16
tubulation, tubule, tubulet etc. 260.6
Tucana 318.6
tuck n. adjunct 39.2
  fold 258.1
  feast 298.37
  life force 359.2
  sweets 396.2
  (delicacy 298.9)
  weapon 727.3
tuck v. 258.3
tuck in eat 29.44
  lodge 184.12
  insert 300.5
tuck on 37.3
tuck up 972.8
tucker n.
  neckpiece 225.33
  food 298.5, 6
  fatigue 688.1
tucker v. 688.5
tucker bag 191.5
tufa 342.4
tuft bundle 72.5
  hair 256.3
  feathers 256.8
tufted 256.13
tufthunter
  sycophant 886.2
  self-seeker 943.2
tufthunting 886.1
tug n. tugboat 273.4
  pull 285.2
  strain 686.1
tug v. pull 285.4
  strain 686.5
tugboat 273.4

tug of war
  contest 720.2
  game 840.11
tuition 537.1
tuitional, tuitionary
  540.7
tulip 440.2
tulipwood 635.3
Tullian 582.12
Tulu 560.4
tumble n.
  confusion 59.2
  fall 306.2
tumble v. derange 61.2
  perish 162.5
  pitch 267.45
  fall 306.6
  jump about 315.9
  be indiscriminate
    465a.2
  be excited 824.7
tumble down 659.12
tumbler glass 191.11
  acrobat 599.21
tumbrel, tumbril 272.5
tumefaction, tumes-
  cence swelling 194.1
  convexity 250.1, 2
  ailment 655.16
tumescent
  swollen 194.10
  tumorous 250.9
  diseased 655.25
tumid swollen 194.10
  (convex 250.9)
  grandiloquent 577.7
tumidity
  swelling 194.1
  convexity 250.1
tummy 191.7
tumor, tumour
  swelling 194.2
  protuberance 250.2
  ailment 655.16
tumorous
  swollen 194.10
  tumescent 250.9
  diseased 655.25
tump 206.2
tumult turmoil 59.4
  agitation 315.1
  noise 404.2
  excitement 825.3
tumultuary 173.11;
  824.11
  (vehement 825.10)
tumultuous
  troublous 59.11
  turbulent 173.12
  (blustering 887.4)
tumulus 363.13
tun n. paunch 191.7
  receptacle 191.11
  drunkard 959.11
tun v. 959.15
tuna 298.18
tundra 344.1
tune n.
  tone 402.2; 413.4, 13
  attunement 413.1
  air 415.2
  in tune 413.26

out of tune inapt 24.7
  unconformable 83.9
  off-key 414.4
  imperfect 651.4
  impaired 659.12
to the tune of
  quantity 25.8
  payment 807.6
  at a price 812.7
tune v. attune 413.24
  play tunes 416.18
tune down
  decrease 36.4
  moderate 174.5
tune up
  harmonize 413.24
  begin to play 416.21
tuneful
  melodious 413.27
  poetical 597.13
tunefulness 413.4
tuneless 414.4
tungsten 635.6
tungsten lamp 423.3
Tungus, Tunguz 560.4
tunic cloak 225.15
  clerical ∼ 999.1
tuning fork 417.13
tunnage See tonnage
tunnel n. 252.3
  (hole 260.1)
  (conduit 350.1)
tunnel v. 252.9
  (perforate 260.14)
tunneler, tunneller
  252.7
  (workman 690.10)
tup ram 366.8
  male animal 373.6
tupek, tupik hut 189.4
  tent 223.5
Tupi 560.4
tu quoque 468.1, 5
turban 225.26
turbid troublous 59.11
  viscid 352.8
  opaque 426.4
turbinal 248.5
turbinate 312.7
turbination 312.1
turbine propeller 284.6
  rotator 312.4
  engine 633.3
turbinoid 248.5
turbulence
  turmoil 59.4
  (violence 173.1)
  agitation 315.1
  excitement 825.3
  fury 825.4
turbulent
  troublous 59.11
  tumultuous 173.12
  (agitated 315.12)
  (stormy 349.26)
  (blustering 887.4)
  noisy 404.9
  excited 824.11
  (vehement 825.10)
tureen 191.11
turf n. elastic 325.2
  greensward 367.10

fuel 388.1
  horse racing 621.7;
    720.5; 840.11
  race course 728.1
turf v. 371.8
turfman 840.19
turfy 367.14
turgescence
  expansion 194.1
  grandiloquence
    577.2
turgescent 577.7
turgid swollen 194.10
  (overfull 641.6)
  grandiloquent 577.7
turgidity
  expansion 194.1
  grandiloquence
    577.2
Turk horse 271.4
  polygamist 903.5
turkey facts 1.2
  handbag 191.5
  food 298.25
  fowl 366.23
  essentials 642.4
turkey trot 840.7
Turkish bath 382.6
Turkoman 560.4
turmaline See tour-
  maline
turmeric paper 463.5
turmoil confusion 59.4
  (violence 173.1)
  (brawl 713.4)
  agitation 315.1
  excitement 825.3
turn n. state 7.1
  crisis 134.4
  round 138.4
  change 140.1
  turning point 145.2
  tendency 176.1
  obliquity 217.1
  form 240.1
  curvature 245.1
  travel 266.4, 8
  deviation 279.1
  circuity 311.2
  (circle 247.2)
  whirl 312.2
  music 413.10
  aspect 448.4
  start 508.3
  act 599.5
  propensity 602.2
  circuit 629.1
  aptitude 698.2
  aid 707.1
  grace 784.4
  shock 825.2
  penchant 865.1
by turns
  in rotation 138.13
  interchangeably
    148.5
  (reciprocally 12.8)
give a turn
  change 140.6
  startle 508.6; 824.3
  help 707.6
  frighten 860.10

in turn
  consecutively 69.7
  in order 58.8
  in rotation 138.13
take a turn
  change 140.5
  travel 266.13
to a turn
  exactly 494.16
  completed 729.6, 8
turn v. change 140.5
  tend 176.2
  oblique 217.5
  curve 245.3
  convolve 248.3
  blunt 254.2
  turn ship 267.24
  direct 278.4
  deviate 279.4, 6
  go around 311.3, 4
  rotate 312.7
  induce 615.9
turn a deaf ear
  be deaf 419.6
  be inattentive 458.5
  (be insensible 823.3)
  ignore 460.5
  refuse 764.3
  be pitiless 914a.2
turn around one's
  finger
  have influence 175.8
  dominate 737.12
turn away
  turn aside 279.7
  disregard 458.5
  avoid 623.6
  snub 930.7
turn back
  return 104.5
  about-ship 267.24
  about-face 283.6
  (revert 145.4)
  (tergiversate 607.7)
turn color 824.8
turn down 764.2
turn in 683.9
turn into 522.6
turn king's evidence
  527.10
turn off stop 142.7
  electricity 158a.11
  eject 297.8
  extinguish 421.6
  execute 972.8
turn on 158a.11
turn one's coat
  607.8
turn one's hand to
  676.2
  (busy oneself 625.7)
turn out happen 151.3
  put externally 220.5
  clothe 225.42
  navigation 267.69
  evict 297.8, 9
  go on strike 719.4
turn over
  be inverted 218.5
  fold 258.3
  capsize 267.35
  transfer 270.7

urnback — twist 1146

urn (*continued*)
  overthrow 308.5
  transfer 783.3
  give 784.9
urn over a new leaf
  change 140.6
  improve 658.6
  reform 950.4
turn tail 623.10
turn the corner
  change 140.5
  improve 658.6
  succeed 731.5
turn the head
  astonish 870.3
  enamor 897.13
turn the scale
  be unequal 28.2
  have advantage 33.6
  change 140.6
  revert 145.4
  contribute 153.8
  gain influence 175.9
  invert 218.4
  counterevidence
    468.2
  induce 615.9
  predominate 737.12
turn the tables
  have advantage 33.6
  gain influence 175.9
  invert 218.4
  counterevidence
    468.2
  retaliate 718.2
  predominate 737.12
turn the trick 731.5
turn to begin 66.5
  be converted into
    144.8
  set to work 686.7
turn turtle 218.5
turn up happen 151.3
  chance 156.7
  appear 446.2
  come unawares
    508.5
  abandon 624.3
turn up one's toes
  360.6; 363.23
turnback, turncoat
  607.5
  (reversionist 145.3)
  (waverer 605.3)
  (traitor 949.3)
turning point
  crisis 134.4
  reversion 145.2
  (inversion 218.1)
  (regression 283.4)
  climax 210.1
  limit 233.1
turnip timepiece 114.6
  vegetable 298.30
turniplike 245.22
turnkey 753.1
turnmeter 267a.29
turn of mind 820.1
turn of the tide
  turning point 145.2
  (inversion 218.1)
  climax 210.1

turnout assembly 72.2
  attendance 186.6
  wardrobe 225.2
  vehicle 272.8
  strike 719.2
  demonstration 882.3
turnover food 298.12
  overthrow 308.2
turnpike
  roadway 627.3
  obstacle 706.2
turnpiker 268.2
turnspit dog 366.6
  fire iron 386.3
turnstile
  recorder 553.3
  obstacle 706.2
turntable 215.20
turntail 607.5
turnup 448.1
turpentine *n.*
  burnisher 255.3
  oil 356.3
  paint 428.5
turpentine *v.* 428.10
turpitude 945.2
turps turpentine 356.3
  paint 428.5
turquoise, turquois
  blue 438.2, 3
  gem 847.8
turquoise green 435.2
turret 206.3
turret ship 726.11
turtle printing 591.5
  stubbornness 606.4
turtleback 273a.10
turtledove 897.5, 9
turtlelike 275.8
tush *n.* 253.3
tush *int.* 403.9
  (speech 585.6)
tusk 253.3
tussle *n.* 720.2
tussle *v.* 720.8
tut! silence 403.9
  bah! 930.11
  fie! 932.16
tutelage
  teaching 537.1
  pupilage 539.2
  instructorship 540.6
  protectorship 664.2
  tendance 749.2
tutelary *n.*
  guardian 664.3
  deity 979.12
tutelary *adj.* 664.12
tutor *n.* 540.1
  (protector 664.3)
tutor *v.* 537.9
tutorage
  teaching 537.1
  instructorship 540.6
tutoress 540.2
tutorial 540.7
tutorship
  teaching 537.1
  instructorship 540.6
tutta forza 415.30
tutti 415.15
Tuxedo, tuxedo 225.14

tuyère 386.1
twaddle *n.*
  nonsense 517.2, 3
  verbosity 573.1
  chatter 584.2
twaddle *v.*
  talk nonsense 517.6
  be verbose 573.5
  be loquacious 584.4
twaddlement 517.2
twaddler 841.4
twaddly 517.9
twaddy nonsense 517.2
  chatter 584.2
twain *n.* 89.2
  in twain 44.14
twain *adj.* 89.4
twang *n.* taste 390.1
  pungency 392.1
  stridor 410.1
  language 563.5
  accent 580.4
twang *v.* jerk 285.5
  sound harshly 410.6
  strum 416.18
twanger 416.3
twangle stridor 410.1
  speech defect 583.1
twank
  sound harshly 410.6
  strum 416.18
twattle *n.*
  nonsense 517.2
  chatter 584.2
twattle *v.*
  talk nonsense 517.6
  be loquacious 584.4
twattling 517.9
tweak jerk 285.5
  pain 378.4
  ~ the nose 830.5
tweed 219.5
tweedle touch 379.3
  whistle 410.8
  play music 416.18
tweedledee *n.*
  violinist 416.3
  instrument 417.1
tweedledee *v.*
  whistle 410.8
  sing 416.20
tweedledum and
  tweedledee 415.3
tweeds 225.21
'tween-brain 450.2
'tween decks 273.8
tweet 412.2
tweezers 781.2
twelfth 98.22; 99.3
Twelfth-day,
  Twelfth-night,
  Twelfthtide 138.7;
  998.13
twelve 98.7
twelvemonth 108.1
twentieth 98.24
twenty 98.7
twenty-one 820.12
twenty questions
  840.11
twice 90.5
twice-told 104.6

twice-told tale 496.3
  (repetition 104.3)
  (tedium 841.3)
  old joke 842.6
twiddle touch 379.3
  ~ one's thumbs
    681.2; 683.8
twiddle-twaddle
  nonsense 517.2
  chatter 584.2
twig *n.* member 51.4
  foliage 367.4
twig *v.* 441.10
twilight *n.* 126.1
  (morning 125.1)
  (semidarkness
    422.2)
twilight *adj.* 126.5
  (morning 125.3)
  (dim 422.8)
twilight sleep 376.1
twill *n.* 219.5
twine interlace 219.8
  convolve 248.3
  fold 258.3
twin *n.* 17.5
twin *adj.*
  analogous 17.11
  accompanying 88.8
  duplicate 90.3
twine interlace 219.8
  convolve 248.3
twinge *n.* 378.1
twinge of conscience
  scrupulousness
    603.2
  penitence 950.1
  (conscientiousness
    939.2)
  (guilt 947.1)
twinge *v.* 378.5
twinkle *n.*
  instant 113.3
  glitter 420.5
  glimpse 441.2
twinkle *v.* 420.18
twinkly 420.23
twins 89.2
Twins 318.6
twirl *n.* coil 248.2
  (turn 311.2)
  whirl 312.2
  eddy 348.8
twirl *v.* convolve 248.3
  rotate 312.7
twist *n.* girl 129.5
  tendency 176.1
  cord 205.3
  obliquity 217.1
  (circuit 629.1)
  network 219.4
  distortion 243.1
  coil 248.2
  (complexity 59.3)
  turn 311.2
  tobacco 392a.7
  aspect 448.4
  prejudice 481.3
  bent of mind 820.1
  hunger 865.3
twist *v.* oblique 217.5
  interlace 219.8

twisted — unaccountable

distort 243.3
convolve 248.3
deviate 279.5, 6
wiggle 315.9
prejudice 481.8
misinterpret 523.2
misrepresent 555.4
twisted
distorted 243.5
convoluted 248.4
eccentric 503.17
twister
whirlwind 349.13
lie 546.1
twisting 243.1
twit *n.* banter 856.1
gibe 930.3
twit *v.* ululate 412.2
sing 416.20
banter 856.4
scoff 930.6
reproach 938.4
twitch *n.* jerk 285.3
pain 378.1
start 508.3
twitch *v.* jerk 285.5
vellicate 315.11
~ with pain 378.5
~ with excitement 824.7
twitchety, twitchy 315.13
twitter *n.* shake 315.4
trepidation 825.3
in a twitter 315.14
twitter *v.* shake 315.9
chirp 412.2
sing 416.20
be excited 824.7
'twixt 228.13
'twixtbrain 450.2
two 89.2, 4, 6
two bits 800.8
two-by-four *adj.*
little 193.8
paltry 643.12
mediocre 736.3
two-by-four *n.* 635.3
twodecker 189.3
two-edged 253.11
two-faced
dissembling 544.8
treacherous 940.12
two-facedness 544.2
two-fisted 159a.5
twofold *adj.* 90.3
(dual 89.4)
twofold *adv.* 90.4
two-forked 91.7
two-master 273.2
two or three 100.1
twopence 800.8
twopenny-halfpenny 643.12
two-seater 273a.1
two-sided
double 90.3
bilateral 236.7
twosome 89.2
two-spot 643.6
two-step music 415.7
dance 840.7

two-wheeler 272.5
tycoon 745.3
tyg, tig 191.11
tyke, tike dog 366.6
peasant 876.5
tyler See tiler
Tylopoda 206.7
tympan, timpan
drum 417.10
printing 591.5
tympanist 416.7
tympanites 194.2
tympanitis 418.9
tympano See timpano
tympanum top 210.4
drum 417.10
eardrum 418.5
tympany
distention 194.1
swelling 194.2
drum 417.10
tymp stick 417.13
typal 75.6
type *n.* prototype 22.1
kind 75.2
(nature 5.3)
form 240.1
measure 466.2
mark 550.2, 6
print 591.6
(letter 561.1)
type *v.*
exemplify 82.6
typewrite 590.13
type bar 591.9
type face type 591.6
type foundry, type metal 591.5
typer 590.11
typescript
writing 590.3
(copy 21.1)
print 591.2
typeset 591.18
typesetter 591.12
typesetting 591.1
type slug 591.9
typewrite 590.13
typewriter
instrument 590.10
typist 590.11
typewriting 590.1
typhoid, typhus 655.6
typhoon wind 349.9
whirlwind 349.13
typical
classification 75.6
peculiar 79.8
exemplary 82.11
symbolic 521.3
emblematic 550.21
representative 554.9
typify prefigure 511.9
mean 516.5
symbolize 521.2; 550.18
typist 590.11
typographer 591.12
typographic 591.18
typography 591.1
typotelegraph 532a.5
Tyr, Tyrr

heavens 318.2
war-god 722.7
god 979.3
tyrannical 739.5
tyrannize 739.4
tyranny 739.2
(lawlessness 964.3)
tyrant despot 739.3
(usurper 925.4)
potentate 745.2
evildoer 913.1
tyre See tire
tyro, tiro 541.6
(ignoramus 493.1)

U

ubication, ubiety 186.3
Ubiquitarian 984.14
ubiquitous 976.12
ubiquity
omnipresence 186.4
divine attribute 976.2
U-boat 726.11
udder 191.6
udometer, udomograph 348.12
ugh! yes! 488.14
dislike 867.11
uglify 846.5
(deform 243.3)
(blemish 848.2)
ugliness 846
(distortion 243.1)
ugly homely 846.6
(distorted 243.5)
(repulsive 830.14)
irascible 901.7
be ugly 846.4
ugly duckling 846.3
uh-huh! 488.14
uhlan 716.4
Uigur 560.4
ukase 741.3
Ukrainian 560.4
ukulele, ukalele, ukelele 417.2
ulcer sore 655.16
affliction 830.2
ulcerate 659.9
ulema 967.1
uliginose, uliginous
swampy 345.3
muddy 352.9
Ull, Ullr chase 622.2
god 979.3
ullage 53.2
ulster 225.17
ulterior
additional 37.7
extraneous 57.4
future 121.7
distant 196.5
ultimate final 67.8
eventual 151.7
decisive 474.10
ultimately
eventually 121.9; 151.8
at last 133.12

ultimatum
decision 620.1
demand 741.2
offer 763.1
stipulation 770.1
ultimogeniture 775.4
ultramarine blue 438.2
color 438.4
ultramicroscope 445.1
ultramodern 123.11
ultramontane *n.*
alien 57.3
Papist 984.16
ultramontane *adj.*
alien 57.4
distant 196.5
papish 984.25
papal 995.9
ultramontanism 984.6
ultramundane 196.5
ululant crying 412.3
lamenting 839.13
ululate cry 412.2
wail 839.9
ululation, ululu
animal sounds 412.1
wailing 839.1
umber *n.* 433.2
umber *adj.* 433.4
umbilical 222.4
umbilicus 222.2
umbra shadow 422.3
spirit 980a.1
umbrage 900.1
(hate 898.1)
give umbrage 900.10
take umbrage 900.6
umbrageous 422.9
umbrella cover 223.4
(sunshade 424.2)
parachute 273a.7
umpirage 724.1
umpire *n.*
mediator 724.2
judge 967.1
umpire *v.* 724.3
umpteen 100.1
unabashed
fearless 861.8
brazen 885.10
unabated 31.11
unable impotent 158.8
incompetent 699.15
unableness 158.1
unacceptability 830.1
unacceptable
intolerable 649.9
unpleasant 830.10
unaccessibility 471.2
unaccessible 471.7
unaccommodating
uncongenial 24.8
annoying 830.12
uncourteous 895.6
unbenevolent 907.7
unaccountability 964.3
unaccountable
unusual 83.10
ununderstandable 519.6
exempt 748.18
irresponsible 964.6

unaccurate — unbridle 1148

unaccurate 495.14
unaccustomed
 unusual 83.10
 unused 614.3
 (ignorant 491.8)
 (inexperienced 699.14)
unaccustomedly 614.4
unaccustomedness
 nonprevalence 614.1
 inexperience 699.1
unacknowledged
 unavowed 489.6
 anonymous 565.9
 unthanked 917.4
unacquaintance 491.1
unacquainted
 ignorant 491.8
 inexperienced 699.14
unactive v. 683.11
unactive adj. 683.12
unactivity 683.1
unadjusted 699.15
unadmonished 508.7
unadorned
 language 576.3
 unornamented 849.4
unadulterated
 unmixed 42.6
 pure 494.13
unadventurous 864.6
unadvisability 647.1
unadvisable 647.3
unadvised
 inexpectant 508.7
 ill-managed 699.17
unaffected true 494.14
 sincere 543.3
 style 578.4
 obstinate 606.6
 artless 703.4
 unmoved 823.6
 (brazen 885.10)
 simple 849.3
 (tasteful 850.5)
unaided alone 87.8
 unstrengthened 160.15
 (helpless 158.9)
 unassisted 706.10
unalienable 922.6
unalike 18.4
unallayed 159.13
unallied 10.5
unallowed
 unwarranted 925.9
 illegal 964.5
unalloyed
 unmixed 42.6
 pure 494.13
unalluring 830.10
unalterability 323.1
unalterable
 unchangeable 150.7
 inflexible 323.5
unaltered 141.6
unambiguous 518.5
unambitious 866.4
unamiability 907.2
unamiable 907.7
unanimated 823.6
unanimity

consensus 23.5
assent 488.3
 (agreement 709.3)
 (concord 714.1)
unanimously 488.17
 (co-operatively 709.8)
 (concordantly 714.5)
unanswerable
 conclusive 474.10
 exempt 748.18
 irresponsible 964.6
unanswered 478.4
unappetizing
 unsavory 395.5
 (dislikable 867.9)
 unpleasant 830.10
unapprehended 491.14
unapprehensive 861.8
unapprized 491.8
unapproachable
 infinite 105.3
 distant 196.5
unapproached
 unequaled 28.4
 supreme 33.8
unappropriate
 inapt 24.7
 inexpedient 647.3
unappropriated 782.4
unapproved 932.12
unapt
 inappropriate 24.7
 impotent 158.8
 inexpedient 647.3
 unskillful 699.11
**unarmed, unarmored,
 unarmoured** 665.9
unarranged
 disorderly 59.8
 unprepared 674.7
 unornamented 849.4
unarray 226.4
unarrayed 849.4
unarticulated 403.7
unartificial
 artless 703.4
 simple 849.3
unascertainable 491.15
unascertained
 uncertain 475.10
 unknown 491.14
unasked
 voluntary 602.10
 unrequested 766.4
unaspiring
 unambitious 866.4
 unpretentious 881.6
unassailable 664.11
unassertive 725.5
unassisted alone 87.8
 unstrengthened 160.15
 unaided 706.10
unassuming
 veracious 543.3
 artless 703.4
 simple 849.3
 unpretentious 881.6
unatoned 951.4
unattached 44.12

unattackable 664.11
unattainability 471.2
unattainable 471.7
unattended alone 87.8
 neglected 460.10
unattempted 623.12
unattested 468.4
 (untrue 546.6)
unattracted 866.4
unattractive 830.10
 (undesirable 866.5)
unauspicious
 inopportune 135.6
 inauspicious 512.5
unauthentic
 unauthoritative 475.13
 illogical 477.10
 unsound 495.16
 (spurious 545.13)
unauthenticated
 unattested 468.4
 unauthoritative 475.13
 illogical 477.10
 unauthentic 495.16
unauthorized
 prohibited 761.4
 unwarranted 925.9
 illegal 964.5
unavailing
 nugatory 158.11
 useless 645.8
 (abortive 732.8)
unavoidable
 inevitable 601.11
 (requisite 630.3)
 compulsory 744.3
unavoidableness 601.1
unavowed 489.6
unaware
 ignorant 491.8
 unsuspecting 508.7
unawares adj. 508.7
unawares adv.
 unknowingly 491.16
 unexpectedly 508.11
 come unawares 508.5
 take unawares 508.5, 6
 (catch unprepared 674.6)
unawed 861.8
unbalance 503.11
unbalanced
 unequal 28.3
 topheavy 218.7
 insane 503.12
 unjust 941a.3
unbar 750.3
unbearable fetid 401.4
 unacceptable 649.9
 insufferable 830.18
unbecoming inapt 24.7
 inexpedient 647.3
 (unworthy 940.9)
 indecent 961.9
unbefitting inapt 24.7
 inexpedient 647.3
unbegotten 2.9
unbeguile 545a.2
unbegun 674.7

unbelief disbelief 485
 infidelity 989.2
unbelievability 485.3
unbelievable 485.11
 (improbable 473.3)
 be unbelievable 485.8
unbelieve 485.5
unbeliever 989.4
 (doubter 485.4)
 (pagan 984.20)
unbelieving
 faithless 485.9
 (incredulous 487.4)
 infidelic 989.7
unbend
 straighten 246.4
 ~ the mind 452.2
 relax 687.4
unbending
 inflexible 323.5
 unmanageable 704.10
unbenevolence 907.2
unbenevolent 907.7
unbeseeming 851.6
unbesought
 voluntary 602.10
 unasked 766.4
unbiased, unbiassed
 unprejudiced 498.12
 (free 748.16)
 (just 941.3)
 impartial 941.3
unbind disjoin 44.7
 free 750.3
unblamable 946.6
 (vindicable 937.10)
unblemished
 perfect 650.5
 clean 652.14
 preserved 670.6
unblenched 861.8
unblended 42.6
unblest
 unfortunate 735.9
 unpossessed 777a.5
 disapproved 932.12
unblown 674.8
unblushing
 brazen 885.10
 (unaffected 823.6)
 immodest 961.9
unboat 292.9
unboiled 674.7
unbolt 750.3
unbooked, unbookish 491.9
unborn 2.9
unbosom 529.5
unbought unsold 796.8
 gratuitous 815.10
 uncorrupted 946.5
unbound 748.13
unbounded
 infinite 105.3
 unlimited 180.7
 unrestricted 748.15
unbrace unman 158.7
 relax 687.4
unbreathed 526.8
unbred 895.6
unbridle 750.3

unbridled
 unmitigated 173.15
 free 748.13
 (lax 738.7)
 (intemperate 954.4)
 (incontinent 961.10)
unbroken whole 50.7
 continuous 69.6
 preserved 670.6
unbrokenness 69.1
unbuild 162.4
unburden lighten 320.4
 ~ one's mind 529.5
unburdened 705.7
 (unrestrained 748.13)
unbury 363.24
unbuttoned 748.13
uncage 750.3
uncalled-for
 superfluous 641.5
 unrequired 678.7
uncandid false 544.7
 unfair 941.3
uncanny ugly 846.6
 ghostly 980a.4
uncared-for
 neglected 460.10
 unpleasant 830.10
 disliked 867.8
 unloved 898.6
uncase 260.12
uncate 245.8
uncaught 748.13
uncaused 156.12
unceasing
 perpetual 112.4
 constant 136.4
 continuing 143.4
uncensurable 946.6
uncensured 931.10
unceremonious 895.6
uncertain
 irregular 139.2
 inconstant 149.6
 indistinct 447.5
 unsure 475.9
 (doubtful 485.10, 11)
 (equivocal 520.5)
 (irresolute 605.5)
 (speculative 621.19)
 unsafe 665.7
be uncertain 475.6
uncertainly 475.17
uncertainty
 irregularity 139.1
 unsureness 475
 (doubt 485.2)
 (irresolution 605.1)
 (gamble 621.2)
 (fearfulness 860.2)
uncertitude 475.1
unchain disjoin 44.7
 free 750.3
unchained 748.13
unchallengeable 922.6
unchallenged
 uncontradicted 488.13
 right 922.6
unchangeable 150.7
 (durable 110.9)

 (permanent 141.6)
 (infallible 474.14)
 (resolute 604.7)
 (persevering 604a.3)
 (obstinate 606.6)
unchangeableness 150.1
unchanging
 uniform 16.5
 constant 136.4
 permanent 141.6
 continuing 143.4
uncharitable 907.7
 (unfriendly 889.3)
uncharitableness, uncharity 907.2
unchartered
 unwarranted 925.9
 illegal 964.5
unchaste 961.10
 (wicked 945.11)
 (dissipated 954.5)
unchastity 961.2
unchecked
 unchanged 141.6
 free 748.13
uncheerful
 gloomy 421.8
 sad 837.9
unchivalric 940.9
unchristian
 excessive 641.5
 heterodox 984.22
 infidelic 989.7
unchristianity 984.1
uncial
 capital letter 561.9
 writing 590.15
unciform 245.8
uncircumscribed 180.7
uncivil uncouth 851.7
 discourteous 895.6
 (vulgar 851.6)
uncivilized
 savage 173.14
 uncouth 851.7
 ungenteel 895.6
unclad 226.8
unclarity 519.1
unclassical
 speech 579.3
 uncouth 851.7
uncle kinsman 11.3
 Negro 431.4
 pawnbroker 787.2, 3
unclean dirty 653.16
 (untidy 59.9)
 obscene 961.9
be unclean 653.14
uncleanly 653.16
uncleanness 653
 (untidiness 59.1)
unclease 653.15
unclear faint 405.9
 indistinct 447.5
 vague 475.11
 obscure 519.7
unclench 260.12
Uncle Sam
 United States 182.3
 American 188.9
unclever 699.11

uncleverness 699.1
unclipped 50.7
uncloak display 525.2
 disclose 529.3
unclog open 260.12
 disembarrass 705.4
 free 750.3
unclosed 260.15
unclothe 226.4
unclouded light 420.22
 visible 446.4
 manifest 525.4
unclubbable, unclubable 893.9
unclutch open 260.12
 let go 790.3
uncoif 226.4
uncoil 313.2
uncolored, uncoloured
 colorless 429.6
 true 494.13
uncombed untidy 59.9
 uncouth 851.7
uncombined
 unmixed 42.6
 incoherent 47.3
un-come-at-able 471.7
uncomely 846.6
uncomfortable
 displeased 828.14
 distressing 830.11
uncommon
 unusual 83.10
 (peculiar 79.8)
 infrequent 137.2
uncommonly
 remarkably 31.21
 infrequently 137.3
uncommunicated 781.6
uncommunicative 585.4
 (secretive 528.22)
uncommunicativeness 585.1
uncompact 322.4
uncompanionable 893.9
uncompassionate
 unbenevolent 907.7
 pitiless 914a.3
uncompleted
 incomplete 53.4
 unfinished 730.3
 (frustrated 732.9)
uncompounded 42.6
uncompromising
 conservative 141.7
 resolute 604.7
 bigoted 606.7
 strict 739.5
 (orthodox 82.10)
unconcealable 525.6
unconcealed
 open 260.15
 visible 446.4
 manifest 525.4
 disclosed 529.7
unconceived 2.9
unconcern
 apathy 823.1
 indifference 866.1
 (incuriosity 456.1)

unconcerned
 tolerant 740.4
 apathetic 823.5
 indifferent 866.6
 (incurious 456.3)
unconcocted 674.7
uncondemned
 forgiven 918.6
 acquitted 970.4
unconditional
 unqualified 52.10
 unlimited 748.15
 unprohibited 760.6
unconditionally
 absolutely 31.16
 certainly 474.16
unconditioned 748.15
unconfident 475.10
unconfined 748.13
unconfirmed 475.10
unconformable 83.9
 (disagreeing 24.6)
 (disorderly 59.8)
 (capricious 608.5)
 (unaccustomed 614.3)
 (lawless 964.6)
 (unorthodox 984.22)
be unconformable 83.8
unconformity 83
 (irrelation 10.1)
 (nonuniformity 16a.1)
 (disagreement 24.1)
 (dissent 489.1)
unconfuted
 demonstrated 478.4
 true 494.10
uncongenial inapt 24.8
 (irrelevant 10.6)
 insalubrious 657.4
unconnected
 irrelative 10.5
 disjoined 44.12
 discontinuous 70.4
 illogical 477.10
unconscionable
 immense 31.9
 dishonest 940.8
unconscious
 physically ~ 376.5
 inattentive 458.11
 ignorant 491.8
 involuntary 601.14
 asleep 683.16
 emotionally ~ 823.5
unconsciousness
 physical ~ 376.1
 ignorance 491.1
 emotional ~ 823.1
unconsidered 452.4
unconsonant 24.6
unconspicuous 447.4
unconstitutional 964.5
unconstitutionality 964.1
unconstrained
 free 748.13
 (unprejudiced 498.12)
 (lax 738.7)

unconstraint — underprop

unconstrained (cont'd)
  inexcitable 826.9
unconstraint 748.1
unconsumed 40.6
uncontested
  indubious 474.12
  believed 484.14
uncontradicted 488.13
uncontrollable
  inevitable 601.11
  obstinate 606.6
  (irrepressible 173.16)
  unmanageable 704.10
  impulsive 825.11
uncontrolled
  capricious 608.5
  free 748.13
  impulsive 825.11
uncontroverted 488.13
unconventional
  unconformable 83.9, 11
  (unaccustomed 614.3)
  language 563.15
  uncouth 851.7
unconventionality 83.2
unconversable 585.4
unconversant
  ignorant 491.8
  (unaccustomed 614.3)
  inexperienced 699.14
unconverted
  dissentient 489.5
  infidelic 989.7
unconvinced
  uncertain 475.10
  dissentient 489.5
uncooked 674.7
uncork open 260.12
  free 750.8
uncorrupted
  authentic 494.12, 13
  honest 939.7
  virtuous 944.4
  (undefiled 652.14)
  (pure 960.2)
  innocent 946.5
uncounted 475.10
uncourteous 895.6
uncourtly speech 579.3
  uncourteous 895.6
uncouth speech 579.3
  awkward 699.12
  homely 846.8
  vulgar 851.7
  (slovenly 59.9)
  (countrified 183.3)
  (unformed 241.6)
  (plebeian 876.11)
uncover divest 226.4
  open 260.12
  discover 481a.3
  display 525.2
  disclose 529.3
  tip the hat 894.9
uncovered
  unhidden 525.4
  unprotected 665.9

uncreated 2.9
uncritical
  undiscriminating 465a.3
  uncensorious 931.9
uncrown
  dethrone 738.5
  depose 756.5
unction
  lubrication 332.1
  ointment 332.2
  emotion 821.2; 824.1
  divine function 976.6
  chrism 998.4
  (sanctification 987.2)
unctional 894.13
unctuous oily 355.3
  (smooth 255.5)
  (lubricant 332.5)
  suave 894.13
  flattering 933.3
  sanctimonious 988.11
unctuousness
  oiliness 355
  (lubrication 332.1)
  flattery 933.1
uncultivated
  rustic 183.3
  unlearned 491.9
  unprepared 674.8, 10
  uncouth 851.7
unculture 674.2
uncultured
  unlearned 491.9
  unrefined 674.8
  uncouth 851.7
uncurbed 748.13
  (intemperate 954.4)
  (incontinent 961.10)
uncurl 246.4
uncurtain open 260.12
  display 525.2
  disclose 529.3
uncurtained 525.4
uncustomary 83.10
  (unfamiliar 614.3)
uncut whole 50.7
  formless 241.5
  unprepared 674.8
undamaged 650.5
undamped 340.7
undate 248.7
undated 115.3
undaunted
  persevering 604a.3
  fearless 861.8
undazzled
  unprejudiced 498.12
  unamazed 871.3
undeceivable 487.4
undeceive 545a.2
  (disclose 529.3)
  (tell the truth 543.2)
undeceived 490.13
undeceiving n. 545a.1
undeceiving adj. 545a.3
undeception 545a
  (disclosure 529.1)

undecided
  uncertain 475.10
  (doubtful 461.25)
  irresolute 605.5
undecipherability 519.1
undecipherable 519.6
undefeated 731.11
undefended 665.9
undefiled
  authentic 494.12, 13
  clean 652.14
  (uncorrupt 944.5)
  (innocent 946.5)
  (pure 960.2)
undefinable
  vague 475.11
  inexpressible 517.11
undefined
  indistinct 447.5
  vague 475.11
  anonymous 565.9
undelectable
  unsavory 395.5
  unpleasant 830.10
undemonstrable 475.14
  (untenable 485.11)
undemonstrated 475.10
undemonstrative 826.9
undeniability 474.1
  (demonstration 478.1)
undeniable 474.10
  (demonstrative 478.3)
  (true 494.10)
undeniably 474.16
undenied 478.4
undependability 940.3
undependable
  unauthentic 495.16
  fickle 608.6
  untrustworthy 940.1
undeprived 781.6
under less 34.7
  below 207.11
  in subjection 749.7
underage 127.5
underagent 758.2
underbid 794.5
underboard 528.24
underbody 225.25
underbreath
  faint sound 405.2
  muted voice 581.3
underbrush 367.8
undercarriage 273a.10
underclothes, underclothing 225.25
undercoat 428.5
undercolor 428.1
undercooked 298.50
undercover 528.21
undercover man
  informer 527.6
  secret agent 528.8
undercovert 530.2
undercurrent
  counteractant 179.2
  current 348.2
  airflow 349.1

latency 526.1
  hidden danger 667.1
  opposition 708.1
underdone 298.50
underdraw 555.4
underestimate 483.3
  (misjudge 481.5)
  (detract 934.3)
underestimation 483
  (misjudgment 481.1)
  (modesty 881.1)
  (detraction 934.1)
underfed 640.9
underfoot 207.11
undergarment 225.25
undergo
  experience 151.4
  feel 821.3
undergraduate 541.4
underground n.
  cellar 191.20
  subway 252.3
  train 272.18
  railway 627.5
underground adj.
  subterranean 208.10
  concealed 528.17
  secret 528.21
underground adv.
  below 207.11
  beneath the sod 363.28
  secretly 528.24
undergrowth 367.8
underhand, underhanded adj. 528.21
  (cunning 702.6)
underhand, underhandedly adv. 528.24
underlay 590.5
underlet 787.6
underlie
  lie under 207.5
  be latent 526.3
underline
  underscore 550.19
  emphasize 642.9
underling inferior 34.3
  (nonentity 643.6)
  (servant 746.1)
  commoner 876.3
underlining 550.7
underlying 5.6
undermine
  disable 158.6
  impair 659.8
  intrigue 702.5
  thwart 706.7
undermost
  lowest 207.10
  bottom 211.5
underneath
  under 207.11
  in subjection 749.7
undernourished 640.9
underpass 627.2
underpin 215.26
underpinning
  foundation 215.3
  leg 266.11
underplot 626.6
underprop 215.26

underrate — undying

underrate 483.3
underrating 483.1
underscore n. 550.7
underscore v.
 underline 550.19
 emphasize 642.9
undersea 208.11
undersell 796.5
underset 215.26
undershirt 225.25
undershoot 267a.34
undershrub 367.8
undersign
 endorse 488.10
 sign 550.19
undersized 193.9
underskirt 225.19, 25
undersong
 repetend 104.2
 tierce 990.7
understand
 know 490.9
 suppose 514.6
 comprehend 518.4
 (be intelligent 498.7)
 interpret 522.6
 (be informed 527.11)
 be concordant 714.2
 sympathize with 888.2
 not understand 519.5
 (be ignorant 491.6)
 (misunderstand 523.2)
 (wonder 870.2)
understandability 518.1
understandable
 knowable 490.18
 comprehensible 518.5
 not understandable 519.6
understandably 518.7
understanding n.
 agreement 23.4
 intellect 450.1
 joint assent 488.3
 intelligence 498.1
 concord 714.1
 compact 769.1
 beyond understanding 519.6
 come to an understanding
 concur 488.8
 be reconciled 723.5
 with the understanding 8.8; 469.8
understanding adj.
 knowing 490.12
 intelligent 498.9
understate 555.4
understood
 implied 526.7
 conventional 852.8
understrapper 34.3
understudy
 substitute 147.2
 actor 599.19

undertake
 engage in 676.2
 (begin 66.5)
 (intend 620.3)
 (pursue 622.6)
 (busy oneself 625.7)
 (attempt 675.3)
 promise 768.3
undertaker 363.6
 (workman 690.10)
undertaking
 enterprise 676
 (intention 620.1)
 (pursuit 622.1)
 (business 625.1)
 (project 626.1)
 promise 768.1
undertone tone 402.2
 faint sound 405.2
 muted voice 581.3
undertow
 current 348.2
 hidden danger 667.1
undervaluation 483.1
undervalue 483.3
undervest 225.25
underwater 208.11
underwear
 undergarments 225.25
 merchandise 798.3
underwood 367.8
underworld 982.1
underwrite 488.10
 (guarantee 771.6)
underwriter 758.2
undescribable 83.10
undeserved 925.9
undesigning 703.4
undesirability
 inexpedience 647.1
 unpleasantness 830.1
undesirable
 inexpedient 647.3
 unpleasant 830.10
undesirous 866.4
undetermination
 uncertainty 475.1
 irresolution 605.1
undetermined
 aoristic 109.5
 chance 156.12
 uncertain 475.10
 (doubtful 461.25; 485.10)
 irresolute 605.5
undeveloped 674.8
undevelopment
 immaturity 674.2
 rough diamond 674.3
undeviating
 uniform 16.5
 unchangeable 150.7
 straight 246.5
 (direct 278.8)
 persevering 604a.3
undevout 989.6
undies 225.25
undigested 674.8
undigestible 657.4

undignified
 colloquial 563.16
 speech 579.3
 unworthy 940.9
undiminished
 unreduced 31.11
 increased 35.5
 whole 50.7
 unweakened 159.13
undine
 elemental spirit 979.7
 water nymph 979.10
undirect 311.6
undirected
 disorderly 59.8
 deviative 279.8
 purposeless 621.21
undiscernible 446.4
undiscerning
 blind 442.6
 inattentive 458.10
 stupid 499.12
undisciplined 608.5
undisclosed
 unknown 491.14
 unrevealed 528.18
undiscoverable
 unknowable 491.15
 ununderstandable 519.6
undiscovered
 unknown 491.14
 unrevealed 528.18
undiscriminating 465a.3
undisguised
 true 494.14
 manifest 525.4
 sincere 543.3
undismayed 861.8
undisposed
 unused 678.7
 unforfeited 781.6
undisputed
 indubious 474.12
 believed 484.14
undissolved
 whole 50.7
 unliquefied 321.9
undistinguishable
 coincident 13.7
 without distinction 465a.3
undistinguished 465a.3
undistorted
 straight 246.5
 true 494.14; 543.3
undisturbed
 quiescent 265.7
 unexcited 826.11
undiversified 16.5
undividable 321.10
undivided
 coherent 46.10
 whole 50.7
 (undiminished 31.11)
 (complete 52.9)
undividedness 87.1
undivulged
 unknown 491.14

unrevealed 528.18
undo disjoin 44.7
 revert 145.4
 destroy 162.4
 counteract 179.4
 open 260.12
 defeat 731.9
undogmatic 498.12
undoing 732.3
undone
 unfinished 674.8
 uncompleted 730.3
 defeated 732.12
 dejected 837.13
 hopeless 859.7
undoubted
 indubious 474.12
 (true 494.10)
 believed 484.14
undoubtedly 474.16
 (actually 1.9)
 (truly 494.15)
undoubting 484.12
 (certain 474.8)
undrape undress 226.4
 open 260.12
 display 525.2
 disclose 529.3
undress n.
 dishabille 225.23
 (nudity 226.2)
 unadornment 849.1
undress v. 226.4
undressed
 unclad 226.8
 unadorned 849.4
undubitable 474.10, 12
undubitably 474.16
undue
 exaggerated 549.3
 excessive 641.5
 inexpedient 647.3
 (wrong 923.4)
 (unmeet 925.8)
 (unjust 941a.3)
be undue 925.5
undueness
 redundance 641.1
 no right 925
 (inexpedience 647.1)
 (wrong 923.4)
 (injustice 941a.1)
undulant 314.12
undulatance 314.1
undulate v.
 aviate 267a.31
 oscillate 314.8
 billow 348.22
undulate, undulating adj. 248.7
 (flowing 348.26)
undulation
 convolution 248.1
 oscillation 314.1
undulatory wavy 248.7
 oscillatory 314.12
undutiful
 unduteous 927.5
 impious 988.10
undying eternal 112.4
 (continuing 143.4)
 unchangeable 150.7

unearned — unforgettable 1152

unearned 925.9
unearth eject 297.17
  disinter 363.24
  discover 481a.3
unearthly
  immaterial 317.6
  righteous 944.3
  supernatural 976.14
  uncanny 980a.4
  heavenly 981.7
  spiritual 987.10
uneasiness 828.2
uneasy restless 149.6
  difficult 704.8
  displeased 828.14
uneatable
  unsavory 395.5
  unpleasant 830.10
uneath 704.8
unedifying 538.4
uneducated 491.9
  (unskilled 699.13)
unembodied 317.6
unemotional 823.5
unemployed
  unused 678.7
  idle 683.12
unemployment 683.2
unencumbered 705.7
unending eternal 112.4
  unlimited 180.7
unendowed
  impotent 158.8
  untalented 699.13
unendurable 830.18
unenlightened 491.8
  (unintelligent
   499.11)
unenlightenment 491.1
unenterprising 864.6
unentertaining 843.5
unenvied 929.6
unequal
  disparate 28.3
  (differing 15.7)
  irregular 139.2
  insufficient 640.8
  unequitable 941a.3
be unequal 28.2
  (be inferior 34.4)
unequaled, unequalled
  unmatched 28.4
  supreme 33.8
unequality 28.1
unequitable 941a.3
unequivocal
  absolute 31.12
  limited 233.3
  certain 474.8
  clear 518.5
unequivocally
  absolutely 31.16
  certainly 474.16
unerring
  infallible 474.14
  accurate 494.11
  constant 939.10
  sinless 946.5
unessential
  extrinsic 6.2
  irrelevant 10.6
  unimportant 643.10

unestablished 185.4
uneven
  ununiform 16a.2
  unequal 28.3
  irregular 139.2
  rough 256.12
unevenness
  nonuniformity 16a.1
  inequality 28.1
uneventful 643.10
unexact 495.14
unexacting 738.7
unexampled
  unimitated 20.3
  unequaled 28.4
  unusual 83.10
unexcelled 33.8
unexceptionable
  tolerable 648.11
  mediocre 736.3
  satisfactory 831.7
  right 922.6
  inculpable 946.6
unexcited
  unaffected 823.6
  unruffled 826.11
unexciting 174.6
unexclusive 76.5
unexempt
  answerable 462.12
  amenable 926.11
unexercised 678.7
unexpanded
  contracted 195.6
  narrow 203.9
unexpectant 508.7
unexpected
  unusual 83.10
  unanticipated 508.8
  (sudden 113.5)
  (premature 132.8)
  accidental 621.20
be unexpected 508.5
unexpectedly 508.11
  (suddenly 113.7)
  (prematurely
   132.12)
  (unpreparedly
   674.12)
unexpectedness 508.1
unexpedient 647.3
unexpensive 815.8
unexperience 699.1
unexperienced 699.14
unexplained
  unknown 491.14
  unrevealed 528.18
unexplored
  unexamined 460.11
  unknown 491.14
  unrevealed 528.18
unexposed
  unknown 491.14
  unrevealed 528.18
  (unexpressed 526.8)
unexpressed 526.8
  (unmeant 517.10)
  (unrevealed 528.18)
unexpressive 517.8
unextinguished
  unmitigated 173.15
  burning 382.17

unfading eternal 112.4
  unchanged 141.6
unfailing
  unchanged 141.6
  infallible 474.14
  faithful 939.10
unfair false 544.7
  unjust 941a.3
  (unconscientious
   940.8)
be unfair 941a.2
unfairness 941a.1
unfaithful false 544.7
  apostate 607.11
  nonobservant 773.5
  untrue 940.10
unfaltering
  resolute 604.7
  persevering 604a.3
unfamiliar
  unusual 83.10
  (unknown 491.14)
  new 123.8
  unaccustomed 614.3
  ∼ with 699.14
unfashionable
  unconventional
   83.11
  old-fashioned 124.9
unfashioned
  formless 241.5
  unprepared 674.8
unfasten 750.3
unfathomable
  infinite 105.3
  abysmal 208.9
  ununderstandable
   519.6
unfavorable, unfavourable
  inopportune 135.6
  inauspicious 512.5
  hindering 706.8
  opposed 708.4
unfeasibility 471.2
unfeasible 471.7
unfeeling n.
  physical ∼ 376.1
  numbness 381.1
  emotional ∼ 823.1
unfeeling adj.
  physically ∼ 376.5
  numb 381.3
  emotionally ∼ 823.5
  heartless 907.8
unfeigning
  veracious 543.3
  artless 703.4
  simple 849.3
unfelt
  insensible 376.5
  numb 381.3
  emotionally ∼ 823.7
unfeminine
  virile 159a.5
  unladylike 851.6
  unpolite 895.6
unfertile 169.4
unfetter 750.3
  (loose 44.7)
unfettered 748.13
unfinished

incomplete 53.4
  unprepared 674.8
  unskilled 699.13
  uncompleted 730.3, 4
unfit v. 158.6
unfit adj.
  unsuitable 24.7
  impotent 158.8
  inexpedient 647.3
  (useless 645.8)
  unprepared 674.7
  incompetent 699.15
render unfit 674.5
  (render useless
   645.7)
unfitness
  unsuitability 24.3
  impotence 158.1
  inexpedience 647.1
  (wrong 923.1)
  (undueness 925.1)
  unpreparedness
   674.1
unfitting inapt 24.7
  inexpedient 647.3
unfixed
  inconstant 149.6
  uncertain 475.10
unflagging
  unweakened 159.13
  persevering 604a.3
  (sedulous 682.19)
unflattering
  true 494.14
  frank 703.4
  simple 849.3
unflavored, unflavoured 391.2
unfledged
  youthful 127.5
  immature 674.8
unfleshly 317.6
unflexible 323.5
unflinching
  resolute 604.7
  persevering 604a.3
  fearless 861.8
unfold
  straighten 246.4
  open 260.12
  unroll 313.2
  display 525.2
  disclose 529.3
unfolding
  flowering 161.4
  appearance 448.1
unfoldment
  evolution 161.5
  unrolling 313.1
  appearance 448.1
  manifestation 525.1
unfool 545a.2
unforced 748.13
  (volitional 600.4)
  (voluntary 602.10)
unforeseen
  unexpected 508.8
  accidental 621.20
unforgettable
  rememberable
   505.20
  notable 642.10

unforgiving 919.6
unforgotten 505.18
unformed
 formless 241.5
 unprepared 674.8
unfortified
 unmixed 42.6
 unprotected 665.9
unfortunate
 inopportune 135.6
 inauspicious 512.5
 inexpedient 647.3
 unlucky 735.9
 (evil 649.8)
 (in trouble 704.11)
 (unsuccessful 732.7)
 (poor 804.7)
 be unfortunate 735.6
unfortunately 735.10
unfounded 546.6
 (unattested 468.4)
unfrequency 137.1
unfrequent 137.2
unfrequented 893.10
unfrequently 137.3
unfriend 891.1
unfriended
 helpless 158.9
 friendless 893.10
unfriendliness 889.1
 (unsociability 893.1)
unfriendly
 opposed 708.4
 inimical 889.3
 (disliking 867.7)
 (unsociable 893.9)
 (hating 898.5)
 (uncharitable 907.7)
 be unfriendly 889.2
unfrock depose 756.5
 degrade 874.7
 disbar 968.4
unfrozen 382.15
unfruitful 169.4
unfruitfulness 169.1
 (inutility 645.1)
unfulfilled 730.3
unfulfillment, unfulfilment
 noncompletion 730.1
 failure 732.1
unfurl
 ~ sails 267.16
 ~ a banner 267.41;
  550.20
 unroll 313.2
 display 525.2
unfurnished 674.7
ungainly
 awkward 699.12
 homely 846.8
ungallant
 uncourageous 862.4
 uncourteous 895.6
ungarnished 849.4
ungenerous 819.4
 (selfish 943.4)
ungenial 657.4
ungenteel vulgar 851.6
 uncivil 895.6
ungentle savage 173.14
 uncourteous 895.6

ungentlemanly
 vulgar 851.6
 uncourteous 895.6
 unbecoming 940.9
ungifted
 unintelligent 499.11
 untalented 699.13
unglue 47.2
ungodliness 989.1
ungodly
 atrocious 649.8
 wicked 945.11
 irreligious 989.6
ungovernable
 obstinate 606.6
 (unmitigable
  173.16)
 unmanageable
  704.10
 insubordinate 742.6
 impulsive 825.11
ungoverned
 anarchic 738.8
 free 748.14
 impulsive 825.11
ungraceful
 inelegant 579.3
 awkward 699.12
 homely 846.8
 uncouth 851.7
ungracious
 uncourteous 895.6
 unbenevolent 907.7
ungrammatical 568.3
 (inelegant 579.3)
ungrammaticism 568
 (barbarism 563.1)
 (malapropism
  565.2)
 (inelegance 579.1)
ungrateful 917.3
 be ungrateful 917.2
ungratefulness 917.1
ungratifying 832.6
ungrounded
 unsubstantial 4.5
 illogical 477.10
 unauthentic 495.16
ungrudgingly 816.5
unguarded
 unwary 460.9
 impulsive 612.4
 unprotected 665.9
 (helpless 158.9)
 shiftless 674.11
unguent, unguentum n.
 lubricant 332.2
 balm 662.6
unguent adj. 355.3
unguided
 unlearned 491.9
 impulsive 612.4
 unskillful 699.17
unguiform 245.8
unguilty 946.5
unguis, ungula 781.3
unhallowed
 unsanctified 988.10
 unholy 989.6
unhampered
 unburdened 705.7

free 748.13
unhand 750.3, 6
unhandled 123.8
unhandsome 940.9
unhandy 699.12
unhappiness 837.1
 (wretchedness
  828.3)
 make unhappy 837.8
 (pain 830.4)
unhappy
 inopportune 135.6
 inexpedient 647.3
 unfortunate 735.9
 sad 837.9
 (wretched 828.16)
unharbored, unharboured 185.4
unharmonious
 disagreeing 24.6
 (quarrelsome 901.9)
 discordant 414.4
unharmoniousness
 24.1
unharness 750.3
unhazardous 664.10
unhealthful 657.3
unhealthfulness 657.1
unhealthy
 infirm 655.24
 insalubrious 657.3
 unsafe 665.7
unheard-of
 unusual 83.10
 (unexpected 508.8)
 new 123.8
 infrequent 137.2
 improbable 473.3
 unknown 491.14
 wonderful 870.7
 renownless 874.10
unheeded 460.10
unheeding
 inattentive 458.10
 careless 460.8
unheroic 862.4
unhesitating
 believing 484.12
 resolute 604.7
unhewn
 formless 241.5
 unfinished 674.8
unhidden visible 446.4
 manifest 525.4
 disclosed 529.7
unhide 529.3
unhindered
 unburdened 705.7
 free 748.13
unhinge displace 61.3
 disable 158.6
 dislocate 185.2
 dement 503.11
unhinged
 impotent 158.8
 insane 503.12
 frustrated 732.9
unholy sinful 945.11
 ungodly 989.6
unhook 750.3
unhoped-for 508.8
unhorse

dismount 292.8
 get down 306.5
unhospitable 893.9
unhouse 297.9
unhoused 185.4
unhuman 907.9
unhurried 685.4
unhurt perfect 650.5
 preserved 670.6
unicorn monster 83.7
 team 272.9
Unicorn 318.6
unideaed 452.3
unideal real 1.8
 true 494.14
unidentical
 dissimilar 18.4
unifying 87.9
unification
 combination 48.1
 (unity 87.1)
 association 709.2
uniflorous, unifoliate
 87.9
uniform n. 225.8
uniform adj. even 16.5
 (alike 17.10)
 (agreeing 23.9)
 (regular 80.3)
 (conformable 82.9)
 (monotonous 104.7;
  841.8)
 (stable 150.5)
 (measured 466.13)
 simple 42.5
 orderly 58.7
 symmetrical 242.4
 smooth 255.5
 be uniform 16.3
 (conform 82.4)
uniformity
 evenness 16
 (similarity 17.1)
 (agreement 23.1)
 (rule 80.1)
 (conformity 82.1)
 (monotony 841.3)
 order 58.1
 symmetry 242.1
uniformly 16.6; 82.12
unify join 43.5
 combine 48.3
 render one 87.5
unifying 87.9
 (conjunctive 43.13)
unigenital, uniglobular 87.9
unijugate 89.5
uniliteral unific 87.9
 one-sided 236.7
unilluminated 421.7
unimaginable
 unusual 83.10
 impossible 471.6
 improbable 473.3
 wonderful 870.7
unimaginative 576.3
unimagined real 1.8
 true 494.14
unimodular 87.9
unimpaired
 perfect 650.5

unimpeachability — unloosen

unimpaired (*cont'd*)
  preserved 670.6
unimpeachability 474.1
unimpeachable
  conclusive 474.10
  (true 494.10)
  perfect 650.5
  right 922.6
  praiseworthy 931.11
  inculpable 946.6
unimportance 643
  (smallness 32.1)
unimportant 643.10
  (inconsiderable 32.8)
  (inferior 34.5)
  (nugatory 158.11)
  (vain 645.8)
  (mediocre 736.3)
  (ignoble 876.11)
be unimportant 643.7
unimpressed 823.6
unindebted 807.10
  (solvent 800.22)
uninfected 652.14
uninflammable 385.8
uninfluenced
  unprejudiced 498.12
  (biased 748.16)
  obstinate 606.6
  impartial 941.3
uninfluential 175a.2
  (powerless 158.8)
uninformed 491.8
  (immature 674.8)
uningenuous
  false 544.7
  dishonest 940.8
uninhabitable 187.12
uninhabited 187.11
uninitiated
  ignorant 491.8
  unskilled 699.13, 14
uninjured
  perfect 650.5
  unscathed 654.5
  preserved 670.6
  (safe 664.10)
uninquisitive 456.3
uninspired 823.6
uninstructed 491.9
unintellectual 499.11
  (incogitant 452.3)
unintellectuality
  mindlessness 450a.1
  (incogitance 452.1)
  unintelligence 499.1
unintelligence 499
  (ignorance 491.1)
unintelligent 499.11
  (mindless 450a.2)
  (incogitant 452.3)
  (ignorant 491.8)
be unintelligent 499.8
unintelligibility 519
  (complexity 59.3)
  (obscurity 475.3)
  (unmeaningness 517.1)
  (enigma 533.2)
  (imperspicuity 571.1)

unintelligible 519.6
  (enigmatic 533.6)
  (imperspicuous 571.2)
  (inarticulate 583.5)
be unintelligible 519.3
render unintelligible 519.4
unintentional 621.20
  (chance 156.12)
  (involuntary 601.14)
unintentionally 621.22
  (by chance 156.13)
uninterested
  apathetic 823.5
  bored 841.9
  indifferent 866.4
  (incurious 456.3)
uninteresting 843.5
  (boring 841.8)
unintermitting, unintermitted
  continuous 69.6
  perpetual 112.4
  constant 136.4
  continuing 143.4
  persevering 604a.3
uninvited 893.10
uninviting
  unsavory 395.5
  unpleasant 830.10
union agreement 23.1
  junction 43.1
  fastening 45.2
  combination 48.1
  contiguity 199.1
  association 709.2
  society 712.4
  concord 714.1
  marriage 903.1
union down 550.13
unionize 48.4
union jack 550.13
union suit 225.25
unipersonalist 984.14
unique unequaled 28.4
  classification 75.6
  rare 83.10
  (dissimilar 18.4)
  (unimitated 20.3)
  (peculiar 79.8)
  (novel 123.10)
  sole 87.7
uniqueness 83.3
unison agreement 23.1
  unisonance 413.1
  unanimity 488.3
  concord 714.1
in unison
  agreeing with 23.1
  unisonant 413.26
unit one 87.2
  ~ of weight 319.4
  military 726.7
Unitarian 984.14
unitarianism 451.19
Unitarianism 984.4
unitary 87.9
unite join 43.5
  (unify 87.5)
  combine 48.3, 4

enter into 56.2
  assemble 72.10, 11
  concur 178.2
  converge 290.2
  co-operate 709.4, 5
  (~ with 712.8)
united joined 43.10
  (unseparated 46.1)
  concordant 714.4
United States 182.3
uniting 87.9
unity identity 13.1
  uniformity 16.1
  completeness 52.1
  oneness 87
  (whole 50.1)
  (individuality 79.2)
  ~ of time 120.1
  concord 714.1
  divine ~ 976.2
univalve 368.6
universal
  general 78.11
  (extensive 31.7)
  (general 372.6)
  (well-known 490.17)
  (common 613.11)
  (unlimited 180.7)
  cosmic 318.15
universal council 696.3
universality
  completeness 52.1
  generality 78.1
universalize 78.8
universal joint 272.16
universal language 560.5
universe
  boundlessness 180.4
  world 318.1
university 542.1
unjust 941a.3
  (inexpedient 647.3)
  (wrong 923.4)
  (undue 925.8)
  (unconscientious 940.8)
unjustifiable 941a.4
  (wrong 923.4)
  (undue 925.8)
  (blameworthy 932.14)
  (wicked 945.11)
unjustified 925.9
  (unjust 941a.3)
unjustness 941a.1
unkempt untidy 59.9
  scattered 73.4
  rough 256.12
  uncouth 851.7
unkennel evict 297.9
  disclose 529.3
unkind, unkindly 907.7
unkindness 907.2
unknowability 519.1
unknowable
  incognizable 491.15
  inunderstandable 519.6
unknowing 491.8
unknowingly 491.16
unknown

unapprehended 491.14
  (unfamiliar 83.10)
  (unrevealed 528.18)
  renownless 874.10
  (ignoble 876.11)
unknown quantity 491.2
unlabored, unlaboured
  style 578.4
  unprepared 674.8
unlade 297.21
unladylike
  vulgar 851.6
  uncourteous 895.6
unlash, unlatch 750.3
unlawful 964.5
unlawfulness 964.1
unlearned 491.9
unlearnedness 491.1
unleash 750.3
unleavened 674.8
unless *conj.* 8.8; 469.8
unless *prep.* 55.7
unlettered 491.9
unlevel 256.12
unlicensed 761.4
unlicked
  undeveloped 674.8
  uncouth 851.7
  (unformed 241.6)
unlicked cub
  unformed 241.3
  undevelopment 674.3
  unrefined person 851.4
unlighted 421.7
unlikable
  unpleasant 830.10
  dislikable 867.9
unlike 18.4
be unlike 18.2
  (be contrary 14.3)
  (differ 15.5)
render unlike 18.3
  (change 140.6)
unlikelihood 473.1
  (small chance 156.4)
unlikely 473.3
unlikeness 18.1
unlimber 323.5
unlimited
  infinite 105.3
  (vast 31.8)
  unending 180.7
  free 748.15
  (unprejudiced 498.12)
unliterary 563.16
unload unpack 297.21
  (displace 185.2)
  lighten 320.4
  sell 796.5
unlock disjoin 44.7
  open 260.12
  solve 481a.4
  free 750.3
unlooked-for 508.8
unloose disjoin 44.7
  free 750.3
unloosen 750.3

1154

unloved — unprecedented

unloved 898.6
  (disliked 867.8)
unlovely 846.6
unloyal 773.5
unlucky
  inopportune 135.6
  inauspicious 512.5
  unfortunate 735.9
unmade 2.9
unmake 145.4
unmalleable 323.5
unman geld 38.7
  devitalize 158.7
  (effeminize 160a.4)
  grieve 837.8
  frighten 860.10
unmanacle 750.3
unmanageable
  obstinate 606.6
  awkward 699.12
  perverse 704.10
unmanliness 160a.1
unmanly
  effeminate 160a.5
  (female 374.11)
  cowardly 862.4
  unbecoming 940.9
unmanned
  devitalized 158.10
  dejected 837.13
  terrified 860.14
unmannered, unmannerly 895.6
unmarked blind 442.6
  neglected 460.10
unmarred
  perfect 650.5
  unscathed 654.5
  preserved 670.6
unmarried 904.5
  be unmarried 904.4
unmarry 905.4
unmask display 525.2
  disclose 529.3
  (undeceive 545a.2)
unmasked 525.4
unmatched
  different 15.7
  dissimilar 18.4
  unimitated 20.3
  unequaled 28.4
  supreme 33.8
unmeaning 517.8
unmeaningness 517
  (foolishness 499.6)
  (unintelligibility 519.1)
unmeant 517.10
  (unexpressed 526.8)
unmeasured
  infinite 105.3
  unlimited 180.7
  indiscriminated 465a.3
  abundant 639.7
unmeditated 612.4
unmeet, 647.1
  (undue 925.8)
  (unjust 941a.3)
unmelodious 414.4
unmentionable
  inexpressible 517.11

disreputable 874.8
unmentionables 225.21
unmerciful 914a.3
  (heartless 907.8)
unmerited 925.9
unmethodical
  disorderly 59.8
  (purposeless 621.21)
  irregular 139.2
  inconstant 149.6
unmindful
  inattentive 458.10
  neglectful 460.8
  forgetful 506.8
  insensible 823.5
  indifferent 866.4
  ungrateful 917.3
unmingled 42.6
unmistakable
  distinct 446.5
  certain 474.8
  understandable 518.5
  manifest 525.4
  positive 535.6
unmistakably 474.16
unmitigated
  absolute 31.12
  unqualified 52.10
  violent 173.15
unmixed
  unmingled 42.6
  pure 494.13
unmodifiable 150.7
unmolested safe 664.10
  content 831.6
unmoneyed 804.7
unmoor 267.15
unmoral
  insensible 823.5
  without morals 945.11
unmourned 898.6
unmoved
  quiescent 265.7
  obstinate 606.6
  unaffected 823.6
unmusical 414.4
unmuzzle 750.3
unnamable 31.10
unnamed 565.9
unnatural
  unusual 83.10
  eccentric 503.17
  affected 853.6
  heartless 907.8
unnavigable 471.7
unnecessary, unneeded 641.5
unneighborly, unneighbourly 895.6
unnerve unman 158.7
  disorder 655.22
unnerved
  unmanned 158.10
  (weak 160.10)
  heartstricken 837.13
unnoticed
  neglected 460.10
  renownless 874.10
unnumbered 105.3
unobscured 420.22

unobservance
  inattention 458.1
  nonfulfillment 773.1
unobservant
  inattentive 458.10
  unwary 460.9
  unfaithful 773.5
unobserved 460.10
unobserving 442.6
unobstructed
  disembarrassed 705.7
  free 748.13
unobtrusive 881.6
unobtrusiveness 881.1
unobtainable 471.7
unobjectionable
  tolerable 648.11
  mediocre 736.3
  satisfactory 831.7
  warrantable 937.10
  inculpable 946.6
unoccupied
  empty 187.11
  incogitant 452.3
  idle 683.11
  (leisured 685.3)
unoffending 648.13
unofficial
  unauthoritative 475.13
  illegal 964.5
unoften 137.3
unopened 261.3
unordinary 83.10
unorganic 358.4
unorganized
  inorganic 358.4
  unprepared 674.7
unornamented
  language 576.3
  inornate 849.4
unorthodox
  unauthoritative 475.13
  heterodox 984.22
  (unconformable 83.9)
unorthodoxy 984.1
  (nonconformity 83.2)
unostentatious 881.6
unowed 807.10
unown 789.11
unowned 782.4
unpack 297.21
unpaid 806.9
  (defaultant 808.11)
  (gratis 815.10)
unpalatability
  unsavoriness 395.1
  unpleasantness 830.1
unpalatable
  unsavory 395.5
  unpleasant 830.10
unparagoned 33.8
  (perfect 650.5)
unparalleled
  unimitated 20.3
  unequaled 28.4
  supreme 33.8

  (best 648.9)
  unusual 83.10
unpardonable 941a.4
unpardonable sin 947.2
unpassable
  unpierceable 261.5
  impracticable 471.7
unpassionate 826.9
unpatriotic 910.3
unpatriotism 910.1
unpeered 28.4
unpeople evict 297.10
  depopulate 893.8
unperceived
  neglected 460.10
  unknown 491.14
  unrevealed 528.18
unperceptible 447.4
unperforated 261.4
unperturbed 826.11
unphilanthropic 907.7
unphilosophical 477.10
unpin, unpinion 750.3
unpitied 932.12
unpitying 914a.3
unplace 185.2
unplaced 185.4
unpleasant
  unsavory 395.5
  displeasing 830.10
  (ugly 846.9)
  (undesirable 866.5)
  (dislikable 867.9)
unpleasantness 830.1
unpleasing
  unsavory 395.5
  unpleasant 830.10
unpliable 323.5
  (unmanageable 704.10)
unplumbed 105.3
unpoetic prosaic 598.4
  matter-of-fact 703.4
  plain 849.3
unpointed 254.3
unpolished
  rough 256.12
  speech 563.15; 579.3
  unfinished 674.8
  inornate 849.4
  uncouth 851.7
  uncourteous 895.6
unpolite 895.6
unpoliteness 895.1
unpopular
  unpleasant 830.10
  disliked 867.8
unpossessed 777a.3
  (vacant 187.11)
unpossibility 471.1
unpossible 471.6
unpracticability 471.2
unpracticable 471.7
unpracticed, unpractised 699.13, 14
unpragmatic 498.12
unpraiseworthy 932.13
  (unworthy 940.9)
unprecedented
  unusual 83.10
  infrequent 137.2

unprejudiced — unruly 1156

unprejudiced
  unbiased 498.12
  (unrestricted 748.16)
  (just 941.3)
  impartial 941.3
unpremeditated 612.4
  (involuntary 601.14)
  (accidental 621.20)
  (unprepared 674.7)
unprepare 674.5
unprepared
  unready 674.7
  (incomplete 53.4)
  (inexpectant 508.7)
  (unpremeditated 612.4)
  (imperfect 651.4)
  unskilled 699.13
be unprepared 674.4
unpreparedly 674.12
  (unexpectedly 508.11)
  (impulsively 612.5)
unpreparedness 674.1
unprepossessing 846.8
unpresentable 851.6
unpretending
  veracious 543.3
  artless 703.4
  simple 849.3
  unassuming 881.6
unpretentious 881.6
unpreventable 601.11
unprevented 748.13
unprimed 699.13
unprincipled 940.8
  (evildoing 945.13)
unprivileged 925.9
unprized 483.4
unproclaimed 526.8
unproduced 2.9
unproductive 169.4
  (impotent 158.8)
  (useless 645.8)
be unproductive 169.3
unproductiveness, unproductivity 169
  (impotence 158.1)
  (inutility 645.1)
unproficiency 699.1
unproficient 699.11
unprofitable 645.8
  (unproductive 169.4)
  (inexpedient 647.3)
  (bad 649.8)
unprofitableness 645.1
  (unproductiveness 169.1)
unprogressive 141.7
unpromising 512.5
  (hopeless 859.8)
unpronounced
  silent 403.7
  unexpressed 526.8
unpropitious
  inopportune 135.6
  inauspicious 512.5
  (hopeless 859.8)
  (unfavorable 708.4)
unprosperous 735.9

  (poor 804.7)
unprotected 665.9
  (helpless 158.9)
  (liable to 177.3)
unproven 477.10
unprovided
  unsupplied 640.12
  unprepared 674.7
unprovincial 498.12
unprovision 674.1
unpublished 526.8
unpunctual late 133.8
  (untimely 135.6)
  irregular 139.2
unpure 961.9
unqualification
  certainty 474.1
  unfitness 674.1
  incompetence 699.1
unqualified
  thorough 52.10
  impotent 158.8
  certain 474.8
  true 494.13
  unfit 674.7
  incompetent 699.15
  unlimited 748.15
  unwarranted 925.9
unquenchable 865.20
unquestionability 474.1
unquestionable 474.10
  (credible 484.15)
unquestionably
  certainly 474.16
  (actually 1.9)
  to be sure 488.14
unquestioned
  indubious 474.12
  believed 484.14
  uncontradicted 488.13
unquestioning 484.12
unquiet
  troublous 59.11
  restless 149.6; 682.21
  (moving 264.8)
  turbulent 173.12
  agitated 315.13
  excitable 825.9
unravel
  disentangle 60.9
  straighten 246.4
  unroll 313.2
  solve 481a.4
  (explain 522.6)
  disembarrass 705.4
unread 491.9
unreadiness 674.1
unready 674.7
unreal nonexistent 2.8
  (unsubstantial 4.5)
  (supposititious 514.9)
  (imaginary 515.12)
  erroneous 495.12
unreasonable
  illogical 477.10
  (improbable 473.3)
  (prejudiced 481.10)
  (absurd 497.4)
  (foolish 499.15)

  (fanatical 503.18)
  exaggerated 549.3
  capricious 608.5
  exorbitant 814.6
  unjustifiable 941a.4
unreasonableness 477.5
  (absurdity 497.1)
unreasonably 31.20
unreasoning
  incogitant 452.3
  unintelligent 499.11
unrecognizable
  indistinct 447.5
  unintelligible 519.6
unrecorded 552.4
unreduced
  undiminished 31.11
  increased 35.5
  whole 50.7
unrefined
  unlearned 491.9
  speech 563.15; 579.3
  (barbarous 563.15)
  crude 674.8
  vulgar 851.6
unrefinement 851.1
unreformed 951.4
unrefreshed 688.6
unrefuted
  demonstrated 478.4
  true 494.10
unregarded
  neglected 460.10
  unrespected 929.6
unregenerate 988.10
unregistered 552.4
unregular 149.6
unrelated 10.5
  (different 15.7)
unrelenting 919.6
unreliability
  uncertainty 475.4
  untrustworthiness 940.3
unreliable
  inconstant 149.6
  uncertain 475.14
  (untenable 485.11)
  unauthentic 495.16
  tergiversating 607.10
  fickle 608.6
  unsafe 665.7
  untrustworthy 940.11
unrelieved 835.4
unreligious 989.6
unremembered 506.7
unremitting
  continuous 69.6
  perpetual 112.4
  constant 136.4
  continuing 143.4
  persevering 604a.3
unremoved 184.17
unremunerated 806.9
unremunerative 645.8
unrepealed 141.6
unrepentant 951.3
unrepressed 173.15
unrequited

  unpaid 806.9
  unthanked 917.4
unresentful 918.5
unreserved
  sincere 543.3
  frank 703.4
unresisting
  submissive 725.5
  obedient 743.3
  meek 826.10
unresolved 605.5
unrest
  restlessness 149.3
  agitation 315.1
  excitement 825.3
unrestrained
  capricious 608.5
  free 748.13
  (unburdened 705.7)
  (intemperate 954.4)
  (incontinent 961.10)
  lawless 964.6
unrestraint 954.1
unrestricted
  undiminished 31.11
  unqualified 52.10
  open 260.15
  free 748.13, 15
  (unprejudiced 498.12)
unrevealed
  unknown 491.14
  concealed 528.18
  (unexpressed 526.8)
unrevenged 918.6
unrevoked 143.4
unrewarded
  unpaid 806.9
  unthanked 917.4
unrhymed 598.4
unriddle 481a.4
unriddling 481a.2
unrig demolish 162.4
  render useless 645.7
unrighteous 945.11
unripe youthful 127.5
  sour 397.6
  ignorant 491.8
  immature 674.8
  inexperienced 699.14
unrivaled, unrivalled
  unequaled 28.4
  supreme 33.8
unroll unfold 313.2
  display 525.2
  disclose 529.3
unrolling 313.1
unromantic 494.14
unroot 301.5
unrooted 498.12
unruffled
  equable 174.6
  quiescent 265.7
  unaffected 823.6
  inexcitable 826.9
  (philosophical 451.38)
  unexcited 826.11
unruliness 742.1
unruly
  turbulent 173.12
  obstinate 606.6

unmanageable
  704.10
 anarchic 738.8
 disobedient 742.6
 lawless 964.6
unsaddle 756.5
unsafe 665.7
unsaid 526.8
unsaintly 945.11
unsalable, unsaleable
 useless 645.8
 unmarketable 796.8
unsanctified
 impious 988.10
 unholy 989.6
unsanctioned 925.9
unsane 503.12
unsatisfaction 832.1
unsatisfactory
 inexpedient 647.3
 intolerable 649.9
 dissatisfactory 832.6
 (disappointing
  509.5)
unsatisfied 832.5
unsatisfying 832.6
unsavoriness, un-
 savouriness 395
 (pungency 392.1)
unsavory, unsavoury
 tasteless 391.2
 unpalatable 395.5
 (pungent 392.5)
 (dislikable 867.9)
 unpleasant 830.10
 be unsavory 395.4
 (repel 830.7)
unsay 607.9
unscathed
 perfect 650.5
 uninjured 654.5
 preserved 670.6
unscented 399.5
unschooled 491.9
unscience 491.1
unscientific 477.10
unscreen display 525.2
 disclose 529.3
unscreened
 unhidden 525.4
 unprotected 665.9
unscrupulous 940.8
unseal 260.12; 529.3
unseasonable
 inapt 24.7
 untimely 135.6
 (inexpedient 647.3)
unseasonableness
 135.1
unseasoned
 unhabituated 614.3
 immature 674.8
 inexperienced 699.14
unseat unplace 185.2
 depose 756.5
unseconded 706.10
unseeing 442.6
unseemliness 846.1
unseemly
 foolish 499.15
 ungrammatical
  568.3

inelegant 579.3
inexpedient 647.3
 ugly 846.6
 untasteful 851.6
 indecent 961.9
unseen invisible 447.4
 neglected 460.10
 unrevealed 528.18
unseldom 136.5
unselfish
 generous 816.4
 disinterested 942.5
 (charitable 906.7)
 be unselfish 942.4
unselfishness
 liberality 816.1
 disinterest 942
 (benevolence 906.1)
unseparated 46.10
 (united 43.10)
 (combined 48.5)
unserviceability 645.1
unserviceable 645.8
unsettle
 discompose 61.4
 confuse 458.9
 startle 508.6
unsettled
 irregular 139.2
 inconstant 149.6
 unplaced 185.4
 uncertain 475.10, 16
 unprejudiced 498.12
 insane 503.12
 irresolute 605.5
unsettlement
 confusion 458.4
 irresolution 605.1
unsevered 50.7
unshackle 750.3
unshackled 748.13
unshaded
 visible 446.4
 manifest 525.4
unshaken 159.13
unshape derange 61.2
 destroy form 241.4
unshapely 846.6
unshapen 241.5
unsharpened 254.3
unshaven 256.13
unsheathe open 260.12
 ~ the sword 722.9
unsheltered 665.9
unship 297.21
unshipment 185.1
unshod 226.9
unshorn whole 50.7
 bearded 256.13
unshrinking
 resolute 604.7
 fearless 861.8
unshroud
 display 525.2
 disclose 529.3
unsightly 846.6
unsignificancy 517.1
unsignificant 517.8
unsincere
 hypocritical 544.8
 affected 853.6
unsincerity 544.2

unsinew 158.6
unskilled 699.13, 14
 (uneducated 491.9)
 (unaccustomed
  614.3)
unskillful, unskilful
 699.11
be unskillful 699.6
unskillfulness, unskil-
 fulness 699
 (ignorance 491.1)
 (stupidity 499.2)
 (inutility 645.1)
unsociability 893.1
 (unfriendliness
  889.1)
unsociable, unsocial
 893.9
 (unfriendly 889.3)
unsoiled 652.14
unsoldierlike 862.4
unsolicited 766.4
unsolicitous
 neglectful 460.8
 undesirous 866.4
unsolvable 471.7
unsolved 528.18
unsophisticate 703.2
unsophisticated
 unmixed 42.6
 pure 494.13
 artless 703.4
 (simple 849.3)
unsophistication 703.1
unsought
 voluntary 602.10
 evasive 623.12
 unasked 766.4
unsound weak 160.13
 (impaired 659.12)
 illogical 477.10
 unauthentic 495.16
 insane 503.12
 deceptive 545.13
 imperfect 651.4
 unhealthy 655.24
 unsafe 665.7
 morally 945.12
 unorthodox 984.22
unsounded 403.7
 (phonetic 561.10)
 (mute 581.8)
unsparing
 abundant 639.7
 severe 739.5
 liberal 816.4
unspeakable
 immense 31.10
 inexpressible 517.11
 wonderful 870.8
unspecified
 general 78.14
 anonymous 565.9
unspent 678.7
unspiritual
 material 316.8
 worldly 989.9
unspoiled perfect 650.5
 preserved 670.6
unspotted
 perfect 650.5
 clean 652.14

unstable
 inconstant 149.6
 (irresolute 605.5)
 (fickle 608.6)
 frail 160.11
 weak 160.13
 topheavy 218.7
 uncertain 475.14
 unsafe 665.7
 morally ~ 945.12
unstaid 149.6
unstained 652.14
unsteadfast 149.6;
 940.10
unsteadiness 160.1
unsteady
 irregular 139.2
 inconstant 149.6
 weak 160.12
 (infirm 655.24)
 (impaired 659.12)
 topheavy 218.7
 uncertain 475.16
 unsafe 665.7
 morally ~ 945.12
unstinting
 lavish 639.7
 liberal 816.4
unstirred
 unaffected 823.6
 unexcited 826.11
unstop 260.12
unstopped
 constant 136.4
 continuing 143.4
unstored 640.12
unstrained 653.16
unstrap 750.3
unstrength 160.1
unstrengthen 160.8
unstring weaken 160.8
 unnerve 655.22
unstrong 160.10
unstudied 460.11
unsubmissive
 obstinate 606.6
 resistant 719.5
 disobedient 742.6
unsubstantial
 chimerical 4.5
 (unreal 2.8)
 (nugatory 158.11)
 (imaginary 515.12)
 (spectral 980a.4)
 frail 160.11
 weak 160.13
 thin 203.10
 immaterial 317.6
 rare 322.4
 uncertain 475.14
 illogical 477.10
 unauthentic 495.16
 deceptive 545.13
unsubstantiality
 nullity 4
 (nonexistence 2.1)
 frailty 160.1
 immateriality
  317.1, 2
 specter 980a.1
unsubstantialize
 immaterialize 317.5

unsubstantiation — unuttered 1158

unsubstantialize (ctd.)
  spiritualize 994.20
unsubstantiation
  unsubstantiality 4.1
  immateriality 317.1
unsuccess 732.1
unsuccessful 732.7
  (unfortunate 735.9)
  be unsuccessful 732.5
unsuccessfully 732.13
unsuccessive 70.4
unsufficiency 699.1
unsuitability
  unfitness 24.3
  inexpedience 647.1
  (wrong 923.1)
  (undueness 925.1)
unsuitable inapt 24.7
  inexpedient 647.3
  (wrong 923.4)
  (undue 925.8)
  intolerance 649.9
unsuited 24.7
  (untimely 135.6)
unsullied clean 652.14
  natural 674.9
unsung 526.8
unsuperable 471.7
unsupplied 640.12
unsupported
  unstrengthened 160.15
  unattested 468.4
unsuppressed
  unchanged 141.6
  unmitigated 173.15
unsure
  uncertain 475.9
  (irresolute 605.5)
  unsafe 665.7
  untrustworthy 940.11
unsurmountable 471.7
unsurpassed 33.8
  (vast 31.8)
unsusceptible
  unchangeable 150.7
  insensible 823.5
  (inexcitable 826.9)
unsuspected
  believed 484.14
  unknown 491.14
unsuspecting
  confiding 484.13
  (credulous 486.5)
  inexpectant 508.7
  confident 858.9
unsuspicious
  confiding 484.13
  artless 703.4
  fearless 858.10
unsustainable
  uncertain 475.9
  (unauthentic 495.16)
  illogical 477.10
unsustained
  uncertain 475.10
  (unauthentic 495.16)
  illogical 477.10
unswayed 498.12
unsweet

unsavory 395.5
off-key 414.4
unswerving
  straight 246.5
  (direct 278.8)
  resolute 604.7
  persevering 604a.3
unsymmetrical
  disorderly 59.8
  distorted 243.5
unsymmetry 59.1
unsympathetic
  uncongenial 24.8
  unbenevolent 907.7
  pitiless 914a.3
unsystematic
  disorderly 59.8
  irregular 139.2
untactful 465a.3
untainted
  perfect 650.5
  clean 652.14
  (uncorrupt 944.5)
  unscathed 654.5
  preserved 670.6
untalented 699.13
untalked-of 526.8
untamed savage 173.14
  uncouth 851.7
untangle 481a.4
untarnished 652.14
untaste 391.1
untasteful
  unsavory 395.5
  unpleasant 830.10
  inelegant 851.6
untaught 491.9
  (immature 674.8)
untaxed 815.10
unteach 538.2
unteachable 499.12
untenable
  defenseless 158.9
  illogical 477.10
  unbelievable 485.11
  (controvertible 475.9)
untenanted 187.11
  (unpossessed 777a.3)
Unterseeboot 726.11
untether 750.3
unthankful 917.2
unthankfulness 917.1
unthawed
  undissolved 321.9
  unwarmed 383.11
unthinkable 471.6
unthinking
  incogitant 452.3
  involuntary 601.14
  unintentional 621.20
unthought-of 460.10
unthriftiness 818.1
unthrifty
  improvident 674.11
  prodigal 818.4
unthrone
  uncrown 738.5
  depose 756.5
untidiness 59.1
  (uncleanness 653.1)

untidy 59.9
  (deranged 61.6)
  (unclean 653.16)
untie disjoin 44.7
  (disentangle 60.9)
  free 750.3
until 106.8
untilled 674.8
untimeliness 135
  (anachronism 115.1)
  (prematurity 132.2)
  (intrusion 228.3)
  (inexpedience 647.1)
untimely inapt 24.7
  inopportune 135.6
  (anachronous 115.3)
  (premature 132.8)
  (unpunctual 133.8)
  (inexpedient 647.3)
  be untimely 135.3
  (be inexpedient 647.2)
untimeous, untimous 135.6
untiring
  persevering 604a.3
  industrious 682.19
untitled 876.11
untold infinite 105.3
  uncertain 475.10
  unexpressed 526.8
  (unrevealed 528.18)
untouched new 123.8
  natural 674.9
  unused 678.7
  unaffected 823.6
untoward
  inopportune 135.6
  obstinate 606.6
  inexpedient 647.3
  (unworthy 940.9)
  bad 649.8
  unmanageable 704.10
  adverse 735.8
untractable
  inflexible 323.5
  obstinate 606.6
  unmanageable 704.10
untrained 699.13
untrammeled, untrammeled
  unburdened 705.7
  free 748.13
untranslated 20.3
untraveled, untravelled 265.7
untried new 123.8
  undecided 475.10
  inexperienced 699.14
untrimmed
  unprepared 674.7
  matter-of-fact 703.4
  unornamented 849.4
untrodden new 123.8
  unpierced 261.4
  unused 678.7
untroth falsity 544.1
  lie 546.1
untroubled

equable 174.6
peaceful 721.4
unexcited 826.11
untrue
  erroneous 495.12
  false 546.6
  (unattested 468.4)
  (unveracious 544.7)
  (spurious 545.13)
  nonobservant 773.5
  unfaithful 940.10
untruss 750.3
untrustful 940.11
untrustworthiness
  uncertainty 475.4
  unreliability 940.3
untrustworthy
  uncertain 475.14
  unauthentic 495.16
  unsafe 665.7
  unreliable 940.11
untruth error 495.1
  falsity 544.1; 546.1
  (deception 545.1)
untruther 548.5
untruthful 544.7
  (dishonest 940.8)
  be untruthful 544.4
untruthfulness 544.1
  (error 495.1)
untutored
  unlearned 491.9
  artless 703.4
untwine 313.2
untwist
  disentangle 60.9
  unroll 313.2
ununiform
  uneven 16a.2
  (different 15.7)
  (dissimilar 18.4)
  (multiform 81.2)
  rough 256.12
ununiformity
  unevenness 16a.1
  disorder 59.1
ununiformly 16a.3
unused
  remaining 40.6
  unaccustomed 614.3
  unemployed 678.7
  (new 123.8)
  inexperienced 699.14
unusual 83.10
  (dissimilar 18.4)
  (unimitated 20.3)
  (remarkable 31.13)
  (peculiar 79.8)
  (novel 123.10)
  (unknown 491.14)
  (unexpected 508.8)
  (unfamiliar 614.3)
  (superexcellent 648.10)
  (wonderful 870.7)
unusually 31.21
unusualness 83.3
unutterable
  immense 31.10
  inexpressible 517.11
  wonderful 870.8
unuttered 403.7

unvalued — uplift

unvalued
 unprized 483.4
 unpleasant 830.10
 disliked 867.8
 unloved 898.6
unvaried uniform 16.5
 (monotonous) 104.7
 continuing 143.4
 style 575.2
 (speech 576.3)
unvarnished
 true 494.13
 language 576.3
 matter-of-fact 703.4
 unornamented 849.4
unvarying
 uniform 16.5
 constant 136.4
 changing 141.6
 continuing 143.4
unveil open 260.12
 manifest 525.2
 disclose 529.3
unveiled 525.4
unveiling 66.1
unversed 491.8
unvirtuous
 unrighteous 945.11
 unchaste 961.10
unvisible
 imperceptible 447.4
 unrevealed 528.18
unvisited 893.10
unvocal silent 403.7
 aphonous 581.7
unvocalized 403.7
unvoiced 402.11
unwarlike 862.4
unwarned 508.7
unwarped
 unprejudiced 498.12
 (just 941.1)
 impartial 941.3
unwarrantable
 unjustifiable 941a.4
 illegal 964.5
unwarranted
 illogical 477.10
 excessive 641.5
 uncue 925.9
 illegal 964.5
unwary 460.9
 (inexpectant 508.7)
unwashed 653.16
unwatered 340.7
unwavering 604a.3
unwearied
 persevering 604a.3
 industrious 682.19
 untired 689.5
unweave 60.9
unwedded
 ungiven to 614.3
 unmarried 904.5
unweighed 460.11
unwelcome
 unpleasant 830.10
 excluded 893.10
unwell 655.23
unwholesome 657.3
unwholesomeness
 657.1

unwilling 603.5
 (dissenting 489.5)
 (involuntary 601.14)
 (opposed 708.4)
 (refusing 764.5)
be unwilling 603.4
 (dissent 489.4)
 (avoid 623.6)
 (oppose 708.2)
 (refuse 764.2)
unwillingly 603.6
 (necessarily 601.15)
 (compulsorily 744.4)
unwillingness 603
 (dissent 489.1)
 (obstinacy 606.1)
 (opposition 708.1)
 (refusal 764.1)
 (dislike 867.1)
unwind 313.2
unwisdom 499.1
unwise
 unintelligent 499.11
 foolish 499.15
 (ill-managed 699.17)
 inexpedient 647.3
unwitting
 unknowing 491.8
 involuntary 601.14
 unintentional 621.20
unwittingly 621.22
unwomanly 159a.5
 (male 373.7)
unwonted
 unusual 83.10
 unaccustomed 614.3
unworkability 471.2
unworkable 471.7
unworldly
 immaterial 317.6
 righteous 944.3
 supernatural 976.14
 spiritual 987.10
unworn 159.13
unworthy
 paltry 643.12
 inexpedient 647.3
 dishonorable 940.9
 (disreputable 874.8)
 (unpraiseworthy 932.13)
unwrap undress 226.4
 straighten 246.4
 open 260.12
unwrinkled 255.5
unwritten
 traditional 124.8
 unexpressed 526.8
 unrecorded 552.4
 oral 582.10
 (verbal 562.8)
unwritten law
 precept 697.1
 law 963.2
unwrought 674.8
unyielding
 unchangeable 150.7
 inflexible 323.5
 (resolute 604.7)
 (obstinate 606.6)

 (resistant 719.5)
unmanageable 704.10
unyoke 750.3
up *n.* increase 35.1
 improvement 658.1
up *v.* increase 35.3
 ~ and go 293.4
up *adj.* modern 123.11
 frothy 353.10
 fashionable 852.7
be all up 162.5
up against it
 nonplused 475.16
 in difficulty 704.11
up in arms
 prepared 673.11
 busy 682.20
 in opposition 708.4
 at loggerheads 713.8
 on the offensive 716.9
 resistant 719.5
 warring 722.12, 14
 at enmity 889.3
 indignant 900.12
up in the air
 475.15, 16
up to able 157.9
 aware of 490.13
 prepared for 673.11
 competent 698.12
up *prep.*
up a tree
 nonplused 475.16
 cornered 704.11
up the wrong tree
 495.13
up *adv.* aloft 206.19
 vertically 212.9
 upward 305.8
up to 106.5
upalong 305.8
up-and-coming 682.18
up-and-comingness 682.4
up-and-doing 682.20
up-and-down *adj.* 212.8
up and down *adv.* 314.14
Upanishad 986.2
upas 663.6
upbear support 215.26
 bear aloft 307.5
 lend support 707.7
upbeat 413.23
upbraid 932.2
upbraiding 932.3
upcast *n.* 307.1
upcast *v.* 307.5
upcast *adj.* 307.8
 (ascendant 305.7)
upclimb *n.*
 acclivity 217.2
 ascent 305.1
upclimb *v.* 305.5
upcome *n.* 305.1
upcome *v.* 305.4
upcountry *n.*
 the country 183.1

 inland 221.3
upcountry *adj.*
 rustic 183.3
 inland 221.10
updive 309.4
updraft 305.1
upend 212.7
upgang 305.1
upgo *n.*
 acclivity 217.2
 ascent 305.1
upgo *v.* 305.4
upgrade
 acclivity 217.2
 (ascent 305.1)
 convalescence 654.1
 on the upgrade 658.16
upgrow
 become high 206.11
 ascend 305.4
upgrowth
 growth 194.3
 ascent 305.1
upheaval
 outbreak 173.2
 (debacle 162.3)
 elevation 307.1
 (ascent 305.1)
 outburst of passion 825.5
upheave erect 212.7
 ascend 305.4
 raise 307.5
uphelm 267.24, 70
uphill *n.* 217.2
uphill *adj.*
 acclivitous 217.10
 (ascending 305.7)
 laborious 686.10, 11
 difficult 704.8, 12
uphill *adv.* up 305.8
 go uphill 217.6
uphold support 215.26
 upraise 307.5
 corroborate 467.9
 demonstrate 478.2
 preserve 670.3
 (sustain 143.3)
 lend support 707.7
 approve 931.5
 defend 937.6
 preserve 976.8
upholder
 supporter 215.2
 abettor 711.4
 (friend 890.2)
 (benefactor 912.1)
 (sympathizer 914.2)
upholstery 634.1
upkeep *n.*
 support 215.1
 aid 707.1
upkeep *v.* 707.7
upland
 backcountry 183.1, 3
 highland 206.2, 17
upleap *n.* 309.1
 (ascend 305.1)
upleap *v.* 309.4
 (ascend 305.4)
uplift *n.* 217.2

uplift — uselessly

uplift v. erect 212.7
  raise 307.5
  lighten 320.4
  improve 658.8
uplifted 307.8
uplong 305.8
up oars 267.69
upper superior 33.7
  higher 206.15
upper case n.
  letter 561.1
  type 591.6
upper-case adj.
  letter 561.9
  type 591.18
upper crust
  society 852.4
  nobility 875.2
upper-cruster 875.4
upper hand
  advantage 33.2
  dominion 737.2
  gain the upper hand
    advantage 33.2
    (gain influence 175.9)
    ascendancy 731.8
  have the upper hand
    have advantage 33.6
    dominate 737.12
upper house 696.5
uppermost
  supreme 33.8
  higher 206.15
  top 210.6
upper story top 210.2
  head 210.3
  brain 450.2
**upper ten thousand,
  upper ten**
  society 852.4
  nobility 875.2
uppish 885.8
upraise erect 212.7
  raise 307.5
  lighten 320.4
uprear erect 212.7
  raise 307.5
upright n.
  vertical 212.2
  post 215.16
upright adj.
  vertical 212.8
  uplifted 307.8
  honorable 939.7
    (veracious 543.3)
    (right 922.5)
    (ethical 926.12)
    (virtuous 944.4)
    (innocent 946.5)
    (pure 960.2)
upright adv. 212.9
unrighteous 939.7
uprightness 939.1
uprise n. height 206.2
  acclivity 217.2
  ascent 305.1
uprise v. be high 206.9
  become high 206.11
  incline 217.6
  ascend 305.4
uprising n.

acclivity 217.2
revolt 742.2
  (revolution 146.1)
uprising adj.
  acclivitous 217.10
  ascendant 305.7
uproar n. turmoil 59.4
  (violence 173.1)
  noise 404.2
uproar v. 404.6
uproarious
  turbulent 173.12
  noisy 404.9
  excited 824.11
uproot eject 297.17
  extract 301.5
ups and downs
  circumstances 151.2
  luck 156.1
  alteration 314.3
  adversity 735.1
upset n.
  revolution 146.1;
    742.2
  inversion 218.1
  overthrow 308.2
upset v.
  discompose 61.4
  destroy 162.4
  invert 218.4, 5
  capsize 267.35
  overthrow 308.5
  confuse 458.9
  startle 508.6
  thwart 706.7
  defeat 731.9
  revolutionize 742.5
  agitate 824.3
upset adj.
  overthrown 308.9
  overwrought 824.10
upshoot 305.4
upshot result 154.1
  conclusion 480.1
upside 210.2
upside down 218.6
  (in disorder 59.13)
upspear, upspin 305.4
upspring n. 309.1
upspring v.
  ascend 305.4
  leap 309.4
upstage v. 930.7
upstage adj. 599.28
upstairs aloft 206.19
  up 305.8
upstart n. 876.8
  (newness 123.5)
upstart, upstream v.
  305.4
upstream adv. up 305.8
  laboriously 686.11
  with difficulty 704.12
upswarm 305.5
upswing 305.1
upthrust 307.1
**up-to-date, up-to-the-
  minute**
  modern 123.11
  fashionable 852.7
uptown 305.8
upturn n. 308.2

upturn v.
  invert 218.4, 5
  ascend 305.4
  overthrow 308.5
upward adj. 305.7
upward, upwards adv.
  305.8
upwards of 33.9
upway 217.2
upwind 305.4
upwith n. 217.2
upwith adv. 305.8
uraeus 747.1
Ural-Altaic languages
  560.4
uranic 318.16
uranium
  cauterant 384.11
  metal 635.6
**uranographer, ura-
  nographist** 318.12
uranolite, uranolith
  318.3
**uranology, uranome-
  try** 318.10
Uranus 318.3
urban 189.22
urbane 894.12
urbanity 894.1, 3
  (sociality 892.1)
urceole, urceus 998.8
urchin child 129.3
  (offspring 167.4)
  dwarf 193.5
  imp 980.3
urge n. 615.2
urge v. inflame 173.8
  incite 615.7
  (impel 276.7)
  hasten 684.2
  (accelerate 274.10)
  advise 695.4
  entreat 765.5
urgency
  necessity 630.1
  importance 642.2
  haste 684.1
urgent
  important 642.13
    (requisite 630.3)
    (importunate 765.8)
  hasty 684.5
urial 366.8
Uriel 977.1
urinate 297.15
urine 299.3
  (water 337.1)
  (offal 653.6)
urn n. vase 191.10
  receptacle 191.11
  mortuary ~ 363.11
  ceramics 384.14
  boiler 386.1
urn v. 363.20
**Ursa Major, Ursa
  Minor** 318.6
Urth, Urthr 601.4
urticaria 655.17
urus 366.13
U. S. 182.3
usability 644.1
usable 644.8

1160

usage custom 613.2
use 677.2
  (conduct 692.1)
usance 677.1
use n. custom 613.2
  utility 644.1
    (help 707.1)
  employment 677
  estate 780.2
  be of use
    be useful 644.2
    (serve 707.10;
      746.8)
    be benevolent 906.5
  come into use 613.9
  in use 677.7
  of no use 645.8
    (nugatory 158.11)
  of use 644.5
  out of use 678.6
use v. employ 677.5
  (take advantage of
    698.10)
  squander 818.3
  use language 908.5
  use up waste 638.2
  exhaust 677.6
  fatigue 688.5
  squander 818.3
used
  accustomed 613.12
  employed 677.7
  used up
    worn out 659.12
    fatigued 688.6
    satiated 869.6
useful 644.5
  (productive 168.7)
  (conducive 176.3)
  (instrumental 631.4)
  (beneficial 648.12)
  (salubrious 656.5)
  (helpful 707.12)
  (serving 746.9)
  be useful
    be serviceable 644.2
    (subserve 631.3)
  serve 746.8
  render useful 644.4
usefully 644.9
usefulness 644.1
  (use 677.1)
useless 645.8
  (nugatory 158.11)
  (inane 499.15)
  (wasted 638.4)
  (inadequate 640.8)
  (superfluous 641.5)
  (unimportant
    643.10)
  (inexpedient 647.3)
  (impaired 659.12)
  (incompetent
    699.15)
  (abortive 732.8)
  render useless 645.7
    (render powerless
      158.6)
  (unprepare 674.5)
  (disuse 678.2)
uselessly 645.9

uselessness 645.1
 (waste 638.1)
user usufruct 677.1
 employer 677.4
Ushas 979.4
usher n. escort 88.4
 underteacher 540.1
 theater 599.17
 doorkeeper 717.6
 attendant 746.1
 wedding attendant 903.4
usher v. 88.7
 usher in begin 66.5
 prior 116.3
 precede 280.2
 preannounce 511.8
usine 691
U.S.S. 726.11
ustulate 384.23
ustulation 384.3
usual orderly 58.7
 customary 613.11
 (conformable 82.9)
 (frequent 136.3)
usucapion 777.2
usucapt 777.5
usufruct 677.1
usurer 787.2
usurious 819.4
usurp arrogate 737.13
 ~ authority 738.5
 appropriate 789.8
 take from 789.11
 assume 925.6
usurpation
 ~ of authority 737.9
 dethronement 738.3
 assumption 925.3
usurper
 potentate 745.2
 taker 789.6
 arrogater 925.4
 (pretender 548.3)
 (tyrant 739.3)
usury 806.3
utas 98.4
utensil
 receptacle 191.1
 instrument 633.1
utilitarian n. 911.1
utilitarian adj.
 useful 644.5
 public-spirited 906.8
utilitarianism
 philosophy 451.14
 philanthropy 906.3
 (utility 644.1)
 ethics 926.4
utility usefulness 644
 (productiveness 168.1)
 (expedience 646.1)
 (use 677.1)
 (help 707.1)
 utilitarianism 906.3
utility man 599.19
utilization 677.3
 (utility 644.1)
utilize 677.5
utmost n. 52.4; 233.1
 to the utmost 52.14

(extremely 31.19)
utmost adj. 33.8
Utopia 515.6
 (perfection 650.1)
utopian n. 515.7
 (optimist 858.5)
utopian adj.
 visionary 515.12
 optimistic 858.9
utopianism 515.2
utricle 191.6
utter v. disperse 73.3
 divulge 529.4
 publish 531.7
 voice 580.8
 speak 582.6
 issue money 800.19
utter adj.
 absolute 31.12
 unqualified 52.10
utterance word 562.1
 phrase 566.1
 vocal ~ 580.3
 (phonation 402.3)
 (diction 569.1)
 speech 582.1
 statement 582.4
give utterance
 divulge 529.4
 voice 580.8
 speak 582.6
utter bar 968.2
utterer 582.5
utterly 52.14
 (extremely 31.19)
uttermost 52.4; 233.1
uturuncu 980.7
uvular 402.11
uxoricide 361.2
uxorious 807.14
Uzbek, Uzbeg 560.4

V

V fork 91.2
 five 98.1
 crotch 244.2
vacancy
 emptiness 187.3
 (depletion 640.4)
 brainlessness 450a.1
vacant empty 187.11
 (wanting 640.11)
 (unpossessed 777a.3)
 unthinking 452.3
 empty-headed 499.14
 expressionless 517.8
vacate leave 293.4
 (absent oneself 187.8)
 abandon 624.3
vacation n.
 departure 293.1
 evacuation 297.5
 abandonment 624.1
 rest 687.2
 (leisure 685.1)
 resignation 757.1
on vacation 187.10
vacation v. 687.5

vacational 687.7
vaccination, vaccine n. 179.2
vaccine adj. 366.26
vaccinia 655.6
vacillancy 314.1
vacillate
 procrastinate 133.5
 vary 149.4
 (be capricious 608.4)
 be uncertain 475.6
 be irresolute 605.4
 (change 140.5)
 (tergiversate 607.7)
vacillating
 inconstant 149.6
 irresolute 605.5
vacillation
 oscillation 314.1
 uncertainty 475.1
 irresolution 605.1
 (changeableness 149.1)
 (tergiversation 607.1)
vacillatory
 oscillatory 314.12
 irresolute 605.5
vacuity
 emptiness 187.3
 (nonexistence 2.1)
 brainlessness 450a.1
 incogitance 452.1
vacuolar 357.9
vacuolation 161.5
vacuole 357.3
vacuometer 338.8
vacuous empty 187.11
 (unsubstantial 4.5)
 incogitant 452.3
 empty-headed 499.14
vacuum 187.4
vacuum cleaner 652.7
vacuum tube 423.11
vade mecum 694.7
vadium, vadium mortuum, vadium vivum 771.1
vag, vagabond n.
 wanderer 268.2
 vagrant 876.9
 (beggar 767.2)
 (outcast 893.5)
vagabond v. 266.14
vagabond adj. 266.24
vagabondager 268.2
vagabondism 266.2
vagabondize 266.14
vagary
 daydream 458.3
 fancy 515.4
 caprice 608.1
 prank 842.7
vagas See vakass
vaginant 223.29
vagitus 129.6
vagrancy
 wandering 266.2
 deviation 279.1
 indolence 683.3
vagrant n. 268.2; 876.9

vagrant adj.
 inconstant 149.6
 wandering 266.24
 deviative 279.8
 capricious 608.5
vague chimerical 4.6
 dim 422.8
 indistinct 447.5
 uncertain 475.11
 illogical 477.10
 obscure 519.7
 (imperspicuous 571.2)
vagueness 475.3
vail gratuity 784.3
 perquisite 973.2
vain unreal 2.8
 nugatory 158.11
 useless 645.8
 (unimportant 643.10)
 hopeless 859.7
 conceited 880.6
 (overestimated 482.4)
 (proud 878.6)
 (pretentious 882.8)
 (arrogant 885.8)
 (selfish 943.4)
be vain 880.4
in vain 732.13
labor in vain
 shortcoming 304.1
 disappointment 509.1
 uselessness 645.3, 6
 (failure 732.1)
 (attempt the impossible 471.5)
 (waste 638.2)
 (mismanage 699.7)
 (fail 732.5)
render vain 880.5
vainglorious 880.6
 (boastful 884.7)
vainglory 880.1
vairagi 996.8
vakass, vagas 999.1
vakil, vakeel 968.1
valance 231.2
vale n. 252.5
vale int. 293.14
valediction
 leave-taking 293.2
 speech 582.2
valedictorian, valedictory n. 293.2
valedictory adj. 293.8
Valenciennes 847.6
valentine 902.5
valet n. minister 631.2
 retainer 746.1
valet v. 746.8
valet de place 694.6
valetudinarian n. 655.20
valetudinarian adj. 655.24
valetudinarianism 655.1
valetudinarium 662.17
valetudinary 655.24

Valhalla — Varuna

Valhalla, Valhall
  981.3
vali 745.5
Vali 979.3
valiant 861.8
valid
  sound 150.5; 159.12
  potent 157.8
  authentic 494.14
  (real 1.8)
  sufficient 639.6
  remain valid 141.4
validate
  confirm 467.9
  ratify 488.10
validation 488.4
validity potence 157.1
  authenticity 494.2
valise 191.5
vallation fence 232.2
  fortification 717.3
valley 252.5
  (cleft 198.3)
valley of death 360.1
vallum 717.3
valor, valour 861.1
valorization 480.2
valorous 861.8
valse music 415.7
  dance 840.7
valuable useful 644.6
  (beneficial 648.12)
  precious 814
valuate 466.10
valuation
  measurement 466.1
  estimation 480.2
  value 812.3
value n. utility 644.1
  excellence 648.1
  (importance 642.1)
  worth 812.3
  virtue 944.1
  of value 644.6
value v.
  measure 466.10
  estimate 480.7
  rate highly 642.8
  appraise 812.4
  appreciate 931.5
valueless 645.8
value received 810.1
valve stopper 263.2
  (outlet 295.5)
  automobile 272.16
  floodgate 350.2
valvula, valvule 263.2
vambrace 717.2
vamoose, vamose 293.5
vamp n.
  music 415.15, 16
  seductress 617.3
  flirt 902.6
vamp v. change 140.6
  lure 617.4
  repair 660.11
  seduce 897.13
vamp up
  improve 658.10
  repair 660.11
vampire, vampyre
  seductress 617.3

extortionist 789.6
  flirt 902.6
  evildoer 913.4
  fiend 980.2
  witch 992.3
vampirism
  rapacity 789.4
  sorcery 992.1
van front 234.2
  (precession 280.1)
  vehicle 272.3, 10, 15
  vanguard 717.5
  in the van
  before 234.9
  in advance 280.4
vancourier 64.1
vandal destroyer 165.1
  barbarian 876.7
  evildoer 913.1
vandalism 851.1
vandyke n. beard 256.5
  serration 257.2
Vandyke v. 257.5
Vandyke brown
  433.1, 2
Vandyke red 434.2, 6
vane
  changeableness
  149.2
  weather vane 338.9
vanfoss 717.3
vang 273.1
vanguard front 234.2
  (precursor 64.1)
  advanced guard
  717.6
Vanir, Vans 979.3
vanish
  cease to be 2.5
  be transient 111.5
  fade 429.4
  disappear 449.2, 3
  obliterate 552.2
vanishing point
  modicum 32.2
  inextension 180a.1
  diminutive 193.2
  disappearance 449.1
vanity futility 645.2
  vain expectation
  859.1
  conceit 880
  (overestimation
  482.1)
  (pride 878.1)
  (ostentation 882.1)
  (boasting 884.1)
  (arrogance 885.1)
  (selfishness 943.1)
Vanity Fair 852.4
vanquish 731.9
vanquisher 731.4
vanquishment 732.3
Vans See Vanir
vantage, vantage
  ground
  advantage 33.2
  (leverage 175.3)
  (footing 215.4)
vapid insipid 391.2
  feeble style 575.2
  dull 843.5

vapidity
  insipidity 391.1
  ~ of expression
  575.1
vapor, vapour n.
  gas 334.2
  cloud 353.5
  hot water 382.5
  imagining 515.4
vapor, vapour v.
  boast 884.5
  bluster 887.3
vaporability, vapour-
  ability 336.2
vaporarium, vapor
  bath 336.4; 386.6
vaporer, vapourer
  887.2
vaporescence, vapour-
  escence 334.1
vaporization, vapour-
  ization 336
  (gaseity 334.1)
vaporize, vapourize
  336.5
  (gasify 334.6)
vaporizer, vapourizer
  336.3
vapor lamp 423.3
vaporlike, vapourlike
  334.7
  (volatile 336.7)
vaporosity 334.1
  (vaporability 336.2)
vaporous, vapourous
  chimerical 4.6
  gaseous 334.7
  volatile 336.7
  (moist 339.7)
  cloudy 353.11
  imaginary 515.12
vapors, vapours
  blues 837.1
  sullens 901.2
vapory, vapoury 515.12
vaquero cowboy 268.8
  stockman 370.4
vara 200.6
vargueno 191.15
variability
  irregularity 139.1
  changeableness
  149.1
  (fickleness 608.3)
  irresolution 605.1
variable n. 153.1
variable adj.
  irregular 139.2
  changeable 149.5
  (irresolute 605.5)
  (fickle 608.6)
  uncertain 475.16
variance
  difference 15.1
  disparity 24.2
  disagreement 713.2
  (contention 720.1)
  at variance
  disagreeing 24.6
  (dissimilar 18.4)
  dissentient 489.7
  opposed 708.4

at loggerheads
  713.10
  inimical 889.3
variant different 15.7
  disagreeing 24.6
variation
  difference 15.1
  dissimilarity 18.1
  mathematics 84.5
  change 140.1
  deviation 279.1
  music 415.3
  irresolution 605.1
varicella 655.6
varicose 655.25
varicose veins, vari-
  cosis 655.5
varied different 15.7
  dissimilar 18.4
  diversified 81.3
variegate 440.4
  (mix 41.6)
variegated
  diversified 81.3
  divers-colored 440.5
  (mixed 41.9)
  (colorful 428.14)
variegation
  multiformity 81.1
  color 440
  (mixture 41.4)
variety difference 15.1
  kind 75.2
  multiformity 81.1
  unconformity 83.1
  animal kingdom
  366.1
  vegetable kingdom
  367.1
variform 81.2
variola 655.6
variometer
  electricity 158a.6
  aviation 267a.29
variorum 596.5
various
  diversified 81.3
  numerous 102.5
variscite green 435.2
varlet 949.1
varment, varmint
  366.17, 24
varnish n. adherer 46.3
  burnisher 255.3
  paint 428.5
  (coating 223.18)
  pretext 619.1
  extenuation 937.3
varnish v. polish 255.4
  paint 428.10
  (coat 223.23)
  (resin 356a.2)
  sophisticate 477.7
  disguise 544.3
  speech 577.4
  pretext 619.2
  extenuate 937.8
varsity 542.1
Varuna heavens 318.2
  spirit of the sea
  341.2

1162

deity 979.4
vary differ 15.5
 change 140.5, 6
 (dissimilate 18.3)
 be changeable 149.4
 deviate 279.4
 variegate 440.4
 be irresolute 605.4
vascular 260.16
vasculum
 receptacle 191.6
 case 191.8
vase pot 191.10
 ceramics 384.14
vaseline oil 356.2
 balm 662.6
vassal 746.4
vassalage 749.1
vast immense 31.8
 spacious 180.6
 huge 192.15
vastness 31.1
vasty 192.15
vat 191.11
Vaterland
 fatherland 182.2
 Germany 182.3
vates 513.2
Vatican papacy 995.4
 Pope's palace 1000.5
vaticide 361.2
vaticinal 511.11
vaticinate 511.7
vatication 511.1
vaudeville 599.3
vaudevillian n. 599.19
vaudevillian adj.
 599.28
vault n.
 compartment 191.2
 arch 215.18; 245.2
 (convexity 250.6)
 leap 309.1
 ~ of heaven 318.2
 burial place 363.13
 hiding place 530.2
 safe-deposit ~ 802.1
vault v. arch 245.3
 convex 250.7
 leap 309.4
vaulted 245.5
vaulter 309.3
vaulting n. 245.1
vaulting adj. 865.18
vaunt n. 884.1
vaunt v. 884.5
vauntmure 717.3
vavasor, vavasour,
vavassor
 proprietor 779.2
 nobleman 875.5
Vayu wind 349.2
 deity 979.4
veal 298.21
Veda 986.2
Vedanta, Vedantism
 984.11
Vedantist 984.21
vedette 717.6
Vedic 124.7
vee 98.1
veer change 140.5

oblique 217.5
 sidle 236.5
 turn ship 267.24
 deviate 279.4
 ~ round 283.6
 (tergiversate 607.7)
veery 366.22
vega 344.1
vegetable n.
 food 298.30
 plant 367.2
vegetable adj. 367.14
 (vegetative 365.3)
 (botanical 369.11)
vegetable kingdom
 367.1
vegetal n. 367.2
vegetal adj.
 vegetative 365.3
 vegetable 367.14
vegetarian n.
 eater 298.41
 abstainer 953.3
vegetarian adj.
 vegetable-eating
 298.48
 vegetable 367.14
 abstinent 953.6
vegetarianism
 eating 298.1
 abstinence 953.2
vegetate exist 1.4
 be inert 172.2
 grow 194.6; 365.2
 be quiescent 265.5
 cause growth 367.12
 lie idle 683.8
vegetation
 inertness 172.1
 vegetable life 365
 plant life 367.1
 inaction 681.1
vegetation spirit 371.3
vegetative
 vegetal 365.3
 vegetable 367.14
vegetism 365.1
vehemence
 violence 173.1
 loudness 404.1
 ~ of expression
 574.3
 fervor 821.2
 fury 825.4
 violent anger 900.3
vehement
 violent 173.11
 loud 404.8
 style 574.7
 passionate 825.10
 (rampant 824.11)
vehicle n.
 conveyance 272
 painting 428.3
 stageplay 599.3
 medium 631.2
 instrument 633.1
vehicle v. 270.8
vehicular 272.22
vehiculate ride 266.18
 transport 270.8
veil n. cover 223.2

(concealment 530.3)
 (disguise 545.5)
 clothes 225.12, 15
 (shade 424.1)
 screen 424.3
 (hiding 530.3)
 transparency 425.2
beyond the veil 528.24
take the veil
 seclude oneself
 893.6
 take holy orders
 995.8
veil v. shade 424.6
 conceal 528.10
veiled
 indistinct 447.5
 vague 475.11
veiled voice
 faint sound 405.2
 muted voice 581.3
veiling cloth 219.5
 veil 225.12
 transparency 425.2
vein nature 5.3
 tendency 176.1
 thinness 203.5
 filament 205.1
 vessel 350.4
 tone 402.2
 ~ of speech 569.1
 fund 636.2
 mood 820.1
in the vein
 willing 602.8
 disposed 820.4
veined 440.10
veinous 205.7
veinule 205.1
velar 402.11
veld, veldt 344.1
veldschoen, veldt-
schoen 225.27
velleity 600.1
vellicate twitch 315.11
 tickle 380.5
vellication 315.6
vellicative
 agitated 315.13
 ticklish 380.7
 pungent 392.5
vellum
 stationery 590.10
 (paper 635.4)
 bookbinding 593.10
veloce 415.32
velocimeter 274.8
velocipede 272.14
velocity 274
 (transience 111.1)
 (haste 684.1)
velours 219.5
velumen 255.2
velutinous
 smooth 255.5
 nappy 256.15
 velvety 324.8
velvet cloth 219.5
 smooth 255.2
 nap 256.10
 softness 324.3
 well-being 377.2

ease 705.1
 prosperity 734.1
velveteen 255.2
velvety smooth 255.5
 nappy 256.15
 soft 324.8
venal
 parsimonious 819.4
 dishonest 940.8
venality
 parsimony 819.1
 improbity 940.1
vend n. 796.1
vend v. 796.5
vendaval 349.9
vendee 795.2
vendetta feud 720.2
 revenge 919.1
vendibility 796.4
vendible salable 796.7
 commodity 798.1
vendor 797.3
vendue 796.2
veneer n. layer 204.2
 superficiality 209.1
 coating 223.18
 mere show 882.1
veneer v.
 form layers 204.4
 coat 223.24
venenate infect 655.22
 poison 659.10
venenation 655.2;
 659.3
venerable old 124.6
 estimable 928.9
 (sage 500.4)
venerate
 reverence 928.4
 worship 990.9
venerated 928.9
veneration
 reverence 928.1
 (piety 987.1)
 worship 990.1
venerative
 reverential 928.8
 worshipful 990.15
venereal disease 655.7
venery hunting 622.2
 unchastity 961.2
venesect 297.13
venesection
 evacuation 297.5
 bloodletting 662.15
Venetian blind 260.5
vengeance 919.1
 with a vengeance
 extremely 31.22
 utterly 52.14
 violently 173.18
 effectively 175.11
vengeful 919.6
venial 937.10
 (inculpable 946.6)
venin 663.4
venire facias, venire
 969.2
venison 298.26
vennel 627.3
venom poison 663.4
 rancor 907.1

venomous — vertical

venomous
  poisonous 657.3
  gruff 895.7
  malevolent 907.6
venose 205.7
vent *n.* opening 260.1
  (loophole 671.4)
  parachute 273a.7
  outlet 295.5
  (conduit 350.1)
  air passage 351.1
  sale 796.1
  find vent exude 295.7
  (escape 671.6)
  pass through 302.2
  be published 531.9
  give vent to
  let out 297.13
  (exude 295.7)
  divulge 529.4
vent *v.* divulge 529.4
  publish 531.7
  ~ one's spleen 900.8
ventage outlet 295.5
  air passage 351.1
venter origin 153.4
  vessel 191.6
  stomach 191.7
venthole opening 260.1
  outlet 295.5
ventiduct 351.1
  (fan 349.21)
ventilate begin 66.5
  air 338.10
  (blow 349.22)
  (deodorize 399.4)
  cool 385.4
  ~ a question 476.11
  publish 531.7
  discuss 595.4
  disinfect 652.13
ventilation
  airing 338.6
  (wind 349.1)
  argumentation 476.2
  publication 531.1
  disinfection 652.2
ventilator
  aeroator 338.6
  (blower 349.20)
  (fan 349.21)
  (airway 351.1)
  (cooler 387.1)
  air passage 351.1
ventose 349.31
ventricle 191.6
ventricose 250.9
ventricular 191.23
ventriloquism, ventriloquist 580.6
  (resonance 408.1)
ventriloquize 580.10
ventriloquous 580.13
venture *n.*
  gamble 621.2
  (experiment 463.3)
  attempt 675.1
  undertaking 676.1
  (business 625.1)
venture *v.*
  presume 472.3; 748.9
  ~ a guess 514.6

~ to say 535.8
hazard 621.17; 665.4
(experiment 463.10)
attempt 675.3
(speculate 463.10)
undertake 676.2
invest 787.5
dare 861.3
venturer 621.15
  (experimenter 463.6)
venturesome, venturous
  enterprising 682.18
  daring 861.9
  rash 863.7
Venturi tube 267a.29
venue focus 74.1
  position 184.1
venule 205.1
Venus planet 318.3
  a beauty 845.3
  love 897.4
  goddess 979.2
Veps, Vepse 560.4
veracious 543.3
  (artless 703.4)
  honorable 939.7)
veraciously 543.4
veracity 543
  (artlessness 703.1)
  (probity 939.1)
veranda, verandah 191.17
verb 567.2
verbal literal 516.9
  vocabular 562.8
  (spoken 582.10)
verbally
  literally 19.14
  verbatim 562.11
verbatim 19.14
  (exactly 494.16)
  (verbally 562.11)
verbiage
  vocabulary 562.3
  diction 569.1
  verbosity 573.1
verbose 573.7
  (loquacious 584.5)
  (redundant 641.5)
verbosity 573.1
  (verbiage 562.3)
  (loquacity 584.1)
  (redundance 641.1)
verdancy 435.1
verdant herbal 367.14
  green 435.6
  ignorant 491.8
  inexperienced 699.14
verd antique 435.3
verdet 435.2
verdict 480.1
verdigris *n.* 435.2, 3
verdigris *v.* 435.5
verdigrisy 435.6
verditer 435.4
Verdun 722.5
verdure
  vegetation 367.4, 9
  greenness 435.1
verdurous

herbal 367.14
green 435.6
Verein 712.4
verge *n.* 231.1
  (extremity 67.2)
  (limit 233.1)
  beyond the verge 180.7
  on the verge of
  about to 121.11
  near 197.11
verge *v.* tend 176.2
  ~ on 197.5
  edge 231.3
  side 236.4
  direct 278.4
vergent 67.8
verger 996.5
veridical
  evidential 467.11
  genuine 494.11
  authentic 494.12
  veracious 543.3
veridity 543.1
verifiable 467.11
verification test 463.1
  confirmation 467.3
  certification 474.2
  demonstration 478.1
  ratification 488.4
verificative 467.11
verify test 463.8
  confirm 467.9
  certify 474.6
  demonstrate 478.2
  ratify 488.10
verily absolutely 31.16
  truly 494.15
verisimilar 472.5
verisimilitude 472.1
veritable
  unqualified 52.10
  true 494.10
verity 494.1
verjuice 397.1, 2
vermeologist 368.2
vermeology 368.1
Vermes 366.25
vermicious, vermicular 368.15
vermiculation
  enterology 221.6
  ornamentation 847.3
vermiform
  wormlike 248.6
  (cylindric 249.8)
  vermicious 368.15
vermiform process 261.1
vermifugal 662.25
vermifuge 662.11
vermilion *n.* 434.2, 6
vermilion *v.* 434.7
vermilionette 434.6
vermin rodents 366.17
  insects 366.24
  (uncleanliness 653.11)
  riffraff 876.2
vernacular *n.* 560.2
  (colloquialism 563.3)

vernacular *adj.*
  native 188.11
  colloquial 563.16
  (linguistic 560.9)
  common 613.11
vernal 123.8
vernal equinox 126.2; 318.8
vernation 367.4
Verner's law 402.5
vernier 193.7
vernile 886.4
vernility 886.1
Vernunft 450.1
Veronese green 435.2
veronica 993.2
verruca
  protuberance 250.2
  wart 655.16
verrucated, verrucose 250.9
versatile
  changeable 149.5
  proficient 698.11
versatility
  changeableness 149.1
  proficiency 698.1
verse section 51.2
  music 415.15
  passage 593.7
  poetry 597.1
  poem 597.2
  versification 597.6
  stanza 597.7
versecraft 597.5
versed familiar 490.14
  skilled 698.14
verse form 597.6
versicolor, versicolour 440.5
versification 597.5, 6
versifier 597.10
versify 597.12
version 522.2
  (paraphrase 21.4)
vers libre 597.1
vers librist 597.10
verso left 239.2
  reverso 593.7
Verstand
  intellect 450.1
  understanding 498.1
versus
  opposite to 237.7
  toward 278.17
  opposed to 708.5
vertebra 235.4
vertebral 235.12
vertebral column 235.4
vertebrate *n.* 368.9
  (animal life 366.1)
vertebrate *adj.* 368.19
vertex 210.1
Verthandi 601.4
vertical *n.* 212.2
vertical *adj.*
  summital 210.6
  perpendicular 212.8
  (steep 217.12)
  (straight 246.5)

1164

viscera — void

viscera 221.4
visceral 221.11
viscid 352.8
  (coherent 46.9)
  (tough 327.5)
viscidity
  tenacity 46.2
  stickiness 352.1
  (toughness 327.1)
viscidize 352.6
viscidulous 352.8
viscin 45.6
viscoidal 352.8
viscosimeter 267a.29
viscosity
  tenacity 46.2
  stickiness 352.1
viscount 875.5
viscountcy, viscounty 875.9
viscountess 875.6
viscous 352.8
viscum 45.6
vise, vice
  adherer 46.3
  holdfast 781.2
visé See visa
Vishnu 979.4
visibility
  aeronautics 267a.19
  perceptibility 446
  (appearance 448.1)
  (manifestness 525.1)
visibilize
  make visible 446.3
  manifest 525.2
visible
  perceptible 446.4
  (visual 441.18)
  (apparent 448.7)
  manifest 525.4
  become visible 446.2
  (seem 448.6)
  (be disclosed 529.6)
  make visible 525.2
visibly 446.6
  (apparently 448.8)
vis inertiae
  force 157.1
  inertness 172.1
vision sight 441
  apparition 443.9
  dream 515.5
  specter 980a.1
visionary n. 515.7
visionary adj.
  515.11, 12
  (unreal 2.8)
  (chimerical 4.6)
visionless 442.6
visit n. 892.3
  (chat 588.2)
visit v. attend 186.9
  go to 266.22
  call upon 892.10
  (pay respects 894.8)
  punish 972.5
visitant 294.4
visitation illness 655.3
  evil 649.2
  adversity 735.1
  affliction 830.2

visiting 892.3
visiting card 550.11
visitor incomer 294.4
  (alien 57.3)
  supervisor 694.1
  guest 890.7
visor, vizor
  mask 225.11
  disguise 545.5
  armor 717.2
vista 441.6; 448.2
visual ocular 441.18
  visible 446.4
visualize 220.6
vis vitae, vis vitalis, vis viva
  potence 157.1
  life force 359.2
  (energy 171.1)
vital living 359.10
  important 642.14
vital air 359.2
vital force
  life force 359.2
  (spirit 994.11)
  theosophy 994.10
vitality stability 150.1
  strength 159.1
  life 359.1
vitalization 359.4
vitalize 359.8
vital principle
  essence 5.2
  potence 157.1
  life force 359.2
  inmost mind 450.3
  psyche 994.11
vitals 221.4
  (stomach 191.7)
vitascope 445.6
Vitharr, Vithar
  wood 367.7
  god 979.3
  deity 979.11
Vithi 981.3
vitiate
  counteract 179.4
  corrupt 659.9
  demoralize 945.10
vitiated
  diseased 655.25
  corrupt 945.15
vitiation 659.3
viticultural 371.9
viticulture 371.1
viticulturist 371.2
vitreosity 425.1
vitreous hard 323.5
  transparent 425.4
vitrescence 323.2
vitrics 384.14
vitrification 323.2
vitrify 323.4
vitrine 191.15
vittle, vittles etc. See victual etc.
vituperate 932.8
vituperation
  malediction 908.1
  berating 932.3
vituperative rude 895.6
  maledictory 908.6

  abusive 932.11
vituperator 936.2
viva! 931.13
vivacious active 682.16
  gay 836.7
vivacissimo 415.32
vivacity
  animation 682.1
  (life 359.1)
  gaiety 836.2
viva voce 609.3
vive! 883.7
Vivian, Vivien 992.3
vivid forceful 171.9
  violent 173.11
  acute 375.7
  bright 420.22
  colorful 428.14
  remembered 505.18
  graphic 518.6
  dramatic 599.28
vivificate vitalize 359.8
  refresh 689.2
vivification
  invigoration 159.2
  vitalization 359.4
  (revivification 660.2)
  refreshment 689.1
vivificative 359.11
vivify strengthen 159.8
  vitalize 359.8
  (produce 161.8)
  (revivify 660.13)
  refresh 689.2
viviparous 357.10
vivisection 828.6
vixen fury 173.6
  female animal 374.8
  shrew 901.4
  malevolent woman 913.5
vixenish 901.7
viz. 79.13
vizard mask 225.11
  disguise 545.5
vizier, vizir
  director 694.2
  executive 745.9
vizor See visor
vocable 562.1
vocabular 562.8
vocabularian n. 560.7
vocabularian adj. 562.8
vocabulary
  glossary 86.1
  diction 569.1
  (language 560.1)
  (verbiage 562.3)
  dictionary 593.4
vocabulist 560.7
vocal n. sound 402.2
  voice 580.1
vocal adj.
  sounded 402.11
  musical 415.28
  oral 580.11
  spoken 582.10
vocal cords 580.2
vocalion 417.5
vocalise 415.18

vocalism 415.10
vocalist 416.10
vocality 580.1
vocalization
  vocal music 415.10, 18
  utterance 580.3
vocalize sing 416.20
  express 566.3
  utter 580.8
vocal resonance 408.1
vocation 625.5
vocational 625.11
vocational training 537.4
voce tone 402.2
  voice 413.14; 580.1
voce velata 581.3
vociferate 411.7
  (be noisy 404.6)
  (exclaim 580.9)
  (wail 838.9)
vociferation
  clamor 404.2
  outcry 411.2
  (exclamation 580.5)
vociferous noisy 404.9
  clamorous 411.8
vociferousness 411.4
vodka 959.6
vogue fashion 852.1
  popularity 873.1
  come into vogue 873.12
voice n. tone 402.2
  music 413.14
  singer 416.10, 12
  human ~ 580
  vote 609.3
  give one's voice for assent 488.6
  consent 762.2
  one voice 488.3
  raise one's voice dissent 489.4
  insist upon 535.5
  speak out 582.6
  oppose 708.2
  censure 932.7
  with one voice concurrently 178.5
  unanimously 488.17
voice v. tune 413.24
  announce 531.7
  express 566.3
  utter 580.8; 582.6
voice box
  windpipe 351.3
  vocal organs 580.2
voiced 402.11
  (vocal 580.12)
voiceful 580.11
voiceless
  phonetics 402.11
  silent 403.7
  aphonous 581.7
voicelessness 581.1
voice part 415.13
void n. 187.4
  (nonexistence 2.1)
void v. 297.14
void adj.

voidance — waddle

void (*continued*)
 nonexistent 2.7
 incomplete 53.4
 empty 187.11
 abrogated 756.6
 become void 67.6
 make void 756.3
voidance 297.5
voidness 187.3
voile 219.5
voiture 272.4
voiturier driver 268.9
 carrier 271.1
voivode, voivod 745.3
Volans 318.6
volant 267a.37
Volapük, Volapuk 560.5
volatile n. 334.2
volatile adj.
 transient 111.6
 brief 111.7
 inconstant 149.6
 aeronautical 267a.37
 light 320.7
 gaseous 334.7
 vaporous 336.7
 scatterbrained 458.13
 fickle 608.6
volatile alkali 334.2
volatility
 transience 111.1
 navigation 267.1
 levity 320.1
 gaseity 334.1
 vaporability 336.2
volatilization 336.1
volatilize 336.5
volation
 aeronautics 267a.1
 flight 267a.23
volcanic
 turbulent 173.12
 plutonic 382.23
 excitable 825.11
 hot-tempered 901.7
volcanic water 382.5
volcanic wind 382.4
volcano outbreak 173.2
 fire 382.8
 furnace 386.1
volcanology 382.12
volitant 267a.37
volitate 267a.30
volitation
 aeronautics 267a.1
 flight 267a.23
 volitational 267a.37
volition 600.1
volitional 600.4
 (self-determined 748.17)
volitionally 600.5
volitionate 600.2
volitive 600.4
Volkslied 415.10
volley horde 72.4
 shot 284.4; 406.2
 barrage 716.2
 ~ of arrows 727.6
volplane n. 267a.24

volplane v. 267a.30
Volstead Act 761.1
volt, voltage 158a.5
 (measurement 466.3)
voltaic 158a.12
voltaic pile 158a.6
voltaism 158a.1
voltameter 158a.6
voltametric 158a.12
volt-coulomb 158a.5
volte-face n.
 regression 283.1
 tergiversation 607.1
volte-face v. 283.6
volubility 584.1
voluble 584.5
volume
 quantities 31.3
 size 192.1
 book 593.1
voluminous 192.11
voluntarily 600.5
 (willingly 602.11)
 (optionally 609.17)
 (intentionally 620.5)
voluntarism 600.1
voluntaristic 600.4
voluntary n.
 prelude 64.2
 music 415.15
 volunteer 602.5
voluntary adj.
 volitional 600.4
 spontaneous 602.10
 (optional 609.14)
 (free 748.17)
volunteer n.
 voluntary 602.5
 soldier 726.6
volunteer v. 763.3
 (be willing 602.6)
volunteer adj. 602.10
voluptuary 954a.1
 (libertine 962.1)
voluptuous
 pleasure 377.7
 pleasureableness 829.7
 sensual 954.4; 961.11
voluptuousness, volupty 954.1
volutate 311.5
volutation 311.1
volute coil 248.2
 ornament 847.4
volution 311.2
vomit emit 295.7
 disgorge 297.18
 spout 348.20
vomiting 297.5
vomitive n. 662.10
vomitive adj.
 vomitory 297.22
 emetic 662.25
vomitory n.
 opening 260.1
 outlet 295.5
vomitory adj.
 vomitive 297.22
 emetic 662.25
voodoo n.

sorcery 992.1
voodooist 992.2
fetish 993.2
voodoo v. 992.4
voodoo adj. 992.5
voog See **vug**
voortrekker 64.1
voracious
 greedy 865.20
 gluttonous 957.4
voracity greed 865.4
 gluttony 957.1
vorant 298.48
Vorspiel 415.15
Vorstellung 515.4
vortex whirl 312.2
 eddy 348.8
vortical rotating 312.8
 gulfy 348.26
vorticism 556.6
vorticist 559.1
vorticose 312.8
votary advocate 711.4
 devotee 840.19
 enthusiast 865.7
vote n. 609.3
Vote n. 560.4
vote v. 609.10
 vote against 708.2
 vote for assent 488.6
 consent 762.2
voter 609.4
voting 609.3
votive 768.6
votive offering 990.6
vouch testify 467.8
 depose 535.4
 promise 768.3
voucher
 credential 467.4; 550.11
 record 551.1
 security 771.1
 money order 800.7
 receipt 807.4
vouchsafe permit 760.3
 consent 762.2
 pray do 765.9
 give 784.8
vouchsafement
 permission 760.1
 gift 784.3
voussoir 215.18
vow n. oath 535.2
 promise 768.1
vow v. swear 535.4
 promise 768.3
vowel, vowellike 402.2
 (letter 561.1)
vox 580.1
vox et praeterea nihil
 impotent 158.3
 egoist 880.3
 boaster 884.3
vox populi
 public opinion 484.3
 unanimity 488.3
 publicity 531.3
 popular vote 609.3
voyage n.
 journey 266.8
 cruise 267.6

 (passage 302.1)
voyage v. 267.10
voyager, voyageur 268.1
vriddhi 402.2
vrouw 374.2, 3
vs. 237.7
V-shaped
 bifurcate 91.7
 crotched 244.5
vug, vugg, vugh 252.2
Vulcan fire 382.8
 smith 690.6
 god 979.2
vulgar
 grammar 563.15; 579.3
 unrefined 851.6
 (shocking 830.13)
 (plebeian 876.11)
 (uncivil 895.6)
 obscene 961.9
 be vulgar 851.5
vulgarian
 vulgar speaker 579.2
 unrefined person 851.4
 (slattern 59.5)
vulgarism
 vulgar word 563.1
 vulgar speech 579.1
 bad taste 851.1
vulgarity
 language 579.1
 (barbarism 563.1)
 (incivility 895.1)
 obscenity 961.1
vulgate
 vernacular 560.2
 colloquialism 563.3
Vulgate 985.2
vulnerability 665.2
vulnerable
 helpless 158.9
 pregnable 665.9
vulnerary n. 662.6
vulnerary adj. 662.25
Vulpecula 318.6
vulpine 702.6
vulture bird 366.22
 tyrant 739.3
 taker 789.6

W

Wa 560.4
Waac 726.7
wabble, wabbly See **wobble** etc.
wacke 342.3
wad n. quantities 31.3
 lump 192.5
 ~ of money 800.11, 12
wad v. fill 52.7
 weight 319.9
wadding
 contents 190.1
 stopper 263.1
 softness 324.3
waddle 275.5

1168

waddy — wanting

waddy 727.7
Wade n. 192.8
wade v. bathe 267.46
  wade into
    set to work 686.7
    attack 716.5
  wade through
    study 539.4
    labor 686.6
wafer cement 45.6
  thinness 203.5
  lamina 204.2
waffle 298.12
waffle iron 386.1
waft transport 270.8
  blow 349.22
  ~ a sigh 839.7
waftage 270.2
wag n.
  oscillation 314.5
  wit 844
wag v. walk 266.16
  depart 293.4
  oscillate 314.8
  shake 315.8, 9
  ~ the tongue 582.6
wage 722.9
wager n.
  ~ of law 467.2
  bet 621.3
wager v. 621.18
wagerer 621.15
wages 973.2
wageworker 690.2
waggery 842.2
waggish
  playful 836.10;
    840.23
  prankish 842.9
waggle n. 314.5
waggle v. vary 149.4
  oscillate 314.8
  shake 315.8, 9
wagon, waggon n.
  272.2, 7, 11
wagon, waggon v.
  270.8
wagoner, waggoner
  268.9
Wagoner, Waggoner
  318.6
wagonette, waggon-
  ette 272.4
wagonload, waggon-
  load 190.1
wagonwright, wag-
  gonwright 690.7
wagwit 844
Wahabi, Wahabee,
  Wahhabi 984.18
Wahabiism, Wahab-
  ism 984.8
waif derelict 782.2
  vagabond 876.9
  castaway 893.5
wail n. 839.1
  (cry 411.3)
wail v. blow 349.22
  sough 405.5
  stridulate 410.5
  ululate 412.2
  lament 839.9

  (cry 411.6)
wain 272.2
wainscot n. base 211.1
  lining 224.1
wainscot v. 224.2
wainscoting, wain-
  scotting 224.1
wainwright 690.7
waist shirt 225.18
  garment 225.34
waistband 225.34
waistcloth 225.22, 34
waistcoat 225.16
wait n. 416.10
wait v. 133.4, 7
  (not do 681.2)
  wait on
    accompany 88.6
    await 507.5
    help 707.10
    serve 746.8
    toady 886.3
    pay respects 894.8
  waiter plate 191.12
    servant 746.1
  waiter on Providence
    neglector 460.3
    idler 683.7
    contented person
      831.2
waiting n. delay 133.2
  expectation 507.3
waiting adj. 746.9
waiting maid 746.2
waiting room 191.17
waive postpone 133.4
  have no choice
    609a.2
  relinquish 624.3;
    782.3
  not use 678.5
wake n. afterpart 65.2
  aeronautics 267a.16
  funeral 363.4
  track 550.4
  party 892.5
  in the wake of 281.5
wake v. 824.2
wakeful
  attentive 457.9
  vigilant 459.8
  sleepless 682.24
wakefulness 682.9
waken 824.2
waldgrave 875.5
Waler 271.4
Walhalla See Val-
  halla
wali, vali 745.5
walk n. beat 181.4
  travel 266.4, 8
  (exercise 686.2)
  slow motion 275.2
  (gait 266.5)
  ~ of life 625.3
  path 627.2
  career 692.3
  arena 728.1
walk v.
  travel 266.13, 16
  (move 264.6)
  go slow 275.5

  walk one's chalks
    depart 293.5
    flee 623.10
  walk out 719.4
  walk over 731.6
  walk the chalk 82.5
walker 268.6
walking beam 273a.10
walking delegate
    negotiator 758.3
    deputy 759.1
walking gentleman,
    walking lady 599.19
walking papers 297.4
walking part 599.7
walking stick
    staff 215.15
    cane 727.7
walkist 268.6
walk-on 599.7, 19
walkout 719.2
walkover 731.3
walk-up 191.21
wall n.
  precipice 212.3
  lining 224.1
  partition 228.6
  fence 232.2
  (obstacle 706.2)
  fortification 717.3
  go to the wall
    perish 162.5
    fail 732.5
    go bankrupt 808.6
wall v.
  wall in confine 751.8
  circumscribe 229.2
wallaby 309.3
wallah, walla
  person 372.3
  man 373.2
wallboard 635.3
wallet 802.2
walleye 443.4
walleyed 443.14
wallop strike 276.8
  bubble 353.8; 405.7
  whip 972.6
wallow n. 343a.1
wallow v. grovel 207.5
  pitch 267.45
  welter 311.5
  (submerge 310.5)
  luxuriate in 377.4
  ~ in the mire 653.14
  delight in 827.6
Wall Street 799.3
walnut nut 298.33
  wood 635.3
walnut tree 367.6
walrus 366.21
Waltonian 622.5
waltz music 415.7
  dance 840.7
wamble vary 149.4
  go slow 275.5
  oscillate 314.8
wambly 160.12
wame 191.7
wampum 800.3
wan v. 429.4
wan adj. pale 429.6

  sad 837.16
wand staff 215.15
  divining rod 511.5
  scepter 747.1
  magic ~ 993.3
wander rove 266.14
  deviate 279.5
  be inattentive 458.5
  be uncertain 475.6
  err 495.7
  ~ in delirium 503.9
wanderer 268.2
  (idler 683.7)
  (beggar 767.2)
wandering n.
  roving 266.2
  deviation 279.1
  delirium 503.3
wandering adj.
  unconformable 83.9
  nomadic 266.24
  deviative 279.8
  (circuitous 629.3)
  preoccupied 458.11
  delirious 503.14
Wandering Jew 268.2
wanderlust 266.2
wane n.
  subsidence 36.2
  deterioration 659.1
  on the wane
    decreasingly 36.6
    sickly 655.24
    deteriorating 659.11
    unprosperous 735.9
wane v. decrease 36.3
  recede 287.2
  deteriorate 659.6
  (age 128.7)
wanga voodoo 992.1
  spell 993.1
wangateur 992.2
wanigan, wangan,
  wangun 273.4
waning 128.8
want n. deficiency 53.2
  requirement 630.1
  lack 640.3
  (shortcoming 304.1)
  poverty 804.1
  desire 865.1
  for want of 640.13
  in want 804.7
  (wanting 640.11)
  in want of
    empty 187.11
    needful 630.3
want v.
  be inferior 34.4
  fall short 304.2
  require 630.2
  lack 640.6
  be poor 804.4
  desire 865.11
want ad 531.4
wantage
  deficiency 53.2
  want 640.3
wanting
  incomplete 53.4
  absent 187.10
  short of 304.3

wanton — wash ball

wanting (*continued*)
  feeble-minded
    499.13
  lacking 640.11
  deprived of 776.6
  be found wanting
    be unequal 28.2
    be small 32.4
    be inferior 34.4
    fall short 304.2
    be insufficient 640.6
wanton *n.* 962.2
wanton *v.*
  carouse 840.21
  make love 902.7
  dissipate 954.3
wanton *adj.*
  unconformable 83.9
  inconstant 149.6
  capricious 608.5
  reckless 863.7
  wicked 945.11
  unchaste 961.10
wantonness 961.2
wapentake 181.2
wapiti 366.11
war *n.* contest 720.2
  warfare 722
  at war
    disagreeing 24.6
    at loggerheads
      713.10; 720.11
    in opposition 708.4
    warring 722.14
    at enmity 889.3
  declare war
    quarrel 713.7
    wage war 722.9
war *v.* 722.9
  (attack 716.5)
  (fight 720.8)
war bag 191.5
war bird 269a.1
warble twitter 412.2
  sing 416.20
warbler bird 366.22
  songster 416.10, 11
war club 727.7
warcraft 722.2
war cry alarm 669.1
  defiance 715.1
  battle cry 722.3
ward *n.* part 51.1
  territory 181.2
  hospital 662.17
  protectorship 664.2
  asylum 666.3
  guard 717.1
  stronghold 717.4
  dependent 746.3
  custody 751.4
ward *v.* protect 664.6
  guard 717.7
ward off repulse 289.2
  avert 706.5
  fend off 717.8
warden guardian 664.3
  guard 717.6
  official 745.9
  jailer 753.1
wardenship 664.2

warder guardian 664.3
  guard 717.6
  jailer 753.1
ward heeler 886.2
wardmote 966.2
war dog 726.3
wardrobe 225.2
  (outfit 634.1)
wardship 664.2
ware! 864.3, 9
**warehouse, ware-
  room** *n.*
  storehouse 636.4
  shop 799.1
warehouse *v.* 636.7
wares 798.1
warfare *n.* 722
  (broil 713.4)
  (attack 716.1)
  (contention 720.1)
warfare *v.* 722.9
warfarer 726.4
warful 722.13
war game 722.1
war gas gas 334.2
  weapon 727.15
war-god, war-goddess
  722.7
war hatchet 722.3
war horse crone 130.3
  veteran 700.3
  soldier 726.4, 12
warlike 722.13
  (defiant 715.3)
  (courageous 861.8)
  (quarrelsome 901.9)
warlikeness 722.6
  (irascibility 901.1)
warlock 992.2
warm *v.* heat 384.16, 19
  impassion 824.2
  become excited
    824.8
  ~ the heart 829.5
  whip 972.6
warm up
  improve 658.10
  revive 660.13
warm *adj.* near 197.8
  calid 382.15
  (califactive 384.22)
  orange 439.5
  red 434.9
  near 481a.8
  vehement 574.7
  wealthy 803.8
  fervent 821.6
  excited 824.9
  friendship 888.4
  angry 900.13
  hot-tempered 901.7
warm-blooded 382.16
warmed-over
  repeated 104.6
  reheated 384.23
  trite 843.6
warmhearted
  hearty 821.6
  tender 822.7
  friendly 888.4
  benevolent 906.6
warming *n.* 384.1

warming *adj.* 384.22
**warming house,
  warming pad** 386.1
warming pan
  substitute 147.2
  heater 386.1
warm spring
  hot water 382.5
  health resort 662.17
warmth heat 382.1
  color 428.1
  vehemence 574.3
  passion 821.2
  hot temper 900.1
  benevolence 906.1
warn *n.* 668.1
warn *v.*
  advise against 616.2
  caution 668.6
  (tipoff 527.9)
  (signal 550.20)
  (sound alarm 669.3)
  (threaten 909.2)
  ~ off 761.2
warner 668.4
  (watcher 444.1)
warning *n.* 668
  (omen 512.1)
  (tip 527.3)
  (indication 550.1, 2)
  (danger 665.1)
  (alarm 669.1)
  (caution 864.1)
  (threat 909.1)
without warning
  508.11
warning *adj.* 668.9
  (alarming 669.5)
  (threatening 909.3)
warp *n.* tendency 176.1
  obliquity 217.1
  distortion 243.1
  ~ and woof 329.1
  prejudice 481.1
  bent of mind 820.1
  partiality 941a.1
warp *v.* change 140.5
  tend 176.2
  contract 195.4
  distort 243.3
  navigate 267.10
  deviate 279.6
  prejudice 481.8
  corrupt 659.8
war paint 225.13
  in war paint 673.11
warpath 722.6
  go on the warpath
    722.9
warped distorted 243.5
  (imperfect 651.4)
  partial 941a.3
  perverted 945.14
warplane 273a.2
warrant *n.*
  authority 467.4
  pledge 535.2
  record 551.1
  writ 741.3
  commission 755.1
  permit 760.2
  promise 768.1

  guarantee 771.1
  money order 800.7
  justification 937.1
warrant *v.*
  testify 467.8
  confirm 467.9
  acknowledge 488.9
  vouch 535.4
  permit 760.4
  (authorize 737.10)
  promise 768.3
  guarantee 771.6
  justify 937.5
warrantable 937.10
warranted 924.10
  (permissible 760.6)
warrantee 771.2
warrant officer 745.11
warranty
  permission 760.1
  promise 768.1
  guarantee 771.1
  (authority 467.4)
warren 168.3
warrior 726.4
warship 726.11
Wars of the Roses
  722.4
war song song 415.10
  martial music 722.3
wart
  diminutive 193.2, 5
  protuberance 250.2
  (blemish 848.1)
  tumor 655.16
wart hog 366.7
war to the knife
  death struggle 720.2
  warfare 722.1
warty 250.9
war whoop
  alarm 669.1
  defiance 715.1
  battlecry 722.3
wary 864.6
  (careful 459.7)
wash *n.* cavity 252.2
  aeronautics 267a.16
  marsh 345.1
  paint 428.5
  cleanser 652.8
wash *v.* swash 348.19
  murmur 405.5
  paint 428.10
  clean 652.9
  (water 337.5)
**wash a blackamoor
  white** 471.5
  (labor in vain 645.6)
wash down 298.47
wash one's hands of
  abandon 624.3
  (resign 757.2)
  (recant 607.9)
  discard 678.3
  discountenance
    764.3
  relinquish 782.3
wash out 649.5
wash up 67.7
wash ball 356.5

wash basin, wash
  boiler, washbowl
  652.5
wash brush, wash-
  cloth 652.7
wash-colored, wash-
  coloured 428.13
washday 652.2
washdish 652.5
washed-out
  colorless 429.6
  impaired 659.12
washerman, washer-
  wife, washer-
  woman 652.6
washery, washhouse
  652.4
washin 273a.10
washing 652.2
washing machine
  652.7
washing maid,
  washmaid 652.5
washing powder 356.5
washing soda 652.8
Washington's Birth-
  day 138.7
washout
  destruction 162.2, 3
  crack-up 267a.27
  airplane 273a.10
  shortcoming 304.1
  overflow 348.3
  cleansing 652.2
  failure 732.1
washpot 652.5, 6
washrag 652.7
washroom, washshed
  652.4
washtub
  receptacle 191.11
  washbasin 652.5
wash-up, washwork
  652.2
washy
  wishy-washy 160.14
  unmeaning 517.9
  feeble style 575.2
wasp 366.24
waspish savage 173.14
  irascible 901.7
wassail n. spree 959.3
  alcoholic drink
  959.8
wassail v. 959.17
  (revel 840.21)
wassailer 959.11
wastage waste 638.1
  rubbish 645.4
waste n. decrease 36.1
  decrement 39a
  wasteland 169.2
  (plain 344.1)
  consumption 638
  (decomposition
  49.1)
  (destruction 162.1)
  (inutility 645.1)
  (deterioration
  659.1)
  (misuse 679.1)
  (loss 776.1)

  rubbish 645.4
  (dregs 40.2)
  (offal 653.6)
  decay 659.2
  prodigality 818.1
  gone to waste 638.4
waste v. decrease 36.3
  shrink 195.4
  consume 638.2
  damage 659.8
  ~ time 683.8
  (pass time 106.3)
  (lose an opportu-
  nity 135.5)
  squander 818.3
waste away
  decrease 36.3
  decompose 49.3
  shrink 195.4
  sicken 655.21
  decay 659.7
wastebasket
  rubbish 645.4
  discard 678.3
waste bin 645.4
wasted
  gone to waste 638.4
  (useless 645.8)
  impaired 659.12
  (unsound 160.13)
wasteful 818.4
wastefulness 818.1
  (waste 638.1)
wasteland 169.2
wastepaper, waste-
  paper basket 645.4
waster, wastethrift
  818.2
wasteyard 645.4
wasting 195.1
wastrel
  vagabond 268.2;
  876.9
  (outcast 893.5)
  spendthrift 818.2
  (neglector 460.3)
wastry, wastrie, wast-
  ery 818.1
watch n. company 72.3
  timepiece 114.6
  lookout 441.2
  vigil 459.2
  sentinel 668.4
  guard 717.6
  keep watch
  be vigilant 459.4
  (watch 441.11)
  (defend 717.7)
  safeguard 664.7
on the watch
  attentive 457.9
  expectant 507.7
  (vigilant 459.8)
  cautious 864.3
watch v. look at 441.11
  (attend 186.9)
  be vigilant 459.4, 6
  (be attentive 457.4)
  wait 507.5
watch and wait
  wait 507.5
  prepare 673.9

  do nothing 681.2
  watch for 507.4
  (look 441.11)
  (keep watch 459.4)
watch one's step
  be careful 459.3
  be cautious 864.3, 9
watch out
  be attentive 457.4, 10
  be careful 459.4
  care for 459.6
  expect 507.4
  beware 864.3, 9
watch over
  care for 459.6
  protect 664.6
watch and ward
  vigil 459.2
  protectorship 664.2
  sentinel 668.4
  guard 717.1
watchdog dog 366.6
  guard 717.6
watcher 444.1
watchet n. 438.2
watchet adj. 438.6
watch fire 382.8
watchful
  attentive 457.9
  vigilant 459.8
watchfulness 459.2
watchhouse 752.1
watching n. 459.2
watching adj. 267.50
watchmaker 690.8
watchman
  sentinel 668.4
  (watcher 444.1)
  guard 717.6
watchman's rattle
  signal 550.14
  alarm 669.1
watchtower
  observatory 441.5
  landmark 550.10
watchword sign 550.11
  battlecry 722.3
water n.
  weakness 160.5
  sounding 208.4
  drink 298.4
  urine 299.3
  perspiration 299.4
  H₂O 337.1
  (drink 298.4)
  (fluid 333.2)
  transparency 425.2
above water
  safe 664.10
  unindebted 807.10
water v. dilute 160.9
  wet 337.5
  (moisten 339.5)
  tend stock 370.7
water-bearer 348.16
Water Bearer 318.6
water butt 252.2
water carrier
  water boy 348.16
  (workman 690.10)
  cloud 353.5
water closet 653.9

  (room 191.16)
  (lavatory 652.4)
water color
  paint 428.5
  painting 556.9
water-colorist, water-
  colourist 559.2
watercourse
  stream 348.1
  channel 350.1
watercraft 273.1
water dog 269.1
watered 440.10
waterfall hair 256.3
  cataract 348.7
waterflood 348.3
waterfowl 366.22
water gap 350.1
water gate 350.1
water glass 428.5
water ice 298.13
watering 337.2
  (cleaning 652.2)
watering can, water-
  ing cart 337.3
watering place 662.17
waterless 340.7
water level 213.3
  at water level 213.10
water line, waterline
  ship 273.7
  watermark 466.5
  at water line 267.61
waterlogged
  impotent 158.8
  encumbered 706.9
Waterloo 722.5
waterman 269.2
watermark 466.5
watermelon 298.32
water nymph 979.10
water pistol 840.16
waterproof n. 225.17
waterproof adj.
  seaworthy 273.15
  moistureproof
  340.11
  secure 664.10, 11
water qualm 655.13
waterscape view 448.2
  picture 556.10
watershed range 206.2
  summit 210.1
waterside 342.2
Water Snake 318.6
waterspout rain 348.11
  whirlwind 349.13
  conduit 350.1
water sprite 979.10
  (spirit of the sea
  341.2)
watertight close 261.6
  seaworthy 273.15
  waterproof 340.11
  proof 664.11
waterway
  seaway 267.8
  ship 273.7
  channel 350.1
water wing 666.1, 4
waterwork 350.1

watery — wearisomeness

watery
  wishy-washy 160.14
  aqueous 337.6
  (liquid 333.7)
  (moist 339.7)
  feeble style 575.2
  be watery 337.4
watt, wattage 158a.5
wattle 219.4
wattmeter 158a.6
wave *n.*
  convolution 248.1
  oscillation 314.1, 5
  billow 348.10
  (swell 194.2; 250.2)
  ornamentation 847.3
  greeting 894.4
wave *v.* oscillate 314.8
  shake 315.8
  (brandish 314.11)
  signal 550.20
  flaunt 882.7
  ~ a wand 992.4
wave the bloody shirt 722.10
wavelet 348.10
waver *n.* 314.5
waver *v.* vary 149.4
  oscillate 314.8
  flutter 315.10
  glitter 420.18
  be uncertain 475.6
  demur 485.7
  be irresolute 605.4
waverer 605.3
  (equivocator 477.6)
wavering *n.* 475.1
wavering *adj.*
  irregular 139.2
  inconstant 149.6
  uncertain 475.16
  irresolute 605.5
waveson 73.2
wavy 248.7
  (flowing 348.26)
wax *n.* burnisher 255.3
  softness 324.3
  cerate 356.6
  record 417.9; 551.6
  candle 423.7
  modeler's ~ 557.8
wax *v.* increase 35.4
  ~ and wane 140.5
  be converted into 144.8
  grow 194.6
  polish 255.4
  rub 331.3
  lubricate 332.4
waxwork 554.4
waxworker 690.9
waxy cerate 355.3
  angry 900.23
way condition 7.1
  degree 26.1
  extent 180.1
  distance 196.1
  portal 260.4
  navigation 267.7
  headway 282.1
  ~ in 294.5
  ~ out 295.5; 671.4

  channel 350.1
  custom 613.2
  vocation 625.5
  method 627
  (plan 626.1)
  (means 632.1)
  (conduct 692.1)
  (fashion 852.1)
  procedure 692.1
be in the way of 177.2
by way of 278.16; 631.5
get under way 267.16
  (embark 293.6)
go out of one's way 311.3
  (deviate 279.4)
  (go round about 629.2)
have one's own way
  have one's will 600.2
  be obstinate 606.5
  dominate 737.12
  be free 748.8
have way upon 267.16
in a way as if 17.17
  displeased 828.14
in no way 87a.3
in one way or another
  somehow 155.7
  by some means 627.10
in the way 706.8
keep out of the way
  be absent 187.8
  avoid 623.6
lose one's way
  stray 279.5
  bungle 699.7
  be in difficulty 704.6
  fail 732.5
on the way
  en route 270.13
  (in passing 302.4)
  approaching 286.5
show the way 693.4
the Way 976.5
under way
  moving 264.10
  afloat 267.54
  forward 282.5
wayback 122.2
way car 272.19
way enough! 267.69
wayfare 266.12
wayfarer 268.1
waylay ambush 530.5
  be cunning 702.5
way of all flesh 360.1
go the way of all flesh 360.6
ways distance 196.1
  means 632.1
  conduct 692.1
ways and means
  method 627.1
  means 632.1
  assets 780.7
  funds 800.2
wayward
  inconstant 149.6

  obstinate 606.6
  capricious 608.5
  disobedient 742.6
  sinful 945.11
waywardness 481.3
way-weary, wayworn
  travel-worn 266.26
  fatigued 688.6
waywode See **voivode**
wayzgoose 840.2
w.c. 653.9
W. C. T. U. 953.4
weak
  strengthless 160.10
  (impotent 158.8)
  (effeminate 160a.5)
  (watery 337.6)
  (infirm 655.24)
  (impaired 659.12)
  insipid 391.2
  phonetics 402.11
  faint 405.9
  pale 429.6
  illogical 477.10
  feeble-minded 499.13
  language 575.2
  weak-willed 605.6
  lax 738.7
  compassionate 914.6
  morally ~ 945.12
  of easy virtue 961.10
  be weak 160.6
weaken decrease 36.4
  become weak 160.6
  unstrengthen 160.8
  (render powerless 158.6)
  (moderate 174.5)
  (impair 659.8)
  blunt 254.2
  evidence 468.2
  sicken 655.21, 22
weakening 160.2
weaker sex 374.5
weak-eyed 443.15
weakhearted 862.4
weakliness 160.1
  (infirmity 655.1)
weakling 160.4
  (impotent 158.3)
  (mollycoddle 160a.3)
weakly *adj.* 160.10
  (infirm 655.24)
weakly *adv.* 32.12
weak-minded 499.13
weakness
  strengthlessness 160
  (impotence 158.1)
  (fault 651.2)
  ~ of expression 575.1
  weak will 605.2
  desire 865.1
  ~ of the flesh 945.4
weak point
  sophism 477.2
  fault 651.2
  vice 945.4
weak sister
  weakling 160.4

  mollycoddle 160a.3
weak-willed 605.6
weal good 648.2
  prosperity 734.1
weald 344.1
wealth riches 803
  (abundance 639.2)
  (prosperity 734.1)
  (prosperous 734.7)
  (assets 780.7)
  (funds 800.2; 803.8)
weapon 727.1
  (safeguard 717.2)
weaponless 665.9
  (helpless 158.9)
wear *n.*
  decomposition 49.1
  clothes 225.1
  waste 638.1
  deterioration 659.2
  use 677.1
wear *v.* decrease 36.3
  decompose 49.3
  have on 225.45
  turn ship 267.24
  decay 659.7
wear off cease 142.6
  ~ ~ a habit 614.2
wear on 110.7
  (elapse 109.3)
wear one's heart on one's sleeve
  manifest oneself 525.2
  be artless 703.3
wear out
  waste away 638.2
  decay 659.7
  tire out 688.5
wear the breeches 737.12
wear the willow 839.12
wearable 225.3
wearables 225.1
wear and tear
  decrease 36.1
  decomposition 49.1
  waste 638.1
  deterioration 659.2
weariful
  fatigued 688.6
  fatiguesome 688.8
  boresome 841.8, 9
weariness
  fatigue 688.1
  ennui 841
  (languor 683.4)
  (sadness 837.1)
  (dullness 843.1)
  (satiety 869.1)
wearing
  fatiguing 688.8
  irksome 841.8
wearing apparel 225.1
  (merchandise 798.3)
wearisome
  fatiguesome 688.8
  (laborious 686.10)
  annoying 830.12
  irksome 841.8
wearisomeness 841.3

1172

weary v. fatigue 688.5
  bore 841.5
  (sate 869.4)
weary adj.
  fatigued 688.6
  dismal 837.10
  bored 841.9
  (languid 683.14)
  (disgusted 828.14)
  be weary 841.7
  become weary 688.4
weary-footed 688.6
wearying
  fatiguing 688.8
  boring 841.8
  (dull 843.5)
weary-laden, weary-looking 688.6
Weary Willie
  slow goer 275.4
  idler 683.7
weary-winged, weary-worn 688.6
weasand gullet 350.4
  windpipe 351.3
weasel n.
  animal 366.17
  eye 441.9
weasel v. 544.5
weasel words
  meaningness 517.1
  equivocation 544.1
weather n. side 236.3
  windy ~ 338.4
  hot ~ 382.3
  cold ~ 383.3
weather v.
  weather the storm
    be stable 150.3
    navigate 267.31
    recover 660.15
    be safe 664.4
    (escape 671.6)
    surmount 731.7
weather-beaten 659.12
weatherboard n.
  coating 223.18
  side 236.3
weatherboard v. 223.24
weather-bound 229.4; 751.11
weathercock
  changeableness 149.2
  weakling 160.4
  weathervane 338.9
  waverer 605.3
  (tergiversator 607.4)
weathered 659.12
weather eye eyes 441.7
  vigilance 459.2
weather gauge,
  weatherglass 338.8
weather-going tide,
  weather helm 236.3
weathermaker,
  weatherman 513.3
weatherproof
  sound 159.12
  impregnable 664.11
weather prophet

barometer 338.8
prophet 513.3
weather-tight 664.11
weather vane
  changeableness 149.2
  weathercock 338.9
  (wind gauge 349.17)
  (weather prophet 513.3)
weather-wise 511.11
weave n. 219.4
weave v. produce 161.8
  interlace 219.8
weazen v. 195.4
weazen, weazened,
  weazen-faced,
  weazeny adj.
  shrunk 195.6
  (dwarfed 193.9)
  thin 203.11
web filament 205.1
  network 219.4
  (texture 329.1)
web-footed 219.11
webwork
  complexity 59.3
  network 219.4
webworm 366.25
wed 903.12, 13
wedded 903.14, 16
wedded to
  addicted to 613.12
  in love with 897.15
wedding 903.3
wedding ring 902.5
wedge n. angle 244.2
  cutter 253.6
wedge v. attach 43.6
  ~ **in** 228.8, 10
wedge-shaped 244.5
wedlock 903.1
wee 193.8
weed n. horse 271.6
  plant 367.2
  tobacco 392a.1, 3
weed v. excise 38.5
  segregate 55.4
  cultivate 371.8
  clean 652.10
weed out
  eliminate 42.4
  exclude 55.3
  eject 297.17
  extract 301.5
weeds clothes 225.6
  useless 645.4
  mourning 839.4
  widow's ~ 905.2
weedy thin 203.11
  paltry 643.12
week 108.1
week-end 106.3
weekly n. 593.6
weekly adj. 138.11
week of Sundays 110.3
  for a week of Sundays 110.11
ween judge 480.6
  think 484.8
  know 490.9
  suppose 514.6

weep rain 348.25
  lament 839.6
  sob 839.8
  (cry 411.5)
  pity 914.3
weepers 225.6
weeping n. 839.2
weeping adj. 214.7
weet-weet 727.5
weevil 366.24
weewow, weewaw
  unsteady 160.12
  crooked 217.13
weigh
  have influence 175.7
  be heavy 319.8
  ponder 451.27
  compare 464.2
  discriminate 465.2
  measure 466.10
  evince 467.7
  decide between 609.7
  be important 642.7
weigh anchor 267.15
  (embark 293.6)
weigh down
  weight 319.8, 9, 10
  aggrieve 649.6
  encumber 706.6
  subjugate 749.5
weigh beam, weighbridge 319.5
weighed 466.13
weighing 319.3
weight n.
  influence 175.1
  gravity 319.1, 4
  (measure 466.3)
  vigor 574.1
  importance 642.1
  impediment 706.2
  authority 737.2
  oppression 837.4
  have weight 467.7
weight v. load 52.7
  weigh 319.8, 9
weightless 320.7
weighty
  influential 175.10
  heavy 319.12
  evidential 467.11
  language 574.9
  important 642.12
  cumbrous 830.16
weir fence 232.2
  floodgate 350.2
  obstruction 706.2
weird n. 993.1
weird adj.
  unusual 83.10
  ghostly 980a.4
  necromantic 992.5
Weird Sisters
  Fates 601.4
  sorceresses 992.3
Weismannism 161.5
welch, Welch etc. See welsh etc.
welcome n. 892.4; 894.3
  (arrival 292.5)
  (greeting 894.4)

welcome v. 892.11
  (greet 894.9)
welcome adj. 829.7
welcome int. 292.13
weld n. 43.3
weld v. 46.7
  (attach 43.6)
welding blowpipe 386.1
welfare good 648.2
  (benevolence 906.1)
  prosperity 734.1
  public ~ 906.3
welfare work 602.4
welfare worker 602.5
welkin heavens 318.2
  atmosphere 338.1
  make the welkin ring 411.7
well n. fountain 153.2
  depth 208.2
  cavity 252.2
  pool 343a.1
  source of supply 636.2
  health resort 662.17
well v.
  ~ **out** 295.7
  jet 348.20
  ~ **over** 641.2
well adj.
  in health 654.4
  satisfactory 831.9
  all's well 664.14
  get well 660.15
  well and good
  yes! 488.14
  satisfactory 831.9
well adv. 648.14
  (skillfully 698.16)
  (commendably 931.12)
wellaway!, welladay! 839.18; 870.11
well-advised 498.11
well-affected
  favorable 707.13
  friendly 888.4
  benevolent 906.6
well-armed
  well-prepared 673.11
  heavy-armed 717.9
  armed 722.12
well-arranged 845.16
well-balanced 242.4
well-behaved 894.12
well-being
  comfort 377.2
  good 648.2
  health 654.1
  prosperity 734.1
well-beloved 897.16
wellborn 875.10
well-bred noble 875.10
  civil 894.12
well-composed 845.16
well-conned 490.15
well-cooked 298.50
well-defined
  distinct 446.5
  accurate 494.11

well-disposed — wheel of fortune 1174

well-disposed
　willing 602.8
　favorable 707.13
　friendly 888.4
　benevolent 906.6
well-doing 944.1
well-done 298.50
well-drawn 594.7
well-educated 490.15
well enough
　somewhat 32.14
　tolerable 648.11
well-equipped 634.3
well-expressed 578.4
well-favored, well-
　favoured
　shapely 242.5
　comely 845.10
well-fed 192.12
well-fitted 634.3
well-formed
　shapely 242.5
　comely 845.10
well-founded
　substantial 3.4
　stable 150.5
　plausible 472.6
　assured 474.9
　logical 476.16
　valid 494.14
well-groomed 847.14
well-grounded
　substantial 3.4
　stable 150.5
　plausible 472.6
　assured 474.9
　logical 476.6
　well-informed
　　490.15
　valid 494.14
　skilled 698.14
well-grouped 845.16
wellhead 153.2
well-heeled
　well-equipped 634.3
　well-prepared 673.11
　moneyed 803.8
well-informed 490.15
　be well-informed
　　490.10
wellingtons 225.27
well-intentioned
　favorable 707.13
　friendly 888.4
　benevolent 906.6
　virtuous 944.3
well-invented 472.6
well-judged 498.11
well-knit 159.10
well-known
　known 490.17
　(trite 843.6)
　distinguished 873.16
well-laid 611.6
well-liked
　popular 928.9
　approved 931.10
well-made
　made 161.13
　shapely 242.5
　comely 845.10
well-mannered 894.12

well-marked 446.5
well-meaning, well-
　meant
　favorable 707.13
　friendly 888.4
　benevolent 906.6
well-natured 906.6
well-nigh
　almost 32.15
　nearly 197.12
well off, well-off
　prosperous 734.7
　wealthy 803.8
well-ordered 58.7
well-paying 775.12
well-posted 490.15
well-prepared 673.11
well-proportioned
　shapely 242.5
　comely 845.10
well-provided 634.3
　(plenty 639.7)
well-put 578.4
well-rated 805.6
well-read 490.14, 15
well-regulated 58.7
　(conformable 82.9)
well-rounded 650.5
well-set, well-set-up
　242.4
well-speaking 582.11
well-spent 731.11
well-spoken
　speaking 582.11
　courteous 894.12
wellspring
　source 153.2
　source of supply
　　636.2
well-stocked, well-
　supplied 634.3
well-timed 134.7
well-to-do, well to do
　prosperous 734.7
　wealthy 803.8
well-trimmed 267.51
well-trodden 613.11
well-varied 845.16
well-watered 339.8
well-wisher
　favorer 711.4
　(friend 890.2)
　(sympathizer 914.2)
　philanthropist 911.1
Welsh, Welch n. 560.4
welsh, welch v.
　avoid 623.8
　not pay 808.5
Welsh, Welch adj.
　188.11
welsher, welcher
　shirker 623.4
　swindler 792.8
　defaulter 808.3
Welshman, Welch-
　man 188.9
Welsh rabbit 298.29
welt n. 231.2
welt v. 972.6
welter grovel 207.5
　pitch 267.45
　wallow 311.5

wen
　protuberance 250.2
　tumor 655.16
wench girl 129.5
　negress 431.4
　jade 949.4
　strumpet 962.2
wend move 264.6
　travel 266.12
werefolk, werewolf
　980.7
wergild, weregild
　974.1
werowance 745.3
weskit 225.16
Wesleyan 984.14
west n. 278.2
west v. 278.5
west adj. 278.10
wester n. 349.11
wester v. 278.5
wester adj. 278.10
westerly n. 349.11
westerly adj. 278.10
western n. 594.2
western v. 278.5
western adj. 278.10
westerner 594.2
Westerner 57.3
westing 196.1
wet n. moisture 339.1
　rain 348.11
　swig of liquor 959.10
wet v. perspire 295.7
　urinate 297.15
　dampen 337.5
　(moisten 339.5)
　rain 348.25
　drink to 959.17
wet one's whistle
　drink 298.47
　tipple 959.15
wet adj. moist 339.7
　(watery 337.6)
　(rainy 348.27)
　soaked 339.8
　mistaken 495.13
wet blanket
　discouragement
　　616.1
　marplot 706.3
　spoilsport 837.5
　bore 841.4
wether ram 366.8
　male animal 373.6
wet nurse n. 664.3
wet-nurse v. 707.9
wetting 337.2
wettish 339.7
　(rainy 348.27)
whack n. condition 7.1
　agreement 23.1
　piece 51.3
　blow 276.3
　attempt 675.1
　share 778.1; 786.2
　in whack 58.7
　out of whack
　　disagreeing 24.6
　　disorderly 59.8
　　impaired 659.12
whack v. cut 44.8

　strike 276.8
　bang 406.7
whack down
　fell 213.7
　cut down 308.5
whack up
　cut up 44.9, 10
　apportion 786.3
whacker 192.6
whacking vast 31.8
　huge 192.15
whale n.
　largeness 192.6, 8
　animal 366.21
whale v. 972.6
whalebone 325.2
whale oil 356.4
whaler
　large thing 192.6
　ship 273.1
whaling vast 31.8
　huge 192.15
whang fastening 45.2
　piece 51.3
　lump 192.5
　cord 205.3
whap, whapper See
　whop etc.
wharf anchorage 666.4
　dockyard 691
wharfage 812.2
wharf hand 269.7
what adv. 461.27
what int. 870.11
whatever 26.5; 78.6
what not 102.5
what's-its-name,
　what-you-may-
　call-it 565.4
　(object 316.3)
wheat 367.9
wheedle
　persuade 615.9
　flatter 933.2
wheedler
　instigator 615.6
　flatterer 935.2
wheedling 933.3
wheel n. cycle 272.14
　rotation 312.2, 4
　(circle 247.2)
　rack 975.3
　on wheels 705.8
wheels within wheels
　complexity 59.3
　wheel 312.4
　mechanism 633.2
wheel v.
　~ about 218.5
　ride 266.18
　turn round 283.6
　turn 311.4
　rotate 312.7
wheelbarrow, wheel
　chair 272.11
wheeler, wheele horse
　271.3
wheelman 269.5
wheel of fortune
　changeableness
　　149.2
　chance 156.1

wheelwork — white flag

wheel 312.4
  fate 601.3
wheelwork 633.2
wheelwright 690.7
wheeze n.
  novel idea 453.1
  deception 545.3
wheeze v.
  breathe 349.23
  sibilate 409.3
wheezy 409.4
whelk
  protuberance 250.2
  pustule 655.16
whelm 641.4
whelp n.
  youngling 129.4, 7
  dog 366.6
  scoundrel 949.1
whelp v. 161.9
when whereupon 106.6
  inquiry 461.29
whence
  hence 155.5; 293.10
  inquiry 461.30
whenever when 106.6
  at any time 119.3
where n. 184.1
where adv.
  whither 186.18
  inquiry 461.30
whereabouts, where-
  about where 186.18
  inquiry 461.30
whereanent 9.10
whereas while 106.9
  since 115.8
whereat 117.4
whereaway
  where 186.18
  inquiry 461.30
whereby 631.5
wherefore n. 615.1
wherefore adv.
  hence 155.5
  why 155.6
  inquiry 461.28
  this being so 480.14
wherein apropos 9.10
  internally 221.12
whereness
  location 184.1
  presence 186.3
whereof, whereon 9.10
wheresoever, where-
  soe'er 186.19
whereto apropos 9.10
  inquiry 461.30
whereunto
  apropos 9.10
  inquiry 461.30
whereupon when 106.6
  subsequently 117.4
wherever 186.19
wherewith, where-
  withal n.
  means 632.1
  money 800.1
wherewith, where-
  withal adv. 632.2
wherry 273.4
whet a.

appetizer 298.38
  stimulus 615.3
whet v. stimulate 171.7
  inflame 173.8
  sharpen 253.9
  excite 824.2
  ~ the appetite
    617.4; 865.14
whether 469.8
whether or not
  provided 469.8
  optionally 609.17
whetrock, whetstone
  253.7
which 461.27
whiff n. puff 349.4
  ~ of passion 825.5
whiff v. puff 349.22
  fish 622.8
whiffet
  youngling 129.1
  puff 349.4
  insignificancy 643.6
whiffle 349.22
whiffy odorous 398.8
  fetid 401.4
Whig 712.6
while n. 109a.1, 111.3
  after a while 132.15
while v.
  while away the time
    spend time 106.3
    do nothing 681.2
    (leisure 685.2)
    idle 683.8
    pleasure 840.21
while, whileas,
  whiles conj. 106.9
whiles adv. 109a.3
whilom adj. 122.10
whilom adv. 122.14
whilst 106.9
whim fancy 515.4
  caprice 608.1
  (notion 453.1)
  (quirk 481.3)
  (craze 503.7)
  (desire 865.8)
  humor 842.1
whimper n. 839.1
whimper v. 839.8
whimsey, whimsy
  fancy 515.4
  caprice 608.1
whimsical
  fanciful 515.12
  capricious 608.5
  witty 842.9
  ridiculous 855.5
whimsicality, whimsi-
  calness
  capriciousness 608.2
  facetiousness 842.2
whin 367.8
whine n. 839.1
whine v. sough 405.5
  stridulate 410.5
  ululate 412.4
  wail 839.9
whinny 412.2
whip n.
  collector 72.9

rider 268.8
  driver 268.9
  blow 276.3
  pennant 550.13
  incentive 615.3
  scourge 975.1
whip v. agitate 315.8
  ~ a horse 370.7
  urge 615.7
  hasten 684.2
  defeat 731.9
  beat 972.6
  strike 276.8
whip in gather 72.11
  insert 300.5
whip off 293.5
whip the cat 683.8
whip and spur 274.14
whipcord 205.3
whip hand
  advantage 33.2
  dominion 737.2
whipped 732.12
whipped cream 298.12
whipper-in 72.9
whippersnapper
  youngling 129.1
  insignificancy 643.6
whipping 972.3
whipping post 975.3
whipsaw 257.3
whipster 129.1
whir, whirr n. 312.2
whir, whirr v. 405.6
whirl n.
  travel 266.4, 7, 8
  rotation 312.2
  eddy 348.8
  attempt 675.1
  excitement 825.3
whirl v. rotate 312.7
  eddy 348.2
whirlabout n. 312.2, 4
whirlabout adj. 312.8
whirlblast, whirlicane
  349.13
whirligig n. 312.2, 4
whirligig v. 312.7
whirligig adj. 312.8
whirlpool n. 348.8
  (danger 667.1)
whirlpool v. 312.7
whirlwind 349.13
whirly n. 312.4
whirly adj. 312.8
whirry 312.2
whisht 403.9
whisk n. 652.7
whisk v.
  transport 270.8
  speed 274.9
  agitate 315.8
  rustle 405.5
  sweep 652.12
whisk off eject 297.8
  discard 678.3
whisker boom 273.12
whiskered 256.13
whisker jumper 273.10
whiskers chin 234.5
  beard 256.5
whisket See wisket

whisky, whiskey 959.6
whisper n.
  faint sound 405.2
  tip 527.3
  rumor 532.3
  muted voice 581.3
in a whisper
  sotto voce 405.11
  secretly 528.24
whisper v. blow 349.22
  tell privately 527.9
  speak covertly
    528.12
  divulge 529.4
  rumor 531.7
  (gossip 532.7)
  speak softly 581.6
whispered 405.9
whispering n. 405.2
whispering adj. 405.10
whist n. silence 403.1
  game 840.12
whist v. 403.5
whist adj. 403.6
whist int. 403.9
whistle n.
  noisemaker 404.4
  high tone 410.2
  stridor 410.4
  music instrument
    417.4
  signal 550.14
  alarm 669.1
whistle v. blow 349.22
  rustle 405.5
  sibilate 409.3
  toot 410.8
  warble 412.2
  ~ a tune 416.18
  music 416.20
whistle at 930.6
whistle down the
  wind 476.11
whistle for
  ask for 765.4
  solicit 865.13
whistle-pig 366.17
whistler horse 271.6
  animal 366.17
whit 32.2
not a whit 536.4
white n. horse 271.5
  color 430.1
white v. 430.6, 7
white adj. color 430.8
  excited 824.9
  honest 939.7
  render white 430.6
white book 551.2
whitecap 348.10
Whitechapel cart 272.5
whited sepulcher 545.6
white elephant
  bane 663.1
  possession 780.1
  gift 784.3
white feather 862.1, 2
  show the white
    feather 862.3
white flag 723.3
  hoist the white flag
  make peace 723.4

Whitefriars — will 1176

white flag (cont'd)
  surrender 725.4
Whitefriars 791.8
white goods 798.3
white heat 382.2
white horse 348.10
white-hot 382.16
White Lady 980a.1
white lead 430.4
white lie 546.3
  secrecy 528.2
  (pretext 619.1)
  tell a white lie 619.2
white-livered 862.4
white magic 992.1
white man
  whiteness 430.3
  honest man 939.5
  good person 948.1
white matter 450.2
white meat 298.25
white metal 545.6
whiten pale 429.4, 5
  make white 430.6
  turn color 824.2
whiteness
  heat flush 382.7
  color 430
whitening
  albification 430.2
  (decoloration 429.2)
  whitewash 430.5
white plague 655.2, 10
whites
  clothes 225.8, 21
  leucorrhea 299.1
white slave 962.2
white slaver 962.4
White Sunday 138.7
whitetop 223.5
whiteware 384.14
whitewash n.
  whitening 430.5
  pretext 619.1
  defeat 732.3
  clearing debt 808.1
  extenuation 937.3
whitewash v.
  whiten 430.7
  (paint 428.10)
  disinfect 652.13
  defeat 731.9
  clear of debt 808.8
  extenuate 937.8
  exculpate 970.3
white wine 959.7
white wing 652.6
whither where 186.18
  hither 278.12
  inquiry 461.30
whiting fish 298.18
  whitewash 430.5
whitish 430.9
  (light-colored 429.7)
  (gray 432.4)
Whitmonday 138.7
Whitsunday, Whitsun Day
  anniversary 138.7
  holyday 998.13

Whitsuntide, Whitsun Tide 998.13
whittle n. 253.6
whittle v. 44.8
whiz, whizz n.
  agreement 23.4
  bargain 769.1
whiz whizz v.
  speed 274.9
  hum 405.6
  sibilate 409.3
  sound harshly 410.6
whiz-bang, whizz-bang firework 382.9
  noisemaker 404.4
whizgig, whizzer 404.4
who 461.27
whoa! 142.8
whole n. 50
  (completeness 52.1)
  (unity 87.1)
as a whole 50.10
make whole 660.8
on the whole
  mainly 50.11
  finally 476.20
  all considered 480.14
whole adj. entire 50.6
  (complete 52.9)
  healthy 654.4
whole-footed 703.4
whole hog n. all 50.2
  limit 52.4
whole-hog adj. 52.10
wholesale n. 796.1
by wholesale
  greatly 31.15
  wholly 50.10
wholesale v. 796.5
wholesale adj.
  extensive 31.7
  (abundant 639.7)
  commercial 794.10
wholesaler 797.1
wholeness 52.1
whole show 50.2
wholesome sane 502.5
  salubrious 656.5
wholesomeness 656.1
whole-souled 944.3
wholly 50.10
  (fully 31.17)
  (completely 52.13)
whoop n. 197.2
whoop v. 411.5
  whoop it up
  be violent 173.7
  be noisy 404.6
whooping 31.8
whooping cough 655.9
whop, whap n. 276.3
whop, whap v.
  strike 276.8
  bang 406.7
whopper, whapper
  large thing 192.6, 7
  lie 546.2
  (exaggeration 549.1)
whopping, whapping
  vast 31.8
whore 962.2

whoredom 961.6
whoremonger 962.1
whorish 961.10
whorl 248.2
whortleberry 298.31
Who's Who 551.2
why n. puzzle 533.2
  reason 615.1
why, for why, forwhy etc.
  wherefore 155.6
  inquiry 461.28
why int. 535.8
wick village 189.17
  lighter 388.4
wicked difficult 704.8
  sinful 945.11
  (dishonest 940.8)
  (unjustifiable 941a.4)
  (impure 961.9)
the wicked 949.5
wickedly 945.20
wickedness 945.1
  (impiety 988.1)
  (irreligion 989.1)
wicker, wickerwork 219.4
wicket 260.5
wickiup, wikiup 189.4
wide extensive 31.7
  (inclusive 76.5)
  spacious 180.6
  broad 202.6
  phonetics 402.11
wide of the mark
  afield 196.9
  deviatively 279.9
  erroneous 495.12
  (abortive 732.8)
wide-arched 202.6
wide-awake, wide-awake hat n. 225.26
wide-awake adj.
  attentive 457.9
  vigilant 459.8
  sagacious 498.10
  alert 682.17
widely greatly 31.15
  broadly 196.10
wide-minded 498.12
widen expand 194.5, 8
  broaden 202.4
wide-open
  expanded 194.10
  open 260.15
wide-spaced, wide-spanned 202.6
widespread
  extensive 31.7
  (prevalent 78.10)
  (abundant 639.7)
  scattered 73.4
  spacious 180.6
  expanded 194.10
widow 905.3
widowed 905.5
widower 905.3
widowerhood, widowhood 905.2
widowly 905.5
widowman 905.3

widow woman 905.3
width
  proportions 180.5
  breadth 202.1
wield brandish 315.8
  handle 379.3
  employ 677.5
wield the scepter 737.11
wieldy 705.6
wife 903.8
wig 256.4
wigging 932.3
wiggle vary 149.4
  waggle 315.9
  be excited 824.7
wight 372.3
wigmaker
  stageman 599.17
  craftsman 690.8
wigwag n.
  alternation 314.3
  signal 550.14
wigwag v. 314.10
wigwam hut 189.4
  tent 223.5
wikiup See wickiup
wild n. waste 169.2
  woods 367.7
wild adj.
  turbulent 173.12
  savage 173.14
  luxuriant 365.4
  rabid 503.13
  overwrought 824.10
  passionate 825.10
  uncouth 851.7
  reckless 863.7
  enamoured 897.15
  infuriated 900.13
  licentious 961.10
wild ass 271.10
wildcat 366.3
wildebeest 366.10
wild-eyed rabid 503.13
  overwrought 824.10
wilderness
  complexity 59.3
  waste 169.2
  (plain 344.1)
  woods 367.7
wildfire 382.8
wild flower, wildflower 845.4
wild fowl, wildfowl 366.22
wild-goose chase
  bootless errand 645.3, 6
  difficulty 704.7
  failure 732.1
  go on a wild-goose chase 699.7
wild West 183.1
wildwood 367.7
wile deceit 545.3
  artifice 702.3
will n. volition 600
  resolution 604.1
  purpose 620.1
  testament 771.1
  bequest 784.6

at will 600.5
  (freely 748.21)
  (permission 760.7)
 have a will of one's
  own
  have one's will 600.2
  be independent 748.8
  with a will 602.11
will v.
  exercise volition
   600.2
  (choose 609.7)
  resolve 604.6
  bequeath 784.13
 will he, nill he;
  will I, nill I 601.15
willed minded 600.3
  willing 602.8
willful, wilful 606.6
willing volitional 600.4
  well-disposed 602.8
  (assenting 488.11)
  (teachable 539.7)
  (consenting 762.3)
 be willing 602.6
  (assent 488.6)
  (consent 762.2)
willingly 602.11
  (permissibly 760.7)
  (consentingly 762.4)
  (with pleasure
   827.13)
willingness 602
  (assent 488.1)
  (eagerness 682.3)
  (consent 762.1)
will-o'-the-wisp 420.11
willow tree 367.6
  emblem of sorrow
   839.4
will power 604.2
  (will 600.1)
willy-nilly
  in disorder 59.13
  necessarily 601.15
wilt 688.4
wilted 659.12
wily 702.6
wimble 262
wimple 225.26
win n. 731.3
win v. triumph 731.6
  gain 775.6
 win one's spurs
  triumph 731.6
  acquire honor 873.12
 win over
  convince 484.10
  induce 615.9
  reconcile 831.4
 win through 731.5
wince
  suffer physically
   378.4
  shrink 623.9
  be sensitive 822.4
  suffer mentally 828.9
winch 307.2
wind n. speed 274.6
  windstorm 349.11
 against the wind
  267.56

 betwixt wind and
  water 267.63
 have the wind of
  267.20
 in the wind
  going on 151.5
  imminent 152.3
  bewildered 475.16
 in the wind's eye
  navigation 267.56
  intoxicated 959.21
wind v. zigzag 217.8
  convolve 248.3
  about-ship 267.24
  deviate 279.5
  (turn 311.4)
  air 338.10
  toot 410.8
  ~ a horn 416.18
 wind up end 67.5
  cease 142.6
  strengthen 159.8
  prepare 673.6
  finish 729.3, 4
windbag
  chatterer 584.3
  boaster 884.3
windbound
  bound 229.4; 751.11
  encumbered 706.9
wind cone 267a.29
winded 688.7
wind eddy 349.13
windfall benefit 648.2
  gain 775.2
wind gauge
  weathervane 338.9
  anemometer 349.17
wind gun 727.10
wind indicator 267.29
windiness 349.14
winding n. 248.1
  (circuit 629.1)
winding adj. 248.4
windingly 248.8
winding sheet 363.8
wind instrument 417.4
wind-instrumentalist
  416.2
windjammer
  mariner 269.1
  ship 273.2
  musician 416.2
  chatterer 584.3
  boaster 884.3
windlass ship 273.14
  lifter 307.2
windless 688.7
windmill
  gyroscope 273a.10
  rotator 312.4
windmill plane 273a.1
window opening 260.5
  transparency 425.2
  eye 441.7
windowpane
  window 260.5
  glass 384.14
  transparency 425.2
window shade 260.5
window-shop 795.4
window-shopper 795.2

windowshut
  window 260.5
  shutter 424.3
window shutter 260.5
window sill
  base 215.3
  window 260.5
windpipe 351.3
  (conduit 350.4)
windshield 272.16
windstorm 349.11
wind-swept 349.25
windup 67.1
windward n. 236.3
  (navigation 267.1)
windward adj. 236.8
  (direction 278.14)
windy blowy 349.25, 31
  (airy 338.11)
  grandiloquent 577.7
  loquacious 584.5
  boastful 884.7
wine n. 959.7
wine adj. 434.9
winebibber 959.11
winebibbing n. 959.1
winebibbing adj.
  959.23
wine cooler 387.1
winery 959.14
wing n. addition 39.3
  member 51.4
  side 236.1
  airplane 273a.10
  ~ of fowl 298.25
  lever 307.4
  stage 599.12, 15
  flight 623.2
  military unit 726.9
 on the wing
  moving 264.10
  on the way 270.13
  departing 293.10
wing v. fly 267a.30
  transport 270.8
wing and wing 267.55
wing chair 215.22
wing cover 223.17
wingcut 599.15
winged adjunct 39.4
  fast 274.13
 Winged Horse 318.6
wink n. instant 113.3
  signal 550.3
  ~ of sleep 683.5
wink v. blink 443.11
  signal 550.20
 wink at
  not look 442.5
  disregard 460.4
  connive at 760.3
  not observe 773.3
  condone 918.3
winker eye 441.7
  blinkard 443.6
winking 443.6
winkle 223.16
winner
  good thing 648.4
  victor 731.4
winning n. 731.3
winning adj.

 alluring 617.5
  delightful 829.8
  winsome 894.12
winnings 775.2
winnow segregate 55.4
  fan 338.10
  analyze 461.17
  select 609.7
  refine 652.10
  (eliminate 42.3)
winsome alluring
  617.5
  (likable 897.17)
  delightful 829.8
  cheerful 836.11
  courteous 894.12
winter season 126a.5
  old age 128.2
  cold weather 383.3
winterlike 383.8
wintertide, wintertime
  126a.5
wintry, wintery
  seasonal 126a.6
  cold 383.8
wipe n. blow 276.3
  gibe 930.3
wipe v. strike 276a.8
  dry 340.5
  clean 652.9
  beat 972.6
 wipe out excise 38.5
  destroy 162.4
  kill 361.10
  obliterate 552.2
 wipe the slate clean
  clear of debt 808.8
  forgive 918.3
 wipe up 162.4
wire n. fastening 45.4
  cord 205.3
  airplane 273a.10
  telegram 532a.3
  pickpocket 792.6
wire v. 532a.8
wiredrawn 205.7
wireless n. speed 274.6
  telephony 532a
 by wireless 684.7
wireless v.
  telegraph 532a.8
  radiobroadcast
   532a.9
wireless adj. 532a.10
wireless telegraph,
  wireless telephone
  532a.5
wirepull 175.6
wirepuller
  influence 175.5
  politician 694.4
  schemer 702.4
wirepulling
  influence 175.4
  intrigue 626.6
  cunning 702.1
wiresmith 690.6
wireway 627.6
wireworker 690.9
wireworks 691
wireworm 366.25

wiry — womanhood

wiry strong 159.10
  stringy 205.7
wis believe 484.8
  suppose 514.6
wisdom
  wise saying 496.2
  sagacity 498.3
  (intellect 450.1)
  (judgment 480.1)
  (knowledge 490.1)
  (foresight 510.1)
  (farsightedness 510.1)
  (experience 698.4)
  (prudence 864.1)
wise *n.*
  the ~ 500.3
  way 627.1
wise *adj.*
  ~ to 490.13
  sagacious 498.11
  (philosophical 451.38)
  (judicial 480.12)
  (knowing 490.12)
  (informed 490.15)
  (sage 500.4)
  (expedient 646.4)
  (experienced 698.15)
wiseacre sciolist 493.2
  wise person 500.2
  (fool 501.1)
wisecrack *n.* 842.4
wisecrack *v.* 842.8
wisecracker 844
wise guy sciolist 493.2
  wiseacre 500.2
  insolent person 885.3
wiseman, wise man 500.1
wise men of Gotham 501.1
wisenheimer, wiseheimer 500.2
wish *n.* will 600.1
  desire 865.1
  (intention 620.1)
wish *v.* 865.11
  best wishes
  hail! 894.15
  congratulation 896.1
  benevolence 906.1
  meet one's wishes
  consent 762.2
  please 829.4
  (gratify 865.15)
wishbone
  wish-bringer 865.9
  wish-giver 993.4
wisher 865.7
wishful 865.16
wishing cap
  wish-bringer 865.9
  wish-giver 993.4
wish-wash 517.3
wishy-washy
  weak 160.14
  insipid 391.2
  unmeaning 517.9
  style 575.2

mediocre 736.3
wisket, whisket 191.9
wisp 72.5
wisteria 438.3
wisteria blue 438.2
wistful
  thoughtful 451.35
  eager 821.6
  desirous 865.16
wistfully 865.22
wit *n.* **intellect** 450.1
  intelligence 498.1
  skill 698.4
  humor 842
  humorist 844
  at one's wit's end
  nonplused 475.16
  at an impasse 704.11
wit *v.* 490.9
  to wit 79.13; 522.9
witan 696.4
witch *n.* fury 173.6
  ugly person 846.3
  shrew 901.4
  malevolent woman 913.5
  sorceress 992.3
witch *v.* 992.4
witch-charmed 992.7
witchcraft 992.1
witch doctor 992.2
witchery
  allurement 617.1
  sorcery 992.1
  spell 993.1
witch-finder 992.2
witch hazel 511.5
witch-hunter 992.2
witching 992.6
witchlike 992.5
witch of Endor
  sorceress 992.3
  medium 994.14
witch-ridden 992.7
witch stick 993.3
witchwork 992.1
witenagemot, witenagemote 696.4
with in addition 37.9
  in conjunction 88.9
  in company with 88.9
  (jointly 43.14)
  by means of 632.4
withal *adv.* 88.9
withal *prep.* 37.9
withdraw deduct 38.4
  go back 283.5
  recede 287.2
  depart 293.4
  (absent oneself 187.8)
  extract 301.5
  recant 607.9
  abandon 624.3
  resign 757.2
withdrawal
  exclusion 55.1
  progression 283.1
  recession 287.1
  departure 293.1
  (absence 187.1)

extraction 301.1
  recantation 607.3
  rejection 610.1
  abandonment 624.1
  resignation 757.1
  seclusion 893.2
withdrawment 757.1
withdrawn 44.12
withe fastening 45.2
  handle 215.7
wither age 128.7
  shrink 195.4
  dry 340.5
  deteriorate 659.6
withered shrunk 195.6
  thin 203.11
  dried 340.9
  time-worn 659.12
withering
  tyrannical 739.5
  desolating 830.17
  scornful 930.8
  censorious 932.11
withers 250.2
withhold
  keep secret 528.11
  restrain 751.6
  prohibit 761.2
  hold back 781.4
  stint 819.3
  abstain 953.5
within 221.12, 13
  from within 221.12
  within an ace of
  almost 32.15
  near 197.11
withindoors, withinforth, withinside, withinward 221.12
without *adv.*
  lacking 187.16
  externally 220.8
  around 227.5
  wanting 640.11
  be without 777a.2
without *prep.*
  minus 38.11
  excluding 55.7
without *conj.* 8.8
withstand 719.3
  (counteract 179.3)
  (oppose 708.2)
withy 45.2
witless
  mindless 450a.2
  scatterbrained 458.13
  ignorant 491.8
  unintelligent 499.11
witling wiseacre 500.2
  fool 501.1
  humorist 844
witness *n.*
  spectator 444.1
  testimony 467.2
  deponent 467.6
  (litigant 969.9)
  informant 527.5
  voucher 550.11
  bear witness
  testify 467.8
  depose 535.4

promise 768.3
witness *v.* **attend** 186.9
  see 441.10
  (be spectator 444.3)
  testify 467.8
witness box 966.6
wits intellect 450.1
  intelligence 498.1
witticism 842.4
  (maxim 496.1)
wittingly 620.5
witty 842.9
  (amusing 840.22)
wive 903.13
wivern, wyvern 83.7
wizard
  learned man 492.2
  sage 500.1
  proficient 700.1
  sorcerer 992.2
wizen *v.* **shrink** 195.4
  wither 659.6
wizen, wizened, wizenfaced *adj.*
  shrunk 195.6
  thin 203.11
wobble, wabble *n.* 605.1
wobble, wabble *v.*
  vary 149.4
  go slow 275.5
  oscillate 314.8
  flounder 315.9
  be irresolute 605.4
wobbler, wabbler 605.3
wobbly, wabbly 605.5
Woden paternity 166.2
  war 722.7
  god 979.3
woe, wo evil 649.2
  (bane 663.1)
  mental suffering 828.1
  affliction 830.2
  sorrow 837.3
woeful, woful
  deplorable 649.8
  wretched 828.16
  grievous 830.11
  sad 837.9
woefully, wofully 31.23
wold 344.1
wolf *n.* 366.5
  wolf at the door
  danger 667.1
  poverty 804.1
Wolf *n.* 318.6
wolf *v.* 957.3
wolfhound 366.6
wolfish 789.15
woman
  mollycoddle 160a.3
  female 374.2
  (girl 129.5)
  (adult 131.3)
  womankind 374.5
  good ~ 948.2
  prostitute 962.2
womanbody, womanfolk 374.2
womanhood

womanish — work of art

adulthood 131.1
womankind 374.5
womanish 160a.5
  (female 374.11)
womanishness 160a.1
womanism 374.9
womanist 374.10
womanization 160a.2
womanize 160a.4
womankind 374.5
womanlike 160a.5
womanliness 160a.1
womanly
  effeminate 160a.5
  (adult 131.5)
  female 374.11
woman suffrage 374.9
woman-suffragist 374.10
womb 153.4
womera, womerah 727.5
wonder *n.*
  nonesuch 648.4
  astonishment 870
  (surprise 508.2)
  prodigy 872.1
  do wonders
    try one's best 675.5
    be industrious 682.12
    succeed 731.5
  no wonder 871.5
wonder *v.*
  be uncertain 475.6
  be ignorant 491.6
  marvel 870.2
  (not understand 519.5)
wonderful
  unusual 83.10
  astonishing 870.7
  (stupendous 31.8)
  be wonderful 870.5
wonderfully
  remarkably 31.21
  astonishingly 870.9
wonderless 871.3
wonder of the world 872.1
wonder-struck 870.6
  (surprised 508.10)
wonder-worker 992.2
wonder-working 870.7
wondrous
  remarkably 31.21
  astonishing 870.7
wont *n.* custom 613.2
  usage 677.2
wont *v.*
  habituate 613.8
  be accustomed 613.10
wont *adj.* 613.12
  be wont 613.10
wonted
  customary 613.11, 12
  conventional 852.8
wonting 613.2
woo solicit 865.13
  court 902.7
wood backwoods 183.1

saddle 215.23
woods 367.7
firewood 388.3
lumber 635.3
(tree 367.6)
wood chopper 371.2
woodchuck 366.17
woodchuck day 138.7
woodcut
  engraving 558.3
  screen 599.15
woodcutter 371.2
wooded rough 256.12
  arboraty 367.15
wooden 367.15
wood engraving 558.1, 3
woodenhead 501.1
wooden horse 975.3
wooden spoon 493.1
wooden walls
  fortification 717.4
  battleships 726.10, 11
woodland *n.*
  backwoods 183.1
  woods 367.7
woodland *adj.* 183.3
wood louse 366.24
woodmote 966.2
wood-note 412.1
woodpeck, woodpecker 366.22
woodsman 371.2
wood turpentine 356.3
wood winds 417.4
woodworker
  craftsman 690.5
  worker 690.9
woody 367.15
wooer 897.6
wooing 902.2
wool thread 205.5
  cloth 219.5
  hair 256.3, 10
  softness 324.3
woolen, woollen
  rustic 183.3
  rude 851.7
woolgathering *n.* 458.3
woolgathering *adj.* 458.11
woolly, wooly *n.* 225.25
  nappy 256.15
  (smooth 255.5)
  downy 324.7
woolly-headed 256.13
woolpack 353.5
woolsack
  official seat 747.5
  seat of justice 966.1
woon, wun 745.7
woozy 458.12
wop alien 57.3
  Italian 188.9
woppish 188.11
word *n.*
  testimony 467.2
  maxim 496.1
  report 527.1
  news 532.1

message 532.2
affirmation 535.1, 2
vocable 562
  (name 564.3)
statement 582.4
talk 588.1
promise 768.1
give one's word
  testify 467.8
  promise 768.3
in a word 572.4
in other words 522.9
keep one's word
  keep faith 772.4
  be honorable 939.6
the Word Deity 976.5
  Bible 985.2
upon my word
  I'll warrant 535.8
  I promise 768.8
word for word 19.14
  (exactly 494.16)
word to the wise
  reminder 505.5
  tip 527.3
  advice 695.1
word *v.* phrase 566.3
  talk 582.6
wordbook 593.4
word-bound 585.4
word-catcher 936.1
wordcraft 582.3
wordiness 573.1
  (verbiage 562.3)
wording 569.1
wordless 581.7
word of command
  call 550.16
  battle cry 722.3
  command 741.1
word of honor 768.1
word of mouth 582.1
  by word of mouth 582.13
word painter
  author 593.15
  storyteller 594.4
word painting 594.1
wordplay 842.5
  (equivoque 520.2)
words speech 582.1
  quarrel 713.3
have words with
  quarrel 713.7
  reprove 932.8
word-seller 593.15
word-slinger 584.3
wordy 573.7
work *n.* product 161.6
  agency 170.1
  musical ~ 415.3
  writing 590.3
  book 593.1
  business 625.1, 5
  task 625.2
  labor 686.1, 3
  (difficulty 704.1)
at work
  operative 170.4
  busy 682.20
  (acting 680.7)
  (**laboring** 686.9)

be at work 625.7
work *v.* produce 153.7
  operate 170.2
  leaven 320.6
  ferment 353.8
  employ 677.5
  act 680.5
  do 680.6
  labor 686.6, 8
  (busy 625.6)
  (be busy 682.13)
  embroider 847.11
work for aid 707.8
  serve 746.8
work in
  foist in 10.4
  interject 228.8
  intrude 228.10
work on 175.6
work one's way
  advance 282.2
  pass 302.2
  forge ahead 682.12
  labor 686.6
  succeed 731.5
  prosper 734.5
work out solve 481a.4
  do 680.6
  complete 729.2
work up form 240.6
  excite 824.2
  enrage 900.11
work well
  go easily 705.3
  succeed 731.5
workability 470.2
workable
  operative 170.4
  practicable 470.6
workaday, workday
  businesslike 625.11
  working 686.9
  ordinary 849.3
worked up 900.13
worker bee 366.24
workman 690.2
workfellow 890.3
workgirl, workhand 690.2
work horse
  horse 271.3
  laborer 690.2
workhouse
  workshop 691
  prison 752.1
working *n.*
  agency 170.1
  workings of the mind 451.1
working *adj.*
  tending to 176.3
  busy 682.20
  laboring 686.9
workingman, workman 690.2
workmanship
  production 161.1
  handiwork 680.3
work of art 556.8
  (production 161.6)
  (beauty 845.4)
  (**virtue** 847.10)

workout — wrinkle 1180

workout 463.1
  give a workout 463.8
works
  the ~ 50.2
  workshop 691
  good ~ 906.2
  give the works 361.10
workshop 691
workwoman 690.2
world
  quantities 31.3
  affairs 151.2
  boundlessness 180.4
  universe 318
  people 372.2
  fashionable ~ 852.4
  a world of 102.5
  the world beyond 121.3
  come into the world 359.7
worldling person 372.3
  self-seeker 943.2
  irreligionist 988.4; 989.4
worldly
  earthly 318.14
  unspiritual 989.9
  (selfish 943.4)
worldly-minded 989.9
worldly-wise 698.8, 15
world-self, world soul, world spirit 359.3
  (God 976.2)
World War 722.4
world-wide
  universal 78.11
  (extensive 31.7)
  unlimited 180.7
world-wise 698.15
world without end 112.5
worm n.
  diminutive 193.2
  coil 248.2
  insect 366.25
  (larva 129.8)
  blight 663.2
  (destroyer 165.1)
  (decay 659.2)
worm in the apple
  evil 649.2
  blight 663.2
  source of distress 830.2
worm v.
  convolve 248.3
  creep 275.6
worm in
  foist in 10.4
  interject 228.8
  intrude 228.10
worm out
  pump 461.15
  discover 481a.3
worm-eaten 659.13
wormer 622.5
wormlike 248.6
wormwood 395.3
worn impaired 659.12
  (unsound 160.13)
  (used 677.7)

exhausted 688.6
worried 828.15
worry n.
  annoyance 828.4
  trouble 830.2
worry v. fuss 825.6
  fret 828.10
  harass 830.5
worrying 830.12
worse
  impaired 659.12
  aggravated 835.4
become worse 659.6
go from bad to worse
  deteriorate 659.6
  (be aggravated 835.3)
  fail 732.5
render worse 835.2
worse and worse
  unsatisfactory 832.7
  aggravated 835.6
worship n.
  (reverence 928.1)
  (obeisance 928.2)
  (piety 987.1)
worship v.
  venerate 928.4
  ~ God 990.9
  (revere 928.4)
  (idolize 991.6)
worshiper, worshipper 990.8
worshipful
  noble 873.18
  devout 990.15
  (reverent 928.8)
  (pious 987.10)
worst 731.9
worsted n. 219.5
worsted adj. 732.12
wort 367.2
worth n.
  consideration 147.2
  excellence 648.1
  utility 644.1
  value 812.3
  virtue 944.1
worth adj. 777.7
for all one is worth 274.15
not worth a straw
  paltry 643.12
  (useless 645.8)
  poor 804.7
not worth one's salt 645.8
worth one's salt 644.6
worth the whistle 815.8
worthless
  paltry 643.12
  (nugatory 158.11)
  useless 645.8
worthlessness 645.2
worth-while 646.4, 6
not worth-while 643.12
worthy n.
  personage 642.5
  great man 873.9
  good person 948.1

worthy adj.
  reputable 873.15
  entitled 924.5, 11
  praiseworthy 931.11
  honorable 939.7
  virtuous 944.3
would-be
  so-called 565.7
  upstart 876.8
  arrogant 885.8
wound n. injury 659.4
  (sore 655.16)
  mental pain 830.2
wound v. pain 378.4
  harm 649.6
  (be malevolent 907.5)
  injure 659.8
  (afflict 655.22)
  pique 824.5
  ~ the feelings 830.3
  offend 900.10
wounded
  distressed 828.13
  offended 900.12
woven 219.11
wrack
  destruction 162.1
  wreck 162.3
  seaweed 367.3
go to wrack and ruin 162.5
wraith 980a.1, 2
wraithlike 980a.4
wrangle argue 476.11
  demur 485.7
  object 489.4
  quarrel 713.7
  (contend 720.8)
  find fault 932.7
wrangler arguer 476.9
  learned man 492.1
  student 541.4
  oppositionist 710.2
  disputant 726.1
wranglesome 901.9
wrangling
  argumentation 476.2
  quarreling 713.3
wrap n. covering 223
  (warmth 384.13)
  cloak 225.15
wrap v. cover 223.23
  clothe 225.41
  close 261.2
wrap up cover 223.23
  clothe 225.41
wrap-around 225.15, 17
wrapper cover 223.11
  (enclosure 232.1)
  garment 225.15, 23
  undergarment 225.25
wrapping 223.11
wraprascal, wrap-round, wrap-up 225.15, 17
wrath 900.1
wrathful 900.13
wreak inflict 739.4
  ~ vengeance 919.4

wreath n.
  network 219.4
  tail 235.6
  circle 247.2
  flowers 400.4
  trophy 733.1
  decoration 847.5
Wreath n. 318.6
wreath, wreathe v. 219.8
  (convolve 248.3)
wreathy 248.4
wreck n.
  destruction 162.3
  deterioration 659.5
  accident 735.3
go to wreck 162.5
wreck v. destroy 162.4
  shipwreck 267.33
wrecked 732.10
wrecker 792.3
Wren 726.10
wrench n.
  extraction 301.2
  turn 311.2
  tool 781.2
wrench v. distort 243.3
  jerk 285.5
  ~ from 789.11
wrest distort 243.3
  extract 301.6
  force from 744.2
  seize 789.9, 11
wrestle 720.8
wrestler
  strong man 159.6
  combatant 726.1
  (player 840.17)
wrestling 720.7
  (sports 840.10)
wretch sufferer 828.8
  beggarly fellow 876.9
  reprobate 949.1
wretched paltry 643.12
  deplorable 649.8
  miserable 828.16
  (sorrowful 837.11)
  (mournful 839.13)
  (in despair 859.7)
  disreputable 874.8
wretchedly 32.12
wretchedness 828.3
  (sorrow 837.3)
  (despair 859.1)
wriggle wiggle 315.9
  be excited 824.7
  wriggle into 294.6
  wriggle out of 671.6
wright 690.7
wring distort 243.3
  convolve 248.3
  extract 301.6
  pain 378.4
  clean 652.9
  force from 744.2
  take 789.11
  extort 791.13
  torture 830.6
  ~ one's hand 839.11
wringing-wet 339.8
wrinkle n. fold 258.1

(furrow 259.1)
novel idea 453.1
wrinkle *v.* age 128.7
  contract 195.4
  convolve 248.3
  roughen 256.11
  fold 258.3
wrinkled aged 128.8
  angular 244.5
  rough 256.12
wrinkly rough 256.12
  folded 258.4
wristband 225.31
writ decree 741.3
  law 969
  (warrant 467.5)
write
  ~ music 415.26
  pen 590.13
  (dramatize 599.25)
  correspond 592.6
  ~ poetry 597.11
  ~ prose 598.3
  write down 551.8
  (write 590.13)
writer penman 590.11
  (recorder 553.1)
  correspondent 592.5
  author 593.15, 16
  (producer 164.1)
  (annalist 553.2)
  (narrator 594.4)
  (poet 597.10)
  (playwright 599.22)
  notary 968.1
write-up
  publicity 531.3
  writing 590.3
  commentary 595.2
writhe distort 243.3
  wiggle 315.9
  suffer physically 378.4
  be excited 824.7
  suffer mentally 828.9
writing
  written language 590
  (record 551.1)
  (production 161.6)
  book 593.1
  in writing 590.15
  put in writing 551.8
  (write 590.13)
writing frame 442.2
writing paper 590.10
writ of error 969.6
writ of protection 969.2
written
  in writing 590.15
  (literal 561.9)
  (destined 601.13)
  it is written 601.16
written law 697.1
wrong *n.* error 495.1
  evil 649.2
  impropriety 923
  (inexpedience 647.1)
  (undueness 925.1)
  (improbity 940.1)

(injustice 941a.1)
sin 945.1
misdeed 947.2
be in the wrong 495.7
do wrong 941a.2
in the wrong
  mistaken 495.13
  wrong 923.4
wrong *v.* 649.6
wrong *adj.*
  erroneous 495.12, 13
  unseemly 647.3
  bad 649.8
  morally ~ 923.4
  (inexpedient 647.3)
  (undue 925.8)
  (reprehensible 932.14)
  (unjustifiable 941a.4)
  unjust 941a.3
  wicked 945.11
be wrong err 495.7
  be improper 923.3
wrong *adv.* 649.11; 923.5
wrongdoer 949.2
  (evildoer 913.1)
wrongdoing vice 945.6
  misdeed 947.2
wrongful
  improper 923.4
  unjust 941a.3
  unlawful 964.5
wrongheaded 481.9
wrongly 923.5
wroth 900.13
wrought 729.6
wrought iron 635.6
wrought-up
  excited 824.9
  angry 900.13
wry 217.13
make a wry face
  suffer physical pain 378.4
  suffer mental pain 828.9
  express discontent 832.3
  grieve 839.11
  show dislike 867.4
  disapprove 932.5
wung-out 267.55
wynd square 189.19
  yard 232.1
wyvern See **wivern**

X

x 491.2
X 219.6
xanthein, xanthin 436.4
xanthic 436.6
Xanthippe, Xantippe 901.4
xanthocarpous 436.6
xanthochroia, xanthochromia 436.2
xanthoderma 436.2

xanthophyll, xanthophyl 436.4
xanthosis 436.2
  (discoloration 440a.1)
xebec 273.2
xenodochium 189.8
xenogamy, xenogenesis 161.2
xenogenetic 161.11
xerophagy 956.2
xiphoid 253.15
xiphopagus 83.7
Xmas 138.7
X ray light ray 420.3
  picture 556.12
X-ray photography 556.4
xyloglyphy 557.1
xylograph 558.3
xylographer 559.6
xylography 558.1, 2
xylophone 417.10

Y

y 491.2
Y fork 91.2
  crotch 244.2
yacht *n.* 273.2
yacht *v.* 267.10
yachting 267.1
yaffle 25.2
yager See **jäger**
Yahoo 876.7
yak 366.13
yam 298.30
Yama 979.4
yammer 839.8
yank *n.* 285.3
yank *v.* 285.5
Yankee alien 57.3
  American 188.9
Yankeeland 182.3
yap *n.* 260.2
yap *v.* yelp 411.5
  bark 412.2
yard thousand 98.10
  length 200.6
  enclosure 232.1
  (plot 181.3)
  (square 189.19)
  spar 273.12
  workshop 691
yardarm 273.12
yardarm to yardarm
  side by side 236.9
  alongside ship 267.62
yardstick 466.2, 4
yare 682.17
yarn thread 205.2
  falsehood 546.1
  narrative 594.2
  joke 842.4
yarr 412.2
yashmak, yashmac 225.12
  (shade 424.1)
yataghan, yatagan 727.3

yaup See **yawp**
yaw *n.*
  aeronautics 267a.6
  deviation 279.2
yaw *v.*
  navigate 267.23, 24
  (deviate 279.4)
  aviate 267a.31
yawl *n.* 273.2
yawl *v.*
  yowl 411.5; 412.2
  wail 839.9
yawmeter 267a.29
yawn gape 260.13
  be sleepy 683.9
  (be fatigued 688.4)
  be bored 841.7
yawning *n.* 260.9
yawning *adj.*
  abysmal 208.9
  gaping 260.15
yawny sleepy 683.15
  fatiguing 688.8
yawp, yaup 411.5; 412.2
y-clept, y-cleped 564.8
Ydalir 981.3
yea *n.* 488.1
yea *adv.*
  still more 33.10
  yes 488.14
yean 161.9
year 108.1
in years 128.8
year after year
  repeatedly 104.8
  long 110.11
  constantly 136.6
yearbook
  record 551.2, 3
  journal 593.6
yearling infant 129.6
  calf 366.12
yearly 138.11
yearn pine 837.6
  ~ for 865.11
yearning desire 865.2
  (love 897.1)
  compassion 914.1
year-old 129.6
years long time 110.3
  age 128.1
yeast 320.3
yeasty 320.8
yegg, yeggman 792.2
yell *n.* cry 411.1
  cheer 838.4
yell *v.* shout 411.5, 7
  cheer 838.8
  wail 839.9
yellow *n.* 436.1
yellow *v.* 436.5
yellow *adj.*
  golden 436.6
  sensational 824.12
  cowardly 862.4
  jealous 920.3
yellow book 551.2
yellow boy 800.5, 6
yellow-cross liquid 334.2

yellow-eyed — zincograph 1182

yellow-eyed
  poor-sighted 443.14
  jealous 920.3
yellow-faced 436.6
yellow fever 655.6
yellow flag 668.3
  (alarm 669.1)
yellow jack
  disease 655.6
  warning sign 668.3
yellow jacket 366.24
yellow journalism 824.1
Yellowknife 434.5
yellow madder 436.1
yellowness 436
yellow ocher, yellow peril, yellow race 436.4
yellow streak 862.1
  have a yellow streak 862.3
yelp yap 411.5
  bark 412.2
  wail 839.9
  ~ at 932.8
yen n. money 800.8
  desire 865.2
yen v. 865.11
Yenisei 560.4
yeoman seaman 269.3
  agriculturist 371.2
  soldier 726.4, 7
  retainer 746.1
yeoman of the guard
  guard 717.6
  soldier 726.4, 7
yeomanry 726.6
yep 488.14
yerk n. 276.3
yerk v. strike 276.8
  jerk 285.5
  ~ out 416.21
yes n. 488.1
yes v. 488.6
yes adv. 488.14
  (certainly! 474.16)
  (affirmation 535.8)
  (permission 760.7)
  (consent 762.4)
yes man 886.2
yesterday, yesteryear 122.2
yet notwithstanding 30.8
  additionally 37.8
  still 106.7
  previously 116.5
  until now 118.4
  (formerly 122.14)
  nevertheless 469.7, 8
yew tree 367.6
  wood 635.3
yew green 435.2
Yid 188.9
Yiddish 188.11
yield n. product 161.6
  crop 636.3
yield v. bear 161.9
  (be profitable 775.10)
  be pliant 324.5

(be elastic 325.3)
  assent 488.6
  acknowledge 488.9
  relinquish 624.3; 782.3
  provide 637.4
  submit 725.3
  consent 762.2
  (be induced 615.10)
  part with 784.11
  bring in 810.4
  (be received 785.4)
  sell for 812.6
yield the ghost 360.6
yield the palm
  be inferior 34.4
  surrender 725.4
yielding n.
  submission 725.1
  consent 762.1
yielding adj.
  flexible 324.6
  (manageable 705.6)
  submissive 725.5
  (meek 826.10)
Ymir, Ymer 192.8
yodel, yodle 416.20
yoga, Yoga 955.1; 994.1
yogi, yogin
  ascetic 955.2
  (religious 996.11)
  Hindu 984.21
  occultist 994.13
  priest 996.8
yogism 994.1
yogist 984.21
yo-ho v. 411.5
yo-ho int. 457.10
yoick 411.5
yoicks! 622.12
yoke n. fastening 45.2
  pair 89.2
  frame 215.8
  fetter 752.2
  (subjection 749.1)
shake off the yoke
  escape 671.6
  go free 750.4
yoke v. attach 43.6
  pair 89.3
  ~ horses 370.7
yokefellow 890.3
yokel oaf 501.1
  awkward fellow 701
  rustic 876.5
yokeldom 183.1
yokelish 183.3
yokemate 903.5
yolk 436.3
yon, yond, yonder
  that 79.10
  distance 196.5, 7, 8
yore, yoretime 122.2
of yore
  formerly 122.14
  old 124.6
Yorktown 722.5
Yoshiwara 961.7
you
  you are welcome! 784.17

you bet! 535.8
  (yes! 488.14)
young n. 167.3
young adj. 127.5
younger 127.8
younglet 129.7
youngling n. 129
  (offspring 167.4)
youngling adj. 127.5
young man 897.6
youngster, younker 129.1
yours truly 79.4
youth youthhood 127
  youngling 129.1, 4, 7
youthful 127.5
  make youthful 127.4
youthhead, youthheid 127.1
youthy 127.5
yowl howl 411.5; 412.2
  wail 839.9
Ypres 722.5
yucca 253.2
Yuga 108.2
yule log 388.3
yuletide
  anniversary 138.7
  holytide 998.13
yummy 394.7
Yurak 560.4

Z

z 491.2
Z 67.1
Zadkiel
  weather prophet 513.3
  angel 977.1
zaffer, zaffre 438.4
zag n. zigzag 217.4
  angle 244.2
zag v. zigzag 217.8
  angle 244.4
zambo mongrel 41.5
  Negro 431.4
zamindar, zemindar 779.2
zamindari, zamindary 780.4
zany fool 501.1
  comedian 599.20
  buffoon 844
zarabanda See saraband
zeal eagerness 682.3
  (resolution 604.1)
  fervor 821.2
  ambition 865.2
zealot fanatic 504.2
  (dogmatist 474.4)
  (opinionist 606.3)
  (live wire 682.10)
  (religious 983a.6)
  devotee 840.19
  votary 865.7
zealotic 503.18
  (dogmatic 474.15)
zealotry 503.7
  (dogmatism 474.3)

(hyperorthodoxy 983a.5)
zealous eager 682.18
  ardent 821.6
  pious 987.10
zebra 440.2
  (animal 366.2)
zebrass 41.5
  (animal 366.2)
zebrawood 635.3
zebrula, zebrule 41.5
zebu 366.12
Zechariah 513.2
zemindar, zemindari
  See zamindar
zemstvo 696.1
Zenaga 560.4
zenana harem 374.7
  abode of love 897.10
Zend-Avesta 986.1
zendik 984.20
zenith 210.1
  in the zenith
  great 31.6
  paramount 642.14
  eminent 873.18
zenithal 210.6
Zephaniah 513.2
zephyr n. 349.5
Zephyr, Zephyrus n. 349.2
zephyr v. 349.22
Zeppelin, zeppelin 273a.5
zero 87a.1
  (nothing 2.2)
zero hour crisis 134.4
  attack 716.1
zest pleasure 377.1
  relish 394.2
  (taste 390.1)
zetetic n. inquiry 461.1
  investigation 461.9
  inquirer 461.12
zetetic adj. 461.24
Zeus paternity 166.2
  god 979.2
zig n. zigzag 217.4
  angle 244.2
zig v. zigzag 217.8
  angle 244.4
ziganka music 415.7
  dance 840.7
zigzag n.
  obliquity 217.4
  (deviation 279.2)
  (circuit 629.1)
  angle 244.2
  ornamentation 847.3
zigzag v. stagger 217.8
  angle 244.4
  alternate 314.10
zigzag adj. 217.16
  (angular 244.5)
  (deviate 279.8)
  (circuitous 311.6; 629.3)
zigzag adv. 314.14
zinc 635.6
zinc green 435.2, 4
zincograph 558.3

zincographer 559.6
zincography 558.1
zinc orange 439.3
zinc white 430.4
zingaro, zingano 268.2
Zion 981.1
zip *n.* 392.1
zip *v.* speed 274.9
  sibilate 409.3
zippy 392.5
zircon 847.8
zircon light light 420.7
  lamp 423.3
zither 417.2
zitherist 416.3
zocle See socle
zodiac zone 230.2
  circle 247.2
  constellation 318.6
  signs of the zodiac
    constellation 318.6
  astrology 318.8
zodiacal light 420.12
zoetic 359.10

zoic 366.26
Zoilus 936.1
Zollverein
  society 712.4
  treaty 769.2
zonar, zonnar
  zone 230.2
  circle 247.2
zone region 181.1
  latitude 181.5
  layer 204.1
  circuit 230.2
  (enclosure 232.1)
  circle 247.2
zoo 370.3
zoogloea, zooglea
  microbe 193.4
  germ 357.4
zoogloeal 357.10
zoogonidium 193.4
zoographer 368.2
zoography 368.1
zooid *n.* 357.4
  (animal 366.2)

zooid *adj.*
  organic 357.8
  animal 366.26
zoological 368.11
  (animal 366.26)
zoological garden
  370.3
zoologist 368.2
  (naturalist 357.7)
zoology 368
  (science 357.5;
  490.8)
zoom *n.* 267a.24
zoom *v.* 267a.31
zoon 357.4
  (animal 366.2)
zoophobia 860.4
zoophorus 210.4
Zoophyta, zoophytes
  366.1
zoospore
  microbe 193.4
  sperm 357.4
zootomist 368.2

zootomy 368.1
zoril animal 366.3
  malodor 401.2
Zoroaster 986.3
Zoroastrian *n.*
  382.11 ; 991.5
Zoroastrian *adj.* 984.21
Zoroastrianism
  fire worship 382.11;
  991.1
  religion 984.11
Zouave 726.4
zounds! 870.11
zucchetto 999.1
Zulu 876.7
Zulu-Kaffir 560.4
zwieback 298.11
zygospore 193.4
zygote microbe 193.4
  germ 357.4
zyme 320.3
zymic, zymogenic,
  zymological, zy-
  molytic 320.8

ABBREVIATIONS USED IN THIS BOOK

abbr.	abbreviation	Gram.	grammar
adj.	adjective	Heb.	Hebrew
adv.	adverb	Her.	heraldry
Aeronaut.	aeronautics, aeronautical	Hind.	Hindustani
Alg.	algebra	Hist.	history, historical
Amer.	America, American	Hunt.	hunting
Anat.	anatomy	illit.	illiterate
Antiq.	antiquity	Ind.	India, Indian
Arab.	Arabian	*int.*	interjection
arch.	archaic	Ir.	Irish
Arch.	architecture	iron.	irony, ironical
Archaeol.	archaeology	It.	Italian
Astrol.	astrology	Jap.	Japanese
Astron.	astronomy	joc.	jocose, jocular
Austral.	Australia	journ.	journalistic
Biogeog.	biogeography	L.	Latin
Biol.	biology	*masc.*	masculine
Bot.	botany	Math.	mathematics
Calif.	California	meas.	measure
Can.	Canada	Mech.	mechanics
Carp.	Carpentry	med.	medical
Chem.	Chemistry	Med.	medicine
Ch.	church	Metal.	metallurgy
Chin.	China, Chinese	Meteorol.	meteorology
coll.	colloquial	Mil.	military
Com.	commerce	Min.	mineralogy, mining
conj.	conjunction	ML.	medieval Latin
crim.	criminal	Moham.	Mohammedan
Criminol.	criminology	Mongol.	Mongolia
Cryst.	crystallography	Mus.	music
Dent.	dentistry	Myth.	mythology
derog.	derogatory	*n.*	noun
dial.	dialect	N.Afr.	North Africa
Du.	Dutch	N.Amer.	North America
Eccl.	ecclesiastical	Naut.	nautical
Econ.	economics	Nav.	naval
Elec.	electricity	NL.	New Latin
Eng.	England, English	North.	northern
erron.	erroneous	Numis.	numismatics
etc.	etcetera	obs.	obsolete
exc.	except	obsoles.	obsolescent
F.	French	orig.	original (ly)
fem.	feminine	Per.	Persian
fig.	figurative	Pg.	Portuguese
Fort.	fortification	Pharm.	pharmacy
G.	German	Philos.	philosophy
Geol.	geology	Phonet.	phonetics
Geom.	geometry	*phr.*	phrase
Gr.	Greek	Phys.	physics

Abbreviations

Physiol.	physiology	Southwest.	southwestern
Phytogeog.	phytogeography	Sp.	Spanish
P.I.	Philippine Islands	spec.	special(ly)
pl.	plural	Sport.	sporting
Polit.	politics, political	Surg.	surgery
Pr.	Provençal	Tech.	technology, technical
prep.	preposition	Teleg.	telegraphy
Print.	printing	Teut.	Teutonic
Pros.	prosody	Theat.	theatrical
Psychol.	psychology	Theol.	theology
R.C.Ch.	Roman Catholic Church	Turk.	Turkish
Railroad	railroading	Univ.	university
Rel.	religion	U.S.	United States
Rom.	Roman	usu.	usually
Russ.	Russian	*v.*	verb
S.Afr.	South Africa	Vet.	veterinary
S.Amer.	South America	vulg.	vulgar
Scot.	Scotland, Scotch, Scottish	West.	western
sing.	singular	W.Ind.	West Indies
South.	southern	Zool.	zoology

AUTHORS QUOTED IN THIS BOOK

Abercrombie, L[ascelles]. 1888–1938.
Adams, F[ranklin] P[ierce]. 1881–
Adams, H[enry Brooks]. 1838–1918.
Addams, J[ane]. 1860–1935.
Addison, [Joseph]. 1672–1719.
Ade, G[eorge]. 1866–1944.
Adler, [Alfred]. 1870–1937.
Aeschylus. 525–456 B.C.
Aesop. Circa 620–560 B.C.
Agesilaus [the Great, King of Sparta]. 444–360 B.C.
Aguecheek [pseudonym of Charles B. Fairbanks]. 1827–1859.
Aiken, C[onrad]. 1889–
Akenside, [Mark] 1721–1770.
Alcott, A[mos] B[ronson]. 1799–1888.
Alcott, L[ouisa May]. 1832–1888.
Aldrich, T[homas Bailey]. 1836–1907.
Allen, E[lizabeth] A[kers]. 1832–1911.
Allen, H[ervey]. 1889–1949.
Allingham, W[illiam]. 1824–1889.
Amiel, [Henri-Frédéric]. 1828–1881.
Anacharsis. Floruit circa 600 B.C.
Archimedes. 287–212 B.C.
Aristotle. 384–322.
Arnold, M[atthew]. 1822–1888.
Atterbury, [Francis]. 1662–1732.
Ausonius, [Decimus Magnus]. Floruit 310–394.
Austen, J[ane]. 1775–1817.
Austin, A[lfred]. 1835–1913.
Bacon, [Francis]. 1561–1626.
Bacon, L[eonard]. 1887–1954.
Bagehot, W[alter]. 1826–1877.
Bagster, S[amuel]. 1800–1835.
Bailey, P[hilip] J[ames]. 1816–1902.
Baillie, [Joanna]. 1762–1851.
Bain, [Alexander]. 1818–1903.
Balfour, [Arthur James]. 1848–1930.
Balzac, [Honoré de]. 1799–1850.
Bangs, J[ohn] K[endrick]. 1862–1922.
Barbauld, A[nna] L[etitia]. 1743–1825.

Barham, [Richard Harris]. 1788–1845.
Baring-Gould, S[abine]. 1834–1924.
Barrie, [Sir James Matthew]. 1860–1937.
Barthélemy, [Auguste Marseille] 1796–1867.
Barton, B[ernard]. 1784–1849.
Baum, V[icki]. 1888–
Bayly, T[homas] H[aynes]. 1797–1839.
Beattie, [James]. 1735–1803.
Beaumont and Fletcher. See Beaumont, [Francis]; Fletcher, [John].
Beaumont, [Francis]. 1584–1616.
Becon, [Thomas]. 1512–1567.
Beecher, H[enry] W[ard]. 1813–87.
Behn, A[phra]. 1640–1689.
Bellinghausen, [Eligius von Münch-]. 1806–1871.
Belloc, [Hilaire]. 1870–1953.
Benét, S[tephen] V[incent]. 1898–1943.
Benét, W[illiam] R[ose]. 1886–1950.
Bennett, A[rnold]. 1867–1931.
Bentham, [Jeremy]. 1748–1832.
Benton, T[homas] H[art]. 1782–1858.
Béranger, [Pierre Jean de]. 1780–1857.
Bergson, [Henri]. 1859–1941.
Berkeley, G[eorge]. 1685–1753.
Bias. Floruit circa 566 B.C.
Bible. Authorized Version.
Bickerstaff, [Isaac]. Circa 1735–circa 1812.
Bierce, A[mbrose]. 1842–?1914.
Bion. Floruit 280 B.C.
Bismarck, [Otto Eduard Leopold, Prince von]. 1815–1898.
Blackmore, [Richard Dodderidge]. 1825–1900.
Blackstone, [Sir William]. 1723–1780.
Blake, W[illiam]. 1757–1827.
Blunt, W[ilfrid] S[cawen]. 1840–1922.

BOETHIUS, [ANICIUS MANLIUS SEVERINUS]. 480?–524.
BOGART, J[OHN B.]. 1845–1921.
BOHN, H[ENRY] G[EORGE], compiler. 1796–1884.
BOILEAU[-DESPRÉAUX, NICHOLAS]. 1636–1711.
BOKER, G[EORGE] H[ENRY]. 1823–1890.
BOLITHO, [WILLIAM, pseudonym of WILLIAM BOLITHO RYALL]. 1890–1930.
BOSSUET, [JACQUES BÉNIGNE]. 1627–1704.
BOSWELL, [JAMES]. 1740–1795.
BOVEE, C[HRISTIAN] N[ESTELL]. 1820–1904.
BRATHWAITE, [RICHARD]. 1588?–1673.
BRETON, N[ICHOLAS]. 1545?–?1626.
BRIDGES, [ROBERT]. 1844–1930.
BRIGHT, J[OHN]. 1811–1889.
BRONTË, E[MILY JANE]. 1818–1848.
BROOKE, R[UPERT]. 1887–1915.
BROOKS, P[HILLIPS]. 1835–1893.
BROOME, [WILLIAM]. 1689–1745.
BROWN, T[HOMAS] E[DWARD]. 1830–1897.
BROWNE, T[HOMAS, SIR]. 1605–1682.
BROWNING, [ROBERT]. 1812–1889.
BRUNO, [GIORDANO]. 1548?–1600.
BRYANT, [WILLIAM CULLEN]. 1794–1878.
BUCKINGHAM, DUKE OF [GEORGE VILLIERS]. 1628–1687.
BUFFON, [GEORGE LOUIS LECLERC DE]. 1707–1788.
BULLEIN, W[ILLIAM]. ?–1576.
BULWER-LYTTON, [EDWARD GEORGE EARLE LYTTON, FIRST BARON LYTTON]. 1803–1873.
BUNYAN, [JOHN]. 1628–1688.
BURGESS, G[ELETT]. 1866–1951.
BURKE, [EDMUND]. 1729–1797.
BURNS, [ROBERT]. 1759–1796.
BURROUGHS, [JOHN]. 1837–1921.
BURTON, R[OBERT]. 1577–1640.
BUSSY-RABUTIN, [ROGER, COMTE] DE. 1618–1693.
BUTLER, N[ICHOLAS] M[URRAY]. 1862–1947.
BUTLER, [SAMUEL]. 1600–1680.
BUTTERWORTH, H[EZEKIAH]. 1839–1905.
BYNNER, W[ITTER]. 1881–
BYROM, [JOHN]. 1692–1763.
BYRON, [GEORGE GORDON, SIXTH BARON]. 1788–1824.
CAESAR, [CAIUS JULIUS]. 102?–44 B.C.

CALDERÓN, [DE LA BARCA, PEDRO]. 1600–1681.
CALLIMACHUS. 3rd century B.C.
CAMDEN, [WILLIAM]. 1551–1623.
CAMPBELL, T[HOMAS]. 1777–1844.
CARLYLE, [THOMAS]. 1795–1881.
CARMAN, [WILLIAM] B[LISS]. 1861–1929.
CARNEY, J[ULIA] F[LETCHER]. 1823–1908.
CARPENTER, H[ENRY] B[ERNARD]. 1840–1887.
CARROLL, [LEWIS, pseudonym of CHARLES LUTWIDGE DODGSON]. 1832–1898.
CATHER, W[ILLA SIBERT]. 1876–1947.
CATO, [DIONYSIUS]. Circa 3rd century A.D.
CATO, [MARCUS PORCIUS] THE ELDER. 234–149 B.C.
CENTLIVRE, S[USANNAH]. 1667?–1723.
CERVANTES, [MIGUEL DE]. 1547–1616.
CHAPMAN, G[EORGE]. 1559?–1634.
CHARLES I, KING [OF ENGLAND]. 1600–1649.
CHAUCER, [GEOFFREY]. 1340?–1400.
CHESTERFIELD, [PHILIP DORMER STANHOPE, FOURTH EARL OF]. 1694–1773.
CHESTERTON, [GILBERT KEITH]. 1874–1936.
CHURCHILL, C[HARLES]. 1731–1764.
CHURCHILL, W[INSTON LEONARD SPENCER]. 1874–
CIBBER, [COLLEY]. 1671–1757.
CICERO, [MARCUS TULLIUS]. 106–43 B.C.
CLARKE, J[OHN], compiler. Published Paroemiologia Anglo-Latina, 1639.
CLAUDEL, P[AUL LOUIS CHARLES]. 1868–1955.
CLAUDIAN(US). Floruit 365–408.
CLEANTHES. Circa 300–220 B.C.
CLEMENCEAU, [GEORGES B. E.]. 1841–1929.
CLEVELAND, [STEVEN GROVER]. 1839–1908.
COBB, I[RVIN SHREWSBURY]. 1876–1944.
COFFIN, R[OBERT] P[ETER] T[RISTRAM]. 1892–1955.
COHAN, G[EORGE MICHAEL]. 1878–1942.
COKE, [SIR EDWARD]. 1552–1634.
COLBY, F[RANK MOORE]. 1865–1925.
COLERIDGE, [SAMUEL TAYLOR]. 1772–1834.
COLERIDGE, H[ARTLEY]. 1796–1849.

Authors Quoted

COLLINS, [WILLIAM]. 1721–1759.
COLLINS, J[OHN] C[HURTON]. 1848–1908.
COLTON, C[HARLES C.]. 1780–1832.
CONFUCIUS. 551–478 B.C.
CONGREVE, [WILLIAM]. 1670–1729.
CONRAD, [JOSEPH]. 1857–1924.
COOKE, R[OSE] T[ERRY]. 1827–1892.
COPELAND, [CHARLES TOWNSEND]. 1860–1952.
COPLAND, [ROBERT]. 1508–1547.
CORNEILLE, [PIERRE]. 1606–1684.
COTTON, N[ATHANIEL]. 1705–1788.
COUÉ, [ÉMILE]. 1857–1926.
COWLEY, [ABRAHAM]. 1618–1667.
COWPER, [WILLIAM]. 1731–1800.
CRABBE, [GEORGE]. 1754–1832.
CRANE, N[ATHALIA]. 1913–
CREIGHTON, [MANDELL]. 1843–1901.
CROMWELL, [OLIVER]. 1599–1658.
CRONIN, A[RCHIBALD] J[OSEPH]. 1896–
CURRAN, J[OHN PHILPOT]. 1750–1817.
CURTIS, G[EORGE WILLIAM]. 1824–1892.
DACRE, H[ARRY]. Floruit 1892.
DANIEL, S[AMUEL]. 1562–1619.
DANTE, [ALIGHIERI]. 1265–1321.
DARWIN, [CHARLES ROBERT]. 1809–1882.
DAVIDSON, J[OHN]. 1857–1909.
DAVIES, J[OHN, SIR]. 1569–1626.
DAY, C[LARENCE]. 1874–1935.
DEFOE, [DANIEL]. 1661?–1731.
DEKKER, [THOMAS]. 1570?–?1641.
DE LA MARE, [WALTER], 1873–1956.
DELONEY, [THOMAS]. 1543?–?1607.
DEMOCRITUS. Floruit circa 400 B.C.
DEMOSTHENES. 385–322 B.C.
DENHAM, J[OHN, SIR]. 1615–1669.
DE QUINCEY, [THOMAS]. 1785–1859.
DESCAMPS, [JEAN BAPTISTE]. 1714–1791.
DESCARTES, [RENÉ]. 1596–1650.
DESTOUCHES, [PHILIPPE N.]. 1680–1754.
DIBDIN, T[HOMAS]. 1771–1841.
DICKENS, [CHARLES]. 1812–1870.
DICKINSON, E[MILY]. 1830–1886.
DIDEROT, [DENIS]. 1713–1784.
DIGBY, K[ENELM HENRY]. 1800–1880.
DILLON, G[EORGE]. 1906–
DIOGENES. Circa 412–323 B.C.
DISRAELI, [BENJAMIN]. 1804–1881.
DOBSON, [HENRY AUSTIN]. 1840–1921.
DONNE, [JOHN]. 1573–1631.
DOSTOEVSKI, [FYODOR]. 1821–1881.

DOUGLAS, [LORD] A[LFRED] B[RUCE]. 1870–1945.
DOYLE, A[RTHUR] CONAN, [SIR]. 1859–1930.
DRAXE, T[HOMAS], compiler. ?–1618.
DRINKWATER, [JOHN]. 1882–1937.
DRYDEN, [JOHN]. 1631–1700.
DUMAS, [ALEXANDRE]. 1824–1895.
DUNSANY, [LORD, EDWARD JOHN MORETON DRAX PLUNKETT]. 1878–1957.
EDISON, T[HOMAS] A[LVA]. 1847–1931.
EINSTEIN, [ALBERT]. 1879–1955.
ELIOT, G[EORGE, pseudonym of MARION ANN EVANS CROSS]. 1819–1880.
ELIOT, T[HOMAS] S[TEARNS]. 1888–
ELIZABETH, QUEEN [OF ENGLAND]. 1533–1603.
ELLIS, H[AVELOCK]. 1859–1939.
EMERSON, [RALPH WALDO]. 1803–1882.
ENGLISH, T[HOMAS] D[UNN]. 1819–1902.
EPICTETUS. 60?–?120.
ERASMUS, [GERARD DIDIER]. 1465–1536.
ESTROM, D. A. Floruit 1897.
EURIPEDES. 480–406 B.C.
EUWER, A[NTHONY]. 1877–
EVANS, A[RTHUR] B[ENONI]. 1781–1854.
EVERETT, D[AVID]. 1769–1813.
EYTINGE, M[ARGARET]. Floruit 1883.
FALCONER, W[ILLIAM]. 1732–1769.
FARQUHAR, [GEORGE]. 1678–1707.
FAWCETT, [JOHN]. 1789–1867.
FÉNELON, [FRANÇOIS DE SALIGNAC DE LA MOTHE]. 1651–1715.
FIELDING, [HENRY]. 1707–1754.
FIRMIN, G[ILES]. 1614–1697.
FITZGERALD, [EDWARD]. 1809–1883.
FLETCHER, J[OHN]. 1579–1625.
FLETCHER, P[HINEAS]. 1582–1650.
FLORIO, [JOHN]. 1553?–1625.
FOOTE, S[AMUEL]. 1720–1777.
FORD, L[ENA] G[UILBERT]. Floruit 1915.
FOSS, S[AM] W[ALTER]. 1858–1911.
FOWLER, E[LLEN] T[HORNEYCROFT]. 1860–1929.
FRANCE, A[NATOLE, pseudonym of JACQUES ANATOLE THIBAULT]. 1844–1924.
FRANCK, R[ICHARD]. 1624?–1708.
FRANKLIN, [BENJAMIN]. 1706–1790.

FREDERICK [II] THE GREAT, [KING OF PRUSSIA]. 1713–1754.
FROST, [ROBERT]. 1875–
FROUDE, [JAMES ANTHONY]. 1818–1894.
FULLER, [THOMAS], compiler. 1654–1734.
FULLER, M[ARGARET]. 1810–1850.
GALILEO. 1564–1642.
GALSWORTHY, [JOHN]. 1867–1933.
GANDHI, MOHANDAS [KARAMCHAND]. 1869–1948.
GARNETT, R[ICHARD]. 1835–1906.
GARRISON, [WILLIAM LLOYD]. 1805–1879.
GARTH, [SIR SAMUEL]. 1661–1719.
GASKELL, E[LIZABETH CLEGHORN, MRS.]. 1810–1865.
GAUGUIN, [EUGÈNE HENRI PAUL]. 1848–1903.
GAVARNI, [PAUL, pseudonym of SULPICE GUILLAUME CHEVALIER]. 1801–1866.
GAY, J[OHN]. 1685–1732.
GAYNOR, W[ILLIAM JAY]. 1849–1913.
GEORGE V, KING [OF ENGLAND]. 1865–1936.
GIBBON, [EDWARD]. 1737–1794.
GIBRAN, [KAHLIL]. 1833–1931.
GIBSON, W[ILFRID] W[ILSON]. 1878–
GIFFORD, W[ILLIAM]. 1756–1826.
GILBERT, [SIR WILLIAM SCHWENCK]. 1836–1911.
GILMAN, C[HARLOTTE] P[ERKINS STETSON]. 1860–1935.
GLADSTONE, [WILLIAM EWART]. 1809–1898.
GLASGOW, E[LLEN]. 1874–1945.
GOETHE, [JOHANN WOLFGANG VON]. 1749–1832.
GOGARTY, [OLIVER ST. JOHN]. 1878–1957.
GOLDONI, [CARLO]. 1707–1793.
GOLDSMITH, [OLIVER]. 1728–1774.
GOULD, G[ERARD LOUIS]. 1885–1936.
GRAFTON, [RICHARD]. ?–?1572.
GRAHAME, J[AMES]. 1765–1811.
GRANT, U[LYSSES] S[IMPSON]. 1822–1885.
GRAY, [THOMAS]. 1716–1771.
GREELEY, H[ORACE]. 1811–1872.
GREEN, M[ATTHEW]. 1696–1737.
GREENE, R[OBERT]. 1560?–1592.
GREGORY [I], SAINT. 590–604.
GUICHARD, [JEAN FRANÇOIS]. 1731–1811.

GUITERMAN, [ARTHUR]. 1871–1943.
HAGEMAN, S[AMUEL MILLER]. 1848–1905.
HALE, N[ATHAN]. 1755–1776.
HALIBURTON, [THOMAS CHANDLER]. 1796–1865.
HALLECK, [FITZ-GREENE]. 1790–1867.
HARDY, [THOMAS] 1840–1928.
HARINGTON, [SIR JOHN]. 1561–1612.
HARPER, R[OBERT GOODLOE]. 1765–1825.
HARRIS, W[ILLIAM] T[ORREY]. 1835–1909.
HARRISON, F[REDERIC]. 1831–1923.
HAWTHORNE, [NATHANIEL]. 1804–1864.
HAY, J[OHN]. 1838–1905.
HAYS, W[ILL H.]. 1879–1954.
HAZLITT, [WILLIAM]. 1778–1830.
HAZLITT, W[ILLIAM] C[AREW]. 1834–1913.
HEBER, [REGINALD]. 1783–1826.
HEGEL, [GEORG WILHELM FRIEDRICH], 1770–1831.
HEMANS, F[ELICIA] D[OROTHEA]. 1793–1835.
HEINE, [HEINRICH]. 1797–1856.
HELPS, A[RTHUR, SIR]. 1813–1875.
HEMINGWAY, [ERNEST]. 1898–
HEMMINGER, G[RAHAM]. 1896–1946.
HENLEY, W[ILLIAM] E[RNEST]. 1849–1903.
HENRY, M[ATTHEW]. 1662–1714.
HENRY, O. [pseudonym of WILLIAM SYDNEY PORTER]. 1862–1910.
HENRY, P[ATRICK]. 1736–1799.
HERBERT, A[LAN] P[ATRICK]. 1890–
HERBERT, G[EORGE]. 1593–1633.
HERFORD, O[LIVER]. 1863–1935.
HERGESHEIMER, [JOSEPH]. 1880–1954.
HERODOTUS. 484–?424 B.C.
HERRICK, [ROBERT]. 1591–1674.
HESIOD. Circa 735 B.C.
HEYWOOD, J[OHN]. 1497?–?1580.
HIGGINSON, T[HOMAS WENTWORTH]. 1823–1911.
HIPPOCRATES. Circa 460–357 B.C.
HITCHCOCK, R[OSWELL] D[WIGHT]. 1817–1887.
HOBBES, [THOMAS]. 1588–1679.
HODGSON, R[ALPH]. 1871–
HOFFENSTEIN, [SAMUEL GOODMAN]. 1890–1947.
HOLCROFT, [THOMAS]. 1745–1809.
HOLMES, [OLIVER WENDELL]. 1809–1894.

Authors Quoted

Homer. Various dates ascribed, from 1200 B.C to 850 B.C.
Hood, [Thomas]. 1799–1845.
Hope, A[nthony, pseudonym of Anthony Hope Hawkins]. 1863–1933.
Hopkins, G[erald] M[anley]. 1844–1898.
Horace, [Quintus Horatius Flaccus]. 65–8 B.C.
Housman, [Alfred Edward]. 1859–1936.
Hovey, R[ichard]. 1864–1900.
Howard, F[rederick, fifth Earl of Carlisle]. 1748–1825.
Howe, N[athaniel]. 1764–1837.
Howell, J[ames]. 1594?–1666.
Howell, T[homas]. Floruit 1568.
Howells, [William Dean]. 1837–1920.
Hubbard, E[lbert]. 1859–1915.
Hughes, T[homas]. 1822–1896.
Hugo, [Victor]. 1802–1885.
Huneker, [James Gibbons]. 1860–1921.
Hunt, L[eigh]. 1784–1859.
Huxley, [Thomas Henry]. 1825–1895.
Huxley, A[ldous]. 1894–
Ibsen, [Henrik]. 1828–1906.
Ingelend, [Thomas]. Floruit 1560.
Ingelow, [Jean]. 1820–1897.
Ingersoll, [Robert Green]. 1833–1899.
Irving, W[ashington]. 1783–1859.
James I of Scotland. 1394–1437.
James, H[enry]. 1843–1916.
James, W[illiam]. 1842–1910.
Jeffers, R[obinson]. 1887–
Jefferson, [Thomas]. 1743–1826.
Jerrold, [Douglas William]. 1803–1857.
Jewel, J[ohn]. 1522–1571.
Johnson, [Samuel]. 1709–1784.
Jones, J[ohn] P[aul]. 1747–1792.
Jonson, [Ben]. 1573?–1637.
Joubert, [Joseph]. 1754–1824.
Jowett, [Benjamin]. 1817–1893.
Junius [pseudonym, possibly of Sir Philip Francis (1740–1818)].
Juvenal, [Decimus Junius]. 60?–?140 A.D.
Karr, A[lphonse]. 1808–1890.
Keats, [John]. 1795–1821.
Keble, [John]. 1792–1866.
Key, T[homas] H[ewitt]. 1799–1875.
Kilmer, A[line Murray]. 1888–1941.
Kingsley, [Charles]. 1819–1875.

Kipling, [Rudyard]. 1865–1936.
Kossuth, [Louis]. 1802–1894.
Kreymborg, [Alfred]. 1883–
La Bruyère, [Jean de]. 1644–1754.
La Fontaine, [Jean de]. 1621–1695.
Lamb, [Charles]. 1775–1834.
Landor, [Walter Savage]. 1775–1864.
Langland, [William]. 1330?–?1400.
Lanier, [Sidney]. 1842–1881.
Lao-tsze. Floruit 6th century B.C.
La Rochefoucauld, [François, Duc de]. 1613–1680.
Lawrence, D[avid] H[erbert]. 1885–1930.
Lear, E[dward]. 1812–1888.
Le Gallienne, R[ichard]. 1866–1947.
Lemierre, [Antoine Marie]. 1723–1793.
Le Sage, [Alain René]. 1668–1747.
Lessing, [Gotthold Ephraim]. 1729–1781.
L'Estrange, [Sir Roger]. 1616–1704.
Lewes, G[eorge] H[enry]. 1817–1878.
Lewis, C[ecil] D[ay]. 1905–
Lewis, S[inclair]. 1885–1951.
Lewisohn, [Ludwig]. 1883–1955.
Lincoln, [Abraham]. 1809–1865.
Lindbergh, [Charles Augustus]. 1902–
Lindsay, V[achel]. 1879–1931.
Lippmann, W[alter]. 1889–
Livy, [Titus Livius]. 59 B.C.–17 A.D.
Lloyd, D[avid]. 1752–1838.
Locke, [John]. 1632–1704.
Lodge, T[homas]. 1558?–1625.
Longfellow, [Henry Wadsworth]. 1807–1882.
Louis XIV, [King of France]. 1638–1715.
Louis XV, [King of France]. 1710–1774.
Lovelace, [Richard]. 1618–1658.
Lowell, [James Russell]. 1819–1891.
Lowell, A[my]. 1874–1925.
Lucan, [Marcus Annaeus Lucanus]. 39–65 A.D.
Lucian. Circa 120–180.
Lucretius, [Titus Lucretius Carus]. 95–55 B.C.
Luther, [Martin]. 1483–1546.
Lydgate, [John]. 1370?–?1451.
Lyly, [John]. 1554?–1606.
Lyttleton, [George]. 1709–1773.
Lytton Strachey, [Giles]. 1880–1932.

MacCall, W[illiam]. 1812–1888.
MacDonald, G[eorge]. 1824–1905.
McFee, W[illiam]. 1881–
McKinley, [William]. 1843–1901.
MacLeish, A[rchibald]. 1892–
Macaulay, [Thomas Babington]. 1800–1859.
Maeterlinck, [Maurice]. 1862–1949.
Maintenon, Mme. de [Françoise d'Aubigne, Marquise de Maintenon]. 1635–1719.
Mahomet. Circa 570–632.
Mann, H[orace]. 1796–1859.
Mann, T[homas]. 1875–1955.
Mansfield, K[atherine, pseudonym of Kathleen Beauchamp Murry]. 1888–1923.
Marcus Aurelius, [Antoninus]. A.D. 121–180.
Markham, E[dwin]. 1852–1940.
Marlowe, [Christopher]. 1564–1593.
Marquis, D[onald Robert Perry]. 1878–1937.
Marryat, [Frederick]. 1792–1848.
Marshall, T[homas] R[iley]. 1854–1925.
Martial, [Marcus Valerius Martialis]. 43–104.
Marvell, A[ndrew]. 1621–1678.
Mary [Stuart], Queen of Scots. 1542–1587.
Marx, K[arl]. 1818–1883.
Masefield, [John]. 1878–
Massey, G[erald]. 1828–1907.
Massinger, [Philip]. 1583–1640.
Maugham, [William Somerset]. 1874–
Maupassant, [Guy] de. 1850–1893.
Mazzini, [Giuseppe]. 1805?–1872.
Melbancke, B[rian]. Floruit 1583.
Melville, [Herman]. 1819–1891.
Menander. 342–291 B.C.
Mencken, H[enry] L[ouis]. 1880–1956.
Meredith, [George]. 1828–1909.
Meredith, O[wen, pseudonym of Edward Robert Bulwer-Lytton]. 1831–1891.
Meriton, [George]. 1634–1711.
Merrick, J[ames]. 1720–1769.
Metrodorus. Floruit 168 B.C.
Michelangelo, [Michelangelo Buonarroti]. 1475–1564.
Middleton, [Thomas]. 1570?–1627.
Mill, J[ohn] S[tuart]. 1806–1873.
Millay, [Edna St. Vincent]. 1892–1950.

Milne, A[lan] A[lexander]. 1882–1956.
Milnes, R[ichard] M[onckton]. 1809–1885.
Milton, [John]. 1608–1674.
Mirbeau, [Octave]. 1850–1917.
Mitchell, S[ilas] W[eir]. 1829–1914.
Molière [pseudonym of Jean Baptiste Paquelin]. 1622–1673.
Montaigne, [Michel Eyquem de]. 1533–1592.
Montgomery, J[ames]. 1771–1854.
Moody, W[illiam] V[aughn]. 1869–1910.
Moore, E[dward]. 1712–1757.
Moore, F[rank]. 1855–1931.
Moore, G[eorge]. 1853–1933.
Moore, T[homas]. 1779–1852.
Morley, C[hristopher Darlington]. 1890–1957.
Morley, J[ohn, Viscount]. 1838–1923.
Morris, G[eorge] P[ope]. 1802–1864.
Morris, L[ewis, Sir]. 1833–1907.
Morris, W[illiam]. 1834–1896.
Morse, [Samuel Finley Breese]. 1791–1872.
Napoleon, [Napoleon Bonaparte]. 1769–1821.
Nash, O[gden]. 1902–
Nathan, G[eorge] J[ean]. 1882–1958.
Neale, [John Mason]. 1818–1866.
Neihardt, J[ohn Gneisenau]. 1881–
Nepos, [Cornelius]. 1st century B.C.
Newman, [John Henry, Cardinal]. 1801–1890.
Newton, A[lfred] E[dward]. 1863–1940.
Nietzsche, [Friedrich Wilhelm]. 1844–1900.
Noyes, A[lfred]. 1880–1958.
Omar Khayyám. 1070–1123.
Onasander. Floruit 49 A.D.
O'Neill, E[ugene]. 1888–1953.
O'Shaughnessy, A[rthur]. 1844–1881.
Osler, [Sir William]. 1849–1919.
Ovid, [Publius Ovidius Naso]. 43 B.C.–18 A.D.
Paine, T[homas]. 1737–1809.
Palmer, G[eorge] H[erbert]. 1842–1933.
Palmerston, Lord [Henry John Temple]. 1784–1865.
Palsgrave, [John]. 1480–1554.

Authors Quoted

PARKER, D[OROTHY]. 1893–
PARNELL, T[HOMAS]. 1679–1718.
PARSONS, T[HOMAS] W[ILLIAM]. 1819–1892.
PASCAL, [BLAISE]. 1623–1662.
PATER, [WALTER]. 1839–1894.
PATMORE, [COVENTRY]. 1823–1896.
PAYNE, J[OHN] H[OWARD]. 1791–1852.
PEABODY, J[OSEPHINE PRESTON]. 1874–1922.
PEACOCK, [THOMAS LOVE]. 1785–1866.
PEARSON, E[DMUND LESTER]. 1880–1937.
PEGLER, W[ESTBROOK]. 1894–
PENN, W[ILLIAM]. 1644–1718.
PEPYS, [SAMUEL]. 1633–1703.
PERCY, T[HOMAS], compiler. 1729–1856.
PERRY, N[ORA]. 1832–1896.
PERSIUS, [AULUS PERSIUS FLACCUS]. 34–62 A.D.
PÉTAIN, [HENRI PHILIPPE]. 1856–1951.
PETRARCH, [FRANCESCO PETRARCA]. 1304–1374.
PETRONIUS, [CAIUS (ARBITER)]. Died A.D. 66.
PHAEDRUS. Floruit A.D. 20.
PHILLIPS, C[HARLES]. 1789–1859.
PHILLIPS, W[ENDELL]. 1811–1884.
PHOCYLIDES. Floruit 560 B.C.
PIAVE, [F.M.]. Floruit 1850.
PILPAY [or BIDPAI]. 3rd century A.D.
PINDAR. Circa 522–442 B.C.
PINERO, [SIR ARTHUR WING]. 1855–1934.
PITT, [WILLIAM, FIRST EARL OF CHATHAM]. 1708–1778.
PITT, W[ILLIAM, THE YOUNGER]. 1759–1806.
PITTACUS. Circa 652–569 B.C.
PLATO. 428–347 B.C.
PLAUTUS, [TITUS MACCIUS]. Floruit 254–184 B.C.
PLINY THE ELDER, [CAIUS PLINIUS SECUNDUS]. Floruit 62–113.
PLUTARCH. Floruit 66 A.D.
POE, [EDGAR ALLAN]. 1809–1849.
POPE, [ALEXANDER]. 1688–1744.
PORTER, H[ENRY]. Floruit 1596–1599.
POUND, E[ZRA]. 1885–
POWYS, J[OHN] C[OWPER]. 1872–
PRESCOTT, [WILLIAM HICKLING]. 1796–1859.
PRESTON, K[EITH]. 1884–1927.
PRESTON, M[ARGARET] J[UNKIN]. 1820–1897.
PRIOR, [MATTHEW]. 1664–1721.
PROPERTIUS, [SEXTUS AURELIUS]. Floruit 50 B.C.
PROTAGORAS. 490?–?415 B.C.
PROUST, [MARCEL]. 1871–1922.
PUBLILIUS, [SYRUS]. 1st century B.C.
QUARLES, F[RANCIS]. 1592–1644.
QUINTILIAN, [MARCUS FABIUS QUINTILIANUS]. Floruit 35–95.
RABELAIS, [FRANÇOIS]. 1494–1553.
RACINE, [JEAN BAPTISTE]. 1639–1699.
RALEIGH, [SIR WALTER]. 1552?–1618.
RAMSAY, A[LLAN]. 1686–1758.
RANDS, W[ILLIAM BRIGHTY]. 1823–1882.
RAY, J[OHN], compiler. 1628–1705.
REESE, L[IZETTE] W[OODWORTH]. 1856–1935.
RENAN, [JOSEPH ERNEST]. 1823–1892.
REPPLIER, A[GNES]. 1855–1950.
RHODES, C[ECIL JOHN]. 1853–1902.
RICH, B[ARNABE]. 1540?–1617.
RILEY, [JAMES WHITCOMB]. 1849–1916.
RIVAROL, [ANTOINE]. 1753–1801.
ROBINSON, E[DWARD] A[RLINGTON]. 1869–1935.
ROGERS, S[AMUEL]. 1763–1855.
ROGERS, W[ILL]. 1879–1935.
ROMAINE, H[ARRY]. Floruit 1895.
ROOSEVELT, F[RANKLIN] D[ELANO]. 1882–1945.
ROOSEVELT, T[HEODORE]. 1858–1919.
ROSSETTI, C[HRISTINA]. 1830–1894.
ROSSETTI, D[ANTE] G[ABRIEL]. 1828–1882.
ROUSSEAU, [JEAN JACQUES]. 1712–1778.
ROWE, [NICHOLAS]. 1674–1718.
RUSKIN, [JOHN]. 1819–1900.
RUSSELL, B[ERTRAND ARTHUR WILLIAM]. 1872–
RUSSELL, J[OHN] F[RANCIS] S[TANLEY, SECOND EARL]. 1865–1931.
ST. AUGUSTINE. 354–430.
SAINTE-BEUVE, [CHARLES AUGUSTIN]. 1804–1869.
ST. FRANCIS OF ASSISI. 1182–1226.
SAINT-GAUDENS, [AUGUSTUS]. 1848–1907.
ST. JOHN, [HENRY, SECOND VISCOUNT BOLINGBROKE]. 1678–1751.
SAKI [pseudonym of H. H. MUNRO]. 1870–1916.
SALLUST, [CAIUS SALLIUSTIUS CRISPUS]. 86–34 B.C.
SANDBURG, [CARL]. 1878–
SANTAYANA, [GEORGE]. 1863–1952.
SASSOON, S[IEGFRIED]. 1886–
SAVILE, [SIR GEORGE]. 1633–1695.

Authors Quoted

SAXE, J[OHN GODFREY]. 1816–1887.
SAYCE, [ARCHIBALD HENRY]. 1845–1933.
SCHELLING, [FRIEDRICH WILHELM JOSEPH VON]. 1775–1854.
SCHILLER, [JOHANN CHRISTOPH FRIEDRICH VON]. 1759–1805.
SCHOPENHAUER, [ARTHUR]. 1788–1860.
SCHREINER, O[LIVE]. 1855–1920.
SCHURZ, [CARL]. 1829–1906.
SCOTT, [WALTER, SIR]. 1771–1832.
SEEGER, [ALAN]. 1888–1916.
SELDEN, [JOHN]. 1584–1654.
SENECA, [LUCIUS ANNAEUS]. Circa 54 B.C.–A.D. 39.
SEWELL, [WILLIAM]. 1804–1874.
SHAFTESBURY, [LORD (ANTHONY ASHLEY COOPER)]. 1671–1713.
SHAKESPEARE, [WILLIAM]. 1564–1616.
SHAW, [GEORGE BERNARD]. 1856–1950.
SHEDD, J[OHN] A. 1859–
SHELLEY, [PERCY BYSSHE]. 1792–1822.
SHENSTONE, [WILLIAM]. 1714–1763.
SHERIDAN, [RICHARD BRINSLEY]. 1751–1816.
SHERMAN, S[TUART] P[RATT]. 1881–1926.
SHERMAN, W[ILLIAM TECUMSEH]. 1820–1891.
SHIRLEY, J[AMES]. 1596–1666.
SIDNEY, [SIR PHILIP]. 1554–1586.
SIENKIEWICZ, [HENRIK]. 1846–1916.
SILL, E[DWARD] R[OWLAND]. 1841–97.
SMILES, [SAMUEL]. 1812–1904.
SMITH, A[LEXANDER]. 1830–1867.
SMITH, A[LFRED] E[MANUEL]. 1873–1944.
SMITH, H[ORACE] and J[AMES]. 1779–1849, 1775–1839.
SMITH, L[OGAN] P[EARSALL]. 1865–1946.
SMITH, S[YDNEY]. 1771–1845.
SMOLLETT, [TOBIAS GEORGE]. 1721–1771.
SOCRATES. 469–399 B.C.
SOPHOCLES. 496?–406 B.C.
SOUTHEY, [ROBERT]. 1774–1843.
SOUTHWELL, R[OBERT]. 1561?–1595.
SPENCER, [HERBERT]. 1820–1903.
SPENSER, [EDMUND]. 1552?–1599.
SPINOZA, [BENEDICT DE]. 1632–1677.
SPOFFORD, H[ARRIET] P[RESCOTT]. 1835–1921.
SPURGEON, C[HARLES] H[ADDON]. 1834–1892.
STAËL, MME. [ANNE LOUISE GERMAINE] DE. 1766–1817.

STARRETT, V[INCENT]. 1886–
STEELE, [SIR RICHARD]. 1672–1729.
STEPHENS, J[AMES]. 1882–1950.
STERLING, [JOHN]. 1806–1844.
STERNE, [LAURENCE]. 1713–1768.
STEVENS, W[ALLACE]. Floruit 1913.
STEVENSON, [ROBERT LOUIS]. 1850–1894.
STOLBERG, B[ENJAMIN]. **1891–1951.**
STOUT, G[EORGE] F[REDERICK]. 1860–
STOWE, H[ARRIET] B[EECHER]. 1812–1896.
SUCKLING, [SIR JOHN]. 1609–1642.
SUMNER, C[HARLES]. 1811–1874.
SUN YAT-SEN. 1866–1925.
SUTRO, [ALFRED]. 1863–1933.
SWEDENBORG, [EMANUEL]. 1688–1772.
SWIFT, [JONATHAN]. 1667–1745.
SWINBURNE, [ALGERNON CHARLES]. 1837–1909.
SYMONDS, [JOHN ADDINGTON]. 1840–1893.
TACITUS, [CAIUS CORNELIUS]. Circa 55–117 A.D.
TAGORE, [RABINDRANATH]. 1861–1941.
TALLEYRAND [-PERIGORD, CHARLES MAURICE DE]. 1754–1838.
TARKINGTON, [BOOTH]. 1869–1946.
TAYLOR, B[AYARD]. 1825–1878.
TAYLOR, B[ERT] L[ESTON]. 1866–1921.
TAYLOR, H[ENRY, SIR]. 1800–1886.
TAYLOR, J[EREMY]. 1613–1667.
TEASDALE, S[ARA]. 1884–1933.
TEMPLE, W[ILLIAM, SIR]. 1628–1699.
TENNYSON, [ALFRED, LORD]. 1809–1892.
TERENCE, [PUBLIUS TERENTIUS AFER]. 185–159 B.C.
THACKERAY, [WILLIAM MAKEPEACE]. 1811–1863.
THEOBALD, L[EWIS]. 1688–1744.
THOMAS À KEMPIS. 1380–1471.
THOMPSON, F[RANCIS]. 1859–1907.
THOMSON, J[AMES]. 1700–1748.
THOREAU, [HENRY DAVID]. 1817–1862.
THORNBURY, [GEORGE WALTER]. 1828–1876.
THUCYDIDES. 471–401 B.C.
TIBERIUS, [CLAUDIUS NERO]. 42 B.C.–37 A.D.
TICKELL, [THOMAS]. 1686–1740.
TIECK, [LUDWIG]. 1773–1853.
TIERNEY, G[EORGE]. 1761–1830.
TIMROD, H[ENRY]. 1829–1867.
TOLSTOY, [COUNT LEO NIKOLAEVICH] 1828–1910.

Authors Quoted

Torrence, [Frederic Ridgely]. 1875–1950.
Trollope, [Anthony]. 1815–1882.
Trowbridge, J[ohn] T[ownsend]. 1827–1916.
Tupper, [Martin F.], compiler. 1810–1889.
Turgenev, [Ivan Sergeyevich]. 1818–1883.
Tusser, T[homas]. 1524?–1580.
Twain, Mark [pseudonym of Samuel Langhorne Clemens]. 1835–1910.
Tydings, M[illard E.]. 1890–
Tyndall, [John]. 1820–1893.
Uhland, [Johann Ludwig]. 1787–1862.
Underhill, E[velyn]. 1875–1941.
Untermeyer, [Louis]. 1885–
Vandiver, W[illiam] D[uncan]. 1854–1932.
van Dyke, [Henry]. 1852–1933.
van Loon, [Hendrik Willem]. 1882–1944.
Vergil, [Publius Vergilius Maro]. 70–19 B.C.
Victoria, Queen [of England]. 1837–1901.
Voltaire, [François Marie Arouet]. 1694–1778.
Walpole, R[obert, Sir]. 1676–1745.
Walton, I[zaak]. 1593–1683.
Warburton, [William]. 1698–1779.
Ward, A[rtemus; pseudonym of Charles Farrar Browne]. 1834–1867.
Ward, Mrs. H[umphrey]. 1851–1920.
Ward, T[homas]. 1652–1708.
Washington, [George]. 1732–1799.
Washington, B[ooker] T[aliaferro]. Circa 1859–1915.
Watson, W[illiam, Sir]. 1858–1935.
Watts, I[saac]. 1674–1748.
Webb, M[ary]. 1881–1927.
Webster, D[aniel]. 1782–1852.
Weiss, J[ohan]. 1818–1879.
Wellington [Duke of (Arthur Wellesley)]. 1769–1852.
Wells, H[erbert] G[eorge]. 1866–1946.

Wesley, [John]. 1703–1791.
West, G[ilbert]. 1703–1756.
Wharton, E[dith]. 1862–1937.
Whately, [Richard]. 1787–1863.
Wheelock, J[ohn] H[all]. 1886–
Whicher, G[eorge Meason]. 1860–1937.
Whistler, [James Abbott McNeill]. 1834–1903.
Whitman, [Walt]. 1819–1892.
Whittier, [John Greenleaf]. 1807–1892.
Wilberforce, S[amuel]. 1805–1873.
Wilcox, E[lla] W[heeler]. 1855–1919.
Wilde, [Oscar O'Flahertie Wills]. 1856–1900.
Wilder, T[hornton Niven]. 1897–
Wilkins, J[ohn, Bishop (of Chester)] 1614–1672.
Wilkinson, M[arguerite]. 1883–1928.
William III, Prince of Orange. 1650–1702.
Wilmot, J[ohn, second Earl of Rochester]. 1647–1680.
Wilson, [Thomas] W[oodrow]. 1856–1924.
Wither, [George]. 1588–1667.
Wolfe, T[homas]. 1900–1938.
Woodward, W[illiam E.]. 1874–1950.
Wordsworth, [William]. 1770–1850.
Wycherley, [William]. 1640?–1716.
Wylie, E[linor]. 1885–1928.
Xenophanes. Circa 576–480 B.C.
Yates, J[ohn] H[enry]. 1837–?
Ybarra, T[homas] R[ussell]. 1880–
Yeats, [William Butler]. 1865–1939.
Young, [Edward]. 1683–1765.
Zangwill, I[srael]. 1864–1926.
Zeno. Circa 355 B.C.
Zenobius. 117–138 A.D.
Zeuxis. Floruit 5th century B.C.
Zola, [Émile]. 1840–1902.

chance—charlatan 752

chance (continued)
  (at random 59.12)
  (accidentally 621.22)
  possibly 470.7
 good chance 156.3
  (possibility 470.1)
  (probability 472.1)
  (certainty
  (assurance
 have a chan
 have no cha
  156.11
  (be impossi
  471.4)
 take one's c
  gamble 621.
  attempt 675
chance v.
 happen 156.7
 risk 621.17
 chance upon 156.8
chance, chanceful
 adj. 156.12
  (accidental 621.20)
chancel 1000.3
chancellor 745.9
chance-medley 156.1
chancery 966.1, 2
chancre 655.16
chancy
 chance 156.12
 uncertain 475.14
 risky 665.7
  (hazardous 621.19)
chandelier 423.10
chandelle n. 267a.24
chandelle v. 267a.31
Chandi 979.4
chandler 797.1
change n.
 alteration 140
  (modification 15.4)
  (novelty 123.1)
  (conversion 144.1)
  (dislocation 185.1)
  (transference 270.1)
  (tergiversation 607.1)
 money 800.14
change v
 alter 140.5, 6
  (differentiate 15.6)
  (dissimilate 18.3)
  (disturb 61.4)
  (convert 144.6)
  (vacillate 605.4)
  (tergiversate 607.7)
 interchange 148.3
 move 264.6
 transfer 270.6
 barter 794.4
change color
 get excited 824.8
 blush 881.4
change hands
 interchange 148.3
 be transferred 783.4

change one's mind 607.7
change sides 607.7, 8
  (abandon 624.3)
changeability 139.1
changeable
 irregular 139.2
 interchangeable

THIS IS HOW IT WORKS

1. Look up your word in the Index Guide.
2. Choose the reference you want.
3. Look up the reference in the text part.
4. Find your word in a group of synonyms.

  (irresolution 605.1)
  (tergiversation 607.1)
  (fickleness 608.3)
changeably 149.7
changeful
 inconstant 149.6
  (tergiversating 607.10)
 uncertain 475.16
changefulness 149.1
changeless 141.6
changelessness 141.1
changeling
 substitute 147.2
 simpleton 501.1
 elf child 980.6
change of life 128.3
changer 797.7
channel n. bed 211.3
 isthmus 203.3
 conduit 350.1
  (trench 259.2)
  (stream 348.1)
 path 627.2
channel v. 259.3
chant n. song 415.10
 religious ~ 990.2
chant v. 416.20
  (glorify 990.10)
chantecler
 cock 366.23
 male animal 373.6
chanter
 singer 416.10
 bagpipe 417.4
chanticleer
 cock 366.23
 male animal 373 6
chantry 1000.1
chaos confusion 59.2
 anarchy 738.2
chaotic
 confused 59.8
 anarchic 738.8
 lawless 964.6
chap cleft 198.2
 man 373.2
chaparajos 225.28
chaparral 367.7
chaparreras 225.28

chapatty, chupatty 298.12
chapbook 593.1
chapeau 225.26
chapel, chapellany 1000.1
chaperon n.
 escort 88.4

flowers 400.4
trophy 733.1
ornament 847.5
chapman 797.1, 3
chaps 225.28
chapter n. section 51.2
 subject 454.1
 ~ in a book 593.7
 council 696.3
chapter v. 44.10
chapter and verse 494.15
chapter of accidents
 circumstances 151.2
 luck 156.1
chaqueta 225.16
char burn 384.18
 do chars 746.8
charabanc 272.4
character n.
 nature 5.3
 (kind 75.2)
 (particularity 79.2)
 (tendency 176.1)
 state 7.1
 constitution 54.1
 oddity 83.4
 number 84.1
 notation 415.23
 eccentric 504.3
 earmark 550.6
 letter 561.1
 (writing 590.9)
 role 599.7
 disposition 820.1
character v.
 engrave 558.5
 letter 561.6
characteristic n.
 particularity 79.2
 (nature 5.3)
 earmark 550.6
 trait 820.1
characteristic adj.
 differentiative 15.8
 peculiar 79.8
 (intrinsic 5.7)
 (characterized 820.3)
 typical 550.21
characterization 599.7
characterize
 personate 554.8

name 564.6
describe 594.5
charade riddle 533.2
 drama 599.3
 game 840.11
charbon 655.18
charcoal residue 40.2
 carbon 384.15
  3, 9, 16
  625.2
  693.2
  276.2)
  1.1
commission 755.1
price 812.1
accusation 938.1
curacy 995.3
in charge
 in control 693.7
 in custody 751.12
without charge 815.10
charge v. fill 52.7
 enjoin 695.5
 attack 716.5
 command 741.4
 commission 755.4
 bargain 794.5
 receive credit 805.5
 assess 812.5
 accuse 938.4
chargeability 947.1
chargeable
 liable 806.8
 assessable 812.5
 blameworthy 932.14
 (guilty 947.4)
charge account 811.1
chargé d'affaires 759.2
charger horse 271.3
 war horse 726.12
chariot 272.1, 4
charlotee 272.4
charioteer 268.9
Charioteer 318.6
charitable
 almsgiving 784.15
 philanthropic 906.7
 (liberal 816.4)
 (merciful 914.6)
charitableness 906.2
 (liberality 816.1)
charitably 906.9
charity
 almsgiving 784.2
 benevolence 906.1, 2
 (aid 707.1)
 (mercy 914.1)
charivari noise 404.2
 discord 414.2
charlatan n.
 impostor 548.3
 (sciolist 493.2)
 (affector 853.4)
 (boaster 884.3)